Romanian
Practical Dictionary
Romanian-English/
English-Romanian

Romanian

Practical Dictionary

Romanian-English/
English-Romanian

Mihai Miroiu

HIPPOCRENE BOOKS, INC.
New York

For information, address:
HIPPOCRENE BOOKS, INC.
171 Madison Avenue
New York, NY 10016
www.hippocrenebooks.com

Library of Congress Cataloging-in-Publication Data

Miroiu, Mihai.
Romanian-English, English-Romanian practical dictionary / Mihai Miroiu.
   p. cm.
 ISBN-13: 978-0-7818-1224-5
 ISBN-10: 0-7818-1224-0 (alk. paper)
 1. Romanian language--Dictionaries--English. 2. English language--Dictionaries--Romanian. I. Title.
PC779.M59 2009
459'.321--dc22

                                                    2008013273

Printed in the United States of America.

For my sons, Mihai and Alex,
with love and pride

ACKNOWLEDGMENTS

My work has been inspired by many fine individuals, and it is impossible for me to mention them all. I have been taught to read language and literature by superb teachers, beginning with Mr. Predescu, my fourth-grade teacher, continuing in high school with Traian Cantemir, on to my Bucharest undergraduate days with Leon Levițchi, and then to my London graduate studies with Professor Randolph Quirk. The intellectual dedication and infectious enthusiasm of these humanists have largely contributed to developing my interest in language and in the power of the written and the spoken word.

I am most grateful to my mother for a lifetime of encouragement, support, and sustenance. Always in my memory is my father, forever an exemplary model of hard work, integrity, and resilience.

I am very grateful to Monica Bentley, Senior Editor at Hippocrene for bringing the project the distance it needed in the last stages.

I would like to thank the staff of the Olin Library at Cornell University, and the staff of the Elmira College Library for their assistance and cooperation.

I would especially like to thank my sons, Alex and Mihai, who have shown constant interest and support and whose editorial and computer skills served me well through the final stage of the project.

CONTENTS

KEY TO ROMANIAN PRONUNCIATION

VOWELS

Symbol	Pronunciation	Romanian examples	Similar sounds in English words
a	similar to English vowel sound as in palm or card, but shorter and not so far back	cat, sac	come, done
e	/e/	bem, set	bet, set
i	between /i/ and /i:/	in, bine	keep, seat
ĭ	short, voiceless i	pomi, mari	
o	between /o/ and /o:/	bot, cort	bought, pork
u	between /u/ and /u:/	şut, mult	shoot, boot
ă	between /ă/ and /ă:/	rană, cadă	runner, hurt
â/î	as in reed and rude, uttered with spread lips	râde, coborî	table

DIPHTHONGS AND TRIPHTHONGS

Symbol	Romanian examples	Similar sounds in English words
ea	beat, dumneata	bat, chat
ei	mei, bei	day, beige
ai	mai, nai	my, Cairo
au	sau, dau	out, now
ia	hârtia, Anglia	young, yard
ui	lui, pui	ruinous
ie	ies, miez	yes
io	creion, Ion	yawn, York
iu	iute, fotoliu	you
ou	nou, birou	bowl, Nicole
oa	doar, soare	wonder
oi	doi, soi	noise, toy
ua	ziua, aluat	won
uă	nouă, vouă	work
eu	meu, leu	(falling diphthong)*
ăi	săi, băi	(falling diphthong)*
ău	rău, tău	so, mow
âi	pâine, mâine	(falling diphthong)*
âu	râu, frâu	(falling diphthong)*
eau	vreau, credeau	**
eoa	pleoapă	**
iai	tăiai	**
iau	miau	meow

*These diphthongs have no equivalent in Standard English. Diphthongs may be *falling* (the first element is accented) or *rising* (the second element is accented).

** These have no equivalent sound in Standard English. They are triphthongs, sound groups made up of three vocalic sounds (two semivowels and one vowel) constituting a whole in pronunciation. They are vocalic glides, i.e the tongue moves from one special position to another or to others within one and the same syllable.

CONSONANTS

Symbol	Pronunciation	Romanian examples	Similar sounds in English words
b	/b/	bere	bar
c	/k/	carte	car
d	/d/	dar	deer
f	/f/	frig	frost
g	/g/	gard	garden
h	/h/	hotel	hotel
j	/zh/	ruj	rouge
l	/l/	liber	liberty
m	/m/	mai	my
n	/n/	nod	nod
p	/p/	pot	pot
r	/r/	rai	ray
s	/s/	student	student
ş	/sh/	şi	she
t	/t/	tac	tuck
ţ	/ts/	baţi	bats
v	/v/	verde	very
x	/gz/	exemplu	example
	/ks/	fix	fix
z	/z/	zero	zero

SPECIAL GROUPS OF LETTERS

Symbol	Pronunciation	Romanian examples	Similar sounds in English words
ce	/che/	cec	check
ci	/chi/	cirip	chirp
che	/ke/	schemă	sketch
chi	/ki/	schi	ski
ge	/dje/	general	general
gi	/dji/	gimnastică	gymnastics
ghe	/ge/	ghem	get
ghi	/gi/	ghindă	guilt

BASIC ROMANIAN GRAMMAR

NOUNS

Noun Gender

Masculine/Neuter	Feminine
consonant (lup, tren)	-ă (casă)
-u (codru, teatru)	-e (carte)
-e (frate, nume)	-ie (cheie, familie)
-i (cui, taxi)	-ea (măsea)
-a (pijama)	

Noun Number

Gender	Singular	Plural
masculine	consonant (elev)	-i (elevi)
	-u (metru)	-i (metri)
	-e (perete)	-i (pereți)
neuter	consonant (caiet; tren)	-e; -uri (caiete; trenuri)
	-i (tramvai; taxi)	-e; -uri (tramvaie, taxiuri)
	-u (teatru)	-e (teatre)
	(tablou)	-uri (tablouri)
	-(i)u (fotoliu)	-(i)i (fotolii)
feminine	-ă (fată; lampă)	-e; -i (fete; lămpi)
	-e (floare)	-i (flori)
	-ea (șosea)	-le (șosele)
	-a (basma)	-le (basmale)

Plural endings

Romanian nouns have different plural endings depending on the gender of the noun. Broadly speaking, to mark the plural, masculine nouns take the ending –i, feminine nouns take the endings –e or –i, and neuter nouns take the endings –e or -uri.

Masculine	Feminine	Neuter
-i	-e	-uri
	-i	-e
	-le	-i

Article declension

The definite article

	Masculine	Feminine	Neuter
Singular			
Nom., Acc.	-l, -le, -a	-a	-l, -le
	(calul, fratele, tata)	(casa)	(portul, numele)
Gen., Dat.	-lui, (e)i	-i	-lui
	(calului, fratelui, tatei)	(casei)	(portului, numelui)
Voc.	-le	-	-le
	(calule)		(portule)

	Masculine	Feminine	Neuter
Plural			
Nom., Acc.	-i	-le	-le
	(cai*i*, fraţi*i*, taţi*i*)	(case*le*)	(porturi*le*, nume*le*)
Gen., Dat.	-lor	-lor	-lor
	(cai*lor*, fraţi*lor*, taţi*lor*)	(case*lor*)	(porturi*lor*, nume*lor*)
Voc.	-lor	-lor	-lor
	(cai*lor*, fraţi*lor*, taţi*lor*)	(case*lor*)	(porturi*lor*, nume*lor*)

The indefinite article

	Masculine	Feminine	Neuter
Singular			
Nom., Acc.	un (cal)	o (casă)	un (pod)
Gen., Dat.	unui (cal)	unei (case)	unui (pod)
Plural			
Nom., Acc.	nişte (cai)	nişte (case)	nişte (poduri)
Gen., Dat.	unor (cai)	unor (case)	unor (poduri)

Noun Declension

Masculine nouns with indefinite articles

	Article					
Singular						
Nom.	**un**	tată	om	ochi	fiu	frate
Gen.	**a unui**	tată	om	ochi	fiu	frate
Dat.	**unui**	tată	om	ochi	fiu	frate
Acc.	**un**	tată	om	ochi	fiu	frate
Voc.		tată	-	-	-	frate
Plural						
Nom.	**nişte**	taţi	oameni	ochi	fii	fraţi
Gen.	**a unor**	taţi	oameni	ochi	fii	fraţi
Dat.	**unor**	taţi	oameni	ochi	fii	fraţi
Acc.	**nişte**	taţi	oameni	ochi	fii	fraţi
Voc.		-	-	-	-	-

Feminine nouns with indefinite articles

	Article				
Singular					
Nom.	**o**	mamă	stea	carte	zi
Gen.	**a unei**	mame	stele	cărţi	zile
Dat.	**unei**	mame	stele	cărţi	zile
Acc.	**o**	mamă	stea	carte	zi
Voc.	-	mamă	-	-	-
Plural					
Nom.	**nişte**	mame	stele	cărţi	zile
Gen.	**a unor**	mame	stele	cărţi	zile
Dat.	**unor**	mame	stele	cărţi	zile
Acc.	**nişte**	mame	stele	cărţi	zile
Voc.	-	-	-	-	-

Neuter nouns with indefinite articles

	Article			
Singular				
Nom.	un	pat	pai	nume
Gen.	a unui	pat	pai	nume
Dat.	unui	pat	pai	nume
Acc.	un	pat	pai	nume
Voc.	-	-	-	-
Plural				
Nom.	nişte	paturi	paie	nume
Gen.	a unor	paturi	paie	nume
Dat.	unor	paturi	paie	nume
Acc.	nişte	paturi	paie	nume
Voc.	-	-	-	-

Masculine nouns with definite articles

Singular					
Nom.	tatăl	omul	ochiul	fiul	fratele
Gen.	a tatălui	a omului	a ochiului	a fiului	a fratelui
Dat.	tatălui	omului	ochiului	fiului	fratelui
Acc.	tatăl	omul	ochiul	fiul	fratele
Voc.	-	omule	-	fiule	-
Plural					
Nom.	taţii	oamenii	ochii	fiii	fraţii
Gen.	a taţilor	oamenilor	ochilor	fiilor	fraţilor
Dat.	taţilor	oamenilor	ochilor	fiilor	fraţilor
Acc.	taţii	oamenii	ochii	fiii	fraţii
Voc.	taţilor	oamenilor	-	fiilor	fraţilor

Feminine nouns with definite articles

Singular				
Nom.	mama	steaua	cartea	ziua
Gen.	a mamei	a stelei	a cărţii	a zilei
Dat.	mamei	stelei	cărţii	zilei
Acc.	mama	steaua	cartea	ziua
Voc.	-	-	-	-
Plural				
Nom.	mamele	stelele	cărţile	zilele
Gen.	a mamelor	a stelelor	a cărţilor	a zilelor
Dat.	mamelor	stelelor	cărţilor	zilelor
Acc.	mamele	stelele	cărţile	zilele
Voc.	mamelor	-	-	-

Neuter nouns with definite articles

Singular			
Nom.	patul	paiul	numele
Gen.	a patului	a paiului	a numelui
Dat.	patului	paiului	numelui

Acc.	patu*l*	paiu*l*	nume*le*
Voc.	-	-	-

Plural

Nom.	paturi*le*	paie*le*	nume*le*
Gen.	a paturi*lor*	a paie*lor*	a nume*lor*
Dat.	paturi*lor*	paie*lor*	nume*lor*
Acc.	paturi*le*	paie*le*	nume*le*
Voc.	-	-	-

PRONOUNS

Personal Pronoun Declension

First Person

	Singular	*Plural*
Nom.	eu (eu spun)	noi (noi spunem)
Gen.	-	-
Dat. stressed	mie (mie îmi place)	nouă (nouă ne place)
Dat. unstressed	îmi (îmi dai?)	ne (ne dai?)
	mi (mi s-a spus)	ni (ni s-a spus)
	mi- (mi-l dai?)	ni- (ni-l dai?)
	-mi (dă-mi cadoul)	ne- (ne-ai chemat?)
	-mi (dă-mi-l! dă-mi-o!)	-ne (dă-ne cadoul!)
		-ni- (dă-ni-l)
		-ne- (dă-ne-o!)
Acc. stressed	mine (pe mine)	noi (pe noi)
Acc. unstressed	mă (mă iubeşti?)	ne (ne iubeşti?)
	mă- (mă-mbrac)	ne- (ne-mbrăcăm)
	-mă (întreabă-mă)	-ne (întreabă-ne)
	-mă- (ruga-mă-vei)	-ne- (ruga-ne-vei)
	m- (m-a văzut)	
	-m- (dusu-m-am)	

Second Person

	Singular	*Plural*
Nom.	tu (tu spui)	voi (voi spuneţi)
Gen.	-	-
Dat. stressed	ţie (ţie îţi place?)	vouă (vouă vă place?)
Dat. unstressed	îţi (îţi place?)	vă (vă place)
	ţi (ţi s-a spus?)	vi (vi s-a spus?)
	ţi- (ţi-l dau?)	vi- (vi-l dau?)
	-ţi- (aducându-ţi-l)	-vi- (aducându-vi-l)
	-ţi (ia-ţi cartea!)	-vă (luaţi-vă cartea!)
		vă- (vă-ngădui asta)
		v- (v-o dau?)
		-v- (luaţi-v-o!)
Acc. stressed	tine (pe tine)	voi (pe voi)
Acc. unstressed	te (te iubesc)	vă (vă iubesc)

Singular	*Plural*
te- (te-ntreb)	vă- (vă-ntreb)
-te (întreabă-te)	-vă (întrebați-vă)
-te- (ruga-te-aş)	-vă- (ruga-vă-vor)
	v- (v-am întrebat)
	-v- (vedea-v-aş)

Third person

		Singular		*Plural*
Nom.	*m/n*	el	*m*	ei
	f	ea	*f/n*	ele
Gen.	*m/n*	lui	*m/f/n*	lor
	f	e		
Dat. stressed	*m/n*	lui	*m/f/n*	lor
	f	ei		
Dat. unstressed	*m/f*	îi (îi spun)	*m/f*	le (le spun)
		i (i s-a spus)		le- (le-am spus)
	n	i- (i-am spus)	*n*	-le (dă-le cartea!)
		-i (să-i spui)		-le- (dă-le-o!)
		-i- (datu-i-s-a)		li (li s-a spus)
				li- (li-s drag)
				-li- (datu-li-s-a)
Acc. stressed	*m/n*	el	*m*	ei
	f	ea	*f/n*	ele
Acc. unstressed	*m/n*	îl (îl cunosc)	*m*	îi (îi cunosc)
		l- (l-am văzut)		i- (i-am văzut)
		-l (să-l vezi)		-i (să-i vezi)
		-l- (vedea-l-aş)		-i- (vedea-i-aş)
	f	o (o cunosc)	*f/n*	le (le cunosc)
		o- (o-ncep)		le- (le-ncep)
		-o (pune-o aici!)		-le (pune-le aici!)
		-o- (căuta-o-voi)		-le- (vedea-le-aş)

Possessive Pronouns

Pronoun	*Singular m/n*	*Singular f*	*Plural m*	*Plural f/n*
my/mine	al meu	a mea	ai mei	ale mele
your/yours	al tău	a ta	ai tăi	ale tale
his/hers/its	al său	a sa	ai săi	ale sale
our/ours	al nostru	a noastră	ai noştri	ale noastre
your/yours	al vostru	a voastră	ai voştri	ale voastre
their/theirs	al lor	a lor	ai lor	ale lor

Interrogative-Relative Pronouns

Cine

Case		Singular		Plural
Nom.	m/f	cine	m/f/n	-
	n	-		
Gen.	m/f	(al, a, ai, ale) cui	m/f/n	-
	n	-		
Dat.	m/f/n	cui	m/f/n	-
Acc.	m/f	cine	m/f/n	-
	n	-		

Cât/ă

Case		Singular		Plural
Nom.	m/n	cât	m	câți
	f	câtă	f/n	câte
Gen.	m/f/n	-	m/f/n	câtor
Dat.	m/f/n	-	m/f/n	câtor
Acc.	m/n	cât	m	câți
	f	câtă	f/n	câte

Care

Case		Singular		Plural
Nom.	m/f/n	care	m/f/n	care
Gen.	m/f/n	(al, a, ai, ale) căeui(a)	m/f/n	(al, a, ai, ale) căror(a)
Dat.	m/n	căruia	m/f/n	cărora
	f	căreia		
Acc.	m/f/n	care	m/f/n	care

Cel/Ceea ce

Case		Singular		Plural
Nom.	m	cel ce	m	cei ce
	f	ceea ce	f	cele ce
Gen.	m	celui ce	m/f	celor ce
	f	celei ce		
Dat.	m	celui ce	m/f	celor ce
	f	celei ce		
Acc.	m	cel ce	m	cei ce
	f	ceea ce	f	cele ce

Emphatic Pronouns

	Singular m	Singular f	Plural m	Plural f
1st person	însumi	însămi	înșine	însene
2nd person	însuți	însăți	înșivă	însevă
3rd person	însuși	însăși	înșiși	înseși, însele

ADJECTIVES

Adjective Declension
Adjectives following nouns

	1	2	2	2	2	3	3	4
Singular, All Cases								
m, n	gri	mare	amărui	bălai	feroce	vişiniu	muritor	bun
f	gri	mare	amăruie	bălaie	feroce	vişinie	muritoare	bună
Plural, All Cases								
m	gri	mari	amărui	bălai	feroci	vişinii	muritori	buni
f, n	gri	mari	amărui	bălaie	feroce	vişinii	muritoare	bune

Adjectives preceding nouns with definite articles

	1	2	2	2	2	3	3	4
Singular, Nominative & Accusative								
m, n	griul	marele	amăruiul	bălaiul	ferocele	vişiniul	muritorul	bunul
f	-	mare	amăruia	bălaia	ferocea	vişinia	muritoarea	buna
Singular, Genitive (al, a, ai, ale) & Dative								
m,n	griului	marelui	amăruiului	bălaiului	ferocelui	vişiniului	muritorului	bunului
f	-	marii	amăruiei	bălaiei	ferocei	vişiniei	muritoarei	bunei
Plural, Nominative & Accusative								
m	-	marii	amăruii	bălaii	ferocii	vişinii	muritorii	bunii
f, n	-	marile	amăruile	bălaiele	ferocele	vişiniile	muritoarele	bunele
Plural, Genitive (al, a, ai, ale) & Dative								
m	-	marilor	amăruilor	bălaielor	ferocilor	vişiniiilor	muritorilor	bunilor
f, n	-	marilor	amăruilor	bălaielor	ferocelor	vişiniilor	muritoarelor	bunelor

Adjectives preceding nouns with indefinite articles

	1	2	2	2	2	3	3	4
Singular, Nominative & Accusative								
m, n	-	mare	amărui	bălai	feroce	vişiniu	muritor	bun
f	-	mare	amăruie	bălaie	feroce	vişinie	muritoare	bună
Singular, Genitive (al, a, ai, ale) & Dative								
m, n	-	mare	amărui	bălai	feroce	vişiniu	muritor	bun
f	-	mari	amărui	bălaie	feroce	vişinii	muritoare	bune
Plural, Nominative & Accusative								
m	-	mari	amărui	bălai	feroci	vişinii	muritori	buni
f, n	-	mari	amărui	bălaie	feroce	vişinii	muritoare	bune
Plural, Genitive (al, a, ai, ale) & Dative								
m	-	mari	amărui	bălai	feroci	vişinii	muritori	buni
f, n	-	mari	amărui	bălaie	feroce	vişinii	muritoare	bune

Demonstrative Adjectives

Preceding the noun: this, these (acest)

Case		Singular		Plural
Nom. & Acc.	m/n	acest	m	aceşti
	f	această	f/n	aceste
Gen. & Dat.	m/n	acestui	m	acestor
	f	acestei	f/n	acestor

Following the noun: this, these (acesta)

Case		Singular		Plural
Nom. & Acc.	m/n	acesta	m	aceştia
	f	aceasta	f/n	acestea
Gen. & Dat.	m/n	acestuia	m	acestora
	f	acesteia	f/n	acestora

Preceding the noun: that, those (acel)

Case		Singular		Plural
Nom. & Acc.	m/n	acel	m	acei
	f	acea	f/n	acele
Gen. & Dat.	m/n	acelui	m	acelor
	f	acelei	f/n	acelor

Following the noun: that, those (acela)

Case		Singular		Plural
Nom. & Acc.	m/n	acela	m	aceia
	f	aceea	f/n	acelea
Gen. & Dat.	m/n	aceluia	m	acelora
	f	aceleia	f/n	acelora

Demonstrative Adjectives and Pronouns

This (one), these (ones): ăsta

Case		Singular		Plural
Nom. & Acc.	m/n	ăsta	m	ăştia
	f	asta	f/n	astea
Gen. & Dat.	m/n	ăstuia	m	ăstora
	f	ăsteia	f/n	ăstora

That (one), those (ones): ăla

Case		Singular		Plural
Nom. & Acc.	m/n	ăla	m	ăia
	f	aia	f/n	alea
Gen. & Dat.	m/n	ăluia	m	ălora
	f	ăleia	f/n	ălora

The other (one/ones): celălalt

Case	Singular		Plural	
Nom. & Acc.	m/n	celălalt	m	ceilalţi
	f	cealaltă	f/n	celelalte
Gen. & Dat.	m/n	celuilalt	m	celorlalţi
	f	celeilalte	f/n	celorlalte

The same (one/ones): acelaşi

Case	Singular		Plural	
Nom. & Acc.	m/n	acelaşi	m	aceiaşi
	f	aceeaşi	f/n	aceleaşi
Gen. & Dat.	m/n	aceluiaşi	m	aceloraşi
	f	aceleiaşi	f/n	aceloraşi

This one, that one, these ones, those ones: acesta/acela

Case	Singular		Plural	
Nom. & Acc.	m/n	acesta/acela	m	aceştia/aceia
	f	aceasta/aceea	f/n	acestea/acelea
Gen. & Dat.	m/n	acestuia/aceluia	m	acestora/acelora
	f	acesteia/aceleia	f/n	acestora/acelora

VERBS

Auxiliary Verbs

Fi

Present Indicative

sunt/sânt, -s, s-, îs	suntem/sântem
eşti	sunteţi/sânteţi
este, e, -i, i-, îi	sunt/sânt

Compound perfect (Perfectul compus)

am fost	am fost
ai fost	aţi fost
a fost	au fost

Imperfect (Imperfectul)

eram	eram
erai	eraţi
era	erau

Past Perfect (Mai-mult-ca-perfectul)

fusesem	fuseserăm
fuseseşi	fuseserăţi
fusese	fuseseră

Simple perfect (Perfectul simplu)

fusei, fui	furăm, fuserăm
fuseşi, fuşi	furăţi, fuserăţi
fuse, fu	fură, fuseră

Avea

Present Indicative

am	avem
ai	aveți
are	au

Compound perfect (Perfectul compus)

am avut	am avut
ai avut	ați avut
a avut	au avut

Imperfect (Imperfectul)

aveam	aveam
aveai	aveați
avea	aveau

Past Perfect (Mai-mult-ca-perfectul)

avusesem	avuseserăm
avuseseși	avuseserăți
avusese	avuseseră

Simple perfect (Perfectul simplu)

avui, avusei	avurăm, avuserăm
avuși, avuseși	avurăți, avuserăți
avu, avuse	avură, avuseră

Vrea/Voi

Present Indicative

vreau/voiesc	vrem/voi
vrei/voiești	vreți/voiți
vrea/voiește	vor/voiesc

Compound perfect (Perfectul compus)

am vrut	am vrut
ai vrut	ați vrut
a vrut	au vrut

Imperfect (Imperfectul)

vream/voiam	vream/voiam
vreai/voiai	vreați/voiați
vrea/voia	vreau/voiau

Past Perfect (Mai-mult-ca-perfectul)

vruse(se)m/voisem	vruseserăm/voiserăm
vruse(se)și/voiseși	vruseserăți/voiserăți
vruse(se)/voise	vruseseră/voiseră

Simple perfect (Perfectul simplu)

vrui	vrurăm/voirăm
vruși	vrurăți/voirăți
vru/voi	vrură/voiră

The Indicative Mood

Present tense, 1ˢᵗ conjugation: infinitive -a (ruga, lucra)

-, -ezi (rog, lucrez)	-m, -m (rugăm, lucrăm)
-i, -ezi (rogi, lucrezi)	-ți, -ți (rugați, lucrați)
-ă, -ează (roagă, lucrează)	-ă, -ează (roagă, lucrează)

Present tense, 2nd conjugation: infinitive -ea (cădea)

- (cad)	-m (cădem)
-i (cazi)	-ți (cădeți)
-e (cade)	- (cad)

Present tense, 2nd conjugation: infinitive -ea (veghea)

-ez (veghez)	-m (veghem)
-ezi (veghezi)	-ți (vegheați)
-ează (veghează)	-ează (veghează)

Present tense, 3rd conjugation: infinitive -e (face)

- (fac)   -m (facem)
-i (faci)   -ți (faceți)
-e (face)   - (fac)

Present tense, 4th conjugation:
infinitive -i; -î (dormi, rosti)

-esc (dorm, rostesc)   -m, -m (dormim, rostim)
-i, -ești (dormi, rostești)   -ți, -ți (dormiți, rostiți)
-e, -ește (doarme, rostește)   -, -esc (dorm, rostesc)

infinitive -i; -î (doborî, urî)

-ăsc (dobor, urăsc)   -m, -m (doborîm, urâm)
i-, -ăști (dobori, urăști)   -ți, ți (doborâți, urâți)
-ă, -ăște (doboară, urăște)   -ă, -ăsc (doboară, urăsc)

Imperfect, 1st conjugation: infinitive -a (ruga, lucra)

-m (rugam, lucram)   -m (rugam, lucram)
-i (rugai, lucrai)   -ți (rugați, lucrați)
- (ruga, lucra)   -u (rugau, lucrau)

Imperfect, 2nd conjugation: infinitive -ea (cădea)

-m (cădeam)   -m (cădeam)
-i (cădeai)   -ți (cădeați)
- (cădea)   -u (cădeau)

Imperfect, 2nd conjugation: infinitive -ea (veghea)

-m (vegheam)   -m (vegheam)
-i (vegheai)   -ți (vegheați)
- (veghea)   -u (vegheau)

Imperfect, 3rd conjugation: infinitive -e (face)

-m (făceam)   -m (făceam)
-i (făceai)   -ți (făceați)
- (făcea)   -u (făceau)

Imperfect, 4th conjugation: infinitive -i; -î (dormi, rosti; doborî, urî)

-m (dormeam, rosteam; doboram, uram)   -m (dormeam, rosteam; doboram, uram)
-i (dormeai, rosteai; doborai, urai)   -ți (dormeați, rosteați; doborați, urați)
- (dormea, rostea; dobora, ura)   -u (dormeau, rosteau; doborau, urau)

Simple perfect, 1st conjugation: infinitive -a (ruga, lucra)

-i (rugai, lucrai)   -răm (rugarăm, lucrarăm)
-și (rugași, lucrași)   -răți (rugarăți, lucrarăți)
- (rugă, lucră)   -ră (rugară, lucrară)

Simple perfect, 2nd conjugation: infinitive -ea (cădea)

-i (căzui)   -răm (căzurăm)
-și (căzuși)   -răți (căzurăți)
- (căzu)   -ră (căzură)

Simple perfect, 2nd conjugation: infinitive -ea (veghea)
-i (vegheai) -răm (veghearăm)
-şi (vegheaşi) -răţi (veghearăţi)
- (veghe) -ră (vegheară)

Simple perfect, 3rd conjugation: infinitive -e (face)
-i (făcui) -răm (făcurăm)
-şi (făcuşi) -răţi (făcurăţi)
- (făcu) -ră (făcură)

Simple perfect, 4th conjugation:
infinitive -i (dormi, rosti;)
-i (dormii, rostii) -răm (dormirăm, rostirăm)
-şi (dormişi, rostişi) -răţi (dormirăţi, rostirăţi)
- (dormi, rosti) -ră (dormiră, rostiră)
infinitive -î (doborî, urî)
-i (doborâi, urâi) -răm (doborârăm, urârăm)
-şi (doborâşi, urâşi) -răţi (doborârăţi, urârăţi)
- (doborî, urî) -ră (doborâră, urâră)

Past perfect, 1st conjugation: infinitive -a (ruga, lucra)
-sem (rugasem, lucrasem) -serăm (rugase- răm, lucrase- răm)
-seşi (rugaseşi, lucraseşi) -serăţi (rugase- răţi, lucrase-răţi)
-se (rugase, lucrase) -seră (rugaseră, lucraseră)

Past perfect, 2nd conjugation: infinitive -ea (cădea)
-sem (căzusem) -serăm (căzuserăm)
-seşi (căzuseşi) -serăţi (căzuserăţi)
-se (căzuse) -seră (căzuseră)

Past perfect, 2nd conjugation: infinitive -ea (veghea)
-sem (vegheasem) -serăm (veghease- răm)
-seşi (vegheaseşi) -serăţi (veghease- răţi)
-se (veghease) -seră veghease- ră)

Past perfect, 3rd conjugation: infinitive -e (face)
-sem (făcusem) -serăm (făcuserăm)
-seşi (făcuseşi) -serăţi (făcuserăţi)
-se (făcuse) -seră (făcuseră)

Past perfect, 4th conjugation:
infinitive -i (dormi, rosti)
-sem (dormisem, rostisem) -serăm (dormiserăm, rostiserăm)
-seşi (dormiseşi, rostiseşi) -serăţi (dormiserăţi, rostiserăţi)
-se (dormise, rostise) -seră (dormiseră, rostiseră)
infinitive -î (doborî, urî)
-sem (doborâsem, urâsem) -serăm (doborâserăm, urâserăm)
-seşi (doborâseşi, urâseşi) -serăţi (doborâserăţi, urâserăţi)
-se (doborâse, urâse) -seră (doborâseră, urâseră)

Compound perfect: present tense of avea + participle
(i.e., rugat, lucrat, căzut, vegheat, făcut, dormit, rostit, doborât, urât)

am + participle   am + participle
ai + participle   ați + participle
a + participle   au + participle

Future tense: future tense of voi + infinitive
(i.e., ruga, lucra, cădea, veghea, face, dormi, rosti, doborî, urî)

voi + infinitive   vom + infinitive
vei + infinitive   veți + infinitive
va + infinitive   vor + infinitive

Conditional Mood

Present tense: a variable auxiliary element (aş, ai, ar, am, ați, ar) + infinitive
(i.e., ruga, lucra, cădea, veghea, face, dormi, rosti, doborî, urî)

aş + infinitive   am + infinitive
ai + infinitive   ați + infinitive
ar + infinitive   ar + infinitive

Perfect tense: a variable auxiliary element + fi + participle
(i.e., fi rugat, fi lucrat, fi căzut, fi vegheat, fi făcut, fi dormit, fi rostit, fi doborât)

aş + fi + participle   am + fi + participle
ai + fi + participle   ați + fi + participle
ar + fi + participle   ar + fi + participle

Subjunctive Mood

The subjunctive present is identical with the indicative present in all persons except for the 3rd person singular and plural.

Present Tense, 1st conjugation

să rog	să rugăm
să rogi	să rugați
să roage	să roage

Present Tense, 1st conjugation

să lucrez	să lucrăm
să lucrezi	să lucreze
să lucrați	să lucreze

Present Tense, 2nd conjugation

să cad	să cădem
să cazi	să cădeți
să cadă	să cadă

Present Tense, 2nd conjugation

să veghez	să veghem
să veghezi	să vegheați
să vegheze	să vegheze

Present Tense, 3rd conjugation

să fac	să facem
să faci	să faceți
să facă	să facă

Present Tense, 4th conjugation

să dorm	să dormim
să dormi	să dormiți
să doarmă	să doarmă

Present Tense, 4th conjugation

să dobor	să doborâm
să dobori	să doborâți
să doboare	să doboare

Perfect Tense

să + fi + participle (i.e., rugat, lucrat, căzut, vegheat, făcut, dormit, rostit, doborât)

Irregular Verbs

Bea

Present Indicative

beau	bem
bei	beţi
bea	beau

Simple Perfect

băui	băurăm
băuşi	băurăţi
băsu	băură

Imperfect

beam	beam
beai	beaţi
bea	beau

Past Perfect

băusem	băuserăm
băuseşi	băuserăţi
băuse	băuseră

Da

Present Indicative

dau	dăm
dai	daţi
dă	dau

Simple Perfect

dădui	dădurăm
dăduşi	dădurăţi
dădu	dădură

Imperfect

dădeam/dam	dădeam/dam
dădeai/dai	dădeaţi/daţi
dădea/da	dădeau/dau

Past Perfect

dădusem	dăduserăm
dăduseşi	dăduserăţi
dăduse	dăduseră

Lua

Present Indicative

iau	luăm
iei	luaţi
ia	iau

Simple Perfect

luai	luarăm
luaşi	luarăţi
luă	luară

Imperfect

luam	luam
luai	luaţi
lua	luau

Past Perfect

luasem	luaserăm
luaseşi	luaserăţi
luase	luaseră

Mânca

Present Indicative

mănânc	mâncăm
mănânci	mâncaţi
mănâncă	mănâncă

Simple Perfect

mâncai	mâncarăm
mâncaşi	mâncarăţi
mâncă	mâncară

Imperfect

mâncam	mâncam
mâncai	mâncaţi
mânca	mâncau

Past Perfect

mâncasem	mâncaserăm
mâncaseşi	mâncaserăţi
mâncase	mâncaseră

Sta

Present Indicative		Simple Perfect	
stau	stăm	stătui	stăturăm
stai	stați	stătuși	stăturăți
stă	stau	stătu	stătură

Imperfect		Past Perfect	
stăteam/stam	stăteam/stam	stătusem	stătuserăm
stăteai/stai	stăteați/stați	stătuseși	stătuserăți
stătea/sta	stăteau/stau	stătuse	stătuseră

Usca

Present Indicative		Simple Perfect	
usuc	uscăm	uscai	uscarăm
usuci	uscați	uscași	uscarăți
usucă	usucă	uscă uscară	

Imperfect		Past Perfect	
uscam	uscam	uscasem	uscaserăm
uscai	uscați	uscaseși	uscaserăți
usca	uscau	uscase	uscaseră

Prepositions and Cases

Prepositions that take the genitive

asupra, contra, deasupra, dedesubtul, înaintea, înapoia, îndărătul, împotriva, împrejurul

Examples: contra inamicului, deasupra dealului, înapoia casei, împotriva lui, împrejurul orașului

Prepositions that take the dative

datorită, mulțumită, grație; asemănător, caracteristic, conform, contrar, corespunzător, favorabil, potrivit, specific; asemenea

Examples: datorită ție, grație efortului; conform planului, contrar așteptărilor, potrivit dorințelor; asemenea fratelui

Prepositions that take the accusative

ca, cu, către, de, din, după, fără, în, între, la, lângă, pe, pentru, peste, până, prin, spre, sub; despre, dinspre, dintre, înspre, printre; de la, de către, de pe, fără de, pe la, pe lângă, până la

Examples: ca mine, cu mama, fără scop, în cameră, lângă birou, pentru prieteni, prin curte; despre eroi, printre oameni; de la noi, pe lângă

Abbreviations

Abbreviation	English	Romanian
abbr	abbreviated, abbreviation	abreviere, prescurtare
acc	accusative	acuzativ
adj	adjective	adjectiv
adv	adverb	adverb
agr	agriculture	agicultură
anat	anatomy	anatomie
ant	antonym	antonim
approx	approximately	aproximativ
archit	architecture	arhitectură
art	article	articol
astrol	astrology	astrologie
astron	astronomy	astronomie
auto	automobiles	automobile
aux	auxiliary	auxiliar
avia	aviation	aviaţie
bio	biology	biologie
biochem	biochemistry	biochimie
bot	botany	botanică
chem	chemistry	chimie
cin	cinema	cinematografie
coll	colloquial	termen uzual
com	commerce	comerţ
comp	computing	calculatoare
cond	conditional	condiţional
conj	conjunction	conjuncţie
constr	construction	construcţii
cul	culinary	arta culinară
dat	dative	dativ
def	definite	(articol) definit
dem	demonstrative	demonstrativ
dir	direct	direct
econ	economics	ştiinţe economice
edu	education	învăţământ
eg	for example	de exemplu
elec	electricity	electricitate
emph	emphatic	de întărire
ento	entomology	entomologie
esp	especially	mai ales
f	feminine	feminin
fam	familiar/informal	familiar
fig	figuratively	sens figurat
fin	finance	finanţe
freq	frequentative	frecventativ
frml	formal	termen formal
gen	genitive	genetiv
geog	geography	geografie
geol	geology	geologie
geom	geometry	geometrie

gram	grammar	gramatică
hist	history	istorie
hum	humorous	termen umoristic
hydr	hydrology	hidrologie
icht	ichthyology	ihtiologie
imp	impersonal	impersonal
ind	industry	industrie
indef	indefinite	nedefinit
indic	indicative	indicativ
indir	indirect	indirect
interj	interjection	intejecție
inter	interrogative	interogativ
inv	invariable	invariabil
iro	ironic	ironic
irreg	irregular	neregulat
jur	law, legal	termen juridic
ling	linguistics	lingvistica
lit	literary	termen literar
liter	literature	literatură
log	logics	logică
m	masculine	masculin
math	mathematics	matematică
mech	mechanics	mecanică
med	medicine	medicină
met	meteorology	meteorologie
metal	metallurgy	metalurgie
mil	military	termen militar
min	mining	minerit
miner	mineralogy	mineralogie
mod	modal (verb)	(verb) modal
mus	music	muzică
myth	mythology	mitologie
n	noun	substantiv
nm	masculine noun	substantiv masculin
nf	feminine noun	substantiv feminin
nn	neuter noun	substantiv neutru
naut	nautical, naval	termen de navigație
neg	negative	negativ
nom	nominative	nominativ
num	numeral	numeral
obs	obsolete	termen învechit
opt	optics	optică
orn	ornithology	ornitologie
pass	passive	diateza pasivă
pej	pejorative	peiorativ
pers	personal	personal
pharm	pharmacy	termen farmaceutic
phil	philosophy	filosofie
phot	photography	arta fotografică
phys	physics	fizică
physiol	physiology	fiziologie

pl	plural	plural
pol	politics	ştiinţe politice
poss	possessive	posesiv
prep	preposition	prepoziţie
pres	present	prezent
pron	pronoun	pronume
psych	psychology, psychiatry	psihologie, psihiatrie
rad	radio	radiodifuziune
rail	railroad	transport feroviar
recip	reciprocal	reciproc
ref	reflexive	reflexiv
rel	relative	relativ
relig	religion	religie
s	noun	substantiv
scol	school	termen şcolar
silv	silviculture	silvicultură
sing	singular	singular
sl	slang	termen argotic
smb	somebody	cineva
smth	something	ceva
soc	sociology	sociologie
sp	sport	sport
subj	subjunctive	subjonctiv
sup	superlative	superlativ
tech	technical	termen tehnic
tele	telecommunication	telecomunicaţii
tex	textiles	industria textilă
thea	theatre	teatru
tv	television	televiziune
typ	typography	arta tipografică
usu	usually	de obicei
v	verb	verb
vet	veterinary medicine	medicină veterinară
vi	intransitive verb	verb intranzitiv
voc	vocative	vocativ
vr	reflexive verb	verb reflexiv
vt	transitive verb	verb tranzitiv
vul	vulgar	termen vulgar
zool	zoology	zoologie

ROMANIAN-ENGLISH DICTIONARY

A

a¹ *art def f* the; **maşin~** the car; *art poss* of; **~ casei** of the house.

a² *interj* a(h)! o(h)! (*foarte bine!*) (very) well, *coll* all right!, OK!.

abajur [aba'zhur] *nn* lamp shade/screen; (*de hârtie*) paper shade.

abandon [aban'don] *nn* abandonment; *jur* renunciation; *com* abandonment; *sp* withdrawal; *psych* abandon; (*renunţare*) giving up • **~a** *vt* (*a părăsi*) to quit; (*a renunţa la*) to give up; *mil* to abandon; (*drepturi, pretenţii*) to relinquish; (*un bolnav*) to give up ‖ *vi sp* to quit ‖ *vr* to neglect oneself; (*unui lucru*) to give oneself up to (smth); to become addicted to; to give way to.

abanos [aba'nos] *nm bot* ebony tree; (*lemn*) ebony; **de ~** ebony.

abataj [aba'tazh] *nn min* coal face; (*ca acţiune*) hewing; *silv* felling; (*sacrificare a vitelor*) slaughter; *naut* careening.

abate¹ [a'bate] *nm* abbot, Father Superior.

abate² [a'bate] *vt* (*din drum*) to turn off/aside/away; (*prin forţă*) to push/drive away; (*de la o linie dreaptă*) to deflect; *fig* (*a distrage*) to divert (from); (*prin sfat*) to dissuade (from); (*cu argumente*) to reason/talk smb out of; (*a doborî*) to knock/break down; *silv* to fell; *naut* to steer off ‖ *vr* (*a o lua în altă direcţie*) to go out of one's way.

abatere [a'batere] *nf* turning off/away; (*de la*) deviation (from); (*încălcare a legii*) violation; (*morală*) misdemeanor; (*de la regulă*) exception; (*greşeală, rătăcire*) aberrance; *tech* (*distanţă*) deviation; deflection.

abator [aba'tor] *nn* slaughterhouse, (*public*) abattoir; *fig* bloodshed.

abătut [abă'tut] *adj* (*deprimat*) depressed; *coll* out of sorts; (*descurajat*) dispirited; (*melancolic*) melancholy; gloomy; *coll* in the blues/dumps.

abces [ab'ches] *nn med* abscess, boil.

abdica [abdi'ka] *vi* to abdicate; (*a se retrage*) to retire, to resign • **~re** *nf* abdication, abdicating.

abdomen [abdo'men] *nn* abdomen, belly.

abecedar [abeche'dar] *nn* primer, spelling book.

aberant [abe'rant] *adj bio* deviant, abnormal, aberrant, aberrational; *gram* anomalous, wrong.

aberaţie [abe'ratsie] *nf astron, opt* (*deviere*) *also fig* aberration; *psych* insanity; (*absurditate*) fallacy, absurdity.

abia [a'bia] *adv* (*cu greutate*) hardly; (*nu tocmai*) not quite; (*d. cantitate*) scarcely; (*numai*) only, just; (*d. timp*) not later than.

abil [a'bil] *adj* (*îndemânatec*) skillful, able, capable; (*iute*) quick; (*deştept*) clever; (*uşor de mână*) handy, light-handed; (*cu experienţă*) versatile, experienced in; (*ager şi dibaci*) deft; (*fizic şi intelectual datorită educaţiei*) dexterous; (*capabil*) able, capable; competent, qualified; ingenious, resourceful; artistic; (*în sens negativ*) (*subtil*) subtle; sharp; *fam* smart; (*viclean*) sly, crafty, cunning.

abilitate [abili'tate] *nf* (*pricepere*) ability, skill; (*competenţă*) competence; (*iscusinţă*) cleverness; (*inventivitate*) ingenuity.

abis [a'bis] *nn* abyss; (*prăpastie*) *fig* chasm; (*văgăună*) ravine; (*râpă adâncă*) precipice; (*iad*) hell; (*mister*) mystery.

abject [ab'zhekt] *adj* (*netrebnic*) low, mean; abject,

vile; servile; (*josnic*) base; (*depravat*) depraved; (*infam*) infamous; foul; (*d. comportament*) despicable; **în mod ~** *adv* abjectly.

abjecţie [ab'zhektsie] *nf* (*ticăloşie*) abjection; (*înjosire*) degradation; humiliation.

abnegaţie [abne'gatsie] *nf* self-denial/-sacrifice, abnegation; **plin de ~** selfless, self-denying/sacrificing; **spirit de ~** spirit of abnegation, selflessness.

aboli [abo'li] *vt* to abolish; (*o lege*) to repeal.

abominabil [abomi'nabil] *adj* abominable; dreadful; dire; rank; (*dezgustător*) foul; (*oribil*) horrible; (*odios*) loathsome; (*d. crimă*) heinous; (*d. vreme*) filthy ‖ *adv* abominably, loathsomely, horribly, dreadfully.

abona [abo'na] *vt* (*pe cineva*) to take out a subscription for smb; *vr* to subscribe (to); (*la teatru*) to reserve seats • **~ment** *nn* (*la un ziar*) subscription; (*bilet la teatru*) season ticket; (*la autobuz*) bus pass; (*la tren*) commutation ticket; **cu ~** by subscription.

aborda [abor'da] *vt naut* (*a urca la bord; d. un vas*) to board; (*a se ciocni de*) to collide; *fig* (*pe cineva*) to approach; (*un subiect*) to broach; (*a începe*) to begin on/upon; (*a întreprinde*) to undertake; (*a se ocupa de*) to deal with ‖ *vi also naut* to land; *naut* (*a acosta*) to moor; to cast anchor.

abrevia [abrevi'a] *vt* (*un articol*) to cut down, to shorten; (*o formă gram.*) to contract.

abreviere [abrevi'ere] *nf* abbreviation; shortening; abridgement.

abroga [abro'ga] *vt jur* (*o lege*) to repeal; to abrogate ‖ *vr* to be abrogated/repealed • **~re** *nf jur* abrogation; repeal; reversal.

abrupt [ab'rupt] *adj* abrupt, steep; disjointed; (*d. stil*) harsh ‖ *adv* abruptly; (*brusc*) suddenly.

abrutiza [abruti'za] *vt* to brutalize; (*mintea sau simţirea*) to stupefy; (*mai ales prin băutură*) to besot ‖ *vr* to become brutalized; to become a brute/animal.

absent [ab'sent] *nm* absentee ‖ *adj* absent, missing; (*plecat*) away; (*omis*) omitted; (*pierdut*) lost, gone; *fig* absentminded; (*neatent*) inattentive; (*cufundat în gânduri*) wrapped up in thought; **a fi ~** to be absent; (*a nu fi acasă*) to be out ‖ *adv* absentmindedly; inattentively.

absenţă [ab'sentsă] *nf* (*lipsă la apel*) absence; non-attendance; *jur* default; (*lipsă, nevoie*) lack, shortage; (*neatenţie*) absence of mind.

absolut [abso'lut] *adj* absolute; perfect; complete; (*sigur*) sure, positive; (*afirmativ*) emphatic; (*nelimitat*) unlimited; (*liber*) unrestricted; (*autoritar*) imperative; strict, severe; pure; inalienable ‖ *adv* absolutely, utterly, totally; (*neapărat*) unfailingly; (*categoric*) positively ‖ *interj* absolutely!, to be sure!; **zero ~** *phys, chem* absolute zero • **~ul** *nn* the absolute.

absolvent [absol'vent] *nm* graduate.

absolvi [absol'vi] *vt* (*cursuri*) to finish; (*o şcoală*) to graduate from; *relig* (*de păcate*) to forgive; *jur* to acquit, to find/pronounce not guilty; *fig* to absolve; (*a ierta*) to forgive, to excuse.

absolvire [absol'vire] *nf* graduation; *jur* acquittal; *relig* absolution; *fig* release; (*de obligaţii, datorii*) exoneration; (*iertare*) forgiveness; **examen de ~** final examination.

absorbant [absor'bant] *nm* absorbent ‖ *adj* absorbent, absorptive; *fig* (*captivant*) absorbing, captivating.

absorbi [absor'bi] *vt* to absorb, to suck (in); (*a inhala*) to inhale; *fig* (*a fascina*) to fascinate; *fig* (*a-și insuși*) to drink in; *chem* (*gaz*) to occlude; *econ* (*d. o firmă*) to take over; *fam* to swallow up • ~**re** *nf* absorption, sucking in; *fig* engrossment.

absorbție [ab'sorbtsie] *nf* absorption; **circuit de** ~ (radio) absorption circuit; ~ **a unei firme** takeover.

abstinent [absti'nent] *nm* (*de la băutură*) abstainer, teetotal(l)er; *coll* water drinker; (*de la vot*) abstainer; (*sex*) chaste person || *adj* abstinent; (*de la mâncare și băutură*) abstemious; (*mai ales de la băutură*) temperate; (*sex*) continent, chaste.

abstinență [absti'nentsă] *nf* (*periodică*) abstinence, abstention; (*de durată*) abstemiousness; (*de la băutură*) temperance; (*sex*) continence; (*post*) fast(ing).

abstract [abs'trakt] *adj* abstract; abstract, ideal; remote; (*de neînțeles*) abstract, abstruse; (*teoretic*) general; (*artă*) non-representational || *nn* abstract(ness) || *adv* **în mod** ~ abstractly.

absurd [ab'surd] *nn* absurdity || *adj* absurd; irrational; (*contrar bunului simț sau naturii*) preposterous; (*stăpânit de o idee fixă*) infatuated; (*fără judecată*) unreasonable; (*fără noimă*) foolish, silly; (*ridicol*) ridiculous; (*ilogic*) illogical, incongruous || *adv* absurdly; (*stupid*) ineptly; (*prostesc*) nonsensically, foolishly; **prin** ~ against all reason, contrary to all reason • ~**itate** *nf* absurdity; irrationality; unreasonableness; foolishness; nonsense; incongruity; (*aberație*) fallacy; (*ca act*) foolish thing/notion; nonsense • ~**ul** *lit, phil* the absurd.

abține [ab'tsine] *vr* (*de la*) to abstain/to refrain from (doing smth); (*a refuza*) to decline; (*a-și stăpâni pasiunile*) to control/master one's passions; (*de la băutură*) to keep off.

abunda [abun'da] *vi* to abound; **a** ~ **în** to abound with, to teem/swarm/bristle with.

abundent [abun'dent] *adj* abundant, plentiful; (*îmbelșugat*) liberal; (*bogat*) rich; (*copios*) copious; (*luxuriant*) luxurious; (*amplu*) ample; (*implicând ideea de risipă*) lavish, profuse; (*d. mâncare*) hearty; (*d. păr*) shaggy || *adv* abundantly.

abundență [abun'dentsă] *nf* abundance, plenty; excess, plethora; (*creștere abundentă*) overgrowth; (*bogăție*) richness; (*în sens negativ*) lavishness; **în** ~ *adv* in abundance, plentifully.

abur ['abur] *nm* (*de apă*) steam; (*puternic mirositor sau nociv*) fumes; (*fum*) smoke; (*lichid sau solid vaporizant*) vapor; (*exhalare*) reek; (*ceață umedă*) damp; (*al pământului*) damp; (*suflu*) breath of air/wind, puff; (*răsuflare*) breath; *fig* (*nălucă*) mere phantom.

aburi [abu'ri] *vt* (*a expune la aburi*) to steam; (*a dezinfecta*) to fumigate; to exhale; to give out || *vr* (*a se acoperi cu aburi*) to steam up; *also fig* to mist; (*a se umezi*) to become damp; (*a deveni neclar*) to dim; (*a se înfierbânta*) to become heated; (*a se înroși la față*) to flush (up), to blush.

abuz [a'buz] *nn* abuse, excess; (*obicei rău*) corrupt practice; (*întrebuințare greșită*) misuse; (*maltratare*) mal/ill treatment; (*încălcare*) transgression; *jur* over-indulgence; (*înșelăciune*) deceit; fraud; ~ **de încredere** breach of trust.

abuza [abu'za] *vi* to abuse; (*a întrebuința greșit*) to misuse; **a** ~ **de** (*a înșela*) to deceive; (*a aduce prejudicii*) to encroach upon; to prejudice; (*cineva, ceva*) to take an unfair advantage of smb/smth; (*amabilitatea cuiva*) to intrude upon.

abuziv [abu'ziv] *adj* abusive, excessive || *adv* abusively, improperly; arbitrarily.

ac [ak] *nn* (*de cusut*) needle; (*cu gămălie, de cravată*) pin; (*de siguranță*) safety pin; (*de păr*) hair pin; *med* needle; *zool* (*de arici*) spine; (*de porc mistreț*) quill; *bot* (*frunză aciculară*) needle (leaf); (*ghimpe*) prickle; *ento* sting; (*țeapă*) *also fig* prick; (*de pick-up*) stylus; (*de ceasornic*) hand; *fig* (*stimulent*) spur; (*durere*) pang; (*împunsătură*) hit; (*al conștiinței*) prick; *rail* switches.

acacia [a'kachia] *nf bot* acacia.

acadea [aka'dea] *nf* lollipop; caramel.

academic [aka'demik] *adj* academic(al); *phylos* Academic; scholastic; **an** ~ academic year; *fig* **pictură** ~**ă** an academic style of painting || *adv* **în mod** ~ academically • ~**ian** *nm* academician, member of the Academy.

academie [akade'mie] *nf* Academy; *lit* Academe; ~ **de** **științe** Academy of Sciences; ~ **militară** Military Academy; ~ **navală** Naval College.

acalmie [akal'mie] *nf* (*d. mare*) calm at sea; (*d. sunet*) lull; (*pauză*) pause; (*răgaz*) respite; (*liniște*) quiet; (*armistițiu*) armistice, truce.

acapara [akapa'ra] *vt* to seize, to take hold of; **a** ~ **puterea** to seize power; *com* to buy up • ~**tor** *adj* monopolizing, possessive; (*lacom*) greedy; *fig* (*captivant*) absorbing || *nm com* monopolizer; monopolist; *pej* grabber; (*de alimente*) food hoarder.

acar [a'kar] *nm* (*cel care produce ace*) needle maker; *rail* switchman, pointsman.

acareturi [aka'returi] *nf pl* outhouses; extensions; (*d. lucruri*) chattels; *agr* (*unelte*) implements.

acasă [a'kasă] *adv* (*static*) at home; within, in(doors); (*spre casă*) home, homeward; **ca** ~ *adv* in a homely way.

accelera [akchele'ra] *vt* to accelerate; (*a grăbi*) (*d. pași*) to hasten; (*a iuți*), to speed up; (*a urgenta*) to expedite; (*votarea unei legi*) to rattle || *vi* (*d. puls*) to quicken; *auto* to step on the gas || *vr* to become faster • ~**re** *nf* speeding (up); acceleration; *econ* speed-up • ~**tor** *nn* *tech* accelerator; *auto* throttle || *adj* accelerating.

accent [ak'chent] *nn* accent; (*tonic*) stress; (*particularitate lingvistică*) pronunciation; (*ton*) tone (of voice); (*semn*) mark; *fig* focus, emphasis on • ~**ua** *vt* (*vocale*) to lay stress upon; (*cuvinte*) to emphasize; (*a marca prin accent grafic*) to mark with an accent; (*a sublinia*) to highlight; (*a întări*) to strengthen; (*a scoate în relief*) to point out || *vr* to become more conspicuous; (*se agrava*) to be(come) worse, to worsen; (*a spori*) to increase • ~**uat** *adj* (*d. vocale*) accented; (*d. cuvinte*) emphasized; *fig* stressed, underlined.

accept [ak'chept] *nn econ* (*poliță*) acceptance • ~**a** *vt* to accept; (*a primi*) to receive; (*a lua*) to take; (*o cerere, rugăminte; o ofertă*) to agree to; (*o provocare*) to take up; (*un sfat*) to take the advice; (*un pariu*) to hold; (*a adopta*) to adopt; (*a îmbrățișa*) to embrace; *jur* (*un proiect de lege*) to pass, to adopt || *vi* to agree, to acquiesce; *coll* to okay; **a** ~ **să** *vt* to accept that; (*a presupune*) to assume; *econ* to honor • ~**abil** *adj* acceptable; admissible; passable; satisfactory • ~**are** *nf* acceptance; (*tacită*) acquiescence

acces[1] [ak'ches] *nn* (*intrare*) access; (*contact*) accession; **cod de** ~ access code; **parolă de** ~ password.

acces² [ak'ches] *nn med (de boală)* attack, fit, stroke; *(brusc)* (sudden) seizure; *(de tuse)* coughing fit; *(brusc și violent)* outburst, fit; *(izbucnirea unei boli)* outbreak; *(revenire a bolii)* relapse; impulse.

accesare [akche'sare] *nf comp* accessing.

accesibil [akche'sibil] *adj* accessible (to), approachable; *(d. persoane)* easy to access; **greu** ~ difficult to access; *(d. locuri)* hard to reach, hard to get to; *(d. persoane)* unapproachable; **ușor** ~ easy to access; *(d. locuri)* easy to reach, easy to get to; **preț** ~ affordable price.

accesoriu [akche'soriu] *nn* accessory; appendage; *pl (dependințe)* outbuildings, premises; *pl (podoabe)* accessories; *(și de pescuit)* paraphernalia; *(de teatru)* props; *pl tech* appliances, gear ‖ *adj* accessory; incidental; *(secundar)* secondary, subsidiary.

accident [akchi'dent] *nn* accident; *(întâmplare nefericită)* mishap; *(întâmplare neprevăzută)* casual event; *(nenorocire)* misfortune; *(catastrofă)* casualty; *(dezastru)* disaster; *(pană)* breakdown; *(fenomen trecător)* happening; *med* unexpected symptom; *pl* accidence ‖ *nm mus* accidental • ~a *vt* to wound (in an/by accident); to hurt; *(d. o mașină)* to damage in an accident; *(d. peisaj, teren)* to give variety to ‖ *vi* to be hurt/wounded in an accident; to hurt oneself; to injure oneself • ~al *adj* accidental; *(neprevăzut)* casual, chance …; *(întâmplător)* incidental, random …; *(fortuit)* fortuitous; *(posibil)* contingent; med adventitious ‖ *adv* casually, accidentally; *(din întâmplare)* by (a mere) accident/chance; fortuitously

ace(e)a [a'cheea] *adj dem f* that; ~ **casă, casa aceea** that house; that … there ‖ *pron dem f* that; **ce este ~?** what's that?; *(subliniind comparația sau contrastul)* that one; ~ **este a ei** that one is hers; **de** ~ *adv* therefore, that is why, for that reason; *(în consecință)* consequently, accordingly; whereupon; **după** ~ next, then, afterwards.

aceasta [a'cheasta] *adj dem f* this; **cartea** ~ this book ‖ *pron dem f* this, that; it; *(acest fapt)* this fact; *(acest lucru)* this thing; this one; **pentru** ~ *adv* for this/it; *(pentru a face ~)* in order to do it; *(în acest scop)* for this purpose; *(din această cauză)* for this reason, that is why.

aceeași [a'cheeash] *adj dem f* the same, the very same; *(identică)* identical; ~ … **ca și**… the same … as … ‖ *pron dem f* the same (one).

acei [a'chei] *adj dem m pl* those; those … there; ~ **prieteni** those friends (there).

aceia [a'cheia] *adj dem m pl* those ‖ *pron* those (ones); ~ **care** those that/who.

aceiași [a'cheiash] *adj dem m pl* the same, the very same; identical ‖ *pron dem m pl* the same (ones).

acel [a'chel] *adj dem m* * **acela**.

acela [a'chela] *adj dem m* that, that … there; **omul** ~ that man (there) ‖ *pron dem m* that; ~ **care** he who, the one who.

același [a'chelash] *adj dem m* the same, the very same, the self-same; *(identic)* identical; *(înrudit cu)* akin to; *(asemănător cu)* similar to ‖ *pron dem m* the same (one).

acele [a'chele] *adj dem f* those

acelea [a'chelea] *adj dem f pl* those, those … there; **cărțile** ~ **sunt ale tale** those books (there) are yours ‖ *pron dem f pl* those (ones); ~ **care** those that/who.

aceleași [a'cheleash] *adj/pron dem f pl* the same (ones).

acest [a'chest] *adj dem m* this; ~ **perete** this wall • ~a *adj dem m* this, that, this … here ‖ *pron dem m* this, this one; ~ **din urmă** the latter; he.

aceste [a'cheste] *adj dem f pl* these.

acestea [a'chestea] *adj dem f pl* these, those, these … here; **toate** ~ all this; *(în prezent)* nowadays; *(în trecut)* the other day, a few days ago; *(în viitor)* the next day ‖ *pron dem f pl* these ones; ~ **din urmă** the latter; **cu toate** ~ *adv* however, yet, nevertheless; *(în ciuda acelor lucruri)* in spite of all this.

acești [a'cheshti] *adj dem m pl* these.

aceștia [a'cheshtia] *adj dem m pl* these, those, these … here ‖ *pron dem m pl* these (ones); ~ **din urmă** the latter; *(ei)* they.

achita [aki'ta] *vt (pe cineva de o obligație)* to release smb from; *jur* to acquit (of); *(mai ales d. un judecător de instrucție)* to discharge; to exonerate from; *com (a termina de plătit)* to pay off ‖ *vr (de o îndatorire)* to acquit oneself of (a duty), to do one's duty; *(a îndeplini)* to fulfill ‖ *vi* to pay off; *(a plăti)* to pay • ~re *nf (plată)* payment; *(a unei datorii)* discharge of; *jur* acquittal; *(de către jurați)* deliverance.

achizitor [akizi'tor] *nm* acquirer; buyer, purchaser; collector.

achiziție [aki'zitsie] *nf (descoperire)* finding, discovery; *(acțiune)* (prin efort, mai ales d. ceva folositor) acquisition; purchase; *(lucru dobândit)* acquirement.

achiziționa [akizitsio'na] *vt (prin efort)* to acquire (by purchase); *(a cumpăra)* to buy, to purchase; *(a obține)* to obtain, to get; *(a ~ ceva dificil de obținut)* to secure; *(a aduna)* to collect, to gather.

aci [a'chi] *adv* * **aici**.

acid [a'chid] *nm/adj* acid ‖ *adj* acidic; *(acru)* sour; *fig (d. o persoană)* witty; ~ **dezoxyribonucleic** *chem* deoxyribonucleic acid.

aciua [achu'a] *vr* to take cover/shelter; *(a se ascunde)* to hide (oneself); *(a căuta adăpost)* to seek shelter; *(a se odihni)* to rest (oneself); *(a găzdui)* to harbor, to put up.

aclama [akla'ma] *vt (o persoană, un discurs)* to acclaim, to cheer; to hail ‖ *vi* to cheer, to welcome • ~ție *nf* cheering, ovation.

aclimatiza [aklimati'za] *vt* to acclimate, to acclimatize to; *(a deprinde)* to inure ‖ *vr bot* to acclimate, to acclimatize; *fig (d. oameni)* to accustom oneself to new surroundings • ~re *nf* acclimation, acclimatization.

acnee [ak'nee] *nf med* acne.

acoladă [ako'ladă] *nf typ* brace; *hist, mus, archit* accolade.

acolo [a'kolo] *adv* there, over there; *(în locul acela)* at that place; *lit obs* yonder; *(într~)* there, to that place; **de** ~ *adj* of that place, from there ‖ *adv (din locul acela)* from/of/in that place; **pe** ~ *adv (loc)* there, thereabouts; in those parts; *(direcție)* that way.

acomoda [akomo'da] *vr (cu)* to adjust/accommodate oneself to, to adapt oneself to ‖ *vt* to accommodate, to adapt.

acompania [akompani'a] *vt (a însoți)* to accompany smb; *(o doamnă)* to escort; *(o domnișoară în societate)* obs to chaperon ‖ *vi* to accompany • ~ment *nn (companie)* accompaniment, escorting.

acont [a'kont] *nn (avans)* advance (money); *(arvună)* earnest money; *(plată parțială)* payment on account, part(ial) payment; (*rată*) down/cash payment • **~a** *vt* to pay an installment on; (*a arvuni*) to pay earnest money for

acoperi [akope'ri] *vt* to cover; (*a înveli*) to cover/wrap up; (*pe cineva cu corpul, pt. a proteja*) to shield smb with one's body; (*cu un strat exterior*) to coat; (*în parte*) to overlap; (*cu un capac*) to put a lid on; (*cu o plapumă*) to cover with a blanket; (*cu aur*) to gild; (*cu argint*) to silver; (*cu fier*) to iron; (*cu vopsea*) to paint; (*cu pete*) to spot; (*cu lac*) to varnish; (*cu iarbă*) to cover with turf/sod; (*cu paie*) to cover with straw; (*cu pământ*) to cover with earth; (*cu un îngrăşământ*) to spread manure; (*a îmbrăca*) to dress; (*a împodobi*) to (be)deck; (*a răspândi peste*) to spread over; to scatter over; (*a presăra*) to strew over; *com* to pay off; (*a adăposti*) to shelter; (*a ascunde ceva*) *fig* to hide, to conceal; (*pe cineva*) to harbor; (*a masca*) to mask; (*a pune bine*) to secure; (*a tăinui*) to keep something (a) secret; *lit* to shroud in mystery; *frml* to draw a veil over; (*prin tăcere*) to hush up; (*a ţine ascuns*) to keep concealed; to shroud; (*sub false aparenţe*) to disguise; (*a ascunde privirii*) to screen (from your sight); *mil* to protect; *sp* (*a bloca*) to cover a player; (*a parcurge o distanţă*) to cover a distance • **~re** *nf* covering * **acoperi**; *fig* protection; *fin* reimbursement, remittance; security; *mil* cover; *astron* obfuscation.

acoperiş [akope'rish] *nn* roof; (*mic*) small roof; *fig* lid; (*umbrar*) canopy; (*capotă*) hood.

acord [a'kord] *nn* (*înţelegere*) agreement; (*aranjament*) arrangement; contract; (*unitate*) unity; (*armonie*) harmony, congeniality; (*unanimitate*) accord, union; (*potrivire*) consistency, congruity; (*conformitate*) conformity; (*coincidenţă*) coincidence; (*solidaritate*) solidarity, concordance; (*mai ales d. planuri*) concurrence; *mus* chord; (*armonie*) concord; *pl* (*sunete plăcute*) strains; *rad* tuning; **de ~!** agreed!, granted!, all right!, fair enough!; (*ne-am înţeles*) it's a deal!; **de/în ~ cu** in accordance with, in keeping/conformity with; **a fi de ~ cu** (*ceva*) to agree to smth; (*cineva*) to agree with smb.

acorda [akor'da] *vt* (*a da*) to give, to grant, to confer; (*a binevoi să dea*) to vouchsafe; (*a ataşa*) to attach; (*a permite*) to allow; (*drepturi şi privilegii*) to license; *mus*, *rad* to tune; (*un instrument*) to tune an instrument; *fig* (*a armoniza*) to harmonize; (*a pune de acord*) to bring into accord; (*a face să se potrivească*) to fit; to make agree ‖ *vr mus* to be in tune, to harmonize; *fig* (*a se potrivi*) to agree; (*a fi în acord*) to be in accord • **~re** *nf* granting; *mus* tuning; adjustment.

acordeon [akorde'on] *nm* accordion • **~ist** *nm* accordion/concertina player, accordionist.

acordor [akor'dor] *nm mus* tuner ‖ *nn* tuning key/ hammer; tuning cone.

acosta [akos'ta] *vt* (*pe cineva*) to come up to smb, to accost; to stop; *naut* to dock, to moor; to board; to dock (in space) ‖ *vi* to accost; to land.

acredita [akredi'ta] *vt* to accredit; (*a da crezare*) to believe; to give credit to smb; (*a împuternici*) to authorize ‖ *vr* to get accredited • **~re** *nf* accreditation; *com* opening of a credit line; (*crezare*) credit, credibility • **scrisori de ~re** letters of accreditation, credentials; *com* letters of credit.

acreditiv [akredi'tiv] *nn com* letter of credit; (*împuternicire*) *pol* credentials; *jur* power of attorney.

acri [a'kri] *vt* to make sour; (*puţin, pentru a da gust*) to flavor with an acid ‖ *vr* to get/turn/go sour, to sour; (*d. lapte*) to curdle, to turn sour; *fig* **a i se ~ de** to be fed up with.

acrobat [akro'bat] *nm* acrobat, rope dancer.

acrobaţie [akroba'tsie] *nf* acrobatics.

acroşa [akro'sha] *vt tech* (*a agăţa*) to hang up/on; (*un vehicul*) to couple/hitch on (to); (*a lovi*) to hit; *naut* to grapple; (*a prinde*) to hold ‖ *vr* **a se ~ de** to cling/fasten to.

acru[1] ['akru] *nm* acre (0.4 ha)

acru[2] ['akru] *adj* sour, acid; (*tăios*) (*d. miros*) acrid; sharp; (*ca oţetul*) vinegar(ish); *chem* acetous; (*acrişor*) acidulous; (*necopt*) unripe, green; *fig* (*supărăcios*) sulky, sour; *fig* (*greu*) painful; (*amar*) bitter, pungent ‖ *adv* sourly, morosely.

act [akt] *nn* (*faptă*) act, action; *jur* (*oficial*) document, deed; *pl* judicial acts; *edu*, *jur* records; (*teatru*) act.

activ [ak'tiv] *adj* active; (*harnic*) diligent; (*energic, vioi*) brisk; (*ocupat*) busy; (*operativ*) efficient; potent; (*în funcţie*) acting; *com* due; *pl* assets; credit (account) ‖ *nn pol* the most active members ‖ *adv* actively • **~ist** *nm* activist; militant • **~itate** *nf* activity; (*acţiune*) action; (*lucru, muncă*) work; (*funcţie*) job, function; (*mişcare*) movement; (*treabă*) business; (*eficacitate*) potency; briskness; **în ~** in activity, in progress; (*d. oameni*) working, employed; *mil* on active service/duty.

actor [ak'tor] *nm* actor, player; (*într-un eveniment*) participant.

actriţă [ak'tritsă] *nf* actress; (*de tragedie*) tragedienne.

actual [aktu'al] *adj* (*de acum*) present(-day), existing; contemporary; today; current; modern; (*interesant*) topical • **~itate** *nf* reality; (*stare actuală*) present/ actual state; present (time); (*interes actual*) present interest; (*moda zilei*) fashion of the day/hour; (*eveniment al zilei*) event of the day; (*eveniment actual*) question of the day/of the moment; (*conformitate cu timpul*) up-to-dateness; **de ~** (*al zilei*) of the day; (*de interes*) of present interest; (*adaptat la ~*) coll up-to-date; opportune; (*arzător*) burning, urgent.

acţiona [aktsio'na] *vi* to act, to take action; (*a lucra*) to work; (*a opera*) to operate ‖ *vt tech* to drive, to operate, to run; to set smth in motion/action.

acţionar [aktsio'nar] *nm com* (important) stockholder; shareholder.

acţiune [aktsi'une] *nf* action; (*activitate*) activity; act; (*curajoasă*) feat; (*faptă*) deed, exploit; (*procedeu*) proceeding(s); (*efect asupra*) action/effect on/influence over smth/smb; *liter* (*într-un roman*) story, plot; *jur* law-suit, trial; *com* share; *pl* stock; **în ~** in action; *tech* in gear.

acuarelă [akua'relă] *nf* (*pictură*) aquarelle, watercolor(s); (*vopsea*) watercolor.

acum(a) [a'kum(a)] *adv* now; at present, at this time; (*în zilele noastre*) nowadays; (*astăzi*) today; (*în această clipă*) at this moment; (*adineaori*) just now, a little while ago; (*atunci*) then, that moment; (*în urmă*) ago; (*la rând, după aceasta*) next; (*îndată*) at once, just/right now; (*curând*) soon; **de ~ înainte/ încolo** from now on, henceforward; (*d. un punct de plecare în trecut*) ever since (then), thence(forward); **până ~** till/until now, up to now; **ca ~** (*aşa cum e ~*)

as it is now; (*de parcă ar fi ~*) as if it were now; (*în mod viu*) vividly; (*clar*) clearly.

acumula [akumu'la] *vt* to accumulate; (*în secret*) to hoard up; (*a îngrămădi*) to pile/heap up; (*d. bani*) to amass; (*rezerve*) to pile up; (*d. dobândă*) to accrue; (*a aduna*) to gather up; (*a înmagazina*) to store; (*a spori*) to increase || *vr* to accumulate, to (be) heap(ed) up; (*a se aduna*) to gather up; (*a spori*) to increase.

acumulator [akumula'tor] *nn elec* accumulator, storage battery.

acupla [aku'pla] *vt* to join * **cupla**; (*a împerechea*) to couple, to pair (off with) || *vr* (*a se împerechea*) to mate; to couple, to copulate.

acupunctură [akupunk'turǎ] *nf med* acupuncture.

acuratețe [akura'tetse] *nf* accuracy, precision; exactitude; exactness; **cu** ~ *adv* accurately.

acustic [a'kustik] *adj* acoustic; **izolat** ~ sound-proof.

acut [a'kut] *adj* (*ascuțit, pătrunzător*) (*d. sunet*) acute, sharp; (*d. simțuri*) keen; (*d. curiozitate*) intense; (*d. gelozie*) bitter || *adv* acutely.

acuza [aku'za] *vt* (*ceva*) to blame it on smth; (*de*) to accuse (of); (*a învinovăți*) to charge (with); (*a imputa*) to impute (with); (*a reproșa*) to reproach (with); to blame (for); (*un funcționar, de abuz în serviciu*) to impeach; *jur* to prosecute, to sue; *med, also fig* to indicate, to manifest || *vi* to accuse || *vr* to accuse/blame oneself; (*reciproc*) to accuse/blame each other.

acuzare [aku'zare] *v* * **acuza** || *nf* accusing; accusation; *jur* (*învinuire*) charge; (*vină*) guilt; (*inculpare*) inculpation; (*pt. diverse vini*) indictment; (*de abuz în serviciu*) impeachment; (*penală*) arraignment; (*procuror*) the prosecution, prosecutor; **act de** ~ bill of indictment; **cap de** ~ count of (an) indictment.

acuzativ [akuza'tiv] *nn gram* accusative (case).

acvariu [ak'variu] *nn* aquarium; (*de mici dimensiuni*) fish bowl.

acvatic [ak'vatik] *adj* aquatic, water ….

acvilin [akvi'lin] *adj* aquiline; **nas** ~ Roman nose.

adaos [a'daos] *nn* addition, (*spor, creștere*) increase, rise; (*supliment*) supplement; (*mărire*) enlargement; (*plus*) extra; (*completare*) enclosure (with a letter); (*atașare*) attachment; (*urmare*) sequel; (*interpolare*) interpolation; (*la metale*) alloy; (*anexă*) appendage, extension; (*accesoriu*) accessory; amendment; (*la o lucrare, carte, lege*) addendum, addenda; appendix; (*la o scrisoare*) postscript; (*la o lege, un document*) rider; (*la un testament*) codicil; (*la o poliță*) slip.

adapta [adap'ta] *vt* (*la*) to adapt (to/for); (*a face să coincidă*) to tally; (*a ajusta*) to fit, to set (to); to conform (to); (*timpului, împrejurărilor*) to time (to); (*a acomoda*) to accommodate (to); (*a potrivi*) to fit (to); *telec* to match; to acclimat(iz)e; (*pt. scenă*) to adapt for the stage; (*a deprinde*) to accustom to || *vr* (*la*) to adapt oneself (to); to adjust oneself to; (*timpului*) to conform oneself.

adăpa [adǎ'pa] *vt* (*vite*) to water; (*oameni*) *rare pej* to give smb to drink; (*a uda*) to wet || *vr* (*d. vite*) to drink; (*a bea lacom*) to swill.

adăpost [adǎ'post] *nn* shelter, refuge; *fig* shroud; (*loc sigur*) safe place; (*refugiu*) safe harbor; (*loc retras*) recess; *mil* dug-out; (*al șoferilor de taxi*) rest; (*locuință*) house, lodging(s); (*cămin*) home; (*azil*) asylum; sanctuary; *fig* (*protecție*) protection; (*scut*) shield; (*sprijin*) support; (*acoperire*) cover, screen; **fără** ~ homeless; **la** ~ safe, sheltered • **~i** *vt* to shel-

ter, to harbor; (*a găzdui*) to take in, to accommodate; *mil* (*a încartirui*) to quarter; (*a ascunde*) to hide; (*a apăra*) to protect; (*a înmagazina*) to store; (*a duce într-un loc sigur*) to take to a safe place; (*a păzi*) to safeguard || *vr* (*a căuta adăpost*) to shelter oneself, to seek (a) shelter; (*a găsi adăpost*) to find refuge/shelter; (*a găsi protecție*) to find protection; (*a se ascunde*) to hide oneself.

adăuga [adǎu'ga] *vt* to add; (*a mări*) to enlarge; (*a spori*) to increase; (*a amplifica*) to amplify; to magnify; (*a anexa, a alătura*) to annex, to append to; to include; to enclose; to complete, to fill up; (*a atașa*) to attach; (*a însera*) to insert; to introduce; to interpolate; *math* to add || *vr* to be added/joined; (*d. dobândă*) to accrue || *vi* to add.

adânc [a'dânk] *adj* deep; (*jos*) low; *esp fig* profound; dense, thick; (*înțelept*) wise; (*mare*) great; (*serios, complet*) thorough(going); (*tainic*) secret; (*misterios*) mysterious; obscure || *adv* deeply; (*jos*) lowly; (*extrem de*) profoundly, deeply; (*cu înțelepciune*) wisely; (*departe*) far (away) || *nn* (*adâncime*) depth; (*fund*) bottom; (*apă adâncă*) *obs* deep water(s), ocean.

adânci [adân'chi] *vt* to deepen, to make deeper; (*a scobi*) to hollow (out); (*a săpa*) to dig; (*a face o gaură*) to make a hole; *tech* to ream; (*prin spălare, d. ape*) to wash away; (*a eroda, d. ape*) to wear away; (*a extinde*) to extend; (*a lărgi*) to widen; (*cu dalta*) to scoop out with a gouge; *archit* to groove; *fig* (*a lărgi*) to widen; (*a extinde*) to extend; (*a îmbunătăți*) to improve; (*a spori*) to increase; (*a intensifica*) to intensify; *fig* (*a sonda*) to sound, to fathom; to examine; (*a (s)cufunda*) to sink, to immerse; *fig* to go deeply/thoroughly into, * **aprofunda**; (*a înrăutăți*) to worsen; to further || *vr* to deepen, to grow/become deeper; (*a intra adânc*) to go deep(er); (*a se afunda, d. construcții*) to subside; (*a se (s)cufunda*) to sink (low); (*a se duce la fund*) to go to the bottom; *fig* to be(come) absorbed/engrossed; to plunge • **~me** *nf* depth; *frml, fig* profoundness, profundity; (*lățime*) width, breadth; (*înălțime*) height; (*lungime*) length; (*distanță*) distance; (*fund*) bottom; (*prăpastie*) abyss; (*ungher tăinuit*) (innermost) recess; interior, inside; (*pătrundere*) insight; (*cuprindere*) scope; (*înțelepciune*) wisdom; *fig* intensity; (*putere*) power, force.

addenda [a'denda] *nf pl* addenda, *sg* addendum

adecvat [adek'vat] *adj* adequate, suitable || *adv* adequately, suitably.

ademeni [ademe'ni] *vt* (*a ispiti*) to tempt, to entice; to seduce; (*a amăgi*) to delude; (*a înșela*) to beguile; (*a momi*) to lure; (*a prinde în cursă*) to ensnare; (*cu vorba*) to cajole smb into; (*prin lingușire*) to coax; (*a corupe*) to corrupt; (*a fascina*) to fascinate; (*a duce pe căi greșite*) to lead astray.

adept [a'dept] *nm* follower, supporter; adherent; *pej* hanger-on; (*al unei doctrine*) proponent; (*subliniind dependența*) dependant; (*al unui maestro*) *also relig* disciple; partisan; (*zelos*) zealot; (*prozelit*) proselyte; (*inițiat*) initiate; (*închinător*) votary, worshipper.

adera [ade'ra] *vi* to adhere; (*a fi pentru*) to side with (smb); (*a se înscrie*) to join; (*a intra în*) to enter; (*a trece de partea*) to go over to the side of; to adopt; (*a consimți la*) to consent/agree to; (*a aproba*) to endorse an opinion; (*a îmbrățișa*) to espouse, to

embrace; to cling || ~**re** *nf* adhesion, adhering; *
adera; consent, assent; agreement.

aderent [ade'rent] *adj* (*care se lipește*) adhesive; (*la*)
adherent, adhering to || *nm* adherent; follower; *
adept.

aderență [ade'rentsă] *nf med, tech* adherence; *tech*
(*lipire*) adhesiveness; *metal* linkage; *math* closure;
fig adhesion.

ades(ea), adeseori [a'desea, a'deseori] *adv* often; *lit*
oft; (*de multe ori*) many times; *lit* many a time; time
and again; (*repetat*) repeatedly; (*frecvent*) frequently; (*de cele mai multe ori*) more often than not.

adevăr [ade'văr] *nn* truth; (*conformitate cu adevărul*)
verisimilitude; (*fapt*) fact; (*realitate*) reality; (*veraci-
tate*) veracity, truthfulness; (*sinceritate*) sincerity;
axiom; (~ *banal*) truism || *adv* (*cu adevărat*) indeed,
actually, really; (*în realitate*) in reality; (*de fapt*) in
fact, as a matter of fact • ~**ul adevărat** the plain/
honest truth.

adevărat [adevă'rat] *adj* true; (*veritabil*) genuine;
(*sigur*) certain; (*bun*) good; (*garantat*) warranted;
original; natural; authentic; pure; (*legitim*) legitimate; (*incontestabil*) undeniable; (*conform cu reali-
tatea*) true to fact; real; (*drept, just*) right; (*pozitiv*)
positive; (*cum se cuvine*) proper, right; correct;
(*fidel*) faithful; sincere, frank; (*veridic*) truthful || *adv*
(*sincer*) frankly, sincerely, openly; (*cinstit*) honestly;
(*în realitate*) in truth/reality; (*cu ~*) really, actually;
certainly; (*în mod pozitiv*) positively || *interj* in
truth!, honestly!, that's right! || *inter* really?, is it
true?, do you really mean it?.

adeveri [adeve'ri] *vt* to confirm, to bear out; (*a confirma adevărul*) to ascertain the truth of; (*a întări*) to
corroborate, to prove; (*prin jurământ*) to declare on
oath; (*prin sigiliu*) to seal; (*a atesta*) to (at)test, to
testify; (*a verifica*) to verify; (*a garanta*) to vouch,
to warrant; (*a depune mărturie*) to bear witness; (*a
recunoaște*) to acknowledge; (*a dovedi*) to prove; (*a
motiva suficient*) to substantiate; (*a demonstra*) to
demonstrate || *vr* to prove (to be) true/correct, to hold
true; (*a se realiza*) to come true • ~**nță** *nf* (*de primire*)
receipt, voucher; (*recipisă de depunerea mărfurilor*)
warrant; (*certificat medical*) doctor's certificate;
(*atestat*) attestation; testimonial, certificate; (*cupon*)
counterfoil.

adeziune [adezi'une] *nf phys* adhesion.

adeziv [ade'ziv] *adj/nm* adhesive.

adia [adi'a] *vi* (*d. vânt*) to blow/breeze; (*a flutura*) to
float, to flutter; (*a se mișca*) to move about; (*a foșni*)
to rustle.

adiacent [adia'chent] *adj* (*apropiat, fără a fi în contact*)
adjacent; (*atingându-se într-un loc*) adjoining,
contiguous.

adică [a'dikă] *adv* (*va să zică*) that is to say; (*anume*)
namely; (*ca să spunem așa*) as it were; (*propriu zis*)
properly speaking; (*cu alte cuvinte*) in other words;
(*pe scurt*) in short; (*în texte*) viz., i.e., id est; (*în sens
strict*) strictly speaking; (*exprimat în timpul unei re-
flecții*) … now that is …, well …

adiere [adi'ere] *nf* breath/gust/puff of wind; *lit* gale.

adineaorea, adineaori, adineauri [adi'neaorea,
adi'neaori, adi'neauri] *adv* (*și mai ~*) a little while
ago; (*chiar acum*) just now; (*nu cu mult în urmă*) not
long ago, only just now.

adio [a'dio] *interj* good-bye!, farewell!, adieu! || *nn*

good-bye, farewell, adieu; **a-și lua ~ de la ceva** to
give smth up for lost; *coll* to kiss smth good-bye; (*de
la cineva*) to bid/wish smb good-bye.

aditiv [adi'tiv] *nn chem* additive.

adițional [aditsio'nal] *adj* additional; further; (*suplimentar*) supplementary; (*secundar*) secondary, subordinate.

adjectiv [adzhek'tiv] *nn gram* adjective.

adjudeca [adzhude'ka] *vt jur* to adjudicate, to adjudge;
to confer (on); (*un premiu*) to award (on) || *vr* to be
adjudged (to).

adjunct [ad'zhunkt] *adj* deputy; assistant; adjunct || *nm*
deputy; assistant; adjunct.

administra [admini'stra] *vt* (*a avea grijă de*) to look
after; (*a conduce*) to manage, to administer; (*a gu-
verna*) to govern; (*a avea în grijă să*) to be in charge
of; (*a da, doctorie etc*) to give, to administer • ~**re** *nf*
administration, management • ~**tor** *nm* administrator;
manager, director; trustee; (*supraveghetor*) superintendent; (*al unui spital*) governor; warden; (*al unor
bunuri disputate*) receiver; (*vechil de moșie*) bailiff;
(*într-un colegiu, club*) steward • ~**ție** *nf* (*conducere*)
administration, management; (*direcție*) direction;
(*supraveghere; inspectorat*) superintendence;
(*sarcină, însărcinare*) charge; (*guvernare*) government; *mil* commissariat; (*clădire, birou*) office(s);
consiliu de ~ council board, board of administration;
(*la un teatru*) managing board of a theater; (*la o societate pe acțiuni*) board of directors/trustees.

admira [admi'ra] *vt* to admire; (*pe cineva*) *fig* to look
up to smb; to respect, to revere; (*a venera*) to vener-
ate; (*a prețui*) to praise || *vr* to admire oneself; (*reci-
proc*) to admire each other • ~**bil** *adj* admirable;
excellent; splendid; *coll* great; (*minunat*) wonderful;
lit wondrous; (*neîntrecut*) matchless; *lit* peerless ||
adv admirably || *interj* (*și ironic*) that's wonderful!,
that's splendid!; *coll* great! • ~**ție** *nf* admiration;
(*prețuire*) appreciation, reverence; veneration.

admite [ad'mite] *vt* to admit; to permit; (*a încuviința*)
to allow; (*a îngădui*) to admit of; (*ceva inevitabil*) to
tolerate; (*a aproba*) to approve of; (*a fi de acord cu*)
to agree/consent to; (*în mod public sau deschis*) to
acknowledge; (*păcate*) to confess; (*a concede, a
mărturisi*) to own; (*a primi*) to receive; to adopt; to
accept; (*a lăsa*) to let, to leave; (*a catadicsi*) to
vouchsafe; (*a lăsa să intre*) also *fig* to let in, to
admit; *edu* (*a introduce în*) to matriculate; (*a numi*)
to appoint; (*a conține*) to contain, to hold || *vr* to be
allowed/permitted/admitted.

admonesta [admone'sta] *vt* to admonish, to scold;
(*oficial*) to reprimand.

adnota [adno'ta] *vt* (*o carte*) to annotate; (*un text*) to
comment upon.

adolescent [adoles'chent] *nm* teenager, adolescent; (*im-
berb*) beardless youth; *pej* stripling; (*tânăr*) youth.

adolescență [adoles'chentsă] *nf* adolescence, teens;
(*tinerețe*) youth, youthful age.

adopta [adop'ta] *vt jur* to adopt; *fig* (*a îmbrățișa*) to
embrace, to espouse; (*a lua*) to take; (*a alege*) to
choose; to assume, to put on; (*a-și însuși*) to endorse; (*a imita*) to imitate; (*a primi*) to receive.

adoptiv [adop'tiv] *adj* adoptive; **copil ~** adoptive/foster
child; **tată ~** adoptive/foster father; **familie/mamă
~ă** adoptive/foster family/mother.

adopți(un)e [adoptsi'une] *nf jur* adoption.

adora [ado'ra] *vt also fig* to worship, to adore; (*a preamări*) to glorify; to exalt; (*a idolatriza*) to worship; *lit* to love fervently; *coll* to be crazy/mad about; (*a venera*) to revere; (*un star*) to idolize • ~**bil** *adj* adorable, worshipful; (*admirabil*) admirable; (*încântător*) delightful, charming; (*minunat*) wonderful, lovely; (*demn de a fi iubit*) loveable; (*ales*) exquisite.

adormi [ador'mi] *vt* to send to sleep, to put to bed/sleep; (*prin citit*) to read to sleep; (*prin cântec*) to sing to sleep; (*prin hipnoză*) to hypnotize; (*a potoli*) to assuage; (*a micșora*) to lessen; (*a amorți*) to benumb; *fig* (*a înșela*) to cheat; (*prin promisiuni*) to deceive with fine promises; (*a lega la ochi*) to hoodwink; *fig* (*a plictisi*) to send to sleep, to bore || *vi* to fall asleep, to go to sleep; (*a ațipi*) to doze off; to nod off; *fig lit* (*a se stinge*) to die out/away; *fig* (*a amorți*) to get benumbed; *fig* (*a muri*) to die, to pass away • ~**re** *nf* falling asleep, * **adormi**; *relig* death; *jur* demise, passing away.

adrenalină [adrena'lină] *nf chem, bio* adrenalin.

adresa [adre'sa] *vt* (*o scrisoare*) to address, to direct; (*a pune adresa pe*) to put/write the address on; (*mărfuri*) to forward, to consign; (*a exprima*) to express; *frml* to voice; (*a prezenta*) to present || *vr* **a se ~** to address oneself to; to address smb; (*pt. a cere ceva*) to apply to; (*a apela la*) to appeal to; (*a recurge la*) to resort to; (*a se întoarce către*) to turn back to; (*a vorbi cu*) to speak to; (*a informa*) to inform.

adresă [a'dresă] *nf* (*loc*) address, domicile; (*destinație*) destination; (*pe plic*) direction; (*comunicare*) communication; **pe** ~ to the address of; (*prin grija*) care of, under cover of; **la** ~ **lui** (*împotriva lui*) against him; (*pe socoteala lui*) on his behalf; (*d. el*) about him; (*la domiciliul lui*) at his residence/house/home.

aduce [a'duche] *vt* to bring; (*a se duce să aducă*) to fetch; (*a trimite după*) to send for; (*a duce*) to carry, to take; to transport; (*a produce, a da*) to bring in, to yield; (*a rodi*) to bear; (*a procura*) to get; (*a furniza*) to furnish, to supply; (*a oferi*) to offer; (*a cauza*) to bring about; (*a implica*) to involve; (*a însoți, a conduce*) to accompany; (*a strânge*) to gather, to collect; (*a îndoi*) to bend || *vi* **a ~ cu** to be like, to look like.

adula [adu'la] *vt* to fawn upon, to worship; (*a linguși*) to flatter; (*a lăuda exagerat*) to cajole.

adulmeca [adulme'ka] *vt* (*a lua urma*) to follow the scent of, to trail; (*a mirosi*) *also fig* to sniff, to scent; *fig* to smell; (*a bănui*) to sense, to suspect; (*a simți*) to feel; (*a ghici*) to guess; (*a observa*) to notice; (*a da de urmă*) to trace; (*a presimți*) to foresee.

adult [a'dult] *adj* grown(-up), adult; (*major*) full-aged || *nm* grown(-up) person/man, grown-up, adult.

adulter [adul'ter] *adj* adulterous || *nm* (*persoană*) adulterer || *nn* (*acțiune*) adultery; adulterous intercourse/relationship.

adumbri [adum'bri] *vt* (*a umbri*) to shade; (*a întuneca, a arunca umbră asupra*) to overshadow; *fig* to obscure, to cast aspersions (up)on || *vr* to sit in the shade.

aduna [adu'na] *vt* (*a strânge într-un tot*) to bring/get/draw together; (*la un loc*) to bring together; (*a strânge ceva împrăștiat*) to gather (up); (*grămadă*) to heap/lay up; (*în secret, cu grijă*) to hoard; (*a reuni*) to assemble; (*a colecta/colecționa*) to collect; (*în vederea unei acțiuni comune*) to rally, to muster; (*d. informații*) to glean; (*a mări, a spori*) to amass; (*d. bani sau obiecte*) to store up; (*a recolta*) to har-

vest, *also fig* to reap; (*de jos*) to take/pick up; (*prin colectă*) to collect money/subscriptions; (*impozite*) to levy/collect taxes/money; (*fonduri*) to raise funds; *math* to add || *vr* to assemble, to congregate; (*a se înghesui*) to huddle (up); (*a se însoți cu*) to associate with; (*pt. o trecere în revistă*) *mil* to muster || *vi math* to add • ~**re** *nf* gathering; (*mulțime*) multitude; crowd; (*grup de persoane*) gathering, *also mil* assembly; (*întrunire*) meeting, rally; (*științifică*) conference, congress; (*politică*) convention; *relig* (*conclav*) conclave; (*grup de credincioși*) congregation; (*grămadă*) pile, mass; (*mănunchi*) cluster, bunch; (*colecție*) collection; (*acumulare*) accumulation; *math* addition; (*agregat*) aggregate.

adunătură [adună'tură] *nf* (*mulțime*) crowd, multitude; *pej* mob, riff-raff; (*grup*) group; (*ceată*) troop; *pej* gang; (*adunare*) gathering; (*grămadă*) heap, pile; (*amestecătură*) mixture, medley; *coll* hodge-podge; (*vechituri*) lumber.

adverb [ad'verb] *nn* adverb.

advers [ad'vers] *adj* contrary, adverse, opposite, counter.

adversar [adver'sar] *nm* adversary; (*de idei*) opponent; (*într-o dispută*) disputant; (*în luptă*) antagonist; (*prea puternic*) overmatch; (*atacator*) assailant; (*dușman*) enemy, foe; *jur* counterpart(y); rival.

aer ['aer] *nn* air; look, aspect; (*răsuflare*) breath; (*înfățișare*) appearance; (*prezență*) presence; (*poză*) pose; (*ținută*) carriage, posture; (*maniere*) manner, ways; (*mină*) countenance; *lit* mien; (*asemănare*) likeness, resemblance; (*instalație*) air conditioning; *icht* bladder; ~ **proaspăt** fresh air; ~ **închis** stuffy/confined air; ~ **curat** fresh/pure/open air; ~ **răcoros** cool air; ~ **viciat** foul/tainted air; ~ **vesel** *fig* cheerful air • ~**isi** *vt* to air; to aerate, to weather; (*a împrospăta aerul*) to renew the air; (*a ventila*) to ventilate || *vr* to take air/an airing; to be refreshed.

aerlift ['aerlift] *nn tech* airlift.

aerob [ae'rob] *adj* aerobian, aerobic.

aerodrom [aero'drom] *nn* airport.

aeronautică [aerona'utikă] *nf avia* aeronautics.

aeronavă [aero'navă] *nf avia* airship.

aeroplan [aero'plan] *nn* (air)plane.

aeroport [aero'port] *nn* airport.

aeropurtat [aeropur'tat] *adj* airborne; **trupe ~e** paratroopers.

aerosoli [aero'soli] *nm pl* aerosols.

aevea [a'evea] *adj/adv* * **aievea**.

afabil [a'fabil] *adj* affable, gracious; (*politicos*) polite, civil; (*amabil*) amiable; (*curtenitor*) courteous || *adv* affably, graciously.

afacere [a'fachere] *nf* (*referitor la profit*) business, *pl* dealings; (*referitor la interese majore*; *chestiune*) affair; (*negoț*) trade, commerce; (*tranzacție*) transaction, undertaking; (*încheiată*) bargain; (*speculație*) speculation; (*discuție*) matter; (*chestiune care afectează pe cineva*) concern; *pl* (*treburi, sarcini*) tasks; *pl* (*treburi de stat, particulare*) affairs; *jur* case; **a face o ~** to make/strike a bargain; *coll* to cut a deal.

afacerist [afache'rist] *nm* businessman; *pej* (*speculant*) trafficker, racketeer.

afară [a'fară] *adv* out; (*în exterior*) outside, (*în aer liber*) in the open (air); (*în afara casei*) outdoor(s); (*departe, în străinătate*) abroad; (*la țară*) in the country || *interj* out (with you)!, get out (of here)!; *coll* pack off!; ~ **de** *adv* (*pe lângă*) besides; (*cu excepţia*) except(ing), apart from; *lit* save (for); **a da** ~ *vt* (a izgoni) to drive/turn out.

afâna [afâ'na] *vt* to break up, to make loose/spongy.

afecta[1] [afek'ta] *vt* to affect; (*a simula*) to assume, to put on; (*a imita*) to imitate, to mimic; (*a preocupa*) to concern; (*a tulbura*) to trouble; (*a atinge*) to touch; (*a emoţiona*) to move; (*a supăra*) to offend; (*a mâhni*) to afflict, to grieve; (*a modifica*) to modify, to alter || *vi* to pretend.

afecta[2] [afek'ta] *vt com* (*a aloca o sumă*) to earmark, to allocate to/for; *com* to mortgage; *mil* to detail, to post.

afectare[1] [afek'tare] *nf* affectation; (*simulare*) pretense, dissimulation; (*aer superior*) airs, prudishness; (*preţiozitate*) over-refinement; (*cochetărie*) primness; archness; (*imitare*) imitation.

afectare[2] [afek'tare] *nf com* (*de fonduri*) earmarking, allocation; *mil* assignment, posting; ~ **de fonduri** appropriation of funds.

afectat [afek'tat] *adj* affected; (*studiat*) elaborate; (*în comportament*) prim; (*ipocrit*) demure; theatrical; (*mofturos*) spruce; (*şi curios*) curious; (*exagerat*) gushing; *pej* chi-chi; (*d. stil*) stilted || *adv* with affectation, affectedly; (*cochet*) primly, demurely.

afectiv [afek'tiv] *adj* affective, emotional; (*sensibil, simţitor*) sensitive; (*care denotă afecţiune*) affectionate.

afectuos [afektu'os] *adj* affectionate; (*iubitor*) loving || *adv* affectionately, lovingly.

afecţiune [afektsi'une] *nf* (*dragoste*) affection, love; (*simpatie*) sympathy; (*ataşament*) attachment, liking for; *med* ailment, disorder; (*boală*) disease; *pl* affections, passions.

afemeiat [afeme'iat] *adj* lewd, lecherous || *nm* (*crai*) ladies' man.

aferent [afe'rent] *adj* also *jur* due; *phys* adherent; *anat* afferent.

afet [a'fet] *nn mil* gun-carriage.

afgan [af'gan] *nm/adj* Afghan.

afilia [afili'a] *vt/vr* to affiliate with; to join a party.

afină ['afină] *nf bot* bilberry.

afinitate [afini'tate] *nf* (*asemănare*) resemblance; (*înrudire*) affinity (between), congeniality; (*analogie*) analogy.

afirma [afir'ma] *vt* to affirm; (*a declara*) to state (positively), to declare; (*solemn*) to asseverate; (*cu dârzenie*) to assert; (*a susţine*) to maintain, to contend; (*cu argumente*) to posit; (*a promova o idee*) to advance; (*a spune*) to say; (*a pretinde*) to allege; *log* to predicate || *vr* (*a se face respectat*) to make oneself respected; (*a se distinge*) to distinguish oneself; (*a se impune*) to assert oneself • ~**ţie** *nf* (*declaraţie*) statement; (*spusă*) say(ing); (*solemnă*) asseveration; (*dârză*) assertion; (*asigurare*) assurance; (*alegaţie*) allegation; (*conformă cu realitatea*) affirmation; *log* predication.

afiş [a'fish] *nn* poster, (posting) bill; (*ca reclamă*) advertisement; (*mare, pe şosea sau clădiri*) billboard; (*de teatru*) poster, playbill • ~**a** *vt* to post, to bill; (*a publica*) to publish, to announce; (*pt. vânzare, ca reclamă*) to advertise; (*a etala*) to exhibit, to display; (*a face paradă de*) to show off, to flaunt; (*a proclama*) to proclaim; (*zgomotos*) to puff; (*ignoranţă*) to expose/betray one's ignorance || *vt* to make a show of

oneself; (*a se da în spectacol*) to draw attention to oneself; (*a se pretinde*) to pretend to be, to pose as; (*a trece drept*) to pass oneself off for • ~**ier** *nn* notice board, billboard.

afla [a'fla] *vt* (*a prinde de veste*) to learn, to find out; (*a fi informat despre*) to be informed of/about; (*a şti*) to know; (*a înţelege*) to understand; (*a găsi*) to find; (*din întâmplare*) to come upon/across; to hit upon (an idea); (*a descoperi*) to discover; to invent; (*a vedea*) to see; *math* to determine || *vr* (*a fi*) to be; to be (found), to exist; (*a fi prezent*) to be present; (*a fi aşezat*) to be situated, to lie; (*a se ridica*) to stand; (*a deveni public*) to become known; (*a se dovedi*) to come to light, to turn out; **se află** there is/are || *vi* to hear/learn about smth; (*a găsi*) to find.

afluent [aflu'ent] *nm* tributary, affluent.

afluenţă [aflu'entsă] *nf* (*belşug*) affluence, plenty; (*multă lume*) throng; crowd; (*năvală*) rush; **ore de** ~ rush hour.

aflux [a'fluks] *nn med* afflux, rush; *hydr* inflow of water; *elec* surge.

afon [a'fon] *adj* voiceless; having no ear for music; *coll* stupid, dumb.

aforism [afo'rism] *nn* aphorism; maxim.

afreta [afre'ta] *vt naut* to freight; to charter.

african [afri'kan] *nm/adj* African.

afront [a'front] *nn* affront, slight; *coll* slap in the face; offense; (*jignire*) insult, outrage.

aftă, afte ['aftă, 'afte] *nf med* ulcer(s) in the mouth; *pl* thrush.

afuma [afu'ma] *vt* (*a expune*) to smoke; (*şuncă*) to smoke-dry; (*şi a săra*) to cure; (*peşte*) to kipper; (*a umple de fum*) to fill with) smoke; (*a acoperi cu fum*) to cover with smoke; (*albine*) to smoke out; (*ţânţari, cu foc*) to smudge; (*pt. a dezinfecta*) to fumigate; (*butoaie, cu sulf*) to (fumigate with) sulphur; (*a îmbăta*) *coll* to fuddle || *vr* (*a se îmbăta*) to get fuddled || *vi* (*a fumega*) to smoke.

afunda [afun'da] *vt* (*a scufunda*) to (cause to) sink, to submerge; (*aruncând în apă*) to plunge; (*superficial*) to dip; (*a înmuia*) to soak; (*complet*) to immerse; (*a adânci*) to deepen || *vr* (*a se scufunda, îneca*) to sink; (*a dispărea sub apă*) to dip; (*a plonja*) to plunge; (*a se duce la fund*) to go/sink to the bottom; (*d. înotători*) to dive; *also fig* (*a fi înghiţit*) to be swallowed up; *fig* (*a dispărea*) to vanish, to disappear; (*în umbră/întuneric*) to disappear in/to be swallowed up; (*a pătrunde adânc în*) to become lost in; to go deep into; (*în studiu*) to bury oneself in study.

afurisit [afuri'sit] *nm* rogue, scoundrel || *adj* (ac)cursed; *fig* damned, confounded; *coll* deuced, blessed; (*neascultător*) naughty.

agale [a'gale] *adv* (*încet*) slowly, leisurely; (*leneş*) lazily, idly; (*în voie*) deliberately; (*treptat*) gradually, step by step; (*neatent*) carelessly.

agapă [a'gapă] *nf relig* agape; (*masă comună*) brotherly repast.

agasa [aga'sa] *vt* to plague, to pester; (*a necăji*) to tease, to banter; *coll* to bug; (*a enerva*) to irritate, to annoy.

agăţa [agă'tsa] *vt* (*a atârna*) to hang (up), to put up; (*cu/pe un cârlig*) to hook up; (*a ataşa*) to attach; (*la remorcă*) to couple up; to accost; (*a pune mâna pe*) catch hold of; to capture || *vr* (*a nu se mai desprinde de*) to stick to, to hold on; (*a se folosi de*) to seize (up)on; (a găsi vina) to find fault with;(a se lega de) to nag at, to carp at; (a asalta) to assail; (a nu da pace) to plague, to pester; (a ataca) to attack; (a ridica obiecţii nefondate faţă de) to pick a hole, to pick at smth.

agăţătoare [agătsă'toare] nf (la haină) tab, hanger; pl bot climber, trailer.

agăţător [agătsă'tor] adj climbing, clinging; trailing, creeping.

ageamiu [adjea'miu] nm greenhorn, colt; (începător) beginner, novice, amateur.

agendă [a'djendă] nf (ordine de zi) agenda; (carnet) notebook, pocketbook.

agent [a'djent] nm agent; agency; intermediary, middleman; factor; (împuternicit) proxy; jur mandatory; mil liaison officer; contact man.

agenţie [adjen'tsie] nf (ca întreprindere) agency, company; (sediu) agency office; (intermediu) medium; (forţă) force.

ager ['adjer] adj (pătrunzător) keen, penetrating; (sprinten) quick, agile; (abil) shrewd, clever; coll cute; (dibaci) skillful; (harnic) active, industrious; (viguros) vigorous.

agheasmă [a'giasmă] nf relig holy/consecrated water; (rachiu) coll lush.

aghesmui [ages'mui] vt relig to sprinkle with holy water; (a bate) to thwack, to pepper || vr (a se îmbăta) coll to get/grow fuddled.

agil [a'djil] adj agile, nimble || adv with agility, with nimbleness.

agita [adji'ta] vt (a mişca) to move; (a pune în mişcare) to set in motion; (a clătina) to shake; (un lichid) to stir (up); (o sabie) to wield, to brandish; (a flutura un steag etc) to wave; fig (a tulbura) to disturb, to inflame || vr (a se nelinişti) to fret, to fume; (a fi neliniştit) to be restless; (a nu-şi găsi astâmpăr) to fluster; (a se suci) to squirm • ~t adj agitated; (iritat) irritated; (emoţionat) excited; (neliniştit) restless; (supărat; d. mare sau vânt angry) angry; (cuprins de febră) feverish.

agitaţie [adji'tatsie] nf (emoţie) emotion, excitement; (nerăbdare) impatience; (nelinişte) unrest, nervousness; (zăpăceală) flurry; (febră) fever; (vâlvă) fuss; (aprindere) inflammation; pol agitation, propaganda.

aglomera [aglome'ra] vt to crowd, to throng; (a îngrămădi) to heap up, to pile up; (a acumula) to amass || vr to accumulate; (d. oameni) to crowd, to gather; (a spori) to increase • ~ţie nf agglomeration; (mulţime) crowd, crush; **oră de ~** rush hour.

agonie [ago'nie] nf agony/pangs (of death); death throes; (trecătoare) anguish; (chin) torment; torture.

agonisi [agoni'si] vt (a obţine prin efort) to acquire, to obtain; (a câştiga) to gain, to win; (prin muncă) to earn; (a căpăta) to get.

agoniza [agoni'za] vi also fig to agonize.

agrafă [a'grafă] nf hook, clasp; (pt. hârtie) (paper) clip, clasp; staple; (ac de siguranţă) safety pin; (de păr) hairpin; (copcă, în chirurgie) suture; constr ornamental keystone.

agramat [agra'mat] adj illiterate, unlettered || nm illiterate (person).

agrar [a'grar] adj agrarian; agr agricultural.

agrava [agra'va] vt to make worse, to make more severe, to worsen || vr to grow worse, to worsen, to deteriorate.

agrea [agre'a] vt (a-i plăcea) to like, to love; (a vedea

cu ochi buni) to favor; (ceva) to approve of; coll to sanction; to accept; (a primi favorabil) to receive favorably; (a fi de acord cu) to consent to • ~bil adj (plăcut) agreeable; (d. comportare, vreme etc) pleasant; (ca persoană) pleasing; easy-going; (încântător) delightful, charming; prepossessing || adv agreeably || nn the agreeable.

agregat [agre'gat] nn tech unit, assembly, generating set; chem, geol aggregate.

agrement [agre'ment] nn pleasure; (distracţie) amusement; (sentiment) consent, approval.

agresiune [agresi'une] nf aggression on/upon; unprovoked assault.

agresiv [agre'siv] adj aggressive; all over smb.

agresor [agre'sor] nm aggressor.

agricol [a'grikol] adj agricultural, farming.

agricultor [agrikul'tor] nm farmer; ploughman; (ţăran) peasant.

agricultură [agrikul'tură] nf agriculture, farming, rural economy.

agrişă [a'grişă] nf bot gooseberry; (roşie) barberry; (neagră) black currant.

agronom [agro'nom] nm agronomist, agricultural engineer.

ah [ah] interj (emoţie) ah!; (mirare) oh!, ha(h)!; (lamentaţie) oh!, alas!, oh dear!, oh heavens!, good(ness) gracious!, my goodness!; (satisfacţie, bucurie) oh!; (foarte bine) very well!, all right! || nn sigh, moan, complaint.

aha [a'ha] interj (înţeleg) (oh) I see!; (da) yes.

ahtiat [ahti'at] adj keen on; crazy about.

ai [ai] art poss of; ~ mei my folks, my people; ~ lor theirs, of theirs || interj (cum?) what?, eh?; (ei?) well?

aici [a'ich] adv here; (în acest loc) at this place; in/on this place; (încoace) here; lit hither; (în cele de faţă, alăturat) herein, herewith; (de ~, din aceasta) herefrom; (acolo) there; (în acest punct) at this place; (on) this side; (aici jos, pe pământ) here below, down here; (la noi) with us, in this/our country; present; (la aceste cuvinte) at these words; **de ~** (din acest loc) from here; (din această ţară) of this country; (în consecinţă) hence; **pe ~** here; (la noi) with us; (primprejur) hereabout(s), about here, round here; (trecând prin/intrând) through here, through this place; (pe acest drum) this way; **până ~** (spaţial) so/thus far, as far as here; (în cărţi) down to here; (temporal) till now, until now, so far.

aidoma [a'idoma] adj (quite) alike; identical; ~ cu the very picture of, the spitting image of.

aievea [a'ievea] adv actually, really || adj real, actual.

aisberg ['aisberg] nn iceberg.

aiura [aiu'ra] vt (a vorbi fără sens) to talk nonsense/foolishly; med to rave, to ramble.

aiurea [a'iurea] adj crazy; foolish * **aiurit** || adv (într-un loc nedeterminat) in the middle of nowhere; (în altă parte) elsewhere; anywhere else; (spre un alt loc) to some other place; (în străinătate; în altă parte) abroad || interj coll well, I never!, you don't say so!; (abţine-te!) coll stow it!; (e o minciună) coll that's a stretcher • ~lă nm also med driveling nonsense; (vorbe fără sens) coll twaddle, babble; drivel(ing); (prostie) piece of extravagance; sl bullshit; (lipsă de judecată) thoughtlessness; (absurdi-

tate) absurdity; (*zăpăceală*) confusion; (*zarvă*) coll fuss; (*haos*) chaos; (*amestecătură*) coll jumble.

aiurit [aiu'rit] *adj* (*neatent*) absentminded; heedless, careless; (*confuz*) confused, bewildered; (*uituc*) forgetful; scatterbrained; (*prostuţ*) lightheaded; (*ameţit*) giddy; silly, foolish; hare-brained; (*d. vorbire fără noimă*) coll twaddling, driveling ‖ *nm* coll driveler, scatterbrain; (*pieton distrat*) jaywalker.

ajun [a'zhun] *nn* eve, day/evening before; (*post*) fasting; **în** ~ on the eve of that day, the day before • ~**ul Anului Nou** New Year's Eve.

ajuna [azhu'na] *vi relig* (*a posti*) to fast, to abstain from food; (*a mânca de sec*) to abstain from meat.

ajunge [a'zhundje] *vi* (*a veni, a sosi*) to come; to arrive; (*a fi de ajuns*) to do; (*a deveni*) to become, to get; (*a dobândi*) to obtain; (*a atinge*) to attain; (*a câştiga*) to gain; (*prin efort*) to acquire; (*a accede la o poziţie*) to accede to; (*a dura până la*) to last until/ till; (*a începe*) to begin, to start; (*a fi de ajuns să*) to be enough/sufficient to ‖ *vt* (*pe cineva din urmă*) to catch up with; (*a egala*) *fig* to match, to equal; (*a prinde ceva din urmă*) to catch; (*vânat*) to take; (*un vas*) *naut* to come up with; (*a atinge*) to touch, to reach; (*a apuca*) to seize; (*a nimeri*) to hit; (*a apuca o perioadă, a trăi*) (to live) to see; (*a-l* ~ *oboseala etc*) to be overcome, to be overwhelmed; (*a fi cuprins de*) to be seized with ‖ *vr* (*reciproc*) to meet; (*a fi destul*) to suffice, to be enough/sufficient; *fig* to make one's mark, to come into one's own; (*a parveni*) to be an upstart; **atât** ~ *vi* this much will do; to be enough/sufficient; **a** ~ **să** *vi* (*a reuşi să*) to succeed in; to manage to.

ajura [azhu'ra] *vt* to pierce; to sew in openwork.

ajusta [azhus'ta] *vt* (*a potrivi*) to level, to match; *tech* to fit; (*a adapta*) to adjust smth to; to fit smb/smth up.

ajustor [azhus'tor] *nm* adjuster, adaptor; *tech* engine filler.

ajuta [azhu'ta] *vt* (*pe cineva cu ceva*) to help smb (with smth, in doing smth); (*a contribui la efortul cuiva*) to aid; (*nu ca egal*) to assist; (*a susţine*) to back smb/smth up; (*a sprijini, material şi moral*) to support; (*a veni în ajutorul cuiva*) coll to succour; (*a da o mână de ajutor*) to lend a (helping) hand to; (*a uşura condiţia cuiva*) to relieve; (*a fi de partea*) to side with; (*a susţine o cauză*) to champion; (*verbal*) to plead/argue the cause of; (*a mângâia*) *fig* to comfort; (*a încuraja*) to encourage ‖ *vi* (*a folosi la, a ajuta la*) to help, to serve ‖ *vr* to help oneself, to shift for oneself; (*reciproc*) to help each other; (*a se sprijini*) to support each other; (*a contribui la*) to contribute to; (*a cauza*) to cause, to bring about; (*a promova*) to promote; (*a remedia*) to remedy, to redress.

ajutător [azhută'tor] *adj* (*care ajută*) helping, helpful; (*accesoriu*) accessory; auxiliary; (*suplimentar*) supplementary, additional; (*secundar*) secondary.

ajutor [azhu'tor] *nn* help; helping; (*asistenţă*) assistance; (*sprijin material şi moral*) support; *fig* backing (up); (*colaborare cu un scop*) aid; co-operation, collaboration; (*uşurare*) relief; (*redresare*) redress; (*remediu*) remedy; (*ajutor bănesc*) allowance; (*salvare*) rescue, salvation; (*refugiu*) refuge; **prim** ~ first aid ‖ *nm/nn* helper, aid(er); assistant; (*susţinător*) backer, supporter; (*adjunct*) adjunct; (*locţiitor*) deputy; (*salvator*) rescuer; (*complice*) accomplice; *jur* accessory

al [al] *art poss* of ~ **mamei** mother's; ~ **băiatului** the boy's, of the boy; ~ **meu** mine.

alabastru [ala'bastru] *nn* miner alabaster.

alai [a'lai] *nn* (*suită*) train, suite; (*de onoare*) retinue; cortege; (*procesiune, mai ales religioasă*) procession; escort; (*însoţitori*) followers, retainers; (*slujitori*) attendants, attendance; *fig* cohort; array; (*urmări*) consequences; pomp, (great) show, display; parade; *fig* (*funerar*) funeral train/procession; *fig pej* coll row, hubbub; (*scandal*) fuss.

alaltăieri [a'laltăieri] *adv* the day before yesterday.

alamă [a'lamă] *nf metal* (yellow) brass; *pl* brassware.

alambic [alam'bik] *nn chem* alembic, still.

alandala [alan'dala] *adv* (*în dezordine*) in disorder; coll pell-mell; *sl* all over the show/ballpark; (*pe dos*) wrong, the wrong way; (*fără noimă*) at random.

alarma [alar'ma] *vt* (*a nelinişti*) to worry, to trouble; (*a tulbura*) to disturb; (*a speria*) to startle, to frighten; *mil* to alert; (*a anunţa poliţia*) to warn ‖ *vr* to become alarmed/restless, to be uneasy about.

alarmă [a'larmă] *nf* alarm, panic; (*teroare*) terror; (*nelinişte*) disquiet, uneasiness; ~ **de incendiu** fire alarm; ~ **falsă** false alarm.

alăpta [aləp'ta] *vt* to suckle, to nurse.

alătura [alătu'ra] *vt* (*a pune alături*) to join; to annex to; to append; (*a include*) to enclose; (*a apropia*) to draw near; (*a compara with/to*) to contrast; (*a confrunta*) to confront; (*a colaţiona*) to collate with ‖ *vr* (*a se apropia*) to approach, to draw near.

alături [a'lături] *adv* by, nearby, close by; (*vecin*) next door; (*împreună*) together; (*umăr la umăr*) side by side; *fig* at random; beside the point; ~ **de** by (the side of), beside, close to; (*pe lângă*) past; (*în comparaţie cu*) in comparison with, compared with.

alb [alb] *adj* white; *lit* snowy, silvery; (*curat*) clean, pure; (*brumat*) hoary; (*liber, gol*) blank; *pol* blue, conservative; (*d. glas*) toneless ‖ *nn* white (color) ‖ *nm* (*om* ~) white (man).

albanez(ă) [alba'nez(ă)] *nm/nf* Albanian ‖ *adj* Albanian.

albastru [al'bastru] *adj* blue; (*ca cerul*) sky-blue, azure; (*ca safirul*) sapphire; (*greu*) coll tough ‖ *nn* blue (color); (*al cerului*) azure.

albatros [alba'tros] *nm* albatross.

albăstrea [albăs'trea] *nf bot* cornflower, bluebonnet.

albi [al'bi] *vi* to whiten, to turn/get white; (*d. culori, a se decolora*) to fade; (*d. materii textile*) to bleach; (*a încărunţi*) to turn/become/grow grey; (*a licări*) to gleam, to shimmer; (*a se zări alb*) to gleam white ‖ *vt* to whiten, to blanch; (*textile*) to bleach; (*a acoperi cu ceva alb*) to cover with a white ...; (*a încărunţi pe cineva*) to make smb grow grey; (*a spăla*) to wash; (*a curăţa*) to render clean; (*a vărui*) to whitewash.

albie ['albie] *nf* (*covată*) trough; (*pt. spălat*) trough for washing; (*ciubăr*) tub; (*matcă de râu*) riverbed, bottom.

albină [al'bină] *nf* (*domestică*) (honey/hive) bee; *bot* bee flower/orchis; (*trântor*) (bee) drone; (*regină*) queen, mother bee; (*de pădure*) bumblebee.

album [al'bum] *nn* album; (*pt. decupaje*) scrapbook; (*pt. desene*) sketch book.

albumină [albu'mină] *nf* albumin(e).

albuş [al'bush] *nn* white (of an egg).

alcătui [alkătu'i] *vt* to make (a face); (*a crea*) to create; to form; *pharm* (*o reţetă*) to make up a prescription; (*a construi*) to build; (*a monta*) to put together; to organize, to set up; (*a întocmi*) to make up; (*a redacta, a schiţa*) to draw up, to draft; (*a compune*) to compose; to compile; (*a scrie*) to write; to invent, to devise; (*a constitui*) to incorporate.

alcool [al'kool] *nn* alcohol; (*în comerţ*) spirits; (*băuturi alcoolice*) hard liquor; *coll* the hard stuff.

ale ['ale] *art poss* of; ~ **tatălui** of the father, the father's; ~ **tale** yours; ~ **lui John** John's.

alea ['alea] *adj dem f pl* those; **casele** ~ those houses || *pron dem f pl* those (ones).

alean [a'lean] *nn* (*dor*) longing, yearning; (*nostalgie*) nostalgia, melancholy; (*suferinţă*) sorrow, grief, suffering.

aleatoriu [alea'toriu] *adj also jur* aleatory; chancy, uncertain; *coll* iffy; random.

alee [a'lee] *nf* alley; (*îngustă, între clădiri*) lane; (*potecă*) path; (*printre pomi*) aisle; (*pt. pietoni*) walk; (*pt. trăsuri*) drive; (*pt. auto*) driveway; (*pt ciclişti*) cycleway.

alegător [alegă'tor] *nm pol* voter, elector; (*care îşi schimbă părerea*) floater; chooser.

alege [a'ledje] *vt* to choose; to pick (out), to select; (*oameni, soldaţi*) to draft; (*dintre mai multe obiecte*) to choose from/between several things; (*întâmplător*) to pitch upon; *pol* to elect, to vote for; (*pt. preşedinte*) to vote into the chair; (*a cerne*) to sift, to winnow; (*a se hotărî pentru*) to fix upon; (*a lua partea*) to side with; (*a despărţi*) to separate; (*a distinge*) to distinguish; (*a asorta*) to sort; (*a arăta*) to show; to decide; (*a da la o parte*) to reject; (*a scoate coaja*) to shell, (*legume, fructe*) to peel; (*a spicui*) to glean; (*a înţelege*) to understand || *vr* (*a se despărţi*) to separate; (*a deveni*) to become; (*a se decide*) to settle; (*a avea ca rezultat*) to result; (*a se desprinde*) to come off; *chem* to be disengaged; (*a se deosebi de*) to differ from; (*a rămâne cu*) to be left with; (*a primi*) to get • ~**re** *nf* choosing; choice; (*selecţie*) selection; *phil, pol* election; (*optare*) option; (*dintre două*) alternative; (*prin vot secret sau bile*) ballot(ing), voting by ballot; (*separare*) separation; (*distincţie*) distinction; (*discriminare*) discrimination; (*selectare*) sorting (out), classifying; (*decizie*) decision.

alegorie [alego'rie] *nf* allegory.

alene [a'lene] *adv* (*cu lene*) idly, lazily; carelessly; (*încet*) slowly; (*somnoros*) drowsily, sleepily; (*uşor*) gently; (*treptat*) gradually; (*nonşalant*) nonchalantly || *adj* (*leneş*) idle, lazy; negligent, careless; (*somnoros*) drowsy, sleepy; (*nonşalant*) nonchalant, indifferent; (*uşor*) gentle; (*încet*) slow; (*treptat*) gradual.

alerga [aler'ga] *vi* (*a da fuga*) to run; (*foarte repede*) to race; *coll* to dash off; (*f. repede, în linie dreaptă*) to scud; (*d. tren, maşină*) to go; (*a curge*) to flow; (*a se grăbi*) to hasten, to hurry; (*a da năvală*) to rush; (*a se repezi*) to dash; (*a zbura*) *fig* to fly; *fig* (*d. timp*) to pass, to go by; (*în cursă*) to race; *fig* (*d. nori*) to float; **a ~ după** (*a urmări*) to pursue, to chase; *fig* (*a râvni*) to hunt after/for || *vt* (*a alerga o cursă, o distanţă*) to run; (*a goni, a fugări*) to drive, to chase; (*a cutreiera*) to scour, to wander through • ~**re** *nf* running; (*fugă*) flight; (*cursă*) run(ning); race; (*osteneală*) pains; (*urmărire*) pursuit, chase.

alergător [alergă'tor] *nm* runner, * **alerga**; (*curier*) courier, express messenger || *adj* running, * **alerga**.

alergie [aler'djie] *nf med* allergy.

alert [a'lert] *adj* alert, quick, lively || *adv* alertly, quickly • ~**a** *vt* to alert, to give the alarm to; to warn • ~**ă** *nf* alert, alarm, warning.

ales [a'les] *adj* choice, select; *frml* recherché; *relig* elect; (*d. limbă*) polished; (*distins*) distinguished; rare; (*de primă clasă*) first-class; *coll* prime, capital; excellent, exquisite; supreme; distinct; (*vădit*) obvious; definite, precise || *adv* **mai** ~ (*mai cu seamă*) (e)specially, particularly; (*cu atât mai mult că*) all the more (as) || *nn* choosing, choice, * **alege** || *nm* sweetheart; beau; selected person, nominee; *pl fig* **cei aleşi** the chosen ones, the elite.

alfabet [alfa'bet] *nn* alphabet.

algă ['algă] *nf* alga, *pl* algae.

algebră [al'djebră] *nf* algebra.

algerian [aldjeri'an] *adj/nm* Algerian, Algerine.

alia [ali'a] *vt* to ally, to unite; (*prin căsătorie*) to ally (to/with); (*metale*) to alloy, to mix; *fig* to combine, to unite || *vr* (*a face o alianţă*) to make/form an alliance; (*prin căsătorie*) to be(come) allied; to marry into a family; (*d. fluide*) to mix; (*d. metale*) to alloy • ~**nţă** *nf* (*ligă*) league; (*între state*) alliance; (*confederaţie*) confederation, confederacy; (*coaliţie*) coalition; (*căsătorie*) match; marriage; (*rudenie*) lineage.

alibi [ali'bi] *nn* alibi.

alică [a'likă] *nf* grain of shot, pellet; *esp pl* hail/dust shot.

alienare [alie'nare] *nf jur* alienation, transfer; (*izolare*) estrangement; (*mintală*) insanity.

alienat [alie'nat] *adj jur* alienated; *med* mentally alienated || *nm* psychopath(ic), insane person.

alifie [ali'fie] *nf coll* ointment, salve; (*pt. ochi*) eyesalve; (*mir*) chrism; *fig* (*alinare*) balm.

aligator [aliga'tor] *nm* alligator.

aliment [ali'ment] *nn* food, nutriment; *pl jur* alimony, allowance; (*provizii*) provisions, supplies • ~**a** *vt* (*a hrăni*) to feed, to nourish; (*d. râuri, maşini, piaţă*) to supply; (*o persoană, a întreţine*) to support; (*un sentiment*) to keep alive/up • ~**ar** *adj* (*de alimente*) food ...; alimentary; (*nutritiv*) nutritious • ~**aţie** *nf* (*acţiune*) feeding; nourishment, nutrition.

alina [ali'na] *vt* (*a potoli*) to temper, to mitigate; (*a îndulci*) to appease, to pacify; (*o emoţie, o durere*) to soothe, to allay; *fig* to stanch/staunch; (*a uşura*) to lighten, to relieve; (*a micşora*) to lessen; to dampen, to cool; to satisfy; (*setea*) to quench; (*teama*) to calm, to still; to console, to comfort; *med* to ease; (*d. suferinţă*) to alleviate || *vr* to calm down; (*d. furtună*) to abate; (*d. vânt*) to drop; (*a se opri*) to stop • ~**re** *nf* tempering, appeasing, * **alina**; alleviation; (*uşurare*) relief; (*mângâiere*) comfort, consolation.

alinia [alini'a] *vt* to align, to line up; to range; *mil* to dress; *typ* to align type || *vr* to be in line with, to fall into line; *pol* to follow a line; *mil* to dress.

aliniat [alini'at] *nn* indented line; paragraph || *adj* aligned.

aliniere [alini'ere] *nf* aligning; *mil* alignment; *typ* ranging; (*monetară*) *fin* alignment of currencies.

alinta [alin'ta] *vt* (*a dezmierda*) to caress, to stroke; (*a strânge în braţe, a săruta*) to cuddle, to fondle; (*în joacă*) to cajole; (*cu privirea*) to look affectionately at; (*un animal*) to make a fuss of; (*a răsfăţa*) to spoil; (*a fi prea indulgent cu*) to pamper; (*a mângâia*) to pet; (*a linguşi*) to flatter, to coax || *vr* to coddle oneself; (*a se răsfăţa*) to frolic, to gambol; (*d. îndră-*

gostiţi) to cuddle, to bill and coo; (*a se preface*) to simper; (*a se legăna*) to swing, to rock.

alipi [ali'pi] *vt* to join, to unite; (*a apropia*) to draw near; (*un teritoriu*) to annex ‖ *vr* **a se ~ de** to join; (*a se lipi de*) *fig* to cling to; (*a adera*) to adhere to.

almanah [alma'nah] *nn* almanac.

alo [a'lo] *interj* (*hei!*) hello!

aloca [alo'ka] *vt* to assign, to allocate for; (*a destina*) *econ* to earmark for; (*a da bani pt. a finanţa*) to fund • ~**re** *nf* allocation, granting; *fin* allotment • ~**ţie** *nf* * **alocare**; *jur* allocation, assignment; (*ajutor bănesc*) grant-in-aid, allowance.

alocuţiune [alokutsi'une] *nf* (*solemnă*) address, allocution.

aloe [a'loe] *nf bot* aloe, century plant.

alpinism [alpi'nism] *nn* mountaineering, mountain/alpine climbing.

alpinist [alpi'nist] *nm* mountaineer, alpinist; (mountain) climber, rock climber.

alt(ă) ['alt(ă)] *adj indef* (*diferit*) other; **o ~ă zi** another day; (*încă*) another; (*suplimentar*) further, supplementary.

altar [al'tar] *nn relig* altar, communion table; (*parte a bisericii*) apse, chancel; *fig* shrine, sanctuary.

altădată ['altădată] *adv* (*odinioară*) once, formerly; in the past, in time past; (*în viitor*) some day; one of these days; some time or other; (*în alte rânduri*) at other times.

altceva ['altcheva] *pron indef* something else/different; (*în prop. neg. şi interog.*) anything else.

altcineva ['altcineva] *pron indef* somebody else, (*în prop. neg. şi interog.*) anybody else; (*un altul*) another one.

altcumva ['altkumva] *adv* otherwise, or; else; in a different way; differently.

alte ['alte] *adj f pl* other • ~**le** *pron f pl* others; **între ~** among other things • ~**ori** *adv* (at) other times; (now) ..., now ...

altera [alte'ra] *vt* (*a schimba*) to alter, to modify; (*a strica*) to spoil, to taint; to falsify; (*a contraface alimente*) to adulterate; to impair; (*un text*) to corrupt; (*a denatura*) to garble; to distort; to deprave; to misrepresent; *fig* to forge, to counterfeit; to debase ‖ *vr* to change, to deteriorate; (*d. alimente*) to go/run bad, to be tainted; (*d. culori*) to fade.

altercaţie [alter'katsie] *nf* wrangle, dispute, argument.

alternanţă, alternare [alter'nantsă, alter'nare] *nf* alternation; *agr* rotation.

alternativ [alterna'tiv] *adj* alternative; *phys* rotatory; **curent ~** *elec* alternating current ‖ *adv* alternatively.

alternativă [alterna'tivă] *nf* alternative.

alteţă [al'tetsă] *nf* (His/Her) Highness; prince, princess.

altfel ['altfel] *adv* (*în alt fel*) differently, otherwise; (*dacă nu...*) or; (*de altminteri*) as for the rest; **de ~** in fact, actually; (*în plus*) moreover, besides; further; (*în alte privinţe*) in other respects.

altitudine [alti'tudine] *nf* height, altitude.

altminteri [alt'minteri] *adv* otherwise; or else.

altoi[1] [alto'i] *vt* to (en)graft, to ingraft; (*prin detaşare*) to bud; *fig* to implant, to instill; *med* to inoculate, to vaccinate; *fig* (*a bate*) to beat, to spank; (*cu cureaua*) to lathe ‖ *vr* (*a se îmbăta*) *coll* to get tight/tipsy.

altoi[2] [al'toi] *nn* (*mlădiţă*) graft, cutting; (*plantă altoită*) stock, parent (plant); (*altoire*) grafting, ingraftment; *med* vaccine.

altruism [altru'ism] *nn* altruism.

altruist [altru'ist] *nm* altruist ‖ *adj* selfless, unselfish ‖ *adv* selflessly, altruistically.

altul ['altul] *pron m* another (one) * **alt**.

altundeva ['altundeva] *adv* somewhere else, elsewhere.

alţi ['altsi] *adj m pl* other; ~ **oameni** other people.

alţii ['altsii] *pron m pl* others, other ones.

aluat [a'luat] *nn* (*de pâine*) dough; paste, (cake) batter.

aluminiu [alu'miniu] *nn* aluminum.

alun [a'lun] *nm bot* (hazel)nut tree; ~ **american** peanut, groundnut; ~ **turcesc** filbert (tree).

alună [a'lună] *nf* (hazel)nut; filbert.

aluneca [alune'ka] *vi* to slide, to slip; (*a derapa*) to skid; *avia* to yaw; (*pierzându-şi echilibrul*) to slip, to miss one's footing; (*a se mişca liber*) to shift; *fig* to slip, to lapse; to go astray; to err.

alunecos [alune'kos] *adj* slippery, slippy.

alunga [alun'ga] *vt* to chase, to press on; (*a urmări*) to pursue, to follow; (*a îndepărta*) to drive away, to remove; (*a izgoni*) to chase/drive away/out; to evict; to exile, to banish; (*a concedia*) to dismiss; *coll* to lay off ‖ *vr* (*reciproc*) to chase each other.

alungi [alun'dji] *vt* to elongate; to lengthen; (*a întinde*) to stretch; (*d. haine*) to let down; to prolong ‖ *vr* to lengthen, to thin out.

aluniţă [alu'nitsă] *nf* beauty spot; (*neg*) mole.

alură [a'lură] *nf* (*ţinută*) carriage, bearing; walk; (*d. un cal*) paces of a horse; (*d. persoane*) to have style; (*înfăţişare*) look, air; *sp* pace; speed, rate; *naut* point of sailing.

aluzie [a'luzie] *nf* allusion (to), hint; (*răutăcioasă*) innuendo.

alveolă [alve'olă] *nf anat* alveola, *pl* alveolae, alveolus, *pl* alveoli; (*la faguri*) cell; (*la dinţi*) socket; (*la fructe*) cell; *agr* seed cell.

alviţă [al'vitsă] *nf* nougat.

amabil [a'mabil] *adj* kind, nice; (*d. comportament*) endearing; (*binevoitor*) kind(ly), bland; obliging, helpful ‖ *adv* kindly; amiably; politely.

amabilitate [amabili'tate] *nf* kindness, amiability; obligingness; (*favoare*) favor, politeness; (*compliment*) compliment.

amalgam [amal'gam] *nn chem* amalgam; *fig* blend, mixture; congeries.

amanet [ama'net] *nn* (*ipotecă*) mortgage; (*zălog*) pawn; deposit; (*ostatec*) hostage.

amant [a'mant] *nm* lover, sweetheart; (*curtezan*) suitor, wooer; (*secret*) backdoor man • ~**ă** *nf* lover, sweetheart; (*în sens negativ*) mistress.

amar [a'mar] *adj* bitter; *fig* (*dureros*) painful, sore; (*grozav*) dreadful, severe ‖ *adv also fig* bitterly.

amara [ama'ra] *vt/vi naut* to moor.

amator [ama'tor] *nm* lover (of smth); fan; (*neprofesionist*) amateur, dilettante; (*cunoscător*) connoisseur ‖ *adj* amateur, lay; ~ **de artă** art lover; ~ **de sport** sports fan.

amăgi [amă'dji] *vt* (*a mistifica*) to mystify; (*a păcăli*) to deceive, to fool smb; (*a înşela*) to cheat; (*a ispiti*) to tempt, to entice; to seduce, to lure; to abuse the confidence of; (*a momi cu vorbe dulci*) to wheedle ‖ *vr* to deceive/fool oneself; (*a se înşela*) to be mistaken • ~**tor** *adj* deceptive; seductive; tantalizing; illusory ‖ *nm* deceiver, wheedler.

amănunt [amă'nunt] *nn* detail, particular; small point;

(*împrejurare*) circumstance; **în ~** in detail, minutely; *econ* **cu ~ul** by retail.

amănunţit [amănun'tsit] *adj* detailed; circumstantial; close, thorough; minute || *adv* meticulously, minutely.

amărăciune [amără'chune] *nf* bitterness; *fig* gall; grief.

amărât [amă'rât] *adj* (*abătut*) miserable, downcast; (*supărat*) embittered; (*trist*) sad; ill at ease, heavy-hearted; (*nenorocit*) wretched; (*rablagit*) *sl* beat-up || *nm* wretched/miserable man; *coll* poor devil; (*nenorocit*) wretch.

amărî [amă'rî] *vt* (*a întrista*) to sadden; (*a mâhni*) to distress; (*a supăra*) to (ag)grieve; (*a irita*) to embitter || *vr* to get bitter; *fig* to feel hurt/annoyed; to sadden; *fig* to become embittered.

amâna [amâ'na] *vt* to postpone, to put off; to procrastinate; to adjourn, to defer; to prorogate; *pol* to table; (*o sentinţă*) to suspend a judgement; (*executarea unei sentinţe*) to reprieve a condemned person; (*audierea acuzatului*) to remand the accused; *econ* (*o plată*) to put off, to hold over; *edu* to defer; (*a trage de timp*) to play for time; (*a păsui un debitor*) to respite • **~re** *nf* (*acţiune*) postponing; (*rezultat*) adjournment; (*păsuire*) stay; referring; delay, respite; *mil* deferment.

amândoi, amândouă [amân'doi, amân'două] *pron* both (of us/you/them); the two || *adj* both.

ambala [amba'la] *vt* (*a înveli*) to wrap (up); (*a împacheta*) to pack (up); (*în vid*) to vacuum-pack; (*motorul*) to race; *coll* to rev the engine || *vr* (*d. motor*) to race; (*d. un cal*) to bolt/to run away; *fig* (*a se încinge*) to warm up; to be carried away; to fly into a passion; to get excited (about); to work oneself up; to get worked up || *interj* **nu te ~!** don't get excited!, keep your head!, *coll* keep cool!, cool it! • **~j** *nn* * **ambalare**; wrapper, package • **~re** *nf* packing/wrapping (up); *auto* racing the engine.

ambarcaţi(un)e [ambarkatsi'une] *nf* boat, craft.

ambasadă [amba'sadă] *nf* mission; (*clădire*) embassy; (*personal*) ambassador's staff.

ambasador [ambasa'dor] *nm also fig* ambassador; *fig* envoy; representative; messenger; deputy.

ambele ['ambele] *num/adj f pl* both || *pron* the two, both (of them).

ambianţă [ambi'antsă] *nf* environment, ambience, milieu.

ambiguu [am'biguu] *adj* ambiguous, doubtful; two-edged; (*echivoc*) equivocal || *adv* ambiguously.

ambii ['ambii] *num/adj m pl* both || *pron* both (of them), the two.

ambiţie [am'bitsie] *nf* ambition (of, for); (*dorinţă*) wish; (*aspiraţie*) aspiration, hankering (after smth).

ambiţiona [ambitsio'na] *vt* to arouse the ambition of, to pique || *vr* (*a se încăpăţâna să*) to be bent on smth/doing smth; to be obstinate; to set one's heart on.

ambiţios [ambitsi'os] *adj* ambitious; (*care vrea să parvină*) aspiring; (*încăpăţânat*) obstinate, stubborn; perseverative, tenacious || *nm* ambitious person; *pej* go-getter.

ambreia [ambre'ia] *vt* to engage, to clutch || *vr* to come into gear; *vi* to engage the gear; *auto* to release the clutch pedal.

ambulant [ambu'lant] *adj* itinerant, strolling; **actor ~** strolling actor.

ambulanţă [ambu'lantsă] *nf* ambulance (car).

ambuscadă [ambus'kadă] *nf* ambush, ambuscade.

ambuteiaj [ambute'iadz] *nn* bottling; traffic jam.

ameliora [amelio'ra] *vt/vr* to ameliorate, to improve, to get better • **~re** *nf* (a)melioration, improvement.

amenaja [amena'zha] *vt* to arrange, to lay out; (*o casă*) to decorate; to dispose; (*a utila*) to fit out, to equip (with); (*un oraş*) to plan • **~re** *nf* equipping, arranging; fitting out, * **amenaja**; arrangement, decoration; disposition; *pl* fittings, installations; facilities.

amenda¹ [amen'da] *vt* (*pe cineva*) to fine, to penalize.

amenda² [amen'da] *vt* (*a îmbunătăţi*) to improve; (*o lege*) to amend; *agr* to manure • **~ment** *nn pol* amendment; *agr* (*îmbunătăţire*) improvement.

amendă [a'mendă] *nf* fine, penalty.

ameninţa [amenin'tsa] *vt* (*cu*) to threaten (with); *coll* to bulldoze; (*d. o primejdie*) to hang over || *vi* to menace, to threaten; (*d. un pericol*) to impend • **~re** *nf* threatening, * **ameninţa**; threat, menace; *pl jur* intimidation.

ameninţător [amenintsă'tor] *adj* menacing, threatening; forbidding; lowering; (*rău prevestitor*) foreboding || *adv* menacingly, threateningly.

America [a'merika] *nf* America; the United States of America.

american [ameri'kan] *nm/adj* American; Yankee

amestec [a'mestek] *nn phys* mixture; blend; mix; mingling; *fig* (*un întreg lipsit de coerenţă*) (ad)mixture; (*lucruri amestecate*) medley, congeries; *coll* odds and ends; (*ghiveci*) mess; (*dezordine*) jumble; disarray; *coll* mix-up; (*d. oameni*) medley; *coll* mixed bag; *lit* miscellany; pastiche; (*legătură*) connection; (*participare*) share; (*nedorit*) meddling; (*intervenţie*) interference; (*încrucişare*) crossing • **~a** *vt phys* to mix (up); to merge, to blend; (*lucruri*) to (com)mingle; to muddle up; to combine; (*a încurca*) to entangle; *also fig* to confound, to confuse; (*a confunda două persoane*) to take smb for smb else; (*cărţile*) to shuffle; (*a dilua*) to dilute; (*d. aluat*) to knead; (*a implica*) to involve; to imply; (*a încrucişa*) to cross; (*a uni*) to unite; (*culorile*) to blend colors || *vr* to mix, to mingle; (*a se contopi cu*) to blend (in); (*d. contur*) to blur; (*a se băga*) to interfere with; (*în discuţie*) to join in; (*a interveni în favoarea*) to intercede for; (*a-şi băga nasul unde nu-i fierbe oala*) *coll* to poke one's nose in smb else's business • **~at** *adj* mixed, combined || *adv coll* so-so; not very well.

ametist [ame'tist] *nn miner* amethyst.

ameţeală [ame'tseală] *nf* dizziness, giddiness; *med* vertigo, fear of heights.

ameţi [ame'tsi] *vt* to make dizzy/giddy; to make smb's head turn/swim; (*a ului*) to stun, to daze; to amaze, to stagger; to bewilder; (*cu o lovitură*) to stun; (*cu o substanţă*) to anesthetize; (*d. vin*) to fluster; (*a îmbăta*) to make smb drunk/tipsy; *also fig* to intoxicate; (*a amăgi*) *coll* to diddle, to nab; (*a trage pe sfoară*) to double-cross; (*a potoli*) to ease; (*foamea*) to allay; (*a păcăli*) to take in || *vi* to be(come) dizzy/giddy || *vr* (*cu alcool*) to get drunk/tipsy; *coll* to get tight • **~tor** *adj* (*uluitor*) astounding; (*zăpăcitor*) staggering • (*d. o privelişte*) stunning; (*asurzitor*) deafening; (*d. o înălţime*) giddy, dizzy; (*d. viteză*) breathtaking; breakneck.

amfiteatru [amfi'teatru] *nn* amphitheater; *edu* lecture room, *med* theater.

amfitrioană [amfitri'oană] *nf* hostess.

amfitrion [amfitri'on] *nm* host, amphitryon.

amforă ['amforă] *nf* amphora.
amiabil [ami'abil] *adj* amiable, good-natured, friendly, amicable || *adv* in a friendly way/manner.
amiază, amiazi [a'miază, a'miazi] *nf* noon, midday; **după ~** *nf* afternoon || *adv* in the afternoon; **la ~** at noon; (*zenit*) zenith.
amic [a'mik] *nm* (male) friend; *coll* pal, buddy.
amidon [ami'don] *nn* starch; amidin(e).
amigdală [amig'dală] *nf anat* tonsil.
amigdalită [amigda'lită] *nf med* tonsillitis, amygdalitis.
amin [a'min] *interj relig* amen; *coll* all over!.
aminti [amin'ti] *vt* (*a ~ cuiva să facă ceva*) to remind smb (to do smth); (*ceva, pe cineva*) to remember (smth/smb); to mention; to insinuate; to allude (to), to suggest; (*a evoca*) to evoke; to recall || *vr* (*a-şi ~ de*) to remember, to (re)call smth/smb to mind; (*a rememora*) to reminisce.
amintire [amin'tire] *nf* memory; (*aducere aminte*) recollection; souvenir, memento.
amiral [ami'ral] *nm/adj naut* admiral.
amnar [am'nar] *nn* flint steel; tinder box; *archit* post.
amnezie [amne'zie] *nf* amnesia, loss of memory.
amnistia [amnisti'a] *vt* to grant amnesty.
amnistie(re) [amnisti'ere] *nf* amnesty.
amoniac [amo'niak] *nn* ammonia.
amonte [a'monte] *adv* (*în ~*) upstream.
amor [a'mor] *nn* love; (*legătură*) love affair; (*~ propriu*) self-love, vanity; (*mândrie*) (legitimate) pride, amour-propre; (*persoană iubită*) sweetheart; (*zeu*) Cupid; **a face ~ (cu)** to make love (to).
amorf [a'morf] *adj* amorphous.
amorsa [amor'sa] *vt mil* to prime; to fuse; (*o undiţă*) to bait; *also tech* to set in; to kick off; to start; *elec* to induce || *vr tech* to start.
amortisment [amortis'ment] *nn com* buying up; liquidation; paying off, payment.
amortiza [amorti'za] *vt com* (*un credit*) to liquidate; to pay/clear off; (*o anuitate*) to redeem; *jur* to amortize; (*un şoc*) to absorb, to cushion; (*un zgomot*) to deaden, to muffle; (*o cădere*) to break; (*oscilaţia*) to damp down/out || *vr* (*d. o maşină*) to be amortized • **~re** *nf com* (re)payment; redemption, paying off; *tech* damping; (*atenuare*) breaking; absorption; (*a sunetului*) sound-proofing.
amorţi [amor'tsi] *vi* (*a deveni insensibil*) to grow numb, to be dull/insensible; *coll* to go to sleep; (*a cădea în toropeală*) to become drowsy; (*a împietri*) *fig* to be hardened; (*a amuţi*) to be silent; to be hushed/mute; (*d. un animal care hibernează*) to become dormant || *vt* (*a anestezia*) to (be)numb; *fig* (*a calma o durere*) to temper, to appease.
amperaj [ampe'radz] *nn elec* amperage
amplasa [ampla'sa] *vt* (*a aşeza*) to set, to put || *vi* (*a fi ~t*) (*d. un oraş*) to lie; (*d. birouri*) to locate • **~ment** *nn mil* emplacement, gun pit; position; *constr* location, site.
amplifica [amplifi'ka] *vt/vr* to amplify; to increase; (*a dezvolta*) to develop; to embroider; to exaggerate; (*d. o lentilă*) to magnify.
amplitudine [ampli'tudine] *nf math* amplitude; *lit* vastness; *astron* diurnal arc; range.
amploare [am'ploare] *nf* ampleness, proportions; width, fullness; volume; compass, range; extent; *also fig* scope, amplitude; (*răspândire*) spreading, extension.

amplu ['amplu] *adj* ample, spacious; full; profuse || *adv* amply.
amprentă [am'prentă] *nf also fig* impress(ion), stamp, imprint; (*urmă*) impression; (*digitală*) fingerprint; (*a roţii*) track; mold; *fig* mark
amputa [ampu'ta] *vt* to amputate, to cut off • **~re** *nf* amputation; cutting off.
amuletă [amu'letă] *nf* amulet, talisman, charm.
amurg [a'murg] *nn* dusk, twilight; *fig* old age; decline; **în ~** in the twilight.
amuţi [amu'tsi] *vi* (*a deveni mut*) to be struck dumb, to become mute; *fig* to remain speechless; (*a tăcea*) to be(come) silent/mute || *vt* to dumb(found); to render silent; to hush, to muffle.
amuza [amu'za] *vt* to amuse, to entertain || *vr* to have a good time, to enjoy/amuse/divert oneself; to make merry.
an [an] *nm* year; **~ bisect** leap year; **la mulţi ~i!** A Happy New Year to you!; (*felicitări*) congratulations!; (*aniversare*) Happy Birthday!.
anacronic [ana'kronik] *adj* anachron(ist)ic, outdated.
anafură [a'nafură] *nf* Eucharist bread.
anale [a'nale] *nf pl* annals.
analfabet [analfa'bet] *nm/adj* illiterate (person).
analfabetism [analfabe'tism] *nn* illiteracy.
analgezic [anal'djezik] *nm med* painkiller; *also adj* analgesic, anodyne.
analitic [ana'litik] *adj* (*derivat de la "analiza"*) analytic(al); (*de la "anale"*) annalitic(al).
analiza [anali'za] *vt* to analyze; to examine, to test; to dissect; (*a cântări atent*) to ponder things (carefully); *gram* to parse || *vr* to analyze oneself.
analiză [ana'liză] *nf* analysis; *med* test; synopsis, abstract; *fig* critical examination, review; *gram* parsing.
analog [ana'log] *adj* analogous (to), similar (to) || *adv* analogically, similarly • **~ie** [analo'djie] *nf* analogy (to, with, between).
ananas [ana'nas] *nm bot* pine plant; (*fruct*) pineapple.
ananghie [a'nangie] *nf* hardship, hard condition; difficulty!; (*necaz*) predicament; *coll* mess; (*lipsă*) want, need(iness).
anapoda [a'napoda] *adj* topsy-turvy; wrong-headed || *adv* (*pe dos*) wrong side out; upside down; (*razna*) astray.
anarhie [anar'hie] *nf* anarchy.
anason [ana'son] *nm bot* anise; (*sămânţă*) aniseed, anise seed.
anatemă [a'natemă] *nf relig* anathema.
anatomic [ana'tomik] *adj* anatomical || *adv* anatomically.
anatomie [anato'mie] *nf* anatomy.
ancheta [anke'ta] *vt* to inquire into, to investigate; (*pe cineva*) to cross-examine, to question smb || *vi* to hold an inquiry, to investigate.
anchetă [an'ketă] *nf* inquest; (*poliţie*) investigation; probe; *jur* (cross-)examination; (*parlamentară*) inquiry; **~ Gallup** Gallup poll.
anchiloza [ankilo'za] *vr* to become ankylozed, to grow stiff; *fig* to become hide-bound || *vt* to ankylose, to stiffen • **~re** *nf* stiffening * **anchiloza**.
ancora [anko'ra] *vt* to anchor; *constr* to brace, to tie || *vi naut* to cast/to come to an) anchor; *fig* to pitch one's tent.
ancoră ['ankoră] *nf naut* anchor; *rail* anchor bolt; (*a balonului*) grapnel; *archit* brace; *fig* shift; (*de salvare*) (one's) sheet anchor.

andivă [an'divă] *nf bot* endive.

andosa [ando'sa] *vt econ* to endorse.

andrea [an'drea] *nf* (knitting) needle.

anecdotă [anek'dotă] *nf* funny story, anecdote.

anemic [a'nemik] *adj med* anemic, affected with anemia; (*slab, fără vlagă*) weak, feeble || *adv* weakly, feebly.

anemie [ane'mie] *nf* anemia, want/deficiency of blood; feebleness.

anemonă [ane'monă] *nf* anemone, wind flower.

anestezia [anestezi'a] *vt med* to anesthetize.

anestezic [anes'tezik] *nm/adj med* anesthetic.

anestezie [aneste'zie] *nf med* anesthesis, anesthesia.

anestezist [aneste'zist] *nm med* anesthesiologist, anesthetist.

anevoie [ane'voie] *adv* with difficulty, painstakingly; (*abia*) scarcely, hardly.

anevoios [anevo'ios] *adj* hard, difficult; rough; critical.

anexa [anek'sa] *vt* to annex; to append; to join; (*a alătura într-un plic*) to enclose.

anexă [a'neksă] *nf* annex; (*la un raport*) rider, schedule; (*la o carte*) appendix; (*la o scrisoare*) enclosure; (*d. venituri*) supplementary income; (*dependință*) outbuilding; *fig* appendage.

anexiune [aneksi'une] *nf* annexation.

angaja [anga'dza] *vt* to engage; (*într-o slujbă*) to hire, to employ; (*echipaj*) to sign on; (*recruți*) to enlist; (*a folosi*) to use; *mil* (*o luptă*) to commence; (*a convinge*) to oblige, to pledge; (*a începe*) to begin, to start; to set smth going; to open; to enter, to start upon; *jur* to institute; to invite || *vr* (*a se obliga să*) to pledge/bind oneself (to); (*a-și da cuvântul*) to pledge one's word; (*a promite*) to promise; (*într-un servici*) to take a job, to become employed; (*a porni pe un drum*) to take; *mil* to enlist; (*d. o luptă*) to commence • **~ment** [angazha'ment] *nn* commitment, pledge; (*promisiune*) plight • **~t** [anga'zhat] *nm* employee; *pej* hireling || *adj* pledged, engaged; (*în servici*) hired, employed; *pol* committed, aligned.

angelic [an'djelik] *adj* angelic(al), cherubic || *adv* angelically.

anghinare [angi'nare] *nf bot* artichoke.

anghină [an'ginā] *nf med* angina; quinsy.

angoasă [an'goasă] *nf psych* anguish, anxiety, distress.

angrena [angre'na] *vt* to throw/put into gear; *fig* to rally, to draw || *vr* to get into gear • **~j** *nn* gearing; *fig* wheels.

angro [an'gro] *adj/adv* (by) wholesale || *nn* wholesale market • **~sist** *nm* wholesale dealer.

anihila [anihi'la] *vt* to annihilate, to destroy • **~re** *nf* annihilation.

anima [ani'ma] *vt* to animate, to quicken; (*conversația*) to enliven; (*a însuflți*) to endow with life; (*a pune în mișcare, a împinge*) to drive; *fig* to smarten || *vr* to quicken, to come to life; to smarten; *fig* to become animated; (*d. chip*) to brighten/lighten up; (*d. ceartă*) to wax hot.

animal [ani'mal] *nn* animal, beast; *fig* brute; *coll* blighter; **~ de pradă** predator || *adj* animal.

animat [ani'mat] *adj* animated; (*plin de viață*) full of life; (*vioi*) alive, lively; (*o stradă*) busy.

animozitate [animozi'tate] *nf* enmity, hatred; spite.

anin [a'nin] *nm bot* alder (tree).

anina [ani'na] *vt ver* (*a atârna*) to hang (up); (*d. un cârlig*) to hook; (*a cupla*) to couple, to hitch; *fig* (*pe cineva*) to waylay, to buttonhole || *vr* **a se ~ de** (*d. o*

haină) to get caught on; (*a nu da drumul*) to cling to; (*a acosta*) to waylay; *coll* to buttonhole; (*a căuta pricină*) to find/pick fault with.

aniversa [aniver'sa] *vt* to celebrate || *vr* to be celebrated.

aniversare [aniver'sare] *nf* anniversary; (*a zilei de naștere*) birthday.

anod [a'nod] *nm elec* anode (plate), positive electrode.

anodin [ano'din] *adj* harmless; (*neinteresant*) dull, anodyne.

anomalie [anoma'lie] *nf* anomaly, abnormality; abberation, deviation.

anonim [ano'nim] *nm* anonymous person || *adj* anonymous; (*care nu vrea să-și dea numele*) unnamed • **~at** *nn* anonymity.

anorganic [anor'ganik] *adj* inorganic.

anormal [anor'mal] *adj* (*d. situații*) anomalous; (*d. însușiri*) abnormal; (*cu handicap mental*) mentally challenged; *fig* unjust, unfair || *adv* abnormally.

anost [a'nost] *adj* dull, insipid; *also fig* stale; (*d. persoane*) stodgy; (*d. glume*) pointless; tame.

anotimp [ano'timp] *nn* season.

ansamblu [an'samblu] *nn* ensemble; (*totalitate*) aggregate; (*întreg, tot*) entirety; general effect; *archit* pile; *mus* (vocal) ensemble; **de ~ general.

anșoa [an'shoa] *nn* anchovy.

antagonism [antago'nism] *nn* antagonism.

antagonist [antago'nist] *adj* antagonistic, opposed.

antarctic [an'tarktik] *adj* Antarctic.

antebelic [ante'belik] *adj* pre-war.

antebraț [ante'brats] *nn* forearm.

antenă [an'tenă] *nf* antenna; *coll* feeler; *rad, tel* aerial; *naut* lateen yard.

antepenultim [antepen'ultim] *adj* antepenultimate, last but two.

anterior [anteri'or] *adj* anterior (to); (*d. o dată*) earlier (than); previous; (*d. o perioadă*) former; (*d. o întâmplare*) prior (to), antecedent (to); *ling* front; *anat* fore, anterior || *adv* previously, before, earlier, formerly, prior to this.

anteriu [ante'riu] *nn* surplice.

antet [an'tet] *nn* heading.

antiaerian [antiaeri'an] *adj* anti-aircraft.

antibiotic [antibi'otik] *nn/adj* antibiotic.

antic ['antik] *adj hist, lit* ancient; old; (*d. mobilă*) antique; (*demodat*) old-fashioned, antiquated || *nm* ancient.

anticameră [anti'kameră] *nf* waiting room, anteroom.

anticar [anti'kar] *nm* second-hand bookseller; (*colecționar*) antiquarian, antique dealer || *adj mil* antitank • **~iat** [antikari'at] *nn* second-hand bookstore.

antichitate [antiki'tate] *nf hist* antiquity, ancient times; (*ca obiect*) curio; (*caracter învechit*) antiquatedness; (*vechime, caracter antic*) antiqueness.

anticipa [antichi'pa] *vt/vi* to anticipate, to forestall.

anticoncepțional [antikoncheptsio'nal] *adj* contraceptive, birth-control || *nn pl* contraceptive, birth-control pills.

anticonstituțional [antikonstitutsio'nal] *adj* anticonstitutional.

anticorp [anti'korp] *nm bio* antibody.

antiderapant [antidera'pant] *adj auto* nonskid(ding), antiskid.

antidot [anti'dot] *nn* antidote (for/to, against).

antifascist [antifas'chist] *nm/adj* antifascist.

antigel [anti'djel] *nn auto* antifreeze.
antiguvernamental [antiguvernamen'tal] *adj* antigovernment.
antihrist [anti'hrist] *nm* antichrist, archfiend, foe.
antilopă [anti'lopă] *nf* antelope; *(piele)* shammy.
antioxidant [antioksi'dant] *nm chem* antioxidant.
antipatic [anti'patik] *adj* unlikable; unprepossessing; *(ursuz)* morose; *coll* crabby, ill-natured; **mi-e ~ I** dislike him.
antipatie [antipa'tie] *nf (față de/pentru)* antipathy (to/against), aversion (for/from/to), dislike.
antisemit [antise'mit] *nm* Jew-baiter, anti-Semite || *adj* anti-Semitic.
antiseptic [anti'septic] *nn/adj med* antiseptic.
antisocial [antisochi'al] *adj* antisocial.
antişoc [anti'shok] *adj* shockproof.
antiteză [anti'teză] *nf* antithesis.
antologie [antolo'djie] *nf* anthology.
antonim [anto'nim] *nn* antonym || *adj* antonymous.
antract [an'trakt] *nn* intermission, interval; *also mus* entr'acte.
antrax ['antraks] *nn med* anthrax.
antren [an'tren] *nn* pep, go, liveliness, briskness, vivacity.
antrena [antre'na] *vt sp* to train; *(o echipă)* to coach; *(un biciclist, alergător, auto)* to pace; *(a stimula)* to stimulate; *(a ralia)* to rally; *(a atrage)* to draw; *(a atrage după sine)* to involve, to entail; *(a cauză)* to bring about; *tech* to drive || *vr sp* to train, to undergo training; *(a se înflăcăra)* to get carried away • **~ment** *nn* training; *auto* pace making; *mus* practice.
antrenant [antre'nant] *adj (captivant)* absorbing, captivating; *(d. muzică)* lively, catchy.
antrenor [antre'nor] *nm* coach, trainer; *(al unui boxer)* handler; *(al unui alergător, biciclist)* pacer, pacemaker.
antrepozit [antre'pozit] *nn* warehouse, storehouse; *naut* wharf.
antreprenor [antrepre'nor] *nm* (builder and) contractor, undertaker, entrepreneur.
antrepriză [antre'priză] *nf* private enterprise; *(societate com.)* company; firm; contract.
antreu [an'treu] *nn* anteroom; *(hol)* (entrance) hall, vestibule.
antricot [antri'kot] *nn* rib.
antropologie [antropolo'djie] *nf* anthropology.
anturaj [antu'razh] *nn* company, environment; set, circle of friends; associates, attendants; entourage, suite.
anual [anu'al] *adj* yearly, annual || *adv* yearly, annually, every year.
anuar [anu'ar] *nn* annual, yearbook.
anuitate [anui'tate] *nf fin* annuity.
anula [anu'la] *vt* to annul; *(un testament)* to render void, to rescind; to set aside; *(o lege, un permis)* to repeal/cancel/ rescind a law/permit; *(un aranjament)* to call off; *(un contract, un cec)* to cancel; *(un târg) coll* to call off; *(un vot)* to override; *jur* to overrule.
anume [a'nume] *adj* special; *(niște)* certain || *adv (cu numele de)* named; *(şi ~)* namely, that is to say; *(înadins)* deliberately, on purpose; specially.
anumit [anu'mit] *adj* certain.
anunţ [a'nunts] *nn* announcement, notice; *(reclamă la ziar)* ad(vertisement); *(la jocul de cărţi)* declaration, bid • **~a** *vt (a vesti)* to announce, to give notice of; to break the news to smb; *(a da un anunţ despre)* to ad-

vertise; *(pe cineva, un vizitator)* to announce, to usher in; *(pe cineva că...)* to inform smb of smth; *(a prevesti)* to foretell; *(a făgădui)* to promise; *(a licita, la jocul de cărţi)* to meld || *vr* to announce oneself.
anus ['anus] *nn anat* anus; *sl* arse, ass.
anvelopă [anve'lopă] *nf auto* tire, outer cover (of a tire).
anvergură [anver'gură] *nf avia* span, breadth; *fig* scope, amplitude.
anxietate [anksie'tate] *nf* anxiety.
aoleu [ao'leu] *interj (durere, suferinţă; compătimire; ameninţare)* ah!; *(spaimă)* ah!, bless you!, oh dear!; *(surpriză)* ah!, *coll* oh boy!, oh my!, dear me!, bless me!, blow me!; *(regret)* oh!, alack (the day)!; *(nerăbdare)* oh dear!; *(reproş)* come on!.
aortă [a'ortă] *nf anat* aorta.
aparat [apa'rat] *nn also fig* apparatus; device, appliance; *(maşină)* machine; instrument; gear, mechanism; *anat (digestiv)* system; *(personal)* staff; *(de stat)* machinery; **~ automat** *(cu fise)* slot machine; **~ foto** camera.
aparent [apa'rent] *adj* apparent, seeming; *(nereal)* not real; *(prefăcut)* sham; false; *(vizibil)* visible; evident; *jur (moştenitor)* heir apparent || *adv* apparently, to all appearances.
aparenţă [apa'rentsă] *nf (ivire)* appearance, look; outside; **în ~** apparently, seemingly, ostensibly.
apariţie [apa'ritsie] *nf (ivire)* appearance, coming out; *(sosire)* advent; *(publicare)* publication; *(publicaţie)* issue; *(naştere)* birth; *(înfiinţare)* setting up; *(nălucă)* apparition, ghost.
apartament [aparta'ment] *nn* apartment; suite, set of rooms.
aparte [a'parte] *adj* particular, peculiar, special; unique || *adv* apart; separately; *(în teatru)* aside, stage whisper.
aparteu [apar'teu] *nn* aside.
aparţine [apar'tsine] *vt* to belong to; *jur* to own; to be owned by.
apatic [a'patik] *adj* apathetic, sluggish, listless; *coll* lackadaisical; indolent, slothful; *(nepăsător)* indifferent || *adv* apathetically, passively.
apatie [apa'tie] *nf* apathy, listlessness, sluggishness.
apatrid [apa'trid] *nm* stateless person.
apă ['apă] *nf* water; *coll* Adam's ale; *(curs de ~)* waterway/course, stream; *(râu)* river; *(mare)* sea; ocean; *pl* waters; *(valuri)* waves; *(a unei stofe, pietre preţioase)* luster; *(lacrimi)* tears; saliva; *(sudoare)* sweat, perspiration; *med* dropsy.
apăra [apă'ra] *vt* to defend; to stand up for; *(pasiv)* to protect, to shield (against, from); *(a sprijini)* to support; *(a susţine)* to maintain, to champion; *(verbal, o cauză)* to give lip service to a cause; *(drepturi)* to stick up for one's rights || *vr* to defend oneself; to protect, to shield oneself from/against; *(a riposta)* to hit back.
apărător [apără'tor] *nm* protector, defender; supporter; *jur* counsel for the defense || *adj* protecting, * **apăra**.
apărea [apă'rea] *vi* to appear, to become visible; *(la orizont, prin ceaţă) also fig* to loom, to heave in sight; *(a veni)* to come; *(a se prezenta)* to turn up; *(a-şi face apariţia)* to make one's appearance, to show up; *(d. un actor)* to come on; *(pe scenă)* to walk/to tread the boards; *(la suprafaţă)* to emerge; *(brusc în ochii cuiva)* to break out upon the eyes; *(distinct)* to arise; to appear in public; *(a lua naştere)*

to come into being; (*a se revela*) to reveal oneself; (*a se întâmpla*) to occur, to happen; (*a avea loc*) to take place; (*d. o carte*) to be published.

apăsa [apă'sa] *vt* (*a atârna greu pe*) to weigh (up)on smb, to weigh smb down; (*a presa*) to press; (*a stoarce, a strânge cu putere*) to squeeze; (*butonul*) to push, to press; (*a accentua*) to (lay) stress (on), to emphasize; *fig* (*a asupri*) to oppress; (*a fi o povară pentru*) to lie heavy on; (*a chinui*) to torment, to torture || *vi* to weigh, to lie heavy; **a ~ pe** to press; *fig* to stress.

apăsător [apăsă'tor] *adj* heavy; (*asupritor*) overpowering, oppressive; (*copleşitor*) overwhelming; (*insuportabil*) unbearable; (*chinuitor*) torturing, tormenting; (*aspru*) hard, harsh || *adv* overwhelmingly.

apeduct [ape'dukt] *nn* aqueduct; (*conductă*) water main.

apel [a'pel] *nn* appeal; (*chemare*) call; call-in; (*strigarea catalogului*) *also mil* roll call, call-over; *telec* (tele)phone call; *jur* appeal • **~a** *vi* (la) to appeal (to) • **~ativ** *nn* appelative; name.

apendice [a'pendiche] *nn anat* appendix; (*generic*) appendage; (*într-o carte*) supplement; *fig* tag, tab.

apendicită [apendi'chită] *nf med* appendicitis.

aperitiv [aperi'tiv] *nn* appetizer, hors d'oeuvre || *adj* stomachic.

apetisant [apeti'sant] *adj* appetizing; savory, delicious; *fig* alluring.

apetit [ape'tit] *nn also fig* appetite.

apicultor [apikul'tor] *nm* beekeeper, apiculturist, apiarist.

apicultură [apikul'tură] *nf* beekeeping, apiculture.

aplana [apla'na] *vt* to appease, to settle; (*o ceartă*) to make up a quarrel; (*divergenţe*) to iron/to work out the differences || *vr* to quiet; to straighten out.

aplatiza [aplati'za] *vt tech* to flat(ten), to hammer down; *also fig* to blunt, to render dull.

aplauda [aplau'da] *vi* to clap one's hands, to cheer; (*cu putere*) *coll* to bring the house down; (*furtunos*) to applaud loudly; *coll* to raise the roof || *vt* to applaud, to cheer; (*un actor, în picioare*) to rise at an actor; to receive with applause; *fig* to greet, to welcome; (*a lăuda*) to commend || *vr* (*pentru*) to congratulate oneself (on)..

aplauze [a'plauze] *nf pl* applause, cheers; (*prelungite*) *coll* big hand (for).

apleca [aple'ka] *vt* (*la*) to incline; (*a încovoia*) to bend, to bow; (*a lăsa in jos*) to lower; (*ochii*) to cast down (one's eyes); (*capul, pentru a se feri*) to duck one's head; (*capul, înainte*) to bend, to lean forward; (*umerii*) to stoop; (*un ulcior*) to tilt; (*balanţa*) to tip the scales; (*a se vesteji*) to droop; (*a supune*) to subdue; (*a subjuga*) to enslave; (*a umili*) to humiliate || *vr* to bend, to lean out/over; (*d. un pom plin de rod*) to bend down; (*d. o corabie*) to list, to be heeling over; (*pt. a saluta*) to bow; (*adânc*) to bow down; *fig* (*a se supune*) to bend, to give in • **~re** *nf* bending, leaning, * **apleca** (*într-o parte*) lopsidedness; *also fig* inclination, bent (for/ towards).

aplica [apli'ka] *vt* (*la*) to apply (to); (*ceva, pe ceva*) to lay (smth on smth); (*o ştampilă*) to append (to); (*a da*) to give; to administer; *jur* to enforce; to execute, to carry out || *vr* to be applied; (*cuiva*) to refer to smb • **~bil** *adj* applicable, feasible.

aplică [a'plikă] *nf* bracket (for a lamp, etc); applied ornament.

aplomb [a'plomb] *nn* self-assurance, self-possession; (*neruşinare*) cheek, impudence.

apocalips [apoka'lips] *nn* apocalypse; revelation.

apocaliptic [apoka'liptik] *adj* apocalyptic(al).

apogeu [apo'djeu] *nn* apogee; *fig* height, zenith, climax, summit, peak.

apoi [a'poi] *adv* (*pe urmă*) then; (*după aceea*) afterwards, after that; (*pe lângă asta*) besides (that); (*totuşi*) however; (*în apodoze*) then, in this case; (*dar*) but; (*vezi?*) (do) you see?, well?, why?; (*bagă de seamă*) mind; **şi ~?** and (besides); (*ei şi ce?*) and what of it?

apologet [apolo'djet] *nm* extoller, idolater; apologist • **~ic** *adj* apologetic(al); laudatory || *adv* apologetically.

apometru [apo'metru] *nn* water meter.

apoplexie [apoplek'sie] *nf* (fit of) apoplexy; (*atac*) *coll* stroke.

aport[1] [a'port] *nn* contribution, share; *com* contribution of capital.

aport[2] [a'port] *interj* fetch it!

apos [a'pos] *adj* watery, aqueous.

apostol [a'postol] *nm also fig* apostle; (*carte*) Books/Acts of the Apostles, Acts.

apostrof [apos'trof] *nn* apostrophe • **~a** *vt* to apostrophize.

apoteoză [apote'oză] *nf* coronation; apotheosis, deification.

aprecia [aprechi'a] *vt* to appraise, to estimate the value of; (*greutatea*) to reckon; (*distanţa, temperatura etc*) to determine; (*a măsura*) to measure, to assess; (*a judeca*) to judge; (*a socoti*) to consider; (*a preţui*) to appreciate, to prize.

apreciere [aprechi'ere] *nf* (*estimare*) valuation, estimate; (*favorabilă*) appreciation; (*stimă*) esteem; judgment, opinion; (*măsurătoare*) estimation; (*creştere a valorii*) *fin* rise in value.

apret [a'pret] *nn text* dressing, starch, finishing preparation.

aprig ['aprig] *adj* (*înfocat*) fiery, ardent; (*pătimaş*) passionate; (*năvalnic*) impetuous; (*violent*) acrimonious; (*cu sânge fierbinte*) hot-blooded; (*d. cai*) high-spirited; (*aspru*) harsh; (*d. frig*) brutal; (*crud*) cruel; (*îndârjit*) bitter; (*feroce*) ferocious, fierce; *geog* steep || *adv* passionately; (*cu îndârjire*) bitterly; (*aspru*) harshly.

april(ie) [a'prilie] *nm* April.

aprinde [a'prinde] *vt* (*lampa, focul, pipa*) to light; (*cu ajutorul unui buton*) to switch on; (*a da foc la*) to kindle, to set fire to; (*a incendia*) to set on fire, to set fire to; (*un chibrit*) to strike; *fig* to excite, to inflame; (*a înfuria*) to get smb's temper up; (*imaginaţia*) to fire the imagination || *vr* to kindle; (*a lua foc*) to take/catch fire; (*a lumina*) to light; (*a străluci*) to shine; (*a izbucni*) to break out; (*la faţă*) to blush; (*d. faţă*) to redden; (*în legătură cu un subiect*) to warm up to one's subject; (*de băutură*) to grow excited; (*a se înfuria*) to fly into a passion; *coll* to sprunt, to flare up; *med* to become inflamed.

aprins [a'prins] *adj* alight; burning; (*strălucitor*) fiery; (*fierbinte*) hot; (*viu*) vivid; (*d. culori*) bright; *fig* passionate, hot; violent, vehement; (*focos*) crisp; (*brusc*) sudden; (*năvalnic*) impetuous; (*zelos*) zealous; (*d. o ceartă*) heated; (*d. o dorinţă*) fervent; (*d. dragoste*) ardent; (*la faţă*) flushed || *adv* passionately, heatedly.

aproape [a'proape] *adv* near (by), close (by); (*d. cineva*) within call; (*în vecinătate*) in the vicinity;

(temporal) near; *(în curând)* soon; shortly; *(peste puțin)* in a short time; *(cam)* pretty much, nearly; about, some, approximately; ~ **exact** about right; **pe** ~ near/close by; **de** ~ *(în spațiu)* near/close to; *(imediat lângă)* by, hard by; *(în vecinătatea)* in the vicinity of; *(în timp)* close on, on the point/brink of.

aproba [apro'ba] *vt* to approve of, to sanction; *(o lege, o măsură)* to endorse; *(a fi de acord cu)* to agree with smb to (do) smth; *(a consimți)* to consent to; *(oficial)* to agree formally to smth; *(a ratifica)* to ratify; *(o lege)* to pass a law || *vi (din cap)* to nod in approval; *(cu privirea)* to look with approval || *vr* to be carried.

aprod [a'prod] *nm* usher; *jur* bailiff, process server.

aprofunda [aprofun'da] *vt* to study/consider thoroughly, to go deeply/thoroughly into.

apropia [apropi'a] *vt* to bring/draw near(er); *(un scaun)* to draw up/in; *fig* to bring/draw together; to compare || *vr (de)* to come/draw/get near (to), to approach; *fig (a se împrieteni)* to become (good) friends, to make friends with; *(a fi iminent)* to impend; *(d. noapte)* to draw on.

apropiere [apropi'ere] *nf (ca acțiune)* approaching, * **apropia**; *(ca distanță)* nearness, proximity; *fig pol* rapprochement; *(intimitate)* intimacy; *(metodă la vânătoare)* stalking; **în** ~ close/near by; *(de acest loc)* near here; **prin** ~ somewhere near here/there.

apropo [apro'po] *nn* hint; *(răutăcios)* innuendo || *adv* by the way || *interj* incidentally, by the way, by the by(e).

apropria [apropri'a] *vt* to make appropriate; *(a-și ~)* to appropriate smth to oneself.

aproviziona [aprovizio'na] *vt (cu)* to supply (with); to provide with; to provision, to cater for || *vr* to take/lay in a stock/supply; to buy in, to provide oneself • ~**re** *nf* provisioning, supplies.

aproxima [aproksi'ma] *vt* to approximate, to estimate • ~**tiv** *adj* approximate; *(d. un calcul, o sumă)* rough || *adv* approximately, roughly; *(cam)* about, some • ~**ție** *nf* approximation; **cu** ~ approximately, at a rough guess.

apt [apt] *adj* able, capable; *mil* fit.

aptitudine [apti'tudine] *nf* aptitude, ability; *jur* capacity for.

apuca [apu'ka] *vt* to seize, to catch, to grip; to capture; *(a pune mâna pe)* to take/catch hold of; *(cu ghiarele)* to claw; *(a înșfăca brusc)* to snatch, to grab; *(ținând cu putere)* to grasp; *(cu dorința de a păstra)* to clutch; *(a lua)* to get; *(a surprinde)* to fall upon; *(d. noapte)* to overtake; *fig (a cuprinde cu privirea)* to take in; *(un drum)* to take; *fig (a trece prin)* to experience; *(a fi contemporan cu)* to have known; *(în viitor)* to live to see; *(a înțelege)* to understand; *(d. un sentiment)* to seize || *vr* **a se** ~ **de** *(a se prinde de)* to seize/grip smth; *(a începe)* to take up; *(a întreprinde)* to undertake; *(băutură)* to take to; *(unul pe altul)* to take each other by || *vi* **a** ~ **spre** to make for, to head for.

apune [a'pune] *vi (d. soare)* to set (down), to go down; *fig* to fade; *(a decădea)* to decline; *(a muri)* to die; *(a dispărea)* to vanish, to disappear.

apus [a'pus] *nn* west; *(asfințit)* sunset; *fig (decădere)* decline; *(moarte)* death; *(dispariție)* disappearance; *(trecut)* bygone || *adj fig* dead, faded; *(dispărut)* vanished.

ar [ar] *nm agr* are (100 square meters).

ara [a'ra] *vt/vi* to plough, to till.

arab [a'rab] *nm* Arab(ian) || *adj (d. persoane)* Arab; *(d. obiceiuri)* Arabian; *(d. limbă, literatură)* Arabic; **numere** ~**e** Arabic numerals; **Peninsula** ~**ă** Arabian Peninsula.

arabil [a'rabil] *adj* arable, tillable.

arac [a'rak] *nm* vine prop, stake.

aragaz [ara'gaz] *nn* gas stove, cooker.

arahidă [ara'hidă] *nf bot* ground/pea/earth nut.

aramă [a'ramă] *nf* copper; *(galbenă)* brass, yellow copper; *(roșie)* cuprite, red copper; *pl* copper/brass kitchen utensils; *(clopot)* bell; *(tun)* canon.

aranja [aran'zha] *vt (a pune în ordine)* to (ar)range, to set/put in order; *(cravata)* to straighten; *(părul)* to put straight; *(camera)* to tidy up; *(a înfrumuseța)* to trim (up); to organize; *(o serbare)* to get up; *(a pune la cale)* to plan; *(un program)* to draw up a program; *mus* to set; *fig (a pune la punct)* to settle; *fig (în sens negativ)* *(a falsifica un meci etc)* to fix; *(pe cineva)* *coll* to tear smb's character to rags/shreds; *(a se răfui cu)* *coll* to fix smb || *vr* to be arranged; *(aspectul)* to trim/tidy oneself up; *(a se rezolva)* to be set to rights; *(a ieși bine)* to turn out all right; *(a se stabili)* to settle (down); *(a-și găsi o situație)* to find a situation • **s-a** ~**t** he has settled/steadied down • ~**ment** *nn* also *mus* arrangement; *(și ordin)* order; *(înțelegere)* agreement, settlement.

arar(eori) [a'rareori] *adv* seldom, rarely.

arămiu [ara'miu] *adj* copper-colored, coppered.

arăta [ară'ta] *vt* to show; *(a expune)* to exhibit, to display; *(a indica)* to indicate; *(a marca)* to mark; *(d. contoar)* to read; *(a desemna)* to point out, to point to; *(cuiva un oraș)* to show smb around; *(a învăța)* to teach; *(a dovedi)* to prove; *(a manifesta, a da dovadă de)* to show; *(a trăda emoții)* to betray; *(a revela)* to reveal; *(a vorbi despre)* *fig* to betoken, to speak of || *vi (cu degetul la)* to point at/to; *(a părea)* to look, to seem, to appear || *vr* to show oneself; *(a apărea)* to appear; *(a deveni vizibil)* to come into sight; *(a se înfățișa)* to turn up; *(a se arăta la chip)* to show up; *(d. soare)* to shine out; *(a se vedea)* to be seen; *(a se dovedi)* to show oneself; *(a părea)* to seem, to appear.

arătător [ară'tător] *nn* forefinger; *tech* hand.

arătură [ară'tură] *nf (arat)* plowing; dressing; *(ogor)* ploughland.

arbitra [arbi'tra] *vt/vi jur* to arbitrate; *sp* to referee, to umpire.

arbitrar [arbi'trar] *adj* arbitrary || *adv* arbitrarily.

arbitru [ar'bitru] *nm jur* arbitrator, referee; *sp* umpire; *fig* judge; *(al eleganței)* arbiter of taste; disposer; **liber** ~ free will.

arbora [arbo'ra] *vt (un steag)* to hoist, to raise; *fig* to declare in favor of; to put on, to display.

arbore ['arbore] *nm bot* tree; *(tânăr)* sapling; *(fructifer)* fruit tree; *(verde)* evergreen; *naut* mast; *tech* shaft, spindle, axle; ~ **genealogic** genealogical tree, family tree.

arbust [ar'bust] *nm* bush, shrub.

arc [ark] *nn (armă)* bow; *geom* arc; *archit (boltă)* arch, vault; *tech (resort)* spring.

arcadă [ar'kadă] *nf archit* archway, arcade; *anat* arch.

arctic {'arktik] *adj* arctic.

arcui [arku'i] *vt* to bend, to arch || *vi* to bend.

arcuş [ar'kush] *nn mus* bow; fiddlestick.
arde ['arde] *vi* to burn; (*d. casă*) *also fig* to be on fire, to be alight; (*înăbuşit*) to smolder; (*ca iasca*) to burn like tinder; (*până în temelii*) to burn down; (*a lumina*) to light; (*d. soare*) to scorch; (*a da căldură*) to give heat; (*a fi fierbinte*) to be hot; (*a avea febră*) to be feverish/in a fever; (*d. o rană*) to smart; it's hot (news), it's very important; (*în jocurile de copii*) you are getting warm/hot! ‖ *vt* (*folosind foc, căldură, acid*) to burn; (*superficial*) (*o cămaşă la călcat*) to scorch; (*a pârli, a flamba*) to singe; (*d. carne: a rumeni*) to soar; (*a carboniza*) to char; (*a consuma*) to burn up; (*a da foc*) to set on fire; (*a încălzi*) to heat, to warm up; (*d. mâncare*) to smoke; (*a face scrum*) to burn to cinder; *tech* to calcinate; (*a topi, a sintetiza*) to clinker; (*a distruge*) to destroy (by fire); (*a frige*) to fry; (*a opări*) to scald; (*a pârli*) to singe; (*a cauteriza*) to sear; (*d. soare*) to scorch; (*a bronza*) to (sun)tan; *fig* (*a înţepa*) to lash; *fig* (*a înşela*) to take in; (*a păcăli*) to cheat; (*a păgubi*) to damage; *fig* (*a roade*) to gnaw; (*a îmboldi*) to urge; (*a pedepsi*) to punish; *fig* (*a lovi*) to deal/deliver a blow; *fig* (*a face*) to do, to make; *fig* to brand ‖ *vr* to be/get burnt; (*la soare*) to get/be sunburnt; *fig* to get hurt, to burn one's fingers; to be a loser; (*a se păcăli*) to be deluded, to deceive oneself; *coll* to be taken in; (*a pierde bani*) to be out of pocket.
ardei [ar'dei] *nm bot* pepper, pimento; (*mai ales iute*) chilly, paprika; ~ **gras** green/mild pepper; ~ **iute** hot pepper, cayenne (pepper).
ardezie [ar'dezie] *nf geol* (roof) slate; **de** ~ (*şi de culoarea ardeziei*) slaty.
ardoare [ar'doare] *nf* ardor; eagerness, fervor; (*zel*) zeal; warmth; **cu** ~ *adv* ardently, passionately, zealously.
arenă [a'renă] *nf* arena; ring; (*amfiteatru*) amphitheater; *lit* stand; *fig* field; **în** ~ in the arena.
arenda [aren'da] *vt* to lease; to rent.
arendă [a'rendă] *nf* (*drept*) lease; (*plată*) rent.
arest [a'rest] *nn* arrest; (*întemniţare*) imprisonment; (*închisoare*) prison, jail • ~**a** *vt* to arrest, to take in custody • ~**are** *nf* arrest(ing); capture.
argăseală [argă'seală] *nf* tanning; tannin.
argentinian [ardjentinia'an] *adj/nm* Argentine, Argentinean.
argilă [ar'djilă] *nf* clay, argil.
argint [ar'djint] *nn* (silver) coin, piece of silver; *fig* lucre; silver, *chem* argentum; *fig* (*alb*) argent; (*care conţine* ~) *chem* argentic; ~ **veritabil** sterling silver • ~**a** *vt* to silver; (*a albi*) to whiten; *fig lit* to cast a silver shimmer on.
argou [ar'gou] *nn* argot; slang; (*al lumii interlope*) cant.
argument [argu'ment] *nn* reason, *also math* argument.
arhaic [ar'haik] *adj* archaic; (*demodat, învechit*) obsolete, obsolescent.
arhanghel [ar'hangel] *nm* archangel.
arheolog [arheo'log] *nm* archaeologist.
arhiepiscop [arhie'piskop] *nm* archbishop.
arhiereu [arhie'reu] *nm* bishop.
arhipelag [arhipe'lag] *nn* archipelago.
arhiplin [arhi'plin] *adj* full (to capacity), full to the brim; (*aglomerat*) crowded; (*d. un autobuz, o încăpere*) crammed, packed.
architect [arhi'tekt] *nm* architect • ~**ură** *nf* architecture; *fig* framework.

arhivar [arhi'var] *nm* archivist, town-clerk, keeper of (public) records.
arhivă [ar'hiva] *nf pl* (*locul*) archives; (*obiecte*) archiv(e), records.
arici [a'rich] *nm* hedgehog, (land) urchin; (*de mare*) sea urchin; *zool* porcupine; (*bandă adezivă la îmbrăcăminte*) Velcro.
arid [a'rid] *adj also fig* arid, dry, barren; unproductive.
arie[1] ['arie] *nf* area; (*suprafaţă*) surface; (*zonă*) zone; (*întindere*) extent, expanse; ~ **de lansare** *astron* launching site.
arie[2] ['arie] *nf mus* aria.
arie[3] ['arie] *nf* (*de treierat*) threshing floor/ground.
arierat [arie'rat] *nm* moron, half-wit ‖ *adj* backward, half-witted.
arierate [arie'rate] *nf pl fin* arrears.
ariergardă [arier'gardă] *nf mil* rear guard.
arin [a'rin] *nm* alder (tree).
aripă ['aripă] *nf also fig* wing; *lit* pinion; (*de şoim*) sail; (*de peşte*) fin; *fig* shelter; (*de moară*) (sail) arm; (*de ventilator*) vane; (*de elice*) fan; blade; (*la roata unei trăsuri*) splashboard; *auto* mudguard; *avia* aerofoil; (*flanc*) flank; *pol* wing.
aristocrat [aristo'krat] *nm* aristocrat ‖ *adj* aristocratic.
aristocraţie [aristokra'tsie] *nf* aristocracy; (*oligarhie*) the upper ten (thousand).
aritmetică [arit'metikă] *nf* arithmetic.
arivist [ari'vist] *nm* arriviste, self-seeker; careerist, pusher; *sl* go-getter, place-hunter ‖ *adj* pushy.
arlechin [arle'kin] *nm* harlequin; (*culisă*) wing; (*reflector*) boom, perch.
arma [ar'ma] *vt mil* to cock, to prime; (*o mină*) to timber; *constr* to reinforce, to fortify, to strengthen; to sheathe, to armor; *naut* to commission, to fit out; *min* to prime • ~**ment** *nn* armament; arms, weapon; munition • ~**tă** *nf* army, forces; *fig* host, legion.
armator [arma'tor] *nm* (*proprietar*) shipowner; fitter.
armă ['armă] *nf also fig* weapon; *pl also* arms; (*puşcă*) gun, rifle; (*specialitate militară*) branch; ~ **chimică** chemical weapon; ~ **biologică** biological weapon; ~**e atomice** atomic/nuclear weapons; ~**e de exterminare în masă** weapons of mass destruction.
armăsar [armă'sar] *nm* (*pt. prăsilă*) stallion, stud (horse); (*tânăr*) colt; (*pt. călărie*) steed; *lit* palfrey, courser; *fig sl* (*d. un bărbat*) stud.
armean, armeană [ar'mean, ar'meană] *nm/nf/adj* Armenian; **limba** ~ (the) Armenian language.
armistiţiu [armi'stitsiu] *nn* armistice, *also fig* truce.
armonică [ar'monikă] *nf* accordion; (*hexagonală*) concertina; (*de gură*) mouth organ.
armonie [armo'nie] *nf also fig* harmony; (*înţelegere*) concord, concert.
armonios [armoni'os] *adj* harmonious ‖ *adv* harmoniously.
armoniza [armoni'za] *vt* to harmonize ‖ *vr* (*cu*) to harmonize (with); to be in keeping with; (*d. culori*) to tone (with).
armură [ar'mură] *nf* armor; panoply.
arogant [aro'gant] *adj* arrogant, domineering; *pej* chi-chi; (*dispreţuitor*) contemptuous, scornful ‖ *adv* arrogantly, hautstily.
aroganţă [aro'gantsă] *nf* arrogance, overbearing manner.
aromat [aro'mat] *adj* aromatic, fragrant; (*d. vin*) flavored ‖ *nn* (*mirodenie*) spice.

aromă [a'romă] *nf* aroma, flavor, fragrance; *(puternică)* tang; *(savoare)* relish; *fig* impress, smack.

arpagic [arpa'djik] *nn* chive, scallion; bulb for planting.

arsenal [arse'nal] *nn* arsenal; *fig* stock(-in-trade).

arsenic [ar'senik] *nn* arsenic.

arsură [ar'surǎ] *nf* (*rană*) burn; *(opăreală)* scald; *(durere, de la o rană)* smart, sharp pain; *(la stomac)* heartburn; * **arşiţă.**

arşiţă ['arshitsǎ] *nf* scorching heat; *sl* dog days; *also fig (febră)* fever.

artă ['artǎ] *nf* art; *(măiestrie)* skill, mastery; *(meşteşug)* craft(smanship).

arteră [ar'terǎ] *nf* anat artery; *(drum)* thoroughfare, main highway; *(în ţară)* arterial road/highway.

articol [ar'tikol] *nn (de ziar)* article; *(de lege)* item; clause; *com* commodity; *pl* goods, wares.

articulaţie [artiku'latsie] *nf* anat joint, articulation; *tech* joint.

artificial [artifichi'al] *adj* artificial, factitious; *tech* man-made; *fig* recherché, sophisticated; *(pretins)* sham || *adv* artificially.

artificier [artifichi'er] *nm* pyrotechnist; *mil* artificer; *min* shotsman, shotfirer.

artificiu [arti'fichu] *nn* artifice, artificial means; *(născocire)* (guileful) expedient, contrivance; makeshift; *pl* fireworks.

artilerie [arti'lerie] *nf* mil artillery.

artist [ar'tist] *nm (plastic) also fig* artist; *(în alt domeniu)* artiste; *mus, thea* performer, *(dramatic)* actor • **~ic** *adj (de artă şi de gust)* artistic(al); art-like || *adv* artistically.

artizan [arti'zan] *nm* artisan, handicraftsman, craftsman.

art(e)rită [arte'rita] *nf med* arthritis.

arţar [ar'tsar] *nm* maple tree.

arţăgos [artsă'gos] *adj coll* quarrelsome, acrimonious; *coll* cantankerous, ill-tempered.

arunca [arun'ka] *vt* to throw; *coll* to shy, to chuck; *esp fig* to cast; *(cu putere)* to hurtle; *(a azvârli)* to hurl, to fling; to deliver, to pitch; *(raze)* to dart (forth); *(o scrisoare la cutie)* to drop; *(a lepăda)* to throw off; *(la gunoi)* to throw away || *vi* **a ~ cu ceva în cineva** to throw/fling smth at smb || *vr* to throw/fling oneself; *(înainte)* to throw/fling oneself forward; to precipitate oneself; *(în apă)* to plunge into the water; *(asupra cuiva)* to attack smb.

aruncător [arunkă'tor] *nn/nm* thrower; *(de flăcări)* flamethrower; *(de mine)* (trench) mortar; *tech* kicker; *(de ciocan) sp* hammer thrower.

arvună [ar'vunǎ] *nf* earnest (money).

arzător [arză'tor] *nn* burner || *adj* burning, hot; *(d. vreme)* sultry; *fig* topical, urgent || *adv* ardently; *(intens)* intensely.

as [as] *nm also fig* ace.

asalt [a'salt] *nn* assault, storm; attack, onslaught; *(la scrimă)* bout; *(la lupte)* wrestling bout • **~a** *vt* to storm, to assail; *(a ataca)* to attack, to beset, to pitch; *fig* to assault, to beset.

asambla [asam'bla] *vt tech* to assemble; to fit together; to collate; *comp* to link; *elec* to connect, to join; *mech* to join (up), to couple.

asana [asa'na] *vt agr* to dike in; *(o mlaştină)* to reclaim, to drain; *(un oraş)* to improve the sanitation of; *fig* to improve; to normalize; *(literatura)* to purge; *(finanţele)* to reorganize, to stabilize.

asasin [asa'sin] *nm* murderer, assassin; *coll* zap • **~a** *vt*

to murder, to assassinate; *fig* to annoy, to bother, to pester to death.

ascendent [aschen'dent] *nm* ancestor; *rare* ascendant || *nn* influence (over smb), hold, pull || *adj* ascending, upward.

ascendenţă [ascen'dentsǎ] *nf* ascending line, ancestry; origin, descent, extract(ion).

ascensiune [aschensi'une] *nf* climbing, ascent; rising; *fig* advancement; progress, rise.

ascensor [aschen'sor] *nn* elevator, lift.

ascet [as'chet] *nm also fig* ascetic, hermit, anchorite; austere person; *(om retras)* recluse.

asculta [askul'ta] *vt* to listen to; *(a trage cu urechea)* to eavesdrop; *(un cântăreţ)* to hear; to examine; *(a crede)* to believe, to credit; *(a ţine seama de)* to hear; *(a se supune)* to obey; *med* * **ausculta** || *vi* to listen; **a ~ de** to obey, to heed.

ascultător [askultă'tor] *nm* listener; *(pe furiş)* eavesdropper || *adj* obedient, submissive || *adv* obediently.

ascunde [as'kunde] *vt* to hide, to conceal; *(vederii)* to screen; *(provizii, într-o ascunzătoare)* to cache; *(bani, valori) sl* to stash; to cover; *fig* to dissemble, to keep back; to slur; to keep to oneself; to mask; *(de cineva)* to keep back from smb || *vr* to hide (oneself), to be hiding/hidden; *(a sta la pândă)* to lurch, to lurk; *fig* to lie (behind smth); *(de cineva)* to hide from.

ascuns [as'kuns] *adj* secret, hidden, concealed; *(izolat)* secluded; *(pitit, la pândă)* lurching, lurking; obscure; abstruse; mysterious; unspoken; *(latent, tăinuit)* latent; *fig (secretos)* secretive, cagey; *(prefăcut, fals)* wry || *nn* secret, secrecy || *adv* **în/pe ~** secretly, stealthily, on the sly/the quiet.

ascunzătoare [askunză'toare] *nf* hiding-place, hideout; stash; *fig* by-lane; *(refugiu)* shelter; *(pt. vânat)* covert; haunt; den; nest.

ascunziş [askun'zish] *nn* cache; by-lane; *(loc de pândă)* lurch; *fig* secret.

ascuţi [asku'tsi] *vt also fig* to sharpen; *(pe piatră, cuţitul etc)* to grind; *(la tocilă)* to whet; *(în piele) (briciul)* to strop; to enhance; to intensify; to refine || *vr* to sharpen, to be sharpened; *fig* to be enhanced, to intensify • **~me** *nf* sharpness, acuteness • **~re** *nf* sharpening; *also fig* intensification; *tech* whetting • **~ş** *nn (de cuţit)* (cutting) edge; *(lamă)* blade; prick; *fig* power of expression; sarcasm • **~t** *adj (d. un cuţit, dinte)* sharp(ened); *(la tocilă)* whetted; *(d. unghiuri)* acute; *(d. ghiare)* sharp(-pointed) claws; *fig* keen; intense; bitter; shrewd; shrill; *(d. durere)* stinging; *(d. o remarcă)* witty; *(subtil)* subtle; *(sfredelitor)* piercing; penetrating; caustic.

aseară [a'seară] *adv* last night, yesterday evening; *(peste noapte)* overnight.

asedia [asedi'a] *vt* to besiege, to beleaguer, to beset.

asediu [a'sediu] *nn* siege; **stare de ~** state of siege/ emergency, martial law; **sub ~** under siege.

asemăna [asemă'na] *vt (cu)* to compare smth (to), to liken (to) || *vr (cu)* to resemble, to be/look (a)like; *(a egala)* to compare to; to match • **~re** *nf* similitude; *(între oameni)* resemblance, likeness; *(între idei)* similarity; *(asemuire)* comparison; **fără ~** beyond comparison, peerless.

asemănător [asemănă'tor] *adj* alike, similar || *adv* similarly, likewise.

asemenea, asemeni [a'semenea, a'semeni] *adj* like; *(asemănător)* alike; *(astfel de)* such; *geom* congruent || *adv* **de ~** also, too.

asentiment [asenti'ment] *nn* assent, consent; acquiescence.

aservi [aser'vi] *vt* to enslave, to subject; to subdue, to bind.

asezona [asezo'na] *vt* to season.

asfalt [as'falt] *nn* asphalt; (*mineral*) pitch, bitumen.

asfinţi [asfin'tsi] *vi* to set, to go down; *fig* to be on the wane; to be in decay • ~t *nn* sundown, sunset; (*crepuscul*) twilight; *fig* decline; (*punct cardinal*) west.

asfixia [asfiksi'a] *vt* to asphyxiate ‖ *vr* to choke, to suffocate; (*din cauza oxidului de carbon*) to be poisoned by charcoal fumes.

asiatic [asi'atik] *nm/adj* Asian, Asiatic.

asiduu [a'siduu] *adj* assiduous, relentless ‖ *adv* assiduously.

asigura [asigu'ra] *vt* (*materialiceşte*) to provide (for); (*a garanta*) to secure; to assure; (*un rezultat*) to ensure; (*o ţară*) to make a country secure; (*averea*) to consolidate one's fortune; (*o rentă cuiva*) to settle an annuity on smb; (*verbal: pe cineva de ceva*) to assure of; (*printr-o companie de asigurări*) to insure (against); (*a pune într-o poziţie stabilă*) to make smth firm/ steady; to fix, to fasten; to prop up; to make fast; (*alpinism*) to belay; (*a se ocupa de*) to take care of ‖ *vr* (*a se convinge*) to make sure/certain of; (*contra incendiului*) to insure oneself against, to take out an insurance • ~re *nf* (*acţiune*) making sure/safe; (*dată cuiva*) assurance; (*contra accidentelor*) insurance; (*garantare*) safeguard, guarantee.

asimetrie [asime'trie] *nf* asymmetry.

asimila [asimi'la] *vt/vi* to assimilate; to absorb; (*a compara cu*) to assimilate to; to compare with/to; to class as ‖ *vr* to be assimilated • ~re *nf* assimilation; (*înţelegere*) uptake.

asin [a'sin] *nm* ass.

asista [asis'ta] *vi* (*la*) to attend; to be present at; to watch; to look on ‖ *vt* to help, to assist.

asistent [asis'tent] *nm* assistant, assister, helper; (*în spital*) paramedic, medical social worker; (*universitar*) assistant professor; bystander, spectator ‖ *adj* present.

asistenţă [asis'tentsă] *nf* (*prezenţă*) presence, attendance; (*public*) audience, *relig* congregation; spectators; (*cei de faţă*) those present; (*societate*) company; (*ajutor*) assistance, help; (*juridic*) legal aid.

asmuţi [asmu'tsi] *vt also fig* (*a ~ împotriva*) to set/urge smth/smb on smb, to hound at smb.

asocia [asochi'a] *vt* to associate, to unite; *elec* to connect ‖ *vr* to share in, to join in smth; *econ* to join a corporate body; (*la o părere, iniţiativă*) to endorse; (*la o crimă*) to be a party to; **a se ~ cu** to associate/to join forces with; *econ* to enter into a partnership with • ~t *nm* associate, partner; fellow worker; (*principal*) senior partner; honorary member • ~ţie *nf* (*în diferite sensuri*) association; (*societate*) society, company; fellowship; *econ* partnership; *elec* connecting, coupling.

asolament [asola'ment] *nn* crop rotation, rotation/alternation of crops.

asorta [asor'ta] *vt* to assort, to sort; to match, to fit; (*un magazin*) to stock, to furnish ‖ *vr* to match, to fit/go well together, to suit one another; (*a nu se ~*) to clash with.

asortiment [asorti'ment] *nn* assortment, range, array.

aspect [as'pekt] *nn* (*înfăţişare*) look, appearance; (*ţinută*) bearing; (*şi privinţă*) aspect; (*situaţie, perspectivă*) *fig* complexion.

aspectuos [aspek'tuos] *adj* good-looking, neat; (*încântător*) engaging; (*de efect*) of striking appearance, showy.

asperitate [asperi'tate] *nf* asperity; (*a unei suprafeţe*) roughness, ruggedness; (*a stilului*) crabbedness; (*a caracterului, a vocii*) harshness, sharpness.

aspic [as'pik] *nn* aspic (jelly).

aspira [aspi'ra] *vt* (*a pronunţa aspirat*) to breathe (sound), to aspirate; (*aer, parfum*) to inspire, to breathe in; to sniff up; (*apă*) to suck up/in ‖ *vi* to inspire, to breathe in, to inhale • ~nt *nm* (*la*) aspirant to; *edu* candidate, graduate (student); *naut* midshipman; *mil* officer cadet • ~re *nf* inhalation; inspiration • ~tor *nn* (*de praf*) vacuum cleaner; *tech* aspirator, suction/exhaust fan ‖ *adj* suction, sucking • ~ţie *nf tech* aspiration, sucking up; inspiration, inhaling; *fig* (*la, spre*) striving (for), yearning (for/after); (*către scenă*) hankering after the stage.

aspirină [aspi'rină] *nf* aspirin.

aspri [as'pri] *vt/vr* to harden; *fig* to worsen, to aggravate.

asprime [as'prime] *nf* (*a pielii*) callosity; (*a vocii, vinului*) roughness; (*a vremii*) bitterness; *fig* (*de caracter*) harshness; (*severitate*) severity; rigor; (*a unui reproş*) sharpness; (*a tonului*) asperity.

aspru ['aspru] *adj* (*ant. 'moale'*) hard; (*ant. 'neted'*) rough, rugged; (*d. păr*) shaggy, wiry; (*răguşit*) raucous, gruff; (*d. voce*) rasping; *fig* (*sever*) rigorous; acrimonious; censorious; (*rece, fără inimă*) callous; (*exigent*) exacting; (*d. competiţie*) keen; (*d. condiţii*) rigid, strict; (*d. pământ*) shaggy; (*d. trăsături*) sharp; (*d. disciplină, privire*) severe, stern; (*d. măsuri*) strong; drastic; (*d. iarnă, climă*) inclement; (*tăios*) biting ‖ *adv* severely

asta ['asta] *adj dem f coll* this; that ‖ *pron dem* this one, that one

astăzi ['astăzi] *adv* today; (*acum, în zilele noastre*) now(adays); (*în prezent*) at present, at the present day; now.

astâmpăra [astâmpă'ra] *vt* (*a potoli*) to quiet; (*setea*) to quench; (*foamea*) to stay, to appease ‖ *vr* to calm down, to be at ease.

astea ['astea] *adj dem f pl coll* these ‖ *pron dem f pl coll* these; such things; **cu toate** ~ nevertheless.

astenie [aste'nie] *nf med* asthenia, (*slăbiciune*) debility.

asterisc [aste'risk] *nn* asterisk.

asteroid [astero'id] *nm astron* asteroid; (*planetă mică*) planetoid.

astfel ['astfel] *adv* in this way, thus; like this; (*aşa*) so; (*în felul următor*) in the following way; (*după cum urmează*) as follows; (*prin urmare*) therefore, hence.

astmă, astm ['astmă, 'astm] *nf med* asthma.

astringent [astrin'djent] *adj* astringent, tart.

astrologie [astrolo'djie] *nf* astrology.

astronaut [astrona'ut] *nm* spaceman, astronaut, cosmonaut • ~ică *nf* astronautics.

astronom [astro'nom] *nm* astronomer • ~ie *nf* astronomy.

astru ['astru] *nm* heavenly body; (*stea*) star; (*planetă*) planet.

astupa [astu'pa] *vt* (*o gaură*) to stop (up), to plug; (*o sticlă, cu dopul*) to cork (up); (*gura cuiva*) to gag; *fig also* to silence smb; (*urechile*) *fig* to close one's ears; (*cu degetele*) to stick one's fingers into one's ears; (*a închide*) to close up; (*a zidi*) to wall up; (*o groapă*) to fill up; (*a înveli*) to wrap up; (*o scurgere*) to stop a leak; (*a bloca*) to block; (*o ţeavă*) to clog; (*cu o bară*) to bar ‖ *vr* to be stopped (up); (*cu mâl*) to silt.

asuda [asu'da] *vi* to sweat, to perspire; (*a se aburi*) to steam, to become damp; *fig* to toil, to grind, to labor • ~**t** *adj* sweaty; hot; (*d. mâini*) clammy.

asuma [asu'ma] *vi* to assume, to take upon oneself.

asupra [a'supra] *prep* (*peste*) over; (*despre*) about, on, concerning; (*împotriva*) over; against; (*faţă de*) towards; for; (*spre*) to.

asupri [asu'pri] *vt* to oppress, to crush (down); to grind/bear/weigh down; to persecute; to tyrannize; to exploit; (*a nedreptăţi*) to wrong • ~**re** *nf* oppression, exploitation • ~**tor** *nm* oppressor, exploiter; autocrat ‖ *adj* oppressive; oppressing.

asurzi [asur'zi] *vt* to make smb deaf, to deafen; to din; *fig* to split smb's eardrum ‖ *vi* to grow deaf; (*brusc*) to lose one's hearing ‖ ~**tor** *adj* deafening.

aş [ash] *interj* why no!, not at all!

aşa [a'sha] *adj* such; ~ **ceva** such a thing, something like that; the like (of it); (*asta*) this ‖ *adv* so; (*astfel*) thus, in this way, like this; (*în felul următor*) in the following way; (*după cum urmează*) as follows; (*întocmai*) *coll* that's it/the thing/the stuff; (*bine*) *coll* there (you are); (*desigur*) of course, certainly; (*la întâmplare*) at random; (*oricum*) anyhow; (*interogativ*) really?, indeed? ‖ *interj* there!, OK!, all right!, fine!, that's it!, that's the ticket!; ~ **şi** ~ so so, not so hot, not too well; **cum** ~ how so?, how is that?, how do you mean?; ~ **zis** alleged; ~ **să fie** so be it!, agreed!, all right! • ~**dar** *adv* (*deci*) therefore, hence, consequently; (*astfel*) thus, so, in this way.

aşchia [ashki'a] *vt/vr* to split, to splinter, to be cut.

aşchie ['ashkie] *nf* splinter, chip, sliver, shave; *esp pl* flinders; *pl* shaving, scraping.

aşeza [ashe'za] *vt* (*a plasa*) to place; to posit; (*într-o poziţie sau atitudine*) to posture, to pose; (*a aranja*) to arrange; (*părul*) to smoothe; (*a pune*) to put; (*masa*) to set/lay the table; (*şine*) to lay; (*în ordine*) to put in order; (*grămadă*) to pile (up/on); (*în stive*) to stack; (*lemne*) to stow; (*în picioare*) to stand; (*pe cineva*) to seat; (*a ridica*) to raise; (*a construi*) to build; (*a face*) to make; (*un cort*) to pitch; (*a întemeia*) to found; (*a organiza*) to organize; to fix; (*a stabili*) to establish ‖ *vr* (*pe scaun, în fotoliu*) to sit down; (*a se instala comod*) to make oneself comfortable; (*în rând*) to line/draw up; (*a se stabili*) to settle (down); (*d. casă, teren*) to subside; (*d. precipitaţii*) to fall; (*a poposi*) to make a halt; (*a se potoli*) to calm down; (*a începe*) to begin • ~**re** *nf* (*acţiune*) lying, putting, seating; (*aranjare*) arrangement; (*poziţie*) situation; (*localizare*) location; (*omenească*) settlement; (*loc*) place; (*locuinţă*) dwelling; (*casă*) house; (*orânduire*) system.

aşijderea [a'shidzderea] *adv* likewise, as well, also, too.

aştepta [ashtep'ta] *vt* to wait for, to await; (*cu nerăbdare*) to look forward to; (*a păsui*) to give smb time; (*a spera în*) to hope for, to expect; (*a fi însărcinată*) to expect ‖ *vr* **a se** ~ **la** to expect, to be prepared for ‖ *vi* to wait; (*a pândi*) to lie in wait for, to lurk • ~**re** *nf* waiting; *pl fig* expectations, prospects; anticipation; **în** ~ in abeyance; **în** ~**a** in anticipation of, in the expectation of, pending.

aşterne [ash'terne] *vt* (*a întinde pe jos*) to spread (out), to lay; to strew; (*a scrie*) to write, to put down (in writing); (*a trânti*) to knock down ‖ *vr* to spread; (*d. zăpadă*) to fall; **a** ~ **masa** to lay the table, to lay dinner/supper.

aşternut [ashter'nut] *nn* bed clothes; (*strat*) layer, stratum; *typ* blanket; (*culcuş*) bed(ding).

atac [a'tak] *nn* attack, onslaught; (*al unei bănci*) hold-up; (*asalt*) assault; (*ofensivă*) offensive; (*nedorit, neplăcut*) taint; (*la cărţi*) lead; (*decisiv*) all-out attack; *fig* attack; *med* fit, stroke; bout; brush; (*uşor*) touch; *mus* entry • ~**a** *vt mil* to attack, to assail; to set upon; (*d. acizi*) to corrode, to etch; (*a critica*) to criticize, to run down; (*a începe*) to begin, to start; (*a contesta*) *frml* to impugn smb's motives/authority; *jur* to contest ‖ *vi* to (start an) attack

atare [a'tare] *adj* such; (*ca* ~) (*aşa cum e*) as such; in so many words; (*deci*) therefore, consequently.

ataşa [ata'sha] *vt* to attach, to join ‖ *vr also fig* (*a se* ~ *de*) to become attached to • ~**ment** *nn* (*pentru, faţă de*) attachment (to), affection (for) • ~**t** *nm* attaché.

atavism [ata'vism] *nn* atavism.

atârna [atâr'na] *vt* to hang (up) ‖ *vi* to hang (down); (*d. oameni, a fi spânzurat*) to be hanged; (*a avea o greutate*) to weigh; (*a valora*) to be worth; *also fig* to hang from; (*a depinde de*) to depend on.

atât [a'tât] *adj/adv indef* so much, (*d. timp*) so long • ~**a** *adj indef* so much; (*ca timp*) so long; (*singurul*) the only/sole/unique ‖ *pron indef* so much ‖ *adv* so much; (*ca timp*) so long; ~ **timp** for so long (a time); **numai** ~ just this, only that; no more, this/that much • ~**ea** *adj/pron indef f pl* so many.

atâţi [a'tâtsi] *adj indef m pl* so many.

atâţia [a'tâtsia] *adj/pron indef m pl* so many; ~ **oameni** so many people.

ateism [ate'ism] *nn* atheism.

atelă [a'telă] *nf* splint.

atelier [ateli'er] *nn* (work)shop, workroom; atelier, loft; (*hală*) shopfloor; (*de artă*) studio; (*muncitorii din* ~) shop/workroom staff; (*activitate practică*) workshop.

atemporal [atempo'ral] *adj* timeless, without relation to time.

ateneu [ate'neu] *nn* athenaeum.

atent [a'tent] *adj* (*la*) attentive (to), considerate (of), mindful (of); (*grijuliu*) cautious; (*d. o cercetare*) careful, thorough; (*politicos*) polite, courteous; (*amabil*) amiable; (*grijuliu faţă de ceilalţi*) thoughtful ‖ *adv* carefully, attentively, cautiously.

atenta [aten'ta] *vi* (*a* ~ *la*) to violate; *fig* to encroach/infringe on/upon; **a** ~ **la viaţa cuiva** to make an attempt on smb's life • ~**t** *nn* (criminal) attempt, assault (upon); (*la viaţa cuiva*) attempt (on smb's life), attempted murder; *fig* violation, infringement (on/upon) • ~**tor** *nm* (would-be) assassin.

atenţie [a'tentsie] *nf psych* attention; heed; (*observaţie*) note, notice; (*grijă*) care; *fig* consideration, respect; (*cadou*) present; (*la semafor*) caution ‖ *interj* be careful!, watch out!; caution!, (pay) attention!

atenua [atenu'a] *vt* to reduce, to lessen; to tone down, to soften; (*o pedeapsă, urmări*) to mitigate; (*gravitatea unei fapte*) to extenuate; (*a micşora*) to diminish; to palliate; (*a uşura durerea*) to alleviate, to allay ‖ *vr* to lessen, to diminish; to fade • ~**re** *nf* lessening, diminishing; breaking; mitigation; (*uşurare*) alleviation.

ateriza [ateri'za] *vi* to land, to alight • **~re** *nf* landing, alighting, landfall.

atesta [ates'ta] *vt* to attest, to certify, to certificate.

ateu [a'teu] *nm* atheist.

atinge [a'tindje] *vt* to touch; (*uşor, în treacăt*) to touch lightly, to brush; (*d. păsări*) to skim; (*la suprafaţă*) to brush against; *fig* to scratch the surface; (*a se lovi de*) to knock against; (*a deranja*) to disturb, to trouble; (*a ajunge la; un nivel*) to reach; *naut* (*într-un port*) to touch (at); (*un scop*) to attain; (*a realiza*) to achieve; *fig* (*a mişca*) to move; (*a jigni*) to hurt, to offend; *fig* (*a privi*) to concern; (*a menţiona*) to touch upon; (*a ponegri*) to slander smb ‖ *vr* (*cu*) to be in touch/contact, to be contiguous.

atitudine [ati'tudine] *nf* (*poziţie a corpului*) posture; (*faţă de*) attitude (towards); *fig* stand.

atlas[1] [at'las] *nn* (*geografic*) atlas, book of maps/plates.

atlas[2] [at'las] *nn* anat atlas.

atlet [at'let] *nm* athlete • **~ă** *nf* athlete • **~ism** *nn* athletics.

atmosferă [atmos'feră] *nf phys* atmosphere.

atol [a'tol] *nn* atoll, coral island.

atom [a'tom] *nn* atom; ~ **marcat** tagged/labeled atom • **~ic** *adj* (*d. greutate, teorie*) atomic; (*d. bombă*) atom; **energie ~ă** atomic energy, nuclear power; **centrală ~ă** atomic powerplant/station.

atomizator [atomiza'tor] *nn* atomizer, spray(er).

atomizor [atomi'zor] *nn tech* atomizer, spray; pulverizer.

atotcuprinzător [atotkuprinză'tor] *adj* all-embracing.

atotputernic [atotpu'ternik] *adj* almighty, all-powerful, omnipotent.

atotştiutor [atotshtiu'tor] *adj* omniscient ‖ *nm coll* know-it-all

atractiv [atrak'tiv] *adj* attractive, appealing, alluring, engaging, captivating, enthralling • **~itate** *nf* attractiveness, appeal.

atracţie [a'traktsie] *nf* attraction, pull; *fig* attractiveness, appeal; *pl* amusements, attractions; (*teatru*) variety/cabaret show.

atrage [a'tradje] *vt* (*d. magnet, soare*) *also fig* to attract, to draw; (*a momi*) to (al)lure, to entice; (*a ispiti*) to tempt, to seduce; (*a câştiga*) to win; (*după sine*) to bring about, to trigger; **a-şi ~ ...** to arouse/draw ... upon one; (*critica, elogiile*) to come in for; (*dispreţul*) to fall into smb's contempt; (*mânia*) to bring down smb's anger upon one; (*neplăceri*) to get (oneself) into trouble, *coll* to get (oneself) into a mess; (*ura, cheltuieli, pierderi*) to incur; *recip* to attract one another.

atrăgător [atrăgă'tor] *adj* attractive, winning; *coll* cunning; stirring; lively, catchy; (*ademenitor*) inviting, engaging; (*irezistibil*) compelling; (*frumos*) beautiful, handsome ‖ *adv* attractively, invitingly.

atribui [atribu'i] *vt* to assign (to), to allot (to); (*a acorda*) to confer on, to bestow on; (*a distribui*) to distribute, to assign; (*un rol, teatru*) to cast smb for; (*o faptă, o intenţie, o carte*) to attribute to, to ascribe to; (*un proiect*) to credit smb with a plan, to give smb credit for a plan; (*în sens negativ*) to fasten smth on smb; to impute to; (*importanţă*) to attach; (*o vină*) to pin the guilt on smb; (*a-şi ~*) to assume, to claim ‖ *vr* (*a fi atribuit*) to be assigned/distributed/ attributed.

atribut [atri'but] *nn* attribute; (*calitate*) quality; symbol; (*semn*) sign; (*emblemă*) emblem, hallmark; (*însemne*) *pl* insignia.

atribuţie [atri'butsie] *nf* duty, task, obligation(s); (*putere*) *pl* power, prerogative, competence.

atroce [a'troche] *adj* savage, heinous; (*groaznic*) ghastly, awful; (*durere*) excruciating, agonizing ‖ *adv* heinously, savagely; shockingly, awfully.

atrocitate [atrochi'tate] *nf* atrociousness (of smth); (*ca act*) atrocity, atrocious act; dreadful thing, horrible deed/crime.

atu [a'tu] *nn also fig* trump (card); *fig* the best card.

atunci [a'tunch] *adv* then, at that time; by then; (*până la vremea aceea*) before then; (*în cazul ăsta*) in this/that case; **chiar ~** just/right then; **pe ~** then, at that time, in those days.

aţă ['atsă] *nf* (*în diferite sensuri*) thread; yarn; (*de cusut*) sewing thread; cotton; *bot* fiber, filament.

aţâţa [atsâ'tsa] *vt* (*a aprinde*) to light, to kindle; (*a înteţi*) to stir, to fan; *fig* to stir up, to add fuel to, to arouse; (*a asmuţi*) to set; (*a instiga*) to instigate, to incite; to foment; (*a stimula*) to whet.

aţinti [atsin'ti] *vt* (*ochii*) to direct/to fix/to rivet one's eyes on; (*a concentra*) to focus smth on; (*a ochi*) to aim/point (a gun) at ‖ *vr* to stare, to look fixedly.

aţipi [atsi'pi] *vi* to doze, to drowse off; to get a nap.

au [au] *conj* (*sau*) or ‖ *interj* oh!, ouch!, ah!.

audia [audi'a] *vt jur* to interrogate, to hear; (*cursuri*) to attend; (*un curs, ca oaspete*) to audit; (*a asculta*) to listen to, to give a hearing to; to audition.

audienţă [audi'entsă] *nf* (*la*) audience, hearing (with, of); (public) audience, public.

audiere [audi'ere] *nf* examination, hearing.

audiovizual [audiovizu'al] *adj* audio-visual.

auditor [audi'tor] *nm* listener • **~iu** *nn* (*persoane*) audience, public; (*sală*) auditorium, auditory.

audiţie [au'ditsie] *nf* hearing, audition; concert.

augur [au'gur] *nn* augury, omen; *neg* portent, auspice ‖ *nm* augur; **de bun ~** auspicious, favorable; **de rău ~** of ill omen, ominous.

august[1] ['august] *nm* August.

august[2] [au'gust] *adj* august, stately, majestic.

aulă ['aulă] *nf* lecture room/hall, assembly hall.

aur ['aur] *nn* gold, *chem* aurum; *coll* gold, money, wealth; (*avere, bogăţie*) *fig* Mammon; **de ~** gold; *fig lit* golden.

aureolă [aure'olă] *nf astron* halo, nimbus, ring; glory; charisma.

auriu [au'riu] *adj* golden; *fig* bright, brilliant.

auroră [au'roră] *nf* dawn, daybreak, break of day; aurora; **aurora boreală** the northern lights, aurora borealis.

auster [aus'ter] *adj* (*d. viaţă, condiţii*) austere, temperate; (*d. post*) strict; ascetic; (*d. cineva*) stern, straitlaced; (*d. stil*) severe; *sl* bare-bones • **~itate** *nf* austerity; strictness, sternness.

australian(ă) [australi'an(ă)] *nm/nf/adj* Australian.

austriac(ă) [austri'ak(ă)] *nm/nf/adj* Austrian.

autentic [auten'tik] *adj* authentic, genuine; (*d. o copie*) certified, exemplified • **~itate** *nf* authenticity, genuineness.

autentifica [autentifi'ka] *vt* to authenticate, to notarize, to certify • **~re** *nf* authentication.

autism [au'tism] *nn med* autism.

autoamăgire [autoamă'djire] *nf* self-delusion/complacency, indulging in illusions.

autoanaliză [autoana'liză] *nf* self-examination.

autoapărare [autoapă'rare] *nf* self-defense.

autobiografie [autobiogra'fie] *nf* autobiography; *fig* personal record, background.

autobuz [auto'buz] *nn* (motor)bus.

autocamion [autokami'on] *nn* truck.

autocamionetă [autokamio'netă] *nf* pick-up truck.

autocar [auto'kar] *nn* (motor)coach, touring/sightseeing car.

autocisternă [autochis'ternă] *nf* tank truck, tanker.

autoconservare [autokonser'vare] *nf* self-preservation, self-maintenance.

autocrat [auto'krat] *nm* autocrat, tyrant.

autodeterminare [autodetermi'nare] *nf pol* self-determination, self-government.

autodidact [autodi'dakt] *nm* self-taught/-educated man.

autogară [auto'gară] *nf* bus terminal.

autograf [auto'graf] *nn* autograph || *adj* autographic(al).

autohton [autoh'ton] *adj* autochthonous, aboriginal, local || *nm* native.

automat [auto'mat] *nn* automaton, machine; (*pt. dulciuri*) slot-machine; (*pt. muzică*) juke-box; *mil* tommygun, automatic || *adj* automatic(al), automatous.

automatizare [automati'zare] *nf* automa(tiza)tion.

automobil [automo'bil] *nn* automobile, (motor)car; (*de joacă*) go-kart; (*de bâlci*) bumper car || *adj* self-propelled/-propelling.

autonom [auto'nom] *adj* autonomous, independent; self-contained, self-reliant.

autonomie [autono'mie] *nf* autonomy, independence, self-government; *avia* flight range

autoportret [autopor'tret] *nn* portrait of the artist, self-portrait.

autopropulsie [autopro'pulsie] *nf* self-propulsion.

autopsie [auto'psie] *nf* autopsy, postmortem (examination).

autor [au'tor] *nm* author, maker, originator, founder; (*al unui proiect*) contriver, promoter; (*al unei crime*) perpetrator; *jur* principal; (*arte*) writer, composer, painter.

autoritar [autori'tar] *adj* authoritative, authoritarian, overbearing.

autoritate [autori'tate] *nf* authority; (*caracter autoritar*) authoritativeness; *pl* authorities; *coll* the law; (*specialist*) expert (on).

autoriza [autori'za] *vt* to authorize, to permit; to license; to approve; (*pe cineva*) to empower; *fig* to justify, to sanction • **~ţie** *nf* permit, license, accreditation; permission.

autoservire [autoser'vire] *nf* self-service; *cu* ~ self-service.

autostop [auto'stop] *nn* traffic lights; block signal; (*ca mod de a călători*) hitchhiking.

autostradă [auto'stradă] *nf* highway, freeway.

autoturism [autotu'rism] *nn* (motor)car, vehicle.

autovehicul [autove'hikul] *nn* motor vehicle.

auxiliar [augzili'ar] *adj* auxiliary; (*suplimentar*) supplementary; additional || *nn gram* auxiliary.

auz [a'uz] *nn* hearing • **~i** *vt* to hear; (*a asculta*) to listen; (*a afla*) to learn; (*a i se spune*) to be told; (*din întâmplare*) to overhear || *vi* to hear; (*a afla*) to learn || *vr* to be heard; to get/spread about.

aval [a'val] *nn* lower part of a stream; (*în* ~) downstream; *econ* endorsement on a bill.

avalanșă [ava'lanșă] *nf* avalanche.

avangardă [avan'gardă] *nf mil* advanced detachment/guard; *fig* vanguard.

avanpost [avan'post] *nn mil* outpost.

avanpremieră [avanpremi'eră] *nf* preview; private view; (*teatru*) dress rehearsal.

avans [a'vans] *nn com* advance/earnest (money); loan; *tech* advance; *pl* advances, overtures; encouragement; *sp* start, lead; *fig* advantage; the upper hand; **în** ~ in advance, beforehand • ~**a** *vi* (*a înainta*) to advance, to move/step/go forward; (*d. o corabie*) to make headway; (*spre*) to head towards; (*cu pași mari*) to stride along; (*a-și croi drum*) to make one's way; (*cu greu*) to drag oneself along; to progress; (*a promova în serviciu*) to promote; (*în grad*) to advance in rank || *vt* (*pe cineva*) to promote; (*bani*) to advance; to pay in advance; (*a propune*) to put forward; *mil* (*trupele*) to move the troops forward.

avantaj [avan'tazh] *nn* advantage, benefit; (*folos*) avail; (*față de concurență*) *econ* competitive edge • ~**os** *adj* advantageous, favorable; fruitful; (*potrivit*) becoming (*dress*) || *adv* to great advantage, advantageously • ~**a** *vt* to put/set in advantage; (*a proteja*) to favor.

avar [a'var] *nm* miser, skinflint || *adj* stingy, miserly, avaricious.

avaria [avari'a] *vt* to damage, to spoil || *vr* to deteriorate, to perish, to go bad.

avarie [a'varie] *nf* damage, injury.

avânt [a'vânt] *nn* (*la fugă*) running start; (*la săritură*) running jump; (*la plonjare*) running dive; (*salt*) spring, bound, dash; (*dezvoltare*) raising, development; (*progres*) progress; (*propășire*) advance(ment); (*elan*) élan, upsurge; (*impuls*) momentum, impetus; (*entuziasm*) enthusiasm; (*însuflețire*) animation; (*energie*) dash, swing • ~**a** *vr* to dash, to rush, to dart; to plunge || *vt* to push, to dart, to dash.

avea [a'vea] *vt* to have (got); (*a poseda*) to possess, to be in possession of; (*a se bucura de*) to enjoy; (*a* ~ *în componență*) to consist of, to be composed of; (*a purta*) to carry; (*a fi de o anumită înălțime, vârstă*) to be high/old; (*a simți*) to feel; (*a fi autorul*) to be the author of || *v aux* to have || *vr* (*a se* ~ *bine cu cineva*) to get on/along well, to be on good terms with.

aventura [aventu'ra] *vr* to expose oneself, to take too many risks.

aventură [aven'tură] *nf* adventure; (*sentimentală*) intrigue, (love) affair.

aventurier [aventuri'er] *nm* adventurer; happy-go-lucky fellow; soldier of fortune.

avere [a'vere] *nf* fortune, wealth; (*bani*) money; (*bunuri*) goods; (*proprietate*) property, assets, estate; (*stare*) pile.

aversă [a'versă] *nf* (rain)shower; downfall.

aversiune [aversi'une] *nf* (*față de*) aversion to/for/from, dislike to/for/of, distaste for.

avertisment [avertis'ment] *nn* warning; (*către cititori*) prefatory note, foreword; (*înștiințare*) notice.

avertiza [averti'za] *vt* to warn; (*a înștiința*) to give smb notice, to notify, to advise of smth • ~**re** *nf* warning, notifying.

aviator [avia'tor] *nm* pilot, airman, flier, flyer.

aviație [avi'atsie] *nf* aviation; aircraft; (*forță aeriană*) air force; (*civilă*) civil aviation, airlines.

avid [a'vid] *adj* greedy, grasping, eager || *adv* greedily, eagerly.

avion [avi'on] *nn* aircraft, airplane; (*pentru mărfuri și pasageri*) combination aircraft.

aviz [a'viz] *nn* note, notice, notification; *also com* advice; (*părere*) opinion, judgment; (*punct de vedere*) point of view; *tech* recommendation • ~a *vt* to give smb notice; to inform; to let know; *com* to advise of smth; (*a avertiza*) to warn; (*a aproba*) to endorse, to approve || *vi* to advise, to decide • ~ier *nn* notice board, clipboard, bulletin board, poster board.

avocat [avo'kat] *nm* lawyer, attorney; (*pledant*) barrister(-at-law); (*al apărării*) counsel for the defense; *fig* advocate, champion; (*intermediar*) mediator.

avort [a'vort] *nn* (*spontan*) miscarriage; (*chirurgical*) abortion • ~a *vi* to miscarry, to abort.

avuție [avu'tsie] *nf* riches, wealth, richness.

ax [aks] *nn* axle, spindle • ~ă *nf* axis; *tech* axle, spindle; (*de macara*) pin.

axiomă [aksi'omă] *nf* axiom.

azalee [aza'lee] *nf bot* azalea.

azbest [az'best] *nn* asbestos.

azerbaidjan [azerbaid'zhan] *adj/nm* Azerbaijani.

azi ['azi] *nn/adv* today.

azil [a'zil] *nn* asylum, mental institution, nursing home; *fig* refuge, shelter.

azot [a'zot] *nn* nitrogen, azote.

azur [a'zur] *nn* azure, blue.

azvârli [azvâr'li] *vt* (*a arunca*) to throw, to sling, to fling; (*afară*) to throw out; (*în sus*) to toss, to throw up || *vr fig* to fling oneself (into); (*asupra*) to dash against || *vi* (*d. animale*) to kick.

B

ba [ba] *adv* no, not at all, on the contrary; (*da*) yes, of course, indeed; (*mai mult decât atât*) moreover, even more.

babă ['babă] *nf* old woman; *pej* (old) bag, crone, hag; (*apelativ*) my dear old woman, granny.

babord [ba'bord] *nn naut* port(side).

babuin [babu'in] *nm zool* baboon.

bac [bak] *nn* ferry(boat).

bacalaureat [bakalau'reat] *nm* (*persoană*) school graduate || *nn* school-leaving examination, baccalaureate.

baci ['bach] *nm* (head) shepherd; (*conducător*) leader.

bacil [ba'chil] *nm bio* bacillus, *pl* bacilli.

bacon [ba'kon] *nn* ham.

bacșiș [bak'shish] *nn* tip, baksheesh.

bacterie [bak'terie] *nf* bacterium, *pl* bacteria.

baga [ba'ga] *nf* tortoiseshell.

bagaj [ba'gazh] *nn* luggage; *mil* baggage.

bagatelă [baga'telă] *nf* trifle, unimportant/insignificant matter; *mus* bagatelle.

bagateliza [bagateli'za] *vt* to minimize, to belittle, to make light of.

baghetă [ba'getă] *nf* wand, stick; *mus* baton; (*pt. indicat pe hartă*) pointer; (*pâine*) (long thin) loaf of bread, baguette; *tech* wood casing/strip; *constr* beading, strip of wood.

baie ['baie] *nf* (*îmbăiere*) bathe; (*cameră*) bathroom; (*cadă*) bathtub; (*scăldat*) dip, swim(ming); *pl* (*stațiune*) spa; *tech, chem* bath.

baionetă [baio'netă] *nf* bayonet.

bal [bal] *nn* ball, party.

baladă [ba'ladă] *nf lit, mus* ballad.

balama [bala'ma] *nf* hinge; (*îmbinare, articulație*) joint.

balamuc [bala'muk] *nn* madhouse, lunatic asylum,

bedlam; *coll* booby-hatch; *fig* (*dezordine*) confusion, disorder, muddle, mess.

balans [ba'lans] *nn* balancing, rocking; (*echilibru*) poise • ~a *vt* (*a legăna*) to rock, to swing; (*a ține în echilibru*) to balance, to poise || *vr* to rock, to swing, to sway; (*d. vapoare*) to toss • ~oar *nn* rocking chair; *coll* rocker; seesaw, (child's) swing.

balanță [ba'lantsă] *nf* balance; (*cântar*) (pair of) scales; *astrol* Libra; *econ* balance.

balast [ba'last] *nn* ballast, roadbed; *naut* ballast tank; *fig* lumber, burden.

balaur [ba'laur] *nm* dragon; (*monstru*) monster • ~ul *astron* The Dragon.

balcanic [bal'kanik] *adj geog* Balkan.

balcon [bal'kon] *nn constr* balcony.

bale ['bale] *nf pl* slobber, slaver, (*la animale*) foam, froth.

balenă [ba'lenă] *nf* whale; (*lamelă pt. corset*) whalebone; (corset-)stay; *astron* Balena Cetus.

balerin [bale'rin] *nm* ballet dancer • ~ă *nf* ballerina, ballet dancer.

balet [ba'let] *nn* ballet.

baligă ['baligă] *nf* (cow) dung, droppings; (*băligar*) manure; *coll* muck.

balistic [ba'listik] *adj mil* ballistic • **rachetă ~ă** ballistic missile.

baliverne [bali'verne] *nf pl* twaddle, nonsense; *coll* humbug, bunkum; *sl* crap, bullshit, a pile of rubbish/ crap.

baliză [ba'liză] *nf* (*plutitoare*) buoy; (*luminoasă*) beacon, seamark; *avia* runway light; *auto* (road)sign; (*schi*) marker.

balnear [balne'ar] *adj* balneal • **stațiune ~ă** spa, seaside resort.

balon [ba'lon] *nn* balloon; (*de aer, săpun*) bubble; *sp* (*minge*) ball; (*fulgarin*) raincoat.

balonzaid [balonza'id] *nn* raincoat.

balot [ba'lot] *nn* bale, pack, package, bundle.

balotaj [balo'tazh] *nn sp, pol* tie(break), tiebreaker; *pol* run-off, second ballot.

balsam [bal'sam] *nn* balsam; conditioner; *fig* balm.

baltă ['baltă] *nf* (*băltoacă*) pool, puddle, pond; (*mlaștină*) swamp, marsh, bog.

balustradă [balu'stradă] *nf* (*la balcon, terasă*) balustrade; (*la scară*) rail, railing, banisters; (*pod, balcon*) parapet.

bamă ['bamă] *nf bot* okra (pod).

bambus ['bambus] *nm* bamboo; **muguri de ~** bamboo shoots.

ban [ban] *nm* coin (the hundredth part of a "leu"); *pl* currency; *pl* money.

banal [ba'nal] *adj* (*obișnuit*) (*d. conversație, idei*) banal, trite; (*d. persoană*) ordinary, run-of-the-mill; (*curent*) (*d. știre, incident*) everyday, commonplace; (*d. viață*) humdrum; (*uzat*) (*d. expresii*) hackneyed; (*neimportant*) trivial, platitudinous || *adv* in a commonplace/banal manner.

banan(ier) [ba'nan(i'er)] *nm bot* banana tree.

banană [ba'nană] *nf* banana; *elec* banana plug/jack.

banc[1] [bank] *nn* (*grămadă*) bank, shoal.

banc[2] [bank] *nn* (*glumă*) joke, quip, anecdote, wisecrack.

banc[3] [bank] *nn* (work)bench.

bancă[1] ['bankă] *nf* (*de șezut*) (*în parc*) bench; (*școlară*) desk; (*în biserică*) pew; (*la tribunal*) dock.

bancă[2] ['bankă] *nf econ* bank.

bancher [ban'ker] *nm* banker.

banchet [ban'ket] *nn* banquet, feast.

banchetă [ban'ketă] *nf* bench, settee.

banchiză [ban'kiză] *nf geog* ice bank/floe/pack.

bancnotă [bank'notă] *nf econ* bill.

bancomat [banko'mat] *nn* ATM (Automatic Teller Machine).

bandaj [ban'dazh] *nn* bandage, dressing; (*pt. hernie*) truss; *tech* steel/rubber tire • ~a *vt* to bandage, to dress.

bandă¹ ['bandă] *nf phys, tech* band, belt, strap, strip, tape.

bandă² ['bandă] *nf* (*grup*) band, gang, pack; *fig* clique, coterie.

banderolă [bande'rolă] *nf* banderole.

bandit [ban'dit] *nm* bandit, gangster, brigand; *fig* villain, crook, rogue, swindler • ~esc *adj* criminal, bandit-like; (*de jaf*) predatory; (*la drumul mare*) highway robbery.

banduliera [banduli'eră] *nf* sling, shoulder strap/belt.

bang [bang] *interj* clash, ding-dong, bong.

baptist [bap'tist] *nm/adj* Baptist.

bar¹ [bar] *nn* (*tejghea*) bar; (*local*) café, nightclub.

bar² [bar] *nm phys* bar.

bara [ba'ra] *vt* (*a opri*) to bar; (*a bloca*) to block up, to close; (*un râu*) to dam; *fig* to obstruct, to thwart; (*a trage o bară*) to cross; (*a anula*) to cross out, to strike out.

baracă [ba'rakă] *nf* hut, shed; *coll* shack; (*dugheană*) booth.

baraj [ba'razh] *nn* dam; dike, dyke; (*mic*) weir; *mil* barrage; (*d. competiție*) tiebreak(er); ~ **de poliție** road block, police cordon.

bară ['bară] *nf auto, tech, jur, mus* bar; (*drug*) crowbar; (*tijă*) rod; (*pârghie*) lever; *typ* oblique stroke.

barbar [bar'bar] *nm* barbarian || *adj* barbarian; (*sălbatic*) savage; *fig* barbarous, uncivilized; inhuman, cruel || *adv* savagely, barbarously, cruelly • ~ie *nf* barbarism; *fig* (*sălbăticie*) barbarity; cruelty, savagery; vandalism.

barbă ['barbă] beard; (*bărbie*) chin; (*minciună*) lie, fib, tall story/tale.

barbut [bar'but] *nn* dice, craps.

barcă ['barkă] *nf* boat; (*lată*) punt; (*pneumatică*) dinghy; (*pt. traversare*) ferry; *pl* (*la bâlci*) swing-boats.

bard [bard] *nm* bard, poet.

bardă ['bardă] *nf* (broad) axe, hatchet.

barem¹ ['barem] *adv* at least, if only.

barem² [ba'rem] *nn* standard, quota, norm; (*în școală*) grading scale.

baretă [ba'retă] *nf* strap; (*la încălțăminte*) shoe strap; (*la cască*) chin strap; (*de medalie*) bar of medal, medal ribbon.

baricada [barika'da] *vt* to bar, to block (up) || *vr* to block/barricade oneself (in), to lock oneself (up) in.

baricadă [bari'kadă] *nf* barricade.

barieră [bari'eră] *nf* barrier, bar; (*feroviară*) gate; (*vamală*) toll bar/gate; (*rotitoare*) turnstile; *hist* turnspike; *fig* obstacle, impediment.

baril [ba'ril] *nn* barrel.

bariton [ba'riton] *nm mus* baritone.

barman ['barman] *nm* barman, bartender.

barometru [baro'metru] *nn* barometer; (*cu cadran*) (weather) glass.

baron [ba'ron] *nm* baron • ~easă *nf* baroness.

baros [ba'ros] *nn* sledge(hammer).

barou [ba'rou] *nn jur* bar (association).

barză ['barză] *nf* stork.

bas [bas] *nm mus* bass (singer) || *nn* bass sound/voice; *mus* (*instrument*) bass euphonium, bass saxhorn.

baschet ['basket] *nn* basketball || *pl coll* sneakers.

basculantă [basku'lantă] *nf* dump truck.

baseball ['beisbol] *nn* baseball.

basm [basm] *nn* fairytale; *fig* yarn; *pl* (*minciuni*) lies.

basma [bas'ma] *nf* bandana, (head)scarf; (*de gât*) neckerchief.

basorelief [basoreli'ef] *nn* bas-relief.

bastard [bas'tard] *nm/adj* illegitimate (child), bastard.

bastion [basti'on] *nn mil also fig* bulwark, bastion, stronghold.

baston [bas'ton] *nn* (walking) stick; (*toiag*) staff, cane; (*pt. a bate*) cudgel; (*polițienesc*) truncheon.

baștină ['bashtină] *nf* (*patrie*) homeland, motherland, native land; origin, descent.

batal [ba'tal] *nm zool* wether.

batalion [batali'on] *nn mil* battalion.

bate ['bate] *vt* to beat; (*a lovi*) to strike, to hit; (*a pedepsi*) to punish; (*cu bățul, repetat*) to batter; (*a lovi o singură dată*) to bash, to whack; (*cu biciul*) to lash, to whip; (*cu mâna*) to buffet; (*cu palma*) to slap; (*la fund*) to spank; (*cu pumnul*) to punch; (*ușor, pe spate*) to pat/slap/tap; (*tare, a tăbăci*) *sl* to give smb a good/sound beating; (*a învinge*) to defeat; (*monedă*) to coin money; (*d. pantofi*) to pinch; (*d. lapte, unt*) to churn; (*d. ouă*) to beat/whip/whisk the whites/yolks || *vi* (*d. ceas*) to strike the hour, to tick; (*d. clopot*) to ring, to toll; (*ritmic: d. inimă, puls*) to throb; (*d. ploaie, grindină*) to patter; (*d. vânt*) to blow || *vr* to fight; *fig* to contend; *fig* to be approaching, to be imminent/impending • ~rie *nf elec, mil* battery; *mus* drums, percussion instruments; (*frapieră*) cooler; (*de vin*) a bottle of wine and one of soda.

batic [ba'tik] *nn* (head)scarf; (*de gât*) bandanna, neckerchief.

batistă [ba'tistă] *nf* handkerchief; *coll* hanky.

batjocori [batzhoko'ri] *vt* (*a ridiculiza*) to jeer (at), to make fun of, to ridicule; to profane, to desecrate; (*a disprețui*) to disdain, to flout; (*a necinsti*) to rape, to violate; to abuse.

batjocură [bat'zhokură] *nf* (*bătaie de joc*) insult, jeer, mockery, ridicule; (*lucru făcut prost*) careless work, bungle; (*farsă*) travesty; **în** ~ mockingly.

batog [ba'tog] *nn icht* haddock; smoked carp/salmon/sturgeon fillet.

baton [ba'ton] *nn* bar, roll, stick.

batoză [ba'toză] *nf* threshing machine, thresher, thrasher; *fig* stout woman.

baza [ba'za] *vt* to base, to found, to ground || *vr* **a se** ~ **pe** to depend/rely on, to be based on.

bazaconie [baza'konie] *nf* fancy; maggot.

bazar [ba'zar] *nn* (oriental) bazaar.

bază ['bază] *nf* (*temelie*) base, foundation, groundwork; (*partea de jos*) bottom, foot; *fig* basis, ground; (*sprijin*) support; *pl* A.B.C.s, fundamentals, rudiments; *math* radix.

bazin [ba'zin] *nn* (*de înot*) (swimming)pool; *geog* basin, area; *anat* pelvis; *tech* reservoir, tank.

băcan [bă'kan] *nm* grocer.

băcănie [băkă'nie] *nf* (*prăvălie*) grocery store; (*meserie*) grocery (trade).

bădăran [bădă'ran] *nm* churl, ill-bred/ill-mannered/ rude person.

băga [bă'ga] *vt* to introduce, to put in(to); (*cu forţa, prin împingere*) to force, to push in, to shove in; (*a numi, a angaja*) to find a post/job for, to give smb a job || *vr* (*a intra în*) to come/pop in, to enter; (*nepoftit*) to intrude (upon); (*a interveni*) to interfere, to meddle.

băgăcios, băgăreţ [băga'chos, băgă'reţs] *nm coll* busybody, meddler, intruder || *adj* prying, intruding; (*curios*) inquisitive.

băiat [bă'iat] *nm* boy; (*fiu*) son; (*copil*) child; (*flăcău*) lad, youth, young man; (*om*) guy.

băieţandru [băie'tsandru] *nm* lad, youngster, youth.

băieţaş, băieţel [băie'tsash, băie'tsel] *nm* little boy; (*puşti*) kid; *pej* brat.

băieţoi [băie'tsoi] *nm* hobbledehoy; (*fată băieţoasă*) tomboy, hoyden, romp.

bălai [bă'lai] *adj* * **bălan**.

bălan [bă'lan] *adj* (*d. păr*) blond(e), fair, light, golden; (*d. boi*) white.

bălăbăni [bălăbă'ni] *vt* (*d. picioare*) to dangle; (*d. braţe*) to swing (about) || *vr* to dangle, to swing; to wobble, to sway.

bălăci [bălă'chi] *vr* (*a stropi*) to splash, to paddle, to dabble; (*a merge prin*) to wade (in/through).

bălăngăni [bălăngă'ni] *vr* to dangle; (*d. clopote*) to ring.

bălării [bălă'rii] *nf pl* weeds.

bălegar, băligar [băle'gar, băli'gar] *nn* manure, dung; (*fermentat*) compost.

bălmăji [bălmă'zhi] *vt coll* (*a îndruga*) to mumble; (*a amesteca*) to throw into confusion, to muddle/jumble (up).

bălos [bă'los] *adj* slobbering, slobbery, driveling.

băltoacă [băl'toakă] *nf* puddle; (*mare*) splash; pool.

bălţat [băl'tsat] *adj* motley, variegated; (*în dungi*) (*regulate*) striped; (*aleatorii*) streaked, streaky; (*pătat*) (*aleator*) speckled; (*mai regulat*) spotted, spotty; (*amestecat*) mixed, miscellaneous; (*ţipător*) gaudy.

bănos [bă'nos] *adj* lucrative, paying, profitable; remunerative, yielding

bănui [bănu'i] *vt* (*a presupune*) to presume, to suppose; (*a-şi imagina*) to guess, to imagine; to think; to mistrust, to suspect • **~ală** *nf* (*presupunere*) supposition; (*închipuire*) fancy, notion; (*gând*) hunch, idea, inkling; (*suspiciune*) distrust, mistrust, suspicion; **a avea o ~** (*negativ*) to have a suspicion; (*pozitiv*) to have a hunch/idea • **~tor** *adj* suspicious; (*neîncrezător*) distrustful || *adv* suspiciously, distrustfully.

bărăgan [bără'gan] *nn* (*pârloagă*) moor(land), heath; (*câmpie*) plain, steppe.

bărbat [băr'bat] *nm* man; (*masculul*) male; (*soţ*) husband || *adj* also fig manly; brave, resolute.

bărbătesc [bărbă'tesk] *adj* (*caracteristic bărbaţilor*) male, manly; (*masculin*) masculine; virile; (*curajos*) brave; (*hotarât*) resolute.

bărbăteşte [bărbă'teshte] *adv* like a man, in a manly way, manfully, resolutely.

bărbăţie [bărbă'tsie] *nf* (*ca vârstă*) manhood; (*a firii*) manliness, masculinity, virility; (*hotărâre*) resoluteness; (*bravură*) bravery, gallantry.

bărbie [băr'bie] *nf* (*la om*) chin; (*la bovine*) dewlap.

bărbier [bărbi'er] *nm* barber; *fig* liar, fibber, storyteller • **~i** *vt* to shave, to give smb a shave; *fig* (*a înşela*) to dupe || *vr* (*singur*) to shave (oneself), to have a shave;

(*la bărbier*) to get a shave, to get shaved; *fig coll* (*a se lăuda exagerat*) to fib, to brag • **~t** *nn* shave, shaving || *adj* shaven.

bărbos [băr'bos] *adj* bearded; (*neras*) unshaved, unshaven; *bot, zool* barbate.

băşcălie [băshkă'lie] *nf* mockery, derision.

băşică [bă'shikă] *nf anat* bladder; (*rană*) blister, pustule, vesicle; (*de aer*) bubble; *auto* breathelizer.

băştinaş [băshti'nash] *nm* native, aboriginal; *pl* aborigines, autochthon(s) || *adj* aboriginal, indigenous, native.

bătaie [bă'taie] *nf* beating; (*cu băţul*) cudgeling, drubbing; (*biciuire*) lashing, whipping; (*cu palma*) cuff, slap(ping); (*cu pumnul*) punch(ing), pummel(ling); (*luptă*) battle, fight; (*încăierare*) brawl, scuffle; (*înfrângere*) defeat, licking; (*a ceasului*) tick(ing), stroke; (*a clopotelor*) ringing, peal, toll; (*ciocănitură*) knock, (*uşoară*) tap(ping); (*rapidă şi uşoară*) rap(ping); (*puls*) pulsation; *mus* beat, time; (*a ploii*) beating; (*din picior*) stamping; (*pe umăr*) patting; **~ de cap** trouble, anxiety; (*parodie*) travesty; (*lucrare proastă*) botchery.

bătăios [bătă'ios] *adj* fighting, pugnacious, bellicose; (*agresiv*) truculent; (*certăreţ*) quarrelsome; feist, contentious.

bătălie [bătă'lie] *nf* battle.

bătător [bătă'tor] *nn* (*de covoare*) carpet beater; (*pt. lapte*) churn staff.

bătători [bătăto'ri] *vt* to tread, to stamp down || *vr* to be trodden/beaten; (*d. mâini*) to have hardened/ calloused hands • **~t** *adj* beaten, trodden; *also fig* **drum ~** beaten path/track; (*d. mâini*) callous.

bătătură[1] [bătă'tură] *nf anat* (*la picior*) corn; (*la palmă*) hard skin, callosity; *vernac* (*curte*) front yard, court.

bătătură[2] [bătă'tură] *nf tex* filling, weft.

bătăuş [bătă'ush] *nm* brawler, bully, rowdy || *adj* contentious, pugnacious.

bătrâior [bătrâ'ior] *adj* elderly, oldish.

bătrân [bă'trân] *nm* **un ~** an old/aged man; *coll* gaffer • **~e!** (*amical*) old man/fellow || *adj* old, aged; (*cărunt*) hoary; (*foarte vechi, antic*) ancient • **~ă** *nf* old/aged woman • **~el** *nm* elderly man • **~esc** *adj* old, aging; (*demodat*) old(-fashioned); (*d. datina*) traditional, popular • **~eşte** *adv* in the old (people's) way; (*cumpătat*) sedately; traditionally • **~eţe** *nf* old age • **~ică** *nf* an old lady.

băţ [băts] *nn* stick, rod; (*baston*) cane; (*pt. arătat pe hartă*) pointer.

băutor [bău'tor] *nm* (*heavy*) drinker; (*beţiv*) drunkard.

băutură [bău'tură] *nf* drink; *coll* booze; (*la culcare*) nightcap; (*alcoolică*) liquor; *frml* (*orice băutură cu excepţia apei: lapte, ceai*) beverage; (*beţie*) drinking spree; *med* potion, decoction.

bâigui [bâigu'i] *vt* to mumble, to stutter || *vi* (*a vorbi nedesluşit*) to jabber; to falter; (*a aiura*) to rave, to ramble; (*a vorbi alandala*) to drivel.

bâjbâi [bâzhbâ'i] *vi* (*prin întuneric*) to grope (about), to fumble; (*a mişuna*) to teem, to swarm.

bâlbâi [bâlbâ'i] *vt* to stammer, to stutter || *vr* to stammer, to stutter; (*a vorbi neclar*) to speak confusedly, to jabber; (*a vorbi repede*) to sp(l)utter (out) • **~ală** *nf* stutter(ing), stammer(ing) • **~t** *nm* stammerer, stutterer || *nn* stutter, stammer || *adj* stuttering, stammering.

bâlci ['bâlchi] *nn* fair; *fig* (*gălăgie*) hubbub; **de ~** low (class); shameful.

bântui [bântu'i] *vt* (*d. stafii*) to haunt; (*a pustii*) to lay waste, to ravage; (*d. animale*) to infest, to overrun; (*d. molime*) to rage, to sweep (over) ‖ *vi* to rage, to be rife, to wreak havoc.

bârfă ['bârfă] *nf* gossip(ing); small talk; tittle-tattle.

bârfi [bâr'fi] *vt* to gossip (about); (*pe cineva*) to gossip about smb; to tittle-tattle; (*pe la spate, calomnios*) to revile, to slander ‖ *vi* to chat, to chatter, to gossip; (*malițios*) to backbite, to speak ill of; to talk scandal.

bârlog [bâr'log] *nn* (*d. animale*) den, lair, hole; *fig* (*casă*) home; (*locuință improvizată*) hovel; (*cotlon*) corner, nook.

bârnă ['bârnă] *nf* beam; (*grindă*) joist; (*de dimensiuni mari*) girder.

bâtă ['bâtă] *nf* (*lucrată*) cudgel, club, heavy stick.

bâtlan [bât'lan] *nm* heron.

bâțâi [bâtsâ'i] *vi/vr* (*o mișcare bruscă a capului*) to jerk, to jitter; (*în pat*) to toss about; (*d. copii*) to wriggle; (*a tremura*) to shiver, to tremble; (*a se agita*) to fidget, to be restless; (*a dansa prost*) to jig about, to jiggle (about).

bâzâi [bâzâ'i] *vi* (*d. insecte*) to buzz; (*d. albine*) to hum; (*d. bondari*) to drone; (*a țiui*) to sound; (*d. urechi*) to ring; (*a se smiorcăi*) to whimper • ~t *nn* hum, buzz; (*al bondarilor*) drone; (*plâns(et)*) whimpering, whining.

bea ['bea] *vt* to drink; (*a consuma*) to have, to take; (*a adăpa*) to water; (*totul, până la fund*) to drink up; (*pe nerăsuflate*) to drink down, to drink all at once; (*cu înghițituri mari*) to swig, to swill; (*a sorbi, cu încetul*) to sip ‖ *vi* to drink; *coll* to be fond of the bottle; (*mult*) to booze, to drink hard/heavily.

beat ['beat] *adj* drunk; drunken; **e** ~ drunk; inebriated, intoxicated; *coll* tight; (*foarte beat*) plastered, sizzled, loaded; (*afumat*) tipsy, mellow; (*puțin beat*) merry, happy, tiddly; *sl* squiffy; ~ **de bucurie/fericire** drunk/delirious/intoxicated with joy/delight.

beatitudine [beati'tudine] *nf* beatitude, bliss, supreme/perfect happiness.

bebeluș [bebe'lush] *nm* baby; *lit* babe, nurs(e)ling; (*alintător*) chickabiddy.

bec [bek] *nn* (*electric*) bulb; (*de gaz*) gas burner, gas jet.

becață [be'katsă] *nf* *orn* snipe.

beci ['bechi] *nn* cellar; (*subsol*) basement, (*apartament de subsol*) basement apartment; (*închisoare*) dungeon; *sl* (*arest*) can.

begonie [be'gonie] *nf* *bot* begonia.

behăi [behă'i] *vi* (*oaie*) to baa, to bleat.

bej [bezh] *nn/adj* beige.

belciug [bel'chug] *nn* hook; metal ring.

belea [be'lea] (*persoană*) nuisance, a real pain, bother; (*bucluc*) mess, scrape; (*necaz*) trouble, misfortune; (*povară*) burden, encumbrance.

belgian, belgiană [bedji'an, beldji'ană] *nm/nf/adj* Belgian.

belicos [beli'kos] *adj* warlike, bellicose, aggressive.

beligerant [belidje'rant] *adj* belligerent, aggressive.

belșug [bel'shug] *nn* abundance, plenty; (*bogăție*) wealth, opulence; (*surplus*) profusion, exuberance; **din** ~ copiously, abundantly, in abundance.

benchetui [benketu'i] *vi* to feast, to banquet.

benefic [be'nefik] *adj* beneficent, beneficial to, favorable to • ~**ia** [benefichi'a] *vi* (*a* ~ *de*) to benefit/profit from; (*a avea dreptul*) to enjoy; to derive advantage/profit from; to gain (from/by); to turn smth to (good)

account/profit • ~**iar** [benefichi'ar] *nm* *econ* beneficiary.

beneficiu [bene'fichu] *nn* benefit; advantage; (*câștig*) gain, profit.

benevol [bene'vol] *adj* voluntary, spontaneous; unpaid ‖ *adv* voluntarily; at one's pleasure; of one's own accord/will.

benign [be'nign] *adj* *med* benign.

benzină [ben'zină] *nf* *auto* gas(oline), petrol; (*neofalină*) benzene • ~**rie** *nf* gas station.

berărie [beră'rie] *nf* (*local*) ale house; (*grădină de vară*) beer house; *rare* (*fabrică*) brewery.

berbec [ber'bek] *nm* ram; (*batal*) wether; (*carne*) mutton; *astron* The Ram, Aries; *hist, mil* battering ram.

bere ['bere] *nf* beer, ale.

beregată [bere'gată] *nf* windpipe, throat, gullet; (*la animale*) throttle.

beretă [be'retă] *nf* beret, cap; (*scoțiană*) tam-o'shanter.

berlină [ber'lină] *nf* *auto* sedan.

bernă ['bernă] *nf* **în** ~ flag at half mast.

bestial [besti'al] *adj* brutish, beastly, ferocious; savage ‖ *adv* brutishly, ferociously, savagely • ~**itate** *nf* brutishness, beastliness, ferocity, savagery.

bestie ['bestie] *nf* (*wild*) beast; *fig* brute, (ferocious) beast.

beșteli [beshte'li] *vt* to scold, to censure; (*cu vehemență*) to haul smb over the coals.

beteală [be'teală] *nf* tinsel.

betegi [bete'dji] *vt* to cripple, to maim ‖ *vr* to be crippled, to become an invalid; (*a se îmbolnăvi*) to be taken ill.

beton [be'ton] *nn* concrete.

beție [be'tsie] *nf* (*amețeală*) intoxication, drunkenness; (*obicei*) drinking, boozing; (*chef*) drinking bout/party; *coll* booze; *also fig* inebriation, intoxication, delirium, frenzy.

betiv [be'tsiv] *nm* drunkard, hard drinker; *coll* boozer; (*alcoolic*) sot ‖ *adj* addicted to drink(ing) • ~**an** *nm* drunkard, hard drinker, sot.

bezmetic [bez'metik] *nm* madcap, giddy-head ‖ *adj* crazy, giddy, brainless.

beznă ['beznă] *nf* *also fig* dark(ness), gloom, obscurity.

biban [bi'ban] *nm* perch.

bibelou [bibe'lou] *nn* figurine.

biberon [bibe'ron] *nn* baby bottle; (*suzetă*) dummy.

bibilică [bibi'lika] *nf* guinea-fowl/hen.

Biblie ['biblie] *nf* Bible, Holy Scripture(s).

bibliografie [bibliogra'fie] *nf* bibliography.

bibliotecar [bibliote'kar] *nm* librarian.

bibliotecă [biblio'tekă] *nf* (*instituție, cameră*) library; (*mobilă*) bookcase; (*rafturi*) bookshelves; (*volantă*) bookmobile.

bicarbonat [bikarbo'nat] *nn* *chem* bicarbonate; ~ **de sodiu** baking soda.

bicentenar [bichente'nar] *adj/nn* bicentenary, bicentennial.

biceps ['bicheps] *nm* biceps.

bici [bich] *nn* (horse) whip; *fig* scourge.

bicicletă [bichi'kletă] *nf* bicycle; *coll* bike; wheel.

biciclist [bichi'klist] *nm* cyclist, bicyclist.

biciui [bichu'i] *vt* to flog, to whip; *also fig* to lash; (*a pedepsi*) to castigate, to censure • ~**tor** *adj* lashing; biting, harsh, scathing.

bidinea [bidi'nea] *nf* mason's brush, whitewashing brush.

bidon [bi'don] *nn* canteen; container; (*de apă*) *mil* soldier's canteen; (*de lapte*) milkcan; (*cilindric*) drum.

biet [biet] *adj* (*sărac*) poor, needy; (*nenorocit*) miserable, unfortunate • ~ul de el! poor fellow/soul; *coll* poor devil/beggar.

bifa [bi'fa] *vt* to check off.

biftec ['biftek] *nn* (beef) steak.

bifurca [bifur'ka] *vr* to fork, to branch off/out • ~re, ~tie *nf* bifurcation, fork, crossroads.

bigam [bi'gam] *nm* bigamist || *adj* bigamous • ~ie *nf* bigamy.

bigot [bi'got] *nm* bigot || *adj* bigoted; religious, overdevout • ~ism *nn* bigotry.

bigudiu [bigu'diu] *nn* (hair) curler.

bijuterie [bizhute'rie] *nf* jewel; *pl* jewelry; *fig* gem.

bijutier [bizhuti'er] *nm* jeweler.

bilanț [bi'lants] *nn fin* balance sheet; statement of account; schedule of assets and liabilities; *fig* survey; (*rezultat*) evaluation, assessment.

bilă[1] ['bilă] *nf med* bile.

bilă[2] ['bilă] *nf* ball; *pl* (*pietricele pt joc*) marbles; (*cap*) *coll* nut.

bilet [bi'let] *nn* ticket; (*scrisoare*) note, short letter; (*costul călătoriei*) fare; *econ* bill; ~ simplu single; ~ dus și întors roundtrip ticket.

biliard [bili'ard] *nn* (*variante*) pool, snooker, billiards.

bilion [bili'on] *nn* trillion.

bilunar [bilu'nar] *adj* bimonthly; bimestrial.

bine ['bine] *nn* good, right; (*avantaj*) advantage, benefit; (*câștig*) gain, profit; (*noroc*) fortune, blessing; (*cu ~*) safely, all right; (*cu succes*) successfully; (*la revedere*) good-bye, so long || *adj* fine, nice, good-looking; respectable, honorable || *adv* well, all right, OK; correctly, properly, rightly; mergi cu ~ take care!, have a pleasant journey!; rămâi cu ~ good-bye, I hope to see you again; la ~ și la rău for better or for worse; ~ zis well said || *interj* excellent, well, good, (all) right; fine; OK; *coll* deal.

binecrescut [binekres'kut] *adj* well brought up, well-bred, well-behaved.

binecuvânta [binekuvân'ta] *vt* to bless.

binefacere [bine'fachere] *nf* (*avantaj*) advantage; (*fericire*) blessing, boon; (*faptă bună*) charity, good/kind action.

binefăcător [binefăkă'tor] *nm* benefactor || *adj* (*caritabil*) charitable; beneficent; (*pentru sănătate*) beneficial; (*d. vânt*) bracing.

bineînțeles [bineîntse'les] *adv* certainly, naturally, (as a matter) of course.

binevenit [bineve'nit] *adj* welcome; (*oportun*) timely, seasonable.

binevoi [binevo'i] *vi* to condescend, to be willing • ~tor *nm* well-wisher || *adj* benevolent, kind, agreeable.

binoclu [bi'noklu] *nn* binoculars; (*de teatru*) opera glasses.

biochimie [bioki'mie] *nf* biochemistry.

biografie [biogra'fie] *nf* biography.

biolog [bio'log] *nm* biologist • ~ie [biolo'djie] *nf* biology.

bioxid [biok'sid] *nn chem* dioxide; ~ de carbon carbon dioxide.

biped [bi'ped] *nm* biped || *adj* bipedal, two-footed.

bir [bir] *nn hist* tax, tribute, impost.

birjar [bir'zhar] *nm* coachman, coachdriver.

birocrat [biro'krat] *nm* bureaucrat.

birocratism, birocrație [birokra'tism, birokra'tsie] *nn/nf* bureaucracy, red tape; officialdom.

birou [bi'rou] *nn* (*cameră*) study; (*public*) office; (*politic*) bureau; (*mobilă*) (writing) desk/table.

birui [biru'i] *vt* to conquer, to defeat, to vanquish; (*a supune*) to subdue; *fig* to overcome, to overwhelm || *vi* to triumph, to be victorious • ~tor *nm* victor, conqueror || *adj* victorious, triumphant || *adv* victoriously, triumphantly.

biruință [biru'intsă] *nf* victory, triumph, conquest.

bis [bis] *nn* encore || *interj* encore!, repeat!, again!, once more!

biscuit [bisku'it] *nm* biscuit, cracker.

biserică [bi'serikă] *nf* church; (*capelă*) chapel; (*clerul*) the clergy.

bisturiu [bistu'riu] *nn med* scalpel, lancet.

bivol ['bivol] *nm* buffalo • ~iță *nf* buffalo cow.

bizantin [bizan'tin] *nm/adj* Byzantine.

bizar [bi'zar] *adj* bizarre, quaint • ~erie *nf* queerness, oddity, extravagance; (*pitoresc*) quaintness.

bizon [bi'zon] *nm* bison; (~ american) buffalo.

bizui [bizu'i] *vr* a se ~ pe to count/depend/rely/bank (up)on; (*a se încrede în*) to trust (in).

blajin [bla'zhin] *adj* kind, mild, gentle, calm, good-hearted, kindhearted; (*la vorbă*) soft-spoken || *adv* kindly, mildly, etc.

blam [blam] *nn* blame, reprimand, censure.

blama [bla'ma] *vt* to blame; (*a critica*) to criticize, to censure; to reprove.

blană ['blană] *nf* (*par*) fur; (*piele de animal*) skin, hide; (*scândură*) board.

blasfemie [blasfe'mie] *nf* blasphemy.

blat [blat] *nn* (*aluat pt. prajituri*) layer.

blaza [bla'za] *vr* to be blasé/indifferent; (*a fi sătul*) to be weary/fed up || *vt* to pall, to weary • ~t *adj* blasé, tired/weary (of life); indifferent, jaded.

blazon [bla'zon] *nn* coat of arms, armorial (bearings); heraldry, armory.

blănar [blă'nar] *nm* furrier, fur dealer.

blând [blând] *adj* (*d. oameni*) mild, kind, gentle, sweet; good-/soft-hearted, good-natured; (*liniștit*) calm, quiet; (*supus*) docile, meek; (*d. glas*) soft; (*d. animale*) tame; (*d. cai*) steady || *adv* mildly; (*cu delicatețe*) gently, gingerly • ~ețe *nf* sweetness, gentleness; docility, tameness; (*bunătate*) kindness, kindheartedness; cu ~ gently, gingerly; (*amabil*) kindly.

bleg [bleg] *nm* (*prost*) blockhead, fool; *coll* dolt, noodle, ninny; (*indolent*) lazybones; (*om moale*) *coll* milksop; (*om timid*) sheepish fellow || *adj* (*prost*) stupid, foolish; *coll* soft, soft-minded; indolent, lazy; (*lăsător*) languid, negligent; *coll* lackadaisical; timid, shy; (*moale*) weak(ly); (*care atârnă*) drooping, flabby; (*d. urechi*) floppy, lop-eared.

blenoragie [blenora'djie] *nf med* blennorrhagia, gonorrhoea, V.D.; *sl* clap.

blestem [bles'tem] *nn* curse; *lit* oath, damnation; (*prin invocarea spiritelor*) imprecation; *relig* anathema; (*blasfemie*) blasphemy; *fig* scourge; calamity • ~a *vt* to put a curse on, to damn; to utter imprecations against; *relig* to anathemize; to blaspheme || *vi* to curse • ~ăție *nf* villainy; knavish act; (*josnicie*) baseness, meanness; (*trăsnaie*) mischief, prank; frolic.

bleu [bleu] *nn/adj* (light) blue, azure • ~marin *nn/adj* navy blue, dark blue, ultramarine blue.

blindat [blin'dat] *adj* armored; iron-clad.

bliț [blits] *nn* flash gun; flashlight.

bloc [blok] *nn* (*bucată*) bloc; (*clădire*) block of apartments, apartment house; *pol* group, coalition; (*grămadă*) lump; (*un tot*) whole, unit; **în ~** (*d. lucruri*) altogether, wholesale; (*d. oameni*) together.

bloca [blo'ka] *vt* (*a împiedica*) to block (up), to shut off, to obstruct; **a ~ circulația** to block traffic; *mil* to blockade; *econ* (*un capital*) to lock up; *tech* (*roți, un mecanism*) to lock ‖ *vr* to be stopped, to be blocked; to be shut off; (*d. un motor*) to become stuck, to lock; *fig* to be shocked/stunned • **~dă** *nf mil* blockade.

blocnotes [blok'notes] *nn* note pad, jotter.

blond [blond] *nm* fair-/light-haired man/boy, blond ‖ *adj* (*d. păr*) blond, fair-haired; (*d. ten*) fair-/light-skinned, of a fair complexion • **~ă, ~ină** *nf* fair-/light-haired woman/girl; blonde ‖ *adj* blonde, fair-haired.

bluf [bluf] *nn* bluff, hoax.

blugi ['bludji] *nm pl coll* blue jeans.

bluză ['bluză] *nf* blouse.

boa ['boa] *nm* boa.

boabă ['boabă] *nf bot* berry; bacca; (*bob*) grain; (*sămânță*) seed; (*de strugure*) grape; (*picătură de apă, sudoare*) bead; *fig* whit, bit; trifle, trifling matter; (*deloc, nimic*) (not) at all; (*nici un cuvânt*) not a word, not a bit (of it).

boală ['boală] *nf* illness, sickness; (*de durată*) disease; (*indispoziție*) ailment, indisposition; (*locală*) complaint; (*tulburare*) trouble, disorder; *vet* distemper; *fig* passion.

boare ['boare] *nf* breath (of wind); gentle breeze.

boarfă ['boarfă] *nf* old coat; rag; *pl* old clothes, shabby/threadbare clothes; *sl* (*femeie ușoară*) hooker, slut.

bob[1] [bob] *nn* (*de grâu, porumb*) grain, seed ‖ *nm* bean; (*plantă*) horse bean.

bob[2] [bob] *nn sp* bobsleigh, bobsled.

bobârnac [bobâr'nak] *nn* flick, fillip.

bobină [bo'bină] *nf text* bobbin, spool; (*mosor*) reel; *elec* coil; (*film*) reel.

boboc [bo'bok] *nm bot* bud; (*de rață*) duckling; (*de gâscă*) gosling; (*student*) freshman.

Bobotează [bobo'tează] *nf* Epiphany, twelfth day/night.

bocanc [bo'kank] *nm* boot; *mil* ankle boot.

bocăni [bokă'ni] *vi* to knock, to thump; (*cu ciocanul*) to hammer; (*în mers*) to clamp, to stamp one's feet.

boccea [bok'chea] *nf* (*legătură*) bundle.

bocet ['bochet] *nn* lament, lamentation; (*plânset*) moaning, wailing; (*ritual la înmormântări*) dirge.

boci [bo'chi] *vt* to bemoan, to bewail; *fig* to mourn for; to lament ‖ *vi/vr* to wail, to lament • **~toare** *nf* (hired) mourner, lamenter.

bodegă [bo'degă] *nf* tavern, public house; pub, bodega.

bodogăni [bodogă'ni] *vi* to mutter, to grumble, to murmur.

boem [bo'em] *nm/adj* bohemian.

bogat [bo'gat] *nm* rich/wealthy man.

bogătaș [bogă'tash] *nm* (very) rich man, man of means; *coll* moneybags.

bogăție [bogă'tsie] *nf* (*avere*) wealth, opulence; *pl* riches; (*abundență*) abundance, profusion; (*splendoare*) splendor.

bogății [bogă'tsii] *nm pl* the rich (people), the wealthy, the well-to-do; *coll* the upper crust ‖ *adj* rich; (*cu bani*) moneyed; (*avut*) prosperous, wealthy, well-off; *coll* rolling in money; *fig* (*îmbelșugat*) abundant in, plentiful; (*amplu*) ample, copious; rich, fertile; (*d. vegetație*) luxuriant; (*valoros*) valuable, precious;

(*luxos*) luxurious, sumptuous; (*măreț*) magnificent ‖ *adv* richly, abundantly; (*din plin*) fully; (*foarte*) very, highly.

boia [bo'ia] *nf* (*de ardei*) paprika; (*vopsea*) dye.

boicot [boi'kot] *nn* boycott • **~a** [boiko'ta] *vt* to boycott.

boier [bo'ier] *nm hist* boyar; (*nobil*) nobleman, aristocrat; (*dregător*) court official; (*moșier*) landowner, gentleman farmer; *fig* lord, master; (*persoană importantă*) man of distinction; *coll* big shot.

boiler ['boiler] *nn tech* boiler.

bolborosi [bolboro'si] *vt* to mutter, to mumble ‖ *vi* (*a vorbi repede*) to babble, to gabble; (*d. apă*) to bubble; (*d. curcani*) to gobble.

bold [bold] *nn* (*ac*) pin; (*pt. vite*) goad; (*stimulent*) stimulus, incentive.

boli [bo'li] *vi* to be ill/ailing/sickly; *coll* to be poorly; to ail.

bolnav [bol'nav] *nm* sick man; *pl* the sick; *med* patient ‖ *adj* ill; (*suferind*) ailing, in bad/poor health; *coll* poorly, off color; (*fără vlagă*) feeble; (*care nu se simte bine*) unwell; (*deranjat mintal*) deranged; *coll* crazy.

bolovan [bolo'van] *nm* boulder, heavy stone; block.

boltă ['boltă] *nf archit* vault, arch(way), colonnade; (*de verdeață*) bower, arbor; (*a cerului*) *fig lit* the vault/canopy of heaven, celestial vault/dome.

bolti [bol'ti] *vt* to arch, to vault ‖ *vr* to form a vault, to (form an) arch.

bomba [bom'ba] *vt* to make smth bulge/jut out ‖ *vr* to bulge, to swell out, to jut out.

bombarda [bombar'da] *vt* (*din avion*) to bomb; (*cu artilerie*) to shell, to strafe; *phys* to bombard (with neutrons); *fig* to pester, to bother; to besiege, to importune • **~ment** *nn* (*aerian*) air raid, bombing; (*de artilerie*) shell/gun fire, shelling.

bombastic [bom'bastik] *adj* bombastic, high-flown ‖ *adv* bombastically.

bombă ['bombă] *nf* bomb; (*obuz*) shell; projectile, torpedo.

bombăni [bombă'ni] *vi* to grumble, to mumble, to growl ‖ *vt* (*pe cineva*) to grumble at/to smb; (*a cicăli*) to nag smb.

bombeu [bom'beu] *nn* toe cap.

bomboană [bom'boană] *nf* candy, sweet; (*acadea*) lollipop; *pl* confectionery, sweetmeats

bon [bon] *nn* ticket, note, bill; order, voucher, coupon; (*de plată*) sales slip; (*chitanță pt. bani*) receipt; *com* bond.

bonă ['bonă] *nf* nanny, nurse maid, (nursery) governess.

bondar [bon'dar] *nm* bumblebee.

bondoc [bon'dok] *nm* stumpy man, short and stout man ‖ *adj* stumpy, thickset.

bonetă [bo'netă] *nf* (woman's/child's) bonnet; cap; *naut* studding sail.

bonier [boni'er] *nn econ* bill-book, order book; voucher book, receipt book.

bonificare, bonificație [bonifi'kare, bonifi'katsie] *nf* allowance, bonus.

bonitate [boni'tate] *nf econ* reliability.

bonom [bo'nom] *nm* good-natured/genial guy ‖ *adj* genial, good-natured ‖ *adv* genially, good-naturedly.

bont [bont] *adj* blunt, stumpy; (*d. lamă*) edgeless.

borangic [boran'djik] *nn* floss silk, raw silk.

borcan [bor'kan] *nn* (glass) jar, bottle; (*vas*) pot, vessel.

bord [bord] *nn* (*margine*) edge, border; *auto* dashboard; *avia* (*tabloul cu instrumente*) instrument panel; *avia*, *naut* board; **la ~** aboard; **peste ~** overboard.

bordei [bor'dei] *nn* cottage, cabin; (*colibă*) hut, shelter; (*de scânduri*) booth; (*de pământ*) earth house.

bordel [bor'del] *nn* brothel, whorehouse.

borderou [borde'rou] *nn* docket, statement; invoice; account; note; (*stat de plată*) pay packet.

bordo [bor'do] *nn* Bordeaux (wine), claret || *adj* dark red.

bordură [bor'dură] *nf* (*la trotuar*) curbstone; (*la haine*) trimming, border.

borfaş [bor'fash] *nm* thief; (*hoţ de buzunare*) pickpocket; (*escroc*) cheat; crook; *fig* jerk.

bornă ['bornă] *nf* (*piatră de hotar*) landmark, boundary mark/stone; *elec* terminal, clamp.

borş [borsh] *nn* (sour) bran and water; (*ciorbă*) bortsch; sour soup.

borţos [bor'tsos] *adj* big-bellied, pot-bellied.

boschet [bos'ket] *nn* bower, arbor; (*tufiş*) bush; (*desiş*) thicket.

boscorodi [boskoro'di] *vt* to nag at smb || *vi* to babble; to grumble; (*a bodogăni*) to mutter; (*a întinde vorba*) *coll* to rattle/reel off.

bostan [bos'tan] *nm* pumpkin; (*pepene verde*) (water)-melon; *sl* (*cap*) nut, pate.

bosumfla [bosum'fla] *vr* to pout; (*a se îmbufna*) to sulk, to be sulky.

boşorog [bosho'rog] *nm* person suffering from hernia; *fig* (*bătrân*) old fogey; decrepit/helpless old man; *coll* old blighter; dodderer, totterer || *adj* suffering from hernia; *fig* doddery, tottering.

bot [bot] *nn* muzzle; (*rât*) snout; (*gură*) mouth; *coll* chops, jaw; (*grimasă*) pout; (*vârf*) point; (*capăt*) end.

botanică [bo'tanika] *nf* botany.

botez [bo'tez] *nn relig* baptism; (*al copiilor*) christening • **~a** [bote'za] *vt relig* to baptize; (*copii*) to christen; (*ca naş*) to act as godfather/godmother; to convert; (*a numi*) to name, to call, to baptize; (*a porecli*) to nickname, to dub; (*a stropi*) *coll* to sprinkle, to wet; (*a amesteca cu apă băuturi*) *coll* to doctor || *vr* to be baptized/christened || *vi* (*a face un botez*) to perform a christening ceremony; (*ca naş/ă*) to stand as godfather/godmother.

botniţă ['botnitsă] *nf* muzzle; *fig* (*gură*) *coll* chops, jaw.

boţ [bots] *nn* (*de pâine, hârtie*) ball; (*mic*) pellet; (*de pământ*) clod ball.

bou [bou] *nm* ox; *fig* (*prost*) dolt, idiot, moron, blockhead.

box[1] [boks] *nn* (*sport*) boxing; (*antrenament*) sparring; (*pumnar*) knuckle duster.

box[2] [boks] *nn* (*piele*) calfskin.

boxa [bok'sa] *vt/vi* to box; (*la antrenament*) to spar.

boxă ['boksă] *nf* dock, box; (*pt. cai*) horse box.

boxer [bok'ser] *nm* boxer, (*ironic*) pugilist, prizefighter.

braconaj [brako'nazh] *nn* poaching.

braconier [brakoni'er] *nm* poacher.

brad [brad] *nm* fir (tree), pine (tree).

bragă ['bragă] *nf* millet beer.

brambura ['brambura] *adv* at random, aimlessly.

brancardă [bran'kardă] *nf* stretcher.

brancardier [brankardi'er] *nm* stretcher bearer.

branşa [bran'sha] *vt* to connect, to plug in • **~ment** *nn* *elec* lead, branch circuit; *tech* branching, service line.

branşă ['branshă] *nf* branch, line; (*domeniu*) field, domain, sphere.

bras [bras] *nn sp* breaststroke.

braserie [brase'rie] *nf* brasserie, restaurant with bar.

brasieră [brasi'eră] *nf* (*adulţi*) undershirt; (*pt femei*) halter top; body(stocking); (*de copii*) child's sleeveless vest.

braţ [brats] *nn anat also fig* arm; (*cantitate*) armful; *pl fig* hands, workers; (*forţă*) strength, power.

brav [brav] *nm* hero, brave man || *adj* brave; (*viteaz*) valiant, gallant; (*curajos*) plucky, courageous; (*îndrăzneţ*) bold, daring || *adv* bravely, valliantly.

brava [bra'va] *vt* (*a sfida pe cineva*) to defy, to stand up to; (*ceva*) to face, to fly in the face of.

bravadă [bra'vadă] *nf* bravado, brag(ging), swashbuckling.

bravo ['bravo] *nn/interj* bravo, excellent, well done; *coll* attaboy; hear, hear; **~ ţie!** good for you!

bravură [bra'vură] *nf* bravery, heroism, valor, courage; daring.

brazdă ['brazdă] *nf* (*şanţ de plug*) furrow; (*strat*) bed; (*pt. legume*) drill; (*între două ogoare*) balk; ridge between two fields; (*de pământ, bucată*) clod; (*de iarbă cosită*) window, swath; *fig* (*urmă*) track, trail; (*de corabie*) wake; (*de roată*) trace; *fig* (*rid*) wrinkle.

brăţară [bră'tsară] *nf* bracelet, bangle; *tech* clamp(s), band.

brăzda [brăz'da] *vt* (*cu plugul*) to furrow, to trace/draw furrows across; (*a cresta*) to notch, to indent; to traverse, to cross; (*marea*) to plough; (*a lăsa dâre*) to leave traces/tracks (on); (*a zbârci*) to wrinkle (up).

brânduşă [brân'dushş] *nf bot* (*ca gen*) colchicum; (*de primăvară*) spring crocus; (*de toamnă*) meadow saffron.

brânză ['brânză] *nf* cheese.

brâu [brâu] *nn* girdle; belt; (*la femei*) band, waistband; (*eşarfă*) sash; *archit* frieze, molding, cornice; (*talie*) waist; (*dans*) girdle dance.

bre [bre] *interj* (hei!) you!; I say, look here, listen; (*vai*) man (alive); (*mirare*) ah!, indeed!, you don't say so!.

breaslă ['breaslă] *nf* guild, trade, corporation, company.

breaz [breaz] *adj* (*d. animale*) (*cu o pată albă*) white spotted on the head; (*vărgat*) dappled, piebald; (*d. vaci*) brindled; (*cu pete*) spotted, speckled; *fig* (*ironic: deştept, iscusit*) smart, skilled at, good at.

brebenel [brebe'nel] *nm bot* hollowwort.

brec [brec] *nn* (*trăsură*) shooting brake; (*auto*) estate car; station wagon.

breloc [bre'lok] *nn* trinket; (*la ceasuri*) fancy ornament, charm.

breşă ['breshă] *nf* breach, gap, break, opening.

bretea [bre'tea] *nf* (shoulder) strap; *pl* suspenders.

breton [bre'ton] *nn* (*coafură*) bangs, fringe (of hair).

brevet [bre'vet] *nn* license, patent, certificate • **a ~a** *vt* to patent.

briceag [bri'cheag] *nn* (pen) knife, pocketknife.

brichetă [bri'ketă] *nf* (cigarette) lighter; (*de cărbune*) briquette.

brici ['brichi] *nn* razor.

bridge ['bridge] *nn* (*joc de cărţi*) bridge.

brigadă [bri'gadă] *nf mil* brigade; (*de lucru*) team, crew; **~ mobilă** (*de poliţie*) flying squad.

brigadier [brigadi'er] *nm* (*membru*) member of a team, crew; (*şef*) foreman; *mil* brigadier; (*silvic*) ranger, forester.

briliant [brili'ant] *nn* brilliant.
britanic [bri'tanik] *adj* British, English.
brizant [bri'zant] *adj* shattering, disruptive, high-explosive ‖ *nm pl naut* breakers, combers.
briză ['briză] *nf* breeze.
broască ['broaskă] *nf zool* (*de apă*) frog; (*de uşă*) lock.
broboadă [bro'boadă] *nf* (head)kerchief.
brocart [bro'kart] *nn* brocade.
broda [bro'da] *vt* to embroider; *fig* to invent; (*o poveste*) to embellish, to make up; *fig* to spin a yarn.
broderie [brode'rie] *nf* (piece of) embroidery, embroidering; *mus* grace notes.
brodi [bro'di] *vt* (*a nimeri*) to hit (right); (*a ghici*) to guess ‖ *vr* to chance, to happen, to occur.
bronşită [bron'shită] *nf med* bronchitis.
bronz [bronz] *nn* bronze.
bronza [bron'za] *vt* to bronze; (*d. soare*) to tan, to brown ‖ *vr* to tan, to get a (sun)tan, to be tanned; to sunbathe.
broşă ['broshă] *nf* brooch.
broşură [bro'shură] *nf* (*plachetă*) brochure, booklet, pamphlet.
brotac, brotăcel [bro'tak, brotă'chel] *nm* green/tree frog.
bruftului [bruftulu'i] *vt* to rough plaster; to treat harshly/roughly, to bully.
bruia [bru'ia] *vt* to jam (broadcasts) • ~j *nn* jamming.
bruion [bru'ion] *nn* draft, rough copy.
brumă ['brumă] *nf* (white) hoar frost; *lit* rime; (*pe fructe*) dust; *fig* (*cantitate mică, spoială*) a little, a (little) bit, a smattering • ~riu *adj* (light) grey, grayish.
brun [brun] *adj* brown; (*d. oameni*) dark, dark-haired, dark-skinned • ~et [bru'net] *nm* dark-haired man; (*cu pielea oacheşă*) swarthy man/boy, dark-skinned man/boy ‖ *adj* (*la păr*) dark(-haired); (*la ten*) of dark/swarthy complexion • ~ă *nf* brunette; dark-haired girl/woman/lady, dark-skinned girl/woman/lady.
brusc [brusk] *adj* (*neaşteptat*) sudden, unexpected; (*pripit*) rash, sharp, abrupt ‖ *adv* suddenly, unexpectedly, all of a sudden, abruptly, sharp(ly).
brusca [brus'ka] *vt* (*a trata brutal*) to treat harshly, to bully; (*a se răsti*) to speak harshly/rudely (to), to snub; (*a trata aspru*) to treat rudely/harshly; to be curt/brusque; (*a grăbi lucrurile*) to press; to push on; (*o intrare*) to break/force open.
brut [brut] *adj* (*în stare naturală, neprelucrat*) raw, crude; (*neterminat*) rough, unfinished; *econ* gross.
brutal [bru'tal] *adj* brutal, savage, violent; (*bădărănos*) rude, boorish, rough ‖ *adv* brutally, cruelly, savagely • ~itate *nf* brutality, violence, cruelty; ill-treatment; cu ~ roughly • ~iza *vt* to handle. roughly; to brutalize, to ill-treat; (*a teroriza*) to bully.
brutar [bru'tar] *nm* baker.
brutărie [brută'rie] *nf* bakery.
bubă ['buba] *nf* sore; (*umflătură*) bump, swelling; (*vânătaie*) bruise; (*puroi, abces*) boil, abscess, ulcer; *fig* difficulty; (*obstacol*) hindrance; (*neajuns*) drawback; (*necaz*) trouble; *coll* rub; (*durere*) sorrow, grief; (*punct slab*) weak point.
bubonic [bu'bonik] *adj med* bubonic.
bubui [bubu'i] *vi* (*d. tunet*) to thunder, to rumble; (*d. tunuri*) to boom, to roar.
buburuză [bubu'ruză] *nf ento* ladybug.
bucată [bu'kată] *nf* piece, bit; part, portion; fragment;

(*căpeţel*) end; (*extras*) passage, excerpt; (*îmbucătură*) mouthful, morsel; (*vită*) head of cattle.
bucă ['bukă] *nf* (*a şezutului*) buttock, *esp pl* buttocks; (*a obrazului*) chubby cheek; *esp pl* cheeks • ~lat [bukă'lat] *adj* chubby, chubby(-cheeked/-faced).
bucătar [bukă'tar] *nm* (male) cook; (*într-un restaurant*) chef.
bucătăreasă [bukătă'reasă] *nf* cook.
bucătărie [bukătă'rie] *nf* (*odaie*) kitchen; *naut* galley; *fig* (*arta culinară*) cuisine, cooking.
buchet [bu'ket] *nn* bouquet, bunch of flowers, nosegay; (*de vin*) bouquet.
buchisi [buki'si] *vt* to grind, to cram; (*a bate*) to drub, to flog, to pummel.
buclă ['bukla] *nf* curl, lock, ringlet; *avia, tech, fig* loop.
bucluc [bu'kluk] *nn* (*necaz*) trouble, bother; *coll* scrape, mess; tight spot; (*nenorocire*) adversity, misfortune, predicament.
buclucaş [buklu'kash] *adj* quarrelsome, captious; (*supărător*) troublesome; (*neplăcut*) unpleasant, ticklish; difficult; intricate ‖ *nm* troublemaker.
bucşa ['buksha] *nf elec* jack.
bucura [buku'ra] *vt* to delight, to fill with joy, to please ‖ *vr* (*a fi bucuros*) to rejoice, to be happy/glad/pleased; to be filled with joy; (*a avea drepturi*) to enjoy, to possess, to have; **mă bucură** I'm happy (that).
bucurie [buku'rie] *nf* joy, happiness, gladness, exultation; (*veselie*) gaiety, glee, joyfulness.
bucuros [buku'ros] *adj* (*mulţumit*) glad, happy, pleased; (*vesel*) cheerful, merry; (*exprimând veselie*) gay ‖ *adv* gladly, willingly, with pleasure.
budincă [bu'dinkă] *nf* pudding.
buf [buf] *interj* bam.
bufet [bu'fet] *nn* (*mobilă: de sufragerie*) sideboard; (*de bucătărie*) cupboard; buffet; (*la teatru, gară*) refreshment room/bar; (*cârciumă*) pub.
bufni [buf'ni] *vt* (*a lovi producând un zgomot înfundat*) to thump, to thud; to bang; (*a izbucni în râs*) to burst out laughing, to burst/break into laughter ‖ *vi* (*a produce un zgomot înfundat*) to thud, to thump; (*a ricoşa*) to bounce, to rebound; (*d. flăcări, a răbufni*) to blaze up; (*a izbucni*) to spring up, to break out; (*d. lichide*) to gush forth; to grumble • ~tură *nf* bang, thud, thump.
bufniţă ['bufnitsă] *nf* owl.
bufon [bu'fon] *nm* (*mai ales la circ*) clown, fool, buffoon • ~erie *nf* clowning, foolishness, antics, buffoonery; (*în teatru, film*) slapstick (humor/comedy).
buget [bu'djet] *nn* budget.
buhai [bu'hai] *nm* bull; (*broască*) toad.
buimăceală [buimă'cheală] *nf* (*ameţeală*) dizziness; (*uluială*) dismay, bewilderment, perplexity, confusion.
buimăci [buimă'chi] *vt* (*prin lovire*) to stun, to stupefy; (*prin ceva neobişnuit, neaşteptat*) to amaze, to astonish, to astound; (*a stupefia*) to dumbfound, to bewilder, to put out (of countenance); *coll* to flabbergast, to flummox.
bujie [bu'zhie] *nf tech* spark plug.
bujor [bu'zhor] *nm bot* peony.
bulă ['bulă] *nf* (*pecete*) bull; (*aer*) bubble.
bulb [bulb] *nm bot* bulb, bulbous root; *anat* bulb.
bulboană [bul'boană] *nf* whirlpool, eddy, vortex.
bulbuc [bul'buk] *nm* water bubble; (*de săpun*) soap bubble; *bot* marsh marigold, caltha; *bot* globe flower.

buldog ['buldog] *nm* bulldog.

buldozer [bul'dozer] *nn constr* bulldozer.

buletin [bule'tin] *nn* (*scos de o organizație*) bulletin; ~ **de identitate** I.D., identity card/paper; ~ **de știri** news bulletin.

bulevard [bule'vard] *nn* avenue, boulevard.

bulgar(ă) [bul'gar(ă)] *nm/nf/adj* Bulgarian.

bulgăre ['bulgăre] *nm* ball.

bulină [bu'lină] *nf* pill, tabloid.

bulion [buli'on] *nn* (*sos de roșii*) tomato sauce; (*în bacteriologie*) bouillon, culture medium for bacteria.

buluci [bulu'chi] *vr* to push/jostle one another; (*a da năvală*) to flock to; (*a se îngrămădi*) to crowd.

bulumac [bulu'mak] *nm* post, pole, stake.

bulversa [bulver'sa] *vt* to upset, to unsettle, to bowl (*smb*) over.

bum [bum] *interj* bang, boom.

bumbac [bum'bak] *nn* cotton (plant); *text* cotton.

bumbăceală [bumbă'cheală] *nf* thrashing, beating, pummeling.

bumerang [bume'rang] *nn* boomerang.

bun [bun] *nm* (*bunic*) grandfather, grandparent ‖ *nn* (*avere*) property, fortune; (*al statului*) domain; (*pământ*) estate, manor; *pl* goods, one's belongings/effects/possession; *also fig* assets ‖ *adj* good; profitable; (*sănătos*) sound, wholesome, beneficial; (*potrivit*) fit, proper, right; favorable, fortunate; noble; (*cinstit*) honest, upright; (*drept*) just, right(eous); (*iubitor*) affectionate, loveable; (*plăcut*) nice, pleasant; (*amabil*) kind, obliging; (*priceput*) skillful, clever; veritable, genuine, true, real; (*în bună stare*) perfect, in good repair; (*norocos*) lucky, auspicious ‖ *interj* good, all right, OK, splendid.

Bunavestire [bunaves'tire] *nf relig* Annunciation.

bună-credință [bunăkre'dintsă] *nf* good faith.

bună-cuviință [bunăkuvi'intsă] *nf* decorum, decency; (*politețe*) politeness, good manners.

bunăstare [bună'stare] *nf* welfare, well-being.

bunătate [bună'tate] *nf* goodness, excellence; (*calitate*) first/top quality/rate; (*suflet bun*) kindness, kindliness; *pl* (*d. mâncare*) dainties; delicatessen.

bunăvoie [bună'voie] *nf* **de** ~ willingly, freely.

bunăvoință [bunăvo'intsă] *nf* goodwill, benevolence.

buncăr ['bunkăr] *nn mil* blockhouse, stronghold; *tech* also bunker.

bunic [bu'nik] *nm* grandfather; *coll* grandpa • ~**ică** *nf* grandmother; *coll* grandma, gran(ny), grannie.

bura [bu'ra] *vi* to drizzle.

burduf [bur'duf] *nn* (*bășică*) bladder; (*sac*) skin; (*foale*) bellows.

burduși [burdu'shi] *vt* (*a îndesa, a umple*) to cram, to stuff; *fig coll* (*a bate*) to sandbag, to thrash/flog soundly.

burete [bu'rete] *nm bot* (*ciupercă*) mushroom, fungus; *zool* sponge; (*de stors*) sponge.

burghez [bur'gez] *nm/adj* bourgeois • ~**ie** *nf* the middle classes, the bourgeoisie.

burghiu [bur'giu] *nn* borer; (*mare*) auger; (*lung*) churn drill, wimble; (*sfredel*) gimlet.

buric [bu'rik] *nn anat* navel, umbilicus; (*al degetului*) tip.

burlac [bur'lak] *nm* bachelor ‖ *adj* single.

burlan [bur'lan] *nn* (rain)pipe; (*coș*) flue, stovepipe.

burlesc [bur'lesk] *nn* burlesque ‖ *adj* burlesque, ludicrous, ridiculous ‖ *adv* comically, ridiculously, ludicrously.

burnița [burni'tsa] *vi* to drizzle.

burniță ['burnitsă] *nf* drizzle.

bursă[1] ['bursă] *nf* scholarship; grant.

bursă[2] ['bursă] *nf* (*de acțiuni, valori*) stock exchange; (*de mărfuri*) commodity exchange; ~ **neagră** black market.

bursier [bursi'er] *nm edu* scholar, scholarship/grant holder, grantee.

bursuc [bur'suk] *nm zool* badger; *fig coll* (*om grăsuț*) dumpy/stumpy guy; *fig coll* (*om ursuz*) growler, grumbler.

burtă ['burtă] *nf* (*pântec*) belly, stomach, abdomen; (*mare*) paunch; (*mâncare*) tripe; (*partea mai umflată a unui lucru*) bilge; pot-belly.

buruiană [buru'iană] *nf* weed; (*de leac*) medicinal plant/herb.

burzului [burzulu'i] *vr* (*d. păr*) to stand (up) on end; (*ca peria*) to bristle up; *fig coll* to fire up, to fly into a passion; (*d. vreme*) to break (up).

busculadă [busku'ladă] *nf* scuffle, bustle, jostling.

busolă [bu'solă] *nf* compass; *fig* guide.

bust [bust] *nn* bust (statue).

busuioc [busu'iok] *nn bot* sweet/common basil.

buși [bu'shi] *vt* (*a înghionti*) to push, to elbow; (*cu o armă*) to thrust; (*cu piciorul*) to kick; (*a da lovituri*) to punch, to thump; *coll* to knock about ‖ *vr* to jostle each other.

bușon [bu'shon] *nn tech* stopper; *elec* fusible plug.

buștean [bush'tean] *nm* (*copac tăiat*) log; (*ciot*) stump of a tree.

butadă [bu'tadă] *nf* quip, witticism, sally.

butaș [bu'tash] *nm* cutting, slip, layer.

butelie [bu'telie] *nf* bottle; ~ **de aragaz** gas cylinder.

butoi [bu'toi] *nn* cask, barrel; (*mic*) keg; (*mare*) butt, hogshead.

buton [bu'ton] *nm* (*nasture*) button; (*de manșetă*) cufflink; wristband button; (*de guler*) collar stud ‖ *nn* (*de sonerie*) bell/push button; (*la radio*) knob; (*comutator*) *elec* switch.

butonieră [butoni'eră] *nf* buttonhole.

butuc [bu'tuk] *nm* (*copac tăiat*) log, block of wood; (*ciot*) tree stump, tree trunk; (*de viță*) vine; (*la roată*) hub; (*pentru tăiat*) (chopping) block; *pl* (*cu găuri pt. tortură*) stocks.

butucănos [butukă'nos] *adj* thick, stumpy; (*grosolan*) boorish; (*stângaci*) clumsy.

buturugă [butu'rugă] *nf* tree-stump, block of wood.

buză ['buză] *nf anat* lip.

buzdugan [buzdu'gan] *nn* mace.

buzunar [buzu'nar] *nn* pocket, pouch; (*pentru ceas*) fob; *zool, bot* sac.

C

ca [ka] *adv* (*la fel ca*) as, like; **alb** ~ **zăpada** (as) white as snow, snow-white; **nu e** ~ **mine** he is not like me; ~ **altădată** as before; ~ **atare** as such; (*decât*) than; **e mai înalt** ~ **mine** he is taller than me; (*aproximativ*) about; **e** ~ **și mort** he is as good as dead; (*în calitate de*) as; **a vorbit** ~ **profesor** he spoke as a teacher; (*de exemplu*) for instance, such as; (*în privința*) as for; (*de asemenea*) as well as ‖ *conj* (*scopul*) ~ **să** in order to; so that; with a view to; **citesc cartea** ~ **să înțeleg intriga** I'm reading the book (in order) to understand the plot; ~ **nu cumva să** in order not to, so that, for fear that; (*comparație ireală*) ~ **și cum** as if.

cabană [ka'banâ] *nf* hut; (*la munte*) chalet; *pej* shack.

cabaret [kaba'ret] *nn* nightclub, cabaret.

cabină [ka'binâ] *nf* box, cabin, booth; (*carlingă de avion*) cockpit; (*telefonică*) telephone booth; (*de vapor*) cabin berth; (*de lux*) stateroom; (*la plajă*) beach hut; (*la piscină*) changing cubicle/room.

cabinet [kabi'net] *nn* (*guvern*) cabinet, government; (*birou*) office; (*dentar*) dental office; (*medical*) consulting room, surgery.

cablu ['kablu] *nn* cable, rope.

cabotin [kabo'tin] *nm* ham (actor), third-rate actor; **a face pe ~ul** to strike a pose, to act (badly), to attitudinize.

cabra [ka'bra] *vt* to prance, to rear (up).

cabrioletă [kabrio'letâ] *nf* cabriolet, gig.

cacao [ka'kao] *nf* cocoa; (*arbust*) cocoa tree.

cacealma [kacheal'ma] *nf* (*la jocul de cărți*) *also fig* bluff.

cacofonie [kakofo'nie] *nf* cacophony.

cactus ['kaktus] *nm bot* cactus.

cadavru [ka'davru] *nn* corpse, (dead) body, cadaver; (*de animal*) body, carcass.

cadă ['kadâ] *nf* tub, vat.

cadență [ka'dentsâ] *nf mus* cadence; (*ritm*) rhythm; (*în vorbire*) modulation; (*a pasului*) step, pace; **în ~ cu** *also fig* keeping pace/step with.

cadet [ka'det] *nm* cadet.

cadou [ka'dou] *nn* gift, present; ~ **publicitar** freebie, free gift.

cadran [ka'dran] *nn* dial, face of a clock/watch; (*solar*) sundial.

cadrilat [kadri'lat] *adj* chequered, checked.

cadru ['kadru] *nn* (*ramă*) frame; (*tablou*) picture, painting; (*de cinema*) still; (*mediu*) environment; (*de desfășurare a unei acțiuni*) setting; ~ **social** social environment, milieu; *fig* framework, background • **în ~ul** within the framework of, as part of; (*printre*) among; (*persoană*) worker, specialist; *pl* staff, personnel; *pol, mil* cadre(s).

caduc [ka'duk] *adj* decaying, falling, crumbling; fragile, frail, shaky, flimsy; (*d. persoane*) decrepit; *jur* null, void; (*d. un acord, testament etc*) lapsed; out of date.

cafea [ka'fea] *nf* coffee.

cafe-bar [ka'fe 'bar] *nn* café, coffeehouse.

cafenea [kafe'nea] *nf* café, coffeehouse.

cafeniu [kafe'niu] *adj* brown, coffee-colored.

caftan [kaf'tan] *nn* caftan, mantle, (velvet) gown.

cagulă ['kagulâ] *nf relig* cowl; (*de penitent*) hood; *mil* hood.

caiac [ka'iak] *nn* kayak.

caier ['kaier] *nn* bundle; (*de lână*) flock of wool; (*de in*) flax tress.

caiet [ka'iet] *nn* (*pt. școlari*) exercise book, writing book, copybook; (*de note*) notebook; (*de desen*) drawing book; (*la vânzare*) terms and conditions.

caimac [kai'mak] *nn* skin of milk; (*smântână*) *also fig* cream.

cais [ka'is] *nm* apricot tree • ~**ă** *nf* apricot.

cal [kal] *nm zool* horse; (*armăsar pt. călărie*) steed; (*armăsar pt. reproducere*) stallion; (*la șah*) knight; (*jucărie*) rocking-horse; ~ **de bătaie** (*ca subiect predilect de discuție*) hobbyhorse; (*țintă a ironiei*) laughing stock, butt of people's jokes.

calabâlc [kalaba'lâk] *nn* caboodle; (*catrafuse*) belongings, things, stuff; *coll* one's traps/sticks, luggage.

calambur [kalam'bur] *nn* pun, play on words; *rare* quibble.

calamitate [kalami'tate] *nf* calamity, disaster; misfortune; ~ **naturală** natural disaster; *fig* nuisance.

calapod [kala'pod] *nn* (shoemaker's) last; (*pt. pălării*) hat block; *fig* pattern, type, cliché.

cală[1] ['kalâ] *nf naut* (*pt. încărcătură*) hold; (*de lansare*) stocks, slip(way); (*de ridicare*) hauling-up slip.

cală[2] ['kalâ] *nf bot* calla.

calc [kalk] *nn* tracing; (*hârtie*) tracing paper; (*lingvistic*) loan translation; *fig* imitation, copy.

calcan[1] [kal'kan] *nm icht* turbot, ray.

calcan[2] [kal'kan] *nn* blank/blind wall.

calcar ['kalkar] *nn* limestone, chalky/calcareous stone.

calciu ['kalchu] *nn chem* calcium.

calcul[1] ['kalkul] *nn math* calculus; calculation, estimation; (*în mare*) reckoning; (*apreciere*) estimate; *pl fig* plans, speculations, calculations.

calcul[2] ['kalkul] *nm med* calculus, stone; ~ **biliar** biliary calculus; *coll* gallstone.

calcula [kalku'la] *vt math* to calculate, to reckon; to work out; (*a aduna*) to sum up, to total up; (*a estima*) to estimate, to consider, to rate • ~**tor** *nn* (personal) computer; ~ **portabil** *nn* laptop || *adj* calculating, computing, reckoning.

cald [kald] *nn* warmth, heat || *adj* warm; (*fierbinte*) hot; (*căldut*) lukewarm, tepid; *fig* (*afectuos*) affectionate; (*nou*) fresh || *adv* warmly, affectionately.

caldarâm [kalda'râm] *nn* paving; road surface; cobblestone.

cale ['kale] *nf* road; (*stradă*) street; way, course; (*trecere*) passage; (*rută*) route; (*de rulare*) traffic lane; (*depărtare*) distance, long way; (*mijloc*) means.

caleidoscop [kaleido'skop] *nn* kaleidoscope.

calendar [kalen'dar] *nn* calendar; (*program pe ziua/săptămâna în curs*) agenda, schedule

calibra [kali'bra] *vt tech* to calibrate, to gauge; to measure.

calibru [kali'bru] *nn mil* caliber, bore; *tech* gauge; (*diametru*) diameter; (*mărime*) size; *fig* stature.

caliciu [ka'lichu] *nn bot* calyx, cup.

califica [kalifi'ka] *vt* to qualify; (*a numi*) to call, to name, to describe (smth/smb as) || *vr* to acquire skill; (*d. sport, concurs*) to qualify • ~**re** *nf* (*pregătire*) skill, training; *sp* qualification; ~**tiv** *nn* name; *ling* modifier; (*stil*) epithet; (*notă*) grade, rating || *adj* qualifying, modifying.

caligrafie [kaligra'fie] *nf* calligraphy; (*scris*) handwriting, penmanship.

calin [ka'lin] *adj* (*d. ton, privire, comportament*) cuddly, loving, affectionate.

calitate [kali'tate] *nf* quality, attribute; (*însușire*) feature, property; (*poziție*) capacity, position; (*fel*) sort, kind, brand.

calitativ [kalita'tiv] *adj* qualitative || *adv* qualitatively; **salt ~** qualitative leap.

calm [kalm] *nn* calm(ness), quiet(ness); peace; (*d. aer, noapte*) stillness; peacefulness; (*al caracterului*) coolness; (*indiferență*) indifference || *adj* (*liniștit*) quiet; tranquil, unruffled; (*cu sânge rece*) cool; (*stăpânit*) composed, even-tempered; (*care nu se* *grăbește*) unhurried; (*d. natură*) serene, peaceful; (*d. aer, noapte*) still; (*d. mare*) smooth; (*d. viață*) uneventful ‖ *adv* calmly, quietly • ~**a** *vt* to calm (down), to set at ease; (*a alina*) to alleviate, to soothe, to appease; (*durerea*) to ease, to relieve; (*nervii*) to steady; (*mulțimea*) to pacify ‖ *vi* to have a soothing effect ‖ *vr* (*d. persoane*) to calm down, to take it easy; (*d. vânt, mare*) to be(come) calm/still, to die out/ down; (*d. durere*) to ease, to subside.

calmant [kal'mant] *nn* sedative ‖ *adj* soothing, sedative.

calmar [kal'mar] *nm cul* calamari; sleeve-fish.

calomnia [kalomni'a] *vt* (*a defăima*) to defame, to slander; (*în scris*) to libel; to discredit, to bring into disrepute • ~**tor** *nm* slanderer; (*în scris*) libeler, scandalmonger ‖ *adj* libelous, slanderous.

calomnie [kalom'nie] *nf* (*orală*) slander; (*inventată*) calumny; (*în scris, publică*) libel; (*defăimare*) defamation; **proces de** ~ libel suit, action for libel.

calomnios [kalomni'os] *adj* slanderous, defamatory; *jur* libelous ‖ *adv* slanderously.

caloric [ka'lorik] *adj phys* heat, heating, caloric.

calorie [kalo'rie] *nf* calorie.

calorifer [kalori'fer] *nn* radiator; (*încălzire centrală*) central heating.

calvar [kal'var] *nn relig* calvary, agony, ordeal.

cam [kam] *adv* about, around, some, approximately; (*aproape*) nearly, almost; (*oarecum*) rather, pretty, somewhat; **e ~ același lucru** it's nearly the same thing, it amounts to much the same thing; ~ **așa ceva** approximately, like this, somewhat like this; **e ~ târziu** it's rather late; **sunt ~ la fel** they are almost identical.

camarad [kama'rad] *nm* (*tovarăș*) comrade, fellow, mate; (*coleg de școală*) schoolmate, schoolfriend, schoolfellow; (*de clasă*) classmate; (*de arme*) brother in arms • ~**erie** *nf* camaraderie; comradeship; *mil* esprit de corps; (*bună tovărășie*) good fellowship, companionship.

camarilă [kama'rilă] *nf* court clique, camarilla.

camătă ['kamătă] *nf* (*afacere ilegală*) usury, usurious/ exorbitant interest.

cambie ['kambie] *nf com* promissory note, bill of exchange.

cameleon [kamele'on] *nm zool* chameleon; *fig* (*d. persoană*) chameleon, turncoat, weathercock.

camelie [ka'melie] *nf bot* camellia.

cameră ['kameră] *nf* (*odaie*) room; (*locuință*) apartment; (*de bicicletă*) inner tube; (*de minge*) bladder.

cameristă [kame'ristă] *nf* (*la hotel*) chambermaid; lady's maid.

camfor ['kamfor] *nn* camphor.

camion [kami'on] *nn* (*cu tracțiune mecanică*) truck; (*basculant*) dump truck; (*pt. mobilă*) van; (*cu tracțiune animală: cai*) dray • ~**etă** *nf* pick-up (truck), van.

campanie [kam'panie] *nf mil* campaign; *pol also fig* drive.

camping ['kamping] *nn* camping ground/site, holiday camp.

campion [kampi'on] *nm* (*as*) champion, ace; (*apărător al unei cauze*) defender • ~**at** *nn* (*supremație*) championship; (*concurs*) championship(s); (*tenis, șah*) tournament.

campus ['kampus] *nn* campus.

camufla [kamu'fla] *vt mil* to camouflage; (*ferestre*) to black out; *fig* (*a masca*) to disguise; (*a ascunde*) to

hide, to conceal; (*o greșeală*) to cover up ‖ *vr mil* to camouflage oneself; *fig* (*a se masca*) to disguise oneself; (*a se ascunde*) to hide (oneself).

canadian [kanadi'an] *nm/adj* Canadian (male) • ~**ă** *nf* Canadian (female).

canal [ka'nal] *nn* (*natural*) channel; (*artificial*) canal; (*pt. scurgere reziduuri*) sewer, drain; (*rigolă*) gutter; spout, conduit; *anat, bot* duct, tube • ~**ul Mânecii** The (English) Channel.

canalie [ka'nalie] *nf* rascal, scoundrel, villain, rogue.

canaliza [kanali'za] *vt* (*o regiune, râu*) to supply with sewerage system; *fig* (*a direcționa spre*) to channel, to guide, to direct • ~**re** *nf* sewerage, piping conduit.

canapea [kana'pea] *nf* couch, sofa, settee.

canar [ka'nar] *nm* canary (bird).

canat [ka'nat] *nn* (*de ușă, la o masă extensibilă*) leaf, fold; (*de fereastră*) wing.

canava [kana'va] *nf tex* canvas; *fig* sketch, groundwork, outline.

cană ['kană] *nf* (*mare*) pitcher, decanter, jug; (*de metal, cu capac*) tankard; (*ceașcă*) cup, mug.

cancan [kan'kan] *nn* (*dans*) cancan; (*bârfă*) scandal, gossip, tittle-tattle.

cancelar [kanche'lar] *nm* chancellor.

cancelarie [kanche'larie] *nf* (*birou*) office; (*la școala*) teachers' room; staff room.

cancer ['kancher] *nn med* cancer, carcinoma; neoplasm.

candelabru [kande'labru] *nn* chandelier, candelabrum.

candelă ['kandelă] *nf* icon lamp, votive light.

candid [kan'did] *adj* candid, sincere, frank, open ‖ *adv* candidly, sincerely, frankly, openly

candida [kandi'da] *vi* (*în alegeri*) to run/stand (for); *fig* to aspire (to) • ~**t** *nm* (*la un post*) applicant; (*la un examen*) candidate, examinee; *pol* (*în alegeri*) nominee • ~**ură** *nf* candidature; *coll* candidacy.

candoare [kan'doare] *nf* (*sinceritate*) candor, sincerity, frankness; (*puritate*) purity, innocence, guilelessness.

canelură [kane'lură] *nf tech* groove; *archit* fluting.

cangrena [kangre'na] *vi/vr med* to go/become gangrenous; *also fig* to canker; to corrupt, to become corrupt.

cangrenă [kan'grenă] *nf med* gangrene; mortification; *fig* blight, canker, corruption.

cangur ['kangur] *nm* kangaroo.

canibal [kani'bal] *nm* cannibal, man-eater; *fig* savage, ferocious person.

caniculă [ka'nikulă] *nf* dog days.

canin [ka'nin] *adj* (*d. câine*) canine, dog-like ‖ *nm* eye-tooth, canine (tooth).

canion [kani'on] *nn* canyon.

canistră [ka'nistră] *nf* can, canister.

canoe [ka'noe] *nf* canoe.

canon [ka'non] *nn* (*regulă*) dogma, tenet; *relig* canon, church decree; *relig* (*pedeapsă*) penance; (*chin*) torment, torture, ordeal.

canotaj [kano'tazh] *nn* boating, canoeing, rowing, sailing.

cant [kant] *nn* edge, edging.

cantalup [kanta'lup] *nm* (*cantaloupe*) melon.

cantată [kan'tată] *nf mus* cantata.

cantină [kan'tină] *nf* canteen; *scol* cafeteria, refectory; (*sală de mâncare*) eating-hall.

cantitate [kanti'tate] *nf* quantity, amount; *math* number.

cantitativ [kantita'tiv] *adj* quantitative ‖ *adv* quantitatively.

canto ['kanto] *nn mus* vocal music, singing.

canton [kan'ton] *nn adm, geog* canton; *rail* block station, watchman's cabin; (*de șosea*) gatekeeper's cabin.

cantonament [kantona'ment] *nn mil* quartering, billeting; *sp* training camp.

cap [kap] *nm* (*conducător*) chief, leader; *pej* ringleader || *nn anat* head; (*țeastă*) skull; (*al unui os*) apophysis; *sl* pate, noodle; (*minte*) mind, brains; *geog* cape, promontory; (*început*) start, beginning; (*capăt*) end; (*vârf*) top.

capabil [ka'pabil] *adj* capable, able; (*talentat*) talented, gifted; *jur* qualified, competent.

capac [ka'pak] *nn* lid; (*care se înșurubează*) cap; top; (*cu filet*) screw cap/top.

capacitate [kapachi'tate] *nf* volume; (*aptitudine*) ability; capability; talent, gift; (*competență*) competence; (*somitate*) authority, outstanding person; (*putință*) power; *tech, elec* capacity; *jur* legal competence.

capăt ['kapăt] *nn* (*extremitate*) end, extremity; limit, bottom; (*început*) beginning, start; (*bucățică*) bit, piece.

capcană [kap'kană] *nf* trap, snare; *fig* pitfall; *coll* catch.

capelă [ka'pelă] *nf* (*bisericuță*) chapel; *mil* (peaked) cap.

caperă ['kaperă] *nf bot* caper.

capilar [kapi'lar] *adj* capillary.

capital [kapi'tal] *nn econ* capital, assets; (*bani*) money, cash; ~ **bancar** banking capital; ~ **fix** fixed capital; ~ **social** share/registerd capital || *adj* capital, chief, principal, main; **importanță** ~**ă** paramount/utmost importance • ~**ă** *nf* capital.

capitalism [kapita'lism] *nn* capitalism.

capitalist [kapita'list] *adj* capitalist(ic) || *nm* capitalist, employer.

capitol [ka'pitol] *nn* (*de carte*) *also fig* chapter; (*chestiune*) matter, subject.

capitona [kapito'na] *vt* to upholster, to pad, to quilt.

capitula [kapitu'la] *vi mil* to capitulate; *fig* to surrender.

capodoperă [kapo'doperă] *nf* masterpiece.

caporal [kapo'ral] *nm mil* private first class.

capot [ka'pot] *nn* dressing gown, bathrobe, robe; *naut* hood, tarpaulin • ~**ă** *nf* (*a motorului*) hood; *avia* cowl(ing); (*de piele*) top; (*pliantă*) folding top.

capră ['kapră] *nf* (she) goat, nanny goat; (*de munte/sălbatică*) chamois; (*de trăsură*) dicky; (*de tăiat lemne*) trestle; (*de gimnastică*) vaulting horse; (*joc*) leap frog.

capricios [kapri'chios] *adj* whimsical, freakish, capricious; (*încăpățânat*) wayward || *adv* capriciously, freakishly, whimsically.

capriciu [ka'prichiu] *nn* caprice, whim, fancy; *mus* capriccio, caprice.

capricorn [kapri'korn] *nn astrol* Capricorn, the Goat.

capsa [kap'sa] *vt* to staple.

capsă ['kapsă] *nf mil* detonator, primer; (*pt. hârtii*) staple.

capsulă [kap'sulă] *nf anat, zool, bot* capsule; (*păstaie*) pod; *tech* cap, seal of bottle.

capta [kap'ta] *vt phys* to capture, to catch; (*apă, energie*) to collect; (*curent electric*) to pick up; *fig* to captivate, to win smb over; (*atenția*) to gain, to capture • ~**re** *nf tech* collecting, piping; *elec* picking up (of current).

captiv [kap'tiv] *nm/adj* captive, prisoner.

captiva [kapti'va] *vt* to captivate; (*d. cărți, filme*) to enthrall, to thrill; (*a fermeca*) to charm, to fascinate;

(*atenția*) to capture • ~**nt** *adj* (*d. persoane*) captivating, charming, fascinating; (*d. cărți*) gripping, thrilling, enthralling.

captivitate [kaptivi'tate] *nf* captivity.

captura [kaptu'ra] *vt* to capture, to catch, to seize, to take.

captură [kap'tură] *nf* capture, seizure, catching; prize.

car [kar] *nn* cart, wagon; *hist* chariot; (*încărcătură*) cartful; ~ **alegoric** float, pageant.

carabină [kara'bină] *nf mil* carbine, rifle.

caracatiță [kara'katitsă] *nf zool* octopus.

caracter [karak'ter] *nn psych* character, nature, disposition; aspect; (*trăsătură*) feature, characteristic; **lipsă de** ~ lack of principle; fickleness of character, spinelessness; **tărie de** ~ strength of character; (*semn grafic*; *literă*) letter; *typ* (metal) type • ~**istic** *adj* (*pentru*) characteristic (of); typical (of); specific (to), illustrative (of); distinctive • ~**istică** *nf* specific/ salient feature, characteristic (feature) • ~**iza** *vt* to characterize; to describe, to mark, to distinguish || *vr* to be characterized/distinguished/marked • ~**izare** *nf* character(ization); (*referință*) reference, testimonial.

carafă [ka'rafă] *nf* decanter, carafe, water bottle.

caraghios [kara'gios] *nm* (*bufon*) buffoon, funny guy; (*prost*) fool, dolt; ridiculous person; (*poznaș*) practical joker; (*original*) eccentric; *coll* crank || *adj* (*ridicol*) ridiculous; (*prostesc*) foolish, ludicrous; (*comic*) funny, comical; (*ciudat*) singular, queer, odd || *adv* ridiculously, foolishly, comically, oddly

caramea, caramelă [kara'mea, kara'melă] *nf* caramel, toffee.

carantină [karan'tină] *nf* quarantine.

carapace [kara'pache] *nf* shell, carapace.

caras [ka'ras] *nm* crucian (carp).

carat [ka'rat] *nn* carat.

caravană [kara'vană] *nf* caravan, desert convoy.

carbid [kar'bid] *nn chem* calcium carbide.

carbon [kar'bon] *nn chem* carbon; **bioxid de** ~ carbon dioxide.

carbonifer [karboni'fer] *adj* coal-bearing, carboniferous; **bazin** ~ coal basin/field.

carburant [karbu'rant] *nm* (motor)fuel, carburant.

carburator [karbura'tor] *nn* carburetor.

carcasă [kar'kasă] *nf* (*schelet*) carcass; (*cadru*) frame(work), framing; skeleton (of a ship).

carceră ['karcheră] *nf* lock-up room.

card [kard] *nn econ* card.

cardiac [kardi'ak] *nm* cardiac patient || *adj* cardiac, heart…; **afecțiune** ~**ă** heart disease; **stop** ~ cardiac arrest.

cardinal [kardi'nal] *adj* cardinal; **punct** ~ cardinal point; *fig* chief || *nm relig* cardinal; (*zool*) cardinal (bird).

cardiolog [kardio'log] *nm* cardiologist, heart specialist.

care ['kare] *pron rel* (*pt. pers.*) who, that; (*pt. lucruri*) which, that; ~ **încotro** everywhere, in all directions; ~ **va sa zică** that is to say, therefore || *pron inter* which; ~ **dintre ei?** which of them?; what; (*cine*) who; ~ **e numele ei?** what is her name? ~ **ești?** who is there? || *pron rel* (*unii*) some || *adj rel, inter* which; ~ **băiat a luat-o?** which boy took it?

carență [ka'rentsă] *nf* default, deficiency in/of.

careu [ka'reu] *nn also mil* square; (*la pocher*) four (of a kind); (*de cuvinte încrucișate*) crossword puzzle; *sp* field, sportsground; (*de tenis, volei, baschet*) court.

cargobot [kargo'bot] *nn naut* cargo boat, freighter, tramp (steamer).

caria [kari'a] *vt* to rot, to decay || *vr* to rot, to decay, to grow carious.

caricatură [karika'tură] *nf (şi desen)* cartoon; *fig* caricature; *(imitare)* take-off.

caricaturiza [karikaturi'za] *vt* to caricature; *(a imita)* to take off.

carie ['karie] *nf med* caries, decay.

carieră[1] [kari'eră] *nf (profesiune)* career.

carieră[2] [kari'eră] *nf (de piatră)* quarry, (stone) pit; *(la suprafaţă)* open pit.

carierist [karie'rist] *nm* self-seeker, careerist; *(social)* climber; *coll* go-getter.

caritabil [kari'tabil] *adj* charitable, open-handed, benevolent.

caritate [kari'tate] *nf* charity, philanthropy, benevolence.

carlingă [kar'lingă] *nf* cockpit.

carnaj [kar'nazh] *nn* massacre, slaughter, carnage.

carnal [kar'nal] *adj* carnal, bodily; sensual, sensuous.

carnaval [karna'val] *nn* carnival.

carne ['karne] *nf (vie)* flesh; *fig* body; **în ~ şi oase** in person, in the flesh; *(tăiată, de mâncat)* meat; *bot* pulp.

carnet [kar'net] *nn (legitimaţie)* card; *(permis)* license; **~ de cecuri** checkbook; *(de notiţe)* notebook.

carneţel [karne'tsel] *nn* notebook, jotter, pocketbook.

carnivor [karni'vor] *nn* carnivore, predator || *adj* carnivorous.

caro [ka'ro] *nn (jocul de cărţi)* diamonds.

carosabil [karo'sabil] *adj* **partea ~ă** carriage way, roadway.

caroserie [karose'rie] *nf auto* bodywork, coachwork.

carou [ka'rou] *nn* square • **în ~uri** check(er)ed.

carpen ['karpen] *nm bot* hornbeam.

carpetă [kar'petă] *nf* rug.

cart [kart] *nn naut* watch; go-cart.

cartare [kar'tare] *nf (poştă)* sorting; *geog* plotting, mapping, map-drawing.

cartă ['kartă] *nf* charter.

carte ['karte] *nf* book; *(de joc)* playing card; *(învăţătură)* learning, schooling; *(legitimaţie)* card; *(scrisoare)* letter; **~ poştală** postcard; **~ de credit** credit card; **~ de telefon** telephone book/directory.

cartel [kar'tel] *nn com* cartel, trust; combine; *pol* coalition.

cartelă [kar'telă] *nf* card; *(de telefon)* phone card; ration book/card; *hist (de îmbrăcăminte)* clothing coupons.

cartier [karti'er] *nn* neighborhood, district, quarter.

cartilaj [karti'lazh] *nn anat* cartilage; *culin coll* gristle.

cartof [kar'tof] *nm bot (plantă)* potato plant; *(tubercul)* potato.

cartografie [kartogra'fie] *nf* cartography, mapping.

carton [kar'ton] *nn (de calitate, pt. planşe etc)* cardboard, pasteboard card.

cartotecă [karto'teka] *nf* card index.

cartuş [kar'tush] *nn (de ţigări)* carton; *mil* cartridge; *archit* cartouche.

carusel [karu'sel] *nn* merry-go-round.

casa [ka'sa] *vt* to repeal; *jur* to annul.

casant [ka'sant] *adj* breakable; *(fragil)* fragile.

casă ['kasă] *nf* house; *(clădire)* building; *pej (sărăcăcioasă)* hovel; *(mare şi luxoasă)* mansion; *(conac)* manor; *(locuinţă)* dwelling; *(cămin)* home; *(gospodărie)*

household; *(cei care locuiesc în casă)* a houseful of people; *(familie)* family; *(pt. plată în magazine)* cash register; *(general)* payment counter; *(bancă)* teller; *(ghişeu)* window; *(de bilete)* ticket office; *(teatru)* box office; **Casa Albă** The White House (U.S.).

cascadă [kas'kadă] *nf also fig* cascade, falls, waterfall.

cascador [kaska'dor] *nm* stuntman, stand-in.

cască ['kaskă] *nf mil* helmet; *(de radio)* headphones, earphones; *(de înot)* bathing-cap; *(de baie)* bath cap; *(de protecţie)* crash helmet; *sp* baseball cap.

caschetă [kas'ketă] *nf* cap.

caserolă [kase'rolă] *nf* casserole.

casetă [ka'setă] *nf (film)* audio/videocassette; *(pt. bani, birou)* cash box; *(pt. bijuterii)* jewel box, casket; *typ* font (cassette); column.

casetofon [kaseto'fon] *nn* tape recorder.

casier/ă [kasi'er/ă] *nm/nf* cashier; *rail* booking clerk.

casierie [kasie'rie] *nf (pt. salarii)* pay office; *(magazin)* cash register; payment counter.

casnic ['kasnik] *adj (de casă)* home…; *(de gospodărie)* household; domestic; *(de familie)* family, married • **~ă** *nf* homemaker.

cast [kast] *adj* chaste.

castan [kas'tan] *nm* chestnut tree • **~ă** *nf (sălbatică)* horse chestnut; *(comestibilă)* sweet chestnut.

castă ['kastă] *nf* caste.

castel [kas'tel] *nn* castle.

castitate [kasti'tate] *nf* chastity; virtue.

castor ['kastor] *nm zool* beaver.

castra [kas'tra] *vt* to castrate, to emasculate; *(d. animale)* to geld, to neuter, to spay.

castravecior [kastrave'chor] *nm* gherkin.

castravete [kastra'vete] *nm* cucumber.

castron [kas'tron] *nn (supieră)* tureen; bowl, soup-plate.

caş [kash] *nm/nn* sweet/unsalted sheep's cheese; green ewe cheese.

cataclism [kata'klism] *nn* disaster, calamity, cataclysm.

catacombă [kata'kombă] *nf* catacomb.

catadicsi [katadik'si] *vt* to deign.

catafalc [kata'falk] *nn* catafalque; **pe ~** (lie) in state.

catalizator [kataliza'tor] *adj chem* catalytic || *nn* catalyst, catalyser, accelerator.

catalog [kata'log] *nn* catalogue, list; *com* stocklist, inventory; *(şcoală)* roll, roster • **a striga ~ul** to call the roll.

cataloga [katalo'ga] *vt* to catalog, to register, to put/enter in a catalog; to label.

cataplasmă [kata'plasmă] *nf med* cataplasm, poultice.

cataractă [kata'raktă] *nf geog* falls, cataract; *med* cataract.

cataramă [kata'ramă] *nf* buckle, clasp.

catarg [ka'targ] *nn* mast.

catastrofă [katas'trofă] *nf* catastrophe, disaster, calamity.

catâr [ka'târ] *nm zool also fig* mule.

catedrală [kate'drală] *nf* cathedral.

catedră [ka'tedră] *nf (mobilă)* teacher's desk; *edu* department.

categoric [kate'gorik] *adj (d. răspuns)* categorical, definite, positive; *(d. refuz)* flat, pointblank || *adv* categorically, definitively, positively

categorie [katego'rie] *nf* category; *(fel)* kind, sort; class, order; *sp* weight.

categorisi [kategori'si] *vt* to categorize, to classify; to qualify.

catifea [kati'fea] *nf* velvet.

catod [ka'tod] *nm elec* cathode.

catolic [ka'tolik] *nm/adj* Catholic.

catolicism [katoli'chism] *nn* Catholicism.

catrafuse [katra'fuse] *nf pl* kit; *coll* kit and caboodle • **a-şi lua/strânge ~le** to pack one's bags and get out; *mil* to pack up one's kit.

catran [ka'tran] *nn* tar.

caucazian [kaukazi'an] *nm/adj* Caucasian.

cauciuc [kau'chuk] *nn* rubber; *(auto)* tire.

caustic [ka'ustik] *adj chem* caustic, burning; *fig* biting, cutting ‖ *adv* caustically, bitingly.

cauteriza [kauteri'za] *vt med* to cauterize, to sear, to burn out.

cauţiune [kautsi'une] *nf jur* bond, bail; *(pt. un împrumut)* security.

cauza [kau'za] *vt* to cause, to bring about, to determine; to produce; *(a da naştere la)* to call forth.

cauză ['kauză] *nf* cause; motive, reason, ground(s); **în ~** involved, concerned; *jur* case.

cavaler [kava'ler] *nm hist* knight; **~ rătăcitor** knight errant; *(călăreţ)* rider, horseman; **~ii Mesei Rotunde** the Knights of the Round Table; *(însoţitor)* companion, escort; *(la dans)* male partner in dancing; *(admirator)* admirer, beau; *(om bine crescut)* gentleman; *(holtei)* bachelor; **~ de onoare** best man ‖ *adj* gallant • **~ie** *nf mil* cavalry.

cavernă [ka'vernă] *nf* cave, cavern; *med* cavity.

caviar [kavi'ar] *nn* caviar.

cavitate [kavi'tate] *nf* cavity, hollow.

cavou [ka'vou] *nn* tomb, burial vault.

caz [kaz] *nn also gram* case; *(întâmplare)* happening, event, occurrence; *(exemplu)* instance; *(zarvă)* fuss; *(problemă)* issue; *med* patient; *jur* test case; **în ~ de** in the event of; **în orice ~** in any case, at all events.

caza [ka'za] *vt* to accommodate, to put (smb) up; *mil* to billet, to quarter.

cazan [ka'zan] *nn* boiler; *(de rufe)* copper, cauldron; *(de ţuică)* still, alembic.

cazare [ka'zare] *nf* accommodation; *mil* billeting, quartering.

cazarmă [ka'zarmă] *nf* barrack(s).

cazier [kazi'er] *nn jur* (criminal/police) record; *(mobilă)* (set of) pigeonholes.

cazinou [kazi'nou] *nn* casino.

cazma [kaz'ma] *nf* spade.

caznă ['kaznă] *nf* torture; *fig* torment, ordeal; *(martiriu)* martyrdom; *(suferinţă)* agony; *(strădanie)* strain, pains; effort, trouble.

cazon [ka'zon] *adj* soldierly, soldier's, military; *fig* rigid, stiff, harsh.

că [ka] *conj* that; **cred ~ va veni** I think (that) he will come; *(fiindcă)* for, because; **să mergem ~ e târziu** let's go because it's late; *(altfel)* or (else), otherwise; **grăbeşte-te ~ nu-l mai găseşti** hurry up or/otherwise you won't find him; *(încât)* that; **cu toate ~** although; **pentru ~** because, for, since, as.

căci ['kăch] *conj* for, because, as.

căciulă [kă'chulă] *nf* (fur) cap; *fig* **de ~** per head.

căciuli [kăchu'li] *vr (a se umili)* to cringe, to bow low; *(a cere)* to cadge, to scrounge, to sponge.

cădea [kă'dea] *vi* to fall (down); *(a se desprinde)* to fall off; *(a lăsa să cadă)* to drop; *fig (a se prăbuşi)* to collapse, to break down; *(la examen)* to flunk, to fail; *(a avea loc)* to be, to happen; *(d. frunze)* to fall; *(d. păr)* to lose one's hair; *(a eşua)* to come to noth-

ing; to fall flat; *(d. un guvern)* to bring down, to topple; *(a se lăsa să cadă într-un fotoliu)* to drop/sink/ flop into an armchair; *(d. vânt)* to subside, to die down; *(d. conversaţie)* to flag; *(d. entuziasm)* to wane, to decline; *(d. temperatură afară)* to go down; *mil (a ~ asupra inamicului)* to fall on, to attack; *fig (d. dificultăţi)* to be plagued/beset by; *(d. păr)* to hang loose; *(d. draperii)* to come (down to the ground); *(d. ploaie)* to rain, to come down; *(d. grindină)* to hail; *(d. zăpadă)* to snow ‖ *vr* **a i se ~** to get no more than one's due, to fully deserve.

cădelniţă [kă'delnitsă] *nf relig* censer, thurible.

cădere [kă'dere] *nf* (down)fall; *fig* collapse, ruin; *(distrugere)* destruction: *(eşec)* failure; *(pricepere)* capacity, competence.

căi [kă'i] *vr* to repent, to regret, to be contrite.

căina [kăi'na] *vt (a compătimi)* to sympathize/commiserate with, to pity; *(a deplânge)* to deplore, to lament (over), to mourn (for) ‖ *vr* to lament, to wail, to moan.

căinţă [kă'intsă] *nf (remuşcare)* repentance, remorse, contrition; regret; *(pt. păcate)* penitence.

călăreţ [kălă'rets] *nm* horseman, rider.

călări [kălă'ri] *vi* to ride; to gallop; *(la pas)* to amble; *fig* to tyrannize • **~e, ~t** *nf/nn* horseback riding, equitation; *(plimbare călare)* ride.

călător [kălă'tor] *nm* traveler; *(pe mare) obs* voyager; *(pasager)* passenger, tourist ‖ *adj* traveling, itinerant; migratory; *(nomad)* vagrant, nomadic.

călători [kălăto'ri] *vi* to travel (about), to tour; *(pe uscat, cu o destinaţie)* to (make a) journey; *(pe apă)* to voyage; *(a rătăci)* to wander, to roam; **a ~ cu trenul** to go/travel by train/rail; **a ~ pe jos** to go on foot, to hike ‖ *vr (a pleca)* to go away; *(a muri)* to pass away • **~e** *nf* travel; *(cu destinaţie precisă)* journey; *(scurtă)* trip, tour; *(pe apă)* voyage; *(cu maşina)* ride.

călău [kă'lău] *nm* executioner; hangman; *fig* butcher, tyrant.

călăuză [kălă'uză] *nf* guide; adviser; *(carte)* guidebook; *fig* guiding principle.

călăuzi [kălău'zi] *vt* to guide, to show/take smb around; *(a sfătui)* to advise; *(a învăţa)* to teach ‖ *vr* **a se ~ (după)** to take as a guide, to follow.

călca [kăl'ka] *vt* to step, to tread (on), to trample (on); *(a zdrobi)* to crush; *(în picioare)* to trample underfoot; *(cu maşina)* to run over; *(a vizita)* to visit, to drop in/on; *(d. hoţi)* to rob, to break into; *(cu fierul)* to iron, to press; *fig (a încălca)* to violate, to infringe; *(o promisiune)* to break; *(a năvăli peste)* to fall upon ‖ *vi (a păşi)* to take a step back/forward/towards; to set foot on dry land; **a ~ strâmb** *(propriu)* to stumble; *fig (moral)* to step/be out of line; to be out of bounds, to overstep the bounds/limits.

călcâi [kăl'kâi] *nn anat also fig; pantof* heel.

căldare [kăl'dare] *nf (găleată)* bucket, pail; *(cazan)* boiler; *geol* hollow.

căldură [kăl'dură] *nf* heat, warmth; *phys* heat; *fig* ardor, fervor, zeal; *(febră)* fever(ishness); **cu ~** warmly, ardently, passionately; *pl zool* rut; *(d. oameni) vulg* to be horny.

călduros [kăldu'ros] *adj* warm, hot; *fig* ardent, passionate ‖ *adv* warmly, ardently, passionately.

călduţ [kăl'duts] *adj* lukewarm, tepid; *fig* lukewarm, halfhearted.

Calea Robilor *n astron* The Milky Way.

căli [kă'li] *vt* (*fier*) to temper, to harden; *fig* to strengthen; (*varză, ciuperci, ceapă, carne*) to stir-fry ‖ *vr* to be(come) tempered/hardened; *fig* to harden/steel/ brace oneself; (*fizic*) to toughen oneself up.

călimară [kăli'mară] *nf* ink-pot; (*ca suport*) inkstand.

călugăr [ka'lugar] *nm* monk, friar • **~iță** *nf* nun; *pl* (*pension pt. fete*) convent (school); *ento* praying mantis • **~i** [kălugă'ri] *vr* (*d. bărbați*) to enter a monastery; (*d. femei*) to enter a convent/nunnery, to take the habit; (*femei, bărbați*) to take vows, to take the veil.

căluș [kă'lush] *nn* gag; *fig* to stop smb's talk; *mus* bridge (of a violin); (*pictură*) easel.

călușari [kălu'shari] *nm pl* Romanian men's folk dance (similar to the morris dance); group of dancers performing.

călușei [kălu'shei] *nm pl* merry-go-round; roundabout.

căluț [kă'luts] *nm* little horse; pony; *ento* grasshopper.

cămară [kă'mară] *nf* pantry, larder.

cămașă [kă'mashă] *nf* (*pt. bărbați*) shirt; *tech* (*înveli-toare*) casing, sheath(ing); *bot* pellicle, peel; (*a bobului*) husk; (*de damă*) nightie, nightdress, night-gown.

cămătar [kămă'tar] *nm* moneylender, usurer, loan shark.

cămilă [kă'milă] *nf zool* camel; (*cu o cocoașă*) drome-dary.

cămin [kă'min] *nn* (*sobă*) fireplace, hearth; (*casă*) home; **fără** ~ homeless.

căpăstru [kă'păstru] *nn* bridle, halter.

căpăta [kăpă'ta] *vt* to get, to obtain, to receive; (*în dar*) to get as a present; (*a câștiga*) to acquire; (*prin muncă*) to earn; (*a se îmbolnăvi*) to catch.

căpătâi [kăpă'tâi] *nn* (*la pat*) head; (*capăt*) end; (*cămin*) shelter, roof, home; **de** ~ basic, essential.

căpătui [kăpătu'i] *vr* to settle (down), to get employ-ment; to do well for oneself; to get married ‖ *vt obs* (*a numi*) to appoint (to a good job).

căpățână [kăpă'tsână] *nf coll* noodle, pate, head; (*țeastă*) skull; bothead, bulb.

căpcăun [kăpkă'un] *nm* ogre; *fig* monster, brute.

căpetenie [kăpe'tenie] *nf* chief, head, leader; (*coman-dant*) commander; (*de trib*) chieftain.

căpiat [kă'piat] *adj* sturdied; *coll* cracked, dotty.

căpitan [kăpi'tan] *nm mil* captain; *naut, sp* skipper; *naut, also fig* commander, chief; (*de bandă*) leader, head; master.

căpiță [kă'pitsă] *nf* cock, rick, stack.

căprar [kă'prar] *nm obs mil* corporal; (*păzitor de capre*) goatherd.

căprioară [kăpri'oară] *nf* deer, roe (deer), doe; (*tânără*) (little) kid.

căprior [kăpri'or] *nm zool* roebuck; *archit* rafter.

căprui [kă'prui] *adj* hazel.

căpșun [kăp'shun] *nm* strawberry plant • **~ă** *nf* straw-berry.

căptușeală [kăptu'sheală] *nf* lining; *archit* facing; (*la pălărie*) hat tip; *tech* coating; *min* timbering.

căptuși [kăptu'shi] *vt* to line; (*a umple*) to stuff; *archit* to face; (*cu scânduri*) to board; to render; (*a tapisa*) to wainscot; *min* to timber; (*a păcăli*) to cheat, to take in ‖ *vr* to be lined, to be stuffed; (*a căpăta/ cumpăra ceva nedorit și neplăcut*) to get oneself.

căpușă [kă'pushă] *nf* sheep louse/tick; *bot* castor-oil plant.

căra [kă'ra] *vt* to carry, to transport; (*cu sine*) to carry

out, to take away; (*a îndepărta*) to carry away/off; to remove ‖ *vr* to go away; to pack off.

cărare [kă'rare] *nf* (*potecă*) path; *fig* way; (*în păr*) parting.

cărăbuș [kără'bush] *nm ento* scarab beetles.

cărămidă [kără'midă] *nf* brick.

cărămiziu [kărămi'ziu] *adj* brick-colored.

cărăuș [kără'ush] *nm* carter, waggoner.

cărbune [kăr'bune] *nm* coal; (*mangal*) charcoal; (*jar, tăciuni*) ember(s); *bot* smut; *med* anthrax; *elec* car-bon; (*artă*) crayon.

cărpănos [kărpă'nos] *adj* stingy, mean, close-fisted.

cărturar [kărtu'rar] *nm* scholar, learned/well-read man.

cărucior [kăru'chor] *nn tech* truck, trolley; (*de copil*) baby carriage, stroller; (*la aeroport, pt. bagaje*) trolley.

cărunt [kă'runt] *adj* grey, grey-haired; grizzled.

căruță [kă'rutsă] *nf* wagon, cart; (*încărcătură*) cartful, cartload.

căsăpi [kăsă'pi] *vt* to slaughter, to butcher, to kill; *fig* to slay, to massacre, to mangle.

căsători [kăsăto'ri] *vt* to marry (away), to give away in marriage; to join in marriage ‖ *vr* **a se** ~ **cu cineva** to marry (smb); *coll* to tie the knot • **~t** *adj* married, wedded.

căsătorie [kăsăto'rie] *nf* marriage, match; (*religioasă*) wedding; (*căsnicie*) wedlock, married life; matrimony.

căsca [kăs'ka] *vt* (*a deschide gura*) to open (wide); (*a întredeschide*) to open slightly, to half-open ‖ *vi* (*de somn*) to yawn ‖ *vr* to open; *fig* (*d. o prăpastie*) to gape, to yawn.

căsnicie [kăsni'chie] *nf* married/wedded life, wedlock, family life.

căsuță [kă'sutsă] *nf* little house; (*cutie poștală într-o instituție*) pigeon hole; ~ **poștală** P.O.B., Post office box, post box.

căşuna [kăshu'na] *vt* (*a pricinui*) to determine, to cause ‖ *vi* **a-i** ~ **pe** (*a prinde ură pe*) to begin/come to hate; (*a tăbărî*) to fall upon, to rush upon, to attack.

cătrăni [kătră'ni] *vt* (*a unge cu catran*) to tar; (*a amărî*) to grieve, to vex, to afflict ‖ *vr* to grow sad/angry/ furious.

către ['kătre] *prep* (*spațial*) to, towards; ~ **sud** to the south, southwards; (*temporal*) about, towards, by, against; ~ **sfârşitul anului** by the end of the year; ~ **ora 10** about ten o'clock; (*față de*) to; (*de* ~) by; **scrisă de** ~ **el** written by him.

cătun [kă'tun] *nn* hamlet, small village.

cătușe [kă'tushe] *nf pl* handcuffs; *fig* fetters, chains.

căţăra [kătsă'ra] *vr* to climb; (*cu trudă*) to clamber; to scramble up; (*d. plante*) to creep, to twine.

căţea [kă'tsea] *nf zool also fig* bitch; *fig* hussy, slut.

căţel [kă'tsel] *nm* (*ca mărime*) doggie, little dog; (*pui*) puppy; *fig coll* toady, flunkey; ~ **de usturoi** clove of garlic.

căuş [kă'ush] *nn* (*lingură mare*) dipper, ladle, scoop; (*pt. barcă*) bailer • **~ul palmei** *nn* the hollow of the hand.

căuta [kău'ta] *vt* to look for, to seek for/after; (*a sco-toci*) to search for; (*în dicționar*) to look up; (*a dori*) to want; (*a provoca*) to get at, to pick on; (*a îngriji*) to take care, to look after; (*bolnav*) to nurse; (*a se strădui*) to try, to endeavor • *vr* **a fi ~t** to be required/ wanted/demanded; *com* to be in great demand; (*a se îngriji*) to look after oneself.

căzni [kăz'ni] *vr* (*a se chinui*) to torment/torture oneself; (*a se trudi*) to endeavor, to strive, to take pains, to be at pains.

câine ['kâine] *nm zool* dog; (*de vânătoare*) hound, retriever; (*mic*, *tânăr*) puppy, whelp; *fig* (*javră*) cur; beast • **~sc** *adj* (*de câine*) doggy, canine; (*aspru*) dog's, beastly.

câmp [kâmp] *nn* field; (*câmpie*) plain, flat/level country; *fig* domain, range, sphere, scope • **~enesc** *adj* (*de șes*) of the field/plain; (*țărănesc*) rustic, rural, country • **~ie** *nf* plain, field, flats; (*țară de jos*) lowland.

când [kând] *adv* when(ever); ~ **vine?** when is he coming? ~ **și** ~ now and then, occasionally; **de** ~ since when, how long; **de** ~ **e aici?** how long has he been here?, since when has he been here?; **din** ~ **în** ~ from time to time, now and then, occasionally || *conj* when; **spune-mi** ~ **să vin** tell me when to come; (*pe când*) while, as, when; **l-am văzut pe** ~ **pleca** I saw him while he was leaving; (*ori de câte ori*) whenever; (*după*) after; **ca și** ~ as if; **ca și** ~ **nu ar ști** as if he didn't know; **de** ~ since; **citește de** ~ **a venit** he has been reading since he came; **până** ~ until.

cândva [kând'va] *adv* (*în viitor*) some day; (*în trecut*) once, one day, formerly; ever.

cânepă ['kânepă] *nf bot* hemp; **de** ~ hempen.

cânta [kân'ta] *vt* (*din gură*) to sing; (*la un instrument*) to play; (*la un instrument de suflat*) to blow; (*încet și solemn*) to chant; **a** ~ **din flaut** to play the flute; **a** ~ **o melodie** to sing/play an air/tune; (*a slăvi*) to extol, to praise; (*victoria*) to exult; *coll* to crow; *sl* (*a spune*) to chirp || *vi* (*din gură*) to sing; (*la un instrument*) to play; (*d. păsări*) to warble; (*d. cocoși*) to crow.

cântar [kân'tar] *nn* balance, (pair of) scales; (*mare*) weighing machine; (*cântărire*) weighing.

cântăreață [kântă'reatsă] *nf* singer, chanteuse, vocalist; (*de operă*) opera singer.

cântăreț [kântă'rets] *nm* singer, vocalist; opera singer; (*corist*) chorister; *relig* psalm reader; *fig lit* bard.

cântări [kântă'ri] *vt* to weigh; *fig* (*a cumpăni*) to weigh/balance (in one's mind); (*a chibzui*) to consider, to ponder (over); to reflect, to deliberate upon; to examine; (*a aprecia*) to estimate, to value; to appraise || *vi* to weigh, to have a weight of || *vr* to weigh oneself; to be weighed.

cântec ['kântek] *nn* song; tune, air, melody; *relig* hymn, chant/canticle; (*festiv*) carol.

cârâi [kârâ'i] *vi* (*d. corbi*) to croak; (*d. ciori*) to caw; *fig* to bleat || *vt* to nag, to pester || *vr* to bicker.

cârcel [kâr'chel] *nm bot* tendril; *med* cramp.

cârciumar [kârchu'mar] *nm* publican, innkeeper.

cârciumă ['kârchumă] *nf* pub, bar, tavern; (*la țară*) inn.

cârcotaș [kârko'tash] *nm* pettifogger, carper || *adj* caviling, querulous, fault-finding; (*nemulțumit*) grumbling, grumpy, cantankerous.

cârd [kârd] *nn* (*de păsări, rațe*) flock; (*stol*) bevy, flight; (*de gâște*) gaggle; *pej* (*grup de oameni*) group; (*ceată*) band, bunch, gang; (*mulțime*) crowd.

cârdășie [kârdă'shie] *nf* coterie; (*clică*) clique; **în** ~ **cu** in collusion with, in league with.

cârjă ['kârzhă] *nf* (*pt. infirmi*) crutch; (*de pastor*) staff; *relig* crozier; *fig* support.

cârlig [kâr'lig] *nn* hook; (*pt. rufe*) peg; (*de undiță*) fish hook; *naut* grappling iron, grapple; *fig* lure.

cârlionțat [kârlion'tsat] *adj* curled; (*ondulat*) waved; (*mărunt*) frizzled, crimpy.

cârmaci [kâr'mach] *nm naut* helmsman, steerman; *sp* coxswain/cox; **fără** ~ coxless; *fig* leader, pilot.

cârmă ['kârmă] *nf naut* helm, rudder, tiller; (*guvernare*) head, lead.

cârmi [kâr'mi] *vt/vi* to steer, to veer; to bring round, to turn about/round.

cârmui [kârmu'i] *vt/vi* to govern, to rule; (*a îndruma*) to direct, to guide.

cârn [kârn] *adj* (*d. nas*) snub, turned-up; (*d. cineva*) snub-nosed.

cârnat [kâr'nat] *nm* sausage.

cârpaci [kâr'pach] *nm* shoe repairer, cobbler; *fig* (*lucrător prost*) bungler, botcher.

cârpă ['kârpă] *nf* (*zdreanță*) rag; (*pânză*) cloth; (*de praf*) duster; (*de vase*) dish cloth; *fig* (*om moale*) milksop, weakling.

cârpi [kâr'pi] *vt* to mend, to repair; (*a petici*) to patch (up); (*a coase la un loc*) to piece/sew together; (*ciorapi*) to darn; (*a lucra prost*) to bungle, to botch.

cârti [kâr'ti] *vi* to grumble (about/at/over); to cavil (at/about), to murmur (at/about)

cârtiță ['kârtitsă] *nf zool* mole.

câștig [kâsh'tig] *nn* gain; (*prin muncă*) earnings; (*venit*) income; profit, advantage; *com* returns; (*neașteptat*) windfall, godsend; (*folos*) use, benefit; (*la loterie*) prize • **~ător** *nm* winner • **~a** *vt* to gain; (*prin muncă, efort*) to earn; (*prin noroc, perseverență*) to win; (*a căpăta, a obține*) to obtain, to get; (*a dobândi*) to acquire || *vi* to win; (*muncind*) to earn; *fig* to profit.

cât¹ [kat] *nn* quotient.

cât² [kât] *adj* how much, what; **de** ~ **ulei ai nevoie?** how much oil do you need? || *pron* how much, what || *adv* how (much/long); ~ **ai stat acolo?** how long did you stay there?; ~ **de** ~ (*afirm.* și *interog*) a little; *neg* at all; **cu** ~ **mai repede, cu atât mai bine** the sooner the better || *prep* as ... as, like; **înalt** ~ **un copac** tall like a tree, as tall as a tree || *conj* (*modal*) as much as; **fă** ~ **poți** do as much as you can; (*temporal*) as long as; ~ **trăiești înveți** you learn as long as you live; (*concesiv*) although, however; ~ **de bun este și totuși** however good he is and yet; ~ **despre** as to, as for.

câtă ['kâtă] *adj indef* what, how much || *pron* how much; ~ **vrei?** how much do you want? || *pron inter* **a câta?** which?

câte ['kâte] *adj* how many || *pron* those, they; how many; ~ **vrei?** how many do you want? || *adv* by; **unul** ~ **unul** one by one; ~ **doi** by twos, two in a row.

câteodată [kâteo'dată] *adv* sometimes, at times, now and then/again.

câteva [kâte'va] *adj/pron indef* (*nu multe*) some, a few; (*un număr de*) several.

câtva [kât'va] *adj/pron indef* some, a little; ~ **timp** some/a little time || *adv* a little.

câți ['kâtsi] *adj* how many; ~ **ani au trecut!** so many years have passed || *pron* those, they; (*indef., inter.*) how many; ~ **vrei?** how many do you want?.

câțiva [kâtsi'va] *adj/pron* (*nu mulți*) some, a few; **am** ~ **prieteni** I have a few friends; (*un număr de*) several; ~ **băieți jucau fotbal** several boys were playing football.

ce [che] *nm* **un** ~ something || *adj inter* what; ~ **oră e?** what time is it?; which; (*exclamație*) what; ~ **casă**

(mare) what a (big) house! || *pron inter* what; ~ **e?** what's the matter? || *pron rel* **cel** ~ he who; **ceea** ~ what; **cei** ~ those who || *adv* how; ~ **bine!** how well!; ~ **de oameni!** how many people!; **cât pe** ~ almost, nearly.

cea [chea] *art* the; ~ **mai bună** the best; ~ **care** she who; *(pt. lucruri)* that which || *interj* ho!

ceafă ['cheafă] *nf* nape (of the neck), scruff of the neck.

ceai ['cheai] *nm bot (plantă)* tea plant/shrub || *nn (băutură)* tea; *(petrecere)* tea party • ~**nic** *nn* teapot.

cealaltă [chea'laltă] *adj* the other; ~ **carte** the other book || *pron* the other (one); **dă-mi-o pe** ~ give me the other one.

ceapă ['cheapă] *nf bot* onion.

ceară ['cheară] *nf* (bees)wax; *(din urechi)* ear wax, cerumen.

cearcăn ['chearkăn] *nn* dark ring, circle.

cearşaf [chear'shaf] *nn* bedsheet; *(de plapumă)* coverlet.

ceartă ['cheartă] *nf* quarrel, squabble; *coll* falling out; *(schimb de cuvinte)* argument, dispute; *(luptă)* fight, brawl, row; *(disensiune)* dissension, feud.

ceas [cheas] *nn* hour, time, o'clock; *fig (moment)* time; *(de mână)* (wrist)watch; *(de masă)* clock • ~**ornicări** *nf (atelier)* watchmaker's (shop); *(meserie)* watch-making

ceaşcă ['cheashkă] *nf* cup; *(conţinutul)* cupful.

ceată ['cheată] *nf (de oameni)* band, group; *(bandă)* gang, clique, ring; *(de animale)* pack, flock.

ceaţă ['cheatsă] *nf* mist; *(deasă)* fog; *(uşoară)* haze; *fig* mist, veil, cloud.

ceaun [chea'un] *nn* cast-iron kettle.

cec [chek] *nn* check.

ceda [che'da] *vt* to yield, to give up; *(a abandona)* to surrender; *jur* to make over to; **a** ~ **teren** to give/lose ground; **a** ~ **trecerea** to yield, *(d. o construcţie, frânghie)* to give way || *vi* to yield, to give in; *(a se supune)* to submit (oneself) to; *(unei tentaţii)* to succumb.

cedru ['chedru] *nm bot* cedar.

cegă ['chegă] *nf icht* starlet.

ceh [cheh] *nm/adj* Czech.

cei [chei] *art* the; ~ **bogaţi** the rich || *pron* those; ~ **ce** *(pt. persoane)* those who; *(pt. lucruri)* those which.

ceilalţi [chei'laltsi] *adj* the other || *pron* the others, the other ones.

cel [chel] *art* the; ~ **mai bun** the best || *pron* that; ~ **ce/ care** *(pt. persoane)* he who; *(pt. lucruri)* that which.

celălalt [chelă'lalt] *adj* the other; ~ **capăt** the far(thest) end || *pron* the other (one).

cele ['chele] *art* the; ~ **mai bune** the best || *pron* those; ~ **ce** *(pt. persoane)* those who; *(pt. lucruri)* those which, the things which.

celebra [chele'bra] *vt* to celebrate; *(a comemora)* to commemorate || *vr* to be celebrated.

celebritate [chelebri'tate] *nf (persoană)* celebrity, illustrious/famous person; *(faimă)* fame, renown.

celebru [che'lebru] *adj* famous, renowned, celebrated.

celelalte [chele'lalte] *adj* the other || *pron* the others, the other ones.

celibat [cheli'bat] *nn* celibacy, celibate.

celibatar [cheliba'tar] *nm* bachelor, single man || *adj* single, unmarried • ~**ă** *nf* single/unmarried woman; spinster.

celofan [chelo'fan] *nn* cellophane.

celt [chelt] *nm* Celt • ~**ă** *nf (limba)* Celtic; *(femeie)* Celt (woman).

celulă [che'lulă] *nf bio, pol, mil* cell; *anat* cell, (blood) corpuscle.

celuloid [chelulo'id] *nm* celluloid.

celuloză [chelu'loză] *nf* cellulose.

cenaclu [che'naklu] *nn* literary circle.

cent [chent] *nm* cent.

centenar [chente'nar] *nm* centenarian || *nn* centenary (celebration) || *adj* centennial, centenary.

centigrad [chenti'grad] *nn* centigrade.

centigram [chenti'gram] *nn* centigram.

centilitru [chenti'litru] *nm* centiliter.

centimetru [chenti'metru] *nm* centimeter; *(de măsură)* tape measure.

centra [chen'tra] *vt sp* to center; *fig* to center, to focus || *vi sp* to center.

central [chen'tral] *adj* central, principal, main || *adv* in the center.

centrală [chen'trală] *nf (întreprindere)* head/central office; *(staţie, uzină)* station.

centraliza [chentrali'za] *vt* to centralize • ~**tor** *nn* synoptic table || *adj* centralizing.

centru ['chentru] *nm anat, sp* center || *nn geom* center, central point, middle; *fig* focus; *com* shop, unit.

centură [chen'tură] *nf* belt, girdle.

cenuşă [che'nushă] *nf* ash(es), cinders; *relig* (mortal/ earthly) remains.

cenuşăreasă [chenushă'reasă] *nf* Cinderella, cinderella; *fig* domestic drudge; *hist* scullion.

cenuşiu [chenu'shiu] *nn/adj* grey; *(ca cenuşa)* ash (colored); *(d. păr)* grizzled, grizzly.

cenzura [chenzu'ra] *vt* to censor, to expurgate.

cenzură [chen'zură] *nf (cenzurare)* censorship, expurgation; the Board of Censors.

cep [chep] *nn* spigot; *(canea)* tap, plug; *tech* tenon.

cer [cher] *nn* sky; *fig* heaven, paradise; *(soartă)* providence • ~**ul gurii** *anat* the palate, the roof of the mouth.

ceramică [che'ramikă] *nf* pottery, ceramics.

cerb [cherb] *nm zool* stag, hart, buck.

cerc [cherk] *nn geom* circle; *(de butoi, pt. copii)* hoop; *(de plită)* ring; *(în apă)* ripple; *fig* sphere, domain, range.

cercel [cher'chel] *nm* earring • ~**uş** *nm* small earring; *bot* lily-of-the-valley; fuchsia.

cerceta [cherche'ta] *vt* to examine; to study; to inspect; to go (thoroughly) into; to inquire/search/look into; to explore; *(a sonda)* to sound out; *(o carte)* to peruse; *jur* to try; to examine; *(a ancheta)* to inquire into; to conduct inquiries into; *mil* to reconnoiter • ~**re** *nf (ştiinţifică)* investigation, research; *jur (audiere)* trial, hearing; *(anchetă)* inquiry.

cercetaş [cherche'tash] *nm (membru al cercetăşiei)* (boy) scout; *mil* scout, skirmisher; *(deschizător de drum)* pathfinder, pioneer.

cercetător [cherchetă'tor] *nm* researcher, research worker; investigator; examiner, inspector; explorer; searcher; scholar || *adj* investigating; curious, inquisitive; *(scrutător)* scrutinizing; searching || *adv* inquisitively, curiously, searchingly.

cercevea [cherche'vea] *nf* frame; *(de fereastră)* window frame; sash.

cerdac [cher'dak] *nn (pridvor)* veranda(h), porch; *(de fântână)* well roof.

cere ['chere] *vt* to demand, to ask, to request; *(a revendica)* to claim; *(a necesita)* to require; to call for; *(a* *îndemna*) to urge; (*a dori*) to want, to desire; (*a cere insistent, a cerşi, a implora*) to beg || *vr* com to be in (great) demand; to be necessary/needed/required.

cereală [chere'ală] *nf* grain, cereal (plant).

cerebel [chere'bel] *nn anat* cerebellum.

cerebral [chere'bral] *adj* cerebral, mental || *nn* rationality; intellectual/rational/cerebral nature.

ceremonie [cheremo'nie] *nf* ceremony, ritual, rite; (*politeţe*) solemnity.

cerere ['cherere] *nf* demand; (scrisă) petition, application (form); (*revendicare*) claim; (*rugăminte*) request; (*făcută cu umilinţă*) supplication; *com* demand; ~ şi ofertă supply and demand.

ceresc [che'resk] *adj* heavenly, celestial; *fig* heavenly, divine, sublime.

cerinţă [che'rintsă] *nf* (*nevoie*) want, lack, need; desideratum; (*necesitate*) necessity, requirement; (*cerere*) demand; (*condiţie necesară*) prerequisite.

cerne ['cherne] *vt* (*prin sită*) to sift/sieve; *fig* to make out, to sort, to discern; (*a supune unui test pt. a depista o boală etc*) to screen || *vi* (*a bura*) to drizzle, to sprinkle.

cerneală [cher'neală] *nf* ink.

cerni [cher'ni] *vt* (*a înnegri*) to blacken, to make black; (*a întuneca*) *also fig* to darken || *vr* (*a se înnegri*) to go/turn black; (*a se îmbrăca*) to dress in black/ mourning; (*a se întuneca*) to grow dark/dim/dusky; *fig* (*a se posomorî*) to become gloomy; to grow/ become sad.

cerşetor [chershe'tor] *nm* beggar; *coll* cadger; *frml* mendicant; tramp, vagabond.

cerşi [cher'shi] *vt* to beg || *vi* to go begging/cadging.

cert [chert] *adj* sure, certain, undoubted || *adv* doubtless, surely, certainly, undoubtedly.

certa [cher'ta] *vt* (*un copil*) to scold, to tell smb off; (*un adult*) to reprove, to rebuke, to censure; (*uşor/cu simpatie*) to chide; (*a învinui*) to blame || *vr* to quarrel.

certăreţ [chertă'rets] *nm* quarrelsome/querulous person || *adj* quarrelsome; querulous, peevish.

certifica [chertifi'ka] *vt* to certify; to attest; (*o semnătură*) to authenticate • ~t *nn* certificate; attestation.

certitudine [cherti'tudine] *nf* certainty, assurance; cu ~ certainly, positively.

cerui [cheru'i] *vt* to wax; (*duşumeaua*) to polish.

cesiona [chesio'na] *vt jur* (*cuiva*) to assign (to smb), to transfer, to make over (to smb).

cetate [che'tate] *nf* fortress; *mil* stronghold; *obs* (*oraş*) citadel, walled city, fortified town.

cetăţean [chetă'tsean] *nm* citizen, denizen; (*în evul mediu*) burger, burgess • ~că *nf* citizen; (*în evul mediu*) burger, burgess.

cetăţenesc [chetătse'nesk] *adj* civic, civil.

cetăţenie [chetătse'nie] *nf* citizenship.

ceţos [che'tsos] *adj* foggy, misty, hazy; (*neclar*) vague, dim.

ceva [che'va] *nn* some(thing) || *adj* a little, some; any; am ~ timp I have some time; ai ~ zahăr? have you got any sugar? || *pron* (*în prop. afirm.*) something; (*în prop. inter.*) anything.

cezariană [chezari'ană] *nf med* caesarian section/ operation.

cheag [keag] *nn* rennet; (*de sânge*) clot; *fig* funds, stock, money; (*economii*) savings.

chef [kef] *nn* (*petrecere*) feast, banquet; *coll* (fine) spread; (*dispoziţie*) desire, mind; (*capriciu*) whim,

fancy • ~liu *nm* (*om vesel*) jolly/good fellow; *coll* brick; (*băutor*) drinker, boozer || *adj* (*bine dispus*) sociable; (*căruia îi place să bea*) fond of the bottle • ~ui [kefu'i] *vi* to revel, to booze, to go on a spree.

chei [kei] *nn* quay, embankment, pier; (*de mărfuri*) wharf.

cheie ['keie] *nf* key; *mus* clef; *fig* key, clue, solution; (*problemă*) crux (of the matter); *pl geog* gorge(s), narrow pass/strait; *tech* wrench, spanner || *adj* key, staple.

chel [kel] *nm* bald-headed person || *adj* bald(-headed).

chelălăi [kelălă'i] *vi* to yelp.

chelfăneală [kelfă'neală] *nf* thrashing, licking, spanking.

chelfăni [kelfă'ni] *vt* to drub, to spank, to thrash || *vr* (*d. câini*) to fight.

chelie [ke'lie] *nf* baldness, bald head.

chelner ['kelner] *nm* waiter; barman; (*pe vapor*) steward • ~iţă *nf* waitress; (*la bar*) barmaid.

cheltui [keltu'i] *vt* to spend, to expend; *fig* to consume; (*a risipi*) to waste, to squander || *vi* to spend (much) || *vr* to be spent, to be wasted, to be squandered • ~ală *nf* expense; *fin* expenditure, outlay; *fig* (*pierdere*) loss; (*risipă*) waste.

chema [ke'ma] *vt* (*a striga*) to call; to invite, to ask; (*a trimite după*) to send for; (*la telefon*) to call/ring up; (*a evoca*) to call up; (*duhuri*) to raise; to conjure; (*a convoca*) to convene, to summon; to assemble; *jur* to summon, to cite || *vi* (*a striga*) to cry; to call out; to shout || *vr* (*a se numi*) to be called/named, to go by the name; (*a avea semnificaţie*) to signify.

chem(i)oterapie [kemiotera'pie] *nf med* chemotherapy.

chenar [ke'nar] *nn* (*cadru*) frame, framing; *archit* cornice; (*de fereastră*) ledge; (*margine*) border, edging; (*la covor*) border; *text* list, festoon; *typ* border.

chepeng [ke'peng] *nn* trap door.

chercheli [kerke'li] *vr* to booze, to get fuddled/tipsy/lit up.

cherestea [kere'stea] *nf* timber, lumber; *fig* build, frame.

chestiona [kestio'na] *vt* to ask, to question, to examine.

chestionar [kestio'nar] *nn* questionnaire, survey; (*formular*) form.

chestiune [kesti'une] *nf* (*întrebare*) question; issue, problem; (*lucru*) matter, thing.

chetă ['ketă] *nf* collection; (*banii*) takings.

chezăşie [keză'shie] *nf* pledge, guarantee; *jur* surety, bail; *com* security, collateral.

chiar [kiar] *adv* (*până şi*) even; ~ dacă ar veni even if he came; (*însuşi*) oneself; ~ el he himself, the very man; (*tocmai*) just, right; (*exact*) exactly, precisely, the very; ~ acum right now, just now; ~ aşa exactly, just like that.

chibiţ [ki'bits] *nm* kibitzer.

chibrit [ki'brit] *nn* match.

chibzui [kibzu'i] *vt* (*a judeca*) to consider (thoroughly), to ponder (over); (*a gândi bine*) to think over; (*a cumpăni*) to weigh; (*a pune la cale*) to plan; (*a complota*) to plot || *vi* to think, to ponder || *vr* (*cu cineva*) to deliberate/consult with • ~ală *nf* thinking, consideration || cu ~ considerately; (*gândit*) deliberately; (*înţelept*) wisely.

chichiţă [ki'kitsă] *nf* creep hole; excuse, pretext; pretence, dodge, subterfuge.

chicinetă [kichi'netă] *nf* little kitchen, kitchenette.

chiciură [ki'chiură] *nf* hoar frost.

chicot ['kikot] *nn* (*râs înfundat*) giggle, titter, chuckle;

(*hohot*) burst of laughter • ~i [kiko'ti] *vi* (*a râde în-fundat*) to giggle, to titter, to chuckle; (*cu hohote*) to laugh out loud, to roar with laughter.

chiflă ['kiflă] *nf* (French) roll.

chiftea [kif'tea] *nf* groundmeat ball.

chilie [ki'lie] *nf* (*mănăstire*) cell; (*cămăruţă*) small room.

chilipir [kili'pir] *nn* (*cumpărătură ieftină*) (good) bargain; (*noroc*) godsend, windfall.

chiloţi [ki'lotsi] *nm pl* (*ca rufărie*) drawers, knickers; *coll* (*pt. bărbaţi*) pants, (*pt. femei*) panties; (*de baie*) bathing/swimming trunks, swimsuit.

chimen ['kimen] *nn bot* caraway.

chimic ['kimik] *adj* chemical || *adv* chemically.

chimie [ki'mie] *nf* chemistry.

chimion [kimi'on] *nn bot* cumin.

chimioterapie [kimiotera'pie] *nf med* chemotherapy.

chimist [ki'mist] *nm* chemist.

chimono [kimo'no] *nn* kimono.

chin [kin] *nn* torture, torment; *fig* (*suferinţă*) agony; (*sufletesc*) affliction, distress; (*trudă*) labor(s), pains, effort.

chinez [ki'nez] *nm* Chinese, Chinaman || *adj* Chinese • ~ă *nf* Chinese (woman); Chinese, the Chinese language || *adj* Chinese.

chingă ['kingă] *nf* girth, band.

chinină [ki'ninã] *nf* quinine.

chintă ['kintă] *nf* (*de tuse*) coughing fit; (*la poker*) flush.

chintesenţă [kinte'sentsă] *nf* quintessence.

chinui [kinu'i] *vt also fig* to torture, to torment; (*a nu da pace*) to harass, to worry; (*a fi o pacoste*) to plague, to harry; **a-şi ~ creierii** *vr* (*a trudi*) to moil and toil, to labor; to try hard, to strive (to do smth); (*ca o corvoadă*) to drudge, to slave; (*singur*) to torment/torture oneself; (*a fi neliniştit*) to be uneasy, to fret, to worry.

chiolhan [kiol'han] *nn coll* spree, booze, blow-out.

chior ['kior] *nm* person with only one eye; *coll* boss-eyed person || *adj* one-eyed, blind in/of one eye; (*miop*) short-sighted; *fig* blind; (*d. lumină*) dim.

chiorăi [kioră'i] *vt* to rumble • ~ală, ~t *nn* rumbling.

chiorâş [kio'râsh] *adv* askance, askew, awry.

chioşc ['kioshk] *nn* (*în parc*) kiosk; (*pt. muzică*) bandstand; (*frunzar*) arbor; (*de ziare*) newsstand; (*tutungerie*) tobacconist's; (*de răcoritoare*) soda-fountain.

chiot ['kiot] *nn* (*strigăt*) cry, shout; (*ascuţit*) yell(ing), shriek.

chip [kip] *nn* (*faţă*) face, countenance; (*înfăţişare*) look, appearance, air; (*pe monede*) effigy; (*imagine*) image, portrait; (*poză*) picture; (*fel*) manner, way; (*mijloc*) means.

chiparos [kipa'ros] *nm* cypress.

chipeş ['kipesh] *adj* (*frumos*) good-looking, handsome; (*bine făcut*) well-made.

chipiu [ki'piu] *nn* peaked cap.

chirci [kir'chi] *vr* (*a se ghemui*) to cower, to crouch; (*în creştere*) to be(come) stunted in one's growth.

chiriaş [kiri'ash] *nm* lodger, tenant.

chirie [ki'rie] *nf* rent; (*pt. obiecte*) hire.

chirpici [kir'pich] *nn* adobe.

chirurg [ki'rurg] *nm* surgeon.

chist [kist] *nn med* cyst.

chiştoc [kish'tok] *nn* cigarette end/stump/butt; (*copil*) brat, kid.

chit[1] [kit] *nn* (*pastă*) putty.

chit[2] [kit] *adj* quits; **a fi ~** to be quits.

chitanţă [ki'tantsă] *nf* receipt; (*de predare a unui obiect*) claim check.

chitară [ki'tară] *nf* guitar.

chitarist [kita'rist] *nm* guitar player.

chitic [ki'tik] *nm* (*peşte mic*) small fry.

chiţăi [kitsă'i] *vi* to squeak, to give a squeak.

chiţibuşar [kitsibu'shar] *nm* pettifogger, caviler || *adj* pettifogging, pernickety.

chiui [kiu'i] *vt* to shout; (*ascuţit*) to yell; (*de bucurie*) to shout/yell exultantly, to cheer.

chiul [kiul] *nn* (*absenţă*) truancy, absence without leave; (*lene*) slackness.

chiuretaj [kiure'tazh] *nn* curettage, curettement.

chiuvetă [kiu'vetă] *nf* (*de bucătărie*) sink; (*de baie*) wash bowl.

chivernisi [kiverni'si] *vt* to administer, to manage; (*a economisi*) to save, to lay by || *vr* to get a place, to settle; (*a se îmbogăţi*) to get rich; (*a trăi cu economie*) to live thriftily.

ci [chi] *conj* but; (*înaintea unui imperativ*) do, without fail, by all means.

cianură [cha'nură] *nf chem* cyanide.

cibernetică [chiber'netikă] *nf* cybernetics.

cicatrice [chika'triche] *nf* scar.

cicatriza [chikatri'za] *vr* to heal (up), to skin/scar over • ~re *nf* healing, closing up (of a wound).

cică ['chikă] *adv* (*se zice că*) they/people say, as the story goes; (*chipurile*) as it were, allegedly; (*nici mai mult nici mai puţin*) neither more nor less.

cicăleală [chikă'lealã] *nf* (*reproş*) nagging; (*sâcâială*) vexing; annoying; fault-finding.

cicăli [chikă'li] *vt* to nag, to pester, to annoy; (*a certa*) to bicker • ~tor *adj* nagging; (*sâcâitor*) annoying; fault-finding || *nm* nagger, pesterer, grumbler.

ciclic ['chiklik] *adj* cyclic(al) || *adv* cyclically.

ciclism [chi'klism] *nn* cycling.

ciclist [chi'klist] *nm* cyclist.

ciclon [chi'klon] *nn* cyclone.

ciclu ['chiklu] *nn* cycle, series, course.

cicoare [chi'kware] *nf bot* chicory.

cidru ['chidru] *nn* cider.

cifră ['chifră] *nf* figure, digit; (*număr*) number; numeral; amount, total.

cifru ['chifru] *nn* cipher, code.

cilindru [chi'lindru] *nn geom* cylinder; *tech* cylinder, drum; *obs* top/high hat; opera hat.

cimbru ['chimbru] *nm bot* savory.

ciment [chi'ment] *nn* cement • ~a [chimen'ta] *vt* to cement; (*oţel*) to case-harden; (*substanţe*) to glue/stick/piece together; *fig also* (*a întări*) to strengthen, to fortify || *vr* to be cemented, to be glued; *fig* to consolidate, to grow firm.

cimitir [chimi'tir] *nn* cemetery, graveyard; (*mic*) churchyard.

cimpanzeu [chimpan'zeu] *nm* chimpanzee; *coll* chimp.

cimpoi [chim'poi] *nn mus* bagpipe.

cina [chi'na] *vi* to have supper.

cină ['chină] *nf* supper • **Cina cea de taină** The Last Supper.

cinci ['chinch] *num/adj* five.

cine ['chine] *pron inter* who, whom, (*selectiv*) which || *pron rel* who, he who; ~ **e acolo?** who is there? **cu ~?** with whom, who … with? **pe ~?** whom?

cineast [chine'ast] *nm* filmmaker.

cinefil [chine'fil] *nm* movie fan, moviegoer.

cinema [chine'ma] *nn* cinema, movie(s), motion picture(s); (*clădirea*) movie (theater).

cinematograf [chinemato'graf] *nn* cinema; movies; motion pictures • **~ic** *adj* cinematic; cinematographic • **~ie** *nf* cinema(tography).

cineva [chine'va] *pron indef* somebody, someone; (*în prop. inter. şi neg.*) anyone, anybody; (*persoană importantă*) somebody important, some big shot.

cingătoare [chinga'tware] *nf* girdle, belt.

cinic ['chinik] *adj* cynic(al); (*neruşinat*) shameless; (*sfruntat*) bare-faced; (*d. indecenţă*) brazen ‖ *adv* cynically; shamelessly, brazenly ‖ *nm* cynic; shameless/brazen person.

cinism [chi'nism] *nn* cynicism; shamelessness, effrontery.

cinste ['chinste] *nf* (*onestitate*) honesty, integrity; (*fidelitate*) fidelity, faithfulness, loyalty; (*virtute*) virtue; (*castitate*) chastity, maidenhood; (*preţuire*) appreciation; respect, esteem, consideration; (*vază*) repute, credit, (fair) fame; good name; (*onoare*) honor; glory; (*favoare*) favor; pomp, ceremony; (*cadou*) gift, present; (*trataţie*) treat; (*băutură*) drink.

cinsti [chin'sti] *vt* (*a onora*) to honor; (*a respecta*) to respect; (*a aduce omagiu*) to do/render homage to; (*a dărui*) to present (with); (*a da un bacşiş*) to tip; (*a trata*) to treat; (*a bea*) to drink ‖ *vr* (*a bea*) to drink, to booze • **~t** *adj* (*onest*) honest, honorable, upright; (*în comerţ, jocuri*) fair (dealing); (*de încredere*) reliable; (*credincios*) loyal, faithful; true, sincere; virtuous; (*cast*) chaste; (*respectat*) venerable, respectable ‖ *adv* honestly, sincerely; in all sincerity; honorably.

cinteză, cintezoi ['chinteză, chinte'zoi] *nf, nm* chaffinch.

cioară ['choară] *nf* crow; rook.

ciob [chob] *nn* (*hârb*) crock, shard; (*bucată*) shiver, piece, fragment.

cioban [cho'ban] *nm* shepherd.

ciobăniţă [chobă'nitsă] *nf* shepherdess; shepherd's wife.

cioc¹ [chok] *nn* beak, bill; (*barbă*) goatee, imperial; (*minciună*) fib, shave.

cioc² [chok] *interj* (*bătaie la uşă*) knock!; (*lovitură*) bang!

ciocan [cho'kan] *nn* hammer; (*de lemn, mic*) mallet, gavel; *anat* malleus.

ciocănel [chokă'nel] *nn* also *mus* hammer, mallet.

ciocăni [chokă'ni] *vt* (*cu ciocanul*) to hammer; (*cu ciocul*) to peck; *fig* to nag ‖ *vi* to hammer (away); (*cu ciocul*) to peck; (*la uşă*) to knock.

ciocănitoare [chokăni'toare] *nf* wood-pecker.

ciocârlie [chokâr'lie] *nf* (sky)lark; Romanian folk song.

cioclu ['choklu] *nm* undertaker; (*gropar*) grave-digger, sexton.

ciocni [chok'ni] *vt* (*de*) to push, to knock (against); to clang; (*pahare*) to touch, to clink; (*a sparge*) to break ‖ *vr* to knock/strike/dash/rush (against); to collide, to run into; *fig* to clash, to be conflicting • **~re** *nf* concussion, knocking; (*de trenuri*) collision; *mil* encounter, clash; *fig* collision, clash, conflict.

ciocolată [choko'lată] *nf* chocolate; (*băutură*) chocolate, cocoa ‖ *nf/adj* (*culoare*) chocolate, dark brown.

ciolan [cho'lan] *nn* (*os*) bone; (*mădular*) limb; *fig* (*o afacere bănoasă*) lucrative business.

ciomag [cho'mag] *nn* (*bâtă*) club, cudgel; (*cu metal la capăt*) bludgeon; (*băţ*) stick; (*lovitură cu ~ul*) blow, whack.

ciomăgi [chomă'dji] *vt* to cudgel, to pummel, to sandbag.

ciondăneală [chondă'neală] *nf* scolding, chiding; (*cicălire*) bickering, nagging; (*ceartă*) row, high/hot/ hard words.

ciondăni [chondă'ni] *vt* to scold, to chide; (*a cicăli*) to nag ‖ *vr* to bicker; to wrangle, to quarrel, to squabble.

ciopârţi [chopâr'tsi] *vt* to cut/hack into pieces/bits; (*cu satârul*) to chop up; (*a dezmembra*) to dismember; (*a mutila*) also *fig* to mutilate, to mangle.

ciopli [cho'pli] *vt* (*lemn*) to carve, to hew; (*piatră*) to cut; (*a cizela*) to chisel; to polish; to fashion ‖ *vr* to be carved, to be chiseled, to be polished; *fig* to become polished/refined • **~tor** *nm* (*în lemn*) carver, hewer; (*în piatră*) stonecutter, stonemason.

ciorap [cho'rap] *nm* (*lung*) stocking; (*scurt*) sock; *pl com* pantyhose, hose, hosiery.

ciorbă ['chorbă] *nf* sour soup; (*borş*) borsch; *fig* (*vorbărie*) twaddle, gas, froth; (*flecar*) gabbler, chatterbox.

ciorchine [chor'kine] *nm* bunch, cluster.

ciordi [chor'di] *vt coll* to nick, to sneak, to pinch.

ciornă ['chornă] *nf* rough copy, (rough) draft.

cioroi [cho'roi] *nm orn* raven, crow; *pej* gypsy.

ciorovăi [chorovă'i] *vr* to squabble * **ciondăni**.

ciot [chot] *nn* (*nod în lemn*) knot, snag, gnarl; (*buturugă*) stump; (*stârpitură*) runt; (*pitic*) dwarf, midget.

circ [chirk] *nn* circus; *geol* circus, basin; *fig* mockery.

circa ['chirka] *adv* about, approximately, some, ... or so.

circă ['chirkă] *nf* police station; (*medicală*) medical center.

circuit [chirku'it] *nn elec* circuit; *sp* round; *fin* turnover; (*de curse auto-moto*) racing circuit, racing track.

circula [chirku'la] *vi* (*d. oameni, vehicule*) to circulate, to move about; (*a face naveta*) to ply; *fin* (*d. bani*) to be in circulation; (*d. zvonuri*) to be about/afloat; (*a curge*) to flow; (*d. ştiri*) to spread • **~ţie** *nf* (*a aerului, sângelui; monetară*) circulation; traffic.

circular [chirku'lar] *adj* circular.

circulară [chirku'lară] *nf* circular (letter), memo(random).

circumferinţă [chirkumfe'rintsă] *nf geom* circumference; (*suprafaţa exterioară*) outer surface; (*a taliei, pomului*) girth; (*a unui oraş*) perimeter, boundaries.

circumscripţie [chirkum'skriptsie] *nf adm* district, area, division; (*medicală*) health center circuit; (*de poliţie*) (police) precinct; *pol* constituency.

circumspect [chirkum'spekt] *adj* wary, cautious, circumspect ‖ *adv* warily, cautiously, prudently.

circumstanţă [chirkum'stanstă] *nf* circumstance, case, occasion; **de ~** for the occasion, occasional, improvised.

circumvoluţi(un)e [chirkumvolutsi'une] *nf anat* convolution.

cireadă [chi'readă] *nf* herd/drove of cattle.

cireaşă [chi'reaşă] *nf* (sweet) cherry; **~ amară** bitter/wild cherry, morello.

cireş [chi'resh] *nm bot* (sweet) cherry tree.

ciripi [chiri'pi] *vt/vi* to twitter, to chirp; (*a cânta*) to warble.

ciroză [chi'roză] *nf med* cirrhosis.

cisternă [chis'ternă] *nf* tank, reservoir, cistern.

cistită [chis'tită] *nf med* cystitis.

cişmea [chish'mea] *nf* (water) pump, hydrant; (*robinet*) faucet, tap.

cita [chi'ta] *vt* (*autor*) to quote; to cite; (*a menţiona*) to mention; *jur* to subpoena, to summon • **~re** *nf* quoting, citing, summoning • **~t** *nn* quotation, quote • **~ţie** *nf* subpoena, summons.

citadelă [chita'delă] *nf* citadel.

citadin [chita'din] *nm* townsman; *pl* townsfolk, townspeople || *adj* town …, city …, urban.

citeţ [chi'tets] *adj* legible || *adv* legibly.

citi [chi'ti] *vt* to read; (*a silabisi*) to spell; (*atent*) to peruse; (*complet*) to read through; (*superficial*) to skim, to scan; *fig* (*gânduri*) to read; (*a studia*) to read up, to study || *vi* to read; (*a silabisi*) to spell; (*cu grijă*) to peruse; (*fără grabă*) to read slowly || *vr* to read, to be read • **~re** *nf* reading; (*descifrare*) deciphering; **carte de** ~ reading book, reader • **~t** *nn* reading || *adj* read; (*având multă lectură*) well-read • **~tor** *nm* reader

citronadă [chitro'nadă] *nf* lemon squash, lemonade.

ciubăr [chu'băr] *nn* tub.

ciubuc [chu'buk] *nn* hookah; *archit* cornice; *fig coll* (*câştig*) gain, profit; (*bacşiş*) tip; (*pt. a corupe*) bribe.

ciucure ['chukure] *nm* tassel.

ciudat [chu'dat] *adj* (*straniu*) strange, curious; (*neobişnuit*) singular, unusual; (*aparte*) peculiar, quaint; bizarre, weird, odd, queer; eccentric, whimsical || *adv* strangely, curiously, unusually, peculiarly, weirdly, oddly.

ciudă ['chudă] *nf* (*mânie*) anger, rage, fury; (*pică*) grudge, malice, spite; (*ranchiună*) rancor, resentment; **cu** ~ out of spite, in anger; **în ciuda** in spite of, despite; (*cu toate acestea*) for all that; (*în* ~ *cuiva*) in defiance/spite of smb; (*înfruntând*) in the teeth of.

ciudăţenie [chudă'tsenie] *nf* singular/strange/curious thing; (*raritate*) curio; (*purtare ciudată*) strange behavior; (*întâmplare ciudată*) strange occurrence; (*aspect neobişnuit*) peculiarity; (*aspect straniu*) strangeness, oddity; (*excentricitate*) eccentricity; (*capriciu*) whim; freak.

ciufuli [chufu'li] *vt* (*părul*) to ruffle, to tousle; (*a trage de păr*) to seize by the hair || *vr* (*d. păr*) to be/get disheveled; (*reciproc*) *fig coll* to have a set to.

ciuguli [chugu'li] *vt* (*d. păsări*) to peck, to pick; (*din mâncare*) to pick at; (*a muşca din*) to nibble at || *vr coll* to bill and coo.

ciuli [chu'li] *vt* (*urechile*) to prick up one's ears.

ciulin [chu'lin] *nm bot* thistle.

ciumă ['chumă] *nf med* pestilence, plague; *hist* black death; (*femeie rea*) *coll* fury, shrew, vixen; (*femeie urâtă*) fright; scarecrow; (*femeie bătrână şi rea*) old hag/crone.

ciung [chung] *nm* one-armed person || *adj* one-armed/handed; (*schilod*) crippled; (*d. pomi*) pruned, lopped.

ciunti [chun'ti] *vt* (*a scurta*) to cut short, to curtail; (*urechile*) to crop; (*coada*) to dock; (*aripile*) to clip; (*pomii*) to prune, to lop; (*mustaţa, barba*) to trim; (*tăişul*) to take the edge off; (*a schilodi*) to cripple, to maim; to cut down, to reduce; (*un discurs*) to truncate, to mangle; (*un text*) to curtail || *vr* to be/get cut short; (*a se toci*) to grow blunt.

ciupercă [chu'perkă] *nf* (*cu pălărie*) mushroom; *med, bio* fungus; (*de ţesut ciorapi*) darning egg/mushroom.

ciupi [chu'pi] *vt* (*a pişca*) to pinch, to tweak; (*a înţepa*) to sting; (*d. pureci*) to bite; *fig* (*a fura*) to filch, to pilfer; (*dintr-o sumă*) to dock smth off a sum.

ciur [chur] *nn* sieve, screen; (*mare*) riddle.

ciurui [churu'i] *vt* (*d. gloanţe*) to riddle; (*a găuri peste tot*) to pierce || *vi* (*a se scurge*) to drip; (*a şiroi*) to stream, to gush.

ciută ['chută] *nf zool* hind, doe, female hart.

civic ['chivik] *adj* civic, civil.

civil [chi'vil] *nm* civilian; **în** ~ in civvies || *adj* civilian; *jur* civil.

civiliza [chivili'za] *vt* to civilize; *fig* to polish up || *vr* to become civilized/refined • **~ţie** *nf* civilization.

cizela [chize'la] *vt* (*aur*) to chase; (*lemn*) to chisel; (*a şlefui*) to polish; *fig* to polish up || *vr* to be chased; *fig* to polish (oneself).

cizmar [chiz'mar] *nm* shoemaker; (*cârpaci*) shoe-repairer, cobbler.

cizmă ['chizmă] *nf* high/top boot; (*mai înaltă de genunchi*) jack boot; *fig* blockhead.

claca [kla'ka] *vi* to break down; *fig* to fail; *sp* to strain a tendon, to rupture/tear a ligament; (*d. voce*) to go.

claie ['klaie] *nf* (*de fân*) hayrick, haystack; (*de grâu*) corn stack; (*grămadă*) pile, heap; (*de păr*) a shock of hair.

clamă ['klamă] *nf* hook, fastener; (*agrafă*) hair pin; (*pt. hârtie*) paper clip.

clan [klan] *nn* clan.

clandestin [klande'stin] *adj* clandestine, secret, illicit || *adv* clandestinely, secretly, in a secret manner, illicitly.

clanţă ['klantsă] *nf* (*de uşă*) door handle; *fig vulg* trap.

clapă ['klapă] *nf* (*de pian, maşină de scris*) key; (*la instrum. de suflat*) piston; (*de orgă*) stopple; *tech* flap; (*la o pompă*) clack; *typ* gripper; (*pt. urechi*) ear(f)lap; (*de la buzunar*) flap.

clapon [kla'pon] *nm* capon.

clar [klar] *adj* clear, transparent; pure; *fig* (*limpede*) obvious; (*desluşit*) distinct; (*care se înţelege*) intelligible; evident, manifest; simple, plain; (*luminos*) bright, serene; (*d. stil*) lucid || *adv* clearly, evidently, obviously, etc.

clarifica [klarifi'ka] *vi* to elucidate, to explain (away); to resolve, to solve, to clear up, to clarify || *vr* to become clear.

clarinet [klari'net] *nn* clarinet.

claritate [klari'tate] *nf* clearness, clarity; (*transparenţă*) transparency; (*caracter desluşit*) distinctness; (*a stilului*) lucidity.

clarvăzător [klarvăză'tor] *adj* clear-sighted, far-sighted/seeing.

clarviziune [klarvizi'une] *nf* clear-sightedness, far-sightedness.

clasa [kla'sa] *vt* (*a clasifica*) to classify, to class; (*a sorta*) to sort out; (*documente*) to file, to arrange; (*a evalua pe cineva*) to size smb up; *jur* to stop, to quash; (*o acţiune*) to close || *vr* to be classified, to be/rank among; *sp* to place.

clasament [klasa'ment] *nn* classification, position, place, alphabetical/chronological order.

clasă ['klasă] *nf* (*sală*) classroom; (*de elevi*) class, form, grade; category, division; *bot* order; *bio, soc, avia, rail* class.

clasic ['klasik] *nm* classic; classicist || *adj* classic; (*tradiţional*) classical; (*cunoscut*) well-known; (*d. lupte*) Graeco-Roman || *adv* classically • **~ism** [klasi'chism] *nn* classicism.

clasifica [klasifi'ka] *vt* to classify, to arrange in classes;

(*a sorta*) to sort (out); (*la şcoală*) to rate, * **clasa** • ~**re, ~ţie** *nf* classification; (*la şcoală*) ratings.
clasor [kla'sor] *nn* stamp book; (*sertar*) filing drawer; (*dulap*) filing cabinet.
clauză ['klauză] *nf* clause, provision, stipulation, rider.
claviatură [klavia'tură] *nf* keyboard, clavier.
claviculă [kla'vikulă] *nf anat* clavicle, collarbone.
claxon [klak'son] *nn* horn, klaxon, hooter • ~**a** *vi* to honk (one's horn), to toot one's horn.
clăbuc [klă'buk] *nm* (*spumă*) foam; (*de săpun*) soap suds, lather.
clădi [klă'di] *vt* (*o casă*) to build, to construct; (*a ridica*) to set up, to erect; *fig* (*a întemeia*) to found, to develop, to build up; (*a aranja în grămezi*) to stack/pile up; (*în straturi*) to arrange in layers || *vr* to be built, to be constructed, to be set up, etc • ~**re** *nf* building; (*publică*) edifice.
clănţăni [klăntsă'ni] *vi* (*cu dinţii*) to chatter (one's teeth); (*a tremura*) to tremble; (*cu un obiect metalic*) to clink, to clank, to rattle.
clăpăug [klăpă'ug] *adj* (*d. oameni*) flap-eared, lop-eared; (*d. urechi*) flapping, loppy; *fig* (*prost, bleg*) thick-headed.
clăti [klă'ti] *vt* (*vase, mâini, rufe, păr*) to rinse; (*a spăla*) to wash; (*gâtul*) to gargle; (*cu un curent de apa*) to flush || *vr* to rinse (one's mouth).
clătina [klăti'na] *vt* to shake, to toss; (*a legăna*) to rock || *vi* **a ~ din cap** (*negativ*) to shake one's head; (*afirmativ*) to nod || *vr* to shake; (*pe picioare*) to stagger, to reel; (*d. dinţi*) to be loose; (*a se legăna*) to rock; (*d. o clădire, pământ, sticlă*) to shake; (*d. un vas*) to pitch and toss; (*d. un guvern, regim*) to totter; (*d. o bancă, un scaun*) to rock
clătită [klă'titâ] *nf* pancake.
clefăi [klefă'i] *vi* (*a molfăi*) to chomp, to munch, to crunch.
clei [klei] *nn* glue; (*din făină*) paste • ~**os** *adj* (*lipicios*) sticky, gluey, adhesive; *also med* clammy; (*d. pâine*) slack, half-baked; (*neştiutor*) *sl* dumb.
clemă ['klemă] *nf tech* clamp; *elec* terminal, connector.
clemenţă [kle'mentsă] *nf* clemency, mercy.
clepsidră [klep'sidră] *nf* sandglass, hourglass.
cleptoman [klepto'man] *nm/adj* kleptomaniac • ~**ie** *nf* kleptomania.
cler [kler] *nn* clergy.
cleşte ['kleshte] *nm* (pair of) tongs; (*cu buze late*) (pair of) pliers; (*mic*) (pair of) pincers; (*de perforat*) punch, clippers; (*de nuci*) nutcracker; (*pt. zahăr*) sugar tongs; (*pt. sobă*) fire tongs; *zool* (*de rac*) claw.
cleveti [kleve'ti] *vi* to gossip, to slander, to backbite.
clică ['klikă] *nf* clique, coterie, cabal, set, faction, gang.
clichet ['kliket] *nn tech* catch, pawl, ratchet.
client [kli'ent] *nm com* customer, client; *jur* client; (*individ*) fellow; (*la taxi*) fare; (*hotel*) guest; (*fără rezervare*) chance guest, walk-in; (*publicitate*) account • ~**elă** *nf com* customers; *jur* clients, practice; *med* patients.
climat [kli'mat] *nn also fig* climate; *fig* atmosphere.
climatizare [klimati'zare] *nf tech* air-conditioning; climate control system.
climă ['klimă] *nf* climate; *lit* clime.
clin [klin] *nn* gusset.
clinchet ['klinket] *nn* (*de clopoţei*) tinkling; jingling; (*de pahare*) clinking.
clinică ['klinikă] *nf* clinic.

clinti [klin'ti] *vt* (*a mişca*) to move, to shift; (*a atinge*) to touch; *fig* to move, to stir || *vr* (*a se mişca*) to move, to stir; (*în prop. neg.*) to budge; *fig* (*a se abate*) to swerve, to flinch.
clipă ['klipă] *nf* moment, instant.
clipi [kli'pi] *vi* (*din ochi*) to blink; (*a face cu ochiul*) to wink; *physiol* to nictitate; (*a licări*) to blink, to twinkle; **cât ai ~ din ochi** in a jiffy, in no time.
clipoci [klipo'chi] *vi* to ripple; *lit* to murmur, to purl • ~**t** *nn* rippling; purl(ing), murmuring.
cliring ['kliring] *nn com* clearing.
clismă ['klismă] *nf med* enema.
clişeu [kli'sheu] *nn phot* negative; *fig* cliché, stock phrase.
cloacă ['kloakă] *nf* sewer, cesspool; *fig* cloaca, morass.
cloci [klo'chi] *vt* (*d. păsări*) to hatch; (*artificial*) to incubate; *fig* (*a pune la cale*) to hatch; (*a medita*) to brood over || *vi* (*d. păsări*) to brood; *fig* (*a tândăli*) *coll* to idle; (*a sta acasă*) to be a regular stay at home || *vr* (*a ieşi din ou*) to hatch; (*a se strica*) to become bad/stale; (*d. apă*) to be foul.
clocot ['klokot] *nn* bubbling (up); *fig* excitement, agitation.
clocoti [kloko'ti] *vi* (*a fierbe*; *d. un sentiment*) to boil; to seethe, to rage; (*d. mare*) to roar, to surge; (*a face vârtejuri*) to whirl, to eddy; *fig* (*a fi în plină desfăşurare*) to be in full swing || ~**tor** *adj also fig* (*care fierbe*) boiling, seething, bubbling; (*fierbinte*) hot; (*învolburat*) whirling, ebbing; (*înspumat*) foaming; (*mugind*) roaring; (*d. activitate*) tumultuous, tireless.
clona [klo'na] *vt bio* to clone.
clonă ['klonă] *nf bio* clone.
cloncăni [klonkă'ni] *vi* (*d. cloşti*) to cluck, to chuck; (*a croncăni*) to croak; *fig* (*a flecări*) to jabber.
clonţ [klonts] *nn* (*cioc*) beak.
clopot ['klopot] *nn* bell.
clopotniţă [klo'potnitsă] *nf* (*turlă*) steeple; (*separată*) belfry.
clopoţel [klopo'tsel] *nm* small bell, hand bell; *bot* bell-flower; *pl* (*ghiocei*) snowdrops.
clor [klor] *nn chem* chlorine.
clorofilă [kloro'filă] *nf bot* chlorophyll.
cloroform [kloro'form] *nn* chloroform.
closet [klo'set] *nn* lavatory, toilet; *coll* men's/ladies' room, bathroom; latrine.
cloşcă ['kloshkă] *nf* hatching hen; *pej* (*om inactiv*) idler, loafer; (*Cloşca*) *astron* the Pleiades, the seven stars.
clovn [klovn] *nm* clown; *hist* jester; *fig* buffoon.
club [klub] *nn* (*asociaţie*) club; (*local*) clubhouse.
coacăză ['koakăză] *nf* gooseberry, black currant.
coace ['koache] *vt* (*în cuptor*) to bake; (*d. soare*) to ripen, to mature; *fig* (*a chinui*) to burn, to torture; *fig* (*a urzi*) to plot, to hatch || *vi med* to gather (to a head) || *vr* (*d. plante*) to ripen; (*în cuptor*) to be baking; *med* to gather; *fig* (*a se maturiza*) to (grow) mature; *fig* (*la soare*) to bask, to sunbathe.
coadă ['koadă] *nf zool* tail; (*de vulpe*) brush; (*de cerb, iepure*) scut; (*de cal*) horse tail; (*pieptănătură*) pigtail; (*d. coafură*) pony tail; plait; *bot* stalk; (*mâner*) handle, helve; (*trenă*) train; (*capăt*) end; (*şir*) line, file.
coafa [koa'fa] *vt* to dress (smb's hair) || *vr* (*la coafor*) to have a hairdo, to have one's hair done; (*singur*) to do one's hair.

coafeză [koa'feză] *nf* hairdresser.

coafor [koa'for] *nm* (*persoană*) hairdresser; (*salon de coafură*) hairdresser's.

coafură [koa'fură] *nf* hairdo, hairstyle.

coagula [koagu'la] *vt* to coagulate; (*lapte*) to curdle || *vr* to coagulate; (*d. lapte*) to turn to curds; (*d. sânge*) to clot • ~re *nf* coagulation, curdling, clotting.

coajă ['koazhă] *nf* (*de copac*) bark; (*de pâine*) crust; (*de brânză*) rind; (*de fruct*) skin, peel; (*de ouă, nucă*) shell; (*de semințe*) husk, hull; *med* (*de rană*) crust, scab.

coală ['koală] *nf* sheet (of paper).

coaliție [koa'litsie] *nf* coalition, union, league; *pej* conspiracy.

coamă ['koamă] *nf zool* (*de cal, leu*) mane; (*de zid*) coping; (*culme*) ridge

coapsă ['koapsă] *nf* thigh, haunch.

coardă ['koardă] *nf* cord, chord; *mus* string; (*pt. joacă*) skipping rope; *tech* (*arc*) spring; *geom* chord.

coasă ['koasă] *nf* scythe; (*cosit*) haymaking; mowing.

coase ['koase] *vt/vi* to sew, to stitch; (*a însăila*) to baste; *med* to stitch.

coastă ['koastă] *nf anat* rib; (*povârniș*) slope, declivity; (*a unei coline*) side, gradient; (*latură*) flank; (*țărm*) sea coast/shore.

coautor [koau'tor] *nm* co-author; *jur* accomplice.

cobai ['kobai] *nm zool* guinea-pig.

cobalt ['kobalt] *nn* cobalt.

cobe ['kobe] *nf* (*rău augur*) ill omen, portent; (*pasăre cobitoare*) bird of ill omen; (*corb*) evil-boding raven; *fig* croaker, calamity prophet; (*la găini*) pip.

cobi [ko'bi] *vi* to be a prophet of evil; *coll* to be a Cassandra || *vt* to forebode.

cobiliță ['kobilitsă] *nf* yoke.

coborâre [kobo'râre] *nf* descent; (*scădere*) lowering; (*dintr-un vehicul*) getting off; (*ieșire*) exit; *fig* degradation, decline; (*la schi*) downhill run/race; (*cu parașuta*) parachute jump.

coborî [kobo'rî] *vt* (*a da jos*) to take/put down; (*a trage jos*) to draw down; (*a lăsa jos*) to let down; (*a aduce jos*) to bring/carry down; to lower; to reduce, to cut; (*a degrada*) to degrade, to debase; (*a deprecia*) to depreciate, to disparage || *vr* (*din*) to get/go out of; (*a se înjosi*) to debase/demean oneself || *vi* (*a se da jos*) to go/get down; (*a veni jos*) to come down(wards); (*în grabă*) to hurry/run down; (*din vehicul*) to get out/off/down from; (*a descăleca*) to dismount; (*a asfinți*) to set/go down; (*d. prețuri*) to go down, to drop; *fig* to be degraded, to fall; (*a descinde din*) to descend from; (*d. temperatură, barometru*) to drop, to fall; (*d. ceață*) to come down; (*d. râu*) to flow down to; (*d. pace, liniște, calm*) to come over smb; (*d. drum, potecă, stradă*) to go down(hill), to slope down; **a-și ~ vocea** *vt* to lower one's voice.

cobra ['kobra] *nf zool* cobra.

coc [kok] *nn* chignon, bun (of hair).

coca ['koka] *nf bot* coca.

cocaină [koka'ină] *nf* cocaine.

cocardă [ko'kardă] *nf* rosette, cockade.

cocă¹ ['kokă] *nf* (*aluat*) dough, paste; (*clei*) paste.

cocă² ['kokă] *nf naut, avia* hull.

cocârja [kokâr'zha] *vr* to crook, to bend.

coccis ['kokchis] *nn anat* coccyx.

cocean [ko'chean] *nm* (*tulpină*) stalk; (*știulete*) (corn) cob; (*de varză*) cabbage head.

cochet [ko'ket] *adj* elegant, smart, stylish; (*care caută să placă*) coquettish, flirtatious || *adv* smartly, stylishly; (*ca atitudine*) coquettishly, demurely • ~a *vt* (*cu*) to flirt with, to play the coquet(te); to put on affected airs/fine graces; *fig* to toy/trifle with.

cochilie [ko'kilie] *nf* shell.

cocină ['kochină] *nf* pigsty.

cocioabă [ko'choabă] *nf* hut, hovel, shanty.

cocleală [kok'leală] *nf* (*rugină de aramă*) verdigris; (*gust rău*) foul taste, bitter taste.

cocli [kok'li] *vr* to rust, to be(come) covered/coated with verdigris; (*a avea gust de cocleală*) to taste of verdigris.

cocoașă [ko'koashă] *nf* (*om, cămilă*) hump(back), hunch(back); *fig* clog.

cocoli [koko'li] *vt* (*a înfofoli*) to muffle, to wrap up; (*a răsfăța*) to spoil, to pamper; (*a proteja*) to wrap smth in cottonwool.

cocoloș [koko'losh] *nn* (*bulgăre*) ball; (*mic*) pellet; lump.

cocoloși [kokolo'shi] *vt* (*a mototoli*) to crumple; *fig* (*a mușamaliza*) to hush up; (*a răsfăța*) to spoil; (*a înfofoli*) to wrap up || *vr* (*a se înfofoli*) to muffle oneself up; (*a se face cocoloș*) to ball.

cocon [ko'kon] *nm ento* cocoon.

cocor [ko'kor] *nm orn* crane.

cocos [ko'kos] *nm bot* coconut tree.

cocostârc [koko'stârk] *nm orn* stork.

cocoș [ko'kosh] *nm* (*domestic*) rooster, cock; (*în fabule*) chanticleer; (*de munte*) grouse, capercaillie || *nn* (*la o armă*) cock • ~el *nm* (*cocoș tânăr*) young cock, cockerel; *fig* cockalorum; (*bani*) gold coin.

cocoșat [koko'shat] *nm* humpback, hunchback || *adj* humpbacked, hunchbacked.

cocotă [ko'kotă] *nf* cocotte, tart.

cocotier [kokoti'er] *nm bot* coconut tree.

cocoța [koko'tsa] *vt* to perch, to put on the top || *vr* (*a se cățăra*) to climb/clamber (up); (*pe o creangă*) to perch, to alight; *fig* to obtain quick promotion.

cocs [koks] *nn* coke.

coctail ['kokteil] *nn* (*băutură*) cocktail; (*recepție*) cocktail party.

cod¹ [kod] *nm* (*pește*) cod(fish).

cod² [kod] *nn jur* code; (*lege*) law; **~ civil** civil code; **~ penal** criminal/penal code; **~ de acces** access code; **~ poștal** zip code.

codană [ko'dană] *nf* teenage girl, bobby soxer.

codaș [ko'dash] *nm* lagger, laggard, slacker || *adj* (*din urmă*) last; (*din coadă*) lagging behind; (*înapoiat*) backward.

codi [ko'di] *vr* to waver, to vacillate; *coll* to dilly-dally.

codicil [kodi'chil] *nn jur* codicil.

codobatură [kodo'batură] *nf orn* wagtail.

codoș [ko'dosh] *nm pej* (*proxenet*) pander, procurer, pimp; (*pârâtor*) informer, telltale.

codru ['kodru] *nm* forest; (*bucată*) hunk.

coechipier [koekipi'er] *nm sp* fellow member.

coeficient [koefichi'ent] *nm phys, math* coefficient, value.

coercitiv [koerchi'tiv] *adj jur* coercive.

coerent [koe'rent] *adj* coherent; *fig* integrated || *adv* coherently.

coerență [koe'rentsă] *nf* coherence.

coexista [koegzis'ta] *vi* to coexist.

coexistență [koegzis'tentsă] *nf* coexistence; ~ **pașnică** peaceful coexistence.

cofetar [kofe'tar] *nm* confectioner; (*patiser*) pastry cook.

cofetărie [kofetă'rie] *nf* confectioner's, confectionery.

coif [koif] *nn* helmet.

coincide [koin'chide] *vi* to coincide (with), to concur with; (*a se potrivi*) to tally, to dovetail; *math* (*două figuri geometrice*) to match, to agree.

coincidență [koinchi'dentsă] *nf* coincidence, concurrence; (*simultaneitate*) simultaneous occurrence, simultaneity; **o ~ fericită** a happy coincidence.

coji [ko'zhi] *vt* to skin; (*cartofii*) to peel; (*copacii*) to bark, to peel off; (*fructe*) to shell, to husk ‖ *vr* (*d. piele*) to peel off, to scale; *med* to desquamate; (*d. pomi*) to shed the bark; (*a se desprinde*) to come off.

cojoc [ko'zhok] *nn* sheepskin coat.

colabora [kolabo'ra] *vi* to co-operate in; (*la un proiect*) to take part in, to assist in; *hist* to collaborate; (*la o publicație*) to contribute • ~**re** *nf* cooperation, collaboration; (*la o publicație*) contribution • ~**tor** *nm* co-worker, collaborator; (*la o publicație*) contributor • ~**ționist** *nm pol* collaborationist, quisling.

colac [ko'lak] *nm* (*de pâine*) knot-shaped bread, twist; (*cerc*) ring, circle; (*de closet*) closet belt.

colant [ko'lant] *adj* (*d. substanțe*) sticky; (*d. persoane*) *coll* clinging ‖ *nm pl* tights, pantyhose.

colaps [ko'laps] *nn* collapse.

colateral [kolate'ral] *nm* collateral relative ‖ *adj* collateral.

colaționa [kolatsio'na] *vt* to collate, to compare (one copy with another), to check.

colcăi [kolkă'i] *vi* (*de*) to be alive with, to teem with, to swarm with.

colecta [kolek'ta] *vt* to gather, to collect ‖ *vi* (*d. răni*) to gather • ~**re** *nf* gathering, collecting.

colectă [ko'lektă] *nf* collection; subscription.

colectiv [kolek'tiv] *nn* group, collective; (*într-o instituție*) staff, personnel ‖ *adj* collective, joint; **contract ~** collective agreement; *jur* **recurs ~** class action suit ‖ *adv* collectively, jointly.

colector [kolek'tor] *nm hist* purveyor ‖ *nn tech* collector, collecting main/pipe ‖ *adj* collecting, collector.

colecție [ko'lektsie] *nf* collection; (*de cărți*) series; anthology, selection; (*de ziare*) newspaper file.

colecționa [kolektsio'na] *vt* to gather, to collect; (*plante*) to botanize • ~**r** *nm* collector; (*de timbre*) stamp collector, philatelist; (*de antichități*) antiquary • ~**re** *nf* collecting.

coleg [ko'leg] *nm* co-worker, fellow (worker), mate.

colegiu [ko'ledju] *nn* (*instituție de învățământ*) school, college; (*colectiv*) body, board.

colesterol [koleste'rol] *nm med* cholesterol.

colet [ko'let] *nn* parcel; package.

colibă [ko'libă] *nf* hut, hovel, cabin, shack, shanty.

colică ['kolikă] *nf med* colic; *pl* gripes.

colier [koli'er] *nn* necklace.

colină [ko'lină] *nf* hill, hillock; (*ridicătură de pământ*) elevation, eminence.

colind [ko'lind] *nn* (Christmas) carol.

colinda [kolin'da] *vt* to go/walk/stroll all over, to rove, to wander ‖ *vi* to go carol-singing.

colivie [koli'vie] *nf* cage.

colizi(un)e [kolizi'une] *nf* collision.

coloană [ko'lwană] *nf archit* column, pillar; support; *typ, phys, mil* column.

colocatar [koloka'tar] *nm* inmate; co-tenant, joint tenant.

colocvial [kolokvi'al] *adj* colloquial.

colocviu [ko'lokviu] *nn* (*universitate*) oral (examination); scientific debate, colloquium.

colon [ko'lon] *nn anat* colon.

colonel [kolo'nel] *nm* colonel.

colonial [kolo'nial] *adj* colonial.

colonie[1] [kolo'nie] *nf* colony, settlement; (*de vară*) summer camp.

colonie[2] [ko'lonie] *nf* (eau de) cologne.

coloniza [koloni'za] *vt* to colonize.

colora [kolo'ra] *vt* to color; (*a da culoare*) to lend color to; (*a păta*) to stain, to tint, to tinge; (*a vopsi*) to dye; (*a rumeni*) to bring color to the cheeks; *fig* (*a înflori*) to color, to exaggerate; *mus* to ornament with flourishes ‖ *vr* to color; (*la față*) to color up, to blush.

colorant [kolo'rant] *nn* dye (stuff), coloring matter ‖ *adj* coloring.

colorit [kolo'rit] *nn* coloring, color, hue; *lit* brilliance/richness/vividness of style.

colos [ko'los] *nm* colossus, giant • ~**al** [kolo'sal] *adj* colossal, huge, gigantic; *coll* (*grozav*) awesome, grand ‖ *adv* immensely, enormously; *coll* capitally, admirably.

colporta [kolpor'ta] *vt* (*știri*) to circulate, to spread about; *obs* (*a vinde*) to peddle, to hawk.

colportor [kolpor'tor] *nm* (*de știri*) newsmonger; *pej* (*de bârfe*) scandalmonger; *obs* (*negustor*) hawker, pedlar.

coltuc [kol'tuk] *nm* crust of bread.

colț [kolts] *nn* (*al străzii, camerei, gurii, ochiului*) corner; (*cotlon*) nook; (*unghi*) angle ‖ *nm* (*dinte canin*) (eye)tooth, canine; (*de măsea/dinte*) (tooth) stump/cusp; *zool* fang; (*de stâncă*) crag • ~**os** *adj* sharp-tongued, cantankerous • ~**uros** *adj* angular; (*d. stânci*) craggy; (*d. linii, contururi*) jagged, ragged; (*osos*) bony.

columnă [ko'lumnă] *nf* column.

comanda [koman'da] *vt* (*a porunci*) to command, to be in command/charge of; (*a ordona*) to order; (*locuri*) to book, to secure; *com* to order ‖ *vi* to command, to be in command; (*la restaurant*) to order, to give one's order; *fig* to order (smb) about.

comandant [koman'dant] *nm mil* commander, commanding officer; (*de batalion*) major; commandant; *naut* (*de navă*) captain; executive officer; first lieutenant; *avia* (*de bord*) captain; ~ **suprem** commander-in-chief.

comandă [ko'mandă] *nf* (*ordin*) command, order; *fig* **la ~** ostentatiously, to order; (*la ordinul cuiva*) at smb's order; *com* order; *tech* control, operation; *mil* command; *naut* (*locul*) bridge deck; ~ **(de) la distanță** remote control.

comasa [koma'sa] *vt* to amalgamate, to merge, to fuse • ~**re** *nf* amalgamating, merging, fusion.

comă ['koma] *nf med* coma.

combaină [kom'bainǎ] *nf* combine.

combatant [komba'tant] *nm* fighter, combatant ‖ *adj* fighting.

combate [kom'bate] *vt* to combat, to struggle/fight against; (*dăunători, boală*) to control; *fig* to discourage.

combativ [komba'tiv] *adj* fighting, combative • ~**itate** *nf* combative spirit, fighting ability.

combina [kombi'na] *vt chem* to combine, to blend;

(*cifre, idei*) to arrange, to group; (*a pune la cale*) to contrive, to devise || *vr* to combine; to start an affair with • ~**ţie** *nf* also *chem* combination; *fig* plan, scheme; (*calcul*) calculation; maneuvre.

combină [kom'bină] *nf* combine.

combinezon [kombine'zon] *nn* (*de damă*) slip, petticoat, chemise; (*de aviator*) overalls.

combustibil [kombus'tibil] *nm* fuel, combustible || *adj* combustible, inflammable.

combustie [kom'bustie] *nf* combustion, burning.

comedie [kome'die] *nf* comedy; *fig* farce, sham, make-believe.

comemora [komemo'ra] *vt* to commemorate • ~**re** *nf* commemoration.

comensurabil [komensu'rabil] *adj math* commensurable, measurable.

comenta [komen'ta] *vt* to comment upon, to discuss; to criticize, to annotate || *vr* to be commented upon.

comentariu [komen'tariu] *nn lit, pol* commentary; (*adnotare*) annotation; *fig* comment, remark.

comentator [komenta'tor] *nm* commentator; (*exeget*) annotator; (*la ziar*) columnist.

comercial [komerchi'al] *adj* trade, trading, commercial; *naut* merchant …; (*d. afaceri*) business || *adv* commercially • ~**iza** *vt* to market, to commercialize.

comerciant [komerchi'ant] *nm* merchant, trader, dealer; shopkeeper.

comerţ [ko'merts] *nn* trade, commerce.

comesean [kome'sean] *nm* table companion; *pl* guests.

comestibil [komes'tibil] *adj* edible, eatable.

cometă [ko'metă] *nf* comet.

comic ['komik] *nm* comic actor; comedian || *adj* comic; (*nostim*) comical, funny, laughable; (*spiritual*) humorous, witty || *adv* comically, humorously, ludicrously, funnily • ~**ul** *nn* (*generic*) the comic; (*particular*) the comic part.

comisar [komi'sar] *nm* commissar, commissary; (*poliţist*) police inspector, (police) captain.

comisie [ko'misie] *nf* committee, board, commission.

comision [komisi'on] *nn com* commission, allowance; (*serviciu*) errand, service.

comisionar [komisio'nar] *nm* (*persoană care face servicii*) errand boy, commissionaire.

comitat [komi'tat] *nn* county.

comite [ko'mite] *vt* to commit, to perpetrate, to do, to make.

comitet [komi'tet] *nn* committee, commission, board.

comoară [ko'moară] *nf* treasure; *fig* treasury, mine, wealth.

comod [ko'mod] *adj* comfortable, convenient, easy; (*la îndemână*) handy; indolent, easy-going, lazy || *adv* comfortably, conveniently, easily; (*la îndemână*) handily; indolently.

comodă [ko'modă] *nf* chest of drawers, commode.

comoditate [komodi'tate] *nf* comfort, comfortableness, ease; (*indolenţă*) indolence, laziness.

comoţi(un)e [komotsi'une] *nf* commotion, disturbance; (*şoc*) *med* shell-shock, concussion.

compact [kom'pakt] *adj* compact, dense, close; ~ **disc** compact disc, CD || *adv* compactly, densely.

companie[1] [kompa'nie] *nf* (*tovărăşie*) company, companionship; (*prezenţă*) presence; (*grup*) group, party, company.

companie[2] [kom'panie] *nf mil* company.

compara [kompa'ra] *vt* (*noţiuni similare*) to compare

with; (*noţiuni diferite*) to compare to; (*a asemăna*) to draw a parallel between || *vr* to compare (oneself) with • ~**tiv** *nn gram* comparative (degree) || *adj* comparative || *adv* comparatively (speaking), by way of comparison • ~**ţie** *nf* comparison; (*literară*) simile; analogy; **în ~ cu** in/by comparison with; **prin ~** by comparison.

compartiment [komparti'ment] *nn* compartment, division; *rail* compartment; *also fig* (*casetă*) pigeonhole; *fig* branch, department, province.

compas [kom'pas] *nn math* (pair of) compasses; (*pt. măsurat distanţe*) dividers.

compasiune [kompasi'une] *nf* sympathy, compassion, pity; **cu ~** compassionately.

compatibil [kompa'tibil] *adj* (*cu*) compatible (with), consistent (with) • ~**itate** *nf* compatibility, consistence.

compatriot [kompatri'ot] *nm* fellow countryman, compatriot.

compătimi [kompăti'mi] *vt* to pity, to commiserate • ~**re** *nf* sympathy, pity, compassion • ~**tor** *adj* sympathetic, compassionate || *adv* sympathetically, compassionately.

compensa [kompen'sa] *vt* to compensate for; (*a despăgubi*) to make up for, to make good; *jur* to balance; (*datorii*) to set off (debts), to offset; (*a regla*) to adjust; **a ~ o pierdere** to make good a loss || *vr* to be compensated, to make up for each other • ~**ţie** *nf* compensation, offset, indemnity; (*despăgubire*) damages, reparations.

competent [kompe'tent] *adj* competent, qualified; (*versat*) conversant (with).

competenţă [kompe'tentsă] *nf* competence, ability, proficiency; *also jur* jurisdiction.

competitor [kompeti'tor] *nm* competitor.

competiţie [kompe'titsie] *nf* competition, rivalry; *sp* contest, match.

compila [kompi'la] *vt* (*a reuni*) to compile; *pej* to plagiarize.

complăcea [komplă'chea] *vr* (*în*) to indulge in, to delight in; (*a se mulţumi cu*) to be content/satisfied with.

complement [komple'ment] *nn geom* complement; *gram* object.

complementar [komplemen'tar] *adj* complementary.

complet [kom'plet] *adj* (*întreg*) complete, entire, whole; (*cuprinzător*) comprehensive; (*profund*) thorough; (*plin*) full (up) || *adv* completely, entirely, thoroughly, fully.

completa [komple'ta] *vt* to complete, to make smth complete; (*un formular*) to fill out/up; (*a întregi*) to round (a number), to make up; **a ~ o sumă** to make up a sum of money || *vr* to complete (each other), to complement.

complex [kom'pleks] *nn* complex; ~ **comercial** (shopping) mall || *adj* complex; *math* compound; complicated, intricate • ~**at** *adj* inhibited, self-conscious; *coll* mixed up • ~**itate** *nf* complexity, intricacy.

complezenţă [komple'zentsă] *nf* kindness, obligingness; **de ~** perfunctory, perfunctorily; out of kindness.

complica [kompli'ka] *vt* to complicate || *vr* to become complicated/involved • ~**t** *adj* complicated, elaborate; (*d. mecanism*) intricate; (*d. stil*) tangled, involved; (*dificil*) difficult • ~**ţie** *nf* complication(s); *fig* intricacy, complexity.

complice [kom'pliche] *nm* accomplice, accessory (to), party (to), abettor.

complicitate [komplichi'tate] *nf* complicity; *jur* aiding and abetting; **a acţiona în ~ cu** to act in collusion/complicity with.

compliment [kompli'ment] *nn* compliment; *pl (salutări)* regards, respects, compliments.

complini [kompli'ni] *vt* to complete, to finish, to fulfil, to accomplish.

complot [kom'plot] *nn* plot, conspiracy, scheme • **~a** *vi* to plot, to conspire, to hatch a plot.

component [kompo'nent] *nn* component (part), constituent, element || *adj* component, constituent.

comporta [kompor'ta] *vt* to require, to call for; *(a implica)* to entail, to involve; *(a admite)* to allow, to admit || *vr* to behave/conduct oneself, to act • **~ment**, **~re** *nn*, *nf* behavior, conduct, demeanor.

composta [kompos'ta] *vt* to (date) stamp, to punch (a ticket); to obliterate.

compot [kom'pot] *nn* compote, stewed fruit.

compozitor [kompozi'tor] *nm mus* composer; *typ* compositer, typesetter.

compoziţie [kompo'zitsie] *nf* composition; structure, make-up; construction; *(şcolară)* essay; *(pictură)* genre/subject painting; *typ* typesetting; writing, making up.

compresă [kom'presă] *nf med* compress.

comprima [kompri'ma] *vt (d. gaze)* to compress, to condense; *fig (a concedia)* to lay off, to fire || *vr* to be pressed together • **~t** *nn* tablet || *adj* compressed.

compromis [kompro'mis] *nn* compromise, arrangement || *adj* disgraced, discredited.

compromite [kompro'mite] *vt* to compromise; to discredit, to disgrace; *(autoritatea)* to impair; *fig (a periclita)* to menace, to endanger, to jeopardize || *vr* to compromise/discredit oneself.

compromiţător [kompromitsă'tor] *adj* compromising; disreputable.

compune [kom'pune] *vt* to compose; to make up, to form; *(a redacta)* to draft, to draw up; *typ* to set (type) || *vi* to compose || *vr a se ~ din* to consist of, to be made up of • **~re** *nf* composition; *(alcătuire)* structure.

computare [kompu'tare] *nf* computation.

computer [kom'puter] *nn* computer.

comun [ko'mun] *nn* common || *adj* common, joint; *(obişnuit)* common, everyday, ordinary; vulgar, gross, coarse; *(banal)* commonplace; *(reciproc)* mutual.

comună [ko'mună] *nf (diviziune teritorială)* commune, village.

comunica [komuni'ka] *vt (a transmite)* to communicate, to convey; *(a face cunoscut)* to inform, to apprise; *(oficial)* to notify; *(în secret)* to impart smth to smb; *(a spune)* to tell || *vi* to be connected, to communicate with; to be in touch/contact with || *vr* to be transmitted/communicated/informed • **~re** *nf* communication, message; *(ştire)* piece of news; *(lucrare ştiinţifică)* paper, essay • **~t** *nn* official statement/announcement, press release • **~tiv** *adj* communicative, talkative • **~ţie** *nf* communication; *(legătură)* connection, intercourse.

comunist [komu'nist] *nm/adj* communist.

comunitate [komuni'tate] *nf coll (d. idei, interese)* similarity; *(societate)* community; *(proprietate)*

common ownership; *(urbană)* urban community; *(religioasă)* community, congregation.

comuta [komu'ta] *vt jur (în)* to commute; *elec (d. curent)* to switch/change over • **~re** *nf jur* commutation • **~tor** *nn elec* switch, commutator.

con [kon] *nn (de vulcan, lumină)* cone; *(de brad)* fir cone; **în formă de ~** cone-shaped.

conac [ko'nak] *nn* manor, mansion.

concav [kon'kav] *adj* concave.

concedia [konchedi'a] *vt (a destitui)* to dismiss; *(neutru)* to discharge; *(a reduce personalul)* to lay off, to make redundant; *coll* to downsize, to fire; *(a îndepărta)* to send away, to send about one's business.

concediere [konchedi'ere] *nf* dismissal, discharge, layoff.

concediu [kon'chediu] *nn* vacation, holiday; *also mil* leave (of absence); furlough; **în ~** on vacation, on leave.

concentra [konchen'tra] *vt* to concentrate; *(d. raze, atenţie)* to focus, to center; *(d. lapte)* to condense; *(d. stil)* to compress; *mil* to call up || *vr* to concentrate (on), to focus • **~re** *nf* concentration, focusing; *mil* call-up; *(d. companii etc)* integration, merging, merger • **~t** *nn* concentrate, extract || *adj* concentrated; *(d. lapte)* condensed; *fig (asupra)* intent (on), engrossed (in); *(d. stil)* concise, terse; *mil* drafted || *adj/nm mil* called-up (reservist).

concepe [kon'chepe] *vt (a zămisli; a imagina)* to conceive; *(a născoci)* to devise, to imagine; *(a formula)* to formulate, to word; *(a compune)* to compose, to write; *(a schiţa)* to sketch, to draft || *vr* to be conceived, to be devised, etc.

concept [kon'chept] *nn phil (concepţie)* notion, concept; rough draft/copy.

concepţie [kon'cheptsie] *nf (zămislire)* conception, conceiving; *(idei)* view, idea; *(generală)* outlook.

concern [kon'chern] *nn com* concern.

concert [kon'chert] *nn (spectacol)* concert; *(bucată muzicală)* concerto.

concesie [kon'chesie] *nf* concession, granting; *(cedare)* yielding.

concesiona [konchesio'na] *vt econ* to lease, to grant, to license • **~r** *nm econ* concessionaire, license holder; *com* agent, dealer.

concesiune [konchesi'une] *nf econ* concession; *(drept de vânzare)* license, licensing; *(privilegiu)* granting, patent.

conchide [kon'kide] *vt (că)* to come to the conclusion that, to conclude that; to deduce that, to gather that.

concilia [konchili'a] *vt* to reconcile || *vr* to be reconciled.

conciliator [konchilia'tor] *adj* conciliating, conciliatory || *nm* conciliator, peacemaker.

conciliere [konchili'ere] *nf* (re)conciliation.

concis [kon'chis] *adj* concise, brief, terse || *adv* concisely, briefly, tersely.

concizie [kon'chizie] *nf* concision, conciseness, brevity.

conclav [kon'klav] *nn* conclave.

concludent [konklu'dent] *adj (d. argumente)* conclusive; *(convingător)* cogent, convincing.

concluzie [kon'kluzie] *nf* conclusion, inference; *jur* conclusion, finding, decision.

concomitent [konkomi'tent] *adj* concomitant, concurrent, simultaneous || *adv* concomitantly, concurrently, simultaneously (with).

concorda [konkor'da] *vi* to correspond (to), to be in

accordance with, to accord with; *gram* to agree, to concord.

concordie [kon'kordie] *nf* agreement, concord, harmony, accord.

concret [kon'kret] *adj* concrete; real, actual; *(precis)* definite, precise, specific || *adv* concretely, definitely.

concretiza [konkreti'za] *vt* to materialize; *(a realiza)* to effect, to carry out || *vr* to materialize, to come true; to take shape.

concubinaj [konkubi'nazh] *nn* cohabitation, concubinage.

concubină [konku'binə] *nf* mistress, concubine.

concura [konku'ra] *vi (a coopera)* to combine, to unite; *(în vederea unui success)* to work towards, to contribute || *vi sp* to compete (with) || *vt com* to rival, to compete with.

concurent [konku'rent] *nm* rival; *(participant la o întrecere)* competitor, contestant || *adj* competing, competitive, rival; *math* concurrent, converging.

concurență [konku'rentsə] *nf* competition, rivalry.

concurs [kon'kurs] *nn (întrecere)* competition, contest, event; *(examen)* competitive examination; *(colaborare)* cooperation; *(ajutor)* assistance, help, aid, support.

condamna [kondam'na] *vt jur* to sentence, to convict; *(la amendă)* to fine; *fig* to blame, to censure, to condemn; *lit* to doom • **~bil** *adj* blamable, blameworthy • **~re** *nf jur* conviction, judgment, sentence; *fig (dezaprobare)* blame, reproof, censure.

condei [kon'dei] *nn (toc)* penholder; *fig (scris)* penmanship; *(caligrafie)* handwriting.

condensa [konden'sa] *vt phys*, *chem* to condense; *(prin presiune)* to compress; *fig* to boil down, to cut down; *(a concentra)* to concentrate || *vr* to condense, to become condensed • **~re** *nf* condensation; *(prin presiune)* compression; *(concentrare)* concentration.

condescendent [kondeschen'dent] *adj* condescending, patronizing.

condescendență [kondeschen'dentsə] *nf* condescension, patronizing attitude.

condică ['kondikə] *nf* register, book; *scol* roll, class register.

condiment [kondi'ment] *nn* condiment, seasoning, spice.

condiție [kon'ditsie] *nf (împrejurare)* condition, circumstance; *(clauză)* condition, provision; *pl* terms; ~ **esențială** prerequisite; *(rang)* position, status, rank; *(stare)* state; *(situație)* situation; **în ~ bună** in good order/state; *(d. un sportiv)* to be in shape; *(d. o clădire)* in good repair.

condiționa [konditsio'na] *vt (aerul; a subordona unor condiții)* to condition; *(lemnul)* to season; *(a trata)* to treat; to depend on smth || *vr* to be conditioned • **~l** *nn gram* conditional (mood) || *adj* conditional.

condoleanțe [kondole'antse] *nf pl* condolences.

conducător [kondukə'tor] *nm* leader; *(șef)* chief, head, ruler; *(călăuză)* guide; *phys* conductor || *adj* ruling; *(călăuzitor)* guiding; principal, leading; *phys* conducting, transmitting.

conduce [kon'duche] *vt* to lead; *(a călăuzi)* to guide, to direct; *(mașina)* to drive; to pilot; *(a cârmi)* to steer; *(a administra)* to manage, to control; *(a guverna)* to govern, to rule, to run; *(a însoți)* to accompany, to escort; *(la ușă)* to see to the door; *(pe cineva acasă)* to see smb home; *(la gară)* to see smb off; to drive, to take; *mus* to conduct; *mil* to command || *vi sp* to lead, to be in the lead; *auto* to drive || *vr* **a se ~ după**

to take as a guide, to be guided • **~re** *nf* leadership, management; *(guvern)* government; *(persoane)* leaders; *(călăuzire)* guidance.

conductă [kon'duktə] *nf tech* pipe(line), conduit; ~ **de apă/gaz** water/gas pipe.

conduită [kondu'itə] *nf* conduct, demeanor, behavior; *pl* manners, manner of life.

conecta [konek'ta] *vt* to connect, to link • **~re** *nf elec* connecting, connection.

confecție [kon'fektsie] *nf* manufacture; *pl* ready-made clothes, ready-to-wear clothes.

confecționa [konfektsio'na] *vt* to make, to manufacture; *(o rochie)* to make (a dress) || *vr* to be manufactured, to be made (up).

confederație [konfede'ratsie] *nf* (con)federation, union.

conferențiar [konferentsi'ar] *nm* speaker, lecturer; *(invitat)* guestspeaker; *(grad univ.)* associate professor.

conferi [konfe'ri] *vt* to award, to confer, to grant || *vi* **a ~ (asupra)** to consult together; *(a discuta cu cineva despre ceva)* to talk with smb over smth.

conferință [konfe'rintsə] *nf (discurs)* speech, lecture; *(consfătuire)* conference, meeting.

confesiune [konfesi'une] *nf (mărturisire)* confession, admission; *relig* denomination, faith, religion.

confident [konfi'dent] *nm* confidant, confidential friend || *adj* trusting, trustful; *(d. fire)* confident, optimistic.

confidențial [konfidentsi'al] *adj* confidential, secret || *adv* confidentially, privately, in confidence; **strict ~** in strict confidence; *(d. un document)* top secret.

configurație [konfigu'ratsie] *nf (d. calculatoare)* configuration, outline, form.

confirma [konfir'ma] *vt (și o rezervare, ordin)* to confirm, to establish; *(a întări)* to strengthen; *(a adeveri)* to corroborate; to acknowledge || *vr* to be confirmed, to be established; *(d. știri)* to prove to be true • **~re** *nf (also relig)* confirmation; *(d. știri)* corroboration; *(de primire)* acknowledgement.

confisca [konfis'ka] *vt* to confiscate, to seize, to forfeit.

conflict [kon'flikt] *nn* conflict, struggle, strife, clash.

conform [kon'form] *adj* concordant, true, consistent (with); ~ **cu originalul** certified (true) copy || *prep* ~ **cu** *(în acord cu)* in accordance/keeping/agreement with, in compliance with; *(în virtutea)* by virtue of, on the strength of.

conforma [konfor'ma] *vr* to conform, to comply with, to abide by.

conformist [konfor'mist] *nm* conformist, conventionalist || *adj* conformist, conventional, time-serving.

confort [kon'fort] *nn* comfort, convenience(s) • **~abil** *adj* comfortable; *coll* comfy, snug, cozy || *adv* comfortably, snugly, cozily.

confrate [kon'frate] *nm* colleague, fellow member.

confrunta [konfrun'ta] *vt* to confront, to contrast; to compare; *(d. manuscrise)* to collate || *vr* to confront each other; to confront an opponent.

confunda [konfun'da] *vt* to mix up, to mistake for || *vr* to be mixed; *(d. interese)* to merge, to be identical; *(cu)* to be apt to be confused with; *(a fi identic)* to be identical (with); to be indistinct.

confuz [kon'fuz] *adj (amestecat)* confused, mixed; *(nedeslușit)* dim, blurred, vague, hazy; muddled; *(rușinat)* abashed, ashamed, embarrassed; *(uimit)* perplexed, bewildered || *adv* confusedly, dimly, vaguely

confuzie [kon'fuzie] *nf* confusion; (*dezordine*) disorder, jumble; (*a spiritului*) distraction, perplexity; (*eroare*) mistake, misunderstanding, error.

congela [kondje'la] *vt* to freeze, to deep-freeze; to congeal ‖ *vr* to freeze • ~**tor** *nn* deep-freeze, freezer.

congestie [kon'djestie] *nf med* congestion; ~ **cerebrală** stroke.

congestiona [kondjestio'na] *vt* to congest; (*circulația*) to jam, to block ‖ *vr* to be(come) congested; (*la față*) to turn red in the face, to flush.

conglomerat [konglome'rat] *nn geol, econ* conglomerate; *fig* mixture, congeries.

congolez [kongo'lez] *adj* Congolese ‖ *nm* native/inhabitant of the Congo, Congolese.

congregație [kongre'gatsie] *nf relig* congregation, brotherhood, community; *hist* The Congregation (under the French Restoration).

congres [kon'gres] *nn* congress, convention, conference; **membru al ~ului** congressman.

coniac [ko'niak] *nn* cognac, brandy.

conic ['konik] *adj* conic, conical; *tech* coned, tapering, cone-shaped.

conifer [koni'fer] *nn* conifer, coniferous tree ‖ *adj* coniferous.

conjuga [konzhu'ga] *vt gram* to conjugate; *fig* to combine, to unite ‖ *vr* to be conjugated.

conjugal [konzhu'gal] *adj* conjugal, married; **viață ~ă** married life.

conjunctură [konzhunk'tură] *nf* situation, circumstances, juncture.

conjuncție [kon'zhunktsie] *nf gram* conjunction.

conlucra [konlu'kra] *vi* to cooperate with, to collaborate, to concur (in); (*a contribui la*) to contribute (to).

conopidă [kono'pidă] *nf bot* cauliflower.

conotație [kono'tatsie] *nf* connotation.

consacra [konsa'kra] *vt* (*a consfinți*) to sanction, to establish; (*a dedica*) to devote (to), (*also relig*) to dedicate ‖ *vr* to devote oneself to, to devote one's time/abilities to.

consătean [konsă'tean] *nm* countryman; *pl* fellow villagers • ~**ă** *nf* woman living in the same village.

consecință [konse'chintsă] *nf* consequence; (*rezultat*) result, outcome; **în ~** in consequence, consequently, (*deci*) therefore, as a result

consecutiv [konseku'tiv] *adj* consecutive, running ‖ *adv* consecutively, in succession, running; **două zile ~** two days running/in a row.

consecvent [konsek'vent] *adj* consistent, steadfast ‖ *adv* consistently, steadfastly.

consemna [konsem'na] *vt* (*bani*) to deposit; (*a înregistra*) to register, to write down, to record; *mil* to confine; (*un elev*) to keep after hours, to keep in ‖ *vr* (*d. bani*) to be deposited; (*un fapt*) to write down, to record.

consens [kon'sens] *nn* consensus; accord, agreement, concord.

conserva [konser'va] *vt* (*fructe*) to preserve, to can, to tin; (*a păstra*) to keep ‖ *vr* to be preserved • ~**re** *nf* preserving, preservation; conservation, conserving • ~**tor** *nn mus* school/academy of music, conservatoire, conservatory.

conservă [kon'servă] *nf* preserve, preserved food; (*cutie*) tinned food, canned food.

consfătuire [konsfătu'ire] *nf* (*conferință*) conference;

(*întrunire*) meeting; (*dezbatere*) discussion, debate; (*deliberare*) deliberation.

considera [konside'ra] *vt* (*a cerceta atent*) to consider; (*a cumpăni*) to weigh/balance (in one's mind); to examine; (*a crede*) to think, to deem, to ponder (upon); (*a privi*) to look upon, to regard ‖ *vr* (*a se socoti*) to consider/hold oneself • ~**bil** *adj* considerable, significant, great; (*substanțial*) appreciable; important; (*mare*) large; (*întins*) extensive ‖ *adv* considerably, significantly, very much.

consignație [konsig'natsie] *nf* antique shop; (*cu obiecte de calitate inferioară*) junk shop; consignment.

consilier [konsili'er] *nm* (*sfătuitor*) counselor, adviser, consultant.

consiliu [kon'siliu] *nn adm* board, council, committee; ~ **de administrație** board of directors; ~ **de Securitate** Security Council.

consimțământ [konsimtsă'mânt] *nn* agreement; (*aprobare*) approval, consent, acquiescence.

consimți [konsim'tsi] *vt* to accept ‖ *vi* to consent (to), to give one's consent; (*a fi de acord*) to agree (to), to approve of.

consistent [konsis'tent] *adj* firm, solid; dense, thick; (*hrănitor*) nourishing, rich, substantial.

consoană [kon'soană] *nf ling* consonant.

consoartă [kon'soartă] *nf* wife, spouse; *coll* the missis/ missus; *hum* the better half.

consola [konso'la] *vt* to comfort, to give comfort to ‖ *vr* to console oneself (with), to find comfort in.

consolă [kon'solă] *nf archit* console, bracket; (*la cămin*) mantelpiece; (*mobilă*) pier table.

consolida [konsoli'da] *vt* (*also fig*) to consolidate, to strengthen, to reinforce; to brace; to put on a solid basis; *com* (*o datorie*) to fund ‖ *vr* to be consolidated/strengthened/reinforced; (*a se întări*) to grow firm.

consorțiu [kon'sortsiu] *nn econ* consortium, syndicate, corporation.

conspecta [konspek'ta] *vt* to summarize, to make a summary/abstract of.

conspira [konspi'ra] *vi* to plot, to conspire (against) • ~**tiv** *adj* conspiring, conspiratorial; (*tainic*) secret; illegal, clandestine, underground ‖ *adv* secretly; illegally • ~**ție** *nf* conspiracy, plot; **a urzi o ~** to hatch a plot.

consta [kons'ta] *vi* (*din*) to consist of, to be made up of; (*în*) to consist in, to lie in.

constant [kon'stant] *adj* (*statornic*) constant, steadfast; (*neschimbat*) unchanging, invariable ‖ *adv* constantly, invariably.

constata [konsta'ta] *vt* (*a descoperi*) to find, to see; (*a stabili*) to establish, to ascertain; (*a nota*) to note; (*a înregistra*) to record, to state ‖ *vr* to be found.

constelație [konste'latsie] *nf* constellation.

consternat [konster'nat] *adj* (*îngrozit*) horrified, dismayed; (*uluit*) amazed, astounded, dumbfounded; *coll* flummoxed, flabbergasted; perplexed.

constipat [konsti'pat] *adj med* constipated, costive; *coll fig* narrow-minded; *fig* (*ursuz*) sullen, morose; (*acru*) crabbed, sour(-tempered).

constipație [konsti'patsie] *nf med* constipation, costiveness.

constitui [konstitu'i] *vt* to constitute; to form, to make/set up; (*a fi*) to be; (*a reprezenta*) to represent; (*a fi considerat*) to be considered as, to be looked upon as; (*a înființa*) to set up, to establish || *vr* to be formed, to be made up, to be set up.

constituție[1] [konsti'tutsie] *nf pol* constitution.

constituție[2] [konsti'tutsie] *nf* constitution, structure, build, frame.

constrânge [kon'strândje] *vt* (*a forța*) to force, to compel; (*a sili*) to constrain, to oblige; *jur* to coerce • **~re** *nf* compulsion; (*morală*) constraint, restraint; (*obligație*) obligation; (*restricție*) restriction; *jur* coercion.

constructor [kons'truktor] *nm* builder, constructor.

construcție [kons'truktsie] *nf also fig* construction, structure; (*cladire*) building; (*construire*) construction; *gram* structure.

construi [konstru'i] *vt* (*a face*) to make; (*o casă*) to build; (*a înălța*) to erect, to raise; (*un oraș*) to found; (*un drum*) to lay out; (*o teorie*) to put together; *gram* to frame (a sentence); *math* to construct; (*a desena*) to draw; *fig* to build up; to form || *vr* to be made/built/erected, etc || *vi* to build.

consul ['konsul] *nm* consul.

consulta [konsul'ta] *vt* (*o persoană, o lucrare*) to consult; (*a întreba*) to ask || *vr* to confer, to consult each other • **~nt** *nm* (*care dă sfaturi*) counselor, adviser, consultant; (*care cere sfaturi*) consulter || *adj* consulting • **~nță** *nf* consultancy, (expert/specialized) advice • **~ție** *nf med* consultation, medical advice; (*sfat*) advice; *jur* (legal) opinion.

consum [kon'sum] *nn* consumption.

consuma [konsu'ma] *vt* to consume; (*a mânca*) to eat; (*a devora*) to devour; (*a bea*) to drink; (*a coroda*) to eat away, to corrode; (*a distruge*) to destroy; (*a epuiza*) to exhaust, to wear out; (*d. puteri: a istovi*) to drain; (*a folosi*) to use; (*a risipi*) to waste; (*d. energie*) to consume || *vr* to be consumed/eaten; *fig* to fret, to waste/pine away; (*a se istovi*) to exhaust oneself.

conștient [konshti'ent] *adj* (*de*) aware (of); *also med* conscious (of) || *adv* consciously.

conștiincios [konshtiin'chos] *adj* conscientious, thorough, scrupulous || *adv* conscientiously, thoroughly, scrupulously.

conștiinciozitate [konshtiinchiozi'tate] *nf* conscientiousness, thoroughness, scrupulousness.

conștiință [konshti'intsă] *nf* (*stare conștientă*) awareness, consciousness; (*etică*) conscience; ~ **de sine** self-awareness; **problemă de** ~ matter of conscience.

cont [kont] *nn com* account; ~ **personal** personal account; ~ **de active** assets account; ~ **bancar** bank account; ~ **curent** checking account; ~ **creditor** account payable; ~ **debitor** account receivable; *fig* account, consideration.

conta [kon'ta] *vi* (*a se bizui pe*) to count (on), to rely (on), to depend (on); (*a avea importanță*) to count, to matter.

contabil [kon'tabil] *nm* accountant, bookkeeper || *adj* bookkeeping • **~itate** *nf* bookkeeping, accounting.

contact [kon'takt] *nn* contact, touch; (*legătură*) connection; *auto* ignition; *elec* connection, contact.

contagios [kontadji'os] *adj* contagious, catching, infectious.

container [kon'tainer] *nn* container.

contamina [kontami'na] *vt* to contaminate, to infect; (*d. apă*) to pollute || *vr* to become contaminated • **~re** *nf* contamination, pollution, contagion; *ling* contamination.

conte ['konte] *nm* count; (*în Anglia*) earl.

contempla [kontem'pla] *vt* to contemplate, to gaze at.

contemporan [kontempo'ran] *nm* contemporary || *adj* (*actual*) contemporary, present-day • **lumea ~ă** today's world; (*cu*) contemporaneous with.

conteni [konte'ni] *vt/vi* to cease, to stop.

contesta [kontes'ta] *vt* to dispute, to contest, to challenge; *pol* to protest • **~ție** *nf jur* appeal; (*legal*) contest/dispute, complaint.

context [kon'tekst] *nn* context.

continent [konti'nent] *nn* continent.

contingent [kontin'djent] *nn* contingent.

continua [kontinu'a] *vt* to continue, to carry on, to keep (on); (*a relua*) to resume || *vi* to continue, to go/carry on; (*a dura*) to last || *vr* to be continued.

continuitate [kontinui'tate] *nf* continuity.

continuu [kon'tinuu] *adj* continuous, permanent, uninterrupted; (*repetat*) continual || *adv* continuously, permanently, continually.

contondent [konton'dent] *adj* blunt.

contopi [konto'pi] *vt* to blend, to fuse, to melt || *vr* to merge, to blend, to melt into each other; (*a fi una*) to become one.

contor [kon'tor] *nn* meter, counter.

contorsiona [kontorsio'na] *vt* to contort (one's body/face) || *vr* to contort, to writhe.

contra ['kontra] *adj* counter, negative || *adv* counter || *prep* (*împotriva*) against, contrary to, in opposition to; *jur, sp* versus, vs; (*în schimbul*) in exchange for.

contraatac ['kontraa'tak] *nn mil* counterattack.

contrabalansa ['kontrabalan'sa] *vt* to counterbalance, to compensate, to set off; (*a contracara*) to counteract.

contrabandă [kontra'bandă] *nf* (*acțiunea*) smuggling, contraband; (*de băuturi alcoolice*) bootlegging; (*de arme*) gunrunning; (*marfă*) contraband/smuggled goods.

contrabandist [kontraban'dist] *nm* smuggler; (*de băuturi alcoolice*) bootlegger.

contrabas [kontra'bas] *nn mus* double bass, contrabass.

contracara [kontraka'ra] *vt* to counteract; (*a zădărnici*) to cross, to thwart, to oppose.

contract [kon'trakt] *nn com, jur* contract, agreement, deed.

contracta [kontrak'ta] *vt com* (*un împrumut*) to contract; (*o datorie*) to incur; (*un obicei*) to develop, to acquire; (*o boală*) to catch; (*mușchii*) to tense || *vr* to be contracted; to be incurred, to be developed, to be acquired; to be caught; (*d. mușchi*) to contract, to tense up.

contradictoriu [kontradik'toriu] *adj* contradictory; (*d. știri*) conflicting || *adv* **în ~** contradictorily.

contradicție [kontra'diktsie] *nf* contradiction; opposition; contrariness.

contraface [kontra'fache] *vt* to counterfeit, to forge; (*a imita*) to imitate.

contraindicație ['kontraindi'katsie] *nf med* contra-/counter-indication.

contramanda [kontraman'da] *vt* to call off; to cancel; (*un ordin*) to countermand; (*un contract*) to revoke.

contraofensivă [kontraofen'sivă] *nf* counteroffensive.

contrapunct [kontra'punkt] *nn mus* counterpoint.

contrar [kon'trar] *adj* contrary; (*opus*) opposite; (*potrivnic*) adverse; (*deosebit*) different; (*invers*) reverse, **în caz** ~ otherwise, or; (*dacă nu*) if not; **în**

sens ~ in the opposite direction || *prep* contrary to; (*împotriva*) against; (*în ciuda*) despite, in spite of • **~ul** *nm* the contrary.

contrarevoluție ['kontrarevo'lutsie] *nf* counterrevolution.

contraria [kontrari'a] *vt* to vex, to irritate, to upset, to annoy; *coll* to put out.

contraspionaj ['kontraspio'nazh] *nn* counterespionage.

contrast [kon'trast] *nn* contrast; **în ~ cu** in contrast with/to, unlike smth, in contradiction/opposition to.

contrasta [kontras'ta] *vt* to contrast, to put/set smth in contrast || *vi* (*cu*) to contrast with/to, to stand in contrast with/to.

contravenient [kontraveni'ent] *nm* offender, trespasser || *adj* contravening.

contravenție [kontra'ventsie] *nf* contravention, trespass, infringement, (minor) offense.

contrazice [kontra'ziche] *vt* to contradict; *fig* to belie, to refute; (*ceva*) to be contrary to || *vr* to contradict oneself; (*reciproc*) to contradict each other; (*a se afla în contradicție*) to be contradictory/conflicting.

contribuabil [kontribu'abil] *nm* taxpayer.

contribui [kontribu'i] *vi* (*la*) to contribute (to), to be instrumental in (doing smth).

contribuție [kontri'butsie] *nf* contribution; (*rol*) part, role; (*participare*) participation; (*parte*) portion; (*bănească*) share, quota; *fin* (*impozit*) tax, rate, duty.

control [kon'trol] *nn* control; (*verificare*) checking, check-up, verification; (*inspecție*) inspection; (*examinare*) examination; (*supraveghere*) supervision, control; (*cenzură*) censorship; (*la obiecte prețioase*) hallmark; *fin* auditing • **~or** *nm* controller; (*de bilete*) ticket collector; *fin* auditor; *avia* (*de zbor*) flight controller.

controla [kontro'la] *vt* (*o activitate*) to control, to supervise; (*bilete*) to check; *fin* to audit; (*a examina*) to examine; (*a verifica*) to verify, to check up; (*a domina*) to master || *vr* to control oneself.

controversă [kontro'versă] *nf* controversy, disputation; (*chestiune controversată*) matter in dispute/point at issue.

contur [kon'tur] *nn* outline, contour; (*linii*) lines; (*margine*) edge; (*formă*) form.

contura [kontu'ra] *vt* to outline, to sketch || *vr* (*a apărea*) to appear, to come into view; (*clar, pe un fond*) to stand out; (*neclar*) to loom.

contuzie [kon'tuzie] *nf* contusion, bruise.

conține [kon'tsine] *vt* to contain, to include; (*concret*) to hold; (*a fi alcătuit din*) to be composed of, to be made up of.

conținut [kontsi'nut] *nn* content; (*capacitate*) capacity; volume; (*fond*) contents, matter, substance; subject matter; (*semnificație*) significance; (*tablă de materii*) (table of) contents.

convalescență [konvales'chentsă] *nf* convalescence.

convenabil [konve'nabil] *adj* convenient, suitable, fit; (*d. prețuri*) affordable, cheap; fair; (*d. salarii*) adequate; (*mulțumitor*) satisfactory, acceptable || *adv* conveniently, suitably; affordably, cheaply, fairly; adequately.

conveni [konve'ni] *vi* (*asupra*) to agree (up)on/about; (*a fi convenabil*) to be convenient/suitable, to fit; to be agreeable to; **îi convine** it suits him; **dacă îți convine** if that is agreeable to you, if that is OK with you • **~ența** *nf* convenience, suitability; **căsătorie de**

~ marriage of convenience; (*bună cuviință*) decency, decorum; *pl* social conventions, etiquette, proprieties.

convenție [kon'ventsie] *nf* convention; (*înțelegere*) agreement; *pol* convention, assembly.

conversa [konver'sa] *vi* (*cu*) to talk (with smb); to converse (with); *coll* to chat • **~ție** *nf* talk, conversation; chat.

converti [konver'ti] *vt* (*a preface în*) to convert smth into, to change; *com* to convert; *also relig* to convert to a faith/point of view; (*a aduce la vederile sale*) to win over (to one's opinions) || *vr* to become converted.

conviețui [konvietsu'i] *vi* to live together; (*d. un cuplu*) to cohabit

convinge [kon'vindje] *vt* to convince, to persuade || *vr* to make sure, to see for oneself • **~re** *nf* (*credință*) conviction, belief; (*acțiune*) persuasion; *pl* principles; **cu ~** with conviction; (*ferm*) firmly; (*cu entuziasm*) with enthusiasm, enthusiastically; **fără ~** halfheartedly, without enthusiasm.

convoca [konvo'ka] *vt* to summon, to convene; to invite smb (to an interview); to call.

convoi [konvo'i] *nn* convoy, caravan, train; procession; ~ **de mașini** motorcade.

convorbire [konvor'bire] *nf* talk, conversation; (*telefonică*) telephone call; ~ **cu taxă inversă** collect call; ~ **interurbană** long-distance call.

convulsi(un)e [konvulsi'une] *nf med* convulsion, spasm, contraction; *pol* upheaval.

coopera [koope'ra] *vi* to cooperate; (*a contribui*) to contribute (to); (*a participa*) to participate in • **~re** *nf* cooperation, participation • **~tor** *nm* cooperator, cooperative farmer || *adj* cooperative, cooperating.

coopta [koop'ta] *vt* to co-opt.

coordona [koordo'na] *vt* to coordinate.

copac [ko'pak] *nm* tree.

copcă ['kopkă] *nf* clasp, hook; (*cataramă*) belt buckle; *med* wound clip.

copertă [ko'pertă] *nf* cover.

copia [kopi'a] *vt* (*a transcrie*) to write out, to copy out; (*pe curat*) to make a clean/fair copy; (*a imita*) to ape, to imitate; to reproduce; (*a mima*) to mimic; (*a plagia*) to plagiarize; (*a contraface*) to forge, to counterfeit; (*muzică, pe film*) to dub (off); (*d. calculatoare, pe dischetă, pe hard*) to copy, to back up; *scol* to crib || *vi* to crib.

copie ['kopie] *nf* (*reproducere exactă*) copy, transcription; ~ **a unui document** duplicate; ~ **autentificată** certified copy; ~ **calculator, pe hârtie** printout; ~ **pe dischetă** diskcopy; (*transcriere*) transcript; (*imitație*) imitation; *typ* copy; (*a unei statui*) replica.

copil [ko'pil] *nm* child; *coll* kid, little one; (*mic*) infant, baby; (*pici*) brat, urchin; (*urmaș*) descendant, offspring; (*fiu*) boy, son; (*fiică*) girl, daughter; (*produs al minții*) brainchild, baby • **~aș** *nm* baby, babe; *coll* kiddy • **~ă** *nf* (little) girl; (*fiică*) daughter • **~ăresc** *adj* (*de copil*) child's, children's, childlike; childish; infantile; naïve • **~ăros** *adj* childish; *fig* foolish • **~ări** *vi* to spend one's childhood || *vr* to behave childishly • **~ărie** *nf* (*vârstă*) childhood, girlhood, boyhood, infancy; (*comportare*) childishness.

copilot [kopi'lot] *nm* copilot.

copios [kopi'os] *adj* abundant, plentiful, rich; (*d. mâncare*) sumptuous, copious; *coll* square || *adv* abundantly, plentifully, etc.

copist [ko'pist] *nm* clerk; copyist, transcriber.

copită [ko'pită] *nf* hoof.

copleşi [kople'shi] *vt* to overwhelm, to overcome, to overpower.

copoi [ko'poi] *nm* greyhound, bloodhound; *fig also pol* sleuthhound; *(poliţist) coll* cop.

copt [kopt] *nn* maturation, ripening; *(la cuptor)* baking || *adj* ripe, mature; *(pârguit)* mellow; *(dezvoltat)* fully developed/grown; *(în cuptor)* baked; *fig* mature, ripe.

copulaţie [kopu'latsie] *nf* copulation.

cor [kor] *nn (în ~)* in chorus; **toţi în ~!** all together! *(ansamblu)* choir.

corabie [ko'rabie] *nf* ship, vessel, sailing boat/ship.

coral[1] [ko'ral] *adj* choral || *nn* choral (song).

coral[2] [ko'ral] *nm (mărgean)* coral; **recif de ~** coral reef.

corb [korb] *nm orn* raven; *fig* vulture, bird of prey.

corcitură [korchi'tură] *nf bio* crossbreed, hybrid; *coll* cross; *(javră) also fig* mongrel.

corcoduşă [korko'dushă] *nf* wax cherry.

cord [kord] *nn anat* heart; **transplant de ~** heart transplant.

cordial [kordi'al] *adj* cordial, hearty, heartfelt; sincere, true; *(amabil)* kindl(y) || *adv* cordially, kindly, wholeheartedly • **~itate** *nf* cordiality, heartiness, warmth.

cordon [kor'don] *nn* girdle, belt; *(şnur)* flex(ible cord), cord, string; *(panglică a unui ordin)* ribbon of an order; *med* cord, cordon; **~ ombilical** umbilical cord.

corect [ko'rekt] *adj (fără greşeli)* correct, faultless; exact, accurate; *(ireproşabil)* proper, impeccable; *(cinstit)* fair, just, honest || *adv* correctly, accurately, etc.

corecta [korek'ta] *vt* to correct, to amend; *(a îndrepta)* to rectify, to improve; *(şpalturi)* to revise, to read (proofs); *(extemporale)* to grade, to correct; *typ* to proofread; *(ziare, reviste)* to sub-edit, to sub; *naut, mil* to adjust || *vr* to grow better, to improve; *(în comportare)* to mend (one's ways); *(în vorbire)* to correct oneself.

corectitudine [korekti'tudine] *nf* correctness; **~ politică** political correctness (PC); *(cinste)* uprightness, honesty.

corector [korek'tor] *nm* corrector; *scol* examiner; *typ* proofreader || *nn tech* corrector; *(la calculator)* (spell/grammar) check.

corectură [korek'tură] *nf typ* proofreading.

coreean, -ă [kore'ean(ă)] *nm/nf/adj* Korean.

coregraf [kore'graf] *nm* choreographer • **~ie** *nf* choreography.

corela [kore'la] *vt* to correlate, to link || *vi* to be correlated/linked.

coresponda [korespon'da] *vi* to correspond with, to write to, to be in correspondence with.

corespondent [korespondent] *nm* correspondent; *(la ziar)* reporter, correspondent, contributor; **~ local** local correspondent || *adj* corresponding.

corespondenţă [korespon'dentsă] *nf* correspondence; *(poştă)* mail; *(la ziar)* report; *(potrivire)* agreement, conformity; **prin ~** by correspondence.

corespunde [kores'punde] *vi* to correspond to/with, to agree with, to tally with, to fit, to square with.

corespunzător [korespunză'tor] *adj (potrivit)* adequate, suitable; *(conform)* corresponding to, according to; **în mod ~** adequately || *adv* accordingly.

coriandru [kori'andru] *nm bot* coriander.

coridor [kori'dor] *nn* corridor, passage, hall.

corija [kori'zha] *vt* to correct, to improve || *vr* to mend (one's ways); * **corecta**.

cormoran [kormo'ran] *nm orn* cormorant.

corn[1] [korn] *nn* horn; *(de cerb)* antler; *(de vânătoare)* hunting horn, bugle; *(specialitate de patiserie)* croissant, roll; *(de plug)* plough tail/handle; *mus* (French) horn.

corn[2] [korn] *nm bot* cornel tree.

cornee [kor'nee] *nf anat* cornea, corneous tunic.

cornet [kor'net] *nn* cornet; **~ acustic** ear trumpet.

coroană [ko'roană] *nf (cunună)* wreath, garland; *(regală) also fig* crown; *(ducală)* coronet; *(monedă)* crown; *bot* corona; *(a unui pom)* top crown of a tree.

corobora [korobo'ra] *vt* to corroborate, to confirm.

coroda [koro'da] *vt tech, chem* to corrode, to erode, to eat/wear away.

coroiat [koro'iat] *adj (d. nas)* hooked, aquiline.

corolă [ko'rolă] *nf bot* corolla.

coronarian [koronari'an] *adj anat* coronary.

coroziune [korozi'une] *nf* corrosion.

corp [korp] *nn (trup)* body; **~ de balet** corps de ballet; *geom.* solid (body/figure); *lit (~ ceresc)* celestial/heavenly body • **~ul omenesc** human body; *(cadavru)* dead body, corpse; *(de animal)* carcass; *mil, pol* corps; *typ (literă)* size of type; group.

corpolent [korpo'lent] *adj* corpulent, fat, portly.

corporal [korpo'ral] *adj (trupesc)* bodily; *(d. pedepse)* corporal.

corporaţie [korpo'ratsie] *nf* corporation; *hist* (trade) guild.

corsaj [kor'sazh] *nn* bodice.

corset [kor'set] *nn* corset, stays.

cort [kort] *nn* tent; *(mare)* marquee, pavilion.

cortegiu [kor'tedju] *nn* convoy, train, retinue; *(procesiune)* procession.

cortină [kor'tină] *nf* curtain; *(laterală)* tab.

corupe [ko'rupe] *vt* to corrupt; to deprave; to pervert; *(a vicia)* to defile, to taint; to seduce; *(a mitui)* to bribe; *(martori)* to suborn || *vr* to be(come) corrupted, etc.

corupţie [ko'ruptsie] *nf* corruption, depravity; *(influenţă negativă) fig* ulcer.

corvoadă [kor'voadă] *nf hist* corvee, forced/statute labor; *mil* fatigue (duty); *fig* chore, drudgery, irksome task/job; **ce ~!** what a drag/bind!.

cosaş [ko'sash] *nm* mower, reaper; *ento* grasshopper.

cosi [ko'si] *vt* to mow, to cut (with a scythe), to reap; *fig* to mow down, to destroy, to kill || *vr* to be mown, to be cut, to be reaped.

cositor[1] [kosi'tor] *nn* tin.

cositor[2] [kosi'tor] *nm* * **cosaş**.

cosmetică [kos'metikă] *nf* cosmetics; beauty parlor/salon.

cosmeticiană [kosmetichi'ană] *nf* cosmetician, beautician.

cosmic ['kosmik] *adj* cosmic, space; **spaţiu ~** (outer) space.

cosmonaut [kosmona'ut] *nm* spaceman, astronaut, cosmonaut.

cosmopolit [kosmopo'lit] *nm* cosmopolitan, cosmopolite || *adj* cosmopolitan.

cosmos ['kosmos] *nn* cosmos, outerspace.

cost [kost] *nn* cost; *(preţ)* price; *(valoare)* value • **~a** *vt* to cost || *vi* to cost; *(a valora)* to be worth.

costisitor [kostisi'tor] *adj* expensive, dear, costly.

costiță [kos'titsă] *nf* chop; bacon.

costum [kos'tum] *nn* (*bărbătesc*) suit (of clothes); (*de damă*) (woman's) suit/costume; (*îmbrăcăminte*) costume, dress.

coș¹ [kosh] *nn* basket; (*pt. mâncare*) hamper; *sp* basket; (*horn*) stovepipe, chimney, stack, funnel.

coș² [kosh] *nn* (*bubuliță*) pimple; (*negru*) blackhead; acne.

coșar [ko'shar] *nm* chimney sweep(er).

coșciug [koshchug] *nn* casket.

coșcovi [koshko'vi] *vr* (*d. tencuială*) to come off; (*a se scoroji*) to shrink; (*a se umfla*) to swell (out); (*a se coji*) to peel off.

coșmar [kosh'mar] *nn* nightmare.

cot [kot] *nm* (*măsură*) ell || *nn anat* elbow; (*ghiont*) nudge, jab; (*cotitură*) bend, curve, turn; ~ **la** ~ shoulder to shoulder.

cota [ko'ta] *vt* to quote, to rate, to consider • ~**re** *nf* quotation, rating • ~**ție** *nf fin* quotation, quoting.

cotă ['kotă] *nf* (*parte*) share, portion, quota; (*contribuție*) contribution; *fin* quotation; *geog* height, elevation, altitude; *mil* hill; (*la curse*) odds; (*a unei cărți*) press mark.

cotcodăci [kotkodă'chi] *vi* also *fig* to cackle, to chatter.

coteț [ko'tets] *nn* (*de păsări*) hen/chicken coop; (*de porci*) pigsty; (*de câine*) (dog) kennel; (*pt. porumbei*) dovecot.

coti [ko'ti] *vi* to turn right/left, to turn to; (*d. râuri*) to meander.

cotidian [kotidi'an] *nn* daily (paper) || *adj* daily, everyday.

cotitură [koti'tură] *nf* turn(ing); (*a unui râu*) bend, curve, meander; *fig* turning point; (*schimbare*) sudden change; (*criză*) crisis.

cotiza [koti'za] *vi* to pay one's (membership) dues • ~**ție** *nf* dues; (*la un club*) subscription; (*parte*) quota, share.

cotlet [kot'let] *nn* chop, cutlet.

cotlon [kot'lon] *nn* (*ascunzătoare*) hiding place, nook, recess; (*ungher*) corner; (*bârlog*) den, lair; (*firidă*) niche.

cotoi [ko'toi] *nm* tomcat, male cat.

cotonogi [kotono'dji] *vt coll* to thrash, to beat (black and blue), to drub; to pound into a jelly.

cotor [ko'tor] *nn* (*ciot*) stub, tab; *bot* stalk, stem; (*de chitanțier*) counterfoil; (*de carte*) spine; (*băț, coadă*) stick.

cotoroanță [koto'roantsă] *nf* hag, old woman/witch; *coll* old crock/jade.

cotrobăi [kotroba'i] *vt* to rummage, to ransack || *vi* to fumble (in, about), to rummage (in, about).

cotropi [kotro'pi] *vt* (*a invada*) to invade, to overrun; (*a ocupa*) to occupy, to take possession of; (*a cuceri*) to conquer.

coțofană [kotso'fană] *nf orn* magpie.

covârși [kovâr'shi] *vt* (*a copleși*) to overwhelm, to overcome; (*a înfrânge*) to defeat, to overpower; (*a întrece*) to surpass, to get the better of • ~**tor** *adj* overwhelming.

covor [ko'vor] *nn* carpet; (*carpetă*) rug • ~**ul fermecat** the magic carpet.

covrig [ko'vrig] *nm* pretzel, ring-shaped biscuit; *fig* coil.

cowboy ['kauboi] *nm* cowboy.

cozonac [kozo'nak] *nm* sponge cake.

cozoroc [kozo'rok] *nn* (cap) peak; visor.

crab [krab] *nm zool* crab.

crah [krah] *nn* (financial) crash, bankruptcy, failure.

crai [krai] *nm* (*împărat*) emperor; (*rege*) king; (*om desfrânat*) rake, philanderer, wanton.

crainic ['krainik] *nm* (radio) announcer, broadcaster; *hist* herald, town crier.

cramă ['kramă] *nf* wine cellar.

crampă ['krampă] *nf med* cramp, spasm, convulsion.

crampon [kram'pon] *nn* cramp (iron); (*cârlig*) hook; (*la bocanci*) cleat, calk; (*pt. fotbal*) stud; *fig* cling • ~**a** *vr* (*de*) to cling to, to hang on to.

craniu ['kraniu] *nn anat* cranium, skull, brain pan.

crap [krap] *nm icht* carp.

cras [kras] *adj* crass, gross • **ignoranță ~ă** crass/gross ignorance.

crater ['krater] *nn* crater.

cratiță ['kratitsă] *nf* saucepan.

craul [kraul] *nn sp* crawl.

cravașă [kra'vashă] *nf* horse whip.

cravată [kra'vată] *nf* (neck)tie; (*la lupte*) headlock.

Crăciun [kră'chun] *nn* Christmas, X-mas; **Moș** ~ Father Christmas, Santa (Claus).

crăpa [kră'pa] *vt* (*a despica*) to crack, to split, to cleave; (*cu toporul*) to chop; (*ușa*) to open slightly, to half open; (*a mânca*) *pej coll* to wolf down, to gorge, to guzzle || *vi* (*a despica*) to crack, to split, to cleave; (*a sparge*) to burst, to break; (*a muri*) *pej* to die; *sl* to croak, to peg out; (*a mânca*) *pej coll* to (stuff and) gorge || *vr* to crack; (*d. piele*) to be chapped.

crăpătură [krăpă'tură] *nf* crack, split; (*a pielii*) chap; (*în metal*) flaw; (*în zid*) cranny; (*scurgere*) leak; (*a unui automat*) slot; (*lunguiață*) slit; (*a ușii*) chink; (*deschizătură îngustă*) narrow opening; *fig* breach, leak.

crâcni [krâk'ni] *vi* to protest, to grumble.

crâmpei [krâm'pei] *nn* fragment.

crâncen ['krânchen] *adj* terrible, grim, dreadful; (*aprig*) fiery; (*feroce*) ferocious || *adv* terribly, grimly, etc.

crâng [krâng] *nn* grove; (*desiș*) thicket.

crea [kre'a] *vt* to create, to bring into life/existence; to make, to produce; to invent, to devise; (*a întemeia*) to set up, to found, to create; (*a stârni*) to create, to arouse, to bring about || *vi* to create || *vr* to be created, to be set up • ~**tor** *nm* creator; author; (*fondator*) founder || *adj* creative • ~**tură** *nf* creature; (*persoană*) person, individual; (*ființă*) being • ~**ție** *nf* creation.

creangă ['kreangă] *nf* branch, bough; (*parte dintr-o creangă*) twig.

creastă ['kreastă] *nf* (*la păsări*) crest, comb; (*moț*) tuft; (*de munte*) crest, ridge; (*de val*) crest.

crede ['krede] *vt* (*a considera*) to think, to consider; (*a da crezare*) to believe (in), to give credence to; (*a-și închipui*) to imagine || *vi* (*a se considera*) to consider/think oneself; (*a fi îngâmfat*) to be conceited; *imp* **se** ~ people think that || *vi* to believe in, to have faith in.

credincios [kredin'chos] *nm* believer || *adj* (*care are o credință*) believing, faithful, pious; (*loial*) loyal, devoted; (*cinstit*) honest; (*de nădejde*) reliable.

credință [kre'dintsă] *nf* (*religioasă*) faith, belief; (*confesiune*) denomination; (*convingere*) conviction; (*părere*) opinion, view; (*loialitate*) loyalty, faithfulness; (*încredere*) trust, faith, confidence; **de bună ~** in good faith, well-meaning; **de rea ~** ill-meaning/-intentioned.

credit ['kredit] *nn fin also fig* credit; (*împrumut*) loan; *fig* influence, repute; (*prestigiu*) prestige • **~or** *nm* creditor • **~a** *vt* to credit.

credo ['kredo] *nn* credo, creed.

credul [kre'dul] *adj* credulous, gullible • **~itate** *nf* credulity, credulousness, gullibility.

creier ['kreier] *nm anat* brain, cerebrum; *cul* brains; *fig* (*minte*) brains, mind, intelligence; (*rațiune*) reason; (*judecată*) judgment; (*al unui proiect*) mastermind • **~ul mic** little brain, cerebellum;.

creion [kre'ion] *nn* pencil.

crem [krem] *adj* cream-colored.

crematoriu [krema'toriu] *nn* crematory, crematorium.

cremă ['kremă] *nf* cream; *fig* flower; pick; **~ de față** cold cream; **~ hidratantă** moisturizing cream; **~ de ras** shaving cream; **~ de ghete** shoe polish.

cremene ['kremene] *nf* flint, quartz.

crenvurșt ['krenvursht] *nm* frankfurter.

creol [kre'ol] *nm/adj* Creole.

crepuscul [kre'puskul] *nn* twilight, dusk, crepuscle.

crescător [kreskă'tor] *nm* breeder ‖ *adj* growing • **~ie** *nf* nursery, farm.

creson [kre'son] *nn bot* garden/town cress(es).

cresta [kres'ta] *vt* to dent, to indent, to notch; (*a tăia*) to cut.

creșă ['kreshă] *nf* day care, nursery.

crește ['kreshte] *vt* (*d. copii*) to bring up, to raise, to educate; (*a pregăti*) to train; (*d. animale*) to breed, to rear; (*d. plante*) to grow, to cultivate ‖ *vi* to grow; (*d. copii*) to grow up; (*a spori*) to increase; (*a se dezvolta*) to develop, to mature; (*a se ridica*) to rise; (*a se umfla*) *also fig* to swell • **~re** *nf* growth, (*sporire*) increase; (*dezvoltare*) rise, development; (*a animalelor*) breeding, raising; (*educație*) upbringing, education; (*a apelor*) rising, tide; **bună ~** good breeding, good manners; **în~** growing, on the increase.

creștet ['kreshtet] *nn* crown, top; head.

creștin [kresh'tin] *nm/adj* Christian • **~a** *vt* to christianize ‖ *vr* to become (a) Christian • **~ism** *nn* Christianity.

cretă ['kretă] *nf* chalk.

cretin [kre'tin] *nm* idiot, moron, cretin, imbecile, dolt.

creț [krets] *nn* (*cârlionț*) lock; (*păr creț*) curly hair, crimp; (*cută*) crease, pleat; (*rid*) wrinkle ‖ *adj* (*d. păr*) curly, frizzy; (*d. cineva*) curly-haired; (*plisat*) pleated.

crevasă [kre'vasă] *nf* crevasse, crevice.

crevetă [kre'vetă] *nf* shrimp.

crez [krez] *nn* creed, credo.

cric [krik] *nn tech* jack(screw), winch, windlass.

crimă ['krimă] *nf* crime; *jur* felony, criminal offense; (*asasinat*) murder, homicide.

criminal [krimi'nal] *nm* criminal, murderer; felon ‖ *adj* criminal; murderous ‖ *adv* criminally.

crin [krin] *nm bot* lily.

criogenie [kriodje'nie] *nf tech* cryogenics.

criptă ['kriptă] *nf* vault, tomb, crypt.

criptic ['kriptik] *adj* cryptic(al), abstruse, esoteric, obscure.

crisalidă [krisa'lidă] *nf ento* chrysalis, pupa.

crispa [kris'pa] *vt* to contract, (*fața*) to screw up; (*pumnii*) to clench (fists) ‖ *vr* to contract.

cristal [kris'tal] *nn* crystal • **~in** [krista'lin] *nn* crystalline lens ‖ *adj* crystal clear, (as) clear as crystal.

cristaliza [kristali'za] *vt/vr* to crystallize; *fig* to materialize.

criteriu [kri'teriu] *nn* criterion, *pl* -ria

critic ['kritik] *nm* critic ‖ *adj* critical; (*hotărâtor*) crucial, decisive; (*dificil*) difficult; *coll* ticklish ‖ *adv* critically • **~a** *vt* to criticize; *also fig* to censure, to find fault with; (*a defăima*) to defame • **~ă** *nf* criticism; (*literară*) critique; (*criticii*) the critics.

crizantemă [krizan'temă] *nf bot* chrysanthemum.

criză ['kriză] *nf* crisis; (*economică*) crisis, depression, slump; (*lipsă*) shortage; *med* attack, fit.

croat [kro'at] *nm* Croat ‖ *adj* Croatian.

croazieră [kroazi'eră] *nf* cruise, trip.

crocant [kro'kant] *adj* crisp, crunchy.

crochet [kro'ket] *nn sp* croquet.

crocodil [kroko'dil] *nm zool* crocodile; *elec* crocodile clip.

croi [kro'i] *vt* to cut (to measure), to cut out; (*a plănui*) to plan, to devise; (*a deschide*) to open, to lay open; (*a bate*) to strike, to lash, (*cu palma*) to slap • **~tor** *nm* tailor; *ento* Capricorn beetle • **~toreasă** *nf* dressmaker, seamstress.

crom [krom] *nn phys* chrome, chromium.

cromozom [kromo'zom] *nm bio* chromosome.

croncăni [kroncă'ni] *vt/vi* (*also fig*) to croak, to caw.

cronic ['kronik] *adj* chronic ‖ *adv* chronically.

cronicar [kroni'kar] *nm* (*istoric*) chronicler; (*ziarist*) columnist, commentator, reporter.

cronică ['kronikă] *nf* chronicle; (*de ziar*) news, report, column; (*literară*) book review.

cronologic [krono'lodjik] *adj* chronological ‖ *adv* chronologically.

cronometra [kronome'tra] *vt* to time.

cronometru [krono'metru] *nn* chronometer; **cursă contra ~** timed race.

cros [kros] *nn sp* cross-country race/run(ning).

crosă ['krosă] *nf sp* hockey stick; golf club.

croșeta [kroshe'ta] *vt/vi* to crochet.

croșetă [kro'shetă] *nf* crochet, hooked needle.

cruce ['kruche] *nf* cross; (*intersecție*) intersection, crossing, crossroads; **în ~** crossways, crosswise • **~a** Roșie the Red Cross.

cruci [kru'chi] *vr* to cross oneself, to make the sign of the cross; *fig* to be dumbfounded, to be struck dumb.

cruciadă [kruchi'adă] *nf* crusade.

crucial [kruchi'al] *adj* crucial, decisive.

crucifix [kruchi'fiks] *nn* crucifix.

cruciș [kru'chish] *adj* (*d. ochi*) squint(ing), squint-eyed; *coll* boss-eyed; (*d. drumuri*) crossing ‖ *adv* crossways, crosswise; (*oblic*) slantwise, slantways, aslant; **a se uita ~** to squint; to be squint-eyed.

crucișător [kruchishă'tor] *nn naut* battleship, cruiser.

crud [krud] *adj* (*neprelucrat*) raw; (*nefiert*) raw, uncooked; (*necopt*) *also coll* green; *fig* immature, callow, young; (*nemilos*) cruel, brutal, violent; (*sălbatic*) savage ‖ *adv* cruelly, brutally, violently, savagely.

crunt [krunt] *adj* (*crud*) cruel, savage, brutal, grim; (*sângeros*) bloody; (*aspru*) bitter; (*groaznic*) awful, dreadful, terrible ‖ *adv* cruelly, savagely, etc.

crupă ['krupă] *nf* (*a calului*) croup(e), crupper.

crupe ['krupe] *nf pl* groats, grits.

crupier [krupi'er] *nm* (*la bursă*) broker's backer; (*la cazino*) croupier.

crustaceu [krusta'cheu] *nn zool* crustacean, shellfish.

crustă ['krusta] *nf* crust; (*de rac*) mail.

cruţa [kru'tsa] *vt* to spare, to have mercy on smb ‖ *vr* to spare oneself; not to overburden oneself.

cruzime [kru'zime] *nf* cruelty, brutality.

ctitor ['ktitor] *nm* founder • ~**ie** *nf* foundation.

cu [ku] *prep* (*asociere, instrumentul*) with; **te-am văzut** ~ **el** I saw you with him; (*şi*) and; **pâine** ~ **unt** bread and butter; (*d. îmbrăcăminte*) in; **îmbrăcată** ~ **o rochie albă** dressed in a white frock; (*posesia*) with; **o fată** ~ **ochi albaştri** a girl with blue eyes, a blue-eyed girl; (*conţinutul*) of, with; **o ceaşcă** ~ **ceai** a cup of tea; (*modul*) with; ~ **grijă** with care, carefully; (*durata*) for; ~ **anii** for years (on end); (*raportul, proporţia*) by; ~ **miile** by the thousands; (*concesiv*) with, in spite of, despite.

cuantifica [kuantifi'ka] *vt* to quantify; *phys* to quantize.

cuarţ [kuarts] *nn* quartz.

cub [kub] *nn* cube; (*jucărie*) (toy) brick ‖ *adj* cubic.

cubanez, -ă [kuba'nez(ă)] *nm/nf/adj* Cuban.

cubic ['kubik] *adj* cubic; **zahăr** ~ lump of sugar.

cuc [kuk] *nm orn* cuckoo.

cuceri [kuche'ri] (*o ţară*) to conquer; (*a supune*) to subdue, to subjugate; *fig* to captivate; (*pe cineva*) to make a conquest of; (*inima cuiva*) to win; (*de partea sa*) to win over; (*a obţine*) to gain; (*a dobândi*) to obtain.

cucernic [ku'chernik] *adj* pious, devout ‖ *adv* piously, devoutly.

cucoană [ku'koană] *nf* lady; (*vocativ*) madam, ma'am; *coll* (*soţie*) spouse, wife.

cucui [ku'kui] *nn* bump.

cucurigu [kuku'rigu] *interj* cock-a-doodle-doo!.

cucută [ku'kută] *nf bot* hemlock.

cucuvaie [kuku'vaie] *nf orn* (little) owl.

cufăr ['kufăr] *nn* chest, trunk, box.

cufunda [kufun'da] *vt also fig* (*în*) to sink (into), to plunge (into) ‖ *vr* to sink (into), to plunge (into), to duck; (*d. submarine*) to submerge, to dive; *fig* to be plunged/absorbed/buried in; * **scufunda**.

cugeta [kudje'ta] *vi* to think (over), to ponder/brood (over).

cugetător [kudjetă'tor] *nm* thinker; **liber** ~ free thinker.

cui [kui] *nn* nail.

cuib [kuib] *nn* nest; *fig* (*casă*) home, house; (*ascunzătoare*) den; *agr* hole; (*de insecte*) nidus, *pl* -di; (*de viespi*) hornets nest.

cuibări [kuibă'ri] *vi* (*d. păsări*) to nest ‖ *vr fig* to nestle.

cuier [ku'ier] *nn* (hat/coat) peg; (*mobilă*) hallstand.

culca [kul'ka] *vt* (*în pat*) to put to bed; (*a aşeza jos*) to lay down, to put down; (*a trânti*) to knock down; (*a doborî arbori*) to fell, to hew down; (*a ucide*) to kill ‖ *vr* to go to bed; *coll* to turn in; (*a se întinde*) to lie down; **a se** ~ **cu cineva** to sleep with smb • ~**re** *nf* going to bed, turning in; **a merge la** ~ to go to bed.

culcuş [kul'kush] *nn* bed; (*adăpost*) shelter.

culegător [kulegă'tor] *nm* collector; *typ* typesetter, compositor; *agr* reaper.

culege [ku'ledje] *vt* (*a aduna*) to gather, to collect; (*flori, fructe*) to pick up, to cull; (*d. recoltă*) to reap, to harvest; (*d. informaţii*) to collect, to glean; *typ* to typeset ‖ *vr* to be gathered, etc.

culinar [kuli'nar] *adj* culinary.

culise [ku'lise] *nf pl thea* wings, backstage; *fig* **în** ~ behind the scenes; **de** ~ backstairs.

culme ['kulme] *nf* summit, top, peak; *fig* climax, highest point, acme • **asta-i** ~**a!** *coll* that beats everything/the devil!, that's the limit!, that crowns it all!.

culminant [kulmi'nant] *adj* culminating, highest, climactic; **punct** ~ culminating/highest point, climax.

culoar [ku'lwar] *nn* passage, corridor; *sp* lane.

culoare [ku'lware] *nf* color, tint; (*nuanţă*) shade, hue; (*vopsea*) paint, dye; (*la cărţi*) suit; (*la pocher*) straight flush.

culpabil [kul'pabil] *adj* guilty.

culpă ['kulpă] *nf* guilt.

cult[1] [kult] *nn relig* cult, creed; (*religie*) religion; *fig* worship.

cult[2] [kult] *adj* (well-)educated, cultured, well-read.

cultiva [kulti'va] *vt also fig* to cultivate; (*pământul*) to farm, to till; (*cereale*) to raise, to grow; (*a dezvolta*) to develop; (*mintea*) to improve ‖ *vr* to improve/ broaden one's mind; to educate oneself • ~**tor** *nm* farmer, grower, cultivator ‖ *nn* cultivator.

cultură [kul'tura] *nf* culture, education; *agr* crop; (*cultivare*) cultivation, growing; (*creştere*) breeding, rearing; *bio* (*de bacterii*) colony.

cum [kum] *adv* (*ref. la verb*) how; ~ **o mai duci?** how are you?; (*poftim?*) I beg your pardon?, (*zău?*) really?; (*ref. la subst.*) what ... like; ~ **e noul profesor?** how is the new teacher like?; ~ **te cheamă?** what is your name? ‖ *conj* (*completivă*) how; **nu ştiu** ~ **să încep** I don't know how to begin; (*deoarece*) as, since, because; ~ **nu era gata am plecat fără el** as he was not ready we left without him; (*precum*) as; **fă** ~ **îţi spun** do as I tell you; (*în timp ce*) as, while; ~ ... **şi** no sooner ... than, hardly ... when ‖ *interj* why; what.

cuminte [ku'minte] *adj* (*liniştit*) quiet; (*ascultător*) good, obedient, dutiful; (*rezonabil*) wise, sensible, reasonable; (*precaut*) cautious; chaste; **a fi** ~ to behave oneself, to stay out of trouble ‖ *adv* (*liniştit*) quietly; (*ascultător*) obediently; (*rezonabil*) wisely, sensibly.

cumnat [kum'nat] *nm* brother-in-law • ~**ă** *nf* sister-in-law.

cumpănă ['kumpănă] *nf* (*echilibru*) balance, poise; (*de fântână*) sweep; (*pt. găleţi*) yoke; *fig* moderation, discretion; (*încercare*) ordeal; (*ezitare*) hesitation.

cumpăni [kumpă'ni] *vt* (*a cântări*) to weigh; (*a balansa*) to balance; *also fig* to consider, to weigh, to ponder.

cumpăra [kumpă'ra] *vt* to buy, to purchase; (*a mitui*) to bribe, to buy off; (*martori*) to suborn ‖ *vr* to be bought • ~**re** *nf* buying, purchasing; (*mituire*) bribing; (*a martorilor*) subornation.

cumpărător [kumpără'tor] *nm* buyer, purchaser; (*client*) customer; *jur* vendee.

cumpăt ['kumpăt] *nn* balance, equilibrium, poise • ~**are** *nf* temperance, moderation, sobriety.

cumplit [kum'plit] *adj* ferocious, cruel, grim, terrible ‖ *adv* ferociously, cruelly, terribly.

cumsecade [kumse'kade] *adj* (*d. oameni*) decent, honest, amiable; (*d. lucruri*) fit, proper, suitable ‖ *adv* decently, properly.

cumva [kum'va] *adv* (*oarecum*) somehow, anyhow; (*poate*) perhaps, maybe; by chance/accident.

cunoaşte [ku'noashte] *vt* to know, to be aware of; (*a fi familiarizat cu*) to be acquainted with, to be familiar/ conversant with; (*a fi versat în*) to be versed in; (*a trece prin*) to experience, to witness || *vr* to meet, to be acquainted; (*a se observa*) to be seen, to be perceptible/ noticeable • **~re** *nf* knowledge; *phil* cognition; **~ de sine** self-knowledge; *jur* cognizance.

cunoscător [kunoskă'tor] *nm* expert, connoisseur || *adj* expert (in), experienced (in), versed (in).

cunoscut [kunos'kut] *nm* acquaintance || *adj* (well)-known, renowned; acquainted; (*d. figură*) familiar.

cunoştinţă [kunosh'tintsă] *nf* (*persoană*) acquaintance; (*cunoaştere*) knowledge; *jur* cognizance; (*conştienţă*) consciousness; **a fi fără ~** to be unconscious.

cununa [kunu'na] *vt* (*a fi naşi*) to be godfather/godmother/godparents to; to wed, to marry || *vr* to wed, to marry.

cununie [kunu'nie] *nf* wedding, marriage ceremony.

cupă[1] ['kupă] *nf* cup, bowl, goblet; *relig* chalice; *tech* bucket; *bot* crown.

cupă[2] ['kupă] *nf* (*la cărţi*) hearts.

cupla [ku'pla] *vt tech* to couple.

cuplu ['kuplu] *nn* couple, pair.

cupolă [ku'polă] *nf* cupola, *archit* dome.

cupon [ku'pon] *nn* coupon; (*de stofă*) remnant.

cuprinde [ku'prinde] *vt* to include, to comprise, to contain; to involve; (*a copleşi*) to overwhelm, to overcome; (*a îmbrăţişa*) to embrace; (*a cuceri*) to overrun, to occupy; (*cu privirea*) to see, to take in || *vr* (*în*) to be included in, to be comprised in.

cuprins [ku'prins] *nn* (*conţinut*) content(s); (*tablă de materii*) table of contents; (*suprafaţă*) surface, area; (*întindere*) extent, stretch; (*al apelor*) expanse; (*regiune*) part(s), region || *adj* comprised, included; *fig* seized.

cupru ['kupru] *nn* copper.

cuptor [kup'tor] *nn* oven; *tech* furnace; (*de var*) kiln; (*cantitatea de pâine*) batch; *fig* heat; (*iulie*) *vernac* July.

curabil [ku'rabil] *adj med* curable.

curaj [ku'razh] *nn* courage, valor; nerve, pluck; **a prinde ~** to take courage/heart; *interj* cheer up!, buck up! • **a-şi pierde ~ul** to lose courage/heart • **~os** *adj* courageous, brave || *adv* courageously, bravely.

curat [ku'rat] *adj* clean; (*îngrijit*) tidy, neat; (*fără amestec*) pure; (*nediluat*) straight, neat; (*senin*) clear; (*proaspăt*) fresh; (*veritabil*) genuine; net; pure; (*cinstit*) honest, frank, fair; (*neprihănit*) chaste, immaculate; (*impecabil*) faultless; (*simplu, complet*) sheer, downright; *fig* (*deschis*) open; (*lămurit*) distinct || *adv* (*îngrijit*) neatly; (*cinstit*) honestly.

cură ['kură] *nf* cure, course of treatment; **~ de slăbire** slimming cure, diet.

curăţa [kură'tsa] *vt* to clean; (*a spăla*) to scour, to rinse; (*cu peria*) to brush; (*a freca*) to scrub; (*îmbrăcămintea*) to launder; (*de ceva*) to clear; (*a decoji*) to peel; (*d. mazăre*) to shell, to pod; (*d. pomi*) to prune, to trim; *coll* (*de bani*) to fleece, to skin; *coll* (*a omorî*) to do for; (*a elibera*) to clear; (*de duşmani*) to mop up || *vr* to clean, to wash, to brush oneself; to trim up; *coll* (*de bani*) to be ruined, to be cleaned out; (*a se debarasa*) to get rid of.

curăţătorie [kurătsăto'rie] *nf* (dry-cleaning) laundry, dry cleaner's.

curăţenie [kură'tsenie] *nf* cleanliness; (*îngrijire*) neat-

ness; (*puritate*) purity; clarity, clearness; (*acţiunea*) cleaning; *med* purge, purgative.

curând [ku'rând] *adv* soon (afterwards), before long; (*îndată*) at once, immediately; (*repede*) quickly; **pe ~** see you soon; (*mai degrabă*) rather, sooner; **de ~** recently, of late, lately.

curba [kur'ba] *vt* to curve, to bend.

curbă ['kurbă] *nf* curve; (*viraj*) turn, bend.

curcan [kur'kan] *nm orn* turkey (cock); *sl* (*poliţist*) cop; *hist* footslogger.

curcă ['kurkă] *nf orn* turkey hen.

curcubeu [kurku'beu] *nn* rainbow.

curea [ku'rea] *nf* (*cordon*) belt; (*de ceas*) strap; (*de atârnat*) strap, thong, sling.

curent [ku'rent] *nm* stream, current, flow; (*d. aer*) *met* air current, draft; *elec* current || *nn* current; *fig* trend, tendency || *adj* current; **opinie ~ă** current opinion; fluent; (*d. cheltuieli, preţuri*) running; (*obişnuit*) customary; (*d. lună*) instant, present, current || *adv* (*obişnuit*) currently, usually, generally; fluently.

curenta [kuren'ta] *vt* to shock; to produce an electric shock || *vr* to get a shock.

curgător [kurgă'tor] *adj* (*d. apă*) running, flowing; (*d. vorbire*) fluent || *adv* fluently.

curge ['kurdje] *vi* to flow, to run; (*d. un recipient*) to leak; (*a picura*) to drip; (*d. nas*) to run; (*d. sunete*) to flow; (*d. timp*) to pass (by), to elapse; (*repede*) to fly.

curier [kuri'er] *nm* messenger, courier; (*corespondenţă*) mail; (*la radio*) listener's letter box.

curios [kuri'os] *nm* a nosy person, snoop; (*voaior*) Peeping Tom || *adj* curious; (*băgăreţ*) inquisitive; (*ciudat*) strange, odd, peculiar; (*neobişnuit*) uncommon; (*rar*) rare; original || *adv* curiously, inquisitively, strangely, oddly, etc.

curiozitate [kuriozi'tate] *nf* curiosity, interest; (*exagerată*) inquisitiveness; *coll* nosiness; (*obiect*) curio; (*ciudăţenie*) oddity, peculiarity; **de/din ~** out of curiosity.

curma [kur'ma] *vt* (*a întrerupe*) to interrupt, to break off; (*a înceta*) to cease; (*a sfârşi*) to end; (*a opri*) to stop, to put an end to; to break; **a ~ tăcerea** to break the silence.

curmal [kur'mal] *nm bot* date tree/palm • **~ă** *nf* date.

curmeziş [kurme'zish] *adv* across, crosswise; **în ~** crossways; **de-a ~** across.

curs[1] [kurs] *nn* (*de apă*) flow, course; current, stream; (*al gândurilor*) train; (*desfăşurare*) course; (*al povestirii*) thread; (*direcţie*) trend; (*d. timp*) lapse, duration; *fin* rate of exchange; ; **în ~** under way; **~ de apă** river/water course • **~ul evenimentelor** the course of events • **în ~ul** during, in the course of.

curs[2] [kurs] *nn* (*prelegere*) lecture; (*serie de lecţii*) course of lectures; (*manual*) textbook.

cursă[1] ['kursă] *nf auto* ride; *naut* cruise, voyage; *rail* local (train); *sp* (*întrecere*) race, racing; (*drum*) run; (*însărcinare*) errand; *tech* motion, stroke.

cursă[2] ['kursă] *nf* (*capcană*) trap, snare; *also fig* pitfall.

cursiv [kur'siv] *adj* (*d. scriere*) cursive, running; (*d. vorbire*) fluent; *typ* italic || *adv* cursively, fluently.

cursor [kur'sor] *nn* slider, cursor.

curta [kur'ta] *vt* to court, to pay court to, to woo.

curte ['kurte] *nf* (*palat*) court; (*a casei*) yard, courtyard; (*pătrată*) quad(rangle); *jur* tribunal; (*atenţie acordată cuiva*) courting, courtship; **a face ~ cuiva**

to court smb, to pay court to smb; *fig* to curry favor with smb.
curtean [kur'tean] *nm* courtier.
curtenitor [kurteni'tor] *adj* courteous; (*politicos*) polite || *adv* courteously, politely.
curtezană [kurte'zană] *nf hist* courtesan.
curtoazie [kurtoa'zie] *nf* courtesy, courteousness.
curvă ['kurvă] *nf* whore, hooker, streetwalker, tart, trollop.
cusătoreasă [kusăto'reasă] *nf* seamstress.
cusătură [kusă'tură] *nf* (*la haină*) seam; (*cusut*) sewing; *tech* joint, junction, *metal* seam.
custode [kus'tode] *nm* caretaker, custodian; (*d. muzeu*) curator.
custodie [kusto'die] *nf* custody.
cusur [ku'sur] *nn* defect, shortcoming, flaw; **fără ~** perfect, faultless, flawless • **~giu** *nm* fault-finder || *adj* picky, choosy, fastidious.
cuşcă ['kushkă] *nf* (*pt. animale*) cage; (*de câine*) kennel; (*de găini*) coop; (*pt. suflor*) prompter's box.
cuşetă [ku'shetă] *nf rail* couchette, berth; *naut* bunk.
cutare [ku'tare] *pron* so and so || *adj* (this or) that, such and such.
cută ['kuta] *nf* (*pliu*) fold, pleat; (*rid*) wrinkle.
cuteza [kute'za] *vt/vi* to dare, to venture.
cutezător [kutezǎ'tor] *adj* daring, bold, audacious || *adv* daringly, boldly, fearlessly.
cutie [ku'tie] *nf* box; **~ de chibrituri** box of matches; **~ de scrisori** letter box; **~ poştală** postbox; *tech* **~ de viteze** gear box.
cutră ['kutră] *nf* double-dealer, weathercock.
cutreiera [kutreie'ra] *vt/vi* to wander, to scour, to travel all over; *coll* to knock about.
cutremur [ku'tremur] *nn* earthquake.
cutremura [kutremu'ra] *vr* to tremble, to shiver, to shake; (*a se înfiora*) to shudder.
cutremurător [kutremură'tor] *adj* awful, terrible; (*mişcător*) moving, touching, breathtaking.
cutumă [ku'tumă] *nf* common law.
cutumiar [kutumi'ar] *adj jur* common/customary law.
cuţit [ku'tsit] *nn* knife; (*bisturiu*) lancet, bistoury.
cuvă ['kuvă] *nf* tub, vat.
cuvânt [ku'vânt] *nn* word; (*discurs*) speech, address, (*la şedinţă*) floor; reason, motive; (*promisiune*) promise; (*părere*) opinion; *pl* (*ceartă*) quarrel; (*învăţătură*) teaching; (*sfat*) advice; **~ cu ~** word for word • **~are** *nf* speech; (*scurtă*) address.
cuveni [kuve'ni] *vr* **a se ~ sa** to be fit(ting); ought to; **a i se ~** to be one's due, to deserve.
cuvertură [kuver'tură] *nf* coverlet, bedspread, counterpane.
cuviincios [kuviin'chos] *adj* decent, decorous; (*cum se cuvine*) proper, becoming; (*politicos*) polite, civil || *adv* decently, decorously, etc.
cuviinţă [kuvi'intsă] *nf* decency, decorum, propriety.
cuvios [kuvi'os] *adj* pious, devout.
cvadrimotor [kvadrimo'tor] *nn avia* four-engined aircraft.
cvartet [kvar'tet] *nn* quartet.
cvasi ['kvasi] *adv* quasi.
cvintet [kvin'tet] *nn* quintet.
cvorum ['kvorum] *nn jur* quorum.

D

da[1] [da] *vt* to give, to offer, (*a înmâna*) to hand (over); (*a dărui*) to present smb with smth; (*a acorda*) to grant, to award, to confer; (*a furniza*) to supply smth for/to smb, to provide, to deliver; (*a plăti*) to give, to pay (for); to yield, to produce || *vi* (*a lovi*) to strike, to hit; (*înspre*) to open out on, to look out on.
da[2] [da] *adv* yes; **~ or ba?** yes or no?; **ba ~** oh, yes, of course; **cred că ~** I think so || *interj* really?, is that so?.
dac [dak] *nm/adj* Dacian.
dacă ['dakă] *conj* (*în prop. completive*) if, whether; (*când*) when; (*în prop. condiţ.*) if, in case, suppose, supposing, provided (that).
dactilografă [daktilo'grafă] *nf* typist.
dactilografie [daktilogra'fie] *nf* typewriting.
dafin ['dafin] *nm bot* daphne, laurel, bay (tree).
dală ['dală] *nf* flagstone, paving stone, flooring tile.
dalie ['dalie] *nf bot* dahlia.
daltă ['daltă] *nf* chisel.
damă ['damă] *nf* (*doamnă*) iron lady; *sl* (*cocotă*) broad, tart; (*la şah, cărţi*) queen; *pl* (*joc*) checkers, (game of) draughts.
damigeană [dami'djeană] *nf* demijohn.
damnat [dam'nat] *adj/nm* damned.
dană ['dană] *nf naut* berth, anchoring place, wharf.
dandana [danda'na] *nf* (*tărăboi*) hubbub, racket; (*belea*) mess, scrape.
danez [da'nez] *nm* Dane || *adj* Danish • **~ă** *nf* Dane, Danish woman; Danish, the Danish language.
dangăt ['dangăt] *nn* ring/peal of bells, chime, toll, (*de înmormântare*) (funeral) knell.
dans [dans] *nn* dance; (*ca acţiune*) dancing; *coll* hop.
dansa [dan'sa] *vi* to dance; *coll* to hop; (*d. un vas pe apă*) to bob (up and down) on the water || *vt* to dance • **~toare** *nf* dancer; (*balerină*) ballerina, ballet dancer; (*de varieteu*) chorus girl • **~tor** *nm* dancer; (*balerin*) ballet dancer.
dantelă [dan'telă] *nf* lace; (*lucrătură*) fancy work; *fig* tracery.
dantură [dan'tură] *nf* (set of) teeth; **~ falsă** denture(s).
dar[1] [dar] *nn* (*cadou*) gift, present; (*talent*) gift; **în ~** as a present; (*obicei*) habit • **are ~ul beţiei** he likes a drink or two, he is fond of the bottle.
dar[2] [dar] *conj* but; **~ ce să vezi?** but guess what?; (*pe când*) while; (*şi totuşi*) and yet, still, however.
darămite ['dărămite] *adv* more than that, besides, to say nothing of, let alone.
darnic ['darnik] *adj* liberal, generous, open-handed; *fig* fruitful, fertile, rich.
dascăl ['daskăl] *nm* (*profesor*) teacher, schoolmaster; (*învăţat*) scholar; *relig* psalm reader.
dat [dat] *nn* (*acţiune*) giving, * **da**; (*obicei*) custom, habit; destiny; (*element*) donnee, datum || *adj* given.
data [da'ta] *vt* to date || *vi* **a ~ din** to date back to, to go back (to), to come from.
dată]'dată] *nf* date, day; **ce ~ e azi?** what's the date today?; (*oară*) time; **de data asta** this time; (*noţiune*) donnee, datum, *pl* data; *pl* (*fapte*) data, facts.
datină ['datină] *nf* custom, tradition.
dativ [da'tiv] *nn gram* dative.
dator [da'tor] *adj* (*faţă de*) indebted (to); **a fi ~** to be in debt; *fig* (*obligat*) obliged (to), under an obligation to.

datora [dato'ra] *vt* to owe ‖ *vr* to be due (to smb) • **~t** *adj* (*d. bani*) owed; (*cuvenit*) due.

datorie [dato'rie] *nf* (*de bani*) debt; *pl* liabilities; credit; *fig* (*morală și*) duty, obligation, responsibility.

datorită [dato'rită] *prep* (*din cauza*) because of, owing to, on account of; (*mulțumită*) thanks to.

datornic [da'tornik] *nm* debtor, person in debt.

daună ['daună] *nf* (*pagubă*) damage, havoc, ravages; *fig* (*prejudiciu*) harm, prejudice; *pl* (*despăgubiri*) damages, compensation.

dădacă [dă'dakă] *nf* dry nurse, nanny, nurse/nursery maid.

dăinui [dăinu'i] *vi* to last, to endure; (*a continua*) to continue, to go on.

dăltui [dăltu'i] *vt* to chisel, to carve out; *fig* to mold, to fashion.

dărăpăna [dărăpă'na] *vr* to deteriorate, to fall/go to ruin, to fall into decay/disrepair, to ruin.

dărăpănătură [dărăpănă'tură] *nf* ramshackle/tumble-down/dilapidated old house

dărâma [dără'ma] *vt* (*d. clădiri*) to demolish, to pull down; (*d. mecanism*) to dismantle; (*a distruge*) to destroy, to shatter; *fig* to crush, to overpower.

dărnicie [dărni'chie] *nf* generosity, lavishness; (*abundență*) plenty, abundance; **cu** ~ generously, lavishly, bountifully.

dărui [dăru'i] *vt* to give smth as a present, to make smb a present of; (*cu generozitate*) to lavish; (*a înzestra*) *also fig* to gift, to endow smb with ‖ *vr* to devote oneself to, to dedicate oneself to • **~re** *nf* offering, presenting; * **dărui**; (*abnegație*) ~ **de sine** abnegation, self-denial/-sacrifice; (*pasiune*) dedication.

dăscăli [dăskă'li] *vt obs* (*a face morală*) to lecture, to scold, to reprimand; to teach, to instruct, to coach (in a subject).

dăuna [dău'na] *vi* to harm, to injure, to damage; to prejudice.

dăunător [dăună'tor] *nm agr* pest ‖ *adj* injurious (to), harmful, detrimental, prejudicial; **caracter** ~ harmfulness, (ob)noxiousness.

dâmb [dâmb] *nn* hill(ock), elevation (of the ground), mound.

dânsa ['dânsa] *pron f* she.

dânsele, dânșii ['dânsele, dânshii] *pron f, m, pl* they.

dânsul ['dânsul] *pron m* he.

dâră ['dâră] *nf* (*urmă*) trail, track; (*fâșie*) streak; (*semn*) mark; (*în apă, a unei corăbii*) wake; (*vânătoare*) scent; *fig* trace.

dârdâi [dârdâ'i] *vi* to tremble, to shiver; (*d. dinți*) to chatter.

dârz [dârz] *adj* (*ferm*) firm, steadfast, unflinching; (*încăpățânat*) obstinate, stubborn; (*curajos*) bold, courageous • **~enie** *nf* (*fermitate*) firmness, steadfastness; (*încăpățânare*) obstinacy, stubbornness; (*îndrăzneală*) daring, boldness.

de [de] *adv* so, as ‖ *prep* (*din*) of; **o casă** ~ **lemn** a wooden house; (*cu*) **un pahar** ~ **vin** a glass of wine; (*despre*) about, of, on; **vorbește-mi** ~ **el** tell me about him; (*de către*) by; **scris** ~ **Poe** written by Poe; (*de la*) from; (*timp de*) for; (*din cauza*) out of, for, from, with; **a plânge** ~ **bucurie** to weep with/for joy ‖ *conj* (*dacă*) if ‖ *interj* (*păi*) well!.

deal [deal] *nn* hill; (*înălțime*) elevation; eminence; height; **la** ~ uphill.

deasupra [dea'supra] *adv* above; (*peste*) over; **pe** ~ (*în*

plus) moreover, besides ‖ *prep* (*static*) above; **lampa era** ~ **mesei** the lamp was above the table; (*peste*, *implicând mișcare*) over.

debandadă [deban'dadă] *nf* disorder, confusion; *mil* rout.

debara [deba'ra] *nf* lumber room.

debarasa [debara'sa] *vt* (*de*) to relieve, to rid of ‖ *vr* (*de*) to get rid of, to free oneself from.

debarca [debar'ka] *vt* (*mărfuri*) to unload, to unship; (*pasageri*) to land, to disembark; (*din autobuz*) to set down; *fig* to dismiss; (*un guvern, o putere*) to overthrow ‖ *vi* (*de pe navă*) to land; (*din tren*) to get off • **~der** *nn* landing place/ stage, wharf; (*chei*) pier, jetty • **~re** *nf* landing, disembarkation, unshipping.

debil [de'bil] *nm* ~ **mintal** a mental defective ‖ *adj* mentally ill/retarded; non compos mentis; (*bolnăvicios*) sickly; (*plăpând*) feeble, weak(ly), delicate, frail.

debit ['debit] *nn* (*de apă*) flow, discharge; *fin* debit; (*chioșc*) newsstand, newsstall; (*de tutun*) tobacconist's (shop); *fig* gabble.

debloca [deblo'ka] *vt tech* to unblock, to unjam; *fin* to free, to relieve; (*a curăța*) to clear away; (*a concedia*) *mil* to discharge.

deborda [debor'da] *vt* (*d. ape*) to overflow; (*a vărsa*) to vomit, to throw up; *fig* to gush, to burst with • **~nt** *adj* overflowing, gushing, brimming over.

debușeu [debu'sheu] *nn* outlet, market.

debut [de'but] *nn* (*început*) beginning, debut, first appearance.

debuta [debu'ta] *vi* (*a începe*) to begin, to start; to make one's debut/first appearance.

debutant [debu'tant] *nm* beginner; debutant; *coll* deb; tyro • **~ă** *nf* beginner, debutante; *coll* deb.

decadă [de'kadă] *nf* (period of) ten days/years; (*deceniu*) decade.

decadență [deka'dentsă] *nf* decadence; decay; (*decrepitudine*) decline.

decalaj [deka'lazh] *nn* difference; *fig* discrepancy; (*rămânere în urmă*) lagging behind, gap; (*avans*) lead, headstart; ~ **orar** time difference.

decan [de'kan] *nm edu* dean; (*de vârstă*) senior, doyen.

decapita [dekapi'ta] *vt* to behead, to decapitate • **~re** *nf* beheading, decapitation.

decapotabil [dekapo'tabil] *adj auto* convertible.

decar [de'kar] *nm* (*la cărți*) ten.

decatlon [deka'tlon] *nn sp* decathlon.

decădea [dekă'dea] *vi* (*d. lucruri*) to decline, to (fall into) decay; (*d. clădiri*) to deteriorate, to fall/be out of repair; (*d. o persoană: a scăpăta*) to go down (in the world); to be ruined; (*moral*) to fall, to disgrace oneself.

decădere [dekă'dere] *nf* decline, decay; (*degradare*) debasement, degradation; (*corupere*) corruption.

decăzut [dekă'zut] *adj* degenerate, (*also fig*) debased; *fig* low-down, fallen, corrupt.

decât [de'kât] *adv comp* than; **e mai înalt** ~ **mine** he is taller than me; (*în afară de*) but; **nimeni altul** ~ **el** none/no other but he ‖ *conj* (rather) than, instead of; **râdea mai mult** ~ **plângea** he was laughing rather than crying; (*în prop. afirm.*) only; **nu mă ajuta** ~ **când îl rugam** he helped me only when I asked him.

deceda [deche'da] *vi* to decease, to die, to pass away; *coll* to kick the bucket • **~t** *adj/nm* deceased, dead, defunct.

decembrie [de'chembrie] *nm* December.

deceniu [de'cheniu] *nn* decade.

decent [de'chent] *adj* decent, decorous, proper ‖ *adv* decently, decorously, properly.

decență [de'chentsă] *nf* decency, decorum, propriety.

decepție [de'cheptsie] *nf* disappointment; *coll* let down.

decepționa [decheptsio'na] *vt* to disappoint, to let down.

decerna [decher'na] *vt* (*un premiu*) to award; (*un titlu*) to confer (on) • ~re *nf* award(ing) of prizes, prize giving.

deces [de'ches] *nn* death, demise.

deci ['dech] *conj* therefore, consequently, then, accordingly, hence.

decide [de'chide] *vt* to decide, to make/take a decision, to resolve; (*a stabili*) to settle, to fix; (*a convinge*) to persuade, to determine, to make, to cause ‖ *vi/vr* to decide, to determine, to resolve; to bring oneself to (do smth).

decima [dechi'ma] *vt* to decimate; (*în război*) to slaughter, to massacre; (*d. boli*) to waste, to decimate, to finish off.

decisiv [dechi'siv] *adj* (*d. voce*) decisive, ultimate, crucial; **rol** ~ decisive role.

decizie [de'chizie] *nf* (*hotărâre*) decision, resolution, determination; *jur* verdict, sentence.

declama [dekla'ma] *vt/vi* to recite, to declaim.

declanşa [deklan'sha] *vt* to initiate; (*un război, proteste*) to unleash; (*un atac*) to launch; (*focul*) to open; *tech* (*un mecanism*) to release, to set, to start; to set in motion; to activate, to trip; (*ceas deşteptător*) to set off; *fig* (*d. critici, întrebări*) to trigger ‖ *vr* (*d. război, epidemie*) to break out.

declara [dekla'ra] *vt* to declare, to state; (*a mărturisi*) to admit; (*d. impozite*) to enter; *jur* to pronounce; (*a înregistra*) to register ‖ *vr* to declare oneself; (*d. un proces, fenomen*) to break out, to start, to become manifest • ~ție *nf* declaration; (*oficială*) statement; (*proclamaţie*) proclamation; *jur* (*sub jurământ*) affidavit; (*de naştere, deces, domiciliu*) notification; (*din partea unei oficialităţi*) (important) announcement; ~ fiscală/de impozit tax return; ~ falsă perjury • **Declaraţia de Independenţă** Declaration of Independence.

declic [de'klik] *nm tech* (*care blochează un mecanism*) pawl, catch; (*care declanşează un mecanism*) trigger; (*zgomot*) click(ing) sound.

declin [de'klin] *nn* decline, declension; **a fi în** ~ to be on the decline/wane; (*al frumuseţii*) fading; (*al zilei*) close.

declina [dekli'na] *vt gram* to decline; (*a refuza*) to refuse ‖ *vr* to be declined.

decoda, decodifica [deko'da, dekodifi'ka] *vt* to decode.

decola [deko'la] *vi avia* to take off • ~re *nf* take-off.

decolonizare [dekoloni'zare] *nf* decolonization.

decolora [dekolo'ra] *vt* to discolor; (*a albi*) to bleach ‖ *vr* to lose color, to fade • ~t *adj* discolored, colorless; *fig* drab.

decoltat [dekol'tat] *adj* (*d. rochii*) low-necked, low-cut; (*d. femei*) bare-shouldered; *fig* high-kilted, blue; (*d. limbaj*) free, licentious; indecent, improper, indecorous.

decolteu [dekol'teu] *nn* décolletage, low-cut neck, neck-opening/line of dress.

deconcerta [dekoncher'ta] *vt* to disconcert, to put out of countenance, to confound.

deconecta [dekonek'ta] *vt tech* to disconnect ‖ *vr fig* to relax, to unwind.

decongela [dekondje'la] *vt* to thaw (out); (*d. congelator*) to defrost; (*d. alimente*) to defreeze.

decont [de'kont] *nn fin* reimbursement; discount, deduction; settlement • ~a *vt fin* to reimburse, to discount; to deduct • ~are *nf fin* discount, deduction, settlement.

decor [de'kor] *nn* (*teatru, natural*) scenery, décor; (*d. film*) **în ~ natural** on location; (*imprejurimi*) surroundings; (*fundal*) background; *fig* setting, background; decoration, ornament; (*înfrumuseţare*) embellishment; *archit* ornamental/decorative work

decora [deko'ra] *vt* (*a împodobi*) to decorate, to adorn; (*a ilumina*) to illuminate; *coll* to do up (a house); *mil* to decorate • ~tiv *adj* decorative, ornamental • ~tor *nm* (interior) decorator; *thea* scene/stage painter, stage designer; **pictor** ~ *nm* stage designer.

decoraţie [deko'ratsie] *nf* decoration, medal, award.

decrepit [dekre'pit] *adj* (*d. cineva*) decrepit, senile; (*d. casă, zid*) tumbledown, dilapidated.

decret [de'kret] *nn* decree, order, fiat • ~a *vt* to decree, to enact; (*a hotărî*) to decide, to ordain.

decupa [deku'pa] *vt* to cut out/up; (*d. metal*) to cut, to punch; to stamp out; (*d. piele*) to pink.

decupla [deku'pla] *vt* (*d. vagoane*) to uncouple; *telec* to decouple; to disconnect ‖ *vr* to be uncoupled/decoupled.

decurge [de'kurdje] (*a se desfăşura*) to happen, to unfold; (*din*) to follow, to ensue, to result (from).

decurs [de'kurs] *nn* (*curs*) course; lapse; (*durată*) duration; interval.

deda [de'da] *vr* (*a se dedica*) to dedicate oneself to; (*a se apuca de*) to set about to; to take to, to indulge in.

dedesubt [dede'subt] *adv* below, beneath, under, underneath; **vezi ~** see below ‖ *nn* (*partea de jos*) bottom • ~uri *fig only pl* unseen/covert/hush-hush details/facts.

dedica [dedi'ka] *vt* to dedicate; (*d. timp, viaţă*) to devote, to consecrate ‖ *vr* to devote oneself to.

deduce [de'duche] *vt* to infer, to deduce; (*a conchide*) to conclude, to gather.

deducţie [de'duktsie] *nf* deduction; inference; conclusion; **prin ~** by (way of) inference; deductively; inferentially.

defavorabil [defavo'rabil] *adj* unfavorable, detrimental, disadvantageous.

defăima [defăi'ma] *vt* to defame, to slander, to libel • ~re *nf* defamation, slander, libel.

defăimător [defăimă'tor] *nm* defamer, slanderer, libeler ‖ *adj* defamatory, slanderous, libelous ‖ *adv* slanderously.

defect [de'fekt] *nn* defect, imperfection; (*cusur*) deficiency, drawback, shortcoming; *also tech* flaw, fault; ~ **fizic** infirmity; deformity; **fără ~** faultless, flawless ‖ *adj* defective, faulty, in disrepair, out of order • ~a *vt* to spoil, to put (a mechanism) out of order ‖ *vr* to be out of order, to break down, to go wrong.

defecţiune [defektsi'une] *nf* breakdown, flaw, defect.

defensiv [defen'siv] *adj* defensive ‖ *adv* defensively • ~ă *nf* defensive.

deferent [defe'rent] *adj* deferential, respectful.

deferi [defe'ri] *vt jur* (*un caz*) to submit/refer (to).

deficienţă [defichi'entsă] *nf* deficiency, insufficiency; (*lipsă*) shortcoming, drawback; ~ **alimentară** malnutrition; ~ **mintală** mental deficiency; **cu ~ fizică** challenged (person); **persoană cu ~ de vedere** visually impaired person.

deficit [defi'chit] *nn* deficit, shortage; ~ **bugetar/ comercial** budget/trade deficit • **~ar** *adj* (*sărac*) scanty, poor; (*d. mărfuri*) scarce; (*d. an agricol*) lean; (*d. recoltă*) short crop; *fin* (*d. buget*) in a deficit, showing a deficit; (*d. cont*) showing a debit (balance), in the red; (*d. o fabrică*) loss-making, unprofitable.

defila [defi'la] *vi* to parade, to march past; to walk in procession; *mil* to march off; (*în șir*) to file off • **~re** *nf* mil parade, (a) march past; (*în șir*) file; defiling; procession.

defileu [defi'leu] *nn* (*îngust*) defile; (*trecătoare*) pass; (*gât*) gorge; canyon.

defini [defi'ni] *vt* (*a descrie*) to define, to characterize, to describe; (*a stabili*) to determine, to delineate.

definitiv [defini'tiv] *adj* definitive, final, ultimate, conclusive; irrevocable, irreversible; incontestable, irrefutable || *adv* definitively, finally, ultimately, conclusively; (*pentru totdeauna*) for good (and all); irrevocably, irreversibly; incontestably, irrefutably • **~a** *vt* (*a desăvârși*) to finalize, to finish off/up, to complete; (*în slujbă*) to appoint permanently.

definiție [defi'nitsie] *nf* definition; (*la cuvinte încrucișate*) clue; **prin ~** by the very fact, logically, by definition; **televiziune de înaltă ~** high definition television.

deflagrație [defla'gratsie] *nf* combustion, deflagration.

deflora [deflo'ra] *vt* to deflower.

deforma [defor'ma] *vt* to deform, to put (smth) out of shape; to deface, to disfigure; (*d. lemn, metal*) to warp, to buckle; *fig* (*a denatura*) to distort || *vr* to be(come) deformed, to get out of shape; to warp, to be warped, to buckle • **~re, ~ție** *nf* deformation; (*d. imagini*) also *fig* distortion; (*urâțire*) disfigurement; (*d. lemn, metal*) warping, buckling.

defrauda [defrau'da] *vt jur* to embezzle, to defraud.

defrișa [defri'sha] *vt* to clear/grub (land) • **~re** *nf agr* deforestation; grubbing, clearing.

defunct [de'funkt] *adj* late, deceased, defunct || *nm* the defunct, the deceased, the departed.

degaja [dega'zha] *vt* (*a emana*) to emit, to give off, to exhale; (*d. căldură*) to liberate, to give out; (*a curăța*) to clear (up); (*a elibera*) to relieve, to disengage; *sp* to clear || *vr* (*a se emite*) to be emitted, to escape, to emanate; (*a se elibera*) to get rid of smth, to free oneself, to break loose; *fig* (*a se desprinde*) to come out/off; (*a se limpezi*) to clear up.

degeaba [de'djeaba] *adv* (*gratis*) for free; *com* free of charge; for nothing; *coll* for love, for a song; (*inutil*) in vain, to no avail, uselessly; (*fără motiv*) for no reason (whatever).

degenera [dedjene'ra] *vi* (*d. calitate*) to degenerate into; *fig* to deteriorate • **~re** *nf* degeneration; (*morală*) degeneracy; deterioration.

degera [dedje'ra] *vi* to be benumbed with cold, frost-bitten, to suffer from frostbite; *fig* (*a tremura*) to tremble/shiver with cold, to freeze; (*d. plante, pomi*) to be killed/nipped by the frost.

degerătură [dedjeră'tură] *nf* chilblain, kibe.

deget ['dedjet] *nn* (*de la mână*) finger; ~ **arătător** forefinger, index finger; ~ **mare** thumb; ~ **mic** little finger; ~ **mijlociu** middle finger; (*de la picior*) toe; *obs* (*măsură*) inch; (*măsură*) finger, fraction; fingers.

degetar [dedje'tar] *nn* thimble; *bot* foxglove.

deghiza [degi'za] *vt* to disguise, to dress (smb) up; to mask; (*a ascunde*) to conceal; to dissimulate || *vr* to disguise oneself, to dress up, to put on a mask • **~re** *nf* disguise, get-up; fancy dress/costume; dissimulation.

degrabă [de'grabă] *adv* (*repede*) quickly; (*curând*) soon; before long, presently; (*pe dată*) at once, readily; **mai ~** rather, sooner.

degrada [degra'da] *vt* (*din funcție*) *esp mil* to demote, to downgrade; (*a înjosi*) to depreciate; (*d. suprafață*) to deface || *vr* (*a se deteriora*) to fall into disrepair, to wear out; *fig* (*a se înjosi*) to lower/demean/abase oneself • **~re** *nf* degradation; downgrading; (*dintr-o funcție*) demotion; (*moral*) degradation; defacement; dilapidation; *geol* degradation, weathering.

degresa [degre'sa] *vt* (*a curăța*) to remove the grease marks from, to clean; to remove the fat from, to defat.

degringoladă [degringo'ladă] *nf frml fig* downfall, collapse; decline, decay; (*d. prețuri*) slump.

degusta [degus'ta] *vt* to taste, to sample; (*a savura*) to savor, to relish.

deîmpărțit [deîmpăr'tsit] *nm math* dividend.

deînmulțit [deînmul'tsit] *nm math* multiplicand.

deja [de'zha] *adv* (*în prop. afirm.*) already; **a venit ~** he's already come; before; (*în prop. inter.*) yet; ~ **trebuie să pleci?** do you have to go just yet?

dejuca [dezhu'ka] *vt* (*d. planuri*) to thwart, to frustrate, to foil.

dejun [de'zhun] *nn* lunch (time); *frml* luncheon; **micul ~** breakfast.

dejuna [dezhu'na] *vi* to (eat/have one's) lunch.

delapida [delapi'da] *vt jur* to misappropriate (funds), to embezzle, to peculate • **~re** *nf jur* embezzlement, peculation, misappropriation • **~tor** *nm jur* embezzler, peculator.

delator [dela'tor] *nm* informer, delator.

delăsa [delă'sa] *vr* to neglect one's duties, to slack off; to be/get slack; to be remiss.

delecta [delek'ta] *vt* (*a desfăta*) to delight; (*pe cineva*) to amuse, to entertain || *vr* to take delight in (doing) smth; to enjoy oneself; to indulge (in), to delight (in) • **~re** *nf* (*desfătare*) delight, pleasure, enjoyment; amusement, entertainment, fun.

delega [dele'ga] *vt* to delegate, to commission; (*a autoriza*) to authorize • **~t** *nm* (*reprezentant*) delegate, representative; *coll* rep; (*locțiitor*) deputy; (*împuter-nicit*) mandatory • **~ție** *nf* (*misiune*) delegation; (*autorizație*) delegation (of authority), mandate, authorization; (*grup*) delegation, body of delegates.

delfin [del'fin] *nm zool* dolphin • **~ul** *astron* Delphinus.

delibera [delibe'ra] *vi* (*asupra*) to deliberate (on/over); to confer with (smb) on • **~re** *nf* deliberation, consultation; reflection, consideration • **~t** *adj* deliberate, intentional; *jur* premeditated, deliberate; **în mod ~** deliberately, on purpose || *adv* deliberately, intentionally.

delicat [deli'kat] *adj* delicate; (*d. piele*) soft, sensitive; (*d. culori*) subdued; (*slab*) weak; (*plăpând*) frail, fragile; (*subțire*) thin, slender, slim; (*fin*) fine, dainty, refined; (*gingaș*) gentle, tender; (*dificil*) ticklish, knotty; (*prevenitor*) amiable || *adv* delicately, softly, etc.

delicatese [delika'tese] *nf pl* delicatessen, dainties, delicacies.

delicatețe [delika'tetse] *nf* (*gingășie*) delicacy, gentle-ness, tenderness; (*fragilitate*) frailty, fragility; (*finețe*) fineness; (*a culorilor*) softness; (*a gustului*) refinement; (*d. o situație*), difficulty, awkwardness; tactfulness, thoughtfulness.

delicios [deli'chios] *adj* (*d. mâncare*) delicious, savory, nice; *fig* (*d. ceva/cineva*) charming, delightful.

deliciu [de'lichiu] *nn* delight, relish; great joy, extreme pleasure.

delict [de'likt] *nn* offense, misdemeanor; (*grav*) felony; **prins în flagrant** ~ caught in the act; caught red-handed.

delimita [delimi'ta] *vt/vr* to delimit; (*un teritoriu*) to demarcate, to limit, to mark the limits of; (*responsabilități*) to define, to determine.

delicvent [delik'vent] *nm* offender, delinquent, malefactor.

delicvență [delik'ventsă] *nf jur* delinquency, offense, criminality.

delir [de'lir] *nn med* delirium; (*aiureală*) raving; **a fi în** ~ to be delirious; *fig* frenzy, ecstasy, rapture.

delira [deli'ra] *vi* to be delirious, to rave; to be frantic • ~**nt** *adj* (*d. febră, boală*) delirious, raving, frantic, frenzied.

deloc [de'lok] *adv* not at all, by no means, on no account, not in the least.

deltă ['deltă] *nf geog* delta.

deluros [delu'ros] *adj* hilly.

demagog [dema'gog] *nm* demagogue.

demara [dema'ra] *vi* (*d. mașină*) to start, to move off; (*d. șoferi*) to drive away/off; *sp* to put on a spurt || *vt naut* to unmoor, to cast off.

demarca [demar'ka] *vt* to mark (by), to delimit || *vr sp* to break free from one's opponent • ~**ție** *nf* demarcation, delimitation; **linie de** ~ demarcation/boundary line.

demasca [demas'ka] *vt* to expose; to unmask, to lay bare/open, to reveal || *vr* to take off one's mask, to be unmasked; to be exposed, to show one's true face/colors.

dement [de'ment] *nm* lunatic, madman, demented/insane person || *adj* demented, mad, insane, mentally deranged.

demență [de'mentsă] *nf* madness, insanity, lunacy; *med* dementia.

demențial [dementsi'al] *adj* insane, mad, demented, rabid.

demers [de'mers] *nn* approach, step, measure.

demilitariza [demilitari'za] *vt* to demilitarize.

demina [demi'na] *vt mil* to clear of mines.

demisie [de'misie] *nf* resignation.

demisiona [demisio'na] *vi* to resign, to step down, to tender one's resignation; *fig* to give up • ~**r** *adj* resigning, who has resigned; (*d. cabinet*) outgoing || *nm* resigner.

demisol [demi'sol] *nn* semi-basement.

demistifica [demistifi'ka] *vt* to undeceive, to disabuse; *coll* to debunk smth.

demite [de'mite] *vt* to dismiss, to discharge, to remove; (*din funcție înaltă*) to depose.

demn [demn] *adj* honorable, decent, dignified, respectable; (*semeț*) haughty; ~ **de** worthy of, deserving; ~ **de atenție** worthy of note, noteworthy; ~ **de laudă** praiseworthy; laudable; ~ **de milă** pitiable || *adv* in a dignified manner, with dignity, worthily • ~**itate** *nf* dignity, self-respect; (*mândrie*) pride; (*post*) office, high position.

demnitar [demni'tar] *nm* dignitary, high official; *sl* big gun.

demobiliza [demobili'za] *vt mil* to demob(ilize), to disband; *fig* to discourage, to dishearten • ~**re** *nf* demobilization.

democrat(ă) [demo'krat(ă)] *nm/nf* democrat || *adj* democratic.

democratic [demo'kratik] *adj* democratic || *adv* democratically.

democrație [demokra'tsie] *nf* democracy; ~ **populară** people's democracy.

demodat [demo'dat] *adj* old-fashioned, out of fashion, obsolete; *fig* unfashionable, superannuated; *hum* worm-eaten; *coll* back number.

demografic [demo'grafik] *adj* demographic.

demola [demo'la] *vt* to demolish, to pull down, to tear down; (*o masă, cu o lovitură de picior*) to kick (a table) down; *fig* (*un argument, o teorie*) to demolish; (*d. reputația, onoare, viață*) to ruin.

demon ['demon] *nm* demon, devil, fiend.

demonstra [demon'stra] *vt* to demonstrate; (*a arăta*) to show; (*a dovedi*) to prove, to bear testimony to; (*d. afirmație, teorie*) to substantiate, to bear out || *vi* (*d. oameni: a manifesta*) to demonstrate • ~**tiv** *adj gram* demonstrative; **pronume** ~ demonstrative pronoun; (*d. cineva*) expansive; illustrative, graphic • ~**ție** *nf* (*manifestație*) demonstration; (*dovadă*) proof, evidence; *mil* ~ **de forță** show of force.

demonta [demon'ta] *vt* to dismantle; (*d. un mecanism*) to take down, to take apart; *fig* (*a descuraja*) to discourage; (*a tulbura*) to put out of countenance; to discountenance.

demoraliza [demorali'za] *vt* to demoralize; to discourage, to dishearten || *vr* to become demoralized, to lose heart • ~**t** *adj* discouraged, dejected, depressed, disheartened.

demult [de'mult] *adv* (*moment trecut terminat*) long ago; **mai** ~ formerly, once || *adv* (*durată neterminată*) for (quite) a long time; *coll* for ages.

denatura [denatu'ra] *vt* (*a interpreta fals*) to misrepresent, to misinterpret, to distort, to misconstrue; (*d. substanțe*) to denature (alcohol).

denie ['denie] *nf relig* evening service during Passion week (in Eastern Orthodox churches).

denigra [deni'gra] *vt* to denigrate, to put smb down; to backbite, to slander • ~**tor** *adj* denigrating, disparaging || *nm* denigrator, disparager.

denivelare [denive'lare] *nf geog* making uneven; change of level.

denota [deno'ta] *vt* to denote, to show, to indicate.

dens [dens] *adj* dense, thick, compact; (*d. stil*) concise, condensed || *adv* densely, thickly, compactly • ~**itate** *nf phys* density.

dentar [den'tar] *adj* tooth …, dental.

dentist [den'tist] *nm* dentist, dental surgeon.

denuclearizat [denukleari'zat] *adj* atom-free, nuclear-free.

denumi [denu'mi] *vt* to name, to call, to term, to designate.

denunț [de'nunts] *nn* denunciation; *sl* squeal.

denunța [denun'tsa] *vt* to denounce; (*a dezvălui*) to expose; (*a pârî*) to denounce, to inform against, to tell on smb; *sl* to squeal (on smb), to snitch.

deoarece [deware'che] *conj* because, since, as.

deocamdată [deokam'dată] *adv* for the time being, for the moment.

deochiat [deo'kiat] *adj* bewitched by the evil eye; (*rău famat*) ill famed; (*d. glume*) ribald, blue.

deodată [deo'dată] *adv* (*brusc*) suddenly, all of a sudden, unexpectedly; (*prin surprindere*) unawares; (*în același timp*) (all) at once, at the same time, simultaneously; **au plecat** ~ they left at once.

deodor(iz)ant [deodori'zant] *nn* (*pt. persoane*) deodorant; (*pt. cameră*) air freshener; (*pt. WC*) deodorizer.

deoparte [deo'parte] *adv* aside; **a lăsa** ~ to leave aside; **a sta** ~ to keep/stand aside/aloof; (*a nu se băga*) to sit out; *coll* to sit on the fence.

deopotrivă [deopo'trivă] *adv* alike; the same.

deosebi [deose'bi] *vt* to distinguish, to differentiate; to discern; (*a vedea*) to make out, to distinguish; to tell apart, to tell (one from the other) || *vr* to differ (from), to be different (from one another); *fig* (*a se distinge*) to be distinguished, to distinguish oneself, to stand out • ~**re** *nf* difference, distinction; *fig* (*d. păreri*) divergence, difference; ~ **de vederi** divergence/difference of opinion; **fără** ~ indiscriminately; **fără** ~ **de** irrespective of, regardless of; **spre** ~ **de** unlike, in contrast with/to • ~**t** *adj* (*diferit*) different, unlike; distinct, remarkable; (*ciudat*) peculiar, singular, strange; (*ales*) exquisite, choice || *adv* (*extrem de*) highly, extremely, particularly; (*în afară de*) apart from, besides.

depana [depa'na] *vt tech* to troubleshoot, to repair, to mend • ~**re** *nf tech* troubleshooting; (emergency) repairs • ~**tor** *nm* troubleshooter; breakdown mechanic; (*d. televizoare*) (television) repairman.

departament [departa'ment] *nn* department, ministry.

departe [de'parte] *adv esp inter, neg* far (away/off), at a great distance; (*în prop. afirm.*) a long way; from far, from a distance; (*superior*) by far, easily; (*d. aluzie*) by way of a hint/suggestion; **mai** ~ (*spațial*) farther away/down; (*temporal*) later on; (*în continuare*) on; **citește mai** ~ read on, go on reading; (*mai profund, mai mult*) further.

depăna [depă'na] *vt* to reel (on), to wind, to spin, to spool up.

depărta [depăr'ta] *vt* (*a îndepărta*) to remove, to clear away; (*dintr-o funcție*) to oust smb; (*a izgoni*) to drive smb away; (*d. picioare*) to spread || *vr* to depart, to go away/off; to distance/estrange oneself from; (*a se abate de la*) to deviate from • ~**re** *nf* distance, remoteness; **în** ~ in the distance, far off/away; **din** ~ from a distance, *lit* from afar • ~**t** *adj* remote, distant, far off/away; a long/great way off.

depăși [depă'shi] *vt* (*a trece de*) to pass/go beyond, to go past; (*într-o cursă*) to get ahead of, to overtake, to outrun; (*d. o sumă*) to top; (*d. bani, timp*) to overrun; *fig* to surpass, to exceed, to excel; **a ~ limitele/măsura** *fig* to overstep the bounds, to overdo it; • ~**t** *adj* (*d. un plan*) overfulfilled; (*învechit*) obsolete, old-fashioned, out of date, dated.

dependent [depen'dent] *adj* (*de*) dependent (on); addicted to; ~ **de droguri** drug addict.

dependență [depen'dentsă] *nf* (*de*) dependence (on); (*a unei țări*) dependency; (*subordonare*) subordination, subjection.

depila [depi'la] *vt* to depilate, to remove (the) hair from; *ind* to grain (skin).

depinde [de'pinde] *vi* (*de cineva/ceva*) to depend on

smb/smth, to be dependent on; (*a fi în puterea*) to be in smb's power; ~! that depends!; we shall see!, maybe!; (*a ține de*) to belong to; (*a fi supus*) to be subordinate/subject to.

depista [depis'ta] *vt* (*a descoperi*) to find out, to discover; (*un criminal*) to track down; to hunt/ferret out; (*d. o boală*) to detect.

deplasa [depla'sa] *vt* to move (away), to displace, to shift || *vr* to move around, to walk; (*a călători*) to travel, to move about; to shift, to be displaced.

deplânge [de'plânje] *vt* (*ceva*) to deplore, to lament (for/over); (*pe cineva*) to pity, to sympathize with.

deplin [de'plin] *adj* thorough(going); (*întreg*) whole, entire; (*plin*) full; *fig* absolute, perfect, complete || *adv* wholly, thoroughly; **pe** ~ entirely, wholly, completely.

deplora [deplo'ra] *vt rare* to deplore, to lament, to regret deeply • ~**bil** *adj* lamentable, deplorable; (*d. un incident*) regrettable.

deporta [depor'ta] *vt* (*un deținut*) to transport; (*d. un străin*) to deport; to exile, to banish; to send (prisoner) to concentration camp • ~**re** *nf* (*a unui străin*) deportation; (*a unui deținut*) transportation; internment • ~**t** *nm* deported (person), transported (convict); deportee, internee, prisoner.

deposeda [depose'da] *vt* to dispossess (of), to deprive (of), to bereave (of); to oust smb (from) • ~**re** *nf* dispossession, deprivation.

depou [de'pou] *nn rail* depot.

depozit [de'pozit] *nn* warehouse, storehouse, storage room; *mil* dump, stores, depot; *com* deposit; (*sediment*) sediment; (*la vin*) dregs; (*într-un recipient de apă*) scales • ~**a** *vt* to deposit, to store (up) || *vr* to settle, to form a deposit, to be deposited.

depoziție [depo'zitsie] *nf jur* statement, deposition, testimony; (*sub jurământ*) affidavit.

deprava [depra'va] *vt* to deprave, to corrupt, to pervert || *vr* to become depraved • ~**re** *nf* depravation; (*morală*) depravity, corruption, debauchery • ~**t** *nm* degenerate, depraved; debauchee || *adj* depraved, debauched, dissolute.

deprecia [deprechi'a] *vt* (*d. monedă*) to depreciate, to devalue; (*a subevalua*) to underrate; to undervalue; (*a discredita*) to disparage, to belittle || *vr* (*d. lucruri*) to fall in value, to lose its value; (*d. persoane*) to belittle oneself, to make oneself cheap • ~**tiv** *adj* disparaging, derogatory.

depresiune [depresi'une] *nf geog* depression, hollow (ground), dip; *met* low, trough; *econ* slump; (*a valorii*) fall.

deprima [depri'ma] *vt* (*a descuraja*) to dishearten, to discourage; (*d. moral*) to lower; (*a întrista*) to sadden, to grieve • ~**nt** *adj* depressing, disheartening • ~**re** *nf* depression, dejection • ~**t** *adj* depressed, despondent, downcast, low-spirited; *coll* down in the mouth.

deprinde [de'prinde] *vt* to adopt, to acquire; (*d. un obicei*) to fall into a habit || *vr* to be/get used to, to become accustomed to; *coll* to get the hang of smth • ~**re** *nf* (*obicei*) habit; *pl* (*maniere*) manners; **din** ~ out of habit; (*abilitate*) skill, dexterity, knack.

deprins [de'prins] *adj* (*experimentat*) experienced, skilled; accustomed, used to, inured.

depune [de'pune] *vt* to lay/put/set down; (*d. bani*) to deposit, to put aside/away/by; (*a sedimenta*) to deposit; **a ~ armele** *mil* to lay down one's arms; to surrender; *fig* to give it up; to acknowledge one's defeat || *vr* to settle; to deposit.

deputat [depu'tat] *nm* deputy, delegate; *pol* Representative; Member of Parliament, M.P.

deraia [dera'ia] *vi* to derail, to become derailed; *fig* to go off the track, to talk nonsense/rubbish; to drivel; to rave; *coll* (*grav, pe fond senil*) to go ga-ga.

deraiere [dera'iere] *nf* derailment.

deranj [de'ranzh] *nn* (*dezordine*) disorder; *fig* trouble, disturbance, inconvenience; **nu e nici un ~** it's no trouble at all.

deranja [deran'zha] *vt* (*pe cineva*) to disturb, to trouble, to put smb out; (*d. lucruri, hârtii*) to disarrange, to throw into disorder; (*a strica*) to spoil; (*d. stomac*) to upset || *vr* to trouble oneself, to put oneself out; to go out of one's way; **nu te ~** please don't trouble/disturb yourself • **~ment** *nn tech* damage; *elec* fault; *med* (*mintal*) mental derangement; (*stomacal*) stomach trouble; *pl telec* Service Department.

derapa [dera'pa] *vi* to skid, to sideslip • **~re** *nf* skid(ding), sideslip(ping).

derâdere [de'râdere] *nf* derision, scoff(ing), mocking, mockery; **în ~** in mockery, mockingly.

derbedeu [derbe'deu] *nm* guttersnipe; vagabond, tramp; scallywag; cad, loafer, loiterer.

derbi ['derbi] *nn sp* derby.

derdeluş [derde'lush] *nn* slide.

deregla [dere'gla] *vt* to disturb, to trouble; *tech* (*d. un mecanism*) to put out of balance, to disarrange; (*d. minte*) to unsettle || *vr* (*d. un mecanism*) to go out of order, to go wrong; (*d. minte*) to become unsettled • **~re** *nf* disordered/unsettled state; (*d. ceas, motor*) malfunctioning; *med* (*a pulsului*) irregularity; (*mentală*) mental derangement; (*hormonală*) hormone disorder; *psych* (*comportamentală*) dissolute behavior.

deriva [deri'va] *vt* to derive; (*d. cursul unei ape*) to divert, to tap the course of; *elec* to branch; *rail* to shunt, to switch || *vi ling* to be derived from; (*a proveni*) to descend from; (*a izvorî*) to spring (from); *naut* to drift.

derivă [de'rivă] *nf naut* drift, leeway; *avia, fin* drift; *fig* **a fi în ~** to be left to drift, to drift

derizoriu [deri'zoriu] *adj* derisory, laughable; **preţ ~** ridiculously low price.

dermatolog [dermato'log] *nm* dermatologist • **~ie** *nf* dermatology.

derogare [dero'gare] *nf jur* derogation; (*de la un examen, o cerinţă*) waiver; *fin* (*de la plata unor taxe*) exemption.

derula [deru'la] *vt* (*un sul*) to unfurl, to unroll; (*un cablu*) to unwind, to uncoil || *vr* (*d. sul*) to come unrolled, to unroll; (*d. cablu*) to come unwound; *fig* to unfold, to develop, to take place.

deruta [deru'ta] *vt* to baffle, to confuse, to mislead, to put smb off • **~nt** *adj* baffling, confusing, disconcerting, misleading.

derută [de'rută] *nf mil* rout, disorderly retreat; (*zăpăceală*) confusion, bewilderment, perplexity.

des [des] *adj* dense, thick; numerous, abundant; **iarbă deasă** thick grass; **păr ~** thick hair; (*frecvent*) repeated, frequent; **vizite ~e** frequent visits || *adv* often, frequently, repeatedly; **a se întâlni ~ cu cineva** to see smb quite often; (*dens, strâns*) closely, thickly, densely; **a scrie ~** to write closely together.

desăvârşi [desăvâr'shi] *vt* (*a perfecţiona*) to perfect, to

improve; (*a termina*) to finish, to complete, to bring to perfection; to achieve, to carry through || *vr* to perfect oneself; to be perfected • **~re** *nf* (*perfecţionare*) perfection, improvement; (*terminare*) termination, finishing, completion, accomplishment; **cu ~** totally; utterly, completely, entirely, wholly • **~t** *adj* (*perfect*) perfect, consummate, thorough, accomplished; (*terminat*) finished, complete || *adv* perfectly.

descalifica [deskalifi'ka] *vt* to disqualify, to deprive (of); (*d. avocaţi*) to disbar || *vr* to be disqualified • **~re** *nf* also *sp* disqualification.

descălţa [deskăl'tsa] *vt* to take off smb's shoes || *vr* to take off one's shoes • **~re, ~t** *nf, nn* taking off one's shoes.

descărca [deskăr'ka] *vt* (*d. greutate*) to unload; to discharge, to unship; to tip/dump; (*a goli*) to empty; (*d. armă*) to unload; to let/fire off one's gun; (*pe cineva de*) to exempt (from), to relieve of; (*d. o sarcină*) to let off; *jur* to exonerate (from); *econ* to receipt; *fig* to unburden || *vr* (*d. greutate*) to be unloaded; (*d. armă*) to go off; *elec* (*d. baterie*) to run down, to discharge; *fig* to get smth off one's chest.

descătuşa [deskătu'sha] *vt* also *fig* to unfetter, to unchain, to unbind || *vr* also *fig* to free oneself, to break loose (from).

descâlci [deskâl'chi] *vt* (*a descurca fire*) also *fig* to disentangle, to unravel; (*a clarifica*) to clear up; (*d. o problemă*) to puzzle out, to work out; (*a pune ordine*) to arrange, to settle.

descântec [des'kântek] *nn* (*farmec*) magic, charm, magic formula/spell; (*împotriva bolii*) disenchantment; (*în sens rău*) evil spell.

descendent [deschen'dent] *nm* descendant; *pl* offspring, progeny, issue || *adj* descending, downward • **linie ~ă** descending line; (*genealogie*) line of descent.

descendenţă [deschen'dentsă] *nf* (*origine*) descent, lineage, origin; (*descendenţi*) descendants, offspring, progeny; (*posteritate*) posterity.

descentraliza [deschentrali'za] *vt* to decentralize || *vr* to be decentralized • **~re** *nf* decentralization.

descheia [deske'ia] *vt* (*o haină*) to unbutton; (*un nasture*) to undo || *vr* (*d. cineva*) to unbutton oneself; (*d. nasture*) to come undone.

deschide [des'kide] *vt* to open; (*a descuia*) to unlock, to unfasten; (*a forţa*) to force open; (*a scoate dopul*) to uncork; (*robinetul*) to turn on; (*ceva sigilat*) to unseal; (*un aparat electric*) to turn on, to switch on; (*a inaugura*) to open (up), to inaugurate; (*a întreprinde*) to start, to establish; (*o discuţie*) to open, to begin; *med* (*un abces*) to lance || *vr* to open, to be opened; (*d. vreme*) to be clearing up; (*d. persoane*) to open out; (*d. prăpastie: a se căsca*) to yawn; (*d. flori*) to come out; to blossom; (*a crăpa*) to break/burst open • **~re** *nf* (*d. uşă, cont*) opening; (*început*) beginning; **cuvânt de ~** opening speech/address; (*d. pod*) span; *constr* opening, aperture; (*d. o peşteră*) mouth, entrance; *fig* open-mindedness; (*francheţe*) openness.

deschis [des'kis] *adj* open; *fig* (*d. cineva*) frank, open-minded, outspoken; **un om ~** a frank/outspoken person; (*d. atitudine*) undisguised; (*clar*) clear, evident; (*d. culori*) light; **verde ~** light green; **larg ~** wide open; **vot ~** vote by show of hands || *adv* openly; (*limpede*) plainly; (*sincer*) above-board • **păr de**

culoare ~ă light/fair hair; *fire* ~ă frank, open nature; **şedinţă** ~ă public meeting; **vot** ~ vote by show of hands.

descifra [deschi'fra] *vt* to make out, to read, to interpret; *fig (a rezolva)* to unravel, to solve; *telec* to decode.

descinde [des'chinde] *vt (a se da jos din)* to descend (from), to come down; *coll (din tren, avion, autobuz)* to get off; *(din maşină)* get out of; *(de pe cal)* to dismount; *(a sosi)* to arrive, to come; *(a-şi avea originea)* to descend from; *(a trage la un hotel)* to put up at; *(d. poliţie: a se deplasa la)* to descend on; to raid.

descoase [des'koase] *vt (o cusătură)* to undo, to unstitch; *fig (a iscodi)* to pump, to sound, to worm (a secret) out of smb; *(o chestiune)* to search, to pry into ‖ *vr* to come undone.

descoji [desko'zhi] *vt (d. coajă)* to remove the skin/bark from; *(d. mazăre)* to shell, to husk; *(d. fructe, cartofi)* to peel, to skin ‖ *vr (d. pomi)* to shed the bark, to be barked; *(d. piele)* to peel (off), to come off.

descompune [deskom'pune] *vt* to decompose, to break up, to disintegrate; *(a strica)* to decay, to rot ‖ *vr* to decompose, to disintegrate, to crumble; *(a putrezi)* to decay, to rot; *(d. trăsăturile feţei)* to be/become distorted/contorted.

desconsidera [deskonside'ra] *vt* to disregard, to slight; to despise; *(a nu da ascultare)* to disobey; *(a nu ţine seama de)* to ignore, to pay no heed to • **~re, ~ţie** *nf* disregard, lack of consideration, contempt.

descoperi [deskope'ri] *vt (a dezveli)* to uncover, to (lay) bare; *fig (a afla)* to discover, to find out; *(a se afla)* to be discovered/disclosed, to come to light; *(a detecta)* to detect; *(a dezvălui)* to reveal, to disclose ‖ *vr (a-şi scoate pălăria)* to uncover/bare one's head; to take off one's hat; **cine a ~t America?** who discovered America? • **~re** *nf* discovery; *(dezvăluire)* disclosure, revelation, exposure • **~t** *adj* open, uncovered; *(cu capul gol)* bareheaded; *fig* exposed, unprotected; *(d. cont)* overdrawn.

descotorosi [deskotoro'si] *vt (de)* to rid of ‖ *vr* to get rid of, to rid oneself of.

descreierat [deskreie'rat] *nm fig* scatter-brain; *coll* harum-scarum ‖ *adj* crazy, mad, reckless, hare-brained.

descreşte [des'kreshte] *vi* to diminish, to decrease, to dwindle; *(a se scurta)* to grow shorter; *(d. flux)* to recede; *(a scădea)* to abate, to go down; *fin* to depreciate.

descrie [des'krie] *vt geom* to describe, to draw; *(a prezenta)* to depict, to sketch; *(a portretiza)* to portray; **a ~ amănunţit** to give a minute description of • **~re** *nf* description; *lit* narrative, sketch, picture, portrayal.

descuia [desku'ia] *vt* to unlock, to unfasten; *(a deschide)* to open ‖ *vr* to be unlocked/opened; *fig* to become broad-minded.

descult [des'kults] *adj/adv* barefoot(ed).

descumpăni [deskumpă'ni] *vt* to upset, to unsettle, to confound, to bewilder; to disorient; *(a descuraja)* to discourage.

descuraja [deskura'zha] *vt (a demoraliza)* to discourage, to dishearten ‖ *vr* to lose heart/courage • **~re** *nf* discouragement, despondency • **~t** *adj* dejected, depressed; downhearted • **~tor** *adj* discouraging, disheartening, depressing.

descurca [deskur'ka] *vt (a descâlci)* to disentangle, to unravel; *fig (a rezolva)* to resolve, to solve, to clear

up, to puzzle out ‖ *vr* to be disentangled; *fig* to fend for oneself, to shift for oneself; *coll* to get by.

descurcăreţ [deskurkă'rets] *adj* resourceful, versatile, ingenious.

deseară [de'seară] *adv* tonight, this evening.

desemna [desem'na] *vt (a numi într-o funcţie)* to appoint; *(un candidat)* to nominate; *(a indica)* to designate; *(o dată)* to set a date; *jur* to assign.

desen [de'sen] *nn (artă)* drawing; *(tablou desenat)* drawing, sketch(ing), draft; *(model pe material)* design, pattern.

desena [dese'na] *vt* to draw, to sketch ‖ *vr* to loom; to outline; to stand out, to take shape • **~tor** *nm* drawer, sketcher; *tech* draftsman, designer.

deseori ['deseori] *adv* often, frequently, repeatedly.

desert [de'sert] *nn* dessert, pudding, sweet; *(prăjituri)* sweets.

deservi [deser'vi] *vt (a face un deserviciu)* to damage, to harm, to be detrimental to; to work for a community • **~ciu** *nn* bad-/ill-turn, disservice, harm • **~re** *nf* * **deserviciu**; working for a community.

desface [des'fache] *vt (a dezlega)* to undo, to unbind, to untie; *(a deschide)* to unwrap, to unpack; *(d. haină)* to unfasten; *(d. fermoar)* to unzip; *(d. şireturi)* to unlace; *(d. cusătură)* to unpick; *(d. păr)* to let one's hair down; *(a desfăşura: o hartă)* to spread (out); *(a vinde)* to sell off one's goods, to market; *(a anula)* to break (off), to cancel; *(a destrăma)* to dissolve ‖ *vr (a se dezlega) (d. şireturi, nod)* to come undone; *(d. păr)* to come down; *(d. nasturi)* to come/tear off; *(d. un obiect, animal)* to come/get/break loose; *(a se deschide)* to open; *(d. flori)* to burst (open).

desfăşura [desfăshu'ra] *vt (a întinde un ziar)* to unfold; *(d. un steag)* to unfurl; to spread out; *(a înfăptui)* to carry on; to display ‖ *vr (d. un cablu)* to come unwound; to uncoil; *(d. o privelişte)* to open up; *(a decurge)* to go on; *(a avea loc)* to proceed, to take place • **~re** *nf (înaintare)* unfolding, progress, development; *(etalare)* display; **în curs de** ~ in progress.

desfăta [desfă'ta] *vt* to please, to delight, to give pleasure to ‖ *vr (cu)* to delight in, to enjoy oneself • **~re** *nf* relish, delight, pleasure, enjoyment; *(veselie)* merriment, mirth; *(bucurie)* joy, glee, rejoicing; *pl* pleasures, enjoyments.

desfide [des'fide] *vt (a provoca)* to defy, to dare, to challenge; *(a înfrunta)* to brave, to face.

desfigura [desfigu'ra] *vt* to disfigure; *(a poci)* to deface, to deform; *(a mutila)* to maim, to mutilate.

desfiinţa [desfiin'tsa] *vt (a face să înceteze)* to abolish, to break up; to suppress; *(a anula)* to annul, to cancel, to revoke; *jur (a abroga)* to repeal, to abrogate, to rescind; *(a lichida)* to eliminate, to do away with; *fin (d. o companie, un cont)* to wind up.

desfrânat [desfrâ'nat] *nm* profligate, rake, libertine ‖ *adj* debauched, dissipated, dissolute, licentious.

desfrâu [des'frâu] *nn* dissipation, licentiousness, debauchery, dissoluteness; *(sexual)* fornication.

desfrunzi [desfrun'zi] *vt* to defoliate, to strip/denude of leaves ‖ *vr* to shed the leaves.

deshidrata [deshidra'ta] *vt/vr* to dehydrate, to desiccate • **~re** *nf med, chem* dehydration, desiccation.

deshuma [deshu'ma] *vt* to exhume, to disinter.

desigur [de'sigur] *adv* certainly, by all means, of course, naturally, surely.

desiş [de'sish] *nn* thicket.

deslușı [deslu'shi] *vt* (*a distinge*) to distinguish, to discern, to perceive; (*a explica*) to explain, to clear up, to solve || *vr* to loom/heave in sight, to become distinct/visible; (*a se lămuri*) to become explicit, to be explained • ~t *adj* (*ușor de distins*) distinct; (*clar*) clear, plain, intelligible; evident; (*citeț*) legible || *adv* distinctly.

despacheta [despake'ta] *vt* (*a deschide*) to open; (*un geamantan, o cutie*) to unpack; to unwrap; (*mărfuri*) to uncase.

despăduri [despădu'ri] *vt* to deforest, to clear (land) of trees.

despăgubi [despăgu'bi] *vt* to compensate (for); to reimburse, to remunerate || *vr* to make up for smth; to cover a loss; to make amends (for smth).

despărți [despăr'tsi] *vt* to separate, to sever; (*a detașa*) to detach, to put asunder; (*a dezbina*) to split, to divide || *vr* (*a se separa*) to part company; (*d. asociați*) *com* to dissolve a partnership; to (get a) divorce, to separate, to split up; (*d. drumuri*) to fork, to branch off; (*a se lipsi de*) to part with.

despera, dispera [despe'ra, dispe'ra] *vt* to drive/reduce to despair || *vi* to despair, to be in despair, to give way to despair • ~re, ~re *nf* despair, desperation, despondency.

despica [despi'ka] *vt* to split, to cleave; (*a face tăieturi*) to slit || *vr* to split, to cleave, to slit; (*a se bifurca*) to bifurcate, to branch out.

despot ['despot] *nm* absolute ruler, tyrant, despot • ~ism *nn* despotism, tyranny, absolutism.

despovăra [despovă'ra] *vt also fig* to unburden, to unload, to discharge.

despre ['despre] *prep* about, of; (*cu privire la*) on, about, concerning; (*în legătură cu*) in connection with; **cât** ~ as for, as to.

desprinde [des'prinde] *vt* (*a desface*) to detach, to separate; to unbind, to unfasten; (*d. tren*) to uncouple, to undo; (*d. concluzie*) to infer, to draw || *vr* (*a se desface*) to detach; (*d. un nasture*) to come/ tear off; (*d. părți*) to come apart; to separate, to break off, to break loose; (*d. vopsea de pe tablouri, pereți*) to flake, to come away/off; (*d. coaja de pe copaci*) to peel off; *pol* (*d. un concurent*) to break away, to pull ahead; (*d. cineva*) to tear oneself away; *fig* (*din*) to result (from).

despuia [despu'ia] *vt* (*a dezbrăca*) to strip, to undress; (*d. pielea animalelor*) to skin, to flay; (*d. pomi*) to despoil, to defoliate; (*a selecta fragmente*) to extract, to excerpt; (*a jefui*) to rob, to strip smb of smth || *vr* (*a se dezbrăca*) to strip oneself, to take off one's clothes; (*d. pomi*) to shed the leaves.

destăinui [destăinu'i] *vt* (*a dezvălui*) to reveal, to disclose; to divulge; *coll* to blab, to let out || *vr* to confess (one's secrets); to open one's heart (to smb) • ~re *nf* confession, confidence.

destin [des'tin] *nn* destiny, fate; (*ursită*) lot, fortune • ~a *vt* to destine; to mean (for), to intend || *vr* to devote oneself; to be destined/meant/intended • ~atar *nm* addressee, recipient; (*al unui mandat poștal*) *com* consignee • ~ație *nf* destination; (*a unei clădiri, sume de bani*) destination, (intended) purpose.

destinde [des'tinde] *vt* to ease, to slacken, to release; (*a întinde*) to spread, to extend, to stretch out || *vr* to become slack, to slacken; to relax, to take it easy • ~re *nf* (*slăbirea încordării*) relaxing, slackening; *fig*

relaxation; (*răgaz*) leisure; (*distracție*) entertainment; *pol* détente, easing of tension; (*d. gaze*) expansion.

destitui [destitu'i] *vt* to discharge, to dismiss, to remove, to relieve.

destoinic [des'toinik] *adj* capable, efficient, competent.

destrăbălare [destrăbă'lare] *nf* dissoluteness, dissipation, debauchery; (*sexuală*) fornication.

destrăma [destră'ma] *vt* (*ceva țesut*) to unweave, to unravel; (*a purta*) to fray; (*a rupe*) to tear; *fig* to dissolve, to break up; (*d. visuri*) to shatter || *vr* to come off, to be torn; to ravel out; *fig* to disintegrate, to break up; (*d. ceață*) to clear away.

destul [des'tul] *adj* enough, sufficient || *adv* enough; sufficiently; rather/pretty late || *interj* enough (of that), that will do.

destupa [destu'pa] *vt* (*o sticlă*) to uncork; (*a deschide*) to open; (*a curăța*) to clear.

desuet [desu'et] *adj* obsolete, antiquated, out-of-date.

deșănțat [deșăn'tsat] *adj* (*dezordonat*) disorderly, untidy, careless; (*nelalocul lui*) indecent, improper; (*rușinos*) shameful, brazen.

deșert [de'shert] *nn* desert, wasteland, wilderness; (*gol*) vacuum, void; **în** ~ in vain, vainly || *adj* (*gol*) empty; *geog* (*pustiu*) waste; (*d. o regiune*) desolate; (*inutil*) useless; (*d. vorbire*) idle; (*d. încercare*) futile • ~a *vt* to empty; (*d. cutie, sertar*) to clear; (*a bea*) to drink up.

deșertăciune [deshertă'chune] *nf* vanity; (*inutilitate*) futility, uselessness.

deșeu [de'sheu] *nn usu pl* refuse, waste (material), rubbish • ~ri radioactive radioactive waste.

deși [de'shi] *conj* (al)though; *frml* albeit.

deșira [deshi'ra] *vt* (*d. ață*) to unwind, to unravel; (*d. mărgele*) to unstring; (*d. ciorapi*) to ladder || *vr* to unwind, to be unwound; (*d. mărgele*) to come off; (*a se destrăma*) to ravel, to fray out; (*d. ciorapi*) to ladder.

deștept [desh'tept] *nm* clever/wise man; *iro* wise guy, a clever Dick; *pej* dolt, blockhead, num(b)skull || *adj* clever, bright, sharp; *coll* brainy; cute; (*treaz*) (wide) awake || *adv* cleverly.

deștepta [deshtep'ta] *vt* (*a trezi*) to wake (up), to rouse smb from sleep; *fig* to awaken, to arouse || *vr* (*a se trezi*) to awake, to wake up; *fig* to grow wise • ~re *nf* awakening, waking; *mil* reveille.

deșteptător [deshteptă'tor] *nn* alarm clock.

deșuruba [deshuru'ba] *vt* to unscrew || *vr* to get/come unscrewed.

detalia [detali'a] *vt* to detail, to relate/describe in detail || *vr* to appear, to stand out.

detaliu [de'taliu] *nn* (*amănunt*) detail, particular; **în** ~ in detail, minutely, at length; *econ* retail trade; **în** ~ *com* by the piece, by retail.

detașa [deta'sha] *vt* to detach, to unfasten; (*d. vagoane*) to uncouple; (*a separa*) to separate; (*pe cineva*) to transfer temporarily || *vr* (*a se desprinde*) to separate, to detach oneself (from); (*a se distinge*) to stand out • ~re *nf* (*a unui obiect*) detaching, cutting off (of smth); (*a cuiva*) transfer (to another job), assignment of a mission; (*a unui ofițer*) *fig* indifference, lack of interest, detachment • ~ment *nn* detachment, draft (of troops); (*echipă*) team, group.

detecta [detek'ta] *vt telec* to detect, to discover, to notice.

detectiv [detek'tiv] *nm* detective, plainclothes (police) man; (*la hotel*) house/hotel detective; *coll* private eye.

detector [detek'tor] *adj* detecting, sensing ‖ *nn* detector, indicator, sensor.

detenţie, detenţiune [de'tentsie, detentsi'une] *nf jur* detention, imprisonment.

detergent [deter'djent] *nm* detergent.

deteriora [deterio'ra] *vt* to impair, to spoil, to damage ‖ *vr* to deteriorate, to get out of order, to spoil, to worsen.

determina [determi'na] *vt* (*a stabili*) to determine, to establish; (*a hotărî*) to fix, to decide on; (*a cauza*) to make, to induce, to cause; (*a convinge*) to persuade, to convince • **~re** *nf* determination, fixing; *med* (*a grupei sanguine*) typing (of blood).

detesta [detes'ta] *vt* to detest, to hate, to loathe • **~bil** *adj* hateful, detestable, awful, loathsome ‖ *adv* hatefully, detestably, awfully, loathsomely; *fig* extremely badly.

detona [deto'na] *vt* to detonate; to explode • **~ţie** *nf* detonation.

detracat [detra'kat] *adj* deranged, unbalanced, corrupt, dissolute.

detractor [detrak'tor] *nm* detractor, disparager.

detriment [detri'ment] *nn* detriment, loss, disadvantage • **în ~ul** (*cuiva*) to the detriment/prejudice of smb; to smb's detriment/disadvantage.

detrona [detro'na] *vt* to depose, to dethrone, to overthrow.

deturna [detur'na] *vt* to embezzle, to misappropriate; (*d. un avion*) to hijack • **~re** *nf* embezzlement, misappropriation; hijacking.

deţinător [detsină'tor] *nm* holder, owner.

deţine [de'tsine] *vt* (*o funcţie*) to hold, to occupy; (*a avea*) to hold, to own, to have, to possess; (*în închisoare*) to detain/keep smb prisoner.

deţinut [detsi'nut] *nm* detainee, convict, prisoner; *coll* jailbird; ~ **politic** political prisoner

deunăzi [de'unăzi] *adv* the other day; (*acum câteva zile*) a few days ago.

devaloriza [devalori'za] *vt* (*d. bani*) to devalue, to devaluate; (*d. mărfuri*) to mark down; to depreciate ‖ *vr* to be/get devalued; to depreciate; to grow cheaper.

devansa [devan'sa] *vt* (*a întrece*) to outrun, to outdistance, to overtake; to precede, to go/come before smb/smth.

devasta [devas'ta] *vt* (*a distruge*) to devastate, to destroy, to lay waste; (*a jefui*) to rob, to pillage, to sack • **~tor** *adj* devastating ‖ *nm* devastator.

developa [develo'pa] *vt phot* to develop.

deveni [deve'ni] *vi* to become, to grow; to get; (*a se întâmpla cu cineva*) to become of • **~re** *nf* becoming, evolution; • **în~** in the making.

dever ['dever] *nn* turnover, business (done); (*vânzare*) sale.

deversa [dever'sa] *vt* to empty, to discharge ‖ *vr* to empty, to flow (into).

devia [devi'a] *vt* to deviate (from), to swerve (from), to diverge.

deviere [devi'ere] *nf* deviation, aberration.

deviz [de'viz] *nn* estimate, quotation, specification.

deviză [de'viza] *nf* motto; (*lozincă*) slogan, watchword; *fig* device, standard.

devora [devo'ra] *vt* (*d. animale*) to devour; (*d. oameni*)

to wolf down, to gobble up; (*d. flăcări*) to consume, to destroy • **~nt** *adj* (*d. poftă, foame*) ravenous.

devota [devo'ta] *vr* to dedicate oneself (to), to devote oneself (to) • **~ment** *nn* devotion, self-sacrifice • **~t** *adj* devoted, staunch, loyal.

devreme [de'vreme] *adv* early.

dexteritate [deksteri'tate] *nf* dexterity, skill, skillfulness.

dezabuzat [dezabu'zat] *adj* world-weary, disillusioned, disenchanted, disappointed.

dezacord [deza'kord] *nn* (*neînţelegere*) disagreement, variance, discord; *mus* discord, dissonance, disharmony.

dezagreabil [deza'greabil] *adj* disagreeable, unpleasant; (*d. cineva*) surly, grumpy.

dezamăgi [dezamă'dji] *vt* to disappoint, to disillusion, to let down • **~re** *nf* disappointment, disillusionment.

dezamorsa [dezamor'sa] *vt also fig* to defuse.

dezaproba [dezapro'ba] *vt* to disapprove, to deprecate; (*a aduce obiecţii*) to object (to); (*a condamna*) to blame.

dezarma [dezar'ma] *vt mil also fig* to disarm; *mil* to demobilize; to unload ‖ *vi* to disarm • **~re** *nf* disarmament.

dezarticula [dezartiku'la] *vt* to put out of joint, to dislocate ‖ *vr* to be disjointed.

dezastru [de'zastru] *nn* disaster, calamity • **~os** *adj* disastrous, calamitous; appalling.

dezavantaj [dezavan'tazh] *nn* disadvantage; (*neajuns*) drawback, shortcoming, handicap.

dezavantaja [dezavanta'zha] *vt* to disadvantage, to put smb at a disadvantage, to harm, to handicap.

dezavua [dezavu'a] *vt frml* (*a dezaproba*) to disapprove of, to repudiate; (*a nu recunoaşte*) to disown, to deny, to disclaim.

dezaxat [dezak'sat] *nm* unbalanced person, desperado ‖ *adj tech* eccentric (cam); *tech* (*d. o roată*) out of alignment; *fig* unbalanced.

dezbate [dez'bate] *vt* (*a discuta*) to discuss, to debate (upon), to argue; (*a recenza*) to review, to comment (upon) • **~re** *nf* debate, discussion; *pl* proceedings.

dezbăra [dezbă'ra] *vt* **a ~ pe cineva de ceva** to rid smb of, to break smb of (a habit) ‖ *vr* **a se ~ de** to get rid of; (*un obicei*) to give up, to break oneself of; (*maturizându-se*) to grow out of smth.

dezbina [dezbi'na] *vt* to split, to divide; (*a separa*) to separate, to sever; (*a diviza*) to disconnect ‖ *vr* to fall apart, to fall out with one another; (*a se separa*) to separate, to part; *com* to dissolve a partnership • **~re** *nf* (*separare*) separation, split; (*duşmănie*) discord, feud, disagreement.

dezbrăca [dezbră'ka] *vt* (*ceva*) to take off; (*pe cineva*) to undress, to strip ‖ *vr* to undress (oneself), to take off one's clothes, to strip oneself.

dezechilibra [dezekili'bra] *vt* to unbalance, to throw (smb) off balance ‖ *vr* to lose one's balance/poise • **~t** *adj* out of balance; *fig* unbalanced, unhinged ‖ *nm* unbalanced person.

dezechilibru [dezeki'libru] *nn* want/lack of balance/poise; imbalance; *psych* unbalance, maladjustment.

dezerta [dezer'ta] *vi mil, also fig* to desert, to abandon, to defect • **~re** *nf also fig* desertion; defection.

dezertor [dezer'tor] *nm mil* deserter; *fig* deserter, quitter, defector.

dezgheţ [dez'gets] *nn* thaw • **~a** *vt* to defrost, to thaw, to melt; *fig* to warm; (*a înviora*) to enliven ‖ *vr* to thaw; *fig* to warm (up), to grow warm; (*a se înviora*) to brighten up.

dezgoli [dezgo'li] *vt* (*capul*) to bare, to uncover; to denude, to divest ‖ *vr* to bare/uncover one's head; to strip (oneself); to denude/divest oneself.

dezgropa [dezgro'pa] *vt* to dig up/out; (*a deshuma*) to disinter, to exhume.

dezgust [dez'gust] *nn* disgust (at, for), distaste (for), aversion (to, for), dislike (of, for) • ~a *vt* to disgust, to sicken ‖ *vr* to sicken (oneself), to grow sick (of) • ~ător *adj* disgusting, nasty, nauseating, repulsive; (*d. miros*) offensive; (*d. laudă, complimente*) fulsome.

deziluzie [dezi'luzie] *nf* disillusion, disillusionment, disappointment.

dezinfecta [dezinfek'ta] *vt* to disinfect.

dezinforma [dezinfor'ma] *vt* to misinform • ~re *nf* misinformation.

dezinteres [dezinte'res] *nn* lack of interest, indifference, unconcern.

dezinvolt [dezin'volt] *adj* easy-going; (*d. mișcări*) easy, free; (*d. maniere*) detached, unselfconscious • ~ură *nf* offhandedness; (*d. maniere*) lack of constraint, unselfconsciousness, ease; **cu** ~ in a offhand/casual way.

dezlănțui [dezlăntsu'i] *vt* to unleash, to unbridle ‖ *vr* to break loose, to burst; (*d. furtună*) to break out; (*d. molimă*) to rage, to play havoc/destruction; (*d. vânt*) to rage, to sweep along; (*d. oameni*) to rage/fly at.

dezlânat [dezlâ'nat] *adj* teased, unraveled; *fig* loose ‖ *adv* loosely.

dezlega [dezle'ga] *vt* (*a desface un nod*) to untie, to undo, to unfasten; (*d. șireturi*) to unlace the shoes; (*a slăbi*) to loosen; (*a elibera*) to unfetter; (*a rezolva*) to resolve; (*a elucida*) to clear up; (*a absolvi*) *also relig* to absolve; (*a ierta*) to forgive; to exonerate, to exempt ‖ *vr* (*d. nod*) to get/come undone/untied; to disentangle; (*a se elibera*) to get free, to make oneself free; to wrench oneself free.

dezlipi [dezli'pi] *vt* (*d. ceva lipit*) to unglue, to tear off; (*a detașa*) to detach, to get smb apart; (*a despărți*) to separate, to sever; *fig* to tear off ‖ *vr* (*a se desprinde*) to come off/ undone; *fig* to separate, to sever (from), to tear oneself away (from).

dezmăț [dez'măts] *nn* (*nerușinare*) shamelessness, dissipation, debauchery; (*debandadă*) confusion, riot, anarchy; revelry • ~at *nm* (*nerușinat*) shameless fellow ‖ *adj* negligent; (*destrăbalat*) profligate, wanton.

dezmembra [dezmem'bra] *vt* to dismember, to cut up, to dissect; (*un stat*) to divide up.

dezmetici [dezmeti'chi] *vt* to waken, to bring smb back to their senses ‖ *vr* (*din somn*) to wake up; *also fig* to come to (one's senses), to recover one's reason/ senses; (*din leșin*) to regain one's consciousness, to come round.

dezmierda [dezmier'da] *vt* (*a mângâia*) to caress, to fondle, to stroke; (*a alinta*) to spoil, to pamper; *fig* (*a desfăta*) to delight; (*ochiul*) to please.

dezminți [dezmin'tsi] *vt* to deny, to contest, to disavow; (*d. fapte*) to refute, to belie ‖ *vr* to go back on one's word • ~re *nf* denial; refutation.

dezmorți [dezmor'tsi] *vt* to take the chill off, to re-move stiffness/numbness from; (*palmele*) to chafe (hands) ‖ *vr* (*a se întinde*) to stretch oneself; to lose

one's numb feeling; *fig* (*a se încălzi*) to warm up, to cheer/liven up.

dezmoșteni [dezmoshte'ni] *vt* to disinherit; *coll* to cut smb off without a penny; *fig* to disown.

deznădăjdui [deznădăzhdu'i] *vi* to despair, to sink into despair; to be/grow desperate.

deznădejde [deznă'dezhde] *nf* despair, desperation, despondency.

deznoda [dezno'da] *vt* to undo, to untie; (*un nod*) to unknot ‖ *vr* to come undone.

deznodământ [deznodă'mânt] *nn* (*rezultat*) result, issue; *coll* upshot, outcome; *lit* denouement.

dezodorizant [dezodori'zant] *adj/nn* (*pt. oameni*) deodorant; (*pt. WC*) deodorizer; (*pt. camere*) air-freshener.

dezolant [dezo'lant] *adj* sad(dening), distressing; (*d. știri*) disheartening; (*d. vreme*) depressing.

dezolat [dezo'lat] *adj* grieved, distressed, desolate; *coll* very sorry.

dezonoare [dezo'noare] *nf* dishonor, disgrace, shame.

dezonora [dezono'ra] *vt* to dishonor, to disgrace, to bring shame on smb ‖ *vr* to disgrace oneself, to lose one's honor.

dezordine [de'zordine] *nf* disorder, confusion, untidi-ness; *pol also pl* disturbance(s), riots; **în** ~ out of order; helter-skelter, hurry-skurry.

dezordonat [dezordo'nat] *adj* (*d. cineva, d. o cameră*) untidy, disorderly, disorganized; (*neglijent*) careless; (*d. viață*) irregular (life); (*d. un discurs*) digressive, desultory ‖ *adv* negligently, untidily.

dezorganiza [dezorgani'za] *vt* to disorganize, to unset-tle, to upset ‖ *vr* to get/become disorganized; *coll* to go to pieces.

dezorienta [dezorien'ta] *vt* to make smb lose his bear-ings, to disorient, to disorientate; *fig* to bewilder, to perplex, to put smb out ‖ *vr* to lose one's bearings, to get confused • ~t *adj* bewildered, puzzled, at a loss.

dezoxiribonucleic [dezoksiribonu'kleik] *adj biochem* deoxyribonucleic (acid).

dezrădăcina [dezrădăchi'na] *vt also fig* to uproot, to tear/pull up by the roots; to tear/uproot smb from • ~t *adj* uprooted; *fig* alienated ‖ *nm* exile, uprooted person.

dezrobi [dezro'bi] *vt* (*d. sclavi*) to emancipate; (*a pune în libertate*) to (set) free, to liberate; *coll* to let off ‖ *vr* to gain one's freedom, to free oneself.

dezumaniza [dezumani'za] *vt/vr* to dehumanize.

dezumfla [dezum'fla] *vt* to deflate, to let air out; *med* to bring down swelling; *fig* to ridicule ‖ *vr* (*d. balon*) to deflate; (*d. anvelope*) to go flat; *med* (*d. umflătură*) to subside, to go down; *fig coll* to fall flat, to be deflated.

dezvălui [dezvălu'i] *vt* (*a descoperi*) to unveil, to uncover; *fig* (*a destăinui*) to reveal, to disclose; to divulge; (*o conspirație*) to unmask, to expose ‖ *vr* to come out, to appear • ~re *nf* revealing, disclosure, revelation.

dezvăța [dezvă'tsa] *vt* to wean smb from a habit; to break smb from a habit ‖ *vr* to get rid of a habit, to leave off a habit.

dezveli [dezve'li] *vt* (*a descoperi*) to uncover; (*un monument*) to unveil; (*capul*) to bare ‖ *vr* to uncover oneself; to be uncovered.

dezvinovăți [dezvinovă'tsi] *vt* to exculpate (from), to exonerate (from) || *vr* to exculpate oneself (from), to clear oneself/one's character.

dezvolta [dezvol'ta] *vt* to develop, to promote; (*a educa*) to form, to mold; (*a emite*) to give off, to emit; (*un subiect*) to enlarge on a matter; *math* to expand || *vr* to develop (oneself), to grow up, to increase; (*a se forma*) to be molded, to form oneself; (*a se întinde*) to spread out, to expand • ~**re** *nf* development, advancement; (*creștere*) growth, increase; *fig* emission.

diabet [dia'bet] *nn med* diabetes, diabetes mellitus.

diabolic [dia'bolik] *adj* diabolical, devilish, fiendish || *adv* diabolically, fiendishly.

diacon [dia'kon] *nm* deacon.

diademă [dia'demă] *nf* tiara, diadem.

diafan [dia'fan] *adj* diaphanous, transparent; *fig* delicate.

diafilm [dia'film] *nn* film strip.

diafragmă [dia'fragmă] *nf anat* diaphragm, midriff; *tech* diaphragm (of telescope); *phot* diaphragm stop.

diagnostic, diagnoză [diag'nostik, diag'noză] *nn/nf med* diagnosis, *pl* diagnoses.

diagnostica [diagnosti'ka] *vt* to diagnose, to diagnosticate.

diagonală [diago'nală] *nf geom* diagonal (line); **în ~** diagonally; *fig* at a glance, in a hurry, hastily; (*la uniformă*) baldric.

diagramă [dia'grama] *nf* diagram.

dialect [dia'lekt] *nn* dialect • ~**ică** *nf* dialectics.

dializă [dia'liză] *nf med, chem* dialysis.

dialog [dia'log] *nn* dialogue.

diamant [dia'mant] *nn* diamond; (*unealtă*) glazier's diamond, diamond point.

diametru [dia'metru] *nn* diameter; (*calibru*) bore.

diapazon [diapa'zon] *nn* (*instrument*) tuning fork; (*înălțime*) pitch, diapason; (*întinderea vocii*) compass/range of voice.

diapozitiv [diapozi'tiv] *nn* (film) slide, transparency.

diaree [dia'ree] *nf med* diarrhea, looseness of the bowels.

diatribă [dia'tribă] *nf* diatribe.

diavol ['diavol] *nm also fig* devil; (*spirit rău*) demon, fiend; (*copil neastâmpărat*) imp.

dibaci [di'bach] *adj* (*îndemânatic*) deft, dexterous, skilled; (*priceput*) clever, ingenious; (*șiret*) sly, cunning.

dibăcie [dibă'chie] *nf* (*îndemânare*) skill, skillfulness, deftness; *fig* (*pricepere*) cleverness, ingenuity; (*șiretenie*) cunning.

dibui [dibu'i] *vt* (*a pipăi*) to fumble, to grope for; (*a găsi*) to find out; (*a nimeri*) to hit || *vi* to grope/fumble about; to feel one's way.

dichisi [diki'si] *vt* (*a îmbrăca*) to dress up; (*a împodobi*) to adorn, to trim; (*a aranja*) to arrange, to fit/fix up, to tidy up || *vr* to dress oneself up; *coll* to tog oneself up, to adorn oneself; (*a se pregăti*) to get ready, to prepare.

dicta [dik'ta] *vt also fig* to dictate, to order, to command || *vr* to be dictated.

dictare [dik'tare] *nf* dictation.

dictator [dikta'tor] *nm* dictator, autocrat.

dictatură [dikta'tură] *nf* dictatorship.

dicton [dik'ton] *nn* dictum; maxim; adage.

dicționar [diktsio'nar] *nn* dictionary; lexicon.

dicțiune [diktsi'une] *nf* diction, articulation, delivery, enunciation.

didactic [di'daktik] *adj* didactic, teaching.

dietă [di'etă] *nf med* diet, regimen.

dietetic [die'tetik] *adj* dietetic, dietary.

diferend [dife'rend] *nn* disagreement, argument, dispute; difference, variance.

diferență [dife'rentsă] *nf* difference; (*distincție*) distinction.

diferenția [diferentsi'a] *vt* to differentiate, to distinguish; *math* to obtain the differential of || *vr* to be different (from each other), to differ.

diferi [dife'ri] *vi* to differ, to be different, to vary • ~**t** *adj* (*deosebit*) different (from); (*neasemănător*) dissimilar, unlike; (*variat*) varied, various || *adv* differently.

dificil [difi'chil] *adj* (*complicat*) difficult, hard, tough, intricate; (*d. cineva: capricios*) hard to please, choosy, particular; (*nesupus*) unmanageable, unyielding.

dificultate [difikul'tate] *nf* (*greutate*) difficulty, complication, hardness; *fig* crux; (*piedică*) obstacle, hindrance, impediment.

diform [di'form] *adj* deformed, misshapen, unshapely; twisted, monstrous.

difuz [di'fuz] *adj* (*împrăștiat*) diffuse; (*vag*) dim, vague; (*d. lumină*) diffused; (*d. stil*) prolix style • ~**a** *vt* (*d. lumină, căldură*) to diffuse; (*d. idei, știri*) to spread, to disseminate; (*prin radio*) to broadcast; (*d. presă*) to distribute, to circulate || *vr* to be spread/diffused; (*prin radio*) to broadcast • ~**are** *nf* (*d. lumină, căldură*) diffusion, spreading; (*d. radio*) broadcast(ing); distribution • ~**or** *nn* loudspeaker; diffuser; (*la un motor*) mixer || *nm* distributor.

dig [dig] *nn* dam, dike, embankment; (*mare*) breakwater; (*în port*) pier, jetty.

digera [didje'ra] *vt* to digest; *fig* to swallow, to stomach || *vr* to be digested.

digestie [di'djestie] *nf* digestion.

digestiv [didjes'tiv] *adj* digestive.

digit ['didjit] *nm tech* digit, figure, number.

digital [didji'tal] *adj anat* digital, finger; *comp* digital.

digresiune [digresi'une] *nf* digression.

dihanie [di'hanie] *nf* (*animal*) wild animal, beast; (*monstru*) monster, freak of nature.

dihor [di'hor] *nm zool* polecat.

dilata [dila'ta] *vt* to dilate, to expand; *med* (*stomacul*) to distend || *vr* (*d. aer*) to expand; (*d. stomac*) to become distended; (*d. pupilă*) to dilate; (*a se umfla*) to swell.

dilemă [di'lemă] *nf* dilemma.

diletant [dile'tant] *nm* dilettante, amateur; (*profan*) layman || *adj* dilettante, lay.

diligență[1] [dili'djentsă] *nf* diligence, application, industry; *jur* proceeding.

diligență[2] [dili'djentsă] *nf* diligence, stagecoach.

dilua [dilu'a] *vt* to dilute, to weaken; *fig* to attenuate; (*d. băutură*) to water down; (*d. vopsea*) to thin down • ~**nt** *nn chem* diluter.

dimensiune [dimensi'une] *nf* dimension; (*mărime*) size; (*proporție*) proportion.

dimineață [dimi'neatsă] *nf/adv* morning; (*zori*) dawn, daybreak.

diminua [diminu'a] *vt* to diminish, to decrease, to lessen || *vr* to diminish, to decrease, to decline, to dwindle; (*d. profituri*) to fall off.

diminutiv [diminu'tiv] *nn* diminutive, pet name; hypocoristic word/form.

dimpotrivă [dimpo'trivă] *adv* on the contrary; (*opus*) opposite.

dimprejur [dimpre'zhur] *adj/adv* about, around.

din [din] *prep* (*spațial*) in, at, of; **florile ~ parc sunt roșii** the flowers in the park are red; (*indică punct de plecare*) from; **venea ~ sat** he was coming from the village; (*indică extracția*) out of; **scoase cartea ~ servietă** he took the book out of the bag; (*temporal*: *punctul de plecare*) from, since; **îl cunosc ~ 1990** I have known him since 1990; (*exprimă cauza*) out of, because of, through; **~ curiozitate** out of curiosity; (*partitiv*: *aparținând*) of; **unul ~ prietenii mei** one of my friends; (*indică materialul*) of, from; **~ aur** made of gold.

dinadins [dina'dins] *adv* on purpose, intentionally, deliberately; **cu tot ~ul** by all means, at all costs.

dinafară¹ [dina'fară] *prep* outside.

dinafară² [dina'fară] *adv* out, out of doors; *frml* without; **de ~** from outside; **pe ~** on/from (the) outside; externally, outwardly, apparently; *fig* superficially, judging by appearances; *fig* (*în ignoranță*) ignorant, in ignorance.

dinainte [dina'inte] *adv* (*spațial*) before, in front; (*temporal*) (*din timp*) beforehand, in advance || *adj* anterior, previous; former; fore, front; (*primul*) first, foremost.

dinaintea [dina'intea] *prep* before, in front of; (*în față*) in the face of; (*în prezența*) in the presence of.

dinamic [di'namik] *adj* dynamic, lively || *adv* dynamically.

dinamita [dinami'ta] *vt* to dynamite, to blow up.

dinamită [dina'mită] *nf* dynamite.

dinapoi [dina'poi] *adv* (*în urmă*) behind; (*în spate*) in the rear, at the back • **~a** *prep* behind, at the back of.

dinastie [dinas'tie] *nf* dynasty.

dinăuntru [dină'untru] *adv* (*static*) within, inside; (*dinamic*) from within || *adj* inner, inward.

dinăuntrul [dină'untrul] *prep* (*înăuntru*) inside, within, in the interior of; (*din interiorul*) from within.

dincoace ['dinkoache] *adv* (*aici*) (over) here; (*de partea asta*) on this side (of); **~ de zid** on this side of the wall; **pe ~** this way.

dincolo ['dinkolo] *adv* beyond, over there; (*de partea cealaltă*) on the other/further side; (*alături: în cealaltă cameră*) in the next room; (*peste*) across; (*vizavi*) opposite; **~ de** beyond, on the other/further side of; **~ de zid** on the other side of the wall; **de ~** from there, on that side; beyond; in the next room.

dincotro [dinko'tro] *adv* from where, from what place; *obs frml* whence.

dineu [di'neu] *nn* dinner (party).

dinozaur [dino'zaur] *nm zool* dinosaur.

dinspre ['dinspre] *prep* from.

dintâi [din'tâi] *adj* first, greatest; (*anterior*) former || *adv* at first, at the beginning.

dinte ['dinte] *nm* tooth, *pl* teeth; (*colț*) fang; (*de elefant*) tusk; (*de pieptene, ferăstrău*) tooth of comb/saw; (*de roată*) sprocket, cog; (*de furcă*) prong; (*subțire*) tine.

dintre ['dintre] *prep* (*dintre doi*) between; *obs* betwixt; (*dintre mai mulți*) (from) among, of.

dioptrie [diop'trie] *nf opt* diopter.

diplomat [diplo'mat] *nm* diplomat || *adj* (*cu diplomă*) certified; *fig* (*dibaci*) tactful, diplomatic.

diplomă ['diplomă] *nf* diploma.

direct [di'rekt] *adj* (*drept*) direct, straight; (*deschis*) open, sincere, outspoken; (*d. tren*) through train || *adv* (*drept*) straight, directly; (*deschis*) openly, frankly; (*pe șleau*) plainly, in plain English.

directivă [direk'tivă] *nf* direction, norm; *pl* guidelines, instructions, directives.

director¹ [di'rektor] *nm* (*de întreprindere*) manager, managing director; (*de muzeu, închisoare*) warden; (*de școală*) principal; (*de scenă*) stage manager.

director² [direk'tor] *adj* guiding, leading, directing; *geom* directrix; *tech* steering.

direcție [di'rektsie] *nf* (*sens*) direction, way, course; *naut* bearings; (*tendință*) trend; (*conducere*) management, control, directorate; board (of directors); (*birou*) manager's office; (*la școală*) principal's office; *auto* direction, driving, steering.

diriginte [diri'djinte] *nm* (*la poștă*) postmaster.

dirija [diri'zha] *vt* (*a conduce*) to lead, to conduct; (*a ghida*) to guide, to direct, to put right; (*a sfătui*) to advise; (*a administra*) to direct, to control, to manage, to run; *mus* to conduct || *vi mus* to direct, to conduct.

dirijor [diri'zhor] *nm mus* conductor; (*de fanfară*) bandmaster.

disc [disk] *nn* (*de patefon*) record, disc; *sp* discus; *anat* disc; *tech* disc, plate.

discernământ [dischernă'mânt] *nn* discernment, judgment, discrimination.

discerne [dis'cherne] *vt* (*a vedea*) to see, to distinguish, to make out; to discern, to discriminate.

disciplina [dischipli'na] *vt* to discipline, to bring smb under control/discipline || *vr* to discipline oneself.

disciplină [dischi'plină] *nf* discipline; (*ramură de studiu*) branch of science/knowledge, subject (matter).

discipol [dis'chipol] *nm* disciple, follower.

discordant [diskor'dant] *adj* (*d. sunete*) discordant, dissonant; jarring, grating; (*d. culori*) clashing; (*d. opinii*) conflicting, diverging • **notă ~ă** *mus* false/wrong note; jarring sound; *geol* (*d. straturi*) unconformable.

discordanță [diskor'dantsă] *nf* (*nepotrivire*) disagreement, discordance, clash; (*d. culori*) clashing; (*d. sunete*) dissonance; *geol* unconformability.

discordie [dis'kordie] *nf* (*neînțelegere*) discord, difference, disagreement; (*dihonie*) feud; (*ceartă*) quarrel, ill-blood • **mărul ~ei** the apple of discord, the bone of contention.

discotecă [disko'tekă] *nf* discotheque; *coll* disco; record library, library of records; record cabinet, record collection.

discredita [diskredi'ta] *vt* to discredit; (*pe cineva*) to disparage, to run smb down, to compromise || *vr* to compromise oneself, to become discredited, to fall into disrepute.

discrepanță [diskre'pantsă] *nf* discrepancy.

discret [dis'kret] *adj* (*d. atitudine*) discreet, cautious; modest, unobtrusive, reserved, unassuming; (*d. îmbrăcăminte*) simple, plain; (*d. înfățișare*) inconspicuous; (*d. ton*) subdued; (*d. loc*) quiet, secluded; (*d. conversație*) hushed; (*tainic*) secret, private; *math* discrete; discontinuous || *adv* discreetly, cautiously, etc.

discreție [dis'kretsie] *nf* discretion, prudence, reserve; **la ~** (*din belșug*) in abundance, plenty, as much as one pleases.

discreționar [diskretsio'nar] *adj* discretionary.

discrimina [diskrimi'na] *vt* to discriminate (against);

to select, to choose, to distinguish • **~re** *nf* discrimination, differentiation; **~ rasială** racial discrimination, color bar • **~toriu** *adj* discriminating.

disculpa [diskul'pa] *vt* to exculpate, to exonerate, to clear smb (of a crime) ‖ *vr* to exculpate oneself (from), to exonerate oneself (from), to clear oneself (of).

discurs [dis'kurs] *nn* speech; (*solemn*) address, oration; (*demascator*) diatribe, harangue.

discuta [disku'ta] *vt* (*a vorbi despre*) to discuss, to talk about/over; (*a dezbate*) to debate (upon); (*a pune la îndoială*) to question, to dispute; (*a pune în discuție*) to moot ‖ *vi* to discuss, to talk (to/with); (*în contradictoriu*) to argue • **~bil** *adj* (*contestabil*) disputable, controversial, debatable, arguable; (*îndoielnic*) questionable, doubtful.

discuție [dis'kutsie] *nf* discussion, talk, conversation; (*aprinsă*) argument, dispute, altercation; (*dezbatere*) discussion, debate; **fără ~** undoubtedly, indisputably; categorically, beyond question.

diseca [dise'ka] *vt also fig* to dissect.

disecție [di'sektsie] *nf* dissection.

disemina [disemi'na] *vt* to spread, to disseminate.

disensiune [disensi'une] *nf* dissension, discord, variance.

disident [disi'dent] *nm* dissident, dissenter, nonconformist ‖ *adj* dissenting, dissident, dissentient.

disidență [disi'dentsă] *nf* dissidence, difference, disaccord; *pol* split, splinter party.

disimula [disimu'la] *vt* to dissimulate, to dissemble, to hide, to conceal.

disjungere [dis'zhundjere] *nf jur* severance (of causes).

disloca [dislo'ka] *vt anat* to dislocate; (*o articulație*) to sprain, to put out of joint; *mil* to shift, to transfer; *tech* to take to pieces, to dismantle ‖ *vr anat* to dislocate; *mil* to disband; *tech* to fall to pieces, to break up.

disonanță [diso'nantsă] *nf* dissonance, discord, clash.

disparat [dispa'rat] *adj* disparate, dissimilar, ill-assorted.

dispariție [dispa'ritsie] *nf* disappearance, vanishing; (*moarte*) demise; (*pierdere*) loss.

dispărea [dispă'rea] *vi* (*din vedere*) to disappear, to vanish; (*a nu se mai vedea*) to vanish from sight, to disappear from view; (*treptat*) to fade away; (*a muri*) to pass away, to die.

dispărut [dispă'rut] *nm* dead person, deceased, the late; *pl* the dead, the departed; *pl mil* the missing ‖ *adj* missing, lost; (*d. specie*) extinct; (*d. lume*) vanished.

dispensa [dispen'sa] *vt* (*de*) to excuse smb from, to exempt smb from ‖ *vr* to dispense with, to do without (smth), to renounce.

dispensar [dispen'sar] *nn med* dispensary, surgery

dispensă [dis'pensă] *nf* license; (*de*) exemption (from), dispensation; certificate of exemption.

dispera [dispe'ra] *vi* * **despera**.

dispersa [disper'sa] *vt* to disperse, to scatter, to spread; (*o mulțime*) to break up; (*o armată*) to rout an army ‖ *vr* to disperse, to scatter; (*d. nori, mulțime*) to break up.

displăcea [displă'chea] *vi* to dislike, to displease, to be displeased/dissatisfied.

disponibil [dispo'nibil] *nn fin* available funds, available/liquid assets ‖ *adj* (*la îndemână*) available; vacant, unoccupied; (*liber*) free • **~itate** *nf* (*rezervă*) availability, reserve.

dispozitiv [dispozi'tiv] *nn tech* device, contrivance, appliance.

dispoziție [dispo'zitsie] *nf* (*la îndemână*) disposal; **la ~** available; (*prevedere legală*) provision, condition, stipulation; (*hotărâre*) order; (*aranjare*) arrangement, disposition, distribution; (*ordine*) order; (*stare sufletească*) mood, frame/state of mind; (*ordin*) order, measure, step.

dispreț [dis'prets] *nn* contempt, scorn, disdain; **cu ~** scornfully, disdainfully.

disprețui [dispretsu'i] *vt* to scorn, to despise, to hold in contempt; (*a sfida primejdiile*) to defy • **de ~t** contemptible, despicable; abject, vile, mean • **~tor** *adj* contemptuous, disdainful, scornful ‖ *adv* scornfully, contemptuously, disdainfully.

disproporție [dispro'portsie] *nf* disproportion, want/lack of proportion; (*nepotrivire*) disparity, incongruity.

dispune [dis'pune] *vt* (*a ordona*) to order, to decide, to dispose; (*a prevedea*) to prescribe; (*a aranja*) to set (out), to lay, to arrange; (*a înveseli*) to cheer up ‖ *vi* (*a avea la dispoziție*) to dispose; *sp* to defeat, to outplay.

disputa [dispu'ta] *vt* to dispute, to contest; (*a pretinde*) to claim; to contend (with smb) for smth ‖ *vr sp* to be fought/played

dispută [dis'pută] *nf* dispute, controversy; altercation, quarrel; *sp* contest, competition.

distant [dis'tant] *adj* distant; *fig* aloof, reserved.

distanță [dis'tantsă] *nf* (*depărtare*) distance; range, reach; (*deosebire*) difference; (*în timp*) interval; **la ~** at (a) distance; in the distance; off; away; (*unul de altul*) far between; *fig* aloof.

distila [disti'la] *vt* to distill.

distinct [dis'tinkt] *adj* (*deosebit*) distinct, separate; (*clar*) clear, distinct; (*marcat*) marked; (*d. contur*) unblurred; (*lizibil*) legible ‖ *adv* distinctly, clearly.

distincție [dis'tinktsie] *nf* (*deosebire*) distinction, difference; (*rafinament*) refinement, elegance; (*decorație*) decoration; (*cinste*) honor; **cu ~** with honors

distinge [dis'tindje] *vt* (*a deosebi de*) to distinguish (from), to tell apart; (*a vedea*) to discern, to perceive, to make out; (*a acorda*) to award a distinction ‖ *vi* **a ~ între** to tell one from the other ‖ *vr* (*d. ceva*) to stand out, to be conspicuous; (*d. cineva*) to distinguish oneself.

distonant [disto'nant] *adj* discordant, dissonant; (*d. culori*) clashing.

distra [dis'tra] *vt* to amuse, to entertain ‖ *vr* to enjoy oneself, to have a good time.

distracție [dis'traktsie] *nf* entertainment, amusement, pastime; (*lipsă de atenție*) absent-mindedness, lack of attention, abstraction.

distrage [dis'tradje] *vt* to distract, to divert, to turn off (from); (*a abate*) to sidetrack.

distrat [dis'trat] *adj* absentminded, inattentive, scatterbrained; **aer ~** absent/vacant look ‖ *adv* absentmindedly, inattentively.

distribui [distribu'i] *vt* to distribute, to deal/give out, to allot; (*a împărți*) to divide, to share; *thea* to cast (smb in a part/role); (*d. scrisori: a preda*) to deliver, to hand out.

distribuție [distri'butsie] *nf* division, allotment; *thea* cast.

district [dis'trikt] *nn* district; (*regiune*) region, area.

distructiv [distruk'tiv] *adj* destructive.

distrugător [distrugă'tor] *nm* destroyer; exterminator ‖

nn (*navă*) destroyer || *adj* (*d. agent*) destroying; (*d. război*) destructive, devastating.

distruge [dis'trudje] *vt* to destroy; (*a desfiinţa*) to abolish; (*a extermina*) to exterminate, to extirpate; (*a nimici*) to annihilate; (*a ruina*) to ruin, to wreck; (*a dărâma clădiri*) to pull down, to raze; (*a pustii*) to lay waste, to ravage; (*a devasta*) to devastate; *fig* (*a nărui speranţele*) to shatter, to dash || *vr* to be destroyed, to fall into decay; to destroy oneself.

diurnă [di'urnă] *nf* daily allowance/fee.

divaga [diva'ga] *vi* to wander (away from the point; in one's speech); to ramble; to digress (from); to depart from the subject/question; to be discursive • ~ţie *nf* digression, digressing; rambling.

divan [di'van] *nn hist* divan; (*sală*) *obs* council-room; (*mobilă*) sofa, couch, divan, ottoman.

divă ['divă] *nf* diva, star.

divergenţă [diver'djentsă] *nf* divergence, discrepancy, difference; *bio, math* divarication.

divers [di'vers] *adj* (*variat*) diverse, various, different; (*banal*) trite, common; (*d. opinii*) varied • ~ifica *vt/vr* to diversify, to vary, to variegate • ~itate *nf* variety, diversity; difference.

diversiune [diversi'une] *nf mil* diversion; distraction; (*sabotaj*) sabotage, *pol* red-herring; *fig* side-tracking.

divertisment [divertis'ment] *nn* entertainment, diversion, amusement; *mus* divertimento, divertissement.

dividend [divi'dend] *nn fin* dividend.

divin [di'vin] *adj also fig* divine, sacred, heavenly.

diviza [divi'za] *vt* to divide, to share; (*a semăna discordie*) to set (people) at variance || *vr* to be divided, to break up (into).

divizie [di'vizie] *nf mil* division; *sp* league.

diviziune [divizi'une] *nf* division, partition; (*separare*) separation; portion, part.

divizor [divi'zor] *nm math* divisor, factor || *nn elec* divider.

divorţ [di'vorts] *nn* divorce; *jur* separation.

divorţa [divor'tsa] *vt* to divorce || *vi* to divorce, to get a divorce, to be divorced; **a ~ de cineva** to divorce smb.

divulga [divul'ga] *vt* (*un secret*) to disclose, to reveal, to let out; (*a trăda pe cineva*) to give away, to betray.

dizenterie [dizente'rie] *nf med* dysentery.

dizertaţie [dizer'tatsie] *nf* * **disertaţie**.

dizgraţie [diz'gratsie] *nf* disfavor, disgrace.

dizgraţios [dizgratsi'os] *adj* (*lipsit de graţie*) unseemly, ungraceful; awkward; inelegant; (*diform*) ungainly, unsightly, homely, ugly; (*ruşinos*) disgraceful, shameful, offensive.

dizolva [dizol'va] *vt* (*o substanţă*) to dissolve, to melt; (*parlamentul*) to dissolve; (*o tovărăşie*) to break || *vr* (*a se topi*) to dissolve, to melt; (*d. o adunare*) to break up, to disband.

do [do] *nm mus* C, do, doh; **~ major** C major.

doagă ['doagă] *nf* stave.

doamnă ['doamnă] *nf* lady, woman; (*ca formă de adresare*) madam, ma'am; (*în scris, împreună cu numele*) Mrs; (*indiferent de starea civilă*) Ms; (*profesoară*) school mistress; (*femeie bătrână*) old/aged woman, matron; (*principesă*) princess.

doar ['doar] *adv* (*numai*) only, just, but; (*poate*) perhaps, maybe, probably; (*desigur*) surely; (*ştii*) you see/know.

dobândă [do'bândă] *nf com* interest; (*cămătărească*) usury; (*câştig*) gain, profit.

dobândi [dobân'di] *vt* (*a căpăta*) to get, to obtain, to acquire; (*şi a câştiga*) to gain; (*a-şi procura*) to secure, to find || *vr* to be obtained/gotten.

dobitoc [dobi'tok] *nn* beast, animal; (*prost*) blockhead, dolt, num(b)skull, addlebrained, addlepated (man).

doborî [dobo'rî] *vt* to throw down; **a ~ la pământ** to knock down, to throw down; (*a învinge*) to overcome; (*a înfrânge*) to defeat; *fig* to overthrow.

doc[1] [dok] *nn naut* dock, warehouse.

doc[2] [dok] *nn tex* duck (cloth), canvas.

docher [do'ker] *nm naut* docker, stevedore.

docil [do'chil] *adj* (*ascultător*) meek, submissive, tractable; (*care poate fi învăţat*) teachable.

doct [dokt] *adj* erudite, learned.

doctor ['doktor] *nm* (*medic*) doctor; (*clinician*) physician; (*chirurg*) surgeon; (*de medicină generală*) General Practitioner, G.P.; (*apelativ*) **domnule ~!** doctor!; (*în ştiinţă*) master, doctor; **~ în medicină** M.D., Doctor of/in Medicine; (*în ştiinţe*) D.Sc., Doctor of Science; (*în litere*) Master of Arts.

doctorie [dokto'rie] *nf* drug, medicine.

doctrină [dok'trină] *nf* doctrine.

document [doku'ment] *nn* (*act*) document, deed, act; (*proces verbal*) record • **~a** *vt* to document; to support with documentary evidence || *vr* to gather evidence.

documentar [dokumen'tar] *nn* documentary || *adj* reference, documentary.

dogar [do'gar] *nm* cooper.

dogmă ['dogmă] *nf* dogma, tenet.

dogoare [do'goare] *nf* (*a focului*) (red) heat, glow; (*a soarelui*) blazing heat, blaze; *fig* (*a inimii*) ardor, fervor.

dogori [dogo'ri] *vt* (*a arde*) to burn, to scorch; (*a coace*) to ripen, to mellow; (*a înroşi*) to redden; (*d. faţă*) to flush || *vi* to burn; (*d. foc*) to glow; (*d. soare*) to scorch, to be burning hot.

doi [doi] *num/adj/nm* two; **cei ~** the two (of them); **~ câte ~** by twos, two by two, in couples.

doică ['doikă] *nf* wet nurse.

doime [do'ime] *nf math* half; *mus* minim.

doisprezece ['doisprezeche] *num/adj/nm* twelve.

dojană [do'zhană] *nf* reproach, reprimand, reproof, rebuke.

dojeni [dozhe'ni] *vt* to reproach, to reprimand, to reprove • **~tor** *adj* reproachful, reproving, chiding.

dolar [do'lar] *nm* dollar; *coll* buck, greenback.

doldora [do'ldora] *adj* chock-a-block, crammed; (*cu bani*) well-lined.

doleanţă [dole'antsă] *nf* (*plângere*) complaint, grievance; (*cerere*) request.

doliu ['doliu] *nn* mourning.

dolofan [dolo'fan] *adj* plump, pudgy; (*d. obraz*) chubby.

dom [dom] *nn* dome, cathedral, cupola; *geol, tech* dome.

domeniu [do'meniu] *nn* (*moşie*) domain, (real) estate, (landed) property; (*nedat în arendă*) demesne; (*sferă de activitate, de cunoaştere*) domain, field, area; *phys* range.

domestic [do'mestik] *adj* (*ce ţine de casă*) domestic, household, family; *fig* private, intimate; (*d. animale*) tame.

domiciliu [domi'chiliu] *nn* (place of) residence, abode, home; *jur* domicile; **la ~** at home; at one's private house.

domina [domi'na] *vt* (*d. cineva*) to dominate; (*a stăpâni*) to rule (over), to govern; (*d. o clădire, înălţime*) to tower over/above, to rise above, to overlook; (*d. voce*) to overpower ‖ *vi* (*a stăpâni*) to rule, to hold sway; (*a predomina*) to be prevalent, to prevail, to be predominant.

dominant [domi'nant] *adj* (*care domină*) ruling, dominating, dominant; (pre)dominant, prevailing, prevalent; characteristic.

domn [domn] *nm* gentleman, man; (*împreună cu numele*) Mr.; (*ca formă de adresare*) sir; (*domnitor*) prince, ruler, count; (*stăpân*) lord, master, owner • ~**ul** *relig* The Lord, God Almighty.

domni [dom'ni] *vi* to reign, to rule; *fig* to live in clover.

domnişoară [domni'shoară] *nf* young lady; (*cu numele, ca formă de adresare*) Miss; (*însoţitoare*) maid of honor.

domol [do'mol] *adj* (*încet*) slow, leisurely; (*d. oameni, animale: liniştit*) quiet, calm; (*d. sunet, glas: blând*) hushed, low, gentle ‖ *adv* (*uşor, încet*) gently, softly; (*treptat*) slowly, gradually, by degrees • ~**i** *vt* (*a calma*) to calm (down), to quiet, to set at ease; (*a împăca*) to appease; (*d. sete*) to quench; *frml* to slake; (*d. foame*) to stay; (*a alina*) to comfort, to assuage, to soothe ‖ *vr* (*a se calma*) to quiet down, to calm down, to compose oneself; (*d. furtună, vânt*) to abate.

dona [do'na] *vt* to donate; (*a da*) to give • ~**re** *nf* donation, contribution • ~**tor** *nm* giver, donor • ~**ţie** *nf* donation, gift.

doniţă ['doniţă] *nf* (wooden) pail/bucket; (*conţinutul*) bucketful, pailful.

dop [dop] *nn* (*de plută*) cork; (*de sticlă*) stopper; (*de lemn*) plug; (*de butoi*) bung.

dor [dor] *nn* (*dorinţă*) longing, yearning (for/after), hanker(ing) (after/for); (*tristeţe*) melancholy, grief, sorrow; ~ **de casă/ţară** homesickness • ~**i** *vt* (*ceva*) to want, to wish (for), to desire; to long/yearn/crave for; (*a intenţiona*) to intend; (*într-o rugăminte, preferinţă*) to like; (*pe cineva*) to want, to desire; (*a ura*) to wish • ~**inţă** *nf* wish (for), desire (for); (*către un ideal, scop*) striving (for/after), aspiration (for/after); (*arzătoare*) longing, yearning.

dormi [dor'mi] *vi* to sleep, to be asleep; *lit* to slumber; (*a aţipi*) to take a nap; (*uşor*) to doze; *coll* to snooze; (*a-şi petrece noaptea*) to put up for the night; *fig* (*d. lucruri*) to lie dormant • ~**ta** *vi* to doze; *coll* to snooze, to have a nap.

dormitor [dormi'tor] *nn* bedroom; (*la internat*) dormitory.

dornic ['dornik] *adj* desirous (of), eager (for); (*însetat*) thirsty (for); (*râvnitor*) covetous (of); (*nerăbdător*) anxious, longing.

dos [dos] *nn* (*spate*) back(side); *pe* ~ (*invers*) upside down; (*d. haine*) inside out • **în** ~**ul** behind; (*şezut*) behind, buttock(s), bottom; *coll* butt; back, reverse.

dosar [do'sar] *nn* file, dossier; (*cu clape*) folder; (*personal*) record; *jur* case, brief.

dosi [do'si] *vt coll* to hide, to conceal; (*a fura*) to steal ‖ *vr* to hide/conceal oneself.

dosnic ['dosnik] *adj* hidden, isolated, secluded; (*depărtat*) remote.

dota [do'ta] *vt* (*a utila*) to endow, to equip, to supply; *fig* to bestow (upon); (*d. mirese*) to dower.

dotă ['dotă] *nf* dowry, marriage portion.

douăzeci [două'zech] *nm/adj/num* twenty, a score.

dovadă [do'vadă] *nf* (*fapt*) proof; *pl jur* evidence;

(*indicaţie*) sign, manifestation; (*exemplu*) instance, example, illustration; (*act*) certificate.

dovedi [dove'di] *vt* (*a demonstra*) to prove, to show, to demonstrate; (*a manifesta*) to evince; (*a atesta*) to certify, to attest, to confirm ‖ *vr* to be proved; to prove (oneself), to turn out.

dovleac [dov'leak] *nm bot* pumpkin; *fig coll* pate, nut.

dovlecel [dovle'chel] *nm bot* (marrow) squash.

doză ['doză] *nf* dose, proportion, amount.

drac [drak] *nm* devil • ~**ul** *nm* Satan, The Evil One; *coll* Old Nick; (*drăcuşor*) imp, dickens; *fig* demon, fiend.

drag [drag] *nm* love, lover; darling ‖ *nn* love; (*consideraţie*) sake, eagerness ‖ *adj* dear, beloved, cherished; (*preferat*) favorite, pet • ~**ul mamei** my dear good boy/child; the apple of her eye • ~**ul meu** my dear/love/darling.

draga [dra'ga] *vt* to drag, to dredge.

dragă[1] ['dragă] *nf* love, sweetheart, darling ‖ *interj* honey!, (my) dear!.

dragă[2] ['dragă] *nf tech* dredger.

dragon [dra'gon] *nm mil* dragoon ‖ *nn* sword knot/tassel.

dragoste ['dragoste] *nf* (*sentiment*) love, affection; (*iubit/ă*) love; **cu** ~ lovingly, affectionately.

dramatic [dra'matik] *adj thea also fig* dramatic.

dramatiza [dramati'za] *vt thea also fig* to dramatize; to adapt for the stage.

dramă ['dramă] *nf thea* (*gen*) drama; (*piesă*) play; *fig* tragedy, catastrophe.

drapel [dra'pel] *nn* flag, banner; *mil* colors • ~**ul american** the Stars and Stripes, the Star-Spangled banner.

draperie [drape'rie] *nf* curtains, drapes, draperies.

drastic ['drastic] *adj* drastic.

drăcesc [dră'chesk] *adj* devilish, diabolical, fiendish; *fig* infernal.

drăcuşor [drăku'shor] *nm* little/young devil; *fig* imp.

drăgălaş [drăgă'lash] *adj* lovely, cute, sweet; graceful.

drăgăstos [drăgăs'tos] *adj* loving, affectionate, tender ‖ *adv* lovingly, with love, affectionately.

drăguţ(ă) [dră'guts(ă)] *nm/nf coll* sweetheart, beloved (one) ‖ *adj* (*frumuşel*) pretty, good-looking; (*amabil*) kind(ly), gentle, nice.

drege ['dredje] *vt* (*a repara*) to mend, to repair; (*d. încălţăminte*) to cobble, to vamp; (*d. haine*) to patch up; (*d. ciorapi*) to darn; (*a întrema*) to cure; *fig* (*a îndrepta*) to correct; (*o nedreptate*) to make restitution; (*vinul*) to doctor; (*mâncarea*) to season, to flavor ‖ *vr* (*a se îmbunătăţi*) to mend, to improve; (*a se întrema*) to recover, to get over; (*d. vreme*) to clear up, to improve.

drena [dre'na] *vt* to drain.

drept [drept] *adj* (*ant stâng; just*) right; (*ca însuşire morală*) *also relig* righteous; (*echitabil*) fair, equitable; (*direct, neocolit*) straight; (*d. drumuri etc*) direct; (*în picioare*) erect, upright; (*adevărat*) true, real; (*abrupt*) steep; *jur* lawful; (*cinstit*) honest, just; correct; (*ant fals*) straightforward; (*potrivit*) proper, suitable ‖ *adv* (*direct, spaţial*) straight ahead; (*exact*) rightly, justly; (*de fapt*) in fact, as a matter of fact; (*făţiş*) openly; (*chiar*) right ‖ *nn* right, privilege; *jur* law; jurisprudence; (*dreptate*) justice; (*permisiune*) permission; (*retribuţie*) royalties; **de** ~ by right(s), under the law; (*în mod natural*) naturally; (*legitim*) legitimately.

dreptate [drep'tate] *nf* justice, righteousness; *(justeţe)* fairness, fair-mindedness; *(nepărtinire)* impartiality.

dreptunghi [drept'ungi] *nn geom* rectangle • **~ular** *adj geom* right-angled; rectangular.

dresa [dre'sa] *vt (d. animale)* to tame, to train; *(d. cai)* to break in.

dresor [dre'sor] *nm* tamer, trainer; *(de cai)* horse breaker.

dribla [dri'bla] *vt/vi sp* to dribble.

dric [drik] *nn* hearse, funeral car.

drog [drog] *nn* drug; *coll* dope • **~a** *vt* to drug; *(cu stupefiante)* to dope || *vr* to take medicine; *(cu stupefiante)* to dope oneself, to take drugs, to be on smth.

drogherie [droge'rie] *nf* drugstore, druggist's (shop).

drojdie ['drozhdie] *nf* dregs, sediment; *(de cafea)* grounds; *(de băutură)* lees.

dromader [droma'der] *nm zool* dromedary.

drug [drug] *nm* (crow) bar.

drum [drum] *nn (concret)* road; *(stradă)* street; *(şosea)* highway; *(arteră)* thoroughfare; *(rută)* route; *(scurt)* (short)cut; *(trecere)* passage; *(cale) fig* way, path; *(călătorie)* journey, trip; *(pe apă)* voyage; *astron (al stelelor)* course; *(al planetelor)* orbit; *(al unei comete)* track; *(carieră)* career; **~ bun!** (I wish you) a good/ safe journey!, farewell!; **~ greşit** wrong way.

drumeţ [dru'meţ] *nm* traveler, wayfarer • **~ie** *nf* wandering, excursion, wayfaring.

dubă ['dubă] *nf* (police) van.

dubios [dubi'os] *adj (îndoielnic)* doubtful, dubious; questionable, problematic; *(nesigur)* uncertain || *adv* doubtfully, etc.

dubiu ['dubiu] *nn* doubt, uncertainty; *(şovăială)* vacillation, hesitation, wavering.

dubla [du'bla] *vt* to double; *(d. efort)* to redouble (one's efforts); *(d. pas)* to quicken (one's pace); *(a căptuşi)* to line (a coat); *(d. actor)* to stand in (for); *cin (d. un film)* to dub; *(d. nave)* to make, to weather || *vr* to double, to increase twofold.

dublet [du'blet] *nn* duplicate; *ling, phys* doublet.

dublu ['dublu] *adj* double, twofold || *adv* twice (as much), double, doubly.

dublură [du'blură] *nf thea* understudy; *cin* stand-in; *(cascador)* stuntman; *(la îmbrăcăminte)* lining.

ducat [du'kat] *nn (teritoriu)* duchy; *(demnitate)* dukedom.

duce[1] ['duche] *nm (teritoriu)* duke • **~să** *nf* duchess.

duce[2] ['duce] *vt (a conduce)* to lead, to take; *(a călăuzi)* to guide; *(a mâna)* to drive; *(a căra)* to bear, to carry; *(d. activitate)* to carry on; *(d. viaţă)* to live; *(a suporta)* to resist; *(a întreţine)* to entertain, to carry on; *(un război)* to wage; *(a păcăli) coll* to fool, to take smb in || *vi (a rezista)* to resist; *(a conduce)* to lead (to) || *vr (a merge)* to go; *(şi a aduce)* to fetch; *(a pleca)* to leave; *(a dispărea)* to pass away, to die.

dud [dud] *nm bot* mulberry tree • **~ă** *nf* mulberry.

dudui [dudu'i] *vi (d. foc, sobă)* to roar; *(d. maşini)* to drone, to whir(r); *(a se zgudui)* to throb.

duduie [du'duie] *nf* young lady.

duel [du'el] *nn* duel; encounter; single combat; *(polemică)* polemics, battle of words.

duet [du'et] *nn mus* duet, duo.

duh [duh] *nn (suflet, spirit)* soul, spirit, ghost; *(strigoi)* ghost, genie, *pl* genii; **~ bun** kind genie; **~ rău** evil spirit; *(inteligenţă)* wit.

duhni [duh'ni] *vi* to stink, to reek.

duhoare [du'hoare] *nf* stench, stink, reek.

duios [du'ios] *adj (gingaş)* tender, gentle; *(iubitor)* affectionate, loving; *(blând)* soft; *(înduioşător)* sad, melancholy; *(jalnic)* woeful, sorrowful || *adv* tenderly, sadly, etc

dulap [du'lap] *nm* plank || *nn* cupboard, case; *(pt. haine)* wardrobe.

dulăpior [dulă'pior] *nn* locker; *(noptieră)* bedside table; commode.

dulău [du'lău] *nm* mastiff; sheepdog.

dulce ['dulche] *nn* dessert; *pl* sweets; *relig* meat || *adj also fig* sweet, sugared, honeyed; *(drăguţ)* sweet, lovely, dear, lovable; *(plăcut)* nice; *(măgulitor)* flattering || *adv* sweetly, kindly, charmingly; *(drăgăstos)* lovingly, amorously.

dulceag [dul'cheag] *adj* sweetish, mellow; *(d. linguşire)* greţoasă* fulsome, nauseous; *fig (d. versuri)* soppy, mawkish.

dulceaţă [dul'cheatsă] *nf (farmec)* sweetness; *(blândeţe)* mildness; *(a glasului)* softness; *(aliment)* jam, preserve; *pl (bunătăţi) also fig* sweets, dainties; *(voluptate)* voluptuousness.

dulgher [dul'ger] *nm* carpenter, joiner.

dulie [du'lie] *nf elec* socket, lamp socket; *mil (de cartuş)* cartridge case.

dumbravă [dum'bravă] *nf* grove, coppice, copse.

dumeri [dume'ri] *vt* to enlighten, to clear up || *vr (a înţelege)* to understand, to see.

duminică [du'minikă] *nf* Sunday; *relig* the Lord's Day, Sabbath.

dumneaei [dumnea'ei] *adj poss* her; **casa ~** her house || *pron pers* she; **mi-a dat-o ~** she gave it to me; (to) her; **întreab-o pe ~** ask her.

dumnealor [dumnea'lor] *adj poss* their; **vecinul ~** their neighbor || *pron pers* they; **m-au întrebat ~** they asked me; (to) them; **i-am văzut pe ~** I saw them || *pron poss* theirs; **al ~** theirs.

dumnealui [dumnea'lui] *adj poss* his; **casa ~** his house || *pron pers* he; **~ e aici** he is here; (to) him; **întreabă-l pe ~** ask him || *pron poss* his; **al ~** his.

dumneata [dumnea'ta] *pron pers* you; **te întreb pe ~** I am asking you.

dumneavoastră [dumnea'voastră] *adj poss* your; **fratele ~** your brother || *pron pers* you; **~ ne puteţi ajuta** you can help us; (to) you; **vă rog pe ~** I am asking you || *pron poss* yours; **al ~** yours.

dumnezeiesc [dumneze'iesk] *adj* divine, godlike; *fig* heavenly, wonderful.

Dumnezeu [dumne'zeu] *nm* God, the Lord; *fig (zeu)* god, idol, divinity; **~ să-l ierte!** God rest his soul!; **~ ştie!** goodness knows!; **mulţumesc lui ~** thank goodness/God.

dună ['dună] *nf* dune, sand hill.

dunărean [dună'rean] *adj* Danubian.

dungat [dun'gat] *adj* striped.

dungă ['dungă] *nf (linie)* stripe, streak; *(zbârcitură)* wrinkle; *(brazdă)* furrow; *(margine)* edge, border.

după ['după] *prep (îndărătul)* behind; *(timp)* after; **~ aceea** after that, afterwards; *(apoi)* then; subsequently, *(mai târziu)* later on; *(succesiune)* after; **~ mine** follow/after me; *(scop)* for; *(mod: conform cu)* according to, in accordance/conformity with, by; **~ alfabet** alphabetically.

duplicat [dupli'kat] *nn* duplicate, identical copy.

duplicitar [duplichi'tar] *adj* duplicitous, double-faced, deceptive.

dur [dur] *adj* (*tare*) hard; (*aspru*) harsh; (*nemilos*) callous, unfeeling; (*sever*) stern, strict;(*dificil*) difficult; (*obositor*) troublesome, laborious || *nm coll* a tough guy, a hard nut.

dura¹ [du'ra] *vt* to build, to make, to construct.

dura² [du'ra] *vi* to last • **~bil** *adj* lasting, durable • **~tă** *nf* length (of time), duration; *mus* length, value.

durduliu [durdu'liu] *adj* plump; (*d. copii, obraji*) chubby; (*d. femei*) buxom.

durea [du'rea] *vt* (*fizic*) to ache, to hurt, to be sore; (*sufletește*) *fig* to pain, to give/cause pain; to make suffer; to grieve, to distress, to afflict; to regret, to feel sorry.

durere [du'rere] *nf* (*fizică*) ache, pain; *fig* (*suferință*) suffering; (*sufletească*) grief, sorrow; *lit* woe; (*chin*) torture; **cu** ~ sadly, sorrowfully, with regret; **de** ~ with pain.

dureros [dure'ros] *adj* (*fizicește*) painful, aching, sore; **loc** ~ (*pe corp*) sore place, tender/sensitive/raw spot.

duritate [duri'tate] *nf* (*a unei substanțe*) hardness; *fig* harshness, callousness, sternness, severity.

durui [duru'i] *vi* to rumble • **~t** *nn* rumble.

duș [dush] *nn* shower (bath); *fig* cold water.

dușcă ['dushkă] *nf* draught, gulp; (*mică*) sip, thimbleful.

dușman [dush'man] *nm* enemy; *lit* foe; opponent, adversary.

dușmăni [dushmă'ni] *vt* to hate, to bear a grudge to || *vr* to hate each other • **~e** *nf* enmity, hostility, bad-blood; (*pică*) rancor, grudge, ill-feeling; **în** ~ (*fără voie*) unwillingly.

dușmănos [dushmă'nos] *adj* (*față de*) hostile (to), inimical, unfriendly || *adv* hostilely, in a hostile manner.

dușumea [dushu'mea] *nf* floor(ing).

duză ['duză] *nf tech* nozzle, bean.

duzină [du'zină] *nf* dozen; **de** ~ ordinary.

E

ea [ia] *pron pers* she; *accus* her.

ebonită [ebo'nită] *nf* ebonite, vulcanite.

ebraic [e'braik] *adj* Hebrew • **~ă** *nf ling* Hebrew.

ebrietate [ebrie'tate] *nf* (state of) inebriation, intoxication, drunkenness.

ecartament [ekarta'ment] *nn rail* gauge (of track).

echer [e'ker] *nn* square; (*colțar*) corner plate, angle iron.

echidistant [ekidis'tant] *adj* equidistant.

echilibra [ekili'bra] *vt* (*a cumpăni*) to balance, to equilibrate; (*un vas, un avion*) to trim; *fig* to counter-balance || *vr* to balance, to be in equilibrium, to equilibrate.

echilibru [eki'libru] *nn also fig* equilibrium, balance, (equi)poise; (*d. avion*) stability.

echinocțiu, echinox [eki'noktsiu, eki'noks] *nn astron* equinox.

echipa [eki'pa] *vt* to equip, to fit out; (*a găti*) to dress up, to trim || *vr* to equip/provide oneself with; (*a se găti*) to dress up, to get dressed; (*a cumpăra lucruri*) to fit/rig oneself out; (*a se îmbrăca*) to dress for • **~j** *nn naut, avia* crew; (*cai cu trăsură*) (*doi cai*) carriage and pair; (*patru cai*) carriage and four; *tech* equipment, gear • **~ment** *nn tech, mil* equipment, outfit; kit, rigging; *sp* outfit, gear.

echipă [e'kipă] *nf sp* team, squad; group; (*schimb*) shift.

echitabil [eki'tabil] *adj* fair, just, equitable; impartial || *adv* fairly, justly, equitably, impartially,.

echitate [eki'tate] *nf* fairness, impartiality; (*dreptate*) justice, equity, equitableness.

echitație [eki'tatsie] *nf* equitation, (horseback) riding.

echivalent [ekiva'lent] *nn* equivalent; (*sinonim*) synonym || *adj* equivalent (to), worth || *adv* equally.

echivoc [eki'vok] *nn* ambiguity; (*îndoială*) doubt; (*neînțelegere*) misunderstanding || *adj* equivocal, ambiguous, evasive; (*îndoielnic*) doubtful, dubious; questionable, suspicious; (*obscen*) smutty, risqué.

eclipsa [eklip'sa] *vt astron also fig* to eclipse; *fig* to put (smb) in the shade; to overshadow, to outshine; (*în teatru*) *also fig* to upstage || *vr* to avoid/shun public attention; to vanish, to make off.

eclipsă [e'klipsă] *nf astron* eclipse; ~ **de soare** solar eclipse, eclipse of the sun; *fig* obscurity, oblivion.

ecluză [e'kluză] *nf* (*canal*) lock, sluice (gate); (*între mare și râu*) tide gate.

ecolog [eko'log] *nm* ecologist • **~ic** *adj* ecological, environmental • **~ie** *nf* ecology.

econom [eko'nom] *nm* (*într-o organizație*) treasurer, bursar; (*al unei moșii*) agent; *hist* steward || *adj* (*chibzuit*) economical, sparing; (*d. mese sau comportament*) frugal; (*între* ~ *și zgârcit*) parsimonious, thrifty • **~ic** *adj* (*din domeniul economiei*) economic; economical, thrifty; inexpensive; (*rentabil*) cheap, profitable || *adv* economically, thriftily • **~icos** *adj* economical, inexpensive || *adv* economically, sparingly.

economie [ekono'mie] *nf* economy; ~ **de piață** market economy; (*știință*) economics; (*cumpătare*) economy, thrift, frugality; **cu** ~ thriftily, economically, sparingly; *pl* savings; *coll* nest egg.

economisi [ekonomi'si] *vt* (*d. bani, timp, energie*) to save; (*d. bani*) to lay/put by; (*d. resurse*) to conserve; to husband.

economist [ekono'mist] *nm* (*comentator, professor etc*) economist.

ecosistem [ekosis'tem] *nn bio* ecosystem.

ecou [e'kou] *nn also fig* echo; response.

ecran [e'kran] *nn* screen; *comp* monitor • **~iza** *vt* to film, to screen • **~izare** *nf* film version, filming.

ecuator [ekua'tor] *nn geog* equator.

ecuație [eku'atsie] *nf math* equation.

ecuson [eku'son] *nn* crest, coat of arms, shield; *mil* badge; tab; (*collar*) patch; *auto* parking permit; (*cu numele*) name-badge.

ecvestru [ek'vestru] *adj* equestrian.

eczemă [ek'zemă] *nf med* eczema.

edifica [edifi'ka] *vt* (*a construi*) to build (up), to construct, to create; (*a stabili*) to establish; (*a lămuri*) to enlighten || *vr* to be enlightened, to understand • **~tor** *adj* enlightening, self-evident, telling.

edificiu [edi'fichu] *nn* (*clădire*) building, edifice; *fig* fabric, structure.

edita [edi'ta] *vt* to publish; to bring out; (*a îngriji*) to edit; (*a tipări*) to print; (*o revistă*) to run; (*un disc*) to produce; (*pe calculator*) to edit.

editor [edi'tor] *nm* publisher; (*îngrijitor de ediție*) editor (of text) • **~ial** *nn* editorial, leading article || *adj* publishing, editorial; (*d. un articol*) leading.

editură [edi'tură] *nf* publisher, publishing house.

ediție [e'ditsie] *nf* edition, issue.

educa [edu'ka] *vt* (*a instrui*) to educate; (*de către părinți*) to bring up; (*a forma*) to train • **~re** *nf* education, training, bringing up • **~tiv** *adj* instructive, educational • **~tor** *nm* educator, teacher; nursery school teacher || *adj* educative, educational • **~tie** *nf* education; (*pregătire*) training; (*în copilărie*) upbringing; (*maniere*) (good) manners, (good) breeding.

efect [e'fekt] *nn* (*urmare*) effect, result, consequence; *pl jur* (*proprietate*) goods, property; (*impresie*) impression; *com* bill (of exchange), draft; *pl* (*haine*) clothes, possessions, belongings; *mil* equipment, effects; *tech* power; **~ de seră** greenhouse effect • **~e speciale** special effects.

efectiv [efek'tiv] *nn mil* effective force/strength; *com* balance in cash || *adj* effective, actual, real || *adv* actually, really, in actual fact.

efectua [efektu'a] *vt* to perform, to accomplish, to carry out; to put into effect, to bring about; *econ* to make (a payment); (*a se produce*) to take place; to be carried out/through.

efemer [efe'mer] *adj* ephemeral, short-lived, fleeting.

efeminat [efemi'nat] *adj* effeminate, womanish, unmanly.

eficace [efi'kache] *adj* (*d. un remediu, mijloc*) effective, effectual; (*d. medicamente*) efficacious.

eficacitate [efikachi'tate] *nf* efficiency, effectiveness, efficacy.

eficient [efichi'ent] *adj* efficient, efficacious; (*măsuri ~*) appropriate measures/actions.

eficiență [efichi'entsă] *nf* efficiency.

efort [e'fort] *nn* effort, exertion, endeavor; *mech* strain, stress.

efuziune [efuzi'une] *nf* effusion; *fig* outpour(ing), overflow, gush.

egal [e'gal] *adj* (*la fel*) equal, alike; even, uniform; identical, the same; *math* equal to; (*cu aceleași drepturi*) enjoying the same rights; proportionate, commensurate; indifferent, all the same; (*cu fire blândă*) even tempered; *sp* (*d. meci, rezultat*) drawn || *nm* equal, peer, fellow, match • **~a** *vt* to make (smth) equal (to), to equal(ize); *fig* to match || *vi sp* to tie, to draw • **~itate** *nf* equality; uniformity, regularity; (*paritate*) parity; identity, sameness; (*asemănare*) similarity; *sp* tie; (*la tenis*) deuce; regularity, evenness; *math* equation.

egiptean [edjip'tean] *nm/adj* Egyptian; **limba ~ă** (the) Egyptian (language) • **~că** *nf* Egyptian (woman/girl).

egocentric [ego'chentrik] *adj/nm* egocentric, self-centered (person).

egoism [ego'ism] *nn* selfishness, egoism, self-centeredness.

egoist [ego'ist] *nm* egoist, selfish person || *adj* selfish, egoistic(al), self-seeking/-centered.

egotism [ego'tism] *nn* egotism.

egretă [e'gretă] nf (*pană*) aigret(te), plume; *orn* egret.

ei¹ [iei] *pron pers pl* they; *accus pl* them; **i-am întrebat pe ~** I asked them || *pron pers sg f* (to) her; **dă-i cartea ~** give the book to her, give her the book || *pron poss* **a(i), ai, ale ~** hers; **cartea e a ~** the book is hers || *adj pron* her **cartea ~** her book.

ei² [ei] *interj* (*ascultă!*) hey (you)!, I say!; (*ai văzut?*) well?; (*concesiv*) well; (*cum?*) eh, what (do you mean?); (*nici pomeneală*) not at all, not in the least.

ejacula [ezhaku'la] *vt* to ejaculate • **~re, ~ție** *nf* ejaculation.

ejecție [e'zhektsie] *nf* ejection.

el [iel] *pron pers m* he; (*d. animale, obiecte*) it.

elabora [elabo'ra] *vt* to elaborate; to work out, to develop; (*a redacta un plan*) to draw up; (*o antologie, dicționar*) to compile.

elan¹ [e'lan] *nm zool* elk, moose.

elan² [e'lan] *nn* élan, enthusiasm; (*avânt*) impetus; (*al spiritului*) buoyancy; (*vioiciune*) briskness; impulse, a burst of energy.

elastic [e'lastik] *nn* elastic; rubber band || *adj* elastic; (*care sare*) springy, rebounding; *fig* (*d. pași*) buoyant; resilient; (*d. reguli, legi*) flexible || *adv* elastically.

elasticitate [elastichi'tate] *nf* elasticity, springiness, resilience; flexibility.

ele ['iele] *pron pers f* they.

electoral [elekto'ral] *adj* electoral, elective.

electorat [elekto'rat] *nn hist* electorate, rank of Elector; *pol* electorate, (body of) electors.

electric [e'lektrik] *adj* electric(al), power.

electrician [elektrichi'an] *nm* electrician, electrical fitter.

electricitate [elektrichi'tate] *nf* electricity; (electric) current, (electric) power.

electrocardiogramă [elektrokardio'gramă] *nf med* electrocardiogram.

electrocuta [elektroku'ta] *vt* to electrocute, to execute/kill by electricity.

electron [elek'tron] *nm phys* electron.

electronică [elek'tronikă] *nf* electronics.

electrotehnică [electro'tehnikă] *nf* electrotechnics, electrical engineering.

elefant [ele'fant] *nm zool* elephant.

elegant [ele'gant] *adj* elegant; neat; smart, well-dressed; (*la modă*) stylish, fashionable; *fig* graceful, neat; (*d. stil, maniere*) polished, distinguished; (*d. gesturi, comportament*) courteous.

eleganță [ele'gantsă] *nf* elegance, grace, refinement; (*modă*) smartness, fashionableness.

elegie [ele'djie] *nf* elegy; (*cântec de jale*) plaintive/mournful song, dirge.

element [ele'ment] *nn* element, factor; *pl* (*principii*) elements, rudiments, first principles; *elec* cell; (*de calorifer*) radiator rib • **~ar** *adj* (*de bază*) elementary, elemental, rudimentary; (*la școală*) lower.

eleșteu [elesh'teu] *nn* (small) pond.

elev [e'lev] *nm* (*școlar*) schoolboy; (*generic*) pupil, trainee; (*om studios*) student; (*discipol*) disciple, follower.

elevat [ele'vat] *adj* noble, lofty; (*d. stil*) elevated, high.

elevă [e'levă] *nf* student, schoolgirl, pupil.

elibera [elibe'ra] *vt* to liberate, to (set) free, to release; to unfetter; (*o cameră de hotel*) to vacate; (*d. instincte, pasiuni*) to unleash; (*d. un act*) to issue, to deliver || *vr* to free/liberate oneself • **~re** *nf* liberation; (*din captivitate*) release; (*după război*) demobilization; (*a unui soldat; de energie*) discharge; (*predare*) delivery; **~ condiționată** *jur* parole • **~tor** *nm* liberator, deliverer || *adj* liberating, delivering.

elice [e'liche] *nf geom, anat, archit* helix; *avia, naut* prop(eller).

elicopter [elikop'ter] *nn* helicopter; *coll* chopper.

eligibil [eli'djibil] *adj* eligible.

elimina [elimi'na] *vt* to eliminate; (*a îndepărta*) to remove, to cross out; (*d. bănuieli*) to clear up; (*d. obstacole*) to do away with; (*d. o ipoteză*) to rule out; to exclude; (*d. un sportiv*) to knock out; (*a* *şterge*) to erase; *scol* to expel; *chem* to reduce, to isolate • **~toriu** *adj* eliminatory.

elipsă [e'lipsă] *nf geom* ellipse; *ling* ellipsis.

elită [e'lită] *nf* elite; (the) pick (of), flower; **de** ~ top-notch, picked.

elixir [elig'zir] *nn* elixir; *fig* balm.

elocvenţă [elok'venţsă] *nf* eloquence.

elogia [elodji'a] *vt* to extol, to praise to the skies, to speak highly of.

elogios [elodji'os] *adj* eulogistic, laudatory ‖ *adv* highly, eulogistically.

elogiu [e'lodju] *nn* (*discurs*) eulogy, panegyric; (*laudă*) praise, commendation.

elucida [eluchi'da] *vt* to elucidate, to clarify, to clear up.

elucubraţie [eluku'bratsie] *nf* fallacy; aberration.

eluda [elu'da] *vt* to elude, to evade; to shirk; *coll* to dodge.

elveţian [elvetsi'an] *nm/adj* Swiss • **~că** *nf* Swiss (*female*).

e-mail ['imeil] *nn* E-mail; **a transmite/trimite un** ~ to (send an) email.

email [e'mail] *nn* enamel.

emana [ema'na] *vt* to give off, to discharge; (*a răspândi*) to spread; to produce ‖ *vi* to emanate, to issue, to flow; *fig* (*de la*) to emanate (from), to proceed (from).

emancipa [emanchi'pa] *vt* to emancipate ‖ *vr* to become emancipated, to free oneself (from) • **~t** *adj* emancipated; full-fledged.

embargo [embar'go] *nn* embargo.

emblemă [em'blemă] *nf* emblem, badge; *fig* symbol, sign; (*de marcă*) brand mark.

embrion [embri'on] *nm bio also fig* embryo; *fig* germ, bud; **în** ~ in embryo, in the bud.

emfatic [em'fatik] *adj* pompous; bombastic, grandilo-quent; (*d. stil*) turgid ‖ *adv* pompously, etc.

emfază [em'fază] *nf* pomposity, bombast, grandilo-quence; **cu** ~ pompously.

emigra [emi'gra] *vi* (*d. oameni*) to emigrate; (*d. păsări*) to migrate • **~nt** *nm* emigrant, émigré • **~re** *nf* (*d. oameni*) emigration; (*d. păsări*) migration • **~ţie** *nf* emigration; emigrants.

eminent [emi'nent] *adj* excellent; eminent; (*distins*) distinguished, outstanding; (*foarte priceput*) proficient.

emisar [emi'sar] *nm* emissary, messenger.

emisferă [emis'feră] *nf* hemisphere; ~ **australă** (the) southern hemisphere; ~ **boreală** (the) northern hemisphere.

emisie [e'misie] *nf phys* emission.

emisiune [emisi'une] *nf physiol* (*emitere*) emission; *opt* emission; *fin* (*de bani*) issue; (*radio, TV*) broadcast-(ing), transmission.

emite [e'mite] *vt* to emit; (*d. căldură*) to give out; (*d. miros*) to give off, to send forth; (*a rosti*) to utter; (*d. o teorie*) to put forward; *rad, TV* to transmit, to broadcast; *fin* (*a pune în circulaţie*) to issue.

emiţător [emiţsă'tor] *nn tech* transmitter, emitter ‖ *adj* transmitting, issuing, broadcasting.

emolient [emoli'ent] *nn/adj pharm* emollient.

emotiv [emo'tiv] *adj* emotional, shy; emotive.

emoţie [e'motsie] *nf* (*sentiment*) emotion, excitement; (*tulburare*) agitation (of mind), commotion.

emoţiona [emotsio'na] *vt* (*a impresiona*) to excite, to thrill; (*a mişca*) to move, to touch ‖ *vr* (*a fi mişcat*) to be touched/moved; (*a se nelinişti*) to get excited/

alarmed/upset • **~l** *adj* emotional • **~nt** *adj* (*mişcător*) moving, touching; (*tulburător*) exciting, thrilling • **~t** *adj* (*mişcat*) moved, thrilled; (*tulburat*) excited, agitated, nervous.

empiric [em'pirik] *adj* empiric(al) ‖ *adv* empirically.

emulaţie [emu'latsie] *nf* rivalry, competitiveness.

emulsie [e'mulsie] *nf biochem* emulsion.

enciclopedie [enchiklope'die] *nf* encyclopedia.

enclavă [en'klavă] *nf geol, pol* enclave.

energetică [ener'djetikă] *nf* energetics.

energic [e'nerdjik] *adj* (*d. cineva*) energetic, full of energy; *coll* having plenty/lots of go; *sl* full of beans; (*apăsat*) emphatic; (*d. limbaj*) forcible; drastic, strong; (*viguros*) vigorous, forceful ‖ *adv* energeti-cally, strongly, vigorously, forcefully.

energie [ener'djie] *nf* energy; strength, force; (*vigoare*) vigour; (*vioiciune*) liveliness; *coll* push, go; (*ştiinţă*) *phys* energy, power.

enerva [ener'va] *vt* to vex, to annoy; *coll* to aggravate, to get on smb's nerves ‖ *vr* to be annoyed/chafed; to be/grow impatient; to get angry (with smb/at smth) • **~nt** *adj* annoying, irritating; nerve-racking ‖ *adv* annoyingly, irritatingly • **~re** *nf* annoyance, irritation, vexation.

englez [en'glez] *nm* Englishman ‖ *adj* English • **~ă** *nf* English, the English language • **~esc** *adj* English • **~eşte** *adv* English, like an Englishman • **~oaică** *nf* Englishwoman, English girl.

enigmatic [enig'matik] *adj* enigmatic(al), puzzling; (*neînţeles*) unintelligible, mysterious ‖ *adv* enigmati-cally, mysteriously.

enigmă [e'nigmă] *nf* enigma, puzzle, riddle; (*cu scop distractiv*) conundrum.

enoriaş [enori'ash] *nm* parishioner; *pl* flock.

enorm [e'norm] *adj* enormous, huge, immense, vast, colossal; (*uimitor*) astonishing; (*îngrozitor*) awful, dreadful; (*înspăimântător*) outrageous, tremendous ‖ *adv* enormously, hugely, immensely, tremendously • **~itate** *nf* (*imensitate*) enormousness, vastness, hugeness; (*prostie*) stupid thing; (*monstruozitate*) monstrosity, dreadful deed, outrageousness.

entitate [enti'tate] *nf* entity.

entorsă [en'torsă] *nf med* sprain, twist, wrench.

entuziasm [entuzi'asm] *nn* enthusiasm, eagerness; (*încântare*) elation; **cu** ~ enthusiastically, with enthu-siasm; **fără** ~ halfheartedly • **~a** *vt* to fill/fire (smb) with enthusiasm, to enthuse, to enrapture ‖ *vr* to be full of enthusiasm, to go into raptures (over); to be keen on smth.

entuziast [entuzi'ast] *nm* enthusiast, enthusiastic ad-mirer ‖ *adj* enthusiastic, *coll* gushing.

enumera [enume'ra] *vt* to enumerate, to count.

enunţ [e'nunts] *nn also math* statement, utterance; *also phil* enunciation.

epata [epa'ta] *vt* to astound, to amaze, to dumbfound; *coll* to flabbergast, to bowl over.

epavă [e'pavă] *nf naut* wreck, derelict; (*d. cineva*) human wreck.

epic ['epik] *adj* epic.

epidemie [epide'mie] *nf* epidemic.

epidermă [epi'dermă] *nf* epidermis.

epigramă [epi'gramă] *nf lit* epigram; (*vorbă înţepătoare*) witty sting, quip.

epila [epi'la] *vt* * **depila**.

epilepsie [epilep'sie] *nf med* epilepsy.

epilog [epi'log] *nn liter* epilogue.

episcop [e'piskop] *nm relig* bishop • **~ie** *nf relig* (*eparhie*) bishopric, diocese; (*demnitate*) episcopate, episcopal office.

episod [epi'sod] *nn* episode; (*incident*) incident; (*întâmplare*) occurrence, event.

epistolar [episto'lar] *adj* epistolary.

epitaf [epi'taf] *nn* epitaph.

epitet [epi'tet] *nn liter* epithet.

epocă ['epokă] *nf* epoch; (*timp*) time; (*perioadă*) age, period; era.

epolet [epo'let] *nn mil* epaulet(te).

epopee [epo'pee] *nf liter* epic (poem), epos.

eprubetă [epru'betă] *nf chem* test tube.

epuiza [epui'za] *vt* (*a seca*) to exhaust, to drain, to empty; (*a obosi*) to exhaust, to tire out; (*a termina*) to exhaust, to spend, to use up; (*a risipi*) to waste; (*d. resurse*) to deplete, to run low on smth; (*d. vânzări*) to sell out; (*d. o sursă*) to run dry, to dry up || *vr* to be/become exhausted; (*a se obosi*) to exhaust oneself, to wear oneself out; (*d. cărți*) to get out of print; (*d. o marfă*) to be/get out of stock; (*d. provizii*) to run out, to give out • **~re** *nf* (*oboseală*) exhaustion; (*sfârșeală*) *fig* lassitude, weariness; (*terminare*) exhausting; (*a unei cărți*) getting out of print; (*secare*) emptying, draining, depletion.

epurare [epu'rare] *nf* cleansing, purifying, filtering; *pol* purge.

erată [e'rată] *nf* erratum, *pl* errata.

eră ['eră] *nf* era; *geol* period; **era noastră** A.D. (Anno Domini).

erbicid [erbi'chid] *nn chem, agr* weed killer, herbicide.

erecție [e'rektsie] *nf archit, physiol* erection.

ereditar [eredi'tar] *adj* hereditary.

ereditate [eredi'tate] *nf bio* heredity; *jur* heirship, right of inheriting, inheritance.

eretic [e'retik] *nm* heretic || *adj* heretical, unorthodox || *adv* heretically, unorthodoxly.

erezie [ere'zie] *nf* heresy, heterodoxy; (*greșeală*) *fig* fallacy.

ermetic [er'metik] *adj* tight, airtight, watertight; *fig* hermetic || *adv* hermetically.

eroare [e'roare] *nf* error, mistake, blunder; (*scăpare din vedere*) oversight, slip; miscalculation.

eroda [ero'da] *vt geog, geol* to erode, to eat/wear away • **~re** *nf* eroding, erosion, wearing away.

eroic [e'roik] *adj* (*vitejesc*) heroic(al), courageous, brave; *lit* epic || *adv* heroically, courageously, bravely.

eroină [ero'ina] *nf* heroine.

eroism [ero'ism] *nn* heroism; courage, bravery.

eronat [ero'nat] *adj* erroneous; (*inexact*) incorrect, wrong; (*d. cineva*) mistaken; (*indus în eroare*) misled.

erotic [e'rotik] *adj* erotic, amatory; **film** ~ sex/porn movie.

erou [e'rou] *nm* hero; (*luptător pt. o cauză*) champion; *liter* main character.

eroziune [erozi'une] *nf* erosion, denudation, wearing away.

erudit [eru'dit] *nm* scholar, learned man || *adj* erudite, learned, scholarly.

erudiție [eru'ditsie] *nf* erudition, learning, scholarship.

erupe [e'rupe] *vi* to erupt, to burst forth, to be in eruption; *med* to break out || *vt* to eject, to throw out.

erupție [e'ruptsie] *nf geol* eruption; *med* (*urticarie*) rash, breaking out.

escadrilă [eska'drilă] *nf naut* flotilla; *avia* flight of aircraft.

escadron [eska'dron] *nn avia, naut, mil* squadron.

escalada [eskala'da] *vt* to climb (over), to scale; *mil* to escalate • **~re** *nf* climbing (over), scaling; *mil* escalation.

escalator [eskala'tor] *nn tech* escalator.

escală [es'kală] *nf naut, avia* (*loc*) stopover, port/place of call; (*oprire*) call, stop.

escapadă [eska'padă] *nf* escapade; outing.

eschimos [eski'mos] *nm/adj* Eskimo.

eschiva [eski'va] *vr* (*a se sustrage de la*) to shirk, to dodge, to evade; (*a se retrage*) to slip away/out/off; *coll* to make oneself scarce.

eschivă [es'kivă] *nf sp* dodging, ducking, slip away/ aside.

escorta [escor'ta] *vt* to escort; (*a însoți*) to accompany.

escortă [es'kortă] *nf* (*suită*) escort, train, retinue; *mil* guard, convoy.

escroc [es'krok] *nm* rogue, swindler, crook; *coll* conman • **~a** *vt* to cheat, to swindle, to take in; *coll* to fleece, to con • **~herie** *nf* swindle, swindling, fraud.

eseist [ese'ist] *nm* essayist, essay-writer.

esență [e'sentsă] *nf* essence, being; nature, substance; (*parfum*) perfume, oil; **în** ~ essentially, in essence.

esențial [esentsi'al] *nn* essence, pith || *adj* (*ținând de esență*) essential; indispensable, necessary; material, important; (*de bază*) basic, fundamental • **~ul** *nn* the main/chief/essential point.

eseu [e'seu] *nn liter* essay; *sp* (*rugbi*) try.

esofag [eso'fag] *nn anat* esophagus.

esplanadă [espla'nadă] *nf* esplanade.

est [est] *nn* East, Orient; **de** ~ east(ern), easterly; **spre** ~ eastward, towards the east.

estet [es'tet] *nm* esthete • **~ic** *adj* (a)esthetic(al) || *adv* aesthetically.

estima [esti'ma] *vt* to estimate, to assess, to appraise; to calculate • **~re** *nf* estimation, appraising, assessment; estimate, valuation • **~tiv** *adj* estimated.

estompa [estom'pa] *vt* (*artă*) to stump; *fig* to blur, to tone down || *vr* to grow dim, to be/grow blurred, to fade away • **~t** *adj* soft, indistinct, dim, blurred, faded.

estradă [es'tradă] *nf* platform, stage; (*tribună*) rostrum; (*gen de spectacol*) music hall.

estuar [estu'ar] *nn geog* estuary.

eșafod [esha'fod] *nn* scaffold.

eșalon [esha'lon] *nn mil* echelon.

eșalona [eshalo'na] *vt* to stagger, to phase, to space out; *mil* to echelon • **~re** *nf* staggering, phasing; *mil* echeloning.

eșantion [eshanti'on] *nn* sample, pattern, specimen; population sample.

eșapament [eshapa'ment] *nn auto* exhaust; escapement.

eșarfă [e'sharfă] *nf* scarf; (*șal*) shawl; sash; *med* arm sling.

eșec [e'shek] *nn* failure, setback, defeat.

eșua [eshu'a] *vi* (*d. nave*) to strand, to run aground; (*cu intenție*) to ground; to fail, to fall through, to miscarry.

etaj [e'tazh] *nn constr* (*pe dinăuntru*) floor; (*pe dinafară*) stor(e)y; **la** ~ upstairs; *geol* layer, stratum; (*într-o grădină*) terrace; (*al unei prăjituri*) tier; *tech* stage.

etajeră [eta'zheră] *nf* bookstand; (*poliță*) shelf; rack; (*pentru diverse*) what-not.

etala [eta'la] *vt com* to display, to exhibit, to expose; *fig* to show off, to flaunt || *vr fig* to show off • ~t on display.

etalon [eta'lon] *nn* standard (of measures).

etanș [e'tansh] *adj* tight; airtight, watertight, impervious • ~eitate *nf tech* tightness, imperviousness.

etapă [e'tapă] *nf* (*stadiu*) stage; (*oprire*) stop, halting place; stage of a journey; *sp* leg, lap.

etate [e'tate] *nf* age; în ~ elderly, aged.

eter [e'ter] *nn chem, fig* ether; (*aer*) air; (*cer*) sky.

etern [e'tern] *adj* eternal; (*nesfârșit*) everlasting, endless; (*perpetuu*) perpetual || *adv* eternally, forever • ~ul *nn* the eternal • ~itate *nf* eternity.

eterogen [etero'djen] *adj* heterogeneous; incongruous; dissimilar, different; mixed.

etic ['etik] *adj* ethic(al), moral • ~ă *nf* ethics.

eticheta [etike'ta] *vt* to label, to attach a label to; (*d. mărfuri*) to ticket; *fig* to classify.

etichetă [eti'ketă] *nf* label; (*pentru mărfuri*) ticket; *fig* (*politețe*) etiquette, formality; fără ~ *fig* informally.

etimologie [etimolo'djie] *nf ling* etymology.

etiopian [etiopi'an] *nm/adj* Ethiopian.

etnic ['etnik] *adj* ethnic(al).

etnograf [etno'graf] *nm* ethnographer.

etolă [e'tolă] *nf* stole.

etos ['etos] *nn* ethos.

etuvă [e'tuvă] *nf* drying stove/oven; sterilizer.

eu [ieu] *nn* ego, self || *pron* myself; *coll* me, number one.

eufemism [eufe'mism] *nn* euphemism.

euforic [eu'forik] *adj* euphoric, elated, exulting.

euforie [eufo'rie] *nf* euphoria, elation.

eunuc [eu'nuk] *nm* eunuch.

Europa [eu'ropa] *nf* Europe.

european(ă) [euro'pean(ă)] *nm/adj/nf* European.

eutanasie [euta'nasie] *nf med* euthanasia.

evacua [evaku'a] *vt* to evacuate, to remove; *med* to eject; to throw out; (*d. abur*) to exhaust; (*d. apă*) to drain off; (*d. chiriași*) to evict; (*d. trupe*) to withdraw; (*a lăsa liber*) to clear; (*d. un apartament*) to vacate • ~re *nf* evacuation, voiding, draining off; discharge; (*a chiriașilor*) eviction; (*a populației*) evacuation; (*a trupelor*) withdrawal; clearing; *tech* exhaust.

evada [eva'da] *vi* to escape (from), to get away, to evade • ~re *nf* escape, break-out; *fig* escapism • ~t *nm* fugitive, escaped prisoner.

evalua [evalu'a] *vt* to estimate, to reckon, to evaluate; (*d. venit, proprietate*) to assess, to appraise • ~re *nf* estimate, evaluation; (*a proprietății*) valuation, appraisement.

evanghelic [evan'gelik] *adj relig* (*privitor la evanghelie*) evangelic(al), Gospel ...; Evangelical, Protestant.

evanghelie [evan'gelie] *nf relig also fig* Gospel.

evantai [evan'tai] *nn* fan; în ~ fan-shaped.

evapora [evapo'ra] *vt phys* to evaporate || *vr phys* to evaporate; *fig* to vanish (into thin air); to make oneself scarce • ~re *nf phys* evaporation.

evazat [eva'zat] *adj* (*d. fuste*) flaring, flared.

evazionist [evazio'nist] *nm* escapist; ~ fiscal tax dodger.

evaziune [evazi'une] *nf* evasion, dodge; ~ fiscală tax evasion.

evaziv [eva'ziv] *adj* evasive, vague, cagey || *adv* evasively, vaguely, cagily.

eveniment [eveni'ment] *nn* event, development; (*întâmplare*) happening, experience, incident, occurrence.

eventual [eventu'al] *adj* possible, likely; (*întâmplător*) random, casual, accidental || *adv* possibly; (*la nevoie*) in case of need; (*dacă e cazul*) if so, if such be the case • ~itate *nf* possibility, contingency; (*probabilitate*) likelihood • în ~a in the event of.

evident [evi'dent] *adj* clear, evident, obvious || *adv* clearly, evidently, obviously.

evidență [evi'dentsă] *nf* (*realitate*) evidence, reality; *com* (*situație*) situation, record, account.

evidenția [evidentsi'a] *vt* (*a lăuda*) to praise, to distinguish; (*a sublinia*) to emphasize, to point out, to spotlight || *vr* to stand out, to make oneself conspicuous.

evita [evi'ta] *vt* to avoid, to shun; (*a ocoli*) to obviate, to sidestep; to give (smb) a wide berth, to keep/stay clear of; to elude, to escape; (*o lovitură*) to dodge; (*a-și feri capul, a se lăsa în jos*) to duck.

evlavie [e'vlavie] *nf relig* piety, devoutness, devotion; reverence, respect.

evlavios [evlavi'os] *adj* pious, devout, religious; bigoted.

evoca [evo'ka] *vt* to evoke, to conjure up, to recall • ~re *nf* evocation, calling/conjuring up • ~tor *adj* evocative, suggestive, reminiscent.

evolua [evolu'a] *vi* (*d. un plan*) to evolve; to develop, to advance; (*a crește*) to grow; (*în public*) to perform; (*d. o boală*) to take its course.

evoluție [evo'lutsie] *nf* evolution, advance, development; (*d. o boală*) course.

evreică [e'vreikă] *nf* Jewess, Jewish girl/woman.

evreiesc [evre'iesk] *adj* Jewish; *ling* Yiddish.

evreu [e'vreu] *nm* Jew.

exact [eg'zakt] *adj* exact, accurate, correct; (*fidel*) faithful, close; precise, punctual; (*minuțios*) minute, punctilious; (*adevărat*) true; strict, rigorous; (*pe măsură*) closely fitting || *adv* exactly, accurately, correctly; punctually, precisely; (*minuțios*) minutely; (*la fel*) just, the same || *interj* that's it!, right (you are)!, (that's) right! • ~itate *nf* (*acuratețe*) exactness, accuracy; punctuality; (*grijă*) carefulness; cu ~ accurately; punctually.

exagera [eksadje'ra] *vt* to exaggerate, to overdo, to overstate; *coll* to pile it on; (*a supraestima*) to overestimate, to overrate || *vi* to exaggerate • ~re *nf* exaggeration, overstatement • ~t *adj* exaggerated; (*d. cineva*) given/prone to exaggeration; *fig* colored; (*dramatic*) histrionic.

exalta [egzal'ta] *vt* (*a ridica în slăvi*) to exalt, to extol, to praise highly; (*a înflăcăra*) to excite, to warm/work up || *vr* to be exalted, to grow excited/enthusiastic • ~re *nf* elation, exaltation • ~t *nm* enthusiast, hothead; fanatic || *adj* enthusiastic, excited, heated || *adv* enthusiastically.

examen [eg'zamen] *nn* (*cercetare*) examination; inspection; investigation, inquiry; (*verificare*) verification; *edu* exam.

examina [egzami'na] *vt* (*d. elev, pacient*) to examine; (*a cerceta*) to investigate, to search, to scrutinize; (*a judeca*) to weigh, to consider; to inspect; to scan, to survey; *jur* to inquire into • ~re *nf* examination, scrutiny, investigation • ~tor *nm* examiner, investigator || *adj* examining || *adv* examiningly, searchingly.

exaspera [egzaspe'ra] *vt* to exasperate, to irritate, to annoy; *coll* to aggravate, to drive smb crazy/nuts • **~nt** *adj* exasperating, irritating, annoying; *coll* aggravating • **~re** *nf* exasperation, irritation.

excava [ekska'va] *vt tech* to excavate, to dig out • **~tor** *nn tech* excavator, digger, steam shovel.

excedent [eksche'dent] *nn* surplus, overplus; *anat* excess • **~ar** *adj* excess, surplus.

excela [eksche'la] *vi* to excel (in/at).

excelent [eksche'lent] *adj* excellent, capital; *coll* first rate; splendid || *adv* excellently || *interj* capital!, great!.

excelenţă [eksche'lentsă] *nf* excellence, superiority; *(mai presus de orice)* above all; *(ca titlu)* Excellency.

excentric [eks'chentrik] *adj geom also fig* eccentric; *(nebun)* mad, crazy || *nm* eccentric, odd/strange fellow || *nn tech* cam • **~itate** *nf astron, geom, phys* eccentricity; *fig* oddity, peculiarity, singularity.

excepta [ekschep'ta] *vt* to leave out, to except, to bar.

excepţie [eks'cheptsie] *nf* exception • **cu ~a** except(ing), with the exception of.

excepţional [ekscheptsio'nal] *adj* exceptional, out of the ordinary; outstanding, extraordinary; *(neobişnuit)* uncommon || *adv* exceptionally, extremely, exceedingly; *(minunat)* wonderfully, rarely.

exces [eks'ches] *nn (lipsă de cumpătare)* excess; *(depăşire)* transgression; *(la mâncare)* gluttony; *(la băutură)* intemperance; *(sexual)* debauchery; *(violenţă)* violence, abuse • **~iv** *adj* excessive, exorbitant; extreme; enormous, monstrous; *(nemoderat)* immoderate; *(violent)* outrageous || *adv* too much/hard; exceedingly, extremely, excessively.

excita [ekschi'ta] *vt (a stimula)* to excite, to stimulate; *(a aţâţa)* to stir up; to thrill; to arouse, to work up; *(d. pofta de mâncare)* to sharpen, to whet; *(sexual)* to turn on; *elec* to energize || *vr* to get excited, to get worked up; *(sexual)* to be aroused/excited • **~bil** *adj* excitable, irritable, irascible.

exclama [ekskla'ma] *vt/vi* to exclaim, to cry out; *lit* to ejaculate • **~re** *nf* exclamation; *lit* ejaculation.

exclude [eks'klude] *vt* to exclude (from), to shut out; *(a împiedica)* to preclude; *(a nu lua în considerare)* to rule out; *(a da afară din şcoală, organizaţie)* to expel, to bar; *(din barou)* to disbar; *(din biserică)* to ban, to excommunicate; *(a nu se potrivi)* to be incongruous, to be inconsistent; *(dintr-o funcţie publică)* to remove; *(ca alimente dintr-un regim)* to cut out; *recip* to exclude each other.

exclusiv [eksklu'siv] *adj* exclusive, sole || *adv* exclusively, only.

excomunica [ekskomuni'ka] *vt relig* to excommunicate; *fig* to cast out, to expel • **~re** *nf relig* excommunication; *fig* expulsion.

excremente [ekskre'mente] *nn pl bio* feces, excreta, excrement, dejecta.

excrescenţă [ekskres'chentsă] *nf* excrescence, outgrowth.

excreta [ekskre'ta] *vt bio* to excrete.

excreţie [eks'kretsie] *nf physiol, bio* excretion, excreted matter, secretion; *(eliminare)* elimination.

excursie [eks'kursie] *nf* excursion, trip, outing; *(pe jos)* hike; *fig* investigation, digression, dissertation.

excursionist [ekskursio'nist] *nm* excursionist, tourist; *coll* tripper; *(pe jos)* hiker.

execrabil [ekse'krabil] *adj* execrable; abominable, detestable || *adv* execrably, abominably, detestably.

executa [egzeku'ta] *vt (a îndeplini)* to fulfil, to carry out/through, to implement; *(a face)* to do, to accomplish; *(a asculta)* to execute, to obey; *mus* to perform; *(a ucide)* to put to death; *jur* to distrain || *vr (a se supune)* to submit, to comply with • **~nt** *nm mus* performer, executant; accomplisher, doer; agent.

executiv [egzeku'tiv] *adj* executive; *jur* executory || *nn* executive committee/power.

executor [egzeku'tor] *nm* performer, doer, accomplisher; *jur* executor.

execuţie [egze'kutsie] *nf* execution; *(a unei ipoteci)* foreclosure; *(meşteşug)* workmanship; *(îndeplinire)* fulfillment, implementation.

exemplar [egzem'plar] *adj* exemplary, worthy of imitation || *adv* exemplarily || *nn (model)* sample, pattern; *(de carte)* copy, number.

exemplifica [egzemplifi'ka] *vt* to exemplify, to illustrate by/with examples.

exemplu [eg'zemplu] *nn (pildă)* example; instance; *(mostră)* sample, pattern; *(comparaţie)* comparison; model; **(ca) de ~** (as) for instance, such as, e.g.

exercita [egzerchi'ta] *vt (a practica o meserie)* to practice, to exercise, to pursue; *(a întrebuinţa)* to use, to perform; *(a influenţa)* to exert, to bring … to bear; *(puterea)* to wield.

exerciţiu [egzer'chitsiu] *nn* practice; study; *mil* drilling; *pl* athletics; *mus* study; *edu* exercise; *pl (temă)* homework; *(al funcţiilor)* discharge.

exersa [egzer'sa] *vt/vi* to practice.

exhaustiv [egzhaus'tiv] *adj* exhaustive, complete.

exhibiţionism [ekshibitsio'nism] *nn* exhibitionism.

exhuma [ekshu'ma] *vt* to exhume, to disinter, to dig up.

exigent [eksi'djent] *adj* demanding, exacting, hard to satisfy.

exigenţă [eksi'djentsă] *nf* exigency, exigence; demand, requirement.

exil [eg'zil] *nn* exile, banishment.

exila [egzi'la] *vt* to exile, to banish; *(a proscrie)* to outlaw; to proscribe || *vr* to exile/exclude oneself; *(a se izola)* to withdraw, to seclude oneself • **~t** *adj* exiled || *nm* exile.

exista [egzis'ta] *vi (a fiinţa)* to be, to exist; *(a trăi)* to live, to have life; *(a fi disponibil)* to be available; *(a dăinui)* to last, to endure.

existent [egzis'tent] *adj* existent, existing, living; *(păstrat)* extant.

existenţă [egzis'tentsă] *nf* existence, being; *(trai)* living, livelihood; *(viaţă)* life, existence.

exmatricula [eksmatriku'la] *vt* to expel • **~re** *nf* expulsion.

exod [ek'sod] *nn relig* exodus; *(al unui popor)* migration; *lit* exode.

exorbitant [eksorbi'tant] *adj* exorbitant, excessive, unreasonable, outrageous.

exotic [eg'zotik] *adj* exotic.

expansiune [ekspansi'une] *nf phys* expanse, dilation; *anat, bot* expansion, enlargement; *fig* spread.

expansiv [ekspan'siv] *adj* expansive; effusive, exuberant || *adv* expansively.

expatria [ekspatri'a] *vt* to expatriate, to banish || *vr* to settle abroad, to go into exile • **~t** *nm* expatriate, exile.

expectora [ekspekto'ra] *vt/vi* to expectorate.

expedia [ekspedi'a] *vt (a trimite)* to send (off), to dispatch, to forward; *(mărfuri, mai ales pe apă)* to ship;

(*scrisoare*) to mail; (*a executa repede ceva*) to expedite; (*a se debarasa de cineva*) to get rid of, to get smb out of the way; *coll* to send smb packing.

expedient [ekspedi'ent] *nn* expedient, (make) shift.

expeditiv [ekspedi'tiv] *adj* quick, speedy, swift; (*d. cai, mijloace*) expeditious || *adv* expeditiously, quickly.

expeditor [ekspedi'tor] *nm* sender; *econ* (*de mărfuri*) consigner, forwarder, forwarding agent.

expediție [ekspe'ditsie] *nf* (*trimitere*) sending, dispatch(ing); (*călătorie*) expedition; *mil* campaign.

experiență [eksperi'entsă] *nf* (*înțelepciune*) experience, knowledge, skill; **cu** ~ experienced; **fără** ~ inexperienced; (*probă de laborator*) experiment, test, trial; (*întâmplare*) experience(s), trial.

experiment [eksperi'ment] *nn* experiment; ~ **pe om** human experiments, tests on humans • **~a** *vt* to experiment, to test, to try out • **~al** *adj* experimental; tentative || *adv* experimentally; tentatively.

expert [eks'pert] *nm* expert, authority, appraiser; *fig* adept (at).

expertiză [eksper'tiză] *nf* (expert) examination, survey; *com* expert appraisement, valuation; (*raport*) expert's report.

expira [ekspi'ra] *vt anat* to expire, to breathe out || *vi anat* to breathe out, to exhale; (*a-și pierde valabilitatea*) to expire, to end; *com* to fall/become due, to be up • **~re** *nf* expiration, breathing out; (*scadență*) expiry, end, expiration.

expletiv [eksple'tiv] *adj/nn* expletive.

explica [ekspli'ka] *vt* (*a clarifica*) to explain, to clarify, to clear up; (*mai ales un text literar*) to explicate; (*o doctrină, o problemă*) to expound, to elucidate; to interpret; to comment upon; to justify, to account for || *vi* to explain, to give an explanation; to be explained/justified || *vr* to explain oneself; (*a fi clar*) to be clear/manifest • **~bil** *adj* explainable, explicable • **~tiv** *adj* explanatory.

explicație [ekspli'katsie] *nf* explanation; (*interpretare*) exegesis; (*justificare*) justification, vindication; (*cauză*) reason, cause; (*discuție*) show-down; (*a unui text literar*) explication.

explicit [ekspli'chit] *adj* explicit, clear, plain || *adv* explicitly, clearly, plainly.

exploata [eksploa'ta] *vt* (*ceva*) to exploit; (*pământul*) to cultivate; (*o mină*) to work; (*cărbune*) to win/get coal; (*o linie ferată*) to operate; (*oameni*) to grind down; to use; (*a profita de pe urma*) to take (unfair) advantage of, to profit; (*a înșela*) to impose upon; (*ignoranța, răbdarea cuiva*) to trade on; (*a nedreptăți*) to wrong; *fig* (*un succes*) to make the best of; (*talentul*) to make the most of one's talent • **~re** *nf* exploitation; taking (unfair) advantage of; *econ* (*funcționare*) operation, running • **~tor** *nm* exploiter, oppressor || *adj* exploiting, oppressing.

exploda [eksplo'da] *vi chem* to explode, to blow up; *fig* to burst out; *coll* to go off.

explora [eksplo'ra] *vt* to explore; *fig* to fathom, to probe; (*a pătrunde în*) to penetrate, to dive into; *coll fig* to go to the bottom of smth; *mil* to scout, to reconnoiter • **~tor** *nm* explorer.

explozie [eks'plozie] *nf* explosion, detonation, blast; *fig* outburst.

exploziv [eksplo'ziv] *nn also fig* explosive || *adj chem* detonating; *ling* plosive.

exponat [ekspo'nat] *nn* exhibit, item exhibited/displayed.

export [eks'port] *nn* (*acțiune*) exportation; (*marfă*) export • **~a** *vt* to export • **~ator** *nm* exporter || *adj* exporting.

expoziție [ekspo'zitsie] *nf* exhibition, show.

expres [eks'pres] *nn rail* express train; (*bufet*) snackbar, cafeteria || *adj rail* express; (*intenționat*) intentional; (*clar*) explicit, clear || *adv* (*clar*) expressly, explicitly; (*înadins*) intentionally, deliberately, on purpose.

expresie [eks'presie] *nf* (*manifestare*) *also math* expression; manifestation, show; (*locuțiune*) phrase, idiom; (*termen*) term; (*a feței*) countenance.

expresionism [ekspresio'nism] *nn* expressionism.

expresiv [ekspre'siv] *adj* expressive; (*grăitor*) eloquent, suggestive; (*plastic*) graphic || *adv* expressively, eloquently • **~itate** *nf* expressiveness.

exprima [ekspri'ma] *vt* to express, to convey; (*a formula*) (*oral*) to utter, to put into words; *frml* to set forth in words; (*în scris*) to write, to put down; to manifest || *vr* to express oneself • **~re** *nf* expression, utterance; (*dicție*) diction; (*stil*) style; language.

expropria [ekspropri'a] *vt jur* to expropriate, to take over.

expropriere [expropri'ere] *nf jur* expropriation, taking over.

expulza [ekspul'za] *vt* (*din țară*) to expel, to banish, to exile; to eject; (*a da afară*) to exclude • **~re** *nf* expulsion; ejection, evacuation, discharge.

expune [eks'pune] *vt* (*a arăta*) (*mărfuri, tablouri*) to exhibit, to display; (*vederii*) to put out/forth; (*a lăsa descoperit*) *also fig* to expose; (*a pune în pericol*) to endanger; (*o teză, teorie etc*) to explain, to expound; to set forth; (*o situație*) to state, to lay before; (*un mort*) to lay out; *phot* to expose || *vr* to expose oneself (to); (*a-și primejdui viața*) to put oneself in danger; (*a risca*) to run a risk; to risk (one's life); *coll* to put one's life on the line • **~re** *nf* (*aranjare etc*) exposition, display; (*discurs*) speech, lecture; (*relatare*) account, narration; *lit* exposition.

extaz [eks'taz] *nn* ecstasy, rapture; enthusiasm.

extensibil [eksten'sibil] *adj* extensible, stretchable; tensile.

extensiv [eksten'siv] *adj* extensive; (*larg*) wide, broad; (*de întindere*) extending, of extension.

extensor [eksten'sor] *nm anat* extensor || *nn* (*aparat de gimnastică*) chest expander, exerciser; *avia* shock-absorber || *adj anat* extensor.

extenua [ekstenu'a] *vt* to exhaust, to wear out || *vr* to tire oneself out, to work oneself to death • **~re** *nf* exhaustion, fatigue • **~t** *adj* exhausted, worn/tired out; *coll* done in.

exterior [eksteri'or] *nn* outside, exterior; (*înfățișare*) appearance, look; (*străinătate*) foreign countries; *cin* exterior (shot); **în** ~ (*în afară*) outside; (*afară din casă*) outdoors; (*în străinătate*) abroad || *adj* exterior, external, outer, outside; *pol* foreign.

extermina [makestermi'na] *vt* (*un popor*) to exterminate, to wipe out; (*a eradica*) to eradicate, to root out; (*un rău*) to stamp out.

extern [eks'tern] *nm scol* day student; *med* extern, non-resident || *adj* external, outside, outer; *pol* foreign; *geom* exterior.

extinctor [ekstin'ktor] *adj* extinguishing || *nn* fire-extinguisher.

extinde [eks'tinde] *vt/vr* to spread, to extend, to expand • **~re** *nf* extension; proportions, expansion.

extirpa [ekstir'pa] *vt med* to extirpate; *fig* to eradicate, to root out, to remove • **~re** *nf* extirpation, eradication, removal.

extorcare [ekstor'kare] *nf* extortion.

extra ['ekstra] *adv* extra (fine), superior, first-rate/-class.

extracție [eks'traktsie] *nf min* extraction, digging out; (*extragere*) drawing out; origin.

extrafin [ekstra'fin] *adj* superfine, of a special vintage.

extrage [eks'tradje] *vt* to extract, to draw out; (*un dinte*) to pull out; *chem* to derive; (*a alege*) to select; *min* to dig out.

extraordinar [ekstraordi'nar] *adj* (*neobișnuit*) unusual, extraordinary; (*minunat*) wonderful, amazing; special ‖ *adv* extraordinarily, extremely, uncommonly.

extras [eks'tras] *nn* extract; (*fragment*) excerpt, passage; offprint.

extrașcolar [ekstrashko'lar] *adj* extracurricular.

extraterestru [ekstrate'restru] *adj* extraterrestrial.

extravagant [ekstrava'gant] *adj* extravagant; eccentric, odd, weird; (*nebunesc*) crazy, wild, foolish; (*risipitor*) thriftless; (*exagerat*) exaggerated ‖ *adv* extravagantly, etc.

extravaganță [ekstrava'gantsă] *nf* (*purtare*) extravagance; (*fapt*) folly, oddity; exorbitance; (*risipă*) waste.

extravertit [ekstraver'tit] *adj psych* extravert, extrovert.

extrăda [ekstră'da] *vt* to extradite, to hand over • **~re** *nf* extradition.

extrem [eks'trem] *adj* extreme, utmost; (*în gradul cel mai înalt*) most, greatest, highest; excessive; (*cel mai depărtat*) extreme, remotest, farthest, furthest ‖ *adv* (**~ de**) extremely, highly, exceedingly ‖ *nn* extreme; **la ~** to the extreme/-utmost • **~ist** *nm* extremist • **~itate** *nf* (*capăt*) end, extreme, limit; (*vârf*) tip, end; (*culme*) extremity, climax, highest degree; excess • **~ul Orient** the Far East.

extrovertit [ekstrover'tit] *nm* extrovert ‖ *adj* extroverted.

exuberant [eksube'rant] *adj* exuberant, exultant, buoyant.

exulta [eksul'ta] *vi* to exult, to rejoice • **~re** *nf* exultation, elation, jubilation.

ezita [ezi'ta] *vi* to hesitate, to waver, to vacillate; *coll* to hem and haw • **~nt** *adj* hesitating, vacillating, wavering; *coll* shilly-shally • **~re** *nf* hesitation, wavering, vacillation; (*în vorbă*) stammer.

F

fabrica [fabri'ka] *vt* to manufacture, to make, to produce; (*d. bani*) to coin; (*d. bere*) to brew; (*a falsifica*) to forge; (*a inventa*) to concoct, to fabricate; (*o poveste*) to make up, to invent • **~nt** *nm* manufacturer, maker, factory/mill owner.

fabrică ['fabrikă] *nf* factory; (*din industria ușoară*) mill; (*de cărămizi, cherestea*) yard.

fabula ['fabula] *nf* fable; fiction, invention.

fabulos [fabu'los] *adj* fabulous; mythical, legendary; *fig* fabulous, incredible, enormous, prodigious.

face ['fache] *vt* (*concret: a crea*) to make, to create; to fabricate, to make, to manufacture; (*a clădi*) to make, to build; (*a găti*) to make, to cook, to prepare, to bake; (*abstract*) to do; (*a comite*) to perpetrate, to

commit; (*a executa*) to perform, to effect; (*un desen*) to draw, to paint; (*a compune*) to write, to compose; to make, to determine; (*a alcătui*) to make up, to compose, to form; (*a preface*) to turn, to render, (*a numi într-o funcție*) to appoint; (*a măsura*) to amount to, to come to; (*a imita*) to act, to play; **a ~ afaceri** to do business; **ce mai faci?** how are you doing?; **nu ~ nimic** it's all right, it's nothing, it doesn't matter in the least, never mind ‖ *vi* (*a merita*) to be worth (while) ; **nu ~** it isn't worth it; it doesn't pay; **cât ~?** how much does it cost?; how much does it come to?; (*a acționa*) to do; (*a se îndrepta către*) to turn round (to); **fă la dreapta** turn (to the) right; (*a proceda*) to do ‖ *vr* (*a deveni*) to become, to get, to grow, to turn; **se ~ târziu** it is getting late; (*a se preface*) to feign, to pretend, to sham, to fake; (*a avea loc*) to take place, to happen, to come about; (*a se matura*) (*d. brânză*) to ripen; (*d. vin*) to age; (*d. bolnav*) **a se ~ bine** to recover • **s-a făcut!** OK!, all right!, that's settled; *com* deal, that's a bargain.

facil [fa'chil] *adj* (*ușor*) easy, facile; superficial, shallow.

facilitate [fachili'tate] *nf* facility, ease, easiness; *pl* (*înlesniri*) facilities.

facsimil [faksi'mil] *nn* facsimile, exact copy.

factor ['faktor] *nm math* factor; **~ comun** common factor; *fig* factor, agent, element; (*poștaș*) postman.

factura [faktu'ra] *vt* to invoice (goods), to make an invoice of.

factură [fak'tură] *nf com* invoice, bill.

facțiune [faktsi'une] *nf* faction, splinter group, clique.

facultate [fakul'tate] *nf* (*aptitudine*) ability, aptitude; *edu* faculty, college.

fad [fad] *adj* (*fără gust*) tasteless, flavorless, insipid; (*plicticos*) dull, flat, vapid.

fag [fag] *nm bot* beech (tree).

fagot [fa'got] *nn mus* bassoon.

fagur(e) ['fagur(e)] *nm* honeycomb.

faianță [fa'iantsă] *nf* faience; glazed earthenware; tile.

faimă ['faimă] *nf* fame, renown, reputation; *pej* notoriety.

faimos [fai'mos] *adj* famous, renowned, celebrated; *pej* notorious.

fală ['fală] *nf* glory; (*faimă*) fame, celebrity; (*mândrie*) pride, arrogance; (*lăudăroșenie*) boast, vaunt.

falcă ['falkă] *nf anat* jaw(bone), jowl; *tech* jaw, cheek.

fald [fald] *nn* fold, pleat, crease.

faleză [fa'leză] *nf* cliff, sea-wall; embankment.

falie ['falie] *nf geol* fault.

faliment [fali'ment] *nn fin* bankruptcy; (*numai pt. companii*) insolvency; crash; *fig* failure, ruin.

falit [fa'lit] *adj fin* bankrupt; (*numai pt. companii*) insolvent; *coll* broken ‖ *nm* bankrupt, defaulter.

falnic ['falnik] *adj* lofty, stately, splendid; (*trufaș*) haughty ‖ *adv* proudly.

fals [fals] *nn* false(hood), error; (*înșelăciune*) cheating, deception; (*d. document*) fake, forgery; (*d. bijuterii*) imitation ‖ *adj* (*greșit*) false, fallacious, wrong; (*mincinos*) spurious, untrue; (*ipocrit*) hypocritical, double-dealing; (*prefăcut*) treacherous, sham; (*d. bani*) forged, counterfeit; fake(d), artificial ‖ *adv* falsely, treacherously; (*greșit*) mistakenly; *mus* out of tune.

falsifica [falsifi'ka] *vt* to falsify; (*alimente, băuturi*) to adulterate, to doctor; (*bani, un document*) to forge, to counterfeit; (*un text*) to fake, to alter • **~tor** *nm* falsifier; (*de bani, documente*) forger, counterfeiter; (*de alimente*) adulterator.

familial [famili'al] *adj* family ..., household ..., domestic.

familiar [famili'ar] *adj* (*obişnuit*) familiar, intimate ‖ *adv* familiarly, informally • **~iza** *vt* to familarize/ acquaint smb (with); (*cu frigul*) to inure smb to (cold) ‖ *vr* to be/get acquainted (with), to be/get accustomed/used/inured to.

familie [fa'milie] *nf also* ling, bot, zool family; *coll* folks, people; **familia Brown** the Brown family, the Browns.

fana [fa'na] *vr* to wither, to wilt, to droop, to fade.

fanatic [fa'natik] *nm* fanatic, enthusiast; zealot ‖ *adj* fanatical, enthusiastic.

fanatism [fana'tism] *nn* fanaticism, zealotry.

fandare [fan'dare] *nf* lunge, thrust.

fandoseală [fando'seală] *nf* (*afectare*) affectation, airs and graces; (*mândrie*) pride, haughtiness.

fanfară [fan'fară] *nf* fanfare; brass band.

fantasmagorie [fantasma'gorie] *nf* phantasmagoria; weird spectacle.

fantastic [fan'tastik] *adj* fantastic(al), fanciful, weird; (*ciudat*) queer, odd; (*straşnic*) capital, tremendous ‖ *adv* fantastically ‖ *nn* fabulousness • **~ul** the fantastic, the uncanny.

fantă [fantă] *nf tech* slit.

fante ['fante] *nm coll* (*la cărţi*) knave; (*filfizon*) dude.

fantezie [fante'zie] *nf* (*imaginaţie*) imagination, fancy; (*capriciu*) whim; freak; *pl* inventions; (*minciuni*) lies; *mus* fantasia, reverie.

fantezist [fante'zist] *adj* fanciful, fantastic(al); (*neadevărat*) untrue, invented ‖ *adv* fancifully.

fantomatic [fanto'matik] *adj* ghost-like, phantom-like; *fig* sporadic; (*vag*) vague.

fantomă [fan'tomă] *nf* (*stafie*) phantom, ghost; (*apariţie*) (ghostly) apparition; (*himeră*) chimera.

fapt [fapt] *nn* fact; (*acţiune*) deed, action; (*realitate*) reality, truth; (*întâmplare*) happening, occurrence; certainty; **de ~** actually, as a matter of fact; strictly speaking; (*la urma urmei*) after all; *jur* de facto; **în ~** actually, in effect, in actual fact.

faptă ['faptă] *nf* act, action, deed; (*eroică*) exploit, feat.

far [far] *nn* lighthouse, beacon; *fig* beacon; *auto* headlight, headlamp.

fard [fard] *nn* make-up, paint, rouge • **~a** *vt/vr* to make (oneself) up, to use makeup.

farfurie [farfu'rie] *nf* dish, plate, saucer; (*conţinutul*) plateful (of).

faringe [fa'rindje] *nn anat* pharynx; *coll* gullet.

farmacie [farma'chie] *nf* (*magazin*) drugstore; (*în spital*) dispensary; pharmacy; (*ştiinţă*) pharmaceutics.

farmacist [farma'chist] *nm* druggist, pharmacist.

farmec ['farmek] *nn* charm, spell; (*vrajă*) magic; (*încântare*) attraction, fascination; (*al unei femei*) glamour.

farsă ['farsă] *nf thea* farce; (*festă*) practical joke, trick, prank, hoax.

farsor [far'sor] *nm* (*ghiduş*) jester, (practical) joker, trickster; (*înşelător*) humbug, swindler, cheat.

fascicul [fas'chikul] *nn* fascicle, bundle; pencil • **~ă** *nf* fascicle, section, (serial) installment; (*broşură*) brochure; leaflet.

fascina [faschi'na] *vt* to fascinate, to captivate, to delight

• **~nt** *adj* fascinating • **~ţie** *nf* fascination, spell, charm.

fascism [fas'chism] *nn pol* fascism.

fascist [fas'chist] *nm/adj* fascist.

fasole [fa'sole] *nf bot* (kidney/haricot) bean; ~ **verde** French/string/green bean.

fasona [faso'na] *vt* to shape, to fashion; (*după un model*) to mold; (*a dăltui*) to chisel ‖ *vr* to become refined.

fast [fast] *nn* pomp, splendor, ostentation; (*lux*) luxury • **~uos** *adj* pompous, magnificent, gorgeous.

fasung [fa'sung] *nn tech* socket.

faşă ['fashă] *nf* (*bandaj*) dressing, bandage; roller; (*scutece*) swaddling clothes.

fatal [fa'tal] *adj* fatal, fateful; destined; inevitable; deadly, mortal, disastrous ‖ *adv* inevitably, fatally • **~itate** *nf* (*soartă*) fate, fatality, destiny; (*nenorocire*) misfortune, mischance.

fată ['fată] *nf* girl, young woman; (*domnişoară*) miss, young lady; *lit* damsel; *dial* lass; (*fecioară*) virgin, maiden; (*fiică*) daughter; (*servitoare*) maid, (female) servant.

faţadă [fa'tsadă] *nf archit* front (side), façade, frontage; *fig* appearance, show, ostentation; **de** ~ *fig* sham, window dressing.

faţă ['fatsă] *nf* (*obraz*) face; *lit* visage; *sl* mug; (*înfăţişare*) look, appearance; (*ten*) complexion; (*expresie*) air, countenance; *lit* mien; (*suprafaţă*) surface; (*a unei pietre*) facet; (*a apei*) expanse; (*exterior*) front, outside; (*partea din faţă*) front, foreground; *archit* façade, front side; (*a unei monede*) obverse; aspect; (*parte a unui disc, a unui poliedru*) side; ~ **în** ~ (*cu*) face to face (with); **în** ~ in front; (*peste drum*) opposite, across the road/street; (*drept înainte*) right ahead; (*sincer*) in smb's face; **pe** ~ openly, above board; in smb's face • **în faţa** in front of the.

faţetă [fa'tsetă] *nf* (*de piatră, preţ, personalitate*) facet; side; *typ* plate; *metal* bevel.

fault [fault] *nn sp* foul play, offense.

faună ['faună] *nf* fauna.

favoare [fa'voare] *nf* favor, benevolence, kindness; (*cadou*) gift, hand-out.

favorabil [favo'rabil] *adj* (*d. cineva*) favorable; (*binevoitor*) benevolent; (*d. ceva*) (*propice*) propitious, auspicious; (*convenabil*) convenient, opportune; (*avantajos*) advantageous ‖ *adv* favorably, propitiously.

favorit [favo'rit] *adj/nm* favorite, pet, darling.

favoriţi [favo'ritsi] *nm pl* side-burns, (side) whiskers.

favoriza [favori'za] *vt* (*a avantaja*) to favor; to be partial to; (*a promova*) to promote, to forward; (*a sprijini*) to support, to patronize; (*a înlesni*) to encourage; (*ilegal*) to abet, to connive.

fazan [fa'zan] *nm orn* pheasant; *fig* dupe.

fază ['fază] *nf* (*stadiu*) also astron phase; stage, period; flashlight.

făcăleţ [făkă'lets] *nn cul* stirring stick.

făclie [făk'lie] *nf* torch; *fig* luminary, star, beacon.

făgaş [fă'gash] *nn also fig* rut, track; routine, path; *fig* direction, orientation.

făgădui [făgădu'i] *vt* to promise, to pledge, to vow ‖ *vr* to bind/pledge oneself • **~ală** *nf* promise, pledge, vow.

făină [fă'ină] *nf* (*de grâu*) flour; (*de porumb*) (corn)meal.

fǎli [fǎ'li] *vr* to boast (of/on), to pride oneself (on); *coll* to talk big; (*a face pe grozavul*) to swagger, to brag.

fǎlos [fǎ'los] *adj* haughty, proud, bumptious.

fǎptaş [fǎp'tash] *nm* (*fǎptuitor*) doer, performer; author; (*rǎufǎcǎtor*) evil-doer, culprit; (*al unei crime*) perpetrator.

fǎptui [fǎptu'i] *vt* (*a face*) to do, to make; (*un delict*) to commit, to perpetrate.

fǎpturǎ [fǎp'turǎ] *nf* (*fiinţǎ*) being, creature; nature; (*trup*) body, figure, form.

fǎraş [fǎ'rash] *nn* dust pan; (*pt. sobǎ*) fire shovel.

fǎrǎ ['fǎrǎ] *prep* without, -less; ~ **dinţi** toothless; ~ **onoare** without honor; (*minus*) minus/less; **patru** ~ **doi fac doi** four minus two is two; (*cu excepţia*) except(ing), besides; **eram trei** ~ **Tom** we were three besides Tom; (*pt. a indica ora*) to, before; **e cinci** ~ **zece** it's ten before five; (*introduce o condiţie*) but for; ~ **ajutorul lui n-am fi putut termina** but for his help we couldn't have finished || *adv* unwillingly, willy-nilly || *conj* without.

fǎrǎdelege [fǎrǎde'ledje] *nf* offense, crime, felony; trespass, contravention; (*încǎlcare*) infringement; (*hulǎ*) blasphemy, sacrilege.

fǎrâmǎ [fǎrâ'mǎ] *nf* (*de pâine*) crumb; bit, small piece, scrap; *pl* smithereens, shivers; *fig also* grain, bit, jot.

fǎrǎmicios [fǎrǎmi'chios] *adj* crumbling away; breakable; (*d. sticlǎ*) brittle; (*d. mǎrfuri*) fragile.

fǎrǎmiţa [fǎrǎmi'tsa] *vt* to crumble; (*d. o ţarǎ*) to dismember.

fǎt [fat] *nm* fetus; (*bǎiat*) boy; (*copil*) child.

fǎta [fǎ'ta] *vt* to drop, to bring forth, to give birth to; (*d. lupoaicǎ*) to cub; (*d. cǎţea, ursoaicǎ*) to whelp; (*d. scroafǎ*) to farrow; (*d. iapǎ*) to foal; (*d. vacǎ*) to calve || *vi* to cub, to whelp, to farrow, to foal, to calve.

fǎţarnic [fǎ'tsarnik] *nm* double-dealer, hypocrite || *adj* hypocritical, dissembling, two-faced.

fǎţǎrnicie [fǎtsǎrni'chie] *nf* hypocrisy, double-dealing, pretense.

fǎţiş [fǎ'tsish] *adj* open, frank, sincere; (*fǎrǎ ascunzişuri*) outspoken, undisguised; (*drept*) downright; (*obraznic*) shameless, bold || *adv* frankly, outspokenly, above-board; (*fǎrǎ ruşine*) shamelessly, to smb's face.

fǎuri [fǎu'ri] *vt* (*a crea*) to create, to forge, to make; (*a plǎnui*) to devise, to plan; (*a nǎscoci*) to concoct, to invent.

fâlfâi [fâlfâ'i] *vi* (*d. pǎsǎri*) to flutter, to flap/clap one's wings; (*în vânt*) to fly, to wave, to float.

fân [fân] *nn* hay.

fântânǎ [fân'tânǎ] *nf* (draw-)well; (*cişmea*) fountain; *fig* source, origin.

fârnâi [fârnâ'i] *vi* to snuffle, to twang.

fâsâi [fâsâ'i] *vi* (*d. apǎ, gaze*) to fizz(le); to sing; to swish; (*d. gâşte*) to hiss.

fâstâci [fâstâ'chi] *vr* to lose one's head, to be/get flurried/perplexed/confused; (*în vorbire*) to be put out.

fâşâi [fâshâ'i] *vi* to rustle, to move/glide along with a rustling noise, to whiz along.

fâşie [fǎ'shie] *nf* (*de stofǎ*) band; (*de hârtie*) slip; (*de pǎmânt*) strip; (*de luminǎ*) streak.

febrǎ ['febrǎ] *nf med also fig* fever.

febril [fe'bril] *adj med* feverish, febrile; *fig* ardent || *adv* feverishly.

februarie [feb'ruarie] *nm* February.

fecale [fe'kale] *nf pl* feces, excreta, excrements.

fecioarǎ [fe'choarǎ] *nf* virgin, maiden; (*fatǎ bǎtrânǎ*) old maid, spinster; *relig* Virgin (Mary); (*zodiac*) Virgo; **de** ~ maidenly, virginal, maidenlike.

fecior [fe'chor] *nm* boy; (*flǎcǎu*) lad; (*fiu*) son; (*servitor*) footman, valet.

fecund [fe'kund] *adj* (*roditor*) fertile, fruitful, rich; *fig* fecund, prolific, inventive.

federal [fede'ral] *adj* federal.

federaţie [fede'ratsie] *nf* (con)federation.

feeric [fe'erik] *adj* fairy(like); *fig* magical, enchanting || *adv* magically.

fel [fel] *nn* (*mod*) manner, way; **în ~ul acesta** in this way/manner, thus, so, like this; **într-un** ~ **sau altul** in one way or another; (*tip*) kind, sort; ~ **de** ~ all kinds/sorts of; (*tip de mâncare*) dish, (*ca ordine*) course; (*fire*) nature, disposition, character; (*obicei*) custom, tradition; **de** ~ not at all, by no means; **în ce** ~? how?; **la** ~ (*identic*) *adj* identical || *adv* identically, alike; (*asemenea şi ţie*) the same to you.

felicita [felichi'ta] *vt* to congratulate smb (on), to compliment; *recip* to congratulate each other || *vr* to congratulate oneself • **~re** *nf* congratulation; (*carte poştalǎ*) greeting card.

felie [fe'lie] *nf* slice; (*de carne*) cut, steak; (*subţire, de slǎninǎ*) rasher; *fig* domain.

felin [fe'lin] *adj zool* feline; *fig* catlike, graceful.

felinar [feli'nar] *nn* street lamp; (*de mânǎ*) lantern; *sl* (*ochi*) headlight(s), daylights, glamps.

femeie [fe'meie] *nf* woman; *coll* womankind, the gentle sex; *vernac* (*soţie*) wife, spouse; *coll hum* better half • **~sc** *adj* womanly, women's; (*d. sex*) female; feminine.

femeiuşcǎ [feme'iushkǎ] *nf pej* skirt, flirt, a bit of fluff.

femelǎ [fe'melǎ] *nf zool* female; *bot* female, pistillate.

feminin [femi'nin] *nn/adj also gram* feminine.

feminism [femi'nism] *nn pol, soc* feminism, women's lib(eration) movement, suffragette movement; *med* femin(il)ism.

feminist(ǎ) [femi'nist(ǎ)] *nm/nf* feminist || *adj* of/ related to feminism.

feminitate [femini'tate] *nf* femininity, womanhood; (*la un bǎrbat*) effeminacy, womanishness.

femur [fe'mur] *nn anat* femur, thighbone.

fenomen [feno'men] *nn* phenomenon, *pl* phenomena; (*fapt*) fact; (*minune*) wonder, marvel, prodigy.

fenomenal [fenome'nal] *adj* phenomenal; extraordinary, outstanding, amazing || *adv* phenomenally, etc.

fentǎ ['fentǎ] *nf sp* feint.

ferǎstrǎu [ferǎs'trǎu] *nn* saw.

ferealǎ [fe'realǎ] *nf* (*precauţie*) wariness, precaution; (*grijǎ*) care, guard; (*adǎpost*) shelter.

fereastrǎ [fe'reastrǎ] *nf* window; (*geam*) window pane; (*vitrinǎ*) shop window; (*gol*) gap, void; *scol* (*interval liber între ore*) window; (*la calculator*) window.

fereca [fere'ka] *vt* (*a încuia*) to lock (up); (*a lega*) to bind, to hoop; (*a înlǎnţui*) to chain, to fetter.

ferfeniţi [ferfeni'tsi] *vt* to tear to/in rags and tatters, to shred || *vr* to be torn to shreds.

feri [fe'ri] *vt* (*a apǎra de*) to shelter, to protect (from/ against), to guard (from); (*a scǎpa, a salva*) to save/keep (from) || *vi* (*lateral*) to step/stand aside; (*printr-un salt lateral*) to dodge; (*a sǎri înapoi*) to recoil; (*prin aplecare*) to duck || *vr* (*a se da în lǎturi*) to step/stand aside; (*a evita*) to avoid, to shun, to keep clear of; (*a fi atent*) to be on one's guard.

feribot [feri'bot] *nn naut* ferryboat.

fericire [feri'chire] *nf* happiness, bliss, felicity; *(noroc)* good luck/chance/fortune; **din ~** fortunately, luckily, happily.

fericit [feri'chit] *nm* happy man/fellow/person; *relig* His Holiness || *adj* happy, blissful, blessed; *(norocos)* lucky, fortunate; *(favorabil)* propitious, favorable || *adv* happily, etc.; **un an nou ~!** a Happy New Year!.

ferigă ['ferigă] *nf bot* fern, bracken.

ferm [ferm] *adj* firm, steadfast, steady; *(dârz)* unyielding; *(hotărât)* resolute, unswerving || *adv* firmly, etc.

fermă ['fermă] *nf* farm, farmhouse; **~ de lapte** dairy (farm).

fermeca [ferme'ka] *vt* (*a încânta*) to enchant, to charm; (*a fascina*) to fascinate; (*a vrăji*) to bewitch, to cast a spell on • **~t** *adj* (*încântat*) delighted, enchanted, fascinated; *(vrăjit)* bewitched, under a spell.

fermecător [fermekă'tor] *adj* charming, delightful || *adv* charmingly, delightfully.

fermenta [fermen'ta] *vi* to ferment • **~ție** *nf* fermentation, effervescence; *fig* tumult, agitation, ferment, commotion.

fermier [fermi'er] *nm* farmer.

fermitate [fermi'tate] *nf* firmness; *(tărie)* solidity; *(fixitate)* steadiness; *(de caracter)* steadfastness, staunchness; **cu ~** firmly, unswervingly.

fermoar [fer'moar] *nn* zipper.

feroce [fe'roche] *adj* fierce, ferocious; *(crud)* cruel; brutal, savage; *(setos de sânge)* bloodthirsty; *(inuman)* inhuman, barbarous; *(nemilos)* ruthless, pitiless, merciless; terrible, dreadful, awful, fearful || *adv* fiercely, savagely, grimly; *(fără milă)* ruthlessly, pitilessly, mercilessly.

ferocitate [ferochi'tate] *nf* ferocity, fierceness; *(sete de sânge)* bloodthirstiness; *(cruzime)* cruelty; *(sălbăticie)* savagery; *(neîndurare)* ruthlessness, inhumanity.

fertil [fer'til] *adj* fertile, productive, fruitful; *fig also* prolific.

fervent [fer'vent] *adj* fervent, devout, ardent || *adv* fervently, devoutly, ardently.

fes [fes] *nn* fez, Turkish cap.

fesă ['fesă] *nf* buttock; *pl* behind, buttocks, posterior.

festă ['festă] *nf* (nasty) trick, prank, practical joke, hoax.

festiv [fes'tiv] *adj* festive; *(solemn)* solemn • **~al** *nn* festival • **~itate** *nf* festivity, solemnity, celebration.

feston [fes'ton] *nn* festoon; scallop.

feștilă [fesh'tilă] *nf* (*fitil*) wick; *(lumânare)* candle.

fetid [fe'tid] *adj* fetid, stinking, foul, malodorous, rank.

fetiș [fe'tish] *nn* fetish; idol.

fetișcană [fetish'kană] *nf* teenage/adolescent girl.

fetiță [fe'titsă] *nf* little girl; *(fiică)* daughter.

fetru [fe'tru] *nn* felt.

fetus ['fetus] *nm anat* fetus.

feudal [feu'dal] *nm* feudal lord || *adj* feudal.

fezanda [fezan'da] *vt* to hang (meat, game).

fi [fi] *vi* to be, to exist; **sunt mulți** there are many; (*a se afla*) to be (found), to lie; **Suedia este în nord** Sweden lies in the north; (*a trăi*) to live, to be alive; (*a consta din*) to lie/to consist (in); (*a aparține*) to belong (to); (*a se simți*) to be, to feel; **mi-e foame/sete/somn** I'm hungry/thirsty/ sleepy; (*a costa*) to be, to cost; **cât e metrul?** how much does a meter cost?; (*a se întâmpla*) to happen, to occur; **mi-a spus cum a fost** he told me how it happened; (*v. copulativ*) to be; **filmul e interesant** the movie is interesting || *v aux*

to be; **romanul e scris de Faulkner** the novel is written by Faulkner; (*pt. formarea perfectului*) to have; **aş fi citit-o** I should have read it; **până la 10 îşi va fi terminat temele** he will have finished his homework by ten o'clock; *(modal)* to be to; **dacă e să vină** if he is to come, if he should come.

fiabil [fi'abil] *adj tech* reliable, dependable • **~itate** *nf tech* reliability.

fiară ['fiară] *nf* (wild) beast; *fig* brute.

fiasco [fi'asko] *nn* failure; *coll* flop.

fibră ['fibră] *nf anat also fig* fiber; *bot* filament; *(de carne)* fiber; *text* yarn.

fibrom [fi'brom] *nn med* fibroma.

ficat [fi'kat] *nm anat* liver.

fictiv [fik'tiv] *adj* fictitious, imaginary, false.

ficțiune [fiktsi'une] *nf* fiction, imagination; *(invenție)* fabrication, concoction.

ficus ['fikus] *nm bot* ficus.

fidea [fi'dea] *nf* vermicelli.

fidel [fi'del] *adj* (*credincios*) faithful, true; *(devotat)* devoted, loyal || *adv* faithfully, truly, devotedly, loyally • **~itate** *nf* fidelity; *(loialitate)* loyalty, attachment; trustworthiness; *(devotament)* devotion, faithfulness; *(exactitate)* accuracy, exactness; (*a memoriei*) retentiveness, tenacity; *phys* **înaltă ~** high fidelity, hi-fi; **cu ~** truly, faithfully, loyally.

fiecare [fie'kare] *adj* (*separat*) each; *(global)* every; *(oricare)* any; *(din doi)* either; **de ~ dată** every time; **în ~ an** year by year, yearly, year in, year out; **în ~ zi** every (single) day, day after day; **la ~ doi ani** every other/second year || *pron* (*separat*) each (one); **~ dintre ei** each of them; *(global)* everybody, everyone; **~ poate înțelege asta** everybody can see this; *(oricine)* anybody, anyone; *(din doi)* either.

fier [fier] *nn* iron; *(de călcat)* pressing/flat iron; *(al croitorului)* goose; *(de coafat)* curling tongs; *pl* chains, fetters, shackles; **de ~** *fig* made of iron, stern, unwavering.

fierar [fie'rar] *nm* blacksmith.

fierbe [fi'ferbe] *vt* to boil; *(la foc mic)* to simmer; *(de obicei la cuptor)* to stew; *(a găti)* to cook; *(cafea)* to make; *fig* to torture, to torment || *vi* to boil; *(la foc mic)* to simmer, to stew; *(d. vin: a fermenta)* to ferment, to work; *(a produce efervescență)* to effervesce; *fig (d. mare)* to be seething/rough, to rage, to roar; *fig (d. cineva)* to seethe, to boil over.

fierbinte [fier'binte] *adj* hot, boiling/piping hot; *(arzător)* scorching, torrid; *fig (înflăcărat)* burning, hot, ardent, fiery.

fiere ['fiere] *nf anat* bile, gall; *fig* venom, bitterness; *(necazuri)* troubles, sorrows.

figura [figu'ra] *vi* (*a apărea*) to appear, to occur; *thea* to play.

figurant(ă) [figu'rant(ă)] *nm/nf thea* extra; *(balet)* figurant; *fig* dummy, puppet.

figurativ [figura'tiv] *adj* figurative, emblematic.

figură [fi'gură] *nf* (*față*) face; *(mină)* countenance, look; *(chip)* image; *(pe o monedă)* effigy; *(pe o carte de joc)* picture; *(persoană)* figure, person; *(tip)* type; character; *fig* picture, shape, form; *geom* (geometrical) figure; (*la șah*) chess piece; *(de dans)* (dance) figure; *(farsă)* (nasty) trick; **~ de stil** figure of speech.

fiică [fi'ikă] *nf* daughter, girl.

fiindcă [fi'indkă] *conj* because, since, as; for.

ființă [fi'intsă] *nf* (*vietate*) being, creature; (*om*) man, human, being, person; (*existență*) existence, being; (*viață*) life; (*fire*) nature, character; (*esență*) essence, substance; **în** ~ (*existent*) extant, existing, present; *jur* valid, legal; ~ **vie** living creature.

fila [fi'la] *vt text* to spin; (*cărțile de joc*) to fan out slowly; (*a urmări*) to shadow, to tail; *naut* to pay/run out.

filament [fila'ment] *nn elec, bot* filament; *anat* fiber.

filantrop [filan'trop] *nm* philanthropist, a do-gooder.

filarmonică [filar'monikă] *nf* philharmonic orchestra.

filatelie [filate'lie] *nf* philately, stamp collecting.

filatelist [filate'list] *nm* philatelist, stamp collector.

filatură [fila'tură] *nf* spinning mill.

filă ['filă] *nf* (*de carte*) leaf; (*coală*) sheet (of paper).

fildeș ['fildesh] *nn* ivory; (*colț de elefant*) tusk.

file [fi'le] *nn* sirloin, fillet; chine.

filet [fi'let] *nn tech* thread; *anat* small fiber.

fileu [fi'leu] *nn* (*de pescuit*) (fishing) net; (*pt. păr*) hairnet, (*pt. păr lung*) snood; *sp* net.

filfizon [filfi'zon] *nm* coxcomb, dandy, fop.

filial [fili'al] *adj* filial.

filială [fili'ală] *nf* branch (office), subsidiary.

filieră [fili'eră] *nf text* spinning nozzle; *metal* draw/die plate; *tech* screw/die stock; *fig* (*făgaș*) way, channel(s); (*de traficanți, teroriști*) network.

filigran [fili'gran] *nn* filigree; (*la bancnote*) watermark.

film [film] *nn phot* (*peliculă*) film; *cin* motion picture; *coll* movie, flick(s); ~ **artistic** feature film; ~ **vorbit** sound film; ~ **mut** silent movie.

filma [fil'ma] *vt* to film; (*d. o scenă*) to shoot.

filologie [filolo'djie] *nf* philology.

filon [fi'lon] *nn* lode, vein.

filozof [filo'zof] *nm* philosopher • **~ic** *adj* philosophical • **~ie** *nf* philosophy; *fig* sophistication.

filtra [fil'tra] *vt* to filter, to strain; (*informații, pacienți*) to screen || *vr* to be filtered; (*d. lumină*) to filter, to steal (through).

filtru ['filtru] *nn* filter; (*strecurătoare*) strainer, percolator.

fin¹ [fin] *nm* godchild, godson.

fin² [fin] *adj* fine; (*subțire*) thin, slender; (*d. forme: grațios*) graceful; delicate; (*ales*) choice, first-class; (*rafinat*) refined, sophisticated; **gust** ~ refined taste; (*mărunt*) fine; (*subtil*) subtle || *adv* finely; (*subțire*) thinly; (*delicat*) delicately; (*subtil*) subtly.

final [fi'nal] *nn* (*sfârșit*) end; (*rezultat*) result; *mus* finale; **în** ~ (*în cele din urmă*) finally, ultimately, eventually; (*într-un târziu*) at last; (*într-un cuvânt*) in a word, to put it briefly || *adj* final, decisive, ultimate • **~iza** *vt* to finalize, to finish, to complete.

financiar [financhi'ar] *adj* financial, finance; fiscal; **an** ~ fiscal year || *nm/nf* (*specialist în finanțe*) financier.

finanța [finan'tsa] *vt* to finance, to subsidize; to fund.

finanțe [fi'nantse] *nf pl* finance(s); (*venituri*) means, resources; **Minister de** ~ Treasury.

fină ['fină] *nf* goddaughter.

finețe [fi'netse] *nf* fineness; (*subțirime*) thinness; (*calit. super.*) high quality; (*delicatețe*) delicacy, nicety; (*rafinament*) refinement; (*d. auz*) keenness; (*subtilitate*) fineness, subtlety, shrewdness.

finisa fini'sa] *vt* to finish • **~j,** ~**re** *nn, nf* finishing (off).

finlandez [finlan'dez] *nm* Finn || *adj* Finnish • **~ă** *nf* Finn, Finnish woman/girl; Finnish, the Finnish language.

fiolă [fi'olă] *nf* ampule, phial; *auto* breathalyzer.

fior [fi'or] *nm* (*de frig, frică*) shiver, shudder; (*plăcut*) thrill.

fiord [fi'ord] *nn geog* fjord.

fioros [fio'ros] *adj* fierce, ferocious, grim, horrible; (*sălbatic*) savage, cruel, wild || *adv* fiercely, etc.

fir [fir] *nn* (*de ață*) thread; (*de păr*) hair; (*de sârmă*) wire; (*de iarbă*) blade; (*tulpiniță*) stalk; *fig* (*al povestirii*) thread; *fig* (*iotă*) grain, bit, jot, whit; ~ **cu** ~ bit by bit, piece by piece.

firav [fi'rav] *adj* frail, feeble, weak; (*șanse, speranțe*) slender, slim; (*d. copii*) puny; (*d. sănătate*) delicate; *fig* insubstantial, tenuous.

fire ['fire] *nf* (*natură*) nature, world; temper, character, disposition.

firesc [fi'resk] *adj* natural.

firește [fi'reshte] *adv* certainly, naturally, (as a matter) of course.

firimitură [firimi'tură] *nf* crumb; *fig* bit.

firmament [firma'ment] *nn* firmament, sky.

firmă ['firmă] *nf* (*denumirea*) sign, doorplate; (*întreprindere*) (business) firm, concern; *fig* disguise, screen.

fisă ['fisă] *nf* nickel, coin; (*pt. automate de dulciuri, țigări* etc) token; (*pt. joc*) counter.

fisc [fisk] *nn* fisc, Internal Revenue, the Treasury • **~al** *adj* fiscal, tax, revenue.

fisiune [fisi'une] *nf phys* fission.

fisura [fisu'ra] *vt/vr* to cleave, to split, to crack.

fisură [fi'sură] *nf* fissure, crack, cleft; **fără** ~ flawless, faultless.

fișă ['fisha] *nf* slip of paper, docket; (*la bibliotecă*) library/catalog card; ~ **personală** (personal) record; ~ **medicală** record; *elec* plug.

fișet [fi'shet] *nn* locker.

fișier [fishi'er] *nn* (*catalog*) card index, file; (*dulap*) card index cabinet.

fitil [fi'til] *nn* (*de lampă*) wick; (*de tun*) *mil obs* slow match; *fig* intrigue.

fițuică [fi'tsuikă] *nf* note, slip/scrap of paper; *scol* crib; *pej* (*ziar*) rag.

fiu [fiu] *nm* (*fecior*) son, boy; (*copil*) child; descendant.

fix [fiks] *adj* fixed, set, immobile; steady, constant; (*neschimbat*) fixed, unchanging; exact, precise; (*fără țintă*) vacant looking || *adv* fixedly, constantly; (*privind în gol*) vacantly; (*d. oră: exact*) sharp.

fixa [fik'sa] *vt* (*de ceva*) to fix, to fasten (to); (*cu un cui*) to nail; (*cu un ac cu gămălie*) to pin; (*a nitui*) to rivet; (*a întări*) to strengthen, to make secure; (*a lega*) to tie, to bind; (*a stabili*) to settle, to appoint; (*condiții*) to lay down, to stipulate; (*a preciza*) to determine; (*a măsura*) to measure; (*latitudinea*) to find, to ascertain; (*prețul*) to state; (*a aranja*) to settle, to arrange || *vr* (*a se întări*) to fasten, to fix; (*a se decide*) to fix on, to decide for/against; (*a se stabili*) to settle down.

fizic ['fizik] *nn* (*înfățișare*) physique, appearance, look; (*trup*) frame, body, figure || *adj* physical; (*trupesc*) bodily.

fizică ['fizikă] *nf* physics; ~ **atomică/nucleară** nuclear physics.

fizician [fizichi'an] *nm* physicist.

fizionomie [fiziono'mie] *nf* physiognomy, countenance; *fig* aspect, configuration.

flacără [fi'flakără] *nf* flame; (*puternică*) blaze; *fig* flame, heat (of passion).

flacon [fla'kon] *nn* (stoppered) bottle, flask, phial.

flagel [fla'djel] *nn* scourge • ~a *vt* to scourge, to flog, to whip, to lash.

flagrant [fla'grant] *adj* glaring, flagrant.

flamingo [fla'mingo] *nn orn* flamingo.

flanc [flank] *nn mil* flank, wing, side.

flanelă [fla'nelă] *nf* (*material, stofă*) flannel; (*pulover*) jersey, sweater; (*de corp*) vest; (*mai ales sportivi*) undershirt.

flasc [flask] *adj* limp, flabby, flaccid.

flash [flash] *nn elec, phot* flash.

flașnetar [flashne'tar] *nm* organ-grinder.

flașnetă [flash'netă] *nf mus* barrel organ, hurdy-gurdy.

flata [fla'ta] *vt* to flatter, to fawn (upon).

flaut ['flaut] *nn mus* flute • ~ist *nm mus* flutist, flute player.

flăcău [flă'kău] *nm* (country) lad, youth; (*holtei*) bachelor.

flămând [flă'mând] *adj* hungry; (*înfometat*) famished, starving, ravenous; *fig* thirsty (for), greedy (after).

flămânzi [flămân'zi] *vt* to starve, to famish || *vi* to be hungry/ravenous; to suffer from hunger, to starve.

fleac [fleak] *nn* trifle; (*prostie*) foolish/silly stuff; (*obiect*) trinket; (*persoană*) a (mere) nobody/cipher; *pl fig* nonsense, gas, bunkum, tittle-tattle.

fleașcă ['fleashkă] *nf* flop; (*molâu*) weakling; *coll* milksop; **ud** ~ dripping wet; (*palmă peste obraz*) slap in the face.

flecăreală [flekă'realä] *nf* idle/empty talk, gossip, tittle-tattle.

flegmatic [fleg'matik] *adj* phlegmatic, stolid, calm || *adv* phlegmatically, calmly.

flegmă ['flegmă] *nf med* phlegm; *fig* imperturbability, stolidity.

fler [fler] *nn* (*adulmecare*) scent; *fig* flair, nose, intuition.

fleșcăi [fleshkă'i] *vi* to squelch || *vr* to wilt, to become flabby/soft; to be played out.

flexibil [flek'sibil] *adj* flexible, pliable, pliant • ~itate *nf* flexibility, pliancy, pliability.

flirta [flir'ta] *vi* to flirt.

floare ['floare] *nf* flower; (*eflorescență*) bloom; (*d. arbore*) blossom; *fig* bloom; *fig* (*elită*) elite, cream, pick; (*mucegai*) mold, mildew; **în** ~ in bloom; ~ **la ureche** *fig* (it's a) piece of cake.

floral [flo'ral] *adj* floral.

floră ['floră] *nf* flora.

florăreasă [floră'reasă] *nf* florist; flower girl.

florărie [floră'rie] *nf* flowershop.

floretă [flo'retă] *nf* (fencing) foil.

floricea [flori'chea] *nf* little flower, tiny blossom, floweret; *pl* (*de porumb*) popcorn; *fig pl* flourishes.

florii [flo'rii] *nf pl* Palm Sunday.

flotant [flo'tant] *nm* floating person; *coll* drifter || *adj* floating.

flotă ['flotă] *nf naut* fleet; *mil* navy.

fluctua [fluktu'a] *vi* to fluctuate, to oscillate • ~ție *nf* fluctuation; (*oscilație*) oscillation; (*a cadrelor*) turnover.

fluent [flu'ent] *adj* fluent || *adv* fluently.

fluid [flu'id] *adj/nn* fluid • ~itate *nf* fluidity, liquidity.

fluier ['fluier] *nn* whistle; *mus* pipe, flute; *anat vernac* shinbone.

fluiera [fluie'ra] *vt* to whistle; (*dezaprobator*) to boo, to hoot (at) || *vi* to whistle; (*a vâjâi*) to whiz; (*dezaprobator*) to boo.

fluorescent [fluores'chent] *adj chem* fluorescent.

flușturatic [flushtu'ratik] *nm* giddy fellow, madcap || *adj* lightheaded, thoughtless; (*nestatornic*) fickle, flighty.

flutura [flutu'ra] *vt* (*batista*) to wave; (*brațele*) to swing; (*amenințător*) to brandish || *vi* to flutter; (*în vânt*) to fly, to float, to wave; *fig* to flit.

fluturaș [flutu'rash] *nm* (*ornament*) spangle, sequin • **cu** ~**i** spangled.

fluture ['fluture] *nm ento* butterfly; *tech* throttle.

fluviu ['fluviu] *nn* river; *fig* stream, flood.

flux [fluks] *nn naut* (high) tide, high water; *fig* (*val*) wave, rising tide; (*revărsare*) flood; flow, stream; ~ **și reflux** high tide and low tide; ebb and flow; *med* menstruation; *phys* flux.

foaie ['foaie] *nf* (*filă*) leaf; (*coală*) sheet; (*pagină*) page; (*ziar*) newspaper; *pl* (*fustă*) skirt; ~ **de pontaj** check/time sheet.

foaier [foa'ier] *nn* foyer.

foame ['foame] *nf* hunger; (*foamete*) famine, starvation; *fig* (*de*) thirst (for), craving • ~**te** *nf* starvation, famine.

foarfecă ['foarfekă] *nf* (pair of) scissors; (*mare*) shears; *zool* (*la rac*) claws.

foarte ['foarte] *adv* very; (*extrem de*) most, extremely, highly; (*cu participii trecute*) (very) much, well.

fobie [fo'bie] *nf* phobia, morbid fear/dread.

foc [fok] *nn* fire; (*vâlvătaie*) blaze; (*de tabără*) bonfire; (*mare*) conflagration; *jur* arson; (*împușcătură*) shot; (*detunătură*) report; (*tir*) firing; (*căldură*) heat; *fig* (*pasiune*) ardor, passion; (*durere*) grief, sorrow; (*necaz*) trouble, worry; (*mânie*) anger, fury, wrath.

focaliza [fokali'za] *vt opt* to focus.

focar [fo'kar] *nn med, phys* focus, *pl* foci/focuses; *tech* furnace; (*de locomotivă*) firebox; *fig* center, hotbed.

focă ['fokă] *nf zool* seal.

focos [fo'kos] *adj* (*d. oameni*) fiery, ardent, passionate; (*năvalnic*) impetuous; (*d. cai*) spirited || *nn mil* fuse; ~ **atomic/nuclear** atomic/nuclear warhead.

foe(h)n [fen] *nn met* foehn (wind); *elec* hairdryer.

fofila [fofi'la] *vr* to slink, to slip, to sneak; *fig* to dodge, to evade.

foi [fo'i] *vi* (*a fi plin de*) to abound (in), to teem (with) || *vr* to fuss, to bustle (about); (*nervos*) to fidget; (*a se codi*) to hesitate.

foios [fo'ios] *adj* (*frunzos*) leafy; (*din mai multe foi*) foliated || *nn bot* deciduous tree.

foișor [foi'shor] *nn* (*turn de pază*) watchtower; (*terasa unei clădiri înalte*) look-out (tower); belvedere; balcony; (*chioșc, umbrar*) arbor, pavilion.

foiță [fo'itsă] *nf* thin paper; small leaf; leaflet.

folclor [folk'klor] *nn* folklore.

folos [fo'los] *nn* use, utility; gain, profit; (*beneficiu*) benefit, advantage; **ce** ~? what is the use of it?, to what purpose?; **cu** ~ usefully, profitably • **în/spre** ~**ul** in behalf of.

folosi [folo'si] *vt* to use, to utilize, to make use of; (*a profita de*) to profit by, to capitalize on || *vi* to be of use, to be useful || *vr* to use, to avail oneself of • ~**tor** *adj* useful, advantageous, profitable.

fond [fond] *nn* (*conținut*) content, substance, essence; *fin* fund, capital; (*caracter*) nature; (*bază*) fundamentals, stock; (*artă*) background; (*al unei stofe*) foundation; *sp* long distance; **în** ~ (*de fapt*) actually, in fact, as a matter of fact; basically, essentially, fundamentally.

fonda [fon'da] *vt* to set up, to establish, to found • **~tor** *nm* founder ‖ *adj* founding.

fonetică [fo'netikă] *nf* phonetics.

fonic ['fonik] *adj* phonic.

fontă ['fontă] *nf* cast iron; (*brută*) pig iron.

fora [fo'ra] *vt* to drill, to bore • **~j** *nn* drilling, boring; bore/drill hole.

foraibăr [fo'raibăr] *nn* latch.

forceps ['forcheps] *nn med* forceps.

forestier [foresti'er] *adj* forest, forested; (*de cherestea*) timber ‖ *nm* forest ranger.

forfotă ['forfotă] *nf* agitation, bustle, fuss.

forfoti [forfo'ti] *vi* to bustle, to fuss; (*a mișuna*) to teem.

forja [for'zha] *vt* to forge.

forjă ['forzhă] *nf* forge.

forma [for'ma] *vt* (*a alcătui*) to form, to build (up); (*a constitui*) to set up, to found; (*a educa*) to train, to educate ‖ *vr* to form, to develop; (*a se înființa*) to be set up, to be founded; (*a lua forma*) to assume/take a form/shape; (*a se instrui*) to train oneself.

formal [for'mal] *adj* formal, proper, in due form; official, solemn; (*de formă*) perfunctory; express ‖ *adv* formally, specifically; (*de formă*) perfunctorily • **~ist** *nm* formalist, stickler for etiquette ‖ *adj* ceremonious, punctilious; formal, precise • **~itate** *nf* formality; (*procedură*) form, ceremony; (rule of) etiquette.

formație, formațiune [for'matsie, formatsi'une] *nf* formation; (*educație*) training; (*orânduire*) system, structure; *mil* unit; *sp* disposition; (*echipă*) team.

formă ['formă] *nf* form; *also geom* shape; (*înfățișare*) appearance; (*croială*) cut, make; (*format*) size; *naut pl* (*ale unei nave*) lines; *pl* (*siluetă*) figure; *pl* (*ale unei femei*) curves; form(ality), ceremony; (*calapod*) (*pt. pantofi*) last; (*pt. pălării*) block; (*de topit metale*) mold, cast; (*fel, mod*) way, manner; *sp also* condition, fettle; **de ~** perfunctory, superficial; **fără ~** shapeless, without form; **sub ~ de** under the form of, in the shape of; **sub nici o ~** by no means, on no account, in no way.

formidabil [formi'dabil] *adj* formidable; wonderful; *coll* tremendous, fantastic ‖ *adv* formidably; wonderfully ‖ *interj* great, super; you don't say so!, well, I never!.

formula [formu'la] *vt* to formulate; (*a exprima*) to express, to couch, to put; (*a întocmi un act*) to draw up; **a ~ o plângere** to lodge a complaint; *math* to formulize.

formular [formu'lar] *nn* (printed) form, blank.

formulă [for'mulă] *nf chem, math, also fig* formula; (*mijloc*) means; (*soluție*) solution; method.

fort [fort] *nn* fort, stronghold • **~ăreață** *nf* fortress, stronghold • **~ifica** [fortifi'ka] *vt mil* to fortify, to strengthen; to consolidate; *fig* to invigorate ‖ *vr* to grow strong(er), to gain (in) strength • **~ificație** *nf* fortification, defense works.

fortuit [fortu'it] *adj frml* fortuitous; (*întâmplător*) casual, chance, accidental.

forța [for'tsa] *vt* (*pe cineva*) to force, to oblige, to compel; (*a deschide, a separa cu efort*) to force open, to prize; **a ~ nota** to overdo it, to exaggerate ‖ *vr* to strain oneself, to exert oneself; (*a se căzni*) to endeavor; *fig* to affect.

forță [for'tsă] *nf* force, strength; (*putere*) power, might; (*intensitate*) intensity; (*vigoare*) vigor; (*violență*)

force, violence; *mil* (armed) force(s); *fig* appeal, attractiveness.

fosforescență [fosfores'chentsă] *nf phys* phosphorescence.

fosilă [fo'silă] *nf* fossil; *fig* fossil, stick-in-the-mud.

fost [fost] *nm coll* has-been ‖ *adj* former, past, ex-; (*defunct*) late.

foșnet ['foshnet] *nn* (*al vântului*) rustle, sough; (*al unei rochii*) rustle, swish.

foșni [fosh'ni] *vi* (*d. vânt*) to rustle, to sough; (*d. rochie*) to rustle, to swish.

fotbal ['fotbal] *nn* (association) football; *coll* soccer.

fotocopie [foto'kopie] *nf* photocopy.

fotogenic [foto'djenik] *adj* photogenic.

fotograf [foto'graf] *nm* cameraman; (*la atelier*) photographer.

fotografia [fotografi'a] *vt* to photograph, to take photographs ‖ *vr* to have a/one's photo taken.

fotografie [fotogra'fie] *nf* (*poză*) photo(graph), picture; (*dintr-un film*) still; (*ca artă*) photography.

fotoliu [fo'toliu] *nn* armchair, easy chair; (*la teatru*) (orchestra) stall.

fotoreporter [fotore'porter] *nm* newspaper/magazine photographer.

fox(terier) [foksteri'er] *nm zool* fox-terrier.

frac [frak] *nn* tail coat, tails, dresscoat.

fractura [fraktu'ra] *vt med* to fracture, to break.

fractură [frak'tură] *nf med, geol* fracture.

fracție ['fraktsie] *nf* fraction.

fracțiune [fraktsi'une] *nf* fraction, fragment; *pol* faction, splinter (party), group.

fragă ['fragă] *nf* wild strawberry.

fraged ['fradjed] *adj* (*moale*) soft; (*d. carne*) tender; (*delicat, plăpând*) frail, delicate; *fig* (*necopt*) unripe; (*d. vârstă*) early.

fragil [fra'djil] *adj* (*d. sticlă*) fragile, brittle; (*ca aviz*) **~!** handle with care!; *fig* (*delicat*) frail, tender; (*d. autoritate*) weak, unstable • **~itate** *nf* (*d. sticlă*) fragility, brittleness; *fig* frailty.

fragment [frag'ment] *nn* fragment; (*de piatră*) chip; (*de lemn*) splinter; (*pasaj*) passage, excerpt; (*de conversație, cântec*) snatch • **~ar** *adj* fragmentary ‖ *adv* fragmentarily.

fraht [fraht] *nn fin* bill of consignment/lading, waybill, freight.

fraier(ă) ['fraier(ă)] *nm/nf/adj* sucker, dupe.

fraieri [fraie'ri] *vt coll* to dupe, to sucker.

franc [frank] *adj* (*deschis*) frank, open, candid ‖ *adv* frankly, openly, candidly.

franca [fran'ka] *vt* to stamp.

francez [fran'chez] *nm* Frenchman, *pl* the French ‖ *adj* French • **~ă** *nf* French, the French language.

franchețe [fran'ketse] *nf* frankness, candor, openness.

francmason [frankma'son] *nm* freemason.

franj [franzh] *nn* fringe.

franțuzesc [frantsu'zesk] *adj* French.

frapa [fra'pa] *vt* to strike; to surprise, to shock; (*d. băuturi*) to ice; to chill • **~nt** *adj* striking, surprising, glaring.

frapieră [frapi'eră] *nf* ice bucket.

frasin ['frasin] *nm bot* ash (tree).

frate ['frate] *nm* brother; (*confrate*) brother, *pl* brethren; *relig* friar; *fig* comrade, fellow; *coll* pal, buddy • **~rn** *adj* brotherly, fraternal • **~rnitate** *nf* brotherhood, fraternity.

frauda [frau'da] *vt jur* to defraud, to cheat, to swindle.

fraudă ['fraudă] *nf* fraud, embezzlement; *(înşelăciune)* swindle, cheating.

fraudulos [fraudu'los] *adj* fraudulent; **în mod** ~ by fraud, by false pretenses || *adv* fraudulently.

frază ['frază] *nf mus* phrase; *gram* (compound/complex) sentence.

frăgezi [frădje'zi] *vt* to make tender/soft || *vr* to become tender/soft.

frământa [frămân'ta] *vt (aluat)* to knead, to work; *(lut)* to temper; *(ceară)* to mold; *(în picioare)* to tread, to stamp; *fig (a preocupa)* to worry, to torment; *fig (a discuta)* to debate, to turn over; **a-şi ~ capul/creierul cu** to rack/worry one's brains with/about || *vr (a se agita)* to fuss, to bustle; *(a se chinui)* to worry, to fret, to torment oneself.

frăţesc [fră'tsesk] *adj* brotherly, fraternal.

frăţie [fră'tsie] *nf* brotherliness, brotherly affection/feeling, fraternity, brotherhood.

frâna [frâ'na] *vi* to put on the brake; *(la căruţe)* to put on the drag || *vt* to brake, to apply the brake/drag to; *fig* to curb, to check, to impede, to be a drag on.

frână ['frână] *nf* brake; *(la căruţă)* drag; *fig* hindrance, obstacle, impediment.

frânge ['frân'dje] *vt* to break; *(în bucăţi)* to break up, to break to pieces; *(în bucăţi mici)* to shiver (to atoms), to smash (up); *coll* to break to smithereens; to fracture; *fig* to defeat || *vr* to break.

frânghie ['frângie] *nf* rope; *(subţire)* line; *(odgon)* cable.

frâu [frâu] *nn* rein; *fig (conducere)* rein(s), helm; **fără** ~ *fig* uncurbed.

freamăt ['freamăt] *nn (al frunzelor)* rustling; *(al vântului)* sigh; *(al unei ape curgătoare)* murmur, purling; *(agitaţie)* bustle, tumult; *(fior)* thrill.

freca [fre'ka] *vt* to rub; *(pt. a curăţa)* to scrub out; *med* to massage; *fig* to censure, to take to task; *coll* to give smb a dressing-down; to criticize harshly, to slate || *vr* to rub against/on/over; *(d. persoane)* to be rubbed; to rub oneself.

frecţie ['frektsie] *nf* massage; *(la frizer)* shampoo.

frecvent [frek'vent] *adj* frequent || *adv* frequently, often.

frecventa [frekven'ta] *vt* to frequent, to visit frequently; *(cursuri)* to attend.

frecvenţă [frek'ventsă] *nf* frequency, frequent occurrence; *(participare)* attendance; *elec, med* frequency.

fredona [fredo'na] *vt* to hum, to croon.

fremăta [fremă'ta] *vi (a foşni)* to rustle; *lit* to sigh; *(d. ape)* to murmur, to purl; *(d. valuri)* to roar; *(a se agita)* to bustle, to fuss; *(a fi înfiorat)* to be thrilled.

frenetic [fre'netik] *adj* frantic, frenzied, wild || *adv* frantically, passionately.

frenezie [frene'zie] *nf* frenzy, excitement.

frescă ['freskă] *nf* fresco; *also fig* picture.

freză ['freză] *nf (frizură)* haircut.

frezie ['frezie] *nf bot* freesia.

friabil [fri'abil] *adj* friable, crumbly.

frică ['frikă] *nf* fear, fright; panic; *(nelinişte)* anxiety; **fără** ~ fearless.

fricos [fri'kos] *nm* coward || *adj* fearful, cowardly, gutless.

frig [frig] *nn* cold; *(ger)* frost; *pl* ague; *also fig* fever.

frigare [fri'gare] *nf* spit, broach, (meat) jack.

frige ['fridje] *vt (pe frigare)* to roast on a spit; *(în cuptor)* to bake; *(la grătar)* to grill, to broil; *(în tigaie)* to fry, to braise; *(a arde)* to burn; *fig (a înşela)* coll to take in, to diddle || *vi* to be/get burnt; to burn oneself; *fig (a fi înşelat)* coll to be cheated/diddled/taken in.

frigid [fri'djid] *adj* frigid; cold, icy.

frigider [fridji'der] *nn* refrigerator; *coll* fridge.

friguros [frigu'ros] *adj* cold, chilly; *(d. cineva)* chilly.

friptură [frip'tură] *nf (la grătar)* steak, grilled meat; *(la cuptor)* roast (meat); ~ **de porc/de vită** roast pork/beef.

frison [fri'son] *nn* (cold) shiver.

frişcă ['frishkă] *nf* whipped cream.

frivol [fri'vol] *adj* frivolous, wanton; superficial, shallow; *(d. limbaj)* flippant || *adv* frivolously.

frizer [fri'zer] *nm* hairdresser; *(bărbier)* barber • **~ie** *nf* barber's (shop), hairdresser's.

front [front] *nn mil, met, pol, fig* front; *min* (working) front; *archit* front(age), front side • **~al** *adj* frontal || *adv* in front.

frontieră [fronti'eră] *nf pol* frontier, border; *fig* boundary.

fruct [frukt] *nn* fruit • **~ifer** *adj* fructiferous, fruit (bearing).

fructifica [fruktifi'ka] *vt* to fructify, to turn to (good) account.

frugal [fru'gal] *adj* frugal.

frumos [fru'mos] *adj* beautiful, fine; *lit* beauteous; *(ca trăsături)* *(d. femei)* fair, lovely; *(drăguţ)* nice; *(d. bărbaţi)* handsome, good-looking; *(amabil)* kind; noble, generous; honorable || *adv* beautifully, finely, handsomely; *(amabil)* kindly; *(binişor, încet)* slowly, nicely.

frumuseţe [frumu'setse] *nf* beauty; *(fată, femeie)* beauty, beautiful girl/woman.

frumuşel, frumuşică [frumu'shel, frumu'shikă] *adj* nice, pretty, good-looking || *adv* slowly, gently.

fruntaş [frun'tash] *nm (în muncă)* front-ranker; *pol* leader || *adj* front-ranking; remarkable; *(la învăţătură)* proficient.

frunte ['frunte] *nf* forehead, brow; *(cap)* also fig head; *fig* elite, cream, pick; **de** ~ top, first-rate/class; prominent, eminent, excellent • **~a sus!** also fig chin up!, cheer up!.

frunză ['frunză] *nf* leaf; *(frunziş)* foliage.

frunzări [frunză'ri] *vt (o carte)* to leaf (through), to thumb (through); *(un ziar)* to glance cursorily at.

frunziş [frun'zish] *nn* foliage, leafage.

frustra [frus'tra] *vt* to frustrate, to deprive • **~re** *nf* frustration.

fudul [fu'dul] *adj* haughty, conceited; *(mândru)* proud; arrogant || *adv* haughtily, etc.

fuduli [fudu'li] *vr* to give oneself airs, to take pride in, to show off; *(prin vorbire)* to brag; *coll* to talk big; *(prin mers)* to strut, to stalk • **~e** *nf* haughtiness, pride, arrogance; *pl vernac* testicles of a ram.

fugar [fu'gar] *nm (evadat)* fugitive, runaway || *adj* fleeting; casual; transient.

fuga ['fuga] *adv* quickly, running || *interj* be quick!, hurry on!, make haste!.

fugar [fu'gar] *nm (evadat)* fugitive; *(refugiat)* refugee; *(exilat)* exile; runner || *adj (trecător)* transient, fleeting; *(grăbit)* hasty; *(d. o remarcă)* passing, desultory; *(la întâmplare)* casual.

fugă ['fugă] *nf* run, flight; *(cursă)* race; escape; *(de acasă pt. a se căsători)* elopement; *mil* rout; **din** ~ in passing, passingly; **în ~** in a hurry, hurriedly; **pe ~** hastily, in a hurry ‖ *vi (oameni, animale)* to stampede ‖ *vt mil* to put (troops) to rout, to rout; *(duşmanul)* to send flying.

fugări [fugă'ri] *vt* to (give) chase, to pursue; *(a izgoni)* to drive out/away; *recip* to chase one another.

fugi [fu'dji] *vi (a alerga)* to run, to fly, to race; *(a se grăbi)* to rush (along); *(a o şterge)* to run away/off, to make off; to decamp, to flee; *(cu cineva)* to elope; *(d. timp: a se scurge)* to pass, to elapse, to go by.

fugitiv [fudji'tiv] *adj* fleeting, transient, transitory; *(întâmplător)* casual.

fular [fu'lar] *nn* scarf; *(călduros)* comforter, muffler; *text* foulard.

fulg [fulg] *nm* flake; **~ de zăpadă** snowflake; *(puf)* fluff; *(pană)* feather; *(de plante)* down; *(de lână)* flock; *(de stofă)* nip • **~i de ovăz** oatmeal, porridge.

fulgarin [fulga'rin] *nn* waterproof (coat), mac(kintosh).

fulger ['fuldjer] *nn* lightning; *(un ~)* a flash of lightning; *fig* flash.

fulgera [fuldje'ra] *vt* to strike; *(pe cineva, la pământ)* to dash to the ground ‖ *vi* to lighten, to flash; *fig (a sclipi)* to flash, to glitter, to sparkle.

fulgerător [fuldjeră'tor] *adj (instantaneu)* quick, flashing, instantaneous.

fulgui [fulgu'i] *vi* to snow lightly with tiny flakes.

fum [fum] *nn* smoke; *pl fig* conceit; airs and graces.

fuma [fu'ma] *vt/vi* to smoke, to have a smoke • **~t** *nn* smoking • **~ul oprit/interzis** no smoking; smoking is not allowed here.

fumător [fumă'tor] *nm* smoker.

fumega [fume'ga] *vi* to smoke.

fumoar [fu'moar] *nn* smoking room.

funciar [funchi'ar] *adj* land(ed); *fig* fundamental, deep-rooted/-seated, innate.

funcţie ['funktsie] *nf* function; *(slujbă)* job; post, position; role, part; **în ~ de** depending on, in terms of; *(conform cu)* in accordance/keeping with, according to.

funcţiona [fuktsio'na] *vi (a-şi exercita funcţia)* to function; *tech* to run, to work, to operate; **a nu ~** to be out of order • **~l** *adj* functional ‖ *adv* functionally • **~re** *nf* work(ing); **în stare de ~** in working order, in good repair.

funcţionar [funktsio'nar] *nm (lucrător de birou)* office worker; *(de stat)* public/civil servant; official, functionary; *(angajat)* employee; *(comercial)* clerk; *(înalt)* office holder.

funcţionăresc [funktsionă'resk] *adj* bureaucratic, red tape ....

funcţiune [funktsi'une] *nf* function.

fund [fund] *nn (partea de jos)* bottom; *(al mării)* ground; *(spate)* behind, back(side); *(suport de lemn)* wooden board/platter/trencher; *(capăt)* end; *(şezut)* buttocks;, behind, backside.

funda [fun'da] *vt* to found, to start, to set up.

fundal [fun'dal] *nn* background.

fundament [funda'ment] *nn (al unei construcţii)* foundation, base; *fig* basis, ground, foundation; *typ* letter board • **~al** *adj* fundamental, essential, vital, basic.

fundaş [fun'dash] *nm sp* fullback.

fundaţie [fun'datsie] *nf (temelie)* foundation; *(instituţie)* foundation, endowed establishment/institution.

fundă ['fundă] *nf* bow.

fundătură [fundă'tură] *nf* blind alley; cul-de-sac.

funebru [fu'nebru] *adj (ceremonie, marş)* funeral; *fig* funereal, gloomy, dismal.

funeralii [fune'ralii] *nn pl* obsequies, funeral (ceremony).

funerar [fune'rar] *adj* funeral, funerary.

funest [fu'nest] *adj* ill-fated, fatal, fateful, disastrous.

funicular [funiku'lar] *nn* cable car, cable way, telepher.

funie ['funie] *nf* rope; *(mai subţire)* line, cord; *(odgon)* cable.

funingine [fu'nindjine] *nf* soot.

fura [fu'ra] *vt* to steal; *(a şterpeli)* to pilfer, to filch; *sl* to nick; *(a jefui)* to rob; *(a delapida)* to embezzle; *(o persoana)* to kidnap; *(a plagia)* to plagiarize; *fig (a lipsi de)* to rob, to deprive of ‖ *vi* to steal, to thieve.

furaj [fu'razh] *nn* fodder, forage.

furcă ['furkă] *nf agr* pitchfork; *(de tors)* distaff; *(la telefon)* cradle, hook.

furculiţă [furku'litsă] *nf* fork.

furgonetă [furgo'netă] *nf auto* van, delivery car/van.

furibund [furi'bund] *adj* frenzied, furious, mad (with fury).

furie ['furie] *nf* fury, rage, passion; *(mânie)* wrath; *(acces)* fit of temper/rage; *(violenţă)* violence; *(nebunie)* madness, frenzy; *fig* impetuosity, violence; *(femeie rea)* shrew; *myth* Fury; **cu ~** furiously, with a vengeance.

furios [furi'os] *adj* furious, angry, enraged, frantic; *(d. vânt)* raging, howling.

furiş [fu'rish] *adj* stealthy, furtive.

furişa [furi'sha] *vr* to creep, to slip (along); *(a se strecura)* to sneak, to skulk; *(încet)* to slink; *(în întuneric)* to prowl (about); *(a o şterge)* to steal away.

furnal [fur'nal] *nn* furnace.

furnicar [furni'kar] *nm zool* anteater ‖ *nn* ant hill; *fig* crowd, throng, multitude.

furnică [fur'nikă] *nf ento* ant; *pl (furnicături)* tingling, pins and needles.

furnir [fur'nir] *nn* veneer.

furnitură [furni'tură] *nf pl* supplies, requisites; *(de birou)* office equipment; stationery; *(croitor)* accessory material in tailoring; furnishings, trimmings.

furniza [furni'za] *vt (a procura)* to supply, to provide, to furnish; *(a livra)* to deliver.

furnizor [furni'zor] *nm* supplier; *(de alimente)* provider, caterer; contractor.

furou [fu'rou] *nn* slip, chemise.

fursec [fur'sek] *nn usu pl* fancy cakes.

furt [furt] *nn* theft, stealing, robbery; *(prin efracţie)* burglary; *(mărunt)* pilfering; *(din magazine)* shoplifting; *(delapidare)* embezzlement; *lit* plagiarism; **~ calificat** aggravated theft.

furtun [fur'tun] *nn* hose.

furtună [fur'tună] *nf also fig* storm, tempest, hurricane; *(cu descărcări electrice)* thunderstorm; *(zbucium)* tumult, commotion, unrest.

furtunos [furtu'nos] *adj* stormy, tempestuous; *(d. mare)* rough; *(agitat)* agitated; violent; vehement, impetuous.

furuncul [fu'runkul] *nn med* furuncule, boil.

fus [fus] *nn (pt. tors)* spindle; *archit* shaft/trunk; *(la maşini)* axle; *bot* stem; *naut* anchor shank; **~ orar** time zone.

fustă ['fustă] *nf* skirt; *(jupon)* petticoat; *fig coll* a bit of fluff.

fuzelaj [fuze'lazh] *nn avia* fuselage.

fuzibil [fu'zibil] *adj* fusible, easily melted, meltable.

fuziona [fuzio'na] *vi* to fuse; *fig* to merge, to blend, to coalesce.

fuziune [fuzi'une] *nf* fusion, melting; *metal* smelting; *phys* (nuclear) fusion; *fig* merging (of companies), merger.

G

gabarit [gaba'rit] *nn naut* (*al unui vas*) model; (*parţial*) mold; *constr* outline; *tech* template; (*sub un pod*) clearance; (*al ecartamentului*) rail/track gauge; (*dimensiuni mari*)) size, dimensions; ~ **depăşit** outsize.

gafă ['gafă] *nf* blunder, gaffe.

gag [gag] *nn cin* gag.

gagică [ga'djikă] *nf coll, sl* girl, chick, bird, babe; mistress.

gaică ['gaikă] *nf* (*bentiţă*) strap; (*butonieră*) buttonhole; (*pt. curea*) loop; (*pt. atârnat*) eye.

gaiţă ['gaitsă] *nf orn* jay; *fig* jabberer, clacker, rattler, telltale, sieve.

gaj [gazh] *nn com* deposit, security, mortgage; (*chezăşie*) pledge; *pl* (*joc*) forfeits.

galant [ga'lant] *adj* (*d. bărbaţi*) gallant, gentlemanly; (*d. gesturi*) courteous, polite; generous, liberal ǁ *adv* gallantly, courteously, etc.

galantar [galan'tar] *nn* shop window.

galanterie [galante'rie] *nf* (*politeţe*) gallantry, courtesy, politeness; (*magazin*) haberdasher's, hosier's; (*obiecte*) notions.

galaxie [galak'sie] *nf astron* galaxy.

gală ['gală] *nf* gala, state; (*festivitate*) festivity, celebration, fete.

galben ['galben] *nn* (*culoare*) yellow; (*vopsea*) yellow dye/ coloring ǁ *adj* yellow; (*bătând în cafeniu*) fallow, buff; (*palid*) pale; (*de boală*) wan; (*icteros*) jaundiced; fair, blond(e).

galeră [ga'leră] *nf naut* galley.

galerie [gale'rie] *nf* corridor; (*expoziţie*) gallery; (*de mină*) drift, level; *thea* circle, the upper circle; (*spectatori*) audience; (*de la galerie*) the gallery; *sp* spectators; (*a unei echipe*) fans; *archit* cornice, molding; beading; (*de sobă*) fender, fireguard; (*suport de perdea*) curtain rack/holder.

galon [ga'lon] *nn* braid, galloon; (*de aur*) gold lace; *pl mil* stripes; (*unitate de măsură*) gallon.

galop [ga'lop] *nn* gallop; **în** ~ at a gallop; *fig* rapidly, fast approaching; (*dans*) gal(l)opade.

galoş [ga'losh] *nm* overshoe, galosh, rubber(s).

galvaniza [galvani'za] *vt phys, metal, physiol* to galvanize, to electroplate; *fig* to stimulate, to excite, to energize.

gamă ['gamă] *nf mus* scale, gamut; *fig* range, assortment.

gambă ['gambă] *nf anat* shank.

gamelă [ga'melă] *nf mil* mess kettle/tin.

gang [gang] *nn* (*pasaj*) passage; corridor, gangway; (*galerie*) gallery; *min* adit.

ganglion [gangli'on] *nm anat* ganglion.

gangrenă [gan'grenă] *nf med also fig* gangrene, canker.

gangster ['gangster] *nm* gangster.

gara [ga'ra] *vt auto* to garage; (*un tren*) to shunt on to a siding; (*un avion*) to park, to put a plane in the hangar.

garaj [ga'razh] *nn auto* garage; *rail* siding.

garant [ga'rant] *nm* guarantor, surety, bail.

garanta [garan'ta] *vt* to warrant, to guarantee; (*a asigura verbal pe cineva*) to assure; (*faptic*) to ensure ǁ *vi* to warrant, to vouch for.

garanţie [garan'tsie] *nf com* (*a calităţii*) warranty, guarantee; (*de plată*) guaranty; (*a executării unui contract*) pledge; (*gaj*) security; (*cauţiune*) bail; *fin* also collateral; *fig* warrant, token, earnest.

gară ['gară] *nf* railroad station, depot.

gard [gard] *nn* fence; (*uluci*) paling; (*viu*) hedge; *sp* hurdle.

gardă ['gardă] *nf also mil, sp* guard; (*pază*) watch; (*apărătoare la sabie, spadă*) (hilt) guard.

gardenie [gar'denie] *nf bot* gardenia.

garderob [garde'rob] *nn* wardrobe, clothes-press.

garderobă [garde'robă] *nf* (*cameră*) cloakroom; (*haine*) clothes, wardrobe.

gardian [gardi'an] *nm* guard(ian), warder, watchman; (*poliţist*) policeman.

gargară [gar'gară] *nf med* gargle.

garnisi [garni'si] *vt* (*o mâncare*) to garnish; (*o rochie*) to trim, to do up; (*pietre preţioase*) to set.

garnitură [garni'tură] *nf* (*grup de obiecte*) set, assortment; (*de unelte*) tool outfit; *cul* garnish(ing), trimmings; (*podoabe*) ornaments, decorations; *rail* set of cars forming a train; *tech* fittings.

garnizoană [garni'zoană] *nf mil* garrison.

garoafă [ga'roafă] *nf bot* carnation, clove pink.

garsonieră [garsoni'eră] *nf* one-room/studio apartment, bachelor's rooms.

gastrită [gas'trită] *nf med* gastritis, inflammation of the stomach.

gastronomie [gastrono'mie] *nf* gastronomy.

gaşcă ['gashkă] *nf coll pej* coterie; (*clică*) clique; set, lot, pack, gang.

gata ['gata] *adj* (*pt. acţiune*) ready; (*încheiat*) finished; (*pregătit*) prepared; (*dispus*) *coll* game; (*în ordine*) in order ǁ *adv* ready, finished; ~ **de** ready for smth; ready to do smth; ~ **să** within an inch of.

gater ['gater] *nn tech* sawmill, frame-/reciprocating saw.

gaură ['gaură] *nf* hole, aperture; (*prelungă*) slit, slot; (*cavitate*) cavity, hollow; (*crăpătură*) crack, chink; (*loc gol*) gap, opening; (*vizuină*) den, burrow; **gaura cheii** keyhole.

gaz [gaz] *nn phys, chem* gas; *med* flatus; *coll* wind(s); (*petrol lampant*) kerosene, lamp oil • ~**a** *vt* to gas • ~**are** *nf* gasification; **cameră de** ~ *hist* gas chamber.

gazdă ['gazdă] *nf* (*bărbat*) host; (*femeie*) hostess; (*proprietar*) landlord, landlady; (*locuinţă*) lodging(s); *bio* host.

gazelă [ga'zelă] *nf zool* gazelle.

gazetar [gaze'tar] *nm* journalist, newspaperman.

gazetă [ga'zetă] *nf* newspaper, journal, gazette.

gazon [ga'zon] *nn* turf, sod.

găgăuţă [găgă'utsă] *nm coll* ninny, milksop, scatterbrain.

găinar [găi'nar] *nm obs* poacher; (*borfaş*) pilferer, thief, pickpocket.

găinaţ [găi'nats] *nn* droppings.

găină [găi'nă] *nf orn* hen; fowl; (*puică*) pullet; (*pui*) chicken.

găinărie [găină'rie] *nf fig* (*hoţie*) pilfering, petty theft.

găinuşă [găi'nushă] *nf orn* hazel, hen, grouse; blackgame; *ento* cockchafer; *bot* meadow rue; *astron* the Pleiades.

gălăgie [gălă'djie] *nf* noise, hubbub, uproar; (*scandal*) racket; *coll* row; (*ţipete*) clamor; (*agitaţie*) bustle; (*zarvă*) tumult, rioting; (*cu bătaie*) brawl(ing).

gălăgios [gălădji'os] *adj* noisy, riotous, blustering || *nm* noisy/riotous person, rioter.

gălbenuş [gălbe'nush] *nn* yolk (of egg).

gălbui [găl'bui] *adj* yellowish.

găleată [gă'leată] *nf* bucket, pail; (*conţinut*) bucketful, pailful.

găligan [găli'gan] *nm* (*lungan*) *coll* beanpole, lamppost.

gămălie [gămă'lie] *nf* (pin)head, head of a pin; **ac cu ~** pin.

gărgăriţă ['gărgăritsă] *nf* ento corn weevil; grain moth; ladybug.

gărgăun [gărgă'un] *nm* ento hornet, yellow jacket; *pl fig* cranks, maggots.

găselniţă [gă'selnitsă] *nf* *fig* happy solution; *fig* lucky find; (*idee*) brainwave.

găsi [gă'si] *vt* to find; (*a descoperi*) to discover, to find out, to come up with; (*a da de*) to come across/upon, to find by chance; (*idee, metodă*) to hit on; (*a întâmpina*) to meet with; to think, to consider || *vr* (*într-o situaţie*) to be, to find oneself; to feel; (*a se afla*) to be (situated); (*d. obiecte întinse*) to lie; (*d. obiecte înalte*) to stand; (*a se pomeni*) to find one-self; (*a fi disponibil*) to be (found/ available).

găteală [gă'teală] *nf* ornament; (*toaletă*) dressing, adornment; (*îmbrăcăminte*) finery, elegant attire.

găti [gă'ti] *vt* (*mâncare*) to cook, to prepare; (*a fierbe*) to boil; (*a îmbrăca*) to dress up; (*a termina*) to end, to finish || *vi* to cook || *vr* to get ready; (*a se îmbrăca*) to smarten (oneself) up.

găunos [gău'nos] *adj* (*scorburos*) hollow; (*gol*) empty; *fig* shallow.

găuri [gău'ri] *vt* to pierce, to go through; to make a hole/holes in; (*a perfora*) to drill, to bore; (*cu gloanţe*) to riddle || *vr* to be torn/pierced; (*d. ciorapi*) to hole; (*a se rupe*) to tear, to wear through.

găzdui [găzdu'i] *vt* to lodge, to accommodate, to put up; *fig* to play host to.

gâdila [gâdi'la] *vt also fig* to tickle; to titillate; (*a măguli*) to flatter || *vr* to be ticklish.

gâfâi [gafa'i] *vi* to pant, to puff, to wheeze • **~ală, ~t** *nf, nn* pant, panting.

gâgâi [gâgâ'i] *vi* to gaggle • **~t** *nn* gaggle.

gâlcă ['gâlkă] *nf* vernac (*umflătură*) swelling, wen; (*amigdale*) *pl* tonsils; *med* (*amigdalită*) quinsy, tonsillitis.

gâlceavă [gâl'cheavă] *nf* vernac discord, quarrel; **a căuta ~** to pick a quarrel with smb; to be spoiling for a fight.

gâlcevitor [gâlchevi'tor] *adj* quarrelsome, contentious, cantankerous || *nm* brawler, wrangler, quarrelsome person.

gâlgâi [gâlgâ'i] *vi* to gurgle; (*a ţâşni*) to bubble, to gush/flow forth; (*a clipoci*) to murmur, to babble • **~t** *nn* gurgling, etc.

gând [gând] *nn* thought; idea, notion; (*minte*) mind, brains; (*intenţie*) thought, intention; plan, scheme; (*părere*) opinion; *pl* (*gândire*) thinking, thoughts; (*închipuire*) imagination; *pl* (*griji*) worry, anxiety; (*dorinţă*) wish, will; (*convingere*) idea, conviction; (*presimţire*) presentiment, anticipation.

gândac [gân'dak] *nm* ento beetle, chafer; (*de bucătărie*) cockroach.

gândi [gân'di] *vi* to think; to reflect; (*a raţiona*) to

reason || *vt* to think (that), to consider (that); (*a spera*) to hope; (*a estima*) to believe; to imagine, to picture; (*a concepe*) to think out || *vr* to think; to con-sider; (*a socoti*) to deem; to ponder, to reflect; (*a plănui*) to plan; (*a-şi închipui*) to imagine, to fancy; (*a ezita*) to hesitate, to waver; **a se ~ la** (*a medita*) to think of, to consider; (*a-şi aduce aminte de*) to think of, to remember; **a se ~ să** (*a avea în vedere*) to mean, to aim at; (*a intenţiona*) to be going to, to in-tend; **a se ~ bine** to think hard/twice, to think smth over • **~re** *nf* (*ca proces*) thinking; (*ca sistem*) thought, idea; (*deliberare*) deliberation, considera-tion; (*visare*) reverie • **~rea modernă** modern thought • **~tor** *nm* thinker || *adj* pensive; thoughtful, wistful; (*absorbit*) absorbed/engrossed in thought.

gânganie [gân'ganie] *nf* bug, (small) insect.â

gângăvi [gângă'vi] *vi/vt* to stammer, to stutter.

gânguri [gângu'ri] *vi* (*d. copii*) to babble, to prattle; (*d. porumbei*) to coo.

gârbov(it) [gârbo'vit] *adj* stooping, bent; (*cocoşat*) hunchbacked, round-shouldered.

gârbovi [gârbo'vi] *vr* to stoop, to become bent/round-shouldered.

gârlă ['gârlă] *nf* stream(let), river, rivulet, brook || *adv* galore, profusely, in profusion.

gâscan [gâs'kan] *nm* gander.

gâscă ['gâskă] *nf* orn goose; *fig* simple-minded woman/girl; *coll* silly goose.

gât [gât] *nn* anat neck; (*gâtlej*) throat, windpipe, gullet; (*înghiţitură*) draught, sip; *coll* pull, drop; (*guler*) collar; (*de sticlă*) neck; *tech* groove.

gâtui [gâtu'i] *vt* to throttle, to strangle; to garotte; *fig* to nip.

geam [djeam] *nn* (*de fereastră*) windowpane; (*fereastră*) window; (*sticlă*) sheet of glass.

geamandură [djeaman'dură] *nf* naut buoy; (*de balizare*) beacon.

geamantan [djeaman'tan] *nn* suitcase, portmanteau; (*mic*) valise; (*cufăr*) trunk.

geamăn(ă) [djeamăn(ă)] *adj* twin || *nm* twin brother/boy || *nf* twin sister/girl.

geană ['djeană] *nf* eyelash; (*de lumină*) streak (of light).

geantă ['djeantă] *nf* bag; (*poşetă*) handbag; (*servietă*) briefcase.

gel [djel] *nn* chem, phys gel.

gelatină [djela'tină] *nf* gelatin(e); (*ca mâncare*) jelly.

gelos [dje'los] *adj* (*pe*) jealous (of smth); (*pizmaş*) envious (of smb).

gelozie [djelo'zie] *nf* jealousy; (*invidie*) envy.

gem [djem] *nn* jam.

geme ['djeme] *vi* to groan, to moan; (*a suspina*) to sigh; *fig* (*de*) to be crowded (with), to swarm (with).

gen [djen] *nn* (*fel*) kind, sort, type; (*mod*) manner, way; *gram* gender; *bio* genus; family; (*în expresii*) like; **de acest ~** of this kind, such.

genă ['djena] *nf* bio gene.

genealogie [djenealo'djie] *nf* genealogy; descent.

genera [djene'ra] *vt* to generate, to engender; to produce; to give birth to; to breed.

general [djene'ral] *nm mil* general || *adj* general, uni-versal; (*comun*) common; **director ~** general man-ager; **în ~** in general; (*în ansamblu*) on the whole; (*în linii mari*) generally/roughly speaking; (*de obicei*) as a (general) rule, usually; (*vag*) generally, vaguely || *nn* general.

generaliza [djenerali'za] *vt/vi* to generalize || *vr* to become general, to spread • **~re** *nf* generalization; general conclusion; (*răspândire și*) spreading

generator [djenera'tor] *adj* generating || *nn* generator.

generație [djene'ratsie] *nf* generation.

generic [dje'nerik] *nn cin* credits; credit/main titles || *adj* generic (term).

generos [djene'ros] *adj* generous, liberal, lavish; (*nobil*) kindhearted || *adv* generously, liberally.

generozitate [djenerozi'tate] *nf* (*dărnicie*) generosity, liberality; (*noblețe*) kindness, nobility; **cu** ~ generously.

genetic [dje'netik] *adj* genetic

geneză [dje'nezǎ] *nf* genesis, origin; **Geneza** (*biblie*) The Book of Genesis.

genial [djeni'al] *adj* (*strălucit*) brilliant; of genius; (*înzestrat*) gifted, ingenious || *adv* brilliantly, with genius.

genital [djeni'tal] *adj anat* genital.

genitiv [djeni'tiv] *nn/adj gram* genitive.

geniu ['djeniu] *nn* (*cu calități excepționale*) genius; (*spirit*) genie, *pl* genii; *mil* engineer(s).

genocid [djeno'chid] *nn* genocide.

genom [dje'nom] *nn bio* genome.

gentil [djen'til] *adj* (*amabil*) kind, obliging; (*politicos*) polite, courteous, amiable; (*drăguț*) nice, gentle || *adv* politely, courteously, nicely • **~ețe** *nf* (*amabilitate*) kindness; (*politețe*) politeness, courteousness, amiability.

gentilom [djenti'lom] *nm* gentleman.

genunchi [dje'nunki] *nm* knee; **în** ~ on one's (bended) knees, on bended knee.

geofizică [djeo'fizikǎ] *nf* geophysics.

geografic [djeo'grafik] *adj* geographical || *adv* geographically.

geografie [djeogra'fie] *nf* geography.

geolog [djeo'log] *nm* geologist • **~ie** *nf* geology.

geometrie [djeome'trie] *nf* geometry.

georgian [djeordji'an] *nm/adj* Georgian.

ger [djer] *nn* frost, frosty weather, severe cold.

geriatrie [djeria'trie] *nf med* geriatrics, gerontology.

german [djer'man] *nm* German • **~ă** *nf ling* German, the German language || *adj* German.

germen ['djermen] *nm* embryo, germ, seed.

germina [djermi'na] *vi bio, fig* to germinate; to shoot, to spring up, to sprout.

geros [dje'ros] *adj* frosty.

gest [djest] *nn also fig* gesture; (*violent*) gesticulation; (*mișcare*) movement, motion.

gestație [djes'tatsie] *nf physiol* gestation, pregnancy.

gesticula [djestiku'la] *vi* to gesticulate, to gesture; *hum* to saw the air.

gestiona [djestio'na] *vt* to administrate, to manage • **~r** *nm* administrator, manager || *adj* administrative.

gestionare, gestiune [djestio'nare, djesti'une] *nf* (financial) administration, management, control.

gheară ['gearǎ] *nf zool, tech* claw; (*la păsări de pradă*) pounce, talon; *pl fig* clutches, grip, grasp, jaws.

gheată ['geatǎ] *nf* boot.

gheață ['geatsǎ] *nf* ice; *pl* drift ice;(*grindină*) hail; *fig* coldness, indifference.

gheb [geb] *nn* (*cocoașă*) hump, hunch; (*ridicătură*) hillock, mound, knoll • **~os** *adj* hunched, hump-backed, hunchbacked.

ghem [gem] *nn* ball (of thread), clew; *zool* third stomach of the ruminates.

ghemotoc [gemo'tok] *nn* ball, pellet; (*de hârtie*) crumpled paper.

ghemui [gemu'i] *vt* to roll/coil up || *vr* to roll/coil oneself up; (*pe vine*) to crouch, to squat; (*de frică*) to cower.

ghepard [ge'pard] *nm zool* cheetah, hunting cat, leopard.

gheretă [ge'retǎ] *nf* (*a portarului*) lodge; *mil* sentry box; (*chioșc*) booth.

gherilă [ge'rilǎ] *nf mil* guerilla.

ghetou [ge'tou] *nn* ghetto.

ghetre ['getre] *nf pl* spats, gaiters.

ghețar [ge'tsar] *nm* glacier; (*aisberg*) iceberg || *nn coll* ice box, fridge.

ghețuș [ge'tsush] *nn* (*concret*) ice (tract), ice-covered ground; (*polei*) glazed frost; (*derdeluș*) slide.

ghici [gi'chi] *vt* to guess, to conjecture; (*a prezice*) to predict, to foretell; (*a prevedea*) to foresee; (*a proroci*) to prophesy; (*a citi*) to read; (*a simți*) to feel || *vi* to divine, to practice divination; (*în cărți*) to tell smb's fortune; (*în stele*) to read in the stars || *vr* to be guessed/sensed; (*a se întrevedea*) to peep (behind smth); (*a apărea*) to loom • **~toare** *nf* (*prezicătoare*) fortune-teller, soothsayer; riddle, puzzle; conundrum; *fig* enigma • **~tor** *nm* guesser; (*prezicător*) diviner, soothsayer, fortune-teller.

ghid [gid] *nm also fig* guide || *nn* (*carte*) guidebook, travelers guidebook/handbook • **~a** *vt* to guide, to direct, to lead || *vr* (*după*) to be guided (by smth), to go by, to take as a guide.

ghidon [gi'don] *nn* handlebars.

ghiduș [gi'dush] *nm* wag, sport, joker || *adj* merry, funny, joking • **~ie** *nf coll* (*glumă*) joke; (*farsă*) farce, prank.

ghiftui [giftu'i] *vt coll, pej* to stuff, to cram || *vr* to stuff oneself with, to gorge oneself (on smth).

ghilimele [gili'mele] *nf pl* (*pt. subliniere*) inverted commas; (*semnele citării*) quotation marks; *coll* quotes; (*pentru repetiție*) ditto marks • **a deschide ~le** to quote; **a închide ~le** to unquote.

ghilotina [giloti'na] *vt* to guillotine.

ghilotină [gilo'tinǎ] *nf* guillotine.

ghimber [gim'ber] *nm bot* ginger.

ghimpe ['gimpe] *nm bot* thorn, thistle; *zool* spine, quill; *fig* (*pentru cineva*) eyesore.

ghindă ['gindǎ] *nf bot* acorn; (*la cărți*) clubs.

ghinion [gini'on] *nn* bad luck; *coll* hoodoo; **ce ~!** how unlucky! • **~ist** *nm* unlucky man/person || *adj* unlucky.

ghioagă ['gioagǎ] *nf* club, mace.

ghioc [giok] *nn icht* cowry/cowrie (shell).

ghiocel [gio'chel] *nm bot* snowdrop; *pl fig* the first white hairs.

ghiont [giont] *nn* nudge, poke, dig (in the rib), jab • **~i** *vt* to nudge, to poke, to jab.

ghiozdan [gioz'dan] *nn* satchel, bag.

ghips [gips] *nn miner* gypsum; plaster of Paris; *med* plaster cast.

ghirlandă [gir'landǎ] *nf* garland, wreath, festoon.

ghișeu [gi'sheu] *nn* window, desk; (*casă*) ticket office; (*teatru*) box office (window); (*gară*) booking office.

ghitară [gi'tarǎ] *nf mus* guitar; ~ **havaiană** Hawaiian guitar, ukulele.

ghiulea [giu'lea] *nf* cannonball.

ghiveci[1] [gi'vech] *nn* flowerpot.

ghiveci[2] [gi'vech] *nn cul* (vegetable) hodge-podge; (*amestec*) *coll* hodhepodge, farrago, potpourri.

ghivent [gi'vent] *nn tech* thread.

gigantic [dji'gantik] *adj* gigantic, titanic, enormous, huge, colossal.

gimnast(ă) [djim'nast(ă)] *nm/nf* gymnast.

gimnastică [djim'nastikă] *nf* gymnastics; *coll* gym.

gimnaziu [djim'naziu] *nn* gymnasium, *pl* gymnasia.

gin [djin] *nn* gin.

ginecolog [djineko'log] *nm med* gynecologist • **~ie** *nf* gynecology.

ginere ['djinere] *nm* son-in-law; *vernac* (*mire*) bridegroom.

gingaş [djin'gash] *adj* (*afectuos*) tender, loving; (*dulce*) sweet; (*plăpând*) frail, fragile; delicate, dainty; (*d. voce*) gentle; (*dificil*) ticklish || *adv* tenderly, gingerly, gently, delicately.

gingăşie [djingă'shie] *nf* (*delicateţe*) delicacy, gentleness; (*fragilitate*) fragility, frailty.

gingie [djin'djie] *nf anat* gum.

gioarsă ['djoarsă] *nf coll* tatters, rag.

gips [djips] *nn* * **ghips**.

gir [djir] *nn* endorsement • **~a** *vt com* to endorse; *fig* to guarantee, to warrant; **a ~ un cec** to endorse a check

girafă [dji'rafă] *nf zool* giraffe; *tech, cin* boom (of microphone).

giratoriu [djira'toriu] *adj* gyratory, gyrating, rotary; **sens ~** rotary, traffic circle.

giroscop [djiro'skop] *nn* gyroscope.

giruetă [djiru'etă] *nf met, avia* weathervane, weathercock.

giugiuli [djudju'li] *vt coll* to fondle, to neck, to cuddle || *vr* to bill and coo, to neck, to pet.

giulgiu ['djuldju] *nn* shroud, pall; *fig* (*văl*) veil.

giumbuşluc [djumbush'luk] *nn* prank, farce, antics; (*glumă*) joke, jest.

giuvaer [djuva'er] *nn* jewel; *fig* gem • **~giu** *nm* jeweler.

glacial [glachi'al] *adj* icy, frosty; *fig* chilly, frigid || *adv* icily, frigidly.

glaciar [glachi'ar] *adj geol* glacial, ice.

gladiator [gladia'tor] *nm* gladiator.

gladiolă [gladi'olă] *nf bot* gladiolus.

glandă ['glandă] *nf anat* gland.

glas [glas] *nn* voice; (*sunet*) sound; *mus* key.

glaspapir ['glaspapir] *nn* emery paper.

glastră ['glastră] *nf* flowerpot, flower vase; bowl.

glasvand ['glasvand] *nn* door; glass partition.

glazura [glazu'ra] *vt* to glaze.

glazură [gla'zură] *nf* (*pentru tort*) icing; (*pentru faianţă*) glaze.

gleznă ['gleznă] *nf anat* ankle.

glicerină [gliche'rină] *nf chem* glycerin(e), glycerol.

glie [glie] *nf lit, fig* (*pământ*) land, earth; (*pământ natal*) native land; (*patrie*) homeland; (*brazdă*) furrow.

glisa [gli'sa] *vi tech* to slide, to slip (over); *avia* to glide.

glisant [gli'sant] *adj* gliding, sliding.

gloabă ['gloabă] *nf* (*mârţoagă*) jade, nag, crock; *obs* (*despăgubire*) damages; (*amendă*) fine; (*impozit*) tax.

gloată ['gloată] *nf* crowd; mob.

glob [glob] *nn astron* globe, sphere; (*de sticlă*) glove; glass.

global [glo'bal] *adj* total, global, aggregate, overall.

globulă [glo'bulă] *nf* globula; *anat* cell, (blood) corpuscle.

glod [glod] *nn* (*noroi*) mud; (*bulgăre de pământ*) clod/ lump of earth.

glonţ [glonts] *nn* bullet || *adv* directly; (*imediat*) at once.

glorie ['glorie] *nf* glory, renown, fame.

glorifica [glorifi'ka] *vt* to glorify, to praise, to extol, to exalt || *vr* to be glorified.

glorios [glori'os] *adj* glorious || *adv* gloriously.

glosar [glo'sar] *nn* glossary; *obs* vocabulary.

glucoză [glu'koză] *nf chem* glucose.

glugă ['glugă] *nf* hood.

glumă ['glumă] *nf* joke, jest, quip; (*farsă*) practical joke, farce; prank; (*spirit*) wit(ticism); **~ nesărată** flat joke; **~ grosolană** coarse joke; **~ răsuflată** stale joke; **în ~** joking(ly), in jest; (meaning it) as a joke.

glumeţ [glu'mets] *nm* wag, wit; joker || *adj* funny, joking; (*vesel*) jolly, merry; (*spiritual*) witty.

glumi [glu'mi] *vi* to joke, to jest; *coll* to kid; *fig* (*cu ceva*) to trifle (with smth).

goană ['goană] *nf* (*fugă*) run(ning); (*cursă*) race; (*urmărire*) pursuit, chase; (*viteză*) speed, gallop; **în ~** in a hurry.

goarnă ['goarnă] *nf* bugle; trumpet.

gogoaşă [go'goashă] *nf* (*prăjitură*) doughnut; (*cocon*) cocoon; *pl fig* lies; *coll* fibs, talltales.

gogoman [gogo'man] *nm coll pej* fool, booby, ninny || *adj* foolish; *coll* addle-brained/pated.

gogomănie [gogomă'nie] *nf coll pej* stupidity; silly act/thing.

gogoşar [gogo'shar] *nm bot* (green/red/sweet) pepper.

gol [gol] *adj* (*dezbrăcat*) naked, bare(-bodied), stripped; *coll* in the buff; (*fără conţinut*) empty; (*găunos*) hollow; (*pustiu*) desert, deserted; (*fără vegetaţie*) barren; (*fără podoabe*) plain; (*desfrunzit*) leafless; *fig* (*fără sens*) idle, shallow, wanton; *fig* (*curat*) pure; (*veritabil*) genuine; *fig* (*aidoma*) like, the very image of || *nn* (*spaţiu gol*) gap, void; (*într-un text*) blank; (*vid*) vacuum, void; (*abis*) abyss; desert; (*teren necultivat*) barren ground; *sp* goal; (*lipsă*) want, deficiency; deficit.

golan [go'lan] *nm* bum, tramp, vagabond; (*ticălos*) rascal, knave; (*mitocan*) cad, boor; (*huligan*) ruffian, hooligan; (*sărac*) beggar, ragamuffin; (*nenorocit*) wretch || *adj* boorish, caddish.

golaş [go'lash] *adj* (*fără pene*) featherless; (*fără vegetaţie*) barren; (*fără păr*) hairless.

golf[1] [golf] *nn geog* bay, gulf; creek.

golf[2] [golf] *nn sp* golf.

goli [go'li] *vt* (*a deşerta*) to empty; (*a bea*) to drink up; (*a sorbi*) to quaff; (*a evacua*) to evacuate, to clear, to vacate || *vr* to get/grow empty/void • **~ciune** *nf* nudity, nakedness; *fig* emptiness, barrenness.

gologan [golo'gan] *nm* copper (coin); (*monedă mică*) penny; *pl* money; *sl* dough, bread.

gondolă [gon'dolă] *nf* gondola.

gong [gong] *nn mus* gong.

goni [go'ni] *vt* (*a fugări*) to chase, to pursue, to hunt; (*a izgoni*) to cast out, to drive out/away; *fig* to banish || *vi* to run, to race; (*d. vite*) to couple, to mate.

gorilă [go'rilă] *nf zool* gorilla.

gorun [go'run] *nm bot* common oak; evergreen oak.

gospodar [gospo'dar] *nm* (*stăpân al casei*) householder, master of the house; (*administrator*) (good) manager; (*ţăran*) peasant || *adj econ* thrifty.

gospodărie [gospodă'rie] *nf* (*la ţară*) farm(stead); (*casă*)

household; (*menaj*) housekeeping; administration; husbandry; economy.
gospodină [gospo'dină] *nf* homemaker, housewife; (*menajeră*) housekeeper.
gotic ['gotic] *adj* Gothic.
grabă ['grabă] *nf* hurry, haste; (*iuțeală*) speed; **fără** ~ at leisure, leisurely; **în** ~ in a hurry, in haste.
grabnic ['grabnik] *adj* (*repede*) quick, speedy; urgent, pressing || *adv* quickly, speedily; urgently.
grad [grad] *nn gram, math, tech* degree; (*rang*) rank, dignity; (*măsură*) measure, extent; **în ce** ~? to what extent/degree?; (*rudenie*) remove.
grada [gra'da] *vt* (*un termometru*) to graduate, to calibrate; *fig* to grade, to sort • ~t *nm nil* non-commissioned officer, non-com, NCO || *adj* (*d. o riglă*) graduated; (*treptat*) gradual, progressive || *adv* gradually, by degrees • ~**ție** *nf* gradation, gradual process; (*stil pictură*) gradation.
grafic ['grafik] *nn* graph, diagram, chart; (*orar*) timetable, schedule || *adj* graphic • ~**ă** *nf* graphics, graphic arts.
grafit [gra'fit] *nn* graphite; (*artă*) graffito.
grafologie [grafolo'djie] *nf* graphology.
grai [grai] *nn* (*vorbire*) speech; (*limbă*) language, idiom; dialect; (*glas*) voice.
grajd [grazhd] *nn* stable; *fig* pigsty.
gram [gram] *nn* gram.
gramatică [gra'matikă] *nf* grammar; grammar book.
gramofon [gramo'fon] *nn* gramophone, record-player.
granată [gra'natâ] *nf bot* pomegranate.
grandilocvent [grandilok'vent] *adj frml* grandiloquent.
grandios [grandi'os] *adj* grand, impressive; (*măreț*) magnificent; lofty, sublime || *adv* impressively, magnificently.
grandoare [gran'doare] *nf* greatness, magnificence; (*măreție*) grandeur, splendor, majesty.
grangur(e) ['grangur(e)] *nm orn* oriole; *fig pej sl* big gun/shot.
granit [gra'nit] *nn* miner granite; *fig* adamant; monolith.
graniță ['granitsă] *nf* frontier, boundary, border(s); **de** ~ frontier; *fig* limit, bound, confines.
granulă [gra'nulă] *nf* granule, grain.
grapă ['grapă] *nf* harrow.
gras [gras] *adj* (*unsuros*) greasy, oily; (*cu grăsime*) fat; (*corpolent*) stout, burly; (*obez*) obese; (*d. o pasăre*) plump; (*îngrășat*) fattened; rich, fertile || *adv fig* liberally, well, handsomely.
graseia [grase'ia] *vi* to roll one's r's, to trill, to burr.
gratie ['gratie] *nf* (*la case*) lattice, trellis; *pl* grating, latticework; (*la închisoare*) bar.
gratifica [gratifi'ka] *vt* to confer, to bestow; (*a răsplăti*) to reward.
gratis ['gratis] *adv* free (of charge), gratis; **pe** ~ free(ly), free of charge; *coll* for free.
gratitudine [grati'tudine] *nf* gratitude, gratefulness, thankfulness.
gratuit [gratu'it] *adj* (*pe gratis*) free (of charge); (*nejustificat*) unjustified, unfounded; (*neprovocat*) wanton, unwarranted || *adv* gratis, free of charge; (*nejustificat*) groundlessly, wantonly.
grația [gra'tsia] *vt* to pardon, to grant a pardon, to reprieve.
grație ['gratsie] *nf* (*farmec*) grace, gracefulness, charm; (*favoare*) favor; **cu** ~ gracefully || *prep* thanks to, owing to.

grațios [gratsi'os] *adj* graceful, charming, winsome || *adv* gracefully.
graur [graur] *nm orn* starling.
grav [grav] *adj* (*d. față, greșeală*) grave, serious; (*d. ton*) solemn; (*d. notă, voce*) deep, low(-pitched); (*d. rană*) severe; critical; (*sever*) stern; important, weighty || *adv* severely, sternly.
grava [gra'va] *vt* to engrave, to cut, to carve; (*cu apă tare*) to etch; (*în relief*) to emboss.
gravidă [gra'vidă] *nf* pregnant woman || *adj* pregnant; *coll* (big) with child, in the family way.
graviditate [gravidi'tate] *nf* pregnancy.
gravita [gravi'ta] *vi* (*spre*) to gravitate to/towards; (*în jurul*) to revolve (round) • ~**te** *nf* (*seriozitate*) gravity, seriousness; *coll* bumptiousness; (*severitate*) sternness; (*stare gravă*) severity • ~**ție** *nf phys* gravity, gravitation.
gravură [gra'vură] *nf* engraving; (*în lemn*) woodcut, wood engraving; (*cu apă tare*) etching; (*lucrare*) print.
grăbi [gră'bi] *vt* to hasten, to hurry; to speed up, to accelerate; to precipitate; (*pe cineva*) to press, to hurry || *vr* to hasten, to hurry (up), to make haste.
grădinar [grădi'nar] *nm* gardener.
grădină [gră'dină] *nf* garden; (*de zarzavat*) kitchen/-vegetable garden; (*livadă*) orchard; (*publică*) park, gardens • ~**ri** *vi* to garden.
grădiniță [grădi'nitsă] *nf* small/little garden; (*de copii*) kindergarten, daycare.
grăi [gră'i] *vt vernac* to say || *vi* to speak, to talk.
grăitor [grăi'tor] *adj* eloquent, graphic, telling || *adv* eloquently, graphically.
grăjdar [grăzh'dar] *nm* stable man, groom; *mil* farrier.
grămadă [gră'madă] *nf* (*de obiecte disparate*) heap; (*masă*) mass; (*îngrămădire*) cluster, clump; (*așezate simetric*) pile; (*de oameni*) crowd; (*mulțime*) multitude, host; (*cantitate mare*) a lot of, lots of, heaps (of); *coll* loads (of), tons of, umpteen || *adv* **claie peste** ~ topsy-turvy, pell-mell, helter-skelter.
grănicer [grăni'cher] *nm* frontier guard; *naut* coast guard.
grăpa [gră'pa] *vt/vi* to harrow.
grăsime [gră'sime] *nf* fat; (*unsoare*) grease; (*corpolență*) fatness, burliness, stoutness.
grăsun [gră'sun] *adj* fattish, plump || *nm* (young) pig, porker.
grăsuț [gră'suts] *adj* fattish; (*d. femei*) plump.
grătar [gră'tar] *nn* (*pentru fripturi*) gridiron; (*fel de mâncare*) grill; (*de sobă*) fire-grate, fire-guard; (*de șters picioarele*) scraper; *min* screen, grate; *hydr* grating.
grăunte, grăunț, grăunță [gră'unte, gră'unts, gră'untsă] *nm, nn, nf* grain, seed; (*pentru cai*) nosebag.
grânar [grâ'nar] *nn also fig* granary.
grâne ['grâne] *nf pl* grains, cereals.
grâu [grâu] *nn bot* wheat, grain.
greabăn ['greabăn] *nn* withers; *fig* (*spate*) back; *fig* (*deal*) crest, top.
greață ['greatsă] *nf* (*senzație de vomă*) nausea, sickness, queasiness; (*scârbă*) disgust, loathing, revulsion.
grebla [greb'la] *vt/vi* to rake.
greblă ['greblă] *nf* rake.
grec [grek] *adj* Greek; *archit* Grecian; *hist* Hellenic.
grefa [gre'fa] *vt* to graft.

grefă ['grefă] *nf med (ţesut)* graft(ing); *(organe)* transplant || *nf jur* court clerk's office.

grefier [grefi'er] *nm jur* court clerk.

greier ['greier] *nm ento* cricket.

grenadă [gre'nada] *nf mil* (hand) grenade.

greoi [gre'oi] *adj (d. persoane)* heavy; *(d. lucruri)* cumbersome, awkward; *(d. stil)* heavy, turgid; *(neîndemânatic)* clumsy, unwieldy; *(d. minte)* dull, slow || *adv* heavily, clumsily.

grep(frut) ['grepfrut] *nn bot* grapefruit.

gresa [gre'sa] *vt* to grease, to lubricate, to oil.

gresie ['gresie] *nf* miner gritstone; *(de ascuţit)* whetstone.

greş [gresh] *nn obs (greşeală)* mistake; *(eroare)* error; *(eşec)* failure; *(a se înşela)* to make a mistake in one's calculations; *(a nu nimeri ţinta)* to miss (one's aim); **fără ~** correctly, faultlessly; *(negreşit)* without fail, by all means.

greşeală [gre'sheală] *nf* mistake; *(eroare)* error; *(gafă)* blunder; *(omisiune)* oversight; *(boacănă) coll* howler, glaring mistake; **~ de calcul** miscalculation; **~ de tipar** misprint; **~ de vorbire** a slip of the tongue; **din ~** by mistake, inadvertently; *(vină)* fault; *(păcat)* sin; *(lipsă)* deficiency; defect, flaw, blemish; failing, drawback; **fără ~** faultlessly, perfectly, impeccably.

greşi [gre'shi] *vt* to mistake; *(a lua drept)* to mistake for; to miss, to fail; **a ~ drumul** to lose one's way; **a ~ ţinta** to miss the mark || *vi* to err, to be mistaken/wrong, to make a mistake; *coll* to slip up, to goof; *(a fi vinovat)* to be guilty, to be at fault; *(a păcătui)* to sin, to trespass; *(a nu nimeri)* to be wide off the mark; to miss one's aim/mark • **~t** *adj* mistaken, wrong, false; *(eronat)* erroneous, fallacious, incorrect; *(nedrept)* wrong, unjust, unfair; illegal, illicit, unlawful.

greţos [gre'tsos] *adj* nauseating, sickening, disgusting; *fig* fulsome.

greu [greu] *adj (la cântar)* heavy, weighty; *(greoi)* clumsy, unwieldy; *(apăsător)* oppressive, onerous; *(dificil)* difficult, hard; *(obositor)* fatiguing, wearisome; *(complicat)* involved, troublesome; *(neplăcut)* unpleasant; *(grav)* severe; *(aspru)* severe, harsh || *adv (greoi)* heavily, weightily; *(serios)* seriously, gravely; *(periculos)* dangerously; *(cu greutate)* with difficulty; *(de-abia)* hardly, scarcely; *(anevoie)* reluctantly, unwillingly; **cu ~** with difficulty, at great pains; **din ~** hard || *nn* weight; *(povară)* burden; *fig* difficulty, brunt || *nm* heavyweight boxer.

greutate [greu'tate] *nf* weight; *(povară)* burden; *(încărcătură)* load; *fig* encumbrance, charge; difficulty, hardship; *(complicaţie)* intricacy; *(necaz)* trouble, bother; authority, influence; *sl* pull; *sp* dumb-bell; **cu ~** *adj (important)* important, influential; *(de-abia)* hardly, scarcely; **fără ~** without trouble/difficulty.

grevă ['grevă] *nf* strike, walk-out; **în ~** on strike; **~ generală** general strike; **~ spontană** wildcat strike.

grevist [gre'vist] *nm* striker || *adj* strike.

gri [gri] *adj* grey.

grijă [grizhă] *nf* care, anxiety, worry; *(necaz)* trouble; **a avea ~ de** *(cineva)* to look after smb, to take care of smb; *(ceva)* to take care of smth, to attend to smth; **nici o ~!** don't worry!, have no fear!; *(atenţie)* care, attention; **ai ~!** take care!, look out!; **cu ~ care**-

fully, with care; *(conştiincios)* conscientiously; *(scrupulos)* elaborately; *(precaut)* cautiously; **fără ~** careless, unconcerned.

grijuliu [grizhu'liu] *adj* careful, mindful; *(precaut)* wary, cautious; *(socotit)* thoughtful, considerate; scrupulous.

grilaj [gri'lazh] *nn* lattice work, grating.

grilă ['grilă] *nf elec* grid; *constr* grate; *mil* grating; *fig* frame; rating.

grimasă [gri'masă] *nf* grimace.

grindă ['grindă] *nf constr* beam, girder.

grindină ['grindină] *nf* hail, hailstone; *fig* hail, shower, volley.

gripat [gri'pat] *adj* ill; *coll* down with the flu.

gripă ['gripă] *nf* influenza; *coll* flu, grip(pe).

griş [grish] *nn* semolina.

grizonat [grizo'nat] *adj* grizzled; turning/going grey.

groapă ['groapă] *nf* pit; hole; *(adâncitură)* hollow; excavation; *(mormânt)* grave.

groază ['groază] *nf* horror, fright, dread; *coll (grămadă, mulţime)* heap(s), lot(s).

groaznic ['groaznik] *adj* awful, frightful, terrible; *coll* scary || *adv* awfully, etc.

grohăi [grohă'i] *vi* to grunt.

gropar [gro'par] *nm* gravedigger; sexton.

gropiţă [gro'pitsă] *nf* small hole; *(în obraz)* dimple.

gros [gros] *adj* thick; big; bulky, voluminous; *(gras)* fat, stout; dense; compact || *adv* thickly; *(mult)* much, highly, largely; *(amplu)* amply; densely; *(din belşug)* abundantly, profusely • **~ul** *nn (cea mai mare parte)* the majority, the bulk of; *coll (închisoare) sl* jug, can, limbo • **~ier** *adj* coarse, rough || *nn pl* fibrous fodder • **~ime** *nf* thickness, bulkiness; *(corpolenţă)* corpulence, stoutness; *(lăţime)* breadth, width; caliber; *(adâncime)* depth.

grosolan [groso'lan] *adj (aspru)* rough, gross; *(nepoliticos)* rude, impolite; vulgar, coarse, common; *(d. o greşeală)* glaring, flagrant || *adv* roughly, grossly, rudely.

grosolănie [grosolă'nie] *nf* rudeness, coarseness; *(acţiune sau vorbă)* incivility.

grotă ['grotă] *nf* grotto, cave.

grotesc [gro'tesk] *nn/adj* grotesque, ludicrous; bizarre, odd, peculiar; *typ* sans-serif.

grozav [gro'zav] *adj (sens pozitiv)* terrific, brilliant; admirable; consummate; distinguished; exceptional, extraordinary; fabulous, fantastic; first-class; outstanding; tremendous; *(uriaş)* colossal; *(îngrozitor)* terrible, horrid, awful, dreadful || *adv* terribly; *coll (echivalent cu "foarte")* awfully, extremely, exceedingly, tremendously, brilliantly, admirably, exceptionally, extraordinarily, fabulously, fantastically, outstandingly.

grozăvi [groză'vi] *vr coll pej* to put on airs; to talk big; *(a se făli)* to boast (of), to brag (of) • **~e** *nf* horror, atrocity; monster; *(minune)* marvel.

grumaz [gru'maz] *nm vernac (gât)* neck; *(ceafă)* nape.

grund [grund] *nn (artă)* prime color; grounding; *constr* plaster rough cast.

grunjos [grun'zhos] *adj* large-grained, rough-grained; rough.

grup [grup] *nn* group, party; *(pâlc)* cluster, *(d. pomi)* clump.

grupa [gru'pa] *vt* to group (together); *(a clasifica)* to classify || *vr* to group (together), to form (a group); (*a se clasifica*) to be classified.

grupă ['grupă] *nf mil, chem* group; ~ **sanguină** blood group.

gudron [gu'dron] *nn* tar.

gudura [gudu'ra] *vr* (*d. câini*) to fawn (upon smb); (*d. oameni*) to toady, to cajole.

guguștiuc [gugu'shtiuk] *nm orn* ring-dove, wood pigeon; *coll* pigeon, dupe, noodle, ninny.

guița [gui'tsa] *vi* to squeak.

guler ['guler] *nn* collar; (*la bere*) head.

gulie [gu'lie] *nf bot* turnip.

gumă ['gumă] *nf* (*cauciuc*) gum; ~ **de mestecat** chewing gum; (*radieră*) eraser; (india) rubber.

gunoi [gu'noi] *nn* (*murdărie*) garbage, rubbish, waste, dirt; (*pe stradă*) litter; **a face** ~ to litter; **ladă de** ~ trash can; (*bălegar*) manure, dung; *coll* muck; *fig* scum, dregs • ~**er** *nm* dustman, garbage collector; scavenger.

guraliv [gura'liv] *adj* talkative, garrulous, loquacious.

gură ['gură] *nf* mouth; *sl* trap; (*buze*) lips; *zool* stoma; (*îmbucătură*) mouthful; (*înghițitură*) draught, sip; *tech* (*de armă*) muzzle; (*deschizătură*) aperture, opening; (*de aer*) vent; orifice; (*vorbire*) speech; (*scandal*) row, quarrel, squabble; (*vorbărie*) gossip; (*sărutare*) kiss; *coll* smack; (*cicăleală*) nagging, pestering; ~ **de incendiu** fire hydrant, fireplug; ~ **de metrou** subway entrance; ~ **spartă** loud mouth.

gureș ['guresh] *adj* talkative, garrulous; (*d. păsări*) chirpy, twittery.

gurmand [gur'mand] *nm* glutton, gourmet || *adj* greedy; (*amator de mâncăruri bune*) fond of dainties.

gust [gust] *nn* taste; (*aromă*) flavor; (*d. vin*) bouquet; (*savoare*) relish, savor; *lit* taste; (*dorință*) desire, appetite; (*înclinație*) inclination, taste; **de bun** ~ in good taste/style; **de prost** ~ in bad/poor taste, unsavory; **după** ~ to taste; **fără** ~ tasteless, unsavory; in bad/poor taste • ~**os** *adj* tasty, savory, appetizing; *coll* nice, good.

gusta [gus'ta] *vt* to taste; (*a sorbi*) to sip; (*a savura*) also *fig* to relish, to enjoy; (*a trece prin*) to experience, to try • ~**re** *nf* tasting; (*mic dejun*) breakfast; (*aperitiv*) snack, light meal.

gușă ['gushă] *nf med* goiter, struma; *orn, zool* crop, dewlap; *fig* double chin, dewlap.

gută ['gută] *nf med* gout.

gutui [gu'tui] *nm bot* quince tree • ~**e** *nf* quince.

guturai [gutu'rai] *nn med* cold (in the head), running (of the) nose, catarrh.

gutural [gutu'ral] *adj* guttural, throaty; (*d. consoane*) velar || *nf ling* guttural.

guvern [gu'vern] *nn* government, cabinet.

guverna [guver'na] *vt* to govern, to rule || *vi* (*a stăpâni*) to rule, to reign; (*d. miniștri*) to govern • ~**mental** *adj* government, state • ~**nt** *adj* ruling, governing; (*d. partid*) in power • ~**nți** *nm pl* the party in power • ~**ntă** *nf* governess, (dry) nurse, au-pair • ~**tor** *nm* governor.

guvid [gu'vid] *nm icht* goby, gudgeon, chub.

guzgan [guz'gan] *nm zool* rat.

H

ha [ha] *interj* (*exprimând surprinderea*) ha(h)!; (*dezgust*) yah!; (*satisfacție*) ha-ha!; (*întrebător*) what?; (*onomatopee imitând râsul*) ha ha!

habitat [habi'tat] *nn bio* biotope; habitat, accommodation.

hai [hai] *interj* (*vino*) come on!, come along!; (*să mergem*) let's go; (*încearcă*) give it a shot/try.

haide ['haide] *interj* (*vino*) come on!, (*să mergem*) let's go!; (*încearcă*) have a try!; (*exprimând neîncredere, dezaprobare*) ~ ~! get along with you!; no kidding!.

haiduc [hai'duk] *nm* outlaw.

haimana [haima'na] *nf* tramp, loafer || *adv* roamingly; **a umbla** ~ (*a rătăci*) *vi* to rove/roam/wander aimlessly.

hain [ha'in] *adj* (*rău*) heinous, wicked; (*crud*) cruel, merciless; (*dușmănos*) hostile, vicious; (*aspru*) harsh || *adv* heinously, cruelly.

haină ['hainǎ] *nf* coat; (*jachetă*) jacket; (*palton*) top coat, overcoat; *pl* clothes, clothing, garments; *lit* raiment, attire.

haită ['haită] *nf* (*de lupi, câini*) pack; (*ceată*) gang.

halat [ha'lat] *nn* (*de lucru*) overalls; (*de casă, de baie*) bathrobe; dressing gown.

hală ['halǎ] *nf* hall; (*piață*) marketplace.

halbă ['halbă] *nf* mug; (*cu capac*) tankard; (*cantitate*) pint.

halcă ['halkǎ] *nf* hunk, chunk.

haltă ['haltă] *nf* rail halt, small station; (*oprire*) stop, stopover; (*loc de popas*) halting/stopping/resting place.

haltere [hal'tere] *nf pl* (*de exercițiu*) dumbbell(s), barbell(s); *sp* weightlifting.

halucinație [haluchi'natsie] *nf* hallucination, delusion.

halva [hal'va] *nf* halva(h), halavah.

ham [ham] *nn* harness.

hamac [ha'mak] *nn* hammock.

hamal [ha'mal] *nm* (*feroviar*) porter; *naut* docker, stevedore.

hambar [ham'bar] *nn* barn, granary, storeroom.

hamei [ha'mei] *nn bot* hops.

han [han] *nn* inn, roadhouse.

handbal ['handbal] *nn sp* handball.

handicap [handi'kap] *nn* handicap, disability; *fig* hindrance, obstacle • ~**at** *nm/adj* disabled person.

hangar [han'gar] *nn avia* hangar.

hanorac [hano'rak] *nn* anorack.

haos ['haos] *nn also fig* chaos, confusion, jumble.

haotic [ha'otik] *adj* chaotic, confused || *adv* chaotically, in a jumble, in confusion.

hapsân [hap'sân] *adj* (*lacom*) grabbing, greedy; (*hain*) hardhearted, wicked, cruel.

har [har] *nn* gift, talent; *relig* grace.

harababură [haraba'bură] *nf* jumble, confusion, pell-mell, (*zarvă*) hullabaloo, hubbub.

harnic ['harnik] *adj* hard-working, industrious, diligent || *adv* industriously, diligently.

harpă ['harpă] *nf* harp; **a cânta la** ~ to play the harp.

harpon [har'pon] *nn* harpoon.

hartă ['hartă] *nf* map; *also naut* chart.

hașiș [ha'shish] *nn* hashish.

haz [haz] *nn* (*glumă*) fun, wit; (*veselie*) fun, spirit, gaiety; (*farmec*) charm, relish; (*miez*) point.

hazard [ha'zard] *nn* hazard, chance; (*risc*) risk • ~**a** *vt* to venture, to take (too many) risks.

hazliu [haz'liu] *adj* funny, amusing, droll; (*distractiv*) entertaining; (*vesel*) merry; (*spiritual*) witty, waggish.

hăitui [hăitu'i] *vt* (*la vânătoare*) to beat up; *fig* to hunt, to chase.

hămăi [hămă'i] *vi* to bark, to bay; (*d. căței*) to yelp, to yap.

hămesit [hăme'sit] *adj coll* starving, famished, sharpset.

hărăzi [hără'zi] *vt* (*a da*) to bestow (upon smb), to give, to grant; (*a sorti*) to destine.

hărmălaie [hărmă'laie] *nf* hubbub, commotion; *coll* hullabaloo; (*învălmăşeală*) bustle, jumble.

hărnicie [hărni'chie] *nf* diligence, zeal, industry; **a munci cu** ~ to work zealously.

hărțui [hărtsu'i] *vt* to nag, to tease; *mil, fig* to harass, to hassle • ~**ală, ~re** *nf* harassing, nagging; hassle, brawl, wrangle; *mil* attrition; **război de** ~ war of attrition.

hăț [hăts] *nn* bridle, *pl* reins.

hău [hău] *nn* chasm, gulf; (*abis*) abyss.

hârâi [hârâ'i] *vi* (*a respira greu*) to rattle, to wheeze; (*d. câini*) to growl; (*d. maşini*) to grate || *vt/vr* (*a sâcâi*) to tease.

hârb [hârb] *nn* (*ciob*) crock, shiver, fragment; (*vas spart*) broken pot; *pl* (*vechituri*) lumber; *fig* old crock, wreck.

hârdău [hâr'dău] *nn* tub, bucket.

hârjoni [hârzho'ni] *vr* to gambol, to frolic, to frisk; *coll* to skylark, to play pranks.

hârleț [hâr'lets] *nm* spade, spud.

hârşâi [hârshâ'i] *vi/vt* to scrape, to grate; (*cu penița*) to scratch.

hârtie [hâr'tie] *nf* paper; ~ **cretată** coated paper; ~ **de copiat/carbon** carbon paper; ~ **de împachetat** packing/wrapping paper; ~ **de calc** tracing paper; ~ **de filtru** filter paper; ~ **de muşte** fly paper; ~ **de toaletă/igienică** tissue paper; ~ **milimetrică** graph paper; ~ **pergament** wax paper, greaseproof paper; **bucată de** ~ piece of paper; **coală de** ~ sheet of paper; (*bancnotă*) (bank)note; **bani de** ~ paper money; paper, document; ~ **cu antet** headed (note)paper.

hârtop [hâr'top] *nn* pothole, rut.

hâtru ['hâtru] *nm* (*mucalit*) wag, wit; (*deştept*) clever man; sly/cunning man || *adj* (*glumeț*) waggish; (*isteț*) clever, cute; (*viclean*) sly, cunning.

hâțâna [hâtsâ'na] *vt* to shake (up); (*a legăna*) to rock, to swing || *vr* to rock (to and fro), to swing, to sway.

hectar [hek'tar] *nn* hectare.

hegemonie [hedjemo'nie] *nf* hegemony.

hei [hei] *interj* heigh!, hey!, hi!, hello!; (*exprimă bucurie*) whoopee!; (*nu e nimeni acolo?*) nobody there?, I say!, hello!.

heleşteu [helesh'teu] *nn* (fish)pond.

helicopter [helikop'ter] *nn avia* helicopter, *coll* chopper.

heliu ['heliu] *nn chem* helium.

hematom [hema'tom] *nn med* haematoma.

hemisferă [hemi'sferă] *nf* * **emisferă**.

hemofilie [hemofi'lie] *nf med* hemophilia.

hemoglobină [hemoglo'bină] *nf med* hemoglobin.

hemoragie [hemora'djie] *nf med* hemorrhage.

hemoroizi [hemoro'izi] *nm pl med* hemorrhoids; *coll* piles.

hepatită [hepa'tită] *nf med* hepatitis; *miner* hepatite.

herghelie [herge'lie] *nf* stud; herd of horses.

hering [he'ring] *nm icht* herring.

hermină [her'mină] *nf zool* hermine; (*blană*) ermine.

hernie [her'nie] *nf med* hernia, rupture.

heroină [hero'ină] *nf chem* heroin.

herpes ['herpes] *nn med* herpes; (*la buze*) cold sore; serpigo.

heterosexual [heteroseksu'al] *adj* heterosexual.

hexagon [heksa'gon] *nn geom* hexagon.

hiat [hi'at] *nn ling* hiatus.

hibernare [hiber'nare] *nf also fig* hibernation.

hibrid [hi'brid] *nm/adj bio, ling* hybrid.

hidos [hi'dos] *adj* hideous; (*dezgustător*) repulsive || *adv* hideously.

hidrant [hi'drant] *nn* hydrant, fire-plug.

hidratant [hidra'tant] *adj* (*d. cremă*) moisturizing.

hidraulică [hidra'ulikă] *nf* hydraulics, fluid mechanics.

hidroavion [hidroavi'on] *nn* hydroplane, seaplane.

hidrocarbură [hidrokar'bură] *nf chem* hydrocarbon.

hidrocentrală [hidrochen'trală] *nf* hydroelectric/ hydropower station.

hidrogen [hidro'djen] *nn* hydrogen.

hienă [hi'enă] *nf zool* hyena; *fig* vulture.

hieroglifă [hiero'glifă] *nf* hieroglyph.

hilar [hi'lar] *adj* (*umoristic*) hilarious, mirthful.

himen ['himen] *nn anat* hymen; *coll* maidenhead.

himeră [hi'meră] *nf myth* chimera; fancy; (*iluzie*) illusion.

hinduism [hindu'ism] *nn relig* Hinduism.

hingher [hin'ger] *nm* dogcatcher.

hiperbolă [hi'perbolă] *nf geom* hyperbola; *liter* hyperbole; exaggeration.

hipertensiune [hipertensi'une] *nf med* hypertension, high blood pressure.

hipic ['hipik] *adj* equine, horse; **concurs** ~ horse race/ show.

hipism [hi'pism] *nn* riding, horseracing.

hipnotiza [hipnoti'za] *vt* to hypnotize, to mesmerize; *also fig* to fascinate, to entrance.

hipnoză [hip'noză] *nf* hypnosis, mesmerism, (hypnotic) trance.

hipodermic [hipo'dermik] *adj* hypodermic.

hipodrom [hipo'drom] *nn* racetrack; (the) turf; *hist* hippodrome.

hipopotam [hipopo'tam] *nm zool* hippopotamus; *coll* hippo.

hipotensiune [hipotensi'une] *nf med* hypotension, low blood pressure.

hirotonisi [hirotoni'si] *vt* to ordain || *vr relig* to take holy orders.

hitlerism [hitle'rism] *nn* Hitlerism.

hlizi [hli'zi] *vr* to titter, to giggle; (*a se zgâi*) to stare.

hm [hm] *interj* humph!, (a)hem!

hoardă [ho'ardă] *nf* horde.

hobby ['hobi] *nn* hobby.

hochei [ho'kei] *nn sp* hockey; (*pe gheață*) ice hockey; (*pe iarbă*) field hockey.

hocus-pocus ['hokus'pokus] *nn* hocus-pocus.

hodorog [hodo'rog] *nm coll* (old) dodderer; ~ **bătrân** *coll* old fart.

hodorogi [hodoro'dji] *vi* to rumble, to rattle; (*a trăncăni*) to babble || *vr* (*a se strica*) to deteriorate; (*d. mobilă*) to get/become rickety; *fig* (*d. cineva*) to decline in health.

hohot ['hohot] *nn* (*de râs*) roar/peal of laughter, guffaw; (*de plâns*) burst of tears, sob(bing).

hohoti [hoho'ti] *vi* (*de râs*) to roar (with laughter), to guffaw; (*de plâns*) to cry one's eyes out, to sob.

hoinar [hoi'nar] *nm* loiterer, rover, wanderer ‖ *adj* loitering, roving, wandering • **gânduri ~e** wandering thoughts.

hoinări [hoină'ri] *vi* to rove, to stroll, to wander (about).

hoit [hoit] *nn* corpse, dead body; (*de animal*) carcass.

hol [hol] *nn* (entrance) hall; (*la hotel*) lounge.

holba [hol'ba] *vt* (*ochii*) to open wide, to stare; *vr* (*la*) to stare (at), to goggle.

holdă ['holdă] *nf* cornfield.

holding ['holding] *nn econ* holding (company).

holeră [ho'leră] *nf med* cholera.

holocaust [holo'kaust] *nn* holocaust.

holtei [hol'tei] *nm* bachelor.

homar [ho'mar] *nm icht* lobster.

homeopat [homeo'pat] *nm* homeopath(ist).

homosexual [homoseksu'al] *adj* homosexual; *coll* gay ‖ *nm* homosexual; *sl pej* faggot, pansy • **~itate** *nf* homosexuality.

hop [hop] *nn* pothole; *pl* pits and bumps; (*salt*) hop; *fig* (*dificultate*) obstacle, difficulty, trouble; *coll* rub ‖ *interj* (*exclamație însoțind o săritură*) hop!, jump!, go!; (*copăcel*) up-a-daisy; (*deodată*) pop!; (*însoțind o cădere*) bang!.

horă ['horă] *nf* hora, reel, Romanian circle dance; music accompanying the hora.

horcăi [horkă'i] *vi* (*d. un muribund*) to rattle (in one's throat); *reg* to snore; (*d. cai*) to snort • **~t** *nn* (*al muribunzilor*) (death) rattle; (*sforăit*) snore, snoring.

hormon [hor'mon] *nm physiol* hormone.

horn [horn] *nn* chimney, funnel, (smoke)stack.

horoscop [horo'skop] *nn* horoscope.

hortensie [hor'tensie] *nf bot* hydrangea.

horticultură [hortikul'tură] *nf* horticulture, gardening.

hotar [ho'tar] *nn* frontier, boundary, border line; *fig* limit, bound(s) • **fără ~e** boundless, without limits; infinite; immense, immeasurable; excessive, unbounded.

hotărî [hotă'rî] *vt* (*a decide*) to decide, to settle, to re-solve; (*a convinge*) to persuade, to convince; (*a stabili*) to fix, to determine; (*a numi*) to name • **~re** *nf* decision; **cu ~** (*cu fermitate*) firmly, resolutely; (*fără îndoială*) certainly, surely; (*scrisă*) resolution; (*ordin*) order, decree; *jur* ruling, judgment; (*finală*) sen-tence; (*siguranță*) resolve; (*fermitate*) determination; (*caracter hotărât*) peremptoriness • **~t** *adj* (*clar*) def-inite; (*decis*) determined, resolute; categorical; (*stabilit*) settled; (*sigur*) sure, certain; (*ferm*) firm, unflinching; **~ lucru** beyond/without (the shadow of) doubt; **un om ~** a resolute man; **la ora ~ă** at the set-tled/appointed time; **ton ~** firm/peremptory tone ‖ *adv* (*categoric*) positively, definitely, certainly; pre-cisely, exactly; (*ferm*) firmly, categorically • **~or** *adj* decisive, conclusive; **într-un moment ~** at a criti-cal/decisive moment; **vot ~** casting vote.

hotel [ho'tel] *nn* hotel.

hoț [hots] *nm* thief; (*de buzunare*) pickpocket; (*tâlhar*) robber; (*spărgător*) burglar; *coll* cracksman; *fig* rascal, villain • **~ie** *nf* theft, stealing; (*tâlhărie*) rob-bery; (*spargere*) burglary; *jur* larceny; (*escrocherie*) swindle.

hrană ['hrană] *nf* food, nourishment; (*întreținere*) up-keep, maintenance; (*masă*) board, fare; (*pt. vite*) fodder, forage.

hrăni [hră'ni] *vt* to feed, to nourish; (*un sugar*) to suckle, to nurse; (*a întreține*) to provide for; *fig* to harbor, to cherish ‖ *vr* (*cu*) to eat, to live on • **~tor** *adj* nourishing, nutritious.

hrăpăreț [hrăpă'rets] *adj* grasping, grabbing, greedy.

hrean [hrean] *nm bot* horseradish.

hrișcă ['hrishkă] *nf bot* buckwheat.

hublou [hu'blou] *nn naut, avia* porthole.

huhurez [huhu'rez] *nm orn* eagle owl; *fig* night owl.

huidui [huidu'i] *vt* to boo, to hoot (after); (*la teatru*) to boo/hoot off the stage • **~ală** *nf* booing, hooting.

huilă [hu'ilă] *nf geol* pit-coal, mineral coal.

hulă ['hulă] *nf naut* swell, surge of sea.

huli [hu'li] *vt/vi vernac* to blaspheme; (*a blestema*) to curse, to swear at; (*a ocărî*) to abuse; *coll* to run down.

huligan [huli'gan] *nm* hoodlum, hooligan, rowdy.

humă ['humă] *nf* clay.

humor [hu'mor] *nn* * **umor**.

hurduca [hurdu'ka] *vt/vi/vr* to jerk, to jolt.

hurui [huru'i] *vi* to roll, to rumble, to rattle • **~t** *nn* rattle, rattling, roar(ing).

husă ['husă] *nf* (*slip*) cover, covering; (*la mașină*) seat cover.

huzur [hu'zur] *nn* (life of) leisure, comfort, ease.

huzuri [huzu'ri] *vi* to lead an easy/comfortable life, to live off the fat of the land.

I

ia [ia] *interj* now, now then; (*haide*) come; (*introduce un răspuns*) why; well; (*cu sens conj. dacă*) it should; (*cu sens adv. doar*) but, only, just; (*nu mai mult decât*) not more than, a matter of; **~ ascultă!** look here!; **~ să vedem** let us see.

iad [iad] *nn also fig* hell.

iadeș ['iadesh] *nn* wishbone; (*pariu*) bet, wager.

iaht [iaht] *nn naut* yacht.

ianuarie [ia'nuarie] *nm* January.

iapă ['iapă] *nf zool* mare.

iar [iar] *adv* (*once*) again; **a venit ~** he's come again; **~ și ~** (*mereu*) ever, over and over again ‖ *conj* (*dar*) but; (*în timp ce*) while; **el vorbea ~ ei nu ascultau** he was speaking but they were not listening; (*și*) and; **el vorbea ~ ei ascultau** he was speaking and they were listening.

iarăși ['iarăsh] *adv* (*once*) again.

iarbă ['iarbă] *nf* grass; *pl* herbs; **fir de ~** blade of grass; **smoc de ~** tuft of grass.

iarnă ['iarnă] *nf* winter; **astă ~** last winter; **la ~** next winter ‖ *adv* in winter.

iască ['iaskă] *nf* tinder, touchwood.

iasomie [iaso'mie] *nf bot* jasmine, jessamine.

iată ['iată] *interj* (*aproape*) here is/are; **~ cartea** here is the book; (*departe*) there is/are; **~ copiii la joacă** there are the children at play; (*privește*) look, behold; **~ că ...** and so, but, and yet; **~ ce** here is what.

iaurt [ia'urt] *nn* yogurt.

iaz [iaz] *nn* (fish)pond; (*lac*) lake.

ibidem ['ibidem] *adv* ibidem, ibid.

ibric [i'brik] *nn* (*de ceai*) teakettle; (*de cafea*) coffeepot.

ici ['ichi] *adv* here; **~ colo** here and there; (*pe alocuri*) in places; **pe ~ pe colo** here and there, in some places.

icoană [i'koană] *nf* icon, (sacred) image; *fig* picture.

icre ['ikre] *nf pl (după fecundare)* spawn; *(ca mâncare)* (salted) roe; *(negre)* caviar.

icter ['ikter] *nn med* icterus, jaundice.

ideal [ide'al] *nn/adj* ideal || *adj* perfect || *adv* ideally • **~ism** *nn* idealism.

idealiza [ideali'za] *vt* to idealize.

idee [i'dee] *nf* idea; notion; *(părere)* view, opinion; *(concepție)* conception; *(gând)* thought, thinking; *(intenție)* intention; plan, scheme; **~ fixă** idée fixe, fixed idea/notion, monomania.

idem ['idem] *adv* idem, ditto.

identic [i'dentik] *adj* identical || *adv* identically, likewise.

identifica [identifi'ka] *vt (cu)* to identify (with) || *vr* to identify oneself (with) • **~re** *nf* identification.

identitate [identi'tate] *nf also math, fig* identity; **buletin de ~** identity card.

ideolog [ideo'log] *nm* ideologist • **~ic** *adj* ideological || *adv* ideologically.

idilă [i'dila] *nf also fig* idyll.

idiom [idi'om] *nn (limbă)* language; dialect, idiom.

idiot [idi'ot] *nm* idiot, imbecile; *coll* fool, silly ass; *sl* clot, dope || *adj* idiotic, foolish; *(d. o glumă)* senseless.

idioțienie [idio'tsenie] *nf (ca atitudine)* rank stupidity; *(ca acțiune)* piece of rank stupidity.

idiș ['idish] *nn* Yiddish.

idol ['idol] *nm* idol, graven image; *fig* idol • **~atrie** *nf* idolatry; *fig* worship • **~atriza** *vt* to worship, to idolize, to adore; to lionize.

ie ['ie] *nf* embroidered (peasant) blouse.

ied [ied] *nm zool* kid.

iederă ['iedera] *nf bot* ivy.

ieftin [ieftin] *adj* cheap; *(d. preț: rezonabil)* affordable, fair; *fig (fără valoare)* worthless; *(banal)* commonplace || *adv* cheap(ly), at a moderate price; *fig* unscathed.

ieftini [iefti'ni] *vt* to cheapen, to reduce/diminish the price of || *vr* to cheapen, to fall in price.

ienibahar [ieniba'har] *nn bot* juniper berry; allspice.

ienupăr [ie'nupar] *nm bot* juniper tree.

iepuraș [iepu'rash] *nm* leveret, young hare, bunny, young rabbit.

iepure ['iepure] *nm zool* hare; *(tânăr)* leveret, young hare; *(de casă)* rabbit; *coll* bunny; **fricos ca un ~** chicken-hearted.

ierarhie [ierar'hie] *nf* hierarchy.

ierbicid [ierbi'chid] *nn* weed-killer, herbicide || *adj* herbicidal.

ierbivor [ierbi'vor] *adj* herbivorous.

ieri ['ieri] *adv* yesterday; *(în ajun)* on the eve; *(în trecut)* formerly, once.

ierna [ier'na] *vi* to winter, to pass/spend the winter; *(a hiberna)* to hibernate • **~t** *nn* wintering, hibernation.

ierta [ier'ta] *vt* to forgive, to pardon; *(a scuza)* to excuse, to condone; *(a trece cu vederea)* to overlook; *(a scuti de)* to exempt (from); *relig* to absolve; *(a cruța)* to spare • **~re** *nf* forgiveness, pardon; *(scuză)* excuse; *(scutire)* exemption; *relig* absolution • **iartă-mă!** excuse me!, I apologize!, I beg your pardon!.

iesle ['iesle] *nf* manger.

ieși [ie'shi] *vi (dintr-un loc)* to come out, to go out; *(orice verb de deplasare + out =* **a ieși** *+ sensul dat de verb)* to creep out, to drive out, to ride out, to rush out, to sail out, to stagger out, to steal out, to stumble out; **a ~ afară** to go out (for a walk); *med* to have a stool; **a ~ bine** *(d. ceva)* to turn out well; *(d. cineva)* to succeed, to do well; **a ~ cu bine (din)** to get over a difficulty; **a ~ din comun** to be distinguished; *mus* **a ~ din măsură** to be/get out of time; **a-i ~ din minte (ceva)** to slip one's mind; **a-și ~ din minți** to go out of one's mind/senses; to go mad; **a ~ din uz** to be/fall/go out of use; *(a se demoda)* to become obsolete; **a ~ în afară** to protrude; to stand out (in bold relief); to be prominent/salient; **a ~ în evidență/relief** to jut out, to be prominent; *(d. cineva)* to stand out; **a ~ în lume** to go out; **a ~ la pensie** to retire; **a ~ la plimbare** to take a walk; **a ~ pe furiș** to steal/sneak out; **a ~ prost/rău** *(d. cineva)* to fail; *coll* to come a cropper; *(d. ceva)* to turn out/end badly; **a ~ victorios** to come off victorious/with flying colors; to carry/win the day; *(la lumină, la suprafață)* to emerge; **a ~ la iveală** to come to light; *(a apărea)* to appear; **a ~ de sub tipar** to come off the press; *(a avea ca rezultat)* to result; *(a se decolora)* to fade; *(d. pete)* to come out; *(d. culori)* to run; *(a deveni)* to become • **~re** *nf* going out, emergence, way out; *(cinema, teatru)* exit; *(izbucnire)* outburst; *(soluție)* solution.

iezer ['iezer] *nn* mountain lake.

igienă [idj'iena] *nf* hygiene.

igienic [idj'ienik] *adj* hygienic, healthy, sanitary; *(de toaletă)* toilet • **hârtie ~ă** tissue paper.

igliță ['iglitsa] *nf* crotchet, lacer.

iglu ['iglu] *nn* igloo.

ignifug [igni'fug] *adj* fireproof, fire-resistant || *nn* fireproof material.

ignora [igno'ra] *vt* to be ignorant/unaware of; *(a nu ține cont)* not take into account; *(a trece cu vederea)* to overlook; *(pe cineva)* to slight • **~nt** *nm* ignoramus, dunce || *adj* ignorant, illiterate • **~nță** *nf* ignorance; **din ~** from/out of ignorance.

igrasie [igra'sie] *nf* damp(ness).

ilar [i'lar] *adj* ridiculous • **~iant** *adj* hilarious, laughable; **gaz ~** laughing gas • **~itate** *nf* hilarity, mirth, laughter.

ilegal [ile'gal] *adj* unlawful, illegal; clandestine, underground || *adv* illegally, unlawfully; clandestinely, underground • **~itate** *nf* illegality, unlawfulness; *(ca act)* unlawful act; clandestine/secret/underground activity.

ilegitim [ile'djitim] *adj (copil)* illegitimate; *(căsătorie)* unlawful; *(pretenții)* unwarranted.

ilicit [ili'chit] *adj* illicit, unlawful || *adv* illicitly, unlawfully.

ilizibil [ili'zibil] *adj frml* illegible, unreadable.

ilogic [i'lodjik] *adj* illogical.

ilumina [ilumi'na] *vt* to light up, to shine (upon); *(o serbare) also fig* to illuminate; *fig* to enlighten || *vr* to light up (with); *(a se înșela)* to brighten up • **~re** *nf* illumination, lighting, * **ilumina**; *fig* inspiration.

iluminism [ilumi'nism] *nn phil* the Enlightenment.

ilustra [ilus'tra] *vt (o carte)* to illustrate; *(a exemplifica)* to exemplify; *(a arunca lumină asupra)* to throw/shed light upon || *vr (a se distinge)* to become famous/well-known; to be illustrated • **~re** *nf* illustration, proof; **o ~ grăitoare** a telling proof • **~ție** *nf* picture, illustration.

ilustru [i'lustru] *adj* famous, illustrious; *(celebru)* celebrated, renowned.

iluzie [i'luzie] *nf* illusion; *fig* empty dream; (*înşelare*) delusion; ~ **optică** optical illusion.

iluziona [iluzio'na] *vt* to delude, to deceive || *vr* to delude/deceive oneself.

iluzoriu [ilu'zoriu] *adj* illusory, illusive.

imaculat [imaku'lat] *adj* immaculate, spotless; *fig* unblemished, undefiled.

imagina [imadji'na] *vt* to imagine, to fancy; (*a născoci*) to invent, to devise; (*a concepe*) to conceive; (*a-şi închipui*) to think, to suppose • ~r *adj* imaginary; (*fantezist*) fancied; *math* (*d. numere*) imaginary • ~tiv *adj* imaginative • ~ţie *nf* imagination; (*fantezie*) fancy, invention; ~ **vie** lively fancy; **e pură** ~ it's only fancy, it's baseless/unfounded; **lipsit de** ~ unimaginative.

imagine [i'madjine] *nf* image; (*reflectare în apă*) reflection (in water); (*reprezentare*) representation; *cin, TV* frame, picture; ~ **reală/virtuală** real/virtual image; ~ **de sinteză** computer-generated image; (*tablou*) picture; (*fotografie*) photograph; (mental) picture, idea, impression; *liter* metaphor, figure of speech; *pl* imagery.

imaterial [imateri'al] *adj* immaterial, unsubstantial.

imatur [ima'tur] *adj* immature, callow; *fig* unfledged; (*d. fructe*) unripe.

imbatabil [imba'tabil] *adj* invincible, unbeatable; irresistible.

imbecil [imbe'chil] *nm* imbecile, idiot, fool || *adj* idiotic, silly, foolish • ~itate *nf* imbecility, idiocy, stupidity.

imbold [im'bold] *nn* impulse, impulsion, impetus; incentive, stimulus.

imediat [imedi'at] *adj* immediate, instant; urgent; *jur* (*d. cauză, succesor*) direct; (*apropiat*) close, near || *adv* immediately, at once; *coll* in a jiffy.

imens [i'mens] *adj* immense; colossal, tremendous, huge; vast; (*nemăsurat*) immeasurable; (*nemărginit*) boundless; profound, deep || *adv* immensely, vastly, hugely • ~itate *nf* immensity; (*vastitate*) vastness; (*infinitate*) infinity; (*nemărginire*) boundlessness; (*mărime*) colossal/huge size, hugeness.

imersiune [imersi'une] *nf* immersion, dipping; (*a unui submarin*) submergence, submersion; *astron* occultation.

imigra [imi'gra] *vi* to immigrate • ~nt *nm* immigrant; ~ **legal** legal immigrant • ~re, ~ţie *nf* immigration; ~ **ilegală** illegal immigration.

iminent [imi'nent] *adj* impending, imminent.

imita [imi'ta] *vt* to imitate; to copy; to mimic, to ape; *thea* to impersonate; (*o semnătură*) to forge || *vi* to imitate, to mimic, to forge • ~tor *nm* imitator; *thea* impersonator • ~ţie *nf* imitation; mimicry; (*fals*) counterfeit, forgery; **bijuterii** ~ imitation/costume jewelry, rhinestone.

imixtiune [imiksti'une] *nf* interference.

imn [imn] *nn* (national) anthem; *relig and fig* hymn; *liter* song (of praise), patriotic song.

imobil[1] [i'mobil] *nn* house, building; block.

imobil[2] [imo'bil] *adj* (*nemişcat*) motionless, still, unmoved; *jur* (*imobiliar*) real; **bunuri** ~ real estate.

imobiliar [imobili'ar] *adj* real (property/estate) • **agenţie** ~ă estate agency, real estate office • **bunuri** ~e real property/ estate • **societate** ~ă building society.

imobiliza [imobili'za] *vt* to immobilize, to bring to a standstill; *com* (*d. capital*) locking up, tying up.

imoral [imo'ral] *adj* immoral; corrupt; (*desfrânat*) dissolute, dissipated, profligate.

imortaliza [imortali'za] *vt* to immortalize.

impacienta [impachien'ta] *vr* to lose patience, to grow/get impatient (at smth, with smb).

impar [im'par] *adj* odd, uneven; **număr** ~ odd number.

imparţial [impartsi'al] *adj* impartial, unbiased; (*corect*) fair-minded, unprejudiced; objective || *adv* impartially • ~itate *nf* impartiality, fairness.

impas [im'pas] *nn* deadlock, stalemate; dilemma.

impasibil [impa'sibil] *adj* impassive, imperturbable, unmoved.

impecabil [impe'kabil] *adj* impeccable; (*d. stil, gust*) faultless; infallible; (*d. tehnică*) flawless || *adv* impeccably, faultlessly, flawlessly.

impediment [impedi'ment] *nn* impediment, obstacle, hindrance.

impenetrabil [impene'trabil] *adj* impenetrable, impervious; (*d. faţă*) inscrutable; (*d. un mister*) unfathomable; (*complicat*) intricate.

imperativ [impera'tiv] *adj* imperative, imperious; (*d. ton*) peremptory || *nn phil* imperative, requirement.

imperceptibil [imperchep'tibil] *adj* imperceptible, slight || *adv* imperceptibly.

imperfect [imper'fekt] *adj* imperfect, defective, deficient, faulty || *adv* imperfectly || *nn gram* (*timp*) imperfect.

imperfecţiune [imperfektsi'une] *nf* imperfection, defect, flaw, fault.

imperial [imperi'al] *adj* imperial • ~ism *nn* imperialism • ~ist *nm* imperialist.

imperios [imperi'os] *adj* imperious, imperative; (*d. ton*) peremptory || *adv* imperiously, urgently, imperatively.

imperiu [im'periu] *nn* empire; *fig* dominion, rule, sway.

impermeabil [imperme'abil] *nn* raincoat, mackintosh; *coll* mac(k) || *adj* waterproof; impervious (to); (*d. ţesături*) water-repellent.

impertinent [imperti'nent] *adj* impertinent, rude, insolent || *adv* impertinently, rudely, insolently.

impertinenţă [imperti'nentsă] *nf* impertinence, rudeness, insolence; **cu** ~ impertinently.

imperturbabil [impertur'babil] *adj* imperturbable, calm, unruffled || *adv* imperturbably.

impetuos [impetu'os] *adj* impetuous, impulsive, rash || *adv* impetuously, impulsively, rashly.

impieta [impie'ta] *vi* (*asupra*) to cast aspersions/a slur/a shadow on; (*a încălca drepturi*) to encroach (upon smth), to infringe (upon) smb's rights; (*a aduce daune*) to harm, to damage • ~te *nf* impiety, ungodliness; (*nelegiuire*) lawlessness; (*ca act*) ungodly act; blasphemy.

implacabil [impla'kabil] *adj* implacable, inflexible, relentless || *adv* implacably, inflexibly, relentlessly.

implant [im'plant] *nn med* implant.

implanta [implan'ta] *vt* to implant, to instill, to insert || *vr* to take root, to become rooted; to be implanted, to set up.

implica [impli'ka] *vt* (*a amesteca*) to involve, to implicate; (*a necesita*) to entail; (*a presupune*) to imply || *vi* (*în*) to be/get involved in; (*a se consacra*) to devote oneself to • ~ţie *nf* implication, involvement.

implicit [impli'chit] *adj* implicit; (*d. intenţie*) implied; (*d. încredere*) absolute || *adv* implicitly.

implora [implo'ra] *vt* to beseech, to implore, to entreat.

impoliteţe [impoli'tetse] *nf* rudeness, lack of manners; (*ca act*) act of rudeness, incivility, discourtesy.

imponderabil [imponde'rabil] *adj* imponderable, imperceptible || *nn* imponderable; ~**itate** *nf* imponderability, weightlessness.

import [im'port] *nn* import; (*acţiunea*) importation.

importa[1] [impor'ta] *vt com* (*din*) to import (from), to bring in (from).

importa[2] [impor'ta] *vi* (*a conta*) to matter, to be of importance/consequence • ~**nt** *adj* important; (*semnificativ*) significant, major; (*mare*) large, considerable; **un obiectiv** ~ a major target; **nimic** ~ nothing important, nothing of consequence; **puţin** ~ unimportant, immaterial; historic, momentous; (*d. cineva*) consequential; (*of* consequence • **sumă** ~**ă** considerable sum (of money).

importanţă [impor'tantsă] *nf* importance; (*semnificaţie*) significance; moment; (*proporţii*) scope; (*mărime*) extent; (*valoare*) consequence, value; (*poziţie socială*) position, standing; **n-are** ~ it doesn't matter, never mind.

importuna [importu'na] *vt rare* to importune, to bother, to pester.

imposibil [impo'sibil] *adj* impossible, out of the question; (*care nu se poate face*) unfeasible; (*d. cineva*) (*nesuferit*) unbearable; *coll* absurd, ridiculous || *interj* impossible!, out of the question! • ~**itate** *nf* impossibility • ~**ul** *nn* one's utmost/best.

impostor [impos'tor] *nm* impostor; *coll* fake, fraud, cheat.

impostură [impos'tură] *nf* imposture, deception, trickery.

impotent [impo'tent] *nm* impotent || *adj* helpless; (*sexual*) impotent.

impotenţă [impo'tentsă] *nf* impotence, impotency; helplessness.

impozabil [impo'zabil] *adj* (*d. venit*) taxable; subject to taxation; (*d. proprietate*) assessable, rat(e)able.

impozant [impo'zant] *adj* (*d. figură, ceremonie*) imposing, grand, impressive.

impozit [im'pozit] *nn* tax, duty; ~ **direct** direct tax; ~ **fiscal** stamp duty; ~ **pe venit** income tax.

impracticabil [imprakti'kabil] *adj* impractical; (*d. un plan*) unpractical; (*d. drumuri*) impassable; *fig* unfeasible, unworkable.

imprecaţie [impre'katsie] *nf* imprecation, curse.

imprecis [impre'chis] *adj* imprecise, inexact, inaccurate.

imprecizie [impre'chizie] *nf* imprecision; (*a unei declaraţii*) vagueness; (*a unui termen*) looseness; inaccuracy.

impregna [impreg'na] *vt also fig* (*de*) to impregnate (with); to permeate || *vr* (*de*) to become saturated (with), to become impregnated/permeated (with); *fig* to become imbued with.

impresar [impre'sar] *nm* impresario, business manager, agent.

impresie [im'presie] *nf* impression, feeling; **a face** ~ to make an impression; **a face** ~ **bună** to cut a good/fine figure; **a face** ~ **proastă** to cut a sorry/poor figure; (*greşită*) delusion.

impresiona [impresio'na] *vt* (*a produce o impresie*) to impress; (*a emoţiona*) to move, to make an impres-

sion on; to act (on the retina); *phot* to expose (film) || *vr* to be strongly affected, to be easily upset • ~**nt** *adj* impressive, spectacular; (*emoţionant*) moving.

impresionism [impresio'nism] *nn* (*artă*) impressionism.

imprevizibil [imprevi'zibil] *adj* unpredictable, unforeseeable; incalculable.

imprima [impri'ma] *vt* (*a lăsa urme*) to imprint, to stamp; (*a tipări*) to print; (*a înregistra*) to register, to record; (*în minte*) to implant; *fig* (*a da*) to lend (to), to inculcate (upon, in); *also fig* (*o mişcare*) to impart || *vr* to be printed, to be imparted; (*în minte*) to linger (in one's memory) • ~**ntă** *nf comp* printer.

imprimat [impri'mat] *nn* (*formular*) form; *pl* printed matter || *adj* print(ed); (*d. o rochie*) print; *elec* **circuit** ~ printed circuit.

imprimeu [impri'meu] *nn text* print.

improbabil [impro'babil] *adj* improbable, unlikely.

impropriu [im'propriu] *adj* improper, unsuitable, inadequate.

improviza [improvi'za] *vt also mus* to improvise; (*un discurs*) to make an impromptu/extempore speech || *vi* to speak extempore; *coll* to speak off the cuff, to ad-lib • ~**ţie** *nf* improvisation, makeshift; (*d. discurs*) extempore speech; (*d. poezie*) impromptu poem.

imprudent [impru'dent] *adj* imprudent, rash, incautious || *adv* imprudently, rashly, incautiously.

imprudenţă [impru'dentsă] *nf* imprudence, rashness, recklessness; imprudent act; **a comite o** ~ to act rashly/imprudently.

impudic [im'pudik] *adj* indecent, shameless; lewd.

impuls [im'puls] *nn* impulse; (*imbold*) impetus, stimulus, spur.

impulsiona [impulsio'na] *vt* to impel, to give an impulse to, to stimulate.

impulsiv [impul'siv] *adj* impulsive, rash, impetuous || *adv* impulsively.

impunător [impună'tor] *adj* imposing, grand, stately.

impune [im'pune] *vt* to impose, to prescribe; (*o regulă*) to enforce, to lay down; (*tăcere*) to enjoin; (*o părere*) to thrust; to inspire ... with respect; (*a obliga la*) to require; (*un impozit*) to tax; (*a cere, a reclama*) to call for || *vi* to be impressive || *vr* to be(come) established; (*d. un scriitor*) to assert oneself, to compel recognition; (*a fi necesar*) to be necessary/imperative; (*a fi de dorit*) to be called for.

impur [im'pur] *adj also chem* impure, tainted, foul; *relig* unclean.

imputa [impu'ta] *vt* to impute, to attribute; to charge, to reproach; *com* (*bani*) to charge smth to || *vr* **a i se** ~ **ceva** to be charged with smth • ~**re** *nf* imputation; (*repros*) reproach; (*vină*) blame; (*bănească*) charge, charging.

imuabil [imu'abil] *adj* immutable, unchanging • ~**itate** *nf* immutability.

imun [i'mun] *adj* (*la o boală*) immune (to/against/from) • ~**itate** *nf med, pol* immunity.

in [in] *nn bot* flax; **de** ~ linen; flaxen; (*sămânţă*) linseed, flaxseed.

inabordabil [inabor'dabil] *adj* out of one's reach; (*d. persoane*) unapproachable; (*d. un preţ*) prohibitive; (*d. un punct strategic*) unattackable.

inacceptabil [inakchept'abil] *adj* unacceptable.

inaccesibil [inakche'sibil] *adj* inaccessible, unapproachable.

inactiv [inak'tiv] *adj* inactive; (*leneş*) idle, indolent;

chem inert • ~**itate** *nf* inactivity, idleness, indolence; sluggishness; (*d. cineva*) **în** ~ out of work; *com* dead period; *chem* inertness.

inadaptabil [inadap'tabil] *nm* misfit || *adj* maladjusted.

inadaptat [inadap'tat] *adj/nm* misfit.

inadecvat [inadek'vat] *adj* inadequate, insufficient.

inadmisibil [inadmi'sibil] *adj* inadmissible; (*de neconceput*) inconceivable.

inadvertență [inadver'tentsă] *nf* inadvertence, inadvertency; (*scăpare*) oversight; (*greșeală*) mistake; slip; lapse; **din** ~ inadvertently, unguardedly, by mistake.

inalienabil [inalie'nabil] *adj* inalienable, untransferable; *jur* (*d. drepturi*) indefeasible.

inamic [ina'mik] *nm* enemy; *lit* foe || *adj* enemy, inimical, hostile.

inamovibil [inamo'vibil] *adj* irremovable; (*d. cineva*) holding an appointment for life; (*d. un post*) held for life.

inaniție [ina'nitsie] *nf* inanition, starvation.

inapt [i'napt] *adj* (*pentru*) inappropriate, unfit (for); *mil* unfit for military service.

inaugura [inaugu'ra] *vt* to inaugurate; (*a dezveli o statuie*) to unveil; (*a deschide*) to open; *fig* to usher in || *vr* to be inaugurated, to open • ~**re** *nf* inauguration, opening.

incandescent [inkandes'chent] *adj also fig* incandescent, glowing, red-hot.

incandescență [inkandes'chentsă] *nf* incandescence, glow.

incapabil [inka'pabil] *adj* incapable, inefficient, unfit, incompetent || *nm* **e un** ~ he is useless, he is no use.

incapacitate [inkapachi'tate] *nf* incapacity, incompetency, inability; *jur* disability, invalidity.

incarna [inkar'na] *vt* to incarnate, to embody, to personify; to become incarnate.

incasabil [inka'sabil] *adj* unbreakable, non-breakable.

incaso [in'kaso] *nn fin* collection (of a sum), proceeds.

incendia [inchendi'a] *vt* to set (smth) on fire, to set fire to; *fig* to set (smth) ablaze, to fire • ~**r** *adj* incendiary; *fig* (*d. un discurs*) inflammatory; *fig* (*roșu*) red, purple • ~**tor** *nm/adj* arsonist, pyromaniac; *fig* instigator.

incendiere [inchendi'ere] *nf* arson, setting on fire.

incendiu [in'chendiu] *nn* (outbreak of) fire, conflagration; *jur* (*provocat*) arson.

incert [in'chert] *adj* uncertain, doubtful • ~**itudine** *nf* uncertainty, incertitude; (*îndoială*) doubt.

incest [in'chest] *nn* incest.

inchiziție [inki'zitsie] *nf* inquisition.

incident [inchi'dent] *nn* incident; (*întâmplare*) occurrence, happening; difficulty, hitch • ~**al** *adj* incidental, fortuitous || *adv* incidentally, fortuitously, by chance.

incidență [inchi'dentsă] *nf phys* incidence.

incinera [inchine'ra] *vt* to cremate, to incinerate.

incintă [in'chintă] *nf* precincts; (*spațiu îngrădit*) enclosure, enclosed space.

incipient [inchipi'ent] *adj* incipient.

incisiv[1] [inchi'siv] *nm anat* incisor (tooth).

incisiv[2] [inchi'siv] *adj fig* biting, incisive, cutting, sharp.

incita [inchi'ta] *vt* to incite, to urge, to stir up • ~**ție** *nf frml* instigation, incitement.

incizie [in'chizie] *nf* incision, cut(ting); (*d. furunculul*) lancing; (*d. copac*) tapping (of tree for resin).

include [in'klude] *vt* to include, to contain; (*într-un plic*) to enclose; (*a insera*) to insert || *vr* to be included, etc.

inclusiv [inklu'siv] *adv* included; **toți erau elevi, ~ Tim** all were students, Tim included; (*d. date*) inclusive; **de luni până vineri** ~ from Monday through Friday inclusive.

incoerent [inkoe'rent] *adj* incoherent, inarticulate, rambling || *adv* incoherently.

incoerență [inkoe'rentsă] *nf* incoherence, incoherency.

incognito [in'kognito] *adj* incognito; *coll* incog.

incolor [inko'lor] *adj also fig* colorless.

incomensurabil [inkomensu'rabil] *adj* immeasurable, huge, vast; *math* incommensurable, incommensurate.

incomod [inko'mod] *adj* (*d. un scaun*) uncomfortable; inconvenient; (*d. o cameră*) incommodious; (*d. ceva greoi*) clumsy, unhandy; (*d. cineva*) troublesome, disagreeable || *adv* uncomfortably • ~**a** [inkomo'da] *vt* to bother, to inconvenience, to put out.

incomparabil [inkompa'rabil] *adj* incomparable, peerless, unrivalled || *adv* incomparably, beyond compare.

incompatibil [inkompa'tibil] *adj* (*cu*) incompatible (with), inconsistent, at variance (with).

incompetent [inkompe'tent] *adj* incompetent, inefficient.

incompetență [inkompe'tentsă] *nf* incompetence, inefficiency.

incomplet [inkom'plet] *adj* incomplete, unfinished || *adv* incompletely.

inconsecvent [inkonsek'vent] *adj* (*d. comportament*) inconsistent, unsteady; (*d. persoane*) fickle, inconstant.

inconsecvență [inkonsek'ventsă] *nf* inconsistency, inconstancy, fickleness.

inconstant [inkon'stant] *adj* unsteady, inconsistent, erratic.

inconștient [inkonshti'ent] *adj* (*act*) unconscious; (*mișcare*) automatic; (*care și-a pierdut cunoștința*) unconscious; *fig* irresponsible || *adv* unconsciously • ~**ul** *nn* the unconscious (mind), the subconscious.

inconștiență [inkonshti'entsă] *nf* (*pierderea cunoștinței*) unconsciousness, blackout; *fig* recklessness, irresponsibility.

incontestabil [inkontes'tabil] *adj* unchallenged, incontestable, indisputable || *adv* incontestably, indisputably, undeniably.

inconvenient [inkonveni'ent] *nn* difficulty; (*dezavantaj*) drawback, disadvantage; inconvenience.

incorect [inko'rekt] *adj* (*greșit*) incorrect, wrong, inaccurate, faulty; (*necinstit*) dishonest, unfair; (*nepotrivit*) unsuitable, improper || *adv* (*greșit*) incorrectly, inaccurately; (*necinstit*) unfairly; (*nepotrivit*) unsuitably.

incorigibil [inkori'djibil] *adj* (*d. copii*) incorrigible; (*bețiv*) hopeless.

incoruptibil [inkorup'tibil] *adj* incorruptible, untouchable • ~**itate** *nf* incorruptibility, integrity.

incredibil [inkre'dibil] *adj* incredible, unbelievable; *coll* marvelous || *adv* incredibly.

incredul [inkre'dul] *adj* incredulous; *relig* unbelieving.

incrimina [inkrimi'na] *vt* to charge, to incriminate, to accuse • ~**re** *nf* incrimination, charge, accusation • ~**t** *adj* accused • ~**tul** *nm* (the) accused, (the) defendant.

incrusta [inkrus'ta] *vt* to inlay, to encrust; *fig* to imprint || *vr* to be(come) encrusted; (*d. țevi, boiler*) to scale • ~**ție** *nf* inlay, inlaid work; encrusting; *phys, chem* incrustation; (*depunere*) furring up/scale.

incubator [inkuba'tor] *nn* incubator.

inculca [inkul'ka] *vt* to inculcate.

inculpa [inkul'pa] *vt* to indict, to charge, to inculpate • **~t** *nm* defendant, person indicted • **~tul** the defendant, the accused.

incult [in'kult] *adj* uneducated, unlearned; (*analfabet*) illiterate.

incurabil [inku'rabil] *adj* incurable; *fig* helpless.

incursiune [inkursi'une] *nf* foray, raid, inroad; *fig* excursion

indecent [inde'chent] *adj* indecent, offensive; (*neruşinat*) shameless, immodest; (*nepotrivit*) unseemly, unbecoming || *adv* improperly.

indecenţă [inde'chentsă] *nf* indecency, immodesty.

indecis [inde'chis] *adj* wavering, indecisive, undecided.

indefinit [indefi'nit] *adj* indefinite; (*vag*) vague, undefined || *adv* indefinitely, vaguely.

indemnizaţie [indemni'zatsie] *nf* indemnity, pay, compensation.

independent [indepen'dent] *adj* independent; (*liber*) free (of || *adv* independently (of smth); ~ **de** independent of; (*indiferent de consecinţe*) whatever the consequences || *nm pol* independent.

independenţă [indepen'dentsă] *nf* independence; (*libertate*) freedom, self-sufficiency.

indescifrabil [indeschi'frabil] *adj* undecipherable; (*ilizibil*) illegible; unintelligible, incomprehensible.

indescriptibil [indeskrip'tibil] *adj* indescribable, beggaring description.

indestructibil [indestruk'tibil] *adj* indestructible.

indeşirabil [indeshi'rabil] *adj* ladder-proof.

index ['indeks] *nn* forefinger, index finger; (*d. carte*) index; **a pune la** ~ (*d. o carte*) to put on the index, *fig* to put on the prohibited list, (*pe cineva*) to blacklist smb, *fig* (*pe cineva, ceva*) to shelve smb.

indexa [indek'sa] *vt econ* (*salarii*) to index-link; to peg • **~re** *nf econ* adjustment payment, pegging, indexation.

indezirabil [indezi'rabil] *nm* intruder; *coll* gate-crasher || *adj* undesirable, objectionable.

indian [indi'an] *nm/adj* Indian; **în şir** ~ in Indian/single file • **~că** *nf* Indian (woman/girl).

indica [indi'ka] *vt* to indicate, to give directions; to point to/out; (*a marca*) to mark; (*a arăta*) to show; (*a prescrie*) to lay down, to prescribe; (*a recomanda*) to recommend • **~tiv** *nn gram* indicative; (**modul**) ~ the indicative (mood); *mil* code; *telec* dialing code; ~ **de apel** call sign/signal || *adj* eloquent, indicative (of) • **~tor** *nn* indicator, sign; (*ac indicator*) pointer; (*d. plan*) index; ~ **al străzilor** street directory; ~ **de nivel** *tech* level indicator/gauge; ~ **de presiune** *tech* pressure indicator; ~ **rutier** guide post || *nm* *

indice || *adj* indicatory • **~ţie** *nf* indication, directive; *pl* instructions • **~ţii de regie/scenice** stage directions.

indice ['indiche] *nm math, phys, chem* index, factor, rating, value; ~ **de preţuri** price index.

indiciu [in'dichiu] *nn* sign, indication, mark, evidence; (*idee*) clue.

indiferent [indife'rent] *adj* indifferent; (*netulburat*) unconcerned; (*apatic*) apathetic; (*rece*) cold, unresponsive; (*fără importanţă*) immaterial, unimportant || *adv* indifferently; ~ **de** regardless of, whatever.

indiferenţă [indife'rentsă] *nf* indifference (to), lack of concern/interest (in); (*pasivitate*) listlessness; (*apatie*) apathy.

indigen [indi'djen] *nm* aborigine, native || *adj* native, indigenous.

indigestie [indi'djestie] *nf* indigestion; **a avea** ~ to have an attack of indigestion.

indigna [indig'na] *vt* to (a)rouse smb's indignation, to anger || *vr* (*de*) to be/become indignant (at smb/with smb) • **~re** *nf* indignation.

indigo [indi'go] *nn* (*vopsea*) indigo; (*hârtie*) carbon paper || *adj* indigo blue.

indirect [indi'rekt] *adj* indirect, devious, evasive; (*ocolit*) roundabout, circuitous; **complement** ~ *gram* indirect object || *adv* indirectly, deviously, evasively.

indisciplină [indischi'plină] *nf* indiscipline, lack of discipline.

indiscret [indis'kret] *adj* indiscreet, imprudent; (*curios*) inquisitive; (*d. o persoană, o întrebare*) tactless; *coll* nosy || *adv* indiscreetly || *nm* indiscreet/tactless person.

indiscreţie [indis'kretsie] *nf* indiscretion; (*ca act*) an indiscreet act/remark.

indiscutabil [indisku'tabil] *adj* indisputable, unquestionable || *adv* indisputably, unquestionably, beyond doubt.

indispensabil [indispen'sabil] *adj* indispensable (to), essential; (*d. un obiect*) not to be dispensed with.

indispensabili [indispen'sabili] *nm pl* (*lungi*) drawers; (*scurţi*) pants; (*glumeţ*) unmentionables.

indisponibil [indispo'nibil] *adj jur* (*proprietate*) inalienable, entailed; (*d. cineva*) unavailable, not available.

indispoziţie [indispo'zitsie] *nf* (*boală uşoară*) indisposition, ailment; *fig* (*proastă dispoziţie*) low spirits, ill-humor; *coll* dumps.

indispune [indis'pune] *vt* to trouble, to put out || *vr* to be upset, to be put out; to become depressed.

indispus [indis'pus] *adj med* (*uşor bolnav*) unwell, indisposed; *coll* poorly, out of sorts; (*prost dispus*) low-spirited.

individ [indi'vid] *nm* (*persoană*) individual; (*tip*) person, fellow; *coll* guy.

individual [individu'al] *adj* individual; (*particular*) private; personal || *adv* individually, one by one • **~ist** *adj* individualistic || *nm* individualist • **~itate** *nf* individuality; (*personalitate*) personality.

indiviziune [indivizi'une] *nf* severalty.

indolent [indo'lent] *adj* indolent, lazy, idle.

indolenţă [indo'lentsă] *nf* indolence, laziness, idleness.

indonezian(ă) [indonezi'an(ă)] *nm/nf/adj* Indonesian.

indubitabil [indubi'tabil] *adj* indubitable, undoubted, beyond doubt.

induce [in'duche] *vt* to lead, to tempt (smb to do smth); *elec* to induce; (*logică*) to infer, to deduce.

indulgent [indul'djent] *adj* indulgent, lenient, tolerant; (*bun*) kind || *adv* indulgently, etc.

indulgenţă [indul'djentsă] *nf* indulgence, lenience; (*bunătate*) kindness; *relig* indulgence.

industrial [industri'al] *adj* industrial, industry • **~izare** *nf* industrialization.

industriaş [industri'ash] *nm* manufacturer, industrialist.

industrie [in'dustrie] *nf* industry; ~ **grea** heavy industry; ~ **uşoară** light industry; ~ **prelucrătoare** processing industry.

inechitabil [ineki'tabil] *adj* inequitable, unfair, unjust || *adv* unfairly, unjustly.

inechitate [ineki'tate] *nf* inequity, unfairness, injustice.

inedit [ine'dit] *adj* unpublished; (*nou*) novel, new; original; undiscovered || *nn* novelty • **~ul** the new.

ineficace [inefi'kache] *adj* inefficient; (*d. o măsură*) ineffective, ineffectual; (*d. un remediu*) inefficacious.

ineficacitate [inefikachi'tate] *nf* ineffectiveness, inefficacy, inefficiency.

inegal [ine'gal] *adj* unequal; (*cu asperități; d. caracter*) uneven; (*neregulat*) irregular ‖ *adv* unequally, etc. • **~abil** *adj* unrivaled, matchless, peerless ‖ *adv* incomparably • **~itate** *nf* inequality, unevenness.

inel [i'nel] *nn* ring; (*verighetă*) wedding ring; *bot* grain; *bio* annulus; (*buclă*) ringlet, curl of hair; *tech* collar, hoop • **~e** *sp nn* the rings.

inepție [inep'tsie] *nf* stupidity, ineptitude, nonsense.

inepuizabil [inepui'zabil] *adj* inexhaustible, endless, unfailing.

inerent [ine'rent] *adj* inherent, intrinsic ‖ *adv* inherently, intrinsically.

inert [i'nert] *adj* inert, limp, inactive, dull; *chem* unreactive ‖ *adv* inertly, etc.

inerție [iner'tsie] *nf* inertness, inactivity, passivity; *phys* inertia.

inestimabil [inesti'mabil] *adj* inestimable, invaluable, priceless.

inevitabil [inevi'tabil] *adj* (*d. un accident*) unavoidable; (*d. un rezultat*) inevitable; inescapable ‖ *adv* unavoidably, inevitably ‖ *nn* the inevitable • **~itate** *nf* inevitability.

inexact [ineg'zakt] *adj* inaccurate, inexact, incorrect ‖ *adv* inaccurately, incorrectly • **~itate** *nf* inaccuracy, inexactitude; (*greșeală*) mistake; unpunctuality.

inexistent [inegzis'tent] *adj* absent, non-existent.

inexistență [inegzis'tentsă] *nf* absence, lack, want, non-existence.

inexplicabil [inekspli'kabil] *adj* unaccountable, inexplicable; (*nejustificat*) unreasonable ‖ *adv* inaccountably, inexplicably, unreasonably.

inexpresiv [inekspre'siv] *adj* (*d. un cuvânt*) inexpressive; (*d. chip*) expressionless ‖ *adv* inexpressively.

inexprimabil [inekspri'mabil] *adj* inexpressible, indescribable, beyond words.

infailibil [infai'libil] *adj* infallible, unerring; (*sigur*) certain, sure, unfailing.

infam [in'fam] *adj* infamous, horrible; (*d. faptă*) foul; (*d. crimă*) unspeakable ‖ *adv* infamously, horribly • **~ie** *nf* infamy, disgrace; (*ca act*) infamous act, vile deed.

infanterie [infan'terie] *nf mil* infantry, foot soldier.

infantil [infan'til] *adj* infantile, infant, child; puerile, childish.

infarct [in'farkt] *nn med* infarct, infarction; **~ mio-cardic** myocardial infarction.

infatuat [infatu'at] *adj* infatuated, conceited, vain ‖ *nm* infatuate.

infect [in'fekt] *adj* horrible, awful; (*respingător*) loathsome; (*d. aer*) foul; (*mârșav*) vile; miserable, wretched; (*d. miros*) stinking.

infecta [infek'ta] *vt* to infect; (*atmosfera*) to poison; to contaminate, to taint; (*apa*) to pollute; *fig* to corrupt ‖ *vr* to be(come) infected; (*d. rană*) to rankle, to fester.

infecție [in'fektsie] *nf* infection; (*miros urât*) stink, stench; *fig* (*porcărie*) awful thing; *fig* (*contagiune morală*) moral corruption/contamination.

infecțios [infektsi'os] *adj* infectious, catching, contagious.

inferior [inferi'or] *nm* subordinate, inferior ‖ *adj*

inferior; lower, bottom; (*d. calitate, mărfuri*) poor • **~itate** *nf* inferiority; humility.

infern [in'fern] *nn also fig* (*iad*) hell; *myth* underworld, (the) inferno • **~al** *adj* infernal, hellish; *fig* (*rău*) (*d. căldură*) devilish, diabolical; **e ~!** it's hellish!, it's sheer hell! ‖ *adv* infernally, etc.

infesta [infes'ta] *vt* to infest, to overrun.

infidel [infi'del] *adj* unfaithful, false, disloyal; (*d. memorie*) untrustworthy; (*d. o traducere*) inaccurate • **~itate** *nf* infidelity, betrayal, unfaithfulness; *fig* (*față de cineva*) disloyalty (to); (*în traducere*) inaccuracy.

infiltra [infil'tra] *vt/vr* (*d. lichid*) to infiltrate, to seep, to filter (in, through); *fig* (*d. idei*) to trickle; to soak; (*a se furișa*) to creep, to slink; *med* to inject.

infim [in'fim] *adj* tiny, minute; (*d. o majoritate*) infinitesimal.

infinit [infi'nit] *adj* infinite; (*nemărginit*) boundless; (*d. spațiu*) immeasurable; *fig* eternal, endless, never-ending; (*nenumărate*) innumerable ‖ *adv* infinitely, extremely • **~ul** *nn* the infinite.

infinitiv [infini'tiv] *nn/adj gram* infinitive.

infirm [in'firm] *nm* cripple, invalid ‖ *adj* infirm; (*schilod*) crippled; (*invalid*) disabled.

infirma [infir'ma] *vt* to refute; (*dovezi*) to invalidate, to quash, to nullify.

infirmerie [infirme'rie] *nf* infirmary, sickroom; (*pe o navă*) sick-bay.

infirmieră [infirmi'eră] *nf* nurse.

inflama [infla'ma] *vr* to swell, to become inflamed; (*d. o rană*) to fester, to rankle; *fig* (*d. cineva*) to flare up • **~bil** *adj* flammable, combustible; *fig* irritable, easily excited • **~re** *nf* inflammation • **~t** *adj* inflamed; (*d. gât*) sore; (*d. o rană*) angry • **~tor** *adj* inflammatory.

inflație [in'flatsie] *nf fin* inflation.

inflexibil [inflek'sibil] *adj also fig* inflexible, obstinate, unyielding ‖ *adv* inflexibly, etc.

inflexiune [infleksi'une] *nf mus* modulation.

inflorescență [inflores'chentsă] *nf bot* inflorescence.

influent [influ'ent] *adj* influential, weighty.

influența [influ'entsa] *vt* to influence; (*opinia publică*) to sway; (*negativ*) to affect • **~bil** *adj* weak, susceptible to influence.

influență [influ'entsă] *nf* influence; (*putere*) authority; (*greutate*) weight; (*ascendent*) ascendancy.

informa [infor'ma] *vt* (*pe cineva, despre ceva*) to inform smb of smth, to tell, to apprize (of); *coll* to let smb know (about smth); (*a încunoștința*) to acquaint smb (with smth); (*oficial*) to give notice to smb (about smth) ‖ *vr* (*despre*) to ask about smth; to inquire into smth, to investigate • **~re** *nf* report, information, notice; *jur* preliminary investigation • **~tor** *nm* informer; (*delator*) informant; *sl* snitch.

informatică [infor'matikă] *nf* computer science, data processing, information science.

informație [infor'matsie] *nf* (piece of) information; *pl* information; *coll* info; *mil* intelligence; (*știre*) item/piece of news; (*cunoștințe*) knowledge; (*la gară*) information desk.

infractor [infrak'tor] *nm* offender; delinquent.

infracțiune [infraktsi'une] *nf* offense, infraction, breaking of the law.

infuzie [in'fuzie] *nf* infusion, steeping.

ingenios [indjeni'os] *adj* ingenious, clever, skillful ‖ *adv* ingeniously, cleverly, skillfully.

ingeniozitate [indjeniozi'tate] *nf* ingenuity, ingeniousness, cleverness.

ingenuu, ingenuă [in'djenuu, in'djenuă] *adj* ingenious, artless, simple ‖ *nf thea* ingénue, artless girl.

ingenuitate [indjenui'tate] *nf* ingenuity, artlessness, simplicity, naivety.

ingera [indje'ra] *vt* to ingest, to swallow.

ingerinţă [indje'rintsă] *nf* encroachment, unwarrantable interference.

inginer [indji'ner] *nm* engineer; ~ **agronom** agronomist; ~ **chimist** chemical engineer; ~ **constructor** civil engineer • ~ie *nf* engineering.

ingrat [in'grat] *nm* ungrateful person ‖ *adj* (*d. cineva*) ungrateful, undutiful; (*d. o sarcină*) thankless; (*neplăcut*) disagreeable; (*dificil*) unrewarded; (*anevoios*) laborious.

ingratitudine [ingrati'tudine] *nf* ingratitude, ungratefulness.

ingredient [ingredi'ent] *nn* ingredient; constituent.

ingurgita [ingurdji'ta] *vt* to ingest, to swallow; *coll* to gorge, to guzzle, to gulp down.

inhala [inha'la] *vt* to inhale, to breathe.

inhiba [inhi'ba] *vt* to inhibit, to hold in/back, to check.

inhibiţie [inhi'bitsie] *nf* inhibition, repression, blocking.

inimă ['inimă] *nf also fig* heart; **în formă de** ~ heart-shaped; **boală de** ~ heart disease; (*suflet*) soul; (*conştiinţă*) conscience; character, nature; ~ **bună** kind/tender heart; ~ **de aur** a heart of gold; ~ **de piatră** a heart of stone/flint, callousness; **bun la** ~ kindhearted, with a heart of gold; **cu inima deschisă** open-hearted; **cu inima grea** with a heavy/sore heart; **cu inima sărită** scared to death; *coll* in a blue funk; **cu inima uşoară** lighthearted, with a free heart; **cu** ~ (*energic*) heartily, with a will; **cu dragă** ~ (*dispus*) willingly, with all one's heart, (*cu plăcere*) with pleasure; **a-şi descărca inima** to get smth off one's chest, (*d. o taină*) to unbosom oneself (of a secret), (*a vorbi*) to open one's heart; **din adâncul inimii** from the bottom of one's heart; **din** ~ wholeheartedly; **din toată inima** with all one's heart, whole-hearted; **după pofta inimii** to one's heart desire/content; **a-l durea inima** *fig* to feel sick/sore at heart; **mă doare inima** it grieves me to the (very) heart, it makes my heart ache; **a-şi face** ~ **rea, a pune ceva la** ~ to take smth to heart; **a i se face** ~a **cât un purice** to have one's heart in one's boots; **a-şi lua inima în dinţi** to pluck up courage/heart, to take heart; **a lua cuiva o piatră de pe** ~ to take a load off/from smb's mind/chest, to unburden one's heart; **a muri de** ~ **rea** to die of a broken heart, to die of grief; **a nu pune (ceva) la** ~ to take it easy; **a râde din toată inima** to have a good laugh, to laugh heartily; **mi s-a umplut inima de bucurie** my heart filled with joy; **a unge la** ~ to go to/in the heart; **a-şi uşura inima** to unburden one's heart, to pour one's heart out (to smb); *coll* to get smth off one's chest; **a-i veni anima la loc** *approx* to feel relieved; (*miez, mijloc*) core, middle, center; **în inima pădurii/ codrului** in the depth/thick/heart of the forest.

inimitabil [inimi'tabil] *adj* inimitable, unique, matchless.

inimos [ini'mos] *adj* (*curajos*) brave, courageous; (*bun*) kind, kind-hearted; (*mărinimos*) generous.

iniţia [initsi'a] *vt* (*în*) to initiate (in); (*a începe*) to start,

to begin ‖ *vr* to become initiated, to learn • ~**tor** *nm* initiator, originator, pioneer • ~l *adj* (*d. literă, cost*) initial; (*d. preţ*) starting ‖ *adv* initially, at the beginning • ~**tivă** [initsia'tivă] *nf* initiative.

iniţiere [initsi'ere] *nf* initiation.

injecta [inzhek'ta] *vt* to inject ‖ *vr* to be injected; (*d. ochi*) to become bloodshot/injected.

injecţie [in'zhektsie] *nf med* injection; *coll* shot.

injurie [in'zhurie] *nf* insult; abuse; outrage.

injurios [inzhuri'os] *adj* insulting, abusive, injurious.

injust [in'zhust] *adj* unjust, unfair ‖ *adv* unjustly, unfairly.

inocent [ino'chent] *adj* (*nevinovat*) innocent, not guilty, blameless; (*curat*) pure, naïve, guileless; *iro* simple-minded, green.

inocenţă [ino'chentsă] *nf* innocence; (*nevinovăţie*) guiltlessness; (*curăţenie*) purity, naivety, chastity; *iro* simple-mindedness.

inocula [inoku'la] *vt med* to inoculate (against); *fig* to imbue (with).

inodor [ino'dor] *adj* inodorous, odorless.

inofensiv [inofen'siv] *adj* harmless, inoffensive, innocuous.

inopinat [inopi'nat] *adj* sudden, unexpected, unforeseen.

inoportun [inopor'tun] *adj* unseasonable, ill-timed, untimely • ~**itate** *nf* inopportuneness, inopportunity, untimeliness.

inospitalier [inospitali'er] *adj* inhospitable, unfriendly.

inovator [inova'tor] *nm* innovator, inventor ‖ *adj* innovating.

inovaţie [ino'vatsie] *nf* innovation.

inoxidabil [inoksi'dabil] *adj* stainless, rustless, rust-resistant.

ins [ins] *nm* guy; individual.

insalubru [insa'lubru] *adj* insanitary, unhealthy, unwholesome.

insatisfacţie [insatis'faktsie] *nf* dissatisfaction.

inscripţie [in'skriptsie] *nf* inscription.

insectar [insek'tar] *nn* insectarium.

insectă [in'sektă] *nf* bug; (*dăunătoare*) vermin.

insecticid [insekti'chid] *nn* insecticide ‖ *adj* insecticidal.

insectivor [insekti'vor] *adj* insectivorous ‖ *nn* insectivore, insect eater.

insensibil [insen'sibil] *adj* insensible; (*la impresii*) insensitive; *fig* unfeeling, callous; (*nepăsător*) indifferent; imperceptible.

inseparabil [insepa'rabil] *adj* inseparable ‖ *adv* inseparably.

insera [inse'ra] *vt* to insert; (*a pune*) to put in; to introduce, to interpolate.

insesizabil [insesi'zabil] *adj* imperceptible, subtle, elusive; *jur* (*d. o proprietate*) not distrainable, not attachable.

insidios [insidi'os] *adj* insidious, perfidious, deceitful.

insignă [in'signa] *nf* badge, insignia.

insignifiant [insignifi'ant] *adj* insignificant, unimportant, trivial.

insinua [insinu'a] *vt* to insinuate, to hint (at); to suggest ‖ *vr* to insinuate oneself (into), to slink (in) • ~**re** *nf* insinuation; (*aluzie*) hint; (*răutăcioasă*) innuendo.

insipid [insi'pid] *adj* insipid, vapid; (*fără gust*) tasteless; (*d. o conversaţie*) dull, flat, boring; (*d. o poveste, un final*) *coll* wishy-washy.

insista [insis'ta] *vi (asupra)* to insist (on, upon); to dwell (on, upon).

insistent [insis'tent] *adj* insistent, urgent; *(d. persoane, rugăminţi)* pressing || *adv* insistently, etc.

insistenţă [insis'tentsă] *nf* insistence, importunity; **cu ~** insistently, urgently.

insolaţie [inso'latsie] *nf* insolation; sunstroke.

insolent [inso'lent] *adj* insolent, impudent, disrespectful; *coll* cheeky || *adv* insolently, etc.

insolenţă [inso'lentsă] *nf* insolence, impudence, impertinence; insolent remark/action.

insolit [inso'lit] *adj* unusual, strange, out of the ordinary.

insolubil [inso'lubil] *adj (d. substanţe)* insoluble; *(d. probleme)* insolvable.

insolvabil [insol'vabil] *adj econ* insolvent.

insomnie [insom'nie] *nf* insomnia, sleeplessness.

inspecta [inspek'ta] *vt* to inspect; to examine, to survey; *(a verifica)* to check (up).

inspector [ins'pektor] *nm* inspector • **~at** *nn* Education Board; inspectorate.

inspecţie [ins'pektsie] *nf* inspection, examination; survey.

inspira [inspi'ra] *vt (aer)* to inspire, to breathe in; *(a insufla)* to inspire smb with smth; *(a provoca)* to fill with || *vr (din)* to draw one's inspiration (from), to draw upon • **~ţie** *nf physiol* inhaling, breathing; *fig* inspiration; *coll* brainstorm, flash of inspiration; *fig* mastermind.

instabil [insta'bil] *adj* unsteady, unstable; *coll* wobbly; *(d. cineva)* unreliable, inconstant • **~itate** *nf* instability, unsteadiness; inconstancy, fickleness.

instala [insta'la] *vt (într-un post)* to install; *(o maşină)* to set up; *(a fixa)* to fix; *(a pune)* to put, to place; *(a aranja)* to arrange; *(pe cineva)* to install, to settle || *vr* to be set up; to be fixed; to be arranged; to install oneself; *(a se stabili)* to settle (down), to make oneself at home • **~tor** *nm* fitter; *(de apă)* plumber • **~ţie** *nf* installation; *tech* equipment, outfit; *(de apă)* plumbing; *(de canalizare)* sewerage; *(ansamblu de construcţii)* plant.

instantaneu [instanta'neu] *nn phot* snapshot || *adj* momentary, sudden || *adv* instantaneously, suddenly.

instanţă [ins'tantsă] *nf jur* (magistrates) court.

instaura [instau'ra] *vt (a institui)* to establish; *(a fonda)* to found, to set up; *(a iniţia)* to initiate || *vr* to be found, to be set up; *(a se statornici)* to strike root.

instiga [insti'ga] *vt* to instigate, to incite, to stir up; to abet • **~re** *nf* instigation, incitement • **~tor** *nm* instigator || *adj* instigating.

instila [insti'la] *vt* to instill.

instinct [ins'tinkt] *nn* instinct • **~iv** *adj* instinctive, instinctual || *adv* instinctively, instinctually, naturally.

institui [institu'i] *vt* to institute, to set up, to establish || *vr* to be instituted, to be set up, to be established.

institut [insti'tut] *nn* institute, institution, establishment.

instituţie [insti'tutsie] *nf* institution, office, establishment, institute.

instructaj [instruk'tazh] *nn* briefing, instructing.

instructiv [instruk'tiv] *adj* instructive, useful.

instructor [ins'truktor] *nm* instructor, teacher; *sp* coach, trainer.

instrucţie [ins'truktsie] *nf* instruction, teaching, education, schooling; *mil* training, drill; *jur* (preliminary) investigation.

instrucţiune [instruktsi'une] *nf* instruction; *pl* directions, orders, rules • **până la noi instrucţiuni** until further notice.

instrui [instru'i] *vt (a învăţa)* to instruct, to teach, to educate, to train; to inform, to brief; *mil* to drill; *jur* to investigate, to examine || *vr* to learn, to acquire knowledge, to educate oneself • **~re** *nf* instruction, teaching; briefing.

instrument [instru'ment] *nn* instrument; *(unealtă)* tool, implement; *(musical)* instrument; *fig (d. cineva)* dupe; *gram* function word.

instrumentist [instrumen'tist] *nm* instrumentalist.

insucces [insuk'ches] *nn* failure; *coll* flop.

insuficient [insufichi'ent] *adj* insufficient; inadequate, deficient; *(d. nutriţie)* low; *(d. greutate)* (short) weight || *adv* insufficiently, inadequately.

insuficienţă [insufichi'entsă] *nf* also *med* insufficiency, deficiency, shortage.

insufla [insu'fla] *vt* to breathe (air into smth), to blow; *med* to spray; *fig* to inspire smb with smth.

insular [insu'lar] *adj* insular || *nm* islander.

insulă ['insulă] *nf* island; *(în denumiri)* isle • **Insulele Britanice** the British Isles.

insulină [insu'lină] *nf med* insulin.

insulta [insul'ta] *vt* to insult, to abuse, to offend || *vr* to insult/abuse each other.

insultă [in'sultă] *nf* insult, abuse • **~tor** *adj* insulting, insolent, offensive.

insuportabil [insupor'tabil] *adj (d. durere)* unbearable; *(d. cineva)* insufferable; *coll* aggravating; *(d. conduită)* intolerable; **e ~!** this is infuriating!, this is the limit! || *adv* unbearably, intolerably, insufferably.

insurecţie [insu'rektsie] *nf* insurrection, insurgence, rebellion.

insurgent [insur'djent] *nm* insurgent, rebel.

intact [in'takt] *adj* intact, untouched, unbroken, undamaged; *fig* unimpaired; *(d. reputaţie)* unsullied, unblemished.

intangibil [intan'djibil] *adj* intangible, impalpable; *(sacru)* sacred, taboo.

integra [inte'gra] *vt* to integrate, to incorporate; *fig* to absorb (into) || *vr (în)* to integrate, to fit in, to become integrated (in); *(a face parte din)* to form part of; *(a aparţine)* to belong to • **~re** *nf* integration.

integral [inte'gral] *adj* integral, complete, whole; *math* integral; *(d. pâine)* wholemeal; *(d. un text)* unabridged || *adv* wholly, completely, entirely.

integritate [integri'tate] *nf* integrity, completeness; *fig* honesty, uprightness.

integru [in'tegru] *adj* incorruptible, upright, honest.

intelect [inte'lekt] *nn* intellect, mind, understanding.

intelectual [intelektu'al] *adj* intellectual, mental; *coll* highbrow || *nm* intellectual; *(cărturar)* scholar; *coll pej* highbrow • **~itate** *nf* intellectuals, (the) intelligentsia.

inteligent [inteli'djent] *adj* intelligent, bright, clever; *coll* brainy || *adv* intelligently, cleverly, wisely.

inteligenţă [inteli'djentsă] *nf* intelligence, understanding; intellect, mind, brains; wit.

inteligibil [inteli'djibil] *adj* intelligible, understandable; *(clar)* clear, distinct || *adv* intelligibly, etc.

intemperie [intempe'rie] *nf* bad weather, inclemency (of weather).

intempestiv [intempes'tiv] *adj* ill-timed, untimely, inappropriate; *(neaşteptat)* unexpected; stormy, tempestuous.

intendent [inten'dent] *nm* administrator, manager, steward.

intens [in'tens] *adj* intense; (*d. durere*) severe; (*puternic*) strong, powerful; (*d. culori*) deep (blue); (*d. tir*) heavy; (*d. circulație*) heavy, dense || *adv* intensely.

intensifica [intensifi'ka] *vt/vr* to intensify • ~re *nf* intensification.

intensitate [intensi'tate] *nf* intensity, intenseness; (*a luminii*) brightness; (*a sunetului*) loudness; (*a vântului*) force; (*a culorilor*) depth; (*a frigului*) severity; (*a curentului*) strength.

intenta [inten'ta] *vt* (*o acțiune cuiva*) to take action against smb; to bring smb to law; to sue smb (at law); to open an action/case against smb.

intenție [in'tentsie] *nf* intention, design; *jur* intent; (*țel*) purpose, aim; (*dorință*) wish, will; **cu** ~ deliberately.

intenționa [intentsio'na] *vt* to plan, to intend, to mean • ~l *adj jur* intentional, deliberate.

interacțiune [interaktsi'une] *nf* interaction.

interbelic [inter'belik] *adj* interwar.

intercala [interka'la] *vt* to insert, to interpolate || *vr* to be inserted/interpolated • ~re *nf* insertion, interpolation.

intercepta [interchep'ta] *vt* to intercept, to tap • ~re *nf* interception, tap(ping).

interdicție [inter'diktsie] *nf* interdiction, ban, prohibition; *jur* incapacity, interdict.

interes [inte'res] *nn* interest; (*beneficiu*) benefit; (*avantaj*) advantage; importance, significance.

interesa [intere'sa] *vt* to interest; (*a privi*) to concern, to bear on; to implicate; (*a fi interesant pentru*) to be interesting to || *vi* to matter, to be material || *vr* (*a arăta interes pentru*) to be interested (in smth); (*a se ocupa cu/de*) to concern oneself with; (*a băga în seamă*) to take notice of; (*a se informa d. cineva*) to inquire for/after smb; (*a se informa de ceva*) to inquire about.

interesant [intere'sant] *adj* interesting; (*amuzant*) amusing; (*atrăgător*) attractive; (*ciudat*) strange; **puțin** ~ dull, uninteresting.

interfață [inter'fatsă] *nf chem, phys, comp* interface.

interimar [interi'mar] *adj* ad interim, temporary.

interior [interi'or] *nn* interior, inside; (*locuință*) dwelling; (*casă*) house; (*teritoriul*) inland; (*la telefon*) extension || *adj* internal; (*d. un spațiu*) interior, inner; (*lăuntric*) inward; **comerț** ~ home trade • **în** ~**ul (casei)** inside (the house), within;.

interjecție [inter'zhektsie] *nf gram* interjection.

interlocutor [interloku'tor] *nm* interlocutor, collocutor; (*vorbitor*) speaker.

interludiu [inter'ludiu] *nn* interlude.

intermedia [intermedi'a] *vt* * **mijloci**.

intermediar [intermedi'ar] *nm* intermediary, mediator; *com* middleman; *pej coll* pander(er), pimp || *adj* intermediate, intermediary.

intermediu [inter'mediu] *nn* agency, mediation, intercession.

interminabil [intermi'nabil] *adj* endless, interminable || *adv* endlessly, interminably.

intermitent [intermi'tent] *adj* intermittent, periodic; (*neregulat*) irregular || *adv* intermittently, periodically, irregularly.

intern [in'tern] *nm* (*elev*) boarder; *med* resident, intern || *adj* internal; (*lăuntric*) inner, interior; *pol* home, domestic • ~**a** *vt* (*în spital*) to hospitalize, to admit to a hospital; (*a închide la ospiciu*) to confine || *vr* to go

to hospital • ~**at** *nn edu* boarding school; *med* internship, residency || *adj* interned, hospitalized.

internațional [internatsio'nal] *adj* international, world; *mus* the Internationale.

internist [inter'nist] *nm med* internist, specialist in internal medicine.

interoga [intero'ga] *vt* to examine; *jur* to interrogate, to question, to cross examine; *edu* to give an exam; *coll* to grill; to query • ~**re** *nf jur* interrogation, examination; *edu* oral test • ~**toriu** *nn jur* interrogatory, cross-examination, questioning.

interpela [interpe'la] *vt* to interpellate • ~**re**, ~**ție** *nf* interpellation, question(ing).

interpola [interpo'la] *vt* to interpolate, to insert, to introduce • ~**re** *nf* interpolation, insert, insertion.

interpret [inter'pret] *nm* interpreter; (*traducător*) translator; (*artist*) performer • ~**a** *vt* to interpret; to construe; **a** ~ **bine/corect** to interpret/understand correctly; (*a explica*) to explain; (*un text*) to expound; (*a juca teatru*) to perform • ~**are** *nf* interpretation, explanation; *mus* interpretation, rendition; *also thea* acting.

interpune [inter'pune] *vr* to interpose, to intervene; (*a se amesteca*) to interfere, to meddle.

intersecta [intersek'ta] *vt/vr* to intersect, to cross.

intersecție [inter'sektsie] *nf* intersection, crossing (point), crossroad.

interurban [interur'ban] *adj* interurban; (*d. convorbiri telefonice*) long-distance (call).

interval [inter'val] *nn* interval, distance; (*spațiu*) space; *mus* interval; (*de timp*) period, lapse of time; (*loc gol*) gap; (*culoar*) aisle.

interveni [interve'ni] *vi* to intervene; (*a se interpune*) to interpose, to step in; (*într-o conversație*) to break in (on); *coll* to chime/cut/butt in; (*a se băga*) to interfere, to meddle; (*în favoarea*) to intercede; to plead with smb for smb/smth; (*a se întâmpla*) to happen, to occur; *med* (*a opera*) to operate.

intervenție [inter'ventsie] *nf* intervention; (*în favoarea cuiva*) intercession; *coll* wangle; *med* ~ **chirurgicală** surgery, surgical operation; (*luare de cuvânt*) speech.

interviu [inter'viu] *nn* interview.

interzice [inter'ziche] *vt* to forbid, to bar; *jur, relig* to interdict; (*un partid, o organizație*) to ban; (*vânzarea unui produs*) to prohibit || *vr* to be forbidden, etc. • ~**re** *nf* ban, prohibition, interdiction.

interzis [inter'zis] *nm jur* convict under judicial disability || *adj* forbidden, prohibited; (*în constr. eliptice*) **no ... fumatul** ~ no smoking • **parcarea** ~**ă** no park(ing here); **staționarea** ~**ă** no stopping/waiting; **zonă** ~**ă** prohibited area; (*subiect* ~) taboo.

intestin [intes'tin] *nn anat* intestine, bowel; *coll* gut || *adj frml* internal, domestic, civil.

intim ['intim] *nm* close friend || *adj* intimate; (*apropiat*) close; familiar; (*prietenos*) friendly; (*retras*) private; (*lăuntric*) interior, innermost; (*d. un înțeles*) inner; (*d. o convingere*) inward, deep-seated || *adv* intimately, closely; (*îndeaproape*) familiarly, well; (*retras*) privately.

intimida [intimi'da] *vt* to intimidate, to frighten, to bully; (*a amenința*) to threaten || *vr* to get nervous, to become self-conscious • ~**re** *nf* intimidation; * **intimida**.

intimitate [intimi'tate] *nf* intimacy, privacy; (*apropiere sufletească*) closeness; *pl* secrets.

intitula [intitu'la] *vt* to entitle, to give a title to || *vr* to be entitled; to call oneself.

intolerabil [intole'rabil] *adj* intolerable, unbearable, insufferable || *adv* intolerably, unbearably, insufferably.

intoleranță [intole'rantsă] *nf* intolerance; *med* inability to tolerate a remedy.

intona [into'na] *vt* to strike up, to break into (song) • ~ție *nf* intonation.

intoxica [intoksi'ka] *vt* to intoxicate, to poison || *vr* to be(come) intoxicated/poisoned.

intoxicație [intoksi'katsie] *nf* intoxication, poisoning.

intra [in'tra] *vi* to enter, to go in, to come in, to walk/step in; a ~ în acțiune *mil* to go into action/battle; *fig* to start operating; a ~ în funcțiune (*d. cineva*) to take up one's duties/post; to enter upon/begin one's duties; (*d. o instalație*) to be set/going into motion; (*a fi dată în folosință*) to be commissioned; to be put into commission; a ~ în vigoare to come into effect; to take effect; to become effective/operative • intră! come in!.

intransigent [intransi'djent] *adj* relentless, strict, uncompromising; (*d. ton*) peremptory.

intranzitiv [intranzi'tiv] *adj gram* intransitive.

intrare [in'trare] *nf* entrance, entry; (*hol*) entrance hall; (*acces*) admittance, admission; (*acțiunea*) entering, coming; (*fundătură*) (blind) alley • ~a interzisă (*pt. public*) Private; ~a interzisă (*pe un teren*) No trespassing, Trespassers will be prosecuted; ~a în vigoare coming into force/effect.

intrepid [intre'pid] *adj* intrepid, dauntless, bold, fearless.

intriga [intri'ga] *vt* to intrigue, to puzzle • ~nt *nm* schemer • *adj* designing, intriguing, scheming.

intrigă ['intrigă] *nf* machination, intrigue, scheme; *liter* (*acțiune*) plot.

intrinsec [intrin'sek] *adj* intrinsic || *adv* intrinsically.

introduce [intro'duche] *vt* to introduce; (*a insera*) to insert; (*a pune*) to put; (*mărfuri*) to bring in; (*a lăsa să intre*) to admit, to let in; (*un străin*) to present, to show/usher in; (*o modă*) to launch || *vr* to enter, to get in; (*a fi introdus*) to be introduced, etc. • ~re *nf* introduction; insertion, admission; (*prefață*) preface, foreword; (*la o scrisoare*) salutation.

introvertit [introver'tit] *adj psych, med* introvert(ed) || *nm* introvert.

intrus [in'trus] *nm* intruder, interloper; *coll* gate-crasher; *jur* trespasser.

intui [intu'i] *vt* to infer, to intuit, to guess.

intuiție [intu'itsie] *nf* intuition.

inuman [inu'man] *adj* (*care nu e uman*) inhuman; (*crud*) inhumane, cruel, savage || *adv* inhumanely, savagely.

inunda [inun'da] *vt* to flood, to inundate, to overflow; *fig* (*d. piață*) to glut; (*d. lumină*) to flood; (*a copleși*) to overwhelm • ~bil *adj* liable to inundation/flooding; easily flooded • ~ție *nf* flood, flooding.

inutil [inu'til] *adj* (*d. muncă*) useless; (*fără profit*) unprofitable; (*zadarnic*) unavailing, futile; (*d. eforturi*) vain; (*d. cheltuieli*) wasteful; e ~! it's no good! || *adv* uselessly, needlessly, in vain • ~itate *nf* inutility, uselessness, futility; (*lipsă de necesitate*) needlessness.

inutilizabil [inutili'zabil] *adj* unusable, useless, worthless; (*d. cineva*) unemployable.

invada [inva'da] *vt* (*o țară*) *also fig* to invade, to overrun; (*o sală*) to break into; (*d. apă*) to flood; (*d.*

buruieni) to overrun; (*a încălca*) to encroach (upon); (*a acoperi*) to cover • ~tor *nm* invader.

invalid [inva'lid] *nm* cripple, invalid || *adj* invalid, infirm; (*d. un soldat*) disabled.

invalida [invali'da] *vt jur* (*alegeri*) to invalidate, to quash; (*un membru*) to unseat.

invaliditate [invalidi'tate] *nf* invalidity, disability.

invariabil [invari'abil] *adj* invariable, unchanging || *adv* invariably.

invazie [in'vazie] *nf* invasion, inroad; infestation.

invectivă [invek'tivă] *nf* invective, *pl* abuse.

inventa [inven'ta] *vt* to invent; (*a descoperi*) to discover; (*o mașină, un plan*) to devise, to contrive; *fig* (*o poveste, minciună*) to fabricate, to make up; (*o acuzație*) to trump up; (*o scuză*) to dream up; (*o expresie*) to coin.

inventar [inven'tar] *nn* inventory; list; catalog; *com* stocklist; survey • ~ia *vt* to catalog, to inventory, to take stock; to take an account of; to be inventoried.

inventator [inventa'tor] *nm* inventor, discoverer.

inventiv [inven'tiv] *adj* inventive, ingenious, resourceful • ~itate *nf* inventiveness, resourcefulness, adroitness.

invenție [in'ventsie] *nf* invention; (*descoperire*) discovery; inventiveness, imagination; *fig* (*minciună*) fabrication, lie, (false) story.

invers ['invers] *adj* inverse, inverted, reverse; (*opus*) opposite, converse || *adv* conversely, inversely; (*pe dos*) the wrong/other way (round); (*d. o haină*) inside out, the wrong side on; (*cu fundul în sus*) upside down; (*cu spatele în față*) back to front; ~ proporțional cu in inverse proportion to, inversely proportional to • ~a *vt* to invert, to reverse || *vr* to be inverted • ~are *nf* inversion, reversal.

investi [inves'ti] *vt* (*bani*) to invest; (*în funcție*) to install; (*cu drepturi*) to vest (smb) • ~ție *nf* investment; *pl* vested interests.

investiga [investi'ga] *vt* to investigate, to examine, to inquire (into) • ~ție *nf* investigation, inquiry.

inveterat [invete'rat] *adj* inveterate, confirmed, ingrained; *coll* die-hard.

invidia [invidi'a] *vt* to envy, to be envious of; (*a râvni*) to covet.

invidie [in'vidie] *nf* envy, covetousness.

invidios [invidi'os] *adj* (*pe*) envious (of); (*pizmaș*) covetous || *adv* enviously.

invincibil [invin'chibil] *adj* invincible, unconquerable.

inviolabil [invio'labil] *adj* inviolable; (*sacru*) sacred.

invita [invi'ta] *vt* (*la*) to invite (smb to), to ask (to); (*a convoca*) to summon; (*a ispiti*) to tempt • ~t *nm* guest • ~ție *nf* invitation; (*bilet*) invitation card.

invizibil [invi'zibil] *adj* invisible, unseen • ~itate *nf* invisibility.

invoca [invo'ka] *vt* to invoke, to call forth; (*a motiva prin*) to plead; (*o scuză*) to make an excuse • ~re *nf* invocation.

involuntar [involun'tar] *adj* involuntary; (*neintenționat*) unintentional, unwilling || *adv* involuntarily, unintentionally.

involuție [invo'lutsie] *nf* involution.

invulnerabil [invulne'rabil] *adj* invulnerable; *fig* watertight.

iobag [io'bag] *nm hist* serf; villain.

iod [iod] *nn chem* iodine.

iolă ['iolă] *nf* yawl.

ion [ion] *nm phys* ion.
iordanian(ă) [iordani'an(ă)] *nm/nf/adj geog* Jordanian.
iotă ['iotă] *nf* jot; **nici o ~** *coll* not a jot/whit.
ipocrit [ipo'krit] *nm* hypocrite, double-dealer || *adj* hypocritical, false, deceitful || *adv* hypocritically.
ipocrizie [ipokri'zie] *nf* hypocrisy, double-dealing, cant.
ipohondru [ipo'hondru] *nm* hypochondriac.
ipostază [ipos'tază] *nf* hypostasis; aspect; *(stare)* state.
ipoteca [ipote'ka] *vt* to mortgage.
ipotecă [ipo'tekă] *nf* mortgage.
ipotetic [ipo'tetik] *adj* hypothetical, assumed || *adv* hypotehetically.
ipoteză [ipo'teză] *nf* hypothesis, assumption, conjecture.
ipsos ['ipsos] *nn* plaster.
iradia [iradi'a] *vt* to irradiate.
iradiere [iradi'ere] *nf phys* irradiation.
irakian [iraki'an] *nm/adj geog* Iraqi.
iranian [irani'an] *nm/adj geog* Iranian.
irascibil [iras'chibil] *adj* irascible, irritable, testy; *coll* quick-tempered || *adv* irascibly, etc. • **~itate** *nf* irascibility, irritability, testiness, quick temper.
iraţional [iratsio'nal] *adj* irrational, illogical, absurd || *adv* irrationally.
ireal [ire'al] *adj* unreal.
irealizabil [ireali'zabil] *adj* impossible, unattainable.
ireconciliabil [irekonchili'abil] *adj* irreconcilable, incompatible.
irecuperabil [irekupe'rabil] *adj* irretrievable, irremediable.
iredentism [ireden'tism] *nn pol* irredentism.
iregularitate [iregulari'tate] *nf* irregularity.
irelevant [irele'vant] *adj* irrelevant, unimportant.
iremediabil [iremedi'abil] *adj* (*d. pierderi*) irremediable; (*d. boală*) incurable; (*d. un rău*) irreparable || *adv* irremediably, irreparably, beyond/past reprieve.
ireparabil [irepa'rabil] *adj/nn* (*d. un rău*) irreparable; (*d. pierderi, greşeli*) irretrievable; beyond repair.
ireproşabil [irepro'shabil] *adj* irreproachable; faultless, flawless || *adv* irreproachably, faultlessly, perfectly.
iresponsabil [irespon'sabil] *adj* irresponsible, reckless.
ireverenţios [ireverentsi'os] *adj* impolite, irreverent, disrespectful || *adv* impolitely, irreverently, disrespectfully.
ireversibil [irever'sibil] *adj* irreversible, irrevocable.
irevocabil [irevo'kabil] *adj* irrevocable, unalterable || *adv* irrevocably.
irezistibil [irezis'tibil] *adj* irresistible, overpowering, fascinating || *adv* irresistibly.
iridiu [i'ridiu] *nn chem* iridium.
iriga [iri'ga] *vt agr* to irrigate, to water; *med* to spray || *vr* to be irrigated • **~re** *nf agr* irrigation; *med* spraying.
iris ['iris] *nm bot* iris, flag || *nn anat* iris.
irita [iri'ta] *vt* (*a enerva*) to annoy, to irritate, to provoke; (*nervii*) to get on (one's nerves); (*d. o rană*) to inflame || *vr* (*a se supăra*) to get annoyed/angry with smb/at smth; to fret; (*d. o rană*) to become irritated/ inflamed • **~bil** *adj* irritable, petulant • **~nt** *adj* irritating, exasperating; *coll* aggravating; *med* irritating • **~re** *nf* irritation, annoyance, anger; *med* inflammation; (*prin frecare*) chafe; soreness.
irlandez [irlan'dez] *nm* Irishman || *adj* Irish • **~ă** *nf* Irishwoman; (*limba*) Irish.
ironic [i'ronik] *adj* ironical || *adv* ironically.
ironie [iro'nie] *nf* irony, banter, chaff.

ironiza [ironi'za] *vt* to banter, to speak ironically, to be ironical.
irosi [iro'si] *vt* to waste, to squander, to fritter away.
irupe [i'rupe] *vi* to irrupt, to intrude; to erupt, to burst out; to overflow.
irupţie [i'ruptsie] *nf* eruption, irruption; (*d. apă*) overflow, flood, inrush.
isca [is'ka] *vt* to arouse, to cause; (*a începe*) to begin, to start || *vr* to arise; (*a începe*) to begin, to start, to break out.
iscăli [iskă'li] *vt/vi* to sign || *vr* to sign; to be signed • **~tură** *nf* signature.
iscoadă [is'koadă] *nf* (*spion*) spy; *mil* lookout.
iscodi [isko'di] *vt* to probe, to pry (into); to examine (closely); (*a spiona*) to spy; (*a născoci*) to invent, to imagine; (*a scorni*) to fabricate; (*a descoase*) to sound, *coll* to pump || *vi* to investigate, to inquire; (*cu ochii*) to peer, to scan.
iscusinţă [isku'sintsă] *nf* skill, ability; talent; art.
iscusit [isku'sit] *adj* skillful, adroit; (*deştept*) cute, clever; (*învăţat*) learned; (*d. lucruri*) clean || *adv* skillfully.
islam [is'lam] *nn* Islam.
islandez(ă) [islan'dez(ă)] *nm/nf geog* Icelander || *nf ling* Icelandic.
islaz [is'laz] *nn* common.
ispăşi [ispă'shi] *vt* to atone (for), to expiate • **~re** *nf* atonement, expiation.
ispită [is'pită] *nf* temptation.
ispiti [ispi'ti] *vt* to tempt; (*a ademeni*) to lure • **~tor** *adj* tempting, luring, enticing; (*atrăgător*) attractive.
ispravă [is'pravă] *nf* (*faptă*) deed; (*faptă eroică*) feat; (*aventură*) adventure; *iro* business, job; (*realizare*) success, achievement; (*poznă*) prank, trick; **de ~** (*vrednic*) worthy, reliable; capable; (*cinstit*) honest; (*bun*) kindhearted.
isprăvi [ispră'vi] *vt* to finish, to end; (*un discurs*) to wind up; (*o lucrare*) to complete; (*a pune capăt*) to put an end to; (*a epuiza*) to run out of || *vi* to finish up; (*cu*) to be through with || *vr* to be all over, to end.
israelit [izrae'lit] *adj* Israeli, Hebrew, Jewish; (*din statul Israel*) Israeli || *nm* Israelite, Hebrew, Jew.
isteric [is'terik] *adj* hysteric(al) || *adv* hysterically || *nm* hysteric, hysterical person.
isterie [iste'rie] *nf med* hysteria; **~ colectivă** mass hysteria.
isteţ [is'tets] *adj* clever, bright, smart; *coll* brainy, sharp; cunning; *iro sl* wise.
istm [istm] *nn geog* isthmus.
istoric [is'torik] *nm* historian || *adj* (*privind istoria*) historical; (*de importanţă istorică*) historic, momentous.
istorie [is'torie] *nf* history; (*poveste*) story, tale, narrative; (*încurcătură*) sad tale.
istorisi [istori'si] *vt* to narrate, to tell • **~re** *nf* narration, narrative.
istovi [isto'vi] *vt* (*a epuiza*) to exhaust; (*a obosi*) to wear out, to tire out; *coll* to fag out || *vr* to be(come) exhausted/tired/worn out; *coll* to be knocked up • **~tor** *adj* exhausting, weary, tiring.
Isus [I'sus] *nm* Jesus • **~e Hristoase!** God Almighty!.
italian [itali'an] *nm/adj* Italian • **~ă** *nf ling* Italian, the Italian language • **~că** *nf* Italian (woman/girl).
italic [i'talik] *adj typ* italic.
itinerant [itine'rant] *adj* itinerant.
itinerar [itine'rar] *nn* itinerary, route, way.

iţă ['itsă] *nf* thread; (*dispozitiv*) heddle, heald.

iubi [iu'bi] *vt* to love, to be in love with; (*a-i plăcea*) to like, to care for; **a ~ la nebunie (pe cineva)** to love madly, to love to distraction; to be madly/passionately in love with; to have a crush on; to be nuts over, to be crazy about, to be infatuated with || *vr* (*reciproc*) to be in love (with each other) • **~re** *nf* love, affection, passion • **~t** *nm* sweetheart, lover || *adj* beloved; (*drag*) dear; favorite • **~tă** *nf* sweetheart; *coll* flame • **~tor** *adj* loving, affectionate || *adv* lovingly, affectionately.

iulie ['iulie] *nm* July.

iunie ['iunie] *nm* June.

iureş ['iuresh] *nn* (*goană*) rush, race, chase; (*asalt*) assault, storm; (*atac*) attack.

iută ['iută] *nf text* jute.

iute ['iute] *adj* (*vioi, sprinten*) swift, brisk; agile, nimble; (*de scurtă durată*) quick; (*care se termină repede*) fast; (*pripit*) rash, hasty; (*nervos*) quick-/hot-tempered; (*ardeiat*) hot, spicy; (*piperat*) peppery; (*d. brânză*) strong || *adv* swiftly, quickly, fast.

iuţeală [iu'tseală] *nf* speed, swiftness; *fig* cleverness; **~ de mână** sleight of hand.

iuţi [iu'tsi] *vt* to speed up, to hasten; **a ~ pasul** to quicken one's pace; (*d. mâncare*) to pepper || *vr* to quicken, to become fast/quicker; (*d. gust*) to go bad, to spoil; (*a se mânia*) to go into a temper, to fly off the handle.

ivi [i'vi] *vr* (*a-şi face apariţia*) to make one's appearance; to turn up; (*a se arăta*) to show oneself; (*neclar*) to loom; (*brusc*) to pop.

ivoriu [i'voriu] *nn* ivory.

iz [iz] *nn* reek, smack; *fig* touch, taste, flavor.

izbăvi [izbă'vi] *vt* to deliver, to save, to rescue; *relig* to redeem || *vr* to be saved • **~re** *nf* salvation; *relig* redemption.

izbândă [iz'bândă] *nf* success, victory, triumph.

izbândi [izbân'di] *vt* to succeed (in), to be successful.

izbi [iz'bi] *vt* (*a lovi*) to hit, to strike; (*cu pumnul*) to punch; (*la pământ*) to knock (down); (*a azvârli*) to throw, to fling; *fig* to strike || *vr* (*de*) to strike (against); *fig* to come up against • **~tor** *adj* striking.

izbitură [izbi'tură] *nf* knock(ing), blow.

izbucni [izbuk'ni] *vi* (*d. incendii, război, furtună*) *also fig* to break out; (*d. flăcări*) to burst/blaze out • **~re** *nf* outbreak; (*de mânie*) outburst.

izbuti [izbu'ti] *vt* to manage (to do smth), to succeed (in doing smth) || *vi* to succeed, to be successful.

izgoni [izgo'ni] *vt* to drive away/out; (*din casă*) to turn out; (*a surghiuni*) to banish.

izlaz [iz'laz] *nn* (village) common.

izmă ['izmă] *nf bot* horsemint, peppermint.

izmeni [izme'ni] *vr* to mince, to be finical/finicky.

izola [izo'la] *vt* (*de*) to isolate (from); *med* to quarantine; *elec* to insulate; (*acustic*) to sound proof || *vr* to live in seclusion; to separate/seclude oneself; to live apart; *pass* to be isolated/secluded; *elec* to be insulated • **~nt** *adj* ling isolating; *elec* insulating || *nm* insulator • **~re** *nf* isolation; (*singurătate*) loneliness, seclusion; *elec* insulation; **~ acustică/fonică** sound proofing • **~ţie** *nf elec* insulation.

izvor [iz'vor] *nn* spring; (*sursă*) source.

izvorî [izvo'rî] *vi* to rise, to spring; (*a ţâşni*) to gush out; (*a curge*) to flow; *fig* (*a proveni din*) to arise (from); to derive (from); to rise; (*a apărea*) to appear.

î

îhî [î'hî] *interj coll* yah, yeah, yes.

îmbarca [îmbar'ka] *vt naut* (*călători*) to embark; (*mărfuri*) to ship; (*în tren*) *mil* to entrain; (*călători*) to put on; *avia* to emplane || *vr* to embark, to ship, to board; *avia* to emplane, to board aircraft • **~re** *nf* embarking; shipment, shipping; *mil* (*în tren*) entrainment; boarding, going on board.

îmbăia [îmbă'ia] *vt* to wash, to give (smb) a bath || *vr* to bathe, to take/have a bath.

îmbălsăma [îmbălsă'ma] *vt* (*aerul*) to scent, to perfume; (*un cadavru*) to embalm • **~t** *adj* balmy, fragrant, scented; **aer ~** balmy air; (*d. cadavre*) embalmed.

îmbărbăta [îmbărbă'ta] *vt* to encourage, to cheer up.

îmbăta [îmbă'ta] *vt* to make smb drunk; *fig* to intoxicate, to elate || *vr* to get drunk/intoxicated/inebriated; *coll* to get screwed/tight/fuddled.

îmbătător [îmbătă'tor] *adj fig* (*ameţitor*) intoxicating, heady; (*încântător*) entrancing.

îmbătrâni [îmbătrâ'ni] *vt* to age || *vi* to age, to grow/get old; (*a arăta bătrân*) to look old(er); (*d. vin*) to mature.

îmbâcsi [îmbâk'si] *vt* to make (smth) stuffy/stale; (*a umple*) to fill up, to cram || *vr* to be/get stuffy/stale • **~t** *adj* (*d. aer*) close, stuffy; (*murdar*) dirty; (*prăfuit*) dusty; (*îndesat, ticsit*) crammed.

îmbelşugare [îmbelshu'gare] *nf* plenty, abundance, wealth.

îmbelşugat [îmbelshu'gat] *adj* plentiful, abundant; (*bogat*) rich; (*roditor*) fruitful.

îmbia [îmbi'a] *vt* (*a îndemna pe cineva să facă ceva*) to urge; (*să primească ceva*) to invite; (*a atrage*) to attract; (*a ispiti*) to lure; *recip* to invite each other.

îmbiba [îmbi'ba] *vt* to soak, to steep (into), to imbue (with) || *vr* (*cu/de*) to soak (in), to sink in, to be imbued (with).

îmbietor [îmbie'tor] *adj* inviting; (*atrăgător*) attractive; (*ademenitor*) alluring, enticing.

îmbina [îmbi'na] *vt* to join, to unite; to combine, to blend; (*a lega*) to connect, to tie; (*a potrivi*) to arrange || *vr* to join, to blend, to combine; (*a se potrivi*) to fit, to dovetail.

îmblăni [îmblă'ni] *vt* to line with fur, to cover/coat with fur.

îmblânzi [îmblân'zi] *vt* to tame, to domesticate; (*a dresa*) to train; *fig* to subdue; (*un copil*) to make tractable; (*a linişti*) to calm, to placate; (*a face mai sociabil*) to make more sociable || *vr* to become/grow tame; to become tractable; to calm down • **~tor** *nm* tamer.

îmboboci [îmbobo'chi] *vi* (*a face boboci*) to bud, to be out; *fig* to blossom.

îmbogăţi [îmbogă'tsi] *vt also phys* to enrich || *vr* to grow rich(er); to make a fortune; to coin/make money; to feather one's nest; (*d. o limbă*) to grow/become richer • **~re** *nf* enrichment, enriching; *phys* enrichment (of uranium).

îmboldi [îmbol'di] *vt* (*d. animale*) to goad (on), to spur; *fig* to urge (on), to hurry; to stimulate, to prod.

îmbolnăvi [îmbolnă'vi] *vt* to render/make sick, to sicken || *vr* to sicken, to fall ill.

îmbrăca [îmbră'ka] *vt* (*o haină*) to put on; (*pe cineva*) to dress, to clothe; *lit* (*luxos, elegant*) to array; (*a acoperi, a înveli*) to cover, to wrap (up) || *vr* to dress (oneself); (*d. profesori, judecători*) to robe; (*a se costuma*) to dress up.

îmbrăcăminte [îmbrăkă'minte] *nf* clothes, clothing, garments; *constr* covering, lining.

îmbrățișa [îmbrătsi'sha] *vt* to hug, to embrace, to clasp smb in one's arms; *fig* (*a cuprinde*) to take in; (*a învălui*) to wrap; (*d. idei*) to uphold; (*o profesie, carieră*) to take up; *recip* to embrace, to hug one another.

îmbrânci [îmbrân'chi] *vt* to jostle, to push, to thrust; *recip* to push/jostle one another.

îmbrobodi [îmbrobo'di] *vt* to wrap (up) one's head; *coll* (*a înșela*) to dupe, to take in || *vr* to wrap up (one's head).

îmbuca [îmbu'ka] *vt* to clamp; (*a mânca*) to eat, to have; (*a înfuleca*) to gobble up; (*a înghiți*) to swallow || *vr* (*a se îmbina*) to dovetail; *recip* to interlock; (*d. roți*) to catch, to mesh.

îmbucățți [îmbukătă'tsi] *vt* to cut into pieces; (*a mărunți*) to mince; (*a parcela*) to parcel out; (*a împărți*) to divide.

îmbucurător [îmbukură'tor] *adj* glad(dening); (*plăcut*) pleasant, gratifying; (*bun*) good.

îmbufna [îmbuf'na] *vr coll* to sulk, to be sulky, to pout • ~t *adj* sulky, pouting, sullen.

îmbuiba [îmbui'ba] *vt* to gorge, to stuff, to cram; *frml* to satiate || *vr* to gorge/stuff/cram oneself; *coll* to tuck in; *frml* to surfeit oneself with • ~t *adj* satiated, surfeited.

îmbujora [îmbuzho'ra] *vr* to blush, to flush, to redden • ~t *adj* blushing, flushed, glowing; florid; (*roșu*) red; hectic.

îmbulzeală [îmbul'zeală] *nf* crush, crowd, throng, cram.

îmbulzi [îmbul'zi] *vr* to throng, to crowd, to press; (*a se repezi*) to rush; (*a se împinge*) to jostle/push one another.

îmbuna [îmbu'na] *vt* (*a liniști*) to appease, to placate; to quieten down; to tone down; (*a îmblânzi*) to tame, to subdue; (*a împăca*) to reconcile || *vr* to calm down, to compose oneself; (*d. vreme*) to cheer/clear up.

îmbunătăți [îmbunătă'tsi] *vt* to improve, to better || *vr* to improve, to get/become better; to mend • ~re *nf* improvement, improving, bettering.

îmbutelia [îmbuteli'a] *vt* to bottle.

împacheta [împake'ta] *vt also med* to pack; (*a înfășura*) to wrap • ~re *nf* (*ambalare*) packing (up); *med* (*învelire*) pack.

împăca [împă'ka] *vt* (*a îmbuna*) to pacify, to calm down, to placate; (*persoane*) to reconcile; (*un diferend*) to settle; (*a satisface*) to satisfy; to console, to soothe, to comfort || *vr* (*a redeveni prieteni*) to become reconciled; *coll* to make it up; to bury the hatchet; (*a cădea de acord*) to agree; (*a se înțelege cu*) to get along/on with; (*a se resemna cu*) to reconcile oneself with; **a se ~ cu** (*a nu mai fi certat cu*) to be reconciled with; (*d. idei*) to agree with, to chime in with; (*a se obișnui cu*) to accustom oneself to, to get used/accustomed to • ~re *nf* reconciliation * **împăca**.

împăciuitor [împăchui'tor] *adj* conciliatory, placatory, propitiatory.

împăduri [împădu'ri] *vt* to afforest • ~re *nf* afforestation.

împăia [împă'ia] *vt* to stuff (a dead animal).

împăienjeni [împăienzhe'ni] *vr* to cover with cobweb(s); *fig* (*d. ochi, vedere*) to grow dim/hazy/blurred.

împământeni [împământe'ni] *vi* to naturalize || *vr* to naturalize; to take root; to adapt/adjust/accommodate oneself.

împăna [împă'na] *vt* to put strips/pieces of fat/garlic cloves into; (*cu slănină*) to lard; *fig* to interlard; to fill, to cram; *tech* to key, to wedge, to shim.

împărat [împă'rat] *nm* emperor; (*rege*) king.

împărăteasă [împără'teasă] *nf* empress; (*regină*) queen.

împărăție [împără'tsie] *nf* empire; (*regat*) kingdom; *obs* sway; *fig* realm.

împărtășanie [împărtă'shanie] *nf relig* Eucharist, sacrament.

împărtăși [împărtă'shi] *vt* (*a comunica*) to impart; (*bucurii, soarta, păreri*) to share; *relig* to give smb the eucharist || *vr relig* to receive the eucharist.

împărți [împăr'tsi] *vt math* (*la*) to divide (by); (*în, între, la*) to divide (into, between, among); (*profituri*) to share (out); (*proprietate*) to apportion, to parcel out; (*a distribui*) to distribute; (*a aloca*) to allot; (*scrisori*) to deliver; (*cărțile de joc*) to deal out; (*pomană*) to give hand-outs; (*premii*) to give out; (*roluri*) to cast; (*a împărtăși*) to share (in) || *vr* to divide, to separate; to fall into categories • ~re *nf math* division; distribution • ~tor *nm math* divisor.

împătri [împă'tri] *vt* to quadruple, to quadruplicate || *vr* to quadruple • ~t *adj/adv* fourfold, quadruple, quadruplicate.

împături [împătu'ri] *vt* to fold (up); (*a înveli*) to wrap up.

împăuna [împău'na] *vr* to boast, to brag, to swagger.

împerechea [impere'kea] *vt* to pair, to match; (*animale*) to couple, to mate; to twin || *vr* to pair, to mate.

împerechere [impere'kere] *nf* pairing, matching; *zool* mating; twinning.

împestrițat [împestri'tsat] *adj* mottled, speckled, spotted.

împiedica [împiedi'ka] *vt* (*un cal*) to hobble; (*a frâna*) to brake; *fig* to hinder, to prevent, to impede || *vr* also *fig* (*de*) to stumble over/against smth, to trip (over smth).

împielițat [împieli'tsat] *nm* the devil; *coll* Old Nick || *adj* devilish, accursed; (*neastâmpărat*) naughty.

împietrit [împie'trit] *adj* (*prefăcut în piatră*) turned to stone; *fig* callous, insensible; (*încremenit*) dumbfounded, flabbergasted, stunned.

împila [împi'la] *vt* to oppress, to grind down, to tyrannize.

împinge [îm'pindje] *vt* to push, to shove, to thrust; *fig* (*a îndemna*) to goad, to drive, to urge; *recip* to jostle/push one another.

împlânta [împlân'ta] *vt* (*în*) to thrust, to shove (into); to stick (into).

împleti [împle'ti] *vt* (*a tricota*) to knit; (*a țese*) to weave; (*părul*) to braid; (*o cunună*) to wreathe, to twine; (*nuiele*) to wattle; *fig* to interweave || *vr* to be knitted/woven; *fig* (*a se îmbina*) to intertwine, to interweave, to blend.

împletici [împleti'chi] *vr* (*la mers*) to stagger, to totter; to titubate; (*la vorbă*) to mumble; (*a se bâlbâi*) to stammer, to stutter.

împlini [împli'ni] *vt* (*un gol*) to fill; to complete; (*a îndeplini*) to carry out, to achieve, to accomplish; (*a face*) to perform; (*a satisface*) to fulfil, to satisfy; (*o vârstă*) to be ... years old || *vr* (*a se adeveri*) to come true; (*d. timp: a se scurge*) to pass, to go by; (*a se îngrăşa*) to fill out, to gain/put on weight • ~t *adj* (*d. timp*) full, complete; (*d. cineva*) well filled out, plump.

împodobi [împodo'bi] *vt* to adorn, to decorate; * **înzorzona**; (*d. cineva*) to dress up, to smarten (oneself) up.

împopoţona [împopotso'na] *vt* to adorn (heavily), to dress up gaudily || *vr* to titivate, to trick oneself out.

împotmoli [împotmo'li] *vr* (*d. o roată*) to get stuck; *fig* to come to a dead end; (*într-o explicaţie, discurs*) to flounder • ~re *nf* sinking/sticking in the mud.

împotriva [împo'triva] *prep* against, counter; *jur, sp* versus, vs, v.

împotrivi [împotri'vi] *vr* to oppose, to object, to resist • ~re *nf* opposition, resistance, objection.

împovăra [împovă'ra] *vt* (*cu*) to burden (with), to load (with); (*a copleşi*) to overwhelm.

împovărător [împovără'tor] *adj* burdensome, burdening, overwhelming.

împrăştia [împrăshti'a] *vt* to spread; (*a presăra*) to sprinkle; (*a răspândi*) to disseminate; (*a risipi*) to scatter; (*d. o mulţime*) to disperse, to break up; (*duşmani*) to drive away; (*o armată*) to rout; *fig* (*a alunga: griji*) to dispel || *vr* to spread, to scatter, to disperse; (*d. nori*) *also fig* to dissipate, to break up; (*d. ceaţă*) to lift, to clear away; (*a dispărea*) to vanish • ~t *adj* (*d. populaţie*) scattered, sparse; (*d. case*) straggling; (*distrat*) absentminded, scatterbrained; (*zăpăcit*) giddy, confused; (*dezordonat*) disorderly; (*d. gânduri*) disconnected, incoherent.

împrăştiere [împrăshti'ere] *nf* scattering, spreading; (*d. oameni*) dispersion, dispersal; (*d. o mulţime*) breaking up; (*d. armată*) rout; *phys* diffusion; (*răspândire*) dissemination; (*risipire*) dissipation, vanishing; (*zăpăceală*) absentmindedness, confusion.

împrejmui [împrezhmu'i] *vt* to enclose, to fence in/off; (*a înconjura*) to surround • ~re *nf* enclosure, fence, paling.

împrejur [împre'zhur] *adv* around, about; **de jur ~** round about, all (a)round/about, full circle.

împrejurare [împrezhu'rare] *nf* circumstance, event; (*fapt*) fact; (*întâmplare*) occurrence, incident.

împrejurime [împrezhu'rime] *nf pl* neighborhood, vicinity; (*suburbii*) outskirts.

împresura [împresu'ra] *vt* (*a încercui*) to close in on/upon, to surround; (*a asedia*) to besiege.

împreuna [împreu'na] *vt* to unite, to join; (*a împerechea*) to pair, to couple || *vr* (*a se uni*) to unite; (*a se strânge*) to gather; (*a se împerechea*) to couple, to copulate.

împreună [împre'ună] *adv* (*cu*) together (with); (*a se potrivi*) to go together; to be paired/matched; to match.

împricinat [împrichi'nat] *nm jur* litigant, plaintiff; accused, defendant.

împrieteni [împriete'ni] *vr* (*cu*) to make/become friends (with); *coll* to pal up (with).

împroprietări [împroprietă'ri] *vt* to put in possession of land • ~re *nf* land reform; allotment/distribution of land.

împrospăta [împrospă'ta] *vt also fig* to refresh; (*a înviora*) to revive, to enliven; (*d. cunoştinţe*) to brush up, to polish up.

împroşca [împrosh'ka] *vt* to splash, to spatter, to sprinkle; (*cu pietre*) to rain (stones on); (*cu noroi*) to spat-

ter; *fig* to sling/fling (mud at); to blemish, to blot; to insult, to offend.

împrumut [împru'mut] *nn* borrowing; loan, credit; **a da cu ~** to lend; **a lua cu ~** to borrow • ~a *vt* (*cuiva*) to lend (to smb); **a ~ bani** to lend money; (*de la*) to borrow (from); (*a imita*) to imitate || *vr coll* (*la*) to borrow smth from.

împunge [îm'pundje] *vt* (*a înţepa*) to sting, to prick; (*cu acul pentru a coase*) to stitch; (*cu spada*) to thrust; (*un animal*) to goad, to prod; (*d. un animal*) to horn, to toss; *fig* to nettle, to pique, to taunt; *fig* **a ~ pe cineva** to taunt, to tease smb.

împunsătură [împunsă'tură] *nf* (*înţepătură*) prick, sting; (*de cusătură*) stitch; **o ~ de ac** a stitch; *fig* taunting/spiteful remark, sneer.

împurpura [împurpu'ra] *vr* to purple, to become purple; to blush, to turn crimson.

împuşca [împush'ka] *vt* to shoot (down); (*a trage în*) to shoot at; (*a omorî*) to shoot dead; to execute || *vi* to shoot, to fire; *tech, constr, etc* to blast, to blow up || *vr* to shoot oneself; (*a-şi zbura creierii*) to blow out one's brains.

împuşcătură [împushkă'tură] *nf* shot; (*ca sunet*) report; *tech, constr, min* blast, blow-up.

împuternici [împuterni'chi] *vt* to authorize; (*a delega*) to vest, to commission • ~re *nf* mandate, commission, authorization • ~t *nm* commissioner, authorized agent; representative, proxy.

împuţi [împu'tsi] *vt* to make smth stink, to spoil || *vr* to become stale/foul/offensive, to reek.

împuţina [împutsi'na] *vt* to lessen, to diminish, to decrease; (*d. corp*) to emaciate; (*d. populaţie*) to thin out || *vr* to diminish, to decrease; to thin out, to whittle down; (*d. profituri*) to fall off; to dwindle.

în [în] *prep* (*spaţial*) (*static*) in, at; **e ~ casă** he is in the house; (*dinamic*) into; **vino ~ casă** come into the house; (*într-un spaţiu*) in, within; (*temporal*) (*pt. date, zile, părţi ale zilei*) on; **~ ziua aceea** (on) that day; **~t-ro zi** (*în trecut*) one day, once; (*în viitor*) some day; (*pt. lună, anotimp, an*) in; **~ iunie** in June; (*după*) in, after; (*în decursul*) within; (*instrument, relaţie*) in.

înadins [îna'dins] *adv* purposely, on purpose, deliberately.

înainta [înain'ta] *vt* to advance; (*o propunere, cerere*) to submit, to put forward; (*o plângere*) to lodge; (*a trimite*) to send (off); (*a promova*) to promote || *vi* (*a avansa*) *also fig* to advance; to head towards; to progress, to make headway; *mil* to be on the offensive; (*a promova*) to be promoted; (*d. un promontoriu*) to jut out.

înaintaş [înain'tash] *nm* precursor, forerunner, predecessor; *sp* forward; trail-blazer, pioneer.

înainte [îna'inte] *adv* (*spaţial*) forward; (*în faţă*) ahead, in front; (*temporal*) (*în trecut*) before; (*mai departe*) on; **~ de** before, prior to; *lit* ere; (*mai devreme*) earlier.

înaintea [îna'intea] *prep* (*spaţial*) before; (*în faţa*) in front of; (*temporal*) before, prior to; (*în avans faţă de*) ahead of.

înalt [î'nalt] *nn* high || *adj* high; (*d. oameni, copaci*) tall; (*d. stânci, clădiri*) towering; *mus* high(-pitched); *elec, tech* high; *fig* lofty; grand, superior, eminent.

înapoi [îna'poi] *adv* (*în spate*) back; (*ca direcţie*) backwards; (*a regresa*) to decline, to retrogress; (*a ceda*)

to give in, to yield; to give back, to return; (*ceasul*)
to put/set back; *auto* to reverse • ~**at** *adj* backward •
~**ere** *nf* (*întoarcere*) return; *fig* backwardness, backward state.

înaripat [înari'pat] *adj* winged; inspired; enthusiastic.

înarma [înar'ma] *vt* to arm; *fig* to fortify, to equip ‖ *vr*
to arm (oneself); *fig* to brace oneself • ~**re** *nf* arming,
armament.

înăbuşi [înăbu'shi] *vt* to suffocate, to smother, to stifle;
(*a îneca*) to choke; (*un sunet*) to drown, to deaden;
a ~ un strigăt to stifle/smother a cry; (*d. plante*) to
grow over; (*d. alimente*) to stew, to braise; (*a
reprima*) to put down, to suppress ‖ *vr* (*d. cineva*) to
choke, to suffocate, to gasp (for breath) • ~**tor** *adj*
stifling, choking, suffocating; (*d. atmosferă*) stuffy;
(*d. vreme*) sultry, oppressive, muggy.

înăcrit [înă'krit] *adj* (*d. lapte*) soured; (*d. cineva*) sour,
morose, grumpy.

înălbi [înăl'bi] *vt* to whiten, to blanch; (*d. rufe*) to bleach.

înălţa [înăl'tsa] *vt* (*a ridica*) to raise, to lift; (*o statuie*)
to erect, to set up; (*un steag*) to hoist; *fig* to uplift ‖
vr to rise.

înălţător [înăltsă'tor] *adj* elevating, uplifting.

înălţime [înăl'tsime] *nf also geog* height; *geog* (*altitudine*) eminence; altitude; (*loc înalt*) ridge, elevation;
(*vârf*) top, summit; *fig* (*măreţie*) loftiness; superiority; (*grad*) high rank; *mus* pitch; (*ca titlu*) Highness.

înăspri [înăs'pri] *vt* to harden, to make hard; (*a înrăutăţi*) to worsen; (*a agrava*) to aggravate; (*a înrăi*)
to embitter; to intensify; (*a ascuţi*) to sharpen ‖ *vr* to
harden (oneself); (*a se înrăutăţi*) to worsen; (*a se înrăi*)
to become embittered; (*a se agrava*) to aggravate; to
intensify; (*a se ascuţi*) to sharpen; (*d. oameni*) to
grow/become hard/tough; (*d. piele, faţă*) to coarsen.

înăuntru [înă'untru] *adv* in, inside, within.

încadra [înka'dra] *vt* (*a pune în ramă*) to frame (a
picture); (*a înconjura*) to surround; (*a împrejmui*) to
enclose; (*a mărgini*) to border; (*într-un cerc*) to encircle; (*a numi*) to appoint; (*într-un post*) to staff, to
take smb on the staff; *mil* (*d. artilerie*) to bracket, to
straddle ‖ *vr* (*a se integra în*) to join (a group), to
affiliate with; (*a se angaja*) to take a job; *fig* to
harmonize (with), to fit, to be in keeping with.

încarnat [înkar'nat] *adj* incarnated, incarnate,
embodied.

încartirui [înkartiru'i] *vt* to quarter, to billet.

încasa [înka'sa] *vt* (*a primi*) to receive, to get, (*un cec*)
to cash; (*a strânge*) to collect; (*impozite*) to raise;
(*datorii*) to recover; *coll* (*o lovitură*) to suffer • ~**tor**
nm (tax) collector; (*taxator*) conductor.

încă ['înkă] *adv affirm, inter* still; **e ~ aici** he is still
here; **mai e ~ aici?** is he still here?; *neg* yet; **~ nu** not
yet; **nu a venit ~** he hasn't come yet; (*în plus*) in
addition; (*din nou*) again; (*mai mult*) some/any
more; **~ doi** another two, two more; **~ o dată** all over
again, once more/again; **~ unul** another, one more;
(*pe lângă asta*) besides, in fact; **şi ~** besides, at that;
(*până acum*) so far, until now; (*chiar*) even.

încăiera [înkăie'ra] *vr* to skirmish, to come to grips
with smb; to have a (bit of a) tussle/scuffle; *coll* to
have a set-to.

încălca [înkăl'ka] *vt* (*un teritoriu*) to invade, to overrun; (*domeniu cuiva*) to encroach (upon), to trespass
(upon); (*drepturi*) to violate, to infringe; **a ~ legea** to
break/violate the law; *fig* to scorn, to defy.

încăleca [înkăle'ka] *vt* to mount, to ride; *fig* to subdue,
to subjugate; *recip* to overlap ‖ *vi* to mount.

încălţa [înkăl'tsa] *vt* to put on; to supply/fit smb with
footwear; *fig coll* to cheat, to diddle; *tech* to shoe ‖
vr to put on one's shoes.

încălţăminte [înkăltsă'minte] *nf* footwear.

încălţător [înkăltsă'tor] *nn* shoehorn.

încălzi [înkăl'zi] *vt also fig* to warm; to heat; (*d.
mâncare*) to warm/heat up; (*d. o haină*) to keep smb
warm; (*a însufleţi*) to animate ‖ *vr* (*d. cineva*) to
warm oneself; (*la soare*) to bask in the sun; (*a-i fi
cald*) to get heated; *fig* to get excited; (*d. un
vorbitor*) to warm up; (*d. obiecte*) to become hot/
warm; (*d. o maşină*) to run hot; (*d. un cablu*) to
chafe; *fig* (*d. atmosferă*) to become animated; (*d. o
discuţie*) to get hot; (*d. vreme*) to be (getting) warm
• ~**re** *nf* heating * **încălzi**; *fig* warming (up).

încăpător [înkăpă'tor] *adj* (*d. o maşină*) roomy; (*d. o
cameră*) spacious; (*mare*) large, big.

încăpăţâna [înkăpătsâ'na] *vr* to be obstinate/stubborn;
(*a stărui*) to persist (in), to stick (stubbornly) to smth
• ~**re** *nf* obstinacy, stubbornness; *coll* pig-headedness;
cu ~ obstinately, stubbornly • ~**t** *nm* obstinate/
stubborn person; *coll* mule ‖ *adj* obstinate, stubborn,
pig-headed; (*d. rezistenţă*) dogged; inflexible, die-
hard.

încăpere [înkă'pere] *nf* room.

încărca [înkăr'ka] *vt* (*d. un camion*) to load; (*prea
mult*) to overload; *also fig* to burden, to clutter (up);
elec (*d. baterie*) to charge; (*o armă*) to load; *fin* to
(over)charge; **a ~ nota de plată** to charge the bill too
high; *fig* to exaggerate; *pass* to be loaded, etc ‖ *vr* to
load/burden oneself.

încărcătură [înkărkă'tură] *nf* load, loading; **~ utilă**
payload; (*mărfuri*) goods; *naut* freight, cargo; *mil,
min* charge of powder; *metal, elec* charge.

încărunţi [înkărun'tsi] *vt* to make smb's hair go/turn
grey; (*a îmbătrâni*) to age ‖ *vi* to go/grow/turn grey,
to grizzle.

încătuşa [înkătu'sha] *vt* to shackle, to fetter; (*în
lanţuri*) to chain, to put into chains; *fig* to bind.

încâlceală [înkâl'cheală] *nf* tangle, entanglement;
confusion, muddle, jumble.

încâlci [înkâl'chi] *vt* (*d. fire*) to tangle, to ravel; (*d.
păr*) to tousle; *fig* to confuse; *coll* to muddle, to mix
up ‖ *vr also fig* to be tangled, to get entangled.

încânta [înkân'ta] *vt* to delight, to enrapture, to be
carried away; (*a amăgi: cu iluzii*) to delude • ~**re** *nf*
delight, rapture, enchantment.

încântător [înkântă'tor] *adj* delightful, pleasing,
ravishing ‖ *adv* delightfully.

încât [în'kât] *conj* (*rezultativ*) that, so (much) … that;
era atât de furios ~ nu putea vorbi he was so
angry that he could not speak; **a ajunge până acolo
~ să** to go as far as to; (*final*) so that; **a vorbit rar ~
toţi să-l înţeleagă** he spoke slowly so that everybody could understand him.

încăpător [închepă'tor] *nm* beginner, novice; *coll*
greenhorn ‖ *adj* beginning; early.

începe [în'chepe] *vt* to start, to begin; *elev* to com-
mence; (*a se apuca*) to set about (smth), to take to ‖
vi to begin, to start; **a ~ bine** to make a good start.

început [înche'put] *nn* beginning, start, outset; *elev*
commencement; origin, source • ~**uri** *nn pl*
beginnings.

încerca [încher'ka] *vt* to try, to attempt; (*a se strădui*) to endeavor; (*a testa: o mașinărie*) to test; (*a pune la încercare*) to put to the test; (*o haină*) to try on; (*pe altcineva*) to fit; (*a simți*) to go through, to experience; (*a suferi*) to undergo • **~re** *nf* trial, attempt; (*strădanie*) endeavor, effort; (*probă: a unei mașini*) test; (*ispitire*) tempting; (*greutate*) hardship, difficulty; (*chin*) ordeal, suffering • **~t** *adj* (hard) tried; (*experimentat*) experienced; (*priceput*) skilled, skillful; (*călit*) hardened || *nn* trying, test(ing).

încercănat [încherkă'nat] *adj* (*d. ochi*) ringed.

încercui [încherku'i] *vt also mil* to encircle; (*a înconjura*) to surround, to enclose; (*a împresura*) *mil* to besiege.

încet [în'chet] *adj* (*domol*) slow; leisurely; *coll* dawdling; **~ ca melcul** slow as a snail; (*greoi*) dull; (*leneș*) lazy, slack; (*prost*) silly; (*d. sunete*) low, soft; (*slab*) faint, weak; (*liniștit*) still; (*blând*) gentle; (*ușor*) light || *adv* (*fără grabă*) slowly; (*greoi*) idly, sluggishly; (*ușor*) gently, lightly.

înceta [înche'ta] *vt* to stop, to cease; to leave off; (*a pune capăt*) to put an end to; to suspend; (*prietenia*) to break off; **a ~ lucrul/munca** to stop/leave off work; (*în uzină*) to quit work; to down tools; (*temporar*) to knock off work || *vi* to cease, to stop; (*a se potoli*) to abate • **~re** *nf* ceasing, stoppage; **fără ~** incessantly, continually, ceaselessly.

încetini [încheti'ni] *vt* to slow down; (*a întârzia*) to delay; *tech* to decelerate; (*ritmul*) to slacken; (*viteza*) to reduce; **a ~ pasul** to go slow(er), to slacken one's pace || *vi* to slow down.

încetoșat [închetso'shat] *adj* foggy; *fig* dim, misty.

închega [înke'ga] *vt* to coagulate, to curdle; to condense; (*a îngroșa*) to thicken; *fig* to unite, to form; (*a începe*) to begin || *vr* to coagulate, to curdle; (*d. sânge*) to clot; to unite.

încheia [înke'ia] *vt* to close, to finish; (*o cuvântare*) to wind up; (*o înțelegere*) to conclude; (*o alianță*) to enter into; (*o căsătorie, un împrumut*) to contract; (*un târg*) to strike; (*cu nasturi*) to button/do up; (*a îmbina*) to combine || *vr* (*a se sfârși*) to end, to close, to come to an end; (*la haine*) to button (oneself) up.

încheiere [înke'iere] *nf* (*sfârșit*) conclusion, end; final part; (*a unui acord*) settlement; (*la nasturi*) buttoning up; **în ~** in conclusion, by way of conclusion.

încheietură [înkeie'tura] *nf* joint, articulation.

închide [în'kide] *vt* to close, to shut; (*cu zăvorul*) to fasten, to bolt; (*cu cheia*) to lock; (*a pune sub cheie*) to put under lock and key; (*pe jumătate*) to half shut, to leave ajar; **a ~ fereastra** to close/shut the window; (*pe cineva*) to confine; (*a întemnița*) to put into prison; (*oile în țarc*) to fold; (*o curte*) to fence (in); (*a împrejmui*) to enclose; (*a bara*) to block; (*a cuprinde*) to include, to contain; (*un aparat, lumina*) to turn/switch off; **a ~ radioul/televizorul** to turn off/switch off the radio/TV; (*școli, uzine*) to close/shut down; **a ~ ghilimelele** to unquote; **a ~ ochii** (*pentru a dormi*) to close one's eyes to sleep; (*a muri*) to pass away || *vr* to close, to shut, to be closed; (*a înceta, a se sfârși*) to be over; (*a se închia*) to lock oneself up; (*a se retrage*) to seclude oneself; (*a se întuneca: d. cer, culori*) to darken; (*d. o rană*) to heal.

închina [înki'na] *vt* (*a dedica*) to devote, to dedicate; (*a preda*) to yield, to surrender; (*a supune*) to subdue, to subjugate; (*paharul*) to raise || *vi* to toast, to

propose a toast || *vr* (*a-și face cruce*) to cross oneself; (*a se ruga*) to pray; (*a saluta*) to bow; (*a se prosterna*) to prostrate oneself; (*a se supune*) to submit.

închipui [înkipu'i] *vt* to imagine, to fancy; (*a născoci*) to invent, to make up; (*a proiecta*) to plan; (*a reprezenta*) to symbolize • **~ește-ți!** just think of that!, just fancy that!, only think! • **~re** *nf* imagination, imagining; (*fantezie*) fancy; (*iluzie*) delusion; (*himeră*) chimera; idea; (*gând*) thought; (*părere*) opinion.

închiria [înkiri'a] *vt* (*a da cu chirie*) to let, to rent; (*obiecte*) to hire; (*a lua cu chirie*) to rent.

închis [în'kis] *adj* closed, shut, * **închide**; (*întemnițat*) imprisoned; (*d. caracter*) reserved; *coll* buttoned up; (*d. expresia feței*) inexpressive, impassive; (*d. aer: apăsător*) close; (*d. culoare*) dark; (*d. cer: înnorat*) cloudy, dull; (*d. un club*) exclusive • **~oare** *nf* prison, jail, gaol; *sl* jug, quod; **la ~** in prison/jail; jailed; *sl* in quod, in the (stone) jug.

închistare [înkis'tare] *nf bio, med* encystment; *fig* seclusion, isolation; confinement, rigidity.

închizătoare [înkiză'toare] *nf* (*la fereastră*) fastener; (*la ușă*) catch, hasp; (*de colier*) clasp; (*de poșete*) snap.

încinge [în'chindje] *vt* (*cu un brâu*) to gird, to girdle; (*a înconjura*) to surround; (*a încălzi*) (*o sobă, mâncare*) to heat (up) || *vr* to heat up; (*d. foc*) to envelop; (*a aprinde*) to (en)kindle; *fig* (*a aprinde*) (*d. sentimente*) to seize; (*cu cingătoare*) to gird(le) oneself; (*d. o sobă, mâncare*) to heat up; (*d. mașină*) to run hot; (*d. foc*) to catch, to flame up; (*d. cineva*) (*a-i fi cald*) to be hot; (*la față*) to flush (crimson), to glow; *fig* (*a începe*) to arise, to begin; (*d. o ceartă*) to flare up; (*d. o discuție*) to break out; *fig* to be animated; (*a se înfierbânta*) to become inflamed; (*d. sentimente*) to run high, to flare up; (*d. cereale*) to mildew, to grow moldy.

înciudat [închu'dat] *adj* spiteful, vexed, angry; *coll* nettled.

încleia [înkl'ia] *vt* to glue/paste together, to stick || *vr* to stick together, to be glued/pasted together.

încleșta [înklesh'ta] *vt* (*a strânge*) to grip, to grasp, to clutch; (*d. pumni*) to clench; **a-și ~ dinții** to clench/set one's teeth; **a-și ~ pumnii** to clench/close one's fists || *vr* (*a se strânge: d. dinți*) to clench, to lock; (*a se încăiera*) to be clasped/entangled in a struggle, to be locked.

înclina [înkli'na] *vt* to incline, to tilt; (*capul*) to bend, to bow || *vr* to bow, to incline; (*o scândură*) to tilt, to tip up; (*a se apleca*) to bend (over, down); (*a saluta*) to bow (down); (*a fi înclinat*) to slant, to tilt; (*d. un țărm*) to shelve, to slope away; (*d. o navă*) to list, to heel (over); (*d. un avion*) to bank; (*a ceda*) to yield, to bow; **a ~ să** to be/feel ready/inclined to; **a ~ spre** to incline to/towards • **~re** *nf* inclination; tilting, canting; (*a capului*) nod; (*a corpului*) bow(ing); (*d. deal*) incline, gradient; (*d. acoperiș*) pitch, slant; (*d. navă*) heel, list; (*d. catarg*) rake; (*d. ac magnetic*) dip; (*~ laterală a drumului la curbe*) *tech* camber; (*d. traiectorie*) angle; *fig* inclination, bent, propensity; (*vocație*) vocation.

încoace [în'koache] *adv* here; *obs* hither; **~ și încolo** to and fro, up and down, back and forth; **mai ~** closer, nearer.

încolăci [înkolă'chi] *vt* to coil, to wind; (*a împleti*) to twine; (*a face ghem*) to roll; (*picioarele*) to cross || *vr* to curl/roll up; (*d. şarpe*) to coil up; (*a se face ghem*) to roll oneself up into a ball; (*d. o frânghie*) to coil; (*a şerpui*) to wind; (*d. un râu*) to meander.

încolo [în'kolo] *adv* (far)away/off; (*la o parte*) aside; (*în direcţia aceea*) in that direction, that way; *obs* thither; **mai** ~ (*spaţial*) farther on; (*temporal*) later on; (*altfel*) otherwise.

încolţi [înkol'tsi] *vt* (*a muşca*) to bite; (*a ataca*) to attack; (*cu colţii*) to dig its teeth into; *fig* (*a prinde la strâmtoare*) to corner smb, to drive hard || *vi bot* (*d. plante*) to sprout, to spring up; *fig* (*d. idee, bănuială*) to arise • ~t with one's back against the wall.

înconjur [în'konzhur] *nn* detour, roundabout way; **fără** ~ plainly, straightforward • **a face ~ul lumii** to travel/go round the world • ~a *vt* to surround; (*a împrejmui*) to enclose, to fence in; (*a da ocol*) to go round; (*a străbate*) to go/walk over; (*a asedia*) to besiege; (*a încercui o armată*) to encircle.

încorda [înkor'da] *vt also fig* to strain; **a-şi ~ auzul** to strain one's ears; **a-şi ~ mintea** to rack one's brains; **a-şi ~ privirile** to strain one's eyes; **a-şi ~ (toate) puterile** to strain every nerve (to do smth), to summon up all one's strength; (*d. relaţii*) to worsen; *mus* to stretch, to pitch || *vr* to strain/exert oneself; (*d. relaţii*) to become strained/tense • ~t *adj* (*d. muşchi*) strained; (*d. nervi*) tense, strung up; concentrated; (*febril*) feverish, strenuous || *adv* feverishly, strenuously, hard.

încornorat [înkorno'rat] *adj* (*d. animale*) horned; *fig* (*d. soţi*) betrayed, cuckolded; *fig* (*d. o minciună*) *coll* whopping • ~ul *adj/nm* the devil; cuckold.

încoronare [înkoro'nare] *nf* coronation; *fig* crowning.

încorpora [înkorpo'ra] *vt* to incorporate (into); to blend; *mil* to draft, to conscript, to call up.

încotoşmăna [înkotoshmă'na] *vt* to wrap up, to muffle up || *vr* to muffle/wrap oneself up.

încotro [înko'tro] *adv* where, which way; *obs* whither.

încovoia [înkovo'ia] *vt* to bend, to curve, to arch || *vr* to bend, to bow, to arch; *fig* to submit, to crouch.

încovoiere [înkovo'iere] *nf* bending, curve, arching; *tech* flection, flexure; (*de drum*) camber; (*de grindă*) sagging.

încrâncenat [înkrânche'nat] *adj* obstinate, stubborn, bitter.

încrede [în'krede] *vr* to confide (in), to trust smb; (*a se baza pe*) to rely on • ~re *nf* confidence, trust; (*bizuire*) reliance (on); ~ **în sine** self confidence; ~ **oarbă** blind/implicit confidence/faith.

încredinţa [înkredin'tsa] *vt* (*cuiva ceva*) to entrust; (*a preda*) to commit, to deliver; (*a da*) to give; (*a mărturisi*) to confide, to disclose; (*a asigura*) to assure smb of smth || *vr* to make certain/sure (of smth).

încremeni [înkreme'ni] *vi* to stand stock-still; (*a fi uluit*) to be dumbfounded/flabbergasted; (*în nemişcare*) motionless, still, unmoved.

încreţi [înkre'tsi] *vt* (*părul*) to wave, to curl; (*a undui: apa*) to ripple, to ruffle; (*a zbârci*) to wrinkle, to crease; (*d. rochie*) to pleat, to fold || *vi* (*d. sprâncene*) to frown, to knit one's brows || *vr* (*d. păr*) to wave, to curl; (*d. apă*) to ripple; (*d. piele*) to be wrinkled, to get/become lined • ~tură *nf* wave, wrinkle; (*în stofă*) kink; * **încreţi**.

încrezător [înkreză'tor] *adj* confident (in); (*nebănuitor*) unsuspicious; (*credul*) credulous.

încrezut [înkre'zut] *adj* conceited, presumptuous, arrogant; *coll* high and mighty.

încropi [înkro'pi] *vt* (*a încălzi*) to make tepid/lukewarm, to warm; *fig coll* to scrape up/together, to knock (smth) together.

încrucişa [înkruchi'sha] *vt* to cross, to intersect; *bio* to cross(breed), to interbreed || *vr* (*d. drum, scrisori*) to cross, to intersect; (*a se întâlni*) to meet; *fig* to clash • ~re *nf* (*de drumuri*) crossing, crossroads; (*nod feroviar*) junction; *bio* crossbreeding, interbreeding.

încrunta [înkrun'ta] *vt* (*sprâncene*) to knit || *vr* to frown, to scowl • ~t *adj* frowning, scowling; (*ursuz*) sullen, morose.

încuia [înku'ia] *vt* to lock (up); (*a închide*) to shut; *fig* to stump, to nonplus || *vr* to lock, to be locked; (*d. cineva*) to lock oneself up; *vernac* (*a se constipa*) to grow costive; **a ~ casa** *vt* to lock up one's house.

încuietoare [înkuie'toare] *nf* bolt; (*la o cutie*) hasp; (*de poşetă, brăţară*) snap; *fig* puzzling question; *coll* poser.

încumeta [înkume'ta] *vr* to venture, to dare.

încunoştinţa [înkunoshtin'tsa] *vt* to inform (of), to acquaint smb with smth; (*oficial*) to notify; *coll* to let smb know • ~re *nf* informing, notification.

încuraja [înkura'zha] *vt* (*pe cineva*) to encourage; (*a înviora*) to cheer up; (*a îmboldi*) to urge; to stimulate; (*ceva: arta*) to foster, to promote; (*a sprijini*) to support; *recip* to encourage one another • ~re *nf* encouragement • ~tor *adj* encouraging, cheering, hopeful.

încurca [înkur'ka] *vt* (*fire*) to tangle; *fig* (*a confunda*) to confuse, to mix up, to muddle; *fig* (*a împiedica, a stânjeni*) to encumber, to hinder; *fig* (*a deranja*) to trouble, to inconvenience; (*a complica*) to complicate; (*o chestiune*) to muddle up; **a ~ lucrurile** to make a mess of things; to mess (things) up; **a ~ planurile cuiva** to upset smb's plans; (*a pune pe cineva în încurcătură*) to perplex, to puzzle; (*a jena*) to confuse || *vr* (*d. fire*) to get entangled; to kink; (*a se prinde*) to be caught in; (*d. cineva: a se zăpaci*) to be perplexed, to get muddled/confused; (*la vorbă/examen*) to flounder; (*a-şi pierde capul*) to lose one's head; (*cu cineva*) to get involved/entangled with smb; (*d. o problemă*) to be getting intricate.

încurcătură [înkurkă'tură] *nf* confusion, mess, muddle; (*harababură*) jumble, mishmash; ~ **de circulaţie** traffic jam, hold-up; ~ **de maţe** *med* intestinal occlusion; *fig* tangled skein; (*necaz*) trouble, mess, scrape; (*dificultate*) difficulty; **a fi în** ~ to be in a tight spot; **a intra într-o** ~ to get into trouble; **a vârî pe cineva în** ~ to make trouble for smb, to get smb into trouble; (*zăpăceală*) confusion, embarrassment.

încuviinţa [înkuviin'tsa] *vt* (*a fi de acord*) (*cu*) to consent, to agree (to); to allow, to permit • ~re *nf* consent, agreement, permission.

îndată [în'dată] *adv* immediately, instantly; ~ **ce** as soon as; **de** ~ at once, immediately, straight away || *interj* (I'm) coming!.

îndatorire [îndato'rire] *nf* duty, obligation.

îndatoritor [îndatori'tor] *adj* obliging, kind.

îndărăt [îndă'răt] *adv* back(wards); *naut* astern.

îndărătnic [îndă'rătnik] *adj* stubborn, obstinate || *adv* stubbornly, obstinately.

îndârji [îndâr'zhi] *vt* to irritate; (*a face să se încăpăţâneze*) to make stubborn/obstinate || *vr* to be/become embittered/hardened; (*a se încăpăţâna*) to be stubborn/obstinate; (*a deveni inflexibil*) to stiffen.

îndeajuns [îndea'zhuns] *adv* enough, sufficiently; quite.

îndelete [înde'lete] *adv* leisurely, at leisure; (*treptat*) gradually, little by little.

îndeletnici [îndeletni'chi] *vr* (*cu*) to deal with, to be engaged in; (*din când în când*) to dabble • ~re *nf* occupation, pursuit; (*lucru*) employment, work, business.

îndelungat [îndelun'gat] *adj* long, long-standing.

îndemânare [îndemâ'nare] *nf* skill, dexterity, skillfulness; cleverness; (*prestidigitaţie*) sleight of hand; (*capacitate*) ability.

îndemânatic [îndemâ'natik] *adj* deft, dexterous; (*dibaci*) skillful, handy; (*măiestrit*) masterly; (*deştept*) clever; (*abil*) able, capable.

îndemn [în'demn] *nn* impulse, stimulus, incentive; goad, spur; (*apel*) appeal; (*sfat*) advice • ~a *vt* to urge, to stimulate; (*a aţâta*) to goad, to spur, to egg on; (*în sens rău*) to incite, to instigate; (*a sfătui*) to advise • **din/la ~ul** prompted by; (*la chemarea*) at the call of, (*în sens negativ*) at/on smb's instigation.

îndeobşte [înde'obshte] *adv* generally, usually, as a rule; ~ **cunoscut** commonly known.

îndeosebi [îndeo'sebi] *adv* especially, particularly, in particular.

îndepărta [îndepăr'ta] *vt* (*a înlătura ceva*) to remove; to take off; **a ~ o pată** to remove a stain; (*pe cineva*) to send away; (*a concedia*) to dismiss; *fig* to eliminate; *fig* (*a înstrăina*) to estrange (from smb) || *vr* to go away, to move off/away; (*d. corabie*) to sail away; (*călare*) to ride away; (*d. maşină*) to drive away; (*a pleca*) to take oneself off; (*a se retrage*) to retire, to withdraw; *fig* to fade away; (*de la subiect*) to wander/stray from the subject; *fig* (*de*) to estrange oneself from • ~t *adj* (*spaţial, temporal*) far off, remote; (*d. rude*) distant; (*d. călătorie*) long.

îndeplini [îndepli'ni] *vt* to fulfil, to carry out; to accomplish, to realize; (*îndatoriri*) to discharge || *vr* to materialize; (*a se adeveri*) to come true • ~re *nf* achievement, fulfillment, implementation.

îndesa [înde'sa] *vt* to cram, to stuff, to pack (with); (*a înfige*) to thrust || *vr* to cluster, to crowd, to flock.

îndesi [înde'si] *vt* to thicken; to make more frequent || *vr* to become thicker/denser; to become more frequent.

îndestulare [îndestu'lare] *nf* providing; (*belşug*) plenty, abundance; **cu ~** plenty, plentifully.

îndestulător [îndestulă'tor] *adj* plentiful, ample, copious; (*de ajuns*) sufficient, enough || *adv* plentifully, etc.

îndigui [îndigu'i] *vt* (*d. pământ*) to dyke, to dam up; (*un râu*) to embank; to impound.

îndobitocit [îndobito'chit] *adj* stupefied, stultified, idiotic.

îndoctrina [îndoktri'na] *vt* to indoctrinate; *coll* to brainwash.

îndoi [îndo'i] *vt* to bend, to curve; (*a împături*) to fold; **a ~t ziarul** he folded the newspaper; (*colţul unei pagini*) to turn down, to fold down; (*prin uzare*) to dog-ear; (*a dubla*) to (re)double; *vr* (*a se gârbovi*) to bend, to bow, to stoop; (*a se dubla, a spori*) to double; (*de ceva*) to doubt, to question • ~ală *nf* doubt, uncertainty, misgiving(s); (*şovăială*) hesitation,

wavering; **fără ~** undoubtedly, without/beyond doubt • ~**elnic** *adj* (*d. lucruri*) doubtful, uncertain, questionable; (*d. persoane*) dubious, suspicious.

îndopa [îndo'pa] *vt* to cram, to stuff; (*o pipă*) to fill; (*o pasăre*) to fatten || *vr* to guzzle, to stuff oneself.

îndrăgi [îndră'dji] *vt* to grow fond of, to take a fancy to; (*a se îndrăgosti de*) to fall in love with.

îndrăgosti [îndrăgos'ti] *vr* (*de*) to fall in love (with), to be infatuated (with); *coll* to be nuts on; *recip* to fall in love with each other • ~t *nm* lover || *adj* (*de*) in love (with), infatuated (with); *fig* fond of.

îndrăzneală [îndrăz'neală] *nf* (*curaj*) daring, courage, audacity; (*obrăznicie*) boldness, impudence, insolence; *coll* cheek; **cu ~** boldly.

îndrăzneţ [îndrăz'nets] *adj* daring, courageous, audacious; (*obraznic*) bold, insolent, impudent; *coll* cheeky || *adv* boldly, etc.

îndrăzni [îndrăz'ni] *vt* to dare, to venture, to presume.

îndrepta [îndrep'ta] *vt* to straighten, to make straight; *fig* to correct, to rectify; (*a repara*) to repair, to mend; (*a îmbunătăţi*) to improve; **a ~ o greşeală** to redress/rectify an error; (*a armă spre*) to aim at; (*a îndruma*) to direct, to guide; **a-şi ~ paşii spre** to turn/direct one's steps || *vr* to straighten oneself, to become straight; (*pe picioare*) to stand up/erect; *fig* (*a se îmbunătăţi*) to improve; (*moraliceşte*) to mend one's ways; (*a se însănătoşi*) to recover; (*a arăta mai bine*) to look better; (*spre*) to make/head for; *lit* to wend one's way to.

îndreptăţi [îndreptă'tsi] *vt* to justify, to entitle; (*o acţiune*) to warrant.

îndruga [îndru'ga] *vt* (*d. lână*) to spin; to utter; (*a trăncăni*) to chatter.

îndruma [îndru'ma] *vt* to guide, to lead • ~re *nf* guidance, direction; (*povaţă*) advice.

îndrumător [îndrumă'tor] *nm/nn* guide || *adj* guiding.

înduioşa [înduio'sha] *vt* to move, to touch || *vr* to be moved/touched; to take pity on smb.

înduioşător [înduioshă'tor] *adj* touching, moving, pathetic || *adv* touchingly, movingly, pathetically.

îndulci [îndul'chi] *vt* to sweeten; (*a mulţumi*) to satisfy; (*a desfăta*) to delight; (*a înmuia*) to soften; (*a micşora*) to diminish, to lessen; (*a potoli*) to alleviate; (*a îmblânzi*) to tame || *vr* to be/become sweet; *fig* (*d. voce*) to grow softer; (*d. vreme*) to grow milder; (*d. ger*) to yield; (*a se potoli*) to abate, to calm down.

îndupleca [înduple'ka] *vt* to persuade, to talk smb into (doing smth) || *vr* to relent, to yield, to give in.

îndura [îndu'ra] *vt* to bear, to suffer, to experience || *vr* (*a se îndupleca*) to give in, to relent, to yield; (*a-i fi milă de*) to take pity on smb; (*a catadicsi*) *iro* to condescend to • ~re *nf* (*milă*) pity, compassion; (*cruţare*) mercy; **fără ~** merciless(ly), ruthless(ly).

îndurera [îndure'ra] *vt* to grieve, to sadden, to pain || *vr* to grieve, to be pained.

înec [î'nek] *nn* drowning; (*inundaţie*) flood • ~a *vt* to drown; (*d. un vas*) to sink; (*a inunda*) to flood, to overflow; *fig* (*a copleşi*) to overwhelm; (*a înăbuşi*) to stifle || *vr* to get drowned; (*d. un vas*) to sink; (*a se sinucide*) to drown oneself; *fig* to ruin oneself; (*d. lucruri*) to go to ruin; (*cu ceva: a se înăbuşi*) to choke on smth.

înfăptui [înfăptu'i] *vt* to achieve, to accomplish, to fulfil || *vr* to come true, to materialize, to be carried out.

înfăşa [înfă'sha] *vt* to swaddle; * **bandaja**.

înfăşura [înfăshu'ra] *vt* to wrap up, to muffle up || *vr* to wrap/muffle oneself up • **~re** *nf* wrapping (up); *elec* (*bobină*) winding.

înfăţişa [înfătsi'sha] *vt* to present; (*a reprezenta*) to represent; (*a descrie*) to describe; (*a zugrăvi*) to depict; (*a arăta*) to produce; (*a aduce*) to bring; (*a închipui*) to imagine || *vr* to come up, to present oneself; *mil* to report (to smb); *jur* to appear (before).

înfăţişare [înfătsi'share] *nf* presentation * **înfăţişa**; (*exterioară*) appearance; aspect; *coll* looks; (*descriere*) description; appearance, presence.

înfia [înfi'a] *vt* to adopt (a child).

înfiera [înfie'ra] *vt also fig* to brand; *fig* to stigmatize.

înfierbânta [înfierbân'ta] *vt* to heat (up); *fig* to vex, to provoke || *vr* (*de căldură*) to get heated; (*de vin*) to get flushed; (*d. maşini*) to run hot; *fig* to warm up, to get excited; (*a se înfuria*) to get into a temper.

înfigăreţ [înfigă'rets] *adj* pushy; intrusive; insinuating.

înfige [în'fidje] *vt* to thrust || *vr* to thrust oneself forward.

înfiinţa [înfiin'tsa] *vt* to set up, to establish; (*a fonda*) to found; to organize; (*a crea*) to create; (*a face*) to make; (*a alcătui*) to form || *vr* to be set up, to be established, to be found; (*a-şi face apariţia*) to turn up, to appear; *fig* to intrude • **~re** *nf* setting up, establishment * **înfiinţa**.

înfiora [înfio'ra] *vt* to thrill; (*a speria*) to frighten; (*a face să tremure*) to shake || *vr* to thrill, to be thrilled; (*a tremura*) to shudder, to tremble, to shiver.

înfiorător [înfioră'tor] *adj* terrible, dreadful, awful || *adv* dreadfully; **~ de** terribly, dreadfully, awfully.

înfiripa [înfiri'pa] *vt* (*a înjgheba*) to scrape/knock together || *vr* to take shape.

înflăcăra [înflăkă'ra] *vt* to fire (up), to inflame || *vr* to get excited, to become inflamed • **~t** *adj* (*fierbinte*) fiery, hot; *fig also* ardent, passionate || *adv* ardently.

înflori [înflo'ri] *vi* to flower, to burst (out) into flower; (*d. flori*) *also fig* to bloom; (*d. pomi*) *also fig* to blossom; *fig* (*a prospera*) to prosper, to flourish, to thrive; *fig* (*a exagera*) to embellish • **~re** *nf* flowering; *fig* flourishing, prosperity • **~t** *adj* blooming, in bloom/blossom; *fig* (*d. stil*) florid • **~tor** *adj* flowering, blooming * **înflorit**; *fig* flourishing, thriving, prosperous.

înfocat [înfo'kat] *adj* (*fierbinte*) hot, heated, fiery; (*scânteietor*) bright; *fig* passionate, ardent || *adv* passionately.

înfofoli [înfofo'li] *vt* to wrap/muffle up || *vr* to wrap/ muffle oneself up.

înfoia [înfo'ia] *vt* (*a umfla*) to swell; (*obrajii*) to blow out; (*a afâna*) to break up || *vr* to swell, to be blown; *fig* to give oneself airs; (*d. păsări*) to ruffle up its feathers.

înfometa [înfome'ta] *vt* to starve • **~t** *adj* starved; (*flămând*) hungry, famished.

înfrăţi [înfră'tsi] *vt* to unite (like brothers) || *vr* (*cu*) to fraternize (with), to become good/close friends; (*d. două oraşe*) to twin • **~re** *nf* fraternity, fraternization, union; (*a două oraşe*) twinning.

înfrâna [înfrâ'na] *vt* (*un cal*) to bridle; (*a îmblânzi*) to tame; *fig* to restrain, to curb, to control || *vr* to restrain/control oneself.

înfrânge [în'frândje] *vt* to defeat, to vanquish; *fig* to conquer; (*a înăbuşi*) to stifle; (*a înfrâna*) to curb • **~re** *nf* defeat.

înfricoşa [înfriko'sha] *vt* to scare, to frighten || *vr* to get scared, to be frightened.

înfricoşător [înfrikoshă'tor] *adj* frightening, dreadful, terrifying || *adv* dreadfully, awfully, horribly.

înfrigurare [înfrigu'rare] *nf* feverishness, excitement; **cu ~** excitedly.

înfrigurat [înfrigu'rat] *adj* shivering, trembling with cold; *fig* anxious, excited, eager.

înfrumuseţa [înfrumuse'tsa] *vt* to embellish, to adorn; (*a găti*) to trim up • **~re** *nf* embellishing, improving, beautifying; adornment, ornament; (*cosmetică*) cosmetology, beautification.

înfrunta [înfrun'ta] *vt* to face (out), to confront; (*a sfida*) to defy, to dare; (*un duşman*) to encounter.

înfrunzi [înfrun'zi] *vi* to leaf (out), to come into leaf.

înfrupta [înfrup'ta] *vr* (*din*) to partake (of), to treat oneself (to); *fig* (*din*) (*a gusta*) to taste (of); (*a se bucura de*) to indulge (in); (*a mânca de dulce*) to break one's fast.

înfuleca [înfule'ka] *vt* to gobble, to guzzle, to gulp (down).

înfumurat [înfumu'rat] *adj* conceited, haughty, arrogant.

înfunda [înfun'da] *vt* (*o deschizătură*) to stop up, to plug; (*o ţeavă*) to clog, to choke (up); (*un butoi*) to bung up; (*a băga*) to shove, to stick; (*pe cineva*) to nonplus; (*la examen*) to pluck; to get/have the best of smb || *vr* to be stopped; (*d. o ţeavă*) to clog; (*a se îngloda: în noroi*) to be/get stuck; (*a se îngropa în*) to bury oneself in.

înfuria [înfuri'a] *vt* to anger, to irritate, to infuriate || *vr* to get/grow/become angry, to lose one's temper; *coll* to fly off the handle • **~t** *adj* furious, angry, infuriated || *adv* angrily, furiously.

îngădui [îngădu'i] *vt* to permit, to allow; (*a tolera*) to tolerate; to admit; (*a păsui*) to grant smb a delay; *neg* to brook || *vi* to be patient || *vr* **a-şi ~** to be allowed/permitted • **~tor** *adj* lenient, tolerant; (*bun*) kind; (*răbdător*) patient || *adv* leniently, tolerantly • **~nţă** *nf* (*indulgenţă*) tolerance, leniency; (*permisiune*) permission, leave; (*aprobare*) approval.

îngăima [îngăi'ma] *vt* to mumble, to stutter.

îngălbeni [îngălbe'ni] *vt* to yellow || *vi* to turn yellow; (*d. oameni*) to grow pale || *vr* (*d. frunze*) to turn yellow, to wither, to wilt; *fig* (*d. oameni*) (*de*) to grow/ turn pale (with); **a ~ de frică** to become as white as chalk, to be in a funk.

îngâmfat [îngâm'fat] *nm* cockscomb, fop || *adj* conceited, arrogant, vain, supercilious; *coll* high and mighty || *adv* conceitedly, arrogantly, vainly, superciliously.

îngâna [îngâ'na] *vt* (*a imita*) to mimic, to imitate; to murmur; (*a băigui*) to mumble, to stammer; (*a fredona*) to hum; *recip* to imitate/mimic one another || *vr* (*a se îmbina*) to combine, to blend; (*a se împleti*) to interweave; (*a se amesteca*) to mix up.

îngândurat [îngându'rat] *adj* (*dus pe gânduri*) thoughtful, pensive, musing; (*îngrijorat*) worried, concerned, anxious || *adv* pensively, musingly.

îngemăna [îndjemă'na] *vt* to twin, to join, to combine; (*strâns*) to blend.

îngenunchea [îndjenun'kea] *vt also fig* to bring down to one's knees; *fig* to subjugate, to subdue || *vi* to kneel (down).

înger ['îndjer] *nm* angel; **~ păzitor** *nm* guardian angel.

înghesui [îngesu'i] *vt* to crowd, to press, to pack; *recip* (*a se înghionti*) to jostle one another || *vr* to crowd, to squeeze.

înghesuială [îngesu'ială] *nf* crowd, crush, squash.

înghet [în'gets] *nn* (hard) frost; *coll* freeze-up • ~a *vt* to freeze || *vi also fig* (*de*) to freeze (with); *fig* to grow stiff/tense/rigid • ~a **salariilor** wage freeze • ~are *nf* freezing, freeze • ~ată [înge'tsată] *nf* ice(-cream).

înghionti [îngion'ti] *vt* to push, to shove, to jostle; (*cu cotul*) to nudge, to jog; *recip* to push/jostle one another.

înghiti [îngi'tsi] *vt* to swallow; (*lacom*) to gulp (down); (*repede*) to bolt; (*repede şi cu zgomot*) to gobble; to inhale, to breathe in; *fig* (*a devora: o carte*) to devour; to absorb; *fig* (*pe cineva*) to stomach; *fig* to check, to curb; (*mânia*) to swallow down; (*o minciună*) to swallow; (*un afront*) to pocket • ~tură *nf* (*de hrană*) mouthful, gulp; (*de lichid*) drink, draught; (*mică*) sip; **dintr-o** ~ at a draught, at one gulp.

îngloba [înglo'ba] *vt* to include, to take smth in.

îngrădi [îngră'di] *vt* to enclose, to fence in, to wall in; to bar, to block up; *fig* to restrict (smb on his rights); (*a pune limite*) to limit.

îngrămădi [îngrămă'di] *vt* (*a aduna*) to assemble, to gather; (*unul peste altul*) to pile/heap up; (*a presa*) to press, to squeeze || *vr* (*d. oameni*) to crowd; (*d. lucruri*) to pile up; (*a se acumula*) to accumulate.

îngrăşa [îngră'sha] *vt* (*animale*) to fatten; *agr* (*pământul*) to fertilize, to manure || *vr* to grow/get fat; (*a câştiga în greutate*) to put on/gain weight, to fill out.

îngrăşământ [îngrăshă'mânt] *nn* (*chimic*) fertilizer; (*natural*) manure.

îngreuna [îngreu'na] *vt* (*a face mai greu*) to make heavy/heavier; (*a împovăra*) to burden; (*a face mai dificil*) to render/make more difficult; (*a agrava*) to worsen || *vr* (*a se face mai greu*) to grow/become heavier; *fig* (*a se face mai dificil*) to become more difficult.

îngriji [îngri'zhi] *vt* to take care of, to look after; (*d. doctor*) to attend; (*un bolnav, copil mic*) to nurse || *vr* (*de*) to take care of (smb/smth), to attend to, to look after; (*pe sine*) to look after oneself; (*a-şi procura*) to secure; (*a procura*) to provide smb with; (*a fi îngrijorat de*) to trouble about; **a se ~ de toate** to see to everything • ~re *nf* taking care of; * **îngriji;** (*grijă*) care; (*atenţie*) attention, attendance; (*supraveghere*) supervision; (*acurateţe*) accuracy • **sub ~rea** under smb's care/control; (*d. cărţi*) edited by • ~t *adj* (*ordonat*) neat; (*d. înfăţişare*) well-groomed; (*curat*) clean; (*frumos*) beautiful; correct; exact; (*d. o lucrare*) accurate; (*minuţios*) elaborate; (*atent*) careful || *adv* neatly, accurately, carefully.

îngrijitor [îngrizhi'tor] *nm* intendant; caretaker; (*servitor*) man-servant.

îngrijora [îngrizho'ra] *vt* to worry, to make anxious/uneasy, to trouble || *vr* to worry, to be anxious/uneasy • ~re *nf* worry, anxiety, uneasiness; (*teamă*) fear, alarm.

îngrijorător [îngrizhoră'tor] *adj* alarming, disquieting, upsetting; (*grav*) serious.

îngropa [îngro'pa] *vt also fig* to bury, to inter || *vr* to to live in seclusion.

îngroşa [îngro'sha] *vt* to thicken, to make thick(er); (*a mări*) to increase; *fig* to worsen; *fig* to exaggerate || *vr* to thicken, to become thicker; to worsen.

îngrozi [îngro'zi] *vt* to horrify, to terrify, to scare || *vr* to be scared/frightened; to take fright; (*a se cutremura*) to shudder • ~t *adj* frightened, terrified, horrified • ~tor *adj* dreadful, awful, horrible || *adv* dreadfully, awfully, horribly; ~ **de** dreadfully.

îngust [în'gust] *adj* narrow; (*subţire*) thin; (*zvelt*) svelte, slim, slender; (*strâmt*) tight; *fig* (*la minte*) narrow-minded, parochial • ~a *vt* to narrow; (*a strâmta*) to tighten || *vr* to get/grow narrow(er); (*către vârf*) to taper; *fig* to shrink.

înhăita [înhăi'ta] *vr* to gang up, to band (together).

înhăma [înhă'ma] *vt* to harness, to hitch up.

înhăţa [înhă'tsa] *vt* to snatch, to seize; (*de guler*) to collar; (*a lua*) to take; (*cu dinţii*) to snap.

înhuma [înhu'ma] *vt* to bury, to inter • ~re *nf* burial, interment.

înjgheba [înzhge'ba] *vt* (*a aduna*) to gather, to collect; (*o sumă*) to raise; (*a încropi*) to knock/scrape together; to form, to set up; (*a întemeia*) to found.

înjosi [înzho'si] *vt* to humble, to belittle, to humiliate || *vr* to demean oneself, to belittle oneself, to humble oneself • ~tor *adj* humiliating, degrading, lowering.

înjuga [înzhu'ga] *vt* to yoke; *fig* to harness || *vr* to yoke.

înjumătăţi [înzhumătă'tsi] *vt* to halve, to divide into halves; (*a micşora*) to diminish || *vr* to diminish, to halve.

înjunghia [înzhungi'a] *vt* to stab, to knife; (*animale*) to kill; *recip* to stab each other || *vr* to stab oneself.

înjura [înzhu'ra] *vt* (*pe cineva*) to swear (at smb), to curse, to abuse; *recip* to abuse one another || *vi* to swear, to curse.

înjurătură [înzhură'tură] *nf* oath, swearword, abuse.

înlăcrimat [înlăkri'mat] *adj* (all) in tears, tearful.

înlănţui [înlăntsu'i] *vt* (*de*) to link up, to connect; (*pe cineva*) to chain, to fetter; (*a îmbrăţişa*) to hug, to hold/take in one's arms; to twine one's arm(s) round; *fig* (*a captiva*) to fascinate || *vr* to be linked, to link up; to hang together; to be interdependent; (*a se înşirui*) to come after one another.

înlătura [înlătu'ra] *vt* (*a îndepărta*) to remove; (*a elimina*) to eliminate; (*obstacole*) to stave off, to avert; (*a concedia*) to dismiss, to fire; (*a aboli*) to do away with.

înlemni [înlem'ni] *vi* to be perplexed, to be astounded, to be stunned • ~t *adj* dumbfounded; ~ **de groază/spaimă** dumb/speechless/dumbfounded with terror/fright.

înlesni [înles'ni] *vt* to facilitate, to make easy/easier • ~re *nf* facility; *pl* favorable terms; (*ajutor*) help, aid.

înlocui [înloku'i] *vt* to replace, to substitute for; (*a lua locul*) to take the place of; (*pe cineva*) to act for, to deputize for; (*a îndepărta: din funcţie*) to dismiss; **a ~ un lucru vechi cu altul nou** to substitute a new thing for an old one; *recip* to be substituted for one another • ~tor *nm* substitute, deputy; (*al unui doctor*) locum (tenens).

înmagazina [înmagazi'na] *vt com* to store (up), to stock; *fig* to store up, to accumulate • ~re *nf* storage, storing up.

înmatricula [înmatriku'la] *vt* to enroll, to matriculate, to register • ~re *nf* registering; (*d. maşină, studenţi*) registration; enrollment.

înmărmuri [înmărmu'ri] *vi* to be taken aback, to be flabbergasted, to be dumbfounded/astounded.

înmâna [înmâ'na] *vt* to hand (over), to deliver (to).

înmiresmat [înmires'mat] *adj* fragrant, perfumed, scented.

înmormânta [înmormân'ta] *vt also fig* to bury, to entomb, to inter • ~re *nf* funeral, burial, entombment.

înmuguri [înmugu'ri] *vi* to bud (forth/out), to burgeon (out/forth) • ~re *nf* budding, burgeoning; *fig* beginning.

înmuia [înmu'ia] *vt* (*a face mai moale*) to soften; (*într-un lichid*) to dip, to soak; (*a uda*) to wet; (*a înduplea*) to persuade, to mollify ‖ *vr* (*d. ger*) to thaw; (*a se încălzi*) to get/grow warm/milder; (*a deveni moale*) to become soft; (*a se îmblânzi*) to relent; (*a se calma*) to calm down; (*d. voce*) to grow softer; (*d. caracter*) to mellow; (*a deveni ud*) to become/get wet; (*a se pătrunde de un lichid*) to get soaked.

înmulți [înmul'tsi] *vt math* (*cu*) to multiply (by); (*a spori*) to increase; (*a mări*) to augment; (*a îmbogăți*) to enrich ‖ *vr bio* to multiply, to reproduce, to breed; (*a spori*) to increase • ~re *nf also math* multiplication; (*sporire*) increase; *bio* reproduction • ~tor *nn math* multiplier, factor.

înnămoli [înnămo'li] *vr* to get stuck, to sink in the mud; (*d. un râu*) to silt up.

înnăscut [înnăs'kut] *adj* inborn, innate.

înnebuni [înnebu'ni] *vt also fig* to drive (smb) mad/crazy, to drive (smb) out of one's mind ‖ *vi* to lose one's mind/wits, to go mad/crazy; *coll* to go off one's rocker; *sl* to go nuts; **a ~ după** to be mad/nuts/crazy about • ~tor *adj* maddening, exasperating.

înnegri [înne'gri] *vt* to black, to blacken ‖ *vr* to turn/become black, to darken; (*a se bronza*) to (get a) tan, to go brown.

înnegura [înnegu'ra] *vt* to dim, to cover with mist; *fig* to obscure, to eclipse ‖ *vr* to darken, to grow dark; (*d. cer*) to cloud over; to become/grow misty; *fig* (*d. vedere*) to grow dim; *fig* (*a se posomorî*) to grow gloomy.

înnobila [înnobi'la] *vt also fig* to ennoble; (*pe cineva*) to raise to the nobility/peerage; (*spiritul*) to uplift, to elevate ‖ *vr* to become ennobled/elevated.

înnoda [înno'da] *vt* to knot, to tie; (*șireturi*) to lace; (*a înnădi*) to piece together; (*a încropi*) to scrape up/together ‖ *vr* to knot; (*d. ață*) to become knotted, to kink.

înnoi [înno'i] *vt* to renovate; (*garderoba*) to renew; (*a împrospăta*) to refresh; (*a face ca nou*) to make as good as new; (*d. un abonament*) to renew one's subscription; (*d. un gen literar*) to revive; (*o metodă, cadre*) to change completely ‖ *vr* to be/get renewed/renovated; (*d. cineva*) to put on smth for the first time • ~re *nf* renovation, renewal, restoring; (*de utilaje*) replacement; (*a sistemului*) reform, improvement.

înnopta [înnop'ta] *vi* to stay overnight, to put up for the night; (*a dormi*) to sleep; (*a fi surprins de noapte*) to be overtaken by the night ‖ *vr* to get/grow dark.

înnora [înno'ra] *vi/vr* to cloud (over) ‖ *vt* to cloud, to darken • ~t *adj* clouded, cloudy, overcast; *fig* clouded, dark.

înota [îno'ta] *vi* to swim; (*a pluti*) to float.

înotătoare [înotă'toare] *nf* swimmer; *zool* fin.

înotător [înotă'tor] *nm* swimmer; ~ **subacvatic** frogman ‖ *adj* swimming.

înrădăcinat [înrădăchi'nat] *adj* (deeply) rooted, implanted; ingrained.

înrăi [înră'i] *vt* to embitter, to exasperate ‖ *vr* to become callous/wicked; (*a se înrăutăți*) to become/grow worse, to deteriorate.

înrăit [înră'it] *adj* embittered, wicked; inveterate, confirmed; *coll* hopeless; **bețiv** ~ inveterate drunkard.

înrăma [înră'ma] *vt* (*un tablou*) to frame, to set in a frame.

înrăutăți [înrăută'tsi] *vt* to worsen, to deteriorate; (*d. o boală*) to aggravate ‖ *vr* to get/grow/become worse, to deteriorate.

înrâurire [înrâu'rire] *nf* influence, impact.

înregistra [înredjis'tra] *vt* (*fapte, în scris*) to record; (*naștere*) to register; (*o comandă*) to enter up; (*bagaje*) to book; (*a memora*) to memorize; **a ~ o cerere** to file a petition; **a-și ~ mașina** to register one's car; (*a imprima*) to record; **a ~ pe bandă** to tape, to record on (magnetic) tape; *fig* (*succese, progrese*) to score ‖ *vr* to register oneself.

înregistrare [înredjis'trare] *nf* registration, registry, registering; recording; booking; (*imprimare*) (sound) recording; ~ **pe bandă/casetă** tape/cassette recording.

înrobi [înro'bi] *vt* to enslave, to subjugate; to subdue; *obs* to enthrall.

înrola [înro'la] *vt mil* to enlist; *fig* (*membri*) to enroll, to recruit ‖ *vr mil* to enlist; *fig* to enroll oneself.

înroși [înro'shi] *vt* to redden, to turn smth red; (*d. fața*) to flush; (*buzele*) to paint ‖ *vr* to grow/become red, to turn red; (*d. cineva*) to flush up, to blush; (*a se coace*) to ripen.

înrourat [înrou'rat] *adj* covered with dew.

înrudi [înru'di] *vr also fig* (*cu*) to be/become related (to) • ~re *nf* relationship, kinship; *fig* relationship, similarity • ~t *adj* related, kindred; *fig* kindred, allied; (*d. limbă*) cognate, kindred.

însă ['însă] *conj* (*dar*) but; however, yet, nevertheless, nonetheless, all the same; (*pe de altă parte*) on the other hand.

înșăila [înșăi'la] *vt* to stitch, to tack; *fig* (*o poveste*) to make up; to imagine, to fancy.

însămânța [însămân'tsa] *vt agr* to sow; *bio* to inseminate, to impregnate.

însănătoși [însănăto'shi] *vt* to cure, to heal; *fig* to reform; (*atmosfera*) to cleanse, to purify; (*literatura*) to purge ‖ *vr* to recover, to be cured • ~re *nf* recovery, healing, curing.

însărcina [însărchi'na] *vt* (*cu*) to charge (with), to commission; (*a încredința cuiva*) to entrust smb with smth, to assign; (*a da instrucțiuni*) to instruct ‖ *vr* to undertake; to take it upon oneself to.

însărcinată [însărchi'nată] *adj* pregnant, (big) with child, expectant; *coll* in the family way.

însângerat [însândje'rat] *adj* blood-stained, stained with blood; bloody; *fig* purple, red, sanguine.

înscăuna [înskău'na] *vt* to enthrone; *fig* to establish, to set up ‖ *vr* to ascend the throne; *fig* to become established.

înscenare [însche'nare] *nf* staging; (*judiciară*) frame-up, set-up.

înscrie [în'skrie] *vt* (*a nota*) to write down, to put down; (*a înregistra*) to register; (*pe o listă*) to place on a list, to enter smb's name; (*la un curs*) to enroll; **a ~ un nume în** (registru) to register/enter a name; (*a* *grava*) to engrave; *geom* to inscribe ‖ *vr* to register/ enter one's name, to enroll; to sign up; **a se ~ la un curs** to register for, to sign up for • **~re** *nf* writing (down), entering; registration, enrollment; inscription; **formular de ~** entry form.

înscris [în'skris] *nn* act, document, certificate; written record.

însemna [însem'na] *vt* to note, to write/put down; (*repede*) to jot down; (*a înregistra*) to record; (*a marca*) to mark ‖ *vi* to mean, to signify; (*a reprezenta*) to represent, to stand for; (*a constitui*) to be; **a nu ~ nimic** to mean/be nothing; *coll* not to be worth a fig • **~re** *nf* noting, * **însemna**; (*notă*) note; (*semn*) sign, mark • **~t** *adj* significant, important; (*de vază*) of note; (*faimos*) noted, famous; considerable, remarkable; (*mare*) large; **puțin ~** immaterial, unimportant.

însemnătate [însemnă'tate] *nf* importance, consequence; (*semnificație*) significance; (*valoare*) value.

însenina [înseni'na] *vt* (*pe cineva*) to cheer up; (*d. față*) to brighten ‖ *vr* (*d. vreme*) to clear up; (*d. fața cuiva*) to brighten/light up; (*d. cineva*) (*a se înveseli*) to cheer up.

însera [înse'ra] *vi* (*a-și petrece seara*) to spend the evening ‖ *vr* to get/grow dark • **~re** *nf* nightfall; (*amurg*) dusk, twilight.

însetat [înse'tat] *adj* (*de*) thirsty (for), craving (for); **~ de sânge** thirsty for blood, blood-thirsty.

însingurat [însingu'rat] *adj* secluded, lone, lonesome.

însorit [înso'rit] *adj* sunny, sunlit.

însoți [înso'tsi] *vt* to accompany; to escort; (*o fată tânără*) to chaperone; (*a conduce*) to show/see off; (*a anexa*) to enclose, to annex; to attend, to follow ‖ *vr* (*cu*) to associate (with), to consort; *vernac* (*a se căsători*) to marry • **~re** *nf* accompaniment; matching; (*căsătorie*) marriage, wedding.

însoțitoare [însotsi'toare] *nf* companion; (*a unei tinere*) chaperone; (*ghid*) guide; **~ de bord** flight attendant, air hostess.

însoțitor [însotsi'tor] *adj* accompanying, attendant ‖ *nm* companion; attendant; (*suită*) retinue; (*turistic*) guide; (*de vagoane*) conductor.

înspăimânta [înspăimân'ta] *vt* to frighten, to terrify, to scare ‖ *vr* to be/get frightened, to be panic-stricken.

înspăimântător [înspăimântă'tor] *adj* dreadful, frightful, terrible ‖ *adv* dreadfully, frightfully, terribly.

înspre ['înspre] *prep* towards; **a da ~** (**curte**) to look on to (the yard).

înstărit [înstă'rit] *adj* well-off, well-to-do; (*bogat*) rich, wealthy.

înstelat [înste'lat] *adj* (*d. cer*) starry, starlit; bespangled.

înstrăina [înstrăi'na] *vt jur* (*d. proprietate*) to alienate, to transfer; (*d. bani*) to embezzle; *fig* to estrange, to alienate ‖ *vr* (*de cineva*) to become estranged (from smb), to become a stranger (to) • **~re** *nf jur* (*de bunuri*) alienation, transfer; estrangement.

însufleți [însufle'tsi] *vt* to give life to (smb, smth); to animate; (*a pune în mișcare*) to actuate; (*a înviora*) to enliven; **a ~ o conversație** to enliven/keep up the conversation; (*a stimula*) to inspire, to urge on ‖ *vr* to become/grow (more) animated/lively; **fața i se ~** his face lit up • **~re** *nf* (*entuziasm*) enthusiasm, fervor; (*vioiciune*) liveliness, briskness; **cu ~** enthusiastically; (*cu căldură*) warmly; (*din inimă*) heartily • **~t** *adj* (*viu*) alive, living; *fig* (*animat*) lively, spirited, brisk.

însuma [însu'ma] *vt* to totalize, to total; to include, to comprise.

însura [însu'ra] *vt* to marry ‖ *vr* (*cu*) to marry (smb), to get married to; *coll* to tie the knot.

însuși [însu'shi] *vt* (*un bun*) to appropriate, to take possession/hold of; *fig* (*a asimila*) to assimilate, to acquire; (*a stăpâni*) to master; *coll* to get the hang of • **~re** *nf* (*trăsătură*) feature; (*calitate*) quality; (*preluare*) appropriation * **însuși**; (*asimilare*) acquisition, mastery.

înșela [înshe'la] *vt* to cheat, to deceive; (*a trage pe sfoară*) to take in, to diddle; (*a escroca*) to swindle, to defraud; (*a minți*) to lie (to), to mislead; (*a trăda: în căsnicie*) to betray, to be unfaithful to; **a ~ așteptările** to let smb down ‖ *vi* to cheat ‖ *vr* (*a nu avea dreptate*) to be wrong, to be mistaken; (*a greși*) to make a mistake.

înșelăciune [înshelă'chune] *nf* fraud, cheat, cheating; fraudulence, deceit; *fig* hoax, humbug; (*minciună*) lie, deception; **prin ~** fraudulently, under false pretences.

înșelător [înshelă'tor] *nm* swindler, cheater, cheat; (*mincinos*) liar ‖ *adj* deceptive, delusive •**~ie** *nf* deception; cheat.

înșeua [înshe'ua] *vt* to saddle.

înșfăca [înshfă'ka] *vt* to seize, to grasp, to grab, to snatch.

înșira [înshi'ra] *vt* (*pe o ață: mărgelele*) to string, to thread; (*a alinia*) to align, to draw up; (*a pune*) to put, to lay; (*a enumera*) to list, to enumerate; *fig* (*povești*) to tell, to spin (yarns) ‖ *vr* to string; to stretch; to follow.

înștiința [înshtiin'tsa] *vt* to inform (of), to advise (of), to apprise (of); (*oficial*) to notify (of), to give notice of; *coll* to let know, to give out • **~re** *nf* notice, notification, announcement.

înșuruba [înshuru'ba] *vt/vr* to screw (on).

întărâta [întără'ta] *vt* (*a instiga*) to incite, to instigate; (*un câine*) to tease, to set (barking); to excite, to set irritate; (*a supăra*) to vex, to anger, to annoy; (*a stimula*) to stimulate, to goad on ‖ *vr* to get excited, to get worked up.

întări [întă'ri] *vt constr* (*d. zid*) to strengthen, to reinforce; (*d. grindă*) to truss; (*a face mai dur*) to harden; *metal* to temper; *mil* (*a fortifica*) to fortify; (*d. poziție, autoritate*) *also fig* to consolidate; to legalize; (*a sublinia*) to stress; (*a corobora*) to corroborate; (*o afirmație*) to back up; to confirm; (*cu autoritate*) to sanction; (*sănătatea*) to build up; (*d. aer*) to invigorate, to brace ‖ *vr* (*a se învârtoșa*) *also fig* to become/ grow hard; (*d. ciment*) to set; (*a se intensifica*) to strengthen, to intensify; to gain/gather strength; (*d. cineva*) to become fit/tough • **~re** *nf* reinforcement, strengthening, consolidation; **pronume de ~** emphatic pronoun • **~tor** *nn* tonic, cordial; *coll* pick-me-up ‖ *adj* fortifying, bracing * **întări**.

întâi [în'tâi] *num* (the) first; (*d. lecții, capitole*) one; **lecția ~** lesson one ‖ *adv* (*la început*) at first, first of all, in the beginning, firstly; **~ și** ~ first and foremost, above all, in the first place • **~etate** *nf* priority; (*preferință*) preference.

întâlni [întâl'ni] *vt* to meet; (*întâmplător*) to run into, to come across/upon; (*a găsi*) to find; *fig* (*dificultăți*) to meet, to come up against; *sp* to encounter ‖ *vr* to meet • **~re** *nf* (*întâmplătoare*) meeting; (*stabilită* *dinainte*) appointment; *coll* date; (*tainică*) assignation; (*sportivă*) encounter, contest, match, (*box*) fight; (*luptă*) fight, skirmish.

întâmpina [întâmpi'na] *vt* to meet; (*a saluta*) to greet, to welcome; (*a da de*) to come across/upon; (*greutăţi*) to face, to come up against • ~re *nf* (*primire*) meeting, welcome • **în ~rea** in anticipation of; contestation, objection.

întâmpla [întâm'pla] *vr* (*a avea loc*) to happen, to occur, to come about; *obs lit* to befall; (*a se alege cu*) to become of • ~re *nf* (*eveniment*) event, occurrence, incident; (*soartă*) chance, hazard, accident; ~ **norocoasă** streak of luck; *coll* fluke.

întâmplător [întâmplă'tor] *adj* accidental, fortuitous; (*d. câştiguri*) odd ‖ *adv* accidentally, by chance/accident.

întârzia [întâr'zia] *vt* to delay, to hold up ‖ *vi* (*la*) to be late (for), to come late (for); (*d. un tren*) to be overdue; (*cu plata chiriei*) to be back/behindhand; (*a zăbovi*) to linger.

întârziere [întârzi'ere] *nf* (*amânare*) delay, retardation; (*la ore*) coming/being late, lateness; *phys, elec* lag; **a fi în ~ (cu)** to be late, to be in arrears.

întemeia [înteme'ia] *vt* (*oraş, afaceri*) to found; (*afaceri, ziar*) to set up; (*a crea*) to create; *fig* (*pe*) to base (on) ‖ *vr* (*d. cineva*) to rely on; (*d. ceva*) to be based/grounded on.

întemeietor [întemeie'tor] *nm* founder.

întemniţa [întemni'tsa] *vt* to jail, to put smb in prison; to imprison.

înteţi [înte'tsi] *vt* to intensify ‖ *vr* to grow strong/stronger.

întina [înti'na] *vt* to defile, to tarnish, to taint; **a ~ reputaţia cuiva** to tarnish/damage smb's reputation.

întinde [în'tinde] *vt* (*a trage*) to pull, to draw; (*un elastic*) to stretch; (*a lungi*) to lengthen; (*a dilata*) to dilate, to expand; (*mâna*) to hold/reach/stretch out; (*a oferi: ziar*) to hold out; (*a aşterne*) to spread (out); (*a pune*) to lay, to put; (*a aranja*) to arrange; *fig* (*a lungi*) to drag out ‖ *vr* (*a se lungi*) to stretch (oneself); (*a se dilata*) to dilate, to expand; (*a se culca*) to lie down; (*a se tolăni*) to sprawl; (*a cădea lat*) to go sprawling; *fig* (*a se lungi*) to be dragged out, to linger; (*a dura*) to last • ~re *nf* (*acţiune*) stretching, * **întinde**; extent, expanse, stretch; (*suprafaţă*) surface, area.

întineri [întine'ri] *vt* to rejuvenate ‖ *vi* to grow younger, to look younger ‖ *vr* to make oneself look younger.

întipări [întipă'ri] *vt also fig* (*în*) to imprint (upon), to stamp (upon); to inculcate ‖ *vr* to stamp/impress oneself (upon); to be branded/graven.

întoarce [în'toarche] *vt* (*a învârti*) to turn; (*a înapoia*) to return; (*ceasul*) to wind up; (*pe dos*) to reverse, to revert; (*fânul*) to toss up; (*a ara din nou*) to turn up (for the second time); (*a replica*) to retort; **a ~ capul** to turn away one's head; **a ~ cuiva spatele** to sit/stand with one's back to smb; *fig* to give smb the cold shoulder, to turn one's back on smb ‖ *vr* (*a se înapoia*) to return, to come back; (*a se răsuci*) to twist, to swing; (*pe loc*) to turn round; (*a se îndrepta spre*) to turn to; (*a se răzgândi*) to change one's mind.

întocmai [în'tokmai] *adv* exactly, precisely; (*chiar aşa*) just so; (*la fel*) (just) the same; (*bineînţeles*) naturally, of course, certainly; (*da*) yes.

întocmi [întok'mi] *vt* (*a elabora*) to draw up, to work out; (*a scrie*) to write; (*a compune*) to compose; (*a

pregăti) to prepare; **a ~ o listă** to draw up a list, to make a list; to organize, to set up; (*a aranja*) to arrange

întorsătură [întorsă'tură] *nf* turn, curve, bend; *fig* contingency; **a lua o ~ fericită/proastă** to take a turn for the better/worse.

întortocheat [întorto'keat] *adj* winding, sinuous, tortuous; (*neclar*) confused, obscure; (*d. stil*) involved, intricate.

întotdeauna [întotdea'una] *adv* always, ever.

întovărăşi [întovără'shi] *vt* (*a însoţi*) to accompany; *recip agr* to form an agricultural association ‖ *vr* (*cu*) to associate (with), to come together.

între ['între] *prep* (*pt. două elemente*) between; *obs lit* betwixt; (*pt. mai multe elemente*) among, amongst; *lit* amid, amidst.

întreba [între'ba] *vt* to ask, to question, to inquire; to examine; **a ~ pe cineva ceva** to ask smb smth ‖ *vi* (*a se interesa de*) to ask about, to inquire after/about/for ‖ *vr* to ask oneself, to wonder • ~re *nf* question, query; matter, question, problem.

întrebător [întrebă'tor] *adj* inquiring, questioning ‖ *adv* inquiringly, questioningly.

întrebuinţa [întrebuin'tsa] *vt* to use, to make use of ‖ *vr* (*a se folosi*) to be in usage, to be used • ~re *nf* use, utilization; **mod de ~** directions for use.

întrece [în'treche] *vt* (*a lăsa în urmă*) to leave behind, to outrun; *fig* (*a depăşi*) to surpass, to exceed; (*a fi superior cuiva*) to excel; **a ~ toate aşteptările** to exceed smb's expectations ‖ *vr* to compete/vie (with) • ~re *nf* competition, emulation; *sp* contest.

întredeschis [întredes'kis] *adj* half-open; (d. uşă) ajar.

întreg [în'treg] *nm* whole; *math* integer ‖ *adj* whole, entire, all; complete, full; (*neprescurtat*) unabridged; (*neştirbit*) undivided; throughout the world • **pe de-a ~ul** entirely, totally, completely • ~**i** [între'dji] *vt* to complete, to round off ‖ *vr* to be completed/rounded off.

întreit [între'it] *adj* treble, triple, threefold ‖ *adv* trebly, triply, threefold.

întrema [între'ma] *vr* to recover, to be/get well again, to pick up (strength).

întreprinde [între'prinde] *vt* to undertake, to embark upon, to venture; (*a organiza*) to organize; (*un studiu*) to enter upon; (*a începe*) to begin • ~re *nf* enterprise; industry, factory; (*comercială*) store, shop; *fig* undertaking; ~ **bancară** bank.

întreprinzător [întreprinză'tor] *adj* enterprising, go-ahead.

întrerupător [întrerupă'tor] *nn elec* switch.

întrerupe [între'rupe] *vt* to interrupt, to discontinue; (*a opri brusc*) to break off; (*d. tăcere, călătorie*) to break; (*d. circulaţie*) to stop; (*d. curent*) to cut/switch off ‖ *vr* to break off, to stop • ~re *nf* interruption; (*încetare*) stoppage, cessation; (*oprire*) break; (*a negocierilor*) breaking off; **fără ~** uninterruptedly, without cessation, continually.

întretăia [întretă'ia] *vt* to cross, to intersect; (*d. linii*) to cut; (*a întrerupe*) to interrupt, to break; *recip* to cross, to intersect.

întretăiere [întretă'iere] *nf* crossing; (*de drumuri*) crossing, crossroads, intersection.

întreţine [între'tsine] *vt* (*pe cineva*) to support; (*a păstra*) to keep; (*d. corespondenţa*) to keep up; **a ~ o conversaţie** to keep up a conversation; (*d. agitaţie*) to foster; (*a alimenta*) to feed ‖ *vr* to support/maintain oneself; (*cu cineva*) to talk with smb (about smth), to converse (with) • ~**re** *nf* (*a cuiva*) support; (*a drumurilor*) maintenance, upkeep; (*la bloc*) rates.

întrevedea [între'dea] *vt* to catch a glimpse of, to catch sight of; (*a prevedea*) to foresee, to contemplate ‖ *vr* to be foreseen/foreshadowed; (*a se zări*) to loom, to be outlined; (*a se aştepta*) to be expected; (*a fi în perspectivă*) to be in prospect.

întrevedere [între've'dere] *nf* meeting, interview, appointment.

întrezări [întreză'ri] *vt* to catch a glimpse of, to catch sight of; (*a prevedea*) to foresee ‖ *vr* to loom.

întrista [întris'ta] *vt* to sadden, to grieve ‖ *vr* to grieve, to be grieved/distressed about smth • ~**re** *nf* grief, sadness, sorrow; **cu** ~ sadly, sorrowfully • ~**t** *adj* sad, grieved, depressed.

întru ['întru] *prep* (*spaţial*) in; into; within; **a locui** ~**un sat** to live in a village; **a intra** ~**o cameră** to enter a room; (*temporal*) in, within; ~**un an** within a year; ~**o clipă** in a moment, in a heartbeat; ~ **totul** wholly, entirely.

întrucât [întru'cât] *conj* as, since, because, for • ~**va** *adv* somehow, to a certain extent, somewhat; (*destul de*) rather.

întruchipa [întruki'pa] *vt* to embody, to impersonate; to represent; to personify; *pass* to be embodied.

întruni [întru'ni] *vt* to bring together; to combine; (*condiţie*) to meet; (*a obţine*) to get ‖ *vr* to rally, to gather, to assemble • ~**re** *nf* meeting, rally, assembly.

întuneca [întune'ka] *vt* *also fig* to cloud; (*a înnora*) to cloud; *fig* to muddle, to obscure ‖ *vr* (*a se însera*) to be getting/growing dark; *also fig* to darken, to become gloomy; (*d. minte*) to grow dim • ~**t** *adj* dark, dim; (*posomorât*) gloomy, bleak; (*înnorat*) clouded, overcast; (*sinistru*) grim.

întunecime [întune'chime] *nf* darkness, gloom(iness), dusk.

întunecos [întune'kos] *adj* dark; *fig* gloomy, somber.

întuneric [intu'nerik] *nm* dark; *fig* darkness, obscurity.

înţărca [întsăr'ka] *vt* to wean; *fig* (*de*) *coll* to wean (from) ‖ *vi* to run dry.

înţelegător [întselegă'tor] *adj* gentle, kind, understanding; broad-minded, tolerant; (*îngăduitor*) lenient ‖ *adv* gently, etc.

înţelege [întse'ledje] *vt* to understand, to make out; (*a pricepe*) to see; (*a-şi da seama de*) to realize; (*o aluzie*) to take the hint; (*a distinge*) to distinguish; (*a vrea să spună*) to mean (to say); **ce înţelegi prin asta?** what do you mean?; *recip* to understand one another; (*a ajunge la o înţelegere*) to come to an agreement/understanding; (*a fi de acord*) to agree; (*a fi în termeni buni*) to get on (well) together; (*a pune la cale, a complota*) to plot, to scheme; *pass* (*a fi clar/de înţeles*) to be clear; (*a fi citeţ*) to be legible • ~**re** *nf* understanding; (*învoială*) agreement; (*compătimire*) sympathy; (*bunăvoinţă*) kindness, goodwill.

înţelepciune [întselep'chune] *nf* wisdom, sagacity; (*prudenţă*) discretion, prudence.

înţelept [întse'lept] *nm* wise man, sage ‖ *adj* wise, sagacious, prudent ‖ *adv* wisely.

înţeles [întse'les] *nn* sense, meaning; **a avea** ~ to make sense; **nu are** ~ it makes no sense; **cu** ~ *adj* significant, meaningful ‖ *adv* significantly, meaningfully; **de** ~ compliant, tractable; (*rezonabil*) sensible.

înţepa [întse'pa] *vt* (*cu acul*) to prick; (*d. o albină*) *also fig* to sting; (*d. purici: a pişca*) to bite; *fig* to taunt, to nettle, to pique; *med* to give smb an injection/shot; **a** ~ **pe cineva** to taunt, to tease ‖ *vi* to prick, to sting, to bite ‖ *vr* to prick/sting oneself, to get stung; to give oneself an injection/shot; *fig* to taunt/nettle each other.

înţepător [întsepă'tor] *adj* pricky, stinging; (*d. gust*) pungent; (*picant*) piquant; tart; *fig iro* sharp, biting, cutting.

înţepătură [întsepă'tură] *nf* sting, prick; (*injecţie*) injection, shot; *pl* * **furnicătură**; *fig* biting remark, taunt.

înţepeni [întsepe'ni] *vt* (*a fixa*) to fasten, to fix ‖ *vi* to stick, to get stuck; *fig* (*de frig*) to become stiff (with); (*de frică/uimire*) to remain stock-still, to be paralyzed (with) ‖ *vr* (*d. roţi*) to stick, to get stuck; to become rigid; (*d. cineva*) to plant oneself, to stand squarely.

înţesa [întse'sa] *vt* to pack, to fill (to capacity), to cram • ~**t** *adj* (*de*) full (of), packed (with), crowded (with).

învălmăşeală [învălmă'sheală] *nf* bustle, jumble, turmoil; (*mulţime*) crowd, throng, hubbub; (*încăierare*) scuffle.

învălui [învălu'i] *vt* to envelop, to cover; (*a înfăşura*) to wrap (up); (*a înconjura*) to surround; (*a încercui*) to encircle; *mil* to outflank.

învăpăiat [învăpă'iat] *adj* inflamed, flaming, aflame; (*înfierbântat*) hot; (*arzător*) ardent; (*scânteietor*) bright; (*aprig*) fiery.

învăţa [învă'tsa] *vt/vi* (*singur*) to learn, to study; **a** ~ **limbi străine** to learn foreign languages; **a** ~ **ceva pe de rost/pe dinafară** to learn smth by heart; (*a preda*) to teach ‖ *vr* to be/get used/accustomed/inured (to); to get into the habit of (doing smth) • ~**t** *nm* scholar, intellectual; *coll* egg-head; *iro* highbrow ‖ *adj* learned; (*cult*) cultured; (*instruit*) educated; (*deprins cu*) accustomed to, used to, inured to.

învăţământ [învătsă'mânt] *nn* education, instruction; (*lecţie*) lesson; (*morală*) moral; ~ **elementar/primar** elementary/primary education; ~ **mediu** secondary education; ~ **mixt** co-education; ~ **superior** college/university education.

învăţătoare [învătsă'toare] *nf* teacher, school-mistress.

învăţător [învătsă'tor] *nm* (school)teacher, schoolmaster; *fig* teacher.

învăţătură [învătsă'tură] *nf* learning, studies; (*ucenicie*) apprenticeship; (*învăţământ*) education, instruction; teaching, moral; (*sfat*) advice; (*lecţie*) lesson; (*cunoştinţe*) knowledge; culture; (*politică*) teaching doctrine.

învârti [învâr'ti] *vt* to spin (round); (*a răsuci*) to twist, to whirl round; (*a dansa*) to dance; (*a mânui*) to wield; (*arme*) to brandish, to flourish; *fig coll* to carry on ‖ *vr* to turn, to spin, to twirl; *astron, tech* to revolve, to rotate; (*a nu mai avea astâmpăr*) to fidget; (*a se căpătui*) to come up/rise in the world; **a i se** ~ **capul** to be/feel giddy/dizzy • ~**tură** *nf* (*întorsătură*) turn, twist, bend; *fig coll* trick.

învârtoşa [învârto'sha] *vt/vr, also fig* to harden.

învechi [înve'ki] *vr* to age, to become old; (*d. cuvânt, obicei*) to become obsolete, to become out of date, to go/fall out of use; (*d. haine: a se uza*) to wear out; (*d. vin*) to mature • ~**t** *adj* old, old-fashioned; (*d. cuvânt*) obsolete; out of date/use, out of fashion •

tehnologie ~tă outmoded technology; (*d. un fumător*) confirmed, inveterate.

învecina [învechi'na] *vr* (*a fi vecin*) to be neighbors, to be adjacent to; *fig* to border on/upon, to verge on • **~t** *adj* neighbor(ing); (*alăturat*) next, adjacent.

înveli [înve'li] *vt* (*a acoperi*) to cover; (*a înfășura*) to wrap (up) ‖ *vr* to wrap/tuck (oneself) up • **~ș** *nn* cover; (*strat*) layer • **~toare** *nf* cover; blanket; *vernac* (*față de masă*) tablecloth.

învenina [înveni'na] *vt also fig* to poison, to envenom; *fig* to embitter.

înverșunare [învershu'nare] *nf* frenzy, fury, rage; (*încăpățânare*) obstinacy, stubbornness; **cu ~** (*aprig*) fiercely; (*frenetic*) frantically; (*încăpățânat*) obstinately, stubbornly.

înverșunat [învershu'nat] *adj* grim, fierce, furious; (*încăpățânat*) stubborn, obstinate.

înverzi [înver'zi] *vt* to make green; (*a vopsi în verde*) to paint smth green ‖ *vi* to go/grow/turn/become green; (*a înfrunzi*) to leaf (out); (*d. oameni*) to turn (ghastly) pale, to turn livid • **~t** *adj* green, verdant.

înveseli [învese'li] *vt* to cheer (smb) up; (*a înviora: conversația*) to brighten up; (*a distra: invitații*) to amuse, to divert; (*a bucura*) to gladden ‖ *vr* to cheer up, to brighten, to rejoice (at, in) • **~re** *nf* rejoicing, merry-making.

investi [înves'ti] *vt* (*cu*) to invest (with), to vest smb (with) • **~re** *nf* (*cu*) investing, investment (with); *jur* authorizing, mandating, giving power of attorney (to).

învia [învi'a] *vt* to raise from the dead, to resurrect; *fig* to revive; (*a anima*) to reanimate ‖ *vi* to rise again, to rise from the dead; *fig* to revive; **Cristos a ~t!** Christ is risen!

înviere [învi'ere] *nf* resurrection; *fig* revival, rebirth.

învingător [învingă'tor] *nm* conqueror, victor ‖ *adj* victorious, triumphant.

învinge [in'vindje] *vt* to defeat, to vanquish; *fig* to overcome, to conquer ‖ *vi* to win, to be victorious, to carry the day.

învinovăți [învinovă'tsi] *vt* (*de*) to accuse (of smth), to charge (with), to find fault (with); *recip* to accuse each other ‖ *vr* to accuse oneself of • **~re** *nf* accusing * **învinovățí**; (*acuzație*) accusation, charge.

învinui [învinu'i] *vt* (*de*) to accuse (of), to charge (with), to blame (for) • **~re** *nf* blame, charge, accusation • **~t** *nm jur esp pl* the defendant, the accused.

înviora [învio'ra] *vt* to animate, to refresh; (*a încuraja*) to cheer up; (*d. culori, o cameră*) to brighten up; (*conversația*) to enliven ‖ *vr* (*d. cineva*) to cheer up, to take heart; (*a se anima*) to become animated • **~re** *nf* enlivening, refreshing, animation; *econ* revival, boom.

învoi [învo'i] *vt* to permit, to allow; to give (smb) leave of absence; *recip* to agree, to come to an agreement; to agree, to consent, to accept; (*de la serviciu*) to take leave of absence • **~re** *nf* leave; (*permisiune*) permission • **~ală** *nf* agreement, contract; (*secretă*) collusion; bargain; **~ scrisă** written agreement; **a cădea la ~** *com* to conclude/strike a bargain; *fig* to come to terms, to come to an agreement.

învrăjbi [învrăzh'bi] *vt* to set against each other, to sow (the seeds of) dissension ‖ *vr* to quarrel, to be at loggerheads • **~re** *nf* feud, discord, quarrel.

învrednici [învredni'chi] *vt* (*cu*) to favor (with), to

honor, to vouchsafe ‖ *vr* (*a binevoi*) to deign; (*a fi în stare să...*) to be able to; (*a reuși*) to succeed (in).

înzăpezit [înzăpe'zit] *adj* snowbound, snowed up.

înzdrăveni [înzdrăve'ni] *vt* to cure ‖ *vr* to recover, to pick up strength.

înzecit [înze'chit] *adj/adv* tenfold.

înzestra [înzes'tra] *vt* (*o industrie*) to endow; (*a echipa*) to equip, to fit out; (*o fată*) to dower; *fig* to endow • **~re** *nf* endowment, equipment, outfit; dowering; *fig* endowments; (*naturală*) gifts; accomplishments, talents • **~t** *adj* endowed; (*talentat*) gifted, talented.

înzorzona [înzorzo'na] *vt* to deck out, to smarten up; *coll* to dress up; *fig* to embroider, to adorn ‖ *vr* to get oneself up, to bedeck oneself.

J

jac [zhak] *nn tech* jack.

jacuzzi [zha'kuzi] *nn* jacuzzi, spa.

jachetă [zha'ketă] *nf* (*pt. bărbați*) sports coat/jacket; (*pt. femei*) jacket.

jad [zhad] *nn* jade.

jaf [zhaf] *nn* plunder, pillage; (*tâlhărie*) robbery; (*jaf armat*) armed robbery; (*la un magazin, o bancă*) hold-up; (*în cantități mici, dar repetat*) pilfering;(*risipă*) extravagance, waste, prodigality.

jaguar [zhagu'ar] *nm zool* jaguar.

jale ['zhale] *nf* (*tristețe*) sorrow; grief; (*disperare*) despair, dismay; (*nenorocire*) misfortune; disaster, tragedy; (*durere*) woe(s), heartache, suffering; (*mizerie, sărăcie*) hardship; deprivation, poverty; (*doliu*) mourning; (*bocete*) keening, wailing; a song of mourning; (*gemete*) moan(ing), groan(ing); **cu ~** (*trist*) sadly, gloomily, mournfully; **de ~** (*d. lucruri*) deplorable, sad, pitiable; (*d. aspect*) doleful; lugubrious; (*care inspiră milă*) pathetic, pitiful, piteous, pitiable.

jalnic ['zhalnik] *adj* (*trist*) sad, grievous, heartbreaking; (*d. voce*) plaintive; melancholy, wistful; (*d. lucruri*) pitiable, deplorable, dispiriting ‖ *adv* sadly, etc.

jalon [zha'lon] *nn* stake, pole; *fig* landmark.

jaluzele [zhalu'zele] *nf pl* blinds.

jambon [zham'bon] *nn* ham.

jandarm [zhan'darm] *nm approx* policeman; **~ călare** mounted policeman.

jantă ['zhantă] *nf auto* wheelrim.

japonez [zhapo'nez] *adj/nm* Japanese • **~ă** *adj/nf* Japanese (woman); (*limba*) Japanese; (*păiniță*) *approx* bread roll.

jar [zhar] *nn* embers; a live brand; coal; (*dogoare*) glow; heat; *fig* ardor, fervor, fire, passion.

jardinieră [zhardini'eră] *nf* window box, jardinière, flower stand.

jargon [zhar'gon] *nn* jargon; cant; (*terminologie specifică unei meserii*) (*numele meseriei*) parlance; **~ gazetăresc/administrativ/medical** newspaper/ official/medical parlance; (*cu conotație negativă*) journalese, officialese.

jartieră [zharti'eră] *nf* garter; **Ordinul Jartierei** the Order of the Garter.

javră ['zhavră] *nf* mongrel, cross-breed, cur; *coll* (*d. o persoană*) tyke, punk; creep; slob; wanker; (*obscen*) bugger; *vulg* shit; jerk.

jaz [zhaz] *nn mus* jazz.

jder [zhder] *nm zool* marten.

jefui [zhefu'i] *vt* (*un ţinut, prin forţă armată*) to plunder, to loot; *obs* to spoil; (*o bancă, un magazin*) to rob; (*în cantităţi mici, dar repetat*) to pilfer; *fig* to fleece, to bleed • **~tor** *nm* plunderer; robber, thief.

jeg [zheg] *coll* slime • **~os** *adj* slimy; dirty, filthy; unwashed.

jeleu [zhe'leu] *nn* jelly.

jeli [zhe'li] *vt* to mourn for, to lament over; to grieve over, to weep for; (*soarta*) to bewail, to bemoan; (*a compătimi*) to pity, to sympathize with || *vi/vr* (*a se tângui*) to lament, to moan, to groan; (*a purta doliu*) to be in mourning for.

jena [zhe'na] *vt* (*a perturba, a împiedica, a incomoda*) to interfere with, to hinder, to impede; (*circulaţia auto*) to hold up, to block; (*a împiedica trecerea/ drumul cuiva*) to be in the way; (*a împiedica vederea*) to obstruct/block the view; (*a strânge*) to be too tight, to pinch; *fig* to embarrass; (*a sta în drumul cuiva*) to be in the way, to inconvenience smb; (*a face să se simtă jenat*) to make smb feel embarrassed; to feel ill at ease || *vr* to be timid, to be bashful • **~nt** *adj* (*d. o persoană*) embarrassing; (*situaţie, linişte*) awkward; (*d. un obiect*) cumbersome; (*incomod*) inconvenient, annoying; (*neplăcut*) unpleasant; delicate, ticklish; (*penibil*) painful, traumatic.

jenă ['zhenă] *nf* (*încurcătură*) embarrassment, perplexity, awkwardness; (*deranj*) inconvenience; (*dificultate fizică*) discomfort, uneasiness; *med* difficulty; (*timiditate*) shyness, timidity, reserve; (*financiară*) want; **fără ~** (*cu neruşinare*) shameless(ly), insolent(ly); (*deschis, pe faţă*) open(ly), frank(ly).

jeratic [zhe'ratik] *nn* live coals; (*ultimii cărbuni aprinşi*) embers.

jerbă ['zherbă] *nf* (*de flori*) spray of flowers; (*de scântei*) shower of sparks; (*de foc*) burst of fire; *mil* cone of fire; (*de apă*) spray/shower of water; *phys* shower.

jerpelit [zherpe'lit] *adj coll* (*d. un obiect*) shabby(-looking), ragged, tattered; (*d. o persoană*) (*fizic*) worn-out, wrecked; (*d. îmbrăcăminte*) worn-out.

jerseu [zher'seu] *nn* (*material*) jersey (cloth); (*obiect de îmbrăcăminte*) jersey.

jertfă ['zhertfă] *nf* offering, sacrifice; victim; (*martir*) martyr; (*pradă*) prey.

jertfi [zhert'fi] *vt* to sacrifice, to immolate; (*a omorî*) to kill || *vr* to sacrifice oneself.

jet [zhet] *nn tech* jet, spurt, spray, splash; **~ de aer** air jet.

jeton [zhe'ton] *nn* (*fisă de telefon*) coin; (*fisă la jocul de cărţi*) chip; (*la maşini de spălat*) token; *com* (*onorariu pt. participarea la o şedinţă*) director's fees.

jgheab [zhgeab] *nn* (*canal pt. scurgerea apei la marginea drumului*) gutter; (*streaşină*) eaves; (*pt. adăpat*) trough; (*în munte*) gully; (*crestătură, adâncitură*) groove.

jigărit [zhigă'rit] *adj coll* skinny, scrawny, bag of bones.

jigni [zhig'ni] *vt* to offend smb, to insult, to hurt/injure (smb's feelings) || *vr* to be offended, to feel offended • **~re** *nf* offense, hurt; affront, insult • **~tor** *adj* offensive, insulting.

jigodie [zhi'godie] *nf vet* distemper; *vet* mange; (*ticălos*) scoundrel, knave; * **jivină**.

jilav [zhi'lav] *adj* (*uşor umed*) moist, damp; (*d. aer şi vreme*) humid; (*asociat cu temperatura scăzută*) dank.

jiletcă [zhi'letkă] *nf* waistcoat.

jindui [zhindu'i] *vt* (*a dori cu intensitate*) to hanker for/after, to crave for; (*a râvni*) to covet; (*a tânji după*) to long/yearn for • **~tor** *adj* covetous, longing for * **jindui** || *adv* covetously, desiringly.

jir [zhir] *nn bot* (oak/beech) mast.

jivină [zhi'vină] *nf* animal, wild beast; (*nedefinit şi posibil peiorativ*) living thing/creature; *fig* (*negativ d. o persoană*) monster, brute, savage.

joacă ['zhoakă] *nf* play(ing); (*distracţie*) fun, pastime; **în ~** (just) for fun, jokingly, as a joke.

joagăr ['zhoagăr] *nn* sawmill.

joardă ['zhoardă] *nf* switch, rod.

joben [zho'ben] *nn* (*la ceremonii, pe scenă*) top hat; crush/opera hat.

joc [zhok] *nn* (*amuzament*) play; **~ cinstit** fair play; (*activitate care presupune un câştigător*) game; **~uri pe calculator** computer games; **~ periculos** dangerous game; (*cărţi de joc*) playing cards; (*ca activitate supusă hazardului*) (*la cazino*) gambling; **~ de bursă** stock market gamble; (*la tenis de câmp*) game; **în ~** in play; *thea* acting; **~ de lumini** lighting effects; (*ca ansamblu*) set; **~ de şah** chess set; **~ de domino** set of dominoes; **~ de cărţi** pack/deck of cards; **~ de popice** set of ninepins; *tech* play, looseness; **are ~** it's rather loose; (*dans*) dance, dancing; **~ popular** folk dance; **~ de lumini** play of light; **~ de cuvinte** play on words, pun.

jocheu [zho'keu] *nm* jockey.

joi [zhoi] *nf* Thursday; **din ~ în Paşti** *coll* once in a blue moon.

joncţiune [zhonktsi'une] *nf* junction; (*acţiunea*) joining.

jongla [zhon'gla] *vi* to juggle (with); (*la circ*) to play tricks by sleight of hand.

jongler [zhon'gler] *nm* juggler • **~ie** *nf* juggling.

jos [zhos] *adj* low; (*josnic*) base, vulgar || *adv* down; (*dedesubt*) below; *lit* beneath, underneath; (*pe pământ*) (down) on the ground; *fig* here, below, on this earth; (*la parter*) on the first floor; downstairs; (*la fund*) at the bottom; (*la poalele dealului*) at the foot of the hill; (*la subsolul unei pagini*) at the bottom/foot of the page; (*ca stare socială*) lowly, humble || *nn* bottom; **în ~** *adv* downwards; **în sus şi în ~** up and down; **~ mâna!** *interj* hands off! • **~nic** *adj* abject, base, despicable || *adv* despicably, basely, shamefully • **~nicie** *nf* baseness, infamy, vulgarity.

jovial [zhovi'al] *adj* cheerful, jolly, joyful || *adv* cheerfully, joyfully, jovially • **~itate** *nf* joliness, joviality, cheerfulness; *coll* jollity.

jubila [zhubi'la] *vi* to jubilate, to be jubilant, to exult; (*cu mulţumire de sine sau cu răutate*) to gloat (over).

jubileu [zhubi'leu] *nn* jubilee.

juca [zhu'ka] *vi* (*a se distra*) to play; *thea* (*d. un actor*) to act; (*a paria*) to gamble; (*care are joc*) to fit loosely || *vt* (*un joc*) to play; (*a dansa*) to dance; (*d. imagine la televizor, calculator etc*) to flicker || *vr* to play; (*a-şi petrece timpul*) to amuse oneself; (*a glumi*) to sport; *pass* to be played; (*la teatru*) to be on.

jucărie [zhukă'rie] *nf* toy, plaything; *fig* easy thing, mere play, trifle.

jucător *nm*, **jucătoare** *nf* [zhukă'tor, zhukă'toare] player; (*la jocuri de noroc, cartofor*) gambler, gamester; (*la bursă*) stockbroker; *vernac* (*dansator*) dancer.

jucăuş [zhukă'ush] *adj* playful, frisky; (*despre ochi*) (*care invită*) rolling; (*inteligenţi, cu interes*) quick.

judeca [zhude'ka] *vt jur* (*un caz*) to try; (*o cerere, un litigiu*) to arbitrate, to adjudicate; (*a-şi da avizul asupra unei situaţii, cărţi*) to judge; (*a crede*) to think, to be of the opinion that; **judecând după** judging by, going by ‖ *vr* (*cu cineva*) to carry on a lawsuit with smb; (*pe sine*) to judge oneself; (*d. un proces*) to be tried; *recip* to judge one another ‖ *vi* to judge • **~tă** [zhude'kată] *nf jur* (*raţiune*) judgment; (*proces*) trial; **a aduce în** ~ to bring smb to trial, to put smb on trial; *jur* (*decizie*) decision; (*într-o afacere juridică*) sentence, verdict; (*opinie*) opinion, view; ~ **sănătoasă** sound judgment, good sense.

judecător [zhudekă'tor] *nm jur* judge; magistrate; justice; (*arbitru*) arbitrator; ~ **de pace** justice of the peace; *fig* judge; connoisseur • **~ie** *nf* (*sediu*) law court; courtroom.

judeţ [zhu'dets] *nn* (*unitate administrativ-teritorială*) county; region; district; *obs* (*judecată*) judgment, trial.

judiciar [zhudichi'ar] *adj* judicial; (*judecătoresc*) judiciary; juridical; **anchetă ~ă** judicial inquiry; **eroare ~ă** miscarriage of justice; **medicină ~ă** forensic medicine; **procedură ~ă** legal proceedings.

judicios [zhudichi'os] *adj* appropriate; sensible, judicious; thoughtful ‖ *adv* judiciously, sensibly, thoughtfully.

judo ['zhudo] *nn sp* judo.

jug [zhug] *nn also fig* yoke; *constr* trimmer.

juli [zhu'li] *vt* to scrape, to graze ‖ *vr* to graze one's skin; to hurt oneself.

jumătate [zhumă'tate] *nf* half; *coll* (*soţie*) (one's) better half; *mus* minim; (*stare incompletă*) halfness; **o ~ de oră** half an hour ‖ *adv* half; ~ **american,** ~ **român** half American, half Romanian.

jumuli [zhumu'li] *vt* (*de pene*) to pluck; *fig* (*de bani, bunuri*) to fleece, to bleed.

juncă ['zhunkă] *nf* heifer.

june ['zhune] *adj obs hum/iro* young; *coll* green, raw ‖ *nm* young man, youth; (*foarte tânăr*) a young guy, stripling; (*băiat*) boy; *coll* youngster; ~ **prim** *thea* (*jeune*) premier.

junghi ['zhunghi] *nn med* shooting/sudden/sharp pain.

junglă ['zhunglă] *nf* jungle.

junioară [zhuni'oară] *nf sp* junior (sportswoman/athlete).

junior [zhuni'or] *nm sp* junior (sportsman/athlete).

jupon [zhu'pon] *nn obs* petticoat; (*modern*) underskirt.

jupui [zhupu'i] *vt* (*pielea*) to skin, to graze, to flay; (*scoarţa*) to bark; (*coaja unui fruct*) to peel; *fig* to bleed, to fleece; to exploit ‖ *vr* to peel off.

jur [zhur] *nn* **în** ~ around; **de** ~ **împrejur** all (a)round, round about; (*în cerc*) in a circle; (*pe toate părţile*) on all sides; (*pretutindeni*) everywhere; in all directions; **în** ~ **de** about, around, approximately.

jura [zhu'ra] *vt* to swear; *lit, frml* to vow; **a** ~ **fidelitate cuiva** to swear/pledge loyalty to smb ‖ *vi* to swear • **~t** *adj* sworn ‖ *nm jur* juryman, juror; *pl* the jury.

jurământ [zhură'mânt] *nn* oath; *fig lit* (*de dragoste*) vow; (*promisiune*) pledge; **a depune** ~ to take an oath; (*de către un juriu, un funcţionar*) to be sworn in; *mil* to be sworn into the army; **a fi sub** ~ to be under oath.

jurisconsult [zhuriskon'sult] *nm* jurisconsult; legal expert.

jurisdicţie [zhuris'diktsie] *nf* (*competenţă*) jurisdiction; (*tribunal*) courts (of law); **a se afla sub** ~ to be in/under the jurisdiction of.

jurisprudenţă [zhurispru'dentsă] *nf* (*doctrină*) jurisprudence; (*decizie*) precedent; (*ansamblu de decizii*) case law.

jurist [zhu'rist] *nm* legal expert, jurist.

juriu ['zhuriu] *nn jur* jury; **membru al ~lui** member of the jury, juror; (*la un concurs, o expoziţie*) (panel of) judges; (*la un examen*) examining board, board of examiners.

jurnal [zhur'nal] *nn* (*publicaţie*) (news)paper; journal; (*cotidian*) daily paper; (*de modă*) fashion magazine; (*intim*) diary; (*de însemnări tehnice, într-un experiment*) record(s); *cin* newsreel; *rad* radio news; TV news; *fin* ledger • **~ist** *nm* journalist, newspaperman, reporter, interviewer.

just [zhust] *adj* (*echitabil, d. o persoană, decizie, pedeapsă*) fair, just, right; (*exact, d. calcul, răspuns*) accurate, correct; (*d. raţionament*) sound; (*potrivit*) suitable; (*drept*) righteous; (*legitim*) legitimate, lawful; **e** ~ it's true, that's right ‖ *adv* justly; correctly; (*cum se cuvine*) properly; (*pe drept*) rightfully ‖ *interj* right, just so • **~ifica** *vt* (*acţiune, comportament, decizie, eroare*) to justify; (*cheltuieli de călătorie, activitate profesională*) to warrant ‖ *vr* to justify oneself; to clear oneself; to clear one's name of an accusation; (*comportament autorizat*) to be authorized to • **~ificare** *nf* (*explicaţie*) justification; (*dovadă*) proof, evidence; **a cere/căuta justificări** to demand/seek justification • **~iţie** *nf* (*echitate*) justice; righteousness; *jur* law.

juvenil [zhuve'nil] *adj* youthful; juvenile; **delincvenţă ~ă** juvenile delinquency.

juxtapune [zhuksta'pune] *vt* to juxtapose, to place side by side ‖ *vr* to be juxtaposed, in juxtaposition • **~re** *nf* juxtaposition.

K

kaki [ka'ki] *adj* khaki.

kamikaze [kami'kaze] *nm* kamikaze.

karate [ka'rate] *nn* karate.

karma ['karma] *nf phil, relig* karma.

karting ['karting] *nn* karting, go-cart racing; **a face** ~ to go carting.

kazah [ka'zah] *nm/adj* Kazak(h).

ketchup ['kechap] *nn cul* (tomato) ketchup.

kilobyte ['kilobait] *nm comp* kilobyte.

kil(ogram) [kilo'gram] *nn* kilo(gram).

kilolitru [kilo'litru] *nm* kiloliter, one thousand liters.

kilometraj [kilome'trazh] *nn* (*distanţă*) mileage; (*instrument de măsurat*) mileage recorder.

kilometru [kilo'metru] *nm* kilometer; **din** ~ **în** ~ every kilometer.

kilo-octet [kilook'tet] *nm comp* * **kilobyte.**

kilowatt [kilo'vat] *nm* kilowatt.

kilt [kilt] *nn* kilt.

kimono [kimo'no] *nn* kimono.

kirghiz [kir'giz] *nm/adj* Kirghiz.

kitsch ['kich] *nn* (*artă*) kitsch.

knock-out ['knokaut] *nn sp* knockout; **a face pe cineva** ~ to knock smb out.

know-how ['nǎuhau] *nn* know-how.
kola ['kola] *nf bot* cola/kola bean.
krypton ['kripton] *nn* krypton.
kurd [kurd] *nm geog* Kurd ‖ *adj* Kurdish • ~ă *nf ling* Kurdish.

L

la[1] [la] *prep (spaţial) (cu verbe de stare pe loc)* at; **este ~ şcoală** he is at school; *(cu verbe de deplasare)* to; **a merge ~ teatru** to go to the theater; *(în direcţia)* towards; *(temporal)* at; **a ajunge ~ timp** to get on/in time; *(în intervalul următor)* next; **~ un an o dată** once a year; *(în timpul)* during; *(distributiv)* **~ duzină** by the dozen; *(arătând diverse relaţii)* on; at; about; over; **a cânta ~** *(un instrument)* to play; *(apartenenţa, eventual temporară)* with; **le-am lăsat ~ secretară** I left them with the secretary.
la[2] [la] *nm mus* A; la.
labă ['labă] *nf (de câine, pisică)* paw; *(de pasăre)* foot; *(de insecte)* leg; *coll (picior la om)* pin; *(mână la om) pej* paw.
labil [la'bil] *adj* unstable, labile.
labirint [labi'rint] *nn (antic, din gard viu etc)* also anat labyrinth; *esp fig* maze.
laborant [labo'rant] *nm* lab(oratory) assistant.
laborator [labora'tor] *nn* laboratory, *coll* lab.
laborios [labori'os] *adj (dificil)* laborious; hard; *(d. stil) pej* labored; *(d. o persoană)* hard-working.
lac[1] [lak] *nn geog* lake; *(în Scoţia)* loch; *(mic, eleşteu)* pond; *(mai ales de agrement)* (boating) lake; *(glaciar)* tarn; *(lacul morii)* mill-pond.
lac[2] [lak] *nn (natural)* lac; varnish; resin solution; *(pt. lemn)* shellac; *(pe picturi)* gloss; lacquer; **a da cu ~** to varnish, to lacquer, to gloss; *(din piele)* patent leather.
lacăt ['lakăt] *nn* padlock; **~ cu cifru** combination lock; **sub ~** under lock (and key).
lacheu [la'keu] *nm* footman; flunkey; *fig (cu dispreţ)* toady; *(servile)* yes-man.
lacom ['lakom] *adj (pasionat)* greedy, avid; *(plin de entuziasm)* eager; hungry; *pej* covetous ‖ *adv* greedily, avidly, hungrily, covetously.
laconic [la'konik] *adj* laconic ‖ *adv* laconically.
lacrimă ['lakrimă] *nf* tear(drop); **în ~i** in tears; *(cantitate f. mică)* drop.
lacrimogen [lakrimo'djen] *adj (d. gaz, bombă)* tear; *fig* mawkish, maudlin; *(uşor sentimental)* namby-pamby; insipid.
lactate [lak'tate] *nf pl* dairy products.
lacună [la'kună] *nf (lipsă)* gap; *anat* lacuna, *pl* lacunae/lacunas; *(de memorie)* blank; *(într-o lege)* loophole; *bot* air cell.
lacustru [la'kustru] *adj (d. floră, faună)* lakeside, lakeshore; *(d. o locuinţă)* lake dwelling, pile dwelling.
ladă ['ladă] *nf (cutie)* case, box; *(cu capac)* chest; *(cufăr)* trunk; **~ de gunoi** trash/garbage can, dust bin.
lagăr ['lagăr] *nn* camp; **~ de concentrare** concentration camp; **~ de exterminare** extermination camp; **~ de muncă** work camp ‖ *nn tech* bearing.
lagună [la'gună] *nf* lagoon.
laic ['laik] *adj* lay, secular ‖ *nm* layman.
lalea [la'lea] *nf bot* tulip.
lamă[1] ['lamă] *nf (de cuţit)* blade; *(de resort)* leaf; *(de metal, sticlă)* strip; *(de microscop)* slide; *(de stor)*

slat; *(de parchet)* strip of parquet flooring; *anat* lamina.
lamă[2] ['lamă] *nf zool* llama.
lambriu [lam'briu] *nn constr* paneling, wainscoting (in wood); casing, lining (in marble).
lamelă [la'melă] *nf* lamella; *(de fier, plastic)* thin strip; *(de mica)* scale; *bot (de ciupercă)* gill; *(de microscop)* cover glass.
lamenta [lamen'ta] *vr* to lament, to wail; to complain • ~bil *adj* deplorable, appalling, dreadful, terrible; *pej* awful; *(d. o persoană)* hopeless, pathetic ‖ *adv* appallingly, etc • ~ţie *nf* lamentation, lament; *(de durere mare)* wail; *pej* moaning, complaining, whining.
lamina [lami'na] *vt/vr metal* to laminate, to roll; *fig (a distruge)* to erode; to destroy, to annihilate.
laminor [lami'nor] *nn metal* rolling mill, flatting mill; *(de hârtie)* plate glazing calendar.
lampadar [lampa'dar] *nn (pe un suport înalt)* floor lamp.
lampă ['lampă] *nf* lamp; **~ de buzunar** torchlight, flashlight; **~ de miner** miner's (safety) lamp; **~ cu petrol** oil lamp; **~ cu halogen** halogen lamp; **~ de birou** desk lamp/light; **~ de noptieră** bedside lamp; **~ de sudură** blowlamp.
lan [lan] *nn (cultivated)* field.
lance ['lanche] *nf* spear, lance.
landou [lan'dou] *nn (un tip de trăsură)* landau; *(pt. copii)* baby carriage.
languros [langu'ros] *adj* sentimental; affectionate; amorous; tender ‖ *adv* sentimentally, amorously.
langustă [lan'gustă] *nf zool* (spiny) lobster.
lanolină [lano'lină] *nf* lanoline.
lansa [lan'sa] *vt (a proiecta înainte)* to throw; *lit* to cast; *(cu violenţă)* to fling, to hurl; *(o săgeata)* to shoot; *(o torpilă)* to launch; *(o bombă)* to drop; *(un balon)* to send up; *(un film)* to release; *(a trimite) (semnale, SOS)* to send out; *(d. navă, proiect, atac, campanie, produs)* to launch; *(moda)* to start; *(o teorie)* to put forward; *(o listă de subscripţie)* to start a fund; *(pe cineva în afaceri)* to set smb up (in business); *fin (titluri de proprietate, un împrumut)* to issue shares/bond; *(a face să meargă) (un motor)* to start up; *(un alergător, un schior)* to get going; *(un tren, vehicul)* to rush along; *(un program pe calculator)* to run ‖ *vr (a alerga)* to rush/dash/shoot forward; *(în politică)* to launch out; *(a se angaja) (afaceri, discuţii, aventură)* to embark on; *(cheltuieli)* to get involved in; *(a se face cunoscut)* to make a name for oneself.
lanternă [lan'terna] *nf* lantern; *(pe construcţii)* skylight.
lanţ [lants] *nn (din metal)* chain; *naut* cable; *(de magazine, hoteluri)* chain; *(muntos)* range; *fig* series, string, train; *mil* line.
lanţetă [lan'tsetă] *nf* lancet.
laolaltă [lao'laltă] *adv* together.
lapida [lapi'da] *vt* to lapidate; to stone to death; *(a bate cu pietre pe cineva)* to stone; *fig (a critica sever)* to throw stones at smb.
lapidar [lapi'dar] *adj (concis, d. stil, replică)* concise, terse, succinct ‖ *nn* lapidary.
lapon [la'pon] *adj* Lapp, Lappish ‖ *nm* Lapp, Laplander • ~ă *nf* Lapp (woman); *(limba)* Lapponic ‖ *adj* Lapp.
lapoviţă ['lapovitsă] *nf* sleet.

lapsus ['lapsus] *nn* slip; (*de memorie*) blank; (*verbal*) slip of the tongue; (*în scris*) slip of the pen.

lapte ['lapte] *nn* milk; ~ **acru** sour milk; ~ **bătut** buttermilk; ~ **concentrat** evaporated milk; ~ **condensat** condensed milk; ~ **dulce/proaspăt** fresh milk; ~ **integral** whole milk; ~ **degresat** skim milk; ~ **praf** powdered/dry milk; ~ **de cocos** coconut milk; ~ **de pasăre** eggnog, egg flip; ~ **de var** limewater, whitewash; ~ **demachiant** cleansing lotion, cleanser.

larg [larg] *adj* (*întins*) (*d. drum, râu, masă*) wide; (*d. față, nas, mâini*) broad; (*d. haine*) loose-fitting; (*d. pantofi*) wide-fitting; **pe** ~ at length, at large; minutely, in detail; generous; (*spațios*) roomy, spacious || *nn* (*spațiu*) room, space; *naut* open sea; **în** ~ in the offing, on the high seas, out at sea.

larghețe [lar'getse] *nf* liberality, open-handedness; (*generozitate*) generosity, largesse; **cu** ~ generously.

laringe [la'rindje] *nn* larynx.

laringită [larin'djită] *nf med* laryngitis.

larmă ['larmă] *nf* tumult, uproar, din; (*d. voci care se ceartă*) row.

larvă ['larva] *nf* larva, *pl* larvae.

lasciv [las'chiv] *adj* (*senzual*) sensual, lascivious; (*lubric*) (*d. comportament*) lewd, lecherous; lustful, randy.

laser ['laser] *nn phys* laser; **rază de** ~ laser beam.

lasou [la'sou] *nn* lasso.

laş [lash] *adj* (*lipsit de curaj*) cowardly; (*care atacă pe la spate*) *also fig* dastardly; (*moale*) weak, feeble || *adv* in a cowardly manner || *nm* coward, dastard • ~**itate** *nf* (*lipsă de curaj*) cowardice, cowardliness; (*slăbiciune*) weakness; **act de** ~ act of cowardice.

lat [lat] *adj* (*între două limite, întins*) wide; (*toată întinderea*) broad; (*mare*) large; (*puțin adânc*) flat, shallow; ~ **în spate** broad-shouldered || *nm* broad; * **lățime**.

latent [la'tent] *adj* latent, dormant; (*ascuns*) hidden || *adv* latently.

lateral [late'ral] *adj* lateral || *adv* laterally; sideways.

latin [la'tin] *adj* Latin; **limbă** ~**ă** Romance/Latin language.

latitudine [lati'tudine] *nf geog* latitude; *fig* (*libertate*) scope, freedom.

latrină [la'trină] *nf* latrines, privy, outhouse.

latură ['latură] *nf* side; *fig* aspect; **în lături** aside || *interj* make way/room; **pe de lături** the wrong way; (*în plus*) extra; indirectly.

laţ [lats] *nn* loop, noose; *fig* trap, snare; (*pt. păsări*) bird trap; **a prinde în** ~ (*propriu*) to trap, to net; *fig* to (en)trap, to (en)snare.

laudă ['laudă] *nf* praise; (*elogiu*) eulogy; *pl* compliments; *relig* (*slavă*) glory; **demn de** ~ praiseworthy, commendable.

laur [laur] *nm* laurel; *bot* * **dafin**.

laureat [lau'reat] *adj* (*prize*)winning; laureate.

lavabil [la'vabil] *adj* washable.

lavabou [lava'bou] *nn* washstand; (*spălător*) lavatory.

lavandă [la'vandă] *nf bot* lavender; (*parfum*) lavender water.

lavă ['lavă] *nf geol* lava.

lavoar [la'voar] *nn* washstand.

laxativ [laksa'tiv] *adj/nn* laxative; ~ **uşor** aperient, mild laxative.

lăbărţa [lăbăr'tsa] *vr* (*a se deforma*) to get out of shape;

(*d. haine: a se lărgi*) to stretch; (*a atârna*) to hang loosely; to droop; (*de picioare*) to spraddle.

lăcaş [lă'kash] *nn obs* dwelling; (*casă*) house, place; *tech* groove.

lăcătuş [lăkă'tush] *nm* locksmith • ~**erie** *nf* (*meserie*) locksmith's trade; (*atelier*) locksmith's shop.

lăcomie [lăko'mie] *nf* greed; cupidity; (*la mâncare*) gluttony; *fig* greediness, avidity; **cu** ~ greedily.

lăcrămioară [lăkră'mioară] *nf bot* lily-of-the-valley; May/wood lily.

lăcrima [lăkri'ma] *vi* to shed tears; (*din cauza unei iritaţii*) to water; (*fals*) (*a se smiorcăi*) to snivel.

lăcustă [lă'kustă] *nf ento* locust; (*cosaş*) grasshopper.

lăfăi [lăfă'i] *vr* (*a sta comod*) to sprawl, to lean back; to loll, to lounge || *vi* * **huzuri**.

lămâi [lă'mâi] *nm bot* lemon-tree • ~**e** *nf* lemon.

lămuri [lămu'ri] *vt* (*a explica şi defini*) to make clear; to set straight; to work out; (*în detaliu*) to explicate; (*prin studiu atent şi efort*) to puzzle out; *coll* to crack; (*un mister, o situaţie*) to clear up; (*a elucida*) to clarify; (*a rezolva*) to solve; (*a arunca lumină asupra*) to throw/shed light upon; (*a stabili*) to settle; to ascertain; to establish; (*pe cineva de ceva*) to enlighten smb; to make smb aware of smth; (*a convinge*) to convince, to persuade; *coll* to bring round || *vr* (*a înţelege*) to figure out; to grasp; *coll* to get to the bottom of; *recip* to come to an agreement; *pass* to be solved, to be cleared up, to be

lăptar [lăp'tar] *nm* milkman.

lăptărie [lăptă'rie] *nf* (*magazin*) dairy, milkshop; (*produse*) dairy products; *sl* (*sâni mari*) melons, big tits.

lăptos [lăp'tos] *adj* (*cu lapte sau ca laptele*) milky; (*d. vacă, care e lapte mult*) that gives a lot of milk.

lărgi [lăr'dji] *vt* (*un drum etc*) to widen; (*o haină*) to let out; (*pantofi*) to stretch; (*o gaură*) to make bigger; (*un diametru, o ţeavă*) to expand; to dilate; (*a amplifica*) to amplify; (*a mări*) to enlarge; (*cunoştinţele*) to extend; (*orizontul, sfera ideilor*) to broaden || *vr* to widen, to extend, to expand, to dilate, to broaden; *pass* to be widened • ~**me** *nf* width, breadth.

lăsa [lă'sa] *vt* (*a permite, a acorda*) to let, to allow, to permit; (*a părăsi*) (*casă, soţ, soţie, urme*) to leave; to abandon; *coll* to walk out on smb; (*a slobozi, a da drumul*) to let loose; to release; (*a pune jos*) to lay/put/set down; (*a întrerupe*) to interrupt; to break; (*a coborî*) to lower; to draw down; to pull down; to omit, to leave out; (*a opri*) to stop; (*a pune alături, ca lucrul de mână*) to lay aside the work; (*a ceda*) to give way; to sit tight; (*a se lărgi, d. pantofi, haine*) to become loose; (*care nu mai rezistă*) to weaken; (*în jos*) to sink; (*d. pământ, casă*) to subside; **a nu** ~ **nici o urmă** to leave no trace; **a nu se** ~ not to give in/way; **a** ~ **o moştenira cuiva** to leave smb a legacy; **a** ~ **ochii în jos** to cast down one's eyes; **a** ~ **lucrul** to stop work; **lăsând la o parte ...** leaving aside; to say nothing of, except for || *vr* **a se** ~ **descurajat** to let oneself become/be discouraged; **a se** ~ **de** (*un obicei*) to quit; (*o meserie*) to retire || *vi* (*d. ceva*) **lasă mult de dorit** it leaves much to be desired.

lăstar [lăs'tar] *nn* offshoot, *pl* copse; *fig* offspring.

lătra [lă'tra] *vi also fig* to bark; to woof; (*furios, mult*) to bay; (*subţire*) to yelp • ~**t** *nn* barking; *v* * **lătra**.

lăturalnic [lătu'ralnik] *adj* side, lateral; (*izolat*) isolated; distant; *fig* roundabout; (*ascuns*) hidden; (*tainic*) secret; (*necinstit*) dishonest.

lături [lă'turi] *nf pl* slops.

lăţime [lă'tsime] *nf* breadth, width; **pe** ~ sideways; widthwise; (*d. pneuri*) width.

lăţos [lă'tsos] *adj* hairy; untidy; (*d. oameni*) (*neîngrijit*) unkempt; (*cu părul lung*) long-haired; (*d. un produs de lână*) shaggy.

lăuda [lău'da] *vt* to praise smb, to speak highly of smb; (*oficial*) to commend; (*de formă*) to give lip-service to; (*a măguli*) to flatter, to compliment || *vr* to boast, to brag; *coll* to talk big • ~**bil** *adj* praiseworthy, commendable || *adv* laudably; commendably.

lăudăros [lăudă'ros] *adj* boastful, bragging || *nm* vaunter; braggart.

lăudăroşenie [lăudăro'shenie] *nf* boastfulness, bragging.

lăutar [lău'tar] *nm vernac* fiddler, musician.

lână ['lână] *nf* wool; (*artificială*) artificial wool; *text* ~ **pură**, ~ **în**~ all wool.

lâncezeală [lânche'zeală] *nf* (*lipsă de vigoare*) languor, listlessness; (*apatie*) apathy, torpor; *fig* dullness.

lâncezi [lânch'zi] *vi* to languish, to pine; to waste away; *fig* to slacken, to stagnate.

lângă ['lângă] *prep* near (to), next to; close to; about; (*nu departe de*) not far from.

leac ['leak] *nn* remedy, cure; (*medicament*) medicine; ~**uri băbeşti** quack medicine; **de** ~ curative, medicinal; **fără** ~ (*nevindecabil*) incurable; (*incorigibil*) incorrigible.

leafă ['leafă] *nf* (*periodic*) salary; (*plata*) wage(s).

leagăn ['leagăn] *nn* (*pt. copii*) cradle, crib; (*scrânciob*) swing; (*pt. copii orfani*) orphanage.

leal [le'al] *adj* honest, fair, upright; straightforward, loyal.

leandru [le'andru] *nm bot* oleander, rose bay.

leaţ [leats] *nn constr* lath, thick slat.

lebădă ['lebădă] *nf orn* swan; (*mascul*) cob swan.

lebărvurst ['lebărvurst] *nm cul* liver sausage, liverwurst.

lector ['lektor] *nm/nf* assistant professor; (*persoană care conferenţiază*) lecturer.

lectură [lek'tură] *nf* (*acţiunea de a citi*) reading; (*materialul pt. lectură*) reading (material); (*interpretare*) interpretation.

lecţie ['lektsie] *nf* (*cursuri*) class; (*ce se învaţă* also *fig* lesson; (*pt. acasă*) assignment, homework.

lecui [leku'i] *vt obs* to cure, to heal || *vr obs* (*a se însănătoşi*) to be healed; to recover; *fig* (*a se sătura de ceva*) to get sick (and tired) of, to be fed up with.

lefter ['lefter] *adj coll* penniless, broke, hard up.

lega [le'ga] *vt* (*de ceva*) to tie (to); (*laolaltă*) to bind, to tie up; (*a prinde, a fixa*) to fasten (to); (*a ataşa*) to attach; (*a conexa*) to link (to); (*a se uni*) to unite; (*a înlănţui*) to chain; (*a încătuşa*) to fetter, to shackle; (*a imobiliza*) to immobilize; (*a priponi, d. un cal*) to tether; (*a pansa*) to dress; (*cu sârmă*) to wire; (*cu frânghie*) to cord; (*a înnoda*) to knot; to buckle up; *elec, comp* (*a conecta la sistem*) (*d. calculator*) to log on to a system; to be on line; (*a căsători*) to marry, to unite in wedlock; (*cu vrăji*) to charm; (*a începe*) to start, to begin; (*idei*) to connect; to oblige; (*a exprima*) to express; *jur* to bequeath || *vr pass* to be tied, to be bound, etc; (*a se obliga*) to bind; (*a se angaja într-o relaţie sentimentală*) to commit oneself; (*a promite*) to promise; (*d. dulceţuri, şerbeturi, sosuri*) to thicken; (*a se coagula*) to clot; **a se** ~ **de** to be connected with; (*a se ţine scai de*) to stick, to cling to; (*a bate la cap*) to bother; (*a nu lăsa în*

pace) not to leave alone; to hassle; to importune; (*a se ataşa de cineva sentimental*) to become/grow fond of; (*a acosta*) to go/come up to smb; (*de vorbele cuiva*) to cavil at; (*a critica*) to find fault || *vi* (*d. plante când prind rod*) to produce.

legal [le'gal] *adj* lawful, legal; (*legitim*) legitimate • **pe căi** ~**e** legally || *adv* legally, lawfully; legitimately • ~**itate** *nf* legality, lawfulness • ~**iza** *vt* (*a face să fie legal*) to legalize; (*a autentifica documente*) to authenticate, to certify || *vr pass* to be certified, to be authenticated.

legaţie [le'gatsie] *nf* legation.

legământ [legă'mânt] *nn* pledge; (*jurământ*) vow; (*înţelegere*) agreement.

legăna [legă'na] *vt* to rock; (*d. barca, leagăn*) to balance; (*a ondula*) to wave, to undulate || *vr* to rock, to swing; (*a se căina*) to stagger, to reel.

legătură [legă'tură] *nf* (*ca o bandă*) band; (*de surcele*) bundle; faggot; (*de fân*) truss; (*de chei*) bunch; (*snop de cereale*) sheaf; (*basma*) (head)kerchief; (*de carte*) binding; (*coperta*) cover; *fig* link; relation, relationship; contact, touch; *elec* coupling; *mil* liaison; *tech* joint, junction; (*amoroasă*) love affair; *rail* connection; **în** ~ **cu** in connection/conjunction with; (*în complicitate cu*) in complicity/collusion with.

lege ['ledje] *nf* law; (*drept*) the law; (*regulă*) rule; * **legalitate**; *relig, pol, jur* act; (~ *nescrisă*) tradition, custom; ~**a junglei** law of the jungle; ~**a gravitaţiei universale** the law of gravity; ~**a cererii şi a ofertei** *econ* law of supply and demand.

legendar [ledjen'dar] *adj* legendary; mythical.

legendă [le'djendă] *nf* (*poveste*) legend; (*mitologică*) myth; *fig* (*minciună*) fairy tale, story; (*pe o medalie*) inscription; (*pe o ilustraţie, fotografie, desen*) caption; (*pe o diagramă, carte*) key; (*pe o hartă*) list of conventional signs.

legifera [ledjife'ra] *vt usu pass* to legislate on, to issue a law on smth.

legislativ [ledjisla'tiv] *adj jur* legislative; **alegeri** ~**e** parliamentary elections; **puterea** ~**ă** the legislature, the legislative power.

legislaţie [ledjis'latsie] *nf* legislation, law(s).

legist [le'djist] *nm* (*medic* ~) forensic pathologist.

legitim [le'djitim] *adj* (*legal*) legitimate; (*în conformitate cu legea*) lawful, rightful; (*justificat*) justified; (*drept*) just, right; **moştenitor** ~ rightful heir; *jur* ~**ă apărare** self-defense • ~**aţie** *nf* identity card, ID; (*de membru al unui club, de serviciu*) card • ~**itate** *nf jur* (*a unui copil, a unei căsătorii*) legitimacy; (*conform legii*) lawfulness; (*corectitudine*) rightfulness.

legumă [le'gumă] *nf* vegetable(s), greens; (*d. o persoană*) vegetable.

leit [le'it] *adj* perfectly similar, quite alike.

lejer [le'zher] *adj* light, comfortable, loose; (*d. îmbrăcăminte şi încălţăminte*) easy-fitting || *adv* lightly.

lemn [lemn] *nn* (*material*) wood; (*butuc*) log; **casă de** ~ log house • ~**ărie** *nf* (*totalitatea părţii lemnoase*) wood; *constr* wainscoting, paneling; (*cherestea*) timber; (*meserie*) woodwork, carpentry; wood cutting; (*grămezi*) lumber • ~**os** *adj* woody; (*din lemn*) wooden; (*d. un fruct, legumă etc*) tough; chewy; (*d. ridichi*) stringy.

lene ['lene] *nf* idleness, laziness, indolence; (*intelectuală*) sluggishness, slowness • ~**ş** *adj* lazy, idle, indolent; (*în gândire*) sluggish; (*lent*) slow(-moving) ||

nm lazybones, lazy person, sluggard • **~şul** *zool* sloth || *adv* lazily, indolently, idly • **~vi** *vi* to idle, to be lazy, to dawdle, to kill time.

lenjerie [lenzhe'rie] *nf* (*de corp*) underwear, lingerie, underlinen; (*de pat*) bedclothes, bedding.

lent [lent] *adj* slow, slow-moving || *adv* slowly.

lentilă [len'tilă] *nf* lens; **~e de contact** contact lenses.

leoaică [le'oaikă] *nf* lioness.

leopard [leo'pard] *nm zool* leopard.

lepăda [lepă'da] *vt vernac* (*a arunca nemaifiind bun*) to throw away, to discard; (*blana, părul, penele, frunzele*) to shed; to cast; *vernac* (*un obiect de îmbrăcămnite*) to take off; *vernac* (*a avorta*) to miscarry; to have an abortion; (*d. animale*) to slink, to cast; *vernac* (*a părăsi*) to abandon; *vernac* (*a renunţa*) to give up; (*un obicei rău*) to break/leave off || *vr* **a se ~ de** (un obicei) to break with; (*de o afirmaţie*) to disown; (*a nega*) to deny; (*solemn, sub jurământ*) to abjure || *vi* (*a avorta*) to miscarry; to have an abortion; (*d. animale*) to cast young.

lepră ['lepră] *nf med* leprosy; *fig* pest; *fig coll* (*d. o persoană fără caracter/scrupule*) scoundrel, villain, jerk.

lepros [le'pros] *adj* leprous || *nm* leper.

lesbiană [lesbi'ană] *nf* lesbian.

lesne ['lesne] *adv* (*uşor*) easily, without effort.

lesnicios [lesni'chios] *adj* (*uşor*) easy, effortless || *adv* easily, in a very easy way.

lespede ['lespede] *nf* plate, slab; (*de pavaj*) flagstone; (*de mormânt*) tombstone, gravestone.

lest [lest] *nn also fig* ballast.

leşie [le'shie] *nf* lye.

leşin [le'shin] *nn* fainting fit, blackout, swoon • **~a** *vi* to faint (away), to black/pass out, to swoon.

letargie [letar'djie] *nf* lethargy; *med* coma; **a cădea în ~** *med* to sink into a coma; *fig* to fall into a state of lethargy.

leton [le'ton] *adj* Lettish; *geog* Latvian || *nm* Lett • **~ă** *nf* (*femeie*) Lett(ish woman); (*limba*) Lettic, Lettish.

leu [leu] *nm pl* lei; *zool* lion; monetary unit of Romania.

leucemie [leuche'mie] *nf* leukemia.

leucoplast [leuko'plast] *nn med* plaster.

leuştean [leush'tean] *nm bot* lovage.

levată [le'vată] *nf* (*la jocul de bridge*) trick.

levănţică [levăn'tsikă] *nf bot* lavender; (*apă de colonie*) lavender (water).

levier [levi'er] *nn tech* lever.

levitaţie [levi'tatsie] *nf* levitation.

lexic ['leksik] *nn ling* lexis, vocabulary • **~ograf** *nm* lexicographer • **~olog** *nm* lexicologist.

leza [le'za] *vt* (*interesele cuiva*) to harm, to damage; (*a nedreptăţi*) to wrong smb; to hurt; *med* (*d. organe*) to injure; **partea ~ă** *jur* the injured party.

leziune [lezi'une] *nf med* lesion, injury, (*rană*) wound.

liană [li'ană] *nf bot* creeper, liana.

liant [li'ant] *nm constr* binder, binding agent/material.

libelulă [libe'lulă] *nf ento* dragonfly.

liber ['liber] *adj* free; independent; autonomous; (*suveran*) sovereign; (*gratuit*) (for) free, free of charge; (*disponibil*) available; (*de timp*) leisure; (*d. un drum*) clear; (*neocupat*) (*d. cameră*) vacant; (*d. linia telefonică*) unengaged; (*d. scaun, loc etc*) not taken; (*d. taxi*) for hire; (*gol*) empty; (*d. persoane*) free; disengaged; (*care nu e la program*) off duty; natural; (*desfăcut*) loose; (*care nu este împiedicat*) unham-

pered; (*spontan*) spontaneous; (*sentimental*) unattached; *chem* uncombined; *sp* (*înot, patinaj, gimnastică*) freestyle • **zi ~ă** day off.

liberal [libe'ral] *adj* (*tolerant*) lenient, liberal || *nm pol* liberal.

libertate [liber'tate] *nf* (*absenţa constrângerii*) freedom; (*sens abstract*) liberty; (*de a alege*) choice; **~ religioasă** freedom of worship; **în ~** at large; **~ provizorie** *jur* (release on) bail; **~ condiţionată** on parole • **~a cuvântului/de expresie** freedom of speech/expression; **~a de asociere** freedom of association; **~a de conştiinţă** liberty of conscience; **~a de a se întruni** freedom of assembly; **~a de opinie** freedom of opinion; **~a presei** freedom of the press.

libertin [liber'tin] *adj* libertine, dissolute; (*d. o carte, limbaj*) licentious || *nm* libertine.

libidinos [libidi'nos] *adj* libidinous, lustful; lewd.

librar [lib'rar] *nm* bookseller.

librărie [libră'rie] *nf* bookstore, bookshop.

libret [li'bret] *nn mus* libretto.

licări [likă'ri] *vi* (*cu intermitenţe*) to sparkle; (*slab*) to flicker, to glimmer; (*cu reflectare*) to shimmer; (*sursă luminoasă pe un fond întunecat*) to gleam; (*strălucire puternică şi scurtă*) to flash; (*ca stelele*) to twinkle; to glint.

licenţă [li'chentsă] *nf* academic degree; (*examene*) graduation examinations, finals; (*permis*) license; **~ poetică** *liter* poetic license.

licenţiat [lichentsi'at] *adj edu* **e ~** he is a graduate; **~ în litere/ştiinţe/drept** bachelor of arts/of science/of law, arts/science/law graduate.

licenţios [lichentsi'os] *adj lit* licentious, lewd; immoral.

liceu [li'cheu] *nn* high school (for students aged 14-18).

lichea [li'kea] *nf* (*d. bărbat*) flunkey, toady, scoundrel.

lichefia [likefi'a] *vt/vr* to liquefy, to liquate.

lichen [li'ken] *nm* lichen.

lichid [li'kid] *nn/adj* liquid, fluid; **bani lichizi** ready money, (hard) cash.

lichida [liki'da] *vt* to liquidate; to end; to abolish; (*o afacere*) to wind up; (*un cont*) to clear; (*o datorie*) to pay off; (*un stoc*) to sell off; *coll* (*a omorî*) to eliminate • **~re** *nf jur* liquidation; *fin* (*de conturi*) settlement, clearing; (*plată la sfârşit de lună*) end-of-month settlement; *v* *** a lichida**.

lichiditate [likidi'tate] *nf usu pl, fin* liquidities, cash.

lichior [li'kior] *nn* liqueur.

licit [li'chit] *adj jur* licit, lawful, permissible.

licitaţie [lichi'tatsie] *nf* (*la vânzare de obiecte*) auction; (*strigare de sume*) bidding.

licoare [li'koare] *nf lit* fine drink, beverage.

licurici [liku'rich] *nm ento* firefly.

lider ['lider] *nm* leader.

lift [lift] *nn* elevator; (*de bucătărie*) rising cupboard, dumb waiter • **~ier** *nm* elevator operator.

lifting ['lifting] *nn* (*cosmetică*) (face)lifting.

ligament [liga'ment] *nn anat* ligament.

ligă ['ligă] *nf* league, confederacy, alliance.

lighean [li'gean] *nn* washbowl, washbasin.

lighioană [li'gioană] *nf lit* (wild) beast, animal.

lignit [lig'nit] *nn* lignite.

lihnit [lih'nit] *adj* starving, famished, dying of hunger.

liliac [lili'ak] *nm bot* lilac; *zool* bat, rearmouse • **~hiu** *adj* lilac(-colored).

liman [li'man] *nn* (*ţărm*) bank; coast; *obs* harbor, port; (*lagună*) lagoon; estuary; *fig* refuge, sanctuary, haven.

limbaj [lim'bazh] *nn* language; (*vorbire*) speech; (*fel de a vorbi*) way/manner of speaking; **~ul corpului/ trupului** body language

limbă ['limbă] *nf anat* tongue; *coll* clapper; language; (*vorbire*) speech; (*element de construcţie din diferite obiecte*) (*de clopot, pantof, cataramă, foc*) tongue; (*de ceasornic*) hand; (*de pendul*) pendulum; (*de încălţat pantofi*) shoehorn; (*lamă*) blade; (*de balanţă*) arm; (*fâşie de pământ*) strip, neck of land; (*flacără*) flame; ~ **maternă** mother tongue; ~ **moartă** dead language; ~ **modernă** modern language; ~ **străină** foreign language; *fig* ~ **ascuţită** sharp tongue; ~ **vorbită** colloquial/spoken language; ~ **vie** living language; ~ **oficială** official language.

limbric [lim'brik] *nm* (*parazit*) belly worm.

limbut [lim'but] *nm* chatterer, talkative fellow/person ‖ *adj* talkative, garrulous; chattering.

limfatic [lim'fatik] *adj med* lymphatic.

limita [limi'ta] *vt* to limit, to restrict; (*drepturile cuiva*) to set bounds/limits to ‖ *vr* to limit/confine oneself to; to keep within limits • **~re** *nf* limitation, restriction, confinement • **~tiv** *adj* limiting, restricting, restrictive.

limită ['limită] *nf* limit; (*a unui teren, a unei ţări etc*) boundary; (*temporal*) deadline, closing date; *math* limiting value; ~ **de vârstă** age limit; *caz* ~ borderline case.

limitrof [limi'trof] *adj* bordering (on), adjacent (to).

limonadă [limo'nadă] *nf* lemonade.

limpede ['limpede] *adj* clear; (*d. stil, explicaţie etc*) clear, lucid; (*desluşit*) distinct; (*d. cer*) bright, cloudless; transparent; (*curat*) pure; obvious, evident; (*sigur*) sure; (*cinstit*) honest; (*d. voce, sunet*) crystal (clear); (*uşor de înţeles*) easily understood; *cul* (*d. supă*) thin ‖ *adv* clearly, etc.

limpezi [limpe'zi] *vt* to clarify, to make clear, to clear (up); (*a curăţi*) to purify; (*rufe*) to rinse, to swill ‖ *vr* (*d. un lichid*) to settle; (*d. vreme*) to clear up; (*o situaţie*) to (become) clear • **~me** *nf* transparency, clarity.

limuzină [limu'zină] *nf* limousine, sedan.

lin [lin] *adj* (*liniştit*) quiet, calm; (*încet*) slow; (*d. o pantă*) gentle; (*neted*) smooth, even ‖ *adv* quietly, calmly ‖ *nm icht* tench.

lindină ['lindină] *nf ento* nit.

lingău [lin'gău] *nm fig* yes-man, flunkey, boot-licker.

linge ['lindje] *vt* to lick (up); (*a linguşi cu slugărnicie*) to flatter; *fig coll* to toady ‖ *vr* (*reciproc, ca felinele*) to lick each other.

lingou [lin'gou] *nn* ingot; ~ **de aur** gold bar/ingot.

lingură ['lingură] *nf* (*obiectul*) (table) spoon; (*conţinutul*) spoonful; *min* bailer; *tech* scoop.

linguriţă [lingu'riţă] *nf* (*obiectul*) teaspoon; (*conţinutul*) teaspoonful.

linguşeală [lingu'şeală] *nf* * **linguşire**.

linguşi [lingu'shi] *vt* to flatter, to fawn (upon); to cringe to ‖ *vr* to fawn (upon), to cringe (to) • **~re** *nf* flattery, cringing, fawning, flattering; *v* * **linguşi** • **~tor** *nm* flatterer, toad-eater ‖ *adj* flattering; *v* * **linguşi**.

lingvist [ling'vist] *nm* linguist • **~ică** *nf* linguistics.

linia [lini'a] *vt* to rule, to mark with lines.

linie ['linie] *nf* (*în diferite sensuri*) line; (*direcţie*) direction; (*chip, mod*) manner; (*contur*) outline; (*riglă*) ruler; (*la jocul de table*) hit; ~ **aeriană** airline, airway; ~ **curbă** curved line; ~ **de atac** *mil* line of attack; ~ **de autobuz** bus line/ route; ~ **de cale**

ferată railroad line; ~ **de conduită** line of conduct, policy; ~ **de forţă** *phys* line of force; ~ **de înaltă tensiune** high tension wire; ~ **de luptă** *mil* battleline; ~ **de ochire** (*la o armă*) sights; ~ **de plutire** *naut* waterline, Plimsoll line; ~ **de producţie** product line; ~ **de produse** range of products; ~ **discontinuă** (*pe drum*) broken line; ~ **dreaptă** straight line; ~ **genealogică** genealogical line/table; ~ **întreruptă** broken line; ~ **maritimă** shipping line; ~ **punctată** dotted line; (line of the) horizon; ~ **telefonică** telephone line; ~ **telefonică directă** (*24 ore din 24*) direct dial telephone, twenty-four-hour hotline; ~ **vizuală** *opt* line of sight • **~a orizontului** skyline.

linişte ['linişte] *nf* (*absenţa zgomotului*) silence, quietness; calm; (*absenţa mişcării*) stillness; (*pace*) peace ‖ *interj* silence!, stop talking!; **în ~** in silence, calmly, quietly.

linişti [lini'shti] *vt* to calm (down); (*a-l face să tacă*) to quiet (down); (*durerea*) to assuage; (*a mângâia*) to comfort; (*a reconforta*) to reassure, to set at rest/ ease; (*un copil*) to quiet; to hush; (*conştiinţa*) to ease; to soothe; (*o mulţime de oameni*) to pacify ‖ *vr* (*a se calma*) to calm/settle/quiet down; (*a-şi reveni dintr-un şoc, surpriză*) to compose oneself; (*a se odihni*) to (have a) rest; (*a înceta*) (*d. vânt, furtună etc.*) to abate, to die down, to subside; (*d. mare*) to become calm; (*d. ploaie*) to ease off; (*d. durere*) to ease.

liniuţă [lini'uţă] *nf* line; (*ortografie*) dash; ~ **de unire** hyphen.

linşa [lin'sha] *vt* to lynch • **~j** *nn* lynching.

linte ['linte] *nf bot* lentil.

lintiţă [lin'tiţă] *nf bot* duckweed, frog foot.

linţoliu [lin'tsoliu] *nn* pall, shroud.

linx [links] *nm zool* lynx.

lipăi [lipă'i] *vt* (*a bea ceva cu zgomot caracteristic*) to lap, to lick (in) ‖ *vi* (*a merge desculţ sau în papuci făcând un zgomo caracteristic*) to scrape/shuffle one's feet.

lipi [li'pi] *vt* (*cu clei*) to glue; (*cu ceară*) to paste; (*cu gumă arabică*) to gum; (*unul de altul*) to glue together; (*un afiş*) to stick, to hang; (*un timbru*) to affix; (*a ataşa*) to attach; (*o casă*) to coat; (*a suda*) to solder; (*autogen*) to weld ‖ *vr pass* to be glued to; (*d. ochi din cauza somnului*) to close; (*a fi lipicios*) to be sticky/clammy; (*a se prinde/agăţa de cineva*) to cling to smb; *vernac* (*d. boli*) to be catching • **~cios** *adj* sticky, clammy; (*atrăgător*) charming; attractive.

lipitoare [lipi'toare] *nf ento also fig* leech; *fig* bloodsucker.

lipsă ['lipsă] *nf* absence; (*insuficienţă*) lack, want; (*neajuns*) shortcoming, drawback; defect, fault; (*greşeală*) mistake, error; (*nevoie*) need; (*jenă financiară*) straitened circumstances; (*sărăcie*) poverty; ~ **de bani** scarcity of money; ~ **de grijă** carelessness; ~ **de gust** lack of taste; ~ **de imaginaţie** lack of imagination; ~ **de răspundere** lack of responsibility, irresponsibility; ~ **la cântar** short weight; **din ~ de** for lack of.

lipsi [lip'si] *vi* (*a fi absent*) to be absent/missing; *jur* to be in default; (*a nu se găsi*) not to be available, not to be found; (*şi insuficient*) to fail, to fall short; (*d. ceva*) to lack, to be lacking in; (*a fi nevoie*) to be needed/wanted; **a-i ~** to lack smth, to want smth; (*a nu-i ajunge, zahărul, pâinea etc*) to be short of; (*a*

duce dorul cuiva) to miss smb || *vr* **a se ~ de ceva/ cineva** to do without smth/smb; (*a renunţa*) to give up, to renounce || *vt* to deprive smb of.
liră¹ ['liră] *nf* (*sterlină*) pound (sterling); *coll* quid.
liră² ['lira] *nf mus* lyre.
liric ['lirik] *adj* lyrical.
lista [lis'ta] *vt comp* to list, to print • **~re** *nf* listing.
listă ['listă] *nf* list; catalog; **~ de aşteptare** wait list; **~ electorală** (*votanţi*) voters' list, electoral roll; (*candidaţi*) list of candidates.
literal [lite'ral] *adj* literal, word for word || *adv* literally • **~mente** *adv* literally; virtually.
literar [lite'rar] *adj* (*d. critică, premiu, limbă etc*) literary.
literat [lite'rat] *nm* man of letters, literary man • **~ură** *nf* literature; (*scris*) writing.
literă ['literă] *nf* letter; (*caracter de ~*) character; (*de tipar*) (printing) type; *pl* letters; literature.
litigant [liti'gant] *nm/adj jur* litigant, party in a law suit.
litigios [litidji'os] *adj jur* litigious, disputed, in dispute; *jur* (*chestiune, caz*) contentious.
litigiu [li'tidjiu] *nn* dispute; *jur* lawsuit, litigation.
litografie [litogra'fie] *nf* lithography.
litoral [lito'ral] *nn* seaside, seashore; **pe ~** at the seaside; coast(line).
litru ['litru] *nm* liter.
lituană [litu'ană] *nf* Lithuanian (language).
lituanian [lituani'an] *nm/adj* Lithuanian.
liturghie [litur'gie] *nf* liturgy; (*la catolici*) mass.
livadă [li'vadă] *nf* orchard.
livid [li'vid] *adj* livid, pale; (*d. ten*) pallid • **~itate** *nf* pallor, pallidness.
livra [li'vra] *vt* (*mărfuri*) to deliver; (*a furniza*) to furnish • **~re** *nf* delivery; furnishing.
livră ['livră] *nf* pound (0,455 kg).
livret [li'vret] *nn* booklet; **~ militar** *nn* service record.
lizibil [li'zibil] *adj* legible, readable.
lizieră [lizi'eră] *nf* (*de pădure*) skirt (of a forest).
lob [lob] *nn* lobe; (*al urechii*) ear lobe; (*la animale*) flap.
lobodă ['lobodă] *nf bot* orache.
loc [lok] *nn* place, spot; (*poziţie, rang*) position; (*spaţiu*) room; (*la teatru, cinema etc*) seat; (*porţiune*) lot, portion; (*de pământ arabil*) plot; (*câmpie*) field; (*ţinut, ţară*) country; (*regiune*) region, part; (*localitate*) locality, place; (*serviciu*) job, post, berth, billet; (*de trecere*) passage; *mil* (*fortificat*) fortified place; fortress; *fig* **~ comun** commonplace, cliché; **~ de casă** house lot; **~ de onoare** place of honor; **~ de naştere** birthplace; **~ de parcare** parking lot; **~ de trecere** *rail* level crossing; **~ liber** (*la un hotel*) vacant room, vacancy.
local [lo'kal] *nn* (*clădire*) building; (*sediu*) premises; restaurant, pub(lic house) || *adj* local; **ziar ~** local newspaper • **~itate** *nf* place; locality; spot; (*oraş*) town; (*sat*) village
localiza [lokali'za] *vt* to localize; (*zgomot, bruiaj etc*) to locate; (*un apel telefonic etc*) to trace; (*în memorie*) to place smth; (*d. foc, inundaţii etc*) to limit; to (bring under) control; (*o epidemie*) to confine, to control || *vr* to confine oneself to.
localnic [lo'kalnik] *nm* native; *usu pl* locals; (*al unui sat*) villager; (*al unui oraş*) inhabitant (of a town).
locaş [lo'kash] *nn lit* dwelling; *tech* groove, slot.
locatar [loka'tar] *nm* (*în spaţii închiriate etc*) tenant,

leaseholder; (*la gazdă*) lodger; (*care locuiesc împreună*) roomer; (*la o pensiune etc*) inmate.
locaţie [lo'katsie] *nf jur* location; (*împrumut de diferite obiecte, staţii etc*) renting (out), hiring (out); rental; **a lua în ~** to rent/hire smth; *rail* hiring.
locomotivă [lokomo'tivă] *nf* engine, locomotive; **~ electrică** electric engine/locomotive.
locotenent [lokote'nent] *nm mil* lieutenant; *avia* first lieutenant; (*în marina comercială*) mate; *avia* wing commander.
locţiitor [loktsii'tor] *nm* acting; deputy; *jur* locum tenens.
locui [loku'i] *vi* to live (in), to reside (in), to inhabit; **a ~ cu** (*părinţii etc*) to live with • **~bil** *adj* (in)habitable, fit for habitation • **~tor** *nm* inhabitant, resident; occupier, occupant • **~nţă** *nf* (*casă*) house, home; residence; **~ de vacanţă** vacation home; (*de obicei luxoasă*) residency.
logaritm [loga'ritm] *nm math* logarithm.
logic ['lodjik] *adj* logical, methodical || *adv* logically • **~ă** *nf phil, math* logic.
logodi [logo'di] *vt obs* to betroth || *vr* to become betrothed/engaged (to smb).
logodnă [lo'godnă] *nf* engagement, betrothal.
logodnic [lo'godnik] *nm* fiancé; *pl* the engaged couple • **~ă** *nf* fiancée.
loial [lo'ial] *adj* (*fidel*) loyal, faithful, true; (*cinstit*) honest, upright; (*d. mijloace de acţiune*) fair • **~itate** *nf* (*cinste*) honesty, fairness, uprightness; loyalty, faithfulness (to), fidelity.
lojă ['lozhă] *nf* (*a spectatorului*) box; (*masonică*) lodge.
lombar [lom'bar] *adj anat* lumbar.
longevitate [londjevi'tate] *nf* (*durată a vieţii*) longevity; (*viaţă lungă*) long life; (*a unui produs*) life.
longitudinal [londjitudi'nal] *adj* longitudinal; lengthwise.
longitudine [londji'tudine] *nf geog* longitude.
lopată [lo'pată] *nf* (*pt. grădinărit etc*) shovel; (*vâslă*) paddle, oar.
lor *adj poss pl* their || *pron poss* **al/a/ai/ale ~** theirs || *pron pers* (to) them
lord [lord] *nm* lord.
lornion [lor'nion] *nn* lorgnette, opera glasses; monocle; pince-nez.
lot [lot] *nn* (*de pământ*) (p)lot, strip; (*d. mărfuri*) transport, lot, batch; (*d. oameni*) group; (*porţiune*) portion; part, share.
loterie [lote'rie] *nf* lottery.
lotus ['lotus] *nn bot* lotus.
loţiune [lotsi'une] *nf* (*general*) also *pharm* lotion; **~ după ras** after-shave (lotion); **~ pentru păr** hair lotion.
lovi [lo'vi] *vt* (*a izbi, a nimeri*) to hit, to strike; (*cu palma*) to slap; (*a bate*) to beat; (*violent şi cu zgomot*) to slam; (*iute şi cu zgomot*) to clap; (*cu cotul*) to nudge; (*uşor*) to pat, to tap; (*cu ceva*) to cuff; (*cu ciocanul*) to hammer; (*cu cureaua*) to leather; (*a biciui*) to whip, to lash; (*cu bastonul*) to cane; (*cu piciorul*) to kick; (*a atinge*) to touch; (*d. fulger*) to strike; (*a ajunge până la*) to reach; (*a ataca*) *mil* to attack; (*a asalta*) to assail; (*din aer*) to raid; (*d. o nenorocire, cutremur etc*) to overtake; to befall; (*a apuca*) to seize; (*a jigni*) to hurt; (*a ofensa*) to offend; (*a răni*) to wound; (*a nedreptăţi*) to wrong; (*a face rău*) to harm; to prejudice; to compromise || *vr* to hurt oneself, to get hurt; (*unul pe altul*) to hit/hurt/wound each other.

lovitură [lovi'tură] *nf* (*și afectiv*) blow; (*de picior*) kick; (*izbitură*) *also fig* stroke; (*în ușă*) knock; (*de bici*) lash; (*atac*) attack, offensive; *sp* hit, drive; (*la fotbal*) shot, kick; (*spargere*) burglary; (*cu cotul*) nudge; (*dezastru*) calamity, disaster; (*ghinion*) piece of ill luck; ~ **aeriană** air raid/strike; ~ **a soartei** a reverse of fortune; ~ **de grație** finishing stroke; ~ **de maestru** a master stroke, a stroke of genius; ~ **de pedeapsă** penalty (kick); ~ **de stat** coup (d'etat); ~ **de teatru** sensational turn of events; *also fig* ~ **de trăsnet** thunderbolt; *fig* a bolt from the blue; ~ **liberă** free kick; ~ **norocoasă** fluke, lucky stroke; ~ **sub centură** foul/deep hit • *sp* ~**cu capul** header.

loz [loz] *nn* lottery ticket.

lozincă [lo'zinkă] *nf* slogan.

lua [lua] *vt* to take; (*brusc*) to snatch smth (up), to seize smth; (*a apuca*) to grab; (*a accepta, a căpăta*) to take; (*a duce cu sine*) to take away; (*a fura*) to steal (smth from smb), to rob smb of smth; (*a cumpăra, a încasa*) to buy, to purchase; to get; (*a rezerva*) to book/reserve (a room); (*a cuceri*) to capture; (*a confisca*) to seize; *mil* to conquer; (*a duce cu sine*) to call for; to collect; to fetch; (*pulsul, temperatura etc*) to take smb's pulse/temperature; (*a bea, a mânca*) to have, to eat; to drink; (*d. o boală, obicei etc*) to get; to catch; (*d. obicei*) to take to the habit of; **a ~t gripa de la fratele său** he got the flu from his brother; (*a călători cu un mijloc de transport*) to take (the bus/train/plane etc); (*a priva*) to deprive, to rob of; (*d. examen*) to pass (an examination); (*a îmbrăca*) to put on; (*în posesie*) to take possession || *vr* (*a se contamina*) *also med* to get, to acquire, to catch; (*a se îngrășa*) to gain weight; (*a se așeza*) to take/have a seat, to sit down; (*a se îmbrățișa*) to put their arms around each other's waists.

lubrifia [lubrifi'a] *vt tech* to lubricate • ~**nt** *adj* lubricating || *nm* lubricant.

luceafăr [lu'cheafăr] *nm astron* Venus; evening/morning star.

lucernă [lu'chernă] *nf* alfalfa; Spanish/Burgundy trefoil.

luci [lu'chi] *vi* to shine, to gleam; (*a scânteia*) to sparkle; (*a licări*) to glisten; (*a străluci de bucurie*) to beam with joy • ~**os** *adj* shiny, glossy, glowing; (*strălucitor*) bright • ~**re** *nf* shining, radiance; brightness • ~**tor** *adj* shining, radiant, bright.

lucid [lu'chid] *adj* lucid, clear, clear-headed || *adv* lucidly, clearly • ~**itate** *nf* (*perspicacitate*) (*d. o analiză, prezentare etc*) lucidity, clearness; (*d. o persoană*) clear-headeaness.

lucra [lu'kra] *vi* to work, to labor, (*din greu*) to toil, to work hard; (*d. o mașină*) to work, to run; (*d. magazine*) to be open; (*cu efect asupra*) to act on, to have effect on; (*d. o navă, un cablu*) to strain; (*d. vin*) to ferment; (*d. lemn*) to warp, to shrink; (*d. pereți*) to crack; (*a fasona*) to fashion, to shape; (*d. un sportiv, muzician, artist*) to practice, to rehearse; (*a submina autoritatea cuiva*) to undermine smb's authority; (*a prelucra*) to process, to work out; **a ~ cu acul** to do needlework; **a ~ la negru** to moonlight; **a ~ pentru** (*o societate, întreprindere*) to work for (a company) || *vt* to work; **a ~ pământul** to work the land, to till, to cultivate; (*a se ocupa cu*) to deal with • ~**re** *nf* (*activitate, scriere*) work; (*acțiune*) working; (*teză etc*) paper.

lucrativ [lukra'tiv] *adj* (*d. o activitate, afacere etc*)

lucrative, profitable; (*d. o slujbă*) well-paid; (*d. o societate, organizație*) **fără scop** ~ not-for-profit (organization); **acțiune cu scop** ~ profit-making activity.

lucrător [lukră'tor] *nm* worker; ~ **social** social worker || *adj* (*în legătură cu lucrul*) working, work; (*harnic*) hardworking, industrious.

lucru ['lukru] *nn* thing, object; (*muncă*) work.

lugubru [lu'gubru] *adj* lugubrious, dreary, dismal; (*înfricoșător*) frightful, dreadful; (*d. un loc*) gloomy, grim; (*d. sunet, țipăt, voce etc*) mournful.

lui [lui] *adj poss* his; its; **al/a/ai/ale** ~ *pron poss* his || *pron pers* (to) him; (to) it.

lujer ['luzher] *nn bot* stem; shoot, tendril.

lulea [lu'lea] *nf* (tobacco) pipe.

lumânare [lumă'nare] *nf* candle, taper; (*aprinsă*) candlelight; (*de ceară*) wax candle; (*de seu*) tallow candle; *sp* (*fotbal*) high ball; *sp* (*tenis*) lob; *sp* (*rugby*) garryowen; up and under; (*gimnastică*) shoulder stand; *avia* vertical climb.

lumbago [lum'bago] *nn med* lumbago.

lume ['lume] *nf* (*univers, umanitate, mediu*) world; (*oameni*) people; (*pământ*) earth; universe, cosmos, solar system; (*omenire*) mankind, humankind; (*societate omenească*) society; (*viață*) life, existence; **om de** ~ society man • ~**a bună** fashionable/high society • **toată** ~**a** everybody, everyone • ~**sc** *adj* worldly, earthly, mundane; (*laic*) secular, lay; (*trupesc*) bodily.

lumina [lumi'na] *vt* to light(en), to illuminate; (*un punct obscur*) *also fig* to shed/throw (a) light on; *fig* (*a lămuri*) to explain, to clear up || *vr* (*în diverse sensuri*) to light/brighten up; (*la minte*) to become clear; (*a înțelege*) to understand || *vi* (*a străluci*) to shine, to light; (*a apărea*) to appear.

lumină [lu'mină] *nf* light; (*înțelegere, învățătură*) learning, education, culture; ~ **electrică** electric light • ~**a lămpii/focului/ chibritului** glow, glimmer; ~**a lunii** moonlight; ~**a ochilor** sight; ~**a soarelui** sunlight; ~**a stelelor** starlight; ~**a zilei** daylight • ~**i de față** *auto* front lights; ~**i de poziție** position lights; ~**i de spate** *auto* rear lights • ~**ile rampei** *thea* floodlights.

luminiș [lumi'nish] *nn* (forest) glade, clearing.

luminos [lumi'nos] *adj* (*d. un corp, cadran*) luminous; (*d. o cameră*) filled with light; (*d. cer*) bright.

lunar [lu'nar] *adj astron* (*în legătură cu luna*) lunar; (*asemănător cu luna*) moonlike; **peisaj** ~ lunar landscape || *adv* monthly.

lună ['lună] *nf astron* moon; ~ **plină** the full moon; ~ **nouă** the new moon || *nf* (*a douăsprezecea parte dintr-un an terestru*) month.

luncă ['lunkă] *nf* waterside, water/river meadow, flood plain; (*zonă inundabilă*) holm.

luneca [lune'ka] *vi* to slip, to skid; (*pe apă*) to glide; (*pe gheață*) to slide; to miss one's footing.

lunecos [lune'kos] *adj* slippery, slick, slithery; (*d. oameni*) sly, wily, shifty.

lunetă [lu'netă] *nf* field-glass, telescope; *archit* groin; *tech* stay; *mil* sighting telescope; *auto* (*geamul din spate al mașinii*) rear window.

lung [lung] *adj* (*d. spațiu*) long, extensive, vast; (*temporal*) prolonged; (*lent*) slow || *adv* long, for a long time • ~**ul** *nn* length; **de-a** ~ **zidului** along the wall.

lungi [lun'dji] *vt* to lengthen, to prolong, to draw out; to dilate; (*a întinde*) to stretch, to extend; *cul* (*supa, mâncarea, vinul etc*) to add water, to dilute || *vr* to lengthen, to become/get/grow longer; (*a se culca*) to lie down • ~**me** *nf* length; (*durată*) duration; ~ **de undă** wave length.

luni ['luni] *nf* Monday; (*lunea*) on Monday, every Monday.

luntre ['luntre] *nf* boat.

lup [lup] *nm* wolf, *pl* wolves.

lupă ['lupă] *nf* magnifying glass.

lupta [lup'ta] *vi* (*cu*) to fight with/against, to struggle with; (*a se război*) to war with/against; *sp* to wrestle; to combat.

luptă ['luptă] *nf* (*în diferite sensuri*) fight; *fig* struggle, battle, warfare; (*concurs*) contest; (*război*) war; (*eforturi*) efforts; *sp* wrestling; ~ **aeriană** air fight; ~ **de interese** conflict of interests; ~ **de clasă** class struggle/conflict • ~**e de stradă** street fight(s); ~**e de tauri** bullfight; ~**e intestine** infighting; ~**e greco-romane** *sp* Graeco-Roman wrestling; ~ **e libere** free-style wrestling; ~ **armată** armed struggle; ~**e parlamentare** parliamentary clashes; • ~**tor** *nm* also *fig* fighter; (*într-un concurs*) champion; (*în război*) warrior; *sp* wrestler || *adj* fighting; * **lupta**.

lupus ['lupus] *nn med* lupus.

lustragiu [lustra'djiu] *nm* shoeblack.

lustră ['lustră] *nf* chandelier.

lustru ['lustru] *nn* polish; also *fig* luster, gloss; (*la pantofi*) shoeshine; superficiality, shallowness.

lustrui [lustru'i] *vt* to glaze, to gloss, to polish; (*de uzură*) to make/become shiny with wear || *vr* to polish one's manners.

lut [lut] *nn* clay, earth.

lux [luks] *nn* luxury, luxuriousness; (*belșug*) abundance.

luxa [luk'sa] *vt* (*o articulație etc*) to sprain, to turn, to wrench; (*cu alte sensuri*) to dislocate • ~**ție** *nf* sprain; dislocation.

luxemburghez(ă) [luksembur'gez(ă)] *adj* Luxemburgish || *nm/nf* Luxemburger.

luxos [luk'sos] *adj* rich; luxurious || *adv* richly; luxuriously.

luxuriant [luksuri'ant] *adj* luxuriant.

M

mac [mak] *nm bot* poppy, white/opium poppy.

macabru [ma'kabru] *adj* (*d. descoperire, poveste etc*) gruesome, grisly, grim; (*d. umor*) macabre.

macadam [maka'dam] *nn* tarmac, macadam.

macagiu [maka'djiu] *nm rail* pointsman, switchman.

macara [maka'ra] *nf* crane; also *naut* derrick; boom; ~ **grea** titan crane; ~ **plutitoare** floating crane; ~ **turn** derrick/tower crane.

macaroane [maka'roane] *nf pl* macaroni.

macaz [ma'kaz] *nn* switch, points.

macedonean [machedo'nean] *adj/nm* Macedonian • ~**că** *nf* Macedonian.

macera [mache'ra] *vt/vi* to steep, to soak.

machetă [ma'ketă] *nf* (*general*) model; also *fig* dummy; (*artă*) clay model; (*a unui afiș, poster, a unei publicații*) paste-up, layout; *tech* scale model.

machia [ma'kia] *vt* to make up || *vr* to make up (one's complexion), to put (one's) make-up on; *coll* to paint • ~**j** *nn* making up; (*ca produs*) make-up; (*pt. ochi*) eyeshadow; eyeliner.

macroeconomic [makroeko'nomik] *adj* macroeconomic.

maculator [makula'tor] *nn* notebook.

maculatură [makula'tură] *nf* waste, spoilt/waste sheets; *typ* mackle; *fig* pulp literature, trash.

maestru [ma'estru] *nm* master; expert || *adj* adept (at/in smth); (*la șah*) **mare** ~ grand master; ~ **de balet** ballet master; ~ **de ceremonii** master of ceremonies, MC; ~ **de dans** dancing master.

mafie ['mafie] *nf* the Maf(f)ia, organized crime; (*grup de interese*) gang.

magazin [maga'zin] *nn* store, shop; (*universal și mare*) emporium; department store; (*mare, cu fel de fel de articole mărunte*) baza(a)r; **lanț de** ~ chain of stores; ~ **alimentar** grocery store; **complex de** ~**e** mall; (*revistă*) magazine, periodical.

magherniță [ma'gerniță] *nf* hovel.

magic ['madjik] *adj* (*d. cuvânt, formulă etc*) magic; (*puteri*) magical • ~**ian** *nm* (*care practică magia, iluzionist*) magician, sorcerer; (*vrăjitor*) wizard.

magistral [madjis'tral] *adj* (*d. o interpretare, demonstrație etc*) masterly; (*d. reușită*) brilliant; (*cu sens negativ*) colossal, monumental || *adv* in a masterly/brilliant manner.

magistrală [madjis'trală] *nf* arterial road; (*șosea*) highway; (*în oraș*) thoroughfare; *rail* main line; *hydr* water main; (*conductă de gaze*) main (gas) pipe line.

magistrat [madjis'trat] *nm jur* (*termen general sau aplicabil uneia din funcțiile menționate*) magistrate; judge; public prosecutor; attorney • ~**ură** *nf* magistrature; (*judecători*) the judges.

magiun [ma'djun] *nn* plum jam; jam.

magmă ['magmă] *nf geol* magma.

magnat [mag'nat] *nm com, ind* magnate, tycoon.

magnet [mag'net] *nm* magnet • ~**ic** *adj* magnetic • ~**ism** *nn phys* magnetism; (*hipnotism*) hypnotism, mesmerism; *fig* ~ **personal** personal magnetism.

magnetofon [magneto'fon] *nn* tape recorder.

magneziu [mag'neziu] *nn chem* magnesium.

magnific [mag'nifik] *adj* magnificent, splendid; (*d. un corp*) superb; (*film, tablou etc*) marvelous, wonderful.

magnolie [mag'nolie] *nf bot* magnolia.

mahala [maha'la] *nf approx* slums, suburb, outskirts; also *fig* low life; **de** ~ suburban; *pej* vulgar, common • ~**giu** *nm* suburbanite; *pej* vulgar-/foul-mouthed fellow; (*bârfitor*) gossip; (*băgăcios*) busy-body.

mahmur [mah'mur] *adj coll* seedy after drinking, with a hangover; (*buimac*) sleepy, prostrate, dizzy; (*indispus*) seedy.

mahomedan [mahome'dan] *adj/nm relig* Mohammedan, Mahometan, Muslim • ~**ism** *nn relig* Mohammedanism, Mahometanism.

mahon [ma'hon] *nm bot* mahogany (tree); (*ca lemn*) mahogany, acajou; (*culoare*) reddish-brown, auburn.

mai[1] [mai] *adv* (*servind la formarea comparativelor*) more; -er; (*aproape*) almost, nearly; (*aproximativ*) approximately, about; (*cât pe ce*) about, on the point of; (*încă*) still; (*nu încă*) not yet; (*iarași*) again; (*încă o dată*) once more/again; (*după aceea*) after(wards); (*și*) and; (*în plus*) besides, in addition; (*pe lângă un pron. nehot.*) else; (*încă un/o*) another; (*în structuri negative*) either (*cu elemente negative*); neither (*cu elemente pozitive*); ~ **apoi** after(wards); (*mai târziu*) later on; (*mai devreme*) earlier; (*cantitativ sau temporal*) no more; (*temporal*) no longer.

mai[2] [mai] *nm* May; **1 Mai** (*ca sărbătoare*) May Day.

maiestate [maies'tate] *nf* majesty; dignity; stateliness, grandeur.

maiest(u)os [maies'tuos] *adj* majestic, stately, dignified; **peisaj** ~ majestic/magnificent landscape || *adv* majestically.

maimuță [mai'mutsă] *nf zool* monkey; (*femelă*) she-monkey; (*antropoidă, fără coadă*) ape; *fig* (*imitator*) ape; (*om asemănător cu o* ~) coll missing link; (*om urât*) freak; monster; fright • **~ri** *vt* to mimic, to ape || *vr* to act/play the ape; (*a se strâmba*) to pull faces.

maioneză [maio'neză] *nf cul* mayonnaise.

maior [ma'ior] *nm mil* (*de infanterie*) major; (*apelativ*) (*din partea unui grad egal sau mai mare*) major; (*din partea unui subordonat*) Sir; *avia* squadron leader; *naut* lieutenant commander.

maiou [ma'iou] *nn* (*care se poartă sub cămașă etc*) undershirt; (*de balerin*) tights; leotard; (*la sportive*) shirt; jersey; T-shirt.

maistru ['maistru] *nm* master; *ind* foreman.

major [ma'zhor] *nm mil* sergeant || *adj* (*la vârsta maturității*) of age; who has come of age.

majora [mazho'ra] *vt* (*prețuri, salarii etc*) to increase, to raise; (*prețul unor servicii, facturi etc*) to put a surcharge on, to put an additional charge on • **~t** *nn* coming of age, (full) age; *jur* majority; **a ajunge la ~** to come of age.

majordom [mazhor'dom] *nm* butler, major-domo, chief steward.

majoritate [mazhori'tate] *nf* majority; ~ **absolută** absolute majority; ~ **covârșitoare** overwhelming majority; ~ **de două treimi** two-thirds majority; ~ **de voturi** majority of votes, a majority vote.

majusculă [ma'zhuskulă] *nf* capital letter; *pl* block letters.

mal [mal] *nn* (*de lac*) lakeside, shore; (*de mare*) coast; (*plajă*) beach; (*de râu*) bank; (*margine*) edge; *lit* brink.

maladie [mala'die] *nf med* illness, disease; **o ~ ușoară/ serioasă** a minor/serious illness; **o ~ letală** a fatal illness/disease; ~ **contagioasă** contagious disease/illness; *vet* (*la câini*) distemper • **~a vacii nebune** mad cow disease.

malaiez [mala'iez] *adj/nm* Malay(an), Malaysian.

malarie [ma'larie] *nf med* malaria, marsh fever; ague (fever).

maldăr ['maldăr] *nn* heap, pile; (*snop*) sheaf; (*mănunchi*) bundle; (*de rufe, de hârtii, de cărți, de lucruri etc*) heaps and heaps of, piles and piles of.

maleabil [male'abil] *adj* soft, pliable, easily modeled; *fig* malleable, tractable, compliant.

malefic [ma'lefik] *adj* harmful; maleficent, baleful, evil.

malformație [malfor'matsie] *nf med* malformation.

malign [ma'lign] *adj med* malignant.

malițios [malitsi'os] *adj* (*răutăcios*) (*d. persoană, zâmbet, remarcă*) mischievous, roguish; *obs* malicious, spiteful || *adv* mischievously; maliciously, spitefully.

malițiozitate [malitsiozi'tate] *nf* malice, maliciousness.

maltez(ă) [mal'tez(ă)] *adj/nm/nf* Maltese.

maltrata [maltra'ta] *vt* to ill-treat, to mistreat, to maltreat; *fig iro* (*limba, gramatica*) to misuse.

malț [malts] *nn* malt.

mamă ['mamă] *nf* mother; *coll* mamma, ma, mum(my).

mamelă [ma'melă] *nf anat* mamma, breast.

mamelon [mame'lon] *nn anat* mamilla; nipple, teat; *geog* mamelon, rounded hillock.

mamifer [mami'fer] *nn zool* mammal || *adj* mammalian.

mamoș ['mamosh] *nm med* (*persoană care asistă la*

nașteri) accoucheur; (*moașă*) midwife; (*medic*) obstetrician.

mamut [ma'mut] *nm* mammoth.

management ['manadjment] *nn* management.

manager [mana'djer] *nm* manager.

mană ['mană] *nf* manna; *bot* blast, blight; *fig* blessing; (*belșug*) plenty.

mandarin [manda'rin] *nm bot* mandarin tree • **~ă** *nf bot* mandarin, tangerine.

mandat [man'dat] *nn* (*procură*) mandate; commission; *jur* warrant; *pol* mandate; ~ **de arestare** *jur* arrest warrant; ~ **de aducere** summons; ~ **de percheziție** search warrant; ~ **de expulzare** eviction order; ~ **prezidențial** president's/ presidential term of office; ~ **poștal** money order; ~ **de plată** money order • **~ar** *nm com* authorized agent.

mandibulă [man'dibulă] *nf zool* mandible.

mandolină [mando'lină] *nf mus* mandolin(e).

manechin [mane'kin] *nn* (*figură de lemn, ceară, plastic folosită în croitorie, simulări etc*) dummy; (*femeie*) model; *obs* mannequin; cover girl; (*arte*) manikin; *fig* (*mere*) puppet; lay figure.

manej [ma'nezh] *nn* riding school, manege; (*acoperit*) riding house/hall; *agr* horse gear; horse-driven mill.

manetă [ma'netă] *nf tech* handle, hand lever.

manevra [mane'vra] *vt* to manipulate, to maneuver; (*o mașină*) to operate, to run; *naut* (*pânzele*) to handle || *vi mil, naut* to maneuver; *rail* to shunt; *fig* to maneuver, to scheme, to plot.

manevră [ma'nevră] *nf mil, naut* exercise, drill; (*în război*) *also fig* maneuver; *rail* shunting, marshaling; *naut* (*frânghie*) rope; *pl* rigging; *fig* scheme, intrigue.

mangal [man'gal] *nn* charcoal.

mangan [man'gan] *nn chem* manganese.

mango ['mango] *nn bot* (fruit of) mango tree.

mangustă [man'gustă] *nf zool* mangoose, mongoose.

maniabil [mani'abil] *adj* manageable; (*d. un vehicul*) easy to handle/control/drive; (*d. un instrument*) handy.

maniac [mani'ak] *adj med* maniac; (*cu diferite fixații*) fussy, finicky, persnickety || *nm/nf* (*nebun*) madman, maniac; ~ **sexual** sex maniac.

manichiură [mani'kiură] *nf* manicure.

manie [ma'nie] *nf psych, med* mania, obsession; *obs* mental derangement; (*pasiune*) craze; odd habit.

manieră [mani'era] *nf* (*conduită*) *pl* manners; (*fel*) manner, way; (*artă*) **în maniera** (*cuiva*) after the manner of.

manifest [mani'fest] *nn* (*program*) manifesto; (*distribuit*) leaflet || *adj* obvious.

manifesta [manifes'ta] *vt* (*interes, intenții etc*) to manifest, to show; (*a arăta*) to show, to reveal; (*a da glas*) to voice; (*a exprima*) to express; (*bucuria etc*) to give vent to; (*curajul*) to display || *vr* to appear, to crop up; (*a se arăta*) to show oneself; *med* (*o boală*) to manifest itself || *vi* to demonstrate; to make a public demonstration • **~re** *nf* demonstration • **~ție** *nf* demonstration.

manipula [manipu'la] *vt* to manipulate, to handle; to operate • **~nt** *nm also tech* operator; (*robotică*) manipulator; (*al banilor*) handler; (*la tramvai*) streetcar driver.

manivelă [mani'velă] *nf tech* handle; *auto* crank (handle); *metal* handhold.

manometru [mano'metru] *nn phys* manometer, pressure gauge; ~ **cu mercur** aneroid gauge.

manoperă [ma'noperă] *nf* manual labor; *fig* * **manevră**.
mansardă [man'sardă] *nf* (*cameră*) attic; (*numai pod*) garret; (*tip de acoperiş*) mansard roof.
manşă ['manshă] *nf avia* (*pârghie*) club, stick control; *sp, pol* round.
manşetă [man'shetă] *nf* (*la mânecă*) cuff; (*la pantalon*) turn-up; (*de ziar*) headline; shoulder note; *tech* cup.
manta [man'ta] *nf* mantle, cloak; *mil* great-coat; *tech* casing; shell, bonnet.
mantou [man'tou] *nn* (lady's) cloak, coat.
manual [manu'al] *adj* manual, hand, hand-made ‖ *adv* manually ‖ *nn scol* textbook; manual; (*ghid; indicator*) handbook, guide.
manufactură [manufak'tură] *nf hist* manufacture.
manuscript, manuscris [manu'skript, manu'skris] *nn* manuscript, MS; (*dactilografiat*) typescript.
mapă ['mapă] *nf* paper case; (*servietă*) folio case, portfolio.
maramă [ma'ramă] *nf* (very thin home-spun raw silk) headkerchief (part of the folk costume in Romania).
maraton [mara'ton] *nn sp* marathon (race), long-distance race.
marca [mar'ka] *vt* to mark, to write; (*a bifa*) to (mark with a) check; (*o ladă etc*) to stencil; (*un obiect de metal preţios*) to hallmark; (*a stigmatiza*) to brand; (*vitele, oile*) to brand cattle; (*a nota*) to make a note of; (*a înregistra*) to register, to record; (*d. orologiu*) to say; to tell the time; (*a delimita*) to mark; (*a arăta*) to show, to indicate; (*a dovedi*) to prove; (*a sublinia*) to underline; **a ~ măsura** *mus* to beat time; *sp* (*un punct*) to score (a goal); (*adversarul*) to mark the opponent ‖ *vr pass* to be marked, etc ‖ *vi sp* to score.
marcant [mar'kant] *adj* outstanding, remarkable, significant.
marcă ['markă] *nf* mark; (*semn*) sign; (*tip, model*) brand; (*fabricaţie*) make; (*poştală*) (postage) stamp; *obs* (coat of) arms; *rail* marking sign; **~a fabricii** (de produs) trademark, brand name; **marcă înregistrată** registered trademark; **~ depusă** registered trademark.
marchetărie [marketă'rie] *nf* (*arte decorative*) inlaid work.
marchiz [mar'kiz] *nm* marquis, marquess • **~ă** *nf* (*în Anglia*) marchioness; (*în Franţa*) marquise; *constr* awning, canopy; marquee; (*ca încăpere*) porch; (*din sticlă, deasupra intrării etc*) glass awning, roof; *rail* driver's cab.
mare[1] ['mare] *adj* (*ca durată, grad, însemnătate, valoare; în sens abstract*) great; (*ca întindere, număr sau conţinut*) large; (*ca volum*) big; (*înalt şi lung, d. oameni, pomi etc*) tall; (*adânc*) deep; (*amplu*) ample; (*enorm*) enormous; (*gras*) fat; (*gros*) thick; infinite; (*înalt*) high; (*încăpător*) roomy; (*larg*) wide; (*lat*) broad; massive; (*măreţ*) grand; numerous; vast, immense; (*voluminos, corpolent*) bulky; (*puternic*) powerful, mighty; adult, grown-up; violent; (*aspru*) hard; (*vestit*) famous, renowned; (*marcant*) outstanding; important; (*hotărâtor*) decisive; (*uimitor*) amazing; stupendous; (*ca intensitate*) (*zgomot*) loud; (*frig*) severe; intense; strong; high; (*ploaie*) heavy.
mare[2] ['mare] *nf also fig* sea; *lit* main; (*oceanul planetar*) ocean • **~a Albă** the White Sea; **~a Neagră** the Black Sea.
maree [ma'ree] *nf* tide; (*flux şi reflux*) ebb and flow; (*flux*) flow; (*reflux*) ebb.
mareşal [mare'shal] *nm mil* marshal.

marfă ['marfă] *nf* commodities, goods, merchandise; *obs* wares.
margaretă [marga'retă] *nf bot* (dog) daisy, moonflower.
margarină [marga'rină] *nf* margarine, artificial butter.
marginal [mardji'nal] *adj* marginal • **~iza** *vt* to marginalize, to cast out.
margine ['mardjine] *nf* edge; (*a unui recipient etc*) brim, rim; (*de prăpastie etc*) brink; (*a trotuarului*) curb; (*a câmpului*) border; (*a unei farfurii, a unui biscuit, a mesei, a pădurii etc*) skirt; (*mal*) bank, coast; (*graniţă*) border, frontier (line); (*extremitate*) end, extremity; (*periferie*) periphery; (*a oraşului*) outskirts; (*la o carte, foaie de hârtie*) margin; (*parte laterală sau circumferinţa unui obiect*) side; limit, bounds; **de ~** peripheral, peripheric; **fără margini** boundless, limitless, infinite.
mariaj [mari'azh] *nn* marriage, match; (*ceremonie*) wedding.
marijuana [mari'huana] *nf chem, med* marijuana; *coll* grass.
marin [ma'rin] *adj* marine, sea.
marina [mari'na] *vt* to marinate, to pickle.
marinar [mari'nar] *nm* sailor, seaman; *obs* mariner.
marinată [mari'nată] *nf* marinade.
marină [ma'rină] *nf* (*flotă*) navy; sea service; **~ comercială** merchant navy; (*navigaţie*) seamanship.
marionetă [mario'netă] *nf* marionette, puppet; *fig* tool.
maritim [ma'ritim] *adj* maritime; sea.
marketing ['marketing] *nn econ* marketing.
marmeladă [marme'ladă] *nf* jam, candied fruit jelly; (*magiun*) plum jam; (*de citrice*) marmalade.
marmotă [mar'motă] *nf zool* marmot.
marmură ['marmura] *nf* marble.
maro [ma'ro] *adj* chestnut(-color), maroon; (*cafeniu*) brown.
marochinărie [marokină'rie] *nf* (*produse*) morocco (leather) goods; (*ca magazin*) (fancy) leather shop; (*meserie*) morocco-leather tanning; (*atelier*) morocco-leather tannery; (*prelucrarea pielii*) leather working.
marsupiu [mar'supiu] *nm zool* marsupium, pouch.
marş [marsh] *interj mil* forward!, march!; *coll* away!, get away!, get out (of here)! ‖ *nn mil, mus* march.
marşarier [marshari'er] *nn auto* reverse (gear); **în ~** in reverse gear.
martie ['martie] *nm* March.
martir [mar'tir] *nm also fig* martyr • **~iza** *vt relig* to martyr; *fig* to martyrize, to torment; (*a face să sufere*) to torture.
martor ['martor] *nm jur, fig* witness; spectator, onlooker; **~ ocular** eyewitness.
marţi [marts] *nf* Tuesday ‖ *adv* on Tuesday.
marţial [martsi'al] *adj* martial, warlike; war • **lege ~ă** martial law; **curte ~ă** court martial.
marxism [mark'sism] *nn* Marxism.
masa[1] [ma'sa] *vt* (*a strânge soldaţi*) to mass, to concentrate; (*a strânge persoane*) to gather together, to assemble ‖ *vr also mil pass* to be massed/concentrated; to mass, to concentrate
masa[2] [ma'sa] *vt* (*a face masaj*) to massage, to shampoo • **~j** *nn* massage, shampooing.
masacra [masa'kra] *vt* to massacre, to slaughter; *fig* to spoil, to bungle; (*muzica etc*) to murder; (*haine*) to ruin.
masacru [ma'sakru] *nn* slaughter, massacre; * **masacra**.

masă¹ ['masă] *nf (mobilă)* table; *(bucătărie)* cooking, cuisine; *(cină)* dinner, supper; *(întreținere)* board; *(mâncare)* meal; *(ospăț)* feast; *(prânz)* lunch, dinner.

masă² ['masă] *nf phys* mass; *(mulțime)* crowd; **de ~** mass; **în ~** in a body; **~ monetară** money supply, money in circulation; **~ de aer** air mass; **~ electrică** electric mass; **~ plastică** plastic mass.

masca [mas'ka] *vt* to mask, to put a mask on; *fig (a ascunde)* to hide, to conceal; *(o fereastră)* to blind; *(lumina)* to shade; *(a disimula)* to disguise || *vr* to mask oneself, to put a mask on • **~radă** *nf* masquerade; mask; *fig* sham, farce.

mască ['masgă] *nf (în diferite sensuri)* mask; *mil* gas mask; *(pentru a proteja respirația)* breathing/protection mask; *(contra ridurilor)* face pack; *thea* masque; *(machiaj)* make-up; *fig* cloak; *(paravan)* screen; *(prefăcătorie)* disguise; *fig (expresie)* face, countenance; *(față care nu exprimă nimic)* straight face; *(persoană în ~)* masker, masquerader.

mascotă [mas'kotă] *nf* mascot, charm, amulet.

mascul [mas'kul] *nm* male; *pej sl* stud • **~in** *adj* male; *gram* masculine; **genul ~** *gram* the masculine gender.

maseză [ma'seză] *nf* masseuse.

masiv [ma'siv] *adj* massive, bulky; solid; *(greu)* heavy; *(trupeș)* stout, heavily built, portly; *(plin)* full; voluminous; substantial; **aur ~** solid gold || *adv* massively, solidly || *nn geog* massif, mountain; *(morman)* heap, pile.

masochism [maso'kism] *nn med* masochism.

mason [ma'son] *nm* freemason • **~erie** *nf* (free)masonry.

masor [ma'sor] *nm* masseur.

masturbație [mastur'batsie] *nf med* masturbation; self-eroticism/-stimulation.

mașinal [mashi'nal] *adj* mechanical, involuntary, unconscious || *adv* mechanically, involuntarily, unconsciously.

mașinație [mashi'natsie] *nf* machination, scheme, intrigue.

mașină [ma'shină] *nf* machine; engine; locomotive; *(batoză)* thrashing machine; car, automobile; *(camion)* truck; *fig* machinery; **~ automată** automatic machine; **~ cu abur** steam engine; **~ de asamblat** assembling machine; **~ de calculat** computer, computing machine, *tech* calculating machine; **~ de cusut** sewing machine; **~ de copiat** (photo)copier, Xerox; **~ de frezat** milling machine; **~ de gătit** cooking stove; **~ de găurit** boring machine; **~ de muls** milking machine; **~ de război** *fig* war machine; **~ de scris** typewriter; **~ de spălat** washing machine; **~ de tocat carne** meat chopper, mincing machine; **~ de tors** spinning machine/frame; **~ de tricotat** knitting machine; **~ de tuns** hair clippers; **~ electrică** electric machine; **~ hidraulică** hydraulic engine; **~ infernală** explosive device; **~ pneumatică** pneumatic machine; **~ termică** heat engine, thermomotor • **~rie** *nf also fig* machinery; plant; engine; *(mașina)* machine, *pl* machines.

mat¹ [mat] *nn (la jocul de șah)* (check)mate.

mat² [mat] *adj (d. un metal)* matt, unpolished, dull; *(d. culori)* flat, pale; *(d. sunete)* dead, thud; *(d. sticlă)* frosted; *(d. ten)* mat.

matahală [mata'hală] *nf (colos)* colossus, giant; *(ceva uriaș)* huge thing; *(monstru)* monster; *sl (sperietoare)* bugbear, bogy, bugaboo.

matcă ['matkă] *nf (a albinelor)* queen; *(de râu)* bed, bottom; *anat* womb.

matelot [mate'lot] *nm* sailor, seaman.

matematică [mate'matikă] *nf scol* mathematic(s); *coll* math.

matematician [matematichi'an] *nm* mathematician.

material [materi'al] *adj* material; *(fizic)* physical; real, concrete || *nn* stuff, material; *(țesătură)* fabric • **~ism** *nn* materialism • **~iza** *vt* to materialize; *(a înfăptui)* to carry out; to realize || *vr* to materialize, to be materialized.

materie [ma'terie] *nf* matter; substance; material; *(stofă)* stuff, fabric; *scol* subject (matter); *(domeniu)* domain, sphere; **~ cenușie** *anat* grey matter; **~ primă** raw material.

matern [ma'tern] *adj* mother's, maternal, *(grijă etc)* motherly || *adv* maternally, in a motherly way • **limbă ~ă** mother tongue, native language • **~itate** *nf* maternity, motherhood; *(spital)* maternity hospital.

matinal [mati'nal] *adj* morning; *(devreme)* early.

matineu [mati'neu] *nn frml* morning; **în ~** in the morning; *thea* matinee/afternoon showing/screening.

matlasat [matla'sat] *adj* quilted, padded.

matrapazlâc [matrapaz'lâk] *nn* fraud, swindle.

matriarhat [matriar'hat] *nn* matriarchate.

matrice [ma'triche] *nf anat* uterus, womb; *math, phys* matrix.

matrimonial [matrimoni'al] *adj* matrimonial, connubial • **agenție ~ă** marriage agency/bureau.

matriță [ma'tritsă] *nf metal, etc* die, mold; *typ* type mold.

matroană [ma'troană] *nf pej* matron, stout/portly woman.

matroz [ma'troz] *nm* sailor, seaman.

matur [ma'tur] *adj (d. persoane)* adult, grown-up; *(d. vârstă, gândire etc)* mature; *(copt)* ripe • **~itate** *nf* maturity; *also fig* ripeness; **a ajunge la ~** *(d. persoane)* to come to maturity; *(d. fructe etc)* to mature • **~iza** *vr (d. fructe etc)* to mature; to ripen; *(d. persoane)* to become mature, to grow up.

maț [mats] *nn anat coll* gut, bowel.

maur [ma'ur] *adj* Moorish; *archit* Moresque, Mauresque || *nm* Moor.

maus [maus] *nn comp* mouse.

mausoleu [mauzo'leu] *nn* mausoleum.

maxilar [maksi'lar] *adj* maxillary || *nn* jaw bone, jaw.

maxim ['maksim] *adj* maximum; highest • **~al** *adj* maximum, top • **~ă** *nf* maxim, adage; aphorism; *phys, etc* maximum • **~um** *nn* maximum, upper limit || *adv* at the most/highest.

mazăre ['mazăre] *nf bot, cul* pea(s).

măcar [mă'kar] *adv (cel puțin)* at least; at any rate; *(chiar)* even; *(nici chiar)* not even, not so much as; **~ că** (al)though; **~ dacă/de** if only, at least if.

măcăi [măkă'i] *vi* to quack.

măcăleandru [măkă'leandru] *nm orn* robin (redbreast).

măcel [mă'chel] *nn also fig* massacre; *(d. animale)* butchery, slaughter • **~ar** *nm also fig* butcher • **~ări** *vt* to slaughter, to massacre || *vr recip* to slaughter each other.

măc(i)eș [mă'chiesh] *nm bot* wild rose/briar, hip rose/tree.

măcina [măchi'na] *vt (grâu, cafea, piper etc)* to grind, to mill; *(a fărâmița)* to crumble; *(a zdrobi)* to crush; *(d. ziduri)* to erode, to eat away || *vr pass* to be ground, etc; (*d. ziduri*) to crumble; (*d. stânci*) to weather.

măciucă [mă'chiukă] *nf* club, bludgeon; (*lovitură de ~*) bludgeon stroke; *fig* staggering blow.

măciulie [măchiu'lie] *nf* (*de baston*) knob; (*de cui, de ac etc*) head; *bot* capsule, head.

măduvă ['măduvă] *nf anat also fig* marrow; *med* medulla; *bot* pith; (*sevă*) sap; *fig* core; essence; **transplant de ~ *med*** marrow transplant.

măgar [mă'gar] *nm zool also fig* donkey, ass; *fig* (*încăpățânat*) mule; (*om rău intenționat*) swine, scum.

măguli [măgu'li] *vt* to flatter, to compliment, to praise; *coll* to butter up; to play up to • ***~tor*** *adj* flattering || *adv* flatteringly.

măgură ['măgură] *nf* hill; (*movilă*) hillock.

măi [măi] *interj* (*nepoliticos când se adresează unei persoane*) hey!, hey you!; **hei ~!** hey you!

măiestrie [măies'trie] *nf* great art, craftsmanship, artistry; (*artă*) art; (*îndemânare*) skill.

măiestrit [măies'trit] *adj* masterly, exquisite, skillful || *adv* skillfully; artfully.

mălai [mă'lai] *nn* (*făină de porumb*) cornmeal.

măluros [mălu'ros] *adj* (*d. plante, care suferă de mălură*) smutty; (*d. maluri înalte și abrupte*) steep, sheer.

mămăligă [mămă'ligă] *nf approx* polenta.

mămică, mămițică [mă'mikă, mămi'tsikă] *nf coll* mom, ma, mommy.

mănăstire [mănăs'tire] *nf* monastery, cloister, (*de obicei de maici*) convent.

mănos [mă'nos] *adj also fig* fruitful, fertile; (*bogat*) rich; (*d. afaceri*) profitable, lucrative.

mănunchi [mă'nunki] *nn* (*de spice, fire etc*) bundle, bunch; (*cât se poate lua cu mâna*) a handful of.

mănușă [mă'nushă] *nf* glove; (*la armură*) gauntlet; (*cu un deget*) mitt(en).

măr [măr] *nm bot* (*pom*) apple tree || *nn* (*fructul*) apple.

mărar [mă'rar] *nm bot* dill.

mărăcine [mără'chine] *nm* bramble, briar, brake.

măreț [mă'rets] *adj* grand, stately, magnificent, majestic, splendid, glorious, gorgeous, impressive || *adv* magnificently, etc. • ***~ie*** *nf* greatness, grandeur, (*maiestate*) majesty, splendor; **~ și decădere** (a unui imperiu etc) the rise and fall (of an empire, etc).

mărgăritar [mărgări'tar] *nn* pearl; *bot* lily of the valley; *bot* loranth; (*pietriș*) gravel.

mărgea [măr'djea] *nf* (glass) bead, glass pearl; *pl* (*la curcan*) wattle.

mărgean [mar'djean] *nn zool* coral.

mărginaș [mărdji'nash] *adj* (*învecinat*) neighboring, adjacent; (*de margine*) peripheral, border; (*depărtat*) remote.

mărgini [mărdji'ni] *vt* to border, to line, to bound; (*a îngrădi*) to enclose; *fig* to limit, to set bounds/limits to || *vr* **a se ~ cu** to be contiguous to, to border (up)on • ***~t*** *adj* bordered, limited; *fig* (*d. disponibilitățile intelectuale*) stupid, obtuse, narrowminded.

mări [mă'ri] *vt also med* to enlarge, to grow; (*a spori*) to increase; (*cu lupa etc*) to magnify; (*a ridica*) to raise; to intensify; (*a lărgi*) to widen, to extend; (*prețul, valoarea etc*) to put up; to enhance; (*a dilata*) to expand; (*o gaură*) to open out || *vr* to grow/get/become large; to become greater; (*a spori*) to increase; (*a se înmulți*) to multiply; (*a crește*) to grow; (*d. prețuri*) to go up; (*d. durere*) to aggravate

• **~me** *nf* size; volume; (*dimensiuni*) dimensions; (*proporții*) proportions; (*întindere*) extent; *pl* dignitaries; *pej coll* big guns/shots.

mărinimie [mărini'mie] *nf* magnanimity, generosity, benevolence.

mărinimos [mărini'mos] *adj* magnanimous, benevolent; (*darnic*) generous, open-handed || *adv* magnanimously, etc.

mărita [mări'ta] *vt* (*d. o femeie*) to marry off, to give (away) in marriage; *fig* (*a vinde ieftin*) *coll* to sell cheap; (*a se debarasa de*) to get rid of || *vr* (*d. o femeie*) (*cu*) to marry smb, to get married (to); *frml* to wed.

măritiș [mări'tish] *nn* (*numai femei*) marriage, matrimony.

mărșălui [mărshălu'i] *vi* to march.

mărturie [mărtu'rie] *nf* testimony, evidence; (*dovadă de prietenie, stimă etc*) token, sign; (*martor*) witness; (*ca delict*) perjury.

mărturisi [mărturi'si] *vt* to confess, to admit; to affirm, to assert; to declare; (*a recunoaște*) to confess, to own; (*pe deplin*) to make a clean breast of; (*a susține*) to maintain || *vr relig* to confess one's sins || *vi* to confess • ***~re*** *nf* confession, admission.

mărțișor [mărtsi'shor] *nn* trinket worn to celebrate March 1, March amulet.

mărunt [mă'runt] *adj* (*mic*) small; fine; (*micuț*) tiny, little; (*neînsemnat*) trifling; (*d. cheltuieli*) petty; (*d. bani*) (small) change; (*scund*) low, short || *adv* small, fine.

măruntaie [mărun'taie] *nf pl* entrails, intestines; (*de vită*) pluck; *fig* bowels; depths.

mărunțiș [mărun'tsish] *nn pl* trifles; (*bani mărunți*) (small) change; *pl* (*obiecte mici*) small goods, petty/small ware(s).

măscărici [măskă'rich] *nm* buffoon, fool; clown.

măsea [mă'sea] *nf anat* molar (tooth), grinder; (*dinte*) tooth; (*la roata morii*) wooden tooth.

măslin [măs'lin] *nm bot* olive (tree) • ***~ă*** *nf* olive • ***~iu*** *adj* olive (colored).

măslui [măslu'i] *vt* (*cărțile*) to make the cards (for a foul play); to chisel; (*alegerile*) to gerrymander, to fix elections.

măsura [măsu'ra] *vt* to measure; (*grâul etc*) to measure out; (*haine etc*) to measure off; (*pământul etc*) to measure up, to survey; (*carburant*) to meter; *fig* to calculate; (*a cântări, cuvintele etc*) to weigh; (*a evalua*) to estimate; (*a înfrâna*) to curb; to proportion; *fig* (*a străbate*) to cross; *fig* (*cu privirea*) to size smb up; to eye smb; *fig* (*a bate*) *coll* to lick, to drub || *vr pass* to be measured, etc; (*cu cineva*) to measure/pit oneself against smb; (*a se lupta*) to fight; (*reciproc, cu privirea*) to look/eye each other up and down || *vi* to be ... long, wide, etc • ***~t*** *adj* measured, calculated, estimated, * **măsura**; (*limitat*) limited; moderate, temperate, reasonable.

măsură [mă'sură] *nf* measure; (*măsurare*) measurement; measuring; (*întindere*) extent; (*cantitate*) quantity, amount; limit; (*metrologie*) foot; *mus* bar; *com* fitting; size; *pl* measures, steps; (*valoare*) value; (*acțiune*) step, action; (*forță*) force.

măsuță [mă'sutsă] *nf* small/little table.

mătase [mă'tase] *nf* silk, *pl* silks; (*a porumbului*) tassel.

mătăsos [mătă'sos] *adj* silky, fine; (*catifelat*) velvety.

mătreaţă [mă'treatsă] *nf* dandruff; scuff.

mătura ['mătura] *vt* to sweep; (*camera etc*) to sweep out; (*murdăria etc*) to sweep up; *fig* to clear out, to make a clean sweep of; (*a alunga*) to drive away; (*a îndepărta*) to sweep away.

mătură ['mătură] *nf* broom; (*de pene*) feather broom; (*târn*) besom; *pl bot* Caffre corn, sorghum; **coadă de** ~ broomstick • **~tor** *nm* sweeper; (~ *de stradă*) street sweeper, scavenger.

mătuşă [mă'tushă] *nf* aunt; old woman; (*ca adresare*) *approx* mother.

mâhni [mâh'ni] *vt/vr* to grieve, to sadden, to distress • **~re** *nf* grief, sorrow; (*tristeţe*) sadness • **~t** *adj* sad, mournful, wistful.

mâine ['mâine] *adv* tomorrow; (*cândva*) some time; (*în viitor*) in the future.

mâl [mâl] *nn* silt, ooze, mud.

mâna [mâ'na] *vt* to drive; (*calul, ca să meargă mai repede*) to urge on; (*a duce*) to carry; (*a împinge*) to push; *fig* to drive on; to urge; to goad.

mână ['mână] *nf anat also fig* hand; *sl* paw; (*la jocul de cărţi*) lead; (*scris*) hand(writing); (*parte*) side.

mânca [mân'ka] *vt* to eat; (*a servi*) to have, to take; (*a pişca*) to sting; *fig* (*a roade*) to eat up/away, to corrode; *fig* (*a mistui*) to consume, to devour; *fig* (*a chinui*) to torment, to torture || *vr pass* to be eaten, etc || *vi* to eat, to have/take dinner • **~re** *nf* eating; feeding; lunching, dining; (*de-ale mâncării*) food; (*merinde*) victuals; (*fel de mâncare*) dish; (*de peste zi*) meal.

mâncăcios [mânkă'chos] *adj* gluttonous, voracious || *nm* (*mâncău*) glutton.

mâncărime [mânkă'rime] *nf* itching.

mâncău [mân'kău] *nm pej* greedyguts, glutton.

mândreţe [mân'dretse] *nf* beauty, splendor.

mândri [mân'dri] *vr* (*cu*) to take pride (in); (*a se făli*) to boast (of/about); (*a se fuduli*) to be haughty • **~e** *nf* pride; (*orgoliu*) vaingloriousness, bumptiousness; (*trufie*) haughtiness, arrogance; vanity.

mândru ['mândru] *adj* proud; (*încrezut*) conceited; (*trufaş*) arrogant; (*frumos*) handsome; (*minunat*) wonderful; (*falnic*) stately; splendid || *nm* (*iubit*) lover; (*dragul meu*) my dear(est).

mânecă ['mânekă] *nf also tech* sleeve; arm.

mâner [mâ'ner] *nn* handle; (*de sabie, pumnal*) hilt; *auto* handgrip.

mângâia [mângâ'ia] *vt* to stroke; (*a dezmierda*) to fondle; *fig* (*ochii*) to caress; *fig* (*a linişti*) to comfort; (*a desfăta*) to delight || *vr* to console oneself; **a se ~ cu** to take comfort in, to seek consolation in, (*cu speranţa*) to flatter oneself with.

mângâiere [mângâ'iere] *nf* stroking, * **mângâia**; (*consolare*) consolation; (*satisfacţie*) satisfaction; (*plăcere*) pleasure; (*sprijin*) support; (*mulţumire*) contentment; gratification.

mângâietor [mângâie'tor] *adj fig* comforting, consoling.

mânia [mâni'a] *vt* to anger, to infuriate || *vr* to get angry, to lose one's temper; (*pe sine*) to be angry with oneself.

mânie [mâ'nie] *nf* rage, fury, (*supărare*) anger; (*ciudă*) spite; (*urgie*) wrath; **iute la ~** quick-/hot-tempered; **la ~** in anger, in a moment of anger/rage.

mânios [mâni'os] *adj* furious, enraged, in a rage, (*supărat*) angry; **a fi ~ pe** to be angry with || *adv* furiously, in a rage.

mânji [mân'zhi] *vt* to soil, to dirty; *fig* to sully, to tarnish || *vr* to soil oneself; to become dirty/soiled.

mântui [mântu'i] *vt (a salva) also relig* to save, to redeem; (*a elibera*) to free, to liberate; (*a termina*) to terminate, to finish, to end || *vr pass* to be saved; to be redeemed; to come to an end • **~re** *nf relig* salvation, redemption; (*salvare*) rescue; (*eliberare*) liberation; (*terminare*) ending • **~tor** *adj* liberating || *nm* liberator; *relig* Savior.

mânui [mânu'i] *vt* to handle, to manipulate; (*condeiul, spada*) to wield; (*bani*) to handle • **~re** *nf* handling; manipulating, manipulation.

mânuşă [mâ'nushă] *nf* glove.

mânz [mânz] *nm* foal, colt; *fig* colt.

mârâi [mârâ'i] *vi* to snarl; (*d. un câine, un urs*) to growl; *fig* to grumble.

mârlan [mâr'lan] *nm* boor, churl, clown.

mârşav [mâr'shav] *adj/adv* * **ticălos**.

mârşăvie [mârshă'vie] *nf* * **ticăloşie**.

mârţoagă [mâr'tswagă] *nf* jade, hack.

mâţ [mâts] *nm zool* (*motan*) (tom)cat, tom, (*mic*) kitten • **~ă** *nf* (*pisică*) cat; *min* safety brake; ~ **blândă** *fig* demure person; sneak; *coll* slyboots • **~işori** *nm pl* kittens; *bot* catkins.

mâzgă ['mâzgă] *nf* slime; *bot* (*sevă*) sap.

mâzgăleală [mâzgă'lealǎ] *nf* * **mâzgălitură**.

mâzgăli [mâzgă'li] *vt* to daub, to smear; (*faţa*) to dirty; (*hârtia*) to blot; *fig* to scribble (off), to scrawl || *vr* to soil oneself • **~tură** *nf also fig* scrawl(ing), scribbling, scribble.

mecanic [me'kanik] *nm auto* mechanic; *rail* engine driver; ~ **de bord** *avia* flight engineer; **inginer** ~ mechanical engineer; **şef** ~ master mechanic, *tech* chief engineer || *adj* mechanical, machine-like || *adv* mechanically • **~ă** *nf phys* mechanics.

mecanism [meka'nism] *nn also fig* mechanism, machinery; device; contrivance; gear; (*tehnică*) technique; (*de ceas*) works.

mecanizare [mekani'zare] *nf* mechanization.

mecena [me'chena] *nm* maecenas, patron (of art, letters).

meci ['mechi] *nn* (*în toate sporturile de echipă*) *also fig* match; ~ **jucat acasă** home match; ~ **jucat în deplasare** away match.

mediat [medi'at] *adj* meda(l)led; (*d. un militar*) decorated || *nm* (*olimpic etc*) gold medalist, recipient of a medal.

medalie [me'dalie] *nf* medal; ~ **de aur** gold medal; **reversul ~i** the reverse of the medal; (*insignă oficială: de poliţist etc*) badge.

medalion [medali'on] *nn* (*bijuterie şi medalie*) medallion; (*cu fotografie*) locket; (*în ziare, la TV*) inset, inset portrait; *cul* medallion.

media [medi'a] *vi/vt* to mediate • **~tor** *adj* mediating, mediatory || *nm* mediator, intermediate, go-between.

medic ['medik] *nm* doctor, physician || *adv* medically; ~ **chirurg** surgeon; ~ **consultant** consultant, consulting physician; ~ **de bord** *naut* ship's doctor; ~ **de familie** family doctor; ~ **legist** forensic/medical expert; ~ **militar** army medical officer, M.O., medical examiner; ~ **veterinar** veterinary surgeon, veterinarian • **~al** *adj* medical; **ajutor** ~ medical aid; **certificat** ~ medical certificate; **examen** ~ (*complet*) medical examination/check-up • **~ament** *nn* medicine, drug, medication • **~aţie** *nf* medication, medical treatment • **~ină** *nf* medicine; **~ legală** forensic/legal medicine, medical jurisprudence; **~ veterinară** veterinary medicine; **~ preventivă** preventive medicine; **~ generală** general medicine.

medie [ˈmedie] *nf* average, medium; *math* mean; **în ~** on an/the average, (taken) one with another.

mediere [mediˈere] *nf* mediation, intercession.

medieval [medieˈval] *adj* medieval.

mediocritate [mediokriˈtate] *nf* mediocrity; (*d. cineva*) second-rater.

mediocru [mediˈokru] *adj* poor, mediocre; (*d. o lucrare*) indifferent; (*d. posibilități*) moderate, second-rate; (*d. o persoană*) nonentity.

medita [mediˈta] *vi* to meditate on, to ponder (over); (*a se gândi*) to think (of), to reflect (up)on || *vt* (*un elev*) to prepare, to coach; to contemplate • **~tiv** *adj* meditating, thoughtful || *adv* meditatively, musingly • **~tor** *nm* private teacher, tutor • **~ție** *nf* meditation; (*a unui elev*) coaching; (*lecție*) lesson.

mediteranean [mediteraˈnean] *adj/nm* Mediterranean.

mediu [ˈmediu] *adj* average, medium || *nn chem* medium; surroundings, environment; (*societate*) society.

meduză [meˈduză] *nf zool* medusa, jellyfish.

megafon [megaˈfon] *nn* loudspeaker, megaphone.

megaloman [megaloˈman] *adj/nm* megalomaniac.

mei [mei] *nn bot* millet || *adj poss m pl* my; **ai ~** mine.

melancolic [melanˈkolik] *adj* melancholy; gloomy; (*înclinat spre melancolie*) melancholic, low-spirited; *coll* under the weather || *adv* melancholically.

melancolie [melancoˈlie] *nf* melancholy; gloom; *med* melancholia.

melanj [meˈlanʒ] *nn* mixture.

melasă [meˈlasă] *nf* molasses, treacle.

melc [melk] *nm zool* snail; *anat* cochlea; *tech* worm gear, slug; (*prăjitură*) Chelsea bun • **ca ~ul** (as) slow as a snail, at a snail's pace.

meleag [meˈleag] *nn* part, region; country • **~uri natale** native country/country.

melodie [meloˈdie] *nf* melody, tune.

melodios [melodiˈos] *adj* melodious, musical, tuneful || *adv* melodiously, tunefully.

melodramatic [melodraˈmatik] *adj* melodramatic || *adv* melodramatically.

melodramă [meloˈdramă] *nf* melodrama.

meloman [meloˈman] *nm* melomaniac, lover of music, music fan, concertgoer.

melon [meˈlon] *nn* bowler (hat).

membrană [memˈbrană] *nf anat, etc* membrane; *rad* diaphragm.

membru [ˈmembru] *nn anat* limb; *anat* male member, penis || *nm* (*într-o societate, consiliu etc*) member.

memento [meˈmento] *nn* memento, reminder; (*carte*) synopsis.

memora [memoˈra] *vt* * **memoriza** • **~bil** *adj* memorable, noteworthy || *adv* memorably • **~ndum** *nn* memorandum, *pl* memoranda; *coll* memo.

memorie [meˈmorie] *nf also comp* memory; (*amintire*) remembrance; **din ~** from memory; **extensie de ~** memory expansion • **în ~a** in memory of, to the memory of.

memoriu [meˈmoriu] *nn* (*raport*) report; *jur* (*la un proces*) (written) statement; *pl* memoirs; (*ale unei societăți etc*) transactions.

memoriza [memoriˈza] *vt* to memorize, to commit to memory; *comp* to write to memory.

menaj [meˈnaʒ] *nn* housekeeping, housewifery; (*familie*) household, family; family life; **a face ~ul** to keep house for smb, (*a face curat*) to clean house.

menaja [menaˈʒa] *vt* (*a folosi cu parcimonie*) to use sparingly, to spare; (*a trata cu grijă pe cineva*) to deal gently/tactfully with; to be too soft to smb || *vr* to spare oneself, to take care of oneself, to look after oneself.

menajer [menaˈʒer] *adj* domestic; pertaining to the house • **~ă** *nf* housewife, housekeeper.

menajerie [menaʒeˈrie] *nf* menagerie.

menghină [menˈgină] *nf* (screw)vice.

meni [meˈni] *vt* to destine; (*a predestina*) to foredoom; (*a prezice*) to foretell; (*a blestema*) to curse • **~re** *nf* mission; (*sarcină*) task; (*soartă*) fate.

meningită [meninˈdʒită] *nf med* meningitis.

meniu [meˈniu] *nn* menu, bill of fare; **~ fix** ordinary.

menopauză [menoˈpauză] *nf physiol* menopause.

menstruație [menstruˈatsie] *nf physiol* menstruation, menses; *coll* period(s).

mental [menˈtal] *adj* * **mintal**.

mentalitate [mentaliˈtate] *nf* mentality, outlook, mindset.

mentă [ˈmentă] *nf bot* peppermint.

mentor [ˈmentor] *nm* mentor.

menține [menˈtsine] *vt* to maintain, to uphold; (*o hotărâre*) to abide by; (*pacea*) to keep; to preserve; (*un obiect într-o anumită poziție*) to keep/hold in position || *vr* to continue; (*a rămâne*) to remain; (*d. prețuri*) to keep/hold up, to remain steady; (*a nu ceda*) to hold out; (*în post*) to keep one's job.

menționa [mentsioˈna] *vt* to mention, to make mention of; (*a specifica*) to specify • **~t mai sus** mentioned above, above-mentioned, aforesaid.

mențiune [mentsiˈune] *nf* mention; (*pe plic*) endorsement; *scol* certificate of good work and conduct; (*la un concurs*) (honorable) mention.

mercantil [merkanˈtil] *adj* mercantile, commercial • **~ism** *nn* mercantilism.

mercenar [mercheˈnar] *adj/nm mil, also fig* mercenary.

mercerie [mercheˈrie] *nf* small wares, haberdashery; (*prăvălie*) small-ware shop.

mercur [merˈkur] *nn chem* mercury, quicksilver.

mereu [meˈreu] *adv* always, permanently, constantly; (*tot timpul*) all the time, time and again; (*neîncetat*) ceaselessly; (*veșnic*) forever.

merge [ˈmerdʒe] *vi* (*în diferite sensuri, d. oameni și animale*) to go; (*pe jos*) to walk; (*a păși*) to step; (*în marș*) to march; (*a se îndrepta*) to repair; (*a se mișca*) to move, to stir; (*a trece*) to pass; (*cu un vehicul*) to drive, to ride, to go by; to go by train/car/bus, etc; (*d. lucruri etc*) to work; to be good for; (*d. puls*) to beat; (*d. monede*) to be current; (*d. afaceri etc*) to go on (well); (*a pleca*) to leave, to set out; (*a se vinde*) to be in demand; (*a fi nevoie*) to be necessary; (*a se potrivi*) (*d. culori*) to go well; to match; to suit; (*d. veșminte*) to fit; to become; **a ~ până la** to go as far as; **a ~ cu** (*împreună cu*) to go with, (*a însoți*) to accompany; (*a se potrivi*) to suit, to belong with; (*a funcționa*) to work; **cum ~?** how are things?, how is it?; **nu ~!** that won't do!, that's a no go!

meridian [meridiˈan] *nn geog, astron* meridian.

merinos [meriˈnos] *adj* **oaie ~** merino sheep.

merit ['merit] *nn* merit, deserve; (*pricepere*) skill •
~**oriu** *adj* praiseworthy, meritorious, deserving • ~**uos**
adj deserving; (*valoros*) valuable, rewarding • ~**a** *vt*
to deserve, to be worth || *vi* to be worth while.

mers [mers] *nn* going, walking, etc * **merge**; (*fel de a
merge*) gait; *fig* course, development, march; ~
înainte progress, advance; ~ **înapoi** *tech* backing,
reverse; backward motion.

mesager [mesa'djer] *nm also fig* messenger; *lit* harbinger, herald • ~**ie** *nf* (*birou*) parcels office.

mesaj [me'sazh] *nn* message; (*chemare*) call, appeal.

mesă ['mesă] *nf relig, mus* mass.

meschin [mes'kin] *adj* (*d. caracter etc*) paltry, petty;
(*d. acțiuni etc*) mean, base, stingy || *adv* meanly,
basely, stingily • ~**ărie** *nf* meanness, pettiness; paltriness; (*ca act*) piece of meanness.

meserias [meseri'ash] *nm* tradesman, artisan, craftsman.

meserie [mese'rie] *nf* trade, handcraft; (*profesie*)
profession.

mesia [me'sia] *nm relig* Messiah.

mesteacăn [mes'teakăn] *nn bot* birch (tree).

mesteca [meste'ka] *vt/vi* to chew, to masticate; (*d. vite*)
to ruminate; (*a mânca*) to eat; *fig* (*a pune la cale*) to
plot, to scheme; (*d. lichide*) to stir.

meșă ['meshă] *nf* lock (of hair); *med* tent.

meșter ['meshter] *nm also fig* master; (*meseriaș*)
craftsman, artisan; (*muncitor calificat*) qualified
worker; artist; expert || *adj* skillful, expert.

meșteri [meshte'ri] *vt* to work; (*a aranja*) to arrange,
to fix; (*a drege*) to set right.

meșteșug [meshte'shug] *nn* (*meserie*) trade; (*profesie*)
profession; (*ocupație*) occupation; (*pricepere*) skill;
talent; art; (*metodă*) method; (*mijloc*) means, device;
(*ingeniozitate*) ingeniousness; (*viclenie*) cunning •
~**ar** *nm* * **meseriaș** • ~**ăresc** *adj* artisan's; handmade
• ~**it** *adj* executed artistically; (*măiestrit*) masterly;
(*ingenios*) ingenious; (*priceput*) skillful || *adv* artisti-
cally; in a masterly way; ingeniously; skillfully.

metabolism [metabo'lism] *nn bio* metabolism.

metafizică [meta'fizikă] *nf* metaphysics.

metaforă [me'taforă] *nf* metaphor.

metaforic [meta'forik] *adj* metaphorical; (*figurat*)
figurative || *adv* metaphorically, figuratively.

metal [me'tal] *nn* metal.

metalic [me'talik] *adj also fig* metallic.

metalurgie [metalur'djie] *nf* metallurgy.

metamorfoză [metamor'foză] *nf* metamorphosis;
complete transformation/change.

metan [me'tan] *nn chem* methane (gas), marsh gas.

meteahnă ['meteahnă] *nf* defect, short-coming; (*boală*)
disease, illness; (*supărare*) trouble; (*slăbiciune*)
weakness; (*pasiune*) passion; (*viciu*) vice; (*păcat*) sin.

meteorit [meteo'rit] *nm astron* meteorite.

meteorolog [meteoro'log] *nm* meteorologist, weather-
man • ~**ic** *adj* weather, meteorologic(al); **buletin** ~
weather report/forecast; **stațiune** ~**ă** meteorologi-
cal/weather station • ~**ie** *nf* meteorology.

meticulos [metiku'los] *adj* meticulous, punctilious ||
adv meticulously, punctiliously.

meticulozitate [metikulozi'tate] *nf* meticulousness,
punctiliousness.

metis [me'tis] *nm* half-caste, mestizo.

metodă [me'todă] *nf* method, system, (*mod*) way.

metodic [me'todik] *adj* methodical, systematic || *adv*
methodically, systematically, by line (and level).

metodist [meto'dist] *nm* methodologist; *relig* Methodist.

metonimie [metoni'mie] *nf lit* metonymy.

metresă [me'tresă] *nf* (kept) mistress; *obs* paramour.

metronom [metro'nom] *nn mus* metronome.

metropolă [me'tropolă] *nf* metropolis; (*capitală*)
capital, city; (*față de o colonie*) parent state, mother
country.

metropolitan [metropoli'tan] *nn* * **metrou** || *adj relig*
metropolitan.

metrou [me'trou] *nn* the subway; underground.

metru ['metru] *nm* meter; (meter) rule; ~ **cub** cubic
meter; ~ **pătrat** square meter.

meu [meu] *pron/adj poss m* my; **al** ~ mine.

mexican [meksi'kan] *adj/nm* Mexican.

mezalianță [mezali'antsă] *nf frml* misalliance.

mezanin [meza'nin] *nn* mezzanine (floor), entresol.

mezeluri [me'zeluri] *nn pl* salami and sausages.

mezin [me'zin] *nm* youngest child.

mi [mi] *nm mus* (the note) E, mi || *pron* to me.

miasmă [mi'asmă] *nf* miasma; (*miros rău*) stench.

miau ['miau] *interj zool* mew, meow, miaow.

miazănoapte [miază'noapte] *nf* north; **de** ~ north(ern).

miazăzi [miază'zi] *nf* south; **de** ~ south(ern).

mic [mik] *adj* (*tânăr, de vârstă mică*) (*mai ales oameni*)
little; (*animale*) young; (*implicând comparația; ant
big, large*) small; (*mititel, minuscul*) minute, tiny;
(*ca statură; scurt*) short; (*și neînsemnat*) minor; insignificant; unimportant; *pej* petty; (*pitic*) dwarfish;
(*și îndesat*) podgy; (*și slab*) chitty; (*în creștere*)
undergrown; imperceptible; (*d. haine: strâmt*) tight;
(*puțin adânc*) shallow; (*scund, jos*) low; (*slab*) weak,
feeble; (*d. lumină*) dim; (*tânăr*) young; (*neînsemnat*)
trifling; (*ușor de suportat etc*) light, slight; (*de dis-
prețuit*) contemptible; (*limitat*) limited.

mica ['mika] *nf* miner mica.

micime [mi'chime] *nf* smallness, littleness; *fig* meanness, pettiness, paltriness.

microb [mi'krob] *nm* microbe, germ.

microbuz [mikro'buz] *nn* minibus.

microcosm [mikro'kosm] *nn* microcosm.

microfon [mikro'fon] *nn* microphone; *coll* mike.

micron [mi'kron] *nm phys* micron, micromillimeter.

microscop [mikro'skop] *nn* microscope.

microundă [mikro'undă] *nf* microwave.

micșora [miksho'ra] *vt* to make smaller, to reduce, to
diminish; to cut down; (*meritul cuiva etc*) to belittle,
to detract from; (*puterea cuiva*) to lessen; (*a scurta*)
to shorten, to make shorter; (*a strâmta*) to make smth
narrower; (*viteza unei mașini*) to slow down; to re-
duce speed || *vr* to become/grow smaller, to dimin-
ish; (*a se scurta*) to get shorter; (*d. zile*) to close in;
(*d. prețuri*) to decrease; to go down; (*puterile fizice
ale unei persoane*) to decline.

mie [mie] *num/adj/nf* thousand || *pron* (to) me.

miel [miel] *nm* lamb.

miercuri ['mierkuri] *nf* Wednesday || *adv* on Wednes-
day; every Wednesday.

miere ['miere] *nf also fig* honey.

mierlă ['mierlă] *nf orn* blackbird, ouzel.

mieros [mie'ros] *adj* honeyed, sugary; (*d. zâmbet*)
bland; (*d. cineva*) soapy, mealy-mouthed || *adv*
blandly.

mieuna [mieu'na] *vi zool* to mew, to meow; (*d. mai
multe pisici*) to caterwaul • ~**t** *nn* mewing, cater-
wauling; mew.

miez [miez] *nn* (*mijloc*) middle; (*inimă*) *also fig* heart; (*al unui fruct*) *also fig* core; pulp; (*de pâine*) crumb; (*de nucă*) *also fig* kernel; *fig* (*toi*) depth; thick; essence; pith; **cu** ~ substantial, pithy, *fig* (*cu tâlc*) significant; **fără** ~ coreless, *fig* empty, idle, futile.

migălos [migă'los] *adj* scrupulous; *pej* finical, finicking ‖ *adv* scrupulously

migdal [mig'dal] *nm bot* almond (tree) • ~**at** *adj* almond-shaped • ~**ă** *nf bot* almond.

migra [mi'gra] *vi* to migrate • ~**tor** *adj* migratory.

migrați(un)e [migratsi'une] *nf* migration.

migrenă [mi'grenă] *nf* headache, migraine.

miji [mi'zhi] *vi* (*a apărea*) to appear; (*la suprafață sau brusc*) to crop up; (*în depărtare*) to loom; (*a licări*) to gleam; (*a răsări*) to rise; (*d. plante*) to come up/out, to sprout; (*d. muguri*) to shoot (out); (*d. ochi*) to screw up (one's eyes); *imp* to be dawning.

mijloc [mizhlok] *nn* middle; (*centru*) center; (*jumătate*) half; (*talie*) waist, middle; (*șale*) loins; (*mod de acțiune*) means; (*metodă*) method; (*cale*) way; instrument; (*resursă*) resource; (*posibilitate*) possibility; (*vehicul*) vehicle; medium; fortune, wealth; reproduction.

mijlocaș [mizhlo'kash] *nm sp* halfback, midfielder ‖ *adj* middle.

mijloci [mizhlo'chi] *vt* (*a media*) to mediate, to intercede/intervene in; (*a contribui la*) to contribute (to) • ~**tor** *nm* mediator, intermediary; (*în negocieri*) negotiator; (*și în sens rău*) go-between; (*codoș*) pander; pimp, procurer.

mijlociu [mizhlo'chiu] *adj* middle; (*d. calitate*) medium; (*d. capacitate etc*) middling; moderate; (*intermediar*) intermediate; (*d. prețuri, viteză, nivel etc*) average; mediocre; (*de mâna a doua*) second-rate; (*d. fiu*) second-born ‖ *nm* second-born (child); **degetul** ~ the middle finger .

milă¹ ['milă] *nf* pity, compassion; (*caritate*) charity; (*bunătate*) kindness; (*dragoste*) love; (*bunăvoință*) goodwill; *relig* grace; (*pomană*) alms; (*mizerie*) misery, wretchedness; (*sărăcie*) poverty; (*jale*) grief; **cu** ~ compassionately; **din** ~ out of pity; **fără** ~ *adj* pitiless, merciless, ruthless ‖ *adv* pitilessly, mercilessly, ruthlessly.

milă² ['milă] *nf* mile; ~ **terestră** statute mile (= 1609,3 m.); ~ **marină** nautical mile (= 1852 m).

milenar [mile'nar] *adj* millennial, millenary.

mileniu [mi'leniu] *nn* the thousand years; *also fig* millennium.

miliard [mili'ard] *num/adj/nn* billion, a thousand millions • ~**ar** *nm* billionaire, multi-millionaire.

miligram [mili'gram] *nn* milligram.

mililitru ['mili'litru] *nm* milliliter.

milimetru [mili'metru] *nn* millimeter; **la** ~ to a hair's breadth.

milion [mili'on] *num/adj/nn* million • ~**ar** *nm* millionaire.

milita [mili'ta] *vi* (*pentru*) to militate (in favor of); to support; to struggle for.

militant [mili'tant] *adj* militant, active ‖ *nm* militant; (*luptător*) (*pentru*) fighter (for); champion (of).

militar [mili'tar] *nm* military man, serviceman, soldier ‖ *adj* military; (*de soldat*) soldierly, soldier-like; ~ **de carieră** career/professional soldier; **serviciu** ~ military service; **vehicul** ~ army vehicle • **acțiune** ~**ă** action; **garnizoană** ~**ă** station • ~**ii** the military, the armed forces • ~**iza** *vt* to militarize.

milog [mi'log] *nm* beggar, cadger.

milos [mi'los] *adj* compassionate; (*caritabil*) charitable • ~**tenie** *nf* (*pomană*) alms, charity; (*danie*) gift, donation • ~**tiv** *adj* (*îndurător*) merciful, (*bun*) kind, (*iertător*) forgiving, (*darnic*) bountiful, generous, liberal • ~**tivire** *nf* * **milă**; (*dărnicie*) bounty, generosity.

mim [mim] *nm* mime • ~**a** *vt* to mime; (*a imita*) to mimic, to ape • ~**etism** *nn zool* mimicry.

mimoză [mi'moză] *nf bot* mimosa; ~ **senzitivă** mimosa, sensitive plant.

mina [mi'na] *vt* to mine; *fig* to undermine.

mină ['mină] *nf* (*în diferite sensuri*) *also fig* mine; (*puț*) pit; (*carieră*) quarry; (*de creion*) lead ‖ *nf* (facial) expression, mien.

mincinos [minchi'nos] *adj* (*d. cineva*) lying, mendacious; (*deșert*) vain, illusory; untrue, false ‖ *nm* liar; *coll* fibber, fibster.

minciună [min'chună] *nf* lie, untruth, falsehood; *coll* fib; (*născocire*) fabrication; (*faptul de a minți*) lying; ~ **gogonată** *coll* whopping lie, whopper; ~ **grosolană** thumping lie; ~ **nevinovată** white lie.

miner [mi'ner] *nm* miner, mine worker.

mineral [mine'ral] *adj* mineral.

minereu [mine'reu] *nn* ore; ~ **de fier** iron ore.

minge ['mindje] *nf* ball.

miniatură [minia'tură] *nf* miniature; **în** ~ in miniature.

minier [mini'er] *adj* of mines; of mining.

minim ['minim] *adj/nn* minimum • ~**aliza** *vt* to minimize, to belittle, to disparage.

minister [mini'ster] *nn* ministry; department; cabinet; government; **Ministerul Afacerilor Externe** State Department; **Ministerul Afacerilor Interne** Department of the Interior; **Ministerul Apărării Naționale** Defense Department; **Ministerul Comerțului** Department of Commerce; **Ministerul de Finanțe** Treasury Department; **Ministerul Justiției** Department of Justice • ~**ial** *adj* ministerial.

ministru [mi'nistru] *nm* (cabinet) minister; ~ **adjunct** deputy minister; ~ **fără portofoliu** minister without portfolio; ~ **de finanțe** Treasury Secretary; ~ **de justiție** Attorney General; ~ **plenipotențiar** Minister Plenipotentiary • ~**l afacerilor externe** Secretary of State, State Secretary; ~**l afacerilor interne** Secretary of the Interior.

minor [mi'nor] *adj* *also mus* minor; minor lesser; *also jur* under full legal age ‖ *nm* minor; *jur* infant • ~**itate** *nf* minority; **în** ~ in the minority.

mintal [min'tal] *adj* mental ‖ *adv* mentally.

minte ['minte] *nf* mind; (*rațiune*) reason, brains; (*judecată*) judgment; (*cugetare*) thinking; *pl* wits, senses; (*înțelepciune*) wisdom; discretion; (*judecată sănătoasă*) (sound) common sense, good sense; **a nu avea** ~ to lack (good) judgment; (*inteligență*) intelligence; (*istețime*) wit; quick wits; (*imaginație*) imagination; **fără** ~ ~ unwise, (*nesăbuit*) rash, reckless, careless, (*prost*) silly, foolish, (*fără cap*) addle-brained, (*ușuratic*) light-minded.

minți [min'tsi] *vi* to lie, to tell a lie/lies; (*a fi înșelător*) to deceive, to be deceptive ‖ *vt* to lie to (smb), to tell smb a lie/lies; (*a înșela*) to deceive; to cheat; to fool; to delude ‖ *vr* **a se** ~ (pe sine) to fool oneself, to deceive oneself.

minuna [minu'na] *vt* to amaze, to astonish, to astound, to fill with wonder/admiration ‖ *vr* (*de*) to marvel (at), to be amazed (at); (*a se întreba*) to wonder • ~t *adj* wonderful, marvelous, splendid; (*încântător*) charming, delightful; *coll* (*bun*) very good; exceptional; (*desăvârşit*) perfect; (*fără pereche*) peerless; (*în basme*) magic; (*făcător de minuni*) wonder-working || *adv* charmingly, delightfully || *interj* great!, perfect!, superb!.

minunăţie [minună'tsie] *nf* marvel, wonder.

minune [mi'nune] *nf* miracle; (*lucru uimitor*) wonder, marvel; wonderful thing; prodigy; **ca prin** ~ miraculously, by some miracle; **de** ~ excellently.

minus ['minus] *adv* minus || *nn* minus; deficit.

minuscul [mi'nuskul] *adj* small, tiny, minute.

minut [mi'nut] *nn* (*în diferite sensuri*) minute; **într-un** ~ in a minute, *coll* in a jiffy, in a heartbeat • ~**ar** *nn* minute hand.

minută [mi'nută] *nf jur* record (of a judgment); (*a unei şedinţe*) minutes; (*cartografie*) draft map.

minuţios [minutsi'os] *adj* (*d. cineva*) scrupulously careful; (*d. o cercetare*) close minutethorough || *adv* minutely, thoroughly, meticulously.

mioară [mi'oară] *nf* lamb; (*oaie*) sheep, ewe.

miop [mi'op] *adj* shortsighted || *nm* shortsighted person, myope.

miorlăi [miorlă'i] *vi/vr* to caterwaul; (*a mieuna*) to mew, to miaow, to meow; (*d. oameni*) to whine, to whimper • ~t *adj* whining, whimpering || *nn* caterwauling, caterwaul.

mir [mir] *nn relig* chrism, consecrated oil.

mira [mi'ra] *vt* (*a surprinde*) to surprise, to astonish, (*a uimi*) to amaze, (*a ului*) to astound || *vr* to wonder (at) • ~**re** *nf* wonder; (*surprindere*) surprise, astonishment; **de** ~ (*uimitor*) astonishing; admirable, wonderful • ~t *adj* astonished, amazed, astounded • ~**col** *nn* (*minune*) miracle, wonder; **ca prin** ~ miraculously, by a miracle • ~**culos** *adj* miraculous; *coll* marvelous.

miraj [mi'razh] *nn* mirage; Fata Morgana; (*farmec*) charm.

mire ['mire] *nm* bridegroom; *pl* bride and groom • ~**asă** *nf* bride.

mireasmă [mi'reasmă] *nf* perfume; (*a florilor*) scent, fragrance.

miriapod [miria'pod] *nn ento* myriapod.

mirişte ['mirishte] *nf* stubble/stumps (in a harvested field).

mirodenie [miro'denie] *nf* spice, seasoning; relish, dressing; * **mireasmă**.

mironosiţă [mirono'sitsă] *nf* sanctimonious woman, prude; species of butterfly.

miros [mi'ros] *nn* smell, odor; perfume; (*al florilor*) fragrance, scent; (*neplăcut*) reek, stench, stink; *pl* condiments, spices; **fără** ~ (*fără simţul mirosului*) destitute of smell, free from smell, (*fără parfum*) scentless • ~i *vi* (*a*) to smell (of); (*urât*) to reek/stink (of); (*a adulmeca*) to scent; (*d. câini*) *also fig* to sniff || *vt* to smell; (*a adulmeca*) *also fig* to scent; to be aware/conscious of • ~**itor** *adj* smelling; (*plăcut* ~) sweet-smelling; (*d. flori*) fragrant; (*urât*) stinking, fetid.

mirt [mirt] *nm bot* myrtle.

mirui [miru'i] *vt* to anoint; *fig* to punch smb's head || *vr* to be anointed.

misionar [misio'nar] *nm/adj* missionary.

misit [mi'sit] *nm* broker; (*mijlocitor*) intermediary, go-between.

misiune [misi'une] *nf* mission; role, part; (*sarcină*) task; (*delegaţie*) delegation, deputation.

misivă [mi'sivă] *nf* missive, epistle.

misogin [miso'djin] *nm* misogynist, woman hater.

mister [mis'ter] *nn* mystery; (*taină*) secret; *thea* mystery (play) • ~**ios** *adj* mysterious; (*tainic*) secret; (*ascuns*) hidden; (*enigmatic*) enigmatic || *adv* mysteriously; secretly; enigmatically.

mistic ['mistik] *adj* mystic(al), esoteric || *adv* mystically || *nm* mystic • ~**ism** *nm* mysticism.

mistifica [mistifi'ka] *vt* to mystify, to baffle; (*a înşela*) to hoax, to fool smb; to take smb in • ~**re** *nf* mystification; hoax; * **mistifica**.

mistreţ [mis'trets] *adj* wild; wood || *nm* **porc** ~ *zool* wild boar.

mistrie [mis'trie] *nf* (mason's) trowel, brick trowel.

mistui [mistu'i] *vt* to digest; *fig* (*a suporta*) to bear, to stand; *fig* (*d. foc*) to consume, to burn up; *fig* (*a irosi*) to squander away, to use up || *vr pass* to be digested, to be consumed, to be burned up; (*d. cineva*) to waste/pine away (with grief) • ~**tor** *adj* consuming, devouring.

mişca [mish'ka] *vi* to stir, to move, to budge; (*dintr-un loc într-altul*) to shift; (*a trăi*) to live; (*a se strădui*) to endeavor; (*a se descurca*) to shift for oneself; *fig* to thrive, to prosper || *vt* to move; (*a deplasa*) to remove, to shift; (*a împinge*) to push; (*a pune în mişcare*) to set in motion; *fig* to excite; (*a atinge*) to touch; (*a stârni*) to stir; to upset; to rouse || *vr* to move; (*a fi în mişcare*) to be in motion; (*a se clinti*) to budge, to stir; (*înainte*) to advance, to move on; (*încoace şi încolo*) to move to and fro, to fidget; (*repede*) to whirl, to whisk; (*din loc*) to change one's place.

mişcare [mish'kare] *nf* motion; (*socială etc*) *also mil* movement; (*gest*) gesture; (*schimbare*) change; (*activitate*) activity; (*acţiune*) action; (*plimbare*) walk(ing), exercise; (*circulaţie*) circulation; (*forfotă*) bustle, stir; (*la şah*) move; (*acţiune revoluţionară*) revolutionary action; (*agitaţie*) agitation; (*răscoală*) revolt, upheaval, uprising; *rail* traffic management; (*de retragere, de spaimă*) recoiling.

mişcător [mishkă'tor] *adj* moving, mobile; *fig* touching, appealing; stirring.

mişel [mi'shel] *adj* (*ticălos*) mean, low; (*laş*) cowardly || *nm* (*ticălos*) rascal, knave, villain; (*laş*) coward • ~**ie** *nf* meanness, baseness; (*ca act*) mean action, vile deed; cowardly trick.

mişmaş [mish'mash] *nn* (*amestec*) hotchpotch, hodgepodge, mishmash; *fig* (*amestecătură*) mishmash, medley; pell-mell; all sorts of things/stuff.

mişuna [mishu'na] *vi* (*de*) to swarm (with), to teem (with).

mit [mit] *nn* myth; legend • ~**ic** *adj* mythical, legendary.

mită ['mită] *nf* graft, bribery; (*concret*) bribe.

miting ['miting] *nm* rally, meeting.

mititei [miti'tei] *nm pl* highly seasoned forcemeat small sausages broiled on the gridiron.

mitocan [mito'kan] *nm* cad, boor, lout; *coll* clodhopper.

mitocănie [mitokă'nie] *nf* boorishness, churlishness; (*ca act*) boorish/churlish action.

mitologie [mitolo'djie] *nf* mythology.

mitoman [mito'man] *nm* mythomaniac; liar; boaster || *adj* mythomaniac; lying; boastful.

mitralieră [mitrali'eră] *nf* machine-gun.
mitropolie [mitropo'lie] *nf relig* bishopric; metropolitan church.
mitropolit [mitropo'lit] *nm relig* bishop.
mitui [mitu'i] *vt* to bribe; to buy smb • **~tor** *nm* briber.
mițos [mi'tsos] *adj* fleecy, fluffy; (*cu păr lung*) long-haired.
mixa [mik'sa] *vt* to mix.
mixt [mikst] *adj* mixed, joint.
mixtură [miks'tură] *nf pharm* mixture.
miza [mi'za] *vt* (*pe*) to stake (on) || *vi* **a ~ pe** to stake on; (*a se bizui pe*) to rely/count on.
mizantrop [mizan'trop] *nm* misanthropist, manhater.
miză ['miză] *nf* stake, staking; (*rămăşag*) bet; object of dispute.
mizer [mi'zer] *adj* wretched, miserable • **~abil** *adj* (*d. cineva*) despicable, mean; * mizer; (*d. o clădire*) wretched, sorry; (*d. o faptă*) low; (*d. vreme*) horrible, atrocious || *adv* despicably, etc. • **~ie** *nf* misery, squalor; (*sărăcie*) poverty; (*lipsă*) want; *pl* (*necazuri*) troubles; (*murdărie*) dirt, squalor; **de ~** of misery; miserable; **în ~** in poverty, in misery.
mlaştină ['mlashtină] *nf* swamp, bog, marsh; (*băltoacă*) pool, quagmire; mire, slough.
mlădia [mlădi'a] *vt* (*vocea*) to modulate; (*trupul*) to twist; (*a îndoi*) to bend || *vr* (*d. voce*) to modulate; to twist, to bend; (*d. trup: a deveni mlădios*) *also fig* to become lithe/supple; (*a deveni flexibil*) to become flexible.
mlădios [mlădi'os] *adj* flexible, pliant; (*d. trup*) lithe, supple; (*zvelt*) svelte, slender, slim; (*d. sunete*) melodious; harmonious; *fig* yielding, pliable; adaptable.
mlădiță [mlă'ditsă] *nf bot* (off)shoot, sprout; *fig* offspring, scion.
mlăştinos [mlăshti'nos] *adj* marshy, boggy, swampy.
moale ['moale] *adj* (*d.voce, lumină* etc) soft; (*d. mână*) flabby, flaccid; (*catifelat*) velvety; (*mătăsos*) silky; flexible; (*slab*) loose; (*d. ouă*) soft-boiled; (*proaspăt*) fresh; (*început*) gentle; (*plăcut*) pleasant; (*fără intensitate*) dim; (*palid*) pale; (*d. vreme*) close, muggy; (*de dezgheţ*) thawy; (*d. paşi*) light; (*d. cineva*) weak, languid; *coll* spineless; (*apatic*) apathetic; (*indolent*) slack; lax || *adv* leniently, indulgently.
moară ['moară] *nf* mill.
moarte ['moarte] *nf* death; (*deces*) decease; (*dispariţie*) disappearance; end; (*omor*) murder; (*măcel*) slaughter, massacre; **fără ~** deathless • **de ~** *adj* mortal, deadly; (*teribil*) terrible, awful || *adv* mortally; (*teribil*) terribly.
moaşă ['moashă] *nf* midwife.
moaşte ['moashte] *nf pl* relic(s) of a saint; *fig* relics.
mobil [mo'bil] *adj* mobile, movable; (*instabil*) unstable, inconstant; (*schimbător*) changeable; (*detaşabil*) detachable; (*d. o ţintă, expresie, privire, populaţie*) moving, shifting; (*vioi*) lively; *sp* (*box*) nimble/quick on his feet || *nn* motive; (*corp în mişcare*) moving body; body in motion.
mobila [mobi'la] *vt* to furnish || *vr pass* to be furnished.
mobilă ['mobilă] *nf* furniture; (*ca articol separat*) piece of furniture.
mobiliza [mobili'za] *vt mil also fig* to mobilize; (*rezervişti*) to call up; (*sindicate, electorat*) to rally.
mochetă [mo'ketă] *nf text* moquette.
mocirlă [mo'chirlă] *nf* * **mlaştină**; *fig* morass, gutter.
mocni [mok'ni] *vi also fig* to smolder; *fig* * **lâncezi** •

~t *adj* (*d. foc, sentimente*) smoldering; (*d. cineva*) reserved; (*tăcut*) taciturn; *fig* (*întunecat*) dark, gloomy; *fig* inactive, slack.
mocofan [moko'fan] *nm coll* blockhead, dolt.
mod [mod] *nn* mode, manner, way; method; *gram* mood; **~ de viaţă** way of life • **~al** *adj* modal.
modalitate [modali'tate] *nf* possibility; (*metodă*) method; mode; *ling, phil* modality; *mus* form of scale.
modă ['modă] *nf* fashion; (*obicei*) custom; (*individual*) habit; **de ~ veche** antique; (*demodat*) outmoded, old-fashioned; **la ~** in fashion, fashionable, all the rage.
model [mo'del] *nn art, ling, math* model; (*exemplu*) example; (*ca unei rochii*) style; (*de tricotaj*) pattern • **~a** *vt* (*caracterul, destinul, corpul*) *also fig* to shape; to model, to fashion; (*argila*) *also fig* to mold; to adapt; (*a influenţa*) to influence || *vr pass* to be modeled, etc.
modem [mo'dem] *nn comp* modem.
modera [mode'ra] *vt* to moderate, to restrain; (*a înfrâna*) to curb; to temper; (*a micşora*) to lessen, to diminish; to reduce; (*ambiţia*) to lower one's sights; (*preţuri*) to restrict • **~tor** *nm* moderator, person leading a public debate or a talkshow • *nn tech* speed governor • **~ţie** *nf* moderation; (*măsură*) measure; restraint.
modern [mo'dern] *adj* modern; (*contemporan*) contemporary; (*la zi*) up-to-date • **~ism** *nn* modernism • **~iza** *vt/vr* to modernize; (*ceva*) to bring up-to-date.
modest [mo'dest] *adj* modest; (*d. un prânz*) frugal; (*fără pretenţii*) unassuming; (*d. haine*) simple; (*sărac*) poor; (*ieftin*) cheap; (*d. o persoană*) humble || *adv* modestly • **~ie** *nf* modesty.
modic ['modik] *adj* slender, modest, (s)light; reasonable.
modifica [modifi'ka] *vt* to modify, to change, (*a revizui, a îmbunătăţi*) to amend; (*a schimba*) to alter || *vr* to change, to alter.
modistă [mo'distă] *nf* milliner.
modul [mo'dul] *nm math* modulus.
modulaţie [modu'latsie] *nf* modulation.
mofluz [mo'fluz] *adj* discontent, sullen, sulky; *obs* bankrupt || *nm* discontented guy.
moft [moft] *nn* (*fleac*) trifle; (*toană*) whim • **~uri!** (stuff and) nonsense!, (such) rubbish!, trifles!; *sl* bullshit!; (*exclamativ*) no nonsense!.
mofturos [moftu'ros] *adj* fastidious, finical, finicky; (*la mâncare*) choosy, fastidious (over); picky, squeamish.
mogâldeaţă [mogâl'deatsă] *nf* midget, small-sized person; indistinct form/shape.
mohorât [moho'rât] *adj* dark; *also fig* gloomy; dreary; (*trist*) sad; (*abătut*) downcast; depressed, down-hearted; (*d. vreme*) dull, overcast.
moină ['moină] *nf* thaw; *agr* fallow (land).
mojar [mo'zhar] *nn* (grinding) mortar, pestle mortar.
mojic [mo'zhik] *nm* (*fără maniere*) ill-bred/mannered, unmannerly; unpolished; (*lipsit de rafinament*) boorish, churlish; (*necivilizat*) wild, uncivil(ized) • **~ie** *nf* rudeness; (*ca act*) incivility; (*numai ca vorbire*) gross abuse; *pl* abusive words.
molar [mo'lar] *nm* molar.
molatic [mo'latik] *adj* (*încet*) slow; (*d. caracter*) flabby; (*d. cineva*) soft; (*leneş*) idle; (*slab*) weak; (*greoi*) heavy || *adv* slowly, softly, idly.
molâu [mo'lâu] *adj* weak; flabby, spiritless; *vulg* shitless.

molcom ['molkom] *adj (încet)* slow; *(liniștit)* still, quiet; *(în surdină)* low; *(gingaș)* gentle; *(blând)* mild.

moleculă [mole'kulă] *nf* molecule.

molesta [moles'ta] *vt* to molest.

moleșeală [mole'sheală] *nf* torpor; drowsiness; *(lipsă de vigoare)* lack of vigor; slackness, flabbiness, lifelessness.

moleși [mole'shi] *vt* to enervate, to weaken; to make sleepy || *vr* to become enervated, to become weak, to lose one's vigor; to be sleepy • **~t** *adj* dull, soft, flabby; *(slab)* weak; *(obosit)* tired; *(fără viață)* lifeless, drooping.

molfăi [molfă'i] *vt* to munch, to mumble; *(d. țigară)* to chew; *fig* to mutter.

molid [mo'lid] *nm bot* common spruce.

molie ['molie] *nf ento* moth.

molimă ['molimă] *nf* epidemic.

molipsi [molip'si] *vt med also fig* to infect, to contaminate || *vr also fig* to be infected; **a se ~ de** to be infected by, to catch • **~tor** *adj also fig* infectious, contagious; **râs ~** infectious laughter.

moloz [mo'loz] *nn* debris; *(plaster)* rubbish.

moluscă [mo'luskă] *nf icht* shellfish, mollusk; *pl* mollusca.

momâie [mo'mâie] *nf* scarecrow; *fig* fright; *fig* dummy, puppet, man of straw.

momeală [mo'meală] *nf* lure, bait, enticement.

moment [mo'ment] *nn* moment; *(provizoriu)* provisional; temporary; **din ~ ce** since, as; seeing that; **în acest ~** at the/this moment, just now, at present • **~an** *adj* momentary || *adv* just now.

momi [mo'mi] *vt* to lure, to bait; *(a părăsi)* to decoy; *fig* to allure, to entice; *(a ispiti)* to tempt; *(foamea)* to satisfy for a short time; *(setea)* to quench for a short time.

monah [mo'nah] *nm* monk • **~al** *adj* monac(h)al, monastic.

monarh [mo'narh] *nm* monarch, *(suveran)* sovereign, *(rege)* king • **~ie** *nf* monarchy.

monastic [mo'nastik] *adj* monastic(al).

monden [mon'den] *adj* of society; fashionable; modern.

mondial [mondi'al] *adj* world, worldwide, universal, international.

monedă [mo'nedă] *nf (piesă metalică)* coin; *(de hârtie)* paper money; *(bani)* money, currency.

monetărie [monetă'rie] *nf* mint.

mongol [mon'gol] *adj/nm* Mongol.

monitor [moni'tor] *nn naut* monitor || *nm* adviser || *nn* image device.

monoclu [mo'noklu] *nn* monocle.

monocotiledonat [monokotiledo'nat] *adj bot* monocotyledonous || *nn* monocotyledon.

monogamie [monoga'mie] *nf* monogamy.

monografie [monogra'fie] *nf* monograph.

monolog [mono'log] *nn* monologue; *(interior)* soliloquy; *(adresare către spectatori)* solo address; *(aparte)* aside.

monopol [mono'pol] *nn also fig* monopoly • **~ist** *adj econ* monopolistic • **~iza** *vt also fig* to monopolize.

monoteism [monote'ism] *nn relig* monotheism.

monoton [mono'ton] *adj* monotonous; *coll* humdrum || *adv* monotonously, all in the same key • **~ie** *nf* monotony.

monstru ['monstru] *nm also fig* monster; *(om foarte urât)* fright || *adj* monstrous, huge, colossal • **~os** *adj* monstrous, *(uriaș)* huge, colossal; *(îngrozitor)* awful, shocking • **~ozitate** *nf* monstrosity; *(a unei crime)* monstrousness.

monta [mon'ta] *vt (pietre prețioase)* to set; *(o fotografie, un tun)* to mount; *(un cauciuc)* to fit; *(un aparat)* to set/fit up; *(o ușă)* to hang; *(un atelier)* to fit out, to equip; *thea* to stage; *fig (împotriva)* to set (against/ at), to provoke (against); to wind up || *vr pass* to be mounted, etc; *fig* to warm up; *(a se enerva)* to get worked/wound up • **~j** *nn* * **montare**; *rad* montage; *cin* editing, cutting • **~re** *nf* assembling, mounting, installing.

montagne russe [mon'tain 'rius] *nf* roller coaster; switchback.

montură [mon'tură] *nf* setting of a precious stone; *tech* enclosure, socket.

monument [monu'ment] *nn also fig* monument; memorial, cenotaph • **~al** *adj* monumental; *fig (enorm)* enormous, huge, colossal.

moral [mo'ral] *nn (stare de spirit)* morale, moral condition; *(curaj)* courage, spirits; *(dispoziție)* mood || *adj* moral; *(d. filozofie)* ethical; intellectual • **~ă** *nf* morals; *(norme ~e)* morality; *(etică)* ethics; *(concluzie moralizatoare)* moral; *fig* lecture.

morar [mo'rar] *nm* miller; *ento* meal beetle.

moratoriu [mora'toriu] *adj jur* moratory || *nn* moratorium.

moravuri [mo'ravuri] *nn pl* customs; morals and manners; manners; *(individuale)* habits.

morbid [mor'bid] *adj* morbid.

morcov ['morkov] *nm bot* carrot.

morfină [mor'finä] *nf* morphine, morphia.

morfinoman [morfino'man] *nm* morphinist, morphine addict.

morfoli [morfo'li] *vt* to munch.

morfologie [morfolo'dje] *nf gram, bio* morphology.

morgă ['morgă] *nf* morgue, mortuary; haughtiness, conceit(edness), arrogance, standoffishness.

morișcă [mo'rishkă] *nf (de mână)* handmill; *(de cafea)* coffee mill; *agr* fanning/winnowing machine; *avia* windmill; **~ de vânt** weather vane.

morman [mor'man] *nn* heap, pile.

mormăi [mormă'i] *vi (d. urși)* to growl; *fig* to mumble, to mutter; *(nemulțumit)* to grumble; *coll* to grouch || *vt* to mumble; to grumble (out) • **~t** *adj* muttered || *nn* growl; *fig* grumbling, muttering.

mormânt [mor'mânt] *nn* grave; *(mai ales ca monument)* tomb; *lit* sepulcher.

mormoloc [mormo'lok] *nm zool* tadpole; *fig (copilaș)* *coll* mite, kiddie.

mormon [mor'mon] *adj/nm relig* Mormon.

morocănos [morokă'nos] *adj* sullen; *(bombănitor)* grumbling, grumbly.

morsă]'morsa] *nf* walrus.

mort [mort] *adj* dead, *(decedat)* deceased; defunct; *(fără viață)* lifeless • **~al** *adj* mortal, deadly, lethal, fatal; great || *adv* mortally; fatally || *interj* cool • **~alitate** *nf* death rate, mortality.

mortar [mor'tar] *nn constr* mortar, binder.

mortier [morti'er] *nn mil* mortar.

mortuar [mortu'ar] *adj* mortuary.

morun [mo'run] *nm icht* beluga, white sturgeon, housen.

moschee [mos'kee] *nf* mosque.

mosor [mo'sor] *nn* reel, bobbin, spool.

mostră ['mostră] *nf* sample; *fig* example, model, foretaste.

moș [mosh] *nm* old man; *coll* greyhead, graybeard; (*bunic*) grandfather; *coll* grandpa; *pl relig* Saturday before Whitsuntide; *coll* Fun Fair; **Moș Crăciun** Santa (Claus); **Moș Ene** the Sandman, the Dustman.

moșie [mo'shie] *nf* estate; *obs lit* (*patrie*) homeland, motherland, fatherland • ~**er** *nm* landowner, landlord; *pl* landed gentry.

moșmondi [moshmon'di] *vi/vr* to mess/putter about; to dawdle.

moșneag [mosh'neag] *nm* old man.

moșteni [moshte'ni] *vt also fig* to inherit || *vr pass* to be inherited • ~**re** *nf* inheritance, heritage, legacy; (*intrare în posesie*) succession; patrimony; *fig* heritage; **prin** ~ by inheritance, hereditary, by right of succession • ~**toare** *nf* heiress • ~**tor** *nm* heir, successor.

motan [mo'tan] *nm zool* tomcat, he-cat; (*bătrân*) gib cat, grimalkin; *fig* silent/hidden/hypocritical person.

motel [mo'tel] *nn* motel.

motiv [mo'tiv] *nn* reason, motive, cause; ground; *mus* theme, motto; (*artă*) motif; (*broderie*) design; pattern • ~**a** *vt* to motivate; (*a justifica un refuz*) to state the reason of; (*a justifica*) to justify; to warrant; (*a întemeia*) to base, to ground • ~**ație** *nf psych* motivation.

moto ['moto] *nn* motto.

motocicletă [motochi'kletă] *nf* motorcycle.

motonavă [moto'navă] *nf naut* motor ship.

motor [mo'tor] *adj* motive, driving; *anat, psych* motor; **nerv** ~ motor nerve; **arbore** ~ *tech* drive shaft, main shaft || *nn* motor, engine; *fig* mover; (*imbold*) stimulus; ~ **cu aburi** steam engine; ~ **cu explozie** *auto* spark-ignition engine; ~ **cu ardere internă** (internal) combustion engine; ~ **cu reacție** *avia* jet engine; ~ **de avion** aircraft engine; ~ **electric** electric motor; ~ **în doi timpi** two stroke engine; ~ **în stea** radial engine; ~ **termic** heat engine; ~ **turbocompresor** turbocharged engine; ~ **în V** vee engine • ~**etă** *nf* moped.

motorină [moto'rină] *nf* gasoline, diesel oil.

mototol [moto'tol] *nn* ball, clew; (*de hârtie*) pellet || *adj coll* slack, sluggish; (*leneș*) idle, lazy; (*adormit*) sleepy, drowsy || *nm* mollycoddle, milksop.

mototoli [mototo'li] *vt/vr* to crumple.

moț [mots] *nn* (*la păsări*) topknot, crest; corona; (*șuviță în față*) forelock; kiss-me-quick; *pl* (curl)papers, papillotes; (*ciucure*) tassel; **cu** ~ crested, tufted; *fig coll* (*obraznic*) cheeky; *fig coll* (*deștept*) cute.

moțăi [motsă'i] *vi* to doze, to nod • ~**ală** *nf* doze, dozing.

moțiune [motsi'une] *nf gram* inflection denoting gender; *pol* motion, proposal.

mov [mov] *adj* mauve, lavender.

movilă [mo'vilă] *nf* knoll, hillock; (*morman*) heap, pile.

mozaic [moza'ik] *nn* mosaic, inlay.

mreajă ['mreazhă] *nf* net trap; *fig* net, meshes, toils.

muc [muk] *nn* wick; (*capăt de lumânare*) candle end; (*de țigară*) cigarette end/butt; (*de trabuc*) cigar stub/stump.

mucalit [muka'lit] *adj* funny, droll || *nm* wag, joker, jester.

muced ['muched] *adj* musty, mildewy, mildewed; (*d. pâine*) moldy.

mucegai [muche'gai] *nn* mold(iness), must(iness).

mucegăit [muchegă'it] *adj* * **muced**; *fig* musty, antiquated.

mucezi [muche'zi] *vi/vr* to mold, to get/grow/go moldy; *fig* * **lâncezi**.

muchie ['mukie] *nf* edge; (*creștet*) top, summit; *tech* margin, border; fin; lip; rib.

mucos [mu'kos] *adj coll* (*cu muci la nas*) snotty; mucous, mucilaginous; *fig* wet behind the ears || *nm* greenhorn; sniveler; brat; sucker.

mufă ['mufă] *nf tech* coupling; (*pentru fixarea capsei*) muff.

muget ['mudjet] *nn zool* low(ing); (*de vacă, și*) moo; (*de bou, și*) bellowing; (*al mării, furtunii, motoarelor*) roar; (*al furtunii*) bluster.

mugi [mu'dji] *vi zool* to low, (*d. vacă, și*) to moo; (*d. bou, și*) to bellow; (*d. vițel*) to bleat; (*d. mare, vânt*) to howl.

mugur ['mugur] *nm* bud, burgeon; (*de frunză, și*) gemma; *med* (small) excrescence; *fig* (*copii*) offspring.

muia [mu'ia] *vt* to soak, to dip; (*a uda*) to wet; (*inul, cânepa*) to ret; (*a băga în apă*) to douse; (*a scălda*) to bathe; (*a face mai moale*) to soften down; (*a încetini*) to slow down; * **îndupleca**; *ling* to palatalize || *vr* (*a deveni ud*) to become/get wet; (*a se pătrunde de un lichid*) to get soaked; (*d. vreme*) to thaw; (*a se încălzi*) to get warm; (*a se calma*) to calm down; (*a deveni mai înțelegător*) to soften, to relent.

muiere [mu'iere] *nf* woman; (*soție*) wife, *coll* one's better half.

mula [mu'la] *vt* to mold, to cast || *vr pass* to be molded/cast; (*d. o rochie*) to fit tightly • ~**j** *nn* molding, casting; (*concret*) (thing) cast.

mulatru [mu'latru] *nm* mulatto.

mulgătoare [mulgă'toare] *adj* milch || *nf* milkmaid; milking machine, milker.

mulgător [mulgă'tor] *nm* milker.

mulge ['muldje] *vt* to milk; *fig* to milk, to drain; (*a exploata*) to exploit || *vr pass* to be milked, to be drained.

muls [muls] *nn* milking.

mult [mult] *adv* much; (*departe*) far; (*multă vreme*) long; **cel** ~ at (the) most; **cu** ~ by far; **de** ~ long ago, for a long time, long since; **mai** ~ more, (*pe lângă asta*) moreover, besides, in addition; **foarte** ~ very much; **mai** ~ **sau mai puțin** more or less || *adj* much; a great deal of, a lot of; (*enumerativ*) several || *pron indef* much, a great deal.

multicolor [multiko'lor] *adj* multicolored.

multimilionar [multimilio'nar] *nm* multimillionaire.

multiplica [multipli'ka] *vt/vr* to multiply.

multisecular [multiseku'lar] *adj* centuries-old.

multitudine [multi'tudine] *nf frml* multitude.

mulți ['multsi] *adj m pl* many; **la** ~ **ani** (*aniversare*) happy birthday; (*sărbătoare*) Happy New Year • ~**me** *nf* multitude, crowd, throng, host, mass.

mulțumi [multsu'mi] *vi/vt* to thank (**mulțumesc** thanks); (*a răsplăti*) to reward, to recompense; (*a satisface*) to satisfy, to content || *vr* to have enough • ~**re** *nf* content(ment), contentedness; satisfaction; (*plăcere*) pleasure; (*bucurie*) joy; (*răsplătire*) reward, recompense; (*recunoștință*) gratitude; *pl* thanks • ~**t** *adj* (*de*) contented (with), satisfied (with); (*încântat*) pleased (with).

mumie [mu'mie] *nf* mummy; *fig coll* bag of bones.

muncă ['muncă] *nf* work, labor; *(anevoioasă)* toil; *(osteneală)* pains; *(bătaie de cap)* trouble; *(eforturi)* efforts; *(activitate)* activity; *(ocupație)* job, work, employment; *pl obs* tortures; ~ **de birou** office work; ~ **fizică** manual labor; ~ **forțată** forced labor; ~ **grea** hard work; ~ **intelectuală** mental/brain work; ~ **la domiciliu** homework, working at home; ~ **manuală** manual work; ~ **obștească** social/public work, man power; ~ **salariată** wage labor.

munci [mun'chi] *vi* to work, *(a trudi)* to toil, to work hard, to labor; **a ~ ca un sclav** to work like a slave, to slave away; **a ~ la negru** to moonlight || *vt (pămân-tul)* to work the land; *fig* to torment; *(a munci)* to toil, to labor; *(a se strădui)* to endeavor; *(a depune eforturi)* to make efforts; *(a-și frământa creierii)* to rack one's brains; *(a se osteni)* to take pains; *(a suferi)* to suffer; *(a se chinui)* to torment oneself; *(a se necăji)* to worry • ~**tor** *adj* working; *(harnic)* hard working, industrious || *nm* worker, workman; ~ **agricol** agricultural worker, farm hand, laborer; ~ **calificat** skilled worker; ~ **industrial** industrial worker; ~ **necalificat** unskilled worker; ~ **portuar** waterside worker, stevedore; *(fer-oviar)* railroad worker, railwayman; ~ **sezonier** seasonal worker; ~ **cu ziua** day laborer, jobber • **clasa** ~**toare** the working class • ~**toresc** *adj* working; labor, worker's; workers; working-class • **mișcare** ~**torească** working-class movement.

municipal [munichi'pal] *adj* municipal • ~**itate** *nf* municipality, municipal authority

municipiu [muni'chipiu] *nn* municipality, municipal town; *(palat municipal)* town-hall; *(la romani)* municipium.

muniție [mu'nitsie] *nf mil* ammunition.

munte ['munte] *nm* mountain; hill; mountain region, mountains; *fig* heap, pile.

muntos [mun'tos] *adj* mountainous; hilly.

mur [mur] *nm bot* bramble, blackberry bush • ~**ă** *nf* blackberry, brambleberry; demberry; *naut* tack.

mura [mu'ra] *vt cul* to pickle; to drench (to the skin) || *vr pass* to be pickled.

murătură [mură'tură] *nf* pickle.

murdar [mur'dar] *adj* dirty, filthy; *(plin de noroi)* muddy, miry; *(d. mâini)* grimy; *(d. pahar și)* thick; *(d. muncă)* slovenly, untidy; *fig* dirty, foul; *(d. o afacere)* unsavory; obscene, bawdy; indecent; *(d. cineva)* mean, base; **rufe** ~**e** washing || *adv* meanly, basely, indecently.

murdări [murdă'ri] *vt* to soil, to dirty; *(a face gunoi)* to litter; *(a păta)* to stain; *(apa)* to pollute; *fig* to sully, to tarnish || *vr* to soil oneself; *(d. lucruri)* to become dirty • ~**e** *nf also fig* dirt, filth; *(corupție)* corruption.

murg [murg] *adj* dark-bay || *nm* dark-bay horse.

muri [mu'ri] *vi* to die, to pass away; *coll* to be called to account; to be dead; *coll* to kick the bucket; *frml* to join the (great) majority; *(a-și da duhul)* to give up the/one's ghost; *(a se ofili)* to wither away; *(d. senti-mente)* to die down/off/away; *(d. un obicei, o civi-lizație)* to die out • ~**bund** *nm* person at the point of death, dying man .

murmur ['murmur] *nn (de protest)* murmur; *(al unui pârâu)* purl(ing), babble, babbling • ~**a** *vi* to murmur; *(a șopti)* to whisper; *(a mormăi)* to mutter, to mumble;

(a bombăni) to grumble, to growl; *(d. un izvor)* to purl, to babble; *(a susura)* to bicker.

musafir [musa'fir] *nm* guest, visitor.

muscă ['muscă] *nf ento* fly; *ento (albină)* bee; *(arti-ficială pt. undiță)* badger fly; *sp (la tir)* bull's-eye.

muson [mu'son] *nm* monsoon.

must [must] *nn* must (of grapes); unfermented wine; juice.

mustață [mus'tatsă] *nf* mustache; *pl ento* feelers, antenna; *bot* tendrils; *(la grâu)* awns, beard; *icht* barbels; *zool* whiskers.

musti [mus'ti] *vi (d. lichide)* to spread, to filter; *(în in-terior)* to soak; *(cu picătura)* to trickle (through); *(la exterior)* to ooze, to leak; *(de)* to be imbibed (with).

mustos [mus'tos] *adj* juicy; *(d. pământ)* fat.

mustra [mus'tra] *vt* to reprove, to reprimand; *coll* to take to task • ~**re** *nf* reprimand, reproof, remonstrance; *coll* wigging, talking to.

mustrător [mustră'tor] *adj* blaming, reproachful • *adv* reproachfully.

musulman [musul'man] *adj/nm* Muslim, Moslem.

mușama [musha'ma] *nf* oilcloth, waxcloth.

mușamaliza [mushamali'za] *vt fig* to hush up.

mușca [mush'ka] *vt/vi also fig* to bite; to bite of; *(d. albine)* to sting; *(cu bucățica)* to nibble.

mușcată [mush'kată] *nf bot* storksbill, geranium.

mușcătură [mushkă'tură] *nf* bite; *(rană)* wound.

mușchetar [mushke'tar] *nm hist* musketeer.

mușchi ['mushki] *nm bot* moss; *anat* muscle; *(carne)* sirloin, fillet.

mușețel [mushe'tsel] *nm bot* wild chamomile.

muștar [mush'tar] *nn* mustard; *bot* white mustard.

mușteriu [mushte'riu] *nm* customer, client; *(cumpără-tor)* buyer.

muștiuc [mush'tiuk] *nm mus* embouchure, lip; *tech* mouthpiece.

muștrului [mushtrulu'i] *vt* to drill, to discipline; *(a mustra)* to lick into shape • ~**ală** *nf* drilling; * **mustrare** *(bătaie)* coll licking, drubbing.

mușuroi [mushu'roi] *nn* hill, heap, mound (of earth).

mut [mut] *adj* dumb; *fig* silent; *(d. un sentiment)* mute; *(fără grai)* speechless; *(înmărmurit)* struck dumb; *thea (rol* ~*)* non-speaking || *nm* dumb person, mute || *adv* mutely, silently.

muta [mu'ta] *vt* to move; to remove, to shift; *(a schimba)* to change || *vr (la)* to move (to); *(în)* to move in • ~**re** *nf* moving * **muta**; *(concret)* removal, moving out; *(la șah)* move • ~**ție** *nf bio* mutation; *(deplasare)* shifting; *(schimbare)* change, alteration; *jur* change of ownership; transfer of property.

mutila [muti'la] *vt* to maim; to mutilate.

mutră ['mutră] *nf* face, mug; *(strâmbătură)* grimace, wry face(s).

mutual [mutu'al] *adj* mutual.

muză ['muză] *nf also fig* muse.

muzeu [mu'zeu] *nn* museum; **de** ~ rare, valuable; *(vechi)* antiquated.

muzical [muzi'kal] *adj* musical; **ureche** ~**ă** musical ear, ear for music || *adv* musically.

muzicant [muzi'kant] *nm* musician.

muzică [muzi'kită] *nf* music.

muzician [muzichi'an] *nm* musician.

muzicolog [muziko'log] *nm* musicologist, music expert.

muzicuță [muzi'kutsă] *nf* harmonica, mouth organ; *coll (gură)* jaw, potato.

N

na [na] *interj coll (iată)* here!; *(poftim)* here you are; *(ia lucrul acesta)* here, take it; *(exprimă nemulțumire)* well I never!; *(la naiba)* the deuce!; damn!
nacelă [na'chelă] *nf avia* balloon car, nacelle, gondola.
nadă ['nadă] *nf also fig* bait, lure; *(vierme în undiță)* angleworm; *fig* enticement.
nadir [na'dir] *nn astron* nadir.
naftalină [nafta'lină] *nf chem* naphthaline; *com coll* mothballs.
nai [nai] *nn mus* syrix, panpipe, reed pipe.
nailon ['nailon] *nn chem* nylon.
naiv [na'iv] *adj* naïf, naive; ingenuous; innocent; sincere; *(credul)* credulous; gullible; *(sărac cu duhul)* simple-minded || *adv* naively, etc || *nm* unsophisticated person; simpleton • **~itate** *nf* naivety, naivete, simplicity; sincerity; credulity; simple-mindedness.
nalbă ['nalbă] *nf bot* (common/country) mallow, round dock; *bot (și ~ de grădină)* hollyhock, rose mallow; *(~ mare)* marshmallow.
namilă ['namilă] *nf* monster, colossus.
naos ['naos] *nn archit (de biserică)* nave; *(de vechi templu grecesc)* naos.
nap [nap] *nm bot* turnip-rooted cabbage.
narator [nara'tor] *nm* narrator.
narați(un)e [naratsi'une] *nf* narrative, narration; *(povestire)* story.
nară ['nară] *nf anat* nostril; *(a balenei)* blowhole; *naut* hawse.
narcisă [nar'chisă] *nf bot* narcissus; *bot (galbenă)* daffodil.
narcisism [narchi'sism] *nn* narcissism, self-love.
narcotic [nar'kotik] *nn* narcotic; *coll* dope.
nas [nas] *nn anat, tech* nose; *coll* beak, conk; *sl* scent box, smeller; *pej* snout; *constr* nib.
nasture ['nasture] *nm* button.
naș [nash] *nm (de botez, de cununie)* godfather, godparent • **~ă** *nf (de botez, de cununie)* godmother.
naște ['nashte] *vt* to bear, to give birth to; *(speranțe)* to give rise to, to arouse; *(un surâs)* to raise; *obs* to bear; *fig* to give rise/birth to || *vr* to be born; *fig* to come into being, to (a)rise, to spring up; *(a apărea)* to appear; *(d. începutul unei zile)* to dawn || *vi* to be confined • **~re** *nf also fig* birth; childbearing, confinement; conception; inception.
natal [na'tal] *adj* native.
natalitate [natali'tate] *nf* birthrate, natality.
natație [na'tatsie] *nf sp* swimming.
nativ [na'tiv] *adj* native, innate, inborn.
natural [natu'ral] *adj (care provine din natură, este ca în natură)* natural; *(d. corp)* bodily; simple; *(veritabil)* genuine; *(înnăscut)* innate; *(d. mătase)* real, pure || *adv* naturally || *interj* naturally!, of course!, certainly!.
natură [na'tura] *nf (în diferite sensuri)* nature; *(fel)* kind, character; temperament, disposition; *(peisaj)* landscape; environment.
național [natsio'nal] *adj* national • **~ism** *nn* nationalism • **~ist** *adj* nationalist(ic) || *nm* nationalist • **~itate** *nf* nationality • **~iza** *vt* to nationalize • **~izare** *nf* nationalization.
națiune [natsi'une] *nf* nation; *(popor)* people; **Națiunile Unite** the United Nations, the UN.
naufragiat [naufradji'at] *adj naut* (ship)wrecked;

(aruncat pe o insulă) castaway || *nm* shipwrecked person.
naufragiu [nau'fradju] *nn* (ship)wreck.
nautic [na'utik] *adj* nautical.
naval [na'val] *adj* naval, nautical, sea.
navă ['navă] *nf naut* vessel, ship; *relig* nave; **~ aeriană** airship, aircraft; **~ amiral** flagship; **~ comercială** merchant ship; **~ de război** warship, man-of-war; **~ de salvare** salvage vessel; **~ fluvială** river boat/vessel; **~ maritimă** sea ship; **~ port-avioane** aircraft carrier; **~ spațială** spaceship, spacecraft.
navetă [na'vetă] *nf* *** suveică**; *rail* commuter train.
naviga [navi'ga] *vi* to sail, to navigate • **~ție** *nf* navigation, sailing.
navlosi [navlo'si] *vt naut* to freight.
nazal [na'zal] *adj anat, ling* nasal.
nazism [na'zism] *nn* Nazi(i)sm.
nazist [na'zist] *adj/nm hist, pol* Nazi.
nazuri ['nazuri] *nn pl* whims, caprice; **a face ~** to be fastidious/squeamish, to be hard to please.
năbădăios [năbădă'ios] *adj (iute la mânie)* peppery; capricious; *(d. animale)* vicious.
nădăjdui [nădăzhdu'i] *vt (că; să)* to hope (that/to); *(a visa)* to dream, to aspire.
nădejde [nă'dezhde] *nf (speranță)* hope; **cu ~** vigorously, diligently, forcibly; **de ~** reliable.
năduf [nă'duf] *nn (astmă)* asthma; *(sufocare)* asphyxia; *(respirație gâfâitoare)* short breath; *** zăpușeală** *(ciudă)* spite; *(supărare)* anger, fury.
nădușeală [nădu'sheală] *nf* perspiration, sweat.
năduși [nădu'shi] *vi* to perspire, to sweat || *vt (a sufoca)* to suffocate, to stifle; *cul* to stew, to steam.
nălucă [nă'lukă] *nf* apparition, ghost; *(iluzie)* illusion; *(himeră)* chimera.
nălucire [nălu'chire] *nf* *** nălucă**; *(halucinație)* hallucination.
nămete [nă'mete] *nm* snowdrift.
nămol [nă'mol] *nn* mud.
năpastă [nă'pastă] *nf* calamity; plague; *(dezastru)* disaster; *obs* calumny, slander; *(nedreptate)* injustice, wrong.
năpădi [năpă'di] *vt (a umple)* to fill; *(a acoperi)* to cover; *(a inunda)* to flood; *(d. buruieni)* to overgrow; *(cu griji)* to beset (with); *(a copleși)* to overwhelm || *vi (d. lichide)* to gush out; *(a se revărsa)* to overflow.
năpăstui [năpăstu'i] *vt (a asupri)* to oppress; to persecute; *(a fi o pacoste pentru)* to pester, to plague; *(a ponegri)* to denigrate; *(a calomnia)* to calumniate, to slander.
năpârli [năpâr'li] *vi (d. animale)* to shed/cast one's coat; *(d. păsări)* to molt; *(d. șerpi)* to slough.
năprasnic [nă'prasnik] *adj (brusc)* sudden; *(neașteptat)* unexpected; violent; *(năvalnic)* impetuous; *(aprig)* fiery; *(grozav)* terrible, tremendous; *(uluitor)* amazing || *adv* suddenly, all of a sudden.
năpusti [năpus'ti] *vr (asupra)* to rush (at/upon); to pounce (upon).
nărav [nă'rav] *nn (obicei rău)* bad habit; *(viciu)* vice; *(patimă)* passion.
nărăvaș [nără'vash] *adj* vicious, restive, randy.
nărui [năru'i] *vr* to crumble, to come/tumble down; *fig* to crumble away, to go to rack and ruin; to end (up) in smoke.
născoci [năsko'chi] *vt* to invent; *(a descoperi)* to

discover; (*a plănui*) to plan; to imagine; (*minciuni*) to fabricate • ~**re** *nf* (*ca acţiune*) invention; * **născoci**; (*descoperire*) discovery; (*minciună*) lie, fib; (*poveste*) story, tale, yarn.

născut [năs'kut] *nm/adj* born; **nou** ~ newborn child.

năstruşnic [năs'trushnik] *adj* extraordinary; (*straşnic*) terrible; (*uimitor*) amazing; (*ciudat*) strange, queer, odd.

nătăfleţ [nătă'flets] *adj* (*prost*) silly, foolish || *nm* (*prost*) blockhead, duffer.

nătărău [nătă'rău] *adj/nm* * **nătăfleţ**.

nătâng [nă'tâng] *adj* (*prost*) silly, foolish; (*stângaci*) awkward, clumsy; (*îndărătnic*) stubborn, obstinate || *nm* (*prost*) duffer, blockhead.

năuc [nă'uk] *adj* (*cu înclinaţii necontrolate*) giddy, silly, scatterbrained; (*cu o senzaţie de ameţeală*) dizzy, reeling; (*cu mintea neclară*) bewildered, perplexed, confused, puzzled; (*uluit*) dumbfounded; (*nebun*) crazy; (*prost*) foolish || *nm* blockhead • ~**i** *vt* (*a zăpăci*) to confuse; *coll* to muddle smb's brain; (*a pune în încurcătură*) to confuse, to puzzle; (*a lăsa perplex*) to perplex; (*a ului*) to amaze, to stun • ~**itor** *adj* stunning, amazing.

năut [nă'ut] *nn bot* ckickpea.

năvală [nă'vală] *nf* (*invazie*) invasion; (*agresiune*) aggression; attack, onslaught; (*asalt*) assault.

năvalnic [nă'valnik] *adj* impetuous; (*furtunos*) stormy || *adv* impetuously || *nm bot* hart's tongue.

năvăli [năvă'li] *vi* (*asupra*) to rush (at), to pounce (upon); (*a ataca*) to attack; to invade, (*a se revărsa*) to overflow.

năvod [nă'vod] *nn* trawl, sweep, net.

năzări [năză'ri] *vr* **a i se ~ (că)** (*a crede*) to think (that); (*a-şi închipui*) to fancy (that); (*a-şi reprezenta*) to picture; (*a-i veni o idee*) to cross one's mind, to dawn upon one.

năzbâtie [năz'bâtie] *nf* prank, trick; mischief; farce; (*glumă*) joke, quip, jest; (*prostie*) mad action/prank.

năzdrăvan [năzdră'van] *adj* supernatural; magic; (*făcător de minuni*) wonder-working; (*de basm*) fairy; extraordinary, matchless, peerless; (*glumeţ*) funny, droll || *nm* magician; (*vrăjitor*) wizard.

năzdrăvănie [năzdrăvă'nie] *nf* (*lucru minunat*) marvel, prodigy; (*glumă*) joke, jest; (*prostie*) mad action/ prank; (*vicleşug*) cunning.

năzui [năzu'i] *vi* (*spre, către*) to aspire (to, after), to strive (for) • ~**nţă** *nf* (*spre, către*) aspiration (for, after).

năzuros [năzu'ros] *adj* self-willed, capricious; (*la mâncare*) dainty, fastidious; squeamish.

nea [nea] *nf* (*zăpadă*) snow.

neabătut [neabă'tut] *adj* firm, steadfast, unflinching.

neadevăr [neade'văr] *nn* untruth, falsehood, (*minciună*) lie.

nedormit [nedor'mit] *adj also fig* awake; (*atent*) attentive; vigilant, alert; active; (*neobosit*) tireless.

neagresiune [neagresi'une] *nf* non-aggression.

neajuns [nea'zhuns] *nn* (*necaz*) trouble; (*dificultate*) difficulty; (*lipsă*) shortcoming; defect.

neajutorat [neazhuto'rat] *adj* (*sărac*) poor, needy, destitute; (*stângaci*) helpless, awkward, inept; (*care stârneşte mila*) pathetic, pitiful, pitiable.

neam [neam] *nn* (*popor*) people, nation; family; origin, extraction, descent; (*rudă*) relative, relation; *frml* kin; species; (*varietate*) variety; (*fel*) kind, sort; *fig* tribe.

neamestec [nea'mestek] *nn* non-interference, non-intervention • ~**at** *adj* unmixed; unmingled.

neamţ [neamts] *nm coll* German; Austrian.

neangajat [neanga'zhat] *adj* non-aligned.

neant [ne'ant] *nn* nothingness, naught, nought; (*nefiinţă*) non-being.

neaoş ['neaosh] *adj* native; (*d. cineva*) true-born; authentic, genuine, pure.

neapărat [neapă'rat] *adj* indispensable, absolute; (*fără aparare*) defenseless; unprotected || *adv* without fail, certainly; necessarily; absolutely.

neascultător [neaskultă'tor] *adj* disobedient; (*greu de stăpânit*) unruly.

neasemuit [neasemu'it] *adj* incomparable, matchless, peerless.

neastâmpăr [neas'tâmpăr] *nn* agitation, bustle; (*nelinişte*) disquietude • ~**at** *adj* agitated, fretting; (*d. copii*) naughty; (*vioi*) lively, vivid; * **nebunatic**.

neaşteptat [neashtep'tat] *adj* unexpected, (*brusc*) sudden, (*neprevăzut*) unforeseen.

neatent [nea'tent] *adj* inattentive || *adv* inattentively, absentmindedly.

neatenţie [nea'tensie] *nf* inattention, absentmindedness.

neatrăgător [neatrăgă'tor] *adj* unattractive.

neautorizat [neautori'zat] *adj* unauthorized.

neavenit [neave'nit] *adj jur* **nul şi** ~ null and void.

neavizat [neavi'zat] *adj* * **neinformat**.

nebănuit [nebănu'it] *adj* unsuspected, beyond/above suspicion; (*de nădejde*) trustworthy; *fig* undreamt of; unforeseen, unexpected.

nebulos [nebu'los] *adj* nebulous || *adv* nebulously.

nebun [ne'bun] *adj* insane, mad, crazy; *fig* (*de durere*) frantic; beside oneself; (*d. iluzii*) wild; (*prostesc*) foolish; extravagant; reckless; (*nestăpânit*) unruly; (*grozav*) terrible, extraordinary, fantastic, tremendous, wild; enormous || *nm* madman, lunatic; (*prost*) *bufon*) fool; *obs* jester; (*la şah*) bishop • ~**esc** *adj* foolish; (*de nebun*) madman's, mad; (*nesăbuit*) reckless • ~**atic** *adj* playful, frolicsome, frisky • ~**ie** *nf* madness, insanity; *fig* folly, act/piece of folly; (*năzdrăvănie*) mad trick; (*manie*) mania, hobby.

necalificat [nekalifi'kat] *adj* unqualified, unskilled.

necaz [ne'kaz] *nn* trouble; (*amărăciune*) sorrow; (*suferinţă*) suffering; (*bătaie de cap*) nuisance; (*impas*) deadlock; (*ciudă*) spite, grudge.

necăji [nekă'zhi] *vt* (*a supăra*) to anger; (*a jigni*) to vex, to tease; (*a irita*) to irritate; (*a deprima*) to depress || *vr* (*a se supăra*) to be/grow angry; (*a se amări*) to be pained; (*a-şi da osteneala*) to endeavor, to take pains.

necăsătorit [nekăsăto'rit] *adj* unmarried, single.

necesar [neche'sar] *adj* necessary, needful; (*d. o informaţie*) requisite; (*cerut*) required; indispensable, essential || *nn* outfit.

necesita [nechesi'ta] *vt* to necessitate, to require • ~**te** *nf* necessity, (*nevoie*) need, want; **cu** ~ of necessity.

nechemat [neke'mat] *adj* (*nepoftit*) unbidden, uninvited, uncalled for; inopportune; *fig* (*neştiutor*) ignorant; incompetent; (*nepriceput*) unskillful.

necheza [neke'za] *vi zool* to neigh, to whinny • ~**t** *nn* *zool* neigh(ing).

nechibzuit [nekibzu'it] *adj* thoughtless, reckless, unwise.

necinste [ne'chinste] *nf* disgrace, dishonor; (*ruşine*) shame; insult.

necinsti [nechin'sti] *vt* to disgrace, to dishonor; to profane; (*o femeie*) to rape, to violate • ~t *adj* dishonest, unfair || *adv* dishonestly.

neciteţ [nechi'tets] *adj* illegible, unreadable.

neclar [ne'klar] *adj* (*vag*) vague, indefinite; (*ceţos*) hazy; obscure; (*greu*) difficult; (*încâlcit*) intricate; ambiguous || *adv* vaguely, etc.

neclintit [neklin'tit] *adj* motionless, still; *fig* inflexible, unbending, unflinching; (*ferm*) firm; **de** ~ firm, stable.

necomestibil [nekomes'tibil] *adj* unedible.

necompetent [nekompe'tent] *adj* * **incompetent**.

neconcludent [nekonklu'dent] *adj* unconvincing.

necondiţionat [nekonditsio'nat] *adj* (*fără rezerve*) unreserved, unhesitating; (*fără condiţii*) absolute; unconditioned; unreserved; (*d. capitulare*) unconditional || *adv* unreservedly, unhesitatingly, unconditionally.

neconfirmat [nekonfir'mat] *adj* unconfirmed.

neconformist [nekonfor'mist] *nm* dissenter || *adj* nonconformist.

neconsolat [nekonso'lat] *adj* unconsoled, uncomforted.

neconstituţional [nekonstitutsio'nal] *adj* unconstitutional.

necontenit [nekonte'nit] *adj* continual, ceaseless, never-ending || *adv* continuously, without cessation, without a break.

necontestat [nekontes'tat] *adj* unquestionable, indisputable; **de** ~ unquestionable.

necontrolat [nekontro'lat] *adj* uncontrolled.

neconvenabil [nekonve'nabil] *adj* inconvenient, unsuitable.

neconvingător [nekonvingă'tor] *adj* unconvincing.

necopt [ne'kopt] *adj* unripe, raw; (*d. o plăcintă*) *also fig* half-baked; *fig* immature; *coll* green, callow.

necorespunzător [nekorespunză'tor] *adj* inadequate; incongruous; inappropriate, unsuitable || *adv* inadequately, etc.

necredincios [nekredin'chos] *adj* unfaithful, disloyal; *relig* unbelieving, irreligious || *nm relig* non-believer, atheist.

necrolog [nekro'log] *nn* obituary (notice), necrology.

necromanţie [nekroman'tsie] *nf* necromancy.

necruţător [nekrutsă'tor] *adj* merciless, ruthless, relentless.

nectar [nek'tar] *nf bot, myth* nectar.

nectarină [nekta'rină] *nf* nectarine.

necugetat [nekudje'tat] *adj* thoughtless, reckless, rash; (*lipsit de consideraţie pentru alţii*) inconsiderate; (*fără grijă, atenţie*) careless, heedless || *adv* thoughtlessly, etc.

necultivat [nekulti'vat] *adj* (*d. pământ*) untilled, uncultivated; waste; *fig* (*d. persoane*) uneducated.

necumpătat [nekumpă'tat] *adj* (*d. cineva*) intemperate; incontinent; wild, uncontrolled; (*d. lucruri*) immoderate, excessive.

necunoscut [nekunos'kut] *adj* unknown; unfamiliar || *nm* stranger • ~ul *nn* the unknown.

necurat [neku'rat] *adj* unclean; (*blestemat*) (ac)cursed; (*diavolesc*) devilish; (*necinstit*) dishonest; dubious, shady; (*d. o afacere*) funny, dark • ~ul *nm* the Evil one.

necuviincios [nekuviin'chios] *adj* (*nerespectuos*) disrespectful, irreverent, uncivil; (*dar sincer*) bluff(y); (*fără ruşine*) brazen, shameless; (*deplasat*) misplaced;

indecent, unseemly; improper, untoward || *adv* disrespectfully, etc.

necuviinţă [neku'viintsă] *nf* impropriety, indecency; (*ca act*) improper act/utterance, breach of manners.

nedecis [nede'chis] *adj* (*care nu a fost decis*) undecided, not settled; (*d. cineva*) irresolute; (*d. o problemă*) undetermined.

nedefinit [nedefi'nit] *adj* indefinite; (*vag*) vague.

nedemn [ne'demn] *adj* (*de*) unworthy (of); (*ruşinos*) shameful.

nedeprins [nede'prins] *adj* (*cu*) unaccustomed (to), unused (to).

nedescoperit [nedeskope'rit] *adj* undiscovered.

nedescris [nedes'kris] *adj* **de** ~ indescribable, unspeakable.

nedesluşit [nedeslu'shit] *adj* * **neclar**.

nedespărţit [nedespăr'tsit] *adj* inseparable.

nedeterminare [nedetermi'nare] *nf also math* indetermination; indeterminateness.

nedezminţit [nedezmin'tsit] *adj* firm, steadfast; (*consecvent*) consistent.

nedisciplinat [nedischipli'nat] *adj* undisciplined.

nedisimulat [nedisimu'lat] *adj* sincere, frank.

nedorit [nedo'rit] *adj* undesirable, unexpected; **oaspete** ~ uninvited guest.

nedrept [ne'drept] *adj* incorrect; illegal; unjust; (*greşit*) wrong; **pe** ~ unjustly, (*nemeritat*) undeservedly, (*samavolnic*) arbitrarily • ~ate *nf* injustice; (*rău*) wrong, iniquity • ~ăţi *vt* to wrong, to do smb an injustice.

nedumeri [nedume'ri] *vt* to surprise, to amaze || *vr* to wonder • ~re *nf* bewilderment, perplexity • ~t *adj* puzzled, perplexed, bewildered.

neesenţial(ă) [neesentsi'al(ă)] *adj* unessential.

neexplorat [neeksplo'rat] *adj* unexplored.

nefamilist [nefami'list] *nm* single, bachelor.

nefast [ne'fast] *adj* (*d. o zi*) ill-fated; (*d. influenţă*) baneful, baleful; (*rău*) bad, evil, nefarious.

nefavorabil [nefavo'rabil] *adj* unfavorable; inauspicious.

nefăcut [nefă'kut] *adj* not done/made, unfinished.

nefericire [neferi'chire] *nf* misfortune; **din** ~ unfortunately, unhappily.

nefericit [neferi'chit] *adj* unhappy; (*fără noroc*) unlucky; (*nenorocit*) miserable; * **nefast** • *nm* wretch.

nefiresc [nefi'resk] *adj* unnatural, artificial, affected.

nefolositor [nefolosi'tor] *adj* useless.

nefondat [nefon'dat] *adj* groundless, indefensible.

nefumător [nefumă'tor] *nm* non-smoker || *adj* non-smoking.

neg [neg] *nm anat* wart.

nega [ne'ga] *vt* to deny, to negate; *jur* to traverse || *vi* to deny a charge • ~re *nf* denial, denying, negation • ~ţie *nf* negation • ~tiv *adj* negative || *adv* negatively || *nn phot* negative.

neghină [ne'gină] *nf bot* cockle, cockweed.

neghiob [ne'giob] *adj* (*prost*) silly, stupid, foolish; (*neîndemânatic*) clumsy || *nm* (*prost*) blockhead • ~ie *nf* (*prostie*) foolish/stupid thing.

neglija [negli'zha] *vt* to take no care of, to disregard, (*îndatoririle*) to be neglectful of; (*pe cineva*) to slight, to ignore; (*a lăsa nefăcut*) to leave undone • ~bil *adj* negligible.

neglijent [negli'zhent] *adj* careless, remiss, neglectful;

indolent, slothful; **stil** ~ loose/slipshod/floppy style ‖ *adv* carelessly, etc.

neglijenţă [negli'zhentsă] *nf* negligence; **din** ~ through an oversight.

negocia [negochi'a] *vt* to negotiate; (*la bursă*) to trade • ~**tor** *nm* negotiator.

negociere [negochi'ere] *nf* negotiation, negotiating; *pl* negotiations; *com* transaction.

negoţ [ne'gots] *nn* trade, commerce.

negresă [ne'gresă] *nf* Negro woman/girl.

negreşit [negre'shit] *adv* (*neapărat*) by all means; (*sigur*) of course, certainly; **du-te** ~ you must go, make sure you go.

negricios [negri'chios] *adj* blackish, darkish; (*oacheş*) dark-haired; dark-skinned; (*d. ten*) swarthy; dusky, dark.

negru ['negru] *adj* black; (*d. piele, ten*) dark, swarthy; (*înnegrit*) blackened; (*ars de soare*) sunburnt; (*ca cerneala*) inky (black); (*bronzat, cafeniu, brun*) brown; (*murdar*) dirty, grimy; (*fără lumină*) dark; obscure; *fig* (*misterios*) mysterious; (*ascuns*) hidden; (*d. gânduri*) gloomy; (*privitor la negri*) Negro.

negură ['negură] *nf* fog; *fig* (*beznă*) dark(ness); (*noapte*) night; *fig* (*mulţime*) multitude, host.

negustor [negus'tor] *nm* merchant, dealer; (*care are prăvălie*) shopkeeper; (*ambulant*) pedlar; ~ **de** dealer in • ~**ie** *nf* trade, commerce; (*afacere*) business.

nehotărâre [nehotă'râre] *nf* hesitation, indecision.

nehotărât [nehotă'rât] *adj* undecided, irresolute; (*şovăitor*) hesitating; (*vag*) vague; *gram* indefinite.

neidentificat [neidentifi'kat] *adj* unidentified.

neiertător [neiertă'tor] *adj* unforgiving, ruthless.

neigienic [nei'djienik] *adj* unhygienic.

neimportant [neimpor'tant] *adj* unimportant, of no account.

neimpozabil [neimpo'zabil] *adj* tax free, not liable to taxation.

neinformat [neinfor'mat] *adj* uninformed.

neinstruit [neinstru'it] *adj* uneducated.

neintenţionat [neintentsio'nat] *adj* unintentional.

neinteresant [neintere'sant] *adj* uninteresting; (*d. viaţă*) uneventful.

neintervenţie [neinter'ventsie] *nf* non-intervention, non-interference.

neinvitat [neinvi'tat] *adj* uninvited.

neisprăvit [neispră'vit] *adj* (*neterminat*) unfinished; endless, infinite; *coll* incapable; *coll* (*prost*) silly; (*necopt*) callow • *nm coll* blockhead, dolt.

neizbutit [neizbu'tit] *adj* unsuccessful, lame; **încercare** ~**ă** lame attempt.

neîmblânzit [neîmblân'zit] *adj* (*sălbatic*) also *fig* wild; savage; (*cumplit*) terrible; (*crud*) cruel, pitiless.

neîmpăcat [neîmpă'kat] *adj* (*nemulţumit*) dissatisfied, discontented; (*aprig*) fierce; irreconcilable, implacable.

neîmpărtăşit [neîmpărtă'shit] *adj* (*d. dragoste*) unrequited.

neîmplinit [neîmpli'nit] *adj* unfulfilled; (*crud*) raw, immature; (*neterminat*) unfinished.

neînarmat [neînar'mat] *adj* unarmed; (*fără apărare*) defenseless.

neîncetat [neînche'tat] *adj* ceaseless, unceasing, continual ‖ *adv* ceaselessly, continually, without cease.

neînchipuit [neînkipu'it] *adj* unimaginable; ~ **de**

unspeakably, inconceivably; (*extrem de*) extremely, exceedingly; **de** ~ unthinkable, inconceivable.

neîncredere [neîn'kredere] *nf* distrust, mistrust; (*bănuială*) suspicion; **cu** ~ distrustfully, suspiciously.

neîndemânare [neîndemâ'nare] *nf* want of skill; clumsiness, awkwardness.

neîndemânatic [neîndemâ'natik] *adj* awkward, clumsy ‖ *adv* awkwardly, clumsily; * **stângaci**.

neîndeplinire [neîndepli'nire] *nf* non-fulfilment; failure to execute/carry out/comply with.

neîndestulător [neîndestulă'tor] *adj* insufficient; scarce; (*sărac*) poor; (*redus*) small, reduced.

neîndoios [neîndo'ios] *adj* sure, certain; doubtless; (*limpede*) clear, obvious ‖ *adv* sure(ly), etc.

neînduplecat [neînduple'kat] *adj* inflexible, unyielding, rigid, adamant.

neînfrânt [neîn'frânt] *adj* unvanquished; **de** ~ invincible.

neînfricat [neînfri'kat] *adj* undaunted, fearless ‖ *adv* fearlessly

neîngrijit [neîngri'zhit] *adj* neglected; (*d. o grădină*) overgrown.

neînsemnat [neînsem'nat] *adj* insignificant, unimportant; (*d. o pierdere*) trivial, trifling.

neînsufleţit [neînsufle'tsit] *adj* inanimate, lifeless.

neîntemeiat [neînteme'iat] *adj* groundless, unfounded.

neîntârziat [neîntârzi'at] *adv* immediately, at once.

neîntrecut [neîntre'kut] *adj* unsurpassed; (*fără pereche*) matchless, peerless.

neîntrerupt [neîntre'rupt] *adj* uninterrupted, unbroken ‖ *adv* uninterruptedly.

neînţelegere [neîntse'ledjere] *nf* (*între persoane*) misunderstanding, disagreement; (*a unui lucru*) lack of understanding.

neînţeles [neîntse'les] *adj* (*d. cineva*) misunderstood; (*tainic*) secret; (*misterios*) mysterious; obscure; **de** ~ incomprehensible, inexplicable, unaccountable, (*ciudat*) strange.

neînvins [neîn'vins] *adj* unvanquished.

nejust [ne'zhust] *adj* unrightful • ~**ificat** *adj* unjustified; unreasonable.

nelămurire [nelămu'rire] *adj* doubt, question.

nelămurit [nelămu'rit] *adj* vague, obscure, uncertain; indefinite; (*d. cineva*) unenlightened ‖ *adv* vaguely, etc.

nelegitim [nele'djitim] *adj* illegitimate.

nelegiuire [neledju'ire] *nf* unlawfulness; (*ca act*) unlawful action; (*impietate*) impiety; (*nedreptate*) iniquity; (*crimă*) crime.

nelegiuit [neledju'it] *adj* infamous, foul; (*ticălos*) villainous, wicked ‖ *nm* scoundrel, villain.

nelimitat [nelimi'tat] *adj* boundless, unbounded.

nelinişte [ne'linishte] *nf* disquiet; (*neodihnă*) restlessness; (*grijă*) anxiety, uneasiness; (*agitaţie*) agitation.

nelinişti [nelini'shti] *vt* to worry, to distress, to alarm ‖ *vr* to worry, to be anxious • ~**t** *adj* uneasy; (*fără astâmpăr*) restless; (*îngrijorat*) upset, anxious, uneasy; *coll* worried; (*d. somn*) troubled, broken; (*agitat*) agitated ‖ *adv* uneasily, anxiously.

nelipsit [nelip'sit] *adj* never-failing; (*obişnuit*) habitual, customary.

nelocuit [neloku'it] *adj* uninhabited; **de** ~ uninhabitable.

nemaipomenit [nemaipome'nit] *adj* unprecedented, unparalleled; extraordinary; ~ **de** extremely, exceedingly.

nemaivăzut [nemaivă'zut] *adj* unprecedented, unparalleled.

nemărginit [nemărdji'nit] *adj* infinite, unlimited, boundless.

nemăritată [nemări'tată] *adj f* unmarried.

nemăsurat [nemăsu'rat] *adj* beyond measure; unmeasurable; (*enorm*) huge, enormous; (*exagerat*) exaggerated.

nemeritat [nemeri'tat] *adj* undeserved.

nemernic [ne'mernik] *adj* knavish; (*josnic*) mean, base; (*infam*) infamous, foul; (*jalnic*) miserable, wretched ‖ *nm* scoundrel, villain, rascal.

nemijlocit [nemizhlo'chit] *adj* immediate, direct.

nemilos [nemi'los] *adj* pitiless, merciless, ruthless ‖ *adv* pitilessly, mercilessly.

nemișcat [nemish'kat] *adj* motionless, steady, stock-still.

nemțesc [nem'tsesk] *adj* German.

nemulțumi [nemultsu'mi] *vt* to displease, to annoy • ~re *nf* dissatisfaction, displeasure; (*necaz*) trouble • ~t *adj* (*de*) displeased (with), dissatisfied (with) ‖ *adv* with displeasure ‖ *nm* malcontent.

nemurire [nemu'rire] *nf* immortality; *relig* eternal life; **la** ~ (*veșnic*) endless; *coll* (*foarte mult*) enormous.

nemuritor [nemuri'tor] *adj* undying; (*veșnic*) eternal.

nenatural [nenatu'ral] *adj* unnatural; (*afectat*) affected.

nenăscut [nenăs'kut] *adj* unborn.

nene ['nene] *nm approx* (*unchi*) uncle.

nenoroc [neno'rok] *nn* ill-luck; (*necaz*) trouble; (*nefericire*) unhappiness • ~i *vt* (*a face nefericit*) to make unhappy; (*a distruge*) to destroy, to ruin; (*a schilodi*) to cripple; (*a fi o pacoste pentru*) to pester, to plague • ~ire *nf* misfortune; accident; (*dezastru*) disaster; (*năpastă*) calamity, affliction; bale; *lit* bane; din ~ unfortunately • ~it *adj* miserable; (*nefericit*) unhappy, unfortunate; (*dureros*) grievous; (*trist*) sad ‖ *nm* wretch.

nenumărat [nenumă'rat] *adj* innumerable, numberless, countless.

neobișnuit [neobishnu'it] *adj* (*cu*) unaccustomed, unused (to); unusual; outstanding, remarkable, exceptional; out of the common.

neobosit [neobo'sit] *adj* indefatigable, tireless; (*harnic*) hard-working; (*susținut*) sustained, continual ‖ *adv* tirelessly.

neobrăzare [neobră'zare] *nf* (*nerușinare*) impudence; *coll* cheek.

neobrăzat [neobră'zat] *adj* bold, impudent, cheeky.

neobservat [neobser'vat] *adj* unobserved, unnoticed.

neocupat [neoku'pat] *adj* unoccupied.

neoficial [neofichi'al] *adj* unofficial, informal; (*d. discuții*) off the record.

neofit [neo'fit] *nm* neophyte; (*începător*) beginner, novice; *coll* tyro.

neologism [neolo'djism] *nn* neologism.

neon [ne'on] *nn chem* neon; **lampă cu** ~ (glow-)lamp.

neorânduială [neorându'ială] *nf* disorder, confusion.

neospitalier [neospitali'er] *adj* inhospitable.

neostoit [neosto'it] *adj* tireless, untired.

nepărtinitor [nepărtini'tor] *adj* impartial, unprejudiced ‖ *adv* impartially.

nepăsare [nepă'sare] *nf* indifference, carelessness; (*lene*) idleness; (*apatie*) apathy; **cu** ~ indifferently, carelessly.

nepăsător [nepăsă'tor] *adj* indifferent, careless; (*apatic*) apathetic ‖ *adv* indifferently, etc.

nepătat [nepă'tat] *adj* stainless, spotless; *fig* immaculate, untainted.

nepătruns [nepă'truns] *adj* (*și de* ~) impenetrable; *fig* mysterious, secret; (*ascuns*) hidden, abstruse.

nepedepsit [nepedep'sit] *adj* unpunished.

nepermis [neper'mis] *adj* forbidden, unlawful, illicit.

nepieritor [nepieri'tor] *adj* unfading, everlasting.

neplată [ne'plată] *nf* non-payment.

neplăcere [neplă'chere] *nf* (*silă*) displeasure; (*scârbă*) disgust, repugnance; (*necaz*) trouble, nuisance.

neplăcut [neplă'kut] *adj* disagreeable, painful, unpleasant; regrettable, unfortunate; (*d. miros*) nasty, obnoxious; (*d. gust*) unpalatable.

nepoată [ne'poată] *nf* (*de unchi*) niece; (*de bunic*) granddaughter.

nepoftit [nepof'tit] *adj* (*neinvitat*) uninvited, unbidden; (*nechemat*) uncalled for; inopportune; (*nedorit*) undesirable ‖ *nm* intruder.

nepoliticos [nepoliti'kos] *adj* uncivil.

nepopular [nepopu'lar] *adj* unpopular; *coll* at a discount.

nepot [ne'pot] *nm* (*de unchi*) nephew; (*de bunic*) grandson; (*urmaș*) descendent; (*la vocativ*) (my) boy!

nepotolit [nepoto'lit] *adj* unabated, unquenched.

nepotrivire [nepotri'vire] *nf* discrepancy; (*dezacord*) discord, disagreement; contrast; contradiction; (*neasemănare*) dissimilarity.

nepotrivit [nepotri'vit] *adj* discordant, dissonant; (*inegal*) unequal; (*neconvenabil*) inconvenient; (*impropriu*) unfit, inadequate; (*deplasat*) out of place; (*d. o remarcă*) unwarranted, uncalled for.

nepregătit [nepregă'tit] *adj* unprepared.

neprelucrat [neprelu'krat] *adj tech* raw, crude, rough.

nepretențios [nepretentsi'os] *adj* unpretentious.

neprețuit [nepretsu'it] *adj* inestimable, invaluable, priceless.

neprevăzător [neprevăză'tor] *adj* improvident, imprudent, unwise.

neprevăzut [neprevă'zut] *adj* unforeseen; (*neașteptat*) unexpected ‖ *nn* contingency, emergency.

nepricepere [nepri'chepere] *nf* (*neștiință*) ignorance; (*lipsă de înțelegere*) incomprehension; incapacity, inability.

nepriceput [nepriche'put] *adj* ignorant; incapable; (*prost*) silly, stupid ‖ *nm* blockhead; *coll* dolt.

neprielnic [nepri'elnik] *adj* unfavorable, inauspicious.

neprietenesc [nepriete'nesk] *adj* unfriendly.

neprietenos [nepriete'nos] *adj* unfriendly; (*ostil*) hostile ‖ *adv* in an unfriendly manner; hostilely.

neprihănit [neprihă'nit] *adj* immaculate, pure, (*cast*) chaste.

neproductiv [neproduk'tiv] *adj* unproductive; **muncă** ~ă wasted work.

neproliferare [neprolife'rare] *nf pol* non-proliferation, non-dissemination.

nepublicat [nepubli'kat] *adj* unpublished.

neputincios [neputin'chios] *adj* powerless, helpless, impotent.

neputință [nepu'tintsă] *nf* powerlessness, helplessness; impotence, impotency; **cu** ~ impossible.

nerambursabil [nerambur'sabil] *adj* irredeemable.

nerăbdare [nerăb'dare] *nf* impatience; (*neliniște*) anxiety; (*ardoare*) eagerness; **cu** ~ impatiently.

nerăbdător [nerăbdă'tor] *adj* impatient; (*doritor*) eager; desirous.

nerealizabil [nereali'zabil] *adj* unrealizable, unattainable.

nerecunoscător [nerekunoskă'tor] *adj* ungrateful.
nerecunoştinţă [nerekuno'shtintsă] *nf* ingratitude, ungratefulness.
neregularitate [neregularitate] *nf* irregularity; (*a scrisului, terenului*) unevenness.
neregulat [neregu'lat] *adj* irregular; (*d. puls*) erratic; (*d. somn*) broken; (*d. viaţă*) disorderly, loose.
neregulă [ne'regulă] *nf* disorder; **în** ~ out of order, amiss.
nerentabil [neren'tabil] *adj* unprofitable.
nerespectare [nerespek'tare] *nf* non-observance.
nerespectuos [nerespek'tuos] *adj* irreverent.
nereuşit [nereu'shit] *adj* unsuccessful, lame.
nereuşită [nereu'shită] *nf* failure, ill success, setback.
nerezolvat [nerezol'vat] *adj* unsolved, unsettled, undecided; **de** ~ insoluble, unsolvable.
nerod [ne'rod] *adj* (*prost*) silly, foolish; (*inutil*) useless; absurd, nonsensical || *nm* (*prost*) blockhead, dolt.
neroditor [nerodi'tor] *adj* unfruitful; (*sterp*) barren, sterile, fruitless.
nerozie [nero'zie] *nf* (*prostie*) stupidity; (*ca act*) foolish action.
neruşinare [nerushi'nare] *nf* impudence, insolence, effrontery; *coll* sauce, cheek.
neruşinat [nerushi'nat] *adj* impudent, insolent; **minciună** ~**ă** outrageous/blatant lie || *nm* impudent fellow.
nerv [nerv] *nm anat* nerve; *pl* fit of nerves; *coll* tantrums; (*isteric*) hysterics; *fig* vim, energy, vigor • ~**os** *adj anat* nervous; (*d. stil*) vigorous; (*d. cineva*) excitable, highly strung; *coll* nervy, on edge; (*agitat*) fidgety; (*d. râs*) hysterical; (*iritat*) irritated || *adv* irritably, impatiently; **sistem** ~ *physiol* nervous system • ~**ozitate** *nf* nervousness, irritability; *coll* fidgets, jumpiness.
nervură [ner'vură] *nf bot, ento* nervure, vein; *tech, constr* rib.
nesatisfăcător [nesatisfăkă'tor] *adj* unsatisfactory || *adv* unsatisfactorily.
nesatisfăcut [nesatisfă'kut] *adj* frustrated.
nesăbuinţă [nesăbu'intsă] *nf* recklessness; (*prostie*) stupidity; (*ca act*) reckless action; (*prostie*) foolish action; rashness.
nesăbuit [nesăbu'it] *adj* reckless, rash; (*nebunesc*) foolish || *adv* recklessly, foolishly.
nesănătos [nesănă'tos] *adj* (*d. climă*) unhealthy; (*d. hrană etc*) unwholesome; (*d. o locuinţă*) unsanitary.
nesărat [nesă'rat] *adj* unsalted; *fig* insipid, dull, flat.
nesătul [nesă'tul] *adj* hungry; (*nesăţios*) insatiable.
nesăţios [nesă'tsios] *adj* insatiable; *fig* greedy, grasping.
neschimbat [neskim'bat] *adj* unchanged, unaltered; (*fix*) fixed, permanent.
nesemnificativ [neseminifika'tiv] *adj* insignificant, unimportant || *adv* insignificantly, unimportantly.
neserios [neseri'os] *adj* (*d. cineva*) not serious; frivolous; (*neîntemeiat*) unfounded, ungrounded; (*neimportant*) unimportant, insignificant; (*copilăros*) childish.
neseriozitate [neseriozi'tate] *nf* lack of seriousness or sense, levity, frivolity.
nesfârşit [nesfâr'shit] *adj* endless, infinite; age-long || *nn* infinite; **la** ~ endlessly, without end.
nesigur [ne'sigur] *adj* uncertain, unsafe, insecure • **mână** ~**ă** unsteady hand • ~**anţă** *nf* uncertainty, incertitude, (*îndoială*) doubt.

nesilit [nesi'lit] *adj* unconstrained, free || *adv* of one's own will, of one's own accord.
nesimţire [nesim'tsire] *nf* (*leşin*) fainting fit, swoon; (*lipsă de sensibilitate*) insensitiveness; *fig* indifference, callousness.
nesimţit [nesim'tsit] *adj* thick-skinned, callous; **pe** ~**e** imperceptibly; (*pe furiş*) stealthily || *nm* thick-skinned fellow.
nesimţitor [nesimtsi'tor] *adj* (*nepăsător*) indifferent, careless; (*insensibil*) insensitive, unfeeling, * **nesimţit**.
nesincer [ne'sincher] *adj* insincere || *adv* insincerely.
nesociabil [nesochi'abil] *adj* unsociable, unfriendly, antisocial.
nesocoti [nesoko'ti] *vt* to overlook; to neglect; (*a nu ţine seama de*) not to take into consideration; to omit; (*a desconsidera*) to disregard; (*a dispreţui*) to scorn; (*a brava*) to defy; to ignore.
nesomn [ne'somn] *nn* sleeplessness, insomnia.
nestabil [nesta'bil] *adj also chem* unstable; (*pe care nu te poţi bizui*) unreliable.
nestatornic [nesta'tornik] *adj* inconstant; (*pe care nu te poţi bizui*) unreliable • ~**ie** *nf* inconstancy, fickleness, (*a caracterului*) flightiness.
nestăpânit [nestăpâ'nit] *adj* unrestrained, unruly, lacking self-control; passionate; fiery; impetuous.
nestăvilit [nestăvi'lit] *adj* irresistible; (*năvalnic*) impetuous.
nestânjenit [nestânzhe'nit] *adj* unhampered.
nestemată [neste'mată] *nf* gem, precious stone.
nesuferit [nesufe'rit] *adj* (*şi de* ~) unbearable, intolerable || *nm* unbearable person.
nesupunere [nesu'punere] *nf* insubordination.
nesupus [nesu'pus] *adj* disobedient, unruly.
neşansă [ne'shansă] *nf* ill-luck, mischance.
neşovăielnic, neşovăitor [neshovă'ielnik, neshovăi'tor] *adj* unhesitating.
neştiinţă [neshti'intsă] *nf* ignorance; unfamiliarity.
neştirbit [neshtir'bit] *adj* untouched; whole, intact.
neştiut [neshti'ut] *adj* un(be)known; (*tainic*) secret; (*ascuns*) hidden • **pe** ~**e** stealthily; *coll* unbeknownst • ~**tor** *adj* ignorant || *nm* ignorance.
net [net] *adj* (*clar*) *also com* clear; net; (*d. o deosebire*) clear-cut; (*d. un răspuns*) plain; **refuz** ~ flat refusal || *adv* plainly; flatly, pointblank; distinctly; **a refuza** ~ to refuse pointblank/flatly.
neted ['neted] *adj* smooth; (*d. drumuri*) even; (*d. piele etc*) sleek; *fig* (*clar*) clear, obvious; precise || *adv* smoothly.
neterminat [netermi'nat] *adj* unfinished.
netezi [nete'zi] *vt* to make smooth/even; to smooth out/down; (*d. drum*) to level; (*cu fierul*) to press, to iron; (*a aranja*) to arrange; (*a mângâia*) to stroke.
neto ['neto] *adv* net.
netot [ne'tot] *nm* * **neghiob**; dolt || *adj* silly, stupid.
netrebnic [ne'trebnik] *adj* (*bun de nimic*) worthless; (*inutil*) useless; (*ticălos*) knavish; (*nenorocit*) miserable, wretched || *nm* rascal, knave, villain.
netulburat [netulbu'rat] *adj* untroubled; (*liniştit*) quiet; unruffled, imperturbable || *adv* quietly, imperturbably.
neuitat [neui'tat] *adj* unforgotten, not forgotten; **de** ~ unforgettable, never to be forgotten.
neurastenic [neura'stenik] *adj/nm med* neurasthenic.
neurolog [neuro'log] *nm med* neurologist, nerve specialist.

neutralitate [neutrali'tate] *nf* neutrality.

neutraliza [neutrali'za] *vt* to neutralize || *vr pass* to become neutralized; *recip* to cancel each other out.

neutru [ne'utru] *adj* neutral; **zonă ~ă** neutral zone; *gram, bot* neuter (gender).

neuzitat [neuzi'tat] *adj* unusual; not in common use.

nevandabil [nevan'dabil] *adj* unsalable, unmarketable.

nevastă [ne'vastă] *nf* married woman; (*femeie*) woman; (*soție*) wife; *coll* one's good lady, one's better half.

nevăstuică [nevăs'tuikă] *nf zool* common/beach marten; *zool* weasel.

nevătămat [nevătă'mat] *adj/adv* unharmed, safe (and sound), woundless.

nevăzător [nevăză'tor] *adj/nm* blind (person).

nevăzut [nevă'zut] *adj* unseen, invisible; **pe ~e** blindly.

neverosimil [nevero'simil] *adj* improbable, unlikely.

nevertebrat [neverte'brat] *adj/nn* invertebrate.

nevinovat [nevino'vat] *adj* innocent; (*cast*) chaste; naïve; simple; (*curat*) pure; (*neprihănit*) immaculate; (*d. o glumă*) harmless || *nm* innocent.

nevinovăție [nevinovă'tsie] *nf* innocence, chastity, naivete; simplicity; artlessness; harmlessness.

nevoiaş [nevo'iash] *adj* needy; (*sărac*) poor; (*nenorocit*) wretched, miserable || *nm* needy person; * **becisnic**.

nevoie [ne'voie] *nf* (*necesitate*) need, necessity; **de/din nevoia** because of, on account of; **de voie, de ~** willy-nilly; **la ~** in an emergency; (*lipsă*) want; (*sărăcie*) poverty; penury; (*strâmtoare*) straits; (*necaz*) trouble; (*dificultate*) difficulty; *coll* (*încurcătură*) scrape, (nice) fix; *pl* business, affairs.

nevoit [nevo'it] *adj* obliged, bound; (*constrâns*) constrained, forced.

nevolnic [ne'volnik] *adj* incapable; * **becisnic**.

nevralgie [nevral'djie] *nf med* neuralgia.

nevrednic [ne'vrednik] *adj* unworthy; (*fără valoare*) worthless.

nevricos [nevri'kos] *adj coll* nervy, jumpy, jittery.

nevrotic, nevrozat [nev'rotik, nevro'zat] *adj/nm* neurotic.

nevroză [ne'vroză] *nf med* neurosis.

newyorkez [niuior'kez] *adj* New York || *nm* New Yorker.

nezdruncinat [nezdrunchi'nat] *adj* unshaken; **de ~** unshakable; * **neclintit**.

nicăieri [nikă'ieri] *adv* nowhere, not ... anywhere; **de ~** from nowhere.

nichel ['nikel] *nn metal* nickel.

nici ['nichi] *adv* (*chiar*) even; (*nici chiar*) not even; **~un/o** no; not one; **~ unul** (*din noi*) neither (of us); (*din mai mulți*) none || *conj* nor • **~când** *adv* never; * **niciodată** • **~cum** *adv* not at all, not in the least • **~decum** *adv* not at all, by no means; *coll* not a bit of it • **~odată** *adv* never, nevermore, at no time.

nicotină [niko'tină] *nf chem* nicotine.

nicovală [niko'vală] *nf* anvil; *anat* incus.

nimb [nimb] *nn* nimbus, halo, glory.

nimeni ['nimeni] *pron* nobody; not ... anybody, no one, not ... anyone; (*nici unul*) none.

nimeri [nime'ri] *vt* (*a lovi*) to hit; (*a ghici*) to guess; (*a reuşi*) to succeed || *vr* (*a fi*) to be; (*a se pomeni*) to find oneself; *imp* (*a se întâmpla*) to happen || *vi* (*undeva*) to get; (*a se pomeni*) to find oneself; (*a sosi*) to come.

nimfă ['nimfă] *nf myth* nymph; *ento* pupa, chrysalis.

nimfomană [nimfo'manã] *nf med* nymphomaniac.

nimic [ni'mik] *pron* nothing; not ... anything; **de ~**

worthless; **mai ~** hardly anything; nothing much || *nn* trifle; (*chestiune neimportantă*) trifling matter; *fig* (*neant*) nothingness; *fig* (*om fără valoare*) non-entity; (*găteală*) knick-knack • **~i** [nimi'chi] *vt* to reduce to nothing, to crush; (*a distruge*) to annihilate, to destroy, to smash, to shatter, to wreck; (*a extermina*) to kill, to finish, to slay.

nimicnicie [nimikni'chie] *nf* nothingness; (*deşertăciune*) vanity.

ninge ['nindje] *vi* to snow; (*a se cerne*) to sift.

ninsoare [nin'soare] *nf* snowfall; (*zăpadă*) snow.

nipon [ni'pon] *adj* Nippon, Japanese.

nirvana [nir'vana] *nf* nirvana.

nisetru [ni'setru] *nm* (common) sturgeon.

nisip [ni'sip] *nn* sand; (*fin*) fine sand; *med* gravel, urinary sand • **~os** *adj* sandy.

nişă ['nishă] *nf archit* niche, recess; *chem* basket funnel.

nişte ['nishte] *art indef* some || *inter* any.

nit [nit] *nn tech* rivet.

niţel [ni'tsel] *adv* a little.

nivel [ni'vel] *nn* level; **~ul mării** sea level; leveling instrument; *fig* standard • **~a** *vt* to level, to even up; *fig* to level down, to level up || *vr pass* to become level; *fig* to be leveled.

noapte ['noapte] *nf* night; (*întuneric*) dark(ness); (*seară*) evening; (*căderea nopții*) nightfall; (*perioadă întunecată*) darkness || *adv* (*noaptea*) at/by night; (*frecventativ*) nights.

nobil ['nobil] *adj* noble; (*distins*) distinguished; (*impunător*) imposing, lofty || *adv* nobly || *nm* noble(man) • **~ime** *nf* nobles, nobility, aristocracy.

nobleţe [no'bletse] *nf also fig* nobility; (*ca naştere*) noble birth; * **nobilime**; *fig* nobleness.

nociv [no'chiv] *adj* noxious, harmful • **~itate** *nf* harmfulness, (ob)noxiousness.

noctambul [noktam'bul] *nm* somnambulist, sleepwalker.

nocturn [nok'turn] *adj* nocturnal, night.

nod [nod] *nn* (*de sfoară etc*) also *tech, naut* knot; (*de cravată*) tie knot; *naut also* bend, hitch; *tech, rail* junction; *geom, phys, astron, bot* node; (*în lemn*) knur(l); *fig* crux, nodus • **~ul gordian** Gordian knot • **~ul vital** *anat* the vital center.

noduros [nodu'ros] *adj* knotty, nodulous; (*d. părţi ale corpului*) skinny, bony.

noi [noi] *pron* we; *coll* us.

noian [no'ian] *nn* (*mulţime*) multitude; (*nemărginire*) immensity; vastness; (*hău*) abyss.

noiembrie [no'iembrie] *nm* November.

nomad [no'mad] *adj* nomadic, wandering || *nm* nomad, ambulatory.

nomenclator [nomenkla'tor] *nn* classified list.

nomenclatură [nomenkla'tură] *nf* nomenclature; list, catalog; system of classification; *pol* (*comunistă*) nomenklatura.

nominal [nomi'nal] *adj* nominal; **apel ~** roll call; **preţ ~** nominal price, face value; **valoarea ~ă** nominal cost; *tech* rated.

nominaliza [nominali'za] *vt* to name, to nominate; to point out.

nominativ [nomina'tiv] *adj/nn gram* nominative.

nonagenar [nonadje'nar] *nm* nonagerian.

nonconformist [nonkonfor'mist] *adj/nm* nonconformist.

nonsens [non'sens] *nn* nonsense, absurdity.

nonstop [non'stop] *adj/adv* nonstop, round-the-clock.
nonșalant [nonsha'lant] *adj frml* nonchalant.
nonșalanță [nonsha'lantsă] *nf* nonchalance.
noptieră [nopti'eră] *nf* nightstand, bedroom/bedside table.
nor [nor] *nm also fig* cloud; ~ **artificial** smokescreen; ~ **de fum** *mil* smoke cloud; **~i cirrus** fleecy clouds, cirri; **~i cumulus** cumulus; **~i de furtună** cumulonimbus; **~i stratus** stratus.
noră ['noră] *nf* daughter-in-law; (*mireasă*) bride.
nord [nord] *nn* north; **la ~ de** north of, to the north of, northwards of • **~est** *nn* northeast • **~estic** *adj* northeast, northeastern • **~vest** *nn* northwest • **~vestic** *adj* northwest, northwestern • **~american** [nordameri'kan] *nm/adj* North American.
normal [nor'mal] *adj* normal; (*sănătos psihic*) sane || *adv* normally; (*obișnuit*) ordinarily • **~iza** *vt* to normalize || *vr* to be(come) normalized.
normativ [norma'tiv] *adj* normative || *nn tech* norm, standard.
normă ['normă] *nf also math* norm; standard; (*regulă*) rule; ~ **de conduită** rule of conduct; (*în producție*) quota; **~e tehnice** technical standards.
noroc [no'rok] *nn* (good) fortune, blessing, (*într-o împrejurare dată*) (good) luck; (*reușită*) hit, success; (*întâmplare favorabilă*) (lucky) chance; (*caracter norocos*) luckiness; hazard; (*prosperitate*) prosperity; (*fericire*) happiness; ~ **neașteptat** godsend; **la ~** at random, hit-or-miss; (*la revedere*) *coll* bye-bye; (*salut*) hi, hello; (*ridicând paharul*) your health! • **~orb** drunkard's luck • **~os** *adj* fortunate, lucky; happy; (*prosper*) thriving, prosperous, (*de succes*) successful.
noroi [no'roi] *nn* mud, mire, slush; (*murdărie*) filth, dirt.
norvegian [norvedji'an] *adj/nm* Norwegian • **~ă** *nf* Norwegian (woman or girl); Norwegian, the Norwegian language.
nostalgic [nos'taldjik] *adj* nostalgic, (*d. priviri*) wistful || *adv* nostalgically, wistfully.
nostalgie [nostal'djie] *nf* nostalgia; (*dor*) longing, yearning; (*melancolie*) melancholy, anguish; (*dor de țară*) homesickness.
nostim ['nostim] *adj* funny, (*amuzant*) amusing; (*interesant*) interesting; (*plăcut*) pleasant; (*atrăgător*) attractive; (*drăguț*) pretty, lovely; *coll* not bad-looking.
nostru ['nostru] *pron/adj poss m* our; **al ~** ours.
noștri ['noshtri] *pron/adj poss m pl* our; **ai ~** ours.
nota [no'ta] *vt* (*a însemna*) to put/jot down, to note; to observe, to notice; (*a ține seama de*) to take into account; *mus* to write down/out || *vr pass* to be put down, etc. • **~bil** *adj/nm* notable • **~re** *nf* putting down, * **nota** • **~bilitate** *nf* notability.
notar [no'tar] *nm* notary; ~ **public** notary public • **~iat** *nn* notary office.
notă ['notă] *nf* (*însemnare scrisă*) note, memo(randum); (*adnotare*) annotation; *pl* notes, commentaries; *mus* note; (*sunet*) sound; *scol* grade; ~ **de comandă** order; ~ **de plată** bill, account.
notes ['notes] *nn* notebook, jotter.
notifica [notifi'ka] *vt* to notify • **~re, ~ție** *nf* notification.
notiță [no'titsă] *nf esp pl* note.
notorietate [notorie'tate] *nf* notoriety, notoriousness.

notoriu [no'toriu] *adj* well-known; (*în sens negativ*) notorious.
noțiune [notsi'une] *nf* notion; idea; concept; *pl* rudiments, ABCs.
nou [nou] *adj* new; (*proaspăt*) fresh; recent; (*un alt*) another, further, additional; (*cel mai recent*) the latest; (*inexistent mai înainte*) novel; (*fără experiență*) inexperienced.
nouă [nouă] *num* nine || *pron* (to) us • **~sprezece** *num* nineteen • **~zeci** *num* ninety; **are ~ de ani** she is ninety years old.
noutate [nou'tate] *nf* novelty; freshness; change, innovation; new book, article, etc; (*știre*) piece of news; information.
novator [nova'tor] *nm* innovator, inventor || *adj* innovating.
novice [no'viche] *adj* (*în*) new (to, in); unpracticed; inexperienced || *nm/nf* inexperienced/unskilled person, (*începător*) beginner; *coll* tyro; greenhorn; (*în perioada de probă*) probationer; (*ucenic*) apprentice; (*în viața monahală*) novice, lay brother/sister.
nu [nu] *adv* not; (*alipit la v. aux. și modale*) don't, hasn't, can't, etc; (*negând altă parte de prop. decât predicatul*) not; (*niciodată*) never; (*nimeni*) nobody; (*nimic*) nothing; (*interjecțional și ca răspuns la întrebări generale*) no.
nuanța [nuan'tsa] *vt* to nuance, to tinge; (*culori*) to gradate; (*prin tonuri de culoare*) to shade, to tone; (*a schimba foarte puțin*) to modulate/vary slightly/subtly; (*personaje etc*) to differentiate subtly; *mus* to modulate • **~re** *nf* nuancing, etc., * **nuanța**; gradation, modulation; subtle differentiation.
nuanță [nu'antsă] *nf* (*a culorii*) also fig nuance, tone, shade; (*culoare*) color; slight/subtle difference; *fig* (*trăsătură particulară*) touch, tinge; *mus* fine shade of feeling; *ling* shade (of meaning), connotation.
nuc [nuk] *nm* (wal)nut (tree); **lemn de ~** walnut (wood), nutwood • **~ă** *nf* nut.
nuclear [nukle'ar] *adj* nuclear; **arme ~e** nuclear weapons/devices; **fizică ~ă** nuclear physics; **reactor ~** nuclear reactor; **reacție ~ă** nuclear reaction.
nucleu [nu'kleu] *nn* also fig nucleus, center, (*miez*) core; (*sâmbure*) kernel; ~ **atomic** *phys* atomic nucleus.
nucșoară [nuk'shoară] *nf* nutmeg.
nucșor [nuk'shor] *nm bot* nutmeg tree.
nud [nud] *adj* (*gol*) also fig naked; (*artă*) nude; (*dezbrăcat*) unclothed; (*d. corp*) bare; (*simplu*) plain; (*curat*) pure || *nn* nude • **~itate** *nf* nudity.
nufăr [nu'făr] *nm bot* (~ *alb*) white water lily, nenuphar; (~ *galben*) yellow water lily; water can.
nuia [nu'ia] *nf* (*rămurea*) twig, switch; (*de salcie*) osier/willow twig.
nul [nul] *adj jur* null; (*fără valoare*) null, of no value, worthless; (*inexistent*) non-existent; (*d. meci*) tie, draw • **~a** ['nula] *nf* zero, naught, cipher; (*într-o cifră*) dummy letter • **~itate** *nf* (*d. cineva*) nonentity, nothing, nought; *jur* nullity.
numai ['numai] *adv* only; (*nimic altceva decât*) but; exclusively, solely; (*nu mai mult decât*) merely; (*pur și simplu*) simply; (*singur*) alone; ~ **așa** for the form's sake; ~ **că** (*cu diferența că*) with the only difference that, (*dar*) but; ~ **dacă** only if, provided.
numaidecât [numaide'kât] *adv* immediately, at once.
număr ['număr] *nn* number; (*cifră*) figure; (*mulțime*) multitude; group; list; (*de ziar etc*) issue; (*la hotel*)

apartment, room; (*la un spectacol*) act, turn; (*la încălțăminte*) size; *text* count; *auto* license; ~ **atomic** *phys* atomic number; ~ **cu soț/par** *math* even number; ~ **de circulație** *auto* registration number; ~ **de loterie** lottery ticket; ~ **fără soț/impar** *math* odd number.

numără [numă'ra] *vt* to count, to compute, to reckon; to enumerate; to consider || *vi* to count || *vr pass* to be counted, etc; *fig* to count.

nume ['nume] *nn also fig* name; (~ *de familie*) last name, family name; *gram* noun, substantive; ~ **bun** good name; (*faimă*) fame, renown.

numeral [nume'ral] *nn gram* numeral, number; ~ **cardinal** cardinal number; ~ **ordinal** ordinal number.

numerar [nume'rar] *nn* current coin; (*bani lichizi*) cash; **în** ~ cash.

numeros [nume'ros] *adj* numerous; (*d. îndatoriri*) manifold; (*variat*) varied, various.

numerota [numero'ta] *vt* to number.

numi [nu'mi] *vt* to name; to call; (*a da un nume*) to give a name to; (*a menționa*) to mention by name; (*a supranumi*) to surname; (*a porecli*) to nickname; (*într-o funcție*) to appoint; *mil* to commission || *vr pass* to be named/called.

numismatică [numis'matika] *nf* numismatics, numismatology.

numitor [numi'tor] *nm math* denominator; ~ **comun** common denominator.

nuntă ['nuntă] *nf* wedding; (*nuntași*) wedding party; (*ceremonia*) wedding festivities; (*petrecerea*) wedding feast; ~ **de argint** silver wedding; ~ **de aur** golden wedding.

nupțial [nuptsi'al] *adj* nuptial, bridal.

nurcă ['nurkă] *nf zool* mink; (*blană*) mink (fur).

nuri ['nuri] *nm pl* sex appeal, looks.

nutreț [nu'trets] *nn* forage, fodder.

nutri [nu'tri] *vt* to feed, to nourish; *fig* (*gânduri*) to harbor; (*speranțe*) to cherish, to entertain || *vr* to eat; (*a se întreține*) to keep oneself.

nutrie ['nutrie] *nf zool* nutria; nutria fur.

nutritiv [nutri'tiv] *adj* nourishing, nutritive; (*privind nutriția*) food.

nuvelă [nu'velă] *nf liter* short story, novelette.

O

o *art indef f* a, an || *pron* her, it || *interj* (*folosită ca invocație*) O!; (*exprimând mirare, bucurie, dorință, groază, mânie*) O!, Oh!, O (dear) me!, O my!.

oac [oak] *interj* croak!

oacheș ['oakesh] *adj* (*brun*) swarthy, dark; (*încercănat*) black-speckled; (*d. animale*) spectacled.

oaie ['oaie] *nf zool* sheep; ewe; (*carne*) mutton; (*blană*) sheepskin, lambskin; *fig pl* flock, sheep.

oală ['oală] *nf* pot, crock; *pl* earthenware; (*conținutul*) pot(ful); *tech* jar, crucible, melting pot.

oară ['oară] *nf* time; **prima** ~ the first time; **ultima** ~ the last time.

oare ['oare] *adv/inter* really?, indeed?, is it?; (*exclamativ*) no!, you don't say so!, indeed!, (now) really!.

oarecare [oare'kare] *adj indef* (*niște*) some; (*anumit*) certain; (*neînsemnat*) little, some; poor, small || *nm* somebody; nobody.

oarecum [oare'kum] *adv* somehow, rather, somewhat.

oaspe(te) ['oaspete] *nm* visitor, guest.

oază ['oază] *nf also fig* oasis.

obârșie [o'bârshie] *nf* (*punct de plecare*) starting point; origin, stock, descent; (*loc de baștină*) native place; (*izvor*) source, spring.

obedient [obedi'ent] *adj* obedient; submissive, gentle, obsequious, servile.

obelisc [obe'lisk] *nn* obelisk.

oberlic(h)t ['oberliht] *nn* transom (window), top/fan light; (*fereastră de subsol*) casement window.

obez [o'bez] *adj* fat, obese • **~itate** *nf* fatness, obesity.

obicei [obi'chei] *nn* (*deprindere*) custom, habit; **de** ~ usually, habitually, generally; **ca de** ~ as usual; **din** ~ out of habit; *pl* (*datină*) customs; usage; *jur obs* common law.

obiect [obi'ekt] *nn* object, thing; (*de studiu*) subject (matter); cause, reason, motive; (*scop*) aim, end; (*marfă*) article, item; *pl* goods; *phil* nonego.

obiecta [obiek'ta] *vt* (*că*) to object (that) || *vi* (*împotriva*) to object (against); *jur* to take exception (to).

obiectiv [obiek'tiv] *nn opt* object glass/lens; *phot* objective; *mil* target; objective (point); (*scop*) object, design || *adj phil* objective; (*artă*) realistic; (*nepărtinitor*) impartial, fair || *adv* impartially, objectively • **~itate** *nf* (*caracter obiectiv*) objectiveness, objectivity; (*imparțialitate*) fairness, impartiality.

obiecți(un)e [obiektsi'une] *nf* objection; *jur* exception.

obișnui [obishnu'i] *vt* (*a deprinde*) (*cu*) to accustom (to), to inure (to) || *vr* (*a se deprinde*) (*cu, să*) to get accustomed (to); (*a se practica*) to be in use, to be customary/habitual • **~nță** *nf* habit, usage; **din** ~ out of (mere) habit • **~t** *adj* usual, habitual, customary; (*comun*) common, ordinary • **~cu/să** used/accustomed (to) || *nm* habitué || *adv* usually, habitually, commonly.

oblădui [oblădu'i] *vt* (*a cârmui*) to rule, to govern, to manage; (*a ocroti*) to protect, to defend || *vi* to rule, to reign.

oblic ['oblik] *adj* (*pieziș*) slanting, sloping, inclined; *geom* oblique || *adv* obliquely, aslant, athwart.

obliga [obli'ga] *vt* (*a sili*) to compel, to oblige; to make, to determine; (*a îndatora*) to make/render indebted || *vr* to oblige/bind oneself, to pledge oneself • **~ție** *nf* (*îndatorire*) indebtedness, obligation; commitment; *jur* (legal) obligation; *jur* contract; *fin* (*obligațiune*) bond • **~tor(iu)** *adj* compulsory, obligatory, binding.

oblon [o'blon] *nn* (window) shutter.

oboi [o'boi] *nn mus* oboe, hautboy.

obol [o'bol] *nn* (*contribuție*) contribution; *relig* offertory; (*modestă*) mite.

obor [o'bor] *nn* (*târg*) cattle fair, stock market; (*ocol*) (cattle) pen, enclosure, stockyard.

oboseală [obo'seală] *nf* tiredness, weariness, fatigue.

obosi [obo'si] *vi* to get tired, to tire, to weary || *vt* to tire out, to weary || *vr* to tire oneself; (*a se deranja*) to take the trouble; (*a face eforturi*) to make efforts • **~tor** *adj* tiresome, wearisome, tiring; (*plicticos*) tedious, irksome.

obraz [o'braz] *nm* cheek, jowl; (*față*) face, countenance; (*îndrăzneală*) cheek(iness), impudence; (*înfățișare*) appearance; aspect; *fig* (*suprafață*) (sur)face.

obraznic [o'braznik] *adj* insolent, brazen(-faced), saucy, impudent; (*neascultător*) naughty, bad, unruly; rebellious || *nm* bold/brazen-faced/saucy fellow || *adv* brazenly, cheekily, boldly.

obrăznicie [obrăzni'chie] *nf* cheek(iness), impudence; *sl* gall; * **obraznic**; (*ca act*) (piece of) impudence, insolence; (*pozna*) blunder, misdeed; (*neastâmpăr*) naughtiness.

obscen [ob'schen] *adj* obscene, filthy, smutty • **~itate** *nf* obscenity, indecency; (*ca act*) dirty joke, broad jest.

obscur [ob'skur] *adj* obscure; (*întunecos*) dark, gloomy; (*nedeslușit*) dim, indistinct; *fig* (*neclar*) confused; *fig* (*necunoscut*) unknown; *fig* (*neînsemnat*) mean, worthless • **~itate** *nf* obscurity; (*întunecime*) dark(ness), murkiness; (*neclaritate*) indistinctness; (*viață modestă*) humble condition, modesty; **a trăi în ~** to lead a(n) obscure/secluded life.

obseda [obse'da] *vt* to haunt, to obsess, to torment.

observa [obser'va] *vt* (*a băga de seamă*) to notice, to observe; to remark, to mention; (*a cerceta*) to examine, to study; (*a privi*) to watch; (*a pândi*) to survey, to keep eyes on ‖ *vr pass* to be noticed; (*pe sine*) to control oneself • **~tor** *nm* (*delegat*) observer, envoy; (*privitor*) onlooker, spectator; (*cercetător*) observer, student; commentator, correspondent ‖ *nn astron* observatory; *mil* observation post, lookout • **~ție** *nf* (*cercetare*) observation; inspection; (*remarcă*) remark; (*constatare*) comment; (*obiecție*) objection; (*dojană*) reprimand, reproof; (*supraveghere*) watching, survey; *med* medical care.

obsesie [ob'sesie] *nf* obsession; *med* fixed idea, (mono)mania.

obstacol [ob'stakol] *nn* (*piedică*) also *sp* obstacle, impediment.

obstetrică [obs'tetrikă] *nf med* obstetrics, tocology.

obstrucție [ob'struktsie] *nf* obstruction, opposition; (*în parlament*) filibuster(ing).

obstrucționa [obstrultsio'na] *vt* to obstruct.

obște ['obshte] *nf* (*colectivitate*) community, mass, people; (*consiliu*) council, board, assembly; *hist* commune.

obtuz [ob'tuz] *adj geom* obtuse; *fig* dull, stupid, dense.

obține [ob'tsine] *vt* to get, to obtain; (*a dobândi*) to acquire; to secure ‖ *vr pass* to be obtained, etc.

obuz [o'buz] *nn mil* shell.

ocară [o'kară] *nf* abuse, insult, outrage; (*rușine*) shame.

ocazie [o'kazie] *nf* (*prilej*) opportunity, occasion, juncture; (*împrejurare*) circumstance.

ocazional [okazio'nal] *adj* occasional, incidental, accidental ‖ *adv* occasionally.

ocărî [okă'rî] *vt* (*a certa*) to upbraid, to reproach; to abuse, to insult; (*a vorbi de rău*) to speak ill of, to censure ‖ *vi* to rail, to inveigle, to curse.

occident [okchi'dent] *nn* West • **~al** *adj* west(ern); **puterile ~e** Western Powers ‖ *nm* Western(er).

ocean [o'chean] *nn* ocean; *fig* sea, flood.

ochean [o'kean] *nn* spy glass, telescope, field glass.

ochelari [oke'lari] *nn pl* glasses, spectacles; (*de soare*) sunglasses; (*de protecție*) goggles; (*de cal*) blinkers, blinders; *fig* narrow-mindedness, parochialism.

ochi[1] ['oki] *nm* eye; *coll* light; *pl* (*văz*) (eye)sight; *pl* (*priviri*) looks, glances; *pl* (*față*) face, cheek; (*mugur de cartof*) leafbud; (*la zaruri, domino*) pip, spot; **~ căprui** hazel/brown eyes; **din ~** at a glance, approximately; **între patru ~** between you and me ‖ *nn* (*de geam*) glass pane; bull's-eye; (*ferestruică la pod*) garret/dormer window; (*luminiș*) glade, clearing; (*de baltă*) pool; (*bulboană*) whirlpool; (*laț*) loop, noose;

(*verigă, za*) ring, link; (*de aragaz*) burner; *pl* (*ouă*) fried eggs; (*românești*) poached eggs; (*pată pe coada păunului*) spot; (*grăsime în supă*) speck of grease; (*de cer*) clear spot ‖ *adv* (*plin*) ~ brimful, full to the brim.

ochi[2] [o'ki] *vi* (*a duce arma la ochi*) to (take) aim; (*a ținti*) (*în*) to (take) aim (at), to level one's gun (at), to train a gun on smb ‖ *vt* to take aim at; to shoot at; (*a nimeri*) to shoot (down); (*a fixa cu privirea*) to watch, to stare at; (*a remarca*) to notice, to single out; (*a râvni la*) to covet, to set one's heart on; (*a căuta*) to be in search of; (*a privi lung*) to look intently at; (*a zări*) to perceive, to catch sight of; to eye suspiciously, to suspect.

ocnaș [ok'nash] *nm* convict, jailbird.

ocnă ['oknă] *nf* (*salină*) salt-mine/-pit, saline; (*temniță*) salt works; convict prison; *fig* hard labor; forced labor; *sl* (*glumă*) side-splitter, wisecrack; *sl* (*persoană*) wag.

ocol [o'kol] *nn* (*înconjur*) detour, round-about way; (*circumferință*) circumference; (*cuprins*) space; (*cotitură*) turn, turning (point); (*îngrăditură*) enclosure; (*împrejurimi*) surrounding(s); (*de vite*) cattle pen, stockyard; (*curte*) (court)yard, grounds; *obs* district, ward; **fără ~** straight, *fig* straightforwardly; circuit • **~ul pământului** the tour of the world; • **~i** *vi* to take a roundabout way, to make a detour; to wander, to ramble ‖ *vt* (*a înconjura*) to round; *naut* to circumnavigate; *fig* to avoid, to shun, to sidestep; (*a împrejmui*) to enclose, to pen ‖ *vr recip* to avoid/shun each other.

ocroti [okro'ti] *vt* (*a apăra*) to protect, to safeguard, to shield; (*a adăposti*) to shelter • **~re** *nf* (*apărare*) protection, (safe)guard(ing), defense; (*adăpost*) shelter, asylum.

ocru ['okru] *nn* ochre.

octavă [ok'tavă] *nf mus* octave.

octombrie [ok'tombrie] *nm* October.

ocular [oku'lar] *adj* ocular, visual, eye; **martor ~** eye-witness ‖ *nn* eyeglass, eyepiece.

oculist [oku'list] *adj* oculistic ‖ *nm* eye doctor, oculist, ophthalmologist

ocult [o'kult] *adj* occult, secret, hidden; supernatural, mystic; (*inaccesibil*) recondite, abstruse, mysterious.

ocupa [oku'pa] *vt* (*a cuceri*) to conquer, to seize, to occupy; (*a umple*) to fill, to take up; (*mintea*) to absorb, to fill; (*a întrebuința*) to engage; (*a locui în*) to reside/live in; (*a reține*) to book; (*a lua în stăpânire*) to take possession of ‖ *vr* (*a se îndeletnici cu*) to do; to busy/occupy oneself (with); **a se ~ de** to take care of, to look after; (*d. un autor*) to deal with.

ocupant [oku'pant] *nm* occupant, invader ‖ *adj* occupying, invading.

ocupați(un)e [oku'patsi'une] *nf* (*îndeletnicire*) occupation; (*muncă*) work, pursuit; (*profesie*) profession; (*meserie*) trade; (*activitate*) activity; (*slujbă*) position, job, employment; (*stăpânire*) occupation, occupancy, holding.

odaie [o'daie] *nf* room.

odată [o'dată] *adv* (*cândva în trecut*) once, at one time, in the old days; (*într-o zi*) one day; (*simultan*) at the same time as, all at once; (*în viitor*) some day/time; (*brusc*) suddenly, all of a sudden; (*imediat*) at once, immediately, in a jiffy; (*în sfârșit*) finally, after all;

a fost ~ ca niciodata once upon a time; ~ și ~ in the end, eventually, at last.
odă ['odă] *nf* ode.
odgon [od'gon] *nn* cable, rope.
odihnă [o'dihnă] *nf (repaus)* rest, repose; *(răgaz)* leisure; *(pauză)* pause, intermission; *(tihnă)* calm, peace, ease; *fig (moarte)* eternal/everlasting rest, quietus; *(palier)* landing/resting place; **fără ~** *adj* restless, active ‖ *adv* restlessly; *(neobosit)* tirelessly, untiringly; *(neîncetat)* incessantly.
odihni [odih'ni] *vt* to rest, to give rest to ‖ *vr/vi* to rest, to repose, to relax; *(a dormi)* to sleep, to be asleep; *(a zăcea)* to lie; *(a se potoli)* to quiet down; *(d. lucruri: a sta)* to lie, to rest, to stand; **odihnească-se-n pace** *fig* may his soul rest in peace.
odinioară [odini'oară] *adv* formerly, once, in the old days.
odios [odi'os] *adj* hateful, loathsome, repulsive.
odisee [odi'see] *nf* odyssey, long adventurous journey.
odor [o'dor] *nn (giuvaer)* jewel, treasure, gem; *fig* precious, darling, dear; *pl relig* ecclesiastical objects and sacerdotal attire.
odraslă [o'draslă] *nf (copil)* child, issue, progeny, *(vlăstar)* offspring, scion, *(urmaș)* descendant.
of [of] *interj* oh!, ah!, alack!, oh dear!, dear me! ‖ *nn (oftat)* sigh, groan, moan; *(durere)* grief, sorrow, complaint.
ofensa [o'fensa] *vt* to offend, to insult; *(a jigni)* to wound, to hurt ‖ *vr* to take offense, to be hurt.
ofensă [o'fensă] *nf* offense, insult, abuse.
ofensivă [ofen'sivă] *nf (atac)* also *fig* offensive, attack, onslaught, *(agresiune)* aggression, raid.
oferi [ofe'ri] *vt (a da)* to offer (up), to present; *(a pune în vânzare)* to put up for sale; *(a plăti)* to tender; *fig* to present, to show ‖ *vr (să)* to offer (oneself to); *(d. ocazii)* to offer/present itself.
ofertă [o'fertă] *nf (propunere)* offer, proposal; *(de mărfuri)* supply; **cerere și ~** supply and demand.
oficia [ofici'a] *vt relig* to celebrate, to perform; *(a celebra)* to solemnize ‖ *vi relig* to celebrate, to say mass.
oficial [ofichi'al] *adj* official; government(al); state; authoritative; *(d. documente)* formal; *(d. discuții)* on the record; legal, authorized; formal, ceremonial ‖ *adv* officially; legally; on the record; *(distant)* stiffly, coldly, formally • **~itate** *nf* official person; *pl* official-dom, authorities.
oficiu [o'fichu] *nn (birou)* office, agency; *(cameră)* pantry; *(îndatorire)* duty; *(slujbă)* position, job; *(funcție)* function; *esp pl (ajutor)* service, assistance • **din ~** *adj* ex officio, official ‖ *adv* ex officio, officially.
ofili [ofi'li] *vt* to wither, to parch; *(a moleși)* to enervate ‖ *vr also fig* (a-și pierde frumusețea) to fade (away); *(a se usca)* to wilt; *(d. plante: a-și lăsa frunzele în jos)* to droop; *(a muri)* to die; to perish; *(a păli)* to lose color, to blanch, to turn/grow pale.
ofițer [ofi'tser] *nm mil* officer; **~ activ** officer in/on active service; *(ordonanță la un grad militar înalt)* orderly officer; *(mai înalt în grad)* senior officer; *(funcționar)* public officer, official; **~ al stării civile** registrar (of births, marriages, and deaths).
ofrandă [o'frandă] *nf (jertfă)* offer(ing), sacrifice; *(dar)* donation, gift; *(prinos)* homage; *(pomană)* (works of) charity, alms.

ofsaid ['ofsaid] *nn sp* offside.
ofta [of'ta] *vi* to sigh (out), to sob; *fig* to moan; **a ~ după** to sigh/yearn for • **~t** *nn* sigh(ing), moan, sob; *fig* wail, lament, complaint.
oftalmolog [oftalmo'log] *nm med* ophthalmologist, eye doctor, occulist.
oftică ['oftika] *nf* tuberculosis, *coll* consumption; *(ciudă)* spite, grudge, fury.
ofticos [ofti'kos] *adj* consumptive, wasted; *fig (d. oameni)* lean, lank; *coll* rawboned; *(d. lucruri)* poor, scanty; *coll* ramshackle; dry ‖ *nm* consumptive/phthisical person/patient.
ogar [o'gar] *nm zool* greyhound, borzoi.
oglindă [o'glindă] *nf* (looking)glass, mirror; speculum; *(imagine)* image, mirror reflection; *(suprafață lucioasă)* smooth surface.
oglindi [oglin'di] *vt* to mirror, to reflect; to present, to describe ‖ *vr pass* to be reflected/mirrored; *pass fig* to be echoed/mirrored/reflected; *(a se privi în oglindă)* to look at oneself in a glass/mirror.
ogor [o'gor] *nn (țarină)* (plowed) field; *(teren agricol)* land; *(pământ nedesțelenit)* fallow land/field/soil; *(arătură)* early plowing.
ogradă [o'gradă] *nf (curte)* court(yard), yard, grounds.
oho [o'ho] *interj* oh!, ah!, dear me!.
oiște ['oishte] *nf (la căruță)* shaft, pole, beam; *(la moară)* main post.
olan [o'lan] *nn* hallow/gutter tile.
olandez [olan'dez] *adj* Dutch ‖ *nm* Dutchman, Hollander, Netherlander • **~ii** *nm pl* the Dutch • **~ă** *nf* Dutchwoman; Dutch girl; Dutch, the Dutch language.
olar [o'lar] *nm (meseriaș)* potter.
olărie [olă'rie] *nf (ca meșteșug)* pottery; *(ca atelier)* pottery (shed); *(ca marfă)* pots, ceramics.
olfactiv [olfak'tiv] *adj anat, physiol* olfactory, olfactive.
oligarhie [oligar'hie] *nf also fig* oligarchy; **~ financiară** financial oligarchy.
olimpiadă [olimpi'adă] *nf sp* Olympiad, the Olympic games; *hist* Olympiad.
olimpic [o'limpik] *adj hist sp* Olympic; **Jocuri ~e** Olympic Games ‖ *adv* majestically, with a dignified air.
oliță [o'litsă] *nf sl* potty.
olog [o'log] *adj (de un picior)* one-legged; *(de două picioare)* legless; *(șchiop)* also *fig* lame; *(infirm)* crippled; unsatisfactory; imperfect; *bot* without tendrils ‖ *nm* one-legged person; legless person; lame person, cripple; *coll* duck.
om [om] *nm* man, *pl* men; human being; *(persoană)* person, individual; *(suflet)* soul; *(cineva)* one, somebody; *(muritor)* mortal; *(ființă rațională)* rational being; *(cu calități deosebite)* real man, good fellow; grown up, adult; *(bărbat)* male, spouse, *(soț)* husband; *(muncitor)* workman; hand, laborer; *mil* soldier; *pl (oameni)* people; they; **~ de afaceri** businessman; **~ de litere** man of letters, author, writer; **~ de lume** man of the world; **~ de nimic** ne'er-do-well, good-for-nothing (fellow); **~ de onoare** honorable man; **~ de paie** dummy, man of straw; **~ de rând** ordinary/average man; **~ de stat** statesman; **~ de succes** a successful man; **~ de știință** scientist, man of science • **~ul** *(generic: umanitatea)* man, the human race, mankind.
omagia [omadji'a] *vt* to do/pay/render homage (to).

omagiu [o'madju] *nn* homage; *pl* respects, regards; (*prinos*) gift; *hist* homage, act of fealty.

ombilic [ombi'lik] *nn anat* navel; umbilical cord.

omenesc [ome'nesk] *adj* (*uman*) human(-like); (*obişnuit*) common, usual, ordinary; (*cum se cuvine*) decent, proper; correct; intelligible; (*citeţ*) legible || *nn* (*caracterul uman*) human character/essence.

omeneşte [ome'neshte] *adv* (*după puterile omului*) humanly, as much as lies in man's power; (*cum se cuvine*) decently, properly.

omeni [ome'ni] *vt* (*a primi bine*) to entertain/receive hospitably; to welcome; (*a ospăta*) to treat, to feed; (*a trata cu băutură*) to pay for a drink; (*a onora*) to honor, to revere || *vr* to eat, to help oneself to food.

omenire [ome'nire] *nf* (*umanitate*) humanity, mankind; (*mulţime*) multitude, mob.

omidă [o'midă] *nf ento* caterpillar; *fig* blood-sucker, leech, extortioner.

omisiune [omisi'une] *nf* omission, oversight; (*lipsă*) lack, flaw, deficiency.

omite [o'mite] *vt* to omit, to skip (over), to leave out, to leave undone.

omletă [om'letă] *nf* omlette.

omnibuz [omni'buz] *nn* (omni)bus.

omniprezent [omnipre'zent] *adj* ubiquitous.

omogen [omo'djen] *adj* homogeneous; unitary, equal.

omologa [omolo'ga] *vt* to ratify, to approve; (*a recunoaşte*) to confirm, to acknowledge || *vr pass* to be ratified, etc.

omonim [omo'nim] *adj ling* homonymous || *nn/nm ling* homonym || *nm* namesake, homonym(ous person).

omoplat [omo'plat] *nm anat* shoulder blade/bone, scapula.

omor [o'mor] *nn* murder, manslaughter, homicide; (*măcel*) massacre, carnage; ~ **cu premeditare** willful/premeditated murder • **~î** *vt* (*a ucide*) to kill, to murder, to slay; (*a masacra*) to slaughter, to butcher; *fig* (*a distruge*) to destroy, to put out; *fig* (*a chinui*) to torture, to torment; *fig* (*a istovi*) to tire to death, to exhaust; *fig* (*a plictisi*) to bore to death || *vr* (*a se sinucide*) to kill oneself, to commit suicide; (*a se istovi*) to ruin/destroy one's health || *vi* to be killing/destructive.

omucidere [omu'chidere] *nf* manslaughter, murder.

omuşor [omu'shor] *nm* man(n)ikin, dwarf; *anat* uvula.

onanism [ona'nism] *nn med* self-abuse; masturbation.

oncologie [onkolo'djie] *nf med* oncology.

onctuos [onktu'os] *adj chem*, *fig* unctuous, greasy, oily || *adv* unctuously.

ondula [ondu'la] *vi* (*a se undui*) to undulate, to wave; (*a şerpui*) to wind || *vt* (*a bucla*) to wave, to curl; *metal* to corrugate • **~ţie** *nf phys* undulation; (*buclă*) wave, curl; *geog* unevenness; accident.

onest [o'nest] *adj* honest, honorable, upright • **~itate** *nf* honesty, integrity, probity.

onoare [o'noare] *nf* (*cinste*) honor, integrity, probity; (*prestigiu*) reputation, repute; (*mândrie*) pride; (*stimă*) esteem; (*favoare*) favor, distinction; glory; boast.

onomastică [ono'mastikă] *nf* name day; *ling* onomastics.

onomatopee [onomato'pee] *nf* onomatopoeia, echoism; echo-word.

onor [o'nor] *nn pl* honors, homage; *mil* salute || *interj* to the colors! • **~a** *vt* to respect, to honor, to revere; (*a plăti*) to pay; (*a fi o cinste pentru*) to be an honor,

to do credit to || *vr recip* to honor/respect/revere each other; (*pe sine*) to honor oneself; to win honor and respect • **~bil** *adj* honorable, worthy; (*cinstit*) honest, upright; (*merituos*) creditable || *adv* honorably, honestly, creditably || *nm* honorable person/citizen • **~ariu** *nn* fee, honorarium • **~ific** *adj* honorary.

opac [o'pak] *adj* opaque, impervious to light; (*întunecat*) dark, obscure; *fig* dense, stupid, obtuse.

opări [opă'ri] *vt* to scald; to soak in boiling water; (*a fierbe*) to boil || *vr pass* to be scalded, etc; (*a face o iritaţie*) to develop diaper rash.

opera [ope'ra] *vt* (*a face*) to do, to make; to perform; *mil* to operate; (*a manipula*) to manage, to manipulate; *med* to operate upon, to perform an operation; to produce, to effect, to bring about; (*a comite*) to commit || *vr pass* (*d. ceva*) to be effected/operated; (*d. cineva*) to undergo an operation || *vi* (*a acţiona*) to work, to operate; *med* to operate, to perform an operation; *coll* (*d. hoţi*) to be busy, to work at it.

operativ [opera'tiv] *adj* operative, effective, quick || *adv* operatively, etc. • **~itate** *nf* efficiency, efficacy, promptness.

operator [opera'tor] *nm* operator; driver; *cin* cameraman; *med* surgeon.

operaţie [ope'ratsie] *nf* (*lucrare*) also *med*, *mil* operation; work, action; *math* arithmetical operation; *fin* financial operation, transaction; (*calcul*) calculation.

operă ['operă] *nf* (*acţiune*) work, deed, action; (*lucrare*) literary/artistic/musical production; *pl* works; (*creaţie*) creation; *mus* opera; ~ **bufă** opera buff; ~ **comică** comic opera; (*teatru de operă*) opera house.

operetă [ope'retă] *nf mus* musical comedy.

opinie [o'pinie] *nf* opinion, idea, view; notion; statement, judgment; sentiment, feeling.

opinti [opin'ti] *vt* to heave, to lift; *fig* to stimulate, to encourage; to urge, to drive || *vr* (*a face un efort*) to exert/strain oneself; *recip* to heave/lift each other.

opiu ['opiu] *nn* opium.

oploşi [oplo'shi] *vt* (*a adăposti*) to shelter, to house; (*a ocroti*) to protect, to shield; to favor || *vr* to find/take refuge/shelter; *fig* to worm one's way (to).

oponent [opo'nent] *nm* opponent, adversary, antagonist.

oportun [opor'tun] *adj* timely, opportune, convenient • **~itate** *nf* opportuneness; timeliness; advisability, desirability • **~ist** *adj* time-serving, opportunistic || *nm* time-server, opportunist.

opozant [opo'zant] *nm* opponent, adversary; *pol* member of the opposition.

opoziţie [opo'zitsie] *nf* opposition; antithesis; (*piedică*) obstacle, impediment; (*împotrivire*) resistance.

oprelişte [o'prelishte] *nf* prohibition, interdiction; (*piedică*) obstacle, stumbling block.

opresiune [opresi'une] *nf* oppression; tyranny.

opri [o'pri] *vt* to stop, to halt; (*mai ales treptat*) to check; (*mişcarea, înaintarea, răspândirea*) to arrest; (*a înceta*) to cease; (*a pune capăt*) to end; (*a împiedica*) to hinder; (*a înfrâna*) to curb; (*a păstra, a reţine*) to withhold; (*locuri*) to book; (*a interzice*) to prohibit; (*a nu îngădui*) not to allow/permit || *vr* (*a sta pe loc*) to stop, to halt; (*a înceta*) to cease; to come to a(n) end/halt; to pause; (*a vânt*) to subside; (*a se reţine*) to abstain; to dwell/insist (up)on || *vi* to stop, to halt, to come to a stop.

oprima [opri'ma] *vt* to oppress, to grind/crush/bear down; (*a exploata*) to exploit.

oprire [o'prire] *nf* stopping, * **oprit**; stop, halt, pause; (*încetare*) cease; (*capăt*) end; (*haltă*) station; (*interzicere*) prohibition, ceaselessly; (*haltă*) station; (*interzicere*) prohibition, ban.

oprit [o'prit] *adj* forbidden, prohibited, banned; **fumatul** ~ no smoking; **intrarea** ~**ă** private, no admittance; **parcarea** ~**ă** no parking.

oprobriu [o'probriu] *nn* scorn, contempt.

opt [opt] *num* eight || *nn sp* figure eight, eight curve • ~**sprezece** eighteen • ~**zeci** eighty.

opta [op'ta] *vi* to choose, to make one's choice, to opt.

optic ['optik] *adj* optic(al); **nerv** ~ *anat* optic nerve • ~**ă** *nf phys* optics; perspective, view; (*viziune*) concept(ion), outlook, angle • ~**ian** [optichi'an] *nm* optician.

optim ['optim] *adj* optimum, most favorable, best • ~**ism** *nn* optimism • ~**ist** *adj* optimistic, sanguine || *nm* optimist.

opţiune [optsi'une] *nf* option, choice, (liberty/freedom of) choosing.

opune [o'pune] *vt* to oppose (to), to set off; to compare (with/to); (*a aduce argumente împotriva*) to put up || *vr* (*a ţine piept*) to oppose, to withstand; *fig* to object (to), to make/raise an objection(to); *geom* to be opposed (to).

opus [o'pus] *adj* opposite (to/from), contrary (to); (*faţă în faţă*) opposite to; facing smb/smth || *nm* opposite, contrary, antagonist.

or [or] *conj* (*dar*) but; (*sau*) or.

oracol [o'rakol] *nn* oracle.

oral [o'ral] *adj* (*referitor la gură*) oral; (*prin viu grai*) oral, viva voce; verbal, oral; (*d. examene*) viva voce || *adv* orally, viva voce, by word of mouth || *nn* viva voce, oral (examination).

oranj [o'ranzh] *adj* orange(-colored) || *nn* orange • ~**adă** *nf* orange juice.

orar [o'rar] *adj* hour; of hours || *nn* (*program*) timetable, schedule; (*ac de ceas*) hour hand.

oraş [o'rash] *nn* town, city; (*orăşenii*) townspeople, townsfolk.

orator [ora'tor] *nm* orator, public speaker.

oră ['ora] *nf* hour; **cât e ora?/ce** ~ **e?** what's the time?, what time is it?; class, lesson.

orăcăi [orăkă'i] *vi* (*d. broască*) to croak; *pej* (*d. copii*) to cry, to whine, to squeal.

orăşean [oră'shean] *nm* townsman, town/city dweller; *pl* townspeople, townsfolk • ~**că** *nf* townswoman.

orătănii [oră'tănii] *nf pl* fowls, poultry.

orândui [orându'i] *vt* (*a aranja*) to arrange, to set; to set in order; to classify; to organize; (*a hotărî*) to decide; (*a îndruma*) to direct; (*a numi*) to appoint || *vr pass* to be arranged, etc; (*a se aranja*) to arrange (oneself) • ~**re** *nf* social system/order; (*grupare*) arrangement; setting in order; (*organizare*) organization; (*stabilire*) assessment.

orb [orb] *adj* (*fără vedere*) blind, sightless; *fig* (*întunecos*) dim, black, dark; *fig* (*iraţional*) blind(folded), thoughtless, reckless; *fig* ignorant; *fig* violent, mad, crazy; *fig* (*nemărginit*) boundless, colossal • ~**ecăi** *vi* to grope, to feel one's way (about); (*a bâjbâi*) to grope/poke/fumble (about) • ~**i** *vi* to become blind || *vt* (*a lua vederea*) to blind; to put out smb's eyes; *fig* (*a lua ochii*) to dazzle, to bewilder; *fig* (*a lua minţile*) to deprive of judgment; *fig* (*a înşela*) to deceive, to blind(fold).

orbită [or'bită] *nf astron, anat* orbit; *fig* range, sphere, scope; *anat* eye socket.

orbitor [orbi'tor] *adj* dazzling || *adv* dazzlingly.

orchestra [orkes'tra] *vt mus* to orchestrate, to score.

orchestră [or'kestră] *nf* orchestra; (*mică*) band; (*în teatru*) orchestra (seats).

ordin ['ordin] *nn* (*poruncă*) *also mil* order, command; (*scris*) written disposition; (*decoraţie*) order; *bot, zool, archit, math* order; category, class; (*tip*) type; *fin* check.

ordinar [ordi'nar] *adj* (*obişnuit*) ordinary, regular, common, usual; frequent; (*de rând*) commonplace, trivial; of little merit; (*grosolan*) coarse, vulgar; caddish, boorish.

ordinator [ordina'tor] *nn* computer.

ordine ['ordine] *nf* order, succession; (*rânduială*) tidiness; (*linişte*) discipline, quietness; (*lege*) rule, regulation; (*orânduire*) system, regime; *mil* disposition of troops.

ordona [ordo'na] *vt* (*a porunci*) to order, to command; to prescribe; to direct; (*a rândui*) to put/set in order || *vi* to command • ~**nţă** *nf* (*dispoziţie*) order, command; *jur* statute, ruling; *fin* order; (*reţetă*) prescription || *nf mil obs* orderly.

oreion [ore'ion] *nn med* mumps, paroti(di)tis.

orez [o'rez] *nn bot* rice.

orfan [or'fan] *adj* orphan; motherless; fatherless; bereaved of parents || *nm* orphan, motherless/fatherless child.

orfelinat [orfeli'nat] *nn obs* orphanage, orphan asylum.

organ [or'gan] *nn anat* organ; *tech* mechanism, device; *fig* (*exponent*) mouthpiece, spokesman; (*ziar*) journal; (*mijloc de comunicare*) agency, medium/means of communication; (*autoritate*) body, authority; ~ **legislativ** legislative body || ~**ic** *adj* organic, structural; vital, fundamental || *adv* organically.

organism [orga'nism] *nn bio* organism, body, being; *fig* whole, organical structure.

organiza [organi'za] *vt* (*a pune în ordine*) to organize, to arrange; (*a înfiinţa*) to set up; (*a înjgheba*) to build up || *vr pass* to be organized, etc; to organize (oneself), to put some order in one's affairs • ~**tor** *adj* organizing || *nm* organizer • ~**toric** *adj* organizational, organizing • ~**ţie** *nf* organization, society, body; structure, make-up, constitution.

orgasm [or'gasm] *nn physiol* orgasm.

orgă ['orgă] *nf mus* organ.

orgie [or'djie] *nf* orgy, revel(ry), debauch(ery).

orgolios [orgoli'os] *adj* vainglorious, (*trufaş*) haughty, (*încrezut*) conceited, self-important; (*mândru*) proud.

orgoliu [or'goliu] *nn* vainglory, self-pride, (*trufie*) haughtiness, (*înfumurare*) self-importance; (*mândrie*) pride.

orhidee [orhi'dee] *nf bot* orchid, orchis; *pl* orchidaceae.

ori ['ori] *conj* (*sau*) or.

oribil [o'ribil] *adj* horrible, horrid, hideous || *adv* horribly, hideously.

oricare [ori'kare] *pron indef* any; (*oricine*) anyone, anybody || *adj indef* any.

oricând [ori'kând] *adv* (*în orice moment*) at any time, no matter when, at all times; (*mereu*) always, ever || *conj* (*ori de câte ori*) whenever.

oricât [ori'kât] *adv* as much as one likes/says; *coll* the sky's the limit; as long as one likes/can; * **oricum**;

~ de however, no matter how ‖ *conj* however much, no matter how much.

orice [ori'che] *pron indef* anything ‖ *adj indef* any.

oricine [ori'chine] *pron indef* (*oricare*) anybody, anyone; (*acela care*) whoever.

oricum [ori'kum] *adv* (*în orice fel*) anyhow, no matter how, in any way; (*în orice caz*) in any case, anyway; (*totuşi*) for all that, still, nevertheless.

orient [ori'ent] *nn* (*punct cardinal*) East; **Orientul Apropiat** the Near East; **Orientul Mijlociu** the Middle East; **Extremul Orient** the Far East.

orienta [orien'ta] *vt* to orient(ate); (*a îndruma*) to direct; to show smb the way ‖ *vr* to find one's whereabouts, to find one's way about; *fig* (*după*) to be guided (by), to take one's cue (from).

oriental [orien'tal] *adj/nm* Eastern, oriental, Levantine.

orificiu [ori'fichu] *nn* orifice, aperture, vent.

original [oridji'nal] *adj* original, firsthand; (*de la origine*) innate; authentic, genuine, true; (*unic*) unique; (*nou*) new-fangled, initial; inventive, creative; eccentric ‖ *nn* original, first/top copy; model ‖ *nm* eccentric person, *coll* quite a character.

originar [oridji'nar] *adj* (*de baştină*) (*din*) native (of); (*de la naştere*) original, innate; initial, primary.

origine [o'ridjine] *nf* origin, source, spring; (*neam*) birth, descent; (*cauză*) cause, starting point; etymology; **la ~** originally, at the beginning;.

orişicum [orishi'kum] *adv* * **oricum.**

ori(şi)unde [orishi'unde] *adv* anywhere, no matter where ‖ *conj* wherever.

orizont [ori'zont] *nn* (*ca linie*) horizon, skyline; (*zare*) sky; distance; *fig* extent, sphere, scope; mental outlook; (*atmosferă*) atmosphere; **min** level • **~al** *adj* horizontal, plane, level ‖ *adv* horizontally; (*la cuvinte încrucişate*) across.

orna [or'na] *vt* (*a împodobi*) to adorn, to ornament, to deck • **~ment** *nn* decorative pattern/design, ornament; *mus* ornament; **ca ~** by way of ornament • **~menta** *vt* to ornament, to adorn, to decorate.

ornitologie [ornitolo'djie] *nf* ornithology.

oroare [o'roare] *nf* (*sentiment*) horror, aversion; (*lucru oribil*) horrible thing, eyesore.

orologiu [oro'lodjiu] *nn* timepiece, clock.

oropsit [orop'sit] *adj* (*prigonit*) persecuted; (*asuprit*) oppressed; (*chinuit*) tormented; (*nenorocit*) unfortunate; (*părăsit*) forsaken; (*d. copii*) orphan; (*fără adăpost*) homeless.

ortac [or'tak] *nm* bud(die), fellow, chum.

ortodox [orto'doks] *adj relig* orthodox, Eastern; *fig* approved, established; conventional ‖ *nm relig* member of the orthodox/Eastern Church.

ortografie [ortogra'fie] *nf* spelling, orthography.

ortopedie [ortope'die] *nf med* orthopedics.

orz [orz] *nm bot* barley; (*ca aliment*) barley(-corn); (*lan*) barley field.

os [os] *nn anat* bone; *pl* (*oseminte*) bones; (*trup*) body.

osândă [o'sândă] *nf* (*condamnare*) condemnation, sentence; (*pedeapsă*) punishment; *fig* doom; *fig* misfortune, catastrophe.

osândi [osân'di] *vt* (*a condamna*) to sentence, to convict; (*a pedepsi*) to punish; *fig* to doom; (*a judeca*) to judge; (*a învinui*) to blame; (*a sili*) to force, to coerce.

osânză [o'sânză] *nf* lard; *fig coll* (*bani*) fat, grease; *coll* (*bunăstare*) well-being, welfare, ease; (*mijloace*) means.

oscila [oschi'la] *vi* to oscillate, to swing; *fig* (*a şovăi*) to hesitate, to waver, to (dilly-)dally.

oseminte [ose'minte] *nn pl lit, obs* bones.

osie ['osie] *nf* axle (tree), spindle; **~ cuplată** *rail* couple axe.

osificat [osifi'kat] *adj* ossified; *fig* (*scheletic*) rawboned.

osmoză [os'moză] *nf* osmosis, osmose.

osos [o'sos] *adj* osseous, bony; (*ciolănos*) big-boned; (*slab*) raw-boned, gaunt.

ospăta [ospă'ta] *vt* (*a primi*) to receive hospitably, to entertain smb as a guest; (*a trata*) to treat, to feed ‖ *vr* to have a treat; to feast, to regale ‖ *vi* to eat, to take a meal • **~r** *nm* waiter.

ospăț [os'păts] *nn* banquet, feast; *coll* spread; (*mâncare*) meal, repast.

ospiciu [os'pichiu] *nn pej sl* (*lunatic*) asylum, madhouse.

ospitalier [ospitali'er] *adj* hospitable.

ospitalitate [ospitali'tate] *nf* hospitality, hospitableness.

ostaş [os'tash] *nm mil* soldier, warrior, trooper; man; *mil* (*grad*) private; *fig* militant, champion.

ostatic [os'tatik] *nm* hostage.

osteneală [oste'neală] *nf* (*oboseală*) lassitude, weariness; exhaustion, tiredness; effort, trouble, exertion; **nu merită osteneala** it isn't worthwhile.

osteni [oste'ni] *vt* to tire out, to weary ‖ *vr* (*a se strădui*) to take great pains/trouble, to put oneself out ‖ *vi* (*a obosi*) to grow/get tired/weary, to weary; (*a-şi da osteneala*) to take great pains, to put oneself out; (*a munci*) to toil.

ostentativ [ostenta'tiv] *adj* ostentatious ‖ *adv* ostentatiously; for show.

ostentație [osten'tatsie] *nf* ostentation; show, display; **cu ~** ostentatiously.

osteoporoză [osteopo'roză] *nf med* osteoporosis.

ostil [os'til] *adj* hostile, inimical ‖ *adv* hostilely, inimically • **~itate** *nf* hostility, enmity; **cu ~** hostilely; *pl, fig* hostilities, warfare.

ostraciza [ostrachi'za] *vt* to ostracize, to expel, to banish.

ostrov ['ostrov] *nn* (*insulă*) island; (*mică*) isle(t); *fig* (*de iarbă*) patch; oasis; (*prag*) bank.

osuar [osu'ar] *nn* ossuary, charnel house, bone urn.

oştire [osh'tire] *nf* army; *fig* multitude, host.

otavă [o'tavă] *nf* aftermath.

otită [o'tită] *nf med* otitis.

otravă [o'travă] *nf also fig* poison, bane; (*venin*) venom, bitterness; *fig* (*doctrină primejdioasă*) baneful doctrine.

otrăvi [otră'vi] *vt* (*a omorî*) to poison; (*a pune otravă în*) to infect; *fig* (*a învenina*) to embitter, to envenom; *fig* to corrupt, to pervert ‖ *vr pass* to be poisoned, etc; to poison oneself; *fig* to embitter one's life • **~tor** *adj* poisonous, venomous; noxious; corrupting; mortal, fatal, killing, lethal ‖ *nm* poisoner.

otreapă [o'treapă] *nf* (*cârpă*) rag, shred; *fig* (*om de nimic*) ne'er-do-well; characterless/spineless person.

oțel [o'tsel] *nn* steel; **de ~** steely, (as) hard as steel; (*din ~*) of steel; (*culoarea oțelului*) grey/colored, steelgray; *fig* steely, inflexible • **~ărie** *nf* mill • **~i** *vt* (*a căli*) *also fig* to steel, to temper; (*a cimenta*) to harden, to reinforce; *fig* (*a întări*) to fortify, to strengthen ‖ *vr pass* to be steeled, etc; *fig* to be(come) steeled/tempered, to steel oneself.

oțet [o'tset] *nn* vinegar • **~i** *vr* to turn sour, to acetify.

ou [ou] *nn* orn, icht, ento egg; bot ovum, germ cell; (*obiect ovoid*) egg(-shaped); *vernac* ball • **~a** *vt/vi/vr* to lay eggs.

oval [o'val] *adj* oval, egg-shaped, ellipsoidal ‖ *nn* oval.

ovar [o'var] *nn anat* ovary.

ovație [o'vatsie] *nf esp pl* applause, cheers, ovations.

ovaționa [ovatsio'na] *vt/vi* to cheer, to applaud, to acclaim.

ovăz [o'văz] *nn bot* oat, oatplant; oats; (*lan*) oat field.

ovul [o'vul] *nn bot, zool* ovule.

oxid [ok'sid] *nm chem* oxide • **~a** *vt/vr* to oxidize, to oxidate.

oxigen [oksi'djen] *nn* oxygen • **~s** *vt chem* to oxygenate, to oxygenize; to oxydize; *text* to bleach; (*părul*) to peroxide ‖ *vr pass* to be oxygenated, etc; *chem* to combine with oxygen, to be(come) oxygenized

ozon [o'zon] *nn chem* ozone.

P

pa [pa] *interj coll approx* bye-bye, see you later, tata!.

pace ['pache] *nf* peace, harmony; calm; (*liniște*) quiet, silence; (*seninătate*) serenity; *coll* (*nimic*) nothing.

pachebot [pake'bot] *nn naut* steamer, steamship; packetboat.

pachet [pa'ket] *nn* packet, package, (*ambalaj*) parcel, (*teanc de rufe*) bundle; (*de scrisori*) batch; (*de cărți de joc*) pack (of cards); (*de cafea*) bag.

pacient [pachi'ent] *nm med* patient.

pacifica [pachifi'ka] *vt* (*o țară*) to pacify; (*mintea, sufletul*) to appease, to calm ‖ *vr pass* to be pacified.

pacoste ['pakoste] *nf* calamity, misfortune; disaster; *fig* nuisance.

pact [pakt] *nn* pact, agreement, treaty.

padelă [pa'delă] *nf* (double-bladed) paddle.

paf [paf] *interj approx* bang!

pager ['peigiăr] *nn* pager, beeper.

pagina [padji'na] *vt* to page, to paginate.

pagină ['padjină] *nf* page; **~ albă** blank page.

pagubă ['pagubă] *nf* damage, harm, injury; detriment; (*pierdere*) loss.

pahar [pa'har] *nn* glass; (*fără picior*) tumbler; (*conținutul*) glassful; *pl med* (*ventuze*) cupping glasses.

pai [pai] *nn also pl* straw; **de ~e** straw; (*d. acoperiș*) thatched; **om de ~** dummy; *fig* man of straw.

paisprezece ['paisprezeche] *num* fourteen.

paj [pazh] *nm* page (boy).

pajiște ['pazhishte] *nf* lawn; meadowland, grassland.

pajură ['pazhură] *nf orn* (royal/golden) eagle; (*pe monedă*) tails; **cap sau ~** head or tails, pitch and toss; (*stemă*) arms; (*personaj fantastic în povești*) griffin.

pal [pal] *adj* pale, wan; (*d. culori*) light.

palat [pa'lat] *nn* palace; *anat* palate.

palavragiu [palavra'djiu] *nm* windbag, chatterer; (*bârfitor*) gossip, tattler.

paleontologie [paleontolo'djie] *nf* paleontology.

palestinian [palestini'an] *nm/adj* Palestinian.

paletă [pa'leta] *nf* (*pictura*) palette; *sp* bat; *sp* racket; *tech* blade.

paliativ [palia'tiv] *adj/nn* palliative

palid ['palid] *adj* pale, wan; *med* pallid, off-color; *fig* colorless; (*d. lumină*) faint; (*d. zâmbet*) wan.

palmă ['palmă] *nf anat* palm (of the hand); (*lovitură*) slap, box (on the ear).

palmier [palmi'er] *nm bot* palm tree.

paloare [pa'loare] *nf* pallor.

palpabil [pal'pabil] *adj* palpable, tangible; (*clar*) clear, obvious, plain.

palpita [palpi'ta] *vi* (*d. inimă*) to throb; to flutter; *med* to palpitate; (*a se înfiora*) to thrill; (*a tremura*) to tremble; (*de furie*) to quiver; (*d. lumină*) to flicker • **~nt** *adj* thrilling, exciting.

palton [pal'ton] *nn* winter coat, greatcoat, top/warm coat; (*de damă*) (winter) coat.

pamflet [pam'flet] *nn* lampoon, skit, satirical tract • **~ar** *nm* pamphleteer, lampoonist.

pană ['pană] *nf* (*de pasăre*) feather; (*de gâscă*) quill; (*condei, peniță*) pen; *fig* pen(manship); (*stil*) style; manner of writing; (*de lemn*) wedge; *tech* key; (*ca piesă de mașină*) cotter; *naut* afterpiece (of a rudder); (*de ciocan*) hammer edge; (*de ferăstrău*) tongue; **categoria ~ sp** feather weight; (*defecțiune*) breakdown; **~ de cauciuc** puncture.

pancartă [pan'kartă] *nf* placard.

pancreas [pan'kreas] *nn anat* pancreas.

panda ['panda] *nf zool* panda.

pandantiv [pandan'tiv] *nn* pendant; *archit* pendentive.

pandemie [pande'mie] *nf med* pandemic (disease); pandemia.

pandișpan [pandish'pan] *nn* pain d'Espagne, sponge cake.

panel [pa'nel] *nn* plywood panel, lumber; core plywood; blackboard.

panglică ['panglikă] *nf* ribbon; (*pt. păr*) fillet; (*de pălărie*) hatband; *tech* band, tape; *med, zool* tapeworm.

panicard [pani'kard] *nm* panicmonger, scaremonger ‖ *adj* alarmist.

panică ['panikă] *nf* panic, scare; (*fugă în dezordine*) stampede; (*groază*) terror.

panoramă [pano'ramă] *nf* panorama; wide prospect.

panou [pa'nou] *nn, also archit* panel; poster.

pansa [pan'sa] *vt* (*o rană*) to dress, (*un membru*) to bandage; to put a plaster cast on; (*cai*) to groom, to rub down • **~ment** *nn* dressing; * **pansa**; (*concret*) bandage, (sticking) plaster.

pansea, panseluță [pan'sea, panse'lutsă] *nf bot* pansy, call-me-to-you.

pantaloni [panta'loni] *nm pl* (*lungi*) pants, (pair of) trousers; (*izmene*) pants; (*de călătorie*) breeches; (*scurți*) shorts; knicker-bockers; (*de golf*) plusfours; (*pescărești*) jeans, Capri pants; (*strâmți*) tight pants, tights.

pantă ['pantă] *nf* slope, incline, gradient; *phys, tech* slope.

panteră ['panteră] *nf zool* panther.

pantof [pan'tof] *nm* shoe; (*cu toc jos*) flat shoe; (*cu toc înalt*) high-heel shoe; (*de casă*) slipper; (*de gimnastică*) gym shoe.

pantomimă [panto'mimă] *nf* pantomime.

papagal [papa'gal] *nm orn* parrot; *fig* glib tongue; **a avea ~** to have the gift of the gab • **~icește** *adv* parrot-like, by heart.

papalitate [papali'tate] *nf* papacy.

papă¹ ['papă] *nm* Pope.

papă² ['papă] *nf* chow, food; *sl* grub.

papetărie [papetă'rie] *nf* stationer's; *(magazin)* stationery.

papion [papi'on] *nn* butterfly bow, bowtie.

papiotă [papi'otă] *nf* spool of sewing silk; *(de hârtie)* curl paper, papillote.

papițoi [papi'tsoi] *nm coll* dude, fop, dandy.

papuc [pa'puk] *nm* slipper, mule; *obs (pantof)* shoe.

papură ['papură] *nf bot* club rush, mace reed; cat('s) tail, black cap; bulrush.

par¹ [par] *adj* even; **număr ~** even number.

par² [par] *nm* pole; *(ascuțit)* stake, picket; *(bâtă)* club; *(creangă)* (thick) branch.

para¹ [pa'ra] *nf fig* penny, farthing; *pl* money; *coll* beans.

para² [pa'ra] *vt (un atac, o lovitură)* to fend off, to ward off; *also fig* to parry; *(prin eschivă)* to dodge.

parabolă [pa'rabolă] *nf (alegorie)* parable; *geom* parabola.

paraclis [para'klis] *nn (capelă)* chapel; bidding prayer • **~er** *nm* sexton, candle lighter.

paradă [pa'radă] *nf mil* parade; *(scrimă)* parry; *fig* show, ostentation; **de ~** showy; *(d. zâmbet, aer)* insincere, forced; *(echitație)* stopping, pulling up.

paradis [para'dis] *nn* paradise; *also fig* heaven.

paradox [para'doks] *nn* paradox • **~al** *adj* paradoxical ‖ *adv* paradoxically.

parafa [para'fa] *vt* to initial; *(a sigila)* to seal; *(a semna un document)* to sign; to conclude.

parafină [para'fină] *nf* paraffin; **ulei de ~** *med* liquid paraffin.

parafrază [para'frază] *nf* paraphrase.

paragină [pa'radjină] *nf (pârloagă)* heath; fallow land; ruin; *(stare de părăsire)* dereliction, neglect; dilapidation.

paragraf [para'graf] *nn* paragraph; section (mark).

paralel [para'lel] *adj (cu)* parallel (to/with); simultaneous (with), concomitant; *(asemănător)* similar ‖ *adv* in parallel; simultaneously, at the same time.

paralelă [para'lelă] *nf also fig* parallel; *(comparație)* comparison; *pl sp* parallel bars.

paraliza [parali'za] *vt* to paralyze, to incapacitate; *fig* to render powerless; to stun; to cripple; to bring to a standstill ‖ *vi* to be stricken with paralysis.

paralizie [parali'zie] *nf med* paralysis; *coll* palsy; **~ progresivă** *med* creeping paralysis.

parametru [para'metru] *nm math* parameter.

paranoia [para'noia] *nf med* paranoia.

paranoic [para'noik] *adj med* paranoic.

paranteză [paran'teză] *nf (rotundă)* parenthesis, round bracket; *(dreaptă)* (square) bracket; *fig* interlude, digression; **în ~** in a parenthesis, in brackets, between parentheses; *fig* by the way.

parapet [para'pet] *nn* parapet; *naut* bulwark.

parastas [paras'tas] *nn* requiem, office for the dead.

parașuta [parashu'ta] *vt* to parachute.

parașută [para'shută] *nf* parachute; *fig sl* whore, prostitute.

parașutist [parashu'tist] *nm* parachutist, skydiver; *mil* paratrooper; parachuter, *pl* paratroops.

paratrăsnet [para'trăsnet] *nn* lightning rod.

paravan [para'van] *nn* folding screen; *fig* screen.

parazit [para'zit] *adj bio* parasitic; *fig* unnecessary, superfluous ‖ *nm bio* parasite, *ento* guest; *fig* sponger, freeloader.

pară ['pară] *nf bot* pear; *min* swage; *tech* switch.

parbriz [par'briz] *nn* windshield.

parc [park] *nn* park; *(grădină)* garden; enclosure; *(de mașini)* car park, parking place; *(de vânătoare)* park • **~a** *vt* to park • **~aj** *nn* parking lot/place • **~are** *nf* parking; *(loc)* parking lot; **~area interzisă** no parking.

parcă ['parkă] *adv* it seems/seemed (that); *(de ~)* as if/though.

parcela [parche'la] *vt* to divide into lots, to parcel (out).

parcelă [par'chelă] *nf* (p)lot, parcel.

parchet [par'ket] *nn constr* parquet floor(ing); *(lamă de ~)* parquetry fillet; *agr* cutting area; public prosecutor's office.

parcurge [par'kurdje] *vt (o regiune)* to cross, to travel through; *(o distanță)* to cover; *(străzi)* to wander; to read/run through/over; to examine (curiously); *(o listă)* to look down; *(documente)* to go over; *(superficial)* to skim (over).

parcurs [par'kurs] *nn* course; circuit; distance covered; *(drum)* route; way; track; *(itinerar)* itinerary.

pardesiu [parde'siu] *nn (de ploaie)* raincoat, mackintosh, waterproof coat; overcoat.

pardon [par'don] *interj* pardon!; excuse me!, (I am) sorry; *(numai ca scuză sau cu indignare)* I beg your pardon!; *(interogativ, solicitând repetarea informației)* I beg your pardon? (I didn't quite catch that).

pardoseală [pardo'seală] *nf* floor(ing).

parfum [par'fum] *nn* perfume, scent, fragrance, *(al vinului)* bouquet • **~a** *vt* to scent ‖ *vr* to wear/use perfume • **~at** *adj* scented, perfumed; *(d. aer)* balmy; *(d. gust)* sweet-tasting • **~erie** *nf* perfume shop, *(raion într-un magazin)* perfume counter, *(magazin)* perfumer's shop.

paria [pari'a] *vi (pe)* to bet, to wager, to lay a bet.

paritate [pari'tate] *nf* parity.

pariu [pa'riu] *nn* bet, wager; **a face un ~** to make/lay a bet/wager.

parlament [parla'ment] *nn* Congress; parliament • **~ar** *adj* parliamentary ‖ *nm* Congressman, member of parliament.

parodia [parodi'a] *vt* to parody, to burlesque.

parodie [paro'die] *nf* parody; *also fig* travesty.

paroh [pa'roh] *nm* rector • **~ie** *nf* parish, *(enoriași)* flock.

parolă [pa'rolă] *nf* password, watchword; parole.

parșiv [par'shiv] *adj* lousy; *(mârșav)* mean, dirty.

partaj [par'tazh] *nn* partition.

parte ['parte] *nf* part, partition; *(care revine cuiva)* share, lot; *(bucată)* piece, fragment; *(capitol)* chapter, section; *(regiune)* region, *(loc)* place; *(direcție)* direction; *(latură)* side; aspect; *(șansă)* chance; *(soartă)* fate; *(persoană sau grup implicat într-o afacere)* party; *jur* side.

partener [parte'ner] *nm* partner • **~iat** *nn* partnership.

parter [par'ter] *nn thea* the pit; *(primele rânduri)* the stalls; *(spectatorii)* audience (in the pit); *constr* first floor.

participa [partichi'pa] *vi (la)* to participate (in), *(a lua parte)* to take part (in); *(la un concurs)* to enter; *(a fi prezent)* to be present (at); *(la un complot)* to be a party (to), to be involved in; *(a juca într-un spectacol)* to appear in; *fig* to contribute (money to); *fig* to share, to sympathize • **~nt** *adj* participating ‖ *nm (la)* participant (in); participator (in); *sp* competitor.

participație [partichi'patsie] *nf com* share, interest.

participiu [parti'chipiu] *nn gram* participle.

particular [partiku'lar] *adj (deosebit)* peculiar,

characteristic; particular, special; (*neobişnuit*) unusual; exceptional; private; personal, individual; **în** ~ privately, in particular || *nm* private person • ~**itate** *nf* peculiarity; characteristic; special nature.

particulă [par'tikulă] *nf* particle; *coll* atom; *gram* particle.

partid [par'tid] *nn pol* party.

partidă [par'tidă] *nf sp* match, game, contest; (*de şah*) game; ~ **de dublu** (*tenis*) doubles match; (*căsătorie*) match; (*şi ca persoană*) party, marriageable person.

partitură [parti'tură] *nf mus* score.

partizan [parti'zan] *nm* partisan, guerilla; *fig* supporter; follower; (*susţinător*) advocate.

parţial [partsi'al] *adj* partial, incomplete || *adv* part(ial)ly, in part.

parveni [parve'ni] *vi* to start, to spring up; (*d. ştiri*) to come in || *vt* (*a reuşi*) **a ~ să** to succeed in • ~**t** *nm* parvenu; upstart.

pas [pas] *nm also fig* step; (*mare*) stride; (*mers*) pace, gait; (*zgomot de paşi*) tread, footsteps; (*urma de* ~) footprint; (*de dans*) pas; *tech* (*dimensiune*) distance; (*longitudinal, între zimţi*) pitch; thread; move || *nn* (mountain) pass; passage; (*cheie*) gorge, straits; *interj* (*la pocher*) pass!; (*la bridge*) no bid!.

pasa [pa'sa] *vt sp* to pass the ball; (*fotbal*) to (deliver a) pass; *coll* (*a da, a transmite*) to pass, to hand over; *cul* (*cartofi, zarzavat*) to mash; to strain.

pasager [pasa'djer] *nm* passenger || *adj* transitory, temporary, short-lived, (*d. durere*) momentary, (*d. frumuseţe*) fleeting.

pasaj [pa'sazh] *nn also mus, constr* passage; piece; (*extras*) excerpt; way; (*cu magazine*) arcade; mall; *rail* crossing.

pasarelă [pasa'relă] *nf constr* footbridge; *naut* gangway.

pasă ['pasă] *nf sp* pass; handball; (*la jocul de cărţi*) round.

pasăre ['pasăre] *nf* bird, (*de curte*) fowl; *pl* (*colectiv*) poultry.

pasibil [pa'sibil] *adj* liable (to), subject (to).

pasienţă [pasi'entsă] *nf* solitaire.

pasiona [pasio'na] *vt* to carry away, to fascinate; to grip || *vr* **a se ~ pentru** to become passionately fond of, to be fired by • ~**l** *adj* love, passional • **crimă** ~**lă** love tragedy, crime passionnel • ~**nt** *adj* gripping; thrilling, exciting; (*d. persoane*) fascinating • ~**t** *adj* passionate, impassioned || *nm* enthusiast; *sp* fan.

pasiune [pasi'une] *nf* passion; **cu** ~ passionately; **fără** ~ dispassionately.

pasiv [pa'siv] *adj* passive || *adv* passively || *nn com* liabilities, debts; *gram* passive voice.

paspartu [paspar'tu] *nn* (*speraclu*) skeleton/master/pass key; (*artă*) slip (in) mount; passé partout (frame).

pastă ['pastă] *nf* paste.

pastel [pas'tel] *nn* pastel; crayon; colored chalk; (*desen*) picture in pastel/crayon, pastel; *liter* (lyrical) descriptive poem; (*d. culori*) light.

pasteuriza [pasteuri'za] *vt* to pasteurize, to sterilize.

pastilă [pas'tilă] *nf* lozenge, tablet, pill; *tech* bearing disc.

pastişă [pas'tishă] *nf* parody.

pastor ['pastor] *nm relig* pastor, (*protestant*) minister.

pastramă [pas'tramă] *nf* pastrami.

paşaport [pasha'port] *nn* passport; *naut* sea letter; *coll* (*concediere*) walking paper.

paşnic ['pashnik] *adj* peaceful, peaceable; (*iubitor de pace*) peace-loving; (*liniştit*) quiet; undisturbed || *adv* peacefully, quietly.

paşte ['pashte] *vi/vt* to feed, to graze; (*a duce la păscut*) to drive/take to pasture; (*d. animale*) to browse, to feed upon; (*iarba*) to crop; *fig* to lie in wait for, to be in store for || *nn* * **Paşti**.

Paşti ['pashti] *nm* Easter; Easter day; (*iudaic*) Passover, Pasch; holy bread distributed in the church on Easter day.

pat [pat] *nn* bedstead; (*cu aşternut*) *also tech* bed; pad, sack; (*sărăcăcios*) pallet; (*de copii*) cot, crib; (*pliant*) folding bed; (*targă*) litter, stretcher; (*culcuş*) couch; (*strat*) layer; (*de puşcă*) butt (stock); *agr* (*pt. flori*) mulch; (*la şah*) stalemate.

pată ['pată] *nf also fig* stain, spot, blot; (*de cerneală*) blob; **fără** ~ spotless, stainless; (*curat*) pure; (*pe reputaţia cuiva*) blemish; (*ruşinoasă*) stigma.

patefon [pate'fon] *nn* gramophone.

patent [pa'tent] *adj* evident, obvious, manifest; *tech* safe, solid; (*d. lacăte*) patent || *nn* patent, license; * **cleşte**.

patern [pa'tern] *adj* paternal, a father's || *adv* paternally • ~**itate** *nf* paternity, fatherhood; (*a unei cărţi*) authorship.

patetic [pa'tetik] *adj* moving, touching || *adv* pathetically.

pateu [pa'teu] *nn* pie, meat pie, fish pie.

patimă ['patimă] *nf* passion; * **părtinire**; bias; (*suferinţă*) ordeal, suffering.

patina [pati'na] *vi* to skate; (*d. roţi*) to slip, to skid • ~**tor** *nm* skater • ~**j** *nn* skating; ~ **artistic** figure skating.

patinoar [pati'noar] *nn* skater rink.

patiserie [patise'rie] *nf* pastry, cakes; (*ca magazin*) pastrycook's shop; cake shop.

patologic [pato'lodjik] *adj* pathological || *adv* pathologically.

patos ['patos] *nn* pathos; enthusiasm; (*afectare*) affected pathos; *coll* bombast.

patriarh [patri'arh] *nm also fig* patriarch • ~**al** *adj* patriarchal; (*d. un loc*) bucolic, idyllic, rustic.

patrie ['patrie] *nf* (one's) native land/country, homeland, mother country, (one's) fatherland, birthplace; *fig* home.

patrimoniu [patri'moniu] *nn* heritage, inheritance; *fin* property, personal assets.

patriot [patri'ot] *nm* patriot • ~**ic** *adj* patriotic || *adv* patriotically, like a patriot • ~**ism** *nn* patriotism.

patron [pa'tron] *nm* employer; (*al unei întreprinderi*) chief, head; (*al unui hotel*) owner, proprietor; (*stăpân*) master; *coll* boss, governor; patron, protector; (*sfânt*) patron saint • ~**at** *nn* employers.

patru ['patru] *num/adj/nm* four • ~**sprezece** *num/adj/nm* fourteen • ~**zeci** *num/adj/nm* forty.

patrula [patru'la] *vi* to patrol.

patrulă [pa'trulă] *nf* patrol.

patruped [patru'ped] *adj* quadrupedal || *nn* quadruped.

pauperiza [pauperi'za] *vt* to pauperize.

pauză ['pauză] *nf* pause; (*la şcoală*) break; interval, intermission; *mus* rest.

pava [pa'va] *vt* to pave, to macadamize • ~**j** *nn* paving; (*concret*) pavement.

pavăză ['pavăză] *nf also fig* shield.

pavilion [pavili'on] *nn* pavilion; (*chioşc de vară, în grădină*) summer house; (*împodobit cu verdeaţă*) pergola; (de vânătoare) shooting lodge; (de spital) block; wing; (steag în marină) colors, flag.

pavoaza [pavoa'za] vt to deck with flags; (a împodobi) to decorate, to adorn.

pază ['pază] nf also fig guard, watch; (atenţie) care, attention.

paznic ['paznik] nm (la o întreprindere, muzeu, parcare) attendant; (la un imobil) janitor; (de noapte) nightwatchman; (de închisoare) guard; turnkey.

păcat [pă'kat] nn sin, transgression; (vină) guilt; (greşeală) mistake, error; (nenorocire) misfortune, ill-luck.

păcăli [păkă'li] vt to hoax, to play a practical joke upon; coll (a înşela) to take in, to diddle || vr to be deceived, to make a mistake.

păcăni [păkă'ni] vi to click, to rattle.

păcătos [păkă'tos] adj sinful; (d. gânduri etc) guilty; (ticălos) mean; (rău) wicked; (nenorocit) miserable, wretched; (defectuos) faulty, defective || nm sinner.

păcătui [păkătu'i] vi to (commit a) sin.

păcură ['păkură] nf fuel/black/crude oil.

păduche [pă'duke] nm ento louse, pl lice; ento wood/ tree louse; fig parasite, sponger.

păduchios [pădu'kios] adj lousy.

pădurar [pădu'rar] nm woodman, forester, forest guard.

pădure [pă'dure] nf wood(s); (mai mare, mai bătrână) forest.

pădureţ [pădu'rets] adj wild.

păgân [pă'gân] adj/nm heathen, pagan; fig wicked/ cruel person.

păgubaş [păgu'bash] nm victim, loser.

păgubi [păgu'bi] vi/vr to lose || vt to harm, to injure, to cause/do damage to • ~tor adj harmful, injurious.

păi [păi] adv/interj (exprimând aprobarea) well, why; (ascultă) I say; (şi) and; what!; (exprimând ezitare) well.

păianjen [pă'ianzhen] nm ento spider; pl cobweb, spider's web; min grab.

pălărie [pălă'rie] nf hat; coll topper; (de dans) (lady's) hat, bonnet; (de paie) straw hat; (panama) Panama hat; (tare) bowler; (cu boruri înguste) narrow-brimmed hat; (de fetru) felt hat; (de fetru, moale) squash hat; (de ciuperci) cap, top; min safety cover.

pălăvrăgi [pălăvră'dji] vi to chatter, to babble, to twaddle; to tattle.

păli [pă'li] vt (a lovi) to strike, to hit; (a cuprinde) to overcome; (a arde) to burn || vr (a se lovi) (de) to strike (against), to hit (against); (a se veşteji) to wither || vi to become/turn pale; (d. surse luminoase) to grow dim.

pălmui [pălmu'i] vt to slap smb in the face, to smack smb.

pămătuf [pămă'tuf] nn feather broom, whisk, duster; (pt. bărbierit) shaving brush; relig aspergillum, sprinkler.

pământ [pă'mânt] nn ground, earth, (uscat) land; (sol) soil; (lumea) the world; (globul) the globe; (câmp) field; (moşie) estate; (regiune) region; (teritoriu) territory; (ţară) country; **Pământul Făgăduinţei** The Promised Land • ~esc adj earthly, terrestrial; earth.

pănuşă [pă'nushă] nf corn husk; husk.

păpădie [păpă'die] nf bot dandelion, lion's tooth, hawkbit.

păpuşar [păpu'shar] nm puppeteer, puppet man/master; (cabotin) sorry player.

păpuşă [pă'pushă] nf (d. o fată) also fig dolly; fig (marionetă) puppet, tool; (de tutun) tobacco hand; ento chrysalis, pupa.

păr [păr] nm bot pear tree; hair; tex nap.

părăgini [părădji'ni] vr to run wild; * **dărăpăna**.

părăsi [pără'si] vt (a pleca) to leave, to quit; to abandon; (a se despărţi de) to part with; (a renunţa la) to give up; (un obicei) to break off; (a înceta) to cease; (a neglija) to neglect; (o cameră de hotel) to vacate; to check out; (drumul: d. o maşină) to go off the road.

părea [pă'rea] vi to seem, to look, to appear; (a-şi închipui) to imagine.

părere [pă'rere] nf opinion, (point of) view; (convingere) conviction; (credinţă) belief; idea, notion; illusion.

părinte [pă'rinte] nm also fig, relig father; pl parents, mother and father; coll folks; (strămoşi) ancestors, forefathers; (întemeietor) founder; (preot) priest • ~sc adj fatherly, paternal.

păros [pă'ros] adj hairy, hirsute; (flocos) shaggy.

părtinire [părti'nire] nf favoring; partiality, bias; (pică) spite, acrimony, bitterness.

părtinitor [părtini'tor] adj partial, biased, unfair.

păruială [păru'ială] nf brawl, fray, tussle; coll scrap.

păsa [pă'sa] vi a-i ~ to care; a-i ~ de (a se interesa de) to care for; (a ţine cont de) to mind.

păsărică [păsă'rikă] nf orn birdie.

păscut [păs'kut] nn grazing, * **paşte**.

păstaie [păs'taie] nf pod.

păstârnac [păstâr'nak] nm bot (common) parsnip.

păstor [păs'tor] nm also fig shepherd • ~i vt to graze; also fig to shepherd || vi to be a shepherd; fig to be a priest.

păstra [păs'tra] vt to keep, to save, to preserve; (a ţine) to hold; (a respecta) to observe; (în memorie) to retain; (a menţine) to maintain; (a păzi) to guard || vr pass (a rămâne) to remain; (d. cineva) to be well-preserved.

păstrăv ['păstrăv] nm icht (common) trout.

păsui [păsu'i] vt to grant smb a delay • ~ală, ~re nf delay, respite.

păşi [pă'shi] vt (pragul) to cross the line || vi to step; (a merge) to walk; (pe vârfuri) to tiptoe; fig to advance; (a se dezvolta) to develop; a ~ în to step in(to), to walk in(to).

păşune [pă'shune] nf pasture, grazing (field).

păta [pă'ta] vt also fig to spot, to stain, to blot.

pătimaş [păti'mash] adj (pasionat) impassioned; (înflăcărat) ardent, fervent || adv passionately, ardently, fervently.

pătimi [păti'mi] vi to endure, to bear, to undergo || vi to suffer; (a fi chinuit) to be tortured/tormented.

pătlagină [păt'ladjină] nf bot plantain, roadweed.

pătlăgea [pătlă'djea] nf bot (roşie) tomato; ~ **vânătă** eggplant.

pătrar [pă'trar] nn quarter, fourth; (al lunii) quarter.

pătrat [pă'trat] adj/nn square.

pătrime [pă'trime] nf fourth; (sfert) quarter; mus crotchet.

pătrunde [pă'trunde] vi to penetrate; to grasp; (a străbate) to cross; (a umple) to fill, to pervade; (a ajunge în) to reach; (d. lichide: a se scurge prin) to trickle through || vt to pervade, to fill; (d. frig) to pierce; (a înţelege) to grasp, to understand; (a mişca) to move;

a ~ în to penetrate, to get into ‖ *vr* **a se ~ de** to be imbued with; (*d. cineva*) to imbue one's mind with; to be filled with the sense of.

pătrunjel [pătrun'zhel] *nm bot* parsley.

pătrunzător [pătrunză'tor] *adj* (*d. frig*) piercing; (*d. privire*) searching; (*d. sunete*) shrill; (*d. minte*) sharp; (*d. cineva*) shrewd; (*mişcător*) touching; **spirit** ~ keenness of perception, insight.

pătul [pă'tul] *nn* (*hambar*) barn; (*pt. porumb*) corn barn; (*pt. fân*) hayloft; (*pt. găini*) hen coop/house; * **răsadniţă**; (*pat mic*) little bed.

pătură ['pătură] *nf* blanket; (*cuvertură*) counterpane; (*strat*) layer, bed; *fig* stratum, *pl* strata; section.

păţanie [pă'tsanie] *nf* accident; incident, (*întâmplare*) happening, occurrence; (*necaz*) trouble, predicament; *pl* adventures.

păţi [pă'tsi] *vt* to experience, to undergo.

păun [pă'un] *nm orn* peacock, peafowl • **~iţă** *nf orn* peahen.

păzi [pă'zi] *vt* to look after, to mind, to (keep) watch over, to take care of; (*a aştepta*) to wait for; (*a urmări*) to watch; (*a apăra*) to defend; (*a păstra*) to keep; (*a respecta*) to observe; (*a se ocupa de*) to deal with ‖ *vr* to take care/heed (of oneself); (*a avea grijă de sine*) to take care of oneself • **~tor** *adj* înger ~ guardian angel ‖ *nm* guardian, keeper; (*al unei clădiri publice*) caretaker; (*de închisoare*) warden.

pâclă ['pâklă] *nf* mist, haze; * **zăpuşeală**; *geol* mud volcano.

pâine ['pâine] *nf* bread; (*de o anumită formă*) loaf (of bread), *pl* loaves; (*aluat*) dough; (*hrană*) food; (*trai*) living; (*slujbă*) job; ~ **albă** white/wheat bread; ~ **de casă** home-made bread; ~ **de secară** rye bread; ~ **integrală** wholemeal bread; ~ **neagră** brown bread.

pâlc [pâlk] *nn* group, troop; (*stol*) flight, bevy; (*turmă*) herd, flock; (*de pomi*) cluster, bunch.

pâlnie ['pâlnie] *nf* funnel; (*crater de obuz*) shell hole; (*de mină*) mine crater.

pâlpâi [pâlpâ'i] *vi* (*d. lumină*) to flutter, to flicker; (*d. foc*) to flare, to bicker; *fig* to glimmer, to gleam.

până ['până] *conj* till, until; by the time; (*mai înainte ca*) before; *lit* ere; (*atâta timp cât*) as/so long as ‖ *prep* (*temporal*) till, until; (*implicând discontinuitatea*) by; ~ **acum** till now, so far, as yet; ~ **azi** to date, to this day; ~ **la** (*temporal*) till, until; (*spaţial*) as far as.

pândă ['pândă] *nf* guard, watch.

pândi [pân'di] *vt* to watch; (*a spiona*) to spy; (*a aştepta*) to wait for ‖ *vi* to be on the watch; to lie in ambush.

pângări [pângă'ri] *vt* to defile; to desecrate; (*un mormânt*) to violate; (*o femeie*) to dishonor; (*a mânji*) to besmear ‖ *vr pass* to be defiled, etc.

pântece ['pânteche] *nn* abdomen, belly, stomach; (*uter*) uterus, womb; *fig* heart, depths, womb.

pânză ['pânză] *nf* linen, cloth; (*de sac*) sackcloth; (*pictură*) canvas; (*tablou*) picture, painting; (*giulgiu*) shroud; *naut* sail; (*de păianjen*) cobweb; *tech, geom* sheet; (*metalică*) wire gauze/cloth; *geol* layer sheet; (*lamă*) blade.

pârâ ['pârâ] *nf* denunciation; *sl* squeal.

pârâi [pârâ'i] *vi* to crack; (*d. lemne, pe foc*) to crackle.

pârâiaş [pârâ'iash] *nn* rivulet, creek, stream.

pârât [pâ'rât] *nm* the accused.

pârâu [pâ'râu] *nn* brook, rivulet; *fig* stream, flood.

pârghie ['pârgie] *nf* lever; *fig* key factor.

pârgui [pârgu'i] *vr* (*to begin*) to ripen.

pârî [pâ'rî] *vt* to denounce; to inform on/against.

pârjoli [pârzho'li] *vt* to set fire, to set on fire; (*a arde*) to burn; *fig* to devastate, to ravage, to lay waste.

pârleaz [pâr'leaz] *nn* stile.

pârli [pâr'li] *vt* (*porcul etc*) to singe; (*a arde*) to burn; (*a bronza*) to tan; (*a usca*) to dry, to scorch; *fig coll* (*a înşela*) to take in ‖ *vr* to burn oneself; *fig coll* to get one's fingers burned; *coll* (*a fi înşelat*) to be taken in.

pârloagă [pâr'loagă] *nf* fallow (ground).

pârnaie [pâr'naie] *nf reg* large-brimmed pot used for cooking; *vernac* prison, quod, pen.

pârtie ['pârtie] *nf* (*cărare*) path; (*trecere*) passage; *sp* track.

pe [pe] *prep* (*spaţial*) on; (*şi cu verbe de mişcare*) upon, onto; (*de pe*) from; (*peste*) over; (*prin*) through; (*spre*) to, towards; in; (*temporal: în timpul*) during; (*cât timp e*) as long as it is; as long as there is; (*înspre*) towards; by; (*în fiecare zi etc*) a, per; (*împotriva*) against; (*pentru*) for, in exchange for; (*potrivit cu*) in accordance with; (*cu*) with; (*într-o limbă oarecare*) in; (*din cauza*) for, because of; ~ **când** (*temporal*) while; (*adversativ*) whereas.

pecete [pe'chete] *nf* also *fig* seal, stamp.

pecetlui [pechetlu'i] *vt* to affix/attach a seal to; (*a sigila*) to seal; to fix; *fig* to ratify, to confirm.

pechinez [peki'nez] *nm zool* Pekin(g)ese, pug; *coll* peke.

pectoral [pekto'ral] *adj* pectoral.

pecuniar [pekuni'ar] *adj* pecuniary, monetary.

pedagogie [pedago'djie] *nf* pedagogy, pedagogics.

pedala [peda'la] *vi* to pedal; to work a treadle; *fig* to insist; **a ~ asupra** to emphasize.

pedală [pe'dală] *nf* (*de pian, bicicletă*) pedal; (*de tocilă etc*) treadle.

pedant [pe'dant] *adj* pedantic, priggish; punctilious ‖ *adv* pedantically ‖ *nm* pedant, prig • **~erie, ~ism** *nf/nn* pedantry, pedantism.

pedeapsă [pe'deapsă] *nf* punishment, penalty; *lit* chastisement; (*sancţiune*) sanction; (*nenorocire*) misfortune; (*năpastă*) calamity; (*ispitire*) ordeal; (*necazuri*) trouble; (*şoc*) imposition; (*d. cineva*) cuss.

pedepsi [pedep'si] *vt* to punish; (*o crimă*) to avenge.

pederast [pede'rast] *nm* paederast, sodomite.

pediatrie [pedia'trie] *nf med* pediatry, pediatrics.

pedichiură [pedi'kiură] *nf* chiropody.

pedigriu [pedi'griu] *nn* pedigree.

peiorativ [peiora'tiv] *adj* (*d. sufixe etc*) deprecating, disparaging; pejorative, derogatory ‖ *adv* deprecatingly.

peisaj [pei'sazh] *nn* landscape, scenery.

pelerin [pele'rin] *nm* pilgrim • **~aj** *nn* pilgrimage.

pelerină [pel'rină] *nf* pelerine, cape; (*manta*) mantle.

pelican [peli'kan] *nm orn* (common) pelican.

peliculă [pe'likulă] *nf phot etc* film; (*pieliţă*) pellicle, thin skin.

pelin [pe'lin] *nn bot* wormwood, mugwort; *fig* bitterness, grief; (*vin*) wormwood wine.

peltea [pel'tea] *nf* fruit jelly; *fig coll* long rigmarole.

peltic [pel'tik] *adj* lisping ‖ *nm* lisping person.

peluză [pe'luză] *nf* lawn, greensward; *sp* grounds, public enclosures.

penaj [pe'nazh] *nn* feathering, plumage.

penal [pe'nal] *adj* penal, criminal; **cod** ~ criminal/penal code; **drept** ~ criminal law • **~iza** *vt jur* to punish; *sp* to penalize.

penar [pe'nar] *nn* pencil case/box.

pendul [pen'dul] *nn* pendulum • **~a** *vi* to swing, to oscillate, to pendulate • **~ă** *nf* grandfather's clock, timepiece, pendulum clock.

penel [pe'nel] *nn also fig* brush.

penetra [pene'tra] *vt* to penetrate.

peni ['peni] *nm* (*monedă*) penny.

penibil [pe'nibil] *adj* painful, clumsy, awkward.

penicilină [penichi'linǎ] *nf* penicillin.

peninsulă [pe'ninsulǎ] *nf* peninsula, half island/isle.

penis ['penis] *nn anat* penis, membrum virile.

penitenciar [penitenchi'ar] *nn* prison, penitentiary.

penitent [peni'tent] *nm* penitent, person doing penance.

penitență [peni'tentsǎ] *nf* penance; (*căință*) penitence, repentance.

peniță [pe'nitsǎ] *nf* pen, nib; *bot* water milfoil.

pensă ['pensǎ] *nf med* forceps; clip; (*la rochii*) pleat.

pensetă [pen'setǎ] *nf* tweezers, nippers, pincers.

pensie ['pensie] *nf* pension; *jur* alimony, child support.

pension [pensi'on] *nn* (private) boarding school.

pensiona [pensio'na] *vt* to pension (off) || *vr* to retire (upon a pension), to be pensioned off • **~r** *nm* retiree, pensioner; (*al unei instituții de ocrotire socială etc*) inmate; (*casă de bătrâni*) resident; (*la o pensiune etc*) boarder; lodger; paying guest.

pensiune [pensi'une] *nf* (*localul*) boarding house; board and lodging; (*cu mic dejun*) bed and breakfast.

pensulă ['pensulǎ] *nf* brush.

pentagon [penta'gon] *nn geom* pentagon.

pentru ['pentru] *prep* (*cu scopul*) for; (*în vederea*) with a view to; (*din cauza*) because of; (*datorită*) owing to; (*în interesul*) for; (*în favoarea*) in favor of; (*în apărarea*) in defense of; (*în numele*) on behalf of; (*de dragul*) for the sake of; (*cu direcția*) for; bound for; (*cu privire la, față de*) for; (*în legătură cu*) in connection with; (*în schimbul*) in exchange for, in return for; (*în locul*) instead of; ~ **ca** (*in order*) to, so (that); ~ **că** for, because, since, as; ~ **ce** why.

penultim [pen'ultim] *adj* last but one, penultimate.

penurie [penu'rie] *nf* penury, scarcity.

pepene ['pepene] *nm bot* (~ *galben*) melon; (~ *verde*) watermelon.

pepinieră [pepini'erǎ] *nf also fig* nursery, seed bed.

pepit [pe'pit] *adj* quadrilled, checked.

pepită [pe'pitǎ] *nf* nugget (of gold).

percepe [per'chepe] *vt* to perceive, to discern; (*a auzi*) to hear; (*impozite etc*) to collect, to levy.

perceptibil [perchep'tibil] *adj* perceptible, discernible; (*cu urechea*) audible; (*d. impozite*) collectable.

perceptiv [perchep'tiv] *adj* perceptive.

perceptor [perchep'tor] *nm* tax gatherer/collector.

percepție [per'cheptsie] *nf psych* perception; revenue office; ~ **senzorială** *psych* sense perception.

percheziție [perke'zitsie] *nf* search; (*domiciliară*) house search; **mandat de** ~ search warrant.

percheziționa [perkezitsio'na] *vt* to search.

perciune [per'chune] *nm* (side) ringlet, side curl.

percuție [per'kutsie] *nf* percussion.

perdea [per'dea] *nf* curtain; (*de ușă*) door curtain; *fig* reserve, restraint; *fig* veil, screen || *adj fig* veiled, discreet; **fără** ~ *adj* curtainless; *fig* improper, scurrilous || *adv* without glossing over anything; (*necuviincios*) improperly, scurrilously.

pereche [pe'reke] *nf* couple, pair; (*de păsări*) brace; (*de boi*) yoke; one of a pair; match; **fără** ~ matchless, peerless || *adj* (*d. numere etc*) even.

peregrinare [peregri'nare] *nf* wanderings, traveling (far and wide).

peren [pe'ren] *adj bot* perennial; evergreen; *fig* everlasting.

perete [pe'rete] *nm* wall.

perfect [per'fekt] *adj* perfect, faultless, flawless; (*ireproșabil*) irreproachable; (*d. o operă de artă etc*) consummate; accomplished; total; complete; thorough; absolute; (*d. reputație, nume*) unsullied || *adv* perfectly, etc || *nn gram* perfect.

perfecționa [perfektsio'na] *vt* to perfect; (*a îmbunătăți*) to improve || *vr* to improve, to gain in skill/quality.

perfecțiune, perfecție [perfektsi'une, per'fektsie] *nf* perfection.

perfid [per'fid] *adj* treacherous, perfidious; (*d. un prieten etc*) false-hearted; (*d. o promisiune etc*) false || *adv* treacherously, etc • **~ie** *nf* treachery, perfidy; (*ca act*) treacherous act.

perfora [perfo'ra] *vt* to perforate, to bore (through); (*un bilet etc*) to punch, to clip || *vr* to be perforated/bored (through) • **~tor** *nn telec* perforator; drilling machine; *ind* casing perforator || *nm* driller, borer; (*de bilete*) punch; clippers.

performanță [perfor'mantsǎ] *nf* (notable) feat, performance.

performer [perfor'mer] *nm sp* performer; (*artist*) entertainer.

perfuzie [per'fuzie] *nf* perfusion.

pergament [perga'ment] *nn* parchment; (*la cărți*) vellum.

perhidrol [perhi'drol] *nn* perhydrol, (hydrogen) peroxide.

peria [peri'a] *vt* to brush; *text* to comb; *fig coll* to curry favor with || *vr* to brush one's clothes/hair.

periclita [perikli'ta] *vt* to endanger, to jeopardize.

pericol [pe'rikol] *nn* peril, danger, jeopardy, hazard, risk.

periculos [periku'los] *adj* dangerous, perilous, hazardous, (*riscant*) risky; **om** ~ rough customer || *adv* dangerously.

perie ['perie] *nf* brush.

periferic [peri'ferik] *adj* (*d. un ținut etc*) outlying; *geom* peripher(ic)al, peripheric; *fig* secondary, subordinate; *anat* peripherical, external.

periferie [perife'rie] *nf* outskirts (of a town); *geom* periphery; **la** ~ on the outskirts; in the suburbs.

perifrază [peri'frazǎ] *nf* periphrasis, circumlocution.

perima [peri'ma] *vr* to be/become obsolete/out-of-date; *jur* to lapse.

perimetru [peri'metru] *nn* perimeter, periphery.

perinda [perin'da] *vr* to succeed each other; (*aproape*) to follow close upon the other; (*a trece*) to pass, to file past.

periniță [peri'nitsǎ] *nf* a lively Romanian folk dance.

perioadă [peri'oadǎ] *nf* period (of time); *geol* cycle; epoch, age, era; (*timp*) time; *mus* phrase.

periodic [peri'odik] *adj* periodical; *astron, mus* periodic; **fenomen** ~ recurrent phenomenon || *nn* periodical magazine.

peripeție [peripe'tsie] *nf* mishap; adventure, episode.

perisabil [peri'sabil] *adj* perishable • **mărfuri ~e** perishable goods, perishables.

periscop [peris'kop] *nn* periscope.
periuță [peri'utsă] *nf* small brush; (*de dinți*) toothbrush; *fig coll* toady, lickspittle, sycophant.
perlă ['perlă] *nf* (*în diferite sensuri*) pearl; *fig* gem.
permanent [perma'nent] *adj* permanent; (*d. o armată, un comitet etc*) standing; (*d. pace etc*) abiding || *adv* permanently, indelibly || *nn* (*al părului*) perm(anent wave); (*legitimație*) pass, card.
permanență [perma'nentsă] *nf* permanence; (*concret*) office permanently open to the public; permanent service; **în** ~ permanently.
permeabil [perme'abil] *adj* permeable, pervious.
permis [per'mis] *adj* permitted, allowed || *nn* permit, authorization, license; ~ **de conducere** driver's license; ~ **de portarmă** gun license; ~ **de muncă** work permit; ~ **de ședere** (*într-o țară*) residence permit.
permisie [per'misie] *nf mil* leave of absence.
permisiune [permisi'une] *nf* leave, permission.
permite [per'mite] *vt* (*în sens pasiv*) to allow; (*în sens activ*) to permit, to give permission.
pernă ['pernă] *nf* pillow; (*de divan, mașină etc*) cushion; (*cu aer*) air cushion.
perniță [per'nitsă] *nf* cushion.
peron [pe'ron] *nn* platform.
perora [pero'ra] *vi* to hold forth || *vt* to debate, to fervently support.
perpeli [perpe'li] *vt* to fry; *fig* to torture, to torment || *vr* to worry, to fret.
perpendicular [perpendiku'lar] *adj* perpendicular.
perpetua [perpetu'a] *vt* to perpetuate || *vr* to endure, to last.
perplex [per'pleks] *adj* puzzled, perplexed.
persecuta [perseku'ta] *vt* to persecute, to victimize.
persecuție [perse'kutsie] *nf* persecution, victimization.
persevera [perseve'ra] *vi* to persevere.
perseverent [perseve'rent] *adj* persevering, assiduous || *adv* perseveringly.
perseverență [perseve'rentsă] *nf* perseverance; **cu** ~ perseveringly, assiduously.
persifla [persi'fla] *vt* to taunt, to banter • ~**re** *nf* bantering; (*ca act*) banter.
persista [persis'ta] *vi* (*în*) to persist (in); to continue (its course).
persistent [persis'tent] *adj* persistent, lasting, enduring.
persoană [per'soană] *nf* individual, person.
personaj [perso'nazh] *nn* personage, character; (*într-o piesă etc*) *pl* dramatis personae.
personal [perso'nal] *adj* personal; individual; (*particular*) private; **efecte** ~**e** personalia || *adv* personally, in person || *nn* personnel, staff; *rail* passenger/slow train • ~**itate** *nf* personality, person of consequence.
personifica [personifi'ka] *vt* to personify; (*a întruchipa*) to impersonate • ~**re** *nf* personification; impersonation.
perspectivă [perspek'tivă] *nf* (*arte etc*) perspective; (*priveliște*) view, sight; *fig* prospect, outlook; expectation.
perspicace [perspi'kache] *adj* perspicacious, shrewd.
pertinent [perti'nent] *adj* pertinent, relevant.
perturba [pertur'ba] *vt* to perturb, to disturb.
perucă [pe'rukă] *nf* wig; periwig.
peruzea [peru'zea] *nf* turquoise.
pervaz [per'vaz] *nn* (*de ușă, fereastră*) jamb; (*de ușă*) doorcase; (*de fereastră*) sash, window frame; (*la un lambriu*) ogee.

pervers [per'vers] *adj* perverse, depraved; (*d. gust*) vicious || *adv* perversely || *nm* pervert • ~**itate** *nf* perversity, perverse(ness) • ~**iune** *nf* perversity.
perverti [perver'ti] *vt* to pervert, to corrupt || *vr* to become perverted/corrupted.
pescar [pes'kar] *nm* fisher(man); (*cu undița*) angler; *orn* (sea-)gull, sea-mew.
pescărie [peskă'rie] *nf* (*pescuit*) fishing; (*ca negoț*) fish trade; (*piață de pește*) fish market; (*produse*) fish; (*cherhana*) fishery.
pescăruș [peskă'rush] *nm orn* common tern; (*~ albastru*) kingfisher.
pescui [pesku'i] *vi* to fish; (*cu undița*) to angle; (*balene*) to whale || *vt also fig* to fish for; (*cu undița*) to angle; (*balene*) to hunt; (*păstrăv*) to catch; (*perle etc*) to dive for.
pesemne [pe'semne] *adv* probably, as it seems, possibly.
pesimism [pesi'mism] *nn* pessimism.
pesimist [pesi'mist] *adj* pessimistic || *nm* pessimist.
pestă ['pestă] *nf* plague; ~ **bovină** cattle plague.
peste ['peste] *prep* over; (*de-a curmezișul*) across, athwart; (*de jur împrejurul*) all around; (*pe tot cuprinsul*) throughout; (*deasupra, pe verticală*) above; (*după*) (*temporal*) after; in; (*în cursul*) during; (*modal*) over; above; beyond; (*mai mult de*) over, more than; ~ **măsură** beyond measure; ~ **tot** everywhere, all over (the place).
pesticid [pesti'chid] *nn* pesticide, pest-killer.
pestilențial [pestilentsi'al] *adj* pestilential.
pestriț [pes'trits] *adj* motley, variegated; (*în mai multe culori*) parti-colored; *fig* mixed.
pește ['peshte] *nm* fish; *pl* **Pești** *astron* Pisces; *fig coll* fancy-man, pimp.
peșteră ['peshteră] *nf* cave, cavern; grotto.
petală [pe'tală] *nf bot* petal.
petardă [pe'tardă] *nf* petard.
petic ['petik] *nn* rag, shred; (*de cârpit o haină*) patch.
petiție [pe'titsie] *nf* petition.
petiționar [petitsio'nar] *nm* petitioner.
petrecăreț [petrekă'rets] *nm* * **chefliu.**
petrece [pe'treche] *vi* (*a se distra*) to amuse oneself, to enjoy oneself; (*bine*) to have a good/great time; (*a se veseli*) to cheer (up); (*a sta*) to stay; (*a locui*) to live || *vt* (*timpul etc*) to spend; (*a însoți*) to accompany; (*la plecare*) to see smb off; (*a îndura*) to undergo; (*cu ochii*) to follow with one's eyes; (*a urmări*) to watch || *vr* (*a se întâmpla*) to happen, to occur; (*a avea loc*) to take place; (*a se sfârși*) to end, to come to an end.
petrecere [pe'trechere] *nf* feast; *coll* (*chef*) spree, blow-out; (*distracție*) amusement, entertainment; (*serată*) party.
petrol [pe'trol] *nn* petroleum; (*mineral*) oil • ~**ier** *adj* mineral oil || *nn naut* tanker, tank ship/steamer, oiler • ~**ifer** *adj* petroliferous, oil-bearing • ~**ist** *nm* oil industry worker.
petunie [pe'tunie] *nf bot* petunia.
peți [pe'tsi] *vt* to ask in marriage; to woo.
pezevenchi, pezevenghi [peze'venki, peze'vengi] *nm* (*escroc*) cheat, swindler; (*ticălos*) rascal, knave, (*glumeț*) rogue; *obs* pimp, pander.
pian [pian] *nn* piano; pianoforte; (*cu coadă*) grand piano; (*de concert*) concert grand piano • ~**ină** *nf* cabinet/upright piano • ~**ist** *nm* pianist, piano player.
piatră ['piatră] *nf* rock, stone; (*bolovan*) boulder; (*pe*

dinți, de vin) tartar; (*de căldare*) scale; (*la rinichi*) stone, calculus; (*la vezica biliară*) gallstone; (*grindină*) hail; (~ *prețioasă*) precious stone, gem.

piață ['piatsă] *nf* market(place); *fig* market; (*loc public*) square; (*rotundă, cu artere radiale*) circus.

pic [pik] *nn* (*picătură*) drop, dripping; (*fărâmă*) bit, grain; **nici un** ~ *coll* not a bit, not an ounce; (*de loc*) not at all; (*câtuși de puțin*) not in the least; **un** ~ just a bit, (just) a little.

pica [pi'ka] *vi* (*a cădea*) to fall (down); (*a picura*) to drip; (*a sosi*) to come (unexpectedly); to turn up, to drop by; (*la examen*) to fail (in); *coll* to be plucked/plowed ‖ *vt* (*a murdări*) to (be)spot; *fig coll* (*la examen*) to flunk.

picant [pi'kant] *adj* (*d. sos etc*) pungent; (*savuros*) savory, *fig* piquant, snappy; (*atrăgător*) attractive.

pică ['pikă] *nf* pique, ill feeling; (*ciudă*) spite; (*dușmănie*) enmity, acrimony; (*la jocul de cărți*) spades.

picătură [pikă'tură] *nf* drop; *pl coll* drops; ~ **cu** ~ drop by drop, little by little.

pichet [pi'ket] *nm* (*joc de cărți*) piquet ‖ *nn tex* pique; *mil, etc* picket; ~ **de grevă** (strike) picket ‖ *nm* (*țăruș*) post, stake.

picheta [pike'ta] *vt* to stake/mark out.

pici ['pichi] *nm* urchin; (*băiețaș*) boy; *coll* kid(dy).

picior [pi'chior] *nn* leg; (*laba ~ului*) foot; *pl* legs, feet; *sl* pins, stumps, trotters; (*de compas*) branch; *constr* abutment; *tech, etc* end, pillar, stand; (*bază*) base, toe; *geom* foot (=30,48 cm).

picnic ['piknik] *nn* picnic.

picoteală [piko'teală] *nf* doze, drowse.

picoti [piko'ti] *vi* to doze, to drowse; (*șezând*) to nod.

pricomigdală [prikomig'dală] *nf* bitter almond.

picta [pik'ta] *vt also fig* to paint, to depict; *also fig* to portray; *fig* to describe.

pictor ['piktor] *nm* painter, artist • **~iță** *nf* painter; woman artist.

pictură [pik'tură] *nf* painting; (*concret*) picture.

piculină [piku'linã] *nf mus* piccolo (flute).

picup ['pikup] *nn elec* record-player.

picura [piku'ra] *vi* to drip, to dribble; *fig* to (re)sound; to vibrate ‖ *vt* to pour out drop by drop.

piedestal [piede'stal] *nn* pedestal, base, plinth.

piedică [piedikă] *nf* obstacle, impediment; (*greutate*) difficulty; (*pt. cal*) hobble; (*la roata carului*) brake shoe; (*frână*) brake; *tech* stopping device; (*la armă*) detent; *sp* tipping; (*cu piciorul*) trip.

piele ['piele] *nf* skin; (*și de animale mari*) hide; (*a unui animal cu blană*) pelt, fur; (*lepădată de șarpe*) slough; snakeskin; (*material*) leather.

pieliță ['pielitsă] *nf med* pellicle; (*a fructelor*) peel; *bot* tunicle; (*pe lichide*) film.

piept [piept] *nn* chest; (*de vițel etc*) *also lit* breast; bust, (*sâni*) bosom; (*de vită*) brisket (beef); (*de deal etc*) slope.

pieptăna [pieptă'na] *vt* (*părul*) to comb; (*a dărăci*) to card; (*inul și cânepa*) to hackle; *fig* to finish, to trim up; (*stilul*) to smooth (out) ‖ *vr* to comb one's hair.

pieptănătură [pieptănă'tură] *nf* hair-do, coiffure; (*la bărbați*) hair-cut.

pieptene ['pieptene] *nm also text* comb; (*des*) tooth comb.

pierde ['pierde] *vt* to lose; (*trenul, filmul, ocazia etc*) to miss; (*terenul*) to feel the ground slipping away; (*o potcoavă*) to cast; (*timpul*) to waste; (*a fi lipsit de*) to be deprived of; (*a distruge*) to destroy ‖ *vr* to be/get lost; (*a dispărea*) to disappear; (*a nu lăsa nici o urmă*) to leave no trace; (*a fi uitat*) to be forgotten; (*în mulțime*) to be lost; (*a se rătăci*) to lose one's way; *fig* to lose one's head; to be confused ‖ *vi* to lose.

pieri [pie'ri] *vi* to perish; (*a muri*) to die; (*a dispărea*) to disappear, to vanish.

piersic ['piersik] *nm bot* peach tree • **~ă** *nf* peach.

pierzanie [pier'zanie] *nf* (*pierdere*) loss; (*perdiție*) perdition; (*ruină*) undoing.

piesă ['piesă] *nf* (*bucată*) *also tech, mil etc* piece; specimen; (*exemplar*) copy; (*de mașină*) part; (*de teatru*) play; (*la șah*) chessman; (*monedă*) coin.

pietate [pie'tate] *nf* piety, godliness; *fig* affectionate devotion.

pieton [pie'ton] *nm* pedestrian.

pietriș [pie'trish] *nn* gravel; (*drumuri*) road metal.

pietros [pie'tros] *adj* full of stones, stony; (*d. o plajă*) flinty, pebbly; *fig* (as) hard as stone, stone-hard.

pietrui [pietru'i] *vt* (*a pava*) to pave; (*cu pietriș*) to metal.

pieziș [pie'zish] *adj* slanting, skew; (*strâmb*) wry; (*d. pământ*) steep; (*d. ochi*) squint(ing); (*d. privire*) sidelong glance; (*d. scriere etc*) sloping; *fig* indirect ‖ *adv* obliquely, slantwise; *fig* indirectly.

piftie [pif'tie] *nf* aspic of pig's feet; meat jelly; *chem* gel.

pigment [pig'ment] *nn* pigment • **~a** *vt/vr* to pigment, to color, to dye.

pigmeu [pig'meu] *nm also fig* pigmy.

pijama [pizha'ma] *nf* pajamas.

pilaf [pi'laf] *nn* pilaw, pilau, pilaf(f).

pilă ['pilă] *nf* file; (*de mână*) hand file; (*de mașină*) machine file; (*de unghii*) nail file; *elec* cell, battery; (*teanc*) pile; (*poduri*) pier; *fig coll* backstairs influence.

pildă ['pildă] *nf* model; (*culme a perfecțiunii*) paragon; instance, example; (*parabolă*) parable. **pili** [pi'li] *vi* to file; *coll* (*a bea*) to tipple, to guzzle ‖ *vr coll* (*a se îmbăta*) to be in one's cups.

pilon [pi'lon] *nm archit etc* pillar; (*de pod*) pier.

pilot [pi'lot] *nm naut, avia* pilot ‖ *adj* (*experimental*) pilot, pioneer • **~a** *vt naut, avia* to pilot, to fly (a plane); *rail* to hand signal ‖ *vi naut* to steer; *rail* to slow (down/up).

pilotă [pi'lotă] *nf* eiderdown.

pilulă [pi'lulă] *nf* pill.

pin [pin] *nm bot* pine(tree).

pingea [pin'djea] *nf* sole.

pingeli [pindje'li] *vt* to heel, to sole; to tap.

ping-pong ['pingpong] *nn sp* ping-pong, table tennis.

pinguin [pingu'in] *nm* penguin, auk.

pinion [pini'on] *nn tech* pinion.

pinten ['pinten] *nm also orn* spur.

pion [pi'on] *nm also fig* pawn.

pionier [pio'nier] *nm* pioneer; *mil* engineer, sapper • **~at** *nn* pioneer's work, breaking new ground.

pios [pi'os] *adj* pious, devout ‖ *adv* piously, devoutly.

pipă ['pipă] *nf* (tobacco) pipe.

pipăi [pipă'i] *vt* to feel, to touch; to fondle, to neck ‖ *vr* to feel one's muscle; to feel for a sore spot, etc.

piper [pi'per] *nm bot* pepper • **~a** *vt also fig* to pepper ‖ *vi* to be peppery • **~at** *adj* peppery; *fig coll* indecent, licentious, indecorous; *fig coll* (*d. prețuri*) stiff.

pipernicit [piperni'chit] *adj* stunted (in one's growth), dwindling.

pipetă [pi'petă] *nf* pipette, dropper.

pipotă ['pipotă] *nf* gizzard.

piramidă [pira'midă] *nf* pyramid.

pirat [pi'rat] *nm* pirate, sea rover, buccaneer.

pireu [pi'reu] *nn* puree; (*de cartofi*) mashed potatoes, potato mash.

piromanie [piroma'nie] *nf* pyromania, incendiarism.

piron [pi'ron] *nn* spike.

pironi [piro'ni] *vt* (*cu piroane*) to nail down/up; to immobilize; (*a fixa*) to fix, to rivet; to concentrate || *vr* to stick, to stay put.

pirotehnic [piro'tehnik] *adj* pyrotechnic(al).

pirotehnie [piroteh'nie] *nf* pyrotechnics.

pirpiriu [pirpi'riu] *adj* feeble, frail; (*subțire, slab*) thin.

piruetă [piru'etă] *nf* pirouette.

pisa [pi'sa] *vt* to pound; *fig* (*a bate*) to pommel; *fig coll* (*a plictisi*) to pin oneself on; to bother, to bore to death.

pisălog [pisă'log] *adj coll* bothersome || *nn* pestle || *nm* importuner; *coll* (*regular*) bore, pest.

pisc [pisk] *nn* peak, summit.

piscicultură [pischikul'tură] *nf* pisciculture, fish breeding.

piscină [pis'chină] *nf* (*pentru înot*) swimming pool; fish pond.

pisică [pi'sikă] *nf zool* cat; *coll* puss(y); *rare* tib/tabby cat; (*cărucior*) traveling crab; *tech* releasing gear.

pisicuță [pisi'kutsă] *nf coll* pussy(cat); kitten.

pisoi [pi'soi] *nm* kitten.

pistă ['pistă] *nf* running track; race/racing track; *avia* runway, flight strip; *fig* course, channel; *elec* radio track.

pistil [pis'til] *nn* bot pistil; *chem* pestle.

pistol [pis'tol] *nn* pistol, revolver • ~et *nn* pistol.

piston [pis'ton] *nn tech* piston.

pistrui [pis'trui] *nm* freckle • ~at *adj* freckled.

pișa [pi'sha] *vr sl, vulg* to piss, to urinate || *vt sl vulg* to piss (on), to wet.

pișca [pish'ka] *vt* to pinch, to tweak; (*d. ger, purici etc*) to bite; (*d. albine, urzică etc*) to sting; (*a gâdila*) to tickle; *fig* to prick; *fig coll* to filch, to nick || *vi* (*a ustura*) to be hot/peppery; to be sharp.

pișcot [pish'kot] *nn* sweet biscuit; wafer.

piti [pi'ti] *vt* to hide || *vr* to hide, to skulk, to nestle.

pitic [pi'tik] *adj* dwarfish, dwarf-like || *nm* dwarf, pygmy.

piton [pi'ton] *nm zool* python || *nn sp* (ice) piton, peg.

pitoresc [pito'resk] *adj* picturesque, quaint; (*d. haine*) gay; (*d. stil*) graphic || *adv* picturesquely, etc || *nn* picturesqueness.

pitula [pitu'la] *vr* to crouch; * **ascunde**.

pitulice [pitu'liche] *nf orn* (jenny/common) wren; garden warbler, white throat.

pițigăiat [pitsigă'iat] *adj* high-pitched, squeaky.

pițigoi [pitsi'goi] *nm orn* titmouse, tomtit.

piui [piu'i] *vi* (*d. pui etc*) to cheep, to peep; * **țiui**.

piuliță [piu'litsă] *nf* mortar; *tech* (screw) nut.

piuneză [piu'neză] *nf* thumbtack, drawing pin.

pivniță ['pivnitsă] *nf* cellar.

pivot [pi'vot] *nn* pivot, spindle, axis; *bot* tap root.

pix [piks] *nn* clutch pencil, push button pencil.

pizmă ['pizma] *nf* envy.

pizmui [pizmu'i] *vt* to envy; (*a dușmăni*) to show enmity to.

plac [plak] *nn* pleasure.

placa [pla'ka] *vt* (*metale*) to plate; (*cu furnir*) to veneer; to placate; *sp* to tackle.

placardă [pla'kardă] *nf* placard, poster.

placă ['plakă] *nf* plate; (*de patefon*) record; (*de ardezie, marmură etc*) slate; *med* (*dentară*) plaque.

placid [pla'chid] *adj* placid, calm; apathetic || *adv* placidly, calmly.

plafon [pla'fon] *nn* ceiling; *fig* extreme limit; *auto, avia* roof.

plagă ['plagă] *nf* (*rană*) wound, sore; *fig* evil, calamity.

plagia [pla'djia] *vt* to plagiarize; *coll* to crib from • ~t *nn* plagiarism • ~tor *nm* plagiarist.

plai [plai] *nn* flat mountain region covered with lawns; mountain road/path; (*câmpie*) field; *lit* (*ținut*) realm; region, part(s).

plajă ['plazhă] *nf* beach.

plan [plan] *nn* (*proiect*) blueprint; plan, scheme; (*al unei construcții etc*) draft; program; *geom* plane; *cin* shot; level; ~ **apropiat** *cin* close shot; ~ **de în-văţământ** curriculum; ~ **general** general layout; **prim** ~ foreground; ~ **secund** middle ground.

plana [pla'na] *vi* (*d. păsări*) to soar, to hover; (*d. avioane*) to glide; *fig* (*deasupra*) to hang (over) || *vt* to smooth, to make even.

planetă [pla'netă] *nf* planet; (*planeta*) the globe, the earth.

planifica [planifi'ka] *vt* to plan || *vr pass* to be planned • ~re *nf* planning.

planor [pla'nor] *nn avia* glider • ~ism *nn* avia gliding.

planșă ['planshă] *nf* (*de desen*) drawing board; (*schiţă*) sketch; (*gravură*) plate; (*lespede*) slab.

planșetă [plan'shetă] *nf* small board/plank; plane table; (*de desen*) drawing board.

planșeu [plan'sheu] *nn* floor.

planta [plan'ta] *vt* to plant, to set; (*a fixa*) to set up, to fix; to stick in the ground || *vr* to take one's stand.

plantație [plan'tatsie] *nf* plantation.

plantă ['plantă] *nf* plant.

planturos [plantu'ros] *adj* stout, portly, burly.

plapumă ['plapumă] *nf* (*de lână*) blanket; (*tighelită*) counterpane; (*de puf*) eiderdown.

plasa [pla'sa] *vt* to place; to put (in a certain place); (*bani*) to invest; (*a vinde*) to sell; (*pe cineva*) to seat; to find a post for; (*un cuvânt*) to put in; to get a word in; *sp* to place(-kick) || *vr* (*într-o ierarhie*) to rank, to range; (*d. mărfuri etc*) (*a se vinde*) to sell • ~ment *nn com* sale; (*investiție*) investment; (*slujbă*) post, situation; *sp* placement • ~toare *nf* usherette • ~tor *nm* thea etc ticket collector; *com* placer, seller.

plasă ['plasă] *nf* net; (*de prins pește*) (fishing) net; (*în compartiment*) rack; string bag; *text* heddle.

plastic ['plastik] *adj* plastic; *fig* graphic(al), suggestive || *adv* graphically, suggestively.

plastilină [plasti'lină] *nf* plasticine.

plastografia [plastografi'a] *vt* to forge, to falsify.

plastografie [plastogra'fie] *nf* forgery.

plasture ['plasture] *nm* plaster.

plat [plat] *adj also fig* flat; level; (*neted*) even; banal, commonplace, trite.

platan [pla'tan] *nm bot* (true) plane (tree).

plată ['platã] *nf* pay(ment); (*onorar*) fee; wages; *fig* (*răsplată*) reward; (*pedeapsă*) punishment; (*ce i se cuvine cuiva*) due.

platcă ['platkă] *nf* inset.

platformă [plat'formă] *nf (în diferite sensuri)* platform.

platfus ['platfus] *nn* flat foot.

platină ['platină] *nf chem* platinum; *opt* stage.

platitudine [plati'tudine] *nf* flatness, dullness; *(banalitate)* banality, commonplace; *(concret)* platitude.

platonic [pla'tonik] *adj* platonic; ideal; abstract.

platou [pla'tou] *nn (podiş)* tableland, plateau; *(tavă)* tray; *tech* plate, disk; *cin* (film) set, (sound) stage.

plauzibil [plau'zibil] *adj* plausible, credible.

plăcea [plă'chea] *vi (d. o interpretare etc)* to go down well; *(d. un roman etc)* to appeal || *vt* to like, to care for; *(a iubi)* to love.

plăcere [plă'chere] *nf* pleasure; *(gust)* liking, taste; *(încântare)* delight; *(distracţie)* amusement, enjoyment.

plăcintă [plă'chintă] *nf* pie.

plăcut [plă'kut] *adj* pleasant, agreeable; *(simpatic)* nice || *adv* pleasantly, agreeably, nicely.

plămân [plă'mân] *nm anat* lung.

plănui [plănu'i] *vt* to plan, to contemplate; *(a intenţiona)* to intend; *(a urzi)* to plot || *vr pass* to be planned, etc.

plăpând [plă'pând] *adj* frail, delicate, *(slab)* weak, feeble; *(blând)* gentle.

plăsea [plă'sea] *nf (de cuţit)* knife handle; *(de sabie)* sword hilt.

plăsmui [plăsmu'i] *vt* to create, to produce; to invent, to devise; *(a falsifica)* to forge, to falsify.

plăti [plă'ti] *vt* to pay; *(în natură)* to pay in kind; *(în bani)* to pay in cash; *(ca răzbunare etc)* to pay back; *(a achita)* to settle a debt; to pay the bill; *(moraliceşte)* to repay smb || *vi* to pay.

plânge ['plândje] *vi* to weep, to cry; *(cu suspine)* to sob; *(a se mâţâi)* to whine || *vt* to weep/cry for, to mourn for; *(a-i fi milă de)* to pity || *vr* to complain; to murmur, to grumble.

pleavă ['pleavă] *nf* chaff, husk; *fig* scum, dregs, riffraff.

plebeu [ple'beu] *nm* plebeian || *adj* plebeian; *(sărac)* destitute.

pleca [ple'ka] *vi* to leave, to depart, to go off/away; *(d. nave)* to sail off; *(d. tren)* to steam off; *(d. cineva)* to walk off/away; *(d. un călăreţ)* to ride off; *(a porni)* to set out; **a ~ la** to leave for || *vt* to bend; *(ochii)* to drop one's eyes; *(capul)* to bow; *(capul, abătut)* to hang; *fig* to subdue || *vr (a se pleca)* to bend; *(pt. a saluta)* to bow; *fig* to submit, to yield, to give in.

plecăciune [plekă'chiune] *nf (low)* bow.

pled [pled] *nn* rug; *(scoţian)* plaid.

pleda [ple'da] *vi* to plead.

pledoarie [pledoa'rie] *nf* pleading.

plenar [ple'nar] *adj* plenary.

plenipotenţiar [plenipotentsi'ar] *adj* plenipotentiary.

plenitudine [pleni'tudine] *nf* plenitude, fullness.

pleoapă ['pleoapă] *nf* eyelid.

pleonasm [pleo'nasm] *nn* pleonasm, redundancy.

pleoşti [pleosh'ti] *vt* to flatten || *vr* to become flat; *fig (d. cineva)* to become depressed; to be in low spirits; *coll* to have the blues.

plescăi [pleskă'i] *vi (d. apă)* to splash; *(d. cineva)* to champ.

plesni [ples'ni] *vi* to break, to burst; *(a crăpa)* to split; *fig (de)* to burst (with) || *vt (a lovi)* to hit, to strike.

pleşuv [ple'shuv] *adj* bald, bald-headed; *(d. sol)* barren; *(d.arbori)* bare.

plete ['plete] *nf pl* locks (of hair), plaited hair.

pletos [ple'tos] *adj* long-haired; *(şi cu părul despletit)* shaggy.

plevuşcă [ple'vushkă] *nf icht* (fish) fry; *fig* small fish.

plia [pli'a] *vt* to fold • **~nt** *adj* folding, that folds || *nn* leaflet.

plic [plik] *nn* envelope; **~ galben** *(oficial)* buff envelope; *fig coll* walking papers/ticket.

plicticos [plikti'kos] *adj/adv* * **plictisitor**.

plictiseală [plikti'seală] *nf* weariness, boredom; *lit (urât)* spleen; *(necaz)* trouble; annoyance; *(a unei călătorii lungi)* the tedium/boredom of a long journey.

plictisi [plikti'si] *vt* to bore, to bother || *vr* to be bored • **~tor** *adj* boring, tedious; *(d. o muncă)* irksome || *adv* boringly, tediously.

plimba [plim'ba] *vt* to take (out) for a walk, to drive; *(un obiect)* to pass; to run || *vr* to walk, to go for a walk/drive • **~re** *nf* walk(ing), stroll; *(cu maşina)* motor run; *(călare, cu bicicleta, maşina)* ride; *(cu trăsura)* drive; *(cu barca)* row, sail.

plin [plin] *adj (de)* full (of), filled (with); *(~ ochi)* brimful, full to the brim; *(ticsit)* packed; crammed; *(masiv)* compact; *(gras)* fat; *(durduliu)* plump; *(întreg)* full, entire, whole.

plisat [pli'sat] *adj* pleated.

plisc [plisk] *nn orn* beak; nib; *fig coll (gură)* pecker; *(vârf)* tip; *fig (greşeală)* blunder, mistake.

plită ['plită] *nf* kitchen range.

pliu [pliu] *nn* fold, pleat.

plivi [pli'vi] *vt* to weed.

ploaie ['ploaie] *nf* rain; *(torenţială)* shower, pouring/pelting rain; *(măruntă)* drizzle; *(cu descărcări electrice)* thunder rain/shower; *(cu băşici)* spill.

ploconi [ploko'ni] *vr (înaintea)* to bow down; *fig* to grovel (before), to kowtow (to).

plod [plod] *nm (copil mic)* baby, babe in arms; *coll hum* snipper-snapper; *pej coll* scrub, dot; embryo; *(sămânţă)* seed; *(germene)* germ.

ploios [plo'ios] *adj* rainy.

plomba [plom'ba] *vt* to stop; *med* to fill a cavity.

plombă ['plombă] *nf* stopping; *med (dentară)* filling.

plonja [plon'zha] *vi sp (înot)* to dive; *(fotbal etc)* to plunge, to dive (at full length).

plonjon [plon'zhon] *nn sp* plunge; *(înot)* dive.

plop [plop] *nm bot* poplar (tree).

ploscă ['ploskă] *nf* canteen; *med* bedpan.

ploşniţă ['ploshnitsă] *nf ento* (bed)bug; *sl* flat.

ploua [plo'ua] *vi* to rain; *(mărunt)* to drizzle; *fig* to shower || *vt* to shower, to rain • **~t** *adj* wet with rain; *fig* crestfallen, downcast.

plug [plug] *nn* plow; *(arat)* plowing; *(la schi)* stern; snowplow • **~ar** *nm* plowman.

plumb [plumb] *nn* miner lead; *(glonte)* slug, bullet.

plumburiu [plumbu'riu] *adj* leaden(-hued); *(d. cer)* murky.

plural [plu'ral] *adj/nn* plural • **~ism** *nn phil* pluralism.

plus [plus] *nn math* plus; extra, addition; surplus; *(avantaj)* advantage; **în ~** in addition, besides.

plută ['plută] *nf* raft; *bot* Lombardy poplar; *(de undiţă)* cork; *(pt. ceruire)* waxing cork.

pluti [plu'ti] *vi* to float, to drift; *(d. nave)* to sail; *(cu o navă)* to navigate; *(cu barca)* to boat; *(a înota)* to swim; *(d. păsări)* to soar, to hover; *fig* to wander.

pluton [plu'ton] *nn mil* platoon; *sp* group; *(la curse)* field.

plutonier [plutoni'er] *nm mil* first sergeant.

plutoniu [plu'toniu] *nn chem* plutonium.

pneu [pneu] *nn* (pneumatic) tire.

pneumatic [pneu'matik] *adj* pneumatic ‖ *adv* pneumatically.

pneumonie [pneumo'nie] *nf med* pneumonia.

poală ['poală] *nf (de cămașă)* hem; *(de haină)* coattail; *(între brâu și genunchi)* lap; *pl (fustă)* skirt; *(de deal etc)* foot.

poamă ['poamă] *nf* fruit, *pl* fruits; *fig coll* bad lot/egg/ hat; *coll (d. o femeie)* hussy, bit of skirt.

poantă ['poantă] *nf* point of a joke; gist of a story; quibble; sting of an epigram, etc; *fig* highlight, high point; *(la balet)* toe(-dancing).

poartă ['poartă] *nf also fig* gate; *(ca intrare)* gateway; portal.

pocăi [pokă'i] *vr relig* to do penance; *(a-i părea rău)* to repent, to regret • ~**nță** *nf relig* penance; repentance.

pocher ['poker] *nn* poker.

poci [po'chi] *vt* to disfigure, to mutilate, to cripple; *(a strica)* to mar, to spoil; *(o limbă)* to murder; *(a cârpăci)* to bungle; *coll* to make a mess of ‖ *vr* to grow ugly; to lose one's good looks; *(a se strâmba)* to mop and mow, to make (wry) faces.

pocinog [pochi'nog] *nn* nasty trick.

pocnet ['poknet] *nn* crack, burst of an explosive; *(plesnitură)* snap; *(izbitură)* smash.

pocni [pok'ni] *vi* * **plesni** ‖ *vt* to hit, to strike • ~**tură** *nf* bang, pop; *(lovitură)* swat; *(din degete)* snap.

pocnitoare [pokni'toare] *nf* cracker, rattler.

pod [pod] *nn* bridge; *(de casă)* garret; *(la șură)* loft; *tech* platform; *sp (podul)* bridge position.

podea [po'dea] *nf* floor; *(scândură de ~)* floor board.

podeț [po'dets] *nn* footbridge.

podgorie [pod'gorie] *nf* hill planted with vines; vineyard.

podidi [podi'di] *vt (d. somn etc)* to overcome.

podiș [po'dish] *nn* plateau, tableland.

podium ['podium] *nn* platform, podium; *(mai ales pt. ocazii solemne)* dais/pedestal of honor.

podoabă [po'doabă] *nf* ornament, adornment; a thing of great value; *(bijuterie)* jewel.

poem, poemă [po'em, po'emă] *nn/nf* poem.

poet [po'et] *nm* poet • ~**ic** *adj (d. o lucrare etc)* poetical; *(d. talent, inspirație, licență)* poetic ‖ *adv* poetically.

poezie [poe'zie] *nf (ca artă, ca totalitate a lucrărilor poetice ale cuiva etc) also fig* poetry; *obs* poesy; *(ca bucată separată)* poem; *(rimată, scurtă)* rhyme; *(frumusețe)* beauty; *(farmec)* charm.

poftă ['poftă] *nf (de mâncare)* appetite; *(chef)* mind (to); *(dorință) (de)* appetite (for), desire (for).

pofti [pof'ti] *vt (a dori)* to wish, to want; *(a invita)* to ask; *(a ruga)* to beg; *(a binevoi)* to condescend; *(a îndrăzni)* to dare.

pofticios [pofti'chios] *adj (lacom) (de)* greedy (of), covetous (of); *(doritor) (de)* desirous (of); *(d. priviri)* wanton; *(lasciv)* lustful ‖ *adv* greedily, etc.

poftim [pof'tim] *interj (invitând pe cineva să intre etc)* please, come in; *(vă rog)* please; *(ca răspuns la o cerere)* here you are!; *(cum ați spus?)* I beg your pardon, say that again; *(ei ~!)* good God!, goodness gracious!, *(asta-i bună!)* coll there now!; here's/that's a fine/nice ....

pogrom [po'grom] *nn* pogrom, massacre.

poiană [po'iană] *nf* clearing, glade.

poimâine ['poimâine] *adv* the day after tomorrow.

pojar [po'zhar] *nn med* measles.

pojghiță [pozh'gitsă] *nf* film, pellicle; crust.

pol [pol] *nm* pole • ~**ar** *adj* polar, arctic.

polariza [polari'za] *vt* to polarize.

polaroid [polaro'id] *nm opt, phot* Polaroid.

polcă ['polkă] *nf* polka.

polei¹ [po'lei] *nn* glazed/block frost; silver thaw; ice sheet.

polei² [pole'i] *vt also fig* to polish.

polemic [po'lemik] *adj* polemic(al), controversial • ~**ă** *nf* polemic, controversial discussion; dispute.

polen [po'len] *nn* pollen.

policlinică [poli'klinikă] *nf* polyclinic, dispensary; *approx* general hospital.

poliester [polies'ter] *nm chem* polyester.

poligam [poli'gam] *adj* polygamous ‖ *nm* polygamist • ~**ie** *nf* polygamy, plural marriage.

poliglot [poli'glot] *nm* polyglot.

poligon [poli'gon] *nn geom* polygon; *mil* shooting/rifle range, practice/shooting ground(s).

poligraf [poli'graf] *nn* polygraph.

poliomielită [poliomie'lită] *nf med* poliomyelitis; *coll* polio.

polistiren [polisti'ren] *nn chem* polystyrene.

politehnic [poli'tehnik] *adj* polytechnic • ~**ă** *nf* polytechnic.

politețe [poli'tetse] *nf* politeness, good manners/breeding; mannerliness; *(amabilitate)* civility, courtesy.

politic [po'litik] *adj* political • ~**ă** *nf (ca sistem, viața politică etc)* politics; *(atitudine, diplomație)* policy • ~**ian** *nm* politician • ~**ianism** *nn* petty politics, politicking.

politicos [politi'kos] *adj* polite, civil, *(curtenitor)* courteous ‖ *adv* politely, etc.

poliță ['politsă] *nf (raft)* shelf; *com (la purtător)* note of hand, promissory note; *(cambie)* bill (of exchange); *(de asigurare)* policy; ~ **în alb** *com* blank check.

poliție [po'litsie] *nf* police; *(ca local)* police precinct/ station.

polițist [poli'tsist] *nm/adj* police ‖ *nm* policeman, police officer; *coll* the law, cop.

polivalent [poliva'lent] *adj chem* polyvalent, multivalent; *fig* multipurpose.

polizor [poli'zor] *nn tech* grinder, grinding machine.

polo ['polo] *nn sp* polo.

polonez [polo'nez] *adj* Polish ‖ *nm* Pole • ~**ă** *nf* Pole, Polish woman/girl; Polish, the Polish language; *(dans)* polonaise.

polonic [polo'nik] *nn* ladle, skimmer.

poltron [pol'tron] *adj* cowardly; dastardly ‖ *nm* poltroon, coward.

polua [polu'a] *vt* to pollute • ~**nt** *nn* polluting substance; *(lichid)* effluent • ~**re** *nf* pollution.

pom [pom] *nm* (fruit) tree.

pomadă [po'madă] *nf* pomade; ointment; *(și pentru păr)* pomatum.

pomană [po'mană] *nf* alms, charity; handout; *relig* funeral repast/feast; *fig* good deed; gratis; *(zadarnic)* uselessly; *(fără scop)* to no purpose, for nothing.

pomeni [pome'ni] *vt (a menționa)* to mention, to make mention of; *(a vorbi despre)* to speak of; *(a ține minte)* to remember; *(a întâlni)* to meet with; *(a auzi de)* to hear of; *(a vedea)* to see; *relig* to pray for ‖ *vr (a se întâmpla)* to happen, to occur; *(a se găsi)* to find oneself; *(a veni)* to come; *(a fi)* to be; **a ~ de** *vi* to mention, to make mention of.

pomicultură [pomikul'tură] *nf* fruit growing.
pompa [pom'pa] *vt* (*a umple*) to pump full; (*a scoate*) to pump out.
pompă ['pompă] *nf phys* pump; pomp, ceremony.
pompier [pompi'er] *nm* firefighter.
pompon [pom'pon] *nn* pompon, ornamental tuft.
pompos [pom'pos] *adj* pompous; (*d. cuvinte, stil*) high-flown.
ponderat [ponde'rat] *adj* cool, level-headed.
pondere ['pondere] *nf* weight; *fig* share; gravity.
ponegri [pone'gri] *vt* to slander, to cast aspersions on; *coll* to run down.
ponei [po'nei] *nm* pony, Shetland horse.
ponosi [pono'si] *vt* (*haine*) to wear out/away/off.
pont [pont] *nn* tip, clue, hint.
ponta [pon'ta] *vt* to clock ‖ *vi* to check in; (*la cărţi*) to punt; **a ~ la sosire** to clock on/in; **a ~ la plecare** to clock off/out • **~j** *nn* clocking; **foaie de ~** time/check sheet • **~tor** *nm* timekeeper; player (in games of chance).
pontif [pon'tif] *nm* pontiff; *fig* pundit.
ponton [pon'ton] *nn naut* pontoon; (*pod*) pontoon bridge.
pop [pop] *nm constr* prop, stav ‖ *nn/adj* kind of music.
popas [po'pas] *nn* halt, stop; (*ca loc*) halting place.
popă ['popă] *nm coll* (*preot*) parson; (*la cărţi de joc*) king; *sp* (*la popice*) king pin, middle pin.
popic [po'pik] *nn* (nine)pin, skittle; *pl* (nine)pins, bowling; *constr* stud; *pl coll* (*picioare*) pins, pegs • **~ărie** *nf* bowling alley.
popor [po'por] *nn* nation, people; (*ţărănime*) peasantry, peasants; (*mulţime*) people, crowd.
poposi [popo'si] *vi* to (come to a) halt.
popotă [po'potă] *nf* officers' mess.
popri [po'pri] *vt* to stop; (*a interzice*) to forbid; (*a sechestra*) to sequester; to arrest.
popula [popu'la] *vt* to people, to populate • **~ţie** *nf* population, (*locuitori*) inhabitants.
popular [popu'lar] *adj pol* people's; (*folcloric*) folk-(lore); (*simpatizat*) popular • **~itate** *nf* popularity • **~iza** *vt* to popularize ‖ *vr pass* to be popularized.
por [por] *nm anat* pore.
porc [pork] *nm zool* hog, pig, *pl* swine ; *coll* grunter; (*vier*) boar; *fig coll* hogger; *coll* (*om lacom*) greedy hog • **~ar** *nm* swineherd.
porcărie [porkă'rie] *nf* piggishness; (*murdărie*) filth; *coll* (*ca act*) dirty/foul trick; *pl coll* (*obscenităţi*) smut; ribaldries; *coll* (*d. mâncare*) pigwash.
poreclă [po'reklă] *nf* nickname.
porecli [pore'kli] *vt* to nickname.
porni [por'ni] *vi/vr* to start, to be off; (*la drum*) to set out; (*a pleca*) to leave; (*d. tren*) to start/steam off; (*d. nave*) to sail away; (*d. un călăreţ*) to ride off; (*a se pune în mişcare*) to come in(to) play; (*a fi în mişcare*) to be in gear; (*a începe*) to begin; (*a izbucni în*) to burst out ‖ *vt* to begin, to start; (*a pune în mişcare*) to move, to bring on; (*o conversaţie etc*) to set going; (*o maşină*) to throw into gear; (*a se avânta*) to embark on; (*a îmboldi*) to urge; (*a aţâta*) to goad.
pornografic [porno'grafik] *adj* pornographic, scurrilous.
pornografie [pornogra'fie] *nf* pornography.
poros [po'ros] *adj* porous, spongy.
port [port] *nn* (*purtare*) carrying, carriage; costume, garb; *fig* conduct; (*radă*) port, harbor; (*maritim*) seaport; (*ca oraş*) port (town).

portabil [por'tabil] *adj* portable.
portal [por'tal] *nn* portal, principal door; *constr* tunnel front.
portar [por'tar] *nm* janitor, doorkeeper; *sp* goalkeeper; *coll* goalie.
portativ [porta'tiv] *nn mus* staff, stave ‖ *adj* portable, hand, pocket.
portavion [portavi'on] *nn naut* aircraft carrier.
portavoce [porta'voche] *nf naut* speaking trumpet.
portăreasă [portă'reasă] *nf* janitress, porter; porter's/janitor's wife.
portărel [portă'rel] *nm jur* bailiff.
portbagaj [portba'gazh] *nn* luggage rack; *auto* trunk.
portchei [port'kei] *nn* keyring.
portdrapel [portdra'pel] *nm mil* color/standard bearer ‖ *nn* stirrup socket/shoe.
portieră [porti'eră] *nf* (*uşă*) door; (*draperie*) door curtain, portiere.
portiţă [por'titsă] *nf* wicket (gate); (*la o grădină etc*) gate; (*de la sobă*) damper.
portjartier [portzharti'er] *nn* suspender belt/girdle.
portmoneu [portmo'neu] *nn* (change) purse; pocketbook; * **portofel**.
portocal [porto'kal] *nm bot* orange tree, citrus • **~ă** *nf* orange • **~iu** *adj* orange.
portofel [porto'fel] *nn* wallet.
portofoliu [porto'foliu] *nn* ministry, portfolio.
portret [por'tret] *nn* portrait; (*tablou*) picture.
portţigaret [portsiga'ret] *nn* (*tabacheră*) cigarette case; (*în care se fixează ţigara*) cigarette holder/tube.
portughez [portu'gez] *adj/nm* Portuguese • **~ă** *nf* Portuguese (woman or girl); Portuguese, the Portuguese language.
portvizit [portvi'zit] *nn* pocketbook.
porţelan [portse'lan] *nn* china(ware), porcelain.
porţie ['portsie] *nf* helping, portion.
porţiune [portsi'une] *nf* portion, part, (*bucată*) piece, fragment.
porumb [po'rumb] *nm bot* corn; **făină de ~** cornmeal.
porumbar [porum'bar] *nm bot* sloe tree, blackthorn ‖ *nn* (*coşar*) granary, corncrib; (*coteţ pentru porumbei*) dovecote, pigeon house.
porumbel [porum'bel] *nm orn* pigeon; *lit* dove; **~ călător** carrier pigeon; **~ mesager** homing pigeon, homer.
poruncă [po'runkă] *nf* order, injunction; **cele zece ~i** the Ten Commandments, the Decalogue.
porunci [porun'chi] *vt* to order, to command ‖ *vi* to rule.
posac [po'sak] *adj* sullen, gloomy ‖ *adv* sullenly, gloomily.
poseda [pose'da] *vt* to own, to possess; (*a avea*) to have; *fig* to be master of; to be conversant with.
posesi(un)e [posesi'(un)e] *nf* possession; (*pământ*) land; (*moşie*) estate.
posesiv [pose'siv] *adj gram* possessive.
posesor [pose'sor] *nm* owner, possessor.
posibil [po'sibil] *adj* possible ‖ *adv* possibly, maybe, perhaps; *coll* in the cards • **~itate** *nf* possibility; *pl* (*mijloace*) means; (*resurse*) resources.
posomorât [posomo'rât] *adj* (*d. vreme, cer*) dull, cloudy; (*d. cineva*) sullen, morose; (*dezolant*) gloomy, dreary ‖ *adv* gloomily, drearily.

pospai [pos'pai] *nn* flour dust; (*strat subţire*) thin layer; *fig* smattering.

post [post] *nn also mi, tech* post; appointment; (*slujbă*) job; (*situaţie*) position; *tech* station; fast(ing).

postament [posta'ment] *nn* pedestal, base.

poster ['poster] *nn* poster; sticker; billboard.

posterior [posteri'or] *adj* posterior; (*de dinapoi*) hinder, hind; (*temporal*) subsequent; (*mai târziu*) later.

posteritate [posteri'tate] *nf* posterity; descendants, issue.

posti [pos'ti] *vi* to fast.

postmortem [post'mortem] *adv* postmortem.

post-restant [postres'tant] *nn/adj/adv* poste restante, general delivery.

postum [pos'tum] *adj* posthumous || *adv* posthumously.

postură [pos'tură] *nf* (*a corpului*) posture, attitude; position, situation.

poşetă [po'shetă] *nf* purse, handbag.

poştal [posh'tal] *adj* postal, post || *adv* by post.

poştaş [posh'tash] *nm* postman, letter carrier.

poştă ['poshtă] *nf* post; (*clădirea, birourile*) post office; *hist* mail coach; *hist* (*distanţă*) post mile; ~ **aeriană** air mail; **prin** ~ by post.

pot [pot] *nn* sweepstake(s), stake.

potabil [po'tabil] *adj* drinkable, fit to drink.

potârniche [potâr'nike] *nf* orn partridge.

potcoavă [pot'koavă] *nf* horseshoe; (*la bocanci*) clout.

potcovi [potko'vi] *vt* to shoe; *fig coll* to diddle, to take in.

potecă [po'tekă] *nf* path.

potent [po'tent] *adj* potent, vigorous.

potenţial [potentsi'al] *nn* potential; (*capacitate*) scope || *adj* potential, prospective.

poteră ['poteră] *nf* hist posse.

poticni [potik'ni] *vr* (*de*) *also fig* to stumble (over); (*şi d. cai*) to flounder.

potir [po'tir] *nn* cup, bowl; *relig* chalice; *bot* calyx.

potlogar [potlo'gar] *nm* swindler, cheat, deceiver.

potlogărie [potlogă'rie] *nf* cheating; (*ca act*) cheat, fraud.

potoli [poto'li] *vt* (*a uşura*) to relieve; (*a micşora*) to diminish; (*a modera, a îndulci*) to mitigate; (*a linişti*) to appease; (*o răscoală*) to suppress; (*patimi*) to assuage; (*vântul*) to lay; (*a face să tacă*) to hush; (*mânia*) to calm; (*a pacifica*) to pacify; (*o durere*) to soothe; (*marea, valurile*) to still; (*furtuna*) to lull; (*setea*) to quench || *vr* (*d. vânt*) to abate; (*d. cineva*) to calm down; to settle down; (*a se micşora*) to diminish.

potop [po'top] *nn* flood; *fig* (*de lacrimi*) flow; (*de ocări etc*) torrent; *fig* (*pustiire*) ravage; (*distrugere*) destruction || *adv* in floods/torrents.

potou [po'tou] *nn sp* post.

potpuriu [potpu'riu] *nn mus* potpourri, medley; *fig* hotch-potch.

potrivi [potri'vi] *vt* (*a pune*) to put, to set; (*a aranja*) to arrange; (*perna etc*) to adjust; (*a pune cum trebuie*) to set/put straight; (*părul*) to smooth; (*a aplica*) (*la*) to apply (to); (*a face să se potrivească*) (*la*) to suit (to); (*a găti*) to trim up; (*cu*) to compare (with/to); (*a asimila*) (*cu*) to assimilate (with/to); (*a pune de acord*) (*cu*) to make agree (with); to harmonize; (*a ajusta*) (*la*) to adjust, to fit (to); (*la*) to adapt (to); (*a acorda*) to tune; (*o mâncare*) to season; (*a nimeri*) to hit || *vr* (*cu*) to agree (with); to coincide (with); to tally (with); (*a corespunde*) to match; (*a fi potrivit*)

to fit in; (*a corespunde scopului*) to suit/answer one's purpose; (*a fi pe măsură*) to fit; to conform (to).

potrivit [potri'vit] *adj* fit, suitable; (*d. un moment*) right; (*corespunzător*) corresponding; (*de mijloc*) average || *adv* moderately, in moderation; (*aşa şi aşa*) so and so.

potrivnic [po'trivnik] *adj* hostile, inimical; (*opus*) opposed (to), contrary (to).

poţiune [potsi'une] *nf med* potion, draught.

povară [po'vară] *nf* burden, load; (*greutate*) weight; *fig* (*chin*) torture.

povaţă [po'vatsă] *nf* (*sfat*) advice, counsel.

poveste [po'veste] *nf* story, tale; (*minciună*) fib; (*cu zâne, basm*) fairytale; (*născocire*) invention; *fig* (*chestiune*) matter • **~lungă** long rigmarole.

povesti [poves'ti] *vt* to tell, to recount • **~re** *nf* telling, recounting • **~tor** *nm* (story)teller, narrator; raconteur.

povârniş [povâr'nish] *nn* slope; (*abrupt*) steep.

poza [po'za] *vi* (*pt. portret etc*) to pose, to sit; *fig* to attitudinize || *vt* to photograph, to take a photograph of.

poză ['pozā] *nf* pose, attitude; *coll* (*fotografie*) picture, photograph.

pozitiv [pozi'tiv] *adj* positive; actual, real; (*util*) useful; (*realist*) practical, matter-of-fact || *adv* positively || *nn phot* positive; *gram* positive (degree).

poziţie [po'zitsie] *nf* position; (*a unei localităţi, case etc*) situation, site; (*a corpului etc*) posture; (*socială*) condition, status; *mil* tactical position; *mus* shift; *fig* attitude, stand; (*punct de vedere*) (point of) view, standpoint.

poziţionare [pozitsio'nare] *nf tech* positioning.

poznaş [poz'nash] *adj* tricky, fond of playing tricks; (*glumeţ*) funny, amusing; (*ciudat*) strange || *nm* practical joker, (*glumeţ*) wag.

poznă ['poznă] *nf* (*glumă*) joke; (*farsă*) farce, trick; (*ştrengărie*) prank, mischief; *coll* lark, frolic; (*prostie*) foolish act; (*pagubă*) damage; (*vătămare*) injury, hurt.

practic ['praktik] *adj* (*folositor*) useful, practical; (*d. cineva*) matter-of-fact; (*priceput*) experienced || *adv* in actual fact, as a matter of fact.

practica [prakti'ka] *vt* to practice, to put into practice; (*a folosi*) to use, to employ || *vr pass* to be practiced.

practică ['praktikă] *nf* practice; (*aplicare*) application; (*uzaj*) usage, use; (*metodă*) method; **a pune în** ~ to put into practice; to implement.

pradă ['pradă] *nf* booty; (*jaf*; *pradă luată prin jaf*) plunder; (*în război*) loot, spoil(s) (of war); (*în război pe mare*) prize; (*a vânătorului, pescarului*) bag, catch.

praf [praf] *nn* dust; (*pudră*) powder; *pharm* cachet, powder.

prag [prag] *nn also fig* threshold; (*de râu*) rapid(s).

pragmatic [prag'matik] *adj* pragmatic || *adv* pragmatically.

praştie ['prashtie] *nf* sling; (boy's) catapult.

praz [praz] *nm bot* leek.

praznic ['praznik] *nn* (*după înmormântare*) funeral repast, burial feast; (*la hram etc*) wake; (church) festival; *fig* feast, banquet.

prăbuşi [prăbu'shi] *vr* to fall suddenly/heavily, to tumble down, to fall in, to come down with a crash; *also fig* to break down, to collapse; *coll* (*d. proiecte etc*) to go wrong • **~re** *nf* (sudden or heavy) fall; collapse; *fig* breakdown, collapse.

prăda [pra'da] *vt* to plunder, to rob; *esp mil* to pillage; (*a devasta*) to ravage; (*un oraș*) to sack, to loot; (*pe cineva*) to rob, to strip.

prăfuit [prăfu'it] *adj* dusty; *also fig* stale; old-fashioned.

prăji [pră'zhi] *vt* (*în tigaie*) to fry; (*la foc*) to roast, to broil; (*pe grătar*) to grill; (*a coace*) to bake; (*a căli*) to stir-fry; (*pâine*) to toast; (*a arde*) to burn; (*a bronza*) to tan; *fig coll* to diddle, to gull ‖ *vr* to fry, to roast, to broil; (*la soare*) to bake/bask in the sun; *fig coll* to be diddled/gulled.

prăjină [pră'zhină] *nf* pole; (*de rufe*) crotch; *fig coll* lamppost; *tech* drill pipe; *sp* (vaulting) pole.

prăjitură [prăzhi'tură] *nf* cake; (*uscată*) biscuit.

prăpastie [pră'pastie] *nf* precipice; *also fig* abyss, gulf; (*strungă*) ravine; (*dezastru*) disaster, ruin.

prăpăd [pră'păd] *nn* disaster, calamity; destruction; *fig* flood • ~i *vt* to destroy, to annihilate; (*a ucide*) to kill; (*a irosi*) to waste; (*a da iama în*) to play havoc with; (*a pustii*) to lay waste ‖ *vr pass* to be destroyed, etc; (*a muri*) to die; (*a pieri*) to perish • ~t *adj* broken, deteriorated; (*distrus*) destroyed; (*nenorocit*) wretched, miserable ‖ *nm* wretch.

prăpăstios [prăpăsti'os] *adj* precipitous, steep; (*d. cineva*) pessimistic; (*fricos*) fearful.

prăși [pră'shi] *vt* to weed, to hoe • ~t *nn* weeding, hoeing.

prăvăli [prăvă'li] *vt* to throw down, to overthrow; (*a trânti*) to knock down ‖ *vr* (*a se prăbuși*) to fall down.

prăvălie [prăvă'lie] *nf* shop.

prânz [prânz] *nn* lunch(eon), midday meal; (*servit uneori seara, dar fiind o masă consistentă*) dinner • ~i *vi* to lunch, to dine, to have dinner ‖ *vi* to have lunch/dinner.

prea [prea] *adv* too; (*în construcții negative*) very.

preajmă ['preazhmă] *nf* surrounding(s), vicinity; **din** ~ near, around; **în** ~ (*spațial*) around, about; (*temporal*) about; (*către*) towards; (*în ajunul*) on the eve of.

prealabil [prea'labil] *adj* previous, preceding; **în** ~ beforehand, to begin with.

preamări [preamă'ri] *vt* to exalt, to extol, (*a lăuda*) to praise.

preambul [pream'bul] *nn* preamble.

preasfințit [preasfin'tsit] *adj relig* very reverend, all holy/saintly.

preaviz [prea'viz] *nn* (previous) notice.

precar [pre'kar] *adj* precarious; (*greu*) hard.

precaut [preka'ut] *adj* (pre)cautious, wary ‖ *adv* cautiously, warily.

precauție [preka'utsie] *nf* precaution; (*prudență*) caution, wariness; **cu** ~ cautiously.

precădere [prekă'dere] *nf* priority, preference; **cu** ~ preeminently, especially, particularly.

preceda [preche'da] *vt/vi* to precede, to go before.

precedent [preche'dent] *adj* (*ultimul dinainte*) preceding; (*de demult*) former, previous ‖ *nn* precedent; **fără** ~ unprecedented, unparalleled, unheard of.

precipita [prechipi'ta] *vt* to hurry, to hasten; *chem* to precipitate ‖ *vr* (*d. evenimente*) to rush, to escape control; *chem* to precipitate • ~ții *nf pl* precipitations; (*ploaie*) rainfall; ~ **radioactive** *met* fallout.

precis [pre'chis] *adj* precise, exact; (*d. un termen etc*) unambiguous ‖ *adv* exactly, precisely; (*sigur*) by all means, definitely; (*referitor la ore*) sharp.

preciza [prechi'za] *vt* to specify, to state precisely ‖ *vr pass* to be specified, to be stated precisely.

precizie [pre'chizie] *nf* precision, preciseness, accuracy ‖ *adj* **de** ~ accurate.

precoce [pre'koche] *adj* precocious.

preconceput [prekonche'put] *adj* preconceived.

precum [pre'kum] *conj* as; ~ **și** as well as; ~ **urmează** as follows.

precupeț [preku'pets] *nm* petty trader; (*de stradă*) street vendor.

precupeți [prekupe'tsi] *vt* to spare.

precursor [prekur'sor] *nm* forerunner, precursor.

preda [pre'da] *vt* to hand over, to deliver; (*a încredința*) to entrust smb with; (*a da*) to give; *scol* to teach ‖ *vr pass* to be handed (over), etc; (*d. cineva*) to surrender; (*ca prizonier*) to yield oneself; to capitulate.

predecesor [predeche'sor] *nm* predecessor, forerunner.

predestinare [predesti'nare] *nf* predestination.

predica [predi'ka] *vi/vt* to preach.

predicat [predi'kat] *nn gram, log* predicate.

predică ['predikă] *nf* sermon.

predilecție [predi'lektsie] *nf* predilection, partiality; **de** ~ *adj* favorite; preferable ‖ *adv* preferably; (*mai ales*) particularly.

predispoziție [predispo'zitsie] *nf* predisposition, propensity; *med* idiosyncrasy.

predomina [predomi'na] *vi* to predominate, to prevail • ~nt *adj* prevailing, predominant.

preemțiune [preemtsi'une] *nf jur* pre-emption, option.

prefabricat [prefabri'kat] *nn constr* prefabricated part, prefab.

preface [pre'fache] *vt* to transform, to change, (*o haină*) to alter; (*a face din nou*) to do/to make anew; **a** ~ **în** to turn into ‖ *vr pass* (*a simula*) to pretend; *esp mil* to malinger.

prefață [pre'fatsă] *nf* foreword, preface, introduction.

prefăcătorie [prefăkăto'rie] *nf* simulation, pretence; (*ipocrizie*) hypocrisy, dissimulation.

prefect [pre'fekt] *nm hist* prefect; ~ **de poliție** chief commissioner of the police • ~ură *nf hist* prefect's office.

prefera [prefe'ra] *vt* to prefer, to like better • ~bil *adj* preferable; (*mai bun*) better ‖ *adv* preferably.

preferință [prefe'rintsă] *nf* preference; **de** ~ preferably.

prefigura [prefigu'ra] *vt* to foreshadow • ~re *nf* premonition, foreshadowing.

prefix [pre'fiks] *nn* prefix.

pregăti [pregă'ti] *vt* to get/make ready, to prepare; (*a instrui*) to train; (*o lecție*) to do; (*pt. un examen*) to coach; (*un sportiv*) to train; (*o surpriză*) to make preparations; to arrange; to have smth in store for smb; (*masa*) to cook/fix the meal ‖ *vr pass* to be trained, etc; to prepare, to get/ make ready; (*a fi pe punctul de a se petrece*) to be about to take place; (*d. un pericol etc*) to be imminent/threatening.

preget ['predjet] *nn* cessation; (*răgaz*) leisure; (*odihnă*) rest; **fără** ~ ceaselessly, continuously, (*imediat*) at once, immediately.

preîntâmpina [preîntâmpi'na] *vt* to prevent, to avert.

prejudecată [prezhude'kată] *nf* prejudice, preconceived idea.

prejudicia [prezhudichi'a] *vt* to be detrimental/prejudicial to.

prejudiciu [prezhu'dichiu] *nn* prejudice; (*moral*) injury, wrong; (*pagubă*) damage; (*rău*) harm.

prelat [pre'lat] *nm* prelate.

prelată [pre'lată] *nf* tarpaulin.

prelegere [pre'ledjere] *nf* lecture.

preleva [prele'va] *vt* to draw.

preliminar [prelimi'nar] *adj* preliminary; explanatory, tentative • **~ii** *nn pl* preliminaries; preamble.

prelinge [pre'lindje] *vr* to trickle, to ooze (out), to drop out.

prelua [pre'lua] *vt* to take over; (*a lua*) to take.

prelucra [preluk'ra] *vt* (*a reface*) to remake; to transform; *tech* to process (into); (*o chestiune*) to debate upon; (*a studia*) to study; (*un plan*) to work out; (*pe cineva*) to brief; to carry on explanatory work with || *vr pass* to be remade, to be transformed.

prelungi [prelun'dji] *vt* to prolong, to extend || *vr* to be delayed, to be dragged out; (*a dura*) to last • **~re** *nf* prolongation, extension.

prematur [prema'tur] *adj* premature, untimely.

premedita [premedi'ta] *vt* to premeditate • **~re** *nf* premeditation; **cu** ~ deliberately, willfully; *jur* with malice/aforethought.

premergător [premergă'tor] *adj* precursory || *nm* forerunner, precursor.

premia [premi'a] *vt* to award a prize (to); (*un funcţionar etc*) to give a bonus to.

premier [premi'er] *nm* premier, prime minister.

premieră [premi'eră] *nf thea* premiere, first performance/night, opening night.

premisă [pre'misă] *nf log, also fig* premise.

premiu [premiu] *nn* prize; (*răsplată*) reward; (*al unui funcţionar etc*) premium, bonus.

prenume [pre'nume] *nn* first name, Christian name.

preocupa [preoku'pa] *vt* to concern, to preoccupy || *vr* **a se** ~ **de** to concern oneself with, to attend to.

preot [preot] *nm* (*catolic şi protestant*) minister, (*ortodox etc*) priest; (*om al bisericii*) clergyman; (*beneficiar al venitului bisericesc*) rector, incumbent; (*idem, o jumătate din venit*) vicar; pastor; (*teolog*) divine.

preoţi [preo'tsi] *vt* to ordain || *vr relig* to take/receive holy orders.

prepara [prepa'ra] *vt* * **pregăti**.

prepelicar [prepeli'kar] *nm zool* (land) spaniel.

prepeliţă ['prepelitsă] *nf orn* quail.

preponderent [preponde'rent] *adj* preponderant; (*d. un rol*) leading.

prepoziţie [prepo'zitsie] *nf gram* preposition.

prerie [pre'rie] *nf* prairie.

prerogativă [preroga'tivă] *nf* prerogative.

presa [pre'sa] *vt* to press, to compress; *fig* to beset, to ply; (*a zori*) to urge • **~nt** *adj* pressing, urgent.

presă ['presă] *nf tech* press, pressing machine; *typ* printing press; (*ziare*) newspapers.

presăra [presă'ra] *vt* to strew; (*cu pudră de zahăr*) to sugar; (*cu nisip*) to sand; (*cu sare*) to salt; (*cu făină*) to sprinkle with flour; (*a împrăştia*) to scatter || *vr pass* to be strewn, etc.

presbitism [presbi'tism] *nn* long-sightedness.

prescrie [pres'krie] *vt* to prescribe, to lay down || *vr jur* to be lost by limitation or prescription.

prescripţie [pres'kriptsie] *nf med* prescription; direction, regulation.

prescurta [preskur'ta] *vt* to abbreviate, to shorten.

presentiment [presenti'ment] *nn* presentiment.

presimţi [presim'tsi] *vt* to sense, to have a premonition/foreboding of • **~re** *nf* foreboding, premonition.

presiune [presi'une] *nf also fig* pressure.

prestabilit [prestabi'lit] *adj* pre-established; *fig* cut-and-dried.

prestanţă [pres'tantsă] *nf* imposing/dignified/impressive appearance.

prestidigitator [prestididjita'tor] *nm* juggler, conjurer, prestidigitator.

prestigios [prestidji'os] *adj* impressive, imposing.

prestigiu [pres'tidjiu] *nn* prestige, high reputation.

presupune [presu'pune] *vt* to presume, to assume, to suppose, (*a implica*) to imply • **~re** *nf* assumption, supposition.

presuriza [presuri'za] *vt* to pressurize.

preş [presh] *nn* carpet, runner; (*la uşă*) door mat.

preşedinte [preshe'dinte] *nm* president; (*al unei adunări etc*) chairman.

preşedinţie [preshedin'tsie] *nf* presidency; chairmanship.

preta [pre'ta] *vr* **a se~ la** (*a se potrivi la*) to be suited to, to lend itself to; (*d. cineva*) to lend/commit oneself to; (*a fi de acord cu*) to agree to; (*la o escrocherie*) to countenance.

pretendent [preten'dent] *nm* pretender; (*la o moştenire etc*) claimant; applicant, candidate; (*la mâna cuiva*) wooer, suitor.

pretenţie [pre'tentsie] *nf* (*la*) claim (to), pretension (to); *pl* pretensions, airs.

pretenţios [pretentsi'os] *adj* exacting, exigent; pretentious, affected || *adv* pretentiously.

pretext [pre'tekst] *nn* pretext, excuse • **sub ~ul** under the pretext of, on the pretence of • **~a** *vt* to pretext, to offer/give as a pretext; to feign, to sham.

pretinde [pre'tinde] *vt* (*ca pe un drept*) to claim, to lay claim to; to mean; (*a cere*) to require; to aspire to; (*a insista asupra*) to insist on; (*a avea nevoie de*) to need; (*a susţine*) to maintain || *vr* **a se ~** to claim to be.

pretutindeni [pretu'tindeni] *adv* everywhere; here, there and everywhere, high and low; (*oriunde*) anywhere.

preţ [prets] *nn also fig* price; cost; *fig* value, worth • **~ios** *adj* precious; *fig* valuable; (*drag*) dear; (*afectat*) affected || *adv* preciously, in an affected manner • **~ui** *vt also fig* to value, to estimate; to appreciate; (*mult, pe cineva*) to think much of; (*mult, ceva*) to set much store by || *vi* to be worth; to cost.

prevăzător [prevăză'tor] *adj* far-seeing/-sighted, provident; prudent, cautious, wary.

prevedea [preve'dea] *vt* to foresee, to forecast; (*în buget etc*) to provide for; (*a înzestra*) to equip || *vr* to be foreseen; *pass* to be provided for; to be stipulated; to be equipped.

preveni [preve'ni] *vt* to inform, to apprise; (*a avertiza*) to warn; (*a preîntâmpina*) to prevent • **~tor** *adj* obliging, amiable || *adv* amiably, politely.

preventiv [preven'tiv] *adj* preventive; *med* prophylactic.

prevesti [preves'ti] *vt* to foreshadow, to presage; *lit* to herald; *rare* to forebode • **~tor** *adj* foreboding.

previzibil [previ'zibil] *adj* predictable, foreseeable.

prezbit [prez'bit] *adj* long-sighted, presbyopic || *nm* long-sighted/presbyopic person.

prezbiterian [prezbiteri'an] *adj/nm* Presbyterian.

prezent [pre'zent] *adj* present; (*acesta*) this || *nn* present; *gram* present (tense).

prezenta [prezen'ta] *vt* to present; (*a oferi*) to offer; (*a da*) to give; (*fapte*) to put/lay before smb; (*concluzii*) to bring up; (*a arăta*) to show; (*a recomanda*) to recommend; (*a avea, a se bucura de*) to have; (*un* *raport*) to make; (*dovezi*) to produce; (*a reprezenta*) to represent; *thea* to perform ‖ *vr* (*a se ivi*) to present oneself; (*d. o situație etc*) to arise; to offer; *coll* to crop up; (*la*) to present oneself (for); (*d. un candidat*) to come forward as a candidate; (*cuiva*) to introduce oneself (to smb).

prezentabil [prezen'tabil] *adj* presentable, of good appearance.

prezentator [prezenta'tor] *nm* entertainer, announcer, presenter.

prezență [pre'zentsă] *nf* presence; (*la școală etc*) attendance ‖ *adj* (*în ochii*) in smb's sight; (*înaintea*) before.

prezervativ [prezerva'tiv] *nn* condom; sheath.

prezice [pre'ziche] *vt* to predict, to forecast, to prophesy.

prezida [prezi'da] *vt* to preside at/over, to chair ‖ *vi* to be in the chair, to preside.

prezidiu [pre'zidiu] *nn* presidium, presidency.

prezumtiv [prezum'tiv] *adj* presumptive.

prezumție [pre'zumtsie] *nf* (*presupunere*) assumption, suspicion; (*îndrăzneală*) presumption.

pribeag [pri'beag] *adj* (*rătăcitor*) wandering, vagrant; (*fugar*) fugitive; (*singur*) solitary, lonely.

pricepe [pri'chepe] *vt* (*a înțelege*) to understand ‖ *vr* to be skilled in smth.

priceput [priche'put] *adj* capable, able; (*îndemânatic*) skillful, skilled; (*deștept*) clever; (*experimentat*) experienced.

prichindel [prikin'del] *nm* dwarf; runt; *coll* Tom Thumb, whipper-snapper.

pricină ['prichină] *nf* reason, cause, motive; (*ceartă*) quarrel; (*chestiune*) matter, affair; (*necaz*) trouble.

pricinui [prichnu'i] *vt* to cause, to bring about, to produce.

prididi [pridi'di] *vt* to overcome, to get over ‖ *vi* **a ~ cu** to bring to a close/conclusion/end; (*a face față*) to cope with.

pridvor [prid'vor] *nn* church porch; verandah, balcony; hallway.

prielnic [pri'elnik] *adj* favorable, propitious; auspicious.

prieten ['prieten] *nm* friend, pal, buddy • **~esc** *adj* friendly, amicable • **~ește** *adv* like a friend; in a friendly way/manner • **~os** *adj* friendly, amicable ‖ *adv* in a friendly way/manner; like a friend • **~ie** *nf* friendship; *frml* amity .

prigoni [prigo'ni] *vt* to persecute; (*a asupri*) to oppress.

prihăni [prihă'ni] *vt* to spoil, to smear; (*o dată*) to undo; to violate.

prii [pri'i] *vi* **a-i ~ cuiva** to be favorable to smb, to suit smb; (*d. climă etc*) to agree with smb.

prilej [pri'lezh] *nn* occasion; (*favorabil*) opportunity; motive, reason • **~ui** *vt* to occasion, to cause, to bring about.

prim [prim] *num/adj* first, initial, inaugural, maiden; (*timpuriu*) early; principal, main; *math* prime.

primar [pri'mar] *adj* primary, elementary; primitive, primeval; **era ~ă** *geol* the primary period ‖ *nm hist* mayor; (*de sat*) (village) magistrate, headman.

primate [pri'mate] *nf pl zool* primates.

primă ['primă] *nf* premium, bonus.

primărie [primă'rie] *nf hist* town hall, mayoralty.

primăvară ['primăvară] *nf* spring.

primejdie [pri'mezhdie] *nf* danger, jeopardy.

primejdios [primezhdi'os] *adj* dangerous, perilous ‖ *adv* dangerously, perilously.

primejdui [primezhdu'i] *vt* to endanger, to jeopardize; (*a risca*) to risk.

primi [pri'mi] *vt* to receive, to get; (*a i se conferi*) to be awarded; (*a i se da*) to be given; (*a întâmpina*) to meet; to admit; to include; to accept; (*a fi de acord*) to agree; to consent to; (*la hotel*) to accommodate.

primitiv [primi'tiv] *adj* primitive, (*primar*) primeval; (*d. o metodă etc*) crude ‖ *adv* primitively.

primitor [primi'tor] *adj* hospitable ‖ *adv* hospitably.

primordial [primordi'al] *adj* primordial, essential ‖ *adv* primordially, essentially.

prin [prin] *prep* through; *coll* thru; in; (*în preajma*) about, around; (*în timpul*) during; **~ care** by/through which, whereby.

princiar [princhi'ar] *adj* princely.

principal [princhi'pal] *adj* chief, principal, main.

principat [princhi'pat] *nn* principality.

principial [princhipi'al] *adj* of principle; *fig* principled ‖ *adv* (*din principiu*) on principle; (*în esență*) in essence, in the main.

principiu [prin'chipiu] *nn* principle, fundamental truth; rule of conduct, conviction.

prinde ['prinde] *vt* to catch; (*a lua*) to take; (*a pescui*) to fish; (*cu năvodul*) to net; (*a apuca, a înșfăca*) to grip, to grasp, to clutch; (*a înhăța*) to grab; to snatch off/up; (*a se agăța de*) to cling to; (*a pune mâna pe, a captura*) to seize; (*a ajunge din urmă*) to catch up; (*a îmbrățișa*) to embrace; (*a prinde în brațe*) to take/clasp/fold in one's arms, to put one's arms round; *fig* (*a cuprinde cu ochiul*) to take in; (*a înțelege, a sesiza*) to comprehend; (*a surprinde*) to surprise; (*a lua pe neașteptate*) to take unawares; (*o privire*) to catch the eye; (*o conversație*) to overhear; (*a fixa, a lega*) to fasten; (*o broșă, o panglică etc*) to pin; (*cu acul*) to sew/stitch together; (*cu boldul*) to fasten/attach with a pin; (*în cui*) to hang; (*în cuie*) to nail; (*în cuie de lemn*) to peg; (*a căpăta, a dobândi*) to acquire; to find; to regain; to recruit; (*a lua cu sila, a răpi*) (*o femeie*) to abduct; (*copii*) to kidnap ‖ *vr* (*a-și asuma o obligație*) (*să*) to pledge one's word (to); (*a face o prinsoare*) to lay a bet; (*a se întări, d. ciment*) to set; (*d. piftie*) to congeal; (*d. lapte*) to curdle; (*d. sânge*) to clot; (*d. râuri*) to freeze up ‖ *vi* (*a reuși, a izbuti*) to succeed; (*o piesă*) to be a success; *coll* to be a hit; (*d. un roman etc*) to have appeal; (*d. un truc*) to come off; (*d. o modă*) to catch on; (*d. plante, arbori etc*) to take root.

prinsoare [prin'soare] *nf* (*rămășag*) *nf* bet, wager.

printre ['printre] *prep* among; (*în mijlocul*) in the middle of; amidst; through; **~ altele** among other things.

prinț [prints] *nm* prince • **~esă** *nf* princess.

prioritate [priori'tate] *nf* priority; (*la circulație*) right of way.

pripă ['pripă] *nf* haste, hurry.

pripi [pri'pi] *vt* to burn ‖ *vr* to hurry (too much), to be in (too great) a hurry; to act rashly/thoughtlessly.

pripon [pri'pon] *nn* (*funie*) tether; (*țăruș*) stake, peg; row of fishing lines • **~i** *vt* to tether; to fix; (*a lega*) to tie, to bind.

prismă ['prismă] *nf geom* prism; *also fig* point of view, angle.

prisos [pri'sos] *nn* surplus; (*belșug*) abundance, plenty.

prispă ['prispă] *nf approx* porch, veranda; (*baraj*) dam.

priva [pri'va] *vt* (*de*) to deprive smb (of) ‖ *vr* **a se ~ de** to do without, to deprive oneself of.

privat [pri'vat] *adj* private, personal, individual.

privată [pri'vata] *nf* privy, latrine.

privatiza [privati'za] *vt* to privatize • **~re** *nf* privatization.

privațiune [privatsi'une] *nf* deprivation, loss; (*lipsă*) privation; (*greutate*) hardship.

priveghea [prive'gea] *vi* to watch; (*a fi treaz*) to be awake; (*intenționat*) to keep vigil || *vt* to watch; (*a îngriji*) to take care of; (*un mort*) to wake.

priveliște [pri'velishte] *nf* view, sight; (*peisaj*) landscape; (*marină*) seascape.

privi [pri'vi] *vi* to look; (*fix*) to gaze; (*în gol sau fix*) to stare; to gawp; (*cu uimire*) to gape; (*cu mânie*) to glare; (*cercetător*) to peer; (*în sus*) to look up; **a ~ la** to look at/on/upon, to gaze at; (*a-și aținti privirea asupra*) to fix one's eyes upon || *vt* to look at; (*fix*) to gaze at/on/upon; (*cercetător*) to peer for; (*a interesa*) to concern; to interest; to consider || *vr recip* to look at each other.

privighetoare [privige'toare] *nf orn* nightingale.

privilegiu [privi'ledju] *nn* privilege; preference; (*favoare*) favor; (*avantaj*) advantage; (*concret*) license.

privință [pri'vintsă] *nf* **în această ~** in this respect, on that score; **în ~a** with regard to, concerning, regarding.

privire [pri'vire] *nf* sight; (*ochi*) eyes; examination; consideration.

priză ['priză] *nf elec* connection, plug; *tech* taking, device; (*de tutun*) pinch of snuff; *fig* influence, popularity; (*greutate*) weight.

prizonier [prizoni'er] *nm* prisoner, captive.

proaspăt ['proaspăt] *adj* fresh, new; (*d. pâine etc*) new; (*înviorător*) bracing; (*rece*) cold; recent; (*nou*) new; (*viu*) living.

proba [pro'ba] *vt* (*a dovedi*) to prove, to demonstrate; to (put to the) test; (*o rochie etc*) to try on; (*un metal etc*) to assay; (*a încerca*) to try || *vr pass* to be proved, to be demonstrated, to be tested, to be tried on.

probabil [pro'babil] *adj* probably, likely || *adv* probably, in all likelihood • **~itate** *nf* probability, likelihood.

probă ['probă] *nf* proof, test; (*încercare*) trial; (*a unui metal*) assay; (*verificare*) verification; check-up, control; examination; (*mostră*) sample; (*de stofă*) pattern; (*dovadă*) evidence; argument; (*a unei haine*) trying on; (*făcută pe altul*) fiting; *sp* event.

probitate [probi'tate] *nf* uprightness, probity, integrity.

problematic [proble'matic] *adj* problematical, doubtful || *adv* problematically.

problemă [pro'blemă] *nf* problem, question; (*chestiune*) matter; (*obiect al unei discuții, controverse*) issue; **~ litigioasă** moot point, vexed question.

proceda [proche'da] *vi* to act; (*la*) to proceed (to); to go on (to).

procedeu [proche'deu] *nn* proceeding, dealing; line of action; (*metodă*) method; (*formulă*) device; (*comportare*) behavior.

procedură [proche'dură] *nf* procedure, proceedings.

procent [pro'chent] *nn* percentage, rate (percent); (*dobândă*) interest • **~aj** *nn* percentage.

proces [pro'ches] *nn* process; (*dezvoltare*) development; (*curs*) course; *jur* action at law; (*civil*) (law)suit; (*penal*) (criminal) trial.

procesa [proche'sa] *vt* to process • **~re** *nf* processing • **~t** *adj* processed; typewritten.

procesiune [prochesi'une] *nf* procession.

proclama [prokla'ma] *vt* to proclaim, to declare; to

publish || *vr pass* to be proclaimed, etc; to proclaim oneself • **~ție** *nf* proclamation.

procrea [prokre'a] *vi* to procreate, to beget; *coll* to have children.

procura [proku'ra] *vt* to procure, to obtain; (*bani*) to raise; (*o clientelă*) to work up a connection; to produce || *vr pass* to be procured, etc.

procuratură [prokura'tură] *nf* prosecuting, magistracy; (*clădirea*) prosecutor's office.

procură [pro'kură] *nf* procuration, proxy; mandate; power of attorney; **prin ~** by proxy.

procuror [proku'ror] *nm* public prosecutor; district attorney.

prodigios [prodidji'os] *adj* prodigious, stupendous || *adv* prodigiously, stupendously.

producător [produkă'tor] *adj* producing, productive || *nm* producer.

produce [pro'duche] *vt* to produce, to yield; (*a face*) to make; (*a crea*) to create; to turn out; (*a da naștere la*) to bring forth; (*a genera*) to generate; (*a livra*) to deliver; to manufacture; (*a cauza*) to bring about || *vr pass* to be produced, etc; (*a avea loc*) to take place; (*a se întâmpla*) to occur, to happen; *thea etc* to appear before the public || *vi* to bring in an income; (*d. o ocupație etc*) to be profitable.

productivitate [produktivi'tate] *nf* productivity, productiveness; productive/yield capacity; (*randament*) efficiency.

producție [pro'duktsie] *nf* (*producere*) production, producing, * **produce**; (*industrială*) output; manufacture; (*agricolă*) yield; *cin* production.

produs [pro'dus] *nn* (*natural*) produce; (*industrial*) product; manufactured article; *fig* result, outcome.

proeminent [proemi'nent] *adj* prominent, jutting out; *fig* remarkable, exceptional.

profan [pro'fan] *adj* profane, secular || *nm* layman, uninitiated person; *coll* outsider.

profana [profa'na] *vt* to profane, to defile; (*un mormânt*) to violate; (*o biserică*) to desecrate; (*talentul etc*) to misuse.

profera [profe'ra] *vt* to utter.

profesi(un)e [pro'fesie] *nf* profession, occupation, trade.

profesional [profesio'nal] *adj* professional.

profesionist [profesio'nist] *adj/nm* professional, expert.

profesoară [profe'soară] *nf* teacher; (*la elementar*) (school-)mistress; (*univ.*) (woman) professor.

profesor [pro'fesor] *nm* teacher; (*la elementar*) (school)master; (*univ.*) professor.

profet [pro'fet] *nm* prophet; (*prezicător*) prophesier • **~ic** *adj* prophetic(al) || *adv* prophetically.

profeție [profe'tsie] *nf* prophecy.

profil [pro'fil] *nn* profile, side face; silhouette; *tech* contour, shape; *fig* type; structure, make-up • **~a** *vt* to profile; *tech* to shape || *vr* to be outlined/silhouetted; *fig* (*pentru/pe un anumit domeniu*) to specialize (in).

profilactic [profi'laktik] *adj med* prophylactic, preventive.

profit [pro'fit] *nn* profit, benefit; (*venit*) income • **~or** *adj* profiteering || *nm* profiteer • **~a** *vi* to profit; **a ~ de** to profit by, to take advantage of, to avail oneself of.

profund [pro'fund] *adj* (*adânc*) deep, profound; (*d. somn*) deep, sound || *adv* deeply, profoundly.

profunzime [profun'zime] *nf* profoundness, depth.

prognostic [pro'gnostik] *nn med* prognosis; forecast • **~a** *vt* to prognose, to forecast.

prognoză [prog'noză] *nf* forecast, prognostication.

program [pro'gram] *nn* program; *fig* bill of fare; (*al unui partid*) platform; (*de studii etc*) syllabus, curriculum; (*de spectacol*) program, playbill; *sp* entry • ~**a** *vt* to program; (*a anunța*) to bill, to announce; to schedule; to plan; (*un dispozitiv*) to set • ~**are** *nf* programming, planning • ~**ator** *nm comp* programmer.

progres [pro'gres] *nn* progress • ~**a** *vi* to progress; (*d. o boală*) to grow (progressively) worse • ~**ist** *adj* progressive; (*d. scriitori, savanți*) progressive-minded; (*avansat*) advanced || *nm* progressionist, progressive • ~**iv** *adj* progressive, gradual || *adv* progressively, gradually.

prohibiție [prohi'bitsie] *nf* prohibition.

proiect [pro'iekt] *nn* project, design; (*document*) draft; *fig* plan, scheme • ~**a** *vt* (*a elabora un proiect pentru*) to project, to design; (*a arunca*) to throw; (*o umbră*) to cast; (*un film*) to show on the screen; (*o rază*) to flash; *fig* to plan, to contemplate || *vr pass* to be projected, etc. • ~**ant** *nm* planner, designer, draftsman.

proiectil [proiek'til] *nn* projectile, missile; (*glonte*) bullet; (*obuz*) shell.

proiector [proiek'tor] *nn* searchlight; projector.

proiecție [pro'iektsie] *nf* projection.

proletar [prole'tar] *adj* proletarian || *nm* proletarian • ~**iat** *nn* proletariat(e).

prolifera [prolife'ra] *vt* to proliferate, to disseminate • ~**re** *nf* proliferation.

prolific [pro'lifik] *adj* prolific.

prolix [pro'liks] *adj* prolix, diffuse; *coll* longwinded || *adv* prolixly, diffusely.

prolog [pro'log] *nn* (*la*) prologue (to).

promenadă [prome'nadă] *nf* * **plimbare**; promenade; (*public*) walk.

promiscuitate [promiskui'tate] *nf* promiscuity, promiscuousness.

promisiune [promisi'une] *nf* (*făgăduială*) promise.

promite [pro'mite] *vt* (*a făgădui*) to promise || *vi* to promise; to be promising.

promițător [promitsă'tor] *adj* promising.

promontoriu [promon'toriu] *nn* promontory, head(land).

promotor [promo'tor] *nm* promoter.

promova [promo'va] *vt* to promote • ~**re** *nf* promotion.

prompt [prompt] *adj* prompt, ready, quick || *adv* promptly • ~**itudine** *nf* promptitude, readiness.

pronostic [pronos'tik] *nn* prognostication.

pronume [pro'nume] *nn gram* pronoun.

pronunța [pronun'tsa] *vt* to pronounce, to articulate; (*a rosti*) to utter; (*o sentință*) to pass, to deliver || *vr pass* to be pronounced, etc; to declare one's opinion; to give one's verdict.

pronunție [pro'nuntsie] *nf* pronunciation.

propaga [propa'ga] *vt* to propagate, to spread (abroad); to popularize || *vr pass* to be propagated, to be spread; (*d. boli*) to spread.

propagandă [propa'gandă] *nf* propaganda.

propășire [propă'shire] *nf* prosperity, flourishing.

propice [pro'piche] *adj* propitious (to), favorable (to).

proporție [pro'portsie] *nf* proportion, ratio; *pl* size; *fig* scope, amplitude; **în ~ cu** in proportion to; (*după*) according to, by.

proporțional [proportsio'nal] *adj* (*cu*) proportional (to) || *adv* proportionally, proportionately.

propovădui [propovădu'i] *vt* to preach, to propagate; (*a învăța*) to teach.

propoziție [propo'zitsie] *nf gram* (*independentă*) sentence; (*parte dintr-o frază*) clause; ~ **principală** main/head clause.

proprietar [proprie'tar] *nm* owner, proprietor; (*funciar*) landowner; (*al unei case, față de chiriași*) landlord.

proprietate [proprie'tate] *nf* property; (*moșie*) estate; (*calitate*) quality; (*trăsătură*) feature, characteristic.

propriu ['propriu] *adj* personal, my/your own; (*potrivit*) proper, fit(ting), appropriate; peculiar to, characteristic of • ~**zis** *adj* proper, properly || *adv* strictly speaking.

propti [prop'ti] *vt* to prop up; (*o casă*) to shore || *vr pass* to be propped up; to support oneself.

propulsa [propul'sa] *vt* to propel, to impel.

propulsie [pro'pulsie] *nf* propulsion, impulsion.

propune [pro'pune] *vt* to suggest, to propose; (*o teorie*) to propound || *vr pass* to be proposed/suggested • ~**re** *nf* proposal, suggestion; (*ofertă*) offer, proposition; (*scrisă*) submission.

proră ['proră] *nf naut* bow, head, prow.

proroci [proro'chi] *vt* to prophesy, to predict.

proscris [pro'skris] *adj* proscribed || *nm* outlaw, prescript.

proslăvi [prosla'vi] *vt* to revere, to extol, to praise.

prosop [pro'sop] *nn* (bath) towel.

prospect [pros'pekt] *nn* prospectus; brochure; plan.

prospecta [prospek'ta] *vt min* to prospect.

prosper [pros'per] *adj* prosperous, thriving, flourishing • ~**itate** *nf* prosperity, thriving, flourishing • ~**a** *vi* to thrive, to prosper, to flourish.

prost [prost] *adj* (*ant "deștept"*) silly, stupid, dull; (*mărginit*) narrow-minded; (*neștiutor*) ignorant; (*naiv*) simple; (*nerafinat*) common; (*rău*) bad, poor; (*dăunător*) harmful; (*nefavorabil*) unfavorable || *adv* badly, poorly || *nm* fool, blockhead, dolt; *coll* noodle, ninny, ass; *sl* sucker; idiot, born fool; *coll* nitwit.

prostată [pros'tată] *nf anat* prostate (gland).

prostănac [prostă'nak] *adj/nm* * **prost**.

prosterna [proster'na] *vr* to prosternate oneself.

prostesc [pros'tesk] *adj* foolish.

prosti [pros'ti] *vt* to stultify, to stupefy, to make stupid; *coll* to fool, to make a fool of || *vr* to grow/get stupid; *coll* to fool (about), to play the fool/ape • ~**e** *nf* folly, stupidity; (*comportare prostească*) foolishness; (*ca act*) foolish/stupid thing; (*absurditate*) nonsense; *coll* rubbish, stuff and nonsense.

prostitua [prostitu'a] *vt also fig* to prostitute || *vr* to prostitute oneself • ~**tă** *nf* prostitute, harlot; *vulg* whore, hooker; *frml* white slave.

prostituție [prosti'tutsie] *nf* prostitution.

protagonist [protago'nist] *nm* protagonist.

protector [protek'tor] *adj* protecting || *nm* protector; *fig coll* sugar daddy; (*al științelor*) patron.

protecție [pro'tektsie] *nf* protection; (*sprijin*) support; (*ajutor*) aid; ~**a muncii** labor protection.

protecționism [protektsio'nism] *nn* protectionism.

proteină [prote'ină] *nf chem* protein.

proteja [prote'zha] *vt* to protect; (*a sprijini*) to support; (*a ajuta*) to aid • ~**t** *nm* protégé || *adj* protected.

protest [pro'test] *nn* protest • ~**a** *vi* (*împotriva*) to protest (against); to object (to/against) || *vt* **a ~ o poliță** *econ* to protest a promissory note.

protestant [protes'tant] *adj/nm* Protestant.

proteză [pro'teză] *nf* prosthesis, prosthetic appliance; (*a membrelor*) artificial limb; (*dentară*) (set of) plates, denture; *ling* prothesis.

protipendadă [protipen'dadă] *nf* aristocracy, nobility.
protocol [proto'kol] *nn* proceedings; ceremonial, protocol.
protoplasmă [proto'plasmă] *nf bio* protoplasm, cell body.
protopop [proto'pop] *nm* archbishop, rector.
prototip [proto'tip] *nn* prototype; *fig* archetype.
protuberanţă [protube'rantsă] *nf* protuberance.
provă ['provă] *nf naut* prow.
proveni [prove'ni] *vi* a ~ din to come/result/proceed from, to originate in.
proverb [pro'verb] *nn* proverb, (*zicală*) saying, maxim, (*vorbă din bătrâni*) adage.
providenţă [provi'dentsă] *nf* providence.
providenţial [providentsi'al] *adj* providential ‖ *adv* providentially.
provincial [provinchi'al] *adj* provincial, country; *coll* countrified ‖ *nm* provincial.
provincie [pro'vinchie] *nf* province; (*ant.* "*oraş*") the provinces, the country; de ~ country, provincial.
provizie [pro'vizie] *nf* provision, store, supply; *pl* provisions, eatables; (*merinde*) victuals.
provizoriu [provi'zoriu] *adj* provisional, temporary.
provoca [provo'ka] *vt* to provoke; to challenge smb to duel; (*a instiga*) to instigate; to cause, to bring about; (*somnul etc*) to induce; (*o nemulţumire*) to give rise to; (*a crea*) to create; (*sentimente*) to call forth; (*un surâs*) to raise; (*a stârni*) to rouse ‖ *vr pass* to be provoked, etc. • ~**tor** *adj* instigating; (*sfidător*) defiant; (*d. zâmbet*) tantalizing.
proxenet [prokse'net] *nm* procurer, pander, pimp.
proximitate [proksimi'tate] *nf* proximity, nearness.
prozaic [pro'zaik] *adj* prosaic(al), philistine; banal, commonplace; (*practic*) matter-of-fact ‖ *adv* prosaically.
prozator [proza'tor] *nm* prose writer, fiction writer.
proză ['prozǎ] *nf also fig* prose.
prozelit [proze'lit] *nm* proselyte.
prudent [pru'dent] *adj* careful, cautious, prudent ‖ *adv* carefully, etc.
prudenţă [pru'dentsă] *nf* prudence, care(fulness).
prun [prun] *nm bot* plum tree • ~**ă** *nf* plum.
prunc [prunk] *nm* baby, babe, infant in arms.
prund [prund] *nn* gravel, grit; bank.
psalm [psalm] *nm* psalm.
pseudonim [pseudo'nim] *nn* pseudonym, pen name, sobriquet.
psihanalist [psihana'list] *nm* (psycho-)analyst.
psihanaliză [psihana'lizǎ] *nf* psychoanalysis.
psihiatrie [psihia'trie] *nf* psychiatry, mind healing.
psihiatru [psihi'atru] *nm* psychiatrist, mind healer.
psihic ['psihik] *adj* psychic(al), mental.
psiholog [psiho'log] *nm* psychologist • ~**ie** *nf* psychology.
psihopat [psiho'pat] *nm* psychopath; neurotic patient; *coll* crank.
psihoză [psi'hozǎ] *nf med* psychosis.
pubertate [puber'tate] *nf* puberty; *coll* awkward age.
pubian [pubi'an] *adj anat* pubian.
public ['publik] *adj* public; (*spectatori*) audience; (*de stat*) State ‖ *adv* publicly ‖ *nn* public.
publica [publi'ka] *vt* to publish, to issue ‖ *vr pass* to be published/issued • ~**ţie** *nf* publication, published work; (*periodică*) periodical; (*carte*) book; (*revistă*) magazine; (*broşură*) brochure, pamphlet.

publicitar [publichi'tar] *adj* (pertaining to) publicity, advertising.
publicitate [publichi'tate] *nf* publicity.
puc [puk] *nn sp* puck.
puci [puch] *nn* putsch.
pudel [pu'del] *nm zool* poodle.
pudic ['pudik] *adj* modest.
puding ['puding] *nn cul* pudding.
pudoare [pu'doare] *nf* chastity, modesty; (sense of) decency; bashfulness.
pudra [pud'ra] *vt* to powder ‖ *vr* to powder (oneself), to powder one's face.
pudră ['pudrǎ] *nf* powder, toilet/face powder.
pudrieră [pudri'erǎ] *nf* powder case, compact.
pueril [pue'ril] *adj* puerile, childish ‖ *adv* puerilely, childishly.
puf [puf] *nn orn* down; *bot* villosity, bloom; (*pt. pudrat*) (powder) puff.
pufăi [pufǎ'i] *vi* (*a respira greu*) to puff and blow/pant; (*dintr-o ţigară*) to puff away at a cigar.
pufni [puf'ni] *vi* to burst out; a ~ în râs to burst out laughing.
pufoaică [pu'foaikǎ] *nf* padded coat.
pufos [pu'fos] *adj* downy, fluffy.
puhoi [pu'hoi] *nn* torrent, rushing stream; *fig* flood.
pui [pui] *nm de pasăre domestică* chicken; (*de pasăre*) nestling; (*de curcan, fazan etc*) poult; (*de animal salbatic*) cub; (*de câine, leu, tigru, urs, lup etc*) whelp; (*copil*) chick(-abiddy), little one; (*dragul meu*) (my) dear, darling; (*de pernă*) small pillow/ cushion • ~**et** *nm bot* seedling, sapling • ~**şor** *nm* chick; (*ca alintare*) chickabiddy; small pillow or cushion.
pulbere ['pulbere] *nf* (*praf*) dust; powder.
pulmonar [pulmo'nar] *adj* pulmonary, of the lungs.
pulover [pu'lover] *nn* sweater, pull-over.
pulpă ['pulpǎ] *nf anat* calf of the leg; (*de animale*) leg, joint; (*de porc*) gammon; (*dentară*) *also bot* pulp.
puls [puls] *nn* pulse • ~**a** *vi also fig* to pulse, to pulsate, to throb • ~**aţie** *nf* throb, heartbeat; *also fig* pulsation.
pulveriza [pulveri'za] *vt* to pulverize, to grind; (*lichide*) to spray ‖ *vr pass* to be pulverized, etc. • ~**tor** *nn* pulverizer; atomizer, sprayer.
puma ['puma] *nf zool* puma, cougar, American panther.
pumn [pumn] *nm* fist; (*ca lovitură*) blow with the fist, buffet, punch; (*conţinutul unui* ~) handful.
pumnal [pum'nal] *nn* dagger, stiletto, poniard.
punct [punkt] *nn* point, spot; place; (*în punctuaţie*) full stop, period; (*deasupra literelor*) *also mus* dot; (*în diferite sensuri*) point; (*în depărtare etc*) speck; (*grad*) extent; (*chestiune*) question; (*articol*) item; (*de program*) number; (*de cusătură, tricotaj*) stitch ‖ *vt* a pune la ~ (*a regla*) (*un dispozitiv*) to tune; (*un mecanism*) to adjust; (*aparat foto*) to focus; (*un proiect, plan*) to finalize ‖ *adv* sharp, exactly, precisely ‖ *interj* period! • ~**a** *vt* to dot; to mark by dots; (*a sublinia*) to point out, to emphasize; (*a înregistra*) to record, to score • ~**aj** *nn sp* score; outline (of a speech).
punctualitate [punktuali'tate] *nf* punctuality.
punctuaţie [punktu'atsie] *nf* punctuation.
puncţie ['punktsie] *nf med* puncture.
pune ['pune] *vt* (*a aşterne*) to put, to lay; (*într-un anumit loc*) to set; *coll* (*repede*) to clap (down); (*a ataşa*) to attach; (*a anexa*) to append; (*în scrisoare*) to

enclose; (*a adăuga*) to add; *med* (*a aplica*) to apply; (*bani, a depune*) to deposit; (*a îmbrăca*) to put on; (*a semăna*) to sow; (*a planta*) to plant; (*a atârna*) to hang; (*a turna*) to pour out; (*o piesă*) to stage; *fig* (*a ridica*) to raise; (*a face*) to cause; to oblige; (*a îmbrăca*) to put on || *vr pass* to be laid, to be set, to be attached, etc; (*a se aşeza*) to sit down; (*a se culca*) to lie down.

pungaş [pun'gash] *nm* pickpocket; (*hoţ*) thief; (*mărunt*) pilferer; (*escroc*) swindler; (*la jocuri de noroc*) cheat; *fig coll* rogue.

pungă ['pungă] *nf* purse; (*de hârtie*) paper bag; (*răsucită*) screw; *zool* pouch; (*săculeţ, în diferite sensuri*) bag; *mil* pocket.

pungăşie [pungă'shie] *nf* (*furt*) (petty) theft; (*mai mic*) pilferage; (*escrocherie*) swindle, fraud.

punitiv [puni'tiv] *adj* punitive.

punte ['punte] *nf* small bridge, footbridge, bridge; *naut* deck; (*de ferăstrău*) summer; (*de butoi*) bottom bar.

pupa [pu'pa] *vt* (*a avea putinţa să*) to kiss; *coll* to buss; (*cu zgomot*) to smack || *vr* to kiss one another • **~t** *nn* kissing; (*ca act*) kiss; *coll* buss; (*zgomotos*) smack(er).

pupă ['pupă] *nf naut* poop, stern; *ento* pupa, chrysalis.

pupăză ['pupăză] *nf orn* hoopoe, hoopoo; *fig coll* (*flecar*) chatterbox, windbag.

pupilă [pu'pilă] *nf anat* pupil (of the eye), eyeball; *jur* ward.

pupitru [pu'pitru] *nn* (*bancă*) desk; (*suport*) stand; *mus* music desk/stand.

pur [pur] *adj* pure; (*curat*) clean; (*limpede*) clear; (*nepătat*) stainless; *fig* pure, chaste, stainless; (*simplu*) mere.

purcea [pur'chea] *nf zool* sow, young sow.

purcede [pur'chede] *vi* (*a porni*) to set out, to start; (*a începe*) to begin; (*a proceda la*) to proceed (to); (*a lua naştere*) (*din*) to originate (in), to come (from).

purcel [pur'chel] *nm zool* piggling, piglet; (*în limbajul copiilor*) piggy(-wiggy).

purgativ [purga'tiv] *nn* purgative.

purgatoriu [purga'toriu] *nn also fig* purgatory, limbo.

purica [puri'ka] *vt* to clean of fleas; *fig* to sift to the bottom; to examine closely.

purice ['puriche] *nm ento* flea; *constr* raising piece; (*cui mic*) small nail || *adj sl coll* sharp.

purifica [purifi'ka] *vt* to purify, to cleanse || *vr* to become pure.

puritan [puri'tan] *adj* puritanic(al); *fig* prudish || *nm* puritan • **~ism** *nn* Puritanism.

puritate [puri'tate] *nf* purity, pureness.

puroi [pu'roi] *nn* pus; *coll* matter.

purpuriu [purpu'riu] *adj* purple.

purta [pur'ta] *vt* to carry; (*ceva greu, a suporta*) to bear; (*a mâna, d. vânt etc*) to drive; (*a conduce*) to lead; (*îmbrăcăminte, un inel etc*) to wear; (*un ceas, bani, arme etc*) to carry || *vr pass* to be carried, to be borne, to be driven, to be lead, to be worn, to be carried; (*a se comporta*) to behave; (*d. o stofă*) to wear; (*a fi la modă*) to be in fashion • **~re** *nf* conduct, behavior; (*a hainelor*) wear.

pustietate [pustie'tate] *nf* * **pustiu**; isolated/secluded place; solitude, seclusion.

pustii [pusti'i] *vt* to lay waste, to ravage, to devastate.

pustiu [pus'tiu] *adj* (*sălbatic*) wild; (*nelocuit*) uninhabited; deserted; (*gol*) empty; (*fără rost*) senseless;

(*inutil*) useless; (*singur*) lonely || *nn* waste(land), wilderness; *fig* solitude; (*plictiseală*) weariness.

pustnic ['pustnik] *nm* hermit, anchorite, recluse.

pustulă [pus'tulă] *nf med* pustule; *coll* pimple.

puşcaş [push'kash] *nm mil* fusilier; (*vânător*) marksman, shot; *coll* gun.

puşcă ['pushkă] *nf* gun, musket; (*ghintuită*) rifle, rifled gun; (*cu ţeava netedă*) smoothbore; arm, weapon.

puşcăriaş [pushkări'ash] *nm* prisoner, convict; *coll* jailbird.

puşcărie [pushkă'rie] *nf* prison, jail; *coll* can.

puşculiţă [pushku'litsă] *nf* money box.

puşlama [pushla'ma] *nf coll pej* good-for-nothing, scapegrace, loafer.

puşti ['pushti] *nm coll* kid; (*flăcăiandru*) lad.

puştoaică [push'toaikă] *nf* flapper, bobbysoxer; chit, lassie.

putea [pu'tea] *vt* (*a avea putinţa să*) can, to be able (to); to be in a position (to); (*a fi capabil*) to be capable (of); (*a avea voie*) (*să*) may; to be permitted/allowed (to); (*a avea posibilitatea*) to have the possibility (to); (*a fi posibil*) may; to be possible (to).

putere [pu'tere] *nf* power; might; (*mecanică, fizică, mai ales în sens activ*) force; (*tărie, în sens pasiv*) strength; (*rezistenţă*) stamina; (*vigoare*) vigor; (*spirituală sau musculară*) nerve; (*tărie de caracter*) backbone; (*energie*) energy; *coll* vim; (*eficacitate*) efficacy; *fig* ability; (*valoare*) value; (*drept*) right; (*capacitate*) capacity; (*toi*) depth; (*influenţă*) power; (*autoritate*) sway; (*stat*) power.

puternic [pu'ternik] *adj* strong; (*d. un motor etc*) powerful; (*d. căldură*) fierce; (*d. frig*) bitter; (*d. aer*) hard; (*d. o dorinţă*) ardent; (*d. mânie etc*) towering; (*d. influenţă etc*) potent; (*d. o lovitură*) hard; (*d. ploaie, furtună, un atac etc*) heavy; (*d. miros*) strong; (*mare*) great; virulent; drastic; important; (*autoritar*) authoritative; solid; resistant || *adv* strongly, etc • **~ii** *nm* the mighty/powerful.

putină ['putină] *nf* vat; (*butoi*) cask, barrel.

putinţă [pu'tintsă] *nf* possibility; **după ~** according to one's possibilities; **peste ~** impossible.

putoare [pu'toare] *nf* stink, stench; *fig coll* (*leneş*) idler, slacker.

putred ['putred] *adj* rotten; (*descompus*) putrid, decomposed; *fig* rotten, corrupt.

putregai [putre'gai] *nn* rot, decay.

putrezi [putre'zi] *vi* to rot, to decay; (*d. cânepă*) to ret.

puturos [putu'ros] *adj* (*rău mirositor*) stinking, fetid; (*leneş*) awfully lazy; *coll* bonelazy || *nm coll* lazybones, slugabed.

puţ [puts] *nn* well; *min* well, shaft.

puţi [pu'tsi] *vi* (*a*) to stink (of); to have a foul/fetid smell.

puţin [pu'tsin] *adj* (*nu mult*) little; (*ceva*) a little; some; (*puţini*) few, some few; (*mic*) small; (*scurt*) short; **pentru ~** you're welcome! || *adv* (*în mică măsură*) little; (*într-o oarecare măsură*) a little; (*cam*) rather; (*temporal*) a little while, for a short time.

puzderie [puz'derie] *nf text* boon; (*praf*) dust; (*gunoaie*) litter; (*fulgi*) flakes; (*stropi*) drops; *fig* multitude, host, legion; (*grămadă*) heap.

R

rabat [ra'bat] *nn* rebate.

rabatabil [raba'tabil] *adj* folding.

rabin ['rabin] *nm* rabbi.

rac [rak] *nm icht* crayfish, crawfish; crab; *astrol* the Cancer, the Crab; (*tirbuşon*) corkscrew; *tech* claw coupling; *min* (*opritor de burlane*) casing dog; *naut* anchor.

rachetă [ra'ketă] *nf also avia* rocket; *pl also* rocketry; *sp* (*tenis*) racket; (*ping pong*) bat; (*pt. zăpadă*) snowshoe, racket.

racilă ['rachilă] *nf* (*meteahnă*) drawback, shortcoming; chronic disease; (*duşmănie*) feud, ill-blood, enmity.

racletă [rak'letă] *nf tech* scraper, wiper.

racola [rako'la] *vt* to tout (for business, vote); (*o prostituată*) to solicit, to accost; (*un spion*) to recruit.

racorda [rakor'da] *vt tech* to connect, to join (up).

radar ['radar] *nn* radar.

radă ['radă] *nf naut* roadstead, roadway.

rade ['rade] *vt* (*a răzui*) to scrape; (*cu guma*) to rub out; to erase; (*pe răzătoare*) to grate; (*cu raşpel*) to rasp; (*a bărbieri*) to shave; (*de la pământ*) to raze; (*a dărâma*) to pull/take down; (*a distruge*) to do for (smb) || *vr* to have/get a shave.

radia [radi'a] *vt* (*d. soare*) to radiate, *also fig* to beam; (*a iradia*) to irradiate; (*a răspândi*) to stream; (*a şterge*) to erase; (*de pe o listă*) to strike/cross off || *vi* to radiate, to beam (with joy, etc) • ~**ţie** *nf* radiation.

radiator [radia'tor] *nn* radiator; (*de răcire*) (cooling) radiator; (*de încălzire*) hot-water radiator.

radical [radi'kal] *nm also pol* radical || *nn* radical; root; sign; *chem, math* radicle || *adv* radically; wholly, entirely.

radieră [radi'eră] *nf* India rubber, eraser.

radiere [radi'ere] *nf jur* erasing, crossing off; (*a unei datorii*) cancellation.

radio ['radio] *nn* radio, wireless; broadcasting; (*aparat*) radio/wireless set; (*portativ*) portable radio.

radioactiv [radioak'tiv] *adj chem, phys* radioactive.

radiografie [radiogra'fie] *nf* radiography; (*film*) X-ray photograph.

radiojurnal [radiozhur'nal] *nn* news (bulletin).

radiolocaţie [radiolo'katsie] *nf* radar, radio location.

radiologie [radiolo'djie] *nf* radiology.

radios [radi'os] *adj* beaming, radiant || *adv* beaming; gladly.

radioscopie [radiosko'pie] *nf* X-ray (examination), radioscopy.

radiotransmisiune [radiotransmisi'une] *nf* radiobroadcasting.

radiu ['radiu] *nn* radium.

radius ['radius] *nn anat* radius.

radon [ra'don] *nn chem* radon.

rafală [ra'fală] *nf* squall, gust, blast of wind; (*de ploaie*) rain fall; (*de mitralieră*) volley of shots, strafing; *mil* burst/storm of gunfire.

rafie ['rafie] *nf bot* raffia.

rafina [rafi'na] *vt also fig* to refine; *fig also* to polish; *tech* to clean || *vr* to become/grow refined; (*d. zahăr, ulei*) to refine • ~**t** *adj* (*d. zahăr*) refined; *also fig* delicate, fine; (*deştept*) subtle, clever; sophisticated • ~**ment** *nn* refinement; subtlety.

rafinărie [rafină'rie] *nf* (*de zahăr*) (sugar) refinery; (*de petrol*) oil distillery, refinery.

raft [raft] *nn* shelf.

rage ['radje] *vi* to (bel)low, to moo; (*d. leu*) *also fig* to roar; *fig* to bellow.

rahat [ra'hat] *nn* Turkish delight/paste; *fig* (*om de nimic*) dud, failure; (*fleac*) beans || *interj* rot!, (bull)shit!.

rahitic [ra'hitik] *adj* rickety.

rahitism [rahi'tism] *nn med* rickets.

rai [rai] *nn also fig* paradise, eden; *naut* pulley wheel.

raid [raid] *nn mil* (air)raid.

raion [ra'ion] *nn* (*în magazin*) department; (*regiune*) district.

raită ['raită] *nf* walk, round; (*vizită*) visit; (*scurtă*) call, short visit; (*rond*) beat.

ralia [rali'a] *vr* **a se ~ la** to join; to rally to; (*o părere*) to come round to, to concur in.

raliu [ra'liu] *nn sp* rally.

ramă ['ramă] *nf* frame; (*de tablou şi*) mat; (*de pantofi*) welt; (*de ochelari*) rim; (*la parchet*) skirting board; (*vâslă*) oar.

ramburs [ram'burs] *nn* (*rambursare*) (re)payment, reimbursement; (*plată*) payment; **contra** ~ cash on delivery (C.O.D.).

rambursa [rambur'sa] *vt* to reimburse, to repay, to refund.

ramifica [ramifi'ka] *vr* to branch out, to ramify • ~**ţie** *nf* ramification, (*concret*) branch(ing).

ramoli [ramo'li] *vr* to grow soft in one's mind, to grow decrepit; (*d. minte*) to soften • ~**t** *nm* old fogey/driveller, dotard || *adj* soft-minded, doddering, decrepit; (*la minte*) stultified, soft-witted/headed.

rampă ['rampă] *nf* rail grade; platform; *mil* landing; (*mobilă*) groundrow; (*barieră*) turnpike; (*balustradă*) handrail; (*teatru*) footlights.

ramură ['ramură] *nf also fig* branch; (*groasă*) limb; (*crenguţă*) bough, twig.

rană ['rană] *nf also fig* wound.

ranchiună [ran'kiună] *nf* spite, rancor, grudge.

ranchiunos [rankiu'nos] *adj* rancorous, spiteful, vindictive.

randament [randa'ment] *nn* efficiency; (*folos*) benefit; (*producţie*) output, productivity.

rang [rang] *nn* rank; position; *math* order.

rangă ['rangă] *nf* crowbar.

raniţă ['ranitsă] *nf* knapsack, haversack; *mil* kitbag, pack.

rapace [ra'pache] *adj* grasping, greedy, rapacious.

rapid [ra'pid] *adj* fast, swift, quick, hasty || *nn* fast/express train || *adv* fast(ly).

rapiţă ['rapitsă] *nf bot* rape(seed).

raport [ra'port] *nn* report; (*dare de seamă*) account, statement; *mil* orderly hour/call, daily parade for the issue of orders; (*relaţie*) relation(ship); *pl* terms; (*şi sexual*) intercourse; *math* ratio; (*comparaţie*) comparison • ~**a** *vt* (*a da un raport despre*) to report on, to give an account of; to relate; to produce, to bring in, to yield || *vr* **a se ~ la** to refer/relate to; to have/make reference to.

rapsod [rap'sod] *nm* rhapsode, rhapsodist; (*bard*) bard.

rar [rar] *adj* rare; (*puţin*) little, scarce; *pl* few; (*d. păr*) thin; (*neobişnuit şi*) unusual; *fig* rare, exceptional; (*neîntrecut*) matchless; (*lent*) slow || *adv* rarely, seldom; (*lent*) slowly; **vorbea** ~ (*d. viteză*) he spoke rarely, (*rareori*) he seldom/scarcely spoke • ~**efiat** *adj* rarefied, thin, tenuous • ~**eori** *adv* seldom, rarely; exceptionally; (*din când în când*) now and then • ~**itate** *nf* (*obiect rar*) rarity, curio(sity); (*eveniment*) rare occurrence; (*lipsă*) scarceness, scarcity.

ras [ras] *nn* shave ‖ *adj* shaven.

rasă]'rasă] *nf* (*omenească*) (human) race; (*descendenţă*) ancestry, descent; **de** ~ of noble race; (*d. cai*) thoroughbred; (*d. câini*) pure-bred, pedigree; *fig* first-rate, remarkable; (*de călugăr*) frock.

rasial [rasi'al] *adj* racial.

rasism [ra'sism] *nn* racism, racial discrimination.

rasist [ra'sist] *nm* racist.

rasol [ra'sol] *nn cul* boiled meat; (*rasoleală*) scamping, mucking.

rasoli [raso'li] *vt* to botch, to bungle.

raşcheta [rashke'ta] *vt tech* to scrape.

rata [ra'ta] *vt* to miss ‖ *vi* to misfire, to fail (to go off) ‖ *vr* to become a human failure; to get nowhere • ~**t** *nm* human failure, wash out; *coll* loser, flop, dud ‖ *adj* failing, ineffectual; (*d. oameni*) washed out.

rată ['rată] *nf* installment, part payment; rate.

ratifica [ratifi'ka] *vt* to ratify; (*a aproba*) to approve, to confirm • ~**re** *nf* ratification.

raton [ra'ton] *nm zool* raccoon.

raţă ['ratsă] *nf orn* duck.

raţie ['ratsie] *nf* ration, portion, allowance; rate; stint; *math* ratio.

raţiona [ratsio'na] *vi* to reason, to argue • ~**l** *adj* rational, reasonable; (*incontestabil*) cogent ‖ *adv* rationally, reasonably • ~**liza** *vt* to rationalize; to ration • ~**lizare** *nf math, phys* rationalization; (*a alimentelor*) rationing • ~**ment** *nn* reasoning, argument, judgment; • ~**re** *nf* reasoning, judgment; rationing.

raţiune [ratsi'une] *nf* reason; (*motiv şi*) grounds, motive.

rază ['rază] *nf also fig* beam, ray, streak of light; (*strălucire*) brightness; (*radiaţie*) radiation; *geom* radius; (*slabă*) gleam • ~ **de acţiune** range of action/operation (of an aircraft); (*a unei campanii publicitare*) coverage/range of an advertising campaign.

razie ['razie] *nf* police raid, round-up.

răbda [răb'da] *vt* (*a trece prin*) to suffer, to endure; (*a suporta*) to bear, to stand; to tolerate; to permit, to allow; to accept ‖ *vi* to have patience; (*a suferi*) to suffer, to endure.

răbdător [răbdă'tor] *adj* patient, suffering, enduring ‖ *adv* patiently.

răboj [ră'bozh] *nn* tally, notched stick; *fig* score; (*însemnare*) notch.

răbufni [răbuf'ni] *vi* (*a izbucni*) to break/burst out; (*implicând zgomot*) to bang; to thunder, to peal.

răceală [ra'cheală] *nf* freshness, cool; (*frig, boală*) cold; *fig* chillness, coldness; indifference.

răchită [ră'kită] *nf bot* (basket) osier, osier willow; (*împletitură şi*) wickerwork.

răci [ră'chi] *vt* to cool (off), to chill; (*după călire*) to quench; *fig* to damp ‖ *vr* to get/grow cool/cold ‖ *vi* to catch cold, to take/catch a chill • ~**tor** *nn* ice-box, refrigerator; *tech* cooler; (*pt. vin*) wine cooler • ~**t** *adj* down with a cold.

răcnet ['răknet] *nn* roar; (*zbierăt*) yell.

răcni [răk'ni] *vi/vt* to roar; (*a zbiera*) to yell; (*a striga*) to shout; (*a mugi*) to low.

răcoare [ră'koare] *nf* coolness, freshness; (*frig*) cold; *pl* shiver, shudder; *sl* (*închisoare*) beanery.

răcori [răko'ri] *vt* to cool (down), to refresh; to calm

(down) ‖ *vr* to cool (down), to refresh oneself; (*d. mâncare*) to become cooler.

răcoritoare [răkori'toare] *nf pl* cooling drinks/beverages.

rădăcină [rădă'chină] *nf* root.

răfui [răfu'i] *vr also fig* (*cu*) to settle/square accounts with, to get even with.

răgaz [ră'gaz] *nn* leisure; (*repaus*) rest; (*pace*) peace; **moment de** ~ respite, breathing space; **fără** ~ without a moment's respite.

răget ['rădjet] *nn* roar; low, bellow.

răguşeală [răgu'sheală] *nf* hoarseness; *med* sore throat.

răguşi [răgu'shi] *vi* to get/become hoarse.

rămas-bun [ră'mas bun] *nn* farewell, adieu, valediction.

rămăşag [rămă'shag] *nn* wager, bet.

rămăşiţă [rămă'shitsă] *nf* remainder, rest; leftover, *coll* shank; (*de material*) remnant; *pl* remains; (*d. mâncare*) leftover; *chem* residuum.

rămâne [ră'mâne] *vi* to remain; (*a sta mai mult timp*) to stay; (*a fi lăsat*) to be left; (*peste noapte*) to stay overnight; to continue; (*a dura*) to endure, to last; (*a* ~ *în continuare*) to stay on; (*a trăi*) to live on.

rămuros [rămu'ros] *adj* branchy, ramose.

răni [ră'ni] *vt* to hurt, to wound, to injure; *fig* to offend, to wound/hurt the feelings of; (*a nedreptăţi*) to wrong ‖ *vr* to get hurt/wounded; to injure oneself.

răpăi [răpă'i] *vi* (*d. ploaie, în geam*) to patter, to lash/whip against the window; (*d. grindină, mitralieră*) to rattle • ~**ală** *nf* pattering, rattle.

răpi [ră'pi] *vt* to ravish, to carry off; *jur* to abduct; (*a fugi cu o femeie*) to elope with; (*minori*) to kidnap; (*d. moarte*) to carry/take off/away; (*lucruri*) to bear/snatch away; (*a fura*) to steal, to rob; (*a lipsi de*) to deprive of; (*a încânta*) to ravish, to enchant • ~**tor** *nm* kidnapper; abductor ‖ *adj* (*vorace*) ravenous; (*d. păsări şi animale*) predatory; (*d. frumuseţe*) ravishing, enchanting.

răposat [răpo'sat] *nm* the late (lamented), the deceased, the dear departed ‖ *adj* dead, deceased, late.

răpune [ră'pune] *vt* (*a înfrânge*) to defeat, to worst; (*a omorî*) to kill; (*a distruge*) to destroy.

rări [ră'ri] *vt* to thin (out); (*a dilua*) to dilute; *agr* (*d. cultură*) to weed out; (*puieţi*) to single out seedings; (*d. pădure*) to thin out; (*vizite, a împuţina*) to make scarce; *mil* (*focurile*) to slacken the rate of fire; *mus* (*măsura*) to slacken the time; *fig* to space out ‖ *vr* to thin out; to grow rarer; to become rarefied.

răsad [ră'sad] *nn* nursery transplant; *fig* seed, race • ~**niţă** *nf agr* hotbed; *fig* shelter, harbor • ~**i** *vt also fig* to transplant.

răsări [răsă'ri] *vi* (*d. aştri*) to rise; (*d. plante*) to spring, to sprout; (*a se ivi*) to come in sight, to appear; (*pe neaşteptate*) to turn up • ~**t** *nn* (*de soare*) sunrise; rising; (*est*) east; orient; **spre** ~ eastward ‖ *adj* risen; (*înalt*) tall(ish), high; (*deştept*) clever; (*valoros*) valuable; (*deosebit*) outstanding; (*bogat*) rich; (*frumos*) beautiful.

răscoală [răs'koală] *nf* (up)rising, revolt, rebellion; (*mai ales d. marinari*) mutiny.

răscoli [răsko'li] *vt* to rummage, to ransack; to rake; (*răvăşi*) to turn upside down; to clutter (up); *also fig* (*a mişca de la loc*) to remove; (*a scurma*) to dig up; (*a ara*) to plow; (*focul*) to stir, to poke; *fig* to stir up, to agitate, to disturb; (*amintiri*) to rake up; (*a mişca*) to move.

răscrăcărat [răskrăkă'rat] *adj* straddling, with legs wide apart.

răscruce [răs'kruche] *nf* crossroad(s), crossing; *also fig* moment of choice, crucial/decisive moment.

răscula [răsku'la] *vr* to rise in arms/rebellion • ~t *nm* rebel, insurgent; (*soldat, marinar*) mutineer ‖ *adj* insurgent, mutinous.

răscumpăra [răskumpă'ra] *vt* to redeem; (*o vină*) to expiate, to atone for; (*un captiv*) to ransom; (*ceva vândut*) to buy back; (*a compensa*) to compensate for, to make up for; (*o datorie*) to pay off • ~re *nf* redemption; compensation; (*plată*) ransom.

răsfăţ [răs'fats] *nn* (*al cuiva*) pampering, spoiling; (*mângâiere*) caressing; (*ca atitudine*) fondling; (*nazuri*) whims; (*desfătare*) delight(s) • ~a *vt* to spoil; *fig* to fondle, to caress; (*a cocoli*) to pamper; (*a înveseli*) to amuse ‖ *vr* to play the spoiled child; to lead an easy life; (*d. îndrăgostiţi*) to bill and coo; to pamper oneself.

răsfira [răsfi'ra] *vt* (*a împrăştia*) to scatter, to spread; to unfold; (*picioarele*) to spread out ‖ *vr* (*d. funie*) to unwind, to uncoil; to disperse; (*a se risipi*) to scatter (about).

răsfoi [răsfo'i] *vt* to turn over; (*a cerceta în grabă*) to look/skim through; (*o carte*) to leaf through; to riffle through a book.

răsfrânge [răs'frândje] *vt* (*d. lumină, imagine*) to reflect, to reverberate; (*mânecile*) to roll/turn up; (*gulerul*) to turn down ‖ *vr* to be reflected; to influence.

răspândi [răspân'di] *vt* to spread, to distribute; to stream; (*idei*) to disseminate; (*a împrăştia*) to scatter, to disperse; (*a presăra*) to strew about; (*hârtii pe jos*) to litter paper about the floor; (*a propaga*) to float; (*zvonuri*) to set afloat; (*un film, o carte*) to release; (*a radia*) to radiate; (*a arunca*) to throw; to shed (light) ‖ *vr* to spread, to stream; (*d. lichide*) to run over; (*d. zvonuri*) to get abroad; (*a se risipi*) to disperse; (*a deveni obişnuit*) to come into general use.

răspântie [răs'pântie] *nf* crossroad(s); *fig* turning point.

răspicat [răspi'kat] *adj* plain, outright, flat ‖ *adv* plainly, flatly, bluntly.

răsplată [răs'plată] *nf* reward; (*pedeapsă*) penalty, punishment.

răsplăti [răsplă'ti] *vt* to reward, to recompense; (*a pedepsi*) to punish.

răspopi [răspo'pi] *vt* to unfrock.

răspunde [răs'punde] *vt* to reply, to answer; (*a riposta*) to retort ‖ *vi* (*la*) to answer to, to reply to; (*prin acţuni*) to respond to; (*obraznic*) to answer back; (*a fi responsabil de*) to be responsible for; (*a garanta*) to guarantee; **a ~ la** (*sentimentele cuiva*) to return; (*salutul cuiva*) to acknowledge; (*apel*) to answer the roll; (*telefon*) to answer the phone; (*o cerere*) to comply with • ~re *nf* responsibility; *econ* liability.

răspuns [răs'puns] *nn* response, answer; (*replică*) reply, retort; (*scurt, sec*) rejoinder.

rǎstǎlmǎci [rǎstǎlmǎ'chi] *vt* to misconstrue, to misinterpret; (*adevărul*) to distort, to pervert.

răsti [răs'ti] *vr* to shout, to bark, to snap; *coll* to huff/snub smb, to fly at smb.

răstigni [răstig'ni] *vt* to crucify; to harangue smb • ~re *nf* crucifixion.

răstimp [răs'timp] *nn* interval, (lapse of) time, duration.

răsturna [răstur'na] *vt* to overturn, to tipple, to topple over; (*paharul*) to turn upside down; (*a doborî*) to knock down/over, (*găleata*) to upset; (*o barcă, o trăsură*) to capsize; (*d. vânt*) to blow down; (*casa cu susul în jos*) to turn everything upside down/topsy-turvy; (*cu picioarele în sus*) to knock over; (*a inversa*) to reverse; (*un stat, o teorie*) to overthrow; (*ordinea lucrurilor*) to overset things ‖ *vr* to overturn, to tip over; (*d. bărci, trăsuri*) to capsize; (*a cădea*) to fall down/over; (*în fotoliu*) to lean/lie/loll back.

răsuci [răsu'chi] *vt* (*fire*) to spin, to twist; (*a roti*) to turn; (*mustăţi*) to turn up; (*a stâlci, a deforma*) to warp; (*a mânui*) to wield; (*a întoarce*) to wring; to dislocate, to put out (of joint); (*piciorul*) to sprain ‖ *vr* (*a se învârti*) to turn (round); (*brusc, pe călcâie*) to spin round; (*a se mişca de colo-colo*) to fidget; (*în pat*) to toss/tumble (about); (*a se torsiona*) to roll.

răsufla [răsu'fla] *vi* to respire, to breathe; (*a-şi recăpăta răsuflarea*) to get/catch one's breath; (*a ofta*) to heave a sigh; *fig* (*uşurat*) to breathe freely; (*din nou*) to breathe again; (*a face un popas*) to make a halt; (*a se odihni*) to (have a) rest; *fig* (*un secret*) to leak out; *fig* (*d. recipiente*) to leak • ~re *nf* breathing; breath, wind; **dintr-o ~** in a/one breath; **fără ~** breathless, (*mort*) dead.

răsuflat [răsu'flat] *adj* (*d. o glumă*) flat; banal, trite; (*d. băutură şi*) stale, flat.

răsuna [răsu'na] *vi* to (re)sound, to ring (out); (*a se auzi*) to be heard; (*a vibra*) to vibrate.

răsunător [răsună'tor] *adj* resounding, resonant; (*d. voce*) stentorian, loud; *fig* resounding, famous; thundering; (*mare*) great.

răsunet [ră'sunet] *nn* sound, echo; (*zgomot*) noise; *fig* also response.

răşină [ră'shină] *nf* resin.

rătăci [rătă'chi] *vt* (*un lucru*) to lose, to misplace; (*drumul*) to lose ‖ *vi* to stray/wander about; (*a vagabonda*) to tramp; (*fără ţintă*) to meander ‖ *vr* (*d. cineva*) to lose one's way, to get lost.

răţoi¹ [ră'tsoi] *nm* drake, male duck.

răţoi² [rătso'i] *vr* to bluster, to swashbuckle.

răţuşcă [ră'tsushkă] *nf orn* duckling.

rău [rău] *adj* bad; (*necorespunzător*) poor, worthless; (*ticălos*) wicked; (*care face rău*) evil(-minded), malicious; (*cu însuşiri rele*) ill, poor; (*nedemn*) unworthy; (*josnic*) mean; (*nărăvaş*) vicious; (*aspru*) unkind; (*d. copii*) naughty; (*strict*) corrupt; (*desfrânat*) profligate; (*mizerabil*) vile; (*scârbos*) foul; (*la inimă*) bad-hearted ‖ *adv* badly; (*cu răutate*) wickedly; (*prost*) poorly ‖ *nn* evil, ill; (*necaz*) harm, wrong; (*boală*) sickness ‖ *nm* scoundrel, villain.

răufăcător [răufăkă'tor] *nm* evildoer, malefactor.

răutate [rău'tate] *nf* wickedness, malice; (*faptă*) misdeed; wrong; (*d. cineva*) malicious person; (*vocativ*) rogue! ‖ *adv* **cu ~** wickedly, viciously, maliciously, spitefully.

răutăcios [răută'chios] *adj* malignant; (*maliţios*) malicious, acrimonious, wicked ‖ *adv* malignantly, maliciously.

răuvoitor [răuvoi'tor] *adj* ill-willed, malicious; hostile ‖ *adv* malevolently, unkindly.

rǎvǎşi [rǎvǎ'shi] *vt* to rummage, to turn upside down; (*a împrăştia*) to scatter about • ~t *adj* helter-skelter, scattered; (*d. păr*) disheveled; *fig* troubled, confused, upset.

răzătoare [răză'toare] *nf* grate, rasp; (*la uşă*) shoe/boot/door scraper.

răzbate [răz'bate] *vi* (*a înainta*) to advance; *fig* to force/cut/make one's way; (*a reuşi*) to succeed; * **răzbi**; (*a trece prin*) to go/pass through, to come through; (*d. apă: a se prelinge*) to ooze through; (*prin mulţime*) to squeeze through; (*a străbate*) to cross; (*a cutreiera*) to scour; (*a străpunge*) to pierce.

răzbi [răz'bi] *vi* * **răzbate**; (*a se auzi*) to be heard; (*a se răspândi*) to spread; *fig* (*a reuşi*) to manage || *vt* to beat, to overcome; (*d. foame*) *fig* to seize.

război [răz'boi] *nn* war, (*ostilităţi*) warfare; (*de ţesut*) weaving loom || [războ'i] *vr* (*cu*) to be at war (with), to wage war (against); *fig* (cu) to war (with).

răzbuna [răzbu'na] *vt* to avenge, to vindicate || *vr* (*pe cineva*) to revenge oneself (on); (*verbal*) to take it out on smb; (*pt. o jignire*) to take vengeance.

răzbunător [răzbună'tor] *adj* revengeful, vindictive || *nm* avenger.

râzgâia [râzgâ'ia] *vt* to spoil, to pamper • ~t *adj* spoiled, pampered.

răzgândi [răzgân'di] *vr* to change one's mind, to think better of it.

răzleţ [răz'leţ] *adj* (*rătăcit*) stray, lost; (*d. un sat*) out-of-the-way; (*singur*) lonely; sporadic || *adv* here and there.

răzmeriţă ['răzmeritsă] *nf* uprising, rebellion.

răzui [răzu'i] *vt* to scrape.

răzvrăti [răzvră'ti] *vr* to rebel (against) • ~re *nf* mutiny.

râcâi [râcâ'i] *vt* to scrape, to scratch; *fig* to gnaw at, to torment.

râde ['râde] *vi* to laugh; (*înfundat*) to chuckle; (*a chicoti*) to titter, to snigger; (*prosteşte*) to giggle; (*dispreţuitor*) to sneer; (*afectat*) to smirk; (*răutăcios*) to grin (at smb); (*ameninţător*) to snarl; (*silit*) to give (vent to) a forced laugh.

râgâi [râgâ'i] *vi* to belch (wind); to retch.

râie ['râie] *nf* scab; itch; (*la animale*) mange; *fig* plague, pest.

râios [râ'ios] *adj* scabby, mangy; *fig* haughty.

râma [râ'ma] *vt/vi* to rout, to root.

râmă ['râmă] *nf zool* earth/dew worm.

rânced ['rânched] *adj* (*d. grăsime*) rancid; (*mucegăit*) musty, moldy; (*d. miros*) fusty; (*respingător*) rank; (*stricat*) foul.

râncezi [rânche'zi] *vi*, *vr* to become rancid/musty.

rând [rând] *nn* (*şir de scaune etc*) row (of); (*alăturat*) *also mil* rank; (*spate în spate*) file, bank (of oars); tier (of seats on a slope); (*ordonată*) range; series; (*succesiune*) succession; (*în text*) line; (*de băuturi*) round; **de** ~ common, ordinary, everyday, habitual.

rândui [rându'i] *vt* to arrange, to (put in good) order; (*prin cameră*) to tidy (up) • ~ală *nf* (good) order, arrangement; system; (*datină*) custom; ceremonial.

rândunea, rândunică [rându'nea, rându'nikă] *nf orn* swallow, martin(et).

rânjet ['rânzhet] *nn* grin, snarl.

rânji [rân'zhi] *vi* to grin; (*prosteşte*) to smirk; (*agresiv*) to show one's teeth, to snarl.

râpă ['râpă] *nf* steep, precipice; (*formată de apă*) gully, cliff.

râs¹ [râs] *nn* laughter, laugh; (*satisfăcut*) chuckle; (*grosolan*) hee haw; (*chicot*) snigger; (*prostesc*) smirk; (*hohot*) peal/outburst of laughter.

râs² [âs] *nm zool* lynx.

râşni [râsh'ni] *vt* to grind • ~ţă *nf* coffee mill/grinder; (*de piper*) quern; (*rablă*) jalopy.

rât [rât] *nn* snout.

râu [râu] *nn* river.

râvnă ['râvnă] *nf* ardor, zeal, fervor, diligence.

râvni [râv'ni] *vi* **a** ~ **la** to covet after/for; to strive for, to aspire to/after.

râzgâia [râzgâ'ia] *vt* to spoil • ~t *adj* spoilt, spoiled.

re [re] *nm mus* D, re.

reabilita [reabili'ta] *vt/vr* to rehabilitate (oneself), to redeem one's good name.

reacredinţă [reakre'dintsă] *nf* dishonesty, insincerity.

reactiva [reakti'va] *vt* to reactivate; to quicken anew || *vr mil* to come back for active service; *chem* to be reactivated.

reactor [reak'tor] *nn elec* reactor; *chem* reaction vessel; *tech* jet engine; *avia* jet plane; *phys* pile.

reactualiza [reaktuali'za] *vt* to bring up-to-date.

reacţie [re'aktsie] *nf chem* reaction; *fig also physiol* (*răspuns*) response.

reacţiona [reaktsio'na] *vi* (*la ceva*) to react (upon smth), to respond (to smth); (*a acţiona*) to act • ~r *nm/adj* reactionary.

readuce [rea'duche] *vt* to bring back.

reafirma [reafir'ma] *vt* to reassert, to reaffirm; (*a reformula*) to restate • ~re *nf* reassertion, reaffirmation.

real [re'al] *adj* real, actual; (*înaintea unui substantiv*) great || *nn* real(ness).

realege [rea'ledje] *vt* to re-elect.

realist [rea'list] *nm* realist || *adj* realistic || *adv* realistically.

realitate [reali'tate] *nf* reality; **în** ~ in (actual) fact, as a matter of fact • ~a *nf* the facts.

realiza [reali'za] *vt* (*a obţine*) to achieve, to realize; (*a îndeplini*) to carry out, to implement; to make a profit; (*a înţelege*) to work out; *cin* to produce || *vr* (*d. un proiect etc: a se adeveri*) to come true, to materialize; (*d. cineva*) to fulfill oneself • ~bil *adj* feasible, possible; (*d. un plan*) workable • ~re *nf* realization, carrying out,* **realiza**; (*lucru realizat*) achievement, accomplishment.

realmente [real'mente] *adv* actually, truly, really.

reaminti [reamin'ti] *vt/vi* to recall, (*a-şi aminti*) to remember.

reanima [reani'ma] *vt* to reanimate.

reapărea [reapă'rea] *vi* to reappear, to reemerge.

reavăn [re'avăn] *adj* moist, wet.

reavoinţă [reavo'intsă] *nf* ill-will, wickedness.

reazem ['reazem] *nn* (main)stay; *tech, math also fig* support.

rebegit [rebe'djit] *adj* shrunken (with cold), chilled to the bone.

rebel [re'bel] *nm* rebel || *adj* mutinous, rebellious; (*d. o boală*) stubborn; (*dificil*) obdurate • ~iune *nf* rebellion, rising, revolt.

rebut [re'but] *nn* (factory) reject; *coll* waste, scrap; *fig* reject.

recalcitrant [rekalchi'trant] *adj* hard to manage, recalcitrant.

recalcula [rekalku'la] *vt* to calculate again, to make a fresh computation of.

recalifica [rekalifi'ka] *vr/vr* to requalify.

recapitula [rekapitu'la] *vt* to summarize, to revise, to sum up • ~re *nf* recapitulation, revision, summing up.

recăpăta [rekăpă'ta] *vt* to recover, to regain.

recăsători [rekăsăto'ri] *vr* to remarry, to marry again.

recâştiga [rekâshti'ga] *vt* to regain, to recover.

rece ['reche] *adj also fig* cold; *(răcoros)* cool; *(şi umed)* chilly; *fig* indifferent; *(de piatră)* unmoved; *(neînţelegător)* unresponsive; *(glacial)* icy; *(mod de a fi)* chilly; **a fi ~** *(d. persoane)* to be cold; *(d. pâine)* to be stale || *adv* coldly, frigidly; *(calm) also fig* coolly, calmly; *(glacial)* icily.

recensământ [rechensă'mânt] *nn* census.

recent [re'chent] *adj* recent, latest || *adv* recently, lately.

recenza [rechen'za] *vt (o carte)* to review; to criticize; to take the census of.

recepta [rechep'ta] *vt* to pick up; to intercept; *(a primi)* to receive.

receptiv [rechep'tiv] *adj (la)* responsive (to).

receptor [rechep'tor] *nn (d. radio, telefon)* receiver || *adj* receiving.

recepţie [re'cheptsie] *nf (petrecere)* reception; *coll* party; *(mondenă)* rout; *(la hotel)* reception desk/office; inquiry office; *(a mărfurilor)* checking (on delivery); *(a unei maşini)* taking over; *(de către un inspector)* acceptance; *telec* reception.

recepţiona [recheptsio'na] *vt* to receive; *com* to check (on delivery) and sign for.

recepţioner [recheptsio'ner] *nm* receptionist, reception desk attendant; *com* controller.

recesiune [rechesi'une] *nf econ* recession.

rechema [reke'ma] *vt* to recall, to call back.

rechin [re'kin] *nm icht* (sea) shark; *fig* shark.

rechizitoriu [rekizi'toriu] *nn* (bill of) indictment, (public prosecutor's) charge; *fig* charge, accusation.

rechiziţie [reki'zitsie] *nf* requisition.

rechiziţiona [rekizitsio'na] *vt* to requisition; *(pt. nevoi obşteşti)* to impress; *(pt. armată)* to commandeer.

recicla [rechi'kla] *vt (materiale)* to recycle; *(personal)* to train • **~re** *nf tech* recycling; *(a personalului)* training courses, professional retraining.

recidiva [rechidi'va] *vi jur* to repeat an offense; to relapse (into a crime); *med* to recur.

recidivist [rechidi'vist] *nm* recidivist, hardened offender; *fig* old log.

recif [re'chif] *nn* reef.

recipient [rechipi'ent] *nn* container, receptacle, vessel.

recipisă [rechi'pisă] *nf* receipt.

reciproc [rechi'prok] *adj* mutual; *gram, log* reciprocal; *math* inverse (ratio); *tech* reversible (motion) • **~itate** *nf* reciprocity.

recita [rechi'ta] *vt* to recite.

recital [rechi'tal] *nn* (musical) recital.

reciti [rechi'ti] *vt* to read (over) again, to re-read.

reclama [rekla'ma] *vt (pe cineva)* to denounce; *jur* to sue at law; *fig (a cere)* to claim; *(înapoi)* to claim back; *(a necesita)* to necessitate, to require • **~nt** *nm jur* plaintiff, claimant • **~ţie** *nf* complaint, claim (to, on, upon); *sl* squeal; objection, protest (against).

reclamă [re'klamă] *nf (abstract)* advertising; *(concret)* advertisement, commercial, ad; *(firmă)* (advertisement/neon) sign.

reclădi [reklă'di] *vt* to rebuild, to reconstruct.

recluziune [rekluzi'une] *nf jur* confinement.

recolta [rekol'ta] *vt* to harvest, to gather/get in; *fig* to reap.

recoltă [re'koltă] *nf (abstract)* harvesting, gathering, vintaging; *(concret)* harvest, crop(s), vintage; *(la hectar)* yield; *fig* collection (of medals).

recomanda [rekoman'da] *vt* to recommend; *(a sugera, a propune)* to suggest; *(a prezenta)* to introduce || *vr* to introduce oneself • **~re** *nf* recommendation, testimonial.

recomandată [rekoman'dată] *nf* registered letter.

recompensa [recompen'sa] *vt* to recompense, to reward.

recompensă [rekom'pensă] *nf* recompense, reward.

reconcilia [rekonchili'a] *vt* to reconcile.

recondiţiona [rekonditsio'na] *vt* to recondition • **~re** *nf* reconditioning.

reconfortant [rekonfor'tant] *adj* stimulating, invigorating; *(d. doctorii)* tonic.

reconsidera [rekonside'ra] *vt* to reconsider, to revaluate • **~re** *nf* reappraisal, reassessment, revaluation.

reconstitui [rekonstitu'i] *vt* to reconstitute; to piece together, to reconstruct, to recreate.

reconstrucţie [rekon'struktsie] *nf also med* reconstruction; rebuilding, rehabilitation; *(a oraşelor)* urban renewal.

reconstrui [rekonstru'i] *vt* to reconstruct, to rebuild.

record [re'kord] *nn* record; *(în industrie)* peak output.

recrea [rekre'a] *vt* to recreate; *(a distra)* to entertain || *vr* to amuse/entertain oneself; to take/have a rest; to relax • **~tiv** *adj* entertaining, amusing • **~ţie** *nf* pause, break, interval; recess; *(odihnă)* rest, recreation.

recrudescenţă [rekrudes'chentsă] *nf* recrudescence.

recrut [re'krut] *nm* recruit, draftee; *coll* rookie; *fig* beginner, novice • **~a** *vt* to recruit, to draft; *(susţinători)* to enlist.

rect [rekt] *nn anat* rectum; *coll* passage.

rectifica [rektifi'ka] *vt* to rectify, to amend, to correct; *(o eroare)* to set right; to put right; *(preţuri)* to adjust; *(a îndrepta)* to straighten; *mil* to dress the ranks; *chem* to redistill.

rectitudine [rekti'tudine] *nf* rectitude.

rector ['rektor] *nm* president, rector, chancellor.

recuceri [rekuche'ri] *vt* to reconquer, to regain.

recul [re'kul] *nn (al tunului)* recoil; *(al puştii)* kick; *fig* return.

reculegere [reku'ledjere] *nf* (solitary) meditation, collectedness.

recunoaşte [reku'noashte] *vt (pe cineva, ceva, un adevăr)* to recognize; to admit; *(pe cineva drept fiu)* to acknowledge a child; *(a mărturisi)* to confess; *(sincer)* to make a clean breast of; *mil* to reconnoiter; to explore; *min* to prospect || *vr recip* to recognize each other; *(a fi clar)* to be clear/evident/obvious.

recunoscător [rekunoskă'tor] *adj* grateful, thankful.

recunoştinţă [rekuno'shtintsă] *nf* gratitude, gratefulness || *adv* **cu ~** gratefully

recupera [rekupe'ra] *vt* to recover, to regain; *(o pierdere)* to retrieve, to recoup.

recurge [re'kurdje] *vi* to resort (to smth / to doing smth).

recurs [re'kurs] *nn* (last) appeal.

recuza [reku'za] *vt jur* to challenge, to take exception to • **~re** *nf jur* challenge.

recuzită [reku'zită] *nf* (stage) props, properties; *fig* arsenal.

recviem [rekvi'em] *nn relig, mus* requiem.

reda [re'da] *vt* to restore, to return, to redeem; *(sensul)* to express, to convey; *(d. picturi) also fig* to render, to reproduce • **~re** *nf* giving/rendering back; *mus* rendition; *(la magnetofon)* playback; *(artă)* expression.

redacta [redak'ta] *vt* to draw up, to draft; *(a scrie)* to write; *hum* to indite; (*a exprima*) to word, to couch; (*un ziar*) to edit.

redactor [re'daktor] *nm* (*de carte sau la ziar*) editor; (*al unei secţii*) (sub)editor; (*de film*) continuity man.

redacţie [re'daktsie] *nf* editorial staff/board; (*ca local*) editorial office; (*redactare*) editorship.

redobândi [redobân'di] *vt* to recover, to regain.

redresa [redre'sa] *vt* to straighten out, to redress; to rectify; to adjust; (*a restabili*) to reestablish; *avia* to right; (*a aduce la starea normală*) to bring to a normal state ‖ *vr* to pick up; *coll* to pick up again; (*d. bărci*) to right.

reduce [re'duche] *vt also chem, math* to reduce; (*a micşora*) to decrease, to diminish; (*a restrânge*) to stint; (*cheltuieli, pierderi*) to cut down; (*salariile*) to dock wages; (*o datorie*) to scale a debt; (*preţul*) to lower; (*o vină*) to extenuate; (*pretenţii*) to abate; (*drepturi*) to restrict; (*voltajul*) to step down; **a ~ la** *fig* to reduce to ‖ *vr* to decrease; (*a se micşora*) to diminish; (*d. pretenţii*) to abate; **a se ~ la** (*d. cheltuieli*) to come/boil down to; (*d. o problemă*) to come/amount to • **~re** *nf* reduction, cutback; deficit, shortfall; (*rabat*) allowance; (*de preţ*) discount, rebate; (*a unui text*) cutting.

redundanţă [redun'dantsă] *nf* redundance.

redus [re'dus] *adj* reduced; (*mic*) small; (*restrâns*) scanty; *fig* (*mărginit*) narrow-minded; (*înapoiat*) backward; (*prost*) stupid; *sl* airhead; *fig* (*restrâns, mărginit*) confined.

redutabil [redu'tabil] *adj* redoubtable, strong; (*periculos*) dreaded, dangerous.

reedita [reedi'ta] *vt* to republish, to reissue, (*a retipări*) to reprint; *fig* to repeat, to rake up ‖ *vr* to be republished/reprinted; *fig* to repeat (oneself); to recur.

reeduca [reedu'ka] *vt* to reeducate; to readjust.

reevalua [reevalu'a] *vt* to revaluate, to reappraise.

reface [re'fache] *vt* to remake, to restore; (*a reconstrui*) to reconstruct, to rebuild; (*o haină, o casă*) to do up again; (*a repara*) to repair; (*o frază*) to recast; (*sănătatea*) to recover; (*a schimba*) to change; (*a rescrie*) to rewrite ‖ *vr* (*d. cineva*) to recover (one's health); *coll* to pick up again; (*a se odihni*) to rest.

referat [refe'rat] *nn* paper, essay; (*raport*) invited paper, report (on); (*recenzie*) review; (*conferinţă*) lecture.

referendum [refe'rendum] *nn* referendum.

referent [refe'rent] *nn* reader, reviewer; reporter.

referi [refe'ri] *vi* (*asupra*) to report (on) ‖ *vr* (*la*) to refer (to) ‖ *vt* (*a trimite la*) to relegate (to) • **~re** *nf* reference; **cu ~ la** regarding, with reference to, in regards to • **~tor** *adj* (*la*) concerning, referring to, with regard/reference to ‖ *prep* as to/for, with reference to, in regards to • **~nţă** *nf* reference; information; (*explicaţie*) explanation; (*recomandare*) recommendation; *pl* credentials.

reflecta [reflek'ta] *vt* to reflect; (*lumina, culoarea*) to throw/send back; (*a oglindi*) to mirror; (*a se gândi la*) to think about ‖ *vr* to be reflected/mirrored.

reflector [reflek'tor] *nn cin* spotlight; *also fig* (*lumina rampei*) limelight; *mil* searchlight, reflector.

reflecţie [re'flektsie] *nf* reflection; mirroring; (*gând*) remark; thought.

reflex [re'fleks] *nn* reflex ‖ *adj* reflex; **act ~** reflex action • **~ie** *nf* reflection, meditation; *phys* reflexion •

~iv *adj gram* reflexive, reflexive pronoun/verb; (*d. cineva*) thoughtful; (*substantivat*) reflexive voice.

reflux [re'fluks] *nn* ebb(ing), ebb tide; **flux şi ~** ebb and flow; *fig* withdrawal, retreat; (*al mulţimii*) surging back.

reforma [refor'ma] *vt* to reform; (*a îmbunătăţi*) to improve; (*a înnoi*) to renew; (*a arunca*) to decommission; *mil* to discharge as unfit • **~t** *nm relig* Protestant, Calvinist, Lutheran ‖ *adj also relig* reformed, * **reforma**, *mil* rejected (from the army); (*d. persoane*) invalid; (*d. obiecte de inventar*) decommissioned • **~tor** *nm* reformer ‖ *adj* reforming.

reformă [re'formă] *nf* reform; *relig* Reformation; *mil* discharge; (*a materialelor*) rejection of defective materials.

refracta [refrak'ta] *vt* to refract; to bend ‖ *vr pass* to be refracted, to suffer refraction.

refractar [refrak'tar] *adj* rebellious, unmanageable; (*nedoritor*) reluctant, unwilling; *tech* refractory, fireproof.

refren [re'fren] *nn* refrain, chorus; *fig* old song.

refrigerator [refridjera'tor] *nn* refrigerator.

refugia [refudji'a] *vr* to take refuge/shelter, to shelter (oneself); (*a fugi*) to flee, to escape • **~t** *nm* refugee.

refugiu [re'fudjiu] *nn* refuge (from); (*al scării*) resting place; (*adăpost*) shelter; (*liman*) haven; (*pt. pietoni*) island; curb.

refula [refu'la] *vt* to suppress, to repress • **~t** *adj* pent-up, repressed, inhibited ‖ *nm* inhibited person.

refuz [re'fuz] *nn* refusal; *tech* refuse • **~a** *vt* to refuse; (*o discuţie, o sfidare*) to decline; (*a respinge*) to turn down (smb, smth); *scol* to fail; *jur* (*a recuza*) to impugn.

regal [re'gal] *nn typ* rack, frame; *cul* feat, treat ‖ *adj* royal, kingly; *rare* regal; *fig* majestic, stately.

regat [re'gat] *nn* kingdom.

regată [re'gata] *nf* regatta.

regăsi [regă'si] *vt* to find again, to recover, (*a redescoperi*) to rediscover ‖ *vr* (*d. cineva*) to find one's bearings; *recip* to meet/find each other again.

rege ['redje] *nm* king.

regie [re'djie] *nf* administration, management; (*cheltuieli*) overhead charges/costs; *thea* stage management; *cin* direction.

regim [re'djim] *nn pol* regime, form of government; (*al muncii*) organization; (*condiţii*) conditions; *med* regimen, diet.

regiment [redji'ment] *nn* regiment.

regină [re'djină] *nf* queen.

regional [redjio'nal] *adj* regional.

registratură [redjistra'tură] *nf* registry (office); registrar's (office).

registru [re'djistru] *nn* record, registry book; *econ also* account book; (*mare*) *also mus* register.

regiune [redji'une] *nf* region; (*parte, ţinut*) part(s); area, zone; (*diviziune administrativă*) county, district.

regiza [redji'za] *vt* to direct, to produce; *thea also* to stage; *fig* (*a înscena*) to plot, to set up.

regizor [redji'zor] *nm* (*de teatru*) stage manager; (*de film*) director, assistant producer.

regla [re'gla] *vt* to regulate, to adjust; (*mersul unui ceas*) to set; (*tirul*) to range • **~j** *nn* adjustment • **~re** *nf* adjustment.

reglementa [reglemen'ta] *vt* to settle, to regulate; (*a stabili*) to establish.

reglementar [reglemen'tar] *adj* regular, statutory || *adv* according to regulations.

regn [regn] *nn* kingdom, reign; ~ul animal the animal kingdom.

regres [re'gres] *nn* regress; *bio* retrogression • ~a *vi* to regress, to retrogress.

regret [re'gret] *nn* (*pentru*) regret/sorrow for; (*remușcare*) compunction; *pl* searching of the heart • ~a *vt/vi* to regret; (*că*) to be sorry (that) • ~abil *adj* regrettable, unfortunate.

regrupa [regru'pa] *vt* to regroup, to reshuffle || *vr* to regroup • ~re *nf* regrouping, reshuffling.

regulament [regula'ment] *nn* regulations, rules.

regularitate [regulari'tate] *nf* regularity; (*a mişcării*) steadiness, evenness.

regulariza [regulari'za] *vt* to regularize.

regulat [regu'lat] *adj* regular; (*d. puls*) steady; (*armonios*) harmonious; (*d. mişcare*) even; (*d. viață*) ordered || *adv* regularly, steadily.

regulă ['regulă] *nf* rule; (*principiu*) principle; (*dogmă*) tenet; * regularitate; *pl med* courses, menses; de ~ as a rule; în~ all right, OK; (*în ordine*) in order.

reiat [re'iat] *adj* striped, ribbed.

reieşi [reie'shi] *vi* to result (from), to follow (from).

reintegra [reinte'gra] *vt* to reinstate, to restore smb to his position/office, (*angajați*) to re-hire.

reintra [rein'tra] *vi* to reenter, to come/go in again.

reintroduce [reintro'duche] *vt* to reinstate.

reîmpărţi [reîmpăr'tsi] *vt* to redivide.

reîmprospăta [reîmprospă'ta] *vt* (*memoria*) to jog, to refresh; (*d. o culoare*) to revive; (*garderoba*) to replenish.

reînarma [reînar'ma] *vt/vr* to rearm.

reîncepe [reîn'chepe] *vt* to resume, to start (all over again) || *vi* to begin again, to start afresh.

reînnoi [reînno'i] *vt* to renew, to reaffirm; (*a relua*) to resume.

reîntinerire [reîntine'rire] *nf* rejuvenation.

reîntoarcere [reîn'toarchere] *nf* coming back, return.

reîntregi [reîntre'dji] *vt* to (re)unify, to (re)unite.

reînvia [reînvi'a] *vt* to resurrect, to revive || *vi* to revive, to resuscitate.

rejudecare [rezhude'kare] *nf jur* trial on review.

relansa [relan'sa] *vi* to raise the bid.

relata [rela'ta] *vt* to report, to tell, to recount; (*cu savoare*) to relate smth with unction • ~re *nf* relating, stating, reporting; (*povestire*) account, narrative.

relativ [rela'tiv] *adj* relative; ~ la relating to, in relation to || *adv* relatively, comparatively • ~itate *nf* relativity.

relaţie [re'latsie] *nf* relation(ship), connection; contact; *pl* relation, intercourse; (*cu cineva*) dealings; (*oameni influenți*) influential people/friends; protection; (*informații*) information; (*relatare*) account, report.

relaxa [relak'sa] *vr* to become relaxed; (*d. cineva*) to (have a) rest.

releu [re'leu] *nn* relay.

releva [rele'va] *vt* to point out, to emphasize; to observe, to notice, to remark • ~nt *adj* relevant (to smth); significant, pertinent.

relicvă [re'likvă] *nf* relic; (*urmă*) vestige; *pl* relics.

relief [reli'ef] *nn* relief; (*artă*) relief.

reliefa [relie'fa] *vt* to throw/bring (out) into (bold) relief, to set off; (*a sublinia*) to point out, to stress || *vr* to be outlined.

religie [re'lidjie] *nf* religion, faith.

religios [relidji'os] *adj* religious, believing.

relua [re'lua] *vt* to take back/again; (*a reîncepe*) to resume; (*lucrările la Senat*) to reconvene; (*un spectacol*) to revive.

remania [remani'a] *vt* to reshuffle; (*o lege*) to reframe.

remaniere [remani'ere] *nf pol* (*guvern*) (cabinet) reshuffle, reshuffling.

remarca [remar'ka] *vt* (*a spune ceva*) to remark (on, upon); to observe, to notice || *vr* to distinguish oneself • ~bil *adj* remarkable, noteworthy (for); *coll* awesome; **orator** ~ outstanding/remarkable speaker; (*uimitor*) astonishing || *adv* remarkably.

remarcă [re'markă] *nf* remark.

remedia [remedi'a] *vt* to remedy, to rectify; (*un rău*) to cure || *vr* to be remedied, to be cured • ~bil *adj* remediable, redeemable.

remediu [re'mediu] *nn* remedy (for), cure (for).

reminiscenţă [reminis'chentsă] *nf* reminiscence.

remite [re'mite] *vt* to deliver; (*a înmâna o cerere, o declaraţie*) to hand in/out; (*a preda*) to hand over.

remiză [re'miză] *nf sp* draw game/match; *econ* rebate; allowance.

remonta [remon'ta] *vt* to invigorate; (*a recupera*) to recoup; *fig* to tone; *coll* to buck up; *tech* to refit; *mil* to remount || *vr* to recover one's strength/spirits.

remorca [remor'ka] *vt* (*ambarcaţiuni*) to tug, to haul; (*maşini*) to trail, to tow; *rail* to draw, to pull.

remorcă [re'morkă] *nf* (*vehicul*) trailer; *naut* tow, vessel towed; *naut* (*parâmă*) tow rope/line; (*remorcare*) towing, tugging.

remorcher [remor'ker] *nn naut* tow/tug boat, tug.

remunera [remune'ra] *vt* to pay, to remunerate • ~ţie *nf* pay(ment), remuneration; *fig* emolument(s).

remuşcare [remush'kare] *nf* remorse, pangs of conscience; *pl* searching of the heart; regret.

ren [ren] *nm zool* reindeer.

renal [re'nal] *adj* anat renal.

renaşte [re'nashte] *vi* to revive, to rise (again), to be reborn • ~re *nf* rebirth, revival; (*reînnoire*) renewal; **Renaşterea** the Renaissance.

renega [rene'ga] *vt* (*un prieten, o părere*) to disown; (*o părere*) to deny; to abjure • ~t *nm* renegade, apostate.

renglotă [ren'glotă] *nf bot* greengage (tree or fruit).

renova [reno'va] *vt* to restore, to renovate; to redecorate; (*a repara*) to repair; (*maşini*) to overhaul.

renta [ren'ta] *vi* to be profitable/lucrative, to bring profit; *coll* to be worthwhile • ~bil *adj* advantageous, profitable; *coll* worthwhile • ~bilitate *nf* profitableness, lucrativeness.

rentă ['rentă] *nf* rent; revenue; (*viageră*) life annuity, pension.

rentier [renti'er] *nm* fund holder, rentier.

renume [re'nume] *nn* renown, fame; (good) name.

renumit [renu'mit] *adj* famous, celebrated, renowned; (*bine-cunoscut*) well-known; (*mai ales în sens negativ*) notorious.

renunţa [renun'tsa] *vi* (*la*) to renounce, to give up; *jur* (*la acuzaţii*) to drop charges; *jur* (*fără a cere compensaţii*) to resign simpliciter; (*la cetăţenie*) to expatriate oneself; (*la credinţă*) to abnegate one's faith; (*la iluzii*) to undeceive oneself; (*la religia sa*) to abnegate one's religion; (*la o slujbă*) to turn in a job; (*la un drept*) to waive a right; (*la luptă*) to give up the struggle; *coll* to throw in the sponge; (*la mândrie*) to swallow one's pride; (*la o părere*) to recant; (*la o reclamație*) to withdraw a claim; (*la naivități*) to shed one's naivete; (*la cărți*) to revoke.

reorganiza [reorgani'za] *vt* to reorganize • **~re** *nf* reorganization.

repara [repa'ra] *vt* to repair, to mend; (*mașini și*) to overhaul; (*o navă*) to refit; (*ciorapi*) to darn; (*o greșeală*) to rectify; (*o nedreptate*) to redress a wrong/grievance; (*un rău*) to redress; (*o pagubă/ pierdere*) to make good, to compensate; to make up for, to compensate for • **~ție** *nf* repair, reparation; (*de ceas, pantofi*) mending; (*revizie*) overhauling.

repartiție [repar'titsie] *nf* distribution; (*a voturilor, a părților*) allotment; (*a cheltuielilor*) allocation.

repartiza [reparti'za] *vt* to distribute, to divide; (*o muncă*) to stint; (*a aloca*) to allocate; (*fonduri*) to earmark; (*voturi și*) to allot; *mil* to detail • **~re** *nf* distribution, allocation.

repatriere [repatri'ere] *nf* repatriation.

repaus [re'paus] *nn* rest, repose, (*răgaz*) respite, leisure; *phys* rest.

repede ['repede] *adj* fast, quick, swift; (*vioi*) nimble, brisk; (*grăbit*) speedy, hasty; (*brusc*) sudden; (*precipitat*) rash; (*furtunos*) tempestuous; (*înaripat*) winged; (*d. dealuri*) sloping || *adv* quickly, rapidly; (*ca mers*) briskly; *mil* at the double; (*curând*) soon, shortly; *coll* off-hand; (*devreme*) early.

reper [re'per] *nn* (*în spațiu*) (guide) mark, landmark; *fig* hint; *mil* reference point; marker; benchmark; (*piesă*) piece, part; (*în timp*) reference (to) • **~a** *vt* to mark with a guide mark, to mark; to locate, to spot; *telec* (*o stație*) to log.

repercusiune [reperkusi'une] *nf* repercussion, impact, (consequential) effects.

repercuta [reperku'ta] *vr* to reverberate.

repertoriu [reper'toriu] *nn* (*teatru*) repertory, repertoire; index, list, catalog; (*culegere*) collection.

repeta [repe'ta] *vt* to repeat, to say/do (over) again; (*a recapitula*) to review; (*de mai multe ori*) to reiterate; (*teatru*) to rehearse; (*o lecție, un rol*) to learn; (*un an școlar*) to fail to get one's remove; (*un test*) to repeat a test || *vr* (*d. o persoană*) to repeat oneself; (*d. o acțiune*) to recur (again) || *vi* to repeat; (*teatru*) to rehearse • **~re** *nf* repetition, reiteration; (*a unui eveniment*) recurrence; **~în cor** *scol* choral work.

repetiție [repe'titsie] *nf* repetition; revision; (*teatru*) rehearsal.

repezeală [repe'zeală] *nf* hurry, haste.

repezi [repe'zi] *vt* (*a izbi*) to hit; (*a arunca*) to throw; (*pe cineva*) (*verbal*) to shout at smb; *coll* to fly at smb; (*fizic*) to pounce upon || *vr* to run; (*a se grăbi*) to hurry; (*a ataca*) to attack; (*inamicul*) to prey/ swoop upon.

repeziciune [repezi'chiune] *nf* swiftness, rapidity, speed.

replia [repli'a] *vt* to yield, to give ground; *mil* to fall back, to retreat.

replica [repli'ka] *vt* to retort, to answer back, to reply.

replică ['replikă] *nf* (*răspuns*) retort, repartee; *thea* speech; *fig* cue; *fig* (*ripostă, refuz*) rebuff; **a da o ~** to rebut; (*artă*) replica, replication.

reportaj [repor'tazh] *nn* (feature) report, running commentary; (*literar*) reportage.

reporter [re'porter] *nm* reporter, correspondent.

represalii [repre'salii] *nf pl* reprisals, retaliation.

represiune [represi'une] *nf* repression.

represiv [repre'siv] *adj* repressive.

reprezenta [reprezen'ta] *vt* to represent; (*a descrie*) to describe, to depict; to imagine, to picture; (*grafic*) to plot; (*pe cineva*) to stand for, to act for; (*a însemna*) to mean; (*o piesă*) to perform • **~re** *nf* description; (*grafică*) plotting; (*teatru*) performance • **~tiv** *adj* representative, illustrative • **~ție** *nf thea* performance • **~nt** *nm* representative; *fig* spokesman, spokesperson; official • **~nță** *nf* representation.

reprima [repri'ma] *vt* to suppress, to repress.

reprimi [repri'mi] *vt* to take back; (*a recăpăta*) to get back, to recover; (*a reangaja*) to reappoint, to rehire.

repriză [re'priză] *nf* (*box*) round; (*fotbal*) first/second half; (*scrimă*) bout; (*polo, hockey*) period; *tech* resumption (of work); *metal* flaw, crack; *mus* reentry (of a theme); **în ~e** in successive stages.

reprobabil [repro'babil] *adj* blamable, blameworthy.

reproduce [repro'duche] *vt* to reproduce; (*a imita*) (*o persoană*) to mimic, to ape; (*un obiect*) to imitate, to replicate; (*a copia*) to copy; (*a multiplica*) to multiply || *vr* to reproduce, to multiply • **~re** *nf* reproduction, copy.

reproducție [repro'duktsie] *nf* reproduction, copy.

reprofila [reprofi'la] *vt* to reshape, to adapt || *vr* to (re)adjust oneself.

reproș [re'prosh] *nn* reproach, reproof; (*învinuire*) blame, censure.

reproșa [repro'sha] *vt* to reproach (smb with smth), to upbraid smb with/for smth.

reptilă [rep'tilă] *nf* reptile.

republica [republi'ka] *vt* to republish, (*a retipări*) to reprint.

republican [republi'kan] *nm* republican || *adj* republican; national, all-country.

republică [re'publikă] *nf* republic.

repudia [repudi'a] *vt* to repudiate, to reject, to forswear.

repulsie [re'pulsie] *nf* repulsion, disgust, loathing.

repulsiv [repul'siv] *adj* repellent, repulsive, loathsome.

repune [re'pune] *vt* to put back again, to restore; (*în drepturi*) to reinstate, to rehabilitate.

repurta [repur'ta] *vt* to gain the victory, to carry the day; (*succese*) to score.

reputat [repu'tat] *adj* reputed, well-known, famous; highly esteemed.

reputație [repu'tatsie] *nf* repute, reputation, fame; *coll* character; (*renume*) renown.

resemna [resem'na] *vr* to resign oneself; (*în fața inevitabilului*) to resign oneself to the inevitable • **~re** *nf* resignation, submission.

resentiment [resenti'ment] *nn* resentment, spite, grudge.

resimți [resim'tsi] *vt* to feel, to experience || *vr* to feel the effects of, to be felt.

resort [re'sort] *nn tech* spring; *fig* moral support; (*sferă*) scope, sphere; sector, section.

respect [res'pekt] *nn* respect, regard, *pl* respects, homage, compliments || *adv* **cu ~** respectfully • **~a** *vt* (*pe cineva*) to respect, to revere; *coll* to look up at; (*legea*) to abide by; (*o clauză*) to comply with; (*tradiția*) to be respectful of; (*o regulă*) to observe; (*regulile jocului*) to see fair (play) • **~abil** *adj* honorable, respectable • **~iv** *adj* respective || *adv* respectively • **~uos** *adj* (*d. copii*) dutiful || *adv* respectfully, dutifully; **al dvs ~** yours respectfully.

respingător [respingă'tor] *adj* repellent, loathsome;

(*groaznic*) dreadful, awful || *adv* repulsively, dreadfully, awfully.

respinge [res'pindje] *vt* (*a alunga*) to repel; (*a refuza*) to refuse; (*categoric*) to rebuff; (*o cerere*) to turn down a request; (*o propunere, un candidat*) to reject; (*o moţiune*) to vote down; (*reclamaţii*) to overrule; (*un argument*) to rebut; (*un atac*) to repulse; (*un inamic*) to roll up; (*asaltul*) to stand the storm; (*cu dispreţ*) to spurn; (*a înstrăina*) to alienate; (*a provoca ostilitate*) to antagonize.

respira [respi'ra] *vi* to breathe; (*astmatic*) to wheeze || *vt* to breathe (in), to inhale; *fig* to betoken • ~**ţie** *nf* breathing, repiration, breath.

responsabil [respon'sabil] *nm* chief, person in charge; *econ* manager, executive, official; responsible person; culprit || *adj* (*pentru*) responsible (for), answerable/accountable (for) • ~**itate** *nf* responsibility, accountability, liability (for).

rest [rest] *nn* remainder, rest; (*în bani*) change, odd money; *math* rest; (*rămăşiţă*) remainder; *coll* shank; *pl* remnants, remains; (*de mâncare*) scraps, leftovers.

restabili [restabi'li] *vt* to restore, to reestablish; (*renumele*) to retrieve; (*a reintroduce*) to reintroduce; (*a reabilita*) to rehabilitate; *coll* to even things up || *vr* (*d. cineva*) to recover, to rally from an illness.

restant [res'tant] *adj* outstanding, remaining.

restanţă [res'tantsă] *nf* (*ca impozit*) arrear; (*datorie*) debt.

restaura [restau'ra] *vt* to restore, to repair, (*a restabili*) to reestablish • ~**tor** *nm* (*artă*) restorer • ~**ţie** *nf* restoration.

restaurant [restau'rant] *nn* restaurant, diner; (*bufet*) refreshment room/bar.

restitui [restitu'i] *vt* to restore, to return; (*bani*) to refund.

restrânge [res'trândje] *vt* to restrict, to limit; to reduce; (*a micşora*) to diminish || *vr* to cut down expenses, to scrounge.

restrictiv [restrik'tiv] *adj* restrictive.

restricţie [res'triktsie] *nf* restriction, limitation, restraint.

restrişte [res'trishte] *nf* affliction, distress, tribulation.

restructura [restruktu'ra] *vt* to reshape, to reorganize; (*personalul*) to lay off.

resursă [re'sursă] *nf* resource(s); *pl also* means; *fig* resourcefulness.

resuscita [resuschi'ta] *vt med* to resuscitate, to bring back to life.

reşedinţă [reshe'dintsă] *nf* residence, abode.

reşou [re'shou] *nn* electric boiling ring; (small portable) electric stove.

retehnologiza [retehnolodji'za] *vt* to streamline.

retenţie [re'tentsie] *nf med, chem* retention; *jur* reservation.

reteza [rete'za] *vt* to cut off, to chop off; (*capul cuiva*) to cut smb's head off; (*crengi*) to lop off; (*coada*) to dock; (*a tăia*) to cut; (*a scurta*) to shorten; to reduce.

reticenţă [reti'chentsă] *nf* reticence, reserve, hesitation.

retină [re'tină] *nf anat* retina.

retipări [retipă'ri] *vt* to reprint, (*a republica*) to republish.

retoric [re'torik] *adj* rhetorical || *adv* rhetorically • ~**ă** *nf* rhetoric, oratory.

retortă [re'tortă] *nf* retort; muffle.

retracta [retrak'ta] *vt* to retract, to take back; *coll* to eat humble pie || *vr* (*d. materiale*) to shrink

retrage [re'tradje] *vt* to withdraw; (*de la şcoală*) to remove; (*bani*) to withdraw; (*cuvântul, făgăduiala*) to take back; *coll* to back out; (*din circulaţie, bani, cărţi*) to call in; (*din funcţiune*) (*o maşină, un vas*) to recall; (*de pe piaţă, unele efecte*) to retire; (*a anula*) to revoke || *vr* to retire; to withdraw; to fall back; (*în fugă*) to beat a hasty retreat, to cut and run; (*din lume/societate*) to renounce the world; *mil* (*de pe o poziţie*) to recede from a position; (*dintr-o afacere*) to draw back; (*d. un candidat*) to drop out; (*d. apă*) to subside, to recede • ~**re** *nf* withdrawal, retiring; (*a apei*) subsiding; *mil* retreat; (*izolare*) isolation; (*refugiu*) refuge; (*anulare*) revocation, canceling.

retras [re'tras] *adj* (*d. un loc*) secluded, remote; (*d. viaţă*) retired; (*d. cineva*) solitary, lonely || *adv* in retirement, in seclusion.

retribui [retribu'i] *vt* to pay, to remunerate • ~**re** *nf* remuneration, payment.

retribuţie [retri'butsie] *nf* remuneration, payment; (*leafă*) salary, wages; fee.

retroactiv [retroak'tiv] *adj* retroactive, retrospective || *adv* retroactively.

retroceda [retroche'da] *vt* to resell, to give back • ~**re** *nf* retrocession.

retrograda [retrogra'da] *vt* to demote; *mil* to lower the rank of smb • ~**re** *nf* demoting; *mil* reduction to a lower rank

retrospectiv [retrospek'tiv] *adj* retrospective || *adv* retrospectively, looking back • ~**ă** *nf* retrospect(ion); (*artă*) retrospective exhibition.

retrovizor [retrovi'zor] *nn* rearview mirror.

retur [re'tur] *nn* return; *sp* return match || *adv* back.

retuş [re'tush] *nn* (*artă*) retouch, touch-up • ~**a** *vt* to retouch, to touch up; *fig* to brush up, to give a finish to.

reţea [re'tsea] *nf* net, netting, network; *archit* tracery; *med* plexus; *opt* diffraction grating; (*de drumuri*) system.

reţetă [re'tsetă] *nf* prescription; receipt; *cul* recipe; *fig* device; (*încasări*) proceeds; *thea* takings.

reţine [re'tsine] *vt* to hold back, to keep; (*făcând să întârzie*) to delay; (*atenţia*) to arrest; (*în pat*) to confine (to bed); (*a opri*) to stop; (*a împiedica*) to prevent/deter (from); (*leafa*) to withhold; (*pe dinafară*) to remember by heart, to memorize; (*a ţine minte*) to bear in mind; (*a păstra*) to keep; (*a nu pierde*) not to lose; (*a rezerva*) to book; (*o cameră*) to engage; (*a priva de libertate*) to confine; (*a stăpâni*) to restrain; (*lacrimile*) to hold back; (*un strigăt, un căscat*) to stifle; (*răsuflarea*) to hold one's breath || *vr* to control/restrain/contain oneself.

reţinut [retsi'nut] *adj* reserved, restrained; cautious; prudent || *adv* with restraint, with discretion.

reumatism [reuma'tism] *nn med* rheumatism.

reumple [re'umple] *vt* to refill.

reuni [reu'ni] *vt* to (re)unite, to bring (people) together; (*a convoca*) to convene; (*un comitet*) to call together; (*a întruchipa*) to combine || *vr* (*a se aduna*) to gather, to come together; (*a se întâlni*) to meet; (*d. biserici*) to unite; (*d. bănci*) to amalgamate; (*a se întruchipa*) to combine • ~**une** *nf* reunion; (*adunare*) meeting, assembly; (*pt. a petrece*) social gathering; *coll* party, function; *sp* match, competition; (*ca acţiune*) reuniting, connecting.

reuşi [reu'shi] *vi* (*d. o piesă*) to be a success; (*d. o* *afacere*) to prosper; (*d. un plan*) to thrive; to succeed (in) || *vt* to make a success of • ~t *adj* successful; (*bun*) good; (*potrivit*) fit; (*fericit*) felicitous; (*d. o expresie*) apt || *adv* successfully; (*bine*) well • ~tă *nf* (*rezultat*) result, outcome; success, successful outcome/result.

reutila [reuti'la] *vt* to reequip, to retool.

revalorifica [revalorifi'ka] *vt* to revalue, to reappraise.

revanşa [revan'sha] *vr* (*a se răzbuna*) to have/take one's revenge; (*în sens bun*) to be quits (with); to return a service to smb.

revanşă [re'vanshă] *nf* revenge, retaliation; (*în sens bun*) return, requital; *sp* return match/game.

revărsa [revăr'sa] *vt* to pour out/forth; (*lumină*) to shed, to throw; **a-şi ~** (*mânia*) to vent one's fury/rage over smb; (*inima*) to pour out || *vr* (*d. un lichid*) to spill; (*d. un râu*) to overflow; (*d. valuri*) to break; (*a ţâşni*) to gush out; (*a fi prea plin*) to overfill; (*d. oameni*) to stream; *fig* to pour out/forth; (*a năvăli*) to rush in.

revedea [reve'dea] *vt* to see/meet again; (*a revizui*) to revise, to reexamine; (*corecturi*) to read (proofs); (*un proces*) to review || *vr* to meet again.

revedere [reve'dere] *nf* seeing (each other) again; (*revizie*) revision; (*a unor persoane*) meeting again; **la ~!** good bye!, so long!, see you later/soon!.

revelator [revela'tor] *adj* revealing || *nn phot* developer.

revelaţie [reve'latsie] *nf* revelation.

revelion [reveli'on] *nn* New Year's Eve, New Year's party.

revendica [revendi'ka] *vt* to claim, to demand; (*drepturi*) to insist on, to assert; (*asupra unui lucru*) to lay claims to; (*responsabilitatea pentru ceva*) to assume responsibility for smth • ~re *nf* claim, demand (on); *jur* revindication, action for recovery of property.

reveni [reve'ni] *vi* to return, to come back; (*altă dată*) to come again; (*a se întâmpla repetat*) to occur, to recur; (*d. o problemă*) to come/crop up again; (*d. memorie*) to come back; (*a apărea din nou*) to reappear; to cost; (*a incumba*) to be incumbent (upon smb); **a-şi ~** to recover one's health; (*după un leşin*) to recover consciousness; *coll* to come round; (*a se simţi bine*) to feel better; (*a fi din nou acelaşi*) to feel like oneself; **a ~ asupra** (*unei hotărâri*) to take back one's words; (*unei păreri*) to reconsider; (*unui subiect*) to bring up; *coll* to keep coming back to it; (*a relua*) to resume; **a ~ la** to come/return back to, to revert to; (*a se ridica la*) to amount to.

rever [re'ver] *nn* lapel, flap; *sp* backhand (stroke).

reverberaţie [reverbe'ratsie] *nf* reverberation.

reverend [reve'rend] *nm relig* reverend (father).

reverenţă [reve'rentsă] *nf* reverence, respect (for); esteem; (*plecăciune*) bow, curtsy; **a face o ~** (*d. bărbaţi*) to bow, (*d. femei*) to drop a curtsy (to smb).

reverenţios [reverentsi'os] *adj* ceremonious, respectful || *adv* with much ceremony.

reverie [reve'rie] *nf* reverie, (*visare*) (day)dreaming, musing.

revers [re'vers] *nn* reverse (face/side); (*d. mână*) back side; (*d. material*) wrong side; (*d. o pagină*) other side; (*lovitură*) (*tenis*) backhand stroke; (*scrimă*) reverse.

reviriment [reviri'ment] *nn* sudden change; reversal; revulsion.

revistă [re'vistă] *nf* periodical, review, journal; (*ilustrată*) magazine; (*lunară*) monthly; (*bilunară*) fort-

nightly; (*săptămânală*) weekly; (*publicată pe hârtie lucioasă*) glossy magazine; *thea* revue; *mil* muster inspection.

revizie [re'vizie] *nf* revision, reviewing, control; *tech* inspection; *auto* overhaul(ing); *mil* medical examination; *typ* proofreading.

revizionism [revizio'nism] *nn* revisionism.

revizor [re'vizor] *nm* inspector (general); (*contabil*) auditor; (*corector*) reviser.

revizui [revizu'i] *vt* to revise, to reexamine, to control; (*a repara*) to overhaul; (*o lucrare literară*) to castigate; (*conturi*) to audit.

revoca [revo'ka] *vt* to revoke, to repeal; (*un ordin*) to rescind; (*a destitui*) to dismiss; (*ambasadori*) to recall • ~re *nf* cancellation, annulment; dismissal, recalling.

revolta [revol'ta] *vt* to disgust, to sicken || *vr* to be disgusted; (*a se indigna împotriva*) to revolt at/against; (*a se răscula*) to rebel (against); *fig coll* to kick against/at smth; *mil, naut* to mutiny • ~t *adj* revolted, indignant; (*împotriva cuiva*) up in arms against smb; rebellious || *adv* with indignation, rebelliously || *nm* rebel, insurgent; *mil* mutineer.

revoltă [re'voltă] *nf* revolt; (*răscoală*) rebellion, rising; *mil, naut* mutiny; indignation • ~tor *adj* revolting, sickening; (*d. comportare*) outrageous || *adv* shockingly, outrageously.

revoluţie [revo'lutsie] *nf* revolution; revolt, upheaval.

revoluţiona [revolutsio'na] *vt* to revolutionize • ~r *nm* revolutionist, revolutionary || *adj* revolutionary, radical.

revolver [revol'ver] *nn* revolver, pistol; *coll* gun; (*de troleu*) line wiper support.

rezema [reze'ma] *vt* to prop, to rest || *vr* to lean against/on; *fig* to rely on.

rezemătoare [rezemă'toare] *nf* (*de scaun*) back; (*balustradă*) (hand)rail, railing.

rezerva [rezer'va] *vt* to reserve, to set aside; (*un dans*) to save; (*timp*) to set apart; (*un loc pt. cineva*) to keep; (*din timp, bilete, locuri*) to book; (*d. viitor*) to have/hold in store.

rezervat [rezer'vat] *adj* reserved, * **rezerva**; (*pe masă*) "taken"; (*d. cineva*) modest; prudent, cautious; timid, shy; (*rece*) standoffish; (*posac*) sullen || *adv* with reservation, reservedly.

rezervaţie [rezer'vatsie] *nf* reservation; (*regiune protejată*) (forest, nature) reserve; (game) preserve; (Indian) reservation.

rezervă [re'zervă] *nf also mil, sp* reserve; stock; supply; (*de pix, creion*) refill; *mil pl* reserve forces/troops; (*de spital*) side-room; *fig* (*reţinere*) caution, reticence; *fig* (*condiţie*) condition, reservation.

rezervor [rezer'vor] *nn* tank, cistern; *hydr* reservoir.

rezident [rezi'dent] *nm* resident.

rezidual [rezidu'al] *adj* residual, residuary.

reziduu [re'ziduu] *nn* residue, residuum, *pl* residua.

rezilia [rezili'a] *vt* to cancel, to terminate, to annul.

reziliere [rezili'ere] *nf* cancellation, annulment.

rezista [rezis'ta] *vi* (*la*) to resist (smth), to stand up to; (*la boală*) to resist disease; (*la durere*) to withstand (smth); (*la un atac*) to hold out (against); (*a dura*) to stay.

rezistent [rezis'tent] *adj* resistant; (*d. un material*) strong, tough; (*d. culori*) fast; durable, enduring; **~ la lumină** colorfast; (*d. cineva*) hardy; (*d. organisme*) refractory; ~ **la maladii** *med* resistant; **~la** proof, -fast; ~ **la apă** waterproof.

rezistență [rezis'tentsă] *nf also phys* resistance; opposition; (*a unui material*) *also tech* strength; (*fizică*) stamina, endurance; *elec* (electric) resistance.

rezoluție [rezo'lutsie] *nf* resolution, solution; *phys* resolution (power); *jur* termination, cancellation.

rezolva [rezol'va] *vt* to solve; (*o problemă și*) to work out; *coll* (*cu efort*) to worry out a problem; (*o chestiune*) to settle; (*o dificultate*) to clear up; (*a pune capăt unui lucru*) to put an end to smth.

rezonabil [rezo'nabil] *adj* reasonable; acceptable; (*înțelept și*) wise ‖ *adv* reasonably.

rezonanță [rezo'nantsă] *nf* resonance; *fig* echo, response.

rezulta [rezul'ta] *vi* (*din*) to result/follow/derive from; (*a urma*) to ensue • **~t** *nn* result, outcome; effect; (*produs*) avail • **fără ~** *adv* ineffectually, uselessly ‖ *adj* ineffectual, ineffective, useless.

rezuma [rezu'ma] *vt* to summarize, to sum up; *coll* (*o carte*) to boil down; (*în câteva cuvinte*) to put in a nutshell; to recapitulate ‖ *vr* **a se ~ la** (*d. cineva*) to confine oneself to; (*d. ceva*) to reduce itself to • **~t** *nn* summary, précis; **în ~** in brief/short, to sum up.

ribonucleic [ribonu'kleik] *adj biochem* ribonucleic.

ricin [ri'chin] *nm bot* castor-oil plant • **~ă** *nf* castor oil.

ricoșa [riko'sha] *vi also fig* to rebound; (*d. gloanțe*) to ricochet.

ricoșeu [riko'sheu] *nn* rebound; (*al gloanțelor*) ricochet.

rid [rid] *nn* wrinkle; (*cută*) furrow • **~a** *vr* to become wrinkled/crinkled • **~at** *adj* wrinkled, crinkled.

ridica [ridi'ka] *vt* to raise; (*de la sol*) to lift; (*ochii, mâinile*) to look up; (*capul, nervos*) to bridle (up); (*din umeri*) to shrug one's shoulders; (*ceva greu*) to heave; (*pălăria*) to take off; (*un steag*) to hoist; (*un cort*) to pitch; (*tabăra*) to break camp; (*a culege*) to pick up; (*a da la o parte*) to remove; (*a deschide*) to open; (*a sufleca*) to roll up; (*a pune drept*) to straighten up; *fig* (*moralul cuiva*) to raise smb's spirits; (*a desființa*) to abolish; to suspend, to adjourn; (*a încasa*) to encash; to collect; to arrest; (*a realiza un plan, o hartă*) to draw up; (*a crea*) to create; (*a promova*) to promote; (*a spori*) to increase; *fig* to enhance; (*a clădi*) to build; (*a urca*) to climb; *fig* (*prețuri*) to put up ‖ *vr* to rise; (*în picioare*) to stand up; (*d. păsări, rachete*) to soar; *fig* (*la o poziție*) to climb; (*a se însănătoși*) to recover; *coll* to pick up again; (*a se afla*) to lie; (*d. construcții înalte*) to rise; to spar; (*a se auzi*) to be heard; (*a răsuna*) to resound; (*a se răzvrăti*) to rebel (against); (*a se isca*) to arise; to appear; (*a crește*) to grow (up); *fig* to bother oneself; (*a spori*) to increase; (*d. plante*) to shoot; **a se ~ la** (*d. valoare*) to amount/come to; (*la un anumit nivel, standard*) to come up (to).

ridiche [ri'dike] *nf bot* radish.

ridicol [ri'dikol] *nn* ridicule ‖ *adj* ridiculous, ludicrous ‖ *adv* ridiculously, laughably.

ridiculiza [ridikuli'za] *vt* to (hold up to) ridicule.

rigid [ri'djid] *adj* rigid, stiff; *fig* illiberal ‖ *adv* rigidly, stiffly • **~itate** *nf* rigidity, stiffness.

riglă ['riglă] *nf* rule(r); ~ **de calcul** slide/sliding rule.

rigoare [ri'goare] *nf* rigor, strictness; **la ~** at a pinch, if need be, if really necessary.

rigolă [ri'golă] *nf* drain, gutter; kennel.

riguros [rigu'ros] *adj* strict, rigorous, severe; (*d. raționament*) close ‖ *adv* strictly, rigorously, severely.

rima [ri'ma] *vi* to rhyme (with) ‖ *vt* to put into rhyme, to versify.

rimă ['rimă] *nf* rhyme; (*vers*) line.

rimel [ri'mel] *nn* mascara.

rindea [rin'dea] *nf* (bench) plane.

rindelui [rindelu'i] *vt tech* to plane, to shave.

ring [ring] *nn* ring; (*de dans*) dance floor; *sp* (*box, patinaj*) rink.

rinichi [ri'niki] *nm anat* kidney.

rinocer [rino'cher] *nm zool* rhinoceros; *coll* rhino.

riposta [ripos'ta] *vi* to retort, to rebut; to give a rebuff (to smb); *sp* to counter; *coll* to thrust and parry.

ripostă [ri'postă] *nf* retort, riposte; *sp* return, counter; *fig* counterstroke.

risc [risk] *nn* risk, hazard, cast of the die • **~a** *vt* to risk, to venture; *coll* to chance one's arm, to stake • **~ant** *adj* risky, daredevil, hazardous; rash, reckless.

risipă [ri'sipă] *nf* waste, thriftlessness; prodigality, extravagance; (*risipire*) dissipation, squandering.

risipi [risi'pi] *vt* (*a irosi*) to waste; (*bani*) to squander (away); (*viața*) to make a mess of one's life; (*timpul*) to waste one's time; (*a împrăștia*) to scatter; (*bănuielile*) to dispel; (*a pune pe fugă*) to put to flight/rout; (*a înfrânge*) to defeat; (*a respinge*) to repel; (*a presăra*) to strew; (*a îndepărta*) to remove ‖ *vr* to disperse, to scatter; (*d. nori, teamă*) to dissipate; (*d. ceață, fum*) to clear away; (*a dispărea*) to vanish; (*a se nărui*) to crumble • **~tor** *nm* squanderer, spendthrift ‖ *adj* wasteful, spendthrift, prodigal; **fiul** ~ the prodigal son.

rit [rit] *nn* rite, ritual; (*credință*) religion, faith, persuasion.

ritm [ritm] *nn* rhythm; *fig* rate, speed, tempo • **~ic** *adj* rhythmic(al); regular ‖ *adv* rhythmically; regularly.

ritos [ri'tos] *adv* categorically, openly.

ritual [ritu'al] *nn* ritual, rite ‖ *adj* ritual.

rival [ri'val] *nm* rival, competitor, adversary, opponent ‖ *adj* rival • **~itate** *nf* rivalry, emulation, competition • **~iza** *vi* to vie (with), to compete (with).

riveran [rive'ran] *adj* riparian, river(side) ‖ *nm* riverside resident.

rizom [ri'zom] *nm bot* rhizome.

roabă [ro'abă] *nf* slave, drudge; (*tărăboanță*) wheelbarrow.

roade [ro'ade] *vt* to gnaw (at); (*câte puțin*) to nibble at; (*pesmeți*) to eat; (*oase, d. persoane*) to pick; (*a face ferfeniță*) to eat away; (*a mușca*) to bite; (*lemnul, d. viermi*) to eat into wood; (*d. rugină*) to corrode; (*metal, d. acid*) to gnaw into metal; (*a uza*) to wear (out); (*d. mare*) to erode; (*pielea*) to rub off; (*provocând răni*) to rub sore; *fig* to prey upon, to wear out; to eat ‖ *vr* to wear out/away.

roată [ro'ată] *nf* wheel; (*cerc*) circle, ring, roundabout.

rob [rob] *nm* slave, bond(s)man

robă ['robă] *nf* robe, gown.

robie [ro'bie] *nf* slavery, bondage; (*trudă și*) drudgery; **în ~** in bonds.

robinet [robi'net] *nn* faucet, tap.

robot [ro'bot] *nm* robot, automaton.

roboti [robo'ti] *vi* to work hard, to toil.

robust [ro'bust] *adj* robust, sturdy, hardy • **~ețe** *nf* robustness, sturdiness, hardiness.

rocadă [ro'kadă] *nf* castling.

rocă ['rokă] *nf* rock.

rochie ['rokie] *nf* dress, gown; (*de vară*) frock; (*de casă*) housecoat.

rod [rod] *nn* fruit; (*recoltă*) crop, harvest; *fig* fruit(s), result, outcome; **cu ~** fruit-bearing, fruited; **a da ~** *fig* to bear fruit.

roda [ro'da] *vt* to run in; (*metale*) to grind, to polish • **~j** *nn* running in; grinding, polishing.

rodi [ro'di] *vi* to bear/yield fruit(s).

rodie ['rodie] *nf bot* pomegranate.

roditor [rodi'tor] *adj* fruit-bearing, fruitful; fertile, rich.

rodnic ['rodnik] *adj* fruitful, productive • **~ie** *nf* fruitfulness; fertility, fecundity.

rog. *See* **ruga**

roi ['roi] *nn also fig* swarm; *fig* cloud || [ro'i] *vi* to swarm; (*de*) to swarm/teem (with).

roib [roib] *nm* chestnut/sorrel horse; (*mai ales iapă*) alezan || *adj* sorrel, chestnut.

rol [rol] *nn also fig* part, role; **~ principal** lead(ing part).

rolă ['rolă] *nf* roll; (*de magnetofon*) reel.

rolfilm [rol'film] *nn phot* roll of film.

rom[1] [rom] *nm* Rom(any), Gypsy.

rom[2] [rom] *nn* rum.

roman[1] [ro'man] *nm/adj* Roman.

roman[2] [ro'man] *nn* novel; (*de dragoste*) romance; (*ca pl.*) fiction; (*scurt*) novelette; (*foileton*) serial; **~ cavaleresc/medieval** romance novel; **~ de anticipație/științifico-fantastic** science fiction novel; **~ istoric** historical novel; **~ de aventuri** tale of adventure; **~ polițist** detective story/novel, *coll* whodunit • **~cier** *nm* novelist, fiction writer.

romantic [ro'mantik] *nm* romanticist || *adj* romantic, romance; Romanesque.

romantism [roman'tism] *nn* romanticism.

român [ro'man] *nm/adj* Romanian • **~ă** *nf* Romanian; (*limba*) the Romanian (language) • **~că** *nf* Romanian (woman, girl) • **~esc** *adj* Romanian • **~ește** *adv* Romanian; like a Romanian; **a vorbi ~** (*răspicat*) to speak bluntly, straightforward.

romb [romb] *nn* rhombus, lozenge.

rond [rond] *nn* flowerbed; (*piațetă*) circus; *mil* round(s), beat.

rondelă [ron'delă] *nf tech* washer; (*de carton*) small round disc.

ronțăi [rontsă'i] *vt* to crunch, to nibble (at).

ropot ['ropot] *nn* tramp; (*de pași*) tramping; (*de pași grăbiți*) patter of feet; (*de copite*) thud, clatter; (*de ploaie*) shower, patter; (*de aplauze*) round of applause.

rost [rost] *nn* sense, meaning; (*scop*) aim, purpose; part, role; (*utilitate*) use(fulness); **ce ~ are?** what's the use? || **fără ~** *adj* useless ||*adv* without avail, uselessly; (*situație socială*) condition; (*gospodărie*) household; (*ocupație*) profession; (*rânduială*) order; **pe de ~** by heart/rote.

rosti [ros'ti] *vt* to utter, to pronounce, to say; (*clar, distinct*) to articulate; (*monoton*) to drone out smth; (*plângăreț*) to whine; (*în pripă*) to reel off; (*a povesti*) to express; (*a expune*) to expound, to set out; (*un toast*) to give/propose a toast • **~re** *nf* utterance; (*vorbire*) speech, way of speaking.

rostogoli [rostogo'li] *vt/vi* to roll, to turn; to roll up.

roșcat [rosh'kat] *adj* russet; reddish, sorrel; (*cu părul roșu*) red-/russet-haired.

roșeață [ro'sheatsă] *nf* redness; (*în obraji*) (high) color; (*culoare roșie*) red color; (*a cerului, a obrajilor*) glow.

roși [ro'shi] *vt* to redden, to turn red; (*fața*) to flush; (*a ruja*) to rouge || *vi* to redden, to grow/become red; (*de emoție*) to blush, to flush.

roșie ['roshie] *nf bot* **pătlăgică**.

roșu ['roshu] *adj* red; (*aprins*) crimson, scarlet; (*sângeriu*) blood-red; (*purpuriu*) purple; (*stacojiu*) scarlet; (*cu fața roșie*) red-cheeked; (*emoționat*) flushed; (*arămiu*) copper-colored; (*roșcat*) foxy; *pol* red || *nn* red; (*roșeață*) redness; (*ruj*) rouge, lipstick; (*la cărți*) hearts.

rotar [ro'tar] *nm* wheelwright.

rotativă [rota'tivă] *nf* rotary press.

rotație [ro'tatsie] *nf* rotation.

roti [ro'ti] *vt* to turn (around/about), to revolve; (*a rostogoli*) to roll || *vr* to turn (around), to revolve (around); (*în jurul unei axe*) to swing on an axis; (*repede*) to spin; (*a se răsuci ca un vârtej*) to swirl, to whirl; (*în aer*) to circle (around).

rotile [ro'tile] *nf pl* forecarriage; **patine cu ~** roller skates; **scaun cu ~** wheelchair.

rotocol [roto'kol] *nn* (*de fum*) wreath; (*felie rotundă*) roll; round slice.

rotofei [roto'fei] *adj* plump, dumpy, *coll* chubby; (*gras*) fat.

rotulă [ro'tulă] *nf anat* knee cap/pan; *anat* patella.

rotund [ro'tund] *adj* round, rounded; circular; (*inelar*) ring-shaped; (*dolofan*) plump; *fig* full.

rotunji [rotun'zhi] *vt also fig* to round off; to complete || *vr* to be/become rounded (off).

rouă ['rouă] *nf* dew.

roz [roz] *nn* rose, pink, pinkish red || *adj* pink(ish), rosy.

roză ['roză] *nf bot* rose; * **trandafir**; *archit* Catherine wheel; **~a vânturilor** wind/compass rose.

rozător [roză'tor] *adj* rodent; gnawing || *nn* rodent.

rozeolă [roze'olă] *nf med* roseola.

rozetă [ro'zetă] *nf* rosette; *archit* Catherine wheel.

rozmarin [rozma'rin] *nm bot* rosemary.

rubedenie [rube'denie] *nf* relative, relation, * **rudă**.

rubeolă [rube'olă] *nf med* rubella, German measles.

rubicond [rubi'kond] *adj* ruddy, blushing, red (in the face).

rubin [ru'bin] *nn* ruby.

rublă ['rublă] *nf* ruble.

rubrică ['rubrikă] *nf* heading; *typ* rubric; (*coloană*) column.

rucsac ['ruksak] *nn* knapsack, backpack.

rudă ['rudă] *nf* relative, relation; *pl* kindred, kinsfolk; (*prin alianță*) in-law(s).

rudenie [ru'denie] *nf* relationship, kinship, kindred.

rudimentar [rudimen'tar] *adj* (*d. organe*) atrophied, rudimentary; primitive, crude, barbarous.

rufe ['rufe] *nf pl* underwear, (body) linen, (under)clothes; (*de pat*) bedclothes.

rug [rug] *nn* stake, pyre; (*pt. cărți*) bonfire.

ruga [ru'ga] *vt* to ask, to beg; *obs* to pray; (*stăruitor*) to implore, to entreat; to conjure; to solicit; (*pt. a interveni pt. cineva*) to intercede with (for smb); (*a pofti*) to invite; **te rog să mă ierți!** I beg your pardon!, I apologize || *vr* to pray; (*de cineva*) to ask leave/permission • **mă rog** you see, you know, well; (*cum ar fi*) as it were; (*într-un cuvânt*) in a word; (*ca să zicem așa*) so to say/speak; (*desigur*) certainly, to be sure • **vă rog!** if you please!; (*nici o problemă*) no trouble!, no problem!.

rugă ['rugă] *nf* prayer; (*rugăminte*) request, entreaty •

~ciune [rugă'chiune] *nf* prayer • **~minte** *nf* request, favor; (*puternică*) entreaty, supplication.

rugbi ['ruibi] *nn sp* football; rugby, rugger.

rugină [ru'djină] *nf* rust; *bot* blight, blast; *bot* red robin.

rugini [rudji'ni] *vi/vr* to rust; (*d frunze*) to turn yellow • **~t** *adj* rusty, corroded; *fig* (*înapoiat*) backward, stick-in-the-mud.

ruina [rui'na] *vt* to ruin, to bring to ruin; to undo || *vr* to ruin oneself; (*d. case mari*) to fall into/go to ruin.

ruină [ru'ină] *nf* ruin, ruination; **în ~e** in ruins.

ruj [ruzh] *nn* rouge; (*de buze şi*) lipstick.

rujeolă [ruzhe'olă] *nf med* * **pojar**.

rula [ru'la] *vt* (*a înfăşura*) to roll (up); (*a rostogoli*) to roll; (*bani*) to circulate; (*un film*) to show || *vi* (*d. filme*) to play • **~nt** *adj* rolling.

ruletă [ru'letă] *nf* (*joc de noroc*) roulette; (*pt. măsurat*) tape measure/line, measuring tape.

rulment [rul'ment] *nm* bearing.

rulotă [ru'lotă] *nf* camper; trailer; caravan.

rulou [ru'lou] *nn* roll; (*jaluzea*) roller blind; (*compresor*) road roller.

rumega [rume'ga] *vt/vi* to chew, to ruminate, (*d. oameni*) to masticate; (*a mânca*) to eat; *fig* (*o idee*) to ruminate on/about/over, to brood on/over smth.

rumegător [rumegă'tor] *nn/adj* ruminant.

rumeguş [rume'gush] *nn* sawdust, scraping.

rumen ['rumen] *adj* ruddy, rosy; red (in the face); (*d. friptură*) nice and brown, well-roasted • **~i** *vt* to redden; (*a frige*) to roast, to make nice and brown; (*un peşte*) to roast a fish brown || *vr* to gain color, to blush; (*a se frige*) to be well-roasted; *fig* (*a se bronza*) to tan, to get sunburnt • **~it** *adj* done to a turn; (*d. friptură*) crisp.

rumoare [ru'moare] *nf* commotion, hubbub.

rundă ['rundă] *nf* round.

rupe ['rupe] *vt* (*a sfâşia*) to tear, to rend; (*în bucăţi*) to tear to pieces; (*a smulge*) to tear off; (*cu rădăcină*) to uproot; (*a culege*) to pick; to cull; to gather; (*a frânge, a fractura*) to break; (*a întrerupe*) to break off; (*relaţiile*) to sever; (*a opri*) to stop; (*a despărţi*) to separate; (*a împrăştia*) to scatter || *vr* to break; (*d. haine, sfoară*) to tear; (*a se uza*) to wear out; (*a părăsi*) to leave.

ruptură [rup'tură] *nf* tear, rent; (*gaură*) hole; (*crăpătură*) rift; (*spărtură*) break; (*breşă*) breach; *fig* breaking off; falling out; (*zdreanţă*) rag.

rural [ru'ral] *adj* rural, village, country(side).

rus [rus] *nm/adj* Russian; **limba ~ă** the Russian language, Russian.

Rusalii [ru'salii] *nf pl* Whitsuntide, Pentecost; **Duminica ~lor** Whit Sunday.

rustic ['rustik] *adj* rustic, country(side).

ruşina [rushi'na] *vt* to (put to) shame || *vr* to be ashamed; (*a se sfii*) to feel shy • **~t** *adj* ashamed || *adv* shamefacedly.

ruşine [ru'shine] *nf* shame, disgrace; (*pată*) blot, blemish; (*sfială*) shyness, bashfulness.

ruşinos [rushi'nos] *adj* shy, bashful, timid; (*stângaci*) gawky; (*d. ceva*) shameful, disgraceful; (*nepoliticos*) undignified; (*nepotrivit*) unbecoming || *adv* disgracefully, ignominiously.

rut [rut] *nn bio* rut, mating/rutting period.

rută ['rută] *nf* route, course, itinerary.

rutier [ruti'er] *adj* road.

rutină [ru'tină] *nf* routine, beaten path; experience; (*în sens negativ*: birocraţie) red tape; (*fel de viaţă*) rut.

S

sa [sa] *adj m* his, *f* her; (*pt. lucruri, animale*) its || *pron* **a ~** his, hers.

sabatic [sa'batik] *adj* sabbatical (year).

sabie ['sabie] *nf* sword; *lit* steel; (*de lemn*) (Harlequin's) lath; (*încovoiată, lată*) sabre; (*scurtă*) cutlass; (*scurtă, îndoită*) falchion; (*turcească*) scimitar.

sabot [sa'bot] *nm* (*încălţăminte*) wooden shoe, clog; *tech* sabot; caster socket.

sabota [sabo'ta] *vt* to sabotage; *coll* to botch, to make a mess of • **~j** *nn* (act of) sabotage; *coll* botching, botched (up) job.

sabotor [sabo'tor] *nm* wrecker, saboteur; bungler, botcher.

sac [sak] *nm* bag, sack; (*pungă*) pouch; (*de hârtie*) paper bag; (*desagă*) knapsack; (*conţinut*) bagful, sackful; (*pânză*) sackcloth; (*pt. pescuit*) hoop/poke net; *anat, bot* sac, pouch.

sacadat [saka'dat] *adj* jerky, abrupt.

sacâz [sa'kâz] *nn* rosin; (*răşină*) (gum) mastic.

sacoşă [sa'koshă] *nf* bag, satchel; (*de piaţă*) market bag; (*de cumpărături*) string bag.

sacou [sa'kou] *nn* (sack) coat, (man's) jacket, lounge coat.

sacrifica [sakrifi'ka] *vt* to sacrifice; to offer as victim; (*animale*) to slaughter; *relig also* to immolate; (*timp, bani*) to devote (to smth) || *vr* to sacrifice oneself; to lay down one's life (for); (*a se dedica*) to devote/dedicate oneself.

sacrificiu [sakri'fichiu] *nn* sacrifice; *relig also* offering, oblation; (*ucidere şi*) immolation.

sacrilegiu [sakri'ledjiu] *nn* sacrilege, profanation; *fig* impiety.

sacristie [sa'kristie] *nf relig* vestry, sacristy.

sacru [sakru] *adj* sacred, consecrated; holy, hallowed; *fig* inviolable; venerable; *anat* sacral.

sadic ['sadik] *adj* sadistic || *adv* sadistically || *nm* sadist.

sadism [sa'dism] *nn* sadism.

safir [sa'fir] *nn* sapphire.

salahor [sala'hor] *nm* day laborer; unskilled worker; *fig* hack (worker).

salam [sa'lam] *nn* salami (sausage); kind of mortadella.

salamandră [sala'mandră] *nf zool* salamander.

salariat [salari'at] *nm* wage-earner; *pl* the wage earners; *pej* hireling; (*de stat*) civil servant; (*funcţionar*) employee; (*muncitor*) worker || *adj* paid; stipendiary; wage-earning; (*angajat*) hired; employed.

salariu [sa'lariu] *nn* pay, (*mai ales chenzină*) wages, (*lunar*) salary; (*plată*) reward, recompense.

salarizare [salari'zare] *nf* wages, pay, (*pt. funcţionari*) salary; payment of salaries.

salată [sa'lată] *nf bot* (*verde*) green lettuce, (garden) lettuce; (*fel de mâncare*) salad; *fig coll* mess, fumble.

salatieră [salati'eră] *nf* salad dish/bowl.

sală ['sală] *nf* hall, (large) room; (*mai mică*) drawing room; (*de spectacol*) house; auditorium; (*pt. prelegeri*) lecture room; (*în spital*) ward; (*hol*) hall; (*antreu*) entrance hall; (*public*) audience.

salbă ['salbă] *nf* (*colier*) necklace; *fig* row, chain; (*la vite*) dewlap.

salcâm [sal'kâm] *nn bot* acacia; locust tree, false acacia.

salcie ['salchie] *nf bot* white/silky willow; willow (tree); sallow; *bot* sweet willow; (*răchită*) osier (willow).

sale ['sale] *adj m* his, *f* her ǁ *pron* **ale** ~ his, hers.

salină [sa'linǎ] *nf* (*ocnǎ de sare*) saltworks, saltmine; saline; (*lac*) salt lake; salt marsh.

saliva [sali'va] *vi* to salivate, to secrete saliva.

salivă [sa'livǎ] *nf* saliva, spittle; (*curgând din gură*) drivel, slobber; (*scuipată*) spit.

salon [sa'lon] *nn* (*cameră*) living room, lounge; (*pe vas*) cabin; (*în spital*) ward; (*expoziție*) showroom; art exhibition; *fig liter* salon; *econ* (motor/car/trade) show; (*local public*) saloon; (*pt. serbări*) hall; (*mobilă*) three-/five-piece suite.

salopetă [salo'petǎ] *nf* overalls.

salt [salt] *nn* (*săritură*) jump; spring, bound; (*de pe loc*) also *fig* leap; (*scurt*) skip; (*brusc*) bounce; (*topăit*) hop; (*în aer*) gambol; (*în apă*) dive; (*în lungime*) broad jump; (*în înălțime*) high jump.

saltea [sal'tea] *nf* mattress; (*cu apă*) waterbed; (*cu arcuri*) spring/box mattress; (*cu puf*) feather bed; (*de paie*) straw mattress, pallet.

saltimbanc [saltim'bank] *nm* acrobat, rope dancer; (*scamator*) juggler; clown; *fig* mountebank, humbug.

salubritate [salubri'tate] *nf* salubrity; sanitation (service).

salubru [sa'lubru] *adj* wholesome, healthy.

salut [sa'lut] *nn* greeting(s), salutation; (*plecăciune*) bow; *mil* salute; (*cuvântare*) welcome, address ǁ *interj* hi (there); *coll* howdy!; (*la revedere*) see you later, so long, good-bye • ~**a** *vt* to greet, to salute; (*cu o plecăciune*) to bow to smb; (*din cap*) to nod at smb; (*cu mâna*) to wave to smb; (*ridicând pălăria*) to raise one's hat to smb; (*în scris*) to send one's regards to smb; *avia* to dip; (*cu sabia*) to salute with a sword; (*cu salve de tun*) to fire a salute; (*cu drapelul*) to troop the colors; *naut* to dip (the flag); (*a ura bun venit*) to welcome; (*a aclama*) to greet smb with cheers; *recip* to greet/salute each other; to exchange greetings; (*cu cineva, a se cunoaște*) to be on nodding terms with smb ǁ *vi mil* to salute • ~**ar** *adj* beneficial, salutary; (*sănătos*) wholesome, healthy • ~**are** *nf* salutation; *pl* greetings.

salva [sal'va] *vt* (*pe cineva*) to save; (*dintr-un pericol*) to rescue; *relig* to redeem; (*a elibera*) to set free; to recuperate, to recover; (*a vindeca*) to heal; *naut* (*un vas, mărfuri*) to salvage; (*ce s-a scris, la calculator*) to save ǁ *vr* to save oneself; (*a scăpa*) to break free; *coll* to back out of smth • ~**re** *nf* saving, salvaging; (*dintr-un pericol*) rescue; (*eliberare*) deliverance; (*scăpare*) escape; *naut also* salvage; (*redobândire*) recovery; *relig* (*mântuire*) salvation; (*siguranță*) safety; *med* emergency/ambulance service • ~**tor** *adj* saving; (*care vindecă*) healing ǁ *nm* (*de la un pericol*) rescuer, saver; (*de mărfuri*) salvager.

salvă [sal'vǎ] *nf mil* salvo, volley; (*de tun*) round of cannon.

salvgarda [salvgar'da] *vt* to safeguard.

salvie ['salvie] *nf bot* common/garden sage.

samavolnic [sama'volnik] *adj* arbitrary; despotic ǁ *adv* arbitrarily; despotically.

samsar [sam'sar] *nm* go-between, middleman; (*de bursă*) broker, agent, jobber.

samur [sa'mur] *nm zool* sable, sable fur.

sanatoriu [sana'toriu] *nn* sanitarium.

sanctifica [sanktifi'ka] *vt relig* to sanctify, to canonize, to make holy, to hallow.

sanctitate [sankti'tate] *nf* sanctity, holiness; (*titlu*) Your/His Holiness.

sanctuar [sanktu'ar] *nn* sanctuary, altar; sanctum.

sancționa [sanktsio'na] *vt* to sanction, to attach a penalty to (a decree); (*a aproba și*) to approve, to ratify; (*a pedepsi și*) to punish, to penalize.

sancțiune [sanktsi'une] *nf* sanction; (*aprobare*) assent; (*pedeapsă*) punishment; (*penală*) penalty.

sandală [san'dalǎ] *nf* sandal.

sandviș, sandvici ['sandvish, sandvich] *nn* sandwich, *coll* sub.

sanguin [sangu'in] *adj* (of) blood; **grupă** ~**ă** blood type/group; (*d. oameni*) sanguine, fiery; (*d. ten*) ruddy.

sanie ['sanie] *nf* sled(ge); (*de plăcere*) sleigh; (*de concurs*) luge, skeleton; *tech* slide.

sanitar [sani'tar] *nm* paramedic; hospital attendant ǁ *adj med* medical; health; *tech* sanitarian, sanitary.

santal [san'tal] *nm bot* white sandal.

santinelă [santi'nelǎ] *nf* sentinel, sentry; *fig* guard(ing), watch.

sapă ['sapǎ] *nf* hoe; (*săpăligă*) grubbing axe/hoe, mattock; *min* bit; (*săpare*) hoeing, digging.

sarabandă [sara'bandǎ] *nf mus* saraband; *fig* (*agitație*) agitation, uproar; (*vârtej*) whirling.

sarafan [sara'fan] *nn* sleeveless frock-like overalls.

saramură [sara'murǎ] *nf* (pickling) brine, pickle; pickled fish.

sarcasm [sar'kasm] *nn* sarcasm, sarcastic remark; malice.

sarcastic [sar'kastik] *adj* sarcastic, sneering; (*mușcător*) biting, cutting ǁ *adv* sarcastically, caustically, sneeringly.

sarcină ['sarchinǎ] *nf* (*încărcătură*) load, charge; (*mare și grea*) burden; (*care apasă*) weight; (*supărătoare*) trouble; *fig* bore, bother, drag; (*a unui animal*) pack load; (*de lemne*) bundle; *fig* (*datorie*) responsibility; (*grea*) charge; (*misiune*) mission; *econ* target plan; *pl* taxes, charges; (*graviditate*) pregnancy.

sarcom [sar'kom] *nn med* sarcoma.

sardea [sar'dea] *nf icht* sardine, anchovy; pilchard.

sare ['sare] *nf* salt; *chem* sodium chloride; *fig* spice, wit.

sașiu [sa'shiu] *adj* squinting, cross-eyed.

sat [sat] *nn* village; (*cătun*) hamlet; countryside; (*locuitori*) villagers.

satana [sa'tana] *nf* devil, fiend.

satanic [sa'tanik] *adj* satanic, fiendish, diabolical.

satâr [sa'târ] *nn* (meat) chopper, cleaver; (*al călăului*) executioner's axe.

satelit [sate'lit] *nm also fig* satellite, secondary planet.

satiră ['satirǎ] *nf* (*împotriva*) satire; skit.

satiriza [satiri'za] *vt* to satirize.

satisface [satis'fache] *vt* to satisfy, to please smb; to meet smb's challenge; (*a răspunde la*) to come up to; *fig* (*curiozitatea*) to gratify/satisfy smb's curiosity; (*dorințele*) to gratify (smb's wishes); (*necesități*) to meet; (*o condiție*) to fulfil; (*foamea*) to appease, to allay.

satisfacție [satis'faktsie] *nf* (*mulțumire*) satisfaction, contentment; (*despăgubire*) amends, reparation (for).

satisfăcător [satisfăkǎ'tor] *adj* satisfying, satisfactory ǁ *adv* satisfactorily.

satura [satu'ra] *vt* (*cu, de*) to saturate (with), to imbue • ~**ție** *nf* saturation; *fig also* cloying, surfeit.

sațietate [satsie'tate] *nf* satiety, repletion.

sau [sau] *conj* or; (*altfel*) or else, otherwise.

saună ['saună] *nf* sauna.

savană [sa'vană] *nf* savanna(h).

savant [sa'vant] *nm* learned man; (*om de știință*) scientist; (*mai ales filolog*) scholar; (*fals*) sciolist || *adj* learned (in), studied; erudite, scholarly; (*cult*) knowledgeable (about); clever, expert || *adv* skillfully, cleverly; learnedly, knowingly.

savarină [sava'rină] *nf cul* savarin.

savoare [sa'voare] *nf* savor, flavor; (*gust plăcut*) smack; *fig also* charm, taste; spice, pungency.

savonieră [savoni'eră] *nf* soap box.

savura [savu'ra] *vt also fig* to enjoy, to relish.

savuros [savu'ros] *adj* savory, tasty; relishable; *fig* charming, enjoyable; *fig* (*picant*) racy, piquant; spicy.

saxofon [sakso'fon] *nn* saxophone, sax.

să [să] *conj* (*dacă*) if; ~ **fi aflat mai devreme** if only I had known earlier; (*pt. imperativ*) let; ~ **începem!** let us begin!; (*în prop. finale*) **ca** ~ in order, so as; (*când subiectul nu se schimbă*) **plecăm devreme ca** ~ **ajungem la timp** we leave early in order to get there on time; in order that, so that; (*când subiectul se schimbă*) **plecăm târziu ca ei** ~ **ne ajungă** we leave late so that they may/can/will catch up with us.

sădi [să'di] *vt* (*plante, pomi*) to plant, to bed (in) seedlings, (*semințe*) to sow; (*o grădină, o vie*) to lay out; *fig* to implant.

săgeată [să'djeată] *nf also fig* arrow; dart; (*scurtă*) bolt; *lit* shaft; *geom, tech* sag; *agr* leading branch; *naut* flying jib boom; (*semn, marcă*) direction sign/arrow.

săgeta [sădje'ta] *vt* to shoot (with an arrow), to harpoon; *fig* (*cu privirea*) to dart a look at smb; (*a trece ca o săgeată*) to dart, to cleave.

săi [sai] *adj poss pl m* his; *f* her; (*animale, lucruri*) its; **frații** ~ his/her brothers || *pron* **ai**~ his/hers.

sălaș [să'lash] *nn* (*locuință*) dwelling, abode; (*ascunziș*) hiding place; (*adăpost*) shelter; (*pt animale*) stable.

sălbatic [săl'batik] *adj* wild; (*d. oameni*) savage, primitive; (*brutal*) brutish; (*crud*) cruel; (*însetat de sânge*) bloodthirsty; (*nesociabil*) unsociable; (*ruşinos*) shy; (*nemanierat*) uncouth; (*d. un loc*) uninhabited; (*d. un teren*) rugged; waste; (*greu de condus*) intractable; (*irascibil*) impetuous; (*aprig*) fiery || *nm* savage, wild man; unsociable/retiring person || *adv* wildly, savagely.

sălbătici [sălbăti'chi] *vt* to make savage, to turn wild || *vr* to become wild/savage; (*a deveni prost crescut*) to become brutalized; (*d. copii*) to run wild; (*d. câmpuri*) to become a wilderness; (*d. plante*) to run wild, to run to seed.

sălbăticie [sălbăti'chie] *nf* (*caracter sălbatic*) wild nature, savageness; (*d. un peisaj*) ruggedness; (*peisaj sălbatic*) wilderness; (*d. un teren*) waste; (*pe dealuri*) barelands; (*pustiu*) desert; (*stare*) wild state; (act of) savagery, ferocious deed; (*cruzime*) cruelty; (*brutalitate*) brutality; *fig* unsociability, shyness.

sălbăticiune [sălbăti'chiune] *nf* wild/savage animal/ beast; (*vânat*) game; (*pustiu*) wilderness.

sălciu [săl'chiu] *adj* brackish, briny; (*d. mâncare*) tasteless; *fig* vapid.

sălta [săl'ta] *vt* (*a ridica*) to heave, to lift/raise up; (*cu o pârghie*) to lever; (*a trage în sus*) to pull up; (*pe*

cineva) to help smb up; **a** ~ **capul** to hold up one's head; *fig* (*a omite*) to skip; (*o clasă*) to skip a grade || *vr* (*a sări*) to jump up; (*a creşte*) to grow || *vi* (*a sări*) to spring, to jump/leap up; (*pe un picior*) to hop; (*salturi mari*) to bound; (*înapoi*) to bounce back; (*ca elasticul*) to bounce; (*pe cal*) to jog; (*de bucurie*) to jump/leap up with joy; (*d. cai*) to jolt; (*a se ridica*) to rise; (*d. cai*) to rear; (*d. câini*) to stand up (on its hind legs); (*d. prețuri*) to look up.

sămânță [să'mântsă] *nf* seed; (*neam*) species; *fig* trace; germ; sperm, semen.

sănătate [sănă'tate] *nf* health, wellbeing; (*vigoare*) freshness; (*stare sănătoasă*) (state of) health; (*spirituală*) sanity; *fig* soundness || *interj* ~ **bună!** good-bye!; (*e bine şi aşa*) all right!; (*nimic de făcut*) nothing doing!.

sănătos [sănă'tos] *adj* (*bine*) well, whole; (*la trup şi*) healthy, in good health; *coll* in fine/good/great shape; vigorous, hale, hearty; (*voinic*) strong; (*şi spiritualiceşte*) sound; (*bun pt. organism*) wholesome; (*salubru*) salubrious; *fig* wise; (*folositor*) good || *adv* healthily, heartily || *interj* **rămâi** ~! good-bye!; **du-te** ~! God speed!, pleasant journey!.

sănius [săni'ush] *nn* (*acțiune*) sledging, (bob)sledding; (*locul*) slope for sledging, slide chute, run.

săpa [să'pa] *vt* to dig, to delve; (*cu sapa*) to hoe; (*brazde*) to hollow (out); (*un puț*) to bore/dig a well; *mil* (*tranşee*) to sap; (*a grava*) to engrave; (*a imprima*) to imprint; (*a excava*) to dig out; (*a eroda*) to wear/wash out; *fig* (*pe cineva*) to undermine || *vt* to dig into, to delve into; (*cu hârlețul*) to spade; (*adânc*) to trench; (*a scormoni*) to grub; (*d. animale*) to burrow; *min* to prospect.

săpăligă [săpă'ligă] *nf* grubbing hoe, weed hook, mattock.

săptămânal [săptămâ'nal] *nn/adj/adv* weekly, hebdomadal, hebdomadary.

săptămână [săptă'mână] *nf* week.

săpun [să'pun] *nm* soap; (*bucată de* ~) bar/piece/cake of soap • ~**i** *vt* to soap, to wash with soap, (*la bărbierit*) to lather, (*a freca*) to rub with soap; *fig* to comb smb; *coll* to fly at smb || *vr* to soap oneself; (*pt. bărbierit*) to lather one's face/chin.

săra [să'ra] *vt* to (season with) salt; (*în saramură*) to salt down, to pickle; (*scrumbii*) to cure • ~**t** *adj* salt(y), briny, salted; (*d. apă*) brackish; *chem* saline, salinous.

sărac [să'rak] *nm* poor man, pauper; *pl* the poor || *adj* poor; (*fără bani*) impecunious; *sl* (stone-) broke; (*zdrențăros*) shabby; (*d. scuze*) paltry; (*nevoiaş*) needy; (*strâmtorat*) in want; (*în mizerie*) miserable; (*arid*) barren; (*gol, golit*) empty; (*neproductiv*) unproductive; *fig* meager; (*redus*) scanty; (*biet*) wretched; (*de compătimit*) piteous, pitiful.

sărăcăcios [sărăkă'chios] *adj* poor(ly), miserable; (*d. teren*) infertile, barren; (*d. persoane, haine*) shabby, threadbare; (*d. hrană*) meager; *fig* (*neîndestulător*) stinted; (*d. salariu*) mere pittance (of a wage) || *adv* poorly, shabbily.

sărăci [sără'chi] *vt* to impoverish, to pauperize; to ruin; (*a lipsi de*) to deprive of; *fig* to render dry || *vi* to grow/become poor; (*a da faliment*) to go bankrupt • ~**e** *nf* (extreme) poverty, destitution; (*lipsă*) want, scarcity; (*penurie*) penury; (*nevoie*) need(iness); (*strâmtorare*) narrowness of means; pauperism;

(*avere mică*) little fortune • ~**me** *nf* the poor (and needy); the paupers.

sărbătoare [sărbă'toare] *nf* holiday; (*zi nelucrătoare*) day of rest; high day; *relig* feast (day); ~**a Morţilor** All Souls' Day; (*marcată cu roşu în calendar*) redletter day; (*petrecere*) festivity, festival; (*vacanţă*) vacation; recess.

sărbătoresc [sărbăto'resk] *adj* festive, holiday-like; solemn; pompous; **aer** ~ festive air.

sărbători [sărbăto'ri] *vt* to celebrate; to observe (a feast); (*o căsătorie*) to solemnize.

sări [sa'ri] *vt* to jump/leap (over), to clear; to omit, to skip, to leave out || *vi* to jump, to leap; (*a ţopăi*) to hop; to frolic; to frisk/skip about; (*cu salturi mari*) to bound; (*în sus*) to spring; (*înapoi*) (*d. minge*) to bounce; (*pe ceva*) to pounce on smth; (*în apă*) to dive; (*la cineva*) to fly at; (*d. lichide: a ţâşni*) to gush (out); (*d. sânge*) to spurt; (*a împroşca*) to spout up/out; (*a plesni*) to burst; (*a crăpa*) to crack; (*a se sparge*) to break; to explode, to blow up; (*d. nasturi: a se desprinde*) to come/fly off; (*d. siguranţă*) to blow; *coll* to go; to pop; (*a tresări*) to startle; (*d. inimă*) to flutter; **a face să sară** to blast, to blow up; • ~**tură** *nf* (*salt*) leap, jump, bound.

sărman [săr'man] *nm* pauper; (*cerşetor*) beggar; poor devil || *adj* poor, needy; * **sărac**.

sărut [să'rut] *nn* kiss; *sl* (*zgomotos*) smacker • ~**a** *vt* to kiss; *hum* to peck; *sl* (*cu zgomot*) to smack; *recip* to kiss (one another); *coll* to bill || *vi* to kiss • ~**are** *nf/nn* kiss(ing); *sl* (*zgomotoasă*) smacker.

sătean [să'tean] *nm* villager; countryman • ~**că** *nf* village/country woman.

sătesc [să'tesk] *adj* rural; village.

sătul [să'tul] *adj* satiate(d), full; *fig* bored, (sick and) tired (of); **a fi ~ de cineva** to be sick and tired of smb, (*până în gât*) to be fed up with smb/smth.

sătura [sătu'ra] *vt* to satiate, to fill; to gorge, to glut; *fig* to satisfy || *vr* to satisfy one's appetite; to have one's fill; (*a fi mulţumit*) to be satisfied/content with; *fig* (*a-i fi prea mult*) to have enough (of smth); to get sick/tired of.

sătios [să'tsios] *adj* nourishing, filling; saturating.

său [său] *adj m* his, *f* her; (*pt. lucruri şi animale*) its || *pron poss m* his, *f* hers.

săvârşi [săvâr'shi] *vt* to commit, to perpetrate; to execute, to perform; to put into execution; (*cu efort*) to achieve; (*a face*) to do, to make; to effect; (*o călătorie*) to accomplish; (*a termina*) to finish; (*a încheia*) to terminate; (*a duce la capăt*) to carry through || *vr obs* (*a muri*) to pass away, to die.

sâcâi [sâkâ'i] *vt* to nag, to pester, to plague, to harass • ~**ală** *nf* nagging, teasing • ~**tor** *adj* pestering, nagging, annoying.

sâmbătă ['sâmbătă] *nf* Saturday.

sâmbure ['sâmbure] *nm* (*de nucă*) kernel; (*mare, de cireaşă*) stone; (*mic*) pip; (*miez*) core, kernel; *fig* gist; marrow; (*ce-i mai bun*) flower; *astron* nucleus; body.

sân [sân] *nm anat* breast, *sl* tit, boob; (*piept*) bosom; (*inimă*) heart; (*pântece*) womb.

sânge ['sânĝe] *nn* blood; (*închegat*) gore; (*masacru*) bloodshed, massacre, (*măcel*) slaughter; *fig* birth, origin; (*înrudire*) kinship; (*rasă*) lineage, race • ~**ra** *vi* to bleed || *vt* (*d. un animal*) to stick • ~**riu** *adj* (as) red as blood, blood-red; *lit* purple • ~**ros** *adj* bloody;

(*cu mult sânge*) sanguine(ous); (*care provoacă vărsare de sânge*) sanguinary; (*criminal*) murderous, homicidal, bloodthirsty.

sârb [sârb] *nm/adj* Serbian • ~**ă** *nf* Serbian, the Serbian language.

sârguincios [sârguin'chios] *adj* industrious, hardworking; zealous; regular, constant.

sârguinţă [sârgu'intsă] *nf* diligence, industry; perseverance; devotion (to work).

sârmă ['sârmă] *nf* wire.

sâsâi [sâsâ'i] *vi* (*d. gâşte, şerpi*) to hiss; (*a vorbi peltic*) to lisp • ~**t** *nn* hissing, hiss; (*vorbire peltică*) lisp.

scabie ['skabie] *nf med* scab; itch.

scabros [ska'bros] *adj* nauseating; salacious; indecent.

scadenţă [ska'dentsă] *nf* date of payment, settling day.

scafandru [ska'fandru] *nm* diver; (*cu costum uşor*) frogman || *nn* (*costum*) diving suit; (*autonom*) scuba (self-contained underwater breaking apparatus), aqualung.

scai, scaiete [skai, ska'iete] *nm bot* thistle.

scală ['skală] *nf rad* tuning dial/plate.

scalp [skalp] *nn anat* scalp.

scalpel [skal'pel] *nn med* scalpel.

scamator [skama'tor] *nm* conjurer, juggler, illusionist • ~**ie** *nf* juggling; (*cu cărţile de joc*) conjuring away; *fig* (juggling) trick, sleight-of-hand; *pej* stealing, filching.

scamă ['skamă] *nf* lint; nap.

scanda [skan'da] *vt* to shout, to chant (slogans); to scan (verse); *mus* to stress, to mark.

scandal [skan'dal] *nn* row, shindy; (*tărăboi*) fuss; brawl; (*gălăgie*) hubbub; *fig* shame • ~**agiu** *nm* brawler, rough customer.

scandaliza [skandali'za] *vt* to revolt; to shock || *vr* to be scandalized/indignant at smth.

scandalos [skanda'los] *adj* scandalous, shameful, disgraceful; shocking.

scaner ['skaner] *nn* scanner.

scarabeu [skara'beu] *nm ento* beetle, scarab(aeus).

scară ['skară] *nf* (*mobilă*) also *fig* ladder; (*extensibilă*) extension ladder; (*de frânghie*) rope ladder; (*treaptă*) step, *pl* steps; (*dublă*) pair of steps; (*rulantă*) escalator, moving stairway; (*la trăsură*) footboard; (*la şa*) stirrup; (*fixă, în clădiri*) (flight of) stairs; (*în spirală*) spiral staircase; (*la termometru, hărţi*) also *mus* scale; (*grad*) degree; extent; *fig* (*socială*) social scale.

scarlatină [skarla'tină] *nf med* scarlet fever, scarlatina.

scatoalcă [ska'toalkă] *nf coll* slap in the face, box on the ears.

scaun [skaun] *nn* chair, seat; (*taburet*) also *med* stool; (*tapisat*) padded chair; (*pliant*) folding chair; *mus* bridge (of a violin); *obs* (*tron*) throne; (*reşedinţă*) seat, residence; capital.

scădea [skă'dea] *vt math* to subtract, to deduct; to reduce, to diminish, to lower; to cut down; to step down (voltage); (*preţul*) to reduce; (*sosul, la gătit*) to boil down; (*d. durere: a micşora*) to mitigate || *vi* (*a micşora*) to diminish; (*d. zile*) to grow shorter; (*a da înapoi*) to recede; *fig* to subside; (*ca număr*) to dwindle; (*d. sunet, lumină*) to fade; (*d. ape*) to sink; (*d. febră*) to abate; (*d. frig*) to relax; (*d. barometru*) to drop; (*d. lună*) to (be on the) wane; (*d. preţuri*) to fall; (*d. valoare*) to depreciate; (*d. profituri*) to decline; (*d. intensitate*) to abate; (*d. foc*) to burn down/low; (*d. vedere, memorie*) to fail.

scădere [skă'dere] *nf math* subtraction, deduction; (*micşorare*) diminution, drop; * **scădea**; deficiency, shortcoming, defect; decline, waning, ebbing.

scăfârlie [skăfâr'lie] *nf anat* scull; *coll* pate, nut.

scălâmb [skă'lâmb] *adj* deformed, distorted.

scălâmbăia [skălâmbă'ia] *vr* to make faces, to make a wry face (at smb), to pull a face • **~lă** *nf* contortion; grimace, wry face.

scălda [skăl'da] *vt* to bathe; (*a spăla*) to give (smb) a bath; (*a uda*) to wet; (*d. mare*) to wash; (*d. un râu*) to water; (*d. soare*) to beam (forth) rays ‖ *vr* (*în baie*) to bathe; (*în râu, mare*) to have a swim.

scăpa [skă'pa] *vt* (*din mână*) to drop, to let slip/fall/go; (*a lăsa să-i scape o lacrimă, un secret*) to let fall, to let out; (*o ocazie*) to let slip; (*a spune ceva din greşeală*) to blurt/blab out; *coll* (*a se da în vileag*) to spill the beans; (*a elibera*) to liberate, to set free; (*a salva*) to rescue; (*pe cineva de ceva*) to relieve smb of smth; (*dintr-o încurcătură*) to help smb out of a difficulty; (*a pierde o ocazie, un tren*) to miss; (*a omite*) to slip ‖ *vi* (*dintr-un loc, dintr-o situaţie*) to break free from; (*a se strecura*) to slip out; (*a se elibera*) to save oneself; (*din legături*) to break loose; (*d. animale*) to slip its chain; (*din închisoare*) to escape; (*de*) (*o boală, furtună*) to survive; (*ceva neplăcut*) to get rid of; to extricate; (*a pune capăt*) to put an end to; (*un obicei*) to get out of; (*a evita*) to avoid, to shun.

scăpăra [skăpă'ra] *vt* to strike (a match); (*scântei*) to send out ‖ *vi* to flash; (*d. ochi*) to glare; (*d. diamante, stele: a scânteia*) to sparkle, to glitter; (*a fulgera*) to lighten.

scăpăta [skăpă'ta] *vi* (*d. soare*) to set; *fig* to go down in the world; to decline.

scărmăna [skărmă'na] *vt* (*lână*) to card, to comb; (*a scămoşa*) to nap; (*câlţi/lână*) to pick wool; *fig* to thrash; *coll* to pommel, to whack.

scărpina [skărpi'na] *vt/vr* to scratch; *fig* (*a bate*) to lick, to hide.

scăzământ [skăză'mânt] *nn* deduction; (*rabat*) rebate, discount; (*pierdere*) loss.

scăzător [skăză'tor] *nm math* subtrahend.

scâlciat [skâlchi'at] *adj* (*d. pantofi*) down at the heels.

scâncet ['skânchet] *nn* whine, whimper(ing), feeble groan.

scânci [skân'chi] *vi* to whimper, to whine.

scândură ['skândură] *nf* board, plank; (*îngustă*) lath; (*de raft*) shelf; (*de brad*) deal board.

scânteia [skânte'ia] *vi* (*d. diamante, rouă, ochi*) to sparkle; to scintillate; (*d. stele*) to twinkle; (*d. lumini: a licări*) to twinkle, to glimmer.

scânteie [skân'teie] *nf also fig* spark; *fig* gleam • **~tor** *adj* sparkling, glittering, glistening; flashing; (*strălucitor*) brilliant, bright.

scârbă ['skârbă] *nf* disgust (at/for), repugnance (to), aversion (to/for/from), dislike (of/for), loathing (for/of); (*greaţă*) nausea; (*ticălos*) rip; *coll* bad egg/character.

scârbi [skâr'bi] *vt* to disgust, to provoke disgust in ‖ *vr* (*de*) to be sickened by, to be sick of, to be disgusted with.

scârbos [skâr'bos] *adj* disgusting, loathsome; sickening, nauseating; foul; (*neplăcut*) offensive, nasty; detestable, repugnant, loathsome.

scârnav ['skârnav] *adj* foul, vile; (*murdar*) filthy; obscene, smutty; *relig* unclean; *fig* infamous, mean.

scârnăvie [skârnă'vie] *nf* (*murdărie, gunoi*) dirt, dung; filthy/foul/vile/infamous act; *fig* vileness, infamy; (*d. o persoană*) foul person.

scârţâi [skârtsâ'i] *vi* (*d. uşi, roţi*) to creak, to squeak; (*d. peniţă*) to scratch; (*d. nisip, zăpadă*) to crunch; *fig* (*afaceri: a merge prost*) not to be in good circumstances • **~ală/it** *nf/nn* creaking, squeaking.

scelerat [schele'rat] *nm* scoundrel, rascal; wretch; criminal ‖ *adj* vile, wicked; criminal; desperate.

scenarist [schena'rist] *nm* script-writer.

scenariu [sche'nariu] *nn also fig* scenario; (*film*)script, screenplay.

scenă ['schenă] *nf* (*acţiune, parte dintr-un act*) scene; (*estradă*) stage; *coll* boards; (*producţie*) production; *fig* the stage; (*loc de petrecere al acţiunii*) setting; (*ceartă*) quarrel, row; (*între soţi*) domestic squabble.

scenic ['schenik] *adj* scenic, theatrical; of the stage.

scenograf [scheno'graf] *nm* scenographer, scene-painter.

sceptic ['scheptik] *nm/adj* skeptic ‖ *adv* skeptically • **~ism** *nn* skepticism.

sceptru ['scheptru] *nn* scepter; *fig also* power, authority.

schelă ['skelă] *nf* scaffolding, wooden platform; *min* (*şantier*) oilfield; (*sondă*) oil well/derrick; *naut* gangway.

schelălăi [skelălă'i] *vi* * **chelălăi**.

schelărie [skelă'rie] *nf* scaffolding(s).

schelet [ske'let] *nn anat* skeleton; *fig* (*om slab*) living skeleton; *coll* bag of bones; (*schemă*) structure; outline; *constr* framework.

schematic [ske'matik] *adj* schematic; diagrammatic; *pej* oversimplified.

schemă ['skemă] *nf* scheme; (*schiţă*) draft; project, plan; chart, diagram; arrangement; (*de personal*) staff list.

scheuna [skeu'na] *vi* (*d. câini*) to yelp, to yap.

schi [ski] *nn* (*obiect*) ski; (*acţiune*) ski(ing); (*pe apă*) aquaplane • **~a** *vi* to ski.

schif [skif] *nn* skiff.

schijă ['skizhă] *nf* (*shell*) splinter; (*fontă*) cast/pig iron.

schilod [ski'lod] *nm* cripple ‖ *adj* maimed, crippled; disabled; infirm; *fig* puny • **~i** *vt* to cripple, to maim; *fig* to mispronounce; to murder; to mutilate.

schimb [skimb] *nn also econ* exchange; (*compensaţie*) compensation; (*schimbare*) change; (*troc*) bartering; *coll* swap; (*la lucru*) shift; *min* stint; *pl* clean/fresh linen; *mil* (new) guard; **în** ~ on the other hand; (*în loc de*) in exchange • **cu ~ul** by turns • **în ~ul** in exchange for • **~a** *vt* to change; to alter, to modify; (*în ceva*) to turn/convert into; (*unul cu altul*) to exchange; (*a comuta*) to commute; (*a înlocui*) to substitute; *fig* (*cursul unui lucru*) to avert ‖ *vr* to (undergo) change, to alter; (*a varia*) to vary; to be altered; (*în bine*) to change for the better; (*în rău*) to change for the worse; (*a-şi ~ hainele*) to get changed • **~are** *nf* (*acţiune*) changing; * **schimba** (*rezultat*) change, exchange; (*modificare*) alteration; metamorphosis; (*variaţie*) variability; inconsistency; *edu* (*a clasei, a secţiei*) transfer; (*a mareei*) turn of the tide; (*a vântului*) shift of the wind • **~ător** *adj* changeable, variable; (*d. vreme*) unsteady; (*d. vânt, mare*) choppy; (*şovăitor*) volatile ‖ *nn tech* exchanger; *auto* gear shift.

schimnic ['skimnik] *nm* hermit.

schimonosi [skimono'si] *vr* to pull faces, to make a face || *vt* to contort, to distort; (*a strica*) to spoil; (*un cuvânt*) to corrupt; * schilodi; (*a strâmba*) to writhe, to twist.

schingiui [skindju'i] *vt* to torture, to rack.

schit [skit] *nn* hermitage.

schița [ski'tsa] *vt* to sketch, to map out, to outline; (*a plănui*) to design, to plan.

schiță ['skitsă] *nf* (rough) sketch, drawing; outline; (*proiect*) (rough) plan, draught; (*literară*) sketch.

schizofrenie [skizo'frenie] *nf med* schizophrenia.

sciatică [schi'atikă] *nf med* sciatica.

scinda [schin'da] *vt* to divide, to split up || *vr* to divide, to split.

sciziune [schizi'une] *nf pol* split, division; secession, dissidence; *chem* scission; *phys* fission.

sclav [sklav] *nm* slave; serf; bond(s)man; *fig also* thrall, drudge.

scleroză [skle'roză] *nf med* sclerosis; *fig* soft-mindedness; ossification; mental sclerosis, * ramolisment.

sclifosi [sklifo'si] *vr* (*a se miorlăi*) to whimper, to whine; (*a face nazuri*) to be squeamish; (*a se preface*) to simper.

sclipi [skli'pi] *vi* (*d. stele*) to glimmer, to twinkle, (*d. metale*) to glitter, (*d. ochi*) to shine; (*a scânteia*) to sparkle; (*de mânie*) to flash • ~tor *adj* shining, sparkling, glittering; * sclipi; *fig* bright, brilliant || *adv* brilliantly.

scoabă ['skoabă] *nf* clamp, cramp-iron; (*daltă*) chisel; (*firidă*) niche.

scoarță ['skoartsă] *nf bot* bark, rind; *anat* cortex; *geog* crust; (*de carte*) (book) cover; (*covor*) rug.

scoate ['skoate] *vt* (*a extrage*) to extract, to draw/pull out; *min* to mine; (*piatră*) to quarry; (*apă*) to draw; (*la iveală*) to produce smth; *fig* to reveal; (*în evidență*) to highlight; (*pe cineva*) to single smb out; (*un punct, argument*) to make a point; (*punctele slabe ale unei argumentări*) to knock holes in an argument; (*la lumină*) to bring to light; (*a înfățișa*) to present; (*a îndepărta*) to remove; (*o haină*) to take off; (*mănuși, cizme*) to pull off; (*a smulge*) to tear/ pluck out; (*a da afară, a arunca*) to throw out; (*în stradă*) to evict; (*a alunga*) to drive away; to banish; (*a concedia*) to dismiss; *coll* to fire; (*a elimina, a emite*) , to emit, to give out/off; (*fum*) to smoke; (*aburi*) to steam; (*cuvinte, sunete*) to utter; to produce; to yield; (*pui*) to hatch; (*d. plante*) to put out; (*a publica*) to publish; to edit; (*în serie*) to issue; *fig* (*a câștiga*) to earn; (*a obține*) to get; (*silit*) to extort; to deduce, to conclude; *math* (*a scădea*) to subtract; (*a scăpa*) to deliver.

scobi [sko'bi] *vt* to hollow (out); to dig (up); (*dinții*) to pick || *vi* to dig, to rummage • ~toare *nf* toothpick • ~tură *nf* hollow; cavity; excavation; (*gaură*) hole; *naut* bell; *tech* groove; (*șanț*) rut.

scofâlcit [skofâl'chit] *adj* emaciated, wasted, gaunt, haggard; (*d. obraji*) hollow, sunken.

scoică ['skoikă] *nf* shell; (*stridie*) oyster; (*cu înghețată*) ice-cream cone; *constr* (*deasupra intrării*) (overhanging) shelter; canopy.

scolastică [sko'lastikă] *nf* scholasticism; school theology.

sconcs [skonks] *nm zool* skunk.

scont [skont] *nn fin* discount • ~a *vt fin* to discount.

scop [skop] *nn* goal, purpose, aim.

scopi [sko'pi] *vt* to castrate, to emasculate; (*animale*) to geld.

scor [skor] *nn* score.

scorbură ['skorbură] *nf* hollow; (*peșteră*) cave.

scorburos [skorbu'ros] *adj* hollow.

scorbut [skor'but] *nn med* scurvy.

scormoni [skormo'ni] *vr* (*a căuta*) (*prin*) to rummage (in), to ransack, to go through, to scour.

scorni [skor'ni] *vt* to invent, to fabricate; * stârni.

scoroji [skoro'zhi] *vr* (*a* shrivel; to be dried; (*d. vopsea*) to peel/flake off; to shrink; (*d. lemn*) to warp • ~t *adj* shriveled; flaked.

scorpie ['skorpie] *nf zool* scorpion; *fig* shrew, fury, vixen.

scorpion [skorpi'on] *nm zool* scorpion; *astrol* Scorpio.

scorțișoară [skortsi'shoară] *nf* cinnamon (bark).

scoruș [sko'rush] *nm bot* service tree.

scotoci [skoto'chi] *vt* to rummage, to ransack, to go through; to scour; (*pe cineva*) to search; (*trecutul*) to rake up the past || *vi/vr* to search; to go through one's pockets.

scoțian [skotsi'an] *nm* Scot, Scotsman || *adj* Scottish; Scotch whisky • ~ă *nf* (*d. limbă*) Scottish Gaelic; Scottish dialect, Scots (English).

scrânciob ['skrânchiob] *nn* swing.

scrânti [skrân'ti] *vt* (*piciorul*) to sprain one's ankle; to dislocate; (*brațul*) to put one's arm out of joint; (*gâtul*) to strain one's neck • ~t *adj* sprained; *fig* crazy; *coll* cracked, a bit off; *sl* batty.

scrâșnet [skrâshnet] *nn* gnashing/grinding of teeth; (*d. ușă, roți etc*) creaking, grating.

scrâșni [skrâsh'ni] *vi* to gnash/grind (one's teeth).

screme ['skreme] *vr* to strain (hard); to do one's best/ utmost; to exert oneself.

scrib [skrib] *nm* scribe; *fig* quill driver, scribbler; corrupt journalist.

scrie [skrie] *vt/vi* to write; (*la mașină*) to type; (*a procesa un text*) to word-process; (*un bilet, în grabă*) to scribble; (*a nota*) to write/jot down; (*după dictare*) to write from (smb's) dictation || *vr* to spell, to be spelled; flaked.

scriitor [skrii'tor] *nm* writer, author.

scrijeli [skrizhe'li] *vt* to scratch, to graze, to scuff; (*a cresta*) to notch; (*a zgâria: piciorul*) to scrape one's shins; (*a stria*) to score.

scrimă ['skrimă] *nf* fencing.

scrin [skrin] *nn* chest of drawers, tallboy.

scripcar [skrip'kar] *nm* fiddler.

scripcă ['skripkă] *nf* fiddle.

scripete ['skripete] *nm* pulley, windlass.

scriptură [skrip'tură] *nf relig* the Holy Scripture, Holy Writ.

scris [skris] *nn* (hand)writing; alphabet; (*caligrafie*) hand; în ~ in writing, in written form || *adj* written • ~oare *nf* letter, epistle.

scroafă ['skroafă] *nf zool* sow; *fig* foul woman.

scrobeală [skro'beală] *nf* starch; (*albastră*) blue.

scrobi [skro'bi] *vt* to (clear-)starch.

scrum [skrum] *nn* ashes.

scrumbie [skrum'bie] *nf icht* herring, mackerel; (*afumată*) bloater, red herring; (*sărată*) kipper.

scrumieră [skrumi'erằ] *nf* ashtray.

scrupul ['skrupul] *nn* scruple, compunction, (conscientious) doubt (about) • ~os *adj* scrupulous (about), meticulous || *adv* scrupulously, meticulously.

scruta [skru'ta] *vt* to scrutinize, to examine closely; to scan; to peer into.

scrutător [skrutǎ'tor] *adj* searching, inquisitive; scrutinizing.

scrutin [skru'tin] *nn* ballot (count), poll.

scuar [skuar] *nn* square.

scufă, scufie ['skufǎ, sku'fie] *nf* night cap.

scufunda [skufun'da] *vr* to sink; (*şi a ieşi rapid la suprafaţă*) to duck; (*a se îneca*) to drown; (*d. pământ*) to subside; (*d. o corabie*) to sink || *vt* (*un vas*) to founder; to submerge, to immerse; (*a înmuia*) to dip.

scuipa [skui'pa] *vt/vi* to spit; *coll* to gob; *med* to expectorate • ~t *nn* spit(tle), saliva; *coll* gob.

scuipătoare [skuipǎ'toare] *nf* cuspidor.

scul [skul] *nn* skein, hank.

scula [sku'la] *vt* (*a trezi*) to wake, to awake(n); *fig* to arouse; to incite, to rouse; (*în picioare*) to raise || *vr* to wake up, to awake; to rise; (*a se ridica în picioare*) to stand up; (*cu greu*) to struggle to one's feet; (*a se revolta împotriva*) to rise in arms against.

sculă ['skula] *nf* (*unealtă*) tool, instrument; *coll* (*poamă*) bad lot/egg; *coll* (*d. o femeie*) bright article.

sculpta [skulp'ta] *vt* to sculpture, to sculpt; to cast; (*a modela*) to mold.

sculptor ['skulptor] *nm* sculptor; wood carver.

sculptură [skul'ptura] *nf* (*ca artă*) sculpture; (*în lemn*) wood carving; (*statuie*) statue, sculpture.

scump [skump] *adj* (*costisitor*) expensive, dear; (*drag*) beloved; cherished; ~a **mea** (my) dear, darling; (*preţios*) valuable; (*zgârcit*) miserly || *adv* dearly; expensively; (*mult*) much || *nm* miser • ~ete *nf* dearness; *obs* dearth; expensiveness; ~a **vieţii** the high cost of living; *fig* (*persoană: odor*) jewel; peach (of a girl); (*lucru*) valuable thing; (*zgârcenie*) avarice • ~i *vt* to raise the price of || *vr* to increase in price, to go up; (*a se zgârci*) to be stingy; (*la*) to skimp over smth.

scund [skund] *adj* low; (*de statură*) short; undersized.

scurge ['skurdje] *vt* to drain, to let out; (*a filtra*) to filter, to strain; (*a epuiza*) to exhaust || *vr* to flow/ stream (down); (*a ieşi*) to run/flow out; (*a se prelinge*) to trickle; (*a se infiltra*) to seep; (*printr-o crăpătură*) to leak; (*picătura cu picătură*) to drip; (*cu încetul*) to ebb away; (*de tot*) to ooze away; (*d. mulţime*) to throng; to pour out of; (*d. timp*) to go by; (*repede*) to fly by; (*pe neobservate*) to slip away; (*liniştit*) to lapse away; (*d. o zi*) to wear on • **a ~apa** *vt* to run/drain off the water.

scurma [skur'ma] *vt* (*a sfredeli*) to drill, to bore; (*cu privirea*) to scrutinize; (*focul*) to rake; (*cu ghiarele*) to scratch; (*d. porci*) to root; *fig* to stir up, to fan; (*trecutul*) to dig (up) || *vi* (*a răvăşi*) to rummage; (*a săpa*) to dig out; (*a râcâi*) to stir; (*a scoate la iveală*) to fish out.

scurt [skurt] *adj* short; (*d. fustă*) skimpy; (*d. vedere*) short-sighted; (*ca timp*) brief; (*puţin*) little • ~a *vt* to shorten, to cut/make short; to curtail; **a-şi** ~ **părul** (*d. femei*) to bob; (*bretonul, ramurile unui copac*) to trim; (*un text*) to cut down; (*un cuvânt*) to abbreviate || *vr* to shorten, to grow shorter • ~**ătură** *nf* shortcut • ~**circuit** *nn* short circuit.

scut [skut] *nn also fig* aegis; *also tech, min* shield; (*sprijin*) support; (*paravan*) screen; (*protecţie*) defense.

scutec ['skutek] *nn* diaper; *pl* swaddling clothes.

scuter ['skuter] *nn* moped; (*de apă*) jet-ski.

scuti [sku'ti] *vt* (*a cruţa*) to spare; (*a economisi*) to save; (*de ceva*) to exempt from; to free from; (*a absolvi de*) to absolve of; (*a lăsa în pace*) to let/leave alone • ~er *nm* shield bearer • ~t *adj* exempted, free; ~ **de taxe** tax-free; ~ **de vamă** duty-free.

scutura [skutu'ra] *vt* to shake (up), to agitate; (*d. vânt*) to sway; (*covoare şi*) to dust; (*a zdruncina*) to jolt; *fig* (*a critica*) to haul over the coals; to give a good dressing down; (*a se lepăda de*) to shake off || *vi* to tidy up; to dust || *vr* to shake; (*d. un cal*) to snort; (*d. pomi*) to lose/shed one's leaves.

scuza [sku'za] *vt* to excuse, to pardon; to make excuses for; **scuzaţi-mă**! I beg your pardon!, I apologize! || *vr* to apologize, to excuse oneself • ~**bil** *adj* excusable, pardonable.

scuză ['skuza] *nf* excuse, apology; pretext.

se [se] *pron* oneself; himself, herself, itself; themselves; **a** ~ **lăuda** to flatter oneself; ~ **îmbrăca** he dressed (himself); *imp* it; one; people, they; ~ **spune că** they say, people say, one says; *recip* (*pentru doi*) each other; (*pentru mai mulţi*) one another; ~ **văd zilnic** they see each other every day.

seamă ['seamǎ] *nf* (*socoteală*) reckoning; account; (*cantitate*) amount; **o** ~ **de** many, a lot of; (*grijă*) care; interest; **băgare de** ~ attention; importance; (*vază*) note; **de** ~ outstanding; (*fel*) kind; (*potrivă*) like.

seamăn ['seamǎn] *nm* fellow creature/man, human being; neighbor; like, equal || *adj* **fără** ~ matchless, peerless.

seară ['seara] *nf* evening; *lit* even, vesper; (*târzie*) night; (*înserare*) nightfall; (*amurg*) twilight, dusk || *adv* **seara** in the evening, at night.

searbăd ['searbǎd] *adj* tasteless, flavorless; *fig* dull, tedious; pointless; (*plat*) flat; (*d. oameni*) (*palid*) pale(-faced).

sec [sek] *adj* (*uscat*) dry; (*secătuit*) dried-up; (*arid*) barren; (*gol*) empty; *fig* bald; (*prost*) dull; *coll* empty-headed; (*fără sifon*) neat; *fig* (*rece*) cold, glacial; (*aspru*) harsh; sharp; curt; (*fără rost*) pointless || *adv* dryly, harshly, coldly || *nn* fast(ing) • ~a *vt* (*a drena*) to drain; (*a usca*) to dry (up); (*a goli*) to empty; (*a slei*) to exhaust; (*a chinui*) to torment || *vi* (*a se usca*) to run dry; (*d. provizii*) to run low/short; (*a fi epuizat*) to be exhausted; (*d. corp*) to become emaciated; *fig* (*d. conversaţie, lacrimi*) to cease, to stop • **lăsata** ~**ului** Shrovetide, Shrove Tuesday.

secară [se'karǎ] *nf* rye.

secătui [sekǎtu'i] *vt* to exhaust, to drain; (*a sărăci*) to impoverish.

secătură [sekǎ'tura] *nf* good-for-nothing, ne'er-do-well, a nobody, unreliable person; *coll* rotter, bad lot; *pl* trifles.

secera [seche'ra] *vt* (*a tăia*) to cut down, to mow; (*a recolta*) to harvest; *fig* to carry/cut off/away; *sp* to bring down a man; *mil* to mow down; to sweep ground.

seceră ['secherǎ] *nf* scythe, sickle; * **seceriş**; *fig* (*a lunii*) crescent • ~**toare** *nf* reaper; (*maşină*) reaping/ harvesting machine; (*legătoare*) harvester (binder) • ~**tor** *nm* reaper.

seceriş [seche'rish] *nn* reaping, (*al grânelor*) *also fig* harvest; gathering (of cereal crops); (*epoca recoltei*) harvest (time).

secesiune [sechesi'une] *nf* secession, segregation; **războiul de ~** the U.S. Civil War, the U.S. War of Secession.

sectă ['sechetă] *nf* drought, dryness.

secetos [seche'tos] *adj* droughty, dry, arid.

sechestra [sekes'tra] *vt* to sequester; to keep smb locked up; *jur* to confine smb illegally; *naut* to lay an embargo upon a ship.

secol ['sekol] *nn* century; *(epocă)* age, period.

secret [se'kret] *nn* secret; **în ~** in secret, privately || *adj* secret, confidential; *(nedezvăluit)* undisclosed; *(ascuns)* undercover; hidden; occult; *(nespus)* untold || *adv* secretly.

secreta [sekre'ta] *vt* to secrete; to produce by secretion.

secretar [sekre'tar] *nm* secretary; **~ general** general secretary, secretary general; **~ particular** private secretary; **~ de stat** State Secretary, Secretary of State • **~ă** *nf* secretary • **~iat** *nn (funcție)* secretaryship; *(birou)* secretariate; secretary's office.

secreție [se'kretsie] *nf* secretion.

sectant [sek'tant] *nm* sectarian.

sectă ['sektă] *nf* sect, denomination.

sector [sek'tor] *nn adm* area, district; *mil, math* sector; *tech, mech* quadrant, arc; *fig* sphere, domain.

secție ['sektsie] *nf* section, department; branch; electoral division, ward.

secțiune [sektsi'une] *nf also math* section; cutting; *archit* profile.

secular [seku'lar] *adj (vechi)* age-old, century-old; *(d. un pom)* venerable; centennial; *(laic)* lay.

secularizare [sekulari'zare] *nf* secularization.

secund [se'kund] *nm* principal assistant, second (in command); *naut* first mate/officer || *adj* second(ary) • **~a** *vt* to second; to be second in command; *fig* to back up, to support • **~ar** *nn* secondhand || *adj* secondary; minor; *gram* subordinate clause.

secundă [se'kundă] *nf* second; **într-o ~** in a split second; *coll* in a jiffy.

secure [se'kure] *nf* axe, hatchet; *(de luptă)* battle ax(e); *(halebardă)* halberd.

securitate [sekuri'tate] *nf* security; *(și siguranță)* safety.

secvență [sek'ventsă] *nf (de film)* still; *fig* snapshot.

sedativ [seda'tiv] *nn/adj* sedative.

sedentar [seden'tar] *adj* sedentary; settled; *mil* garrison(ed) (troops).

sediment [sedi'ment] *nn* sediment, deposit • **~are/ație** *nf* sedimentation.

sedițios [seditsi'os] *adj* seditious; rebellious, mutinous.

sediu ['sediu] *nn* residence; *fig* seat, center; *also mil* headquarters.

seducător [sedukă'tor] *nm* seducer, seductor || *adj* seducing, seductive; attractive; captivating; *(fascinant)* fascinating; *(tentant)* appealing || *adv* seductively, entrancingly.

seduce [se'duche] *vt* to seduce; to carry off/away; *(a corupe)* to bribe; *fig* to captivate, to fascinate; to attract smb.

seducție [se'duktsie] *nf* seduction; *fig* charm, magic.

segment [seg'ment] *nm tech* piston/packing ring || *nn math, anat* segment • **~a** *vt* to segment; to partition/section.

segrega [segre'ga] *vt* to segregate • **~ție** *nf* segregation • **~ționism** *nn* (policy of) racial discrimination; Jim Crow.

seif [seif] *nn* safe, strongbox.

seism [se'ism] *nn* earthquake; *lit* upheaval.

select [se'lekt] *adj* select (gathering), choice • **~a** *vt* to select, to pick out; *lit* to cull; *(a alege)* to choose; *comp* to dial.

selecție [se'lektsie] *nf* selection, choice.

selecționa [selektsio'na] *vt* to select, to choose; to sort; *sp* to spot.

semafor [sema'for] *nn* semaphore; *(pe stradă)* traffic lights; *rail* semaphore signal.

semantică [se'mantikă] *nf* semantics.

semăna¹ [semă'na] *vt* to sow, to seed; *(în rânduri)* to drill; *fig (a răspândi)* to spread, to propagate || *vi* to sow.

semăna² [semă'na] *vi* to resemble smb, to look/sound like smb, to be very much alike.

semănătoare [semănă'toare] *nf* sower, seeder, sowing machine.

semestru [se'mestru] *nn* half year; *edu* semester, term.

semeț [se'mets] *adj (falnic)* lofty, stately; haughty, arrogant; *(îndrăzneț)* daring || *adv* stately, haughtily.

semicerc [semi'cherk] *nn* semicircle.

semidoct [semi'dokt] *nm* dabbler, wiseacre || *adj* half-learned.

semifabricat [semifabri'kat] *adj* semifinished || *nn* half-/semi-finished product; *pl* semi-manufactured goods.

smifinală [semifi'nală] *nf sp* semifinal.

semilună [semi'lună] *nf* half moon, crescent moon.

seminal [semi'nal] *adj* seminal.

seminar [semi'nar] *nn* seminar; conference; *relig* seminary; training college.

seminție [semin'tsie] *nf* tribe; family; *(neam)* nation; people; race; *(gen)* kind.

semiobscuritate [semiobskuri'tate] *nf* dimness, dusk.

semiotică [semi'otikă] *nf ling, phil* semiotics.

semipreparat [semiprepa'rat] *adj* oven-ready.

semit [se'mit] *nm* Semite • **~ic** *adj* Semitic.

semitransparent [semitranspa'rent] *adj* semitransparent, translucent.

semn [semn] *nn (indicație)* sign, indication; symbol; *(semnal)* signal; badge; insignia; emblem; *(cicatrice)* scar; *(distinctiv)* mark; *(urmă)* trace; *(gest)* gesture.

semna [sem'na] *vt* to sign, to put one's name on a document; to conclude; *(ca martor)* to witness; **a ~ în condică** *(la venire/plecare)* to sign on/off.

semnal [sem'nal] *nn* signal; sign; *(gest)* gesture; *(exemplar)* re-print; *mil* call; *rad* signature.

semnala [semna'la] *vt (a atrage atenția)* to point out; to call/draw attention to; *(un fapt)* to refer to; *(a înregistra)* to note; *(a raporta)* to report; *avia* to indicate the position of; *comp* to post.

semnaliza [semnali'za] *vi* to signal; to gesture • **~re** *nf* signalization; (road) signs; signposting; *avia* beaconing (of a runway) • **~tor** *nm mil* signaler; *rail* signalman; *tech* signaling device/apparatus; *ling, math* mark || *adj* signaling.

semnătură [semnă'tură] *nf* signature; *(la un articol)* by-line.

semnifica [semnifi'ka] *vt* to signify, to mean • **~iv** *adj* expressive, meaningful, telling; graphic; important, noteworthy, considerable, significant || *adv* significantly, meaningfully • **~ție** *nf* significance; *(înțeles)* meaning; importance; *(valoare)* value.

senat [se'nat] *nn* Senate; *(clădire)* Senate (house) • **~or** *nm* senator.

senil [se'nil] *nm* dotard ‖ *adj* senile, aged; *(ramolit)* decrepit • **~itate** *nf* senility; senile decay.

senin [se'nin] *nn* clear sky; blue; *fig* serenity; peace; **din ~** out of the blue; unwarranted ‖ *adj* serene; *(d. cer)* clear; *also fig* happy, carefree • **~tate** *nf* serenity, candor.

senior [seni'or] *nm* feudal lord, seigneur; *(nobil)* nobleman, *pl* the nobility ‖ *adj* senior.

sens [sens] *nn (înţeles)* meaning, sense; significance; **~ figurat** figurative sense; **~ propriu** literal/basic sense; *(rost)* reason; value; *(folos)* use; *(direcţie)* direction.

sensibil [sen'sibil] *adj* sensitive (to/about); responsive; susceptible (to); aware (of); sympathetic; *(dureros)* painful; tender; *(apreciabil)* sensible; tangible ‖ *adv* appreciably, considerably, obviously • **~ itate** *nf* sensitiveness; sensibility.

sentenţios [sententsi'os] *adj* sententious ‖ *adv* sententiously.

sentiment [senti'ment] *nn* feeling; sentiment; emotion; *(de bucurie, uşurare)* sensation; *(moral, intelectual)* sense; consciousness; *(vedere, opinie)* view; *(sensibilitate)* sensibility.

sentimental [sentimen'tal] *nm* sentimentalist; *pej* milksop ‖ *adj* sentimental, soft-/tender-hearted; *(dulceag)* soppy; mawkish; *(la beţie)* maudlin ‖ *adv* sentimentally, tenderly.

sentinţă [sen'tintsă] *nf jur (a judecătorului)* sentence, decision; *(a unui juriu)* verdict; *(a unui arbitru)* award; *(ca model)* precedent; maxim, aphorism.

senzaţie [sen'zatsie] *nf* sensation; *(sentiment, bănuială)* feeling; *fig* excitement; **de ~** sensational, amazing.

senzaţional [senzatsio'nal] *adj* sensational, amazing; thrilling; *coll* cool; fantastic.

senzitiv [senzi'tiv] *adj* sensitive; *lit* over-sensitive; *(senzorial)* sensory.

senzorial [senzori'al] *adj* sensory, sensorial, sense.

senzual [senzu'al] *nm* sensualist, man of pleasures ‖ *adj* sensual; *(senzorial şi)* sensuous; carnal; lustful • **~ itate** *nf* sensuality, voluptuousness.

sepală [se'pală] *nf* sepal.

separa [sepa'ra] *vt* to separate (from); to sever (from); *(untul)* to churn butter; *com* to unpack; to divide; to keep apart; *(a distinge)* to distinguish (from) ‖ *vr* to separate (from); *(d. drumuri, râuri)* to branch off; to divorce.

sepia ['sepia] *nf* sepia (color); sepia (drawing).

sepie ['sepie] *nf zool* cuttlefish.

sept [sept] *nn anat, bot* septum, *pl* septa.

septembrie [sep'tembrie] *nm* September.

septic ['septic] *adj med* septic • **~emie** [septiche'mie] *nf med* septicemia.

sequoia [se'kuoia] *nm bot* sequoia.

ser [ser] *nn* serum.

seral [se'ral] *adj* evening.

serată [se'rată] *nf* evening party, soirée; *(intimă)* social gathering.

seră ['seră] *nf* greenhouse; glasshouse; *(încălzită)* hothouse; *(de palmieri)* palm house.

serba [ser'ba] *vt* to celebrate, to fete; *(a respecta obiceiul)* to keep, to observe • **~re** *nf* celebration; festival, feast; *(petrecere)* festivity.

serenadă [sera'nadă] *nf* serenade.

sergent [ser'djent] *nm mil* sergeant, non-com.

serial [seri'al] *adj* serial ‖ *nn cin, liter* series; serial.

serie ['serie] *nf (succesiune de)* series; succession; set; range; *com* line; category; *sp* rating; *cin* part; *sp* heat.

seringă [se'ringă] *nf* syringe.

serios [seri'os] *adj* serious-minded, earnest; responsible, reliable; bona fide; grave, serious; important.

seriozitate [seriozi'tate] *nf* earnestness; *(uşurinţă)* levity; *(gravitate)* seriousness, gravity.

serpentină [serpen'tină] *nf* winding; **în ~** meandering; *tech* (serpent) coil; *(din hârtie)* paper streamer.

sertar [ser'tar] *nn* drawer; *tech* sliding/slide valve.

servantă [ser'vantă] *nf* sideboard; *(pe roate)* dumb waiter; tea trolley; *(servitoare)* maid (servant).

servi [ser'vi] *vt* to be a servant to, to serve smb; *(un client)* to attend to; *(pe cineva, la masă)* to help smb to a dish; *(interesele cuiva)* to further; *(mâncare)* to serve up; *(fructe)* to set on; *(a ajuta)* to assist ‖ *vi* to be useful (to smb); to be in use; to serve ‖ *vr* to help oneself; *(cricket)* to bowl; *(cărţi)* to deal; *(în armată)* to serve; *(sub ordinele cuiva)* to serve under.

serviciu [ser'vichiu] *nn (domestic)* service; *(slujbă)* job; position; *(îndatorire)* duty; **de ~** on duty; professional; *fig* routine; *(la hotel)* attendance; *(adus cuiva)* (good) turn; *(favoare)* favor; *(birou, secţie)* department; *mil* corps; *(set de obiecte)* set; *sp* serv(ice); *(cricket)* bowling; divine service.

servietă [servi'etă] *nf* briefcase, *(mare)* attaché case; *(mapă)* foliocase; bag; portfolio.

servil [ser'vil] *adj* servile, cringing; slavish ‖ *adv* servilely; slavishly.

servitoare [servi'toare] *nf* (maid-)servant, help; *(la toate)* char(woman).

servitor [servi'tor] *nm* manservant; footman.

sesiune [sesi'une] *nf jur* session; sitting.

sesiza [sesi'za] *vt* to observe, to notice; *(a remarca)* to note; *(a înţelege)* to realize; to discern; to inform ‖ *vr* to take notice; *(de ceva)* to realize • **~re** *nf* complaint, protest; *(înţelegere)* realization; *(informare)* notification; *(la redacţia unui ziar)* letter to the editor.

set [set] *nn sp (tenis)* set; *(volei)* game; *(de pulovere)* twin set; *tech (de unelte)* kit.

sete ['sete] *nf* thirst; *fig* craving (for); *(lăcomie)* greed (for); *(năzuinţă)* striving (for/after) ‖ *adj* **cu ~** thirstily; *fig* eagerly, passionately; *(cu ciudă)* spitefully.

seu [seu] *nn* suet, tallow.

sevă ['sevă] *nf* sap; *also fig* vigor; spirit.

sever [se'ver] *adj* hard; inclement; *(aspru)* severe, harsh; austere; rigid, strict; *(neînduplecat)* unrelenting ‖ *adv* hard; severely, sternly.

sex [seks] *nn* sex • **~ism** *nn* sexism • **~ist** *adj* sexist • **~ual** *adj* sexual, sex • **~ualitate** *nf* sexuality, sex • **~y** *adj* sexy.

sezon [se'zon] *nn* season • **~ier** *adj* seasonal; temporary.

sfadă ['sfadă] *nf* quarrel, tiff, row; conflict.

sfat [sfat] *nn (îndrumare)* counsel, piece of advice; *(consfătuire)* conference, consultation; *(consiliu)* council.

sfădi [sfă'di] *vt/vr* to quarrel.

sfărâma [sfără'ma] *vt* to crush, to smash, to shatter; *(nuci)* to crack; *(d. lanţuri)* to burst; *(în bucăţi)* to break/smash into/to pieces; *(ţăndări)* to shiver; *(a distruge)* to destroy; *(a ucide)* to kill ‖ *vr* to break (into pieces), to crumble (away).

sfărâmicios [sfărâmi'chios] *adj* brittle, friable.

sfătos [sfă'tos] *adj* (*înțelept*) wise; (*vorbăreț*) talkative; glib(-tongued).

sfătui [sfătu'i] *vt* to advise, to counsel ‖ *vr* to deliberate; to put heads together; *coll* to chat • **~tor** *nm* adviser, counselor.

sfânt [sfânt] *nm* saint; *fig* holy man ‖ *adj* holy, saintly, godly, sanctified, consecrated • **~ă** *nf* saint; *fig* virtuous woman • **Sfânta Sfintelor** the Holy of Holies.

sfârâi [sfârâ'i] *vi* (*d. flacără, lemne*) to sputter; (*d. foc*) to crackle; (*în tigaie*) to sizzle; (*a bâzâi*) to buzz; (*a țârâi*) to chirp • **~t** *nn* sputtering, sizzling; (*de aripi*) fluttering.

sfârc [sfârk] *nn* nipple, teat; (*al urechii*) lobe; (*al biciului*) whiplash.

sfârși [sfâr'shi] *vt* to terminate, to finish, to end; to finish off; (*a încheia*) to conclude; to wind up; to execute, to carry out; (*a epuiza*) to exhaust; (*a înceta*) to cease ‖ *vr* (*a se isprăvi*) to come to an end; to finish; to cease; (*a muri*) to pass away ‖ *vi* to end, to come to an end • **~t** *nn* end; close; *cin* the end; (*încetare*) cessation; termination; expiration; (*moarte*) death; **fără ~** endless, continuous; **în ~** finally, at last ‖ *interj* finally!, it was about time! ‖ *adj* (*terminat*) finished, concluded; (*epuizat*) exhausted; worked out; *fig* (*de oboseala*) worn out; *coll* deadbeat; (*mort*) dead.

sfârteca [sfârte'ka] *vt* to mangle, to tear up; to hack; *fig* to criticize (harshly).

sfâșia [sfâshi'a] *vt* to tear, to rend; to tear up; (*a bârfi*) to backbite; **a ~ inima cuiva** to break smb's heart.

sfâșietor [sfâshie'tor] *adj* heartrending, heartbreaking; harrowing; (*d. durere*) excruciating, agonizing.

sfeclă ['sfeklă] *nf bot* beet (root).

sferă ['sferă] *nf geom* sphere; globe; *fig* domain.

sfert [sfert] *nn* quarter, (*o pătrime*) a fourth.

sfeșnic ['sfeshnik] *nn* candlestick.

sfetnic ['sfetnik] *nm* counselor, adviser, * **sfătuitor**.

sfială [sfi'ală] *nf* shyness, bashfulness, timidity.

sfida [sfi'da] *vt* to defy, to challenge; (*un pericol*) to brave, to face ‖ *vi* to be defiant • **~re** *nf* defiance.

sfidător [sfidă'tor] *adj* (*d. cuvinte*) provoking, challenging; (*d. atitudine*) defiant; (*ademenitor*) inviting.

sfii [sfi'i] *vr* to be timid/shy; **a se ~ să** to shrink from, to scruple to; to put oneself out.

sfințenie [sfin'tsenie] *nf* holiness, sanctity ‖ *adv* **cu ~** (*cu evlavie*) piously; (*cu exactitate*) scrupulously, to the letter.

sfinți [sfin'tsi] *vt* to hallow, to sanctify; to canonize; (*a beatifica*) to beatify; (*a închina*) to consecrate; (*o biserică*) to dedicate; (*un preot*) to ordain; (*apă, pâine*) to bless; (*a unge*) to anoint ‖ *vr relig* to take/receive holy orders.

sfinx [sfinks] *nm myth, fig* sphinx.

sfios [sfi'os] *adj* shy, timid, (*rușinos*) bashful; modest; (*d. fete*) coy.

sfoară ['sfoară] *nf* cord, string, line.

sforar [sfo'rar] *nm* twine manufacturer; *fig* plotter, schemer.

sforăi [sforă'i] *vi* (*în somn*) to snore; (*d. cai*) to snort • **~ală/t** *nf/nn* snoring, snore; (*la cai*) snort(ing) • **~tor** *adj* snort(ing); *fig* blatant, emphatic.

sforărie [sforă'rie] *nf* plotting, scheme.

sforța [sfor'tsa] *vr* to make an effort, to strain (oneself), to exert oneself; to do one's best • **~re** *nf* effort, exertion.

sfredel ['sfredel] *nn* drill, borer; (*de lemn*) gimlet; (*mare*) (ground) auger; (*pt. pământ*) terrier; (*lung*) churn drill, wimble; *min* (drill) bit • **~i** *vt* to drill, to bore; (*un zid*) to make a hole through a wall; *fig* to pierce; to penetrate • **~itor** *adj* piercing; shrill; keen, sharp.

sfriji [sfri'zhi] *vr* to shrivel up, to shrink up; (*a slăbi*) to grow thin; to dwindle away.

sfruntat [sfrun'tat] *adj* shameless, brazen, outrageous, impudent; **minciună ~ă** outrageous/whopping lie, whopper.

show [shou] *nn thea* (variety) show.

si [si] *nm mus* B, si; **~ bemol major** B flat major.

siaj [si'azh] *nn naut* shipwake.

siamez [sia'mez] *nm/adj* Siamese.

sicriu [si'kriu] *nn* casket; (*ladă*) box.

sidef [si'def] *nn* mother-of-pearl; **de ~** nacreous • **~iu** *adj* nacreous.

siderat [side'rat] *adj frml* flabbergasted, astounded, stunned.

siderurgie [siderurdjie] *nf* metallurgy (of iron and steel); iron smelting.

siestă [si'estă] *nf* siesta, midday rest; *coll* nap.

sifilis ['sifilis] *nn med* syphilis.

sifon [si'fon] *nn* siphon(-bottle); (*apă gazoasă*) soda (water); *tech* siphon; (*la canalizare*) drain trap.

sigila [sidji'la] *vt* to seal (up); (*o ușă*) to put/affix a seal to.

sigiliu [si'djiliu] *nn* seal; sigil; (*la inel*) signet; **inel cu ~** signet ring; *fig* stamp, mark.

siglă ['siglă] *nf* set of initials, acronym; abbreviation.

sigur ['sigur] *adj* sure, secure; (*de incredere*) trustworthy, reliable, trusty, true; (*neîndoios*) certain, positive; unquestionable; fixed, stated; **~ de sine** self-assured; **~ pe sine** *coll* sure of one's ground ‖ *adv/interj* sure(ly), certainly; categorically; (*negreșit*) without fail; (*fără îndoială*) undoubtedly, without doubt.

siguranță [sigu'rantsă] *nf* safety, security; safekeeping; *com* surety, guarantee; (*certitudine*) certainty; positiveness; *coll* cocksureness; *elec* fuse; (*încredere*) confidence; (*a mâinii*) sureness; (*a opiniei etc*) soundness; unerringness; (*poliție*) security police ‖ *adv* (*cu hotărâre*) resolutely; **cu ~** *adv* positively, doubtlessly.

sihastru [si'hastru] *nm* recluse, hermit ‖ *adj* lonely, solitary.

silabă [si'labă] *nf* syllable.

silabisi [silabi'si] *vt* to syllabify.

silă ['silă] *nf* (*aversiune*) aversion, loathing; disgust (at/for/towards); repugnance; abhorrence (of); (*antipatie*) dislike (to/for/of), antipathy (to/for); (*ură*) hatred (of); (*săturare*) satiety; (*rea-voință*) reluctance; (*constrângere*) coercion; **~ de viață** taedium vitae.

silențios [silentsi'os] *adj* silent.

sili [si'li] *vt* to force, to oblige, to compel; (*a constrânge*) to constrain; *coll* to twist smb's arm; *jur* to coerce; (*a zori*) to urge; (*a determina*) to determine ‖ *vr* to do one's best, to take pains; (*a se strădui*) to endeavor; (*a căuta*) to try.

siliciu [si'lichiu] *nn chem* silicon, silicium.

silicon [sili'kon] *nn chem* silicone.

silință [si'lintsă] *nf* effort; endeavor; (*osteneală*) pains-(taking); (*hărnicie*) diligence, assiduity; (*zel*) zeal.

silit [si'lit] *adj* obliged; forcible; obligatory, compulsory; *(fals)* forced, unnatural; *(nevoit)* unwilling • ~**or** *adj* diligent, assiduous; active, busy.

silnic ['silnik] *adj* forcible, forced; *(d. muncă)* hard (labor) ‖ *nm bot* glec(h)oma.

silogism [silo'djism] *nn* syllogism.

siloz [si'loz] *nn* silo.

siluetă [silu'etă] *nf* outline, silhouette; *phot* figure; *mil* figure, target; slimness.

silui [silu'i] *vt* to rape, to violate, to abuse • ~**re** *nf* rape, violation.

silvicultor [silvikul'tor] *nm* silviculturist.

silvicultură [silvikul'tură] *nf* forestry.

simandicos [simandi'kos] *adj pej* fine, genteel.

simbioză [simbi'oză] *nf bio* symbiosis.

simbol [sim'bol] *nn* symbol, token ‖ *adj* symbolic(al) ‖ *adv* symbolically • ~**ism** *nn* symbolism • ~**iza** *vt* to symbolize, to epitomize, to stand for.

simbrie [sim'brie] *nf* pay, *(leafă)* wages.

simetric [si'metrik] *adj* symmetrical ‖ *adv* symmetrically.

simetrie [sime'trie] *nf* symmetry; harmony.

simfonic [sim'fonik] *adj* symphonic, symphony.

simfonie [simfo'nie] *nf mus* symphony.

similar [simi'lar] *adj* of the same kind; alike; *(cu)* similar to, allied/analogous (to/with).

simpatic [sim'patik] *adj* likeable, nice, congenial; *anat* sympathetic; *(cerneală)* invisible ‖ *adv* attractively, nicely.

simpatie [simpa'tie] *nf* sympathy; *(atracţie)* instinctive attraction, liking; *(aprobare)* approval; *(înţelegere)* understanding, sympathy; *(persoană)* sweetheart.

simpatiza [simpati'za] *vt* to like, to take a fancy to; to feel drawn to; **a ~ cu** to sympathize with, to be in sympathy with • ~**nt** *nm* follower; *pol* sympathizer.

simplicitate [simplichi'tate] *nf* simplicity; *(a hainelor)* plainness; * **simplitate**.

simplifica [simplifi'ka] *vt* to simplify; *(o fracţie)* to reduce a fraction to its lowest term ‖ *vr* to become simple(r).

simplitate [simpli'tate] *nf* * **simplicitate**; *(naivitate)* artlessness; simpleness, simple-mindedness.

simplu ['simplu] *adj* simple, plain; *(care nu e compus)* single; *(fără altceva)* mere; elementary; *(obişnuit)* ordinary, common; *(uşor)* easy; straightforward; *(modest)* unobtrusive; *(neafectat)* natural; *(naiv)* artless; credulous ‖ *adv* simply, merely; plainly; *(fără afectare)* naturally; **pur şi ~** purely (and simply), simply (and solely).

simpozion [simpo'zion] *nn* symposium.

simptom [simp'tom] *nn* symptom; sign, indication.

simţ [simts] *nn* sense; *(gust)* taste; **~ moral** moral sense, conscience; **~ practic** practical sense; **bun ~** decency, common sense; *(judecată)* judgment; *(înţelepciune)* mother wit.

simţământ [simtsă'mânt] *nn* feeling; sensation.

simţi [sim'tsi] *vt* to feel, to experience; to have a sensation of, to sense; *(a adulmeca)* to scent; **a ~ vânatul** *(d. câini)* to scent out game; **a ~ că** to feel that; *(a fi conştient de)* to be aware/conscious of; *fig (d. sentimente)* to prove; *(a înţelege)* to understand ‖ *vr* to feel, to be; **a se ~ bine** to feel all right; *(foarte bine)* to feel fine; **a nu se ~ bine** to feel funny; **a se ~ prost** to feel sick/unwell; *(stingherit)* to be uncomfortable • ~**re** *nf* feeling; sentiment; *(conştiinţă)* con-

sciousness; *(bun simţ)* common sense; **fără ~** unconscious • ~**tor** *adj* sensitive (to).

simula [simu'la] *vt/vi* to feign, to sham; to affect ‖ *vi* to pretend (to be ill); *(o boală)* also *mil* to malinger • ~**cru** *nn* semblance, mere mockery; simulacrum.

simulaţie [simu'latsie] *nf jur* simulation, pretence.

simultan [simul'tan] *nn* simultaneous match ‖ *adj* simultaneous, concomitant ‖ *adv* simultaneously, concomitantly • ~**eitate** *nf* simultaneousness, concomitance.

sinagogă [sina'gogă] *nf* synagogue.

sincer ['sincher] *adj* frank, sincere, candid; *(adevărat)* heartfelt; *(d. bucurie)* genuine; earnest ‖ *adv* candidly, sincerely, frankly, genuinely • ~**itate** *nf* sincerity, frankness, candor, genuineness.

sinchiseală [sinki'sealã] *nf* care, trouble.

sinchisi [sinki'si] *vr* to care; **a se ~ de** to care for/about, to mind, to heed.

sincopă [sin'kopă] *nf* syncope; *mus* syncopation.

sincronic [sin'kronik] *adj* synchronic.

sincroniza [sinkroni'za] *vt* to synchronize.

sindicalism [sindika'lism] *nn* tradeunionism; *(patronal)* syndicalism.

sindicalist [sindika'list] *nm* trade unionist.

sindicat [sindi'kat] *nn* union; **~ patronal** syndicate, combine.

sindrofie [sindro'fie] *nf coll* spree, frolic.

sindrom [sin'drom] *nn med* syndrome.

sine ['sine] *nf* ego, self ‖ *pron* oneself; *m* himself, *f* herself, *n* itself; *pl* themselves; **de la ~** naturally.

sinecură [sine'kură] *nf* sinecure, safe berth, feathered nest.

singular [singu'lar] *nn* singular (number); **la ~** in the singular ‖ *adj* singular; *(deosebit)* peculiar (to), remarkable; *(ciudat)* odd, strange; *(diferit)* different, conspicuous.

singur ['singur] *adj* alone; *(neînsoţit, neajutat)* by oneself, on one's own; *(singuratic)* lonely, solitary; *(unic)* sole, single; *(numai)* only; *(însumi)* myself; *(însuţi)* yourself; *(însăşi)* herself; *(însuşi)* himself; *(neutru)* itself; *(înşine)* ourselves; *(înşivă)* yourselves; *(înşişi, însele)* themselves ‖ *adv* alone, lonely • ~**atic** *adj* solitary, lonely, lonesome • ~**ătate** *nf* loneliness, solitude; *(sălbăticie)* wilderness.

sinistrat [sinis'trat] *nm* victim (of a calamity/disaster) ‖ *adj* suffering from a calamity; **zonă ~ă** disaster area.

sinistru [si'nistru] *nn* calamity, catastrophe, disaster ‖ *adj (groaznic)* awful, lugubrious; *(prevestitor)* sinister, ominous; *(înfiorător)* dreary, gruesome, macabre.

sinod [si'nod] *nn relig* synod.

sinonim [sino'nim] *nn* synonym ‖ *adj* synonymous (with).

sintactic [sin'taktic] *adj* syntactical ‖ *adv* syntactically.

sintagmă [sin'tagmă] *nf* syntagm.

sintaxă [sin'taksă] *nf* syntax.

sintetic [sin'tetik] *adj* synthetic ‖ *adv* synthetically.

sintetiza [sinteti'za] *vt* to synthesize.

sintetizor [sinteti'zor] *nn* synthesizer.

sinteză [sin'teză] *nf* synthesis, *pl* syntheses; **de ~** synthetic.

sinucide [sinu'chide] *vr* to commit suicide, to kill oneself • ~**re** *nf* suicide.

sinucigaş [sinuchi'gash] *nm* suicide.

sinuos [sinu'os] *adj* sinuous; devious; winding, tortuous.

sinuzită [sinu'zită] *nf med* sinusitis.

sionism [sio'nism] *nn* Zionism.

sirenă [si'renă] *nf* siren, hooter, buzzer; ~ **de ceață** foghorn; *also myth* mermaid; *phys* siren.

sirian [siri'an] *nm/adj* Syrian.

sirop [si'rop] *nn* syrup; fruit cordial; ~ **de arțar** maple syrup; ~ **de tuse** cough syrup, linctus; *fig* (*d. literatură*) sob stuff • **~os** *adj* syrupy; saccharine; *fig* sloppy, slip-slop.

sista [sis'ta] *vt* to cease, to leave off; to suspend, to stop; to interrupt.

sistem [sis'tem] *nn* system; (*metodă*) method; *coll* device; scheme; manner; (*tip*) type; model; set; network • **~atic** *adj* systematic, methodical ‖ *adv* systematically, methodically • **~atiza** *vt* to system(at)ize.

sitar [si'tar] *nm orn* woodcock.

sită ['sită] *nf* sieve, strainer; (*mai ales pentru făină*) bolter; (*mare, la fereastră*) *also typ* screen; wire mesh.

situa [situ'a] *vt* to place, to locate ‖ *vr* to occupy a certain place; (*a se găsi*) to lie; *fig* to (take a) stand.

situație [si'tuatsie] *nf* situation; (*stare*) state, condition; (*stare de lucruri*) state of affairs; ~ **critică** critical state; (*așezare*) position, site; (*dare de seamă*) report, account; ~ **dificilă** an awkward predicament; *coll* a tight spot.

slab [slab] *adj* (*ant. puternic*) weak, feeble; (*d. vânt*) light, gentle; (*fără vlagă*) faint, feeble; (*lejer*) loose, slack; (*fără voință*) weak-willed; (*subțire*) thin, skinny; (*fără grăsime*) lean; (*d. brânză*) skimmed milk cheese; (*deșirat*) lanky; (*prost, rău*) bad, poor; insufficient; small ‖ *adv* weakly, feebly; poorly, insufficiently.

slalom ['slalom] *nn* slalom; ~ **uriaș** giant slalom.

slav [slav] *nm* Slav ‖ *adj* Slav; (*d. limbă și*) Slavic, Slavonic.

slavă ['slavă] *nf* glory, fame; reverence; splendor; ~ **Domnului!** thank God!.

slăbănog [slăbă'nog] *nm* weakling ‖ *adj* lean, meager; weak, weedy; (*d. vite*) hide-bound; (*de nemâncare*) skeletal, skin and bone.

slăbi [slă'bi] *vi* (*a scădea în greutate*) to grow thin, to lose weight, (*prin tratament*) to slim; to slenderize; (*brusc*) to shed; (*a se micșora*) to diminish; (*a descrește*) to decrease; *fig* (*a-și pierde forțele*) to grow weak(er), to lose strength; (*d. vedere, d.curaj*) to fail; (*d. vânt*) to abate; (*a nu mai fi întins*) to loosen ‖ *vt* (*o legătură*) to slacken; (*d. o boală: a face să slăbească*) to make smb thin(ner); (*d. îmbrăcăminte*) to make smb look thinner; (*a lăsa*) to leave, to let (alone).

slăbiciune [slăbi'chiune] *nf* weakness, feebleness; (*cusur*) shortcoming, weakness; (*punct slab*) weak point; (*pentru ceva/cineva*) weakness for, soft spot for.

slănină [slă'nină] *nf* (*slabă*) bacon; (*grasă*) lard.

slăvi [slă'vi] *vt* to glorify, to extol, (*a lăuda*) to praise, to sing the praise of; to honor.

slei [sle'i] *vi* * **seca**; (*a îngheța*) to freeze ‖ *vr* to freeze; to jelly; to thicken; to cake; (*a se epuiza*) to be exhausted, to peter out • **~t** *adj* frozen, cold; (*îngroșat*) thickened; (*d. sânge*) coagulated; (*istovit*) exhausted, drained; tired out.

slinos [sli'nos] *adj* greasy; filthy, dirty, soiled.

slip [slip] *nn* swimsuit, bathing-suit; *naut, avia* slip.

slobod ['slobod] *adj* free, loose; autonomous; (*d. o*

țară) independent; ~ **la mână** lavish, wasteful, too liberal.

slobozi [slobo'zi] *vt* (*a pune în libertate*) to (set) free, to release; *coll* to let off; (*un sclav*) to liberate; to discharge; (*a da drumul*) to let go; (*a descurca*) to disentangle; *jur* to acquit; *mil* to fire off; (*a arunca*) to cast; (*a lansa*) to launch; (*a scoate o exclamație/un cuvânt*) to utter; *relig* to absolve; (*a scuti de*) to exempt from ‖ *vr* (*a se coborî*) to go/climb down; (*a se repezi*) to rush.

slogan [slo'gan] *nn* catch phrase, slogan.

sloi [sloi] *nn* (*de gheață*) floating ice; (*mare*) ice floe/pack; (*țurțur*) icicle; (*gheață*) ice; (*bucată*) cake; (*de ceară*) cake of wax.

slovac [slo'vak] *nm/adj* Slovak.

sloven [slo'ven] *nm* Slovene ‖ *adj* Slovenian.

slow [slău] *nn mus* slow dance tune, slow tune.

slugarnic [slu'garnik] *adj* menial; cringing, obsequious.

slugă ['slugă] *nf* (man-/maid-)servant, domestic; menial; *pej* flunky • **~rnicie** *nf* servility, obsequiousness.

slujbaș [sluzh'bash] *nm* clerk, * **funcționar**; (*la stat*) civil servant.

slujbă ['sluzhbă] *nf* service; (*post*) job, employment; occupation; (*funcție*) public function; (*situație*) situation; berth; **fără** ~ unemployed, out of a job; *mil* military service; *relig* (divine) service.

sluji [slu'zhi] *vt* to serve, to be in the service of; (*la masă*) to wait upon; *relig* to celebrate; (*a ajuta*) to help; (*a fi de folos*) to be of use ‖ *vi* to serve; *relig* to officiate; (*a folosi*) **a** ~ **la** to serve for; **a** ~ **de/drept** to serve/be used as ‖ *vr* **a se** ~ **de** to (make) use (of), to employ; (*a recurge la*) to resort to.

slujnică ['sluzhnikă] *nf* maid servant.

slut [slut] *adj* ugly (man), dowdy (woman); deformed, hideous.

sluți [slu'tsi] *vt* to make ugly; (*a mutila*) to maim, to mutilate ‖ *vr* to grow ugly; (*a se strâmba*) to make faces.

smalț [smalts] *nn* enamel (of teeth); laquer.

smălțui [smăltsu'i] *vt* to enamel, to lacquer; * **smălța**, *fig* to fleck with flowers, to spangle.

smântână [smân'tână] *nf* (sour) cream; *fig* flower; pick.

smârc [smârk] *nn* swamp, marsh; (*băltoacă*) muddy pool.

smead [smead] *adj* swarthy.

smerenie [sme'renie] *nf* meekness, humility; (*evlavie*) devoutness, piety.

smeri [sme'ri] *vr* (*a se supune*) to submit; (*a se umili*) to humble oneself; (*a se căi*) to repent ‖ *vt* (*a supune*) to subdue; (*a umili*) to humiliate • **~t** *adj* humble, meek; pious, devout.

sminti [smin'ti] *vt* (*a strica*) to spoil, to impair; (*a vătăma*) to harm; (*a prăpădi*) to destroy; (*a deranja*) to disarrange; (*a mișca*) to move, to shift; (*a împiedica*) to hinder; (*a opri*) to stop; (*a înșela*) to deceive; (*a induce în eroare*) to mislead; (*a înnebuni*) to turn smb's head/brain ‖ *vr* (*a înnebuni*) to go mad • **~t** *adj* (*nebun*) mad, crazy; *coll* batty, cracked; (*nebunesc*) foolish.

smiorcăi [smiorkă'i] *vr* to whimper, to whine; (*a se smârcăi*) to snivel • **~ală** *nf* whimper(ing).

smirnă ['smirnă] *nf* myrrh.

smoală ['smoală] *nf* pitch, tar; (*solidă*) rosin.

smoc [smok] *nn* (*de păr, lână, pene*) tuft, crest; (*buchet*) bunch; (*legătură*) bundle.

smochin [smo'kin] *nm bot* fig(-tree) • ~**ă** *nf* fig.

smoching ['smoking] *nn* tuxedo, dinner jacket.

smuci [smu'chi] *vt* to jerk; (*a smulge*) to snatch; (*a trage*) to pull; (*a scoate*) to pull out ‖ *vr* to tear oneself away; (*a se zbate*) to struggle ‖ *vi* (*d. arme*) to kick • ~**tură** *nf* jerk.

smulge ['smuldje] *vt* to pull/tear (out/up/away); to draw; (*cu violență, din*) to wrench (off/away); (*ceva, din mâna cuiva*) to snatch; (*a dezrădăcina*) *also fig* to uproot; to eradicate; (*bani*) to extort, to extract; (*un consimțământ, un secret, bani*) to wring ‖ *vr* to tear oneself away; (*a se elibera*) to break loose/away, to escape.

snob [snob] *nm* snob • ~**ism** *nn* snobbishness, snobbery.

snop [snop] *nm* sheaf, pile; (*de raze*) shaft; (*de gloanțe*) cone.

snopi [sno'pi] *vt* to thrash.

soacră ['soakră] *nf* mother-in-law.

soare ['soare] *nm* sun; *fig* radiant, beaming; **e** ~ it's sunny; **zi cu** ~ sunny day; *fig* day of happiness, red-letter day.

soartă ['soartă] *nf* destiny, fate; (*a cuiva*) lot, portion; (*fatalitate*) fatality; (*noroc*) luck; (*șansă*) chance; (*viitor*) future.

sobă ['sobă] *nf* stove; (*cuptor*) oven; (*cămin*) fireplace, hearth.

sobrietate [sobrie'tate] *nf* sobriety, seriousness; (*cumpătare*) temperance; moderation, restraint.

sobru ['sobru] *adj* sober; temperate; restrained; solemn, austere; (*d. haine*) classic ‖ *adv* soberly, temperately.

soc [sok] *nm bot* common elder tree.

sociabil [sochi'abil] *adj* sociable, convivial.

social [sochi'al] *adj* social.

socialism [sochia'lism] *nn* socialism, socialist system.

socialist [sochia'list] *nm/adj* socialist; **stat** ~ socialist state.

societar [sochie'tar] *nm* (full) member, associate.

societate [sochie'tate] *nf* society; (*comunitate*) community; *pol* (social) system; (*asociație*) company, gathering; (*firmă*) association; group, circle; *sp* club; *econ* firm, partnership; *constr* trust; ~ **pe acțiuni** incorporated company; ~ **anonimă** public company; ~ **cu răspundere limitată** limited (liability) company; (*tovărășie, companie*) company, companionship.

sociolog [sochio'log] *nm* sociologist • ~**ie** *nf* sociology.

soclu ['soklu] *nn* socle, pedestal.

socoteală [soko'teală] *nf* counting, calculation; (*operație aritmetică*) operation; (*plată*) account; (*notă de plată*) bill; (*chibzuință*) reflection, consideration; (*părere*) opinion, view; (*bănuială*) supposition; plan, scheme; (*gând*) idea; (*folos*) use; profit; (*măsură*) moderation; (*economisire*) thrift; (*probleme, poveste*) matter; story; **cu** ~ thoughtfully, circumspect(ly), (*cumpătat*) carefully, moderately, (*cu tâlc*) pointedly; **fără** ~ thoughtlessly.

socoti [soko'ti] *vt* (*a calcula*) to calculate, to reckon; (*a aduna*) to sum/total up; (*a lua în considerație*) to take into consideration/account; to examine; (*a chibzui*) to consider, to think; (*a-și închipui*) to guess; (*a privi ca*) to consider/regard as; (*a intenționa*) to intend ‖ *vr* (*a se răfui*) to settle/square accounts with smb; (*a se gândi bine*) to think it over; (*a se consid-*

era) to consider/think oneself (better) ‖ *vi* (*a calcula*) to compute, to calculate; (*a număra*) to count.

socru ['sokru] *nm* father-in-law; *pl* in-laws, parents-in-law.

sodă ['sodă] *nf* (washing) soda; sodium hydroxide.

sodiu ['sodiu] *nn chem* sodium.

sodomie [sodo'mie] *nf med* sodomy.

sofa [so'fa] *nf* sofa, couch, settee.

sofisticat [sofisti'kat] *adj* (*complicat*) sophisticated, advanced; (*rafinat*) refined; (*afectat*) affected.

soft [soft] *nn* text soft fiber; *comp* soft(ware) • ~**ist** *nm comp* software specialist/expert.

soi [soi] *nn* (*fel*) sort, kind; category; (*calitate*) quality; variety; species; (*rasă*) race, breed; (*fire*) nature; ~ **bun** a fine character; ~ **rău** bad lot/egg; **de** ~ (*bun*) fine; (*ales*) choice; **tot** ~**ul de** all kinds/sorts of.

soia ['soia] *nf* soy(bean).

soios [so'ios] *adj* filthy, dirty.

sol[1] [sol] *nm* (*mesager*) messenger; *also fig* herald, harbinger; *mus* G, sol.

sol[2] [sol] *nn* soil; (*pământ*) earth, ground; *chem* colloidal solution.

solar [so'lar] *nn* solarium ‖ *adj* solar.

sold [sold] *nn econ* balance; (*produse rămase nevândute*) surplus stock, remnant; (*vânzare*) clearance (sale), bargain counter; *pl also* sales • ~**a** *vi com* to balance (an account); (*un cont*) to discharge, to settle; (*mărfuri*) to sell off, to clear ‖ *vr* **a se** ~ **cu** to end/result in; to be the result.

soldat [sol'dat] *nm mil* soldier, (*simplu*) G.I., private; marine; *fig* champion, advocate.

solemn [so'lemn] *adj* solemn, official, formal; grave, serious; impressive ‖ *adv* solemnly, gravely; in a solemn manner/tone; with ceremony; impressively • ~**itate** *nf* solemnity, ceremony.

solfegiu [sol'fedjiu] *nn mus* solfège, solfeggio, solfa.

solicita [solichi'ta] *vt* (*a cere*) to request, to ask/apply for; (*pe cineva pentru*) to appeal to smb for; (*voturi*) to canvas for votes; (*o slujbă*) to apply/compete for a job; (*a necesita*) to require; (*puterile*) to challenge; (*a atrage*) to attract, to appeal (to); (*a cauza*) to cause; *tech* to stress • ~**nt** *nm* petitioner, applicant (for).

solicitudine [solichi'tudine] *nf* solicitude, concern, sympathy, understanding.

solid [so'lid] *nn* solid (body); *pl* solid food ‖ *adj* solid; (*tare*) hard, firm; strong; secure; (*d. o persoană*) sturdy; *coll* hefty, strapping; (*d. o masă*) hearty; (*argument*) sound, thorough; (*adânc*) profound; (*trainic*) lasting; (*sigur*) reliable; serious; *com* well-established ‖ *adv* solidly, firmly; *fig* thoroughly, deeply, soundly.

solidar [soli'dar] *adj* united; interdependent; *jur* (*d. răspundere*) joint and several; (*d. cineva*) liable; *tech* forming one piece with another ‖ *adv* in solidarity, jointly • ~**itate** *nf* solidarity, fellowship; *jur* joint responsibility • ~**iza** *vr* to join together in responsibility/liability; (*cu*) to make common cause with; to show solidarity with.

solie [so'lie] *nf* mission, deputation; (*însărcinare*) task, assignment; (*mesaj*) message; *obs* (*ambasadă*) embassy.

solist [so'list] *nm* soloist.

solitar [soli'tar] *nm* hermit, recluse ‖ *adj* solitary, lonesome, lonely; (*loc*) deserted; isolated ‖ *adv* solitarily.

solniţă ['solnitsă] *nf* salt cellar; (*de piper*) pepper box/pot.

solo ['solo] *nm* solo.

solstiţiu [sol'stitsiu] *nn* solstice; ~ **de vară** summer solstice.

solubil [so'lubil] *adj* soluble; (*d. cafea*) instant (coffee).

soluţie [so'lutsie] *nf chem* solution; (*răspuns*) key, answer.

soluţiona [solutsio'na] *vt* to solve.

solvabil [sol'vabil] *adj* solvent; *fin* (financially) solvent • ~**itate** *nf* solvency, solvability.

solz [solz] *nm* scale.

soma [so'ma] *vt* to summon.

somaţie [so'matsie] *nf* summons; *mil* challenge.

somieră [somi'eră] *nf* spring/box mattress.

somitate [somi'tate] *nf* authority; celebrity.

somn¹ [somn] *nm icht* sheatfish, wells.

somn² [somn] *nn* sleep; (*scurt*) nap, short sleep, snooze; (*uşor; toropeală*) doze, (light) slumber; (*letargic*) lethargy, stupor; (*odihnă*) rest, repose; sleepiness, drowsiness • ~**ambul** *nm* sleepwalker, somnambulist; *med* hypnobate • ~**ifer** *nn* soporific || *adj* soporific, somniferous • ~**olent** *adj* drowsy, sleepy, somnolent • ~**olenţă** *nf* drowsiness, sleepiness • ~**oros** *adj* sleepy, drowsy || *nm* sleepy person || *adv* sleepily, in a sleepy voice.

somon [so'mon] *nm icht* salmon.

somptuos [somptu'os] *adj* sumptuous, gorgeous, luxurious || *adv* sumptuously.

sonar [so'nar] *nm telec* sonar.

sonată [so'nată] *nf mus* sonata.

sonda [son'da] *vt naut* to sound, to fathom; *med* to examine, to test; to explore; *fig* to feel one's way, to see how the land lies • ~**j** *nn* ~ **de opinie** public opinion poll • ~**re** *nf naut* taking bearings/soundings; *naut* fathoming, plumbing; *fig* testing, poll, census.

sondă ['sondă] *nf* (*de petrol*) oil derrick, oil well; *naut* sounding line/lead; sound; *med* probe; *med* (*cateter*) catheter; *tech* proof stick; *elec* electrical sounder; sounding rod (for a well); ~ **spaţială** space probe.

sonerie [sone'rie] *nf* (electric) bell.

sonet [so'net] *nn liter* sonnet.

sonor [so'nor] *adj* sonorous; (*d. râs: tare*) loud; (*d. o boltă*) echoing; (*d. voce*) ringing; (*d. un clopot*) clear-toned; (*d. consoane*) voiced; *pej* high-sounding; *fig* (*faimos*) high-sounding; (*nivel de intensitate a sunetului*) sound (intensity) level || *adv* sonorously.

soporific [sopo'rifik] *adj* soporific, sleep-inducing || *nn* soporific.

sopran(ă) [so'pran(ă)] *nn mus* soprano.

soră ['soră] *nf* sister; (*călugăriţă*) nun; (*de caritate*) (hospital/medical) nurse; sister of charity.

sorbi [sor'bi] *vt* to drink; (*câte o înghiţitură*) to sip, to tiff; (*a bea tot*) to drain; (*dintr-o dată*) to drink off/ up, to gulp; (*nesăţios*) to swill down; to absorb; (*a inspira*) to breathe in; *fig* to devour • ~**tură** *nf* sip, draught.

sordid [sor'did] *adj* sordid, squalid; blowsy.

sorg [sorg] *nn* sorghum.

soroc [so'rok] *nn* term; (*limită*) deadline; period, interval; *med* menses, period(s).

sort [sort] *nn* sort, kind; species, category.

sorta [sor'ta] *vt* to sort (out).

sorti [sor'ti] *vt* to (pre)destine, to fate, to foredoom.

sortiment [sorti'ment] *nn* assortment, range (of goods).

sorţi ['sortsi] *nm pl* odds, chances.

sos [sos] *nn* sauce; (*de friptură*) gravy; (*pt. salată*) dressing • ~**ieră** *nf* sauce/gravy boat.

sosi [so'si] *vi* to arrive, to come • ~**re** *nf* arrival, coming; *sp* finish.

soţ [sots] *nm* (*bărbat*) husband, man, *coll* hubby, (*unul din parteneri*) spouse; *pl* couple • ~**ie** *nf* wife; *coll* rib, better-half.

sovietic [sovi'etik] *nm* Soviet citizen || *adj* Soviet • **Uniunea Sovietică** the Soviet Union.

spadă ['spadă] *nf* sword, rapier.

spaghete [spa'gete] *nf pl cul* spaghetti.

spaimă ['spaimă] *nf* (*frică*) fright, fear, dread; (*groază*) terror, horror; *fig* (*monstru*) scourge, monster.

spalier [spali'er] *nn agr* trellis, espalier; (*şir dublu*) double row; (*aparat de gimnastică*) rib stall.

spanac [spa'nak] *nn bot* spinach; *fig coll* rubbish, nonsense.

spaniol [spani'ol] *nm* Spaniard || *adj* Spanish • ~**ă** *nf* (*limba*) Spanish.

spăranghel [spa'rangel] *nn* (a stick of) asparagus.

sparge ['spardje] *vt* (*a sfărâma*) to break, to crack; (*a zdrobi*) to crush; (*cu putere, în bucăţi mici*) to smash to pieces; to dash/smash (in)to smithereens; (*o uşă*) to break/burst (a door) open; (*un lacăt*) to force; to pick; (*a despica*) to split; (*lemne*) to chop; (*o rană*) to open; *coll* (*pe cineva*) to smash/kick smb's face; (*a nimici*) to destroy; (*a pune pe fugă*) to put to flight || *vr* to break; (*d. cauciucuri*) to burst; (*a crăpa*) to split; (*a plesni*) to snap; (*d. valuri*) to break (against the shore); (*în spume*) to break into foam; (*d. sticlă, porţelan*) to be smashed/shattered; (*d. o adunare*) to break up; (*brusc, cu zgomot*) to go snap || *vi* (*d. o rană*) to break open.

spasm [spasm] *nn* spasm; colic; pang; grimace.

spată ['spată] *nf anat* shoulder blade; *pl* shoulders; (*carne*) spare-rib; *text* reed, comb.

spate ['spate] *nn anat* back; (*umeri*) shoulders; (*spetează*) back (of a chair); ~ **în** ~ back to back; *fig* support, backing; *coll* prop; *mil* logistics.

spatulă [spa'tulă] *nf* spatula.

spaţia [spatsi'a] *vt* to space; (*litere*) to space/set (out); (*rânduri*) to lead/to white out • ~**l** *adj* spatial.

spaţios [spatsi'os] *adj* roomy, spacious.

spaţiu ['spatsiu] *nn* space; (*loc*) room; (*distanţă*) distance, interval; (*regiune*) area, region; (*oficiu*) housing office; (*vid*) void; (*cer*) sky; ~ **cosmic** outer space; (*loc liber*) *typ* blank, gap; (*cadru*) framework.

spăla [spă'la] *vt* to wash; *lit* to lave; (*a curăţa*) to wash off/away; (*cu multă apă*) to swill; (*a face baie*) to bathe; (*aur, din nisip*) to pan off/out; (*o pată*) to wash out a stain; (*cu benzină*) to take out a stain; (*o rană*) to bathe/cleanse a wound; (*rufele*) to launder; (*vasele*) to wash the dishes, to do the dishes; (*cu săpun*) to soap; (*cu buretele*) to sponge; (*cu peria*) to scrub; (*d. o apă, un râu*) to water; *fig* (*a îndepărta*) to wash away; (*a dilua culoarea*) to dilute || *vr* (*d. oameni*) to wash oneself; (*pe cap*) to wash one's hair; (*pe dinţi*) to brush/clean one's teeth; (*a se decolora*) to fade || *vi* to wash • ~**re** *nf geog* washing, water erosion • ~**rea banilor** money laundering.

spălăcit [spălă'chit] *adj* watery, colorless, washed-out.

spălătoreasă [spălăto'reasă] *nf* laundress, washerwoman.

spălătorie [spălăto'rie] *nf* laundry, washhouse.

spărgător [spărgă'tor] *nm* burglar; housebreaker || *nn* breaker, cracker.

spărtură [spăr'tură] *nf* breach; *also fig* dissension, split.

spăşit [spă'shit] *adj* contrite, repentant.

spătar [spă'tar] *nn* back (of a chair).

spân [spân] *nm* glabrous man ‖ *adj* glabrous, smooth.

spânzura [spânzu'ra] *vt* (*pe cineva*) to hang smb; (*a agăţa*) to hang; (*într-un cârlig*) to hook; *coll* (*a cheltui*) to play ducks and drakes with ‖ *vi* to hang from ‖ *vr* to hang oneself.

spânzurătoare [spânzură'toare] *nf* gallows, gibbet.

special [spechi'al] *adj* special, particular; (*deosebit*) peculiar; specialized • **cursă ~ă** (*poştă*) special delivery; **în ~** especially, particularly ‖ *adv* especially, purposefully; (*dinadins*) on purpose • **ist** *nm/adj* specialist in, expert on • **~itate** *nf* speciality, specialization; (*branşă*) special subject; (*a studenţilor*) major (subject), main subject • **~a zilei** today's special • **~iza** *vr/vt* to specialize in, to make a special study of.

specie ['spechie] *nf* species; (*fel*) kind, type, variety • **~a umană** mankind.

specific [spe'chifik] *nn* specific character/nature; essential feature; *fig* share, portion ‖ *adj* (*pentru*) typical of ‖ *adv* specifically • **~a** *vt* to specify, to state definitely; to detail, to particularize • **~aţie** *nf* specification.

specimen [spechi'men] *nn* specimen; example, sample.

spectacol [spek'takol] *nn* performance; show; (*teatral*) play; (*măreţ*) pageant; *fig* spectacle, scene, sight.

spectaculos [spektaku'los] *adj* spectacular ‖ *adv* spectacularly ‖ *nn* spectacularity.

spectator [spekta'tor] *nm* spectator; *pl* (*la teatru*) audience, public; (*martor*) onlooker, bystander; witness.

spectral [spek'tral] *adj* spectral.

spectru ['spektru] *nn* spectrum; **~ solar** solar spectrum; (*fantomă*) specter, ghost, apparition.

specula [speku'la] *vt* (*mărfuri*) to speculate in; (*a profita de*) to profit by ‖ *vi* to speculate, to cogitate (on/about smth), to ponder over • **~nt** *nm* speculator, racketeer • **~ţie** *nf* (*asupra*) speculation, cogitation (upon/on); (*ipoteză*) hypothesis, theory; supposition.

speculă ['spekulă] *nf* speculation, racket, jobbing.

speluncă [spe'lunkă] *nf* den, dive.

speolog [speo'log] *nm* speleologist.

spera [spe'ra] *vt* to hope ‖ *vt* (*că*) to hope for/that • **~nţă** *nf* hope; (*aşteptare*) expectation; (*anticipare*) anticipation; (*încredere*) trust, confidence.

speria [speri'a] *vt* to scare, to frighten; (*a îngrozi*) to terrify, to horrify; to alarm; (*a face să tresară*) to startle ‖ *vr* to be/get scared; to be terrified, to be struck with horror; *coll* to get in a funk; (*a se alarma*) to be alarmed; (*a tresări*) to startle; (*d. cai*) to startle, to shy.

sperietoare [sperie'toare] *nf* fright; scarecrow.

sperios [speri'os] *adj* frightened, fearful; (*d. cai*) shy.

sperjur [sper'zhur] *nm* perjurer ‖ *nn* perjury.

spermă ['spermă] *nf* sperm, semen.

spetează [spe'tează] *nf* back (of a chair); *naut* (sail) arm; (*de fierăstrău*) saw handle; *text* crossbeam.

speti [spe'ti] *vt* (*a deşela*) to break the back of; (*a obosi*) to exhaust ‖ *vr* to break one's back (doing smth); to work oneself to death.

spic [spik] *nn* *bot* ear; *vernac* (*pisc*) peak.

spicher ['spiker] *nm* announcer • **~iţă** *nf* woman announcer.

spicuire [spiku'ire] *nf* gleaning; *pl* quotations.

spilcuit [spilku'it] *adj* *coll* dressed to the nines, just out of the bandbox.

spin [spin] *nm* (*pe tulpină*) thorn; (*pe coajă*) prickle; (*arici*) spine; (*scai*) thistle; *math, phys* spin.

spinare [spi'nare] *nf* back; (*a calului*) saddle back; (*de munte*) mountain crest/ridge; (*de val*) crest.

spinos [spi'nos] *adj* thorny, spiky; (*peşte*) spiny; *fig* hard, difficult; painful; delicate.

spinteca [spinte'ka] *vt* to rip (up/open); (*în două*) to cut asunder; (*a deschide*) to lay/slit/tear open; (*a despica*) to split; (*stâncă*) to fissure; (*pământul*) to crack ; (*cu forţa*) to cleave; (*a tăia*) to cut; (*peşte*) to gut; (*păsări*) to draw; (*a sfâşia*) to rend; (*aerul, valurile*) to cleave; (*cu braţele*) to saw the air; (*d. sunet*) to rend the air.

spion [spi'on] *nm* spy; secret agent; *tech* feeler gauge • **~a** *vt* to spy upon ‖ *vi* to (play the) spy; (*a se băga*) to pry (about) • **~j** *nn* espionage, spying.

spirală [spi'rală] *nf* spiral (line), volute; (*la ceas*) spiral (spring).

spiriduş [spiri'dush] *nm* elf, goblin, (*drăcuşor*) imp, little fiend.

spirit ['spirit] *nn* *also relig* spirit; (*suflet*) soul; (*opus materiei*) mind; intellect, wits; (*duh, fantomă*) ghost, specter; *coll* spook; (*spiriduş*) hobgoblin; (*fantomă*) phantom; (*umbră*) shadow; (*viziune*) vision; (*ingeniozitate*) ingenuity; (*duh*) *fig* wit, spirit; (*umor*) brilliancy; (*glumă*) joke, jest; (*joc de cuvinte*) pun; (*vioiciune*) briskness • **~ism** [spiri'tism] *nn* spiritism, necromancy • **~ual** *adj* spiritual; (*muzică*) sacred; (*eclesiastic*) ecclesiastical; (*cu simţul umorului*) witty; (*deştept*) clever; mental • **~ualitate** *nf* spirituality, spiritualness; intellectual/moral nature; *phil* intellectuality, intellectualness.

spirt [spirt] *nn* alcohol, spirits ‖ *adj* *fig* *coll* quick, agile.

spital [spi'tal] *nn* hospital; infirmary; **navă ~** hospital ship • **~iza** *vt* to hospitalize • **~izare** *nf* hospitalization.

spiţă ['spitsă] *nf* (*de roabă*) spoke (of a wheel); (*neam*) kin; race; (*descendenţă*) (line of) descendants; line, lineage, genealogy.

splendid ['splendid] *adj* splendid; (*măreţ*) magnificent; (*d. un amurg, o zi:* *strălucitor*) glorious, gorgeous; (*d. soare*) brilliant; (*minunat*) wonderful, excellent ‖ *adv* splendidly; wonderfully.

splendoare [splen'doare] *nf* splendor, glory; *lit* radiance, brightness.

splină ['splină] *nf* *anat* spleen; *icht* milt; (*mâncare*) beefbread; *bot* goldensaxifrage.

spoi [spo'i] *vt* to paint; (*a vărui*) to whitewash; (*a cositori*) to tin; (*a auri*) to gild; (*a arginta*) to silver; (*a polei*) to polish; (*a mânji*) to besmear; (*a machia*) to make up ‖ *vr coll* (*a se machia*) to fashion/polish oneself • **~ală** *nf* painting; (*văruială*) whitewashing; *coll* (*machiaj*) make-up; *fig* varnish, gloss; (*pospai*) smattering; *coll pej* (*cunoştinţe superficiale*) smack.

spondiloză [spondi'loză] *nf med* spondylosis.

spongios [spon'djios] *adj* spongy; foamy.

spontan [spon'tan] *adj* spontaneous; (*involuntar*) unwilling ‖ *adv* spontaneously • **~eitate** *nf* spontaneity.

spor¹ [spor] *nm bot* spore.

spor² [spor] *nn* efficiency; output; profit, benefit; progress, headway; (*prosperitate*) prosperity; (*belşug*) abundance; (*creştere*) growth; (*adaos*) addition; (*sporire*) increase.

sporadic [spo'radik] *adj* discontinuous, intermittent ‖ *adv* sporadically.

spori [spo'ri] *vt* to increase, to enhance; to step up; (*a înmulți*) to multiply, to accumulate ‖ *vi* to grow, to increase; (*a avea spor*) to make progress/headway; (*a se înmulți*) to multiply • **~re** *nf* increase, growth; multiplication; (*intensificare*) enhancement.

spornic ['spornik] *adj* efficient, productive, useful; *com* economical, advantageous; profitable, beneficial; (*harnic*) active, diligent; (*îmbelșugat*) abundant, plentiful.

sporovăi [sporovă'i] *vi* to prate, to prattle; (*a flecări*) to chatter • **~ală** *nf* prating, prattle; chatter(ing).

sport [sport] *nn* sport • **~iv** *nm* sportsman, athlete ‖ *adj* sport(ing), sportive • **~ivă** *nf* sportswoman • **~ivitate** *nf* sportsmanship, fair play.

spovedanie [spove'danie] *nf relig* confession (of sins).

spovedi [spove'di] *vt relig* to confess, to shrive ‖ *vr relig* to confess (one's sins); *fig* to open one's bosom, to confide one's secrets.

sprânceană [sprân'cheană] *nf* (eye)brow; *fig* (*culme*) top, summit; (*de deal*) brow; *fig* (*bucată*) piece; (*fâșie*) strap.

spre [spre] *prep* towards; to; ~ **vest** westwards; (*temporal*) against; (*pe la*) about, towards; ~ **ora trei** towards three o'clock; (*pentru*) with a view to, for; ~ **exemplu** for example, for instance.

sprijin ['sprizhin] *nn* support; prop; (*ajutor*) help, aid, assistance; protection • **~i** *vt* to support; (*a propti*) to prop up, to stay; to lean, to rest; *constr* to buttress; *fig* to back up, to endorse; (*moral*) to encourage, to countenance; (*verbal*) to advocate for; (*o rezoluție*) to second; *fig* (*cu argumente*) to buttress up by arguments ‖ *vr recip* to support each other; (*de/pe*) (*cineva*) to lean on smb; (*ceva*) (*pe orizontală*) to lean/rest on; (*pe coate*) to lean on one's elbows; (*pe verticală*) to lean against; *fig* to rely on, to lean upon (smb); (*a se întemeia pe*) to be grounded/based upon.

sprint [sprint] *nn sp* sprint • **~a** *vi sp* to sprint.

sprinten ['sprinten] *adj* agile, nimble, lithe; brisk; (*d. mers*) jaunty; quick; (*vioi*) lively, sprightly; *coll* clean, clever ‖ *adv* quick, nimbly, lightly.

sprințar [sprin'tsar] *adj* sprightly, lively, frisky; (*jucăuș*) playful; (*cochet*) skittish; (*nestatornic*) fickle; (*ușuratic*) wanton.

spulbera [spulbe'ra] *vt* to sweep (off/away); (*a risipi*) to scatter; *fig* to dispel, to dissipate; (*speranțe*) to shatter; (*a distruge*) to ruin, to destroy; (*un mit*) to debunk ‖ *vr* to go up in smoke, to be shattered.

spumă ['spumă] *nf* foam, spume; (*albă*) froth; (*murdară*) scum; (*de bere*) head; (*de săpun*) (soap)suds; (*pt. bărbierit*) lather.

spumega [spume'ga] *vi* to foam; *fig* to foam at the mouth.

spumos [spu'mos] *adj* foamy, frothy; (*d. vin*) sparkling.

spune ['spune] *vt* to say; (*cuiva*) to tell; to relate; (*din nou*) to reiterate; (*a rosti*) to utter; to recite; to declare, to state, to assert; (*a explica*) to explain; *fig* (*a ~ baliverne*) to tell stories; **a ~ da/nu** to say yes/no; (*a numi*) to name, to call; (*a denunța*) to denounce ‖ *vr* to be said.

spurcat [spur'kat] *adj* unclean, dirty, foul.

sst [sst] *interj* hush!, hist!.

sta [sta] *vi* (*în picioare*) to stand, to be about; (*pe vârfuri*) to stand on tiptoe; (*așezat*) to sit; (*la masă*)

to be (seated) at the table; (*ghemuit*) to lie low; (*a se afla*) to lie; (*a rămâne pe loc*) to stay; (*a ~ locului*) to stay put; (*a locui*) to live; (*a se opri*) to stop (short).

stabil [sta'bil] *adj* stable, steady, firm; durable, (long)-lasting; permanent; solid; (*d. prețuri*) steady; (*d. vreme*) settled.

stabili [stabi'li] *vt* to establish, to prove; to set out/down; (*a fixa*) to determine, to settle; (*a institui*) to create, to lay down; (*a se aranja*) to arrange; (*a regla*) to regulate; (*a decreta*) to decree; (*a înființa*) to set up; (*a realiza*) to draw up, to work out; (*a afla*) to find out; (*a verifica*) to verify ‖ *vr* (*a se așeza într-un loc*) to settle (down); (*a se înființa*) to be founded/established.

stabiliment [stabili'ment] *nn* establishment; (*clădire*) premises.

stabilitate [stabili'tate] *nf* stability, constancy; *fig* steadfastness, steadiness; permanence, persistence.

stabiliza [stabili'za] *vt* (*moneda*) to stabilize, to steady ‖ *vr* to be stabilized.

stacană [sta'kană] *nf* tankard, mug.

stadion [stadi'on] *nn* stadium; sports ground.

stadiu ['stadiu] *nn* stage, phase, period.

stafidă [sta'fidă] *nf* raisin; (*fără sâmbure*) sultana; (*mică*) currant; plum.

stafidi [stafi'di] *vr* to dry (up); *fig* to shrivel, to shrink, to dwindle.

stafie [sta'fie] *nf* ghost, phantom; (*apariție*) apparition; (*umbră*) shadow.

stagiar [stadji'ar] *nm* trainee, probationer ‖ *adj* (period of) probation/instruction; training (period).

stagiu ['stadju] *nn* probation/instruction/training period; training course; (*al unui profesor*) teaching practice; (*al unei infirmiere*) probationary period; (*vechime*) seniority, length of service.

stagiune [stadji'une] *nf* (theatrical) season.

stagna [stag'na] *vi* (*d. apă, comerț*) to stagnate, to clog; *fig* (*a lâncezi*) to slacken, to languish; (*a se opri*) to come to a standstill/deadlock; (*a nu curge*) to stop flowing; to flag • **~re** *nf* stagnation, slack time; standstill, stop(page); (*oprire*) cessation; (*lipsă de acțiune*) inaction, suspension; (*a afacerilor*) lull.

stai [stai] *interj* halt!; ~ **pe loc!** stay put!, hold it!.

stal [stal] *nn thea* stalls; (*în expoziție*) stand.

stalactită [stalak'tită] *nf geol* stalactite.

stalagmită [stalag'mită] *nf geol* stalagmite.

stamină [sta'mină] *nf bot* stamen.

stand [stand] *nn* stall, stand; * **stal**.

standard ['standard] *nn* standard, norm ‖ *adj* standard-(ized); *constr* prefabricated • **~iza** *vt* to standardize, to normalize.

staniol [stani'ol] *nn* tinfoil.

staniu ['staniu] *nn chem* tinfoil.

star [star] *nn cin, sp* star; *naut* two-seat sports boat.

stare ['stare] *nf* (*situație*) situation, state, condition; (*proastă*) predicament, plight; (*poziție socială*) social status/standing; (*dispoziție*) mood, frame of mind; (*avere*) wealth; estate, (*mare*) (large) fortune, comfortable position; class, standing; *hist* estate; (*ședere*) remaining, stay(ing); (*poziție*) position; (*repaus*) rest, repose; (*în picioare*) standing; **în ~ bună** in good order/condition, (*d. o casă*) in good repair; (*d. un vapor*) seaworthy; (*d. un sportiv*) in good shape; **în ~ proastă** out of repair/order.

stareț ['starets] *nm* abbot, superior • ~**ă** *nf* abbess, lady superior.

start ['start] *nn* start.

stat¹ [stat] *nn pol* government, state.

stat² [stat] *nn* list; ~ **de salarii** payroll, paylist, paysheet.

stat³ [stat] *nn* (*faptul de a sta*) standing; (*rămânere*) staying, remaining; (*oprire*) stopping; (*statură*) stature, figure; (*înălțime*) height.

static ['statik] *adj* static.

statistic [sta'tistik] *adj* statistical • ~**ă** *nf* (*știință*) statistics; (*dată*) statistic.

stativ [sta'tiv] *nn* stand.

statornic [sta'tornik] *adj* constant, steady, steadfast; firm, unshaken; invariable, permanent; (*stabil*) stable, lasting ‖ *adv* constantly, steadily, invariably.

statornici [statorni'chi] *vt* to settle, to fix, to determine ‖ *vr* (*într-un loc*) to settle (down), to take up one's abode/residence; (*a se întemeia*) to be founded/established.

statuetă [statu'etă] *nf* statuette.

statuie [sta'tuie] *nf* statue.

statură [sta'tură] *nf* stature, figure, height.

statut [sta'tut] *nn* statute, ordinance; by-law, rule(s), regulations; (*situație*) condition, status • ~**ar** *adj* statutory.

stație ['statsie] *nf also rail* station; (*finală*) terminus; (*de metrou*) subway station; (*de tramvai, autobuz*) stop; (*de taxi*) taxi rank; (*de birje*) (coach/cab/taxi) stand; (*popas*) halting/resting place; halt; *obs* (*loc de oprire a diligenței*) stage; (*de benzină*) gas station.

staționa [statsio'na] *vi* (*d. trupe*) to be stationed; (*d. mașini*) to stand; (*a se opri*) to stop, to pull up.

stațiune [statsi'une] *nf* station; (*de recreere*) resort.

staul ['staul] *nn* cow house, stable; stall/shed for cattle.

stavilă ['stavilă] *nf* weir, *fig* obstacle, hindrance, opposition.

stăpân [stă'pân] *nm also fig* master; owner, landlord, proprietor; (*patron*) employer, *coll* boss; (*suveran*) sovereign, lord; (*conducător*) ruler • ~**ă** *nf* mistress of the house; (*proprietăreasă*) landlady • ~**i** *vt* to master; (*a conduce*) to rule over, to govern; (*d. regi*) to be the sovereign/king of; (*tiranic*) to rule with an iron rod; (*despotic*) to dominate over; *fig* (*a stăvili*) to suppress; to control, to keep in check; to hold/keep back; (*a potoli*) to calm down; (*a depăși*) to overcome; (*a poseda*) to possess, to own; (*a se bucura de*) to enjoy; (*a ocupa*) to occupy; (*a ști*) to master; (*o limbă*) to have a thorough command of ‖ *vi* to rule, to reign, to govern; (*a predomina*) to reign, to prevail; (*a bântui*) to rage ‖ *vr* to be master of oneself, to keep one's temper • ~**ire** *nf* mastership, mastery; (*dominare*) domination, dominion; reign, rule; sovereignty; command; (*posesiune*) possession, ownership; (*asociată*) condominium; (*de sine*) self-possession/-control; *obs* government, the authorities.

stărui [stăru'i] *vi* to insist on (smth / doing smth), to persist in (one's claims); (*asupra unui fapt*) to dwell on, to lay stress on a fact; to persevere; to continue; (*a dura*) to endure, to last; to exist; (*în ciuda obstacolelor*) to subsist; (*a zăbovi*) to linger • ~**nță** *nf* insistence, persistence; (*asiduitate*) perseverance; (*răbdare*) patience; (*silință*) diligence; *fig* (*intervenție*) intercession, mediation.

stătător [stătă'tor] *adj* (*d. apă*) stagnant; (*stabil*) stable;

(*care stă în același loc*) stationary, steady; fixed; (*permanent*) standing.

stătut [stă'tut] *adj* stuffy, close; (*d. apă*) foul; (*mucegăit*) musty, moldy; rancid, rank; *fig* (*d. cineva*) aged, old.

stăvilar [stavi'lar] *nn* dam, weir; (*în port*) (harbor) boom; (*ecluză*) lock, sluice.

stăvili [stăvi'li] *vt* to dam (in/off/up), to embank; *fig* (*a înăbuși*) to stifle, to strangle; to quell, to put down; (*a reține*) to hold back, to check; to calm; (*a întârzia*) to delay; (*a încetini*) to slack(en); (*a bloca*) to block; (*a bara*) to bar, to obstruct; (*a împiedica*) to prevent (from), to preclude; (*a opri*) to stop, to arrest.

stâlci [stâl'chi] *vt* (*a bate*) to beat, to pommel; (*rău*) to beat black and blue; (*cu pumnii*) to cuff, to punch; (*cu bățul*) to thrash with a stick, to drub; (*a zdrobi*) to crush; *coll* to squash, to squelch; (*a schilodi*) to mutilate, to cripple; (*o limbă*) to mangle; to murder; (*un text, un cuvânt*) to corrupt; *coll* to bungle, to spoil; (*muzica*) to massacre; (*a denatura*) to distort, to pervert.

stâlp [stâlp] *nn* pillar, pole, stake; (*de poartă*) post, jamb; (*de pod*) pier; (*pilastru*) pilaster, column; (*în mine*) prop; (*de lemn*) (upright) wooden pillar; support, stud, stanchion; (*lateral*) side post; (*indicator*) signpost; *sp* goalpost; (*rugby*) prop forward; *fig* supporter, pillar; (*susținător*) adherent; (*d. o persoană*) (*al bisericii*) staunch supporter.

stână ['stână] *nf* sheepfold, pen.

stâncă ['stâncă] *nf also fig* rock, boulder; (*mică*) rocklet; (*artificială*) rockery; (*ascuțită*) crag; (*abruptă*) bluff; (*pisc*) tor; (*bloc de* ~) large piece of rock; (*faleză*) cliff; (*recif*) reef.

stâncos [stân'kos] *adj* rocky, craggy; (*plin de stânci*) full of rocks; (*ca stânca*) rock-like; (*colțuros*) craggy • **Munții Stâncoși** the Rocky Mountains, *coll* the Rockies.

stâng [stâng] *nn* left leg; *fig* wrong leg ‖ *adj* left • **partea** ~**ă** left side/hand; (*heraldică*) sinister; *thea* prompt side; *naut* port; (*a râului*) left bank; *pol* left(-wing) • ~**a** *nf* the left hand; the left (side); **la** ~ (*spre*) to the left; (*pe*) on the left; *mil* left turn!; *pol* the left • ~**aci** *nm* left-handed person; *fig* lubber, botcher, bungler ‖ *adj* left-handed; clumsy, gauche; *coll* gawky; awkward; bungling ‖ *adv* clumsily, awkwardly • ~**ăcie** *nf* leftness; clumsiness, awkwardness, gaucherie; (*ca act*) blunder; lubberliness.

stânjeneală [stânzhe'neală] *nf* uneasiness, embarrassment; (*piedică*) hindrance, obstacle; disturbance; inconvenience.

stânjenel [stânzhe'nel] *nm bot* iris.

stânjeni [stânzhe'ni] *vt* (*a jena*) to embarrass, to inconvenience; (*a deranja*) to disturb, to trouble; (*a întrerupe*) to interrupt; (*a împiedica*) to hinder, to prevent; *recip* to embarrass each other • ~**t** *adj* uncomfortable, embarrassed.

stârc [stârk] *nm orn* heron.

stârni [stâr'ni] *vt* to (a)rouse; (*a ațâța*) to incite, to stir (up), to provoke; (*dubii*) to raise; (*pasiuni*) to loose; (*interesul cuiva*) to tickle smb's interest; (*a mișca*) to remove; (*a deplasa*) to displace; (*a trezi*) to wake up ‖ *vr* (*d. cineva*) to fly into a rage; (*d. o furtună*) to break (out/forth); (*a apărea*) to appear, to rise.

stârpi [stâr'pi] *vt* to uproot, to eradicate, to destroy, to exterminate; (*a desființa*) to abolish ‖ *vr* to be uprooted, etc; (*d. femei*) *vernac* to become barren.

stârpitură [stârpi'tură] *nf* dwarf, midget; Lilliputian; monster.

stârv [stârv] *nn* carrion, carcass; *pej* (putrid/decaying) carcass.

stea [stea] *nf astron* star; *(mică)* starlet; **~ua polară** the Northern Star, the pole star; *fig* one's lodestar; *thea, cin* (movie) star; *(destin)* fate, destiny; *(pe fruntea unui cal)* (white) blaze, white face/star; *fig* remarkable, prominent; *(pe unghie)* white (spot on the fingernail); *coll* sweetheart; *typ* asterisk; *mil* pip, braid.

steag [steag] *nn* (national) flag; **~ul american** the stars and stripes, the star spangled banner; **a arbora un ~** to hoist a flag; *also mil* colors; *(drapel) also fig* banner; *(stindard)* standard; *naut* pavilion; *(mic)* pennant; *(al cavalerilor, purtat în vârf de lance)* lance pennon.

stegar [ste'gar] *nm* standard-/color-bearer.

stejar [ste'zhar] *nm* oak (tree); **~ verde** evergreen oak, holm oak.

stelar [ste'lar] *adj* stellary, starry, star.

stemă ['stemă] *nf* (coat of) arms, escutcheon, armorial bearings; *(coroană)* crown; *(diademă)* diadem.

stenograf(ă) [steno'graf(ă)] *nm/nf* stenographer.

stenografia [stenografi'a] *vt* to take down in shorthand.

step [step] *nn* tap dancing.

stepă ['stepă] *nf* steppe.

stereofonic [stereo'fonik] *adj* stereophonic.

stereotip [stereo'tip] *adj typ* stereotype; *(d. o ediție)* stereotyped; *fig* cliché, trite ‖ *nn* stereotype plate.

steril [ste'ril] *adj* sterile; barren; infertile; *also fig* fruitless; * **sterp** ‖ *nn* barren gangue.

steriliza [sterili'za] *vt* to sterilize; *(un animal)* to neuter.

stern [stern] *nn anat* breastbone.

sterp [sterp] *adj* barren; sterile; childless; infertile; *also fig* fruitless; unprofitable; *(viață)* useless.

stetoscop [steto'skop] *nn med* stethoscope.

steward(esă) ['stiuard(esă)] *nm/nf* flight attendant.

sticlar [stik'lar] *nm* glassmaker, glassblower; *(geamgiu)* glazier.

sticlă ['stiklă] *nf* *(material)* glass; *(pt. ferestre)* window glass; *(pt. oglinzi)* plate glass; *(ochi de geam)* window pane; *(de lampă)* lamp chimney; *(recipient)* bottle; *(pt. experiențe chimice)* flask; *med (flacon)* vial; *(de murături)* pickle bottle; *(conținutul sticlei)* bottle(ful); *pl (ochelari)* glasses, spectacles.

sticlete [stik'lete] *nm orn* thistlefinch; *fig* policeman, cop.

stigmat [stig'mat] *nn* brand, stigma; mark (with an iron); *(cicatrice)* scar; *fig* stain, blemish; *(urmă)* mark, spot • **~iza** *vt* to mark with an iron; *coll* to badge; *fig* to stigmatize, to brand, to sear.

stih [stih] *nn lit* verse, line, *pl* verses, lines; *relig* verse.

stihie [sti'hie] *nf (fenomen al naturii)* element; Nature; wilderness; solitude; class; *(spectru)* specter, ghost.

stil [stil] *nn lit* style; *(mod)* manner, way; **în ~ul** in the style of, after the manner of • **~at** *adj* stylish; (highly) polished, refined; *(bine-crescut)* well-bred; *(instruit)* well-schooled/trained (in), educated.

stilet [sti'let] *nn* stilet(to), short pointed dagger; *med* stylet, probe.

stilist [sti'list] *nm* stylist, accomplished writer.

stilou [sti'lou] *nn* fountain pen; *(cu pastă)* ball(-point) pen.

stima [sti'ma] *vt* to esteem, to respect; *(f. mult)* to revere, to have a high opinion of; *(a aprecia)* to value,

to prize • **~bil** *nm* honorable ‖ *adj* honorable, estimable, worthy of respect • **~t** *adj* esteemed, respected, revered.

stimă ['stimă] *nf* esteem, regard, respect; **cu ~** *(în scrisori)* yours truly/faithfully/respectfully.

stimul ['stimul] *nm med* stimulus, *pl* stimuli • **~a** *vt* to stimulate; *(pofta)* to whet; *also fig* to activate, to energize; *coll* to kindle, to fillip; *(a îndemna)* to spur, to incite; *(a încuraja)* to encourage; *(afacerile)* to give a stimulus to; *(a învior a)* to cheer, to enliven • **~ator** *nm chem* growth promoter; **~ cardiac** pacemaker • **~ent** *nn* incentive, stimulus, spur; *(solicitare)* challenge; *med* stimulant.

stindard [stin'dard] *nn* standard, banner, * **steag.**

stingător [stingă'tor] *nn* fire extinguisher.

stinge ['stindje] *vt (focul, lumina)* to put out, to extinguish; *(o lumânare)* to blow out; *elec* to switch/turn off; *(a acoperi)* to quench; *(gazul)* to turn off; *(un furnal)* to draw the fires of a furnace; **a ~ un incendiu** to put out a fire, to fight down a fire; **a-și ~ setea** to quench/slake/allay one's thirst; *(a reduce la tăcere)* to reduce to silence, to hush; *fig (a calma)* to appease, to allay; *(un sunet)* to muffle; *fig (a șterge)* to blot out, to efface; *(a anula)* to cancel; *fig (a extermina)* to eradicate; *(a distruge)* to destroy ‖ *vr (d. foc)* to burn out; *(d. foc, lumină)* to die/go out; *(d. o candelă)* to sputter out; *(a se întuneca)* to grow dark/dim; *(d. culori)* to fade; *(d. sunet)* to die down/away; *fig (de dor)* to pine/languish away; *(a muri)* to die; *(a dispărea)* to be over/gone/dead; *(d. o familie)* to become extinct; *(d. plante)* to wither; *fig (a fi în declin)* to be on the decline.

stingher [stin'ger] *adj (desperecheat)* odd, incomplete; only one; alien; *(și necăsătorit)* single; *(singuratic)* lonely, solitary; *(izolat)* isolated • **~eală** *nf (jenă)* embarrassment, uneasiness • **~i** *vt (a jena)* to inconvenience, to embarrass; *(a deranja)* to disturb, to trouble; *(a întrerupe)* to interrupt; *(a împiedica)* to hinder, to impede.

stinghie ['stingie] *nf* perch, pole, rod; *(subțire)* lath, slat; *(pt. găini)* roost; *anat* groin.

stipendia [stipendi'a] *vt* to stipend, to subsidize, to grant financial aid to; to support; to keep in one's pay.

stipula [stipu'la] *vt* to stipulate, to lay down; to provide for/that • **~ție** *nf* stipulation, provision.

stivă ['stivă] *nf* stack, pile, heap.

stivui [stivu'i] *vt* to heap/stack/pile up (books); *tech* to staple; to layer.

stoarce ['stoarche] *vt (lichid din ceva)* to squeeze out; *(prin presare)* to press (out/forth); *(prin zdrobire)* to crush out; *(rufe, prin răsucire)* to wring; *fig (a epuiza)* to wear out; *(a sărăci)* to eat up, to deplete; **a-și ~ creierii** to rack one's brains; *fig (a obține) (bani)* to squeeze (money) out of smb; *coll (a jecmăni)* to fleece, to bleed white; *(lacrimi)* to squeeze/wring tears from smb.

stoc [stok] *nn* stock(pile), supply, store; *(fond)* fund; *(rezervă)* reserve • **~a** *vt* to stock(pile), to store, to hoard.

stofă ['stofă] *nf also fig* stuff, fabric, (woven) material, cloth; *(pt. costum)* suiting.

stog [stog] *nn* rick, stack; *(de fân)* haystack, hayrick.

stoic [stoik] *nm* stoic, disciple of Zeno ‖ *adj* stoical ‖ *adv* stoically • **~ism** *nn* stoicism, endurance.

stol [stol] *nn orn* (*de păsări*) bevy, flock, flight; (*de potârnichi*) covey; (*de insecte*) cloud; **în ~uri** in flocks/throngs; (*mulţime*) throng, multitude; (*ceată*) troop; (*de fete*) band; (*de inamici*) host.

stomac [sto'mak] *nn* stomach, *coll* tummy; (*în limbajul boxerilor*) bread basket; **boală de ~** stomach complaint; *frml* gastropathy; (*la animale*) maw; (*primul ~ al rumegătoarelor*) first stomach of ruminants, paunch; (*al doilea ~*) honeycomb (stomach), bonnet; (*al treilea ~*) manyplies; (*al patrulea ~*) rennet bag; (*la păsări*) gizzard.

stomatolog [stomato'log] *nm* stomatologist • **~gie** *nf* stomatology.

stop [stop] *nn* traffic light(s); (*roşu*) stop (sign), red light; (*la maşini*) stop/brake light; (*în telegrame*) stop ‖ *interj* stop!; **~ cardiac** *med* cardiac arrest (*în telegrame*) stop; *interj* stop! • **~a** *vt* to stop; (*o stofă, ciorapi*) to close, to fine darn ‖ *vi* to stop, to pull up; to come to a stop.

stor [stor] *nn* (roller/Venetian) blind, sunblind, shade; (*în exterior*) awning.

strabism [stra'bism] *nn med* strabism(us), anorthopia.

strachină ['strakină] *nf* dish, basin, bowl; (*adâncă*) tureen.

stradă ['stradă] *nf* street; (*mică*) short/narrow street; (*alee*) lane, alley; (*largă*) avenue; (*înfundată*) dead end, blind alley.

strajă ['strazhă] *nf mil* (*santinelă*) sentry, sentinel; (*patrulă*) patrol; (*pază*) watch, guard; *fig* shield, protection; *naut* ridge rope ‖ *vt* (*ca santinelă*) to stand sentry.

strană ['strană] *nf* (*pt. public*) pew; (*pt. dascăli, cântăreţi*) lectern.

strangula [strangu'la] *vt* to strangle; *tech* to throttle • **~re** *nf* strangling, strangulation; *tech* throttling; constriction, narrowing (of smth); (*a râurilor*) narrow part; (*a străzii*) bottleneck.

straniu ['straniu] *adj* strange, weird, odd, bizarre; peculiar; (*neobişnuit*) unusual; (*sinistru*) uncanny ‖ *adv* strangely, weirdly, oddly.

strapontină [strapon'tină] *nf thea* flap/bracket seat; (*în maşină*) cricket seat.

stras [stras] *nn* rhinestone, shinestone, imitated diamond.

straşnic ['strashnik] *adj* terrible; severe, stern, rigorous; (*aspru*) harsh; (*oribil*) horrible, dreadful; excessive, extreme; violent; (*minunat*) excellent; *coll* great, cool; considerable; (*colosal*) tremendous; sound, solid; (*măreţ*) magnificent ‖ *adv* severely; terribly, awfully; wonderfully.

strat [strat] *nn geol* seam, stratum, *pl* strata; (*de unt*) layer; (*de vopsea*) coat(ing); *fig* (social) stratum; section; (*de flori*) bed.

stratagemă [strata'djemă] *nf mil* stratagem; *fig* ruse, maneuvre, masterstroke; (*truc*) trick.

strategic [stra'tedjik] *adj* strategic ‖ *adv* strategically.

strategie [strate'djie] *nf* strategy.

stratifica [stratifi'ka] *vt/vr* to stratify • **~re/ţie** *nf* stratification, bedding.

străbate [stră'bate] *vt* (*a parcurge*) to cover, to traverse; (*a cutreiera*) to wander/roam/rove through; (*a merge prin*) to go through/over; (*a pătrunde*) to pierce, to go through, * **străpunge**.

străbun [stră'bun] *nm* ancestor, forefather; *pl* progenitors, ancestry ‖ *adj* ancient, antique; ancestors', fore-

fathers' • **~ic** *nm* great-grandfather • **~ică** *nf* great-grandmother • **~ici** *nm pl* great-grandparents.

strădanie [stră'danie] *nf* endeavor, effort, strain, pains.

strădui [strădu'i] *vr* to strive to do smth, to do one's best, to endeavor, to take (great) pains (to).

străduinţă [strădu'intsă] *nf* * **strădanie**.

străfulgera [străfuldje'ra] *vi* to flash (through one's mind); (*a-şi da seama*) to dawn on smb.

străfund [stră'fund] *nn* also *pl* innermost depths.

străin [stră'in] *nm* foreigner; (*necunoscut*) stranger ‖ *adj* (*din altă ţară*) foreign; (*necunoscut*) unknown, unfamiliar; (*de altă natură*) alien, strange; (*ciudat*) odd; *med* heterogenous • **~ătate** *nf* foreign countries; foreign/strange land; **în ~** abroad; **din ~** from abroad.

străluci [strălu'chi] *vi* to shine; (*a arunca raze*) to beam; (*d. ochi, bijuterii*) to gleam; (*a scânteia*) to sparkle, to flash; to scintillate; (*d. stele*) to twinkle, to glitter; (*d. faţă, jar*) to glow; (*d. metale*) to glisten; to gleam; (*d. apă, lumânare*) to glimmer; (*d. lună, satin*) to shimmer; (*d. faruri*) to glare; (*a fi luminat*) to be bright; (*a lumina*) to light; (*ca fulgerul, focul*) to blaze out, to flare; (*brusc*) to glance; (*orbitor*) to dazzle; *fig* (*d. cineva*) to be conspicuous • **~re** *nf* brilliance, vividness; glitter, luster; (*slabă*) glow; (*metalică*) glint; **fără ~** dull, lusterless; lackluster; *fig* magnificence, brilliance • **~t** *adj also fig* brilliant; sparkling, * **străluci**; splendid, gorgeous ‖ *adv* brilliantly, splendidly • **~tor** *adj* brilliant, radiant, beaming (with); splendid, gorgeous, * **străluci**.

strămoş [stră'mosh] *nm* ancestor, forefather, great-grandfather; *pl also* forebears, ancestors.

strănepoată [stråne'poată] *nf* great-granddaughter.

strănepot [stråne'pot] *nm* great-grandson.

strănut [stră'nut] *nn* sneeze • **~a** *vi* to sneeze.

străpunge [stră'pundje] *vt* to pierce, to go/pass through; (*hârtia, cu un ac*) to prick, to puncture; (*a perfora*) to drill, to bore (a hole); (*a înjunghia*) to stab; (*cu lancea*) to transfix; (*cu baioneta*) to bayonet; *fig* to break through.

strávechi [stră'veki] *adj* ancient, old, antique.

străveziu [stråve'ziu] *adj* transparent, translucent, clear; *fig* obvious.

strâmb [strâmb] *adj* crooked; curved, twisted; bent, buckled; (*înclinat*) slanting, askew; *fig* wrong, false; warped ‖ *adv* crookedly, obliquely, slantwise; *fig* falsely, unjustly; wrongly, mistakenly • **~a** *vt* to crook; *also fig* to distort; (*gura, tocurile*) to twist; (*a curba*) to curve; (*a îndoi*) to bend, to buckle ‖ *vr* (*a deveni strâmb*) to become/get crooked/bent/lopsided; (*a face o grimasă*) to make a wry face.

strâmt [strâmt] *adj* (*îngust*) narrow; (*d. spaţiu*) cramped, confined; (*mic*) small; (*strâns*) tight, close; (*d. haine*) skimpy, tight(-fitting); *fig* (*mărginit*) ~ **la minte** narrow-minded • **~a** *vt* to (make) narrow; to make tight(er); (*hainele*) to take in; to reduce, to diminish ‖ *vr* to get narrow/tight; (*d. haine: a intra la apă*) to shrink; to be reduced; (*a se micşora*) to diminish.

strâmtoare [strâm'toare] *nf* (*defileu*) gorge(s); *naut* straits, narrows; *fig* tight spot; (*încurcătură*) embarrassment; (*constrângere*) constraint; (*neplăcere*) awkwardness; scrape, quandary; (*bănească*) straitened circumstances; (*necaz*) trouble; *coll* mess, fix; **la ~** high and dry; **a fi la ~** to be cramped for room; *fig* to be in a tight spot.

strâmtorat [strâmto'rat] *adj* hard-up, in need.

strângător [strângă'tor] *adj* economical, thrifty, sparing ‖ *nm* collector, gatherer; thrifty person.

strânge ['strândje] *vt* (*a înşuruba, a fixa*) to tighten; (*o velă*) to furl; (*un şurub*) to screw up; (*d. pumn, dinţi*) to clench (one's fist/teeth); (*d. sprâncene*) to knit (one's brows); (*a apăsa*) to squeeze; (*a comprima*) to compress; (*a înăbuşi*) to stifle; (*în mână*) to grasp smth; (*în braţe*) to clasp in one's arms; **a ~ mâna** to shake smb's hand; (*a aduna, a scurta*) to fold; to press close together; *mil* to close (ranks); (*a împături*) to fold/make up; (*a strâmta hainele*) to take in; (*a contracta*) to shrink; (*a micşora*) to reduce, to diminish; (*a restrânge*) to restrain; (*a retrage*) to draw in/back; (*a aduna*) to gather; (*a recolta*) to harvest; (*a culege*) to pick up; (*cu greu*) to glean; (*la un loc*) to bring together; to assemble; (*a acumula*) to hoard; (*a colecţiona*) to collect; (*mărfuri, în magazin*) to store; (*bani, fonduri, impozite*) to raise; (*a economisi*) to save; (*a pune în ordine*) to put in order; (*a întări*) to strengthen; (*d. pantofi*) to pinch ‖ *vr* (*a se aduna*) to gather, to assemble; *mil* to concentrate; (*într-un punct*) to converge; (*a se înghesui*) to crowd; (*laolaltă*) to band together; (*unii lângă alţii*) to huddle together; (*lângă cineva*) to snuggle up to smb, to cling close to smb; (*a se ghemui*) to crouch; (*d. lichide*) to freeze; (*d. lapte*) to curdle; (*d. haine, stofă*) to shrink ‖ *vi* (*a apăsa*) to press.

strânsoare [strân'soare] *nf* grip; pressure; (*constrângere*) restraint; constraint; strictness; * **înghesuială**.

streaşină ['streashină] *nf* eave(s); window roof; (*jgheab*) gutter; (*creasta unui zid*) coping.

strecura [streku'ra] *vt* (*lichide*) to strain, to filter; to sift, to screen; (*făină*) to bolt; (*a scurge*) to drain; (*a spăla*) to wash; (*a lăsa să treacă*) to let pass; (*a furişa cu greu*) to squeeze in/out; (*o vorbă*) to put in edgewise; (*un bilet*) to slip ‖ *vr* to filter (in); to glide, to creep; (*a pătrunde în*) to penetrate (into); (*d. lichide*) to seep (through), to trickle through; (*a se furişa*) to steal/sneak away/in/out/by, to slip by; (*cu greu*) to squeeze past/through/in/out; *fig* (*d. neîncredere, frică*) to creep into; (*neobservat*) to slip away; (*d. greşeli*) to slip in.

strecurătoare [strekură'toare] *nf* strainer, colander; (*sită*) riddle.

stres [stres] *nn* stress.

striat [stri'at] *adj* ridged.

strica [stri'ka] *vt* to spoil, to mar; to injure, to damage; to deteriorate; (*a distruge*) to destroy, to ruin; (*o clădire*) to pull down; (*cu lovituri*) to batter; (*a polua*) to pollute; to vitiate; (*a nimici*) to wreck; (*a sparge*) to break (to pieces); (*a sfărâma*) to crush; (*a dezorganiza*) to disorganize; (*a frustra*) to dash; (*a corupe*) to corrupt ‖ *vr* to deteriorate, to go bad; (*d. dinţi*) to decay; (*a putrezi*) to rot; (*a nu funcţiona*) to break down; (*d. ceasuri*) to go wrong; to be out of order; (*moral*) to become corrupted ‖ *vi* (*a face rău*) to harm, to hurt; (*a aduce prejudicii*) to prejudice • ~**t** *adj* spoilt, spoiled, * **strica**; damaged, broken; marred; (*putred*) rotten; (*d. carne*) tainted; (*mucegăit*) moldy; (*d. pâine*) stale; (*d. aer*) polluted; (*d. apă*) foul; (*d. persoane*) corrupt; (*imoral*) unchaste; (*depravat*) debauched; (*d. un copil*) vicious ‖ *adv* badly ‖ *nm* debauchee, rake.

stricăciune [strică'chiune] *nf* (*vătămare*) harm, damage;

(*deteriorare*) deterioration; *pl* damage; (*corupţie*) corruption, immorality.

stricnină [strik'nină] *nf* strychnine.

strict [strikt] *adj* strict; (*d. cineva*) severe, rigid, exact • ~**ul necesar** *nn* no more than is necessary, the bare necessities • ~**eţe** *nf* strictness, severity, rigor, exactness.

strident [stri'dent] *adj* strident, shrill, jarring; (*d. culori*) loud, garish; (*d. voce*) piercing; *fig* (*flagrant*) blatant ‖ *adv* stridently, shrilly; *fig* blatantly.

stridie ['stridie] *nf zool* oyster.

striga [stri'ga] *vt* to call ‖ *vi* to call (out), to cry, to shout; (*a ridica vocea*) to raise one's voice; (*puternic*) (*de bucurie*) to roar; (*vociferând*) to clamor, to bellow; (*a ţipa*) to shriek, to scream; (*a zbiera*) to yell, to howl.

strigăt ['strigăt] *nn* call, cry, shout, yell, * **striga.**

strigoi [stri'goi] *nm* ghost, phantom; (*vrăjitor*) wizard.

stringent [strin'djent] *adj* urgent, acute; pressing.

striptease ['striptiz] *nn* striptease; **persoană care face ~** stripper.

strivi [stri'vi] *vt also fig* to crush; (*ceva moale*) to squash, to bruise; (*d. o cutie*) to flatten out; (*d. o clădire*) to dwarf; (*d. o maşină*) to run (smb/smth) down; **a ~ în picioare** to trample under foot; (*a distruge*) to destroy; (*a copleşi*) to (over)whelm ‖ *vr recip* to crush one another; (*d. avioane: a se zdrobi*) to crash.

strofă ['strofă] *nf lit* stanza, verse, strophe.

strop [strop] *nm* drop; *fig* (*cantitate mică*) whit, jot, bit; sip; **~ cu ~** drop by drop; (*de culoare*) spot/splash; (*pată*) speck, fleck.

stropi [stro'pi] *vt* to sprinkle (with); (*florile*) to water; (*a păta*) to (be)smear ‖ *vi* (*d. foc: a împroşca*) to sputter ‖ *vr* (*a se murdări*) to smear one's clothes • ~**toare** *nf* (watering) can.

structura [struktu'ra] *vt* to structure, to organize.

structură [struk'tură] *nf* structure.

strugure ['strugure] *nm* (bunch/cluster of) grapes; *pl* grapes.

strună ['strună] *nf* (*coardă*) string, cord; (*de arc*) bow string; (*de maţ*) catgut, catling; (*la cal*) bit; *med* whitlow, felon; (*frâu*) bridle, rein; *fig* (*linie dreaptă*) straight line.

strung [strung] *nn* lathe • ~**ar** *nm* turner, lathe operator.

strungă ['strungă] *nf* pen, sheepfold; (*poartă*) wicket, turnstile; *geog* gorge, ravine; (*deschizătură*) opening; (*spărtură*) breach.

struni [stru'ni] *vt* (*d. un cal*) to bridle; *fig* to curb, to restrain, to control, to keep in check.

strunji [strun'zhi] *vt* to (turn/shape/fashion on a) lathe.

struţ [struts] *nm orn* ostrich.

student [stu'dent] *nm* student, undergraduate; (*în primul an*) freshman; (*în anul doi*) sophomore; (*în anul trei*) junior.

studenţime [studen'tsime] *nf* the student body, the students.

studia [studi'a] *vt* to study; to apply oneself to; (*autorii greci*) to explore; (*dreptul etc*) to read; (*a pregăti*) to prepare; (*a reflecta asupra*) to meditate/reflect on; (*a cerceta*) to inquire into; *coll* to look into; to examine; to make a study of ‖ *vi* to study, to learn; (*până târziu*) to burn the midnight oil; (*cu zel*) to be a studious/assiduous reader • ~**t** *adj* (well-)studied, * **studia**; (*d. maniere*) affected, artificial; (*d. un efect*) studied, elaborate.

studio [studi'o] *nn (artă, cin)* studio; *(mobilă)* couch bed.

studios [studi'os] *adj* studious, diligent, hard-working.

studiu ['studiu] *nn* study; *(studiere)* studying; *(cercetare)* research; examination; survey; *pl* studies; *(învățătură)* education, learning; *mus* etude; *(pictură)* sketch.

stuf [stuf] *nn bot* reed, rush • **~ăriș** *nn* reed thicket, brake, spinney • **~os** *adj* bushy; *(d. copaci)* leafy; *(des)* thick; *fig (d. o carte)* solid, abstruse.

stup [stup] *nm also fig* beehive; family/colony of bees.

stupefacție [stupe'faktsie] *nf* stupefaction, amazement, astonishment.

stupefia [stupe'fia] *vt* to stupefy, to stun, to astound • **~t** *adj* dumbfounded, stupefied, stunned, flabbergasted, staggered • **~nt** *nn* intoxicant, narcotic, drug || *adj* stupefying, astounding.

stupid [stu'pid] *adj* stupid, dull(-witted), silly; *(prostesc)* foolish; *(monoton)* monotonous || *adv* stupidly, foolishly • **~itate** *nf* stupidity, foolishness; *(ca act)* foolish/silly action.

stupoare [stu'poare] *nf* stupor.

sturion [sturi'on] *nm icht* sturgeon.

sturz [sturz] *nm orn* thrush.

suav [su'av] *adj* suave; sweet, pleasant; soft; smooth || *adv* pleasantly; suavely.

sub [sub] *prep (în dosul)* under; *(mai jos de)* below; *lit* beneath, underneath; *(la poalele)* at the foot of; *jur* without prejudice; *(temporal)* under, during; *(înspre)* towards; *(d. număr)* below, less than.

subacvatic [subak'vatik] *adj (lumină)* subaqueous; *(cercetare)* subaquatic.

subalimentare [subalimen'tare] *nf* malnutrition, undernourishment.

subaltern [subal'tern] *nm* underling || *adj* subordinate, subaltern.

subaprecia [subaprechi'a] *vt* to underrate, to undervalue, to underestimate.

subconștient [subkonshti'ent] *adj* subconscious; *med* subliminal || *nn* the subconscious; *med* subliminal depths.

subcutanat [subkuta'nat] *adj* hypodermic, subcutaneous.

subdezvoltat [subdezvol'tat] *adj* underdeveloped.

subdirector [subdi'rektor] *nm* deputy manager; *(de școală)* vice-principal, deputy headmaster.

subdiviziune [subdivizi'une] *nf* subdivision.

subestima [subesti'ma] *vt* to underestimate, to underrate.

subevalua [subevalu'a] *vt* * **subaprecia**.

subiect [subi'ekt] *nn also gram* subject; *(al unei cărți)* plot; *(temă)* theme; *(de conversație)* topic; *(chestiune)* matter; *(obiect/cauză de ceartă)* object, cause; *(pacient)* patient; *coll* guinea pig; *(individ)* individual; **~ de milă** object of pity.

subiectiv [subiek'tiv] *adj* subjective; *(părtinitor)* biased, partial || *adv* subjectively • **~ism** *nn* subjectivism • **~itate** *nf* subjectivity; *(părtinire)* bias, partiality.

subit [su'bit] *adj* unexpected, sudden || *adv* unexpectedly, suddenly, all of a sudden.

subînchiria [subînkiri'a] *vt (d. chiriașul principal)* to sublet, to sublease; *(d. al doilea chiriaș)* to rent from the tenant.

subînțelege [subîntse'ledje] *vr* to go without saying, to be implied/meant/understood.

subînțeles [subîntse'les] *nn* implication, connotation; **cu ~** meaningful(ly) || *adj* implied.

subjonctiv [subzhonk'tiv] *nn gram* subjunctive.

subjuga [subzhu'ga] *vt* to subjugate, to subdue; to master; *fig* to captivate, to fascinate.

sublim [su'blim] *adj* sublime, lofty, exalted || *adv* divinely, wonderfully || **~ul** *nn* the sublime, sublimity.

subliminal [sublimi'nal] *adj psych* subliminal.

sublinia [sublini'a] *vt* to underline, to underscore; *fig* to emphasize; *(a pune accent pe)* to focus on, to stress; *(a scoate în evidență)* to highlight.

sublinire [sublini'ere] *nf* underlining; *fig* stress, emphasis; *(accent)* stress.

sublocotenent [sublokote'nent] *nm* junior lieutenant; *naut* second-/sub-lieutenant; *avia* pilot officer.

submarin [subma'rin] *nn naut* submarine, *coll* sub || *adj* submarine; submerged; *(d. curenți)* deep-sea; underwater.

submina [submi'na] *vt* to undermine, to sap.

subnutrit [subnu'trit] *adj* underfed.

subnutriție [subnu'tritsie] *nf* malnutrition; underfeeding.

subofiter [subofi'tser] *nm* non-com(missioned officer), N.C.O.

subordona [subordo'na] *vt* to subordinate • **~re** *nf* subordination.

subpopulat [subpopu'lat] *adj* underpopulated.

subprodus [subpro'dus] *nn* by-product, secondary product.

subscrie [sub'skrie] *vt (a semna)* to sign; *(o sumă)* to subscribe; *(acțiuni)* to apply (for); *fig (a susține o părere)* to endorse || *vi* to subscribe.

subscripție [sub'skriptsie] *nf* subscription (list).

subsecretar [subsekre'tar] *nm* undersecretary.

subsemnatul [subsem'natul] *nm* the undersigned; *hum* yours truly.

subsidiar [subsidi'ar] *adj* subsidiary.

subsol [sub'sol] *nn archit* basement; *geog* subsoil; *(al paginii)* foot.

substantiv [substan'tiv] *nn gram* noun, substantive.

substanță [sub'stantsă] *nf* substance; *(materie)* matter, stuff; *(esență)* essence, gist.

substanțial [substantsi'al] *adj* substantial; *(nutritiv)* nourishing; *fig* pithy, cogent || *adv* substantially, considerably.

substitui [substitu'i] *vt* to substitute (a new thing for the old one), to replace (an old thing with a new one); *jur* to appoint || *vr* to serve as a substitute for • **~re** *nf* substitution; *jur* entail.

substituție [substi'tutsie] *nf* substitution.

subsuoară [subsu'oară] *nf* armpit || *adv* under one's arm.

subteran [subte'ran] *nn* underground, depth; *(mină)* mine || *adj* underground.

subterfugiu [subter'fudjiu] *nn* subterfuge, dodge; *(ascunziș)* creephole.

subtil [sub'til] *adj* subtle, fine; delicate; *(d. miros, auz)* keen, acute; *(d. o diferență)* nice; *(d. argumente)* ingenious; *(d. cineva: perspicace)* shrewd, discerning; sophisticated || *adv* subtly, finely, etc • **~itate** *nf* subtlety, shrewdness; acuteness; nicety; subtle argument • **~iza** *vt (a argumenta cu subtilitate)* to subtilize; *coll (a sustrage)* to make away (with), to lift, to sneak.

subtitlu [sub'titlu] *nn* subtitle; *(la un articol)* cross head(ing).

subtitra [subti'tra] *vt* to subtitle.

subția [subtsi'a] *vt* to (make) thin; *(lemn)* to thin down; *(metal)* to machine down; *(a dilua)* to dilute; *fig* to refine, to polish ‖ *vr* to get thinner/slimmer; (*spre capăt*) to taper (off); *fig* to become refined/genteel.

subțire [sub'tsire] *adj* thin; (*îngust*) narrow; (*zvelt*) svelte, slight, slim, slender; (*d. față*) (*de nemâncare*) pinched; (*slabă și palidă*) gaunt; (*tras*) drawn; lank, lean; fine; (*d. haine*) light(weight), flimsy; (*nerezistent*) weak, delicate; **fir** ~ thin/fine thread; (*diluat*) watery; (*d. vânt*) biting; (*d. voce*) shrill; (*rafinat*) refined; (*ales*) choice; (*insuficient*) meager; (*subtil*) shrewd; (*șiret*) cunning; (*dificil*) squeamish ‖ *adv* thinly; (*ușor*) lightly, finely.

suburban [subur'ban] *adj* suburban.

suburbie [subur'bie] *nf* suburb, suburbia; (*împrejurimi, cartiere murdare*) purlieus; **în** ~ in the suburbs.

subvenție [sub'ventsie] *nf* subsidy, subvention, stipend.

subvenționa [subventsio'na] *vt* to subsidize, to grant financial aid to.

subversiv [subver'siv] *adj* subversive, seditious, undermining.

subzista [subzis'ta] *vi* to subsist, to continue, to exist.

subzistență [subzis'tentsă] *nf* sustenance, subsistence.

suc [suk] *nn* juice.

succeda [sukche'da] *vt* to succeed (to smb), to follow after ‖ *vr* to succeed each other, to alternate.

succes [suk'ches] *nn* success; *coll* (good) luck; favorable result; (*triumf*) triumph; *pl* victories; (*șlagăr, piesă*) hit.

succesiune [sukchesi'une] *nf* succession, sequence, series; *jur* succession inheritance.

succesiv [sukche'siv] *adj* successive ‖ *adv* successively.

succesor [sukche'sor] *nm* successor, heir.

succint [suk'chint] *adj* succinct, concise, brief.

suci [su'chi] *vt* (*a răsuci*) to twist; (*a face sul*) to roll; (*a întoarce*) to turn; (*frânghia*) to kink; (*mâna*) to wrench; (*a disloca*) to sprain; (*a mânui*) to wield; (*a îndoi*) to bend; (*a strâmba*) to crook ‖ *vr* (*a se răsuci*) to twist; (*a se învârti*) to turn; (*a se îndoi*) to bend; (*a se strâmba*) to be crooked.

sucomba [sukom'ba] *vi* to succumb, to die.

suculent [suku'lent] *adj* juicy; (*hrănitor*) nutritious; (*gustos*) toothsome; substantial.

sucursală [sukur'sală] *nf* branch.

sud [sud] *nn* south; ~**ul** the South; ~**vest** southwest; **de** ~ southern; **la** ~ in the south; **la** ~ **de** south of, southwards; **spre** ~ southwards.

suda [su'da] *vt/vr* to solder; (*autogen*) to weld; (*oase*) to knit, to join; *fig* to blend, to fuse.

sudoare [su'doare] *nf* sweat, perspiration; **cu** ~**a frunții** *fig* by the sweat of one's brow.

sudor [su'dor] *nm* welder.

sudură [su'dură] *nf* welding.

suedez [sue'dez] *nm* Swede ‖ *adj* Swedish.

suferi [sufe'ri] *vt* to suffer; (*a suporta*) to stand, to put up with; (*a tolera*) to tolerate, to bear, to brook; (*a trece prin*) to undergo; to allow, to permit ‖ *vi* to suffer from; to feel pain; (*pagube*) to suffer injury, to be damaged • ~**nță** *nf* suffering, pain; (*necaz*) trouble, tribulation.

suficient [sufichi'ent] *adj* enough, sufficient; (*adecvat*) adequate; (*satisfăcător*) satisfactory; (*d. cineva*) self-satisfied ‖ *adv* sufficiently, enough ‖ *interj* that will do!, that will be (more than) enough!.

sufix [su'fiks] *nn ling* suffix.

sufla [su'fla] *vi* to respire, to breathe; (*cu greu*) to gasp, to pant; (*cu zgomot*) to wheeze; **a** ~ **din greu** to be

short of breath; (*adânc*) to draw a long breath; (*d. animale*) to snort; (*cuiva*) to prompt; (*d. vânt*) to blow; (*a adia*) to breathe; (*cu furie, turbat*) to blow a gale ‖ *vt* (*a îndepărta*) to blow away/off; (*a stinge*) to blow out; (*d. o explozie*) to blast; (*sticlă*) to blow; to blow up; (*a șopti*) to whisper; (*la școală, teatru*) to prompt; *fig* (*a fura*) to steal; *coll* to pinch smth from smb; (*a acoperi cu aur/ argint*) to gild, to plate with gold, to silver.

sufleca [sufle'ka] *vt* **a-și** ~ **mânecile** to roll up one's sleeves; *fig* to take off one's coat to work.

sufler [su'fler] *nm thea* prompter.

suflet ['suflet] *nn* soul; (*conștiință*) conscience; (*spirit*) mind; (*inimă, simțire*) heart, feeling; (*om*) man, human being; individual; (*cap*) head; *fig* (*viață*) life, inspiration; prime mover, moving spirit; (*suflare*) breathing; (*respirație*) breath; *fig* heartless(ly), callous(ly) • **din** ~ *adj* heartfelt ‖ *adv* from the bottom of one's heart • ~**esc** *adj* soul; spiritual; moral; (*psihic*) mental • ~**ește** *adv* spiritually, morally.

sufleu [su'fleu] *nn cul* soufflé.

suflu ['suflu] *nn* (*explozie*) explosion, blast; (*respirație*) breath.

sufoca [sufo'ka] *vt also fig* to stifle, to smother; (*d. vești*) to stagger; *fig* (*a înăbuși*) to quell, to suppress; (*d. un sunet*) to muffle ‖ *vr* to stifle, to choke; (*de sete*) to be parched with thirst • ~**nt** *adj* stifling, smothering.

sufragerie [sufradje'rie] *nf* (*cameră*) dining room; (*mobilă*) dining-room furniture.

sufragiu [su'fradju] *nn* suffrage, vote; (*aprobare*) approval.

sugaci, sugar [su'gach, su'gar] *nm* suckling; nurseling.

sugativă [suga'tivă] *nf* blotting paper; *fig* (*bețiv*) toper; *coll* boozer.

suge ['sudje] *vt* to suck; to absorb, to soak up; to imbibe; *fig* to sponge off; *fig* to extort; (*a slei*) to wear out ‖ *vi* to suck; *coll* (*a bea*) to guzzle, to swill.

sugera [sudje'ra] *vt* to suggest; (*a propune*) to propose; (*a insinua*) to insinuate; (*a face aluzie*) to hint.

sugestie [su'djestie] *nf* suggestion; (*idee*) idea, thought; (*propunere*) proposal; incitement; hypnosis.

sugestiv [sudjes'tiv] *adj* suggestive, effective; evocative; (*plastic*) graphical ‖ *adv* in a suggestive way; graphically, eloquently.

sughiț [su'gits] *nn* hiccup; (*de plâns*) sob • ~**a** *vi* to hiccup; (*de plâns*) to sob.

sugruma [sugru'ma] *vt* to strangle; (*a sufoca*) *also fig* to stifle, to choke; to suppress.

sui [su'i] *vt* (*a urca*) to climb; to mount; *frml* to ascend ‖ *vr/vi* to climb up; (*a se cățăra*) to climb up; (*cu dificultate*) to clamber; (*folosindu-se de mâini*) to scramble; (*d. plante*) to creep; **a se** ~ **în** (*mașină*) to get into the car; (*autobuz, tren*) to get on the bus/ train • ~**ș** *nn* (*urcare*) climbing (up); (*tendință*) uptrend.

suită [su'ită] *nf* (*și alai*) retinue, train; series; (*înlănțuire*) succession, chain; (*la jocul de cărți*) suit; (*la pocher*) straight; *mus* suite.

sul [sul] *nn* roll, scroll; (*de hârtie*) bundle; (*de stofă*) bolster; *metal* pinch bar; *text* beam; (*de fum*) puff; (*de praf*) cloud; (*la mașina de scris*) (feed-)roller, platen.

sulă ['sulă] *nf* awl.

sulemenit [suleme'nit] *adj* made-up.

sulf [sulf] *nn chem* sulphur, brimstone.

sulfuric [sul'furik] *adj chem* sulphuric (acid).

suliţă ['sulitsă] *nf* javelin; *hist* spear.

sultan [sul'tan] *nm* sultan.

sumar [su'mar] *nn* summary, abstract; synopsis, digest; *(conţinut)* table of contents ‖ *adj* concise, short *(scurt)* brief; *(grăbit)* hasty ‖ *adv* summarily, scantily • **instanţă ~ă** summary court.

sumă ['sumă] *nf* sum; amount; *(număr)* (great/large) number.

sumbru ['sumbru] *adj* somber, gloomy; *(d. cer)* overcast, dull; *(d. oameni, priviri)* surly, sullen; *(de rău augur)* grim ‖ *adv* gloomily, somberly.

sumedenie [sume'denie] *nf* lot, multitude, host; a great/good deal of.

suna [su'na] *vi* to ring; to sound; *(a răsuna)* to resound; *(d. clopote)* to toll; *(d. zurgălăi)* to jingle; *(d. trompete)* to blare; *(d. pahare)* to clink; *(d. ceas)* to strike; *(a zice)* to say; *(d. ceva scris: a glăsui)* to run, to read ‖ *vt (d. clopote)* to ring; *(d. ore)* to strike; *(la telefon)* to call up smb.

sunătoare [sună'toare] *nf (jucărie)* rattle; *bot* all-saints' wort, hardhay.

sunet ['sunet] *nn* sound; *(de clopote şi)* ring, peal, chime; *(de clopot mare)* clang; *(de tobă)* beat; *(de trompetă)* blare; *(de sirenă)* blast; *(funebru)* knell; *(ecou)* echo; *(foşnet)* rustle; *(în urechi)* ringing; *mus* tone.

supapă [su'papă] *nf* valve.

supă ['supă] *nf cul* soup; *(concentrată)* broth.

supăra [supă'ra] *vt* to make angry, to anger; *(a irita)* to irritate, to irk; *(a plictisi)* to annoy; *(a tachina)* to tease; *(a cicăli)* to nag; *(a înfuria)* to infuriate; *(a exaspera)* to put out; *(a deranja)* to disturb ‖ *vr (pe)* to be angry with; *(din cauza)* to be angry about/at; *(a se enerva)* to get irritated/annoyed; to take offense at; *(a se înfuria)* to fly into a rage/temper; *(a se întrista)* to be sad; *(a se certa)* to quarrel, to fall out with smb • **~re** *nf* anger, sorrow; rage, fury; *(ciudă)* spite; resentment; *(necaz)* trouble; *(rău)* harm; *(povară)* burden; *(pagubă)* damage; *(pierdere)* loss; *(lipsă)* want; *(ofensă)* offense; *(mâhnire)* sadness; *(amărăciune)* bitterness; *(suferinţă)* grief, suffering; *(ceartă)* quarrel, argument; **fără ~** no offense meant • **~t** *adj* angry, cross (with smb, at a thing); *(mânios)* irritated, furious, infuriated; *(trist)* grieved, sad.

supărăcios [supără'chios] *adj* ill-tempered, grumpy, touchy; irritable; short-tempered, petulant.

supărător [supără'tor] *adj* annoying, irritating, vexatious; *(dezamăgitor)* disappointing; *(regretabil)* unfortunate.

superb [su'perb] *adj* superb, splendid; *(de prima calitate)* first-rate; *(măreţ)* magnificent, stately ‖ *adv* superbly, magnificently.

superficial [superfichi'al] *adj* superficial, shallow; *(d. răni)* skin-deep; perfunctory • **~itate** *nf* shallowness, flimsiness, perfunctoriness.

superflu [super'flu] *adj* superfluous, redundant; unnecessary, unwanted.

superior [superi'or] *adj* superior (to); *(d. clase, etaje, membre)* upper; *(d. şcoli, matematică)* higher; *(calitativ)* of superior/highest quality; *(încrezut)* condescending ‖ *nm* superior, one's better; chief; *relig* head of a convent • **~itate** *nf* superiority.

superlativ [superla'tiv] *nn/adj* superlative.

supermagazin [supermaga'zin] *nn* supermarket, superstore.

superman ['superman] *nm* superman, Superman.

supersonic [super'sonik] *adj* supersonic.

superstiţie [super'stitsie] *nf* superstition; *(eres)* old wives' tale.

superstiţios [superstitsi'os] *adj* superstitious.

superviza [supervi'za] *vt* to supervise.

supeu [su'peu] *nn* supper.

supieră [supi'eră] *nf* soup tureen.

supleant [suple'ant] *nm* deputy; substitute ‖ *adj* alternate.

supleţe [su'pletse] *nf* suppleness, litheness, flexibility.

supliciu [su'plichiu] *nn* torture, ordeal; *fig also* torment, agony.

supliment [supli'ment] *nn* supplement (of a magazine), addition; *(încă un/o)* extra • **~a** *vt* to supplement • **~ar** *adj* supplementary, additional; *(d. muncă)* overtime; **ore ~e** overtime.

suplini [supli'ni] *vt* to replace, to be a substitute for; *(o lipsă)* to make up for • **~re** *nf* substitution, replacement; *(a unei lipse)* compensation • **~tor** *nm/nf* substitute (teacher); deputy.

suplu ['suplu] *adj* supple, flexible; *(d. corp)* slim, slender; *(în mişcări)* lithe, nimble; *(moale)* soft; *fig* elastic, easily molded, pliable, tractable; versatile.

suport [su'port] *nn* support, prop; *(pt. scule)* rest; *(pt. lampă)* stand; *(pt. blocnotes)* holder • **~a** *vt (a susţine)* to support, to sustain; *fig* to back; to bear; *(greutăţi)* to withstand; to endure; to be equal to; to weather (a storm); *(d. băutură)* to carry (one's drink); *(a admite)* to tolerate • **~abil** *adj* tolerable, bearable, endurable ‖ *adv* tolerably • **~er** *nm sp* supporter, fan.

supozitor [supozi'tor] *nn* suppository.

supoziţie [supo'zitsie] *nf* supposition, assumption; *(ipoteză)* hypothesis.

supraabundenţă [supraabun'dentsă] *nf* superabundance; *com* glut.

supraaglomerare [supraaglome'rare] *nf* overcrowding.

supraaprecia [supraaprechi'a] *vt/vr* to overrate, to overestimate, to overvalue.

supracopertă [suprako'pertă] *nf (carte)* jacket, dust cover.

supradoză [supra'doză] *nf* overdose.

supraestima [supraesti'ma] *vt/vr* to overestimate.

supraevalua [supraevalu'a] *vt* to overestimate, to overvalue.

suprafaţă [supra'fatsă] *nf* surface; *(întindere)* area.

supraîncălzi [supraînkălzi] *vt* to overheat; *(aburul)* to superheat • **~re** *nf phys* overheating, superheating.

supraîncărca [supraînkăr'ka] *vt* to overload, to overcharge.

supralicita [supralichi'ta] *vi* to overbid.

supranatural [supranatu'ral] *adj* supernatural.

supranumerar [supranume'rar] *adj* supernumerary.

supraom [supra'om] *nm* superman.

supraomenesc [supraome'nesk] *adj* superhuman.

suprapopulat [suprapopu'lat] *adj* overpopulated.

suprapune [supra'pune] *vt* to super(im)pose (upon/on) ‖ *vr* to overlap (one another).

suprarealism [suprarea'lism] *nn* surrealism.

suprasaturaţie [suprasatu'ratsie] *nf chem* supersaturation; *fig* satiation.

suprasolicita [suprasolichi'ta] *vt* to overtax.

suprastructură [suprastruk'tură] *nn phil* superstructure.

suprataxă [supra'taksă] *nf econ* extra tax, surtax, supertax.

supraveghea [suprave'gia] *vt* to oversee, to supervise, to superintend; to observe; *edu* to proctor; (*o mașină*) to tend; (*pe cineva*) to watch; to monitor; (*copii*) to keep an eye on; (*a urmări*) to follow ‖ *vr* to keep oneself in hand.

supraveghetor [suprave'tor] *nm* overseer, supervisor; shopwalker; *rail* inspector; (*paznic*) watchman, guardian; sentry.

supraviețui [supravietsu'i] *vi* to survive (smth); to out-live (smb); to live on • **~re** *nf* survival, outliving • **~tor** *nm* survivor ‖ *adj* surviving.

suprem [su'prem] *adj* supreme, paramount, ultimate; (*ultim*) last; (*d. eforturi*) crowning; (*d. grad*) highest • **~ație** [suprema'tsie] *nf* supremacy.

suprima [supri'ma] *vt* (*a elimina*) to omit, to leave out; *comp* to delete; (*o obiecție*) to dispose of; (*abuzuri*) to put down; (*pe cineva*) to kill; *coll* to do for; (*o dificultate*) to remove; *jur* to conceal; (*a înăbuși*) to quell; (*a anula*) to cancel; (*taxe, legi: a desființa*) to repeal; (*un ziar*) to suppress; (*un titlu*) to withdraw.

supune [su'pune] *vt* to subdue, to subjugate; (*a învinge*) to defeat; (*a câștiga*) to win; (*a stăpâni*) to master; (*a sili*) to force; (*unei influențe*) to subject to; (*unei amenzi*) to fine; (*unui examen*) to examine; to submit, to present ‖ *vr* (*a se resemna*) to resign; (*a asculta*) to obey; (*a capitula*) to surrender; (*unei rugăminți*) to comply with; (*a trece prin*) to undergo • **~re** *nf* submission; (*devotament*) allegiance; (*cucerire*) conquest; respect.

supura [supu'ra] *vi med* to fester, to suppurate, to run.

supus [su'pus] *adj* submissive, subdued; (*umil*) humble; (*ascultător*) obedient; (*d. copii*) dutiful; **~ la** subject to, *econ, jur* (*pasibil*) liable to ‖ *nm* subject ‖ *adv* dutifully, submissively.

sur [sur] *adj* grey, gray; (*cărunt*) grizzled, hoary.

surâde [su'râde] *vi* to smile; (*afectat*) to smirk, to simper; (*disprețuitor*) to sneer; (*forțat*) to force a smile; (*larg*) to beam; (*răutăcios*) to grin.

surâs [su'râs] *nn* smile; (*ironic, răutăcios*) grin, sneer; (*afectat*) smirk, simper.

surâzător [surâză'tor] *adj* smiling, beaming; (*prietenos*) friendly.

surcea [sur'chea] *nf* chip, sliver.

surclasa [surkla'sa] *vt* to surpass, to outdo, to outperform.

surd [surd] *nm* deaf person ‖ *adj* deaf; *ling* voiceless, mute; (*d. zgomot: înăbușit*) muffled, dull; (*dogit*) hollow; (*îndepărtat*) distant; (*d. strigăt*) low; *fig* (*ascuns*) hidden, secret; (*d. sentimente*) veiled; (*nelămurit*) obscure, vague • **~ină** [sur'dină] *nf* mute; în ~ in an undertone • **~omut** *nm* deaf-mute ‖ *adj* deaf and dumb.

surescita [sureschi'ta] *vt* to (over)excite • **~re** *nf* excitement, *med* overstimulation.

surf [surf] *nn* surf; **scândură de ~** surf-board; **a face ~** to surf.

surghiun [sur'giun] *nn* exile, banishment.

surioară [suri'oară] *nf* little sister; *coll* sissy, sis.

surlă ['surlă] *nf* trumpet; fife.

surmena [surme'na] *vt* to overwork, to work too hard ‖ *vr* to over-exert oneself; *coll* to work oneself to death • **~j** *nn* overwork(ing).

surogat [suro'gat] *nn* substitute (for), ersatz; *fig* imitation, counterfeit.

surpa [sur'pa] *vt* to pull down; to make smth fall; to crumble; *fig* (*a distruge*) to destroy; (*a submina*) to undermine ‖ *vr* (*d. un zid, o clădire*) to fall/cave in, to collapse; to slide; (*d. o stâncă*) to slip; *fig* to fall to the ground.

surplus [sur'plus] *nn* surplus, excess • **~ul** *nn* the rest, what is left over.

surprinde [sur'prinde] *vt* to surprise; (*a lua pe nepregătite*) to catch unawares; (*d. noapte*) to overtake; (*o conversație*) to overhear; (*o scrisoare, o privire*) to intercept; (*a descoperi*) to detect; (*a găsi*) to find; (*a sesiza*) to grasp; (*a prinde, a reda*) to catch, to render; (*a mira*) to astonish, to amaze ‖ *vr* to find/catch oneself (doing smth).

surprins [sur'prins] *adj* surprised, astonished; * **surprinde**.

surprinzător [surprinză'tor] *adj* surprising, astonishing; (*neașteptat*) unexpected ‖ *adv* surprisingly, amazingly.

surpriză [sur'priză] *nf* surprise; (*mirare*) astonishment, wonder; (*cadou*) (unexpected) present; *sp* upset.

sursă ['sursă] *nf* source; supply; *fig* origin.

surveni [surve'ni] *vi* to occur, to happen.

surzeală [sur'zeală] *nf* deafness.

surzi [sur'zi] *vt* to deafen ‖ *vi* to grow deaf.

sus [sus] *nn* upper part ‖ *adv* high (up), up; (*deasupra*) above; (*în casă*) upstairs; (*în vârf*) on top; *interj* ~ **mâinile!** hands up!; **capul ~**! chin up! ‖ *adv* from above/on high, from upstairs.

susan [su'san] *nm* sesame.

susceptibil [suschep'tibil] *adj* susceptible; (*țâfnos*) testy, touchy • **~itate** *nf* susceptibility, sensitiveness.

suscita [suschi'ta] *vt* to arouse, to cause, to give rise (to).

suspans [sus'pans] *nn* suspense.

suspect [sus'pekt] *nm* suspect, doubtful person ‖ *adj* suspicious, doubtful, suspect • **~a** *vt* to suspect (smb/smth), to question, to doubt smb.

suspenda [suspen'da] *vt* (*a atârna*) to hang up; to sling; (*a amâna*) to defer; *jur* to adjourn, to postpone; (*a opri*) to suspend; to stop; (*un ordin*) to rescind • **~re** *nf jur* suspension, delay; (*amânare*) postponement; (*oprire*) interruption; stoppage; abeyance; (*a unui ordin*) rescinding; (*din funcție*) dismissal.

suspensie [suspen'sie] *nf* suspension.

suspicios [suspichi'os] *adj* suspicious.

suspiciune [suspichi'une] *nf* suspicion, doubt.

suspin [sus'pin] *nn* sigh, sob • **~a** *vi* to sigh, to sob • **~are** *nf* sighing; (*suspin*) sigh.

suspus [sus'pus] *adj* high-placed.

sustrage [sus'tradje] *vt* (*bani*) (*a fura*) to embezzle, *jur* to defalcate; to take away; (*a ascunde*) to hide ‖ *vr* to elude; (*din sfială*) to shrink (from) • **~re** *nf* embezzlement; avoidance.

susținător [sustsină'tor] *nm* upholder, supporter; (*al unei teze, idei*) advocate; (*al familiei*) breadwinner.

susține [sus'tsine] *vt* to support (smb/smth), to hold (smb/smth) up; *fig* (*a sprijini*) to back (up), to endorse; to back smb (financially); (*a încuraja*) to encourage; (*o hotărâre*) to second; (*a apăra*) to defend; (*o teză; o părere*) to maintain; (*o cauză*) to champion; to affirm, to assert; (*în discuție*) to contend; (*a pretinde*) to allege; (*a menține*) to keep up; (*un examen: a trece prin*) to undergo; to take.

susținut [sustsi'nut] *adj* sustained; (*d. un argument*) supported; (*d. eforturi*) constant, permanent; (*d.*

interes) unflagging; (*d. atenție*) unremitting; (*d. alergare, piață*) steady ‖ *adv* constantly, unceasingly.

susur [su'sur] *nn* murmur, purl(ing), babble; (*foșnet*) rustle • ~a *vi* to murmur, to purl, to ripple; (*a foșni*) to rustle.

sutană [su'tană] *nf relig* cassock.

sută ['sută] *nf/adj/num* hundred.

sutien [suti'en] *nn* bra, brassiere.

sutura [sutu'ra] *vt med* to suture, to sew, to stitch up.

sutură [su'tură] *nf med* suture; *anat* suture, join.

suveică [su'veikă] *nf* shuttle.

suvenir [suve'nir] *nn* souvenir, keepsake, (*amintire*) memory, remembrance.

suveran [suve'ran] *nm* sovereign, monarch ‖ *adj* sovereign, paramount • ~itate *nf* sovereignty.

suzetă [su'zetă] *nf* baby's comforter.

swing [suing] *nn sp, mus* swing.

Ş

șa [sha] *nf also geog* saddle.

șablon [sha'blon] *nn* stencil, pattern; *tech also* template; mold; *text* gauge; *fig* cliché; commonplace ‖ *adv* in a hackneyed/commonplace fashion; unimaginatively; mechanically ‖ *adj* staple, standard(ized); *pej* hackneyed, humdrum; (*nediferențiat*) indiscriminate.

șacal [sha'kal] *nm zool* jackal, golden wolf; *fig also* vulture.

șah [shah] *nm* shah ‖ *nn sp* chess; (*atac*) check.

șaibă ['shaibă] *nf tech* (*rondelă*) washer; (*roată*) sheave.

șaisprezece ['shaisprezeche] *nm/adj/num* sixteen • ~lea *adj/num* the sixteenth.

șaisprezecime [shaispreze'chime] *nf also mus* one/ sixteenth.

șaizeci [shai'zechi] *nm/adj/num* sixty.

șal [shal] *nn* shawl; (*fular*) comforter; muffler.

șalău [sha'lău] *nm icht* pike perch, zander.

șale ['shale] *nf pl anat* loins.

șalter ['shalter] *nn tech* switch.

șalupă [sha'lupă] *nf naut* (ship's) boat; (*cu motor*) (motor)boat.

șaman [sha'man] *nm relig* shaman.

șambelan [shambe'lan] *nm hist* chamberlain.

șampanie [sham'panie] *nf* champagne.

șampon [sham'pon] *nn* shampoo • ~a *vt* to shampoo.

șan [shan] *nn* last, boot/shoe tree.

șandrama [shandra'ma] *nf reg* (*baracă*) booth; *coll* ramshackle/tumbledown building.

șansă ['shansă] *nf* chance; (*noroc*) luck, fortune; (*ocazie*) opportunity; possibility, likelihood; *pl* odds.

șantaj [shan'tazh] *nn* blackmail • ~ist *nm* blackmailer.

șantier [shanti'er] *nn* (building/construction) site, yard, depot; road works; *naut* shipyard; *mil* dockyard.

șanț [shants] *nn* ditch; (*de scurgere pentru apă*) kennel, drain; (*de cetate*) *obs* fosse, moat; *mil* entrenchment, trench; *tech* groove.

șapcă ['shapkă] *nf* peaked cap.

șapte ['shapte] *num* seven • **al ~lea** the seventh • ~sprezece seventeen • ~zeci seventy.

șaradă [sha'radă] *nf* puzzle, enigma, charade.

șaretă [sha'retă] *nf* gig; *lit* chariot.

șarjă ['sharzhă] *nf tech, mil* charge, *fig* attack; cartoon, caricature.

șarlatan [sharla'tan] *nm* charlatan, cheat, fraud; (*pretins*

medic) quack; impostor; *coll* humbug • ~ie *nf* quackery, imposture; *coll* flam.

șarpantă [shar'pantă] *nf constr* framework.

șarpe ['sharpe] *nm zool also fig* snake, serpent.

șase ['shase] *nm/adj/num* six; **al ~lea** the sixth.

șasiu [sha'siu] *nn tech* chassis, frame.

șaten [sha'ten] *adj* (*d. păr*) (chestnut-)brown; (*d. oameni*) brown-haired

șatră ['shatră] *nf* Gypsy camp; Gypsy tribe; (*cort*) tent; (*baracă*) booth.

șăgalnic [shă'galnik] *adj* droll; playful, jocular; comical, funny ‖ *adv* humorously.

șchiop [shkiop] *nm* lame man/boy; *coll* lame duck ‖ *adj* lame; limp; (*d. raționament*) halting; *fig* deficient, imperfect • ~ăta *vi* to limp, to hobble; to walk lamely; *fig* to be lame; to be deficient; not to be up to standard; (*d. versuri*) to be halting.

școală ['shkoală] *nf* school; (*clădire*) school(house); (*învățătură*) schooling, training, education; (*elevi*) scholars.

școlar [shko'lar] *nm* schoolboy, student; *pl* schoolchildren ‖ *adj* school; educational; *frml* scholastic • ~iza *vt* to (put to) school • ~izare *nf* education, schooling.

școlăresc [shkolă'resk] *adj* school, schoolboy; (*simplu*) oversimplified.

școlăriță [shkolă'ritsă] *nf* schoolgirl.

școli [sh'koli] *vt* (*pe cineva*) to teach ‖ *vr* to educate, to instruct.

ședea [she'dea] *vi* to sit; (*d. păsări, pe ram*) to be perched; (*a se așeza*) to sit down; (*a sta, a rămâne*) to stay, to remain; (*a fi*) to be; (*a zăbovi*) to lag; (*a locui*) to live; (*a se odihni*) to (take a) rest.

ședere [she'dere] *nf* stay.

ședință [she'dintsă] *nf* sitting; (*adunare*) meeting, gathering; (*conferință*) conference; *jur* session.

șef [shef] *nm* chief, head; (*al unui trib*) chieftain; superior; (*conducător*) leader; principal; foreman; founder.

șelar [she'lar] *nm* saddler, saddlemaker; harnessmaker.

șemineu [shemi'neu] *nn* chimney; fireplace.

șenilă [she'nilă] *nf auto* caterpillar, chain track.

șeptel [shep'tel] *nn* livestock.

șerbet [sher'bet] *nn cul* sherbet.

șerif [she'rif] *nm* sheriff, law marshall.

șerpoaică [sher'poaikă] *nf* female snake; *fig* shrew, vixen.

șerpui [sherpu'i] *vi* to wind, to sinuate; (*a se încolăci*) to wriggle; (*d. râuri*) to meander • ~tor *adj* winding, meandering; (*d. un râu: sinuos*) crisp.

șervet [sher'vet] *nn* napkin, serviette; (*prosop*) towel.

șervețel [sherve'tsel] *nn* napkin; paper serviette; (*pt. copii*) baby's diaper.

șes [shes] *nn geog* plain ‖ *adj* flat, even, plane.

șevalet [sheva'let] *nn* easel.

șezătoare [sheză'toare] *nf* (literary) social/soiree, bee.

șezlong [shez'long] *nn* deck/lounge/long chair.

șezut [she'zut] *nn anat* seat; *coll* butt, bottom, buttocks.

șfichi ['shfiki] *nn* whiplash; (*lovitură*) stroke/cut with a whip, flick with a whip; (*capăt*) end; (*vârf*) tip; *fig also* sting; hit • ~ui *vt* to whip, to lash, to flog; *fig* to scourge, to lash at; *coll* to slate • ~tor *adj fig* biting, cutting.

și [shi] *conj* and ‖ *adv* (*de asemenea*) too, also, as well; ~ **eu** I too; (*chiar*) even; (*deja*) already.

șic [shik] *nn* elegance, smartness, style; (*haz*) point, grace ‖ *adj* chique, smart, elegant.

șicana [shika'na] *vt* to tease smb, to put spokes in (smb's) wheels; (*a face șicane*) to cavil at, to find fault with; *recip* to tease each other.

șicană [shi'kană] *nf* cavil, trick.

șifona [shifo'na] *vt* to ruffle, to wrinkle, to crease; *fig coll* (*onoarea*) to besmirch; to rumple smb ‖ *vr* to crease; *fig coll* (*a se bosumfla*) to take it badly, to blow one's top.

șifonier [shifoni'er] *nn* wardrobe; (*mic*) chiffonier.

șiling ['shiling] *nm fin* shilling.

șină ['shină] *nf rail* rail; (*de roată*) tire; (*de sanie*) runner.

șind(r)ilă [shin'd(r)ilă] *nf* clapboard, shingle, splinter.

șipcă ['shipkă] *nf* slat, lath.

șipot ['shipot] *nn* (*izvor*) (gushing) spring; (*jgheab*) chute; (*burlan*) pipe.

șir [shir] *nn* (*unul lângă altul*) row; (*unul în spatele altuia*) line; tier; *mil* file; *geog* range, chain; series, succession; range; (*număr*) number; (*listă*) list; (*scurgere*) course; *fig* (*al gândurilor*) train; (*legătură*) connection; **în ~** in a row/line, in a string, in single file; in files; in succession, successively; (*neîntrerupt*) incessantly.

șirag [shi'rag] *nn* necklace, chain; (*de mărgele*) string of beads.

șiră ['shiră] *nf* (*de paie*) hayrick, stack; (*a spinării*) *anat* spine, backbone, spinal column.

șiret[1] [shi'ret] *nn* (shoe)lace/string; (*șnur*) cord; *pl* lace.

șiret[2] [shi'ret] *nm coll* slyboots, sly dog ‖ *adj* sly, canny; (*viclean*) cunning, sharp; (*ștrengar*) mischievous ‖ *adv* cunningly, artfully • **~enie** *nf* cunning, art(fullness) • **~lic** *nn* (*truc*) trick, dodge, artifice, ruse.

șiroi [shiro'i] *vi* to stream, to flow (in great volume), to gush; (*a se prelinge*) to drip; (*a curge repede*) to stream/run swiftly ‖ *nn* flow, stream; torrent, flood; agony (of tears).

șist [shist] *nn geol* shale, schist, slate.

șiștar [shish'tar] *nn* milk pail.

șiță ['shitsă] *nf* clapboard, shingle.

șlagăr ['shlagăr] *nn mus* hit; pop(ular) song.

șleahtă ['shleahtă] *nf* (*clică*) gang, clique, set; (*ceată*) troop; *hist* Polish gentry, lower aristocracy.

șleampăt ['shleampăt] *adj coll* (*neglijent*) slovenly, slatternly; *coll* (*d. femei*) dowdy(ish), sluttish, untidy.

șleau ['shleau] *nn* (*drum*) road, highway, highroad; (*curea*) (rope of the) trace; **pe ~** upfront, openly, straightforwardly.

șlefui [shlefu'i] *vt tech* to grind; (*prin pilire*) to file; (*a lustrui*) *also fig* to polish; (*a îndepărta rugina*) to furbish; *fig* (*un text*) to brush up • **~t** *adj also fig* polished; (*d. stil*) elaborate.

șlep [shlep] *nn naut* barge.

șliț [shlits] *nn tech* slot, groove; (front) slit, fly.

șmecher ['shmeker] *nm* slyboots, dodger, artful/sly dog; *coll* (*escroc*) sharp dealer ‖ *adj* (*șiret*) sly, arch; (*viclean*) cunning, crafty; *coll* deep; (*care găsește soluții prompte*) quick-witted; (*isteț*) clever, sharp; *coll* cute; (*prefăcut*) slippery; (*d. copii: ștrengar*) mischievous • **~esc** *adj coll* of a slyboots/dodger • **~i** *vt* to dupe, to swindle; *coll* to take in ‖ *vr* to grow wise • **~ie** *nf* slyness; cunning, art(fullness); (*artificiu*) trick, dodge; (*înșelătorie*) cheat, swindle; *sl* whiz.

șmen [shmen] *nn coll, sl* (tricky) deal in foreign currency.

șmenar [shme'nar] *nm coll, sl* trickster, crook, con man.

șmirghel ['shmirgel] *nn tech* emery powder; (*ca hârtie*) emery board, sand paper.

șnapan [shna'pan] *nm* charlatan, rogue, scoundrel.

șnițel ['shnitsel] *nn cul* schnitzel, battered steak.

șnur [shnur] *nn* cord; *agr* garden rope; (*al soneriei*) bellpull; (*șiret*) shoelace, shoestring.

șoaptă ['shoaptă] *nf* whisper, (*susur*) murmur, gurgle, purl; **în ~** in a whisper; below/under one's breath.

șoarece ['shoareche] *nm zool* mouse.

șobolan [shobo'lan] *nm zool* rat.

șoc [shok] *nn* (*izbire*) shock, impact, collision; percussion; repercussion, reaction; *auto* choke • **~a** *vt* to shock, to astonish; (*bunul simț*) to offend, to be contrary to • **~ant** *adj* shocking, lurid.

șodou [sho'dou] *nn* eggnog, eggflip, posset.

șofa [sho'fa] *vi* to drive (a car).

șofer [sho'fer] *nm* (*car*) driver; (*al cuiva*) chauffeur; (*de taxi*) taxi driver.

șofran [sho'fran] *nm bot* saffron (crocus); crocus; meadow saffron.

șoim [shoim] *nm orn* falcon, hawk; *fig* champion, hero; (*d. un pilot*) daring hawk; ace; *fig* (*cal aprig*) fiery horse • **~ar** *nm* falconer, hawker.

șold [shold] *nn anat* hip, haunch; (*povârniș*) slope.

șoldan [shol'dan] *nm zool* young hare, leveret; *fig* young man; (*copil*) child; *fig* (*mânz*) colt.

șolticărie [sholtikă'rie] *nf* * **ghidușie**; * **ștrengărie**.

șoma [sho'ma] *vi* to be unemployed, to be out of work; *coll* to be on the dole; to be jobless; (*parțial*) to work (on) short hours; to be/lie idle; (*d. câmp*) to lie fallow • **~j** *nn* unemployment.

șomer [sho'mer] *nm* unemployed worker; *pl* the unemployed ‖ *adj* unemployed, out of work, idle; on the dole.

șonticăi [shontikă'i] *vi* to limp, to hitch, to halt.

șopârlă [sho'pârlă] *nf zool* lizard.

șopoti [shopo'ti] *vi* (*a susura*) to murmur, to purl; (*a foșni*) to rustle; (*a șopti*) to whisper.

șopron [sho'pron] *nn* shed; penthouse.

șopti [shop'ti] *vt* to whisper ‖ *vi* to whisper; (*a susura*) to murmur, to purl, to gurgle; (*a foșni*) to rustle.

șorecar [shore'kar] *nm orn* buzzard.

șoricar [shori'kar] *nm zool* ratter, rat terrier; *orn* kite, forktail.

șorici [sho'rich] *nn* skin of bacon, rind.

șoricioaică [shori'chioaikă] *nf chem, vernac* ratsbane.

șort [short] *nn* shorts.

șorț [shorts] *nn* apron; (*de fetiță și*) pinafore.

șosea [sho'sea] *nf* highroad, main road, macadam road; (*autostradă*) highway.

șosetă [sho'setă] *nf* sock; *com* half-hose.

șoșon [sho'shon] *nm* high overshoe; (*de cauciuc*) high galosh/boot.

șotie [sho'tie] *nf* trick, practical joke, (*poznă*) prank; (*șiretlic*) stratagem, artifice.

șotron [sho'tron] *nn* hop-scotch.

șovăi [shovă'i] *vi* to hesitate, to waver, to dilly-dally; *coll* to go seesaw, to shilly-shally; (*în vorbe*) to stint • **~re** *nf* hesitation, wavering, vacillation; *coll* shilly-shally; **fără ~** unhesitatingly, without faltering • **~tor** *adj* hesitating, wavering; (*d. atitudine*) halting; (*d. glas*) faltering; (*tremurat*) tremulous ‖ *adv* hesitatingly, waveringly.

şovin [sho'vin] *adj* chauvinistic, *pej* jingoistic ‖ *nm* chauvinist, *pej* jingo • ~**ism** *nn* chauvinism, jingoism.

şpaclu ['shpaklu] *nn constr* spatula.

şpagă ['shpagă] *nf sl* * **şperţ**.

şpalt [shpalt] *nn typ* (*planşetă*) galley; (*probă*) galley proof, slip.

şpan [shpan] *nn tech* chip, splinter; *pl* chipping, shavings.

şparli [shpar'li] *vt sl* (*a fura*) to angle, to prig, to swipe.

şperaclu [shpe'raklu] *nn* skeleton/master key.

şperţ [shperts] *nn sl* bribe; *coll* graft, kickback • ~**ar** *nm sl* grafter • ~**ui** *vt sl* to bribe, to grease/oil the palm of smb, to buy smb.

şpiţ [shpits] *nm zool* spitz (dog), Pomeranian (dog) ‖ *nn coll* (*vârf*) tip; *coll* (*ţigaret*) (short) cigarette holder.

şpriţui [shpritsu'i] *vt tech* to sprinkle.

şrapnel [shrap'nel] *nn* shrapnel.

şrot [shrot] *nn agr* gri(s)t, groats.

ştachetă [shta'ketă] *nf* lath; *sp* (jumping) lath; *fig* to have higher demands.

ştafetă [shta'fetă] *nf obs* courier; *sp* relay race; (*persoană*) relay racer.

ştaif [shtaif] *nn* collar stiffener; (*la pantof*) heel counter; **cu** ~ *fig* stiff.

ştampila [shtampi'la] *vt* to stamp; to tag; (*a pecetlui*) to seal.

ştampilă [shtam'pilă] *nf* stamp; *fig* tag, cliché.

ştangă ['shtangă] *nf* bar, rod.

ştanţa [shtan'tsa] *vt tech* to punch, to stamp.

ştecăr [shtekăr] *nn elec* plug.

ştecher ['shteker] *nn* * **ştecăr**.

ştergar [shter'gar] *nn* towel.

ştergătoare [shtergă'toare] *nf* doormat.

ştergător [shtergă'tor] *nn* * **ştergar**; (*cârpă*) rag; (*de praf*) duster; (*de podea*) house flannel; *auto* (windshield) wiper.

şterge ['shterdje] *vt* to wipe; (*a usca*) to (wipe) dry; (*vasele*) to wipe up; (*a îndepărta, a curăţa*) to wipe off; (*a curăţa*) to clean; (*de praf*) to dust; (*ceva ud*) to mop/wipe up; (*ceva scris*) to erase, to blot out; (*a tăia din text*) to strike/cross/cut out; *fig* (*a distruge*) to destroy; to expunge ‖ *vr* to wipe oneself; to dry oneself; (*a deveni banal*) to become threadbare; (*d. culori*) to run; *fig* (*a dispărea*) to vanish, to fade.

şterpeli [shterpe'li] *vt coll* (*mărunţişuri, mici sume de bani*) to pilfer, to filch; *sl* to pinch, to lift.

ştevie ['shtevie] *nf bot* patience, garden sorrel.

şti [shti] *vt* (*a cunoaşte*) to know; (*a-şi da seama de*) to be aware of; (*a avea cunoştinţă de*) to be acquainted with; (*a putea*) can; (*a înţelege*) to understand, to see; (*a-şi aminti ceva*) to remember ‖ *vi* to know, to be conversant (with a subject); **a** ~ **de** (*a cunoaşte*) to know; (*a-i fi teamă de*) to fear; (*a asculta de*) to obey; (*a avea parte de*) to enjoy ‖ *vr* (*a se simţi*) to feel; (*a se considera*) to consider oneself.

ştift [shtift] *nn tech* peg, pin, plug.

ştiinţă [shti'intsă] *nf* science; (*cunoaştere*) knowledge; acquaintance; (*învăţătură*) learning, erudition.

ştiinţific [shtiin'tsifik] *adj* scientific.

ştir [shtir] *nm bot* amaranth.

ştirb [shtirb] *nm* toothless person ‖ *adj* toothless; (*bont*) dull, blunt; (*cu ştribituri*) jagged • ~**i** *vt* to jag, to notch; (*a toci*) to dull; *fig* to encroach upon, to curtail; (*a micşora*) to diminish; (*a vătăma*) to harm;

to prejudice; (*a strica*) to break ‖ *vr* (*a se toci*) to dull; (*a se micşora*) to diminish.

ştire ['shtire] *nf* (*veste*) piece/item of news; *pl* tidings, information; (*cunoaştere*) knowledge.

ştiucă ['shtiukă] *nf icht* pike, jack, river pirate.

ştiulete [shtiu'lete] *nm* corn cob.

ştraif [shtraif] *nn tech, cin* stripe.

ştrand [shtrand] *nn* swimming pool, piscine.

ştrasuri ['shtrasuri] *nn pl* rhinestone.

ştreang ['shtreang] *nn* (*frânghie*) rope; (*pt. spânzurătoare*) noose; *coll* halter; *sl* neckcloth; (*la cai*) trace(s).

ştrengar [shtren'gar] *nm* scapegrace, colt; madcap, romp; naughty child; scamp ‖ *adj* prankish; (*jucăuş*) playful, rouguish; (*neascultător*) naughty.

ştrengărie [shtrengă'rie] *nf* merry prank, gambol; *pl* frolics; (*nebunii*) follies.

ştrengăriţă [shtrengă'ritsă] *nf* playful/frolicsome girl; (*neascultătoare*) naughty/mischievous girl.

ştrudel ['shtrudel] *nn cul* strudel.

ştuţ [shtuts] *nn tech* connecting piece.

şubler ['shubler] *nn tech* sliding/vernier calipers.

şubred ['shubred] *adj* (*firav*) frail; (*d. obiecte*) *also fig* flimsy; (*instabil*) unstable; (*nedurabil*) not solid/ durable; (*d. case*) ramshackle; (*slab*) weak; (*bolnăvicios*) sickly.

şubrezi [shubre'zi] *vt* (*a slăbi*) to weaken ‖ *vr* (*a slăbi*) to weaken, to become frail * **şubred**; (*d. case*) to dilapidate.

şuetă [shu'etă] *nf* gossip, chat.

şugubăţ [shugu'băts] *nm* wag, joker, wit ‖ *adj* waggish, playful, funny.

şui [shui] *adj* (*ţicnit*) doltish; *coll* cracked (up); (*zvelt*) slender; (*îngust*) narrow • ~**er** *nn* whistle; (*al vântului, al glonţului*) singing; (*al glonţului*) whiz • ~**era** *vt* to whistle; (*d. vânt, gloanţe*) to whiz, to ping • ~**erat** *nn* whistling * **şuiera**; pinging, zip ‖ *adj* whistling.

şuncă ['shunkă] *nf cul* ham.

şură ['shură] *nf* shed; penthouse; barn; (*şiră*) stack, rick.

şurub [shu'rub] *nn elec, tech* screw.

şurubelniţă [shuru'belnitsă] *nf tech* screwdriver, turnscrew.

şuşoteală [shusho'teală] *nf* whispering.

şuşoti [shusho'ti] *vi* to whisper; (*a susura*) to murmur.

şut [shut] *nn sp* shot, kick; *min* shift.

şuta [shu'ta] *vi* to shoot.

şuti [shu'ti] *vt sl* to steal, to filtch, to pinch.

şuviţă [shu'vitsă] *nf* lock/strand of hair; (*smoc*) tuft; (*cosiţă*) tress; (*fâşie*) stripe; (*de lumină*) streak.

şuvoi [shu'voi] *nn* stream; flood, torrent.

şvaiţer ['shvaitser] *nn cul* Swiss cheese.

T

ta [ta] *adj poss f* your; *obs* thine; **camera** ~ your room.

tabac [ta'bak] *nn bot* tobacco (plant).

tabacheră [taba'keră] *nf* tobacco box, cigarette box/ case; *obs* snuff-box; *constr* (hinged) skylight.

tabără ['tabără] *nf camp*; *also mil* (en)campment, bivouac; (*popas*) halting place; (*de care*) striking of carts; (*ceată, grup*) group; all of a heap, aheap.

tabel, tabelă [ta'bel, ta'belă] *nn, nf* table; chart; synopsis; index; (*planşă*) plate, picture; (*listă*) list; (*orar*) schedule.

tabiet [tabi'et] *nn (obicei)* habit, mania; comfort.

tablă ['tablă] *nf* tin/iron plate; *(de metal)* sheet; *(de lemn)* board; *(pt. pictor)* panel; *(lespede)* slab; *(de ardezie)* slate; *(la şcoală)* blackboard; *(tabel)* table; *(avizier)* notice board; *pl (joc)* backgammon.

tabletă [ta'bletă] *nf* tablet; *(pilulă)* pill, lozenge; *(de ciocolată)* bar, slab.

tabloid [tablo'id] *nn* tabloid.

tablou [ta'blou] *nn also fig* picture, image; *(artă)* painting, canvas; portrait; figure; *thea* scene; *(descriere)* description; fresco; aspect; list; *(de nume)* roll; *tech* board; *(în hotel)* key rack; *coll* flabbergasted, thunderstruck.

tabu [ta'bu] *nn/adj* taboo.

taburet [tabu'ret] *nn* ottoman, stool; *(pt. picioare)* foot/buffet stool.

tac [tak] *nn (biliard)* cue || *interj* smack!, crack!, slap!.

tacâm [ta'kâm] *nn (pt. o persoană)* cover; *(garnitură)* set; *(pt. o masă)* table linen; set of table linen; *pl* (silver)plate.

tachet [ta'ket] *nm tech* lug, peg.

tachina [taki'na] *vt* to tease, to banter; *coll* to chaff.

tacit [ta'chit] *adj* tacit, implicit, understood || *adv* tacitly.

taciturn [tachi'turn] *adj* reserved, uncommunicative, silent.

tact [takt] *nn mus* beat; time; measure; *fig (delicateţe)* light hand, tact(fullness); *cu* ~ tactfully; *fără* ~ tactless(ly) • **~ic** *adj* tactical.

tactică ['taktikă] *nf mil also fig* tactic(s).

tacticos [takti'kos] *adj* leisurely, slow, steady; *(liniştit)* calm || *adv* leisurely, steadily, calmly.

tactil [tak'til] *adj* tactile.

tagmă ['tagmă] *nf (breaslă)* guild, caste; *(clică)* clique, coterie, set; *(clasă)* class.

tahicardie [tahikar'die] *nf med* tachycardia.

taifas [tai'fas] *nn* chat, prattle, chit-chat, small talk.

taifun [tai'fun] *nn met* typhoon.

tain [ta'in] *nn (raţie)* ratio, portion, share; *(nutreţ)* feed; *(întreţinere)* sustenance, maintenance; *fig* quota, share.

taină ['tainā] *nf* mystery, secret; *relig* mystery; *relig (cuminecătură)* Holy Communion; *fig* skill, knack; *în* ~ secretly, in secret.

tainic ['tainik] *adj* secret, mysterious; *(ascuns)* hidden, recondite, *pej* collusive; *(nespus)* untold, unsaid || *adv* secretly, mysteriously.

taior [ta'ior] *nn* tailor-made suit, costume.

talangă [ta'langă] *nf (a vacii etc)* bell.

talaş [ta'lash] *nn* sawdust, shavings.

talaz [ta'laz] *nn* billow, surge; *(val care se sparge)* breaker, surf.

talc [talk] *nn* mineral talc; *(pudrā)* talcum (powder).

talcioc [tal'chiok] *nn* fair.

tale ['tale] *adj poss f* your; **cărţile** ~ your books || *pron poss* **ale** ~ yours.

talent [ta'lent] *nn* talent; faculty; *(aptitudini)* aptitude; *pl* parts; *(har şi)* gift, knack; *(înclinaţie)* lurch; *(persoană)* genius, virtuoso • **~at** *adj* talented, gifted, endowed with talent.

taler ['taler] *nm hist* dollar || *nn (farfurie)* plate; *(de lemn)* wooden platter; *(mare)* large plate; *(adânc)* soup plate; *(tavă)* tray; *(conţinut)* plateful; *(la cântar)* scale/pan/dish; *mus* cymbals; *pl sp* skeet, clay pigeons.

talger ['taldjer] *nn* dish, plate; *pl mus* cymbals.

talie ['talie] *nf* waist(line); *(mărime)* size; stature; *(corsaj)* bodice, corsage.

talisman [talis'man] *nn* talisman, amulet, charm; *(pt. a avea noroc)* lucky charm.

talmeş-balmeş ['talmesh'balmesh] *adv* helter-skelter, pell-mell, topsy-turvy; in a jumble, in a tumble || *nn* hotch-potch, jumble, medley; confusion.

talon [ta'lon] *nn* coupon; check; *(chitanţă)* stub, counterfoil; *(la cărţi)* talon, stock; *(la ciorapi)* heel • **~a** *vt sp* to heel (out) • **~etă** *nf sp* heel piece, heel sock lining.

talpă ['talpă] *nf anat* sole, planta pedis; *(la pantof)* sole (leather); *(la sanie)* runner; *(la leagăn)* rocker; *(temelie)* foundation; *tech* bed plate.

taluz [ta'luz] *nn* gradient, slope, batter.

tamarin [tama'rin] *nm bot* tamarind (tree).

tamariscă [tama'riskă] *nf bot* tamarisk (plant).

tambur [tam'bur] *nn archit* porch, door vestibule, lobby; *tech* barrel, drum; cylinder; roll, reel.

tamburină [tambu'rinā] *nf* tambourine.

tampon [tam'pon] *nn* rail, *pol, chem* buffer; *(de vată)* swab, pad, wad; *med* tampon; *(de sugativă)* blotter; *min* liquid blanket • ~a *vt* to collide/clash with, to run into, *coll* to bump into; *med* to wad over, to tampon; *(a astupa)* to plug; *chem* to buffer || *vr recip* to run into each other; to collide.

tam-tam [tam'tam] *nn mus* tom-tom, tam-tam; *fig* fuss, to-do, hubbub.

tanc [tank] *nn* tank; *mil* armored car; *(rezervor şi)* container, *** rezervor**; *(petrolier)* tank ship/steamer, tanker • ~**hist** [tan'kist] *nm mil* tanker.

tandem [tan'dem] *nn* tandem.

tandreţe [tan'dretse] *nf* tenderness, affection; *(dragoste)* love, fondness; *cu* ~ lovingly.

tandru ['tandru] *adj* tender, fond, loving || *adv* tenderly, fondly, lovingly.

tangaj [tan'gazh] *nn naut* rocking, pitch(ing).

tangentă [tan'djentă] *nf geom* tangent.

tangibil [tan'djibil] *adj* tangible, touchable; definite, concrete; accessible, reachable.

tangou [tan'gou] *nn* tango.

tanin [ta'nin] *nn chem* tannin.

tanti ['tanti] *nf* aunt; *(proxenetă)* madam, procuress.

tapa [ta'pa] *vt (o scrisoare)* to type; *fig (de bani)* to strike (for); *lit* to cadge smb for smth; *(părul)* to tease/fluff (out) || *vr* to tease one's hair.

tapaj [ta'pazh] *nn (scandal)* fuss, uproar; *(zgomot)* noise, racket.

tapet [ta'pet] *nn* wall paper, tapestry.

tapir [ta'pir] *nm zool* tapir.

tapisa [tapi'sa] *vt (pereţi)* to hang with tapestry; *(la paper; (mobilă)* to upholster.

tapiserie [tapise'rie] *nf* tapestry; *(lucru de mână)* tapestry work.

tapiţa [tapi'tsa] *vt* *** tapisa**.

tapiţer [tapi'tser] *nm* upholsterer • **~ie** *nf* upholstery; upholsterer's (shop).

tarabagiu [taraba'djiu] *nm* shopkeeper, retailer.

tarabă [ta'rabă] *nf* stall, stand; *(tejghea)* counter; *(gheretă)* booth; retail shop.

taraf [ta'raf] *nn* folk music band.

tarantelă [taran'telă] *nf* tarantella.

tarantulă [taran'tulă] *nf ento* tarantula spider.

tară ['tară] *nf* tare; *fig* defect, flaw, evil; (*lipsă*) short-coming; (*viciu*) vice.

tardiv [tar'div] *adj* belated, tardy; late ‖ *adv* belatedly, tardy.

tare ['tare] *adj* (*ant. moale*) hard; (*d. carne, lemn*) tough; solid; (*puternic*) strong; stout; (*d. fiinţe*) vigorous; (*d. colectivităţi*) powerful, mighty; (*zdravăn*) sturdy; durable, enduring; (*ţeapăn*) stiff; (*împietrit*) steeled; (*d. pânza*) starched; (*dârz*) firm; (*neşovăitor*) unflinching; (*aprig*) fierce; violent; vehement; intense; (*neîndurător*) relentless; (*fortificat*) fortified; (*bine instruit*) well-informed; (*concludent*) convincing; (*d. sunete*) loud; (*d. aer*) bracing, invigorating; (*d. fenomenele naturii*) violent; (*d. băuturi*) heavy; (*d. culori*) vivid; (*d. persoane*) as strong as a horse/lion/ox; (*neclintit*) (as) firm as a rock ‖ *adv* (*foarte*) very much, extremely, exceedingly; *coll* badly; heavily, strongly, violently; (*intens*) quickly.

targă ['targă] *nf* stretcher, litter; (*pat mobil*) portable bed/couch; (*pt. lucruri*) barrow.

tarhon [tar'hon] *nm bot* tarragon.

tarif [ta'rif] *nn* tariff; price list; (*taxă, curs*) rate.

tartan [tar'tan] *nn* tartan (cloth); tartan (plaid).

tartă ['tartă] *nf* (fruit/cream) tart; flan.

tartină [tar'tină] *nf* sandwich.

tartor ['tartor] *nm* devil, arch-fiend; *fig* ringleader • ~iţă *nf* she-devil; she-tartar; *fig* shrew, scold.

tartru ['tartru] *nn* tartar; (*dentar*) tophus; (*în sticlă, cazan*) fur.

tas [tas] *nn* plate of a scale.

tasa [ta'sa] *vr* (*d. fundaţii*) to settle, to subside, to set; (*a se afunda*) to sink.

tastatură [tasta'tură] *nf* keyboard; (*de la telecomandă*) keypad.

tastă ['tastă] *nf* (*la calculator*) (function) key.

tată ['tată] *nm* father, *coll* dad; (*în limbajul copiilor*) papa; (*apelativ*) sir; (*apelativ*) my boy, my son; old man; (*străbun*) forefather; *fig* originator, begetter.

tatona [tato'na] *vt* to probe, to sound, to explore ‖ *vi* to grope; to proceed cautiously/tentatively.

tatua [tatu'a] *vt/vr* to tattoo (oneself) • ~j *nn* tattoo (marks), tattooing.

taur [taur] *nm zool* bull; *astrol* Taurus, the Bull.

tautologic [tauto'lodjik] *adj* redundant, tautological.

tavan [ta'van] *nn* (*de cameră*) ceiling; (*de biserică*) roof; (*de pivniţă*) vault; (*în mină*) hanging roof.

tavă ['tavă] *nf* tray; (*pt. servit*) waiter; (*de copt*) griddle, baking tin; shelf.

tavernă [ta'vernă] *nf* tavern, pub(lic house), speak-easy.

taxa [tak'sa] *vt* to tax, to impose a tax on; to regulate the price (of); (*o scrisoare*) to surcharge; (*a amenda*) to fine; *fig* (*a eticheta*) to label, to style; (*a socoti*) to consider.

taxă ['taksă] *nf econ, jur* duty; (*impozit*) tax; ~ **pe valoarea adaugată** value added tax (VAT); (*şcolară*) school/tuition fee; (*cotizaţie*) dues; (*pt. un serviciu*) charge, tariff; (*la electricitate*) rate; (*poştală*) postage; **cu** ~ **inversă** *telec* collect.

taxi [tak'si] *nn* taxi(-cab), cab • ~**metru** *nn* taxi(-cab); (*aparat de taxat*) taximeter.

taxonomie [taksono'mie] *nf bio* taxonomy, (science/method of) classification.

tăbăcar [tăbă'kar] *nm* tanner, leather dresser; (*de piei fine*) tawer.

tăbăci [tăbă'chi] *vt* (*cu tanin*) to tan, to curry, to dress; (*piei fine*) to taw.

tăbărî [tăbă'rî] *vi* (*asupra*) to swoop/fall/pounce (upon), to spring at, to prey upon; (*a ataca*) to attack, to set upon.

tăblie [tă'blie] *nf constr* (*de uşă, de lambriu*) panel(ing), pane.

tăbliţă [tă'bliţă] *nf* plate; (*de scris*) slate; (*inscripţie pe o uşă*) door plate.

tăcea [tă'chea] *vi* to be/keep silent; (*a nu spune nimic*) to hold one's tongue, to say nothing; (*a înceta de a vorbi*) to stop talking, to pause; (*d. zgomote*) to stop, to cease.

tăcere [tă'chere] *nf* quiet, silence; (*pauză*) pause; (*linişte*) stillness; quietness, tranquility; (*după furtună*) *also fig* calm, peace, lull; reticence; *mus* rest ‖ *interj* silence!, hush!; **în** ~ silently.

tăciune [tă'chiune] *nm* (smoldering/fire) brand; *pl* embers; *bot* blight, blast, mildew.

tăcut [tă'kut] *adj* silent, quiet, still; (*rezervat*) reserved, discreet, reticent.

tăgadă [tă'gadă] *nf* denial, negation; (*îndoială*) doubt • **fără** ~ *adj* doubtless, unquestionable ‖ *adv* no doubt, undoubtedly.

tăgădui [tăgădu'i] *vt* to deny, to disavow; to contest; (*a contrazice*) to gainsay; (*a nu recunoaşte*) to disown, to disclaim.

tăi [tăi] *adj poss pl* your; **ai** ~ yours, your folk.

tăia [tă'ia] *vt* to cut (up); (*a deschide prin tăiere*) to cut/rip/break open; (*a despica*) to split, to cleave; (*a elibera prin tăiere*) to cut loose; (*a spinteca*) to rip; (*a cresta*) to notch; (*a reteza*) to stint; (*a răni prin tăiere*) to wound by cutting; (*în bucăţi*) to chop; (*mărunt*) to mince; (*felii*) to slice; (*fâşii*) to shred; (*grosolan*) to cut coarsely/grossly; (*în zigzag*) to zigzag; (*la capete*) to clap; (*a dezmembra*) to quarter; (*a reteza*) to chop/strike off; (*a castra*) to geld; (*în două*) to divide; *tech* to plane; (*a cosi*) to mow; (*a ara*) to plow; (*a brăzda*) to furrow; (*a săpa*) to dig; (*a grava*) to (en)grave; (*cu ferăstrăul*) to saw; (*a scurta*) to shorten; (*un text*) to cross out; (*afară*) to cut out; (*a separa*) to separate; (*a micşora*) to cut down; *med* to operate, to incise, to dissect, to amputate; (*a rezeca*) to resect; (*a ucide*) to kill; to decapitate, to behead; (*un animal*) to slaughter; (*a întrerupe*) to break off; (*o convorbire telefonică etc*) to cut off; (*o discuţie*) to cut/break in; (*a opri*) to cut short; (*a suprima*) to suppress; *geom* to bisect; to intersect; (*un drum*) to open; (*pe un drum mai scurt*) to cut across; *fig* to stitch, to sting ‖ *vr* to cut oneself, to get cut; (*d. ţesături*) to rend; (*d. lapte*) to curdle.

tăietură [tăie'tură] *nf* cut(ting), scission; *med* cut, incision; (*rană*) wound; (*adâncă*) slash, gash; (*cicatrice*) scar; (*într-un text*) passage crossed out; (*din presă*) press-clippings, newspaper cutting; (*deschizătură*) slit, cleft; (*bucată tăiată*) piece, score; (*croială*) cut, style, fashion; (*la haine*) make, set; (*pe copac*) carve.

tăifăsui [tăifăsu'i] *vi* to prattle; *coll* to chat.

tăinui [tăinu'i] *vt* to conceal, to keep secret, to harbor; (*un obiect*) to secrete, to hide; (*lucruri furate*) to receive; (*a vorbi*) * **tăifăsui** • ~**re** *nf jur* (*a cuiva*) abetting; (*a ceva*) concealment; concealment of truth/evidence; hiding.

tăios [tă'ios] *adj* sharp, cutting; (*d. ger, vânt*) biting; (*d. ton*) rough, peremptory; (*d. critică*) severe; (*d. o* *remarcă, părere*) trenchant; (*d. răspuns*) curt ‖ *adv* sharply, roughly; severely.

tăiş [tă'ish] *nn* (cutting) edge, blade; (*de daltă*) chisel bit.

tăiţei [tăi'tsei] *nm pl cul* noodles.

tălmăci [tălmă'chi] *vt* to interpret, to translate; to explain, to comment(ate); (*un text*) to expound, to gloss; to express.

tămădui [tămădu'i] *vt* (*o rană*) to heal, to medicine; (*o boală*) to cure, to remedy; (*suferinţe*) to allay ‖ *vr* to recover (from), to be healed (of) • ~tor *adj* healing, curing.

tămâia [tămâ'ia] *vt relig* to incense; *fig* to perfume, to scent; *fig* (*a preamări*) to extol; (*a linguşi*) to flatter, to curry favor with ‖ *vr* (*a se îmbăta*) to get tight/ fuddled, to get lit up.

tămâie [tă'mâie] *nf* (frank)incense; *fig* perfume, odor; *fig* (*linguşire*) fulsome praise, flattery.

tămbălău [tămbă'lău] *nn* to-do; rumpus, hubbub; (*vacarm*) row, din; fuss, scandal; (*publicitate*) hype; (*chef*) junket.

tăpşan [tăp'shan] *nn* flat piece of ground; * **maidan**; (*pantă*) slope; (*şes*) plain.

tărăboanţă [tără'boantsă] *nf* (wheel)barrow.

tărăboi [tără'boi] *nn coll* (*zgomot*) row, rumpus; racket, din.

tărăgăna [tărăgă'na] *vt* to dally, to tarry, to drag out; (*a amâna*) to put off, to procrastinate; (*vorba*) to drawl; (*picioarele*) to shuffle ‖ *vi* to dilly-dally, to shilly-shally; (*d. timp*) to drag on; (*pe drum*) to trail, to linger, to dawdle • ~re *nf* protraction, postponement; (*în vorbire*) drawl • ~t *adj* protracted; dragging along; dallied; (*d. vorbă*) drawling.

tărăşenie [tără'shenie] *nf coll* story, thing; *coll* (*bucluc*) scrape, mess.

tărâm [tă'râm] *nn* (*regiune*) realm, region, parts; (*lume*) world; *fig* sphere, domain, field (of activity); *lit* clime.

tărâţe [tă'râtse] *nf pl* husk, chaff; (*fine*) bran; (*cu făină*) pollard; (*de lemn*) sawdust.

tărcat [tăr'kat] *adj* (*cu dungi*) striped; (*d. animale*: *pătat*) spotted; (*pestriţ*) motley, variegated.

tărie [tă'rie] *nf* (*forţă fizică*) strength, force, vigor; (*rezistenţă*) firmness, hardiness; energy; intensity; (*dârzenie*) moral force; (*autoritate*) power, authority; (*trăinicie*) resistance, solidity; (*alcoolică*) concentration; *lit* vault/dome of heaven; (*văzduh*) air; (*înălţime*) height; (*vârf*) peak, top ‖ *adv* **cu** ~ forcibly, firmly, steadily.

tărtăcuţă [tărtă'kutsă] *nf bot* gourd; (*mare*) squash; *fig* pate, noddle; *coll* nut.

tătar [tă'tar] *nm/adj* Tartar.

tătic [tă'tik] *nm coll* dad(dy), papa.

tău [tău] *adj poss m* your; *obs lit* thy, thine; **al** ~ yours; **numele** ~ your name; **e al** ~ it's yours.

tăun [tă'un] *nm ento* gadfly.

tăvăleală [tăvă'leală] *nf* rolling; (*luptă*) wrestling, fighting; thrashing, licking; *coll* tanning, drubbing; *fig* wear and tear.

tăvăli [tăvă'li] *vt* (*a rostogoli*) to roll, to trundle; (*iarba*) to tread upon, to trample; (*a murdări*) to soil, to (be)smear ‖ *vr* (*a se da tumba*) to turn somersaults, to roll; *fig* to wallow.

tăvălug [tăvă'lug] *nn* (road/steam)roller; *agr* clod crusher/breaker.

tâlc [tâlk] *nn* sense, meaning, significance; interpretation, explanation; (*pildă*) example; comparison; allegory; (*parabolă*) parable; moral; (*glumă*) joke; **cu** ~ meaningful, witty ‖ *adv* meaningfully.

tâlhar [tâl'har] *nm* thief, robber, bandit; *fig* (*ştrengar*) scoundrel; (*ticălos*) rascal, rogue; (*şarlatan*) crook.

tâlhări [tâlhă'ri] *vi* to be a thief, to lead a thief's life ‖ *vt* **a** ~ **pe cineva** to rob smb • ~e *nf* robbery, hold-up.

tâmpenie [tâm'penie] *nf* stupidity, idiocy, silliness; (*ca faptă*) foolish act; (*greşeală, gafă*) blunder, stupid mistake; *also pl* (*absurditate*) nonsense; (*lucru de nimic*) trifle.

tâmpit [tâm'pit] *nm* idiot, imbecile, moron; airhead, airbrain ‖ *adj* stupid, idiotic, imbecilic; dull, blunt, dim.

tâmplar [tâm'plar] *nm* carpenter; (*de mobilă*) joiner; (*de lux*) cabinetmaker.

tâmplă [tâmplă] *nf anat* temple; *relig* * **catapeteasmă**.

tâmplărie [tâmplă'rie] *nf* carpentry; (*de mobilă*) joinery; (*atelier*) joiner's shop; (*obiecte*) woodwork.

tânăr ['tânăr] *nm* youth, young man; lad; teenager, adolescent; (*necopt*) shaveling, stripling ‖ *adj* young; *pej* juvenile; childish; immature; unfledged • ~ă *nf* young girl/lady/woman; teenager.

tândăli [tândă'li] *vi* to idle, to dawdle, to loiter.

tângui [tângu'i] *vr* to weep, to mourn, to lament, to wail, to cry ‖ *vt* to lament (over), to moan, to bewail, to mourn (for), to weep (for) • ~tor *adj* wailing, mournful, sorrowful; (*d. un cântec*) plaintive, doleful ‖ *adv* mournfully, etc.

tânji [tân'zhi] *vi* to languish (away), to ail; (*după*) to long (after/for), to crave/pine (for); (*d. plante*) to wilt, to droop; (*a lâncezi*) to slacken; to stagnate.

târâi, târî [târâ'i, tâ'rî] *vt also fig* to drag, to pull, to trail; (*după sine*) to lug smth about; **a** ~ **picioarele** to shuffle, to drag one's feet; (*a înainta cu greu*) to trudge along ‖ *vr* to crawl, to creep (along); *coll* to trudge (away); (*încoace şi încolo*) to lurk about; (*a rămâne în urmă*) to lag, to dawdle; (*d. nori*) to drift; (*d. obiecte*) to hang low, to scrape the ground; (*d. plante*) to creep.

târâtoare [târâ'toare] *nf* reptile.

târâtură [târâ'tură] *nf* human rag, lickspittle, toady; (*ticălos*) mean/base fellow; (*stricată*) baggage; *pej* bitch, slattern, slut.

târfă ['târfă] *nf vulg* whore, harlot, slut, bitch; *coll* broad, dame.

târg [târg] *nn* (*bâlci*) fair; market; (*piaţă*) market(place); (*tranzacţie*) bargain, deal; (*tocmeală*) haggle, haggling; (*înţelegere*) agreement, understanding; (*vânzare*) sale; (*comerţ*) trade, business; (*ruşinos*) collusion; (*oraş*) borough, market town; small town, townlet • ~ui *vt* to shop, to buy, to purchase ‖ *vr* (*a se tocmi*) to haggle (over smth), to bargain ‖ *vi* to buy; to go shopping • ~uială *nf* buying, purchasing; (*cumpărătură*) shopping, purchase; (*tocmeală*) bargaining, haggling; squabble.

târlă ['târlă] *nf* sheep fold/pen.

târnăcop [târnă'kop] *nn* pick mattock.

târşâi [târshâ'i] *vt* to drag; (*picioarele*) to (walk with a) shuffle ‖ *vr* * **târî**.

târtiţă ['târtiţă] *nf* rump; *coll* pope's nose.

târziu [târ'ziu] *adj* late, belated, tardy; (*îndepărtat*) remote; (*ultimul*) the last ‖ *adv* late; **cel mai** ~ at the latest; **mai** ~ later, further on, afterwards.

te [te] *pron pers* you; *obs, lit* thee; *ref* yourself; *obs, lit* thyself.

teacă ['teakă] *nf (pt. arme)* sheath, case; *(de sabie)* scabbard; *(de cuțit)* knife case; *bot* pod, cod, silique.

teafăr ['teafăr] *adj* healthy, in good condition/health; *(la minte)* sane, sound; *(neatins)* unharmed, safe.

teamă ['teamă] *nf* fear, apprehension (of); *(spaimă)* fright; *(groază)* dread; *(față de ceva măreț)* awe; *(neliniște)* anxiety, concern, worry; **din/de** ~ of/through/for fear.

teanc [teank] *nn com* bale; *(grămadă)* pile, heap; *(de lemne)* stack; *(legătură)* bundle.

teasc [teask] *nn typ* printing/letter press; *(de struguri)* wine press.

teatral [tea'tral] *adj* theatrical; *(de scenă)* stage-like, stagey; (melo)dramatic, scenic; *pej* histrionic; *also fig* affected, theatrical, stagey; **gest** ~ theatrical/histrionic gesture.

teatru ['teatru] *nn* theater; *also fig* stage; *(clădire)* playhouse; *(genul dramatic) also fig* drama; *fig (profesiune)* acting; *(scenă a acțiunii)* scene, set.

tec [tek] *nm bot* teak.

tegument [tegu'ment] *nn anat, bot* tegument.

tehnic ['tehnik] *adj* technical; technological ‖ *adv* technically.

tehnică ['tehnikă] *nf* technique(s); technology; technicalities; skill, craft, art; *(îndemânare)* technical execution; *mus* execution.

tehnician [tehnichi'an] *nm* technician, technical expert; *fig* practitioner.

tehnocrat [tehno'karat] *nm* technocrat.

tehnocrație [tehnokra'tsie] *nf* technocracy.

tehnologie [tehnolo'djie] *nf* technology; technique.

tei [tei] *nm bot* lime/linden tree; *(coardă, funie)* bast (fiber).

teios [te'ios] *adj bot* fibrous.

teism [te'ism] *nn phil* theism.

tejghea [tezh'gea] *nf* counter, table; *(cu cărți)* (book)stall; *(de tâmplar)* joiner's bench; *(în bar)* bar.

tel [tel] *nn* egg-whisk; *(la pat)* spring.

telecomandat [telekoman'dat] *adj tech* operated by remote control.

telecomandă [teleko'mandă] *nf* remote/distant control.

telecomunicație [telekomuni'katsie] *nf* telecommunication.

telefax [tele'faks] *nn telec* telefacsimile, (tele)fax, fax.

teleferic [tele'ferik] *nn* cable railway; cable car, funicular; ski-lift.

telefon [tele'fon] *nn* telephone (set), *coll* phone; *(apel)* (phone-)call; **cartelă de** ~ phone card; ~ **interurban** trunk line; *(convorbire)* long-distance call; ~ **mobil** mobile phone; **prin** ~ by/over the phone; ~ **public** payphone • ~**a** *vt* to (tele)phone, *(cuiva)* to call smb up, to give smb a call • ~**ist** *nm* telephone operator.

telegenic [tele'djenik] *adj* telegenic.

teleghida [telegi'da] *vt* to operate by remote control.

telegraf [tele'graf] *nn* telegraph(y); telegraph-apparatus ‖ *nm bot* telegraph plant • ~**ia** *vt* to telegraph, to cable, to wire.

telegramă [tele'gramă] *nf* telegram, *coll* wire; *(peste ocean)* cable.

teleimprimator [teleimprima'tor] *nn* start-stop teleprinter, telewriter; *(marcă înregistrată)* teletypewriter.

telejurnal [telezhur'nal] *nn* TV/television news (bulletin).

teleobectiv [teleobiek'tiv] *nn phot* telelens, telescopic lens, telephoto lens.

telepatie [telepa'tie] *nf* telepathy.

telescop [tele'skop] *nn* telescope.

telespectator [telespekta'tor] *nm* (tele)viewer, TV spectator.

televiza [televi'za] *vt* to televise, to telecast, to show on television/TV.

televiziune [televizi'une] *nf* television.

televizor [televi'zor] *nn* TV set, television.

telex ['teleks] *nn telec* telex (machine); telex.

tematică [te'matikă] *nf* theme(s), subject(s).

temă ['temă] *nf* theme; *(de conversație)* topic; subject (matter), thesis; *mus* motif; *ling* root, radical, stem; *pl* homework, exercise(s); task; composition; assignment; *mil* problem, scheme.

temător [temă'tor] *adj* cowardly, fearful, timorous; *coll* yellow; distrustful, suspicious, suspecting.

tembel [tem'bel] *nm* indolent, dawdler; *coll* slacker ‖ *adj* indolent, sluggish.

teme ['teme] *vr* to be afraid of, to fear; to be apprehensive of; *(foarte tare)* to dread smth; *(a se îngrijora)* to worry about.

temei [te'mei] *nn also fig (temelie)* foundation, base, basis; *(motiv)* ground, reason; occasion; wherefore; *(fund)* bottom; *(toi)* thick, depth ‖ *adj* **cu** ~ *(întemeiat)* well-grounded; *(serios)* thorough, solid ‖ *adv* thoroughly; properly; **fără** ~ groundless, unfounded.

temeinic [te'meinik] *adj* solid, earnest; deep, profound; thorough.

temelie [teme'lie] *nf* foundation, basis, ground; *also fig* cornerstone.

temenea [teme'nea] *nf* bow; curtsey, bob; *esp fig* kowtowing.

temerar [teme'rar] *adj* bold, fearless, audacious; *(nechibzuit)* reckless, rash, imprudent, brazen.

temere ['temere] *nf* fear, dread; suspicion, doubt.

temeritate [temeri'tate] *nf* temerity, daring; *(nesocotință)* recklessness, rashness.

temnicer [temni'cher] *nf* jailer, warder, turn-key.

temniță ['temnitsă] *nf* dungeon; *(închisoare)* jail(house), prison; *sl* can, quod; *(izolată)* solitary confinement.

tempera[1] ['tempera] *nf (artă)* tempera, tempora.

tempera[2] [tempe'ra] *vt* to moderate, to mitigate; to damp(en) ‖ *vr* to abate, to calm down.

temperament [tempera'ment] *nn (moral)* temperament, disposition; vigor, zest, pep; *(elan)* life, spirit.

temperat [tempe'rat] *adj* temperate, moderate ‖ *adv* temperately, moderately.

temperatură [tempera'tură] *nf* temperature; *(febră și)* fever.

templu ['templu] *nn* temple; *(protestant)* church, chapel; sanctuary; *(mic, deschis)* monopteron; ~ **mozaic** synagogue.

tempo ['tempo] *nn mus* tempo, pace, time, rhythm.

temporal [tempo'ral] *adj gram* temporal; *anat* temporal.

temporar [tempo'rar] *adj* temporary; transient; provisional ‖ *adv* temporarily, transitorily, provisionally.

temporiza [tempori'za] *vt* to temporize, to delay, to dally.

ten [ten] *nn* complexion, color.

tenace [te'nache] *adj* tenacious; persevering; *fig* dogged, stubborn; *(d. culori)* wearing; *(tare)* strong;

(*d. parfum*) clinging; (*d. memorie*) retentive; (*d. speranță*) fond hope ‖ *adv* tenaciously.

tenacitate [tenachi'tate] *nf* tenacity, mettle, perseverance.

tencui [tenku'i] *vt* to plaster, to parget, to roughcast • ~**ală** *nf* mortar, plaster, roughcast.

tendențios [tendentsi'os] *adj* tendentious, tendencious; biased, partial; *jur* leading.

tendință [ten'dintsă] *nf* tendency, trend; (*înclinație*) bent (for), propensity (to/against, for doing smth); bearing; impulse; (*aspirație*) striving; (*părtinire*) bias • **cu** ~ *adj* tendentious ‖ *adv* tendentiously.

tendon [ten'don] *nn anat* tendon; (*implicând forță*) sinew.

tenebros [tene'bros] *adj* dark, gloomy, somber; *fig* shady, dubious, mysterious.

tenie ['tenie] *nf zool* tape-worm.

tenis ['tenis] *nn* (*de câmp*) lawn tennis; (*de masă*) table tennis, ping-pong.

tenor [te'nor] *nm* tenor.

tensiune [tensi'une] *nf* tension, pressure; (*încordare*) strain; *elec* voltage; (*arterială*) blood pressure; (*nervoasă*) overtension; (*a mușchilor*) stretching; *fig* strain, tenseness.

tenta [ten'ta] *vt* to tempt (into doing smth); (*a ademeni, a ispiti*) to (al)lure, to entice; *fig* to appeal to smb • ~**ție** *nf* temptation, lure.

tentacul [ten'takul] *nn* tentacle, tentaculum.

tentativă [tenta'tivă] *nf* attempt, trial, endeavor; bid.

tentă ['tenta] *nf* tinge, tint; (*nuanță*) hue, shade; touch, tone; **o** ~ **de ironie** a touch/tinge of irony.

teolog [teo'log] *nm* theolog(ue), student of divinity • ~**ie** *nf* theology.

teoremă [teo'remă] *nf* theorem.

teoretic [teo'retik] *adj* theoretical; ideological; *pej* unpractical.

teorie [teo'rie] *nf* theory; *mil* theoretical instruction.

teracotă [tera'kotă] *nf* terracotta.

terapeutic [terape'utik] *adj* therapeutical.

terapie [tera'pie] *nf* therapy.

terasament [terasa'ment] *nn* embankment, earthwork.

terasă [te'rasă] *nf constr* veranda, balcony; *constr, geol* terrace; (*de stâncă*) ledge; offset; bank.

terci ['terchi] *nn* (thin) hominy; (*fiertură*) gruel, porridge; mash • ~**ui** *vt* to crush, to mash.

terebentină [tereben'tină] *nf* turpentine, *coll* turps.

teren [te'ren] *nn* (piece of) ground, plot of land; (*loc*) (house) lot; *sp* sportsground; *sp* (*de tenis, volei, baschet*) court; *sp* (*de fotbal, cricket*) field; *sp* (*de golf*) links, course; *sp* (baseball) champ; *mil* terrain; *geog* country; (*sol*) soil; *fig* domain, province; scene, location; (*loc de întâlnire*) venue.

terestru [te'restru] *adj* land; ground; *astron* terrestrial; earthly.

terfeli [terfe'li] *vt* to soil, to defile; *also fig* to sully, to profane; (*a mânji*) to (be)smear.

tergiversa [terdjiver'sa] *vt* to equivocate, to dally, to delay; *coll* to beat around the bush; to dodge.

tergiversare [terdjiver'sare] *nf* procrastination, shuffling; beating around the bush, evasiveness.

teribil [te'ribil] *adj* terrible, dreadful; (*strașnic*) thumping; (*groaznic*) horrible, awful; appalling; formidable ‖ *adv* terribly, dreadfully, awfully.

terier [teri'er] *nm zool* terrier.

teritorial [teritori'al] *adj* territorial.

teritoriu [teri'toriu] *nn* territory, district, area.

termal [ter'mal] *adj* thermal.

termen ['termen] *nm* term(s), word; expression; relations; *pl* (*condiții*) conditions ‖ *nn* term, time; end, time limit; (*fix*) appointed day/date/hour; (*pt. piață*) quarter day; *com* (*amânare*) delay (granted), respite; *jur* summons; *jur* court day.

termic ['termik] *adj* thermic, thermal; heat.

termina [termi'na] *vt* to (bring to an) end, to finish, to conclude; (*a desăvârși*) to complete; (*munca*) to be through with; (*o ceartă*) to settle; (*o discuție/ședință*) to wind up; (*un tablou*) to finish off; (*a întrerupe*) to break off; (*a absolvi*) to graduate (from); (*la o școală*) to leave school ‖ *vi* to finish, to get done • ~**l** *nn comp, avia* terminal; *ind* terminal pipeline ‖ *adj* terminal, final • ~**ție** *nf* termination, ending.

terminologie [terminolo'djie] *nf* terminology, vocabulary.

terminus ['terminus] *nn* terminus.

termită [ter'mită] *nf ento* termite, white ant.

termocentrală [termochen'trală] *nf* thermo-electric power station.

termometru [termo'metru] *nn* thermometer.

termonuclear [termonukle'ar] *adj* thermonuclear.

termos ['termos] *nn* thermos(-bottle).

termostat [termo'stat] *nn* thermostat.

tern [tern] *adj* dull, tarnished, lusterless; *fig* flat.

teroare [te'roare] *nf* terror, dread; persecution; (*d. o persoană*) terror.

terorism [tero'rism] *nn* terrorism.

terorist [tero'rist] *nm* terrorist.

teroriza [terori'za] *vt* to terrorize; *fig* to bully, to cow.

tertip [ter'tip] *nn* trick, stratagem; (*gând ascuns, invenție*) contrivance, device; creephole; (*șiretlic*) artifice; (*capcană*) catch.

terț [terts] *nm* third party/person ‖ *adj* third.

terțiar [tertsi'ar] *adj* tertiary; **era** ~**ă** tertiary era ‖ *nn geol* the Tertiary.

tescui [tesku'i] *vt* to press fruit (for obtaining juice); to tread; to throng; to pack, to stuff.

test [test] *nn* test, trial • ~**a** [tes'ta] *vt* (*ceva, pe cineva*) to test; *jur* (*a lăsa moștenire*) to bequeath, to (make one's) will • ~**ament** *nn* (last) will; *also relig* testament; *fig* artist's/statesman's testament; **Noul Testament** the New Testament; **Vechiul Testament** the Old Testament • ~**amentar** *adj* testamentary.

testicul [tes'tikul] *nn* testicle, testis, *coll* ball, stone.

testimoniu [testi'moniu] *nn jur* testimony, evidence; ~ **fals** *jur* false witness/evidence, perjury; *jur* (*audiere*) hearing (of witness).

testosteron [testoste'ron] *nm physiol* testosterone.

teșit [te'shit] *adj* flat(tened); (*înclinat*) sloping, slanting; (*bont*) rounded, blunted.

tetanos [te'tanos] *nn med* tetanus.

tetină [te'tină] *nf* (*la biberon*) (rubber) nipple (of feeding bottle); (*detașabilă*) baby's pacifier.

teu [teu] *nn* T(ee)-square, drawing rule; *tech* (*armătură*) T-joint.

tevatură [teva'tură] *nf* agitation, fret; (*gălăgie*) hubbub, noise; row; *coll* shindig; (*bucluc*) trouble; *coll* scrape.

text [tekst] *nn* text, written passage; *mus* lyrics; *thea* (actor's) lines; *typ* text (hand), double pica.

textil [teks'til] *adj* textile • ~**ist** *adj* textile ‖ *nm* textile worker.

textual [tekstu'al] *adj* word-for-word, literal ‖ *adv* to the letter, word for word, literally; in so many words.

textură [teks'tură] *nf* texture, consistency; *geol* (rock) structure.

tezaur [te'zaur] *nn* (*comoară*) treasure; (*monede*) hoard; (*vistierie*) treasury; (*bogăție*) fortune, riches; *fig* thesaurus; *fin* public finances/money • **~iza** *vt* to hoard, to save up, to amass.

teză ['teză] *nf* thesis, proposition, argument; dissertation; (*examen*) written paper; (*idee și*) idea, theory.

ti [ti] *interj* (*phii!*) gee!; (*păcat*) oh!, alas!; *coll* dear me!, goodness (me)!, good gracious!, oh my!.

tiară [ti'ară] *nf* (papal) tiara, triple crown.

tibia ['tibia] *nf anat* tibia, shin, shank bone.

tic [tik] *nn* (spasmodic) tic.

ticăi [tikă'i] *vi* (*d. inimă: a bate*) to beat; (*a palpita*) to throb, to go pit-a-pat; (*d. ceasornice*) to tick ‖ *vr* to dally, to tarry, to dawdle • **~t** *nn* (*al inimii*) throb, pit-a-pat; (*al ceasornicului*) tick(ing) ‖ *adj* inefficient, slow; (*nenorocit*) wretched, miserable.

ticălos [tikă'los] *nm* (*nemernic*) scoundrel, knave, rascal; (*nenorocit*) wretch ‖ *adj* wicked, knavish; mean, vile, base; *coll* riff-raff; good-for-nothing; (*nenorocit*) wretched, miserable.

ticăloșie [tikălo'shie] *nf* baseness, wickedness, meanness; (*acțiune*) mean/vile/base/ action; (*mizerie*) wretchedness, misery.

tichet [ti'ket] *nn* ticket; *rail* reserved seat ticket; (*la garderobă etc*) check; coupon.

tichie [ti'kie] *nf* (skull)cap; (*de noapte*) night cap; (*de copil*) bonnet.

ticlui [tiklu'i] *vt* to arrange, to put/knock together; to make up; *fig* to fabricate, to plot, to devise; to be up to smth.

ticsi [tik'si] *vt* to fill, to cram; (*a aglomera*) to crowd, to huddle • **~t** *adj* crammed, crowded; stuffed with; (chock-)full, packed tight.

tictac [tik'tak] *nn* tick(ing); (*al inimii*) pit-a-pat.

tifon [ti'fon] *nn med* gauze; lint.

tifos ['tifos] *nn med* typhoid fever.

tigaie [ti'gaie] *nf* pan; (*mică, cu coadă*) skillet; basinet.

tighel [ti'gel] *nn* stitch, backstitch • **~i** *vt* to stitch, to quilt.

tigroaică [ti'groaikă] *nf* tigress.

tigru ['tigru] *nm zool* tiger; *fig* fierce person.

tigvă [ti'gvă] *nf anat* (*țeastă*) skull, brain pan; *coll* (*cap*) nut, pate; *bot* bottle gourd.

tihnă ['tihnă] *nf* quiet, repose, rest; (*răgaz*) leisure; peace of mind; **în ~** quietly, at leisure.

tihnit [tih'nit] *adj* quiet, calm, peaceful, restful; uneventful, peaceable.

tijă ['tizhă] *nf* rod; *bot* stem, stalk.

tildă ['tildă] *nf* tilde, swung dash, mark of repetition.

timbra [tim'bra] *vt* to stamp, to stick a stamp on.

timbru ['timbru] *nn* (postage/fiscal) stamp; (*jubiliar*) jubilee stamp; *mus* timbre, color; (*fonetică*) tamber.

timid [ti'mid] *adj* shy, timid, coy, (*rușinos*) bashful; hesitating; (*temător*) timorous; (*neîncrezător*) diffident (with); (*supus*) meek, demure; gentle ‖ *adv* timidly, shyly • **~itate** *nf* timidity, shyness, bashfulness; modesty; delicacy.

timonă [ti'monă] *nf naut* helm, (steering) wheel.

timonier [timoni'er] *nm naut* helmsman, steersman; quartermaster; signalman.

timora [timo'ra] *vt* to cow, to browbeat • **~t** *adj* timorous, fearful ‖ *adv* timorously, fearfully.

timp [timp] *nm mus* time, measure, movement, beat ‖ *nn astron* time; (*personificat*) Father Time; *myth* Saturn; moment; (*oră*) hour; (*zi*) day; (*anotimp*) season; (*epocă*) epoch, times, day; (*perioadă*) age, period; (*ocazie*) occasion, opportunity; *gram* tense; *med* stage (of an operation); **cât ~?** how long?; **din ~** in advance, beforehand; **în ~ ce** while, as; (*pe câtă vreme*) while, whilst; **între ~** meanwhile, (in the) meantime; **la ~** in/on time.

timpan [tim'pan] *nn anat* ear drum, tympanum; *mus* tymbal, timbale; *mus pl* timpani; *archit* tympanon.

timpuriu [timpu'riu] *adj* early; matinal; precocious, untimely; hasty; (*necopt*) unripe; **de ~** (too) at an early hour; (*dimineața*) (early) in the morning.

tină ['tină] *nf* (*noroi*) mud, slime; (*țărână*) earth, dust.

tinctură [tink'tură] *nf pharm* tincture, infusion; (*culoare*) tinge.

tindă ['tindă] *nf* entrance room/hall, vestibule, parlor.

tinde ['tinde] *vi* **a ~ la** to tend to; (*a năzui spre*) to seek, to strive for; to yearn for.

tine ['tine] *pron* you; *obs, lit* thee; **cu ~** with you.

tinerel [tine'rel] *nm* shaveling, youngster; stripling ‖ *adj* young(ish).

tineresc [tine'resk] *adj* youth(ful), juvenile; (*proaspăt*) fresh.

tineret [tine'ret] *nn* youth, young people; **de ~** youth(ful).

tinerețe [tine'retse] *nf* youth; *fig* youthfulness.

tinerime [tine'rime] *nf* young people, youth.

tingire [tin'djire] *nf* (sauce)pan.

tinichea [tini'kea] *nf* (*tablă*) sheet; (*cositorită*) tin (plate); (*vas de ~*) vessel of tin plate; (*cutie*) tin box/ canister; *pej* (*decorație*) decoration.

tinichigerie [tinikidje'rie] *nf* (*atelier*) tinsman's shop.

tinichigiu [tiniki'djiu] *nm* tinker, tinsman, tinsmith.

tip [tip] *nm* individual, character; *coll* guy, fellow ‖ *nn* type, prototype; standard model; (*și tipar*) pattern; (*fel*) kind, sort; category; symbol.

tipar [ti'par] *nn* printing (press), print; (*arta tipăritului*) typographic(al) art, typography; (*industrie*) printing industry; (*șablon*) pattern, model; (*mulaj*) mold, cast; (*materiale nobile*) skillet; **sub ~** in press; (*urmă*) impress(ion), imprint.

tipări [tipă'ri] *vt* to print, to publish; (*la mașina de scris*) to type; (*a întipări*) to imprint, to impress ‖ *vr* to be printed/published • **~tură** *nf* (*acțiune*) printing, publication; (*lucrare tipărită*) printed work; (*imprimat*) print; *pl* printed matter.

tipesă [ti'pesă] *nf coll* jade; *sl* flossy; woman.

tipic¹ ['tipik] *nn* typical character, (quint)essence ‖ *adj* typical (of), characteristic (of).

tipic² [ti'pik] *nn* pattern, template; tradition, rule, norm; *relig* (*carte*) church formulary; *relig* (*rânduială*) ritual; ritual law.

tipicar [tipi'kar] *nm* formalist, stickler; dogmatist; person who sticks to routine, *coll* person stuck in a rut ‖ *adj* fussy, stiff, meticulous, formal(istic).

tipiza [tipi'za] *vt* to typify; to standardize.

tipograf [tipo'graf] *nm* printer, printing worker; (*zețar*) typesetter; typographer • **~ie** *nf* printing works/house; (*arta tiparului*) typography.

tiptil [tip'til] *adv* on tiptoe, lightly; (*pe furiș*) stealthily, furtively; (*încet*) slowly; (*binișor*) gently.

tir [tir] *nn mil* fire, shooting; gunnery; *sp* target shooting; (*poligon*) shooting ground, (rifle) range; (*acoperit*) shooting gallery.

tiradă [ti'radă] *nf* tirade; monologue.

tiraj [ti'razh] *nn* circulation; (*publicare*) printing (off); (*la sobă*) draft.

tiran [ti'ran] *nm* tyrant, despot; *fig* autocrat, bully • *adj* autocratic, despotic • **~ie** *nf* tyranny; despotism, autocracy • **~iza** *vt* to tyrannize; to terrorize, to bully.

tirbușon [tirbu'shon] *nn* corkscrew.

tiribombă [tiri'bombă] *nf* firecracker.

tiroidă [tiro'idă] *nf anat* thyroid.

tisă ['tisă] *nf bot* yew (tree).

titan [ti'tan] *nm myth* Titan; *fig* genius; *chem* titanium.

titanic [ti'tanik] *adj* titanic, titanesque, tremendous.

titirez [titi'rez] *nm* (spinning/humming) top, whirligig; *fig* fidget; (*la moară*) clack.

titlu ['titlu] *nn* title; (*de capitol*) heading; *jur* right, legal basis; section, chapter of a law book; *fig* claim; act, deed; *com* warrant, bond; (*grad și*) degree; (*rang*) rank; *edu* diploma, certificate; *chem* (*probă la metale*) titre; *cin* (*generic*) credit titles; **cu ~ de** by way of, as a, by right of.

titra [tit'ra] *vt chem* to titrate; *cin* to subtitle.

titrat [tit'rat] *n* university graduate; title holder ‖ *adj* having a degree; certified; qualified (teacher); *chem* standard (solution); (*d. text*) titled.

titular [titu'lar] *nm* holder; (*al unei funcții*) occupant; (*al uni act*) bearer; *relig* incumbent ‖ *adj* full; permanent, official; appointed; **profesor ~** tenured professor; **rol ~** *thea* title/leading role.

titulatură [titula'tură] *nf* title; entitling.

tiv [tiv] *nn* hemstitch; selvedge; seam • **~i** *vt* to hemstitch, to selvedge, to seam; *tech* to edge; to lap-joint; *fig* to fringe, to border.

tiz [tiz] *nm* namesake.

tizană [ti'zană] *nf* herbal tea.

toaletă [toa'letă] *nf* toilet; (*îmbrăcăminte*) outfit, dress; (*măsuță de ~*) toilet/dressing table; *fig* covering, dressing; (*lavabou*) washstand; (*closet*) restroom; (*încăpere*) washroom, bathroom; ladies'/men's room; (*fără canalizare*) backhouse.

toamnă ['toamnă] *nf* fall; (*timpul recoltei*) harvesttime; (*anotimpul fructelor*) fruit time.

toană ['toană] *nf* whim, fancy, caprice; fad; freak; mood, disposition; (*clipă*) moment; *coll* jiffy; *med* (*atac*) fit; **cu ~e** moody, whimsical, freakish.

toarce ['toarche] *vt/vi* to spin; (*d. pisici*) to purr.

toartă ['toartă] *nf* (*a unui vas*) ear, handle; (*a cratiței*) panhandle; (*cârlig*) hook; (*de găleată*) bail; (*de lacăt*) shackle; (*cercel*) earring.

toast [to'ast] *nn* toast • **~a** *vt* to give/propose a toast, to toast.

toată ['toată] *adj f* all; (*întreagă*) whole, full ‖ *adv* fully, completely, all.

toate ['toate] *adj f pl* all; (*fiecare*) every.

tobă ['tobă] *nf mus, tech* drum; *cul* mosaic salami; (*la cărți*) diamonds; **~a mare** kettle drum.

tobogan [tobo'gan] *nn* slide, chute.

toboșar [tobo'shar] *nm* drummer, drum player.

toc [tok] (*de scris*) penholder; pen; (*de pantofi*) heel; (*cutie*) case, box; (*teacă*) scabbard, sheath; (*de ochelari*) glass case; (*de revolver*) holster; (*de cartușe*) cartridge case; (*de ușă*) frame, jamb.

toca [to'ka] *vt* (*legume, carne*) to hash, to hack; to chop, to hew; (*cu mașina*) to grind; (*a cresta*) to notch; *fig coll* (*d. bani: a irosi*) to waste; (*a cheltui*) to spend; (*a stoarce*) to sweat; *fig* (*a pisa*) to bother, to pester smb; **a ~ carne** to hash/grind meat ‖ *vi* (*a*

vorbi mult) to prattle, to chatter; (*a clămpăni*) to clack, to rattle; (*d. barză*) to clatter; (*a ciocăni*) to knock; *relig* (*a bate toaca*) to hammer on the bellboard.

tocană [to'kană] *nf cul* goulash, stew, ragout.

tocător [tokă'tor] *adj* hacking, * **toca** ‖ *nn* (*cuțit de tocat*) (meat) chopper, cleaver; (*scândură de tocat*) chopping/cutting board.

tocătură [tokă'tură] *nf* ground meat; (*de plante*) chopped herbs.

toceală [to'cheală] *nf edu* cramming.

toci [to'chi] *vt* to blunt, to jag; to take the edge off; *fig* to dull, to wear out; (*a uza*) to wear away/ off/out ‖ *vi fig* to cram ‖ *vr* to get blunt/dull; to wear out; (*d. o unealtă*) to lose its point/edge; (*d. brici*) to get dull • **~lar** *nm* whetstone grinder, whetter; *edu* crammer • **~lă** *nf* grindstone • **~lărie** *nf* whetstone grinding; whetter's/grinder's shop.

tocit [to'chit] *adj* blunted, jagged; dulled; (*uzat*) worn(out); threadbare.

tocmai ['tokmai] *adv* just; exactly, precisely; (*chiar*) even; (*numai*) only; (*în mod deosebit*) particularly; **nu ~** not quite/exactly; (*de curând*) recently, lately; scarcely; **~ așa** exactly/precisely like that; **~ azi** today of all days; (*d. friptură*) done to a turn.

tocmeală [tok'meală] *nf* bargaining; negotiation; (*târguială*) haggling; (*învoială*) agreement; (*înțelegere*) understanding.

tocmi [tok'mi] *vt* (*a angaja*) to hire, to engage; *com* to order; (*a închiria*) to rent ‖ *vr* (*a se târgui*) to bargain, to haggle, to negotiate; (*a discuta*) to argue; (*a se angaja*) to engage/pledge/commit oneself (to do smth).

togă ['togă] *nf* toga, *pl* togae.

toi [toi] *nn* height; (*punct culminant*) climax; (*mijloc*) middle; **în ~** in full swing/blast, at its height.

toiag [to'iag] *nn* staff; (*ca semn de autoritate*) wand, rod, baton; scepter; (*baston*) (walking) stick; *fig* prop, mainstay.

tolăni [tolă'ni] *vr* to sprawl; to recline, to lie down; (*la căldură, soare*) to bask.

tolbă ['tolbă] *nf* (game) bag, satchel; (*cu săgeți*) quiver; (*de vânătoare*) sportsman's bag; (*pt. păsări*) fowling bag.

tolera [tole'ra] *vt* to tolerate, to suffer; to allow, to permit; (*a suporta*) to bear, to stand • **~nt** *adj* tolerant, liberal; indulgent, lenient • **~nță** *nf* tolerance; indulgence; (*religioasă*) toleration; (*indulgență*) connivance; *tech* tolerance; limit, margin; **~ zero** zero tolerance.

tom [tom] *nn* volume, tome, (part of a) book.

tomată [to'mată] *nf* tomato; **suc de ~e** tomato juice.

tomberon [tombe'ron] *nn* dumping cart, tumbrel.

tombolă [tom'bolă] *nf* tombola, raffle.

tomnatic [tom'natik] *adj* autumnal; *fig* elderly; middle-aged.

tomografie [tomogra'fie] *nf med* tomography.

ton [ton] *nm* tuna (fish) ‖ *nn mus* tone, note; (*timbru*) timbre, (*tonalitate*) key; (*înălțime*) pitch; (musical) sound; (*al vocii*) accent; (*intonație*) intonation; (*de culoare*) tone (of color), (*nuanță*) shade, tint; *fig* fashion; (*la telefon*) dialing tone, signal.

tonaj [to'nazh] *nn naut* tonnage; **~ net** register tonnage.

tonalitate [tonali'tate] *nf mus* tonality, intonation; (*culoare*) shade, hue; prevalent feature, characteristic.

tonă ['tonă] *nf* (metric) ton.

tonetă [to'netă] *nf* stall; (*cu cărți*) stand.

tonic ['tonik] *adj med, mus* tonic; (*întăritor*) invigorating; cordial; *fig* bracing || *nn* tonic.

tonifiant [tonifi'ant] *adj* tonic, bracing || *nn med* tonic (medicine).

tonomat [tono'mat] *nn* juke-box.

tont [tont] *nm pej* booby, dullard, simpleton, moron; (*neîndemânatic*) gawk, lout || *adj* stupid, dull; silly, simple; (*neîndemânatic*) gawky, awkward.

top [top] *nn* (*de hârtie*) ream; (*clasament*) top (chart).

topaz [to'paz] *nn* topaz; (*fumuriu*) cairngorm || *adj* topaz-colored.

topi [to'pi] *vt* to (cause to) melt; (*d. metale*) to (s)melt, to fuse; (*o masă sticloasă*) to frit; (*cânepa*) to ret; (*zăpadă*) to thaw; (*a dizolva*) to dissolve; to consume; *fig* to destroy, to ruin; to soften || *vr* to melt; (*d. metale*) to smelt, to fuse; (*d. zăpadă*) to thaw; *fig* to soften, to relent; (*a dispărea*) to dissolve; (*a se evapora*) to make oneself scarce; (*a se mistui*) to consume • ~re *nf* melting; *metal* smelting; (*a zăpezii*) thaw(ing); (*a cânepii*) retting, rotting.

topografie [topogra'fie] *nf* topography, land survey; (*așezare*) location.

toponimie [toponi'mie] *nf* toponymy.

topor [to'por] *nn* axe, hatchet; (*la indieni nord-americani*) tomahawk; **din** ~ unrefined; uncouth.

toporaș [topo'rash] *nm bot* violet.

toporișcă [topo'rishkă] *nf* * **bardă.**

torace [to'rache] *nn anat* chest, thorax.

toreador [torea'dor] *nm* bullfighter, toreador.

torent [to'rent] *nn* torrent; mountain stream.

torențial [torentsi'al] *adj* torrential, pouring.

torid [to'rid] *adj* (*d. zonă*) torrid; sultry; (*d. căldură*) scorching.

tornadă [tor'nadă] *nf met* tornado.

toropeală [toro'peală] *nf* torpor, dullness; reverie; apathy; (*arșiță*) scorching heat.

toropi [toro'pi] *vt* (*a adormi*) to make drowsy; to cause to become dull/torpid; to make languid; (*a slăbi*) to enervate; to unnerve, to overpower.

torpedo [tor'pedo] *nn* back pedal, coaster brake.

torpila [torpi'la] *vt* to (sink by a) torpedo; *fig* to frustrate, to wreck; (*a submina*) to undermine.

torpilă [tor'pilă] *nf mil* torpedo; *icht* torpedo, electric ray.

tors [tors] *nn* spinning; (*la pisici*) purring; *anat* torso; trunk || *adj* spun • ~**iona** *vt* to twist, to produce torsion in ~**iune** *nf* torsion, torque.

tort ['tortă] *nf* cake (fancy/cream/birthday/wedding).

tortura [tortu'ra] *vt* to torture, to persecute; *fig* to torment • ~t *adj* tortured, tormented; ~ **de gânduri** thought-ridden.

tortură [tor'tură] *nf* torture, suffering; *fig* torment.

torță ['tortsă] *nf* torch.

torționar [tortsio'nar] *adj/nm frml* torturer.

tot [tot] *adj* all; (*întreg*) whole, entire; (*fiecare*) every; (*destul*) enough || *pron* everything; (*partitiv*) all (of it); (*întreg*) whole; the whole (of it); unit; total; *fig* the (quint)essence || *adv* (*temporal*) still; even now; (*în prop. negative*) not yet, not even now; ~ **n-au venit** they haven't arrived yet; (*în continuare*) further, still, on; (*încă*) still; ~ **mai lipsesc două** there are still two missing, two are still missing; (*mereu*) always, all the time; ~ **mai sus** higher and higher;

invariably; (*repetat*) repeatedly; (*crescând*) more; (*la fel*) also, likewise; (*tocmai*) precisely, just; (*iar*) again, anew; the same as usual; (*numai*) only; (*complet*) wholly, completely; **s-a stricat de** ~ it's completely broken.

total [to'tal] *nn* (sum) total; **în** ~ (all) in all, altogether || *adj* whole, entire; general, universal; absolute, complete; *econ* all-out, overall || *adv* totally, utterly, completely • ~**itarism** *nm* totalitarianism • ~**itate** *nf* total, ensemble, whole; totality; **în** ~ entirely, wholly; **luat în** ~ taken as a whole • ~**iza** *vt* to totalize, to tote; to add up (to); (*a centraliza*) to summarize; (*a se ridica la*) to amount to • ~**mente** *adv* absolutely, utterly, totally.

totdeauna [totdea'una] *adv* always, ever; invariably; usually, as a rule; (*oricând*) at all times, at any time; (*continuu*) continually, all along; **ca** ~ as always, as usual; **din** ~ *adj* old, constant || *adv* always, constantly, all the time; **pentru** ~ for good (and all), definitively, for ever (and ever).

totem [to'tem] *nn* totem.

totodată [toto'dată] *adv* at the same time, simultaneously; (*pe de altă parte*) on the other hand.

totuna [to'tuna] *adv* all the same; **mi-e** ~ it makes no difference to me, it's all the same to me.

totuși ['totush] *conj* still, however; nevertheless, nonetheless; **și** ~ and yet, for all that.

toți ['totsi] *pron* all (people), everybody, every man || *adj* all, every; **au venit** ~ they all came; ~ **invitații** all the guests; **noi** ~ all of us.

tovarăș [to'vărăsh] *nm* comrade, pal, mate; associate; (*de afaceri, de viață*) partner; (*însoțitor*) companion.

toxic ['toksik] *nn* toxic (substance) || *adj* toxic, noxious, poisonous; **gaz** ~ poison gas • ~**itate** *nf* toxicity.

toxicoman [toksiko'man] *nm* drug addict • ~**ie** *nf* drug addiction.

toxină [tok'sină] *nf* toxin.

trabuc [tra'buk] *nn* cigar.

trac[1] [trak] *nn coll* fright, funk; *thea* stage fright.

trac[2] [trak] *nm/adj* Thracian.

tracasa [traka'sa] *vt frml* to bother, to plague, to pester.

tracta [trak'ta] *vt tech* to draw along • drag, to tow, to haul.

tractabil [trak'tabil] *adj* manageable, pliant; kindly, amiable.

tractor [trak'tor] *nn* tractor • ~**ist** *nm* tractor driver/ operator.

tracțiune [traktsi'une] *nf* traction, pulling; drive; draft; haulage.

tradiție [tra'ditsie] *nf* tradition, custom; **de** ~ traditional.

tradițional [traditsio'nal] *adj* traditional; usual, habitual; (*d. scuză, echipament*) standard; standing || *adv* traditionally.

traducător [tradukă'tor] *nm* translator, interpreter.

traduce [tra'duche] *vt* to translate (from … to), to render (into another language); to interpret; *fig* to express, to represent; *jur* to sue; to bring to justice/law; *coll* (*a înșela*) to cheat on smb; (*a înfăptui*) to carry out, to bring/carry into effect • ~**re** *nf* translation; interpretation; version.

trafic ['trafik] *nn* traffic, circulation; trade, commerce; *pej* traffic, illicit trade; communication • ~**a** *vi* (*cu*) to traffic/deal (in); to trade illicitly (in); to make illicit profit out of smth • ~**nt** *nm* trafficker, dealer; ~ **de alcool** bootlegger; ~ **de stupefiante** dope dealer/

peddler, drug trafficker; ~ **de carne vie** slave dealer, white slaver.

traforaj [trafo'razh] *nn* fret-saw, jigsaw.

trage ['tradje] *vi* to pull (on); (*cu arma*) to shoot, to fire; **a ~ în** to shoot/fire at; (*a cântări*) to weigh; (*a se opri*) to stop/halt at; to check in at a hotel; (*d. vânt*) to blow gently; (*a avea tiraj*) to draw; (*a tinde spre*) to feel attracted towards; (*a bea*) to drink heavily; *coll* to booze, to swill; (*a fi pe punctul de a*) to be about to; (*d. vreme*) to look like.

tragedie [tradje'die] *nf* tragedy; *fig also* misfortune, catastrophe.

tragere ['tradjere] *nf* drawing, pulling; (*tir*) shooting, firing; musketry; (*artilerie*) gunnery; (*la loterie*) lottery drawing; *metal* wire drawing; (*a unei frânghii*) tugging; towing.

tragic ['tradjik] *adj* tragic; sad, mournful; unfortunate; dreadful || *nn* tragic side (of an event); **în ~** tragically, dramatically || *adv* tragically, sadly.

trahee [tra'hee] *nf anat* trachea; *bot* air vessel, duct.

trai [trai] *nn* life; (*mod de viaţă*) living; existence; (*material şi*) livelihood.

traiect [tra'iekt] *nn* route; line; course; (*de proiectil*) *also elec* path • **~orie** *nf* trajectory; path.

trainic ['trainik] *adj* (long-)lasting, durable; solid, resistant; firm || *adv* solidly, durably.

traistă ['traistă] *nf* (beggar's) bag, purse, pack; (*desagă*) wallet; knapsack; bread bin; (*conţinut*) bagful, sackful.

trambulină [trambu'linǎ] *nf also fig* springboard; (*la înot*) diving board; (*la ski*) ski jump; (*la circ*) trampoline.

trampă ['trampǎ] *nf* bargain; exchange (in kind), barter.

tramvai [tram'vai] *nn* street car.

tranchilizant [trankili'zant] *nn/adj pharm* tranquilizer, sedative.

trandafir [tranda'fir] *nm bot* rose (flower/bush/tree); *cul* thin spiced pork sausage • **~iu** *adj* pink(-colored), rosy; (*d. vin*) rose; *also fig* sanguine, optimistic; bright, cheerful.

transatlantic [transat'lantik] *nn* (Atlantic) liner, transatlantic steamer || *adj* transatlantic.

transă ['transǎ] *nf* (hypnotic) trance; *usu pl* fright, fear.

transborda [transbor'da] *vt naut* to transship; to reload; to transfer (passengers/goods) from one train/plane to another.

transcendent [transchen'dent] *adj* transcendental, metaphysical.

transcrie [tran'skrie] *vt* to transcribe, to copy (officially); *mus* to arrange; *jur* to register; (*dintr-un alfabet în altul*) to transliterate • **~re** *nf* transcription, transcribing, transliteration (into); transcript, copy.

transept [tran'sept] *nn archit, relig* transept, cross aisle.

transfer [trans'fer] *nn* transfer(ring), change of job; (*de populaţie*) resettlement; *jur* assignment, making over; (*de proprietate*) conveyance; transfer of property; *phys* transference; *sp* transfer of players • **~a** *vt* (*o persoană*) to transfer; (*un obiect*) to shift; (*un sediu etc*) to move; (*a atribui*) to make over; *jur* (*drepturi*) to convey; (*o proprietate*) to cede || *vr* to move; to change one's job; *mil* to join another regiment.

transfocator [transfoka'tor] *nn* zoom.

transforma [transfor'ma] *vt* to transform, to change; to metamorphose; to turn/change into; (*a îmbunătăţi*)

to improve; (*a comuta*) to commute; *log* to convert; *sp* to convert a try; to map || *vr* to change, to be changed; (*a deveni*) to become • **~re** *nf* transformation, conversion, make-over; **staţie de ~** *elec* transformer station • **~tor** *nn* transformer || *adj* changing, innovating.

transfug [trans'fug] *nm pol, mil* deserter (to the other side); *fig* defector

transfuzie [tran'sfuzie] *nf* transfusion (esp. of blood).

transgresiune [transgresi'une] *nf* transgression.

transistor [tranzis'tor] *nn elec* transistor; **cu ~i** transistorized; (*computer etc*) solid-state.

translator [trans'lator] *nm* translator, interpreter.

translucid [translu'chid] *adj* translucent.

transmisie, transmisiune [trans'misie, transmisi'une] *nf* transmission; passing on, sending; imparting; handing down; *jur* conveyance, transfer(rence); *rad* broadcast; *also tech* drive, gear(ing).

transmite [trans'mite] *vt* (*căldură etc*) to transmit; to pass on, to convey; to impart; *rad* to broadcast; (*a răspândi*) to spread; to disseminate; (*a transfera*) to transfer; *jur* to assign; (*a preda*) to hand over; (*a încredinţa*) to confer; (*a lăsa*) to leave; (*tradiţii*) to hand down; *tech* to feed || *vi* to broadcast || *vr* to spread; (*d. boli*) to be contagious; (*ereditar*) to run in the family; to be handed down.

transoceanic [transo'cheanik] *adj* transoceanic.

transparent [transpa'rent] *nn* (*pt. scris*) black/ink/writing lines, guide (for writing pad); (*la retroproiector*) transparency || *adj* transparent, translucent; clear (as crystal); (*d. ţesături*) light; diaphanous; *fig* obvious, evident; (*d. un pretext*) flimsy.

transparenţă [transpa'rentsǎ] *nf* transparence, transparency; limpidity, lucidity; **~a cerului** the limpidity of the sky.

transperant [transpe'rant] *nn* Venetian blind, roller blind, shutter, shade; (*afară*) (outside) awning.

transpira [transpi'ra] *vi* (*şi d. plante*) to sweat, to perspire; (*d. geamuri*) to be(come) blurred/steamed; (*d. pereţi*) to be moist/damp; *fig* to leak, to come to light • **~ţie** *nf* sweat, perspiration.

transplant [trans'plant] *nn* transplant • **~a** *vt* (*pomi*) *also fig* to transplant; to replant; (*o inimă*) to perform a heart transplant operation; (*flori*) to bed/pot • **~are** *nf* transplantation, transplanting; *med* (heart) transplant.

transport [trans'port] *nn also pl* transport(ation), conveyance; (*de mărfuri*) carriage; haulage; *naut* shipping; (*cantitate*) supply, consignment; (*cu vaporul*) shipment; *jur* transfer, conveyance; assignment; *psych* rapture, outburst; transports ecstasy; burst • **~a** *vt* to transport, to convey; (*a trimite mai departe*) to forward; (*a duce cu un vehicul*) to carry; (*cu camionul*) to haul; (*a furniza*) to deliver; to deport; *jur* to transfer; to assign; *com* (*în acte*) to carry/bring forward; *fig* (*a încânta*) to delight, to carry away.

transpune [trans'pune] *vt* to transpose; (*d. un curs*) to refurbish, to rehash || *vr fig* to imagine oneself.

transsexual [transeksu'al] *adj/nm* transsexual.

transversal [transver'sal] *adj* transversal, transverse, cross(-cut); (*oblic*) oblique, slanting || *adv* crosswise, across; *also naut* thwartship(s).

transversală [transver'salǎ] *nf geom* transversal (line).

tranşa [tran'sha] *vt* (*d. carne*) to trench, to carve; (*d. pâine*) to slice, to cut; *fig* to resolve/settle (a matter, an issue) once and for all; to dispose of; to make short work of a problem.

tranşant [tran'shant] *adj* categorical, firm, decisive; (*d. cuvinte*) clear-cut; (*d. ton*) peremptory; (*refuz*) blunt; (*d. cineva*) self-assertive.

tranşă ['transhă] *nf fin* part, portion; (*rată*) installment; (*de carne*) section; (*la cărţi, top de hârtie*) (cut) edge.

tranşee [tran'shee] *nf* trench; ditch; line of approach; *agr* drain.

tranzacţie [tran'zaktsie] *nf* transaction; *pl* dealings, deals; agreement; compromise.

tranzistor [tranzis'tor] *nn elec, telec* transistor; *coll* transistor/portable radio; **cu ~i** transistor(ized) • **~izat** *adj elec* transistorized; (*d. computer etc*) solid-state.

tranzit ['tranzit] *nn* transit; **în ~** in transit • **~a** *vt* to convey in transit; to forward || *vi* (*d. mărfuri*) to be in transit.

tranzitiv [tranzi'tiv] *adj gram* transitive.

tranzitoriu [tranzi'toriu] *adj* transitory, transient, transitional, temporary; intermediary; provisional.

tranziţie [tran'zitsie] *nf* transition.

trap [trap] *nn* trot.

trapă ['trapă] *nf* trap(-door), flap floor; trap, pitfall.

trapez [tra'pez] *nn* trapeze; *geom* trapezium.

trapeză [tra'peză] *nf relig* refectory.

trasa [tra'sa] *vt* (*o linie*) to draw; (*a schiţa*) to sketch; to trace, to outline; (*o curbă, un grafic*) to plot; to mark; (*un teren, un drum*) to map/lay out; (*o sarcină*) to assign, to set.

traseu [tra'seu] *nn* route, tract; *rad* plot.

trasor [tra'sor] *nn* tracer; *phys* tracer atom.

trata [tra'ta] *vt* (*o boală*) to treat; (*a se ocupa de un pacient*) to attend; (*a se purta cu*) to behave (towards); (*oaspeţi*) to entertain, to wine and dine; to banquet; (*a face cinste*) to stand a treat; *chem* to treat; to spray; (*lentile*) to coat; (*un subiect*) to deal with; to discuss, to handle; (*a negocia*) to negotiate, to transact a business deal; (*a discuta*) to debate upon, to argue || *vi* to negotiate, to discuss, to deal • **~ment** *nn* treatment; (*mânuire*) handling; *also med* cure, medical attendance/care; attitude, behavior.

tratat [tra'tat] *nn* treaty, pact, agreement; (*carte*) treatise (on); handbook; dissertation, paper • **~ive** *nf pl* negotiations, talks.

trataţie [tra'tatsie] *nf* treat, entertainment.

trauler ['trauler] *nn naut* trawler.

traumatic [trau'matik] *adj* traumatic.

traumatism [trauma'tism] *nn med* trauma.

traumatiza [traumati'za] *vt* to traumatize.

traumă ['traumă] *nf med* trauma.

travaliu [tra'valiu] *nn* work, labor; effort(s); *med* travail, *coll* labor, throes.

traversa [traver'sa] *vt* to cross (over), *lit* to traverse; (*munţii, o ţară*) to cross; (*un râu*) to pass; (*prin vad*) to ford; *also fig* (*a trece prin*) to go/pass through; (*înot*) to swim across; (*navigând*) to sail over/across; (*d. un râu*) to run across/through || *vi* to cross/go/pass over; to step across • **~re** *nf* crossing; (*pasaj*) crosswalk; *naut* fishing; bearing (of sails) to the windward.

traversă [tra'versă] *nf constr* traverse, transom; (*la o scară*) rung; *rail* tie; *auto* cross member (of a frame).

travesti [traves'ti] *vt* to dress up, to disguise; (*a masca*) to mask; to travesty, to parody || *vr* to disguise oneself, to masquerade; *thea* to make up || *nn* disguise;

sl drag • **~re** *nf* disguising; disguise; mask; *thea* make-up • **~t** *adj* disguised, masqued || *nm* transvestite.

trăda [tră'da] *vt* to betray; (*a înşela*) to deceive; to play smb false; *coll* to let smb down; to sell; (*o cauză*) to abandon; (*a da în vileag*) to disclose; *coll* to give away; **a ~ un secret** to let out a secret, *coll* to let the cat out of the bag, (*din greşeală*) to blurt out a secret; *fig* to manifest, to show || *vr* to give oneself away, to betray oneself • **~re** *nf* (*acţiune*) betraying; (*rezultat*) betrayal; treachery, perfidy; *fig* unfaithfulness.

trădător [trădă'tor] *nm* traitor; *thea* the villain || *adj* treacherous, faithless; (*revelator*) tell tale.

trăgaci [tră'gach] *nn* trigger.

trăgător [trăgă'tor] *nm* puller; (*ţintaş*) shot, marksman; **~ de elită** sharpshooter, sniper; *com* drawer (of a bill of exchange) || *nn* drawing/road pen (for maps).

trăi [tră'i] *vi* (*a fi în viaţă*) to live, to be alive/living; to exist, to be; to respire, to breathe; (*a dura*) to last, to live; (*a-şi ~ viaţa*) to lead one's life; (*a duce o viaţă de*) to live a life of; **a ~ bine** (*a petrece*) to lead a pleasant/easy life; *coll* to have a good time of it; (*a fi bogat*) to be well off; (*a mânca bine*) to keep a good table; **a ~ din** (*a se hrăni cu*) to live on; (*d. animale*) to feed on; (*prin, datorita*) to live/subsist by.

trăinicie [trăini'chie] *nf* permanence, solidity.

trăire [tra'ire] *nf* living; (life) experience; (*simţire*) feelings.

trăncăni [trănkă'ni] *vt* to babble, to prattle || *vi* (*a pălăvrăgi*) to chat, to chatter, to prattle; to tell stories; *sl* to yak; (*a bârfi*) to gossip; (*a vorbi tot timpul, incoerent*) to ramble on, to jabber; (*a spune prostii*) to talk nonsense; (*a zăngăni*) to clink, to clack.

trăpaş [tră'pash] *nm* trotter.

trăsătură [trăsă'tură] *nf* (*element*) feature; trait; (*linie trasă dintr-o singură mişcare*) touch, stroke; (*liniuţă de unire*) hyphen.

trăsnaie [trăs'naie] *nf* whim, fad, craze; merry prank; trick, farce; (*prostie*) foolish act, piece of folly.

trăsneală [trăs'neală] *nf* whim; freak, oddity.

trăsnet ['trăsnet] *nn* (thunder)bolt; **lovitură de ~** thunderbolt; **femeie ~** stunner.

trăsni [trăs'ni] *vt* to thunder; to strike down, to blast; (*a izbi*) to strike, to hit || *vi imp* to thunder, to strike; *coll* to fulminate; *fig* to occur (to smb); to appear unexpectedly.

trăsnit [trăs'nit] *nm* (*nebun*) madman, *sl* loony || *adj also fig* thunderstruck; *fig* (*uluit*) flabbergasted, dumbfounded; (*zănatic*) cranky; *coll* cracked; (*nebun*) crazy, nuts; *coll* (*beat*) corky, afflicted.

trăsură [tră'sură] *nf* coach, carriage; (*de mărfuri*) cart; (*uşoară*) gig, dog cart; (*birjă*) cab, hackney coach.

trâmbă [trâm'bă] *nf* (*vârtej*) (*de praf*) whirlwind; (*de vânt*) eddy of wind; (*de apă*) waterspout; (*de nisip*) sandstorm; (*de fum*) roll; (*de zăpadă*) flurry; (*rând, şir*) row, line; (*dungă, fâşie*) stripe; (*ceată, pâlc*) troop; (*de material, rulat*) roll of material; (*adverbial*) in troops/crowds.

trâmbiţa [trâmbi'tsa] *vt* to announce, to proclaim; to trumpet a piece of news, to herald; to advertise || *vi* to blow/sound the trumpet, to sound the bugle.

trâmbiţă ['trâmbitsă] *nf* clarion, bugle, trumpet.

trândav [trân'dav] *adj* idle, slothful, unoccupied; (*d. minte, stomac*) sluggish || *nm* idler, drone, sluggard, *coll* lazybones.

trândăveală [trândă'veală] *nf* * **trândăvire**.

trândăvi [trândă'vi] *vi* to loiter, to dilly-dally, to laze about/around, to slug, to lounge, *coll* to dawdle • ~re *nf* idling.

trântă [trântă] *nf* wrestle, wrestling match; quarrel, row.

trânteală [trân'teală] *nf coll* (*bătaie*) licking, drubbing; *coll* (*încăierare*) scuffle.

trânti [trân'ti] *vt* to fling, to cast (to the ground); to throw down; (*a doborî*) to fell; to knock/push over; (*a izbi*) (*uşa*) to slam; (*a scăpa*) to drop; (*la examen*) to flunk; (*verbal*) (*o înjurătură*) to rap out; (*a răspunde obraznic/răstit*) to snap (at smb); (*a divulga un secret*) to blurt/blunder out || *vi* to fling things about || *vr* to fling/throw oneself about; (*a se culca*) to lie down

trântor [trântor] *nm ento* drone(bee); *fig also* idler, loafer, sluggard, *coll* lazybones.

treabă ['treabă] *nf* business, activity; (*muncă*) work; (*slujbă*) job; occupation; (*chestiune*) problem, issue, matter; (*situaţie*) situation; *pl* business affairs; things to do.

treaptă ['treaptă] *nf* step, stair, tread (of step); rung (of ladder); *pl* flight (of steps); *fig* degree, level, stage; (*rang*) rank.

treaz [treaz] *adj* (wide-)awake, astir, not asleep; (*vioi*) quick, alive; (*atent*) vigilant; (*de veghe*) watchful; (*nebăut*) sober; *coll* dry.

trebălui [trebălu'i] *vi* to putter (about the house); to do small/odd jobs; to bustle about.

trebui [trebu'i] *vi* (*obligaţie*) must, to have to, to be obliged/compelled to, ~e **făcut** it must be done; (*necesitate*) to be necessary/required; to need; to lack, **bluza** ~e **călcată** the blouse needs ironing, **cât îţi** ~e? how much do you need?, how much must you have?; (*datorie*) should, (*mai puternic*) ought to, ~e **să-ţi ajuţi prietenii** you should/ought to help your friends; (*în viitor*) to be to, to have to, to be due to, ~e **să plec mâine** I am/have to leave tomorrow); (*părere exprimată, probabilitate*) must, ~e **să fie obosiţi** they must be tired; (*repros*) **nu** ~a **să-i spui** you shouldn't have told him; (*interdicţie*) **nu** ~e **să mergi acolo** you are not (supposed) to go there; (*a merita*) **aşa îţi** ~e! serves you right! • ~ncios *adj* necessary, needful, useful • ~nţă *nf* need, necessity, want; utility, usefulness, service • **de** ~nţă needful, necessary.

trecătoare [trekă'toare] *nf* (*în munţi*: defileu, cheie) mountain pass; gorge; (*loc de trecere*) passage.

trecător [trekă'tor] *nm* passer-by; (*pieton*) pedestrian || *adj* passing, transient, temporary; (*d. frumuseţe, fericire*) fleeting, short-lived; (*d. durere*) momentary; (*perisabil*) perishable.

trece ['treche] *vi* to pass; (*pe lângă*) to pass by, to go past, to fly by; (*ca un fulger*) to flash past; (*ca o săgeată*) to dart/fly by, to shoot past; (*ca vântul*) to sweep/whisk past/by; (*huruind în goană*) (*d. vehicule*) to rattle along; (*fără a se opri*) (*d. trenuri*) to pass a station; (*pe la cineva*) to drop by; (*repede pe lângă cineva*) to brush past smb; (*a-şi face loc*) to get by/past; (*d. timp*) to fly; (*d. ape*) to flow; (*d. vânt*) to blow; (*d. boli*) to heal; (*a expira*) to run out; (*pe nesimţite*) to slip by; (*cu greu*) to lie/hang heavy; (*a face să treacă timpul*) (*a lenevi*) to while away; (*în mod plăcut*) to beguile; (*a se mişca*) to move; (*mai departe*) to leave behind; *also fig* to go (on);

(*de un punct*) to pass; (*înainte*) to go forward/along; (*a se termina*) to be over; (*a fi avut loc*) to go off; (*a dispărea*) to disappear; (*a muri*) to pass away; (*a străpunge*) to break/come through; to penetrate; (*a depăşi*) to go beyond; (*a accepta*) (*o lege*) to carry; *fig* to experience, to go through, to undergo || *vt* to traverse, to cross; (*a lăsa ceva în urmă*) to leave behind; (*a transmite*) to hand down; (*a moşteni*) to bequeath; (*a nota*) to put down; (*pe o listă*) to enter; (*pe o hartă*) to plot; (*în jurnalul de bord*) to write up the log; (*în procesul verbal*) to enter in the minutes; (*un examen*) to pass an examination; *coll* (*cu brio*) to pass with flying-colors/ honors; *coll* (*cu greu*) to scrape through an exam; (*o lege*) to pass a law; (*a filtra*) to filter; (*prin sită*) to strain; (*a cerne făină*) to sift; (*a cerne nisip*) to screen || *vr* (*a muri*) to pass away; (*a îmbătrâni*) to grow old; (*a se ofili*) to wither; (*d. fructe*) to grow overripe; (*a se sfârşi*) to die away/off; (*a se stinge*) to go/die out; to fade; to diminish; **a** ~ **peste** to traverse, to cross; to go/fly/pass over; (*a călca*) to tread on; (*o dificultate*) to get over; (*a omite*) to overlook; (*a neglija*) to neglect; to ignore; (*a ierta*) to forgive; **a** ~ **la** (*un alt subiect*) to pass on, to turn to; *coll* (*brusc*) to fly/go off on a tangent; (*a fi dat*) to be handed over, to be given to; **a** ~ **în** (*catalog*) to (put/enter in a) catalog; (*condică*) to enter/register (in a roll); **a** ~ **în revistă** to review/survey smth; (*evenimente trecute*) to review the past; (*situaţia*) to survey the situation; (*în minte*) to go over smth in one's mind; *mil* (*trupele*) to inspect/review.

trecere ['trechere] *nf* (*deplasare*) passing (over/across), crossing; **drept de** ~ (*prioritate*) right of way; (*de colo-colo*) going (to and fro); (*înregistrare*) (*în acte*) entering; (*la hotel*) checking in; (*de bani*) transferring; (*în alt post*) reassignment; (*transformare*) transition; (*zonă de acces*) way (through), thoroughfare; *naut* channel; *rail* crossing passage; *fig* pull, influence; (*greutate*) weight; (*d. mărfuri: a fi căutate*) to be in demand; (*expirare a unui termen*) expiry, termination.

trecut [tre'kut] *nn* the past, former times; *gram* past tense, preterite; (*al cuiva*) record, background; (*vechi, ca vârstă*) old, elderly, advanced in years; (*ofilit*) wilted, withered; (*fanat*) faded; (*învechit*) old, obsolete; (*de odinioară*) former; (*anterior*) previous, prior; (*ultim*) last; (*apus*) by-gone; (*mort*) dead.

treflă ['treflă] *nf* clubs.

trei [trei] *nm/adj/num* three; *num ord* **al** ~**lea** the third; ~ **iunie** the third of June; **ora** ~ three o'clock; **câte** ~ by threes, three at a time • ~**sprezece** *num* thirteen • ~**zeci** *num* thirty.

treiera [treie'ra] *vt* to thresh, to thrash; (*bumbac*) to gin; (*cânepă*) to ripple, to boll; (*porumb, mazăre*) to shell • ~**t** *nn* thrashing, threshing(-time).

treierătoare [treieră'toare] *nf agr* threshing/thrashing machine, thresher.

treieriş [treie'rish] *nn* * **treierat**.

treiler ['treiler] *nn* trailer.

treime [tre'ime] *nf* one-third; third part; *relig* Trinity.

tremă ['tremă] *nf* trema, umlaut; di(a)eresis.

tremur ['tremur] *nn* trembling, quivering, shaking; (*al vocii*) quavering; (*de teamă etc*) tremor; (*fior*) shiver; (*scuturătură*) jerk; (*de aripi, frunze*) flutter, rustle; *fig* vibration; thrill • ~**a** *vi* to tremble, to shake;

(*uşor*) to quiver; (*de frig*) to shiver (with cold); (*a se înfiora*) to shudder; (*a vibra*) to vibrate; (*d. apă*) to ripple; (*d. lumină*) to flicker; (*a pâlpâi*) to shimmer; (*d. voce*) to quaver.

tren [tren] *nn rail, mil, tech* train.

trena [tre'na] *vi* to drag on, to linger.

trenă ['trenă] *nf* train.

trenci ['trench] *nn* trench coat, raincoat, waterproof coat, mackintosh.

trening ['trening] *nn* training suit; sports outfit/suit.

trepăduş [trepă'dush] *nm* errand boy, runner; *fig* menial, stooge.

trepida [trepi'da] *vi* to vibrate, to shake; (*d. cineva*) to fidget, to fret; *tech* to chatter; *fig* to be thrilled/eager • ~nt *adj* trepidating, trembling; bustling, agitated; hectic • ~ţie *nf* (*d. maşini*) trepidation, vibration; (*d. braţe etc*) trembling; *fig* bustle, flurry; state of alarm.

trepied [trepi'ed] *nn* three-legged stool; tripod; (*pt. vase, în bucătărie*) trivet.

treptat [trep'tat] *adj* gradual, successive || *adv* gradually, step by step, little by little.

tresă ['tresă] *nf* braid, galloon; *mil* (*arătând gradul*) pip, star; shoulder strap; *mil pl* stripes, gold braids; *naut* (officer's) stripes; bands.

tresălta [tresăl'ta] *vi* * **tresări.**

tresări [tresă'ri] *vi* to (give a) start/jump; to be startled; (*de bucurie*) to leap, to be thrilled; (*de durere*) to wince; (*de teamă*) to shudder; (*de indignare*) to leap up in indignation; (*a tremura*) to quiver; (*d. inimă*) to throb, to flutter.

trestie ['trestie] *nf bot* (common) reed, rush, cane.

trezi [tre'zi] *vt* to wake, to awaken, *fig* to (a)rouse; (*a stârni*) to stir up || *vr* to rise, to get up; (*din beţie*) to become sober; (*din leşin*) to come to; *fig* to become conscious; (*a-şi da seama*) to realize smth; (*d. băuturi*) to grow stale/flat • ~e *nf* (*stare de veghe*) watchfulness, wakeful state; consciousness; sobriety.

trezorerie [trezore'rie] *nf* treasury; treasurer's office.

trezorier [trezori'er] *nm* treasurer; paymaster, paymistress.

tria [tri'a] *vt* (*scrisori*) to sort, to classify; (*haine*) to go through one's wardrobe; *text* (*lână*) to pick; *rail* (*vagoane*) to marshall; (*a selecţiona*) to select; to pick/sort out; *mil* to comb; (*de mână*) to handpick.

triadă [tri'adă] *nf* triad.

triaj [tri'azh] *nn* sorting, selection; *rail* (*gară*) marshaling yard.

trial [tri'al] *nn* trial.

trib [trib] *nn* tribe • ~al *adj* tribal.

tribulaţie [tribu'latsie] *nf* tribulation, trial.

tribun [tri'bun] *nm* tribune; spokesman (of the people); popular orator/speaker.

tribunal [tribu'nal] *nn jur* law court, tribunal, court of justice; *jur* (*judecătorii*) the bench, judge's seat; ~ **civil** civil court.

tribună [tri'bună] *nf* (*stadion*) stand, elevated stalls; public/strangers' gallery; (*pt. discursuri*) rostrum; platform; (*ziar*) tribune; forum, discussion; ~ **de onoare** grandstand.

tribut [tri'but] *nn* tribute, duty, tax; contribution; * **omagiu.**

tributar [tribu'tar] *adj* tributary; dependent; (*d. râuri*) tributary.

tricicletă, triciclu [trichi'kletă, tri'chiklu] *nn* tricycle.

tricolor [triko'lor] *nn* tricolor || *adj* threecolor(ed).

tricot [tri'kot] *nn* (*material*) knitting, knitted fabric, knitwear; *text* stockinet; (*obiect de îmbrăcăminte*) (knitted) jersey/jumper • ~a *vt/vi* to knit • ~aje *nf pl* knitwear, knitted goods.

tricou [tri'kou] *nn* T-shirt; sweater, jumper.

trident [tri'dent] *nn* trident; fish spear.

tridimensional [tridimensio'nal] *adj* three-dimensional, 3-D.

trienal [trie'nal] *adj* triennial; appointed for three years; three-year.

triere [tri'ere] *nf* sorting (out); picking, selecting; *mil* comb-out; * **tria.**

trifoi [tri'foi] *nm bot* trefoil, clover.

trigonometrie [trigonome'trie] *nf* trigonometry.

tril [tril] *nn* trill.

trilogie [trilo'djie] *nf* trilogy.

trimestrial [trimestri'al] *adj* quarterly || *adv* once a term, quarterly.

trimestru [tri'mestru] *nn* quarter, trimester; *edu* term.

trimis [tri'mis] *nm* (government) envoy; (*mass media*) (special) correspondent; messenger, delegate; representative, spokesperson; *fig* messenger, missionary, apostle.

trimite [tri'mite] *vt* to send; (*prin cineva*) to send by hand; (*bani*) to remit; (*prin poştă*) to mail; (*a expedia*) to ship; (*a înainta*) to forward; (*a transmite*) to convey; (*la un text*) to refer to • ~re *nf* dispatch, consignation; (*poştală*) mail.

trinitate [trini'tate] *nf relig* (Holy) Trinity.

trio [trio] *nn mus* trio.

tripartit [tripar'tit] *adj* tripartite.

tripla [tri'pla] *vt* to treble, to triple, to increase three-fold.

triplet [tri'plet] *nn* third copy; third form.

triplicat [tripli'cat] *nn* triplicate, third copy.

triplu ['triplu] *adj* treble, threefold, triple || *nn* treble; *sp* hop, skip and jump.

tripod [tri'pod] *nn* tripod.

tripou [tri'pou] *nn* tripot, gambling house, gambling den.

triptic [trip'tik] *nn* triptych; three-part, three-phase plan.

trist [trist] *adj* sad; (*întristat*) sorry, unhappy, (ag)grieved; sorrowful; (*abătut*) depressed; woebegone; (*d. viaţă, vreme*) dreary; (*monoton*) dull; (*sumbru*) gloomy; (*d. peisaj*) bleak; (*jalnic*) doleful; (*dureros, penibil*) painful; (*regretabil, nenorocit*) wretched • ~eţe *nf* sadness, sorrow, grief; (*amărăciune*) bitterness; gloom; (*profundă*) heartache; (*a unui peisaj*) bleakness; (*a unei camere*) dullness; **cu** ~ sadly.

trişa [tri'sha] *vi* (*la jocul de cărţi*) to trick, to cheat; (*a înşela*) to cheat (over), to lie (about); *coll* to cheat a bit.

trişor [tri'shor] *nm* trickster, cheat, (card) sharper, rook.

triumf [tri'umf] *nn* (*asupra*) triumph over; *fig* success, victory; **în** ~ triumphantly • ~a *vi* (*a fi victorios*) to triumph, to be victorious; (*a se bucura*) to exult/glory in (smth) • ~al *adj* triumphant; *fig* solemn, stately || *adv* triumphantly • ~ător *adj* triumphant, victorious; *fig* successful; *also fig* radiant.

triunghi [tri'ungi] *nn also mus* triangle • ~ular *adj* triangular; *pol* three-cornered.

trivial [trivi'al] *adj* (*obişnuit, comun*) trivial, commonplace; hackneyed; (*d. cuvinte: vulgar*) coarse, vulgar; smutty, obscene • ~itate *nf* triteness; (*grosolănie*) (*ca trăsătură*) vulgarity, coarseness; (*ca termen*) coarse (expression), smut.

troacă ['troakă] *nf* tub, trough; *pl* old/worn/shabby clothes; old shoes.

troc [trok] *nn* truck, barter, exchange (in kind).

trofeu [tro'feu] *nn* trophy; *(pradă)* prey, booty.

troglodit [troglo'dit] *nm* troglodyte, cave-dweller; *fig* primitive man.

troian [tro'ian] *nn* snowdrift, snow heap; *(morman)* heap, pile; *(întăritură)* wall ‖ *adj* Trojan; **cal ~** Trojan horse.

troieni [troie'ni] *vt* to bury in snow, to cover with snow; to snow up.

troiţă [tro'itsă] *nf* roadside crucifix, triptych.

troleibuz [trolei'buz] *nn* trolley-bus.

troleu [tro'leu] *nn* trolley; *coll* trolley-bus.

trombă ['trombă] *nf* waterspout; *(de vânt)* whirlwind; *(de apă)* cloudburst.

trombon [trom'bon] *nn* *mus* trombone.

tromboză [trom'boză] *nf* *med* thrombosis.

trompă ['trompă] *nf* *(de elefant)* trunk; *(la insecte)* proboscis; probe; *anat* tube; *pl anat* fallopian tubes; *tech* shaft tube; *archit* trumpet.

trompetă [trom'petă] *nf* trumpet; *mil* bugle.

trompetist [trompe'tist] *nm* trumpet-player, trumpeter.

tron [tron] *nn* throne; *fig* scepter, sway; *reg (sicriu)* coffin.

trona [tro'na] *vi* to rule, to reign; to sit enthroned; *fig* to dominate; to occupy a place of honor; *pej* to lord it.

tronson [tron'son] *nn* *constr* section (of any roughly cylindrical object); *(în transporturi)* section/portion of a line.

trop [trop] *interj* trop, trop tramp! ‖ *nm* trope.

tropăi [tropă'i] *vi* to clatter (along), to thump; *(a umbla cu paşi grei)* to bump along, to stamp one's feet.

tropic ['tropik] *nn* tropic; *pl also* tropical zone • **~al** *adj* tropical; *(cald)* torrid • **~ul Capricornului** Tropic of Capricorn • **~ul Racului** Tropic of Cancer.

tropot ['tropot] *nn* tramping; *(al ploii)* rattle; *(de copite)* clatter of hoofs.

trosc [trosk] *interj* bang!, thud!, thump!, slap!; **~ pleosc!** slap!, smack!, slap-bang!, whack!.

trosnet ['trosnet] *nn* *vernac* crash; *(d. podea, lemn)* crack; *(d. ramuri, oase)* snap; *(d. frunze uscate)* crackling; *(d. zăpadă)* crunching.

trosni [tros'ni] *vi/vt* to crack; *(d. bici)* to smack; *(d. frunze uscate, lemne, pe foc)* to crackle; *(d. zăpadă)* to crunch.

trotinetă [troti'netă] *nf* (child's) scooter.

trotuar [trotu'ar] *nn* sidewalk, footpath.

trubadur [truba'dur] *nm* troubadour.

truc [truk] *nn* *(meşteşug, pricepere)* knack (of doing smth); trick, dodge; stratagem, artifice.

truca [tru'ka] *vt* to fake, to rig; *cin* to use special effects • **~j** *nn cin* trick picture, special effects.

trudă ['trudă] *nf (muncă grea)* toil, hard work, labor; *(osteneală)* effort(s), pains; *(oboseală)* tiredness, *lit* fatigue; *(suferinţă)* suffering(s); *(necaz)* trouble; *(folos)* use, profit, gain.

trudi [tru'di] *vi/vr* to toil, to labor; to take great pains; *(a se istovi)* to work oneself to death ‖ *vt* to torture; *(a exploata)* to grind; to work smb to the bone.

trufanda [trufan'da] *nf* hasting, hothouse fruit/vegetable; early fruit/vegetable.

trufaş [tru'fash] *adj* haughty, arrogant, proud; overbearing; *(încrezut)* conceited, *coll* stuck up; *fig* majestic, stately; imposing ‖ *adv* haughtily, arrogantly.

trufă ['trufă] *nf* truffle; *bot* truffle; *(la câini)* nose.

trufie [tru'fie] *nf* arrogance, haughtiness; **cu ~** overbearingly.

trunchi ['trunki] *nn* trunk; *anat* main stem (of an artery); *(ciot)* stump; *(butuc)* block, stub; *archit* drum (of a column); *geom* frustum.

trunchia [trun'kia] *vt* to cut/chop off; *fig (a reduce)* to cut down; *(un text)* to maim; *(a denatura)* to distort, to twist.

trup [trup] *nn* body; *(cadavru)* cadaver, (dead) body; *fig* clay; *(trunchi)* trunk.

trupă ['trupă] *nf* troop, band; gang; *(de cercetaşi)* (scout) troop; *mil* unit, *(soldaţi de rând)* rank and file, privates, *pl* troops; *thea* troupe, company.

trupesc [tru'pesk] *adj* bodily; *(fizic)* physical, corporal; carnal, sexual • **cunoaştere ~ească** carnal knowledge.

trupeş ['trupesh] *adj* strong, well-built; stout, corpulent.

trusă ['trusă] *nf* (surgeon's instrument) case; kit.

trusou [tru'sou] *nn* (bride's) trousseau; hope chest.

trust [trust] *nn (capitalist)* corporation, trust; *(socialist)* association/group of industries.

tţ [tts] *interj* tut-tut-tut!.

tu [tu] *pron* you; *obs* thou; **şi ~?** you too?; **eşti chiar ~?** is it really you?.

tub [tub] *nn* tube; *(de pastă)* tube of pasta; *(ţeavă şi)* pipe; *anat* duct.

tubă ['tubă] *nf* *mus* tuba.

tuberculos [tuberku'los] *nm* consumptive/tubercular patient ‖ *adj* consumptive, phthisical.

tuberculoză [tuberku'loză] *nf* tuberculosis, *coll* consumption.

tuciuriu [tuchiu'riu] *adj* swarthy, dark-skinned ‖ *nm* gypsy; black, *pej* nigger.

tufă ['tufă] *nf* shrub, bush; *(creangă)* branch.

tufiş [tu'fish] *nn* (cluster of) bushes/shrubs; *(desiş)* thicket; *(lăstăriş, tufăriş)* underwood; boscage.

tuia ['tuia] *nf bot* (American) arbor vitae, white cedar.

tul [tul] *nn text* tulle, net (fabric).

tulbura [tulbu'ra] *vt (pe cineva)* to trouble; *(a îngrijora)* to worry; *(a emoţiona)* to move; *(a zăpăci)* to confuse; to throw smb into confusion; *(mintea)* to obfuscate; *(a deranja)* to disturb; *(a face să se simtă prost)* to make uneasy; *(a supăra)* to upset; *(a stârni)* to stir; *(liniştea)* to break in (upon); to spoil; *(o activitate)* to interfere with; *(a întrerupe)* to interrupt; *(a împiedica)* to impede; *(mintea)* to cloud; *(a zăpăci)* to flurry; *(d. un lichid)* to make muddy/cloudy; *(d. apă)* to muddy; *(d. vânt)* to ripple (the water)) ‖ *vr (d. un lichid)* to grow turbid/dim; *(d. vin)* to get cloudy; *(d. mare)* to get rough; *(d. cer)* to become overcast; *(d. o imagine, vedere)* to become blurred; *(d. voce)* to break; *(d. oameni)* to become confused/flustered; to fly into a temper; to become excited/worked up; *(a se emoţiona)* to flutter, to be flurried.

tulburător [tulbură'tor] *adj* troubling; *(sinistru)* uncanny; *(emoţionat)* exciting, thrilling; *(d. frumuseţe)* alluring, tantalizing; *(care dă fiori)* thrilling; *(mişcător)* moving.

tulbure ['tulbure] *adj* troubled; *(d. o situaţie)* confused; *(în vârtej)* eddying; *(d. apă)* muddy; turbid; *(d. vin)* thick; *fig (neclar)* dim, vague; *(d. ochi)* filmy; *(d. cer)* overcast; *(difuz)* hazy; *fig* muddled; *(neliniştit)* worried, uneasy.

tulei [tu'lei] *nn* down; downy beard.

tuli [tu'li] *vt coll* **a o ~** to decamp, to clear out/off; *(în* *viteză*) to bolt, to cut and run; (*pe furiş*) to slip away ‖ *vi* to go, to proceed.

tulpină [tul'pină] *nf bot* stem, stalk; (*de copac*) trunk; *med* strain.

tumbă ['tumbă] *nf* somersault; caper.

tumefia [tume'fia] *vr med* to tumefy, to swell; to distend • ~t *adj med* tumefied, swollen.

tumoare [tu'moare] *nf* tumor, *coll* growth; ~ **benignă** benign tumor; ~ **malignă** malignant tumor; swelling.

tumult [tu'mult] *nn* tumult; (*zarvă*) din, riot, uproar, commotion; thunder, clash; turmoil; hustle and bustle; **în** ~ in an uproar, in confusion • ~**uos** *adj* tumultuous, stormy; impetuous; uproarious, riotous ‖ *adv* tumultuously, stormily.

tun [tun] *nn mil* cannon, gun.

tuna [tu'na] *vi imp* to thunder; (*d. arme*) to boom; *fig* to roar, to blast.

tunar [tu'nar] *nm mil* artillery man, gunner.

tunător [tună'tor] *adj* (*d. voce*) thunderous; stentorial; (*care ceartă*) scolding, grumbling; (*d. furtună*) rumbling, roaring.

tunde ['tunde] *vt* (*pe cineva*) to cut the hair of; (*părul, blana, gardul*) to clip; (*a potrivi*) to trim; (*băieţeşte/ scurt*) to crop; (*chilug*) to crop close; (*la animale*) to shear; (*iarba*) to mow; (*pomii*) to lop; (*vârful*) to top ‖ *vr* (*singur*) to cut one's hair; (*la coafor/frizer*) to have one's hair cut.

tundră ['tundră] *nf geog* tundra.

tunel [tu'nel] *nn* tunnel.

tunet ['tunet] *nn* thunder; *fig* peal, roar (of applause).

tunică [tu'nikă] *nf* (*cu diferite sensuri*) tunic, coat, jacket; skin.

tuns [tuns] *nn* hair-cutting; (*scurt*) crop, shingle(d hair); (*la oi*) shearing; (*al pomilor*) pruning ‖ *adj* cut, trimmed; (*d. o persoană*) short-haired; (*d. păr*) short; (*băieţeşte*) tomboy crop; (*d. mustaţă; d. un gard viu*) clipped; (*d. iarbă*) mown; (*d. copaci*) pruned; (*d. animale*) shorn • ~**oare** *nf* haircut.

tupeu [tu'peu] *nn* impudence, audacity, effrontery, *coll* gall.

tupila [tupi'la] *vr* (*a se ghemui*) to crouch, to squat; (*a se ascunde*) to hide; (*a se furişa*) to slink, to sneak/ steal up; to thread one's way.

tur [tur] *nn* tour; round; (*ocol*) roundabout (way); (*cotitură*) turn; (*plimbare*) walk; (*scurtă*) stroll; *sp* (*de pistă*) lap; (*la pantaloni*) seat; (*rând de băuturi*) stand • ~**aţie** *nf* revolution, rotation, turn.

tură ['tură] *nf* shift; (*la şah*) castle, rook.

turba [tur'ba] *vi med* to grow rabid; *fig* to (fret and) fume, to fly into a rage.

turban [tur'ban] *nn* turban.

turbare [tur'bare] *nf med* rabies, hydrophobia; *fig* passion, temper; rage, mad fury.

turbat [tur'bat] *adj med* rabid; **câine** ~ mad dog; ~ **de furie** *fig* mad, crazy, furious; (*grozav*) tremendous; (*sălbatic*) wild; (*d. viteză*) break-neck ‖ *adv* rabidly, madly.

turbă ['turbă] *nf geol* peat.

turbină [tur'bină] *nf tech* turbine; (*acţionată de aer*) air/wind turbine; (*acţionată de apă*) water turbine/ wheel.

turboreactor [turboreak'tor] *nn avia* turbojet.

turbulent [turbu'lent] *adj* turbulent, riotous; (*nesupus*) mutinous; (*neliniştit*) restless; (*d. copii*) boisterous; (*d. vreme, vânt*) stormy.

turbulenţă [turbu'lentsă] *nf* turbulence, riot; boisterousness.

turc [turk] *nm* Turk; *relig* Mohammedan, Moslem ‖ *adj ling* Turkish; *hist* Ottoman • ~**ă** *nf ling* Turkish, the Turkish language • ~**esc** *adj* Turkish.

turcoază [tur'koază] *nf geol* turquoise.

turelă [tu'relă] *nf* turret; *naut* cupola, (gun) turret.

turism [tu'rism] *nn* tourism, tourist trade; touring; (*maşină*) motor car.

turist [tu'rist] *nm* tourist, excursionist; (*holiday*) visitor; *pej* tripper; (*pedestru*) globetrotter.

turlă ['turlă] *nf constr* tower; donjon, dungeon; *archit* spire, steeple; (*la sondă*) oil derrick; headgear.

turmă [tur'mă] *nf zool* herd, drove, *orn* flock, (*d. lei*) pride; *fig* (*mulţime, gloată*) mob, rabble, riff-raff; *pej* horde; *fig relig* sheep.

turmenta [turmen'ta] *vr* (*a se îmbăta*) to get intoxicated/ drunk.

turn [turn] *nn constr* tower, turret; (*la şah*) rook, castle.

turna [tur'na] *vt* (*un lichid*) to pour; (*picătura cu picătură*) to drop (oil) into smth; (*un metal*) to cast; (*în formă*) to mold; (*la strung*) to turn (on a lathe); (*un film*) to shoot a film; (*d. actori: a juca într-un film*) to play/star in a film; *fig* to mold, to shape; (*a denunţa*) to denounce; to inform; *coll* to tell on smb ‖ *vi met* to pour; *fig sl* to inform, to squeal.

turnant [tur'nant] *adj* revolving, rotating; **fotoliu** ~ swivel chair/seat; *fig* hub, center; **scenă** ~**ă** revolving stage; **uşă** ~**ă** revolving door • ~**ă** *nf* revolving bookcase; (*curbă*) curve, bend; (street) corner.

turnător [turnă'tor] *nm* metal foundry-worker, founder; *fig* squeak, informer; denunciator; *scol* sneak, blab(ber) • ~**ie** *nf* metal foundry (works), smelting house; delation, blabbing.

turnesol [turne'sol] *nn chem* litmus.

turneu [tur'neu] *nn* tour.

turnichet [turni'ket] *nn* turnstile.

turnir [tur'nir] *nn hist* tournament.

turnură [tur'nură] *nf* (*direcţie*) turn, direction, course; *ling* locution; phrase; *obs* bustle (of a woman's dress).

turtă ['turtă] *nf* bread; cake.

turti [tur'ti] *vt* to batter, to crush, to squash; to flatten, to make flat ‖ *vr* to be battered/crushed; to become flat; (*d. fundaţii: a se tasa*) to settle, to set • ~**t** *adj* flattened; (*plat*) flat; (*d. casă*) battered; (*zdrobit*) crushed; (*strivit*) squashed; (*d. nas*) bashed in; (*d. sferă*) oblate.

turturea, turturică [turtu'rea, turtu'rikă] *nf orn* turtle dove.

turui [turu'i] *vi* to chatter, to yak; (*d. păsări*) to coo • ~**ală** *nf* verbiage; flow of language.

tuse ['tuse] *nf med* cough(ing).

tuspatru [tus'patru] *num* all four (of them).

tustrei [tus'trei] *num* all three (of them).

tuş [tush] *nn* China ink; *sp* touch • ~**ă** *nf* (*de pensulă*) (brush) stroke; (*manieră de a crea*) manner, style; *sp* (*hochei*) roll-in; touch-line.

tuşi [tu'shi] *vi med* to cough; (*a-şi drege glasul*) to clear one's throat.

tuşieră [tushi'era] *nf* ink pad.

tuşit [tu'shit] *nn med* coughing.

tutelar [tute'lar] *adj* upper, higher; (*d. un zeu*) tutelary; (*d. îngeri*) guardian.

tutelă [tu'telă] *nf* guardianship; wardship, patronage; protection; *pol* trusteeship.

tutore [tu'tore] *nm* guardian; (*al unui minor*) tutor; protector.

tutui [tutu'i] *vt/vr* to be on familiar terms with smb.

tutuială, tutuire [tutu'ială, tutu'ire] *nf* * **tutuit**.

tutun [tu'tun] *nn* tobacco (plant) • **~gerie** *nf* tobacco shop, tobacconist's.

twist [twist] *nn mus* twist.

Ț

țambal [tsam'bal] *nn mus* cembalo, dulcimer.

țanc [tsank] *nn* pointed cliff/crag; (*stâncă*) crag, rock; **la ~** in the nick of time, (*la fix*) on the dot.

țandără ['tsandără] *nf* chip, splinter; flake; (*cioburi*) broken/flying glass; (*bucată*) fragment, shred.

țanțoș ['tsantsosh] *adj* proud, haughty ‖ *adv* proudly, haughtily.

țap [tsap] *nm zool* he-goat, billy goat; (*măsură*) half-pint, small mug (of beer); **~ ispășitor** scapegoat; *coll* whipping boy; *astrol* Capricorn.

țar [tsar] *nm* czar, tzar, tsar.

țară ['tsară] *nf* country, land; (*patrie*) homeland, fatherland; state; (*regiune*) region; (*rurală*) country(side), village; (*popor*) people; (*țărani*) peasantry.

țarc [tsark] *nn* pen, fold, enclosure, paddock; (*de oi*) sheep pen, sheepfold; (*de nuiele*) wattle enclosure; reservation; (*pt. copii*) playpen.

țarină ['tsarină] *nf* field, upturned land, tilled/fallow land, field under cultivation.

țăcălie [tsăcă'lie] *nf* goatee, short (pointed) beard.

țăcăni [tsăcă'ni] *vi* to rattle, to snap; (*d. mașini, mori*) to clack; (*d. copite*) to click ‖ *vr* to go nuts/crazy/mad • **~t** *nn* click; clacking; rattling ‖ *adj* crazy, mad, crack-brained.

țăran [tsă'ran] *nm* peasant, countryman; farmer; (*sătean*) villager • **~că** *nf* peasant woman/villager; countrywoman.

țărănesc [tsără'nesk] *adj* peasant, rustic, rural, country-like.

țărănime [tsără'nime] *nf* peasantry, peasants.

țărănoi [tsără'noi] *nm pej* churl, country bumpkin.

țărână [tsă'rână] *nf* dust; (*pământ*) earth, ground; *fig* clay, dust.

țărm [tsărm] *nn* (*de râu*) bank, riverside; (*de mare*) coast, (sea)shore; (*plat*) beach, foreshore; (*margine de apă*) waterside; (*tărâm*) realm; *fig* refuge, haven.

țăruș [tsă'rush] *nm* stake, peg, pile; (*pt. cai*) wooden plug.

țâfnă ['tsâfnă] *nf vet* pip; ill-humor, petulance; (*ifose*) airs; (*dispoziție*) mood, frame of mind; arrogance, haughtiness.

țâfnos [tsâf'nos] *adj* testy, peevish, quick-tempered; haughty, arrogant.

țânc [tsânk] *nm coll* chit, mite; brat; kid(die), tot.

țânțar [tsân'tsar] *nm ento* gnat, mosquito.

țârâi [tsără'i] *vi* (*ca sunet*) to ring; (*d. greieri*) to chirp; (*a picura*) to drip, to trickle; (*d. ploaie*) to drizzle • **~t** *nn* ringing, chirping; dripping, trickling, drizzling.

țârcovnic [tsâr'kovnik] *nm relig* sacristan.

țâșni [tsâsh'ni] *vi* (*d. apă*) to gush (out), to spout up; to well/spring forth; (*d. sânge*) to spurt; (*d. scântei*) to fly; (*d. lumină*) to flash; *fig* (*d. animale*) (*a ieși brusc*)

to spring out; (*a se ivi brusc*) to spring up, to pop up; (*a se repezi*) to rush out, to dash off.

țâșnitoare [tsâshni'toare] *nf* drinking fountain.

țâști ['tsâshti] *interj* hist!, hush!, ssh!, silence!.

țâță ['tsâtsă] *nf vernac anat* teat, nipple, boob; breast, bosom; (*uger*) udder.

țâțâi [tsâtsâ'i] *vi* (*de frică*) to tremble, to quiver (with fear); (*de bucurie*) to frisk (about); (*d. greier*) to chirp.

țâțână [tsă'tsână] *nf tech, vernac* (door) hinge.

țeapă ['tseapă] *nf* (*așchie*) chip, splinter; (*spin*) thorn, prick(le); (*de animal*) spine, spike; (*pt. tortură*) stake; (*vârf de par*) point of a pole/stake; prick.

țeapăn ['tseapăn] *adj* rigid, stiff; *anat* (*fără viață*) numb, lifeless; (*de durere*) (be)numbed; *fig* (*neîndemânatic*) awkward; rigid, inflexible; straight-laced; stiff; (*ceremonios*) formal; *fig* robust, sturdy ‖ *adv* stiffly, rigidly.

țeastă ['tseastă] *nf coll* skull; *frml* cranium; (*cap*) head, *coll* pate, noodle.

țeavă ['tseavă] *nf* pipe, tube, conduit, duct; (*de armă*) barrel, stock.

țel [tsel] *nn* goal, object, aim; (*scop*) purpose, design; (*obiectiv*) objective; *mil* target, objective.

țelină ['tselină] *nf bot* (*tulpină*) celery; (*rădăcină*) celeriac; *agr* (*teren nedesțelenit*) fallow land, unplowed land.

țepos [tse'pos] *adj* spiky; bristly; *bot* thorny, prickled; *zool* spiny, spinous; *fig* stinging, caustic.

țepușă [tse'pushă] *nf* stake; (*așchie*) splinter, chip; (*ghimpe*) thorn.

țesală 'tse'sală] *nf* currycomb; *agr* chain harrow.

țesăla [tsesă'la] *vt* (*cai*) to curry(comb); *fig coll* to whack, to pommel; *fig* (*a șlefui, a cizela*) to polish, to brush up.

țesător [tsesă'tor] *nm* weaver • **~ie** *nf* (*meșteșug*) weaving, weaver's trade; (*fabrică*) weaving mill.

țesătură [tsesă'tură] *nf* also *fig* texture, fabric; (woven) material, *pl* wools, woolens; *anat* also *fig* tissue.

țese [tse'se] *vt* to weave; (*a cârpi ciorapi*) to darn, to mend; (*a broda*) to embroider; (*a lucra goblenuri*) to work; (*a împleti*) to knit; (*a urzi*) (*paie*) to plait; (*in*) to warp; (*d. păianjeni*) to spin; *fig* to hatch/weave (a plot), to plot, to fabricate ‖ *vi* to weave, to work at the loom.

țiclean [tsi'klean] *nm orn* nuthatch.

țicneală [tsik'neală] *nf coll* craze, folly, madness; (*manie*) monomania, (inveterate) habit, idiosyncrasy; *coll* hobby.

țicni [tsik'ni] *vr coll* to go mad/crazy/dotty • **~t** *adj coll* batty, crazy, dotty, cracked.

ție [tsie] *pron* (to) you.

țigan [tsi'gan] *nm* Gypsy, Zingaro; (*mai ales în scris*) Romany • **~că** *nf* gypsy woman; folk dance, the tune of this dance.

țigară [tsi'gară] *nf* cigarette; (*de foi*) cigar.

țigaret [tsiga'ret] *nn* cigarette holder • **~ă** *nf* * **țigară**.

țigănesc [tsigă'nesk] *adj* gypsy(like); (*d. limbă*) Romany.

țiglă ['tsiglă] *nf* (roofing) tile.

țiitoare [tsii'toare] *nf* kept mistress/woman, concubine.

ține ['tsine] *vt* to hold (in one's hand); (*a conține*) to hold; (*a purta*) to carry; (*a mânui*) to wield; (*a păstra*) to keep; (*a reține*) (*pe cineva*) to stop; *sp* (*un adversar*) to collar; (*lacrimile, mânia*) to check; (*a în-*

treţine şi) to keep up; (*a avea*) to have; (*a stăpâni*) to own; to administer, to manage; (*a sprijini*) to support; (*a susţine*) to hold up; (*a respecta*) to observe; to consider; (*a trata*) to treat as; to continue; to insist on; (*a face să aştepte*) to keep waiting/hanging about; (*a privi*) to concern; **a ~ la** to be fond of, (*a pune preţ pe ceva*) to value ‖ *vr* (*pe picioare*) to hold oneself (erect); to stand; (*a se stăpâni*) to refrain/ contain oneself; (*a avea loc*) to take place; (*a nu ceda*) to stand firm; (*unul de altul*) to hold together; (*a urma*) to follow; (*a se socoti*) to think oneself; (*a se întreţine*) to maintain oneself; (*a trăi*) to live; (*cineva*) to stick/cling to; (*a face*) to do.

ţintaş [tsin'tash] *nm* marksman; shooter, firer.

ţintă ['tsintă] *nf* target; (*punct alb*) white, bull's eye; *fig* aim, goal, end; (*intenţie*) intention, design; (*a unui atac*) receiving end; (*cui*) nail; (*pt. tapiţerii*) (tin) tack; (*de lemn*) peg, plug; (*de bocanci*) spike; (*pt. alpinişti*) clinker, weltnail; (*pată pe fruntea animalelor*) blaze; **fără ~** aimless(ly), (at) random ‖ *adv* fixedly.

ţinti [tsin'ti] *vt* to aim at; to take aim at/for; (*cu puşca*) to point/level one's gun at; (*cu tunul*) to train (the cannon) at; (*a dori ceva*) to set one's sights on smth; (*a se referi la*) to have smth in view, to relate to smth ‖ *vi* to aim (at smth); to point at; (*a se referi la*) to refer/allude to; *fig* (*a năzui*) to strive for/after, to aspire to.

ţintui [tsintu'i] *vt* to nail, to rivet; to clinch; (*a bate în ţinte*) to fasten with nails; (*complet*) to nail up (to); (*cu ţinte de lemn*) to peg (to); to fix; (*d. atenţie*) to rivet; (*ochii cuiva*) to arrest; (*cu ochii plini de reproş*) to fasten smb with a reproachful eye; (*a captiva*) to fascinate, to captivate.

ţinut [tsi'nut] *nn* region, country(side), province; *fig* (*tărâm*) realm ‖ *adj* kept, bound; (*forţat*) obliged.

ţinută [tsi'nută] *nf* (*a corpului*) carriage, bearing; (*demnă*) port, deportment; (*mers*) gait; (*purtare*) conduct, demeanor; attitude; (*haine*) suit, clothes; *mil* uniform; **de** (*mare*) ~ full dress, formal; **de ~** *fig* decorous, decent; *mus* holding/sustained note.

ţipa [tsi'pa] *vi* to shout, to cry out; (*tare*) to scream; (*a zbiera*) to yell; (*ascuţit*) to shriek, to screech; (*d. culori*) to clash ‖ *vt* to shout (at), to cry, to scream.

ţipar [tsi'par] *nm icht* loach; *also fig* (*anghilă*) eel.

ţipăt ['tsipăt] *nn* scream, shout, (*puternic*) yell, (*sinistru*) screech, shriek.

ţipător [tsipă'tor] *adj* strident, blatant, harsh; (*d. voce*) shrill; (*d. culori*) glaring, loud; (*d. haine*) flashy; (*d. flori*) showy; meretricious; (*d. o nedreptate*) flagrant.

ţiplă ['tsiplă] *nf* ox bladder; cellophane paper; celluloid; *tech* gold-beater('s) skin.

ţiţei [tsi'tsei] *nn* crude oil, petroleum.

ţiui [tsiu'i] *vi* to whiz; (*d. vânt*) to whistle; (*d. glonţ*) to ping • **~t** *nn* whizz(ing sound); (*de glonţ*) ping; (*al urechilor*) tingle.

ţoapă ['tsoapă] *nf coll* (*bărbat*) cad, lout, yokel; (*femeie*) frump, slut.

ţol [tsol] *nm* inch.

ţop [tsop] *interj* hop!, jump!, go! • **~ăi** *vi* to hop (about); to leap, to jump; **~ăind** hippety-hoppety; *pej* to dance • **~ăială, ~ăit** *nf, nn coll* hopping, jumping; *pej* dancing.

ţopârlan [tsopâr'lan] *nm* lout, country bumpkin, uncouth fellow.

ţuguia [tsugu'ia] *vt/vr* to taper; (*d. buze*) to purse (up) • **~t** *adj* tapering, pointed; **cap ~** pointed head.

ţuică ['tsuikă] *nf* plum brandy.

ţumburuş [tsumbu'rush] *nn* salience, protuberance.

ţurţure ['tsurtsure] *nm* icicle.

U

ucenic [uche'nik] *nm* apprentice, trainee; *jur* articled clerk; novice, beginner, tiro; (*în meserie*) probationer; (*în mănăstire*) novice; (*elev*) pupil; *fig* disciple, apostle • **~ie** [ucheni'chie] *nf* (*în meserie*) (term of) apprenticeship; (*în profesii liberale*) articles; (*contract*) indenture; (*instruire*) instruction; (*noviciat*) novitiate.

ucide [u'chide] *vt* to kill, *lit* to slay; (*d. animale*) to slaughter, to butcher; (*a asasina*) to murder; (*mai ales o persoană politică*) to assassinate; to execute; (*a strangula*) to strangle; (*prin înăbuşire*) to suffocate; (*în bătaie*) to beat/thrash within an inch of smb's life; (*aruncând cu pietre*) to stone smb to death; (*cu o lovitură de cuţit*) to stab smb to death; (*prin împuşcare*) to shoot smb to death; *fig* to destroy ‖ *vr* (*a se sinucide*) to commit suicide; *recip* to kill/strike one another.

ucigaş [uchi'gash] *adj* murderous; guilty of murder; mortal, deadly, lethal; (*însetat de sânge*) bloodthirsty; *fig* (*d. un zâmbet*) provocative, bewitching ‖ *nm* murderer ‖ *nf* murderess; assassin, (*plătit*) hired assassin, *sl* hit man; **~ de copii** child murderer; **~ de frate** fratricide; **~ de mamă** matricide; **~ de tată** patricide .

ucigător [uchigă'tor] *adj* * **ucigaş**; (*groaznic*) terrible, dreadful.

ucrainean [ukrai'nean] *nm/adj* Ukrainian • **~ă** *nf* Ukrainian (woman); *ling* Ukrainian.

ud [ud] *adj* wet, soaked, watery, drenched (with); (*umed*) damp, moist; *chem* humid • **~a** *vt* to wet, to drench; (*a umezi*) to moisten, to damp; (*a înmuia*) to soak, to souse; to dip; (*a stropi*) to sprinkle; (*a împroşca*) to splash; (*cu rouă*) to bedew; (*d. rău: a trece prin*) to flow through; (*florile*) to water (the plants); (*a iriga*) to irrigate ‖ *vr* to get/become wet/ soaked.

uf [uf] *interj* (*exprimând durerea*) ah!, oh!; (*vai*) alas!; (*Doamne!*) dear me!; ugh!, well!

uger ['udjer] *nn* udder.

ugui [ugu'i] *vi* to coo • **~t** *nn* cooing.

uhu [u'hu] *interj* tu-whit!, to-whoo!.

uimi [ui'mi] *vt* to surprise, to astonish, to amaze • **~re** *nf* amazement, astonishment, wonder • **~tor** *adj* surprising, astonishing, amazing; (*grozav*) prodigious, stupendous.

uita¹ [ui'ta] *vt* to forget; (*a neglija*) to neglect; (*a scăpa din vedere*) to overlook; (*a omite*) to leave smth out; (*a lăsa în urmă*) to leave behind; (*a lăsa în părăsire*) to forsake; (*a ierta*) to forgive ‖ *vi* to forget, to be forgetful.

uita² [ui'ta] *vr* (*a privi*) to look at (smth/smb); to eye; to face; (*cu atenţie*) to view; (*a urmări*) to watch; (*fix*) to stare at; (*cu admiraţie*) to gaze at; (*prosteşte*) to gape at; (*cu mânie*) to glare at; (*pe furiş*) to peep; (*a scruta*) to peer at; (*pieziş, chiorâş*) to look askance/ awry; (*cruciş*) to squint; (*încruntat*) to frown/scowl at smb; (*la cineva*) to squint/skew at smb; (*pe sine*) to forget oneself; (*a-şi pierde controlul*) to lose all self-control; **a se ~ la** (*a ţine seama de*) to mind, to be mindful of; to examine.

uitare [ui'tare] *nf* forgetting, forgetfulness; oblivion; (*iertare*) forgiveness; **~ de sine** self-denial.

uitătură [uită'tură] *nf* look, glance; (*admirativă*) gaze; (*pe furiş*) peep; (*furioasă*) glare.

uituc [ui'tuk] *adj* forgetful, oblivious; (*distrat*) absent-minded || *nm* scatterbrain, forgetful person; (*neatent*) neglectful.

ulcer [ulcher] *nn med* ulcer, abscess, (*rană deschisă*) running sore • **~aţie** *nf med* ulceration.

ulcică [ul'chikă] *nf* small pot; mug; pitcher.

ulcior [ul'chior] *nn* pitcher, jug.

ulei [u'lei] *nn* oil; (*comestibil*) salad oil; (*pictură*) oil painting, canvas • **~os** *adj* oily, oleaginous, oleous; (*d. vin*) ropy.

ulicioară [uli'chioară] *nf* (village) lane; by-street; narrow alley; (*fundătură*) dead end, blind alley.

uliţă ['ulitsă] *nf* lane, narrow street, alley; street.

uliu ['uliu] *nm orn* sparrow-hawk, goshawk.

ulm [ulm] *nm bot* elm (tree).

ulterior [ulteri'or] *adj* ulterior, subsequent (to); further; (*următor*) following; (*viitor*) future; (*anterior*) posterior, later || *adv* after(wards), then, subsequently; (*mai târziu*) later on; (*curând după aceea*) soon after.

ultim ['ultim] *num/adj* last, final, ultimate; closing; (*din doi*) latter; (*din capăt*) final, end; (*cel mai recent*) latest; *also fig* (*cel mai de jos*) the lowest; (*cel mai din spate*) the hindmost; (*regretatul*) the late; supreme, utmost.

ultimatum [ulti'matum] *nn* ultimatum.

ultragia [ultradji'a] *vt* to outrage, to abuse, to insult; to attack scurrilously.

ultraj [ul'trazh] *nn* outrage, insult; flagrant insult; (*la pudoare*) indecent assault; *jur* insulting behavior; *jur* (*faţă de un magistrat*) contempt of court.

ultra-liberal [ultralibe'ral] *adj/nm* ultra-liberal.

ultramarin [ultrama'rin] *adj/nn* ultra-marine.

ultrascurt [ultra'skurt] *adj* ultra-short.

ultrasensibil [ultrasen'sibil] *adj* oversensitive.

ultrasunet [ultra'sunet] *nn* ultrasound; *pl* ultrasonic waves.

ultraviolet [ultravio'let] *adj* ultraviolet.

ulucă [u'lukă] *nf* thick plank/board; *pl* board fence.

ului [ulu'i] *vt* to astound, to stagger, to perplex, to stupefy, to stun, to amaze; * **uimi** || *vr* to be astounded, etc; (*a se zăpăci*) to become perplexed • **~ală** *nf* amazement, astonishment, (*zăpăceală*) bewilderment, perplexity • **~re** *nf* wonder • **~t** *adj* (*uimit*) amazed, astonished, staggered; (*încurcat*) taken aback, at a loss; (*zăpăcit*) flurried • **~tor** *adj* amazing, astonishing, astounding, bewildering, flabbergasting.

uman [u'man] *adj* human, man's; **fiinţe ~e** human beings, humans, mankind; (*omenos*) humane, decent || *adv* humanely, decently • **~ism** *nn* humanism .

umanistică [uma'nistikă] *nf* humanities, humane studies.

umanitar [umani'tar] *adj* humanitarian • **~ist** *nm* humanitarian.

umanitate [umani'tate] *nf* (*fire omenească*) humanity; human nature; (*omenie şi*) humaneness, kindness; (*omenire*) mankind.

umaniza [umani'za] *vt* to humanize || *vr* to become human/humane.

umăr ['umăr] *nn anat* shoulder; (*de haine*) dress-hanger; *fig* (*de deal*) crest, ridge; **~ la ~** shoulder to shoulder, side by side.

umbla [um'bla] *vi* (*a merge*) to go; (*a se mişca*) to move; (*pe jos*) to walk; to go on foot; (*cu un vehicul public, călare*) to ride; (*cu automobilul*) to drive; (*a călători*) to travel; (*d. vapoare*) to sail; (*a rătăci*) to wander; (*a vagabonda*) to ramble/roam about; to function, to work; to circulate; (*d. bani*) to be in current use; (*a fi îmbrăcat*) to be dressed; to utilize, to use; (*a recurge la*) to resort to; (*a scotoci*) to rummage, to go through; (*a căuta să, a fi interesat de*) to try to, to be after; (*a falsifica*) to falsify, to forge || *vt* (*a cutreiera*) to scour, to wander; **a ~ cu** *vi* to tamper with; **a ~ aiurea** *vi* to fool about/around; (*a rătăci*) to wander/tramp aimlessly; (*a pierde timpul*) to idle/loaf about • **umblă sănătos!** God speed!, pleasant journey!.

umbrar [um'brar] *nn* arbor, bower; (*construit*) summer house; (*acoperiş de frunze*) leafy roof, canopy of leaves.

umbră ['umbră] *nf* (*de copaci*) shade; **la ~** in/under the shade; (*a cuiva*) shadow; *astron* umbra; (*frig*) coolness; (*întuneric*) dark, gloom.

umbrelă [um'brelă] *nf* (*de ploaie*) umbrella; (*de soare*) sunshade, parasol; (*pe plajă*) beach umbrella.

umbri [um'bri] *vt* (*a da umbră*) to shade; (*a arunca umbră asupra*) to cast a shadow on; *fig* (*pe cineva*) to eclipse; to overshadow; *coll* to put smb in the shade; (*d. pictură*) to tint; (*a apăra*) to screen; (*a ascunde*) to obscure • **~t** *adj* shadowy, shady; *fig* eclipsed, thrown/put into (the) shade.

umbros [um'bros] *adj* shady, giving/affording shade; shaded; (*des*) thick.

umed ['umed] *adj* moist, damp; humid; (*ud*) wet, watery; (*mlăştinos*) boggy.

umeraş [ume'rash] *nn* (coat)hanger.

umezeală [ume'zeală] *nf* dampness, humidity, moisture.

umezi [ume'zi] *vt* to moisten, to make damp; to wet; (*tare*) to drench, to soak || *vr* to become moist/damp.

umfla [um'fla] *vt* (*a umple*) to fill; (*suflând*) to inflate, to pump up; (*obrajii*) to puff out; (*orez*) to puff; (*a bomba*) to swell (out/up); (*pieptul*) to stick/thrust out one's chest; (*pânzele*) to belly (out) the sails; (*tare*) to (cause to) swell; (*ca un sac*) to bag; (*a spori*) to grow; to extend; (*a lărgi*) to widen; (*a exagera*) to exaggerate; to embroider; (*a înşfăca*) to seize, to grab; *coll* (*a fura*) to lift, to pinch; *fig coll* (*a bate*) to tan smb's hide || *vr* to swell (out); to expand; (*d. faţă*) to swell/puff up; (*d. o rochie*) to swell/puff out; (*d. lichide, râuri, pâine*) to rise; (*d. vopsea*) to blister; *fig* (*a se îngâmfa*) to puff up; (*a se balona*) to bulge (out); *fig* (*a mânca mult, cu lăcomie*) to gobble/guzzle • **~t** *adj* swollen; (*tumefiat*) tumescent; (*d. ape*) turgid; (*d. critică*) rich.

umflătură [umflă'tură] *nf med* swelling, inflammation.

umiditate [umidi'tate] *nf* humidity, moisture.

umil [u'mil] *adj* (*smerit*) humble, low(ly); (*supus*) submissive, meek; (*sărac*) humble, poor || *adv* humbly, meekly • **~i** *vt* to humiliate, to humble, *coll* to take smb down a peg; to oppress || *vr* to humiliate oneself, to stoop (low); to kowtow (before smb); (*a se supune*) to submit • **~inţă** *nf* humility, meekness;

(rușine) shame, slight; *(supunere)* submissiveness • **~it** *adj* humiliated, humble(d); *(umil, simplu)* modest, self-effacing; *(laș, bătut)* craven, mean • **~itor** *adj* humiliating, degrading.

umor [u'mor] *nn* humor; *(scris)* facetiae; ~ **ieftin** slapstick; ~ **macabru** grim humor; ~ **negru** sick humor, bitter/sardonic humor; ~ **sec** dry humor; **fără** ~ humorless • **~ist** *nm* humorist, humorous writer • **~istic** *adj* humorous; *(glumeț)* facetious.

umple ['umple] *vt (cu ceva)* to fill (up) with; *(a ghiftui, a îndesa)* to cram; *(prea tare)* to overcrowd; *(din nou)* to refill (a glass) with; *(un șanț, o groapă)* to fill (up)/(in); *(ardei etc)* to stuff; *(a completa spații libere)* to fill out; *(a cuprinde)* to contain; *(a aproviziona)* to stock ‖ *vr* to fill (up), to become full; to be filled.

umplutură [umplu'tură] *nf cul (tocătură)* stuffing, filling; filling (in); filling material; earth; *fig (substitut)* substitute, makeshift.

un [un] *art indef* a, an; one; *pl* some; ~ **om** a man • **~ii oameni** some people ‖ *pron (cineva)* somebody, someone; *pl (unii)* some • **~ii spun că** some say that • **~l câte ~l** one by one, singly, in singles • **~l din ei** one of them ‖ *num* * **unu**.

una ['una] *pron* one thing; * **un** ‖ *num* one; **am doar** ~ I have only one; ~ **din ele** one of them.

unanim [una'nim] *adj* unanimous, univocal; of one mind ‖ *adv* unanimously, to a man, with one voice/consent, by common consent.

unanimitate [unanimi'tate] *nf* unanimity; concord, agreement; **în** ~ unanimously.

unchi ['unki] *nm* uncle.

uncie [unchie] *nf* ounce.

undă ['undă] *nf* wave, billow, tide; *elec, telec* wave; ~ **de simpatie** *fig* wave of sympathy; *(flux)* high tide/water.

unde ['unde] *adv* where; *(încotro)* where (to), whither, to what place; *(în care direcție)* in what direction; *(când)* when; then; *(deodată)* at once; *(deoarece)* as, for, because.

undeva [unde'va] *adv* somewhere, in some place (or other); elsewhere; *(în interogații sau negații)* anywhere; **mergi** ~? are you going anywhere?; *(indicând direcția)* to some place.

undiță ['unditsă] *nf* fishing-/angling-rod/line.

undui [undu'i] *vi* to wave, to undulate; to float, to flutter; *(d. apă)* to ripple; *(în vânt)* to float on the breeze; *(d. steag)* to billow; *(d. perdea)* to flow • **~os** *adj* undulous, wavy, * **undui**; *(d. trestie)* waving; *(d. voce, sunete)* inflected, modulated; *(d. mișcări)* swaying • **~re** *nf* waving, undulation; *fig (a glasului)* modulation, inflection.

unealtă [u'nealtă] *nf* tool, instrument, utensil; *fig* stool pigeon, decoy.

unele ['unele] *adj f pl* some, certain ‖ *pron* some; ~ **cărți** some books; ~ **din ele** some of them; ~ **sunt noi** some are new.

unelti [unel'ti] *vt* to plot, to intrigue, to scheme; *(a pune la cale)* to concoct; to hatch (out); *(a născoci)* to devise, to contrive ‖ *vi* to plot (against smb), to hatch out plots • **~re** *nf (conspirație)* conspiracy, plot; conjuration; *(intrigă)* intrigue.

uneori [une'ori] *adv* sometimes, occasionally; *(din când în când)* at times, (every) now and then/again, once in a while.

unge ['undje] *vt* to smear; *(cu ulei)* to oil; *(cu grăsime)* to grease; *(cu săpun)* to soap; *(cu smoală)* to peck; *(cu alifie)* *(o rană)* to salve; *(a vopsi)* to paint; *(a vărui)* to whitewash; *fig (a mitui)* to bribe; *coll* to tickle smb's palm; *(domn)* to anoint.

ungher [un'ger] *nn (în casă) also fig* corner, nook, (retired) spot; *(margine)* edge.

unghi ['ungi] *nn also fig* angle; *fig* point of view.

unghie ['ungie] *nf anat* nail; *(de animal)* claw; *(de pasăre de pradă)* talon; *(copită)* hoof.

unguent [ungu'ent] *nn* ointment, salve, unguent.

ungur, unguresc ['ungur, ungu'resk] *adj* Hungarian, Magyar.

uni¹ [u'ni] *pref* (single) ‖ *adj* plain; plain (color).

uni² [unifi'ka] *vt* to unite; *(a lega)* to join, to link; *also fig (a amesteca)* to blend; to combine; *(a pune de acord)* to reconcile ‖ *vr* to unite, to join together; *econ (a fuziona)* to merge; *mil* to effect a junction; *(d. râuri)* to meet; *(din nou)* to reunite; *mil* to rally; *(a se învoi)* to agree.

unic ['unik] *adj* one, single, only; *(d. moștenitor)* sole; *(deosebit)* special, unique, unparalleled, unrivaled; *pol* united • **de ~ă folosință** single use • **~itate** *nf* oneness, singleness.

unicorn [uni'korn] *nm myth* unicorn.

unifica [unifi'ka] *vt* to unify, to amalgamate; to consolidate; to standardize (weights and measures) ‖ *vr* to merge, to combine • **~re** *nf* unification, union; amalgamation; *pol, econ, jur* merger.

uniform [uni'form] *adj* uniform, homogeneous, unvarying; regular; *(neted)* even; smooth ‖ *adv* uniformly, homogeneously; evenly, plainly.

uniformă [uni'formă] *nf* uniform; *mil* regimentals.

uniformitate [uniformi'tate] *nf* uniformity, sameness, evenness.

unii ['unii] *adj* some, certain; ~ **oameni** some people ‖ *pron* some; ~ **au venit deja** some have already arrived.

unilateral [unilate'ral] *adj* unilateral, one-sided; *fig* narrowminded.

uninominal [uninomi'nal] *adj* uninominal; **vot** ~ *pol* voting for a single member, for one member only.

unipolar [unipo'lar] *adj elec* unipolar, homopolar, single-pole; *bio* unipolar (cell).

unire [u'nire] *nf* union; *(coaliție)* coalition, alliance; confederacy; agreement, accord; concord; *(armonie)* harmony; *econ (fuzionare)* merger; *(a unor râuri)* confluence; *(a culorilor)* blending; combination (of).

unisex [uni'seks] *adj* unisex (shop).

unison [uni'son] *nn* unison; **la** ~ in unison (with); in keeping (with).

unit [u'nit] *adj* united; *(d. o comunitate)* tight-knit.

unitar [uni'tar] *adj* unitary, unitarian, integrated.

unitate [uni'tate] *nf math, mil, med* unit; *(unire)* unity, union; accord, agreement; *(omogenitate)* uniformity, conformity; identity; consistency.

uniune [uni'une] *nf* union; *(unire)* alliance, confederation, association; *(societate)* society, club; *(căsătorie)* marriage; *econ* corporation; syndicate, monopoly union.

univers [uni'vers] *nn* universe, cosmos; world • **~al** *adj* universal, world; *(bun la toate)* all-purpose; *(d. un magazin)* department store ‖ *adv* universally, generally • **~alitate** *nf* generality, universality.

universitar [universi'tar] *adj* university, academic(al) || *nm* member of the teaching profession; academic.
universitate [universi'tate] *nf* college; university.
unsoare [un'soare] *nf (grăsime)* grease, fat; *(alifie)* salve, ointment; pomade.
unsprezece ['unsprezeche] *nm/adj/ num* eleven • **al ~lea** the eleventh.
unsuros [unsu'ros] *adj* greasy, smeary, *(uleios)* oily, *(gras)* fatty; *(murdar)* filthy; *(lipicios)* sticky; *(d. vin: uleios)* ropy.
unt [unt] *nn* butter, *(de gătit)* cooking butter; *(ulei)* oil • **~delemn** *nn* (edible) oil; *(de floarea-soarelui)* sunflower oil; *(de măsline)* olive oil; *(de salată)* salad oil • **~ieră** *nf* butter dish • **~os** *adj* buttery; greasy • **~ură** *nf* grease, fat; **~ de porc** lard.
unu, una ['unu, 'una] *num card* one.
ura¹ ['ura] *interj* hurrah!, hurray!, hooray!.
ura² [u'ra] *vt* to wish, to offer one's good wishes; *(a felicita)* to congratulate.
uragan [ura'gan] *nn met* hurricane; tornado.
urale [u'rale] *nf pl* hurrays, ovations, cheers.
urangutan [urangu'tan] *nm zool* orangutan.
uraniu [u'raniu] *nn* uranium.
urare [u'rare] *nf* wish; well-wishing; *pl* good wishes, congratulations.
ură ['ură] *nf* hatred (of/for); *frml* hate; detestation; *(dușmănie)* enmity, ill-blood; **cu ~** with (bitter) hatred.
urătură [ură'tură] *nf* * **urare**.
urâcios [ură'chios] *adj* hateful, unpleasant, nasty; *(urât)* ugly, plain(-looking); *(rău)* wicked; *(nesuferit)* disagreeable; *(supărăcios)* irritable; *(ursuz)* surly; *(grosolan, țâfnos)* rude; *(scârbos)* disgusting; *(josnic)* mean; immoral.
urâciune [ură'chiune] *nf* ugliness, ungainliness; *(monstru)* monster; *(pocitanie)* freak of nature, fright; *(d. o femeie)* homely woman; ugly duckling.
urât¹ [u'rât] *nn (plictiseală)* ennui, boredom, tediousness; *lit* spleen.
urât² [u'rât] *adj (aspect)* ugly, plain, hideous; dowdy; *(d. față)* homely; *(d. figură)* deformed; *(d. haine)* unbecoming; *(d. caracter: rău)* wicked; *(urâcios)* hateful; *(imoral)* foul; *(josnic)* mean; *(d. miros)* bad; stinking; *(murdar)* filthy; *(dezgustător)* disgusting; rotten || *adv* unfairly, foully; *(cu răutate)* wickedly, meanly.
urățenie [ură'tsenie] *nf* ugliness, plainness, homeliness.
urâți [ură'tsi] *vt* to render/make ugly; to disfigure || *vr* to become/grow ugly/plain, to lose one's good looks.
urban [ur'ban] *adj* town, city; *(politicos)* civil, urbane • **~ism** *nn* town-planning; *ling* urbanism • **~istică** *nf* town-planning • **~itate** *nf* urbanity; **cu ~** urbanely.
urbe ['urbe] *nf frml* town, city.
urca [ur'ka] *vt* to climb (up), to go/come up; to mount; to ascend; to scale; *(a înălța)* to fly (a kite); *(a spori)* to raise || *vi* to rise, to go up; to mount; *(a merge sus)* to go upstairs; *(d. păpușari)* to soar; *(d. avion)* to climb; *(a se ridica la)* to amount to; *(a crește)* to grow; to increase; *(la bord)* to board; *(într-un vehicul)* to go in(to a car), to go on (a bus, train) || *vr* to climb up; *(a se înălța)* to rise, to soar.
urcior [ur'chor] *nn* pitcher, jug, ewer; *(la ochi)* sty(e).
urcuș [ur'kush] *nn* climb, ascent; *(urcare)* going up; *(pantă)* slope.
urdoare [ur'doare] *nf* bleary eyes.
urduros [urdu'ros] *adj* bleary-eyed, rheumy.

ureche [u'reke] *nf anat* ear; *(auz)* ear, hearing; *mus* ear for music; *(de ac)* eye of a needle; *(de căciulă)* ear tab; *(toartă)* handle.
urechea [ure'kea] *vt* to pull/tweak smb's ear; to castigate (by pulling one's ears) • **~lă** *nf* tweaking/pulling smb's ears, thrashing, beating.
urechelniță [ure'kelnitsă] *nf ento* earwig; *bot* houseleek.
urechiușă [ure'kiushă] *nf bot* chanterelle.
uree [u'ree] *nf med* urea.
uretră [u'retră] *nf anat* urethra.
urgent [ur'djent] *adj* urgent, pressing; quick, fast, prompt || *adv* urgently, quickly, immediately • **~a** *vt* to speed up, to haste(n), to rush; to expedite.
urgență [ur'djentsă] *nf* urgency, emergency; **de ~** immediately, urgently.
urgie [ur'djie] *nf* wrath, *lit* ire; *(a soartei)* scourge; *(blestem)* curse.
urgisit [urdji'sit] *adj* unfortunate, star-crossed.
uriaş [uri'ash] *nm* giant, titan; Goliath; *(căpcăun)* ogre || *adj* enormous, huge, immense.
urina [uri'na] *vt anat* to urinate, to pass/make water; *vulg* to piss • **~r** *adj* urinary.
urină [u'rină] *nf* urine; water.
urî [u'rî] *vt* to hate, to have a grudge against; to detest, to loathe || *vr* to hate each other.
urla [ur'la] *vi (d. vânt, valuri, furtună)* to roar, to moan; *(d. lupi, câini)* to howl; *(d. copii)* to squall; *(a țipa)* *(d. oameni, de furie)* to yell; *(a geme)* to wail || *vt* to roar/bawl out.
urlător [urlă'tor] *adj* howling.
urlet ['urlet] *nn* roar; *(țipăt și)* howl(ing); yell(ing); roar(ing); moan(ing); scream(ing); *coll* yawl.
urma [ur'ma] *vt* to follow (close); *(a merge pe urmele)* to follow (in smb's footsteps); *(foarte aproape)* to shadow smb; *(a se ține strâns de)* to cling/stick to; *(a succeda)* to succeed; *(a asculta)* to obey; *(o regulă)* to observe; *(cursuri, școală)* to attend; to continue; *(a duce, a executa)* to carry on || *vi* to continue; *(după)* to come after, to follow • **~re** *nf* following, * **urma**; *(a unei cărți)* continuation, sequel; *(rezultat)* result, outcome; repercussion; consequential effects; after effects; *(imitare)* imitation; **prin ~** therefore, consequently, accordingly.
urmaş [ur'mash] *nm* descendant, successor (to smb); *(care urmează)* after-comer; *(moștenitor)* heir; *(unic)* sole heir; *jur* inheritor; *(vlăstar)* offspring; *pl* posterity; *(discipol)* disciple (of); adherent; *pl fig* future generations, the generations to come.
urmă ['urmă] *nf* trace, trail; *(întipărire)* imprint; *(de picior)* footprint; *(de roată)* rut; *(de vapor)* wake; *(de vânat)* track; *(miros)* scent; *(de obuz)* path; *(semn)* sign; mark; *pl (resturi)* remains, debris; *(de rană)* scar; *fig* marks (of suffering); furrow; *(cantitate mică)* (slight) trace; **cel din ~** the last, *(din doi)* the latter; **din ~** *(spațial)* from behind; *(temporal)* last, past; **fără ~** without a trace; **în cele din ~** finally, at last/length, *coll* in the long run; **până la ~** eventually; *(ca urmare)* as a result of; **în ~** *(spațial)* behind; *(temporal)* before; **la ~** *(înapoi)* behind; *(la sfârșit)* at the end; **a rămâne în ~** *(cu o activitate)* to be behind (the schedule); *(cu chiria)* to be in arrears with the rent; *(d. ceas)* to be slow; *(a fi demodat)* to be behind the times; *(d. plată)* to be overdue/outstanding; *(mental)* to be backward, to be retarded; *(d. idei)* to be old-fashioned; *(d. țară)* to be underdeveloped.

urmări [urmă'ri] *vt* (*a merge în urma cuiva*) to pursue; to follow; to go after; (*a lua urma*) to track (down); (*a fila*) to shadow; (*a alerga*) to chase; (*cu privirea*) to follow (with one's eyes); to persecute; (*pentru un motiv*) to press hard; (*un criminal*) to hunt down; (*a asculta atent*) to listen; *coll* to hang on smb's words; (*în timp*) to watch; to follow up (a clue); (*a participa regulat la*) to attend (concerts/lectures) (regularly); (*a avea de gând*) to mean; to aim at; *jur* to sue (at law), to bring an action against; (*a supraveghea*) to keep an eye on; *edu* to proctor (exam) • ~**re** *nf* chase, pursuit; (*judiciară*) proceedings; (*în justiție*) prosecution; (*supraveghere*) surveillance; (*spionare*) shadowing • ~**tor** *nm* pursuer; (*la vânătoare de animale, fig de oameni*) tracker; persecutor.

următor [urmă'tor] *adj* next, following; (*d. lucruri*) subsequent, ensuing; successive.

urnă ['urnă] *nf* urn; (*electorală*) ballot box.

urni [ur'ni] *vt* (*a mișca*) to move; (*a pune în mișcare*) to set in motion; to start; (*a da la o parte*) to move/push/shove out of the way ‖ *vr* to move; (*a se clinti*) to budge; (*d. tren: a porni*) to start; (*d. o procesiune*) to move off.

urs [urs] *nm zool* bear; *fig* (*om care bombăne*) grumbler, growler; (*stângaci*) numb hand • ~**ă** *nf* **Ursa Mare** the Great Bear, the Big Dipper; **Ursa Mică** the Lesser Bear, the Little Dipper.

ursită [ur'sită] *nf* (*soartă*) fate, lot, destiny; predestined wife; * **ursitoare**.

ursitoare [ursi'toare] *nf* Fate, Parca.

ursoaică [ur'soaikă] *nf* she-bear, female bear; *archit* dormet window; funnel, chimney.

ursuleț [ursu'leț] *nm* bear's cub/whelp; (*jucărie*) teddy bear.

ursuz [ur'suz] *adj* sulky, sullen; (*care bombăne*) grumbling, grumpy; (*arțăgos*) peevish ‖ *nm* grumpy person, growler, grumbler ‖ *adv* grumpily, sullenly.

urticarie [urti'karie] *nf med* rash, urticaria.

urui [uru'i] *vi* * **hurui**.

urzeală [ur'zeală] *nf text* warp(ing); weft; (*mașinație*) machination, intrigue, plot, conspiracy.

urzi [ur'zi] *vt* to warp; *fig* (*a mașina*) to plot, to hatch, to frame; (*a provoca*) to provoke, to cause.

urzica [urzi'ka] *vt* to prick, to sting, to bite; *fig* to sneer at, to tease smb; to offend ‖ *vr* to nettle, to sting, to prick (oneself); to get stung ‖ *vi* to prick, to sting.

urzică [ur'zikă] *nf bot* (stinging) nettle; (*moartă*) dead nettle • ~**tură** *nf* nettle rash, urtication.

usca [us'ka] *vt* to dry; (*a pune la uscat*) to lay/hang out to dry; (*fân*) to ted; (*lemn*) to season; (*pământul*) to dry up; (*gura*) to parch; (*corpul, de boală*) to emaciate; (*a șterge*) to wipe (dry); (*la aer*) to air; (*a epuiza*) to exhaust; (*a arde*) to scorch; (*a seca*) to drain ‖ *vr* to (become) dry; (*a pieri*) to fade away; (*a seca*) to run dry; to drain; (*d. plante*) to wither; to droop • ~**t** *nn* drying; (*pământ*) land; (*continent*) mainland, continent ‖ *adj* dry; (*d. lemn*) well-seasoned; (*ofilit*) withered, drooping; barren, arid; (*ars*) scorched; (*scorojit*) shrunken; (*slab*) thin; (*fără carne*) fleshless.

uscăciune [uskă'chiune] *nf* dryness; (*secetă*) drought; *fig* aridity, bareness.

uscător [uskă'tor] *nn* drier, drying device/apparatus; (*de păr*) hair dryer; (*pt. rufe*) drying cupboard; (*cu aburi*) steam dryer • ~**ie** *nf* drying room/floor/yard/stove.

uscățiv [uskă'tsiv] *adj* bony, scraggy; (*d. trup*) lank, skinny; (*d. copaci*) bare.

uscior [us'chior] *nn* * **ușor**.

ustensile [usten'sile] *nf pl* utensils, tools, implements.

ustura [ustu'ra] *vt* to smart, to burn; (*a mânca*) to itch; *fig* to sting, to bite.

usturător [usturǎ'tor] *adj* (*d. durere*) smarting; (*d. căldură*) scorching, parching; *fig* itching, itchy; (*arzător*) burning; sarcastic; (*amar*) bitter.

usturime [ustu'rime] *nf* smarting pain; burning.

usturoi [ustu'roi] *nm bot* garlic; **cățel de** ~ clove of garlic.

usuc [u'suk] *nn* (*în lâna oilor*) yolk, wool oil.

ușă ['ushă] *nf* (*și portieră*) door; (*de intrare*) front door; (*de ieșire*) *also fig* way out; (*de serviciu*) back door; (*prag*) threshold; (*deschizătură*) doorway; (*intrare*) entrance; *also fig* gate.

ușier [ushi'er] *nm* usher; *jur* (*la tribunal*) bailiff, usher of the court; (*portar*) doorman, doorkeeper; janitor.

ușor [u'shor] *nm* door jamb ‖ *adj* (*d. greutate*) light; (*de făcut*) easy (to do); (*mic, neimportant*) slight; (*abia simțit*) gentle; (*subțire*) thin; superficial; fluent; mild; (*d. cafea etc*) weak; (*d. sunet etc*) faint; (*d. pierderi*) trivial; free; (*d. haine*) comfortable; (*d. moravuri*) lax; (*d. dispoziție*) lighthearted ‖ *adv* lightheartedly.

ușura [ushu'ra] *vt* (*o povară*) to lighten; to unburden; (*a alina*) to soothe, to comfort, to calm, to pacify; (*a micșora*) to diminish; to reduce; to ease; to mitigate; (*a înmuia*) to soften; (*a facilita*) to facilitate ‖ *vr* (*la stomac*) to relieve oneself; (*a-și face nevoile*) to relieve nature; (*a naște*) to deliver; *fig* (*a-și lua o piatră de pe inimă*) to ease up • ~**re** *nf* (*alinare*) relief; (*sentimentul de*) release; **oftat de** ~ sigh of relief.

ușuratic [ushu'ratik] *adj* flippant, careless; lightminded, shallow; (*frivol*) frivolous, flighty; (*schimbător*) volatile ‖ *adv* wantonly, flippantly; carelessly.

ușurel [ushu'rel] *adv* slowly, gently, easily ‖ *interj* steady!; **mai** ~! take it easy!.

ușurime [ushu'rime] *nf* facility; lightmindedness.

ușurință [ushu'rintsă] *nf* (*pondere*) lightness; (*facilitate*) easiness (of task); ease (with which smth is done); (*frivolitate*) flippancy; shallowness; (*nechibzuință*) carelessness; (*lipsă de seriozitate*) levity; (*îndemânare*) agility; **cu** ~ easily, readily; (*neserios*) recklessly, with indifference.

uter ['uter] *nn anat* uterus, womb • ~**in** *adj* uterine.

util [u'til] *adj* useful, of use, helpful; reasonable; (*bun la ceva*) available, serviceable ‖ *adv* usefully, profitably.

utila [uti'la] *vt* to equip, to fit out; to supply (with) • ~**j** *nn* equipment, outfit; gear; plant stock.

utilitar [utili'tar] *adj* utilitarian; service.

utilitarism [utilita'rism] *nn phil* utilitarianism.

utilitate [utili'tate] *nf* use(fullness), utility; useful purpose; (*folos*) use, avail.

utiliza [utili'za] *vt* to use, to make use of, to resort to • ~**tor** *nm* user.

utopic [u'topik] *adj* Utopian.

utopie [uto'pie] *nf* Utopia; fancy; (*plan utopic*) Utopian scheme.

uvertură [uver'tură] *nf mus* overture.

uvulă [u'vulă] *nf anat* uvula.

uz [uz] *nn* usage; (*întrebuințare*) use, using; utilization,

employment; (*obicei*) custom, tradition; old practice/usage • ~a *vt* to use, to make use of; to utilize; (*d. ţesături, haine*) also *vr* to fray; (*a purta*) to wear out/off; *fig* to wear out || *vi* a ~ de to resort to, to use || *vr* to wear (out/away) • ~are *nf* wear and tear.

uzanţă [u'zantsă] *nf* usage, tradition, custom; după ~ according to custom.

uzat [u'zat] *adj* worn out; (*d. haine*) threadbare, shabby; (*d. o funie*) frayed; (*d. un lucru*) trite.

uzină [u'zină] *nf* works, plant, mill, (*fabrică*) factory.

uzitat [uzi'tat] *adj* in (current) usage/use, current; (*obişnuit*) customary, usual; (*acceptat*) accepted.

uzual [uzu'al] *adj* usual, customary, common || *adv* usually.

uzură [u'zură] *nf* wear (and tear); ~ prin frecare attrition, abrasion, (*acţiune*) wearing (away), erosion.

uzurpa [uzur'pa] *vt* to usurp (from); (*drepturile*) to encroach upon, to usurp (smb's rights) • ~re *nf* usurpation; encroachment • ~tor *nm* usurper || *adj* usurping; encroaching.

V

vacant [va'kant] *adj* (*d. post*) vacant; vacancy; (*gol*) empty (space); (*liber*) vacant, unoccupied.

vacanţă [va'kantsă] *nf* vacation, holiday(s); *jur, pol* recess; (*slujbă*) vacancy; vacant office/post.

vacarm [va'karm] *nn* din, racket, uproar, hubbub.

vacă ['vakă] *nf* cow; *fig* goose; swine, beast; *sl pej* old cow, bitch.

vaccin [vak'chin] *nn* vaccine, *coll* shot, vaccination, inoculation • ~a *vt* to vaccinate, to inoculate • ~are *nf* vaccination, inoculation.

vacuum ['vakuum] *nn* vacuum; vacuum apparatus.

vad [vad] *nn* ford; (*trecere*) crossing; (*albie*) bed (of a river); (*d. un magazin, bancă*) high street shop, store bank; frequented place; (*drum*) road; (*cale*) way; *fig* headway.

vafă ['vafă] *nf cul* waffle.

vag [vag] *adj* vague, indefinite; (*d. cunoştinţe*) sketchy; (*d. memorie etc*) dim; (*d. vedere etc*) blurred; (*d. o imagine*) fuzzy; *fig* (*neclar*) dim, hazy, indistinct.

vagabond [vaga'bond] *nm* wanderer, vagabond; *pej* bum, hobo || *adj* vagabond, wandering • ~a *vi* to wander (about), to ramble; *coll* to be on the road/loose; (*a hoinări*) to prowl the streets • ~j *nn* wandering(s); *pej* vagrancy.

vagin [va'djin] *nn anat* vagina.

vagon [va'gon] *nn rail* car (for passengers); (*de marfă*) truck, wagon; (*deschis*) freight car; (*de tramvai*) streetcar, trolley • ~et *nn* truck, trolley; *min* tram.

vai [vai] *interj* oh dear!, poor me!, *obs* alas!; (*nu se poate*) you don't say so!; (*ce nenorocire*) what a pity!.

vaier ['vaier] *nn* cry, lament; * **vaiet**.

vaiet ['vaiet] *nn* groan, moan, lamentation.

vajnic ['vazhnik] *adv* vigorous, hearty; (*aprig*) fiery; (*neînfricat*) dauntless; (*straşnic*) terrible, fearful.

val [val] *nn* wave; (*mare*) billow; (*mic*) small wave, ripple; (*care se sparge*) breaker; *fig* torrent, stream; crowd (of people); (*de dantelă*) cascade ; ~ de căldură heat wave; ~ de entuziasm wave of enthusiasm; ~ de mânie surge of anger; *typ* roller.

valabil [va'labil] *adj* valid, good; *jur* available; legal(ly binding), lawful; (*îndreptăţit*) justified, legitimate;

authentic; (*curent şi*) current, passable • ~itate *nf* validity, justification.

vale ['vale] *nf* valley, *lit* vale; (*vâlcea*) dale, dell; (*curs de apă*) stream; (*pe deal*) downhill; (*pe râu*) downstream.

valenţă [va'lentsă] *nf chem* valence; *fig* aptitudes, capacity.

valet [va'let] *nm* valet, man-servant; (*la grajduri*) groom, stableboy; (*însoţitor*) flunky, footman; (*la cărţi*) knave, jack.

valid [va'lid] *adj* able-bodied, fit (for service); *jur* valid • ~a *vt* to validate, to ratify, to authenticate • ~itate *nf* validity; availability.

valiză [va'liză] *nf* (small) portmanteau, (*mare*) suitcase; *naut* gripsack.

valoare [va'loare] *nf* value; (*sumă*) amount; *fig* worth; *fig* merit, dessert; (*virtute*) virtue; (*sens*) meaning; significance; importance; *mus* (time) value; de ~ valuable; *also fig* worthy; fără ~ of no value; *fig* worthless.

valora [valo'ra] *vi* to be worth; to cost.

valorifica [valorifi'ka] *vt fin* to capitalize, to turn to (good, the best) account; (*d. bani*) to invest one's money to good account; *econ* to revaluate; (*d. pământ*) to enhance the value of; (*d. un teren*) to develop/farm; (*d. o cădere de apă, vânt*) to harness; (*d. o mlaştină*) to reclaim.

valoriza [valori'za] *vt phil* to valuate.

valoros [valo'ros] *adj* valuable, precious; of great value; important; *fig* worthy, deserving; (*distins*) distinguished; (*talentat*) talented; (*cu greutate*) weighty.

vals [vals] *nn* waltz • ~a *vi* to waltz.

valută [va'lută] *nf* (foreign) currency; ~ forte hard currency.

valvă ['valvă] *nf bot, tech* valve.

valvârtej [valvâr'tezh] *adv* quick, nervously, anxiously; in a jumble || *nn* jumble, bustle; tumult.

vamal [va'mal] *adj* custom (house), customs.

vamă ['vamă] *nf* customs, custom-house; (*taxă*) (custom) duty, custom, toll; scutit de ~ duty-free.

vameş ['vamesh] *nn* customs officer; *naut* tide-waiter, tidesman; *relig* publican.

vampă ['vampă] *nf* vamp, gold-digger.

vampir [vam'pir] *nm myth* vampire; *fig* blood sucker, extortioner; mass murderer; *zool* vampire bat.

van [van] *adj* futile, fruitless, ineffectual; (*d. efort etc*) unavailing; (*d. laudă*) vainglorious; (*d. vorbe etc*) empty; flimsy; (*d. o femeie*) coquettish; (*lumesc*) worldly; în ~ vainly, in vain; of no avail, of no use.

vană ['vană] *nf* tub; *tech* valve.

vandabil [van'dabil] *adj econ* marketable, salable.

vandal [van'dal] *nm* vandal • ~ism *nn* vandalism.

vanilie [va'nilie] *nf bot* vanilla (plant); vanilla.

vanitate [vani'tate] *nf* vanity, (*mândrie*) pride, (*îngâmfare*) conceit; futility.

vanitos [vani'tos] *adj* vain, vainglorious, conceited.

vapor[1] [va'por] *nm* vapor; haze; fumes (of wine/petrol).

vapor[2] [va'por] *nn* steamship, steamer, steamboat, vessel.

vaporiza [vapori'za] *vt* to vaporize; to spray, to atomize || *vr* to become vaporized, to vaporize; to rise as vapor • ~tor *nn* vaporizer; (*de parfum*) atomizer; *agr* sprayer.

vaporos [vapo'ros] *adj* vaporous, filled with steam, steamy; (*eteric*) ethereal; (*ceţos*) misty, hazy.

var [var] *nn* chalk, lime.

vară ['vară] *nf* summer; **de** ~ summer(ly); **la** ~ next summer.

vargă ['vargă] *nf* (*nuia*) rod, wand; switch; (*dungă*) stripe, streak.

varia [vari'a] *vt* to vary, to change; to diversify; to variegate || *vi* to change, to alter; to take place alternately, to come alternately; *econ* to fluctuate.

variabil [vari'abil] *adj bio, math, gram* variable, changeable; (*schimbător*) changing; unsteady; (*d. viteză*) varying; (*d. vreme*) unsettled; (*nestabil*) inconstant; (*nestatornic*) fickle • ~ă *nf* variable • ~itate *nf bio, gram* variability; changeability, mutability, fluctuation.

variantă [vari'antă] *nf* variant; alternative.

variat [vari'at] *adj* varied, varying, various; variegated; miscellaneous; diverse; manifold, multiple.

variație [vari'atsie] *nf* variation; (*a timpului*) change in the weather.

variațiune [variatsi'une] *nf mus* variation; (*a compasului*) compass error.

varice [va'riche] *nf med* milk leg, varicose vein.

varicelă [vari'chelă] *nf med* chickenpox, varicella.

varietate [varie'tate] *nf* variety, diversity.

varieteu [varie'teu] *nn* music hall, variety show.

variolă [vari'olă] *nf* smallpox, variola.

varză ['varză] *nf bot* cabbage.

vas [vas] *nn* vessel; (*rotund*) bowl; (*de lut*) flower pot; (*oală și*) pot, receptacle; (*farfurii*) plates and dishes, crockery; china; (*butoi*) cask; *anat, bot* canal, duct; *naut* craft, (*corabie*) ship.

vasal [va'sal] *nm/adj* vassal • ~itate *nf* vassalage.

vascular [vasku'lar] *adj anat* vascular, vasculiferous.

vaselină [vase'lină] *nf* vaseline, petroleum jelly.

vast [vast] *adj* vast, immense, huge, large; wide; extensive.

vată ['vată] *nf med* cotton(-wool); (*de croitorie*) wadding, padding.

vatman [vat'man] *nm* motor-man; driver (of electric train).

vatră ['vatră] *nf* fireplace, hearth; (*casă*) house, home; dwelling place; (*arie*) area.

vază ['vază] *nf* (*renume*) renown, fame, prestige; (*vas*) (flower) vase; (*autoritate*) authority, esteem; (*influență*) influence; **cu** ~ renowned, outstanding.

vă [vă] *pron pers* you (*ex.* ~ **sun mâine** I'll call you tomorrow); (to) you (*ex.* ~ **spun totul** I'll tell [to] you everything) || *pron ref* yourself, *pl* yourselves (*ex.* **v-ați distrat bine?** did you enjoy yourself/yourselves?) || *pron recip* (*doi*) each other; (*mai mulți*) one another (*ex.* ~ **cunoașteți?** do you know each other?, do you know one another?).

văcar [vă'kar] *nm* cowboy; cowherd.

văcsui [văksu'i] *vt* to black, to polish • ~**tor** *nm* bootblack; shoeblack.

vădană [vă'dană] *nf coll* widow.

vădi [vă'di] *vt* to show; (*a dovedi*) to manifest, to prove; (*a denunța*) to denounce || *vr* to turn out, to prove; (*a ieși la lumină*) to become known, to come to light • ~**t** *adj* obvious, evident, manifest || *adv* obviously, etc.

văduv ['văduv] *nm* widower, widowed man • ~ă *nf* widow, widowed woman; (*bogată*) dowager • ~**i** *vt* to deprive of, to rob (of); to bereave of || *vi* to become a widow/widower.

văicăreală [văikă'reală] *nf* lamentation, wailing.

văicări [văikă'ri] *vr* to wail, to lament.

văita [văi'ta] *vr* to lament, to wail, to groan.

văl [văl] *nn* veil; *text* voile; (*la arabi*) yashmak; *fig* film, haze, mist (before one's eyes); (*care protejează*) shroud.

vălmășag [vălmă'shag] *nn* confusion, jumble; (*zarvă*) tumult, hubbub; (*mulțime*) crowd, throng; medley; clutter.

vămui [vămu'i] *vt* to make (smth) clear customs; *fig* to take a toll of • ~**re** *nf* clearing customs.

văpaie [vă'paie] *nf* flame, blaze, blazing fire; heat; glare; *fig* fire, glow, passion, ardor.

văr [văr] *nm* cousin.

văratic [vă'ratik] *adj* summer; summery, estival.

vărgat [văr'gat] *adj* striped, streaked, streaky.

vărsa [văr'sa] *vt* (*a turna*) to pour (out); (*din greșeală*) to spill; (*sânge, lacrimi*) to shed; (*a depune bani*) to deposit; to vomit; *coll* to throw/bring up; (*a răsturna*) to upset || *vr* (*d. râuri*) (*în*) to flow (into the sea); (*a se revărsa*) to overflow (its banks); *pass* to be spilled, to be upset || *vi* to vomit, to be sick; (*d. ploaie*) to be pouring.

vărsat [văr'sat] *nn* smallpox; (*vărsătură*) vomit(ing); ~ **de vânt** chicken pox; ~ **negru** variola, cow pox || *adj* (*d. mărfuri*) bulk, retailing.

vărsământ [vărsă'mânt] *nn fin* payment.

Vărsător [vărsă'tor] *nm astrol* Aquarius, the Water carrier.

vărui [văru'i] *vt* to whitewash; to limewash; (*copaci*) to cover with lime/chalk, to chalk.

vătăma [vătă'ma] *vt* to harm, to damage; (*a răni*) to wound, to hurt; *fig* (*a prejudicia*) to prejudice, to be prejudicial to; to wrong, to injure || *vr* to injure/hurt oneself; (*a face hernie*) to get a rupture.

vătămător [vătămă'tor] *adj* harmful, injurious, hurtful; (*otrăvitor*) noxious; detrimental, prejudicial (to).

vătămătură [vătămă'tură] *nf med* wound; *vernac* rupture, hernia; colic.

vătrai [vă'trai] *nn* (*de sobă*) poker, fire rake/hook; (*de oiște*) pole hook.

vătui [vătu'i] *vt* to wad, to pad; to quilt, to line with wadding; *fig* (*pașii*) to tread softly, to deaden one's footsteps.

văz [văz] *nn* sight; (*vedere și*) eyesight, vision.

văzduh [văz'duh] *nn* air; atmosphere.

vâj [vâzh] *interj* (*d. aripi, elice, obuz*) whirr!; (*d. glonț, mașină în viteză*) whiz!

vâjâi [vâzhâ'i] *vi* (*d. vânt*) to whiz, to whistle; to roar; to howl, to rage; (*d. paie*) to rush, to swish; (*d. valuri*) to hiss; (*d. motor*) to purr, to throb; (*d. glonț, săgeată*) to ping; (*d. urechi*) to buzz; (*a bâzâi*) to hum, to whirr • ~**ală** *nf* * **vâjâit** • ~**t**, ~**tură** [vâzhâ'it, vâzhâi'tură] *nn/nf* whiz(zing); roar(ing) * **vâjâi**.

vâlcea [vâl'chea] *nf* glen, dale; small/narrow valley.

vâltoare [vâl'toare] *nf* eddy, whirlpool; *fig* whirl.

vâlvă ['vâlvă] *nf* commotion, stir; (*agitație*) agitation; (*renume*) fame, renown.

vâlvătaie [vâlvă'taie] *nf* blaze, *coll* flare.

vâlvoi [vâl'voi] *adj* disheveled, frowsy; (*d. păsări*) ruffled.

vâna [vâ'na] *vt* to hunt, to chase; to drive, to pursue; (*cu câini*) to course; (*vulpi*) to go foxhunting; (*iepuri*) to go rabbiting; (*cu dihorul*) to ferret; (*păsări din* *zbor*) to shoot flying; (*a împuşca*) to shoot; (*a urmări*) to hound; to hunt down; *fig* to hunt after ‖ *vi* to hunt, to go a-hunting.

vânat [vâ'nat] *nn* game; (*mâncare*) venison; (*vânătoare*) hunting; (*cu blană*) ground game; (*de apă*) wildfowl; (*păsări*) game birds; (*animale al căror vânat e permis*) fair game.

vână ['vână] *nf anat, geol, bot* vein; (*vas de sânge*) blood vessel; (*tendon*) sinew; *bot* nerve; nervure; *min* lode, seam; reef; (*de apă*) (*pânză freatică*) water table; (*în pietre preţioase*) flaw; (*în piatră*) streak; *fig* inspiration, humor.

vânăt ['vânăt] *adj* bluish, purple; purplish-/violet-blue; (*albăstrui*) bluish-grey; *fig* (deadly) pale, livid.

vânătaie [vână'taie] *nf* bruise; (*la ochi*) black eye.

vânătă ['vânătă] *nf* (*plantă*) eggplant, aubergine.

vânătoare [vână'toare] *nf* hunting; *also fig* hunt; *obs* sport; (*goană*) chase; pursuit; (*cu puşca*) shooting; (*în desiş*) cover shooting; (*participanţii, cu câini, cai*) field.

vânător [vână'tor] *nm* hunter, huntsman; (*braconier*) poacher; *mil* rifleman, light infantryman • **~esc** *adj* hunter's.

vânjos [vân'zhos] *adj* robust, strong, sturdy; sinewy; (*sănătos*) healthy

vânos [vâ'nos] *adj* (*cu vine*) full of veins; (*cu tendoane*) sinewy; (*puternic*) * **vânjos**; (*d. pietre preţioase*) clouded.

vânt [vânt] *nn* wind; (*adiere*) breeze; (*zefir*) zephyr; **rafală de ~** squall, gust of wind; (*puternic*) gale, high wind; storm; hurricane; *med* windy colic • **~os** *adj* (*d. vreme*) windy; windswept.

vântura [vântu'ra] *vt* to winnow, to fan; (*a flutura*) to flutter, to wave; (*a împrăştia*) to scatter (to the four winds); (*o idee*) to ventilate; (*lumea*) to roam ‖ *vr* to wander, to roam; to go about.

vântură-lume ['vântură'lume] *nm* adventurer; stroller; *coll* (*flecar*) gassy/windy fellow, gas bag.

vânzare [vân'zare] *nf* sale; (*acţiune*) selling; (*trădare*) treason, treachery; perfidious act; **de ~** for sale.

vânzătoare [vânză'toare] *nf* clerk, shop assistant, saleswoman.

vânzător [vânză'tor] *nm* (*comerciant*) seller, dealer, (*mic*) retailer, retail dealer; (*in magazin*) clerk, salesman, shop assistant; (*pe stradă*) street vendor; *jur* vendor; **~ de ţară** *fig* traitor (to one's country); (*al unui secret*) betrayer.

vânzoleală [vânzo'leală] *nf* bustle, turmoil, commotion.

vânzoli [vânzo'li] *vt* to stir ‖ *vr* to fuss, to bustle, to go to and fro.

vârcolac [vârko'lak] *nm* werewolf, wolfman; vampire; ghoul; ghost; lycanthrope.

vârf [vârf] *nn* (*culme*) summit; (*pisc*) peak; (*partea cea mai de sus*) top; (*d. val*) crest; (*d. cap*) crown; (*ascuţit*) point(ed end), spike; needle; (*al părţilor corpului*) tip; (*stâncos*) spine; (*d. limbă etc*) tip; head; toe; *fig* climax, meridian; culminating point; pinnacle; (*loc dominant*) head; (*capăt*) end; *geom* vertex; **cu ~** (*d. vase*) brimful; (*sală plină*) overcrowded, packed ‖ *adv* (*de ajuns*) enough.

vârî [vâ'rî] *vt* (*a băga*) (*în*) to put (into); (*a împinge*) to push; (*a introduce*) to shove, to thrust into; to poke (into); (*adânc*) to bury; *also fig* to get, to put; (*a implica*) to involve; to invest ‖ *vr* to get in, to enter; (*a se strecura*) to creep; (*în pat*) to creep/tumble into

bed; (*a se amesteca*) to interfere (with); (*ca mijlocitor*) to intercede; (*ca un intrus*) to pry; *coll* to poke one's nose into; (*a se angaja*) to enter (into), to engage (in).

vârstă ['vârstă] *nf* age; (*bătrâneţe*) old age; **ce ~ ai?** how old are you?; (*generaţie*) generation; (*epocă*) epoch, period.

vârstnic ['vârstnik] *adj* ripe, mature; old, of age; elderly; senior ‖ *nm* grown-up, adult.

vârtej [vâr'tezh] *nn* (*de apă*) eddy, whirlpool; vortex; (*cotitură*) meander; (*de vânt*) whirlwind; (*puternic*) tornado; *fig* (*rotaţie*) whirl, twirl; *fig* (*ameţeală*) dizziness; (*zarvă*) bustle; (*toi*) thick; *tech* lifting jack; winding gear of an elevator.

vârtos [vâr'tos] *adj* solid, firm; (*tare*) strong, hard; sinewy; stout; (*ţeapăn*) stiff; *also fig* (*d. caracter*) stern; tough ‖ *adv* strongly, vigorously; rigidly, firmly.

vâsc [vâsk] *nn* *bot* mistletoe.

vâscos [vâs'kos] *adj* viscous, viscid; (*lipicios*) gluey, clammy; *coll* sticky, tacky; adhesive; slimy; thick.

vâslaş [vâs'lash] *nm* oarsman, rower; (*în doi*) sculler.

vâslă ['vâslă] *nf* oar; (*padelă*) (*canoe*) paddle; (*la dublu*) double-banked oars; (*de galeră*) sweep.

vâsli [vâs'li] *vi* to row; to pull at the oar; (*în doi*) to scull; (*cu padela*) to paddle.

veac [veak] *nn* century; (*epocă*) age, period, epoch; (*viaţă*) life; (*eternitate*) eternity.

vecernie [ve'chernie] *nf* vespers.

vechi ['veki] *adj* old; (*d. istorie etc*) ancient; past; early; (*demodat*) obsolete, antique; (*din bătrâni*) old-established • **~me** *nf* (old) age, oldness; (*mare*) antiquity; (*în slujbă*) seniority, length of service; **din ~** (from days) of yore, from ancient times • **~tură** *nf* old thing/dress; rubbish, frippery; *pl* old clothes; (*zdrenţe*) rags; *pl* (*mobile*) lumber; second-hand furniture; (*hârţoage*) old papers/manuscripts; old books.

vecin [ve'chin] *nm* (next-door) neighbor ‖ *adj* neighboring; (*mărginaş*) bordering, adjacent (to), contiguous (to) • **~ătate** *nf* (*zonă*) neighborhood, surrounding district; (*apropiere*) proximity; nearness, vicinity.

vector [vek'tor] *nm math* vector.

vedea [ve'dea] *vt* to see; to set eyes on; (*a zări*) to sight; to perceive, to catch sight of, to catch a glimpse of; (*a privi*) to look at; (*a asista*) to witness; (*a observa*) to notice; (*a înţelege*) to understand; (*a socoti, a considera*) to consider; (*a întâlni*) to meet; (*a vizita*) to visit ‖ *vi* to see; (*a avea grijă*) to look after, to see to/about ‖ *vr* (*a fi lumină*) to be light; to be seen/visble; (*a se ivi*) to show; (*a se pomeni*) to find oneself; *recip* to see each other, to see one another; (*a se întâlni*) to meet.

vedenie [ve'denie] *nf* vision, hallucination; fantasy; phantom, ghost, specter.

vedere [ve'dere] *nf* (*acţiune*) seeing * **vedea**; (*văz*) eyesight; vision; (*privelişte*) view, sight; panorama; (*tablou*) picture; (*ilustrată*) postcard; (*părere*) opinion, conception; (*întâlnire*) meeting, visit; **în ~a** with a view to; (*pentru*) for, in order to; **la ~a** at the sight of.

vedetă [ve'detă] *nf* star, leading actor/actress/man/lady; *naut* vedette, gunboat, small motor boat, patrol boat; *mil* mounted guard/sentry.

vedetism [vede'tism] *nn* swashbucklery, swagger.

vegeta [vedje'ta] *vi* (*d. plante*) to grow; (*d. persoane*) to vegetate; to lead an aimless/uneventful life; to be a vegetable.

vegetal [vedje'tal] *adj* vegetable, vegetal.

vegetar(ian)ism [vedjetaria'nism] *nn* vegetarianism; (*radical*) veganism.

vegetarian [vedjetari'an] *nm/adj* vegetarian; (*strict*) vegan.

vegetație [vedje'tatsie] *nf* vegetation; *pl med* vegetations; adenoids growths, *coll* adenoids.

veghe ['vege] *nf* (*ca stare*) wakefulness, wakeful state; sitting/staying up; (*şi strajă*) *mil* (night) watch; *naut* lookout; **de ~** vigilant, alert, on one's guard; (*diviziune a nopții*) night watch; *relig* vigil • **~a** *vt* to watch || *vi* to be awake; (*a sta până târziu*) to stay up late, to stay up till small/wee hours; (*a sta de pază*) to watch; (*a fi cu ochii în patru*) to be on the lookout; *fig* to be vigilant; *mil* to stand by; *relig* to keep vigil; **a ~ asupra** to watch over, to keep an eye on.

vehement [vehe'ment] *adj* vehement, heated; passionate, bitter || *adv* vehemently; ardently, passionately.

vehemență [vehe'mentsă] *nf* vehemence, passion, bitterness.

vehicul [ve'hikul] *nn* vehicle, conveyance; *fig* medium.

veioză [ve'ioză] *nf* side-lamp.

velă ['velă] *nf* sail.

veleitate [velei'tate] *nf* slight desire/inclination; starry impulse; (*ambiție*) ambition, striving.

velocitate [velochi'tate] *nf* velocity, speed, swiftness.

velodrom [velo'drom] *nn* cycling/cycle-racing track.

velur [ve'lur] *nn text* (corduroy) velvet.

venal [ve'nal] *adj* venal, mercenary, corruptible; corrupt • **~itate** *nf* venality, corruption.

venă ['venă] *nf med* vein.

vendetă [ven'detă] *nf* vendetta, murderous revenge.

venera [vene'ra] *vt* to revere, to reverence, to worship • **~bil** *adj* venerable, honorable.

veneric [ve'nerik] *adj* venereal; **boli ~e** venereal diseases, V.D.

venetic [vene'tik] *adj* alien, foreign || *nm* foreigner; newcomer; intruder.

veni [ve'ni] *vi* (*a sosi*) to come, to arrive; (*a apărea*) to turn up; (*a fi adus*) to be brought; (*a vizita*) to drop by; (*a urma*) to follow; (*arătând originea*) to be/ come from; to inherit; (*a se întâmpla*) (*dintr-o cauză*) to result from; (*a ajunge*) to come up (to); **a ~ pe lume** to be born.

venin [ve'nin] *nn* venom, poison (of snake); *also fig* (*răutate*) spite, malice; fury, rage; (*fiere*) gall, bile • **~os** *adj* venomous, poisonous; (*rău*) noxious; (*răutăcios*) spiteful; full of venom/malice.

venit [ve'nit] *nn* income, revenue; rent; (*salariu*) salary, wages; (*venire*) arrival, coming || *nm* newcomer.

ventil [ven'til] *nn tech* valve.

ventila [venti'la] *vt* to air, to fan, to ventilate • **~tor** *nn* ventilator; (*rotativ*) fan; electric fan • **~ție** *nf* ventilation, airing.

ventriloc [ventri'lok] *nm* ventriloquist.

ventuză [ven'tuză] *nf* cupping glass; *zool* sucker; suction cap/disc.

verandă [ve'randă] *nf* porch, veranda(h).

verb [verb] *nn gram* verb • **~al** *adj* verbal, oral || *adv* verbally, orally; by word of mouth; personally.

verde ['verde] *nn* green (color); (*verdeață*) verdure, greenness; (*la cărți*) spades || *adj* green; (*verzui*) greenish; (*necopt*) raw; (*d. vin*) young; *fig* (*d. oameni*)

inexperienced; (*începător*) greenhorn; (*d. lemn*) sappy; (*proaspăt*) fresh; (*viguros*) vigorous; (*zdravăn*) stout; (*d. pers. în vârstă*) hale and hearty || *adv* plainly, openly; (*obraznic*) boldly • **~ață** *nf* green, greenery; (*culoare*) greenness; (*şi plante*) verdure; *pl* greens, vegetables; green goods/stuff.

verdict [ver'dikt] *nn also jur* verdict; *jur* ruling.

vergea [ver'djea] *nf* rod, wand; *naut* yard.

veridic [ve'ridik] *adj* truthful, veridical, *lit* veracious || *adv* truthfully, veridically, veraciously • **~itate** *nf* veracity, truthfulness; lifelikeness.

verifica [verifi'ka] *vt* to check (up); to verify; to examine, to inspect; to overhaul; to audit; to scrutinize; to prove, to confirm • **~bil** *adj* verifiable • **~re** *nf* verification; inspection, examination; scrutiny • **~tor** *adj* verifying; * **verifica** || *nm* examiner, controller, inspector; (*aparat*) testing machine; (*instrument*) gauge, calipers.

verigă [ve'rigă] *nf* link (of chain); chain loop; (*inel*) ring.

verighetă [veri'getă] *nf* wedding ring.

verişoară [veri'shoară] *nf* cousin; * **vară**.

verişor [veri'shor] *nm* cousin; * **văr**.

veritabil [veri'tabil] *adj* genuine, real, actual, authentic, true; (*credincios*) staunch, loyal; (*pur*) pure, sterling; natural.

vermut [ver'mut] *nn* vermouth.

vernisa [verni'sa] *vt* to varnish.

vernisaj [verni'sazh] *nn* private view, preview; inauguration.

verosimil [vero'simil] *adj* plausible, credible; probable, likely • **~itate** *nf* verisimilitude, probability, likelihood.

vers [vers] *nn also pl* verse; *pl* poetry; (*rând*) line; *relig* (Bible) verse; *mus* lyrics.

versant [ver'sant] *nn* slope, mountainside; bank (of a canal).

versat [ver'sat] *adj* expert, adept (at), well-versed.

versatil [versa'til] *adj* inconstant, vacillating, wavering • **~itate** *nf* inconsistency, vacillation, versatility.

versifica [versifi'ka] *vt/vi* to versify, to put into verse.

versiune [versi'une] *nf* version; (*traducere*) translation.

verso ['verso] *nn* back (of the page); **pe ~** overleaf.

vertebrat [verte'brat] *adj/nn* vertebrate.

vertebră [ver'tebră] *nf anat* vertebra.

vertical [verti'kal] *adj* vertical, perpendicular, upright || *adv* vertically; straight up; (*în rebus*) down.

vertiginos [vertidji'nos] *adj* breathtaking, breakneck, staggering; (*amețitor*) dizzy, giddy || *adv* dizzily, rapidly.

vertij [ver'tizh] *nn med* vertigo; fear of heights; dizziness, giddiness.

vervă ['vervă] *nf* verve, zest; *coll* go.

verzui [ver'zui] *adj* greenish.

vesel ['vesel] *adj* merry, cheerful, joyful, in good spirits, cheery; *lit* blithe; (*fericit*) happy; (*d. culori*) gay; (*d. o conversație*) amusing; (*d. o petrecere*) lively || *adv* joyfully, merrily, cheerfully, gaily, brightly.

veselă [ve'selă] *nf* plates and dishes, crockery, china.

veselie [vese'lie] *nf* joy, cheerfulness; daftness; merry-making; gladness; delight; (*bucurie*) rejoicing, merriment; (*petrecere*) feast.

vest [vest] *nn* (the) West; **de ~** Western, westerly • **~ic** *adj* western.

vestă [ve'stă] *nf* vest, waistcoat.

veste ['veste] *nf* (piece of) news, news (item); *pl* information, news (of/about); (*zvon*) rumor, report; **fără ~** unawares, unexpectedly, suddenly.

vesti [ves'ti] *vt* (*pe cineva*) (*despre*) to inform/advise (of); to let smb know (about smth); (*a preveni*) to warn, to notify; (*ceva*) to announce; to herald; (*a semnala*) to signal, to report smth.

vestiar [vesti'ar] *nn* (*la teatru, restaurant*) checkroom; (*la internat*) wardrobe room; (*în sala de sport*) changing/locker room; *jur* robing room; (*cu dulapuri*) locker room.

vestibul [vesti'bul] *nn* (entrance) hall; *thea* lobby; *anat* vestibule.

vestigiu [ves'tidjiu] *nn* vestige, remains; trace.

vestimentar [vestimen'tar] *adj* clothing, dress.

vestit [ves'tit] *adj* renowned, well-known, famous; *pej* notorious, ill-famed, in bad repute.

vestitor [vesti'tor] *nm* announcer, bearer of news; (*de rele*) harbinger of evil, bearer of bad news; (*care anunță public*) proclaimer, herald; (*la curte*) crier; (*în oraș*) town crier; (*sol*) messenger || *adj* heralding.

veston [ves'ton] *nn* jacket, coat; *naut* monkey jacket.

veșmânt [vesh'mânt] *nn* attire, garment, garb; coat; *relig* canonicals, vestment.

veșnic ['veshnik] *adj* eternal, everlasting; (*nesfârșit*) endless, ceaseless; (*neîntrerupt*) continuous, unceasing || *adv* always, incessantly • **~ie** *nf* eternity; immortality; perpetuity; *fig* ages, long time.

veșted ['veshted] *adj* withered, drooping, wilted.

veșteji [veshte'zhi] *vr* (*d. plante*) to wither, to droop, to wilt; *also fig* to fade, to dry (up) || *vt* to wither, to wilt, to fade; (*a usca*) to parch; to dry (skin); (*a înfiera*) to brand, to stigmatize.

veteran [vete'ran] *nm mil* veteran, old campaigner; *fig* old-timer; *pol* elder statesman.

veterinar [veteri'nar] *nm* veterinarian, *coll* vet; veterinary surgeon; *mil* farrier || *adj* veterinary.

veto ['veto] *nn* veto.

vetust [ve'tust] *adj* stale, dusty; obsolete, old-fashioned; decrepit, decayed.

veveriță ['veveritsă] *nf zool* squirrel.

vexa [vek'sa] *vt* (*a jigni*) to vex, to hurt, to offend; (*a supăra*) to annoy, to upset • **~t** *adj* vexed; *coll* miffed.

vezică [ve'zikă] *nf anat* vesicle; *coll* bladder.

vi [vi] *pron* (to) you.

via ['via] *prep* via, through, by way of.

viabil [vi'abil] *adj* viable, fit to live, capable of living • **~itate** *nf* viability; practicability.

viaduct [via'dukt] *nn* viaduct.

viager [via'djer] *adj* life(long), for life.

viață ['viatsă] *nf* life; (*biografie*) biography; (*ca durată*) lifetime, lifespan; existence; way of life/living, lifestyle; vitality; (*vioiciune*) liveliness; (*realitate*) reality; **fără ~** lifeless; **în ~** (*viu*) alive; above ground; (*în timpul vieții*) during one's life; **pe ~** for life.

vibra [vi'bra] *vi* to vibrate; (*a face să vibreze*) to make smth vibrate; (*a emoționa*) to thrill • **~nt** *adj* vibrating, resonant; *fig* stirring, rousing; vibrant • **~ție** *nf* vibration; resonance.

vicar [vi'kar] *nm* dean; locum tenens.

vicepreședinte [vichepreshe'dinte] *nm* vice-president, vice-chairman, deputy chairman.

vicerege [viche'redje] *nm* viceroy.

viceversa [viche'versa] *adv* vice versa.

vicia [vichi'a] *vt* to vitiate; to spoil; to corrupt; (*aerul*)

to pollute; *jur* to invalidate • **~t** *adj* corrupt(ed), vitiated; tainted; poor, thin; (*d. aer*) polluted, foul.

vicios [vichi'os] *adj* depraved, corrupt; defective, faulty; wrong, incorrect; vicious; **cerc ~** vicious circle; tricky, restive.

vicisitudine [vichisi'tudine] *nf* vicissitude, hardship.

viciu ['vichiu] *nn* vice, bad habit; depravity, corruption; fault, defect, flaw.

viclean [vi'klean] *adj* cunning, astute, wily, sly; captious; (*trișor*) cheating, tricky; **cel ~** the Evil One || *adv* slyly.

viclenie [vikle'nie] *nf* craftiness, cunning, slyness; (*înșelăciune*) fraud, cheating; (*perfidie*) perfidiousness.

vicleșug [vikle'shug] *nn* sly trick, fraud.

viconte [vi'konte] *nm* viscount • **~să** *nf* viscountess.

victimă ['viktimă] *nf* victim; sufferer; prey; *pl* casualties.

victorie [vik'torie] *nf* victory, triumph; success.

victorios [viktori'os] *adj* victorious, triumphant || *adv* victoriously, triumphantly.

vid [vid] *nn* vacuum, *pl* vacua, vacuums; *fig* void, emptiness • **~a** *vt* to void, to empty; *tech* to vacuum.

videocasetă [videoka'setă] *nf* videocassette, videotape.

videocasetofon [videokaseto'fon] *nn* videocassette recorder, VCR.

videoconferință [videokonfe'rintsă] *nf* video conference.

videodisc [video'disk] *nn* videodisk.

vidră ['vidră] *nf zool* otter.

vie [vie] *nf* vineyard.

vienez [vie'nez] *nm/adj* Viennese.

vier[1] [vi'er] *nm* wine grower, vintager.

vier[2] [vi'er] *zool* boar; (*mistreț*) wild boar.

vierme ['vierme] *nm ento* (*de pământ*) (earth)worm; (*de nisip, de pescuit*) lug(worm); (*larvă*) grub, maggot, larva; *fig lit* worm, poor little wretch.

viespar [vies'par] *nn* wasps' nest; *fig* hornets' nest, swarm.

viespe ['viespe] *nf ento* hornet, wasp; *fig* shrewd, scold.

vietate [vie'tate] *nf* creature, living being.

viețui [vietsu'i] *vi* to live; * **trăi**.

viețuire [vietsu'ire] *nf* (way of) living; (*viață*) life.

viețuitoare [vietsui'toare] *nf* * **vietate**.

viețuitor [vietsui'tor] *adj* living, animate.

vifor ['vifor] *nn met* (*vânt puternic*) gale; *met* (*furtună de zăpadă*) snowstorm.

viforniță [vi'fornitsă] *nf* * **vifor**.

vigilent [vidji'lent] *adj* vigilant, watchful, alert.

vigilență [vidji'lentsă] *nf* vigilance, watchfulness.

vigoare [vi'goare] *nf* vigor, strength, zing; **cu ~** vigorously; **fără ~** (*d. persoane*) exhausted, washed out, (*d. stil*) flat, lifeless; **în ~** in force; (*valabil*) valid, operative.

viguros [vigu'ros] *adj* vigorous, forceful; (*solid*) stout, big; (*bine clădit*) robust, sturdy.

viitor [vii'tor] *nn also gram* future; (*timp*) future times; coming ages; **în ~** in (the) future; **pe ~** from now on || *adj* future; (*următor*) next, following.

viitură [vii'tură] *nf* high flood; rising, swell; (*revărsare*) freshet.

vijelie [vizhe'lie] *nf* gale, storm; (*uragan*) hurricane.

vijelios [vizheli'os] *adj* (*d. vreme, cer*) thundery, stormy; lowering; *fig* tempestuous, high-spirited; heated.

vilă ['vilă] *nf* villa; house (in a residential area); (*mică, de țară*) cottage.

vilegiatură [viledjia'tură] *nf* stay, vacation.

vilegiaturist [viledjiatu'rist] *nm* vacationer, holiday maker.

vin [vin] *nn* wine.

vină ['vină] *nf* guilt, fault, blame; *(mică, uşoară)* peccadillo; *jur* offense, misdemeanor.

vinci [vinch] *nn* winch, windlass.

vinde ['vinde] *vt* to sell, to deal in; *(mărfuri)* to dispose of; *fig (a trăda)* to betray, to sell out ‖ *vi/vr* to sell; *fig* to sell oneself.

vindeca [vinde'ka] *vt* to heal, to cure (of) ‖ *vr* to recover (from), to get over; *(d. o rană)* to heal.

vindecător [vindekă'tor] *adj* healing ‖ *nm* healer; *(şarlatan)* charlatan, quack (doctor).

vindicativ [vindika'tiv] *adj* vindictive, revengeful, spiteful.

vineri ['vineri] *nf* Friday.

vinicultură [vinikul'tură] *nf* wine-growing.

vinovat [vino'vat] *nm* culprit; guilty man/person/party ‖ *adj* guilty, culpable; responsible; *(dator)* in debt.

vinovăţie [vinvă'tsie] *nf* guilt(iness).

vintre ['vintre] *nf* anat loins.

vioară [vi'oară] *nf* violin; *(scripcă)* fiddle.

vioi [vi'oi] *adj* lively; *(plin de viaţă)* full of life; brisk; vivacious; hot; high-spirited; *(vesel)* cheerful; *(d. culori)* bright, vivid; rapid, quick; impulsive; *(ager)* quick of apprehension; *coll* quick in/on the uptake ‖ *adv* briskly, eagerly; cheerfully • ~ciune *nf* liveliness, vivacity, animation; briskness; fire; joyfulness, cheerfulness; blitheness; agility.

viol [vi'ol] *nn* rape, abuse, ravishment; violation; *jur* assault • ~a *vt* to violate; to infringe, to break; *(a profana)* to defile; to trespass; *(o femeie)* to rape; *jur* to assault, to violate • ~ator *nm jur* transgressor, law-breaker; *(de teritoriu)* trespasser, offender; violator; ravisher.

violă [vi'olă] *nf mus* viola.

violent [vio'lent] *adj* violent; impetuous; *(d. vânt)* high; fierce; *(d. măsuri)* drastic; *(d. miros)* pungent; *(d. culori)* loud; *(nervos)* irritable; *(fierbinte)* hot(-blooded); ardent; vehement ‖ *adv* violently, stormily.

violenţă [vio'lentsă] *nf* violence; *jur* duress; force; irritation; fierceness; **prin ~** by violence/force, forcibly.

violet [vio'let] *adj* violet, purple, mauve.

violoncel [violon'chel] *nn mus* cello.

violonist [violo'nist] *nm mus* violinist, violin player.

viorea [vio'rea] *nf bot* violet.

viperă ['viperă] *nf zool* viper, adder; *fig* (rattle)snake.

vira [vi'ra] *vt com* to transfer (money); to clear (checks); *phot* to tone ‖ *vi* to turn, to sweep round; *(d. vânt)* to veer; *auto* to take a turn/corner, to corner • ~j *nn* turning, bend; *avia (în jurul axei verticale)* yaw • ~ment *nn* (credit) transfer.

viran [vi'ran] *adj* waste, vacant; *loc* ~ waste/vacant land.

virgin [vir'djin] *adj* chaste; maiden; virgin; blank; unexposed; *(nepătat)* immaculate, stainless • ~al *adj* virginal, maiden(ly); *mus* type of harpsichord • ~ă *nf* maiden, virgin • ~itate *nf* maidenhood, virginity; *fig* purity.

virgulă ['virgulă] *nf gram* comma; *(la cifre, procente)* decimal point.

viril [vi'ril] *adj* manly, virile • ~itate *nf* manliness, virility.

viroagă [vi'roagă] *nf* ravine.

viroză [vi'roză] *nf med* virosis.

virtual [virtu'al] *adj* virtual; **realitate ~ă** virtual reality, VR; potential.

virtuos [virtu'os] *adj* virtuous; chaste; honest.

virtuoz [virtu'oz] *nm* virtuoso, eminent artist, great master • ~itate *nf* virtuosity; proficiency; artistic perfection; *(desăvârşire)* consummation; accomplishment.

virtute [vir'tute] *nf* virtue; *(şi castitate)* chastity, continence; *(curaj)* courage, valor; **în ~a** by virtue of, under.

virulent [viru'lent] *adj* virulent; powerful.

virus ['virus] *nn bio, comp* virus.

vis [vis] *nn* dream; *(fantezie)* illusion; fancy; *(viziune)* vision; apparition; *(himeră)* chimera; *(coşmar)* nightmare; daydream, reverie • ~a *vt (în somn)* to dream (of/about smth/smb) ‖ *vi (a medita)* to daydream; to meditate; to be dreaming/wistful; *(a năzui)* to dream of • ~are *nf* (day)dream, wistfulness; musing • ~ător *nm* dreamer; *fig* visionary, wishful thinker; muser ‖ *adj* dreamy, wistful, wishful; musing.

visceral [vische'ral] *adj anat* visceral; deep-seated; innermost.

viscol ['viskol] *nn met* blizzard, snowstorm • ~eală *nf* * **viscol**.

visterie [viste'rie] *nf* treasury, treasure house; exchequer.

vişin ['vishin] *nm bot* (morello/sour) cherry tree • ~ă *nf* morello/sour cherry • ~iu *adj* cherry-colored.

vital [vi'tal] *adj* essential, vital.

vitalitate [vitali'tate] *nf* zing, vitality, liveliness.

vitamină [vita'mină] *nf* vitamin.

vită ['vită] *nf zool (bou)* ox, *(vacă)* cow, *pl* cattle; *fig* brute, beast.

viteaz [vi'teaz] *nm* hero, brave man ‖ *adj* brave, valiant, heroic, courageous, bold; *(îndrăzneţ)* daring, gallant; stout.

vitejie [vite'zhie] *nf* bravery, gallantry, valor, courage; *lit* prowess; *(faptă)* feat, achievement.

viteză [vi'teză] *nf* speed; *phys* velocity; *auto* gear; *(rapiditate)* rapidity; quickness; *(a unei corăbii)* headway; *(de expediere)* dispatch, promptness.

vitezometru [vitezo'metru] *nn* speedometer, tachometer.

viticultor [vitikul'tor] *nm* wine grower.

viticultură [vitikul'tură] *nf* viticulture, wine growing.

vitraliu [vi'traliu] *nn* stained/colored glass window; leaded glass window.

vitreg ['vitreg] *adj* step/half (brother); *fig* unjust, unfair; *(crud)* cruel; *(nenorocit)* miserable; *(nefavorabil)* inauspicious; hostile; *(rău)* wicked; *fig* unnatural/cruel mother ‖ *adv* cruelly, harshly.

vitrină [vi'trină] *nf* shop window; *(în casă)* glass case/cabinet; *(în muzeu)* display cabinet.

vitriol [vitri'ol] *nn chem* vitriol.

viţă ['vitsă] *nf bot* vine; *(origine)* extract, stock; *(neam)* descent, race; descendant, offspring; *(fel)* kind, sort; *(şuviţă)* lock; *(fâşie)* strip.

viţea [vi'tsea] *nf zool* heifer.

viţel [vi'tsel] *nm zool* calf; *(carne)* veal.

viu [viu] *adj* living, alive; *(d. plante)* green; vigorous; *fig* vivacious; brisk; *(d. foc)* hot; *(d. limbi)* modern; animated, lively; *(puternic)* strong; *(d. lumină, culori)* bright, intense; eternal; *(vioi)* vivid; quick ‖ *adv* vividly, briskly; strongly, intensely.

vivace [vi'vache] *adj* lively, vivid, full of life; *bot* perennial; *mus* vivace.

vivacitate [vivachi'tate] *nf* liveliness, animation, vivacity.

vivisecţie [vivi'sektsie] *nf* vivisection.

viza [vi'za] *vt* to visa; to countersign, to stamp; (*a aproba*) to sanction, to okay; *also fig* (*a ţinti la*) to (take) aim at; to covet; (*pe cineva*) to hint at, to refer to.

vizavi [viza'vi] *nn* counterpart; person opposite (at table); (*la cărţi*) partner; **de** ~ opposite; across the street || *adv* opposite; across the street; over against smth; ~ **de** (*în relaţie cu*) towards, in relation to, as regards.

viză ['viză] *nf* visa; stamp; sanction; initials.

vizetă [vi'zetă] *nf* peephole.

vizibil [vi'zibil] *adj* visible; perceptible; obvious, evident || *adv* visibly, perceptibly; obviously, evidently • ~**itate** *nf* visibility.

vizieră [vizi'eră] *nf* visor; peak.

viziona [vizio'na] *vt* to see, to view (a film).

vizionar [vizio'nar] *nm* visionary, dreamer || *adj* visionary.

vizita [vizi'ta] *vt* (*pe cineva*) to go to see smb; (*oficial*) to pay/make a call on; (*cu un scop*) to pay a visit to smb, to visit smb; (*neanunţat*) to drop by, to walk in; (*un loc*) to call at; to visit; (*d. doctor*) to attend; to inspect; to survey • ~**tor** *nm* caller, visitor, *lit* visitant; (*musafir*) guest; (*des*) frequenter; *sp pl* the visitors, the visiting team.

vizită ['vizită] *nf* (*vizitare*) *also med* visit; (*socială*) call.

vizitiu [vizi'tiu] *nm* coachman; driver.

viziune [vizi'une] *nf* vision; imagination; (*concepţie*) opinion; (*fantomă*) apparition, fantasy.

vizor [vi'zor] *nn* peephole; *mil* sight; *phot* view finder.

vizual [vizu'al] *adj* visual; of view.

vizuină [vizu'ină] *nf* (*de animale mari*) lair, den; kennel; (*gaură*) burrow; (*de iepure*) hutch; (*de vulpe*) earth; set; *fig* hovel; retreat; (*cocioabă*) hole.

vlagă]'vlagă] *nf* strength; vitality, energy, force; (*sevă*) sap.

vlăgui [vlăgu'i] *vt* to exhaust, to drain, to wear out; (*a slăbi*) to weaken; (*pământul*) to exhaust; (*resursele*) *also fig* to deplete || *vr* to tire/wear oneself out; to drain/lose one's strength; to grow/become weak(er)/ feeble(r); (*a slăbi*) to grow/become thin/emaciated; (*d. resurse*) to run low; (*d. sol*) to be impoverished/ emaciated.

vlăjgan [vlăzh'gan] *nm* strapping/sturdy/stout fellow.

vlăstar [vlăs'tar] *nn bot* shoot, offshoot; (*ramură tânără*) twig; (*din rădăcină*) runner; (*urmaş*) offspring, descendant.

voal [voal] *nn* veil; * **văl**; *phot* fog (on negative) • ~**a** *vt* to veil; (*d. sunete*) to muffle; *phot* to fog; *fig* to veil, to dim || *vr* to become fogged; (*d. ochi*) to mist over • ~**at** *adj* veiled, dim; obscure; (*d. paşi*) muffled; (*d. voce*) husky; *phot* fogged.

voastră, voastre ['voastră, 'voastre] *adj f* your; **a(le)** ~**(e)** yours.

vocabular [vokabu'lar] *nn* vocabulary, word list.

vocal [vo'kal] *adj* vocal, relating to the voice || *adv* vocally.

vocală [vo'kală] *nf* vowel.

vocaţie [vo'katsie] *nf* vocation, calling; (*înclinaţie*) propensity, proclivity; *relig* divine call.

voce ['voche] *nf* voice; (*bună*) good voice; *mus* part.

vocifera [vochife'ra] *vi* to clamor, to vociferate; (*a striga*) to shout, to yell.

vodevil [vode'vil] *nn* vaudeville, light comedy; topical, satirical song (with refrain).

vogă ['vogă] *nf* fashion, vogue; **în** ~ en/in vogue, in fashion; *coll* all the rage/go.

voi[1] ['voi] *pron* you.

voi[2] [vo'i] *vt* to want; (*a dori*) to desire, to wish (for); (*a intenţiona*) to intend; (*a cere*) to request || *vi* to will, to want; (*a dori*) to wish.

voiaj [vo'iazh] *nn* trip; (*pe uscat*) journey; (*pe mare*) voyage • ~**a** *vi* to travel; to tour, to be/go touring; (*destinaţie menţionată*) to journey; (*pe mare*) to voyage, to cruise • ~**or** *nm* traveler; (*pe mare*) voyager.

voie ['voie] *nf* (*voinţă*) will; (*dorinţă*) wish; desire; (*plăcere*) pleasure; liking; (*alegere*) free choice; (*dispoziţie*) frame of mind; (*permisiune*) permission; ~ **bună** good mood/humor, high spirits; **cu** ~ voluntarily, willingly, of one's own free will; **de bună** ~ of one's own accord, willingly; **după** ~ at will, as one wishes, (*cantitativ*) as much as one wishes; **în** ~ at will, free and easy; **fără** ~ *adj* unintentional, involuntary; (*fără plăcere*) unwilling || *adv* unintentionally, involuntarily; reluctantly, unwillingly.

voievod [voie'vod] *nm hist* voivode, ruler, prince.

voinic [voi'nik] *nm* hero; courageous/brave man; (*flăcău*) lad, young man; (*în basme*) Prince Charming || *adj* strong, robust; (*zdravăn*) stout; (*sănătos*) sound, healthy.

voinţă [vo'intsă] *nf* will; (*dorinţă*) desire, wish; (*intenţie*) intention; (*putere*) willpower; determination; **după** ~ at will/pleasure, as much as one wishes; **fără** ~ without a will of one's own, (*slab*) weak(-minded), (*nehotărât*) irresolute, undecided.

voios [vo'ios] *adj* merry, cheerful, bright, in good spirits || *adv* merrily, cheerfully.

voioşie [voio'shie] *nf* cheerfulness, joyousness, gaiety; alacrity; liveliness, briskness; blitheness.

voit [vo'it] *adj* deliberate, intentional, willful; premeditated || *adv* deliberately, intentionally.

volan [vo'lan] *nn* steering wheel; (*la rochie*) flounce.

volatil [vola'til] *adj* volatile • ~**itate** *nf* volatility.

volbură ['volbură] *nf* whirlwind; (*bulboană*) eddy, whirlpool; *bot* bindweed.

volei ['volei] *nn* volleyball.

voleu [vo'leu] *nn* (*artă*) leaf (of a polyptych); *sp* volley; (*la fereastră*) blind, shutter.

volt [volt] *nm elec* volt • ~**aj** *nn elec* voltage.

volubil [vo'lubil] *adj* talkative, voluble • ~**itate** *nf* talkativeness, volubility.

volum [vo'lum] *nn* volume; (*mărime*) bulk, size, mass; quantity; (*carte*) volume, book; work.

voluminos [volumi'nos] *adj* bulky, sizable, large; unwieldy; (*întins*) wide; (*d. persoane*) stout; (*d. cărţi: gros*) thick

voluntar [volun'tar] *nm* volunteer, voluntarily enlisted man || *adj* (*hotărât*) voluntary; determined; (*încăpăţânat*) obstinate, stubborn; (*neascultător*) self-willed; (*năravaş*) ornery || *adv* voluntarily, willingly; deliberately, intentionally.

voluntariat [voluntari'at] *nn* volunteering.

voluptate [volup'tate] *nf* voluptuousness; lust, sensual pleasure; (*desfătare*) delight, relish; great pleasure.

voluptuos [volup'tuos] *adj* voluptuous; lustful.

vomă ['vomă] *nf* vomiting, nausea, throwing up.

vomita [vomi'ta] *vt* to vomit, to bring/throw up || *vi* to vomit, to be sick.

vopsea [vop'sea] *nf* (*ulei*) paint; (*chimică*) dye; (*culoare*) color.

vopsi [vop'si] *vt* (*cu pensula*) to paint; (*a vărui*) to whitewash; (*cu soluție*) to color; (*lână, material, păr*) to dye; (*hârtie, sticlă*) to stain ‖ *vr* (*părul*) to have one's hair dyed/colored; (*singur/ă*) to dye/color one's hair; (*șuvițe*) to highlight one's hair; (*a se machia*) to make up, to paint one's face • ~**tor** *nm* painter; dyer.

vorace [vo'rache] *adj* voracious, rapacious, ravenous; (plant) that exhausts the soil.

voracitate [vorachi'tate] *nf* voracity, voraciousness, ravenousness.

vorbă ['vorbă] *nf* (*cuvânt*) word; (*expresie*) expression; (*ant. faptă*) saying; (*discuție*) conversation, talk, chat; (*vorbărie*) prating; (*ceartă*) quarrel; proverb, saying; (*fel de a vorbi*) manner/way of speaking, speech; (*promisiune*) promise; (*înțelegere*) agreement; (*chestiune*) question; matter; subject; (*zvon*) rumor; (*obiecție*) objection; *pl* words; (*bârfă*) gossip, small talk; ~ **lungă** (*persoană*) *coll* great babbler, chatterbox; (*poveste*) rigmarole, a long yarn • ~**reț** *nm* chatterbox, windbag, prattler ‖ *adj* talkative, garrulous • ~**rie** *nf* idle talking, talkativeness, tittletattle; ~ **goală** talky-talk; *pej* hot air.

vorbi [vor'bi] *vt* to speak, to talk; (*a rosti*) to utter; (*a spune*) to say ‖ *vr* to agree to; to make an appointment with smb; (*a complota*) to plot, to scheme; (*a discuta*) to talk (to/with); (*a flecări*) to chat (with); (*în public*) to give a lecture (on smth); (*a ține un discurs*) to make a speech; (*a pleda*) to plead; **a ~ deschis/pe șleau** to speak one's mind; to speak bluntly/plain(ly); to use plain language; (*cu cineva*) to be open with smb • ~**re** *nf* speech; speaking; (*manieră*) manner of speech • ~**tor** *nm* speaker, talker ‖ *nn* parlor, visiting room ‖ *adj* speaking, talking.

vostru, voștri ['vostru, 'voshtri] *adj* your; **e dreptul ~** it's your right; **al/ai ~** yours; **sunt ai ~** they are yours.

vot [vot] *nn* vote; (*drept de~*) suffrage, franchise; (*votare*) polling, voting, ballot(ing) • ~**a** *vt* to vote; (*o lege*) to pass, to carry; (*și a alege*) to elect • ~**are** *nf* vote, ballot, poll(ing); **cabină de ~** polling booth; **secție de ~** polling station/place.

votcă ['votka] *nf* vodka.

votiv [vo'tiv] *adj* votive.

vrabie ['vrabie] *nf* sparrow.

vrac [vrak] *nn* bulk goods.

vraci ['vrachi] *nm* (*vrăjitor*) sorcerer, wizard; (*la indienii americani*) medicine man; (*șaman*) shaman; (*șarlatan*) quack, charlatan; (*medic*) physician.

vraf [vraf] *nn* pile, heap; stack, ream; bale, pack; file; packet, bundle; wad.

vraiște ['vraishte] *nf* confusion; *coll* mess ‖ *adj* topsy-turvy, helter-skelter; (*deschis*) (wide) open.

vrajă ['vrazhă] *nf* charm, spell; (*magie*) magic, enchantment; (*neagră*) black magic, evil spell, (*vrăjitorie*) sorcery.

vrajbă ['vrazhbă] *nf* feud, dissension; (*dușmănie*) enmity.

vrăbioară [vrăbi'oară] *nf cul* sirloin.

vrăji [vră'zhi] *vt* to bewitch, to cast/put a spell upon; to enchant; *fig* to charm, to enrapture; (*a atrage*) to fascinate, to captivate • ~**toare** *nf* witch, sorceress; beldam(e); (*ghicitoare/ prezicătoare*) sibyl • ~**tor** *nm*

wizard, conjurer; (*african*) obi man; *fig* charmer, enchanter • ~**torie** *nf* witchcraft; black magic/art; (*Africa*) obi.

vrăjmaș [vrăzh'mash] *nm* enemy, foe ‖ *adj* hostile (to), opposed (to); unfriendly; cruel (to/towards); terrible; dreadful; (*d. natură*) inhospitable, unfavorable.

vrea [vrea] *vt/vi* * **voi**; will; (*a dori*) to want, to wish (for), to desire; (*cu subiect abstract*) to demand, to require.

vrednic ['vrednik] *adj* (*merituos*) worthy, deserving (of); (*plin de demnitate*) dignified; (*harnic*) hardworking; diligent; (*capabil să/de*) able (to), capable (of); (*potrivit*) fit, suitable • ~**ie** [vredni'chie] *nf* merit; worth; (*hărnicie*) diligence, industry; assiduity; (*capacitate*) capability, capacity; (*vitejie*) bravery, valor; (*cinste*) honor.

vrej [vrezh] *nn* creeping stalk/stem, bine.

vreme ['vreme] *nf* time; moment; (*ocazie*) opportunity, occasion; (*răgaz*) respite; *pl* times; age; *met* weather; **de ~ ce** since, as, because; **la ~** on time, in due time • ~**lnic** *adj* temporary; (*provizoriu*) provisional; (*trecător*) transitory, transient; transitional ‖ *adv* temporarily, for some time, for a short while.

vreo [vreo] *adj* some; (*adverbial*) *approx* about; **acum ~ cinci ani** about five years ago; **peste ~ lună** in about a month, in a month or so; (*interogativ, negativ*) any; **ai ~ veste**? (have you) any news?; **să nu faci ~ prostie** don't do anything stupid.

vreodată [vreo'dată] *adv* ever; at any time; (*cândva*) sometime.

vreun [vre'un] *adj* some ‖ *inter* any; **ai ~ indiciu**? have you any clue?

vreuna, vreunul [vre'una, vre'unul] *pron* one (of them); somebody ‖ *inter* any(body); **te-ai întâlnit cu ~**? have you met any of them?

vui [vu'i] *vi* (*d. mașini*) to hum; (*d. arme*) to boom; (*d. pădure*) to rustle; (*d. vânt: a mugi*) to roar; (*d. tunet*) to rumble; (*d. valuri*) to thunder; (*d. mulțime*) to murmur; (*d. voci*) to drone; (*d. urechi*) to ring; (*a fi plin de sunete*) to (re)sound, to echo • ~**et** *nn* rumble, rumbling, boom(ing); (*de mașini*) din; (*de motoare*) hum(ming); (*de voci*) murmur(ing); (*muget*) roaring; howling; buzzing in the ears.

vulcan [vul'kan] *nm geog* volcano • ~**ic** *adj* (d. roci) volcanic; *fig* fiery, ardent; (d. imaginație) vivid.

vulcaniza [vulkani'za] *vt* to vulcanize, to cure • ~**re** *nf* vulcanization.

vulg [vulg] *nn* the common/low people, vulgus; *pej* rabble, mob.

vulgar [vul'gar] *adj* (*josnic*) low, mean, base; (*ordinar*) coarse; (d. limbaj) unkempt; (*comun*) common, ordinary; (*neștiințific*) vulgar ‖ *adv* vulgarly, coarsely • ~**itate** *nf* vulgarity, coarseness; vulgar expression; vulgarism • ~**iza** *vt* (*a populariza știința*) to popularize; (*a face vulgar*) to coarsen, to vulgarize ‖ *vr* to grow vulgar.

vulnerabil [vulne'rabil] *adj* vulnerable, weak, easily wounded/hurt; **loc ~** weak point, sore spot; *fig* Achilles' heel • **itate** *nf* vulnerability.

vulpe ['vulpe] *nf zool* (red) fox, vixen; (*pui*) cub; *fig* cunning/sly fox.

vulpoaică [vul'poaikă] *nf zool* she-fox, vixen; *fig* sly/cunning fox.

vulpoi [vul'poi] *nm zool* he-fox; *fig* sly/cunning fox; *coll* artful dodger.

vultur ['vultur] *nm orn* eagle, *also fig* vulture; *astron* the Eagle, Aquila; (*stindard*) standard.
vulvă ['vulvă] *nf anat* vulva.

W

wagnerian [vagneri'an] *adj* belonging/referring to Wagner('s music)
wagon-lit [vagon'li] *nn rail* sleepingcar, sleeper.
warant ['uarant] *nn econ* warrant.
waterpolo ['uotărpolo] *nn sp* water polo.
watt [vat] *nm phys, elec* watt • ~**oră** *nf phys* watt-hour.
w.c. [ve'che] *nn* restroom, lavatory, ladies'/men's room.
week-end ['wikend] *nn* week-end.
western ['western] *nn* western.
whig [wig] *nm hist, pol* Whig.
whisky ['wiski] *nn* whisky.
wolfram ['volfram] *nn miner* wolfram(ium), tungsten.

X

xenofob [kseno'fob] *nm/adj* xenophobe • ~**ie** *nf* xenophobia.
xerocopie [ksero'kopie] *nf* photocopy.
xerografie [kserogra'fie] *nf* xerography, Xerox copying.
xerox ['kseroks] *nn coll* (trademark) Xerox (machine), copying machine, photocopier; Xerox copy • ~**a** [kserok'sa] *vt* to photocopy.
xilen [ksi'len] *nm chem* xylene.
xilofon [ksilo'fon] *nn mus* xylophone.
xilografia [ksilografi'a] *vi* to carve in wood, to engrave on wood.
xilografie [ksilogra'fie] *nf* wood carving/engraving; (*gravură*) xylography, wood cut.
xilogravură [ksilogra'vură] *nf* wood cut.

Y

yală ['ială] *nf* safety-lock.
yancheu [ian'keu] *nm/adj* Yankee.
yard ['iard] *nm* yard.
yemenit [ieme'nit] *nm/adj geog* Yemenite.
yen [ien] *nn fin* yen (Japanese monetary unit).
yoga ['ioga] *nf* yoga.
yoghin [io'gin] *nm* yogi(n), (Indian) ascetic.
yuan ['iuan] *nn fin* yuan (Chinese monetary unit).
yucca ['iuka] *nf bot* yucca.

Z

za [za] *nf* link (of chain); coat of mail, hanbeck.
zadarnic [za'darnik] *adj* (*inutil*) useless, vain, futile; (*superfluu*) superfluous; (*fără rezultat*) fruitless; ineffectual; unnecessary || *adv* in vain, uselessly.
zahana [zaha'na] *nf* slaughterhouse; shamble, abattoir; (*specialități*) choice meat cuts; restaurant serving special dishes of fried meat.
zaharină [zaha'rină] *nf* saccharine.
zaharisi [zahari'si] *vr* to candy; (*d. miere*) to crystallize; *fig* to dodder, to soften || *vt* to (sweeten with) sugar; (*d. fructe*) to candy • ~**t** *adj* candied; *fig* (*d. persoane*) doddering, doting, senile.
zaharniță [za'harnisă] *nf* sugar box/bowl/basin.
zahăr ['zahăr] *nn* sugar; *chem* saccharum; (*brut*) raw/ crude sugar; ~ **candel** sugar candy; ~ **cubic** lump

sugar; ~ **de trestie** cane sugar; ~ **farin** icing sugar; ~ **praf/pudră** powder sugar, glazing sugar; ~ **tos** granulated sugar; *fig* moonshine; **de** ~ sugar(y); *fig* wonderful.
zaiafet [zaia'fet] *nn* (*cul*) clam bake; drinking bout; *coll* (*petrecere*) blow-out, spree; (*masă*) (rich) meal; *coll* (fine) spread.
zambilă [zam'bilă] *nf bot* hyacinth.
zar [zar] *nn* die, *pl* dice; *pl* (*joc*) game of dice.
zare ['zare] *nf* horizon, skyline; vista; **în** ~ in the distance; (*lumină*) light; (*slabă*) subdued (gleam of) light; *coll* shine; *lit* sheen; (*strălucire*) brilliancy; (*culme de munte*) summit.
zarvă ['zarvă] *nf* (*zgomot*) noise, hubbub, racket; (*larmă*) uproar, tumult; (*agitație*) bustle, agitation; combustion; fuss, scandal; ado; (*ceartă*) quarrel, dispute; (*cu gălăgie*) brawling, squabble; **fără** ~ *fig* without a fuss, without any fanfares.
zarzavagiu [zarzava'djiu] *nm* greengrocer.
zarzavat [zarza'vat] *nn bot* vegetables, greens; (*de bucătărie*) pot/green herbs; greengrocery; *fig* hotchpotch.
zarzăr ['zarzăr] *nm bot* ungrafted apricot tree.
zaț [zats] *nn typ* matter; (*de cafea*) lee, grounds; dregs, sediments.
zăbală [ză'bală] *nf* (curb) bit, (bridle) bit.
zăbavă [ză'bavă] *nf* (*întârziere*) delay, dalliance; respite, repose; (*tergiversare*) shuffling; amusement, pastime; **cu** ~ late • **fără** ~ *adv* without delay, there and then, forthwith || *adj* instant, immediate, prompt.
zăbovi [zăbo'vi] *vi* (*a rămâne în urmă*) to linger, to lag behind; (*a întârzia*) to be/come too late; (*a-și pierde timpul cu*) to waste one's time on.
zăbrea [ză'brea] *nf* iron bar, rail; *pl* trellis, lattice; *archit* screen; (*gratii*) grating; (*de sârmă, pt. plante*) wire netting; (*la sobă*) fender, guard; (*grilaj*) rail(ing); (*gard*) fence.
zăbreli [zăbre'li] *vt* to surround with a grating/railing/ wire netting; to lattice; to fit a grill(e) on the window.
zăcământ [ză'cământ] *nn geol, min* deposit(s), bed, layer, lode, vein; lie of the lodes.
zăcea [ză'chea] *vi* (*a sta întins*) to lie, to rest; (*și a se afla*) to be situated; (*a fi bolnav*) to lie in bed, to be confined (to one's bed).
zădărî [zădă'rî] *vt* to incite, to rouse; (*un câine*) to tease, to harass.
zădărnici [zădărni'chi] *vt* (*a dejuca planurile*) to thwart, to frustrate; to sabotage; to overset; (*a înfrânge*) to defeat; (*a distruge*) to ruin; (*a nimici*) to annihilate • ~**e** *nf* (*inutilitate*) futility, uselessness; wantonness; (*deșertăciune*) vanity.
zăduf [ză'duf] *nn* (*căldură mare*) sultry/stifling heat; sultriness; scorching heat; (*caniculă*) heat wave; *fig* (*supărare*) grief, sorrow; worry.
zăgaz [ză'gaz] *nn* dam, barrier, dike; (*pe râu*) bank, embankment; (*în port*) mole, jetty; (*dig*) sea wall; (*ecluză*) weir; (*canal*) lock; *fig* barrier, obstacle.
zăgăzui [zăgăzu'i] *vt* to dam up, to (em)bank; to impound; *fig* to stem, to check.
zălog [ză'log] *nn* (*obiect*) deposit, guarantee, pawn; (*în bani*) (collateral) security; *obs* (*ipotecă*) mortgage; (*la unele jocuri*) forfeit; (*ostatic*) hostage; surety.
zămisli [zămis'li] *vt* (*un copil*) to conceive, to beget; to bear, to give birth (to); *fig* to imagine; to create; to invent; to form.

zănatic [ză'natik] *adj* (*nebun*) crazy, foolish, flighty; (*aiurit*) thoughtless; *coll* scatterbrained, harebrained.

zăngăneală [zăngă'neală] *nf* clanking, clashing; * **zăngănit**.

zăngăni [zăngă'ni] *vt* to clang, to clatter; *also fig* to brandish || *vi* (*d. chei*) to rattle, to clank; (*d. săbii etc*) to click; (*d. pahare, monede*) to clink, to chink; to jingle, to jangle • ~t *nn* clang(ing), clink; rattling; (*d. lanţuri*) clanking; (*d. săbii*) clash; (*d. pahare*) clink(ing); (*d. chei*) jingling.

zăpadă [ză'padă] *nf* snow; *pl* masses of snow.

zăpăceală [zăpă'cheală] *nf* (*dezordine*) confusion, disorder; (*agitaţie*) flurry, agitation; (*încurcătură*) entanglement; embarrassment; (*nedumerire*) bewilderment, perplexity.

zăpăci [zăpă'chi] *vt* (*pe cineva*) to dumbfound, to perplex, to disconcert, to stupefy, to puzzle, to stun; (*mintea*) to obfuscate; (*hârtii*) to muddle/mix up; to ravel/tangle || *vr* to lose one's head, to be perplexed; to be at a loss • ~t *nm* scatterbrain || *adj* flighty, harebrained, scatterbrained, thoughtless; irresponsible, reckless, rash; (*nebun*) crazy; (*ameţit*) dizzy; daft; (*uimit*) bewildered.

zăpuşeală [zăpu'sheală] *nf* sultry/burning/scorching heat.

zăpuşi [zăpu'shi] *vi* (*d. soare*) to burn (hot).

zăpuşitor [zăpushi'tor] *adj* searing, sultry.

zări [ză'ri] *vt* (*pt. prima dată*) to catch sight of, to get/ catch a glimpse of; to discover; (*a vedea*) to view; *naut* to sight; to observe, to notice; to discern, to perceive; (*a-şi da seama de*) to realize || *vr* (*a apărea*) to appear, to come to light; (*a deveni vizibil*) to become visible; *naut* to heave in sight; (*a deveni clar*) to become clear/evident.

zău [zău] *interj* (*cu adevărat*) really, truly, in fact, actually; (*chiar aşa*?) really?, indeed?, are you serious?; (*pe cuvânt*) upon my word!, on my soul!, by/upon my faith!, by Jove!; *coll* and no mistake; (*exprimând neîncrederea şi indignarea*) indeed.

zăvoi [ză'voi] *nn* riverside coppice; * **luncă**.

zăvor [ză'vor] *nn* bolt, bar; **sub** ~ (safely) locked up, under lock and key, in safe custody • ~î *vt* to (bar and) bolt (up); to lock (a door); to bolt smb in, to lock smb up; *fig* to close; (*a ascunde*) to conceal, to hide || *vr* to bolt oneself in; *fig* to shut oneself up (in one's shell).

zâmbet ['zâmbet] *nn* smile; (*rânjet*) grin; (*dispreţuitor*) scornful smile, sneer; (*afectat*) simper, smirk.

zâmbi [zâm'bi] *vi* to smile (at); (*a rânji*) to grin (at); (*cu dispreţ*) to sneer (at); (*afectat*) to simper, to smirk • ~tor *adj* smiling || *adv* smilingly.

zână ['zână] *nf* fairy; (*zeiţă*) goddess.

zâzanie [ză'zanie] *nf* (*ceartă*) quarrel, feud; discord; machination.

zbate ['zbate] *vr* to toss, to writhe; *also fig* to struggle; (*cu picioarele*) to kick about; (*în apă*) to flounder, to splash (about) in the water; *fig* to strain.

zbârci [zbâr'chi] *vt* to wrinkle; (*d. frunte*) to become lined; (*d. piele, un măr*) to shrivel (up); (*d. apă*) to ripple || *vr* to get/form wrinkles, to crumple • ~tură *nf* wrinkle.

zbârli [zbâr'li] *vt* (*penele*) to ruffle; (*d. o pasăre*) to raise/ruffle up its feathers, to put up its feathers; (*părul*) to tousle || *vr* (*d. păr*) to bristle up; *fig* to get on one's hind legs • ~t *adj* (*d. pene, păr*) tousled, disheveled; *fig* (*d. oameni*) irritated, angry.

zbârr [zbâr] *interj* whirr!

zbârnâi [zbârnâ'i] *vi* (*d. insecte*) to buzz, to hum, to whirr • ~ală *nf* buzz(ing noise) • ~t *nn* buzz(ing), whirr(ing).

zbengui [zbengu'i] *vr* to gambol, to frolic; * **hârjoni** • ~ală *nf* gamboling, frolic(king).

zbiera [zbie'ra] *vi* (*d. cineva*) (*la*) to yell (at), to bellow, to bawl (at); (*d. măgar*) to bray; (*d. vite*) to low, to moo.

zbierăt ['zbierăt] *nn* yell, bellow, roar; bray; moo, low.

zbir [zbir] *nm* tyrant, brute; (*asupritor*) oppressor; satrap; rigid and severe person.

zbor [zbor] *nn* flight; (*planat*) gliding; (*înălţare*) soar(ing); (*al păsărilor*) *frml* vol(it)ation; (*de şoim*) career; (*ca acţiune*) flying; (*avânt*) soaring; *fig* (*fugă*) race, run; ~ **cosmic** space flight; **în/din** ~ on the fly, on/upon the wing, (*în aer*) in the air; *fig* quickly, rapidly.

zbucium ['zbuchum] *nn* agitation, fret(ting); turmoil; (*nelinişte*) anxiety, uneasiness; torment; (*zbatere*) struggle.

zbuciuma [zbuchu'ma] *vr* to be agitated/nervous, to fret, to be anxious/uneasy, to worry; to struggle • ~t *adj* agitated, nervous, uneasy, anxious; (*d. viaţă*) tumultuous, eventful, turbulent.

zbughi [zbu'gi] *vt* **a o** ~ to rush/scuttle away; *coll* to scamper/scour/scud away/off.

zbura [zbu'ra] *vi* to fly; (*a-şi lua zborul*) to take one's flight; (*a se înălţa în zbor*) *also avia* to soar; (*peste ceva*) to fly over; (*razant*) to skim the ground; (*f. repede*) to dart through the air; (*cu avionul*) to go by airplane/air; (*d. insecte, păsări*) to flit; (*d. perdele*) to flutter; *fig* (*a se mişca repede*) to dash; to travel fast; (*ca săgeata*) to dart; *fig* (*a trece repede*) to fly (away); *fig* (*a se pierde*) to be gone/lost; (*a dispărea*) to vanish; (*a pleca*) to flee.

zburătăci [zburătă'chi] *vt* to cast/fling smth at || *vr* to grow (up) || *vi* (*d. zburătoare*) to take one's flight; (*d. pui*) to grow; (*d. copii*) to grow up.

zburătoare [zbură'toare] *nf* bird; *pl* feather.

zburător [zbură'tor] *nm* pilot, flier, flyer; (*la trapez*) trapeze artist, trapezist; (*duh*) *approx* goblin; (*pânză*) *naut* fore-top gallant sail || *adj* flying; (*înaripat*) winged.

zburda [zbur'da] *vi* to frisk (about), to frolic, to romp, (*d. iezi*) to gambol; to leap; • ~lnic *adj* frisky, gamboling; lively, exuberant; (*jucăuş*) playful.

zburdălnicie [zburdălni'chie] *nf* sporting; sportiveness; liveliness, exuberance; playfulness; *pl* * **nebunie**.

zburli [zbur'li] *vt* to ruffle || *vr* to become ruffled/ entangled; * **zbârli**.

zdranc, zdrang [zdrank, zdrang] *interj* crash!, smash!

zdravăn ['zdravăn] *adj* strong; (*voinic*) sturdy, sinewy; (*sănătos*) healthy; (*la minte*) sane; (*întreg*) whole; (*tare*) solid; (*straşnic*) terrible || *adv* terribly, awfully, mightily.

zdrăngăni [zdrăngă'ni] *vi* to jingle, to rattle; (*la; din*) to thrum • ~t *nn* rattling, thrumming.

zdreanţă ['zdreantsă] *nf* rag, tatter; *fig* human rag, flop.

zdrenţăros [zdrentsă'ros] *nm* ragamuffin || *adj* ragged, tattered.

zdrenţui [zdrentsu'i] *vr* to tear; to be frayed/torn, to be worn out / *vt* to tear, to rend.

zdrobi [zdro'bi] *vt* to crush, to bruise; (*a sfărâma*) to break; (*a turti, ceva moale*) to squash; to swat; to flatten out; *fig* to crash; (*a învinge*) to defeat; (*a distruge*) to destroy; (*o inimă*) to break; (*un proiect*) to quench the smoking flax; (*o revoltă*) to stamp out a rebellion || *vr* to crash; to be crushed • ~t *adj* crushed, defeated; * **zdrobi**; *fig* (*istovit*) exhausted, tired/worn out; deadbeat; (*de durere*) overwhelmed/prostrate with grief • ~tor *adj* crushing; overpowering; (*numeros*) overwhelming.

zdruncina [zdrunchi'na] *vt* to shake; (*d. vânt*) (*o barcă*) to buffet; (*d. căruță*) to jolt; *fig* (*a submina*) to undermine; (*a slăbi*) to weaken; (*convingerile*) to shatter || *vi* to jolt, to bump, to shake; **o maşină care** ~ă a bumpy car.

zdruncinătură [zdrunchină'tură] *nf* jolt.

zdup¹ [zdup] *nn sl* (*închisoare*) quod, can; jug.

zdup² [zdup] *interj* thud!, thump!, bump!, smash!, bang!.

zdupăi [zdupă'i] *vi* to tread heavily, to trample.

zeamă ['zeamă] *nf* (*de fructe*) juice; (*de carne*) gravy, sauce; (*supă*) soup; (*sevă*) sap.

zebră ['zebră] *nf zool* zebra; *coll* (*trecere pietoni*) zebra/pedestrian crossing.

zece ['zeche] *n/adj/num* ten • ~lea *adj/num* tenth.

zecimal [zechi'mal] *adj* decimal • ~ă *nf math* decimal fraction.

zecime [ze'chime] *nf* tenth; *pl* tens.

zefir [ze'fir] *nm* zephyr, soft wind/breeze, west wind, balmy breeze.

zeflemea [zefle'mea] *nf* mockery, banter, raillery.

zeflemisi [zeflemi'si] *vt* to ironize; to scoff/sneer (at); to rail/mock at; to ridicule, to make fun of.

zeflemist [zefle'mist] *nm* scoffer, railer, mocker; joker; *coll* chaffer, quizzer.

zeflemitor [zeflemi'tor] *adj* quizzical, bantering, teasing, ironical.

zeitate [zei'tate] *nf myth* deity, god.

zeiță [ze'iتă] *nf* goddess.

zel [zel] *nn* zeal, ardor, fervor; zest; eagerness; **cu** ~ eagerly, zealously; **exces de** ~ false/misguided zeal • ~os *adj* zealous, eager; ardent, fervent; (*să facă un serviciu*) officious; (*harnic*) diligent, hardworking || *adv* zealously, eagerly; diligently.

zemos [ze'mos] *adj* juicy, rich in juice || *nm* melon.

zenit [ze'nit] *nn astron* zenith; *also fig* summit; climax, vertex.

zer [zer] *nn* whey.

zero ['zero] *nn/nm/num math* zero; (*cifră*) cipher, nought; (*punct de îngheț*) freezing point; (*în sport*) nil; (*tenis*) love; (*nimic*) nothing; *fig* (*d. o persoană*) a mere cipher/nobody, a nonentity.

zestre ['zestre] *nf* dowry, dower; (*trusou*) trousseau; (*ladă*) hope chest.

zețar [ze'tsar] *nm typ* compositor, typesetter.

zeu [zeu] *nm myth* god.

zevzec [zev'zek] *nm* idiot, nit(wit), *coll* pinhead, blockhead || *adj* silly, stupid, empty-headed, addle-brained.

zgardă ['zgardă] *nf* dog collar; (*lesă*) leash, lead.

zgâi [zgâ'i] *vr* to stare (at), to gape (at), *coll* to goggle (at).

zgâlțâi [zgâltsă'i] *vt* to jolt, to jerk; (*a scutura*) to shake; * **zdruncina** || *vr* to shake, to tremble (with); (*a se smuci*) to jerk • ~ală *nf* shaking; * **zgâlțâi** • ~tură *nf* shake, jog; (*smucitură*) jerk.

zgândări [zgândă'ri] *vt* (*focul*) to rake; (*o rană*) to irritate; *fig* to rub it in(to); (*a înțepa*) to prick; *fig* to revive; (*o situație*) to aggravate; (*a agrava*) to anger;

(*a aţâţa*) to incite; to stir up; (*nemulțumirea*) to fan; (*pofta*) to whet.

zgârcenie [zgâr'chenie] *nf* avarice, meanness, stinginess.

zgârci¹ ['zgârchi] *nn* cartilage.

zgârci² [zgâr'chi] *vr* (*de căldură*) to shrivel, to shrink; (*a fi zgârcit*) to be stingy/niggardly; (*la ceva*) to skimp over; to grudge || *vt* (*d. căldură*) to shrivel; (*a încorda*) to strain • ~t *nm* skinflint, scrape-penny || *adj* stingy, niggardly, greedy, skimpy, mean.

zgâria [zgâri'a] *vt* to scratch; to scrape; to graze; (*d. pisici*) to claw; *fig* (*hârtia*) to scrawl || *vr* to get a scratch.

zgârie-brânză ['zgârie'brânză] *nm coll* scrooge, skinflint.

zgârie-nori ['zgârie'nori] *nm* skyscraper.

zgârietură [zgârie'tură] *nf* scratch, scrape.

zglobiu [zglo'biu] *adj* sprightly; * **zburdalnic**; (*jucăuş*) playful, coltish.

zgomot ['zgomot] *nn* noise, sound; (*agitaţie*) bustle; (*strigăte*) shouting, clamor; (*ceartă*) brawl(ing); (*scandal*) riot, din; (*tărăboi*) hubbub, uproar; (*zarvă*) fuss, ado; *med* cardiac/respiratory murmur; ~ **surd** thud, thump; **fără** ~ quietly, silently • ~os *adj* noisy, boisterous, uproarious || *adv* noisily, etc.

zgribuli [zgribu'li] *vr* to shrivel, to shrink; (*de frig*) to tremble (with); (*a se ghemui*) to squat (down), to cower (down) • ~t *adj* shriveling, shrinking; huddled (up), trembling.

zgripţoroaică, zgripţuroaică [zgriptso'roaikă, zgriptsu'roaikă] *nf fig* (old) hag, (old) crone.

zgrunţuros [zgruntsu'ros] *adj* (*d. o suprafaţă*) rough, uneven; (*d. lapte*) curdled; (*d. sos*) lumpy; (*d. pară*) gritty.

zgudui [zgudu'i] *vt also fig* (*a zdruncina*) to shake (violently); to disturb smb || *vr* to shake, to totter, * **zdruncina**.

zguduială [zgudu'ială] *nf* commotion; quake, shake; *fig* shock.

zguduitor [zgudui'tor] *adj* shaking; *fig* terrible; thrilling; staggering; (*emoţionant*) touching, moving.

zguduitură [zgudui'tură] *nf* shake, jerk, jolt, jog.

zgură ['zgură] *nf* slag, *also fig* dross; (*la terenuri de sport*) cinders.

zi [zi] *nf* day; (*lumină*) daylight; (*dată*) date, time; *pl* (*vremuri*) times, years; life; ~ **de naştere** birthday; ~ **de plată** pay day; ~ **liberă** day off; **la** ~ up to date.

ziar [zi'ar] *nn* (news)paper, journal; (*oficial*) gazette; (*zilnic*) daily paper, *pl* dailies • ~ist *nm* journalist, newspaperman, pressman; reporter; (*comentator*) columnist; correspondent; (*vânzător*) newspaper boy/man • ~istică *nf* journalism.

zibelină [zibe'lină] *nf zool* sable; (*ca haină*) sable cape/cloak.

zibetă [zi'betă] *nf zool* civet cat.

zicală [zi'kală] *nf* saying, adage, maxim.

zicătoare [zikă'toare] *nf* * **zicală**.

zice ['ziche] *vt* to say (smth); (*ceva cuiva*) to tell smb smth; to relate, to tell; to declare; to affirm; (*a rosti*) to utter; to recite; (*a citi*) to read; *vernac* (*a cânta*) to sing; (*dintr-un instrument*) to play || *vr* **se** ~ **că** they/people say, it is said || *vi* to say; (*a cânta la un instrument*) to play • ~re *nf* saying, quotation, utterance, speech; communication.

zid [zid] *nn constr, also fig* wall; *fig* barrier • ~ar *nm constr* bricklayer, (stone)mason; builder; (*tencuitor*) plasterer • ~**ărie** *nf* (*lucru*) brickwork, bricklaying; (*ca meserie*) masonry; (*de piatră*) stonework • ~**i** *vt constr* (*a clădi*) to build (up), to construct, (*a ridica*) to erect, to raise (up); (*a închide*) to wall in/up; to block up; (*a crea*) to create.

zigzag [zig'zag] *nn* zigzag (line); **în** ~ (in) zigzag.

zilier [zili'er] *nm* day-laborer.

zilnic ['zilnik] *adj/adv* daily, everyday.

zimț [zimts] *nm* (*de ferăstrău*) tooth, dent; (*de roată*) cog; *pl* (*la monedă*) milled edge; * **crenel** • ~**a** *vt tech* * **zimțui** • ~**at** *adj tech* toothed; indented; (*d. monezi*) milled; (*crestat*) notched, jagged; (*d. roți*) cogged; *bot* dentate(d), serrated; denticulate(d); (*crenelat*) crenel(l)ated • ~**ui** *vt tech* to jag, to notch • ~**uit** *adj* * **zimțat**.

zinc [zink] *nn chem* zinc, spelter; *typ* cliché.

zis [zis] *adj* named, called; **așa** ~ would-be, so-called; **bine** ~ what is more.

zloată ['zloată] *nf* sleet.

zmeoaică [zme'oaikă] *nf* dragon's mother; dragon's wife/sister; fiery mare.

zmeu[1] [zmeu] *nm* dragon.

zmeu[2] [zmeu] *nn* (*jucărie*) kite.

zmeur [zmeur] *nm bot* raspberry (bush), hindberry (bush) • ~**ă** *nf* raspberry.

zoaie ['zoaie] *nf* (*apă cu săpun*) soap suds; (*lături*) dirty water; dish water; *coll* slops; *vernac* hog wash.

zobi [zo'bi] *vt* (*a fărămița* to crumb; (*a zdrobi*) to crush.

zodiac [zodi'ak] *nn astrol* zodiac.

zodie ['zodie] *nf astrol* (*semn*) sign of the zodiac, star/sun sign; (*constelație*) zodiacal constellation; *fig* fate, star.

zonal [zo'nal] *adj* zonal, area.

zonare [zo'nare] *nf* zoning, division into zones.

zonă ['zonă] *nf* zone; (*regiune*) area, region.

zoolog [zoo'log] *nm* zoologist • ~**ic** *adj* zoological; **grădină** ~**ă** zoological gardens; *coll* zoo • ~**ie** *nf* zoology.

zootehnie [zooteh'nie] *nf* livestock/animal breeding.

zor [zor] *nn* hurry, haste; efficiency; dispatch; (*viteză*) speed.

zorea [zo'rea] *nf bot* * **zorele**.

zorele [zo'rele] *nf pl bot* morning glory.

zori [zo'ri] *vt* to hurry, to hasten, to (*a îndemna*) to urge, to goad; (*a precipita*) to precipitate; (*a grăbi*) to speed up; to expedite || *vr* to make haste, to hurry, to hasten; (*a se arăta zorile*) to be dawning || ['zori] *nm pl* (early) dawn, daybreak; *mil* reveille; **în** ~ at dawn/daybreak.

zornăi [zornă'i] *vt/vi* (*d. lanțuri, pinteni, geamuri*) to rattle, to clank, to clink; (*d. bani*) to jingle; (*d. clopoței*) to jingle, to tinkle • ~**t** *nn* clang; (*de lanțuri*) clank.

zorzoane [zor'zoane] *nf pl* gewgaws, cheap ornaments, trinkets, knick-knack; paraphernalia.

zugrav [zu'grav] *nm* house painter; *obs* (*pictor*) painter.

zugrăveală [zugră'veală] *nf* painting.

zugrăvi [zugră'vi] *vt* to paint; (*în ulei*) to paint in oils; (*a vărui*) to whitewash; (*a împodobi*) to decorate; *also fig* to describe, to depict, to portray.

zuluf [zu'luf] *nm* lock, curl, ringlet.

zumzăi [zumză'i] *vi* (*d. insecte*) to buzz; (*d. avion*) to hum; (*d. motor*) to purr.

zumzet ['zumzet] *nn* buzz(ing), humming, purr(ing).

zurbagiu [zurba'djiu] *nm coll* noisy/riotous fellow/child; rowdy; brawler || *adj* riotous; noisy; rebellious, unruly; (*d. copii*) unbiddable.

zurgălău [zurgă'lău] *nm* little bell; *pl* (set of) bells; (*la cal*) bell harness; (*la sanie*) sleigh bells.

zurliu [zur'liu] *adj coll* crazy, potty, cracked.

zurui [zuru'i] *vi* to jiggle.

zvastică ['zvastikă] *nf* swastika.

zvăpăiat [zvăpă'iat] *adj* frolicsome, gamboling; (*zăpăcit*) dizzy, giddy, empty-headed.

zvâcni [zvâk'ni] *vi* (*d. inimă*) to throb, to beat; (*d. tâmple, sprâncene*) to twitch; (*a sări*) to jump; (*în picioare*) to spring up, to spring to one's feet; (*a tresări*) to start; (*d. alergători, mașini: a se lansa brusc*) to rush/dash off; (*d. pușcă: a avea recul*) to kick • ~**re** *nf* throb, pulse; jerk, twitch; (*tresărire*) start; (*a puștii*) kick.

zvânta [zvân'ta] *vt* to air, to dry; (*a bate*) to beat, to thrash.

zvârcoleală [zvârko'leală] *nf* writhing, tossing, squirming.

zvârcoli [zvârko'li] *vr* to writhe, to wriggle, to squirm; (*în pat*) to toss (about); (*a se lupta*) to struggle; (*a se frământa*) to fret • ~**re** *nf* writhing, convulsion; (*stare de agitație*) fretting.

zvârli [zvâr'li] *vt* to fling, to hurl, * **azvârli** • ~**tură** *nf* fling, throw.

zvelt [zvelt] *adj* svelte, slender, slim; willowy, lithe; supple; clean-limbed; (*armonios*) harmonious • ~**ețe** *nf* slimness, slenderness.

zvon [zvon] *nn* rumor; hearsay; (*zgomot*) noise, din, hubbub; (*de clopote*) toll, peal, chime; ~ **fals** false rumor • ~**i** *vr* to be rumored, to get about; to murmur, to purl.

ENGLISH-ROMANIAN DICTIONARY

A

A, a¹ s (*letter*) a; (*musical note*) la; film n nepotrivit pentru copiii sub 14 ani; nota f 10 ‖ adj prim, (de categoria) întâi.

a² *art* un, o.

aback *adv* înapoi; pe spate; în spate.

abandon *vt* a abandona; a părăsi; (*hope, etc*) a renunța la ‖ *vi* a abandona ‖ s abandon n • ~ment s abandonare f, părăsire f; abandon n; singurătate f.

abashed *adj* stingherit, jenat; rușinat.

abate *vt* a micșora, a reduce; a abroga, a anula ‖ *vi* (*courage*) a scădea, a se micșora; (*storm*) a slăbi.

abbatoir s abator n.

abbey s abație f, mănăstire f; catedrală f.

abbot s stareț m.

abbreviate *vt* a abrevia, a prescurta; a rezuma; a scurta.

abbreviation s abreviere f, abreviație f, prescurtare f; rezumat n

ABC s ABC, alfabet n; abecedar n

abdicate *vt* a abdica de la, a renunța la ‖ *vi* (*king, etc.*) a abdica (de la).

abdication s abdicare f.

abdomen s abdomen n, pântece n, burtă f.

abduct *vt* a răpi • ~ion s răpire f.

aberration s aberație f; abatere f, deviere f; rătăcire f; defecțiune f.

abet *vt* a încuraja • ~tor s complice m.

abeyance *to be in* ~ a fi în suspensie; **to fall into** ~ a cădea în desuetudine.

abhor *vt* a detesta • ~rence s aversiune f.

abide *vt/vi* (*tolerate*) a suporta, a toler; ~ **by** (~ *a rule*) a respecta regula, (~ *a promise*) a-și respecta cuvântul/ promisiunea.

ability s capacitate f; talent n.

abject *adj* abject, mizerabil; (*apology*) jalnic; **in ~ poverty** în neagră sărăcie.

able *adj* (*capable*) în stare (*de ceva*); (*clever*) competent.

abnegation s dăruire f de sine.

abnormal *adj* anormal.

aboard *adv* la bord ‖ *prep* la bordul; **to go** ~ a se îmbarca.

abode s (*house*) locuință f; (*domicile*) domiciliu n.

abolish *vt* a desființa, a aboli; a suprima.

abolition s desființare f, suprimare f.

A-bomb s bombă f atomică.

abominable *adj* abominabil, îngrozitor, oribil; urât.

aboriginal *adj* indigen, autohton.

abort *vt* (~ *a pregnancy*) a avorta; (~ *a plan, project*) a abandona, a eșua; *comp* a renunța • ~ion s med avort n, avorton m, stârpitură f; monstru m; eșec n, nereușită f; insucces n; **have an** ~ a face un avort.

abound *vi* a abunda, a fi din belșug.

about *adv* (de jur) împrejur; în jur/preajmă; în toate părțile; pe aici/aproape, prin apropiere; cam; aproximativ; (*around*) în jur de; aproape, ca și ‖ *prep* în jurul/preajma; în toate direcțiile; (pe) lângă; pe la; prin; pe; din jurul, dimprejurul; la, asupra; (*concerning*) despre, de, cu privire la, în ceea ce privește; **what is it** ~? despre ce este vorba? ‖ *adj* sculat, în picioare; activ, prezent; pe aici, prin preajmă; ~ **to** *adj* pe punctul de a, gata să; cât pe ce să • ~**face** s *fig* schimbare f radicală.

above *adv* sus; mai sus; deasupra; deasupra capului; pe deasupra; mai sus, mai înainte, anterior; în cer, pe cer; pe o treaptă mai înaltă; mai mult/mulți ‖ *adj* de

mai sus/înainte, anterior; precedent ‖ s **the** ~ cele de mai sus/înainte.

abrasion s răzuire f; *tech* șlefuire f.

abrasive *adj tech* abraziv; (*character*) aspru; (*voice*) caustic; (*criticism, wit*) ascuțit, tăios.

abreast *adv* în același rând, alături; **keep** ~ **of** a se ține la curent cu.

abridge *vt* a prescurta; a rezuma; a abrevia; a scurta; a micșora, a limita.

abroad *adv* în străinătate, peste hotare; pretutindeni; departe de țintă.

abrogate *vt* a abroga, a desființa.

abrupt *adj* abrupt, prăpăstios; accidentat; brusc; aspru, tăios; nepoliticos.

abscess s abces n; bubă f.

abscond *vi* a fugi; a se ascunde de.

absence s absență f, lipsă f.

absent *adj* absent; neatent, distrat; inexistent • ~ee s absent m; absenteist m • ~minded *adj* distrat, neatent, preocupat.

absolute *adj* absolut, deplin, total, perfect; complet; necondiționat; nelimitat; pur, curat; categoric, sigur, incontestabil • ~ly *adv* (în mod) absolut; în întregime; pe deplin, întru totul; necondiționat; nelimitat; categoric, sigur, indiscutabil.

absolution s iertare f a păcatelor.

absolve *vt* **to** ~ **smb (from)** a scuti pe cineva de.

absorb *vt* a absorbi, a absoarbe; a consuma; a amortiza; a aspira • ~ing *adj* (*book, etc.*) pasionant.

abstain *vi* a se abține, a se reține (de la); a se stăpâni.

abstention s abținere f.

abstinence s abstinență f.

abstract *adj* abstract; dificil; abscons; abstrus ‖ s (*cuvânt*) abstract n; abstracțiune f; sumar n; (*summary*) rezumat n; compendiu n; conspect n ‖ *vt* a separa, a despărți; (*extract*) a extrage; a abstrage; a abstractiza; (*summarize*) a rezuma; a conspecta • ~ion s abstragere f; abstracți(un)e f; noțiune f abstractă.

absurd *adj* absurd, (*meaningless*) lipsit de sens, irațional, ilogic; (*silly*) prostesc; nesăbuit; (*ridiculous*) caraghios, ridicol.

abundance s abundență f, (*profusion*) prisos n, (*plenty*) belșug n; (*wealth*) bogăție f.

abundant *adj* (*profuse*) abundent, (*rich*) îmbelșugat • ~ly *adv* (*obviously*) extrem de; (*to grow*) din belșug.

abuse *vt* a abuza de, a face abuz de; a ultragia; (*treat badly*) a maltrata; a profera injurii; a înjura; a vorbi de rău; (*insult*) a insulta, a ofensa ‖ s abuz n, exces n; (*misuse*) folosire f abuzivă/greșită; ultraj n; (*mistreatment*) maltratare; invective f pl, insulte f pl. • **abusive** *adj* insultător; abuziv.

abyss s abis n, prăpastie f.

academic *adj* academic; universitar; teoretic, savant; pretențios; pedant; scolastic ‖ s membru m al unei universități sau al unui colegiu; profesor m; cadru m de predare.

academy s academie f; universitate f.

accede *vi* (*agree*) **to** ~ **to** a consimți, a fi de acord; (*monarch*) **to** ~ **to the throne** a urca pe tron.

accelerate *vt* a accelera; a grăbi ‖ *vi* a se accelera, a prinde viteză.

acceleration s accelerare f; *auto* accelerație f.

accelerator s *tech* accelerator n.

accent s accent n; (*emphasis*) subliniere f; fel n particular de a vorbi/a pronunța; trăsătură f distinctivă, particularitate *f* || *vt* (*emphasize*) a accentua; a sublinia, a scoate în evidenţă • **~uate** *vt* a accentua; a sublinia, a scoate în relief.

accept *vt* a accepta, a primi; a recunoaşte, a admite; a lua asupra sa || *vi* a accepta, a primi; a fi de accord • **~able** *adj* acceptabil; convenabil • **~ance** *s* accepţie *f*, semnificaţie *f*; (*club, position*) admitere *f*.

access *s* acces *n*; intrare *f*; criză *f*; atac *n* • **~ible** *adj* (*place*) accesibil; disponibil.

accession *s* avansare *f*, promovare *f*; urcare *f*; ~ **to the throne** urcare pe tron; suplimentare *f*; adaos *n*, spor *n*; sporire *f*, creştere *f*.

accessory *adj* accesoriu, secundar, auxiliar, adiţional || *s* accesoriu *n*; piesă *f* auxiliară; adaos *n*; complice *m*.

accident *s* accident *n*; întâmplare *f*; nenorocire *f*; accident *n* de teren • **~al** *adj* accidental, întâmplător; fortuit.

acclaim *s* elogii *n pl* || *vt* a lăuda.

acclamation *s* ovaţii *f pl*.

acclimatize *vi* **to** ~ **to** a se adapta la.

acclivity *s* coborâş *n*.

accolade *s hist* acoladă *f*; răsplată *f*, premiu *n*, distincţie *f*; *mus* acoladă *f*.

accommodate *vt* a acomoda, a potrivi; a găzdui; a adăposti; a avea grijă de; a încartirui; a cuprinde || *vi/vr* (*adapt*) a se acomoda (cu, la), a se adapta (la).

accommodating *adj* grijuliu, atent.

accommodation *s* acomodare *f*; potrivire *f*; ajustare *f*; ajutor *n*; înlesnire *f*; loc *n* (la hotel etc).

accompaniment *s* acompaniament *n*.

accompanist *s mus* acompaniator *m*.

accompany *vt* a acompania, a însoţi; a conduce || *vi* a acompania.

accomplice *s* complice *m*.

accomplish *vt* a face, a efectua, a realiza; a desăvârşi; a duce la capăt • **~ed** *adj* (*skilled*) înzestrat, dotat • **~ment** *s* efectuare *f*, realizare *f*, facere *f*, săvârşire *f*; ducere *f* la bun sfârşit; *pl* talent(e) *n*; pregătire *f* artistică.

accord *vt* a pune de acord (cu); a face să concorde (cu); (*grant*) a acorda || *s* acord *n*, unanimitate *f*; sentiment *n*, aprobare *f*; concordanţă *f*.

according *adv* (**to**) conform, potrivit.

accordion *s mus* acordeon *n*.

accost *vt* a acosta; (*prostitute*) a racola.

account *s* (*rendition*) relatare *f*; (*report*) raport *n*; dare *f* de seamă; (*narrative*) povestire *f*; istorisire *f*; descriere *f*; prezentare *f*; socoteală *f*; (*explanation*) explicaţie *f*; *fin* cont *n*; factură *f*; notă *f* de plată; profit *n*, folos *n*, beneficiu *n* || *vt* a considera, a socoti, a declara || *vr* a se considera, a se socoti; **by all ~s** după spusele tuturor; **on** ~ **of** din cauza; **on no** ~ în nici un caz, nicidecum; ~ **for** a explica, a justifica; **take into** ~ a lua în considerare • **~able** *adj* răspunzător • **~ancy** *s* contabilitate *f* • **~ant** *s* contabil *m*.

accredit *vt* a avea încredere în; a împuternici • **~ed** *adj* acreditat.

accretion *s* sporire *f*; **capital** ~ *s* majorare *f* de capital.

accrue *vi fin* a spori, a creşte.

accumulate *vt* a acumula, a aduna, a strânge, a colecţiona || *vi* a se acumula, a se aduna, a spori.

accumulation *s* acumulare *f*, colecţionare *f*.

accumulator *s tech* acumulator *n*; colecţionar *m*.

accuracy *s* acurateţe *f*, precizie *f*, exactitate *f*; acribie *f*.

accurate *adj* (*report, etc.*) exact; (*weapon, number, typist*) precis.

accusation *s* acuzaţie *f*.

accusative *s/adj* acuzativ *n*.

accuse *vt* a acuza, a învinui (*de*) || *vi* a acuza, a învinovăţi • **~d** *s* acuzat *m*.

accustom *vt* (**to**) a obişnui cu, a deprinde cu • **~ed** *adj* obişnuit, uzual; obişnuit cu, deprins cu.

ace *s* as *m*.

ache *s* durere *f* || *vi* a-l durea, a avea dureri de; a-i fi dor de

achieve *vt* (*do a task*) a realiza, a efectua, a face, a înfăptui; a duce la capăt; (*aim for*) a atinge (un scop) • **~ment** *s* (*completion*) realizare *f*, efectuare *f*, îndeplinire *f*; creaţie *f*.

acid *adj* acid, acru; caustic, aspru, || *s chem* acid • **~ic** *adj* acid, de acid

acknowledge *vt* a recunoaşte, a admite; a accepta, a aproba; a mărturisi; (*letter, etc.*) a confirma; a certifica, a adeveri; a fi recunoscător • **~ment** *s* recunoaştere *f*; (*of error*) mărturisire *f*.

acme *s* apogeu *n*.

acne *s med* acnee *f*.

acorn *s* ghindă *f*.

acoustic *adj* acustic • **~s** *s pl* acustică *f*.

acquaint *vt* (*inform*) a aviza, a aduce la cunoştinţă, ~ **with** a pune la curent cu; **be ~ed with** (~ *a fact*) a şti; (~ *a place or person*) a cunoaşte • **~ance** *s* cunoaştere *f*, cunoştinţe *f pl*, informaţii *f pl*; cunoştinţă *f*; cunoscut *m*.

acquiesce *vi* (**to**) a fi (până la urmă) de acord.

acquiescence *s* acceptare *f*, consimţire *f*.

acquire *vt* a căpăta, a dobândi; a-şi însuşi; (~ *fame*) a câştiga (faimă etc).

acquisition *s* achiziţie *f*.

acquisitive *adj* strângător; acaparator; lacom; receptiv; studios; asiduu.

acquit *vt jur* a achita • **~tal** *s jur* achitare *f*.

acre *s* acru *m*, pogon *n*.

acrid *adj* (*taste, smell*) înţepător, usturător; *fig* acerb.

acrimony *s* amărăciune *f*; ciudă *f*

acrimonious *adj* aspru, caustic, acrimonios.

acrobat *s* acrobat *m* • **~ics** *s pl* acrobaţie *f*, arta *f* acrobatică; acrobaţii *f pl*.

across *adv* de-a curmezişul, în curmeziş; transversal; dincolo; pe partea cealaltă; pe malul opus; cruciş, în cruce || *prep* peste; deasupra; de la o margine la alta; dincolo.

acrylic *s/adj* acrilic *n*.

act *s* (*deed*) act *n*, fapt *n*, faptă *f*; (*action*) acţiune *f*, manifestare *f*; curs *n*; (*theater*) act *n*; proces *n*, desfăşurare *f*; document *n*; *jur* lege; număr *n* || *vt* (*perform*) a interpreta, a juca rolul; a juca rolul de, a face pe || *vi* a juca; (*pretend*) a interpreta un rol, a juca teatru, a se preface; (*work*) a funcţiona; a acţiona; (*behave*) a se comporta, a se purta; a proceda • **~ing** *s* (*performance*) interpretare *f* || *adj* (*temporary*) interimar, suplinitor; ~ **the fool** a face pe prostul.

action *s* (*deed*) acţiune *f*, faptă *f*; (*happening*) manifestare *f*; măsură *f*; purtare *f*, comportare *f*; comportament *n*, funcţionare *f*; influenţă *f*; eficacitate *f*; efect *n*, rezultat *n*; activitate *f*; *jur* proces *n*; *mil* luptă *f*, bătălie *f*; *jur* punere *f* sub acuzare.

active *adj* activ; energic; vioi; eficient; plin de viaţă; neobosit; productiv.

activist *s* activist *m.*

activity *s* activitate *f;* mişcare *f;* funcţionare *f;* energie *f;* dinamism *n;* acţiune *f;* influenţă *f.*

actor *s* actor *m;* interpret *m;* realizator *m;* participant *m.*

actress *s* actriţă *f;* interpretă *f.*

actual *adj* real, adevărat; efectiv; actual, prezent • **~ly** *adv* într-adevăr, în realitate; de fapt; oricât ar părea de ciudat; în ciuda aşteptărilor; totuşi; în momentul de faţă, în prezent.

actuary *s* actuar *m,* statistician *m* al unei societăţi de asigurări; *jur* grefier *m.*

actuate *vt (machine)* a pune în mişcare; *frml (person)* a activa, a impulsiona; a stimula; a împinge; a determina.

acuity *s* acuitate *f,* agerime *f,* ascuţime *f.*

acumen *s* pătrundere *f,* perspicacitate *f,* discernământ *n.*

acupressure *s* presopunctură *f.*

acupuncture *s* acupunctură *f.*

acute *adj (sharp)* ascuţit; *(keen)* ager, *(perceptive)* pătrunzător; *(pain)* acut, ascuţit; *(intense)* puternic; pronunţat; la ordinea zilei, arzător.

ad *s* reclamă *f;* anunţ *n.*

adamant *adj* **to be ~** a fi inflexibil.

adapt *vt (adjust)* a adapta; *(fit)* a potrivi, a ajusta (la) || *vr (get used to)* a (se) adapta (la) || *vi* a se adapta; a se ajusta (la) • **~able** *adj (person)* adaptabil, suplu • **~ation** *s* adaptare *f.*

add *vt* a adăuga (la); a aduna (cu); *(numbers)* a adiţiona || *vi* a aduna, a face o adunare.

addendum *s (pl* **addenda)** addenda *f,* adaos *n* (la o lucrare); anexă *f;* econ completare *f,* act *n* adiţional.

adder *s* viperă *f.*

addict *s also fig* vicios *m;* **drug ~** *s* drogat *m;* dependent *m* de droguri • **~ed to** *adj (care s-a)* dedat unui viciu; pradă unui viciu; căruia îi place (lectura etc) • **~ion** *s* dependenţă *f (de alcool* etc).

addition *s* adunare *f;* adaos *n;* plus *n;* spor *n;* completare *f;* întregire *f;* adăugire *f.*

additive *s* aditiv *n.*

addled *adj (eggs)* stricat; *(confused)* confuz.

address *vt* a adresa (scrisoare etc cuiva); a se adresa (cuiva); a vorbi (cuiva) || *s* adresă *f;* cuvântare *f; (talk)* discurs *n;* tact *n,* îndemânare *f;* comportare *f;* ţinută *f* • **~ee** *s* destinatar *m.*

adenoids *s pl anat* vegetaţii *f pl* adenoide, polipi *m pl.*

adept *adj* **(at)** expert/specialist (în).

adequate *adj* corespunzător, adecvat; exact; destul, suficient (pentru); acceptabil, mulţumitor.

adhere *vi* a se lipi (la); a adera (la) • **~nt** *adj* aderent, adeziv; *(sticky)* lipicios || *s frml* aderent *m,* susţinător *m,* partizan *m.*

adhesion *s* adeziune *f;* aderenţă *f;* lipire *f; fig* adeziune *f;* consimţământ *n.*

adhesive *adj* adeziv; lipicios; insistent || *s* adeziv *n;* **~ tape** *s* leucoplast *n,* bandă *f* adezivă.

adieu *interj* adio!.

adjacent *adj* învecinat, vecin (cu); apropiat (de); adiacent.

adjective *s* adjectiv *n;* lucru *n* secundar, accesoriu *n* || *adj* adjectival, atributiv, relativ; secundar; accesoriu; dependent.

adjoin *vt frml* a se învecina cu || *vi* a se învecina • **~ing** *adj* învecinat, vecin, alături de.

adjourn *vt* a amâna || *vi (~ meeting)* a suspenda.

adjudge *vt (rule)* a declara; *(decide)* a adjudeca; *(award)* a atribui.

adjudicate *vt jur (trial)* a judeca; a adjudeca, a atribui; *jur (sentence)* a da.

adjunct *s* adjunct *m;* ajutor *n;* **(to)** complinire *f,* adaos *n* (la); *gram* complement *n* circumstanţial || *adj* subordonat; conexat (cu).

adjure *vt* a conjura, a ruga stăruitor.

adjust *vt* a ajusta (la); a potrivi (după; la); *(regulate)* a regla (după); a pune în ordine; a sistematiza || *vr/vi (adapt)* a se adapta (la); **~ to** adaptare la • **~ment** *s* modificare *f; tech* reglare *f.*

ad-lib *adj* improvizat || *adv* după/în voie || *s* improvizaţie *f* || *vi* a improviza.

administer *vt (~ a company, business)* a administra, a conduce; *(~ a punishment)* a aplica, a supune, *(~ drugs)* a administra.

administration *s* conducere *f,* administrare *f;* prestare *f;* administraţie *f;* luare *f;* **the Administration** administraţia *f,* guvernul *n* SUA.

administrative *adj* administrativ; executiv.

administrator *s* administrator *m;* (bun) organizator *m; (state, firm)* conducător *m; jur* executor *m* testamentar.

admirable *adj* admirabil, minunat, splendid.

admiral *s* amiral *m.*

admiration *s* admiraţie *f.*

admire *vt* a admira, a preţui în mod deosebit; a privi cu admiraţie.

admission *s* acces *n,* intrare *f;* taxă *f* de intrare; admitere *f,* primire *f;* acceptare *f;* recunoaştere *f;* **~ ticket** *s* bilet *n* de intrare.

admit *vt* a recunoaşte; **(that)** a recunoaşte că; *(allow entry)* a admite || *vi* **~ to (doing smth)** a recunoaşte că, a admite că.

admonish *vt* a admonesta.

admonition *s* avertisment *n;* admonestare *f;* sfat *n.*

ado *s (bother)* agitaţie *f,* tevatură *f ; (delay)* întârziere *f* ; **without more ~** fără întârziere.

adolescence *s* adolescenţă *f;* tinereţe *f.*

adolescent *adj* adolescent, pueril || *s* adolescent *m.*

adopt *vt* a adopta; a înfia, a lua de suflet; a îmbrăţişa, a accepta, a primi; a lua; a aproba • **~ion** *s* adoptare *f;* acceptare *f;* aprobare *f;* îmbrăţişare *f.*

adorable *adj* adorabil, fermecător, extraordinar.

adoration *s* adorare *f;* adoraţie *f.*

adore *vt* a adora; a venera; a idolatriza; a iubi cu pasiune.

adorn *vt* a orna.

adrenalin *s* adrenalină *f.*

adrift *adj* în derivă || *adv fig* **to go ~** a merge în derivă.

adroit *adj* priceput, iscusit, îndemânatic, abil.

adulation *s* adulare *f,* adulaţie *f,* linguşire *f,* flatare *f.*

adult *adj* adult; matur; copt || *s* (om) adult *m,* om matur *m;* animal *n* adult; plantă *f* adultă.

adulterate *vt (with)* a amesteca (cu); a falsifica, a contraface; *coll* a boteza (cu) • **~d** *adj* amestecat; falsificat, contrafăcut.

adulterer *s* soţ *m* adulter.

adultery *s* adulter *n.*

advance *vt* a împinge în faţă; a muta, a mişca, a avansa; a promova; a prezenta; a formula; a ridica, a mări, a urca; a spori; a da bani ca avans || *vi* a înainta, a avansa; a progresa, a promova; a creşte, a se urca || *s* înaintare *f,* mers *n* înainte; avans *n;* avansare *f,* promovare *f;* progres *n,* dezvoltare *f;* acont *n;* urcare *f.* • **~d** *adj* din faţă; din frunte; avansat; înaintat; vârstnic.

advantage *s* avantaj *n;* profit *n;* beneficiu *n;* folos *n;*

privilegiu *n*; situație *f* privilegiată; superioritate *f* || *vt* a avantaja; a fi în avantajul cuiva • **~ous** *adj* folositor, avantajos.

advent[1] *s* apariție *f*.

Advent[2] *s relig* a doua venire *f* a lui Christos.

adventure *s* aventură *f* • **~r** *s* aventurier *m*.

adventurous *adj* aventuros.

adverb *s gram* adverb *n*.

adversary *s* adversar *m*, oponent *m*; (*foe*) inamic *m*, dușman *m*.

adverse *adj* defavorabil • **~ly** *adv* nefavorabil; (în mod) ostil.

adversity *s* adversitate *f*; necazuri *n pl*; nenorocire *f*, calamitate *f*.

advertise *vt com* a face reclamă/publicitate; (~ *in a newspaper, etc.*) a da un anunț • **~ment** *s com* reclamă *f*; (*newspaper*) anunț *n*.

advice *s* sfat *n*; recomandare *f*; îndemn *n*.

advisable *adj* recomandabi, oportun.

advise *vt* a sfătui; a recomanda cuiva; a îndemna; a informa, a notifica || *vi* a da sfaturi; a se sfătui, a se consulta (cu) • **~r** *s* consilier *m*.

advisory *adj* consultativ.

advocate *vt* a preconiza, a sprijini || *s jur* avocat *m*; susținător *m*.

aerial *adj* aerian.

aerobics *s* aerobic *n*

aerodynamics *s pl* aerodinamică *f*; (*qualities*) aerodinamism *n*.

aeronautics *s pl* aeronautică *f*.

aerosol *s* aerosol *m*.

aesthetic *adj* estetic.

affair *s* afacere *f*, chestiune *f*, problemă *f*; *pl* afaceri *f*; poveste *f*; legătură amoroasă *f*; încăierare *f*, luptă *f*; serată *f*, șezătoare *f*.

affect *vi* a simula; a afișa; a-i plăcea; a influența (în rău), a afecta; a folosi (expresii pompoase); a supăra; a emoționa || *s* afect *n* • **~ation** *s* prefăcătorie *f* • **~ed** *adj* afectat, studiat, prefăcut.

affection *s* afecțiune *f* • **~ate** *adj* afectuos, tandru.

affidavit *s* afidavit *n*, depoziție *f* sub jurământ.

affiliate *vt* a primi ca membru; a stabili originea/ paternitatea || *vr* a se asocia (cu), a se afilia (la).

affiliation *s* primire *f* ca membru; calitate *f* de membru; apartenență *f*; (**to**) afiliere *f*, înscriere *f* (la); *jur* stabilirea *f* paternității.

affinity *s* afinitate *f*.

affirm *vt* a afirma; a declara, a susține (cu tărie); a confirma • **~ation** *s* afirmare *f*, susținere *f*; confirmare *f*; ratificare *f*; afirmație *f*; declarație *f*.

affix *vt* (*stamp*) a lipi.

afflict *vt* a chinui; a năpăstui || *vr* a fi tulburat profund • **~ion** *s* nenorocire *f*; durere *f*; chin *n*; năpastă *f*; jale *f*.

affluent *adj* bogat, avut; abundent, îmbelșugat || *s* afluent *m*.

afford *vt* a-și permite, a-și îngădui; a da (satisfacții etc); a oferi; a prilejui; a aduce (un câștig etc) • **~able** *adj* disponibil; posibil.

afield *adv* departe; rătăcit; pe/la câmp.

afloat *adj* also *fig* plutitor.

afoot *adj* în plină activitate; *lit, obs* (*on foot*) pe picioare.

aforementioned *adj* mai sus amintit/menționat.

affront *vt* a aduce un afront cuiva, a ofensa, a jigni; a înfrunta, a sfida || *s* afront *n*, insultă *f*, jignire *f*.

afraid *adj* temător, care se teme; speriat.

afresh *adv* din nou.

Africa *s* Africa *f* • **~n** *adj/s* african *m*.

aft *adv naut* pe/la pupa.

after *prep* după; la sfîrșitul; în urma; unul după altul; în șir; în spatele; înapoia; ca/drept urmare; în maniera/ stilul; conform cu; în conformitate cu || *adv* după aceea; mai târziu, ulterior, pe urmă || *conj* după ce; când || *adj* viitor; ulterior; de mai târziu; din spate, din/ de la urmă • **~effect** *s* efect *n* ulterior, repercusiune *f*.

aftermath *s* consecințe *f pl*, urmări *f pl*.

afternoon *s* după amiază *f*.

afterthought *s* idee *f* tardivă; răspuns *n* tardiv; truc *n*; tertip *n*.

afterward *adv* după aceea, ulterior, mai târziu.

again *adv* (*over*) din nou, iar(ăși); (*once more*) încă o dată; (*besides*) în afară de asta, (*furthermore*) pe lângă acestea.

against *prep* împotriva, (în) contra; în comparație cu; prin contrast cu; pentru; în vederea.

age *s* (*of person, tree, etc.*) vârstă *f*, etate *f*; (*period*) perioadă *f* a vieții; (*old age*) bătrânețe *f*, vârstă *f* înaintată; vechime *f*; (*epoch*) epocă *f*; eră *f* || *vt* a îmbătrâni, a face să îmbătrânească; a lăsa să se învechească || *vi* (*person*) a îmbătrâni; (*wine*) a se învechi • **~old** *adj* străvechi.

ag(e)ing *s* îmbătrânire *f*; maturizare *f*; uzură *f*.

agency *s* agenție *f*; organ *n*; organizație *f*; instituție *f*; agent *m*; factor *m* activ; forță *f*, putere *f*; influență *f*.

agenda *s* agendă *f*, ordine *f* de zi; plan *n*.

agent *s* agent *m*; reprezentant *m*; intermediar *m*, mijlocitor *m*; persoană *f* de încredere; spion *m*; factor *m*; mijloc *n*.

aggravate *vt* (*worsen*) a agrava, a înrăutăți; a îngreuna; (*increase*) a intensifica, a mări, a spori; a plictisi, (*annoy*) a bate la cap; a scoate din sărite.

aggravation *s* (*deterioration*) agravare *f*; îngreunare *f*; (*irritation*) supărare *f*; necaz *n*.

aggregate *adj/s* total *n*.

aggression *s* agresiune *f*; atac *n*; agresivitate *f*.

aggressive *adj* agresiv; bătăios; pornit; ofensiv; energic; activ; întreprinzător; amenințător.

aggrieved *adj* ofensat; nedreptățit; îndurerat.

aghast *adj* ~ (**at smth**) înspăimântat, înfricoșat (de).

agile *adj* agil, vioi, sprinten, activ, iute.

agitate *vt* (*shake*) a agita; (*worry*) a tulbura || *vi* a face agitație/propagandă (pentru) • **~d** *adj* agitat.

agitation *s* (*emotional*) agitație *f*, neliniște *f*; (*protest*) manifestație *f*.

agitator *s* agitator *m*; propagandist *m*; *tech* agitator *n*, amestecător *n*.

agnostic *adj* agnostic.

ago *adv* acum, în urmă (cu).

agog *adj* (**on/upon/for/about**) pasionat (de, după), dornic (de); surexcitat; înnebunit; nerăbdător.

agonizing *adj* chinuitor, foarte dureros.

agony *s* agonie *f*; suferință *f* grozavă, chin *n* cumplit; izbucnire *f*, acces *n*.

agrarian *adj frml* agrar.

agree *vi* a accepta, a consimți, a subscrie; a fi de acord, a fi de aceeași părere; a cădea de acord || *vt* a accepta, a consimți, a aproba • **~able** *adj* plăcut, agreabil; dispus să accepte/aprobe; favorabil; bun, adecvat, corespunzător, potrivit • **~ment** *s* acord *n*; înțelegere *f*; învoială *f*.

agricultural *adj* agricol.

agriculture s agricultură f; agronomie f.

aground adv naut eşuat; **to run** ~ a eşua.

ahead adv/adj înainte, în faţă; în frunte; din faţă/frunte; dinainte; pe viitor; de viitor.

aid vt a ajuta, a sprijini, a da ajutor || vi a ajuta, a da ajutor || s ajutor n; sprijin n; proteză f; pl trupe f pl auxiliare; ajutoare f pl; întăriri f pl.

aide s consilier m; ajutor n.

AIDS s sida f, sindromul n deficienţei imunitare dobândite.

ail vi a fi bolnav • ~**ing** adj suferind, bolnav • ~**ment** s boală f, afecţiune f.

aim vi a ochi, a ţinti (în); a ataca; a urmări; (strive) a năzui (la, spre) || vt a ochi cu (în); (~ a gun) a în-drepta (spre) || s (target) ţintă f, obiectiv n; (purpose) scop n; intenţie f; **take** ~ **at** a ţinti, a viza • ~**less** adj (person) fără ţintă; (action) inutil • ~**lessness** s lipsă f de scop; inutilitate f.

air s aer n; văzduh n; atmosferă f; înfăţişare f; mină f; mediu n; mers n; arie f, melodie f; cântec n; pl aere n, importanţă f, poză f || vt a aerisi, a aera; a ventila; a zvânta, a usca; a exprima, a expune (în public); **by** ~ par avion; ~ **force** s aviaţia f militară; ~ **mail** s poştă f aeriană || vt a expedia par avion.

airbed s saltea f pneumatică.

airborne adj aeropurtat.

air-conditioned adj cu aer condiţionat, climatizat

air-conditioner s aparat n de aer condiţionat.

aircraft s avion n; ~**carrier** portavion n.

airfield s aerodrom n.

air-hostess s însoţitoare f de bord, stewardesă f.

airing s aerisire f.

airlift s pod n aerian || vt a transporta pe un pod aerian.

airline s companie f aeriană.

airplane s avion n; aeroplan n.

airport s aeroport n.

air-raid s atac n aerian.

airship s aeronavă f.

airsick adj rău de avion.

airtight adj etanş la aer, ermetic.

aisle s alee f; (on plane) culoar n.

ajar adj întredeschis.

akin adj înrudit; apropiat, asemănător.

alabaster s alabastru n.

alacrity s frml entuziasm n.

alarm s alarmă f; semnal n de alarmă; panică f; teamă f || vt a alarma; a speria; a nelinişti, a tulbura; a avertiza, a preveni; ~ **clock** s ceas n deşteptător.

alas excl vai!

Albania s Albania f • ~**n** adj albanez || s (person) albanez m; (language) albaneză f.

albatross s albatros m.

albeit conj deşi; cu toate că; chiar dacă.

albino s albinos m; suferind m de albinism.

album s album n.

albumen s albuş n, albumină f.

alchemist s alchimist m.

alchemy s alchimie f.

alcohol s alcool n; spirt n • ~**free** adj fără alcool • ~**ic** adj alcoolic.

alcove s alcov n.

alderman s consilier m municipal.

ale s bere f (englezească).

alert adj sprinten, ager, vioi, alert; atent, prevăzător;

vigilent || s alarmă f, alertă f || vt a alarma; a alerta, a preveni.

alfalfa s bot lucernă f.

alga s (pl **algae**) algă f.

algebra s algebra f.

Algeria s Algeria f • ~**n** adj algerian || s algerian m.

alias s nume n de împrumut n; nume fals || adj alias, numit şi, cunoscut şi ca.

alibi s alibi n, scuză f, pretext n.

alien s străin m; extraterestru m || adj străin, din altă ţară; al altuia; ciudat, straniu; extraterestru • ~**ate** vt a aliena, a înstrăina • ~**ation** s alienare f; alienaţie f; îndepărtare f; boală f mintală.

alight vi a coborî; a se aşeza; a ateriza || adj luminat; aprins; arzând.

align vt a alinia • ~**ment** s aliniere f; reglare f; tech aliniament n, centrare f; tech direcţie f; paralelism n; grupare f, aliniere f.

alike adj la fel, asemenea; asemănător(i) || adv în mod egal, aproape egal, (aproape) la fel.

alimony s pensie f alimentară.

alive adj viu, în viaţă; activ, energic, vioi; existent; valabil; viabil || adv cu însufleţire.

alkali s, chem (pl ~**s**/-**es**) alcaliu m • ~**ne** adj alcalin.

all adj tot, toată, toţi, toate; întreg; fiecare; oricare; orice || pron tot, toate; toţi, toată lumea || adv cu totul, complet, în întregime || s tot n, bunuri n pl, avere f.

allay vt frml a aplana; (~ suspicion) a risipi, a îndepărta.

allegation s speculaţie f, afirmaţie f, declaraţie f (pe bază de deducţii); presupunere f.

allege vt a pretinde, a invoca • ~**d** adj pretins; bănuit; neconfirmat; aşa-zis • ~**dly** adv după cum se pretinde.

allegiance s supunere f; loialitate f.

allegory s alegorie f.

allergy s alergie f.

alleviate vt a uşura; a alina, a îndulci.

alley s alee f; cărare f; uliţă f; stradă f (îngustă); trecere f; interval n; culoar n; fundătură f.

alliance s alianţă f; aliat m; colaborare f; înţelegere f; înrudire f; uniune f; federaţie f.

allied adj aliat; similar, apropiat.

alligator s zool aligator m.

alliteration s aliteraţie f.

allocate vt (allot) a aloca; (share) a repartiza.

allocation s alocare f; distribuire f; repartizare f; alocaţie f.

allot vt (~ position, task) a repartiza; (~ money, time, resources) a aloca • ~**ment** s grădină f; lot n de pământ; atribuire f; parte f.

all over adv peste tot; la capăt; terminat; leit; din toate punctele de vedere.

allow vt a permite, a îngădui; a da voie (să); a recunoaşte; a nu contesta; ~ **for** a ţine cont de, a lua în considerare.

allowance s (money) îndemnizaţie f; bani n pl de buzunar; (excuse) **to make** ~**s for smb** a da dovadă de indulgenţă faţă de cineva.

alloy s aliaj n.

allude vi a face aluzie (la).

allure vt a atrage, a seduce

alluring adj atrăgător, seducător.

allusion s (hint) aluzie f.

alluvium s aluviune f.

ally vt a alia; a uni; a înrudi || vi a se alia || s aliat m.

almanac s almanah n.

almighty adj coll atotputernic; extraordinar.

almond *s (tree)* migdal *m*; *(fruit)* migdală *f* || *adj* (ca) de migdală, migdalat.

almost *adv* aproape (că); cât pe ce/mai-mai/gata-gata.

alms *s pl frml* pomană *f*.

aloft *adv* în aer, în sus.

alone *adj* singur; stingher; neînsoțit; neajutat (de nimeni); el însuși, ea însăși etc; doar, numai.

along *prep* de-a lungul; în lungul; în cursul/timpul || *adv* înainte; mai departe; în lung; în rând; încoace; aici.

aloof *adv* **(from)** departe (de); *also fig* la distanță (de) || *adj* depărtat; îndepărtat; *fig* distant, rece; rezervat.

aloud *adv* tare; zgomotos; cu hohote.

alphabet *s* alfabet *n*; elemente *n pl* de bază; rudimente *n pl*.

already *adv* deja; și.

also *adv* de asemenea; și; în plus, pe lângă acestea.

altar *s* altar *n*.

alter *vt* a transforma, a modifica, a schimba || *vi* a se schimba, a se transforma • *~ation s* modificare *f*, transformare *f*.

alternate *adj* alternativ, alternant, schimbător; intermitent; de rezervă; suplimentar, adițional || *s* locțiitor *m*, înlocuitor *m*; supleant *m* || *vi* a alterna, a se schimba; a se succeda || *vt* a alterna, a face să alterneze.

alternative *s* alternativă *f*.

alternator *s elec* alternator *n*.

although *conj* deși, cu toate că, în ciuda faptului că; chiar dacă.

altitude *s* altitudine *f*.

alto *s mus (voice, instrument)* alto *n*; contralto *n*; *(singer)* altist *m*.

altogether *adv* cu/întru totul, complet, total; în întregime; în general; până la urmă || *s* întreg *n*, tot *n*.

altruism *s* altruism *n*.

altruistic *adj* altruist.

aluminum *s* aluminiu *n*.

always *adv* (în)totdeauna, veșnic; mereu, încontinuu; fără întrerupere.

am *v aux* sunt.

amalgamate *vt (companies)* a fuziona; *(metals)* a amalgama.

amalgamation *s (companies)* fuzionare *f*; *(metals)* amalgamare *f*.

amass *vt* a aduna, a acumula, a strânge.

amateur *s* amator *m*, diletant *m*; nepriceput *m*, novice *m*, începător *m* || *adj* de amator(i).

amatory *adj* erotic, amoros.

amaze *vt* a uimi, a ului • *~ment s* uimire *f*, stupefacție *f*.

amazing *adj* surprinzător, uimitor, uluitor; teribil (de), grozav (de); minunat, excelent.

ambassador *s* ambasador *m*; reprezentant *m*, trimis *m*, sol *m*.

amber *adj* de culoarea chihlimbarului || *s* chihlimbar *n*.

ambidextrous *adj* ambidextru.

ambiguity *s* ambiguitate *f*, expresie *f* ambiguă.

ambiguous *adj* ambiguu; cu două înțelesuri; echivoc; vag, neclar; dubios, problematic.

ambition *s* ambiție *f*.

ambitious *adj* ambițios; vanitos; lacom (de); pompos, pretențios.

ambivalence *s* ambivalență *f*.

ambivalent *adj* ambivalent.

amble *vi* a merge agale || *s* mers *n* agale; buiestru *n*.

ambulance *s* ambulanță *f*; spital *n* militar de campanie.

ambush *s* ambuscadă *f*; pândă *f*; atac *n* prin surprindere || *vt* a ataca din ambuscadă || *vi* a ataca/acționa din ambuscadă.

ameliorate *vt* a ameliora, a îmbunătăți || *vi* a se ameliora, a se îmbunătăți.

amelioration *s* ameliorare *f*, îmbunătățire *f*.

amen *interj* amin!.

amenable *adj (cooperative)* docil, supus; *(answerable)* responsabil.

amend *vt (improve)* a îmbunătăți; a perfecționa; a amenda (un text); *(correct)* a corija; *(alter)* a modifica || *vi* a se îndrepta, a se corija • *~ment s* îmbunătățire *f*; corectare *f*, corijare *f*; amendare *f*; amendament *n*.

amenity *s* confort *n*, înlesniri *f pl*; amenajări *f pl*; echipamente *n pl*; *pl* bucurii *f pl*, satisfacții *f pl*; *pl* splendori *f pl*.

America *s* America *f* • *~n adj* american || *s* american *m*; *(language)* engleza *f* americană • *~n* **Dream** visul *n* American.

amethyst *s* ametist *n*.

amiable *adj* binevoitor, prietenos; afabil; amabil.

amicable *adj* amical, prietenesc.

amid *prep* în mijlocul.

amiss *adj (wrong)* în neregulă || *adv* **to take smth ~ a** înțelege greșit, a lua în nume de rău.

amity *s* amiciție *f*.

ammeter *s* ampermetru *n*.

ammonia *s (liquid)* amoniac *n*.

ammunition *s* muniție *f*; stoc *n* de muniție; arsenal *n* (de idei etc).

amnesia *s* amnezie *f*.

amnesty *s* amnistie *f*.

amoeba *s* amibă *f*.

among *prep* printre; între; dintre; în, în mijlocul; unul din(tre); împreună.

amoral *adj* amoral.

amorous *adj* amoros; îndrăgostit; drăgăstos.

amorphous *adj* amorf.

amortization *s* amortizare *f*.

amount *vi* a se ridica la; a atinge; a forma; a alcătui; a echivala cu; a însemna || *s* cantitate *f*; sumă *f*; total *n*.

ampere *s elec* amper *m*.

amphetamine *s pharm* amfitamină *f*.

amphibian *s zool* amfibie *f*.

amphitheatre *s* amfiteatru *n*.

ample *adj* amplu, larg, vast, cuprinzător; abundent; suficient; adecvat, potrivit.

amplifier *s* amplificator *n*.

amplify *vi (~ an idea)* a explica amănunțit/în detaliu; a dezvolta; *(~ power, sound)* a amplifica; a lărgi; a extinde.

amply *adv* din abundență; cu generozitate.

amputate *vt* a amputa.

amputation *s* amputare *f*.

amuse *vt (cause laughter)* a face să râdă; *(entertain)* a distra, a amuza; ~ **oneself** a se amuza/distra • *~ment s* amuzament *n*, distracție *f*; veselie *f*; haz *n*; obiect *n* de amuzament/atracție; plăcere *f*; desfătare *f*.

amusing *adj* amuzant, distractiv; nostim, hazliu.

an *art indef* un, o.

anachronism *s* anacronism *n*.

anagram *s* anagramă *f*.

anal *adj* anal.

analogous *adj* analog.

analogue *s* analog *n*.

analogy *s* analogie *f*; **by ~** prin analogie.

analysis *s* analiză *f*, cercetare *f*, examen *n* minuţios; studiere *f*; studiu *n*.

analyst *s* analist *m*; *chem* chimist *m* analist.

analytical *adj* analitic.

analyze *vt* a analiza, a cerceta, a examina minuţios; a studia; a face psihanaliza (cuiva).

anarchy *s* anarhie *f*.

anathema *s* anatemă *f*.

anatomical *adj* anatomic.

anatomy *s* anatomie *f*; disecţie *f*; analiză *f* amănunţită; critică *f*.

ancestor *s* strămoş *m*, străbun *m*.

anchor *s* ancoră *f*; liman *n*, speranţă *f*; realizator *m* de program (TV) ‖ *vt* a ancora; a prinde, a fixa; a se încrede în ‖ *vi* a ancora; a se linişti.

anchovy *s* anşoa *f*.

ancient *adj* antic; străvechi; din vechime; demodat; bătrân ‖ *s* antic *m*; clasic *m*; bătrân *m*; moşneag *m* .

ancillary *adj* auxiliar.

and *conj* şi, precum şi, atât ... cât şi; dar, însă; sau, ori; fie ... fie; aşa că; de aceea; deci, aşadar; ca să, pentru a; din ce în ce mai, tot mai.

Andorra *s* Andora *f*.

anecdote *s* anecdotă *f*; snoavă *f*; povestire *f*; istorioară *f*.

anemia *s* *med* anemie *f*.

anesthesia *s* anestezie *f*.

anesthetic *s* anestezic *n*; **under** ~ sub anestezie.

anesthetist *s* anestezist *m*.

anesthetize *vt* a anestezia.

anemone *s* *bot* anemonă *f*.

anew *adv* din nou, iar(ăşi); încă o dată; într-un mod nou.

angel *rel* înger *m*; spirit *n* ocrotitor.

angelica *s* *bot* angelică *f*, aglică *f*.

anger *s* supărare *f*, mânie *f*; acces *n* de furie ‖ *vt* a supăra, a înfuria, a mânia.

angina *s* *med* ang(h)ină *f* pectorală.

angle *s* *geom, etc* unghi *n*; (*corner*) colţ *n*; (*viewpoint*) punct *n* de vedere; situaţie *f*; latură *f*; undiţă *f* ‖ *vt* (*twist*) a denatura, a prezenta într-o lumină falsă; a pescui/a prinde cu undiţa.

angling *s* pescuit *n* cu undiţa.

Anglo-Saxon *adj* anglo-saxon; englez(esc) ‖ *s* anglo-saxon *m*; limba *f* anglo-saxonă, engleza *f* veche; englez *m*.

angry *adj* supărat, mânios, înfuriat, furios; ameninţător.

anguish *s* (*agony*) angoasă *f*, (*torture*) chin *n*.

angular *adj* unghiular, colţuros.

animal *s* *zool* animal *n*; dobitoc *n*; fiară *f*; *pej* brută *f*; bestie *f* ‖ *adj* animal, de animal; animalier; bestial; animalic; carnal.

animate *adj* viu, însufleţit, vioi ‖ *vi* a se anima • ~**d** **cartoon** *s* film *n* (de desene animate).

animation *s* animaţie *f*, însufleţire *f*; viaţă *f*; veselie *f*; animare *f*, aducere *f* la viaţă; fiinţare *f*, existenţă *f*; realizarea *f* unui film de desene animate.

animosity *s* animozitate *f*, ură *f* puternică; duşmănie *f*.

aniseed *s* *bot* anason *n*.

ankle *s* *anat* gleznă *f*.

annals *s* *pl* anale *f pl*.

annex *s* anexă *f* ‖ *vt* a anexa • ~**es** *s pl* anexă *f*, supliment *n*.

annihilate *vt* a anihila, a nimici.

annihilation *s* anihilare *f*, nimicire *f*.

anniversary *s* aniversare *f*; sărbătorire *f* ‖ *adj* aniversar, comemorativ.

annotate *vt* a adnota.

announce *vi* a anunţa; a proclama; a declara; a vesti • ~**ment** *s* anunţ *n*, înştiinţare *f*; vestire *f* • ~**r** *s* radio, *tv* crainic *m*, prezentator *m*.

annoy *vt* a supăra, a necăji; a deranja; a plictisi • ~**ance** *s* supărare *f*, iritare *f*; deranj *n*; necaz *n*, neplăcere *f*; om *m* enervant/plictisitor; pacoste *f*, belea *f* • ~**ing** *adj* supărător; enervant; plictisitor; insuportabil.

annual *adj* anual, de fiecare an ‖ *s* plantă *f* anuală; publicaţie *f* anuală; anuar *n*.

annuity *s* anuitate *f*; **life** ~ rentă viageră.

annul *vt* a anula; *jur* a abroga • ~**ment** *s* anulare *f*.

anode *s* *elec* anod *m*.

anodyne *s* analgezic *n* ‖ *adj* calmant; anodin, banal.

anoint *vt* a mirui; a unge.

Annunciation *s* *relig* Buna Vestire *f*.

anomaly *s* anomalie *f*.

anonymity *s* anonimat *n*, caracter *n* anonim.

anonymous *adj* anonim, necunoscut; fără nume; obscur.

anorak *s* hanorac *n*.

another *adj* (*different*) un alt/o altă; (*extra*) încă un/o; un al doilea, o a doua.

answer *s* (*reply*) răspuns *n*; replică *f*, ripostă *f*; (*solution*) soluţie *f*; rezolvare *f*; (*result*) rezultat *n* ‖ *vt* (*respond*) a răspunde, a replica; (*counter*) a riposta; (*fulfill*) a corespunde; a satisface; a rezolva ‖ *vi* a răspunde; a replica; a riposta.

ant *s* *ento* furnică *f*.

antagonist *s* opozant *m*, adversar *m*, potrivnic *m*.

antagonize *vt* a provoca ostilitate.

antecedent *s* antecedent *n*.

antelope *s* *zool* antilopă *f*.

antenna *s* antenă *f*.

anthem *s* imn *n*.

anthology *s* antologie *f*.

anthropology *s* antropologie *f*

anthropological *adj* antropologic.

anti *s* opozant *m* continuu.

anti-aircraft *s* antiaeriană *f*

antibiotic *s* antibiotic *n*.

antibody *s* anticorp *m*.

anticipate *vt* (*expect*) a anticipa; (*foresee*) a prevedea; (*think likely*) a şti dinainte; a bănui; (*forestall*) a premerge; a precipita ‖ *vi* a anticipa; a şti dinainte; a prevedea.

anticipation *s* anticipare *f*, prevedere *f*; **in** ~ **of** anticipând.

anticlimax *s* cădere *f*, declin *n*.

anticlockwise *adj*/*adv* în sens invers acelor de la ceasornic.

antics *s pl* (*of children, animals*) ţopăială *f*; *pej pol* bufonerii *f pl*.

anticyclone *s* *met* anticiclon *n*.

antidote *s* antidot *n*.

antifreeze *s* antigel *n*.

antihistamine *adj* *pharm* antihistaminic.

antipathy *s* antipatie *f*.

antiperspirant *s* deodorant *n*.

antique *adj* vechi; antic, clasic; demodat, învechit ‖ *s* obiect *n* vechi; obiect *n* de artă antic • ~**s** *s* antichităţi *f pl*, obiecte *n pl* de artă.

antiquity *s* (*oldness*) antichitate *f*; vechime *f*; trecut *n* îndepărtat; antichitate *f* clasică; anticii *m pl*; *pl* (*objects*) antichităţi.

anti-Semite *s* antisemit *m.*

antiseptic *adj* antiseptic ‖ *s* dezinfectant *n.*

antisocial *adj* antisocial; nesociabil, sălbatic.

antithesis *s* antiteză *f.*

antitrust *adj* antitrust.

antlers *s pl* coarne *n pl* de cerb.

antonym *s gram* antonim *n.*

anus *s anat* anus *n.*

anvil *s also anat* nicovală *f.*

anxiety *s* (*worry*) grijă *f*, (*concern*) îngrijorare *f*, (*fear*) teamă *f*, (*unease*) neliniște *f*; motiv *n* de neliniște; (*angst*) anxietate *f.*

anxious *adj* (*worried*) îngrijorat, neliniștit; (*worrying*) neliniștitor, îngrijorător; (*eager*) doritor, nerăbdător.

any *adj* orice; oricare; toți; indiferent care; vreo, ceva, niște; puțin ‖ *pron* oricine; oricare, toți; ceva; câțiva; câteva; unii; unele; puțin, câtva; nimic; de nici un fel; nici unul/una.

anybody *pron* toți, toată lumea; oricine; oricare; cineva, vreun om, vreo persoană; nimeni.

anyhow *adv* oricum, la întâmplare; în dezordine; deloc, defel, în nici un caz.

anyone *pron* * **anybody.**

anything *pron* orice; ceva; nimic ‖ *adv* cât de cât.

anyway *adv* oricum; totuși, cu toate acestea.

anywhere *adv* oriunde; în orice loc; peste tot, pretutindeni; indiferent unde; undeva; nicăieri.

apart *adv* (*separated*) separat (de); departe (de); (*in pieces*) în bucăți ‖ *adj* independent; deosebit; separat; (*isolated*) izolat.

apartment *s* cameră *f*, odaie *f*; apartament *n*; locuință *f*; etaj *n*; ~ **house** *s* bloc *n*; imobil *n.*

apathetic *adj* apatic; indiferent.

apathy *s* apatie *f*; indiferență *f.*

ape *s zool* maimuță *f* ‖ *vt* a imita.

aperture *s* (*opening*) deschizătură *f*; (*orifice*) orificiu *n*; (*hole*) gaură *f*; vizor *n.*

apex *s* (*top*) vârf *n*; (*summit*) culme *f*, creștet *n*; (*climax*) apogeu *n*; punct *n* culminant; cap *n.*

aphasia *s med* afazie *f.*

aphonia *s med* afonie *f.*

aphorism *s* aforism *n.*

aphrodisiac *adj/s* afrodisiac *n.*

apiece *adv* bucata, per bucată, de fiecare (persoană).

apogee *s* apogeu *n.*

apologetic *adj* apologetic, de scuză ‖ *s* apologie *f.*

apologize *vi* a se scuza, a cere scuze.

apology *s* scuze *f pl*, iertare *f*; apărare *f*; justificare *f*; explicare *f.*

apoplexy *s med* apoplexie *f*; *coll* dambla *f.*

apostle *s relig* apostol *m.*

apostrophe *s gram* apostrof *n*; apostrofă *f.*

appal *vt* (*shock*) a produce consternare; (*frighten*) a înspăimânta, a șoca • **~ling** *adj* (*dreadful*) înspăimântător.

apparatus *s* aparat *n*, dispozitiv *n*; (*gym*) aparat *n*; (*system, organization*) aparat *n.*

apparent *adj* (*obvious*) evident, clar, aparent, vizibil, indiscutabil; (*seeming*) iluzoriu; fals; pretins • **~ly** *adv* evident.

apparition *s* (*phantom, ghost*) apariție *f*, fantomă *f*; (*vision*) nălucă *f*, nălucire *f*; (*sudden*) apariție *f*, ivire *f* (neașteptată).

appeal *vt* a deferi unei instanțe superioare ‖ *vi* (*request*) a apela (la; pentru); a face (un) apel; (*please*) a

plăcea (cuiva); a face recurs/appel ‖ *s* apel *n*; recurs *n*; drept *n* de apel; chemare *f*; rugăminte *f*; interes *n*; atracție *f* • **~ing** *adj* (*moving*) emoționant, mișcător; (*attractive*) atrăgător.

appear *vi* (*be seen*) a apărea, a se ivi, a se vedea; a se prezenta; (*seem*) a părea, a arăta; a-și face apariția; a se tipări, a se publica; a compărea, a se înfățișa; a se găsi; a exista; a reieși, a rezulta (din) • **~ance** *s* (*act*) apariție *f*, ivire *f*; venire *f*; (*aspect*) exterior *n*; înfățișare *f*; (*publication*) publicare *f*, tipărire *f*; (*look*) aparență *f*, impresie *f.*

appease *vt* a calma, a liniști.

appendicitis *s med* apendicită *f.*

appendix *s* (*pl* **–dixes/-dices**) apendice *n.*

appetite *s* (*hunger*) poftă *f* de mâncare; (*desire*) dorință *f*, poftă *f.*

appetizer *s* aperitiv *n.*

appetizing *adj* care stimulează pofta de mâncare; gustos; delicios; apetisant.

applaud *vt* (*clap*) a aplauda; (*approve*) a aproba, a fi de acord (cu) ‖ *vi* a aplauda.

applause *s* aplauze *f pl.*

apple *s bot* măr *n.*

appliance *s* dispozitiv *n*; instrument *n*; instalație *f*; aparat *n.*

applicable *adj* (**to**) aplicabil (la).

applicant *s* (**for**) (*job*) candidat *m* (la); solicitant *m*, postulant *m.*

application *s* (*use*) aplicare *f*, folosire *f*; aplicabilitate *f*; (*request*) cerere *f*, solicitare *f* (de); (*diligence*) aptitudine *f*; efort *n*; *comp* ~ (**program**) aplicație *f*, program *n.*

apply *vt* a aplica (la); a se folosi de; a recurge la; (*ask*) a se adresa ‖ *vi* (*refer*) a fi aplicabil, a se aplica.

appoint *vt* (*assign*) a numi; a înființa; (*fix*) a stabili, a fixa; (*decide on*) a hotărî • **~ment** *s* (*for job*) numire *f*, desemnare *f*; post *n*, slujbă *f*; întâlnire *f*; **to set up an** ~ a fixa o întâlnire.

apportion *vt* a repartiza.

appraisal *s* evaluare *f.*

appraise *vt* a evalua; a aprecia.

appreciable *adj* considerabil.

appreciate *vi* a aprecia; (*be grateful for*) a fi recunoscător pentru; (*value*) a prețui, a recunoaște; (*be aware of*) a înțelege; (*rise in value*) a crește/spori ca valoare.

appreciation *s* mulțumire *f*; (*sympathy*) înțelegere *f*; (*gratitude*) recunoștință *f.*

apprehend *vt* (*arrest*) a aresta; (*understand*) a înțelege, a presimți; (*fear*) a se teme, a avea temeri.

apprehension *s* (*fear*) neliniște *f*; impacientare *f*; (*understanding*) înțelegere *f.*

apprehensive *adj* neliniștit; **to be ~ about smth** a se teme de ceva; perceptiv, rapid în deslușire sau înțelegere.

apprentice *s* ucenic *m.*

approach *vt* • (*advance*) a se apropia; a veni; a sosi ‖ *vt* a se apropia de; (*speak to*) a aborda, a vorbi cu; a semăna cu; (*tackle*) a trata; (*handle*) a se ocupa de ‖ *s* apropiere *f*; sosire *f*, venire *f*; intrare *f*, acces *n*; abordare *f*; interpretare *f*; (*method*) manieră *f*, mod *n.*

appropriate *vt* (*set aside*) a aloca; a destina; (*take for oneself*) a-și însuși, a fura ‖ *adj* potrivit, adecvat.

approval *s* aprobare *f*, sancționare *f*; consimțământ *n*; asentiment *n*; confirmare *f.*

approve *vt* a aproba, a ratifica ‖ *vi* **to** ~ **(of smth)** a aproba (ceva).
approximate *vt* a se apropia ‖ *adj* aproximativ.
apricot *s* caisă *f.*
April *s* aprilie *m*; april; Prier.
apron *n* şorţ *n.*
apt *adj* (*suitable*) potrivit, nimerit; priceput, isteţ; (*capable*) competent, capabil, apt.
aptitude *s* aptitudine *f*, dispoziţie *f*; **to have an** ~ **for** a avea înclinaţie pentru.
aqualung *s* scafandru *m.*
aquarium *s* (*pl* **–riums/-ria**) acvariu *n.*
Aquarius *s astrol* Vărsător *m.*
aquatic *adj* (*animal, plant*) acvatic; (*sport*) nautic.
aqueduct *s* apeduct *n.*
aqueous *adj* apos.
aquiline *adj* acvilin.
Arab *s/adj* arab *m* • ~**ian** *adj* din Arabia, arăbesc • ~**ic** *adj* arab ‖ *s* (*language*) arabă *f.*
arable *adj* arabil.
arbitrary *adj* (*subjective*) arbitrar, samavolnic; despotic; (*capricious*) capricios; (*random*) accidental, întâmplător.
arbitrate *vt* a arbitra.
arbor *s* frunzar *n*, umbrar *n*; chioşc *n*, pavilion *n*, pergolă *f.*
arc *s tech, gram* arc *n*; *elec* arc *n* electric ‖ *vi tech* a forma un arc; *elec* a produce scântei; a se arcui.
arcade *s* arcadă *f*; pasaj *n.*
arch[1] *s* arc *n*; cupolă *f*; pod *n*, punte *f*; boltă *f*; curcubeu *n.*
arch[2] *vi* a se arcui.
archaic *adj* arhaic.
archbishop *s* arhiepiscop *m.*
archduke *s* arhiduce *m.*
archeology *s* arheologie *f*
archeological *adj* arheologic
archeologist *s* arheolog *m.*
archer *s* arcaş *m.*
archery *s* tir *n* cu arcul.
archetype *s* arhetip *n.*
archetypal *adj* tipic, arhetipal.
archipelago *s* arhipelag *n.*
architect *s* arhitect *m*; planificator *m*; creator *m*; iniţiator *m* • ~**ure** *s* arhitectură *f*; stil *n* arhitectural; structură *f*, construcţie *f.*
archives *s pl* arhivă *f*; arhive *f pl* naţionale.
archivist *s* arhivist *m.*
arctic *adj* arctic.
ardent *adj* (*fervent*) înflăcărat, pătimaş, pasionat; arzător; mistuitor; (*passionate*) înfocat; (*zealous*) aprig.
ardor *s* ardoare *f.*
arduous *adj* (*strenuous*) intens, stăruitor; (*hard*) dificil, anevoios, greu; (*steep*) abrupt; prăpăstios.
are *v* (*to be*) eşti, suntem, sunteţi, sunt.
area *s* arie *f*; suprafaţă *f*; (*section*) zonă *f*; (*region*) regiune *f*; (*subject*) sferă *f*, domeniu *n.*
arena *s also fig* arenă *f.*
argue *vi* (*contend*) a argumenta; a pleda; (*reason*) a judeca; a discuta (cu); (*quarrel*) a se certa (cu) ‖ *vt* (*debate*) a discuta; (*maintain*) a susţine; a aduce argumente.
argument *s* argument *n*; dovadă *f*; (*reasons*) motiv *n*; raţiune *f*; argumentare *f*; (*debate*) discuţie *f*, dispută *f*, ceartă *f*; sumar *n*, rezumat *n.*
aria *s mus* arie *f.*

arid *adj also fig* arid; neinteresant.
Aries *s astrol* Berbec *m.*
arise, arose, arisen *vi* (*appear*) a se ridica, a se ivi, a apărea; *lit* (*sun*) a se înălţa; (*person*) a învia.
aristocracy *s* aristocraţie *f.*
aristocrat *s* aristocrat *m.*
arithmetic *s* aritmetică *f.*
arm[1] *s anat* braţ *n*; mână *f*; mânecă *f*; latură *f*; pârghie *f*; (*section*) ramură *f*, filială *f*; ~ **in** ~ *adv* braţ la braţ.
arm[2] *s* arme *f pl*; armament *n*; *pl* armoarii *f*; blazon *n*; armă (infanterie etc) ‖ *vt* a înarma; a arma, a pune armătura la ‖ *vr/vi* a se înarma (cu) • ~**ed** *adj* înarmat ‖ *v* * **alarm.**
armchair *s* fotoliu *n.*
armistice *s* armistiţiu *n.*
armor *s* (*for person*) armură *f*; (*for army vehicles*) blindaj *n* • ~**y** *s* depozit *n* de arme.
arms race *s* cursa *f* înarmărilor.
army *s* (*military*) armată *f*; organizaţie *f*; (*crowd*) mulţime *f*; puzderie *f.*
aroma *s* aromă *f.*
around *adv* de jur împrejur; peste tot; în toate părţile; prin apropiere; pe ici şi colo; împrejur; în viaţă; existent, disponibil ‖ *prep* în jurul, de jur împrejurul; nu departe de, pe lângă; prin; pe la.
arouse *vt* (*awaken*) a trezi (din somn); (*stir*) a excita.
arrange *vt* (*place*) a aranja, a pune în ordine; a clasifica; (*set up*) a pregăti; (*plan*) a plănui; a prelucra; a adapta ‖ *vr* a se aranja • ~**ment** *s* (*layout*) aranjare *f*, rânduire *f*, punere *f* în ordine; clasificare *f*; ordine *f*, rânduială *f*; (*display*) aranjament *n*; (*agreement*) înţelegere *f*, învoială *f*, acord *n*; adaptare *f*; prelucrare *f.*
array *s* (*objects*) etalare *f*; (*ornaments*) dispunere *f.*
arrears *s pl* (*money owed*) restanţe *f pl*; **to be in** ~ a fi în întârziere, (*loans*) a avea restanţe.
arrest *s* (*capture*) arestare *f*; (*stare de*) arest *n*; interdicţie *f*; oprire *f*; încetare *f* ‖ *vt* (*apprehend*) a aresta; a pune sub interdicţie; (*stop*) a opri, a împiedica; (*engage*) a reţine (atenţia etc), a atrage (privirile etc).
arrival *s* venire *f*, sosire *f*; apariţie *f*, ivire *f*; nou-venit *m*; nou-născut *m.*
arrive *vi* (*get there*) a sosi, a veni; a ajunge; (*succeed*) a fi recunoscut, a se impune; (*be delivered*) a veni pe lume.
arrogance *s* aroganţă *f*; înfumurare *f.*
arrogant *adj* arogant, încrezut, înfumurat, semeţ.
arrow *s* săgeată *f*; semn *n* de direcţie; împunsătură *f.*
arsenal *s* arsenal *n.*
arsenic *s* arsenic *n.*
arson *s* incendiu *n* criminal/voluntar • ~**ist** *s* piroman *m.*
art *s* artă *f*; meşteşug *n*, îndemânare *f*; meserie *f*; pricepere *f*; cunoaştere *f*; (*cunning*) viclenie *f*; şiretlic *n* • ~**ful** *adj* viclean • ~**less** *adj* natural, neprefăcut.
artery *s* arteră *f.*
arthritis *s med* artrită *f.*
artichoke *s bot* anghinare *f.*
article *s* (*item*) articol *n*, obiect *n* de comerţ; (*piece*) articol (de ziar etc); (*paragraph*) paragraf *n*; (*clause*) *pl* prevederi *f*, contract *n* ‖ *vt* a expune/prezenta punct cu punct; a obliga prin contract; a da la ucenicie.
articulate *adj* (*person*) care se exprimă clar; (*speech*) clar, limpede ‖ *vt* (~ *thoughts, wishes*) a formula.

artifact *s* artefact *n*; vestigii *n pl* de cultură materială a omului preistoric; obiect *n* făcut de om.
artifice *s* artificiu *n*.
artificial *adj* (*man-made*) artificial; (*affected*) nesincer, afectat.
artillery *s* artilerie *f*.
artisan *s* artizan *m*.
artist *s* artist *m* plastic; maestru *m*; actor *m*; cântăreț *m* • ~**ic** *adj* artistic.
as *adv* la fel de, tot atât de; nu mai puțin; și; de asemenea; *conj* tot atât de ... ca (și), precum, la fel ca și, ca (și), întocmai ca (și); cum, așa cum; (pe) când, în timp/ vreme ce; deși, cu toate acestea || *prep* ca, în calitate de || *pron* care || ~ ... ~ *adv* la fel de/ca; la fel ca.
a.s.a.p. *abbr coll* (*as soon as possible*) cât mai repede.
asbestos *s* azbest *n*.
ascend *vt* a urca (pe), a sui; a se urca pe || *vi* a (se) urca, a se sui; a se ridica.
ascension *s* (*climb*) suire *f*, ascensiune *f*; (*rising*) progres *n*.
ascent *s* (*climb*) ascensiune *f*; suiș *n*; (*in rank*) avansare *f*.
ascertain *vt* a stabili.
ascetic *adj* ascetic || *s* ascet *m*.
ascribe *vt* a atribui.
ash[1] *s* (*from fire*) scrum *n*; cenușă *f*; *pl* rămășițe *f pl* pământești, pulbere *f*, țărână *f*; ~ **tray** scrumieră *f*.
ash[2] *s* bot (*tree*) frasin *m*.
ashamed *adj* rușinat (de); jenat, care se sfieşte.
ashore *adv* la mal, pe uscat.
Asia *s* Asia *f* • ~**n** *adj/s* Asiatic.
aside *adv* dintr-o parte; aparte; **to move** ~ a se da la o parte; ~ **from** cu excepția || *s thea* aparteu *n*; comentariu *n*, remarcă *f*.
ask *vt* (*inquire*) a întreba; a pune o întrebare; a chestiona; (*request*) a cere (un sfat etc); a ruga (pe cineva); (*demand*) a pretinde; a necesita; (*invite*) a invita || *vi* a întreba; ~ **for** *vi* a cere, a avea nevoie de, a solicita, a necesita, a pretinde; a întreba de, a se interesa de.
askew *adv* pieziș, strâmb.
asleep *adj* adormit; **to fall** ~ *vt* a adormi.
asparagus *s* bot sparanghel *m*.
aspect *s* (*look*) înfățișare *f*, mină *f*; aspect *n*, (*facet*) latură *f*, parte *f*; (*position*) poziție *f*; așezare *f*; (*view*) vedere *f*.
aspen *s* bot plop *m* tremurător.
asperity *s also fig* asprime *f*.
aspersion *s* defăimare *f*; stropire *f*; *pl* insinuări *f pl* răutăcioase.
asphalt *s* asfalt *n*.
asphyxia *s med* asfixiere *f*.
asphyxiate *vt/vi* a (se) asfixia.
aspire *vi* a aspira, a tinde (spre), a năzui (la)
aspiration *s* aspirație *f*
aspiring *adj* ambițios.
aspirin *s* aspirină *f*.
ass *s* măgar *m*; prost *m*, nătâng *m*, idiot *m*; *sl* fund *n*, șezut *n*.
assail *vt* a asalta; a ataca violent; a încerca să învingă; a înfrunta cu hotărâre.
assassin *s* ucigaș *m* • ~**ate** *vt* a ucide, a asasina, a suprima • ~**ation** *s* ucidere *f*, asasinat *n*, asasinare *f*, suprimare *f*.
assault *s mil* (on) asalt *n* asupra, atac *n*; agresiune *f* (împotriva cuiva) || *vt* a agresa.

assemble *vt/vi* (~ *things*) a asambla; (~ *people*) a se aduna; (*put together*) a monta.
assembly *s* (*gathering*) adunare *f*, întrunire *f*, întâlnire *f*; sfat *n*, (*council*) consiliu *n*; (*meeting*) ședință *f*.
assent *s* consimțământ *n*, asentiment *n* || *vi* a-și da consimțământul/asentimentul (la).
assert *vt* (*declare*) a afirma cu putere, (*uphold*) a susține; (*stress*) a sublinia; a arăta, a manifesta || *vr* a se impune/afirma; a se remarca; (~ *rights*) a insista asupra drepturilor sale • ~**ion** *s* afirmație *f*.
assess *vt* (*evaluate*) a evalua, a estima, a aprecia; a stabili; (*measure*) a fixa; (*judge*) a judeca (meritele etc) • ~**ment** *s* evaluare *f*, estimare *f*, apreciere *f*; stabilire *f*, fixare *f* (a valorii); valoare *f*, preț *n*; (*tax*) impozit *n*, taxă *f*; (*judgment*) părere *f*, opinie *f*.
asset *s* bun *n* de preț, lucru *n* valoros; (*quality*)) calitate *f*, însușire *f*; *pl* (*benefit*) bunuri *n*; avere *f*; investiție *f*; *pl* succesiune *f*; moștenire *f*.
assiduity *s* asiduitate *f*, stăruință *f*, perseverență *f*.
assiduous *adj* asiduu, stăruitor, insistent; atent; perseverent.
assign *vt* (~ *a job, etc*) a atribui; a aloca, a destina; a ceda; a acorda; a fixa, a stabili; a preciza; a delimita; (~ *a person*) a numi.
assignation *s* stabilire *f*, fixare *f*; atribuire *f*, alocare *f*; destinare *f*; precizare *f*; delimitare *f*; cedare *f*.
assignee *s* reprezentant *m*; împuternicit *m*; agent *m* (al unei firme); moștenitor *m* de drept.
assignment *s* (*appointment*) numire *f*; (*task*) sarcină *f*, (*duty*) datorie *f*; (*allocation*) alocare *f*; detașare *f*; temă *f*, lecție *f*.
assimilate *vt/vi* (a se) asimila; a se egaliza (cu).
assimilation *s* asimilare *f*.
assist *vt* (*help*) a ajuta; (*back*) a sprijini; (*aid*) a asista, a colabora (cu) || *vi* (*support*) a ajuta; a asista ca martor (la) • ~**ance** *s* ajutor *n*, sprijin *n* • ~**ant** *s* ajutor *n*, asistent *m*; vânzător *m*.
assize *s jur* ședința *f* de tribunal • ~**s** *jur* sesiune *f* judecătorească.
associate *s* a asocia; a stabili o asociație/legătură (cu) || *vi/vr* a se asocia; a se uni (cu); a se alia (cu); a se înhăita (cu) || *adj* asociat; unit; legat || *s* asociat *m*; partener *m*; membru *m* al unei asociații etc.
association *s* asociație *f*; în ~ **with** în colaborare cu.
assortment *s* sortare *f*; grupare *f*, clasificare *f*; asortiment • ~ varietate *f*.
assume *vt* (*suppose*) a presupune, a crede; (*guess*) a bănui; (*infer*) a deduce; a înțelege; (*undertake*) a-și asuma, a lua asupra sa; a-și aroga; (*feign*) a simula, a pretinde că are; a lua, a căpăta (o formă etc); (*affect*) a-și da/lua (aere).
assurance *s* (*pledge*) asigurare *f*; (*self-confidence*) siguranță *f* de sine, încredere *f* în sine.
assure *vt* a asigura, a încredința || *vr* a se convinge (de).
asterisk *s* aterisc *n*.
asteroid *s* asteroid *m*.
asthma *s med* astm *n*.
astir *adj/adv* în mișcare; sculat.
astonish *vt* a mira • ~**ed** *adj* uimit, surprins || *v* * **astonish** • ~**ing** *adj* uimitor • ~**ment** *s* uimire *f*.
astound *vt* a ului; a surprinde peste măsură; a șoca.
astray *adj* rătăcit || *adv* pe căi greșite; **to go** ~ a se rătăci; **to lead smb** ~ a deturna pe cineva de la calea dreaptă.
astride *adv* călare || *prep* călare pe.

astringent *adj* astringent || *s* substanță *f* astringentă.
astrologer *s* astrolog *m*; cititor *m* de stele.
astrology *s* astrologie *f*.
astronaut *s* astronaut *m*.
astronomer *s* astronom *m*.
astronomy *s* astronomie *f*.
astute *adj* abil, viclean.
asunder *adv* (*in two*) în două; (*in pieces*) în bucăți.
asylum *s* azil *n*.
asymmetric(al) *adj* asimetric, nesimetric.
at *prep* (*place*) la; ~ **school** la școală; (*direction*) către, spre; **to smile** ~ **smb** a surâde cuiva; (*a certain moment*) la; ~ **midnight/noon** la miezul nopții; ~ **night** noaptea; (*age, speed*) la; ~ **twenty** (**years of age**) la 20 de ani; ~ **60 miles per hour** la șaizeci de mile pe oră; (*price*) la; ~ **30 dollars a pair** la 30 dolari perechea; (*state, condition*) în; ~ **peace/war** în timp de pace/război; (*after adjectives*) la, de; **good/bad** ~ **smth** bun/rău la; ~ **all** *adv* (*response to question*) deloc, nicidecum; **anything** ~ **all will do** merge orice.
atheism *s* ateism *n*.
atheist *s* ateu *m*.
Athens *s* Atena *f*.
athlete *s* sportiv *m*, atlet *m*.
athletics *s* atletism *n* || *adj* de atletism.
Atlantic *adj* atlantic; **the** ~ (**Ocean**) *s* Oceanul *n* Atlantic.
atlas *s* atlas *n*.
ATM *s* bancomat *n*.
atmosphere *s* atmosferă *f*; aer *n*; ambianță *f*.
atmospheric *adj* atmosferic.
atoll *s geog* atol *m*.
atom *s* atom *m*; strop *m* • ~**ic** *adj* atomic.
atomizer *s* atomizor *n*.
atone *vi* a ispăși; a răscumpăra.
atrocious *adj* atroce, îngrozitor.
atrocity *s* (*violence*) atrocitate *f*; (*act of violence*) faptă *f* cumplită/bestială.
attach *vt* (*fasten*) a atașa (de); (*join*) a prinde, a lega, (*stick*) a fixa (de); (*assign*) a da, a acorda, a atribui (importanță etc) • ~**ment** *s* atașament *n*; fixare *f*.
attaché case *s* servietă *f* diplomat.
attack *vt* a ataca; (*assault*) a asalta; (*criticize*) a critica; (*tackle*) || a se apuca de || *vi* (*hit*) a ataca, a întreprinde un atac || *s* (*strike*) atac *n*, asalt *n*; *med* criză *f*; critică *f*; început *n*; abordare *f*.
attain *vt* (*reach*) a atinge, a ajunge la; (*achieve*) a realiza.
attempt *vt* (*try*) a încerca; a încerca să facă; a atenta la (viața cuiva) || *s* (*shot*) încercare *f*; tentativă *f*; (*endeavor*) experiență *f*, probă *f*; (*challenge*) atentat *n*.
attend *vt* (~ *a meeting*) a fi prezent la; (~ *a school*) a frecventa; *frml* (*accompany*) a însoți; a escorta; a avea parte de; a urmări; a trata; (*look after*) a îngriji; a sluji || *vi* (*be present*) a fi prezent; a frecventa; ~ **to** a se ocupa de • ~**ance** *s* (*presence*) prezență *f*, frecvență *f*; (*number of persons*) asistență *f*, public *n* • ~**ant** *adj* (*problem*) care decurge din || *s* paznic *m*, gardian *m*; (*gas station*) vânzător *m*.
attention *s* atenție *f*; concentrare *f*; îngrijire *f*; preocupare *f*; interes *n*.
attic *s* pod *n*, mansardă *f*.
attire *s lit* straie *n pl*, veșminte *f pl* || *vt lit* a înveșmânta.
attitude *s* atitudine *f*, (*stance*) ținută *f*; comportare *f*, purtare *f*; (*approach*) părere *f*; poziție *f*; punct *n* de vedere; poză *f*.
attorney *s jur* avocat *m*.

attract *vt* (*draw*) a atrage; a ademeni, a ispiti; a fi urmat de; a fi ascultat de; (*be attractive*) a atrage; a avea farmec • ~**ion** *s* (*pull*) atragere *f*; atracție *f*; (*appeal*) forță *f* de atracție; punct *n* de atracție; (*charm*) farmec *n* • ~**ive** *adj* (*pretty*) atractiv; atrăgător; frumos; (*appealing*) plăcut; agreabil; simpatic; (*interesting*) interesant.
attribute *vt/vi* (*ascribe*) a atribui (ceva, cuiva) || *s* (*quality*) atribut *n*, însușire *f*; *gram* atribut *n*.
attrition *s* (*wearing down*) uzură *f*.
atypical *adj* atipic.
aubergine *s bot* (*pătlăgea*) vânătă *f*.
auburn *adj* cafeniu-roșcat, roșu-închis.
auction *s* licitație *f* || *vt* a vinde la licitație.
audacious *adj* (*daring*) îndrăzneț, curajos.
audacity *s* (*daring*) îndrăzneală *f*; (*impudence*) obrăznicie *f*, nerușinare *f*.
audible *adj* audibil, care se aude; *phys* fonic; acustic.
audience *s* (*at lecture*) auditoriu *n*; asistență *f*; public *n*; spectatori *m pl*; *frml* (*meeting*) audiență *f*.
audiovisual *adj* audiovizual.
audit *s* audit *n*, verificarea *f* conturilor || *vt* (*accounts*) a verifica, a controla.
audition *s thea* audiție *f*; *cin* probă *f*; (*hearing*) auz *n*.
auditor *s* (*assessor*) cenzor *m*; (*inspector*) revizor *m*.
auditorium *s* (*pl* –**riums/ria**) sală *f* (de concert); auditoriu *n*.
auditory *adj* auditiv.
augment *vt* (*increase*) a spori, a augmenta.
august[1] *adj* (*dignified*) maiestuos; solemn.
August[2] *s* august *m*, Gustar.
aunt *s* mătușă *f*; tanti *f* • ~**ie** *s coll* tanti *f*.
au pair *s* (persoană *f*) care primește casă, masă și o mică remunerație în schimbul supravegherii copiilor.
aura *s* aură *f*, aureolă *f*; atmosferă *f*.
auspicious *adj* favorabil, prielnic; promițător.
austere *adj* auster, sobru, sever, grav, aspru; simplu, fără ornamente.
austerity *s* austeritate *f*; sobrietate *f*; severitate *f*.
Australia *s* Australia *f* • ~**n** *adj/s* Australian *m*.
Austria *s* Austria *f* • ~**n** *adj/s* austriac *m*.
authentic *adj* (*genuine*) autentic, veritabil, (*accurate*) adevărat; original; (*reliable*) demn de încredere.
author *s* autor *m*; scriitor *m*; creator *m*.
authoritarian *adj* (*strict*) sever; (*controlling*) tiranic || *s* despot *m*, tiran *m*.
authoritative *adj* (*respected*) autoritar; (*reliable*) serios, de încredere.
authority *s* autoritate *f*; (*power*) putere *f*; (*ability*) drept *n*, competență *f*; (*permission*) împuternicire *f*; acreditare *f*; delegație *f*; (*confidence*) prestigiu *n*; (*specialist*) persoană *f* competentă; specialist *m*; expert *m*; (*citation*) sursă *f* autorizată/competentă.
authorize *vt* (*empower*) a autoriza, a împuternici; a delega; (*sanction*) a aproba, a permite; a admite.
autobiography *s* autobiografie *f*.
autocratic *adj* autocratic, autocrat.
autograph *s* autograph *n*.
automatic *adj* (*machine*) automat; automatizat; mecanic; (*smile, answer*) mașinal; involuntar || *s* armă *f* automată.
automation *s* automatizare *f*.
automobile *s* automobil *n*.
autonomous *adj* autonom.
autonomy *s* autonomie *f*.

autopsy *s* autopsie *f.*

autumn *s* toamnă *f.*

auxiliary *adj* auxiliar, ajutător; suplimentar, adițional; *gram* auxiliar || *s* (*person*) ajutor *n*; *pl mil* armate *f pl* aliate; *gram* verb *n* auxiliar.

avail *vt* a da, a oferi; a fi de folos, a folosi || *vi* a ajuta, a fi de folos, a avea rost || *s* folos *n*; (*benefit*) ajutor *n*; (*aim*) efect *n*; **to no** ~ în van, fără rezultat; **money** ~**ed him little happiness** banii i-au dat/oferit prea puțină fericire.

available *adj* (*accessible*) disponibil, existent; (*on hand*) la îndemână; (*existing*) prezent; abordabil; accesibil; (*vacant*) liber.

avalanche *s* also *fig* avalanșă *f.*

avarice *s* avariție *f*, zgârcenie *f.*

avenge *vt* a răzbuna || *vi* (**on/upon**) a se răzbuna (pe).

avenue *s* (*street*) alee *f*; drum *n*, stradă *f* cu pomi; bulevard *n*; magistrală *f*; (*prospect*) cale *f*, posibilitate *f*, mijloc *n.*

average *s* valoare *f* medie; medie *f* || *adj* mediu; obișnuit; normal; mediocru || *vt* a calcula/face media; a ajunge la o medie de.

averse to *adj* care este contra/împotriva; care nu e de acord cu; care se opune.

aversion *s firml* (*dislike*) aversiune *f*, silă *f*, dezgust *n*; antipatie *f*; (*object of dislike*) obiect *n* al aversiunii.

avert *vt* (*avoid*) a preveni; (*turn away*) a îndepărta; (~ *eyes*, *etc*) a feri.

aviary *s* aviariu *n*; coteț *n* sau colivie *f* mare pentru păsări.

aviation *s* aviație *f*

aviator *s* aviator *m*; pilot *m.*

avid *adj* avid (de); lacom; pasionat.

avocado *s bot* avocado *n.*

avoid *vt* (*shun*) a evita, a ocoli; (*evade*) a se feri de; a anula (o decizie etc).

avow *vt* (*declare*) a declara deschis; (*admit*) a recunoaște, a mărturisi.

await *vt* a aștepta; a fi în așteptarea; a-l aștepta (pe cineva) || *vi* a aștepta, a fi în așteptare.

awake, awoke *also* **awaked** *vt* (~ *a person*) a trezi, a deștepta; a scula; (~ *memories*) a evoca; a stimula; (~ *hope*) a stârni || *vi* (*get up*) a se trezi, a se deștepta; a se scula; (*become aware*) a căpăta viață || *adj* (*up*) treaz, sculat (din somn).

awaken *vt/vi* also *fig* a (se) trezi • ~**ing** *s* trezire *f* (la realitate)

award *vi* (*confer*) a da, a acorda (un premiu etc) || *s* (*reward*) răsplată *f*; (*prize*) premiu *n*; *jur* recompensă *f*; acordare *f*, conferire *f*; (*decision*) decizie *f*; hotărâre *f* (a unui arbitru etc).

aware *adj* (*alert*) conștient, (*informed*) care își dă seama de; (*cognizant*) calificat, pregătit, priceput; (*sensitive*) înțelegător, sensibil.

away *adv* departe; în altă parte; încolo; altundeva; la o depărtare de; de mult, de mult timp || *interj* (hai) pleacă de aici!; (hai) să mergem!.

awe *s* uimire *f* și teamă *f* sau venerație *f*; înfiorare *f*; **to be in** ~ **of smth** a fi impresionat de || *vi* a inspira uimire și teamă sau venerație; a copleși • ~**some** *adj* impresionant, inspirând uimire și teamă; sublim.

awful *adj* (*dreadful*) grozav, teribil, cumplit; (*appalling*) îngrozitor; afurisit.

awhile *adv* câtva timp, câtăva vreme.

awkward *adj* (*clumsy*) stângaci, neîndemânatic;

nepotrivit, impropriu; incomod; (*situation*) jenant; apăsător; (*difficult*) dificil, greu; (*inconvenient*) inoportun • ~**ness** *s* stângăcie *f*, neîndemânare *f.*

awl *s* sulă *f.*

awning *s constr* marchiză *f*; (*store*) streașină *f*; (*tent*) cort *n*; tendă *f.*

axe *s* secure *f*, topor *n* || *vt* a tăia de pe listă, a șterge din buget.

axiom *s* axiomă *f* • ~**atic** *adj* axiomatic.

axis *s* (*pl* **axes**) axă *f.*

axle *s tech* ax *n*, arbore *m*, osie *f.*

ay *adv* da.

azalea *s bot* azalee *f.*

azimuth *s astr* azimut *n.*

azure *s lit* azur *n* || *adj* azuriu.

B

B, b *s* (*letter*) b, B; **B** *s mus* si; *scol* calificativ *n*, notă *f.*

babble *vi* a gânguri; (*blather*) a bolborosi; a se bâlbâi; a murmura, a susura; (*jabber*) a pălăvrăgi, a trăncăni || *vt* a îngăima; a da de gol, a divulga || *s* (*voices*) gângurit *n*, uguit *n*; (*prattle*) bolborosit *n*; bâlbâială *f*; murmur *n*, susur *n*; (*chatter*) flecăreală *f*, pălăvrăgeală *f.*

baboon *s zool* babuin *m* (specie de maimuță).

baby *s* copil *m* (mic), copilaș *m*; prunc *m*; sugaci *m*; pui *m* (de animal); *coll* drăguță *f*, fată frumoasă *f* • ~**hood** *s* prima copilărie *f*, pruncie *f* • ~**sitter** *s* persoană care supraveghează copilul cât părinții lipsesc de acasă.

baccalaureate *s* licență *f.*

bachelor *s* celibatar *m*, cavaler *m*, holtei *m*; licențiat *m.*

back *s* (*rear*) spate *n*, spinare *f*; fund *n*; (*backside*) spetează *f*, spătar *n*; străfund *n*; (*support*) sprijin *n* || *adj* din urmă/spate, dindărăt; ultim; vechi; înapoiat || *adv* înapoi, îndărăt, în spate; altădată; din nou || *vt* (*assist*) a sprijini, (*sponsor*) a susține; a încăleca; (*bet on*) a paria (pe un cal) || *vi* (*reverse*) a merge înapoi; a da îndărăt.

backache *s* durere *f* de șale/mijloc.

backbite *vt* a calomnia, a vorbi de rău (în spate) || *vi* a calomnia, a bârfi

backbone *s* șira *f* spinării, coloană *f* vertebrală; *fig* coloană *f* vertebrală, temelie *f*; *fig* tărie *f* de caracter, fermitate *f.*

backdate *vt* a antedata.

backdoor *s* ușă *f* din spate, intrare *f* din dos.

backdrop *s also fig* cortină *f* de fundal.

backfire *vi aut* a da rateuri; (*plan*) a se întoarce (împotriva cuiva).

backgammon *s* (*game*) joc *n* de table || *vt* a face marț.

background *s* fund *n*; fond *n*; (*backdrop*) fundal *n*; loc *n* retras; atmosferă *f*; (*milieu*) mediu *n*; (*setting*) decor *n*; (*experience*) cunoștințe *f pl*; acompaniament *n*; zgomot *n* de fond.

backhand *s* dosul *n* palmei; lovitură *f* dată cu dosul palmei; scriere *f* aplecată spre stânga; *sp* revers *n.*

backlash *s* repercusiune *f*; contralovitură *f.*

backlog *s* (*work*) lucru *n* în întârziat, restanță *f.*

backpack *s* rucsac *n.*

backside *s coll* posterior *n*, dos *n.*

backstage *adv* în culise || *adj* din fundul scenei; din culise; *fig* de culise; secret || *s* culise *f pl.*

backstroke s sp craul n pe spate; tech mers n înapoi; recul n.

backward adj (glance, movement) în urmă, înapoi; (region) slab dezvoltat; (person) înapoiat, întârziat • ~s adv înapoi, îndărăt, în spate; (in reverse order) invers; (back first) de-a-ndoaselea; de-a-ndărătelea; pe spate.

backwater s contracurent n; golf n (de râu); braţ n mort.

bacon s bacon n; slănină f.

bacteria s pl bacterii f pl.

bad adj (awful) rău, (poor) prost; (shoddy) urât; (defective) stricat, (corrupt) imoral, vicios; (rude) necuviincios; stătut; (unhealthy) bolnav; (adverse) neplăcut; nepotrivit; (damaging) dăunător; (flawed) fals; greşit, incorect, inexact; nereuşit, neizbutit; (imperfect) nesatisfăcător || s the ~ cei/oamenii m pl răi || adv rău, prost; greşit; urât; foarte mult, grozav • ~ly adv grav; prost; urât; ~ hurt rănit grav; ~ managed condus prost; behave ~ a se comporta urât.

badge s semn n (distinctiv); marcă f; emblemă f; insignă f; simbol n || vt a însemna, a marca.

badger s zool bursuc m, viezure m || vt ~ smb a bate la cap pe cineva.

badminton s (game) badminton n.

baffle vt a deruta, a zăpaci.

bag s sac m; desagă f; săculeţ n; traistă f; tolbă f; (suitcase) valiză f, geamantan n; geantă f, poşetă f; balon n; muiere f || vt a pune la sac, a îndesa; a face (o colecţie etc); (shoot) a împuşca (vânat); a fura || vi a se umfla; a se pungi • ~gage s (luggage) bagaj n; (gear) echipament n; tren n, convoi n; puştancă f; drăcoaică f; târfă f; palavragiu m, pierde-vară m.

baggy adj umflat, lăbărţat; bufant.

bail s (law) cauţiune f; out on ~ pe cauţiune; put up ~ for a depune garanţie pentru (cineva) || vt ~ out a plăti cauţiune pentru a elibera pe (cineva).

bailiff s (law) uşier m, aprod m.

bait s (fishing) momeală f || vt a momi; (to bother) a necăji.

bake vt a coace (în cuptor); a usca (la soare); a arde || vi a se coace; a se întări; a se prăji (la soare), a se bronza • ~ry s brutărie f.

baking soda s bicarbonat de sodiu n.

balance s (weighing scale) balanţă f, cântar n; (poise) echilibru n; stabilitate f; (weight) greutate f, pondere f; nesiguranţă f; cântărire f, cumpănire f; bilanţ n || vt (weigh) a cântări; (assess) a aprecia, a compara; a contrabalansa; a echilibra, (equalize) a egala || vi a fi în echilibru; a se balansa; ~ sheet econ bilanţ n.

balcony s balcon n.

bald adj chel; gol, golaş; simplu, sărăcăcios; plat; sec, monoton; făţiş, sincer.

bale s minge f; glonţ n; balot n; ~ out vt (boat) a goli || vi (plane) a sări cu paraşuta.

baleful adj (menacing) ameninţător; (vindictive) răzbunător.

ball¹ s sferă f, glob n; bilă f; corp n ceresc; minge f; balon n; glonte n; ghem n; chiftea f || vt a strânge/ face ghem || vi a se face ghem • ~s s sl testicule n pl; curaj n.

ball² s (dance) bal n • ~room s sală f de dans.

ballad s baladă f.

ballast s balast n.

ballet s (art) dans n; (activity) balet n.

balloon s balon n; aerostat n || vt a înălţa, a ridica || vi a se ridica cu balonul; a se umfla.

ballot s bilă f (de vot); (paper) buletin n de vot; vot n, scrutin n; tragere f la sorţi || vi a vota; a trage la sorţi || vt a vota, a alege.

balm s balsam n, elixir n; alinare f • ~y adj (weather) blând.

bamboo s bambus m.

ban vt (forbid) a interzice; (bar) a opri; a blestema; (proscribe) a condamna || s (prohibition) interzicere f, interdicţie f; exilare f, surghiun n; blestem n; opro-briu n.

banal adj banal, ordinar.

banana s (tree) banan m; (fruit) banană f; măscărici m, paiaţă f.

band¹ s ceată f, (group) grup n; bandă f; şleahtă f; detaşament n; (music) orchestră f; mil fanfară f || vi a se uni, a se coaliza.

band² s legătură f; bandă f; (strip) fâşie f; cordon n; centură f; obligaţie f; lungime f de undă • ~aid s leucoplast n • ~age s bandaj n, pansament n.

bandit s bandit m.

bandy adj crăcănat || vt ~ about/around a împrăştia, a face să circule.

bane s (nuisance) belea f; (curse) pacoste f; otravă f • ~ful adj nefast.

bang s (slam) a trânti cu zgomot; (hit) a izbi; (whack) a bate, a lovi || vi a se închide cu zgomot; a pocni, a răsuna || s (crash) lovitură f, izbitură f; (thud) pocnet n || adv cu un bubuit/pocnet; brusc, deodată; drept, direct.

bangle s brăţară f.

banish vt (expel) a expulza; (dismiss) a concedia • ~ment s expulzare f.

banister s balustradă f, bară f (la scară).

bank¹ s (edge) mal n; ţărm n; dig n, zăgaz n; terasament n; (sand) banc n; troian n, nămete n || vt a îndigui, a zăgăzui || vi a se înclina.

bank² s fin bancă f; ~ account s cont n bancar; ~ bill s cambie f bancară; ~ statement s extras n de cont; ~ on vt a conta pe (ceva) • ~er s bancher m • ~note s bancnotă f • ~rate s taxă f de scont.

bankruptcy s faliment n.

banner s drapel n; pancartă f; afiş n.

banquet s banchet n.

banter s ironie f, batjocură f, glumă f.

baptism s botez n.

baptize vt a boteza.

bar s (rod) bară f; drug n; bucată f; lingou n; zăvor n; barieră f, obstacol n, piedică f; (law) discriminare f; banc n de nisip; (for drinks) bar n; (music) măsură f; tact n; dungă f, făşie f || vt (obstruct) a bara, a împiedica, a bloca; a zăvorî; (ban) a interzice, a opri; a despărţi (de); (expel) a exclude; a vărga, a dunga || prep cu excepţia, în afară de; ~ code s cod n de identificare a produselor.

barbarian s/adj also fig barbar m.

barbarism s barbarie f; lipsă f de civilizaţie; purtare f necivilizată; acţiune f barbară.

barbarous adj barbar; crud, feroce; (person) necioplit.

barbecue s petrecere f în aer liber la care se face grătar.

barbed wire s sârmă f ghimpată.

barber s bărbier m • ~'s (shop) frizerie f.

barbiturate s barbiturice n pl.

bard s bard m.

bare *adj* (*naked*) gol, despuiat, neacoperit; (*barren*) pustiu, deşert; desfrunzit; sterp, neroditor; sărac (în); ros, tocit; simplu, numai || *vt* (*uncover*) a dezgoli; (*strip*) a despuia, a dezbrăca; (*expose*) a dezvălui, a da în vileag • **~foot** *adj*/*adv* descult.

bargain *s* (*transaction*) afacere *f*, tranzacţie *f*, târg *n*; (*good buy*) câştig *n*, profit *n*; cumpărătură *f* || *vt* a negocia, a se târgui pentru; a face troc cu; a încheia un târg; a face o afacere; a se tocmi; **~ for** (*expect*) a se aştepta la; **~ with** a se tocmi cu; **into the ~** pe deasupra.

barge *s* şalupă *f* || *vi coll* **~ past smb** a da peste cineva; **~ in (on)** a întrerupe.

baritone *s mus* bariton *m*.

bark[1] *vi* (*dog*) a lătra (la, după) || *s* lătrat *n*.

bark[2] *s* (*tree*) scoarţă *f*.

barley *s bot* orz *n*.

barn *s* (*storage place*) hambar *n*, pătul *n*; (*shed*) şură *f*, şopron *n*; grajd *n*, ocol *n*; depou *n* de tramvaie.

barometer *s* barometru *n*.

baron *s* baron *m*.

barrack *s* baracă *f*; *pl* cazarmă *f*; clădire *f* uriaşă.

barrage *s* (foc de) baraj *n*; (*questions*) avalanşă *f*, potop *n*.

barrel *s* butoi *n*; baril *m*; butoiaş *n*.

barren *adj* steril, arid.

barricade *s* baricadă *f*.

barrier *s* (*obstruction*) barieră *f*; poartă *f*; graniţă *f*, hotar *n*, limită *f*; (*obstacle*) piedică *f*, obstacol *n*.

barrister *s jur* avocat *m*.

barrow *s* roabă *f*.

bartender *s* bufetier *m*, barman *m*.

barter *s* schimb *n* în natură, troc *n* || *vi* a face troc || *vt* a vinde.

base[1] *s* (*basis*) bază *f*, fundament *n*, temelie *f*; (*source*) esenţă *f*; start *n*, punct *n* de plecare || *adj* de la bază; de bază; fundamental || *vt* (*found*) a întemeia; a pune bazele.

base[2] *adj* josnic, inferior.

baseball *s* baseball *n*.

basement *s* fundament *n*, temelie *f*; subsol *n*.

bash *s coll* izbitură *f*; **to have a ~** a face o încercare || *vt* a lovi, a pocni; (*car*) a lovi, a izbi.

bashful *adj* ruşinos, timid, sfios.

basic *adj* de bază, fundamental; *chem* bazic.

basil *s bot* busuioc *n*.

basin *s* (*sink*) chiuvetă *f*; (*wash~*) lighean *n*; (*bathroom*) lavabou *n*; bazin *n*, rezervor *n*; *geog* depresiune *f*.

basis *s* bază *f*, temelie *f*; punct *n* de plecare.

bask *vi* a încălzi; **to ~ in the sun** a face plajă.

basket *s* coş *n*; nacelă *f* || *vt* a arunca la coş.

basketball *s sp* baschet *n*.

bass[1] *adj* (*voice*) jos || *s* (*singer*) bas *m*; contrabas *m*.

bass[2] *s icht* biban *m*.

bassoon *s mus* fagot *m*.

bastard *s* bastard *m*, copil *m* nelegitim; hybrid *m*, corcitură *f*, ticălos *m*, nemernic *m*; tip *m*, individ *m* || *adj* bastard, nelegitim; stricat, fals; monstruos; hidos.

baste *vt cul* a unge, a stropi (carnea) cu unt şi condimente.

bastion *s* bastion *n*.

bat[1] *s* băţ *n*; bâtă *f*, ciomag *n*; *sp* paletă *f*; *infrml* lovitură *f* (cu ciomagul) || *vt* (*strike*) a lovi, a izbi (cu paleta etc) • **right off the ~** pe loc, imediat; fără întârziere.

bat[2] *s zool* liliac *m*.

batch *s* (*loaves*) teanc *n*, grămadă *f*; (*letters*) serie *f*; (*product*) lot *n*.

bath *s* baie *f*, îmbăiere *f*; (*tub*) cadă *f*; cameră *f* de baie; băi *f pl*, staţiune *f* balneară • **~robe** *s* halat *n* de baie • **~room** *s* (cameră de) baie *f* • **~tub** *s* cadă *f*.

bathe *vt* a scălda, a spăla, a uda || *vi* a se scălda

bathing *s* scăldat *n*; **~ suit** *s* costum *n* de baie.

batman *s mil* ordonanţă *f*.

baton *s sp* ştafetă *f*; *mus* baghetă *f*.

battalion *s* batalion *n*.

batter[1] *vt* a bate.

batter[2] *s* pastă *f*; aluat *n*.

battery *s* bătaie *f*; baterie *f*; divizion *n*; acumulator *n*.

battle *s* (*clash*) bătălie *f*, (*fight*) luptă *f*; bătaie *f*; conflict *n*; întrecere *f* || *vi* (*fight*) a (se) lupta (pentru).

batty *adj coll* smintit, ţăcănit.

bawdy *adj* pornografic, obscen.

bawl *vi* a zbiera, a urla.

bay[1] *s* arcadă *f*; deschidere *f*; nişă *f*; golf *n*.

bay[2] *adj* murg || *s* (cal) murg *m*.

bay[3] *vi* a lătra || *s* lătrat *n*.

bay[4] *s* dafin *m*; **~ leaf** *s* frunză *f* de dafin.

bayonet *s* baionetă *f*.

bay window *s* bovindou *n*, nişă *f* cu fereastră arcuită.

bazaar *s* (*market*) bazar *n*.

be, was, were, been *v* a fi, a exista, a fiinţa; a se împlini; a costa, a face.

beach *s* ţărm *n* de mare; litoral *n*; plajă *f*; banc *n* de nisip || *vt* a pune pe uscat; a descărca pe ţărm || *vi* a eşua.

beacon *s* far *n*; *naut* baliză *f*.

bead *s* mărgea *f*, perlă *f*; mărgăritar *n*; bob *n*, boabă *f*; strop *n*.

beak *s* cioc *n*.

beaker *s* pahar *n* fără picior.

beam *s archit* grindă *f*, bară *f*, traversă *f*; rază *f*; nimb *n*, aureolă *f*; (*smile*) zâmbet *n* radios/larg.

bean *s bot* fasole *f*.

bear[1] *vt* (*carry*) a purta, a duce , a căra; (*give birth*) a naşte, a da naştere la; (*tolerate*) a suporta; a suferi || *vr* a se comporta || *vi* a rezista; a naşte; a rodi; **~ right/left** a o lua la dreapta/stânga • **~able** *adj* suportabil • **~er** *s* purtător *m*.

bear[2] *s zool* urs *m*; om *m* ursuz.

beard *s* barbă *f*; radiculă *f*, mustaţă *f* || *vt* a trage de barbă; a înfrunta, a sfida.

bearing *s* (*behavior*) ţinută *f*; (*relation*) legătură *f*, raport *n*; (*direction*) direcţie *f*; **lose one's ~s** a fi dezorientat.

beast *s* animal *n*, dobitoc *n*; vită *f*, fiară *f*, bestie *f*.

beat *vt* a bate; (*hit*) a lovi; (*thrash*) a ciomăgi; a marca; a suna; (*defeat*) a învinge; (*outclass*) a întrece; a depăşi || *vi* a bate, a ciocăni; (*pound*) a lovi, a izbi; a urla || *s* (*blow*) lovitură *f*, (*stroke*) bătaie *f* (a ceasului etc); măsură *f*, (*stress*) ritm *n*; (*police*) rond *n*, patrulare *f*; **~er** *s* bătăuş *m*.

beatitude *s relig* beatitudine *f*.

beating *s* (*as punishment*) bătaie *f*; (*defeat*) înfrângere *f*.

beauteous *adj lit* splendid.

beautiful *adj* frumos; minunat; admirabil; mândru.

beautify *vt* a înfrumuseţa.

beauty *s* frumuseţe *f*; splendoare *f*; femeie *f* frumoasă; graţie *f*; **~ parlor** *s* salon *n* de coafură/cosmetică.

beaver *s zool* castor *m*.

because *conj* pentru că, fiindcă, deoarece, întrucât, cum.

beckon *vt* a face semn || *vi* ~ **to smb** a face semn cuiva.

become *vi* a deveni, a ajunge, a se face || *vt* a i se potrivi, a-i veni bine cuiva.

becoming *adj* (*suitable*) potrivit, care vine bine; corespunzător, cuvenit.

bed *s* pat *n*; așternut *n*; culcuș *n*; (*flowers*) strat *n*; (*coal, etc*) strat *n* || *vt* a culca; a sădi, a planta || *vi* a se culca; a înnopta; ~ **and breakfast** casă și micul dejun.

bedaubed *adj* mânjit.

bedraggled *adj* (*unkempt*) murdar; (*untidy*) neîngrijit.

bedroom *s* dormitor *n*, cameră *f* de culcare.

bee *s* *ento* albină *f*; om *m* harnic; concurs *n* școlar pe disciplline.

beech *s* *bot* (*tree*) fag *m*.

beef *s* carne *f* de vită; forță *f* (mușchiulară); *coll* diferend *n*.

beeper *s* pager *n*.

beer *s* bere *f*; (*glass of beer*) pahar *n* de bere *f*.

beet *s* *bot* sfeclă *f* • ~**root** *s* sfeclă *f* roșie.

beetle *s* *ento* gândac *m*; cărăbuș *m*.

befall *vi* a se întâmpla.

before *adv* înainte, în față; altădată; odinioară; deja; înaintea, dinaintea || *conj* înainte de a, înainte ca; până ce/când.

befriend *vt* a ocroti.

beg *vt* a ruga, a se ruga de, a solicita; a cere cuiva || *vi* a cerși, a cere de pomană; a ruga, a cere (de la) • ~**gar** *s* cerșetor *m* • ~**garly** *adj* mizer.

begin *vt* (*start*) a începe, a porni; (*set out*) a se apuca de; a debuta în || *vi* a începe, a porni • ~**ner** *s* novice *m*, începător *m* • ~**ning** *s* început *n*; debut *n*; pornire *f*; origine *f*; punct *n* de plecare.

begrudge *vi* (*resent*) a avea pică pe; (*envy*) a invidia.

behalf *s* on ~ **of, in** ~ **of** din partea, în numele.

behave *vi* a se purta, a se comporta; a funcționa, a lucra.

behead *vt* a decapita.

behind *adv* în urmă, în spate, îndărăt || *prep* în spatele, îndărătul, în urma; din spatele; după.

behold *vi* *lit* a vedea, a privi, a zări.

beige *adj* bej.

being *s* (*creature*) ființă *f*; **come into** ~ a lua ființă, a lua naștere, a vedea lumina zilei.

belated *adj* întârziat, tardiv.

belch *vi* a râgâi; a vomita, a vărsa; a erupe || *vt* a da afară; a vărsa; a erupe; a rosti; a profera || *s* râgâială *f*, eructație *f*; vomitare *f*; erupție *f*.

belfry *s* clopotniță *f*.

Belgian *adj/s* Belgian.

Belgium *s* Belgia *f*.

Belgrade *s* Belgrad *n*.

belief *s* *relig* credință *f*; încredere *f*; convingere *f*; (*opinion*) părere *f*.

believe *vt* (*think*) a crede; a socoti; (*deem*) a fi de părere || *vi* (*trust*) a crede (în); a socoti • ~**r** *s* credincios *m*; credul *m*; partizan *m*, apărător *m*.

belittle *vt* a subestima, a subaprecia.

bell *s* clopot *n*; sonerie *f*; talangă *f*; pâlnie *f*; halteră *f*; caliciu *n*.

bellicose *adj* belicos.

belligerent *s/adj* beligerant *m*.

bellow *vi* a mugi.

bellows *s* *pl* *tech* foale *f pl*.

belly *s* *anat* burtă *f*, pântece *n*; stomac *n*; (*plane*) fuzelaj *n* || *vt* a umfla || *vi* a se umfla • ~**button** *s* buric *n*.

belong *vi* a aparține (cuiva); ~ **to smth** a fi membru a ceva; a fi la locul său; **this chair** ~**s there** acest scaun e de acolo • ~**ings** *s* *pl* lucruri *n pl*, obiecte *n pl*, bunuri *n pl*; neamuri *n pl*, rude *f pl*; acareturi *n pl*, dependințe *f pl*.

beloved *adj* iubit.

below *adv* dedesubt, jos; mai jos; la subsol(ul paginii); mai departe; în cele ce urmează || *adj* de jos, de mai jos; dedesubt || *prep* dedesubtul, sub; în josul.

belt *s* curea *f*, centură *f*, cordon *n*; cingătoare *f*, brâu *n*; *tech* curea *f* de transmisie; (*land*) regiune *f*, zonă *f*;

bemuse *vt* (*perplex*) a uimi, a năuci, a ului.

bench *s* bancă *f*; banchetă *f*; scaun *n* judecătoresc; zid *n*, val *n*; (*worktable*) banc *n* de lucru.

bend *vt* (*curve*) a îndoi, a încovoia; a apleca; (*twist*) a strâmba; a întinde; a supune || *vi* a se îndoi, a se încovoia, a se strâmba; a se apleca, a se întinde || *s* îndoire *f*, încovoiere *f*; (*bow*) aplecare *f*; strâmbare *f*; (*turn*) cotitură *f*, meandră *f*, curbură *f*.

beneath *adj* mai jos, dedesubt || *prep* dedesubtul, sub, mai jos de; inferior.

benediction *s* binecuvântare *f*.

benefaction *s* binefacere *f*.

benefactor *s* binefăcător *m*; donator *m*.

beneficent *adj* generos; binefăcător, salutar; folositor.

beneficial *adj* binefăcător, folositor, util; avantajos, profitabil.

benefit *s* (*profit*) beneficiu *n*, (*gain*) câștig *n*, folos *n*; (*help*) ajutor *n*; (*advantage*) avantaj *n*; binefacere *f*; privilegiu *n* || *vi* a beneficia || *vt* (*do good to*) a folosi, a aduce foloase.

benevolent *adj* (*kindly*) binevoitor; favorabil; (*charitable*) mărinimos, milostiv. **benevolence** *s* bunăvoință *f*; binefacere *f*.

benign *adj* (*person*) blând; binevoitor; *med* benign.

bent *adj* (*thread*) răsucit, torsionat; (*person, body*) curbat, încovoiat; (*determined*) hotărât || *s* predispoziție *f* (la), înclinație *f* (spre).

benumb *vt* *also fig* a amorți; a toci.

bequeath *vt* *also fig* a lăsa moștenire prin testament.

bequest *s* testament *n*, legat *n*; *also fig* moștenire *f*.

berate *vt* (*rebuke*) a dojeni; (*scold*) a mustra

bereaved *adj* îndoliat, îndurerat || *s* **the** ~ *s* familia *f* îndoliată.

beret *s* beretă *f*.

Berlin *s* Berlin *n*.

Berne *s* Berna *f*.

berry *s* boabă *f*, bob *n*, grăunțe *n pl*.

berserk *adj* nebun furios || **go** ~ *vt* a fi/deveni nebun de furie.

berth *s* cușetă *f*; **give a wide** ~ a evita.

beseech, besought, besought *vt* (*entreat*) a ruga stăruitor, (*implore*) a implora.

beside *prep* lângă, aproape de; pe lângă, față de, în comparație cu; în afară de, mai presus de • ~**s** *adv* în plus, pe lângă asta || *prep* în afară de.

besiege *vt* (*town, fortress*) a asedia; *fig* a hărțui, a asalta.

best *adj* cel mai bun; superior; excelent; neîntrecut; minunat || *adv* cel mai bine, cel mai mult || *s* maximum *n* || *vt* a învinge, a înfrânge, a bate; **at** ~ *adv* în cel mai bun caz; **do one's** ~ *vt* a face tot ce-i stă în puteri.

bestial *adj* (*brutish*) bestial • ~**ity** *s* bestialitate *f*.

bestman *s* cavaler *m* de onoare.

bestow *vt* ~ **smth on smb** a conferi, a acorda ceva cuiva.

bestseller *s* carte *f* de mare succes.

bet *s* pariu *n*, rămăşag *n*, prinsoare *f*; miză *f* || *vt* a face pariu pe; a face pariu cu || *vi* a face pariu/prinsoare (pe).

betray *vt* a trăda.

better *adj* mai bun; superior; preferabil; mai mare || *adv* mai bine || *s* superioritate *f*, avantaj *n* || *vt* (*improve*) a îmbunătăţi, a corija, a îndrepta; (*enhance*) a mări, a spori; a depăşi || *vi/vr* a se îndrepta; (*advance*) a progresa.

between *prep* între; dintre; printre; la mijlocul || *adv* la mijloc; între unul şi altul.

beverage *s* băutură *f* (preparată).

beware *vi* a se păzi/feri (de); ~ **of** ... atenţie la ...

bewildered *adj* dezorientat, năucit.

bewitch *vt* a fermeca, a fascina, a încânta; a vrăji.

beyond *prep* dincolo de; peste; de/pe partea cealaltă; mai presus de; pe lângă, în afară de || *adv* dincolo, pe partea cealaltă; mai departe; mai încolo; la distanţă || *adj* de dincolo; din partea cealaltă, din depărtare.

bias *s* părtinire *f*; prejudecată *f*; (*sewing*) bie *n* • ~**ed** *adj* părtinitor.

bib *s* babetă *f*, bărbiţă *f*.

Bible, the *s* Biblia *f*.

biblical *adj* biblic.

bibliography *s* bibliografie *f*.

bicameral *adj* bicameral.

biceps *s pl* biceps *m*.

bicker *vi* a se certa, a se sfădi.

bicycle *s* bicicletă *f*.

bid *s* licitaţie *f*; (*cards*) cerere *f*; (*attempt*) tentativă *f*, încercare *f* || *vi* (*auction*) a licita; (*in cards*) a cere; (*command*) a ordona; (*greet*) a ura.

bidet *s* bideu *n*.

biennial *adj* bienal.

bier *s* catafalc *n*.

bifocals *s pl* ochelari *m pl* bifocali.

bifurcate *vi* a se bifurca.

big *adj* mare; masiv; gros; solid; înalt; voinic; vârstnic; major; important.

bigamy *s* bigamie *f*.

bigot *s* bigot *m* • ~**ry** bigotism *n*.

bike *s* * **bicycle**.

bikini *s* bikini *n*.

bilberry *s bot* (*plant*) afin *m*; (*fruit*) afină *f*.

bile *s anat* fiere *f*; (*anger*) mâhnire *f*.

bilingual *adj* bilingv.

bill[1] *s pol* proiect *n* de lege, lege *f*; document *n*; listă *f*; inventar *n*; certificat *n*; (*utilities*) factură *f*; notă *f* de plată; cambie *f*; (*poster*) afiş *n*; anunţ *n* || *vt* a înregistra; a factura; a înştiinţa.

bill[2] *s* cioc *n*.

billiards *s pl* biliard *n*.

billion *s* bilion *n*; miliard *n*.

billow *s lit* talaz *n*, brizant *n*, val *n* mare || *vi* a se ridica, a se umfla.

bin *s* dulăpior *n*; (*case*) ladă *f*; cutie *f*; ladă *f* de gunoi; cupă *f*; (*silo*) siloz *n*.

binary *adj* binar.

bind *vt* a lega; a strânge; a uni; (~ *a book*) a lega; a întări; a prinde; (*force*) a obliga; a determina || *s* legătură *f*; panglică *f*; fâşie *f* • ~**ing** *adj* liant, care leagă; *jur* obligator; care obligă || *s* legătură *f*; legare *f*; (*book*) copertă *f*; bandaj *n*; tiv *n*.

binge *s* chef *n*, zaiafet *n* || *vi* a chefui.

binoculars *s pl* binoclu *n* (de câmp).

biodegradable *adj* biodegradabil

biography *s* biografie *f*.

biographer *s* biograf *m*.

biographical *adj* biografic.

biology *s* biologie *f*.

biological *adj* biologic.

biologist *s* biolog *m*.

biopsy *s med* biopsie *f*.

biped *s/adj* biped *m*.

birch *s bot* mesteacăn *m*.

bird *s* pasăre *f*; tip *m*, cetăţean *m*, individ *m*.

birth *s* naştere *f*; facere *f*; început *n*, origine *f*; **give** ~ *vt* a da naştere (la) • ~ **control** *s* măsuri *f pl* anticoncepţionale • ~**day** *s* zi *f* de naştere, aniversare *f* • ~**place** *s* locul *n* naşterii • ~ **rate** *s* natalitate *f*.

biscuit *s* chiflă *f*; biscuit *m*, pesmet *m*.

bisect *vt* a tăia în două.

bishop *s relig* episcop *m*; (*chess*) nebun *m*.

bison *s zool* bizon *m*.

bit[1] *s* (*horse*) zăbală *f*; (*drill*) burghiu; *comp* bit *m*.

bit[2] *s* bucată *f*, fărâmă *f*; pasaj *n*; **a** ~ *adv* puţin, un pic; ~ **by** ~ puţin câte puţin.

bitch *s* căţea *f*; *coll pej* femeie *f* stricată, târâtură *f* • ~**y** *adj* sever; scârbos.

bite *vt* (*nibble*) a muşca; a arde; a coroda; (*smart*) a ustura; a calomnia, a defăima || *vi* (*snap at*) a muşca; a arde; a ustura || *s* muşcătură *f*; ardere *f*, corodare *f*; (*mouthful*) îmbucătură *f*.

biting *adj* ascuţit, usturător; *fig* şfichiuitor.

bitter *adj* amar, dureros; crud, chinuitor; aspru; înverşunat || *s* amar *n*, amărăciune *f*; bere *f* amară.

bizarre *adj* bizar, straniu.

blab *vi* a trăncăni, a cleveti; a bârfi || *s* clevetitor *m*; bârfitor *m* • ~**ber** *vi* a sporovăi.

black *adj* negru; brun; întunecat; închis; supărat; abătut || *s* negru *m*; om *m* de culoare neagră; doliu *n* || *vt* a înnegri; a defăima; ~ **eye** *s* ochi *m* învineţit/umflat; ~ **ice** *s* polei *n*; ~ **market** *s* bursa *f* neagră.

blackberry *s* mură *f*.

blackbird *s* mierlă *f*.

blackboard *s* tablă *f*.

blackcurrant *s* coacăză *f* neagră.

blackhead *s* punct *n* negru.

blackleg *s pej* escroc *m*.

blackmail *s also fig* şantaj *n*.

blackout *s mil* camuflaj *n*; pană *f* de curent electric; *med* leşin *n*, amnezie *f*.

blacksmith *s* fierar *m*; potcovar *m*.

bladder *s* vezică *f*.

blade *s* foaie *f*, frunză *f*; fir *n* (de iarbă); lamă *f*, pană *f*, ic *n*; pală *f*, paletă *f*; pânză *f* (de ferăstrău).

blame *vt* a învinovăţi, a acuza; (*censure*) a blama || *s* mustrare *f*, reproş *n*; vină *f*, învinuire *f*; răspundere *f*.

blanch *vt/vi* a (se) albi.

bland *adj* prevenitor, curtenitor; prietenos; afabil; (*drug*) liniştitor; care nu irită; (*weather*) blând, dulce; stupid, fără haz.

blank *adj* (*empty*) gol, pustiu; liber; curat; (*check*) în alb; (*look*, *expression*) inexpresiv; absorbit; (*page*) nescris; (*outright*) total, complet || *s* (*void*) loc *n*, spaţiu *n* liber; spărtură *f*; ţintă *f*; *metal* bloc *n*, lingou *n*, ţaglă *f*; *min* steril *n*, gol *n*; *econ* formular *n*, blanchetă *f*; *mil* cartuş *n* orb/de exerciţiu; *math* rubrică *f*.

blanket s cuvertură f, pătură f|| vt a acoperi cu o pătură; a stinge, a înăbuși; a cuprinde, a include.

blare vi a urla, a zbiera || s vacarm n; (*trumpet*) sonerie f.

blaspheme vi a blasfema, a huli, a cârti || vt a cârti împotriva (cuiva).

blasphemy s blasfemie f, hulă f.

blast s (*wind*) suflu n, rafală f; vijelie f; (*explosion*) detunătură f, explozie f; distrugere f|| vt (~ hopes, etc) a distruge, a ruina; a arunca în aer, a exploda; fig a blestema || vi a huli, a blasfema; a răsuna.

blatant adj zgomotos, gălăgios; (*obvious*) țipător; ostentativ; (*shameless*) lipsit de jenă; fig strigător la cer, flagrant.

blather s (*chatter*) vorbărie f, vorbe f pl goale, flecăreală f; prostii f pl || vi a vorbi verzi și uscate, a trăncăni; a spune prostii.

blaze s revărsare f de lumină; (*flare*) lumină/culoare f vie; (*large fire*) foc n, flacără f, vâlvătaie f; (*anger*) izbucnire f; fig strălucire f, glorie f|| vt a arde, a pune pe foc; a trâmbița, a da în vileag || vi a arde cu flacără vie; a străluci, a luci; a radia.

blazing adj în flăcări; (*sun*) orbitor, strălucitor; coll furibund.

bleach vt a înălbi, a albi; a vărui; (*hair*) a decolora, a oxigena; a curăța, a spăla || vi a păli || s albire f, decolorare f; decolorant m.

bleak adj (*bare*) gol, pustiu; fără vegetație; (*landscape*) sumbru, deprimant, mohorât, trist; (*prospect*) trist; (*weather*) rece; ofilit; palid; (*wind*) aspru, rece, tăios.

bleat vi (*sheep*) a behăi; fig (*person*) a se plânge, a se văicări || s behăit n.

bleed vi (*lose blood*) a sângera; a fi rănit; a-și vărsa sângele; a muri; a fi jecmănit || vt a lua sânge, a însângera; a răni • ~ing adj also fig care sângerează; rănit.

blemish s cusur n, neajuns n, lipsă f; (*reputation*) pată f rușinoasă, stigmat n; (*fruit*) pată f|| vt a păta, a necinsti, a dezonora.

bleep s semnal n sonor • ~er s pager n.

blend vt a amesteca, a combina, a îmbina; a asorta; (~ colors) a îmbina, a amesteca || vi a se amesteca; a se uni; a se combina, a se îmbina; (~ colors, etc) a se asorta, a se potrivi, a se armoniza; fig a se îmbina || s amestec n, combinație f; îmbinare f; potrivire f, armonie f.

bless vt also fig a binecuvânta, a blagoslovi; (*approve*) a da binecuvântarea; (*exalt*) a ridica în slăvi; a ferici, a face fericit; a fi recunoscător • ~ed adj binecuvântat, care are de toate; fericit; norocos; relig (prea) fericit, slăvit || v * bless • ~ing s binecuvântare f, blagoslovire f; binecuvântare f, noroc n, fericire f; a ~ in disguise partea f bună a unei nenorociri etc.

blight s uscare f; mălură f; mană f; pacoste f|| vt a vătăma; a distruge • ~er s tip m antipatic.

blimp s dirijabil n, zepelin n.

blind adj (*sightless*) orb, nevăzător; obtuz; nechibzuit; neclar; neciteț; (*wall*, etc) orb; mat, nelustruit; bot fără floare, neînflorit || vt a orbi, a lua vederea; a eclipsa || s pl (*roller blinds*) storuri n pl; jaluzele f pl; pretext n, scuză f; phot diafragmă f • ~fold adj/adv cu ochii legați, legat la ochi || vt also fig a lega la ochi || s bandă f (pentru ochi) • ~ness s also fig orbire f.

blink vi (*wink*) a clipi; a privi chiorâș; (*flash*) a sclipi, a

luci || vi a privi printre gene; a închide ochii la; a ocoli || s clipit n, clipire f; privire f furișă; (*flicker*) sclipire f, licărire f.

bliss s fericire f; beatitudine f; extaz n.

blister s bășică f, pustulă f; med vezicator n; emplastru n; tech bulă f de aer, gol n, suflură f|| vt a bășica; a arde, a ustura; med a aplica un vezicator pe; fig a critica aspru/usturător || vi a se bășica.

blizzard s viscol n, furtună f de zăpadă; vifor n, vijelie f.

blob s strop m, picătură f; formă f; a ~ of color o pată f de culoare.

bloc s pol bloc n.

block s (*wood*) butuc n; buștean n; bloc n de piatră, lespede f; (*building*) corp n de case; cvartal n; (*obstruction*) barieră f, obstacol n; carnet n de note; tech scripete m; min bloc n, pilier m; typ clișeu n || vt (*obstruct*) a bloca, a opri, a împiedica; sp a stopa; a bloca; a pune piedici.

bloke s coll tip m.

blond adj blond, bălai || s (*bărbat*) blond m • ~e s/, adj (femeie) blondă, blondină f.

blood s sânge n; neam n, viță f; viață f; omor n; ~ donor s donator de sânge m; ~ group s grupă sanguină f; ~ poisoning s septicemie f; ~ pressure s tensiune arterială f; ~ stream s sânge n; sistem n sanguin n.

bloodcurdling adj înfiorător, care îți dă fiori.

bloodhound s copoi m.

bloodshed s masacru n.

bloodshot adj (*eye*) congestionat, injectat cu sânge.

bloodthirsty adj sângeros, crud, setos de sânge, însetat de sânge.

bloom s înflorire f, floare f; fig culoare f, bujori n pl, roșeață f; fig înflorire f, prosperitate f|| vi a înflori, a fi în floare; fig a înflori, a prospera; in full ~ în (plină) floare • ~er s sl gafă f.

blossom s floare f, inflorescență f; înflorire f|| vi a în-flori; a îmboboci; a se dezvolta.

blot s (*ink*) pată f; fig pată f, stigmat n || vt also fig a păta, a murdări, a mânji; fig a șterge, a spăla.

blotch s (*stain*) pată f; (*mark*) semn n.

blotter s sugativă f.

blouse s bluză f.

blow¹ s (*hit*) lovitură f; to come to ~s a se lua la bătaie.

blow² vi (*wind*) a sufla, a bate; a suna, a răsuna; (*go off*) a exploda, a sări în aer || vt (*fire*) a sufla în, a ațâța; a cânta la; (*inflate*) a umfla || s răsuflare f; suflu n; aut explozie f de cauciuc.

blubber s untură f de balenă || vi pej a plânge cu hohote.

bludgeon s bâtă f; măciucă f|| vt a lovi cu bâta; a ciomăgi.

blue adj albastru; (*azure*) azuriu; vânăt; palid; (*indigo*) învinețit; indecent; (*sad*) abătut; conservator || vt a albăstri; out of the ~ din senin.

blue-collar adj necalificat.

bluish adj albăstrui, albăstriu.

blueprint s plan n, schiță f, proiect n || vt a întocmi un plan.

bluff s (*deception*) bluf n; faleză f|| vt a înșela, a induce în eroare || vi a înșela, a trage o cacialma || adj sincer, direct.

blunder s gafă f, gogomănie f|| vi a face o gafă, a comite o eroare.

blunt adj (*blade*) tocit; (*pencil*) bont; (*object*) contondent, tare; (*person*) direct, necioplit || vt also fig a toci.

blur s formă f confuză, pată f neclară ‖ vt (image) a estompa, a tulbura.

blush vi a roşi ‖ s roşeaţă f.

boa s zool şarpe m boa.

boar s zool vier m; (porc) mistreţ m.

board s scândură f; (meals) masă f; mâncare f, hrană f; poliţă f, raft n; scenă f; (officials) consiliu n; carton n; copertă f; avizier n ‖ vt a acoperi cu scânduri, a pardosi; (lodge) a ţine în pensiune; (ship, plane) a urca pe/la bord.

boast s laudă f de sine; mândrie f ‖ vi a se lăuda, a se făli ‖ vt a lăuda; a dispune de; a se lăuda cu.

boat s ambarcaţiune f; barcă f; luntre f; şalupă f; vas n; corabie f; submarin n.

bob¹ vi (up and down) a ţopăi; (curtsy) a face o reverenţă ‖ s reverenţă f.

bob² vt (~ hair) a tăia scurt; (~ a tail) a scurta.

bobbin s bobină f.

bobsled, bobsleigh s bob n.

bodice s corsaj n.

bodily adv cu totul, în întregime ‖ adj corporal, trupesc, fizic, carnal; ~ **harm** vătămare corporală.

body s corp n, trup n; (corpse) cadavru n; persoană f, individ m, om m; tulpină f; (car) caroserie f; (association) organ n, organizaţie f; (mass) masă f, mulţime f ‖ vt a întruchipa.

bog s mlaştină f • **get ~ged down** vi a se împotmoli • **~gy** adj mlăştinos.

bogus adj fals.

bohemian s/adj boem m.

boil¹ vi a fierbe, a clocoti; a face spume la gură ‖ vt a fierbe, a pune la fiert ‖ s fierbere f; punct n de fierbere.

boil² s med furuncul m.

boisterous adj turbulent, zgomotos, neastâmpărat.

bold adj (daring) îndrăzneţ, curajos; (brash) obraznic; abrupt; stâncos; apăsat; citeţ.

bolster s (pillow) pernă f (de canapea) ‖ vt a sublinia, a susţine; **to ~ up** a susţine, a sprijini.

bolt s săgeată f; fulger n; trăsnet n; zăvor n; lacăt n; fugă f, goană f ‖ vi (run off) a o lua la fugă ‖ vt a zăvorî; (gulp) a înfuleca.

bomb s bombă f ‖ vt a bombarda • **~ard** vt/vi mil, fig a bombarda (cu).

bond s (people) legătură f; (promise) angajament n; fin bon n, titlu n ‖ vt fig (people) a uni ‖ vi (connect) a se lega sufleteşte.

bone s os n, ciolan n; pl schelet n ‖ vt a scoate oasele din.

bonfire s foc n în aer liber.

bonnet s capotă f; bonetă f.

bonus s (money) primă f; gratificaţie f; fig (advantage) bonus n, plus n.

bony adj osos; cu oase.

booby trap s (bomb) capcană f, obiect-capcană n; farsă f.

book s carte f; volum n; broşură f; cânt n; caiet n; listă f; tabel n; inventar n ‖ vt a înregistra; a lua/a elibera bilete; a angaja (un vorbitor etc); (reserve) a rezerva; (order) a comanda.

bookcase s bibliotecă f.

booking s rezervare f.

bookkeeper s contabil m.

booklet s broşură f, cărticică f.

bookmaker s persoană f care ţine registrele de pariuri la curse.

bookmark s semn n de carte.

bookseller s librar m.

bookshop s librărie f.

bookstall s stand n de cărţi.

bookstore s * **bookshop**.

boom s (noise) bubuitură f; (business) avânt n, prosperitate f; naut estacadă f; (microphone) braţ n ‖ vi a bubui; com a fi în plin avânt/creştere.

boomerang s bumerang n.

boon s lucru n foarte util; hatâr n.

boor s necioplit m • **~ishness** s mitocănie f.

boost vt (~ production) a stimula; (~ popularity) a creşte, a spori ‖ s (production) creştere f, sporire f; (economy) creştere f.

boot s (shoe) gheată f; bocanc m; cizmă f; (car) portbagaj n ‖ vi a lovi cu piciorul; a da afară.

booth s tarabă f; dugheană f; baracă f; chioşc n; cabină f.

booze s coll alcool n, băuturi f pl alcoolice ‖ vi a o face lată.

border s (boundary) hotar n; graniţă f, frontieră f; limită f, margine f; mal n, ţărm n; (edging) bordură f; chenar n ‖ vi (be next to) a (se) mărgini (cu).

bore¹ vt (~ a hole) a sfredeli, a perfora; (~ a well) a fora; (~ metal) a aleza ‖ s sfredelitură f; alezaj n.

bore² vt a plictisi, a enerva ‖ s muncă f plicticoasă; persoană f plictisitoare • **~dom** s plictiseală f.

boring adj plicticos, anost, plictisitor.

born adj născut; înnăscut.

borough s orăşel n; arondisment n; circumscripţie f electorală.

borrow vt a împrumuta, a lua cu împrumut; a-şi însuşi • **~ing** s împrumut n.

bosom s piept n, sâni m pl; fig sân m.

boss s şef m; patron m, stăpân m ‖ vt a fi şeful, a conduce ‖ vi a face pe şeful.

botany s botanică f.

both adj amândoi, ambii; cei doi; amândouă, ambele; cele două ‖ pron amândoi; ambii; cei doi; amândouă, ambele, cele două.

bother vt a plictisi; a necăji; a bate la cap; a supăra ‖ s necaz n.

bottle s sticlă f; flacon n; butelie f; băutură f ‖ vt a îmbutelia.

bottom s fund n; capăt n; poale f pl; bază f, fundament n; fond n, miez n ‖ adj de la fund, de jos; din spate; fundamental, esenţial • **~ less** adj fără fund.

bough s ramură f, creangă f.

boulder s stâncă f ascuţită, bolovan m.

boulevard s bulevard n.

bounce vi a sări; a ricoşa; a sălta; a se lăuda ‖ s salt n, săritură f; ricoşeu n; izbitură f; fanfaronadă f.

bound¹ adj legat, ataşat, prins; obligat, silit; **I'm ~ to say** admit, trebuie să spun/recunosc; **be ~ for** vt (person) a fi în drum spre, (train, etc) a avea destinaţia; **~ for** adj cu destinaţia.

bound² vi (leap) a sări ‖ s săritură f, salt n.

bound³ vt a limita, a mărgini • **~s** s pl limite f pl • **~ary** s frontieră f, hotar n, graniţă f; limită f; margine f.

bounty s generozitate f; (prize) premiu n; (gift) dar n; econ (reward) primă f de export.

bouquet s buchet n.

bourgeois s burghez m ‖ adj burghez.

bout s (illness) atac n, criză f; acces n; perioadă f; (boxing) competiţie f.

bow¹ vi a se îndoi; a se încovoia, a se apleca; a se

înclina; a se supune || *vt* a înclina; a pleca fruntea || *s* aplecare *f*, plecăciune *f*.

bow² *s* (*archery*) arc *n*; arcuş *n*; curcubeu *n*; (*ribbon*) fundă *f*.

bow³ *s naut* provă *f*, partea *f* dinainte.

bowels *s pl anat* intestine *n pl*.

bowl¹ *s* vas *n*; vază *f*; strachină *f*; castron *n*; lighean *n*; cupă *f*.

bowl² *vt sp* a lansa/arunca mingea • ~**ing** *s sp* joc *n* de bile.

box¹ *s* cutie *f*; tabacheră *f*; casetă *f*; ladă *f*; boxă *f*; bancă *f*; lojă *f*; gheretă *f*; cabană *f*; cadou *n* || *vi* a pune într-o cutie, a împacheta.

box² *vi sp* a boxa, a face box.

boy *s* băiat *m*; tânăr *m*; fiu *m*, fecior *m*.

boycott *vt* a boicota || *s* boicot *n*, boicotare *f*.

boyfriend *s* prieten *m*.

boyhood *s* copilărie *f*; adolescenţă *f*.

bra *s* sutien *n*.

brace *s* (*dental*) aparat *n* dentar; aparat *n* ortopedic || *vt* a susţine, a consolida.

bracelet *s* brăţară *f*.

bracing *adj* reconfortant.

bracken *s* ferigă *f*.

bracket *vt* a pune între paranteze || *s* suport *n*; paranteză *f* rotundă/dreaptă; **in** ~**s** între paranteze; **age/ income** ~ *s* tranşă *f* de vârstă/venit.

brag *vi* a se lăuda, a se făli, a face paradă de.

braid *s* cosiţă *f*; panglică *f*; împletitură *f*; şnur *n*; şiret *n*; tresă *f* || *vt* a împleti; a lega cu o panglică.

braille *s*/*adj* braille *n*.

brain *s* creier *n* • ~**s** *s pl* inteligenţă *f*, minte *f* • ~**child** *s* idee *f* personală, invenţie *f* personală • ~**teaser** *s coll* problemă *f* grea • ~**wash** *vt fig* a spăla creierul; a îndoctrina • ~**y** *adj* isteţ, deştept, cu cap.

braise *vt* (*meat, etc*) a fierbe înăbuşit.

brake *s* frână *f*; piedică || *vt* a frâna; a împiedica.

bramble *s* (*plant*) mărăcine *m*; (*fruit*) mură *f*, dudă *f*.

bran *s* tărâţe *f pl*.

branch *s* (*bough*) creangă *f*, ramură *f*; ramificaţie *f*; afluent *n*; braţ *n* de râu; (*local office*) filială *f*, sucursală *f*; (*area*) domeniu *n* || *vt* (*divide*) a împărţi, a diviza || *vi* (*bifurcate*) a se ramifica; a se lărgi, a se întinde.

brand *s* marcă *f*, clasă *f*, sort *n*; semn *n*, stigmat *n*; tăciune *m* aprins || *vt* a arde cu fierul roşu, a însemna; a stigmatiza • ~**name** *s* marcă *f* de fabrică.

brandish *vt* a roti (armele) deasupra capului (în semn de ameninţare/victorie).

brandy *s* coniac *n*.

brass *s* (*metal*) alamă *f*, bronz *n*; *mus* **the** ~ instrumente de suflat din alamă, alămuri; ~ **band** *s* fanfară *f*.

brassiere *s* brasieră *f*; sutien *n*.

brat *s* puşti *m*; ştrengar *m*, copil *m* neastâmpărat.

brave *adj* brav, curajos, viteaz; frumos; minunat, splendid || *vt* a brava, a înfrunta; a sfida; a provoca.

bravo *interj* bravo.

brawl *s* tărăboi *n*, ceartă *f*, încăierare *f*.

brawn *s* muşchi *m* • ~**y** *adj* muşchiulos, cu muşchi.

brazen *adj* (*person*) obraznic, insolent; (*lie*) sfruntat; ~ **it out** *vt* a susţine ceva cu neruşinare.

bray *s* răget *n* (de măgar) || *vi* (*donkey*) a rage.

breach *s* (~ *of a law*) infracţiune *f*, violare *f*; (~ *of a promise*) încălcare *f*; ~ **of contract** încălcarea con-

tractului; deschizătură *f*, breşă *f* || *vt* (~ *an agreement*) a încălca; a face o breşă în.

bread *s* pâine *f*; hrană *f*; mâncare *f* || *vt* a găti cu pesmet.

breadth *s* lăţime *f*, lărgime *f*; mărinimie *f*, generozitate *f*.

break, broke, broken *vt* (*smash*) a sparge, a sfărâma; (*sever*) a frânge; (*rupture*) a rupe; a strica; (*shatter*) a zdrobi; a desface; a renunţa la; a îmblânzi, a domestici; (*destroy*) a distruge, a ruina || *vi* a se sparge, a se sfărâma; a se frânge; a se rupe; (*break down*) a se strica; (*stop*) a se opri; a se întrerupe; ~ **into** (~ *a house*) a pătrunde prin efracţie, (~ *a safe, etc*) a forţa; ~ **up** a (se) sfărâma || *s* (*pause*) pauză *f*; ruptură *f*; întrerupere *f* • ~**able** *adj* casabil, fragil • ~**age** *s* spargere *f* • ~**down** *s* pană *f*, (*mental*) depresiune *f* nervoasă; analiză *f* • ~**er** *s* (*wave*) val *n* uriaş • ~**through** *s* descoperire *f* importantă.

breakfast *s* micul dejun *n*, gustare *f* de dimineaţă • *vt* a lua micul dejun.

breast *s* piept *n*; pieptar *n*; platoşă *f* || *vt* a da piept cu, a înfrunta • ~**stroke** *s* bras *n* (la înot).

breath *s* respiraţie *f*, răsuflare *f*, suflu *n* • ~**alyze** *vt* a supune testului pentru alcoolemie • ~**alyzer** *s* aparat *n* pentru măsurarea alcoolemiei.

breathe *vi* a respira || *vt* a respira; a duhni a; ~ **in** *vi* a inspira || *vt* a aspira; ~ **out** a expira • ~**r** *s coll* moment *n* de repaus/odihnă.

breed *s* rasă *f*, specie *f* || *vt* (~ *animals, plants*) a creşte; *fig* (*suspicion*) a naşte, a crea || *vi* a se reproduce.

breeze *s* adiere *f*, boare *f*; ceartă *f* || *vi* a adia, a sufla lin.

brevity *s* scurtime *f*; laconism *n*.

brew *vt* a fierbe, a fabrica (bere); a pune la cale, a urzi || *vi* a fabrica bere etc; a urzi; a se pregăti; a se apropia.

bribe *s* mită *f* || *vt* a mitui.

brick *s* cărămidă *f*; bucată *f*; tabletă *f*; brichetă *f* || *vt* a construi din cărămidă.

bride *s* mireasă *f*.

bridge¹ *s* pod *n*; punte *f*; ponton *n*; covertă *f*; pasarelă *f* || *vt* a construi un pod/o punte; a împăca, a concilia.

bridge² *s* (*cards*) bridge *n*.

bridle *s* căpăstru *n*, frâu *n*.

brief *adj* scurt, concis || *s* rezumat *n*, compendiu *n* || *vt* a rezuma; a da ultimele instrucţiuni cuiva.

brier *s bot* măceş *m*.

brigade *s* brigadă *f*.

brigadier *s* general *m* de brigadă.

bright *adj* strălucitor; luminos; senin; sclipitor; lucitor; viu; limpede, clar; ager; minunat; grozav; vesel; optimist; favorabil.

brilliant *adj* strălucitor; luminos; splendid; măreţ; eminent || *s* briliant *n*.

brim *s* margine *f* || *vi also fig* (**with**) a fi plin de.

brine *s* saramură *f*.

bring *vt* a aduce; a lua, a duce; a cauza, a produce; a intenta; ~ **about** a cauza, a produce; ~ **around** a însănătoşi; ~ **back** (*object*) a restitui, (*person*) a aduce înapoi, a reaminti, a restabili.

brink *s* margine *f*; **on the** ~ **of** pe marginea, la un pas de.

brisk *adj* vioi, iute; (*tone*) hotărât.

bristle *s* păr *m* || *vi also fig* a se zbârli.

Britain *s* Marea Britanie *f*.

British *adj* britanic; **the** ~ *s pl* britanicii *m pl*.

brittle *adj* fragil.

broad *adj* (*wide*) larg, lat, (*extensive*) întins; spaţios; (*obvious*) vădit, clar; tolerant; principal, general ||

adv (openly) pe faţă, deschis; complet • ~**minded** adj liberal.

broadcast vt a transmite (prin radio); a difuza || vi a vorbi, a cânta (la radio) || adj radiodifuzat || s emisiune f radiofonică; program n de radio.

broccoli s bot broccoli n.

brochure s broşură f, prospect n.

broken adj sfărâmat, spart, dărâmat, distrus; nerespectat; întrerupt, întretăiat • ~**hearted** adj deznădăjduit; cu inima frântă/zdrobită, zdrobit (de durere).

broker s agent m de bursă; **insurance** ~ agent m de asigurări • ~**age** s curtaj n.

bronchitis s med bronşită f.

bronze s bronz n || adj (culoare) bronz.

brooch s broşă f.

brood s (animal) pui m pl clociţi || vi fig ~ **over/about** smth a medita asupra, a se frământa.

brook[1] vt a suferi, a suporta; a accepta.

brook[2] s geog pârâu n.

broom s mătură f || vt a mătura.

broth s supă f de carne.

brothel s bordel n.

brother s frate m; confrate m; tovarăş m.

brow s (forehead) frunte f; sprânceană f; (hill) vârf n.

brown adj cafeniu, maron || s hârtie f de ambalaj.

browse vt/vi (book) a răsfoi; (animal) a paşte.

bruise s vânătaie f || vt (~ skin, arms) a-şi învineţi; (~ fruit) a bate; fig (~ pride) a jigni, a călca în picioare.

brunch s gustare f (la ora 10-11).

brunette s brunetă f.

brush s perie f; pensulă f; tufiş n || s periat n || vt a peria; a atinge uşor.

brusque adj brusc.

Brussels s Bruxelles n.

brutal adj brutal • ~**ize** vt a brutaliza.

brute s brută f || adj (force) brutal.

brutish adj animalic; crud, brutal.

bubble s băşică f, bulă f; himeră f || vi a face băşici.

buccaneer s pirat m; aventurier m.

Bucharest s Bucureşti m.

buck vi (horse) a azvârli din picioare || s (animal) mascul; coll dolar m; **to pass the** ~ coll a nu-şi asuma responsabilitatea.

bucket s găleată f.

buckle s cataramă f || vt a încheia cu cataramă.

buckwheat s bot hrişcă f.

bud s mugur m || vi a înmuguri.

budge vt a urni || vi a (se) mişca.

budget s buget n.

buffalo s bivol m.

buffer s tampon n; comp memorie f tampon/amortizoare.

buffet[1] s lovitură f, pumn m || vt a lovi.

buffet[2] s bufet n; bar n.

bug s ploşniţă f; (germ) microb m; microfon n || vt (~ a room) a instala dispozitive de ascultare; (annoy) a necăji, a irita; ~ **off!** şterge-o!, cară-te!.

bugger s vulg tâmpit.

bugle s goarnă f.

build s construcţie f || vt a construi, a clădi; a crea; a făuri treptat; a aduna • ~**ing** s clădire f; construire f, făurire f.

built-in adj (integral) inerent, esenţial; component; **a** ~ **cupboard** dulap în perete; **a** ~ **disadvantage** un dezavantaj inerent.

bulb s bot bulb m; elec bec n.

Bulgaria s Bulgaria f • ~**n** s (people) bulgar m || adj bulgar.

bulge s cocoaşă f || vi (with) a fi umflat (de).

bulk adj angro || s (mass) volum n; (person) corpolent; **in** ~ econ angro.

bull s zool taur m; mascul m.

bulldog s zool buldog m.

bulldozer s buldozer n.

bullet s glonţ n • ~**proof** adj blindat, antiglonţ.

bulletin s buletin n.

bullion s lingou n; **gold** ~ lingou n de aur.

bullish adj econ de creştere, în creştere; (upbeat) entuziast, optimist.

bull's eye s centrul n ţintei.

bully s tiran m || vt a tiraniza, a brutaliza.

bum s vagabond m.

bumble vi coll a mormăi.

bumblebee s ento bondar m.

bump s cocoaşă f; ciocnire f; zgomot n înăbuşit || vt (head) a izbi; aut a ciocni || vi (into) a da peste, coll a se întâlni nas în nas cu (cineva) • ~**er** s pahar n plin, cupă f plină; aut bară f de protecţie; tech amortizor n || adj foarte bogat; neobişnuit de mare, record • ~**ily** adv cu smucituri • ~**y** adj (road) cu hârtoape

bumptious adj îngâmfat.

bun s coc n; chiflă f.

bunch s mănunchi n, legătură f; buchet n de flori; ciorchine m || vt/vi a (se) înmănunchia.

bundle s legătură f; teanc n || vt a lega, a înmănunchia.

bungalow s bungalou n.

bungle vt a strica, a deteriora.

bunion s ceapă f.

bunk s cuşetă f, pat n.

bunker s mil buncăr n; (coal) rezervor n.

bunny s zool iepuraş m.

buoy s geamandură f; ~ **up** vt a susţine.

burden s povară f, sarcină f, greutate f, răspundere f || vt a încărca; a asupri.

bureau s (desk) comodă f, scrin n; (room) birou n.

bureaucracy s birocraţie f, birocratism n; birocraţii m pl.

bureaucrat s birocrat m.

burglar s spărgător m, hoţ m.

burial s înmormântare f.

burn vt (destroy by fire) a arde; a cauteriza; (smart) a ustura; a prăji; (singe) a pârli || vi (be on fire) a arde, a fi aprins; a dogori; a lumina; a avea febră || s arsură f; semn n cu fierul roşu.

burp s râgâială f || vi a râgâi.

burrow s vizuină f || vi a săpa o vizuină; fig a cerceta.

burst vi a plesni, a crăpa; a exploda || vt a arunca în aer; a distruge || s explozie f; ropot n; izbucnire f; apariţie f.

bury vt a îngropa, a înmormânta; a ascunde, a tăinui.

bus s autobuz n.

bush s tufă f, tufiş n; coadă f stufoasă.

business s (transaction) afacere f; tranzacţie f; (commerce) comerţ n; (store) magazin n; chilipir n; (concern) ocupaţie f; (matter) chestiune f, (issue) problemă f; obligaţie f, datorie f; ~ **card** s carte f de vizită; ~ **manager** s director comercial; **on** ~ cu treabă • ~**like** adj de afaceri; practic; metodic; calculat; precis; expeditiv • ~**man** s om m de afaceri; comerciant m.

bust[1] s anat piept m; (statue) bust n.

bust[2] adj coll (broken) terminat; **to go** ~ a da faliment || vt coll a sparge.

bustle *vi* a se agita || *s* (*activity*) agitație *f*.
busy *adj* harnic, activ; ocupat, prins cu; aglomerat; plin, încărcat; plictisitor, sâcâitor, insistent || *vt* a da de lucru cuiva.
but *conj* dar, însă; ci; și; totuși, cu toate acestea; fără să; decât; fără a || *adv* numai, doar || *prep* (în) afară de, cu excepția || *pron* care să nu.
butane *s* butan *n*.
butcher *s* măcelar *m*; călău *m*; lucrător *m* prost || *vt* a înjunghia, a sacrifica; a ucide, a omorî, a măcelări; a masacra.
butler *s* majordom *m*.
butt[1] *s* (*of a cigarette*) muc *n*; (*of a gun*) pat *n* de pușcă; (*for wine, water etc*) butoi *n*; (*target*) țintă *f*.
butt[2] *vt* a lovi cu capul; **to ~ in on smb** *vi* a întrerupe pe cineva.
butter *s* unt *n*; lingușire *f*, lingușeală *f* || *vt* a unge cu unt.
buttercup *s bot* pintenul *m* cocoșului.
butterfly *s* fluture *m*; (stil de înot) fluture *m*; om *m* superficial; femeie *f* frumoasă.
buttocks *s pl* (*of a person*) fese *f pl*; (*of an animal*) crupă *f*.
button *s* nasture *m*, bumb *m*; buton *n*, pastilă *f* || *vt* a coase nasturi; a încheia cu nasturi, a încheia nasturii.
buttress *s* (*arch*) contrafort *n* || *vt* (*bolster*) a consolida.
buxom *adj* (*women*) durdulie, dolofană.
buy *vt* (*purchase*) a cumpăra; a corupe, a mitui; a face cumpărături • **~back** *s* revânzare *f*; *coll* (*believe*) a da crezare • **~er** *s* cumpărător *m*, achizitor *m*.
buzz *vi* a zumzăi || *s* zumzăit *n*.
by *prep* lângă, foarte aproape; alături de; în preajma; până la; prin; cu ajutorul; prin mijlocul || *adv* alături, aproape, în apropiere; **~ and ~** curând (după aceea); treptat, încetul cu încetul; **~ and large** în general (vorbind).
bye-bye *interj coll* pa!.
by(e)-law *s* dispoziție *f* executivă.
by-election *s* alegeri *f pl* parțiale.
bypass *s* ocolire *f* || *vt* (**~ a town**) a ocoli; (**~ a subject**) a evita; *med* **~ operation** *s* grefă *f* vasculară.
by-product *s* derivat *n*; *fig* consecință *f*.
bystander *s* spectator *m*.
byte *s comp* bit *m*.
byword *s* proverb *n*, zicală *f*; (*epitome*) întruchipare *f*, personificare *f*.

C

C, c (litera) C, c; *mus* (nota) do.
cab *s* cabrioletă *f*; birjă *f*; birjar *m*; taxi *n*.
cabal *s* conspirație *f*, complot *n*; clică *f*, camarilă *f* politică.
cabaret *s* (spectacol de) cabaret *n*.
cabbage *s* varză *f*; căpățână *f* de varză; om *m* insensibil/ nepăsător.
cabin *s* casă *f* simplă; bordei *n*; baracă *f* || *vi* a înghesui.
cabinet *s* dulap *n*; vitrină *f*; *pol* cabinet *n* de miniștri.
cable *s* cablu *n*, otgon *n*, frânghie *f* groasă; parâmă *f*; cablogramă *f*; telegramă *f* || *vt* a fixa cu un cablu; a telegrafia || *vi* a telegrafia • **~ TV** *s* cablu TV *n*.
cacao *s bot* cacao *f*.
cackle *vi* (*of a hen*) a cotcodăci; (*of a person*) a trăncăni.
cactus *s* (*pl* **–tuses/ti**) cactus *m*.
cad *s* mojic *m*, bădăran *m*; nemernic *m* • **~ish** *adj* (*person*) infam.

caddie *s* cutie *f* pentru ceai.
cadge *vt coll* a cerși • **~r** *s* cerșetor *m*.
cadence *s* cadență *f*.
cadet *s mil*, *naut* cadet *m*.
cafe *s* ceainărie *f*; cafe *f*, restaurant *n*; bar *n*; cafenea *f*.
cafeteria *s* bufet *n* cu autoservire.
caffeine *s* cafeină *f*.
cage *s* colivie *f*; cușcă *f*; închisoare *f*; (cabină de) lift *n* || *vt* a băga într-o colivie.
cagey *adj coll* (*reticent*) rezervat; (*wary*) precaut; (*evasive*) vag, ocolit.
cajole *vt* a măguli.
cake *s* prăjitură *f*; cozonac *m*; chec *n*; tort *n*; turtă *f*; (*bar*) bucată *f*; (*lump*) bulgăre *m*; brichetă *f*; crustă *f* || *vi* (*encrust*) a se întări, a prinde coajă; a se lipi de.
calamine *s miner* calamină *f*.
calamity *s* calamitate *f*, nenorocire *f*.
calcium *s* calciu *n*.
calculate *vt* a calcula, a socoti, a număra; a chibzui; a presupune; a-și închipui; a prevedea || *vi* a calcula; a număra.
calculating *adj* precaut, prevăzător.
calculation *s* calcul *n*, socoteală *f*; prevedere *f*, estimare *f*.
calculator *s* calculator *n*.
calculus *s* (*pl* **calculi/-es**) *med* calcul *m*, piatră *f*.
calendar *s* calendar *n*; almanah *n*; listă *f*, tabel *n*; catalog *n* || *vt* a trece în calendar.
calf[1] *s zool* vițel *m*.
calf[2] *s anat* pulpa *f* piciorului.
caliber *s* calibru *n*.
call *vt* a chema; (*name*) a numi; a spune; (*term*) a denumi; (*baptize*) a boteza; (*summon*) a convoca; a atrage (atenția); a deștepta; a considera; (*phone*) a telefona cuiva || *vi* (*shout*) a striga; a mieuna; (*yell*) a urla; (*phone*) a telefona; **~ on** a trece (pe la cineva) || *s* chemare *f*; strigăt *n*; (*appeal*) apel *n*; invitație *f*; propunere *f*; (*request*) solicitare *f*; (*phone call*) convorbire *f* telefonică; somație *f*; cauză *f*, motiv *n*.
calligraphy *s* caligrafie *f*.
callous *adj* (*skin*) îngroșat, bătătorit; *fig* împietrit, aspru, dur; crud.
callow *adj* (*inexperienced*) lipsit de experiență.
calm *adj* (*still*) calm; frumos, senin; (*relaxed*) liniștit; (*cool*) cu sânge rece || *s* (*peace*) calm *n*, acalmie *f*; liniște *f*, pace *f* || *vi* (*quiet down*) a calma, a liniști.
calorie *s* calorie *f*.
calumniate *vt* a calomnia.
calumny *s* calomnie *f*.
camcorder *s* cameră *f* de luat vederi.
camel *s zool* cămilă *f*; macara *f*.
camellia *s bot* camelie *f*.
camera *s* aparat *n* de fotografiat; cameră *f* de chibzuință; cameră *f* de televiziune.
camomile *s bot* mușețel *n*.
camouflage *s* camuflaj *n* || *vt* a camufla.
camp[1] *s* (*site*) lagăr *n*, tabără *f*; bivuac *n* || *vi* a campa, a ridica o tabără.
camp[2] *adj* afectat, efeminat.
campaign *s* campanie *f* || *vi* **~ (for/against)** a face campanie (pentru/împotriva).
camphor *s* camfor *n*.
camping *s* drumeție *f*; excursie *f*; camping *n*; campare *f*; campament *n*.
campus *s* cetate *f* universitară, campus *n*.

camshaft *s aut* arbore *m* cu came.

can[1] *v mod* a putea, a fi în stare, a fi capabil; a şti, a se pricepe; a fi posibil, a fi cu putinţă; a avea voie.

can[2] *s (oil)* bidon *n*; canistră *f*; *(beer, fruit)* cutie *f* ‖ *vt* a conserva, a pune în cutii de conserve • ~**ned** *adj* conservat.

Canada *s* Canada *f*.

Canadian *s* canadian(ă) *m*, *f* ‖ *adj* canadian.

canal *s* canal *n*; tub *n*; duct *n*.

canary *s zool* canar *m*.

Canberra *s* Canberra.

cancel *vt* a şterge, a radia; a anula; a rezilia; a neutraliza; a compensa ‖ *s* refacere *f* a unei pagini, retipărire *f*.

cancer *s* cancer *n*, carcinom *n*; *(blight)* pacoste *f*, năpastă *f*; *(bane)* blestem *n*.

candelabrum *s* (*pl* **candelabra**) candelabru *n*.

candid *adj* candid, sincer; ~ **camera** *s* camera *f* ascunsă.

candidacy *s* candidatură *f*.

candidate *s* candidat *m*; pretendent *m*.

candle *s* lumânare *f*; watt *m*.

candor *s* sinceritate *f*.

candy *s* zahăr *n* candel; bomboană *f*; drops *n* ‖ *vt* a fierbe în zahăr; a zaharisi ‖ *vi* a se zaharisi.

cane *s* trestie *f*, stuf *n*; baston *n*; arac *m* ‖ vt a bate, a biciui.

canine *adj* (rasă) canină ‖ *s* (dinte) canin *m*.

canister *s* cutie *f* de tablă; canistră *f*.

cannabis *s* cânepă *f*, marijuana *f*.

cannibal *s* canibal *m*.

cannon *s* tun *n*.

canny *adj* *(clever)* abil, priceput.

canoe s canoe *n*.

canon s canon *n*; regulă *f*.

canopy *s* *(bed)* baldachin *n*; *(chair)* învelitoare *f*; *(branches, trees)* boltă *f*.

cantankerous *adj* *(irritable)* arţăgos; certăreţ.

canteen *s* *(restaurant)* cantină *f*; gamelă *f*.

canter *s* galop *n* mic ‖ *vi* a merge în galop mic.

canton *s* canton *n*.

cantor *s* cantor *m*.

canvas *s* pânză *f* groasă.

canvass *vi pol* (~ *a person*) a umbla după voturi; *(ask an opinion)* a face un sondaj.

canyon *s geog* canion *n*.

cap *s* şapcă *f*; beretă *f*; bonetă *f*; pălărie *f*; înveliş *n*; capac *n*; calotă *f*; şef *m* ‖ *vt* a pune cuiva şapca etc pe cap; *(cover)* a înveli; *(top)* a încununa; a întrece; a limita, a restricţiona.

capability *s* *(ability)* pricepere *f*; *(capacity)* capacitate *f*; aptitudine *f*.

capable *adj* capabil; priceput; competent; eficient.

capacious *adj* încăpător, spaţios.

capacity *s* *(limit)* capacitate *f*; *(ability)* aptitudine *f*.

cape[1] *s* *(cloak)* pelerină *f*; capă *f*.

cape[2] *s geog* promontoriu *n*; cap *n*.

caper *s cul* caperă *f*; *(jump)* salt *n*, tumbă *f*; *(joke)* poznă *f*, ştrengărie *f*; escapadă *f* ‖ *vi (frolic)* a zburda; a face giumbuşlucuri.

capital *s econ* *(funds)* capital *n*; venit *n*; *(city)* capitală *f*; majusculă *f* ‖*adj econ (principal)* principal; excelent; ~ **assets** fonduri fixe; ~ **flight** exod al capitalului; ~ **goods** mijloace de producţie; ~ **letter** majusculă *f*; ~ **market** piaţă financiară.

capitalism *s* capitalism *n*.

capitalist *s* capitalist *m*.

capitalization *s econ* capitalizare *f*.

capitalize *vt* a scrie cu majuscule; *econ* a capitaliza.

capitulate *vi* a capitula.

capricious *adj* capricios.

Capricorn *s astrol* Capricorn *m*.

capsicum *s bot* ardei *m*.

capsize *vt/vi* a (se) răsturna, a (se) da peste cap.

capsule *s* capsulă *f*; **space** ~ capsulă cosmică.

captain *s* conducător *m*, şef *m*; comandant *m*; căpitan *m* ‖ *vt* a fi căpitanul (echipei).

caption *s* legendă *f*; *(title)* subtitlu *n*.

captivate *vt* a captiva, a fermeca.

captive *s/adj* captiv *m*, prizonier *m*.

captivity *s* captivitate *f*.

capture *s* captură *f*; capturare *f*; pradă *f*, trofeu *n* ‖ *vt* a prinde, a captura; a capta.

car *s* maşină *f*, automobil *n*; autoturism *n*; vagon *n*; cabină *f* (de lift).

caramel *s* caramel *n*.

carat *s* carat *n*.

caravan *s* caravană *f*, căruţă *f* cu coviltir.

caraway *s bot* chimen *n*.

carabiner *s* carabinier *m*.

carbohydrates *s pl* hidrocarburi *f pl*.

carbon *s (element)* carbon *n*; ~ **copy** copie *f* cu indigo; *fig* copie *f* fidelă.

carbuncle *s* furuncul *n*, buboi *n*; granat *n*.

carburetor *s* carburator *n*.

carcass *s (animal)* hoit *n*.

card *s* carte *f* de joc; *pl* (joc de) cărţi *f*; carnet *n*; agendă *f*; *(business ~)* carte *f* de vizită; fişă *f*; tichet *n*; bilet *n*; cartonaş *n*; *(ID)* buletin *n* de identitate; felicitare *f*; ~ **phone** *s* telefon *n* cu cartelă; **phone** ~ cartel telefonică • ~**board** *s* carton *n* • **post**~ *s* carte *f* poştală.

cardiac *adj* cardiac; ~ **arrest** *s* stop *n* cardiac.

cardigan *s* vestă/haină *f* tricotată, cardigan *n*.

cardinal *adj* cardinal ‖ *s relig* cardinal *m*.

care *s (nursing)* grijă *f*, îngrijire *f*; *(trouble)* supărare *f*; *(anxiety)* nelinişte *f*; *(attention)* atenţie *f*; *(caution)* prevedere *f* ‖ *vi (look after)* a se îngriji, a avea grijă de; *(mind)* a-i păsa; ~ **about** a-i păsa (de); ~ **for** a avea grijă (de), a-i plăcea (ceva).

career *s* carieră *f*, *(profession)* profesiune *f*; progres *n*; viaţă *f*, *(livelihood)* existenţă *f*; goană *f*, viteză *f*; galop *n* ‖ *vi* a goni, a zbura.

careful *adj (gentle)* atent; *(wary)* prudent; *(thorough)* minuţios, migălos, scrupulos.

careless *adj* fără griji; *(insensitive)* nepăsător; neatent; *(casual)* neglijent; *(sloppy)* indolent; uşuratic; firesc, natural.

caress *vt* a mângâia ‖ *s* mângâiere *f*.

caretaker *s* gardian *m*, paznic *m*.

cargo *s* încărcătură *f*.

caricature *s* caricatură *f*.

caries *s pl* carie *f* (dentară).

caring *adj* protector, ocrotitor; atent, prevenitor.

carnage *s* măcel *n*.

carnal *adj* carnal, trupesc.

carnation *s bot* garoafă *f*.

carnival *s* carnaval *n*

carnivorous *adj* carnivor.

carol *s mus (Christmas)* colind *n*, cântec *n* de Crăciun.

carousal *s* chef *n*, zaiafet *n*.

carpenter *s* *(construction)* dulgher *m*; *(furniture)* tâmplar *m*.

carpentry s tâmplărie f.

carpet s covor n; carpetă f || vt a aşterne cu covoare; a acoperi (cu flori etc).

carriage s (coach) trăsură f; caleaşcă f, echipaj n; vagon n; vagonet n; transport n; cărăuşie f; ţinută f, alură f; aer n, înfăţişare f; executare f.

carrier s com transportator m; med purtător m; ~ **bag** s sacoşă f; ~ **pigeon** s porumbel m mesager.

carrion s hoit n.

carrot s bot morcov m.

carry vt (bear) a duce, a purta, a căra; (move) a transporta; (support) a sprijini, a susţine; a întreţine; a răspândi, (convey) a transmite; a dispune de; (contain) a conţine, a cuprinde; math a reporta; (~ a magazine) a tipări, a publica; a difuza; (involve) a atrage după sine; a impune; a forţa; (stock) a vinde, a ţine; mil a cuceri || vi (reach) a ajunge până la o anumită distanţă; (be pregnant) a fi însărcinată || s distanţă f; sonoritate f; traiectorie f; ~ **out/through** vi a duce la bun sfârşit, a executa (o treabă).

cart s căruţă f, car n; furgon n; cărucior n de transport; roabă f || vt a duce cu căruţa.

cartilage s anat cartilaj n.

cartography s cartografie f.

cartographer s cartograf m.

carton s cutie f de carton; (of cream, yogurt) borcan n; (of milk) cutie f din carton.

cartoon s desen n umoristic; bandă f desenată; (film) desene n pl animate.

cartridge s (gun, pen) cartuş n; phot rolfilm n.

carve vt/vi a tăia, a ciopli; a sculpta, a grava.

cascade s cascadă f.

case[1] s caz n, întâmplare f; incident n; accident n; (situation) situaţie f; problemă f; (law) proces n; pacient m; om m ciudat.

case[2] s (luggage) valiză f; (crate) cutie f; (box) ladă f; (holder) recipient n.

cash s bani m pl; bani m pl gheaţă || vt a încasa; a schimba în bani; a plăti (în numerar) • ~**ier** s casier m || vt a concedia; a elimina.

cashmere s caşmir n.

casing s (covering) înveliş n, învelitoare f; (door) toc n; cercevea f; (carapace) carcasă f, (shell) înveliş n; anvelopă f.

casino s cazinou n.

cask s butoi n.

casket s (for jewel) casetă f, cutie f; (coffin) sicriu n.

casserole s cratiţă f, tocăniţă f.

cassette s casetă f; phot film m.

cassock s sutană f.

cast s (throw) aruncare f; risc n; şansă f; tech matriţă f; thea distribuţie f; (look) înfăţişare f, aspect n; colorit n, nuanţă f; (type) expresie f, mină f; model n; înclinare f || vt (toss) a arunca; a da (votul); (shed) a lepăda; (spread) a răspândi; a îndepărta; tech a turna (în forme etc); thea a distribui; ~ **away** s naufragiat m.

castanets s pl castaniete f pl.

caste s castă f.

castigate vt (criticize) a critica aspru; (reprimand) a înfiera, a blama.

castle s castel n; turn n (la şah) || vi a face rocadă.

castor oil s ulei n de ricin.

castrate vt a castra.

casual adj (indifferent, relaxed) dezinvolt, nepăsător;

nepoliticos, nesimţit; întâmplător; (dress) comod, sport; (work/er) temporar.

casualty s mort m, victimă f; rănit m; accidentat m.

cat s pisică f; felină f; pisica f cu-nouă-cozi; fig femeie f falsă; individ m, tip m || vt a bate cu gârbaciul.

cataclism s cataclism n.

catacomb s catcombă f.

catalogue s catalog n.

catalyst s also fig catalizator n.

catamaran s catamaran n.

catapult s praştie f || vt also fig a catapulta.

cataract s med cataractă f.

catarrh s med catar n, guturai n.

catastrophe s catastrofă f.

catch, caught, caught vt (~ a bus) a prinde, a apuca; (~ a disease) a molipsi; fig a cuceri; a reţine; (understand) a pricepe; a captura; a se îmbolnăvi de; (hunt) a vâna; (fish) a pescui; (discover a mistake, etc) a descoperi || vi (snag) a se prinde, a se agăţa; (~ a infection) a fi molipsitor, a se răspândi; a se aprinde || s (act of catching) prindere f, apucare f; capturare f; captură f, pradă f; câştig n; venit n; folos n; (snag) capcană f, şiretlic n; pauză f, întrerupere f, oprire f.

categorical adj categoric; (definite) absolut; hotărât.

category s categorie f.

cater vi a se ocupa de mâncare, a organiza masa; (~ to customers) a se adresa; (anticipate) a prevedea; ~ **for** vi a satisface • ~**er** s furnizor m de mâncare • ~**ing** s com restaurante n pl, hoteluri n pl.

caterpillar s omidă f.

caterwaul vi a miorlăi, a mieuna.

cathedral s catedrală f, dom n.

cathode s catod n.

catholic adj catolic; universal; larg; tolerant; lipsit de prejudecăţi; **Catholicism** s relig catolicism n.

catkin s mâţişor m.

cattle s vite f pl; bovine f pl.

catty adj pej răutăcios, perfid.

Caucasian adj/s caucazian; (persoană f) cu ten alb şi păr închis la culoare.

cauldron s cazan n.

cauliflower s bot conopidă f.

causal adj cauzal.

cause s cauză f; temei n; motiv n; justificare f; problemă f, chestiune f || vi a cauza, a stârni; a pricinui.

causeway s dig n rutier; şosea f.

caustic adj caustic.

caution s prudenţă f, precauţie f; atenţie f; avertisment n || vt a preveni, a avertiza.

cautious adj prudent.

cavalry s cavalerie f.

cave s (grotto) peşteră f, grotă f, cavernă f; cavitate f; depresiune f; pivniţă f || vt a săpa, a scobi || vi ~ **in** (yield) a ceda.

caveat s avertisment n, prevenire f; jur protest n; suspendare f (a unui proces).

cavern s cavernă f, grotă f.

caviar s caviar n.

cavil vi (complain) a se lamenta; (split hairs) a despica firul în patru; (niggle) a cârti, a bombăni.

cavity s cavitate f.

caw s croncănit n || vi a croncăni.

cayenne s bot ardei m (roşu).

cease vt a înceta || vi a înceta.

CD-ROM s compact disc n, CD n.

cedar *s bot* cedru *m.*

cedilla *s ling* sedilă *f.*

ceiling *s* tavan *n*, plafon *n*; limită *f.*

celebrate *vt* a sărbători, a celebra; a comemora; a oficia

celebration *s* sărbatorire *f*; (*occasion*) festivitate *f*; (*event*) sărbătoare *f.*

celebrity *s* celebritate *f*; faimă *f.*

celerity *s* viteză *f.*

celery *s bot* țelină *f.*

celestial *adj* ceresc, *lit* celest.

celibate *s/adj* celibatar *m.*

cell *s bio*, *comp* celulă *f*; ~ **phone** *s* mobil *n.*

cellar *s* pivniță *f*, beci *n.*

cellist *s* violoncelist *m.*

cello *s* violoncel *n.*

cellular *adj* celular.

cement *s* ciment *n* ‖ *vt also fig* a cimenta.

cemetery *s* cimitir *n.*

cenotaph *s* cenotaf *n.*

censer *s relig* cădelniță *f.*

censor *s* cenzor *m*; supraveghetor *m* ‖ *vt* a cenzura.

censure *s* dezaprobare *f*, blam *n*, critică *f* ‖ *vt* a blama, a critica.

census *s* recensământ *n.*

cent *s* cent *m.*

centenarian *s* persoană *f* (în vârstă) de o sută de ani.

centenary *s/adj* centenar *n.*

center *s* centru *n*; punct *n* central ‖ *adj* central; *pol* de centru, centrist.

centigrade *adj* centigrad.

centigram *s* centigram *n.*

centimeter *s* centimetru *m.*

centipede *s ento* miriapod *m.*

central *adj* (*pivotal*) central; (*vital*) fundamental, esențial, (*main*) principal; accesibil; ~**heating** *s* încălzire *f* centrală.

centrifugal *adj tech* centrifug.

century *s* secol *n*, veac *n*; centurie *f.*

ceramic *adj* din ceramică • ~**s** *s pl* obiecte *n pl* din ceramică.

cereal *s* cereală *f.*

ceremonial *adj* (*dress*) de ceremonie; (*duty*) onorific ‖ *s* ceremonial *n.*

ceremony *s* ceremonie *f*; ceremonial *n*; ritual *n*; solemnitate *f*; formalitate *f*; politețe *f.*

certain *adj* anumit, anume; oarecare; sigur, precis, cert, categoric ‖ *pron* unii, unele.

certificate *s* certificat *n*; ~ **of deposit** *s* recipisă *f* de depunere.

certification *s* certificare *f*, adeverire *f*, atestare *f.*

certify *vt* a certifica, a atesta; a confirma; **this is to** ~ se adeverește prin prezenta.

certitude *s* (*certainty*) certitudine *f*; (*assurance*) siguranță *f*; (*conviction*) convingere *f.*

cervix *s anat* col *n* uterin.

cesspit *s* hazna *f.*

cesspool *s* hazna *f*; *fig* cloacă *f*, mocirlă *f.*

chafe *vt* (*rub*) a irita.

chaff *s* tărâțe *f pl.*

chaffinch *s orn* pițigoi *m.*

chain *s* lanț *n*; *pl* (*shackle*) cătușe *f pl*; robie *f*, sclavie *f*; captivitate *f*; rețea *f*, sistem *n*; (*group*) grup *n*, concern *n* ‖ *vt* a lega cu un lanț; a pune în lanțuri, a fereca; a înrobi; ~ **store** magazin cu sucursale.

chair *s* scaun *n*; catedră *f*; loc *n* de onoare; *jur* scaun *n*

electric ‖ *vt* a așeza (pe un scaun); a instala (într-un post); a purta în triumf.

chalet *s* cabană *f.*

chalice *s rel* potir *n*; *bot* caliciu *n.*

chalk *s* cretă *f.*

challenge *s* provocare *f*, chemare *f* (la întrecere); pretenție *f*; cerere *f*; parolă *f*; somație *f* ‖ *vt (dare)* a provoca, a chema (la luptă etc); a cere, a pretinde; a necesita; a se îndoi de; (*dispute*) a contesta; a soma; a recuza.

challenging *adj* incitant, stimulativ.

chamber *s* cameră *f*; ~ **music** *s* muzică *f* de cameră; ~ **of commerce** *s* cameră *f* de comerț.

chamberlain *s* șambelan *m.*

chameleon *s zool* cameleon *m.*

chamois *s* căprioară *f*; ~ **leather** *s* piele *f* de căprioară.

champagne *s* șampanie *f*, vin *n* spumos.

champion *s* campion *m.*

chance *s* întâmplare *f*; (*luck*) noroc *n*, șansă *f*, soartă *f*; risc *n*; (*prospect*) posibilitate *f* ‖ *vt* (risk) a risca ‖ *adj* (*accidental*) întâmplător, incidental.

chancelor *s* cancelar *m*; *scol* rector *m.*

chancy *adj coll* nesigur, riscant.

chandelier *s* lustră *f*, candelabru *n.*

change *vt* a schimba; (*replace*) a înlocui; (*alter*) a modifica; a transforma ‖ *vi* a se schimba, a se modifica; a se transforma ‖ *s* schimbare *f*, înlocuire *f*; modificare *f*, transformare *f*; variație *f*, noutate *f*; (*coins*) mărunțiș *n*, rest *n.*

channel *s* matcă *f*, albie *f*; canal *n*; șenal *n*; (*ditch*) rigolă *f*; braț *n*; (*means*) făgaș *n* ‖ *vt* a-și face/croi drum; a canaliza, (*direct*) a îndrepta.

chant *vt relig* a psalmodia; (*words, slogans*) a scanda ‖ *s* cânt *n.*

chaos *s* haos *n*; prăpastie *f*, abis *n*; confuzie *f*, anarhie *f.*

chap[1] *vi* (~ *skin*) a crăpa • ~**ped** *adj* (*skin, lips*) crăpat.

chap[2] *s coll* bărbat *m*, tip *m.*

chapel *s* capelă *f.*

chaperon *s* însoțitoare *f* (a unei fete tinere); damă *f* de companie ‖ *vt* a însoți (o fată tânără).

chaplain *s* preot *m*, capelan *m.*

chapter *s* capitol *n*; episod *n*; temă *f*, subiect *n*; (*branch*) filială *f* (a unui club etc); asociație *f* studențească.

char[1] *vi* (*burn*) a carboniza.

char[2] *vi* a face menajul; ~ **woman** *s* femeie *f* de menaj.

character *s* caracter *n*, fire *f*, natură *f*; (*moral fiber*) forță *f* morală; aspect *n*, fel *n*; personaj *n*, erou *m*; caracterizare *f*; (*integrity*) reputație *f*; (*quality*) calitate *f*, rol *n*, funcție *f*; literă *f* • ~**istic** *adj* caracteristic, tipic, specific ‖ *s* caracteristică *f*, particularitate *f.*

charcoal *s* (*drawing*) cărbune *m*; (*fuel*) cărbune *m* de lemn.

charge *s* (*accusation*) învinuire *f*, acuzare *f*; șarjă *f*, atac *n*; preț *n*, cost *n*; sarcină *f*; încărcătură *f*; grijă *f*; păstrare *f*; (*custody*) supraveghere *f* ‖ *vt* a încărca; a alimenta; (*attack*) a ataca; a cere (un preț) ‖ *vi* a cere/pretinde plata ; ~ **account** *s* cont *n* curent; ~ **card** *s* carte *f* de credit pentru cumpărături • ~**able** *adj* răspunzător (de); învinuit (de); impozabil.

chariot *s* car *n* de luptă.

charisma *s* carismă *f.*

charitable *adj* generos, darnic.

charity *s* milă *f.*

charm *s* vrajă *f*, farmec *n*; talisman *n*, fetiș *n* ‖ *vt* a chart 282 chop

fermeca; a vrăji; a fascina • ~ing *adj* fermecător, fascinant, încântător.

chart *s* grafic *n*, diagramă *f*; hartă *f* || *vt* (*plot*) a înscrie pe o hartă; *fig* a reaminti.

charter *s* (*document*) cartă *f* || *vt* (*plane*, *ship*) a navlosi.

chary *adj* (*wary*) prudent, precaut.

chase *vt* a vâna; (*pursue*) a urmări; a alerga după; a îndepărta; a risipi || *vi* a vâna; a alerga, a fugi || *s* (*hunt*) vânătoare *f*; vânători *m pl*; (*game*) vânat *n*; sălbăticiuni *f pl*; (*pursuit*) urmărire *f*, hăituire *f*; animal *n* urmărit.

chasm *s also fig* prăpastie *f*.

chassis *s* șasiu *n*, cadru *n*.

chaste *adj* pur, cast, neprihănit || *s* castitate *f*, puritate *f*.

chastise *vt* a pedepsi aspru.

chastity *s* castitate *f*, puritate *f*.

chat *vi* a sta de vorbă, a sporovăi || *s* șuetă *f*, discuție *f* prietenească • ~**ter** *vi* (*people*) a pălăvrăgi, a sporovăi; (*birds*, *animals*) a cârâi; (*teeth*) a clănțăni || *s* pălăvrăgeală *f*; cârâitură *f*.

chauffeur *s* șofer *m*.

chauvinism *s* șovinism *n*.

chauvinist *s* sexist *m*; șovin *m*.

cheap *adj* (*low-cost*) ieftin; convenabil; banal; (*shoddy*) superficial; (*poor quality*) prost; jenat || *adv* ieftin, convenabil.

cheat *vt* (*deceive*) a înșela; a păcăli || *vi* a înșela, a trișa || *s* înșelăciune *f*, amăgire *f*; escrocherie *f*; înșelător *m*; (*con*) escroc *m*.

check *s* (*stop*) oprire *f*, întrerupere *f*; piedică *f*, frână *f*; șah *n*; (*inspection*) control *n*, verificare *f*; etichetă *f*; semn *n*; (*bill*) bon *n*; recipisă *f*; fisă *f*; carou *n*, pătrat *n* || *vt* a opri brusc, a întrerupe; a frâna; (*impede*) a împiedica, a controla; (*verify*) a verifica; a bifa; a înregistra.

cheek *s anat* obraz *m*; tupeu *n*, neobrăzare *f* • ~**y** *adj* neobrăzat.

cheep *s* piuit *n* || *vi* a piui.

cheer *vt* a bucura; a înveseli; a încuraja; a aclama, a ovaționa || *vi* a se bucura; a prinde curaj; a aclama || *s* aprobare *f*, acord *n*; *pl* urale *f*, aclamații *f*, ovații *f*; încurajare *f*; dispoziție *f* • ~**ful** *adj* voios, vesel; primitor, prietenos; luminos • ~**leader** *s* animator *m*, animatoare *f*.

cheese *s* brânză *f* • ~**cake** *s* plăcintă *f* cu brânză.

cheetah *s zool* ghepard *m*.

chef *s* bucătar *m* șef; bucătar *m*.

chemical *adj* chimic || *s* preparat *n* chimic.

chemise *s* furou *n*; rochie *f* lejeră cu bretele.

chemist *s* chimist *m* • ~**ry** *s* chimie *f*.

chequered *adj* în/cu carouri.

cherish *vt* a îndrăgi; (*hope*) a nutri.

cherry *s* (*tree*) vișin *m*; (*fruit*) vișină *f* || *adj* (*color*) vișiniu.

chess *s* (jocul de) șah *n*.

chest *s* ladă *f*, cufăr *n*; scrin *n*; dulap *n*; *anat* piept *n*.

chestnut *s bot* castană *f*; ~ **tree** castan *m* || *adj* (*color*) castaniu.

chew *vt* a rumega, a mesteca; *fig* a cugeta || *s* rumegat *n*, mestecat *n*; tutun *n* de mestecat • ~**y** *adj* greu de mestecat.

chick *s also fig* puișor *m*; *sl* tipă *f* bine • ~**en** *s* pui *m* (de găină); (*hen*) găină *f*, cocoș *m*; odor *n*, copilaș *m*; tânăr *m*, tânără *f* fără experiență; (*coward*) om *m* laș sau fricos.

chicory *s* (*vegetable*) andivă *f*, cicoare *f* de grădină.

chide *vt* (*scold*) a certa, a mustra || *vi* a se certa, a se sfădi.

chief *s* (*leader*) șef *m*, conducător *m*; ofițer *m* întâi; ofițer *m* secund || *adj* (*foremost*) de frunte; conducător; principal.

chiffonier *s* dulap *n*; scrin *n*.

chilblain *s med* degerătură *f*.

child *s* (*pl* **children**) copil *m*; prunc *m*; sugar *m*; persoană *f* imatură; urmaș *m*; produs *n*, rezultat *n* • ~**hood** *s* copilărie *f* • ~**ish** *adj* naiv; copilăresc; copilăros; prost • ~**less** *adj* fără copii.

chil(l)i *s* (*vegetable*) chilli *m*, ardei *m* iute (de cayenne).

chill *s* (*illness*) răceală *f*; (*fear*) frison *n*, fior *n* || *adj* răcoros || *vt* (~ *drink*, *food*) a pune la rece; (~ *a person*) a face să tremure || *vi* (~ *food*, *drink*) a se răci • ~**y** *adj* rece, răcoros; înfrigurat, înghețat; distant; descurajator; deprimant.

chime *vt* (*clock*) a suna || *vi* (*clock*, *bell*) a bate || *s* (*clock*, *bell*) dangăt *n*.

chimera *s* himeră *f*.

chimney *s* șemineu *n*, cămin *n*; (*smokestack*) coș *n*, horn *n*; crater *n* de vulcan; crăpătură *f* în stâncă.

chimpanzee *s zool* cimpanzeu *m*.

chin *s* bărbie *f* || *vi* a trăncăni, a flecări.

china¹ *s* porțelan *n*.

China² *s* China *f*

Chinese *s/adj* chinez(ă); **the** ~ *s* chinezii *m pl*.

chink¹ *s* (*slit*) crăpătură *f*.

chink² *s* (*sound*) zăngănit *n*, clinchet *n* || *vt* a face să zăngăne.

chip *s* așchie *f*; surcică *f*; șindrilă *f*; șipcă *f*; (*bit*) fărâmă *f*, fragment *n*, ciob *n*; felie *f* subțire; copil *m*, odraslă *f*; *comp* microchip || *vi* a așchia; (*fragment*) a se fărâmița; (*break off*) a se sparge.

chiropodist *s* pedichiurist/ă *m/f*.

chiropody *s* pedichiură *f*

chirp *vi* (*birds*) a ciripi; (*cricket*) a țârâi • ~**y** *adj* voios.

chisel *s* (*for wood*) cuțit *n*, daltă *f*; (*for metal*, *stone*) daltă *f* || *vt* a cizela.

chitchat *s coll* taifas *n*; pălăvrăgeală *f*, trăncăneală *f*.

chivalrous *adj* galant; (*polite*) curtenitor, politicos.

chivalry *s lit* cavalerism *n*; (*good manners*) galanterie *f*, purtare *f* curtenitoare.

chives *s pl bot* arpagic *m*.

chlorine *s chem* clor *n*.

chloroform *s pharm* cloroform *n*.

chlorophyll *s bot* clorofilă *f*.

chockful *adj* arhiplin.

chocolate *s* ciocolată *f*; *pl* bomboane *f* de ciocolată || *adj* de ciocolată; ciocolatiu.

choice *s* alegere *f*, selecție *f*; (*option*) opțiune *f*; preferință *f*; alternativă *f*; (*range*) (a)sortiment *n*; parte *f* aleasă || *adj* (*select*) cel mai bun; superior; (*well-chosen*) elegant; rafinat.

choir *s* cor *n*.

choke *vt* a strangula, a sufoca; (*block*) a astupa || *vi* a se sufoca || *s aut* șoc *n*, clapetă *f* de pornire.

cholera *s med* holeră *f*.

cholesterol *s med* colesterol *n*.

choose, chose, chosen *vt* a alege, a selecta; a hotărî; a prefera; a vrea || *vi* a alege, a putea alege.

chop¹ *vt* a tăia bucăți, a ciopli; (~ *vegetables*) a toca; (*budget*) a reduce || *vi* a ciopli; a despica || *s* lovitură *f* de topor etc.

chop² s *cul* cotlet n • ~**per** s satâr n; *coll avia* elicopter n • ~**s** s pl buze f pl.

chopstick s bețișor n chinezesc de mâncat.

chord s *anat* cord n, inimă f; *mus* acord n.

chore s (*unpleasant task*) corvoadă f; **household** ~**s** s muncile f pl casnice.

choreography s coregrafie f.

chortle vi a chicoti, a râde pe înfundate ‖ s chicotit n.

chorus s (*part of song*) refren n; (*singers*) *also fig* cor n.

chose vt * **choose**.

chosen vt * **choose**.

christen vt a boteza; a numi.

Christian adj/s *relig* creștin m • ~**ity** s religia f creștină • ~**ize** vt a creștina.

Christmas s Crăciun n; ~ **tree** s pom m de Crăciun.

chromatic adj cromatic.

chrome s crom n ‖ adj cromat.

chromium s * **chrome**.

chromosome s cromozom m.

chronic adj (*illness*) cronic; (*liar*) înveterat.

chronicle s cronică f.

chronological adj cronologic.

chronology s cronologie f.

chronometer s cronometru n.

chrysalis s *ento* crisalidă f.

chrysanthemum s *bot* crizantemă f.

chubby adj (*cheek*) bucălat; (*person, hands*) dolofan.

chuck vt *coll* (*throw*) a arunca; (~ *a friend*) a abandona; ~ **away/out** vt (*things*) a se descotorosi, (*chance*) a lăsa să-i scape.

chuckle vi a râde pe înfundate.

chug vi (*train*) a pufăi.

chunk s bucată f mare; (*bread*) codru m.

church s biserică f; capelă f; paraclis n; slujbă f, serviciu n divin; rit n ‖ vt a face o slujbă pentru.

churn s aparat n pentru prepararea untului; (*for cream*) bidon n ‖ vt a bate; **to** ~ **out** a produce în serie.

chute s (*shaft*) jgheab n; plan n înclinat; (*slide*) pantă f; (*waterfall*) cădere f de apă.

cider s cidru n.

cigarette s țigaretă f, țigară f; ~ **end** s chiștoc n; ~ **holder** s țigaret n; ~ **lighter** s brichetă f.

cinch s *coll* (*sure bet*) chestie f sigură, bagatelă f; (*easy task*) treabă f ușoară.

cinders s pl cenușă f.

cine camera s aparat n de filmat.

cinema s cinema(tograf) n; film n; cinematografie f.

cinnamon s scorțișoară f.

cipher s cifru n; cifră f arabă; nulă f, zero n.

circle s cerc n; (*ring*) inel n; manej n; arenă f; rang n; rotație f; curs n; coroană f ‖ vt a se învârti în jurul; (*orbit*) a înconjura, a încercui ‖ vi (*go around*) a se învârti; a se mișca în cerc.

circuit s circuit n; tur n; (*movement*) revoluție f.

circular adj circular; de cerc ‖ s circulară f; reclamă f; prospect n.

circulate vi a circula; a se amesteca printre invitați ‖ vt (~ *a rumor*) a se propaga; (~ *documents*) a face să circule, a circula.

circulating adj circulant; ~ **capital** *fin* capital circulant.

circulation s (*flow*) circulație f; (*distribution*) răspândire f, împrăștiere f.

circumcise vt a tăia împrejur

circumcision s circumcizie f.

circumference s circumferință f.

circumflex adj *ling* accent n circumflex.

circumscribe vt a circumscrie.

circumspect adj circumspect.

circumstance s circumstanță f • ~**s** mijloace n pl financiare; **under no** ~ în nici un caz.

circumstantial adj accidental, întâmplător; ~ **evidence** *jur* probe indirecte.

circus s circ n; piață f (rotundă); arenă f; manej n.

cistern s rezervor n de apă; rezervor n al vasului W.C.

citation s (*quote*) citat n; *jur* citație f.

cite vt a cita.

citizen s cetățean m; orășean m • ~**ship** s cetățenie f.

citrus fruit s citrice f pl.

city s oraș n; ~ **hall** s primărie (a unui oraș).

civic adj (*leader, event*) municipal; (*duty, pride*) civic • ~**s** s pl instrucție f civică.

civil adj (*public*) civil, cetățenesc; (*polite*) politicos, curtenitor; ~ **case** *jur* proces n civil; ~ **law** *jur* drept civil; ~ **rights** drepturi civile; ~ **society** societate civilă • ~**ian** s/adj civil m; *jur* specialist m în dreptul civil; (*clothes*) civil • ~**ity** s politețe f, amabilitate f • ~**ization** s civilizație f; cultură f; lumea f civilizată • ~**ize** vt a civiliza.

clack s trosnet n, pocnitură f; vorbărie f, pălăvrăgeală f; *tech* supapă f, clapetă f.

clad adj *lit* îmbrăcat, înveșmântat.

claim vt (*ask for*) a cere, a pretinde; a reclama; (*demand*) a revendica; (*state*) a afirma, a susține; (*apply for*) a solicita ‖ s (*request*) pretenție f; revendicare f; (~ *a right*) drept n • ~**ant** s pretendent m; reclamant m, solicitant m.

clairvoyant s clarvăzător m.

clam s *icht* scoică f comestibilă.

clamber vi a se cățăra.

clammy adj (*skin*) lipicios; (*weather*) umed și rece.

clamor s (*noise*) țipăt n ‖ vi ~ **for smth** a cere zgomotos ceva.

clamp s clamă f, agrafă f; șurub n; *med* pensă f ‖ vt a strânge; *aut* a acționa sabotul (de blocare).

clan s clan n • ~**nish** adj de clan • ~**sman** s membru m al unui clan.

clandestine adj clandestin.

clap s (*slap*) pocnet n, pocnitură f; tunet n; pl aplauze f ‖ vt a pocni din; a aplauda; a trânti cu zgomot; a bate din ‖ vi a pocni; a trosni; a aplauda • ~**per** s limbă f de clopot.

claret s (*wine*) roșu, de Bordeaux; (*color*) roșu-închis, bordo.

clarification s clarificare f.

clarify vt (*explain*) a clarifica; (*refine*) a purifica; (*filter*) a decanta ‖ vi a se clarifica, a se limpezi; a se purifica.

clarinet s *mus* clarinet n.

clarity s claritate f.

clash vi a se izbi; a se lovi, (*collide*) a se ciocni; (*clang*) a zăngăni; a răsuna; a fi în conflict; (*not match*) a nu se potrivi/asorta; a nu coincide ‖ vt (*bang*) a trânti cu zgomot ‖ s ciocnire f; (*clang*) zăngănit n; conflict n; nepotrivire f.

clasp vt a strânge ‖ s încheietoare f, cataramă f.

class s clasă f, (*set*) categorie f; (*status*) calitate f; (*rank*) rang n; promoție f ‖ vt (*classify*) a clasifica; a aparține unei clase • ~**mate** s coleg m de clasă.

classic adj perfect, desăvârșit; clasic, vestit; (*simple*) simplu, sobru; esențial; (*common*) tradițional, (*typical*) tipic ‖ *s* clasic *m*, autor *m* clasic; (*model*) lucrare *f* clasică.

classification *s* clasificare *f*.

classified *adj* clasificat; confidenţial, secret; ~ **ad** anunţ (în ziar).

classify *vt* a clasifica; a declara/considera secret.

clatter *s* zăngănit *n*, zornăit *n*; (*loud*) bubuit *n*.

clause *s gram* propoziţie *f*; *jur* clauză *f*; punct *n*, articol *n*.

claustrophobia *s* claustrofobie *f*.

claw *s* gheară *f*; cleşte *m*; mână *f*; foarfece *f pl* ‖ *vt* a-şi înfige ghearele; a apuca cu ghearele; (*graze*) a zgâria ‖ *vi* a se apuca cu mâinile de.

clay *s* argilă *f*, lut *n*, humă *f*; pământ *n*, ţărână *f*; noroi *n*; pulbere *f*; trup *n*.

clean *adj* (*neat*) curat, îngrijit; (*pure*) pur; nescris; (*untainted*) nepătat; imaculat; inocent; nevinovat; dibaci; iscusit ‖ *adv* cu desăvârşire ‖ *vt* a curăţi; a curăţa; a lustrui; a spăla; a şterge • ~**er** *s* femeie de serviciu *f* • ~**ing** *s* curăţenie *f*.

cleanse *vt* a curăţa; a dezinfecta; a purga.

clear *adj* (*obvious*) limpede, clar; (*fine*) senin; transparent; curat ‖ *adv* strălucitor; cu totul, total ‖ *vt* (*tidy*) a curăţa; a strânge; a evacua; a elibera; a risipi; a limpezi; (*free*) a achita; a lămuri; a defrişa ‖ *vi* a se limpezi, a se însenina; a se ridica (ceaţa) • ~**ance** *s* (*permission*) autorizaţie *f*; (*approval*) aprobare *f*; (*wood*) defrişare *f*; (*check*) achitare *f*; *econ* lichidare *f* de stoc • ~**ing** *s* suprafaţă *f* defrişată; *econ* cliring *n*; *econ* lichidare *f*, validare *f* • ~**ing house** *s econ* birou *n* de cliring/decontare.

cleave, clove, cleft *vt/vi* a (se despica) • ~**r** *s* satâr *n*.

clef *s mus* cheie *f*.

clench *vt* a strânge.

clergy *s relig* cler *n*; preoţi *m pl* • ~**man** *s* preot *m*.

clerical *adj* (*activity*) de birou; *relig* clerical.

clerk *s* secretar *m*; funcţionar *m*; amploiat *m*; vânzător *m*; cleric *m*.

clever *adj* (*smart*) deştept, inteligent; spiritual; (*astute*) ingenios; (*talented*) talentat; înzestrat; (*cunning*) abil; dibaci.

cliché *s typ* clişeu *n*; *fig* clişeu *n*, banalitate *f*; expresie *f* stereotipă.

click *s* (*of a lock*) păcănit *n*; (*of a tongue*) plescăit *n*; (*of heels*) ţăcănit *n* ‖ *vt* a păcăni, a plescăi ‖ *vi* (*heels*) a ţăcăni; (*camera*) a produce un declic.

client *s* client *m*; cumpărător *m*; favorit *m*; trepăduş *m* • ~**ele** *s* clientelă *f*, clienţi *m pl*.

cliff *s* faleză *f*; ţărm *n* stâncos; stâncă *f* în mare; coastă *f*; terasă *f*.

climate *s* climat *n*.

climatic *adj* climateric.

climax *s* culme *f*, punct *n* culminant; culminaţie *f*; gradaţie *f* ‖ *vi* a culmina.

climb *vt* (*mount*) a (se) urca pe, a sui; a se căţăra; (*scale*) a face o ascensiune ‖ *vi* a se urca, a se ridica ‖ *s* urcare *f*, căţărare *f*, ascensiune *f*.

clinch *vt* (*finalize*) a definitiva; (*settle*) a aplana.

cling, clung, clung *vi* a se agăţa (de); (*clothes*) (**to**) a se lipi.

clinic *s* (*building*) centru *n* medical, clinică *f*.

clink *vi* a bate clopotul, a suna.

clip *vt* a prinde, a ataşa; (~ *nails*) a tăia; a reteza; (~ *word*) a prescurta; (~ *a hedge*) a tunde; (~ *a newspaper article*) a decupa ‖ *s* retezare *f*; *coll* lovitură *f* (cu palma etc); (*paper~*) agrafă *f*; (*hair* ~) clamă *f*.

clitoris *s anat* clitoris *n*.

cloak *s* mantie *f*.

clock *s* ceas *n*; pendulă *f*; orologiu *n*; deşteptător *n* ‖ *vt* a cronometra, a ponta; ~ **maker** *s* ceasornicar *m* • ~**wise** *adv* în direcţia acelor de ceasornic • ~**work** *s* mecanism *n* de ceas.

clog *vt* a astupa; ~ **up** a astupa ‖ *vi* a se astupa, a se înfunda ‖ *s* sabot *m*.

cloister *s* chilie *f*.

clop *s* tropot *n* (de copite).

close *adj* închis; îngrădit; încuiat; ascuns; secret; (*tight*) strâns; (*oppressive*) viciat; sever; (*near*) apropiat, intim; (*minute*) detaliat, minuţios; (*precise*) exact, fidel; ~ **shave** *s* situaţie *s* limită ‖ *adv* strâns, apropiat; aproape, cât pe ce ‖ *vt* a închide; a împrejmui; (*shut down*) a încuia; (*block*) a bloca; (*finish*) a termina; (*end*) a sfârşi, (*conclude*) a încheia • ~**fisted** *adj* zgârcit • ~**out** *s* lichidare *f* de mărfuri • ~**up** *s* prim plan *n*.

closet *s* cameră *f*, odaie *f*; cămară *f*, magazie *f*; dulap *n* (în perete); birou *n*, cabinet *n*; toaletă *f*.

closing *s* închidere *f*.

closure *s* închidere *f*; încheiere *f*.

clot *s* (*blood, milk*) cheag *n*; *coll* nătăfleţ *m* ‖ *vi* (*blood*) a coagula.

cloth *s* pânză *f*, postav *n*; stofă *f*; cârpă *f*; faţă *f* de masă.

clothe *vt* a îmbrăca • ~**s** *s pl* îmbrăcăminte *f*, haine *f*; *pl* rufărie *f*, lenjerie *f*.

clothing *s* îmbrăcăminte *f*, înveliş *n*.

cloud *s* nor *m*; potop *n*; (*shade*) umbră *f*, supărare *f*; (*veil*) văl *n* ‖ *vt* a înnora, a umbri ‖ *vi* a se înnora; a se întunecа • ~**y** *adj* noros; înnorat; tulbure; confuz; înceţoşat.

clove¹ *s* ~**s** (*spice*) cuişoare *f pl*.

clove² *s* (*of garlic*) căţel *m* de usturoi.

clover *s* trifoi *m*.

clown *s* clovn *m*; măscărici *m*; bădăran *m* ‖ *vi* a face pe clovnul/bufonul.

club *s* club *n* ‖ *vi* a se strânge, a se întruni.

clue *s* indiciu *n*; definiţie *f* • ~**less** *adj* *coll* ignorant.

clump *s* (*trees, bushes*) desiş *n*; pâlc *n*; grămadă *f*; grup *n*; şuviţă *f*.

clumsy *adj* (*awkward*) stângaci, neîndemânatic; aspru, grosolan; (*gauche*) lipsit de tact.

clumsiness *s* stângăcie *f*, neîndemânare *f*.

cluster *s* grup *n* ‖ *vi* a se aduna; (*buildings, etc*) a fi grupate, a forma un grup.

clutch *vt* (*grasp*) a apuca, a prinde; (*grip*) a ţine strâns ‖ *s* apucare *f*, strângere *f*, strânsoare *f*; ambreiaj *n*.

clutter *s* dezordine *f* ‖ *vt* a face dezordine.

coach *s* (*bus*) autocar *n*; (*rail*) vagon *n*; (*sport*) antrenor *m*; (*school*) meditator *m*.

coagulate *vi* a (se) coagula.

coal *s* cărbune *m*; huilă *f*; tăciune *m* ‖ *vt* a preface în cărbune, a carboniza; ~ **field** *s* bazin *n* carbonifer; ~ **mine** *s* mină *f* de cărbuni.

coalesce *vi* a se amesteca, a se contopi.

coalition *s* coaliţie *f*.

coarse *adj* aspru, grosolan; brut; inferior; vulgar; nepoliticos.

coast *s* coastă *f*, ţărm *n* de mare; litoral *n*; graniţă *f*, limită *f* ‖ *vt/vi* a naviga de-a lungul coastei.

coat *s* haină *f*; veston *n*; sacou *n*; jachetă *f*; palton *n*, mantou *n*; (*fur* ~) blană *f*; (*wool* ~) lână *f*; (*skin*) piele *f,* penaj *n; (layer)* înveliș *n* ‖ *vt (cover)* a înveli, a acoperi; a vopsi • ~**ing** *s* strat *n; cul* glazură *f.*

coax *vt ~ smb* **(to do smth)** a convinge pe cineva (să facă ceva) (prin lingușiri, alintare etc).

cobble *vt (shoes)* a repara • ~**r** *s* cizmar *m.*

cobblestone *s* piatră *f* de pavaj.

cobra *s* cobră *f.*

cobweb *s* pânză *f* de păianjen.

cocaine *s* cocaină *f.*

cock *s* cocoș *m;* cântatul *n* cocoșului; șef *m;* sfârlează *f;* trăgaci *n* ‖ *vt (raise)* a ridica (trăgaciul etc); a pune pe o ureche (pălăria etc) • ~**eyed** *adj* sașiu • ~**fight** *s* luptă *f* de cocoși • ~**y** *adj* înfumurat, infatuat; arogant.

cockle *s* cochilie *f* de moluscă.

cockpit *s* cockpit *n,* carlingă *f,* locul *n* pilotului.

cockroach *s* gândac *m* de bucătărie.

cocksure *adj* încrezut, sigur de sine.

cocktail *s* cocteil *n;* cal *m* cu coada tăiată.

cocky *adj* încrezut, infatuat.

cocoa *s bot (tree)* arborele *m* de cacao; *(fruit)* cacao *f.*

coconut *s* nucă *f* de cocos.

cocoon *s text* cocon *m,* gogoașă *f* de mătase.

cod *s icht* cod *n,* batog *n.*

code *s* cod *n;* codice *n;* cifru *n;* semnal *n* ‖ *vt* a codifica, a cifra.

codeine *s chem* codeină *f.*

codicil *s* codicil *n.*

codify *vt* a codifica.

coeducation *s* învățământ *n* mixt.

coefficient *s* coeficient *n.*

coerce *vt* a constrânge

coercive *adj* coercitiv.

coexist *vi* a coexista.

coffee *s* cafea *f;* arborele *m* de cafea; *~* **bar** *s* cafenea *f; ~* **break** *s* pauză *f* pentru cafea; *~* **pot** *s* cafetieră *f;* ibric *n* pentru cafea; *~* **table** *s* măsuță *f* joasă.

coffin *s* sicriu *n.*

cog *s (wheel)* dinte *m;* roată *f* dințată.

cogent *adj (forceful)* convingător; *(coherent)* pertinent; *~* **evidence** probe convingătoare.

cognac *s* coniac *m.*

cognate *s* cuvânt *n* înrudit (cu altul) ‖ *adj* înrudit.

cognition *s* cunoaștere *f.*

cognizable *adj jur* care intră în competența curții.

cognizance *s* competență *f;* sferă *f* de cunoștințe; cunoaștere *f.*

cohabit *vi* a coabita.

coherence *s* coerență *f.*

coherent *adj* coerent.

cohesion *s* coeziune *f.*

coil *s (rope)* încolăcire *f;* buclă *f;* *elec* bobină *f; (contraceptive method)* sterilet *n* ‖ *vt* a înfășura ‖ *vi* a se încolăci.

coin *s* monedă *f;* ban *m* ‖ *vt* a bate (monedă); a născoci, a inventa.

coincide *vi* a coincide.

coincidence *s* coincidență *f.*

coke *s* cocs *n;* coca-cola *f; sl* cocaină *f.*

colander *s* strecurătoare *f.*

cold *adj (chilly)* rece; răcoros; înfrigurat; *(aloof)* neprietenos; mort; leșinat ‖ *s* vreme *f* rece; temperatură *f* scăzută; senzație *f* de frig; răceală *f; ~* **cream** *s* cremă *f* de față; *~* **war** *s* război *n* rece • ~**blooded** *adj* cu sânge rece • ~**hearted** *adj* insensibil.

colic *s med* colică *f.*

collaborate *vi* a colabora; a coopera.

collaboration *s* colaborare *f;* cooperare *f.*

collapse *vi (building, person)* a cădea, a se prăbuși; *(marriage)* a eșua; a fi pliant ‖ *s* cădere *f,* prăbușire *f; (marriage)* eșec *n.*

collapsible *adj* rabatabil.

collar *s* guler *n;* zgardă *f;* manșon *n* ‖ *vt* a lua de guler; a încăleca.

collarbone *s anat* claviculă *f.*

collate *vt* a colaționa.

collateral *s econ* garanție ‖ *adj* suplimentar; colateral, secundar.

colleague *s* coleg *m.*

collect *vt (gather)* a strânge; a aduna; *(hoard)* a colecta; a încasa ‖ *vi* a se strânge, a se aduna; a fi colecționar ‖ *adv/adj* (contra) ramburs; cu taxă inversă • ~**ed** *adj* rezervat, calm • ~**ion** *s* strângere *f,* adunare *f;* colecționare *f;* colecție *f;* grămadă *f;* colectă *f* • ~**ive** *adj* colectiv ‖ *s* cooperativă *f* • ~**ive bargaining** *s* negocieri *f pl* colective (asupra contractului de muncă) • ~**or** *s (hobby)* colecționar *m; (debt, rent)* încasator *m.*

college *s* colegiu *n;* facultate *f;* universitate *f;* academie *f;* școală *f* superioară; institut *n;* corporație *f.*

collide *vi* a intra în coliziune (cu)

collie *s zool* collie *m,* câine *m* ciobănesc scoțian.

collision *s* coliziune *f.*

colloquial *adj* familiar.

colloquy *s* discuție *f,* dialog *n;* dezbatere *f.*

cologne *s* (apă) de colonie.

colon *s gram* două puncte *n pl; anat* colon *n.*

colonel *s mil* colonel *m.*

colonial *adj* colonial.

colony *s* colonie *f.*

color *s (of dye)* culoare *f; (tint)* colorit *n;* ton *n; (shade)* nuanță *f; (of paint)* vopsea *f;* pigment *m;* roșeață *f;* caracter *n; pl* steag *n,* drapel *n* • ~**blind** *adj* daltonist • ~**fast** *adj* rezistent la spălat • ~**ful** *adj* pitoresc; plin de culoare.

colossal *adj* colosal.

colossus *s* colos *m.*

colt *s* mânz *m.*

column *s* coloană *f; (article)* rubrică *f.*

coma *s med* comă *f;* **in a** *~* în (stare de) comă.

comb *s* pieptene *m;* meliță *f;* darac *n;* creastă *f;* fagure *m* ‖ *vt* a pieptăna; a dărăci; *(scour)* a scotoci.

combat *s* luptă *f* ‖ *vt* a lupta, a combate.

combination *s* combinare *f;* combinație *f;* unire *f;* combinezon *n;* sintagmă *f;* cifru *n* secret.

combine *vt* a combina; a uni; a amesteca ‖ *vi* a se combina; a se uni; a se amesteca ‖ *s* combină *f;* cartel *n;* sindicat *n.*

combustible *adj/s* combustibil *m.*

combustion *s* combustie *f.*

come, came, come *vi (arrive)* a sosi, a veni; *(reach)* a ajunge; a se apropia; *(happen)* a se întâmpla, a se petrece; a proveni; a se face, a deveni; a se găsi; *~* **about** *vi* a se întâmpla; *~* **across** *vt (find)* a da de/ peste; a întâlni (din întâmplare); *~* **after** *vi* a căuta, a fi în căutarea; *~* **again** *vi* a veni din nou, a se întoarce, a reveni; *~* **along** *vi* a veni cu cineva, a însoți pe cineva ‖ *interj* hai(de)!, haidem!, haideți! *~* **back** *vi* a se întoarce, a reveni; *~* **by** *vi* a dobândi, a căpăta, a câștiga; *~* **down** *vi* a veni, a sosi, *(rain)* a cădea, a coborî, a se lăsa (în jos); (*tradition*) a transmite; *fig* a decădea, a coborî; a se degrada; a se îmbolnăvi; ~ **in** a intra; a pătrunde; (*train*) a sosi; a-şi lua postul în primire; a începe să fie folosit/la modă; *fig* a se maturiza, a se coace; a se dovedi (util etc); a juca un rol, a avea un cuvânt de spus; ~ **off** a se desprinde, a se desface; a se întâmpla, a se petrece, a se desfăşura; a reuşi, a izbuti; a se achita; a se descotorosi; ~ **out** a reieşi, a deveni clar; *thea* a-şi face debutul, a ieşi în public; (*stains, etc*) a ieşi; ~ **to** *vi* (*from faint*) a-şi reveni, a-şi recăpăta cunoştinţa; (*inherit*) a-i reveni (cuiva), a moşteni; (~ *a total*) a se ridica la || *interj* hai!, haide!, ei hai!; (ei hai) lasă! ~ **under** *vi* a ţine de (o categorie), a se subsuma (unei categorii); a fi supus (unei influenţe) • ~**back** *s* revenire (la putere etc); plată *f*; răzbunare *f*; replica *f*, ripostă *f* • ~**down** *s* cădere *f*; scădere *f*, micşorare *f*; înrăutăţire *f*

comedian *s* actor *m* de comedie.

comedy *s* comedie *f*.

comeliness *s* drăgălăşenie *f*, farmec *n*; frumuseţe *f*.

comely *adj* drăgălaş, graţios; frumos; atrăgător.

comet *s* cometă *f*.

comfort *s* (*relief*) mângâiere *f*; sprijin *n*; tihnă *f*; confort *n* || *vt* (*soothe*) a mângâia, a alina; (*console*) a consola • ~**able** *adj* confortabil; tihnit, comod; liniştitor.

comic *adj* (*funny*) comic, amuzant, nostim || *s* (*comedian*) actor *m* de comedie; (*comic book*) bandă *f* desenată.

comma *s gram* virgulă *f*.

command *vt* a comanda; (*demand*) a pretinde; (*rule*) a stăpâni; a dispune de; (*dominate*) a domina; a impune || *vi* a comanda; a cuprinde cu vederea || *s* (*order*) ordin *n*; comandă *f*; (*authority*) autoritate *f*; ordine *f*, dispoziţie *f* • ~**eer** *vt* a rechiziţiona • ~**er** *s* (*army*) comandant *m*; (*navy*) căpitanul *m* echipajului • ~**o** *s* detaşament *n* de diversiune, commando *n*.

commemorate *vt* a comemora.

commence *vt* a începe, a înfiripa || *vi* a începe.

commend *vt* (*praise*) a lăuda; a recomanda; (*entrust*) a încredinţa • ~**able** *adj* lăudabil • ~**ation** *s* laudă *f*; recomandare *f*.

commensurate *adj* proporţional; (**with**) echivalent (cu).

comment *s* comentariu *n*; observaţii *f pl* || *vi* a comenta; a discuta despre.

commerce *s* comerţ *n*.

commercial *s* reclamă *f* || *adj* comercial; ~ **bank** *s* bancă *f* comercială; ~ **law** *s* drept *n* comercial • ~**ize** *vt* a comercializa.

commiserate *vi* (*with smb*) a compătimi, a-i fi milă de.

commiseration *s* compătimire *f*.

commission *s* (*board*) comisie *f*; mandat *n*; (*charge*) comision *n*; comitere *f*, (*task*) însărcinare *f*; funcţie *f*; ordin *n*, brevet *n* || *vt* a împuternici; a autoriza; a comanda; a da în funcţiune.

commit *vt* (~ *a crime*) a comite, a face, a săvârşi; (*promise money, etc*) a aloca || *vr* a se obliga • ~**ment** *s* (*promise*) angajament *n*, obligaţie *f*; (*obligation*) obligaţie *f*, responsabilitate *f*.

committee *s* comitet *n*; comisie *f*.

commodious *adj* (*roomy*) spaţios; convenabil.

commodity *s* articol *n* de comerţ, marfă *f*.

common *adj* (*shared*) comun; general; (*usual*) obişnuit; vulgar, trivial || *s* islaz *n* (comunal); ~ **stock** *s econ* capital/fond *n* iniţial; *fig* fond *n* comun.

commonwealth *s* republică *f*; stat *n*; comunitate *f* de naţiuni; federaţie *f*; bunăstare *f* generală.

commotion *s* freamăt *n*, agitaţie *f*, tulburare *f*; zarvă *f*, zgomot *n*; zguduire *f*.

communal *adj* (*kitchen, garden*) folosit în comun; (*life, etc*) comunitar, colectiv.

commune *vi* (**with**) a fi în strânsă legătură (cu); a comunica, a sta de vorbă intim (cu) || *s* comunitate *f*; *admin* comună *f*.

communicate *vt* a comunica, a transmite

communication *s* comunicare *f*; *tele* legătură *f*; transmitere *f*.

communion *s* comuniune *f*; unire *f*.

communism *s* comunism *n*.

communist *adj/s* comunist *m*.

community *s* (*society*) comunitate *f*; proprietate *f* în comun; (*similarity*) asemănare *f*; opinia *f* publică; ~ **center** *s* cămin *n* cultural; ateneu *n*.

commute *vi* (*travel*) a face navetă; a comuta; *jur* a comuta • ~**r** *s* navetist *m*.

compact *s/adj* compact; dens; concis; înghesuit || *vt* a consolida; a face compact; a condensa || *s* (*make-up*) pudrieră *f*; (*agreement*) contract *n*; ~ **disk** *s* compact disc *n*, CD *n*; ~ **disk player** *s* lector *m* de CD-uri.

companion *s* (*buddy*) tovarăş *m*; (*attendant*) însoţitor *m*; interlocutor *m*; complice *m*; ghid *n*, manual *n*.

company *s* (*friendship*) companie *f*, tovărăşie *f*; vizitatori *m pl*; asociaţi *m pl*; (*business*) societate *f* (comercială).

comparable *adj* comparabil.

comparative *adj* comparat, comparativ; aproximativ || *s* (gradul) comparativ *n*.

compare *vt* (*contrast*) a compara; a face schimb de || *vi* a fi comparabil || *s* comparaţie *f*.

comparison *s* comparaţie *f*; asemănare *f*.

compartment *s* compartiment *n*.

compass *s* busolă *f*; (*scope*) amploare *f* • ~**es** *s pl* compas *n*.

compassion *s* (*sympathy*) compasiune *f* • ~**ate** *adj* compătimitor, milos, plin de compasiune.

compatibility *s* compatibilitate *f*.

compatible *adj* compatibil (cu).

compel *vt* (*force*) a obliga pe cineva (să facă ceva) • ~**ling** *adj* irezistibil.

compensate *vt* a compensa/despăgubi (pe cineva) || *vi* ~ **for smth** a compensa cu, a fi o compensaţie pentru.

compensation *s* compensare *f*; despăgubire *f*.

compete *vi* a concura; a se întrece.

competence *s* competenţă *f*.

competent *adj* competent, calificat.

competition *s* (*rivalry*) concurenţă *f*, rivalitate *f*; (*contest*) competiţie *f*; concurs *n*.

competitor *s* concurent *m*.

compile *vt* a alcătui, a redacta • ~**r** *s* autor *m* (de antologii).

complacency *s* mulţumire *f* de sine, automulţumire *f*.

complacent *adj* mulţumit de sine.

complain *vi* a se plânge de; a aduce o acuzaţie.

complaint *s* nemulţumire *f*; reclamaţie *f*; (*grievance*) plângere *f*; (*illness*) durere *f*; boală *f*.

complement *s* acompaniament *n*; (*number*) efectiv; *gram* complement *n* || *vt* a complini.

complete *adj* complet; total; (*done*) încheiat, terminat || *vt* (*finish*) a sfârşi, a termina, a încheia; (*perfect*) a perfecţiona, a desăvârşi.

complex *adj* complex; complicat; dificil • ~**ity** *s* complexitate *f* • ~**ion** *s* ten *n*, culoare *f* a feţei; configuraţie *f*, profil *n*.

compliant *adj* obedient, supus.

complicate *vt* a complica; a încurca ‖ *vi* a se complica; a se încurca • ~**d** *adj* complicat; complex; dificil.

complicity *s* complicitate *f*.

compliment *s* compliment *n*; laudă *f*; *pl* salutări *f pl* ‖ *vi* a face complimente cuiva; a felicita • ~**ary** *adj* laudativ, măgulitor; de felicitare; gratuit.

comply *vi* (**with**) a ceda; a fi de acord; a se supune.

component *s tech* element *n*, component *n*, reper *n*.

compose *vi* (*write*) a compune; a redacta; a culege; a se domoli; a aplana ‖ *vr* (*calm*) a se stăpâni ‖ *vi* a compune; a culege • ~**r** *s* compozitor *m*.

composition *s* compunere *f*; formare *f*; compoziţie *f*; amestec *n*; constituţie *f*; caracter *n*.

compositor *s* zeţar *m*.

compost *s* compost *n*.

composure *s* calm *n*, sânge *n* rece.

compound[1] *s chem*, *ling* compus *n*; (*number*) complex *n*; incintă *f* ‖ *vt* a compune.

compound[2] *vt* (*make worse*) a agrava, a înrăutăţi.

comprehend *vt* (*grasp*) a înţelege; a cuprinde, a include.

comprehension *s* (*grasp*) capacitate *f* de înţelegere; (*command*) cuprindere *f*.

comprehensive *adj* exhaustiv, cuprinzător, detaliat; (*insurance*) pentru toate riscurile.

compress *vt* a comprima; (*text*) a scurta.

comprise *vt* a cuprinde; **to be ~d of** a consta în, a include.

compromise *s* (*settlement*) compromis *n*; compromitere *f* ‖ *vt* a compromite; a periclita; a ajunge la un compromis; (*give in*) a renunţa la ‖ *vi* a face un compromis.

compromising *adj* compromiţător.

comptroller *s econ* controlor *m*, revizor *m*.

compulsion *s* (*strong wish*) dorinţă *f* nestăpânită; (*obligation*) constrângere *f*, silire *f*.

compulsive *adj* nestăpânit, năvalnic; (*obsessive*) obsedant; (*gripping*) captivant, palpitant; **~ shopper** persoană ahtiată după cumpărături.

compulsory *adj* obligatoriu.

compunction *s* remuşcare *f*.

compute *vt* a calcula.

computer *s* calculator *n*; maşina *f* de calcul; **~ game** *s* joc *n* electronic; **~ graphics** *s pl* grafică *f* computerizată; **~ language** *s* limbaj *n* de programare; **~ port** *s* acces *n*, intrare *f*; **~ program** *s* program *n* informatic; **~ science** *s* informatică *f* • ~**ization** *s* informatizare *f* • ~**ize** *vt* a computeriza • ~**ized** *adj* informatizat.

comrade *s* tovarăş *m*, camarad *m*.

con *s* argument *n* contra; vot *n* contra; **the pros and ~s** voturile pro şi contra.

concave *adj* concav.

conceal *vt* a ascunde, a disimula.

concede *vt* a recunoaşte; a ceda.

conceit *s* (*arrogance*) vanitate *f* • ~**ed** *adj* încrezut, vanitos; îngâmfat.

conceivable *adj* posibil, plauzibil.

conceive *vt* a concepe ‖ *vi med* a concepe, a zămisli; **~ of** *vi* a concepe, a-şi imagina.

concentrate *vt* a concentra, a aduna ‖ *vi* a se concentra, a se strânge ‖ *s* concentrat *n*.

concentration *s* concentrare *f*; strângere *f*; concentraţie *f*.

concentric *adj* concentric.

concept *s* concept *n*.

conception *s* concepţie *f*.

concern *vt* (*relate to*) a privi, (*affect*) a afecta; a preocupa ‖ *s* (*interest*) interes *n*, participare *f*; relaţie *f*; importanţă *f*; (*worry*) preocupare *f*, grijă *f* • ~**ing** *prep* privitor la, despre, referitor la • ~**ed** *adj* implicat; preocupat; îngrijorat; neliniştit.

concert *s* concert *n*; acord *n*, concordanţă *f*, armonie *f* ‖ *vt* a plănui împreună • ~**ed** *adj* (*effort*) concertat, conjugat.

concertina *s mus* concertină *f*.

concerto *s mus* concert *n*; compoziţie *f* muzicală.

concession *s* (*yielding*) concesie *f*; (*special price*) reducere *f*.

conciliation *s* conciliere *f*.

conciliate *vi* a se împăca.

conciliatory *adj* împăciuitor, conciliator.

concise *adj* concis; laconic; scurt, succint.

conclude *vt* (*end*) a încheia, a termina; a conchide; (*settle*) a stabili, a hotărî ‖ *vi* (*close*) a încheia, a termina.

concluding *adj* final

conclusion *s* (*close*) încheiere *f*, terminare *f*, (*end*) sfârşit *n*; concluzie *f*; rezumat *n*; deducţie *f*.

conclusive *adj* definitiv.

concoct *vt* a prepara, a pregăti; *fig* a scorni, a născoci, a inventa.

concomitant *adj* concomitent.

concord(ance) *s* concordanţă *f*.

concourse *s* sală *f* mare, galerie *f*.

concrete *adj* (*real*) concret; făcut din beton ‖ *s* beton *n*.

concubine *s* amantă *f*, concubină *f*.

concur *vi* (*agree*) a fi de acord (cu) • ~**rently** *adv* simultan.

concussion *s med* comoţie *f*, izbitură *f*, lovitură *f*.

condemn *vt* a condamna, a blama.

condense *vi* a condensa, a comprima ‖ *vi* a se condensa.

condescend *vi* (*positively*) a binevoi să, a găsi de cuviinţă să, a se osteni să; (*negatively*) a binevoi să, a catadicsi să; *fig* a coborî până la; a se înjosi până acolo încât să (facă ceva) • ~**ing** *adj* condescendent, binevoitor; (*atmosphere*, etc) protector.

condiment *s* condiment *n*.

condition *s* condiţie *f*; stipulaţie *f*; clauză *f*; stare *f*; situaţie *f* ‖ *vt* a condiţiona; a determina, a produce; a pregăti, a antrena • ~**al** *s gram* condiţional *n* ‖ *adj* condiţionat.

conditioner *s* (*for hair*) balsam *n*; (*for clothes*) balsam *n* de rufe.

condom *s* condom *n*, prezervativ *n*.

condo(minium) *s* apartament *n* într-un imobil în coproprietate; imobil *n* în coproprietate; *pol* condominiu *n*.

condone *vt* a trece cu vederea, a scuza.

conduce *vi* (**to**) a (con)duce (la).

conducive *adj* care contribuie la; **to be ~ to** a duce la.

conduct *s* conductă *f* ‖ *vt* a conduce, a duce (spre); *mus* a dirija • ~**or** *s mus* dirijor *m*; (*on a bus*, *train*) încasator *m*.

conduit *s* conductă *f*.

cone *s* (*~ shape*) con *n*; (*ice cream ~*) cornet *n*; *geom* con *n*; *bot* con *n*.

confabulate *vi* (**with**) a sta de vorbă (cu)
confectioner *s* cofetar *m* • ~'s (**shop**) cofetărie *f* • ~y *s* dulciuri *n pl*, produse *n pl* de cofetărie.
confederacy *s* confederație *f*, ligă *f*; **the Confederacy** *s* Statele *n pl* confederative.
confederate *adj* confederativ, federativ ‖ *s* membru *m* al unei confederații/federații; aliat *m*; complice *m* (la o crimă etc); *hist* partizan *m* al Statelor confederative.
confederation *s* confederație *f*; federație *f*; ligă *f*; alianță *f*.
confer *vt* a conferi ceva (cuiva); a da, a acorda ‖ *vi* (**with**) a discuta, a se sfătui (cu cineva despre ceva) • ~ence *s* conferință *f*; congres *n*; adunare *f*; ședință *f*.
confess *vt* (*own up*) a mărturisi, (*admit*) a recunoaște; a confesa, a spovedi ‖ *vi* a-și recunoaște (vina etc); a face mărturisiri • ~ion *s* mărturisire *f*, recunoaștere *f*; confesiune *f*, spovedanie *f*; credință *f*, crez *n*; rit *n*.
confetti *s* cofeti *n pl*.
confidant *s* confident *m*.
confide *vi* a avea încredere în; a se încrede în.
confidence *s* (*certainty*) convingere *f*; (*assurance*) siguranță *f*; (*trust*) încredere *f*; confidență *f*, secret *n*.
confidential *adj* confidențial, secret; de încredere; încrezător, credul.
confine *vt* (*subject, etc*) a limita, a restrânge; (*imprison*) a închide; a aresta; a priva de libertate ‖ *s pl* limită *f*, hotar *n*, graniță *f*.
confirm *vt* a confirma.
confiscate *vt* a confisca.
confiscation *s* confiscare *f*.
conflate *vt* a împreuna, a îngemăna.
conflict *s* conflict *n*; luptă *f*; ciocnire *f*; contradicție *f* ‖ *vi* a fi în conflict/contradicție (cu).
confluence *s* confluență *f*.
conform *vt* a pune de acord ‖ *vi* a se acorda, a fi în concordanță.
confound *vt* a zăpăci, a ului.
confront *vt* (~ *an issue, enemy*) a înfrunta; (*challenge*) a confrunta pe cineva (cu).
confuse *vt* a confunda; (*mix up*) a amesteca, (*obscure*) a încurca; (*puzzle*) a zăpăci; a intimida.
confusing *adj* derutant.
confusion *s* confuzie *f*, încurcătură *f*; dezordine *f*; zăpăceală *f*, perplexitate *f*.
congeal *vi* (*blood*) a se coagula.
congenial *adj* simpatic, agreabil.
congenital *adj* congenital.
congested *adj* (*street*) aglomerat; *med* congestionat.
conglomerate *s geol, fig* conglomerat *n*.
conglomeration *s* congestionare *f*, aglomerare *f*; amestec *n*, amestecătură *f*, conglomerat *n*.
congratulate *vt* a felicita.
congratulations *interj* felicitări!; bravo!.
congregate *vi* a (se) aduna, a (se) întruni.
congress *s* congres *n*; adunare *f* generală; **the U.S. Congress** congresul *n* SUA.
congruent *adj frml* (*fitting*) corespunzător, adecvat; *math* congruent.
conic(al) *adj* conic.
conifer *s bot* conifer *n*.
conjecture *s* (*guess*) presupunere *f*, bănuială *f*; suspiciune *f*; ipoteză *f* ‖ *vt/vi* (*suppose*) a bănui, a presupune.
conjugal *adj* conjugal.
conjugate *vt/vi* a conjuga

conjugation *s* conjugare *f*.
conjunction *s gram* conjuncție *f*.
conjunctivitis *s med* conjunctivită *f*.
conjure *vt* (*invoke*) a invoca, a chema; (*juggle*) a face să apară/dispară prin scamatorii; a vrăji, a fermeca • ~r *s* scamator *m*.
connect *vt* a lega; a uni; a asocia; a conecta ‖ *vi* a fi în legătură (cu) • ~ion *s* (*bond*) legătură *f*, corespondență *f*; (*relation*) rude *f pl*; cunoscuți *m pl*; relații *f pl*.
connive *vi* a complota; (*condone*) a îngădui, a permite; ~ **at smth** *vi* a închide ochii asupra.
connoisseur *s* cunoscător *m*.
connotation *s* conotație *f*.
connubial *adj* conjugal.
conquer *vt* a cuceri, a câştiga ‖ *vi* a învinge • ~or *s* învingător *m*.
conquest *s* cucerire *f*.
conscience *s* conștiință *f*; cuget *n*.
conscientious *adj* conștiincios.
conscious *adj* conștient, lucid; treaz; inteligent; intenționat; voit • ~ness *s* cunoștință *f*; conștiență *f*; conștiință *f*.
conscript *s mil* recrut *m*, recrutat *m*.
consecrate *vt* a consacra.
consecration *s* consacrare *f*.
consecutive *adj* consecutiv, succesiv.
consensus *s* consens *n*.
consent *s* (*permission*) consimțământ *n*, permisiune *f*; acord *n* ‖ *vi* (**to**) a consimți (să); a-și da consimțământul (la; să).
consequence *s* consecință *f*, urmare *f*; importanță *f*, însemnătate *f*.
consequently *adv* drept urmare, în consecință, de aceea.
conservative *adj/s* conservator *n*.
conservatory *s* seră *f*; *mus* conservator *n*.
conserve *vt* (~ *energy, food*) a economisi; (~ *nature, wildlife*) a proteja ‖ *s* dulceață *f*.
consider *vt* (*think*) a se gândi la; (*contemplate*) a intenționa; (*believe*) a considera, a crede ‖ *vr* a se crede, a se considera ‖ *vi* a judeca.
considerable *adj* considerabil, remarcabil.
considerate *adj* (*kind*) prevenitor, amabil; (*thoughtful*) atent (cu); **it's ~ of you to help him** e frumos din partea ta să-l ajuți.
consideration *s* considerație *f*, respect *n*; considerare *f*; apreciere *f*; (*factor*) considerent *n*; argument *n*.
consign *vt* (~ *goods*) a expedia; (*entrust*) a încredința • ~ment *s* expediere *f*, expediție *f* de marfă.
consist *vi* a sta în; a consta în; a se reduce la • ~ent *adj* consistent; (*steady*) solid; des; (*constant*) consecvent; logic; (*in harmony*) compatibil.
consolation *s* consolare *f*.
console *vt* a consola, a mângâia, a încuraja.
consolidate *vt/vi* a (se) consolida.
consolidation *s* consolidare *f*.
consommé *s* consome *n*.
consonant *s gram* consoană *f*.
conspicuous *adj* izbitor; remarcabil.
conspiracy *s* conspirație *f*; uneltire *f*.
conspire *vi* a complota; (*chance*) a contribui la a face ceva.
constable *s* polițist *m*.
constancy *s* constanță *f*; fidelitate *f*.
constant *adj* constant, stabil, permanent; fidel ‖ *s* constantă *f*.

constellation s constelație f.
consternation s consternare f.
constipated adj constipat.
constipation s constipație f.
constituency s circumscripție f electorală; alegători m pl.
constituent adj constitutiv, component; pol constituent ‖ s constituent n, parte f constitutivă/componentă; ling constituent m imediat; pol alegător m.
constitute vt a constitui, a compune; (establish) a constitui, a forma.
constitution s (charter) constituție f; sistem n de guvernământ; organism n; structură f • ~al adj constituțional.
constrain vt a constrânge • ~ed adj fals, afectat.
constraint s (self-control) reținere f, rezervă f; constrângere f.
constrict vt a strânge, a comprima; a contracta.
construct vi (build) a construi, a clădi; a imagina; (create) a crea • ~ion s construire f; construcție f; clădire f; interpretare f • ~ive adj de construcție; constructiv.
consul s consul m • ~ate s consulat n.
consult vt a consulta; a se sfătui cu; a ține cont de; a lua în considerație • ~ant s specialist m, expert m • ~ation s consultare f.
consume vt (eat) a consuma, a mânca sau a bea; (use) a uza, a folosi; (destroy) a irosi, a cheltui ‖ vi a se consuma (din cauza) • ~r s consumator m; ~ credit s credit n de consum; ~ goods s pl bunuri npl de consum.
consuming adj mistuitor.
consummate adj desăvârșit, perfect ‖ vt a finaliza.
consumption s consum; tuberculoză f.
contact s contact n; (~ person) relație f, contact n ‖ vt a contacta, a lua legătura cu; (phone) a lua legătura cu; in ~ (with smb) adv în legătură/contact cu cineva; to make ~ with smb vt a stabili contactul/intra în contact cu cineva.
contagious adj contagios, molipsitor, infecțios.
contain vt (hold) a conține, a cuprinde, a include; (control) a înfrâna, a-și stăpâni.
contaminate vt a murdări, a polua; a strica, a contamina, a corupe.
contemplate vt (consider) a plănui, a intenționa, a contempla ‖ vi a medita.
contemplation s cugetare f, meditație f; reverie f.
contemporaneous adj contemporan.
contemporary adj contemporan; simultan; concomitent; modern ‖ s contemporan m.
contempt s dispreț n; ~ of court jur sfidarea f curții.
contend vi (fight) a se lupta; (compete) a se întrece; (vie) a rivaliza, a fi rivali; (argue) a discuta (în contradictoriu) ‖ vt (that) a susține, a afirma (că) • ~er s competitor m.
content[1] s volum n, capacitate f, conținut n; esență f, miez n; (ant: form) substanță f. • ~s s conținut n; volum n; cuprins n, tablă f de materii.
content[2] adj mulțumit, satisfăcut ‖ vt a mulțumi, a satisface • ~ment s stare f de mulțumire.
contention s controversă f, litigiu n.
contentious adj litigios, contestat.
contest s (fight) luptă f; (race) întrecere f; competiție f; (argument) controversă f ‖ vt (challenge) a contesta, a nega; (dispute) a dezbate, a disputa.

context s context n.
contiguous adj (next) alăturat; adiacent; învecinat.
continent s continent n.
contingency s întâmplare f, accident n; eveniment n neprevăzut.
contingent adj întâmplător, accidental; neprevăzut.
continual adj continuu, neîntrerupt; repetat.
continuance s continuare f; continuitate f.
continuation s continuare f.
continue vt (go on) a continua, a urma; (resume) a relua; a menține ‖ vi a continua; (remain) a rămâne; (last) a dura.
continuous adj continuu, neîntrerupt; progresiv.
contort vi a răsuci, a deforma.
contour s contur n; (map) curbă f de nivel.
contraband s contrabandă f ‖ adj de contrabandă.
contraception s med contracepție f, prevenirea f sarcinii.
contraceptive s/adj anticoncepțional n.
contract s (pact) contract n, (agreement) acord n, înțelegere f ‖ vt (catch) a contracta; (reduce) a prescurta; a contrage • ~or s parte f la un contract • ~ual adj contractual.
contradict vt a contrazice; a fi în contradicție cu; a contraveni.
contralto s mus contralto n.
contraption s coll șmecherie f, drăcie f.
contrariwise adv pe de altă parte; în direcție inversă; dimpotrivă.
contrary adj (opposing) contrar, opus; nefavorabil; (stubborn) încăpățânat ‖ s (reverse) contrar n; (opposite) opus n.
contrast s contrast n, opoziție f; (difference) diferență f ‖ vt a contrasta, a opune; a compara ‖ vi a contrasta, a forma un contrast.
contravene vt (law) a contraveni (legii); fig a contrazice.
contravention s contravenție f.
contribute vt a contribui cu; a colabora cu; a scrie (pentru).
contribution s contribuție f; participare f; colaborare f; articol n.
contributor s factor m determinant; (~ of money) donator m; (~ on paper) colaborator m, corespondent m • ~y adj determinant, contributoriu.
contrite adj pocăit, spășit.
contrition s pocăință f; regret n.
contrivance s (device) dispozitiv n, mecanism n; ingeniozitate f; tertip n.
contrive vt (invent) a descoperi, a inventa; (manage) a găsi mijlocul de a face ceva • ~d adj tras de păr.
control vt (check) a controla, a verifica; (regulate) a reglementa, a norma; (run) a dirija, a conduce; (rule) a stăpâni; a comanda ‖ s control n, verificare f; normare f; reglare f; conducere f.
controller s controlor m; revizor m.
controversial adj controversat; discutabil.
controversy s controversă f, discuție f în contradictoriu.
contusion s contuzie f.
conundrum s șaradă f.
convalesce vi a fi în convalescență • ~nce s convalescență f.
convector s radiator n cu convecție.
convene vt a convoca, a reuni ‖ vi a se reuni, a se strânge.
convenience s comoditate f; confort n; at your earliest

~ cât mai curând posibil; ~ **store** magazin *n* universal în cartier.

convenient *adj* confortabil; comod; (*suitable*) convenabil, avantajos.

convent *s relig* mănăstire *f.*

convention *s* (*meeting*) convenție *f;* (*practice*) obicei *n,* convenție *f* • **~al** *adj* (*typical*) convențional, (*standard*) tradițional; normal; artificial; curtenitor; monden.

converge *vi also fig* a converge.

conversant *adj* (**with**) cunoscător (în ale).

conversation *s* conversație *f,* discuție *f;* purtare *f,* comportare *f.*

converse[1] *vi* a conversa, a sta de vorbă, a discuta.

converse[2] *adj* opus; contrar; invers; reciproc ‖ *s* opus *n,* contrar *n;* parte *f* întregitoare; *math* teoremă *f* reciprocă; *gram* inversiune *f.*

conversion *s* transformare *f,* schimbare *f.*

convert *vt* a transforma, a preface; *relig* a converti; *econ* a converti, a preschimba; *jur* a-și însuși, a-și apropria (ilegal) ‖ *s relig* convertit *m; pol* transfug *m* • **~ible** *s* (*car*) limuzină *f* decapotabilă ‖ *adj* transformabil; *econ, etc* convertibil.

convex *adj* convex.

convey *vt* (*carry*) a transporta; (*express*) a comunica (ceva cuiva).

convict *vt* a dovedi că cineva este vinovat; a declara vinovat; a condamna ‖ *s* condamnat *m,* ocnaș *m* • **~ion** *s* convingere *f; jur* condamnare *f.*

convince *vt* a convinge.

convincing *adj* convingător.

convolution *s* circumvoluțiune *f,* șerpuire *f;* cot *n;* (*involvement*) întortochere *f;* (*intricacy*) complexitate *f.*

convolvulvus *s bot* volbură *f.*

convoy *s* convoi *n.*

coo *vi orn* a gânguri.

cook *s* bucătar *m,* bucătăreasă *f* ‖ *vt* a găti; a fierbe; a coace; a prăji etc ‖ *vi* a găti, a fi bucătar; a se găti; a se fierbe • **~book** *s* carte *f* de bucate • **~er** *s* mașină *f* de gătit • **~ery** *s* artă *f* culinară, gastronomie *f.*

cookie *s* biscuit *m,* fursec *n.*

cool *adj* (*cold*) răcoros; calm; liniștit; nepăsător; indiferent; (*composed*) imperturbabil; (*unfriendly*) rece, neprietenos; (*trendy*) monden ‖ *vt* a răcori ‖ *vi* a se răcori; a se răci; ~ **it!** *coll* las-o mai moale!; **to keep one's** ~ a se ține cu firea.

coop *s* coteț *n* de păsări; **to** ~ **up** *vt coll* a izola, a închide.

cooper *s* dogar *m.*

cooperate *vi* a coopera; a conlucra.

cooperation *s* cooperare *f;* conlucrare *f;* cooperație *f.*

cooperative *adj* cooperatist.

co-opt *vt* a coopta.

coordinate *adj* coordonat; egal, de același fel ‖ *vt* a coordona, a pune de acord.

coordination *s* coordonare *f.*

cop *s coll* polițai *m.*

cope[1] *vi* a face față; a se descurca; a învinge.

cope[2] *s relig* sfită *f;* manta *f,* mantie *f;* acoperământ *n;* boltă *f* (cerească).

Copenhagen *s* Copenhaga.

copier *s* (foto) copiator *n.*

co-pilot *s* copilot *m.*

copious *adj* copios; abundent.

copper[1] *s* (*metal*) cupru *n;* aramă *f;* (*money*) monedă *f* de cupru; cazan *n* de aramă.

copper[2] *s also* **cop** *sl coll* polițai *m.*

coppice, copse *s* crâng *n,* dumbravă *f.*

copulate *vi* a se împreuna, a se împerechea.

copy *s* (*replica*) copie *f,* (*immitation*) imitație *f;* reproducere *f;* manuscris *n;* text *n* ‖ *vt* a copia; a scrie un text; a imita.

copyright *s* drept *n* de autor.

coral *s* coral *m.*

cord *s* sfoară *f;* șnur *n;* șiret *n;* cordon *n;* funie *f;* cablu *n;* coardă *f.*

cordial *adj* cordial, călduros ‖ *s* întăritor *n,* tonic *n.*

cordon *s* cordon *n;* **to** ~ **off** *vt* a bara (cu un cordon de poliție).

corduroy *s* catifea *f* reiată.

core *s* (~ *of fruit*) cotor *n;* (*earth*) miez *n;* (*reactor*) interior *n; fig* (*people*) nucleu *n;* (*issues, politics*) esențial *n* ‖ *vt* a scoate miezul.

cork *s* dop *n;* bușon *n;* plută *f* ‖ *vt* a astupa cu un dop; a ascunde • **~screw** *s* tirbușon *n.*

corn[1] *s* grăunte *m,* bob *n;* grâne *f pl;* cereale *f pl;* grâu *n;* porumb *m* ‖ *vt* a granula; a săra (carnea).

corn[2] *s med* bătătură *f.*

cornea *s anat* cornee *f.*

corner *s* colț *n,* ungher *n;* loc *n* retras ‖ *vt* a încolți.

cornet *s mus* (*also paper*) cornet *n.*

cornflakes *s pl* fulgi *m pl* de porumb.

corny *adj coll* (*joke*) învechit; răsuflat, banalizat; (*story, movie*) siropos.

corollary *s* corolar *n,* concluzie *f.*

coronary *adj* coronarian; ~ **thrombosis** infarct *n* miocardic.

coronation *s* încoronare *f.*

corporal[1] *adj* corporal; ~ **punishment** pedeapsă *f* corporală.

corporal[2] *s mil* caporal *m.*

corporate *adj* corporativ; comun.

corporation *s* corporație *f;* societate *f* pe acțiuni; municipalitate *f.*

corporeal *adj* fizic, material; trupesc, carnal.

corps *s* corp *n* (diplomatic, expediționar etc).

corpse *s* cadavru *n.*

corpulent *adj* corpolent.

corpuscle *s* globulă *f;* **red/white** (**blood**) **~s** globule roșii/albe.

corral *s* țarc *n,* ocol *n;* tabără *f* (înconjurată de căruțe).

correct *adj* (*right*) corect; exact; just; (*proper*) corespunzător ‖ *vt* a corecta; (*rectify*) a îndrepta; a potrivi • **~ion** *s* corectare *f;* corectură *f;* corecție *f;* corectitudine *f;* pedeapsă *f; chem* rectificare *f.*

correlate *vi* a corespunde; a pune în corelație.

correlation *s* corelație *f.*

correspond *vi* a corespunde; a corespunde, a se potrivi, a se armoniza • **~ence** *s* corespondență *f;* concordanță *f;* asemănare *f* • **~ent** *s* corespondent *m* de presă; persoană *f* cu care se corespondează.

corridor *s* coridor *n,* culoar *n.*

corroborate *vt* a corobora, a confirma, a întări.

corroboration *s* coroborare *f;* confirmare *f.*

corrode *vi* a coroda, a roade; a oxida ‖ *vi* a se coroda, a se oxida.

corrosion *s* coroziune *f.*

corrosive *adj* coroziv; *fig* caustic.

corrugated *adj* ondulat, încrețit; ~ **iron** tablă *f* ondulată.

corrupt *adj* (*shady*) corupt, imoral, depravat; venal; viciat ‖ *vt* a corupe; a mitui; a priva de drepturi civile

• **~ion** s putrezire f, descompunere f; corupție f;
depravare f; denaturare f, falsificare f.
corset s corset n.
cosignatory s cosemnatar m; contrasemnatar m.
cosmetic adj fig superficial || s produs n cosmetic.
cosmic adj cosmic.
cosmonaut s cosmonaut m.
cosmopolitan s/adj cosmopolit m.
cosmos s cosmos n.
cost vt a costa, a face; a evalua, a prețui; a cere, a
reclama || s cost n; (price) preț n, valoare f; (outlay)
cheltuieli f pl || adj de cost; ~ **estimate** s deviz n; ~
price s preț n de cost; ~ **of living** costul vieții • **~ly**
adj scump • **~s** spl cheltuieli fpl de judecată.
coster(monger) s vânzător m ambulant de fructe,
legume etc.
costive adj constipat.
costume s costum n; fel n de a se îmbrăca, stil n
vestimentar.
cot s pat n de campanie, pat n pliant.
cottage s casă f țărănească; (hut) bordei n; casă f la
țară; (chalet) vilă f; ~ **cheese** s brânză f de vaci.
cotton s bumbac; țesătură f de bumbac, stambă f; vată
f; ață f (de bumbac); ~ **wool** s vată f, vată f hidrofilă.
couch s sofa f, divan n, canapea f; cușetă f; bârlog n,
vizuină f || vt (express) a exprima, a formula, a
redacta; (put/lay down) a culca; (lower head) a
înclina; (lower spear) a coborî.
cougar s zool cuguar m, pumă f.
cough vi a tuși || vt a expectora || s tuse f; tușit n.
could v mod *can.
council s consiliu n, sfat n; sinod n || adj de consiliu.
counsel s sfat n; avocat m.
count[1] vt (tally) a număra; a socoti; a calcula; (deem) a
considera || vi a număra; a socoti; a fi inclus; a conta
|| s numărătoare f, numărare f; calcul n; considerație
f; total n, sumă f.
count[2] s conte m • **~ess** s contesă f.
counter[1] s (shop, etc) tejghea f, ghișeu n; pion n.
counter[2] adj contrar || vt (~ a blow) a para; **to** ~ **smth**
(with) a riposta.
counteract vt a contracara, a contrabalansa.
counterattack vt/vi a contraataca.
counterbalance vt a contrabalansa; a contracara.
counterespionage s contraspionaj n.
counterfeit adj contrafăcut, fals || s contrafacere f || vt a
contraface, a falsifica.
counterfoil s talon n al unui chitanțier.
counteroffer s contraofertă f.
counterpane s cuvertură f.
counterpart s (person) omolog m; (thing) echivalent n.
countersign vt a contrasemna || s mil etc parolă f;
contrasemnătură f.
countrified adj rustic, pastoral.
country s (nation) țară f, (state) stat n; (motherland)
patrie f; loc n natal; **the** ~ țară f, provincie f; ținut n,
regiune f || adj rural, rustic; provincial; ~ **music** s
muzică f country • **~house** s reședință f la țară • **~man**
s compatriot m.
county s comitat n, district n; județ n; ~ **seat/town** s
reședință f de județ.
coup s pol (revolt) lovitură f (de stat); (success)
lovitură f (de maestru).
couple s (pair) pereche f; cuplu n; soț m și soție f || vt a

împerechea; (fasten) a lega, (join) a uni; (team) a
asocia, a cupla.
coupon s cupon n; talon n; bon n.
courage s (guts) curaj n; (bravery) bravură f, (valor)
viteje f • **~ous** adj curajos; brav; viteaz.
courgette s bot dovlecel m.
courier s curier m; comisionar m; mesager m (diplomatic); agent m.
course s (classes) curs n, desfășurare f; (flow) scurgere
f; durată f, timp n; mers n, direcție f; purtare f, comportare f; mod n, manieră f; fel n de mâncare; pistă f,
teren n; ciclu f, serie f; puls n, tendință f || vi a urma
un curs; a circula; a alerga; a curge.
court s curte f; ogradă f; jur judecătorie f, tribunal n; sp
teren n de sport; avansuri n pl || vt (woo) a curta; (ask
for) a atrage asupra sa; ~ **of law** s tribunal n; ~
martial s curte f marțială • **~room** s sală f de judecată
• **~ship** s curte f (făcută unei femei).
courteous adj curtenitor, manierat, bine crescut.
courtesan s curtezană f.
courtesy s politețe f.
courtier s curtean m.
courtly adj prevenitor, politicos.
courtyard s curte f; ogradă f.
cousin s văr m sau verișoară f; rudă f, neam n.
cove s golf n.
covenant s pact n, acord n, convenție f.
cover vt a acoperi; (conceal) a ascunde; (shield) a
apăra; (include) a cuprinde; (deal with) a trata;
(cross) a parcurge; a cloci; a asigura || vi a forma un
strat gros || s învelitoare f, înveliș n; capac n; toc n;
teacă f, plic n; copertă f; refugiu n; pretext n;
acoperire f; ~ **letter** s scrisoare f de intenție; econ
scrisoare f de trăsură • **~age** s acoperire f.
covert adj ascuns, tainic; latent.
covet vt a râvni; a dori cu înfocare; a invidia • **~ous** adj
(greedy) lacom, ahtiat, avid; (envious) invidios.
cow s zool vacă f; femelă f,
cowboy s cowboy m.
coward s (om) fricos m, laș m || adj fricos, laș • **~ly** adj
laș, fricos.
cower vi a se ghemui.
cowl s glugă f; rasă f de călugăr.
coworker s coleg m de servici.
coxcomb s creastă f de cocoș; tichie f de bufon.
coy adj timid, sfios.
coyote s zool coiot m.
coziness s confort n.
cozy adj comod, confortabil; (room) călduros; intim,
prietenos.
crab s crab m; homar m; rac m; **the Crab** Cancerul n,
Racul n; astrol zodia f Cancerului • **~apple** s măr m
sălbatic • **~by** adj morocănos • **~bed** adj (writing)
neciteț.
crack s (snap) pocnet n; pocnitură f; (crash) trosnet n;
bubuit n; (chink) crăpătură f, fisură f; deschizătură f;
(joke) glumă f || adj de calitate superioara; de elită ||
vt a pocni din, a trosni din; a crăpa; (break) a sparge;
a strica; a întrerupe || vi a pocni; a crăpa.
cracker s biscuit m, fursec n.
crackle vi (fire) a trosni; (radio, etc) a pârâi.
cradle s leagăn n; tech nacelă f || vt (person) a legăna;
(object) a umbla cu grijă.
craft s (skill) meșteșug n; naut ambarcațiune f.
crafty adj viclean.

crag *s* colț *n* de stâncă.

cram *vt* (*stuff*) a îndesa, (*fill up*) umple; a ghiftui; (*force*) a îndopa; a băga în cap; (*study*) a toci (o materie), a învăța mecanic ‖ *s* înghesuială *f*, aglomerație *f*; toceală *f*.

cramp *s med* crampă *f* ‖ *vt* a stânjeni, a împiedica.

cranberry *s bot* merișor *m*.

crane *s* macara *f*.

crank *s tech* manivelă *f*; *coll* (*person*) excentric *m*.

cranny *s* (*crack*) crăpătură *f*; (*crevice*) crevasă *f*.

crap *s vulg* fecale *f pl*, rahat *n*, balegă *f*, tâmpenii *f pl* • ~s *s* barbut *n*.

crash *vi* (*collapse*) a se prăbuși; a se sparge; (*fail*) a da greș; a se ruina; (*go bust*) a da faliment ‖ *vt* a doborî; a sfărâma ‖ *s* (*car* ~) accident *n*; (*train* ~) ciocnire *f*; (*stockmarket* ~) faliment *n*, crah *n*; prăbușire *f*, ruină *f*; bubuit *n*; trosnet *n* ‖ *adj* (*course*) intensiv; riguros; brusc; ~ **helmet** *s* cască *f* de protecție; ~ **land** *vi* a ateriza forțat.

crate *s* coș *n* mare, ladă *f*, hârdău *n*.

crater *s* crater *n*.

cravat *s* cravată *f*; fular *n*; eșarfă *f*.

crave *vt* (~ *affection*) a fi însetat de; (~ *cigarettes*) a fi dependent de ‖ *vi* ~ **for** a dori mult, a fi însetat de; (~ *cigarettes*) a tânji după.

crawl *vi* (*baby*) a merge în patru labe; (*person*) a se târî; (*traffic*) a merge încet ‖ *s sp* **the** ~ craul *n*.

crayfish *s* langustă *f*, rac *m*.

crayon *s* creion *n* colorat.

craze *s* nebunie *f*; mânie *f*.

crazy *adj* (*mad*) nebun, dement, smintit; (*foolish*) nebunesc, prostesc; mânios; (*wild*) dezechilibrat.

creak *vi* (*door*) a scârțâi.

cream *s* frișcă *f*; cremă *f*; spumă *f*; elită *f* ‖ *adj* crem ‖ *vt* a lua crema de pe.

crease *s* cută *f*, încrețitură *f*, pliu *n* ‖ *vt* a încreți ‖ *vi* (*cloth*) a se șifona.

create *vt* (*produce*) a crea; (*make*) a face; a numi; a acorda titlul de; (*generate*) a stârni; a lăsa (o impresie etc).

creation *s* creare *f*, facere *f*; numire *f*, acordare *f* a unui titlu; creație *f*, operă *f*.

creative *adj* creator, inventiv.

creativity *s* creativitate *f*.

creator *s* creator *m*.

creature *s* (*being*) creatură *f*, făptură *f*, ființă *f*; animal *n* domestic; rob *m*, sclav *m*, unealtă *f*.

credential *s* încredere *f*; scrisoare *f* de recomandare; (*permit*) legitimație *f*; *pl* scrisori *f pl* de acreditare.

credibility *s* credibilitate *f*.

credible *adj* credibil, plauzibil.

credit *s* (*recognition*) credit *n*; credibilitate *f*; influență *f*; (*trust*) încredere *f*; (*repute*) reputație *f*, renume *n*; cinste *f*, (*honor*) onoare *f*; aprobare *f* ‖ *vt* a credita; a împrumuta; a crede în; ~ **account** *s* cont *n* creditor; ~ **card** *s* carte *f* de credit; ~ **line** *s* linie *f* de credit • ~**able** *adj* meritoriu • ~**or** *s* creditor *m*.

credulity *s* credulitate *f*.

credulous *adj* credul.

creed *s* principii *n pl*; *relig* credință *f*.

creep *vi* (*crawl*) a se târî; (*sneak*) a se furișa; (*clamber*) a se cățăra; (*skulk*) a se strecura ‖ *s* târâre *f*; furișare *f*; dilatare *f* • ~**er** *s* animal *n* târâtor; plantă *f* agățătoare • ~**y** *adj* înfricoșător.

cremate *vt* a incinera

cremation *s* incinerare *f*.

crematorium *s* (*pl* –**ria**) crematoriu *n*.

crematory *s* crematoriu *n*.

crêpe *s* (*material*) crep *n*; (*pancake*) clătită *f*.

crescent *s* (*moon*) lună *f* nouă, semilună *f*; stradă *f* în semicerc.

cress *s bot* creson *n*, brâncuță *f*.

crest *s* (*of a bird*, *hill*) creastă *f*; (*heraldry*) coamă *f*, panaș *n*.

cretin *s* cretin *m*.

crevice *s* crăpătură *f*, fisură *f*.

crew *s* (*squad*) echipaj *n*; brigadă *f*; (*group*) grup *n*; (*party*) companie *f*; (*team*) echipă *f*.

crib *s* iesle *f*; pătuț *n*, pat *n* (de copil); odăiță *f*; casă *f*, locuință *f*; magazin *n*; furtișag *n* ‖ *vt* a închide; a înghesui; a copia.

cricket[1] *s ento* greier *m*.

cricket[2] *s sp* cricket *n*.

crime *s* delict *n*; infracțiune *f*; crimă *f*; asasinat *n*; mârșăvie *f*.

criminal *adj* criminal, penal ‖ *s* criminal *m*; asasin *m*, ucigaș *m*.

crimson *adj* (*color*) purpuriu, roșu aprins; (*shame*) roșu ‖ *s* carmin *n*.

cringe *vi* a da înapoi.

crinkle *vi* (~ *clothes*) a mototoli; a încreți.

cripple *s* infirm *m*, schilod *m*, invalid *m* ‖ *vt* a schilodi; a mutila; a paraliza; a strica.

crisis *s* criză *f*; moment *n* crucial.

crisp *adj* (*crunchy*) crocant; fragil; (*cool*) rece; (*chilly*) înghețat; (*bracing*) răcoros, (*fresh*) proaspăt; ondulat; vioi; precis, clar; (*brisk*) animat ‖ *vt* a prăji bine; a ondula ‖ *vi* a deveni crocant; a se ondula.

crisscross *s* încrucișare *f*; întretăiere *f*, intersecție *f* ‖ *adj* încrucișat, întretăiat ‖ *vi* a se întretăia ‖ *adv* contrar; aiurea, pe dos.

criterion *s* (*pl* **criteria**) criteriu *n*.

critic *s* critic *m* • ~**ism** *s* critică *f* • ~**al** *adj* critic; decisiv, hotărâtor; culminant; riscant, periculos.

criticize *vt* a critica; a dezaproba.

croak *s* croncănit *n*; orăcăit *n* ‖ *vi* a croncăni; a orăcăi; a bombăni; a vorbi răgușit.

crochet *s* croșetă *f*, lucru *n* croșetat.

crockery *s* faianță *f*; olărie *f*.

crocodile *s zool* crocodil *m*.

crocus *s bot* șofran *n*.

crony *s coll* prieten *m* bun, amic *m*.

crook *s* cârjă *f*; cârlig *n*; cange *f*; cotitură *f*; meandră *f*; cocoașă *f*; (*criminal*) escroc *m* ‖ *vt* a îndoi, a încovoia • ~**ed** *adj* încovoiat, cocoșat; îndoit; necinstit; reprobabil.

crop *s* (*harvest*) recoltă *f*; seceriș *n*; cultură *f*; serie *f*; masă *f*; păr *m* tăiat scurt; bici *n*, cravașă *f* ‖ *vt* (*gather*) a recolta, (*pick*) a culege; a cultiva, a crește; (*clip*) a tunde.

croquet *s* (*game*) crochet *n*.

cross *s* cruce *f*; semnul *n* crucii; crucifix *n*; încrucișare *f*; hibrid *m*; intersecție *f* ‖ *adj* transversal; (*angry*) supărat (pe); contrariu ‖ *vt* a intersecta; a traversa; a hibridiza; (*thwart*) a se opune; a contrazice; ~ **section** *s* (*drawing*) secțiune *f* transversală; (*sample*) eșantion *n*.

cross-examine *vt jur* a supune unui interogatoriu.

cross-eyed *adj med* sașiu.

crossfire *s* foc *n* încrucișat.

crossing *s* traversare *f*; intersecţie *f*.
cross-legged *adv* cu picioarele încrucişate; picior peste picior.
cross-reference *s* notă *f* de trimitere (în cărţi).
crossroads *s pl* intersecţie *f*.
crosswind *s* vânt *n* din lateral.
crosswise *adv* în cruciş.
crossword puzzle *s* joc *n* de cuvinte încrucişate.
crotch *s* şliţ *n*; bifurcare *f*; prăjină *f* (de rufe).
crotchet *s mus* pătrime *f*; idee *f* năstruşnică/ciudată, fantezie *f*.
crouch *vi* a se chirci, a se aşeza pe vine.
crow *s* cioară *f*; corb *m*; cântecul *n* cocoşului, cucurigu *n*; strigăt *n* de bucurie || *vi* (*rooster*) a cânta; (*baby*) a gânguri.
crowd *s* (*mass*) mulţime *f*, masă *f*; înghesuială *f*; (*host*) grămadă *f* || *vt* a umple, (*cram*) a înţesa; a ticsi; (*squeeze*) a presa || *vi* (*gather*) a se îngrămădi; a se înghesui.
crown *s* coroană *f*; (*hill*) culme *f*, creştet *n*; (*hat*) calotă *f* || *vt* (~ *a king*) a încorona; *fig* (*efforts*) a încununa; a încheia, a sfârşi.
crucial *adj* crucial; decisiv; hotărâtor; (*critical*) critic.
crucify *vt* a răstigni, a crucifica.
crude *adj* brut, neprelucrat; necopt; imatur; grosolan; needucat; ţipător.
cruel *adj* crud, nemilos; chinuitor.
cruise *vi* a face o croazieră; a patrula pe mare; a călători || *s* croazieră *f*; navigare *f*, plutire *f* • ~**r** *s* iaht *n*/motonavă *f* de croazieră; crucişător *n*.
crumb *s* fărâmă *f*, fărâmitură *f*; miez *n* de pâine.
crumble *vt* (*crush*) a face fărâme / *vi* (*fall to pieces*) a se face fărâme; a se preface în ruine; a se spulbera; (*collapse*) a se nărui.
crumple *vi* a mototoli.
crunch *vt* a roade, a ronţăi || *vi* a scârţâi || *s* ronţăit *n*; scârţâit *n* • ~**y** *adj* crocant.
crusade *s* cruciadă *f*; campanie *f* || *vi* a lua parte la o cruciadă/campanie; a duce o campanie/luptă.
crush *vt* (*quash*) a strivi; a zdrobi; a şifona; (*subdue*) a supune; a paraliza; a copleşi || *vi* a se înghesui; a-şi croi drum; a se şifona || *s* (*press*) înghesuială *f*; (*squeeze*) strivire *f*; apăsare *f*; lovitură *f*; suc *n* de portocale.
crust *s* coajă *f*; crustă *f*, înveliş *n* || *vt* a acoperi cu o crustă; a prinde coajă.
crutch *s* cârjă *f*; suport *n*; sprijin *n*.
cry *vi* (*yell*) a ţipa; (*weep*) a plânge; (*wail*) a jeli; (*howl*) a urla, a lătra; a zbiera; (*call*) a striga || *vt* (*exclaim*) a exclama; a anunţa cu glas tare || *s* (*shout*) ţipăt *n*; plânset *n*; (*scream*) strigăt *n*.
crypt *s* criptă *f*.
cryptic *adj* ascuns, secret, misterios.
crystal *s* cristal *n*.
cub *s zool* pui *m* de animal; (~ *scout*) lupuşor *m*.
cube *s* cub *n* || *vt* a ridica la cub; a tăia sub formă de cuburi
cubic *adj* cubic; (*in units*) cub.
cubicle *s* (*for changing*) cabină *f*; nişă *f*; alcov *n*.
cuckoo *s* cucu *m*.
cucumber *s* castravete *m*.
cuddle *s* mângâiere *f*, răsfăţ *n* || *vt* a dezmierda, a alinta; (*hug*) a îmbrăţişa || *vi* a se lipi (de cineva); a se strânge/cuibări la pieptul cuiva; a se ghemui, a se încolăci.

cue¹ *s thea, tv* replică *f*, semnal *n*; **on** ~ la momentul potrivit.
cue² *s* (*billiards*) tac *n*.
cuff¹ *s* manşetă *f*; ~ **links** *s pl* butoniere *f pl*.
cuff² *s* cătuşă *f* || *vt* a pune în cătuşe; a pălmui.
culinary *adj* culinar.
cull *vt* (~ *flowers, animals etc*) a strânge, a culege; (~ *text*) a alege, a selecta; a spicui.
culminate *vi* (**in**) a culmina (în, prin), a ajunge la un punct culminant.
culmination *s* punct *n* culminant; *astron* culminaţie *f*.
culprit *s jur* acuzat *m*, pârât *m*; vinovat *m*.
cult *s relig*, *fig* cult *n*.
cultivate *vt* (*plant*) a cultiva; (*grow*) a creşte; (*nurture*) a educa, a instrui.
cultivation *s* cultivare *f* (a pământului); cultură *f* (a plantelor); cultivare *f*, dezvoltare *f* (a intelectului); educaţie *f*; cultură *f*.
culture *s* cultură *f*; semănătură *f*; creştere *f*, cultivare *f*; nivel *n* intelectual || *vt* a cultiva.
cultural *adj* cultural; de cultură.
cumbersome *adj* (*object*) stânjenitor; *fig* greoi.
cunning *adj* (*person*) şiret, viclean; (*plan*, *method*) şiret, ingenios, viclean || *s* (*person*) viclenie *f*; (*plan*, *method*) şiretlic *m*, vicleşug *n*.
cup *s* ceaşcă *f*; cupă *f*; potir *n*; caliciu *n* || *vt* a face mâna căuş.
cupboard *s* bufet *n*, dulap *n*; şifonier *n*, garderob *n*.
curate *s* vicar *m*.
curator *s* (*museum*) custode *m*, conservator *m*.
curb *s* zăbală *f*; strună *f*; frâu *n*; bordură *f* a trotuarului || *vt* a struni; a stăpâni, a înfrâna.
curdle *vi* (*milk*) a se prinde; (*blood*) a se coagula, a se închega.
cure *vt* (*heal*) a vindeca; (*make well*) a îndrepta; a înlătura; a curma; a conserva; a săra, a afuma || *s* cură *f*, (*treatment*) tratament *n*; vindecare *f*; remediu *n*; conservare *f*.
curfew *s mil* interdicţie *f* de a ieşi din casă (după o anumită oră); stingere *f*.
curiosity *s* curiozitate *f*; indiscreţie *f*; ciudăţenie *f*.
curious *adj* curios.
curl *s* buclă *f*; spirală *f*; colac *m*; vârtej *n*; ondulaţie *f* || *vt* (~ *hair*) a ondula; a încreţi; a încolăci || *vi* a se ondula, a se încreţi; ~ **up** *vi* (*person*, *animal*) a se încolăci • ~**y** *adj* creţ, ondulat; încreţit; neregulat.
currant *s* (*dried fruit*) stafidă *f* neagră; *bot* (*berry*) coacăză *f*; (*bush*) coacăz *m*.
currency *s* (*money*) valută *f*; valoare *f*, mijloc *n* de plată; curs *n* (valutar); valabilitate *f*; (*circulation*) circulaţie *f*.
current *adj* curent, comun, răspândit; (*in progress*) în curs; (*present*) actual, prezent || *s* (*stream*) curent *n*; flux *n*; şuvoi *m*; (*flow*) curs *n*, desfăşurare *f*.
curry¹ *s* (*spice*) curry *m*; mâncare *f* gătită cu curry.
curry² *vt* (*horse*) a ţesăla; **to** ~ **favor with smb** a căuta să intre în graţiile cuiva; a se linguşi pe lângă cineva.
curse *s* blestem *n*; înjurătură *f*; pacoste *f*, nenorocire *f* || *vt/vi* a blestema, a injura.
cursor *s comp* cursor *n*.
cursory *adj* superficial.
curt *adj* scurt, concis, categoric.
curtail *vt* (~ *speech*) a (pre)scurta; a scurta, a tăia, a reteza; *fig* (~ *visit, etc*) a scurta; (~ *expenses*) a reduce, a micşora.

curtain *s* perdea *f*; draperie *f*; cortină *f* ecran *n* ‖ *vt* a pune perdele la.

curtsy *s* reverență *f* ‖ *vi* a face o reverență.

curve *s* (*arc*) curbă *f*; curbură *f*; (*arch*) arc *n*; cot *m* ‖ *vt* a curba; (*bend*) a îndoi; a bomba; a arcui, a bolti ‖ *vi* a se curba; a se arcui, a se bolti.

cushion *s* (*pillow*) pernă *f*; saltea *f*; (*pad*) tampon *n*, amortizor *n* ‖ *vt* a pune o pernă sub; (*mitigate*) a amortiza; (*stifle*) a mușamaliza.

custard *s* cremă *f* englezească din ouă și lapte.

custodian *s* (*curator*) custode *m*; (*warden*) tutore *m*; *jur* garant *m*, chezaș *m*; (*janitor*) paznic *m*.

custody *s* custodie *f*; îngrijire *f*; păstrare *f*; pază *f*; arest *n*, închisoare *f*.

custom *s* (*habit*) obicei *n*, datină *f*; (*convention*) obișnuință *f*; uzanțe *f pl*, convenții *f pl*; impozit *n*; taxă *f*; (*trade*) client *m*, cumpărător *m*; vamă *f*, taxe *f pl* vamale • **~ary** *adj* usual, obișnuit • **~made** *adj com* (făcut) de comandă.

customer *s* cumpărător *m*, client *m*; tip *m*, individ *m*.

customize *vt* a confecționa/construi/executa la comandă.

cut *vt* (*slash*) a tăia; a croi; (*chop*) a reteza; (*clip*) a tunde; a cosi; a secera; a recolta; a strânge; a grava; a jigni; (*skip classes*) a lipsi (la școală etc); a biciui; a intersecta ‖ *s* tăietură *f*; (*wound*) rană *f*; (*decline*) reducere *f*; (*slice*) bucată *f*, felie *f*; croială *f*; jignire *f* ‖ *adj* tăiat; retezat; tuns; cosit; secerat; gravat • **~back** *s* reducere *f*.

cute *adj* deștept, isteț; drăguț, atrăgător

cutlery *s* cuțitărie *f*, cuțite *n pl*; tacâmuri *n pl*.

cutlet *s* cotlet *n*, antricot *n*; crochetă *f*.

cutting *adj* (*wind*) tăios; rece, înghețat; *fig* tăios, usturător; (*mind*) acerb; sarcastic; *tech* tăietor, de tăiere ‖ *s* (*plant*) butaș *m*; (*from newspaper*) tăieturi *f pl* (din ziare).

CV *s* (*abbr* curriculum vitae) cv *n*.

cyberspace *s comp* spațiu *n* virtual.

cycle *s* (*sequence*) ciclu *n*; timp *m*; perioadă *f*; serie *f*; bicicletă *f*; tricicletă *f*; motocicletă *f* ‖ *vi* a încheia un ciclu; a merge cu bicicleta etc.

cycling *s* ciclism *n*

cyclist *s* biciclist(ă) *m*, *f*.

cyclone *s* ciclon *n*.

cylinder *s geom*, *etc* cilindru *m*; *aut* cuzinet *m*, cilindru *m*; tăvalug *n*, tambur *n*.

cymbal *s mus* talger *n*; țambal *n*.

cynic *s* (om) cinic *m* • **~ism** *s* cinism *n*.

cynical *adj* cinic; sarcastic; batjocoritor.

cypress *s* chiparos *m*.

Cypriot *s/adj* cipriot *m*.

Cyprus *s* Cipru.

cyst *s med* cist *n* • **~itis** *s med* cistită *f*.

czar *s* țar *m*.

Czech *s/adj* ceh ‖ *s* (*language*) limba *f* cehă.

D

D, d *s* (*letter*) D, d; *mus* (*note*) re.

dab *s* atingere *f* ușoară; tamponare *f*; (*paint*) pată *f* ‖ *vt* a atinge (ușor); (*wound*) a tampona; a unge (cu o alifie etc); a acoperi cu un strat subțire.

dabble *vi* (*in water*) a se bălăci; a se stropi ‖ *vt* a-și bălăci (mâinile etc); a înmuia; a stropi; **to ~ at/in** a se ocupa printre altele (și) de.

dad, daddy *s coll* tăticu(țu) *m*.

daffodil *s bot* narcisă *f*.

daft *adj* natâng, slab de minte; prostănac, tâmpit.

dagger *s* pumnal *n*; hanger *n*.

dahlia *s bot* dalie *f*.

daily *adj* zilnic, cotidian; obișnuit ‖ *adv* zilnic, în fiecare zi ‖ *s* ziar *n* care apare zilnic, cotidian *n*.

dainty *adj* (*pretty*) drăguț, nostim; (*graceful*) grațios; elegant; minunat; mofturos, dificil; (*delicate*) sensibil, gingaș; (*refined*) ales, gustos ‖ *s* delicatesă *f*, trufanda *f*.

dairy *s* lăptărie *f*.

daisy *s* bănuțel *m*, părăluță *f*; margaretă *f*.

dalliance *s* tândăleală *f*; mocăială *f*.

dally *vi* (*linger*) a se mocăi; (**with**) a cocheta (cu), a flirta (cu).

dam *s* baraj *n*, dig *n*; zăgaz *n* ‖ *vt* a zăgăzui, a stăvili.

damage *s* pagubă *f*; (*harm*) rău *n*; (*dent*) stricăciune *f*; *pl* compensație *f*, despăgubiri *f pl* ‖ *vt* (*break*) a deteriora, a defecta; *tech* a avaria; *fig* a discredita

damaging *adj* care aduce prejudicii.

damn *vt* a osândi; a blestema; a înjura; a condamna; a critica ‖ *s* blestem *n*; înjurătură *f* • **~ation** *s relig* (veșnică) osândă *f*, chinurile *n pl* iadului; distrugere *f*, ruină *f* • **~ed** *adj relig* osândit la chinurile iadului, (*ill-fated*) damnat; *coll* afurisit, blestemat ‖ *adv* al naibii de, grozav de • **~ing** *adj* apăsător, insuportabil.

damp *adj* (*moist*) umed; (*wet*) ud; (*soggy*) jilav; deprimat ‖ *s* (*humidity*) umezeală *f*, igrasie *f*; deprimare *f* • **~en** *vt* (*moisten*) a umezi; a stropi; a uda; a stinge (focul); a potoli • **~ness** *s* umiditate *f*.

damper *s* (*constraint*) constrângere *f*; (*restraint*) reținere *f*; (*deterrent*) descurajare *f*, dezamăgire *f*, decepție *f*; mus surdină *f*; *aut* amortizor *n*.

damson *s* (*fruit*) prună *f* renglotă; (*tree*) prun *m*.

dance *vi* a dansa; a juca; a sări ‖ *vt* a dansa; a legăna ‖ *s* dans *n*; joc *n*; horă *f*; muzică *f* de dans; serată *f* dansantă; bal *n* • **~r** *s* dansator *m*.

dancing *s* dans *n*.

dandelion *s bot* păpădie *f*.

dandruff *s* mătreață *f*.

dandy *s* fante *m*.

Dane *s* danez(ă) *m/f*.

danger *s* pericol *n*, primejdie *f* • **~ous** *adj* periculos, primejdios; riscant.

dangle *vt* a legăna, a bălăbăni ‖ *vi* (*be hanging*) a se legăna.

Danish *adj* danez(ă) *m/f*; (*language*) daneză *f*.

dank *adj* umed.

dappled *adj* pătat; bălțat.

dare *v mod* a îndrăzni; a cuteza; a se aventura; (*risk*) a risca ‖ *vt* (*have the guts*) a îndrăzni; (*gamble*) a înfrunta, a risca; (*defy*) a desfide; **I ~ say** presupun că … • **~devil** neînfricat; înfipt.

daring *s* îndrăzneală *f* ‖ *adj* îndrăzneț.

dark *adj* întunecos, întunecat; închis; negru; (*brunette*) cu părul negru, brunet; ascuns; (*dim*) obscur, neclar; (*evil*) urât, ticălos; (*gloomy*) mohorât; (*sad*) trist; jalnic ‖ *s* întuneric *n*; (*night*) noapte *f*; ignoranță *f*; **in the ~** ignorant, neștiutor • **~en** *vi* a se întuneca • **~ness** *s* obscuritate *f*, întuneric *n*.

darling *s* iubit(ă) *m/f*, drag *m*, scump(ă) *m/f*; preferat(ă) *m/f* ‖ *adj* scump, favorit; minunat.

darn *vt* (*socks*) a cârpi ‖ *adj coll* iubit, scump ‖ *adv coll* extrem de, al naibii de.

dart s (*game*) săgeată f mică || vi a se repezi • ~s s pl joc n de săgeți.

dash s (*drop*) strop n; cantitate f infimă; pic n; (*color*) pată f; linie f de dialog || vt a arunca, a azvârli cu putere; (~ *hope*) a se nărui || vi a se grăbi.

dastardly adj ticălos.

data s date f pl, relații f pl; ~ **processing** s comp prelucrarea f datelor • ~**base** s comp bază f de date.

date[1] s dată f; zi f; (*time*) timp n; epocă f, perioadă f; (*meeting*) întâlnire f; băiat m, fată f cu care îți dai întâlnire || vt a data; (*go out with*) a avea o întâlnire cu cineva.

date[2] s (*fruit*) curmală f; (*tree*) curmal m.

dative s gram dativ n.

datum s (pl **data**) dată f, relație f, informație f.

daub vt a mâzgăli.

daughter s fiică f, fată f, copilă f • ~**in-law** s noră f.

daunt vt a descuraja • ~**ing** adj care intimidează; descurajator.

davenport s (*sofa*) canapea f, divan n; șezlong n.

dawdle vi a hoinări; a trena, coll a se mocăi.

dawn vi a se crăpa de ziua; a începe; a se ivi || s zori m pl, auroră f.

day s zi f, pl vreme f, (*time*) timp m; viață f; (*period*) perioadă f, (*era*) epocă f; ~ **after** a doua zi; ~ **before** în ajun; ~ **off** s zi f liberă • ~**dream** vi a visa cu ochii deschiși • ~**light** s lumina f zilei; zori n pl de zi • ~**time** s ziua; timpul m zilei; (*work, flight*) de zi.

daze vt a ului; a zăpăci, a năuci || s uluire f; zăpăceală f.

dazzle vt a orbi cu lumina; a lua vederea.

dazzling adj orbitor, care îți ia vederea.

deacon s diacon m.

dead adj mort; (*deceased*) decedat; (*lifeless*) fără viață; (*silent*) inactiv; (*stiff*) amorțit; (*frozen*) înghețat; total, complet; exact, precis; stricat; (*dull*) monoton; mat, fără luciu; ~ **end** s fundătură f; ~ **heat** s sp sosire f simultană.

deaden vt (*sound*) a înăbuși; (*pain*) a calma.

deadline s limită f; hotar n, margine f; termen n final.

deadlock s impas n.

deadly adj (*enemy*) mortal, de moarte; implacabil || adv (*boring, serious*) extrem (de), teribil (de); ~ **sin** s păcat n capital.

deadpan adj (*face*) lipsit de expresie || adv impasibil.

deadweight s also fig povară f; capacitate f de încărcare a unui vas.

deaf adj surd; care nu vrea să audă/să asculte.

deal, dealt, dealt vt (*distribute*) a împărți, a distribui; a da, a administra || vi (~ *cards*) a da/a face cărțile; ~ **in** a se ocupa cu comerțul de; ~ **with** com a negocia cu, (*handle*) a se ocupa de, (~ *book, report, etc*) a trata || s afacere f; tranzacție f; servit n, datul n cărților; sistem n de măsuri (guvernamentale) • ~**er** s comerciant m; (*cards*) jucător m care dă cărțile; (*drugs*) traficant m • ~**ings** s pl com operațiuni f pl, tranzacții f pl; (*people*) relații f pl.

dean s scol decan m; relig vicar m; preot m paroh.

dear adj scump, costisitor; drag; dragă; stimate m, stimată f || adv scump || s iubit m, iubită f.

dearth s penurie f, criză f.

death s moarte f; ucidere f, asasinat n; sfârșit n; mormânt n; ~ **certificate** s certificat n de deces; ~ **duties** s pl drepturi n pl succesorale; ~ **penalty** s pedeapsa f capitală; ~ **rate** s (procent de) mortalitate f; ~ **tax** s taxe f pl de succesiune; ~ **toll** s numărul n

(total al) morților • ~**ly** adj ca de mort/moarte; mortal; ~ **quiet** liniște mormântală.

debacle s dezgheț n; debandadă f; also fig catastrofă f, dezastru n.

debase vt a degrada; **to** ~ **oneself** a se degrada, a se înjosi.

debatable adj discutabil; contestabil.

debate s dezbatere f; polemică f; controversă f || vt a dezbate, a discuta || vi a discuta; a polemiza.

debauch s dezmăț n; orgie f || vt (*corrupt*) a corupe; a seduce • ~**ee** s stricat m, destrăbălat m • ~**ery** s desfrâu n.

debilitate vt (*weaken*) a slăbi, a epuiza

debility s debilitate f.

debit s debit n || vt a debita.

debonair adj nonșalant; amabil; plăcut.

debris s rămășițe f pl, resturi n pl.

debt s datorie f • ~**or** s datornic m, debitor m.

debug vt comp (*fix*) a depana; a scoate microfoanele (din clădire).

debunk vt (*lay bare*) a dezvălui, a arăta în adevărata sa lumină, (*demistify*) a demitiza.

debut s debut n || vi a debuta.

decade s (grup de) zece; deceniu n, zece ani m.

decadence s decadență f.

decadent adj decadent.

decamp vi coll (*run away*) a o șterge, a se face nevăzut.

decant vt a decanta • ~**er** s carafă f.

decapitate vt a decapita

decapitation s decapitare f.

decay vi (*rot*) a putrezi, (*decompose*) a se descompune; a se strica; (*crumble*) a se ruina; a decădea; a slăbi, a scădea; a se șubrezi; a îmbătrâni || s (*rotting*) putrezire f, descompunere f; (*ruin*) dărăpănare f, ruină f; decădere f, slăbire f; șubrezire f, îmbătrânire f • ~**ing** adj în declin, în (stare de) putrefacție.

decease s deces n, moarte f || vi a deceda, a muri.

deceit s înșelătorie f, șiretlic n.

deceive vt a înșela, a amăgi; a induce în eroare || vr a se înșela, a se minți singur.

December s (luna) decembrie m.

decency s (*politeness*) amabilitate f, politețe f; bun-simț n; (*propriety*) decență f, bunăcuviință f.

decent adj (*polite*) decent, cuviincios; mulțumitor; (*good*) bun; cumsecade; amabil, serviabil; modest; adecvat, corespunzător.

decentralization s descentralizare f.

decentralize vt a descentraliza.

deception s (*cheating*) înșelăciune f; (*sham*) minciună f; (*fraud*) șarlatanie f.

deceptive adj amăgitor, înșelător.

decibel s decibel m.

decide vt a decide, a rezolva; a determina || vi a hotărî, a lua o hotărâre; a se hotărî; a alege

deciding adj decisiv.

deciduous adj foios.

decimal adj zecimal || s (fracție) zecimală f.

decimate vt a decima.

decipher vt a decoda; a descifra.

decision s (*resolution*) hotărâre f, decizie f; (*verdict*) concluzie f; sentință f; (*resolve*) fermitate f, tărie f; energie f.

decisive adj hotărât, ferm; decisiv.

deck s naut punte f; imperială f; (~ *of a bridge*) tablier *n* de pod; (~ *of cards*) pachet *n* (de cărți de joc) ‖ *vt* (*adorn*) a orna, a împodobi.

declaim *vt* (*hold forth*) a perora; a declama, a recita.

declamation *s* pledoarie *f*; tiradă *f*; recitare *f*.

declaration *s* declarație *f*.

declare *vt* a declara.

declassify *vt* a face public (informații secrete).

declension *s gram* declinare *f*.

decline *vt* (~ *responsibility*) a declina; a refuza; *gram* a declina ‖ *vi* (*sun etc*) a apune, a asfinți; a fi în declin, a decădea; (*prices, etc*) a scădea, a se micșora; a se înclina, a se apleca ‖ *s* declin *n*, decădere *f*; prăbușire *f*; *fig* (*life*) amurg *n*, asfințit *n*; pantă *f*.

declivity *s* înclinare *f*, pantă *f*.

decoction *s* decoct *n*, infuzie *f*.

decode *vt* a decoda.

decolonize *vt* a decoloniza.

decompose *vt* a descompune; a analiza; a desface, a destrăma; a dezagrega ‖ *vi* (**into**) a se descompune (în); a se desface (în); (*decay*) a se descompune, (*rot*) a putrezi.

decorate *vt* a împodobi, a ornamenta; a decora; a vărui; a tencui; a tapeta

decorator *s* decorator *m*.

decoration *s* decorați(un)e *f*, ornamentație *f*, ornament *n*; decorare *f*; ornamentare *f*; văruire *f*; tencuire *f*; tapetare *f*.

decorative *adj* decorativ.

decorous *adj* (*well-mannered*) manierat; (*proper*) de bun gust.

decorum *s* bună-cuviință *f*.

decoy *s* (*hunting*) momeală *f*; (*person*) complice *m* ‖ *vt* a atrage în capcană.

decrease *vt* (*lessen*) a micșora, a diminua; a reduce, a scădea ‖ *vi* (*dwindle*) a descrește, a se micșora; a se reduce ‖ *s* (*decline*) descreștere *f*, micșorare *f*, reducere *f*.

decree *s* decret *n* ‖ *vt* a decreta.

decrepit *adj* (*feeble*) ramolit, slăbit de bătrânețe; (*old*) uzat, vechi; (*decaying*) ponosit.

decry *vt* (*deprecate*) a dezavua; (*belittle*) a deprecia, a diminua.

dedicate *vt* a sfinți (o biserică); (*devote*) a consacra, a dedica; a închina

dedication *s* devotament *n*, dedicație *f*, consacrare *f*.

deduce *vt* a deduce, a trage concluzia.

deduct *vt* a deduce; (*numbers*) a scădea; (*from wage*) a reduce • **~ion** *s math* scădere *f*; reținere *f*, scăzământ *n*; deducție *f*.

deed *s* faptă *f*, acțiune *f*; manifestare *f*; ispravă *f*; realitate *f*; act *n*, document *n*.

deejay *s* disc jokey *m*.

deem *vt* (*think*) a considera că, a socoti că.

deep *adj* adânc; profund; complicat, greu; cufundat, adâncit; (*low*) jos; (*intense*) intens; (*secret*) misterios ‖ *s* adâncime *f*, adânc *n* ‖ *adv* adânc, la mare adâncime • **~seated** *adj* adânc înrădăcinat.

deer *s zool* cerb *m*; căprioară *f*.

deface *vt* a mânji, a murdări.

defamation *s* defăimare *f*.

defame *vt* a defăima.

default *s* slăbiciune *f*, lipsă *f*, absență *f*; vină *f*; *jur* neprezentare *f*; contumacie *f*; *comp* funcție *f* prestabilită ‖ *vt* a nu îndeplini (o obligație); *econ* a nu (putea plăti); *jur* a condamna pentru neprezentare;

a condamna în contumacie; *sp* a nu se prezenta la (o probă); a pierde prin neprezentare ‖ *vi* a nu-și îndeplini obligațiile; *econ* a fi în restanță/întârziere cu plata; *jur* a nu se prezenta (la proces); a pierde procesul prin neprezentare.

defeat *vt* (*vanquish*) a învinge; (*crush*) a distruge; a anula; a declara nul și neavenit ‖ *s* (*loss*) înfrângere *f*; anulare *f*.

defect *s* (*flaw*) defect *n*, lipsă *f*, imperfecțiune *f* ‖ *vi* (*desert*) a dezerta; a cere azil politic; (*go over*) a trece în tabăra dușmanului • **~ion** *s* defecțiune *f* • **~ive** *adj* defectuos • **~or** *s* transfug *m*.

defend *vt* a apăra; a proteja; a feri ‖ *vr* a se apăra • **~ant** *s* apărător *m*; *jur* acuzat *m*, inculpat *m* • **~ing** *adj sp* en titre, în apărare.

defense *s* apărare *f*; protecție *f*; scut *n*; pavăză *f*; pledoarie *f* • **~less** *adj* neajutorat; lipsit de apărare.

defensive *adj* defensiv; **on the** ~ în defensivă.

defer *vt* (*postpone*) a amâna; (*suspend*) a suspenda; a întârzia (să) • **~ence** *s* respect *n* • **~ment** *s* amânare *f*; suspendare *f*.

defiance *s* sfidare *f*; ~ **of the law** sfidare/nerespectare a legii.

defiant *adj* (*person*) intransigent, încăpățânat; sfidător; (*action*) provocator.

deficiency *s* lipsă *f*; carență *f*; deficiență *f*.

deficient *adj* insuficient, deficient; **be ~ in smth** *vt* a-i lipsi ceva; **mentally** ~ deficient mintal; ~ **in courage** căruia îi lipsește curajul.

deficit *s econ* deficit *n*.

define *vt* (*delineate*) a defini; a preciza; a caracteriza; (*describe*) a descrie; (*explain*) a explica, a lămuri.

definite *adj* precis, limpede, clar; deslușit, hotărât; definit • **~ly** *adv* categoric, fără nici o îndoială.

definition *s* (*delineation*) definire *f*; precizare *f*; definiție *f*; caracterizare *f*; (*clarity*) claritate *f*; (*focus*) contur *n* clar.

definitive *adj* definitiv, final; decisiv; definitoriu.

deflate *vt* a dezumfla, a goli; a reduce, a scădea ‖ *vi* a se dezumfla, (*shrink*) a scădea, (*decrease*) a se micșora.

deflation *s* dezumflare *f*; *econ* deflație *f*.

deflect *vt* a devia • **~ion** *s* ricoșare *f*.

deflower *vt* a deflora.

deform *vt* (*distort*) a deforma, a sluți, a urâți; a desfigura; a denatura • **~ation** *s* deformare *f*, sluțire *f*, urâțire *f*; *fig* denaturare *f*; deformație *f* • **~ity** *s* malformație *f*.

defraud *vt* (~ *the state*) a delapida; (~ *a person*) a escroca.

defray *vt* (*pay*) a acoperi (cheltuieli) • **~able** *adj* rambursabil • **~al** *s* acoperire *f* a cheltuielilor.

defrock *vt* a răspopi.

defrost *vt* (*refrigerator, etc*) a decongela.

deft *adj* abil • **~ness** *s* abilitate *f*.

defunct *adj* defunct.

defuse *vt also fig* (*resolve*) a dezamorsa.

defy *vt* a desfide; a provoca; a sfida; a încălca (legea); a disprețui; a brava.

degenerate *vi* a degenera ‖ *adj* degenerat.

degrade *vt mil* a degrada; a retrograda (în funcție); a strica, a deteriora; a corupe; (*debase*) a înjosi; (*humiliate*) a umili; *chem, tech* a degrada ‖ *vi* (*decay*) a se degrada; a se înjosi.

degrading *adj* degradant, înjositor.

degree s *(grade)* grad *n*, ordin *n*, *(level)* rang *n*; *(step)* treaptă *f*; *(measure)* măsură *f*; clasă *f*; titlu *n*.

dehumanize *vt* a dezumaniza.

dehydrate *vt* a deshidrata • **~d** *adj* deshidratat.

deice *vt tech* a dejivra, a dezgheța • **~r** *s aut* instalație *f* de dejivraj.

deign *vt* **(to)** a catadicsi (să), a se deranja (să).

deity s divinitate *f*; zeu/zeiță *m/f*.

dejected *adj* abătut

dejection s deprimare *f*, tristețe *f*.

delay *vt* a întârzia; a amâna ‖ *s* întârziere *f*; amânare *f*.

delectable *adj* amuzant, distractiv.

delectation s distracție *f*, amuzament *n*.

delegate *vt* a delega ‖ *s* delegat *m*.

delegation s delegație *f*.

delete *vt* a șterge, a suprima.

deleterious *adj* *(harmful)* dăunător, nociv, *(injurious)* vătămător, nesănătos.

deletion s ștergere *f*; ștersătură *f*.

deliberate *adj* *(intentional)* voit, intenționat; *(planned)* plănuit; *(cautious)* precaut; *(slow)* lent, încet; greoi ‖ *vt* a discuta, a se sfătui ‖ *vi* *(ponder)* a delibera (asupra; cu privire la) • **~ly** *adv* voit, intenționat.

deliberation s *(reflection)* chibzuință *f*, deliberare *f*; ponderație *f*; *(care)* grijă *f*, prudență *f*.

delicacy s *(of object, situation)* delicatețe *f*, *(fineness)* finețe *f*; *(polish)* rafinament *n*; *(frailty)* fragilitate *f*; *(sensitivity)* sensibilitate *f*; *(gracefulness)* gingășie *f*.

delicate *adj* delicat, fin; slăbuț, plăpând; grațios; discret, atenuat; ales; atent; prevenitor; fragil.

delicatessen s delicatese *f pl*, alimente *f pl* fine; alimente *f pl* preparate; bufet *n*; magazin *n* alimentar.

delicious *adj* *(tasty)* delicios, savuros; *(delightful)* încântător, fermecător.

delight s plăcere *f*, bucurie *f*, desfătare *f* • **~ed** *adj* încântat • **~ful** *adj* încântător, fermecător.

delinquency s delincvență *f*.

delinquent *adj* vinovat ‖ *s* delincvent *m*.

delirious *adj* *lit, fig* delirant; frenetic.

delirium s *also fig* delir *n*.

deliver *vt* *(save)* a scăpa, a salva; a elibera; *(~ a message)* a transmite; *(~ letters)* a distribui; *(~ goods)* a livra; *(~ a speech)* a rosti, a ține (un discurs etc); a ceda; *(~ a blow)* a da (o lovitură); *(~ a baby)* a naște • **~ance** s scăpare *f*, salvare *f*; *relig* mântuire *f*, izbăvire *f*; eliberare *f*; declarație *f* (oficială); *jur* verdict *n* • **~y** s *(of goods)* livrare *f*; furnizare *f*; *(of mail)* distribuire *f*; transmitere *f*, predare *f*; *(supply)* alimentare *f*; *(of a speech)* dicțiune *f*; *(of a baby)* naștere *f*.

dell s vale *f*.

delta s deltă *f*.

delude *vt* a induce în eroare, a înșela; **to ~ oneself** a-și face iluzii.

deluge s potop *n* ‖ *vi* a inunda.

delusion s *(illusion)* iluzie *f*, amăgire *f*; *also fig* miraj *n*; înșelăciune *f*, înșelătorie *f*; *med* halucinație *f*; obsesie *f*; manie *f* • **~al** *adj* obsedat, pradă halucinațiilor.

delusive *adj* înșelător, amăgitor.

delve *vt* *(past)* a scormoni, a scotoci; *(bag)* a scotoci (în).

demagogue s demagog *m* • **~ry** s demagogie *f*.

demand *vt* *(ask)* a cere, a pretinde; *(require)* a necesita, a reclama ‖ *s* *(request)* cerere *f*, solicitare *f*, dorință *f*; *(claim)* revendicare *f*; căutare *f*; întrebare *f*; investi-

gație *f*, cercetare *f* • **~ing** *adj* *(person)* exigent(ă); *(work, course)* pretențios; *(schedule)* încărcat.

demarcate *vt* a demarca.

demeaning *adj* înjositor, degradant.

demeanor s comportare *f*, ținută *f*.

demented *adj* nebun, dement.

demerit s deficiență *f*; defect *n*.

demijohn s damigeană *f*.

demilitarization s demilitarizare *f*.

demise s deces *n*; *fig* moarte *f*, sfârșit *n*.

demobilize *vt* a demobiliza.

democracy s democrație *f*.

democrat s democrat *m* • **~ic** *adj* democratic.

demography s demografie *f*.

demolish *vt* a dărâma, a demola; a distruge, a zdrobi.

demolition s demolare *f*.

demon s demon *m* • **~iacal** *adj* demonic.

demonstrate *vt* *(prove)* a demonstra, a dovedi; *(show)* a prezenta; *(protest)* a manifesta.

demonstration s demonstrație *f*; manifestație *f*

demonstrative *adj* demonstrativ.

demonstrator s manifestant *m*.

demoralize *vt* a demoraliza; a slăbi moralul (cuiva); a deprava, a corupe.

demote *vt* a retrograda.

demotion s retrogradare *f*.

demur *vi* *(object)* a protesta (la), a se opune (la), a obiecta ‖ *s* obiecție *f*; protest *n*.

demure *adj* *(shy)* sfios, modest; serios, așezat; *(prim)* afectat; mofturos; care face pe modestul • **~ness** s sfială *f*, modestie *f*; afectare *f*; mofturi *n pl*, nazuri *n pl*; modestie *f* prefăcută.

den s bârlog *n*, vizuină *f*.

denial s negare *f*; contestare *f*; dezmințire *f*; refuz *n*; renegare *f*.

denim s *text* dril *n*; blue-jeans *m*.

Denmark s Danemarca *f*.

denominate *vt* a denumi.

denomination s *(name)* denumire *f*, nume *n*; *(money)* valoare *f* (a banilor); *relig* confesiune *f*, sectă *f*.

denominator s *math* numitor *n*.

denotation s semn *n*, indiciu *n*; conotație *f*.

denote *vt* a denota, a indica, a însemna.

denouement s deznodământ *n*.

denounce *vt* a acuza, a învinui; a denunța.

dense *adj* *(thick)* dens, des; *(compact)* compact; strâns; *(deep)* mare, profund; *(opaque)* opac, obtuz.

density s densitate *f*.

dent s dinte *m*, zimț *m*; semn *n*, urmă *f* ‖ *vt* a tăia, a cresta.

dental *adj* dentar; dental; **~ floss** s mătase *f* dentară; **~ surgeon** s chirurg-dentist *m*.

dentist s dentist *m* • **~ry** s dentistică *f*, stomatologie *f*.

denture s proteză *f* dentară, dantură *f* falsă.

denude *vt* a dezgoli, a dezveli, a despuia; *(trees)* a desfrunzi; **(of)** a lipsi, a priva (de).

denunciation s *(accusation)* acuzare *f*, învinuire *f*; *(condemnation)* denunțare *f*; denunț *n*; *(of a treaty)* denunțare *f*.

deny *vt* a nega; *(refute)* a respinge; a contesta; a renega; *(renounce)* a renunța la; *(refuse)* a refuza ‖ *vi* a nega.

deodorant s dezodorizant *n*.

depart *vi* a pleca; a porni; a muri ‖ *vt* a pleca din; *(deviate)* **~ from** a se îndepărta de.

department *s* raion *n*, secție *f*; departament *n*, minister *n*; catedră *f*; domeniu *n*, ramură *f*.

depend *vi* a fi în suspensie, a fi pendinte; a depinde, a fi condiționat • ~**able** *adj* (*person*) demn de încredere; de nădejde; vrednic de crezare; (*machine*) fiabil.

depict *vt* (~ *in words*) a descrie; (~ *in a painting*) a reprezenta • ~**ion** *s* pictură *f*; reprezentare *f*.

deplete *vt* a goli, a deșerta; a seca; *fig* (~ *forces, etc*) a epuiza.

depletion *s* deșertare *f*, golire *f*; secare *f*; *fig* epuizare *f*; *med* sângerare *f*, emisie *f* de sânge.

deplore *vt* a deplânge, a deplora.

deploy *vt also mil* a desfășura (forțele); a dispune în formație de luptă.

deport *vt* a deporta, a expulza • ~**ation** *s* deportare *f*, expulzare *f*.

depose *vt* (*king*) a detrona; *jur* a depune, a mărturisi (că)

deposit *s geol* zăcământ *n*, depozit *n*, sediment *n*, strat *n*; *econ* depozit *n*, depunere *f*; *chem* sediment *n*; precipitat *n* || *vt chem* a depune; a precipita; *geol* a sedimenta; *econ* a depune, a depozita; a așeza.

depot *s* depozit *n*; gară *f*.

deprave *vi* a se deprava • ~**d** *adj* depravat; vicios; corupt.

depravity *s* depravare *f*; destrăbălare *f*; viciu *n*.

deprecate *vt* a dezaproba, a dezavua.

depreciate *vt* (~ *of money*) a deprecia, a devaloriza; *fig* a deprecia, a subestima || *vi* a se deprecia, a se devaloriza.

depreciation *s fin* depreciere *f*, devalorizare *f*; (*belittling*) subestimare *f*; desconsiderare *f*.

depress *vt* (~ *a button*) a apăsa, a presa; a scufunda; (~ *a person*) a deprima; *fin* a slăbi, a micșora; (*lower prices*) a coborî • ~**ed** *adj* apăsat, presat; (*person*) deprimat; abătut; trist; micșorat; coborât • ~**ing** *adj* demoralizant • ~**ion** *s* (*despair*) depresie *f* nervoasă; (*slump*) criză *f* economică; (*hollow*) depresiune *f*.

deprivation *s* privare *f*, lipsire *f*; pierdere *f*.

deprive *vt* (**of**) a lipsi, a priva (de).

depth *s* (*of hole, water*) adâncime *f*; (*of layer*) grosime *f*; înălțime *f*; (*of color, emotion*) profunzime *f*; (*of crisis*) gravitate *f*; (*of knowledge*) întindere *f*; mizerie *f*; **in** ~ temeinic, în profunzime.

deputize *vi* (**for**) a înlocui (pe)

deputy *s* deputat *m*; reprezentant *m*; delegat *m*.

derail *vt* (*train*) a deraia, a face să deraieze.

deranged *adj* (*unhinged*) dereglat; (*crazy*) nebun.

derby *s sp* derbi *n*; (*hat*) melon *n*.

deregulate *vt* (~ *prices, wages*) a elibera; a ridica restricțiile.

derelict *adj* abandonat, părăsit.

deride *vt* a ridiculiza, a lua în bătaie de joc, a zeflemisi, a ironiza.

derision *s* derâdere *f*, bătaie *f* de joc.

derisive *adj* ironic, zeflemitor; batjocoritor.

derivation *s* derivație *f*.

derive *vt* (*gain*) a obține (ceva); (~ *income*) a căpăta, a câștiga; (~ *satisfaction*) a primi, a căpăta, a dobândi || *vi* (**from**) *ling* a deriva, a proveni (din/de la); a se trage din.

dermatology *s* dermatologie *f*.

derogate *vt* a micșora, a diminua.

derogation *s* micșorare *f*, derogare *f*.

derogatory *adj* (**from, to**) defavorabil, dăunător (pentru); (*meaning*) peiorativ; derogatoriu.

derrick *s min* turla *f* sondei; *tech* macara *f*.

descale *vt* a detartra.

descend *vi* a (se) coborî, a se da jos; a se lăsa în jos || *vt* a coborî • ~**ant/ent** *s* urmaș *m*, descendent *m*.

describe *vt* (*explain*) a descrie, a prezenta; a caracteriza || *vr* a se prezenta (ca).

description *s* descriere *f*.

descriptive *adj* descriptiv.

desegregation *s* abolirea *f* segregației rasiale.

descry *vt* a zări; a detecta.

desert[1] *s* pustiu *n*, deșert *n*; pustietate *f* || *adj* pustiu, nelocuit.

desert[2] *vt* a părăsi, a abandona; a dezerta • ~**ion** *s* dezertare *f*.

desert[3] *s* parte *f* cuvenită; **get one's just** ~**s** a primi ceea ce merită.

deserve *vt* a merita, a fi vrednic de.

desiccate *vt* a deshidrata.

design *vt* a desena; (*plan*) a proiecta, a plănui; a destina || *vi* a desena; a proiecta || *s* (*drawing*) desen *n*; (*project*) proiect *n*; plan *n*; schiță *f*; tip *n*; (*pattern*) model *n*; scop *n*; (*intention*) intenție *f* • ~**er** *s* desenator *m*; proiectant *m*; *fig* intrigant *m*.

designate *vt* (*name*) a desemna, a numi; (*specify*) a indica, a denumi, a marca || *adj* (*elect*) desemnat, numit.

desirable *adj* de dorit, dezirabil; oportun; bun.

desire *vt* a dori, a vrea || *s* dorință *f*; rugăminte *f*; cerere *f*; poftă *f*.

desirous *adj* dornic, doritor; ~ **of fame** dornic de popularitate.

desist *vi* (**from**) a termina (cu), a înceta (să).

desk *s* masă *f* de scris, birou *n*; bancă *f*, pupitru *n*; ~ **clerk** *s* recepționer *m* (la hotel).

desolate *adj* (*place*) pustiu, părăsit; sterp, neroditor; (*person*) singur, nefericit.

despair *s* deznădejde *f*, disperare *f*.

desperate *adj* disperat; nebunesc; nesăbuit; teribil, grozav.

desperation *s* disperare *f*; **in** ~ de disperare.

despicable *adj* josnic; vrednic de dispreț; condamnabil.

despise *vt* a disprețui.

despite *prep* (*in spite of*) în ciuda, cu tot.

despondency *s* disperare *f*, deznădejde *f*; (*dejection*) demoralizare *f*; (*gloom*) melancolie *f*.

despondent *adj* deznădăjduit; deprimat, abătut.

despot *s* despot *m* • ~**ic** *adj* despotic.

dessert *s* desert *n*, dulce *n*.

destination *s* destinație *f*.

destine *vt* a destina, a meni • ~**d for** *adj* destinat pentru (ceva) • ~**d to do smth** destinat pentru a face ceva.

destiny *s* destin *n*, soartă *f*.

destitute *adj* fără mijloace, nevoiaș, sărac.

destroy *vt* a distruge, a dărâma; a demola; a nimici; a ruina; a nărui • ~**er** *s* (*ship*) distrugător *n*.

destruction *s* distrugere *f*, nimicire *f*.

destructive *adj* distrugător, distructiv; nimicitor.

desultory *adj* (*aimless*) dezorganizat, haotic; (*random*) sporadic, răzleț; (*haphazard*) întâmplător.

detach *vt* (*separate*) a detașa, a separa || *vr* a se detașa • ~**able** *adj* detașabil • ~**ed** *adj* detașat; (*unbiased*) obiectiv; indiferent • ~**ment** *s* detașare *f*, desprindere *f*; *mil* detașament *n*.

detail s detaliu n, amănunt n || vt a detalia; a descrie amănunțit.

detain vt (arrest) a reține; (delay) a face să aștepte; (hinder) a împiedica.

detect vt a găsi; a descoperi; a detecta; a constata • ~ive s detectiv m.

detention s detenție f, arest n; scol reținere f a elevilor după cursuri (ca pedeapsă).

deter vt (from) a împiedica, a opri (de la); a face pe cineva să-și schimbe hotărârea; a descuraja.

detergent s detergent m.

deteriorate vt a strica; a deteriora; a înrăutăți || vi a se strica; a se deteriora.

deterioration s deteriorare f, înrăutățire f.

determination s determinare f, stabilire f, precizare f; hotărâre f; decizie f.

determine vt (settle) a determina, a stabili; (find out) a constata; (decide) a hotărî; a convinge; a (se) decide • ~d adj (person) hotărât; (effort) asiduu.

deterrent s mijloc n de intimidare; mil forță f de descurajare.

detest vt a detesta, a urî, a nu putea suferi • ~able adj detestabil, odios, execrabil.

dethrone vt also fig a detrona.

detonate vt a face să explodeze || vi a detona; a exploda.

detour s înconjur n, ocol n.

detract vi (from) a scădea, a diminua, a reduce (din).

detriment s detriment n; pagubă f; **to the ~ of** în detrimentul.

deuce s (on card) doi m; (in tennis) egalitate f; excl coll drace!, la naiba!, ei drăcie!.

devaluate vt econ a devaloriza.

devaluation s econ devalorizare f, depreciere f.

devalue vt econ a devaloriza.

devastate vt a devasta, a pustii.

devastating adj (power) devastator, pustiitor.

develop vt (grow) a dezvolta; (expand) a extinde; (improve) a stimula; (expound) a expune amănunțit; a manifesta || vi (progress) a se dezvolta; (grow) a crește; a evolua • ~ment s dezvoltare f, extindere f, creștere f; mărire f; evoluție f; împrejurare f; întâmplare f.

deviate vi (from) a devia, a se abate (de la).

deviation s abatere f, deviere f.

device s (gadget) mecanism n, dispozitiv n; (apparatus) aparat n; instrument n; econ deviz n; plan n, schemă f, proiect n; procedeu n; (ruse) truc n, șiretlic n; dorință f; voie f.

devil s diavol m, drac m; om m rău; împielițat m || vt a preface într-un drac; a îndrăci; a condimenta puternic • ~ish adj diabolic, malefic.

devious adj (person) nesincer, prefăcut; (plan) lăturalnic, cu subterfugii; fig întortocheat, ocolit.

devise vt a inventa, a născoci; (contrive) a pune la cale.

devoid adj (of) lipsit de, fără.

devolution s (time) scurgere f, trecere f; desfășurare f; (of assets) transmitere f; degenerare f; pol descentralizare f.

devolve vt (transfer) a transmite, a transfera; (decentralize) a descentraliza || vi (on) a reveni, a cădea în sarcina (cuiva).

devote vt a dedica, a consacra • ~d adj (to) devotat || vi credincios, loial; iubitor (de).

devotion s devotament n.

devour vt lit, fig a devora.

devout adj (person) pios, cucernic; (earnest) sincer; devotat.

dew s rouă f; picături f pl; prospețime f.

dexterity s dexteritate f.

dexterous adj abil, îndemânatic.

diabetes s diabet n.

diabetic s/adj diabetic m.

diabolic(al) adj diabolic.

diagnose vt a diagnostica.

diagnosis s diagnostic n.

diagnostic s diagnostic n || adj de diagnostic.

diagonal adj diagonal; oblic || s diagonală f; secțiune f diagonală.

diagram s diagramă f; grafic n; schemă f • ~matic adj grafic.

dial s cadran n; scală f; busolă f; disc n cu numere || vt a forma (un număr); ~ **tone** ton n • ~ing code prefix n.

dialect s dialect n; regionalism n; limbaj n; limbă f.

dialogue s dialog n.

diameter s diametru n.

diamond s (gem) diamant n; (cards) caro n.

diaper s (cloth) pânză f cu desene geometrice; scutec n; șervet n.

diaphragm s anat diafragmă f.

diarrhea s med diaree f.

diary s jurnal n zilnic; jurnal n intim; carnet n de notițe; calendar n de buzunar.

dice s pl (game) zaruri n pl || vt cul a tăia în cuburi; **no** ~ nu.

dick s sl detectiv m; individ m; **a clever** ~ s un arogant • ~head s pej imbecil.

dicky s plastron n.

dictate vt/vi a dicta || s dictat n, ordin n.

dictation s dictare f.

dictator s dictator m • ~ship s dictatură f.

diction s (pronunciation) dicție f; stil n de exprimare.

dictionary s dicționar n.

didactic adj didactic.

die[1] vt a muri, a deceda; a nu mai putea după; a stinge, a pieri; ~ **away** vi bot a se ofili; ~ **down** vi (sound) a slăbi; (wind) a înceta; (fire) a se stinge; ~ **out** vi a se stinge, a dispărea.

die[2] s pl dice zar n; matriță f.

diesel s diesel n; ~ **engine** s aut motor n diesel, (train) locomotivă f diesel.

diet s dietă f; regim n alimentar; hrană f || vt a pune la regim || vr a ține regim alimentar || vi a fi la regim, a respecta un regim alimentar.

differ vi (from) a diferi, a se deosebi, a fi diferit (de); (from, with) a nu fi de acord cu (cineva); (with) a se certa (cu) • ~ence s diferență f, deosebire f; diferend n, neînțelegere f • ~ent adj diferit, deosebit; altfel; neobișnuit, special • ~ential adj diferențial; distinctiv || s tech diferențial n; math diferențială f • ~entiate vt a diferenția, a deosebi, a distinge; a face să se deosebească || vi a se diferenția, a se deosebi, a se distinge.

difficult adj (hard) dificil, greu; (tough) complicat; (problematical) capricios; susceptibil • ~y s dificultate f, greutate f; (trouble) necaz n; problemă f.

diffident adj (person) neîncrezător în sine; (smile, gesture) modest, sfios; rezervat.

diffuse adj difuz || vt/vi a (se) împrăștia, a (se) dispersa.

diffusion s împrăștiere f, dispersare f.

dig, dug, dug vt a săpa; a băga, a vârî; a înghionti; a

scoate, a extrage; a înțelege || *vi* a săpa; a învăța intens || *s* (*in archaeology*) săpătură *f*; (*with elbow*) ghiont *n*; (*jibe*) împunsătură *f*; *pl* bârlog *n*, locuință *f*.

digest *s* rezumat *n*; compendiu *n* || *vt* (~ *food*) a digera; (~ *facts*) a înțelege, a-și însuși; a clasifica; a acapara || *vi* a digera; a se digera • ~**ion** *s* digestie *f*.

digit *s math* cifră *f*; (*finger*) deget *n* • ~**al** *adj* (*clock, etc*) numeric, digital • ~**ize** *vt* a digitaliza.

dignified *adj* demn, plin de demnitate; respectabil.

dignify *vt* (*exalt*) a evidenția, a distinge; (*honor*) a onora, a face vrednic de.

dignity *s* demnitate *f*; prestigiu *n*.

digress *vi* (*from*) a se abate, a devia (de la); a face digresiuni • ~**ion** *s* digresiune *f*.

dike *s geol* filon *n*; șanț *n*, canal *n* de scurgere; val *n*, întăritură *f* de pământ; *fig* piedică *f*, obstacol *n*.

dilapidated *adj* (*house*) în ruină, dărăpănat; (*machine*) stricat; (*clothes*) ponosit, uzat; *fig* stricat; *fig* ruinat.

dilapidation *s* deteriorare *f*, degradare *f*; ruină *f*.

dilate *vt* a dilata; a mări, a extinde || *vi* a se dilata; a se mări, a se extinde.

dilemma *s* dilemă *f*.

diligence *s* sârguință *f*, zel *n*.

diligent *adj* harnic, silitor, sârguincios.

dill *s bot* mărar *n*.

dilly-dally *vi coll* (*dawdle*) a se moșmondi; (*waver*) a ezita.

dilute *vt* a dilua; a slăbi, a atenua, a micșora.

dilution *s* diluat *n*; diluare *f*.

dim *adj* slab; obscur; mat; întunecos; (*light*) estompat, (*sound*) vag; neclar; șters, nebulos • ~**ness** *s* obscuritate *f*.

dime *s* (monedă *f* de) zece cenți; **a ~ a dozen** ieftin ca braga; ~ **novel** *s* roman de duzină.

dimension *s* (*measurement*) dimensiune *f*, măsură *f*; proporții *f pl*.

diminish *vt* (*lessen*) a diminua; (*weaken*) a slăbi || *vi* a se diminua; a se micșora, a slăbi • **law of ~ing returns** legea randamentului scăzut.

diminution *s* diminuare *f*.

diminutive *s* diminutiv *n* || *adj* micuț.

dimple *s* gropiță *f* (în obraz/bărbie).

din *s* vacarm *n*.

dine *vt* a oferi o masă, a ospăta; a da de mâncare; a deservi || *vi* a mânca, a lua masa; a prânzi; a cina.

dinghy *s naut* derivor *n*.

dingle *s* vâlcea *f*.

dingy *adj* (*room*) murdar; plin de funingine; (*clothes*) murdar, soios.

dining room *s* sufragerie *f*.

dinky *adj coll* nostim, drăgălaș; *pej* neînsemnat.

dinner *s* masă *f* (principală); prânz *n*; cină *f*; dineu *n*.

dinosaur *s zool* dinozaur *m*.

diocese *s relig* dioceză *f*, eparhie *f*.

dip *vi* a afunda, a (s)cufunda; a înmuia; a vârî; (~ *by hand*) a băga, a vârî; (~ *in water*) a scoate; (~ *of head*) a pleca, a înclina; *naut* a coborî (pavilionul); *aut* a micșora lumina; *relig* a boteza (în apă); (*sun*) a coborî (la orizont) || *s* (*road, land*) pantă *f*; înclinație *f*; *cul* sos *n*; (*swim*) scăldat *n*.

diphthong *s ling* diftong *m*.

diploma *s* diplomă *f*.

diplomacy *s* diplomație *f*.

diplomat *s* diplomat *m*; persoană *f* plină de tact • ~**ic** *adj pol* diplomatic; *fig* diplomat(ic), abil, dibaci; plin de tact.

dippy *adj coll* (*silly*) candriu.

dipstick *s auto* jojă *f* de ulei.

dire *adj* (*terrible*) groaznic, teribil; (*extreme*) extrem; ~ **poverty** neagră sărăcie.

direct *adj* direct; nemijlocit; personal; (*frank*) sincer; exact || *vt* (*traffic*) a dirija; a conduce; a controla; a îndruma; a ordona || *vi* a ordona; a dirija.

direction *s* direcție *f*; orientare *f*; indicație *f*; normă *f*; conducere *f*; control *n*; îndrumare *f*; sferă *f*, domeniu *n*; tendință *f*; regie *f*.

directive *s* directivă *f*.

director *s* director *m*; conducător *m*; administrator *m*; dirijor *m*; regizor *m* • ~**ate** *s* (*board*) consiliu *n* de administrație; (*position*) post *n* de director.

directory *s* registru *n*, carte *f* de adrese; carte *f* de telefon.

dirge *s* bocet *n*, cântare *f* de mort.

dirt *s* murdărie *f*; gunoi *n*; pământ *n*, sol *n*, teren *n*; *sl* indecență *f*, pornografie *f*, obscenitate *f* • ~**y** *adj* (*unclean*) murdar; (*corrupt*) indecent, obscen; infectat; (*dishonest*) necinstit; urât || *vt* (*soil*) a murdări; a păta || *vi* a se murdări; a se păta.

disability *s* infirmitate *f*, dizabilitate *f*.

disabled *adj* inapt; invalid; infirm.

disadvantage *s* dezavantaj *n*; inconvenient *n*; prejudiciu *n*, pagubă *f* • ~**ous** *adj* dezavantajos; nefavorabil.

disaffected *adj* (*discontented*) nemulțumit; (*disloyal*) rebel, potrivnic.

disagree *vi* a nu corespunde, a nu coincide, a se contrazice; a nu fi de acord; a se certa; a nu se înțelege • ~**able** *adj* dezagreabil, neplăcut • ~**ment** *s* dezacord *n*.

disappear *vi* a dispărea; a se stinge, a muri • ~**ance** *s* dispariție *f*.

disappoint *vt* a dezamăgi, a decepționa; a înșela; a deziluziona • ~**ment** *s* dezamăgire *f*, deziluzie *f*.

disapprove *vt* a dezaproba; a nu fi de acord.

disapproval *s* dezaprobare *f*.

disarm *vi* a dezarma • ~**ament** *s* dezarmare *f*.

disarray *s* (*disorder*) dezordine *f*, neorânduială *f*; (*confusion*) zăpăceală *f*; (*mess*) dezorganizare *f*; neglijență *f* || *vt* a pune în neorânduială; a zăpăci; a dezorganiza.

disaster *s* dezastru *n*, nenorocire *f*, calamitate *f*; sinistru *n*; ~ **area** *s* zonă *f* calamitată.

disastrous *adj* dezastruos.

disavow *vt* (~ *a child, opinion*) a dezavua; (~ *responsibility, faith*) a nega, a nu recunoaște.

disband *vt mil* a demobiliza, a lăsa la vatră; a dizolva, a desființa || *vi mil* a se împrăștia; (~ *an association*) a se dizolva, a se desființa.

disbelief *s* necredință *f*, lipsă *f* de credință; neîncredere *f*.

disbelieve *vt* a nu da crezare la; a nu crede în; a nu se încrede în.

disbursal *s* rambursare *f*; sumă *f* plătită.

disburse *vt* (~ *money*) a plăti.

disc *s* *disk.

discard *vt* (*cast off*) a înlătura; (*remove*) a îndepărta; (*get rid of*) a renunța la.

discern *vt* a discerne, a desluși.

discharge *vt* (~ *a patient*) a da drumul, a externa; (~ *an employee*) a concedia, a da afară (din slujbă); (~ *a* *prisoner*) a elibera; (~ *a gun*) a descărca; (~ *a soldier*) a lăsa la vatră; (~ *cargo*) a descărca, a goli; (~ *a duty*) a îndeplini, a se achita (de o obligație); *jur* a disculpa, a dezvinovăți (de); *elec* a descărca; *econ* a plăti, a achita; (~ *smoke*) a degaja, a emite; (~ *chemicals*) a deversa ‖ *s* (~ *of a patient*) externare *f*; *jur* punere *f* în libertate; *mil* liberare *f*, trimitere *f* la vatră; (~ *of smoke*) degajare *f*; (~ *of waste*) deversare *f*, scurgere *f*; *med* scurgere *f*.

disciple *s* discipol *m*.

disciplinarian *s* adept *m* al disciplinei.

disciplinary *adj* disciplinar.

discipline *s* (*regulation*) disciplină *f*; ordine *f*; (*subject*) ramură *f* (a unei științe); (*punishment*) pedeapsă *f* ‖ *vt* a disciplina; a antrena; (*punish*) a pedepsi.

disclaim *vt* a nu recunoaște (ca al său); (~ *a right*) a renunța (la); a nega; a repudia.

disclose *vt* (*reveal*) a dezvălui; a divulga; a aduce la cunoștință; a arăta, a scoate la lumină, a înfățișa.

disclosure *s* divulgare *f*; dezvăluire *f*.

discolor *vi* a se decolora.

discomfit *vt* (*embarrass*) a face să se jeneze; (*thwart*) a strica (planuri etc) • ~**ure** *s* jenă *f*, stânjeneală *f*.

discomfort *s* (*ache*) durere *f*; (*anxiety*) neliniște *f*, tulburare *f*; (*embarrassment*) jenă, stinghereală *f* ‖ *vt* a deranja, a tulbura, a stingheri; a jena.

discompose *vt* a tulbura liniștea; a stingheri.

disconcert *vt* a deconcerta, a tulbura.

disconnect *vt* a desface; a separa; a detașa; a deconecta.

disconsolate *adj* neconsolat, nefericit; inconsolabil.

discontented *adj* nemulțumit.

discontinue *vt* a înceta, a întrerupe.

discontinuous *adj* intermitent.

discord *s* dezacord *n*, discordie *f*; *mus* disonanță *f*.

discotheque *s* discotecă *f*.

discount *s* (*reduction*) reducere *f*; rabat *n*; scont *n* ‖ *vt* a deconta; (*reduce*) a micșora valoarea; (*disregard*) a nu ține cont de; ~ **rate** *s* taxă *f* de scont.

discourage *vt* a descuraja.

discourse *s* cuvântare *f*; conversație *f*.

discourteous *adj* nepoliticos, necuviincios.

discover *vt* a descoperi; a găsi; a constata • ~**y** *s* descoperire *f*.

discredit *vt* a discredita ‖ *s* discreditare *f*.

discreet *adj* discret; prudent, prevăzător; modest, simplu.

discrepancy *s* discrepanță *f*.

discrete *adj* (*distinct*) diferit, alcătuit din elemente diferite; eterogen; individual, distinctiv; *phil* abstract.

discretion *s* discreție *f*; judecată *f*, discernământ *n*.; libertatea *f* de a dispune/hotărî; maturitate *f* (de gândire).

discriminate *vt* a distinge.

discriminating *adj* discriminatoriu; preferențial.

discrimination *s* discriminare *f*, deosebire *f*, distincție *f*; discernământ *n*, judecată *f*.

discus *s* disc *n*.

discuss *vt* a discuta, a judeca • ~**ion** *s* discuție *f*.

disdain *s* dispreț *n* • ~**ful** *adj* disprețuitor.

disease *s* boală *f* ‖ *vt* a îmbolnăvi, a molipsi, a infecta.

disembark *vi* a debarca.

disembowel *vt* a eviscera.

disenchanted *adj* deziluzionat, decepționat.

disengage *vt* a elibera, a degaja ceva (de); *tech* a declanșa • ~**d** *adj* liber; *aut* debraiat.

disentangle *vt* a descurca; *fig* a lămuri, a clarifica.

disfavor *s* (*disapproval*) dezaprobare *f*; (*disrespect*) dizgrație *f*; **to fall into ~ with smb** *vt* a cădea în dizgrația cuiva.

disfigure *vt* a desfigura; a sluți; a strica, a deforma.

disgrace *s* dizgrație *f*; rușine *f* ‖ *vt* a face de rușine; a dizgrația • ~**ful** *adj* rușinos, de ocară; condamnabil.

disgruntled *adj* nemulțumit.

disguise *vt* (*cover up*) a deghiza, a masca; (*hide*) a ascunde ‖ *s* deghizare *f*; travestire *f*; (*mask*) mască *f*.

disgust *s* dezgust *n*, silă *f* ‖ *vt* a dezgusta; a scârbi • ~**ing** *adj* dezgustător; respingător.

dish *s* (*plate*) farfurie *f*; strachină *f*; vas *n*; fel *n* (de mâncare); *tech* disc *n* ‖ *vt* a pune/servi în farfurie; a înșela • ~**cloth** *s* spălător *n* de vase • ~**washer** *s* mașină *f* de spălat vase; spălător *m* de vase.

dishearten *vt* a descuraja; a demoraliza; a întrista.

disheveled *adj* (*hair*) despletit; încâlcit, ciufulit, nepieptănat; (*person*) dezordonat, răvășit; cu părul despletit.

dishonest *adj* necinstit • ~**y** *s* necinste *f*; rea credință *f*; ticăloșie *f*.

dishonor *s* dezonoare *f*, rușine *f* ‖ *vt* a dezonora, a face de rușine; a înjosi; *econ* a nu onora.

disillusion *s* deziluzie *f*, dezamăgire *f*.

disinfect *vt* a dezinfecta, a steriliza • ~**ant** *s* dezinfectant *n*.

disinflation *s* *econ* deflație *f*.

disingenuous *adj* nesincer; viclean; necinstit.

disinherit *vt* a dezmoșteni.

disintegrate *vt* a dezintegra, a descompune; a dezagrega; (*break up*) a destrăma; a fărâmița ‖ *vi* (*fall to pieces*) a se descompune, a se dezintegra, a se fărâmița.

disinter *vt* a deshuma.

disinterested *adj* dezinteresat; imparțial, obiect; indiferent, nepăsător.

disjointed *adj* dezmembrat; (*writing*) dezarticulat, dezlânat; (*style*) incoerent; *anat* scrântit, luxat.

disk *s* *comp* (*hard*) disc *n*; *comp* (*soft*) dischetă *f* • ~ **drive** *s* *comp* lector *m* de dischete • ~**ette** *s* *comp* dischetă *f*.

dislike *vt* a nu-i plăcea ‖ *s* antipatie *f*, aversiune *f*, repulsie *f*.

dislocate *vt* *med* a scrânti, a disloca, a luxa; a desprinde; *fig* a dezorganiza, a încurca.

dislocation *s* dislocare *f*; *fig* dezorganizare *f*.

dislodge *vt* a îndepărta, a deplasa, a mișca din loc; a scoate (din).

dismal *adj* întunecat, posomorât, mohorât; deprimant; trist; groaznic.

dismantle *vt* *tech* a demonta; *constr* a demola; a dărâma.

dismay *s* (*shock*) spaimă *f*, groază *f*; (*panic*) panică *f*; disperare *f*, exasperare *f* ‖ *vt* a îngrozi, a înspăimânta; (*depress*) a demoraliza.

dismiss *vt* (*fire*) a concedia; (*release*) a da drumul; (*send away*) a îndepărta, a alunga; (*reject*) a respinge • ~**al** *s* concediere *f*, destituire *f*; eliberare *f*; pauză *f*, repaus *n*; *fig* îndepărtare *f*, alungare *f*; *jur* respingere *f*.

dismount *vt* (~ *from a horse, etc*) a da jos; *tech* a demonta; a scoate montura ‖ *vi* a se da jos, a coborî (de pe).

disobedience *s* neascultare *f*; nesupunere *f*.

disobedient *adj* neascultător; nesupus.

disobey *vt* a nu da ascultare, a nu se supune.

disorder *s* (*mess*) dezordine *f*; confuzie *f*; (*turmoil*) tulburare *f*; (*confusion*) zăpăceală *f*; (*illness*) boală *f*; *med* dereglare *f*, deranjament *n* || *vt* a deranja, a dezorganiza; *med* a deregla • **~ly** *adj* neîngrijit, dezordonat; şubred, şubrezit; nedisciplinat, neastâmpărat; turbulent; (*conduct*) necuviincios, urât || *adv* în neorânduială; nedisciplinat; necuviincios, urât.

disorganized *adj* (*person*) dezordonat, aiurit; (*system*) prost conceput.

disown *vt* a nu recunoaşte, a refuza să recunoască; (~ *authority*) a nega; a renega.

disparage *vt* a discredita, a compromite; a denigra.

disparaging *adj* nepoliticos; dispreţuitor.

disparate *adj* disparat; cu totul diferit; incompatibil.

disparity *s* disparitate *f*, deosebire *f*, diferenţă *f*; nepotrivire *f*, neconcordanţă *f*.

dispassionate *adj* calm, liniştit, imperturbabil; imparţial, obiectiv.

dispatch *vt* (*send off*) a trimite, a expedia; *tech* a dispeceriza; a termina repede; *coll* a expedia (o chestiune etc); (*kill*) a ucide || *s* (*message*) trimitere *f*, expediere *f*; depeşă *f*; raport *n* oficial; (*newspaper*) telegramă *f*, corespondenţă *f*; grabă *f*, rapiditate *f*; promptitudine *f*.

dispel *vt* (~ *feelings, clouds*) a împrăştia, a risipi.

dispensary *s* dispensar *n*.

dispense *vt* (~ *justice, drugs*) a administra; (~ *food, etc*) a împărţi, a distribui; (~ *a prescription*) a prescrie; *jur* (*from*) a dispensa; a scuti (de).

dispersal *s* dispersare *f*; împrăştiere *f*; împărţire *f*, distribuire *f*.

disperse *vt* (*scatter*) a împrăştia; (*dissolve*) a dispersa || *vi* a se împrăştia, a se dispersa.

dispersion *s* împrăştiere *f*, răspândire *f*.

dispirited *adj* descurajat; abătut.

displace *vt* a deplasa; a transfera; a înlocui • **~ment** *s* deplasare *f*; înlocuire *f*.

display *vt com* a etala, a expune, a prezenta; (~ *courage, etc*) a manifesta || *s* etalare *f*, expunere *f*, prezentare *f*; expoziţie *f*.

displease *vi* a nu plăcea (cuiva); a nu fi pe placul (cuiva); a nemulţumi.

displeasure *s* nemulţumire *f*.

disposable *adj* disponibil; la îndemână.

disposal *s* dispoziţie *f*, dispunere *f*, aşezare *f*; ordine *f*; (*removal*) evacuare *f*, eliminare *f*; transfer *n*; cedare *f*; (*clearance*) vânzare *f*.

dispose *vt* (*set out*) a dispune, a aşeza; (*arrange*) a aranja; a folosi.

disposition *s* (*temperament*) caracter *n*, fire *f*; (*tendency*) înclinaţie *f*; *pl mil* dispozitiv *n*.

dispossess *vt* (**of**) a deposeda (de); *jur* a expropria • **the ~ed** *s* cei năpăstuiţi *m pl*.

disproportion *s* disproporţie *f* || *vt* a disproporţiona.

disprove *vt* a dovedi/demonstra netemeinicia, slăbiciunea, falsitatea.

disputable *adj* discutabil; litigios.

dispute *vt* (*challenge*) a contesta; a se opune; (*argue*) a disputa; a dezbate, a dezbate || *s* (*argument*) dispută *f*, discuţie *f*, dezbatere *f*, controversă *f*, ceartă *f*; (*industrial*) conflict *n* (de muncă); **beyond ~** incontestabil.

disqualify *vt* a descalifica; *sp* a descalifica.

disregard *vt* (*ignore*) a nu lua în considerare, a nu ţine

seamă de, a neglija; (~ *danger*) a dispreţui; (~ *a warning*) a nu ţine cont de || *s* (**of**) indiferenţă *f*, nepăsare *f* (faţă de), neglijare *f*, desconsiderare *f*; (**for**) lipsă *f* de consideraţie (faţă de cineva).

disreputable *adj* rău famat, de proastă reputaţie; (*object*) urât; uzat.

disrepute *s* faimă *f* proastă.

disrespect *s* (**for**) lipsă *f* de respect/consideraţie (faţă de).

disrupt *vt* a distruge, a sfărâma; (*upset*) a submina; a dezmembra • **~ive** *adj also fig* destructiv, perturbator; *fig* de subminare; *elec* disruptiv.

dissatisfaction *s* nemulţumire *f*, insatisfacţie *f*.

dissatisfied *adj* nemulţumit.

dissect *vt* a diseca; a face o disecţie; *fig* a diseca, a analiza.

dissemble *vt* (*hedge*) a disimula, a masca, a ascunde, a camufla || *vi* a se preface; a simula.

disseminate *vt* a răspândi.

dissension *s* neînţelegere *f*; (*opposition*) disensiune *f*.

dissent *vi* (**from**) a avea o altă părere (decât), a se deosebi în păreri (de), a nu fi de acord (cu); *relig* a fi disident || *s* dezacord *n*; părere *f* diferită; opoziţie *f*; *relig* disidenţă *f*.

dissidence *s* dezacord *n*; părere *f* diferită; opoziţie *f*; *relig, pol* disidenţă *f*.

dissident *s* disident *m*;

dissimilar *adj* (**to**) diferit (de), deosebit (de).

dissimulate *vt* *dissemble.

dissipate *vt* (~ *clouds, fear*) a împrăştia; (~ *fortune, energy*) risipi, a irosi, a cheltui || *vi* (~ *clouds, etc*) a se risipi, a se împrăştia; a duce o viaţă uşuratică.

dissociate *vt* a disocia, a desparţi, a separa; *chem, phys* a disocia || *vr* a se disocia, a se despărţi || *vi chem, phys* a se disocia.

dissociation *s* disociere *f*, despărţire *f*, separare *f*; *psych, chem, etc* disociaţie *f*.

dissolute *adj* uşuratic, frivol.

dissolution *s* (*closure*) desfiinţare *f*; (*termination*) anulare *f*, reziliere *f*; (*ending*) cădere *f*, năruire *f*; (*divorce*) divorţ *n*.

dissolve *vt* (*melt*) a dizolva; a dilua; a evapora; a lichida; a anula; (*disband*) a desfiinţa; a elucida || *vi* a se dizolva; a se dilua; a se evapora; a se anula; (*disappear*) a dispărea.

dissuade *vt* (**from**) a sfătui să nu (facă ceva), a căuta să schimbe părerea (cuiva); a deconsilia.

distaff *s* furcă *f* (de tors).

distance *s* (*space*) distanţă *f*; depărtare *f*; interval *n*; (*coldness*) răceală *f*; (*reserve*) rezervă *f*, perspectivă *f*; perioadă *f* || *vt* (*dissociate*) a se distanţa de.

distant *adj* îndepărtat; vag, aproximativ; rezervat, rece, distant.

distaste *s* antipatie *f*, aversiune *f*, silă *f* • **~ful** *adj* neplăcut, dezagreabil.

distemper *s* boală *f*, indispoziţie *f*, stare *f* maladivă; proastă dispoziţie *f* || *vt med* a îmbolnăvi, a tulbura (o funcţie).

distend *vt* a umfla || *vi* (*stomach*) a se balona; (*sails*) a se umfla • **~ed** *adj med* dilatat.

distil *vt chem* a distila; *fig* a extrage, a scoate; a picura, a lăsa să cadă picătură cu picătură || *vi chem* a se distila; a picura, a cădea picătură cu picătură.

distinct *adj* (*clear*) distinct, clar; (*different*) deosebit, diferit; individual; anume, precis; (*distinctive*) divers, felurit • **~ion** *s* (*difference*) distincţie *f,* diferenţă *f;* (*excellence*) fineţe *f,* eleganţă *f;* originalitate *f;* superioritate *f;* (*worth*) renume *n;* decoraţie *f* • **~ive** *adj* distinctiv, caracteristic, specific.

distinguish *vt* a distinge; a percepe; a vedea; a remarca ‖ *vr* a se distinge, a se remarca.

distort *vt* a deforma, a strâmba, a desfigura; *fig* a denatura; a prezenta într-o lumină falsă • **~ion** *s* deformare *f,* desfigurare *f; fig* denaturare *f.*

distract *vt* (*divert*) a distrage; a zăpăci; a sminti • **~ion** *s* nebunie *f;* zăpăceală *f,* confuzie *f* (a minţii); distragere *f* a atenţiei; absenţă *f;* ceva *n* ce atrage atenţia; (*entertainment*) distracţie *f,* amuzament *n;* **love to** ~ *vt* a iubi la nebunie.

distraught *adj* înnebunit; ~ **with grief** înnebunit de durere.

distress *s* (*suffering*) suferinţă *f,* durere *f;* epuizare *f;* catastrofă *f;* avarie *f;* (*trouble*) nenorocire *f;* pericol *n;* naufragiu *n* ‖ *vt* (*upset*) a face să sufere; a produce suferinţă • **~ing** *adj* (*news, etc*) dureros.

distribute *vt* (*deal out*) a împărţi, a distribui; (*dispense*) a repartiza; a difuza; (*hand out*) a da.

distribution *s* distribuire *f;* repartizare *f;* difuzare *f;* împrăştiere *f* (pe o suprafaţă); distribuţie *f,* clasificare *f.*

distributor *s tech, auto, econ* distribuitor *m; text* depunător *m.*

district *s* district *n,* raion *n,* sector *n;* ţinut *n;* zonă *f;* cartier *n;* domeniu *n;* circumscripţie *f;* ~ **attorney** *s jur* procuror *m;* ~ **court** *s jur* tribunal *n* de instanţă (federală).

distrust *vt* a nu avea încredere în, a se îndoi de; a bănui, a suspecta ‖ *s* neîncredere *f,* suspiciune *f;* bănuială *f* • **~ful** *adj* (*of*) neîncrezător (în), bănuitor (cu privire la).

disturb *vt* a tulbura, a deranja; a incomoda, a stânjeni; a strica ‖ *vr* a se deranja • **~ance** *s* tulburare *f;* nelinişte *f;* perturbare *f;* defectare *f.*

disuse *s* nefolosire *f,* neîntrebuinţare *f;* desuetudine *f;* scoatere *f* din uz; **to fall into** ~ (*factory*) a fi abandonat; (*law*) a fi abandonat • **~d** *adj* dezafectat.

ditch *s* şanţ *n,* canal *n;* rigolă *f;* jgheab *n;* tranşee *f* ‖ *vt* a săpa un şanţ.

ditto *adv* idem.

ditty *s hum* cântec *n.*

divan *s* divan *n.*

dive *vi* a plonja; a se scufunda; a se ascunde ‖ *s* plonjare *f;* scufundare *f.*

diverge *vi* (*from*) a se abate, a devia, a diverge (de la), a diferi (de) • **~nce** *s* divergenţă *f,* dispută *f.*

diverse *adj* diferit; altfel (decât); variat, divers.

diversification *s* diversificare *f;* varietate *f.*

diversify *vt* a diversifica.

diversity *s* diversitate *f,* varietate *f;* nepotrivire *f,* diferenţă *f.*

diversion *s* deviere *f,* abatere *f; tech, etc* branşament *n,* ramificaţie *f;* (*fun*) distracţie *f,* amuzament *n;* (*river, funds*) deturnare *f,* deviere *f; mil, pol* diversiune *f.*

divert *vt* a abate; a devia; a distrage atenţia; a distra, a amuza.

divest *vt frml* (*of*) a dezbrăca (de); a lipsi (de); (*opinion, belief*) a se dezice de; (~ *a coat*) a dezbrăca; (~ *luggage*) a se debarasa de.

divide *vt* (*distribute*) a împărţi, a distribui; (*allot*) a repartiza; (*split*) a diviza; (*separate*) a separa, a izola

‖ *vi* a se despărţi; a se separa; a se izola; a se înstrăina • **~d** *adj* (*country*) dezbinat.

dividend *s econ* dividend *n; math* deîmpărţit *n.*

divider *s math* divizor *m; tech* piesă *f* de ramificaţie; *pl* compas *n.*

dividing *adj* (*wall, etc*) despărţitor.

divine *adj* divin.

divisible *adj* divizibil.

division *s* diviziune *f,* separare *f.*

divorce *s* divorţ *n;* despărţire *f,* separare *f* ‖ *vt* a divorţa; a se despărţi (prin divorţ) • **~e** *s jur* persoană *f* divorţată.

divulge *vt* (*reveal*) a divulga; (*disclose*) a da pe faţă, a dezvălui.

dizzy *adj* ameţit; zăpăcit, năucit; ameţitor ‖ *vt* a ameţi, a zăpăci.

do[1] *s mus* (nota) do.

do[2], **did, done** *v aux* (*in questions*) ~ **you speak English?** vorbiţi englezeşte?; (*with the negative*) **I do not believe him** nu îl cred; (*for emphasis*) **he does know where it is** el ştie sigur unde se află; (*elliptically*) **you know as much as I** ~ ştii tot atât cât ştiu şi eu ‖ *vt* (*be busy with*) a face, a se ocupa cu; (*carry out*) a înfăptui; (*study*) a studia; (*solve*) a rezolva; (*fix*) a aranja; (*clean*) a curăţa; (*finish*) a termina; (*imitate*) a imita; (*cover*) a străbate; *thea* (*perform*) a juca; (*cheat*) a înşela; (*cook*) a pregăti; (*translate*) a reda ‖ *vi* (*perform*) a face, a se descurca; (*referring to health*) a se simţi; (*be active*) a fi activ; (*work*) a lucra; (*act*) a acţiona; (*behave*) a proceda; (*be enough*) a fi suficient; (*be suitable*) a fi bun/potrivit; (*be useful*) a fi util/convenabil; ~ **away with** *vt* a suprima; ~ **up** *vt* (*laces*) a lega, (*buttons*) a încheia, (*room*) a decora, a reface, (*parcel*) a ambala; ~ **with** *vi* a avea nevoie de; ~ **without** *vi* a se lipsi de; **make** ~ *vi* a se descurca; **how are you ~ing?** *coll* ce mai faceţi?; *frml* **how** ~ **you** ~? (*on being introduced*) încântat(ă) ‖ *s* (*party*) chef *n,* petrecere *f;* serată *f;* (*cheat*) înşelătorie *f.*

doc *s coll* doctor *m.*

docile *adj* docil, ascultător; blând.

dock[1] *s naut* bazin *n;* doc *n* ‖ *vt naut* a andoca ‖ *vi naut* a intra în bazin; a acosta • **~er** *s* docher *m* • **~yard** *s* şantier *n* naval.

dock[2] *s jur* boxă *f,* bancă *f* (a acuzaţilor).

dock[3] *vt* a tăia, a scurta (coada); (~ *wages*) a tăia, a reduce, a micşora.

docket *s* fişă *f;* listă *f;* borderou *n;* chitanţă *f;* recipisă *f;* ordine *f* de zi.

doctor *s med* doctor *m,* medic *m* ‖ *vt* a îngriji de; a boteza (vinul etc); a falsifica • **~ate** *s* doctorat *n.*

doctrine *s* doctrină *f.*

document *s* document *n;* act *n;* certificat *n; fig* document *n,* dovadă *f* ‖ *vt* a sprijini/confirma prin acte/documente • **~ary** *adj* documentar *n* ‖ *s* (film) documentar *n* • **~ation** *s* documentare *f.*

dodder *vi coll* a şontăcăi • **~er** *s* babalâc *m* • **~ing** *adj* senil.

dodge *vt* (*avoid*) a evita, a ocoli; (~ *a blow*) a para; (~ *the law*) a eluda; (*get out of*) a scăpa de ‖ *vi* (*duck*) a se eschiva; a se da în lături, a se feri ‖ *s* ferire *f,* evitare *f,* ocolire *f;* salt *n* în lături; *coll* tertip *n,* şmecherie *f;* truc *n; sp* fentă *f.*

doe *s zool* (*deer*) căprioară *f;* (*rabbit*) iepuroaică *f;* (*rat*) şoricioaică *f.*

dog *s* câine *m*; mascul *m*; vulpoi *m*; lup *m*; şacal *m*; individ *m* || *vt* a lua urma; a merge pe urmele; a urmări; ~ **food** *s* hrană *f* pentru câini; ~**eat**~ *adj* nemilos, neînduplecat.

dog-eared *adj* (*book*) cu colţul îndoit/colţurile îndoite.

dogfish *s icht* câine *m* de mare, rechin *m* mic.

dogged *adj* tenace; ~**ly** *adv* cu tenacitate.

dogwood *s bot* corn *m*; sânger *m*.

dogma *s* dogmă *f* • ~**tic** *adj* dogmatic.

do-it-yourself *s* bricolaj *n*.

dole *s* alocaţie *f* de şomaj; subvenţie *f*, ajutor *n* || *vt* a da ceva de pomană; a cheltui împotriva voinţei sale; ~ **out** *vt* a distribui/a împărţi cu economie.

doleful *adj* jalnic, trist; melancolic.

doll *s* păpuşă *f*; fată *f*, femeie *f* frumoasă.

dollar *s* dolar *m*; ~ **sign** *s* simbolul *n* dolarului; ~ **diplomacy** *s* diplomaţia *f* dolarului.

dolor *s* (*sorrow*) supărare *f*; (*grief*) durere *f*.

dolphin *s icht* delfin *m*.

dolt *s* prostănac *m*.

domain *s also fig* domeniu *n*.

dome *s* dom *n*, cupolă *f*; acoperiş *n*; catedrală *f*; capac *n*, calotă *f*.

domestic *adj* (*home*) domestic, casnic; (*internal*) intern; indigen; (*marital*) conjugal; ~ **science** *s* arte *f pl* menajere || *s* servitor *m*.

domicile *s* domiciliu *n*.

dominant *adj* dominant.

dominate *vt* a domina; a ţine sub influenţa sa.

domination *s* dominaţie *f*, stăpânire *f*.

domineering *adj* (*authoritarian*) autoritar, despotic; (*officious*) superior, mândru, îngâmfat; (*mountain*) înalt, care domină (împrejurimile).

dominion *s pol* dominion *n*; *pl* domenii *n pl*; dominaţie *f*, stăpânire *f*; guvernare *f*; teritoriu *n*.

domino *s* (*game*) domino *n*; ~ **effect** *s* efectul *n* dominoului.

don *s scol* profesor *m* universitar; expert *m*, cunoscător *m*, specialist *m*; persoană *f* distinsă.

donate *vt* a dona; a face o donaţie; a contribui.

donation *s* (*bequest*) donare *f*; (*gift*) donaţie *f*; (*contribution*) contribuţie *f*.

done *adj* (*finished*) terminat; (*cooked*) bine gătit/prăjit; *coll* (*exhausted*) obosit, extenuat.

donkey *s zool* măgar *m*; asin *m*; nătărău *m*; încăpăţânat *m*.

donor *s med* donator *m*; (*benefactor*) donator *m*.

doom *s* (*fate*) soartă *f*, destin *n*; (*disaster*) osândă *f*; damnaţiune *f*; (*death*) pieire; (*end*) sfârşitul *n* lumii || *vt* a condamna; a pecetlui (soarta etc) • ~**ed** *adj also fig* condamnat.

door *s* uşă *f*; poartă *f*; acces *n* • ~**bell** *s* sonerie *f* • ~**knob** *s* mâner *n* • ~**mat** *s* preş *n* (de şters picioarele) • ~**step** *s* prag *n* • ~**to**~ *adj/adv* la domiciliu, din uşă în uşă • ~**way** *s* uşă *f*, intrare *f* (în casă etc).

dope *s* lăcuire *f*, emailare *f*; *sl* drog *n*, narcotic *n*, stupefiant *n*; toxicoman *m*; tâmpit *m* || *vt sl* a droga.

dormant *adj* somnolent; (*volcano*) inactiv, latent; (*law*) neaplicat; liniştit; latent, în stare latentă; potenţial.

dormitory *s* dormitor *n* (în internate etc).

dormouse *s zool* alunar *m*.

dosage *s* (*amount*) dozaj *n*; (*prescription*) posologie *f*.

dose *s* doză *f* || *vt* a doza; (*administer medicine*) a administra un medicament.

dot *s* punct *n*; bulină *f* || *vt* a puncta; a preciza detaliile; **on the** ~ la ţanc • ~**ted** *adj* punctat; ~ **with** presărat cu.

dotage *s* senilitate *f*, decrepitudine *f*; *fig* dragoste *f* nebună.

dote *vi* (**upon**) a iubi la nebunie, a adora.

double *adj* (*twofold*) dublu, îndoit; încovoiat; ipocrit, fals || *adv* (*twice*) dublu, îndoit || *s* (*twice as much/many*) dublu *n*; număr *n* dublu; pas *m* alergător; fugă *f*; meandră *f*; viclenie *f*; (*lookalike*) dublură *f* || *vt* a dubla; (*bend*) a îndoi; a duplica || *vi* a se dubla; a coti; a fugi înapoi; ~ **bass** *s mus* contrabas *n*; ~ **bed** *s* pat *n* dublu; ~ **cream** *s* smântână *f*; ~ **entry** *s econ* contabilitate *f* dublă; ~ **glazing** *s* geam *n* dublu; ~ **room** *s* cameră *f* cu două paturi; ~ **sharp** *s mus* dublu diez *n* • ~**barrelled** *adj* (*name*) cu particulă nobiliară, (*gun*) cu două ţevi, *fig* cu dublu tăiş • ~**cross** *vt* a păcăli, a înşela, *coll* a trage pe sfoară • ~**dealer** *s* ipocrit *m* • ~**decker** *s* autobuz *n* cu imperială • ~**digit** *adj* cu două cifre • ~**edged** *adj also fig* cu două tăişuri • ~**faced** *adj* cu două feţe, nesincer, fals, ambiguu, echivoc, reversibil • ~**jointed** *adj anat* cu articulaţii sau membre deosebit de flexibile • ~**quick** *adj/adv* foarte repede/rapid • ~**talk** *s* vorbe *f pl* în doi peri, vorbe cu două înţelesuri • ~**time** *s mil* marş *n* forţat.

doubt *s* (*uncertainty*) îndoială *f*; (*suspicion*) bănuială *f*, suspiciune *f* || *vi* (*distrust*) a se îndoi; (*have reservations*) a ezita, a şovăi || *vt* a se îndoi de, a nu avea încredere • ~**ful** *adj* îndoielnic; incert, nesigur • ~**less** *adv* fără nici o îndoială.

dough *s* aluat *n*, cocă *f*; pastă *f*; *sl fin* bani *m pl* • ~**nut** *s* gogoaşă *f*.

dour *adj* (*sullen*) ursuz, posac; (*stern*) aspru, sever; (*stubborn*) încăpăţânat.

dove *s* porumbel *m* • ~**cote** *s* porumbar *n*, coteţ *n* de porumbei.

dowdy *adj* (*clothes*) neîngrijit; murdar; demodat; (*person*) îmbrăcat fără gust sau neglijent.

down[1] *adv* jos; la parter; pe pământ; coborât || *adj* coborâtor, descendent; situat mai jos; (*depressed*) deprimat; bolnav; în numerar || *s* coborâre *f* || *vt* a coborî; (*drink*) a da de duşcă; (*lay down*) a lăsa, a pune jos (uneltele).

down[2] *s* (*fine hair*) puf *n* • ~**y** *adj* pufos.

downcast *adj* deprimat, abătut; descurajat; (*eyes*) plecat, în pământ/jos.

downfall *s* potop *n*, ploaie *f* torenţială; *also fig* prăbuşire *f*, ruină *f*, distrugere *f*.

downhearted *adj* deprimat, abătut; descurajat.

downhill *adj* în pantă; **go** ~ *vt* a coborî în pantă, (*deteriorate*) a fi în declin, (*business*) a merge prost, a fi periclitat, a se înrăutăţi.

down-home *adj coll* sudist.

download *vt comp* a încărca.

down payment *s* acont *n*, avans *n*.

downplay *vt* a minimaliza.

downpour *s* aversă *f*, ploaie *f* torenţială.

downright *adv* (*utterly*) de-a dreptul, pur şi simplu, cu totul || *adj* (*manner*) sincer; direct, deschis; (*person*) sincer, deschis; onest.

downscale *vt* (*slim down*) a reduce.

downsize *vt* (*underside*) dedesubt *n*; (*disadvantage*) inconvenient *n*, neajuns *n* || *vt* (*slim down*) a reduce.

downstairs *adv* la parter, jos || *adj* de la parter.

downstream *adv* în aval, la vale; **go ~** *vt* a coborî râul.

downtime *s* perioadă *f* de nefuncționare (a unei mașini, uzine).

down-to-earth *adj* pragmatic, cu picioarele pe pământ.

downtown *adv* în sau spre centrul unui oraș || *s* centrul *n* unui oraș.

downtrend *s* tendință *f* de scădere.

downtrodden *adj* oprimat.

downturn *s* (in) scădere *f* (a).

downward *adj* în jos; (*glance*) plecat • **~s** *adv* în jos.

dowry *s* zestre *f*.

doze *vi* a moțăi; a dormi ușor || *s* moțăială *f*; somn *n* ușor.

dozen *s* duzină *f*; **a baker's ~** un grup de 13.

drab *adj* maron-gălbui; *fig* cenușiu; monoton; tern; lipsit de strălucire; trist mohorât.

draft *s* (*of a letter*) ciornă *f*; schemă *f*, schiță *f*; proiect *n*; plan *n*; *com* trată *f*; (*wind*) curent *n*; tiraj *n*; atelaj *n*; sorbitură *f*, înghițitură *f*; **the ~** *mil* recrutarea *f* || *vt* (~ *a speech*) a schița, a face un plan; a face o ciornă; *mil* a recruta; (*personnel*) a detașa.

drag *vt* (*haul*) a scoate cu greutate; (*lug*) a târî; (*go slowly*) a tândăli; a curăța || *vi* a se târî; a se scurge încet; (~ *a river*) a draga || *s* dragă *f*; frână *f*; obstacol *n*; *coll* corvoadă *f*; *coll* (*wearing women's clothing*) **in ~** *adj* în travesti.

dragon *s also fig* dragon *m*

dragonfly *s ento* libelulă *f*.

drain *s* drenaj *n*, golire *f*; canal *n* de scurgere; rigolă *f*; asanare *f*; scurgere *f*; flux || *vt* (*empty*) a seca; a drena; a deseca; (*deplete*) a secătui; (*exhaust*) a epuiza • **~age** *s* (sisteme de) canalizare *f* • **~pipe** *s* țeavă *f* de scurgere.

drake *s orn* rățoi *m*.

drama *s* dramă *f*; teatru *n* • **~tic** *adj* dramatic; (*effect*) teatral • **~tist** *s* dramaturg *m* • **~tize** *vt* a adapta pentru scenă; (*exaggerate*) a dramatiza.

drape *vt text* a drapa; *fig* a împodobi, a decora || *s text* drapaj *n*; *pl* draperii *f pl*, perdele *f pl*.

draper *s* comerciant *m* de manufactură.

drastic *adj* drastic, aspru, sever; extrem.

draught *s* **draft

draw, drew, drawn *vt* (*pull*) a trage, a târî; (*move*) a mișca; (*pull out*) a scoate; (*derive*) a extrage; a deduce; a smulge; (*attract*) a atrage; a inspira; a redacta; (*sketch*) a desena; a termina la egalitate; **~ near** a se apropia (de); **~ out** a prelungi; **~ up** (*plan*) a întocmi, a elabora (un plan) || *s* scoatere *f*, extragere *f*; tragere *f*; loterie *f*; (*lure*) atracție *f*; (*finish equal*) egalitate *f*; (*dead heat*) remiză *f*.

drawback *s* inconvenient *n*, neajuns *n*.

drawbridge *s* pod *n* basculant; pod *n* mobil; *naut* scară *f* de acostare, pasarelă *f*.

drawer *s* sertar *n*; trăgător *m*; desenator *m*; proiectant *m*.

drawing *s* tragere *f*; desen *n*; loterie *f*; **~ board** planșetă *f* de desen.

drawl *vt* a tărăgăna, a rosti tărăgănat || *vi* a vorbi tărăgănat || *s* tărăgănare *f* (în vorbire), vorbire *f* tărăgănată.

dread *vt* a se teme de || *s* teamă *f*; sperietoare *f* • **~ful** *adj* teribil, cumplit, grozav; îngrozitor || *s* roman *n* polițist.

dream, dreamed/dreamt, dreamed/dreamt *vt* a visa; (*fancy*) a-și închipui; (*think*) a se gândi la; (*fantasize*) a năzui || *s* (*wish*) vis *n*, aspirație *f*; (*fantasy*) fantezie

f; (*delusion*) iluzie *f*; (*hallucination*) halucinație *f*; (*delight*) încântare *f* • **~y** *adj* visător.

dreary *adj* (*weather*) mohorât, trist; plictisitor.

dredge *vt/vi* a draga || *s* dragă *f*.

dregs *s pl* drojdii *f pl*, zaț *n*, reziduuri *n pl*; *fig* drojdie *f* (a societății).

drench *vt* (*wet*) a înmuia; (*douse*) a îmbiba; (*soak*) a uda până la piele || *s* înmuiere *f*; îmbibare *f*; *chem* saturare *f*; *tech* baiț *n*.

dress *s* rochie *f*; (*clothes*) îmbrăcăminte *f*, haine *f pl* || *vt* (*put on*) a îmbrăca; a pregăti; (*adorn*) a împodobi; a bandaja; a tăbăci; a finisa || *vi* a îmbrăca.

dressage *s* dresaj *n*.

dresser [1] *s* (*furniture*) bufet *n*; măsuță *f* de toaletă.

dresser [2] *s thea* costumier *m*; *med* soră *f* (medicală); *min* sortator *m*.

dressing *s med* (*bandage*) pansament *n*; *cul* sos *n*; umplutură *f*; *min* îmbogățire *f*; *naut* pavoazare *f*; *coll* muștruluială *f*, chelfăneală *f*; *tech* îndreptare *f*; prelucrare *f*; **~ gown** *s* halat *n*; **~ table** *s* măsuță *f* de toaletă.

dressmaker *s* croitoreasă *f*.

dribble *vi* a picura, a se scurge; a saliva || *vt sp* a dribla.

dried *adj* (*milk*) praf; (*fruit*) uscat.

drier *s* uscător *n*.

drift *vi* a fi dus/purtat de vânt/curent; *naut* a fi în derivă; *avia* a devia; (*sand*) a se îngrămădi, a se face mormane; (*snow*) a se troieni; *fig* a se lăsa în voia soartei || *vt* a lăsa în voia vântului/curentului; (*wind, etc*) a duce cu sine; a abate, a devia, a deplasa || *s* curgere/plutire *f* (înceată); tendință *f*, direcție *f*, sens *n*; (*meaning*) sens *n* general; (*snow*) troian *n*; (*sand*) morman *n*, acumulare *f*; *naut* derivă *f* de curent; *mil* derivă *f*; *geol* aluviune *f*; alunecare *f*; mișcare *f* de alunecare; *tech* poanson *n* de perforat, matriță *f* de perforat; alezor *n*.

drill *vt* (~ *a hole*) a găuri; (~ *teeth*) a freza; (~ *a well*) a fora; *mil* a face instrucție || *vi* a excava, a for a || *s* (*tool*) burghiu *n*; (*dentist's tool*) freză *f*; *min* sfredel *n*; *ling* exercițiu *n*.

drink, drank, drunk *vt* a bea; a sorbi; a absorbi; a-n-spira; a adăpa || *vi* a bea; a se adăpa || *s* băutură *f*; pahar *n*; dușcă *f*.

drip *vi* a picura; a se prelinge || *vt* a picura || *s* picurare *f*; scurgere *f*; strop *m*, picătură *f* • **~dry** *adj* (*on label*) a nu se călca • **~ping** *s* (*fat*) grăsime *f*.

drive, drove, driven *vt* a mâna; a goni; a urmări; a conduce; a acționa; a duce; a împinge; a vârî || *vi* a mâna; a conduce; a merge (cu o mașină) || *s* (*car, etc*) mers *n*, cursă *f*; pasaj *n*, drum *n* carosabil; (*chase*) urmărire *f*; energie *f*, forță *f*; (*stimulus*) imbold *n*; (*trend*) tendință *f*; *fig* întrecere *f*, cursă *f*; *tech* propulsie *f*; acționare *f*; mers *n*; regim *n*; *mil* atac *n*; lovitură *f*; (*campaign*) campanie *f*, efort *n*, strădanie *f*; *comp* lector *m* de dischete.

drive-in *s* (*cinema*) drive-in *n*; (*bank, restaurant*) serviciu *n* oferit în mașină.

drivel *s* salivă *f*, scuipat *n*; *coll* prostii *f pl*, fleacuri *n pl*, idioțenii *f pl*.

driver *s* șofer *m*, conducător *m* auto; vizitiu *m*; birjar *m*; mecanic *m*; văcar *m*; **~'s license** *s* permis *n* de conducere auto.

driveway *s* alee *f*.

driving *adj* (*rain*) torențial; (*wind*) biciuitor || *s tech* comandă *f*; motor *n*; *aut* conducere *f*; **~ instructor** *s* instructor *m* de la şcoala de şoferi; ~ **lesson** *s* lecţie *f* de conducere auto; ~ **school** *s* şcoală *f* de şoferi; ~ **test** *s* examen *n* pentru obţinerea permisului de conducere auto.

drizzle *vi* a burniţa || *s* burniţă *f*.

droll *adj* comic; (*odd*) curios, ciudat • **~ery** *s* caraghioslâc *n*, comicărie *f*.

dromedary *s zool* dromader *n*.

drone *s also fig* trântor *m*; (*sound*) bâzâit *n*, zumzăit *n*; (*traffic, etc*) zumzet *n* || *vi* a bâzâi, a zumzăi; a vorbi monoton.

drool *vi* (*slobber*) a–i curge balele; (*salivate*) a-i lăsa gura apă.

droop *vi* (*head*) a apleca, a înclina; (*eyelids*) a coborî, a lăsa în jos.

drop *s* (*liquid*) strop *m*, picătură *f*; duşcă *f*; bomboană *f*; (*fall*) cădere *f*; reducere *f*; distanţă *f* || *vi* a picura; (*fall*) a cădea; (*price*) a scădea; a se lăsa în jos; a se înclina || *vt* a picura; a stropi; a scăpa; a se lăsa de; a întrerupe; ~ **off** *vi* (*sleep*) a adormi • **~out** *s* marginalizat *m*; student *m* care abandonează facultatea • **~pings** *s pl* ceva *n* ce cade în picuri; ploaie *f*; grăsime *f*; balegă *f*; bălegar *n* • **~s** *s pl med* picături *f pl*.

drought *s* secetă *f*.

drove *s* (*herd*) turmă *f*; cireadă *f*; cârd *n*; (*throng*) mulţime *f*, cârd *n* || *vt* (*cattle*) a mâna • **~r** *s* păstor *m*.

drown *vt* a îneca; (*sink*) a scufunda; (*flood*) a inunda; (*engulf*) a înăbuşi; a astupa; a îndepărta; (*cover*) a acoperi.

drowsiness *s* somnolenţă *f*.

drowsy *adj* somnoros, moleşit; adormitor; vlăguit.

drub *vt* (*defeat*) a învinge (categoric); (*beat with stick*) a ciomăgi; a bate.

drudge *s* salahor *m*; trudă *f* || *vi* a trudi • **~ry** *s* corvoadă *f*, muncă *f* neinteresantă.

drug *s* medicament *n*; drog *n*, narcotic *n*, stupefiant *n* || *vt* a droga; a pune droguri în || *vi* a se droga, a lua droguri.

drum *s mus* tobă *f*; tambur *n*; bidon *n*, canistră *f* || *vi mus* a cânta la tobă; a bate toba || *vt* a executa (muzică) la tobă • **~stick** *s mus* beţisor *n* de tobă; (*chicken*) pulpă *f*, copan *n*.

drunk *adj* beat, îmbătat || *s* om *m* beat • **~ard** *s* beţiv *n* • **~enness** *s* (stare de) beţie *f*.

dry *adj* (*parched*) uscat; (*waterless*) secat; (*arid*) secetos; sec; (*thirsty*) însetat; (*dull*) plictisitor; zvântat || *vt* (*make dry*) a usca; (*rub*) a şterge; (*dessicate*) a seca || *vi* (*parch*) a se usca, a seca; ~ **clean** *vt* a curăţa chimic; ~ **cleaner's** *s* curăţătorie *f* chimică.

dual *adj* dublu • **~ity** *s* dualitate *f*.

dub *vt* (*nickname*) a porecli, a numi; (*movie*) a dubla • **~bing** *s* dublare *f* (a unui film); dublaj *n* • **~bed** *adj* (*film*) dublat.

dubious *adj* îndoielnic; ezitant, nesigur.

duchess *s* ducesă *f*.

duck[1] *s orn* raţă *f*; comoară *f*, odor *n*; scumpete *f*; afundare *f*; scufundare *f*; ferire *f* (a capului).

duck[2] *vt* a cufunda; a ocoli; (*dodge*) a se eschiva de la, a se feri de.

duct *s anat* canal *n*, tub *n*; *tech* canal *n*, conductă *f*, tub *n*.

dud *s* lucru *n* bun de nimic; om *m* bun de nimic, neisprăvit *m*; *mil* bombă *f* care nu explodează || *adj* bun de nimic, inutil; (*check*) fals, fără acoperire; (*bomb*) neexplodat.

dude *s* (*guy*) ins *m*, individ *m*; (*city dweller*) *sl* orăşean *m*.

due *adj* datorat, de plată; (*suitable*) corespunzător; aşteptat || *s* cele cuvenite *f pl*; drept *n* || *adv* drept, direct, exact; **be** ~ *vt* a trebui să sosească; ~ **to** *prep* datorită, din cauza; ~ **process of law** *jur* respectarea garanţiilor legale • **~s** *s pl* cotizaţie *f*.

duel *s* duel *n* || *vi* a se duela, a se bate în duel.

duet *s mus* duo *n*, duet *n*; *fig* dialog *n*; dispută *f*, controversă *f*.

dug *s* mamelă *f*; (*udder of cow, goat*) uger *n* || *v* ***dig**.

duke *s* duce *m*.

dulcet *adj lit* (*sweet*) dulce, suav.

dulcimer *s* ţambal *n*.

dull *adj* (*dense*) stupid; (*obtuse*) obtuz; (*dim*) mat; (*slow*) încet; leneş; insensibil; indiferent; (*weather*) posomorât; (*gloomy*) sumbru; vag, ceţos; (*blunt*) tocit, bont; (*sound*) monoton || *vt* a toci; a amorţi; a potoli; a slăbi || *vi* (*blunt*) a se toci; a se micşora; (*reduce*) a slăbi.

duly *adv* la timpul potrivit; la timp; în timp util; corect.

dumb *adj* mut; tâmpit; necuvântător • **~bell** *s* halteră *f* • **~found** *v* a ului, a consterna, a stupefia • **~ness** *s* muţenie *f*.

dummy *s* manechin *n*; machetă *f*; *fig* manechin *n*, om *m* de paie; *fig* marionetă *f*; unealtă *f*; *sl* nătărău *m* || *adj* fals; fictiv; (*cartridges*) de exerciţiu.

dump *s* morman *n*, grămadă *f*; zgomot *n* surd || *vt* (~ *trash*) a arunca, a azvârli; a bascula; (*unload*) a descărca • **~ster** *s* pubelă *f*.

dumpling *s* găluşcă *f*.

dunce *s* prost *m*, nătâng *m*.

dune *s* dună *f*.

dung *s* balegă *f*; bălegar *n*.

dungarees *s text* stambă *f*; *pl* pantaloni *m pl* de stambă, salopetă *f* de stambă.

dungeon *s* carceră/închisoare *f* subterană.

duo *s mus, thea* duet *n*; (*couple*) pereche *f*, cuplu *n*.

dupe *s* fraier *m*; unealtă *f*, agent *m* || *vt* a escroca.

duplex *s* apartament *n* pe două nivele; apartament *n* pentru două familii.

duplicate *vt* a dubla; (*photocopy*) a copia || *adj* dublu; analog || *s* duplicat *n*; copie *f*; reproducere *f*.

duplication *s* duplicare *f*; copiere *f*; ~ **machine** maşină de multiplicat.

duplicity *s* duplicitate *f*.

durable *adj* durabil, trainic.

duration *s* durată *f*; **for the** ~ **of** până la capătul/ sfârşitul.

duress *s* constrângere *f*; **under** ~ constrâns (fiind).

during *prep* în timpul/cursul; ~ **the day** în timpul zilei.

dusk *s* amurg *n*, crepuscul *n*.

dust *s* pulbere *f*, praf *n*; ţărână *f*; polen *n*; agitaţie *f*; fleac *n* || *vt* a şterge praful, a curăţa, a prăfui; ~ **jacket** *s* (*books*) învelitoare *f* care apără de praf, supracopertă *f* • **~er** *s* cârpă *f* de şters praful • **~y** *adj* prăfuit; *vag*; neinteresant, fad.

Dutch *s/adj* olandez(ă) *m/f*; **the** ~ *s* olandezii *m pl*.

dutiful *adj* (*obedient*) supus, ascultător; (*respectful*) respectuos; conştiincios.

duty *s* (*obligation*) datorie *f*, obligaţie *f*; (*job*) serviciu *n*; (*responsibility*) răspundere *f*; folosire *f*; (*tax*) taxă *f*; *pl* taxe *f pl* (vamale); **off** ~ liber; **on** ~ de serviciu • **~free** *adj* scutit de vamă.

duvet *s* plapumă *f* de puf.

dwarf *s* pitic *m* ‖ *vt* a opri creșterea; a micșora • **~ish** *adj* de pitic; pitic, mic; nedezvoltat; pipernicit.

dwell, dwelled/dwelt, dwelled/dwelt *vi* a locui, a trăi; a rămâne • **~ing** *s* locuință *f*.

dwindle *vi* a se micșora, a se diminua; a-și pierde importanța; a se agrava.

dye *s* colorant *m*; vopsea *f*; culoare *f*; nuanță *f* ‖ *vt* a colora, a vopsi • **~d-in-the-wool** *adj* îmbibat/pătruns de vopsea; *fig* total, perfect, desăvârșit, complet; *fig* înrăit, înveterat.

dying *adj* (*person*) muribund; (*plant, language, industry*) muribund, pe cale de dispariție.

dyke *s* *dike*; *pej* lesbiană *f*.

dynamic *adj* *tech* dinamic; *fig* dinamic, activ, energic; *med* dinamic, funțional.

dynamite *s* dinamită *f* ‖ *vt* a dinamita.

dynamo *s* *elec* dinam *n*; mașină *f* dinamo-electrică.

dynasty *s* dinastie *f*.

dysentery *s* *med* dizenterie *f*.

dysfunction *s* disfuncție *f* • **~al** *adj* disfuncțional.

dyslexia *s* dislexie *f*.

dyslexic *adj* dislexic.

dyspepsia *s* *med* dispepsie *f*, indigestie *f*.

E

e, E *s* (litera) e, E; *mus* (nota) mi.

each *adj* fiecare ‖ *pron* fiecare.

eager *adj* doritor, dornic; pasionat; înverșunat • **~ness** *s* dorință *f* (puternică), poftă *f*, sete *f*; înflăcărare *f*, zel *n*, ardoare *f*.

eagle *s* vultur *n*; monedă *f* de aur de 10 dolari.

ear[1] *s* *anat* ureche *f*; *fig* auz *n*, ureche *f* (muzicală); **to be all ~s** a fi numai urechi, a asculta cu atenție • **~ache** *s* *med* durere *f* de urechi.

ear[2] *s* mâner *n*, toartă *f*; *bot* spic *n*; moț *n* ‖ *vi* a da în spic.

earl *s* conte *m*.

early *adj* timpuriu; (*untimely*) prematur, precoce; urgent.

earmark *vt* (*allocate*) a aloca (o sumă).

earn *vt* (*take home*) a câștiga; (*receive*) a dobândi, a căpăta.

earnest *adj* (*sober*) serios; (*heartfelt*) convins, încredințat; important; (*solemn*) grav; (*intense*) zelos, înfocat, aprins; (*desire*) arzător ‖ *s* seriozitate *f*; **in ~** în (mod) serios; **in all ~** cu toată seriozitatea.

earring *s* cercel *m*.

earth *s* (*globe*) pământ *n*, glob *n*; (*world*) lume *f*; omenire *f*; (*ground*) uscat *n*; țărână *f*; (*mud*) lut *n*; (*soil*) sol *n*, teren *n* ‖ *vt* a îngropa; a săpa • **~quake** *s* cutremur *n*; zguduire *f* • **~shaking** *adj coll* (*event, discovery*) extraordinar

earwig *s* *ento* urechelniță *f*.

ease *s* pace *f*, liniște *f*; tihnă *f*; lenevie *f*; mângâiere *f*; ușurință *f*; naturalețe *f* ‖ *vt* a liniști; a mângâia; a alina; a reduce, a micșora.

easel *s* șevalet *n*.

easily *adv* ușor, cu ușurință; liber, nestingherit; (*without doubt*) fără doar și poate.

east *s* răsărit *n*, est *n* ‖ *adj* estic, răsăritean; oriental ‖ *adv* la răsărit, în est.

Easter *s* Paște *n*, Paști *n pl*.

easy *adj* (*simple*) simplu, ușor; (*comfortable*) comod; (*calm*) liniștit; (*relaxed*) degajat; blând; înțelegător;

(*effortless*) nesilit ‖ *adv* ușor, cu ușurință; fără grabă, liniștit.

eat, ate, eaten *vt* (*have a meal*) a mânca; a se hrăni cu; (*bother*) (**at**) a roade; (*destroy*) a distruge ‖ *vi* a mânca, a lua masa • **~able** *adj* comestibil • **~ery** *s* ospătărie *f*, birt *n*.

eaves *s pl* streașină *f*.

eavesdrop *vi* a trage cu urechea ‖ *vt* a auzi ceva trăgând cu urechea/fără să vrea.

ebb *s* reflux *n* ‖ *vi* (*sea, tide*) a se retrage.

ebony *s* abanos *n* ‖ *adj* (*color*) negru ca abanosul.

ebullient *adj* exuberant, expansiv.

eccentric *adj* excentric, ciudat, straniu ‖ *s* excentric *m*, original *m*.

ecclesiastic *adj* ecleziastic, bisericesc ‖ *s* cleric *m*.

echelon *s* eșalon *n*.

echo *s* ecou *n*, răsunet *n*; urmare *f*, rezultat *n*; imitație *f* ‖ *vi* a avea ecou; a răsuna ‖ *vt* a repeta, a imita.

eclair *s* (*pastry*) ecler *n*.

eclipse *s* *also fig* eclipsă *f* ‖ *vt* a eclipsa.

ecology *s* ecologie *f*.

economic *adj* (*monetary*) economic; (*profitable*) rentabil, profitabil; **~ downturn** recesiune economică; **~ growth** creștere economică • **~al** *adj* cumpătat, chibzuit; economicos • **~s** *s* economie *f*, știința *f* economiei.

economist *s* economist *m*.

economy *s* economie *f*; gospodărie *f*; (*saving*) păstrare *f*; organizare *f*, structură *f*; (*financial system*) sistem *n* economic.

ecstasy *s* extaz *n*, încântare *f*.

eczema *s* *med* eczemă *f*.

eddy *s* (*vortex*) vârtej *n* (de vânt etc)

Eden *s* rai *n*, paradis *n*.

edge *s* (*rim*) margine *f*; (*verge*) muchie *f*; (*limit*) lizieră *f*; (*sharpness*) tăiș *n*, creștet *n*, vârf *n*; (*frame*) chenar *n*; tiv *n*; agerime *f* ‖ *vt* (*sharpen*) a ascuți; a teși; a tăia; a strecura ‖ *vi* a se furișa.

edible *adj* comestibil ‖ *s pl* mâncare *f*, bucate *f pl*.

edification *s* *frml* edificare *f*.

edifice *s* *also fig* edificiu *n*.

edify *vt* *frml* a edifica.

edit *vt* a edita, a publica, a redacta.

edition *s* ediție *f*.

educate *vt* (*tutor*) a educa; a crește; a cultiva; (*train*) a antrena ‖ *vr* a se instrui.

education *s* (*instruction*) educație *f*; (*schooling*) învățătură *f*, pregătire *f*; creștere *f*; cultură *f*; (*teaching*) învățământ *n*.

eel *s* *icht* țipar *m*.

eerie *adj* (*creepy*) neliniștitor, sinistru; (*strange*) ciudat, misterios.

effect *s* (*result*) efect *n*, consecință *f*, rezultat *n*; acțiune *f*; valabilitate *f*; cuprins *n*; (*impression*) impresie *f* ‖ *vt* (*achieve*) a efectua, a executa • **~ive** *adj* (*efficient*) eficace; (*useful*) util, activ; (*in effect*) în vigoare; (*real*) efectiv, real, frapant ‖ *s pl* efective *n pl*.

effeminate *adj* efeminat.

effervescent *adj* (*liquid*) efervescent; (*drink*) gazos.

effete *adj* (*weak*) istovit; (*society*) epuizat; decadent.

efficacious *adj* *frml* eficace.

efficiency *s* (*effectiveness*) eficiență *f*, eficacitate *f*; operativitate *f*; (*competence*) pregătire *f*, calificare *f*; putere *f* de muncă; *tech* productivitate *f*, randament *n*; (*organization*) bună funcționare *f*.

efficient adj (effective) eficient, eficace, operativ; productiv; (proficient) capabil, competent ‖ s cauză f, agent m; math factor m; înmulțitor m.

effigy s efigie f; chip n, figură f.

effort s (exertion) efort n; (endeavor) sforțare f; realizare f, rezultat n.

effrontery s insolență f.

effusive adj (person) expansiv, exuberant, comunicativ; (welcome) călduros; pej exagerat.

egg s ou n; germen m, embrion m; mină f, grenadă f.

egoism s egoism n.

egoist s egoist m • **~ic** adj egoist.

egotism s phil egotism n; egocentrism n.

egregious adj (blatant) flagrant, scandalos; (cowardice etc) extrem; **an ~ lie** s minciună abominabilă; **an ~ error** s greșeală enormă.

egress, egression s ieșire f.

Egyptian s/adj egiptean m.

eiderdown s plapumă f umplută cu puf.

eight num opt ‖ s opt n; formație f de opt • **~een** num optsprezece • **~y** num optzeci.

either pron fiecare, oricare (din doi); amândoi, ambii ‖ adj fiecare, oricare; ambii, amândoi ‖ conj sau ... sau ‖ adv nici.

ejaculate vi a exclama; a striga ‖ vt med a ejacula; (words) a rosti repede.

eject vt (objects) a expulza, a evacua; (persons) a alunga, a expulza.

eke vi (out) a adăuga la; a lungi, a prelungi; a suplimenta, a completa; fig a lungi.

elaborate adj (intricate) complicat; executat cu grijă ‖ vt (develop) a crea, a executa cu grijă; (explain) a da detalii, a explica în detaliu.

elapse vi a se scurge.

elastic adj elastic, flexibil; adaptabil; optimist ‖ s gumă f; elastic n.

elated adj în culmea fericirii; jubilând.

elbow s cot n; cotitura f; curbă f; meandră f ‖ vt a înghionti; a îmbrânci ‖ vi a coti, a șerpui.

elder[1] adj mai mare, mai în vârstă; anterior, premergător ‖ s pl superiori m pl; strămoși m pl, străbuni m pl. • **~ly** adj cam în vârstă, bătrâior.

elder[2] s bot soc m.

eldest adj cel mai mare, cel mai în vârstă, cel mai bătrân.

elect vt a vota, a alege; a numi; a prefera; a decide ‖ adj ales; votat; desemnat; distins • **~ion** s alegeri f pl; scrutin n; jur alegere f, opțiune f; relig predestinare f; **~eer** vi a organiza o campanie electorală.

electric adj electric; electrizant ‖ s corp n electric; izolator n • **~ity** s electricitate f; energie f electrică.

electrify vt a electrifica.

electrocute vt a electrocuta.

electrode s elec electrod m.

electronic adj electronic; **~ mail** (**email**) s poștă f electronică, curier n electronic.

elegant adj (stylish) elegant; (neat) frumos; rafinat; luxos; excelent; (chic) dichisit.

elegy s elegie f.

element s (part) element n, parte f; stihie f; mediu n; fond n; noțiuni f pl de bază • **~al** adj (basic) de bază, fundamental; (nature) dezlănțuit; chem elementar.

elementary adj elementar, primar, primitiv, simplu.

elephant s zool elefant m.

elevate vt also fig (raise) a ridica, a înălța; fig (exalt) a înobila, a înălța sufletește; (promote) a promova, a înainta (în funcție) • **~d** adj ridicat, înălțat; suspendat; fig elevat, înalt, superior; **~ train** s metrou n aerian.

elevation s (rise) ridicătură f (de pământ etc); (promotion) promovare f.

elevator s elevator n; macara f; lift n, ascensor n.

eleven num unsprezece.

elf s gnom m, spiriduș m; zână f; fig drac m, împielițat m, ștrengar m.

elicit vt (draw out) a zmulge, a scoate, a extrage; fig (~ an answer, etc) a zmulge, a reuși să obțină; (~ admiration, etc) a stârni, a provoca.

eligible adj (for) pol eligibil (ca); bun, potrivit, acceptabil; (~ male) bun de însurătoare; (~ female) de măritat.

eliminate vt (get rid of) a elimina, a înlătura; (eradicate) a lichida, a distruge.

elite s elită f, floare f, cremă f.

elixir s elixir n.

elk s zool elan m.

ellipse s math, ling elipsă f.

elm s bot ulm m.

elocution s elocuțiune f, dicțiune f; elocință f, elocvență f, oratorie f; pej emfază f, vorbire f bombastică.

elongate vt a lungi; (~ line) a prelungi • **~ed** adj (in space) alungit; (in time) prelungit.

elope vi a fugi (cu iubitul sau iubita); a fugi pe ascuns.

eloquence s elocință f.

eloquent adj elocvent; fig elocvent, grăitor, semnificativ.

else adv mai, încă, în plus; altul, alt, alta, altă, altfel, altminteri.

elude vt a eluda, (avoid) a ocoli; (evade) a se feri de.

elusive adj (indefinable) insesizabil; evaziv; care-ți scapă printre degete.

emaciated adj vlăguit, epuizat; slăbit; atrofiat.

email, e-mail s curier n electronic ‖ vt a trimite prin curier electronic.

emanation s emanație f; radiație f; exalare f; origine f.

emancipate vt jur a emancipa; a elibera (de prejudecăți, etc).

emasculate vt a castra.

embalm vt a îmbălsăma (un cadavru); a parfuma, a înmiresma.

embankment s taluz n.

embargo s embargo n; sechestru n; interzicere f, prohibiție f; fig piedică f ‖ vt a pune embargo pe; a sechestra, a rechiziționa; fig a opri, a interzice.

embark vt a îmbarca; a încărca pe un vas ‖ vi naut a se îmbarca; **to ~ on/upon** vi a porni (pe calea etc), a se angaja în.

embarrass vt a stânjeni, a jena; a îngreuia, a complica; a împiedica.

embassy s ambasadă f; funcție f de ambasador.

embed vt a băga, a vârî; fig a sădi, a întipări.

embellish vt a înfrumuseța, a împodobi.

ember s cenușă f fierbinte; pl tăciuni m pl aprinși.

embezzle vt a delapida, a deturna, a-și însuși.

embitter vt (make bitter) a înfuria, a supăra; a întrista; (become disillusioned) a fi decepționat/dezamăgit.

emblem s emblemă f, simbol n; stemă f; blazon n; mostră f.

embody vt a întrupa, a încarna; a concretiza; fig a întrupa; a întruchipa; a personifica, a reprezenta; fig a alcătui, a forma.

emboss *vt text* a gofra; a dăltui în relief; (~ *coins*) a stampa, a bate; *fig* a împodobi, a ornamenta.

embrace *vt* (*hug*) a îmbrățișa; a accepta, a primi; a studia; (*contain*) a cuprinde || *s* (*cuddle*) îmbrățișare *f.*

embroider *vt* a broda; a înzorzona.

embryo *s bio* embrion *m*, germen *m*; fetus *m*; *fig* embrion *m*, germen *m.*

emerald *s* smarald *n* || *adj* de smarald; de culoarea smaraldului.

emerge *vi* a se ivi, a apărea; a ieși la iveală.

emergency *s* eventualitate *f*; necesitate *f*; (*crisis*) caz *n* extrem; (*disaster*) pericol *n*; (*urgent situation*) urgență *f*; ~ **room** *s* sală *f* de urgențe.

emery *s* șmirghel *n.*

emetic *adj* vomitiv.

emigrant *s* emigrant *m.*

emigrate *vi* a emigra.

eminence *s* (*prominence*) renume *n*, prestigiu *n*; (*high ground*) ridicătură *f.*

eminent *adj* (*ground*) ridicat, înalt; *fig* eminent, distins, remarcabil.

emir *s* emir *m.*

emissary *s* emisar *m.*

emission *s* emitere *f*, emanare *f.*

emit *vt* (*release*) a răspândi, a emana; (*give out*) a emite, a radia; a scoate (sunete etc).

emolument *s frml* retribuție *f*, remunerație *f.*

emotion *s* sentiment *n*; emoție *f* • ~**al** *adj* (*moving*) sentimental, emoțional, afectiv; (*sensitive*) emotiv.

empathy *s* empatie *f.*

emperor *s* împărat *m.*

emphasis *s ling* accent *n*, accentuare *f*; *fig* accentuare *f*, subliniere *f*; *fig* expresivitate *f*, elocință *f*; *typ* caractere *n pl* cursive/italice sau spațiate.

emphasize *vt* a accentua; a sublinia, a reliefa.

empire *s* imperiu *n*; împărăție *f*; stăpânire *f*, putere *f.*

empirical *adj* empiric.

emplacement *s mil* amplasare *f.*

employ *vt* (*use*) a folosi; (*hire*) a angaja || *vr* a se ocupa • ~**ee** *s* funcționar *m*, slujbaș *m* • ~**er** *s* patron *m*, stăpân *m*; antreprenor *m* • ~**ment** *s* folosire *f*, ocupație *f*, serviciu *n*, slujbă *f.*

empower *vt* a împuternici, a autoriza; a permite, a da posibilitatea (cuiva).

empty *adj* (*unfilled*) gol, neocupat, liber; (*uninhabited*) nelocuit || *vt* (*drain*) a goli; a descărca || *vi* a se goli; a se vărsa (un râu).

emu *s orn* emu *m.*

emulate *vt* a rivaliza cu.

emulation *s* emulație *f*, întrecere *f.*

emulsion *s chem*, *etc* emulsie *f.*

enable *vt* a da posibilitatea de a; a permite; a îndreptăți (pe cineva) să.

enact *vt* (~ *law*) a legifera, a adopta; a hotărî, a decreta; *thea* a pune în scenă, a juca.

enamel *s* smalț *n*, email *n*; (*tooth* ~) smalț *n* || *vt* a smălțui, a emaila; *fig* a smălțui, a împodobi.

enamor *vt* a face sa îndrăgească, a face să se îndrăgostească; *fig* a fermeca, a vrăji.

encase *vt* a împacheta, a ambala; a înrăma; a acoperi, a înveli; *constr* a cofra.

enchant *vt* (*charm*) a încânta, a desfăta.

encircle *vt* a încercui, a înconjura; *mil* a învălui.

enclave *s* enclavă *f.*

enclose *vt* a închide; a îngrădi; a pune (în plic etc); a anexa.

enclosure *s* (*area*) îngrăditură *f*; (*letter*) anexă *f* la o scrisoare.

encore *interj* bis || *s* bis *n* || *vt* a bisa.

encounter *s* întâlnire *f* || *vt* a întâlni.

encourage *vt* (*give confidence*) a încuraja; (*support*) a sprijini, a favoriza; (*promote*) a stimula; a instiga.

encroach *vt* (**on/upon**) a uzurpa, a impieta asupra a ceva.

encumber *vt* (*hinder*) a stânjeni; (*impede*) a împiedica, a îngreuna; (*burden*) a încărca, a împovăra.

encyclopedia *s* enciclopedie *f.*

end *s* capăt *n*, cap *n*; rest *n*; sfârșit *n*; (*garden, table, street*) capăt *n*, extremitate *f*; latură *f*; limită *f*; hotar *n*; moarte *f*; scop *n*; rezultat *n*; concluzie *f*; (*cigarette*) muc *n* || *vt/vi* a (se) sfârși; a se spulbera; **at an** ~ *adj* terminat, sfârșit; **on** ~ *adv* (*upright*) sculat, în picioare, (*continually*) fără întrerupere.

endanger *vt* a pune în pericol, a periclita.

endearing *adj* atrăgător, cuceritor.

endeavor *vt* a se strădui, a încerca || *s* sforțare *f*, efort *n*, strădanie *f.*

endemic *adj med* endemic; (~ boală *f* endemică, endemie *f.*

endive *s bot* andivă *f*; cicoare *f.*

endorse *vt* (*view*) a aproba, a susține; *econ* a andosa; (*check*) a încasa • ~**ment** *s* (*viewpoint*) aprobare *f*, sprijinire *f*, sancționare *f*; *econ* andosare *f*, gir *n.*

endow *vt* (*equip*) a dota, a înzestra; (*give money*) a face donații.

endurance *s* (*stamina*) rezistență *f*; (*fortitude*) suporta-bilitate *f.*

endure *vt* (*bear*) a îndura, a suporta || *vi* (*last*) a dura, a dăinui.

enema *s* clismă *f.*

enemy *s* dușman *m* || *adj* inamic, ostil.

energetic *adj* energic; de energie, energetic.

energy *s* energie *f*, forță *f*, vigoare *f.*

enervate *vt* a epuiza, a slei de putere.

enfold *vt* a înfășura, a înveli; *fig* a cuprinde, a îm-brățișa; a plia, a îndoi.

enforce *vt* a aplica, a face să fie respectat.

engage *vt frml* (*employ*) a angaja; a tocmi; (~ *attention, interest*) a suscita, a trezi; a absorbi; (*hold*) a reține; *tech* a porni (un motor); a obliga; a logodi; a ataca || *vi* a garanta, a se obliga; a promite • ~**d** *adj* angajat; (*in smth*) ocupat (cu ceva); (*phone*) ocupat; (*to be married*) logodit; angrenat • ~**ment** *s* (*commitment*) angajament *n*, obligație *f*; logodnă *f*; ocupație *f*; luptă *f*; (*meeting*) întâlnire *f*, (*date*) rendezvous *n.*

engaging *adj* seducător, cuceritor.

engine *s* mașină *f*; motor *n*; (*train*) locomotivă *f*; dispozitiv *n*; mecanism *n*; ~ **driver** *s* mecanic *m* de locomotivă.

engineer *s* inginer *m*; mecanic *m*, mașinist *m*; tehnician *m*; montor *m* || *vt* a construi, a proiecta; a pune la cale • ~**ing** *s* inginerie *f*; tehnologie *f*; *mil* geniu; *fig* mașinații *fpl.*

England *s* Anglia *f*; în Anglia.

English *adj* englez(esc), britanic || *s* (limba) engleză *f*; *pl* **the** ~ englezii; **translate into** ~ *vt* a traduce în engleză; a angliciza.

engrave *vt* a grava, a tăia; a întipări.

engraving *s* gravură *f.*

engrossed *adj* (**in**) absorbit (de ceva), adâncit (în ceva).

engulf *vt* a înghiți, a scufunda.

enhance *vt* a spori, a intensifica.

enigma *s* enigmă *f*, mister *n*.

enjoy *vt* (*benefit from*) a se bucura de; (*like*) a gusta, a-i plăcea ‖ *vr* (*take pleasure in*) a se distra, a petrece • ~**able** *adj* agreabil • ~**ment** *s* plăcere *f*.

enlarge *vt* a lărgi, a mări; (*upon*) a dezvolta • ~**ment** *s* lărgire *f*, expansiune *f*; *phot* mărire *f*.

enlighten *vt* a lumina, a lămuri • ~**ed** *adj* luminat, instruit • ~**ment** *s* clarificare *f*, lămurire *f*; **the Enlightenment** *s* Secolul *n* Luminilor, Iluminismul *n*.

enlist *vt* *mil* a înrola; a recruta; (*obtain*) a asigura ‖ *vi* *mil* (*in*) a se înrola (în).

enmity *s* ostilitate *f*, dușmănie *f*.

ennui *s* lehamite *f*, plictiseală *f*.

enormity *s* întindere *f*, suprafață *f* vastă.

enormous *adj* enorm, uriaș, colosal; (~ *patience*, *success*) imens; monstruos, îngrozitor.

enough *adj* destul, suficient ‖ *adv* destul, de ajuns, suficient; foarte.

enquire *vt* (**when/if/how**) a se interesa (când/dacă/cum) ‖ *vi* (**about**) a se informa (asupra).

enrage *vt* a înfuria, a exaspera, a scoate din sărite • ~**d** *adj* dezlănțuit; (*animal*) turbat.

enrich *vt* a îmbogăți; a înfrumuseța; a îngrășa, a fertiliza ‖ *vr* a se îmbogăți.

enroll *vt* a înscrie; a înregistra; a înrola; a înregimenta; a împacheta • ~**ment** *s* înscriere *f*; înregistrare *f*.

ensign *s* (*flag*) pavilion *n*, stindard *n*.

enslave *vt* a supune, a transforma în sclav • ~**ment** *s* *also fig* înrobire *f*, subjugare *f*.

ensnare *vt* a prinde în capcană; *fig* a prinde în mreje, a ademeni.

ensue *vi* a urma, a rezulta.

ensure *vt* a asigura, a garanta ‖ *vr* a se asigura.

entail *vt* a antrena, a atrage (după sine).

entangle *vt* (*tangle*) a încurca, a încâlci; a zăpăci; *fig* a vârî în bucluc; *fig* (*ensnare*) a ademeni, a prinde în mreje.

enter *vt* (~ *a room*, *vehicle*) a intra în, a pătrunde în; (~ *a university*, *the army*) a intra în/la; (~ *a school*) a se înscrie în/la; (~ *politics*) a se lansa în politică; (*sign up*) a înscrie pe cineva la ceva; (*write down*) a înscrie; *comp* a introduce; a vârî; a fi admis la; a înainta; a intenta; a iniția ‖ *vi* (*come/go*) a intra; (*register*) a se înscrie (la); ~ **into** *vt* (*negotiations*, *etc*) a începe, a stabili.

enterprise *s* întreprindere *f*; proiect *n*, plan *n*; inițiativă *f*; antrepriză *f*; fabrică *f*, uzină *f*.

enterprising *adj* cu inițiativă, întreprinzător.

entertain *vt* (*have visitors*) a primi, a trata; a întreține, a conversa cu; (*divert*) a distra, a amuza ‖ *vr* a se distra; a petrece ‖ *vi* a primi vizite.

enthrall *vt* a captiva, a fermeca.

enthusiasm *s* (*passion for*) entuziasm *n*; (*interest*) pasiune *f*.

enthusiastic *adj* entuziast, înflăcărat; entuziasmat.

entice *vt* a ademeni, a momi.

entire *adj* întreg, tot, deplin; intact; nealterat • ~**ly** *adv* cu totul, în întregime.

entitle *vt* (~ *to smth*) a da dreptul (cuiva la ceva); (~ *to do smth*) a autoriza (pe cineva să facă ceva) • ~**d** *adj* autorizat; (*named*) intitulat • ~**ment** *s* drept *n*; putere *f*, autorizare *f*.

entity *s* *phil* entitate *f*.

entomology *s* entomologie *f*.

entrails *s pl* *anat* intestine *n pl*, măruntaie *f pl*; *fig* străfund *n*.

entrance¹ *s* intrare *f*, pătrundere *f*; acces *n*; ușă *f*; poartă *f*; debut *n*; început *n*.

entrance² *vt* a vrăji; a fermeca; a aduce în stare de transă.

entrant *s* (*competitions*, *etc*) concurent *m*.

entreat *vt* a implora, a ruga stăruitor.

entrenched *adj* *mil* prevăzut cu tranșee; fortificat; *fig* (*tradition*, *etc*) înrădăcinat; vechi.

entrepreneur *s* antreprenor *m*.

entrust *vt* a încredința (ceva cuiva).

entry *s* intrare *f*, acces *n*; ivire *f*, apariție *f*; ușă *f*; poartă *f*; trecere *f*; vestibul *n*; (*competition*) înscriere *f*; listă *f*; (*dictionary*) articol *n* de dicționar; (*document*) inscripție *f*, înscriere *f*.

entwine *vt* (*interweave*) a împleti, a încolăci; (*embrace*) a îmbrățișa, a cuprinde cu brațele; *fig* a îmbina ‖ *vi* a se împleti, a se încolăci.

enumerate *vt* a enumera.

enunciate *vt* a enunța, a formula.

envelop *vt* a înveli, a înfășur.

envelope *s* plic *n*, înveliș *n*; copertă *f*.

envenom *vt* a învenina.

envious *adj* invidios.

environment *s* înconjurare *f*; (*surroundings*) împrejurimi *f pl*; (*milieu*) mediu *n*, ambianță *f*; atmosferă *f* • ~**al** *adj* (*pollution*) a mediului înconjurător; (*impact*) asupra mediului înconjurător.

environs *s pl* suburbii *f pl*.

envisage, envision *vt* a considera, a prevedea.

envoy *s* trimis *m*, emisar *m*, mesager *m*.

envy *s* invidie *f*; obiect *n* al invidiei ‖ *vt* a invidia, a pizmui.

enzyme *s* *chem* enzimă *f*.

ephemeral *adj* *fig* efemer, trecător.

epic *adj* epic; eroic ‖ *s* poem *n* epic; epopee *f*.

epidemic *s* epidemie *f*.

epidermal *adj* epidermic.

epigram *s* epigramă *f*; sentință *f*; maximă *f*.

epilepsy *s* *med* epilepsie *f*.

epilogue *s* epilog *n*.

Epiphany *s* *relig* Bobotează f; *fig* epifanie *f*, manifestare *f* divină.

Episcopal *adj* episcopal.

episode *s* episod *n*; întâmplare *f*.

epistle *s* epistolă *f*, scrisoare *f*.

epitaph *s* epitaf *n*.

epithet *s* epitet *n*.

epitome *s* (*gist*) sumar *n*, rezumat *n*; **the ~ of** modelul lui.

epoch *s* epocă *f*; ev *n*; perioadă *f*.

equable *adj* egal, constant.

equal *adj* (*on a par*) egal; același; (*like*) asemenea; (*equivalent*) echivalent, corespunzător; echilibrat; uniform; calm; ponderat; imparțial ‖ *s* (*peer*) egal *m*; pereche *f* ‖ *vt* (*match*) a egala, a fi egal cu; a se compara cu • ~**ity** *s* egalitate *f* • ~**izer** *s* *sp* gol *n* egalizator.

equanimity *s* calm *n*, echilibru *n* sufletesc.

equate *vt* (*with*, *to*) a egal(iz)a; *math* a pune în ecuație.

equation *s* ecuație *f*.

equator *s* ecuator *n*.

equestrian *adj* ecvestru.

equidistant *adj* echidistant.

equilateral *adj math* echilateral.

equilibrium *s* echilibru *n*.

equinox *s astron* echinocţiu *n*.

equip *vt* (**with**) a echipa, a înzestra (cu); a utila (cu); *fig* (**with**) a echipa, a înzestra, a prevedea • **~ment** *s* echipare *f*; echipament *n*; utilaj *n*; instalaţie *f*.

equity *s* (*justice*) echitate *f*, dreptate *f*; *jur* lege *f* nescrisă, drept *n* natural; (*impartiality*) imparţialitate *f*; *fin* (*market value*) fond/capital *n* propriu; (*share*) acţiune *f* (cotată la bursă).

equivalent *adj/s* echivalent *n*.

era *s* eră *f*; epocă *f*.

eradicate *vt also fig* a eradica.

erase *vt* a rade, a şterge; a îndepărta.

erect *adj* drept, vertical; ridicat; înălţat, sus; neclintit; mândru ‖ *vt* a ridica, a construi; a monta; a asambla; a înălţa; a stabili • **~ion** *s* (*statue*) ridicare *f*; (*building*) construire *f*; (*penis*) erecţie *f*.

ermine *s* hermină *f*.

erode *vt* (~ *rocks*, *soil*) a eroda; *fig* (~ *confidence*, *rights*) a reduce ‖ *vi* (~ *rocks*, *soil*) a se eroda; *fig* (~ *confidence*) a scădea; (~ *rights*) a se reduce.

erosion *s* (*soil*) eroziune *f*; (*corrosion*) roadere *f*; distrugere *f*, *fig* (*confidence*) scădere *f*; (*rights*) diminuare *f*; (*corrosion*) roadere *f*; distrugere *f*.

erotic *adj* erotic; amoros • **~a** *s* erotism *n*; poezie *f* erotică; senzual *m*.

err *vi* a greşi, a se înşela; *fig* a greşi, a păcătui.

errand *s* cursă *f*, comision *n*; **to go on/run an** ~ a face o cursă.

erratic *adj* (*life*) dezordonat, neregulat; (*behavior*) straniu, ciudat; schimbător; *geol* eratic.

error *s* eroare *f*, greşeală *f*; păcat *n*; abatere *f*.

erudite *adj/s* erudit *m*, învăţat *m*.

erupt *vi* a erupe; a izbucni; a ţâşni; a ieşi.

escalate *vi* (~ *a conflict*) a se intensifica; *fig* a escalada.

escalator *s* escalator *n*, scară *f* rulantă.

escapade *s* escapadă *f*, aventură *f*, ispravă *f*.

escape *vi* a scăpa, a fugi; (~ *from prison*) a evada; (~ *danger*, *a person*) a scăpa de; (*survive*) a o scoate la capăt ‖ *vt* (~ *danger*) a scăpa de ‖ *s* scăpare *f*; fugă *f*; evadare *f*; evacuare *f*, eşapament *n*; (*gas*, *water*) scurgere *f*.

escapism *s* evaziune *f* (din realitate).

escort *s* escortă *f*; pază *f*; însoţitor *m* ‖ *vt* a escorta; a însoţi.

Eskimo *s* eschimos *m*.

esophagus *s anat* esofag *n*.

esoteric *adj* ezoteric; (*person*) iniţiat; secret; confidenţial.

especial *adj* special, deosebit • **~ly** *adv* mai ales; (*more than usual*) îndeosebi; în special.

espionage *s* spionaj *n*.

esplanade *s* esplanadă *f*.

essay *s* încercare *f*, tentativă *f*; *liter* eseu *n*; *scol* lucrare *f*; teză *f*.

essence *s* esenţă *f*, fiinţă *f*; substanţă *f*; parfum *n*; *cul* extract *n*.

essential *adj* esenţial, vital, absolut, extrem ‖ *s* esenţă *f*, substanţă *f*; lucru *n* esenţial; bază *f*.

establish *vt* (*set up*) a stabili, a aşeza; (*institute*) a organiza; a instala; (*confirm*) a consacra; (*found*) a fonda; (*create*) a constitui; (*prove*) a demonstra • **~ment** *s* stabiliment *n*, întreprindere *f*, instituţie *f*; (*organization*, *business*) fondare *f*, constituire *f*; **the**

Establishment *s* ordinea *f* stabilită, cercurile *n pl* conducătoare.

estate *s* clasă *f* (socială), stare *f*, (*property*) domeniu *n*, avere *f*, proprietate *f*; condiţie *f*; *jur* (*inheritance*) bunuri *n pl*; (*housing*) împărţirea *f* în loturi; (*industrial*) zonă *f* industrială.

esteem *s* stimă *f* ‖ *vt* a stima.

estimate *s* (*valuation*) evaluare *f*, apreciere *f*; sumă *f*, total *n*; (*guess*) părere *f*, opinie *f* ‖ *vt* (*assess*) a estima, a aprecia.

estuary *s geog* estuar *n*.

etch *vt* a grava • **~ing** *s* gravură *f*.

eternal *adj* etern; neschimbat; interminabil.

eternity *s* eternitate *f*, veşnicie *f*.

ether *s chem*, *phys* eter *n* • **~eal** *adj chem*, *phys* eteric; *fig* eteric; aerian; diafan.

ethical *adj* moral, etic.

ethics *s pl* etică *f*, morală *f*.

ethnic *adj* (*tradition*, *group*) etnic; (*costume*) popular, folcloric.

etiquette *s* convenienţă *f*, etichetă *f*, norme *f pl* de comportare.

etymology *s* etimologie *f*.

Eucharist *s relig* împărtăşanie *f*, cuminecătură *f*.

eulogize *vt* a elogia.

eulogy *s* elogiu *n*.

eunuch *s* eunuc *m*.

euphemism *s* eufemism *n*.

euphoria *s* euforie *f*.

eureka *interj* evrica!.

Europe *s* Europa *f* • **~an** *adj/s* european *m*.

euthanasia *s* eutanasie *f*.

evacuate *vt* (*vacate*) a evacua, a goli; (*abandon*) a părăsi.

evacuee *s* evacuat *m*.

evade *vt* (*elude*) a eluda; (*avoid*) a ocoli; (*dodge*) a evita ‖ *vi* (*escape*) a evada, a fugi (din).

evaluate *vt* a evalua, a preţui; a aprecia.

evanescent *adj* (*fleeting*) care dispare repede; (*transitory*) trecător, efemer.

evangelical *adj* evanghelic.

evaporate *vi* a se vaporiza; a se evapora; a dispărea ‖ *vt* a vaporiza.

evaporation *s* vaporizare *f*; evaporare *f*.

evasion *s* evaziune *f*; eschivare *f*; ocolire *f*; **tax** ~ *s* evaziune fiscală.

evasive *adj* evaziv, vag, ocolit.

eve *s* ajun *n*; **on the** ~ **of** în ajunul, în preziua, în preajma/ pragul/ajunul.

even *adj* (*smooth*) neted; plan; (*equal*) egal; cu soţ; lichidat; calm; (*balanced*) echilibrat; echitabil; exact ‖ *adv* (*still*) chiar, până şi; întocmai ‖ *vt* a nivela, a egaliza • **~handed** *adj fig* imparţial, nepărtinitor.

evening *s* seară *f*; serată *f*; ~ **dress** rochie *f* de seară, haine *f pl* de seară; ~ **service** *s relig* vecernie *f*.

evensong *s relig* slujbă *f* de seară.

event *s* (*occasion*) întâmplare *f*, accident *n*; (*experience*) eveniment *n*; *sp* probă *f*, competiţie *f*; (*outcome*) eventualitate *f* • **~ful** *adj* memorabil.

eventual *adj* final, decisiv, definitiv; eventual, posibil.

ever *adv* vreodată, cândva; mereu, întotdeauna.

evergreen *adj* peren ‖ *s* plantă *f* perenă (cu frunze mereu verzi).

everlasting *adj* etern.

every *adj* fiecare; toţi, toate.

everybody *pron* fiecare; toți, toată lumea.

everyday *adj* zilnic, cotidian; obișnuit, banal.

everyone *pron* * **everybody**.

everything *pron* tot, toate (lucrurile).

everywhere *adv* pretutindeni, peste tot.

evict *vt* a evacua, a expulza.

evidence *s* (*proof*) dovadă *f*, mărturie *f*; (*facts*) probă *f*; evidență *f* ‖ *vt* (*prove*) a dovedi, a demonstra ‖ *vi* (*testify*) a depune mărturie.

evident *adj* evident, clar.

evil *adj* (*nasty*) rău; (*vile*) nefast, funest, dăunător; trist, jalnic ‖ *s* rău *n*; (*wickedness*) necaz *n*, nenorocire *f*.

evince *vt frml* (*show*) a demonstra, a manifesta; (*quality*) a da dovadă de.

evoke *vt* (~ *a memory*) a evoca; (~ *feelings*) a suscita.

evolution *s* evoluție *f*, dezvoltare *f*, progres *n*; desfășurare *f*.

evolve *vt* (*develop*) a desfășura, a dezvolta; a elabora; a degaja, a emite ‖ *vi* a se dezvolta; a se desfășura.

ewe *s zool* oaie *f*.

exacerbate *vt* (~ *a feeling*) a spori, a accentua; (~ *a problem*) a agrava, a exacerba.

exact *adj* exact, precis; (*strict*) riguros; (*thorough*) metodic; (*meticulous*) punctual; corect ‖ *vt* (*demand*) a pretinde, a cere.

exaggerate *vt* a exagera; a amplifica.

exalt *vt* (*acclaim*) a exalta, a slăvi; a înflăcăra, a aprinde; (*promote*) a înălța, a ridica • **~ed** *adj* exaltat; (*style*) solemn.

exam *s* examen *n*.

examination *s* examen *n*; examinare *f*, cercetare *f*; inspecție *f*; control *n*; revizie *f*; verificare *f*; interogatoriu *n*.

examine *vt* (*look into*) a examina; (*research*) a cerceta; a inspecta; (*check*) a controla; a verifica; a interoga.

example *s* exemplu *n*; model *n*; mostră *f*; precedent *n*; lecție *f*.

exasperate *vt* (*infuriate*) a exaspera, a scoate din sărite; (*annoy*) a irita; (*worsen*) a agrava (o boală, etc.)

excavate *vt* a excava, a săpa, a dezgropa.

excavator *s* excavator *n*.

exceed *vi* a depăși; a întrece.

excel *vt* (*surpass*) a depăși, a întrece; (*stand out*) a fi superior; (*shine*) a excela, a se distinge • **~lence** *s* desăvârșire *f*, perfecțiune *f*, superioritate *f* • **~lent** *adj* (*outstanding*) excelent, minunat, ireproșabil.

except *prep* cu excepția, (în) afară de; mai puțin, minus ‖ *conj* dacă nu ‖ *vt* a excepta, a exclude • **~ion** *s* excepție *f*, abatere *f*; raritate *f*; obiecție *f*; opoziție *f*; rezervă *f* • **~ional** *adj* excepțional.

excerpt *s* extras *n*, fragment *n*, pasaj *n*.

excess *s* (**of**) surplus *n*, exces *n*, prisos *n* (de); abuz *n*; **to** ~ fără (nici o) măsură ‖ *adj* excedentar • **~ive** *adj* (*extreme*) excesiv, exagerat; extravagant; exorbitant.

exchange *s* schimb *n*; bursă *f*; centrală *f* (telefonică) ‖ *vt* a schimba; a face schimb de • **~able** *adj* interșanjabil; înlocuibil; de schimb.

excise *s fin* accize *f pl*.

excite *vt* (*stimulate*) a excita; (*incite*) a provoca; (*stir up*) a emoționa • **~ment** *s* (*enthusiasm*) excitare *f*, excitație *f*; (*thrill*) emoție *f*; (*agitation*) frământare *f*.

exciting *adj* excitant; emoționant, mișcător; captivant.

exclaim *vt/vi* a exclama; a striga.

exclamation *s* exclamație *f*.

exclude *vt* (*keep out*) a exclude, a elimina.

exclusive *adj* (*society*) exclusiv, închis; (*use, news, story*) exclusiv ‖ *s* exclusivitate *f*; ~ **of** *prep* exclusiv, excluzând.

excommunicate *vt relig* a excomunica.

excrement *s* excrement *n*.

excrete *vt physiol* a excreta.

excruciating *adj* (*pain*) atroce; (*noise*) infernal.

excursion *s* (*outing*) excursie *f*; (*expedition*) expediție *f*; (*trip*) călătorie *f*; incursiune *f*; (*digression*) digresiune *f*, divagație *f*.

excuse *s* (*reason*) scuză *f*; (*justification*) justificare *f*; scutire *f* ‖ *vt* (*forgive*) a scuza; (*justify*) a justifica; (*exempt*) a scuti ‖ *vr* (*apologize*) a se scuza, a-și cere iertare.

execrable *adj frml* execrabil.

execute *vt* a executa, a îndeplini; a efectua; a aplica; a redacta, a scrie; a sancționa, a viza; a omorî.

execution *s* (*of person*) execuție *f*; *frml* (*of an order, etc*) executare *f*; *jur* (*of a will, sentence, etc*) executare *f*.

executive *adj* (*power*) executiv; (*job*) administrativ ‖ *s* (*person*) cadru *n*; (*group*) birou *n*.

executor *s jur* (*of will*) executor *m* (testamentar).

exemplary *adj* (*very good*) exemplar, model; (*typical*) tipic; (*reproving*) drastic; ~ **punishment** pedeapsă exemplară.

exemplify *vi* (*characterize*) a exemplifica; (*illustrate*) a exemplifica, a ilustra.

exempt *vt* (*from*) a scuti, a absolvi, a dispensa (de) ‖ *adj* (*from*) scutit (de).

exercise *s* exercițiu *n*, exercitare *f*; (*application*) aplicare *f*; (*working out*) antrenament *n*; dovadă *f*; (*assignment*) temă *f* ‖ *vt* a exersa; (*train*) a antrena; (*bring to bear*) a exercita; a instrui ‖ *vi* a se exersa.

exert *vt* a exersa; (*force*) a întrebuința, a face uz de; **to** ~ **oneself** *vt* a se sili, a se strădui.

exhale *vt* (*give off*) a exala, a emana, a degaja; (*breathe out*) a expira; *fig* (*utter*) a da drumul, a rosti; (*in anger*) a da frâu liber.

exhaust *vt* (*drain*) a goli; a scoate; (*use up*) a epuiza ‖ *s* eșapament *n*, evacuare *f* • **~ed** *adj* epuizat, istovit • **~ing** *adj* epuizant, obositor • **~ion** *s* epuizare *f*, golire *f* • **~ive** *adj* exhaustiv, complet.

exhibit *vt* (~ *art*) a expune; (~ *a skill, etc*) a etala, a da dovadă de; (*show feeling*) a arăta ‖ *s* (*art* ~) exponat *n*, obiect *n* expus; *jur* probă *f* materială • **~ion** *s* expunere *f*, prezentare *f*; (*feelings*) manifestare *f*; (*art*) expoziție *f*, salon *n*; târg *n* de mostre.

exhilarating *adj* (*experience*) amețitor; (*walk, etc*) tonic.

exhort *vt frml* a îndemna • **~ation** *s* stăruința *f*.

exigency *s* (*need*) nevoie/necesitate *f* imperioasă, imperativ *n*; (*emergency*) urgență *f*, situație *f* critică.

exigent *adj frml* urgent; presant; (*exacting*) exigent.

exiguous *adj frml* (*means, income*) neînsemnat, mic, modest.

exile *s* exilare *f*; exil *n*; exilat *m* ‖ *vt* a exila.

exist *vi* (*be*) a fi, a exista; (*live*) a trăi; (*be real*) a se afla.

exit *vi* (*go out*) a ieși, a pleca ‖ *s* (*way out*) ieșire *f*, (*leaving*) plecare *f*; (*door*) ușă *f*; (*death*) moarte *f*.

exonerate *vi* (~ *from blame*) a disculpa; (~ *from obligation*) a elibera (de).

exorbitant *adj* exorbitant.

exorcise *vt* (~ *a ghost*) a exorciza, a alunga.

exotic *adj* exotic ‖ *s* plantă *f* exotică.

expand *vt (inflate)* a dilata; *(develop)* a extinde ‖ *vi* a se dilata; a se extinde; a se desfășura.

expanse *s (area)* întindere *f; (spread)* expansiune *f*, lărgire *f*.

expansion *s (increase)* dilatare *f; (growth)* expansiune *f*, extindere *f*; ~ **of the market** extindere a pieței.

expansive *adj (open)* expansiv, exuberant; *(extensive)* vast, întins.

expatriate *vt* a expatria ‖ *s* expatriat(ă) *m/f* ‖ *adj (community)* de expatriați.

expect *vt* a aștepta; a spera; a se aștepta la; a vrea, a dori.

expectorate *vt/vi med, frml* a expectora.

expedient *adj (suitable)* indicat ‖ *s (means)* expedient *n*, tertip *n*, soluție *f* practică.

expedition *s (journey)* expediție *f; (haste)* promptitudine *f*, grabă *f*.

expeditious *adj frml* expeditiv; prompt, rapid.

expel *vt* a da afară, a exclude, a elimina.

expenditure *s* cheltuială *f*.

expense *s (expenditure)* cheltuiala *f; (price)* preț *n*, cost *n*.

expensive *adj* scump, costisitor; luxos.

experience *s (skill)* experiență *f*; trăire *f; (event)* întâmplare *f; (knowledge)* calificare *f*, cunoaștere *f* ‖ *vt* a experimenta; *(feel)* a simți, *(go through)* a trece prin; *(live through)* a încerca un sentiment.

experiment *s (trial, test)* experiență *f*, experiment *m*, probă *f* ‖ *vi (conduct test)* a experimenta • **~al** *adj* experimental.

expert *s* expert *m*, specialist *m* ‖ *adj* expert, cunoscător • **~ise** *s (know-how)* experiență *f*, *(skill)* competență *f*.

expiate *vt frml* a ispăși.

expire *vt* a expira ‖ *vi* a expira; a muri; a se termina.

expiry *s (of visa, etc)* expirare *f*.

explain *vt (clarify)* a explica; *(explicate)* a interpreta; *(give reasons for)* a motiva ‖ *vr* a se justifica, a se explica ‖ *vi (give explanation)* a da explicații.

explanation *s* explicare *f*; interpretare *f*; motivare *f*; explicație *f*.

expletive *s/adj gram* expletiv *n; (oath)* cuvânt *n* obscen.

explicit *adj (precise)* explicit, *(clear)* clar; *(unequivocal)* evident.

explode *vt (blow up)* a arunca în aer; *(discredit)* a discredita ‖ *vi (go off)* a exploda; *(burst)* a izbucni.

exploit *s (feat)* ispravă *f*, *(heroic act)* faptă *f* eroică ‖ *vt (take advantage of)* a exploata.

explore *vt (travel around)*) a explora, *(delve into)* a cerceta, a studia; *(survey)* a sonda • **~er** *s* explorator *m*.

explosion *s* explozie *f*; izbucnire *f*; hohot *n*.

explosive *adj/s* exploziv *n*.

exponent *s (theory)* exponent, *m*, interpret *m*.

export *vt* a exporta ‖ *s* export *n*; articol *n* de export.

expose *vt* a expune; *(unmask)* a demasca; *(display)* a etala; *(reveal)* a destăinui; a abandona ‖ *vr* a se expune.

exposition *s (explanation)* expunere *f*, prezentare *f; (exhibition)* târg *n*, expoziție *f*.

exposure *s phot* timp *n* de expunere; publicitate *f*; copertă *f; (~ to light, radiation)* expunere *f*; **to die of ~** a muri de frig.

express *vt (state)* a exprima, a formula; *(expedite)* a expedia urgent ‖ *vr* a se exprima ‖ *adj* expres, formal; *(train)* expres; special, exact; intenționat ‖ *s (train)* rapid *n*, expres *n* • **~ion** *s* exprimare *f*; expresie *f*; mină *f*; expresivitate *f*; noțiune *f*.

expropriate *vt* a expropria.

expulsion *s (eviction)* expulzare *f*, *(ejection)* izgonire *f*; *tech* eșapament *n*, evacuare *f*.

exquisite *adj (fine)* splendid, *(superb)* excelent.

extant *adj frml* (încă) existent.

extemporaneous *adj (speech)* improvizat, liber.

extend *vt (expand)* a întinde, a extinde; *(lengthen)* a lungi; *(broaden)* a lărgi; *(prolong)* a prelungi; a răspândi; *(offer)* a oferi.

extension *s (building)* înălțare *f*, *(expansion)* mărire *f*; prelungire *f; (visit)* prelungire *f* în timp; *(visa)* prelungire *f* a termenului; *(deadline)* report; *(power)* creștere *f; (law)* lărgire *f; tele* poștă *f; elec* prelungitor *n*.

extensive *adj (quantity)* considerabil; *(area)* vast; *(discussion)* aprofundat; *(change, use)* considerabil.

extent *s (scope)* întindere *f*, lungime *f; (range)* importanță *f; (degree)* măsură *f*.

extenuate *vt* a atenua.

exterior *adj* exterior; extern ‖ *s (house, car)* exterior *n*, parte *f* exterioară; *(person)* extern, parte *f* exterioară.

exterminate *vt* a extermina.

external *adj* extern.

extinct *adj (vanished)* stins; *(dead)* mort; uitat • **~ion** *s* dispariție *f*, extincție *f*.

extinguish *vt (put out)* stinge; *(quench)* a potoli; a distruge, a nimici; *(settle debt)* a achita • **~er** *s* extinctor *n*.

extirpate *vt frml* a extirpa.

extol *vt frml (praise)* a proslăvi.

extort *vt* a extorca.

extra *adj* extra, suplimentar; superior ‖ *adv* suplimentar, peste; extrem de ‖ *s* plată *f* suplimentară; figurant *m*; calitate *f* extra.

extract *vt (~ coal, oil)* a extrage; *(~ a tooth)* a extrage, a scoate; *(~ confession, information)* **(from)** a-i smulge cuiva, a scoate de la cineva; a alege ‖ *s* extras *n*, pasaj *n*, fragment *n*; esență *f*.

extradite *vt* a extrăda.

extramarital *adj* extraconjugal.

extramural *adj scol* fără frecvență.

extraneous *adj (irrelevant)* colateral, care nu e la obiect, străin; *(from outside)* din afară/exterior.

extraordinary *adj* extraordinar.

extravagance *s* extravaganță *f; (excessive spending)* risipă *f*, cheltuieli *f pl* excesive; *(luxury)* extravaganța *f*, nebunie *f*.

extravagant *adj (person)* risipitor, cheltuitor; *(taste)* costisitor; *(ideas, dress)* extravagant; *(exaggerated, elaborate)* extravagant, bizar.

extreme *adj (radical)* extrem; *(utmost)* maxim, minim; *(excessive)* excesiv; *(ultimate)* din urmă, de sfârșit ‖ *s* extremă *f*, limită *f*, capăt *n*.

extremist *adj/s* extremist *m*.

extremity *s (farthest point)* extremitate *f*, capăt *n; pl anat* extremități *f pl*, membre *n pl; fig* limită *f; fig (end)* agonie *f*, ultimele clipe *f pl; (adversity)* strâmtoare *f*, mizerie *f*, sărăcie *f; usu pl (extreme measure)* măsuri *f pl* excepționale.

extricate *vt* **(from)** a scoate (din); *(difficulty)* a se descurca, a scăpa (de).

extrovert *s/adj* extrovertit *m*.

exuberance *s (excitement)* exuberanță *f; (enthusiasm)* entuziasm *n*.

exuberant *adj (vegetation)* exuberant, luxuriant; *(joy,* *etc*) debordant, excesiv; *fig* rodnic, fertil; (*style*) încărcat, înflorit; prolix; (*person*) exuberant, expansiv.

exude *vt med* a exuda, a elimina; *fig* a iradia, a împrăştia ‖ *vi* a transpira, a asuda.

exult *vi* a jubila, a exulta • **~ant** *adj* entuziasmat.

eye *s anat* ochi *m*; (*needle*) ureche *f*; vizor *n* ‖ *vt* a privi (la); a observa, a urmări.

eyeball *s* glob *n* ocular.

eyebrow *s* sprânceană *f.*

eye-catching *adj* atrăgător, îmbietor, reţinând privirea.

eyedrops *s pl* picături *f pl* de ochi.

eyeglasses *s pl* ochelari *m.*

eyelash *s* geană *f.*

eyelid *s* pleoapă *f.*

eyeliner *s* tuş *n* pentru ochi.

eye-opener *s* revelaţie *f*; *coll* bombă *f.*

eyeshadow *s* fard *n* pentru pleoape.

eyesight *s* vedere *f*, câmp *n* vizual.

eyesore *s med* urcior (la ochi); *fig* spin *m* în ochi; (*ugly thing*) hidoşenie *f.*

eyewitness *s* martor *m* ocular.

F

F, f *s* (litera) F, f; *mus* (nota) fa; notă *f* insuficientă.

fa *s mus* (nota *f*) fa.

fable *s* fabulă *f*; (*parable*) născocire *f*; (*tale*) legendă *f*; (*myth*) mit *n*; fabulaţie *f*; subiect *n* ‖ *vt* a născoci, a inventa; a minţi.

fabric *s* material *n*, (*textile*) ţesătură *f*, (*cloth*) stofă *f*; (*structure*) construcţie *f*; structură *f.*

fabricate *vt* (*make*) a fabrica, a executa; (*make up*) a scorni, a inventa; (*forge*) a falsifica, a contraface.

fabrication *s* (*production*) fabricare *f*, producere *f*; (*lie*) scorneală *f*, născocire *f*; (*forgery*) fals *n*, contrafacere *f.*

fabulous *adj* (*mythical*) fabulos, mitic; *coll* (*extraordinary*) senzaţional, fabulos.

façade *s* faţadă *f.*

face *vt* (*challenge*) a brava, a sfida; (*stand in front of*) a sta în faţă, a aştepta ‖ *s* (*visage*) faţă *f*; (*countenance*) expresie *f*, mină *f*; *pl* grimasă *f*, neruşinare *f*; prezenţă *f*; (*appearance*) aspect *n* exterior; (*dial*) cadran *n*; (*façade*) faţadă *f*; ~ **cream** *s* cremă *f* de faţă; ~ **value** *s* (*coin*, *stamp*) valoare *f* nominală • **~lift** *s* lifting *n*, operaţie *f* plastică • **~saving** *adj* care salvează prestigiul/reputaţia.

facet *s* faţetă *f.*

facetious *adj* (*person*) care face glume când nu trebuie; (*teasing*) glumeţ; poznaş.

facial *adj* facial, al feţei; de faţă ‖ *s* masaj/tratament *n* facial.

facile *adj* (*simplistic*) facil; superficial.

facilitate *vt* (*make easy*) a uşura, a facilita; (*encourage*) a promova, a încuraja.

facility *s* facilitate *f*, uşurinţă *f*; (*characteristic*) aptitudine *f*; (*amenity*) amenajare *f.*

facing *adj* din faţă, opus.

facsimile *s* telecopie *f*, fax *n*; facsimil *n.*

fact *s* (*piece of evidence*) fapt *n*; împrejurare *f*; (*reality*) realitate *f*; (*truth*) adevăr *n*; esenţă *f* **in** ~ *conj* în fapt.

faction *s* facţiune *f*; fracţiune *f*, partidă *f*; bandă *f*, clică *f*; sciziune *f*, dezbinare *f.*

factitious *adj* fictiv; fals.

factor *s* (*cause*) factor *n*; agent *m*, mijlocitor *m*; (*feature*) element *n*; *math* factor *m*; coeficient *m*; divizor *m*; *tech* coeficient *m* (de siguranţă); *bio* genă *f.*

factory *s* fabrică *f*, uzină *f.*

factual *adj* faptic, real, efectiv.

faculty *s* (*sense*) facultate *f*; (*ability*) aptitudine *f*; (*gift*) talent *n*; (*staff*) cadru *n* didactic.

fad *s* (*vogue*) admiraţie *f* exagerată, modă *f*; (*personal*) manie *f*, idee *f* fixă.

fade *vi* (*wilt*) a se ofili; (*become paler*) a păli; (*grow fainter*) a se şterge; (*lose color*) a se decolora; (*die away*) a se stinge.

fag *s pej* homosexual *m*, pederast *m.*

fail *s* eşec *n*; cădere *f* ‖ *vi* (*be unsuccessful*) a nu reuşi; (*go down*) a cădea; a slăbi; a se termina ‖ *vt* a nu reuşi; a omite; (*not pass*) a nu promova • **~ing** *s* hibă *f*, defect *n* ‖ *prep* în lipsa, în absenţa • **~ure** *s* (*lack*) absenţă *f*, lipsă *f*; (*deficiency*) insuficienţă *f*; eşec *n*; (*collapse*) cădere *f*; slăbiciune *f*, pagubă *f*; ratat *m*; (*breakdown*) pană *f.*

faint *adj* (*weak*) slab, sleit; fricos; (*dim*) vag ‖ *s* (*blackout*) leşin *n* ‖ *vi* a slăbi; a ameţi; (*pass out*) a leşina.

fair[1] *adj* (*fine*) frumos, îngrijit; (*weather*) senin; limpede; (*legible*) lizibil; (*clean*) nepătat; (*natural*) firesc; favorabil; (*right*) cinstit; imparţial; (*evenhanded*) corect, echilibrat; (*complexion*) alb; (*hair*) blond ‖ *adv* cinstit; drept; echitabil; direct, sincer.

fair[2] *s com* (*trade event*) târg *n*; (*carnival*) bâlci *n.*

fairy *s* zână *f*, nimfă *f*; elf *m*, gnom *m* ‖ *adj* de zână; fermecat, feeric, de basm.

faith *s* (*belief*) credinţă *f*; convingere *f*; (*trust*) încredere *f*; religie *f*; (*loyalty*) loialitate *f* • **~ful** *adj* credincios; fidel; exact; cinstit.

fake *vt* (*forge*) a falsifica; a înşela; (*simulate*) a simula ‖ *s* (*forgery*) contrafacere *f*; (*fraud*) înşelăciune *f*; (*sham*) impostor *m* ‖ *adj* (*forged*) fals.

falcon *s* şoim *m.*

fall, fell, fallen *vi* (*drop*) a cădea; (*collapse*) a se prăbuşi; (*descend*) a se lăsa; a se ruina; a pieri; a se potoli; (*decrease*) a decădea ‖ *s* (*reduction*) cădere *f*; scădere *f*; (*waterfall*) cascadă *f*; (*slope*) pantă *f*; (*autumn*) toamnă *f*; ~ **apart** *vt* (*cards*, *chairs*) a se dezmembra, *fig* (*country*) a se nărui, (*person*) a se prăbuşi; ~ **back** *vi* (*crowd*) a se retrage; ~ **behind** *vi* (*race*) a rămâne în urmă, (*rent*) a întârzia, (*work*) a rămâne în urmă; ~ **for** *vi* (*love*) a-i cădea cu tronc, (*lie*) a se lăsa păcălit; ~ **in** *vi* (*ceiling*, *roof*) a se surpa, a se prăbuşi, *mil* a se alinia; ~ **off** *vi* (*branches*, *handles*) a cădea, a se rupe, (*numbers*, *applications*) a se diminua, a scădea; ~ **out** *vi* (*hair*, *teeth*) a cădea, (*friends*) a se certa, *mil* a rupe rândurile; ~ **over** *vi* (*person*, *etc*) a cădea; ~ **through** *vi* (*plans*, *business*) a eşua, a nu reuşi.

fallacious *adj* (*erroneous*) eronat; (*deceptive*) înşelător.

fallacy *s* (*erroneous belief*) eroare *f*, sofism *n.*

fallible *adj* supus greşelii, (*weak*) failibil.

fallout *s* emanaţii *f pl* radioactive, radiaţii *f pl.*

fallow *adj* (*land*) părăginit, nedestelenit.

false *adj* (*fake*) fals, greşit; (*untruthful*) neîntemeiat; (*insincere*) necredincios; artificial; ~ **alarm** *s* alarmă *s* falsă; ~ **teeth** *s pl* proteză *f* dentară.

falsetto *s mus* falsetto *n.*

falsify *vt* (~ *a document*) a falsifica, a contraface; (~ *a story*) a răstălmăci, a denatura; (*disappoint*) a deza-măgi; a înşela (speranţele cuiva).

falter *vi (stagger)* a se clătina; *(steps, voice)* a şovăi; *(hesitate)* a ezita.

fame *s* faimă *f*; renume *n*.

familiar *adj (recognizable)* familiar; *(habitual)* obişnuit, *(common)* comun; ireverenţios; *(intimate)* familial ‖ *s* prieten *m* apropiat • **~ity** *s (knowledge)* cunoaştere *f* • **~ize** *vt* a se familiariza (cu).

family *s (relations)* familie *f*, *(line, breed)* neam *n*, clan *n*; *(group)* grup *n*; ~ **doctor** *s* doctor *m* de familie; ~ **planning** *s* planificare *f* familială; ~ **clinic** *s* centru *n* de planificare familială.

famine *s (food shortage)* foamete *f*; *(scarcity)* lipsă *f*; *(want)* absenţă *f*.

famished *adj coll* înfometat; **I'm ~!** mor de foame!.

famous *adj (renowned)* vestit, renumit; grozav • **~ly** *adv coll* excelent, nemaipomenit.

fan¹ *s* evantai *n*; ventilator *n*; vânturătoare *f* ‖ *vt* a face vânt; a vântura; a stârni; a adia.

fan² *s* microbist *m*; amator *m* entuziast; admirator *m* al cuiva.

fanatic *s* fanatic *m*.

fanciful *adj (imaginary)* imaginar; *(whimsical)* capricios, cu toane; *(bizarre)* straniu, ciudat, bizar; *(clothing)* extravagant.

fancy *s (fantasy)* fantezie *f*; imaginaţie *f*; *(desire)* dorinţă *f*, *(whim)* capriciu *n*; *(preference)* preferinţă *f* ‖ *adj* straniu; fantezist; *(whimsical)* capricios; modern; *(food)* rafinat; *(hotels, restaurants: expensive)* de lux; *(price)* exagerat; *(clothes)* extravagant ‖ *vt coll (feel like)* a avea chef de, a dori; *(imagine)* a-şi imagina; a avea impresia; a considera ‖ *vi* a-şi imagina, a-şi închipui; ~ **that!** ei poftim!, imaginează-ţi!.

fanfare *s* fanfară *f*.

fang *s (dog)* colţ *m*; *(snake)* dinte *m* veninos.

fantastic *adj (fanciful)* fantastic; *(imaginary)* închipuit; bizar; excentric; *(whimsical)* capricios.

fantasy *s (dream)* iluzie *f*; *(fancy)* fantezie *f*; imaginaţie *f*; *(whim)* capriciu *n*; bănuială *f*.

far *adv* departe; mult, considerabil ‖ *adj* (în)depărtat; extreme • **~away** *adj* îndepărtat; *fig (look, etc)* dus, absent, pierdut • **~reaching** *adj* de mare răsunet • **~sighted** *adj (person)* clarvăzător, *(plan)* elaborat cu luciditate.

farce *s thea* farsă *f*; *fig* poznă *f*, harababură *f*.

farcical *adj* ridicol.

fare *s* costul *n* unei călătorii; bilet *n*; călător *m*; mâncare *f* ‖ *vi* a o duce; a se simţi.

farewell *s* rămas *n* bun ‖ *interj* adio!.

farm *s (ranch)* fermă *f*, gospodărie *f*; *(farmhouse)* locuinţă *f* de fermier; *(fruit farm)* pepinieră *f* ‖ *vt (till soil)* a lucra (pământul); a arenda ‖ *vi* a cultiva pământul • **~er** *s* fermier *m*; ţăran *m*; arendaş *m* • **~hand** *s* muncitor *m* agricol • **~house** *s* fermă *f* • **~ing** *s* agricultură *f*; creşterea *f* animalelor • **~stead** *s* fermă *f* cu toate acareturile.

fart *s vulg* vânturi *n pl* ‖ *vi vulg* a trage vânturi.

farther *adv* mai departe ‖ *adj* mai depărtat.

farthest *adv* cel mai departe ‖ *adj* cel mai îndepărtat.

farthing *s approx* ban *m*, bănuţ *m*.

fascinate *vt (enthrall)* a fascina, *(charm)* a fermeca; a deochea ‖ *vi (allure)* a fascina, a vrăji.

fascinating *adj (person, country)* fascinant; *(work place)* atrăgător; *(idea)* foarte interesant.

fascination *s* fascinaţie *f*.

fascism *s* fascism *n*.

fascist *s* fascist *m*.

fashion *s (way)* fel *n*, *(mode)* mod *n*, *(manner)* manieră *f*; *(trend)* modă *f*; *(vogue)* vogă *f*; *(style)* stil *n*; gen *n*; *(taste)* gust *n*; croială *f*; *(method)* uzanţă *f* ‖ *vt (shape)* a modela; a transforma.

fast¹ *adj (firm)* tare, *(secure)* solid; *(enduring)* durabil; *(tight)* strâns; *(lasting)* trainic; *(steady)* tenace; dens ‖ *adv* strâns, tare.

fast² *adj (quick)* repede, *(swift)* iute; frivol ‖ *adv (promptly)* repede, iute; ~ **food** *s* fast food *n*, mâncare *f* gata de servit.

fast³ *vi* a ţine post, a posti.

fasten *vt* a fixa; *(tie)* a lega; *(safety belt)* a ataşa; *(clothes, bag)* a încheia, a închide; *(lock)* a încuia ‖ *vi* a se fixa; a se prinde; a se închide • **~ing** *s* închidere *f*.

fastidious *adj (fussy)* mofturos, *(picky)* cusurgiu, *(difficult)* dificil; *(refined)* fin, delicat.

fat *adj (overweight)* gras, dolofan; *(meat)* gras, unsuros; *(wallet)* gros; *(soil)* fertil; abundent; rentabil; mărginit ‖ *s (food)* grăsime *f*; *(cooking)* untură *f*.

fatal *adj* fatal; *(decision, words)* fatidic; *(accident, disease)* mortal.

fate *s (destiny)* soartă *f*, destin *n*; *(fatality)* prăpăd *n*, moarte *f* • **~ful** *adj* fatidic.

father *s* tată *m*; creator *m*; *(parent)* părinte *m*; *(ancestor)* strămoş *m*; *(priest)* preot *m* ‖ *vt (beget)* a crea; a adopta • **~hood** *s* paternitate *f* • **~in-law** *s* socru *m*.

fathom *s naut* stânjen *m*, braţ *n* (măsură *f* egală cu 185 cm).

fatigue *s (tiredness)* oboseală *f*, *(exhaustion)* extenuare *f*; corvoadă *f*; *(metal)* modificare *f* structurală care indică uzura unei piese ‖ *vt* a obosi, a extenua, a istovi.

fatten *vt* a îngrăşa ‖ *vi* a se îngrăşa • **~ing** *adj* care îngraşă.

fatuous *adj (self-important)* infatuat, înfumurat, plin de sine; *(stupid)* prostesc, *(pointless)* fără sens, *(idiotic)* idiot; *(attempt, etc)* inutil, fără sens/rost.

faucet *s* robinet *n*.

fault *s* defect *n*; lipsă *f*; *(error)* eroare *f*; vină *f*; *geol* falie *f* • **~less** *adj* impecabil.

fauna *s zool* faună *f*.

favor *s (good turn)* favoare *f*; *(act of kindness)* serviciu *n*; îndatorire *f*; avantaj *n*; interes *n*; *(support)* ocrotire *f* ‖ *vi* a favoriza; *(assist)* a sprijini • **~ite** *adj* favorit, preferat.

fawn *s (animal)* pui *m* de căprioară ‖ *adj* sălbatic ‖ *vi (over smb)* a se gudura pe lângă cineva.

fear *s (fright)* frică *f*, teamă *f*; *(terror)* groază *f*; *(dread)* temere *f*; *(anxiety)* îngrijorare *f*; *(awe)* veneraţie *f* ‖ *vi (be afraid of)* a se teme; *(be anxious)* a fi îngrijorat ‖ *vt* a se teme.

feasible *adj* realizabil, posibil.

feast *s* sărbătoare *f*; *(banquet)* petrecere *f*; *(delight)* desfătare *f* ‖ *vt (treat)* a ospăta; *(delight)* a desfăta.

feat *s (achievement)* ispravă *f*, *(exploit)* faptă *f* vitejească.

feather *s (quill)* pană *f*; coamă *f*; fel *n*, fire *f* ‖ *vt (adorn)* a împodobi.

feature *s (trait)* trăsătură *f*; *(look)* aparenţă *f*; fizionomie *f*; *(article)* articol *n* de ziar; număr *n* de atracţie ‖ *vt (portray)* a descrie; *(highlight)* a sublinia; a prezenta în rolul principal.

febrile *adj lit, med* febril.

February *s* februarie *m*, Făurar.

feckless *adj* (*ineffectual*) ineficace, incapabil; (*irresponsible*) nesăbuit.

fecund *adj lit* (*woman*) fertil; (*author*) prolific; (*imagination*) bogat.

federal *adj* federal.

federation *s* federație *f*.

fee *s* (*doctor*) onorariu *n*; retribuție *f*; bacșiș *n*; (*membership*) cotizație *f*; (*tuition*) taxă *f* școlară; (*admission*) tarif *n*, preț *n*.

feeble *adj* (*person*) (*weak*) slab, debil, (*frail*) plăpând; (*pulse*) slab; (*meager*) imperceptibil, neînsemnat; infim, neglijabil; (*ineffectual*) inferior, necorespunzător.

feed, fed, fed *vt* (*nourish*) a hrăni; (~ *cattle*) a paște; a încărca; (~ *a fire, fear, etc*) a alimenta, a întreține || *vi* (*eat*) a mânca; a se hrăni || *s* (*food*) hrană *f*; aliment *n*; (*fodder*) nutreț *n*; porție *f*.

feed-back *s* reacții *f pl*; *elec* reacție *f*, retroacțiune *f*.

feel, felt, felt *vt* a pipăi, a atinge; (*experience, sense*) a simți; (*emotion*) a resimți; (*think*) a fi de părere; a considera; a aprecia; a presimți || *vi* a simți; a se simți || *s* senzație *f*; impresie *f*, sentiment *n* • ~ing *adj* (*responsive*) sensibil, simțitor; (*sympathetic*) compătimitor; (*sensitive*) senzitiv || *s* (*sensation*) senzație *f*; (*sense*) simț *n*; (*emotion*) sentiment *n*, emoție *f*; tulburare *f*; (*sensitivity*) sensibilitate *f*.

feet *s pl* * **foot**.

feign *vt* (*pretend*) a simula, (*fake*) a se preface.

felicitous *adj frml* (*happy*) fericit; (*word*) fericit, potrivit; elocvent; expresiv.

feline *s/adj* (*animal*) felin *n*.

fell *vi* * **fall** || *vt* (~ *a tree, person*) a doborî • ~s *s pl* geog teren *n* arid, land *n*.

fellow *s obs* om *m*, ins *m*; (*colleague*) tovarăș *m*, camarad *m*; (*society, college*) membru *m*, asociat • ~ship *s* (*friendship*) prietenie *f*, (*comradeship*) camaraderie *f*; (*society*) asociație *f*, corporație *f*; (*title*) titlu *n* de membru/asociat.

felony *s jur* crimă *f*, nelegiuire *f*.

felt[1] *vt* * **feel**.

felt[2] *s* (*material*) fetru *n*, pâslă *f* • ~tip pen *s* carioca *f*.

female *adj* femeiesc, feminin; al femeilor; pentru femei || *s* femelă *f*.

feminine *adj* de femeie, femeiesc; feminin; efeminat.

feminist *adj* feminist.

fence *s* (*hedge*) gard *n*; (*enclosure*) țarc *n*; parapet *n*; (*railing*) balustradă *f* || *vt* (*enclose*) a îngrădi.

fend *vi* (~ *for oneself*) a se descurca singur • ~ *off vt* (~ *a blow*) a para; (~ *questions, reporters*) a respinge, a îndepărta.

fender *s* apărătoare *f* de foc (la gura sobei); *aut* aripă *f*; (*boat*) apărătoare *f*.

fennel *s bot* chimen *n* dulce.

ferment *vi* a fermenta || *s* (*uproar*) agitație *f*, (*excitement*) efervescență *f*.

fern *s bot* ferigă *f*.

ferocious *adj* feroce.

ferocity *s* (*rage*) ferocitate *f*; (*cruelty*) cruzime *f*.

ferret *s* dihor *m* alb; ~ **about/around** *vi coll* a scotoci, a cotrobăi.

ferris wheel *s* scrânciob *n*.

ferrous *adj* feros.

ferry *s* feribot *n*; pod *n* plutitor; bac *n* || *vt* a transborda cu feribotul/bacul.

fertile *adj* (*land*) (*productive*) fertil; (*prolific*) fecund, (*fruitful*) roditor; (*rich*) bogat; fertilizat; (*imagination*) fertil, fecund; (*women*) fertilă.

fertility *s* fertilitate *f*.

fertilize *vt* a fertiliza; a fecunda.

fervent *adj* (*keen*) fervent; avid.

fester *vi* (*wound*) a supura, a coace.

festival *s* festival *n*; sărbătoare *f* || *adj* festiv.

festive *adj* (*celebratory*) festiv, sărbătoresc; jovial; (*merry*) petrecăreț.

festivity *s* (*party*) petrecere *f*, chef *n*; (*celebration*) festivitate *f*, sărbătorire *f*.

festoon *vt* (*decorate*) a împodobi cu ghirlande || *s* ornament *n*.

fetch *vt* (*bring*) a aduce; (~ *money*) a se vinde la/cu; a da; (*draw*) a atrage || *vi* a se duce să aducă ceva || *s* truc *n*, șmecherie *f* • ~ing *adj* (*enticing*) seducător.

fete *s* sărbătoare *f*, chermeză *f*.

fetid *adj* fetid, urât mirositor.

fetish *s* (*sexual*) fetiș *n*; manie *f*, obsesie *f*.

fetter *vt* a pune în lanțuri || *s* cătușă *f*.

fetus *s* fetus *m*.

feud *s* ceartă *f* || *vi* a se certa.

feudal *adj* feudal.

fever *s* temperatură *f*, febră *f*; friguri *n pl*; (*fervor*) înfrigurare *f*; (*agitation*) nervozitate *f*.

few *adj/pron* puțini, nu mulți.

fiancé *s* logodnic *m*.

fiancée *s* logodnică *f*.

fiasco *s* (*failure*) fiasco *n*.

fiat *s* autorizație *f*; decret *n*, ordonanță *f*.

fib *s coll* minciună *f*, glumă *f* || *vi* a spune gogoși/glume.

fiber (*strand*) fibră *f*, filament *n*; țesătură *f*; structură *f*, caracter *n* • ~**glass** *s* fibră *f* de sticlă.

fickle *adj* (*changeable*) schimbător, (*erratic*) capricios, (*vacillating*) nestatornic.

fiction *s* (*narrative*) ficțiune *f*; (*invention*) invenție *f*; (*literature*) beletristică *f*; (*imagination*) imaginație *f* • ~**al** *adj* (*false*) fictiv.

fictitious *adj* fictiv, imaginar.

fiddle *s mus* vioară *f*; *coll* **fit as a** ~ în formă || *vt/vi mus* a cânta la vioară.

fiddling *adj* (*trivial*) neînsemnat, de mică importanță || *n* (*fidgeting*) neastâmpăr *n*.

fidelity *s* (*faithfulness*) credință *f*, (*commitment*) fidelitate *f*, (*loyalty*) loialitate *f*, (*devotion*) devotament *n*; (*dependability*) acuratețe *f*, precizie *f*; **hi-fi(delity)** *adj elec* de mare precizie/acuratețe.

fidget *s* (*uneasiness*) neastâmpăr *n*; (*person*) neastâmpărat *m* || *vi* (*be restless*) a se agita, a se foi • ~y *adj* agitat, nervos.

field *s* câmp *n*; ogor *n*; *comp* câmp *n*; *sp* teren *n*; bazin *n*; (*study*) domeniu *n*; *mil* câmp *n* de luptă; fond *n*; ~ **trip** *s* călătorie *f* de studii • ~**work** *s* muncă *f* de teren.

fiend *s* (*monster*) monstru *m*; *coll* (*fanatic*) nebun *m*, maniac *m* • ~**ish** *adj* diabolic; *coll* (*intricate*) complicat, complex.

fierce *adj* (*ferocious*) feroce, aprig; (*brutal*) sălbatic; (*aggressive*) fioros, grozav; (*vicious*) cumplit, (*ardent*) energic, activ; (*heat*) torid; (*storm, temperament*) violent.

fiery *adj* (*in flames*) arzând; (*speech*) înflăcărat; (*person, temperament*) aprig, impetuos.

fifteen *num* cincisprezece

fifth *s* cincime *f* || *num* al cincilea

fifty *num* cincizeci.

fig *s* (*tree*) curmal *m*; (*fruit*) curmală *f*.

fight, fought, fought *vt* (*struggle*) a (se) lupta; (*dispute*) a combate; (*clash*) a se bate în; (*defend*) a apăra ‖ *s* (*battle*) luptă *f*; bătaie *f*; (*competition*) întrecere *f*; companie *f* • ~er *s* avion *n* de vânătoare, vânător *m*; (*soldier*) combatant *m*; (*person fighting*) luptător *m* • ~ing *s* încăierare *f*; (*war*) conflict *n*.

figment *s* născocire *f*; **a ~ of smb's imagination** născocirea (rodul) imaginației cuiva.

figurative *adj* (*meaning*) (*sens*) figurat.

figure *s* (*number*) cifră *f*; preț *n*; (*body shape*) siluetă *f*; formă *f*; linie *f*; *geom* figură *f* geometrică; (*stature*) ținută *f*; diagramă *f*; (*personality*) personalitate *f* ‖ *vt* (*think*) a gândi, (*suppose*) a presupune; (*feature*) a reprezenta; (*assume*) a-și imagina; a simboliza; (*reckon*) a considera ‖ *vi* a apărea; ~ **out** *vt* a înțelege, a găsi.

filament *s* fir *n*, firicel *n*; *bot*, *elec* filament *n*.

filbert *s* *bot* (*tree*) alun *m*; (*fruit*) alună *f*.

filch *vt* (*steal*) a șterpeli.

file[1] *s* (*folder*) fișier *n*; arhivă *f*; (*dossier*) dosar *n*; *comp* fișier *n*; (*row*) șir *n* ‖ *vt* a fișa; (~ *documents*) a pune la dosar; a clasa; *jur* (~ *a complaint*) a face, a depune; (~ *a lawsuit*) a intenta ‖ *vi* (*walk in single file*) a merge în șir indian; ~ **clerk** *s* documentarist *m*; **in single** ~ în șir indian; **on** ~ îndosariat, la fișier.

file[2] *s* pilă *f* ‖ *vt* (*whet*) a pili.

filet *s* *cul* fileu *n*.

filial *adj* filial.

filibuster *s* obstrucție *f* parlamentară ‖ *vt* (*legislation*) a obstrucționa, a împiedica • ~er *s* obstrucționist *m*.

filigree *s* filigran *n*.

filing cabinet *s* biblioraft *n*, clasor *n*.

fill *vt* (~ *a glass*) a umple; (~ *a sail*) a umfla; (~ *a tooth*) a plomba; (~ *a hole*) a astupa; (~ *out a form*) a completa; (*satisfy*) a satisface; (*soak*) a satura; (~ *a vacancy*) a ocupa ‖ *vi* a se umple ‖ *s* saț *n*, saturare *f*.

fillet *s* *cul* file *n* ‖ *vt* *cul* a porționa.

fill-in *s* *coll* (*person*) înlocuitor *m*.

filling *adj* care satură, foarte hrănitor ‖ *s* (*of a tooth*) plombă *f*; (*of a sandwich, pie*) garnitură *f*; ~ **station** *s* stație *f* de benzină.

fillip *s* bobârnac *n*; (*boost*) impuls *n*.

filly *s* *zool* mânză *f*.

film *s* film *n* artistic; *phot* peliculă *f*; imagini *f* *pl* ‖ *vi* a filma.

filter *s* filtru *n* ‖ *vt* (~ *coffee, water, oil, air*) a filtra.

filth *s* (*dirt*) murdărie *f*; *fig* (*smut*) obscenități *f* *pl* • ~y *adj* murdar, urât, ticălos, mârșav; imoral, obscen, desmățat.

fin *s* (*fish*) aripioară *f* înotătoare.

final *adj* (*closing*) final; (*last*) ultim; definitv; decisiv; *gram* de scop ‖ *s* partidă *f* decisivă; examen *n* final • ~e *s* parte *f* finală a unei compoziții muzicale; deznodământ *n*; final *n*.

finance *s* venituri *n* *pl* bănești ‖ *vt* a finanța; ~ **company** *s* instituție *f* financiară de credit; **high** ~ *s* marea finanță *f*.

financial *adj* financiar; ~ **advisor** *s* consilier *m* financiar; ~ **director** *s* director *m* financiar.

financier *s* finanțist *m*; bancher *m*.

financing *s* finanțare *f*.

finch *s* *orn* cinteză *f*, cintezoi *m*.

find, found, found *vt* (*hit upon*) a găsi, (*locate*) a afla,

(*discover*) a descoperi; a inventa; a considera; (*get*) a căpăta; (*notice*) a constata ‖ *vr* a se realiza; a se pomeni ‖ *s* (*discovery*) descoperire *f*; **to** ~ **out** *vi* a se documenta ‖ *vt* a se informa în legătură cu; (~ *a truth*) a descoperi, a afla; (*uncover*) a demasca • ~ings *s* *pl* concluzii *f* *pl*.

fine[1] *adj* (*tune*) fin, delicat; (*work*) excelent; (*weather, building*) frumos; (*detail, difference*) subtil; (*slight*) fragil; (*delicate*) gingaș; precis; festiv ‖ *adv* grozav, foarte bine • ~**ly** *adv* subțire, în bucăți mici • ~**ness** *s* (*of gold*) titlu *n*; puritate *f*; eleganță *f* • ~**tune** *vt* (*devices*) a regla.

fine[2] *s* (*penalty*) amendă *f* ‖ *vt* (*punish*) a amenda.

finery *s* găteală *f*.

finesse *s* (*skill*) dibăcie *f*, (*flair*) abilitate *f*, (*adroitness*) îndemânare *f*; (*subtlety*) finețe *f*; tact *n*; (*ingenuity*) viclenie *s*, șiretenie *f*; (*cards*) impas *n*.

finger *s* deget *n*; indicator *n* ‖ *vt* a atinge cu degetele; a lua; a fura • ~**nail** *s* unghie *f* (de la mână) • ~**print** *s* amprentă *f* (digitală) • ~**tip** *s* vârful *n* degetului.

finish *vt* (*conclude*) a sfârși; (*exhaust*) a epuiza; (*destroy*) a distruge; (*kill*) a ucide; (*polish off*) a finisa ‖ *vi* (*draw to a close*) a termina ‖ *s* (*end*) final *n*; (*conclusion*) încheiere *f*; finisaj *n* • ~ **line** *s* linie *f* de sosire.

finite *adj* finit.

fink *s* *sl* (*strikebreaker*) spărgător *m* de grevă; (*informer*) informator *m*; (*nasty person*) antipatic *m*, nesuferit *m*.

Finland *s* Finlanda *f*.

Finn *s* finlandez.

Finnish *adj* finlandez.

fir *s* (*tree*) brad *m*; (*wood*) lemn *n* de brad.

fire *s* (*flames*) foc *n*; (*blaze*) incendiu *n*; (*shooting*) tragere *f*; (*fervor*) căldură *f*, (*passion*) pasiune *f*; temperatură *f* ‖ *vt* a pune pe foc; a incendia; (*shoot*) a împușca; (*dismiss*) a concedia; (*inspire*) a trezi entuziasm ‖ *vi* a se aprinde; a trage cu arma; ~ **alarm** *s* alarmă *f* în caz de incendiu; ~ **brigade** *s* pompieri *m* *pl*; ~ **door** *s* ușă *f* de protecție împotriva incendiilor; ~ **drill** *s* exerciții *n* *pl* de evacuare în caz de incendiu; ~ **engine** *s* mașină *f* de pompieri; ~ **escape** *s* scară *f* de incendiu; ~ **exit** *s* ieșire *f* în caz de incendiu; ~ **extinguisher** *s* extinctor *n*; ~ **station** *s* unitate *f* de pompieri.

firearm *s* armă *f* de foc.

firecracker *s* pocnitoare *f*.

firefighter *s* pompier *m*.

firefly *s* *ento* licurici *m*.

fireguard *s* apărătoare *f* (așezată înaintea sobei).

firehouse *s* unitate *f* de pompieri.

fireman *s* fochist *m*; pompier *m*.

fireplace *s* șemineu *n*, cămin *n*.

firepower *s* *mil* putere *f* de foc.

fireproof *adj* neinflamabil, ignifug.

fireside *s* loc *n* lângă cămin, gura *f* sobei; **by the** ~ la gura sobei.

firewood *s* lemne *n* *pl* de foc.

fireworks *s* *pl* foc *n* de artificii; *fig* (*anger*) foc și pară.

firing *s* *mil* schimb *n* de focuri; salvă *f* de focuri de armă; ~ **squad** *s* pluton *n* de execuție.

firm[1] *adj* (*hard*) dur, tare; (*solid*) ferm; (*structure*) solid; (*proof*) sigur; compact; (*determined*) hotărât; aspru ‖ *adv* ferm • ~**ly** *adv* cu fermitate; neclintit.

firm[2] *s* *com* firmă *f*, societate *f*.

firmament *s* boltă *f* cerească.

first *num* prim, întâi ‖ *adj* prim, întâi; principal ‖ *adv* primul; mai întâi; mai curând ‖ *s* început *n*; ~ **aid** *s* primul ajutor *n*; ~ **lady** *s* prima doamnă *f* a ţării; ~ **name** *s* prenume *n* • ~**born** *s* primul născut *m* • ~ **rate** *adj* excelent

fiscal *adj* fiscal; financiar.

fish *s* peşte *m*; tip *m* ‖ *vt* a pescui; (*catch fish*) a prinde peşte; a scoate ‖ *vi* a pescui; (*scout about*) a umbla după ceva; ~ **bone** *s* os *n* de peşte; ~ **cake** *s* crochetă *f* de peşte; ~ **fingers/sticks** *s pl* crochete *f pl* de peşte pane; ~ **hook** *s* cârlig *n* de undiţă; ~ **oil** *s* ulei *n* de peşte; ~ **shop** *s* pescărie *f*; ~ **slice** *s* cuţit *n* de peşte; ~ **tackle** *s naut* palanc *n* de traversieră; ~ **tail** *s* coadă *f* de peşte; ~ **tank** *s* acvariu *n*.

fisherman *s* pescar *m*.

fishing *s* pescuit *n*; **to go** ~ a merge la pescuit; ~ **tackle** *s* unelte *f pl* de pescuit.

fishmonger *s* negustor *m* de peşte.

fishpond *s* lac *n* de peşte.

fishy *adj* (*smell, taste*) de peşte; (*suspect*) dubios.

fission *s phys* fisiune *f*; ~ **bomb** *s* bombă *f* atomică/de fisiune.

fissure *s* fisură *f*, (*crack*) crăpătură *f*; crăpare *f*; (*fracture*) rupere *f*; *geol* falie *f*.

fist *s* pumn *m*; mână *f* ‖ *vt* a lovi cu pumnul; a strânge în mână.

fit¹ *adj* (*adequate*) adecvat, (*right*) bun, (*suitable*) potrivit; (*proper*) indicat; (*qualified*) competent; vrednic; (*healthy*) sănătos ‖ *vt* (*match*) a se potrivi; (*tally*) a corespunde; (*fix*) a ajusta; (*provide with*) a utila ‖ *vi* a se potrivi ‖ *s* potrivire *f* • ~**ful** *adj* răzleţ, sporadic • ~**ted** *adj* fixat • ~**ting** *s* probă *f* la croitor • ~**tings** *s pl* instalaţii *f pl*, accesorii *n pl*.

fit² *s med* (*convulsion*) acces *n*; (*attack*) criză *f*.

fitness *s* (*suitability*) potrivire *f*; conformitate *f*; (*qualification*) calificare *f*; (*health*) sănătate *f*; condiţie *f* fizică (bună); oportunitate *f*.

fitter *s* instalator-montator *m*.

five *num* cinci.

fix *vt* (*fasten*) a fixa; (*set up*) a stabili; a aţinti; a întipări; (*settle*) a aranja; (*stare*) a se uita fix ‖ *vi* a se fixa ‖ *s* (*quandary*) bucluc *n*; ordine *f* • ~**ation** (**on/about**) *s* obsesie *f* (pentru) • ~**ed** *adj* (*set*) fixat; (*unchanged*) fix; (*smile*) îngheţat, ca o mască • ~**ate** *vt* (*attention*) a atrage, a reţine; (*preoccupy*) a preocupa; a obseda.

fixture *s* (*equipment*) instalaţie *f*; (*permanent*) tradiţie *f* înrădăcinată; *sp* (*match*) întâlnire *f* sportivă.

fizz *vi* (*drink*) a face bule; (*fireworks*) a pârâi, a trosni.

fizzle *vi* (**out**) (*fire*) a se stinge; (*fireworks*) a se termina; (*interest, etc*) a dispărea.

flabbergasted *adj* înmărmurit, năucit.

flabby *adj* (*soft*) moale, flasc; (*flaccid*) flasc.

flag¹ *s* steag *n*; drapel *n*; fanion *n*; pavilion *n* ‖ *vt* a semnaliza cu steagul; a marca cu steguleţe.

flag² *vi* (*person, energy*) a slăbi; (*conversation*) a tărăgăna.

flaggelate *vt* a biciui; a flagela.

flagon *s* garafă *f*, carafă *f*.

flagpole *s* catarg *n*.

flagrant *adj* (*brazen*) flagrant.

flagstone *s* dală *f*, lespede *f*.

flair *s* (*skill*) fler *n*; (*propensity*) perspicacitate *f*; (*knack*) talent *n* înnăscut, (*gift*) înzestrare *f*.

flake *s* fulg *m*; solz *m*; coajă ‖ *vi* a cădea sub formă de fulgi.

flamboyant *adj* (*ostentatious*) extravagant; (*gaudy*) viu colorat, (*glitzy*) sclipitor.

flame *s* flacără *f*; (*fire*) foc *n*; (*passion*) pasiune *f*; (*love*) dragoste *f* ‖ *vi* (*burn*) a arde; (*flare*) a izbucni în flăcări; a se înflăcăra.

flaming *adj* (*burning*) arzător; (*blazing*) în flăcări; (*passionate*) pasional, pătimaş; (*fierce*) furios.

flamingo *s orn* flamingo *n*.

flammable *adj* inflamabil.

flan *s cul* tartă *f* cu fructe.

flank *s anat* parte *f* (a corpului); (*building*) aripă *f*; (*hill*) coastă *f*, pantă *f*, versant *n*; *mil* flanc *n*, extremitate *f* ‖ *vt* *mil* a flanca; a apăra flancurile.

flannel *s text* flannel *n*; (*clothes*) flanel(ă) *n/f*.

flap *s* (*envelope, pocket*) clapă *f*; parte *f* răsfrântă; (*hat*) bor *n* (al pălăriei); (*flutter*) fâlfâit *n*; (*wave*) fluturat *n*; lovitură *f*; pocnitură *f*, pocnet *n* ‖ *vi* a se bălăbăni; a flutura, a fâlfâi ‖ *vt* (*flutter*) a bate din (aripi), a flutura (aripile); a legăna, a mişca; a bate, a lovi (cu ceva lat).

flare *vi* (*blaze*) a arde cu flacără vie; (*flicker*) a pâlpâi; (**up**) (*war, etc*) a se intensifica brusc; (*person*) a se mânia, a se înfuria; (*pants, skirt*) a se lărgi, a se evaza; (*nostrils*) a se dilata ‖ *s* (*flash*) flacără *f* vie; (*flicker*) pâlpâit *n*; trasor *n*; rachetă *f* semnalizatoare; *naut* (*flame*) faclă *f*, (*torch*) torţă *f*.

flash *s* (*blaze*) fulgerare *f*; (*glint*) scânteiere *f*; (*flicker*) licărire *f*; (*smile*) zâmbet *n*; ocheadă *f*; (*instant*) clipă *f*; (*burst*) explozie *f*; instantaneu *n* ‖ *vi* a fulgera; (*glisten*) a scânteia; (*glimmer*) a licări; (*pass quickly*) a zbura; a arunca (o privire).

flashlight *s* bliţ *n*; flaş *n*; far *n* proiector.

flask *s* termos *n*; *chem* balon *n*; retortă *f*.

flat¹ *adj* (*even*) plat, (*level*) întins, (*smooth*) neted; (*tedious*) stătut; trezit; (*unequivocal*) exact; (*downright*) direct; (*tire*) dezumflat; (*refusal*) categoric; (*business*) calm; (*voice*) monoton; (*show, etc*) şters, lipsit de originalitate; (*beer, etc*) trezit; (*price*) fix; *mus* (*person's voice*) care cântă prea grav; (*note*) bemol ‖ *adv* lat, întins; (*unequivocally*) precis; (*utterly*) complet ‖ *s* câmpie *f*; ţărm *n* jos; baltă *f*.

flat² *s* apartament *n*; etaj *n*.

flatter *vt* (*cajole*) a flata; a înfrumuseţa; a încânta (ochii); a satisface ‖ *vi* (*sweet-talk*) a recurge la linguşiri • ~**ing** *adj* măgulitor • ~**y** *s* linguşire *f*.

flatulence *s med* meteorism *n*, gaze *n pl*; *fig* preţiozitate *f*, bombasticism *n*.

flatware *s* (*cutlery*) tacâmuri *n pl*; (*plates*) farfurii *f pl*.

flaunt *vt* (*flag*) a flutura/fâlfâi mândru; (*people*) a umbla ţanţoş, (*show off*) a se grozăvi; a se etala; (*exhibit*) a face paradă de, a se făli cu.

flautist *s mus* flautist *m*.

flavor *s* (*savor*) gust *n* plăcut; (*bouquet*) buchet *n*; (*essence*) parfum *n*; iz *n*; aromă *f*; (*spice*) condiment *n*; atmosferă *f* ‖ *vt* (*to season*) a condimenta.

flaw *s* (*material, character*) defect *n*; (*plan, argument*) fisură *f*, punct *n* slab; *jur, etc* viciu *n* • ~**less** *adj* perfect • ~**lessly** *adv* perfect, desăvârşit.

flax *s bot* in *n*.

flay *vt* (*skin an animal*) a jupui; (*criticize*) a stigmatiza.

flea *s* purice *m*; ~ **bite** *s* pişcătură *f* de purice; ~ **collar** *s* zgardă *f* antipurici; ~ **market** *s* hală *f* de vechituri.

fleck *s* (*speck*) pată *f* pe corp; eczemă *f*; pistrui *m*; (*color, light*) pată *f*; (*scrap*) părticică *f*, particulă *f*, (*crumb*) fărâmă *f* • ~**ed with** *adj* pătat cu.

fled *vi* * **flee**.

flee, fled, fled *vi* (*run away*) a fugi; a dispărea din; a se sfârşi || *vt* (*escape*) a fugi din; a părăsi (o ţară).

fleece *s* lână *f* || *vt coll* a jecmăni, a prăda.

fleet[1] *s* (*vessel*) flotă *f*; (*trucks*) parc *n*.

fleet[2] *adj* alert, sprinten • ~**ing** *adj* (*moment*) scurt, succint; (*look*) fugitiv, în treacăt; (*visit*) fulger.

Flemish *adj* flamand || *s* (*language*) flamandă *f*; **the** ~ *s pl* flamanzii *m pl*.

flesh *s* carne *f*; (*body*) trup *n*; (*mortal*) muritor *m*; (*core*) miez *n*; senzualitate *f* || *vt* a înroşi cu sânge; a îngrăşa; a descărna.

flew *vi* * **fly**.

flex *s elec* fir *n* || *vt* (*bend*) a îndoi, a încovoia • ~**ible** *adj* (*supple*) flexibil, (*elastic*) elastic; (*accommodating*) maleabil; (*adaptable*) adaptabil; (*compliant*) îngăduitor.

flick *s* (*of a whip, towel*) lovitură *f* uşoară; (*of a finger*) bobârnac *n*; *pl coll* film *n* || *vt* (*whip*) a pocni, a atinge; a da un şfichi; (*button*) a apăsa pe • ~**er** *vi* (*candle, light*) a pâlpâi; (*shadow*) a tremura; (*eyelids*) a clipi.

flight *s* zbor *n*; (*birds*) stol *n*; (*volley of arrows, etc*) salvă *f*; şir *n*; (*time*) scurgere *f* rapidă (a timpului); (*fleeing*) fugă *f*; (*haven*) refugiu *n*, adăpost *n*; (*steps*) trepte *f pl* || *vi* a migra; ~ **attendant** *s* steward *m*, stewardesă *f*; ~ **crew** *s* echipaj *m*; ~ **deck** *s* (*aircraft carrier*) punte *f* de decolare; (*plane*) cabină *f* de pilotaj; ~ **recorder** *s* cutie *f* neagră.

flimflam *vt* (*cheat*) a escroca || *s* (*drivel*) trăncăneală *f*.

flimsy *adj* (*dress, material*) lejer; (*building, etc*) şubred; (*excuse*) fără valoare.

flinch *vi* a tresări; (*from*) a se abate, a se clinti (de la datorie etc).

fling, flung, flung *vt* (*throw*) a arunca, (*pitch*) a azvârli || *s sl* (*extra-marital affair*) aventură *f*, idilă *f*.

flint *s* (*stone*) cremene *f*; (*lighter*) piatră *f*.

flip *s* lovitură *f* uşoară; bobârnac *n* || *vt* a lovi uşor; (~ *a burger, etc*) a arunca în aer pentru a întoarce; (~ *a disk*) a întoarce; (~ *a switch*) a apăsa; ~ **over** *vr* a se răsturna (brusc); ~ **through** *vt* a frunzări • ~**flop** *s* (*sandal*) şlap *m*; *coll* (*attitude, policy*) schimbare *f* totală, întorsătură *f*.

flippant *adj* (*frivolous*) uşuratic, (*offhand*) dezinvolt.

flipper *s* (*animal*) înotătoare *f*; (*swimming*) labe *f pl*.

flirt *vi* a flirta, a cocheta; a se mişca încoace şi încolo || *vt* a mişca încoace şi încolo || *s* cochetă *f*; flirt *n* • ~**atious** *adj* care flirtează.

flit *vi* (*birds*) a trece în zbor.

float *vi* (*drift*) a pluti; (*hover*) a se perinda || *vt* (*flood*) a inunda; a face să plutească; a realiza || *s* dop *n*, plută *f*; flotor *n*; (*buoy*) baliză *f*.

flock[1] *s* (*of sheep*) turmă *f*; (*of birds*) stol *n*; (*of people*) gloată *f*, mulţime *f*.

flock[2] *s* (*wool*) smoc *n*; *text* ghemotoc *n*; fulg *m*.

flog *vt* (*lash*) a biciui; *fig* (*reprimand*) a critica aspru • ~**ging** *s* bătaie *f* zdravănă; biciuire *f*; pedeapsă *f* corporală.

flood *s* (*overflow*) inundaţie *f*; (*deluge*) potop *n*; flux *n*; (*torrent*) şuvoi *n* || *vt* (*water, light*) a inunda; a revărsa; (*overwhelm*) a copleşi || *vi* a se revărsa; a se îngrămădi • ~**ing** *s* inundaţii *f pl*.

floodlight *s* proiector *n*.

floor *s* (*ground*) podea *f*; planşeu *n*; (*story*) etaj *n*; (*level* nivel *n*; vatră *f*; (*bottom*) fund *n* (de mare) || *vt* a pardosi; (*baffle*) a încurca.

flop *s coll* fiasco *n*, eşec *n* • ~**py** *adj* (*flower*) ofilit; (*collar*) moale, nescrobit; ~ **disk** *s comp* dischetă *f*.

flora *s* floră *f*.

floral *adj* floral; cu flori; în formă de floare.

florid *adj* (*red*) rumen; (*extravagant*) înflorit, încărcat.

florist *s* florar *m*, cultivator/vânzător *m* de flori.

flotation *s* flotare *f*.

flounce[1] *vi* (*stomp*) a umbla nervos; (*storm*) a se năpusti, a se repezi || *s* mişcare *f* bruscă/nestăpânită.

flounce[2] *s* (*dress*) volan *n*.

flounder[1] *vi* (~ *in water, mud, snow*) a se mişca (cu) greu, a se împotmoli; (*struggle*) a se zbate (în apă); (*dither*) a se încurca la vorbă, (*falter*) a vorbi cu greutate, a se exprima greu || *s* mişcări *f pl* greoaie; (*struggle*) zbatere *f*; luptă *f* (cu valurile etc).

flounder[2] *s icht* plătică *f*.

flour *s* făină *f* || *vt* a măcina.

flourish *vt* (*brandish*) a agita, a flutura; (*display*) a etala; a împodobi || *vi* (*plants, etc*) a creşte din abundenţă; (*children*) a fi sănătos, a fi înfloritor; (*business, etc*) a prospera; (*arts*) a înflori; a vorbi bombastic || *s* agitare *f*; (*wave*) fluturare *f*, parafă *f*; înfloritură *f* retorică.

flout *vt* (*advice, etc*) a respinge, (*ignore*) a nu ţine seama de; (*ridicule*) a ridiculiza, (*scoff*) a-şi râde de; (*treat with contempt*) a privi cu dispreţ || *vi* a fi dispreţuitor; (*mock*) a-şi bate joc.

flow *s* (*run*) curgere *f*, (*gush*) flux *n*, (*stream*) curent *n*; (*of water, information*) circulaţie *f*; vărsare *f*; curs *n*; (*discharge*) debit *n*; (*flood*) revărsare *f*; (*of funds*) fluctuaţie *f*, variaţie *f*; (*of words*) torent *n* || *vi* (*run*) a curge; (*flood*) a inunda; (*traffic, days*) a se scurge; (*hair, clothes*) a atârna, a flutura; ~ **chart/diagram** *s* organigramă *f*.

flower *s* înflorire *f*; (*bloom*) floare *f*; (*best*) elită *f* || *vi* (*blossom*) a înflori || *vt* a împodobi cu flori • ~**bed** *s* strat *n*/răzor *n* de flori • ~**y** *adj* (*dress, material*) cu imprimeu floral; *pej* (*style*) bombastic.

flown *vi* * **fly**.

flu *s* **the** ~ gripă *f*.

fluctuate *vi* a fluctua, a varia.

flue *s* şemineu *n*; (*chimney*) coş *n*; (*shaft*) tiraj *n*, fum *n*; met (*furnace*) tiraj *n*.

fluency *s* uşurinţă *f*, fluenţă *f* (în exprimare).

fluent *adj* fluent, curgător.

fluff *s* puf *n*, tulei *n*; ghemotoc *n* de praf (sub mobile).

fluid *s* fluid *n*; (*cleaning*) lichid *n* || *adj* fluid; (*unstable*) schimbător.

fluke *s coll* întâmplare *f* fericită.

flummox *vt coll* a buimăci, a năuci.

flung *vt* * **fling**.

flunk *vt* (~ *an exam*) a rata, a pica; (~ *students*) a pica la examen.

flunky *s* lacheu *m*; servitor *m*; lingău *m*.

fluorescent *adj* fluorescent.

fluoride *s chem* fluorură *f*.

flurry *s* (*rain, wind, snow*) rafală *f*, *fig* (*objections*) val *n*; (*activities, emotions*) torent *n*, potop *n*.

flush[1] *s* jet *n* de apă; îmbujorare *f*; (*feeling*) avânt *n*, ardoare *f*; (*poker*) culoare *f* || *vt* a trage apa la toaletă || *vi* (*blush*) a se înroşi, a se îmbujora • ~**ed** *adj* (*face*) îmbujorat, roşu; (*excited*) înflăcărat, exaltat.

flush[2] *adj* bogat, abundent; (*river*) umflat; (*blow, etc*) drept, direct; (*with*) darnic, generos (cu); viguros, plin de vigoare, puternic || *adv* (*with*) la acelaşi nivel (cu); (*strike, etc*) drept, direct, exact.

flustered *adj* (*anxious*) neliniştit, (*tense*) agitat, (*worried*) tulburat.

flute *s mus* flaut *n*, fluier *n*.

flutter *s* (*wings*) fâlfâit *n*, fluturare *f*; (*excitement*) emoţie *f*, (*agitation*) nelinişte *f* || *vi* (*birds, insects*) a zbura; (*wings*) a bate; (*flag, dress*) a fâlfâi.

flux *s* schimbare *f*.

fly[1], **flew, flown** *vi* (~ *a plane, kite*) a plana, a zbura; (*birds, insects*) a zbura; (*pilot a plane*) a pilota; (~ *on a plane*) a călători cu avionul; (*run fast*) a alerga, a fugi; (~ *a flag*) a flutura || *vt* a zbura peste; a înălţa; a pilota || *s* zbor *n*; rever *n*; şliţ *n*; clapă *f* • ~**ing** *adj* zburător || *s* aviaţie *f*; ~ **saucer** *s* farfurie *f* zburătoare.

fly[2] *s ento* muscă *f*.

foal *s zool* mânz *m*.

foam *s* spumă *f*; zgură *f*; mare *f* || *vi* a spumega.

fob *s* (*pocket*) buzunăraş *n* la pantaloni; (*chain*) lănţişor *n*; (*ornament*) breloc *n*; ~ **off** a (se) scăpa/debarasa de cineva/ceva.

focal point *s* focar *n*; *fig* punct *n* focal.

focus *s* focar *n*; *phot* focalizare *f*; (*center*) centru *n*; (*epicenter*) epicentru *n*; (*heart*) miez *n* || *vt* (*direct*) a focaliza; (*concentrate*) a concentra || *vi* a se concentra; (*eye*) a se acomoda.

fodder *s* nutreţ *n*.

foe *s liter* duşman *m*.

fog *s* (*haze*) ceaţă *f*, (*mist*) pâclă *f*; (*vapor*) abur *n*; (*smoke*) fum *n*; (*dark*) întuneric *n*; *fig* întunecime *f*, întuneric *n*; (*stupor*) zăpăceală *f*; *tv* văl *n*, voal *n* || *vt* (*cloud*) a înceţoşa.

fogey *s* (*stick-in-the-mud*) om *m* de modă veche, om *m* încuiat; (*reactionary*) înapoiat *m*.

foggy *adj* ceţos; nebulos, neclar; înceţoşat.

foghorn *s naut* sirenă *f* de ceaţă.

foible *s* punct *n* slab; (*weakness*) slăbiciune *f*, (*oddity*) manie *f*, ciudăţenie *f*.

foil[1] *s* frunză *f*; *met* tablă *f* subţire; *typ* filă *f*, foaie *f*; *cul* foaie *f* de aluminiu; *fig* contrast *n*; termen *n* de comparaţie.

foil[2] *vt* (~ *a plan, etc*) a dejuca, a zădărnici.

foil[3] *s* (*fencing*) floretă *f*.

foist *vt* (**on**) (*impose*) a vârî (ceva) pe gât (cuiva); (*wheedle*) a face (pe cineva) să cumpere ceva (netrebuincios).

fold[1] *s* (*crease*) cută *f*, (*wrinkle*) pliu *n*; (*crinkle*) fald *n*; uşă *f*; canat *n* || *vt* a îndoi; a înfăşura; a plisa; (*in arms*) a încrucişa (mâinile) || *vi* (~ *a table, etc*) a se plia; (*petals, etc*) a se închide; (*end a project, etc*) a eşua; *thea* (*close a show*) a nu avea succes; (*go bankrupt*) a da faliment; (*fold paper, etc*) a se împături.

fold[2] *s* (*sheep*) ţarc *n*.

folder *s* mapă *f*, dosar *n*; clasor *n*.

foliage *s* frunziş *n*.

follicle *s* foliculă *f*.

folk *s* oameni *m pl*, lume *f*; popor *n*, naţiune *f* || *adj* (*art*) folcloric; (*medicine*) tradiţional; ~ **music** muzică *f* folk • ~**lore** *s* folclor *n* • ~**sy** *adj* (*unsophisticated*) popular; apropiat de popor; sociabil; prietenos.

follow *vi* (*go along*) a urma; (*go on*) a continua; a frecventa || *vt* (*go after*) a urma după; (*abide by*) a se

ţine de; a imita; (*understand*) a înţelege; ~ **up** (*an idea, etc*) a lua în considerare; (*warning*) a da urmare la • ~**er** *s* discipol *m*.

folly *s frml* (*foolishness*) prostie *f*, absurditate *f*; (*madness*) nebunie *f*.

foment *vt* (*stir up*) a instiga.

fond *adj* (*loving*) iubitor, (*affectionate*) afectuos; indulgent; drag, scump • ~**ly** *adv* cu simpatie, cu afecţiune, cu tandreţe.

fondle *vt* a mângâia.

fondness *s* (*love*) dragoste *f*, (*warmth*) căldură *f*, cordialitate *f*; poftă *f*, apetit *n*; (**for**) (*partiality*) predilecţie/preferinţă *f* pentru, (*attachment*) înclinaţie *f* (spre).

font *s relig* cristelniţă *f*, baptisteriu *n*; *typ, comp* font *n*.

food *s* hrană *f*, alimente *n pl*; alimentaţie *f*; provizii *f pl*; ~ **mixer** *s* mixer *n*; ~ **poisoning** *s* toxiinfecţie *f* alimentară; ~ **processor** *s* robot *n* de bucătărie.

fool *s* (*stupid person*) prost *m*, neghiob *m*; nebun *m*, (*jester*) măscărici *m*, (*clown*) clovn *m* || *vt* (*dupe*) a înşela, a păcăli || *vi* a se prosti; a glumi; a face pozne; ~ **about/around** *vi* a face pe prostul, a fi necredincios/infidel • ~**hardy** *adj* temerar • ~**ish** *adj* idiot, stupid • ~**proof** *adj* infailibil, cert.

foot *s* picior *n*; (*animal*) labă *f*; poale *f pl*; suport *n*; (*of the page, stairs*) partea *f* de jos; piedestal *n*; (*measure*) picior *n* (30,48 cm) || *vi* a dansa || *vt* a trece prin; (*bill*) a plăti (nota); ~**and-mouth disease** *s vet* febră *f* aftoasă.

footage *s* secvenţe *f pl* (de film).

football *s* fotbal *n*; fotbal *n* american; minge *f* de fotbal.

footbrake *s* frână *f* (de picior).

footbridge *s* pasarelă *f*.

footdragging *s* tergiversare *f*; întârziere *f*.

foothold *s* punct *n* de sprijin, priză *f*, loc *n* de pus piciorul.

footing *s* sprijin *n*; **to lose one's** ~ a se împiedica; *fig* (*base*) poziţie *f*.

footlights *s pl* luminile *f pl* rampei.

footnote *s* notă *f* de subsol.

footpath *s* cărare *f*.

footprint *s* amprentă *f* (de picior), urmă *f* de paşi.

footstep *s* pas *m*; călcătură *f*; urmă *f* de picior.

footwear *s* încălţăminte *f*.

for *prep* pentru; spre binele de; de partea; în vederea; împotriva; spre; către; prin; din cauza; în timpul; ca, drept; ca urmare; în ciuda || *conj* pentru că, fiindcă, deoarece, întrucât.

forage *vi* (**for**) (*scavenge*) a fora, (*rummage*) a scormoni, a scotoci.

foray *s liter, fig* incursiune *f* (în).

forbade *vt* * **forbid**.

forbear[1], **forbore, forborne** *vt* (*abstain*) a se abţine de la/a; a căuta să nu || *vi* a se abţine; (*refrain*) a se reţine; a se stăpâni, a se controla • ~**ance** *s* abţinere *f*, (*self-restraint*) reţinere *f*; (*self-control*) stăpânire *f* de sine; (*patience*) răbdare *f*, (*tolerance*) îngăduinţă *f*, indulgenţă *f* • ~**ing** *adj* stăpânit, reţinut; condescendent, indulgent; răbdător.

forbear[2] *s* strămoş *m*.

forbid, forbade, forbidden *vt* (*prohibit*) a opri, a interzice; (*prevent*) a împiedica; (*ban*) a nu permite • ~**ding** *adj* (*unfriendly*) auster; (*threatening*) sinistru || *v* * **forbid**.

force *s* (*power*) forţă *f*, (*strength*) putere *f*; valabilitate *f;* solicitare *f; (influence)* influenţă *f; (intensity)* intensitate *f* || *vt (compel)* a forţa; a viola; a smulge • ~ **feed** *vt* a hrăni cu forţa, a îndopa • ~**ful** *adj (person)* energic, puternic; *(style)* viguros; *(impression)* puternic, deosebit; *(speech)* convingător.

forceps *s pl* forceps *n.*

forcible *adj (by force)* forţat; în forţă; *(argument)* convingător; *(emphatic)* categoric; *(personality)* puternic.

ford *s* vad *n.*

fore *adj naut* spre prova, în faţă || *s* parte din faţă *f;* **to come to the** ~ *vt* a se impune.

forearm *s* antebraţ *n.*

forebears *s pl* strămoşi *m pl,* strămoşi *m pl.*

forebode *vt* * **forbid**.

foreboding *s* presimţire *f.* || *adj* prevestitor (de rău).

forecast *vt (predict)* a prevedea; *(anticipate)* a anticipa || a prevedea; *(project)* a planifica dinainte || *s (prediction)* prognoză *f,* prevedere *f.*

foreclose *vt jur* a popri, a sechestra (un bun ipotecat); a declara prescrisă (o ipotecă).

forecourt *s* partea *f* din faţă; *(building)* curte *f* (închisă) în faţa unei clădiri.

forefathers *s pl* strămoşi *m pl,* strămoşi *m pl.*

forefinger *s* index *n.*

forefront *s* prim plan *n.*

foregone *adj* ştiut/cunoscut dinainte; **it's a** ~ **conclusion** concluzie/hotărâre ştiută dinainte.

foreground *s* prim-plan *n.*

forehand *s (tennis)* lovitură *f* de dreapta.

forehead *s* frunte *f.*

foreign *adj* străin, în străinătate; *(trade)* extern, exterior; impur; ~ **affairs** *s pl* afaceri *f pl* externe; ~ **currency** *s* valută *f,* bani *m pl* străini; ~ **exchange** *s* devize *npl;* ~ **policy** *s* politică *f* externă • ~**er** *s* străin *m,* persoană *f* din altă ţară.

foreleg *s (horse)* membru *m* anterior; *(other animals)* laba *f* din faţă.

foreman *s (worker)* maistru *m; jur* preşedinte *m* al juriului.

foremost *adj* principal || *adv* **first and** ~ în primul rând.

forename *s* nume *n* de botez.

forensic *adj (investigation, etc)* medico-legal.

forerunner *s* precursor *m.*

foresee, foresaw, foreseen *vt* a prevedea • ~**able** *adj* previzibil; **for the** ~ **future** pentru zilele/lunile ce vor veni.

foreshadow *vt* a prevesti.

foresight *s* prevestire *f,* prorocire *f.*

foreskin *s* anat prepuţ *n.*

forest *s (woods)* codru *m;* pădure *f; (multitude)* mulţime *f* || *vt (afforest)* a împăduri.

forestall *vt (prevent)* a împiedica; *(anticipate)* a o lua înaintea cuiva.

foretaste *s* anticipare *f,* "avant gout" *n.*

foretell, foretold, foretold *vt* a prezice.

forethought *s* prevedere *f,* grijă *f;* anticipare *f,* anticipaţie *f* (a viitorului).

forever *adv* pentru totdeauna, pe veci; mereu, într-una.

forewarn *vt* a avertiza.

foreword *s* cuvânt *n* înainte, prefaţă *f.*

forfeit *s* amendă *f; (game)* gaj *n* || *vt* a pierde • ~**ure** *s* jur *(loss)* pierdere *f* prin confiscare; *fig (surrender)* renunţare *f.*

forgave *vt* * **forgive**.

forge[1] *s* met *(furnace)* forjă *f;* fierărie *f* || *vt* met a forja.

forge[2] *vt (counterfeit)* a falsifica, *(fake)* a contraface; a născoci, a inventa • ~**ry** *s* fals *n,* falsificare *f,* contraface *f.*

forge[3] *vi* **(ahead)** a înainta cu greu.

forget, forgot, forgotten *vt (not remember)* a uita || *vr* a-şi pierde cunoştinţa; a uita de sine; a fi altruist || *vi* a uita (de).

forgive, forgave, forgiven *vt (pardon)* a ierta; *(excuse)* a scuza; a renunţa la || *vi* a ierta; a fi iertător • ~**ness** *s* iertare *f.*

forgiving *adj* iertător.

forgo, forwent, forgone *vt* a renunţa la.

forgot *vt* * **forget**.

forgotten *vt* * **forget**.

fork *s (for food)* furculiţă *f; (tool)* furcă *f; (in a road)* bifurcaţie *f; (in a river)* confluenţă *f; mus (for tuning)* diapazon *n* || *vi* a se bifurca.

forlorn *adj (person, face)* nenorocit, trist; *(place)* părăsit; *(attempt)* disperat.

form *s (shape)* formă *f,* aspect *n; (outline)* contur *n; (figure)* siluetă *f;* expresie *f; (manner)* manieră *f; (kind)* specie *f, (variety)* varietate *f,* etichetă *f;* ceremonie *f; (questionnaire)* formular *n;* bancă *f;* clasă *f; (pattern)* model *n* || *vt (fashion)* a da o formă, *(shape)* a modela; *(educate)* a educa; a alcătui; *(found)* a fonda; *(create)* a forma || *vi (take shape)* a se forma; a lua o formă.

formal *adj* formal; de formă; *(party, etc)* oficial; *(person)* formalist; *(language)* elevat; *(clothes)* de ceremonie; *(strict)* categoric, *(precise)* precis; simetric • ~**ity** *s* formalitate *f.*

format *s also comp* format *n* || *vt comp* a formata.

formation *s* formaţie *f; (ideas, plans)* elaborare *f.*

former *adj* fost, trecut || *pron* **the** ~ primul, cel dintâi • ~**ly** *adv* altădată, pe vremuri.

formidable *adj* formidabil.

formula *s (pl* –**as,** -**ae)** formulă *f.*

formulate *vt* a formula.

formulation *s* formulare *f.*

fornication *s* curvie *f;* adulter *n.*

forsake, forsook, forsaken *vt liter (*~ *smb)* a părăsi, a abandona; (~ *a habit)* a renunţa la, a se debarasa de.

forswear, forswore, forsworn *vt frml (renounce)* a renunţa la; *relig* a se lepăda de; *(deny)* a se dezice de || *vr* a fi sperjur, a jura strâmb/fals.

fort *s* mil fort *n.*

forte *s* punct *n* forte.

forth *adv* afară; în afară; înainte; mai departe.

forthcoming *adj (imminent)* pe cale să apară; *(nice)* comunicativ.

forthright *adj (up-front)* deschis, *(frank)* sincer, direct.

forthwith *adv frml* imediat, numaidecât.

fortification *s* fortificaţie *f.*

fortify[2] *vt (strengthen)* a fortifica; *(reinforce)* a întări; *(corroborate)* a corobora; a confirma || *vr* a se fortifica.

fortitude *s* forţă *f* morală, tărie *f* de caracter; curaj *n;* rezistenţă *f.*

fortnight *s* cincisprezece zile *f pl,* două săptămâni *f pl.*

fortress *s* mil fortăreaţă *f.*

fortuitous *adj* fortuit, neprevăzut; accidental, întâmplător.

fortunate *adj* norocos; favorizat; prielnic || *s* om *m* norocos • ~**ly** *adv* din fericire; (în mod) fericit.

fortune *s (luck)* noroc *n; (chance)* şansă *f;* întâmplare *f* fericită; succes *n*; *(fate)* soartă *f*; *(wealth)* avere *f* • **~teller** *s* ghicitor *m*, ghicitoare *f*.

forty *num* patruzeci.

forum *s* *(pl* **fora)** forum *n*.

forward *adj* din faţă, dinainte; *(planning)* pe termen lung; înaintat; *(movement)* de avangardă; fruntaş; isteţ; *(bold)* obraznic; timpuriu ‖ *adv* *(onward)* înainte, mai departe; *(ahead)* în faţă; spre viitor ‖ *s* înaintaş *m* (la fotbal) ‖ *vt* *(send on)* a trimite mai departe; *(dispatch)* a accelera; *(promote)* a promova; *(goods)* a expedia • **~ing** *s* trimitere *f*, expediere *f*; accelerare *f*, grăbire *f*; înaintare *f* • **~looking** *adj* care vede în viitor; prevăzător.

fossil *s* geol *(relic)* fosilă *f*, *fig* fosilă *f*, persoană *f* cu idei învechite ‖ *adj* geol fosilizat, pietrificat; *fig* învechit, înapoiat, închistat.

foster *adj* *(family)* de ocrotire/adopţie ‖ *vt (children)* a ocroti; *fig* a hrăni, a îngriji.

fought *vi* * **fight.**

foul *adj* *(unclean)* murdar; *(coarse)* urât; *(dishonest)* necinstit; *(rotten)* putred; *(polluted)* viciat; *(contagious)* molipsitor ‖ *s* lucru *n* murdar; ciocnire *f*; *sp* fault *n* ‖ *vt (make dirty)* a murdări; *(pollute)* a polua; *(taint)* a păta; *sp* a faulta.

found¹ *vt* * **find.**

found² *vt (city, etc)* a fonda, a întemeia • **~ing father** *s* părinte *m* fondator; **Founding Fathers** *s pl* părinţii *m pl* fondatori (ai statului american).

foundation *s* fundare *f*; *(establishment)* înfiinţare *f*; *(groundwork)* fundaţie *f*; *(charity)* donaţie *f*; *(base)* bază *f*; *(institution)* organizaţie *f*.

founder *s* fondator *m* ‖ *vi (ship)* a se scufunda.

foundling *s* copil *m* abandonat luat în grijă.

foundry *s* topitorie *f*, turnătorie *f*.

fountain *s* izvor *n*; fântână *f* arteziană; rezervor *n*; sursă *f*; obârşie *f*.

four *num* patru ‖ *s* patru, grup *n* de patru • **~teen** *num* patrusprezece ‖ • **~th** *num* al patrulea; **~ of July** patru iulie (sărbătoarea naţională a SUA).

fowl *s* orn orătanie *f*, pasăre *f* de curte.

fox *s* zool vulpe *f*, vulpoi *m*; şmecher *m* ‖ *vi* a se acri; a se trezi; **out ~** *vt (deceive)* a înşela, *(confuse)* a zăpaci.

foyer *s (hotel, theater)* foaier *n*; *(house)* hol *n* la intrare.

fracas *s (brawl)* scandal *n*, ceartă *f*; *(noise)* larmă *f*, zgomot *n*.

fraction *s* fracţie *f* • **~ally** *adv* puţin, un pic.

fracture *s* fractură *f* ‖ *vt* a fractura.

fragile *adj* fragil; gingaş; şubred; trecător.

fragment *s (scrap)* fragment *n*; parte *f*; *(section)* pasaj *n* ‖ *vt (break)* a fragmenta, a fărâmiţa.

fragrance *s* parfum *n*, mireasmă *f*.

fragrant *adj* parfumat.

frail *adj* fragil; *(weak)* slab; *(feeble)* plăpând, *(in poor health)* bolnăvicios • **~ty** *s also fig* slăbiciune *f*.

frame *s (skeleton)* schelet *n*, *(body)* corp *n*; *(construction)* construcţie *f*; *(of window, bicycle, etc)* cadru *n*, *(of picture)* ramă *f*; *(of car)* şasiu *n*; *(of bed)* somieră *f*; *(of glasses)* rame *f pl*, montură *f*; *(border)* chenar *n*; *(structure)* structură *f*; organizare *f*; sistem *n*; imagine *f* ‖ *vt (~ a picture, face)* a încadra, (~ *a picture)* a înrăma; a îmbina; *(elaborate)* a elabora; a forma; a rosti; *(set up)* a înscena; a născoci; **~ of mind** *s* stare *f* de spirit • **~work** *s* structură *f*, *fig (context)* cadru *n*.

France *s* Franţa *f*.

franchise *s* pol *(right to vote)* drept *n* de vot; *com* scutire *f* (de taxe), gratuitate *f*; *econ* franşiză *f* ‖ *vt (license)* a acorda o franşiză.

frank *adj (truthful)* sincer, *(candid)* franc, *(open)* deschis; evident, clar ‖ *vt* a franca; a timbra.

frankincense *s* tămâie *f*.

frantic *adj (activity)* frenetic; *(effort, search)* disperat.

fraternal *adj* fratern, frăţesc.

fraternity *s (community)* confrerie *f*; *(friendship)* fraternitate *f*; club *n* studenţesc.

fraternize *vi (with)* a se asocia (cu).

fraud *s (deception)* înşelătorie *f*; *(impostor)* escroc *m*, *(swindler)* pungaş *m* • **~ulent** *adj (practice, use)* fraudulos; *(signature, check)* fals, contrafăcut; *(earnings)* illicit.

fraught *adj* **(with)** încărcat cu; *(situation, etc)* dificil.

frazzle *vt (exhaust)* a slei, a speti ‖ *s (of clothes)* uzură *f*, roadere *f* • **~d** *adj* epuizat.

fray *vi (material)* a se uza; *(nerves)* a fi încordat răbdării, la capătul răbdării ‖ *s (dispute)* ceartă *f* zgomotoasă, scandal *n*; *(skirmish)* încăierare *f*, *(tussle)* bătaie *f*; *(fight)* luptă *f*, *(conflict)* conflict *n* • **~ed** *adj* ros, tocit.

freak *s (oddity)* ciudăţenie *f*; *(monster)* monstru *m*; *(unusual occurrence)* anormalitate *f*; *coll* fan *m* ‖ *adj (bizarre)* bizar, *(unusual)* insolit; **to ~ out** *coll (panic)* a intra în panică; *(get mad)* a exploda (de furie).

freckle *s* pistrui *m* ‖ *vt* a pistruia ‖ *vi* a se umple de pistrui.

free *adj* liber; *(autonomous)* autonom; *(sovereign)* suveran; *(released)* dezlegat; *(exempt)* scutit de; imparţial; *(spontaneous)* spontan; *(natural)* firesc; *(gratis)* gratuit; generos ‖ *adv (without charge)* gratis, gratuit ‖ *vt (release)* a elibera; *(exempt)* a scuti; **~ enterprise** libera întreprindere; **~ market** economie de piaţă; **~ thinker** liber cugetător; **~ will** liber arbitru • **~dom** *s* libertate *f*; drept *n*; privilegiu *n*; intimitate *f* • **~lance** liber profesionist • **~ly** *adv* în libertate; cu generozitate/mărinimie.

freeway *s* autostradă *f*.

freesia *s* bot frezie *f*.

freeze, froze, frozen *vt* (~ *wages)* a îngheţa; (~ *food)* a congela; *(control)* a stabiliza ‖ *vi (water, pipes)* a îngheţa; *(ice over)* a da îngheţul ‖ *s (weather)* îngheţ *n*; ger *n*; *(wages)* îngheţare *f* • **~r** *s* congelator *n*.

freezing *adj* îngheţat; **I'm ~** îngheţ de frig; **~ point** *s* punct *n* de îngheţ.

freight *s (cargo)* încărcătură *f* (a unui vas); transport *n*; *(cost of shipping)* cheltuieli *f pl* de transport.

French *adj* francez ‖ *s (language)* franceză *f* ‖ *s pl* **the ~** francezii *m pl*; **~ loaf** *s* baghetă *f*; **~ fries** *s* cartofi *mpl* prăjiţi.

frenetic *adj (activity)* frenetic; *(lifestyle)* trepidant.

frenzied *adj (activity)* frenetic; *(attempt)* disperat.

frenzy *s (flurry)* frenezie *f*, *(fury)* furie *f*.

frequency *s* frecvenţă *f*.

frequent *adj (recurrent)* frecvent; *(repeated)* repetat; constant; *(regular)* obişnuit ‖ *vt (visit often)* a frecventa.

fresco *s* frescă *f*.

fresh *adj (newly baked/picked)* proaspăt; *(new)* nou; recent; dulce; *(water)* potabil; *(clean)* curat; *(unsullied)* nefolosit; *(different)* diferit; odihnit; întărit;

actual; neexperimentat • **~en** *vt* (*refresh*) a împrospăta; **to ~ up** *vi* a-şi face toaleta.

freshman *s* student *m* în anul I, boboc *m*.

fret[1] *vi* (*worry*) a se nelinişti, a fi agitat/nervos; (*water*) a se încreţi; **~ and fume** *vt* a spumega de mânie • **~ful** *adj* (*anxious*) neliniştit, agitat; (*irritable*) iritabil, irascibil; arţăgos; (*wind*) violent.

fret[2] *vt* a trafora.

fretsaw *s* ferăstrău *n* pentru traforaj.

fretwork *s* traforaj *n*.

friable *adj* friabil.

friar *s* călugăr *m*.

friction *s* (*rubbing*) frecare *f*, (*chafing*) fricţiune *f*; *fig* (*tension*) fricţiune *f*, (*disagreement*) neînţelegere *f*.

Friday *s* vineri *f*; servitor *m* credincios.

fridge *s* frigider *n*.

friend *s* prieten *m*; cunoscut *m*; coleg *m*; sfătuitor *m*; simpatizant *m* • **~ly** *adj* (*person, behavior*) prietenesc, amical, prietenos; (*match*) amical; favorabil; (*quarrel*) fără consecinţe; (*nation*) prieten || *adv* prieteneşte || *s* meci *n* amical • **~ship** *s* prietenie *f*, amiciţie *f*.

frieze *s archit* friză *f*.

frigate *s naut* fregată *f*.

fright *s* frică *f*; **to give smb a ~** a speria pe cineva • **~en** *vt* (*scare*) a speria, (*terrify*) a băga groaza în • **~ening** *adj* înfricoşător.

frigid *adj* frigid.

frill *s* (*decoration*) volan *n*; *coll* (*bonus*) supliment *n*.

fringe *s* (*tassel*) franjure *m*, ciucure *m*; (*periphery*) margine *f*, (*forest*) lizieră *f*, **~ benefit** *s* recompensă *f*, **~ theater** *s* teatru *n* de avangardă.

frippery *s* (*showy objects*) podoabe *f pl* ieftine, zorzoane *f pl*; (*ostentation*) ostentaţie *f*.

frisk *vt* (*play*) a zburda, a ţopăi; (*search*) a scotoci • **~y** *adj* plin de viaţă.

fritter[1] *s cul* bucată *f* de carne prăjită sau friptă; *approx* clătite *f pl* cu mere; bucată *f*, fragment *n*.

fritter[2] *vt* (**away**) (*~ money, etc*) a pierde, (*squander*) a irosi, (*spend*) a cheltui.

frivolity *s* (*thoughtlessness*) frivolitate *f*.

frivolous *adj* frivol.

frizzy *adj* (*hair*) foarte creţ.

frock *s obs* sutană *f*, rasă *f* (de călugăr); tunică *f*.

frog *s zool* broască *f*; *rail* macaz *n*.

frolic *vi* (*frisk*) a zburda, (*let down one's hair*) a face nebunii.

from *prep* de la, din; de pe; din partea; după; în urma; din cauza; dintre; între || *adv* de sus.

front *adj* (*tooth, etc*) din faţă; (*page*) primul || *s* partea *f* din faţă; (*of a dress, house, etc*) faţă *f*; *mil, met* front *n*; (*sea ~*) litoral *n*; (*appearance: person*) atitudine *f*, ţinută *f*; *pej* (*business*) faţadă *f*; **in ~** *adv* (*walk, push*) în faţă; (*people*) înainte || *prep* în faţa • **~runner** *s* favorit *m* • **~wheel drive** *s* tracţiune *f* pe faţă.

frontier *s* (*boundary*) frontieră *f*, (*border*) graniţă *f*; *fig* (*edge*) limită *f* • **~sman** *s* pionier *m*.

frost *s* (*chill*) ger *n*, (*ice*) îngheţ *n*; (*rime*) chiciură *f*; (*coolness*) asprime *f* || *vt* (*freeze*) a îngheţa; a congela; (*ice*) a glazura.

froth *s* (*beer, ocean*) spumă *f*.

frown *vi* (*glower*) a se încrunta || *s* (*scowl*) încruntătură *f*, (*glare*) privire *f* încruntată.

froze *vi* * **freeze**.

frozen *vi* * **freeze**.

fructify *vt frml* a fructifica || *vi* a da roade.

frugal *adj* (*meal*) frugal; (*person, life*) econom, modest.

fruit *s* fruct *n*; rod *n*; (*result*) rezultat *n*; (*outcome*) urmare *f* || *vi* a rodi • **~ful** *adj* fructuos.

fruition *s* realizare *f*, împlinire *f*.

fruitless *adj* (*plant*) neroditor; (*effort*) zadarnic, inutil; (*soil*) sterp, steril.

frustrate *vt* (*thwart*) a zădărnici; (*foil*) a dejuca; a învinge; (*disappoint*) a înşela; **frustration** *s* (*foiling*) zădărnicire *f*, dejucare *f*; (*disappointment*) înşelare *f* (a aşteptărilor).

frustum *s math* trunchi *n* (de con etc).

fry *vt* a prăji, a frige || *vi* a se prăji; a se frige || *s* carne *f* prăjită; friptură *f* • **~ing pan** *s* tigaie *f*, tingire *f*.

fuchsia *s bot* fuxia *f*.

fuck *vt/vi vulg* a face sex; **~ off!** *vi vulg* cară-te!.

fudge *s cul* caramea *f* (moale).

fuel *s* carburant *m*, combustibil *m* || *vt* (*supply*) a alimenta cu carburant; *fig* (*~ speculation*) a alimenta; (*encourage*) a stimula; **~ pump** *s* pompă *f* de alimentare; **~ tank** *s* rezervor *n* de carburant.

fugitive *s* (*person*) fugar *m*; (*deserter*) dezertor *m*, (*escapee*) evadat *m*; (*refugee*) refugiat *m* || *adj* (*person*) fugit; fugar; (*transitory*) fugitiv, trecător, efemer; (*literary work*) ocazional.

fulfill *vt* (*~ a task, role*) a îndeplini; (*~ hopes*) a împlini; (*~ an ambition*) a realiza; (*~ a need*) a satisface; a termina; a desăvârşi.

full *adj* plin; (*parking*) complet; (*eaten enough*) îndopat, ghiftuit, sătul, săţios, nutritiv; lejer; bogat; (*explanation, day*) întreg, complet; (*volume*) maxim; (*life*) plin; (*schedule*) încărcaţi; (*set*) complet; (*face*) rotund; (*mouth*) cărnos; (*skirt, sleeve*) amplu || *adv* foarte; complet; drept, direct, chiar, tocmai || *vt* a croi larg • **~blown** *adj* (*fully*) pe deplin dezvoltat; matur; (*flowers*) înflorit, în plină floare • **~fledged** *adj* (*bird*) cu pene, în stare să zboare; (*fully*) (pe deplin) dezvoltat, matur; (*person*) cu drepturi depline • **~y** *adv* complet, pe deplin, cu totul; chiar, tocmai; amplu, bogat.

fulminate *vi frml* (**against/at**) a tuna şi a fulgera (împotriva).

fulsome *adj* (*thanks*) exagerat; (*welcome*) plin de efuziune.

fumble *vi* (*grope*) a cotrobăi, (*feel around*) a bâjbâi; (**for**) a scotoci.

fume *vi* (*seethe*) a se înfuria • **~s** *s pl* emanaţii *f pl*; fum *n*; gaze *n pl* de eşapament.

fun *s* glumă *f*, (*enjoyment*) distracţie *f*; (*joy*) veselie *f*; ridiculizare *f*, partea *f* amuzantă || *adj* (*amusing*) amuzant, distractiv; (*pleasurable*) plăcut.

function *s* (*task*) funcţie *f*, (*job*) post *n*; (*occupation*) activitate *f*; (*role*) rol *n*; ceremonie *f*; (*party*) recepţie *f* || *vi* (*operate*) a funcţiona; (*work*) a lucra.

fund *s fin* fond *n*, capital *n*; (*nest egg*) rezervă *f*,; (*stock*) stoc *n* || *vt* a consolida; (*finance*) a finanţa.

fundamental *adj* (**to**) fundamental (pentru).

funeral *adj* funerar, funebru || *s* înmormântare *f*, funeralii *f pl*; procesiune *f* funebră.

funerary *adj* funerar.

funereal *adj* ca de înmormântare; lugubru.

funfair *s* parc *n* de distracţii.

fungus *s* (*pl* **–gi/-guses**) ciupercă *f*.

funicular *s* funicular *n*.

funnel *s* pâlnie *f*; (*of a ship*) coş *n*.

funny *adj* (*amusing*) amuzant, (*comical*) distractiv; (*witty*) nostim; (*droll*) caraghios; (*odd*) ciudat ‖ *s* pagină *f* veselă.

fur *s* blană *f*; piele *f* (de animal) ‖ *vt* a îmblăni.

furious *adj* furios, înfuriat; (*effort*) îndârjit; (*temperament*) dezlănțuit; (*fight*) violent, năpraznic.

furl *vt* (*umbrella, etc*) a închide; *naut* (*sail*) a strânge; a înfășura.

furlough *s mil* permisie *f*; (*laying off*) disponibilizare *f* temporară.

furnace *s tech* cuptor *n*; *met* furnal *n*; *fig* ispitire *f*, încercare *f* grea.

furnish *vt* (*supply*) a aproviziona (cu); (*provide*) a furniza; a mobila; a oferi; a procura.

furniture *s* mobilă *f*, mobilier; utilaj *n*, inventar *n*.

furrow *s* (*land*) brazdă *f*; (*forehead*) rid *n*.

furry *adj* (*animal*) cu blană; (*material*) îmblănit.

further *adj* adițional; ulterior ‖ *adv* mai mult; în plus ‖ *vt* a promova; a încuraja.

furthest *adj* cel mai îndepărtat ‖ *adv* cel mai departe.

furtive *adj* (*person*) ascuns, secret; (*look*) furiș.

fury *s* (*anger*) furie *f*; (*vehemence*) vehemență *f*.

fuse *vi* a se topi; (*blend*) a fuziona; (*mingle*) a se contopi ‖ *vt* (*combine*) a uni prin fuziune; a topi; a fuziona ‖ *s elec* siguranță *f*; (*bomb*) detonator *n*; fitil *n*; (*fireworks*) amorsă *f* • ~**box** cutie *f* cu siguranțe.

fuselage *s* fuselaj *n*.

fusible *adj* fuzibil, topit; ~ **metal** aliaj de lipit.

fusion *s* (*union*) fuziune *f*, (*combination*) fuzionare *f*, (*blending*) contopire *f*.

fuss *s* (*commotion*) agitație *f*; (*excitement*) nervozitate *f* inutilă; (*objection*) obiecție *f*; (*worry*) frământare; pedant *m* ‖ *vt* a plictisi; a enerva ‖ *vi* (*fret*) a se agita; (*be nervous*) a se enerva; (*quarrel*) a se certa • ~**y** *adj* (*person*) agitat, nervos; (*pedantic*) aferat; (*fastidious*) exagerat; înzorzonat.

fustian *s* (*fabric*) barchet *n*, finet *n*; *fig, lit* (*bombast*) stil *n* pompos/bombastic.

fustigate *vt* a bate cu bățul; *fig* a critica aspru.

fusty *adj* (*moldy*) mucegăit; (*rotten*) stricat; (*antiquated*) învechit, (*stuffy*) închistat, (*old-fashioned*) demodat.

futile *adj* (*vain*) zadarnic, (*pointless*) fără rost.

futility *s* (*uselessness*) zădărnicie *f*; (*ineffectiveness*) superficialitate *f*.

futon *s* saltea *f* (de origine japoneză) făcută din straturi de bumbac.

future *adj* (*upcoming*) viitor; (*forthcoming*) următor ‖ *s* viitor *n*; timpuri *n pl* viitoare; (*prospect*) perspectivă *f*; *fin* contract *n* pentru bunuri de perspectivă; **in the** ~ în viitor.

futuristic *adj* futuristic.

fuzz *s* (*down*) puf *n*; (*lint*) scamă *f* • ~**ily** *adv* (în mod) neclar, vag, difuz; ca prin ceață • ~**y** *adj* (*hair*) creț; (*image, etc*) neclar, estompat; (*thoughts*) confuz.; pufos; cu/de puf.

G

G, g *s* (litera) G, g.

gab *s coll* trăncăneală *f* ‖ *vi* a trăncăni • ~**by** *adj* vorbăreț • ~**ble** *vt/vi* a trăncăni, a bolborosi ‖ *s* limbaj *n* neinteligibil/incorect • ~**fest** *s coll* taifas *n*, șuetă *f*.

gable *s* fronton *n*.

gad *vi* (**about**) a umbla creanga, a hoinări • ~**about** *s* teleleu *m*.

gadfly *s ento* tăun *m*.

gadget *s* dispozitiv *n*; truc *n*; șmecherie *f*; fleac *n*.

gaff *s* cange *f*; *naut* pic *n*, vergă *f* ‖ *vt* a prinde (pești) cu cangea.

gaffe *s* (*blunder*) gafă *f*.

gaffer *s hum* bătrânel *m*, bunicuț *m*.

gag[1] *vt* a pune căluș ‖ *s* căluș *n*.

gag[2] *s coll* (*joke*) glumă *f*, efect *n* comic.

gaggle *s* (~ *of geese*) cârd *n* de gâște; (*throng*) gloată *f* ‖ *vi* a gâgâi.

gaiety *s* veselie *f*.

gaily *adv* voios, vesel, jovial; (*brightly*) țipător.

gain *s* câștig *n*; spor *n*; avantaj *n*; răsplată *f* ‖ *vt* a câștiga; a obține; a cuceri; a ajunge la ‖ *vi* a câștiga; a profita; a se îngrășa; a spori, a înainta.

gainsay *vt frml* (*deny*) a nega, a infirma; (*contradict*) a contrazice.

gait *s* (*of a person*) umblet *n*, mers *n*; (*of a horse*) pas *m*.

gaiters *s pl* ghetre *f pl*.

gal *s coll* (*girl*) fetișcană *f*.

gala *s* serată *f* de gală.

galaxy *s astron* galaxie *f*.

gale *s* vânt *n* puternic; furtună *f*; *fig* izbucnire *f*; *fig* hohot *n*.

gall *s* fiere *f*, bilă *f*; amărăciune *f*; invidie *f*; tupeu *n*; scârbă *f*; jupuitură *f* ‖ *vt* a jupui; a roade; a enerva.

gallant *adj* (*brave*) curajos; (*polite*) galant.

gallbladder *s anat* vezică *f* biliară.

galleon *s hist* galion *n*, corabie *f* de război.

gallery *s* galerie *f*; balcon *n*; suporteri *m pl*; sală *f* de expoziție.

galley *s* (*of a ship*) galeră *f*; (*kitchen*) cambuză *f*.

gallivant *vi hum* (**about/around**) a umbla fără rost.

gallon *s* galon *n* (măsură de capacitate = 3,34 l).

gallop *s* galop *n*; alergare/plimbare *f* la galop ‖ *vi* a galopa, a alerga în/la galop.

gallows *s* spânzurătoare *f*; spânzurare *f*.

gallstone *s med* calcul *m* biliar.

galore *adj* din plin, din abundență.

galosh *s* galoș *m*.

galvanize *vt tech* a galvaniza; *fig* a stimula (pe cineva) să facă ceva.

gamble *s* joc *n* de noroc; aventură *f* ‖ *vi* a juca jocuri de noroc; a miza (pe); a risca ‖ *vt* a risca la joc; a miza, a paria • ~**r** *s* jucător *m* de jocuri de noroc, cartofor *m*; escroc *m*; aventurier *m*.

gambol *s* zburdălnicie *f* ‖ *vi* a zburda.

game *s* joc *n*; sport *n*; partidă *f*, meci *n*; (*tennis*) ghem *n*; distracție *f*; farsă *f*; intenție *f*, plan *n*; vânat *n* ‖ *adj* curajos; dispus, pregătit ‖ *vi* a juca jocuri de noroc ‖ *vt* a juca/a miza la cărți etc; ~ **warden** *s* paznic *m* de vânătoare.

gammon *s* șuncă/costiță *f* afumată.

gamut *s mus, fig* gamă *f*.

gander *s orn* gânsac *m*.

gang *s* bandă *f*; echipă *f*; grup *n*; serie *f*; organizație *f* de gangsteri ‖ *vt* a pune laolaltă; a cupla ‖ *vi* a se aduna, a se înhăita.

gangling *adj* (*lanky*) deșirat.

gangrene *s med*, *fig* cangrenă *f*.

gangster *s* gangster *m*; bandit *m*.

gangway *s* pasarelă *f*.

gaol *s* * **jail**.

gap *s* (*loc*) gol *n*; lipsă *f*, lacună *f*; omisiune *f*; pauză *f*; decalaj *n*; abis *n*; chei *n*; întrerupere *f*; spărtură *f*.

gape *vi* (*stare*) a căsca gura (de mirare); (*split, open a gap*) a se deschide, a sta deschis.

garage *s* garaj *n*; atelier *n* de reparaţii auto.

garb *s lit* îmbrăcăminte *f* || *vt* (*clothe*) a înveşmânta.

garbage *s* gunoi *n*; murdărie *f*; *coll* prostii *f pl*.

garble *vt* (*mangle*) a deforma, a trunchia; (*distort*) a denatura; (*muddle*) a încurca.

garden *s* grădină *f*; parc *n*; terasă *f*; arenă *f*; sală *f* mare || *adj* cultivat; de grădină || *vi* a face grădinărit • ~**er** *s* grădinar *m*.

gargle *vi* a face gargară.

gargoyle *s* gargui *n*, burlan *n* scurt ornamentat.

garish *adj* (*color*) strident; (*light*) orbitor.

garland *s* ghirlandă *f* de flori.

garlic *s* usturoi *m*; căpăţână *f* de usturoi.

garment *s* îmbrăcăminte *f*.

garner *s lit* hambar *n* || *vt* (~ *grain*) a înmagazina; *fig* (~ *info*) a strânge, a aduna.

garnish *vt* a garnisi || *s* garnitură *f*.

garret *s* mansardă *f*.

garrison *s mil* garnizoană *f*.

garrulous *adj* (*person*) vorbăreţ; (*style*) prolix.

garter *s* suport *n* pentru şosete; suspensor *n*; jartieră *f*.

gas *s* gaz *n*; abur *m*; benzină *f*; anestezie *f* || *adj* gazos; de gaze || *vt* a gaza || *vi* a pălăvrăgi.

gash *s* spintecătură *f* || *vt* a spinteca.

gasket *s* garnitură *f*, manşon *n*.

gasoline *s* benzină *f*.

gasp *s* răsuflare *f* întretăiată || *vi* a gâfâi; (~ *in shock, surprise*) a avea respiraţia întretăiată.

gastric *adj* gastric.

gastronomic *adj* gastronomic.

gastronomy *s* gastronomie *f*.

gate *s* poartă *f*; pas *n*, trecătoare *f*; ecluză *f*; valvă *f*; spectatori *m pl* (la meciuri); taxă *f* (de intrare) • ~**crash** *vt/vi coll* a lua parte la o reuniune/recepţie fără a fi invitat; a intra nepoftit • ~**crasher** *s* spectator *m* care intră fără bilet; intrus *m*, musafir *m* nepoftit.

gateway *s* intrare *f*; ~ **to** intrare *f*, uşă *f*; *fig* cheie *f*.

gather *vt* a strânge; (~ *flowers, information*) a culege; (~ *courage, strength*) a aduna; (*harvest*) a recolta; a cuprinde; (~ *material*) a plisa; a câştiga; (~ *speed*) a prinde, a spori; (*understand*) a înţelege; a deduce; a afla || *vi* (~ *people*) a se aduna; a se îmbulzi; (*clouds* ~) a a se strânge || *s* pliseu *n* • ~**ing** *s* adunare *f*, întrunire *f*.

gaudy *adj* bătător la ochi.

gauge *s* măsură *f*; ecartament *n*; gabarit *n*; jojă *f*; etalon *n*; reper *n* || *vt* a măsura.

gaunt *adj* (*feeble*) sfrijit; (*desolate*) pustiu.

gauntlet *s* mănuşă *f* (de protecţie sau în sport).

gauze *s* tifon *n*; *text* voal *n*; ceaţă *f*.

gave *vt* * **give**.

gavel *s* ciocănel *n* (la bursă etc).

gawk *vi* (**at**) a se uita prosteşte/zgâi (la).

gawky *adj* (*person*) stângaci; (*movement*) dezordonat.

gawp *vi coll* (**at**) a se holba (la).

gay *adj* vesel; ţipător; petrecăreţ; imoral; afemeiat || *s* homosexual *m*; lesbiană *f*.

gaze *vt* a privi lung; a privi în gol || *s* privire *f* lungă.

gazelle *s zool* gazelă *f*.

gazetteer *s* index *n* geographic.

gear *s* angrenaj *n*; viteză *f*; costum *n*; utilaj *n*; mecanism *n* || *vt* a înzestra cu un mecanism; a adapta.

geese *s pl* * **goose**.

gelatine *s* gelatină *f*.

geld *vt* a castra.

gelignite *s* (exploziv cu) fulmicoton *n*.

gem *s* piatră *f* preţioasă, nestemată *f*; bijuterie *f*; odor *n* || *vt* a împodobi cu nestemate.

Gemini *s pl astrol* Zodia *f* Gemenilor.

gender *s* sex *n*; *gram* gen *n*.

gene *s bio* genă *f*.

genealogy *s* genealogie *f*.

general *adj* general, universal; obişnuit; vag; nedefinit; principal || *s* general *m*; comandant *m* • ~**ization** *s* generalizare *f* • ~**ize** *vt* a generaliza • ~**ly** *adv* în general.

generate *vt* (~ *energy, etc*) a crea, a genera; (~ *power, heat*) a produce; (~ *interest*) a suscita.

generation *s* generaţie *f*; (*of jobs*) creare *f*; (*of interest*) inducere *f*; (*of power*) producere *f*.

generator *s elec* generator *n*.

generic *adj* generic.

generosity *s* generozitate *f*.

generous *adj* generos; nobil; altruist; bogat.

genetic *adj* genetic • ~**ist** *s* genetician *m* • ~**s** *s pl* genetică *f*.

Geneva *s* Geneva; **Lake** ~ Lacul *n* Leman.

genial *adj* amabil şi curtenitor.

genital *adj* genital • ~**s** *s pl* organe *n pl* genitale.

genitive *s gram* genitiv.

genius *s* geniu *n*, genialitate *f*; om *m* genial; dar *n*; talent *n*; particularitate *f*.

gentle *adj* blând; gingaş; amabil; moderat; uşor; distins; galant; onorabil.

gentleman *s* domn *m*, gentleman; bărbat *m*, om *m*.

gently *adv* (*mildly*) uşor, cu menajamente; (*discreetly*) discret; (*gradually*) uşor, treptat; (*slowly*) încet(işor).

gentry *s* mica nobilime *f*.

gents *s sl* bărbaţi *m pl*.

genuine *adj* veritabil; autentic; pur; onest, sincer, deschis, cinstit.

genus *s* (*pl* **genuses, genera**) gen *n*, specie *f*.

geographic *adj* geographic.

geography *s* geografie *f*.

geologic *adj* geologic.

geologist *s* geolog *m*.

geology *s* geologie *f*.

geometric *adj* geometric.

geometry *s* geometrie *f*.

geophysics *s* geofizică *f*.

geopolitics *s* geopolitică *f*.

geranium *s bot* muşcată *f*.

geriatric *adj med* geriatric; *pej* (*person*) decrepit; (*thing*) învechit.

germ *s* microb *m*, germene *m*; bacterie *f*; embrion *m*; nucleu *n*; început *n*; spor *n* || *adj* microbian || *vi* a germina.

germane *adj frml* pertinent, relevant; ~ **to** legat de.

German *s/adj* german *m*; (*people*) german *m*; (*language*) germană *f* • ~**y** *s* Germania *f*.

germinate *vi also fig* a germina.

germination *s* germinare *f*.

gerund *s gram* gerunziu *n*.

gestation *s* gestaţie *f*.

gesticulate *vi* a gesticula.

gesture *s* gest *n*, mişcare *f*; acţiune *f*, act *n* || *vi* a gesticula.

get, got, gotten *vt* (*receive*) a căpăta, a primi; (*obtain*) a obţine; (*fetch*) a procura; (*find*) a găsi; (*take*) a lua;

(*force*) a sili; (*cause*) a determina; (*persuade*) a convinge; (*achieve*) a realiza; (*earn*) a câştiga; (*contract*) a contracta o boală; (*learn*) a deprinde; (*grasp*) a pricepe; (*catch*) a prinde; (*pick up*) a culege; (*conquer*) a cuceri || *vi* (*reach*) a ajunge; (*arrive*) a sosi; (*manage*) a reuşi; (*go*) a se duce, a merge; a nimeri; (*start*) a începe să; (*become*) a deveni • ~ **about/ around** *vi* (*move*) a se deplasa; (*news, etc*) a circula, a se răspândi • ~ **along** *vi* a se descurca; a înainta, a face progrese; a trăi în armonie (cu cineva) • ~ **at** *vt* a ajunge (până) la; (*suggest*) a vrea să spună; *coll* a critica, a denigra • ~ **away** *vi* a pleca; a pleca în vacanţă; a evada, a scăpa • ~**away** *s* fugă *f* • ~ **back** *vi* (**to**) (*return to, resume*) a reveni la; *coll* a telefona • ~ **by** *vi* a se descurca, a o scoate la capăt • ~ **down** *vt* a fi deprimat; (*lower*) a coborî • ~ **in** *vt* a strânge; a stoca; a aduna; a plasa; a educa; a semăna; a planta || *vi* a intra; a ajunge; a reveni, a se urca; a veni la putere • ~ **off** *vt* a scoate || *vi* a pleca de la; (*train, etc*) a coborî; (*punishment*) a scăpa; a pleca • ~ **on** *vt* (*a bus, etc*) a urca în; (*a horse*) a încăleca || *vi* (*a bus, etc*) a urca; a se înţelege, a fi de acord; a avansa, a progresa; (*succeed*) a reuşi • ~ **out** *vt* a scoate, a extrage; a publica; a rosti; a rezolva || *vi* (*of a car, etc*) a coborî; a ieşi (afară); a pleca; (*escape*) a scăpa; (*news*) a se afla, a se răspândi • ~ **up** *vt* a urca, a înălţa; a irita; a pregăti; a elabora; a organiza; a stârni; a născoci; a aranja; a prezenta; a monta || *vi* a se scula; a încăleca; a se înteţi; a se găti; a se agita.

geyser *s* gheizer *n*.

ghastly *adj coll* (*horrible*) înspăimântător; (*macabre*) înfricoşător.

gherkin *s* castravecior *m*, cornişon *m*.

ghetto *s* ghetou *n*.

ghost *s* stafie *f*, duh *n*, fantomă *f*; autor *m* care scrie sub semnătura altuia; suflet *n*; umbră *f*.

giant *adj* uriaş, colosal, gigantic || *s* uriaş *m*, gigant *m*, colos *m*; titan *m*.

gibberish *s* vorbire *f* păsărească, pălăvrăgeală *f* confuză.

gibe *s* insultă *f*.

giblets *s pl* măruntaie *n pl* (de pasăre), potroace *n pl*.

giddy *adj* ameţit.

gift *s* cadou *n*; donaţie *f*; talent *n*; fleac *n*; ~ **certificate** *s* cec-cadou *n*.

gigabyte *s comp* giga-octet *n*.

gigantic *adj* uriaş, gigantic.

giggle *vi* a chicoti || *s* chicoteală *f*; mucalit *m*; glumă *f*.

gigolo *s* gigolo *m*.

gild *vt* a sufla cu aur.

gill *s* (*of a fish*) branhie *f*; (*of a mushroom*) lamelă *f*.

gilt *adj* aurit || *s* aurire *f* • ~**edged** *adj econ* sigur, fără riscuri.

gimmick *s coll* şmecherie *f*, artificiu *n*; expedient *n*.

gin *s* gin *n*.

ginger *s* ghimbir *n*, imbir *n*; elan *n*, însufleţire *f* || *vt* a aromatiza cu ghimbir; a îmboldi; a înviora.

gingerly *adv* prudent, precaut; delicat, tiptil || *adj* precaut, prudent, grijuliu.

gipsy *n* * **gypsy**.

giraffe *s zool* girafă *f*.

girder *s* grindă *f*.

girdle *s* curea *f*; corset *n*.

girl *s* fată *f*, tânără *f*; domnişoară *f*; iubită *f*; fiică *f*; slujnică *f*; vânzătoare *f* • ~**friend** *s* prietenă *f*; iubită *f*; logodnică *f*.

girth *s* (*of a tree*) circumferinţă *f*; (*of a person*) măsură *f* a taliei; (*of a horse*) chingă *f*.

gist *s* esenţă *f*; **get the ~ of** smth a înţelege esenţialul.

give, gave, given *vt* a da; (~ *a present*) a dărui, a oferi; a dona; a atribui; (~ *attention*) a consacra, a acorda; a permite; a distribui; a plăti; a preda; a împărtăşi; a rosti; a emite; a realiza; a dedica; (~ *a message*) a transmite; (*convey*) a comunica; a ura; a interpreta; ~ **away** *vt* (*hand over*) a înmâna; (~ *a bride*) a conduce la altar; (*throw away*) a irosi; (*reveal*) a divulga; (*betray*) a trăda; ~ **back** *vt* (*return*) a restitui, (*reflect image, light*) a reflecta, a oglindi; ~ **in** *vt* a înmâna, a anunţa, a adăuga || *vi* a renunţa, a ceda, a se supune; ~ **off** *vt* (~ *a smell*) a exala, (~ *smoke*) a degaja a face, (~ *heat*) a produce; ~ **or take** *prep* în plus sau în minus; ~ **or take a day** o zi în plus sau în minus || *vi* a ceda; a da de pomană; a se prăbuşi; a se umezi; a ieşi; a se zvânta; ~ **out** *vt* a distribui || *vi* (*supplies*) a se termina; (*machines*) a se defecta; ~ **up** *vt* a abandona; a se retrage; a ceda; a renunţa la; a sacrifica; a se dezice; a preda; a denunţa || *vi* a ceda, a renunţa, a se retrage.

gizzard *s* pipotă *f*.

glacial *adj also fig* glaciar.

glacier *s* gheţar *n*.

glad *adj* bucuros; fericit; voios; dispus (să facă ceva) • ~**ly** *adv* cu bucurie; cu plăcere.

glade *s* luminiş *n*.

gladiator *s* gladiator *m*.

gladiola *s* (pl ~**li**) *bot* gladiolă *f*.

glamor *s* (*person*) farmec *n*; (*clothes*) eleganţă *f*, şic *n*; (*job*) prestigiu *n* • ~**ous** *adj* (*person*) seducător; (*clothes*) elegant; (*job*) prestigios.

glance *s* privire *f* (fugară); licărire *f* || *vi* a se uita în treacăt.

gland *s anat* glandă *f*; ganglioni *m pl* (la gât).

glare *vi* (**at**) a privi crunt (pe cineva / la ceva); (~ *of sun, lamp*) a străluci orbitor || *s* privire *f* aspră/feroce; lumină *f* orbitoare.

glaring *adj* (*light*) orbitor; (*mistake*) grosolan, strigător la cer; (*color*) viu; *pej* ţipător; (*look*) feroce, sălbatic.

glass *s* sticlă *f*; sticlărie *f*; oglindă *f*; ochean *n*, binoclu *n*; lunetă *f* || *adj* de sticlă; ~ **ceiling** *s* obstacol *n* discriminatoriu • ~**es** *s pl* ochelari *n pl*.

glaze *vt* (~ *tile, etc*) a smălţui; (~ *a cake*) a glasa || *s* (*tile*) smalţ *n*; (*cake*) glazură *f*.

glazier *s* geamgiu *m*.

gleam *vi* (*surface, object*) a licări; (*eyes, light*) a străluci || *s* (*of gold*) reflex *n*; (*of fire, sunset*) licărire *f*, *fig* licărire *f*, rază *f*, urmă *f*.

glean *vt* a spicui, a culege.

glee *s* bucurie *f*, jubilare *f*.

glen *s* vale *f* îngustă, ravină *f*, strungă *f*.

glib *adj pej* (*person*) limbut, descurcăreţ (în vorbe); (*excuse, promise*) uşuratic, facil.

glide *vi* (*dancer, ship*) a aluneca; (*person*) a se mişca fără efort; (*fly*) a plana • ~**r** *s* planor *n*.

gliding *s* planorism *n*.

glimmer *vi* (*faint light*) pâlpâire *f*, *fig* semn *n*, licărire *f*.

glimpse *s* privire *f* (fugară), ochire *f*; licărire *f* || *vt* a zări || *vi* a arunca o privire; a licări; a se ivi.

glint *vi* a scânteia || *s* reflex *n*; (*of an eye*) fulgerare *f*.

glisten *vi* a străluci.

glitter *s* sclipire *f*, strălucire *f*; splendoare *f*, fast *n* || *vi* a sclipi, a străluci.

gloat *vi* **(over)** a privi lacom la, a sorbi/mânca din ochi; a privi cu desfătare/nesaţ la; a se bucura de.

global *adj* mondial; ~ **warming** *s* încălzirea *f* planetei.

globe *s* glob *n*, sferă *f*; glob n pământesc; astru *m*.

globule *s* globulă *f*; picătură *f*.

gloom *s* (*dark*) obscuritate *f*; (*unhappiness*) tristeţe *f* • ~**y** *adj* întunecos; sumbru; trist; lugubru.

glorify *vt* (*worship*) a ridica în slăvi; (*honor*) a cinsti, a onora.

glorious *adj* glorios,victorios; splendid, grozav; superb, magnific.

glory *s* (*fame*) glorie *f*; merit *n*; mândrie *f*; nimb *n*; (*beauty*) splendoare *f*, strălucire *f*.

gloss *s* strălucire *f*, luciu *n*; (*paint*) vopsea *f* strălucitoare • ~**y** *adj* (*hair, etc*) lucios; (*book, photo*) pe hârtie lucioasă.

glossary *s* glosar *n*, vocabular *n*.

glove *s* mănuşă *f*; ~ **compartment** *s* torpedou *n*.

glow *s* strălucire *f*, lumină *f*; dogoare *f*; arşiţă *f*; flacără *f*; licărire *f*; ardoare *f*; vioiciune *f*; îmbujorare *f* || *vi* a arde; a scânteia; a (stră)luci; a radia; a se aprinde; a se îmbujora.

glower *vi* (**at**) a se uita fioros (la).

glucose *s* glucoză *f*.

glue *s* clei *n* || *vt* a lipi.

glum *adj* întunecat, sumbru, mohorât; (*unhappy*) ursuz.

glut *s* îndestulare *f*, prisos *n*; *econ* supraabundenţă *f*; excedent *n*.

glutinous *adj* lipicios.

glutton *s* (om) lacom *m*, gurmand *m*, mâncău *m*.

glycerine *s* glicerină *f*.

gnarled *adj* (*tree*) noduros; răsucit, strîmb; (*hand, finger*) noduros, diform.

gnash *vt/vi* a scrâşni (din dinţi).

gnat *s ento* ţânţar *m*.

gnaw *vt* a roade, a mânca; *fig* a distruge, a nimici || *vi* (**at**) a roade (din), a mânca; *fig* (**at**) a roade, a chinui, a frământa; (**into**) (*metal*) a coroda, a roade.

gnome *s* gnom *m*, pitic *m*.

go, went, gone *vi* (*move*) a merge, a umbla; a se duce la; (*travel*) a călători; a ieşi; a circula; (*leave*) a pleca; (*reach*) a se întinde; (*elapse*) a se scurge; (*work*) a funcţiona; (*proceed*) a proceda; (*happen*) a se petrece; (*succeed*) a izbuti; (*intend*) a intenţiona; (*disappear*) a dispărea; (*die*) a muri; (*belong*) a se integra; (*text, bell*) a suna || *vt* a face; a îndura; a accepta || *s* mişcare *f*, acţiune *f*; probă *f*, modă *f*; întâmplare *f*; târg *n*; (*energy*) elan *n*; succes *n*; ~ **ahead** *vi* (**with**) a continua (ceva); a avea loc, a se întâmpla; ~ **along** *vi* a înainta; ~ **along with** (~ *an idea, etc*) a sprijini, a susţine; (~ *a person*) a urma; ~ **at** *vi* a se repezi/năpusti la, a se apuca de; ~ **back on** *vt* (~ *a promise*) a reveni (asupra); ~ **back to** a relua, a reîncepe să; a data din; ~ **by** *vi* (*time*) a trece; (*conduct*) a urma; (*follow*) a se lua după; ~ **down** *vi* (*price*) a scădea; (*be accepted*) a fi bine/rău primit; (*sun*) a apune; (*tire, etc*) a se dezumfla || *vt* a coborî; ~ **in** *vi* a intra; ~ **in for** (*competition*) a lua parte la; (*exam*) a se prezenta la; (*activity*) a îndrăgi; (*partici-pate in*) a face, a se apuca de; ~ **into** *vt* (~ *a study*) a studia, a examina; (~ *a profession*) a ajunge, a deveni; ~ **off** *vi* a exploda; (*alarm*) a suna; (*food*) a se strica; (*light, etc*) a se stinge || *vt* (*lose interest*) a nu mai îndrăgi; ~ **on** *vi* (*occur*) a se întâmpla; (*heat-ing, etc*) a se pune în funcţiune; a se prelungi; a

merge înainte; a continua; a progresa; a avansa; a avea succes; a se petrece; a expira; ~ **out** *vi* a ieşi (afară); (*leave*) a pleca; (*start*) a porni; (*resign*) a demisiona; (*publication*) a apărea; (*run out*) a se termina; (*light, fire, etc*) a se stinge; ~ **through** *vt* (*experience*) a trece prin, a suferi; a examina; (~ *with a threat, etc*) a merge până la capăt; ~ **up** *vi* a urca; (*price*) a creşte || *vt* a urca; ~ **without** *vt* a se lipsi de, a nu avea nevoie de.

goad *vt* a îmboldi; *fig* a stimula, a îmboldi; *fig* a irita, a aţâţa.

goal *s* ţintă *f*, ţel *n*; scop *n*; obiectiv *n*; *sp* poartă *f*; *sp* but *n*; sosire *f*, finiş *n* • ~**keeper** *s sp* portar *m*.

goat *s zool* capră *f*.

gobble *vt* a înghiţi; (**down/up**) a înfuleca.

go-between *s* intermediar *m*.

goblin *s* spiriduş *m*, drăcuşor *m*.

god *s* zeu *m*, zeitate *f*, divinitate *f*; **God knows** numai Dumnezeu ştie; **for God's sake** pentru numele lui Dumnezeu; **thank God** Slavă Domnului; **(my) God!** *excl* Doamne!, Dumnezeule!.

godchild *s* fin *m* (la botez).

goddaughter *s* fină *f*.

godfather *s* naş *m*.

godmother *s* naşă *f*.

godson *s* fin *m*.

goggles *s pl* ochelari *m pl*.

goiter *s med* guşă *f*.

gold *s* aur *n*; avere *f*; odor *n* || *adj* de/din aur; auriu; blond • ~**en** *adj* de aur; auriu • ~ **medal** *s* medalie *f* de aur • ~**mine** *s also fig* mină *f* de aur • ~**smith** *s* giuvaergiu *m*.

golf *s* golf *n* || *vi* a juca golf.

gondola *s* gondolă *f*.

gone *vi* * **go**.

gong *s* gong *n*.

gonorrhea *s med* gonoree *f*, blenoragie *f*.

good *adj* (*fine*) bun; (*strong*) solid; (*sound*) sănătos; (*decent*) cumsecade; (*nice*) frumos; corect; (*attractive*) chipeş; (*kind*) amabil; (*pleasant*) agreabil; (*proper*) potrivit; (*true*) veritabil; (*valid*) valabil; (*clever*) capabil; (*skillful*) priceput; (*able*) abil; (*obedient*) ascultător; (*reliable*) propice; pios; (*ample*) amplu || *adv* tare, destul, foarte; bine, cu adevărat || *s* bine *n*; serviciu *n*; folos *n*; fericire *f*, bunăstare *f* • ~**bye** *in-terj* la revedere!, bun rămas!, drum bun! || *s* rămas *n* bun • ~**looking** *adj* (*person*) frumos • ~**natured** *adj* (*person*) blând (din fire), bonom; prietenos, amabil; (*quarrel, etc*) simplu, naiv.

goodie, goody *s coll* (*sweet*) bomboană *f*; *pl* zaharicale *f pl* cofeturi *f pl*; (*person*) bun *m* || *interj* grozav!, bravo!.

goodness *s* bunătate *f*; valoare *f*, calitate *f* bună; puritate *f*, virtute *f*; evlavie *f* || *excl* (**my**) ~ ! Doamne Dumnezeule!.

goods *s pl* mărfuri *f pl*.

goodwill *s* bunăvoinţă *f*.

goof *s coll* (*fool*) neghiob *m*; (*blunder*) gafă *f* || *vt* a face o gafă.

goon *s* (*thug*) bătăuş *m*; spărgător *m* de grevă.

goose *s* (*pl* **geese**) gâscă *f*; friptură *f* de gâscă; gogoman *m*, gâsculiţă *f* • ~**flesh** *fig* piele de găină

gooseberry *s bot* agrişă *f*.

gopher *s zool* gofer *m*; popândău *m*.

gore *vt* a lua în coarne; a străpunge || *s* sânge *n* închegat/ coagulat.

gorge *s* trecătoare *f*, defileu *n*.

gorgeous *adj* minunat, splendid; abundent, luxuriant.

gorilla *s zool* gorilă *f*.

gorse *s bot* grozamă *f*.

gory *adj* sângeros.

gospel *s* (*doctrine*) învățătură *f*; **Gospel** *s* Evanghelie *f*.

gossip *vi* a pălăvrăgi; a bârfi || *s* taifas *n*; bârfă *f*; flecar *m*; bârfitor *m*; cronică *f* mondenă (în ziare).

got *vt* * **get.**

Gothic *adj* gotic.

goulash *s cul* gulaș *n*.

gourd *s bot* tigvă *f*, tâlv *n*.

gourmet *s* gurmet *m*; gastronomie *f*; (*cook*) expert *m* în gastronomie.

gout *s med* gută *f*.

govern *vt* a guverna; a conduce; a stăpâni || *vi* a fi la putere • **~ment** *s* guvern *n*; stat *n*; guvernare *f*; control *n* || *adj* guvernamental; oficial.

gown *s* rochie *f*; togă *f*, robă *f*, mantie *f*, pelerină *f* || *vt/vi* a (se) îmbrăca în robă.

grab *vt* a înhăța; a șterpeli || *s* înhățare *f*; lăcomie *f*; acaparare *f*.

grace *s* grație *f*, farmec *n*; eleganță *f*; *pl* mofturi *n pl*, aere *n pl*; favoare *f*; politețe *f*; iertare *f*; amânare *f*, păsuire *f*; dispensă *f* de studii || *vt* a împodobi; a onora; ~ **period** *s* perioadă *f* de grație,; răgaz *n* • **~ful** *adj* grațios, elegant.

gracious *adj* (*polite*) amabil; (*kind*) binevoitor; (*merciful*) milostiv; mieros || *excl* (**Good**) ~! Doamne Sfinte!.

gradation *s* gradare *f*; stadiu *n*.

grade *s* rang *n*; grad *n*; clasă *f*; notă *f*; categorie *f*; fel *n*; înclinație *f*; ascensiune *f* || *vt* a grada; a clasa.

gradient *s* pantă *f*.

gradual *adj* treptat, progresiv.

graduate *s* titrat *m*, licențiat *m*, diplomat *m* universitar; absolvent *m* || *vi* a-și lua diploma; a grada; a doza; a conferi o diplomă.

graduation *s* gradare *f*; gradație *f*; dozare *f*; decorare *f*; absolvire *f*; (~ *ceremony*) decernare *f* a diplomelor.

graffiti *s pl* graffiti *n pl*.

graft *s* (*plant*) altoi *n*; *med* grefă *f*; *coll* corupție *f* || *vt* (*plant*) a altoi; (*skin*) a grefa.

grain *s* grăunte *m*, bob *n*; cereale *f pl*, grâne *f pl*; (*wood*) fibră *f*, nervură *f*; (*material*) grăunte *m*; (*marble, etc*) nervură *f*; dram *n*; fire *f* || *vt* a granula, a măcina.

gram *s* gram *n*.

grammar *s* gramatică *f*.

grammatical *adj* gramatical.

gramophone *s obs* gramofon *n*, patefon *n*.

granary *s also fig* grânar *n*, hambar *n*.

grand *adj* mare, important; grandios; splendid; nobil; generos; principal; total; încrezut || *s fin* bancnotă *f* de o mie de dolari.

grandchild *s* (*boy*) nepot *m*; (*girl*) nepoată *f*.

granddad *s coll* bunic(uț) *m*.

granddaughter *s* nepoată *f* de bunică.

grandfather *s* bunic *m*, tată *m* mare.

grandma *s coll* bunicuță *f*.

grandmother *s* bunică *f*.

grandparent *s* bunic *m*/ bunică *f* • **~s** bunici *m pl*.

grand piano *s mus* pian *n* cu coadă.

grandson *s* nepot *m* de bunic.

grand slam *s sp* mare șlem *n*.

grandstand *s* tribună *f*.

grand total *s* sumă *f* totală, total *n* general.

grange *s* (*farm*) fermă *f*; *obs* (*granary*) hambar *n*.

granite *s* granit *n*.

grant *vt* a acorda; a aloca; a ceda; a dona; a permite; a admite; a aproba; a garanta || *s* alocație *f*; bursă *f*; acordare *f*; aprobare *f*; donație *f*; permisiune *f*.

granular *adj* granular, grunjos.

granulate *vt* a granula; a fărâmița • **~d sugar** *s* zahăr *n* tos.

granule *s* granulă *f*; grăunte *m*, fir *n*, bob *n*.

grape *s* bob *n* de strugure; *pl* struguri *m pl*; viță *f* de vie.

grapefruit *s* pom *m* care produce grepfrut; grep *n*.

graph *s* grafic *n*, diagramă *f*; șapirograf *n* || *vt* a multiplica.

graphology *s* grafologie *f*.

grapple *vt* (~ *with person, animal*) a lupta cu; (~ *with problems*) a se zbate, a se lupta cu.

grasp *vt* a apuca; a smulge; a îmbrățișa; a pricepe || *s* înhățare *f*, înșfăcare *f*; pricepere *f*; dominație *f*; mâner *n*.

grass *s* iarbă *f*; pășune *f*, pășunat *n*; buruiană *f*; (*drug*) marijuana *f* || *vt* a paște; a semăna cu iarbă; a trânti || *vi* a se acoperi cu iarbă.

grasshopper *s* lăcustă *f*.

grassroots *s pl fig* bază *f* || *adj* din popor, de la bază.

grate¹ *s* grilă *f*, grilaj *n*; (*stove*) grătar *n*.

grate² *vt* a râcâi; a zgâria; a răzui || *vi* a scârțâi; a scrâșni.

grateful *adj* recunoscător; binevenit; odihnitor; reconfortant.

gratification *s* (*state, action*) satisfacție *f*, plăcere *f*.

gratify *vt* (*person*) a satisface, a mulțumi; a face pe plac; a desfăta; a răsplăti; (*desire*) a satisface, a potoli.

grating *adj* strident; (*voice*) strident, aspru || *s* grătar *n*.

gratis *adj* gratis.

gratitude *s* recunoștință *f*, mulțumire *f*.

gratuitous *adj* gratuit.

gratuity *s* gratificație *f*, primă *f*; bacșiș *n*.

grave¹ *adj* grav; serios; solemn; urgent; sumbru; modest.

grave² *s* mormânt *n* • **~stone** *s* piatră *f*/lespede *f* de mormânt.

gravel *s* pietriș *n*.

gravitate *vi* a gravita.

gravitation *s* gravitație *f*.

gravity *s* (*force*) gravitație *f*, greutate *f*; (*seriousness*) gravitate *f*.

gravy *s* suc *n* de carne; sos *n* de friptură.

graze¹ *vt* (*scrape*) a zgâria, a jupui; a atinge ușor || *s* julitură *f*, zgârietură *f*.

graze² *vi* (*animal*) a pășuna, a paște; (*farmer*) a duce la păscut.

grease *s* grăsime *f*; untură *f*; lubrifiant *m* || *vt* a unge; a gresa; a lubrifia.

great *adj* mare, măreț, grandios; considerabil; intens; uriaș; esențial; ilustru; excelent; iscusit; grozav; nobil; arogant; îndelungat || *s* **the** ~ cei mari; bogații *m pl*; total *n*, întreg *n* || *interj* grozav!, strașnic!.

Greece *s* Grecia *f*; **Greek** || *s*/*adj* grec; (*language*) greaca *f*.

greed *s* (*for food*) lăcomie *f*; (*for money, power*) aviditate *f* • **~y** *adj* lacom, avid; ahtiat; avar, hrăpăreț.

green *adj* verde; crud, necopt; pământiu; proaspăt; nepriceput; nevinovat; viguros; neînvățat || *s*

(culoare) verde *f*; verdeață *f*; pajiște *f*; vigoare *f* || *vt* a
înverzi; a vopsi verde; ~ **card** *s* carte *f* de sejur.
greenhouse *s* seră *f*; ~ **effect** *s* efect *n* de seră.
Greenland *s* Groenlanda *f*.
greet *vt* a saluta; a da onorul; a întâmpina • ~**ing** *s*
salut *n*, salutare *f*; complimente *n pl*; urări *f pl*;
întâmpinare *f*.
gregarious *adj* gregar; de turmă; sociabil.
grenade *s* grenadă *f*; **hand** ~ grenadă *f* de mână.
grenadier *s* grenadier *m*.
grew *vi* * **grow**.
grey *adj* cenușiu, gri; sur; cărunt; palid; mohorât;
monoton || *s* gri *n*; bursuc *m* || *vt* a vopsi în gri; a
încărunți.
greyhound *s zool* ogar *m*.
grid *s* grătar *n*; *tech* grilă *f*; rețea *f*; caroiaj *n*.
grief *s* supărare *f*, durere *f*; necaz *n*; plângere *f*.
grievance *s* plângere *f*, doleanță *f*.
grieve *vt* (*upset*) a mâhni, a întrista || *vi* (**for**) a fi în
doliu, a plânge (pe) cineva/ceva.
grievous *adj* (*causing pain*) dureros, supărător; *lit*
(*grave*) grav, serios; (*loss*) greu; cumplit; (*pain*)
cumplit, chinuitor, crunt.
grill *s* grătar *n*; rotiserie *f*; grilaj *n*; grilă *f* || *vt* a frige
la/pe grătar; a supune unui interogatoriu sever; a
anula || *vi* (*sun*) a arde, a frige; a face plajă; ~ **room** *s*
rotiserie *f*, (restaurant cu) grătar *n* • ~**e** *s* grilă *f*.
grim *adj* (*face*) sever; (*decision*) inflexibil; (*truth*, *news*)
sinistru; (*room*, *wall*) lugubru; (*day*) posomorât, trist.
grimace *s* grimasă *f* || *vi* a se strâmba, a se schimonosi.
grimalkin *s* (*feline*) pisică *f* bătrână; zgripțuroaică *f*,
cotoroanță *f*.
grime *s* jeg *n*, murdărie *f*.
grimy *adj* murdar, jegos.
grin *s* rânjet *n*; zâmbet *n* || *vi* a rânji; a zâmbi; a zâmbi/
râde silit.
grind, ground, ground *vt* a măcina; a mărunți; a
mesteca; a poliza; a șlefui; a scrâșni; a îndopa; a
asupri || *vi* a se măcina; a se freca; a se șlefui; a
scârțâi; a învăța pe rupte || *s* măcinare *f*; scârțâit *n*;
corvoadă *f*; toceală *f*.
grip *s* strânsoare *f*; înhățare *f*; înțelegere *f*; mâner *n*;
atracție *f* || *vt* a apuca/ține strâns; a strânge; a prinde;
a cuprinde.
gripe *s* înșfăcare *f*; strânsoare *f*; *pl med* colici *n pl*,
crampe *f pl*; *pl naut* parâme *f pl*, odgoane *n pl*; *coll*
smiorcăială *f*, plângere *f* || *vi* a apuca, a înhăța; *fig* a
înțelege, a prinde; *naut* a lega de țărm; *coll* ~ **about**
smth a bombăni despre ceva.
grisly *adj* înfiorător, sinistru; macabru; sever, aspru.
gristle *s* zgârci *n*, cartilaj *n*.
grit *s* (*gravel*) pietriș *n*, prundiș *n*; (*dust*) praf *n*; (*sand*)
nisip *n*; (*for fowl*) crupe *f pl*; *coll* (*courage*) îndrăz-
neală *f*; *fig* tărie *f* de caracter, hotărâre *f*; energie *f* || *vi*
a scârțâi, a scrâșni (ca nisipul).
grizzly *adj* (*greyish*) sur, cărunt || *s zool* grizli *m*, urs *m*
cenușiu.
groan *s* (*painful cry*) geamăt *n*; murmur *n* (de dezapro-
bare) || *vi* a geme; *fig* a scârțâi, a geme.
grocer *s* băcan *m* • ~**y** *s* băcănie *f*; *pl* coloniale *f pl*,
articole *n pl* de băcănie.
groggy *adj* (*weak*) slăbit; (*unsteady*) amețit.
groin *s anat* regiune *f* inghinală; *archit* boltă *f*
încrucișată.
groom *s* (*horse*) rândaș *m*, grăjdar *m*; (*bridegroom*)

mire *m* || *vt* (*comb*) a țesăla; *fig* (*prepare*) (**for**) a
pregăti pe cineva (pentru ceva).
groove *s* (*in metal*, *wood*) fisură *f*, scobitură *f*; (*for
pulley*) canelură *f*; (*in a disk*) șanț *n*; *coll* (*rut*) rutină
f; monotonie *f*.
groovy *adj* (*cool*) grozav; (*trendy*) la modă || *interj*
super!.
grope *vi* (**for/after**) a căuta pe bâjbâite; a orbecăi.
gross *adj* grosolan, vulgar; carnal; obscen; măcinat mare;
com global, brut; (*behavior*) șocant; (*negligence*)
vinovat; obez, enorm || *s* gros *n*, toptan *n*.
grotesque *adj* grotesc || *s* **the** ~ grotescul *n*.
grotto *s* grotă *f*.
grouch *vi* a se văicări || *s* văicăreală *f*; văicăreț *m*.
ground¹ *vt* * **grind**.
ground² *s* pământ *n*, sol *n*, teren *n*; poligon *n*; parc *n* de
vânătoare; grădină *f*; fond *n*; temelie *f*; motiv *n* || *vt* a
întemeia; a motiva; a depune; a trânti; a pune temelia;
a grundui || *vi* a ateriza; a eșua; a se împotmoli; ~
crew *s* personal *n* la sol.
grounding *s* (**in**) cunoștințe *f pl* de bază (despre).
groundless *adj* neîntemeiat.
groundswell *s* hulă *f*.
groundwork *s* temelie *f*, fundație *f*; *fig* fundament *n*,
bază *f*.
group *s* grup *n*; grupă *f*; grupare *f*; formație *f* || *vt* a
grupa; a clasifica, a asorta.
grouse¹ *s orn* cocoș *m* de munte.
grouse² *vi* a bombăni, a mormăi, a protesta.
grove *s* crâng *n*, pădurice *f*, dumbravă *f*.
grow, grow, grown *vi* a crește; a se dezvolta; a progresa;
a proveni din; a deveni || *vi* a crește, a produce; a lăsa
să-i crească; ~ **old** *vt* a îmbătrâni; ~ **cold** *vt* a se face
frig; ~ **angry** *vt* a se mânia • ~**er** *s* cultivator *m*;
crescător *m* de animale • ~**ing** *s* creștere *f*.
growl *vi* (*animal*) a mârâi, a mormăi; (*person*) a băigui;
(*thunder*) a tuna, a bubui || *s* mârâit *n*; bâiguială *f*;
bubuit *n* (de tunet).
grown *vi* * **grow**.
grown-up *adj* adult, mare || *s* adult *m*, om *m* mare.
growth *s* creștere *f*; dezvoltare *f*, sporire *f*; ~ **hormone**
hormon de creștere; ~ **rate** rată de dezvoltare.
grub *s* (*insect*) larvă *f*; *coll* mâncare *f*.
grubby *adj* murdar, soios.
grudge *s* pică *f*, ranchiună *f*; răutate *f* || *vi* a se împotrivi,
a se opune; a fi invidios || *vt* a da/ceda ceva cu greu;
a invidia.
gruel *s* terci *n*, fiertură *f* de cereale || *vt* a pedepsi aspru.
grueling *adj* epuizant, extenuant.
gruesome *adj* de groază, înspăimântător.
gruff *adj* (*hoarse*) gros; aspru, morocănos.
grumble *vi* a bombăni, a protesta; a chiorăi || *vt* a
mormăi, a murmura || *s* a bombăneală *f*, mormăit *n*;
bubuit *n* de tunet.
grumpy *adj coll* încruntat.
grunge *s* (*dirt*) murdărie *f*.
grunt *vi* a mormăi || *s* bombănit *n*, mormăit *n*.
guarantee *vt* a garanta; a asigura || *vi* a depune garanție
|| *s* garanție *f*; cauțiune *f*; amanet *n*; garant *m*.
guarantor *s* garant *m*.
guard *s* gardă *f*; pază *f*; vigilență *f*; reținere *f*; rezervă *f*;
neîncredere *f*; corp *n* de gardă; șef *m* de tren || *vt* a
păzi; a-și măsura (cuvintele); a însoți || *vi* a se feri; a
fi prudent; a face de gardă.

guerilla *s* partizan *m* din rezistență; **urban** ~ *s* gherilă *f* urbană.

guess *vt* a ghici; a presupune; a crede ‖ *vi* a face presupuneri ‖ *s* bănuială *f*, presupunere *f*; apreciere *f* • ~**work** *s* presupuneri *f pl*, ipoteze *f pl*.

guest *s* oaspete *m*, invitat *m*; chiriaș *m*; parazit *m*.

guffaw *s* (hohot de) râs *n* ‖ *vi* a râde în hohote, a hohoti de râs.

guidance *s* îndrumare *f*; conducere *f*.

guide *s* călăuză *f*, ghid *m*; îndreptar *n*; consilier *m*; dispozitiv *n* de ghidare ‖ *vt* a îndruma; a dirija, a conduce.

guild *s* corporație *f*, breaslă *f*; asociație *f*.

guile *s* (*trickery*) înșelăciune *f*, înșelătorie *f*; (*cunning*) viclenie *f*, șiretenie *f*.

guillotine *s* (*for beheading*) ghilotină *f*; (*shredder*) mașină *f* de tăiat hârtia ‖ *vt* a ghilotina.

guilt *s* vină *f*, culpă *f*; vinovăție *f*, culpabilitate *f* • ~**y** *adj* vinovat, culpabil.

Guinea *s* Guineea *f*.

Guinea pig *s* *zool* cobai *m*; *fig* cobai *m*, animal *n* de experiență.

guise *s* (*appearance*) aparență *f*, înfățișare *f*; aspect *n* înșelător, mască *f*; (*costume*) veșminte *n pl*, vestimentație *f*.

guitar *s* *mus* chitară *f*, ghitară *f*.

gulf *s* *geog* golf *n*; *fig* abis *n*; volbură *f*, vârtej *n*.

gull *s* *orn* pescăruș *m*.

gullet *s* *anat* esofag *n*.

gullibility *s* credulitate *f*.

gullible *adj* credul.

gully *s* (*valley*) albie *f* de torent; (*ditch*) rigolă *f*.

gulp *s* (*drink*) sorbitură *f*; (*food*) înghițitură *f* lacomă ‖ *vt* a înghiți ‖ *vi* a i se pune un nod în gât; ~ **down** *vi* a înghiți.

gum[1] *s* gumă *f*; cauciuc *m*; gumă *f* de mestecat, chewing-gum *n*; clei *n* de arbore; urdoare *f* ‖ *vt* a lipi; a lua peste picior ‖ *vi* a se lipi; a secreta rășină.

gum[2] *s* *anat* gingie *f*.

gun *s* armă *f* de foc; pistol *n*; revolver *n*; tun *n*; trăgător *m*; vânător *m*; hoț *m* ‖ *vt* a vâna, a împușca; a bombarda cu artileria • ~**man** *s* persoană *f* înarmată • ~**powder** *s* praf *n* de pușcă • ~**shot** *s* foc *n* de armă.

gurgle *vi* a gâlgâi, a bolborosi; (*water*) a clipoci; (*baby*) a gânguri ‖ *s* gâlgâit *n*, bolborosit *n*; clipocit *n*.

gush *vi* a țâșni, a izbucni; a-și revărsa sentimentele; a împroșca cu ‖ *s* șuvoi *n*, torent *n*, jet *n*; revărsare *f* (a sentimentelor).

gusset *s* (*dress*, *etc*) clin *n*.

gust *s* (*of wind*) rafală f; (*of smoke*) pală *f*; (*of laughter*) izbucnire *f*.

gusto *s* elan *n*, antren *n*; poftă *f*.

gut *s* *sl anat* intestin *n*, stomac *n*; poftă *f* (de mâncare); coardă *f* (de vioară); *pl coll* intestine *n pl*; *pl fig* tupeu *n*, curaj *n*; defileu *n* ‖ *vt* a curăța; (*take out*) a goli; (*destroy*) a devasta; a jefui.

gutter *s* (*roof*) jgheab *n*; (*ditch*) rigolă *f*.

guy[1] *s* *coll* tip *m*, individ *m*, băiat *m*; glumă *f*; sperietoare *f*.

guyline *s* (*rope*) coardă *f* de cort.

guzzle *vt coll* (~ *food*) a înfuleca; (~ *a drink*) a bea cu nesaț.

gym(nasium) *s* sală *f* de gimnastică/sporturi; liceu *n*; gimnaziu *n*.

gymnast *s* gymnast *m* • ~**ics** *s pl* gimnastică *f*.

gynecologist *s* ginecolog *m*.

gynecology *s* ginecologie *f*.

gyp *vt* a escroca, a trage pe sfoară ‖ *s* escroc *m*, șarlatan *m*.

gypsum *s* g(h)ips *n*, ipsos *n*.

gypsy *s* țigan *m*, rom *m*; nomad *m*; vagabond *m*; (limba) țigănească ‖ *adj* țigan; țigănesc; câmpenesc ‖ *vi* a vagabonda.

gyrate *vi* a se roti, a se învârti.

gyration *s* învârtire *f*, rotire *f*.

gyroscope *s* giroscop *n*.

H

H, h *s* (litera) H, h.

haberdashery *s* mercerie *f*.

habit *s* obicei *n*; obișnuință *f*; comportare *f*; mentalitate *f*; caracteristică *f*; costum *n* de călărie ‖ *vt* a îmbrăca.

habitable *adj* locuibil.

habitat *s* *bio* habitat *n*, areal *n*; *fig* loc *n*, reședință *f*.

habitual *adj* obișnuit.

hack[1] *s* icht egrefin *m*, morun *m*.

hack[2] *s* (*horse*) cal *m* de povară/ham; mârțoagă *f*, gloabă *f*; *fig* salahor *m*, angajat *m*; *fig* salahor/hamal *m* literar, scrib *m*.

hackneyed *adj* uzat, tocit; banalizat; răsuflat.

had *v aux* * **have**.

haddock *s* *icht* egrefin *m*, morun *m*.

haft *s* (*of knife*, *sword*) mâner *n*.

hag *s* *coll* baborniță *f*; cață *f*, scorpie *f*.

haggard *adj* (*face*) descompus, tras; (*person*) abătut, descurajat.

haggle *vi* (**over/about**) a negocia, a se tocmi.

Hague *s* **The** ~ Haga.

hail[1] *s* grindină *f*; *fig* grindină *f*, ploaie *f* ‖ *vi* a bate piatră/grindină; *fig* a cădea/se abate ca piatra/grindina.

hail[2] *vt* a aclama, a saluta; (~ *a taxi*) a chema; *naut* a semnaliza ‖ *vi* a se saluta; a striga, a exclama.

hair *s* păr *m*; blană *f*; puf *n* ‖ *vt* a depila.

hairbrush *s* perie *f* de păr.

haircut *s* tunsoare *f*, tuns *n*.

hairdo *s* coafură *f*, pieptănătură *f*.

hairdresser *s* coafor *m*; coafeză *f*; frizer *m*.

hair-dryer *s* uscător *n* de păr, foehn *n*; cască *f*.

hairnet *s* fileu *n* pentru păr, plasă *f* pentru păr.

hair-piece *s* perucă *f*.

hairpin *s* ac *n* de păr, agrafă *f* de păr.

hair-raising *adj* care face să ți se ridice părul măciucă; (*voyage*) înspăimântător.

hairspray *s* fixativ *n* pentru păr.

hairstyle *s* coafură *f*.

hairy *adj* din/de păr; păros; hirsut.

Haiti *s* Haiti *f*.

hake *s* *icht* merlan *m*.

hale *adj* sănătos; viguros; ~ **and hearty** *adj* bine sănătos, sănătos și voios.

half *s* jumătate *f*; doime *f*; semestru *n*; repriză *f* ‖ *adj* parțial, incomplet ‖ *adv* pe din două, pe jumătate; parțial, incomplet; oarecum.

half-and-half *adv* jumătate-jumătate, pe din două ‖ *adj* incomplet, parțial, insuficient; în părți egale, jumătate-jumătate.

half-baked *adj coll (food)* pe jumătate crud, necopt; făcut numai pe jumătate; *fig* neisprăvit, necopt.
half-breed *s (person) pej* metis *m,* corcitură *f.*
half-brother *s* frate *m* vitreg.
half-hearted *adj* fără tragere de inimă, lipsit de entuziasm; șovăielnic, șovăitor.
half-hour *s* jumătate *f* de oră.
half-mast *s* bernă *f; (flag)* **at** ~ în bernă.
half moon *s* semilună *f.*
half-open *adj* întredeschis.
half-price *s* jumătate *f* de preț.
half-sister *s* soră *f* vitregă.
half-time *s* jumătate *f* de normă; *sp* pauză *f* între reprize.
halfway *adj* situat la jumătatea drumului; parțial, incomplet ‖ *adv* la jumătatea drumului.
half-wit *s* debil *m* mintal; om *m* redus (la minte).
halibut *s icht* cambulă *f.*
hall *s* coridor *n,* culoar *n;* hol *n;* auditoriu *n;* salon *n;* sală *f* de judecată; edificiu *n* public; cămin *n* studențesc.
hallmark *s (trait)* caracteristică *f,* emblemă *f; (metal)* marcaj *n; fig* pecete *f,* amprentă *f.*
hallowed *adj* sfințit, sfânt, sacru; *fig* sfânt, sacru; venerat, adorat.
Halloween *s* Halloween *n* (sărbătoarea *f* vrăjitoarelor și a fantomelor).
hallucination *s* halucinație *f.*
hallway *s* vestibul *n.*
halo *s* aureolă *f,* nimb *n; astron* halo *n,* cerc *n* luminos.
halt *vt* a se opri (din mers); a înceta să se miște; a face o haltă/un popas; *mil* a opri; a ordona (unei trupe) să facă o haltă ‖ *s* haltă *f,* oprire *f,* popas *n.*
halter *s* ștreang *n;* funie (pentru spânzurătoare); *fig* (moarte prin) spânzurătoare *f;* căpăstru *n;* bluză *f* care lasă spatele gol • **~neck** *adj* cu spatele gol.
halve *vt* a reduce la jumătate, a înjumătăți; *(divide)* a împărți în două.
ham *s cul* șuncă *f,* jambon *n;* cabotin *m;* cabotinism *n; (radio)* radioamator *m;* ageamiu *m* ‖ *vt* a juca prost ‖ *vi* a șarja.
hamburger *s* hamburger *m;* chiftea *f;* sandviș *n* cu tocătură.
hamlet *s* cătun *n.*
hammer *s* ciocan *n* ‖ *vt* a ciocăni; a distruge; a bombarda cu artileria; a dojeni ‖ *vi* a ciocăni; a bocăni.
hammock *s* hamac *n.*
hamper¹ *vt* a stingheri; a limita, a restrânge.
hamper² *s* coș *n* de rufe; *(for food)* coș *n* de nuiele.
hamster *s zool* hamster *m,* hârciog *m.*
hand *s* mână *f;* braț *n;* dibăcie *f;* antrenament *n;* stil *n,* amprentă *f;* scriere *f;* sursă *f;* autoritate *f;* muncitor *m;* ajutor *n;* individ *m;* beneficiu *n* ‖ *vt* a înmâna; a expedia; a conduce; a urca; a manipula.
handbag *s* sac *m* de voiaj; trusă *f,* poșetă *f.*
handbook *s* manual *n; (for tourist)* ghid *n.*
handbrake *s* frână *f* de mână.
handcuff *vt* a pune cătușe (la mâini), a încătușa ‖ *s pl* cătușe *f pl.*
handicap *s* handicap *n;* dezavantaj *n;* obstacol *n* ‖ *vt* a handicapa; a dezavantaja; a stânjeni.
handicraft *s* meșteșug *n,* meserie *f;* artizanat *n,* artă *f* meșteșugărească.
handily *adv (easily)* cu ușurință; *(conveniently)* comod.
handiwork *s* lucru *n,* muncă *f* manuală.
handkerchief *s* batistă *f.*
handle *s* mâner *n; (of a pan, etc)* coadă *f; (of a jug)*

toartă *f;* ocazie *f* ‖ *vt* a mânui; a pipăi; *(be in charge)* a se ocupa de; a conduce; *(~ a problem)* a trata, a rezolva; *(~ an issue)* a discuta; *(~ a difficulty)* a face față.
handmade *adj* lucrat de mână.
hand-out *s (gift)* donație *f; (brochure)* prospect *n.*
hand-pick *vt* a selecționa, a alege cu grijă • **~ed** *adj* ales/sortat/selecționat cu mâna/cu grijă; *fig coll* ales pe sprânceană.
handrail *s* rampă *f.*
handshake *s* strângere *f* de mână.
handsome *adj* frumos, chipeș; drăguț, elegant; generos; însemnat, considerabil.
handstand *s* echilibru *n* (pe mâini).
handwriting *s* scriere *f* de mână.
handy *adj* comod; la îndemână; disponibil; potrivit; abil, priceput.
hang, hung, hung *vt* a atârna; a prinde; a expune ‖ *vi* a atârna; a spânzura; a oscila; a fi în suspensie; a depinde de; a persista • ~ **about/around** *vi* a se învârti fără rost • ~ **on** *vi* (to) a se agăța/a se crampona (de); *coll* a aștepta; *(persevere)* a rezista în condiții dificile • ~ **out** *vi* a pierde timpul • ~ **up** *vt* a agăța ‖ *vi* a pune receptorul în furcă.
hangar *s* hangar *n;* adăpost *n;* șopron *n.*
hanger *s* cuier *n,* umeraș *n.*
hangover *s* mahmureală *f;* vestigii *n pl;* efecte *n pl* târzii.
hanker *vi* **(after/for)** a râvni, a dori mult.
hankie *s coll* batistă *f.*
hansom *s* birjă *f.*
hap *s coll* șansă *f;* întâmplare *f* • **~less** *adj* nefericit.
haphazard *adj* întâmplător, ocazional • **~ly** *adv* întâmplător, din întâmplare.
happen *vi* a se întâmpla; a surveni; a se petrece; a se întâmpla să fie.
happily *adv* fericit; din fericire; **they lived** ~ au trăit fericiți.
happiness *s* fericire *f,* satisfacție *f;* noroc *n;* veselie *f.*
happy *adj* fericit; vesel; bucuros; norocos; grozav.
harangue *s* discurs *m* moralizator; perorație *f* ‖ *vt* a ține un discurs moralizator.
harass *vt* a hărțui, a chinui, a necăji.
harbinger *s* vestitor *m;* prevestitor *m;* precursor *m.*
harbor *s* port *n;* adăpost *n,* refugiu *n* ‖ *vt* a adăposti; a proteja; a conține; a nutri ‖ *vi* a ancora; a se adăposti; a acorda azil.
hard *adj* tare, ferm; dur; solid; rezistent; puternic; dificil; aspru; rău; obositor; silitor; supărător; zgârcit ‖ *adv* greu; sever; cumplit; rău; necruțător; ~ **cash** *s* numerar *n;* ~ **copy** *s comp* copie *f* de hârtie; ~ **disk** *s comp* hard disc *n;* ~ **feelings** *s pl* resentimente *n pl;* ~ **labor** *s* muncă *f* silnică; ~ **luck** *s* ghinion *n* • **~line** *adj* dur.
hardball *s (game)* baseball *n; (ball)* minge *f* de baseball.
hard-hearted *adj* rău, afurisit.
hardiness *s (of person)* robustețe *f, (of plant)* rezistență *f.*
hardly *adv* abia (dacă, de); prea puțin; puțin probabil; tocmai, abia; aspru.
hardship *s* greutăți *f pl* materiale; privațiuni *f pl.*
hardware *s* articole *npl* de metal, feronerie *f; comp* hardware *n; mil* armament *n; coll (guns)* arme *f pl.*
hardy *adj (person, animal)* viguros, robust; *(plant)* rezistent, viguros.
hare *s* iepure *m* de câmp ‖ *vi* a alerga iute/ca un iepure.

haricot *s* fasole *f* uscată.

harlequin *s* arlechin *m.*

harlot *s* femeie *f* uşoară.

harm *s* vătămare *f*; rău *n*; avarie *f*; dăunare *f* || *vt* a dăuna; a face rău; a avaria • **~ful** *adj* nociv, dăunător, rău; periculos • **~less** *adj* inofensiv; inocent; blând.

harmonic *adj mus* armonic; consonant; armonios; *math* armonic.

harmonica *s mus* armonică *f*; muzicuţă *f.*

harmonious *adj* armonios; omogen, uniform; muzical, melodios.

harmonize *vt* a armoniza || *vi* a se armoniza, a fi concordant/armonios.

harmony *s* armonie *f.*

harness *s* (*horse, child*) ham *n* || *vt* (~ *a horse*) a înhăma; (~ *resources, etc*) a exploata.

harp *s* harpă *f* || *vi* a cânta la harpă; **to ~ on** *vi* a insista, a stărui (asupra).

harpoon *s* harpon *n* || *vt* a vâna cu harponul.

harpsichord *s mus* clavecin *n.*

harridan *s pej* baborniţă *f.*

harrowing *adj* (*experience*) sfâşietor; (*movie, story*) deprimant.

harsh *adj* aspru; sever; nemilos; strident; dezagreabil.

harvest *s* seceriş *n*; recoltare *f*, cules *n*; recoltă *f*; rezultate *n pl*; răsplată *f* || *vt* a recolta; a culege.

hasp *s* (*for door*) încuietoare *f*, zăvor *n*; cremonă *f* || *vt* a încuia, a zăvorî.

hassle *s coll* deranjare *f*, sâcâire *f*, supărare *f* || *vt* a sâcâi, a bate la cap.

haste *s* grabă *f*; precipitare *f* || *vi* a se grăbi (să).

hasty *adj* grăbit; pripit; irascibil; nesăbuit.

hat *s* pălărie *f*; rang *n*; individ *m* || *vt* a pune pălăria pe cap; a acoperi cu pălăria.

hatch[1] *vt* (~ *eggs*) a cloci; *fig* (*plan*) a pune la cale, a urzi, a concepe || *vi* (*hen ~es eggs*) a cloci; (*chicken ~es eggs~ chicks*) a ieşi din găoace.

hatch[2] *s* (*opening*) deschizătură *f* în peretele dintre bucătărie şi sufragerie; *naut* tambuchi *n*, bocaport *n*; trapă *f*; zăgaz *n.*

hatchet *s* toporişcă *f.*

hate *vt* a urî; a duşmăni || *s* ură *f*, silă *f*; oroare *f*; persoană *f* antipatică • **~ful** *adj* odios.

hatred *s* ură *f*, silă *f*; oroare *f*; duşmănie *f*; pică *f.*

haughty *adj* semeţ; mândru; arogant; demn.

haul *vt* (*pull*) a trage; (*tow*) a remorca; a transporta • *s* (*pull*) tragere *f*, târâre *f*; (*distance*) parcurs *n*; (~ *in a catch*: *of fishermen*) pradă *f*, *fig* pradă *f*, câştig *n*, profit *n.*

haunch *s anat* şold *n*; coapsă *f*; *cul* pulpă *f* din spate.

haunt *vt* a frecventa; a bântui; a obseda; a chinui || *vi* a rămâne || *s* loc *n* frecventat; vizuină *f*; speluncă *f* de hoţi.

hauteur *s* trufie *f.*

have, had, had *v aux* (*in perfect tenses*) **to ~ finished** a fi terminat; **to ~ left** a fi plecat; **to ~ been/had** a fi fost/avut; **I had known her for years** o cunoşteam de mulţi ani; **I ~ been thinking** mă tot gândesc; (*in tag questions*) **you've read this book, haven't you?** ai citit cartea aceasta, nu-i aşa? || *v mod* (*to show obligation, necessity*) a trebui; a necesita, a cere; **do you ~ to go?, ~ you got to go?** chiar trebuie să plecaţi? || *vt* (*own*) a avea, a poseda; a dispune de; (*show*) a dovedi; (*give birth*) a da naştere; (*be sick*) a avea/suferi de (o boală); (*think*) a concepe; (*keep*) a reţine;

(*allow*) a permite; (*experience*) a suporta; a trece prin; (*receive*) a căpăta; (*consume*) a mânca/bea; (*carry out*) a îndeplini; (*cause*) a determina; (*invite*) a primi; (*assert*) a susţine, a afirma.

haven *s* port *n.*

haversack *s* raniţă *f*, rucsac *n.*

havoc *s* pagubă *f*, stricăciune *f* • **play ~ with** *vt* a devasta; (~ *health*) a se sminti, a detracta; (~ *plans*) a ruina, a distruge.

hawthorn *s bot* păducel *m*, gherghin *m.*

hawk *s* şoim *m*; *om m* hrăpăreţ || *vt* a vâna cu şoimi; a ataca.

hay *s* fân *n*; răsplată *f* (a muncii); sumă *f* infimă || *vt* a usca; a hrăni, a da fân.

haywire *adj* învălmăşit, încurcat; *fig* tulburat, agitat || *adv* aiurea; **go ~** *vt* a o lua razna, a funcţiona prost.

hazard *s* risc *n*, hazard *n* || *vt* a risca • **~ous** *adj* riscant; temerar; bazat pe noroc.

haze *s* ceaţă *f.*

hazel *s bot* (*tree*) alun *m* (turcesc); (*fruit*) alună *f* (turcească); culoare *f* maronie || *adj* (*eyes*) căprui.

hazy *adj* ceţos; înnorat; voalat; cherchelit.

he *pron* el, dânsul || *s* mascul *m*, bărbat *m.*

head *s* cap *n*; minte *f*; inteligenţă *f*; inventivitate *f*; talent *n*; viaţă *f*; persoană *f*; vârf *n*; şef *m*; extremitate *f* || *vt* a fi în fruntea; a aşeza; a se opune || *vi* a se întoarce cu faţa; a merge (spre) • **~ start** *s* (**on/over**) avantaj *n* a supra.

headache *s* durere *f* de cap, nevralgie *f*; complicaţie *f*, dificultate *f.*

headfirst *adv* cu capul înainte.

headlamp *s* far *n.*

headline *s* (*paper, radio, etc*) titlu *n* important; ştiri *f pl* principale.

headlong *adv* (*fast*) impetuos; în mod nechibzuit; cu capul înainte.

headmaster *s* director *m* (de şcoală).

headmistress *s* directoare *f* (de şcoală).

head-on *adj* (*collision*) frontal, din plin; (*confrontation*) faţă în faţă || *adj* direct.

headphones *s pl* căşti *f pl* audio.

headquarters *s* (*business, etc*) sediu *n*; (*army*) stat *n* major, cartier *n* general.

headrest *s* rezemătoare *f* pentru cap.

headroom *s* loc/spaţiu *n* de trecere.

headscarf *s* batic *n*, basma *f.*

headset *s radio* cască *f.*

headstrong *adj* încăpăţânat, voluntar.

headway *s archit* săgeată *f* a arcului; progres *n*; **make ~** *vt* a face progrese.

heady *adj* ameţitor, exaltant; (*intoxicating*) îmbătător.

heal *vt* a vindeca; a remedia; a reface; a întări || *vi* a se vindeca; a se reface • **~ing** *adj* curativ || *s* vindecare *f.*

health *s* sănătate *f*; ~ **food** *s* alimente *n pl* dietetice; ~ **insurance** *s* asigurare *f* de sănătate; ~ **service** *s* (serviciu de) asigurări *f pl* sociale • **~y** *adj* sănătos; viguros; viabil; sigur; prosper; salutar; considerabil.

heap *s* grămadă *f* || *vt* a îngrămădi • **~s** *s pl coll* (*people, things*) o mulţime *f* de; (*time, money*) foarte mult, enorm.

hear, heard, heard *vt* a auzi; a afla; a asculta; a împlini; a audia || *vi* a auzi, a afla de; a primi veşti; a accepta, a permite; ~ **me out** ascultă-mă până la capăt • **~ing** *s* (*sense*) auz *n*; (*process*) audiere *f* • **~ing aid** *s* aparat *n* auditiv, proteză *f* auditivă.

hearsay *s* zvon *n.*

hearse *s* dric *n*, car *n* mortuar.

heart *s* inimă *f*, cord *n*; piept *n*; simțire *f*; suflet *n*; afecțiune *f*; plăcere *f*; dispoziție *f*; conștiință *f*; părere *f*; sinceritate *f* • ~ **attack** *s* atac *n* de cord • ~ **failure** *s* stop *n* cardiac.

heartache *s* durere *f* de inimă.

heartbeat *s* bătaie *f* de inimă; **in a** ~ într-o clipă, cât a bate din palme.

heart-breaking *adj* sfâșietor, chinuitor, cumplit.

heartbroken *adj* cu inima zdrobită.

heartburn *s* arsuri *f pl* la stomac.

heartfelt *adj* sincer.

hearth *s* vatră *f*; (*fireside*) cămin *n*, șemineu *n*; *fig* (*home*) casă *f*, cămin *n*; patrie *f*.

heartless *adj* fără inimă, nemilos.

heart-throb *s* palpitație *f*.

heart-to-heart *adj* (*talk*) deschis, sincer; intim, de la om la om.

heartwarming *adj* reconfortant.

hearty *adj* entuziast; energic; sincer; abundent.

heat *s* căldură *f*; arșiță *f*; caniculă *f*; ardoare *f*; vigoare *f*; toi *n*; foc *n*; efort *n*; (*sports*) serie *f* || *vt* a înfierbânta; a inflama; a irita; ~ **wave** *s* val *n* de căldură, caniculă *f* • ~**ing** *s* încălzire *f*.

heath *s* *bot* iarbă *f* neagră, erica *f*; bărăgan *n*, landă *f*, câmp *n* necultivat.

heathen *adj/s* păgân *m.*

heather *s* *bot* iarbă *f* neagră, buruiană *f*.

heave *vt* a ridica, a înălța, a trage (cu greu, la deal), a împinge (cu greu, la deal); *naut* a trage, a aduce (într-o poziție) || *vi* a se înălța, a se ridica; (*sea*) a se înălța și a coborî; (*chest*) a gâfâi.

heaven *s* cer *n*; rai *n*, paradis *n*; fericire *f*.

heavy *adj* greu; greoi; încărcat; apăsător; stângaci; închis; sumbru; prost; dificil; puternic; ~ **cream** *s* smântână *f* groasă.

heavyweight *adj* *sp* de categorie grea || *s* categorie *f* grea.

Hebrew *s* (*people*) evreu *m*; (*language*) ebraică *f*.

heckle *vt* a interpela (răuvoitor), a bombarda/chinui cu întrebări || *vi* a sâcâi pe cineva cu întrebări repetate • ~**r** *s* persoană *f* care interpelează/care bombardează (pe orator) cu întrebări.

hectare *s* hectar *n.*

hectic *adj* (*feverish*) febril, cu/de febră, fierbinte; (*meeting, day*) agitat, animat; pasionat, neliniștit; palpitant, emoționant.

hector *vt* a teroriza.

hedge *s* gard *n* viu || *vi* a se eschiva.

hedgehog *s* *zool* arici *m*; *mil* herison *n*, obstacol *n* de sârmă ghimpată.

heed *s* atenție *f* || *vt* a acorda atenție; a ține seama de • ~**less** *adj* (**of**) neatent la, care nu ține seama de (ceva).

heel *s* călcâi *n*; toc *n*; gât *n* (de vioară); colț *n* (de pâine).

hefty *adj* vânjos, robust; viguros, puternic; abundent, copios, bogat.

hegemony *s* hegemonie *f*.

heifer *s* *zool* vițică *f*, vițea *f*.

height *s* (*of a person, building, mountain*) înălțime *f*; *avia* altitudine *f*; (*acme*) culme *f*, apogeu *n*.

heinous *adj* atroce; odios, ticălos.

heir *s* succesor *m*; urmaș *m*, moștenitor *m* • ~**ess** *s* moștenitoare *f*.

heist *s* *sl* (*holdup*) furt *n* armat || *vt* a comite un furt armat.

helicopter *s* elicopter *n.*

heliport *s* aeroport *n* pentru elicoptere.

helium *s* *chem* heliu *n.*

hell *s* iad *n*, infern *n* || *interj* drace!, la naiba! || *vi* a alerga repede • ~**bent** *adj* *coll* îndârjit; de neoprit.

Hellene *s* *hist* elen *m*, grec *m.*

hello *interj* (*greeting*) bună!, salut!; (*to answer phone*) alo!, da! || *s* apel *n* || *vi* a striga alo || *vt* a chema.

helm *s* *also fig* cârmă *f*.

helmet *s* coif *n*; cască *f*; bonetă *f*.

help *s* ajutor *n*; servitoare *f*; remediu *n* || *vt* a ajuta; a sprijini; a remedia; a folosi; a servi cu || *vi* a ajuta • ~**er** *s* ajutor *n*; femeie *f* la menaj • ~**ful** *adj* (*person*) serviabil; (*advice*) util • ~**ing** *s* porție *f*; (*pie, etc*) felie *f* • ~**less** *adj* neajutorat, neputincios; (*look, gesture*) de neputință • ~**line** *s* linie *f* de asistență telefonică.

Helsinki *s* Helsinki.

helve *s* mâner *n*, toartă *f*; (*tool*) coadă *f*.

hem *s* tiv *n* || *vt* a tivi; a încorseta.

hemisphere *s* emisferă *f*.

hemlock *s* *bot* cucută *f*.

hemoglobin *s* hemoglobină *f*.

hemorrhage *s* *med* hemoragie *f*.

hemorrhoids *s* *pl* *med* hemoroizi *m pl.*

hemp *s* *bot* cânepă *f*.

hen *s* găină *f*; (*birds*) femelă *f*; cloșcă *f*; femeie *f* agitată.

hence *adv* deci, de unde; de aici/acum înainte/încolo • ~**forth** *adv* *frml* de acum înainte.

henchman *s* (*follower*) acolit *m*; (*right-hand man*) suporter *m.*

henna *s* henna *f*, vopsea *f* (pentru păr) || *vt* a vopsi părul cu henna.

henpecked *adj* ținut sub papuc.

her *adj* ei; său, sa, săi, sale || *pron* pe ea, -o.

herald *s* (*messenger*) crainic *m* || *vt* a anunța.

herb *s* iarbă *f*; plantă *f* medicinală; buruiană *f* • ~**alist** *s* doctor *m* homeopat • ~**icide** *s* ierbicid *n* • ~**ivore** *s* animal *n* ierbivor.

herd *s* turmă *f*; cireadă *f*; gloată *f* || *vi* a se ține împreună; a se asocia || *vt* a paște, a mâna la păscut.

here *adv* aici; încoace; acum || *adj* de aici, aici de față || *s* locul *n* acesta; momentul *n* acesta • ~**after** *adv* în viitor • ~**by** *adv* prin aceasta, prin prezenta.

hereditary *adj* ereditar, moștenit; succesoral.

heredity *s* ereditate *f*.

heresy *s* erezie *f*.

heretic *s* eretic *m.*

heritage *s* moștenire *f*; avere *f*; soartă *f*; drept *n* legitim; tradiție *f*.

hermetic *adj* *also fig* ermetic.

hermit *s* ermit *m*, pustnic *m.*

hernia *s* *med* hernie *f*.

hero *s* erou *m*; viteaz *m*; protagonist • ~**ic** *adj* eroic • ~**ine** *s* eroină *f* • ~**ism** *s* eroism *n* • ~**worship** *s* cultul *n* eroilor.

heroin *s* *chem*, *med* heroină *f*.

heron *s* *zool* bâtlan *m.*

herpes *s* *med* herpes *n.*

herring *s* *icht* hering *m*, scrumbie *f*.

hers *pron* al său, a sa, ai săi, ale sale.

herself *pron* se; (ea) însăși, chiar ea; o, pe ea însăși; ei însăși, chiar ei; ea, dânsa.

hesitant *adj* ezitant, nesigur.

hesitate *vt* a ezita; a șovăi; a se bâlbâi.

hesitation *s* (*indecision*) ezitare *f*, nehotărâre *f*; (*uncertainty*) nesiguranță *f*.

heterogeneous *adj* eterogen; divers, diferit.

heterosexual *s/adj* heterosexual *m*.

hexagon *s* hexagon *n*.

heyday *s* perioadă *f* de înflorire, prosperitate *f*, culme *f*, toi *n*.

hi *interj* hei!, alo!, bună!

hiatus *s* lacună *f*.

hibernate *vi* a hiberna.

hiccup, hiccough *s* sughiț *n* || *vi* a sughița.

hide[1] *, hid, hidden* *vt* a ascunde; a acoperi; a ține secret || *vi* a ascunde; a se refugia || *s* ascunzătoare *f*; observator *n*.

hide[2] *s* piele *f* de animal.

hideous *adj* hidos; (*mistake, conditions*) îngrozitor, cumplit.

hiding[1] *s* ascunzătoare *f*, refugiu *n*.

hiding[2] *s* (*beating*) bătaie *f* (cu biciul); ciomăgeală *f*.

hierarchy *s* ierarhie *f*.

hieroglyph *s* hieroglifă *f*.

hi-fi *s* aparatură *f* (audio) de înaltă fidelitate, hi-fi *n*.

high *adj* înalt; furios; distins; strident; avansat; trecut; intens; neobișnuit; propice; serios; important; arogant; tulburat || *adv* sus; abundent || *s* înălțime *f*; deal *n*; cer *n*; ~ **chair** *s* scaun *n* înalt (pentru copii); ~ **frequency** *s phys* înaltă frecvență *f*; ~ **jump** *s sp* săritură *f* în înălțime; ~ **life** *s* stil *n* de viață al înaltei societăți; ~ **roller** *s* (*spendthrift*) cheltuitor *m*, mână *f* largă, (*gambler*) cartofor *m*; ~ **school** *s* liceu *n*, colegiu *n*, școală *f* secundară; ~ **season** *s* plin sezon *n* (turistic).

highbrow *adj* prețios, pretențios, cu pretenții (intelectuale) || *s* om *m* pretențios, cu pretenții (intelectuale etc).

high-handed *adj* despotic.

high-heeled *adj* (*shoes*) cu toc înalt.

highland *s* regiune *f* muntoasă/deluroasă, platou *n*.

highlight *s* (*event, etc*) moment/punct *n* forte || *vt* a scoate în evidență, a sublinia; (*pencil*) a sublinia un text pentru a-l pune în evidență.

highly *adv* (*manner*) frumos, onorabil; favorabil; **think** ~ **of smb/smth** *vt* a avea o părere bună despre cineva/ ceva; (*degree*) foarte, cât se poate de, extrem/grozav de.

highness *s fig* înălțime *f*; altitudine *f*; (*title*) alteță *f*; **Your Highness** Alteța/Înălțimea Voastră.

high-pitched *adj* (*sound*) înalt, ascuțit, acut, strident; (*roof*) ascuțit, abrupt, țuguiat; *fig* măreț, sublim, înaltă ținută.

high-powered *adj* de (mare) putere; (*prestigious*) de nivel înalt; (*person, job*) important.

high-speed *adj* de mare viteză.

high-spirited *adj* curajos, îndrăzneț, viteaz; nobil, mărinimos.

high-tech *adj* (*method, industry*) de vârf.

highway *s* autostradă *f*; rută *f* principală, drum *n* principal.

hijack *s* deturnare *f* || *vt* a deturna • ~**er** *s* pirat *m* al aerului/șoselei.

hike *s* plimbare *f*, excursie *f*; ridicare *f* || *vt* a ridica; a

spori; a lua la plimbare || *vi* a face o plimbare; a călători; a se ridica.

hilarious *adj* ilar, vesel, zgomotos.

hill *s* deal *n*, colină *f*; movilă *f*; pantă *f* || *vt* a face morman; a îngrămădi.

hilt *s* (*of knife*) mâner *n*, plăsea *f*; (*of gun*) pat *n*; **up to the** ~ *adj* până la maximum.

him *pron* pe el, îl; lui; îi • ~**self** *pron* se; (el) însuși, chiar el; el personal.

hind *s zool* căprioară *f*, femelă *f* a căpriorului || *adj* din spate, posterior.

hinder *vt* a împiedica, a stingheri.

Hindi *s* hindi *f*, limba *f* hindusă || *adj* hindi, în limba hindusă.

hindrance *s* piedică *f*, obstacol *n*.

hindsight *s* (*gun*) înălțător *n*; (*of an occurrence, etc*) înțelegere *f* întârziată/ulterioară.

Hindu *s/adj* hindus *m*, indian *m*.

hinge *s* joncțiune *f*, articulație *f*; *fig* principiu/element *n* de bază || *vt* (**upon**) a depinde de.

hint *s* aluzie *f*; indiciu *n*; sugestie *f*; urmă *f* || *vt* a sugera || *vi* a face aluzie la, a insinua.

hip *s anat* șold *n*; îmbinare *f*.

hippopotamus *s zool* hipopotam *m*.

hire *vt* a închiria; a da cu chirie; a angaja; a lua cu împrumut || *vi* a se angaja || *s* închiriere *f*; angajare *f*; slujbă *f*; salariu *n*.

hirsute *adj* păros; lățos.

his *adj poss* lui, său, îi, -i || *pron* al lui/său, a lui/sa, ai lui/săi, ale lui/sale.

hiss *s* (*snakes, etc*) șuierat *n*; (*crowd*) fluierături *f pl* || *vi* (*snakes*, etc) a șuiera.

historian *s* istoric *m*.

historic *adj* de importanță istorică, epocal, istoric • ~**al** *adj* (cu caracter) istoric; diacronic.

history *s* istorie *f*; cronică *f*; poveste *f*; trecut *n*.

hit, hit, hit *vt* a lovi, a izbi; a se lovi; a găsi; a nimeri; a șoca; a ajunge || *vi* a lovi; a se izbi; a ataca; a se petrece; a reuși || *s* lovitură *f*; șoc *n*; atingere *f*; triumf *n*; șlagăr *n*; noroc *n* • ~**-and-run** *adj* (*accident*) cu fugă de la locul accidentului; (*action*) pripit, rapid, nechibzuit; ~ **driver** *s* șofer care a părăsit locul accidentului.

hitch *s* (*obstacle*) impediment *n*, obstacol *n*, piedică *f*; *tech* cuplare *f*, cuplaj *n* || *vt* a prinde, a fixa || *vi* a se mișca de colo până colo, a se smuci, a se agita.

hitchhike *vi* a face autostop || *vt* a solicita autostop || *s* autostop.

hitherto *adv* până acum/azi/în zilele noastre.

hive *s* stup *m*; roi *n* || *vt* a aduna (ca) într-un stup || *vi* a sta (ca) într-un stup.

hoard *s* stoc *n*, provizie *f*; (*useless things*) morman *n*, grămadă *f* || *vt* a strânge, a aduna; (~ *food, etc*) a face provizii • ~**ing** *s* păstrare *f*, tezaurizare *f*; stocare *f*, adunare *f*, strângere *f*.

hoarse *adj* (*person, voice*) răgușit; (*cry, whisper*) aspru, care îți zgârie auzul.

hoax *s* păcăleală *f*, farsă *f*.

hobble *vt* (~ *a horse*) a împiedica, a priponi; a face să șchiopăteze || *vi* a șchiopăta, a șontâcăi.

hobby *s* pasiune *f*, manie *f*.

hobnob *vi* (**with**) a fi prieten la cataramă (cu); (*consort*) a se asocia (cu)

hobo *s* vagabond *m*.

hock[1] *s* vin *n* alb, riesling *n*.

hock² *s zool* partea *f* mijlocie a piciorului dinapoi ‖ *vt* a pune amanet, a amaneta; **in** ~ amanetat; îndatorat.

hockey *s sp* hochei *n* pe gheaţă; hochei *n* pe iarbă.

hockshop *s coll* casă *f* de amanet.

hocus-pocus *s* scamatorie *f*, înşelătorie *f*, hocus-pocus *n*; (*deceptive talk*) hocus-pocus *n*, formulă *f* magică.

hoe *s* săpăligă *f* ‖ *vt* a săpa; a prăşi.

hog *s* porc *m*; mâncău *m*, gurmand *m*; mitocan *m* ‖ *vt coll* a acapara, a monopoliza.

hoist *vt* a ridica, a înălţa; (~ *a flag*) a înălţa, a ridica ‖ *s* ridicare *f*, înălţare *f*; elevator *n*, macara *f*.

hold¹, **held**, **held** *vt* a ţine; a stăpâni; a deţine; a ocupa; a opri; a reţine; a preocupa; a conţine; a considera; a susţine ‖ *vi* a se ţine; a rezista; a se aplica; a se apuca de ‖ *s* influenţă *f*; sprijin *n*; stăpânire *f*; temniţă *f*; ~ **down** *vt* a ţine plecat/în jos; ~ **forth** *vi* a perora; ~ **in** *vt* a stăpâni, a ţine în frâu; ~ **off** *vt* a ţine la distanţă; ~ **on** *vi* a nu se da bătut, a se ţine tare; ~ **on!** ţine-te bine!; aşteaptă o clipă!; ~ **out** *vt* (*arm, etc*) a întinde; (*offer*) a oferi, a da ‖ *vi* a rezista (până la capăt); a dăinui, a persista; (*supplies*) a ajunge, a ţine; ~ **to** *vt* a face (pe cineva) să respecte, a ţine (pe cineva) legat de (o promisiune etc); ~ **together** *vt* a uni, a lega ‖ *vi* a rămâne uniţi/împreună; ~ **up** *vt* a arăta; a expune; a ţine sus/drept; a opri, a reţine; (a ataca pentru) a jefui; a întârzia, a reţine.

hold² *s naut* cală *f*.

holder *s* posesor *m*; deţinător *m*; concesionar *m*; suport *n*.

holding *s econ* holding *n* ‖ *adj* care deţine; tutelar.

holdover *s* vestigiu *n*.

Holland *s* Olanda *f*; *text* olandă *f*.

hole *s* gaură *f*; defect *n*; vizuină *f*; ascunzătoare *f*; bucluc *n*; gropiţă *f* ‖ *vi* a găuri ‖ *vi* (*golf*) a marca un punct.

holiday *s* sărbătoare *f*; zi *f* de odihnă; *pl* vacanţă *f*; concediu *n* ‖ *adj* vesel, de sărbătoare.

holler *vt/vi* a striga, a ţipa.

hollow *adj* scobit; găunos; gol; scofâlcit; dogit; necinstit ‖ *s* scobitură *f*; depresiune *f* ‖ *adv* zdravăn, rău.

holly *s bot* ilice *n*.

holster *s* toc *n* (de pistol).

holy *adj* sfânt; sfinţit, sanctificat; (*day*) mare; divin, dumnezeiesc; evlavios, religios; înspăimântător, teribil.

homage *s* omagiu *n* (public); deferenţă *f*, respect *n*.

home *s* cămin *n*, casă *f*; domiciliu *n*; patrie *f*; habitat *n*; familie *f*; azil *n*; sediu *n* ‖ *adj* domestic; familial; intern ‖ *adv* acasă; spre casă; la ţintă ‖ *vt* (*provide a* ~) a adăposti; ~ **address** *s* adresă *f* personală (de la domiciliu); ~ **computer** *s* computer *n* personal; ~ **help** *s* femeie *f* de serviciu; ~ **rule** *s* autonomie *f*, independenţă *f* legislativă.

homecoming *s* întoarcere *f* acasă; revenire *f* la un loc de care te leagă amintiri.

home-grown *adj* de casă, domestic.

homeland *s* patrie *f*, ţară *f* natală.

homeless *adj* fără casă/adăpost/cămin, lipsit de adăpost; **the** ~ *s pl* cei fără locuinţă.

homely *adj* familial; simpatic; obişnuit; natural; plat; urât.

home-made *adj* făcut în casă.

homeopath *s* (*doctor*) homeopat *m*.

homesick *adj* plin de dor de casă, cuprins de nostalgie.

homestead *s* fermă *f* acordată unui colonist; fermă *f*, gospodărie *f* ţărănească; casă *f* de ţară (cu acareturi).

homework *s scol* temă *f* pentru acasă; *coll* muncă *f*, lucru *n*.

homicide *s* crimă *f*, omucidere *f*.

homily *s relig, fig* predică *f*.

homogeneous *adj* omogen.

homonym *s* omonim *n*.

homosexual *s/adj* homosexual *m*.

hone *vt* (*sharpen*) a ascuţi; (*analysis*) a aprofunda.

honest *adj* cinstit; adevărat; sincer; onorabil; merituos; virtuos; modest; nevinovat • ~**y** *s* cinste *f*, sinceritate *f*, probitate *f*.

honey *s* miere *f*; dulceaţă *f*, iubită *f* ‖ *interj* scumpo!, iubito! ‖ *vt* a îndulci.

honeymoon *s* luna *f* de miere ‖ *vr* a-şi petrece luna de miere.

honk *vi* (~ *a horn*) a claxona; (*geese*) a gâgâi ‖ *vt* **to** ~ **the horn** a claxona.

honor *s* onoare *f*, cinste *f*; virtute *f*; legământ *n*; faimă *f*; mândrie *f*; stimă *f*; distincţie *f* ‖ *vt* a onora • ~**arium** *s* onorariu *n* • ~**ary** *adj* onorific.

hood *s* glugă *f*; capotă *f*; insignă *f* ‖ *vt* a acoperi cu o glugă.

hoodlum *s coll* gangster *m*, tâlhar *m*.

hoof *s* copită *f* ‖ *vt* a lovi cu copita; a merge pe jos; a ţopăi, a dansa.

hook *s* cârlig *n*; cosor *n*, cuţit *n*; croşetă *f*; copcă *f*; capcană *f* ‖ *vt* a agăţa, a prinde ‖ *vi* a se încovoia.

hooligan *s* huligan *m*.

hoop *s* (*band of metal for tub, etc*) cerc *n*; cerc *n* de jucărie.

hoopla *s coll* (*advertizing*) publicitate *f* zgomotoasă.

hooray *interj* ura!.

hoot *vi* (*owl*) a ţipa ‖ *s* ţipătul *n* bufniţei.

hop(s)¹ *s bot* hamei *n*; drog *n* ‖ *vt* a aromatiza cu hamei; a droga; a stimula.

hop² *vi* a sări într-un picior; (*bird*) a ţopăi ‖ *s* săritură *f*; ţopăit *n* într-un picior.

hope *s* speranţă *f*; încredere *f*; şansă *f*; sprijin *n* ‖ *vi* a spera ‖ *vt* a spera; a-şi pune speranţele în • ~**ful** *adj* (*optimistic*) plin de speranţă; (*promising*) încurajator, promiţător • ~**fully** *adv* cu optimism, cu încredere; (*hoping*) cu noroc, să sperăm că • ~**less** *adj* disperat; (*tears*) de disperare; *coll* (*no good*) de nimic • ~**lessly** *adv* cu disperare; iremediabil, complet.

horde *s hist* hoardă *f*, *fig* hoardă *f*, ceată *f*, bandă *f*.

horizon *s* orizont *n*; orizont *n* intelectual.

horizontal *adj* orizontal; plat, întins, neted.

hormone *s* hormon *n*.

horn *s* corn *n*; antenă *f*; cornet *n*; braţ *n* (de râu) ‖ *vt* a scurta, a reteza; a împunge.

hornet *s* gărgăun *m*, viespe *f*.

horoscope *s astrol* horoscop *n*.

horrendous *adj* cumplit, groaznic.

horrible *adj* oribil, groaznic; odios.

horrid *adj* neplăcut, insuportabil, înspăimântător.

horrific *adj* oribil, înfiorător.

horrify *vt* a îngrozi.

horror *s* groază *f*; oroare *f*; înfiorare *f*; *pl* anxietate *f*; melancolie *f*.

hors d'oeuvre *s* aperitiv *n*, antreu *n*, hors d'oeuvre *n*.

horse *s* cal *m*; armăsar *m*; cavalerie *f*; cal-putere *m* ‖ *vt* a muta cu de-a sila; a supune biciuirii ‖ *vi* a călări; ~ **chestnut** *s* (*tree*) castan *m*; (*fruit*) castană *f*; ~ **hair** *s* păr *m* de cal ‖ *adj* de păr de cal; ~ **race** *s* cursă *f* de cai • ~**back** *s* spinare *f* de cal; şa *f* ‖ *adv* călare • ~**back**

riding s echitație f • **~breaker** s dresor m de cai • **~drawn** adj tras de cai • **~man** s călăreț m, cavalerist m • **~shoe** s potcoavă f de cal; obiect n în formă de potcoavă • **~woman** s călăreață f, amazoană f.

horsepower s fig cal-putere m.

horseradish s hrean n.

horsefly s tăun m.

horticulture s horticultură f.

hose s ciorapi m pl lungi; furtun n ‖ vt a stropi cu furtunul.

hosiery s galanterie f de damă; tricotaje n pl.

hospice s (inn for travelers) casă f de oaspeți; (hospital) spital n.

hospitable adj ospitalier, primitor.

hospital s spital n; clinică f; atelier n de reparații.

hospitality s ospitalitate f.

host s gazdă f; patron m (de local); bio plantă-gazdă f; (crowd) ceată f, mulțime f.

hostage s ostatic m; garanție f; chezaş m.

hostel s han n; cămin n; azil n.

hostess s gazdă f; hangiță f; stewardesă f.

hostile adj ostil; inamic; rece; neospitalier; antagonist.

hostility s ostilitate f.

hot adj fierbinte; iute; aprins; febril; nervos; lacom; nestăpânit; vehement; dornic; lasciv; proaspăt; excitant; la modă; ilicit; periculos; absurd; **~ dog** s crenvurşt m, hotdog m; **~ flash** s val n de căldură, bufeu n • **~bed** s focar n • **~tempered** adj coleric.

hotel s hotel n.

hotline s linie f telefonică directă, fir n scurt; (special) linie f de comunicare continuă (24/24 ore).

hound s zool câine m (de vânătoare), ogar m ‖ vt a urmări, a hăitui.

hour s oră f; ceas n; lecție f; oră f de drum; moment n, timp n.

house s casă f; imobil n; clădire f; domiciliu n; locuință f; gospodărie f; cămin n; adăpost n; local n; sală f; spectacol n; public n; familie f, stirpe f ‖ adj de casă, casnic; domestic • **~boat** s vapor n amenajat pentru locuit • **~bound** adj țintuit în casă; silit să stea în casă • **~breaker** s spărgător m • **~coat** s capot n, halat n • **~hold** s gospodărie f; familie f, locatarii m pl ‖ adj casnic, gospodăresc; (name, word) familiar • **~keeper** s menajeră f • **~maid** s fată f în casă, servitoare f, femeie f de serviciu • **~to~** adj/adv din casă în casă • **~trained** adj (animal) curat • **~warming** s (petrecere f de) inaugurare f a unei case • **~wife** s nevastă f; femeie f de casă • **~work** s menaj n, treabă f în casă.

housing s locuință f, găzduire f; **~ project** s ansamblu n de locuințe.

hovel s cocioabă f; bordel n; baracă f.

hover vi (fly) a plana.

how adv cum, în ce fel; în ce sens; din ce cauză?, de ce?; cât?, în ce măsură? ‖ conj cum, felul cum; după cum, aşa cum; în orice fel ‖ s mod n, fel n, metodă f.

however conj oricum, în orice mod ‖ adv oricât de mult; în orice caz; totuşi, cu toate acestea; pe de altă parte.

howl vi a urla; a râde în hohote ‖ s urlet n; (laugh) hohot n.

hoyden s băiețoi m.

hub s (wheel) butuc n; (activity) centru n, punct n central.

hubbub s (of voices) vuiet n, larmă f; (uproar) vacarm n.

hubby s coll soțior m.

huckleberry s bot afină f.

huckster s (pedlar) vânzător m ambulant; pej autor m de reclame publicitare zgomotoase.

huddle vi a se ghemui, a se chirci ‖ s grup n restrâns.

hue s (color) nuanță f, tentă f.

huff s acces n de furie/mânie, supărare f ‖ vt a teroriza; a forța, a sili ‖ vi a pufăi; a face pe grozavul.

hug vt a strânge în brațe; a iubi ‖ s îmbrățişare f; strângere f puternică.

huge adj uriaş, enorm, imens, colosal.

hulk s (ship) schelet n; (person) matahală f.

hull s naut carcasă f, parte f exterioară.

hullabaloo s debandadă f, scandal n.

hum vi a bâzâi; a fredona; a se bâlbâi; a ezita ‖ vt a fredona ‖ s şovăială f; ezitare f; bâlbâială f; mormăit n ‖ interj hm!.

human adj omenesc, uman; pământesc ‖ s om m, ființă f omenească; **~ resources** s pl resurse f pl umane.

humane adj omenos, uman; indulgent; umanistic.

humanities s pl ştiințe f pl umaniste.

humanity s umanitate f.

humble adj umil; supus; umilit; obscur; modest ‖ vt a umili; a diminua; a submina ‖ vr a se umili.

humbug s sl (person) şarlatan m; (deception) şarlatanie f, înşelătorie f; (nonsense) prostii f pl, fleacuri n pl.

humdrum adj monoton.

humid adj umed • **~ity** s umiditate f, umezeală f.

humiliate vt a umili; a face de ruşine.

humiliation s umilire f.

humility s umilință f.

hummock s (knoll) deal n mic.

humor s dispoziție f, stare f; înclinație f; umor n; veselie f ‖ vt a satisface; a răsfăța; a se supune (cuiva) • **~ous** adj cu/de umor; spiritual; amuzant.

hump s cocoaşă f.

hunch s bucată f groasă/mare; bănuială f, suspiciune f, presentiment n, fler n ‖ vt a curba, a îndoi (înafară).

hundred num sută; sutălea ‖ s sută f.

hung vt * **hang**; **~ over** adj coll to be **~** a fi mahmur.

Hungarian adj unguresc ‖ s (people) ungur m, unguroaică f.

Hungary s Ungaria f.

hunger s foame f; poftă f; înfometare f ‖ vi a-i fi foame; a tânji după ‖ vt a înfometa; **~ strike** s greva f foamei.

hungry adj flămând; avid; sărac, sterp; nerentabil.

hunk s (piece) bucată f mare, halcă f; sl (man) bărbat m bine/sexy.

hunker vi (crouch) a sta pe vine; (squat) a se aşeza pe vine; (animal) a se ghemui, a se ascunde.

hunt vt a vâna, a hăitui; a împuşca; a urmări; a persecuta; a cutreiera ‖ vi a merge la vânătoare; a scotoci ‖ s vânătoare f; teren n de vânătoare.

hurdle s sp obstacol n, gard n; fig obstacol ‖ vt a sări (peste); fig a trece peste, a depăşi.

hurl vt a arunca, a azvârli; a înfige; a împinge înainte ‖ vi a se repezi (înainte).

hurly-burly s (commotion) agitație f, hărmălaie f.

hurray interj ura!.

hurricane s uragan n, furtună f.

hurry s grabă f; urgență f; pripeală f; agitație f; nerăbdare f ‖ vi a se grăbi; a se pripi ‖ vt a grăbi; a rasoli, a face în pripă.

hurt vt a răni; a lovi; a jigni; a strânge; a strica; a dăuna ‖ vi a te durea; a fi dureros ‖ s rană f; lovitură f; nedreptate f; durere f • **~ful** adj jignitor, insultător.

husband *s* soț *m*, bărbat *m*, om *m* ‖ *vt* a economisi; a cruța; a mărita.

hush *s* liniște *f* ‖ *excl* liniște!, sst!.

husk *s* (*grain, seed*) coajă *f*, teacă *f* ‖ *vt* a coji; a decortica.

husky *adj* plin de coji; (*voice*) răgușit; *coll* (*burly*) mătăhălos ‖ *s zool* câine *m* eschimos.

hussar *s hist* husar *m*.

hussy *s sl* (*shameless woman*) otreapă *f*.

hustle *vi* a îmbrânci, a da brânci; *fig* a îmboldi, a împinge din urmă ‖ *s* agitație *f*, îmbulzeală *f*, înghesuială *f*.

hut *s* colibă *f*; baracă *f*; cabană *f*; adăpost *n* ‖ *vt* a caza în barăci ‖ *vi* a locui în baracă.

hutch *s* coteț *n* pentru iepuri.

hyacinth *s bot* zambilă *f*.

hybrid *s/adj* hibrid *m*.

hydraulic *adj* hidraulic.

hydrocarbon *s chem* hidrocarbură *f*.

hydro-electric *adj* hidroelectric.

hydrofoil *s* ambarcațiune *f* cu aripi portante.

hydrogen *s chem* hidrogen *n*.

hyena *s zool* hienă *f*.

hygiene *s* igienă *f*.

hymen *s anat* himen *n*.

hymn *s* imn *n* ‖ *vt* a lăuda, a slăvi; a exprima, a da glas.

hype *s coll* reclamă *f* agresivă ‖ *vt* a face reclamă agresivă.

hypertension *s* hipertensiune f.

hyphen *s gram* liniuță *f* de unire, cratimă *f*.

hypnosis *s* hipnoză *f*.

hypnotic *adj* hipnotic.

hypnotism *s* hypnotism *n*.

hypnotize *vt* a hipnotiza.

hypochondria *s med* ipohondrie *f*.

hypocrisy *s* ipocrizie *f*.

hypocrite *s* ipocrit *m*, prefăcut *m*; mironosiță *f*.

hypocritical *adj* ipocrit, prefăcut.

hypodermic *adj* subcutanat ‖ *s* injecție *f* subcutanată.

hypotenuse *s geom* ipotenuză *f*.

hypothesis *s* (*pl* –ses) ipoteză *f*.

hypothetical *adj* ipotetic.

hysterectomy *s med* incizie *f* a uterului.

hysteria *s med* isterie *f*.

hysterical *adj* isteric.

hysterics *s pl* istericale *f pl*; (*fit*) criză *f* de nervi; *coll* (*laughter*) râs *n* nestăpânit/isteric.

I

I, i *s* (litera) I, i ‖ **I** *pron* eu ‖ *s* eu *n*, ego *n*.

iamb *s ling* iamb *n*.

ibidem *adv* ibidem, tot acolo.

ice *s* gheață *f*; înghețată *f*; glazură *f*; răceală *f*, rezervă *f* ‖ *vt/vi* a îngheța; a răci, a frapa; a se jivra, a se răci • ~cream *s* înghețată *f*.

Iceland *s* Islanda *f*.

icicle *s* țurțure *m*.

icing *s* glazură *f*; *avia* jivraj *n*.

icon *s* imagine *f*; chip *n*; icoană *f*; idol *m*.

icy *adj* de/din/cu gheață; (*aloof*) distant, rezervat.

ID card *s* act *n* de identitate.

idea *s* idee *f*, noțiune *f*; imagine *f*; gând *n*; concepție *f*; bănuială *f*; mod *n* de gândire; mentalitate *f*.

ideal *adj* desăvârșit, ideal, perfect; nereal; mintal ‖ *s* ideal *n*, perfecțiune *f*; țintă *f*.

identical *adj* identic, absolut la fel cu.

identification *s* identificare *f*.

identify *vt* a identifica; (*document*) a permite identificarea • *vi* (**with**) a se identifica cu.

identity *s* identitate *f*; asemănare *f*; unicitate *f*; persoană *f*; ~ **card** *s* legitimație *f*; buletin *n* de identitate.

ideology *s* ideologie *f*.

idiocy *s* idioțenie *f*; stupiditate *f*.

idiom *s* idiom *n*, dialect *n*, grai *n*; limbaj *n*; expresie *f* idiomatică.

idiosyncrasy *s* idiosincrasie *f*, particularitate *f*; manierism *n*; *med* idiosincrasie *f*, (hiper-)sensibilitate *f*, alergie *f*, *fig* aversiune *f*.

idiot *s* idiot *m*, imbecil *m* • ~ic *adj* idiot.

idle *adj* inutil; nefondat; stupid; trândav, indolent; nefolosit, inactiv.

idol *s* idol *m*; ideal *n*; impostor *m*; concepție *f* greșită.

idyllic *adj* idilic.

if *conj* dacă, de, ca; deși, cu toate că; în cazul când; cu condiția ca.

iffy *adj* nesigur, improbabil, incert.

igloo *s* iglu *n*.

ignite *vt* a aprinde; a inflama ‖ *vi* a se aprinde; a se inflama; a arde.

ignition *s* (*action*) aprindere *f*; *aut* scânteie *f*, aprindere *f*; **switch on the** ~ *vt* a porni motorul.

ignoble *adj* (*base*) josnic; (*shameful*) rușinos; (*immoral*) corupt.

ignominious *adj* (*shameful*) rușinos; (*foul*) infam.

ignominy *s* (*shame*) rușine *f*; mârșăvie *f*, infamie *f*.

ignoramus *s* ignorant *m*.

ignorance *s* ignoranță *f*.

ignorant *adj* ignorant, neștiutor.

ignore *vt* a ignora; a refuza să țină seama de.

ill *adj* bolnav; rău, ticălos; aspru; nenorocos; ostil; prost, urât ‖ *adv* rău, prost, urât; aspru; dușmănos; neplăcut ‖ *s* rău *n*; daună *f*; necaz *n*, nenorocire *f*; ~ **feeling** *s* resentiment *n*.

illegal *adj* ilegal, nepermis; ilicit, clandestin.

illegible *adj* ilizibil, neciteț.

illegitimate *adj* nelegitim.

ill-fated *adj* fatal, funest.

illicit *adj* ilicit, interzis; clandestin, nepermis.

illiterate *s/adj* analfabet *m*, neșcolarizat *m*.

illness *s* boală *f*, maladie *f*; indispoziție *f*.

illogical *adj* ilogic.

ill-timed *adj* inoportun, în contratimp.

illuminate *vt* a (i)lumina; a lămuri, a explica; *fig* a lumina/lămuri (pe cineva).

illuminating *adj* edificator.

illusion *s* iluzie *f*, amăgire *f*; înșelăciune *f*.

illusory *adj* iluzoriu.

illustrate *vt* a ilustra; a exemplifica; a explica, a lămuri.

illustration *s* (*picture*) ilustrație *f*; ilustrare *f*.

illustrious *adj* ilustru, celebru.

image *s* imagine *f*, chip *n*; idee *f*; concepție *f*; replică *f*; idol *m*; icoană *f*; simbol *n*; descriere *f*; portret *n* • ~**ry** *s* imagini *f pl* artistice.

imaginary *adj* imaginar.

imagination *s* (*ability*) imaginație *f*; (*fantasy*) invenție *f*.

imaginative *adj* imaginativ; (*solution*) plin de imaginație.

imagine vt a(-şi) imagina; a concepe; a deduce; a presupune.

imbalance s dezechilibru n.

imbecile s pej imbecil m, idiot m.

imbecility s imbecilitate f.

imbibe vt (drink) a bea; (absorb) a acumula.

imbroglio s (mess) încurcătură f.

imbued adj plin; ~ **with** adj înţesat cu.

imitate vt a imita; a copia; a simula; a maimuţări.

imitation s imitare f, imitaţie f.

immaculate adj imaculat, fără pată; pur, curat.

immaterial adj imaterial; spiritual; (to) irelevant, neînsemnat.

immature adj imatur, necopt, crud, nematur.

immeasurable adj infinit, incomensurabil.

immediate adj imediat, direct; instantaneu; urgent; iminent • ~ly adv imediat, pe loc; urgent || conj de îndată ce, curând după ce.

immense adj imens, uriaş, colosal; nemărginit; grozav, straşnic.

immensity s imensitate f.

immerse vt a afunda, a (s)cufunda (în); fig a îngropa, a afunda (în).

immersion s (s)cufundare f, afundare f; imersiune f; fig absorbire f, cufundare f.

immigrant s imigrant m || adj care imigrează.

immigrate vi a imigra, a veni (într-o ţară).

immigration s imigraţie f.

imminent adj iminent, inevitabil.

immobile adj imobil, fix.

immobilize vt a imobiliza.

immoderate adj exagerat, excesiv.

immodest adj indecent, neruşinat; îndrăzneţ.

immoral adj imoral; stricat; ticălos; desfrânat.

immortal adj nemuritor.

immovable adj fix; (resolute) ferm.

immune adj med imun; fig (protected) la adăpost de.

immunity s med imunitate f; fig (protection) siguranţă f (faţă de).

imp s (elf) spiriduş m; sl (child) drăcuşor m, ştrengar m.

impact s ciocnire f; efect n; impact n || vt a lovi, a ciocni; a influenţa.

impair vt a deteriora, a strica, a avaria; a slăbi, a submina; a ruina; (efficiency) a reduce.

impale vt a trage în ţeapă; a înţepa cu suliţa.

impart vt (~ information) a comunica, a împărtăşi; a împărţi (cu).

impartial adj imparţial.

impassable adj impracticabil, de netrecut,

impasse s fundătură f; impas n, situaţie f fără ieşire.

impassioned adj pasionat.

impassive adj impasibil.

impatience s nerăbdare f.

impatient adj nerăbdător; nervos; iritat; intolerant.

impeach vt jur a acuza, a pune sub acuzare; a pune la îndoială, a suspecta.

impeccable adj impecabil, ireproşabil; ferit de păcat/ greşeală.

impede vt a obstrucţiona.

impediment s impediment n.

impel vt (push) a împinge; (drive) a impulsiona.

impending adj iminent.

impenetrable adj also fig de nepătruns.

imperative adj imperios, urgent; necesar || s gram imperativ n.

imperfect adj imperfect; defectuos; incomplet.

imperial adj imperial; maiestuos; suveran • ~ism s imperialism n • ~ist s imperialist m.

imperil vt a primejdui.

impermeable adj impermeabil.

impersonal adj impersonal; detaşat; şters.

impersonate vt a se da drept; a imita; a personifica, a întruchipa.

impersonation s uzurpare f de identitate; (role, play) imitaţie f.

impertinent adj impertinent, obraznic.

impervious adj (to) impenetrabil (pentru), impermeabil (la); fig (to) insensibil (la), impermeabil, inaccesibil (pentru).

impetuous adj impetuos.

impetus s (urge) elan n; (stimulus) impuls n, stimulent n.

impinge vi (on/upon) a avea efect/influenţă (asupra), a influenţa; a se ciocni, a se izbi; a veni în contact cu.

impish adj pus pe rele.

implacable adj neîmpăcat; implacabil.

implant vt med a implanta; (instill) a inspira.

implement s unealtă f; obiect n; mijloc n || vt a aplica; a îndeplini; a utila.

implication s implicare f, amestec n; implicaţie f; aluzie f, sugestie f.

implicit adj implicit; (faith) absolut.

implore vt a implora; a cere, a solicita.

imply vt a presupune; a sugera; a însemna că; a insinua.

impolite adj nepoliticos; fără maniere.

import vt a importa; a însemna || s import n; frml sens n; importanţă f.

importance s importanţă f.

important adj important; influent; pompos.

importunate adj (annoying) enervant, exasperant.

importune vt a importuna.

impose vt (upon) a impune, a pretinde, a solicita insistent; econ (on/upon) a impune, a stabili; (upon) a impune, a face impresie bună; a fi impunător/ impresionant.

imposing adj impunător, falnic.

impossible adj imposibil; insuportabil; inacceptabil; condamnabil.

imposter s impostor m.

impotence s impotenţă f.

impotent adj slab; incapabil; impotent.

impound vt a confisca.

impoverish vt a sărăci, a pauperiza.

impregnate vt a fecunda; a fertiliza, a face să sădească; (with) a satura, a umple; a impregna (cu).

impress vt a imprima; a impresiona || vi a impresiona || s imprimare f; fixare f; amprentă f; sigiliu n; efect n; caracteristică f • ~ion s impresie f; (play, role) imitaţie f; (books, etc) imprimare f, tipărire f; (stamp) ştampilare f • ~ive adj impresionant.

imprint vt a imprima, a ştanţa; fig a imprima, a fixa (în memorie); a băga, a vârî (în capul cuiva) || s (sign) amprentă f, urmă f; numele n editorului (pe o carte).

imprison vt a întemniţa.

improbable adj (story, excuse) improbabil.

impromptu s improvizaţie f; mus impromptu n || adj improvizat || adv ex abrupto, pe neaşteptate, în mod improvizat.

improper adj impropriu; inexact; nepotrivit; indecent; grosolan.

impropriety s (*indecency*) indecenţă f; (*misdeed*) faptă f reprobabilă.
improve vt a perfecţiona; a corecta; a valorifica; a profita de ‖ vi a se ameliora; a progresa • ~ment s îmbunătăţire f; corectare f; amenajare f; valorificare f.
improvise vt/vi a improviza, a face improvizaţii.
imprudent adj imprudent.
impudent adj neruşinat.
impulse s impuls n; imbold n; stimulent n; motivaţie f; impulsivitate f ‖ vt a impulsiona.
impulsive adj impulsiv.
impure adj impur; falsificat, contrafăcut; indecent, imoral, destrăbălat.
imputation s (*charge*) imputare f; (*allegation*) alegaţie f.
in prep în; la; înăuntrul; cu; prin ‖ adv înăuntru, în interior; acasă; la destinaţie ‖ adj (din) interior, dinăuntru; sosit; la modă; în plin sezon; la curent cu ‖ s autoritate f.
inability s incapacitate f; neputinţă f.
inaccessible adj inaccesibil.
inaccurate adj inexact, incorect.
inactive adj inactiv; leneş; retras; sedentar.
inadequate adj nepotrivit, neadecvat, necorespunzător; insuficient.
inadvertent adj neatent; neglijent; necugetat, nechibzuit.
inane adj inept; stupid, prostesc; găunos.
inanimate adj neînsufleţit.
inanity s inepţie f.
inappropriate adj nepotrivit; insuficient.
inapt adj inapt.
inarticulate adj nearticulat, confuz, vag; (*person*) care se exprimă cu dificultate; (*explanation*) prost exprimat, neclar.
inasmuch conj în măsura în care; deoarece, întrucât ‖ adv dat fiind că.
inattentive adj neatent.
inaudible adj abia auzit; care nu poate fi auzit.
inaugurate vt a inaugura; a începe, a iniţia, a deschide.
inauspicious adj nefavorabil, neprielnic.
inborn adj înnăscut, congenital, nativ; natural, ereditar.
incandescent adj incandescent.
incapable adj (of) incapabil (de).
incapacity s incompetenţă f.
incautious adj imprudent.
incendiary adj incendiar; fig revoluţionar, incendiar ‖ s incendiator m; fig revoluţionar m, agitator m; (*bomb*) bombă f incendiară.
incense[1] s tămâie f.
incense[2] vt a înfuria.
incentive s (*stimulus*) motivaţie f, îndemn n; econ recompensă f, primă f.
incertitude s incertitudine f.
incessant adj continuu.
incest s incest n.
inch s ţol m, inci m ‖ vi a înainta treptat ‖ vt a câştiga teren pas cu pas.
inchoate adj incipient; incomplet.
incident s incident n, întâmplare f; luptă f; fapt n; ciocnire f ‖ adj incident; legat (de); inerent (pentru).
incinerate vt a incinera.
incinerator s crematoriu n (de gunoi).
incision s incizie f.
incisive adj also fig incisiv.
incisor s dinte m incisiv.

incite vt a aţâţa, a stârni; a genera; a îndemna, a îmboldi; a stimula; (to) a incita, a instiga (la).
inclement adj (*person*) nemilos, neîndurător, neîngăduitor; (*weather*) aspru.
inclination s înclinare f, înclinaţie f.
incline vt a înclina; a convinge; a decide ‖ vi a se înclina; a tinde (să) ‖ s pantă f, înclinaţie f.
inclosure s îngrăditură f.
include vt a include; a îngrădi; a mărgini.
inclusive adj inclus; incluzând toate costurile.
incognito adv incognito.
incoherent adj incoerent.
income s venit n, câştig n.
incomparable adj incomparabil.
incompatible adj (with) incompatibil (cu).
incompetent adj incompetent; necalificat; nepotrivit.
incomplete adj incomplet.
incomprehensible adj de neînţeles.
inconceivable adj de neconceput.
inconclusive adj neconcludent.
incongruous adj nepotrivit; nearmonios; necorespunzător; nelalocul lui; deplasat; absurd, ridicol.
inconsiderate adj nechibzuit, nesăbuit; (*person*) nepăsător, egoist.
inconsistent adj în opoziţie, contradictoriu; (*person*) inconsecvent; lipsit de logică.
inconspicuous adj neobservat; modest.
incontestable adj incontestabil.
incontinence s lipsă f de stăpânire; depravare f, destrăbălare f, imoralitate f; med incontinenţă f.
inconvenience s neplăcere f, neajuns n ‖ vt a deranja.
inconvenient adj incomod; inoportun.
incorporate vt a integra; a uni; a grupa; a întrupa ‖ adj integrat; îmbinat; unit.
incorrect adj incorect; fals; nepotrivit.
increase vt a spori; a creşte ‖ vi a se mări; a se înmulţi; a se dezvolta ‖ s sporire f; adaos n; dezvoltare f.
incredible adj incredibil; neobişnuit; uluitor.
incredulous adj neîncrezător.
increment s creştere f, dezvoltare f, sporire f; (*salary*, etc) spor n, ridicare f, sporire f; adaos n, supliment n.
incriminate vt jur a pune sub acuzaţie, a acuza, a incrimina, a inculpa; fig a incrimina, a acuza; a condamna.
incubate vt a cloci; a supune la incubaţie ‖ vi a cloci (ouă), a sta cloşcă.
inculcate vt a inculca, a insufla.
incumbent s titular m ‖ adj necesar, care se impune.
incur vt a-şi atrage (asupra sa); a risca, a-şi lua riscuri; (*difficulties*) a întâmpina, a da de.
incurable adj incurabil.
indebted adj also fig îndatorat.
indecent adj indecent, neruşinat.
indecision s nehotărâre f.
indecisive adj nehotărât; neconcludent; nesigur.
indecorous adj de prost gust.
indeed adv într-adevăr; sigur; foarte; extrem de; ba chiar; totuşi ‖ interj ei nu, zău!, chiar aşa!, ţi-ai găsit!.
indefatigable adj neobosit.
indefinite adj nedefinit; nehotărât; vag; nelimitat.
indelible adj de neşters, indelebil; de neuitat, nepieritor.
indemnification s compensaţie f; garanţie f.
indemnify vt a compensa; (*cover*) a asigura.
indemnity s îndemnizaţie f; despăgubire f, compensaţie f; garanţie f, garantare f.

indent *vt* a zimţui; a cresta; a face un duplicat; a angaja ca ucenic ‖ *vi* a face zimţi; a se îmbina ‖ *s* zimţ *m*; dantelare *f*; cupon *n*.

independence *s* independenţă *f*, autonomie *f*.

independent *adj* independent; autonom; înstărit.

indeterminate *adj* imprecis.

index *s* (*book*) index *n*; (*library*) indice *n*, repertoriu *n*, fişier *n*; *econ* indice *n*; ~ **card** fişă *f*; ~ **finger** *s* deget *n* arătător • ~**linked** *adj* indexat.

India *s* India *f*.

Indian *s* indian *m*; indian *m* american ‖ *adj* indian, din India; (de) indian american, de piele roşie; ~ **summer** *s* toamnă *f* lungă, vară *f* târzie.

indicate *vt* a indica; a schiţa; a fixa; a denota; a pomeni.

indication *s* indicaţie *f*, indicare *f*.

indicator *s* indicator *n*.

indict *vt jur* (**for/as**) a inculpa, a pune sub acuzaţie (pentru); *also fig* a acuza.

indifference *s* indiferenţă *f*.

indifferent *adj* indiferent; neînsemnat; banal; mediocru.

indigenous *adj* indigen, băştinaş.

indigent *adj* sărac lipit.

indigestion *s* indigestie *f*.

indignant *adj* indignat, revoltat.

indignation *s* indignare *f*.

indignity *s* ofensă *f*, jignire *f*, insultă *f*; josnicie *f*; infamie *f*; umilinţă *f*, înjosire *f*.

indigo *s/adj* indigo *n*.

indirect *adj* indirect; evaziv; nesincer.

indiscipline *s* indisciplină *f*.

indiscreet *adj* indiscret; nesocotit, necumpătat; neprevăzător, imprudent.

indiscriminate *adj* (*person*) lipsit de discernământ; (*behavior*) confuz; neclar; (*crime*) comis la întâmplare.

indispensable *adj* indispensabil.

indisposed *adj* indispus, prost dispus; *med* indispus; uşor bolnav.

indisputable *adj* indiscutabil.

indistinguishable *adj* imperceptibil; nedesluşit.

individual *s* om *m*, individ *m*; personalitate *f* ‖ *adj* individual; specific; original; separat; (*distinctive*) personal.

indoctrinate *vt* a îndoctrina.

indolent *adj* indolent, nepăsător; *med* nedureros; insensibil.

indomitable *adj* de neabătut, care nu se lasă.

indoors *adv* în casă; în interior.

induce *vt* (**to**) a convinge, a determina, a face să; a îndemna (să), a împinge (la); a stârni, a provoca; a deduce; a conchide; *elec* a produce prin inducţie.

induct *vt* (*install*) a investi; (*initiate*) a iniţia • ~**ion** *s* (*position*) instalare *f*; *jur* punere *f* în posesie; *elec* inducţie *f*; *tech* admisie *f*, aspiraţie *f*; *mil* incorporare *f*; *med* cauză *f* (generatoare); *log* inducţie *f*, metodă *f* inductivă • ~**ee** *s* membru *m* recent primit într-o societate, etc.

indulge *vt* a răsfăţa; a tolera; a păsui; a se consola ‖ *vi* a trage la măsea • ~**nce** *s* plăcere *f*; dorinţă *f*; lux *n*; slăbiciune *f*; abuz *n*.

industrial *adj* industrial; ~ **action** *s* grevă *f*; ~ **park** *s* zonă *f* industrială; ~ **relations** *s pl* relaţii *f pl* patronat-sindicat; ~ **revolution** *s* revoluţie *f* industrială.

industrious *adj* harnic, silitor.

industry *s* industrie *f*; fabrică *f*, uzină *f*; hărnicie *f*.

inebriated *adj also fig* ameţit, beat, îmbătat (de); în stare de ebrietate.

inedible *adj* necomestibil; de nemâncat.

ineffective *adj* ineficace, zadarnic; incapabil, incompetent; (*art*) lipsit de efect, nereuşit; plat, searbăd.

ineffectual *adj* (*action*) fără efect/rezultat/succes; inutil; anost, plat, şters; (*person*) incapabil, ineficient, nepriceput.

inefficiency *s* (*action*) ineficienţă *f*; (*person*) incapacitate *f*, incompetenţă *f*.

inefficient *adj* (*action*) ineficient, ineficace; (*person*) incapabil, incompetent.

inept *adj* stupid, prostesc, absurd, inept; nepotrivit, deplasat; inoportun; *jur* nul (şi neavenit), fără efect; (*person*) idiot, stupid.

inequality *s* inegalitate *f*.

inert *adj* inert • ~**ia** *s* inerţie *f*; indolenţă *f*.

inescapable *adj* inevitabil, fatal.

inevitable *adj* inevitabil; fatal; inerent.

inexcusable *adj* de neiertat, de nescuzat; nejustificabil.

inexhaustible *adj* inepuizabil.

inexpensive *adj* ieftin.

inexperienced *adj* neexperimentat, lipsit de experienţă.

inexpressive *adj* inexpresiv.

inextricable *adj* încâlcit; de nerezolvat.

infallible *adj* infailibil; fără greş, sigur; iminent; inevitabil, de neînlăturat.

infamous *adj* infam; josnic; scârbos; execrabil.

infamy *s* infamie *f*.

infancy *s* (*fragedă*) copilărie *f*, pruncie *f*; *jur* minorat *n*, minoritate *f*; *fig* fază *f* embrionară, început *n*.

infant *s* prunc *m*, sugaci *m*; minor *m* ‖ *adj* infantil; pueril; embrionar • ~**ile** *adj* infantil.

infantry *s mil* infanterie *f*.

infatuated *adj* orbit, înnebunit, scos din minţi; (**with**) îndrăgostit nebuneşte (de), nebun (după).

infect *vt* (**with**) *med* a infecta; *fig* a se propaga la; *fig* a vicia, a otrăvi, a corupe; *jur* a vicia, a lovi (cu, prin) • ~**ion** *s* infecţie *f*; infectare *f*, molipsire *f*; viciere *f* • ~**ious** *adj med* infecţios; *fig* (*enthusiasm, etc*) contagios.

infer *vt* (**from**) a deduce, a conchide, a trage concluzia (din); a presupune, a necesita, a implica; a indica, a arăta.

inferior *adj* inferior; subaltern ‖ *s* inferior *m*; subaltern *m*; subordonat *m*.

infernal *adj* infernal, de iad/infern; *coll* drăcesc, diabolic.

infest *vt* a infesta, a invada, a împânzi; a hărţui, a tulbura, a bântui.

infidelity *s relig* necredinţă *f*; (*of a spouse*) infidelitate *f*; neloialitate *f*, lipsă *f* de devotament.

infighting *s* certuri *f pl* interne, conflicte *n pl* civile.

infiltrate *vt* (**into**) a infiltra, a strecura (în); a îmbiba, a impregna ‖ *vi* (**through/into**) a se infiltra, a se strecura (în, prin) ‖ *s* infiltrare *f*; infiltraţie *f*; *med* infiltrate *n*.

infinite *adj* fără margini; infinit ‖ *s* puzderie *f*, puhoi *n*.

infinitive *s gram* infinitiv *n*, (modul *n*) infinitiv.

infirm *adj* infirm ‖ **the** ~ *s pl* infirmii *m pl*.

inflame *vt* a aprinde; a da foc la; *also fig* a încinge, a înflăcăra; *fig* a aţâţa, a incita; *fig* (*fuel*) a întreţine, a alimenta; *med* a inflama, a face să se inflameze ‖ *vi* a se aprinde, a se inflama, a lua foc; *fig* (**with**) a arde, a se înflăcăra (de); *med* a se inflama.

inflate *vt* (~ *a tire, etc*) a umfla, a umple (cu aer); *econ* (~ *a price, salary*) a creşte, a umfla; (~ *a check, etc*) a încărca (nota); *fig* a se umfla în pene (de) • **~d** *adj* umflat; *fig* infatuat, îngâmfat; *econ* umflat, încărcat, mărit; *fig* bombastic, emfatic.

inflation *s econ* inflaţie *f.*

inflection *s* încovoiere *f*, îndoire *f*, curbare *f*; curbură *f*, îndoitură *f*; *gram* flexiune *f*; *gram* formă *f* flexionară; *mus* modulaţie *f.*

inflict *vt* a izbi, a lovi în; a cauza; a aplica || *vr* a se impune, a se vârî.

influence *s* influenţă *f*; autoritate *f*; forţă *f* || *vt* a influenţa.

influential *adj* influent; puternic.

influenza *s med* gripă *f.*

influx *s* aflux *n.*

inform *vt* a informa; a anunţa; a inspira; a umple de; ~ **on** *vt* a denunţa.

informal *adj* (*person, party*) simplu; (*clothes*) de zi cu zi; (*visit, etc*) neprotocolar; neceremonios; (*meeting*) informal; liber, degajat, familiar, intim.

information *s* informaţii *f pl*; informare *f*, luare *f* de cunoştinţă; **for your** ~ pentru informarea dvs., cu titlu de informaţie; ştiri *f pl*, veşti *f pl*, noutăţi *f pl*; cunoştinţe *f pl*, cultură *f*, informaţie *f*; *jur* denunţ *n*, informare *f*, delaţiune *f*; ~ **desk** *s* birou *n* de informaţii; ~ **technology** *s* informatică *f*; ~ **theory** *s* teoria *f* informaţiei.

informative *adj* (cu caracter) informativ.

informed *adj* informat, în cunoştinţă de cauză, la curent; încunoştiinţat; informat, documentat || *v* * **inform**.

informer *s* informator *m*, om *m* care dă informaţii; *pej* denunţător *m*, delator *m*; *coll* turnător *m.*

infra-red *adj* infraroşu.

infrastructure *s* infrastructură *f.*

infrequent *adj* rar.

infringe *vt* (~ *rights*) a împiedica, a uzurpa; (~ *laws, etc*) a încălca || *vi* (**on**) (~ *rights*) a încălca; (~ *laws, etc*) a contraveni la.

infuriate *vt* a înfuria || *adj* furios, mânios.

infuse *vt* (*instill*) a insufla; (*fill*) a turna, a vărsa (în); (*steep*) a îmbiba (cu), a umple (de).

infusion *s* insuflare *f*, inspirare *f*; turnare *f*; infuzie *f*; injectare *f.*

ingenious *adj* ingenios; inventiv; spiritual.

ingenuity *s* ingeniozitate *f.*

ingenuous *adj* ingenuu, candid, inocent; sincer, franc, deschis; generos, mărinimos.

ingot *s* lingou *n.*

ingrained *adj* vopsit/impregnat/imprimat în fibră/fir; *fig* (*opinion, hate*) (adânc) înrădăcinat/imprimat/ întipărit; *fig* înrăit, înveterat.

ingratiate *vr* (**oneself with**) a intra în graţiile (cuiva), a se vârî sub pielea (cuiva).

ingratitude *s* ingratitudine *f.*

ingredient *s* ingredient *n.*

ingress *s frml* intrare *f.*

inhabit *vt* a locui, a domicilia în; *also fig* a popula.

inhale *vt* a inhala; a inspira; a absorbi; a respira || *vi* a trage în piept (fumul).

inherent *adj* inerent.

inherit *vt* a moşteni; a succede, a urma.

inhibit *vt* a inhiba, a paraliza; (**from**) a opri, a împiedica (să, de la); a interzice, a nu permite.

inhuman *adj* inuman, crud, neomenos; barbar, feroce, sălbatic; rece, indiferent.

inimical *adj* ostil; advers.

iniquitous *adj* (*unjust*) nedrept; arbitrar; (*evil*) criminal, ticălos.

iniquity *s* nedreptate *f*, injustiţie *f*; act *n* arbitrar; ticăloşie *f*, nelegiuire *f*; *relig* păcat *n.*

initial *adj* iniţial; primordial || *s* iniţială *f*; *pl* parafă *f* || *vt* a parafa, a aviza.

initiate *vt* a iniţia; (*talk*) a începe, a deschide; a lua iniţiativa; a inaugura; a lansa, a introduce; *jur* a intenta, a introduce; (**into**) (*teach*) a instrui; (*secret society*) a primi || *vi* a lua/avea iniţiativa; a porni, a începe; (*secret society*) a fi admis/iniţiat/introdus.

initiative *s* iniţiativă *f*; spirit *n* întreprinzător; *pol* drept *n* de iniţiativă legislativă.

inject *vt* a injecta; a insufla; a intercala • **~ion** *s* injecţie *f*; insuflare *f*; sugerare *f.*

injure *vt* a răni; a lovi; a jigni; a păgubi; a dăuna; a avaria || *vr* a se răni.

injurious *adj* (*detrimental*) vătămător; (*insulting*) injurios, defăimător.

injury *s* rană *f*; ofensă *f*; lezare *f*; daună *f*; avarie *f*; prejudiciu *n.*

injustice *s* nedreptate *f.*

ink *s* cerneală *f* || *vt* a scrie cu cerneală; a păta/murdări cu/de cerneală • **~-jet printer** *s comp* imprimantă *f* cu jet de cerneală.

inkling *s* (mică) bănuială *f*, suspiciune *f*; (*hint*) idee/ noţiune *f* vagă.

inland *adj* interior || *adv* în interior.

in-laws *s pl coll* socri *m pl*; rude *f pl* prin alianţă.

inlay *vt* (**with**) a incrusta; a marcheta, a parcheta; a intercala, a insera, a introduce; *fig* a orna; a împodobi || *s* incrustare *f*; incrustaţie *f*; marchetare *f*; plombă *f* dentară; intercalare *f*, inserare *f.*

inlet *s* (*lake, sea*) golfuleţ *n*, sân *n* de mare; *tech* admisie *f*, ştuţ *n* de intrare.

inmate *s* (*of a prison*) deţinut *m*; (*of a mental hospital*) internat *m.*

inn *s* han *n*; birt *n*, ospătărie *f*; cârciumă *f.*

innate *adj* înnăscut, congenital; inerent, ereditar; firesc, natural, instinctiv; *phys* de inerţie.

inner *adj* interior, intern, lăuntric; tainic; slab.

innocence *s* inocenţă *f.*

innocent *adj* inocent; candid; ignorant; simplist; firesc; inofensiv || *s* nevinovat *m*; novice *m.*

innocuous *adj* inofensiv; **render** ~ *vt fig* a goli de conţinut.

innovation *s* inovaţie *f.*

innuendo *s* insinuare *f*, aluzie *f.*

innumerable *adj* nenumărat.

inoculate *vt med* a inocula; a vaccina; *bio* a însămânţa; *fig* a inocula, a inculca, a insufla.

inordinately *adv* excesiv, exagerat; fără moderaţie; (în mod) neregulat/dezordonat.

inorganic *adj chem* anorganic; neorganic, neintegrat; străin, exterior; *ling* nearticulat.

in-patient *s* bolnav/pacient *m* spitalizat/internat.

input *s tech* admisie *f*; intrare *f*; putere *f* consumată; *tech* alimentare *f*, furnizare *f*; *elec* putere *f* de alimentare; contribuţie *f*, sprijin *n*; *comp* intrare *f*, acces *n* || *vt comp* a accesa.

inquest *s* anchetă *f.*

inquietude *s* nelinişte *f*, anxietate *f.*

inquire vt a întreba de; a se interesa ‖ vi a întreba, a se interesa.

inquiry s (*question*) întrebare f, solicitare f de informații; (*inquest*) anchetă f; investigație f; cercetare f.

inquisition s tortură f, chin n; *jur* cercetare f, anchetă f; percheziție f; **the Inquisition** s *hist* Inchiziția f.

inquisitive adj iscoditor, curios; indiscret.

inroad s (*raid*) atac n; (*advance*) incursiune f, invazie f.

inrush s *also fig* năvală f, aflux n, avalanșă f.

insane adj dement, nebun; demențial, nebunesc.

insanity s demență f.

insatiable adj nesățios, avid; nesătul.

inscribe vt *math, etc* a înscrie; (**in/on**) a grava, a săpa, a scrie (pe, în); (**to**) a dedica; *com* a înregistra acționarii.

inscription s inscripție f.

inscrutable adj misterios, greu de înțeles.

insect s insectă f, gâză f; nulitate f; ~ **repellent** s cremă f antiinsecte.

insecure adj (*person*) neliniștit, nesigur; (*jobs, etc*) incert, nesigur; șubred; instabil; critic; periculos.

inseminate vt a insemina.

insemination s *bio* fecundare f; însămânțare f.

insensitive adj (**to**) insensibil, indiferent (la); nepăsător (față de).

inseparable adj de neseparat, inseparabil.

insert vt a insera; a intercala; a înscrie; a vârî ‖ s insert n; inserție f, intercalare f • ~**ion** s inserție f, introducere f.

inshore adj costier, de coastă; care se apropie de țărm ‖ adv la țărm, aproape de țărm/mal; spre țărm/mal.

inside s interior n; dos n; burtă f; gânduri n pl ascunse ‖ adj dinăuntru; secret ‖ adv înăuntru, în interior; ~ **of** prep (*building, etc*) în interiorul • ~**r** s inițiat m; om m bine informat; (*club, etc*) membru m; (*coach*) pasager m, călător m.

insidious adj insidios; prefăcut, viclean; insinuant; perfid, înșelător; subtil.

insight s intuiție f; perspicacitate f; înțelegere f; privire f, ochire f.

insignificant adj neînsemnat.

insincere adj nesincer.

insinuate vt a strecura, a introduce încetul cu încetul; a insinua, a lăsa să se înțeleagă ‖ vr (*into*) a se insinua, a se strecura pe furiș.

insipid adj insipid, fără gust; *fig* nesărat, fără gust, banal, anost, plicticos.

insist vi a insista; a pretinde că; a persista în ‖ vt a pretinde, a susține.

insole s talpă f interioară.

insolent adj insolent, impertinent.

insoluble adj *chem* insolubil; *fig* de nerezolvat, fără soluție/rezolvare.

insomnia s insomnie f.

insolvent s falit m ‖ adj econ, jur insolvabil, falimentar.

inspect vt a inspecta; a cerceta; a verifica • ~**ion** s inspecție f; verificare f; control n; revizie f; examen n.

inspiration s inspirație f.

inspire vt a inspira, a trage în piept, a aspira; *fig* a inspira; a însufleți, a anima.

instability s instabilitate f, lipsă f de echilibru; nestatornicie f, inconstanță f.

install vt a instala; a instaura; a stabili; *tech* a instala; a monta; a amenaja.

installment s *com* rată f, vărsământ n, tranșă f; plată f în rate; (*book*) fasciculă f.

instance s exemplu n, pildă f; dovadă f, probă f, exemplificare f ‖ vt a da de exemplu, a cita ca exemplu, a exemplifica.

instant s clipă f, moment n ‖ adj curent; imediat; urgent; insistent; ușor solubil • ~**aneous** adj instantaneu.

instead adv în schimb; mai degrabă; ~ **of** prep în loc de.

instep s *anat* scobitură f a gleznei.

instigate vt (**to**) a instiga, a incita (la); a ațâța, a provoca.

instill vt a picura, a turna cu picătura; *fig* a inculca, a strecura, a infiltra; a insufla.

instinct s instinct n, simț n; intuiție f.

institute s institut n ‖ vt a institui.

institution s instituție f, organizație f; instituire f, fondare f; precept n, principiu n.

instruct vt a instrui; a informa; a da instrucțiuni; a însărcina; a furniza relații.

instrument s instrument n; unealtă f; dispozitiv n ‖ vt a orchestra; a înfăptui • ~**al** adj *mus, tech* instrumental; (**to/in**) folositor, util (pentru); esențial, indispensabil (pentru).

insubordinate adj nesupus, rebel, refractar, nesubordonat.

insufficient adj insuficient; incomplet; nesatisfăcător, necorespunzător.

insular adj (*perspective*) mărginit; (*person*) limitat.

insulate vt *elec* a izola; (~ *a boiler*) a proteja contra pierderilor de căldură; (*protect*) a proteja.

insulin s *med* insulină f.

insult s insultă f; batjocură f ‖ vt a insulta, a ofensa, a jigni.

insurance s asigurare f; ~ **policy** s poliță f de asigurare.

insure vt *com* a asigura, a încheia o asigurare pentru; a se asigura, a fi sigur ‖ vi (*prevent*) a se asigura, a se proteja de • ~**d** s/adj asigurat m • ~**r** s agent m de asigurare.

insurgent s insurgent m, răzvrătit m, revoluționar m.

insurmountable adj de netrecut, insurmontabil.

insurrection s insurecție f.

intact adj neatins.

intake s *tech* (dispozitiv de) admisie/aspirație f; aspirare f; captare f; *elec* putere f cheltuită/consumată, consum n; (*of food, etc*) rație f; (*recruits*) cei admiși/acceptați.

intangible adj intangibil, de neatins; impalpabil; *fig* imperceptibil, insesizabil; *jur* inviolabil.

integral adj integral, complet, total; integrant, esențial, indispensabil; compus, complex; *math* integral ‖ s întreg n, tot n, totalitate f; *math* integrală f.

integrate vt a integra; a reuni, a strânge laolaltă; a constitui, a alcătui; a cuprinde; a totaliza; a sintetiza.

integrity s (*honor*) integritate f, onestitate f; (*wholeness*) integritate f, totalitate f.

intellect s intelect n, minte f, rațiune f, inteligență f • ~**ual** adj intelectual; mintal ‖ s intelectual m; intelectualitate f.

intelligence s (*ability*) inteligență f; serviciu n de informații; informații f pl, lămuriri f pl.

intelligent adj inteligent, deștept; ~ **card** s cartelă f magnetică • ~**sia** s intelectualitate f.

intelligible adj inteligibil, care poate fi înțeles.

intemperate *adj* necumpătat, nestăpânit; **~ zeal** *s* exces de zel.

intend *vt* a plănui, a intenționa; a urmări; a destina; a vrea să spună.

intense *adj* intens; arzător; acut; iritabil; zelos.

intensification *s* intensificare *f*.

intensify *vt* a intensifica.

intensity *s* intensitate *f*.

intensive *adj* intensiv.

intent *s* intenție *f*, țel *n*, scop *n* ‖ *adj* atent, concentrat; (**on/upon**) încordat, concentrat (asupra), îndreptat (spre, asupra); cufundat în, absorbit de/în.

intention *s* intenție *f*; plan *n*; scop *n*; concept *n*, noțiune *f* • **~al** *adj* intenționat; plănuit; virtual.

inter *vt* a înmormânta, a îngropa, a înhuma.

interact *vi* a fi interdependent, a se influența/condiționa reciproc; (**with**) a comunica (cu cineva).

intercede *vi* (**with**) a interveni (pe lângă cineva); a (inter)media, a mijloci.

intercept *vt* a intercepta.

interchange *s* schimb *n*; intersecție *f* amenajată ‖ *vt* a schimba • **~able** *adj* (**with**) care se poate schimba/înlocui cu.

intercom *s* interfon *n*.

intercourse *s* relații *f pl*, legături *f pl*; comunicare *f* (spirituală), limbaj *n* comun; relații *f pl*/raporturi *n pl* sexuale/intime.

interdict *vt* a interzice.

interest *s* interes *n*, avantaj *n*, profit *n*; (*passion*) pasiune *f*, curiozitate *f*; importanță *f*; punct *n* de atracție; *econ* dobândă *f* ‖ *vt* a interesa, a atrage ‖ *vi* a fi interesat, a prezenta interes; **~ rate** *s* rata *f* dobânzii • **~ed** *adj* interesat, plin de interes • **~ing** *adj* interesant; important; decisiv.

interface *s comp* interfață *f* ‖ *vt* (*connect*) a conecta.

interfere *vi* a interveni; a mijloci; a se amesteca; a interfera.

interim *s* interimat *n*, perioadă *f* interimară ‖ *adj* interimar; temporar, provizoriu.

interior *adj* interior, intern; lăuntric, intim ‖ *s* interior *n*; suflet *n*.

interjection *s gram* interjecție *f*; exclamație *f*.

interlock *vi tech* a se îmbuca ‖ *vt tech* a conexa; a cupla; a sincroniza.

interlocution *s* conversație *f*, discuție *f*.

interlocutor *s* interlocutor *m*.

interloper *s* intrus *m*.

interlude *s* (*pause*) interval *n*; *mus*, *fig* interludiu *n*, intermezzo *n*.

intermediary *s/adj* intermediar *m*.

intermediate *adj* intermediar; mijlocit; mediat; mediu ‖ *vi* a face pe mijlocitorul.

interminable *adj* interminabil, fără sfârșit.

intermission *s* pauză *f*, recreație *f*; antract *n*.

intermittent *adj* intermitent.

intern *vt* a interna ‖ *s* stagiar *m*; *med* rezident *m*; (*in firm*) stagiar *m* • **~ship** *s* stagiu *n* în spital sau la o firmă.

internal *adj* intern; intrinsec; intim; **Internal Revenue** *s* fiscul *n*.

international *adj/s* internațional *m*; *sp* internațional *m*.

Internet *s* Internet *n*.

internist *s med* medic *m* internist.

interplay *s* interacțiune *f*.

interpolate *vt* a interpola, a intercala.

interpose *vi* a se interpune; a media, a juca rol de mediator ‖ *vt* a interpune, pune la mijloc; a opune; a interveni cu, a face uz de.

interpret *vt* a interpreta; a explica; a înțelege; a traduce; a juca ‖ *vi* a fi interpret.

interrelation *s* corelație *f*.

interrogate *vt* a interoga, a întreba.

interrogative *adj* interogativ ‖ *s* interogativ *n*, forma *f* interogativă; întrebare *f*, interogație *f*.

interrupt *vt* a întrerupe; (*silence*) a rupe; a tulbura ‖ *vi* a întrerupe.

intersect *vt* a intersecta ‖ *vi* a se întretăia, a se încrucișa, a se intersecta • **~ion** *s* intersecție *f*, răscruce *f*.

intersperse *vt* (**with**) a presăra, a umple (cu); (**between/among**) a presăra, a răspândi, a amesteca (între, printre).

interstate (highway) *s* autostradă *f*.

intertwine *vt/vi* a (se) întrețese.

interval *s* interval *n*; răstimp *n*; întrerupere *f*; pauză *f*.

intervene *vi* (**~ in an event**) a surveni; (**~ with a person**) a interveni, a se amesteca (în); (*time*) a se scurge, a trece.

intervention *s* intervenție *f*.

interview *s* interviu *n*; întrevedere *f* ‖ *vt* a intervieva.

interwar *adj* interbelic.

intestine *s anat* intestin *n*.

intimate[1] *adj* intim; secret; familiar; profund ‖ *s* intim *m*; confident *m*.

intimate[2] *vt* a sugera, a lăsa să se înțeleagă; *jur* a notifica; a pune în vedere.

intimidate *vt* a intimida.

intimidation *s* intimidare *f*.

into *prep* în; spre, înspre; cu; *coll* (*very interested in*) **he is really ~ music** îl interesează foarte mult muzica.

intolerable *adj* intolerabil, inadmisibil.

intolerant *adj* intolerant.

intonation *s* intonație *f*; *mus also* intonare *f*.

intoxicate *vt* a îmbăta, a ameți.

intractable *adj* refractar, dificil, intratabil; nesupus; (*horse*) năravaș; (*land*) necultivabil; (*material*) ingrat, intratabil.

intransigent *adj* intransigent.

intransitive *s/adj gram* intranzitiv.

intravenous *adj* intravenos.

intrepid *adj* intrepid, îndrăzneț, întreprinzător.

intricate *adj* complicat; încâlcit.

intrigue *s* intrigă *f*; uneltire *f*; dragoste *f* ‖ *vt* a intriga, a mira ‖ *vi* a unelti.

intrinsic *adj* intrinsec.

introduce *vt* a introduce; a iniția; a prezenta; a recomanda ‖ *vr* a se prezenta.

introduction *s* introducere *f*; prefață *f*; inițiere *f*; prezentare *f*.

introspective *adj* introspectiv, cu caracter de introspecție.

introvert *s* introvertit *m* • **~ed** *adj* introvertit.

intrude *vi* a veni nepoftit; a deranja; a impune ‖ *vr* a-și impune prezența • **~r** *s* intrus *m*.

intrusion *s* intruziune *f*; (**on/upon**) intrare *f* nedorită, sosire *f* nedorită, venire *f* nedorită; (**into**) imixtiune *f*, amestec *n*, ingerință *f*; *jur* uzurpare *f*.

intrusive *adj* nepoftit, nedorit; supărător; *geol* intruziv, plutonic, abisal.

intuition *s* intuiție *f*.

inundate *vt* a inunda; (*overwhelm*) a copleși.

invade *vt mil, fig* a invada; (*overrun*) a copleși; (*raid*) a încălca; a viola.

invalid[1] *adj* bolnav; infirm; inapt || *s* bolnav *m*; infirm *m*, invalid *m*; om *m* inapt.

invalid[2] *adj jur* (nul și) neavenit; fără valoare/efect; ineficace, inoperant; nejustificat, neîntemeiat.

invaluable *adj* (*person, aid, advice*) prețios (pentru); valoros (pentru); (*experience, etc*) inestimabil (pentru).

invariable *adj* invariabil, neschimbător.

invariably *adv* (în mod) invariabil; mereu, neîncetat; fără nici o excepție.

invasion *s* invadare *f*; năvălire *f*; încălcare *f*.

invasive *adj mil* invadator, năvălitor; *fig* (*intrusive*) nedorit, deranjant, stânjenitor.

invective *s* invectivă *f*; insultă *f*.

inveigh *vi* (**against**) a profera injurii (la adresa).

inveigle *vt* (**into**) (*entice*) a ademeni (în, să); (*trick*) a îmbrobodi (ca să).

invent *vt* a inventa; a descoperi; a născoci • **~ion** *s* invenție *f*; descoperire *f*; ingeniozitate *f*; născocire *f*.

inventory *s* (*list*) inventar *n*; (*goods*) stoc *n*.

inverse *adj* invers.

inversion *s* inversiune *f*, inversare *f*.

invert *vt* a inversa, a întoarce; a răsturna; a schimba ordinea; *chem* a inverti.

invertebrate *adj zool* nevertebrat; *fig* fără șira spinării; molâu, moale, molatic || *s zool* nevertebrat *n*.

invest *vt* a investi; a împuternici; a instala; a înveșmânta || *vi* a investi • **~ment** *s* investiție *f* • **~or** *s econ* investitor *m*; acționar *m*.

investigate *vt* a investiga; a ancheta || *vi* a face cercetări, a face o anchetă.

investigation *s* investigații *f pl*; cercetare *f*; anchetă *f*.

inveterate *adj* înveterat.

invidious *adj* (*unfair*) nedrept; discriminatoriu; (*unpleasant*) ingrat, neplăcut.

invigorate *vt* a înviora; a împrospăta; a revigora.

invigorating *adj* tonifiant, înviorător.

invincible *adj* (*arms, champions*) invincibil; (*record*) imbatabil.

invisible *adj* invizibil.

invitation *s* invitație *f*; solicitare *f*.

invite *vt* a invita; a solicita; a provoca; a tenta || *vi* a lansa o invitație.

inviting *adj* atrăgător, agreabil; (*food*) apetisant.

invoice *s* factură *f* || *vt* (~ *a customer*) a trimite factura la; (~ *goods*) a factura.

invoke *vt* (~ *a law, etc*) a invoca; (~ *feelings*) a da naștere, a provoca; (*ask for help*) a cere, a implora.

involuntary *adj* involuntar.

involve *vt* a implica; a interesa; a necesita; a complica.

inward *adj* interior; spre interior • **~s** *adv* spre interior.

iodine *s chem* iod *n*.

ion *s phys* ion *n*.

iota *s* iotă *f*, pic *n*.

Iran *s* Iran *n* • **~ian** *s/adj* Iranian *m*.

Iraq *s* Irak *n* • **~i** *s/adj* irakian(ă) *m/f*.

irascible *adj* (*testy*) irascibil; (*touchy*) susceptibil.

irate *adj* furios.

ire *s lit* mânie *f*.

Ireland *s* Irlanda *f*.

iris *s bot* iris *m*.

Irish *s/adj* irlandez(ă) *m/f*; **the** ~ *s* irlandezii *m pl*.

irksome *adj* obositor, plictisitor; supărător, enervant.

iron *s* fier *n*; fier *n* de călcat; sabie *f*; cătușe *f pl*; armă *f* de foc; harpon *n* || *adj* de fier; feros; aspru; viguros; *fig* ferm, neclintit || *vt* a netezi; a călca (cu fierul) • **to** ~ **out** *vt fig* (~ *a difficulty*) a aplana; (~ *a problem*) a rezolva.

ironic(al) *adj* ironic, sarcastic.

irony *s* ironie *f*, sarcasm *n*.

irrational *adj* (*action*) irațional, nelogic; absurd; inexplicabil; (*person*) care nu judecă, irațional.

irreconcilable *adj* de neîmpăcat.

irredeemable *adj econ* nerambursabil, neamortizabil; (*person*) incorigibil; (*loss*) de nerecuperat.

irrefutable *adj* de necontestat, irefutabil.

irregular *adj* neregulat; asimetric; dezordonat; ilicit || *s pl* trupe *f pl* neregulate.

irrelevant *adj* irelevant; neînsemnat.

irreparable *adj* ireparabil.

irreplaceable *adj* de neînlocuit.

irrepressible *adj* (*enthusiasm*) care nu poate fi reprimat.

irreproachable *adj* ireproșabil.

irresistible *adj* irezistibil.

irresolute *adj* nehotărât.

irrespective *prep* (**of**) fără a ține seama de, independent/indiferent de.

irresponsible *adj* iresponsabil, nesăbuit.

irretrievably *adv* ireparabil, iremediabil, definitiv.

irreverent *adj* ireverențios, lipsit de respect/deferență.

irrevocable *adj* irevocabil.

irrigate *vt* a iriga; a uda, a stropi; *med* a spăla (o rană).

irritable *adj* iritabil; susceptibil.

irritate *vt* a irita, a enerva; a stimula; a excita.

irritating *adj* iritant.

irritation *s* (*annoyance*) iritare *f*, supărare *f*; (*inflammation*) iritare *f*, iritație *f*.

irruption *s* irupție *f*, năvălire *f*.

is *v aux* este, e.

Islam *s* islam *n*, lumea *f* islamică/musulmană; popor *n* islamic/musulman; islamism *m*, mahomedanism *n*.

island *s* insulă *f*; zonă *f* izolată; *aut* refugiu *n* pentru pietoni || *vt* (*isolate*) a izola.

isolate *vt* a izola, a separa; *med* a izola, a ține în carantină • **~d** *adj* izolat; separat.

issue *s* ieșire *f*; scăpare *f*; scurgere *f*; sfârșit *n*; (*result*) rezultat *n*; (*offspring*) progenitură *f*; (*publication*) ediție *f*; (*bills*) emisiune *f*; (*document*) eliberare *f*; (*subject*) chestiune *f*; concluzie *f* || *vi* a decurge; a ajunge la un rezultat || *vt* (~ *stocks, bills*) a emite; (*publish*) a edita, a publica; (~ *documents*) a elibera, (*distribute*) a distribui.

isthmus *s geog* istm *n*.

it *pron pers* el, ea || *pron dem* ace(a)sta, ăsta/asta.

Italian *adj* italian || *s* (*person*) italian(că) *m/f*; (*language*) italiană *f*.

italic *adj* italic • **~s** *s pl* caractere *n pl* cursive, litere *f pl* cursive.

Italy *s* Italia *f*.

itch *s* râie *f*; sete *f*, dorință *f* (de), pasiune *f* (pentru) || *vi* a produce mâncărime; a fi nerăbdător să • **~y** *adj* care dă mâncărimi.

item *s* paragraf *n*, alineat *n*, (*news*) articol *n*; (*agenda*) punct *n*; element *n*; număr *n*; subiect *n* || *vt* a bifa, a nota • **~ize** *vt* a detalia; a puncta.

itinerant *adj* itinerant, ambulant.

itinerary *s* itinerar *n*, rută *f*; călătorie *f*; plan *n* de
    călătorie.
its *adj pos* a(l) lui/ei, al său, a sa, ai săi, ale sale.
itself *pron* se; (pe) el însuși, chiar pe el; chiar lui,
    lui/sie însuși; pe ea însăși, chiar (pe) ea; ei/sie însăși.
ivory *s* fildeș *n*, colț *m*; culoare *f* ivorie || *adj* din fildeș;
    ivoriu; **Ivory Coast** *s* Coasta *f* de Fildeș.
ivy *s bot* iederă *f*; **Ivy League** *s* cele opt mari univer-
    sități din estul Statelor Unite.

J

J, j *s* (litera) J, j.
jab *vt* (**into**) a băga/vârî (cu forța), a împinge în || *s*
    lovitură *f* bruscă; împunsătură *f*.
jabber *s* sporovăială *f* || *vi* a sporovăi • **~er** *s* palavragiu
    m.
jack *s tech* cric *n*, vinci *n*; *constr* capră *f*, suport *n*; *naut*
    geac *n*; *min* perforator *n*; *elec* jac *n*, fișă *f* || *vt* a ridica
    cu cricul/vinciul; *fig* **~ up** (*~ a price*) a urca • **~of-
    all-trades** *s* meșter *m* bun la toate • **~o'lantern** *s*
    luminiță *f* rătăcitoare.
jackal *s zool* șacal *m*.
jackass *s* (*donkey*) măgar *m*; *pej* (*imbecile*) nătărău *m*.
jackdaw *s zool* stăncuță *f*.
jacket *s* jachetă *f*, vestă *f*; (*potato*) coajă *f*; înveliș *n*;
    (*book*) supracopertă *f*; (*disc*) învelitoare *f*.
jackpot *s* lozul *n* cel mare.
jade[1] *s miner* jad *n*.
jade[2] *s* (*horse*) gloabă *f*, mârțoagă *f*; *obs* (*shrew*)
    zgripțuroaică *f*.
jaded *adj* blazat, plictisit.
jagged *adj* dantelat, zimțat, crestat.
jaguar *s zool* jaguar *m*.
jail *s* închisoare *f*, temniță *f* || *vt* a închide, a întemnița.
jam[1] *vt* (*door, etc*) a bloca, a înțepeni, a încuia; (*traffic*)
    a bloca circulația; *radio* a bruia; (*switchboard*)
    supraîncărca; a strânge; (**into**) a îndesa; a presa; a
    bruia || *vi* a se strânge; a se presa; a se bloca || *s*
    blocaj *n* de circulație; *tech* blocare *f*; înțepenire *f*;
    gripare *f*; *aut* presare *f*.
jam[2] *s cul* dulceață *f*, gem *n*.
jamboree *s* petrecere *f*, chef *n*; (*scout rally*) jamboree *f*.
jangle *vi* (*rattle*) a suna aspru/discordant || *s* (*jingle*)
    sunet *n* discordant; larmă *f*, gălăgie *f*.
janitor *s* portar *m*; administrator *m*; îngrijitor *m*.
January *s* (luna) ianuarie *m*, Gerar.
Japan *s* Japonia *f* • **~ese** *s/adj* japonez(ă) *m/f*; **the ~**
    japonezii *m pl*.
jape *s* glumă *f*; farsă *f*.
jar[1] *s* borcan *n*; recipient *n*, vas *n*.
jar[2] *vi* a trepida; a scârțâi; a se ciocni || *vt* a lovi || *s*
    sunet *n* discordant; șoc *n*; trepidație *f*; ciocnire *f*.
jargon *s* jargon *n*.
jasmine *s bot* iasomie *f*.
jaundice *s med* icter *n*, gălbenare *f* • **~d** *adj* (*attitude*)
    acru, morocănos.
jaunt *s* plimbare *f* || *vi* a face o plimbare sau o scurtă
    călătorie de plăcere.
jaunty *adj* degajat, dezinvolt; nepăsător; elegant, stilat.
javelin *s mil* lance *f*; suliță *f*; *sp* suliță *f*.
jaw *s* falcă *f*; sporovăială *f* || *vi* a îndruga verzi și uscate
    || *vt* a dădăci.
jay *s orn* gaiță *f*.

jaywalk *vi* a traversa strada în afara trecerii pentru
    pietoni; a fi distrat • **~er** *s* pieton *m* distrat.
jazz *s mus* jazz *n*; **~ up** *vt coll* a se înveseli • **~y** *adj* de
    jaz; țipător; animat.
jealous *adj* gelos; invidios; atent • **~y** *s* gelozie *f*.
jeans *s pl* blugi *m pl*.
jeep *s* jeep *n*, mașină *f* de teren.
jeer *vi* a huidui, a batjocori (în public) || *s* zeflemea *f*,
    batjocură *f*; *fig* împunsătură *f*, înțepătură *f*.
jelly *s* jeleu *n*; peltea *f*; piftie *f* || *vi* a se face jeleu || *vt* a
    face jeleu/piftie • **~fish** *s* meduză *f*.
jeopardize *vt* a compromite, a pune în pericol, a
    periclita.
jeopardy *s* risc *n*; pericol *n*; **put in ~** *vt* a pune în
    pericol.
jerk *s* (*movement*) zguduială *f*, smucitură *f*; *coll* idiot
    m, tâmpit *m* || *vi* (*person*) a tresări; (*vehicle*) a zgâlțâi
    • **~ily** *adv* spasmodic, pe apucate.
jersey *s* jerseu *n*; *text* tricot *n*.
jest *s* glumă *f*; **in ~** in glumă • **~er** *s* bufon *m*.
Jesus (Christ) *s* Iisus, Iisus-Hristos.
jet[1] *s* avion *n* cu reacție; (*liquid*) jet *n*; canal *n*; *aut*
    jiclor *n*; *tech* ajutaj *n*, duză *f* || *vt* a arunca; a pulver-
    iza • **~lag** *s* oboseală *f* din cauza decalajului orar • **~
    propulsion** *s avia* propulsie *f* cu aer cald.
jet[2] *s miner* gagat *n*; lignit *n*.
jettison *vt* (*cargo*) a arunca peste bord; *fig* (*ideas*) a
    renunța la, a abandona.
jetty *s naut* jetea *f*, jetelă *f*; dig *n*; chei *n*; debarcader *n*.
Jew *s* evreu *m* • **~ess** *s* evreică *f*.
jewel *s* bijuterie *f*; nestemată *f*; odor *n*; (*watch*) rubin *n*
    • **~er** *s* bijutier *m* • **~ry** *s* bijuterii *f pl*.
Jewish *adj* evreiesc; evreu; ebraic.
jib[1] *s naut* (*sail*) floc *n*; (*look*) înfățișare *f*, aspect *n*.
jib[2] *s* (*of a crane*) braț *n* de macara.
jib[3] *vi* (*horse balks*) a se cabra; (*person balks*) a refuza
    fi dispus, /a nu fi dispus (să facă ceva), a se opune.
jibe *s* sarcasm *n*, ironie *f*, batjocură *f*.
jiffy *s coll* clipită *f*, moment *n*; **in a ~** cât ai zice pește,
    cât ai clipi din ochi.
jig *s mus* gigă *f*; *tech* gabarit *n*; *tech* capră *f* de montaj;
    naut palanc *n*; *typ* matriță *f*.
jiggle *vt* (*rattle*) a zgâlțâi; (*shake*) a clătina.
jigsaw *s* ferăstrău *n* mecanic; mozaic *n*, puzzle *n*.
jilt *vt* (*~ someone*) a părăsi; *coll* a lăsa cu buza umflată.
jingle *s* (*sound*) clinchet *n*, zornăit *n*; (*melody*) semnal
    n (radiofonic) || *vi* (*~ a bell*) a răsuna; (*~ coins, etc*) a
    zornăi.
jinx *s coll* cobe *f*, piază *f* rea.
jittery *adj coll* (*person*) nervos, agitat; (*situation*)
    tensionat, delicat.
job *s* muncă *f*, lucru *n*, ocupație *f*; post *n*; profit *n*;
    afacere *f*; ocazie *f*; furt *n* || *vi* a munci ocazional; a
    specula || *vt* a angaja; a închiria • **~less** *adj* șomer *m*.
jockey *s* jocheu *m* || *vi* (*for*) a căuta să obțină prin
    tertipuri, viclenie etc.
jockstrap *s sp* suspensor *n*.
jocular *adj* vesel, jovial; amuzant.
jodhpurs *s pl* pantaloni *m pl* de călărie.
jog *s* zgâlțâit *n*; ghiont *n*; obstacol *n*; mers *n* încet || *vt* a
    zgâlțâi; a zgudui || *vi* a se mișca încet; a face jogging
    • **~ging** *s* jogging *n*.
join *vt* a lega, a uni, a cupla; (*~ a party*) a intra în, a
    deveni membru; (*~ a club*) a se înscrie la/în; (*~ the
    army*) a se înrola; (*~ a line*) a se așeza la coadă; a

reveni la; a însoți || *vi* a se uni cu; a deveni membru; (~ *a club*) a se înscrie.

joiner *s* tâmplar *m*.

joint *s anat* articulație *f*, încheietură *f*; *aut* garnitură *f* de etanșare; îmbinare *f*; (*meat*) halcă *f*; *tech* racord *n*; *tech* nod *n*; *rail* joantă *f*; *constr* nod *n*; rost *n*; balama *f*; *met* cusătură *f* || *vt* a cupla; a îmbina, a combina; *constr* a îmbina, a etanșa; a rostui; ~ **venture** *s* între-prindere *f* mixtă • ~**ly** *adv* de comun acord.

joist *s constr* grindă *f*; bară *f*.

joke *s* glumă *f*, farsă *f*; întâmplare *f* hazlie || *vi* a glumi • ~**er** *s* (*person*) glumeț *m*; (*card*) joker *m*.

jolly *adj* (*person*) jovial, vesel; (*time, etc*) agreabil, plăcut.

jolt *vt* a hurduca, a zgâlțâi || *vi* a (se) hurduca; a vibra || *s* hurducătură *f*; smucitură *f*; izbitură *f*; *tech* șoc *n*; *fig* șoc *n*, lovitură *f*.

jostle *s* ciocnire *f*, lovire *f*; înghesuială *f*, aglomerație *f*; înghiontire *f* || *vt* a împinge; a înghesui; a înghionti || *vi* a se împinge; a se înghesui; a se înghionti.

jot *s* iotă *f*, pic *n*, urmă *f* || *vt* (**down**) a nota, a însemna.

journal *s* jurnal *n* zilnic; revistă *f*; ziar *n*.

journalism *s* ziaristică *f*, gazetărie *f*; presă *f*.

journalist *s* ziarist *m*.

journey *s* călătorie *f*, voiaj *n* || *vi* a călători.

journeyman *s* (*apprentice*) calfă *f*, *obs* (*day-worker*) zilier *m*.

jovial *adj* jovial, vesel.

jowls *s pl* obraji *m pl*.

joy *s* bucurie *f*; voioșie *f*; confort *n* • ~**ful** *adj* vesel, voios; mulțumit.

joystick *s avia* manșă *f*; *comp* manetă *f*.

jubilant *adj* (*person*) radios, copleșit de bucurie; (*cry*) de bucurie.

jubilee *s* jubileu *n*.

Judaism *s relig* iudaism *n*.

judge *s jur* judecător *m*; critic *m*; expert *m* || *vt jur* a judeca, a hotărî; a critica; a evalua || *vi jur* a judeca; a crede; a condamna; a cugeta.

judgment *s jur, relig* judecată *f*; *jur* (*verdict*) sentință *f*; (*opinion*) opinie *f*; (*wisdom*) discernământ *n*; pedeapsă *f* divină.

judicial *adj* judiciar, juridic.

judicious *adj* judicios, chibzuit.

judo *s* judo *n*.

jug *s* ulcior *n*; ibric *n*; cană *f*; *sl* închisoare *f* || *vt* a pune în ulcior; a întemnița.

juggernaut *s* camion *n* de mare tonaj.

juggle *vt also fig* a jongla cu || *vi* a jongla • ~**r** *s* jongler *m*; *fig* escroc *m*.

jugular *adj anat* jugular || *s* venă *f* jugulară.

juice *s* suc *n*, zeamă *f*; miez *n*; vigoare *f* || *vt* a scoate sucul din.

juicy *adj* suculent, zemos; umed; picant; grozav; viguros.

jukebox *s* tonomat *n*.

July *s* (luna) iulie *m*; (luna lui) Cuptor.

jumble *s* amestec *n*; (*mess*) harababură *f*; zăpăceală *f*, confuzie *f* || *vt* (*mix up*) a amesteca, a pune de-a valma; (~ *ideas, etc*) a zăpăci, a încurca.

jumbo *s* colos *m*; monstru *m*, dihanie *f*; om *m* oarte mare, animal *n* oarte mare, obiect *n* foarte mare; *coll* elefant *m* || *adj* colosal, uriaș; ~ **jet** *s* avion *n* de mare capacitate.

jump *s* săritură *f*, salt *n*; fior *n*; avantaj *n* || *vt* a sări; a sălta; a zgudui || *vi* a sări; a sălta; a trece repede • ~**er**

s săritor *m*; parașutist *m*; pulover *n*; bluză *f*; ~ **cable** *s* cablu *n* de branșare la baterie • ~**start** *vt* (*car*) a împinge (pentru a porni); a porni utilizând cablu de încărcare a bateriei • ~**y** *adj* nervos, agitat.

junction *s* (*road*) intersecție *f*, răscruce *f*; joncțiune *f*; *rail* nod *n* de cale ferată, încrucișare *f*; asociație *f*; confluență *f*.

juncture *s* moment *n*, clipă *f*; *fig* situație *f*, stare *f* de lucruri; criză *f*, perioadă *f* critică; punct/loc *n* de legătură; *tech* încheietură *f*; cusătură *f* sudată; element *n* de legătură, articulație *f*; **at a critical** ~ într-un moment critic.

June *s* (luna) iunie *m*, Cireșar.

jungle *s* junglă *f*; desiș *n*; mlaștină *f* cu păpuriș.

junior *adj* junior; mai tânăr; (*rank*) subordonat || *s* junior *m*; (*rank*) subaltern *m*; (*age*) mezin *m*, per-soană *f* mai tânără; elev/student *m* în anul 3.

juniper *s bot* ienupăr *m*.

junk[1] *s* vechituri *f pl*, obiecte *n pl* uzate; *met* fier *n* vechi; deșeuri *n pl* || *vt* a arunca la gunoi; ~ **food** *s* pej* mâncare *f* tip fast-food; ~ **mail** *s* reclame *f pl* (sosite prin poștă); ~ **shop** *s* prăvălie *f* cu lucruri de ocazie • ~**yard** *s* depozit *n* de obiecte uzate/fier vechi/deșeuri.

junk[2] *s* (*boat*) joncă *f*.

junket *s coll pej* călătorie *f* pe cheltuiala altuia; *coll* petrecere *f*, chef *n*; *cul* brânză *f* aromatizată.

junkie, junky *s sl* (*drug addict*) toxicoman *m*; *fig* (*football, etc fan*) suporter *m*, admirator *m*.

junta *s pol* juntă *f*.

juridical *adj* juridic.

jurisdiction *s* jurisdicție *f*.

jurist *s jur* jurist *m*.

juror *s jur* jurat *m*.

jury *s jur* jurați *m pl*; juriu *n*.

just *adj* (*fair*) drept, just, corect; meritat; justificat; exact || *adv* (*only*) tocmai, (*exactly*) precis; (*a minute ago*) adineaori; chiar atunci; (*now*) chiar acum; (*barely*) doar; (*simply*) numai.

justice *s* justiție *f*, judecată *f*; dreptate *f*; (*cause*) temei *n*; judecător *m* (de pace).

justifiable *adj* justificabil.

justification *s* justificare *f*.

justify *vt* a justifica; a motiva; a explica; a confirma.

jut *vi* a ieși în afară, a fi proeminent || *s* ieșitură *f*; proeminență *f*; proiectare *f*.

jute *s bot* iută *f*.

juvenile *adj jur* minor, juvenil; (*childish*) pueril || *s jur* minor *m*.

juxtapose *vt* a alătura, a juxtapune.

juxtaposition *s* alăturare *f*; juxtapunere *f*.

K

K, k *s* (litera) K, k.

kaftan *s* caftan *n*.

kaleidoscope *s* caleidoscop *n*.

kamikaze *s*/*adj* kamikaze *m*.

kangaroo *s zool* cangur *m*.

karat *s* carat *n*.

karate *s* carate *n*.

kayak *s* caiac *n*.

kebab *s cul* kebab *n*.

keel *s naut* chilă *f*; *naut* barcă *f* cu velă pătrată; *hydr* carenă *f* || *vi* (**over**) *naut* a naufragia; (*person*) a leșina.

keen *adj* ascuțit; tăios; profund; inteligent; subtil; acut; activ; pasionat; dornic.

keep, kept, kept *vt* (*save*) a păstra; (*prevent*) a împiedica; (*~ prisoner*) a ține; (*~ a promise*) a respecta; (*~ an appointment*) a merge la; (*~ an oath*) a fi fidel; (*~ a diary*) a ține; (*sheep, etc*) a crește; (*own a store*) a ține; (*have a car*) a poseda, a avea; *sp* a apăra; (*have a family*) a se îngriji de; a întreține; (*continue*) a continua ‖ *vi* (*weather continues*) a dura; a rezista; **~ on** *vi* a continua (fără încetare); **~ out** *vt* a împiedica să intre; **~ up** *vt* a continua, a menține • **~er** *s* paznic *m* • **~ing** *s* stăpânire *f*; întreținere *f*; păstrare *f*; pază *f*, supraveghere *f*.

keg *s* butoiaș *n*; butoi *n*.

kennel *s* coteț *n* (de câine); adăpost *n*; vizuină *f*; refugiu *n* ‖ *vt* a ține în coteț.

Kenya *s* Kenia *f* • **~n** *s/adj* kenian(ă) *m, f*.

kept *vt* * **keep**.

kernel *s* (*nut*) sâmbure *m*; miez *n*; (*corn, etc*) grăunte *m*, bob *n*; *phys* nucleu *n*, sâmbure *m*.

kerosene *s* kerosen *n*, petrol *n* lampant.

ketchup *s* ketchup *n*.

kettle *s* ceainic *n*; ibric *n*; oală *f*; vas *n* de fiert; cazan *n*; boiler *n*.

key *s also fig* cheie *f*; zăvor *n*; soluție *f*; cod *n*; ton *n*; cifru *n*; conector *n*; (*typewriter*) tastă *f*; (*piano*) clapă *f*; (*map*) legendă *f*; **~ ring** *s* portchei *n* ‖ *vt* a acorda; a manipula; a închide cu cheia.

keyboard *s also comp* tastatură *f*.

keypad *s comp* tastatură *f* numerică.

khaki *s/adj* (culoare) kaki *f*.

kick *vi* a da din picioare; a da cu copita; a protesta; a sări în sus ‖ *vt* a lovi cu piciorul; a azvârli sus; a da afară ‖ *s* lovitură *f* (cu piciorul); recul *n*; tărie *f*; **~ off** *vi coll* a porni, a demara; *sp* a pune/repune balonul în joc • **~back** *s coll* (*bribe*) șpagă *f*; *tech* recul *n*.

kid¹ *s* (*child*) puști *m*, țânc *m*; (*goat*) ied *m*; (*leather*) piele *f* de ied/capră; *coll* (*brother/sister*) mic; **my ~ sister** sora mea mai mică.

kid² *s* păcăleală *f* ‖ *vt* a păcăli, a trage pe sfoară; a glumi; a se preface • **no ~ding!** fără glumă!.

kidnap *vt* a răpi, a fura (un copil sau un om) • **~ping** *s* răpire *f*.

kidney *s anat* rinichi *m*; fel *n*; natură *f*; temperament *n*; **~ bean** *s* fasole *f* mare.

kill *vt* (*slay*) a omorî; a asasina; a tăia; *fig* (*~ hope*) a pune capăt la; (*~ pain*) a suprima; (*destroy*) a distruge; a îndura; a istovi; (*defeat*) a respinge; (*shock*) a epata; (*stop*) a înăbuși ‖ *s* animal *m* omorât; vânat *n*; omor *n* • **~er** *s* (*person*) ucigaș *m*, asasin *m*; (*animal*) carnivor.

killjoy *s coll* persoană *f* care strică cheful altora.

kiln *s* cuptor *n*.

kilo *s* kilogram *n*; *coll* chil *n*.

kilobyte *s comp* kilooctet *n*.

kilogram *s* kilogram *n*.

kilometer *s* kilometru *n*.

kilowatt *s* kilowat *m*.

kilt *s* kilt *n* (fustanelă purtată de scoțieni).

kimono *s* chimono *n*.

kin *s* rude *f pl*; înrudire *f*; rudenie *f*.

kind¹ *s* rasă *f*; neam *n*; familie *f*; fel *n*; esență *f*; gen *n*; calitate *f*.

kind² *adj* bun, amabil; cordial, sincer, amical • **~hearted** *adj* bun la suflet; generos.

kindergarten *s* grădiniță *f* de copii.

kindle *vi* (*~ a fire*) a aprinde; *fig* (*~ feelings*) a suscita, a trezi.

kindness *s* gentilețe *f*, amabilitate *f*.

kindred *s* (*similar*) asemănător; **~ spirit** *s* spirit *n* înfrățit.

kinetic *adj phys* cinetic.

king *s* rege *m*; domn *m*; monarh *m*; suveran *m*; magnat *m* • **~dom** *s* (*country*) regat *n*; (*animal, plant*) regn *n*.

kingfisher *s orn* pescăruș *m*.

kingsize(d) *adj* (*cigarette*) lung; (*package*) uriaș; (*bed*) mare.

kink *s* (*in a rope*) nod *n*; răsucitură *f*; încovoiere *f*, îndoitură *f*; *physiol* cârcel *m*; spasm *n*; *fig* (*quirk*) ciudățenie *f*; *fig* capriciu *m*, toană *f* ‖ *vi* a se încurca, a se încâlci ‖ *vt* a face un nod sau noduri • **~y** *adj coll* vicios.

kinsfolk *s* rude *f pl*, neamuri *n pl*.

kiosk *s* chioșc *n*.

kipper *s* hering *m* afumat.

kiss *vt* a săruta; a atinge ușor ‖ *vi* a se săruta ‖ *s* sărutare *f*; atingere *f* ușoară; **the ~ of life** *s* (*CPR*) respirație *f* gură la gură.

kit *s* cadă *f*; găleată *f*; echipament *n*; raniță *f*; set *n*; trusă *f* de scule; grup *n*.

kitchen *s* bucătărie *f*; fel *n* de a găti.

kite *s* uliu *m*, erete *m*; zmeu *n*; *om m* hrăpăreț.

kitten *s* pisicuță *f*; pisoi *m*, motănaș *m*.

kitty *s* (*cards*) miză *f*, bancă *f*.

kiwi *s* (*bird*) (pasărea) kiwi *f*; (*fruit*) kiwi *n*.

kleptomania *s* cleptomanie *f*.

knack *s* îndemânare *f*, abilitate *f*, iscusință *f*; talent *n*; deprindere *f*, obișnuință *f*; *coll* chițibuș *n*, truc *n*; *text* cută *f*, încrețitură *f*.

knapsack *s* raniță *f*, rucsac *n*.

knave *s* (*cards*) valet *m*; *obs* șarlatan *m*.

knead *vt* a frământa.

knee *s* genunchi *m*; colțar *n*; legătura *f* ‖ *vt* a lovi cu genunchiul ‖ *vi* a îngenunchea.

kneel, knelt, knelt *vi* a îngenunchea, a sta în genunchi; **~ down** *vi* a îngenunchia, a se așeza în genunchi.

knew *vt* * **know**.

knickers *s pl* pantaloni *m pl* de golf.

knickknack *s* bibelou *n*; bagatelă *f*.

knife *s* cuțit *n*; racletă *f*; bisturiu *n* ‖ *vt* a tăia.

knight *s* cavaler *m*; cal *m* (la șah) ‖ *vt* a face cavaler.

knit *vt* a tricota; a împleti; a lega; a încrunta (sprâncenele) ‖ *vi* a împleti; a tricota; a se lega • **~ting** *s* tricotare *f*, împletitură *f* • **~wear** *s* tricotaje *n pl*.

knob *s* nod *n*; (*tree*) ciot *n*; *geog* dâmb *n*, colină *f*; (*door*) mâner *n*; *tech* proeminență *f*, convexitate *f* • **~by** *adj* noduros, cioturos.

knock *vt* (*hit*) a lovi, a izbi; a bate; a ciocăni; a învinge; (*censor*) a critica aspru; a se izbi cu ‖ *vi* a bate; a se ciocni; a se lovi ‖ *s* lovitură *f*; ciocănit *n*; critică *f* aspră • **~out** *s sp* knock-out *n*; lovitură *f* zdrobitoare.

knoll *s* colină *f*, dâmb *n*.

knot *s* nod *n*; buclă *f*; fundă *f*; miez *n*; legătură *f*; ceată *f* ‖ *vt* a înnoda; a lega • **~ty** *adj* spinos, încurcat, delicat.

know, knew, known *vt* (*~ that*) a ști (că); (*~ how to do smth*) a ști să faca ceva; (*~ a person, place*) a cunoaște; (*~ a profession, job*) a se pricepe la, a fi priceput în; (*meet*) a cunoaște, a face cunoștință cu; (*remember*) a recunoaște, a-și reaminti; (*experience*) a avea experiența; (*regard*) a considera || *vi* a ști; a cunoaște • **~how** *s* pricepere *f*, tehnică *f*, know-how *n* • **~ing** *adj* (*smile*, *look*) cu înțeles, semnificativ • **~ingly** *adv* (*smile*, *look*) subtil; (*deliberately*) conștient.

knowledge *s* cunoaștere *f*; cunoștințe *f pl*; informație *f*; cunoștință *f*, știință *f*; știre *f*, veste *f* • **~able** *adj* (*expert*) bine informat; (*well researched*) bine documentat.

known *vt* * **know**.

knuckle *s anat* articulație/încheietură *f* a degetului; *tech* articulație *f*, încheietură *f*; *tech* clichet *n* de cuplare; *naut* cot *n* || *vt* a lovi cu degetul.

kohlrabi *s bot* gulie *f*.

Korea *s* Coreea *f* • **~n** *adj* coreean || *s* (*person*) coreean(ă) *m/f*; (*language*) coreeană *f*.

kosher *adj* (*food*) cușer; *coll* autentic, veritabil.

kowtow *vi* (**to**) a se ploconi (în fața cuiva).

krypton *s chem* kripton *n*.

kudos *s* (*status*) prestigiu *n*; (*esteem*) onoare *f*.

kung fu *s* kung-fu *n*.

Kurd *s* kurd *m* • **~ish** *s* limba *f* kurdă || *adj* kurd.

Kuwait *s* Kuweit *n*.

L

L, l *s* (litera) L, l.

la *s* (nota) la *f*.

lab *s abbr* laborator *n*.

label *s* etichetă *f*; inscripție *f*; denumire *f*; marca *f* fabricii || *vt* a eticheta; a marca; a califica.

labor *s* muncă *f*; efort *n*; lucru *n*; muncitorii *m pl*; strădanie *f*; *pl* durerile *f pl* facerii || *vt* a trudi; a munci || *vi* a munci la; a elabora; **Labor Day** *s* ziua *f* muncii; **~ camp** *s* lagăr *n* de muncă; **~ force** *s* populație *f* activă; mână *f* de lucru; **~ union** *s* sindicat *n* • **~er** *s* muncitor *m* • **~saving device** *s* aparat *n* electric de uz casnic.

laboratory *s* laborator *n*.

laborious *adj* (*person*) harnic; (*work*) laborios, anevoios; (*style*) greoi.

laburnum *s bot* bobițel *m*; salcâm *m* galben.

labyrinth *s* labirint *n*; *fig* impas *n*.

lace *s* (*material*) dantelă *f*; (*shoe~*) șiret *n*; șnur *n*; panglică *f*; *mil* tresă *f* || *vt* (~ *a shoe*) a lega cu șireturi; a vărga; a biciui; a înfrumuseța; (~ *a drink*) a turna alcool în.

lacerate *vt* a rupe, a sfâșia; a chinui, a tortura.

lack *s* lipsă *f*; neajuns *n* || *vt* a-i lipsi; a-i trebui || *vi* a lipsi, a nu se găsi.

lackadaisical *adj pej* nepăsător, apatic, indiferent.

lackey *s* (*minion*) lacheu *m*; *pej* lingușitor *m*.

lackluster *adj* șters, lipsit de strălucire, spălăcit.

laconic *adj* laconic.

lacquer *s* (*for wood*) lac *n*, vernis *n*; (*for hair*) fixativ *n* || *vt* a lăcui, a lustrui.

lactate *s chem* lactat *n* || *vi* a secreta lapte.

lacteal *adj* lăptos, ca laptele.

lacuna *s* (*in text*) lacună *f*.

lacy *adj* de dantelă; dantelat.

lad *s* băiat *m*; tânăr *m*; flăcău *m*.

ladder *s* scară *f*; (*stocking*) ochi *n* dus, fir *n* dus || *vi* a se deșira.

laden *adj* (**with**) încărcat, plin (de).

lading *s* încărcătură; *naut* caric *n*, navlu *n*.

ladle *s* lingură *f* mare, polonic *n*; cupă *f*, benă *f* || *vt* a scoate cu polonicul.

lady *s* doamnă *f*; stăpână *f*; iubită *f* || *adj* feminin; de femeie • **~in-waiting** *s* doamnă *f* de onoare • **~like** *adj* distins, elegant.

ladybug *s ento* buburuză *f*;

lag *vi* a zăbovi; a întârzia || *s* întârziere *f*; zăbovire *f* || *vt* a pune doage/șipci; *tech* a căptuși cu izolație termică || *s* doagă *f*; șipcă *f*.

lager *s* bere *f* blondă.

laggard *s om m* leneș/încet.

lagoon *s* lagună *f*.

laic(al) *adj* laic.

laid *vt* * **lay**.

laid-back *adj* relaxat, destins.

lain *vi* * **lie**.

lair *s* vizuină *f*, bârlog *n*.

laity *s relig* laici *m pl*, mireni *m pl*.

lake *s* lac *n*; iaz *n*; ghiol *n*; iezer *n*.

lamb *s* miel *m*; (carne de) miel *f*; om *m* blând; ageamiu *m* • **~swool** *s* lână *f* de miel || *adj* din lână de miel.

lame *adj also fig* schilod; șchiop; neconvingător || *vt* a schilodi • **~brain** *s coll* imbecil *m*, cretin *m*.

lament *s* tânguire *f*, bocet *n*; *liter* elegie *f* || *vi* a se lamenta, a se tângui || *vt* a deplânge, a deplora • **~able** *adj* (*woeful*) deplorabil, jalnic; (*poor*) lamentabil; (*regrettable*) regretabil.

laminate *vt* a lamina || *vi* a se lamina.

lamp *s* lampă *f*; felinar *n*; lanternă *f* || *vt* a lumina.

lampoon *s* satiră *f* || *vt* a satiriza.

lance *s* lance *f* || *vt* a străpunge.

lancet *s med* bisturiu *n*.

land *s* (*earth*) pământ *n*; uscat *n*; (*soil*) sol *n*; (*arable*) teren *n*; (*country*) țară *f*; ținut *n*; provincie *f* || *vi* (~ *a plane*, *ship*) a debarca; (~ *a plane*) a ateriza; a sosi; a cădea || *vt naut* a debarca; (~ *a criminal*) a captura; (*hit*) a trage; *coll* (~ *a job*, *etc*) a obține, a câștiga; (*cause trouble*) a atrage necazuri asupra cuiva.

landlady *s* gazdă *f*; proprietăreasă *f*; stăpână *f*; gospodină *f*; hangiță *f*.

landlord *s* moșier *m*; proprietar *m*; gazdă *f*; hangiu *m*.

landmark *s* bornă *f* de hotar; baliză *f*; punct *n* de reper; *fig* moment *n* hotărâtor/marcant.

landscape *s* peisaj *n*.

landslide *s* alunecare *f* de teren; (*rock*) surpare *f*; *fig* triumf *n*, victorie *f* răsunătoare.

lane *s* alee *f*; cărare *f*; străduță *f*; culoar *n*; pasaj *n*; coridor *n*; bandă *f* de circulație.

language *s* limbă *f*; limbaj *n*; vorbire *f*; exprimare *f*, stil *n*.

languid *adj* moale; pasiv, apatic; slab.

languish *vi* a lâncezi.

languorous *adj* (*languid*) languros; (*slow*) încet, lent; (*relaxed*) moale.

lank *adj* (*person*) înalt și slab, deșirat; (*hair*) neted, lins; (*grass*) rar • **~y** *adj* deșirat; lins; rar.

lantern *s* felinar *n*, lanternă *f*.

Laos *s* Laos *n*.

Laotian *s/adj* laoțian(ă) *m/f*.

lap[1] *s* poală *f*; genunchi *m pl*; sân *m*; lob *m* (al urechii); *sp* tur *n* de pistă.

lap[2] *vt* (*drink*) a lipăi || *vi* (*water ~s at shore*) a clipoci.

lapel *s* rever *n*.

Lapland *s* Laponia *f*.

Lapp *s/adj* lapon || *s* (*people of Lapland*) lapon(ă) *m/f*.

lapse *s* eroare *f;* lapsus *n;* delăsare *f;* cădere *f;* curs *n;* interval *n;* întrerupere *f;* declin *n* ‖ *vi* (*document*) a nu mai fi valabil; (*membership*) a lua sfârșit; (*tradition*) a se pierde; *jur* (*right*) a decădea; (*time*) a se scurge, a trece; a pieri.

laptop *adj comp* portabil.

larceny *s* furt *n.*

larch *s bot* zadă *f.*

lard *s* untură *f* (de porc) ‖ *vt* a împăna (cu slănină); a unge; *fig* (*speech*) a presăra.

larder *s* cămară *f;* provizii *f pl.*

large *adj* (*big*) mare; (*liberal*) larg; (*extensive*) spațios, întins, vast; (*important*) mare; (*fat*) gras ‖ *adv* larg; pompos; trufaș; **at ~** *adv* pe larg, pe de-a întregul, (*prisoner, etc*) în libertate; **by and ~** *adv* în ansamblu.

lariat *s* lasou *n.*

lark¹ *s* (*bird*) ciocârlie *f.*

lark² *vi* a glumi ‖ *vt* a tachina; a necăji ‖ *s* glumă *f;* năzbâtie *f;* distracție *f.*

larva *s* (*pl* –**vae**) larvă *f.*

larynx *s anat* laringe *n.*

lascivious *adj* lasciv; provocator.

laser *s* laser *m;* **~ printer** *s comp* imprimantă *f* cu laser.

lash *s* (*eye~*) geană *f;* (*whip*) lovitură *f* de bici ‖ *vt* a biciui; *fig* a critica, a nu cruța; a-și bate joc de; *fig* (*waves ~ the shore*) a lovi, a izbi; **to ~ out** *vi* (**at/against**) a biciui, a critica aspru.

lass *s* fată *f;* fetiță *f.*

lassitude *s* oboseală *f;* lâncezeală *f;* moleșeală *f.*

lasso *s* lasso *n;* arcan *n.*

last¹ *adj* ultim; (*past*) trecut; (*final*) final; (*most recent*) cel mai recent, modern ‖ *adv* ultimul, la sfârșit; ultima oară; **~ name** *s* nume *n* de familie • **~ditch** (**effort**) *adj* ultim, disperat.

last² *vi* a dura; (*food*) a se păstra, a se conserva; (*feelings*) a persista; **~ out** *vi* (*survive*) a supraviețui, a dăinui; (*be enough*) a ajunge, a fi de ajuns.

latch *s* zăvor *n* • **~key** *s* cheie *f* (de la ușă).

late *adj* târziu; (*delayed*) întârziat; (*tardy*) tardiv; ultim; (*recent*) recent; (*former*) fost; (*deceased*) răposat ‖ *adv* (*behind*) târziu, cu întârziere; (*recently*) de curând, recent • **~comer** *s* întârziat *m* • **~ly** *adv* recent, de curând; în ultima vreme.

latent *adj* latent.

lateral *adj* lateral.

lath *s* șipcă *f,* leaț *n;* (*plank*) palplanșă *f.*

lathe *s* strung *n.*

lather *s* spumă *f* (de săpun) ‖ *vt* a face spumă, a săpuni.

Latin *s/adj* latin *m* ‖ *s* (*language*) latină *f.*

latitude *s* latitudine *f;* libertate *f* (de acțiune); lărgime *f.*

latrine *s* latrină *f,* closet *n* fără canalizare.

latter *adj/pron* the **~** cel din urmă, cel de-al doilea, ultimul.

lattice *s* zăbrele *f pl;* grătar *n.*

laudatory *adj* laudativ, omagial.

laugh *s* râs *n* ‖ *vi* a râde; **to ~ at** *vi* a-și bate joc de, a râde de • **~able** *adj* ridicol • **~ter** *s* râs *n,* râsete *n pl.*

launch *vt* a lansa; a da (o lovitură); a întreprinde; a începe ‖ *s* lansare *f; naut* barcaz *m;* șalupă *f;* barcă *f* cu motor.

launder *vt* (*wash*) a spăla; *fig* (*~ money*) a spăla • **~ette** *s* spălătorie *f* publică.

laundress *s* spălătoreasă *f.*

laundry *s* spălătorie *f;* rufe *f pl* spălate.

laureate *s/adj* laureat *m.*

laurel *s bot* dafin *m.*

lava *s* lavă *f.*

lavatory *s* spălător *n;* toaletă *f;* piscină *f.*

lavender *s bot* levănțică *f.*

lavish *adj* generos, darnic; (*praise*) neprecupețit ‖ *vt* a împărți; a acorda.

law *s* lege *f;* regulă *f;* regulament *n; jur* drept *n;* proces *n;* **~ and order** *s* ordine *f* publică; **court of ~** *s* tribunal *n* • **~abiding** *adj* care respectă legea • **~ful** *adj* legal, permis, conform legii • **~less** *adj* fără legi; anarhic; (*person*) ticălos; (*passion*) nestăpânit, neînfrânat • **~maker** *s* legiuitor *m,* legislator *m.*

lawn *s* peluză *f,* pajiște *f* • **~ mower** *s* mașină *f* de tuns iarba • **~ tennis** *s sp* tenis *n* de camp.

lawsuit *s* proces *n;* **bring a ~ against smb** *vt* a intenta proces cuiva.

lawyer *s* avocat *m;* jurist *m.*

lax *adj* liber, destins; (*conduct*) îndoielnic; (*ideas, etc*) vag, neclar.

laxative *s med* laxativ *n.*

lay¹, laid, laid *vt* (*set a table*) a pune, a așeza; (*~ a trap*) a întinde, (*~ out a plan*) a face; (*flatten a crop*) a culca; (*~ eggs*) a oua; (*get rid of*) a scăpa de; (*set*) a situa; (*have sex with*) a se culca (cu); (*refute*) a desminți; (*~ a wager*) a paria ‖ *vi* a oua; a paria ‖ *s* cablare *f;* situare *f;* contur *n;* direcție *f;* **~ aside** *vt* a lăsa deoparte; **~ off** *vt* a disponibiliza; **~ over** *vi* a face o escală; **~ waste** *vt* a devasta • **~over** *s* escală *f.*

lay² *adj* laic • **~man** *s relig* laic *m,* mirean *m;* profan *m,* nespecialist *m.*

lay³ *s* melodie *f;* baladă *f.*

layer *s* strat *n;* banc *n;* matcă *f;* zăcământ *n;* vlăstar *n* ‖ *vt* a stivui.

layout *s* (*of an office, building*) aranjament *n;* (*of a garden*) plan *n;* (*of a page*) punere/aranjare *f* în pagină ‖ *vt* (*arrange*) a amenaja; a amplasa; (*present*) a expune, a arăta; (*design*) a proiecta; (*plan*) a planifica; (*spread out*) a așterne; *coll* (*spend*) a cheltui.

laziness *s* lene(vie) *f,* trândăvie *f.*

lazy *adj* (*person*) leneș, trândav, indolent; (*action*) încet, domol, apatic.

lead¹, led, led *vt* a (con)duce; (*guide*) a ghida; a dirija; (*induce*) a determina ‖ *vi* a fi ghid; a conduce ‖ *s thea* rolul *n* principal; conducere *f;* (*guidelines*) directive *f pl,* îndrumări *f pl;* (*initiative*) comandă *f;* exemplu *n;* (*for a dog*) lesă *f;* (*path*) potecă *f;* (*clue*) indiciu *n,* pistă *f; sp* primul loc *n;* (*in card game*) rând *n* • **~er** *s* conducător *m;* șef *m;* lider *m;* articol *n* de fond; conductă *f* de scurgere • **~ership** *s* (*persons*) conducătorii *m pl;* (*action*) direcție *f,* conducere *f;* (*quality*) calități *f pl* de conducător.

lead² *s* min plumb *n;* (*pencil*) mină *f* • **~ed** *adj* (*gasoline*) cu plumb • **~free** *adj* fără plumb.

leaf *s* (*tree, etc*) frunză *f;* petală *f;* frunziș *n;* (*book*) foaie *f,* pagină *f,* filă *f;* (*table*) tăblie *f;* canat *n* ‖ *vi* a înfrunzi ‖ *vt* a frunzări; **~ through** (*~ a magazine, etc*) *vt* a parcurge, a răsfoi.

league *s* ligă *f; sp* campionat *n;* **be in ~ with** *vt* a fi aliat cu.

leak *vi* a curge; a ieși la iveală ‖ *vt* a scurge; a strecura; (*~ secrets*) a divulga ‖ *s* spărtură *f;* scurgere *f;* **~ out** *vi* (*liquid*) a se scurge; *fig* (*secret, etc*) a transpira, a fi divulgat • **~age** *s* spărtură *f;* scurgere *f* • **~y** *adj* neetanș; care are scurgeri.

lean[1], **leaned/leant, leaned/leant** *vi* a se înclina ‖ *vt* a sprijini, a rezema; ~ **on/against** *vi* a se rezema pe/de.

lean[2] *adj* (*person*) slab, uscățiv; (*meat*) slab, fără grăsime; *fig* slab, sărac, neroditor; neproductiv • ~**ing** *s* (**towards**) înclinație *f* (pentru) ‖ *adj* înclinat, aplecat.

leant *vi* * **lean**.

leap, leaped/leapt, leaped/leapt *vi* a sări; a acționa pripit ‖ *vt* a sări peste; a face să sară ‖ *s* salt *n*, săritură *f*; ~ **year** *s* an *m* bisect • ~**frog** *s* (joc *n*) de-a capra ‖ *vt* a depăși (dintr-o săritură).

leapt *vi* * **leap**.

learn, learned/learnt, learned/learnt *vt* a învăța, a studia; a afla; a auzi; a reține ‖ *vi* a învăța; a exersa • ~**ed** *adj* cult, erudit • ~**er** *s* debutant *m*, elev *m* • ~**ing** *s* cultură *f*, erudiție *f*.

lease *s* arendă *f*; chirie *f*; închiriere *f*; contract *n* de închiriere ‖ *vt* a arenda; a închiria • ~**hold** *s* pământ *n*/teren *n* arendat; casă *f* închiriată.

leash *s* lesă *f*.

least *adj* cel mai mic; cel mai puțin ‖ *adv* cel mai puțin; **at** ~ cel puțin; ~ **of all** cu atât mai puțin; **not in the** ~ câtuși de puțin, absolut de loc.

leather *s* piele *f* ‖ *vt* a acoperi cu piele; a bate.

leave, left, left *vt* (*quit*) a părăsi, (*depart from*) a pleca din; (*abandon*) a lăsa; (*deposit*) a depune; (*forget*) a omite ‖ *vi* (*depart*) a porni spre; (*resign*) a demisiona; (*end*) a termina ‖ *s* (*permission*) învoire *f*; plecare *f*; despărțire *f*; **on** ~ *adj* în concediu.

leaven *s* maia *f*, ferment *m*, drojdie *f*.

leavings *s pl* rămășițe *fpl*.

Lebanese *s*/*adj* libanez(ă) *m*/*f*.

Lebanon *s* Liban;

lecherous *adj* lubric, libidinos.

lectern *s* pupitru *n*; strană *f*.

lecture *s* prelegere *f*; conferință *f*; morală *f* ‖ *vi* a ține o prelegere ‖ *vt* a face morală; a conferenția (despre).

led *vt* * **lead**.

ledge *s* (*window* ~) ramă *f*; (*mountain* ~) cornișă *f*.

ledger *s* registru *n*; *constr* grindă *f* orizontală.

lee *s naut* bordul *n* de sub vânt; protecție *f*, adăpost *n*, apărare *f*.

leech *s zool* lipitoare *f*, *fig* parazit *m*, lipitoare *f*.

leek *s bot* praz *m*.

leer *s* privire *f* răutăcioasă; privire *f* lacomă/ pofticioasă ‖ *vi* (**at**) a se uita chiorâș/strâmb sau pofticios/lacom (la).

lees *s pl* sediment *n*; drojdie *f*, drojdii *f pl*.

leeway *s naut, avia* derivă *f*; *fig* marjă *f* de manevră.

left[1] *vt* * **leave**.

left[2] *adj* stâng; radical; liberal ‖ *adv* de/în/spre stânga ‖ *s* **the** ~ stânga *f* • ~**handed** *adj* (*person*) stângaci; (*tool*) pentru stângaci.

leftover *adj* care rămâne, în plus ‖ *s pl* rămășițe *f pl*, resturi *n pl*.

leg *s* (*of a person, pant*) picior *n*; *anat* gambă *f*; (*of an animal*) labă *f*; *cul* (~ *of lamb*) ciozvârtă *f*; (*pork, chicken* ~) pulpă *f*; (*furniture* ~) picior *n*, suport *n*; piedestal *n*; (*of a trip*) etapă *f*, rundă *f*; (*part of a road*) bretea *f*, ramificație *f* de șosea ‖ *vt* a împinge cu piciorul; *coll* a păcăli.

legacy *s also fig* moștenire *f*.

legal *adj* juridic, legal; judecătoresc; permis; ~ **holiday** *s* sărbătoare *f* legală; ~ **adviser** *s* jurisconsult *m*.

legation *s* legație *f*, misiune *f* diplomatică.

legend *s* legendă *f*; mit *n*; explicație *f*.

legible *adj* citeț, lizibil; clar.

legion *s* legiune *f*; armată *f*, *fig* legiune *f*, mulțime *f* (mare).

legislate *vt jur* a legifera ‖ *vi* a elabora legi.

legislation *s* legislație *f*.

legitimate *adj* legitim; drept ‖ *vt* a adopta, a înfia.

leisure *s* răgaz *n*; timp *n* liber; tihnă *f* ‖ *adv* în tihnă, pe îndelete ‖ *adj* liber; ~ **center** *s* centru *n* de recreere/ distracții.

lemon *s* (*tree*) lămâi *m*; (*fruit*) lămâie *f*; (*color*) culoarea *f* lămâiei; *coll* om *m* antipatic/nesuferit; nereușită *f*, eșec *n*.

lend, lent, lent *vt* a împrumuta; a închiria; a împărtăși ‖ *vi* a da cu împrumut • ~**ing library** *s* bibliotecă *f* de împrumut • ~**ing rate** *s* rată *f*, dobândă *f* de credit/împrumut.

length *s* lungime *f*; distanță *f*; durată *f*; măsură *f*; metraj *n* • ~**en** *vt* (~ *dress, etc*) a întinde, a lungi; (*life*) a prelungi ‖ *vi* a alungi.

leniency *s* (*clemency*) indulgență *f*, toleranță *f*; (*kindness*) blândețe *f*.

lenient *adj* blând; indulgent; binevoitor; răbdător.

lenitive *adj* calmant.

lens *s* lentilă *f*; lupă *f*; obiectiv *n*.

lent[1] *vi* * **lend**.

Lent[2] *s relig* postul *n* mare/Paștelui.

lentil *s bot* linte *f*.

Leo *s astrol* Leul *m*.

leopard *s zool* leopard *m*.

leotard *s* costum *n* purtat de dansatori (dintr-o singură piesă, mulat pe corp).

leper *s* lepros *m*.

leprosy *s* lepră *f*.

leprous *adj* lepros.

lesbian *s* lesbiană *f*.

lesion *s* leziune *f*, rană *f*.

less *adj* mai puțin; mai mic; inferior; minor ‖ *adv* mai puțin; nu atât/așa de ‖ *prep* fără, minus, mai puțin ‖ ~**en** *vt* (~ *risk, chance*) a diminua, a reduce; (~ *pain*) a atenua ‖ *vr* a se micșora; (~ *pain*) a se atenua • ~**er** *adj* mai mic/neînsemnat; minor; inferior.

lesson *s* lecție *f*; prelegere *f*; dojană *f*; tâlc *n* ‖ *vt* a da lecții; a dojeni.

lessor *s jur* persoană *f* care dă cu chirie/în arendă.

lest *conj* ca nu cumva, ca să nu, de teamă/frică să nu; să nu.

let, lent, let *vt* (*allow*) a permite; a lăsa; (*hire*) a închiria ‖ *vi* a se închiria; ~ **alone** *vi* în afară de, ca să nu mai vorbim de; ~ **in** *vt* a lăsa să intre; a primi; ~ **off** *vt* a da drumul la; a descărca; a lansa; a ierta (de); ~ **out** *vt* a lăsa să iasă; a da drumul; (~ *a scream*) a scoate; (~ *clothes*) a lărgi; (~ *a prisoner*) a elibera; ~ **up** *vi* (*stop*) a se opri; (*diminish*) a încetini; (*relax*) a-și acorda un răgaz • ~**down** *s coll* decepție *f*; încetinire *f*, relaxare *f*; declin *n*, regres *n*.

lethal *adj* de moarte; mortal; fatal

lethargy *s* letargie *f*; inerție *f*; apatie *f*; somn *n* adânc/de moarte.

letter *s* literă *f*; caracter *n*; scrisoare *f* ‖ *vt* a imprima litere; a nota; ~ **bomb** *s* scrisoare *f* capcană; ~ **of credit** *s com* scrisoare *f* de credit • ~**head** *s* antet *n* • ~**opener** *s* coupe papier *n*.

lettuce *s bot* lăptucă *f*.

leukemia *s med* leucemie *f*.

level *s tech* nivelă *f* cu bule de aer; cotă *f*; nivel *n*; treaptă *f*; câmpie *f* ‖ *adj (equal)* la același nivel; orizontal; *(flat)* plat, plan; regulat; monoton; calm ‖ *vt (flatten)* a nivela, a netezi; *(raze)* a șterge (de pe fața pământului); a egaliza; ~ **with smb** *vi coll* a fi franc/deschis cu cineva.

lever *s* pârghie *f*; levier *n*; mâner *n*.

levitation *s* levitație *f*.

levity *s* superficialitate *f*; neseriozitate *f*.

levy *s* prelevare *f*, impozit *n*; *jur* sechestru *n* judiciar ‖ *vt* a preleva, a percepe (impozite)

lewd *adj* desfrânat; lasciv; obscen.

lexical *adj* lexical.

lexicon *s* listă *f* de cuvinte; dicționar *n*.

lexis *s* lexic *n*.

liability *s econ* răspundere *f*, responsabilitate *f*; *pl* pasiv *n*, datorii *f pl*; obligație *f*.

liable *adj* obligat să; care poate să; pasibil de; expus la; raspunzător de/pentru.

liaison *s* legătură *f* (amoroasă); pronunțare *f* legată.

liana *s bot* liană *f*.

liar *s* mincinos *m*.

libel *s* calomnie *f* ‖ *vt* a calomnia.

liberal *adj* liberal; generos; degajat.

liberate *vt* a elibera; a degaja.

libertine *s/adj* libertin *m*, depravat *m*.

liberty *s* libertate *f*; permisiune *f*; risc *n*.

Libra *s astrol* Balanța *f*.

librarian *s* bibliotecar *m*.

library *s* bibliotecă *f*.

libretto *s mus* libret *n*.

lice *s pl* * **louse.**

license *s* licență *f*; autorizație *f*; brevet *n*; abatere *f*; libertinaj *n* • **~e** *s* brevet *n*, patent *n*.

licentious *adj* libertin, depravat.

lichen *s bot* lichen *m*.

lick *vt* a linge; a bate ‖ *vi* a fugi ‖ *s* lingere *f*, lins *n*; ciomăgeală *f*; fugă *f* • **~ing** *s (thrashing)* ciomăgeală *f*; *(defeat)* înfrângere *f*.

lid *s* capac *n*; pleoapă *f*; copertă *f*; interdicție *f*.

lie¹, lay, lain *vi* a sta culcat, a zăcea; a locui; a se afla ‖ *s* configurație *f*.

lie² *vi* a minți ‖ *s* minciună *f*; născocire *f*.

Liechtenstein *s* Liechtenstein.

lien *s jur* garanție *f*; privilegiu *n*.

lieu *s* loc *n*; **in ~ of** în loc de.

lieutenant *s mil* locotenent *m*; locțiitor *m*.

life *s (living)* viață *f*; trai *n*; *(existence)* existență *f*; *(biography)* biografie *f*; *(living person)* ființă *f*; *(durability)* durată *f*; *(nature)* natură *f*; *(liveliness)* vioiciune *f*; regn *n*; ~ **insurance** *s* asigurare *f* de viață.

lifebelt *s* centură *f* de siguranță, colac *m* de salvare.

lifeboat *s naut* barcă *f* de salvare

lifeguard *s (at a pool)* profesor *m* de înot; *(at a beach)* salvamar *m*; *(bodyguard)* gardă *f* personală.

life-jacket *s* vestă *f* de salvare.

lifelike *adj (statue, etc)* care pare viu; *(portrait)* veridic, asemănător; viu, plin de viață.

lifeline *s naut* balustradă *f*; frânghie *f*/coardă *f* de salvare; *fig* legătură *f* vitală, ancoră *f* de salvare.

lifelong *adj* pe viață; până la moarte.

lifesaver *s* salvamar *m*; salvator *m*.

lifespan *s (of a person, animal)* speranță *f* de viață; *(of machines, etc)* durată *f* de viață/funcționare.

lifestyle *s* stil *n* de viață.

lifetime *s* viață *f*, durata *f* vieții; *tech* durată *f* de funcționare.

lift *vt* a ridica; a fura; a plagia; a dezgropa; a urca ‖ *vi* a se ridica; a se împrăștia; a decola ‖ *s* ridicare *f*; înălțare *f*; ascensor *n*.

ligament *s anat* ligament *n*.

light¹ *s* lumină *f*; zi *f*; *(instrument)* lampă *f*; *aut* far *n*; felinar *n*; *(cigarette)* foc *n*; *(traffic ~)* semafor *n*, stop *n*; *also fig* astru *m*, stea *f*; *pl* inteligență *f*; *pl* crez *n*, doctrină *f* ‖ *adj (bright)* luminos; *(color)* deschis; *(hair)* blond ‖ *vt* (~ *a cigarette*) a aprinde; a lumina ‖ *vi (face)* a străluci, a se lumina; a se aprinde; a se însenina.

light² *adj* ușor; *(blow, sleep, steps)* ușor; *(wind)* slab; *(movement)* suplu; delicat; *(reading)* recreativ, ușor, amuzant; *(work)* ușor; *(traffic)* fluid; *(correction)* rar ‖ *adv* ușor; cu ușurință.

light³ *vi (bird)* a se lăsa, a coborî; a cădea.

light-headed *adj* delirant; zăpăcit, aiurit.

lighthearted *adj* cu inima ușoară, fără griji; voios.

lighter *s* brichetă *f*; aprinzător *m*; fitil *n*.

lighthouse *s* far *n*.

lightning *s* fulger *n*; ~ **rod** *s elec* paratrăznet *n*.

like¹ *adj* asemănător, asemenea, analog, similar ‖ *s* seamăn *m*, pereche *f* ‖ *adv* (într-un mod) asemănător; în același mod/fel/chip; probabil ‖ *prep* ca, (la fel) ca și, la fel cu; **very** ~ *adj* foarte probabil; întrucâtva, până la un punct; **be or look** ~ *vt* a fi la fel cu cineva, a semăna cu cineva, a se asemăna cu cineva; **it looks** ~ **it** *fig* așa te pare/s-ar părea; **run** ~ **mad** *vt* a alerga ca un nebun/ca ieșit din minți.

like² *vt* a-i plăcea; a ține la; a îndrăgi ‖ *vi* a-i plăcea, a vrea, a dori.

likely *adj* probabil; potrivit, adecvat.

liking *s (taste)* gust *n*, înclinare *f*; *(affection)* simpatie *f*; plăcere *f*; preferință *f*; **take a ~ to/for** *vt* a prinde gust de, a începe să-i placă (ceva, cineva).

lilac *s bot* liliac *m* ‖ *adj (color)* liliachiu, violaceu.

lilt *s* melodie *f* ritmată; ritm *n* cadențat.

lily *s bot* crin *m*.

limb *s (body part)* membru *m*; *(tree ~)* creangă *f*; părtaș *m* ‖ *vt* a dezmembra.

limber *adj (lithe)* flexibil, elastic, *(agile)* agil.

limbo *s relig, lit* pragul *n* iadului; *fig* uitare *f*; stare *f* nesigură, stare *f* de incertitudine.

lime ¹ *s bot* tei *m*; .

lime² *s bot* lămâi *m*.

limelight *s* rampă *f*; *thea* lumina *f* rampei; **be in the ~** *vi* a fi în centrul atracției, a fi în prim plan, a fi punctul de atracție.

limerick *s* limerick *n*, poezie *f* umoristică absurdă.

limit *s* limită *f*; margine *f*; *pl* ținut *n* ‖ *vt* a limita; a fixa prețul • **~ation** *s* limitare *f*; restricție *f*; *jur* prescripție *f* (extinctivă).

limo *s coll* * **limousine.**

limousine *s aut* limuzină *f*.

limp¹ *vi* a șchiopăta.

limp² *adj* mlădios, suplu; neputincios; *(~ clothing, etc)* mototolit; neapretat.

limpet *s zool* melc *m* de apă.

limpid *adj (water, air)* limpede, clar; *fig (style)* limpede, clar, neînzorzonat.

linchpin *s* cui *n* de osie; *tech* fus *n*; fuzetă *f*; *fig (key player)* personaj-cheie *n*.

linden *s bot* tei *m*.

line[1] *s* (*rope*) funie *f*; sfoară *f*; șnur *n*; ață *f*; (*fishing ~*) undiță *f*; *math, phys* linie *f*; (*border*) hotar *n*; (*norm*) regulă *f*; (*written ~*) rând *n*, vers *n*; (*limit*) limită *f*; (*wrinkle*) rid *n*, cută *f*; *naut* parâmă *f*; *mil* front *n*; (*kinship*) neam *n*; (*route*) traseu *n*, rută *f*; *tel* linie *f* || *vt* a linia; (*~ forehead*) a brăzda; (*line up*) a înșirui; *mil* a alinia; **stand in** *~ vt* a sta la coadă.

line[2] *vt* (*~ clothes*) a căptuși.

linen *s* pânză *f*; olandă *f*; lenjerie *f*.

liner *s naut* navă *f* de linie, vas *n* de linie; pachebot *n*; transatlantic *n*; *avia* avion *n* care face curse regulate.

lineup *s sp* echipă *f*; (*suspect ~*) șir *n* de suspecți (care urmează să fie identificați de către un martor).

linger *vi* (*person*) a zăbovi; (*doubt, pain*) a persista, a dura; (*stroll*) a hoinări; (*waiver*) a șovăi; a tânji; (*poison ~s*) a acționa încet || *vt* a-și pierde vremea.

lingerie *s* lenjerie *f*; albituri *f pl*.

linguist *s* lingvist *m*.

liniment *s med* loțiune *f*.

lining *s* (*of clothes, etc*) căptușeală *f*; dublură *f*; (*stomach ~*) mucoasă *f*; *aut* (*brake ~*) garnitură *f*.

link *s* verigă *f*, inel *n*; ochi *n*; legătură *f* || *vt* a înlănțui; a uni || *vi* a se lega.

linoleum *s* linoleum *n*.

linseed *s* ulei *n* de in.

lint *s* puf *n*; scamă *f*; *mil* fitil *n*; fibră *f*, fir *n*.

lion *s zool* leu *m*; *fig* (*celebrity*) celebritate *f*.

lip *s* buză *f*; margine *f*; muchie *f* || *vt* a săruta.

lipstick *s* ruj *n* (de buze).

liquefy, liquify *vt/vi* a (se) lichefia.

liqueur *s* lichior *n*.

liquid *adj* lichid; fluid; senin; schimbător; plăcut || *s* lichid *n*; soluție *f*.

liquidate *vt fig* (*kill*) a lichida; *fin* (*~ debt*) a achita; *jur* (*~ an estate, company*) a lichida, a desființa.

liquor *s* băutură *f*; soluție *f*; suc *n*; sos *n*.

liquorice *s bot* lemn *n* dulce.

Lisbon *s* Lisabona *f*.

lisp *vi* a sâsâi; a se bâlbâi || *vt* a rosti sâsâit || *s* sâsâit *n*; foșnet *n*; susur *n*.

lissome *adj* (*lithe*) zvelt, (*agile*) sprinten.

list[1] *s* listă *f*; tabel *n*; inventar *n*; registru *n*; catalog *n*; rol *n*; stat *n* || *vt* (*make list of*) a nota pe o listă; (*enter in a list*) a înregistra; (*enumerate*) a enumera; (*classify*) a clasa; *comp* a lista.

list[2] *vi naut* a se înclina.

listen *vi* a asculta; a fi atent la || *s* audiție *f*.

listing *s* listă *f*; *comp* listare *f*.

listless *adj* nepăsător, indiferent; apatic.

lit *vt* * **light**.

litany *s relig* litanie *f*, rugăciune *f*.

liter *s* litru *m*.

literacy *s* știință *f* de carte; deprinerea *f* de a citi și a scrie; instrucție *f*.

literal *adj* literal; precis; pedant; prozaic.

literary *adj* literar; de litere.

literate *adj* cu știință *f* de carte; cu carte, cult; învățat || *s* om *m* cu știința de carte; om *m* cu carte, om *m* cult; om *m* învățat; literat *m*.

literature *s* literatură *f*; litere *f pl*; documentație *f*, bibliografie *f*.

lithe *adj* suplu, mlădios.

lithograph *s* litografie *f* || *vt* a litografia • *~y* litografie *f*.

lithosphere *s* litosferă *f*.

litigant *s jur* parte *f* litigiantă || *adj* în litigiu.

litigate *vt* a pune în litigiu || *vi* a se judeca (cu).

litigation *s jur* litigiu *n*; contestație *f*.

litter *s* gunoi *n*; murdărie *f*; dezordine *f*; (*newborn animals*) purcei etc abia fătați || *vt* a murdări; a așterne paie; (*give birth to a litter*) a făta.

little *adj* mic; puțin; câtva, ceva; îngust; meschin || *pron/s* puțin, ceva || *adv* puțin, nu mult; ceva, oarecum, întrucâtva; deloc, de fel.

littoral *s/adj* litoral *n*.

liturgy *s relig* liturghie *f*.

live[1] *vi* a trăi, a exista; a locui; a se întreține || *vt thea* (*~ a role*) a trăi; (*life*) a duce (o viață).

live[2] *adj* viu, în viață; plin de viață, vioi; real, din viață; (*color*) viu, aprins; (*embers*) aprins; *tech* mobil; *elec* sub tensiune; *radio, tv* în direct; (*show*) cu/în public; (*bomb*) nedescărcat, neactivat, neexplodat.

livelihood *s* trai *n*; mijloace *n pl* de existență/trai.

lively *adj* (*mind*) vioi, ager; (*color*) viu; (*person*) plin de viață, vesel; energic; iute; (*debate, etc*) animat, aprins.

liven *vt* (*~ a person*) a anima, a înveseli; (*~ a place*) a anima || *vi* a se însufleți, a se anima.

liver *s anat* ficat *m*.

livery *s* uniformă *f*; livrea *f*.

livestock *s* vite *f pl*; șeptel *n*.

livid *adj* livid; vânăt.

living *adj* viu, în viață; (*color*) viu, aprins, luminos; *fig* vioi; energic; activ, harnic; aidoma, leit || *s* viață *f*, existență *f*; trai *n*; mod *n* de viață; **the ~ image of her mother** leit maică-sa; **~ room** *s* cameră *f* de zi, salon *n*.

lizard *s zool* șopârlă *f*.

load *s* povară *f*, sarcină *f* || *vt* a încărca; a copleși || *vi* a încărca; a lua încărcătură • *~ing* *s* încărcătură *f*, încărcare *f*.

loaded *adj* încărcat; plin; *mil* încărcat; (*~ question*) viclean; *coll* afumat, cherchelit; *coll* plin de bani.

loadstone *s* * **lodestone**

loaf[1] *s* pâine *f*; franzelă *f*; căpățână *f* de zahăr.

loaf[2] *vi* a trândăvi; a hoinări || *s* trândăveală *f*, trândăvie *f*, lene *f*.

loam *s agr* cernoziom *n*; lut *n*; *constr* chirpici *n*.

loan *s* împrumut *n* || *vt* a da cu împrumut, a împrumuta

loath *adj* (*to*) refractar (la); **be ~ to do smth** *vt* a nu fi dispus să facă ceva • *~some* *adj* dezgustător, respingător.

loathe *vt* a detesta, a-i fi silă de; **~ doing smth** *vi* a avea oroare să facă ceva, a detesta să facă ceva.

lob *vi* a merge greu/greoi; (*~ in tennis*) a arunca mingea sus || *vt* (*~ in tennis*) a executa un lob.

lobby *s* vestibul *n*; hol *n*; coridor *n*; *thea* foaier *n*; *naut* culoar *n*; (*pressure group*) lobby *n* || *vt pol* a influența (Congresul).

lobe *s anat* lob *n* (al urechii); alveolă *f* pulmonară; *bot* lob *n*; *tech* petală *f*, lob *n*; camă *f*, lobă *f*.

lobster *s icht* homar *m*.

local *adj* local; îngust || *s* localnic *m*; tren *n* local.

locale *s* (*of a novel, play, movie*) scenă *f* (a acțiunii), cadru *n* (al acțiunii).

locate *vt* (*position*) a situa, a repera; (*~ a source*) a localiza; (*place, etc*) a amplasa; a instala; a poziționa, a așeza || *vi* a se stabili.

location *s* loc *n*; situație *f*; amplasare *f*; locație *f*; **on ~** *cin* în exterior.

lock[1] *s* (*of a door*) lacăt *n*; zăvor *n*; broască *f*; (*canal*)

ecluză *f*; piedică *f* ‖ *vt* (~ *a door, etc*) a încuia; (~ *brakes*) a frâna; (*hug*) a strânge în brațe; *tech* a bloca ‖ *vi* a fi închis/încuiat; (~ *a door, etc*) a se încuia, a se închide; ~ **out** *vt* a încuia afară, a lăsa afară; ~ **one-self out** *vi* a se încuia pe dinafară; ~ **up** *vt* (*imprison*) a întemnița/duce la închisoare; (~ *a house*) a încuia cu cheia; (~ *valuables*) a închide, a pune sub cheie.

lock² *s* (*of hair*) meșă *f*.

locker *s* dulăpior *n*; compartiment *n*; cheson *n* • ~**room** *s* vestiar (cu dulăpioare) ‖ *adj* (~ *joke*) pipărat

locket *s* medalion *n*.

lockout *s* închiderea *f* fabricii.

locomotive *adj* locomotor ‖ *s* locomotivă *f*.

locust *s* ento lăcustă *f*.

lode *s* (*vein of ore*) vână *f*; (*vein of gold, silver*) filon *n*.

lodestar *s* steaua *f* polară; stea *f* călăuzitoare.

lodestone *s* miner magnetită *f*.

lodge *s* (*guardhouse, etc*) gheretă *f*; colibă *f*; căsuță *f*; culcuș *n*; (*hunting* ~) pavilion *n*, chioșc *n*; pavilion *n* de vânătoare; (*Masonic* ~) lojă *f* ‖ *vt* a găzdui; a caza; (~ *a complaint*) a depune ‖ *vi* a poposi; a locui (cu chirie); (*object*) a rămâne pe loc, a se opri • ~**r** *s* locatar *m*; chiriaș *m*.

lodging *s* găzduire *f*; locuință *f*; cameră *f* de închiriat.

loft *s* pod *n*; mansardă *f*; porumbar *n*.

log *s* (*wood*) butuc *n*; buturugă *f*; (*ship record*) jurnal *n* de bord; (*plane's logbook*) carnet *n* de zbor ‖ *vt* a consemna, a înregistra; ~ **in** *vi comp* a deschide o sesiune de lucru; ~ **out** *vi comp* a încheia legătura.

lofty *adj* (*mountain, etc*) foarte înalt, semeț, avântat; *fig* (*ideals, etc*) înalt, nobil, măreț; splendid; elevat, superior; (*person*) mândru, trufaș; arogant.

logarithm *s* math logaritm *m*.

loggerheads *s pl* cineva; **be at** ~ **with smb** *vi* a fi certat cu cineva; *coll* a fi la cuțite cu cineva.

logic *s* logică *f* • ~**al** *adj* logic, rațional.

logistics *s pl* mil logistică *f*; *fig* organizare *f*.

loin *s* anat șale *f*; spate *n*; (*beef*) file *n*.

loiter *vi* a hoinări, a rătăci; a zăbovi; a se mocăi; a tândăli • ~**er** *s* pierde-vară *m*, leneș *m*.

loll *vi* (*lounge*) a se lungi, a se tolăni; (*hang*) a atârna.

lollipop *s* acadea *f*.

London *s* Londra *f* • ~**er** *s* londonez(ă) *m/f*.

lone *adj* singur(atic) • ~**liness** *s* singurătate *f* • ~**ly** *adj* solitar; retras; stingher; singuratic • ~**r** *s* solitar *m*.

long¹ *adj* lung; prelung; mare; ridicat ‖ *s* durată *f* ‖ *adv* mult (timp), multă vreme; în întregime; de mult (timp); **in the ~ term** *adv* pe termen lung • ~**dis-tance** *adj* (*runner*) de cursă lungă; (*call*) interurban • ~**hand** *s* scriere *f* curentă (normală) • ~**haul** *adj* vapor/avion *n* de cursă lungă • ~**life** *adj* (*milk*) con-servare îndelungată; (*battery*) de lungă durată • ~**range** *adj* mil cu bătaie lungă, cu rază mare de acțiune; (*plan, etc*) pe termen lung • ~**shot** *s* încer-care *f* (fără mari sorți de izbândă) • ~**standing** *adj* de demult, vechi • ~**suffering** *adj* (*person*) îndurător, răbdător • ~**winded** *adj* (*person*) vorbăreț; (*speech*) interminabil, lung, plictisitor; *fig* prolix.

long² *vi* (**for**) a tinde spre/către; a dori (cu înfocare), a râvni la; a tânji după.

longevity *s* longevitate *f*.

longing *adj* doritor; plin de dor ‖ *s* dor *n*; năzuință *f*.

longitude *s* geog longitudine *f*.

longshoreman *s* docher *m*.

look *s* privire *f*, uitătură *f*; *also pl* înfățișare *f*, aspect *n*,

figură *f*; expresie *f*, mină *f* ‖ *vi* a se uita, a privi; a părea; ~ **at** *vi* a se uita la; a urmări; a lua în conside-rare; a cerceta; ~ **for** *vi* a căuta; a se aștepta la; ~ **for-ward** *vi* a aștepta cu nerăbdare; ~ **into** *vi* a se uita/a privi înăuntru; a cerceta, a examina, a studia; ~ **on** *vi* (*person* ~*s on*) a privi, a fi spectator; ~ **out** *vi* a fi atent; a privi afară, a se uita afară ‖ *exclam* atenție!; ~ **out on** *vi* (*house* ~*s out on*) a da înspre;~ **up** *vi* a privi în sus; a ridica privirile; (~ *a word*) a căuta (un cuvânt în dicționar); ~ **up to** *vi* a admira; ~ **upon** *vi* a considera, a socoti, a privi, a vedea; ~ **well** (*person*) a avea aerul/înfățișarea; (*clothes*) a sta/ședea bine; (*work, etc*) a merge bine; (*house*) a da înspre ‖ *vt* a exprima (pe față) • ~**alike** *s* (*double*) sosie *f*

loom¹ *vi* a se ivi, a se arăta; a se contura; *fig* a se întrevedea (la orizont); *fig* (*threat, etc*) a fi iminent.

loom² *s text* război *n* de țesut; gherghef *n*.

loon(y) *s/adj coll* țicnit *m*; ~ **bin** *s coll* azil *n* de nebuni.

loop *s* laț *n*, nod *n*; ochi *n*; meandră *f*; buclă *f*; arc *n*; luping *n* ‖ *vt* a înnoda; a ridica ‖ *vi* a șerpui.

loophole *s* deschizătură *f*; crenel *n*; *fig* portiță *f* (de scăpare); fisură *f*.

loose *adj* (*animal*) dezlegat; liber; *fig* (*anger*) dezlănțuit; (*clothes*) larg; (*ideas*) vag; inexact; (*writing*) neciteț; (*earth*) fărâmicios; afânat; (*money*) mărunt; (*person, life*) imoral, depravat ‖ *vt* a dezlega; a despleti; a elibera • ~**ly** *adv* liber; desfăcut; *fig* vag; neprecis; inexact; *fig* neglijent; *fig* în destrăbalare, imoral.

loosen *vt agr* a afâna; *med* a evacua; a slăbi ‖ *vi* (~ *a knot*) a se desface; (~ *a bolt*) a se slăbi.

loot *s* pradă *f*; jaf *n* ‖ *vt/vi* a prăda, a jefui.

lop¹ *vt* (~ *a tree*) a curăța de ramuri; ~ **off** *vt* a tăia.

lop² *vi* (*ears* ~) a atârna; (*animal* ~*s*) a înainta în salturi.

lopsided *adj* strâmb, înclinat, aplecat (într-o parte).

loquacious *adj* limbut; volubil.

lord *s* domn(itor) *m*; stăpân *n*; lord *m*; senior *m*; magnat *m* ‖ *vt* a conferi titlul de lord; a domni peste.

lorry *s* camion *n*.

lose, lost, lost *vt* (~ *a person, object, ground, etc*) a pierde; (~ *an object*) a rătăci; (*watch* ~*s time*) a rămâne în urmă ‖ *vi* a pierde; a suferi pierderi; (*watch* ~*s time*) a întârzia, a rămâne în urmă.

loss *s* pierdere *f*; daune *f pl*; pagubă *f*; impas *n*; scurgere *f*; deșeuri *n pl*.

lost *adj* pierdut.

lot *s* sorți *m pl*; tragere *f* la sorți; soartă *f*; noroc *n*; lot *n*; parte *f*; individ *m*.

lotion *s* loțiune *f*.

lottery *s* loterie *f*.

lotus *s bot* lotus *m*.

loud *adj* (*sound*) puternic, tare; (*laughter*) zgomotos; (*voice*) sonor; (*color*) țipător, strident; vulgar ‖ *adv* tare; pătrunzător; strident.

lounge *vi* a se odihni; a trândăvi ‖ *s* lenevie *f*; fotoliu *n*; șezlong *n*; sofa *f*; foaier *n*; hol *n*.

louse *s* (*pl* lice) păduche *m*.

lousy *adj* (*clothes*) rău, groaznic, prost.

lout *s* mitocan *m*, bădăran *m*.

lovable *adj* atrăgător, simpatic, plăcut.

love *s* (*affection*) iubire *f*; odor *n*; (*darling*) persoană *f* iubită; salutări *f pl*; (*score in tennis*) zero ‖ *vt* (*like*) a iubi; a îndrăgi ‖ *vi* a iubi; **for** ~ de amorul artei; **not for** ~ **or money** pentru nimic în lume; **in** ~ îndrăgostit; **make** ~ **to** *vt* a face dragoste cu; ~ **affair** *s* aventură *f* sentimentală; ~ **life** s viață f amoroasă • ~**making** s amor n, dragoste f; curte f.

lovely adj drăguț; frumos; fermecător; grozav.

lover s îndrăgostit m; iubit m; pețitor m.

loving adj iubitor.

low[1] adj jos, scund, (~ quality) inferior; (~ intelligence) scăzut; (small) mic; redus; (~ voice) încet; șoptit; adânc; (origin) umil, modest; fig deprimat; fig (cheap) ieftin, comun, vulgar; josnic, abject; urât || adv jos; la pamânt; încet; recent • ~**cut** adj (dress) decoltat • ~**key** adj discret • ~**ly** adj modest, umil • ~**lying** adj jos.

low[2] s muget n || vi a mugi.

lower vt a coborî; a reduce || vr a se umili || vi a scădea.

loyal adj loial.

lozenge s (tablet) pastilă f; (shape) romb n.

lubricant s lubrifiant m.

lubricate vt a lubrifia.

lubricious adj lit lubric, lasciv.

lucent adj strălucitor.

lucid adj limpede; clar; lucid; lămurit.

luck s noroc n, șansă f; soartă f, destin n • ~**ily** adv printr-un noroc; din fericire • ~**y** adj (person) norocos; (event) propice, favorabil; care poartă noroc.

lucrative adj lucrativ, rentabil.

ludicrous adj ridicol, grotesc; absurd.

lug s tech toartă f; tech mâner n; tech manivelă f; tech canelură f; constr capră f, consolă f.

luggage s bagaj n.

lugubrious adj lugubru.

lukewarm adj căldut; fig căldut; lipsit de entuziasm.

lull s acalmie f, calm n, liniște f; (in a speech) pauză f || vt (~ a child) a adormi prin cântece; fig (ease pain) a potoli, a alina; (~ suspicion) a adormi || vi (~ wind, pain) a se potoli, a se domoli.

lullaby s cântec n de leagăn.

lumbago s med lumbago n.

lumbar adj anat lombar.

lumber[1] s vechituri f pl; cherestea f || vt a arunca de-a valma; a îngrămădi.

lumber[2] vi a se mișca greoi/stângaci; a hodorogi, a hurui.

luminous adj luminos; limpede; inteligent.

lump s masă f, grămadă f; angro n; (~ of earth) bulgăre m; (~ in throat) nod n (în gât); (~ of sugar) bucată f de zahăr; med umflătură f; cucui n || vt a aduna; a lua în bloc; a înghiți (un afront); • **sum** s sumă f globală

lunacy s nebunie f.

lunar adj lunar.

lunatic adj nebun, alienat; lunatic.

lunch s prânz n; gustare f || vi a prânzi; a lua o gustare || vt a oferi o gustare • ~ **break** s pauză f de prânz.

lung s anat plămân m.

lunge vi (in fencing) a fanda; (horse) a lovi cu copita || vt a izbi/a lovi cu arma (pe cineva) || s (in fencing) lovitură f cu vârful spadei; fandare f; săritură f înainte, salt n înainte; (of a horse) azvârlitură f.

lupus s med lupus n.

lurch[1] vi (person) a sta ascuns; a sta la pândă; a recurge la tertipuri; a se clătina; naut (ship) a se înclina || s ascunziș n, pândă f; naut înclinare f, ambardee f; mers n clătinat/împleticit.

lurch[2] s ascunziș n; pândă f; mers împleticit n; **leave smb in the** ~ vt fig a părăsi pe cineva la nevoie.

lure s nadă f, momeală f; ademenire f, ispită f || vt a ispiti; a fermeca.

lurid adj posomorât, întunecat, întunecos; (light) sumbru; palid; (clothes) în culori țipătoare; (details, etc) sinistru; înfiorător; senzațional.

lurk vi (person) a sta ascuns; a pândi; a spiona; a se furișa; (danger, fear, etc) a dăinui, a persista.

luscious adj suculent; delicios; încărcat; seducător.

lush[1] adj (vegetation) luxuriant, bogat; (fruit) zemos, suculent; fig (description) amplu; (luxurious) somptuos.

lust s senzualitate f; poftă f trupească; sete f (de putere) || vi (for) a dori cu pasiune, a râvni • ~**ful** adj (look) languros, pofticios; (greedy) lacom, avid • ~**y** adj robust.

luster s lustru n; fig renume n, faimă f; lustră f; candelabru n.

lute s mus lăută f.

lux s phys lux n.

Luxembourg s Luxemburg.

luxuriance s (abundance) abundență f; (lavishness) splendoare f; (richness) bogăție f.

luxuriant adj (vegetation) luxuriant; (style) încărcat, prolix.

luxuriate vi (delight in) a se desfăta/delecta (cu); lit (proliferate) a crește luxuriant/bogat.

luxurious adj luxos, bogat, somptuos; risipitor, cheltuitor; sensual, voluptuos.

luxury s lux n; bogăție f; belșug n, abundență f; obiect/ articol n de lux; pompă f; splendoare f.

lyceum s (hall) sală f de conferințe; ateneu n.

lye s leșie f.

lymph s physiol limfă f; ~ **cell** s limfocită f.

lynch vt a linșa.

lynx s zool linx m, râs m.

lyre s mus liră f.

lyrical adj lyric; sentimental.

lyricist s poet m liric; textier m.

lyrics s pl cuvinte n pl, text n (al unui cântec).

M

M, m s (litera) M, m.

ma s coll mămică f.

mac s coll * **mackintosh**.

macabre adj macabru; fioros, cumplit.

macadam s macadam n.

macaque s zool macac m.

macaroni s macaroane f pl, spaghete f pl.

macaroon s pricomigdală f.

macaw s orn papagal m.

mace[1] s (staff) buzdugan n; sceptru n; baston n; tac n.

mace[2] s cul (spice) nucșoară f.

macerate vt/vi a (se) macera.

machination s uneltire f.

machine s mașină f; aparat n; automobil n; mecanism n; motocicletă f; bicicletă f • ~**gun** s mil mitralieră f || vt a mitralia • ~**ry** s mașini f pl; fig mecanism n; utilaj n, aparat n; sistem n de funcționare.

machinist s mecanic m; lăcătuș m, ajustor m.

mackerel s icht scrumbie f.

mackintosh s impermeabil n; haină f de ploaie; manta f de cauciuc.

macrobiotics s macrobiotică f.

macroeconomics s macroeconomie f.

mad adj nebun; turbat; (angry) furios; absurd; turbat; (fierce) cumplit || vt a înfuria.

madam s doamnă f.

madcap s nebun m, zăpăcit m, descreierat m.

madden vt (drive insane) a înnebuni, a scoate din minți; (exasperate) a exaspera, a înfuria.

made adj făcut; clădit; instruit; creat ‖ v * **make**.

madman s nebun m; disperat m.

madness s nebunie f; prostie f; furie f; frenezie f.

Madrid s Madrid n.

mafioso s mafiot m.

magazine s revistă f; magazin n; magazie f; mil deposit n de arme sau provizii.

maggot s larvă f; vierme m.

magic adj magic; de basm, minunat ‖ s magie f; vrajă f, farmec n; fascinație f.

magistracy s magistratură f.

magistrate s judecător m de pace; funcționar m public.

magnanimous adj mărinimos; nobil, generos.

magnate s magnat m; potentat m.

magnesium s chem magneziu n.

magnet s magnet m; punct n de atracție.

magnification s opt mărire f; tel amplificare f; relig glorificare f, preamărire f.

magnificent adj magnific; luxos; grozav.

magnify vt a mări; a amplifica; a exagera • ~**ing glass** s lupă f.

magnitude s mărime f, dimensiune f; importanță f.

magnolia s bot magnolie f.

magpie s orn cotofană f.

mahogany s (lemn de) mahon m.

maid s fată f; fecioară f; servitoare f.

maiden s fată f; fecioară f ‖ adj (flight) primul, de început; inaugural; fig nou • ~ **name** s nume n de fată.

mail[1] s (letters) corespondență f; (postal service) servicii poștale n pl ‖ vt a expedia prin poștă; ~ **order** s vânzare f prin corespondență • ~**man** s poștaș m, factor m poștal.

mail[2] s (armor) zale f pl; carapace f.

maim vt a mutila, a schilodi.

main s continent n; uscat n; conductă f. principală ‖ adj principal; fundamental.

mainframe s comp supercomputer n.

mainly adv mai ales, în special, îndeosebi.

mainstay s temelie f, element n principal.

mainstream adj dominant, majoritar.

maintain vt (keep) a menține; (care for) a întreține; a apăra; (assert) a susține; a afirma.

maintenance s (public order) menținere f; (upkeep) întreținere f; apărare f.

maize s bot porumb m.

majestic adj măreț, maiestuos.

majesty s maiestate f; măreție f.

major adj (important) major, mare; principal; semnificativ; mus major ‖ s major m, persoană f majoră; senior m; mil maior m; scol specialitate/materie f principală.

majority s majorat n; majoritate f.

make, made, made vt (manufacture) a face, a fabrica; (construct) a construi; (create) a produce; (cook) a pregăti; (achieve) a realiza, a înfăptui; (cause) a cauza, a simula; (appoint) a face, a numi (în funcție); a forma; (reach) a ajunge la; (earn) a câștiga; (compel) a obliga; a determina ‖ vi a încerca; a părea; a merge spre; a se întinde; a deveni ‖ s (brand) marcă f (de fabrică); tip n; model n; formă f; talie f; caracter n; ~ **it** vt a sosi la timp; a reuși, a izbuti; ~ **out** vt

(see, hear) a discerne; a înțelege; (check) a emite; (form) a completa; (draw up) a întocmi; a redacta; ~ **up** vt (end a quarrel) a aplana; a farda; a machia; (~ a story, etc) a inventa; a ticlui; a prescrie; a plăti; a recâștiga; a alcătui; (prepare a prescription) a pregăti, a executa; econ (account) a balansa; a încheia (un bilanț); ~ **up for** vi a compensa.

makeshift s expedient n; paliativ n ‖ adj improvizat.

makeup s machiaj n; fard n.

making s (creation) fabricare f, creare f; (manufacture) confecționare f; (construction) construire f; devenire f; **in the** ~ în devenire, în procesul de formare.

maladjusted adj prost adaptat; (person) inadaptabil.

maladroit adj stângaci, neajutorat.

malady s lit maladie f, boală f.

malaria s med malarie f.

malcontent s/adj frml nemulțumit m.

male adj (sex) bărbătesc, masculin ‖ s bărbat m; mascul m.

malediction s frml blestem n.

maledictory adj de blestem.

malefactor s frml răufăcător m.

maleficent adj lit malefic, rău; vătămător.

malevolent adj răuvoitor; invidios; neprielnic.

malfeasance s jur infracțiune f; abuz n.

malformation s malformație f.

malfunction s proastă funcționare f ‖ vi a funcționa prost.

Mali s Mali.

malice s răutate f; pică f, ranchiună f; invidie f; intenție f criminală.

malicious adj rău; răutăcios; răzbunător; invidios; premeditat.

malignant adj rău; dăunător; med malign; ostil; perfid.

malinger vi mil a se preface bolnav.

mall s mall n, centru n comercial.

mallard s orn rață f sălbatică.

malleable adj (substance) maleabil; (person) îngăduitor; flexibil; adaptabil; maleabil.

mallet s mai n, ciocan n de lemn.

mallow s bot nalbă f.

malnutrition s alimentație f defectuoasă; subnutriție f.

malpractice s incompetență f (în serviciu); jur eroare f profesională, neglijență f; med tratament n greșit.

malt s malț n.

Malta s Malta f

Maltese s/adj maltez(ă) m/f; **the** ~ maltezii m pl.

maltreat vt a se purta urât cu.

mammal s mamifer n.

mammoth s geol, zool mamut m ‖ adj gigantic, uriaș, colosal.

man s bărbat m; soț m; prieten m; adult m; individ m; soldat m; jucător m; navă f ‖ vt (~ a ship, etc) a echipa; (staff) a furniza personal pentru; a înarma; a încuraja ‖ interj omule!, măi!; măi, să fie!, extraordinar! • ~**ly** adj bărbătesc.

manacle vt also fig a încătușa; spl cătușe f pl.

manage vt a dirija; a administra, a conduce; a reuși; a îmblânzi; a duce la capăt ‖ vi a reuși; a se descurca • ~**able** adj ușor de mânuit • ~**ment** s (people) conducere f; administrație f; (control) gestionare f; pricepere f; dibăcie f; tertip n; direcție f • ~**r** s director; conducător m; administrator m; șef m; gospodar m; sp, etc manager m • ~**rial** adj directorial.

mandarin s bot (tree) mandarin m; (fruit) mandarină f.

mandate *s jur* mandat *n*; procură *f*; împuternicire *f*; ordin *n*; *pol* mandat *n*.

mandatory *adj* împuternicit; obligatoriu; forțat ‖ *s jur* mandatar *m*.

mandolin *s mus* mandolină *f*.

mane *s (of a horse)* coamă *f*; *(of a person)* chică *f*, coamă *f*.

maneuver *s* manevră *f*; mașinație *f*; uneltire *f* ‖ *vi* a face manevre; a manevra.

manfully *adv* curajos, vitejește, bărbătește.

manganese *s chem* mangan *n*.

mange *s vet* scabie *f*, râie *f*.

manger *s* iesle *f*.

mangle[1] *s* manglu *n*, calandru *n* ‖ *vt* a călca.

mangle[2] *vt* a ciopârți, a sfârteca; a mutila; *fig* a denatura, a deforma.

mango *s bot (fruit)* mango *n*; *(tree)* mangotier *m*, manghier *m*.

manhandle *vt* a transporta cu brațele; *coll* a brutaliza, a se purta grosolan cu.

manhole *s* trapă *f*; deschizătură *f*; gură *f* de canal; *rail* nișă *f*, adăpost *n*; *naut* gură *f* de om; *tech* gură *f* de vizitare.

mania *s* manie *f*; nebunie *f*; delir *n*; idee *f* fixă; pasiune *f*.

manicure *s* manichiură *f*.

manicurist *s* manichiurist(ă) *m/f*.

manifest *adj* clar ‖ *vt* a manifesta ‖ *vi* a manifesta, a demonstra ‖ *vr* a se manifesta • **~o** *s* manifest *n*, proclamație *f*; declarație *f* publică.

manifold *adj* variat, diferit, divers; numeros, multiplu ‖ *s* varietate *f*, diversitate *f*; *min* claviatură *f*; colector *n*.

manikin *s (dwarf)* pitic *m*; omuleț *m*.

manipulate *vt* a manipula, a mânui; *fig* a manevra; a măslui.

manipulation *s (of equipment)* manipulare *f*, mânuire *f*; *fig* manevră *f*; mașinație *f*.

manipulative *adj (person)* viclean, șiret; *(behavior)* abil, subtil.

mankind *s* omenire *f*, umanitate *f*.

man-made *adj* sintetic, artificial.

mannequin *s* manechin *m*.

manner *s* mod *n*, fel *n*; manieră *f*; stil *n*; obicei *n*; ținută *f*; categorie *f* • **~ism** *s* manierism *n*; afectare *f*; manieră *f*, particularitate *f*.

manor *s hist* feudă *f*, moșie *f* feudală; conac *n*.

manpower *s* mână *f* de lucru; *mil* efective *n pl*.

manse *s* casă *f* parohială.

mansion *s* vilă *f*; casă *f* mare; bloc *n*.

manslaughter *s jur* omucidere *f* involuntară.

mantelpiece *s* cămin *n*; poliță *f* deasupra căminului; prichici *n* (de sobă).

mantilla *s* broboadă *f*.

mantle *s* mantou *n*; manta *f*, capă *f*; pelerină *f*; *(of snow)* strat *n*, înveliș *n*; *(of fog)* perdea *f*, văl *n*; *constr* fațadă *f*, parte *f* exterioară; *geol* manta *f* de protecție.

manual *adj* manual ‖ *s* manual *n*; ghid *n*.

manufacture *s* fabricare *f*; prelucrare *f*; produs *n*; *(machinery)* construcție *f*; industrie *f* ‖ *vt* a fabrica; *(machinery)* a construi; *fig* a inventa, a plăsmui.

manure *s* îngrășământ *n* (natural), gunoi *n*, bălegar *n* ‖ *vt* a îngrășa (pământul).

manuscript *s/adj* manuscris *n*.

many *adj* mulți, multe; numeroși, numeroase; o mulțime ‖ *pron* mulți dintre ei/ele.

map *s* hartă *f*; plan *n*; schiță *f*; mutră *f* ‖ *vt (plan)* a elabora; *(schedule)* a stabili; *(task)* a trasa; *(draw)* a întocmi harta; *(record)* a trece pe hartă.

maple *s bot* arțar *m*.

mar *vt* a strica, a deteriora; *(~ pleasure)* a tulbura; *(~ a person)* a distruge.

marathon *s sp* maraton *n*.

marauder *s (person)* jefuitor *m*; *(bird)* răpitor *m*.

marble *s (stone)* marmură *f*; *pl (game)* joc *n* cu bile.

March[1] *s* (luna) martie *m*; *Mărțișor*.

march[2] *vi mil* a mărșălui; a defila; a se scurge; a înainta; a face progrese ‖ *s* marș *n*; mers *n*; scurgere *f*; progres *n*.

marchioness *s (title)* marchiză *f*.

mare *s zool* iapă *f*.

margarine *s* margarină *f*.

margin *s* margine *f*; frontieră *f*; țărm *n*; deosebire *f* ‖ *vt* a mărgini; a adnota • **~al** *adj* marginal, secundar.

marguerite *s bot* părăluță *f*, bănuțel *m*.

marigold *s bot* gălbenea *f*, filimică *f*.

marijuana *s* marijuana *f*, hașiș *n*.

marinade *s cul* marinată *f* ‖ *vt* a marina.

marine *adj* marin; maritim ‖ *s* navă *f* marină; marină *f* comercială; bleumarin *n*.

marionette *s* marionetă *f*.

marital *adj* de soț, a soțului; *(~ happiness)* matrimonial, conjugal; *(~ problems)* matrimonial, marital.

maritime *adj* maritim; marin.

marjoram *s bot* sovârv *n*, origan *n*.

mark *s* urmă *f*; *(sign)* semn *n*; *(blot)* pată *f*; simptom *n*; *(score)* notă *f*; punct *n*; *(target)* țintă *f*; fel *n*; *(impact)* amprentă *f*; *(indicator)* indicator *n*; reper *n* ‖ *vt (stain)* a păta, a marca; *(indicate)* a indica, a nota; a alege; a dovedi • **~er** *s* persoană *f* care marchează; pontator *m*; *(book ~)* semn *n* de carte; *agr* marcator *n*; *constr* reper *n*; *ling* marcă *f*; placă *f* comemorativă; *(pen)* creion *n* care scrie gros.

market *s* piață *f*; târg *n*; cerere *f* ‖ *vt* a vinde; a lansa pe piață ‖ *vi* a comercializa; **~ research** *s* studiu *n* de piață; **~ value** *s* valoare *f* de piață • **~ing** *s* comerț *n*; marketing *n*; vânzare *f*. • **~place** *s* piață *f*.

marksman *s* trăgător *m* de elită.

marmalade *s* gem *n* de portocale.

maroon[1] *adj* castaniu ‖ *s* culoare *f* castanie; petardă *f*.

maroon[2] *vt (person)* a părăsi/lăsa pe o insulă/coastă pustie; *fig* a izola (de restul lumii) • **~ed** *adj* abandonat.

marquee *s* cort *n* mare (în formă de umbrelă); *constr* marchiză *f*.

marquess, marquis *s (title)* marchiză *f*, marchiz *m*.

marquetry *s* marchetărie *f*.

marriage *s* căsătorie *f*; căsnicie *f*; *fig* îmbinare *f*.

married *adj* căsătorit, măritată/însurat; conjugal.

marrow *s (of bone)* măduvă *f*; **~ transplant** *s* transplant *n* de măduvă.

marry *vt* a căsători; a lua în căsătorie, a se căsători cu; *fig* a îmbina, a uni ‖ *vi* a se căsători cu.

Mars *s (planet)* Marte.

marsh *s* mlaștină *f*; pământ/ținut *n* mlăștinos.

marshal *s mil* mareșal *m*; maestru *m* de ceremonii; șerif *m* ‖ *vt* a aranja, a dispune; a conduce/prezenta/introduce (solemn) pe cineva; *rail* a compune, a forma (un tren); a manevra (vagoane).

mart *s (market)* piață *f*.

marten *s zool* jder *m*.

martial *adj* marțial, de război; războinic; ~ **law** *s* legea *f* marțială.

Martian *s* marțian *m*.

martin *s* *orn* lăstun *m*, rândunică *f* de casă.

martinet *s* partizan *m* al disciplinei severe, zbir *m*.

martyr *s* martir *m*; *fig* martir *m* ‖ *vt* a martiriza; a chinui, a tortura • ~**dom** *s* martiriu *n*; *fig* chinuri *n pl*, torturi *f pl*.

marvel *s* minune *f* ‖ *vi* (at) a se minuna, a se mira, a fi uimit (de) • ~**ous** *adj* minunat, uimitor; de necrezut; extraordinar.

marzipan *s* marțipan *n*.

mascara *s* rimel *n*.

mascot *s* mascotă *f*; talisman *n*.

masculine *adj* masculin; bărbătesc; viril.

mash *s* terci *n*; pireu *n* de cartofi; amestec *n*; ghiveci *n* ‖ *vt* a terciui; a face piure.

mask *s* mască *f*; pretext *n* ‖ *vt* a masca; a ascunde ‖ *vi* a se masca; a se ascunde.

masochist *s* masochist *m*.

mason *s* zidar *m*; francmason *m*.

masonry *s* *constr* zidărie *f*; francmasonerie *f*.

masquerade *s* mascaradă *f*, bal *n* mascat; costum *n* de mascaradă; *fig* (*pretence*) mascaradă *f*, farsă *f* ‖ *vt* a masca, a deghiza, a travesti; *fig* a masca, a ascunde ‖ *vi* a fi deghizat/travestit; *fig* a se masca, a se preface.

mass[1] *s* masă *f*, grămadă *f*, mulțime *f*; substanță *f* ‖ *adj* (~ *protest*) în masă, în număr mare; (~ *support, etc*) masiv ‖ *vt* a masa; a strânge ‖ *vi* a se aduna.

mass[2] *s* *relig* mesă *f*; liturghie *f*.

massacre *s* masacru *n* ‖ *vt* a masacra.

massage *s* masaj *n* ‖ *vt* a face masaj.

masseur *s* masor *m*.

masseuse *s* maseză *f*.

massive *adj* masiv; greu; compact; mare; robust; uriaș, grozav; vast.

mast *s* (*ship*) catarg *n*; (*radio, tv*) pilon *n*; stâlp *m*.

master *s* stăpân *m*; patron *m*; domn *m*; maestru *m*; meșter *m*; căpitan *m*; învățător; *m*; licențiat *m*; director *m* ‖ *adj* principal; conducător ‖ *vt* a-si însuși; a subjuga; a învăța; (~ *a difficulty*) a învinge; (~ *a situation*) a fi stăpân pe; (*control*) a conduce • ~**ly** *adj* magistral • ~**mind** *s* fig creier *n* ‖ *vt* (*action*) a organiza, a concepe • ~**piece** *s* capodoperă *f* • ~**'s degree** *s* *edu* licență *f* • ~**y** *s* autoritate *f*, putere *f*; măiestrie *f*, perfecțiune *f*; (*language, etc*) cunoaștere *f* desăvârșită.

masticate *vi/vt frml* (*chew*) a mesteca.

mastiff *s* buldog *m*, câine *m* de pază.

masturbate *vi* a se masturba.

mat *s* covoraș *n*; preș *n*; suport *n*; mușama *f*; păr *m* încâlcit ‖ *vt* a acoperi; a încâlci ‖ *adj* mat, opac; șters.

matador *s* matador *m*.

match[1] *s* chibrit *n* • ~**box** *s* cutie *f* de chibrituri.

match[2] *s* pereche *f*; meci *n*; competiție *f*; pariu *n*; partidă *f*; potrivire *f* ‖ *vt* a potrivi; a împerechea; a egala ‖ *vi* a se potrivi; a se asorta • ~**ing** *adj* asortat, potrivit.

mate *s* coleg *m*; prieten *m*; însoțitor *m*; pereche *f*; ajutor *n*; ofițer *m* ‖ *vt* a căsători; a împerechea ‖ *vi* a se căsători; a se împerechea.

material *adj* material, fizic; trupesc; real; concret ‖ *s* material *n*; materie *f*; subiect *n* • ~**istic** *adj phil, etc* materialist.

materialize *vi* (*offer, threat*) a se concretiza, a se realiza; (*person, object*) a apărea.

maternal *adj* matern.

maternity *s* maternitate *f*; instinct *n* matern.

mathematician *s* matematician *m*.

mathematics *s* matematică *f*.

matinee *s* matineu *n*.

mating *s* împerechere *f*; ~ **season** *s* perioada *f* de împerechere.

matins *s* *relig* slujba *f* de dimineață.

matriarch *s* (*ruler*) matriarh *m*; (*old woman*) *s* matroană *f* • ~**al** *adj* matriarhal.

matrimonial *adj* matrimonial.

matrimony *s* căsatorie *f*; căsnicie *f*, viață *f* conjugală.

matrix *s* *anat* uter *n*; *tech* matriță *f*; ștanță *f*; *typ* matriță *f*; *math* matrice *f*; *geol* rocă-mamă *f*.

matron *s* matroană *f*; mamă *f* de familie; femeie *f* măritată; văduvă *f* remăritată; intendentă *f*.

matt *adj* mat; ~ **paint** *s* vopsea *f* mată.

matted *adj* (*hair, etc*) încâlcit, încurcat; acoperit cu rogojini.

matter *s* *phys* materie *f*; fond *n*; (*issue*) problemă *f*, chestiune *f*; (*material*) materie *f*; (*affair*) afacere *f*, lucru *n*; ocazie *f*; importanță *f*; *med* (*pus*) puroi *n* ‖ *vi* a conta; a însemna, a valora; **what's the** ~? ce s-a întâmplat?; **for that** ~ în acestă privință; **no** ~ **what** orice s-ar întâmpla; **there's something the** ~ **with my leg** am ceva la picior; **it doesn't** ~ nu are importanță; **as** ~**s stand** după cum stau lucrurile; **it's no laughing** ~ e o chestiune serioasă • ~**of-fact** *adj* prozaic; realist; lipsit de imaginație.

mattress *s* saltea *f*; somieră *f*.

mature *adj* matur; copt ‖ *vt* a lăsa să se coacă ‖ *vi* a se coace; a se maturiza.

maturity *s* maturitate *f*.

matzo *s* *cul* pască *f* (evreiască).

maudlin *adj* (exagerat de) sentimental.

maul *s* mai *n* manual ‖ *vt* a lovi cu maiul; a maltrata; a mutila, a schilodi; *fig* (*criticize*) a critica aspru.

mausoleum *s* mausoleu *n*.

mauve *adj* (*color*) mov, liliachiu.

maven *s* expert *m*, specialist *m*.

maverick *s* neconformist *m*, rebel *m*.

maw *s* *zool* stomac *n*; *orn* gușă *f*; *pej* burdihan *n*.

mawkish *adj* (*maudlin*) excesiv de sentimental.

maxim *s* maximă *f*; precept *n*.

maximum *s* maxim *n*.

May[1] *s* (luna) mai *m*, florar; tinerețe *f*; primăvară *f* • ~ **Day** *s* Întâi Mai *n*.

may[2], **might** *v mod* a putea, a avea voie, a-i fi permis; a fi posibil; **if I** ~ **say so** dacă pot spune astfel; **you** ~ **well ask** aveți dreptate să întrebați; **whatever it** ~ **cost** oricât ar costa; **that's as** ~ **be** este posibil; ~ **the best man win** (fie ca) să câștige cel mai bun.

maybe *adv* poate, posibil; poate că; ~ **not** poate că nu; ~ **so, but** … poate că-i așa dar…

mayhem *s* (*chaos*) debandadă *f*; (*turmoil*) panică *f*; teroare *f*.

mayonnaise *s* *cul* maioneză *f*.

mayor *s* primar *m*.

maze *s* *also fig* labirint *n*.

me *pron* pe mine, mă; mie, îmi, mi, -mi.

mead *s* (*drink*) mied *n*.

meadow *s* pajiște *f*, livadă *f*; fâneață *f*; luncă *f*.

meager *adj* slab; rar; sărac; insuficient.

meal¹ *s* masă *f*; mâncare *f*; **eat a ~** *vt* a mânca.

meal² *s* (*flour*) făină *f* • **~y** *adj* (*floury*) făinos; (*pale*) palid; poros; afânat • **~y mouthed** *adj* mieros; onctuos.

mean¹, meant, meant *vt* a însemna; a vrea să spună; a intenţiona, a vrea; a fi gata de || *vi* a însemna; a fi important; **what do you ~?** ce vreţi să spuneţi?; **that doesn't ~ a thing** asta nu înseamnă nimic; **I didn't ~ to hurt you** nu am vrut să vă jignesc; **I ~ what I say** vorbesc serios, nu glumesc.

mean² *adj* (*not generous*) meschin; (*miserly*) zgârcit; egoist; (*shabby*) jalnic, deplorabil, sărăcăcios; (*inferior*) umil; de jos, inferior; (~ *person, behavior*) josnic, ticălos, mârşav, abject; infam; (~ *intellect*) inferior.

mean³ *s* mediu *n*; *math* medie *f* || *adj* mediu.

meander *s* (*river*) meandră *f*; cotitură *f*, cot *n*; *archit* meandră *f* || *vi* a face meandre; a face cotituri; a şerpui; a hoinări.

meaning *adj* semnificativ; intenţionat || *s* înţeles *n*, sens *n* • **~ful** *adj* (*look*) semnificativ; plin de înţeles; (*relations, etc*) important • **~less** *adj* fără sens; inexpresiv.

means *s* (*way*) mijloc *n*, cale *f*; (*method*) metodă *f*; mijlocire *f*, ajutor *n*; (*resources*) mijloace *n pl*, resurse *f pl*, posibilităţi *f pl*; bani *m pl*; avere *f*.

meant *vt* * **mean**.

meanwhile *adv* între timp; deocamdată.

measles *s med* pojar *n*.

measly *adj med* de pojar; *coll* care nu face doi bani, fără valoare, neînsemnat.

measure *s* măsură *f*; volum *n*; mărime *f*; întindere *f*; forţă *f*; limită *f*; grad *n*; ritm *n*; moderaţie *f* || *vt* a măsura; a evalua || *vi* a lua măsuri; a măsura • **~ment** *s* măsurare *f*, măsură *f*.

meat *s* carne *f*; *fig* miez *n*, esenţă *f*.

mechanic *s* mecanic *m*; maşinist *m*; lăcătuş *m*.

mechanism *s* mecanism *n*.

mechanized *adj* mecanizat.

med *adj coll* medical; **~ student** *s* medicinist *m*.

medal *s* medalie *f*; **gold ~** *s* medalie *f* de aur.

meddle *vi* (*interfere*) (**in, with**) a se amesteca, a se vârî (în).

media *s pl* **the ~ mass** media *f*.

median *s math* medie *f*; mediană *f* || *adj* mediu; median.

mediate *adj* intermediar || *vt* a mijloci; a fi mediator.

mediation *s* (*arbitration*) mediere *f*; intermediu *n*.

mediator *s* intermediar *m*.

medical *adj* medical; **~ student** *s* student *m* în medicină; **~ exam** *s* examen *n* medical.

Medicare *s* asistenţă *f* medicală (pentru bătrâni).

medication *s* medicaţie *f*; **to be on ~** a urma un tratament.

medicinal *adj* medicinal; **~ herbs** *s pl* plante *f pl* medicinale.

medicine *s* medicină *f*; medicament *n*; remediu *n*.

medieval *adj* medieval.

mediocre *adj* mediocru; banal, comun.

mediocrity *s* mediocritate *f*.

meditate *vi* a medita || *vt* a plănui.

meditation *s* reculegere *f*, meditaţie *f*.

Mediterranean *adj* mediteranean.

medium *s* (*average*) medie *f*; agent *m*; *bio* mediu *n*, ambianţă *f*; (*means*) mijloc *n*; mijlocitor *m*; metodă *f*; (*spiritualist*) mediu *n* || *adj* mediu; *cul* (*meat*) potrivit; **in the ~ term** pe termen mediu • **~sized** *adj* de mărime mijlocie.

medley *s* amestec *n*; *mus* potpuriu *n*; *liter* varia *f* || *adj* amestecat, divers, eterogen, diferit.

meek *adj* blând; supus; împăciuitor; sfios, umil.

meet, met, met *vt* (~ *a person*) a întâlni; (~ *by appt*) a regăsi, a reîntâlni; (*catch a train, plane*) a merge să aştepte; (~ *needs*) a satisface, a răspunde la; (*solve a problem*) a rezolva; (~ *a challenge*) a răspunde la; (*pay the cost*) a plăti; (*know*) a cunoaşte; a întâmpina; a înfiinţa; a da de; (~ *an obligation*) a onora || *vi* a se întâlni; a se cunoaşte; a se asocia; a se înfrunta; a fi de acord • **~ing** *s* întâlnire *f*; întrunire *f*; şedinţă *f*; confluenţă *f*; întrecere *f*.

megabyte *s comp* megaoctet *n*.

megahertz *s phys* megahertz *m*.

megalomania *s* megalomanie *f* • **~c** *s* megaloman *m*.

megaphone *s* megafon *n*, portavoce *f*.

melancholia *s* melancolie *f*.

melancholic *adj* melancolic.

melancholy *s* melancolie *f*, tristeţe *f* || *adj* melancolic, trist; deprimat; posomorât; dezolant.

meld *vi* (*merge*) a se combina; a se potrivi.

melee *s* încăierare *f*; busculadă *f*.

mellifluous *adj* melodios, dulce.

mellow *adj* copt; suav; delicat; moale; discret || *vt* a înmuia; a îndulci; a atenua || *vi* a se (în)muia; a se coace.

melodious *adj* melodios; dulce; muzical.

melodrama *s* melodramă *f*.

melody *s mus* melodie *f*; arie *f*; cântec *n*; temă *f*; caracter *n* melodic.

melon *s* pepene *m* galben; cantalup *m*; pepene *m* verde.

melt *vt* a topi; a dizolva; a înmuia; a mişca; a amesteca || *vi* a se topi; a se dizolva; a dispărea • **~down** *n* fuziune *f* nucleară.

melting pot *s metal* creuzet *n*; *coll* **~ (of several cultures)** un melanj (de culturi diferite).

member *s* membru *m*; asociat *m*; tovarăş *m* • **~ship** *s* calitate *f* de membru; societate *f*, comunitate *f*.

membrane *s anat* membrană *f*; *tech* membrană *f*, peliculă *f*; coajă *f*, pojghiţă *f*.

memento *s* memento *n*, aducere *f* aminte; amintire *f*, suvenir *n*.

memo *s* notă *f* de serviciu.

memoir *s* memoriu *n*; raport *n*; notă *f* oficială; expunere *f* de fapte; *pl* memorii *f pl*, amintiri *f pl*; (auto)biografie *f*.

memorabilia *s pl* suveniruri *n pl*.

memorable *adj* memorabil, de neuitat.

memorandum *s* (*pl* **–da/dums**) memorandum *n*; notă *f* de serviciu.

memorial *adj* memorial; memorabil || *s* amintire *f*; memorie *f*; memoriu *n*; notă *f*; petiţie *f*.

memorize *vt* a memora; a reţine.

memory *s* memorie *f*; (*event*) amintire *f*; reminiscenţă *f*; *comp* memorie *f*.

men *s pl* * **man**.

menace *s* ameninţare *f*; pericol *n* || *vt* a ameninţa; a periclita, a pune în pericol.

menacing *adj* ameninţător.

menagerie *s* menajerie *f*.

mend *vt* a repara; (~ *clothes*) a cârpi, a coase; a corecta; a vindeca || *vi* a se corija; a se însănătoşi || *s* reparaţie *f*; întremare *f*.

mendacious *adj frml* (*remark*) fals, nesincer; (*person*) mincinos, înşelător.

mendacity *s frml* mitomanie *f;* falsitate *f.*
mendicant *s* cerşetor *m;* călugăr *m* cerşetor || *adj* cerşetor, care cere de pomană.
menfolk *s pl* bărbaţi *m pl.*
menial *adj (task)* casnic, domestic, de gospodărie; *fig* servil; umil; josnic || *s* servitor *m,* slugă *f; fig* om *m* servil, lacheu *m.*
meningitis *s med* meningită *f.*
menopause *s med* menopauză *f.*
menstrual *adj physiol* menstrual; lunar, mensual.
menstruation *s physiol* menstruaţie *f.*
menswear *s* articole *n pl* (de îmbrăcăminte) pentru bărbaţi.
mental *adj* mental; intelectual; spiritual; psihic; ~ **hospital** *s* spital *n* psihiatric • **~ity** *s* intelect *n,* capacitate *f* intelectuală; *(mindset)* mentalitate *f,* mod *n* de a gândi.
menthol *s chem* mentol *n.*
mention *s* menţiune *f* || *vt* a menţiona; a cita; a releva.
mentor *s* mentor *m.*
menu *s* meniu *n,* listă *f* de bucate; *comp* menu *n.*
mercantile *adj* mercantil comercial, negustoresc; *fig* mercantil, interesat; meschin.
mercenary *adj* mercantil, interesat; venal || *s mil* mercenar *m.*
merchandise *s* marfă *f,* mărfuri *f pl.*
merchant *s* comerciant *m;* tip *m.*
merciful *adj* iertător, îndurător; indulgent; compătimitor • **~ly** *adv* din fericire.
merciless *adj* nemilos, crud.
mercurial *adj (shifty)* schimbător, imprevizibil; *(lively)* vioi, ager.
mercury *s chem* mercur *n.*
mercy *s* compasiune *f;* clemenţă *f;* iertare *f;* caritate *f;* indulgenţă *f;* voie *f.*
mere *adj* pur, simplu || *adv* doar, numai • **~ly** *adv* numai, doar; pur şi simplu.
meretricious *adj frml (glamor)* amăgitor; *(impression)* fals; *(jewelry)* ieftin, de prost gust; *(style)* bombastic.
merge *vt* a amesteca, a contopi; a uni; *econ, comp* a fuziona || *vi* a îmbina; *econ (with)* a fuziona cu; a se uni; *(colors)* a se topi || *s comp* fuziune *f* • **~r** *s* fuziune *f.*
meridian *s geog, astron* meridian *n; astron* zenit *n; fig* zenit *n,* apogeu *n,* culme *f.*
meringue *s cul* bezea *f,* bezele *f pl.*
merit *s* merit *n,* valoare *f;* calitate *f* || *vt* a merita.
meritocracy *s* meritocraţie *f.*
mermaid *s myth* sirenă *f.*
merry *adj* vesel, voios; iute; vioi; glumeţ; **Merry Christmas!** Crăciun fericit!.
mesh *s* ochi *m* de sită/plasă; *rail* reţea *f; math* celulă *f; tech* angrenare *f; pl* plasă *f,* reţea *f, pl fig* cursă *f,* capcană *f* || *vt (net)* a împleti; *tech* a angrena; *fig* a prinde în mreje/cursă.
mesmeric *adj* captivant, fascinant.
mesmerize *vt* a hipnotiza, a fascina; *fig* a fascina, a vrăji, a fermeca.
mess[1] *s (filth)* murdărie *f;* gunoi *n; (untidiness)* dezordine *f; (trouble)* necaz *n* || *vt* a murdări; a răvăşi; a face dezordine; a cârpăci.
mess[2] *s mil* popotă *f; naut* careu *n;* comeseni *m pl;* masă *f* comună.
message *s* mesaj *n,* ştire *f;* apel *n;* misiune *f;* scrisoare *f;* comunicare *f* || *vt* a transmite; a semnaliza.

messenger *s* mesager *m,* curier *m;* vestitor *m.*
messiah *s relig* mântuitor *m.*
messy *adj* murdar; dezordonat; răvăşit.
met *vt* * **meet**.
metabolism *s bio* metabolism *n.*
metal *s* metal *n;* macadam *n;* pietriş *n;* balast *n;* zel *n* || *vt* a acoperi cu metal; a macadamiza • **~lic** *adj (sound, mineral)* metalic; *(color, finish)* metalizat • **~lurgy** *s* metalurgie *f.*
metamorphosis *s* metamorfoză *f.*
metaphor *s* metaforă *f.*
metaphysics *s phylos* metafizică *f.*
meteor *s* meteor *m;* meteorit *m;* bolid *m; fig* meteor *m,* bolid *m* • **~ite** *s* meteorit *m.*
meteorologist *s* meteorolog *m.*
meteorology *s* meteorologie *f.*
mete out *vt (~ punishment)* a aplica; *(~ justice)* a împărţi, a distribui.
meter *s* metru *m* || *vt* a stabili consumul de.
methane *s chem* (gaz) metan *n.*
method *s* metodă *f;* sistem *n;* procedeu *n.*
Methodism *s relig* metodism *n.*
Methodist *s relig* metodist *m.*
methylated spirits *s pl chem* alcool *n* metilic, spirt *n* denaturat.
meticulous *adj* meticulos; minuţios.
metonymy *s* metonimie *f.*
metric *adj* metric, măsurat în metri • **~al** *adj* metric; ritmic.
metro *s* metrou *n;* **by ~** cu metroul.
metronome *s mus* metronom *n.*
metropolis *s* metropolă *f;* capitală *f.*
metropolitan *adj* metropolitan || *s* locuitor *m* din metropolă; mitropolit *m,* arhiepiscop *m.*
mettle *s* temeritate *f,* dârzenie *f;* caracter *n,* fire *f;* **show/prove one's ~** a arăta că ce este în stare.
mew *vi* a scânci; a se sclifosi, a se smiorcăi.
Mexican *s/adj* mexican(ă) *m/f.*
mezzanine *s* mezanin *n; thea* balcon *n.*
miasma *s* miasmă *f;* duhoare *f.*
mica *s miner* mică *f.*
mice *s pl* * **mouse**.
microbe *s* microb *m.*
microchip *s comp* microprocesor n.
microfilm *s* microfilm *n.*
microphone *s* microfon *n.*
microscope *s* microscop *n.*
microwave *s (oven)* cuptor *n* cu microunde.
mid *adj* * **middle**.
mid-air *s in ~* în aer liber || *adj* în aer liber.
midday *s* prânz *n,* amiază *f.*
middle *adj* mijlociu; median || *s* mijloc *n;* talie *f* || *vt* a pune la mijloc; **the Middle Ages** *s* Evul *n* Mediu • **~ aged** *adj* de vârstă mijlocie, între două vârste.
midge *s ento* musculiţă *f.*
midget *s* pitic *m,* liliputan *m;* obiect *n* mic.
midnight *s* miezul *n* nopţii; beznă *f.*
midriff *s anat* diafragmă *f;* abdomen *n,* stomac *n.*
midst *s (space)* (parte de) mijloc *n;* interior *n;* **in the ~ of** în mijlocul; **in our ~** printre noi.
midsummer *s* miezul/toiul *n* verii; *astron* solstiţiu *n* de vară.
midway *adv* la jumătate de drum.
midweek *s* mijlocul *n* săptămânii.
midwife *s* moaşă *f* • **~rys** moşit *n;* obstetrică *f.*

midwinter *s* miezul/toiul *n* iernii; *astron* solstițiu *n* de iarnă.

mien *s* (*look*) mină *f*; aspect *n*.

miffed *adj* (*irked*) supărat, vexat.

might[1] *v mod* * **may.**

might[2] *s* putere *f*, autoritate *f*; energie *f* • ~**y** *adj* puternic, tare; mare, întins; grandios.

migraine *s* migrenă *f*, durere *f* de cap.

migrant *adj* (*bird, animal*) migrator; (*worker*) emigrant ‖ *s* (*bird, animal*) migrator *m*; (*worker*) emigrant *m*.

migrate *vi* (*birds, animals*) a migra; (*people*) a emigra.

migration *s* migrațiune *f*.

migratory *adj* migrator.

mike *s coll* (*microphone*) microfon *n*.

mild *adj* moderat; (*voice, weather*) blând; (*metal*) moale; (*weather*) blând, senin; (*attempt, etc*) slab; (*cigarette*) slab, ușor; (*food*) necondimentat; (*light, etc*) slab, domol; lin; odihnitor.

mildew *s bot* mucegai *n*.

mile *s* milă *f* • ~**age** *s* distanță *f* în mile; kilometraj *n*.

milieu *s* mediu *n*, ambianță *f*.

militant *adj* militant, combativ ‖ *s* luptător *m*, combatant *m*; *fig* luptător *m*, militant *m*.

militarize *vt* a militariza.

military *adj* military ‖ *s* **the** ~ armata *f*.

militate *vt* a milita.

militia *s* (*reserve army*) rezerviști *m pl*; (*body of citizens*) miliție *f*.

milk *s* lapte *n* ‖ *vt* a mulge; a stoarce ‖ *vi* a da lapte • ~**shake** *s* băutură *f* rece pe bază de lapte aromatizat • ~**y** *adj* (*color*) lăptos.

mill *s* moară *f*; râșniță *f*; fabrică *f*, uzină *f*, filatură *f* ‖ *vt* a măcina; a șlefui ‖ *vi* a merge în cerc, a se învârti • ~**er** *s* morar *m*; frezor *m*; *tech* freză *f*.

millennium *s* (*pl* –**nia**) mileniu *n*.

millet *s bot* mei *n*.

milligram *s* miligram *n*.

milliliter *s* mililitru *m*.

millimeter *s* milimetru *m*.

milliner *s* modistă *f*.

million *s/num* million *n*.

millipede *s zool* miriapod *n*.

milt *s anat* splină *f*; *icht* lapți *m pl*.

mime *s* mim *m*, clovn *m* ‖ *vi* a mima.

mimic *adj* mimic; imitativ; simulat ‖ *vt* a mima; a imita ‖ *s* imitator *m*.

mimosa *s bot* mimoză *f*; (*drink*) băutură *f* din șampanie și suc de portocale.

minaret *s* minaret *n*.

mince *vt* a mărunți; a toca ‖ *s* carne *f* tocată; tocătură *f*.

mind *s* (*reason*) minte *f*; (*memory*) memorie *f*; amintire *f*; (*psyche*) conștiință *f*; (*intellect*) rațiune *f*, intelect *n*; (*opinion*) opinie *f*; (*desire*) dorință *f*; dispoziție *f* ‖ *vt* (*pay attention to*) a fi atent la; (*look after*) a avea grijă de; (*object to*) a avea ceva împotrivă ‖ *vi* (*be careful*) a fi atent; (*object*) a-i păsa; **I don't** ~ nu am nimic împotrivă; **never** ~ **that now** (*leave it*) lasă asta acum, (*forget it*) nu merită să te ocupi de asta acum • ~**ful** *adj* (*of*) (*risk*) conștient de; atent la; (*responsibility*) preocupat, atent • ~**less** *adj* stupid, absurd • ~**set** *s* mod *n* de a privi viața; convingeri *f pl*.

mine[1] *pron* al meu, a mea, ai mei, ale mele ‖ *adj* meu, mea, mei, mele.

mine[2] *s* mină *f* ‖ *vt* (*excavate*) a săpa; a mina; ~ **detector**

s detector *m* de mine • ~**field** *s* teren *n* minat • ~**r** *s* miner *m*.

mineral *adj* mineral ‖ *s* mineral *n*; minereu *n*.

mingle *vt* a amesteca; a împreuna ‖ *vi* (*sounds, flavors*) a se amesteca cu; (*people*) a se amesteca în.

mingy *adj coll* (*mean*) meschin; zgârcit.

miniature *s* miniatură *f*.

minim *s mus* doime *f*.

minimal *adj* (*cost*) nesemnificativ; (*damage*) minim.

minimize *vt* (*reduce*) a reduce la minimum; (*play down*) a subaprecia, a minimaliza.

minimum *s* minim *n*; valoare *f* minimă ‖ *adj* minim.

mining *s* exploatare *f* minieră ‖ *adj* minier.

minister *s* ministru *m*; preot *m*; slujitor *m*; agent *m*; unealtă *f* ‖ *vi* a fi preot.

ministry *s* slujire *f*; serviciu *n*; *relig* preoție *f*; cler *n*; *pol* minister *n*.

minivan *s* microbuz *n*.

mink *s zool* nurcă *f*; (*fur*) (blană de) nurcă *f*, vizon *n*.

minor *adj* minor, mic, neimportant ‖ *s* minor *m*; materie *f* secundară; ton *n* minor • ~**ity** *s* minoritate *f*; minorat *n*.

minstrel *s hist* menestrel *m*; *lit* rapsod *m*, bard *m*; trubadur *m*.

mint[1] *s bot* mentă *f*.

mint[2] *s* monetărie *f*; sumă *f* mare; sursă *f* ‖ *vt* a bate monedă; a inventa; a născoci; **in** ~ **condition** în perfectă stare.

minuet *s mus* menuet *n*.

minus *prep math* minus, fără; *fig* minus, lipsă ‖ *s math*, *etc* (semnul) minus *n*; *fig* lipsă *f*, neajuns *n*, defect *n*.

minuscule *adj* minuscul.

minute[1] *s* minut *n*; clipă *f*; moment *n*; *pl* proces *n* verbal; notă *f* ‖ *vt* a cronometra.

minute[2] *adj* (*tiny*) minuscule; (*detailed*) amănunțit, detaliat; minuțios; (*slight*) de mică importanță.

minx *s* ștrengăriță *f*, nebunatică *f*.

miracle *s* minune *f*, miracol *n*; model *n*, pildă *f*.

mirage *s* miraj *n*.

mire *s* glod *n*, noroi *n* ‖ *vt lit* (~*d in debt, etc*) a se îngloda; a se împotmoli.

mirror *s* oglindă *f*; reflectare *f* ‖ *vt* a oglindi.

mirth *s* veselie *f*, bucurie *f*; râs *n*.

misadventure *s* accident *n*, nenorocire *f*, ghinion *n*.

misanthropist *s* mizantrop *m*.

misanthropy *s* mizantropie *f*.

misapprehension *s* neînțelegere *f*; înțelegere *f* greșită.

misappropriation *s* deturnare *f*, delapidare *f*.

misbehave *vi* a se comporta urât.

miscalculate *vt* a calcula greșit ‖ *vi* a se înșela.

miscarriage *s jur* eroare *f*, greșeală *f*; eșec *n*, nereușită *f*; *med* avort *n* spontan.

miscarry *vi med* a avorta; (*fail*) a eșua.

miscellaneous *adj* variat, divers; *lit* miscelaneu.

mischief *s* rău *n*; necaz *n*; pagubă *f*; poznă *f*, prostie *f*; trăsnaie *f*.

mischievous *adj* răutăcios; răuvoitor; rău, dăunător; zburdalnic.

misconception *s* neînțelegere *f*, înțelegere *f* greșită; concepție/idee *f* falsă.

misconduct *s* comportare/conduită *f* proastă; infidelitate *f* conjugală; proastă conducere *f*.

misconstrue *vt* a interpreta greșit; a răstălmăci.

miscreant *s* ticălos *m*, tâlhar *m*.

misdeed *s* ticăloșie *f*; fărădelege *f*; crimă *f*.

misdemeanor *s jur* infracţiune *f*; delict *n*.

misdirect *vt* a pune pe o cale greşită; a dezinforma, a induce în eroare.

miser *s* zgârcit *m*.

miserable *adj* jalnic, (*person*) nefericit; (*weather, etc*) prost, rău; trist; (*salary*) derizoriu; groaznic, (*condition*) mizerabil; mizer; abject.

miserly *adj* (*stingy*) avar, cârpănos; (*measly*) foarte mic; de mizerie.

misery *s* (*poverty*) sărăcie *f*; (*grief*) suferinţă *f*; nenorocire *f*; nefericire *f*.

misfire *vi* a nu exploda; a da rateuri; *fig* (*plan*) a eşua, a da greş.

misfit *s* (*dress, etc*) nepotrivire *f*; obiect *n* prost ajustat; inadaptabil *m*.

misfortune *s* nenorocire *f*; adversitate *f*; ghinion *n*.

misgiving *s* presimţire *f* rea, presimţiri *f pl* rele; îndoială *f*.

misguided *adj* (*person*) prost îndrumat; neavizat; (*opinion*) nechibzuit, negândit; (*attempt*) nechibzuit.

mishap *s* nenorocire *f*, accident *n*, ghinion *n*.

misinform *vt* a dezinforma.

misinterpret *vt* a interpreta greşit; a răstălmăci.

misjudge *vt* (~ *time, distance*) a evalua greşit; (~ *a person, etc*) a judeca greşit, a se înşela asupra.

mislay *vt* a aşeza unde nu trebuie; a pierde, a rătăci.

mislead *vt* a induce în eroare • ~ing *adj* greşit, care induce în eroare; înşelător, fals.

mismatch *vt* (*colors*) a asorta prost; (*marriage*) a nu potrivi || *s* (*of colors*) culori *f pl* ce nu se asortează; (*in a marriage*) mezalianţă *f*.

misnomer *s* termen *m* impropriu; nume *n* nepotrivit/ neinspirat.

misogynist *s* misogin *m*.

misplace *vt* a rătăci; a pune greşit.

misprint *s* greşeală *f* de tipar.

misrepresent *vt* (~ *facts*) a denatura, a deforma; (*person*) a prezenta o falsă imagine.

Miss[1] *s* (*term of address*) domnişoară *f*.

miss[2] *vt* (~ *a train, etc*) a scăpa, a pierde; (*forget*) a uita; (*omit*) a omite; a sări; (~ *a person*) a duce lipsa/ dorul; a-i fi dor de || *vi* (*fail to hit target*) a nu nimeri; (*fail to do*) a nu reuşi || *s* (*failure*) eşec *n*.

misshapen *adj* diform, slut, hidos.

missile *s mil* (*weapon*) rachetă *f*; proiectil *n*.

missing *adj* pierdut, rătăcit; care lipseşte, absent.

mission *s* misiune *f*; chemare *f*; scop *n*; sarcină *f*.

misspell *vt* a scrie greşit.

misstep *s* pas *m* greşit.

missus *s coll* consoartă *f*.

mist *s met* ceaţă *f*, pâclă *f*; *fig* ceaţă *f*, văl *n* (în faţa ochilor).

mistake, mistook, mistaken *vt* (~ *the meaning*) a înţelege greşit; (*intention*) a se înşela asupra; a greşi || *s* greşeală *f*, eroare *f*.

Mister *s* (*only* **Mr.**) domnul *m*, domnule *m*.

mistiming *s* inoportunitate *f*.

mistletoe *s bot* vâsc *n*.

mistreat *vt* a maltrata.

mistress *s* stăpână *f*; (*only* **Mrs.**) doamna *f*, doamnă *f*.

mistrust *s* bănuială *f*, neîncredere *f* || *vt* a nu se încrede în; a bănui.

misunderstand *vt* a înţelege greşit; a interpreta greşit; a răstălmăci • ~ing *s* înţelegere *f* greşită; neînţelegere *f*; dezacord *n*.

misuse *s* (*of time, resources*) utilizare *f* greşită; (*of power*) abuz *n*; (*of funds*) deturnare *f* || *vt* (~ *time, resources*) a utiliza greşit; (~ *power*) a abuza; (~ *funds*) a deturna.

mite *s ento* căpuşă *f*; gâză *f*; (*coin*) bănuţ *m*, para *f*; (*little bit*) pic *n*, strop *m*; *coll* (*child*) ţânc *m*, prichindel *m*.

mitigate *vt* (~ *pain*) a atenua, a alina; (~ *zeal, etc*) a tempera, a domoli.

mitigation *s frml* atenuare *f*; reducere *f*.

mitre *s relig* mitră *f*; ongleu *n*.

mitt *s* mănuşă *f* cu un deget; *coll* (*hand*) labă *f*.

mitten *s* mănuşă *f* cu un singur deget.

mix *vt* a amesteca; a combina; *tech* a mixa; *bot, zool* a încrucişa || *vi* a se amesteca; a se asocia || *s* dozaj *n*; *cul* amestec *n*; *mus* mixaj *n*; *constr* dozaj *n*; ~ **up** *vt* a amesteca, a zăpăci, a încurca • ~**ed** *adj* amestecat; eterogen; *scol* mixt • ~**up** *s* zăpăceală *f*, harababură *f*; confuzie *f*.

mixture *s* amalgam *n*, amestec *n*; *med* mixtură *f*; compus *m* chimic.

moan *s* geamăt *n*; suspin *n*; murmur *n* || *vi* a geme; a suspina; a murmura.

moat *s* (*castle, etc*) şanţ *n* de apărare.

mob *s* gloată *f*, mulţime *f*; bandă *f* || *vt/vi* a se îmbulzi.

mobile *adj* mobil; mişcător; schimbător; migrator || *adv* mobil || *s* parte *f* mobilă.

mobility *s* mobilitate *f*.

mobilize *vt/vi* a (se) mobiliza.

moccasin *s* mocasin *m*.

mock *vt* a-şi bate joc de; a sfida; a parodia; a înşela || *adj* prefăcut; înscenat; fals || *s* imitare *f*; ~ **exam** *s* examen *n* de probă, simulare *f* • ~**ery** *s* batjocură *f*; derâdere *f*, ridiculizare *f*; parodie *f*.

modal *s gram* verb *n* modal || *adj* modal.

mode *s* mod *n*, fel *n*; manieră *f*; caracteristică *f*; mod *n*, procedeu *n*; *mus* tonalitate *f*; *gram* mod *n*.

model *s* model *n*; tipar *n*; şablon *n*; tip *n*; mostră *f*; exemplu *n*; sistem *n* || *vt* a modela; a influenţa.

modem *s comp* modem *n*.

moderate *adj* moderat; reţinut; mediu; modic || *vt* a modera || *vi* a se tempera; a arbitra.

moderation *s* moderaţie *f*; (*self-restraint*) reţinere *f*; stăpânire *f* de sine; *phys* frânare *f*, încetinire *f*; **in** ~ moderat; cu moderaţie.

modern *adj* modern; nou; contemporan || *s* om *m* modern.

modest *adj* modest; umil; simplu; ieftin; decent • ~**y** *s* modestie *f*; simplitate *f*; sărăcie *f*; decenţă *f*; puritate *f*; castitate *f*.

modification *s* modificare *f*.

modify *vt* a modifica; a schimba; a transforma || *vi* a se modifica.

modulate *vt phys, etc* a modula || *vi* a se modula.

module *s tech, math* modul *n*.

mohair *s text* mohair *n*.

moist *adj* umed; jilav • ~**en** *vt* a umezi; a uda || *vi* a se umezi.

moisture *s* umezeala *f*, umiditate *f*.

moisturizer *s* cremă *f* hidratantă, lapte *m* hidratant.

molasses *s* melasă *f*.

mold[1] *s* tipar *n*, mulaj *n*, şablon *n*; caracter *n* || *vt* a modela; a turna.

mold[2] *s* (*on bread, etc*) mucegai *n* || *vi* a mucegăi; a se umple de mucegai.

moldy *adj* mucegăit.

mole[1] *s anat* aluniță *f.*

mole[2] *s zool* cârtiță *f.*

molecule *s chem* moleculă *f*, particulă *f.*

molest *vt* (*sexually*) a atenta la pudoarea cuiva; a molesta; (*bother*) a necăji, a supăra.

mollify *vt frml* a domoli, a liniști.

mollusk *s zool* moluscă *f.*

molt *vi* (*birds, animals*) a năpârli.

molten *adj* (*metal*) topit; lichid.

moment *s* moment *n*, clipă *f*; (*importance*) importanță *f.*

momentum *s phys* moment *n*; impuls *n*; *fig* viteză *f*; avânt *n.*

Monaco *s* Monaco.

monarch *s* monarh *m* • **~y** *s* monarhie *f.*

monastery *s* mănăstire *f.*

monastic *adj* monastic; monahal.

Monday *s* luni *f.*

monetary *adj* monetar.

money *s* bani *m pl*; **~ box** *s* pușculiță *f*; **~ grubber** *s* om *m* hrăpăreț/rapace; **~ lender** *s* cămătar *m*; **~ market** *s* piața *f* monetară; **~ order** *s* mandat *n* poștal.

Mongol *adj* mongol || *s* mongol *m*; (limba) mongolă • **~ia** *s* Mongolia.

mongrel *s* (*dog*) corcitură f.

moniker *s coll* (*name*) nume *n*; (*nickname*) poreclă *f.*

monitor *s* (*device*) monitor *n*; *naut* (hidro)monitor *n*; (*person*) sfătuitor *m.*

monk *s* călugăr *m.*

monkey *s zool* maimuță *f*; *tech* cărucior *n* de macara; *constr* berbec *m* (de sonetă).

monocle *s* monoclu *n.*

monogamy *s* monogamie *f.*

monogram *s* monogramă *f.*

monograph *s* monografie *f.*

monologue *s* monolog *n.*

monopolize *vt also fig* a monopoliza.

monopoly *s* monopol *n.*

monosyllable *s* monosilabă *f.*

monotone *s* citire *f* monotonă; repetare *f.*

monotonous *adj* monoton; plictisitor.

monotony *s* monotonie *f.*

monsoon *s met* muson *m.*

monster *s* (*creature*) monstru *m*; dihanie *f*; bestie *f*; (*person, object*) uriaș *m*, colos *m.*

monstrous *adj* (*hideous*) monstruos; (*huge*) enorm, imens; (*atrocious*) odios.

month *s* lună *f*; *coll* in a **~ of Sundays** la sfântu-așteaptă • **~ly** *adj* lunar || *adv* lunar || *s* (*publication*) revistă *f* lunară.

monument *s* monument *n.*

moo *s* muget *n* || *vi* a mugi.

mood[1] *s* dispoziție *f*; mod *n*; stare *f* sufletească; ton *n* • **~y** *adj* capricios, schimbător; prost dispus.

mood[2] *s gram* mod *n.*

moon *s astron* lună *f*; satelit *m* || *vi* a merge ca un somnambul • **~light** *s* clar *n* de lună || *vi* a lucra la negru • **~lighting** *s* muncă *f* la negru.

moor[1] *s* mlaștină f; ținut *n* cu mlaștini de turbă; landă *f.*

moor[2] *vi naut* a se lega; a acosta; a amara.

moose *s zool* elan *m.*

mop *s* spălător *m*; perie *f* cu coadă; pămătuf *n*; smoc *n* || *vt* a spăla pe jos; a șterge.

mope *vi* a fi abătut/indispus.

moped *s* motoretă *f.*

moppet *s coll* fetiță *f* drăgălașă.

moral *adj* moral, etic; spiritual; virtuos || *s* morală *f*, tâlc *n*; pildă *f*; moralitate *f.*

morale *s* moral *n*; stare *f* de spirit; curaj *n.*

moralist *s* moralist *m.*

morass *s* (*marsh*) smârc *n*, mocirlă *f*; (*muddle*) complicație *f*; (*mess*) încurcătură *f*; (*tangle*) hățiș *n.*

moratorium *s* moratoriu *n*; suspendare *f.*

morbid *adj* morbid; patologic; nesănătos; groaznic.

mordant *adj* tăios, acerb, aprig.

more *adj/pron* mai mult(ă); mai mulți/multe || *adv* mai (mult); **~ and ~** din ce în ce; **~ or less** mai mult sau mai puțin; aproape, aproximativ; **all the ~ so** cu atât mai mult.

morello *s* (*cherry*) cireașă *f* amară.

moreover *adv* mai mult decât atât; în plus; pe lângă acestea; de asemenea.

morgue *s* morgă *f.*

moribund *adj also fig* muribund.

Mormon *s* mormon *m.*

morning *s* dimineață *f*; început *n*; zori *pl* || *adj* de dimineață; matinal.

Moroccan *s* marocan(ă) *m/f* || *adj* marocan.

Morocco *s* Maroc *n.*

moron *s coll* cretin-ă *m/f* • **~ic** *adj* cretin.

morose *adj* îmbufnat; morocănos; posomorât.

morphine *s chem* morfină *f.*

morphology *s* morfologie *f.*

morrow *s* ziua *f* de mâine; viitor *n.*

Morse code *s* (codul) Morse *n.*

morsel *s* (*of food*) bucată *f*, bucățică *f*; îmbucătură *f* || *vt* (**out**) a împărți/distribui în porții mici.

mortal *adj* muritor; de moarte; mortal; fatal; teribil || *s* muritor *m* • **~ity** *s* caracter *n* muritor; mortalitate *f*; oameni *m pl*; omenire *f.*

mortgage *s jur* amanetare *f*; ipotecare *f*; amanet *n*; ipotecă *f* || *vt* a amaneta; a ipoteca; a face un împrumut ipotecar.

mortician *s* antreprenor *m* de pompe funebre.

mortify *vt* a chinui, a mortifica; a umili; a jigni; a înăbuși.

mortuary *s* morgă *f.*

mosaic *s constr, fig* mozaic *n.*

Moscow *s* Moscova.

mosey *vi coll* (*amble*) (**along/to**) a merge agale, a se îndrepta agale (spre).

Moslem *s/adj* musulman(ă) *m/f.*

mosque *s relig* moschee *f.*

mosquito *s ento* țânțar *m.*

moss *s* mușchi *m* || *vt/vi* a se acoperi cu mușchi.

most *adj* cel mai mult, cea mai multă; cei mai mulți, cele mai multe || *adv* cel mai/cea mai; cei/cele mai; extrem de, foarte; cel mai mult; îndeosebi; *coll* (*almost*) **~ everybody** aproape toți.

mote *s lit* fărâmă *f*, grăunte *m*; fir *n* de praf.

motel *s* motel *n.*

moth *s ento* fluture *m* de noapte; molie *f*; fluture *m.*

mother *s* mamă *f*; sursă *f*, obârșie *f*; stareță *f* || *vt* a fi mamă; a da naștere; a se îngriji ca o mamă de • **~in-law** *s* soacră *f.*

motif *s art, lit, mus* motiv *n*, temă *f.*

motion *s* mișcare *f*; mers *n*; gest *n*; *tech* funcționare *f*; impuls *n*; *pol* moțiune *f*; *med* scaun *n*, defecație *f* || *vt/vi* a face semn.

motivate *vt* a motiva; a inspira; a stimula.

motivation *s* motiv *n*; motivare *f*, justificare *f*.
motive *s* motiv *n*, mobil *n*; cauză *f* || *adj* motor; stimulator.
motley *adj* amestecat, pestriț.
motor *s* motor *n*; mașină *f* || *vi* a merge cu mașina • ~**boat** *s* barcă *f* cu motor • ~ **vehicle** *s* *auto* vehicul *n* motorizat.
mottled *adj* pestriț; marmorat.
motto *s* moto *n*, deviză *f*.
moult *vt zool* a lepăda (pene etc) || *vi* a năpârli.
mound *s* (*natural*) colină *f*, dâmb *n*, movilă *f*; *geol* tumulus *n*; morman *n*, teanc *n* || *vt* a împrejmui cu un zid de pământ.
mount¹ *s* (*jewelry*) montură *f*; (*photo*) cadru *n*; (*machine*) armătură *f*; *tech* suport *n*; (*horse*) cal *m* înșeuat.
mount² *vt* (~ *a horse, etc*) a se urca pe; a se urca în; a ridica, a sălta; (~ *jewelry*) a fixa, a monta; *thea* a monta; *mil* (~ *an* offensive) a lua (ofensiva); a urca pe (tron) || *vi* a (se) urca; a se cățăra; a încăleca; (*costs* ~) a crește, a se ridica.
mountain *s* munte *m*; grămadă *f* || *adj* colosal.
mourn *vt/vi* a plânge • ~**ing** *adj* de doliu || *s* doliu *n*; durere *f*.
mouse¹ *s* șoarece *m* || *vi* a prinde șoareci • ~**trap** *s* cursă *f* de șoareci.
mouse² *s* *comp* mouse *n*.
mousse *s* *cul* spumă *f*; aspic *n*.
mousy *adj pej* (*shy*) timid, retras.
mouth *s* gură *f*; cioc *n*; bot *n*; orificiu *n*; rât *n* || *vt* a declara; a mesteca; a vorbi tare/afectat.
move *vt* a mișca; (*shift*) a muta; (*push*) a împinge; (*touch*) a emoționa; (*propose*) a propune || *vi* (*go*) a se mișca; (*relocate*) a se muta; (*work*) a funcționa || *s* mișcare *f*; mutare *f*; ~ **away** *vi* a pleca; ~ **in** *vi* a se muta (într-o casă); ~ **on** *vi* a-și continua drumul; (*conversation*) a schimba subiectul; (*time*) a trece, a se scurge; ~ **out** *vi* a se muta (dintr-o casă); ~ **over** *vi* a se da la o parte.
movement *s* mișcare *f*; mutare *f*; deplasare *f*; gest *n*; mers *n*; funcționare *f*; circulație *f*.
movie *s* film *n*.
mow, mowed, mown *vt* a cosi, a secera, a recolta || *s* stog *n*; căpiță *f* • ~**er** *s* secerătoare *f*; mașină *f* de tuns iarba.
moxie *s* *coll* entuziasm *n*, energie *f*.
Mr. *s* * **Mister.**
Mrs. *s* * **mistress.**
Ms. *s* (apelativ pus înaintea numelui unei femei despre care nu știm dacă este sau nu căsătorită).
much *adj* mult(ă) || *adv* prea; foarte; mult; cu mult; de departe; cam, aproximativ.
muck *s* (*manure*) bălegar *n*, gunoi *n*; noroi *n*, nămol *n*; *fig* murdărie *f*, noroi *n* || *vt* a îngrășa cu bălegar; a murdări; a strica.
mucus *s* *anat, etc* mucus *n*; mucozitate *f*.
mud *s* noroi *n*; murdărie *f* || *vt* a murdări; a mânji; a tulbura.
muddle *vt* (*papers*) a amesteca, a încurca; (*person*) a tulbura; a ameți; (*work*) a cârpăci; a strica || *vi* a lucra prost || *s* confuzie *f*, zăpăceală *f*; harababură *f*.
muddy *adj* plin de noroi; tulbure; brunet; confuz; răgușit; vag.
muff *s* manșon *n*; *tech* cuplaj *n*; manșon *n*; bucșă *f*.
muffin *s* *cul approx* brioș *n*.
muffle *vt* a înfășura, a înveli; (~ *a sound*) a înăbuși.

mug *s* cană *f*; pahar *n*; halbă *f*; *coll* mutră *f* || *vt* a pălmui; a jefui • ~**ger** *s* gangster *m* • ~**ging** *s* tâlhărie *f*.
muggy *adj* (*weather*) umed și cald; (*air*) înăbușitor.
mulatto *s* mulatru *m*.
mulberry *s* *bot* (*tree*) dud *m*; (*fruit*) dudă *f*.
mule¹ *s* *zool* catâr *m*; *fig* catâr *m*, (om) încăpățânat *m*; *tech* șablon *n*.
mule² *s* (*slipper*) papuc *m* fără călcâi.
mull *vi* (*over*) a se gândi la, a reflecta la.
mullet *s* *icht* barbun *m*.
mullion *s* cercevea *f* verticală.
multicolored *adj* multicolor.
multifaceted *adj* cu multiple fațete.
multifarious *adj* divers, multiplu.
multilateral *adj* multilateral.
multilingual *adj* plurilingv.
multimedia *adj* multimedia.
multiple *s/adj* multiplu *m*; ~ **choice** *adj* cu mai multe variante de răspuns; ~ **sclerosis** *s* *med* scleroză *f* în plăci.
multiplex *s* sală *f* de cinema cu mai multe ecrane.
multiplication *s* *bio, etc* înmulțire *f*, multiplicare *f*; *math* înmulțire *f*.
multiplicity *s* multitudine *f*.
multiply *vt* a înmulți; a spori || *vi* a spori, a se înmulți.
multi-purpose *adj* multifuncțional.
multiracial *adj* multirasial.
multistory *adj* cu mai multe etaje || *s* parcare *f* etajată.
multitasking *adj* cu operații multiple.
multitude *s* masă *f*, mulțime *f*.
multitudinous *adj* foarte numeros.
mum *s* *coll* mămică *f*.
mumble *vt/vi* a murmura, a mormăi; a molfăi.
mummy¹ *s* (*corpse*) mumie *f*.
mumps *s* *med* oreion *n*.
munch *vt/vi* a clefăi, a plescăi, a mânca cu zgomot.
mundane *adj* lumesc; pământesc, terestru; banal, obișnuit.
municipal *adj* municipal.
munificent *adj* generos.
munitions *s pl* muniție *f*; ~ **factory** *s* fabrică *f* de armament.
mural *adj* mural || *s* pictură *f* murală; frescă *f*.
murder *s* crimă *f*, asasinat *n*; omor *n* || *vt* a ucide; a asasina; a masacra; a stâlci • ~**er** *s* asasin *m*, criminal *m*, ucigaș *m* • ~**ous** *adj* ucigător, criminal.
murky *adj* (*place*) întunecos; (*water*) tulbure; *fig* tulbure.
murmur *s* murmur *n*; susur *n*; foșnet *n*; zumzet *n*; zgomot *n* || *vt* a murmura; a șopti || *vi* a murmura; a șopti; a foșni; a susura.
muscle *s* *anat* mușchi *m*; *fig* greutate *f*, impact *n*.
muscular *adj* (*pain*) muscular; (*person*) mușchiulos.
muse *s* muză *f* || *vi* a medita, a cugeta, a se gândi.
museum *s* muzeu *n*.
mush *s* (*food*) terci *n*, păsat *n*; *coll fig* sentimentalitate *f*.
mushroom *s* ciupercă *f*; parvenit *m* || *vi* a crește ca ciupercile.
music *s* muzică *f*; note *f pl* muzicale • ~**al** *adj* (*event, voice*) muzical; (*skilled at music*) talentat, dotat pentru muzică.
musician *s* muzician *m*; compozitor *m*; muzicant *m*; interpret *m*.
musk *s* mosc *n*, bizam *m*; miros *n* de mosc
musketeer *s* mușchetar *m*.

Muslim *adj/s* musulman *m; mahomedan m.*

muslin *s* muselină *f.*

mussel *s icht* scoică *f.*

must[1] *v mod* a trebui, a fi obligat; a fi sigur/probabil; a nu avea voie, a nu fi permis, a fi interzis ‖ *s* necesitate *f* imperioasă; **I ~ lock the door** trebuie să încui ușa; **you ~ be famished** trebuie să-ți fie foame; **you ~ not smoke** nu e voie să fumezi; **I ~ admit** trebuie să recunosc; **if you ~** dacă trebuie neapărat, dacă nu se poate altfel.

must[2] *s* must *n.*

mustache *s* mustață *f.*

mustang *s* mustang *m,* cal *m* sălbatic.

mustard *s* muștar *n.*

muster *vt* a aduna, a strânge ‖ *vi* a se aduna, a se reuni.

musty *adj* (*smell*) mucegăit, de mucegai; (*room*) neaerisit, care miroase a mucegai.

mutable *adj* schimbător.

mute *adj* mut; tăcut; taciturn ‖ *s* mut *m;* figurant *m;* surdină *f* ‖ *vt* a pune surdină • **~d** *adj* (*color*) șters; (*reaction*) slab; (*protest*) mascat.

mutilate *vt* a mutila, a schilodi; a deforma.

mutineer *s* răzvrătit *m,* rebel *m.*

mutinous *adj* rebel.

mutiny *s* răscoală *f;* rebeliune *f* ‖ *vi* a se răscula.

mutt *s* (*dog*) potaie *f,* cotarlă *f; sl* (*fool*) tâmpit *m.*

mutter *vt* a murmura; a mormăi; (*threat*) a profera ‖ *vi* a murmura; a bombăni ‖ *s* murmur *n;* mormăit *n.*

mutton *s* (carne de) oaie *f.*

mutual *adj* (*feeling, aid*) reciproc, mutual; (*friends, interests*) comun.

muzzle *s* (*dog ~*) bot *n;* botniță *f;* (*~ of a gun*) gură *f* ‖ *vt also fig* a pune botniță, a închide gura (cuiva), a face să tacă.

muzzy *adj* (*person*) zăpăcit, confuz; (*ideas*) confuz; (*picture*) estompat, neclar.

my *adj* meu, mea; mei, mele ‖ *interj* aoleo!, vai!.

mycology *s* micologie *f.*

myopia *s also fig* miopie *f.*

myopic *adj* miop.

myriad *adj lit* nenumărat ‖ *s* mii și mii.

myself *pron ref* mă; însumi, însămi ‖ *pron pers* eu.

mysterious *adj* misterios, tainic; secret.

mystery *s* mister *n;* secret *n;* enigmă *f;* problemă *f.*

mystical *adj* mistic.

mystified *adj* perplex, dezorientat.

mystifying *adj* inexplicabil, înșelător.

mystique *s* mistică *f.*

myth *s* mit *n;* legendă *f* • **~ical** *adj* mitic • **~ological** *adj* mitologic • **~ology** *s* mitologie *f.*

mythomania *s* mitomanie *f.*

N

N, n *s* (litera) N, n.

nab *vt* (*~ a thief*) a pune mâna pe; a înșfăca, a înhăța; (*steal*) a șterpeli.

nadir *s astron* nadir *n; fig* punctul *n* cel mai de jos, limita *f* inferioară.

nag *vt* a cicăli; a sâcâi ‖ *s* cicăleală *f;* sâcâială *f.*

nail[1] *s* unghie *f* ‖ *vt* a țintui; a atinti, a fixa; a înhăța; **~ biting** *s* mania *f* de a-și roade unghiile; *fig* nervozitate *f* ‖ *adj* stresant; sufocant; **~ brush** *s* perie *f* de unghii; **~ file** *s* pilă *f* de unghii; **~ polish/varnish** *s* lac *n* de unghii, ojă *f.*

nail[2] *s* (*metal ~*) cui *n;* țintă *f;* piron *n;* tech știft *n* ‖ *vt* a bate în cuie, a fixa în cuie; a țintui; a pironi; *fig* a atinti, a fixa (atenția); *fig* a înșfăca, a înhăța, a prinde (un hoț etc.).

naive *adj* naiv • **~ty** *s* naivitate *f.*

naked *adj* gol; nud; dezgolit; dezbrăcat; golaș.

namby-pamby *adj coll* (*person*) molâu, mototol; (*style*) afectat, prețios; (*work*) sentimental.

name *s* nume *n;* titlu *n;* denumire *f;* faimă *f;* neam *n; pl* înjurături *f pl* ‖ *vt* a (de)numi; a spune pe nume; a fixa.

nanny *s* doică *f,* bonă *f.*

nanosecond *s* o miliardime *f* de secundă.

nap[1] *s* ațipeală *f;* pui *m* de somn.

nap[2] *s text* scamă *f;* (*velvet*) pluș *n;* (*cloth*) puf *n.*

nape *s anat* ceafă *f.*

napkin *s* șervețel *n.*

narcissus *s bot* narcisă *f.*

narcotic *adj/s med* narcotic *n;* soporific *n.*

narrate *vt* a povesti; a relata; a nara.

narration *s* narațiune *f,* povestire *f.*

narrative *adj* narativ, de povestire ‖ *s* relatare *f,* povestire *f;* narațiune *f.*

narrator *s* narrator *m,* povestitor *m.*

narrow *adj* (*mind, etc*) îngust; strâmt; limitat; (*victory, majority*) strâns; (*exam, etc*) sever; (*control*) strict; (*meaning*) exact ‖ *vi* (*river*) a se îngusta, a se strâmta ‖ *vt* a strâmta, a îngusta; a restrânge; (*eyes*) a închide pe jumătate.

nasal *adj anat* nazal ‖ *s ling* (sunet) nazal *n;* (consoană) nazală *f.*

NASA *s abbr* (**National Aeronautics and Space Administration**) Administrația *f* Națională de Aeronautică.

nascent *adj* care se naște, în devenire; care se înfiripă.

nasturtium *s bot* călțunaș *m.*

nasty *adj* (*foul*) murdar; (*obscene*) obscen; scârbos; (*mean*) josnic; (*harmful*) dăunător; (*impolite*) obraznic; (*wicked*) răutăcios; (*~ smell, feeling*) neplăcut; (*~ weather*) rău, urât; (*unkind*) hain; (*~ problem*) dificil, delicat; (*~ accident*) grav; (*~ fall*) urât.

nation *s* națiune *f;* popor *n;* țară *f* • **~wide** *adj* în întreaga țară; (*campaign, etc*) la scară națională ‖ *adv* pe tot cuprinsul țării.

national *adj* național; (*campaign, etc*) la scară națională; (*tradition*) național ‖ *s* cetățean *m;* **~ anthem** *s* imn *n* național • **~ism** *s* naționalism *n* • **~ity** *s* naționalitate *f;* cetățenie *f;* națiune *f,* popor *n.*

native *adj* (*country*) natal; (*language*) matern; (*plant, animal*) indigen; înnăscut; nativ ‖ *s* băștinaș *m;* indigen *m;* localnic *m;* **Native American** *s* indian *m* american.

nativity *s* naștere *f; relig* Nașterea *f* Domnului, Crăciun *n.*

natty *adj coll* (*person*) spilcuit; (*dress*) elegant; (*device*) ingenios.

natural *adj* natural; normal; firesc; simplu; real; viu; (*instinct*) înnăscut; (*artist, etc*) înnăscut, talentat ‖ *s* dispoziție *f* naturală • **~ly** *adv* firește, bineînțeles; natural, firesc; simplu.

nature *s* natură *f;* univers *n;* fire *f;* fel *n;* esență *f;* dispoziție *f;* **~ reserve** *s* rezervație *f* naturală.

naturist *s* nudist *m.*

naught *s obs, lit* zero *n,* nimic *n* ‖ *adv obs, lit* deloc.

naughty *adj* obraznic, rău; mofturos; urât; şocant; nepoliticos.

nausea *s* greaţă *f*; rău *n* de mare; silă *f* • **~ting** *adj also fig* greţos, dezgustător.

nauseous *adj* greţos.

nautical *adj* nautic, marinăresc.

naval *adj* naval, maritim.

nave *s relig* naos *n*, navă *f*.

navel *s anat* ombilic *n*; *coll* buric *n*; *fig* centru *n*, miez *n*.

navigable *adj* navigabil.

navigate *vt/vi* a naviga, a pilota.

navigation *s* navigaţie *f*, navigare *f*.

navigator *s* navigator *m*.

navy *s naut*, *mil* (*service*) marină *f*; flotă *f* militară; (*fleet*) flotă *f*; ~ **blue** bleumarin.

nay *adv obs*, *hum* chiar, ba mai mult || *s* vot *n* negativ.

Nazi *s/adj* nazist *m*.

near *adv* aproape; în preajmă || *adj* apropiat; intim; greu || *prep* (*space*) lângă; aproape de; spre; (*time*) în jurul, pe la || *vt/vi* a se apropia • **~sighted** *adj* miop • **~by** *adv* aproape, în apropiere || *prep* aproape de || *adj* apropiat • **~ly** *adv* aproape; mai-mai; de aproape; aproximativ.

neat *adj* (*room, etc*) curat, ordonat; (*work*) îngrijit; (*writing*) citeţ; frumos; (*solution*) abil, ingenios; (*liquor*) pur, fără apă; simplu; (*clear*) clar; concis; *coll* straşnic, super • **~ly** *adv* îngrijit; clar, limpede; abil, cu abilitate.

nebulous *adj* nebulos.

necessarily *adv* inevitabil, obligatoriu; **not** ~ nu neapărat; **it's not** ~ **so** nu este neapărat aşa.

necessary *adj* necesar; obligatoriu; esenţial || *s* necesar *n*; toaletă *f*.

necessitate *vt* a necesita.

necessity *s* necesitate *f*; imperativ *n*; lipsă *f*, nevoie *f*.

neck *s anat* gât *n*; (*bottle*) gât *n*; guler *n*; *geog* istm *n*; coş *n* vulcanic.

necklace *s* salbă *f*, colier *n*; cravată *f*.

neckline *s* (*dress*) răscroiala *f* gâtului.

necromancer *s* necromant *m*.

necromancy *s* necromanţie *f*.

nectar *s myth* nectar *n*, licoarea/băutura *f* zeilor; *fig* nectar *n*, licoare *f*.

nectarine *s bot* nectarină *f*.

necktie *s* cravată *f*.

née *adj* născută.

need *s* nevoie *f*; necaz *n*; lipsă *f* || *vt* a avea nevoie de; a trebui || *v mod* a trebui; **if** ~ **be** dacă este cazul; la nevoie.

needle *s* ac *n*; andrea *f*; săgeată *f*; vârf *n*; obelisc *n* || *vt* a coase; a sâcâi.

needless *adj* (*expense, etc*) inutil; (*remark, etc*) deplasat.

nefarious *adj* (*wicked*) abject, infam; (*immoral*) necurat; vicios.

negate *vt* (*deny*) a nega; (*nullify*) a respinge; a anula; (~ *efforts*) a anihila.

negation *s* negaţie *f*; negare *f*.

negative *adj* negativ || *s* negaţie *f*; refuz *n* || *vt* a nega; a respinge.

negativity *s* negativism *n*.

neglect *vt* (*overlook*) a neglija; a omite; (~ *a garden*) a lăsa în paragină || *s* (*of a garden*) proastă întreţinere *f*; (*of children*) lipsă *f* de îngrijire; (*of work*) neglijare *f*; desconsiderare *f*.

negligée *s* neglijeu *n*.

negligence *s* neglijenţă *f*, neatenţie *f*; scăpare *f*, omisiune *f*; nepăsare *f*.

negligent *adj* neglijent; neatent; indolent.

negligible *adj* insignifiant.

negotiable *adj econ* negociabil; (*road*) accesibil; (*river*) navigabil; (*conflict*) aplanabil.

negotiate *vi* a negocia || *vt econ*, *pol* a negocia; a trata; a discuta; (*obstacle*) a învinge.

negotiation *s* negociere *f*.

negotiator *s* negociator *m*.

Negro *s/adj pej* negru *m*.

neigh *vi* (*horse's*) a necheza || *s* nechezat *n*.

neighbor *s* vecin *m*; semen *m* || *vt/vi* a se învecina • **~hood** *s* cartier *n*.

neither *pron* nici unul/una || *adj* nici unul/una || *adv* nici || *conj* ~ ... **nor** nici ... nici.

neologism *s* neologism *n*.

neons neon *n*.

nephew *s* nepot *m*.

nepotism *s* nepotism *n*.

nerd *s coll* (*geek*) încuiat *m*; (*bore*) nesuferit *m*.

nerve *s* nerv *m*; forţă *f*; energie *f*; curaj *n*.

nervous *adj* nervos; agitat; expresiv; enervant.

nervy *adj coll* (*tense*) nervos, agitat; (*cheeky*) obraznic, impertinent.

nest *s* cuib *n*; adăpost *n*; viespar *n*; set *n* || *vt* a cuibări || *vi* a trăi în cuib; ~ **egg** *s* bani *m pl* strânşi la ciorap.

nestle *vi* a se ghemui, a se cuibări.

net[1] *s* plasă *f*; capcană *f*; reţea *f* || *vt* (*fish*) a prinde în plasă; (*money*) a câştiga net; (*business*) a aduce un venit net || *adj* net.

Net[2] *s* **the** ~ Internetul *n*; **to surf the** ~ a naviga pe Internet.

nether *adj obs*, *lit* de jos.

Netherlands *s pl* Olanda.

nettle *vt* a agasa || *s bot* urzică *f* • **~rash** *s med* urticarie *f*.

network *s* (*net*) plasă *f*; (*system*) reţea *f*, sistem *n* || *vi* (*meet people*) a stabili contacte/relaţii.

neuralgia *s med* nevralgie *f*.

neurologist *s* neurolog *m*.

neurology *s* neurologie *f*.

neurosis *s med* nevroză *f*.

neurotic *adj med* nevrotic || *s med* nevrotic *m*.

neuter *adj gram* neutru; *bot* asexuat; imparţial, neutru || *s gram* (genul) neutru *n* || *vt* (~ *an animal*) a castra.

neutral *adj* neutru, neangajat; (*color*) cenuşiu, sur; *phys*, *elec* neutru, neutral; neprecis || *s* stat *n* neutru; cetăţean *m* al unui stat neutru.

never *adv* niciodată; deloc, defel; imposibil.

nevertheless *adv* totuşi, cu toate acestea.

new *adj* nou; recent; proaspăt; novice; **New Delhi** *s* New Delhi; **New Testament** *s relig* Noul Testament *n*; **New Year** *s* Anul *m* Nou; **New Zealand** *s* Noua Zeelandă.

newborn *adj* nou-născut.

newcomer *s* nou-venit *m*; străin *m*, necunoscut *m*.

newfangled *adj coll* ultramodern; de modă nouă.

new-laid *adj* (*egg*) proaspăt.

newlyweds *s pl* tineri *m pl* căsătoriţi.

news *s radio* ştire *f*, informaţie *f*; veste *f*, noutate *f*; ~ **agency** *s* agenţie *f* de presă • **~flash** *s* ştiri *f pl* pe scurt • **~letter** *s* buletin *n* informativ • **~paper** *s* ziar *n*, hârtie *f* de ziar; **~room** *s* redacţie *f* (de ziar) •

~stand s stand n de ziare • **~worthy** adj care merită să fie publicat.

newsy adj (letter) plin de noutăți.

newt s zool triton m.

next adj (page, etc) următor; (room) învecinat; vecin; (month, etc) viitor ‖ adv pe urmă, apoi, după aceea ‖ prep lângă; ca și ‖ s următorul m; ~ **of kin** s rudă f apropiată.

nib s peniță f.

nibble vt a roade, a mușca (din); a ciuguli ‖ s mușcătură f.

nice adj (day, etc) plăcut, frumos; (food) bun; (painting) frumos; (person) amabil, simpatic; (dress) drăguț; (vacation, etc) agreabil; (minute) scrupulous, atent; minuțios; (problem) delicat; (respectable) virtuos; (difference) subtil, dificil; (hearing) fin; ascuțit; (device) sensibil; (style) căutat; afectat • ~**ly** adv cu amabilitate; bine, frumos.

nicety s (precision) precizie f, exactitate f; (subtlety) finețe f, subtilitate f; (refinement) rafinament n; pl ambilități f pl; subtilități f pl, chichițe f pl.

niche s nișă f; fig adăpost n, refugiu n; fig loc n bun, situație f bună.

nick s (notch) crestătură f; tech îngustare f ‖ vt a cresta, a face o crestătură.

nickel s chem nichel n; bănuț m de cinci cenți.

nickname s poreclă f; diminutiv n ‖ vt a porecli.

Nicosia s Nicosia f.

nicotine s nicotină f.

niece s nepoată f.

nifty adj coll (stylish) de mare clasă; (clever) deștept; (neat) măiestrit.

Nigeria s Nigeria • ~**n** adj/s nigerian(ă) m/f.

niggard s zgârcit m, avar m • ~**ly** adj zgârcit, avar; meschin ‖ adv cu zgârcenie.

nigger s pej negru m.

niggle vi (fuss over details) a se ține de fleacuri/nimicuri, a se ocupa de fleacuri/nimicuri; a fi extrem de migălos; (worry) a nu da pace, a roade ‖ vt (nag) a sâcâi, a agasa ‖ s cicăleală f, pisălogeală f; sâcâială f.

niggling adj (nagging) agasant, sâcâitor; (petty) minor, mărunt, insignifiant.

night s noapte f; seară f; beznă f; **at** ~ noaptea; seara; ~ **school** s școală f serală, cursuri n pl serale; ~ **shift** s schimb n/tură f de noapte; ~ **watch** s pază f de noapte; paznic m de noapte.

nightclub s club n de noapte.

nightdress s cămașă f de noapte.

nightfall s înserare f, lăsarea f nopții.

nightgown s cămașă f de noapte.

nightie s coll cămașă f de noapte.

nightingale s orn privighetoare f.

nightlife s viață f de noapte, activitate f nocturnă.

nightly adj de noapte, nocturn ‖ adv noaptea; în fiecare noapte.

nightmare s coșmar n; groază f; obsesie f.

nighttime s (timp de) noapte f; timpul n nopții.

nil s zero n; nimic n.

nimble adj (movement) sprinten, vioi, agil; (mind) vioi, sprinten; ascuțit; (answer) prompt; (listener) receptiv.

nimbus s met nimbus n; (halo) nimb n, aureolă f.

nincompoop s coll tâmpit m.

nine num nouă ‖ s noar m • ~**teen** num nouăsprezece • ~**ty** num nouăzeci.

nip vt (pinch) a pișca, a ciupi; a ciuguli ‖ (bite) a mușca; a apuca, a strânge; (squeeze) a presa, a comprima;

(numb) a atinge, a lovi; ~ **in the bud** vt a înăbuși în fașă ‖ s ciupitură f, pișcătură f; mușcătură f; apucare f; (sip) sorbitură f • ~**ping** adj (cold) tăios; mușcător; fig mușcător, sarcastic, usturător.

nipple s anat sfârc n; (on a baby's bottle) suzetă f; mech duză f; tech niplu n, racord n.

nit s ento lindină f.

nitrogen s azot m, nitrogen n.

no adv nu ‖ adj nici un/o; nu ‖ s negație f; refuz n; vot n contra.

nobility s nobilime f.

noble adj generos; nobil; superb; grandios.

nobody pron nimeni ‖ s nimeni m; nulitate f.

nocturnal adj nocturn.

nod s salut n; moțăit n ‖ vi a da din cap aprobator; a picoti ‖ vt a da din cap; a încuviința.

noise s zgomot n; larmă f; zvon n; intrigă f ‖ vt a răspândi zvonul.

noisome adj lit (smelly) pestilențial; (repellent) dezgustător, respingător.

noisy adj zgomotos; gălăgios; țipător.

nomad s/adj nomad m.

nominal adj econ, gram nominal; convențional; oficial; mic, neînsemnat.

nominate vt (candidate) a propune candidatura; (appoint) a numi.

nomination s numire f, desemnare f.

nominative s gram nominativ n.

nominee s candidat m (la alegeri sau la un post).

nonaggression s neagresiune f.

nonattendance s absentare f.

nonchalant adj nonșalant.

noncommitted adj evaziv.

noncompliance s nesupunere f, nerespectare f.

nonconformist s/adj nonconformist m.

nondescript adj greu de descris/clasificat; oarecare ‖ s persoană f fără o ocupație/profesiune precisă.

none pron nici unul/una; nimeni; nimic.

nonentity s nulitate f; ficțiune f; himeră f; om m fără valoare, nulitate f.

nonetheless adv totuși.

nonexistent adj inexistent.

nonfiction s proză f (dar nu beletristică).

nonintervention s neamestec n.

noninvasive adj care nu deranjează/importunează.

no-no s coll lucru/comportament n inacceptabil.

nonplussed adj derutat, descumpănit.

nonprofit adj cu scop nelucrativ.

nonrefundable adj nerambursabil.

nonresident s nonrezident m.

nonsense s nonsens n; absurditate f ‖ interj prostii!, aiurea!.

nonsensical adj absurd, aberant.

nonsmoker s nefumător m, persoană f care nu fumează.

nonstarter s coll afacere f fără sorți de reușită.

nonstop adj (flight) direct, fără escală; (activity) continuu; (rain) fără oprire ‖ adv (speak, work) fără oprire, neîncetat; (rain) neîncetat.

nonviolence s nonviolență f.

noodle s prost(ănac) m, tont m.

noodles s pl fidea f, tăiței m pl.

nook s cotlon n, loc n retras; **every** ~ **and cranny** s toate aspectele/fațetele.

noon s amiază f; fig apogeu n, culme f.

no-one pron * **nobody**.

noose *s* laț *n*, arcan *n*; ștreang *n*; nod *n*; *fig* laț *n*, capcană *f*.

nor *conj* nici; **neither you ~ I** nici tu nici eu.

Nordic *adj* nordic.

norm *s* normă *f*, etalon *n*, standard *n*.

normal *adj* normal; obișnuit; conform || *s* stare *f* normală; tip *n* normal • **~cy** *s* normalitate *f*.

north *s* nord *n* || *adj* nordic, de nord || *adv* spre nord; **North America** *s* America de Nord; **North American** *s*/*adj* nord-american *m* • **~east** *s* (*direction*) nord est *n*; (*region*) nord-estul *n*, regiunea *f* din nord-est/ nord-estică || *adj* de nord-est, nord-estic || *adv* spre/ către nord-est; la nord-est • **~ern** *adj* nordic, de nord; (*wind*) dinspre/de nord.

Norway *s* Norvegia *f*.

Norwegian *s*/*adj* norvegian(ă) *m*, *f*.

nose *s* *anat* nas *n*; *zool* bot *n*; cioc *n*; *fig* miros *n*; *naut* proră *f* tech camă *f* || *vt*/*vi* a mirosi; a adulmeca; a dibui • **~dive** *s* *avia* picaj *n* || *vi* *avia* a coborî în picaj; *fig* (*prices*) a se prăbuși; (*hopes*) a se nărui.

nostalgia *s* nostalgie *f*, dor *n*.

nostalgic *adj* nostalgic.

nostril *s* *anat* nară *f*.

nostrum *s* leac *n* empiric; *pol* panaceu *n*.

nosy *adj* curios, băgăcios.

not *adv* nu; nici; **~ at all** deloc, câtuși de puțin.

notable *adj* notabil; remarcabil || *s* personalitate *f*.

notably *adv* mai ales; deosebit de.

notarize *vt* a certifica, a atesta.

notary *s* notar *m*.

notation *s* notare *f*; *math* notație *f*; (*jotting*) notă *f*, însemnare *f*.

notch *s* crestătură *f*; tăietură *f*; *tech* canelură *f*; șanț *n*; *elec* ancoșă *f*; *geol* depresiune *f*; *geog* defileu *n*; trecătoare *f*; chei *n* || *vt* a cresta; a tăia; *tech* a dantela; a dința.

note *s* notă *f*; adnotare *f*; bancnotă *f*; semn *n*; sunet *n*; melodie *f*; reputație *f* || *vt* a fi atent la; a observa; a nota; a adnota; a denota • **~book** *s* carnet *n*; agendă *f*.

nothing *pron* nimic || *s* lucru *n* mărunt, nimic *n*, fleac *n*; zero *n*; neființă *f* || *adv* deloc, defel, câtuși de puțin.

notice *s* aviz *n*; anunț *n*; știre *f*; recenzie *f* || *vt* a observa; a recenza; a se referi • **~able** *adj* vizibil, perceptibil; observabil; remarcabil, demn de atenție.

notification *s* notificare *f*, înștiințare *f*.

notify *vt* (*make known*) a notifica, a duce la cunoștință (ceva); (*inform*) a anunța, a informa (pe cineva).

notion *s* noțiune *f*, idee *f*; concept *n*; intenție *f*; capriciu *n*.

notoriety *s* notorietate *f*.

notorious *adj* (*criminal, etc*) notoriu, faimos; (*place*) rău famat.

notwithstanding *conj* deși, cu toate că || *adv* totuși, cu toate acestea || *prep* în ciuda, fără a ține seama de.

nougat *s* nuga *f*.

nought *pron* nimic || *s* nimic *n*, zero *f*; *math* zero *f*, nulă *f*.

noun *s* *gram* substantiv *n*.

nourish *vt* a nutri; a hrăni, a alimenta.

novel[1] *s* roman *n*.

novel[2] *adj* nou, inedit; neobișnuit; straniu || *s* roman *n*.

novelty *s* noutate *f*; inovație *f*; ciudățenie *f*.

November *s* noiembrie *m*.

novice *s* novice *m*, neofit *m*; începător *m*.

noxious *adj* nociv.

now *adv* acum; în prezent; imediat || *conj* acum când; acum că; cum, de vreme ce • **~adays** *adv* în zilele noastre; în ziua de azi, actualmente.

nowhere *adv* nicăieri.

noxious *adj* (*gas*) nociv, vătămător; (*influence*) nefast.

nozzle *s* (*of a teapot, etc*) cioc *n*; *tech* ajutaj *n*; duză *f*; știuț *n*; jiclor *n*; orificiu *n*.

nuance *s* nuanță *f*.

nub *s* (*crux*) esență *f*, miez *n*; (*piece*) bucată *f*.

nubile *adj* sexy.

nuclear *adj* nuclear; **~ bomb** *s* bombă *f* atomica; **~ energy** *s* energie *f* nucleară; **~ fission** *s* fisiune *f* nucleară; **~ fusion** *s* fuziune *f* nucleară; **~ power** *s* energie *f* nucleară; **~ reactor** *s* reactor *n* nuclear.

nucleus *s* (*pl* **nuclei**) nucleu *n* (atomic); *math* nucleu *n*; centru *n*; *fig* nucleu *n*, germene *m*.

nude *adj* gol, nud; clar, evident || *s* nud *n*; goliciune *f*.

nudist *s*, *adj* nudist *m*.

nudge *vt* a înghionti, a atinge cu cotul; a da un ghiont/ cot (cuiva) || *s* ghiont *n*.

nudism *s* nudism *n*.

nudist *s* nudist *m*.

nudity *s* nuditate *f*; trup *n* gol.

nugatory *adj* *coll* zadarnic, inutil; fără valoare; ineficace, fără efect.

nugget *s* *miner* pepită *f*.

nuisance *s* (*annoyance*) neplăcere *f*, (*bother*) bătaie *f* de cap; (*irritant*) pacoste *f*, om *m* cicălitor.

nuke *s* *coll* bombă *f* nucleară || *vt* a detona.

null *adj* *jur* nul; nevalabil; *math* nul, zero; vid; fără valoare/conținut; inexistent; inexpresiv; **~ and void** *adj* nul și neavenit.

numb *adj* amorțit; indiferent || *vt* a amorți.

number *s* număr *n*; numeral *n*; *pl* aritmetică *f*; serie *f*; exemplar *n* || *vt* a număra; a numerota; a însuma; **~ one** *adj* prim, principal || *s* *coll* subsemnatul *m*.

numeracy *s* cunoaștere *f* a matematicii.

numeral *s* *gram* numeral *n*; număr *n*; cifră *f* || *adj* numeric; cifric.

numerate *vt* a număra, a calcula; a enumera; a exprima prin cifre.

numerator *s* *math* numărător *m*.

numerical *adj* numeric; cifric.

numerous *adj* numeros; numeroși, mulți.

numismatic *adj* numismatic.

numismatist *s* numismat *m*.

numskull *s* *coll* nătâng *m*.

nun *s* *relig* călugăriță *f*.

nuptial *adj* nupțial • **~s** *s* *pl* nuntă *f*.

nurse *s* doică *f*; soră *f*, infirmieră *f*; îngrijire *f* || *vt* (~ *a baby*) a alăpta; a crește (un copil); (~ *a patient, cold*) a îngriji; a trata; *fig* (~ *hopes*) a nutri.

nursery *s* (*school*) creșă *f*; *bot* pepinieră *f* • **~ rhyme** poezie *f* pentru copii;

nursing home *s* azil *n* privat de pensionari/bătrâni; sanatoriu *n* particular.

nurture *vt* (~ *children*) a crește; a educa; (~ *plants*) a îngriji; *fig* (~ *hopes, etc*) a nutri || *s* creștere *f*; educare *f*; *bot* creștere *f*, cultivare *f*.

nut *s* nucă *f*; alună *f*; *tech* piuliță *f*; mufă *f*; cap *n*; aiurit *m* || *vi* a culege nuci • **~cracker** *s* spărgător *m* de nuci • **~shell** *s* coajă *f* de nucă; **in a ~** în rezumat; pe scurt.

nutmeg *s* *cul* nucșoară *f*.

nutrient *adj* nutritiv, hrănitor || *s* hrană *f*; nutreț *n*.

nutrition *s* alimentare *f*; hrănire *f*; nutriție *f*; hrană *f* •
~**ist** *s* dietetician *m*.
nutritious *adj* nutritiv, hrănitor.
nuzzle *vi* (*dog*) a-şi freca botul; (*pig*) a râma ‖ *vi* (*nestle*)
a se ghemui, a se strânge, a se face ghem.
nylon *s* nylon *n*.
nymph *s* *also fig* nimfă *f*.
nymphomaniac *s* nimfomană *f*.

O

O, o *s* (litera) O, o; zero *n*; **O!** *interj* ah!, a!, vai!, o(h)!;
hei!, alo ‖ *s* zero *n*.
oaf *s* (*fool*) prostănac *m*; (*boor*) mocofan *m*.
oak *s* *bot* stejar *m*; (lemn de) stejar *m*.
oar *s* vâslă *f*, lopată *f*, ramă *f*; vâslaş *m* ‖ *vt* a vâsli.
oasis *s* oază *f*.
oats *s* *pl bot* ovăz *n*.
oath *s* (*promise*) jurământ *n*; (*swear*) înjurătură *f*.
obdurate *adj* (*heartless*) insensibil, aspru; (*obstinate*)
încăpăţânat, căpăţânos.
obedient *adj* supus; docil; ascultător.
obeisance *s* *lit* (*homage*) omagiu *n*; (*bow*) prosternare *f*.
obelisk *s* obelisc *n*.
obese *adj* obez.
obey *vt* a asculta (de); a se supune; a executa ‖ *vi* a fi
supus; a se supune.
obfuscate *vt fml* (*issue*) a înceţoşa, a întuneca; (*person*)
a deruta, a zăpăci.
obituary *s* necrolog *n*.
object *s* (*thing*) obiect *n*, lucru *n*; (*study*) preocupare *f*;
(*goal*) obiectiv *n*; scop *n*; *gram*, *phil* obiect *n*;
obstacol *n* ‖ *vi* a obiecta, a protesta (împotriva).
objection *s* obiecţie *f*; reclamaţie *f*.
objective *adj* obiectiv; concret; impersonal; imparţial ‖
s obiectiv *n*; scop *n*.
obligation *s* obligaţie *f*; datorie *f*.
obligatory *adj* obligatoriu.
oblige *vt* a obliga; a îndatora ‖ *vi* a fi obligatoriu; a fi de
dorit.
obliging *adj* amabil, îndatoritor.
oblique *adj* oblic, înclinat; (*reference*) indirect ‖ *s typ*
bară *f* oblică; *geom* (*linie*) oblică *f*.
obliterate *vt* a şterge; a rade; *fig* a distruge, a şterge
orice urmă de.
oblivion *s* uitare *f*.
oblivious *adj* (of) care uită/a uitat; (to) orb la, care
nu-şi dă seama de.
oblong *adj* dreptunghiular ‖ *s* dreptunghi *n*.
obloquy *s fml* (*abuse*) defăimare *f*; (*disgrace*) oprobriu
n.
obnoxious *adj* (*person*) insuportabil, respingător, odios;
(*smell*) infect; (*comment*) nepoliticos, răuvoitor.
oboe *s mus* oboi *n*.
obscene *adj* obscen; respingător • ~**ly** *adv* în mod
obscen/dezgustător.
obscenity *s* obscenitate *f*; vorbă *f* sau faptă *f* obscenă.
obscure *adj* obscur; enigmatic; complicat ‖ *vt* a
întuneca; a complica.
obscurity *s* obscuritate *f*; confuzie *f*; anonimat *n*; uitare
f; întunecime *f*.
obsequies *s pl fml* ceremonii *f pl* funerare.
obsequious *adj fml* slugarnic.
observable *adj* vizibil, vădit.

observance *s* (*obedience*) respectare *f*; (*rite*) ceremonie
f, ritual *n*.
observant *adj* atent.
observation *s* observare *f*; examinare *f*; scrutare *f*;
observaţie *f*, constatare *f*; remarcă *f*; supraveghere *f*;
control *n*.
observatory *s* observator *n* astronomic.
observe *vt* a observa; a scruta; a constata; a păstra; a
respecta ‖ *vi* a observa • ~**r** *s* observator *m*.
obsess *vt* a obseda • ~**ive** *adj* (*person*) obsesiv; (*need*,
etc) obsedant; chinuitor.
obsolescent *adj* (*system*, *etc*) care se învecheşte, pe
punctul de a ieşi din uz.
obsolete *adj* învechit, demodat; *bio* atrofiat; purtat, ros,
uzat.
obstacle *s* obstacol *n*, piedică *f*.
obstetrics *s pl med* obstetrică *f*.
obstinate *adj* (*person*) încăpăţânat; (*illness*) persistent.
obstreperous *adj frml*, *hum* (*noisy*) zgomotos; (*disorderly*) turbulent; (*defiant*) rebel.
obstruct *vt* (~ *a road*, *etc*) a împiedica, a bloca; (~ *a
passage*) a astupa, a înfunda; *fig* a îngreuna, a face
dificil • ~**ion** *s* împiedicare *f*, blocare *f*; astupare *f*;
sp, *etc* obstrucţie *f*; *med* constipaţie *f*; piedică *f*,
barieră *f*, obstacol *n*.
obtain *vt* a obţine; a câştiga; a procura; a realiza ‖ *vi* a
exista; a folosi.
obtrusive *adj* (*behavior*) inoportun, supărător; (*person*)
obraznic, impertinent; (*smell*) puternic.
obtuse *adj* obtuz; *fig* mărginit.
obverse *s* (*coin*) avers *n*, faţa *f* unei monede.
obvious *adj* evident, clar, vădit.
occasion *s* ocazie *f*; prilej *n*; motiv *n*; pretext *n* ‖ *vi* a
cauza; a prilejui • ~**al** *adj* (*rain*) pasager, trecător;
(*visit*, *etc*) ocazional; accidental.
occult *adj* ocult.
occupant *s* ocupant *m*; (*tenant*) locatar *m*; (*of vehicle*)
pasager *m*.
occupation *s* ocupaţie *f*; (*job*) profesie *f* • ~**al** *adj*
profesional.
occupier *s* (*tenant*) locatar *m*; ocupant *m*.
occupy *vt* a ocupa, a lua în posesiune; (~ *a house*) a
închiria; (~ *space*, *time*) a ocupa; (~ *time*) a folosi;
(*have a position*) a ocupa.
occur *vi* (*happen*) a se petrece, a avea loc; (*problem*) a
apărea; (*word*, *etc*) a se întâlni, a exista, a fi prezent;
~ **to smb** *vi* a veni în mintea cuiva.
ocean *s* ocean *n*.
ocher *adj* (*color*) ocru.
o'clock *adv* (*time*) ora…; **two** ~ ora două; (*position*)
enemy fighter at 9 ~ avion inamic la stânga.
octagon *s geom* octagon *n*.
octane *s chem* octan *m*.
octave *s mus*, *phys* octavă *f*.
October *s* (luna) octombrie *m*, brumărel.
octopus *s icht* caracatiţă *f*; *fig* caracatiţă *f*; păianjen *m*.
ocular *adj* ocular.
oculist *s med* oculist *m*.
odd *adj* impar, fără soţ; (*irregular*) neregulat; adiţional;
(*volume*, *etc*) desperecheat, răzleţ; (~ *jobs*) de ocazie;
(*moment*, *etc*) liber, neocupat, de răgaz; (*strange*)
straniu, ciudat, curios; excentric • ~**ball** *s coll*
excentric *m*.
odds *s pl* şanse *f pl*, sorţi *m pl* de izbândă; avantaj *n*;

diferență *f*, decalaj *n*; **be at ~ with smb** *vi* a fi în dezacord cu cineva.

ode *s liter* odă *f*.

odious *adj* odios, respingător, detestabil.

odor *s* miros *n*; iz *n*; parfum *n*; *fig* reputație *f*, (re)nume *n*.

odyssey *s* odisee *f*.

of *prep* lui; al, a, ai, ale; de; cu; din cauza; din, de la; în; din partea.

off *adv* departe; încolo; în culise || *prep* de pe; din; de; în largul || *adj* liber; depărtat; (*food*) alterat, stricat; (*milk*) stricat; (*light, etc*) stins; (*engine*) oprit; (*canceled*) anulat; (*absent*) absent || *interj* afară!, pleacă!; **~ chance** *s* șansă *f* minimă.

offal *s* rămășite *f pl* de carne; măruntaie *n pl*; stârv *n*.

off-beat *adj coll* aparte, neobișnuit; extravagant.

off-color *adj* (*unusual*) de o culoare neobișnuită; (*offensive*) nepotrivit, de prost gust; defect, stricat; (*person*) indispus.

offend *vt* a jigni; a răni; a supăra || *vi* a ofensa.

offense *s* (*insult*) ofensă *f*, insultă *f*; (*crime*) delict *n*, crimă *f*; (*hurt*) jignire *f*; *sp*, *mil* atac *n*; ofensivă *f*.

offensive *adj* (*action, weapons*) ofensiv; (*behavior, etc*) jignitor; neplăcut; agresiv || *s* ofensivă *f*.

offer *vt* a oferi; a da; a acorda; (~ *hope*) a da; (*present*) a prezenta; (~ *a service*) a propune || *vr*/*vi* a se ivi || *s* (*price, etc*) ofertă *f*; (*special*) ocazie *f*, ofertă *f* (promoțională); propunere *f* • **~ing** *s* (*peace, etc*) propunere *f*, ofertă *f*; *relig* jertfă *f*, ofrandă *f*.

off-hand *adj* improvizat, nepregătit; nonșalant || *adv* improvizat, fără pregătire; fără ceremonie.

office *s* (*room, staff*) birou *n*; oficiu *n*; cabinet *n*; departament *n*, serviciu *n*; minister *n*; (*position*) post *n*; funcție *f*; datorie *f*; **in ~** în funcție; **take ~** *vt* a intra în funcție.

officer *s mil* ofițer *m*; (*official*) agent *m*, funcționar *m*; membru *m* al unui comitet; (*police ~*) polițist *m*.

official *adj* oficial; formal || *s* funcționar *m* • **~dom** *s* birocrație *f*.

officious *adj* insinuant; servil; oficios, neoficial.

offing *s naut* largul *n* mării; **in the ~** *naut* în larg; *fig* în perspectivă, iminent.

off-line *adj comp* deconectat.

off-peak *adj* (*power*) la ore nesolicitate; (*charge*) redus la ore nesolicitate.

off-putting *adj coll* dezagreabil, respingător.

off-season *s* sezonul *n* mort.

offset *vt* (*loss*) a compensa; a echilibra; *typ* a imprima ofset || *s* compensație *f*; plată *f*; *econ* decontare *f*; *typ* ofset *n*; *constr* terasare *f*; *min* nișă *f* în galerie.

offshoot *s bot* mlădiță *f*, vlăstar *n*; *geog* ramură *f* (muntoasă); *tech* braț *n*, parte *f* alungită; *fig* vlăstar *n*, mlădiță *f*.

offshore *adj naut* depărtat de țărm/coastă; din larg; (*oilrig*) în larg; (*island*) aproape de coastă; (*fishing*) de coastă || *adv* în larg.

offside *adj*/*adv* (*traffic*) (pe) dreapta; (pe) stânga; *sp* în afara jocului || *s* partea *f* dreaptă; partea *f* stângă.

offspring *s* urmaș *m*, vlăstar *n*, odraslă *f*; progenitură *f*; produs *n*, rezultat *n*.

offstage *s thea* spatele *n* scenei; culise *f pl* || *adj* din culise || *adv* în/spre culise.

off-the-cuff *adv*/*adj* improvizat.

off-the-record *adj* oficios || *adv* în mod confidențial.

off-white *adj* alburiu.

often *adv* frecvent; adesea.

ogle *vt* a privi galeș; a face ochi dulci cuiva.

ogre *s also fig* căpcăun *m*.

oh *interj* (*pain, surprise, fear, etc*) ah!, a!, vai!, o(h)!.

oil *s* ulei *n*; petrol *n* || *vt* a unge; a lubrifia; a gresa; **~ can** *s tech* gresor *n*; **~ field** *s* zăcământ *n* de petrol; **~ filter** *s* filtru *n* de ulei; **~ painting** *s* pictură *f* în ulei; **~ pump** *s* pompă *f* de ulei; **~ refinery** *s* rafinărie *f* de petrol; **~ rig** *s* (*offshore*) platformă *f* de foraj, (*well*) schelă *f* de foraj; **~skin** *s* haină *f* impermeabilă; **~ slick** *s* maree *f* neagră; **~ tanker** *s naut* petrolier *n*; camion-cisternă *n*; **~ well** *s* puț *n* de petrol • **~y** *adj* uleios, unsuros; (*food*) gras; *fig* onctuos, mieros, insinuant.

ointment *s* unguent *n*, alifie *f*; pomadă *f*.

OK, okay *interj* foarte bine!, perfect!, în regulă!, de acord!, s-a făcut! || *adj* în regulă/ordine; foarte bine, perfect || *vt* a aproba; a fi de acord cu.

okra *s bot* bamă *f*.

old *adj* bătrân; vechi; antic; priceput || *adv* de altădată, de demult.

old-fashioned *adj* demodat; învechit.

oleander *s bot* leandru *m*.

olfactory *adj* olfactiv.

oligarchy *s* oligarhie *f*.

olive *s* (*fruit*) măslină *f*; (*tree*) măslin *m*.

Olympiad *s* olimpiadă *f*.

olympic *adj* olimpic • **the ~s** *s pl* Jocurile *n pl* Olimpice.

omelet *s cul* omletă *f*.

omen *s* semn *n*, augur *n*, prevestire *f* || *vt* a prevesti.

ominous *adj* (*event, etc*) de rău augur; (*sign*) prevestitor de rău, neliniștitor; (*silence, etc*) amenințător.

omission *s* (*exclusion*) omitere *f*; (*oversight*) uitare *f*, omisiune *f*; lipsă *f*.

omit *vt* a omite; a neglija.

omnibus *s obs* (*bus*) omnibuz *n*; **~ bill** proiect *n* de lege ce înglobează măsuri diverse.

omnipotent *adj* atotputernic, omnipotent.

omniscient *adj* atotștiutor.

omnivore *s* omnivor *m*.

omnivorous *adj* omnivor; (*keen*) pasionat.

on *prep* pe; la; în; spre; cu; despre; cu privire la; din; asupra; pentru; de la; după; **~ and off** *adv* din când în când.

once *adv* o dată; altă dată; niciodată || *conj* odată (ce); dacă; **~ in a while** uneori, când și când; **~ or twice** de câteva ori; **not ~** nici o singură dată, niciodată; **more than ~** nu o dată, de mai multe ori; **~ upon a time there was** a fost odată ca niciodată.

one *num* unu(l), una; un, o; prim, prima, întâi || *pron* unul, una (dintre); cel/cea; cei/cele; **~ and all** toți (fără excepție); **for ~ thing** printre alte motive; **I for ~** în ceea ce mă privește; **~-on-~** *adj* (*talk*) între patru ochi; **~ and the same** unul și același.

onerous *adj frml* (*arduous*) greu, anevoios.

oneself *pron ref* se || *pron emph* însuși, însăși.

one-sided *adj geom* unilateral, având o singură latură; *fig* unilateral; limitat; părtinitor; (*tilted*) aplecat într-o parte.

onion *s bot* ceapă *f*.

online *adj*/*adv comp* conectat, în linie/rețea.

only *adj* unic || *adv* doar, numai || *conj* numai că; dacă nu.

onomatopoeia *s liter* onomatopee *f*.

onslaught *s* (*on*) atac *n* violent (asupra, împotriva).

onus *s* responsabilitate *f*, sarcină *f*, obligație *f*.

onyx *s miner* onix *n*.

ooze *vi* a se prelinge; a se scurge/curge foarte încet || *vt* (*perspiration*) a elimina || *s* mâl *n*, nămol *n*; noroi *n*; aluviune *f*; *geol* infiltrație *f*; curgere/scurgere *f* foarte lentă.

opacity *s* (*murkiness*) opacitate *f*; (*of text*) obscuritate *f*; (*of person*) obtuzitate *f*, mărginire *f*.

opal *s miner* opal *n*.

opaque *adj* opac; întunecat; mat; *fig* opac, obtuz, mărginit; *fig* neclar, abscons, obscur.

open *adj* deschis; (*responsive*) receptiv; (*space, etc*) liber, degajat; (*car*) descoperit, decapotabil; (*meeting*) deschis tuturor; (*honesty, etc*) evident, manifest; (*unsolved*) nerezolvat; neacoperit; (*letter, etc*) desfăcut; (*position*) vacant; (*manner*) sincer; (*quarrel*) fățiș, pe față; *tech* declanșat || *vt* a deschide; a inaugura; a descuia; a desface || *vi* a se deschide; a se desface; ~ **up** *vt* (*develop*) a exploata || *vi* (*possibilities*) a se oferi, a se prezenta; (*doors*) a deschide; ~ **market** *s* piață *f* liberă • **~er** *s* tirbușon *n*; deschizător *n* de conserve; • **~minded** *adj* deschis la minte • **~ness** *s* franchețe *f* • **~ing** *s* deschidere *f*; (*in a fence, etc*) gaură *f*; (*in the clouds*) deschizătură *f*, spărtură *f*; început *n*; (*opportunity*) ocazie *f*, șansă *f*; (*thinly wooded area in forest*) luminiș *n*; *thea* premieră *f*; (*vacancy*) post *n* liber/vacant.

opera *s mus* operă *f*.

operate *vt* a manipula; a acționa; a conduce || *vi* a opera; a funcționa; a lucra; a acționa; a avea efect.

operating room *s med* sală *f* de operații.

operation *s* (*action*) operație *f*, acțiune *f*; muncă *f*, lucru *n*; acționare *f*; *med* operație *f*; *econ* producție *f*; *mil*, *math* operați(un)e *f*; *fig* forță *f*, putere *f*; influență *f* • **~al** *adj* în funcțiune, operațional.

operative *adj* operativ; activ; expeditiv, eficace; *med* operator, chirurgical || *s* muncitor *m* calificat.

operator *s* operator *m*; mecanic *m*; mașinist *m*; șofer *m*; telefonist *m*; manipulant *m*; conductor *m*; *med* operator *m*, chirurg *m*; *econ* director *m*.

ophthalmic *adj med* ocular.

ophthalmologist *s* oftalmolog *m*.

ophthalmology *s* oftalmologie *f*.

opinion *s* părere *f*; opinie *f*; concluzie *f*; ~ **poll** *s* sondaj *n* de opinie.

opium *s* opiu *n*.

opponent *s* adversar *m*.

opportune *adj* oportun, adecvat.

opportunist *s* oportunist *m*.

opportunity *s* prilej *n* favorabil, ocazie *f* favorabilă; moment *n* potrivit.

oppose *vt* a opune, a contrasta (cu); a fi împotriva/ contra || *vi* a se opune, a opune rezistență.

opposing *adj* opus, advers.

opposite *adj* opus; invers || *s* opoziție *f* || *adv* vizavi || *prep* vizavi de.

opposition *s* opoziție *f*.

oppress *vt* a apăsa; a asupri; a prigoni.

opt *vi* a opta (pentru).

optical *adj* optic, ocular; vizual.

optimism *s* optimism *n*.

optimist *s* optimist *m* • **~ic** *adj* optimist.

optimize *vt* a optimiza.

optimum *s* cele mai favorabile condiții *f pl*; *econ* valoare *f* maximă || *adj* optim, cel mai bun; cel mai favorabil.

option *s* opțiune *f*; selecție *f*; alegere *f*; drept *n* • **~al** *adj* facultativ.

opulent *adj* bogat; abundant; (*vegetation*) luxuriant.

or *conj* sau, ori; altfel, altminteri; dacă nu.

oracle *s myth* oracol *n*; *fig* prezicere *f*; profeție *f*; *fig* prezicător *m*; profet *m*.

oral *adj* (*speech*) oral, verbal; *med* bucal || *s scol* (*examen*) oral *n*, probă *f* orală.

orange *s bot* portocal *m*; (*fruit*) portocală *f*; (*color*) portocaliu *n*.

orangutan *s zool* urangutan *m*.

orator *s* orator *m*.

orbit *s* orbită *f*, traiectorie *f*; *anat* orbită *f*; *fig* domeniu *n* de activitate, sferă *f* de activitate; *math* suprafață *f* de tranzitivitate || *vi astron* a se mișca/deplasa pe orbită.

orchard *s* livadă *f*.

orchestra *s* orchestră *f*; parter *n*; fotoliu *n*; stal *n*.

ordain *vt* a hirotonisi; a hărăzi.

ordeal *s* încercare *f* grea; *fig* chin *n*.

order *s* (*succession*) ordine *f*, serie *f*; succesiune *f*; secvență *f*; liniște *f*; rânduială *f*; *econ* comandă *f*; decizie *f*; ordin *n*; fel *n*; poziție *f* || *vt* (*command*) a ordona; *econ* a comanda; (*arrange*) a rândui; a prescrie || *vi* a comanda; **on the ~ of** *prep* aproximativ, de ordinul a; **in ~ that** *conj* ca să, cu scopul să; **in ~ to** *conj* pentru ca să • **~ly** *adj* (*person*) ordonat; (*crowd*) disciplinat; (*room, etc*) în ordine.

ordinal *adj* ordinal || *s* numeral *n* ordinal.

ordinance *s* ordonanță *f*, dispoziție *f*.

ordinarily *adv* în mod normal; de obicei.

ordinary *adj* obișnuit; uzual; cotidian; comun; normal; ordinar.

ordination *s* hirotonisire *f*; ordonare *f*, aranjare *f*.

ordnance *s* artilerie *f*; muniție *f*.

ore *s* minereu *n*.

oregano *s cul* oregano *n*.

organ *s anat* organ *n*; voce *f*; *mus* orgă *f*; ziar *n*.

organic *adj* (*animal, plant*) organic; (*food*) biologic; *chem* organic.

organism *s* organism *n*.

organization *s* organizare *f*; organizație *f*.

organize *vt* a organiza, a forma; a institui; a aranja || *vr* a se organiza • **~r** *s* organizator *m*.

orgasm *s physiol* orgasm *n*.

orgy *s* orgie *f*, desfrâu *n*, dezmăț *n*; *fig* exces *n*.

oriental *adj* oriental.

orientate *vt* a orienta spre est; *fig* a orienta || *vi* a se orienta; *fig* a se orienta.

orifice *s* orificiu *n*, gaură *f*; gură *f*; deschizătură *f*, deschidere *f*;

origin *s* (*birth, etc*) origine *f*; neam *n*; (*of a river*) izvor *n*; obârșie *f*; **country of ~** țară *f* de origine • **~al** *adj* prim, inițial; original; originar; nou; creator; înnăscut || *s* original *n*; excentric *m* • **~ate** *vt* a crea; a făuri; a inventa || *vi* a apărea inițial; (**from**) a proveni (din).

ornament *s* ornament *n* || *vt* a ornamenta.

ornate *adj* bogat împodobit/ornamentat; (*style*) căutat, înflorit; prețios.

ornery *adj* (*nasty*) răutăcios; (*stubborn*) încăpățânat, căpățânos.

ornithologist *s* ornitolog *m*.

ornithology *s* ornitologie *f*.

orphan *s/adj* orfan *m* || *vt* a lăsa orfan.

orthodox *adj relig* ortodox, drept-credincios; *fig* ortodox, corect, tradiţional.

orthopedic *adj* ortopedic.

oscillate *vi* a oscila, a pendula; a vibra; a se legăna; *fig* a oscila, a ezita, a şovăi.

oscillation *s* oscilaţie *f*, legănare *f*; vibraţie *f*; fluctuare *f*; fluctuaţie *f*; *fig* oscilare *f*.

osier *s bot* răchită *f*.

Oslo *s* Oslo *n*.

osmosis *s* osmoză *f*.

ossified *adj* osificat; *fig* rigid.

ossify *vt* a osifica.

ostensible *adj* aparent; (*pretended*) servind ca pretext, de suprafaţă; de ochii lumii.

ostentation *s* ostentaţie *f*.

ostentatious *adj* ostentativ, de paradă.

osteopath *s med* osteopat *m*.

osteoporosis *s med* osteoporoză *f*.

ostracize *vt* a ostraciza, a proscrie.

ostrich *s orn* struţ *m*.

other *adj* alţi; alte; alt; altă; celălalt, cealaltă; ceilalţi, celelalte || *pron* altul, alta; alţii, altele || *adv* altfel • **~wise** *adv* altfel || *conj* sau, dacă nu, altminteri; altfel || *adj* altfel, diferit, altul.

Ottawa *s* Ottawa *n*.

otter *s zool* vidră *f*; (*fur*) blană *f* de vidră.

ought *v mod* a trebui; a se cuveni; a fi probabil.

ounce *s* uncie *f* (28 gr); *coll* strop *m*, urmă *f*.

our *adj* nostru, noastră; noştri, noastre; **~ son** fiul nostru • **~s** *pron* al nostru; a noastră; ai noştri; ale noastre • **~selves** *pron ref* ne || *pron emph* înşine || *pron pers* noi.

oust *vt* a elimina, a exclude; *jur* a evacua.

out *adv* (*not in*) afară; în exterior; (*away*) departe; (*elsewhere*) în altă parte; absent; (*light, etc*) stins; (*tide*) jos; (*bloom*) în floare; (*fashion*) demodat || *adj* excesiv; neobişnuit; depărtat; *tech* deplasat; deconectat; *sp* în deplasare; exterior || *interj* (ieşi) afară!.

outback *s* regiuni *f pl* periferice/mai depărtate; **the ~** interiorul ţării (în Australia).

outbid *vt* a supralicita.

outboard *adj naut* exterior, în afara bordului.

outbreak s (*of war, etc*) izbucnire *f*, declanşare *f*; *med* erupţie *f*.

outbuilding *s constr* dependinţă *f*, acaret *n*.

outburst *s* izbucnire *f*, (*fury*) acces n; *fig* explozie *f*.

outcast *s* proscris *m*, paria *m*.

outclass *vt* a întrece, a depăşi.

outcome *s* urmare *f*, efect *n*, rezultat *n*.

outcry *s* strigăt *n*; ţipăt *n*; exclamaţie *f*; (*public ~*) protest n zgomotos.

outdated *adj* perimat.

outdo, outdid, outdone *vt* a depăşi, a întrece || *vr* a se întrece pe sine.

outdoors *adv* afară, în aer liber.

outer *adj* extern, exterior; periferic; *phil* obiectiv; fizic.

outfit s (*clothes*) costum *n*; echipament *n*; instalaţie *f*; dispozitiv *n*; utilaj *n* || *vt* a echipa; a utila.

outgoing *adj* (*friendly*) deschis, sociabil; (*~ president, etc*) demisionar; (*~ mail*) de expediat; (*~ train*) care pleacă; (*~ traffic*) de ieşire.

outgrow *vt* a deveni prea mare pentru; (*~ childhood*) a ieşi din (vârsta copilăriei), a depăşi (vârsta copilăriei); *fig* (*~ a habit, etc*) a se lepăda de.

outhouse *s* dependinţă *f*; aripă *f* de clădire; latrină *f*.

outing *s* excursie *f*; ieşire *f* (la iarbă verde); picnic *n*; călătorie *f* de plăcere.

outlandish *adj* străin, din altă ţară; ciudat, neobişnuit, straniu; bizar; fantastic; (în)depărtat.

outlast *vt* a rezista mai mult decât.

outlaw *s* proscris *m*; exilat *m*; haiduc *m*; criminal *m* || *vt* a proscrie; a exila.

outlay *s econ* cheltuieli *f pl*.

outlet *s econ* debuşeu *n*; debit *n*; livrare *f*; piaţă *f* de desfacere; *tech* evacuare *f*; *elec* bornă *f* de ieşire, priză *f*; *fig* supapă *f* de siguranţă; uşurare *f*.

outline *s* schiţă *f*, contur *n*; plan *n*; conspect *n* || *vt* a schiţa; a prezenta sumar.

outlive *vt* (*person*) a supravieţui cuiva.

outlook *s* perspectivă *f*; concepţie *f*; prognoză *f*.

outlying *adj* (*village*) îndepărtat, izolat; (*suburb*) periferic.

outnumber *vt* a depăşi/întrece ca număr.

out-of-date *adj* (*passport*) expirat; (*clothes*) demodat; (*ideas*) depăşit, învechit.

outpace *vt* a depăşi.

outpatient *s med* pacient *m* extern/cu tratament ambulatoriu.

outplacement *s* plasare *f* a unui angajat concediat.

outpouring *s also fig* revărsare *f*.

outpost *s* avanpost *n*.

output *s* producţie *f*; *comp* ieşire *f*.

outrage s (*feeling*) indignare *f*; (*act*) crimă *f*, atrocitate *f* || *vt* a ultragia, a jigni grav • **~ous** *adj* atroce; imoral; ruşinos; (*~ prices*) de speculă, excesiv; (*heat, etc*) insuportabil, cumplit.

outright *adv* cu totul/desăvârşire, total; făţiş, direct; deodată; imediat; pe loc; pentru totdeauna || *adj* deschis, făţiş; sincer; (*refusal, etc*) categoric; hotărât; indiscutabil; complet, desăvârşit; (*road, etc*) direct, drept.

outset *s* pornire *f*, plecare *f*; început *n*; **from the ~** de la început.

outside *s* exterior *n*; imperială *f* || *adj* extern; extrem; periferic || *adv* afară; în exterior; în larg || *prep* afară din; în afară; dincolo de • **~r** *s* străin *m* (în afara unui cerc etc); *fig* spectator *m*, privitor *m*; nepoftit, nechemat; nespecialist *m*, amator *m*; profan *m*; *sp* competitor *m* fără şanse.

outsize(d) *adj* (*above normal*) enorm, uriaş; (*~ clothes*) măsură *f* foarte mare, număr *n* foarte mare.

outskirts *s pl* periferie *f*.

outspoken *adj* sincer, deschis, făţiş.

outstanding *adj* (*excellent*) remarcabil, excepţional; (*~ example*) marcant, semnificativ; important; (*unsolved*) în suspensie; neefectuat; (*pending*) pendinte; (*~ debt*) neachitat.

outstay *vt* a sta mai mult decât; **~ one's welcome** *vt* a abuza de ospitalitatea cuiva.

outstrip *vt* a întrece, a depăşi; a devansa (pe cineva).

outward *adj* exterior, extern, din afară; vizibil, material; (*~ journey, etc*) în străinătate, peste hotare || **~s** *adv* spre exterior, în afară; peste hotare; la vedere; la suprafaţă; pe din afară.

outweigh *vt also fig* a întrece în importanţă, a cântări mai mult decât.

outwit *vt* a întrece în isteţime; a întrece în viclenie, a păcăli.

oval *adj/s* oval *n*.

ovary *s anat, bot* ovar *n.*

ovation *s* ovație *f.*

oven *s* cuptor *n;* furnal *n.*

over *prep* peste; (pe) deasupra; în cursul; mai mult de; prin; la; în timpul; pe când ‖ *adv* dincolo; acolo; sus; în plus; gata, terminat; exagerat, excesiv; din nou; **all** ~ *prep* peste tot, în toate ‖ *adv* peste tot, pretutindeni ‖ *adj* terminat; ~ **and above** în afară de; pe lângă.

overact *vt thea* a interpreta afectat/exagerat ‖ *vi* a juca afectat/exagerat.

overage *s* (*surplus*) surplus *n*, excedent *n.*

overall *adj* de ansamblu, general, total ‖ *s* salopetă *f*; halat *n* de lucru ‖ *adv* peste tot, pretutindeni; în întregime, complet.

overawe *vt* a timora, a complexa.

overbalance *vi* a se răsturna.

overbearing *adj* autoritar; arogant.

overboard *adv naut also fig* peste bord.

overblown *adj* exagerat.

overburdened *adj* supraîncărcat.

overcast *adj* (*sky*) acoperit cu nori, înnorat; *fig* mohorât, posomorât, sumbru ‖ *vi* (*sky*) a se înnoura, a se acoperi cu nori; *fig* a se posomorî, a se întuneca.

overcharge *s* suprapreț *n*; preț *n* exagerat/excesiv; *tech* suprasarcină *f* ‖ *vt* a cere suprapreț pentru; *tech* a supraîncărca, a suprasolicita.

overcoat *s* pardesiu *n.*

overcome, overcame, overcome *vt* (~ *difficulties, etc*) a depăși, a învinge; (~ *by feelings*) a copleși; (~ *by fatigue*) a doborî ‖ *vi* a învinge; a câștiga.

overcrowded *adj* supraîncărcat, supraaglomerat.

overdo, overdid, overdone *vt* (*exaggerate*) a exagera; (*overcook*) a arde, a prăji prea tare.

overdose *s* supradoză *f.*

overdraft *s tech* supraîncărcare *f*; supraexcitare *f*; *econ* neacoperire *f.*

overdraw *vt fin* (*check*) a elibera fără acoperire; *tech* a supraîncărca; a supraexcita; *fig* a exagera.

overdue *adj* întârziat; depășit ca termen; (*change is* ~, *etc*) așteptat (de mult).

overestimate *vt* a supraestima.

overexpose *vt phot* a supraexpune, a expune prea mult.

overflow *vt* a se revărsa peste; a inunda; a îneca ‖ *vi* a se revărsa; a deborda; a deversa; (*receptacle*) a fi prea plin ‖ *s* revărsare *f*; scurgere *f*; debit *n*; *tech* deversor *n*; *fig* revărsare *f*; prisos *n*; abundență *f.*

overgrown *adj* (~ *garden*) invadat de buruieni, (lăsat) în paragină.

overhang *vi* a atârna deasupra; *fig* a atârna deasupra, a amenința ‖ *s* ieșitură *f*, proeminență *f*; *tech* consolă *f*; *naut* avântare *f.*

overhaul *vt* a revizui, a examina; a repara; a reconstrui ‖ *s* (*car*) revizie *f*, *fig* (*system* ~) revizie *f*, verificare *f.*

overhead *adj* de sus, superior; aerian; (*price*) global ‖ *adv* sus, deasupra ‖ *s* cheltuieli *f pl* de regie.

overhear *vt* (*conversation, etc*) a auzi fără să vrea, a surprinde.

overheat *vt* a supraîncălzi ‖ *vi* (*engine*) a se încălzi.

overjoyed *adj* încântat la culme, fericit.

overland *adj* (*road, etc*) pe uscat ‖ *adv* pe uscat, pe cale terestră.

overlap *s* acoperire *f*, suprapunere *f*; întretăiere *f*, întrepătrundere *f*; coincidere *f* parțială ‖ *vt* a acoperi în parte; a acoperi, a suprapune; a întretăia; a coincide în parte cu.

overlay *vt* (*paint, etc*) a acoperi ‖ *s* (*paint*) acoperire *f*; (*metal*) strat *n*; față *f* de masă.

overleaf *adv* pe verso, pe pagina următoare.

overload *vt* a supraîncărca, a încărca excesiv ‖ *s* supraîncărcare *f.*

overlook *vt* a se ridica deasupra; a domina; a vedea de sus; (~ *an error*) a omite; (*ignore*) a nu ține seama de; (*examine*) a cerceta; (*watch*) a supraveghea.

overnight *adv* peste noapte, noaptea, în timpul nopții ‖ *adj* (~ *parking, etc*) de noapte; (~ *stay*) de o noapte; *fig* (*sudden*) imediat; ~ **success** succes imediat.

overpower *vt* a copleși; a învinge; a supune; *fig* (*sleep, etc*) a copleși; a doborî, a pune stăpânire pe • ~**ing** *adj* (~ *desire*) irezistibil; (~ *smell*) îmbătător.

overqualified *adj* supracalificat.

overrated *adj* exagerat, supraevaluat.

overreact *vi* (*exaggerate*) a reacționa exagerat; (*panic*) a fi cuprins de panică.

override *vt* a călări peste; a nu lua în seamă; *fig* a călca în picioare; a asupri, a oprima; (~ *a decision*) a anula.

overriding *adj* (~ *need, etc*) primordial.

overrule *vt* a stăpâni peste, a conduce; (~ *a proposal*) a respinge; (~ *a decision*) a anula; (~ *an order*) a nesocoti, a trece peste.

overrun *vt mil* a invada, a ocupa; a inunda; (*time*) a depăși; *fig* (*rats*) a invada; (*weeds*) a năpădi.

overseas *adj* (~ *company*) cu activitate în străinătate, de peste mări; (*visitor, etc*) străin; (~ *market*) extern; (~ *trade*) exterior ‖ *adv* peste mări; peste hotare; în străinătate.

oversee *vt* (*supervise*) a supraveghea, a controla • ~**r** *s* supraveghetor *m.*

oversell *vt* (*person, quality*) a exagera, a supraevalua ‖ *n* (*exaggeration*) laudă *f* exagerată.

overshadow *vt* a arunca umbră asupra/pe; (*building, etc*) a domina; *fig* a pune în umbră, a eclipsa.

overshoot *vt* (~ *a target*) a nu nimeri, a greși; (*exceed*) a depăși; a întrece măsura; (*deviate*) a se abate de la ‖ *vi* a greși ținta, a nu nimeri în țintă; *fig* a greși; a întrece măsura.

oversight *s* omisiune *f*; neglijență *f*; supraveghere *f* atentă.

oversleep, overslept, overslept *vt* a dormi prea mult, a nu se trezi la timp.

overspend *vi* a cheltui prea mult.

overspill *s* supraabundență *f*; revărsare *f*; surplus *n*, exces *n.*

overstay *vi* a rămâne mai mult decât; a depăși timpul; **to** ~ **one's welcome** a abuza de ospitalitatea cuiva.

overstep *vt* a păși peste; *fig* a depăși limitele.

overt *adj* deschis, fățiș; sincer; limpede, clar.

overtake, overtook, overtaken *vt* (~ *a car, etc*) a ajunge din urmă; a depăși; (*happen suddenly*) a surprinde; (*fear, etc* ~s) a cuprinde, a pune stăpânire pe.

over-the-counter *adj* vândut direct/fără intermediar; vândut în magazin.

overthrow *vt* a răsturna, a da jos; a trânti; *fig* (~ *a government, etc*) a răsturna.

overtime *s* ore *f pl* suplimentare; *sp* prelungiri *f pl* ‖ *adj* (~ *pay*) pentru ore suplimentare ‖ *adv* (*work* ~) a face ore suplimentare.

overtone *s mus* sunet *n* secundar; *pl fig* nuanțe *f pl*; subtext *n*; conotație *f*; implicații *f pl.*

overture *s mus* uvertură *f;* propunere *f* oficială; parte *f* introductivă.

overturn *vt (boat, etc)* a răsturna; *fig (plan)* a răsturna; a distruge, a ruina; *fig* a înfrânge, a învinge ‖ *vi (boat, etc)* a se răsturna.

overview *s (outline)* conspect *n,* schiță *f; (impression)* vedere/privire *f* generală.

overweening *adj* arogant; superior; înfumurat.

overweight *s* supragreutate *f,* exces *n* de greutate; preponderență *f* ‖ *adj* prea greu, prea gras; în surplus.

overwhelm *vt (grief, etc)* a copleşi; *mil* a nimici, a zdrobi • **~ing** *adj* copleşitor, imens; *(majority, etc)* zdrobitor.

overwork *s* muncă *f* excesivă; muncă *f* suplimentară, ore *f pl* suplimentare ‖ *vt* a extenua; a suprasolicita ‖ *vi* a se extenua; a munci exagerat.

overwrought *adj* extenuat, la capătul puterilor; surex-citat; *(~ nerves)* suprasolicitat; tocit; *(style)* încărcat de amănunte; elaborat.

ovulation *s physiol* ovulație *f.*

owe *vt* a datora; a fi obligat la; a fi îndatorat ‖ *vi* a fi dator.

owl *s orn* bufniță *f;* pasăre *f* de noapte; *fig* înțelept *m.*

own *adj* propriu; personal; scump; *(relative)* apropiat ‖ *vt* a poseda, a avea; a recunoaşte • **~er** *s* proprietar *m,* stăpân *m* • **~ership** *s* proprietate *f,* posesiune *f;* drept *n* de proprietate.

ox *s (pl* **oxen)** *zool* bou *m;* taur *m;* bivol *m;* bizon *m.*

oxygen *s* oxigen *n;* **~ mask** *s* mască *f* de oxigen.

oyster *s zool* stridie *f,* scoică *f.*

ozone *s chem* ozon *n;* **~ layer** *s* strat *n* de ozon • **~-friendly** *adj* care nu dăunează stratului de ozon.

P

P, p *s* (litera) P, p.

pa *s* tăticu *m,* papa *m.*

pace *s* pas *m;* mers *n;* treaptă *f;* viteză *f* ‖ *vt* a păşi; a ține pas cu ‖ *vi* a păşi; a merge; a umbla • **~maker** *s med* stimulator *n* cardiac, pacemaker *n; sp* persoană *f*/maşină *f*/animal *n* care imprimă ritmul.

Pacific *s* **the ~** Oceanul *n* Pacific, Pacificul *n* ‖ *adj* din Pacific.

pacifier *s* suzetă *f,* tetină *f.*

pacifist *s* pacifist *m.*

pacify *vt (country)* a pacifica, a restabili pacea în; *(~ a child, etc)* a linişti, a calma.

pack *s* legătură *f;* balot *n; mil* raniță *f; (cards, etc)* pachet *n;* ambalaj *n; fig* grup *n;* mănunchi *n; (thieves)* bandă *f; (wolves)* haită *f* ‖ *vt* a împacheta; a balota; a lega; a umple ‖ *vi* a împacheta.

package *s* împachetare *f;* balotare *f;* legare *f; (products, etc)* pachet *n;* cutie *f; fig (proposals, etc)* ansamblu *n,* serie *f; comp* program *n* informatic comercializat ‖ *vt* a ambala; **~ deal** *s* contract *n* global; **~ store** *s* magazine *n* în care băuturile se vând în recipiente închise.

packet *s* pachet *n;* balot *n* ‖ *vt* a împacheta.

pact *s* pact *n;* tratat *n.*

pad[1] *s* căptuşeală *f;* pernă *f; (cotton, etc)* tampon *n;* suport *n;* proptea *f; (paper)* bloc *n* de scris; *phys* rampă *f* de lansare; *(dogs, cats)* perniță *f* ‖ *vt (clothes)* a căptuşi; *(wound)* a tampona; *(furniture)* a capitona; *fig (speech)* a umple/lungi cu cuvinte goale etc.

pad[2] *vi* a merge pe jos; a merge tiptil.

paddle[1] *s* vâslă *f,* ramă *f;* padelă *f;* paletă *f;* lopată *f;* vâslit *n;* canotaj *n* ‖ *vt* a conduce cu vâslele.

paddle[2] *vi* a se bălăci; a merge legănat, a se bălăbăni.

paddock *s* padoc *n,* spațiu *n* îngrădit pentru caii de curse; loc *n* unde se înşeuează caii (la hipodrom).

paddyfield *s* orezărie *f.*

padlock *s* lacăt *n* ‖ *vt* a încuia cu lacăt.

pagan *s/adj* păgân *m.*

page[1] *s* paj *m;* aprod *m,* uşier *m;* comisionar *m* ‖ *vt* a chema, a striga (pe nume).

page[2] *s* pagină *f;* filă *f;* episod *n;* moment *n* ‖ *vt* a pagina.

pageant *s* alai/cortegiu *n* sărbătoresc, procesiune *f* sărbătorească; spectacol *n* grandios; carnaval *n;* mascaradă *f; thea* tablou *n* viu; *fig* strălucire *f* goală, pompă *f* falsă.

paid *vt* *** pay.**

pail *s* găleată *f,* căldare *f;* cuvă *f;* benă *f.*

pain *s* durere *f;* pacoste *f;* osteneală *f;* pedeapsă *f* ‖ *vt* a durea; a mâhni • **~killer** *s* calmant *n,* analgezic *n* • **~ful** *adj* dureros; penibil; sensibil; obositor • **~less** *adj* fără durere; *(easy)* fără dificultate.

paint *s* vopsea *f;* ruj *n;* fard *n* ‖ *vt* a picta; a descrie; a farda; a vopsi ‖ *vi* a picta; a se ruja, a se farda.

painting *s* pictură *f,* tablou *n.*

pair *s* pereche *f;* schimb *n;* cuplu *n* ‖ *vt* a împerechea; a aranja doi câte doi ‖ *vi* a forma o pereche; *zool* a se împerechea.

pajamas *s pl* pijama *f.*

Pakistan *s* Pakistan • **~i** *adj, s* pachistanez(ă) *m/f.*

pal *s coll* prieten *m,* tovarăş *m;* partener *m.*

palace *s* palat *n;* reşedință *f* oficială.

palatable *adj (food)* gustos, plăcut la gust; *fig* plăcut, agreabil, acceptabil.

palate *s anat* palat *n,* cerul *n* gurii.

palaver *s (chatter)* vorbe *fpl* goale, vorbărie *f; (fuss)* tevatură *f.*

pale *adj* palid; deschis; şters; difuz ‖ *vi* a păli; a fi eclipsat ‖ *vt* a face să pălească.

paleontology *s* paleontologie *f.*

Palestine *s* Palestina.

Palestinian *adj/s* palestinian *m.*

palette *s (painter)* paletă *f; fig* paletă *f,* gamă, *f; tech* pieptar *n* de coarbă.

paling *s (fence)* gard *n* (de pari); palisadă *f.*

pall[1] *vi* a nu mai avea/prezenta farmec, a-şi pierde farmecul; a deveni plictisitor.

pall[2] *s* giulgiu *n,* lințoliu *n; relig* acoperământ *n; fig* văl *n;* mantie *f.*

palliative *s/adj* paliativ *n.*

pallid *adj* palid.

pallor *s* paloare *f,* lipsă *f* de culoare.

palm[1] *s anat* palmă *f* ‖ *vt* a atinge cu palma; *(hide)* a ascunde în palmă; *coll* a mitui.

palm[2] *s bot* palmier *m; fig* triumf *n,* victorie *f;* lauri *m pl.*

palpable *adj* palpabil; tangibil; *fig* palpabil, evident, clar.

palpate *vt med* a palpa.

palpitate *vi (throb)* a pulsa, a zvâcni; *(shake)* a palpita, a tremura (de).

palsy *s med* paralizie *f.*

paltry *adj* meschin; derizoriu.

pamper *vt* a răsfăța, a răzgâia.

pamphlet *s* broşură *f;* pamflet *n;* catalog *n;* prospect *n.*

pan *s* tigaie *f*; cratiță *f*; tingire *f*; (*bread, etc*) formă *f*, tavă *f* ‖ *vt* a găti în tigaie; a critica aspru ‖ *vi cin* a filma panoramic.

panacea *s* panaceu *n*.

pancake *s* clătită *f* ‖ *vi* a ateriza brusc.

pancreas *s anat* pancreas *n*.

panda *s zool* panda *f*.

pandemonium *s relig* pandemoniu *n*; *fig* iad *n*; *fig* harababură *f*.

pander *vi* a face proxenetism, a fi proxenet; (**to smb**) a satisface pretențiile (cuiva).

pane *s* (ochi de) geam *n*; panou *n*.

panegyric *s* panegiric *n*; elogiu *n*.

panel *s* panou *n*, tablou *n*; *constr* panel *n*; lambriu *n*; (ochi de) geam *n*; (*dress, etc*) aplicație *f*; *elec* tablou *n* de comandă; (foaie de) pergament *n*; *jur* jurați *m pl*; *tv, radio* invitați *m pl*; (*~ of experts*) comitet *n*; (*wood*) panou *n*; (*car*) tablou *n* de bord.

pang *s* durere *f* bruscă; junghi *n*; spasm *n*; *fig* durere/ suferință *f* cumplită; *pl* remușcări *f pl*; mustrări *f pl* de conștiință.

panic *s* panică *f* ‖ *vi* a fi cuprins de panic • **~y** *adj* (*person*) panicat; (*feeling*) de panică.

panorama *s* panoramă *f*; vedere *f* panoramică; *fig* suită/succesiune *f* de imagini; tablou *n* cuprinzător.

panpipe *s mus* nai *n*.

pansy *s bot* pansea *f*; *coll pej* homosexual *m*.

pant *vi* (*person*) a sufla greu, a gâfâi; a-și trage sufletul; (*locomotive*) a gâfâi; a pufăi; (*heart*) a bate puternic, a zvâcni; (*blood*) a pulsa puternic, a zvâcni ‖ *vt* a spune într-un suflet ‖ *s* gâfâit *n*; pufăit *n*; zvâcnire *f*.

panther *s zool* panteră *f*, pumă *f*, cuguar *m*; jaguar *m*.

panties *s pl* chiloți *m pl* de damă.

pantomime *s thea* pantomimă *f*; mimică *f* ‖ *vt* a mima ‖ *vi* a se exprima prin gesturi sau mimică.

pantry *s* cămară *f*.

pants *s pl* pantaloni *m pl*; chiloți *m pl*.

pantyhose *s pl* colanți *m*, dres *n*.

pap *s cul* păsat *n*; terci *n*; (*drivel*) tâmpenii *f pl*.

papa *s coll* tăticu *m*.

papacy *s* papalitate *f*.

papal *adj* papal.

paper *s* (*writing*) hârtie *f*; (*exam*) lucrare *f* scrisă; (*essay*) eseu *n*; (*newspaper*) ziar *n*; (*article*) articol *n*; (*thesis*) teză *f*; (*report*) referat *n*; (*wallpaper*) tapet *n*; *pl* hârtii *f pl*, documente *n pl*, acte *n pl* ‖ *adj* din hârtie; *fig* (*profit*) teoretic ‖ *vt* a scrie; a tapeta • **~clip** *s* agrafă *f* de birou • **~knife** *s* coupe papier *n* • **~weight** *s* prespapier *n* • **~work** *s* lucrări *f pl* scrise; scris *n*; *coll* hârțogărie *f*, scriptologie *f*.

paprika *s bot* ardei roșu; paprică *f*, boia *f* de ardei.

par *s* egal(itate) *f*; *econ* paritate *f*; valoare *f* nominală; medie *f*; stare *f* normală; (*golf*) par *n*; **to be on a ~ with** a fi la egalitate (cu), a fi la același nivel (cu).

parable *s* parabolă *f*.

parabola *s geom* parabolă *f*.

parachute *s* parașută *f* ‖ *vt* a parașuta ‖ *vi* a coborî cu parașuta.

parachutist *s* parașutist *m*.

parade *s* paradă *f*; defilare *f*; marș *n* ‖ *vt* a face paradă de; a defila.

paradise *s* paradis *n*, rai *n*; cer *n*.

paradox *s* paradox *n*.

paraffin *s chem* parafină *f*; ulei *n* de parafină; gaz *n*, petrol *n* lampant.

paragon *s* (*epitome*) întruchipare *f*; (*ideal*) perfecțiune *f*.

paragraph *s* paragraf *n*; notă *f*, notiță *f*; articol *n* scurt.

parallel *adj* (**to**) paralel (cu); paralel, asemănător, analog ‖ *s geom* (linie) paralelă *f*; *geog* paralelă *f*; latitudine *f*; *fig* paralel; asemănător; analogic ‖ *vt* (**with**) a compara (cu); (*road, etc*) a fi/merge paralel cu.

paralysis *s med* paralizie *f*.

paralyze *vi* a paraliza.

parameter *s* parametru *m*.

paramilitary *adj* paramilitar.

paramount *adj* extrem, suprem, maximum.

paranoia *s med* paranoia *f*.

paranoid *adj med* paranoic.

parapet *s mil* parapet *n*; *constr* parapet *n*; fronton *n*; balustradă *f*; rambleu *n*.

paraphernalia *s pl* bunuri *n pl* personale; accesorii *n pl*; *coll* dichisuri *n pl*.

paraphrase *s* parafrază *f*; interpretare *f* liberă ‖ *vt* a parafraza; a interpreta liber.

paraplegic *adj med* paraplegic.

parasite *s bio*, *also fig* parazit *m*.

parasol *s* umbrelă *f* de soare.

paratrooper *s mil* parașutist *m*.

parcel *s* pachet *n*; colet *n*; parcelă *f* ‖ *vt* a face un pachet; *naut* a înfășura (o parâmă).

parch *vt* a prăji; a coace; a rumeni; (*sun*) a pârjoli; a arde ‖ *vi* a se coace, a muri de căldură; (*lips*) a se usca; a se scoroji.

parchment *s* pergament *n*; hârtie *f* de pergament; manuscris *n* pe pergament.

pardon *s* iertare *f*; scuză *f*; amnistie *f* ‖ *vt* a ierta.

pare *vt* a tăia/a îndepărta partea exterioară; a tăia; (*~ an apple, etc.*) a tăia coaja; (*trim*) a tunde; (*shave*) a rade; (*reduce gradually*) a reduce treptat, a micșora.

parent *s* părinte *m*; tată *m*, mamă *f*; sursă *f*.

parenthesis *s* paranteză *f*.

paring *s* cojire *f*; *pl* (*fruit, etc*) resturi *n pl*, rămășițe *f pl*; (*metal*) pilitură *f*.

Paris *s* Paris *n* • **~ian** *s/adj* parizian(ă) *m/f*.

parish *s relig* parohie *f*; enoriași *m pl*; (*civil*) comună *f*; obște *f*.

parity *s econ* paritate *f*; egalitate *f*; analogie *f*; paralelism *n*.

park *s* parc *n* ‖ *vt/vi* a parca • **~ing lot** *s* parcare *f*.

parley *s* (*discussion*) discuție *f*; *mil* tratative *f pl*, negocieri *f pl* • *vi mil* a duce tratative, a parlamenta.

parliament *s* parlament *n*.

parlor *s* salon *n*; atelier *n*; cabinet *n*.

parochial *adj relig* parohial; *fig* local; provincial; îngust; limitat.

parody *s lit* parodie *f*; *fig* imitație *f* nereușită, parodie *f* ‖ *vt* a parodia, a imita.

parole *s* cuvânt *n* (de onoare); *mil* parolă *f* ‖ *vt* a elibera (din închisoare) pe cuvânt; **on ~** în libertate condiționată.

paroxysm *s* paroxism *n*.

parquet *s constr* parchet *n*.

parrot *s* papagal *m* ‖ *vt* a repeta ca un papagal.

parsimonious *adj* (*thrifty*) econom, strângător; (*stingy*) zgârcit.

parsimony *s* (*prudence*) economie *f*; cumpătare *f*; (*stinginess*) zgârcenie *f*.

parsley *s bot* pătrunjel *m*.

parsnip *s bot* păstârnac *m*.

parson s *relig* pastor *m*, preot *m*.
part s parte *f*; bucată *f*; (*series*) episod *n*; (*component*) piesă *f*; (*body ~*) parte *f*, membru *m*; (*proportion*) măsură *f*; (*~ in hair*) cărare *f*; *typ* număr *n*; *econ* datorie *f*; *tech* reper *n*; *mus* voce *f*; *thea* rol *n*; *fig* punct *n* de vedere || *vt* a separa; a distinge || *vi* a se rupe; a muri; a se despărți de • *~*time *adj* cu normă incompletă, cu jumătate de normă.
partake *vi* (**of**) a participa la, a lua parte la; a împărtăși; (*taste*) a avea.
partial *adj* parțial, incomplet; părtinitor, subiectiv.
participant s participant *m*.
participate *vi* (**in**) a participa (la).
participation s participare *f*.
participle s *gram* participiu *n*.
particle s particulă *f*; corpuscul *m*; granulă *f*; fir *n*; *gram* particulă *f*.
particular *adj* special, deosebit, anumit; ciudat; minuțios; mofturos || s particularitate *f*; detaliu *n*.
parting s (*separation*) despărțire *f*; (*leaving*) plecare *f*; (*roads*) bifurcare *f*; răscruce *f*; (*~ of hair*) cărare *f*.
partisan s partizan *m*, adept *m*; *mil* partizan *m* || *adj* partizan; fanatic; *mil* de partizani.
partition s *constr* perete *m* despărțitor; paravan *n*; (*of a country, etc*) împărțire *f*, divizare *f*; partiție *f* || *vt* (*~ rooms*) a compartimenta; (*~ a country*) a împărți, a diviza; a despărți, a separa.
partner s partener *m*, asociat *m*; soț *m*, soție *f* || *vt* a face partener; a alia cu • *~*ship s parteneriat *n*; asociere *f*.
partridge s *orn* potârniche *f*.
party s *pol* partid *n*; partidă *f*; grup *n*; companie *f*; (*reunion*) reuniune *f*; serată *f*, petrecere *f*; *jur* parte *f*; *mil* detașament *n*; *~* **politics** s politica *f* de partid; **rescue** *~* s echipă s de salvare; *~* **spirit** s spirit *n* de partid.
pass *vi* (*move*) a trece; a merge; (*~ time, etc*) a se scurge; (*~ money*) a circula; (*become outdated*) a se perima; (*pain, etc*) a se sfârși; (*~ a bill*) a fi votat; *sp* a pasa; (*overtake*) a depăși || *vt* (*~ someone*) a trece pe lângă; (*~ time*) a petrece; (*hand in*) a înmâna; (*pronounce*) a spune; (*give a verdict*) a pronunța; (*~ a bill*) a vota; a aproba || s *constr* trecere *f*; pasaj *n*; *geog* defileu *n*; pas *n*; pașaport *n*; (*document*) permis *n*; (*bus, etc ~*) abonament *n*; *sp* pasă *f*; *~* **away** *vi* a se sfârși, a înceta; (*~ time*) a trece; (*die*) a muri; *~* **by** *vi* (*time ~*) a trece, a se scurge || *vt* (*ignore*) a nu băga în seamă, a neglija; *~* **for** *vi* a fi luat drept; a fi considerat • *~*able *adj* acceptabil; (*road*) practicabil; (*river*) care poate fi traversat.
passage s trecere *f*; coridor *n*; scurgere *f*; voiaj *n*; fragment *n*; votare *f*; evoluție *f*; episod *n*; incident *n*; (*sea*) traversare *f*.
passenger s pasager *m*, călător *m*.
passerby s trecător *m*.
passing *adj* (*transitory*) trecător; efemer; (*casual*) superficial || s (*departure*) trecere *f*, scurgere *f*; (*death*) moarte *f*.
passion s pasiune *f*; izbucnire *f*, patimă *f* • *~*ate *adj* pasionat; pătimaș; înflăcărat.
passive *adj* pasiv; inactiv; inert; supus; *gram* pasiv.
passivity s pasivitate *f*.
Passover s *relig* Paștele *n* evreiesc; Mielul *m* pascal.
passport s pașaport *n*.
password s *mil*, *comp* parolă *f*.
past *adj* trecut; scurs; dus; ultim; fost; terminat || s

trecut *n* || *prep* după, trecut de; dincolo de; peste; pe lângă, în dreptul.
pasta s *cul* paste *f pl* făinoase.
paste s pastă *f*; clei *n*; aluat *n*; terci *n* || *vt* a lipi.
pastel s pictură *f* în pastel; (*tablou în*) pastel *n*; (*color*) culoare *f* pastel.
pasteurize *vt* a pasteuriza.
pastime s distracție *f*, divertisment *n*; joc *n*.
pastor s *relig* pastor *m*, preot *m* • *~*al *adj* de pastor; pastoral, idilic; *relig* pastoresc; pastoral.
pastrami s *cul* pastramă *f*.
pastry s patiserie *f*; cofetărie *f*.
pasture s pășune *f*, loc *n* de pășunat, izlaz *n*.
pasty[1] *adj* păstos, cleios; (*~ face*) bolnăvicios.
pasty[2] s *cul* pateu *n* (cu carne).
pat *vt* (*~ on shoulder, etc*) a bate (cu palma) || *vi* (*raindrops ~*) a răpăi || s bătaie *f* ușoară; (*of raindrops*) răpăit *n*; (*of butter*) cantitate *f* mică; cocoloș *n*.
patch s petic *n*; (*material*) bucată *f*; (*eye~*) bandă *f*; (*snow, etc*) petic *n*; (*land*) parcelă *f*, petic *n*; *med* plasture *m*; pată *f*; rest *n*; spațiu *n* verde || *vt* a petici • *~*y *adj* inegal; (*~ knowledge*) insuficient, imperfect.
pate s (*head*) scăfârlie *f*, căpățână *f*.
patent *adj* evident, vădit || s brevet *n* de invenție || *vt* a breveta.
paternal *adj* părintesc, patern.
paternity s paternitate *f*.
path s cărare *f*; pârtie *f*; rută *f*; drum *n*; *fig* cale *f*; traiectorie *f*; **off the beaten** *~* pe o cărare nebătătorită.
pathetic *adj* (*sight, grief*) duios, mișcător; patetic; (*attempt*) disperat; inutil; (*performance*) jalnic.
pathologist s medic *m* patolog.
pathology s patologie *f*.
pathos s patos *n*.
patience s răbdare *f*.
patient *adj* răbdător; stăruitor; rezistent || s *med* pacient *m*, bolnav *m*.
patio s *archit* patio *n*, curte *f* interioară.
patois s idiom *n*, dialect *n*.
patriarch s patriarh *m* • *~*al *adj relig* patriarhal, de patriarh; *fig* patriarhal, venerabil; *fig* patriarhal; simplu; tihnit • *~*ate s patriarhie *f* • *~*y s patriarhat *n*.
patrimony s patrimoniu *n*; avere *f* moștenită.
patriot s patriot *m*.
patrol s rond *n*; patrulare *f*; patrulă *f* || *vt/vi* a patrula.
patron s patron *m*; sfânt *m* protector; spectator *m*; vizitator *m* • *~*age s sprijin *n*, protecție *f*, sponsorizare *f* • *~*ize *vt* a patrona, a sprijini; a trata cu condescendență • *~*izing *adj* condescendent.
patsy s *coll* fraier *m*.
patter[1] *vt* a rosti foarte repede || *vi* a vorbi foarte repede || s jargon *n*; argou *n*; sporovăială *f*.
patter[2] *vi* (*rain*) a bate, a răpăi; (*children, etc*) a merge cu pași repezi, a lipăi || s (*rain*) răpăit *n*, bătaie *f*; (*person*) lipăit *n*, tropăit *n*.
pattern s model *n*, tipar *n*, șablon *n*; mostră *f*; desen *n*; mod *n*; stil *n*; pildă *f*; fel *n* || *vt* a aplica modele.
patty s pateu *n* mic.
paucity s (*scarcity*) lipsă *f*, sărăcie *f*.
paunch s burtă *f* (mare); *zool* burduf *n*.
pauper s sărac *m*, nevoiaș *m*.
pause s pauză *f*; oprire *f*; răgaz *n*; ezitare *f* || *vi* a se opri; a șovăi, a ezita.
pave *vt* (*~ a road*) a pava; a pietrui; *fig* (*facilitate*) a

netezi calea (pentru); a pregăti • ~ment s pavare f;
pardosire f; pavaj n; trotuar n; caldarâm n.

pavilion s pavilion n, chioșc n; *archit* aripă f laterală;
foișor n; balcon n; *anat* pavilionul n urechii.

paw s labă f; mână f || *vt* a lovi cu laba; a scotoci.

pawn[1] s amanet n; ipotecă f; garanție f; ipotecare f || *vt*
a amaneta; a ipoteca.

pawn[2] s, *also fig* (*chess piece*) pion m; *fig* marionetă f;
unealtă f.

pay, paid, paid *vt* (~ *money*) a plăti; a remunera; a
compensa; a achita; (~ *with kindness*) a răsplăti; (~
attention) a da atenție; (*be worth*) a merita; (~ *a
visit*) a face || *vi* a plăti; a merita || s plată f • ~**able**
adj plătibil • ~**back** s amortizare f • ~**check** s plată f,
salariu n • ~**day** s zi f de salariu/leafă • ~**ee** s beneficiar m • ~**er** s plătitor m, platnic m • ~**off** s (*reward*)
plată f; retribuție f; *sl* (*bribe*) șpagă f • ~**ment** s plată
f; sumă f de plată; *fig* răsplată f • ~**roll** s stat n de
salarii.

pea s *bot* mazăre f; bob n de mazăre.

peace s pace f; liniște f; ordine f; odihnă f • ~**able** *adj*
pașnic, liniștit • ~**maker** s conciliator m; pacificator
m • ~**ful** *adj* pașnic; liniștit, calm.

peach s *bot* (*tree*) piersic m; (*fruit*) piersică f; *coll* odor n.

peacock s *orn* păun m; *fig* filfizon m; înfumurat m.

peahen s *orn* păuniță f.

peak s *geog* pisc n; vârf n; culme f; *fig* apogeu n, punct
n culminant • ~**ed** *adj* ascuțit, cu vârf.

peal s (*bell*) sunet n; zgomot n; (*gun*) bubuit n; (*laugh-
ter*) hohot n || *vi* a răsuna; (*bell* ~s) a bate || *vt* a face
să răsune; a bate (clopotele).

peanut s *bot* arahidă f; ~ **butter** s cremă f de arahide.

pear s *bot* (*tree*) păr m; (*fruit*) pară f.

pearl s perlă f; odor n; nestemată f; sidef n || *vt* a
împodobi; a granula; a pescui perle.

peasant s țăran m; fermier m; agricultor m.

peat s turbă f.

pebble s prundiș n; pietricică f; *miner* cremene f, silex n.

peccadillo s (*sin*) păcat n mic; greșeală f neînsemnată.

peck[1] s măsură f de capacitate de 9,09 l; *fig* (*worries,
etc*) mulțime f, grămadă f.

peck[2] s ciugulire f; ciocănire f; *coll* sărut n dat în fugă
|| *vt* a ciuguli; a scobi.

pectoral *adj* pectoral • ~s s mușchii m *pl* pectorali.

peculiar *adj* specific, propriu; distinct; exclusiv; unic;
ciudat • ~**ity** s particularitate f; însușire f, proprietate
f; trăsătură f caracteristică; ciudățenie f, curiozitate f.

pecuniary *adj* pecuniar.

pedagogy s pedagogie f.

pedal s pedală f; suport n || *vi* a pedala.

pedant s pedant m • ~**ic** *adj* pedant • ~**ry** s pedanterie f.

peddle *vt* a face comerț ambulant (cu); (*sell drugs*) a
face trafic; (*spread a rumor*) a colporta || *vi* a se
ocupa de fleacuri; a face comerț ambulant.

pedestal s soclu n, piedestal n; suport n; bază f.

pedestrian *adj* pedestru; *fig* prozaic; plicticos;
neinspirat || s pieton m; ~ **crossing** s trecere f de
pietoni.

pediatrician s (*medic*) pediatru m.

pediatrics s pediatrie f.

pedigree s arbore m genealogic; genealogie f; (*person*)
ascendență f; (*animal*) pedigree n || *adj* (*animal*) de
rasă.

peddler s negustor m ambulant; colportor m.

pedophile s pedofil m.

pee s *coll* pipi n || *vi* a face pipi.

peek *vi* a arunca o privire, a se uita (pe furiș).

peel *vt* a coji; a dezghioca; a jupui || *vi* a se coji; (*paint*)
a se scoroji; (*paper*) a se dezlipi; (*skin*) a se coji || s
(*apple, tomato, etc* ~) coajă f.

peep s privire f furișă, căutătură f; ivire f, apariție f || *vi*
a privi pe furiș, a se uita pe furiș; a apărea, a se ivi •
~**hole** s ferestruică f, vizetă f.

peer[1] *vi* a privi atent (la), a se uita atent (la), a cerceta,
a examina.

peer[2] s egal n, pereche f; **without** ~ fără egal/pereche, a
egala, a fi egalul (cuiva).

peevish *adj* arțagos, certăreț; (*answer, etc*) iritat; acru.

peg s cui n; țintă f; pană f; par m; cârlig n; temă f; pre-
text n || *vt* a bate un cui în; a marca; a stabiliza.

pejorative *adj* peiorativ, depreciativ.

Peking s Beijing.

pelican s *orn* pelican m.

pellet s granulă f; tabletă f; pilulă f; ghemotoc n; (*bread,
etc*) cocoloș n.

pell-mell *adv* în dezordine, alandala; (*headlong*)
val-vârtej; zor-nevoie.

pellucid *adj* *liter* limpede; (*style*) limpede, clar; (*mind*)
limpede, lucid.

pelt[1] *vt* a arunca, a azvârli (în cineva), a bombarda; a
ataca; *fig* (*with*) (~ *questions, etc*) a bombarda || *vi*
(*rain, etc*) a bate, a răpăi || s lovitură f (puternică);
mil rafală f; tir n; grabă f, viteză f, iuțeală f.

pelt[2] s (*animal*) piele f, blană f.

pelvis s *anat* pelvis n, bazin n.

pen[1] s condei n; toc n; stilou n; peniță f; pană f; scris n
|| *vt* a scrie, a compune.

pen[2] s (*enclosure*) țarc n; îngrăditură f || *vt* a închide
într-un țarc.

penal *adj* *jur* penal • ~**ize** *vt* *jur*, *sp* a penaliza; a pedepsi.

penalty s pedeapsă f; amendă f; penalizare f.

penance s *relig* penitență f; *fig* corvoadă f, pedeapsă f.

penchant s înclinație f, predilecție f (pentru).

pencil s creion n; penel n; stil n || *vt* a schița, a desena,
a picta.

pendant s pandantiv n; breloc n; lustră f; *naut* atârnător
n; flamură f.

pending *adj* nedecis, nerezolvat; (*case*) în instanță ||
prep în timpul/cursul; până la; înainte de.

pendulum s pendulă f.

penetrate *vt* a pătrunde, a străpunge, a intra în; a se
infiltra în; (*desire, etc*) a cuprinde; *fig* a înțelege; *fig*
a emoționa, a mișca || *vi* (*into*) a pătrunde, a intra în.

penetrating *adj* pătrunzător.

penetration s penetrare f, pătrundere f.

penguin s *orn* pinguin m.

penicillin s *med* penicilină f.

peninsula s *geog* peninsulă f.

penis s *anat* penis n.

penitence s penitență f, căință f.

penitent *adj* care se pocăiește || s penitent m.

penitentiary *adj* de penitenciar; de corecție || s peni-
tenciar n, închisoare f; casă f de corecție f.

pen-name s pseudonim n.

pennant s flamură f; fanion n.

penniless *adj* lefter; sărac.

penny s peni m; cent m; ~**pinching** *adj* zgârcit.

pension s pensie f || *vt* a pensiona.

pensive *adj* gânditor; trist, melancolic.

pentagon *s geom* pentagon *n*; **the Pentagon** *s* Pentagonul *n* (sediul Departamentului Apărării, în SUA)

penthouse *s archit* apartament *n* de lux (la ultimul etaj).

pent-up *adj (feelings)* refulat, înăbușit; *(energy)* stăpânit.

penultimate *adj* penultim.

penury *s* penurie *f*; *(poverty)* sărăcie *f*.

peony *s bot* bujor *m*.

people *s* popor *n*; națiune *f*; neam *n*; oameni *m pl*, lume *f*; familie *f* || *vt* a popula.

pep *s coll (energy)* energie *f*; *(vigor)* vigoare *f* || *vt (person)* a ridica moralul; *(conversation)* a anima.

pepper *s bot* piper *n*; *cul* boia *f*; ardei *m* iute; *bot* ardei *m* gras || *vt* a pipera; a presăra.

per *prep* per, prin, cu; de (fiecare); pe; ~ **diem** *adv* pe zi; zilnic.

perceive *vt (sense)* a percepe; *(understand)* a remarca, a-și da seama de; a înțelege; a observa; a zări; a vedea; *(view as)* a considera.

percent *s* procent *n*; procentaj *n*.

perceptible *adj* perceptibil; palpabil.

perception *s* percepere *f*; sesizare *f*; percepție *f*; intuiție *f*.

perceptive *adj* perceptiv; receptiv.

perch *s* stinghie *f*; *fig* poziție/situație *f* înaltă || *vt* a așeza sus, a cocoța || *vr* a se așeza (sus), a se cocoța.

perchance *adv obs* probabil; din întâmplare.

percipient *adj (person)* fin, perspicace; receptiv; *(analysis)* pătrunzător; *(choice)* inspirat.

percolate *vt* a filtra, a strecura, a percola || *vi* a se filtra, a se strecura; a pătrunde.

percolator *s* filtru *n* de cafea.

percussion *s* ciocnire *f*, lovire *f*; șoc *n*; *med, mus, mil* percuție *f*.

perdition *s frml* perdiție *f*, pierzanie *f*; ruină *f*; *relig* pierzanie *f*, osândă *f* veșnică.

peremptory *adj (authoritative)* autoritar; *(decisive)* decisiv; *(tone)* imperativ; *(refusal)* categoric.

perennial *adj bot* peren; vivace; *fig* peren, de lungă durată; permanent; persistent; *bot* plantă *f* perenă.

perfect *adj* perfect; excelent; complet; exact || *vt* a perfecționa • ~**ion** *s* perfecționare *f*, desăvârșire *f*; perfecțiune *f*; culme *f*.

perfidious *adj* trădător, perfid.

perforate *vt* a perfora, a străpunge || *vi* **(into)** a pătrunde (în).

perform *vt* a efectua, *(~a role)* a îndeplini; *(~ an occupation)* a ocupa; a executa; *(~ in a play, concert)* a interpreta; a juca || *vi (machines)* a merge, a funcționa; *(actor)* a juca; *(singer)* a cânta; *thea, etc* a se produce • ~**ance** *s* executare *f*; performanță *f*; *(show)* spectacol *n*; *(actor, singer)* interpretare *f*; *(engine, etc)* performanță *f*; *tech* productivitate *f*, randament *n* • ~**er** *s thea, etc* artist *m*, interpret *m*; executant *m*.

perfume *s* parfum *n*, aromă *f* || *vt* a parfuma.

perfunctory *adj* superficial, neglijent.

perhaps *adv* poate (că); probabil; posibil; cumva.

peril *s* pericol *n*, primejdie *f*.

perimeter *s* perimetru *n*; contur *n*; circumferință *f*.

period *s* perioadă *f*; durată *f*; eră *f*; etapă *f*; punct *n*; *scol* lecție *f*; *physiol* ciclu *n* menstrual || *adj (furniture, etc)* de epocă.

peripatetic *adj* itinerant.

peripheral *adj (minor)* secundar; *(marginal)* periferic; extern || *s comp* periferic *n*.

periphery *s* periferie *f*; *(fringe)* margine *f*.

periscope *s opt* periscop *n*.

perish *vi also fig* a pieri; a se sfârși || *vt* a distruge; a muri • ~**able** *adj* perisabil || *s pl* mărfuri *f pl* perisabile.

perjure *vi jur* a jura strâmb.

perjury *s jur* sperjur *n*, mărturie *f* falsă; jurământ *n* fals; călcare *f* a jurământului.

perk *vi* a-și ridica capul/fruntea; a se învdiora, a se anima; a-și recăpăta buna dispoziție • ~**y** *adj coll* vioi, plin de viață; plin de antren; infatuat; arogant.

perm *s abbrev* permanent *n* || *vt* a face un permanent || *vi* a fi ondulat.

permanence *s (durability)* trăinicie *f*; *(stability)* stabilitate *f*, permanență *f*.

permanent *adj* permanent; stabil; durabil || *s* permanent *n*.

permeable *adj* permeabil.

permeate *vt (liquid, smell)* a se infiltra, a pătrunde; *(ideas)* a se răspândi.

permissible *adj frml (allowed)* admis, permis; *(tolerable)* permisibil, admisibil.

permission *s* permisiune *f*, îngăduire *f*.

permissive *adj* tolerant, îngăduitor.

permit *vt* a permite, a încuviința; a da voie; a da posibilitatea || *vi* a permite || *s* permis *n*; *econ* licență *f*; voie *f*.

permutation *s* schimbare *f*; rearanjare *f*; *math* permutare *f*; substituție *f*; transformare *f*.

pernicious *adj* dăunător; fatal; pernicios.

peroxide *s chem* peroxid *n*; apă *f* oxigenată.

perpendicular *adj* perpendicular; abrupt || *s geom* perpendiculară *f*.

perpetrate *vt (~ a crime, etc)* a săvârși, a comite, a înfăptui.

perpetrator *s* făptaș *m*, autor *m*; criminal *m*.

perpetual *adj* perpetuu; pe viață; veșnic; inamovibil; *coll (quarrels, etc)* care nu se mai termină, interminabil.

perpetuate *vt (~ a memory, etc)* a perpetua; *(~ a legacy)* a transmite.

perpetuity *s (eternity)* eternitate *f*; *(annuity)* rentă *f* viageră; *jur* inalienabilitate *f*.

perplex *vt* a nedumeri; a dezorienta; a lăsa perplex.

perquisite *s (bonus)* bonus *n*, supliment *n*; *(advantage)* avantaj *n*.

persecute *vt (hound)* a persecuta, a prigoni; *(~d by mosquitoes, etc)* a nu da pace, a chinui.

persecution *s* persecuție *f*.

perseverance *s* perseverență *f*.

persevere *vi* **(at/in/with)** a persevera, a persista.

persevering *adj* perseverent, sârguincios, tenace.

persist *vi* **(in)** a persista, a stărui; a continua, a dăinui • ~**ent** *adj (rain, noise)* persistent; *(problem)* constant; *(resolute)* tenace, încăpățânat.

person *s* individ *m*; persoană *f*; *(aspect)* înfățișare *f*, aspect *n*; ținută *f*; sine *m*.

personal *adj* personal; *(private)* privat; *(remark)* jignitor; *jur* mobil || *s pl* avere *f* personală, bunuri *n pl* mobile; ~ **computer** *s* computer *n* personal/individual.

personality *s* personalitate *f*; notabilitate *f*.

personification *s* personificare *f*.

personify *vt* a personifica.

personnel *s* personal *n*; salariați *m pl*; *(department)* serviciul *n* resurse umane.

perspective *s* perspectivă *f*.

perspiration *s* transpirație *f.*

perspire *vi* a asuda, a transpira; a exsuda.

persuade *vt* a convinge; a determina, a hotărî să ‖ *vr* a se convinge.

persuasion *s* (*act of convincing*) putere *f* de convingere; (*belief*) convingere *f*, concepție *f*; *relig* credință *f.*

persuasive *adj* convingător.

pert *adj* impertinent, obraznic.

pertain *vi* (**to**) a aparține de; a fi caracteristic/propriu; a se referi la.

pertinacious *adj frml* (*stubborn*) încăpățânat, îndărătnic; (*tenacious*) tenace, stăruitor.

pertinent *adj frml* pertinent; oportun.

perturb *vt* (*silence*) a tulbura, *fig* a tulbura, a mișca, a neliniști.

Peru *s* Peru • **~vian** *adj/s* peruvian(ă) *m/f.*

perusal *s* citire/lectură *f* (atentă).

peruse *vt* a citi cu atenție; a studia.

pervade *vt* a pătrunde (în), a îmbiba; (*smell*) a se răspândi; (*feeling, etc*) a invada; *fig* a pătrunde în, a umple; a se difuza în.

pervasive *adj* atotpătrunzător; *fig* universal.

perverse *adj* (*person*) îndărătnic; (*joy*) răutăcios; (*circumstance*) potrivnic; (*verdict, etc*) greșit; corupt, depravat; pervertit, pervers.

perversion *s* (*sexual*) perversiune *f*; (*of the truth*) denaturare *f*; pervertire *f.*

pervert *vt* a perverti, a corupe; (~ *the truth, meaning*) a denatura, a deforma; (~ *justice*) a împiedica; (*sex*) a perverti ‖ *s* pervertit *m*, pervers *m.*

pesky *adj* sâcâitor, supărător.

pessimism *s* pesimism *n.*

pessimist *s* pesimist *m* • **~ic** *adj* pesimist.

pest *s* dăunător *m*; parazit *m*; pacoste *f* • **~er** *vt* a nu lăsa în pace, a supăra, a hărțui.

pestilence *s* pestă *f*, molimă *f.*

pestle *s chem* mojar *n*; *cul* piuliță *f* (de pisat).

pet *s* răsfățat *m*; favorit *m*; odor *n*; animal *n* favorit ‖ *adj* iubit, favorit ‖ *vi* a se săruta.

petal *s bot* petală *f.*

peter *vi* (**out**) (*provisions, etc*) a se sfârși încetul cu încetul; (*interest*) a se diminua, a scădea; (*tire*) a fi epuizat.

petite *adj* (*small*) mic ‖ *s* (*clothing size*) măsură *f* mică.

petition *s* cerere *f*, petiție *f*; rugăminte *f* ‖ *vt* a înainta cerere; a ruga; a cere.

petrified *adj* (*scared*) paralizat/împietrit de spaimă.

petrify *vt* a petrifica, a fosiliza; *fig* a preface în stană de piatră.

petrol *s* benzină *f.*

petroleum *s* țiței *n*; petrol *n*; gaz *n.*

petticoat *s* jupon *n.*

petty *adj* mic; mărunt; meschin; îngust; ~ **cash** *s econ* cheltuieli *f pl* mărunte, încasări *f pl* mărunte; ~ **officer** *s naut* subofițer *m.*

petulant *adj* (*huffy*) iritabil, irascibil; capricios; nerăbdător.

petunia *s bot* petunie *f.*

pew *s relig* strană *f*; rând/șir *n* de bănci.

pewter *s metal* aliaj *n* de cositor și plumb; vase *n pl* cositorite.

phallus *s* falus *n.*

phantom *s* fantomă *f*, spectru *n*, nălucă *f*; închipuire *f*; imagine *f* mentală; umbră *f* ‖ *adj* fantomatic, spectral.

pharmacist *s* farmacist *m.*

pharmacy *s* farmacie *f*; drogherie *f.*

pharynx *s anat* faringe *n.*

phase *s phys, astron* fază *f*; etapă *f*; stadiu *n* ‖ *vt* a introduce; **to ~ in** *vt* a introduce progresiv; **to ~ out** *vt* a suprima/reduce progresiv.

Ph.D. *s abbr* (**Doctor of Philosophy**) doctor *m* în filosofie.

pheasant *s orn* fazan *m.*

phenomenon *s* (*pl* **–mena**) *phylos* fenomen *n*; fapt *n*; fapt *n* neobișnuit; *fig* fenomen *n*, om *m* extraordinar.

phial *s* fiolă *f*; flacon *n.*

philanthropist *s* filantrop *m.*

philanthropy *s* filantropie *f*; caritate *f*; faptă/instituție *f* filantropică.

philatelist *s* filatelist *m.*

philately *s* filatelie *f.*

philosopher *s* filosof *m.*

philosophy *s* filosofie *f*; calm *n*; răbdare *f*; înțelepciune *f.*

phlegm *s physiol* flegmă *f*, spută *f*; *fig* flegmă *f*, indiferență *f*, calm *n*, sânge *n* rece • **~atic** *adj* flegmatic, indiferent, calm.

phobia *s med* fobie *f.*

phone *s* telefon *n* ‖ *vt/vi* a telefona; ~ **call** *s* apel *n* telefonic; ~ **number** *s* număr *n* de telefon • **~book** *s* carte *f* de telefon • **~card** *s* cartelă *f* telefonică • **~in** *s* radio, tv program *n* de dialog la telefon cu ascultătorii.

phonetic *adj* fonetic • **~s** *s pl ling* fonetică *f*; system *n* fonetic.

phony *adj* (*address, etc*) fals, contrafăcut; (*person*) ipocrit, nesincer.

phosphate *s chem* fosfat *m.*

phosphorescence *s phys* fosforescență *f.*

phosphorous *s chem* fosfor *m.*

photo *s* fotografie *f*; *coll* poză *f.*

photocopier *s* mașină *f* de fortocopiat

photocopy *s* fotocopie *f* ‖ *vt* a fotocopia.

photogenic *adj* fotogenic.

photograph *s* fotografie *f*, poză *f* ‖ *vt/vi* a fotografia.

phrase *s* expresie *f*; vorbărie *f*; limbaj *n*, stil *n*; locuțiune *f* ‖ *vt* a exprima; a defini; a formula; *mus* a fraza.

phrasing *s* terminologie *f*, vocabular *n*; *mus* frazare *f*; (*word choice*) selecția *f* vocabularului..

physical *adj* fizic; trupesc; carnal; (*object, etc*) material ‖ *s med* vizită *f* medicală.

physician *s* doctor *m*, medic *m.*

physicist *s* fizician *m.*

physics *s* fizică *f.*

physiology *s* fiziologie *f.*

physiotherapy *s med* fizioterapie *f.*

physique *s* (*person*) fizic *n.*

pianist *s mus* pianist *m.*

piano *s mus* pian *n.*

piccolo *s mus* piculină *f.*

pick[1] *s* scobitoare *f*; alegere *f* ‖ *vt* a săpa; a scobi; a culege; a ciuguli; a critica ‖ *vi* a fura; a ciuguli; a culege; ~ **on** *vi* a sâcâi, a bate la cap; ~ **out** *vi* a alege; a selecționa; a distinge, a recunoaște; (*meaning*) a înțelege; ~ **up** *vt* a săpa; a ridica (de jos); (~ *someone*) a merge după, a trece să ia pe; (~ *by car*) a lua; (~ *a language, etc*) a învăța; (~ *a habit*) a lua; (~ *a bargain*) a descoperi; (~ *speed*) a lua viteză; *coll* (*sex*) a agăța; *radio, etc* a capta, a recepționa; (*work, etc*) a relua, a continua; (*improve health*) a reface, a restabili; (*improve*) a relua • **~up** *s* camionetă *f.*

pick² *s (tool)* târnăcop *n*; *min* picon *n*; instrument *n* cu vârful ascuțit.

picket *s* țăruș *n*; jalon *n*; pichet *n*; *mil* pichet *n*, post *n* de pază; *(strike)* pichet *n* || *vt* a fixa cu țăruși; *(horse, etc)* a priponi; a îngrădi; *mil*, *pol* a instala un pichet pentru; ~ **line** pichet de grevă.

pickle *vt* a mura, a pune la murat; *metal* a decapa, a băițui || *s* saramură *f*; *pl* murături *f pl*.

pickpocket *s* hoț *m* de buzunare.

picky *adj (fussy)* mofturos, sclifosit.

picnic *s* picnic *n*; amuzament *n*, distracție *f* || *vi* a organiza un picnic; a lua parte la un picnic.

pictorial *adj* pictural; grafic; plastic; ilustrat; *(style)* expresiv || *s* magazin *n*, revistă *f* ilustrată.

picture *s* tablou *n*, pictură *f*; *(mental)* imagine *f*; *(photo)* poză *f*, fotografie *f*; desen *n*; portret *n*; *(movie)* film *n*; *fig* situație *f*; *pl* cinema *n* || *vt* a reprezenta; a picta; a oglindi; a ilustra; a descrie; *fig* a imagina, a închipui.

picturesque *adj* pitoresc; colorat; viu.

piddle *vi coll* a face pipi.

piddling *adj coll (job, etc)* neînsemnat, mărunt.

pidgin *s* limbă *f* stâlcită; ~ **English** engleză stricată.

pie¹ *s orn* coțofană *f*; animal *n* bălțat.

pie² *s cul* plăcintă *f*, pateu *n*; tort *n*.

piece *s* bucată *f*; fărâmă *f*; *(land)* parcelă *f*; *(chess, furniture, etc)* piesă *f*; fragment *n*; *(coin)* monedă *f*; *fig* manifestare *f*; pildă *f*; exemplu *n* || *vt* a repara; a combina; a unifica.

pier *s naut* dig *n*; chei *n*; dană *f*; debarcader *n*; *constr* pilon *n*, stâlp *m*.

pierce *vt* a străpunge; a găuri; a străbate || *vi* a răzbate.

piercing *adj (sound)* ascuțit; *(look)* pătrunzător; *(question)* tăios.

piety *s* pietate *f*, evlavie *f*, cucernicie *f*.

pig *s* porc *m*; mistreț *m*; *coll pej* mâncău *m*; *coll pej* om *m* murdar; *metal* lingou *n*; bloc *n*; bară *f* || *vt/vi* a făta • ~**headed** *adj* greu/tare de cap, prost; încăpățânat • ~**tail** *s* coadă *f*, cosiță *f*.

pigeon *s orn* porumbel *m*; *coll* nerod *m*.

pigment *s anat* pigment *m*; *chem* pigment *m*; colorant *m*.

pigmy *s* pigmeu *m*.

pike *s icht* știucă *f*.

pilaf *s cul* pilaf *n*.

pilchard *s icht* sardea *f*.

pile¹ *s* grămadă *f*; morman *n*; *(papers, etc)* teanc *n*; *(wood)* stivă *f*; maldăr *n*; pachet *n*; *phys* pilă *f* (atomică) || *vt* a îngrămădi; a aduna, a acumula.

pile² *s (post)* pilon *n*, stâlp *n* || *vt* a fixa stâlpi în.

pile³ *s (carpet, etc)* pluș *n*.

piles *s pl med* hemoroizi *m pl*.

pilfer *vt* a fura; *coll* a șterpeli.

pilgrim *s* pelerin *m*; călător *m*.

piling *s (support)* stâlp *n*, pilon *n*.

pill *s* pilulă *f* || *vt* a prescrie pilule.

pillage *s* prădare *f*, jefuire *f* || *vt* a prăda, a jefui.

pillar *s also fig* stâlp *m*; pilon *m*; pilastru *m*; *fig* sprijin *n*; *min* pilier *n*.

pillion *s* șaua *f* însoțitorului; loc *n* în spate; **to ride** ~ a urca în spate.

pillory *s* stâlp *m* al infamiei || *vt (brand)* a stigmatiza, a pune la zid.

pillow *s* pernă *f* || *vt* a pune capul pe pernă; a servi ca/drept pernă (cuiva); ~ **case** *s* față *f* de pernă.

pilot *s naut*, *avia* pilot *m*; ghid *m*, călăuză *f*; *constr*

pilot *m*, stâlp *m*; *tech* supapă *f* auxiliară || *vt naut*, *avia* a pilota; *fig* a conduce, a călăuzi, a ghida.

pimento *s bot* ardei *m* roșu.

pimp *s coll* proxenet *m*, codoș *m* || *vi coll* a fi proxenet/codoș.

pimple *s med* pustulă *f*.

pin *s* ac *n* cu gămălie, cu de păr, cu de siguranță; broșă *f*; *tech* bolț *n*; bulon *n*; *elec* consolă *f*, suport *m*; știft *n*; țăruș *m*; cârlig *n* de rufe; *coll* picior *n*; *(bowling)* popic *n* || *vt* a fixa cu un ac; a străpunge; *fig* a țintui; ~ **smth on smb** *vt* a pune ceva în cârca cuiva; ~ **one's hopes on smb/smth** *vt* a-și pune speranțele în cineva/ceva; ~ **down** *vt* a defini, a identifica; ~ **smb down** *vt* a obliga pe cineva să ia o decizie.

PIN *s abbr* (**personal identifcation number**) număr *n* (cod *n*) confidențial.

pinafore *s (apron)* șorț *n*; șorțuleț *n* (de copii).

pincers *s pl (tool)* clește *m*; pensetă *f*; *zool* clește *m*.

pinch *vt* a ciupi, a pișca; *(shoe)* a strânge; *(need, etc)* a chinui; *fig (cold)* a pișca; *coll* a fura; a aresta || *vi* a strânge; a fi avar || *s* ciupitură *f*; necaz *n*; chin *n*; clește *m*; pic *n*; **in a ~** *adv* la ananghie, strâmtorat.

pine¹ *s bot* pin *m*; conifer *n*.

pine² *vi* a se ofili; a fi nemulțumit; a duce dorul; ~ **after** *vi* a tânji după; ~ **away** *vi* a tânji.

pineapple *s bot* ananas *n*.

ping *vi (bullet)* a șuiera; *(mosquito)* a bâzâi; *(timer)* a suna || *s* șuierat *n*; bâzâit *n*.

ping-pong *s sp* ping-pong *n*, tenis *n* de masă.

pinion *s tech* pinion *n*.

pink *s (culoare)* roz; *bot* garoafă *f* || *adj* trandafiriu, roz.

pinnacle *s archit* turn *n* cu vârf ascuțit; *fig* culme *f*, vârf *n*, punct *n* culminant, apogeu *n*.

pinpoint *vt (~ a cause, etc)* a defini, a pune degetul pe rană; *(~ a position)* a localiza; *mil* a repera/bombarda cu precizie; *fig* a stabili/fixa cu precizie.

pint *s* pintă *f*; halbă *f*.

pioneer *s also fig* pionier *m*; inițiator *m*; *mil* pionier *m* || *vi* a fi un pionier/deschizător de drumuri || *vt fig* a deschide drum/cale; *fig* a face muncă de pionierat.

pious *adj* cucernic, pios; religios; virtuos.

pip¹ *s (seed)* sâmbure *m*; *tech* vârf *n* de pompare; impuls *n* scurt.

pip² *s (signal)* vârf *n* de ecou; pip *n*.

pipe *s* țeavă *f*; conductă *f*; tub *n*; pipă *f*; fluier *n* || *vt* a cânta la fluier || *vi* a piui; a fluiera; a cânta; a plânge; ~ **down** *vi* a coborî tonul; *coll* a o lăsa mai moale; ~ **dream** *s* proiect *n* himeric; ~ **up** *vi* a se face auzit • ~**line** *s* conductă *f* de petrol, pipeline *n*.

piping *s (system)* canalizare *f*; *(sewing)* paspoal *n*; firet *n*; *(of birds)* ciripit *n* || *adj* ascuțit; țipător; ~ **hot** *adj* foarte fierbinte.

piquant *adj cul* picant, înțepător, condimentat, iute; *fig* picant, nostim, plăcut.

pique *s* pică *f*, ciudă *f*; supărare *f*, iritare *f*.

piracy *s* piraterie *f*.

pirate *s naut* pirat *m*, corsar *m*; *fig* plagiator *m*; *radio* ascultător *m* clandestin || *adj (illegally used)* pirat || *vt naut* a ataca, a prăda; *fig* a plagia; *(steal music, etc)* a pirata.

pirouette *s* piruetă *f* || *vi* a face piruete.

Pisces *s astrol* Pești *m pl*.

piss *vi vulg* a urina || *s vulg* urină *f*; urinat *n* • ~**ed** *adj vulg (angry)* mânios, enervat • ~**ed-off** *adj vulg* sătul, căruia i s-a făcut lehamite.

pistachio *s bot* fistic *n.*

pistil *s bot* pistil *n.*

pistol *s* pistol *n*, revolver *n* ‖ *vt* a trage cu pistolul în; a împuşca cu pistolul.

piston *s tech* piston *n*; poanson *n.*

pit[1] *s* groapă *f*; mină *f*; carieră *f*; arenă *f*; parter *n*; fosă *f* ‖ *vt* a îngropa.

pit[2] *s (of fruit)* sâmbure *m* ‖ *vt* (~ *fruit*) a scoate sâmburii din.

pitch[1] *s* înclinare *f*; pantă *f*; *naut, avia* tangaj *n*; *phys (sound)* înălţime *f*; nivel *n*; treaptă *f*; grad *n*; *(throw)* aruncare *f*, azvârlire *f*; *(tent)* ridicare *f*, înălţare *f*; *tech* diviziune *f*, divizare *f* ‖ *vt* (~ *tent*) a ridica, a înălţa; (~ *camp*) a instala; *mus* a acorda; *sp* (~ *a ball*) a servi; *(throw)* a lansa; *(price)* a fixa; *(speech)* a adapta ‖ *vi* a cădea; a se instala, a se stabili; (~ *a ball, etc*) a sări în sus; *naut, avia* a avea tangaj; a ridica cortul; a instala tabăra.

pitch[2] *s* smoală *f*; gudron *n*; catran *n.*

pitcher *s* ulcior *n.*

piteous *adj* jalnic.

pitfall *s* capcană *f*; *fig* capcană *f*, cursă *f.*

pith *s bot, anat* măduvă *f*; *fig* esenţă *f*, miez *n*; importanţă *f*; *fig* putere *f*, energie *f.*

pitiable *adj (wretched)* jalnic, de plâns; *(pitiful)* demn de dispreţ.

pitiful *adj* milos; *(situation)* vrednic de milă; *(excuse, etc)* lamentabil.

pitiless *adj* fără milă, nemilos.

piton *s* piton *m.*

pittance *s* salariu *n* derizoriu/de mizerie.

pituitary *adj anat (gland)* glandă *f* pituitară.

pity *s* milă *f*; păcat *n*; regret *n* ‖ *vt* a-i fi milă de.

pivot *s tech* pivot *n*; ax *n*; *fig* punct *n* central, centru *n* ‖ *vt/vi tech* a pivota.

placard *s* placardă *f*, pancartă *f*; afiş *n* ‖ *vt* a pune afişe/ placarde/pancarte pe/în.

placate *vt (soothe)* a împăca, *(pacify)* a pacifica.

place *s* loc *n*; poziţie *f*; situaţie *f*; adăpost *n*; rang *n*; spaţiu *n* ‖ *vt* a pune; a numi; a plasa; a situa; a fixa; **all over the** ~ *adv* peste tot; **in** ~ *adv* la locul său, *(set)* stabilit; **in** ~ **of** *prep* în locul lui, în loc de; **out of** ~ *adv fig* deplasat.

placenta *s anat, bot* placentă *f.*

placid *adj* paşnic, calm, liniştit.

placing *s* plasare *f.*

plagiarize *vt* a plagia.

plague *s med* ciumă *f*; *fig* molimă *f*; pedeapsă *f*, pacoste *f* ‖ *vt* a îmbolnăvi de ciumă; *fig* a chinui; a supăra; a plictisi.

plaice *s icht* cambulă *f.*

plaid *s text* pled *n*, tartan *n.*

plain *adj* limpede, evident; citeţ; uni; simplu; sincer; cinstit; urât; ordinar ‖ *s geog* şes *n*, câmpie *f* ‖ *adv* limpede, clar.

plaintiff *s jur* reclamant *n.*

plaintive *adj* plângător, jalnic; tânguios.

plait *s (hair)* cosiţă *f*; *(dress)* pliu *n*, fald *n* ‖ *vt* a împleti; a plia, a îndoi.

plan *s* plan *n*; proiect *n*; schemă *f*; intenţie *f* ‖ *vt* a plănui; a proiecta.

plane[1] *adj* plan, neted; întins ‖ *s* şes *n*; platou *n*; plan *n*; *avia* avion *n*; *fig* bază *f*; nivel *n*; *tech* rindea *f* ‖ *vt* a rindelui, a da la rindea; a netezi; a şlefui.

plane[2] *s bot* platan *m.*

planet *s* planetă *f.*

plank *s* scândură *f.*

plankton *s bio* plancton *n.*

plant *s bot* plantă *f*; uzină *f*, fabrică *f*; agregat *n*; capcană *f*; truc *n*; spion *m* ‖ *vt* a planta; (~ *a bomb*) a pune; *fig* (~ *ideas*) a sădi; a propaga; *(establish a colony, etc)* a fonda; (~ *a flag, posts, etc*) a posta; *fig* a vârî, a băga (pe ascuns).

plaque *s* placă *f* (comemorativă); *med* placă *f* dentară.

plasma *s bio* plasmă *f*; *miner* heliotrop *n.*

plaster *s* mortar *n*; ipsos *n* ‖ *vt* a tencui; a ghipsa.

plastic *adj* plastic; elastic; de pictură/sculptură; supus; sugestiv; artificial ‖ *s* material *n* plastic; ~ **surgery** *s* chirurgie *f* plastică.

plasticity *s* plasticitate *f*, maleabilitate *f.*

plate *s* farfurie *f*; *(course)* fel *n* de mâncare; mâncare *f*; *metal* tablă *f*; *phot* placă *f*; *typ* gravură *f*, stampă *f*; *(books)* planşă *f*; ilustraţie *f*; *med* proteză *f* dentară ‖ *vt* a placa; a sulfa; *(metal)* a arginta, a auri, etc; *(paper)* a satina.

plateau *s geog* platou *n*, podiş *n.*

platform *s rail* peron *n*; rampă *f*; *constr* podium *n*, estradă *f*; platformă *f*; planşeu *n*; tribună *f*; *pol* poziţie *f*, platformă *f.*

platinum *s metal* platină *f.*

platitude *s* platitudine *f*, loc *n* comun.

platonic *adj* platonic; spiritual; idealist.

platoon *s mil* pluton *n.*

platter *s (for serving)* platou *n.*

plaudits *s pl frml (applause)* aplauze *f pl*; *(praise)* elogii *n pl.*

plausible *adj* plauzibil.

play *s* joc *n*; piesă *f*; glumă *f*; purtare *f*; acţiune *f*; libertate *f* ‖ *vt thea* a interpreta; a juca; *fig* a juca rolul de; *mus* a cânta, a interpreta, a executa; *sp* a juca cu; *(joke)* a face (o glumă), a juca (o festă) ‖ *vi* a se juca; a se distra, a se amuza; *thea* a interpreta, a juca; *mus* a cânta, a interpreta; *cin (movie)* a rula, a se juca; *tech* a avea joc; ~ **down** *vt* a minimaliza; ~ **upon** *vi (feelings)* a se juca cu (sentimentele cuiva), a specula.

play-back *s tele* reproducere *f*, redare *f.*

playboy *s* vânturã-ţară *m*, playboy *m*; om *m* de viaţă.

player *s* jucător *m*; *thea* actor *m.*

playful *adj (person)* jucăuş; vesel; glumeţ; neastâmpărat; *(dog, etc)* jucăuş.

playground *s* teren *n* de joc.

play-group *s* grădiniţă *f* de copii.

playing card *s* carte *f* de joc.

playing field *s* teren *n* de sport.

playmate *s* tovarăş *m* de joacă, camarad *m.*

play-off *s sp* joc *n* decisiv, meci *n* de baraj.

play-pen *s (for a child)* ţarc *n.*

plaything *s also fig* jucărie *f*; fleac *n*, nimic *n.*

playtime *s* recreaţie *f.*

playwright *s* dramaturg *m.*

plea *s* pretext *n*, scuză *f*; pledoarie *f*; dovadă *f*; *(for help)* apel *n*; *(for pity)* rugăminte *f*; cerere *f*; *jur* protest *n*; excepţie *f*; ~ **bargaining** *s jur* posibilitatea *f* unui inculpat de a primi o pedeapsă mai uşoară dacă se declară vinovat.

plead *vi jur* **(for/against)** a pleda; *fig* a pleda, a stărui, a insista ‖ *vt jur* a invoca; a pleda pentru; a aduce ca argument/justificare.

pleasant *adj* plăcut, simpatic; atrăgător; vesel.

please *vt* a mulţumi ‖ *vi* a vrea; a plăcea; a binevoi • **~d**

adj (with) mulțumit, satisfăcut (de); bucuros, încântat (de).

pleasing adj plăcut, agreabil; atrăgător.

pleasure s plăcere f; distracție f; veselie f.

pleat s pliu n || vt a plisa.

plebeian s/adj plebeu m.

plectrum s mus plectru n.

pledge s garanție f; obligație f; promisiune f; dar n; toast n || vt a promite.

plenary adj (meeting) plenar, lărgit; (power) deplin || s (meeting) plenară f.

plenitude s lit abundență f, bogăție f, belșug n.

plenteous adj lit îmbelșugat, abundent.

plentiful adj abundent; copios; roditor, rodnic.

plenty s belșug n, abundență f; prisos n; bogăție f, mulțime f || adv foarte, cu totul.

plethora s exces n, supraabundență f.

pleurisy s med pleurezie f; pleurită f.

pliable adj (material) pliabil, flexibil; fig (person) maleabil, flexibil; docil.

pliant adj * pliable.

pliers s pl clește m (patent); pensă f.

plight s condiție/stare f proastă.

plinth s constr plintă f; pervaz n; tech soclu n de coloană.

plod vi a merge/înainta cu greutate; (toil) a munci din greu, a trudi || s mers n greoi; corvoadă f, muncă f grea.

plodder s om m de corvoadă/care muncește din greu; om m flegmatic/plictisitor.

plonk vt coll (put down) a trânti cu zgomot.

plop s cădere f în apă; zgomot n al căderii în apă || vi a cădea în apă || interj pleosc!, bâldâbâc!.

plot[1] s conspirație f; complot n; liter intrigă f; subiect n || vt a complota; a urzi, a inventa; (~ a map) a însemna, a stabili; math a trasa, a marca || vi a complota.

plot[2] s (land) parcelă f de pământ, petec n de pământ; teren n; (chart) plan n; schiță f; grafic n; diagramă f || vt (land) a diviza/împărți în parcele; tech a reprezenta grafic; a proiecta; a schița.

plow s plug n || vt a ara; a brăzda; a-și croi drum; scol a trânti la examen || vi a ara; **to ~ into** vi (~ a car) a da peste, a se ciocni.

ploy s (trick) tertip n, stratagemă f.

pluck s tragere f; apucare f; smulgere f; efort n; fig curaj n; îndrăzneală f || vt a trage; a smulge; (~ a flower, etc) a culege; (~ a chicken) a jumuli; mus (~ the strings) a ciupi.

plug s tampon n; dop n; pană f; med plombă f; elec priză f; fișă f; aut bujie f || vt (~ a hole) a astupa; a vârî o pană în; (~ a book, movie) a face publicitate pentru; **to ~ in** vt a conecta.

plum s bot (tree) prun m; (fruit) prună f; stafidă f; delicatesă f.

plumage s pene f pl, penaj n.

plumb s (greutate de) plumb n; fir n cu plumb || vt metal etc a plumbui; naut a sonda; fig a sonda; a înțelege; a descoperi || adv fig vertical; fig exact, tocmai.

plumber s instalator m; sudor m.

plume s pană f; (riding) panaș n; (smoke) dâră f (de fum).

plummet s fir n cu plumb; fig povară f || vi (plane, bird) a plonja; fig a cădea.

plump[1] adj durduliu; bucălat || vt a îngrășa; a umfla; a umple || vi a se îngrășa.

plump[2] adj (refusal, etc) net, categoric; direct || adv net, categoric; direct; brusc || s cădere f (cu zgomot); bufnitură f || vi a cădea brusc/cu zgomot.

plunder vt a prăda, a jefui || s (theft) jaf n; jefuire f; prădare f; deposedare f; (stolen items) pradă f.

plunge s plonjare f; plonjon n; afundare f; fig (fall) cădere f || vi a plonja; fig (diminish) a cădea.

plunk s coll (thud) zgomot n sec; coll (slap) scatoalcă f || vt coll (put down) a trânti; (strum) a zdrăngăni.

pluperfect s gram (tense) mai mult ca perfectul n.

plural adj gram plural; multiplu; gram plural || s gram (număr) plural n; cuvânt n la plural.

plus s math plus n; surplus n; excedent n; prisos n; avantaj n; coll (bonus) atu n, plus n; prep math plus, și cu || adj plus; pozitiv.

plush s text pluș n.

plutonium s chem plutoniu n.

ply[1] s text cută f; fald n; îndoitură f; (wood) strat n; fig înclinație f, atracție f || vt a îndoi, a plia; a împături.

ply[2] vt (tool) a lucra/munci cu (un instrument etc); a fi ocupat/a se îndeletnici cu; naut (ship) a efectua, a face (o cursă); a traversa canalul (dus-întors) || vi (at) a munci, a trudi (la); naut (between) a face naveta (între); a face curse regulate (între).

pneumatic adj pneumatic.

pneumonia s med pneumonie f.

poach[1] vt a acapara; a râma, a scormoni; (crush) a călca, a strivi; (trespass) a încălca; a pescui/vâna fără permis; fig (ideas) a împrumuta, a prelua || vi a se împotmoli, a intra în noroi; a face braconaj.

poach[2] vt cul (~ eggs) a face ochiuri.

pocket s buzunar n; sac n; pungă f; gol n de aer || vt a băga în buzunar; **~ battery** s elec baterie f de buzunar; **~ money** s bani m pl de buzunar • **~book** s carnet n; portvizit n; carte f de buzunar • **~ful** s un buzunar n (plin) • **~knife** s briceag n • **~size** s format n mic; format n de buzunar || adj format de buzunar.

pockmark s urmă f de vărsat

pod s păstaie f; sac n; cocon m || vt a dezghioca.

podiatrist s pedichiurist(ă) m/f.

podium s podium n; relig strană f.

poem s poezie f, poem n.

poet s poet m • **~ry** s poezie f; expresivitate f.

poignant adj fig amar; aspru; usturător; acut; fig (remark, etc) ascuțit; fin; subtil; fig (interest) viu.

point s typ, etc punct n; (edge) ascuțiș n; tăiș n; rail ac n, macaz n; (time) stadiu n, moment n; (detail) chestiune f, detaliu n; (essence) esență f; (viewpoint) punct n de vedere; (degree) grad n; nivel n; geog pisc n, vârf n de munte; (result) rezultat n || vt (sharpen) a ascuți; (direct) a indica; a puncta • **~ed** adj ascuțit; fig (remark) incisiv, tăios; archit (style) gotic • **~er** s (needle) ac n indicator; (sign) semn n, dovadă f; (hint) indicație f, indiciu n, pont n; (dog) prepelicar m • **~less** adj fără sens; inoportun.

poise s echilibru n; calm n; siguranță f; fig ezitare f; postură f; ținută f || vt a echilibra.

poison s otravă f; venin n || vt a otrăvi; med a infecta; fig a învenina; a otrăvi.

poke s ghiont n, împingere f || vt a împinge; a da un ghiont; (~ a fire) a scormoni; a vârî, a băga (~ un ghiont; (~ a fire) a scormoni; a vârî, a băga || vi a căuta, a cerceta.

poker s (game) pocher n; (for a fire) vătrai m; **~ face** s față/expresie f imobilă.

poky adj coll (slow) mocăit, lent.

Poland s Polonia.

polar *adj* polar; ~ **bear** *s* urs *m* polar.

polarization *s elec, etc* polarizare *f.*

polarity *s* polaritate *f;* (*split*) divergență *f.*

pole[1] *s* stâlp *m;* par *m;* țăruș *m;* jalon *n;* oiște *f; naut* vârf *n* de catarg.

pole[2] *s elec, geog* pol *m.*

Pole[3] *s* (*from Poland*) polonez(ă) *m, f*

poleax *vt* (*knock down*) a doborî la pământ.

police *s* poliție *f* ‖ *vt* a păzi ordinea; ~ **officer** *s* polițist *m;* ~ **record** *s* cazier *n* judiciar • ~**man** *s* polițist *m.*

policy *s* politică *f,* tactică *f,* metodă *f;* dibăcie *f;* diplomație *f;* înțelepciune *f.*

polio *s med* poliomielită *f.*

Polish[1] *adj* polon(ez) ‖ *s* (limba) poloneză *f.*

polish[2] *vt* a lustrui; a șlefui; a da cu ceară; a poliza; a cizela; a finisa ‖ *vi* a se lustrui/șlefui ‖ *s* lustru *n;* lac *n;* cremă *f* de ghete; cizelare *f;* eleganță *f;* rafinament *n.*

polite *adj* politicos; amabil; distins; rafinat.

political *adj* politic; statal; de conducere • ~**ly correct** *adj* nediscriminator, corect politic.

politician *s* politician *m.*

politicking *s pej* politicianism *n.*

politics *s* știința *f* politică; politică *f.*

poll *s* vot *n,* scrutin *n;* alegeri *f pl,* votare *f;* centru *n* de votare; sondare *f* a opiniei publice ‖ *vt* a efectua alegeri în; a sonda (opinia publică); (*votes*) a obține ‖ *vi* a vota.

pollen *s bot* polen *n* ‖ *vt* a poleniza.

pollinate *vt* a poleniza.

pollute *vt* a polua; *fig* a murdări; a terfeli; a profana.

pollution *s* poluare *f;* poluție *f.*

polo *s sp* polo *n;* polo *n* pe apă.

polyester *s text* poliester *n.*

polygamy *s* poligamie *f.*

polygon *s geom* poligon *n.*

polygraph *s* poligraf *n;* detector *m* de minciuni.

polystyrene *s chem* polistiren *n.*

polytechnic *adj* politehnic; ~ **school** *s* școală *f* politehnică, institut *n* politehnic.

polythene *s chem* polietilenă *f.*

pomegranate *s* (*fruit*) rodie *f;* (*tree*) rodiu *m.*

pomp *s* pompă *f,* fast *n;* strălucire *f.*

pompous *adj* (*self-important*) plin de sine; (*showy*) infatuat; îngâmfat

pond *s* eleșteu *n;* iaz *n;* bazin *n.*

ponder *vt* a cugeta la, a cumpăni, a cântări ‖ *vi* (**on/ upon/over**) a cugeta, a se gândi, a medita (la, asupra).

pontoon *s naut* ponton *n; constr* cheson *n.*

pony *s* ponei *m,* căluț *m* ‖ *adj* mic, mititel; *tech* ajutător, auxiliar.

poodle *s zool* caniș *m,* pudel *m.*

pooh *interj* (*disgust*) ptiu!; (*distrust*) bah!, ei ași!, da' de unde!.

pool[1] *s* iaz *n;* baltă *f;* bazin *n;* piscină *f; min* puț *n* de cercetare; bulboană *f.*

pool[2] *s econ* cartel *n;* (*money*) fond *n* comun; *sp* totalizator *n* ‖ *vt* (*benefits*) a împărți în comun; (*experience*) a face schimb de; *fig* a unifica, a coordona.

poop *s naut* pupă *f* • ~**ed** (**out**) *coll* istovit.

poor *adj* sărac; biet; nenorocit; sterp; șubred; prost; insuficient; redus • ~**ly** *adj* indispus ‖ *adv* prost, rău; sărăcăcios; fără succes.

pop[1] *s coll* tătic *m;* nene *m.*

pop[2] *vt* a pocni; a plesni; a trosni; (*quickly*) a băga, a vârî; (*gun*) a descărca; (*ask a question*) a pune pe

neașteptate ‖ *vi* a pocni; a plesni; a trosni; a detuna; (*quickly*) a ieși/intra/pleca etc repede; (*eyes* ~) a se holba; a ieși din orbite; (*balloons* ~) a plesni, a pocni; (*cork* ~*s*) a sări ‖ *s* pocnet *n;* trosnet *n;* detunătură *f;* (~ *music*) muzică *f* pop; (*soda*) băutură *f* gazoasă ‖ *interj* poc!, trosc!, pac!.

popcorn *s* floricele *f pl* de porumb.

pope *s* papă *m;* preot *m.*

poplar *s bot* plop *m.*

poplin *s text* poplin *n.*

poppy *s bot* mac *m;* opiu *n.*

populace *s frml* populație *f,* popor *n.*

popular *adj* popular; folcloric; ieftin; de succes; (*opinion*) curent; (*person*) simpatizat; (*name, etc*) la modă.

populate *vt* a popula.

population *s* populare *f;* populație *f;* locuitori *m pl.*

porcelain *s* porțelan *n.*

porch *s* verandă *f;* tindă *f;* portic *n;* (*church*) portal *n.*

porcupine *s zool* porc *m* spinos.

pore[1] *s anat* por *m.*

pore[2] *vi* (**over**) a cerceta/studia cu atenție, a fi cufundat în, a fi absorbit de.

pork *s* (carne *f* de) porc; *pol coll* beneficii *n pl* acordate de guvern pentru considerente politice.

pornography *s* pornografie *f.*

porous *adj* poros, cu pori.

porpoise *s icht* delfin *m.*

porridge *s* porridge *n;* terci *n* de ovăz/porumb, fulgi *m pl* de ovăz/porumb.

port[1] *s* port *n;* liman *n;* refugiu *n;* hangar *n.*

port[2] *s naut* babord *n* ‖ *adv* la babord, la/spre stânga; *comp* acces *n,* intrare *f.*

port[3] *s* (**wine**) (vin de) porto *n.*

portable *adj* portabil; portativ.

portend *vt frml, lit* a prevesti.

portent *s frml* prevestire *f* • ~**ous** *adj lit* (*ominous*) prevestitor; sinistru; (*significant*) minunat, extraordinar; (*serious*) grav, solemn; (*pompous*) infatuat.

porter *s* portar *m,* ușier *m;* hamal *m;* însoțitor *m; tech* grindă *f* de rezistență.

portfolio *s* servietă *f;* mapă *f;* (*file*) portofoliu *n; fin* (*stock, etc*) portofoliu *n.*

porthole *s* hublou *n.*

portion *s* parte *f;* cotă-parte *f;* zestre *f; fig* soartă *f;* (*food*) porție *f;* fragment *n* ‖ *vt* a împărți, a diviza; a distribui; (*dowry*) a da ca zestre.

portly *adj* corpolent.

portmanteau *s* valiză *f* mare; ~ **word** *s* cuvânt *n* telescopat.

portrait *s* portret *n;* poză *f;* imagine *f.*

portray *vt* a picta; a reprezenta; *fig* a zugrăvi; a descrie; *thea, cin* a juca, a interpreta rolul de.

Portugal *s* Portugalia *f.*

Portuguese *s/adj* portughez *m;* (*language*) portugheză *f;* **the** ~ *s pl* portughezii *m pl.*

pose *s phot* poză *f,* atitudine *f; fig* poză *f;* afectare *f;* manierism *n* ‖ *vt phot* a aranja; (~ *a question, etc*) a pune; (~ *a problem*) a ridica; a formula ‖ *vi phot, etc* a poza; *fig* a lua o atitudine afectată, a poza; a se da drept, a se preface.

posh *adj* (*classy*) șic; (*superior*) distins.

position *s* poziție *f;* postură *f;* atitudine *f;* post *n* ‖ *vt* a așeza; a plasa; a instala; a poziționa.

positive *adj* real, pozitiv; valoros; (*definite*) precis, clar;

(*emphatic*) ferm; (~ *person*) sigur, convins; (*sincere*) veritabil; (*proof*) convingător, incontestabil; *phil* empiric; *coll* perfect, absolut, deplin, desăvârşit.

posse *s* poteră *f*.

possess *vt* a poseda, a avea; a stăpâni; a cunoaşte bine ‖ *vr* a se stăpâni • **~ion** *s* posesie *f*; avere *f*; autocontrol *n*.

possibility *s* (*chance*) posibilitate *f*; (*prospect*) oportunitate *f*; *pl* perspective *f pl*.

possible *adj* posibil; acceptabil; admisibil.

possibly *adv* posibil, probabil.

post[1] *s* stâlp *m*; par *m*; pilon *m*; ţăruş *m* ‖ *vt* a afişa; a lipi; a posta; a amplasa.

post[2] *s mil* post *n*, poziţie *f*; fort *n*; funcţie *f*; serviciu *n*; *mil* garnizoană *f*; *econ* curs *n* ‖ *vt mil* a numi.

post[3] *s* poştă *f*; (*mail*) poştă *f*, corespondenţă *f* ‖ *vt* a expedia prin poştă; *coll* a informa, a înştiinţa; ~ **office** *s* oficiu *n* poştal • **~age** *s* tarif *n* poştal; timbre *n pl* • **~card** *s* carte *f* poştală; ilustrată *f*.

poster *s* afiş *n*; placardă *f*; afişor *n*.

posterior *adj* posterior; *anat* posterior, dorsal ‖ *s* posterior *n*, şezut *n*.

posterity *s* posteritate *f*.

postgraduate *adj* postuniversitar ‖ *s* doctorand *m*.

post-haste *adv lit* în mare grabă.

posthumous *adj* postum.

postman *s* poştaş *m*, factor *m* poştal.

post-mortem *adj* post mortem, de după moarte ‖ *s med* autopsie *f*.

postpone *vt* a lăsa pentru mai târziu; a amâna.

postscript *s* postscriptum *n*; *fig* supliment *n*, addenda *f*.

postulate *vt* a postula; a accepta fără dovezi; a pretinde, a reclama ‖ *s* postulat *n*; condiţie *f* prealabilă.

posture *s* postură *f*, ţinută *f*, poziţie *f*; *fig* stare *f*, situaţie *f*.

postwar *adj* postbelic, de după război.

posy *s* bucheţel *n* de flori.

pot *s* vas *n*; oală *f*; cană *f*; borcan *n*; găleată *f*; ulcior *n*; duşcă *f* ‖ *vt* a conserva; a fierbe; a pune în oală.

potable *adj* potabil.

potassium *s chem* potasiu *m*.

potato *s bot* cartof *m*.

potency *s* potenţă *f*.

potent *adj* puternic, tare; (*man*) viril, viguros; (*argument*) puternic, convingător; (*drink*) tare, ameţitor.

potential *adj* potenţial, posibil; *elec*, *phys* potenţial; latent, nedezvoltat ‖ *s elec*, *phys* potenţial *n*; posibilitate *f*.

pot-hole *s* (*road*) groapă *f*, hop *n*.

potshot *s* împuşcătură *f* de aproape, împuşcătură *f* la întâmplare; *fig* atac *n* mişelesc.

potion *s* poţiune *f*.

potter *s* olar *m* • **~y** *s* olărie *f*, ceramică *f*; (*shop*) (atelier de) olărie *f*.

pouch *s* traistă *f*; desagă *f*, sac *m*; săculeţ *n*; (*eyes*) pungă *f*; *mil* cartuşieră *f* ‖ *vt* a pune/vârî în sac etc; *fig* a vârî în pungă/buzunar, a –şi însuşi.

poultice *s* cataplasmă *f*, prişniţă *f*.

poultry *s* orătănii *f pl*, păsări *f pl* de curte.

pounce *s* (*bird*) gheară *f*; salt/atac *n* brusc/neaşteptat ‖ *vt* a prinde în gheare; (*bird of prey*) a se năpusti asupra.

pound[1] *vt* (*grind*) a pisa; (*hit*) a bate, a lovi; a zdrobi, a sfărâma; (*ground*) a bătători ‖ *vi* (*heart* ~s) a bate puternic; (~ *a drum*, *etc*) a bate; (*stomp*) a tropăi ‖ *s* lovitură *f* puternică; izbitură *f*.

pound[2] *s* (*weight*) livră *f*, funt *m*, pound *m*; (*British money*) liră *f* (sterlină).

pour *vt* a turna; a vărsa ‖ *vi* a curge; a ploua cu găleata; *fig* a se revărsa.

pout *vi* a se îmbufna, a se bosumfla ‖ *s* îmbufnare *f*, bosumflare *f*; supărare *f*.

poverty *s* sărăcie *f*; lipsă *f*; absenţă *f*.

powder *s* praf *n*; pudră *f*; (*face* ~) pudră *f*; (*gun* ~) pulbere *f*, praf *n* de puşcă ‖ *vt* (~ *your face*) a pudra; *tech* a pulveriza, a pudra; *cul* a săra, a pudra ‖ *vi* a se pudra.

power *s* putere *f*, forţă *f*; tărie *f*; (*ability*) capacitate *f*; posibilitate *f*; *phys*, *tech* putere *f*, energie *f*; randament *n*; (*impact*) tărie *f*, violenţă *f*; *pol* autoritate *f*; control *n*; guvernare *f*; (*state*) stat *n*; (*mandate*) împuternicire *f*, mandat *n*; *math* putere *f*; grad *n*; *opt* putere *f* măritoare; ~ **station** *s* centrală *f* electrică; ~ **steering** *s aut* direcţie *f* asistată • **~ful** *adj* tare, puternic; viguros; influent; intens; elocvent; eficace • **~-operated** *adj tech* (acţionat) mecanic.

pox *s med* variolă *f*.

practicable *adj* practicabil; accesibil; aplicabil; realizabil; (*usable*) carosabil.

practical *adj* practic; concret; aplicabil; util; realist; comod; economicos; (*plan*, *etc*) realizabil ‖ *s* lucrare *f* practică.

practice *s* practică *f*; aplicare *f*; obicei *n*; rutină *f*; metodă *f*; *sp* antrenament *n*; şedinţă *f* de antrenament; *mus*, *etc* exersare *f*, repetare *f*; *mus*, *etc* repetiţie *f*; (*profession*) exercitare *f*; (*doctor's* ~) cabinet *n*; (~ *of law*) birou *n* ‖ *vt/vi* a practica; a folosi; a profesa; a exersa; a se antrena.

practitioner *s* practician *m*; specialist *m*.

pragmatic *adj* pragmatic; activ, energic; practic ‖ *s phil* pragmatist *m*.

Prague *s* Praga *f*.

prairie *s* preerie *f*.

praise *vt* a lăuda; a glorifica ‖ *s* laudă *f*; slavă *f* • **~worthy** *adj* lăudabil, vrednic de laudă.

prance *vi* (*horse*) a cabra, a se ridica pe picioarele dinapoi; *fig* a face pe grozavul, a se fuduli ‖ *vt* (*horse*) a juca ‖ *s fig* înfumurare *f*.

prank *s* festă *f*; renghi *m*; poznă *f*.

prattle *vi* (*child*) a gânguri; (*stream*, *etc*) a murmura, a susura ‖ *s* gângurit *n*; murmur *n*, susur *n*.

prawn *s icht* crevetă *f* (roz).

pray *vi* a se ruga • **~er** *s* rugăciune *f*; rugăminte *f*; cerere *f*; **~er book** *s* carte *f* de rugăciuni.

preach *vi* a predica; a ţine o lecţie de morală.

preamble *s* preambul *n*, introducere *f*.

precarious *adj* precar, greu; nesigur; riscat; accidental; nefondat.

precaution *s* precauţiune *f*, prevedere *f*.

precede *vt* a preceda; a întrece; a prefaţa ‖ *vi* a precede.

precedence *s* prioritate *f*; anterioritate *f*; întâietate *f*.

precept *s* precept *n*.

precinct *s* margine *f*, limită *f*, hotar *n*; *adm* circumscripţie *f*; *pl* incintă *f*; *fig pl* margini *f pl*, limite *f pl*; **police** ~ circă *f* de poliţie.

precious *adj* preţios; scump; drag; *coll iro* grozav; perfect; (*style*) afectat ‖ *adv coll* grozav de ‖ *s* comoară *f*, iubit *m*.

precipice *s* prăpastie *f*, abis *n*.

precipitate *vt* a precipita, a azvârli; (~ *a crisis*) a accelera, a grăbi; *chem* a precipita ‖ *vi chem* a se precipita; a se depune; *met* a se condensa ‖ *s chem* precipitat *n*; sediment *n*.

precipitation *s met* precipitații *f pl*; (*haste*) grabă *f*; *chem* precipitat *n*.

precipitous *adj* prăpăstios; (*steep*) vertiginous: (*hasty*) pripit.

précis *s* scurtă expunere *f*; conspect *n*; rezumat *n*.

precise *adj* precis, exact; întocmai; corect; fidel; clar; (*minute*) migălos; pedant.

precision *s* precizie *f*, exactitate *f*; fidelitate *f*; claritate *f*.

preclude *vi* a face imposibil; a împiedica; (*interpretation, etc*) a înlătura, a preîntâmpina; (*~ a possibility*) a exclude.

precocious *adj* precoce; prematur.

preconceived *adj* preconceput.

precursor *s* precursor *m*.

predator *s* (*animal, bird*) răpitor *m*, animal *n* de pradă, pasăre *f* de pradă; *coll* (*person*) acaparator *m*, jefuitor *m* • **~y** *adj* (*animal, bird*) de pradă, răpitor; (*person*) jefuitor; acaparator.

predecessor *s* (*person*) predecesor *m*; (*thing*) precedent, anterior.

predestine *vt relig* a predestina, a hotărî dinainte.

predicament *s* situație *f* dificilă/grea; situație *f* neplăcută.

predicate *s gram* predicat *n*.

predict *vt* a prezice; a prevesti; a prevedea • **~able** *adj* previzibil.

predilection *s* predilecție *f*, preferință *f*.

predisposition *s* predispoziție *f*.

predominant *adj* predominant, preponderent • **~ly** *adv* (în mod) predominant, în special.

predominate *vi* a predomina, a avea superioritatea ‖ *vt* a predomina; a întrece.

pre-eminent *adj* proeminent, strălucit, excelent, extraordinar.

preempt *vt jur* a achiziționa prin preempțiune; (*~ an action, decision*) a devansa, a preveni • **~ive** *adj* preventiv • **~ive strike** *s* atac *n* preventiv, lovitură *f* preventivă.

preen *vt* (*bird*) a ciuguli/curăța cu pliscul (penele); *fig* (*person*) a se găti, a se dichisi.

prefab *s sl* prefabricat *n*; casă *f* din prefabricate.

prefabricate *vt* a prefabrica.

preface *s* prefață *f* ‖ *vt* (*~ a book*) a prefața.

prefatory *adj* prefațator; introductiv.

prefect *s scol* monitor *m*; prefect *m*.

prefer *vt* (**to**) a prefera; (*promote*) a avansa, a promova; (*request*) a formula.

preferable *adj* preferabil; mai bun decât.

preferably *adv* preferabil, de preferință, mai bine.

preference *s* preferință *f*; alegere *f*; prioritate *f*; *econ, jur* regim *n* preferențial.

prefix *s gram* prefix *n*.

pregnant *adj* (*woman*) gravidă, însărcinată; (*animal*) gestant; cu pui; *fig* prolific; inventiv; bogat; *fig* pregnant.

prehistoric *adj* preistoric.

prejudice *s* (*damage*) prejudiciu *n*; (*opinion*) prejudecată *f* ‖ *vt* a prejudicia; a dăuna; (*favor*) a înclina, a predispune • **~d** *adj* (*person*) care are prejudecăți; (*opinion*) preconceput.

prejudicial *adj* (**to**) prejudiciabil (pentru); păgubitor (pentru).

preliminary *adj* preliminar.

prelude *s mus* preludiu *n*, uvertură *f*; *fig* preludiu *n*; prolog *n*; introducere *f*.

premarital *adj* dinainte de căsătorie, premarital.

premature *adj* prematur; înainte de vreme; negândit, nechibzuit.

premeditate *vt* a premedita, a pune la cale, a plănui • **~d** *adj* (*crime, etc*) premeditat.

premier *adj* prim, principal; primordial ‖ *s* premier *m*, prim ministru *m*.

premiere *s thea* premieră *f*.

premise *s* premisă *f*; punct *n* de plecare; *pl* clădire/clădiri *f pl* cu acareturi; **on the ~s** pe loc, la fața locului.

premium *s* premiu *n*; primă *f*; recompensă *f*; *econ* primă *f* de asigurare; *econ* premiu *n* de producție; **at a ~** foarte scump, cu mare căutare, foarte solicitat.

premonition *s* prevenire *f*, avertisment *n*; premoniție *f*; presentiment *n*.

preoccupation *s* preocupare *f*.

preoccupied *adj* (**with**) preocupat, absorbit (de); (*land, etc*) ocupat mai înainte.

preoccupy *vt* (*obsess*) a preocupa.

prepaid *adj* plătit cu anticipație; (*letter*) francat.

preparation *s* pregătire *f*; preparare *f*; *scol* pregătire *f*; (*cosmetics, etc*) preparat *n*; *mus* preludiu *n*; uvertură *f*; *tech* prelucrare *f*, pregătire *f*; *pharm* medicament *n*, remediu *m*.

prepare *vt* (*study*) a studia; a pregăti; (*cook*) a găti; (*~ for an expedition*) a echipa; *typ* a redacta; *tech* a executa, a face, a fabrica ‖ *vi* (**for**) a se pregăti, a se instrui (pentru); (**to**) a se pregăti să; a fi gata să.

preponderance *s* preponderență *f*.

preponderant *adj* preponderent.

preposition *s gram* prepoziție *f*.

prepossessing *adj* (*attractive*) agreabil, atrăgător.

preposterous *adj* (*absurd*) absurd, fără noimă, ilogic; (*ridiculous*) ridicol, rizibil.

prerequisite *adj* (**for/to**) cerut (de), necesar (pentru); constituind o condiție (pentru) ‖ *s* premisă *f* (obligatorie).

prerogative *s* prerogativă *f*; privilegiu *n* ‖ *adj* care se bucură de prerogative; privilegiat.

presage *vt* (*foretell*) a prevesti.

presbytery *s* presbiteriu *n*.

prescient *adj* anticipativ, profetic.

prescribe *vt* a prescrie; a recomanda ‖ *vi* a da rețete.

prescription *s* prescripție *f*; rețetă *f*; prescriere *f*; recomandare *f*.

presence *s* prezență *f*; existență *f*; companie *f*; aspect *n*; demnitate *f*; spirit *n*.

present *adj* prezent; actual / *s* actualitate *f*; prezent *n*; cadou *n* ‖ *vt* (*describe*) a prezenta; (*submit*) a înainta; (*apply*) a depune; *thea* a reprezenta, a juca; *mil* a prezenta (arma) ‖ *vr* a se ivi.

presentation *s* prezentare *f*; (*ceremony*) acordare *f* (de recompense/premii); (*speech*) expunere *f*; *thea, etc* reprezentație *f*.

preservative *s* conservant *n* ‖ *adj* conservant, care conservă; *tech* anticoagulant.

preserve *vt* a feri; a păstra; a conserva ‖ *vi* a face conserve ‖ *s pl* conserve *f pl*; rezervație *f*.

preside *vi* a fi în frunte; a prezida; a conduce.

president *s* președinte *m*; rector *m*; (*of a company*) director *m* general.

press *vt* a apăsa, a presa; (*iron*) a călca; (*~ juice from* *grapes, etc*) a stoarce; *tech* a imprima; a aplatiza; *fig* a asupri; *fig* (~ *for time*) a presa, a grăbi; *fig* a insista, a stărui; (*embrace*) a strânge; (*push*) a împinge, a înghesui; (*horse*) a îndemna || *vi* (~ *for time*) a presa; a apăsa, a fi apăsător; a răzbate; *tech* a se imprima; a se îmbulzi, a se înghesui || *s* apăsare *f*; presiune *f*; grabă *f*; **the** ~ ziarele *n pl* presa *f*, (*reporters*) jurnal-iști *m pl*; ~ **release** *s* comunicat *n* de presă.

pressing *adj* urgent.

pressure *s* apăsare *f*, presare *f*; asuprire *f*; forțare *f* || *vt* a exercita presiune.

pressurize *vt* (*coerce*) a constrânge, a sili; a presuriza.

prestige *s* prestigiu *n*; considerație *f*.

presumably *adv* probabil.

presume *vt* (*believe*) a crede, (*suppose*) a presupune; a admite; (*guess*) a bănui; (*assume*) a implica || *vi* a presupune; (*venture*) a fi prea îndrăzneț.

presumption *s* presupunere *f*, supoziție *f*; motiv *n*; *jur* prezumție *f*; (*impudence*) tupeu *n*, aroganță *f*.

presumptive *adj* presupus.

presumptuous *adj* (*conceited*) încrezut; (*bold*) îndrăzneț.

presuppose *vt* a presupune.

pretax *adj* (*profits*, *etc*) brut.

pretend *vt* a invoca, a pretexta; a simula; a susține.

pretense *s* pretext *n*, scuză *f*; cerere *f*.

pretentious *adj* pretențios.

pretext *s* pretext *n*, scuză *f* || *vt* a pretexta.

pretty *adj* drăguț, simpatic; afectat, prețios; *iro* grozav || *adv* destul de; cam.

prevail *vi* (**over**) a prevala; (*silence*) a domni; (*triumph*) a triumfa; (*exist*) a exista; a fi răspândit; ~ **on/upon smb** *vi* a convinge pe cineva (să facă ceva).

prevalent *adj* (*widespread*) larg răspândit; (*frequent*) frecvent; (*current*) actual.

prevaricate *vi frml* (*hedge*) a se eschiva; a recurge la subterfugii; a fi echivoc.

prevent *vt* (*avert*) a preîntâmpina, (*stop*) a împiedica || *vi* a interveni, a se întâmpla • ~**ive** *adj* preventiv; *med* profilactic; *tech* preventiv; prevenitor; *jur* preventiv || *s* măsură *f* preventivă; *med* mijloc *n* profilactic/preventiv.

preview *s* avanpremieră *f*.

previous *adj* anterior, prealabil, precedent.

prey *s* pradă *f*; jertfă *f* || *vi* a ieși să prade; *fig* (*fear*, *etc*) a chinui, a roade, a obseda.

price *s* preț *n*; (*cost*) cost *n*; (*value*) valoare *f*; *fin* curs *n*, cotă *f*; (*reward*) răsplată *f*; (*penalty*) jertfă *f* || *vt* a estima; a fixa prețul; **at a** ~ la un preț mare; ~ **index** *s* indice *m* al prețurilor • ~**less** *adj* valoros • ~**y** *adj* *coll* scump.

pricing *s* stabilire *f* a unui preț.

prick *s* (*needle*) înțepătură *f*, împunsătură *f*; (*pain*) durere *f* usturătoare; *bot* ghimpe *m*, spin *m*; țeapă *f*; *fig* chin *n*; (*conscience*) mustrare *f*; *vulg* penis *n*; *vulg* prost *m*, idiot *m* || *vt* (~ *with a needle*) a înțepa, a împunge (cu acul); a găuri, a face gaură; a sfredeli; *fig* a chinui.

prickle *s* *bot* ghimpe *m*, spin *m*; *zool* ac *n*, ghimpe *m* || *vt* a înțepa || *vi* (*tingle*) a ustura, a furnica.

pride *s* mândrie *f*; satisfacție *f*; orgoliu *n*, amor *n* pro-priu; *fig* fală *f*; *pej* îngâmfare *f*, trufie *f*; *fig* floare *f*, (perioadă de) înflorire *f*.

priest *s* preot *m*, cleric *m*.

prig *s* *pej* pedant *m*, formalist *m*; infatuat, îngâmfat,

încrezut, fudul • ~**gish** *adj* *pej* pedant, formalist; infatuat, îngâmfat, încrezut, fudul.

prim *adj* (*prudish*) sclivisit; formal; afectat; (*picky*) pretențios, mofturos.

primacy *s* primat *n*, prioritate *f*.

primarily *adv* (*mainly*) în primul rând, înainte de toate; (*originally*) inițial, la început.

primary *adj* (*basic*) primar, elementar; (*first*) primitiv; inițial; (*main*) primordial, principal || *s* lucru *n* prin-cipal; *opt* culoare *f* primară; *pol* întrunire *f* preelec-torală a votanților; ~ **school** *s* școală *f* primară.

primate *s* *zool* primate *f pl*; *relig* arhiepiscop *m*.

prime *s* înflorire *f*; *fig* cremă *f*; *math* număr *n* prim || *adj* prim; important; principal; esențial; excelent || *vt* a pregăti; *mil* a încărca; *min* a amorsa; *aut* a șprițui; (*art*) a grundui; *fig* a pregăti, a instrui, a informa în prealabil; ~ **rate** *s* taxă *f* de scont preferențial; ~ **time** *s* (*tv*) oră *f* de mare audiență.

primer[1] *s* *scol* abecedar *n*; îndrumar *n*, ghid *n*.

primer[2] *s* (*paint*) grund *n*.

primeval *adj* (*prehistoric*) primitiv, străvechi.

primitive *adj* primitiv; natural; simplu; barbar || *s* primitiv(ist) *m*.

primordial *adj* primordial.

primrose *s* *bot* ciuboțica *f* cucului, primulă *f*.

prince *s* domn(itor) *m*; principe *m*; prinț *m*; magnat *m*.

princess *s* prințesă *f*.

principal *adj* principal, esențial || *s* șef *m*; conducător *m*; patron *m*; *scol* rector *m*; decan *m*; *scol* director *m*; *econ* capital *n* (de bază); *mus* solist *m*; *thea* protago-nist *m*.

principle *s* lege *f*; principiu *n*; regulă *f*; concepție *f*; origine *f*.

print *vt* a tipări; a publica; a edita || *vi* a se tipări || *s* publicație *f*; *phot* copie *f*; imprimat *n*; *typ* literă *f* de tipar; *text* imprimeu *n*; gravură *f*; imprimare *f*; (*trace*) urmă *f*; amprentă *f* • ~**ed matter** *s* tipăritură *f*, imprimate *f pl* • ~**er** *s* (*person*) tipograf *m*; (*firm*) tipografie *f*; *comp* imprimantă *f* • ~**ing** *s* (*activity*) tipărire *f*, imprimare *f*; (*copies printed*) ediție *f*, tiraj *n* • ~ **out** *vt comp* a imprima • ~**out** *s comp* ieșire *f* la imprimantă, listare *f*.

prior *adj* anterior; precedent || *s* egumen *m*; stareț *m* • ~**ity** *s* prioritate *f*; precedență *f*.

prise *s* *tech* pârghie *f* || *vt* a ridica cu o pârghie.

prism *s* *phys*, *geom* prismă *f*.

prison *s* închisoare *f*; arest *n* • ~**er** *s* captiv *m*; prizonier *m*; arestat *m*; deținut *m*; sclav *m*.

pristine *adj* (*pure*) curat, imaculat; (*original*) primar, primitiv; originar.

privacy *s* izolare *f*; retragere *f*; intimitate *f*; taină *f*.

private *adj* privat, particular; personal; intim; confi-dențial, secret; (*person*, *place*) retras, izolat || *s* *mil* soldat *m*; *pl anat* organe *n pl* genitale; ~ **enterprise** *s* întreprindere *f* privată; ~ **eye** *s* detectiv *m* privat.

privation *s* privațiune *f*; (*poverty*) sărăcie *f*.

privatize *vt* a privatiza.

privet *s* *bot* lemn *n* câinesc, mălin *m* negru.

privilege *s* privilegiu *n*; avantaj *n*, favoare *f*; onoare *f*; patent *n*; imunitate *f* || *vt* a acorda un privilegiu; a scuti; a elibera.

prize *vt* a prețui, a aprecia || *s* premiu *n*; câștig *n*; noroc *n*; plăcere *f*.

pro *s coll sp* profesionist *m*; avantaj *n* || *adj coll sp* profesionist; **the** ~**s and cons** *s* avantajele și dezavantajele; ~ **rata** *adj* proporţional || *adv* distribuit proporţional.

probability *s* probabilitate *f*.

probable *adj* probabil; nesigur; veridic; bănuit || *s* candidat *m* probabil; ~ **cause** *s jur* motive *n pl* suficiente/ întemeiate de suspiciune.

probate *s* autentificare *f* a unui testament || *vt* a valida (un testament).

probation *s jur* eliberare *f* condiţionată; (*test*) probă *f*; test *n*; perioadă *f* de încercare; *relig* noviciat *n*.

probe *s med* sondă *f*, cateter *n*; *tech* sondă *f*; sondare *f*; sondaj *n*; cercetare *f*, examinare *f* || *vt* (*survey*) a sonda; (*look into*) a cerceta atent, a studia, a examina.

probity *s* probitate *f*.

problem *s* problemă *f*; chestiune *f*; caz *n* dificil.

procedure *s* procedeu *n*; (*method*) procedură *f*; *med* operaţie *f*; **legal** ~ procedură legală.

proceed *vi* (*continue*) a continua; (*advance*) a înainta; (*act*) a acţiona • ~**s** *s pl* încasări *f pl*, beneficiu *n* • ~**ing** *s* procedeu *n*; *pl* jur proces *n*, acţiune *f* în justiţie; *pl* (*meeting*) lucrări *f pl* (ale unei comisii etc); (*records*) proces *n* verbal, dare *f* de seamă.

process *s* proces *n*; mers *n*; dezvoltare *f*; evoluţie *f*; progres *n*; (*method*) procedură *f* || *vt* (~ *food, information, etc*) a prelucra; (~ *an application*) a se ocupa de; (*make*) a fabrica; (*prepare*) a prepara • ~**ing** *s* tratament *n*; transformare *f*.

procession *s* procesiune *f*, cortegiu *n*.

processor *s comp* procesor *n*; *cul* robot *n*.

pro-choice *adj* în favoarea avortului.

proclaim *vt* a proclama; a declara; a vesti; a interzice; a arăta, a trăda.

proclamation *s* proclamaţie *f*.

proclivity *s frml* înclinaţie *f*, tendinţă *f*.

procrastinate *vi* a amâna.

procreate *vt* a da naştere, a procrea; *fig* a da naştere la; a da viaţă.

procure *vt* a găsi, a procura; (~ *freedom*) a obţine; a asigura || *vi* a fi proxenet.

prod *s* îndemn *n*; împunsătură *f*; *fig* îndemn *n*, imbold *n* || *vt* a mâna, a îndemna.

prodigal *adj* (*wasteful*) risipitor; darnic, generos; abundent, bogat.

prodigious *adj* imens, colosal; monstruos.

prodigy *s* minune *f*.

produce *s* produs *n*; rezultat *n* || *vt* (~ *proof*) a aduce; (*show*) a arăta; (*effect*) a produce; (*grow*) a creşte; (*have success*) a determina; *thea* a juca, a prezenta || *vi* a produce; a fabrica; a cultiva • ~**r** *s cin* producător *m*; *thea* regizor *m*.

product *s* produs *n*; articol *n*; rezultat *n*; rod *n*; (*production*) producţie *f*; (*result*) randament *n*; *thea* regie *f*; (*show*) producţie *f*; piesă *f*, *fig* operă *f*, lucrare *f*.

production *s* (*process*) producţie *f*, fabricare *f*; producere *f*; (*amount*) producţie *f*; (*presentation*) prezentare *f*; *cin, etc* producţie *f*; (*art*) operă *f*.

productivity *s* productivitate *f*.

profane *adj* profan || *vt* a profana.

profanity *s* caracter *n* profan; blasfemie *f*.

profess *vt* (~ *ideas*) a proclama, a declara; (~ *a belief*) a profesa; a împărtăşi; (*trade, etc*) a exercita, a practica.

profession *s* profesie *f*; ocupaţie *f*; rit *n*; credinţă *f*; confesiune *f* • ~**al** *adj* profesional, profesionist || *s* expert *m*; profesionist *m*.

professor *s* profesor *m*; expert *m*.

proffer *vt frml* (*offer*) a oferi, a prezenta; (~ *advice*) a da; (*put forward idea*) a emite.

proficient *adj* expert în; competent în; priceput la || *s* expert *m*.

profile *s* profil *n*; schiţă *f*, contur *n* || *vt* a desena/schiţa profilul.

profit *s fin* profit *n*, câştig *n*; *fig* folos *n*; rost *n*; *econ* venit *n* net || *vi* a profita; a se folosi || *vt* a fi de folos (cuiva); ~ **and loss** profit şi pierdere; ~ **sharing** *s* participare *f* la beneficii • ~**able** *adj* profitabil; rentabil; util; avantajos • ~**eer** *s* profitor *m*.

profligate *adj frml* (*wasteful*) risipitor, cheltuitor; (*dissolute*) depravat, destrăbălat.

profound *adj* adânc; profund; serios; abscons; complicat || *s* adânc *n*.

profundity *s* profunzime *f*.

profuse *adj* (**of/in**) bogat, abundent (în); generos, darnic (cu, în) • ~**ly** *adv* din abundenţă; (în mod) exagerat.

progeny *s frml* progenitură *f*, urmaş *m*.

prognosis *s* pronostic *n*.

prognostication *s med* pronostic *n*; prognosticare *f*, anticipare *f*; prevestire *f*, prezicere *f*.

program *s* program *n*; afiş *n*; plan *n*; *comp* program *n* || *vt* a programa • ~**mer** *s comp* programator *m* • ~**ming** *s comp* programare *f*.

progress *s* progres *n*; evoluţie *f*; succes *n*; curs *n* || *vi* a progresa; a evolua; a obţine succese.

prohibit *vt* a opri, a interzice; (*alcohol, etc*) a prohibi • ~**ion** *s* interzicere *f*.

project *s* proiect *n*, plan *n* || *vt* a plănui, a proiecta; (*estimate*) a prevedea || *vi* (*protrude*) a se proiecta • ~**ion** *s* proiectare *f*; (*forecast*) proiect *n*; proiecţie *f*; (*outcrop*) proeminenţă *f*, excrescenţă *f*.

proletariat *s* proletariat *n*.

proliferate *vt bio* a prolifera, a înmulţi; *fig* a prolifera, a răspândi || *vi bio* a prolifera, a se înmulţi; *fig* a se răspândi.

prolific *adj bio* prolific, fecund; (**in/of**) prolific, abundent, bogat (în).

prologue *s also fig* prolog *n*.

prolong *vt* a lungi, a prelungi.

promenade *s* loc *n* de plimbare; *frml* plimbare *f*.

prominent *adj* proeminent; evident; remarcabil.

promiscuous *adj* eterogen, amestecat; (*person*) de moravuri uşoare; (*behavior*) imoral; *coll* dezordonat.

promise *s* promisiune *f*; perspectivă *f* || *vt* a promite; a se angaja; a se obliga.

promising *adj* promiţător.

promontory *s geog* promontoriu *n*; cap *n*.

promote *vt* (*advertise*) a promova; a susţine; (*position*) a avansa • ~**r** *s* promotor *m*; iniţiator *m*; *constr* benficiar *m*.

promotion *s* promovare *f*; încurajare *f*; (*job*) avansare *f*, promovare *f*.

prompt *adj* prompt; gata; eficient; imediat || *adv* repede || *vt* a îndemna; a sufla; *fig* a trezi; a sugera; a insufla; *fig* a reaminti • ~**ly** *adv* cu promptitudine; imediat; la fix.

prone *adj* (**to**) înclinat/predispus spre || *adj/adv* cu faţa în jos; aplecat, înclinat.

prong *s* dinte *m* (de furcă); vârf *n*; colţ *n*; corn *n*; furcă *f* || *vt* a străpunge.

pronoun *s gram* pronume *n*.

pronounce *vt* a rosti; a declara || *vi* a pronunţa.

pronunciation *s* pronunțare *f*; pronunție *f*; rostire *f*; accent *n/f*.

proof *s* dovadă *f*; probă *f*; mărturie *f*; verificare *f*; control *n*; (*books, etc*) șpalt *n*; (*alcohol*) grad *n* de tărie ‖ *vt* a cauciuca.

prop[1] *s tech* proptea *f*, suport *n*; *fig* sprijin *n*; stâlp *n* ‖ *vt* (~ *against*) a propti/rezema/sprijini de; *fig* a susține; a ajuta.

prop[2] *s thea* recuzită *f*.

propaganda *s* propagandă *f*.

propagate *vt* a spori; a crește; a propaga; a cultiva ‖ *vi* a se propaga.

propel *vt* a propulsa; *fig* a stimula.

propensity *s frml* (**for**) tendință (spre).

proper *adj* (*suitable*) adecvat, potrivit; (*good*) corespunzător; (*appropriate*) convenabil, indicat; (*real*) adevărat, propriu-zis; (*own*) propriu, personal • **~ly** *adv* decent; propriu-zis; cum trebuie; pe drept cuvânt.

property *s* avere *f*; proprietate *f*; calitate *f*; recuzită *f*; stăpânire *f*; semn *n*.

prophecy *s* profeție *f*.

prophet *s* profet *m*.

propitious *adj* favorabil, propice.

proponent *s* (*advocate*) susținător *m*.

proportion *s* proporție *f*; relație *f* ‖ *vt* a proporționa; a armoniza.

proposal *s* propunere *f*; sugestie *f*; ofertă *f*; proiect *n*; plan *n*; cerere *f* în căsătorie.

propose *vt* (*suggest*) a sugera; a propune; a supune; (*intend*) a intenționa; a-și propune; (~ *a toast*) a închina ‖ *vi* a propune; a plănui; (**to**) a cere pe cineva în căsătorie.

proposition *s* (*offer*) propunere *f*; (*task*) treabă *f*, problemă *f*, chestiune *f*; (*available choice*) soluție *f*; (*offer of sex*) propunere *f* indecentă, avans *n*.

propound *vt frml* (~ *an opinion, etc*) a propune, a supune (spre a fi luat în considerare); (*problem*) a pune.

proprietary *adj* de proprietate; particular.

proprietor *s* proprietar *m*.

propriety *s* (*decency*) bună-cuviință *f*, decență *f*; bune maniere *f pl*.

propulsion *s tech* propulsie *f*; *fig* impuls *n*, imbold *n*.

pro-rate *vt* a repartiza/distribui proporțional.

proscribe *vt* a interzice, a prohibi.

prose *s* prozaism *n*; proză *f*; banalitate *f*.

prosecute *vt* a efectua, a continua; a purta; a da în judecată ‖ *vi* a intenta un proces.

prosecution *s* urmărire *f* în justiție f.

prosecutor *s* (*lawyer*) procuror *m*, avocat *m* al acuzării.

prospect *s* (*view*) vedere *f*; (*scene*) priveliște *f*; (*outlook*) perspectivă *f*; *pl* (*hope*) posibilități *f pl*, șanse *f pl*; viitor *n*; *geol, min* prospecțiune *f* ‖ *vt geol, min* a prospecta, a cerceta.

prospective *adj* viitor; în perspectivă; presupus; așteptat.

prospectus *s typ* prospect *n*; broșură *f*; pliant *n*; catalog *n*; *com* listă *f* de prețuri.

prosper *vi* a prospera; a înflori; a reuși ‖ *vt* a face să prospere • **~ity** *s* prosperitate *f*; succes *n*.

prostate *s anat* prostată *f*.

prosthesis *s med* proteză *f*.

prostitute *s* prostituată *f*; om *m* venal ‖ *vt* a prostitua; *fig* a necinsti.

prostitution *s* prostituție *f*; prostituare *f*.

prostrate *adj* culcat/întins la pământ; (*with pain, etc*) copleșit/mut/paralizat (de); *bot* târâtor, întins la pământ ‖ *vt* a culca la pământ; *fig* a copleși, a doborî; (*illness, etc*) a epuiza, a slei ‖ *vr* a se umili.

prostration *s* prosternare *f*; toropeală *f*.

protagonist *s* protagonist *m*.

protean *adj* (*variable*) variabil; (*artist*) versatil.

protect *vt* (**from/against**) a apăra; *tech* a proteja; a îngrădi; *econ* a accepta; a onora ‖ *vr* a se apăra • **~ion** *s* (**from/against**) protejare *f*; protecție *f*; favoare *f*, patronaj *n*; *econ* protecționism *n*; *econ* acceptare *f*; onorare *f*; *phys* ecranare *f*; *tech* consolidare *f*.

protein *s chem* proteină *f*.

protest *s* protest *n*; opoziție *f*; obiecție *f*; *econ* protestare *f*; *jur* declarație *f* solemnă ‖ *vt/vi* a protesta; *jur* a declara solemn.

Protestant *s/adj relig* protestant *m*.

protocol *s* proces *n* verbal; protocol *n*, uzanță *f* diplomatică.

prototype *s* prototip *n*.

protract *vt* a extinde; a prelungi; *tech* a trasa, a desena • **~ed** *adj* prelungit.

protrude *vt* a scoate afară; *fig* (*idea, etc*) a impune ‖ *vi* a ieși în afară.

protuberance *s* protuberanță *f*.

proud *adj* mândru; măreț; splendid; aprig ‖ *adv* mândru, cu mândrie.

provable *adj* verificabil.

prove *vt* a dovedi; *jur* a legaliza; a atesta; a proba; *math* a verifica ‖ *vi* a se dovedi.

provenance *s* (*origin*) proveniență *f*.

proverb *s* proverb *n*.

provide *vt* (**with**) a înzestra; (*supply*) a aproviziona; a furniza; a asigura; *jur* a prevedea, a prescrie.

provided *conj* (**that**) (numai) dacă, cu condiția (ca) să.

providence *s* (*fate*) providență *f*; (*foresight*) prevedere *f*; chibzuială *f*, chibzuință *f*.

providential *adj* providențial; predestinat; norocos.

province *s* (*country*) provincie *f*; *fig* domeniu *n*, sferă *f*; competență *f*.

provincial *adj* provincial.

provision *s* asigurare *f*; furnizare *f*; pregătire *f*; *jur* prevedere *f*, clauză *f*; dispoziție *f*; *pl* hrană *f* ‖ *vt* a aproviziona • **~al** *adj* provizoriu, temporar.

proviso *s* clauză *f*; condiție *f*.

provocation *s* provocare *f*.

provocative *adj* (*offensive*) provocator; obraznic; (*challenging*) provocator, stimulator (de).

provoke *vt* (*incite*) a ațâța; a provoca; a instiga; (*aggravate*) a supăra, a înfuria; (*cause*) a cauza.

provost *s* decan *m*.

prow *s naut* proră *f*, provă *f*.

prowess *s* curaj *n*, bravură *f*; act *n* de curaj, faptă *f* vitejească; (*skill*) îndemânare *f*.

prowl *vi* (~ *the streets, etc*) a colinda (după pradă), a umbla încoace și încolo ‖ *vi* a da târcoale; a umbla după pradă • **~er** *s* vagabond *m*, hoinar *m*.

proximate *adj* imediat, apropiat; aproximativ.

proximity *s* apropiere *f*, proximitate *f*.

proxy *s* mandat *n*, împuternicire *f*; mandatar *m*; **by** ~ prin delegație; prin procură.

prude *s* om *m* care face pe pudicul; "puritan" *m*.

prudence *s* prudență *f*.

prudent *adj* prudent; chibzuit; atent, grijuliu; econom, calculat.

prudish *adj* (*prim*) sclifosit, fandosit; (*starchy*) scorțos.

prune[1] *s bot* prun *m*; prună *f* uscată.

prune[2] *vt* (*tree*) a tăia, a reteza; (*reduce text*) a scurta, a reduce, a simplifica.

prurient *adj* obscen, nerușinat.

pry[1] *s* pârghie *f*; *fig* mijloc *n* ‖ *vt* a ridica/desface cu o pârghie; *fig* a scoate cu greu; a smulge.

pry[2] *vi* (**into**) a examina, a cerceta; (*meddle*) a se vârî, a se băga; *coll* a-și vârî nasul în ceea ce nu-l privește.

psalm *s* psalm *m*; imn *n*.

pseudonym *s* pseudonim *n*.

psyche *s* suflet *n*, spirit *n*.

psychiatrist *s* psihiatru *m*.

psychiatry *s* psihiatrie *f*.

psychic *adj med* psihic; sufletesc; metafizic; (~ *power*) paranormal ‖ *s* psihic *n*; suflet *n*; intelect *n*; mediu *n*.

psycho *s/adj pej* psihopat *m*.

psychoanalysis *s* psihanaliză *f*.

psychoanalyst *s* psihanalist *m*.

psychological *adj* psihologic.

psychologist *s* psiholog *m*.

psychology *s* psihologie *f*.

psychopath *s med* psihopat *m*.

psychosis *s* psihoză *f*.

psychotherapy *s med* psihoterapie *f*.

psychotic *adj* care suferă de o psihoză ‖ *s* persoană *f* care suferă de o psihoză.

pub *s* tavernă *f*, bodegă *f*, pub *n*, cârciumă *f*; han *n*.

puberty *s* pubertate *f*.

pubic *adj* pubian.

public *adj* public; de stat; popular; comunal; deschis; renumit ‖ *s* public *n*; *thea, etc* asistență *f*; auditoriu *n*; lume *f*; ~ **company** *s fin* societate *f* anonimă (cotată la Bursă); ~ **debt** *s econ* datorie *f* publică; ~ **health** *s* sănătatea *f* publică; ~ **holiday** *s* sărbătoare *f* legală; ~ **library** *s* bibliotecă *f* publică/municipală; ~ **opinion** *s* opinia *f* publică; ~ **relations** *s pl* relații *f pl* publice; ~ **school** *s* școală *f* de stat; ~ **transport** *s* transport *n* în comun; ~ **works** *s pl* lucrări *f pl* publice.

publication *s* publicare *f*, editare *f*; anunțare *f*; publicație *f*; carte *f*.

publicity *s* publicitate *f*; reclamă *f*.

publicize *vt* a face reclamă.

public-spirited *adj* animat de spirit civic.

publish *vt* a publica; a anunța; a edita; a declara ‖ *vi* a se tipări, a fi sub tipar • ~**er** *s* editor *m*; director *m* de ziar.

puck *s sp* puc *n* (la hochei).

pucker *vt* a cuta, a plia; (~ *lips*) a țuguia ‖ *vi* a se îndoi, a se cuta, a face cute.

pudding *s cul* budincă *f*.

puddle *s* baltă *f*, băltoacă *f*; smârc *n*.

pudgy *adj* scund și îndesat; rotofei, durduliu; (*fingers*) gros, butucănos.

puerile *adj* pueril, copilăros; imatur; naiv; banal, trivial.

puff *s* (*wind*) adiere *f*, suflare *f*; (*smoke*) trâmbă *f*; nor *m*; (*engine, etc*) pufăit *n*; *med* umflatură *f*; *fig* laudă *f* exagerată ‖ *vi* (*wind*) a sufla; (*engine, etc*) a pufăi; (**at**) a pufăi (din); a fuma; (*pant*) a respire greu; a gâfâi.

pugilistic *adj sp* pugilistic, de box.

pugnacious *adj frml* bătăios, belicos.

pull *vt* a trage; a târî; a duce; a scoate; a întinde; a smulge ‖ *vi* a trage; a târî ‖ *s* tragere *f*; smucitură *f*; entorsă *f*; efort *n*; ~ **off** *vt* a scoate, a smulge; *fig* a

reuși; ~ **oneself together** a-și reveni, a-și aduna puterile; ~ **out** *vt* (~ *troops, etc*) a retrage ‖ *vi rail* a pleca; a se retrage; ~ **over** *vi aut* a trage pe dreapta; a se da la o parte; ~ **through** *vt* (*danger, etc*) a scăpa, a salva; (*difficulty*) a învinge ‖ *vi* a scăpa, a se salva; a răzbate; ~ **together** *vi* a conlucra; a coopera; ~ **up** *vt* a smulge; a smuci; a apuca, a trage; (*wire, etc*) a întinde ‖ *vi* a se opri; a merge înainte.

pullet *s* pui *m* de găină.

pulley *s tech* scripete *m*, troliu *n*.

pullover *s text* pulover *n*.

pulmonary *adj* pulmonar.

pulp *s* (*fruit*) miez *n*; pulpă *f*; *tech* pastă *f* de lemn; *anat* pulpă *f*; *typ* lucrare *f* de doi bani ‖ *vt* a pisa; a face terci; a curăța de pulpă.

pulpit *s* amvon *n*.

pulsate *vi* (*heart*) a pulsa, a bate; (*air, music*) a vibra.

pulse *s anat* puls *n*; *fig* pulsație *f*; ritm *n*; *fig* îndemn *n*; *fig* dispoziție *f* ‖ *vi* a pulsa, a bate; a vibra.

pulverize *vt* a pulveriza; *fig* a preface în pulbere, a face praf; a nimici.

pumice *s* piatră *f* ponce.

pummel *vt* (*punch*) a lovi cu pumnii; (*massage*) a masa, a palpa.

pump *s* pompă *f* ‖ *vt* a pompa; a umfla; a epuiza.

pumpkin *s bot* dovleac *m*, bostan *m*; *coll* tont *m*, neghiob *m*.

pun *s* joc *n* de cuvinte; calambur *n* ‖ *vi* a face un joc de cuvinte/calambur.

punch[1] *s* (lovitură de) pumn *m* ‖ *vt* a lovi; a bate cu pumnii; a îndemna, a mâna.

punch[2] *vt typ, etc* a perfora; *metal* a ștanța; a puncta ‖ *s typ* poanson *n* de literă; *metal* ștanță *f*; *tech* perforator *n*; *constr* șpiț *n*.

punctilious *adj* (*scrupulous*) minuțios, scrupulous; (*proper*) pedant, formalist.

punctual *adj* punctual; pedant; minuțios.

punctuation *s* punctuație *f*.

puncture *s* (*tire* ~) pană *f*; *med* puncție *f*; *typ* punctură *f* ‖ *vt aut* a găuri; a înțepa; *med* a face o puncție ‖ *vi auto* a se dezumfla, a se perfora.

pundit *s* expert *m*.

pungent *adj* iute; (*smell*) înțepător; (*taste*) picant; *fig* ascuțit.

punish *vt* a pedepsi; a lovi ‖ *vi* a pedepsi, a da o pedeapsă • ~**ing** *adj* (*schedule, etc*) epuizant, istovitor; (*defeat*) usturător • ~**ment** *s* pedeapsă *f*; *mil* represiune *f*; represalii *f pl*.

punitive *adj* (*expedition*) punitiv; (*tax*) prohibitiv.

punk *s* (*music, fashion*) punk *n*; *coll* (*worthless person*) lichea *f*, ticălos *m*.

punt *s* (*boat*) barcă *f* cu fundul lat.

puny *adj* firav, plăpând, mititel.

pup *s zool* cățeluș *m* ‖ *vi* (*bitch*) a făta.

pupa *s ento* pupă *f*, crisalidă *f*.

pupil[1] *s* elev *m*, școlar *m*; discipol *m*.

pupil[2] *s anat* pupilă *f*.

puppet *s* păpușă *f*; marionetă *f*; *fig* unealtă *f*; om *m* de paie; manechin *m*.

puppy *s* cățel *m*; pui *m*; maimuțoi *m*.

purchase *vt* (*buy*) a cumpăra; a dobândi; (*trust*) a câștiga; *tech* a ridica ‖ *s* cumpărare *f*; cumpărătură *f*; preț *n*, valoare *f*; *fig* poziție *f* influență; influență *f*; avantaj *n* • ~**r** *s* cumpărător *m*.

purchasing power *s* putere *f* de cumpărare.

pure *adj* pur, curat; clar; absolut; simplu; perfect; nevinovat; abstract • **~ly** *adv* neamestecat; doar, numai; pur şi simplu; cu inocenţă; complet.

purgative *s/adj* purgativ *n*.

purgatory *s relig* purgatoriu *n*; *fig* purgatoriu *n*; iad *n*; *med* purgativ *n*.

purge *vt* a curăţa; a scăpa de; *med* a purga; *pol* a epura || *vi* a se curăţa || *s med* curăţenie *f*; purgativ *n*; *pol* epurare *f*.

purify *vt also fig* a purifica.

puritan *s/adj relig* puritan *m*; *fig* puritan *m*.

purity *s* puritate *f*.

purl[1] *s text* fir *n*; franjuri *n pl*; broderie *f* || *vt* a lucra/ broda cu fir; a pune franjuri la.

purl[2] *vi* a murmura, a susura || *s* murmur *n*, susur(at) *n*.

purloin *vt frml, hum* a sustrage, a subtiliza.

purple *s* purpură *f* || *adj* purpuriu; (*color*) violet; bogat; luxos || *vt* a împurpura.

purport *s* sens *n*, semnificaţie *f*; conţinut *n*; *jur* text *n* || *vt* a pretinde (că); a afirma/susţine (că).

purpose *s* scop *n*, ţel *n*, ţintă *f*, obiectiv *n*; intenţie *f*; efect *n*; voinţă *f* || *vt* a intenţiona, a avea de gând; **on ~** *adv* dinadins; **to no ~** *adv* inutil, zadarnic; degeaba • **~ful** *adj* oportun; hotărât, decis; consecvent; intenţionat; gândit.

purr *vi* (*cat*) a toarce; *tech* (*engine*) a funcţiona liniştit || *s* (*cat*) tors *n*; *tech* (*engine*) funcţionare *f* bună.

purse *s* portofel *n*; pungă *f*; portmoneu *n*; capital *n*; vistierie *f*; poşetă *f* || *vt* a pungi; a încreţi || *vi* a se pungi.

purser *s* comisar *m* de bord.

pursuance *s frml* îndeplinire *f*, executare *f*; **in (the) ~ of his duties** în exercitarea funcţiei sale.

pursue *vt* (*~ a person*) a urmări, a prigoni; a persecuta; (*~ a goal*) a urmări; (*~ a problem*) a continua; (*~ an issue*) a aprofunda; a studia; a cerceta; (*project*) a da curs || *vi* a urmări • **~r** *s* urmăritor *m*.

pursuit *s* urmărire *f*, preocupare *f*; (*goal*) scop *n*, ţel *n*, ţintă *f*; *sp* cursă *f*.

purvey *vt* (*supply*) a aproviziona; a furniza; (*supply information*) a comunica; (*spread lies, rumors*) a colporta.

purview *s jur* parte *f* esenţială (a unei legi etc); sferă *f* (de activitate), domeniu; competenţă *f*; *fig* orizont *n*.

pus *s med* puroi *n*.

push *vt* (*press*) a împinge; (*~ a button*) a apăsa; (*impel*) a îndemna să; *fig* (*process*) a grăbi; a stimula; a lărgi || *vi* a apăsa; a împinge; (*force*) a presa; *coll* (*promote*) a face reclamă pentru || *s* împingere *f*; ghiont *n*; apăsare *f*, *fig* efort *n*; *fig* sprijin *n*, protecţie *f*; *fig* moment *n* critic; *mil* atac *n*; **to ~ on** *vi* a continua; **to ~ through** *vt* (*bill, etc*) a obţine acordul pentru.

pusher *s sl* (*drug*) traficant *m*.

pushy *adj pej* băgăreţ, obraznic.

pusillanimous *adj frml* (*fearful*) temător; (*cowardly*) laş, poltron.

puss *s* pis; **~y** (*cat*) *s* pisică.

pussyfoot *vi coll* a nu se implica, a sta de o parte.

pustule *s med* pustulă *f*.

put, put, put *vt* (*place*) a pune; (*set*) a aşeza; (*rank*) a plasa; *fig* a numi; *fig* (*say*) a zice; a formula; a aprecia, (*question*) a pune (o întrebare); (*issue*) a ridica; *fig* a evalua, a preţui; *sp* (*ball, etc*) a arunca; a lovi || *s* aruncare *f*; azvârlire *f*; **~ together** *vt* a uni; a îm-

bina; a combina; a asambla; *fig* a-şi aduna (gândurile); a compila; (*sum*) a aduna, a totaliza || **~ through** *vt tele* a transmite, a da legătura || **~ up** *vt* (*build*) a înălţa; (*tent, flag*) a ridica; (*~ an umbrella*) a deschide; (*~ on a wall*) a agăţa; (*~ money*) a furniza; (*~ a candidate*) a propune; a creşte, a spori; (*lodge*) a găzdui; **~ up with** *vt* a suporta.

putative *adj* (*presumed*) prezumtiv.

putrefy *vi* (*corpse*) a se descompune.

putrid *adj* putred; putrezit; rău mirositor.

putsch *s* puci *n*.

putt *s* club *n* de golf || *vt/vi* a lovi mingea la golf • **~er**[1] *s* jucător de golf *m*.

putter[2] *vi coll* a-şi face de lucru; (**at**) a-şi pierde vremea cu; a trăncăni, a flecări.

putty *s* chit *n*; mastic *n* || *vt* a chitui.

puzzle *vt* a nedumeri; a lăsa perplex; a încurca; a complica; a-şi chinui, a-şi frământa (creierii) || *s* enigmă *f*; nedumerire *f*; perplexitate *f*; încurcătură *f*; careu *n*, joc *n* de cuvinte încrucişate; **to ~ over smth** a încerca să înţeleagă ceva; **to ~ out** *vt* a descurca, a descâlci (o situaţie dificilă).

puzzling *adj* (*remark*) care lasă perplex; (*symbol, etc*) de neînţeles, misterios.

pygmy *s also fig* pigmeu *m*.

pylon *s* pilon *n*, stâlp *n*.

pyramid *s geom, etc* piramidă *f*.

pyre *s* (*funeral*) rug *n*.

pyromania *s* piromanie *f*.

pyrotechnic *adj* pirotehnic • **~s** *spl* pirotehnie *f*.

python *s zool* piton *m*.

Q

Q, q *s* (litera) Q, q.

quack[1] *s* (*duck*) măcăit *n* || *interj* mac!, mac! || *vi* a măcăi.

quack[2] *s sl* vraci *m*; impostor *m* || *adj* empiric; băbesc || *vi* a practica medicina empirică; a fi un impostor.

quadrangle *s* patrulater *n*; curte *f* pătrată.

quadrant *s astron* cvadrant *n*; *naut* sector *n* de cârmă.

quadrilateral *s/adj* patrulater *n*.

quadruped *s/adj zool* patruped *m*.

quadruple *adj* cvadruplu, împătrit || *s* cvadruplu *n* || *vt/vi* a înmulţi cu patru..

quadruplet *s* grup *n* de patru • **~s** *s pl* (patru copii gemeni) cvadrupli m pl.

quads *s pl coll* cvadrupli *m pl*.

quaff *vt lit* (*drink*) a bea; (*swill*) a bea lacom.

quagmire *s* (*swamp*) mlaştină *f*; *fig* încurcătură *f*, situaţie *f* dificilă.

quail[1] *s orn* prepeliţă *f*.

quail[2] *vi* (*draw back*) a da înapoi.

quaint *adj* ciudat; nostim; original; demodat.

quake *vi* a se cutremura; a se clătina || *s* cutremur *n* (de pământ).

qualification *s* (*skill*) specializare *f*, calificare *f*; (*ability*) aptitudine *f*, competenţă *f*; (*proviso*) condiţie *f*, rezervă *f*.

qualified *adj* (*trained*) calificat; (*skilled*) priceput; talentat; (*limited*) restrâns.

qualify *vt* (*train*) a califica, a pregăti; *jur* a autoriza (să); (*restrict*) a modifica, a restrânge || *vi* a se pregăti (pentru); a se califica (pentru).

qualitative *adj* calitativ.

quality *s* calitate *f*; natură *f*; capacitate *f*; fire *f*; valoare *f*.

qualm *s* neliniște *f*; *pl* remușcări *f pl*; acces *n*; greață *f*; neputință *f*.

quandary *s* încurcătură *f*, dificultate *f*, impas *n*; dilemă *f*.

quantify *vt math* a cuantifica.

quantitative *adj* cantitativ.

quantity *s* mulțime *f*; cantitate *f*; mărime *f*.

quantum *s* (*pl* **quanta**) cuantum *n*; *phys* cuantă *f*; ~ **mechanics** *s* mecanica cuantică.

quarantine *s* carantină *f* ‖ *vt* a pune/ține în carantină.

quarrel *s* ceartă *f*; conflict *n*; pică *f*; antipatie *f* ‖ *vi* a se certa • **~some** *adj* certăreț.

quarry[1] *s* (*stone, etc*) carieră *f*; *fig* sursă *f*, izvor *n* ‖ *vt* a exploata; *fig* a scormoni, a scotoci, a răscoli.

quarry[2] *s* pradă *f*, vânat *n* urmărit; *fig* persoană *f* urmărită/hăituită; *fig* obiect *n* al unei urmăriri/persecuții.

quart *s* *approx* litru *m*; cuartă *f*.

quarter *s* sfert *n*; pătrar *n* al lunii; loc *n*, parte *f*, monedă *f* de 25 cenți; direcție *f*; *pl* locuință *f* ‖ *vt* (*divide*) a tăia; (*accommodate*) a caza; a cantona ‖ *vi* a locui, a fi cazat.

quartet *s* *mus* cvartet *n*.

quartz *s* *miner* cuarț *n*.

quash *vt* *jur* a anula, a casa; *pol* a invalida; *fig* (~ *a revolt*) a reprima, a înăbuși.

quaver *s* *mus* tremolo *n*; tril *n*; *mus* optime *f*; (*voice*) tremur *n*, vibrație *f* ‖ *vi* (*voice*) a tremura; *mus* a face triluri.

quay *s* *naut* chei *n*, debarcader *n*; dană *f*.

queasy *adj* (*food*) grețos; *fig* delicat; *fig* (excesiv de) scrupulos.

Quebec *s* Quebec.

queen *s* regină *f*; *ento* matcă *f*; (*chess*) damă *f*, regină f; (*cards*) damă *f* ‖ *vt* a face regină ‖ *vi* a domni ca regină.

queer *adj* bizar; excentric; indispus; trăsnit; afumat; dubios; fals ‖ *vt* a strica; a înșela, a păcăli.

quell *vt* *also* *fig* a reprima, a înăbuși.

quench *vt* (~ *a fire*) a stinge; (~ *a thirst*) a potoli; *fig* a înăbuși; (*movement*) a opri ‖ *vi* (~ *a fire*) a se stinge; *fig* a se potoli.

querulous *adj* (*person*) plângăreț; smiorcăit; (*tone, voice*) plângător, jalnic; (*argumentative*) cârcotaș.

query *s* întrebare *f*; nedumerire *f* ‖ *vt* a pune la îndoială, a pune sub semnul întrebării.

quest *s* căutare *f*; urmărire *f* ‖ *vt* a căuta, a urmări ‖ *vi* a căuta.

question *s* (*doubt*) îndoială *f*; (*query*) întrebare *f*; *pol* interpelare *f*; chestiune *f*; șansă *f* ‖ *vt* (*ask*) a întreba; (*doubt*) a se îndoi de; a contesta; *pol* a interpela; a cerceta; ~ **mark** *s* semn *n* de întrebare • **~ing** *s* chestionare *f*, interogare *f* ‖ *adj* interogativ, întrebător • **~naire** *s* chestionar *n*.

queue *s* coadă *f*, rând *n* ‖ *vi* a sta la coadă.

quibble *s* subterfugiu *n*; ambiguitate *f*; calambur *n* ‖ *vi* a recurge la tertipuri/subterfugii/echivoc; a se eschiva de la răspunsuri clare; a despica firul în patru.

quick *adj* rapid; agil; prompt, grăbit; ager; fin ‖ *adv* iute, repede • **~en** *vt* a grăbi; a accelera; a stârni; a stimula ‖ *vi* a se accelera • **~ly** *adv* (*rapidly*) repede, iute, rapid; (*promptly*) prompt, imediat • **~tempered** *adj* irascibil, nervos, iute din fire.

quiescent *adj* *lit* (*passive*) retras, pasiv; (*quiet*) calm, liniștit; *fig* latent.

quiet *adj* (*calm*) liniștit; tăcut; (*peaceful*) pașnic; retras; (*hidden*) secret; (*color*) șters ‖ *s* (*calm*) liniște *f*; calm *n* ‖ *vt* a liniști; a alunga; (*allay*) a potoli ‖ *vi* a se liniști.

quill *s* pană *f* (de gâscă); *fig* condei *n*.

quilt *s* cuvertură *f*; plapumă *f*; pufoaică *f* ‖ *vt* a vătui; a matlasa; a capitona.

quince *s* *bot* (*tree*) gutui *m*; (*fruit*) gutuie *f*.

quinine *s* *chem* chinină *f*.

quinsy *s* *med coll* amigdalită *f*.

quintessence *s* (*essence*) chintesență *f*; (*epitome*) întruchipare f.

quintessential *adj* tipic, caracteristic.

quintet *s* *mus* cvintet *n*.

quintuplet *s* grup *n* de cinci; *pl* (cinci copii gemeni) cvinteți *m pl*.

quip *s* (*witty remark*) (vorbă de) spirit *n*; (*sarcastic remark*) glumă *f* mușcătoare; (*jibe*) zeflemea *f*, batjocură *f*.

quirk *s* calambur *n*; observație *f* spirituală; arabesc *n*; tertip *n*; chichiță *f*.

quisling *s* colaboraționist *m*, trădător *m*.

quit[1] *adj* (**of**) chit, achitat; împăcat; eliberat.

quit[2], **quit, quit** *vt* (*leave*) a părăsi, a lăsa; (*give up*) a abandona; (~ *a job*) a demisiona; (~ *smoking, etc*) a se lăsa de.

quite *adv* total, complet, (pe) deplin; tocmai, exact; (*very*) foarte; (*rather*) destul de, cam ‖ *interj* așa e!, desigur!, firește!.

quits *adj* chit; **we're ~** acum suntem chit.

quiver[1] *vi* a tremura; a vibra; a se înfiora; *tech* a vibra, a trepida ‖ *s* tremurat *n*, freamăt *n*; *tech* vibrație *f*, trepidație *f*.

quiver[2] *s* (*for arrows*) tolbă *f*.

quiz *s* interogare *f*; examen *n* oral; *radio, tv* emisiune-concurs *f* ‖ *vt* a examina; a chestiona ‖ *vi* a ține examene.

quizzical *adj* ironic, batjocoritor, sarcastic; ciudat; original; (înzestrat cu) spirit critic.

quorum *s* *pol, etc* cvorum *n*.

quota *s* *econ* cotă *f* (-parte); dividend *n*; normă *f* de lucru.

quotation *s* citat *n*; moto *n*; deviză *f*; citare *f*; *econ* cotare *f*, curs *n*.

quote *vt* (*cite*) a cita; a menționa, a se referi la; *econ* (*specify*) a stabili, a cota, a specifica, a indica ‖ *s* citat *n*; *pl* ghilimele *f pl*; *com* curs *n*; *econ* (*estimate*) deviz *n*.

quotidian *adj* *frml* cotidian, zilnic; banal.

quotient *s* *math* cât *n*; coeficient *m*.

R

R, r *s* (litera) R, r.

rabbi *s* *relig* rabin *m*.

rabbit *s* *zool* iepure *m*; *fig* laș *m*, fricos *m*; ~ **hutch** *s* coteț *n* pentru iepuri (de casă).

rabble *s* gloată *f*, mulțime *f*.

rabies *s* *vet*, *med* turbare *f*.

raccoon *s* *zool* raton *m*, ursuleț *m* spălător.

race[1] *s* cursă *f*; concurs *n*; carieră *f*; orbită *f* ‖ *vi* a alerga; a concura ‖ *vt* a mâna, a grăbi; a forța

race[2] *s* rasă *f*.

racehorse *s* cal *m* de curse.
racetrack *s* pistă *f.*
racial *adj* rasial; ~ **discrimination** *s* discriminare *f* rasială.
racing *s* alergare *f*, cursă *f*; *aut* ambalare *f*; accelerare *f*; *med* (*pulse*) agitat || *adj* de curse; ~ **car** maşină de curse.
racism *s* rasism *n.*
racist *adj/s* rasist *m.*
rack *s* grătar *n*; raft *n*; suport *n*; stativ *n*; cuier *n* || *vt* a pune pe grătar etc.
racket[1] *s sp* rachetă *f.*
racket[2] *s* (*din*) tărăboi *n*, zarvă *f*; contrabandă *f*; (*swindle*) pungăşie *f.*
racquet *s* rachetă *f.*
racy *adj* (*lively*) în vervă; (*suggestive*) picant; decoltat; scabros; (*wine, fruit, etc*) savuros, cu buchet aromat.
radar *s* radar *n*, radiolocator *n.*
raddled *adj* (*worn*) obosit, istovit.
radial *adj* radial; în formă de stea || *s* pneu *n* cu schelet radial.
radiance *s* strălucire *f.*
radiant *adj phys* iradiant; *fig* strălucitor, radios.
radiate *vt/vi phys* a (i)radia; a emite; a răspândi; *radio* a emite, a difuza; *fig* (*joy, etc*) a răspândi, a radia/a străluci de || *vi* a iradia; (*roads, etc*) a fi dispus radial.
radiation *s phys* radiaţie *f*, *fig* strălucire *f.*
radiator *s* radiator *m.*
radical *adj* radical; esenţial || *s pol* radical *n*; *math*, *chem* rădăcină *f*, radical *n.*
radio *s* radio *n* || *vt* (~ *info*) a difuza prin radio; (~ *a person*) a chema prin radio.
radioactive *adj* radioactiv.
radiography *s* radiografie *f.*
radiology *s med* radiologie *f.*
radiotherapy *s med* radioterapie *f.*
radish *s bot* ridiche *f.*
radium *s chem* radiu(m) *n.*
radius *s geom* rază *f* (de cerc); *fig* distanţă *f*, întindere *f*; *anat* radius *n.*
raffia *s bot* rafie *f.*
raffish *adj* (*dissolute*) destrăbălat, dezmăţat.
raffle *s* tombolă *f* || *vt* a pune la tombolă || *vi* a juca la tombolă.
raft *s naut* plută *f*; *naut* ponton *n* || *vt* a transporta cu pluta • ~**er** *s naut* plutaş *m*; pontonier *m*; *constr* grindă *f*; căprior *m.*
rag[1] *s* zdreanţă *f*; cârpă *f*; *fig pej* fiţuică *f*, ziar *n* prost; *pl* haine *f pl* rupte, zdrenţe *f pl.*
rag[2] *vt* (*tease*) a tachina, a râde de, a necăji.
rage *s* (*ire*) furie *f*; *coll* modă *f* || *vi* a se înfuria; *fig* (*storm, etc ~s*) a urla, a vui.
ragged *adj* zdrenţuit; jerpelit; dinţat; aspru; miţos; neglijent; necizelat.
raging *adj* mistuitor; devastator; însufleţit, animat.
raid *s* raid *n*; razie *f* || *vi* a ataca; a face o razie || *vt* a prăda; a invada; a ataca.
rail *s* şină *f*; cale *f* ferată; drug *n*; (*bar*) bară *f*; (*stair*) balustradă *f*; parapet *n*; grilaj *n*; *naut* bastingaj *n* || *vt* a transporta.
railing *s* (*fence*) grilaj *n*; *naut* bastingaj *n*; (*banister*) balustradă *f*; (*road*) parapet *n.*
railroad *s* cale *f* ferată || *adj* feroviar || *vt* a transporta cu trenul; *pol fig* a forţa votarea unei legi || *vi* a călători cu trenul.

raiment *s* îmbrăcăminte *f.*
rain *s* ploaie *f*; *fig* noian *n*; năvală *f* || *v imp* a ploua || *vi* a şiroi || *vt* a ploua cu; *fig* a revărsa, a copleşi de; ~ **forest** *s* pădure *f* tropicală umedă • ~**y** *adj* ploios.
rainbow *s* curcubeu *n.*
raincoat *s* impermeabil *n*; pelerină *f* de ploaie.
raise *vt* a ridica; (*cause*) a stârni; (*bring up*) a creşte; (~ *crops*) a cultiva; (~ *hopes, etc*) a trezi, a deştepta; a avansa; (*increase*) a spori; a rosti; a aduna (bani) || *s* urcare *f*; sporire *f.*
raisin *s* stafidă *f.*
rake[1] *s* greblă *f*; răzătoare *f*; vătrai *n* || *vt* a grebla; a netezi; a strânge (cu grebla); a răzui; *fig* a scormoni, a căuta/scotoci în.
rake[2] *s* libertin *m* || *vi* a trăi în desfrâu.
rakish *adj* (*jaunty*) şmecheresc; dezinvolt.
rally *s pol* miting *n*, întrunire *f*; *auto* raliu *n*; *sp* repriză *f*; *com* nou avânt *n*, revenire *f* || *vt* a aduna, a ralia, a reuni; *mil* a regrupa || *vi* (*patient*) a-şi reveni; (*price*) a urca; *pol* a se ralia; **to** ~ **round** *vi coll* a veni în ajutor.
ram *s* berbec *m* || *vt* a sparge; a presa; a vârî; a ciocni; a tampona.
RAM *s comp abbr* (**random access memory**) memorie *f* cu acces aleatoriu.
ramble *s* hoinăreală *f*; plimbare *f* fără ţintă; excursie *f*; *fig* incoerenţă *f* || *vi* a hoinări, a rătăci, a umbla fără ţintă; *fig* a divaga, a bate câmpii; a trăncăni; **to** ~ **on** *vi pej* a bate câmpii, a vorbi vrute şi nevrute.
rambling *adj* (*confused*) incoerent, haotic; (*irregular*) întortocheat; neregulat || *s* (*hiking*) hoinăreală *f.*
rambunctious *adj* (*boisterous*) nestăpânit; exuberant; gălăgios, turbulent.
ramification *s* ramificaţie *f.*
ramp *vi* a se urca; a se răsuci; a sări || *s* rampă *f*; pantă *f*; taluz *n*; râpă *f*; bord *n*, margine *f*, bordură *f.*
rampage *s* furie *f*; supărare *f*; **to be on the** ~ a face scandal/tărăboi.
rampant *adj* (*unchecked*) năvalnic, nestăpânit; (*wild*) violent, turbat; excesiv; (*overgrown*) luxuriant.
rampart *s mil* metereze *f pl*, (sistem de) fortificaţie *f*; *also fig* pavăză *f*; bastion *n*; *tech* valţ *n*; ax *n.*
ramshackle *adj* dărăpănat; improvizat; şubred.
ran *vi* * **run**.
ranch *s* fermă *f* • ~**er** *s* fermier *m*, proprietar *m* de ranch; crescător *m* de vite.
rancid *adj* râncezit; (*smell, taste*) acrit, acru, înăcrit; *fig* dezgustător, respingător.
rancor *s* ranchiună *f*, pică *f.*
random *s* întâmplare *f*, hazard *n*; bătaie *f* a puştii; **at** ~ la întâmplare || *adj* întâmplător; *math* aleatoriu; ~ **access memory** *s comp* memorie *f* cu acces aleatoriu.
randy *adj coll* excitat (sexual), lasciv.
rang *vt* * **ring**.
range *s* (*series*) şir *n*, rând *n*; *geog* lanţ *n*; ordine *f*; categorie *f*; (*array*) gamă *f*; (*scope*) anvergură *f*; traseu *n*; excursie *f*; sită *f*; plită *f* || *vt* a rândui; a clasa; a sorta || *vi* a hoinări; (*people, animals* ~) a hoinări, a rătăci, a colinda; *zool, bot* a se întinde, a fi răspândit • ~**r** *s* pădurar *m.*
rangy *adj* (*lanky*) cu membre lungi şi subţiri; (*roomy*) spaţios.
rank[1] *s mil* rând *n*, front *n*, linie *f*; rang *n*; titlu *n*; clasă *f*; grad *n* || *vt* a rândui; a evalua; a ataşa || *vi* a ocupa o funcţie; a avea un grad/rang (înalt etc) • ~**ing** *s* (*posi-*

tion) clasament *n*; rang *n* || *adj* (*prominent*) eminent, de valoare; *mil* de grad superior.

rank² *adj* (*plants*) rodnic; luxuriant; (*soil*) mănos, fertil; (*land*) năpădit/acoperit de buruieni; părăginit; (*smell*) rău mirositor, împuțit; rânced

rankle *vi* a supura; *fig* a roade pe cineva, a fi chinuitor/ dureros, a durea.

ransack *vt* (*search*) a scormoni, a scotoci; (*loot*) a jefui, a prăda.

ransom *s* răscumpărare *f*; eliberare *f*; amendă *f* || *vt* a răscumpăra.

rant *vi* a vorbi bombastic, a vorbi cu emfază; a fierbe de furie; a tuna și a fulgera (de mânie).

rap *s* lovitură *f* (ușoară); *mus* rap *n*; ciocănit *n* ușor; învinuire *f* || *vi* a bate, a ciocăni; a striga, a țipa; a înjura || *vt* a lovi, a ciocăni (în); a dojeni; a critica aspru.

rapacious *adj* rapace, acaparator.

rapacity *s* rapacitate *f*.

rape *vt* a viola; a răpi; a seduce || *s* viol *n*; răpire *f*; violare *f*; amestec *n*.

rapid *adj* rapid, iute; abrupt || *s* fugar *m*; vârtej *n* • ~s *s pl* praguri *n pl* (ale unui râu)

rapier *s* spadă *f*; ~ **wit** minte brici/ascuțită.

rapist *s* violator *m*.

rapport *s* raport *n*.

rapprochement *s* reconciliere *f*.

rapt *adj* (*engrossed*) transpus, fascinat.

rapture *s* extaz *n*; răpire *f*, rapt *n*.

rare¹ *adj* rar; excelent; neasemuit; rărit; crud; nefiert • ~ly *adv* (a)rareori.

rare² *adj* (*meat*) în sânge.

rarity *s* (*scarcity*) raritate *f*; (*uncommonness*) curiozitate *f*; piesă *f* rară.

rascal *s* ticălos *m*; hoțoman *m*; ștrengar *m* || *adj* slab; prăpădit.

rash¹ *adj* pripit, iute; impetuos; temerar, nesăbuit • ~ly *adv* pripit, grăbit; nechibzuit • ~ness *s* pripă *f*, grabă *f*; nechibzuință *f*, nesocotință *f*.

rash² *s med* erupție *f*.

rasher *s cul* feliuță *f*, felioară *f*.

rasp *s* rașpă *f* || *vt* (*scrape*) a răzui • ~y *adj* răgușit.

raspberry *s bot* zmeură *f*.

rat *s* șobolan *m*; delator *m*; spion *m*; transfug *m* || *vi* a stârpi șobolanii; a fi transfug.

rate *s* preț *n*, tarif *n*, curs *n*; rată *f*; normă *f*; porție *f*; calcul *n*; taxă *f*; procent *n*; ritm *n*; viteză *f* || *vt* a prețui, a evalua; a cota.

rather *adv* mai bine/curând; mai exact; oarecum; destul de; tare, prea, foarte.

ratify *vt* a ratifica; a valida.

rating *s* (*evaluation*) evaluare *f*, estimare *f*; (*ranking*) clasare *f*; *TV, radio* audiență *f* la public, rating *n*.

ratio *s math* raport *n*; proporție *f*.

ration *s* rație *f*; *pl* alimente *f pl* || *vt* a distribui; a aproviziona; a raționaliza.

rational *adj* logic, rațional; lucid, moderat.

rationale *s* rațiune *f* (de a fi/exista); analiză *f* rațională; expunere/explicare *f* rațională.

rattle *s* morișcă *f*; răpăit *n*; (*clatter*) zăngănit *n*; flecar *m*; flecăreală *f*; zarvă *f* || *vi* a zornăi; a dudui; *fig* a flecări || *vt* a grăbi.

ratty *adj coll* (*shabby*) ponosit; (*irritable*) irascibil.

raucous *adj* (*voice, etc*) răgușit; (*behavior*) zgomotos.

ravage *vt* a devasta || *vi* a face ravagii || *s* devastare *f*, distrugere *f*.

rave *vi* (*ramble*) a delira; (*storm, etc*) a mugi || *vt* a lăuda excesiv || *s* reclamă *f* exagerată; **to** ~ **about** *vi* a vorbi cu entuziasm despre.

raven *s orn* corb *m* || *adj* negru ca pana corbului.

ravenous *adj* (*person*) hămesit, lihnit, mort de foame; (*animal*) lacom, vorace.

ravine *s* râpă *f*, viroagă *f*.

ravish *vt* a silui, a viola; *fig* a încânta, a seduce, a fermeca • ~ing *adj* încântător, fermecător, seducător; captivant.

raw *adj* crud; necopt; (*unprocessed*) brut; natural; jupuit; (*inexperienced*) novice; sensibil; pur; (*air, etc*) rece și umed; vulgar || *s* rană *f*; materie *f* primă; **become** ~ || *vt* a vătăma; ~ **deal** *s* purtare *f* necivilizată; tratament *n* aspru; **get a** ~ **deal** a fi defavorizat.

ray *s* rază *f*; dâră *f*; (*hope*) licărire *f* || *vi* a (i)radia || *vt* a iradia.

rayon *s text* viscoză *f*.

raze *vt* (*destroy*) a nimici.

razor *s* brici *n*; aparat *n* de ras || *vt* a rade.

re *s mus* (nota) re *f* || *prep* în legătură cu; despre.

reach *vt* a ajunge; a sosi la; a înmâna || *vi* a ajunge, a se întinde || *s* atingere *f*; acces *n*; talent *n*; sferă *f* de influență; silință *f*; curs *n*.

react *vi* a reacționa • ~ion *s chem, etc* reacție *f*; mod *n* de a reacționa; efect *n* reciproc.

read, read, read *vt* (~ *a book*) a citi; (*interpret*) a interpreta; (*translate*) a traduce || *vi* (*study*) a citi; a studia; a se citi; (~ *a meter, etc*) a indica || *s* lectură *f*; citit *n*, citire *f* • ~**er** *s* cititor *m*; recenzent *m*; redactor *m*; *typ* corector *m*; carte *f* de citire; antologie *f*; recitator *m*, declamator *m* • ~**ership** *s* număr *n* de cititori.

readily *adv* prompt, rapid, iute; (*gladly*) bucuros, cu dragă inimă; ușor.

readiness *s* (*preparedness*) pregătire *f*; (*promptness*) promptitudine *f*.

reading *s* (*activity*) citit *n*, citire *f*; (*interpretation*) interpretare *f*; (*variant*) variantă *f* || *adj* de citit.

readjust *vt* a readapta, a reajusta; (~ *an instrument*) a regla din nou; (~ *a mirror*) a îndrepta; (~ *a policy*) a rectifica || *vi* (*person*) a se readapta (la).

ready *adj* pregătit, disponibil; dispus; amabil; prompt; eficace || *adv* gata; repede || *vt* a pregăti; a corupe; a antrena; ~ **cash** *s* bani *m pl* gheață; ~ **money** *s* bani *m pl* gheață.

real *adj* real, existent; adevărat; autentic; curat; pur; sincer; imobiliar || *adv* efectiv, într-adevăr; grozav de; ~ **estate** *s* bun *n* imobiliar • ~**ism** *s* realism *n* • ~**ist** *s* realist *m* • ~**istic** *adj* realist.

reality *s* realitate *f*; adevăr *n*; realism *n*.

realization *s* (*fulfillment*) realizare *f*, împlinire *f*; (*awareness*) înțelegere *f*; conștiință *f* (a unei realități).

realize *vt* a înțelege; a realiza; a obține.

really *adv* efectiv, cu adevărat; de fapt • *interj* zău!, serios!, pe cuvânt!.

realm *s* regat *n*; țară *f*; împărăție *f*; tărâm *n*; domeniu *n*.

realtor *s* agent *m* imobiliar.

reap *vt* a secera; (*harvest*) a recolta, a culege; *fig* (~ *glory, etc*) a culege, a recolta.

reappear *vi* a reapărea.

rear¹ *s* spate *n*, dos *n*; coadă *f*; fund *n* || *adj* din spate, dinapoi; de la coadă/sfârșit.

rear[2] s (*bring up*) a creşte; a clădi.

rearrange vt a rearanja; (*plan*) a schimba; (~ *a meeting*) a reprograma.

reason s raţiune f, (*sanity*) minte f; (*good sense*) bun simţ n; motiv n; (*cause*) cauză f || vi a raţiona, a gândi; a medita || vt a judeca; a medita; a convinge; a deduce • **~able** adj rezonabil; moderat; echitabil • **~ably** adv destul de; cu bun simţ; cu moderaţie • **~ed** adj motivat; chibzuit • **~ing** s raţionament n.

reassess vt a reevalua; fig a reconsidera; econ a reimpozita.

reassure vt a asigura (în vorbe); (*comfort*) a linişti, a potoli, a calma.

rebate s com rabat n, reducere f; archit rebord n, prag n; tech scobitură f.

rebel s rebel m; răsculat m || adj răzvrătit, rebel || vi a se revolta; a protesta; a se opune.

rebound vi a ricoşa; a se întoarce (ca un bumerang); (*recoil*) a avea un recul || s recul n; ricoşeu n; *also fig* salt n înapoi.

rebuff s ripostă f; refuz n; eşec n neaşteptat || vt a respinge; a refuza categoric.

rebuild vt a reconstrui.

rebuke s mustrare f, dojană f || vt a dojeni, a mustra.

rebuking adj mustrător.

rebut vt jur, fig a refuta, a respinge; a dezaproba || vi jur a riposta • **~tal** s jur refutare f, respingere f.

recall vt a rechema; a abroga; a retracta; a evoca || s rechemare f; abrogare f; destituire f; amintire f.

recant vt a retracta; a dezaproba || vi a retracta; relig a abjura, a se dezice.

recap vt coll a recapitula || s recapitulare f, revedere f.

recapture vt a recâştiga, a recupera || s recâştigare f, recuperare f.

recast vt (*redraft*) a reface, a remodela; (~ *a play*) a schimba distribuţia; tech a turna din nou.

recede vi a se îndepărta; fig a-şi pierde importanţa; econ a se deprecia.

receipt s primire f; chitanţă f; reţetă f.

receive vt a primi; a găzdui; a admite; a confirma; a stabili || vi a primi vizite • **~r** s primitor m; destinatar m; econ încasator m; com consignator m; jur tăinuitor m; executor m judecătoresc; (*phone*) receptor n; tech rezervor n.

recent adj recent.

receptacle s recipient n.

reception s primire f; acceptare f; întâmpinare f; recepţie f • **~ist** s recepţioner m.

receptive adj receptiv.

recess s cotlon n; nişă f; alcov n; pl adâncuri n pl; pauză f; vacanţă f || vt a ascunde || vi a face o pauză.

recession s retragere f; econ recesiune f.

recharge vt a reîncărca.

recidivist s recidivist m.

recipe s reţetă f; soluţie f; remediu n.

recipient s (*of a letter*) destinatar m; (*of a check*) beneficiar m; (*of a prize*) câştigător m.

reciprocal adj reciproc.

reciprocate vt a plăti cu aceeaşi monedă, a întoarce; (~ *feelings, etc*) a împărtăşi.

recital s mus recital n; (*narration*) povestire f, relatare f.

recite vt a recita; (*list*) a enumera.

reckless adj temerar; nesăbuit; imprudent; nepăsător.

reckon vt a socoti; a evalua; a aprecia || vi a calcula; ~

on vi a se baza pe; ~ **with** vi a se aştepta la • **~ing** s calcul n.

reclaim vt a repara, a corecta; (*land*) a asana; chem a regenera; a recupera, a recâştiga; fig a vindeca, a îndrepta.

recline vi a sta aplecat; a sta culcat; a se rezema || vt a înclina, a apleca.

recluse s pustnic m, sihastru m || adj retras, izolat, singuratic.

recognition s (*credit*) recunoaştere f; (*fame*) renume n; (*gratitude*) recunoştinţă f.

recognize vt a recunoaşte; a admite; a accepta; a înţelege.

recoil s recul n, retragere f; fig oroare f, silă f || vi mil a avea recul; (*from*) a se da înapoi (de la); fig a-i fi silă (de).

recollect vt a-şi aminti • **~ion** s (*recall*) amintire f, (*memory*) memorie f, aducere f aminte.

recommend vt a recomanda; a sfătui • **~ation** s sfat n; stimă f; favoare f.

recompense s recompensă f, răsplată f; compensaţie f || vt a recompensa.

reconcile vt a împăca; a aplana || vr a se împăca; a se resemna.

reconnaissance s mil recunoaştere f, cercetare f.

reconnoiter vi mil a merge în recunoaştere.

reconsider vt a reconsidera.

reconstitute vt a reconstitui.

reconstruct vt a reconstrui; a reface, a restaura; (*crime, etc*) a reconstitui.

record s (*evidence*) mărturie f; (*note*) raport n; act n; registru n; dosar n; cazier n; (*past performance*) record n; disc n || adj (*best*) record || vt (*note down*) a nota; (*make a recording*) a înregistra; a imprima; ~ **holder** s deţinător m al unui record • **~ing** s înregistrare f.

recount vt a povesti, a relata.

recoup vt (*for*) a compensa (pentru); fin a defalca || s jur scăzământ n, reţinere f.

recourse s recurs n; **have ~ to** vt a recurge la.

recover vt a încasa; (*get back*) a redobândi; a recâştiga; a recupera; a scoate || vr (*get well*) a-şi reveni || vi a se reface • **~y** s (*retrieval*) redobândire f, recăpătare f; (*healing*) restabilire f, vindecare f.

recreation s recreare f, destindere f; distracţie f; schimbare f.

recrimination s (*blame*) incriminare f.

recruit s recrut m; novice m || vt a recruta; a completa; a recupera, a redobândi.

rectangle s geom dreptunghi n.

rectify vt a rectifica; a îndrepta; a regla; a potrivi.

rectitude s rectitudine f.

rector s relig paroh m; pastor m; scol rector m.

rectum s anat rect n.

recumbent adj lit culcat, întins, lungit.

recuperate vt (*recover*) a se reface, a se restabili; (*get back*) a recupera.

recur vi (*error, etc*) a se repeta; (*dream*) a reveni; (*pain*) a reapărea • **~rence** s revenire f, repetare f.

recycle vt a recicla, a reutiliza.

red adj roşu; (*hair*) roşcat; rumen; roib; revoluţionar; sângeros || s roşu m; comunist m; extremist m.

redecorate vt a redecora || vi a reface zugrăveala şi tapetul.

redeem vt (*compensate for*) a compensa; (*cash in*) a

recupera; *econ* a amortiza; (*release*) a scăpa, a răscumpăra; *relig* a mântui, a izbăvi.

redemption *s* răscumpărare *f*; eliberare *f*; salvare *f*; *relig* mântuire *f*; *econ* achitare *f*; amortizare *f*.

redirect *vt* (~ *a letter, etc*) a trimite mai departe; (~ *energy, money*) a reorienta; (~ *traffic*) a devia.

redo *vt* (*do again*) a reface; (*rebuild*) a reconstrui.

redolent *adj lit* evocator; (*scented*) mirositor.

redoubt *s* redută *f*.

redraft *vt* a reface, a rescrie; a reformula.

redress *vt* (*restore*) a restabili, a reface; (~ *a wrong*) a îndrepta, a corecta || *s* (*compensation*) îndreptare *f*, corijare *f*; reparare *f*; reparație *f*; ușurare *f*, alinare *f*.

reduce *vt* (*cut*) a reduce; (*decrease*) a scădea; (*trim down*) a scurta; a preface; a schimba; a dilua || *vi* a urma/ține un regim de slăbire.

reduction *s* reducere *f*, micșorare *f*; *com, fin* reducere *f*; rabat *n*; remiză *f*; *tech* rectificare *f*, corecție *f*.

redundancy *s* redundanță *f*, pleonasm *n*; (*job loss*) șomaj *n*; exces *n*, surplus *n*.

redundant *adj* (*superfluous*) superfluu, excesiv; de prisos; (*tautologous*) pleonastic; prolix; *comp, ling* redundant.

reed *s bot* trestie *f*; stuf *n*; săgeată *f*; registru *n*; caval *n* || *vt* (*to thatch/decorate with* ~) a acoperi cu stuf.

reef *s* recif *n* (de coral); *min* filon *n*.

reek *vi* a fumega; a duhni; a avea un iz || *s* miros *n* urât; duhoare *f*; evaporare *f*; căpiță *f*, claie *f*.

reel¹ *s* (*spool*) mosor *n*, bobină *f*; *elec, cin* bobină *f*; *typ* rulou *n*; *naut* tambur *n*; *text* vârtelniță *f*; *tech* șanț *n*, rilă *f* || *vt* a desfășura, a deșira, a depăna; *fig* (*story, etc*) a depăna, a debita; *tech* a bobina.

reel² *vi* a se învârti; a se clătina || *s* legănare *f*, clătinare *f*; amețeală *f*.

re-enact *vt* a reconstitui, a reproduce.

refectory *s* sală *f* de mese, sufragerie *f*, refectoriu *n*.

refer *vt* (**to**) a referi; a înainta, a supune; a trimite la, a îndruma la/către/spre; a atribui; *scol* a amâna; a reporta; *econ* a imputa || *vi* a se referi la, a face aluzie la; a menționa; a apela/recurge la.

referee *s sp* arbitru *m* || *vt sp* a arbitra || *vi sp* a fi arbitru.

reference *s jur* referire *f*; competință *f*; raport *n*; (*recommendation*) referință *f*; citare *f*; atribuire *f*; (*allusion*) aluzie *f*; referent *m*; *pl* recomandație *f*.

referendum *s* referendum *n*.

refill *vt* a reumple || *vi* a se alimenta din nou || *s* (*pen*) rezervă *f*.

refine *vt* a rafina; a șlefui; a ameliora || *vi* a se rafina; a se purifica • ~**ment** *s* perfecționare *f*; rafinament *n*, eleganță *f* • ~**ry** *s* rafinărie *f*; distilerie *f*.

reflect *vt* a reflecta; *fig* a oglindi; *fig* (**on/upon**) a răsfrânge, a proiecta (asupra) || *vi* a se reflecta; (**on/upon**) (*think*) a reflecta asupra, a se gândi la.

reflex *s* reflectare *f*; reflecție *f*, reflex *n* || *adj* reflex; introspectiv.

reform *vt* a reforma, a îndrepta; a stârpi; a amenda || *vi* a se corija; a amenda || *s* reformă *f*; amendare *f* • **the Reformation** *s* Reforma *f* • ~**er** *s* reformator *m*.

refract *vt phys* a refracta.

refrain¹ *vt* a se abține; a se stăpâni; a se păzi (de).

refrain² *s* refren *n*.

refresh *vt* a înviora, împrospăta; a răcori; a întări; a anima; a odihni || *vi* a se reface; a se odihni .

refreshment *s* gustare *f*; aperitiv *n*; răcorire *f*; băutură *f* răcoritoare.

refrigerator *s* frigider *n*.

refuel *vi* a se (re)alimenta cu combustibil; a se aproviziona.

refuge *s also fig* refugiu *n*, adăpost *n*; adăpostire *f*; *fig* salvare *f*, mântuire *f*; **to take ~ in** a se refugia în • ~**e** *s* refugiat *m*.

refund *vt* a rambursa; a compensa || *s* rambursare *f*.

refurbish *vt* a renova • ~**ment** *s* renovare *f*.

refusal *s* refuz *n*; respingere *f*; *jur* drept *n* la preempțiune.

refuse¹ *vt* a refuza; a respinge, a nu accepta; *mil* a replia, a retrage.

refuse² *s* rebut *n*, deșeu *n*; gunoi *n*.

refute *vt* a dezminți, a respinge, a refuta.

regain *vt* (~ *shape, health*) a redobândi; (*get back*) a recâștiga.

regal *adj* maiestuos, regal.

regard *s* (*look*) privire *f*; privință *f*; părere *f*; (*respect*) deferență *f*; *pl* salutări *f pl* || *vt* (*look upon*) a privi; a ține cont; (*consider*) a socoti; (*relate to*) a viza, a se referi la • ~**less** *adj* nepăsător || *adv* oricum; ~ **of** *prep* indiferent de.

regatta *s* regată *f*, concurs *n* de canotaj.

regent *s* regent *m*; *scol* membru *m* al consiliului de conducere.

regime *s pol* regim *n*.

regimen *s med* regim *n*.

regiment *s mil* regiment *n*; *fig* mulțime *f*, masă *f* || *vt mil, fig* a înregimenta.

region *s* regiune *f*; ținut *n*; domeniu *n*; sector *n*, district *n*; zonă *f*.

register *s* (*list*) registru *n*; tabel *n*; catalog *n*; contor *n*; cargou *n* || *vt* (*enter*) a înregistra; a marca; a înscrie; (*reveal*) a exprima || *vi* (*enlist*) a se înscrie; a se instala.

registrar *s* arhivar *m*; *jur* grefier *m*; ofițer *m* de stare civilă; *scol* secretar *m* general.

registration *s* înregistrare *f*; înscriere *f*; *auto* înmatriculare *f*.

regress *vi* a regresa, a da înapoi.

regret *s* regret *n*; căință *f* || *vt* a regreta.

regroup *vi* a se regrupa.

regular *adj* regulat; precis; riguros; fix; (*ordered*) ordonat; reglementar; (*usual*) obișnuit, normal; simetric || *s* (*customer*) client *m*, mușteriu *m*.

regulate *vt* (~ *with rules*) a reglementa; (*control*) a regla; (*adjust*) a potrivi.

regulation *s* ordin *n*; *pl* statut *n*; reglare *f*; ordonare *f*; reglementare *f*.

rehab *s* dezalcoolizare *f*; dezintoxicare *f* • ~**ilitate** *vt* (~ *an ex-con*) a reabilita, a reintegra; (~ *a patient*) a recupera.

rehash *vt* (*rework*) a transforma; a remania; (*repeat*) a relua; a reitera.

rehearsal *s thea* repetiție *f*; *fig* repovestire *f*, reluare *f*; recitare *f*, declamare *f*.

rehearse *vt* a repeta; a recita; a enumera; a repovesti || *vi* a repeta.

rehouse *vt* a instala în locuință nouă, a da o nouă locuință.

reign *s* domnie *f*; putere *f* || *vt* a domni; a guverna; a predomina.

reimburse *vt* a restitui, a rambursa; (**for**) a despăgubi (pentru).

rein *s* frâu *n*; hăț *n*; **to give (a horse/smb) a free ~** a da frâu liber (calului/cuiva).

reincarnation *s* reîncarnare *f*, reîntrupare *f*.
reindeer *s zool* ren *m*.
reinforce *vt* a întări, a consolida; *mil* a aduce întăriri, a întări; *constr* a arma.
reinstate *vt* (*~ an employee*) a reinstala în funcții, a reintegra; (*restore*) a reface, a restabili.
reinvest *vt* a îmbrăca/acoperi din nou; *econ* a investi din nou.
reissue *s* (*~ a book*) reeditare *f* || *vt* (*~ a book*) a reedita; (*~ discs, etc*) a scoate din nou pe piață.
reiterate *vt* a reitera, a repeta.
reject *vt* a respinge; a lepăda; a evacua || *s* rebut *n*; lepădătură *f*.
rejoice *vi* a se bucura, a jubila || *vt* a bucura; a înveseli.
rejoin *vi* a replica, a riposta.
rejoinder *s* răspuns *n*, replică *f*, ripostă *f*.
rejuvenate *vi* a reîntineri.
rekindle *vt also fig* a reaprinde.
relapse *vi* (*into*) a reveni (la); a recădea (în); *med* a recidiva || *s* (*habit*) reluare *f*; recădere *f*; repetare *f*; *med* recidivă *f*, reșută *f*, recădere *f*.
relate *vt* (*tell*) a relata, a povesti; a descrie; (*to, with*) (*connect*) a lega (de), a asocia (cu), a raporta (la) || *vi* (*with*) (*interact*) a fi în raport/relație (cu); a se înrudi (cu).
relation *s* relație *f*; analogie *f*; privință *f*; rudă *f*; relatare *f*; expunere *f* • **~ship** *s* relație *f*, raport *n*; referire *f*.
relative *adj* relativ; respectiv; reciproc || *s* rudă *f*; *gram* pronume/adjectiv *n* relativ.
relax *vt* (*people*) a destinde; a odihni; (*body, etc*) a decontracta; (*loosen*) a desface; a atenua || *vi* (*people*) a se relaxa; a se odihni; (*body, etc*) a se decontracta; (*loosen*) a se desface; *fig* a se îndupleca, a se înmuia.
relay *s sp* ștafetă *f*; *elec* releu *n*; *radio* retransmisie *f* || *vt sp* a schimba; *radio* a retransmite.
release *s* (*relief*) eliberare *f*; scutire *f*; *com* livrare *f*; *cin, mus* lansare *f*, difuzare *f*; *chem* emitere *f*; *mil* lansare *f*; *elec* decuplare *f*; *auto* debreiere *f* || *vt* (*free*) a elibera; a scuti; *jur* a ceda; *mus* a lansa; *cin* a difuza; *tech* a decupla; a declanșa; (*~ a report, etc*) a publica.
relegate *vt* a referi, a trimite; *fig* a clasa; a remite, a supune (spre rezolvare).
relegation *s* (*demotion*) retrogradare *f*; (*referral*) trimitere *f*, referire *f*; remitere *f*.
relent *vi* (*person*) a se îndupleca; (*let up*) a se domoli • **~less** *adj* neînduplecat.
relevant *adj* relevant, important; pertinent; (*info*) util.
reliability *s* siguranță *f*; credibilitate *f*.
reliable *adj* (*person*) demn de încredere, de nădejde, (*machine, etc*) fiabil; sigur; trainic; (*info, etc*) serios.
reliance *s* sprijin *n*, reazem *n*, suport *n*.
reliant *adj* (*on*) încrezător în.
relic *s* urmă *f*; *pl* relicve *f pl*, vestigii *n pl*; amintire *f*.
relief *s* (*comfort*) ușurare *f*; destindere *f*; reducere *f*; (*aid*) ajutor *n*; *jur* reparație *f*.
relieve *vt* (*allay*) a ușura; (*ease*) a degreva; (*help*) a ajuta; *mil* a schimba; a distra; a relaxa; *tech* a debloca.
religion *s* religie *f*, cult *n*; credință *f*, crez *n*; evlavie *f*; călugărie *f*.
religious *adj* pios, religios, evlavios; monahal || *s* călugăr *m*, călugăriță *f*.
relinquish *vt* (*~ power*) a abandona; (*~ a plan, etc*) a renunța la; (*~ a job*) a părăsi.
relish *s* savoare *f*; aromă *f*; condiment *n*; *fig* farmec *n*;

poftă *f*, plăcere *f* || *vt* a condimenta; a mânca/bea cu poftă/plăcere; *also fig* a savura, a se desfăta/delecta cu.
relive *vt/vi* a retrăi, a trăi din nou.
reluctance *s* nehotărâre *f*; împotrivire *f*.
reluctant *adj* ezitant, șovăitor; care se opune; fără chef/poftă • **~ly** *adv* fără tragere de inimă, contrar voinței; cu repulsie.
rely *vi* (**on/upon**) a se bizui pe, a se încrede în.
remain *vi* a rămâne; a zăbovi; a se menține • **~s** *s pl* vestigii *f pl*, urme *f pl*; rămășițe *f pl*.
remake *vt* a reface || *s* versiune *f* nouă.
remand *vt jur* a trimite din nou la închisoare || *s* reîntemnițare *f*; retrimitere *f* la închisoare; **to ~ into custody** a cerceta în stare de arest.
remark *s* observație *f*; remarcă *f*; replică *f* || *vt* a observa; a declara; a replica || *vi* a face o remarcă.
remarkable *adj* remarcabil, deosebit; uluitor.
remarry *vi* a se recăsători.
remedial *adj* curativ; care remediază/corectează; de îndreptare; *tech* de întreținere.
remedy *s* remediu *n*; medicament *n*; corectiv *n*; compensație *f* || *vt* a remedia.
remember *vt* a-și aminti; a răsplăti; a memora || *vi* a-și aminti; a nu uita.
remembrance *s* memorie *f*, amintire *f*; comemorare *f*; **in ~ of smb** în amintirea/memoria cuiva.
remind *vt* a aminti, a reaminti; **to ~ smb of smth** a-i aminti cuiva de ceva.
reminisce *vi* (**about**) a-și aminti (de), a evoca (ceva) • **~nt** *adj* care reamintește de; (*smile*) nostalgic • **~nce** *s* reminiscență *f*; *pl* memorii *f pl*, amintiri *f pl*.
remiss *adj* neglijent; nepăsător; **to be ~** a da dovadă de neglijență.
remission *s relig* iertare *f*, absolvire *f*; *econ* scutire *f*; *jur* renunțare *f*; (*pain, etc*) atenuare *f*, diminuare *f*.
remit *vt* a remite, a transmite; *com* a plăti, a achita; *jur* a retrimite, a înainta; *jur* a suspenda; *jur* a repune în drepturi; *relig* a ierta, a absolvi de • **~tance** *s* (*money*) vărsământ *n*; *com* lichidare *f*, plată *f*.
remnant *s* rest *n*; deșeu *n*; gunoi *n*; vestigiu *n*; fragment *n*.
remonstrance *s frml* protest *n*; nemulțumire *f*.
remorse *s* căință *f*, remușcare *f*.
remote *adj* izolat; (*time, place*) îndepărtat; (*person*) distant; (*aloof*) separat; străin; minim; (*chance, etc*) vag; **~ control** *s* telecomandă *f*.
removal *s* deplasare *f*.
remove *vt* a muta; a îndepărta; (*~ a stain*) a scoate; (*~ a problem*) a rezolva; (*~ suspicion*) a risipi; (*fire an employee*) a concedia; a demite; (*~ clothes*) a scoate, a schimba; a șterge; a aboli; a suprima || *vi* a se muta; a se retrage || *s* treaptă *f*, grad *n*; interval *n*; etapă *f*; neam *n*; mutare *f*.
remunerate *vt* a remunera, a retribui; *fig* a răsplăti.
remuneration *s* remunerație *f*, retribuire *f*.
renaissance *s* renaștere *f*; reînnoire *f*; **the Renaissance** *s hist* Renașterea *f*.
rename *vt* a schimba numele, a da un nou nume.
rend, rent, rent *vt* (*rip*) a sfâșia; (*slit*) a crăpa; *fig* (*heart, etc*) a frânge, a sfâșia || *vi* a se rupe; a se crăpa || *s* sfâșiere *f*.
render *vt* a da, a remite, a înmâna; *com* a livra; *mil* a preda; *fin* (*account*) a preda; (*aid*) a aduce, a oferi; *thea, mus* a interpreta; a executa; (*arts*) a exprima, a reda.

rendezvous *s* întâlnire *f*, randevu *n*; *mil*, *naut* adunare *f* a efectivului.

rendition *s* *mus* interpretare; *(text)* traducere *f*.

renegade *s* renegat *m*.

renew *vt* a reînnoi; a renova; a restaura; a reface; a relua ‖ *vi* a se reînnoi; a renaşte; a reîncepe • **~able** *adj* care poate fi reînnoit.

rennet *s* cheag *n* (pentru lapte).

renounce *vt* a renunţa la; a repudia, a nu recunoaşte ‖ *vi* a se da bătut.

renovate *vt* a renova, a repara, a restaura; a înviora.

renown *s* renume *n*, faimă *f*; reputaţie *f* • **~ed** *adj* **(for)** renumit, vestit, celebru (pentru).

rent *s* chirie *f*; rentă *f*; închiriere *f* ‖ *vt* a închiria; a arenda ‖ *vi* a fi închiriat • **~al** *s* *(car, etc)* taxă *f* de închiriere; *(house)* chirie *f* ‖ *adj* de închiriat; cu chirie.

reopen *vt* a redeschide.

reorganize *vt* a reorganiza.

rep *s* *coll* reprezentant *m*.

repair *vt* a repara; a remedia; a vindeca; a renova ‖ *s* reparaţie *f*; depanare *f*; renovare *f*; stare *f*, condiţie *f*.

reparation *s* despăgubire *f*, compensaţie *f*.

repartee *s* replică *f*.

repast *s* *frml* *(meal)* masă *f*; *(feast)* banchet *n*.

repatriate *vt* a repatria ‖ *s* persoană *f* repatriată.

repay *vt* a plăti, a achita, a restitui; *fig* a răsplăti, a recompensa.

repeal *vt* *jur* a abroga, a revoca; a anula ‖ *s* *jur* abrogare *f*, revocare *f*; anulare *f*.

repeat *vt* a repeta; a recita ‖ *vi* a repeta ‖ *vr* a se repeta; a reveni ‖ *s* repetare *f*; bis *n*; repetenţie *f*.

repel *vt* a respinge; a para; *fig* a nu primi/accepta, a respinge; *fig* a dezgusta.

repent *vt* a regreta, a se căi ‖ *vi* a-i părea rău • **~ance** *s* regret *n*, căinţă *f*, penitenţă *f*, remuşcări *f pl*.

repercussion *s* repercusiune *f*, urmare *f*; reverberaţie *f*; represalii *f pl*.

repertoire *s* *thea*, *mus* repertoriu *n*.

repertory *s* catalog *n*; *thea* repertoriu *n*; depozit *n*, magazie *f*.

repetition *s* repetare *f*; recitare *f*.

replace *vt* a pune la loc; a înlocui; a restitui.

replay *vt* *sp* a rejuca; *(movie, etc)* a relua ‖ *s* *sp* rejucare *f*; meci *n* rejucat; *(movie, etc)* reluare *f*.

replenish *vt* a reumple; **(with)** a completa (cu); a aproviziona din nou (cu)

replete *adj* *frml* *(full)* întesat (de); *(person)* îmbuibat.

replica *s* *(arts)* reproducere *f*, copie *f* (exactă), reproducere *f*; replică *f*; *mus* reluare *f*, repetare *f*.

reply *s* răspuns *n*; replică *f* ‖ *vi* a răspunde, a replica.

report *s* *(account)* raport *n*; ştire *f*; faimă *f*; reportaj *n* ‖ *vt* *(give account)* a raporta; a face un reportaj ‖ *vi* *(turn up)* a raporta; a se prezenta; a informa • **~edly** *adv* după cum se pare/spune • **~er** *s* reporter *m*; raportor *m*.

repose *s* odihnă *f*, repaus *n*; calm *n*; somn *n* ‖ *vi* a se odihni; a sta culcat.

repository *s* *(storehouse)* depozit *n*, magazie *n*; *fig* mină *f*, izvor *n* nesecat.

repossess *vt* a repune în posesie • **~ion** *s* repunere *f* în posesie.

reprehensible *adj* reprobabil, condamnabil.

represent *vt* a (re)prezenta; a denota; a descrie; a juca • **~ative** *adj* tipic; reprezentativ; grăitor ‖ *s* reprezen-

tant *m*; trimis *m*; deputat *m*; membru *m* al Camerei Reprezentanţilor; exemplu *n*.

repress *vt* a reprima, a înăbuşi; *fig* a-şi stăpâni, a-şi reţine • **~ion** *s* represiune *f*; *(sexual)* refulare *f*.

reprieve *vt* *jur* a acorda o suspendare; *com* a amâna; *(delay payment)* a acorda un termen ‖ *s* *jur* graţiere *f*; suspendare/comutare *f* a pedepsei; *com* amânare *f*; *fig* răgaz *n*, amânare *f*.

reprimand *s* mustrare *f*, dojană *f* ‖ *vt* a mustra, a dojeni.

reprint *vt* a retipări, a reedita ‖ *s* retipărire *f*, reeditare *f*.

reprisal *s* represalii *f pl*.

reproach *s* reproş *n*; imputare *f* ‖ *vt* a certa • **~ful** *adj* *(look, etc)* de reproş.

reproduce *vt* *(copy)* a reproduce ‖ *vi* *(have children)* a se reproduce, a se înmulţi.

reproduction *s* *(breeding)* reproducere *f*, înmulţire *f*; *(copy)* copie *f*, imitaţie *f*; înregistrare *f*.

reproof *s* mustrare *f*; dezaprobare *f*.

reprove *vt* *(person)* a condamna; a mustra; *(deed)* a blama.

reptile *s* reptilă *f*; lingău *m*; linguşitor *m* ‖ *adj* târâtor; linguşitor; corupt.

republic *s* republică *f*; cerc *n*, grup *n*.

republican *s/adj* republican *m*; **Republican** *s* membru *m* al Partidului Republican.

repudiate *vt* *(~ an offer, etc)* a respinge; *(~ friends)* a repudia.

repugnance *s* dezgust *n*, silă *f*.

repugnant *adj* antipatic; ostil; opus.

repulsion *s* repulsie *f*, aversiune *f*.

repulsive *adj* refractar; ostil; repulsiv.

reputable *adj* reputat, prestigios.

reputation *s* reputaţie *f*; faimă *f*.

repute *s* reputaţie *f*; **of good ~** cu reputaţie bună.

request *s* *(appeal)* cerere *f*; întrebare *f*; rugăminte *f*; dorinţă *f* ‖ *vt* *(ask for)* a cere; a ruga; a pretinde; a invita.

requiem *s* *mus*, *relig* recviem *n*.

require *vt* a cere, a pretinde; a solicita; *(need)* a necesita; *(oblige)* a impune, a obliga • **~ment** *s* cerinţă *f*, nevoie *f*.

requisite *s* *frml* lucru *n* necesar ‖ *adj* cerut, necesar.

requisition *s* *mil* rechiziţie *f*; cerere *f*, revendicare *f* ‖ *vt* *mil* a rechiziţiona

reread *vt* a reciti, a citi încă o dată.

re-route *vt* *(~ a bus, etc)* a schimba traseul.

rerun *vt* *(~ a race)* a reorganiza; *(~ a tv program)* a redifuza; *(~ a tape)* a pune din nou, a relua ‖ *s* *thea*, *cin*, *tv* reluare *f*, redifuzare *f*; *fig* repetare *f*.

rescind *vt* *(annul)* a anula; *(overturn)* a abroga, a revoca.

rescue *s* salvare *f*; eliberare *f* ‖ *adj* salvator ‖ *vt* a salva; a mântui; a elibera.

research *s* cercetare *f*; căutare *f*; studiere *f* ‖ *vi* a face cercetări ştiinţifice.

resemblance *s* **(to)** asemănare *f*, similitudine *f* (cu).

resemble *vt* a semăna cu; a fi similar cu.

resent *vt* a-i displăcea; a fi jignit/iritat • **~ful** *adj* plin de resentimente/nemulţumire.

reservation *s* rezervare *f*; *(proviso)* rezervă *f*; *(condition)* restricţie *f*; rezervaţie *f*.

reserve *s* rezervă *f*; stoc *n*; reţinere *f*; păstrare *f*; rezervaţie *f* ‖ *vt* a rezerva; a nu se pronunţa.

reservoir *s* bazin *n*, rezervor *n*; sursă *f*; stoc *n*; lac *n* de acumulare.

reset, reset, reset vt (~ *a watch*) a potrivi; (~ *a meter*) a pune la zero; *comp* a reseta, a reinițializa.

reshape vt (*remake*) a reface; (*redesign*) a remodela; *pol* a reorganiza; *fig* a prelucra.

reshuffle vt *pol* a remania; (*restructure*) a regrupa, a reface || s *pol* remaniere *f*; regrupare *f*

reside vi a locui, a domicilia.

residence s reședință *f*; domiciliere *f*.

resident s rezident *m*; locuitor *m* permanent; *med* medic *m* rezident || adj rezident (în); inerent, propriu.

residual adj rezidual

residue s reziduu *n*; depunere *f*; excedent *n*.

resign vt (*quit*) a demisiona din; a ceda; (*hope*) a renunța la || vi a demisiona; (*accept*) a se resemna • ~ation s demisie *f*; resemnare *f*.

resilience s *phys* reziliență *f*; elasticitate *f*; *fig* mobilitate *f*, adaptabilitate *f*; *fig* energie *f*; curaj *n*.

resilient adj *phys* rezilient, elastic; *fig* elastic, mobil, adaptabil; *fig* (*person*) energic; viguros.

resin s rășină *f*.

resist vt a rezista; a se abține || vi a rezista || s strat *n* protector • ~ance s rezistență *f*; opoziție *f*; *elec* rezistență *f*; reostat *n*; *tech* rezistență *f* la temperature înalte • ~ible adj căruia i se poate rezista.

resolute adj decis, hotărât; ferm.

resolution s (*decree*) hotărâre *f*, rezoluție *f*; decizie *f*; (*resolve*) fermitate *f*; *chem* descompunere *f*; dizolvare *f*; *phys* descompunere *f*; *math*, *fig* (*solution*) rezolvare *f*, soluționare *f*.

resolve s hotărâre *f*, decizie *f* || vt a decide; a rezolva; a risipi || vi a se desface; a se decide.

resonance s rezonanță *f*.

resonant adj răsunător, sonor.

resort s resursă *f*, mijloc *n*; recurgere *f*; *jur* instanță *f*; (*spa*) stațiune *f* || vi a recurge la; a apela la; a face uz de.

resound vi a răsuna; (**with**) a răsuna (de); *fig* a avea răsunet/ecou || vt a glorifica.

resource s (*source*) resursă *f*; remediu *n*; soluție *f*; truc *n*; distracție *f*; agrement *n* • ~**ful** adj inventiv, ingenios; plin de resurse.

respect s respect *n*; atenție *f*; privință *f*; relație *f*; *pl* omagii *n pl* || vt a acorda atenție; a respecta; **with** ~ **to** cu privire la, referitor la • ~**able** adj onorabil, respectabil; decent; demn; prezentabil; considerabil • ~**ive** adj respectiv, corespunzător.

respiration s respirație *f*.

respirator s *med* respirator *n*; mască *f* de gaze.

respite s *frml* răgaz *n*.

resplendent adj strălucitor, splendid.

respond vt a riposta, a răspunde.

response s (*answer*) răspuns *n*; replică *f*; (*reaction*) reacție *f*; **in** ~ **to** ca urmare a ...

responsibility s răspundere *f*, responsabilitate *f*; **sense of** ~ simț de răspundere.

responsible adj (**for**) responsabil (pentru); vinovat (de); (*job, etc*) de (mare) răspundere; competent, capabil; demn de încredere, pe care se poate conta.

responsibly adv (în mod) responsabil.

responsive adj (**to**) sensibil (la); (*open*) impresionabil, simțitor; (*alert*) inimos, cordial, entuziast; (*engine*) nervos; (*radio*) selectiv.

rest[1] s odihnă *f*; tihnă *f*; somn *n*; pauză *f*; suport *n*; adăpost *n* || vi a se odihni; a se sprijini; a se bizui; a

se fixa; a depinde de || vt a odihni; a(-și) sprijini; a baza.

rest[2] s (*remainder*) rest *n*, rămășiță *f*; *com* (*account*) încheiere *f* || vi a rămâne.

restaurant s restaurant *n*.

restitution s (*refund*) restituire *f*, returnare *f*; (*amends*) reparații *f pl*, despăgubiri *f pl*.

restive adj (*restless*) neliniștit; (*edgy*) nervos.

restless adj agitat, nervos; (*night*) de nesomn/insomnie.

restore vt (~ *confidence*) a reda; (*give* back) a restitui; (*reinstate*) a restabili; a reface; (*refurbish*) a restaura.

restrain vt (~ *your temper, etc*) a stăpâni, a reține; (~ *feelings*) a-și înăbuși, a-și stăpâni • ~**t** s (*limit*) constrângere *f*; restricție *f*; piedică *f*; (*self-control*) rezervă *f*, reținere *f*; cumpătare *f*; interdicție *f*; (*captivity*) detențiune *f*, reținere *f*.

restrict vt a restrânge; a constrânge.

restroom s closet *n*, toaletă *f*.

result s rezultat *n*; sfârșit *n* || vi a rezulta; a se termina; (**in**) a ajunge la.

resume[1] vt a relua; a continua; a recupera; a recâștiga; a recapitula || vi a reîncepe.

resume[2] s rezumat *n*; curriculum vitae *n*; CV *n*.

resumption s reluare *f*; reîncepere *f*.

resurgence s reapariție *f*; reînviere *f*.

resurrect vt a reînvia || vi a reînvia, a renaște • ~**ion** s înviere *f*; reînviere *f*; *fig* renaștere *f*, reînviere *f*.

resuscitate vt a reanima; a resuscita || vi a reînvia, a renaște.

resuscitation s reanimare *f*; renaștere *f*, reînviere *f*.

retail s *com* vânzare *f* cu amănuntul || adv *com* cu amănuntul/bucata; ~ preț *n* cu amănuntul • ~**er** s negustor *m* cu amănuntul.

retain vt a reține; (*keep*) a păstra; (*maintain*) a menține; a angaja.

retake vt a recaptura; a relua; (*test*) a repeta || s *cin* reluare *f*; (*of exam*) repetare *f*.

retaliate vt (**upon**) a se răzbuna pentru || vi (**on**) a recurge la represalii; a se răzbuna (pe).

retaliation s răzbunare *f*, revanșă *f*; represalii *f pl*.

retaliatory adj represiv, punitiv.

retarded adj întârziat; *med*, *fig* arierat.

retention s *med* retenție *f*; reținere *f*; păstrare *f*; *psych* (capacitate de) memorare *f*; **retentive** adj (*memory*) bun, sănătos; *anat* retentiv.

reticent adj reținut, rezervat; reticent; tăcut, taciturn; necomunicativ.

retina s *anat* retină *f*.

retinue s cortegiu *n*, alai *n*, suită *f*.

retire vi a pleca; a se retrage; a demisiona || vt a retrage; a pensiona.

retool vt a reutila; a reprofila, a reorganiza.

retort[1] s riposta *f*, replică *f* || vt a riposta || vi a riposta (**on**) a replica, a riposta.

retort[2] s *chem* retortă *f* || vt a distila în retortă.

retouch vt a retușa.

retrace vt a reconstitui, a reface; a se înapoia/întoarce pe același drum.

retract vt (*draw in*) a-și retrage; (~ *words*) a retracta, a nega; (*take back*) a-și lua înapoi || vi a se retrage; a se dezice, a retracta.

retreat vt a se retrage; a se refugia || vt a retrage || s retragere *f*; stingere *f*; refugiu *n*.

retrial s *jur* rejudecare *f*.

retribution s (*payback*) recompensă f; (*vengeance*) pedeapsă f, răzbunare f.

retrieval s *comp* cercetare f și extragere f;

retrieve vt (*recover*) a recupera; a regăsi; *comp* a salva, a căuta, a extrage; a remedia; a-și reface ‖ vr a se reabilita • ~r s *zool* câine m de aport.

retrograde adj retrograd, înapoiat.

retrospect s privire f retrospectivă • ~ive s (*art*) retrospectivă f.

return vi (*come back*) a reveni, a se întoarce; a replica ‖ vt (*give back*) a restitui; (*put back*) a repune; a răspunde; a oglindi; *jur* a declara ‖ s (*homecoming*) revenire f; repetare f; *sp* retur n; *com* profit n; refacere f; oglindire f; răsplată f; schimb n; *pol* alegere f.

reunion s adunare f, reuniune f, întrunire f

reunite vt a uni din nou, a reuni; *fig* a aduna, a strânge, a ralia ‖ vi a se reuni.

rev s *coll abbr* (**revolution**) tură f; ~ **the engine** vt a ambala motorul; ~ **up** vi a se ambala.

revamp vt *coll* (*systems, etc*) a restructura; (~ *a house*) a renova; *tech* a reutila/reechipa parțial.

reveal vt a dezvălui; a divulga; a dovedi.

reveille s *mil* deșteptarea f.

revel vi a chefui, a benchetui.

revenge s răzbunare f; *sp, fig* revanșă f ‖ vt a răzbuna ‖ vr a se răzbuna.

revenue s venit n.

reverberate vi (*sound*) a reverbera; a răsuna; a se răsfrânge ‖ vt a face să reverbereze; a reflecta, a răsfrânge.

reverberation s (*of sound, light*) reverberație f; *fig* repercusiune f.

revere vt a respecta profund; a venera.

reverence s venerație f; respect n, stimă f ‖ vt a venera, a adora; a stima, a respecta.

reverend s reverend m.

reversal s schimbare f totală; (*ill luck*) schimbare f a norocului; *jur* anulare f, casare f; *tech* inversare f, reversare f.

reverse adj invers, opus ‖ s (*coin*) revers n; (*back*) verso n; (*opposite*) opus n; năpastă f; *auto* marșarier n ‖ vt a inversa; (*overturn*) a răsturna; (*undo*) a schimba.

revert vi *jur* a reveni unui ascendent ‖ vt (*look, etc*) a întoarce (privirea etc).

review s (*magazine*) revistă f; *com* bilanț n; (*situation*) analiză f, examinare f; (*book, etc* ~) critică f, recenzie f ‖ vt (~ *a salary*) a revizui; a revedea; a corecta; a analiza; (~ *a book, etc*) a recenza; *mil* (*troops*) a trece în revistă; (*recap*) a recapitula • ~er s critic m.

revile vt *lit* (*insult*) a insulta, a ultragia.

revise vt a revedea, a revizui; a corecta.

revision s revizuire f, revedere f; (*change*) schimbare f • ~ist s/adj revizionist m.

revival s renaștere f; (*habit*) reluare f; recăpătare f; (*trade, etc*) relansare f; (*interest*) redeșteptare f.

revive vt (~ *a person*) a reanima; *fig* (~ *the economy*) a relansa; (~ *interest*) a redeștepta; (~ *a tradition*) a restabili; (~ *a show*) a relua; (~ *memories*) a redeștepta ‖ vi (~ *person*) a-și veni în fire; *fig* (~ *hopes, etc*) a renaște.

revoke vt a revoca; a anula, a abroga.

revolt s revoltă f; rebeliune f ‖ vi a se revolta; a se răscula ‖ vt a revolta.

revolution s *pol* revoluție f; *tech* rotație f, revoluție f.

revolve vi a se roti, a se învârti; a gravita; (*ideas*) a circula.

revolver s revolver n.

revolving adj (*rotating*) rotitor; care se rotește; *tech* turnant, pivotant; ~ **scene** scenă rulantă.

revue s *thea* revistă f.

revulsion s dezgust n; repulsie f; *med* revulsiune f.

reward s răsplată f, premiu n ‖ vt a răsplăti, a premia, a recompense • ~ing adj (*work*) plin de satisfacții; (*book*) care merită să fie citită.

rewind vt (~ *a tape*) a rebobina; (~ *a watch*) a întoarce; *text* a depăna.

rewire vt (*electrical*) a reface instalația electrică.

rewrite, rewrote, rewritten vt a rescrie.

Reykjavik s Reykjavik.

rhapsody s *liter, mus* rapsodie f; discurs n pompos; frazeologie f (*goală*).

rhetoric s retorică f, oratorie f; *pej* vorbărie/frazeologie f goală.

rheumatism s *med* reumatism n.

rhinoceros s *zool* rinocer m.

rhododendron s *bot* rododendron m, smârdar m.

rhubarb s *bot* rubarbă f.

rhyme s rimă f ‖ vi a rima; a scrie poezii ‖ vt a rima.

rhythm s ritm n; cadență f.

rib s *anat* coastă f; *bot, zool* nervură f; *coll* nevastă f; (*umbrella*) arc n ‖ vt *tech* a întări cu grinzi; *coll* a tachina.

ribald adj (*lewd*) obscen, vulgar • ~ry s limbaj n vulgar.

ribbon s panglică f; cordon n; șnur n; fâșie f; zonă f; teren n ‖ vi a șerpui.

rice s *bot* orez n ‖ vt a pasa.

rich adj bogat; (*soil*) fertil; copios; (*clothes*) luxos; elegant; (*color*) intens; (*food*) consistent; (*sound*) puternic; (*wine*) tare; (*smell*) pătrunzător; *coll* (*incident*) nostim, amuzant, hazliu • ~**ly** adv somptuos; bogat; din abundență; cu dărnicie; pe deplin • ~**ness** s bogăție f.

rick s (*of hay*) căpiță f ‖ vt (*wrench*) a luxa, a scrânti.

rickets s *med* rahitism n.

rickety adj *med* rahitic; *fig* șubred.

rickshaw s ricșă f, trăsurică f trasă de un om.

ricochet s ricoșare f; ricoșeu n ‖ vi a ricoșa.

rid, rid, rid vt a debarasa; a salva; a scăpa de ‖ adj liber, eliberat.

ridden vi * **ride**.

riddle[1] s ghicitoare f; mister n ‖ vt a rezolva, a explica ‖ vi a vorbi enigmatic.

riddle[2] s sită f, ciur n; stăvilar n ‖ vt a cerne, a trece prin sită/ciur; (~ *with bullets*) a ciurui, a perfora; a argumenta în contradictoriu cu.

ride, rode, ridden vi a călări; a domina; a cuprinde; a înfrunta; a enerva ‖ s plimbare f călare; cursă f; călătorie f cu mașina • ~r s călăreț m; călător m; jocheu m; biciclist m; *typ* intercalare f; *jur* anexă f; *geol, min* filon n.

ridge s (*hills*) lanț n, șir n; (*edge*) creastă f, culme f; (*fold*) încrețitură f, cută f.

ridicule s ridicol n ‖ vt a ridiculiza, a lua în râs ‖ vi a-și bate joc.

ridiculous adj ridicol; caraghios.

rife adj răspândit; frecvent; curent; ~ **with** adj plin de, bogat în.

riffle vt (*pages*) a răsfoi; (*cards*) a amesteca, a face.

riff-raff *s* rămăşiţe *f pl*, resturi *n pl*; (*people*) drojdia *f* societăţii, lepădături *f pl*, scursuri *f pl*.

rifle[1] *s* (*weapon*) puşcă *f*, ghint *n*, carabină *f*, şanţ *n* ‖ *vt* a împuşca; a ghintui ‖ *vi* a trage cu arma.

rifle[2] *vt* (*ransack*) a jefui; a devaliza.

rift *s* (*crack*) crăpătură *f*; *geol* fisură *f*; (*division*) deza-cord *n* ‖ *vt* a spinteca, a despica, a crăpa; *also fig* a sfâşia, a rupe.

rig *vt naut* a echipa, a arma; *fig* (*election, etc*) a falsifica ‖ *s naut* velatură *f*; *fig* ţinută *f*, toaletă *f*, îmbrăcă-minte *f*; **oil ~** (*land*) schelă *f*, (*sea*) platformă *f* de foraj..

right *adj* drept; (*answer, time*) corect; just; (*true*) adevărat; curat; (*idea, decision, direction*) bun; (*suit-able*) convenabil ‖ *s* drept *n*; dreptate *f*; justiţie *f*; partea *f* dreaptă ‖ *adv* drept; îndată; chiar; exact; just; perfect; (*utterly*) cu totul ‖ *vt* a redresa; **~ away** imediat, pe loc; **~ of way** prioritate de trecere; **on the ~** la dreapta; **~ angle** unghi drept • **~eous** *adj* (*person*) drept, cinstit; (*feeling*) justificat, îndreptăţit **~ful** *adj* legitim, legal; cuvenit • **~handed** dreptaci • **~hand man** om de încredere, mâna dreaptă (a cuiva) • **~ist** *s pol* persoană *f* de dreapta • **~ly** *adv* (*properly*) cum se cuvine; (*correctly*) (în mod) corect/just/cinstit; (*for certain*) pe drept cuvânt • **~ness** *s* justeţe *f* • **~minded** cu mintea la cap.

rigid *adj* rigid; dur; aspru; statornic; strict, sever.

rigmarole *s coll* trăncăneală *f*, sporovăială *f*, vorbărie *f* goală.

rigor *s* rigoare *f*, stricteţe *f*; asprime *f*, duritate *f* • **~ous** *adj* sever; strict; exact; minuţios.

rim *s* (*edge*) margine *f*; (*glasses*) ramă *f*; (*wheel*) jantă *f*, obadă *f* ‖ *vt* a încercui; a obăda.

rind *s bot* scoarţă *f*; (*fruit*) coajă *f*; (*cheese*) crustă *f*; (*meat*) şorici *n* ‖ *vt* a coji; a jupui.

ring[1] *s* inel *n*; cerc *n*; verigă *f*; cearcăn *n*; ring *n*; arenă *f*; cartel *n* ‖ *vi* a alerga în cerc ‖ *vt* (*encircle*) a încercui.

ring[2], **rang, rung** *vi* a suna; a răsuna ‖ *vt* (*peal*) a suna; (*alarm*) a anunţa, a vesti ‖ *s* (*bell*) dangăt *n*; (*phone, etc*) ţârâit *n*; (*voice*) timbru *n*; intonaţie *f*; *fig* impresie *f*, aparenţă *f*; (*group*) cerc *n*; (*finger*) inel *n*; (*boxing*) ring *n*.

ringlet *s* (*curl*) cârlionţ *m*.

rink *s* patinoar *n* ‖ *vi* a patina; a face patinaj.

rinse *vt* a clăti; a spăla ‖ *s* clătire *f*; spălare *f*; alcool *n*; loţiune *f* capilară.

riot *s* tărăboi *n*; răscoală *f*; dezmăţ *n*; exces *n*; bogăţie *f*; nebunie *f* ‖ *vi* a face tărăboi; a face excese; a se revolta • **~ous** *adj* (*crowd*) zgomotos; (*behavior*) răzvrătit; (*party*) gălăgios.

rip *vt* a despica, a tăia; a inciza ‖ *vi* a se zbengui; a înjura ‖ *s* tăietură *f*; sfâşiere *f*; spintecare *f*; deşirare *f*.

ripe *adj* copt; în vârstă; dispus să; înţelept; complet • **~n** *vt/vi* a (se) coace.

rip-off *s coll* escrocherie *f*, înşelătorie *f*.

ripple *s* val *n* mic, undă *f*; clipocit *n*; murmur *n*, susur *n* ‖ *vi* (*water*) a se încreţi; (*river*) a clipoci, a susura; (*hair*) a se ondula.

rise, rose, risen *vi* a se urca, a se sui; (*stand up*) a se ridica; (*wake up*) a se scula; (*prices, etc*) a creşte; (*sun, etc*) a răsări; (*rebel*) a se răscula; (*emerge*) a se ivi; (*originate*) a se trage din ‖ *s* ridicare *f*, *fig* par-venire *f*; creştere *f*; (*sun*) răsărit *n*; (*source*) origine *f*.

risen *vi* * **rise**.

rising *adj* (*wave, etc*) care se înalţă; (*prices, etc*) în

creştere; (*artist, etc*) în ascensiune ‖ *s* (*revolt*) răs-coală *f*, revoltă *f*, răzmeriţă *f*; (*of sun, etc*) ridicare *f*, înălţare *f*; (*of prices*) creştere *f*; **~ damp** igrasie *f*.

risk *s* risc *n* ‖ *vt* a risca; a încerca; a îndrăzni să • **~y** *adj* riscant; riscat; decoltat, picant.

risqué *adj* periculos, îndrăzneţ.

rite *s* ritual *n*, ceremonie *f*.

ritual *s* ritual *n*, ceremonial *n*; *relig* tipic *n*, liturghier *n* ‖ *adj* ritual; conform ritului.

rival *s* rival *m* ‖ *adj* rival; opus ‖ *vt* a concura ‖ *vi* a rivaliza cu • **~ry** *s* rivalitate *f*.

riven *adj* (*split*) dezbinat.

river *s* râu *n*; fluviu *n*; potop *n* ‖ *adj* fluvial • **~bank** *s* mal *n*, ţărm *n* • **~bed** *s* albie *f* (de râu/fluviu)

rivet *s* nit *n*; nituire *f* ‖ *vt* a nitui; *fig* a ţintui, a întări; (**to/on**) a-şi pironi/aţinti (privirea etc) asupra, a fixa cu privirea.

Riviera *s* **the French ~** Coasta *f* de Azur; **the Italian ~** Riviera *f* italiană.

rivulet *s* pârâiaş *n*.

roach *s icht* babuşcă *f*; *ento* gândac *m*.

road *s* drum *n*; cale *f*; şosea *f*; stradă *f*; mijloc *n*; radă *f*; **~block** *s* baraj *n* rutier; **~ map** *s* hartă *f* rutieră; **~ safety** *s* siguranţă *f* rutieră; **~ sign** *s* panou *n* rutier de semnalizare; **~ work** *s* lucrări (de reparare a dru-murilor); construcţii/lucrări *f pl* rutiere.

roam *vi* a hoinări; a rătăci; a străbate • **~er** ‖ *s* hoinar *m*, rătăcitor mcutreier(at) *n*; hoinăreală *f*.

roar *vi* (*wind ~s*) a urla; (*people, lions ~*) a răcni; a zbiera; (*thunder ~s*) a tuna; (*sea ~s*) a mugi; a vâjâi; a hohoti ‖ *vt* a răcni ‖ *s* urlet *n*; ţipăt *n*; răcnet *n*; vuiet *n*; hohot *n*; muget *n* • **~ing** *adj* (*person*) care urlă; (*~ wind*) care vuieşte; (*deafening*) asurzitor; (*thriving*) prosper; (*~ business*) înfloritor; (*~ success*) monstru, răsunător.

roast *vt* a frige; a coace; a prăji; *coll* a tachina ‖ *vr* a se încălzi ‖ *vi* a se frige; a se coace; a se prăji ‖ *s* frigere *f*; coacere *f*; prăjire *f*; friptură *f*; barbecue *n*; **~ beef** *s* friptură *f* de vită, rosbif *n*.

rob *vt* a jefui; a fura; a priva de ‖ *vi* a face jaf • **~ber** *s* tâlhar *m*; haiduc *m*.

robe *s* robă *f*; mantie *f*; costum *n* de ceremonie; garderob *n* ‖ *vt* a îmbrăca într-o robă.

robin *s orn* prihor *m*, măcăleandru *m*.

robot *s* robot *m*; automat *n*.

robust *adj* robust; tare; violent, aprig; intens.

rock[1] *s* stâncă *f*; *geol* rocă *f*; cap *n*; acadea *f*; piatră *f*; **~ bottom** *s* fundul *n* ‖ *adj* (*prices*) foarte scăzut; **on the ~s** *adv* (*drink*) cu gheaţă/cuburi de gheaţă; (*marriage*) aproape de despărţire.

rock[2] *vt* (*sway*) a legăna; a balansa; (*stun*) a zgudui ‖ *vi* a se balansa; **~ and roll** *s* rock-and-roll *n*.

rocket *s* rachetă *f* ‖ *vi* a zbura cu o rachetă; a lansa o rachetă; a creşte vertiginos ‖ *vt* a bombarda cu rachete; **~ launcher** *s* lansator *n* de rachete.

rocky *adj* (*road, etc*) stâncos, pietros; *fig* (*economy, marriage*) instabil, precar.

rod *s* vargă *f*; vergea *f*; băţ *n*; năpastă *f*; sceptru *n*.

rode *vt* * **ride**.

rodent *s/adj zool* rozător *n*.

roe[1] *s zool* ciută *f*; căprioară *f*.

roe[2] *s icht* icre *f pl*.

rogue *s* (*rascal*) pungaş *m*, tâlhar *m*; (*scoundrel*) pezevenghi *m*, năzdrăvan *m*.

role *s thea, cin, etc* rol *n*.

roll *s* (*paper*) rulou *n*; (*reel*) film *n*; balot *n*; (*bread*) chiflă *f*; (*list*) listă *f*; (registru *n*; tabel *n*; bubuit *n*; ruliu *n* || *vt* (*revolve*) a roti; a rula; a netezi || *vi* a se roti; a rula; a bubui; a se legăna; ~ **over** *vi* a se întoarce pe partea celalaltă; ~ **up** *vt* (*paper, etc*) a rula; (*sleeves*) a sufleca.

roller *s* tăvălug *n*; sul *n*; rulou *n*; compresor *n*; ~ **coaster** *s* montagne russe *n*; ~ **skate** *s* patină *f* cu rotile.

rollicking *adj coll* (*joyful*) vesel, exuberant; (*noisy*) zgomotos.

rolling *s* rostogolire *f*; rulare *f*; ruliu *n*; laminare *f* || *adj* (*bridge*) rulant; (*slope*) lin; (*reform*) lent şi susţinut.

romaine *s bot* (*lettuce*) salată *f* verde.

Roman *s/adj* roman *m*; ~ **alphabet** *s* alfabet *n* latin.

romance *s* roman *n*; idilă *f*; romantism *n*; basm *n*; poezie *f*; feerie *f*; fantezie *f*; farmec *n*; ficţiune *f* || *vi* a scrie romane; a inventa; a exagera || *adj* romantic.

Romania *s* România *f* • ~**n** *adj* român || *s* român(că) *m/f*; (*language*) română *f*.

romantic *adj* romantic; romanţios; romanesc; pitoresc || *s* romantic *m*.

Rome *s* Roma.

romp *s* zbenguială *f* || *vi* a se zbengui, a zburda • ~**ing** *adj* zburdalnic, nebunatic.

roof *s* acoperiş *n*; boltă *f*; plafon *n*; imperială *f* || *vt* a acoperi; a adăposti.

rook *s orn* cioară *f* de câmp; (*chess*) turn *n*, tură *f*.

rookie *s coll* (*recruit*) boboc *m*, începător *m*.

room *s* cameră *f*; *pl* locuinţă *f*; loc *n*, spaţiu *n*; ocazie *f* || *vi* a locui la comun || *vt* a găzdui • ~**mate** *s* coleg *m* de cameră.

roost *s* (*perch*) stinghie *f*, cracă *f* || *vi* (*birds*) a se cocoţa pe stinghie; a se cuibări; *fig* a-şi găsi adăpost.

rooster *s orn* cocoş *m*.

root[1] *s bot* rădăcină *f*; *fig* sursă *f*; *math* radical *n*; strămoşi *m pl*; fond *n* || *vt* a împlânta; a ţintui || *vi* a se înrădăcina; (*pig*) a râma.

root[2] *vi coll* (**for**) a încuraja, a suţine; a da ajutor/ sprijin.

rope *s* frânghie *f*; odgon *n*; lasou *n*; coardă *f* || *vt* a lega cu o funie; a prinde cu lasoul.

rosary *s relig* mătănii *f pl*.

rose[1] *vi* * **rise**.

rose[2] *s bot* trandafir *m*, roză *f*; bujor *m*; rozetă *f*; roşeaţă *f*; roz *n* || *adj* trandafiriu.

rosemary *s bot* rozmarin *n*.

rosette *s* rozetă *f*, ornament *n*.

rostrum *s* (*pl* ~**s**/**rostra**) tribună *f*.

rosy *adj* (*pink*) roz; (*blushing*) rumen; îmbujorat; (*optimistic*) idilic.

rot *vi* a putrezi; a se strica; a zăcea; a degenera || *vt* a descompune; a rata || *s* cădere *f*; putrezire *f*; descompunere *f*.

rota *s* programare *f* prin rotaţie; (*roster*) listă *f*, registru *n*.

rotary *adj* rotativ; turnant, pivotant.

rotate *vi* a se roti || *vt* a roti; a alterna, a varia.

rotating *adj* care se roteşte; prin rotaţie.

rotation *s* rotaţie *f*.

rote *s* memorie *f*; **by** ~ pe de rost, în mod mecanic.

rotor *s tech* rotor *n*; *math* corn *n* de rotaţie.

rotten *adj* putred, stricat; clocit; cariat; corupt.

rotund *adj* (*shape*) rotund, rotunjit; (*person*) gras; plinuţ; (*style*) bombastic, emfatic.

rouge *s* ruj *n*; fard *n* || *vi* a se ruja; a se farda || *vt* a ruja; a farda.

rough *adj* (*coarse*) aspru; brut; grosolan; (*road, etc*) pietros; ţepos; (*hair*) zbârlit; (*voice*) alterat; *mus* discordant; (*weather*) vijelios; (*draft*) neprelucrat || *s* dezordine *f*; stare *f* brută; bătăuş *m* || *vt* a schiţa; a bruftui || *vi* a se purta aspru || *adv* dur, aspru.

roulette *s* ruletă *f*.

round *adj* rotund; sferic; circular; (*number*) întreg; (*rhythm, etc*) vioi; (*voice*) sonor; (*style*) fluent || *s* cerc *n*; (*police* ~*s*) rond *n*; plimbare *f*; (*cycle*) ciclu *n*; (*set*) rând *n*; (*series*) serie *f*; (*drinks*) rând *n*; ocol *n*; *sp* rundă *f*; *mil* foc *n* (de armă); cartuş *n*; (*cards*) levată *f*; (*applause*) ropot *n* || *vt* a rotunji; a ocoli || *vi* a se rotunji; a se învârti || *adv* în cerc, în jur; ~ **up** *vt* (~ *people, cattle*) a strânge laolaltă; (~ *criminals*) a aresta; *math* a rotunji (în sus); • ~**about** *adj* ocolit, indirect; întortocheat; pe ocolite || *s* cale *f* ocolită • ~**ed** *adj* rotunjit; întregit, completat • ~**ly** *adv* (*utterly*) complet; (*plainly*) pe faţă, direct • ~**the-clock** non-stop • ~**trip** *n* călătorie *f* dus-întors.

rouse *vt* (*wake up*) a trezi, a deştepta; (*stir*) a îndemna, a îmboldi; (*feeling*) a deştepta, a provoca.

rousing *adj* (*speech*) vibrant, pasionat; (*reception*) entuziast.

rout *s mil* debandadă *f*, derută *f*; **put to** ~ *vt* a pune pe fugă, a înfrânge.

route *s* itinerar *n*; rută *f*; *fig* cale *f*, drum *n* || *vt* a dirija; a repartiza.

routine *s* rutină *f*; pricepere *f* || *adj* curent, normal; *pej* banal, şablon; cotidian.

rove *vi* a hoinări; a rătăci || *vt* a cutreiera la întâmplare.

roving *adj* itinerant, hoinar.

row[1] *s* (*line*) şir *n*, rând *n*, linie *f*; şir *n* de case; străduţă *f*; **in a** ~ la rând, în şir.

row[2] *s* (*paddle*) a vâsli || *s* vâslit *n*, canotaj *n*; plimbare *f* cu barca.

row[3] *s* (*noise*) scandal *n*, zarvă *f*; (*disagreement*) ceartă *f*; tapaj *n*; dojană *f*; (*fight*) încăierare *f* || *vi* a se certa || *vt* a certa.

rowdy *adj* gălăgios; scandalagiu.

royal *adj* regesc, regal; princiar; măreţ || *s coll* membru *m* al familiei regale; coală *f* mare de hârtie • ~**ty** *s* regalitate *f*; regat *n*; monarhie *f*; arendă *f*; redevenţă *f*; *pl* drepturi *n pl* de autor.

rub *vt* a freca; a roade; a reduce; a copia un model; a şterge; a lustrui || *vi* a se freca; a se uza || *s* frecare *f*; frecţie *f*; piedică *f*.

rubber *s* cauciuc *n*; gumă *f*, radieră *f* || *adj* din cauciuc; ~ **band** *s* elastic *n*; ~ **stamp** *s* ştampilă *f* || *vt fig* a aproba fără discuţii.

rubbish *s* gunoi *n*; moloz *n*; *coll fig* fleacuri *n pl*, prostii *f pl*.

rubble *s* moloz *n*, dărâmături *f pl*; pietriş *n*, prundiş *n*.

rubicund *adj* rubicond.

ruby *s* rubin *n* || *adj* rubiniu.

rucksack *s* rucsac *n*.

rudder *s naut* cârmă *f*; *fig* principiu *n* conducător/ călăuzitor, călăuză *f*.

ruddy *adj* (*rosy*) rumen; (*flushed*) îmbujorat; (*reddish*) roşcat, roşcovan.

rude *adj* rudimentar; (*boorish*) grosolan; (*impolite*) nepoliticos; brusc; aspru; insolent; violent; (*foul*) vulgar.

rudiment *s* rudiment *n; pl* cunoştinţe *f pl* elementare; baze *f pl* • **~ary** *adj* rudimentar.
rueful *adj* trist; lamentabil.
ruff *s* (*dress*) guler *n* încreţit; *orn, zool* guler *n*.
ruffian *s* ticălos *m*, bandit *m*; brută *f* ‖ *adj* ticălos, mârşav; brutal, sălbatic.
ruffle *vt* (~ *hair*) a ciufuli; (*water* ~*s*) a tulbura; (~ *person*) a ofensa; (~ *patience*) a pierde.
rug *s* carpetă *n*; pled *n*.
rugby *s sp* rugbi *n*.
rugged *adj* (*rocky*) accidentat; (*rough*) aspru; (*strong*) viguros, robust; (*vehicle, etc*) solid, masiv.
ruin *s* ruină *f*; pieire *f* ‖ *vt* a ruina; a nărui; a prăda ‖ *vi* a se ruina; a decădea.
rule *s* regulă *f*; lege *f*; normă *f*; domnie *f*; decizie *f*; riglă *f* ‖ *vt* a conduce; a linia; a decide; **to ~ out** *vt* a exclude, a elimina • **~d** *adj* (*paper*) liniat • **~r** *s* (*leader*) conducător *m*; (*monarch*) domnitor *m*; (*measure*) riglă *f*.
rum *s* rom *m*
rumble *s* (*of traffic, etc*) vuiet *n*, bubuit *n*; (*of a stomach*) chioraială *f* ‖ *vi* a vui, a bubui; (*guts*) a ghiorăi, a chiorăi.
rumbling *s* bubuit *n*; chiorăit *n*; *pl* cârteli *f pl*, crâcneli *f pl*.
rumbastious *adj coll* exuberant.
ruminant *s/adj* rumegător *n*.
ruminate *vi zool* a rumega; *fig* (**on/over/about**) a medita, a reflecta (la).
rummage *vt* a răscoli, a scotoci.
rumor *s* zvon *n*, ştire *f* ‖ *vt* a răspândi zvonuri despre.
rump *s* (*animal*) crupă *f*; (*bird*) târtiţă *f*; *coll* (*people*) şezut *n*.
rumple *vt* (~ *clothes*) a şifona; (~ *hair*) a ciufuli.
rumpus *s* (*furor*) vacarm *n*.
run, ran, run *vi* (*sprint*) a fugi, *sp* a alerga; a se grăbi; *naut* a pluti; (*machine*) a funcţiona; (*river, etc*) a curge; a şiroi; (*turn*) a deveni; (*color*) a se şterge; (*text, etc*) a glăsui; *jur* a fi în vigoare; (*bus, train*) a circula; *fig* (*rumor, etc*) a circula; (*nose*) a curge; (*plant*) a se căţăra; (*engine*) a se învârti; *pol* (**for**) a candida; (*continue*) a dura; (*play*) a se juca; (*time*) a trece, a se scurge ‖ *vt* (*manage*) a conduce; a administra; (*water, etc*) a face să curgă; (*machine, etc*) a acţiona; a vârî; (*distance*) a străbate; (*errand*) a face, a îndeplini; *sp* (*points*) a realiza ‖ *s* fugă *f*; (*jog*) alergare *f*; cursă *f*; *tech* etapă *f*; *tech* serie *f*; *tech* demaraj *n*; *rail* parcurs *n*; traseu *n*; (*machine*) mers *n*, funcţionare *f*; (*outing*) plimbare *f*; (*sequence*) şir *n*, succesiune *f*; serie *f*; (*course*) curs *n*, mers *n*; (*category*) categorie *f*, clasă *f*; *typ* tiraj *n*; ~ **across** *vi* a da peste; ~ **away** *vi* (**from**) a fugi (de); ~ **down** *vi* (*machine*) a se opri; (*battery, etc*) a se descărca; (*spring*) a se destinde ‖ *vt* (*device*) a opri; (*car*) a răsturna, a da peste; (*output*) a restrânge; a reduce activitatea; ~ **into** *vi* (*problems*) a se izbi de; (*people*) a da peste; (*car*) a da peste, a lovi; ~ **off** *vi* a fugi; **~off** *s pol* balotaj *n*; ~ **out** (*supplies, time*) a se epuiza; (*license, etc*) a expira; ~ **over** *vt* (*text*) a parcurge cu privirea; (*car*) a călca; ~ **through** *vi* a se infiltra ‖ *vt* (*read*) a parcurge; (*practice*) a repeta; ~ **to** *vi* (*amount*) a atinge, a urca, a se ridica până la; ~ **up** *vi* (*plant*) a creşte repede; (*price, etc*) a creşte, a se urca, a se mări; *sp* a sosi al doilea; ~ **up against** *vi* a întâlni pe cineva din întâmplare.

runaway *adj* (*horse*) năvalnic; (*victory*) facil; (*inflation*) galopant ‖ *s* fugar *m*, dezertor *m*.
rung¹ *vt* * **ring.**
rung² *s* treaptă *f*.
runner *s sp* alergător *m*; (*seller of drugs, etc*) traficant *m*; (*of a sled*) talpă *f*; (*of a chair, drawer*) şine *f pl* pe care culisează mecanismul; ~ **up** *s sp* câştigătorul *m* de pe locul doi.
runny *adj* (*food*) lichid; (*nose*) care curge.
runty *adj* (*stunted*) pipernicit; (*dwarfish*) pitic, mic.
runway *s* albie *f*, matcă *f*; *avia* pistă *f*, câmp *n* de rulaj; *sp* pistă *f* de curse.
rupture *s* rupere *f*, ruptură *f*; *med* hernie *f*; *elec* străpungerea *f* izolaţiei ‖ *vt* a sparge, a perfora; *fig* a rupe, a desface ‖ *vi med* a produce o hernie.
rural *adj* rural, de ţară, rustic; ţărănesc.
ruse *s* şiretlic *n*, vicleşug *n*, viclenie *f*.
rush¹ *vi* a se grăbi; a năvăli; a se ivi; a ţâşni ‖ *vt* a grăbi; a face repede; a năvăli în ‖ *s* grabă *f*; năvală *f*; cursă *f*; asalt *n*; salt *n*; afluenţă *f*; ~ **hour** *s* oră *f* de vârf.
rush² *s bot* papură *f*; *bot* trestie *f*; rogoz *n*; stuf *n*.
rusk *s* pesmet *m*; biscuit *m*.
russet *adj* maro-roşcat.
Russia *s* Rusia *f* • **~n** *adj* rus ‖ *s* (*person*) rus *m*; (*language*) rusă *f*.
rust *s* rugină *f* ‖ *vt* a rugini; a lăsa în părăsire ‖ *vi* a (se) rugini; *fig* a se prosti; a regresa; a deveni leneş • **~y** *adj* ruginit.
rustic *adj* rustic, provincial, rural; necioplit, grosolan ‖ *s* ţăran *m*.
rustle *vi* (*leaves* ~) a foşni, a fremăta; (*paper* ~*s*) a fâşâi ‖ *vt* (~ *cattle*) a fura.
rustling *s* (*of leaves*) foşnet *n*; (*of cattle*) furt *n* de vite.
rut *s* (*wheel*) făgaş *n*, urmă *f*; (*furrow*) brazdă *f*; *fig* făgaş *n*, direcţie *f*; *fig* deprindere *f*, obicei *n*, rutină *f*; *tech* şanţ *n*; canelură *f*; falţ *n*; **to be in a** ~ a se cufunda în rutină.
ruthless *adj* crud, nemilos.
rye *s* secară *f*; ~ **flour** *s* făină *f* de secară.

S

S, s *s* (litera) S, s.
Sabbath *s relig* sabatul *n*.
sabbatical *s* an *m* sabatic; *relig* fiecare al şaptelea an *m*.
sable *s zool* zibelină *f*, samur *m*.
sabotage *s* sabotaj *n* ‖ *vt* a sabota.
saboteur *s* sabotor *m*.
saber *s* sabie *f* ‖ *vt* a tăia cu sabia; ~ **rattle** *vi fig* a zăngăni armele.
saccharin *s chem* zaharină *f*.
sachet *s* pliculeţ *n*.
sack *s* sac *n* ‖ *vt* a pune într-un sac; (*fire*) a concedia • **~ing** *s* pânză *f* de sac.
sacrament *s relig* sacrament *n*; *relig* împărtăşanie *f*; *fig* semn *n*, simbol *n*.
sacred *adj* sacru; sfinţit; religios; scump; de neatins; inviolabil.
sacrifice *s* sacrificiu *n*; jertfă *f*; ofrandă *f*; lipsă *f*; abnegaţie *f* ‖ *vt/vi* a jertfi ‖ *vr* a se jertfi.
sacrilege *s also fig* sacrilegiu *n*, profanare *f*, pângărire *f*.
sad *adj* trist; mâhnit; abătut; melancolic; mohorât; regretabil; tragic; jalnic • **~ness** *s* tristeţe *f*.

saddle *s* ş(e)a *f;* coamă *f* || *vt* a înşeua; a îngreuia, a împovăra.

sadism *s* sadism *n.*

sadistic *adj* sadic • **~ally** *adv* sadic, cu sadism.

safari *s* safari *n.*

safe *adj* ferit; (*secure*) sigur; (*not dangerous*) fără risc; (*protected*) protejat; eficace; teafăr; (*sound*) solid; convins; prudent || *s* seif *n;* frigider *n;* ~ **sex** *n* sex *n* protejat.

safeguard *s* (**against**) pază *f,* apărare *f* (împotriva); garanţie *f* (împotriva); prevedere *f; tech* dispozitiv *n* de siguranţă || *vt* (**against**) a proteja (împotriva), a feri (de).

safekeeping *s* siguranţă *f,* securitate *f.*

safely *adv* în siguranţă; cu siguranţă; **we can ~ say** putem spune în deplină siguranţă.

safety *s* siguranţă *f,* securitate *f;* ~ **pin** *s* ac *n* de siguranţă.

saffron *s bot* şofran *m.*

sag *vi* (*bend*) a se îndoi; (*slump*) a se lăsa; (*droop*) a se încovoia; a atârna; (*wilt*) a se ofili; a se târî; (*prices* ~) a coborî; (*conversation* ~s) a trena, a lâncezi || *vt* a face să se îndoaie || *s* îndoire *f;* (*drop*) lăsare *f;* tasare *f;* (~ *in prices*) scădere *f,* coborâre *f.*

saga *s liter* saga *f;* legendă *f.*

sagacious *adj* înţelept.

sage[1] *adj* (*wise*) înţelept; inteligent || *s* (om) înţelept *m;* om *m* inteligent.

sage[2] *s bot* salvie *f.*

Sagittarius *s astrol* Săgetător *m.*

sago *s bot* sago *n;* ~ **palm** *s* sagotier *m.*

said *vt* * **say**.

sail *s naut* velă *f,* pânză *f,* velier *n;* plimbare *f* cu un vas || *vi naut* a naviga; a pluti; (*birds, etc*) a zbura; a luneca; *fig* a plana; a se legăna || *vt* a pluti; a naviga pe; a străbate; ~ **through** *vi* a reuşi să facă ceva fără nici un efort • **~ing** *s sp* iahting *n;* plecare *f* în larg • **~or** *s* marinar *m;* matelot *m;* pălărie *f* marinar.

saint *s/adj* sfânt *m* || *vt* a sanctifica.

sake *s* **for the ~ of** pentru, de dragul cuiva, din consideraţie pentru cineva.

salacious *adj* senzual; lasciv; lubric; obscen; desfrânat, destrăbălat

salad *s cul* salată *f.*

salamander *s zool* salamandră *f.*

salami *s* salam *n.*

salary *s* salariu *n.*

sale *s* (*transaction*) vânzare *f;* (*rebate*) sold *n;* (*auction*) licitaţie *f;* **~s clerk** *s* vânzător *m;* **~sman** *s* (*store*) vânzător *m,* (*agent*) comisionar *m,* reprezentant *m* comercial, angrosist *m;* **~sroom** *s* sală *f* de vânzări; **~s rep** *s coll* reprezentant *m* comercial; **~s slip** *s* bon *n* de vânzare; **~s tax** *s* impozit *n* pe cifra de afaceri.

salient *adj* proeminent, ieşit în afară; *fig* proeminent, frapant, izbitor.

saline *adj* sărat; *min, etc* salin, de sare || *s* lac *n* sărat/ salin.

saliva *s physiol* salivă *f.*

sallow[1] *s bot* salcie *f.*

sallow[2] *adj* (*face, etc*) galben; palid; bolnăvicios || *s* culoare *f* palidă/pământie.

sally *s mil* atac *n,* ieşire *f* (din încercuire); (*quip*) remarcă *f* spirituală; ~ **forth/out** *vi lit* a ieşi (la plimbare).

salmon *s icht* somon *m* || *adj* (*color*) roz-portocaliu.

salon *s* (*shop, art*) salon *n.*

saloon *s* (*bar*) cârciumă *f;* berărie *f; naut* salon *n.*

salt *s* sare *f; fig* farmec *n,* haz *n* || *adj* sărat; piperat; picant; nostim; marin || *vt* a săra; a păstra în saramură • **~y** *adj* (*food*) sărat; (*water*) saramură *f.*

salubrious *adj* (*healthy*) sănătos, benefic; (*decent*) curat, salubru.

salutary *adj* (*helpful*) binevenit, oportun; (*beneficial*) binefăcător, benefic.

salutation *s* (*greeting*) salut *n,* salutare *f.*

salute *s* salut *n* || *vi* a saluta; a întâmpina.

salvage *s naut* salvare *f* a unui vas; *naut* bun/obiect *n* recuperat || *vt naut* a salva; *naut* a recupera.

salvation *s* salvare *f; relig* mântuire *f,* izbăvire *f;* **the Salvation Army** *s* Armata *f* Salvării.

salve *s* pomadă *f,* alifie *f.*

salver *s* tavă *f.*

same *adj* acelaşi; aceeaşi; aceleaşi; identic; neschimbat; monoton; indiferent || *pron* acelaşi lucru; aceeaşi persoană; acesta; aceasta; aceştia; acestea || *adv* la fel, în acelaşi mod.

sample *s* mostră *f;* eşantion *n;* exemplar *n;* probă *f;* model *n;* şablon *n* || *vt* a proba; a gusta; a lua probe de; a alege; a compara.

sampling *s* eşantionare *f;* testare *f,* sondare *f.*

sanatorium *s* sanatoriu *n.*

sanctify *vt relig* a canoniza; a sfinţi; a purifica; *fig* a consfinţi.

sanctimonious *adj* ipocrit, făţarnic; moralizator.

sanction *s* sancţiune *f;* confirmare *f* || *vt* a aproba; a confirma; a susţine.

sanctity *s relig* sanctitate *f; relig, etc* sfinţenie *f.*

sanctuary *s relig* sanctuar *n;* templu *n;* biserică *f;* altar *n; fig* adăpost *n,* refugiu *n;* azil *n;* rezervaţie *f.*

sand *s* nisip *n;* curaj *n; pl* plajă *f* || *vt* a presăra nisip; (*polish*) a şlefui • **~castle** *s* castel *n* de nisip • **~paper** *s* hârtie *f* abrazivă, glaspapir *n,* şmirghel *n* || *vt* a şlefui.

sandal *s* sanda(lă) *f.*

sandalwood *s bot* santal *n.*

sandman *s* Moş *m* Ene.

sandwich *s* sandviş *n* || *vt* a intercala; a înghesui.

sane *adj* sănătos la minte; raţional; (*sensible*) judicios; normal.

sang *vt* * **sing**.

sanguine *adj lit* rubicond; optimist.

sanitary *adj* (*system, etc*) sanitar; (*clean*) igienic; ~ **napkin** *s* şerveţel *n* igienic.

sanitation *s* igienizare *f;* salubrizare *f.*

sanity *s* integritate *f* mintală; moderaţie *f,* măsură *f.*

sank *vt* * **sink**.

Santa Claus *s* Moş *m* Crăciun.

sap *s bot* sevă *f;* suc *n; fig* sevă *f,* energie *f,* vigoare *f* || *vt fig* a vlăgui, a epuiza.

sapphire *s* safir *n.*

sarcasm *s* sarcasm *n.*

sarcastic *adj* sarcastic; caustic.

sarcophagus *s* (*pl* **sarcophagi**) sarcofag *n.*

sardine *s icht* sardea *f.*

Sardinia *s* Sardinia.

sardonic *adj* sardonic; sarcastic; diabolic.

sartorial *adj* vestimentar.

sash[1] *s* eşarfă *f,* eşarfă *f;* bandaj *n.*

sash[2] *s* (*frame*) toc/cadru *n* (mobil) de fereastră.

sass *s* tupeu *n* • **~y** *adj* obraznic, impertinent.

sat *vi* * **sit**.

SAT *s abbr* (**Scholastic Aptitude Test**) examen *n* de intrare la universitate.

Satan *s* Satana *f*, diavolul *m*.

satchel *s* ghiozdan *n*.

sated *adj* (**with**) sătul (de)

satellite *s astron* satelit *m*; *tech* satelit *n*, pinion *n* planetar; *fig* satelit *m*, acolit *m*; ~ **dish** *s* antenă *f* pentru satelit/parabolică.

satiate *vt lit* (~ *hunger*) a sătura; (~ *thirst*) a potoli.

satin *s text* satin *n*, atlas *n* ‖ *adj* satinat, de satin.

satire *s* (**on**) satiră *f* (împotriva, la adresa).

satirical *adj* satiric.

satirize *vt* a satiriza

satisfaction *s* (*approval*) satisfacție *f*; (*redress*) compensare *f*.

satisfactory *adj* satisfăcător; plăcut; acceptabil.

satisfy *vt* (*please*) a satisface; (*fulfill*) a îndeplini; a plăti; a compensa; a acoperi; (*convince*) a convinge; (~ *hunger*) a astâmpăra; a ispăși; (~ *a need*) a acoperi.

saturate *vt* a satura, a îmbiba, a impregna; *chem*, *fig* a neutraliza.

saturation *s also fig* saturație *f*.

Saturday *s* sâmbătă *f*; **on ~(s)** sâmbătă; **every ~** în fiecare sâmbătă.

saturnine *adj fig* posomorât; taciturn.

sauce *s cul* sos *n*; suc *n* de fructe; compot *n*; *fig* picanterie *f*; *coll* nerușinare *f* ‖ *vt cul* a asezona; *fig* a atenua; *fig coll* a vorbi obraznic.

saucepan *s* cratiță *f*, oală *f*.

saucer *s* farfurioară *f*; suport *n*.

saucy *adj* (*person*) obraznic, impertinent; (*action*) provocator.

sauerkraut *s cul* varză *f* acră/murată.

sauna *s* saună *f*, baie *f* de aburi.

saunter *vi* a se plimba; a lua aer; a hoinări ‖ *s* plimbare *f*.

sausage *s* cârnat *m*; salam *n*; crenvurșt *m*.

savage *adj* sălbatic, primitiv; barbar; crud, nemilos, fioros ‖ *s* sălbatic *m*; brută *f*; fiară *f*; *fig* necioplit ‖ *vt* a ataca cu ferocitate.

savannah *s geog* savană *f*.

save[1] *vt* (**from**) (*rescue*) a salva de, a feri, (~ *trouble*) a scuti de; *relig* a izbăvi; (~ *time*) a câștiga; (~ *food*) a păstra; *comp* a înregistra, a salva; *sp* a para; a recupera ‖ *vr* a se cruța ‖ *vi* (*put aside*) a economisi; a salva; *relig* a mântui ‖ *s sp* apărare *f*, parare *f*.

save[2] *prep lit* (*except*) fără; cu excepția.

saving *s* (*thrift*) economie *f*; *pl* economii *f pl* ‖ *adj* de economie/economii; **~s bank** *s* bancă *f* de economii.

savior *s* salvator *m*; *lit* izbăvitor *m*.

savor *s* savoare *f*; (*taste*) gust *n*; aromă *f*; nuanță *f* ‖ *vt* a asezona; (*relish*) a savura; a avea gust de; a aminti de • **~y** *adj* gustos; delicios.

savvy *s coll* (*know-how*) cunoaștere *f*, (*ability*) pricepere *f*, înțelegere *f* ‖ *adj* (*well-informed*) priceput, cunoscător; (*shrewd*) perspicace, isteț.

saw[1] *vt* * **see**.

saw[2], **sawed**, **sawn** *vt* a tăia cu ferăstrăul; a cânta la vioară ‖ *vi* a tăia cu ferăstrăul ‖ *s* ferăstrău *n*.

saxophone *s mus* saxofon *n*.

saxophonist *s mus* saxofonist *m*.

say, **said**, **said** *vt* (*speak*) a spune, a zice; (*utter*) a rosti; a articula; a pronunța; (*state*) a afirma; (*admit*) a admite; (*recite*) a recita; (*promise*) a promite ‖ *vi* a vorbi; a sta scris ‖ *s* cuvânt *n*; (*right to be heard*)

părere *f* ‖ *adv* aproximativ, cam; **to ~ the least** ca să nu spun mai mult, fără nici o exagerare; **that is to ~** cu alte cuvinte; adică; **there is no ~ing** nu se poate ști; **whatever you ~** cum vrei tu!, fie!; **when all is said and done** la o adică • **~ing** *s* dicton *n*; enunț *n*.

scab *s med* crustă *f*; *med* râie *f*; *fig* spărgător *m* de grevă; *bot* rugină *f* ‖ *vi med* a forma o crustă.

scabbard *s* (*for sword*) teacă *f*.

scabrous *adj lit* (*skin*) aspru; (*joke*, *subject*) scabros, obscen.

scaffold *s* eșafod *n*; *constr* schelă *f*.

scalawag *s coll* (*rascal*) ștrengar *m*; ticălos *m*.

scald *vt* a opări, a frige; a pasteuriza ‖ *vi* a se opări ‖ *s* arsură *f* (cauzată de un lichid).

scale[1] *s* (*fish, etc*) solz *m* ‖ *vt* a curăți de solzi.

scale[2] *s* (*level*) scală *f*, scară *f*; (*balance*) cântar *n*, balanță *f*; (*range*) gamă *f*; (*size*) mărime *f*; riglă *f* ‖ *vt* (*climb up*) a urca; a asalta ‖ *vi* a (se) urca.

scales *s pl* balanță *f*.

scallion *s bot* (*spring onion*) ceapă *f* verde; (*leek*) praz *m*; (*shallot*) arpagic *m*, eșalot *m*.

scallop *s zool* scoică *f* marină comestibilă; *text* feston *n* ‖ *vt text* a festona.

scallywag *s* **scalawag**.

scalp *s anat* scalp *n*; *fig* trofeu *n* ‖ *vt* a scalpa; a scoate coaja.

scalpel *s med*, *tech* scalpel *n*.

scalper *s coll* speculant *m* de bilete de spectacol.

scam *s coll* escrocherie *f*; inginerie *f* financiară.

scamp *s* (*imp*) ștrengar *m*; (*rascal*) nemernic *m* ‖ *vt* (*work*) a face de mântuială.

scamper *vi* (*dash*) a alerga/fugi cât îl țin picioarele; (*run*) a merge foarte repede ‖ *s* fugă *f*, grabă *f*; mers *n* grăbit; lectură *f* grăbită; călătorie *f* rapidă.

scampish *adj* ticălos, mârșav, josnic, murdar.

scan *s med* tomografie *f*, ecografie *f* ‖ *vt* (*scrutinize*) a examina/cerceta cu grijă; (*read quickly*) a parcurge în grabă; *tech* a baleia, a exploda; *comp* a scana.

scandal *s* scandal *n*; zarvă *f*; ocară *f*; calomnie *f*.

Scandinavia *s* Scandinavia.

scant(y) *adj* limitat, mărginit; redus; restrâns; insuficient.

scapegoat *s also fig* țap *m* ispășitor.

scapula *s anat* (*pl* **scapulas/-ae**) omoplat *m*.

scar *s* cicatrice *f*; rană *f*; urmă *f* ‖ *vt* a umple de răni ‖ *vi* a se cicatriza.

scarab *s ento* scarabeu *m*.

scarce *adj* rar; puțin ‖ *adv* chiar, tocmai; nu tocmai; nu prea.

scarcity *s* (*lack*) lipsă *f*, puținătate *f*; (*shortage*) deficit *n*; penurie *f*; (*rarity*) raritate *f*.

scare *vt* a îngrozi; a speria; a alunga ‖ *vi* a se speria ‖ *s* spaimă *f*; panică *f* ‖ *adj* înfiorător; de groază.

scarf *s* eșarfă *f*; șal *n*; fular *n*; batic *n*.

scarlet *s* culoarea *f* stacojie ‖ *adj* stacojiu, (de un) roșu aprins; **~ fever** *s med* scarlatină *f*.

scarp *s* râpă *f*, coastă *f* abruptă.

scary *adj coll* înfricoșător, înspăimântător.

scathing *adj* (*critique*) acerb; (*reply*) caustic.

scatter *vt* (*disperse*) a risipi; (*spread*) a presăra; a răvăși; (*break up*) a strica; a despărți; a alunga ‖ *vi* a se risipi ‖ *s* risipire *f*; difuzare *f*; împrăștiere *f* • **~brained** *adj coll* zăpăcit.

scavenger *s* animal *n* necrofag; (*person*) gunoier *m*, măturător *m* de stradă.

scene *s thea*, *etc* scenă *f*; *fig* priveliște *f*; tablou *n*;

(*setting*) decor *n*; (*landscape*) peisaj *n*; (*incident*) scandal *n*; spectacol *n*; *liter* episod *n* • ~**ry** *s thea* decor *n*; culise *f pl*; *fig* decor *n*; peisaj *n*, tablou *n*, privelişte *f*.

scenic *adj thea* scenic; (*attractive*) spectaculos; pitoresc; ~ **route** traseu *n* turistic.

scent *s* (*of a flower*) mireasmă *f*; (*of an animal*) miros *n*; (*of perfume*) parfum *n*; (*on a trail*) urmă *f* ‖ *vt* (*sniff*) a mirosi, a adulmeca.

sceptic *adj* sceptic; neîncrezător ‖ *s* sceptic *m* • ~**al** *adj* sceptic; neîncrezător.

scepter *s* sceptru *n*; *fig* sceptru *n*; domnie *f*; putere *f*.

schedule *s* program *n*; (*timetable*) orar *n*; (*plan*) plan *n*; listă *f*; tabel *n*; grafic *n* ‖ *vt* a înregistra; (*arrange*) a programa; a adăuga; ~**d flight** *s* zbor *n* regulat(ă), cursă *f* regulat(ă).

scheme *s* (*plan*) schemă *f*, plan *n*; (*system*) sistem *n*; program *n*; diagramă *f*; *pej* combinaţie *f*, maşinaţie *f*; aranjament *n* ‖ *vi pej* a unelti, a conspira.

schist *s geol* şist *n*.

schizophrenic *s*/*adj med* schizofrenic *m*.

scholar *s* (*expert*) erudit *m*, savant *m*; (*student*) şcolar *m*, elev *m*; bursier *m*; om *m* studios • ~**ship** *s* (*stipend*) bursă *f* (de studii); (*learning*) erudiţie *f*.

scholastic *adj hist* scolastic; *fig* scolastic, dogmatic, pedant; (*educational*) şcolar, academic, universitar.

school *s* şcoală *f*; lecţii *f pl*; elevii *m pl*; instrucţie *f*; concepţie *f* ‖ *vi* a da la şcoală; (*train*) a instrui; (*educate*) a educa; *fig* (*feeling, etc*) a-şi stăpâni; ~ **age** *s* vârstă *f* şcolară; ~ **book** *s* manual *n*; ~ **bus** *s* autobuz *n* şcolar; ~ **year** *s* an *m* şcolar • ~**ing** *s* şcolarizare *f*, instruire *f* • ~**mate** *s* camarad *m* de şcoală • ~**teacher** *s* (*elementary*) învăţător *m*; (*high school*) profesor *m*.

schooner *s naut* goeletă *f*.

sciatica *s med* sciatică *f*.

science *s* ştiinţă *f*; artă *f*; măiestrie *f*; ~ **fiction** *s* science fiction; literatură *f* ştiinţifico-fantastică.

scientific *adj* ştiinţific.

scientist *s* om *m* de ştiinţă.

scimitar *s* iatagan *n*.

scintillating *adj* (*dazzling*) scânteietor; (*brilliant*) strălucitor.

scion *s bot* altoi *n*; *fig* vlăstar *n*, urmaş *m*, descendent *m*.

scissors *s pl* foarfece *f*.

scoff *vt* a-şi râde de, a batjocori.

scold *vt* (*rebuke*) a mustra/dojeni/certa aspru ‖ *vi* a dojeni aspru; a ocărî.

sconce *s mil* întăritură *f*, tranşee *n pl*; adăpost *n* ‖ *vt* a adăposti; a proteja; a îngrădi.

scoop *s* lopată *f*; cupă *f*; (*digging*) excavare *f*; (*ladle*) căuş *n*; (*news story*) ştire *f* senzaţională ‖ *vt* (*dig*) a săpa; a curăţa; (*shovel*) a scoate cu lopata.

scooter *s* (*child's* ~) trotinetă *f*; (*moped*) scuter *n*.

scope *s* orizont *n*; (*range*) gamă *f*; (*extent*) libertate *f*; amploare *f*, sferă *f* de acţiune; diapazon *n*; câmp *n*; (*capacity*) posibilităţi *f pl*.

scorch *vt* a pârjoli; a pârli; (~ *skin*) a arde (superficial); (~ *grass, land, etc*) a usca • ~**er** *s* (*hot day*) zi *f* caniculară; (*smth exciting*) ceva remarcabil • ~**ing** *adj* (*hot*) canicular; (~ *criticism*) necruţător; (*fast speed*) mare.

score *s* urmă *f*; (*notch*) dungă *f*; tăietură *f*; socoteală *f*; *sp* scor *n*; (*mark*) însemnare *f*; spirit *n*; (*cause*) motiv *n*; (*twenty*) grup *n* de douăzeci; succes *n*; *mus* partitură *f* ‖ *vt* (*notch*) a cresta; (*cut*) a tăia; *sp* a marca; a

zgâria; (*achieve*) a câştiga; a estima; (*keep count*) a înregistra ‖ *vi sp* a marca • ~**board** *s* tabela *f* de marcaj • ~**r** *s sp* marcator *m*.

scorn *s* (*contempt*) dispreţ *n*; batjocură *f*; desconsiderare *f* ‖ *vt* (*show contempt*) a zeflemisi, a dispreţui • ~**ful** *adj* dispreţuitor.

Scorpio *s astrol* Scorpion *m*.

scorpion *s zool* scorpion *m*.

Scot *s* scoţian *m* • ~**ch** *adj* scoţian ‖ *s* whisky *n*, scotch *m* • ~**land** *s* Scoţia *f* • ~**tish** *adj* scoţian.

scoundrel *s* om *m* de nimic, ticălos ‖ *adj* josnic, ticălos.

scour[1] *vt* (*rub*) a curăţa, a freca.

scour[2] *vt* (*search*) a străbate, a colinda, a cutreiera.

scourge *s* dezastru *n*, calamitate *f* ‖ *vt fig* a pedepsi; a cauza nenorociri (cuiva).

scout *s* cercetaş *m*; *mil* cercetaş *m*; observator *m* ‖ *vt* a urmări îndeaproape; a căuta; (*explore*) a cerceta ‖ *vi mil* (*reconnoiter*) a pleca în recunoaştere.

scowl *vi* (*glare*) a se încrunta, a privi supărat ‖ *s* (*frown*) privire *f* încruntată; privire *f* furioasă; aer *n* ameninţător.

scrabble *vi* (*scratch*) a zgâria; a râcâi; (*grope*) a cotrobăi, a scotoci (după) ‖ *s* (*scramble*) bătaie *f*, luptă *f*.

scraggy *adj* (*thin*) sfrijit, scofâlcit; (*jagged*) neregulat, asimetric.

scramble *vi* (*climb*) a se urca; a se târî; (*plant*) a se agăţa ‖ *vt* (*mix up*) a amesteca; a strânge; (~ *eggs*) a face jumări ‖ *s* (*clamber*) căţărare *f*; agăţare *f*; (*rush*) busculadă *f*, îmbulzeală *f*; bătaie *f* (pentru ceva).

scrap *s* (*of paper*) bucată *f*; rest *n*; (*of info*) fragment *n*; (*of conversation*) frântură *f*; (*of metal*) deşeu *n*; tăietură *f* (de ziar); *pl* fărâmituri *f pl*, resturi *n pl*; *fig* pic *n*, fărâmă *f* ‖ *vt metal* a da la fier vechi; a arunca; *fig* (*plan, etc*) a abandona, a lăsa baltă • ~**book** *s* album *n* cu decupaje (din ziare).

scrape *vt* (*grate*) a răzui; (*scratch*) a zgâria; (*rasp*) a hârşâi, a scârţâi; a nivela; (*rub*) a freca; (*graze*) a şterge; a scobi; a râcâi ‖ *vi* a rade; a zgâria; a scârţâi ‖ *s* răzuire *f*; hârşâit *n*; scârţâit *n*; (*fix*) necaz *n*; ~ **through** *vt* a reuşi cu greu • ~**r** *s* răzătoare *f*, racletă *f*.

scratch *vt* (*grate*) a juli; a zgâria; a mâzgăli; (*graze*) a şterge; a râcâi; a scărpina; (*rub*) a freca ‖ *s* (*cut*) zgârietură *f*; parafă *f*; semn *n*; scărpinat *n*; scârţâit *n*.

scrawl *vt* a mâzgăli; a scrie neciteţ ‖ *s* mâzgălitură *f*, scris *n* neciteţ.

scrawny *adj* (*thin*) slab, sfrijit, uscăţiv.

scream *vi* (*shout*) a ţipa; a râde cu hohote; a vui; a striga; (*wind* ~*s*) a şuiera ‖ *s* (*cry*) ţipăt *n*; (*screech*) sunet *n* strident; (*howl*) şuierat *n*; (*laughter*) hohot *n*.

scree *s* pietriş *n*, prundiş *n*; grohotiş *n*.

screech *vt*/*vi* (*shriek*) a ţipa; (*tires* ~) a scâşni, a scârţâi ‖ *s* (*scream*) ţipăt *n*; (*of tires*) scârţâit *n*; sunet *n* strident.

screen *s* (*monitor*) ecran *n*; scut *n*; (*partition*) paravan *n*; *fig* perdea *f*; adăpost *n*; sită *f* ‖ *vt* a apăra; a cerne; (*check*) a controla minuţios; a cerceta; a ecraniza; (*hide*) a ascunde, a masca; *fig* a selecta, a alege.

screw *s* (*bolt*) şurub *n*; *avia* elice *f*; *tech* spirală *f*; cornet *n*; sul *n*; *fig* avar *m* ‖ *vt* (*turn*) a înşuruba; (*attach*) a fixa; a presa; a sili; a stoarce; **to** ~ **up** *vt* *tech* a înşuruba; *fig* a şifona, a mototoli; (*face*) a se strâmba; *coll* a strica, a face de mântuială • ~**driver** *s* şurubelniţă *f*.

scribble *vt* a mâzgăli; a murdări ‖ *vi* a scrie în grabă; a mâzgăli ‖ *s* scris *n* neciteţ; mâzgălitură *f*.

scrimmage *s sp* grămadă *f*; (*brawl*) încăierare *f*.

scrimp *vi* (**on**) a fi econom/zgârcit (cu).

script *s cin, radio* scenariu *n*; (*handwriting*) scriere *f* (de mână), scris *n*; (*system*) scriere *f*.

scripture *s* scriere *f*; manuscris *n*; document *n*; **the Scriptures** *s pl relig* Sfânta Scriptură *f*.

scroll *s* (*roll*) sul *n* (de hârtie); pergament *n*; *math, phys* spirală *f*; *tech* filet *n* plan ‖ *vt comp* a rula pe ecran conţinutul unui fişier.

scrooge *s coll* zgârcit *m*, zgârciob *m*.

scrounge *vt* (~ *for money*) a tapa (pe cineva) de bani • **~r** *s coll* parazit *m*, întreţinut *m*.

scrub[1] *vt* (*rub*) a freca; (*clean*) a curăţa ‖ *vi* a freca; (**for**) a trudi pentru ‖ *s* frecat *n*, frecare *f* cu peria; salahor *m*; perie *f*.

scrub[2] *s bot* arbust *m*; tufă *f*; *bot* arbore *m* pitic; *zool* animal *n* pitic.

scruff *s anat* ceafă *f*; **take by the ~ of the neck** *vt* a apuca de ceafă.

scruffy *adj* neîngrijit, neglijent.

scrum *s sp* (*rugby*) grămadă *f*.

scrumptious *adj* gustos, delicios.

scrunch *vt* a mesteca cu zgomot ‖ *vi* (*gravel, snow*) a scârţâi • **~y** *adj* crocant.

scruple *s* scrupul *n*, considerent *n* moral; (*qualm*) remuşcare *f*.

scrupulous *adj* cinstit, scrupulos; meticulos.

scrutinize *vt* a scruta, a cerceta atent.

scrutiny *s* examinare *f* atentă/minuţioasă; privire *f* cercetătoare.

scuba-diving *s* înot *n* subacvatic cu echipament special.

scuff *vi* a merge târşâind/târând picioarele ‖ *vt* (*graze*) a râcâi; (~ *shoe*) a roade, a strica.

scuffle *s* (*brawl*) încăierare *f*, bătaie *f* ‖ *vi* (*fight*) a se încăiera, a se lua la bătaie.

scull *s naut* vâslă *f*, ramă *f*, lopată *f*; barcă *f* (cu vâsle) ‖ *vi* (*paddle a* ~) a vâsli, a rama.

scullery *s* cameră *f* de spălat vase, spălător *n*.

sculpt *vt* a sculpta; a modela, a forma • **~or** *s* sculptor *m* • **~ure** *s* sculptură *f*.

scum *s* (*froth*) spumă *f*; *metal* depunere *f*, crustă *f*; *fig pej* ticălos *m*; *coll pej* (*person*) drojdie *f*, scursură *f*, lepădătură *f*.

scurf *s med, bot* mătreaţă *f*, coajă *f*, crustă *f*.

scurrilous *adj* (*insulting*) injurios, abuziv; indecent; obscen; (*defamatory*) calomnios.

scurry *vi* (*dash*) a fugi, a goni ‖ *vt* a mâna, a goni ‖ *s* (*dash*) fugă *f*; (*rush*) alergătură *f*, agitaţie *f*.

scurvy *s med* scorbut *n*; ticălos *m*, nemernic ‖ *adj* infam, murdar, ticălos.

scuttle[1] *vt naut* a saborda ‖ *s naut* bocaport *n*, tambuchi *n*; *auto* torpedo *n*; chepeng *n*, deschizătură *f*.

scuttle[2] *s* coş *n* pentru cărbuni, găleată *f* pentru cărbuni.

scuttle[3] *s* fugă *f*, goană *f*; plecare *f* bruscă; **to ~ away** *vi* a fugi; *fig* a fugi de o răspundere etc; a se grăbi.

scythe *s* coasă *f* ‖ *vt* a cosi.

sea *s geog* mare *f*; larg *n*; **at ~** pe mare, la apă; **by ~** pe mare, pe cale maritimă; **~ bed** *s* fund *n* de mare, fundul *n* mării; **~ breeze** *s* briza *f* mării; **~ change** *s* schimbare *f* radicală/profundă; **~ eagle** *s orn* vultur *m* de mare; **~ level** *s* nivelul *n* mării; **~ lion** *s zool* leu *m* de mare.

seaboard *s naut* coastă *f* (marină), ţărm *n* de mare.

seafaring *s* viaţă *f* de marinar; călătorie *f* pe mare.

seafood *s cul* fructe *n pl* de mare.

seafront *s* faleză *f*.

seagull *s orn* pescăruş *m*.

seahorse *s icht* căluţ *m* de mare.

seal[1] *s* (*stamp*) sigiliu *n*; marcă *f*; ştampilă *f* ‖ *vt* a sigila; a ştampila; (*clinch*) a ratifica; a izola; (*settle*) a parafa.

seal[2] *s zool* focă *f*.

seam *s text* cusătură *f*; cută *f*; tiv *n* ‖ *vt* a coase; a încreţi ‖ *vi* a crăpa; a se încreţi.

seaman *s* marinar *m*, matelot *m*.

seamstress *s* cusătoreasă *f*.

seamy *adj* cu multe cusături; *fig* (*sordid*) cu aspect neplăcut, sordid.

séance *s* şedinţă *f* de spiritism; (*meeting*) întrunire *f*.

sear *vt* a usca; a vesteji; a ofili; (*scorch*) a pârjoli; (*burn*) a arde; (*singe*) a arde cu fierul roşu; *fig* a întări ‖ *s* uscare *f*; ofilire *f*.

search *vt* (*look for*) a căuta; a scotoci; a cerceta; a urmări ‖ *vi* a căuta; a examina ‖ *s* căutare *f*; examinare *f*; (*for a person, luggage, house*) control *n*, percheziţie *f* • **~ing** *adj* (*inquiry*) aprofundat; (*look*) pătrunzător.

seascape *s* (*painting*) peisaj *n* marin.

seashell *s* scoică *f*.

seaside *s* ţărm *n*; litoral *n*.

season *s* (*period*) anotimp *n*; sezon *n*; (*time*) timp *n*; moment *n* potrivit ‖ *vt* a asezona, a condimenta ‖ *vi* a se aclimatiza, a se adapta; *tech* a se usca; a se coace; **in ~** de sezon; **out of ~** în afara sezonului • **~al** *adj* sezonier • **~ed** *adj* (*traveler, etc*) experimentat; (*soldier*) călit, oţelit.

seasoning *s* uscare *f*; asezonare *f*; preparare *f*; condiment *n*.

seashore *s* ţărm *n* de mare; litoral *n*.

seawall *s* dig *n*.

seaway *s* cale *f* maritimă.

seaweed *s bot* algă *f* marină.

seat *s thea, etc* loc *n*; (*chair*) scaun *n*; spate *n*, dos *n*; (*base*) reşedinţă *f* ‖ *vt* a pune/aşeza pe un scaun; a oferi un scaun; (*provides seating*) a avea locuri pentru; a plasa ‖ *vr* a lua loc.

seaworthy *adj* în stare bună pentru navigaţie.

sec *s coll* (*second*) secundă *f*, clipă *f*; **in a ~!** o secundă!.

secede *vi* (**from**) a se separa de; (*withdraw*) a ieşi, a se retrage din.

secession *s* secesiune *f*.

secluded *adj* izolat; depărtat; retras.

seclusion *s* (*chosen*) solitudine *f*; (*imposed*) izolare *f*; loc *n* retras/izolat.

second[1] *s* secundă *f*; moment *n*, clipă *f*.

second[2] *num* doilea ‖ *adj* doilea, al doilea; suplimentar, adiţional; (**to**) inferior; mai prejos de ‖ *adv* în al doilea rând ‖ *s* ajutor *n*; adjunct *m*; *naut* (ofiţer) secund *m*; *mus* secundă *f*; *pl* marfă *f* de calitatea a doua ‖ *vt* (*support*) a ajuta; a seconda; (~ *motion, etc*) a susţine • **~ary** *adj* secundar; subordonat; minor; inferior; *scol* secundar, mediu; *geol* mezozoic; *chem* secundar • **~hand** *adj* uzat, vechi; de la a doua mână ‖ *adv* de ocazie; de la a doua mână • **~rate** *adj* de calitatea/clasa/categoria a doua; *pej* mediocru.

secrecy *s* izolare *f*; singurătate *f*; caracter *n* ascuns/secret; discreţie *f*.

secret *adj* secret; confidenţial; ascuns; izolat ‖ *s* secret *n*; mister *n*; discreţie *f*.

secretary *s* secretar *m*; secretară *f*; birou *n* de scris; *pol* ministru *m*; **Secretary of State** *s* Ministrul *m* Afacerilor Externe.

secrete *vt* (*from*) a ascunde (de); a feri (de); *bio* a secreta ‖ *vr* a se ascunde.

secretive *adj* secretos, rezervat.

sect *s relig* sectă *f*; *fig* sectă *f*; grup *n*.

section *s* secțiune *f*; (*part*) parte *f*; (*slice*) tăietură *f*; segment *n*; fâșie *f*; paragraf *n*; secție *f*; capitol *n* ‖ *vt* a secționa; a diviza.

sector *s* sector *n*; zonă *f*; parte *f*; *math* arc *n* de cerc; *tech* culisă *f*.

secular *adj* (*lay*) laic, *relig* secular; (*worldly*) lumesc; străvechi.

secure *adj* (*safe*) sigur; apărat; (*fixed firmly*) solid; (*dependable*) de nădejde; (*confident*) încrezător ‖ *vt* (*make safe*) a asigura; a apăra; a fixa; (*attain*) a realiza; (*obtain*) a face rost de; a se asigura de.

securities *s pl fin* titluri *n pl*, valori *f pl*.

security *s* (*safety*) securitate *f*, siguranță *f*; (*safety measures*) pază *f*; apărare *f*; *econ* garanție *f*; girant *m*; garant *m*.

sedan *s* sedan *n*, autoturism *n*; **~ chair** *s* lectică *f*.

sedate *adj* calm, potolit ‖ *vt* a administra un sedativ.

sedation *s* administrare *f* de sedative.

sedative *s/adj med* sedativ *n*.

sedentary *adj* sedentar; *zool* fix, stabil.

sediment *s chem, etc* sediment *n*, precipitat *n*; *geol* noroi *n*; reziduu *n*.

sedition *s* revoltă *f*, răzvrătire *f*.

seditious *adj* subversiv, sedițios.

seduce *vt* (*sexually*) a seduce; a corupe; (*attract*) a atrage; a ademeni.

seduction *s* seducție *f*; corupere *f*.

seductive *adj* (*person*) seducător; (*smile*) ademenitor; (*voice*) ispititor.

see[1], **saw**, **seen** *vt* a vedea, a observa; a zări; (*visit*) a vizita; (*understand*) a pricepe; a întâlni; (*find out*) a descoperi; a afla; (*imagine*) a-și închipui; (~ *a doctor*) a consulta; (*escort*) a însoți; (*meet*) a primi ‖ *vi* a (se) vedea; (*understand*) a pricepe; (*look at*) a privi; a afla; (*think about*) a se gândi; (*make sure*) a cerceta; **~ about** *vi* a se ocupa de; (*find out*) a cerceta; (*object*) a obiecta; **~ through** *vi* a nu se lăsa înșelat.

see[2] *s relig* eparhie *f*, episcopie *f*; arhiepiscopat *n*; reședință *f* episcopală.

seed *s* sămânță *f*; germen(e) *m*; început *n*; *bio* spermă *f*; *pl fig* sămânță *f*, germene *m*; început *n* ‖ *vt* a semăna; a însămânța; a alege ‖ *vi* a semăna; a sădi • **~iness** *s coll* jerpeleală *f*; aspect *n* zdrențăros • **~y** *adj* cu semințe; *text* cu impurități vegetale; *coll* jerpelit.

seek, sought, sought *vt* a căuta; a cere ‖ *vi* a căuta; a cerceta.

seem *vi* a (se) părea • **~ingly** *adv* aparent • **~liness** *s* bunăcuviință *f*; decență *f*.

seen *vt* * **see**.

seep *vt* a se prelinge; a se strecura ‖ *s* fisură *f*.

seesaw *s* balans *n*, legănare *f*; scrânciob *n* ‖ *vt* a legăna ‖ *vi* a se legăna.

seethe *vi* a fierbe, a clocoti; *fig* a fi cuprins de furie, a clocoti de furie.

segment *s* parte *f*; bucată *f*; segment *n*; secțiune *f* ‖ *vt* a segmenta.

segregate *vt* a separa ‖ *vi* a se separa; a se segrega; a se scinda.

segregation *s* separare *f*; discriminare *f*.

seize *vt* (*grab*) a apuca, a prinde; (*confiscate*) a confisca; (*take control*) a cuceri; *fig* (~ *an idea*) a pricepe; (*arrest*) a aresta; *fig* (*panic*) a cuprinde; *fig* (~ *an opportunity*) a profita de, a se folosi; *jur* a lua în posesiune.

seizure *s* (*confiscation*) confiscare *f*; (*capture*) captură *f*; *med* acces *n*, atac *n*; *tech* gripare *f*.

seldom *adv* rar(eori); când și când.

select *adj* select; ales; selectiv; mofturos ‖ *vi* a selecta; a sorta • **~ion** *s* alegere *f*; selecționare *f*; antologie *f*.

self *s* eu *n*, sine *m*; identitate *f*; ego *n*; subiect *m* ‖ *adj* același; identic.

self-absorbed *adj* individualist, egotist.

self-adhesive *adj* autoadeziv.

self-assured *adj* sigur de sine, încrezător în sine.

self-centered *adj* egocentric.

self-colored *adj* de o aceeași culoare, de o culoare uniformă.

self-confident *adj* sigur de sine, încrezător în sine.

self-command *s* stăpânire *f* de sine, calm *n*.

self-conscious *adj* sfios, timid, stângaci; conștient de sine.

self-contained *adj* independent; autonom; retras, nesociabil; *mil* prevăzut/aprovizionat cu toate cele necesare.

self-control *s* autocontrol *n*; stăpânire *f* de sine.

self-defense *s* autoapărare *f*.

self-denial *s* renunțare *f*, privațiune *f*.

self-discipline *s* autodisciplină *f*.

self-doubt *s* neîncredere *f* în sine.

self-employed *adj* care lucrează pe cont propriu.

self-esteem *s* respect *n* față de sine; sentimentul *n* propriei demnități.

self-effacing *adj* modest.

self-evident *adj* clar, evident; axiomatic.

self-explanatory *adj* de la sine înțeles, evident.

self-expression *s* libera *f* exprimare.

self-important *adj* suficient, arogant, care-și dă importanță.

self-indulgent *adj* care nu-și refuză nimic.

self-interest *s* interes *n* personal/propriu; egoism *n*.

selfish *adj* egoist • **~ness** *s* egoism *n*.

selfless *adj* dezinteresat; altruist.

self-made *adj* făcut singur; (~ *man*) care s-a realizat prin sine însuși.

self-opinionated *adj* încrezut, înfumurat; încăpățânat.

self-pity *s* autocompătimire *f*.

self-portrait *s* autoportret *n*.

self-possessed *adj* stăpânit, calm, stăpân pe sine.

self-reliant *adj* independent.

self-respect *s* respect *n* față de sine, sentimentul *n* demnității personale.

self-righteous *adj* sigur de sine; convins că are dreptate; fățarnic, fariseic.

self-rising flour *s* făină *f* în amestec cu drojdie.

self-sacrifice *s* sacrificiu *n* de sine; abnegație *f*.

selfsame *adj* același, identic.

self-satisfied *adj* suficient, mulțumit de sine.

self-seeking *adj* egoist.

self-service *s* autoservire *f*.

self-starter *s* persoană *f* independentă și ambițioasă.

self-sufficient *adj* independent; autonom; încrezător în sine; prezumțios; îngâmfat, încrezut.

self-taught *adj* autodidact.

self-willed *adj* încăpățânat, îndărătnic.

self-worth s amor n propriu.

sell, sold, sold vt (vend) a vinde; a desface; fig a trăda; (advertise) a populariza; a înşela ‖ vi a (se) vinde; (~ an idea, etc) a avea succes ‖ s decepţie f; regret n; hoţie f.

sell-out s com lichidare f; (betrayal) trădare f.

semantic adj semantic.

semaphore s semafor n.

semblance s (façade) înfăţişare f (exterioară), (air) aspect n; asemănare f; copie f; reproducere f; (veneer) aparenţă f; formă f înşelătoare.

semen s bio spermă f, sămânţă f.

semester s semestru n.

semibreve s mus notă f întreagă.

semicircle s semicerc n.

semicolon s gram punct şi virgulă.

semi-conscious adj pe jumătate conştient.

semi-detached house s casă f care are zid/perete comun cu alta.

semifinal s sp semifinală f.

seminal adj anat seminal; (major) prestigios.

seminar s seminar n.

seminary s relig seminar n.

semi-precious adj semi-preţios.

semiquaver s mus semioctavă f.

Semitic adj semit(ic).

semitone s mus semiton n.

semolina s griş n.

senate s pol, scol senat n; **the United States S~** s Senatul n SUA.

senator s senator m.

send, sent, sent vt a trimite; radio a difuza; (mail) a expedia; (throw a ball, etc) a arunca, a azvârli ‖ vi radio a transmite; a emite; a porunci; ~ **for** vi (person) a chema, a aduce; (by mail) a comanda prin corespondenţă; ~ **in** vt (report, etc) a trimite, a înainta; ~ **off** vt (mail) a expedia; sp a elimina din joc • ~**er** s trimiţător m; expeditor m; emiţător n.

senile adj senil; bătrân.

senior adj senior; mai în vârstă ‖ s bătrân; scol student m în ultimul an; persoană f importantă/marcantă; ~ **citizen** s persoană f în vârstă/de vârsta a treia.

sensation s emoţie f; senzaţie f; impresie f; vâlvă f.

sense s (feeling) simţ n; pl (brains) minte f; (logic) luciditate f; (~ of duty) constiinţă f; (wisdom) înţelepciune f; tendinţă f; (meaning) înţeles n; fig esenţă f; fig dispoziţie f ‖ vt (grasp) a pricepe; (feel) a simţi; a detecta.

sensibility s sensibilitate f, simţire f.

sensible adj logic; raţional; inteligent; sensibil; practic; perceptibil.

sensitive adj sensibil; susceptibil; emotiv; simţitor; supărăcios.

sensitivity s sensibilitate f.

sensitize vt text, etc a sensibiliza.

sensory adj sensorial, de simţ.

sensual adj (bodily) senzual.

sensuous adj senzual, senzorial; care apelează la simţuri; estetic.

sent vt * **send**.

sentence s jur, etc sentinţă f; verdict n; gram propoziţie f; frază f ‖ vt a condamna.

sententious adj sentenţios, grav, solemn.

sentiment s sentiment n; atitudine f; patos n; sensibili-tate f; dispoziţie f; sentimentalism n • ~**al** adj senti-mental; emotiv; dulceag.

sentinel, sentry s santinelă f.

separate adj (unconnected) separat; (different) diferit; (discrete) distinct; particular ‖ vt a separa; (break away) a desprinde; (divide) a diviza; a izola ‖ vi a se separa; a divorţa.

separation s separare f, despărţire f.

sepia s/adj sepia f.

September s septembrie m; **in** ~ în septembrie; **last** ~ septembrie trecut.

septic adj med septic; ~ **tank** s fosă f septică.

septicemia s med septicemie f.

sepulchral adj (funereal) funerar; (voice) cavernos, grav; (atmosphere) lugubru.

sequel s (to a book, movie) urmare f.

sequence s ordine f, succesiune f; secvenţă f; rezultat n; episod n.

sequester vt jur a sechestra; frml a izola.

sequin s paietă f.

sequoia s bot secvoia m.

Serbia s Serbia • ~**n** adj sârb, sârbesc ‖ s (person) sârb m; (language) sârbă f.

serenade s serenadă f ‖ vt a cânta o serenadă.

serendipitous adj lit întâmplător.

serene adj (calm) senin; (quiet) liniştit.

serf s şerb m, iobag m; sclav m, rob m.

sergeant s mil sergent m; (police) ofiţer m de poliţie, poliţist m.

serial adj în serie; math curent ‖ s roman n serial/în serie; cin (film) serial n; ~ **number** s număr n (de ordine), serie f; ~ **rapist** s violator m în serie.

series s serie f; progresie f; succesiune f.

serious adj serios, important; (acute) grav; periculos; (grave) sobru; sever; aşezat; (earnest) real; sincer; (provocative) adânc, profund.

sermon s relig predică f, fig predică f, lecţie f, morală f.

serpent s şarpe m; fig şarpe m, viperă f.

serrated adj zimţat, crenelat; bot serat.

serum s (pl ~s/**sera**) ser n.

servant s servitor m; funcţionar m; sclav m.

serve vt (dish up) a servi; (provide) a deservi; a aduce; (supply) a aproviziona; a trata; fig a sluji; (~ time) a face, a ispăşi ‖ vi (work) a servi; (assist) a fi de folos; a funcţiona; sp a servi ‖ s sp serviciu n • ~**r** s (waiter) chelner m; sp persoană f la serviciu; relig ministrant m; comp server n.

service s serviciu n; funcţie f; relig slujbă f; muncă f; (help) ajutor n; aut revizie f, depanare f; (machine) întreţinere f; (favor) favoare f; ordin n; servire f ‖ vt (provide) a deservi; auto a face revizia; (machine) a întreţine; ~ **charge** s comision n; ~ **station** s benzi-nărie f • ~**able** adj folositor, util; (clothes) rezistent; durabil.

serviette s şerveţel n (de masă).

servile adj fig servil, slugarnic.

serving s porţie f (de mâncare).

session s şedinţă f; conferinţă f; sesiune f; an m şcolar; semestru n; curs n.

set, set, set vt (put) a pune, a aşeza; (establish) a fixa, a stabili; (~ a jewel) a monta; (adjust) a regla; (plant) a sădi; (stake, etc) a vârî; (device) a repara; a pregăti; (~ a trap) a întinde; (~ an example) a da; (~ fashion, etc) a lansa; (~ a task, etc) a da; (~ out a problem) a pune; (record) a stabili; med (~ bones, etc) a pune la loc || *vi* (*cement, etc ~s*) a se întări; (*henfowl*) a cloci; (*color*) a prinde; a se fixa; (*sun ~s*) a apune; a se modela; a porni; a se îndrepta || *adj* (*inflexible*) rigid; fix; stabilit; (*firm*) ferm; clădit; (*ready*) gata; întărit || *s* sens *n*; contur *n*; (*collection*) grup *n*; serie *f*; set *n*; *tv*, *radio* aparat *n*; *cin* platou *n*; *thea* decor *n*; ~ **about** *vi* (*begin*) a întreprinde, a începe să; ~ **aside** *vt* (*save*) a pune deoparte; (*dismiss*) a înlătura, a da de o parte; ~ **back** *vt* a împiedica, a opri; a reține; a da înapoi; ~ **off** *vt* a scoate în evidență, a reliefa; a contrasta; a înfrumuseța; a contracara; a separa; (*bomb*) a declanșa; ~ **out** *vt* a delimita; a preciza; a defini; *constr* a jalona; (*display*) a etala; a expune; (*explain*) a prezenta || *vi* (*trip*) a porni, a pleca; ~ **up** *vt* (~ *an organization*) a fonda, a crea; (~ *a committee, etc*) a constitui; (~ *a meeting*) a organiza, a aranja; (*erect a statue, etc*) a ridica, a înălța; (~ *a roadblock*) a plasa, a instala; (~ *equipment*) a instala, a monta; *coll* a înscena o lovitură contra cuiva.

setback *s* piedică *f*, obstacol *n*; oprire *f*; *mil* recul *n*.

settee *s* canapea *f*, banchetă *f*.

setting *s* așezare *f*; decor *n*; montură *f*; apus *n*; montare *f*; direcție *f*.

settle *vt* a stabili; (*rent, etc*) a fixa; (*steady*) a stabiliza; (*come to terms*) a hotărî; (~ *a conflict*) a aplana; (~ *a doubt*) a risipi; (*pay*) a plăti || *vr* (*stay*) a se instala || *vi* (*snow, etc ~s*) a se așeza; (*become peaceful*) a se domoli; (*liquid*) a se limpezi; (*sink*) a se tasa; ~ **down** *vt* a stabili; a coloniza; a regla, a rezolva || *vi* a se așeza; a se liniști; *tech* a decanta; (*weather*) a deveni stabil; ~ **for** *vi* a accepta, a se mulțumi cu; ~ **in** *vi* a se adapta; ~ **on** *vi* a se hotărî, a se decide în privința • ~**ment** *s* stabilire *f*; colonizare *f*; instalare *f*; *tech* sedimentare *f*; amplasare *f*; (*resolution*) reglare *f*; rezolvare *f*; (*deadline*) fixare *f*, stabilire *f*; (*payment*) achitare *f*, tranzacție *f*.

seven *num* șapte || *s* șapte *m*, șeptar *m* • ~**teen** *num* șaptesprezece • ~**th** *num* al șaptelea, a șaptea • ~**ty** *num* șaptezeci.

sever *vt* (*cut*) a tăia; (~ *links*) a rupe; *also fig* a despărți; a dezbina; a desface.

several *adj* mai mulți/multe; câțiva; diferiți, diverși; fiecare; respectiv; separat; individual.

severance *s* (*of relations*) rupere *f*, încetare *f*; (*of contact, etc*) întrerupere *f*; (*division*) separare *f*; *jur* disjungere *f*; ~ **pay** *s* îndemnizație *f* de concediere.

severe *adj* (*harsh*) sever; strict; (~ *illness*) grav; (*plain*) sobru; (*acute*) caustic; (~ *weather*) aspru; (~ *shock*) puternic, dur; (~ *pain*) puternic.

severity *s* (*gravity*) gravitate *f*; (*difficulty*) dificultate *f*; (*harshness*) severitate *f*.

sew, sewed, sewn *vt/vi* a coase.

sewage *s* canalizare *f*; ape *f pl* reziduale, ape *f pl* uzate.

sewer *s* canal *n* colector.

sewn *vt* * **sew**.

sex *s* sex *n*; sexualitate *f*; viață *f* sexuală; ~ **maniac** *s* obsedat *m* sexual • ~**ism** *s* discriminare *f* sexuală.

sextet *s* *mus* sextet *n*.

sexton *s* paracliser *m*.

sexual *adj* sexual; ~ **harassment** *s* hărțuire *f* sexuală; ~ **intercourse** *s* raporturi *n pl* sexuale.

sexy *adj coll* sexi, atractiv

shabby *adj* (*clothes*) ros, jerpelit; (*furniture*) sărăcăcios, jalnic; (*person, etc*) amărât, jalnic; (*behavior*) meschin, josnic.

shack *s* cocioabă *f*; baracă *f*.

shackle *vt* a încătușa; *fig* a împiedica, a pune obstacole • ~**s** *s pl* lanțuri *n pl*; *fig* piedică *f*, obstacol *n*.

shade *s* umbră *f*; răcoare *f*; colorit *n*; nuanță *f*; iluzie *f*; abajur *n* || *vt* a umbri; a hașura; a întuneca; a ascunde.

shadow *s* umbră *f*; spirit *n*; fantomă *f* || *vt* a umbri; a fila; a întrista.

shady *adj* (*shaded*) umbros, umbrit; dubios; (*dishonest*) necinstit; necurat.

shaft *s* (*tool*) mâner *n*, coadă *f*; puț *n*; (*elevator*) cabină *f*; *tech* ax *n*, osie *f*; (*light*) rază *f*.

shaggy *adj* păros; flocos; (*hair*) aspru; zburlit; (*person*) nepieptănat.

shake, shook, shaken *vt* (*agitate*) a scutura; a zgâlțâi; a clătina; (*brandish*) a agita; a slăbi; a distruge; (*unsettle*) a zdruncina || *vi* (*tremble*) a tremura; a se zgudui; a se clătina || *s* (*jiggle*) tremur *n*; zguduire *f*; ~ **down** *vt* (~ *from a tree*) a scutura; *coll* (*rob*) a extorca/stoarce de bani || *vi coll* a se acomoda/obișnui.

shaky *adj* (*voice*) tremurător; (*person*) nesigur (pe picioare); (*chair, etc*) șubred; (*argument*) șubred, care nu stă în picioare; (*insecure*) instabil; oscilant; (*weak*) slab; precar.

shale *s geol* șist *n*.

shall *v aux* voi; vom; o/am să; o/avem să; vei; veți; o/ai să; o/aveți să || *v mod* trebuie; trebuie să || *v aux mod* vei; o/ai să; o/are să; veți; o/aveți să.

shallot *s bot* hașmă *f*.

shallow *adj* mic, puțin adânc; de suprafață; deșert.

sham *adj* prefăcut; simulat; fals || *s* simulare *f*, impostură *f*; *om m* fățarnic.

shaman *s* șaman *m*, vraci *m*.

shamble *vi* (*shuffle*) a merge târșâind picioarele • ~**s** *s pl* abator *n*; *fig* măcel *n*; dezordine *f*, harababură *f*.

shame *s* rușine *f*; ocară *f*; pată *f*; necinste *f* || *vt* a face de rușine; a rușina; a necinsti • ~**ful** *adj* rușinos, scandalos • ~**less** *adj* nerușinat, neobrăzat.

shampoo *s* șampon *n* || *vt* a spăla cu șampon.

shamrock *s bot* trifoi alb *m*.

shank *s anat* gambă *f*, fluierul *n* piciorului, tibie *f*; (*of tool*) mâner *n*; *bot* (*stem*) tulpină *f*, tijă *f*.

shanty[1] *s* (*hut*) cocioabă *f*, bordei *n*.

shanty[2] *s* (*song*) cântec *n* marinăresc.

shape *s* formă *f*; figură *f*; model *n*; imagine *f*; tipar *n*; mostră *f*; configurație *f* || *vt* a modela; a produce; a aranja || *vi* a se contura.

shard *s* ciob *n*, țandără *f*, spărtură *f*.

share *s* parte *f*; aport *n*; contribuție *f*; participare *f*; cotă-parte *f* || *vt* a diviza; a distribui; a împărtăși; ~ **out** *vt* a împărți, a repartiza • ~**holder** *s* acționar *m*.

shark *s icht* rechin *m*; *om m* rapace; (*swindler*) tâlhar *m*.

sharp *adj* (*pointed*) ascuțit; ironic; (*harsh*) incisiv; (*clear*) precis; (*abrupt*) brusc; (*quick*) iute; (*sour*) acru; ager; șiret; (*severe*) aprig; energic; (~ *voice*) tăios; (~ *cry*) pătrunzător; (~ *pain, etc*) pătrunzător; (~ *taste*) picant || *s escroc m* || *adv* brusc; (*exactly*) precis, fix • ~**en** *vt* a ascuți • ~**ener** *s* (*for a pen*) ascuțitoare *f*; (*for a knife*) dispozitiv *n* de ascuțit cuțite • ~**ly** *adv* (*harshly*) aspru, cu asprime; (*suddenly*) brusc.

shatter *vt* (*smash*) a sfărâma, a zdrobi; *fig* (*ruin health*) a distruge, a ruina; (~ *nerves*) a zdruncina; (~ *hopes*) a nărui, a spulbera.

shave *vt* a bărbieri, a rade; a tunde; a tăia; a răzui ||

vr/vi a se rade; a se tunde; a se tăia ǁ *s* ras *n*, bărbierit *n*; apropiere *f*; brici *n*.

shavings *s pl* talaș *n*.

shawl *s* șal *n*.

she *pron* ea; dânsa ǁ *s* fată *f*; femeie *f*; femelă *f*.

sheaf *s* (*corn*) snop *n*; (*letters, etc*) teanc *n*, vraf *n*.

shear *vt* (~ *sheep*) a tunde; ~ **off** *vt* a tăia ǁ *vi* a se desprinde • ~**s** *s pl* (*for gardening, for sheep*) foarfece *f pl*.

sheath *s* (*knife*) teacă *f*; (*cable*) izolație *f*; *tech* husă *f*; manta *f*; *anat* membrană *f* • ~**e** *vt* (~ *a sword, etc*) a băga în teacă/toc; *fig* a acoperi, a îmbrăca.

shed[1] *vt* (*drop*) a vărsa, a lăsa să cadă; (~ *hair*) a pierde; *fig* (~ *light, etc*) a revărsa, a emana ǁ *vi* (~ *leaves, etc*) a cădea; (*animal* ~*s*) a năpârli; a-i cădea părul.

shed[2] *s* șopron *n*; magazie *f*; remiză *f*; atelier *n*; *avia* hangar *n*; *text* rost *n*.

sheen *s lit* strălucire *f*; sclipire *f*; lucire *f*, luciu *n*; îmbrăcăminte *f* bogată.

sheep *s* oaie *f*; persoană *f* timidă; enoriași *m pl* • ~**ish** *adj* sfios, timid; fricos; prostuț, bleg.

sheer[1] *adj* (*fine*) diafan; (*pure*) curat; transparent; complet; (*steep*) abrupt ǁ *adv* vertical; complet.

sheer[2] *vi naut* a se legăna, a se clătina; a devia, a se abate ǁ *s naut* legănare *f*, clătinare *f*; deviere *f*, abatere *f*.

sheet *s* cearșaf *n*; coală *f*; pânză *f*; strat *n*; înveliș *n* ǁ *vt* a acoperi; a înveli; a placa.

sheik(h) *s* șeic *m*.

shelf *s* raft *n*; etajeră *f*; stâncă *f*; prag *n*.

shell *s* scoarță *f*, valvă *f*; (*egg, nut* ~) coajă *f*; (*snail*) cochilie *f*; (*tortoise*) carapace *f*; scoică *f*; *mil* obuz *n* ǁ *vt* a coji, a decortica; a bombarda ǁ *vi/vr* a se coji; a se desprinde.

shelter *s* adăpost *n*; refugiu *n*; apărare *f*; azil *n*; paravan *n*; grânar *n* ǁ *vt* a adăposti; a găzdui; a ascunde; a apăra ǁ *vi* a se adăposti; a se ascunde • ~**ed** *adj* (*from weather*) la adăpost de; (~ *from life, etc*) fără griji.

shelve *vt* a pune/așeza pe raft; *fig* (~ *a project*) a amâna; a pune la dosar; *fig* a destitui, a concedia; a suspenda din serviciu.

shepherd *s* cioban *m*, păstor *m*; *fig* păstor *m* (spiritual); preot *m*; a paște (oile); *fig* a păstori (turma).

sheriff *s* șerif *m*.

sherry *s* sherry *n* (vin *n* de Xeres).

shield *s* scut *n*; ecran *n*; apărător *m*; paravan *n*; blindaj *n* ǁ *vt* a apăra; a tăinui.

shift *vt* (*remove*) a (stră)muta; a deplasa; a comuta; *bot* a răsădi; a înlocui ǁ *vi* (*move*) a se muta; a se mișca; a se întoarce; a (se) feri; *auto* a schimba viteza; *fig* a se descurca ǁ *s* mutare *f*; (*change*) schimbare *f*; pretext *n*; (*period*) schimb *n*; mijloc *n*; viclenie *f*; truc *n*.

shilly-shally *vi pej* a ezita, a șovăi; a tărăgăna.

shimmer *vi* a licări; a sclipi; a luci; a pâlpâi ǁ *s* licărire *f*; lucire *f*; sclipire *f*; pâlpâit *n*.

shin *s anat* tibie *f*.

shine, shone, shone *vi* (*glow*) a (stră)luci; a lumina; (*excel*) a se remarca ǁ *vt* (*polish*) a lustrui; a face să (stră)lucească ǁ *s* luciu *n*; (*sheen*) strălucire *f*; lumină *f*; lustru *n*; *fig* măreție *f*; farmec *n*.

shingle *s* șindrilă *f*; șiță *f*; (*gravel*) pietriș *n*, prundiș *n*.

shinny *vi* (*climb*) a se cățăra.

shiny *adj* strălucitor; lucios; senin; lucitor.

ship *s* navă *f*; vapor *n*; avion *n* ǁ *vt* a îmbarca; a expedia ǁ *vi* a se îmbarca • ~**ment** *s naut* navlu *n*, fraht *n* •

~**per** *s naut* expeditor *m*; *tech* încărcător *m* • ~**ping** *adj* de navigație; maritim; naval ǁ *s* expediere *f*, transport *n*; flotă *f* comercială; vase *f pl* • ~**shape** *adj/adv* în perfectă ordine • ~**wreck** *s* naufragiu *n*; epavă *f* • ~**yard** *s* șantier *n* naval.

shirk *vi* (**from**) a se eschiva de la ǁ *vt* (*evade*) a se eschiva/sustrage de la.

shirt *s* cămașă *f*; cămașă *f* de noapte; bluză *f*.

shit *s vulg* căcat *n*; excrement *n*; defecare *f*; prostii *f pl*; om *m* de nimic; calabalâc *n* ǁ *vi vulg* a se defeca ǁ *vt* a minți; a exagera.

shiver *vi* a tremura; a se înfiora ǁ *s* tremur *n*.

shoal *s* (~ *of fish*) banc *n*.

shock *s* (*upset*) șoc *n*; ciocnire *f*; lovitură *f*; *med* comoție *f*; atac *n* ǁ *vt* a șoca; (*stun*) a ului; a ofensa; (*scandalize*) a scârbi; (*traumatize*) a zgudui; a izbi • ~**ing** *adj* (*news, etc*) îngrozitor; zguduitor; scandalos; revoltător, respingător; rușinos.

shod *vt* * **shoe**.

shoddy *adj* (*work, etc*) de calitate proastă; (*behavior*) nedemn, grosolan.

shoe, shod, shod *vt* a încălța; a potcovi ǁ *s* pantof *n*; gheată *f*; talpă *f*; potcoavă *f*; sabot *m* • ~**lace** *s* șiret *n* de pantofi.

shone *vi* * **shine**.

shook *vt* * **shake**.

shoot, shot, shot *vt* (*gun down*) a împușca; (*aim*) a ținti; (*fire*) a trage; a marca; a arunca; a traversa ǁ *vi* a trage în; (*spurt*) a țâșni; (*dart*) a trece iute; a vâna; a se ivi; *bot* a încolți; *sp* a șuta; (*pain* ~*s*) a durea; (~ *a film*) a filma; *phot* a fotografia ǁ *s* vlăstar *m*; boboc *m*; tir *n*; ~**ing** *s* împușcare *f*; vânare *f*, vânătoare *f*; *cin* filmare *f*; ~ **gallery** *s* pavilion *n* de tir sportiv; ~ **star** *s* stea *f* căzătoare.

shop *s* magazin *n*; atelier *n* ǁ *vi* a face cumpărături • ~**per** *s* cumpărător *m* • ~**ping** *s* cumpărături *f pl*; ~ **mall** *s* centru *n* comercial.

shore *s* țărm *n*; coastă *f*; uscat *n*; ~ **up** *vt* a propti; a sprijini; *fig* a consolida.

shorn *vt* * **shear**.

short *adj* (*small*) scurt; scund; puțin; (*concise*) redus; incomplet; (*curt*) sec; fraged; tăios; deficitar ǁ *adv* (*abruptly*) brusc; pe termen scurt ǁ *s* lipsă *f*; scurtime *f*; ~ **list** *s* lista *f* candidaților selectați; ~ **story** *s liter* nuvelă *f*; ~ **wave** *s* (*radio*) unde *f pl* scurte.

shortage *s* lipsă *f*, criză *f*.

shortbread *s* prăjitură *f* uscată.

short-change *vt* a nu da restul corect; *fig* a înșela.

short-circuit *s elec* scurt circuit *n*.

shortcoming *s* neajuns *n*, lipsă *f*, defect *n*, deficiență *f*.

shortcut *s* (*road*) drum *n* scurt, scurtătură *f*; *fig* soluție *f* miraculoasă.

shortfall *s* deficit *n*.

shorthand *s* stenografie *f*.

short-lived *adj* de scurtă durată; efemer; care nu trăiește mult.

shortly *adv* (*soon*) curând; imediat; (*curtly*) *adj* răstit.

short-range *adj* (*weapon*) cu rază scurtă (de acțiune); (*outlook*) pe termen scurt.

shorts *s* șort *n*; chiloți *m pl* bărbătești; rebut *n*.

short-sighted *adj* miop; obtuz; neprevăzător.

short-tempered *adj* irascibil, nervos.

short-term *adj* (*effects, etc*) pe termen scurt; (*problem*) de scurtă durată.

shot[1] *vt* * **shoot**.

shot² *s mil* foc *n* de armă; (*person*) trăgător *m*; *sp* şut *n*; *phot* poziţie *f*, poză *f*; *pl cin* succesiune *f* de imagini luate într-o singură filmare; *coll* încercare *f*; şansă *f*; *med* (*injection*) injecţie *f*.

should *v aux* aş; am; voi; vom; o/am să; o/avem să; trebuie să ‖ *v mod* ar fi bine; ar trebui, s-ar cuveni.

shoulder *s* umăr *n* ‖ *vt* a împinge cu umărul; a-şi asuma.

shout *s* strigăt *n*; ţipăt *n* ‖ *vt/vi* a striga; a ţipa.

shove *vt* a împinge; a urni; a îmbrânci; a îndesa; a lovi; a aşeza ‖ *s* împingere *f*; trântire *f*; îndesare *f*; ghiont *n*; lovire *f*; punere.

shovel *s* lopată *f*; cupă *f* de excavator ‖ *vt* a săpa; a înfuleca; a căra cu nemiluita.

show, showed, shown *vt* a arăta; a indica; (*prove*) a dovedi; (*display*) a etala; a conduce; a îndruma; (*explain*) a lămuri ‖ *vr* a se arăta; a se dovedi; *jur* a pretinde; a pleda în favoarea ‖ *vi* a se ivi; a se vedea; a juca; a arăta ‖ *s* manifestare *f*; acces *n*; tablou *n*; (*performance*) spectacol *n*; pompă *f*; aparenţă *f*; aspect *n*; semn *n*; ~ **business** *s* industria *f* de divertisment; ~ **off** *vi* a-şi da aere; ~ **of hands** (*vote*) ridicare de mâini; ~ **up** *vi* a se ivi, a-şi face apariţia; **good** ~! *coll* bună treabă!.

showdown *s* arătarea *f* cărţilor (de joc); *fig* (*facts, etc*) dare *f* în vileag, expunere *f*; reglare *f* de conturi; (*person*) explicaţie *f*.

shower *s* aversă *f*; ploaie *f* torenţială; răpăială *f*; abundenţă *f*; duş *n*; jerbă *f* ‖ *vt* a stropi, a inunda; a copleşi; a bombarda.

showgirl *s* artistă *f* de music hall;

showing *s* (*of art*) expoziţie *f*; (*of film*) spectacol *n*; (*performance*) performanţă *f*, realizare *f*.

shown *vt* * **show**.

showroom *s* sală *f* de expoziţie.

showy *adj* de efect, care sare în ochi.

shrank *vt* * **shrink**.

shred *s* (*material*) fâşie *f*; petic *n*; zdreanţă *f*; cârpă *f*; *fig* fărâmă *f*, grăunte *m* ‖ *vt cul* a rade; (*paper*) a tăia fâşii, a toca; a sfâşia • ~**der** *s* maşină *f* de tocat hârtia documente, de distrus documente.

shrew *s zool* şoarece *m* de câmp; *fig* scorpie *f*, cată *f*, femeie *f* rea de gură.

shrewd *adj* ager; şiret; subtil; răutăcios; violent; aspru; iscusit.

shriek *vi* a ţipa ‖ *s* ţipăt *n*, sunet *n* strident.

shrill *adj* (*sound, voice*) ascuţit; (*whistle*) strident.

shrimp *s icht* crevete *m*; pitic *m*.

shrine *s* mormânt *n*, loc *n* sfânt; sanctuar *n*.

shrink, shrank, shrunk *vi* a se strâmta; a se scurta; a se contracta; a intra la apă; (*diminish*) a scădea; (**from**) (*cower*) a se da înapoi, a se retrage; a ezita ‖ *vt* a strânge; a strâmta; a scoroji ‖ *s* strângere *f*; strâmtare *f*; *coll* psihiatru *m* • ~**age** *s* îngustare *f*; *fig* scădere *f*, diminuare *f* • ~**wrap** *vt* a ambala în foiţă de plastic.

shrivel *vi* a se contracta; a se încreţi; a se ofili ‖ *vt* a contracta; a încreţi.

shroud *s* giulgiu *n*; înveliş *n*, văl *n* ‖ *vt* a înfăşura în giulgiu; *fig* a înveli; a învălui; a ascunde.

Shrove Tuesday *s relig* sărbătoare *f* din ultima marţi înainte de Postul Paştelui.

shrub *s* arbust *m*, tufă *f*.

shrug *vt* a ridica din umeri ‖ *s* ridicare *f* din umeri.

shrunk *vt* * **shrink**.

shuck *s* (*pod*) coajă *f* de nucă/castană; (*of oyster*) cochilie *f*; valvă *f* ‖ *vt coll* (*discard*) a se debarasa de.

shudder *vi* (*shake*) a se cutremura, a se înfiora; (~ *with fear, etc*) a tremura ‖ *s* cutremurare *f*, tremur *n*, fior *m*.

shuffle *vt* (~ *feet*) a târşi, a târî; (~ *cards*) a amesteca, a face, a da ‖ *s* târşire *f*, mers *n* târşit; (*of cards*) amestecare *f*.

shun *vt* a evita; a se abţine de la; a se feri.

shunt *vt rail* a manevra, a trece pe altă linie; a gara; *elec* a şunta, a deriva; (*project, etc*) a nu da curs; a amâna; a întrerupe.

shush *interj* sst!.

shut, shut, shut *vt* (*close*) a închide; a astupa; a opri; a întrerupe; a strânge; a împiedica ‖ *vi* (~ *door, etc*) a se închide; ~ **down** *vt* a închide; *tech* a întrerupe; a decupla • ~**down** *s tech* pană *f*; avarie *f*; *econ* întreruperea *f* funcţionării; oprirea *f* exploatării; sistare *f*.

shutter *s* (*window*) oblon *n*; (*camera*) obturator *n*.

shuttle *s text* suveică *f*; (*service*) navetă *f* ‖ *s* (*train, bus, plane*) mijloc *n* de transport pentru navetişti.

shy *adj* timid; rezervat; prudent; ruşinos; sperios ‖ *vi* a tresări • ~**ness** *s* timiditate *f*, sfială *f*,.

shyster *s coll* (*crook*) şarlatan *m*, escroc *m*.

Siamese *adj* (*cat, twin*) siamez ‖ *s* siamez *f*; (*limba*) siameză *f*.

sibling *s* (*brother*) frate *m*; (*sister*) soră *f*.

sick *adj* bolnav; indispus; dezgustat; palid; abătut; galben; de boală; nesănătos.

sickle *s* seceră *f*.

sickness *s* maladie *f*, boală *f*; greaţă *f*.

side *s* latură *f*, parte *f*; aspect *n*; faţă *f*; pantă *f*; secţie *f*; descendenţă *f*; echipă *f*; opinie *f*; pagină *f*; ~ **effect** *med* efect *n* secundar nedorit; (*consequence*) efect *n* secundar, repercusiune *f* ~ **issue** *s* problemă *f* colaterală; ~ **street** *s* străduţă *f*; stradă *f* laterală.

sideboard *s* (*furniture*) bufet *n*.

sidecar *s* ataş *n*.

sidelight *s auto* lumini *f pl* de poziţie.

sideline *s* activitate *f* secundară ‖ *adj* (*tangential*) secundar.

sidelong *adj/adv* oblic, pieziş; înclinat.

sideshow *s thea* completare *f* (la spectacol); intermezzo *n*; *fig* problemă *f* secundară/adiacentă.

sidestep *vi* a se da/a păşi într-o parte ‖ *vt* a se da la o parte din calea; *fig* (*issue*) a evita.

sidetrack *vt rail* a trece pe o linie de rezervă; a gara; *fig* a abate, a devia.

sidewalk *s* trotuar *n*.

sideways *adv* într-o parte; pe o parte; pieziş, oblic.

siding *s rail* linie *f* secundară; *rail* macaz *n*, ac *n*; perete *m* lateral.

sidle *vi* (**along**) (~ *an edge*) a merge înclinat (într-o parte).

siege *s* asediu *n* ‖ *vt* a asedia.

siesta *s* siestă *f*.

sieve *s* sită *f*; ciur *n*; flecar *m* ‖ *vt* a strecura; a cerne.

sift *vt* (*sieve*) a cerne; a strecura; (*examine*) a analiza; a presăra; a selecta ‖ *vi* a se cerne.

sigh *vi* a suspina; a geme ‖ *s* suspin *n*, oftat *n*.

sight *s* (*act*) vedere *f*, privire *f*; (*sense*) văz *n*, vedere *f*; prezenţă *f*; (*scene*) privelişte *f*, scenă *f*; (*mess*) apariţie *f*; (*spectacle*) spectacol *n* ‖ *vt* a vedea; a urmări; a observa; a zări; a ţinti.

sign *s* semn *n*; marcă *f*; gest *n*; indiciu *n*; firmă *f*; simptom *n*; reclamă *f*; indicator *n* ‖ *vt* a semna; a marca; ~

on *vt* (*hire*) a angaja; *mil* a se înrola; *scol* a se înscrie; **~ up** *vt* (*worker*) a angaja; *mil* a înrola ‖ *vi* *mil* a se înrola; *scol* a se înscrie.

signal *s* (*sign*) semnal *n*; semn *n*; indicator *n* ‖ *vt* (*indicate*) a semnala; a vesti ‖ *vi* *auto* a semnaliza ‖ *adj* remarcabil.

signature *s* semnătură *f*, iscălitură *f*.

significance *s* (*meaning*) semnificaţie *f*; importanţă *f*.

significant *adj* important; semnificativ.

signify *vt* a indica.

signpost *s* stâlp *m* indicator.

silage *s* *agr* grâne *f pl* însilozate.

silence *s* linişte *f*; uitare *f* ‖ *vt* a înăbuşi; a face să tacă.

silent *adj* tăcut; rezervat; taciturn; reticent ‖ *s* *cin* film *n* mut.

silica *s* *chem* silice *f*.

silicon *s* *chem* siliciu *n*.

silicone *s* silicon *n*.

silhouette *s* siluetă *f*.

silk *s* mătase *f* ‖ *adj* mătăsos; de mătase.

sill *s* pervaz *n*.

silly *adj* neghiob; prost; nătâng; stupid; absurd; necugetat; **~ person** ‖ *s* prost *m*, neghiob *m*.

silo *s* siloz *n*.

silt *s* mâl *n*, nămol *n*.

silver *s* argint *n*; argintărie *f* ‖ *adj* argintat; de argint; argintiu ‖ *vt* a arginta; a încărunţi ‖ *vi* a albi.

similar *adj* analog, asemănător; identic; similar ‖ *s* obiect *n* asemănător.

simile *s* *liter* comparaţie *f*.

simmer *vt* a fierbe la foc mic ‖ *vi* a clocoti; a fierbe la foc mic ‖ *s* fierbere *f* (la foc mic).

simper *vi* (*sneer*) a zâmbi prosteşte sau afectat.

simple *adj* simplu; (*easy*) uşor; modest; natural; cinstit; (*clean*) curat; sincer; primitiv; (*plain*) de rând; naiv; elementar; inferior.

simplicity *s* simplitate *f*.

simplification *s* simplificare *f*.

simplify *vt* a uşura; a simplifica.

simply *adv* absolut; neapărat; simplu, uşor; modest; numai; **~ wonderful** absolut minunat; **you ~ must see it** trebuie neapărat să-l vezi; **~ furnished** mobilat simplu; **I ~ noticed that** numai am observat că.

simulate *vt* a simula; a afecta; a imita; a lua înfăţisarea de.

simulacrum *s* (*pl* **simulacra**) simulacru *n*.

simulation *s* simulare *f*.

simulcast *vt* *tv, radio* a transmite simultan la radio şi televiziune ‖ *adj* radiotelevizat.

simultaneous *adj* simultan.

sin păcat *n*; ofensă *f*; crimă *f*; sacrilegiu *n* ‖ *vi* a păcătui.

since *adv* de atunci ‖ *prep* de; de la; din ‖ *conj* de când; din clipa (vremea) când; deoarece, întrucât, fiindcă.

sincere *adj* sincer; credincios; cinstit; adevărat.

sincerity *s* sinceritate *f*.

sinew *s* *anat* tendon *n*; *fig* putere *f* fizică, forţă *f*; *fig* rezerve *f pl* de energie.

sing, sang, sung *vt* a cânta; a lăuda; a intona ‖ *vi* a cânta; a ciripi; a susura; a ţârâi; a şuiera; **to ~ along** *vi* a cânta în grup • **~er** *s* cântăreţ *m*, cântăreaţă *f*.

singe *vt* (*scorch*) a pârli; a arde uşor.

single *adj* unic; separat; singur; celibatar ‖ *s* bilet *n* simplu ‖ *vt* a selecta; a distinge; a remarca; **~ combat** *s* luptă *f* între două persoane; **~handed** *adj* făcut

de un singur om ‖ *adv* singur, fără ajutor; **~minded** *adj* hotărât; **~ room** *s* cameră *f* simplă.

singly *adv* separat; singur.

singular *adj* (*odd*) neobişnuit, ciudat ‖ *s* *gram* singular *n*.

sinister *adj* din partea stângă, stâng; (*creepy*) funest; sinistru; dezastruos; cumplit.

sink, sank, sunk *vi* (*go under*) a se afunda; a se scufunda; (*sag*) a se lăsa; (*drop*) a cădea; (*diminish*) a coborî; a se nărui; a se potoli; (*decline*) a apune; (*subside*) a slăbi ‖ *vt* a scufunda; a coborî; a apleca; (dig) a săpa; a achita ‖ *s* chiuvetă *f*; cloacă *f*; canal *n* de scurgere.

sinuous *adj* sinuos; cotit; şerpuit; ondulat; *fig* încurcat, încâlcit, întortocheat; (*person*) imprevizibil.

sinus *s* *anat* sinus *n* • **~itis** *s* *med* sinuzită *f*.

sip *vt* a înghiţi, a sorbi ‖ *s* înghiţitură *f*.

siphon *s* sifon *n* ‖ *vt* (**~** *money*) a transfera; a deturna.

sir *s* domnule *m*.

siren *s* *tech, also myth* sirenă *f*.

sirloin *s* *cul* muşchi *m* (de vacă).

sissy *s* (*coward*) fricos *m*; (*effeminate person*) fătălău *m* ‖ *adj* fricos, timid.

sister *s* soră *f*; infirmieră *f*; călugăriţă *f* • **~in-law** *s* cumnată *f*.

sit, sat, sat *vi* (*person ~s*) a şedea; a sta; (*court, etc ~s*) a fi în şedinţă/lucrări; (*pose for art*) a poza; *fig* a se potrivi; (*assemble*) a se reuni ‖ *vt* a aşeza; a rezema; a sta pe ‖ *vr* a se aşeza; **~ back** *vi* a se aşeza comod; **~ by** *vi* a sta cu mâinile în sân; **~ down** *vi* a se aşeza; **~ in on** *vi* a asista la; **~ up** *vi* a sta drept; a sta până noaptea târziu.

sitcom *s* comedie *f* de situaţie.

site *s* loc *n*; aşezare *f*; (*building, etc*) amplasament *n*, poziţie *f*; *constr* şantier *n*; *archeol* sit *n* ‖ *vt* a situa, a plasa.

sitter *s* babysitter *m*; (*hen*) cloşcă *f*.

sitting *s* (*for meal*) capacitate *f* de servire a mesei, serie *f*; (*for portrait*) şedinţă *f*; (*of committee*) sesiune *f*; **~ duck** *s* *coll* ţintă *f* uşoară; **~room** *s* salonaş *n*; cameră *f* de zi.

situate *vt* a amplasa.

situation *s* (*location*) poziţie *f*, aşezare *f*; (*state of affairs*) situaţie *f*; (*job*) serviciu *n*, slujbă *f*.

six *num* şase • **~teen** *num* şaisprezece • **~ty** *num* şaizeci.

size *s* (*clothes, etc*) măsură *f*; talie *f*; volum *n*; (*building*) dimensiune *f*; *econ* număr *n*; format *n*; statură *f*; *mil* calibru *n*; mărime *f* ‖ *vt* a sorta; a clasa; a potrivi • **~able** *adj* mare, voluminos, de mărime considerabilă.

sizzle *vi* (*crackle*) a sfârâi (în tigaie) ‖ *s* sfârâială *f*.

skate[1] *s* patină *f* ‖ *vi* a patina • **~board** *s* skateboard *n*, planşă *f* cu rotile • **~r** *s* patinator *m*.

skate[2] *s* *icht* calcan *m*.

skating *s* patinaj *n*; **~ rink** *s* patinoar *n*.

skedaddle *vi* (*run off*) a-şi lua tălpăşiţa.

skein *s* (*of wool, silk*) scul *n*.

skeletal *adj* scheletic.

skeleton *s* schelet *n*; schemă *f*; schiţă *f*; cadru *n*; **~ key** *s* şperaclu *n*.

skeptic *adj* sceptic.

sketch *s* desen *n*; schiţă *f*; crochiu *n*; *thea* sceneci *n*, scenetă *f*; (*outline*) plan *n*, rezumat *n*, privire *f* generală ‖ *vt* (*draw*) a desena; a schiţa; *fig* a descrie sumar.

skew *vt* (*distort*) a denatura ‖ *vi* a devia, a se abate.

skewer *s* *cul* frigăruie *f* ‖ *vt* a pune la frigare.

ski s schi n ǁ vi a schia.

skid s tech talpă f; patină f; sabot m; auto derapare f; naut șină f de alunecare ǁ vi auto, etc a derapa, a aluneca; avia a glisa.

skiff s sp schif n.

skill s pricepere f; deprindere f; măiestrie f.

skillet s tigaie f.

skillful adj (clever) iscusit, abil, priceput.

skim vt (~ milk) a smântâni; (~ over a book) a răsfoi; a atinge ușor; fig a rasoli ǁ vi a trece în zbor; (glide) a pluti.

skimp vt (stint) a face economie la ǁ vi a se zgârci • ~y adj coll redus; sărăcăcios; zgârcit; calic.

skin s anat piele f; (crust) crustă f; (casing) înveliș n; (on fruit) coajă f ǁ vi (peel) a se jupui; a se cicatriza ǁ vt (flay) a jupui; a stoarce • ~deep adj superficial • ~ diving s înot n subacvatic • ~flint s zgârie-brânză m • ~tight adj strâmt.

skinny adj slab; sărăcăcios.

skip s salt n ǁ vi (hop) a sări; a o întinde; fig a divaga ǁ vt a omite; a sări (ceva).

skipper s naut comandant m, căpitan m; fig conducător m, șef m; sp căpitan/șef m de echipă

skirmish s mil ambuscadă f; hărțuială f; (tussle) încăierare f; fig ceartă f, altercație f ǁ vi (fight) a se încăiera; mil a angaja o ambuscadă.

skirt s fustă f ǁ vt (evade) a evita; a ocoli ǁ vi a fi la periferie.

skit s parodie f; satiră f; scheci n; schiță f.

skitter vi (bird) a flutura/a bate din aripi; (animal) a se mișca cu repeziciune.

skittish adj (playful) jucăuș; (wary) nervos; sperios.

skittle s popic n • ~s s (game) popice n pl.

skulk vi (lurk) a se pitula; (sneak) a se furișa, a se fofila.

skull s anat țeastă f, craniu n.

skullduggery s coll malversație f, cotcărie f.

skunk s zool sconcs m.

sky s cer n ǁ vt a ridica.

skylark s orn ciocârlie f.

skyscraper s zgârie-nori n.

slab s lespede f; dală f; tabletă f; bucată f; parte f ǁ vt a pava; a acoperi cu dale.

slack adj (loose) destins; slăbit; (person) neglijent, neserios; fig încet, lent; (weather) staționar; (wind) moderat; tech (fixat) slab; cu joc ǁ s com, etc (perioadă de) acalmie f; inactivitate f; tech joc n; naut mare f staționară ǁ vi a slăbi, a ceda; a se des-tinde • ~en vt (~ a grip) a slăbi; (~ the reins) a lăsa mai liber; (step) a micșora; (slow down) a încetini ǁ vi (rope ~s) a se lăsa; (activity ~s) a stagna; (speed ~s) a se micșora/diminua; (wind ~s) a slăbi; (person ~s) a se lăsa pe tânjală.

slacks s pantaloni m pl largi.

slag s metal zgură f; scorie f.

slain vt * **slay.**

slake vt lit (~ one's thirst) a potoli; (~ one's desire) a domoli.

slalom s sp slalom n.

slam vt (bang) a trânti ǁ vi a se închide cu zgomot ǁ s zgomot n; izbitură f.

slander s calomnie f; jur defăimare f ǁ vt a calomnia; jur a defăima.

slang s slang n; jargon n; argou n.

slant vi (incline) a se înclina ǁ vt a înclina; a falsifica ǁ

s (angle) înclinare f; (viewpoint) opinie f; tendință f, înclinație f.

slap vt a pălmui ǁ s palmă f; insultă f ǁ adv brusc; direct.

slash s (gash) tăietură f; rană f ǁ vt (cut) a cresta; (re-duce prices) a reduce drastic; (~ budget, etc) a reduce mult; fig a critica aspru.

slat s (plank) stinghie f; șipcă f.

slate s geol gresie f; șist n; ardezie f; tăbliță f, plăcuță f; pol listă f de candidați/electorală.

slattern s femeie f murdară/neglijentă.

slaughter s masacru n, măcel n; tăiere f ǁ vt a ucide; a măcelări; a tăia.

Slav s/adj slav m • ~onic adj slav; slavon ǁ s ling grupul n limbilor slave.

slave s sclav m ǁ vi a munci ca un rob.

slavish adj (habits) de sclav; fig servil, slugarnic.

slay, slew, slain vt (kill) a omorî, a ucide.

sleazy adj (seedy) rău famat, îndoielnic; (corrupt) imoral; ~ bar s bar n deocheat/rău famat.

sled s sanie f; târnăcop n; mai n ǁ vt a duce cu sania ǁ vi a merge cu sania.

sledge s (sled) sanie f; tech ciocan n de mână; text tachet m.

sledgehammer s (mallet) baros n; ciocan n de forjă.

sleek adj (hair, fur) neted, lucios; (shape) cu linii precise, bine conturat.

sleep, slept, slept vi a (a)dormi; a fi adormit; a hiberna; fig a lâncezi ǁ vt a dormi; a adăposti ǁ s somn n; somnolență f; hibernare f; ~ around vi a-și face de cap; ~ in vi a se scula târziu; a dormi în casă; ~ off vi a uita de (griji etc) dormind; a îneca în somn; ~ with vi a se culca cu (cineva) • ~er s (~ train) cușetă f, tren n cu vagoane de dormit • ~ing bag s sac n de dormit • ~ing pill s somnifer n • ~less adj fără somn, nedormit; fig neobosit • ~walker s somnambul m • ~y adj (drowsy) somnoros; (sluggish) indolent; fig apatic; (fruit) răscopt.

sleet s lapoviță f • ~y adj cu lapoviță.

sleeve s mânecă f; manșon n ǁ vt a pune mâneci la.

sleigh s (sled) sanie f (trasă de cai).

sleight s (skill) îndemânare f, dexteritate f; ~ of hand s (trick) iuțeală f de mână.

slender adj (slim) zvelt; tăios; (small) redus; (lean) slab; fig (income, etc) modest, mic; (hopes, etc) slab.

slept vi * **sleep.**

sleuth s coll detectiv m.

slew s coll grămadă f, sumedenie f ǁ v * **slay** ǁ vi (skid) a derapa; (turn, veer) a vira.

slice s felie f; parte f ǁ vt a tăia felii.

slick adj (glossy) lucios; (smooth) neted, isteț; (efficient) abil; (polished) rafinat; grozav; pej (~ talk) superficial, (~ person) șiret ǁ adv direct; perfect ǁ vt a aranja ǁ vr a se găti.

slide, slid, slid vi a (a)luneca; a se scurge; a se furișa ǁ vt a furișa ǁ s alunecare f; lamă f; pantă f.

sliding adj glisant; ~ door s ușă f glisantă.

slight adj (small) slab; ușor; fragil; (slim) subțire; superficial ǁ vt (insult) a ofensa ǁ s (snub) afront n; desconsiderare f • ~ly adv ușor, oarecum.

slim adj (slender) zvelt; redus; (thin) slab, frugal; (faint) ușor ǁ vi (diet) a slăbi.

slime s nămol n; noroi n; mâl n; tech șlam n; substanță f vâscoasă.

slimy adj (greasy) vâscos; noroios; murdar; fig slugar-nic; dezgustător.

sling, slung, slung vt (toss) a arunca, a azvârli; tech a lansa; med a pune (brațul) în eșarfă ‖ s laț n; mil bandulieră f; praștie f; med bandaj n, eșarfă f; fig lovitură f (a soartei etc).

slink, slunk, slunk vi (creep) a se strecura, a se furișa.

slip vi (slide) a aluneca; a se deplasa; a se scurge; (sneak) a se furișa; a se repezi; a se vârî; (fall) a se surpa; (blunder) a greși ‖ vt a scăpa din; a dezlega ‖ s pas m greșit; greșeală f; gafă f; ghinion n; alunecare f; bilețel n; foaie f.

slipper s papuc m de casă, pâslar m.

slippery adj (sneaky) șiret; nesigur; (greasy) alunecos.

slit vt a despica ‖ s crăpătură f; semn n; fantă f; fisură f; crestătură f.

slither vi (person) a aluneca; (snake) a se târî.

sliver s (of glass, etc) ciob n, așchie f; (of meat, etc) bucățică f.

slob s persoană f leneșă și îngâlată.

slobber vi (drool) a-i curge balele; a saliva; fig (work) a strica; a cârpăci ‖ s salivă f; bale f pl.

sloe s bot porumbar m.

slog s (grind) corvoadă f; (drag) bătaie f de cap ‖ vi (trudge) a munci ca un sclav.

slogan s lozincă f; slogan n; motto n; deviză f.

slop vt (spill) a vărsa; a scurge; (splash) a stropi ‖ s baltă f, smârc n; pl lături f pl.

slope s versant m; pantă f; taluz n; înclinare f ‖ vi a se înclina ‖ vt a înclina.

sloppy adj (shoddy) neîngrijit, neglijent; (~ food) rar, apos; (sappy) dulceag, sentimental.

slosh vt coll (spill) a vărsa ‖ vi (~ liquid) a da pe dinafară; a se revărsa/împrăștia.

slot s crăpătură f; crestătură f; tăietură f; fantă f ‖ vt a cresta, a tăia.

slouch vi (droop) a se pleoști, a se turti; (stoop) a umbla greoi; a atârna.

slough¹ s (bog) mlaștină f; (mud pool) mocirlă f.

slough² vt (~ off skin) a lepăda; fig ~ off vi a se debarasa de.

slovenly adj neîngrijit, neglijent; murdar ‖ adv neglijent.

slow adj încet; leneș; agale; greoi; neglijent; ~ down vi a încetini • ~down s încetinire f • ~ly adv lent, încet.

sludge s (mud) nămol n, mâl n; noroi n; (sewage) reziduuri n pl lichide menajere.

slug s zool melc m, limax m; coll glonț n; tech bară f, bloc n; fig leneș m, trântor m.

sluggish adj (person) apatic; (growth, etc) lent; (business) care stagnează.

sluice s ecluză f.

slum s cartier n sărac, mahala f.

slumber s lit somn n ‖ vi a dormi.

slump s econ (in prices, etc) prăbușire f, scădere f bruscă; criză f, depresiune f; (fall) cădere f bruscă; constr tasare f ‖ vi econ a scădea brusc; a se prăbuși; (activity) a scădea, a se reduce; (drop) a cădea brusc, a se prăbuși.

slung vt * **sling**.

slunk vt * **slink**.

slur s (smear) lezare f; (insult) afront n, insultă f; (stain) pată f, murdărie f; mânjire f ‖ vt (slight) a nu ține seama de, a lăsa de o parte; fig a discredita; a defăima; (~ words) a articula prost/neclar.

slurp vt/vi a sorbi, a bea cu lăcomie ‖ s sorbitură f.

slush s noroi n, nămol n; zloată f; lapoviță f; sentimen-

talism n exagerat • ~y adj cu zloată; noroios; mocirlos; fig dulceag.

slut s pej femeie f murdară/neglijentă; (whore) târfă f, târâtură f.

sly adj (wily) viclean; glumeț; (devious) ascuns; ironic; (furtive) furiș.

smack¹ s (slap) lovitură f; (whip) pocnet n; plesnitură f; (kiss) sărut n zgomotos; (of lips) plescăit n ‖ vt (slap) a pălmui, a trage o palmă; (whip) a pocni, a plesni; (~ lips) a plescăi ‖ adv cu putere; zgomotos; drept, direct

small adj (little) mic; ușor; slab; puțin; (~ person) sărac; redus; umil; subțire; (~ income) modest; (cares, etc) mărunt; fig meschin; josnic ‖ adv mic; încet.

smart adj usturător, dureros; rapid; aspru; vioi; isteț; priceput; modern; șic ‖ s usturime f; durere f acută ‖ vi a ustura; a suferi; a înțepa.

smash vt (crash) a izbi; a pocni; a trânti; (shatter) a sparge; a distruge ‖ vi a se izbi; a se sparge; a eșua ‖ s izbitură f; sfărâmare f; ciocnire f.

smattering s (scrap) crâmpei n, fărâmă f; **a ~ of French** puține cunoștințe de franceză.

smear vt a păta; a unge; (sully) a murdări; (spread) a etala; (insult) a defăima ‖ s (mark) pată f; murdărie f; (slur) defăimare f.

smell, smelt, smelt vt a mirosi; a simți; a adulmeca; a presimți ‖ vi a mirosi; a adulmeca; a duhni ‖ s miros n; duhoare f; mireasmă f.

smile vi a zâmbi, a surâde; fig (upon) a fi favorabil/prielnic (cuiva) ‖ vt a spune zâmbind ‖ s zâmbet n.

smirk s surâs n superior/malițios.

smite, smote, smitten vt lit, obs (strike) a lovi, a pocni; (afflict) a copleși; **be smitten with remorse** vt a fi cuprins de remușcări.

smith s fierar m; potcovar m • ~y s fierărie f.

smitten vt * **smite**.

smock s bluză f de lucru; salopetă f.

smog s smog n, ceață f deasă.

smoke s fum n; țigară f ‖ vi a fumega, a fuma ‖ vt a fuma; a afuma; a bănui • ~r s fumător m; vagon n pentru fumători.

smoking s fumat n; tabagism n; **no ~** fumatul interzis.

smolder vi a arde încet/mocnit; fig a mocni, a dospi ‖ s fum n gros; also fig foc n mocnit/înăbușit.

smooch vi coll (kiss) a se săruta; (pet) a se mângâia.

smooth adj (flat) neted; (soft) lin; lucios; (easy) calm; (charming) plăcut; omogen; (steady) fluent ‖ s netezire f ‖ vt (flatten) a netezi; a șlefui; a întinde; a liniști; a scuza; a ușura • ~ly adv (gently) lin, egal; (flow freely) fluent.

smote vt * **smite**.

smother vt (suffocate) a sufoca; (stifle) a înăbuși; (overwhelm) a stinge ‖ vi a se sufoca.

smudge s murdărie f; pată f; mâzgălitură f ‖ vt a păta, a murdări.

smug adj (conceited) încrezut, infatuat, îngâmfat.

smuggle vt a face contrabandă cu ‖ vi a face contrabandă; a fi contrabandist.

smuggling s contrabandă f.

smut s coll (filth) obscenități f pl, porcării f pl.

snack s gustare f; aperitiv n; înghițitură f.

snag s (problem) inconvenient n, obstacol n; protuberanță f, ieșitură f.

snail s zool melc m.

snake s zool șarpe m; viperă f ‖ vt a încolăci.

snap s (bite) muşcătură f; clănţănit n; pocnet n; fig energie f; fermoar n || adv brusc, deodată || vt a apuca; a ciocni; (break) a frânge; a ţăcăni; phot a face un instantaneu; a pocni || vi a înşfăca; a plesni; (yell) a ţipa; a se frânge.

snappy adj (fashionable) şic, elegant; (lively) animat, vioi; (unfriendly) arţăgos, iritat, enervat.

snare s capcană f; laţ n || vt a prinde în capcană.

snarl s mârâit n || vi a mârâi, a-şi arăta colţii; fig a mormăi, a mârâi.

snatch vt a înşfăca; a smulge || s înşfăcare f; fărâmă f; interval n scurt.

snazzy adj coll (stylish) modern şi de bun gust.

sneak vt a duce pe furiş; a fura || vi a se furişa; a pârî || s pârâtor m; laş m.

sneakers s pl pantofi m pl de tenis; bascheţi m pl.

sneer vi surâs n dispreţuitor; rânjet n || vi (at) (scorn) a zâmbi/surâde batjocoritor (la).

sneeze s strănut(at) n || vi a strănuta

snicker s coll chicotit n || vi (at) a lua în râs.

snide adj (sarcastic) răutăcios; meschin.

sniff vt a pufni; (snivel) a smiorcăi || vt (inhale) a aspira; a priza; fig a mirosi; a bănui || s (smell) miros n; prizare f; aspirare f.

snifter s (glass) pahar n pentru degustare.

snigger vi (giggle) a chicoti; a râde pe înfundate || s chicotit n, râs n pe înfundate.

snip vt (cut) a tăia (cu foarfeca) || s tăietură f (cu foarfeca).

snipe s orn becaţă f.

sniper s mil trăgător m de elită.

snippet s fragment n; (clip) extras n; frântură f.

snitch s coll pârâcios || vi (on) a pârî.

snivel vi (sob) a geme; (whimper) a se smiorcăi, a scânci.

snob s snob m • **~bery** s snobism n • **~bish** adj snob.

snooker s (game) joc n de biliard.

snoop vi coll (sneak) a cotrobăi; (pry) a-şi vârî nasul unde nu-i fierbe oala; (meddle) a se amesteca în treburile altcuiva.

snooty adj coll (snobbish) preţios, pedant.

snooze vi (doze) a dormita, a aţipi || s pui m de somn; moţăială f, aţipeală f.

snore vi a sforăi || s sforăit n.

snorkel s (for a swimmer) tub n de oxigen.

snort s (of a person) sforăit n; (of a horse) sforăitură f || vi (inhale) a respira anevoie, a respira cu zgomot; (horse ~s) a sforăi; (engine ~s) a gâfâi.

snot s coll muc(i) m/pl • **~ty** adj plin de muci.

snout s rât n; bot n.

snow s zăpadă f || vi a ninge || vt a troieni; a înzăpezi • **~ball** s bulgăre m de zăpadă || vi a se umfla, a se mări rapid • **~flake** s fulg m de zăpadă • **~man** s om m de zăpadă • **~plow** s dispozitiv n de curăţat zăpada • **~storm** s furtună f de zăpadă, viscol n.

snowdrop s bot ghiocel m.

snub s (rebuff) mustrare f, dojană f || vt a ignora, a umili; a dojeni.

snuff s tutun n de prizat || vt a priza tutun; a aspira/ inhala cu putere/zgomotos.

snuffle vi (sniffle) a fornăi; a rosti pe nas.

snug adj (cozy) călduţ, comod; confortabil; (~ clothes) bine ajustat.

snuggle vi a se ghemui; (nestle) a se cuibări || vt (cuddle) a strânge în braţe.

so adv aşa/atât de; atât de mult etc; extrem de; foarte; astfel, aşa; în felul acesta; la fel, de asemenea; aşadar, deci; prin urmare; de aceea.

soak vt a uda (leoarcă); a îmbiba; a stoarce || vi a fi ud; a trage la măsea || s udare f.

soap s săpun n; fig linguşire f || vt a săpuni; fig a linguşi; **bar of ~** s calup n de săpun; **~ opera** s tv spectacol n melodramatic serial; **~ powder** s detergent m; **~ suds** s pl clăbuci m pl de săpun • **~y** adj cu săpun; plin de săpun; fig linguşitor.

soar vi a zbura sus; a se înălţa; avia, etc a pluti; a plana; fig a se avânta (spre culmi).

sob s suspin n; hohot n; plâns n cu hohote || vi a plânge cu suspine/hohote.

sober adj sobru; calm; moderat; treaz || vt a trezi; a dezmetici || vi a se trezi.

sobriety s sobrietate f; seriozitate f; (non-drunkenness) (stare de) trezie f.

soccer s sp fotbal n.

sociable adj intim; sociabil; (friendly) prietenos, jovial.

social adj (communal) social; sociabil; monden; public || s (party) serată f; reuniune f, întrunire f • **~ite** s persoană f mondenă.

socialism s socialism n.

socialize vt a socializa; a naţionaliza; (meet people) a frecventa lume.

society s societate f (mondenă); companie f; asociaţie f; club n.

sociologist s sociolog m.

sociology s sociologie f.

sociopath s bolnav m mintal.

sock s şosetă f, ciorap m scurt.

socket s elec dulie f; priză f; (eye ~) orbită f; anat (tooth ~) alveolă f.

soda s chem sodă f calcinată; (~ water) sifon n; (beverage) băutură f acidulată.

sodden adj ud; plin de apă; îmbibat; (soggy) necopt, crud; fig abrutizat.

sodium s chem sodiu n; **~ carbonate** s sodă f.

sodomy s sodomie f, homosexualitate f.

sofa s sofa f, divan n, canapea f.

Sofia s Sofia f.

soft adj moale; fin; slab; blând; delicat; plăcut; politicos; liniştit; milos || adv moale; încet; liniştit; **~ drink** s băutură f nealcoolică; **~hearted** adj milos; blând; bun; **~ pedal** vi fig a încetini || vt fig a atenua, a minimaliza; **~spoken** adj încet; (words) convingător.

soften vt (moderate) a micşora; (substance) a atenua, a înmuia; (skin) a catifela; (impact) a atenua, a îndulci; (attitude) a modera, a îmblânzi || vi (person, etc) a se îmblânzi, a se înduioşa.

software s comp software n.

soggy adj ud leoarcă; muiat.

soil vt a murdări; a păta || s sol n, pământ n; pată f; fig corupţie f.

sojourn s lit sejur n || vi a sta/rămâne un timp.

solace s lit (comfort) consolare f, (relief) alinare f || vt a consola.

solar adj solar.

sold vt * sell.

solder s sudură f || vt a suda.

soldier s soldat m.

sole[1] adj (only) singur; exclusiv.

sole[2] s talpă f; pingea f.

sole[3] s icht sol m.

solemn adj solemn; venerabil; sacru; festiv; serios.

solicit *vt* (*seek*) a solicita, a cere ‖ *vi* (~ *a prostitute*) a-şi oferi serviciile • **~ous** *adj* serviabil, săritor • **~or** *s* solicitant *m*, petiţionar *m*; *jur* avocat *m*; consilier *m* judecătoresc; agent *m* (electoral etc).

solicitude *s* solicitudine *f*; grijă *f*, atenţie *f*; preocupare *f*; grijă *f* exagerată.

solid *adj* solid; dens; compact; omogen; masiv; sigur; robust; tare; puternic ‖ *s* solid *n*.

solidarity *s* solidaritate *f*.

soliloquy *s* monolog *n*.

solitaire *s* (*card game*) pasienţă *f*; (*gem*) solitar *n*.

solitary *adj* (*lone*) singur; (*isolated*) izolat; (*private*) retras; (*unique*) unic; depărtat ‖ *s* solitar *m*.

solitude *s* izolare *f*; singurătate *f*.

solo *s* solo *n*.

solstice *s astron* solstiţiu *n*.

soluble *adj* solubil.

solution *s* (**to**) soluţie *f*; (*liquid* ~) soluţie *f*.

solve *vt* a rezolva; a descifra; a dezlega.

solvent *adj fin* solvabil ‖ *s* dizolvant *m*, solvent *m*.

somber *adj* (*dull*) sumbru, întunecat; (*sad*) trist.

some *adj* ceva, câtva, nişte, puţin; câţiva, unii ‖ *pron* ceva, câtva; câţiva, unii ‖ *adv* vreo, cam; ceva, câtva, întrucâtva • **~body** *pron* cineva ‖ *s* cineva *m*, persoană *f* importantă • **~day** *adv* într-o (bună) zi • **~how** *adv* cumva; oricum; pentru un motiv oarecare • **~one** *pron/s* * **~body**.

somersault *s* săritură *f*, tumbă *f*, dare *f* peste cap ‖ *vi* a face o tumbă/săritură; a se da peste cap.

something *pron* ceva ‖ *adv* cam, întrucâtva, într-o oarecare măsură, puţin.

sometimes *adv* uneori, câteodată; când şi când; din când în când.

somewhere *adv* undeva; în jurul; într-un loc oarecare.

somnambulist *s* somnambul *m*.

son *s* fiu *m*; copil *m*; fecior *m* • **~-in-law** *s* ginere *m*.

sonata *s mus* sonată *f*.

song *s* cântec; ciripit *n*; melodie *f*; cânt *n*; cântare *f*.

sonic *adj* sonic.

sonnet *s liter* sonet *n*.

sonorous *adj* (*resonant*) sonor; (*style*) bombastic.

soon *adv* curând; îndată; devreme; **as** ~ **as** îndată ce; **the ~er the better** cu cât mai devreme, cu atât mai bine.

soot *s* funingine *f*.

soothe *vt* (*calm*) a linişti; (*alleviate*) a calma; (*comfort*) a alina.

soothing *adj* alinător, liniştitor.

soothsayer *s* profet *m*, prezicător *m*.

sophisticated *adj* sofisticat; (*urbane*) rafinat; versat; nenatural; (*complex*) complicat; experimentat.

sophomore *s edu* student *m* în anul II.

soporific *s*, *adj* somnifer *n*, soporific *n*.

sopping *adj* (*drenched*) ud leoarcă.

soppy *adj* (*drenched*) (ud) leoarcă; (*rainy*) ploios.

soprano *s/adj mus* soprană *f*.

sorcerer *s* vrăjitor *m*.

sorceress *s* vrăjitoare *f*.

sorcery *s* vrăjitorie *f*.

sordid *adj* (*squalid*) sordid; (*base*) dezgustător.

sore *adj* dureros; suferind; inflamat; supărat ‖ *s* rană *f*; punct *n* sensibil.

sorghum *s bot* sorg *m*.

sorority *s edu* comunitate *f* de fete, club *n* de fete.

sorrel *s bot* măcriş *n*.

sorrow *s* (*grief*) supărare *f*; necaz *n*; durere *f*; (*regret*) regret *n* ‖ *vi* a-şi face griji; a fi trist; a plânge după.

sorry *adj* (*regretful*) mâhnit; (*wretched*) jalnic; mizer; amărât; **I'm so/very/terribly** ~ îmi pare foarte rău.

sort *s* fel *n*, gen *n*; sort *n*; caracter *n*; specie *f*; calitate *f* ‖ *vt* a sorta; a alege.

sortie *s mil* raid *n*; raită *f*, tur *n*; (*foray*) tatonare *f*.

soubriquet *s* (*alias*) poreclă *f*; (*name*) denumire *f*.

soufflé *s cul* sufle *n*.

sought *vt* * **seek**.

soul *s* suflet *n*; spirit *n*; energie *f*; simţire *f*.

sound[1] *s* sunet *n*; glas *n*; (*noise*) zgomot *n*; sens *n*; ton *n* ‖ *vi* (ră)suna; (*seem*) a părea ‖ *vt* a suna; a exprima; (*announce*) a vesti; a rosti; a declara; a părea.

sound[2] *adj* (~ *body*, *etc*) sănătos, zdravăn; (*reliable*) judicios, înţelept; (~ *investment*) sigur; (*thorough*) temeinic; (*good*) solid.

sound[3] *vt* (*depth*) a sonda.

soup *s cul* supă *f*.

sour *adj* acru; acid; stătut; fără calcar; sterp; neroditor; *fig* posac, supărăcios ‖ *vt* (*milk* ~s) a acri; *fig* a învenina; a irita ‖ *vi* (*milk* ~s) a se acri; (*feelings* ~s) a se răci.

source *s* sursă *f*; izvor *n*; origine *f*.

souse *vt cul* a marina; a mura; (*immerse*) a scufunda; (*drench*) a îmbiba, a înmuia; *coll* (*make drunk*) a îmbăta.

south *s* sud *n*, miază-zi *n* ‖ *adj* de/din sud.

souvenir *s* amintire *f*.

sovereign *adj* suveran ‖ *s* (*ruler*) suveran *m* • **~ty** *s* suveranitate *f*.

sow[1], **sowed**, **sown** *vt* a semăna; a însămânţa; a imprima; a sădi ‖ *vi* a semăna.

sow[2] *s zool* scroafă *f*.

soya *s bot* soia *f*.

spa *s* staţiune *f* balneo-climaterică.

space *s* spaţiu *n*; câmp *n*; (*area*) domeniu *n*; (*room*) loc *n*; aer *n*; (*gap*) gol *n*; (*time*) răstimp *n*; (*cosmos*) univers *n*; atmosferă *f* ‖ *vt* a rări; a spaţia; a distanţa • **~craft** *s* navă *f* spaţială • **~man** *s* astronaut *m*, cosmonaut *m* • **~ship** *s* navă *f* spaţială • ~ **shuttle** *s* navetă *f* spaţială • **~suit** *s* costum *n* de astronaut.

spacious *adj* spaţios.

spade[1] *s* hârleţ *n*; cazma *f*, lopată *f* ‖ *vt* a săpa.

spade[2] *s* (*cards*) pică *f*.

spaghetti *s pl cul* spaghete *f pl*.

Spain *s* Spania *f*.

spamming *s comp* trimitere *f* de materiale publicitare prin Internet.

span *s* (*period*) durată *f*; *avia*, *etc* anvergură *f*; *constr* deschidere *f*; *tech* distanţă *f*, interval *n*; (*duration*) durată *f*; (*extent*) evantai *n*, gamă *f* ‖ *vt* (*time*) a cuprinde, a acoperi; (*bridge*) a trece peste.

spangle *s* paietă *f* ‖ *vt* (**with**) a garnisi cu paiete.

Spaniard *s* spaniol *m*.

spaniel *s zool* câine *m* prepelicar, spaniel *m*.

Spanish *adj* spaniol ‖ *s* (*language*) spaniolă *f*.

spank *vt* a bate la fund.

spanner *s tech* cheie *f* de piuliţe.

spar *vi* (*train*) a se antrena (la box); (*argue*) a se sfădi, a avea un schimb de cuvinte • **~ring match** *s* meci de antrenament • **~ring partner** *s* partener de antrenament.

spare *adj* disponibil; (*extra*) de rezervă; liber; simplu; sobru; frugal ‖ *s* piesă *f* de schimb ‖ *vt* (*show mercy*) a cruța; a scuti; (give up) a renunța; (save) a economisi ‖ vi a fi econom ‖ vr a se cruța.

sparingly adv (use ~) cu moderație; (spend ~) cu zgârcenie.

spark s scânteie f; strop m; sclipire f ‖ vi a scânteia.

sparkle s (of eyes, jewelry) strălucire f; (of stars) sclipire f ‖ vi (shine) a străluci, a sclipi.

sparkling adj also fig sclipitor; (~ wine) spumos.

sparrow s orn vrabie f.

sparse adj (thin) rar, răsfirat; puțin.

spasm s med spasm n; convulsie f; (cough, etc) acces n, criză f; (emotion) acces n.

spastic adj med spastic ‖ s med handicapat m motor.

spat vi * **spit.**

spate s revărsare f a apelor; fig (words, etc) potop n; (crises, etc) serie f.

spatial adj spațial; cosmic.

spatter vt (splash) a împroșca, a stropi ‖ vi (rain ~s) a răpăi ‖ s stropitură f, împroșcătură f; răpăit n; pată f.

spatula s med, cul spatulă f.

spawn s icre n pl; plevușcă f; fig pej progenitură f, odrasle f pl; bot miceliu n ‖ vt icht a depune icre/ouă; fig pej (people) a se prăsi.

spay vt (neuter an animal) a castra.

speak, spoke, spoken vi (talk) a vorbi; a conversa ‖ vt (tell) a spune; a enunța; (express) a exprima; (be fluent in) a cunoaște (o limbă); ~ **easy** hist s local n clandestin (pe vremea prohibiției); ~ **for smb** vi a vorbi în numele cuiva; ~ **of** vi a aminti, a menționa; ~ **out** vi a vorbi deschis; ~ **to** vi a vorbi cu; a confirma (ceva); a se referi la; ~ **up** vi (louder) a vorbi tare/deslușit; (be frank) a vorbi (deschis), a se exprima; a nu tăcea • **~er** s vorbitor m; crainic m; orator m; purtător m de cuvânt; (amplifier) megafon n; **the Speaker of the House** spicherul m Camerei Reprezentanților în Congresul SUA.

spear s lance f; țeapă f; cange f; harpon n ‖ vt (impale) a străpunge cu lancea/sulița.

special adj (particular) special; deosebit; (singular) excepțional; (unique) aparte; urgent; formal ‖ s ediție f specială; tren n special • **~ist** s expert m, specialist m • **~ize** vt a specializa; a specifica; a distinge ‖ vi a se specializa.

specialty s specific n; specialitate f; înțelegere f; caracteristică f.

species s inv bio, etc specie f; (class) clasă f, categorie f; rasă f; soi n; varietate f.

specific adj (particular) tipic; (explicit) specific; (exact) precis; concret ‖ s (fact) detaliu n, amănunt n.

specify vt a preciza, a specifica.

specimen s specimen n; (blood, etc) probă f; mostră f; exemplar n; tip n.

specious adj specios, înșelător; fals.

speck s (fleck) pată f mică; fărâmă f; (dust) fir n; grăunte m ‖ vt a păta • **~le** s pată f de culoare ‖ vt a păta; a împestrița.

spectacle s thea, etc spectacol n; fig spectacol n, scenă f, priveliște f.

spectacular adj spectaculos, impresionant; (huge) impunător.

spectator s spectator m; martor m.

specter s also fig spectru n, fantomă f.

spectrum s phys spectru n; (range) gamă f.

speculate vi (wonder) a specula, a face speculații; a medita; com a specula.

speculation s (theory) speculație f; (guess) presupunere f, ipoteză f; com, fin speculă f.

sped vi * **speed.**

speech s vorbire f; limbă f; rostire f; discurs n; articulare f; conferință f.

speed, sped, sped vt a accelera; a grăbi; a trimite ‖ vi a goni; a se grăbi ‖ s viteză f; grabă f; turație f • **~way** s autostradă f • **~y** adj rapid.

speleologist s speolog m.

speleology s speologie f.

spell[1], **spelt, spelt** vt (write) a ortografia; (letters) a silabisi; (mean) a însemna ‖ vi a ortografia; a se scrie; ~ **out** vt a spune literă cu literă; (decipher) a descifra; (make explicit) a explica.

spell[2] s also fig farmec n, vrajă f • **~binding** adj captivant.

spell[3] s (period of time) răstimp n, interval n; pauză f; repaus n; schimbare f, alternare f.

spelt vt * **spell.**

spend, spent, spent vt a cheltui; (fritter) a risipi; (finish) a termina; (~ time) a petrece; (make an effort) a consacra ‖ vr a se epuiza ‖ vi a cheltui; a se termina; a se uza.

sperm s physiol spermă f.

spew vt/vi a vomita, a voma.

sphere s (ball) sferă f; glob n; (area) domeniu n; limită f; (orb) astru m; competență f; specialitate f.

spherical adj sferic.

sphinx s sfinx m.

spice s condiment n; gust n; savoare f; spirit n ‖ vt a condimenta.

spicy adj (hot) picant; condimentat; piperat; fig echivoc; fără perdea.

spider s ento păianjen m.

spiffy adj șic, elegant și modern.

spigot s (in cask) cep n; (faucet) robinet n.

spike s (metal) vârf n, lance f; (plant) spic n, țep m.

spill, spilt, spilt vt a vărsa; a răsturna; a arunca ‖ vi a vărsa; a se împrăștia ‖ s pată f.

spin, spun, spun vt a toarce; a depăna; (turn) a răsuci; a învârti; text (weave) a țese; a dansa ‖ vi a toarce; a depăna; a se învârti ‖ s (turn) răsucire f; avia vrilă f; tech patinare f; phys spin m; (drive) plimbare f scurtă și rapidă.

spinach s bot spanac n.

spinal adj spinal; ~ **column** s coloană vertebrală.

spindle s text fus n; tech arbore m, ax n; tijă f; bot lujer m; constr balustru n ‖ vi a se întinde, a se lungi; bot a crește drept și subțire.

spindly adj fusiform.

spine s anat coloană f vertebrală; (of a book) dos n; (of a plant, etc) ghimpe m; fig miez n; esență f.

spinster s torcătoare f; fată f bătrână; celibatară f.

spiral s spirală f ‖ adj în spirală ‖ vi (smoke, etc ~s) a urca în spirală.

spire s clopotniță f; turn n; constr fleșă f, săgeată f; bot pai n; lujer n.

spirit s spirit n; suflet n; minte f; intelect n; geniu n; cuget n; demon m; fire f; energie f; alcool n; sens n real; tendință f; spiriduș m ‖ vt a încuraja; a înflăcăra.

spiritual adj spiritual; transcendental; sacru; intelectual; sufletesc ‖ s mus, relig cântec n religios popular.

spit[1], **spat, spat** vt a scuipa; a ploua slab ‖ vt a scuipa ‖ s scuipat n; expectorare f; ploiță f.

spit[2] s cul frigare f; geog banc n de nisip ‖ vt cul a pune pe frigare.

spite *s* (*malice*) ranchiună *f* ‖ *vt* a contraria; **in ~ of** *prep* în ciuda • **~ful** *adj* răuvoitor; dușmănos.

splash *vt* (*splatter*) a împroșca; (~ *with mud*) a murdări; a presăra; a vărsa; a bălăci; a împodobi ‖ *vi* (*dash*) a țâșni; (*spray*) a stropi; a se împroșca; a se murdări; a pleoscăi ‖ *s* stropire *f*; strop *m*; pleoscăit *n*; pată *f*.

splatter *vt* a stropi, a împroșca; a murdări, a mânji ‖ *vi* (*rain ~s*) a răpăi ‖ *s* stropire *f*; pată *f*; răpăit *n*.

spleen *s* anat splină *f*; *fig* (*ill temper*) proastă dispoziție *f*.

splendid *adj* superb; splendid; strălucitor.

splendor *s* splendoare *f*, frumusețe *f*.

splice *vt* tech a îmbina cap la cap; *naut* a matisa; *agr* a altoi ‖ *s* tech îmbinare *f*; *naut* matisare *f*; *elec* conexiune *f* directă.

splint *s* med atelă *f*; *tech* splint *n*.

splinter *s* așchie *f*; surcea *f* ‖ *vt* a sparge ‖ *vi* a se despica; a așchia; a crăpa.

split, split, split *vt* a despica; (*rip*) a rupe; (*break up*) a sfărâma; (*divide*) a dezbina ‖ *vi* a crăpa; a se sfărâma; a se scinda; a da greș; (*leave*) a pleca ‖ *s* (*tear*) ruptură *f*; rupere *f*; fisură *f*; (*division*) sciziune *f*; sfărâmare *f*; **~ second** *s* fracțiune *f* de secundă.

splodge *s* (*of paint, ink*) pată *f*.

splutter *vi* (*person*) a murmura, a îngăima; (*engine*) a tuși, a se îneca; (*fire*) a trosni.

spoil, spoiled/spoilt, spoiled/spoilt *vt* (*ruin*) a strica; a distruge; (*indulge*) a răsfăța ‖ *vi* (*decay*) a se strica; a se învechi • **~s** *s* trofeu *n*; pradă *f*; jertfă *f*; premiu *n*.

spoke¹ *vt* * **speak**.

spoke² *s* spiță *f*; *naut* cavilă *f* de cârmă ‖ *vt* a pune spițe; a pune frână la.

spoken *vt* * **speak**.

spokesman *s* purtător *m* de cuvânt.

spokesperson *s* purtător *m* de cuvânt, purtătoare *f* de cuvânt.

sponge *s* burete *m*; curățare *f*; parazit *m*; bețiv *m* ‖ *vt* a spăla cu buretele; a absorbi; a da uitării ‖ *vi* a se îmbiba; a absorbi.

sponsor *s* naș *m*, nașă *f*; (*backer*) sponsor *m*; inițiator *m*; garant *m* ‖ *vt* (*back*) a sponsoriza, a patrona; a susține; a finanța.

spontaneity *s* spontaneitate *f*.

spontaneous *adj* spontan; firesc; direct; reflex.

spoof *s* (*mockery*) parodie *f*, satiră *f*, (*trick*) înșelătorie *f*, tragere *f* pe sfoară.

spook *s* (*ghost*) stafie *f*; *sl* (*spy*) spion *m* ‖ *vt* a înspăimânta • **~y** *adj* înfricoșător.

spool *s* mosor *n*; bobină *f* ‖ *vt* a înfășura, a bobina.

spoon *s* lingură *f* ‖ *vt* a lua cu lingura; a scobi • **~ful** *s* conținutul *n* unei linguri.

spoor *s* urmă *f* (a vânatului).

sporadic *adj* rar; sporadic; izolat.

spore *s* bot spor *m*.

sport *s* distracție *f*; *pl* sport *n*; sportiv *m* ‖ *vt* a expune ‖ *vi* a face sport; a glumi; a juca; a petrece • **~s car** *s* mașină *f* sport.

spot *s* (*place*) loc *n*; (*mark*) pată *f*; semn *n*; urmă *f*; colț *n*; (*bit*) strop *n*; localitate *f* ‖ *vt* a păta; a murdări; a înjosi; (*notice*) a distinge ‖ *vi* a păta; a se murdări.

spouse *s* soț *m*, soție *f*; mire *m*, mireasă *f*.

spout *s* burlan *n*; canal *n* de scurgere; trombă *f*; jgheab *n*; (*jet*) țâșnire *f* ‖ *vt* a împroșca; a scuipa; a vărsa; a recita ‖ *vi* (*spurt*) a țâșni; a gâlgâi; (*talk*) a perora.

sprain *vt* a suci; a luxa ‖ *s* entorsă *f*, luxație *f*.

sprang *vi* * **spring**.

sprawl *vi* (*person*) a cădea lat; (*town*) a se întinde, a se lăți.

spray¹ *s* stropi *m pl*; lichid *n* pulverizat; ceață *f*; pulverizator *n* ‖ *vt* a stropi; a pulveriza ‖ *vi* a se pulveriza.

spray² *s* (*bunch*) buchet *n*.

spread, spread, spread *vt* (*cover, etc*) a întinde; a așterne; a desfășura; (*smell*) a exala; a presăra; (~ *a rumor, etc*) a răspândi, a propaga; (~ *resources*) a distribui, a repartiza; a difuza; a extinde ‖ *vi* a se întinde; a se difuza; a se împrăștia ‖ *s* (*range*) anvergură *f*; (*distribution*) difuzare *f*; desfacere *f*; față *f* de masă; cuvertură *f* • **~sheet** *s* comp foaie *f* de calcul tabelar.

spree *s* coll chef *n*, petrecere *f*.

sprig *s* rămurea *f*, crenguță *f*; mlădiță *f*; lăstar *m*; *fig iro* flăcăiandru *m*.

sprightly *adj* (*lively*) animat; voios, vesel ‖ *adv* vioi; cu însuflețire.

spring¹, sprang, sprung *vi* (*jump*) a sări; a se ivi; a țâșni; a răsări; a crăpa; a izvorî ‖ *vt* a exploda ‖ *s* (*coil*) resort *n*; (*leap*) salt *n*; izvor *n*; cauză *f*; elasticitate *f*.

spring² *s* primăvară *f*.

sprinkle *vt* (*spray*) a stropi; a pulveriza; a risipi; (*strew*) a presăra ‖ *vi* a stropi; a se cerne; (*rain*) a bura ‖ *s* burniță *f*; stropitură *f*.

sprinkling *s* (*dash*) strop *m*, pic *n*.

sprint *s* sprint *n*; finiș *n* ‖ *vi* a sprinta.

sprite *s* myth spiriduș *m*; gnom *m*; zână *f*.

sprocket *s* (*wheel*) roată *f* dințată.

sprout *s* bot germen *m*; lăstar *m*; *pl* varză *f* de Bruxelles ‖ *vi* bot a germina; a încolți.

spruce¹ *s* bot molid *m*, molift *m*.

spruce² *adj* îngrijit; afectat; elegant ‖ *vt* a dichisi ‖ *vi* a se dichisi.

sprung *vi* * **spring**.

spud *s* coll (*potato*) cartof *m*.

spume *s* lit spumă *f* de val.

spun *vt* * **spin**.

spunky *adj* coll (*person*) dârz; (*fight*) curajos.

spur *s* pinten *m*; *tech* echiu *n*; *constr* contrafort *m* ‖ *vt* (~ *a horse*) a da pinteni.

spurious *adj* (*interest, etc*) simulat; (*argument, etc*) fals.

spurn *vt* (*repulse*) a împinge; *fig* (*reject*) a refuza cu dispreț ‖ *s fig* refuz *n*; disprețuire *f*.

spurt *s* țâșnire *f*, jet *n*; (*burst*) efort *n* brusc; (*speed*) accelerare *f* ‖ *vi* (*gush*) a țâșni; a izbucni; *fig* (*surge*) a crește, a spori.

sputter *vi* (*spit*) a scuipa; (*stammer*) a bolborosi, a bâlmăji; (*pop*) a trosni; a pârâi; a fâsâi.

sputum *s* med (*pl* **sputa**) spută *f*.

spy *s* spion *m*; spionaj *n* ‖ *vt* a spiona; a zări; a cerceta; a descoperi.

squabble *s* (*dispute*) dispută *f*, ceartă *f* ‖ *vi* (*quarrel*) a se certa (cu); a se sfădi (cu).

squad *s* mil detașament *m*; grupă *f*; *sp* echipă *f*; *fig* gașcă *f*; bandă *f* • **~ron** *s* mil escadron *n*; divizion *n*; *naut* escadră *f*; *avia* escadrilă *f*.

squalid *adj* murdar, sordid; *fig* jalnic, mizer; *fig* meschin, ticălos.

squall *s* vijelie *f*, furtună *f*.

squander *vt* a cheltui; a pierde; a risipi ‖ *s* risipă *f*.

squalor *s* (*filth*) mizerie *f*, murdărie *f*; caracter *n* sordid; sărăcie *f*.

square *s* pătrat *n*; scuar *n*; cvartal *n* ‖ *vt* a pune în ordine; a achita; a îndoi; a potrivi || *adj* lat; solid; egal; potrivit; (la) pătrat; onest || *vt* (*reconcile*) a împăca, a pune de acord; (*settle*) a achita; *math* a ridica la pătrat; ~ **dance** *s* cadril *n*.

squash *s sp* squash *n*; *bot* dovlecel *m* || *vt* a strivi; *fig* a înăbuși; a reprima.

squat *adj* ghemuit; strivit, turtit; (*short*) bondoc || *vi* (*crouch*) a se lăsa pe vine.

squawk *vi* (*bird*) a țipa; a cârâi.

squeak *vi* (*squeal*) a chițăi; a țipa; a scârțâi; a scheuna; *fig* a fi turnător || *s* (*screech*) scârțâit *n*; cârâit *n*; țipăt *n* • ~**y** *adj* pițigăiat; scârțâit; ~ **clean** *adj* impecabil.

squeal *s* (*cry*) țipăt *n*; scâncet *n*; guițat n || *vi* (*yell*) a țipa; a schelălăi.

squeamish *adj* (*delicate*) mofturos; (*nauseous*) respingător, scârbos.

squeeze *vt* (*press*) a apăsa; *fig* a smulge; (*squash*) a stoarce; (*pressurize*) a sili; a frământa; a vârî; a furișa || *vi* a se stoarce; a răzbate || *s* apăsare *f*; presiune *f*; smulgere *f*; *fig* șantaj *n*; (*crush*) îmbulzeală *f*; îmbrățișare *f*.

squelch *vi* (*walk in wet terrain*) a lipăi; (*make noise in mud*) a pleoscăi || *vt* (*crush*) a zdrobi; *coll* (~ *a rumor*) a înăbuși; (~ *a person*) a face să tacă.

squid *s icht* calmar *m*.

squiggle *s* (*scribble*) scris *n* neciteț.

squint *s med* strabism *n*; *fig* tendință *f*, înclinație *f* || *vi med* a avea strabism, a se uita sașiu/cruciș.

squirm *vi* (*wriggle*) a se agita; *fig* a nu-și găsi loc; (*feel shame*) a se simți jenat/încurcat.

squirrel *s zool* veveriță *f*.

squirt *vt* a împroșca; a pulveriza; a țâșni || *s* jet *n*; izbucnire *f*; seringă *f*.

squish *vt/vi* (*crush*) a (se) strivi • ~**y** *adj* (*fruit*) fleșcăit, storcit; (*ground*) noroios, moale.

stab *vt* a înjunghia; a tăia; a înfige || *vi* a răni cu || *vr* a se înjunghia || *s* lovitură *f*; durere *f*; junghi *n*.

stability *s* tărie *f*; stabilitate *f*; soliditate *f*.

stabilize *vt* a stabiliza, a fixa; a consolida; *tech* a egaliza.

stable[1] *s* grajd *n* (de cai); staul *n* (de vite) || *vt* a ține în grajd/staul.

stable[2] *adj* stabil; solid; constant; durabil.

staccato *adv/adj mus* stacato.

stack *s* stog *n*; claie *f*; morman *n*; grămadă *f*; potop *n* || *vt* a stivui; a măslui cărțile.

stadium *s* stadion *n*; teren *n* de sport.

staff *s* personal *n*; conducere *f*; stat *n* major.

stag *s zool* cerb *m*.

stage *s thea* scenă *f*; (*platform*) podium *n*; estradă *f*; tribună *f*; arenă *f*; (*phase*) fază *f*; haltă *f*; stagiu *n* || *vt thea* a monta; a plănui; a juca || *vi* a se juca.

stagflation *s econ* stagnare *f* și inflație *f*.

stagger *vi* (*reel*) a se clătina; *fig* a șovăi, a ezita || *vt* (*astound*) a uimi; a descumpăni; (*alternate*) a eșalona, a distribui.

staging *s thea* regie *f*; regizare *f*; *constr* schelă *f*; *naut* debarcader *n*; *min* pod *n* de sondă.

stagnant *adj* inert; stătător.

stagnate *vi also fig* a stagna; a fi inert/inactiv.

stagy *adj thea* scenic, de scenă; teatral; (*affected*) prefăcut; simulat; nesincer.

staid *adj* (*person*) așezat, serios; cumpătat.

stain *s* pată *f*; ocară *f*; murdărie *f*; strop *n* || *vt* a păta; a pângări.

stair *s* treaptă *f*; *pl* scară *f*, scări *f pl* • ~**case** *s* scară *f*, casa *f* scării.

stake[1] *s* par *m*; (*post*) țăruș *m*; stâlp *m*; jalon *n*; *pl* premiu *n* || *vt* a jalona; a bate pari; (*risk*) a risca.

stake[2] *s* (*bet*) miză *f* || *vt* a miza; a pune în joc.

stalactite *s* stalactită *f*.

stalagmite *s* stalagmită *f*.

stale *adj* (*food, water*) vechi, stătut; (*bread*) uscat; rânced; (*beer*) trezit, răsuflat; (*air*) închis; *fig* vechi, trecut, perimat, învechit || *vi* a se învechi; a se strica.

stalemate *s* (*impasse*) impas *n*; (*chess*) pat *n*.

stalk[1] *s* (*of a plant*) tulpină *f*, tijă *f*; (*of a leaf, fruit*) codiță *f*.

stalk[2] *vt* (*hunt*) a vâna mergând tiptil; *fig* (*pursue*) a pândi; a urmări.

stall[1] *s* staul *n*; stand *n*; tarabă *f*; stal *n*; adăpost *n* || *vt* a opri; a îngloda || *vi* a se bloca; a se îngloda.

stall[2] *vt* (*delay*) a întârzia; a face să aștepte; *auto* a opri, a cala; (*animal*) vârî în grajd || *vi* (~ *a motor*) a se cala/bloca; (*delay*) a încerca să câștige timp.

stallion *s zool* armăsar *m*.

stalwart *adj* (*strong*) robust; (*resolute*) hotărât, ferm; (*brave*) viteaz, brav.

stamen *s bot* stamină *f*.

stamina *s* (*energy*) vitalitate *f*, (*vigor*) putere *f*; robustețe *f*; (*resilience*) rezistență *f*.

stammer *s* bâlbâială *f*; gângăveală *f* || *vi* a se bâlbâi; a gângăvi.

stamp *s* (*letter*) timbru *n*; (*object*) ștampilă *f*, sigiliu *n*; *fig* pecete *f*, urmă *f*; amprentă *f*; (*brand*) marcă *f* (a fabricii); *fig* (*character*) caracter *n*, fel *n*, gen *n*, ordin *n* || *vt* (~ *one's foot*) a bate din picior; (*trample*) a călca în picioare; (*imprint*) a imprima, a marca (pe); a întipări; a timbra, a franca; a ștampila.

stampede *s* (*of animals*) fugă *f*; streche *f*; (*of people*) panică *f*, debandadă *f* || *vi* (*animals* ~) a o lua la goană; (*people* ~) a fi cuprinși de panică; a fugi în debandadă/dezordine.

stance *s also fig* poziție *f*, postură *f*.

stand, stood, stood *vi* a sta (în picioare); a se afla; (*halt*) a se opri; (*remain*) a rămâne; (*rise*) a se ridica; (*offer*) a rămâne în picioare; (~ *by a decision*) a rămâne valabil; a rezista || *vt* (*place*) a rezema; a așeza drept; a se opune; (*tolerate*) a suporta; a face cinste || *s* (*stop*) pauză *f*; poziție *f*; ținută *f*; opoziție *f*; suport *n*; raft *n*; cuier *n*; stagnare *f*; tribună *f*; stand *n*; *jur* bară *f*; ~ **back** *vi* a da înapoi; ~ **by** *vi* (~ *a person*) a susține; (~ *a decision, etc*) a menține, a nu da înapoi de la; ~ **down** *vi* a demisiona; ~ **for** *vi* a înlocui; (*signify*) a simboliza, a însemna; *coll* (*tolerate*) a înghiți, a suporta; ~ **out** *vi* a ieși în afară; a ieși în relief; a se distinge clar; ~ **up** *vt coll* a nu veni la o întâlnire fixată || *vi* (*rise*) a se ridica; (**for**) a apăra; (**to**) (~ *heat, etc*) a rezista la; (~ *authority*) a ține piept la.

standard *s* steag *n*; standard *n*; tip *n*; criteriu *n*; grad *n*; regulă *f*; consolă *f*; *arhit* etalon; normal; exemplar; clasic; excelent; ~ **of living** *s* nivel *n* de trai.

standby *s* (*person*) locțiitor *m*, suplinitor *m*; (*ticket, etc*) stand-by *n*; **on** ~ gata să intervină.

standing *adj* (*army, etc*) permanent; (*joke*) continuu || *s* importanță *f*, reputație *f*; **of long** ~ vechi, durabil.

stank *vi* * **stink**.

stanza *s liter* strofă *f*, stanță *f*.

staple[1] *s* (*papers*) capsă *f*; agrafă *f* || *vt* a prinde, a fixa cu cleme.

staple[2] *adj* principal, de bază || *s* produs *n* de bază.

star *s* stea *f*; planetă *f*; noroc *n*; soartă *f*; star *n* || *vt* a străluci; a fi star; **Stars and Stripes** *s* drapelul *n* SUA.

starboard *s naut* tribord *n* || *vt* a vira la dreapta || *adv* la tribord.

starch *s* amidon *n*; formalism *n* || *vt* a scrobi.

stare *s* privire *f* fixă || *vi* (*gaze*) (**at**) a privi fix/ţintă (la), a se uita fix/ţintă (la).

stark *adj* (*bleak*) auster; (*desolate*) dezolat; total, complet, desăvârşit; (*plain*) despuiat, gol; (~ *contrast*) dur || *adv* total, complet.

starling *s orn* sturz *m*.

start *vi* a tresări; (*jump*) a sări; (*begin*) a începe; (*set out*) a pleca || *vt* a speria; a stârni; a începe; a porni; a desface; (*launch*) a lansa; (*create*) a fonda || *s* salt *n*; (*shock*) tresărire *f*; (*beginning*) debut *n*; (*lead*) avans *n*; pornire *f*.

startle *vt* a face să tresară; a surprinde || *s* tresărire *f*; uimire *f*.

startling *adj* surprinzător; senzaţional.

starvation *s* foamete *f*; inaniţie *f*.

starve *vi* a fi lihnit || *vt* a înfometa.

stash *vt* (*hide*) a ascunde, a tăinui || *s* ascunziş *n*.

stasis *s med* stază *f*; (*stagnation*) stagnare *f*.

state *s* (*country*) stat *n*; (*condition*) situaţie *f*; stare *f*; (*ceremonial*) ceremonie *f*; (*grandeur*) pompă *f*; formă *f*; specific *n* || *vt* a fixa; (*utter*) a afirma; a expune; a specifica.

statement *s* afirmaţie *f*; formulare *f*; expunere *f*; relatare *f*; *jur* depoziţie *f*; *fin* extras *n* de cont.

static *adj* static || *s* electricitate *f* statică.

station *s rail* gară *f*; staţi(un)e *f*; *coll* rang *n*; *radio* post *n*; condiţie *f*; (*position*) poziţie *f* socială; postură *f*; imobilitate *f* || *vt* a posta; a aşeza.

stationary *adj* staţionar; imobil.

stationer *s* papetar *m* • **~y** *s* papetărie *f*; (*equipment*) rechizite *n pl* de birou.

statistics *s* (*science*) statistică *f*; (*figures*) date *f pl* (statistice).

statuary *s frml* (grup *n* de) statui *f pl*.

statue *s* statuie *f*; **Statue of Liberty** statuia libertăţii • **~sque** *adj* ca o statuie • **~tte** *s* statuetă *f*.

stature *s* (*build*) statură *f*, talie *f*; (*standing*) anvergură *f*.

status *s jur* statut *n* legal; (*rank*) situaţie *f*; poziţie *f*; (*eminence*) prestigiu *n*.

statute *s* statut *n*; lege *f*.

statutory *adj* statutar; legal; obligatoriu.

staunch *adj* (*loyal*) loial || *vt* (~ *blood, leak*) a opri.

stay *vi* (*reside*) a sta; a locui; (*remain*) a continua; a rămâne; a dura; (*stop*) a se opri; (*wait*) a aştepta || *vt* a opri; a reţine; a aplana; a amâna; a preveni || *s* (*visit*) şedere *f*; (*halt*) oprire *f*; obstacol *n*; vizită *f*; amânare *f*; ajutor *n*; prudenţă *f* • **~ing power** *s* rezistenţă *f*, durabilitate *f*.

stead *s* loc *n*; **in smb's** ~ în locul cuiva.

steadfast *adj* (*firm*) ferm, hotărât; (*loyal*) loial.

steady *adj* (*firm*) ferm; sigur; constant; calm; (*even*) regulat; (*stable*) stabil || *vt* a stabiliza; a întări; (*control*) a calma; a sprijini || *s* suport *n*; *coll* iubit *m*, iubită *f*; logodnic(ă) *m/f*.

steak *s cul* biftec *n*; felie *f*; cotlet *n*; antricot *n*.

steal, stole, stolen *vt* a fura; a răpi; a delapida; *fig* a

cuceri || *vi* a fura; a se furişa || *s* furt *n*; şarlatanie *f*; chilipir *n*.

stealthy *adj* ascuns, secret, tainic.

steam *s* vapori *n pl*; putere *f*; avânt *n* || *vi* a se evapora; a aburi; a fumega || *vt cul* a pregăti la aburi • ~**er** *s* vapor *n*.

steed *s lit* cal *m* de călărie.

steel *s* oţel *n*; spadă *f*, sabie *f*; amnar *n* || *vt* a oţeli.

steep[1] *adj* prăpăstios; (*sheer*) abrupt; extrem; (*excessive*) exagerat || *s* prăpastie *f*.

steep[2] *vt* (*soak*) a înmuia; (*imbue*) a cufunda, a afunda; *fig* (~ *in tears*) a scălda.

steeple *s* clopotniţă *f*; turlă *f*.

steer *vt* a conduce; a dirija; a pilota; a cârmi; a însoţi || *vi* a conduce • ~**ing wheel** *s auto* volan *n*; *naut* timonă *f*, cârmă *f*.

stellar *adj* (*astral*) stelar; *coll* excelent, admirabil.

stem[1] *s* (*stalk*) tulpină *f*; lujer *n*; trunchi *n*; (*of a glass*) picior *n*; (*of a pipe*) gât *n*, ţeavă *f*; suport *n*; coadă *f*; gen *n*; ramură *f*; neam *n*.

stem[2] *vt* (*stop*) a opri.

stench *s* miros *n* urât, duhoare *f*.

stencil *s* şablon *n* || *vt* a executa după şablon; *tech* a matriţa.

stenographer *s* stenograf(ă) *m/f*.

stenography *s* stenografie *f*.

stentorian *adj lit* (*voice*) puternic.

step *s* (*pace*) pas *m*; urmă *f*; drum *n*; (*move*) acţiune *f*; măsură *f*; prag *n*; (*stair*) treaptă *f* || *vt* a călca; a dansa || *vi* (*walk*) a păşi; a merge; a se plimba; a veni, a se duce.

stepbrother *s* frate *m* vitreg.

stepdaughter *s* fiică *f* vitregă.

stepfather *s* tată *m* vitreg.

stepmother *s* mamă *f* vitregă.

steppe *s* stepă *f*.

stepsister *s* soră *f* vitregă.

stepson *s* fiu *m* vitreg.

stereo *adj* stereo || *s* (*set*) combină *f* muzicală.

stereotype *s* stereotip *n*.

sterile *adj* steril; sărac; searbăd; plat; gol.

sterilize *vt* a steriliza.

sterling *s* (*genuine*) veritabil; (*excellent*) excepţional || *s* liră *f* sterlină.

stern[1] *adj* aspru, sever; rigid; riguros.

stern[2] *s naut* pupă *f*.

sternum *s anat* (*pl* ~**s/sterna**) stern *n*.

steroid *s chem* steroid *m*.

stethoscope *s med* stetoscop *n*.

stevedore *s* docher *m*.

stew *vt* (*simmer*) a găti înăbuşit; *cul* a face compot || *vi* a frige/fierbe înăbuşit; a se încălzi || *s cul* tocană *f*; agitaţie *f*.

steward *s* (*warden*) intendent *m*; girant *m*; (*of a college, etc*) econom *m*.

stick[1] *s* (*wood*) baston *n*; (*candy*) baton *n*; (*walking*) baston *n*; *sp* crosă *f*.

stick[2], **stuck, stuck** *vt* (*poke*) a înfige; (*put*) a vârî; a tăia; (*stab*) a înţepa; (*attach*) a lipi; a îndura; a aplica; a învinge || *vi* (**to**) a se prinde; a se lipi; a rămâne; a se bloca; a stărui; ~ **around** *vi* a sta pe aproape/prin preajmă; ~ **out** *vt* (~ *your head*) a scoate; (~ *your hand*) a ridica; (~ *your tongue*) a scoate; ~ **it out** *coll* a ţine piept, a riposta; ~ **to** *vi* (*follow*) a urma; (*promise*) a ţine; (~ *principles*) a rămâne fidel; (~ *a* _decision_) a rămâne la, a fi ferm; ~ **together** a sta împreună, a fi uniţi • **~ing point** s controversă f.

stickler s pedant m; tipicar m.

sticky adj lipicios; vâscos; adeziv; ceţos; umed.

stiff adj (_rigid_) ţeapăn; (_severe_) aspru; fixat; (_strong_) tenace; compact; (_diffcult_) dificil, greu; rece; (_formal_) afectat ‖ s sl (_dead body_) cadavru n • **~en** vt (_harden_) a întări; a fixa; a consolida; (_reinforce_) a face tare; (_thicken_) a îngroşa ‖ vi a se întări; a înţepeni; a se face tare; a se îngroşa; (_breeze_) a se înteţi, fig a se înăspri; a deveni rece/formal.

stifle vt/vi (_smother_) a înăbuşi; (_suppress_) a suprima.

stigma s (_shame_) ruşine f, stigmat n; bot stigmă f.

stile s gard n puţin înalt; barieră f.

stiletto s (_knife_) stilet n; (_heel_) pantof m cu toc cui.

still[1] adj calm; tăcut; blând; rezervat; încet ‖ s pace f; linişte f; tăcere f; cadru n ‖ vt a linişti; a amuţi; ~ **life** s (_art_) natură f moartă.

still[2] adv (_even now_) încă; (_however_) totuşi.

still[3] s fotografie f; alambic n, cazan n.

stillborn adj născut mort;

stilts s pl (_for walking_) cataligge f pl; (_building_) piloni m pl.

stilted adj (_affected_) afectat, nenatural.

stimulate vt a stimula; a îndemna; a excita ‖ vi a stimula.

stimulus s (pl **stimuli**) (_incentive_) stimulent n; bio, psych stimul m.

sting vt a înţepa; a răni; a împunge; a îndemna ‖ vi a înţepa; a durea; a răni ‖ s ac n; înţepătură f; usturime f; provocare f; îndemn n.

stingy adj (_mean_) zgârcit; rar; (_miserly_) sărac; (_small_) insuficient; puţin.

stink, stank, stunk vi a mirosi urât; a avea o proastă reputaţie ‖ s duhoare f, miros n greu • **~ing** adj coll (~ _place_) infect; (~ _weather_) geros; nenorocit.

stint s (_amount of time_) parte f; porţie f; raţie f; (_stretch_) limită f, măsură f; (_shift_) schimb n.

stipend s stipendiu n; bursă f.

stipulate vt a stipula.

stir vt (_agitate_) a agita; (_awaken_) a trezi; a deranja; a urni; (_rouse_) a stârni; (_motivate_) a încuraja ‖ vi a se clinti; a se trezi; a ieşi la iveală ‖ s (_commotion_) agitaţie f; vâlvă f.

stirrup s scară f de şa.

stitch s cusătură f; fir n; junghi n ‖ vt a coase; a tigheli; a broda ‖ vi a coase.

stoat s zool hermină f.

stock s bot trunchi n; butuc n; tulpină f; bio neam n; strămoş m; fin capital n; com stoc n; (_livestock_) şeptel n; (_store_) depozit n ‖ vt (_supply_) a furniza; a culege; a aduna; a spori ‖ vi a înmuguri ‖ adj (_standard_) clasic; ~ **exchange/market** s Bursă f; ~ **phrase** s clişeu n; ~ **taking** s inventar n.

stockholder s acţionar m.

Stockholm s Stockholm n.

stocking s ciorap m.

stockpile s stoc n; depozit n.

stocky adj îndesat, scund şi gras.

stodgy s (_food_) greu de digerat; fig (_heavy_) greoi, încărcat; (_dull_) plicticos.

stoical adj stoic.

stoke vt (~ _a fire_) a întreţine; a alimenta cu combustibil.

stole[1] vt * **steal.**

stole[2] s etolă f.

stolen vt * **steal.**

stolid adj (_impassive_) indiferent; apatic.

stomach s stomac n; abdomen n; dispoziţie f; chef n ‖ vt a suporta, a răbda.

stomp vi a merge cu paşi greoi.

stone s piatră f; dală f; prundiş n; nestemată f; calcul m; grindină f; sâmbure m ‖ vt a lapida; a pietrui • **~cold** adj foarte rece, îngheţat • **~wall** vt pol a obstrucţiona • **~washed** adj spălăcit.

stony adj pietros; fig glaciar; dur; rece.

stood vi * **stand.**

stooge s coll pej cal m de bătaie.

stool s scaun n; taburet n; bot trunchi n; bot butaş m.

stoop vi (_bend down_) a se apleca, a se înclina; (_deign_) a condescinde, a binevoi.

stop vt (_pause_) a opri; (_end_) a sfârşi; a închide; a astupa; (_block_) a bloca; (_prevent_) a reţine, a împiedica ‖ vi a se opri; a se sfârşi; a zăbovi ‖ s (_halt_) oprire f; sfârşit n; piedică f; pauză f; şedere f • **~gap** s fig măsură f provizorie; expedient n • **~page** s grevă f; întrerupere f; med ocluzie f.

storage s depozitare f, înmagazinare f; păstrare f; stocare f; comp memorie f.

store s rezervă f; belşug n; provizie f; depozit n; sursă f; tezaur n; magazin n ‖ vt a aproviziona; a aduna • **~keeper** s comerciant m • **~room** s magazie f.

stork s orn barză f.

storm s furtună f; (_outburst_) zbucium n; izbucnire f ‖ vt a ataca; a asalta ‖ vi (_rage_) a se dezlănţui; a năvăli.

story[1] s (_tale_) poveste f; istorie f; (_article_) relatare f; vorbă f; (_rumor_) zvon n; biografie f; temă f; (_lie_) minciună f; **tell the ~ of** vt/vi a povesti.

story[2] s etaj n; **upper/lower ~** s etaj superior/inferior.

stout adj (_fat_) corpolent; (_sturdy_) solid, rezistent, puternic; (_brave_) curajos, brav.

stove s (_heater_) sobă f; (_oven_) cuptor n; seră f ‖ vt a pune în seră; a dezinfecta.

stow vt naut a arima; a stivui; a aranja; a împacheta; (**with**) a încărca, a umple (cu).

straddle vt (_bestride_) a încăleca pe ‖ vi a fi/merge călare.

strafe vt mil a bombarda intens; a nimici.

straggle vi (_plants_) a creşte, a se dezvolta; (_sprawl_) a se întinde, a se extinde la întâmplare; (_hair_) a fi în dezordine; (_person_) a se mocăi, a se moşmondi.

straight adj direct; drept; corect; precis; exact; sigur; sincer ‖ adv direct; precis; sincer, cinstit • **~forward** adj deschis, cinstit, sincer; (_look, etc_) drept; (_style, etc_) direct; (_task, etc_) simplu, necomplicat.

strain[1] vt a încorda; a forţa; med (~ _a muscle_) a întinde; (~ _eyes_) a obosi; a apăsa; a strânge; (_sift_) a cerne; a încălca; a exagera; (~ _a budget_) a greva ‖ vi (_struggle_) a se încorda; a se forţa; a se cerne ‖ s (_tension_) tensiune f; cernere f; surmenaj n; (_injury_) luxaţie f; (_effort_) efort n • **~ed** adj încordat, tensionat • **~er** s strecurătoare f.

strain[2] s (_breed_) soi n, rasă f; neam n.

strait s geog strâmtoare f; pl fig strâmtoare f, încurcătură f.

strand[1] s şuviţă f; fir n; trăsătură f ‖ vt a răsuci.

strand[2] vt naut a face să eşueze ‖ vi naut a eşua ‖ s lit mal n, ţărm n; plajă f.

strange adj străin; neobişnuit; straniu; nou; bizar • **~r** s străin m, necunoscut m.

strangle vt (_choke_) a strangula; fig a înăbuşi; a strânge; a reprima ‖ vi a se sufoca.

strangulation s strangulare f.

strap *s* curea *f;* cordon *n;* chingă *f;* ştreang *n* || *vt* a bate cu cureaua • **~ped** *adj* strâmtorat • **~ping** *adj* coll vînjos.

stratagem *s* stratagemă *f.*

strategy *s* tactică *f;* strategie *f;* uneltiri *f pl.*

stratification *s* stratificare *f.*

stratify *vt* a stratifica.

stratosphere *s* stratosferă *f.*

stratum *s geol* strat *n,* formaţiune *f; fig* pătură *f* (socială).

straw *s* pai *n.*

strawberry *s bot* căpşun *m;* (*fruit*) căpşună *f;* (*plant*) frag *m;* (*fruit*) fragă *f.*

stray *vi* (*get lost*) a se rătăci; (*wander*) a hoinări; (*drift*) a se abate || *s* animal *n* rătăcit; copil *m* rătăcit || *adj* (*lost*) rătăcit, răzleţ(it); hoinar.

streak *s* linie *f;* dungă *f;* înclinaţie *f;* făşie *f* || *vt* a linia; a dunga || *vi* a alerga.

stream *s* şuvoi *n;* râu *n;* torent *n;* curs *n* de apă; curent *n;* nivel *n* || *vt* a emana; a răspândi; a radia || *vi* a curge; a izvorî; a se răspândi • **~lined** *adj* cu profil aerodinamic; eficient.

street *s* stradă *f* • **~car** *s* tramvai *n.*

strength *s* (*power*) putere *f;* rezistenţă *f;* reazem *n;* efectiv *n;* trăinicie *f;* forţă *f.*

strenuous *adj* (*tiring*) obositor; viguros, înverşunat.

stress *s* (*strain*) încordare *f;* (*tension*) tensiune *f;* forţă *f;* efort *n;* (*pressure*) apăsare *f;* (*emphasis*) accent *n* || *vt* a apăsa; (*emphasize*) a accentua • **~ful** *adj* stresant.

stretch *vt* (*extend*) a întinde; (*widen*) a lărgi; a încorda; a forţa; a doborî; a depăşi; a denatura || *vi* a se întinde; a se mări || *s* întindere *f;* efort *n;* (*section*) zonă *f;* spaţiu *n;* (*spell*) durată *f;* (*period*) perioadă *f;* abuz *n* • **~er** *s* targă *f;* **~bearer** *s* brancardier *m.*

strew *vt lit* a presăra; (*scatter*) a împrăştia; (*cover*) a acoperi.

stricken *adj lit* (*suffering*) rănit; copleşit.

strict *adj* (*severe*) pretenţios, sever; precis, exact.

stricture *s* (*criticism*) critică *f* aspră; (*limit*) restricţie *f,* îngrădire *f; med* strictură *f.*

stride, strode, stridden *vi* a merge cu paşi mari || *s* pas *m* mare.

strident *adj* (*sound, etc*) strident; (*request, attack*) vehement.

strife *s* (*fighting*) luptă *f,* competiţie *f;* (*rivalry*) rivalitate *f;* ceartă *f,* conflict *n;* diferend *n.*

strike, struck, struck/stricken *vt* (*hit*) a lovi; (*beat*) a bate; a izbi; (*fall upon*) a găsi; a frapa; a reuşi; (~ *the hour*) a suna (ora); (~ *a deal*) a încheia || *vi* a lovi; (~ *bells*) a bate; (*attack*) a ataca; (*occur to*) a veni în minte, a trece (prin gând); (*walk out*) a face grevă || *s* grevă *f; mil* raid *n;* (*oil, etc*) descoperire *f, fig* lovitură *f* (norocoasă).

striking *adj* (*arresting*) izbitor, frapant; (*remarkable*) remarcabil, fascinant, extraordinar.

string, strung, strung *vt* (*stretch*) a încorda; (*tie*) a lega; (*excite*) a excita || *s* sfoară *f;* şnur *n;* şiret *n;* coardă *f;* rând *n;* şirag *n;* ~ **along** (*cheat*) a păcăli.

stringent *adj* strict, riguros; imperios, urgent.

strip *vt* a dezbrăca; a jupui; a priva; a înlătura; a goli || *vi* a se despuia; a se coji || *s* bandă *f;* fâşie *f;* pistă *f;* panglică *f;* nimicire *f.*

stripe *s* (*band of color*) dungă *f;* fâşie *f; mil* galon *n;* tresă *f;* fel *n,* soi *n,* specie *f* • **~d** *adj* vărgat, dungat.

strive, strove, striven/strived *vi frml, lit* a năzui; (*endeavor*) a se strădui; (*struggle*) a se lupta.

strode *vi* * **stride.**

stroke *s* lovitură *f;* idee *f;* mişcare *f;* mângâiere *f;* bătaie *f; med* atac *n,* acces *n,* congestie *f* (cerebral) || *vt* a mângâia.

stroll *vi* a cutreiera || *vt* a străbate || *s* hoinăreală *f;* plimbare *f.*

stroller *s* (*walker*) persoană *f* care se plimbă; pieton *m;* (*baby ~pushchair*) cărucior *n* pliabil.

strong *adj* puternic; (*powerful*) viguros; (*stout*) vânjos; robust; iute; (*fervent*) intens; drastic; (*pungent*) înţepător • **~arm** *adj* brutal • **~hold** *s mil* fortăreaţă *f;* redută *f* • **~man** *s* mână *f* de fier • **~minded** *adj* hotărât, care ştie ce vrea • **~willed** *adj* voluntar, hotărât, tenace.

strop *s* curea *f* de ascuţit briciul || *vt* (~ *a razor*) a ascuţi.

strove *vi* * **strive.**

struck *vt* * **strike.**

structural *adj* structural.

structure *s* structură *f;* construcţie *f;* edificiu *n;* organizare *f.*

struggle *vi* a (se) lupta; a se zbate; a răzbi || *s* (*fight*) luptă *f,* conflict *n;* competiţie *f;* concurenţă *f;* (*effort*) sforţare *f;* (*tousle*) încăierare *f.*

strum *vt* (*guitar*) a cânta, a zdrăngăni; (*tune*) a cânta.

strung *vt* * **string.**

strut[1] *vi* (*swagger*) a păşi/merge ţanţoş || *s* mers *n* ţanţoş.

strut[2] *s constr* bară *f,* traversă *f;* (*support*) sprijin *n;* stâlp *m; elec* suport *m; tech* flaminaj *n; avia* lonjeron *n.*

stub *s* (*cigarette*) muc *n,* chiştoc *n;* (*pencil*) capăt *n;* (*check, etc*) talon *n,* cotor *n;* (*stump*) buturugă *f.*

stubble *s agr* mirişte *f;* (*beard*) barbă *f* nerasă/ţepoasă.

stubborn *adj* (*person*) încăpăţânat; refractar; (*stain*) care nu iese; (*reality, etc*) dur, aspru

stubby *adj* (*finger*) scurt şi gros; (*tail*) scurt; (*person*) scund şi îndesat, bondoc.

stuck *vt* * **stick** || *adj* (*trapped*) încolţit; (*wedged*) blocat; (*baffled*) aflat în mare încurcătură; *naut* eşuat, în radă.

stud[1] *s* (*horse*) herghelie *f;* grajd *n;* armăsar *m* de prăsilă.

stud[2] *s* cui *n;* ţintă *f;* ştift *n;* pioneză *f; constr* stâlp *m,* pilastru *m.*

student *s edu* student *m;* elev *m;* (*scholar*) savant *m;* cercetător *m.*

studied *adj* (*affected*) studiat, afectat; (*deliberate*) calculate; intenţionat; premeditat.

studio *s* studio *n;* (*art*) atelier *n.*

studious *adj* studios; chibzuit; silitor; afectat.

study *s* studiu *n;* ţintă *f,* efort *n;* (*zeal*) râvnă *f;* birou *n;* (*report*) eseu *n* || *vt* (*learn*) a studia; a urmări; (*examine*) a observa; a plănui || *vi* (*learn*) a studia.

stuff *s* material *n;* stofă *f;* marfă *f; text* ţesătură *f;* (*things*) haine *f pl,* lucruri *n pl* || *vt* a înţesa; a vârî; cul a împăna; a împăia.

stuffy *adj* (*room*) neaerisit; (*air*) greu; închis; sufocant; (*weather*) înăbuşitor; (*book*) plicticos; (*person*) încuiat; (*nose*) înfundat.

stultifying *adj* (*work, etc*) de abrutizare.

stumble *vi* (*stagger*) a se împiedica; *fig* a greşi; (*hesitate*) a se bâlbâi; a păcătui || *s* poticnire *f;* obstacol *n;* greşeală *f.*

stump *s* (*of a tree*) buştean *m;* (*limbs*) ciot *n* || *vt* (*puzzle*) a încurca, a deruta, a zăpăci.

stun *vt* (*bewilder*) a buimăci, a năuci; (*astonish*) a ului; (*daze*) a orbi; (*shock*) a şoca; (*knock out*) a copleşi.

stung vt * sting.

stunk vi * stink.

stunning adj (dazzling) ameţitor; (astonishing) uluitor; (beautiful) superb, splendid; extraordinar.

stunt[1] vt (inhibit) a opri, a încetini || vi a se pipernici, a se chirci, a se sfriji.

stunt[2] s (feat) ispravă f; tur n de forţă; cin cascadorie f.

stupefy vt a ameţi; a năuci; (stun) a stupefia.

stupendous adj (awesome) extraordinar, formidabil, fantastic; (huge) imens, măreţ.

stupid adj stupid; prost; idiot; prostesc || s idiot m, tâmpit m • ~ity s stupiditate f, prostie f.

stupor s med stupoare f; apatie f; (limbs) amorţeală f, amorţire f.

sturdy adj (strong) robust, voinic; (determined) ferm, hotărât; (durable) solid.

sturgeon s icht sturion m; nisetru m; morun m.

stutter s bâlbâit n, gângăvit n || vt (stammer) a bâigui, a îngăima || vi a se bâlbâi.

sty s (pigpen) cocină f.

style s (method) stil n; manieră f; mod n; ac n; ascuţiş n; arătător n; gen n; modă f; (design) model n; (chic) şic n; (luxury) eleganţă f || vt (~ hair) a coafa; (~ fashion) a modela; (name) a denumi; a porecli; a numi.

stylish adj (person, clothes) modern şi elegant.

stylistic adj stylistic • ~s s stilistică f.

stylus s (tool) ac n (de citire)

stymie vt (block) a împiedica, a înfrâna.

suave adj dulceag, suav.

subconscious adj subconştient, inconştient || s the ~ subconştientul n.

subcontract vt a subcontracta.

subcutaneous adj subcutanat.

subdivide vt a subdiviza.

subdue vt a supune; a cuceri; a îmblânzi; a slăbi.

subhuman adj inuman.

subject adj supus; cucerit || s supus m; (topic) subiect n; (specialty) materie f; individ m; pacient m; motiv n || vt a supune; a cuceri • ~ivism s subiectivism n.

subjugate vt (~ people) a subjuga; (~ feelings) a stăpâni; (~ reaction) a înăbuşi.

subjunctive s gram subjonctiv n.

sublet vt a subînchiria.

sublime adj sublim, măreţ.

submarine s/adj submarin n.

submerge vt a (s)cufunda, a afunda; fig a ascunde || vi a se (s)cufunda.

submit vt a supune spre; a susţine; a propune || vi a se supune; a ceda.

subnormal adj subnormal, înapoiat, retardat || s math subnormală f.

subordinate adj (to) subordonat; inferior; secundar || s subaltern m.

suborn vt jur (~ a witness) a corupe.

subpoena s jur citaţie f || vt a cita.

subscribe vt a subscrie; a favoriza; a sprijini || vi a subscrie; a fi de acord cu; a consimţi să • ~r s abonat m.

subscription s (to a newspaper) abonament n; (to a campaign) contribuţie f; (to a club) cotizaţie; (to an opinion) adeziune f; subscripţie f.

subsequent adj următor, ulterior • ~ly adv ulterior, după aceea, mai târziu.

subservient adj (to) subordonat (cuiva); inferior; servil, slugarnic (faţă de).

subside vi (land) a se tasa; (pain, etc ~s) a se calma, a se atenua; (noise ~s) a se reduce, a se atenua; (building collapses) a se prăbuşi.

subsidiary adj auxiliar, subsidiar || s ajutor n; filială f.

subsidize vt a subvenţiona.

subsidy s subvenţie f.

subsist vi a subzista, a dura.

subsoil s geol subsol n.

substance s esenţă f; substanţă f; materie f; fond n; realitate f.

substandard adj phys, etc subetalon, substandard; ling neliterar.

substantial adj (large) important, considerabil; (meal) copios; (food) hrănitor; (argument) solid; real, material; (rich) avut; (powerful) puternic.

substantiate vt (verify) a dovedi; a confirma, a întări.

substantive s/adj substanţial, real; permanent, durabil; independent; gram substantiv n.

substitute vt a substitui; a înlocui || s surogat n; înlocuitor m; înlocuire f.

subterfuge s subterfugiu n, stratagemă f.

subterranean adj subteran.

subtitle s typ subtitlu n.

subtle adj subtil, fin; ingenios; delicat; dibaci; rafinat.

subtract vt/vi a scădea.

subvention s subvenţie f.

subversive adj (seditious) subversiv; distrugător, distructiv.

subvert vt (undermine) a submina; a răsturna; (corrupt) a corupe, a strica.

suburb s suburbie f; pl margine f.

subway s metrou n; pasaj n subteran; tunel n.

succeed vi a urma, a succeda; a reuşi || vt a succeda.

success s succes n • ~ion s succesiune f • ~ive adj succesiv; consecutiv • ~ful adj reuşit; prosper; înfloritor; (attempt) plin de succes; (book, etc) de succes; (person) care are succes.

succinct adj succint; concis; scurt.

succor s ajutor n || vt a ajuta.

succulent adj suculent; zemos; fig plin de miez; suculent; captivant.

succumb vi (to) a muri (din cauza); (to) a ceda; a nu rezista.

such adj aşa, atare; asemenea; asemănător; cutare || adv aşa de || pron acesta, aceasta, aceştia, acestea; ~-and-~ adj cutare; ~like similar; as ~ ca atare; ~ as de exemplu.

suck vt a suge; a sorbi; a absorbi || vi a suge; a aspira; absorbi || s sugere f, supt n; absorbire f; aspirare f.

sucker s bot lăstar n, mlădiţă f; coll (dupe) fraier m; tech piston n de pompă.

suction s sugere f; aspirare f.

sudden adj brusc; subit; impetuos; iute • ~ly adv brusc, deodată.

suds s pl clăbuci n pl de săpun.

sue vt frml (solicit) a cere; (litigate) a intenta proces; a apela la || vi a intenta proces.

suede s (shoes) piele f întoarsă; (clothes) catifea f.

suet s seu n.

suffer vt (~ pain) a suferi; (bear) a îndura; (~ a loss, etc) a suporta || vi a suferi.

suffice vi frml a fi de ajuns || vt a ajunge (cuiva).

sufficiency s cantitate f satisfăcătoare; belşug n.

sufficient adj suficient; mulţumitor.

suffix s ling sufix n.

suffocate *vt* a sufoca; a stinge; a asfixia ‖ *vi* a se sufoca.
suffocation *s* sufocare *f.*
suffrage *s* (drept de) vot *n.*
suffuse *vt (fill with light, etc)* a inunda, a năpădi.
sugar *s* zahăr *n*; linguşire *f* ‖ *vt* a îndulci; a presăra cu zahăr ‖ *vi* a se zaharisi.
suggest *vt* a sugera; a insinua; a inspira ‖ *vr* a se impune; a-i trece prin minte • **~ion** *s* sugestie *f*; sfat *n*; îndemn *n*; aluzie *f*; ispită *f*; idee *f*; urmă *f.*
suicide *s* sinucidere *f*; sinucigaş *m.*
suit *s (outfit)* costum *n*; *jur* proces *n*; cerere *f*; curte *f* ‖ *vt* a conveni; *(match)* a i se potrivi ‖ *vr* a face cum vrea ‖ *vi (fit)* a se potrivi; a conveni • **~able** *adj (fit)* potrivit; *(proper)* convenabil; adecvat • **~case** *s* valiză *f*, geamantan *n.*
suite *s* suită *f*, cortegiu *n*; *(set)* set *n*; garnitură *f*; *constr* anfiladă *f.*
suitor *s obs* pretendent *m*; *jur* reclamant *m.*
sulk *vi (brood)* a fi supărat/îmbufnat ‖ *s (funk)* îmbufnare *f*; proastă dispoziţie *f.*
sullen *adj (surly)* ursuz; posac; *(look)* aspru, neiertător; *(sky, etc)* închis; apăsător.
sully *vt (dirty)* a murdări; *fig (~ a reputation)* a păta; a compromite.
sulphur *s chem* sulf *n.*
sultan *s* sultan *m.*
sultana *s* stafidă *f.*
sultry *adj (weather)* înăbuşitor; *(temperament, etc)* fierbinte; senzual; erotic.
sum *s* sumă *f*; esenţă *f*; fond *n*; rezultat *n* ‖ *vt* a calcula; a rezuma.
summarize *vt (sum up)* a rezuma; a recapitula.
summary *adj* sumar; concis ‖ *s* conspect *n*; rezumat *n*; recapitulare *f*; expunere *f.*
summation *s (addition)* totalizare *f*; total *n*, sumă *f*; *jur* rezumat *n.*
summer *s* vară *f*; înflorire *f* ‖ *adj* văratic; ~ **resort** *s* staţiune *f* (climaterică) de vară; ~ **school** *s* cursuri *n pl* de vară • **~y** *adj* de vară.
summit *s (peak)* vârf *n*; pisc *n*; *fig* culme *f*; apogeu *n.*
summon *vt jur* a cita; a soma; *(convene)* a convoca; a invita • **~s** *s jur* citaţie *f*; mandat *n*; somaţie *f*; *mil* somare *f*, somaţie *f* ‖ *vt jur* a cita, a convoca.
sump *s tech* colector *n* de apă.
sumptuous *adj (superb)* somptuos, măreţ; *(luxurious)* luxos.
sun *s* soare *m*; zi *f*; vară *f*; lumina *f* soarelui ‖ *vt* a usca la soare; a face baie de soare ‖ *vi* a străluci; a face baie de soare.
sunbathe *vi* a face plajă.
sunbeam *s* rază *f* de soare.
Sunbelt *s* statele *n pl* din sudul SUA.
sunburn *s* arsură *f* de soare; *(tan)* bronzare *f.*
sundae *s* îngheţată *f* cu fructe şi frişcă.
Sunday *s* duminică *f.*
sunder *vt obs* a despica, a sparge.
sundial *s* cadran *n* solar.
sundry *adj* diferit, divers ‖ *s pl* diverse obiecte *n pl*; diverse *f pl.*
sunflower *s bot* floarea *f* soarelui.
sung *vt* * **sing**.
sunglasses *s pl* ochelari *m pl* de soare.
sunk *vi* * **sink** • **~en** *adj (ship)* scufundat; *(cheeks)* supt; *(eyes)* înfundat; *tech* îngropat.
sunless *adj* neînsorit.

sunlight *s* lumina *f* soarelui.
sunlit *adj* însorit
sunny *adj (sunlit)* însorit; *(cheerful)* voios; optimist; fericit.
sunrise *s* răsărit *n* de soare; răsărit *n.*
sunroof *s auto* acoperiş *n* decapotabil.
sunscreen *s* cremă *f* de plajă.
sunset *s* apus *n* de soare; amurg *n*; *fig* declin *n.*
sunshine *s* lumina *f* soarelui; *fig* fericire *f*; spor *n.*
sunstroke *s med* insolaţie *f.*
suntan *s* bronzare *f*; ~ **lotion** *s* loţiune *f* de plajă.
sup *vi obs* a cina.
super *adj* extra, de calitate superioară; *coll* grozav, super.
superannuated *adj* perimat; învechit; demodat.
superb *adj* superb; luxos; somptuos; impunător.
supercilious *adj* încrezut, îngâmfat; superior; dispreţuitor.
superficial *adj (shallow)* superficial; *(surface)* de suprafaţă; *(insincere)* artificial; *(cursory)* rapid; *(trivial)* uşuratic.
superfluous *adj* superfluu, de prisos, inutil.
superhuman *adj* supraomenesc.
superimpose *vt* a suprapune.
superintendent *s* supraveghetor *m*; director *m.*
superior *adj* superior; excelent; încrezut, arogant ‖ *s* superior *m*; director *m*; comandant *m*; *(boss)* şef *m*; *relig* abate *m.*
superlative *adj* suprem, excelent, excepţional, fără egal/pereche; *gram* adjectiv *n.*
supermarket *s* supermarket *n.*
supernatural *adj* supranatural.
superpower *s* supraputere *f.*
supersede *vt (replace)* a înlocui; *(displace)* a elimina, a îndepărta.
supersonic *adj* supersonic.
superstition *s* superstiţie *f.*
superstitious *adj* superstiţios.
superstructure *s* suprastructură *f.*
supervene *vi* a surveni.
supervise *vt (oversee)* a supraveghea; *(~ work)* a superviza; a conduce.
supine *adj lit* culcat, întins pe spate; nepăsător.
supper *s* cină *f.*
supplant *vt (~ a person, thing)* a înlocui.
supple *adj (lithe)* suplu; iute; *(pliant)* supus; docil; acomodabil.
supplement *s* supliment *n.*
supplication *s* rugăminte *f*, implorare *f.*
supplier *s* furnizor *m.*
supply *vt (provide)* a furniza; a aproviziona; a procura; *(deliver)* a livra; a înlocui; *(bring in)* a alimenta ‖ *s* furnizare *f*; aprovizionare *f*; livrare *f*; procurare *f*; stoc *n*; *econ* credit *n*; fond *n*; ~ **and demand** ofertă şi cerere.
support *vt* a susţine; a ajuta; a tolera; a confirma ‖ *s* sprijin *n*; susţinător *m.*
suppose *vt (presume)* a socoti, a presupune; *(imagine)* a crede; a bănui; a implica ‖ *conj (what if)* dacă, în cazul când/că.
supposing *conj* dacă, presupunând.
supposition *s* presupunere *f*, supoziţie *f.*
suppress *vt* a curma; a înăbuşi; a interzice; a ascunde; a reţine • **~ion** *s* reprimare *f*; suprimare *f*, suspendare *f*; interzicere *f.*
suppurate *vi med (wound ~s)* a supura.

supremacy *s* supremaţie *f.*
supreme *adj* suprem; extrem; ultim; fatal.
surcharge *s* supraîncărcare *f;* suprataxă *f; tech* suprasarcină *f* ‖ *vt* a supraîncărca; *tech* a supraalimenta.
sure *adj* sigur; negreşit; cert ‖ *adv* sigur, desigur • **~ly** *adv* desigur, cu siguranţă • **~ty** *s jur* garanţie *f;* cauţiune *f;* certitudine *f;* siguranţă *f.*
surf *s* val *n;* surf *n.*
surface *s* suprafaţă *f;* aparenţă *f;* zonă *f;* arie *f* ‖ *vt* a lustrui; a pietrui; *naut* a aduce la suprafaţă ‖ *vi (rise)* a ieşi la suprafaţă.
surfeit *s* supraabundenţă *f;* exces *n.*
surge *s (people, etc)* mulţime *f,* val *n; elec* supratensiune *f; (emotion, interest)* val *n,* creştere *f; (rage)* acces *n; (sales, etc)* aflux *n* ‖ *vi (sea ~s)* a face valuri; *(people, etc ~)* a se năpusti.
surgeon *s* chirurg; *naut* medic de bord; *mil* medic *m* militar.
surgery *s* chirurgie *f;* sală *f* de operaţii; cabinet *n* medical.
surgical *adj* chirurgical.
surly *adj (gruff)* ursuz, posac, morocănos, posomorât.
surmise *vt (suppose)* a presupune; *(infer)* a deduce; *(conclude)* a conchide; *(guess)* a ghici ‖ *s (guesswork)* presupunere *f,* bănuială *f;* ipoteză *f.*
surmount *vt (overcome)* a învinge; *(~ feelings)* a-şi stăpâni.
surname *s* nume *n* de familie; poreclă *f* ‖ *vt* a da un nume de familie; a porecli.
surpass *vt* a depăşi; a fi superior.
surplice *s relig* sutană *f.*
surplus *s* surplus *n* ‖ *adj* excedentar.
surprise *s* surpriză *f;* uimire *f;* cadou *n* ‖ *vt* a mira; a surprinde.
surreal *adj (strange)* straniu, oniric; supranatural; suprarealist • **~ism** *s* suprarealism *n.•* **~istic** *adj* supranatural.
surrender *vt (give in)* a ceda; *mil* a preda; a părăsi; *(forfeit)* a pierde ‖ *vi* a capitula ‖ *s* capitulare *f;* abdicare *f.*
surreptitious *adj (furtive)* furiş, clandestin; ascuns.
surrogate *s (substitute person)* înlocuitor *m;* locţiitor *m; (substitute thing)* surogat *n;* succedaneu *n.*
surround *vt (enclose)* a înconjura; a îngrădi; *mil (besiege)* a încercui • **~ings** *s pl* împrejurimi *f pl;* ambianţă *f;* anturaj *n;* mediu *n.*
surveillance *s* urmărire *f,* supraveghere *f.*
survey *s (study)* studiu *n; (opinion)* sondaj *n; (ground)* topografiere *f; (buildings)* cadastru *n* ‖ *vt (review)* a trece în revistă; *(examine)* a face un studiu/o anchetă asupra; *(ground)* a măsura; *(buildings)* a inspecta • **~or** *s* controlor *n;* topograf *m;* inspector *m.*
survival *s (endurance)* supravieţuire *f; (relic)* relicvă *f,* rămăşiţă *f.*
survive *vi/vt* a supravieţui.
survivor *s* supravieţuitor *m.*
susceptibility *s (predisposition)* susceptibilitate *f,* predispoziţie *f; (sensitivity)* sensibilitate *f;* impresionabilitate *f.*
susceptible *adj (prone to)* susceptibil; *(responsive)* receptiv, sensibil; *(sensitive)* impresionabil.
suspect *vt* a suspecta; a crede; a simţi; *(distrust)* a se îndoi de; *(think that)* a-şi imagina, a crede; a adulmeca ‖ *vi* a fi bănuitor ‖ *s* suspect ‖ *adj* bănuit; suspect.
suspend *vt (hang)* a agăţa, a atârna; *(postpone)* a suspenda; *(~ an athlete, etc)* a suspenda, a exclude • **~ers** *s pl* bretele *f pl.*
suspense *s* suspensie *f;* aşteptare *f;* încordare *f;* suspans *n;* nesiguranţă *f.*
suspension *s (dismissal)* suspendare *f; scol* eliminare *f; (interruption)* întrerupere *f; (deferral)* amânare *f; tech* suspensie *f; chem* suspensie *f;* **~ bridge** *s* pod *n* suspendat.
suspicion *s* suspiciune *f;* neîncredere *f;* presupunere *f;* umbră *f;* urmă *f.*
suspicious *adj* bănuitor; dubios; neîncrezător.
sustain *vt* a propti; a susţine; *(suffer)* a îndura; a suporta; *(maintain)* a menţine; *thea (role)* a juca; a rezista la; a întări.
sustenance *s (nutrition)* hrană *f,* valoare *f* nutritivă; *(means of subsistence)* mijloace *n pl* de subzistenţă.
suture *s med, bot* sutură *f* ‖ *vt med* a sutura.
suzerainty *s hist* suzeranitate *f.*
svelte *adj* zvelt; mlădios.
swab *s (mop)* pământuf *n;* mătură *f, tech* tampon *n; med* tampon *n.*
swaddle *s* faşă *f,* scutec *n* ‖ *vt* a înfăşa.
swaddling clothes *s pl* scutece *n pl,* feşe *f pl.*
swagger *vi (strut)* a se fuduli, a face pe grozavul; *(boastfulness)* fudulie *f,* mândrie *f;* fanfaronadă *f,* lăudăroşenie *f.*
swain *s obs* flăcău *m,* băiat *m* de la ţară; *(lover)* curtezan *m,* adorator *m,* iubit *m.*
swallow[1] *vt (ingest)* a înghiţi; *(~ tears, etc)* a-şi înăbuşi; *(gulp)* a sorbi; *(~ one's words)* a retracta ‖ *s* gâtlej *n;* sorbitură *f.*
swallow[2] *s orn* rândunică *f.*
swam *vi* * **swim.**
swamp *s* mlaştină *f* ‖ *vt* a scufunda; a doborî; a inunda ‖ *vi* a se scufunda; a se prăbuşi • **~y** *adj* mlăştinos, mocirlos.
swan *s orn* lebădă *f.*
swank *vi coll (show off)* a se grozăvi, a-şi da aere ‖ *s* lăudăros *m; (luxury)* lux *n.*
swap *s* troc *n;* schimb *n* ‖ *vt* a face troc cu; a schimba ‖ *vi* a face schimb.
sward *s obs, lit* pajişte *f.*
swarm *s* roi *n;* mulţime *f;* furnicar *n* ‖ *vi* a roi; a se înghesui; a mişuna ‖ *vt* a ticsi.
swarthy *adj* brunet, oacheş.
swashbuckler *s* fanfaron *m,* lăudăros *m.*
swastika *s* zvastică *f.*
swat *vt (hit)* a pocni, a atinge.
swatch *s* eşantion *n* (de ţesătură).
swathe *s* legătură *f;* bandaj *n* ‖ *vt* a bandaja; a înconjura.
sway *vi (rock)* a se legăna; *(influence)* a influenţa; *(control)* a mânui; a conduce ‖ *vi* a se legăna; a ezita; a se înclina ‖ *s* legănare *f; (power)* putere *f;* domnie f.
swear, swore, sworn *vi* a jura; a înjura ‖ *vt* a (se) jura; a presta jurământ; a declara.
sweat *s* sudoare *f;* corvoadă *f* ‖ *vi* a transpira; a trudi ‖ *vt* a asuda; a exsuda • **~shirt** *s* tricou *n* cu mânecă lungă.
sweater *s* pulover *n.*
Swede *s* suedez(ă) *m/f.*
Sweden *s* Suedia *f.*
Swedish *adj* suedez.
sweep, swept, swept *vt (brush)* a mătura; *(carry)* a duce; a străbate; *(clear)* a şterge ‖ *vi* a mătura; *(speed)* a se năpusti; *(curve)* a şerpui; *(stretch)* a se întinde ‖

s măturat *n*; (*curve*) curbă *f*; curbură *f*; (*bend*) cot *n*; rotire *f*; (*extent*) cuprins *n*; trăsătură *f*; coşar *m*.

sweeping *adj* (*wide*) vast, întins; (*gesture*) larg; (*flight*) planat; (*reform*) radical; (*power*) discreţionar.

sweet *adj* dulce; suav; afabil; melodios; parfumat; proaspăt ‖ *s* dulceaţă *f*; *pl* dulciuri *n pl*; bomboană *f*.

sweetheart *s* iubită *f*, iubit *m*.

swell, swelled, swelled/swollen a umfla ‖ *vi* a se umfla; a creşte; a se mări ‖ *s* umflare *f*; hulă *f*; intensificare *f*; tip *m* elegant ‖ *adj* dichisit; grozav.

sweltering *adj* (*heat*) înăbuşitor, sufocant.

swept *vt* * **sweep**.

swerve *vi* (*veer from*) a se abate (de la) ‖ *s* îndepărtare *f*, abatere *f* (de la).

swift *adj* repede; grăbit ‖ *adv* iute, repede.

swig *vt* a sorbi, a bea lacom ‖ *s* înghiţitură *f*.

swill *vt* a îmbuiba, a ghiftui; a îmbăta ‖ *vi* a bea lacom ‖ *s* lături *f pl*; duşcă *f*.

swim, swam, swum *vi* a înota; a se scălda; a pluti; a avea vertij ‖ *vt* a trece înot; a inunda ‖ *s* înot *n*; scaldă *f*; tumult *n*; vârtej *n* • **~ming pool** *s* bazin *n* de înot, ştrand *n* • **~suit** *s* costum *n* de baie.

swindle *s* escrocherie *f* ‖ *vt* a înşela, a escroca; (*money*) a estorca • **~r** *s* escroc *m*, pungaş *m*, şarlatan *m*.

swine *s* porc *m*.

swing, swang, swung *vi* a se legăna; a se clătina; a oscila; a se roti; a fi spânzurat ‖ *vt* a legăna; a roti; a spânzura; a se bălăbăni; a răsuci; a agita ‖ *s* legănare *f*; leagăn *n*; şvung *n*.

swipe *vt* (*hit*) a pocni, a lovi; (*steal*) a şterpeli, a lăsa pe cineva lefter ‖ *vi* a lovi/da cu putere ‖ *s* (*jab*) observaţie *f* ironică.

swirl *s* (*twirl*) vârtej *n*; *naut* dâră *f*, siaj *n* ‖ *vi* a se învârti; a se roti; a se învolbura.

swish *vi* (*rustle*) a fâşâi, a foşni; (*whisper*) a susura ‖ *vt* a biciui, a şfichiui ‖ *s* fâşâit *n*, foşnet *n*; şuierătură *f*; şfichi *n*; (*whip*) plesnitură *f*.

Swiss *adj* elveţian.

switch *s* nuia *f*; băţ *n*; baston *n*; comutator *n* ‖ *vt* a lovi; a scutura; a manevra; a agita ‖ *vi* a schimba viteza.

Switzerland *s* Elveţia *f*.

swivel *vi* (*spin*) a se învârti, a se roti, a pivota ‖ *s* ax *n*, pivot *m*; *naut* cârlig *n*, verigă *f*; ~ **chair** *s* scaun *n* ergonomic, fotoliu *n* rotitor.

swollen *vi* * **swell**.

swoop *vi* (**upon/on**) a se abate/a se năpusti asupra ‖ *s* năpustire *f*; prăvălire *f*, coborâre *f*; atac *n* (în picaj); **at one** (**fell**) ~ dintr-o singură lovitură, dintr-un singur atac.

swop[1] *vt* (*exchange*) a face schimb de, a schimba ‖ *s* troc *n*, (*switch*) schimb *n*.

sword *s* sabie *f*; spadă *f*; lamă *f*.

swordfish *s* *icht* peşte *m* sabie.

swore *vi* * **swear**.

sworn *vi* * **swear**.

swum *vi* * **swim**.

swung *vt* * **swing**.

sycamore *s* *bot* smochin *m*, sicomor *m*; platan *m*.

sycophant *s* linguşitor *m*.

syllable *s* *ling* silabă *f*; *fig* cuvânt *n*; vorbă *f*, sunet *n*.

syllabus *s* *edu* programă *f* (analitică); plan *n* (de învăţământ).

syllogism *s* silogism *n*.

sylvan *adj* silvic.

symbiosis *s* simbioză *f*.

symbol *s* simbol *n*; emblemă *f*; semn *n*.

symmetry *s* simetrie *f*.

sympathetic *adj* compătimitor, binevoitor; prevenitor; milos; receptiv, sensibil.

sympathize *vi* (**with**) a fi îngăduitor/bun (cu); a fi de partea (cuiva) • **~r** *s* simpatizant *m*.

sympathy *s* milă *f*; compasiune *f*; atracţie *f*; simpatie *f*; condoleanţe *f pl*.

symphony *s* *mus* simfonie *f*.

symposium *s* (*pl* **-siums/-sia**) simpozion *n*.

symptom *s* simptom *n*; indiciu *n*, semn *n* • **~atic** *adj* simptomatic.

synagogue *s* *relig* sinagogă *f*.

sync *s* *coll* sincronizare *f*.

synchopate *vt* *mus* a sincopa; *ling* a contrage/reduce prin eliziune.

synchronic *adj* sincronic; simultan.

synchronize *vt* a sincroniza, a coordona ‖ *vi* a coincide în timp; (*watches*) a arăta aceeaşi oră.

syndicate *s* sindicat *n*; cartel *n*, consorţiu *n* ‖ *vt* a sindicaliza.

syndrome *s* *med* sindrom *n*.

synod *s* sinod *n*.

synonym *s* *ling* sinonim *n*.

synopsis *s* (*pl* **-es**) sinopsis *n*, rezumat *n*.

syntax *s* *gram* sintaxă *f*.

synthesis *s* (*pl* **-ses**) sinteză *f*.

synthesize *vt* a sintetiza • **~r** *s* sintetizor *n*.

synthetic *adj* sintetic; artificial.

syphilis *s* *med* sifilis *n*.

syphon *s*/*vt* * **siphon**.

Syria *s* Siria • **~n** *s*, *adj* sirian(ă) *m*/*f*.

syringe *s* *med* seringă *f*.

syrup *s* sirop *n*.

system *s* (*scheme*) sistem *n*; regim *n*; (*method*) metodă *f*; (*road, etc*) reţea *f*; ~ **disk** *s* *comp* disc *n* de sistem, disc *n* de iniţializare • **~s analyst** *s* *comp* analist *m* programator.

systematic *adj* metodic, sistematic.

systole *s* *med* sistolă *f*.

T

T, t *s* (*letter*) T, t.

tab *s* (*tag*) gaică *f*, agăţătoare *f*; (*bill*) socoteală *f*, calcul *n*; contramarcă *f*, cotor *n*.

tabby *s* (*cat*) pisică *f* tigrată.

table *s* (*furniture*) masă *f*; (*list*) tabel *n*; *frml* (*food*) mâncare *f*; (*chart*) tarif *n*; tablou *n*; *geog* podiş *n*; indicator *n*; (*slab*) placă *f* ‖ *vt* (*put aside*) a pune la dosar; a amâna; (*submit*) a depune; ~ **d'hôte** *adj* masă *f* comună; meniu *n* fix; ~ **tennis** *s* tenis *n* de masă • **~cloth** *s* faţă *f* de masă.

tablespoon *s* lingură *f* de supă.

tablet *s* tăbliţă *f*; tabletă *f*; carnet *n* de note.

tabloid *s* (*newspaper*) ziar *n* de scandal; (*press*) presa *f* populară; tabletă *f*, pastilă *f* ‖ *adj* comprimat, strâns.

taboo *s* tabu *n*, interdicţie *f* ‖ *adj* interzis, prohibit ‖ *vt* a interzice, a prohibi.

tabulate *vt* a prezenta sub formă de tabel.

tacit *adj* tacit, implicit, subînţeles.

taciturn *adj* reticent, taciturn.

tack *s* (*small nail*) cui(şor) *n*; ţintă *f*; *naut* rută *f*, curs *n*, traseu *n*; *fig* tactică *f*, metodă *f* ‖ *vt* (*fix*) a prinde/fixa/ bate în ţinte.

tackle *s* sculă *f; (gear)* echipament *n;* instrument *n; sp* placaj *n* ‖ *vt* a fixa; *(attempt)* a aborda; *(confront)* a ataca; *(block)* a placa.

tacky *adj coll* (~ *movies, etc)* îndoielnic; (~ *jewelry)* fără valoare; *(sticky)* lipicios, umed; (~ *person)* vulgar.

tact *s* tact *n,* delicatețe *f,* abilitate *f •* **~ful** *adj* cu tact, plin de tact, abil.

tactics *s pl (procedure)* tactică *f.*

tactile *adj* tactil.

tadpole *s zool* mormoloc *m.*

taffeta *s text* tafta *f.*

tag *s* capăt *n;* gaică *f; (paper)* etichetă *f; (textile)* marcă *f;* refren *n;* aforism *n;* epilog *n;* înfloritură *f* ‖ *vt* a adăuga; a fi pe urmele.

tail *s* coadă *f;* suită *f;* revers *n* ‖ *vt* a urmări pas cu pas; a adăuga; a atașa; ~ **end** *s* capăt *n,* extremitate *f;* sfârșit *n •* **~gate** *s auto* ușa *f* din spate *•* **~wind** *s* vânt *n* din spate.

tailor *s* croitor *m* ‖ *vt* a croi ‖ *vi* a face croitorie.

taint *vt (infect)* a infecta, *(pollute)* a polua; *fig* a păta, a pângări, a strica ‖ *vi* a se molipsi, a se contamina; a se strica, a se altera ‖ *s (blot)* pată *f;* dezonoare *f;* rușine *f •* **~ed** *adj (person)* compromis, pătat; *(food)* stricat, alterat.

take, took, taken *vt* a lua; a apuca; **(from/out of)** a scoate; *(steal)* a fura; *(conquer)* a ocupa, a cuceri; *(buy)* a cumpăra; a împrumuta; *(carry)* a duce; a susține; *(bear)* a suporta; *(presume)* a presupune; a pricepe; *(get)* a primi; a mânca; *(accompany)* a conduce; *(contain)* a conține; a cuprinde; *(earn)* a încasa; *(set out)* a porni pe; a consuma, a mânca, a bea; a necesita ‖ *vi (succeed)* a reuși; a avea efect; (~ *fire)* a se întinde, *fig* a se însufleți, a se înflăcăra; ~ **after** *vi* a semăna cu; ~ **apart** *vt* a separa, a despărți, a desface (în bucăți); ~ **away** *vt* a răpi, a fura; a suprima, a sustrage; ~ **back** *vt* a lua înapoi, a retrage; a duce înapoi; ~ **down** *vt* a demonta; (~ *notes)* a lua notițe; *(lower)* a coborî; ~ **for** *vt* a lua drept, a confunda cu; ~ **in** *vt* a adăposti; a cuprinde, a include; *(grasp)* a înțelege; *(cheat)* a păcăli, a înșela; ~ **off** *vt* (~ *hat, etc)* a ridica, a scoate; *(remove)* a înlătura; (~ *the price, etc)* a scădea, a reduce; (~ *a list, etc)* a elimina; a suprima ‖ *vi avia* a decola; *coll (leave)* a pleca; ~ **on** *vt* a accepta, a lua; (~ *a shape, etc)* a dobândi, a căpăta; (~ *a passenger)* a lua, a îmbarca; *sp* a juca/concura împotriva ‖ *vi fig (fashion, etc)* a prinde, a se răspândi; ~ **out** *vt* a scoate, a extrage; ~**out** *s* mâncare *f* la pachet; ~ **over** *vt (business, etc)* a prelua, a lua conducerea; *(job)* a înlocui pe cineva ‖ *vi (assume control)* a prelua puterea; ~ **to** *vt* a duce, a transporta ‖ *vi (person)* a avea simpatie pentru, a simpatiza pe; *(activity)* a prinde gust de; *(start)* a se apuca de; ~ **up** *vt* a ridica; *com* a onora; (~ *a problem)* a ridica, a pune; *(wager)* a accepta, a primi; (~ *an idea, etc)* a adopta, a îmbrățișa; *(start a career, etc)* a îmbrățișa; (~ *time)* a ocupa, a absorbi; (~ *room)* a lua, a ocupa; ~ **it easy!** ia-o încet/domol/ușor! *•* **~r** *s (buyer)* cumpărător *m;* amator *m; (user)* consumator *m* de droguri.

takings *spl com* încasări *fpl.*

talcum powder *s* pudră *f* de talc.

tale *s* poveste *f;* basm *n;* legendă *f;* nuvelă *f;* zvon *n;* bârfă *f;* născocire *f.*

talent *s* talent *n;* aptitudine *f;* dar *n.*

talk *vi (speak)* a vorbi; *(confer)* a discuta; a exprima; *(gossip)* a bârfi ‖ *vt (speak a language)* a vorbi; *(discuss)* a discuta ‖ *s (dialogue)* discuție *f; (speech)* vorbire *f; (lecture)* conferință *f; (chitchat)* vorbărie *f;* ~ **show** *s* talk-show *n,* dezbateri *f pl* televizate *•* **~ative** *adj* vorbăreț, locvace.

tall *adj* înalt; ~ **story/tale** *s* poveste *f* vânătorească, basm *n,* fantasmagorie *f.*

tally *s (score)* punctaj *n; (count)* calcul *n;* socoteală *f; com* pontaj *n; sp (score)* scor *n* ‖ *vt* a ponta; a număra, a socoti ‖ *vi (match)* a concorda, a corespunde.

talon *s zool* gheară *f;* talon *n.*

tambourine *s* tamburină *f.*

tame *adj (domestic)* îmblânzit; *(meek)* slab; *pej (person)* supus; cultivat; *(bland)* banal; inofensiv ‖ *vt (break in)* a domestici; a îmblânzi; *(curb)* a domoli; *(train)* a dresa ‖ *vi* a se îmblânzi.

tamper *vi (with)* (~ *files, etc)* a falsifica; a modifica; (~ *a lock)* a deschide cu un șperaclu; (~ *money)* a sustrage; (~ *a witness)* a mitui, a corupe; (~ *a device)* a strica.

tampon *s* tampon *n.*

tan *s* scoarță *f;* tanant *m;* culoare *f* cafenie ‖ *vt* a tăbăci ‖ *vi* a se bronza.

tandem *s* tandem *n* ‖ *adj (legat)* în tandem.

tang *s (taste)* gust *n* iute/picant; *(smell)* miros *n* înțepător/picant.

tangent *s math* tangentă *f.*

tangerine *s bot* mandarină *f.*

tangible *adj* tangibil, palpabil; clar, evident.

tangle *s (muddle)* încurcătură *f; (knot)* încâlceală *f; (mess)* dezordine *f; (dispute)* ceartă *f; (jam)* blocare *f* a traficului ‖ *vt (twist)* a încurca; a complica ‖ *vi* a se încâlci.

tango *s* tango *n* ‖ *vi* a dansa tango.

tank *s* cisternă *f;* tanc *n;* bazin *n;* rezervor *n.*

tankard *s (of beer, etc)* cană cu capac.

tanner *s* tăbăcar *m •* **~y** *s* tăbăcărie *f.*

tannin *s* tanin *n.*

tantalizing *adj (tormenting)* chinuitor; *(alluring)* amăgitor, înșelător; *(tempting)* tentant, ademenitor.

tantamount *adj (to)* echivalent/egal cu.

tantrum *s* furie *f,* isterie *f.*

tap[1] *vt* a lovi ușor, a atinge; a bate ușor ‖ *s* bătaie *f* ușoară; lovitură *f.*

tap[2] *s* robinet *n* ‖ *vt* a găuri; a scoate; a capta; a străpunge; a intercepta.

tape *s (ribbon)* panglică *f;* bandă *f* adezivă; ruletă *f;* casetă *f* ‖ *vt (stick)* a lipi; a măsura; a repera; a tivi; *(record)* a înregistra; ~ **recorder** *s* magnetofon *n.*

taper *s* lumânare *f* subțire ‖ *adj* conic ‖ *vt* a îngusta spre vârf ‖ *vi* a avea formă conică.

tapestry *s* tapiserie *f* ‖ *vt* a tapisa, a decora.

tapioca *s bot, cul* tapioca *f.*

tapir *s zool* tapir *m.*

tar *s* gudron *n,* catran *n.*

tarantula *s ento* tarantulă *f.*

target *s (aim)* țintă *f; (goal)* țel *n; (bomb)* obiectiv *n* ‖ *vt* (~ *a city, etc)* a viza; (~ *a policy)* a se adresa, a viza; a ținti; ~ **practice** *s mil* exerciții *n pl* de tragere/tir.

tariff *s* tarif *n;* taxă *f;* listă *f* de prețuri, tabel *n* de prețuri.

tarmac *s avia* pistă *f.*

tarnish *vt* a păta; a defăima ‖ *vi* a-și pierde luciul ‖ *s* pată *f.*

tarpaulin s pânză f impermeabilă; prelată f; foaie f de cort.

tarragon s bot tarhon n.

tart¹ adj (sharp) acru; picant; (biting) caustic; rigid; muşcător.

tart² s cul tartă f; coll prostituată f.

tartan s stofă f ecosez; pled n scoţian, tartan n.

tartar s cul sos n tartar.

task s (duty) sarcină f; îndatorire f; (chore) corvoadă f; scol temă f || vt a da de lucru; (test) a testa; (tax) a solicita; ~ **force** s mil unitate/trupe f pl de şoc/asalt; unitate f de comando, grup n de comando, grup n operativ • ~**master** s distribuitor m de sarcini; (boss) conducător m, şef m.

tassel s ciucure m; pompon n, moţ n; bot paniculă f terminală; (corn) mătase f.

taste s gust n; aromă f; savoare f; urmă f; fineţe f; preferinţă f; probă f || vt a (de)gusta, a savura, a consuma || vi a avea gust • ~**ful** adj de bun gust.

tasting s (wine, etc) degustare f.

tasty adj savuros; cu bun gust; şic.

tattered adj zdrenţăros, rupt.

tattle s trăncăneală f, pălăvrăgeală f || vi a flecări, a trăncăni, a pălăvrăgi.

tattoo¹ s tatuaj n; tatuare f || vt a tatua.

tattoo² s mil semnal n de stingere; amurg n, înserare f || vi (beat on drum) a bate toba/darabana cu degetul.

tatty adj coll (clothes) ponosit; (person) neîngrijit; (house) dărăpănat, deteriorat.

taught adj * **teach**.

taunt vt (mock) a zeflemisi, (deride) a lua în derâdere; (tease) a necăji; a tachina || s (gibe) zeflemea f, sarcasm n, batjocură f.

taupe s culoare f gri-cafeniu.

Taurus s astrol Taurul m.

taut adj (tense) încordat, întins; (tight) strâns.

tautology s tautologie f.

tavern s cârciumă f.

tawdry adj pej (jewelry) strident; (dress) bătător la ochi, ţipător; (motives) josnic, abject.

tawny adj maro-roşcat, roşiatic.

tax s impozit n; taxă f; solicitare f; tensiune f || vt a taxa; a solicita; a chinui; ~ **cut** s reducere f a impozitului; ~ **evasion** s evaziune/fraudă f fiscală; ~**exempt** adj neimpozabil; ~ **relief** s reducere f fiscală; ~ **return** s declaraţie f de venituri • ~**able** adj impozabil • ~**ation** s impozitare f • ~**payer** s contribuabil m.

taxi s taxi(metru) n || vi a merge cu taxiul; avia a rula pe pistă.

taxidermy s taxidermie f, împăiere f.

taxonomy s taxonomie f.

te s mus (nota) si f.

tea s ceai n; infuzie f; ~ **bag** s pliculeţ n de ceai • ~ **cake** s prăjitură f pentru ceai • ~ **leaf** s bot frunză f de ceai; ~ **room** s ceainărie f, salon n de ceai; ~ **set** s serviciu n de ceai; ~ **towel** s cârpă f de vase; ~ **urn** s samovar m.

teach, taught, taught vt (instruct) a preda; (coach) a instrui, a prepara, a pregăti; (train) a învăţa; (~ a lesson) a da o lecţie || vi (~ at a school) a preda, a fi profesor; (experience) a fi instructiv • ~**er** s profesor m de liceu; învăţător m; pedagog m; institutor m • ~**er certification** s atestat n de învăţământ • ~**ing** s învăţământ n.

teak s bot tec n.

team s (work) brigadă f, echipă f; sp echipă f; ~ **spirit** s spirit n colectiv, spirit n de echipă f • ~**mate** s coechiper m, coleg m de echipă • ~**ster** s căruţaş m; şofer m de camion; ~**work** s lucru n în echipă, colaborare f.

teapot s ceainic n.

tear¹, **tore**, **torn** vt (rip) a sfâşia; (snatch) a smuge; (divide) a despărţi; (sprain) a întinde, a rupe; fig a distruge || vi a se uza; a se rupe; a trage; (dash) a se repezi || s uzură f; defect n; elan n; agitaţie f.

tear² s lacrimă f || vi a lăcrima • ~**ful** adj plângăreţ; plâns; trist, înduioşător.

tease vt (~ wool) a dărăci; a scărmăna; (~ hair) a tapa; (taunt) a tachina; (harass) a hărţui || s (joker) sâcâitor m; vampă f.

teasel s bot scaiete m || vt text a dărăci.

teaspoon s linguriţă f de ceai.

teat s anat sfârc n, mamelon n; tech fus n; pivot m.

technical adj tehnic; ~ **hitch** s defecţiune f tehnică.

technicality s tehnicitate f; detaliu n tehnic.

technician s tehnician m.

technique s (method) tehnică f, metode f pl tehnice, procedee n pl tehnice.

technocrat s tehnocrat m.

technology s tehnologie f.

teddy bear s ursuleţ m de pluş.

tedious adj anost, plicticos; încet; dificil; obositor.

tedium s plictiseală f.

tee s (golf) ţintă f pentru minge, semn n pentru minge.

teem vi (swarm) a mişuna, a foi; (pour) a ploua torenţial.

teenage adj adolescent • ~**r** s adolescent m; adolescentă f; tinerel m; tinerică f.

teepee n * **tepee**.

teeny adj coll foarte mic, minuscul.

teenybopper s sl adolescent(ă) m/f care admiră muzica şi moda de ultima oră.

teeter vi (totter) a se împletici la mers; (see-saw) a se legăna • ~**totter** s scrânciob n, leagăn n.

teeth s * **tooth**.

teethe vi (tooth) a ieşi, a creşte; (child) a-i creşte dinţii, a-i ieşi dinţii.

teetotaler s antialcoolic m, abstinent m (de la băutură).

telecast s transmisie f telvizată; program n de televiziune || vt a transmite la televizor.

telecommunications s pl telecomunicaţii f pl.

telecommuter s persoană f care lucrează la domiciliu utilizând calculatorul.

teleconference s teleconferinţă f.

telegenic adj telegenic.

telegram s telegramă f.

telegraph s telegraf n || vt a telegrafia; ~ **pole** s stâlp m de telegraf.

telemarketing s vânzare f prin telefon.

telepathy s telepatie f.

telephone s telefon n || vi/vt a telefona; ~ **book** s carte f de telefon; ~ **number** s număr n de telefon.

telesales s vânzare f prin telefon.

telescope s telescop n.

teletext s teletext n.

telethon s show n de televiziune programat în scopuri caritabile.

televise vt a televiza.

television s televiziune f; (set) televizor n; **on** ~ la televizor.

telex s telex n || vt a transmite prin telex.

tell, told, told *vt (say to)* a spune; *(convey)* a exprima; *(narrate)* a relata; a prezenta; *(inform)* a anunța; *(show)* a arăta; *(distinguish)* a discerne; *(instruct)* a învăța, a deprinde; a dezvălui, a da în vileag; a prevedea; a invita; a dezvălui ‖ *vi* a spune; a povesti; a avea effect; ~ **apart** *vt* a distinge (între); ~ **off** *vt* *(scold)* a mustra, a dojeni; *(select)* a repartiza, a desemna; ~ **on** *vt (denounce)* a pârî; *(influence)* a afecta, a influența.

teller *s* casier *m* la bancă; bancomat *n*; persoană *f* care numără voturile (în parlament); povestitor *m*.

telling *adj* semnificativ; energic; grăitor, convingător; *(style)* expresiv.

telltale *s coll* pârâcios ‖ *adj* revelator; semnificativ.

temerity *s* impertinență *f*, îndrăzneală *f*.

temp *s* funcționar *m* angajat temporar ‖ *vi coll* a presta temporar o activitate.

temper *s* caracter *n*; dispoziție *f*; furie *f*; calm *n* ‖ *vt* a calma; a alina ‖ *vi* a se tempera.

temperament *s* temperament *n* • ~**al** *adj (unpredictable)* capricios; *(natural)* temperamental.

temperance *s (moderation)* moderație *f*; sobrietate *f*; *(abstinence from alcohol)* abținere *f* de la băutură; antialcoolism *n*.

temperate *adj* temperat, moderat.

temperature *s* temperatură *f*, căldură *f*.

tempestuous *adj also fig* furtunos, vijelios, violent; impetuos.

template *s* tipar *n*, model *n*; *(beam)* traversă *f*.

temple[1] *s relig* templu *n*.

temple[2] *s anat* tâmplă *f*.

tempo *s mus* tempo *n*, timp *m*; ritm *n*, tempo *n*; viteză *f*.

temporal *adj* temporal; pământesc.

temporary *adj* temporar; provizoriu; efemer, trecător.

temporize *vt frml* a temporiza.

tempt *vt* a ademeni; a provoca; a seduce • ~**ation** *s* tentație *f*; seducere *f* • ~**ing** *adj* tentant; atractiv; seducător.

ten *num* zece ‖ *s* nota *f* zece.

tenable *adj (secured)* durabil, solid; *(reasonable)* justificabil, care poate fi apărat.

tenacious *adj* tenace, perseverent.

tenant *s* arendaș *m*; chiriaș *m* ‖ *vt* a închiria.

tench *s icht* lin *m*.

tend[1] *vt* a dirija, a îndruma; a conduce, a însoți; *(~ cattle, etc)* a mâna.

tend[2] *vt* a îngriji; a sluji; a dirija; a-i păsa de.

tendency *s (trend)* tendință *f*; *(propensity)* înclinație *f*; aspirație *f*.

tender[1] *adj (fond)* tandru; *(sensitive)* sensibil, dureros; *(young)* fraged; firav.

tender[2] *vt (offer)* a oferi; a furniza; a propune; a întinde; a înmâna; a decerna; a produce ‖ *s fin (bid)* ofertă *f*; *(proposal)* propunere *f*.

tenderloin *s* (file de) mușchi *m*.

tendon *s anat* tendon *n*.

tendril *s bot* cârcel *m*; lujer *m*.

tenement *s* proprietate *f* arendată; casă *f* închiriată; *jur* privilegiu *n* permanent.

tenet *s* doctrină *f*, dogmă *f*; principiu *n*.

tennis *s* tenis *n*.

tenor *s mus* tenor *m*; *(mood)* sens *n*, semnificație *f*.

tense[1] *adj* încordat; agitat, iritat.

tense[2] *s gram* timp *n*.

tensile *adj tech* extensibil, elastic; ductil.

tension *s* încordare *f*; agitație *f*.

tent *s* cort *n*; umbrar *n*; șopron *n* ‖ *vi* a campa.

tentacle *s zool* tentacul *n*, antenă *f*; *bot* fir *n* exterior, glandă *f* cu tulpină.

tentative *adj* de probă/încercare; empiric; provizoriu, temporar; *(smile)* nesigur.

tenterhooks *s pl (clothes)* copci *f pl*; **to be on** ~ a sta ca pe ghimpi/ace.

tenuous *adj* subțire; *fig* micuț, insuficient; subtil, fin.

tenure *s jur* (drept de) posesiune/stăpânire *f*; *(permanent status)* titularizare *f*.

tepee *s* cort *n* (al pieilor roșii); colibă *f* indiană.

tepid *adj also fig* căldut, căldicel.

term *s* termen *n*; durată *f*; dată *f*; trimestru *n*; sfârșit *n*; *pl* clauze *f pl* ‖ *vt* a numi ‖ *vr* a se intitula.

terminal *adj* fatal; terminal; final; definitiv ‖ *s* capăt *n*; terminal *n*; aerogară *f*.

terminate *vt (end)* a sfârși; a limita; a întrerupe ‖ *vi* a se termina.

termination *s (end)* încetare *f*, suspendare *f*; *(of contract)* reziliere *f*; *(of pregnancy)* avort *n*; *ling* terminație *f*.

terminology *s* terminologie *f*.

terminus *s (pl termini)* țintă *f*, scop *n*; extremitate *f*, capăt *n*; hotar *n*, limită *f*.

termite *s ento* termită *f*.

tern *s orn* rândunică *f* de mare.

terrace *s (patio)* terasă *f*; alee *f*, șir *n* de case; *geol* terasă *f*.

terracotta *s (earthenware)* teracotă *f*.

terrain *s* regiune *f*, teritoriu *n*; *(land)* teren *n*, pamânt *n*.

terrestrial *adj* terestru, pamântesc.

terrible *adj (awful)* teribil; *(horrible)* îngrozitor, groaznic; *(severe)* aspru, violent.

terrier *s (dog)* terier *m*.

terrific *adj (great)* grozav; teribil, oribil; *(enormous)* colosal.

terrify *vt* a speria, a îngrozi, a înspăimânta.

territory *s* sferă *f*; teritoriu *n*; posesiune *f*.

terror *s (horror)* teroare *f*; *(dread)* groază *f*; *coll* tip *m* insuportabil; drac *m* de copil • ~**ist** *s* terorist *m*.

terse *adj (brief)* concis, succinct; laconic.

tertiary *adj* terțiar.

test *s* probă *f*; *(exam)* examen *n*; *(check)* control *n*; *(analysis)* analiză *f*; *(trial)* test *n* ‖ *vt (try)* a proba; a verifica; a analiza; a controla ‖ *vi* a face analize; ~ **case** *s jur* speță *f*/caz *n* care generează jurisprudență; ~**drive** *s* cursă *f* de probă; ~ **flight** *s avia* zbor *n* de încercare/probă; ~ **pilot** *s* pilot *m* de încercare; ~ **run** *s auto* rodaj *n*; ~ **tube** *s* eprubetă *f*; **to** ~ **the waters** a tatona terenul.

testament *s* testament *n*.

testicle *s anat, zool* testicul *n*.

testify *vt (show)* a atesta; a susține ‖ *vi jur (give evidence)* a depune mărturie.

testimonial *s* certificate *n*, atestat n; *(reference)* recomandare *f*; *(tribute)* mărturie *f*.

testimony *s jur* depoziție *f*, *(declaration)* declarație *f*; *(proof)* mărturie *f*; *(certificate)* atestat *n*.

testing *s* testare *f* ‖ *adj* de încercare; experimental.

testy *adj (grumpy)* arțăgos, țâfnos.

tetanus *s med* tetanos *n*.

tetchy *adj (irritable)* urăcios, ursuz.

tether *s* pripon *n*; *fig* limită *f*; capacitate *f* de rezistență ‖ *vt (join)* a atașa.

text *s* text *n*; **~book** *s* carte *f* de școală, manual *n*.

textile *adj* textil || *s* țesătură *f*; material *n*; stofă *f*.

texture *s* țesătură *f*; desime *f*; structură *f*.

than *conj* decât, ca; **he plays tennis better ~ me/I** el joacă tenis mai bine decât mine; **more ~ 10 people** mai mult de zece persoane.

thank *s* recunoștință *f* || *vt* a mulțumi; a fi recunoscător; **~ you** (îți/vă) mulțumesc.

thanks *s pl* mulțumiri *f pl*; *excl* mersi!; **~ to** *prep* datorită, mulțumită; **~ a lot**, **~ very much** (îți/vă) mulțumesc foarte mult; **~ for coming** (îți/vă) mulțumesc că ați venit; **~ for nothing** *iro* mulțumesc; **Thanksgiving (Day)** Ziua *f* Recunoștinței.

that *pron dem* acela/aceea; ăla; aia; aceasta, asta; primul pomenit || *adj* acela, ace(e)a, ăla, aia || *pron rel* care; în care; pe care || *conj* încât; ca, pentru ca; fără ca || *adv* atât de; **after/before ~** după/înainte de aceea; **who's ~?** cine este acela?; **what's ~?** ce-i aia?; **~'s all** asta-i tot; **the house ~ Jack built** casa pe care a construit-o Jack; **it's not ~ far** nu este atât de departe; **and all ~** și toate celelalte, și așa mai departe; **~'s ~** și cu asta basta.

thatched *adj* (*roof*) de paie, de stuf.

thaw *vi* a se dezgheța; a se dizolva; a se încălzi || *s* dezgheț *n*; dizolvare *f*.

the *art def* **~ lamp** lampa; **~ nose** nasul || *adv* cu cât ... cu atât; **~ sooner ~ better** cu cât mai repede, cu atât mai bine.

theater *s* teatru *n*; sală *f* de cinema; amfiteatru *n*.

theft *s* furt *n*; hoție *f*.

their *adj poss* lor; **~ house** casa lor; **~ children** copiii lor.

theirs *pron poss* al/a/ai/ale lor; **that house is ~** acea casă e a lor.

theism *s phil* teism *n*.

them *pron pers* pe ei/ele; li; lor; **I know ~** îi/le cunosc; **many of ~** mulți dintre ei; **we spoke to ~** le-am vorbit (lor).

thematic *adj* tematic.

theme *s* (*topic*) temă *f*; (*subject*) subiect *n*; (*matter*) lucrare *f*; compoziție *f*; *mus* motiv *n*, temă *f*; *n*; *ling* temă *f*.

themselves *pron ref* se; înșiși, însele; singuri, singure; chiar ei/ele; **they are enjoying ~** ei se distrează.

then *adv* atunci; apoi, după aceea; pe atunci; la urma urmei; pe lângă asta || *conj* în acest caz; așadar, deci; pe de altă parte; **by ~** până atunci; **since ~** de atunci; **from ~ on** de atunci încoace; **we went shopping, ~ we had lunch** am făcut întâi cumpărături, apoi am luat masa; **what do you suggest ~?** atunci ce sugerezi?.

thence *adv lit*, *frml* de acolo; de atunci • **~forth** (începând) de atunci.

theologian *s* teolog *m*.

theology *s* teologie *f*.

theorem *s* teoremă *f*.

theoretical *adj* teoretic.

theory *s* teorie *f*; ipoteză *f*; speculație *f* (filosofică).

therapeutic *adj* therapeutic • **~s** *s* terapeutică *f*.

therapy *s* terapie *f*.

there *adv* acolo; aici || *interj* ei! ajunge!; iată, uite • **~by** *adv* prin aceasta; din aceasta; cu aceasta; astfel, în acest mod • **~fore** *adv/conj* de aceea; așadar, deci, prin urmare, astfel.

thermal *adj* termal; cald.

thermodynamics *s phys* termodinamică *f*.

thermometer *s* termometru *n*.

thermonuclear *adj* termonuclear.

thermos *s* termos *n*.

thermostat *s* termostat *n*.

thesaurus *s* dicționar *n* tezaur.

these *pron pl* * **this** aceștia, acestea.

thesis *s* (*pl* **–ses**) (*dissertation*) teză *f*.

thespian *adj* dramatic; **~ art** *s* artă *f* dramatică.

they *pron pers* ei; ele || *pron imp* se.

thick *adj* gros; dens; adânc; vâscos; murdar; excesiv; lipicios || *adv* gros; dens || *s* toi *n*; mijloc *n* • **~en** *vt* a îngroșa, a îndesi || *vi* a se îngroșa • **~ness** *s* grosime *f*; strat *n*; densitate *f*; încâlceală *f*; obtuzitate *f*.

thief *s* hoț *m*; tâlhar *m*.

thieve *vt/vi* a fura.

thigh *s anat* coapsă *f*.

thimble *s* degetar *n* (de cusut).

thin *adj* (*skinny*) slab; (*slim*) subțire; (*air*) rar, rarefiat; (*argument*) neconvingător; (*watery*) diluat || *adv* subțire || *vt* (*dilute*) a dilua; a rări || *vi* a se dilua; a se rări.

thine *adj poss obs* tăi, ta, tale, tău || *pron poss* ai tăi, a ta, ale tale, al tău.

thing *s* (*object*) lucru *n*, obiect *n*; (*item*) articol *n*; (*matter*) chestie *f*; (*point*) detaliu *n*; (*event*) fapt *n*; situație *f*; (*being*) ființă *f*; (*mania*) obsesie *f*; *pl* haine *f pl*; **for one ~** mai întâi, în primul rand; **just the ~** exact ce trebuie.

think, thought, thought *vt* (*reason*) a gândi; a concepe; a reflecta la; (*believe*) a crede; a pricepe; (*suppose*) a-și închipui || *vi* a gândi, a cugeta • **~ing** *s* (*act*) gândire *f*; (*opinion*) părere *f*, opinie *f* || *adj* (*person*) chibzuit, înțelept.

third *num* al treilea; trei || *s* treime *f*; terț *m*, terță *f*; **~ class** clasa a treia; **~ party** *jur* terț, terță persoană; **~ world** lumea a treia.

thirst *s* sete *f*; (*desire*) (**for**) sete (de) • **~y** *adj* (*dehydrated*) însetat; arid; (*eager*) doritor.

thirteen *num* treisprezece.

thirty *num* treizeci.

this *pron dem* acesta, aceasta; ăsta, asta || *adj* acest, aceasta, această || *adv* așa (de), atât (de).

thistle *s bot* ciulin *m*, scai *m*, scaiete *m*.

thong *s* chingă *f*, curea *f*.

thorn *s also fig* spin *m*; ghimpe *m*; mărăcine *m* • **~y** *adj* (*prickly*) țepos; (*difficult*) spinos, dificil, greu.

thorough *adj* minuțios; serios; profund; perfect; ferm; adevărat.

those *pron dem pl* * **that**.

thou *pron obs* tu.

though *conj* deși, cu toate că; chiar dacă || *adv* totuși, cu toate acestea.

thought *s* (*idea*) gând *n*, idee *f*; gândire *f*; (*reflection*) reflecție *f*; (*opinion*) opinie *f*; (*plan*) intenție *f*; (*notion*) noțiune *f*, concepție *f*; (*attention*) grijă *f*; **~ provoking** care te pune pe gânduri • **~ful** *adj* gânditor; profund; meditativ, contemplativ; atent • **~less** *adj* neglijent; necugetat.

thousand *num* o mie || *s* mie *f*; liotă *f*; imensitate *f*.

thrall *s* (*state*) sclavie *f*; (*person*) sclav *m*.

thrash *vt* (*beat*) a ciomăgi; (*thresh*) a treiera; *sp* (*defeat*) a învinge || *vi* a se zvârcoli, a se răsuci.

thread *s* (*yarn*) fir *n*; ață *f*; (*fiber*) fibră *f*; (*drift*) șir *n* (al discuției); logică *f*; *tech* filet *n* || *vt* (*string*) a înșira || *vi* a-și croi drum; **he ~ed his way through the crowd** el și-a făcut loc prin mulțime • **~bare** *adj* (*clothes*) ponosit, uzat; (*joke*) banal, răsuflat.

threat *s* amenințare *f* • **~en** *vt*/*vi* a amenința.

three *num* trei • **~fold** *adj* triplu • **~fourths** *num* trei pătrimi • **~some** *s* grup *n* de trei persoane.

thresh *vt* a treiera; a bate cu îmblăciul

threshold *s* prag *n*; ușă *f*; poartă *f*; început *n*.

threw *vt* * **throw**.

thrice *adv* de trei ori.

thrift *s* (*saving*) economie *f*, cumpătare *f*; (*frugality*) frugalitate *f* • **~y** *adj* econom; prosper; moderat.

thrill *s* fior *m*; emoție *f*; tresărire *f* || *vt* a înfiora; a tulbura; a ameți || *vi* a se înfiora; a fremăta; a zvâcni • **~ing** *adj* înfiorător; senzațional; emoționant; tulburător.

thrive *vi* (*person*) a prospera, a-i merge bine; (*plant*) a crește viguros; (*business*) a prospera.

thriving *adj* înfloritor, prosper; (*plant*) viguros; (*business*) prosper.

throat *s* anat gât *n*; gâtlej *n*; voce *f*.

throb *s* (*heart*) pulsație *f*; palpitație *f*; tremur *n*; fior *n* || *vi* (*heart*) a pulsa, a bate, a palpita; (*engine*) a vibra; (*music*) a bate (ritmul).

throes *s pl* chinuri *n pl*, suferințe *f pl*.

thrombosis *s med* tromboză *f*.

throne *s* tron *n*; templu *n*; coroană *f* || *vt* a așeza pe tron.

throng *s* (*crowd*) mulțime *f*, gloată *f*; îmbulzeală *f* || *vi* a se îmbulzi, a se îngrămădi.

throttle *s tech* supapă *f* de reglaj; regulator *n*, drosel *n* || *vt* a strangula/înăbuși.

through *prep* prin; de la, din; peste; printre; grație, datorită; din cauza; în timpul; inclusiv, până la || *adv* direct || *adj* direct; gata, sfârșit; rupt, ros; **read it ~** citește-o până la sfârșit; **~ and ~** în întregime, complet • **~out** *adv* (*everywhere*) pretutindeni, peste tot; (*all the time*) tot timpul, mereu || *prep* (*in space*) de la un capăt la celălalt; (*in time*) în tot cursul.

throw, threw, thrown *vt* (*fling*) a arunca; (*baffle*) a dezorienta, a deruta; (*money*) a risipi; (*chance*) a pierde; *sp* a trânti; (*party*) a oferi; (*animal*) a făta || *vr* a se arunca || *s* lansare *f*, (*toss*) aruncare *f*, anvergură *f*; **~ away** *vt* (*money*) a risipi; (*chance*) a pierde; (*cards*) a depune, a pune jos; **~ out** *vt* (*eject*) a arunca, a scoate afară; *fig* a scoate în relief; *jur* a respinge; (*expel*) a expulza, a da afară; (*school*) a exmatricula; **~ up** *vt* a abandona, a renunța la; a vomita, a vărsa.

thrown *vt* * **throw**.

thrush *s orn* sturz *m*; *med* aftă *f*.

thrust, thrust, thrust *vt* (*push*) a vârî; a înfige; (*impose*) a impune; (*shove*) a împinge; (*one's way*) a-și croi drum || *vi* a se împinge; a se vârî; a fanda || *s* (*lunge*) fandare *f*; (*push*) îmbrânceală *f*; (*focus*) idee *f* principală, aspect *n* principal; *fig* (*remark*) înțepătură *f*, aluzie *f*.

thud *s* bufnitură *f*, zgomot *n* înăbușit || *vi* a bufni, a face un zgomot surd.

thug *s* bătăuș *m*, cuțitar *m*.

thumb *s* degetul *n* mare || *vt* a mânui stângaci; a murdări; a solicita; **~ through** *vt* a răsfoi, a parcurge • **~tack** *s* piuneză *f*.

thump *s* bufnitură *f*; zgomot *n* surd || *vt* a lovi tare || *vi* a lovi cu un zgomot surd; a bufni; (*heart ~s*) a bate puternic.

thunder *s* tunet *n*; furtună *f*; ropot *n*; amenințare *f* || *vi* a tuna; a vui; a fi mânios • **~storm** *s* furtună *f*.

Thursday *s* joi *f*.

thus *adv* astfel, așa, în acest fel/mod.

thwack *vt* a lovi puternic || *s* lovitură *f* zdravănă.

thwart *vt* a contracara; (*frustrate*) a zădărnici; a dejuca; a înfrânge, a învinge.

thyme *s bot* cimbru *m*.

thyroid *s anat* (glanda) tiroidă *f* || *adj* tiroid; tiroidian.

tiara *s* diademă *f*; *relig* tiară *f*.

tibia *s* (*pl* **tibiae**) *anat* tibie *f*.

tic *s* tic *n* nervos.

tick[1] *vi* (*clock ~s*) a ticăi || *vt* a bate (minutele); (*mark*) a puncta; a bifa || *s* (*of clock*) ticăit *n*; (*a moment*) clipă *f*; bifare *f*.

tick[2] *s ento* căpușă *f*.

ticker *s coll* inimă *f*; ceas *n*; imprimator *n*.

ticket *s* bilet *n*; bon *n*; tichet *n*; anunț *n*; aviz *n*; (*label*) etichetă *f*; (*permit*) permis *n*; dovadă *f*; buletin *n* de vot || *vt* a marca (prețul).

tickle *vt* a gâdila; a amuza; a excita; a măguli || *vi* a fi gâdilitor; a gâdila || *s* gâdilare *f*; iritație *f*.

tidal *adj* referitor la mare; **~ wave** *s* val *n* seismic; aflux *n*; *fig* (*of passion, etc*) val *n* de pasiune etc.

tidbit *s cul* delicatesă *f*; (*of scandal*) detaliu *n* picant/ savuros.

tide *s* maree *f*; flux *n*; soartă *f*; schimb *n*; timp *n* || *vt* a duce || *vi* a se lăsa dus.

tidings *s pl obs, lit* vești *f pl*, știri *f pl*.

tidy *adj* (*neat*) ordonat; îngrijit || *vt* (*arrange*) a aranja; (*neaten*) a curăța; a îngriji || *vi* a face ordine/curățenie; **to ~ up** *vt* a orândui, a aranja || *vi* a face ordine.

tie *vt* a lega; a îmbina; a obliga; a egala || *vi* a egala || *vr* a se obliga || *s* legătură *f*; fundă *f*; nod *n*; cravată *f*; mariaj *n*; obligație *f*; **to ~ up** *vt* a fixa, a lega; *econ* a depune, a consemna; a finaliza; (*obstruct*) a frâna, a bloca.

tier *s* (*row*) rând *n*, șir *n*; (*cake*) etaj *n*; strat *n* (suprapus); **in ~s** straturi, etajat.

tiff *s* (*quarrel*) ciondăneală *f*, ceartă *f*.

tiger *s zool* tigru *m*; *fig* călău *m*, criminal *m*, om *m* crud.

tight *adj* compact; dens; (*firm*) etanș; solid; (*close-fitting*) strâmt; (*tense*) întins; vânjos; apăsător; *coll* beat; *coll* (*difficult*) dificil, greu; (*fixed*) fix || *adv* strâmt; (*strict*) ferm; ermetic; **~fisted** *adj pej* avar, zgârcit; **~lipped** *adj* tăcut; discret; rezervat.

tights *s pl* costum *n* de balerin; dres *n*.

tike *s* (*dog*) javră *f*, potaie *f*; (*child*) țânc *m*.

tilde *s* tildă *f* (~).

tile *s* țiglă *f*; cahlă *f*; cărămidă *f* || *vt* a înveli/acoperi cu țigle/plăci.

till[1] *prep* până (la) || *conj* până (ce, să).

till[2] *s com* sertar *n* la tejghea.

till[3] *vt agr* a ara, a lucra, a cultiva.

tiller *s naut* fusul *n* cârmei; cârmă *f*; *tech* tirant *m*; bielă *f*.

tilt *vt* a răsturna; a apleca || *vi* a se clătina; a se apleca || *s* înclinare *f*; pantă *f*.

timber *s* cherestea *f*; buștean *m*; grindă *f*; pădure *f* || *vt* a propti; a forma; a făuri.

timbre *s mus* timbru *n*.

time *s* timp *n*; (*moment*) răgaz *n*; sezon *n*; (*era*) epocă *f*; durată *f*; (*phase*) stagiu *n*; (*occasion*) ocazie *f*; viață *f*; *mus* măsură *f*; ritm *n* || *vt* (*program*) a fixa; (*count*) a măsura; *sp* a cronometra; a se adapta; a regla; ~ **bomb** bombă *f* cu efect întârziat; ~ **card/ sheet** cartelă *f* de pontaj; ~ **clock** ceas *n* de pontat; **at ~s** *adv* uneori, câteodată; **in** ~ *adv* (*on time*) la timp (pentru); (*finally*) în final, în cele din urmă; (*later*) cu timpul, cu vremea ~ **out** *s sp* timp *m* mort; ~ **switch** *s* comutator *n* automat; ~ **zone** *s* fus *n* orar • ~**less** *adj* etern • ~**ly** *adj* oportun • ~**table** *s* orar *n*.

timid *adj* timid; șovăitor; fricos; sperios.

timing *s* programare *f*; sincronizare *f*; cronometrare *f*.

timorous *adj* (*nervous*) temător, timorat.

timpani *s pl mus* timpane *n pl*.

tin *s* cositor *n*; tablă *f* galvanizată; bidon *n*; cutie *f* de conserve; veselă *f* ‖ *adj* de cositor/tablă ‖ *vt* a cositori; a conserva.

tinder *s* iască *f*; ~ **box** situație *f* explozivă.

tinge *s* (*color*) tentă *f*, nuanță *f*; *fig* ton *n*, iz *n*.

tingle *vi* a amorți; (*with excitement*) a vibra ‖ *s* (*quiver*) furnicătură *f*; tremur *n* (de emoție etc).

tinker *s* spoitor *m*; tinichigiu *m* ‖ *vt* a spoi; (*mess with*) a cârpăci, a repara de mântuială.

tinkle *vt* a țiui; (*ring*) a suna ‖ *s* (*chime*) sunet/dangăt *n* subțirel (de clopot).

tinsel *s* beteală *f*.

tint *s* culoare *f*; tentă *f*, nuanță *f* ‖ *vt* a nuanța, a colora.

tiny *adj* minuscul, micuț.

tip[1] *s* (*point*) vârf *n*, capăt *n*; (*advice*) pont *n*; informație *f* confidențială; (*gratuity*) bacșiș *n* ‖ *vt* (~ *a waiter, etc*) a da bacșiș; ~ **off** *vt coll* a avertiza, a preveni.

tip[2] *vt* (*tilt*) a înclina; a doborî; a deșerta ‖ *vi* a se răsturna; a se înclina ‖ *s* înclinație *f*.

tipple *vi coll* a trage la măsea ‖ *s* (*drink*) băutură *f* alcoolică.

tipsy *adj coll* cherchelit, pilit, amețit.

tiptoe *s* vârf *n* al degetelor de la picioare ‖ *vi* a merge tiptil; **on** ~ în vârful picioarelor.

tirade *s* retorică *f*, tiradă *f*.

tire[1] *vt* a obosi; a extenua; a plictisi ‖ *vi* a obosi; a se plictisi • ~**d** *adj* obosit; istovit; dezgustat • ~**less** *adj* neobosit • ~**some** *adj* sâcâitor, enervant.

tire[2] *s* cerc *n* (de fier) la roată; *auto* pneu *n*, anvelopă *f*, cauciuc *n* ‖ *vt* a schimba cauciuc.

tissue *s* țesătură *f*; voal *n*; țesut *n*; stofă *f* fină; urzeală *f*.

tit *s sl* țâță *f*, sân *m*; sfârc *n*; *pej* tâmpit *m*.

titan *s* titan *m*, uriaș *m* • ~**ic** *adj* titanic.

titanium *s chem* titan *n*.

titillate *s* a ațâța, a excita.

title *s* titlu *n*; rang *n*; drept *n* ‖ *vi* a titra; a denumi; a da drepturi; ~ **deed** *s* titlu *n* de proprietate • ~**holder** *s* posesor *m* al titlului; proprietar *m* de drept; *sp* campion *m*.

titter *s* chicot *n*, chicoteală *f* ‖ *vi* a chicoti, a râde pe înfundate.

tittle-tattle *s coll* bârfă *f*.

titular *adj* titular.

tizzy *s coll* agitație *f*, înfrigurare *f*.

T-junction *s* intersecție *f* în formă de T.

to *prep* spre, către; la; despre; de; în; până (la); pe lângă; potrivit, după; **go** ~ **school** a merge la școală; **from Boston** ~ **Houston** de la Boston până la Huston; **cheek** ~ **cheek** obraz lângă obraz; ~ **his mind** după părerea lui.

toad *s zool* broască *f* râioasă; *coll* canalie *f*, nemernic *m*; *coll* lingușitor *m*.

toast *s* pâine *f* prăjită; pesmet ‖ *vt* a prăji ‖ *vi* a se prăji/ rumeni.

tobacco *s bot* tutun *n*.

toboggan *s* sanie *f* ‖ *vi* a se da cu sania; a coborî o pantă.

today *adv* astăzi; în zilele noastre ‖ *s* ziua *f* de azi.

toddler *s* copilaș/țânc *m* care începe să umble.

to-do *s coll* zarvă *f*, hărmălaie *f*.

toe *s anat* deget *n* de la picior; vârf *n*; bază *f* ‖ *vt* a lovi cu vârful piciorului • ~**nail** *s* unghie *f* de la picior.

toffee *s* caramea *f*; acadea *f*; pralină *f*.

tog *s coll* echipament *n*, uniformă *f*; costum *n*.

together *adv* (*jointly*) împreună (cu); laolaltă; simultan; în șir; consecutiv.

toggle *s* brandenburg *n*; *elec, comp* comutator *n*; **brake** ~ *s* frână *f* cu leviere; ~ **switch** *elec* întrerupător *n*.

toil *vi* a (se) trudi; a se târî; a-și continua munca ‖ *s* trudă *f*; osteneală *f*.

toilet *s* toaletă *f*; îmbrăcăminte *f*; baie *f*; closet *n*; curățire *f*.

token *s* fisă *f*; indiciu *n*; semn *n*; dovadă *f*; simbol *n* ‖ *adj* simbolic; semnificativ ‖ *vt* a dovedi; a denota; ~ **money** *s* monedă *f* fiduciară/divizionară.

tokenism *s pol* politică *f* minimalistă privind angajarea muncitorilor din rândul minorităților.

Tokyo *s* Tokio *n*.

told *vt* * **tell**.

tolerable *adj* suportabil, tolerabil.

tolerance *s* toleranță *f*.

tolerant *adj* tolerant; indulgent.

tolerate *vt* (*abide*) a tolera; a permite; (*bear*) a suporta.

toleration *s* tolerare *f*; toleranță *f*.

toll[1] *s* impozit *n*; taxă *f*; vamă *f*; *fig* plată *f*, vamă *f*; ~ **call** *s* convorbire *f* interurbană; ~ **free** *adj* gratis.

toll[2] *vt* (*ring*) a trage (clopotele) ‖ *vi* (*bell, etc* ~**s**) a bate, a suna ‖ *s* dangăt *n*, sunet *n*.

tomahawk *s* secure *f* (a indienilor din SUA).

tomato *s bot* roșie *f*; tomată *f*.

tomb *s* mormânt *n*; cavou *n*; criptă *f* ‖ *vt* a înmormânta.

tombola *s* tombolă *f*.

tomboy *s* (*girl*) băiețoi *m*.

tomcat *s* motan *m*.

tome *s* tom *n*, volum *n*.

tomfool *s* nătărău *m*, tont *m* • ~**ery** *s* maimuțăreală *f*; nerozie *f*.

tommy gun *s* pușcă *f* automată.

tomorrow *adv* mâine ‖ *s* ziua *f* de mâine.

tom-tom *s* tam-tam *n*, tobă *f*.

ton *s* tonă *f*; grămadă *f*.

tonality *s mus* tonalitate *f*.

tone *s* ton *n*; modulație *f*; intonație *f*; nuanțare *f*; atitudine *f*; inițiativă *f* ‖ *vt* a acorda; a da tonul; a nuanța ‖ *vi* a se armoniza; a se nuanța; ~ **down** *vt* a atenua, a modera; ~ **up** *vt* a tonifia, a întări; ~**deaf** *adj* afon.

tongue *s* limbă *f*; limbaj *n*; grai *n* ‖ *vt* a linge; a sări cu gura ‖ *vi* a trăncăni • ~**tied** *adj* mut; *fig* amuțit, rămas fără glas.

tongs *s pl* clește *m*.

tonic *adj/s med* tonic.

tonight *adv* diseară, astă seară; la noapte ‖ *s* seara/ noaptea *f* asta.

tonsil *s anat* amigdală *f*.

tony *adj coll* (*classy*) șic, la modă.

too *adv* prea; de altfel; foarte; de asemenea, și; pe deasupra.

took *vt* * **take**.

tool *s* unealtă *f*; mijloc *n*; instrument *n*; agent *m* ‖ *vt* a prelucra; a ciopli.

toot *s* (*beep*) sunet *n* de claxon ‖ *vi* (*honk*) a claxona.

tooth *s* dinte *m*; măsea *f*; poftă *f*; gust *n* ‖ *vt* a muşca • **~ache** *s* durere *f* de măsele • **~brush** *s* periuţă *f* de dinţi • **~paste** *s* pastă *f* de dinţi.

tootle *vi* a cânta, a sufla (la un instrument de suflat)

top *s* (*pinnacle*) vârf *n*; pisc *n*; (*car*) capotă *f*; acoperiş *n*; (*lid*) capac *n*; imperială *f* ‖ *adj* (*best*) superior; (*highest*) din vârf; maxim; **in ~ form** în cea mai bună formă; **on ~ of** *prep* (*on*) pe; (*besides*) în plus; **over the ~** depăşind aşteptările; **~ of the line** cel mai bun din serie • **~ping** *s* garnitură *f* ‖ *vt* a fi în frunte, a conduce; (*best*) a întrece; (*surpass*) a depăşi.

topaz *s* topaz *n*.

topiary *s* grădină *f* ornamentală.

topic *s* (*theme*) subiect *n*, temă *f*.

topical *adj* (*current*) la ordinea zilei, de actualitate; *med* local.

topography *s* topografie *f*.

topple *vt* (*bring down*) a răsturna; a rostogoli ‖ *vi* (*fall*) a se răsturna; a se rostogoli.

topsy-turvy *adj* cu susul în jos, anapoda; răvăşit ‖ *adv* invers, pe dos.

torch *s* torţă *f*, făclie *f*; lanternă *f*.

tore *vt* * **tear**.

toreador *s* toreador *m*.

torment *s* tortură *f*; supliciu *n*; chin *n* ‖ *vt* a tortura.

torn *vt* * **tear**.

tornado *s* *met* tornadă *f*.

torpedo *s* torpilă *f*.

torpid *adj* *frml* lent, inert; apatic.

torpor *s* *frml* (*languor*) moleşeală *f*, toropeală *f*.

torque *s* torsiune *f*; *tech* cuplu *n* de torsiune.

torrent *s* torent *n*; *fig* potop *n*, val *n*.

torrid *adj* (*hot*) torid; *fig* arzător.

torsion *s* torsiune *f*.

torso *s* *anat* tors *n*, trunchi *n*.

tort *s* *jur* ofensă *f*, daună *f*, prejudiciu *n*.

tortoise *s* *zool* (broască) ţestoasă *f*.

tortuous *adj* (*convoluted*) întortocheat; (*winding*) sinuos; *fig* nesincer; lipsit de sinceritate.

torture *s* tortură *f*; supliciu *n* ‖ *vt* a tortura.

toss *vt* (*throw*) a azvârli; (*rock*) a legăna; (*head*) a clătina; a alarma ‖ *vi* a se zvârcoli; a se legăna; (*stir*) a se agita; (**~ up**) a trage la sorţi ‖ *s* aruncare *f*; zguduire *f*; tragere *f* la sorţi; scuturare *f*.

tot¹ *s* *coll* (*toddler*) copilaş *m*, ţânc *m*; (*drink*) strop *m*, duşcă *f*, păhărel *n*.

tot² *vt* a aduna, a socoti, a totaliza.

total *adj* total; absolut; întreg ‖ *s* total *n*; întreg *n* ‖ *vt* a însuma; a aduna.

totalitarian *adj* totalitar.

totem *s* totem *n*; **~ pole** *s* stâlp *m* totemic • **~ic** *adj* totemic.

totter *vi* (*falter*) a se clătina, a se bălăbăni.

touch *vt* (*pat*) a atinge; (*feel*) a pipăi; a apăsa; (*affect*) a mişca, a egala; a aborda; a modifica; a retuşa; a marca ‖ *vi* a se lovi; a se atinge ‖ *s* (*pat*) pipăit *n*; tuşeu *n*; (*trace*) nuanţă *f*; atac *n*; pic *n* • **~and-go** *adj* nesigur; riscat • **~down** *s* *avia* aterizare *f*; *sp* gol *n* • **~ing** *adj* impresionant • **~y** *adj* extrem de sensibil, ultrasensibil.

tough *adj* (*rough*) dur; (*difficult*) dificil; inflexibil; tenace; (*strict*) rigid; robust; încăpăţânat ‖ *s* bandit

m; huligan *m*; • **~luck!** ghinion! • **~en** *vt* (*metal*) a întări; (*person*) a căli, a oţeli; (*conditions*) a înăspri.

toupee *s* moţ *n*.

tour *s* călătorie *f*; tur *n*; plimbare *f*; excursie *f*; turneu *n*; cursă *f* ‖ *vi* a voiaja ‖ *vt* a colinda; a face un turneu • **~ism** *s* turism *n* • **~ist** *s* turist *m*.

tournament *s* *hist* turnir *n*; *sp* concurs *n*, competiţie *f*; turneu *n*.

tousled *adj* (*tangled*) ciufulit; cu părul răvăşit; şifonat, boţit.

tout *s* agent *m* de reclamă; vânzător *m* care strigă marfa ‖ *vt* (*peddle*) a vinde la suprapreţ; (*promote*) a atrage clienţii prin reclamă zgomotoasă.

tow *s* cablu *n*; remorcă *f* ‖ *vi* a fi remorcat; **~ truck** *s* maşină *f* de depanare.

toward *prep* (*to*) către, spre; (*regarding*) referitor, faţă de; în scopul de a; aproape de.

towel *s* prosop *n* ‖ *vt* a şterge cu prosopul.

tower *s* turn *n*; reazem *n*; bastion *n*; apărător • **~ing** *adj* impunător; de excepţie, extraordinar.

town *s* oraş *n*; centru *n*; capitală *f*; comună *f* ‖ *adj* urban; citadin; de oraş; **~ hall** *s* primărie *f*; **~ planning** *s* urbanism *n*.

toxic *adj* toxic • **~ology** *s* toxicologie *f*.

toxin *s* toxină *f*.

toy *s* jucărie *f* ‖ *adj* de jucărie; de copii ‖ *vi* a se juca (cu); a se amuza (cu).

trace *s* (*trail*) urmă *f*; (*sign*) semn *n* ‖ *vt* (*draw*) a trasa; a schiţa; (*track*) a urmări • **~able** *adj* detectabil.

trachea *s* *anat* trahee *f*.

tracing *s* (*process*) calchiere *f*; (*result*) desen *n* pe calc, copie *f* pe calc.

track *s* urmă *f* (de paşi); (*path*) făgaş *n*; (*trail*) pistă *f*; şină *f* ‖ *vt* a urmări; a descoperi; **~ record** *s* palmares *n* • **~suit** *s* trening *n*.

tract¹ *s* (*area*) întindere *f*; regiune *f*, ţinut *n*; *anat* tract *n*, traiect *n*.

tract² *s* (*leaflet*) broşură *f*.

tractable *adj* (*person, animal*) docil, blând; maniabil; (*material*) maleabil; (*problem*) rezolvabil.

traction *s* tracţiune *f*.

tractor *s* tractor *n*.

trade *s* (*commerce*) comerţ *n*; (*skill*) profesie *f*; (*exchange*) afacere *f*; rută *f* regulată; (*illicit dealings*) trafic *n* ‖ *vi* (*deal*) a face comerţ ‖ *vt* a negocia; a face schimb de ‖ *adj* comercial; **~ deficit** *s* deficit *n* comercial; **~ fair** *s* târg *n* comercial; **~ in** *vt com* a schimba, a face trafic de; **~in** *s com* schimbare *f* a unui articol vechi cu unul nou; **~ name** *s* nume *n* de marcă; **~off** *s* schimb *n*; compromis *n*; **~ route** *s* rută *f* comercială; **~ school** *s* şcoală *f* profesională; **~ secret** *s* reţetă *n* de fabricaţie • **~r** *s* comerciant *m*; *naut* vas *n* comercial • **~sman** *s* (*trader*) comerciant *m*; negustor *m*; vânzător *m*; (*workman*) meşteşugar *m* • **~mark** *s com* marcă *f* înregistrată; *fig* marcă *f*.

trading port *s* *naut* port *n* comercial.

tradition *s* obicei *n*; tradiţie *f*; legendă *f* • **~al** *adj* tradiţional, legendar.

traduce *vt frml* (*malign*) a calomnia, a defăima.

traffic *s* circulaţie *f*; trafic *n* comercial; comerţ *n* ilicit ‖ *vi* a face comerţ ‖ *vt* a face schimb de; a negocia.

tragedy *s* tragedie *f*; întâmplare *f* tragică.

tragic *adj* tragic; grav; îngrozitor; funest.

trail *vt* a târî; a remorca; a călca pe; a fila ‖ *vi* a se târî ‖ *s* dâră *f*; urmă *f*; trenă *f*; alai *n*; cărare *f*.

train s *rail* tren n; (*procession*) trenă f, suită f;
(*sequence*) lanț n; înlănțuire f; *fig* curs n, mers n;
(*dress*) trenă f || vt (*teach*) a instrui, a învăța, a
pregăti; *sp* a antrena; *mil* (*aim*) a îndrepta, a aținti, a
dirija || vi (*exercise*) a exersa, a se pregăti; *mil* a face
instrucție • ~ee s stagiar m; *mil* recrut m • ~ing s
instruire f, formare f; perfecționare f; antrenament n;
instrucție f.

traipse vi *coll* (*trudge*) a se târî, a merge încet.

trait s trăsătură f.

traitor s trădător m.

trajectory s traiectorie f.

tram s tramvai n || vt a duce cu tramvaiul.

trammel vt *also fig* a împiedica, a înfrâna.

tramp s (*vagrant*) vagabond m; (*long walk*) mers n
lung/obositor, cutreierare f; (*sound*) zgomot n de pași
|| vi (*hike*) a hoinări, a vagabonda; (*traipse*) a merge
greoi.

trample vi *also fig* a călca în picioare, a zdrobi sub
tălpi.

trampoline s plasă f elastică (folosită ca trambulină).

trance s transă f; *med* catalepsie f.

tranquil adj calm, liniștit • ~ity s seninătate f, liniște f •
~izer s tranchilizant n, calmant n.

transact vt (*conduct*) a negocia, a trata; (*conclude*) a
încheia, a executa • ~ion s tranzacție f; gestiune f;
negociere f; *pl* acte n *pl*.

transceiver s aparat n de emisie-recepție.

transcend vt a depăși || vi a excela.

transcribe vt a transcrie, a copia; a reproduce.

transcription s transcriere f.

transept s *archit* transept n.

transfer vt (*shift*) a transfera; (*move*) a muta; (*convey*)
a vira; *jur* a remite; (*displace*) a transpune; a copia ||
s transfer n; (*relocation*) mutare f; predare f; *jur*
cedare f; copiere f; *com* virament n • ~able adj
transferabil; transmisibil; *jur* negociabil, care poate
fi cesionat.

transfixed adj țintuit, încremenit (de groază etc)

transform vt a transforma; a reforma.

transfuse vt a injecta; a face o transfuzie (de sânge).

transfusion s transfuzie f.

transgress vt *frml* (*disobey*) a încălca, a viola; a depăși
(atribuțiile) || vi (*sin*) a păcătui.

transient adj trecător, pasager, efemer; tranzitoriu;
ocazional || s pasager m în tranzit.

transistor s tranzistor m.

transit s tranzit n; transport n; trecere f, traversare f;
parcurs n, drum n.

transition s tranziție f; trecere f; (*evolution*) evoluție f;
(*change*) schimbare f.

transitive adj *gram* tranzitiv.

transitory adj tranzitoriu; efemer; ocazional.

translate vt a traduce; a interpreta; a relua || vi a traduce;
a se explica.

translation s traducere f interpretare f; reluare f;
explicare f.

translator s traducător m.

translucent adj translucid.

transmission s transmitere f; transmisie f.

transmit vt (*convey*) a transmite; (*broadcast*) a transmite, a emite, a difuza.

transmute vt (*change*) a transforma, a schimba.

transom s traversă f, tronson n; oberliht n.

transparency s *also fig* transparență f; (*slide*) diapozitiv
n.

transparent adj transparent; clar; sincer; inefabil;
diafan.

transpire vi a transpira; (*come out*) a se afla, a deveni
de notorietate publică.

transplant vt *med* a grefa, a transplanta; *bot* a răsădi, a
planta || s *med* grefă f, transplant n.

transport s transport n || vt a transporta; *fig* a entuziasma
• ~ation s transport n; mijloc n de transport; bilet n
de călătorie.

transpose vt a transpune; *mus* a transcrie; a transpune.

transverse adj transversal.

trap s capcană f; trapă f; brișcă f || vt a prinde în cursă.

trapeze s (*in circus*) trapez n; ~ **artist** trapezist m.

trapezium s *geom* figură f trapezoidală.

trapezoid s *geom* trapez n; *anat* trapezoid m.

trash s (*garbage*) gunoi n; rebut n; moft n; ratat m;
(*nonsense*) fleac n || vt (*ruin*) a strica, a distruge;
~can s ladă f de gunoi.

trauma s *med* traumă f, traumatism n • ~tic adj traumatic • ~ize vt a traumatiza.

travel vi a călători; a umbla; a se deplasa || vt a străbate
|| s călătorie f; ~ **agency** s agenție f de voiaj; ~ **agent**
s agent m de voiaj • ~ing s călătorie f; deplasare f ||
adj ambulant; nomad; (*crane*) mobil • ~er s călător
m; pasager m; *com* comis voiajor m; ~er's **check** s
cec de voiaj/călătorie.

traverse vt *frml* a străbate || s (*beam*) traversă f.

travesty s travestire f; *thea* travesti n; *fig* parodie f,
caricatură f.

trawl s (*net*) năvod; (*search*) cercetare f, examinare f ||
vi (**for**) a umbla (după) • ~er s *naut* trauler n; dragă
f.

tray s tavă f; scoc n; baie f; compartiment n.

treacherous adj trădător; perfid; fals; nesigur.

treachery s trădare f.

tread s (*tire*) bandă f de rulare; (*shoe*) talpă f; (*walk*)
pas m; (*sound*) zgomot n de pași || vt (*trample*) a
călca (în picioare) || vi (*walk*) a călca, a păși, a merge.

treadle s pedală f.

treason s trădare f de țară; perfidie f.

treasure s comoară f || vt (*object*) a păstra cu grijă, a
păstra ca pe o comoară; (*memory*) a păstra o amintire
frumoasă • ~r s trezorier m.

treasury s trezorerie f; **the Treasury** Ministerul n de
Finanțe; ~ **bill** s *econ* bon n de tezaur; ~ **bond** s
titlu/certificat n de tezaur.

treat vt a trata; a oferi; a îngriji; a dezbate || vi a negocia;
a face cinste || s plăcere f; tratație f.

treatise s (**on**) tratat n (de, despre).

treatment s (*action*) tratament n; tratare f; (*cure*)
tratament n, cură f, îngrijire f.

treaty s tratat n; înțelegere f; convenție f.

treble s număr n triplu; *mus* falset n || adj triplu, întreit;
mus ascuțit, înalt || vt a tripla.

tree s *bot* copac m; arbore m genealogic; (*for shoes*)
calapod n || vt a încolți.

trefoil s *bot* trifoi m.

trek vi (*hike*) a călători || s (*walk*) plimbare f; mutare f
dintr-un loc în altul.

trellis s spalier n; (grătar de) zăbrele f *pl* || vt a acoperi
cu împletitură de nuiele/zăbrele.

tremble vi a tremura; a-i fi teamă; a trepida || s tremur
n; vibrație f.

tremendous *adj* groaznic; uimitor; fantastic.
tremor *s* tremur *n*; vibraţie *f*; trepidaţie *f* ‖ *vi* (*voice*) a tremura; a vibra.
tremulous *adj* (*with fear*) tremurător, tremurând; (*with excitement*) fremătător, vibrant; timid, temător.
trench *s* tranşee *n pl*; şanţ *n*, canal *n*.
trenchant *adj* (*acerbic*) tranşant; (*sharp*) tăios.
trend *s* direcţie *f*; tendinţă *f* ‖ *vi* a tinde către.
trepidation *s* (*alarm*) nelinişte; (*excitement*) înfrigurare *f*.
trespass *vi* a încălca legea; a viola o proprietate ‖ *s* delict *n*; abuz *n*; păcat *n*; violare *f*.
tress *s* (*of hair*) cosiţă *f*; *pl* plete *f pl*, cosiţe *f pl*.
trestle *s constr* capră *f*, suport *n*, postament *n*; piedestal *n*.
triage *s med* triere *f* (a bolnavilor).
trial *s* (*test*) probă *f*; necaz *n*; experienţă *f*; (*pain*) durere *f*; concurs *n*; *jur* proces *n*; (*ordeal*) chin *n*.
triangle *s geom, mus* triunghi *n*.
tribal *adj* tribal.
tribe *s* trib *n*; neam *n*.
tribulation *s* (*affliction*) nenorocire *f*, neajuns *n*; (*ordeal*) calvar *n*.
tribunal *s* tribunal *n*, curte *f* de justiţie, judecătorie *f*.
tribune *s hist* tribun *m*; (*platform*) tribună *f*.
tributary *s* tributar *m*; *geog* afluent *m* ‖ *adj* tributar, care plăteşte tribut.
tribute *s* tribut *n*, bir *n*; *fig* tribut *n*, prinos *n*, omagiu *n*.
trick *s* (*hoax*) farsă *f*; festă *f*; (*ruse*) şiretlic, vicleşug *n*; (*stunt*) şmecherie *f*; chichiţă *f*; secret *n*; (*habit*) manie *f*; (*ploy*) subterfugiu *n* ‖ *adj* (*fake*) trucat ‖ *vt* (*deceive*) a păcăli ‖ *vi* a juca feste • **~ery** *s* viclenie *f*, şmecherie *f*.
trickle *vi* a se prelinge; a se infiltra; a pătrunde ‖ *vt* a picura ‖ *s* şiroi *n*; dâră *f*; prelingere *f*.
tricky *adj* viclean; abil; complicat.
tricolor *s* (*drapel*) tricolor *n*.
tricycle *s* triciclu *n*, tricicletă *f*.
trifle *s* fleac *n*; moft *n*; prostie *f*; amuzament *n*; mic dar *n* ‖ *vi* a glumi; a-şi bate joc.
trifling *adj* minor, neimportant, neînsemnat.
trigger *s* trăgaci *n*; asasin *m* ‖ *vt* a declanşa; a activa.
trigonometry *s* trigonometrie *f*.
trilby *s* (*hat*) pălărie *f* moale.
trill *s* tril *n*; tremur *n* (al vocii).
trilogy *s* trilogie *f*.
trim *adj* îngrijit; cochet ‖ *vt* a aranja; a potrivi; a curăţi; a netezi; a garnisi ‖ *s* ordine *f*; pregătire *f*; tunsoare *f*.
trimester *s* trimestru *n*.
trinity *s* trinitate *f*.
trinket *s* breloc *n*; ornament *n*, bijuterie *f* falsă; bibelou *n* (fără valoare).
trio *s mus* trio *n*; terţet *n*.
trip *s* excursie *f*; drum *n*; pas *m* greşit; piedică *f* ‖ *vi* a se poticni; a greşi ‖ *vt* a pune piedică.
tripe *s cul* burtă *f*; *coll* prostii *f pl*, fleacuri *n pl*; maculatură *f*.
triple *adj* triplu ‖ *vi* a se tripla ‖ *vt* a tripla; **~ jump** *s sp* triplu salt *n*.
triplet *s* trigemeni *m pl*; *mus* terţet *n*.
tripod *s* trepied *n*.
triptych *s* triptic *n*.
trite *adj* (*commonplace*) banal, comun, plat; (*cliched*) uzat, banalizat, răsuflat.
triumph *s* triumf *n*; succes *n* ‖ *vi* a triumfa.

trivia *s pl* (*trifles*) nimicuri *n pl*, fleacuri *n pl*; (*details*) detalii *n pl*, mărunţişuri *n pl*.
trivial *adj* (*slight*) neînsemnat; (*petty*) minor.
trod *vi* * tread.
troglodyte *s also fig* troglodit *m*.
troll *s myth* spiriduş *m* ‖ *vi* (*fish*) a pescui din barcă.
trolley *s elec* troleu *n*; cărucior *n* vagonet; drezină *f*.
trollop *s pej* (*slut*) femeie *f* îngălată; (*whore*) curvă *f*.
trombone *s mus* trombon *n*.
troop *s* trupă *f*; grup *n*; bandă *f*; turmă *f* ‖ *vi* a mărşălui; a se aduna.
trooper *s* (*soldier*) soldat *m* (de cavalerie); poliţist *m* (călare); **state** *~* s jandarm *m*.
trope *s* trop *m*, figură *f* de stil.
trophy *s* trofeu *n*.
tropic *s* tropic *n* ‖ *adj* tropical.
trot *s* trap *n* ‖ *vi* a tropăi, a merge la trap.
trotter *s cul* picior *m* de porc; (*horse*) trăpaş *m*.
trouble *s* necaz *n*; nenorocire *f*; încurcătură *f*; durere *f*; boală *f*; deranj *n*; pană *f* ‖ *vt* a deranja; a incomoda; a supăra; a chinui ‖ *vi* a se deranja • **~maker** *s* producător *m* de tulburări/necazuri • **~shooter** *s* expert *m*, specialist *m*; depanator *m* • **~some** *adj* (*work*) greu, obositor; (*cold*) pătrunzător; (*back, knee*) care doare.
trough *s* (*drainage*) canal *n*; (*animal*) adăpătoare *f*; (*feed*) troacă *f*; *geol* sinclinal *n*.
trounce *vt* (*defeat*) a bate, a nimici.
troupe *s thea* trupă *f*.
trousers *s pl* pantaloni *m pl*.
trout *s icht* păstrăv *m*.
trowel *s* (*for a garden*) plantator *n*; (*for concrete*) mistrie *f*.
truant *s* chiulangiu *m*.
truce *s* armistiţiu *n*; *fig* sfârşit *n*.
truck *s* troc *n*; schimb *n*; fleacuri *n pl* ‖ *vi* a face troc; a cultiva legume ‖ *vt* a face schimb de.
truculent *adj* clonţos; arţăgos; (*hostile*) agresiv.
trudge *vi* (*plod*) a merge greu, a-şi târî picioarele ‖ *s* drum *n* lung/obositor.
true *adj* adevărat; sincer; fidel; exact; original; legal; corect ‖ *adv* adevărat; exact ‖ *interj* aşa e!, adevărat!.
truffle *s bot* trufă *f*; (*candy*) trufă *f*.
truly *adv* cu adevărat, într-adevăr.
trump *s* (*card*) atu *n*.
trumpet *s* trompetă *f*; megafon *n*; porta-voce *f* ‖ *vt* a trâmbiţa ‖ *vi* a suna din trompetă.
truncate *vt* (*shorten*) a (pre)scurta; a reduce; (*abbreviate*) a abrevia; *fig* a trunchia, a deforma; (*text, etc*) a masacra.
truncheon *s* (*club*) baston *n* de poliţist; (*stick*) bâtă *f*.
trundle *vi* (*traipse*) a merge încet cu pas greu ‖ *vt* (*push*) a împinge cu dificultate.
trunk *s* trunchi *m*; butuc *m*; bust *n*; *pl* pantaloni *m pl* scurţi; chiloţi *m pl*; cufăr *n*; trompă *f*; portbagaj *n*.
truss *s med* bandaj *n* suspensor; *constr* grindă *f* ‖ *vt* (*bind*) a lega strâns.
trust *s* încredere *f*; datorie *f*; credit *n*; trust *n*; tutelă *f* ‖ *vt* a încredinţa; a acorda încredere; a spera; a se bizui pe ‖ *vi* a se încrede în; *~* **company** *s* societate *f* fiduciară • **~ful** *adj* încrezător, credul • **~worthy** *adj* de încredere; onest.
trustee *s* tutore *m*, fideicomis *m*; **~ship** *s* tutelă *f*, administrare *f*

trusty *adj obs* de încredere, loial ‖ *s* (*prisoner*) deținut *m* care se bucură de un regim favorizat.

truth *s* adevăr *n*; fidelitate *f*; realitate *f*.

try *vt* (*attempt*) a încerca; (*test*) a verifica; a corija; a deprima; a necăji; (*judge*) a judeca; a decide; a examina; a obosi; a se strădui ‖ *vi* a încerca; a se strădui ‖ *s* (*effort*) încercare *f*; probă *f*.

tryst *s* rendez-vous *n*.

tsar *s* țar *m*.

tsetse fly *s ento* musca *f* țețe.

T-shirt *s* T-shirt *n*, tricou *n*.

T-square *s* teu *n*.

tub *s* cadă *f*; baie *f*; putină *f*; butoi *n* ‖ *vt* a spăla; a îmbăia ‖ *vi* a face baie.

tuba *s mus* tuba *f*.

tubby *adj* (*plump*) dolofan; bondoc.

tube *s* tub *n*; conductă *f*; canal *n*; cameră *f* (auto) ‖ *vt* a drena ‖ *vi* a merge cu metroul.

tuber *s bot* tubercul *m*; rizom *n*.

tuberculosis *s med* tuberculoză *f*.

tuck *s* (*fold*) cută *f*, pliu *n*; pensă *f*; *med* (tip de) operație *f* estetică ‖ *vt* a plisa; a îndoi; (*shorten*) a scurta; (*put*) a băga, a vârî.

Tuesday *s* marți *f*.

tuft *s* smoc *n*; moț *n* • ~**ed** *adj* moțat.

tug *s* smucitură *f*, zvâcnitură *f*; (*ship*) remorcher *n* ‖ *vi* (*pull*) a trage; *naut* a remorca.

tuition *s* (*instruction*) curs *n*, instrucție *f*; ~ **fee** *s* taxă *f* de școlarizare.

tulip *s bot* lalea *f*.

tulle *s* tul *n*.

tumble *s* tumbă *f*; salt *n* mortal; cădere *f* ‖ *vi* a face o tumbă; a cădea ‖ *vt* a trânti; a rostogoli; a răvăși.

tumbler *s* (*glass*) pahar (fără picior); acrobat *m*.

tumescent *adj* tumefiat, umflat.

tummy *s coll* burtă *f*.

tumor *s med* tumoare *f*.

tumult *s* tumult n, vacarm *n*; *fig* neliniște *f* (sufletească), agitație sufletească.

tuna *s icht* ton *n*.

tune *s mus* melodie *f*, arie *f*, cântec *n*; dispoziție *f* ‖ *vt* a acorda; *radio, tv* a regla; ~ **in** *vi radio, tv* a asculta.

tunic *s mil* tunică *f*; *bio, anat* membrană *f*, înveliș *n*.

tunnel *s* tunel *n*; pasaj *n*; galerie *f* ‖ *vt/vi* a săpa un tunel prin.

tunny *s icht* ton *n*.

turban *s* turban *n*.

turbid *adj* tulbure.

turbine *s* turbină *f*.

turbojet *s* turboreactor *n*.

turbot *s icht* calcan *m*.

turbulence *s* turbulență *f* atmosferică; (*unrest*) tulburări *f pl* sociale, dezordini *f pl* stradale.

turbulent *adj* agitat; turbulent; impetuos; violent; zgomotos.

turd *s sl* excrement *n*.

tureen *s* supieră *f*; sosieră *f*; terină *f*.

turf *s* gazon *n*; turf *n*; *sp* curse *f pl* de cai; brazdă *f* de iarbă; *coll* (domeniu de) specialitate *f* ‖ *vt* a acoperi cu brazde de iarbă.

turgid *adj* (*style*) pompos; încâlcit; *med* tumefiat.

turkey *s orn* curcan *m*; curcă *f*; carne *f* de curcan; *sl* eșec *n*, fiasco *n*.

Turkey *s* Turcia.

turmeric *s bot* șofran *n* de India.

turmoil *s* dezordine *f*, harababură *f* ‖ *vt* a deranja; a hărțui ‖ *vi* a fi îngrijorat/tulburat/neliniștit, a se agita.

turn *vt* a întoarce; a învârti; (*twist*) a răsuci; (*curve*) a abate; a răsturna; a ocoli; (*change*) a preface; a acri; *tech* a fasona; *fig* a cizela; (*age*) a împlini, a atinge ‖ *vi* a se răsuci; a se îndrepta; (*wind, etc*) a se schimba; (*become*) a deveni; a se acri ‖ *s* (*twist*) învârtire *f*; (*rotation*) rotire *f*; tur *n*; (*change*) schimbare *f*; tură *f*; (*errand*) serviciu *n*; folos *n*; șoc *n*; (*show*) număr *n*; *med* (*fit*) criză *f*, atac *n*; ~ **away** *vt* a refuza ‖ *vi* a se da la o parte, a renunța; ~ **down** *vt* a refuza, a respinge; (*sound, etc*) a micșora, a da mai încet; ~ **off** *vt* (~ *the road*) a părăsi; (~ *an engine*) a stinge; (~ *a radio, etc*) a închide ‖ *vi* (~ *the road*) a coti; ~ **on** *vt* (~ *an engine, etc*) a aprinde; (~ *a radio, etc*) a deschide; *coll* (*arouse sexually*) a excita ‖ *vi* a se învârti în jurul; a ataca; a depinde de; a se agăța de; ~ **out** *vt* (~ *the light, etc*) a stinge; (~ *a pocket, etc*) a goli, a întoarce pe dos; ~ **out to be** a se adeveri, a se dovedi ‖ *vi* a termina; ~ **up** *vt* (~ *the radio, etc*) a da mai tare; (~ *the gas*) a mări presiunea ‖ *vi* (*person*) a se propti; (*person, object*) a fi regăsit; (*opportunity*) a se prezenta.

turning *s* cotitură *f*, serpentină *f*; răscruce *f*, răspântie *f*; rotație *f*; *astron* (mișcare de) revoluție *f*.

turnip *s bot* nap *m*; rapiță *f* sălbatică.

turnover *s* răsturnare *f*, întoarcere *f*; *tech* culbutare *f*; *econ* cifră *f* de afaceri; randament *n*; *econ* fluctuație *f* a mâinii de lucru.

turnpike *s* autostradă *f* cu taxă; *mil* capră *f* de sârmă ghimpată.

turnstile *s* cruce *f* de barieră.

turpentine *s bot* terebint *m*.

turpitude *s* turpitudine *f*; josnicie *f*, ticăloșie *f*.

turquoise *s* (*stone*) peruzea *f*, turcoaz *n*; (*color*) turcoaz *n* ‖ *adj* turcoaz.

turret *s constr* foișor *n*, turnuleț *n*; *mil* turelă *f*; *tech* cap *n* revolver.

turtle *s zool* (broască) țestoasă *f* de mare.

turtledove *s orn* turturică *f*, turturea *f*;.

tusk *s* (*boar*) colț *n*; (*elephant*) fildeș *n*, colț *n* ‖ *vt* a răni cu colțul.

tussle *s* încăierare *f*, bătaie *f*, luptă *f* ‖ *vi* a se încăiera, a se bate, a se lupta.

tussock *s bot* iarbă *f* înaltă.

tutelage *s frml* tutelă *f*.

tutor *s* profesor *m* (particular); preceptor *m*, meditator *m*, repetitor *m*; *scol* asistent *m*; profesor *m* suplinitor; *jur* tutore *m* ‖ *vt* a instrui, a medita, a învăța, a pregăti.

tuxedo *s* smoching *n*.

twang *s* vorbit *n* pe nas; zdrăngănit *n* ‖ *vt* a zdrăngăni la (chitară etc) ‖ *vi* a scârțâi.

tweak *vt* a trage (de urechi); a aranja, a îndrepta; a regla.

tweed *s text* tuid *n*, tweed *n*.

tweet *s* piuit *n*.

tweeter *s* difuzor *n* de sunete înalte.

tweezers *s* pensetă *f*; cleștișor *n*.

twelve *num* doisprezece ‖ *s* duzină *f*.

twenty *num* douăzeci.

twice *adv* de două ori; repetat.

twiddle *vt* a învârti, a răsuci (în mână) ‖ *vi* (**with**) a se juca cu ‖ *s* răsucire *f*.

twig *s* rămurică *f*, crenguță *f*.

twilight *s* amurg *n*, crepuscul *n*; *fig* amurg *n*, asfințit *n*, declin *n* ‖ *adj* crepuscular.

twin *s* geamăn(ă) *m*, *f*; tiz *n*; pereche *f* ‖ *adj* geamăn; omonim; pereche ‖ *vi* a naște gemeni; a fi pereche (cu) ‖ *vt* a îngemăna.

twine *s* sfoară *f*; șnur *n*; *text* tort *n*; împletitură *f* ‖ *vt* a împleti, a răsuci; a înfășura.

twinge *s* (*pain*) durere *f* bruscă; junghi *n*; (*pang*) spasm *n*; tresărire *f* ‖ *vt also fig* a chinui, a face să doară; (*of conscience*) a mustra, a chinui, a tortura.

twinkle *vi* (*star*, *etc*) a sclipi; a licări; a scăpăra, a scânteia; (*eye*) a clipi ‖ *vt* a aprinde; a face să scânteieze; a clipi din ochi ‖ *s* licărire *f*, (*sparkle*) scânteiere *f*, scăpărare *f*; licăr *n*; clipire *f*, clipit *n*.

twinkling *s* clipită *f*.

twirl *vt* a învârti, a roti repede ‖ *vi* a se învârti, a se roti (repede) ‖ *s* învârtire *f*, rotire *f* (rapidă); vârtej *n*; (*hair*) cârlionț *m*.

twist *s* rotire *f*; twist *n*; cotitură *f*; funie *f*; cornet *n*; amăgire *f*; specific *n* ‖ *vt* a răsuci; a deforma; a stoarce; a păcăli ‖ *vi* a se învârti.

twit *s sl* dojană *f*, mustrare *f*; reproș *n*; zeflemea *f*, batjocură *f*; împunsătură *f*.

twitch *s* spasm *n*; convulsie *f*; tic *n* nervos; smulgere *f*; tragere *f* ‖ *vt* a smulge; a trage; a târî ‖ *vi* a se contracta, a avea o convulsie/un spasm/o contracție.

twitter *vi* a fi agitat/nervos; a frematâ, a trepida (de emoție) ‖ *s* vorbărie *f*, flecăreală *f*, trăncăneală *f*.

twixt *prep obs* între.

two *num* doi/două; doilea ‖ *s* (grup *n* de) doi/două.

tycoon *s* mare industriaș *m*, magnat *m*.

tyke *s coll* javră *f*; țânc *m*, pici *m*.

type *s* tip *n*; clasă *f*; model *n*; gen *n* ‖ *vi* a tipiza • **~setter** *s* zețar *m* • **~writer** *s* mașină *f* de scris.

typhoid *s med* febră *f* tifoidă, tifos *n*.

typhoon *s met* taifun *n*, uragan *n*.

typical *adj* tipic • **~ly** *adv* în mod obișnuit; în mod normal.

typify *vt* a caracteriza; a exemplifica.

typing *s* dactilografiere *f* ‖ *adj* de dactilografie.

typist *s* dactilograf *m*; dactilografă *f*.

typo *s coll* greșeală *f* de ortografie.

typography *s* tipografie *f*.

typology *s* tipologie *f*.

tyrannical *adj* tiranic, despotic.

tyrannize *vt* a tiraniza.

tyranny *s* tiranie *f*.

tyrant *s* tiran *m*.

tyro *s* novice *m*, începător *m*.

tzar *s* țar *m*.

U

U, u *s* (*letter*) U, u.

ubiquitous *adj* omniprezent, nelipsit; obișnuit; frecvent.

ubiquity *s* omniprezență *f*.

udder *s* uger *n*.

ugly *adj* (*unattractive*) urât; (*unpleasant*) neplăcut; (*hostile*) amenințător; (*hideous*) hidos.

ulcer *s med* ulcerație *f*; ulcer *n*; *fig* corupție *f*.

ulterior *adj* ulterior, de mai târziu; (*hidden*) ascuns, tainic, abscons.

ultimate *adj* (*final*) ultim; decisiv; esențial.

ultimatum *s* (*pl* **ultimata**) ultimatum *n*.

ultrasound *s phys* ultrasunet *n*.

ultraviolet *adj* ultraviolet.

ululate *vi frml* (*owl*) a țipa; (*wolf*) a urla.

umber *s* (culoarea) maro închis *f*.

umbilical *adj* ombilical; central.

umbrage *s* umbră *f*; frunziș *n*; umbrar *n*; (*offense*) supărare *f*; resentiment *n*.

umbrella *s* umbrelă *f*.

umpire *s sp* arbitru *m* ‖ *vt* a arbitra.

umpteen *adj* mulți, numeroși; mult, enorm, colosal (de mulți); **~ times** de nenumărate ori.

unabashed *adj* (*undeterred*) liniștit, imperturbabil; (*unashamed*) arogant; mândru, țanțoș.

unabated *adj* neabătut; nepotolit; neclintit.

unable *adj* incapabil.

unabridged *adj* neprescurtat; întreg; neciuntit.

unacceptable *adj* inacceptabil, de neacceptat; intolerabil.

unaccompanied *adj* (*child*) neînsoțit; (*luggage*) nesupravegheat; (*song*) fără acompaniament.

unaccountably *adv* inexplicabil.

unaccustomed *adj* neobișnuit.

unachievable *adj* irealizabil, imposibil.

unadulterated *adj* (*wine*) bun, care nu s-a acrit; (*food*) natural; (*joy*, *etc*) sincer, curat; (*truth*) pur și simplu.

unaffected *adj* neinfluențat, neafectat; sincer, natural.

unaffiliated *adj* neafiliat; independent; neînregimentat politic.

unafraid *adj* liniștit, calm.

unaided *adj* fără ajutorul nimănui, neajutat de nimeni; neajutorat.

unalterable *adj* (*fact*) imuabil; (*decision*) irevocabil; (*truth*) sigur, imuabil.

unaltered *adj* neschimbat.

unambiguous *adj* (*rule*) precis, (*thinking*) clar.

unanimous *adj* unanim • **~ly** *adv* în unanimitate.

unannounced *adj* neinvitat; (*unexpected*) neprevăzut, neașteptat.

unanswerable *adj* (*impossible question*) fără răspuns; (*irrefutable*) incontestabil.

unanticipated *adj* neprevăzut, neașteptat.

unappealing *adj* neplăcut; neatractiv.

unapproachable *adj* (*person*) inaccesibil; distant, rezervat; (*place*) inaccesibil.

unarguable *adj* de necontestat.

unarmed *adj* neînarmat; **~ combat** *s* luptă *f* fără arme.

unashamed *adj* (*brazen*) nerușinat, neobrăzat; (*blatant*) insolent.

unassailable *adj* intangibil; nezdruncinat.

unassuming *adj* modest, fără pretenții.

unattached *adj* (**to**) independent (de); (*free*) liber.

unattainable *adj* (*goal*, *place*) inaccesibil.

unattended *adj* (*luggage*, *etc*) nesupravegheat; (*child*) singur.

unattractive *adj* (*ugly*) neatractiv; (*nasty*) neplăcut.

unauthorized *adj* neautorizat.

unavailable *adj* (*person*) indisponibil; ocupat; (*resources*) ocupat; epuizat.

unavoidable *adj* inevitabil.

unaware *adj* surprins, mirat, uimit; neatent; ignorant, inconștient • **~s** *adv* (*by surprise*) prin surprindere; pe neașteptate; (*by accident*) pe nesimțite; (*unknowingly*) fără voie, inconștient.

unbalanced *adj* (*disturbed*) dezechilibrat; (*biased*) tendențios, părtinitor.

unbearable *adj* insuportabil, de nesuportat.

unbeatable *adj* imbatabil, invincibil.

unbeaten *adj* (*team*) neînvins; (*track*) nebătut.

unbecoming *adj* nepotrivit, neadecvat.

unbeknownst *adj* necunoscut; obscur, neştiut; ~ **to** fără ştirea.

unbelievable *adj* de necrezut, incredibil; (*implausible*) nemaipomenit.

unbelieving *adj* neîncrezător.

unbending *adj* (*will*) neînduplecat; (*metal*) inflexibil.

unbiased *adj* imparţial; nepărtinitor.

unbidden *adj* lit nepoftit, neinvitat.

unblemished *adj* nepătat, ireproşabil.

unblinking *adj* (*impassive*) impasibil; (*fearless*) fără frică/teamă, imperturbabil.

unborn *adj* nenăscut.

unbounded *adj* also fig nemăsurat.

unbreakable *adj* incasabil.

unbridgeable *adj* de nedepăşit/nesurmontat.

unbridled *adj* neînfrânat, nestrunit.

unbroken *adj* (*continuous*) continuu, neîntrerupt; intact, neatins; (*promise*) respectat; (*horse*) nedomesticit; (*record*) neegalat.

unbuckle *vt* (~ *a belt, shoe*) a desface.

unburden *vt lit, frml* a despovăra; ~ **oneself** *vt* a se destăinui.

unbutton *vt* a descheia.

uncalled-for *adj* (*remark*) deplasat; (*criticism*) nejustificat.

uncanny *adj* straniu; ciudat; supranatural.

uncaring *adj* nepăsător.

unceasing *adj* continuu; asiduu.

unceremonious *adj* fără fasoane; (*abrupt*) suspect.

uncertain *adj* (*unsure*) nesigur, îndoielnic; dubios; (*hesitant*) ezitant; capricios, schimbător • ~ty *s* nesiguranţă *f*, incertitudine *f*; (*doubt*) echivoc *n*; (*insecurity*) vicisitudine *f*.

unchallengeable *adj* (*undeniable*) indubitabil; *jur* irecuzabil; (*power*) discreţionar.

unchallenged *adj* necontestat; cu puteri discreţionare; nestânjenit.

unchangeable *adj* imuabil.

unchanging *adj* imuabil; invariabil; etern.

uncharitable *adj* (*unkind*) nemilos; nedrept.

uncharted *adj* (*region*) necunoscut; (*situation*) nesigur.

unchecked *adj* (*unrestricted*) necontrolat, nestăpânit; fără oprire/încetare.

uncivil *adj* nepoliticos.

unclaimed *adj* nerevendicat.

unclassified *adj* (*information*) neclasificat, făcut public.

uncle *s* unchi *m*.

unclean *adj* (*dirty*) murdar; *fig* imund; *relig* necurat, spurcat.

unclear *adj* (*message, etc*) neclar; (*uncertain*) incert.

uncomfortable *adj* (*chair, etc*) inconfortabil; *fig* (*facts, etc*) dezagreabil; (*person*) jenat, care nu se simte în largul său.

uncommitted *adj* (*person*) nedecis; (*literature*) neangajat.

uncommon *adj* rar; neobişnuit; extraordinar.

uncompromising *adj* intransigent, ferm.

unconditional *adj* necondiţionat, fără condiţii.

uncongenial *adj* antipatic; neplăcut.

unconnected *adj* (**with**) fără legătură (cu).

unconscious *adj* med fără cunoştinţă; (*unaware*) inconştient; (*reflex*) involuntar, neintenţionat || *s* psych subconştient *n*.

unconstitutional *adj* neconstituţional.

uncontroversial *adj* necontroversat.

unconventional *adj* neconvenţional, original.

unconvinced *adj* sceptic, plin de îndoieli.

uncooked *adj* nefript; nefiert; nefăcut; necopt, crud.

uncork *vt* (~ *a bottle*) a scoate (dopul).

uncouple *vt* (~ *a carriage*) a decupla.

uncouth *adj* necivilizat; needucat; grosolan, vulgar.

uncover *vt* a descoperi; a dezvălui || *vi* a se descoperi.

unctuous *adj* (*sycophantic*) onctuos, mieros; linguşitor.

uncut *adj* (*hair, etc*) netăiat, întreg; (*uncensored*) necenzurat.

undamaged *adj* neavariat; *fig* nepătat, intact.

undaunted *adj* neabătut, ferm.

undecided *adj* (*person*) indecis, nehotărât; (*problem*) nerezolvat (încă).

undefeated *adj* neînvins.

undefined *adj* nedefinit; nedeterminat.

undemonstrative *adj* rezervat, rece.

undeniable *adj* incontestabil, (de) netăgăduit; irefutabil.

under *prep* sub; într-o, în || *adv* jos, dedesubt || *adj* inferior; pe lângă; subordonat.

underage *adj* minor, care n-a ajuns la majorat; *fig* necopt, imatur.

underbid *vi* a sublicita.

undercarriage *s* avia tren *n* de aterizare.

undercharge *vt* a taxa mai puţin.

underclothes *s pl* lenjerie *f*.

undercoat *s* (*paint*) fundal *n*, strat *n* de fond.

undercover *adj* secret.

undercurrent *s fig* (*tinge*) curent *n* subteran.

undercut *vt* a tăia pe dedesubt; (*cards*) a sublicita; *com* a vinde mai ieftin/sub preţ; *econ* a sublicita.

underdeveloped *adj* subdezvoltat; nedezvoltat.

underdog *s* inferior *m*, subaltern *m*; supus, persoană *f* umilă.

underdone *adj* (*food*) incomplet gătit; (*meat*) în sânge.

underemployed *adj* insuficient utilizat.

underestimate *vt* a subaprecia, a subestima.

underfoot *adv* sub/în picioare.

undergo *vt* (*experience*) a trece prin; (*endure*) a suferi, a suporta; a încerca, a îndura; (~ *an operation, etc*) a i se face, a suferi.

undergraduate *s* student *m*.

underground *adj* subteran; clandestin || *s* metro *n*; subteran *n*; ilegalitate *f*.

undergrowth *s* subarboret *n*; vegetaţie *f* care creşte pe lângă arbori.

underhand *adj* ascuns; clandestin; viclean; necinstit || *adv* în secret/taină; pe ascuns; pe furiş.

underlie *vt* a fi/sta la baza; *fig* (*inspire*) a fundamenta, a susţine, a întemeia.

underline *vt* a sublinia; a reliefa.

undermine *vt* a submina; a slăbi.

underneath *prep* sub, dedesubt; (*move*) în || *adv* sub; *fig* la bază || *adj* dedesubt.

underpaid *adj* prost plătit/remunerat; sub tarif.

underpants *s pl* chiloţi *m pl*; izmene *f pl*.

underpass *s* pasaj *n* subteran.

underprivileged *adj* sărac; persecutat; defavorizat.

underrate *vt* a subestima, a subaprecia.

undershirt *s* maiou *n*, flanelă *f* de corp.

underside *s* partea *f* de dedesubt.

underskirt *s* jupon *n*.

understaffed *adj* cu personal redus/insuficient.

understand, understood, understood *vt* (*grasp*) a
înțelege; (*comprehend*) a deduce; a se înțelege cu; a
subînțelege ‖ *vi* a înțelege • **~ing** *s* (*grasp*) înțelegere
f, pricepere *f*; acord *n*; (*tolerance*) îngăduință *f*;
(*interpretation*) interpretare *f* ‖ *adj* înțelegător,
îngăduitor.

understate *vt* (~ *the truth, etc*) a spune numai pe
jumătate; (*play down*) a diminua, a micșora, a reduce
(din importanță) • **~ment** *s* adevăr *n* spus doar pe
jumătate.

understudy *s thea* dublură *f*.

undertake *vt* a întreprinde, a iniția; a asuma; ~ **to do**
smth *vt* a se angaja să facă ceva.

undertone *s* voce *f* joasă; vorbă/vorbire *f* pe șoptite; *fig*
(*suggestion*) nuanță *f*.

underwater *adj* submarin, subacvatic ‖ *adv* sub apă.

underwear *s* lenjerie *f* intimă; indispensabili *m pl*.

underweight *adj* cu greutate redusă, sub greutatea
normală.

underworld *s* lumea *f* cealaltă; iad *n*, infern *n*; (*gang-
land*) lumea *f* interlopă.

underwrite *vt* a garanta, a gira • **~r** *s econ* girant *m*;
garant *m*; prețuitor *m*; (*title*) emitent *m*.

undeserved *adj* nemeritat.

undesirable *adj* indezirabil ‖ *s* persoană *f* indezirabilă;
intrus *m*.

undetected *adj* neobservat.

undisciplined *adj* nedisciplinat.

undisguised *adj* nedisimulat.

undisputed *adj* necontestat.

undo, undid, undone *vt* (*unfasten*) a desface; a distruge;
a corupe; a strica; (*untie*) a dezlega • **~ing** *s* ruină *f*,
pierdere *f* • **~ne** *adj* (*untied*) desfăcut, dezlegat;
(*work*) neîndeplinit.

undoubted *adj* indubitabil, cert, fără dubii.

undreamed-of *adj* nevisat, nesperat.

undress *vt* a dezbrăca ‖ *vi* a se dezbrăca ‖ *s* neglijeu *n*;
ținută *f* de casă.

undue *adj* necuvenit; nemeritat; nepotrivit, inoportun;
exagerat, excesiv.

undulate *vi* a se undui, a face valuri.

unduly *adv* în mod nedrept/nejustificat/nejust.

unearth *vt* (*dig up*) a dezgropa; (*uncover*) a descoperi •
~ly *adj* (*weird*) straniu; supranatural; (*unreasonable*)
nefiresc; nepotrivit, inoportun.

uneasy *adj* tulburat; jenat; nerăbdător; instabil; speriat
‖ *adv* agitat; incomodat; tulburat; stânjenit.

uneducated *adj* needucat, fără studii; incult, lipsit de
educație.

unemployable *adj* inapt de muncă.

unemployed *adj* (*jobless*) șomer; nefolosit; neangajat.

unemployment *s* șomaj *n*; neutilizare *f*.

unending *adj* nesfârșit; interminabil.

unenthusiastic *adj* lipsit de entuziasm, indiferent,
apatic.

unenviable *adj* de neinvidiat.

unequal *adj* inegal.

unerring *adj* infailibil; exact, precis.

uneven *adj* neregulat; accidentat.

uneventful *adj* calm, tihnit, liniștit; neinteresant.

unexpected *adj* brusc; surprinzător; subit.

unfailing *adj* constant; consecvent; credincios, de
nădejde.

unfair *adj* nedrept; necinstit; nedemn; nesportiv.

unfaithful *adj* necredincios; fals; păgân.

unfamiliar *adj* nefamiliar; straniu; neobișnuit.

unfasten *vt* (*undo*) a desface; (*unlock*) a descuia; (*untie*)
a dezlega.

unfathomable *adj* insondabil; de neelucidat.

unfavorable *adj* nefavorabil.

unfinished *adj* neterminat.

unfit *adj* (**for**) nepotrivit; neadecvat (pentru); (*person*)
inapt ‖ *vt* a face invalid.

unflagging *adj* susținut; inepuizabil.

unflinching *adj* de nezdruncinat.

unfold *vt* (*spread*) a întinde; a desfășura; a dezvolta;
(*reveal*) a dezvălui ‖ *vi* a se desfășura; a se arăta; a se
dezvolta.

unforeseen *adj* neprevăzut; neașteptat.

unforgettable *adj* de neuitat.

unforgivable *adj* de neiertat.

unfortunate *adj* nefericit; nenorocos; supărat ‖ *s*
nenorocit *m*; prostituată *f*.

unfounded *adj* nefondat, neîntemeiat.

unfriendly *adj* ostil; neprietenos; glacial; antipatic;
neospitalier.

unfulfilled *adj* (*person*) frustrat; (*dream*) nerealizat,
neîmplinit; (*promise*) nerespectat.

unfurnished *adj* nemobilat.

ungainly *adj* diform, urât; stângaci, nedibaci; greoi.

ungovernable *adj* (*feelings*) de necontrolat; (*country*)
imposibil de guvernat.

ungrateful *adj* nerecunoscător, ingrat.

unhappy *adj* trist, nefericit; (**with/about**) nemulțumit,
neliniștit; (*incident*) nefericit, regretabil

unharmed *adj* nevătămat.

unhealthy *adj* nesănătos; insalubru.

unheard-of *adj* necunoscut; fără precedent, nemaiauzit,
nou.

unhesitating *adj* (*reply*) prompt; hotărât.

unhurt *adj* teafăr, sănătos.

unhygienic *adj* neigienic.

unicorn *s* unicorn *m* ‖ *adj* unicorn, cu un singur corn.

unidentified *adj* neidentificat.

uniform *adj* omogen; uniform; armonios ‖ *s* uniformă *f*
‖ *vt* a uniformiza.

unify *vt* a uni, a unifica.

unilateral *adj* unilateral.

unimaginative *adj* lipsit de imaginație; îngust la minte,
obtuz.

unimpaired *adj* (*health*) nediminuat, intact.

unimportant *adj* neimportant, fără importanță.

uninhabited *adj* nelocuit.

uninhibited *adj* neinhibat; fără rezerve.

unintelligible *adj* neinteligibil.

unintentional *adj* involuntar, neintenționat.

uninterested *adj* neinteresat.

union *s* unire *f*; uniune *f*; îmbinare *f*; acord *n*; sindicat
n; asociație *f*; mariaj *n* ‖ *adj* sindical • **~ize** *vi* a se
organiza în sindicat.

unique *adj* unic; neobișnuit; straniu.

unisex *adj* unisex, pentru ambele sexe.

unison *s mus* unison *n*, consens *n*.

unit *s* unitate *f*; (*part*) element *n*, parte *f*; (*furniture*)
modul *n*; (*section*) serviciu *n* operativ/funcțional.

unite *vt* a uni; a îmbina; a lega ‖ *vi* a se uni.

unity *s* unitate *f*.

universal *adj* universal.

universe *s* univers *n*; sistem *n*; lume *f*.

university *s* universitate *f* ‖ *adj* universitar.

unjust adj injust.

unkempt adj (clothes, person) neglijent, dezordonat; (hair) nepieptănat.

unkind adj rău, răutăcios; inuman; nedrept, aspru.

unknown adj obscur; necunoscut.

unlawful adj nelegal, ilegal.

unleaded adj (gas, etc) fără plumb.

unlearn vt a dezvăța.

unleash vt (~ a dog) a da drumul din lesă; (~ anger, etc) a dezlănțui.

unless conj dacă nu; în afară de cazul când.

unlike prep spre deosebire de; altfel decât • ~ly adj improbabil; neverosimil.

unlimited adj nelimitat, fără limite.

unload vt a descărca; a debarasa de; a remite || vi a descărca.

unlock vt a descuia.

unlucky adj (person) ghinionist; (choice, etc) nefericit; (number, etc) care aduce ghinion.

unmarried adj necăsătorit, celibatar.

unmask vt a demasca, a deconspira.

unmistakable adj care nu poate fi confundat, clar, evident.

unmoved adj impasibil, indiferent.

unnatural adj nefiresc; inuman; sălbatic.

unnecessary adj inutil, zadarnic; de prisos; exagerat; nedorit.

unnerving adj tulburător.

unnoticed adj neobservat.

unobtainable adj imposibil de obținut.

unobtrusive adj (person) șters; (object) discret; (building) care nu-ți atrage atenția.

unoccupied adj neocupat, liber.

unofficial adj neoficial.

unorthodox adj neortodox.

unpack vt (books) a despacheta; (bag) a desface || vi a despacheta.

unpaid adj neplătit; prost plătit, nerentabil.

unpalatable adj (food) neplăcut la gust; (idea) neplăcut.

unparalleled adj fără precedent.

unpleasant adj neplăcut; grețos; antipatic.

unplug vt elec a scoate din priză.

unpopular adj nepopular.

unprecedented adj fără precedent.

unpredictable adj care nu poate fi prevăzut, imprevizibil.

unprepared adj nepregătit, improvizat.

unprofessional adj neprofesionist; amator.

unprofitable adj nerentabil.

unprotected adj (sex) neprotejat; expus.

unpublished adj nepublicat.

unqualified adj (person) necalificat; (teacher, doctor) nelicențiat; (success) formidabil; (support) necondiționat.

unquestionable adj incontestabil.

unravel vt (untie) a desface; (disentangle) a deșira; (~ thread) a descurca; fig (solve) a clarifica, a soluționa.

unreal adj imaginar; ireal, nereal; nefiresc; fantastic.

unreasonable adj irațional; inexplicabil.

unrecognizable adj de nerecunoscut.

unrecorded adj neconsemnat.

unrelated adj neînrudit; separat; irelevant.

unrelenting adj implacabil, de neoprit.

unreliable adj (car, etc) nefiabil; (person) neserios; nestatornic; nesigur.

unremitting adj perseverent, constant; persistent, insistent.

unrequited adj lit (love) neîmpărtășit.

unrest s neliniște f; agitație f.

unrestrained adj (wild) nemărginit, nelimitat; (anger) necontrolat.

unrivaled adj fără seamăn.

unroll vt/vi a (se) desfășura.

unruffled adj calm, imperturbabil; (hair) întins.

unruly adj nesupus; obraznic; refractar; detracat.

unsafe adj periculos; nesigur.

unsanitary adj nesănătos, insalubru.

unsatisfactory adj nesatisfăcător, care lasă de dorit.

unsavory adj (person) nerecomandabil; (area) rău famat.

unscathed adj nevătămat.

unscrew vt a deșuruba || vi a se deșuruba.

unscripted adj (speech) liber; improvizat.

unscrupulous adj fără scrupule, lipsit de scrupule; ticălos.

unseemly adj lit (improper) deplasat; indecent.

unselfish adj dezinteresat.

unsettle vt (person) a tulbura; (stomach) a deranja.

unsettling adj (disturbing) deconcertant.

unshakable adj (will) ferm, de fier; profund.

unsightly adj urât.

unskilled adj necalificat.

unsolicited adj nedorit.

unsound adj (theory) nefondat; (decision) greșit; (structure) în stare proastă.

unspeakable adj indescriptibil.

unspecified adj nespecificat; neprecizat.

unspoiled adj (person) pur; nerăsfățat; (town) neschimbat, nealterat; (flavor) natural.

unstable adj șubred; instabil; nesigur; inconstant; dezechilibrat.

unsteady adj (hand) tremurând; (weather, etc) instabil; (walk) nesigur, șovăielnic.

unstinting adj generos.

unstoppable adj de neoprit.

unstressed adj ling neaccentuat.

unstuck adj (stamp, etc) dezlipit; fig (plan, etc) care se prăbușește/se năruie.

unsuccessful adj (attempt) în van, fără succes; (meeting) infructuos; (candidate) respins.

unsuitable adj nepotrivit, inadecvat, necorespunzător.

unsure adj nesigur (pe sine); ezitant.

unsurpassed adj fără seamăn.

unswerving adj neclintit, neabătut; ferm.

unsympathetic adj (unfeeling) lipsit de compătimire; nepăsător, indiferent.

untainted adj (water) pur; fig nepătat.

untamed adj (animal) neîmblânzit; sălbatic.

untangle vt a descâlci.

untenable adj (idea) care nu poate fi susținut.

unthinkable adj inimaginabil; de neconceput.

untidy adj neîngrijit; dezordonat.

untie vt (~ a knot, etc) a desface, a deznoda; (~ a prisoner) a dezlega.

until prep până la || conj până (ce).

untimely adj (death) prematur; (arrival) intempestiv; (remark) neinspirat; (moment) prost ales.

untiring adj neobosit.

untouchable adj intangibil.

untoward adj dificil, nedisciplinat; refractar; zurbagiu.

untrue *adj* neadevărat; fals.

untrustworthy *adj* pe care nu te poți bizui.

untruthful *adj* mincinos; neadevărat.

unusual *adj* insolit; nefiresc; excepțional; extraordinar.

unveil *vt* (*uncover*) a etala, a expune; (*reveal*) a dezvălui.

unwanted *adj* (*object*) nefolositor; (*child*) nedorit.

unwarranted *adj* nejustificat; nefondat.

unwelcome *adj* nedorit, inoportun.

unwell *adj* bolnav; indispus.

unwholesome *adj* nesănătos; nociv.

unwieldy *adj* (*person*) greoi; stângaci; (*thing*) greu de mânuit; (*system*) greoi.

unwilling *adj* lipsit de chef/poftă, nedoritor; ostil; refractar.

unwind *vt* (*undo*) a derula; *fig* (*relax*) a se destinde.

unwise *adj* nechibzuit; imprudent.

unwitting *adj* neștiutor, neavizat; nevinovat, inocent, fără nici o vină.

unwonted *adj frml* neobișnuit, neașteptat.

unworthy *adj* (**of**) nedemn (de); rușinos, scandalos; nevrednic, nemernic.

unwrap *vt* a despacheta; a desface.

unyielding *adj* ferm, inflexibil; inebranlabil.

unzip *vt* a trage (un fermoar).

up *adv* (în) sus; vertical; în aer; în picioare; spre/la mine; la suprafață; încolo, departe; vioi; ridicat ‖ *prep* în susul; de-a lungul; contra; spre (mine) ‖ *adj* de/în sus; înalt; treaz; superior; înalt; sfârșit; informat; ridicat.

upbeat *adj* entuziast.

upbringing *s* creștere *f*, educație *f*.

upcoming *adj* care se apropie; care va apărea.

update *vt* a actualiza, a aduce la zi; a moderniza; a pune la curent.

upended *adj* răsturnat.

upfront *adj coll* (*frank*) sincer, cinstit; (*payment*) în avans.

upgrade *s comp* actualizare *f* ‖ *vt* (*improve*) a eficientiza; (*employee*) a promova.

upheaval *s* bulversare *f*; schimbare *f*, răsturnare *f*.

uphill *adj* (*path, etc*) care urcă; *fig* (*task*) greu, dificil.

uphold *vt* (~ *the law*) a menține; (*support*) a susține; a încuraja.

upholstery *s* tapițerie *f*, *auto* capitonaj *n*.

upkeep *s* întreținere *f*.

uplifting *adj* (*inspiring*) înălțător.

upon *prep* pe.

upper *adj* superior; de sus ‖ *s* parte *f* superioară; **the ~ class** *s* înalta societate *f* • **~most** *adj* (*top*) cel mai de sus; (*primary*) primordial; predominant ‖ *adv* deasupra.

upright *adj* drept, vertical; onest; *fig* cinstit, integru ‖ *adv* drept ‖ *s* verticală *f*; perpendiculară *f*.

uprising *s* răscoală *f*.

uproar *s* rumoare *f*; tumult *n*; zarvă *f*.

uproot *vt also fig* a dezrădăcina.

upscale *adj* de lux, select.

upset, upset, upset *vt* (*spill*) a răsturna; (*disturb*) a deranja; (*distress*) a tulbura; a învinge ‖ *vi* a se răsturna ‖ *adj* (*distressed*) tulburat; agitat; neliniștit.

upshot *s* consecință *f*, rezultat *n*.

upside-down *adj* inversat; dezordonat ‖ *adv* în dezordine; invers.

upstage *vt* a eclipsa (pe cineva) ‖ *adv* (*move*) dinspre fundul scenei.

upstairs *adv* la etaj; sus (pe scări) ‖ *adj* de la etaj; de sus ‖ *s* etajul *n* de sus.

upstanding *adj* (*character*) onorabil, integru.

upstart *s* parvenit *m*; proaspăt îmbogățit *m*.

upstream *adv* înspre amonte, în susul apei ‖ *adj* din amonte, în susul apei; *fig* care merge contra curentului.

upsurge *s* creștere *f* rapidă; avânt *n*, elan *n*.

uptake *s bio* absorbție *f*; (*of water*) aducțiune *f*.

uptight *adj coll* neliniștit.

up-to-date *adj* la modă; adus la zi; modern; nou ‖ *adv* la zi; de ultima oră.

uptown *adj* de la periferie ‖ *adv* la periferie.

upturn *s* (*in economy, etc*) înviorare *f*.

upward *adj* ascendent, care se ridică/înalță; de ridicare; îndreptat în sus.

uranium *s chem* uraniu *n*.

urban *adj* urban; orășenesc.

urchin *s* (*rogue*) copil *m* neastâmpărat; ștrengar *m*; pici *m*.

urea *s chem* uree *f*.

urethra *s anat* uretră *f*.

urge *s* îndemn *n*; apel *n*; impuls *n*; stimulent *n* ‖ *vi* a îndemna; a forța; a solicita; a recomanda; a impune.

urgency *s* urgență *f*.

urgent *adj* urgent; necesar; insistent; important.

urinate *vi* a urina.

urine *s* urină *f*.

urn *s* urnă *f* funerară; (*tea*) ceainic *n*.

us *pron pers* noi, pe noi, nouă, ne, ni.

usage *s ling* uzanță *f*, folosire *f*; (*use*) tratament *n*.

use *s* folos *n*; profit *n*; utilitate *f*; valoare *f*; scop *n*; obicei *n* ‖ *vt* (*employ*) a folosi; (*spend*) a consuma; (*treat*) a trata; a uza • **~d** *adj* (*second-hand*) de ocazie; (*object*) folosit, utilizat • **~ful** *adj* folositor; capabil; valoros • **~less** *adj* inutil; fără efect; zadarnic; lipsit de valoare • **~r** *s* utilizator *m*; *sl* narcoman *m* • **~r-friendly** *adj comp* ușor de mânuit.

usher *s* plasator *m* ‖ *vt* a anunța; a introduce; *fig* a inaugura; a conduce.

usual *adj* obișnuit • **~ly** *adv* în mod obișnuit, de obicei.

usurer *s* cămătar *m*.

usurious *adj* cămătăresc.

usurp *vt* a uzurpa, a submina.

utensil *s* ustensilă *f*, instrument *n*.

uterus *s anat* uter *n*.

utilitarian *adj* utilitar, practic; funcțional.

utility *s* utilitate *f*, caracter *n* folositor; serviciu *n* public; *comp* utilitar *n* (pachet de programe de informatică) ‖ *adj* multifuncțional.

utilize *vt* a utiliza; (~ *resources*) a exploata, a utiliza.

utmost *adj* maxim; extrem; suprem ‖ *s* maximum *n*; extrem *n*; efort *n* suprem.

utopia *s* utopie *f* • **~n** *adj* utopic.

utter[1] *vt* a rosti; a pronunța; a exprima • **~ance** *s* exprimare *f*, formulare *f*; pronunțare *f*, rostire *f*; *ling* enunț *n*.

utter[2] *adj* total, complet; neînchipuit • **~ly** *adv* complet, total • **~most** *s* extremă *f* ‖ *adj* cel/cea mai mare.

U-turn *s* întoarcere cu 180; *fig* reviriment *n*.

uvula *s anat* uvulă *f*, omușor *m*.

V

V, v *s* (*letter*) V, v.
vacancy *s* post *n* liber; lapsus *n*.
vacant *adj* vacant; liber; uituc; inexpresiv.
vacate *vt* a lăsa vacant, a elibera.
vacation *s* vacanță *f*; concediu *n* ‖ *vi* a pleca în vacanță/concediu.
vaccinate *vt* a vaccina.
vaccine *s* vaccin *n*.
vacillate *vi* a se clătina; a oscila; a fluctua; a șovăi, a ezita.
vacuous *adj frml* (*eyes, look*) pierdut, absent.
vacuum *s tech, fig* vid *n*; lapsus *n*; (*cleaner*) aspirator *n* ‖ *vt* a curăța cu aspiratorul; **~ cleaner** *s* aspirator *n* (de praf).
vagabond *s* vagabond *m*.
vagaries *s pl* capricii *n pl*; toane *f pl*, hachițe *f pl*.
vagina *s anat* vagin *n*.
vagrant *adj* vagabond, hoinar; rătăcitor ‖ *s* vagabond *m*, haimana *f*.
vague *adj* vag; nedecis.
vain *adj* inutil; stupid; steril; orgolios; de prisos.
valediction *s* rămas-bun *n*.
valet *s* valet *m*, lacheu *m* ‖ *vt* a sluji ca valet.
Valetta *s* Valetta *f*.
valiant *adj* viteaz.
valid *adj* valabil; justificat; întemeiat, temeinic.
valley *s* vale *f*.
valor *s lit* bravură *f*.
valuable *adj* prețios ‖ *s* obiect *n* de valoare.
valuation *s* evaluare *f*; apreciere *f*, prețuire *f*.
value *s* valoare *f*; evaluare *f*; etalon *n*; preț *n*; apreciere *f*; importanță *f*; deviz *n* ‖ *vt* a evalua • **~added tax** *s* taxa *f* pe valoare adăugată • **~d** *adj* prețios, valoros.
valve *s* supapă *f*; lampă *f* de radio.
vamp *s coll* (*woman*) vampă *f*, divă *f*.
vampire *s also fig* vampir *m*.
van *s* furgonetă *f*; camion *n* de mobilă; autodubă *f*; vagon *n* de marfă.
vandal *s* vandal *m*, barbar *m*.
vanguard *s* avangardă *f*.
vanilla *s* vanilie *f*.
vanish *vi* a se șterge; a dispărea.
vanity *s* îngâmfare *f*; frivolitate *f*; capriciu *n*; zădărnicie *f*.
vanquish *vt* a învinge.
vapid *adj* (*remark, style*) insipid, fad.
vapor *s* vapori *m pl*; abur *m* • **~ize** *vt/vi* a (se) evapora.
variability *s* instabilitate *f*; fluctuație *f*.
variable *adj* variabil ‖ *s* variabilă *f*.
variance *s* variație *f*; dezacord *n*; neînțelegere *f*; **be at ~ with** *vi* a fi în dezacord cu
variant *s* variantă *f*.
variation *s* variație *f*, schimbare *f*.
varicose veins *s pl med* varice *n pl*.
varied *adj* variat.
variegated *adj* variat, divers.
variety *s* specie *f*; varietate *f*; (*type*) soi *n*; *thea* varieteu *n*; diversitate *f*.
various *adj* variat; distinct; divers; mulți/multe.
varnish *s* lac *n*; smalț *n*; lustru *n* ‖ *vt* a lăcui; a împodobi; a da lustru.
varsity *adj coll* sport *n* care reprezintă universitatea la cel mai înalt nivel.

vary *vt* a diversifica; a schimba ‖ *vi* a varia; a se abate; a se schimba.
vase *s* vază *f*.
vassal *s* vasal *m*.
vast *adj* vast, imens.
vat *s* cuvă *f*; cadă *f*; butoi *n*.
Vatican *s* Vatican *n*.
vaudeville *s* spectacol *n* de varietăți; music hall *n*; vodevil *n*.
vault[1] *s* (*bank*) trezorerie *f*; (*church*) cavou *n*; (*roof*) boltă *f*.
vault[2] *vi* a sări cu voltă.
vaunted *adj lit* mult trâmbițat.
veal *s cul* carne *f* de vițel.
veer *vi* a vira; a coti.
veg *s coll* legume *f pl*.
vegan *adj* vegetarian (strict) ‖ *s* vegetarian *m* (convins).
vegetable *s* legumă *f* ‖ *adj* vegetal.
vegetarian *s/adj* vegetarian *m*.
vehement *adj* vehement.
vehicle *s* vehicul *n*; (*medium*) modalitate *f*, mijloc *n*.
veil *s* văl *n*; paravan *n*; camuflaj *n* ‖ *vt* a ascunde; a voala; a învălui.
vein *s* vână *f*; toană *f*; nervură *f*; ton *n* ‖ *vt* a stria.
velocity *s* viteză *f*; rapiditate *f*.
velvet *s* catifea *f* ‖ *adj* catifelat; de catifea.
venal *adj* venal, corupt.
vending machine *s* automat *n* (pentru vânzarea dulciurilor, cafelei etc)
vendor *s* vânzător *m*.
veneer *s* (*facing*) furnir *n*; (*appearance*) formă *f*, aparență *f* ‖ *vt* (*cover*) a furnirui; *fig* a da un lustru; a înfrumuseța.
venerable *adj* venerabil.
venerate *vt* a venera, a adora.
venereal *adj* veneric.
venetian blind *s* jaluzea *f*.
vengeance *s* răzbunare *f*.
vengeful *adj* răzbunător.
venison *s cul* carne *f* de vânat.
venom *s also fig* venin *n*.
vent *s* (*opening*) ieșire *f*; supapă *f*; ușurare *f* ‖ *vt* a slobozi; (*emit*) a da frâu liber; (*rage, etc*) a-și vărsa • **~ilate** *vt* a ventila; a aerisi.
ventricle *s anat* ventricul *n*.
ventriloquist *s* ventriloc *m*.
venture *s* (*adventure*) aventură *f*; speculație *f*; hazard *n*; (*firm*) companie *f* ‖ *vt* (*hazard*) a risca; (*offer*) a exprima; (*dare*) a îndrăzni să facă ‖ *vi* a risca; a îndrăzni.
venue *s* (*place*) loc *n* de judecată; loc *n* de întâlnire.
veracity *s* veridicitate *f*.
veranda *s* verandă *f*.
verb *s gram* verb *n*.
verbal *adj* verbal.
verbatim *adj/adv* cuvânt cu cuvânt, textual.
verbose *adj* guraliv; prolix; *fig* înflorit, cu înflorituri.
verdant *adj* verde crud.
verdict *s* verdict *n*; opinie *f*; sentință *f*.
verge *s* (*edge*) margine *f*; (*road*) drum *n* lateral, acostament *n*; **~ on** *vi* (*~ madness, etc*) a se apropia de, a friza.
verger *s relig* paracliser *m*.
verify *vt* a dovedi; a verifica.
verisimilitude *s* autenticitate *f*.

veritable *adj* veritabil, adevărat.
verity *s frml* adevăr *n*.
vermillion *adj* roșu aprins.
vermin *s* insecte *f pl* dăunătoare.
vermouth *s* vermut *n*.
vernacular *s* limbă *f* națională; dialect *n* local; jargon *n* profesional ‖ *adj* neaoș.
vernal *adj lit* (*flowers, breeze*) primăvăratic.
versatile *adj* (*adaptable*) adaptabil; (*multipurpose*) multilateral; (*flexible*) mobil; elastic; inconstant.
verse *s liter* versuri *n pl*, poezie *f*; strofă *f*; vers *n*; verset *n*.
versed *adj* (*experienced*) versat, priceput.
version *s* versiune *f*; traducere *f*.
verso *s* (*of page*) contrapagină *f*; (*of coin*) revers *n*.
versus *prep* contra, împotriva.
vertebra *s* (*pl* **vertebrae**) vertebră *f*.
vertical *adj* cel mai înalt; vertical ‖ *s* verticală *f*.
vertiginous *adj frml* vertiginos.
vertigo *s med* amețeală *f*, vertij *n*.
verve *s* vervă *f*.
very *adv* foarte; chiar; extrem de; prea; tocmai ‖ *adj* precis; adevărat; tocmai acela/aceea/aceia/acelea; ~ **few/little** foarte puțini/puțin; ~ **well** *adv* foarte bine; **the ~ first person** chiar prima persoană; **your ~ own car** propria ta mașină; **I ~ nearly fell** era cât pe aci să cad.
vesicle *s anat* veziculă *f*.
vespers *s pl relig* vecernie *f*.
vessel *s* vas *n*, recipient *n*; *naut* ambarcațiune *f*; vapor *n*; *anat*, *bot* vas *n*; canal *n*; *relig* potir *n*, vas *n*.
vest *s* vestă *f*; maiou *n* ‖ *vt* îmbrăca; a plasa; a investi ‖ *vi* a se îmbrăca; a investi.
vestibule *s* vestibul *n*; antreu *n*.
vestige *s* (*remnant*) vestigiu *n*; (*mark*) semn *n*, (*trace*) indiciu *n*; (*evidence*) dovadă *f*.
vestry *s relig* sacristie *f*; epitropie *f*.
vet *s coll* veterinar *m*; *coll* veteran *m* ‖ *vt frml* a examina; (*treat*) a trata; (*check*) a cerceta, a verifica.
veteran *adj* experimentat ‖ *s mil* fost combatant *m*, veteran *m*; (*experienced person*) veteran *m*.
veterinary *adj* (de) veterinar ‖ *s* medic *m* veterinar.
veto *s* vot *n*; opoziție *f* ‖ *vt* a opune un veto.
vex *vt* (*annoy*) a necăji; (*irk*) a vexa; (*bother*) a plictisi; a contraria • ~**ing** *adj* supărător; plictisitor.
via *prep* prin, via; ~ **satellite** prin satelit.
viable *adj* (*feasible*) viabil.
viaduct *s* viaduct *n*.
vial *s* fiolă *f*.
vibrant *adj* (*bright*) puternic, strălucitor; (*lively*) trepidant; palpitant; emoționant; (*resonant*) cu rezonanță.
vibrate *vi* (*quiver*) a vibra; (*shake*) a se legăna; (*throb*) a palpita; a se agita; a răsuna ‖ *vt* a face să vibreze.
vibration *s* trepidație *f*, vibrație *f*.
vibrator *s* vibrator *n*.
vicar *s relig* preot *m*; vicar *m*; locțiitor *m*, suplinitor *m* • ~**age** *s* casă *f* parohială.
vicarious *adj* indirect, făcut pentru altul/în locul altuia; de substituție; (*power*) delegat.
vice¹ *s* viciu *n*; defect *n*; corupție *f*; nărav *n*.
vice² *s* (*tool*) menghină *f*.
vice-chancellor *s* vice-cancelar *m*; *edu* rector *m*; prorector *m*.
vice-consul *s* viceconsul *m*.
vice-president *s* vicepreședinte *m*.

vice-versa *adv* viceversa, invers.
vicinity *s* vecinătate *f*, împrejurimi *f pl*; *fig* apropiere *f*, preajmă *f*.
vicious *adj* vicios; defectuos; (*cruel*) rău(tăcios); (*animal*) nărăvaș.
vicissitude *s frml* vicisitudine *f*.
victim *s also fig* victimă *f* • ~**ize** *vt* a persecuta, a face o victimă din.
victor *s* învingător *m* • ~**ious** *adj* victorios, biruitor • ~**y** *s* victorie *f*.
victuals *s pl obs* hrană *f*, alimente *f pl*; provizii *f pl*.
video *s* (*medium*) video *n*; (*device*) videocasetofon *n*; (*cassette*) casetă *f* video, video *n*; ~ **game** *s* joc *n* electronic; ~ **tape** *s* casetă *f* video; bandă *f* video ‖ *vt* a filma pe casetă video.
vie *vi* (**with**) a rivaliza (cu); a concura (cu); a se lua la întrecere (cu).
Vienna *s* Viena *f*.
view *s* privire *f*; poză *f*; (*scene*) vedere *f*; (*sight*) priveliște *f*; (*belief*) opinie *f*; esență *f*; imagine *f*; (*aim*) scop *n* ‖ *vt* (*look at*) a privi; a cerceta, a studia; a considera; a inspecta; a vizita; a percepe, a discerne; **on** ~ la vedere, expus • ~**er** *s* telespectator *m*; (*slides*) aparat *n* pentru mărit clișee • ~**point** *s* punct *n* de vedere.
vigil *s* priveghi *n*; *relig* ajun *n* de sărbătoare religioasă.
vignette *s* (*illustration*) vinietă *f*; *phot* bust *n*.
vigor *s* vigoare *f*, putere *f*; vitalitate *f*, energie *f*; eficacitate *f* • ~**ous** *adj* robust; viguros; energic; curajos.
vile *adj* (*unpleasant*) ordinar, vulgar; (*base*) josnic, abject; (*evil*) infam, ticălos.
vilify *vt frml* a denigra, a calomnia.
villa *s* vilă *f*; casă *f* de vacanță *f*.
village *s* sat *n*; comună *f*; localitate *f*.
villain *s hist* iobag *m*; nemernic *m*; răufăcător *m*.
vim *s coll* energie *f*.
vindicate *vt* (*justify*) a justifica; (*claim*) a revendica; (*exculpate*) a dovedi nevinovăția (cuiva).
vindictive *adj* (*unforgiving*) punitiv, de pedeapsă; (*vengeful*) vindicativ, răzbunător.
vine *s* viță *f*; lujer *m* de viță.
vinegar *s* oțet *n*; *fig* acreală *f*.
vintage *s* (*harvesting*) culesul *n* viilor; (*crop*) recoltă *f*, producție *f* (a unui an); (*wine*) vin *n* de calitate superioară ‖ *adj* (*classic*) tipic; (*wine*) de soi nobil; de marcă.
vintner *s obs* negustor *m* de vin; viticultor *m*.
vinyl *s chem* vinilin *n*.
viola *s mus* violă *f* mare; violă *f*.
violate *vt* a viola; a profana; a contraveni.
violation *s* (*of law*) încălcare *f*; (*of property*) intruziune *f*; (*of tomb*) profanare *f*; *jur* infracțiune *f*; *frml* (*rape*) viol *n*.
violence *s* violență *f*; brutalitate *f*; furie *f*.
violent *adj* intens, violent; brutal; aspru; furios; sălbatic; ascuțit.
violet *s bot* viorea *f*, violetă *f*; (*color*) violet ‖ *adj* violet.
violin *s mus* vioară *f* • ~**ist** *s mus* violonist *m*.
viper *s zool* viperă *f*, năpârcă *f*.
virago *s* femeie *f* jandarm, bărbătoi *m*.
virgin *s* fecioară *f*, virgină *f* ‖ *adj* virgin(al), pur; nedeștelenit; neumblat.
Virgo *s astrol* Fecioară *f*, Constelația *f* Fecioarei.
virile *adj* viril; curajos; sclipitor; viguros.

virility *s* virilitate *f.*
virtual *adj* virtual, efectiv, real, de fapt; posibil; ~
   reality *s* realitate *f* virtuală.
virtue *s* virtute *f*; cinste *f*; valoare *f*; însuşire *f*; iscusinţă
   f; putere *f.*
virtuosity *s* virtuozitate *f.*
virtuoso *s* (*pl* ~**s/virtuosi**) virtuoz *m.*
virtuous *adj* virtuos; moral; cast.
virus *s med, bio* virus *n*; *fig* microb *m*, virus *n.*
visa *s* viză *f* ‖ *vt* a viza.
viscount *s* viconte *m.*
viscous *adj* vâscos.
visibility *s* vizibilitate *f.*
visible *adj* vizibil.
vision *s* (*image*) imagine *f*; privelişte *f*; (*dream*) viziune
   f; (*sight*) vedere *f*; (*apparition*) fantomă *f.*
visit *s* (*call*) vizită *f*; inspecţie *f* ‖ *vt* a vizita; a inspecta;
   a pedepsi ‖ *vi* a face o vizită • ~**ation** *s* (*official*)
   vizită *f* oficială; *frml* (*affliction*) calamitate *f*; (*reward*) pedeapsă *f* cerească • ~**or** *s* vizitator *m.*
visor *s* vizieră *f*, cozoroc *n.*
vista *s* (*view*) privelişte *f.*
visual *adj* vizual; ~ **aids** *s pl edu* suporturi *n pl* vizuale.
vital *adj* vital; urgent; fatal; esenţial.
vitamin *s* vitamină *f.*
viticulture *s* viticultură *f.*
vitriol *s chem, fig* vitriol *n.*
vituperation *s* defăimare *f.*
vivacious *adj* (*lively*) vivace, voi; (*cheerful*) în vervă,
   sprinten; (*perennial*) trainic, durabil.
vivid *adj* însufleţit; strălucitor, viu; (*description*) plin
   de viaţă; (*memory*) clar, precis.
vivisection *s* vivisecţie *f.*
vixen *s zool* vulpe *f*, vulpoaică *f.*
viz *adv abbr* (**videlicet**) adică.
V-neck *s* decolteu *n* în formă de V.
vocabulary *s* vocabular *n*; glosar *n*; lexic *n.*
vocal *adj* vocal; zgomotos; sonor.
vocation *s* vocaţie *f* • ~**al** *adj* profesional.
vociferous *adj* zgomotos.
vodka *s* vodcă *f.*
vogue *s* vogă *f*, modă *f.*
voice *s* (*speech*) voce *f*; (*say*) opinie *f*; sonoritate *f*;
   sufragiu *n*; cântăreţ *m* ‖ *vt* (*utter*) a rosti; (*declare*) a
   enunţa.
void *adj* neocupat; (*empty*) pustiu; (*vacant*) liber;
   vacant; *jur* nul ‖ *s* vid *n*; lipsă *f* ‖ *vt* a evacua; a goli;
   a anula.
voile *s text* voal *n.*
volatile *adj chem* volatil; *fig* (*situation*) exploziv;
   (*person*) lunatic; nestatornic; (*market*) instabil.
volcano *s* vulcan *m*; refulare *f.*
volition *s* voinţă *f*, vrere *f.*
volley *s mil* salvă *f*; *fig* potop *n*, torent *n*, grindină *f*; *sp*
   voleu *n* ‖ *vt mil* a trage o salvă de; *fig* a bombarda
   cu; *sp* a prinde/lua mingea din voleu.
volt *s elec* volt *m* • ~**age** *n elec* voltaj *n*, tensiune *f.*
voluble *adj* volubil, comunicativ; vehement.
volume *s phys, chem* volum *n*; (*book*) carte *f*; *pl*
   cantitate *f*; (*capacity*) capacitate *f*; ~ **control** *s*
   potenţiometru *n.*
voluminous *adj* voluminos.
voluntary *adj* voluntar; benevol; spontan.
volunteer *s* voluntar *m* ‖ *adj mil* voluntar; (*unpaid*)
   benevol ‖ *vt* (*offer*) a se oferi voluntar să facă ceva;

(~ *info, etc*) a da de bună voie ‖ *vi* a se oferi voluntar,
   a-şi oferi serviciile (pentru); *mil* a se înrola ca
   voluntar.
voluptuous *adj* voluptuos, senzual.
vomit *vi* a vomita, a voma ‖ *vt* a vomita; *fig* a scoate, a
   vărsa ‖ *s* vomă *f.*
voodoo *s* credinţă *f* în vrăjitorie/farmece/magie;
   vrăjitor *m*, magician *m*; vrajă *f*; farmece *n pl.*
voracious *adj* (*insatiable*) vorace, nepotolit, devorant;
   (*greedy*) lacom, mâncăcios; (*avid*) pasionat.
vortex *s* (*pl* **vortexes/vortices**) vârtej *n.*
vote *s* (*ballot*) vot(are) *n/f*; scrutin *n*; (*motion*) rezoluţie
   f ‖ *vt/vi* (*choose*) a vota; (*suggest*) a propune; ~ **down**
   vt a respinge; ~ **in** a vota, a adopta; ~ **of confidence**
   vot de încredere • ~**r** *s* alegător *m.*
voting *s* votare *f*, scrutin *n.*
votive *adj* votiv.
vouch *vi* (*assure*) a afirma, a susţine; (*guarantee*) a
   garanta; a gira; a dovedi, a confirma • ~**er** *s* martor
   m, garant *m*; (*coupon*) bon *n*, cupon *n.*
vow *s* (*oath*) jurământ *n* ‖ *vt* (*undertake*) a jura ‖ *vi*
   (*swear*) a jura, a se lega.
vowel *s* vocală *f* ‖ *adj* vocalic.
voyage *s* călătorie *f*; croazieră *f* ‖ *vt naut* a străbate ‖ *vi*
   naut a călători cu vaporul • ~**r** *s* călător *m*, voiajor *m.*
voyeur *s* obsedat *m* sexual.
vulcanize *vt* a vulcaniza.
vulgar *adj* (*tasteless*) vulgar; (*rude*) grosolan; obişnuit;
   de rând.
vulnerable *adj* (*weak*) vulnerabil; (*at risk*) expus la;
   criticabil.
vulpine *adj zool* de vulpe; *fig* şiret ca vulpea.
vulture *s orn* vultur *m*; *also fig* pasăre *f* rapace, pasăre *f*
   de pradă.
vulva *s anat* vulvă *f.*

W

W, w *s* (*letter*) W, w.
wacko, wacky *adj coll* trăsnit, smintit.
wad *s* (*of cotton, etc*) tampon *n*; (*of bills, etc*) teanc *n*;
   (*of tobacco*) cocoloş *n* de tutun de mestecat; cocoloş
   n de gumă.
waddle *vi* a merge clătinându-se; a se împletici.
wade *vi* a se bălăci ‖ *vt* a-şi face drum cu greu.
wafer *s* napolitană *f.*
waffle *s cul* vafă *f*; (*blather*) trăncăneală *f* ‖ *vi* (*go on*) a
   trăncăni.
waft *vt* (*carry*) a duce, a purta; *fig* a duce, a purta; a
   aduce ‖ *s* (*floating*) plutire *f*; (*puff*) adiere *f*, boare *f*;
   parfum *n* etc adus de vânt.
wag *vt* (*move*) a mişca, a pune în mişcare; (*dog* ~*s tail*)
   a da din coadă ‖ *vi* a se mişca, a fi în mişcare ‖ *s*
   (*shake*) mişcare *f*; mucalit *m.*
wage *s* salariu *m*; ~ **cut** *s* reducere *f* de salarii; ~ **earner**
   s salariat *m*; ~ **freeze** *s* îngheţarea *f* salariilor; ~ **war**
   (**on/against**) *vt* a duce/purta război (împotriva).
wager *s* pariu *n*, rămăşag *n.*
waggle *vi* (*wave to and fro*) a se clătina, a se bălăbăni;
   a tremura ‖ *vt* (*shake*) a mişca, a agita.
wagon *s* furgon *n*; car *n*; căruţă *f*; camion *n*; vagon *n* de
   marfă ‖ *vt* a transporta.
waif *s* (*rascal*) vagabond *m*, haimana *f*; (*thing*) obiect *n*
   găsit; *jur* bun *n* fără proprietar.
wail *vi* (*howl*) a urla; (*weep*) a plânge; (*complain*) a se

văita || *vt* a deplânge; a jeli || *s* (*moan*) văicăreală *f*; urlet *n*; scâncet *n*.

waist *s* talie *f*.

wait *vi* a aștepta; a servi || *vt* a aștepta; (*delay*) a amâna; a servi (la masă) || *s* (*pause*) așteptare *f*; pândă *f*; expectativă *f*; ~ **list** *s* listă *f* de așteptare.

waiter *s* chelner *m*.

waitress *s* ospătară *f*, chelneriță *f*; servitoare *f*.

waive *vt* (~ *a fee*) a renunța la; (~ *a rule*) a prevedea o derogare de la.

wake[1] *s* naut, *avia* siaj *n*; **in the ~ of** *fig* pe urmele (cuiva); la remorca (cuiva).

wake[2], **woke/waked, woken**) *vi* (*get up*) a se trezi; a se stârni || *vt* (*awaken*) a trezi; (*stir*) a stârni || *s* veghe *f*; ~ **up** *vt/vi* a (se) trezi.

walk *vi* a merge; (*amble*) a umbla; a se plimba; (*stroll*) a hoinări || *vt* (*cover on foot*) a străbate; a cutreiera; (*escort*) a conduce pe jos; (~ *a dog*) a scoate la plimbare || *s* (*stroll*) mers *n* pe jos, plimbare *f*; marș *n*; (*gait*) fel *n* de a merge.

walkie-talkie *s* aparat *n* portativ de emisie-recepție, walkie-talkie *n*.

walkout *s* grevă *f* spontană.

walkway *s* alee *f*, pasaj *n*; pasarelă *f*.

wall *s* zid *n*; (*partition*) perete *m*; (*block*) obstacol *n*; (*dam*) dig *n* || *vt* a zidi; (*enclose*) a închide • ~**ed** *adj* fortificat.

wallet *s* portofel *n*; sac *n*; toc *n*; mapă *f* de piele.

wallflower *s* bot mixandră *f*; *fig* fată *f* nedansată/ neinvitată la dans.

wallop *s* coll (*bash*) bătaie *f*, snopeală *f* || *vt* (*whack*) a snopi/zvânta în bătaie.

wallow *vi* (*flounder*) a se bălăci; (*stagger*) a se legăna; a se tăvăli în noroi || *s* bălăceală *f*.

wallpaper *s* tapet *n* || *vt* a tapeta.

walnut *s* bot nuc *m*; (*fruit*) nucă *f*; lemn *n* de nuc.

walrus *s* zool morsă *f*.

waltz *s* vals *n* || *vi* a valsa.

wan *adj* (*pale*) palid, livid; *fig* șters; mat; (*light*) slab

wand *s* mus baghetă *f*; nuia *f*; baston *n* de comandant.

wander *vi* (*stroll*) a hoinări; (*meander*) a șerpui; (*digress*) a delira; (*stray*) a se rătăci || *vt* a cutreiera • ~**er** *s* pribeag *m*; călător *m* • ~**ings** *s pl* călătorii *f pl*, drumuri *n pl*.

wane *vi* (*interest, etc* ~*s*) a se diminua, a slăbi; (*moon* ~*s*) a descrește.

wangle *vi* coll a izbuti, a reuși; *fig* a înșela || *vt* (*swing*) a trage pe sfoară; a obține prin înșelăciune; (*contrive*) a potrivi, a aranja.

want *vt* (*desire*) a vrea; (*require*) a-i trebui; (*crave*) a pofti; a-i lipsi; (*need*) a necesita; a trebui să || *vi* a fi sărac; a duce lipsă; a lipsi || *s* (*lack*) lipsă *f*; cerere *f*.

wanton *adj* (*gratuitous*) gratuit, nejustificat; (*immoral*) desfrânat, dezmățat.

war *s* război *n*; luptă *f* || *vi* a purta război; a lupta.

warble *s* tril *n*; ciripit *n* || *vi* (*trill*) a scoate triluri; (*chirp*) a ciripi; (*river* ~*s*) a murmura, a susura.

ward *s* apărare *f*; respingere *f*; (*hospital*) secție *f*; sală *f*; tutelă *f*; *jur* pupil *n*; (*district*) circumscripție *f*; cartier *n*; district *n* || *vt* (**off**) a para, a respinge; (~ *illness*) a preveni.

warden *s* îngrijitor *m*; (*custodian*) custode *m*; (*steward*) administrator *m*; (*supervisor*) supraveghetor *m*; (*guardian*) temnicer *m*.

warder *s* (*custodian*) gardian *m*, paznic *m*.

wardrobe *s* garderobă *f*, șifonier *n*.

warehouse *s* depozit *n* de mărfuri; antrepozit *n*.

warily *adv* cu precauție.

wariness *s* (*caution*) precauție *f*; neîncredere *f*.

warlock *s* vrăjitor *m*.

warm *adj* cald; (*hot*) călduros; (*friendly*) prietenos; (*kind*) cordial; (~ *color*) plăcut; (*cheerful*) vesel; (~ *scent*) recent || *vi* a înviora; (*heat*) a încălzi || *vr* a (se) încălzi; a dezmorți.

warn *vt* (*alert*) a avertiza, a preveni • ~**ing** *adj* avertisment *n*; alarmă *f*; semnal *n*; indiciu *n*; înștiințare *f* • ~**ing light** *s* semnal *n* luminos.

warp *s* urzeală *f*; (*twist*) sucire *f*; (*distortion*) deformare *f*; deviere *f* || *vt* a urzi; a suci; a perverti; a deforma || *vi* a se strâmba; a se perverti; a se deforma; a devia; (*wood* ~*s*) a se încovoia, a se strâmba.

warrant *s* motiv *n*; mandat *n*; justificare *f*; drept *n* || *vt* (*justify*) a justifica; (*guarantee*) a garanta; a fi sigur că; (*assure*) a asigura.

warren *s* (*burrow*) vizuină *f*.

warrior *s* luptător *m*; soldat *m*; războinic *m*.

Warsaw *s* Varșovia *f*.

wart *s* anat neg *m*.

wary *adj* (*cautious*) prudent; (*suspicious*) circumspect; prevăzător; (*distrustful*) neîncrezător.

was *v aux* *** be**.

wash *vt* a spăla, a se spăla pe; (*clean*) a curăța; (*river* ~*es*) a uda, a inunda; *text* a albi || *vi/vr* a se spăla || *s* spălat *n*, spălare *f*; stropire *f*; leșie *f*; rufe *f pl* spălate; ~ **bowl** *s* chiuvetă *f* • ~**able** *adj* lavabil • ~**ed-out** *adj* (*faded*) decolorat; *coll* obosit, stors • ~**er** *s* tech șaibă *f*; mașină *f* de spălat; spălător *m* • ~**er-dryer** *s* mașină *f* de spălat vase • ~**ing machine** *s* mașină *f* de spălat.

Washington *s* Washington *n*.

wasp *s* ento viespe *f*.

waste *vt* (*squander*) a risipi; a irosi; (*misuse*) a strica; a distruge || *vi* a se irosi; a cheltui; (*weaken*) a slăbi; a se reduce || *s* irosire *f*; (*debris*) moloz *n*; (*junk*) deșeuri *n pl*; pustietate *f* • ~**ful** *adj* (*person*) cheltuitor; extravagant; (*activity*) nerentabil.

wastrel *s* (*waster*) cheltuitor *m*; pierde-vară *m*.

watch *s* (*timepiece*) ceas *n*; (*guard*) pază *f*; gardă *f*; pândă *f*; (*sentry*) santinelă *f* || *vt* (*guard*) a păzi; (*mind*) a urmări; (*keep an eye on*) a se uita la || *vi* a se uita; a fi atent; a pândi; a veghea.

water *s* apă *f*; mare *f*; inundație *f*; sudoare *f*; urină *f*; (*tears*) lacrimi *f pl*; acuarelă *f* || *vt* (*wet*) a uda; a scălda; (~ *cattle*) a adăpa; (*dilute*) a dilua || *vi* (*dampen*) a se umezi; a lăcrăma • ~**y** *adj* (*tea*) slab; (*food, drink*) prea diluat, apos; (*moist*) umed; ~ **closet** *s* closet *n*, toaletă *f*, WC *n*; ~ **cure** *s med* hidroterapie *f*; ~ **lily** *s bot* nufăr *m*; ~ **main** *s* conductă *f* principală de apă; ~ **pistol** *s* (*toy*) pistol *n* cu apă; ~ **rat** *s zool* șoarece *m* de apă; ~ **tank** *s* rezervor *n* de apă, cisternă *f*.

watercolor *s* (*art*) acuarelă *f*.

watercress *s bot* năsturel *m*, bobâlnic *m*.

waterfall *s* cascadă *f*, cădere *f* de apă

watering can *s* stropitoare *f*.

waterlogged *adj* (*soil*) îmbibat cu apă; (*ship*) cufundat în apă.

watermark *s* (*paper*) filigran *n*; (*level*) semn *n* al nivelului/cotei apei.

watermelon *s bot* pepene *m* verde.

waterproof *adj* impermeabil || *s* haină *f*/manta *f* impermeabilă.

watershed *s* (*divide*) cumpăna *f* apelor; *fig* cumpănă *f*, moment *n* hotărâtor.

waterski *s* ski *n* nautic.

watertight *adj* (*waterproof*) impermeabil; (*excuse*) perfect; (*plan*) infailibil; (*argument*) de necombătut.

waterway *s* cale *f* de navigație.

waterworks *s* sistem *n* hidraulic; stațiune *f* de pompare a apei.

watery *adj* (*wet*) apos; palid; (*color*) pal; (*food, etc*) fără gust.

watt *s elec* watt *m*.

wattle *s* (*sticks*) nuiele *f pl* împletite; (*of bird*) mărgele *f pl*.

wave *s* (*ocean*) val *n*; (*surge*) talaz *n*; ondulație *f*; (*gesture*) semn *n* || *vi* (*flutter*) a se văluri; (*gesticulate*) a face semn; a flutura || *vt* a undui; (*brandish*) a agita; a flutura.

waver *vi* (**between**) a ezita, a oscila (între); (*voice* ~s) a tremura; a fluctua.

wavy *adj* unduios; vălurit; sinuos; ondulat, (*curly*) creț.

wax[1] *s* ceară *f*; lumânare *f*; parafină *f* || *vt* a cerui; ~ **work** *s* figură *f* de ceară; ~ **museum** *s* muzeu *n* al figurilor de ceară.

wax[2] *vi* (*grow*) a crește; (*expand*) a se mări; (*increase*) a spori; (*become*) a deveni; a se face; ~ **angry** *vi* a se supăra.

way *s* (*street*) stradă *f*; (*road*) drum *n*; (*fashion*) mod *n*; (*route*) direcție *f*; (*respect*) privință *f*; (*custom*) uzanță *f*, obicei *n*; stare *f*; domeniu *n* || *adv* mult prea; **no** ~ sub nici un motiv; **by the** ~ apropo; **either** ~ orișicum, oricum ar fi; **one** ~ **or another** într-un fel sau altul; **all the** ~ tot timpul; până la capăt; până la sfârșit; **by** ~ **of** (*via*) prin.

waylay *vt* a pândi; a atrage într-o cursă; a întinde o cursă (cuiva).

wayside *s* margine *f* de drum, marginea *f* drumului.

wayward *adj* (*errant*) capricios, cu toane; (*willful*) îndărătnic; (*rebellious*) nestăpânit, neînfrânat.

we *pron pers* noi.

weak *adj* (*feeble*) slab; (*frail*) delicat; (*brittle*) șubred; difuz; (*watery*) diluat; (*soft*) moale; (*ineffectual*) incapabil; (*irresolute*) șovăitor • **~en** *vt* (*enfeeble*) a slăbi; a potoli; (*water down*) a atenua || *vi* (*decline*) a slăbi; (*subside*) a se potoli; (*diminish*) a se reduce; a scădea; (*abate*) a se înmuia; (*fade*) a se ofili • **~ness** *s* neputință *f*; slăbiciune *f*; moliciune *f*; defect *n*; pornire; șubrezenie *f*.

wealth *s* avere *f*; belșug *n*; abundență *f* • **~y** *adj* bogat.

wean *vt* (~ *a baby*) a înțărca.

weapon *s also fig* armă *f*; mijloc *n*.

wear, wore, worn *vt* (*dress in*) a purta; (*fray*) a toci; (*hold*) a ține; (*tatter*) a uza || *vi* a se strica; a se purta; a rezista; a deveni; a trece || *s* purtat *n*; uzare *f*; modă *f*; (*garments*) confecții *f pl*.

weary *adj* (*tired*) obosit; obositor; (*exhausted*) epuizat || *vt/vi* a (se) plictisi; a (se) obosi.

weasel *s zool* nevăstuică *f*.

weather *s* vreme *f*; timp *n*; furtună *f* || *vt* a aerisi; a decolora; a înfrunta || *vi* a se decolora.

weave, wove, woven *vt* a țese; (*knit*) a împleti; (*unite*) a lega; a urzi; (*make up*) a ticlui || *vi* a țese; a (se) împleti; a croșeta.

web *s* țesătură *f*; pânză *f*; fir *n*; voal *n*; urzeală *f*; rețea *f*; împletitură *f*.

wed *vt* a uni prin căsătorie; a lua de soție pe || *vi* a se căsători • **~ded** *adj* căsătorit; conjugal; (**to**) dedicat (unei îndeletniciri) • **~ded life** *s* viață *f* conjugală • **~ding** *s* cununie *f*, nuntă *f* || *adj* nupțial.

wedge *s* pană *f*, ic *n*; (*slice*) bucată *f* || *vt* (*lodge*) a înțepeni; (*cram*) a vârî, a băga.

Wednesday *s* miercuri *f*.

wee *adj coll* foarte mic; minuscul; foarte puțin.

weed *s* buruiană *f* || *vt* a plivi • **~y** *adj* cu buruieni; (*person*) pirpiriu.

week *s* săptămână *f* • **~day** zi *f* de lucru/lucrătoare • **~end** *s* sfârșit *n* de săptămână, weekend *n* || *vi* a-și petrece weekend-ul • **~ly** *adj* săptămânal || *adv* săptămânal, în fiecare săptămână || *s* săptămânal *n*, hebdomadar *n*.

weeny *adj coll* foarte mic; puțin de tot.

weep, wept, wept *vi* (*cry*) a plânge; a picura; a se aburi; a se prelinge || *vt* a plânge (după); a deplânge.

weevil *s ento* gărgăriță *f*.

weft *s text* urzeală *f*.

weigh *vt* (*mull over*) a cântări; (*ponder*) a chibzui; (*evaluate*) a evalua; (*balance*) a cumpăni || *vi* a conta; a cântări.

weight *s* (*load*) greutate *f*; apăsare *f*; (*burden*) povară *f*; (*power*) cuvânt *n* greu; (*influence*) influență *f*; (*stress*) gravitate *f* || *vt* a îngreuna; a cântări • **~y** *adj* (*heavy*) greu; important, cu greutate.

weir *s* baraj *n*, stăvilar *n*; deversor *n*.

weird *adj* (*strange*) nefiresc, (*odd*) ciudat, (*bizarre*) bizar; (*eerie*) fantomatic; (*unusual*) trăsnit.

welcome *interj* bun venit!, bine ai/ați venit! || *s* bun-venit *n*; salut *n*; (*reception*) primire *f* || *vt* (*greet*) a întâmpina; a lua bun venit; a saluta || *adj* binevenit.

weld *vt* a suda || *s* sudură *f*.

welfare *s* (*wellbeing*) bunăstare *f*; (*benefit*) asistență *f* socială.

well[1] *s* (*fount*) fântână *f*; (*spring*) izvor *n*; (*basin*) bazin *n*; rezervor *n*; *min* puț *n*, gură *f*; sondă *f*; *fig* izvor *n*, (*source*) sursă *f*, origine *f*; *constr* casa *f* scării.

well[2] *adv* (*properly*) (prea) bine; (*suitably*) mulțumitor; (*perfectly*) foarte bine; (*clearly*) mult, cu mult; prea; considerabil || *adj* (*healthy*) sănătos; (*fine*) în ordine; (*fit*) potrivit || *interj* ei poftim!, o!, vai!, asta-i bună!.

well-behaved *adj* bine crescut, manierat; cuminte.

well-being *s* bunăstare *f*.

well-bred *adj* * **well-behaved**.

well-built *adj* bine clădit.

well-groomed *adj* îngrijit; bine întreținut.

well-informed *adj* informat, la curent (cu).

wellington *s* cizmă *f* de cauciuc.

well-known *adj* binecunoscut.

well-meaning *adj* bine intenționat.

wellness *s* stare *f* de bine.

well-nigh *adv* aproape, cât pe ce.

well-off *adj* bogat; înstărit; norocos.

well-paid *adj* bine plătit.

well-rounded *adj* (*person*) rotunjor, rotofei; (*character*) bine conturat; atotcuprinzător.

well-spent *adj* (*time*) folositor.

well-spoken *adj* cu darul vorbirii; bun de gură.

well-timed *adj* oportun; făcut/spus la momentul oportun.

well-to-do *adj* bogat, cu stare.

well-trodden *adj* bătătorit.

well-worn *adj* (*clothes*) purtat; uzat; *fig* banal, comun.

Welsh *adj* velş, galez || *s* (*language*) galeză *f* || *s pl* the ~ galezii *m pl* • **~man** *s* galez *m*, velş *m* • **~woman** *s* galeză *f*, velşă *f*.

welt *s med* inflamaţie *f*; rosătură *f*.

welter *s* (*mess*) confuzie *f*; (*mixture*) amestec *n*; (*muddle*) învălmăşeală *f* || *vi also fig* a se bălăci, a se tăvăli • **~weight** *s* boxer *m* de categoria semimijlocie.

wench *s obs, hum* fetişcană *f*.

wend *vt lit* a o lua/apuca spre; a se îndrepta spre.

went *vi* * **go**.

wept *vi* * **weep**.

were *v aux* * **be**.

werewolf *s* vârcolac *m*.

west *s* vest *n*; occident *n* || *adj* vestic; occidental • **~ern** *adj* de vest; din vest; occidental; apusean || *s* occidental *m*; locuitor *m* din vest; (*movie, novel*) western *n*.

wet *adj* (*damp*) u(me)d; (*rainy*) ploios; (*moist*) lichid; stropit; *coll* (*person*) slab, influenţabil || *vt* (*moisten*) a uda; a înmuia.

wether *s zool* batal *m*.

whack *vt coll* (*thump*) a trage o bătaie, a bate măr || *s* (*slap*) scatoalcă *f*.

whale *s* balenă *f* || *vi* a vâna balene.

whaling *s* vânătoare *f* de balene.

wharf *s naut* chei *n*; debarcader *n*.

what *pron inter* ce?, ce fel?, cum?, cât? || *pron indef* ceva || *pron rel* (ceea) ce || *adj inter* care?, ce? • **~ever** *adj* orice, oricare, indiferent de || *pron inter* ce?; ce anume? || *pron rel* orice; indiferent ce.

wheat *s bot* grâu *n*.

wheedle *vt* (*coax*) a linguşi; a duce cu vorba

wheel *s* roată *f*; volan *n*; timonă *f*; rotire *f*; cerc *n* || *vt* a roti || *vi* a se învârti • **~chair** *s* scaun *n* pe rotile.

wheeler-dealer *s coll pej* afacerist/politician *m* descurcăreţ şi viclean.

wheeze *s* (*sound*) respiraţie *f* şuierătoare || *vi* a respira greu.

whelk *s med* pustulă *f*; coş *n*.

whelp *s* căţel(uş) *m* || *vt* (*of animals*) a făta.

when *adv* când; pe când, în timp ce; (numai) dacă; cu toate că, deşi || *pron rel* când; în care • **~ever** *adv* când (anume) || *conj* (indiferent) când; oricând, ori de câte ori.

where *adv* unde; pe unde; încotro; *fig* cum; în ce poziţie etc; cum, în ce măsură || *conj* unde; pe unde; încotro; (atunci) când; (acolo) unde || *pron* acolo unde, în care; în locul în care • **~abouts** *s* loc *n* unde se află cineva || *adv* unde • **~as** *conj* în timp ce, pe de altă parte • **~by** *conj* cum, pe ce cale, prin ce mijloace • **~upon** *conj* la care, după care • **~ever** *conj* (ori)unde || *adv* oriunde; unde • **~withal** *s* mijloace *n pl* necesare (traiului etc).

whet *vt* (*sharpen*) a ascuţi; *fig* (*stimulate*) a stimula, a aţâţa; a excita.

whether *conj* dacă.

whetstone *s* gresie *f*.

whey *s* zer *n*.

which *pron inter/rel* (pe) care; care/ce/pe care anume || *adj inter/rel* care/ce (anume) • **~ever** *pron, adj* oricare, indiferent care.

whiff *s* (*of perfume*) boare *f*, adiere *f*; (*of food*) miros *n*, iz *n*; (*of smoke*) rotocol *n* de fum.

while *conj* în timp ce, pe când; pe câtă vreme; cât timp; dar, însă; cu toate că, deşi || *s* (răs)timp *n*.

whim *s* (*impulse*) toană *f*, capriciu *n*.

whimper *vi* (*whine*) a scânci; (*sob*) a se smiorcăi; (*dog* ~*s*) a scheuna || *s* (*moan*) scâncet *n*; scheunat *n*.

whimsical *adj* capricios, cu toane; bizar, ciudat, straniu, excentric.

whine *vi* (*whimper*) a scânci; (*moan*) a geme; (*gripe*) a se văita; (*dog* ~*s*) a scheuna || *s* scâncet *n*; geamăt *n*; scheunat *n*; vaiet *n*; plânset *n*.

whinny *vi* a necheza.

whip *s* bici *n*; nuia *f*; cravaşă *f*; vizitiu *m*; aripă *f*; hăitaş *m*; frişcă *f*; organizator *m*. parlamentar || *vt* (*flog*) a biciui; (*whisk*) a bate (lapte); a mânui || *vi* a trece; a răpăi; a fâlfâi; a urla; a se năpusti.

whippet *s zool* (soi de) ogar *m*.

whirl *vt* (*spin*) a învârti || *vi* (*reel*) a se învârti; (*turn*) a se răsuci; (*swivel*) a se învârteji; a goni; a ameţi || *s* vârtej *n*; (*bustle*) agitaţie *f*; (*uproar*) confuzie *f*; răsucire *f*; (*commotion*) zăpăceală *f* • **~wind** *s* tornadă *f*; tumult *n* || *adj* rapid; fulgerător.

whirr *s* (*buzz*) bâzâit *n*, zumzet *n*, zbârnâit *n*; huruit *n* || *vi* (*buzz*) a bâzâi, a zumzăi, a zbârnâi; (*hum*) a hurui; a vibra.

whisk *s* mişcare *f* rapidă; pămătuf *n*; *cul* tel *n* || *vt* (*brush off*) a scutura; a goni; *cul* a bate || *vi* (*move quickly*) a pleca repede.

whiskered *adj* cu favoriţi.

whiskers *s pl* favoriţi *m pl*.

whiskey *s* whisky *n*.

whisper *vi* (*person* ~*s*) a şopti, a şuşoti; *fig* a şopti/şuşoti/bârfi prin colţuri; (*leaves* ~) a fremăta, a foşni; (*water* ~) a murmura; a susura || *s* şoaptă *f*, şuşotit *n*; freamăt *n*, foşnet *n*; murmur *n*; susur *n*.

whist *s* (*game*) whist *n*.

whistle *vi* a fluiera; a şuiera || *s* (*sound*) şuierat *n*; (*object*) fluier *n* • **~blower** *s coll* persoană *f* care reclamă o ilegalitate.

white *adj* (*color*) alb; deschis; argintiu; inocent; onest; sincer; *s cul* albuş *n*; puritate *f*; (*person*) alb *m* || *vt obs* a albi • **~n** *vi/vt* a (se) albi • **~collar** *adj* de funcţionar, funcţionăresc • **~wash** *s* var *n* stins; văruit *n*, spoit *n*; *fig* înăbuşire *f* || *vt* a vărui, a spoi; *fig* a înăbuşi; a ascunde; *sp* a învinge la scor.

whither *adv/conj obs* încotro.

whiting *s icht* merlan *m*.

whitish *adj* albicios.

whittle *vt* (~ *wood*) a ciopli, a tăia; (*carve*) a sculpta || *vi* (~ *wood*) a ciopli.

whiz *vi* (*rush*) a trece val-vârtej || *s* (*expert*) as *m*, expert *m*.

who *pron inter/rel* cine; pe cine; care; pe care || *inter* cine? • **~ever** *pron rel* oricine; acela care/ce; cel care/ce; toţi cei care/ce || *inter* cine oare?.

whole *adj* întreg; tot; complet; integral; total || *s* întreg *n*; tot *n*.

wholewheat *adj* (*bread*) integral.

wholesale *s* vânzare *f* cu ridicata || *adj* (*purchase, sale*) en gros, angro; (*price*) de angro; *pej* (*excessive*) în masă || *adv* en gros, angro; *pej* (*excessively*) cu toptanul.

wholly *adv* în întregime.

whom *pron* * **who** căruia; pe cine; pe care.

whoop *s* (*yell*) strigăt *n*; ţipăt *n* || *vi* a striga; a ţipa.

whooping cough *s med* tuse *f* convulsivă/măgărească.

whoosh *s* fâşâit *n* || *vt* (*whiz*) a porni/trece ca un bolid.

whopper *s coll* namilă *f*, colos *m*; (*lie*) minciună *f*.

whopping *adj coll* uriaş, imens, enorm.

whore *s vulg* târfă *f*, curvă *f*.

whose *adj rel* al, a, ai, ale cărui/cărei/căror || *pron inter/rel* al, a, ai, ale cui(?).

why *adv* de ce?, pentru ce?, din ce cauză?, cu ce scop? || *interj* păi!, păi cum?, cum să/de nu?, desigur!, ca să vezi! || *s* întrebare *f*; motiv *n*, cauză *f*.

wick *s* fitil *n*.

wicked *adj* rău; nemernic; imoral; periculos.

wicker *adj* din nuiele; **made of** ~ de nuiele.

wide *adj* larg; spaţios; întins; schimbător; apreciabil || *adv* extrem; larg.

widow *s* văduvă *f* || *vt* a lăsa văduvă • **~er** *s* văduv *m*.

width *s* lărgime *f*; lăţime *f*; întindere *f*.

wield *vt* (~ *a weapon*) a mânui; (~ *power*) a exercita.

wife *s* soţie *f*.

wig *s* perucă *f*.

wiggle *vt* a mişca din || *vi* a şerpui, a merge şerpuit, a merge în zigzag; a se clătina pe picioare, a şovăi în mers.

wigwam *s* cort *n* (la indieni americani).

wild *adj* sălbatic; crud; barbar; pustiu; primitiv; violent; nelocuit; despletit; nebunesc; fantezist; desmăţat; ~ **card** *s* joker *m* • **~life** *s* animale *npl* sălbatice • **~ly** *adv* frenetic.

wildcat (strike) *s* grevă *f* neautorizată de sindicat.

wilderness *s* regiune *f* sălbatică; pustietate *f*, pustiu *n*; teren/pământ *n* sterp.

wile *s* şiretlic *n*, tertip *n*; vicleşug *n*, şmecherie *f*.

will, would *v aux* vei, veţi, va, vor; o să, ai să, are să, aveţi să, au să; voi, vei, va, vom, veţi, vor || *v mod* vrei, vreţi, vrea, vor; doreşti, doriţi, doreşte, doresc; pot, poţi etc || *s* voinţă *f*; dorinţă *f*; testament *n*.

willful *adj* (*stubborn*) încăpăţânat; (*deliberate*) voit, deliberat, premeditat.

willing *adj* dispus; favorabil; pregătit; înclinat; bucuros; binevoitor.

willow *s bot* salcie *f*.

wilt *vi* (*plant* ~*s*) a se vesteji; (*person* ~*s*) a lâncezi; a se ofili; a slăbi.

wily *adj* şiret, viclean.

wimp *s coll pej* om *m* slab, cârpă *f*.

win, won, won *vi* a învinge; a reuşi || *vt* a câştiga; a căpăta; a convinge || *s* succes *n*; câştig *n*; victorie *f*.

wince *vi* (*flinch*) a tresări; a se înfiora; (*cringe*) a se chirci, a se zgârci || *s* fior *n*; tresărire *f*, convulsie *f*; crispare *f*.

winch *s tech* vinci *n*, troliu *n*.

wind¹, wound, wound *vi* (*coil*) a se răsuci; (*bend*) a coti; a se schimba || *vt* a roti; (*twist*) a răsuci; (~ *a watch*) a întoarce || *s* curbare *f*; meandră *f*; apăsare *f*; cot *n*.

wind² *s met* vânt *n*; (*breath*) suflu *n*; (*gas*) gaz *n* || *vt* a tăia răsuflarea; ~ **instrument** *s mus* instrument *n* de suflat; ~ **tunnel** *s* tunel *n* aerodinamic.

windbreak *s* paravânt *n*.

windfall *s* (*bonus*) chilipir *n*, pleaşcă *f*; moştenire *f* neaşteptată.

windlass *s tech* troliu *n*; vinci *n*; *naut* vinci *n* de ancoră; tambur *n*.

windmill *s* moară *f* de vânt.

windpipe *s anat* trahee *f*.

windshield *s* parbriz *n*.

windswept *adj* bătut de vânturi.

window *s* (*house, etc*) fereastră *f*; *comp* fereastră *f*; (*glass*) geam *n*; (*store*) vitrină *f*; ghişeu *n*; ~ **cleaner** *s* spălător *m* de geamuri; ~ **ledge** *s* pervaz *n* • **~pane** *s* geam *n* • **~sill** *s* pervaz *n*; poliţa *f* ferestrei.

windy *adj* bătut de vânt; vântos; (*verbose*) flecar; fricos.

wine *s* vin *n*; băutură *f*.

wing *s* aripă *f*; flanc *n* || *vt* a grăbi; a da avânt; a zbura prin || *vi* a zbura.

wink *s* clipire *f*; clipă *f*, clipită *f*; licărire *f*, sclipire *f* || *vi* (*person*) a clipi; (*star, etc*) a licări, a sclipi; a pâlpâi || *vt* a clipi din (ochi); a semnaliza prin semnale luminoase.

winkle *s bot* saschiu *m*.

winner *s* câştigător *m*.

winnow *vt* a vântura.

winsome *adj* chipeş, irezistibil.

winter *s* iarnă *f* || *vi* a ierna; a hiberna.

wintry *adj* de iarnă; glacial.

wipe *vt* a curăţa; a şterge; a freca || *s* ştergere *f*.

wire *s* sârmă *f*; fir *n* || *vt* a bobina; a conecta; a telegrafia || *vi* a telegrafia.

wiring *s* instalaţie *f* electrică; cuplare *f*.

wiry *adj* (*person*) subţire şi vânjos; (*hair*) sârmos; (*sound*) metalic.

wisdom *s* judecată *f*; înţelepciune *f*; învăţătură *f*; experienţa *f* vieţii.

wise *adj* înţelept; serios; chibzuit; informat.

wish *vt* (*want*) a dori; a ura || *vi* a aspira; a dori || *vr* a vrea să fie || *s* poftă *f*; (*desire*) dorinţă *f*; (*regards*) urări *f pl*.

wishy-washy *adj* (*color*) spălăcit; (*person*) confuz; şovăielnic.

wisp *s* (*of hair*) smoc *n*; (*of hay, etc*) mănunchi *n*, legătură *f*.

wistful *adj* nostalgic; melancolic; visător.

wit *s* spirit *n*; judecată *f*; isteţime *f*, ironie *f*.

witch *s* vrăjitoare *f*; sirenă *f*; baba-cloanţa *f*.

with *prep* (împreună) cu; alături de; de partea; la; datorită; prin; împotriva; ca şi; la fel cu; în ciuda; în ceea ce priveşte.

withdraw, withdrew, withdrawn *vt* (*remove*) a retrage; (*pull out*) a scoate; a retracta || *vi* (*retire*) a se retrage; (*move back*) a pleca; a retracta; a renunţa.

wither *vt* (*plant* ~*s*) a ofili; a usca; (*body* ~*s*) a îmbătrâni; a istovi; (*hope* ~*s*) a slăbi; a distruge || *vi* a se ofili; a se usca; a tânji • **~ed** *adj* veşted; ofilit; uscat; îmbătrânit • **~ingly** *adv* cu profund dispreţ.

withhold *vt* (*keep back*) (*from*) a reţine, a opri (de la) || *vi* (*from*) a se abţine (de la).

within *adv* înăuntru; în interior; în sinea sa || *prep* în; înăuntru; în interiorul; din, dinăuntrul; pînă la; în limitele.

without *adv* afară; la exterior; în aer liber || *prep* fără; dincolo de; lipsit de.

withstand *vt* a se împotrivi/opune la; a ţine piept; a rezista || *vi* a rezista, a opune rezistenţă, a ţine piept.

witness *s* martor *m*; dovadă *f*; mărturie *f*; probă *f*; exemplu *n* || *vt* a fi martor; a dovedi; a observa || *vi* a depune.

wittingly *adv frml* în cunoştinţă de cauză.

witty *adj* spiritual; plin de duh; mucalit.

wives *s pl* * **wife**.

wizard *s* vrăjitor *m*; magician *m*; scamator *m*.

wizened *adj* (*wrinkled*) zbârcit; (*shriveled*) pipernicit.

wobble *vi* (*shake*) a merge cu paşi nesiguri; a se împletici; a şchiopăta; *fig* a şovăi, a ezita; a da din coadă; a se fâţâi, a se agita.

woe *s* suferinţă *f; pl* necazuri *n pl* • **~ful** *adj* lamentabil; întristat; duios.

woke *vi* * **wake**.

woken *vi* * **wake**.

wolf *s zool* lup *m* || *vi* a vâna lupi; a înfuleca.

woman *s* femeie *f;* fată *f* în casă; soţie *f;* slujnică *f.*

womb *s anat* uter *n;* matcă *f;* pântece *n pl,* vintre *f pl; fig* matcă *f;* sân *m.*

won *vt* * **win**.

wonder *s* (*surprise*) uimire *f;* (*miracle*) miracol *n* || *vi* (*marvel*) a se mira; (*speculate*) a se întreba; a fi uimit • **~ful** *adj* minunat.

wondrous *adj* extraordinar.

wonky *adj* şubred.

wont *s frml* (*habit*) obicei *n,* (*custom*) obişnuinţă *f.*

woo *vt* (*court*) a curta; (*entice*) a încânta prin promisiuni.

wood *s* pădure *f;* lemn *n;* lemne *n pl* (de foc); ~ **lily** *s bot* lăcrămioară *f,* mărgăritar *n;* ~ **pile** *s* grămadă/ stivă *f* de lemne; ~ **pulp** *s* pastă/celuloză *f* de lemn.

woodcock *s orn* sitar *m.*

woodcut *s* gravură *f* în lemn, xilogravură *f.*

wooded *adj* împădurit.

wooden *adj* (*made of wood*) de/din lemn; (*stiff*) împietrit; searbăd; *pej* (*actor*) stângaci, rigid.

woodland *s* ţinut *n* păduros; pădure *f.*

woodpecker *s orn* ciocănitoare *f.*

woodwind *s mus* instrumente *n pl* de suflat, suflători *m pl.*

woodwork *s constr* construcţie *f* de lemn; piese *f pl* de lemn; (*carpentry*) tâmplărie *f,* dulgherie *f.*

woodworm *s* vierme *m* de lemn.

woody *adj* împădurit; de pădure; de lemn; lemnos

woof *s text* bătătură *f;* fir *n* de bătătură.

woofer *s* difuzor *n* de joasă frecvenţă.

wool *s* lână *f;* stofă *f* de lână; fir *n* de lână • **~en** *adj* de/din lână || *s pl* confecţii *f pl* de lână • **~ly** *adj* din/de lână; (*vague*) confuz, neclar, vag.

woozy *adj* (*dazed*) confuz; (*sick*) căruia îi este greaţă.

word *s* (*utterance*) cuvânt *n;* vorbă *f;* (*expression*) exprimare *f,* (*statement*) enunţ *n;* (*remark*) remarcă *f;* (*info*) ştire *f;* (*pledge*) promisiune *f;* ordin *n* || *vt* (*utter*) a exprima; a formula; a redacta; ~ **processing** *s* tehnoredactare *f* computerizată; ~ **processor** *s comp* editor *m* de texte.

wore *vt* * **wear**.

work *s* (*labor*) muncă *f,* lucru *n;* (*effort*) efort *n;* ocupaţie *f; fig* sarcină *f,* datorie *f; pl* uzină *f;* (*opus*) operă *f,* lucrare *f* || *vi* (*toil*) a munci; a lucra; (*succeed*) a reuşi; (*operate*) a funcţiona; (*act*) a acţiona || *vt* a face; a acţiona; a lucra la; a modela; a cauza; a influenţa; a aranja; a convinge; ~ **ethic** *s* etica *f* muncii; ~ **force** *s* forţă *f* de muncă, salariaţi *m pl;* ~ **permit** *s* permis *n* de muncă.

workable *adj* (*plan*) realizabil; (*system*) funcţional.

workaholic *s* persoană *f* împătimită de muncă.

worked up *adj* surescitat, nervos.

worker *s* muncitor *m;* lucrător *m.*

working *s* funcţionare *f;* mecanism *n* || *adj* muncitor, care munceşte; de lucru; (*running*) în stare de funcţionare || *adj* (*running*) care funcţionează; (*employed*) în activitate; (*clothes, etc*) de muncă; ~ **capi-**

tal *s* fond *n* de rulment; ~ **class** *s* clasa *f* muncitoare • **~s** *s pl* (*system, machine*) mecanism *n.*

workload *s* normă *f* de lucru.

workman *s* muncitor *m* • **~ship** *s* meşteşug *n,* măiestrie *f,* pricepere *f.*

workout *s* exerciţii *n pl* de gimnastică.

workshop *s* atelier *n.*

workstation *s comp* computer *n* individual, post *n* de lucru.

workweek *s* săptămână *f* de lucru;.

world *s* (*people*) lume *f;* (*humanity*) omenire *f;* societate *f;* (*globe*) univers *n;* (*life*) viaţă *f;* (*realm*) regn *n* || *adj* mondial; **World Wide Web/www** *s comp* reţeaua *f* Internet • **~ly** *adj* lumesc, pământesc; material.

worm *s zool* vierme *m;* larvă *f; fig* mizerabil *m* || *vt* a smulge un secret; a pătrunde cu greu || *vi* a se târî.

worn *vt* * **wear**.

wornout *adj* (*thing*) uzat, deteriorat, ros; (*person*) epuizat.

worrisome *adj* îngrijorător.

worry *s* (*concern*) îngrijorare *f;* (*anxiety*) nelinişte *f;* (*fear*) teamă *f;* tulburare *f* || *vt* a îngrijora; a nelinişti; (*bother*) a supăra; a chinui; a sfâşia || *vi* (*fret*) a-şi face griji; a se supăra; (*be anxious*) a se nelinişti; (*agonize*) a-i fi teamă de; **don't** ~! nu vă faceţi griji! • **~ing** *adj* enervant, tracasant.

worse *comp* * **bad** mai rău, mai slab, mai prost etc; *comp* (şi) mai rău/slab/prost etc; (şi) mai mult/tare/ rău.

worship *s* (*adoration*) adorare *f,* divinizare *f;* (*reverence*) cult *n,* veneraţie *f* || *vt* (*pray to*) a se închina la; (*revere*) a venera || *vi* (*pray*) a se ruga; a se prosterna.

worst *adj* * **bad** cel mai rău/prost etc || *adv* cel mai rău/prost etc.

worsted *adj text* de lână pieptănată; (*wool*) pieptănat || *s* lână *f* pieptănată.

worth *s also fig* (*value*) valoare *f;* merit *n;* avere *f;* (*import*) reputaţie *f* || *adj* care costă/face; care merită; care are; vrednic de • **~less** *adj* (*valueless*) fără valoare; (*hollow*) fără caracter; inutil; mizerabil.

worthy *adj* (*of*) demn (de, de a, să); vrednic (de); (*reward, etc*) cuvenit, meritat.

would *pret, cond* * **will** || *v aux* ai, aţi, aş, am, ar; vei, va, veţi, vor; o să, am să; vom, o să; *freq* obişnuiam să, obişnuiai să etc.

wound[1] *vt* * **wind[1]**.

wound[2] *s* (*injury*) rană *f;* (*insult*) ofensă *f;* (*cut*) tăietură *f;* cicatrice *f* || *vt* (*injure*) a răni; (*offend*) a jigni.

wove *vt* * **weave**.

woven *vt* * **weave**.

wow *s coll* (*triumph*) mare succes *n* || *vt* a încânta, a fascina, a delecta || *excl* grozav!, extraordinar!.

wraith *s* fantomă *f.*

wrangle *s* (*quarrel*) ceartă *f;* dispută *f* aprinsă; (*squabble*) altercaţie *f* || *vi* (*argue*) a se certa zgomotos; (*bicker*) a se ciondăni; a discuta aprins.

wrap *vt* (*enfold*) a înfăşura; (*package*) a împacheta; (*cover*) a acoperi; a ascunde || *vi* a se acoperi; a se înfăşura || *s* (*bathrobe*) halat *n;* fular *n;* (*covering*) învelitoare *f* • **~per** *s* (hârtie) ambalaj *n.*

wrath *s frml* (*anger*) furie *f,* mânie *f.*

wreath *s* ghirlandă *f;* coroană *f;* cunună *f;* şuviţă *f.*

wreck *s* epavă *f;* (*crash*) năruire *f;* (*shipwreck*) naufragiu *n;* accident *n;* avarie *f;* ruină *f;* (*remains*) resturi *n pl* ‖ *vt* (*destroy*) a distruge; (*demolish*) a dărâma; (*ruin*) a avaria • **~age** *s naut* sfărâmături *f pl*; epavă *f*; dărâmături *f pl*.

wren *s orn* pitulice *f*.

wrench *s* (*tool*) cheie *f* fixă; (*tug*) smulgere *f*; tragere *f* ‖ *vt* (*pull*) a smulge; (*sprain*) a scrânti, a luxa.

wrest *vt* (*wring*) a smulge; (~ *power*) a prelua (prin forță).

wrestle *vi* (*fight*) a se lupta; a se împotrivi ‖ *vt* a (se) lupta cu ‖ *s* luptă *f* greco-romană; trântă *f* • **~r** *s sp* luptător *m*.

wretch *s* nenorocit *m*; nefericit *m*; ticălos *m*, mizerabil *m*.

wriggle *vi* (*wiggle*) a merge/înainta șerpuit; (*twist*) a se încolăci; (*waggle*) a se răsuci; (*writhe*) a se zvârcoli; (*fidget*) a se agita.

wring, wrung, wrung *vt* (*twist*) a suci; (*squeeze*) a stoarce; (*press*) a strânge; (*grasp*) a smulge; a chinui; a frânge ‖ *vi* a se zvârcoli ‖ *s* răsucire *f*; presare *f*; presă *f* • **~ing** *adj* (*drenched*) leoarcă.

wrinkle *s* (*on skin*) rid *n*; (*fold*) încrețitură *f*; cută *f*; pliu *n* ‖ *vt* (*crease*) a încreți; a cuta ‖ *vi* a se cuta • **~ed** *adj* ridat; șifonat

wrist *s anat* încheietura *f* mâinii; manșetă *f*.

writ *s jur* ordonanță *f*; citație *f*.

write, wrote, written *vt* (*jot down*) a scrie; (*compose*) a compune; a redacta ‖ *vi* a scrie; a compune; a redacta; ~ **back** *vi* a răspunde; ~ **down** *vt* a scrie, a nota, a însemna; a deprecia în scris; ~ **off** *vt* (~ *debt*, *etc*) a șterge, a anula; (~ *someone*) a-l considera sfârșit/terminat; (*project*) a-l considera ratat; ~ **up** *vt* (~ *a report*) a întocmi, a redacta; (~ *notes*) a trece pe curat • **~r** *s* scriitor *m*; autor *m*; copist *m*; secretar *m*.

writhe *vi* (*squirm*) a se crispa, a se chirci; (*wriggle*) a se zvârcoli; a suferi cumplit ‖ *vt* (*twist*) a contorsiona; a suci, a răsuci; *fig* a denatura; a răstălmăci.

writing *s* scris *n*; operă *f*; caligrafie *f*; stil *n*.

written *vt* * **write**.

wrong *adj* (*incorrect*) greșit; (*amiss*) fals; (*improper*) nepotrivit; imoral; (*wicked*) rău ‖ *adv* greșit; injust ‖ *s* (*crime*) delict *n*; crimă *f*; (*injustice*) nedreptate *f*; (*harm*) rău *n* ‖ *vt* (*be unfair to*) a nedreptăți; a viola; (*offend*) a jigni; a defăima • **~ful** *adj* (*unfair*) nedrept, injust, incorect; ilegal, nelegitim; culpabil; criminal • **~doer** *s* răufăcător *m* • **~ful** *adj* injust; ilegal • **~ly** *adv* pe nedrept; greșit.

wrote *vt* * **write**.

wrought iron *s metal* fier *n* forjat.

wrung *vt* * **wring**.

wry *adj* (*smile*) forțat; (*face*) acru; (*ironic*) ironic; (*dry*) zeflemitor; *fig* ascuns; prefăcut; fals.

WWW *s abbr* (**World Wide Web**) *s comp* rețeaua *f* Internet.

X

X, x *s* (*letter*) X, x.

xenophobia *s* xenofobie *f*.

Xerox *s* (*machine*) mașina *f* de copiat, xerox *n*; proces *n* de copiere Xerox.

Xmas *s coll abbr* **Christmas** Crăciun *n*.

X-rated *adj* (*of movies*) interzis copiilor sub 18 ani.

X-ray *s phys* rază *f* x; radiografie *f* ‖ *vt* a face o radiografie.

xylography *s typ* xilografie *f*, arta *f* gravurii în lemn; tipar *n* de lemn.

xylophone *s* xilofon *n*.

Y

Y, y *s* (*letter*) Y, y.

yacht *s* iaht *n* ‖ *vi* a călători cu iahtul • **~ing** *s* iahting *n*; călătorie *f* cu iahtul.

yah *interj* ptiu!, brrr!.

yahoo *s* monstru *m*, bestie *f*.

yak *s zool* iac *m*.

y'all *pron abbr* (**you all**) voi toți, voi amândoi.

yam *s bot* ignamă *f*; batat *n*; cartof *m*.

Yank *s coll pej* american *m* yankeu • **~ee** *s coll* american *m* din statele nordice ale SUA; *coll* american *m*.

yap *s* lătrat *n* scurt; *coll* vorbărie *f* ‖ *vi* a lătra scurt.

yard *s* curte *f*; șantier *n*; depozit *n*; cimitir *n*.

yarn *s* fir *n*; poveste *f* lungă; născocire *f* ‖ *vi* a spune povești.

yaw *vi* (*plane, ship*) a se abate din drum.

yawn *vi* a căsca; a se căsca ‖ *s* căscat *n*; prăpastie *f* • **~ing** *adj* imens • **~ing gap** *s* un decalaj *n* imens.

yeah *adv coll* îhî, da.

year *s* an *m*; *pl* vârstă *f* • **~ly** *adj* anual.

yearn *vi* a tânji; (*desire*) a dori cu înfocare/ardoare • **~ing** *s* (**after/for**) dor *n* (de); dorință *f* arzătoare (de); jale *f*.

yeast *s* drojdie *f*; *fig* ferment *n*.

yell *s* răcnet *n*; țipăt *n*; urale *f pl* ‖ *vi* a răcni; a țipa.

yellow *adj* galben; auriu; gălbejit; laș; fricos; ticălos ‖ *s* culoare *f* galbenă; gălbenuș *n*; frică *f* ‖ *vt* a îngălbeni ‖ *vi* a se îngălbeni.

yelp *vi* (*bark*) a lătra; (*yap*) lătrat *n* scurt.

yep *adv coll* îhî, da.

yes *adv* da; firește; desigur ‖ *s* răspuns *n* afirmativ; consimțire *f*; aprobare *f*.

yesterday *s* ieri *f* ‖ *adv* ieri; recent, de curând.

yesteryear *adv* altădată.

yet *adv* încă; acum; deja; măcar; mai ‖ *conj* cu toate acestea, totuși; **he hasn't come** ~ n-a venit încă; **have you finished** ~ ? ai și terminat?; ~ **again** iarăși, din nou.

yew *s bot* tisă *f*.

yield *vt* a produce; a livra; a scoate; a da; a ceda ‖ *vi* a produce a ceda; a se preda ‖ *s* producție *f*; *agr* recoltă *f*; *econ* profit *n*; venit *n*; cedare *f* • **~ing** *adj* supus; ascultător; maleabil; influențabil; (*metal*) elastic, suplu; moale.

yodel *s* iodel *n* ‖ *vi* a cânta ca tirolezii.

yoga *s* yoga *f*.

yogurt *s* iaurt *n*.

yoke *s* jug *n*; *fig* jug *n*, robie *f*, scavie *f*.

yokel *s pej* (*bumpkin*) țărănoi *m*; bădăran *m*.

yolk *s* (*egg*) gălbenuș *n*.

yonder *adj* acel(a), ace(e)a, acei(a), acele(a) de acolo ‖ *adv* acolo ‖ *pron* acela, aceea, aceia, acelea.

yore *s obs*, *lit* **of** ~ de demult.

you *pron pers* tu; mata; dumneata; dvs; voi; ție, îți, ți; matale; dumitale; vouă, vă, vi; pe tine, te; pe mata; pe dumneata; pe voi/dvs, vă.

young *adj* tânăr; junior; (*youthful*) tineresc; (*new*) începător ‖ *s* tineri *m pl*; (*offspring*) pui *m*.

your *adj poss* tău, ta, tăi, tale; matale; dumitale; dvs; vostru, voastră, voștri, voastre • **~self** *pron ref* te; vă ‖ *pron emph* (tu) însuți/însăți; (dvs) înșivă; singur(ă)

• ~selves *pron ref* vă || *pron emph* voi înşivă, voi însevă, chiar voi • by ~selves singuri.

youth *s* tinereţe *f*; tânăr *m*; in his ~ în tinereţea lui; the ~ of today tinerii din ziua de azi • ~ful *adj* tânăr; tineresc; energic; proaspăt; viguros; nou; înfloritor • ~fulness *s* tinereţe *f*; prospeţime *f*.

yowl *s* (*howl*) urlet *n* || *vi* (*howl*) a urla.

yoyo *s* (*toy*) titirez *m* pe sfoară; *sl* (*jerk*) secătură *f*.

yucky *adj coll* (*offensive*) scârbos, dezgustător.

Yuletide *s frml* Crăciun *n*.

yummy *adj coll* delicios.

yuppie *s coll* (*young urban professional*) tânăr *m* de succes.

Z

Z, z *s* (*letter*) Z, z.

Zambia *s* Zambia.

zany *adj coll* (*crazy*) trăsnit, ţăcănit.

zap *vi coll* (*fly, etc*) a omorî, a ucide, a lichida; (*ball, etc*) a lovi, a izbi, a pocni; (*opposing team*) a zdrobi, a bate, a face zob.

zeal *s* zel *n*, râvnă *f*; stăruinţă *f*.

zealot *s* adept *m* fanatic; fanatic *m*.

zealous *adj* zelos; stăruitor; dornic.

zebra *s zool* zebră *f*.

zenith *s astron* zenit *n*; apogeu *n*; culme *f*.

zephyr *s* zefir *n*.

zero *s* zero *n*; nulitate *f*; om *m* de nimic.

zest *s* (*spice*) condiment *n*; (*piquancy*) picanterie *f*; (*passion*) interes *n*; farmec *n*; (*enthusiasm*) energie *f*.

zigzag *s* zigzag *n* || *vi* a face zigzaguri; a merge în zigzag.

zillion *s coll* puzderie *f*.

zinc *s chem* zinc *n*.

zing *s coll* (*vitality*) vioiciune *f*; vervă *f* || *vi* (*travel fast*) a trece ca vântul; (*criticize*) a critica.

Zionism *s* sionism *n*.

Zionist *s* sionist *m*.

zip *s* energie *f*; putere *f*; vigoare *f*; temperament *n* || *vt* (*fasten*) a închide cu fermoarul || *vi* a pârâi; a şuiera; a fi plin de viaţă; ~ code *s* cod *n* poştal • ~per *s* fermoar *n*.

zit *s sl* (*pimple*) coş *n*.

zither *s mus* ţambal *n*.

zodiac *s astrol* zodiac *n*; zodie *f*.

zonal *adj* zonal.

zombie *s coll* fantomă *f*, strigoi *m*.

zone *s* zonă *f*; parte *f*; regiune *f*; sector *n* || *vt* a zona; a înconjura.

zonked *adj sl* istovit, frânt; beat criţă.

zoo *s* grădină *f* zoologică • ~keeper *s* îngrijitor *m* la grădina zoologică • ~logical *adj* zoologic • ~logist *s* zoolog *m* • ~logy *s* zoologie *f*;

zoom *s coll* (*dash*) a porni în trombă; (*plane, fly*) a zumzăi, a zbura || *s phot* zoom *n*; ~ lens *s cin* transfocator *n*.

zucchini *s bot* dovlecel *m*.